The Voice Within

THE VOICE WITHIN

The National Library of Poetry

Cynthia A. Stevens, Editor
Melisa S. Mitchell, Associate Editor

The Voice Within

Library of Congress
Cataloging in Publication Data

ISBN 1-57553-008-2

Manufactured in The United States of America by
Watermark Press
11419 Cronridge Dr., Suite 10
Owings Mills, MD 21117

Editor's Note

Upon reviewing the artistry within this anthology, ***The Voice Within,*** you will be taken upon an intimate journey of emotional enlightenment. The broad assortment of poems presented is wonderfully overwhelming. Each of the poets featured within this anthology has succeeded in crafting an exceptional work of art. As one of the editors and judges of the contributing entries, I had the rewarding opportunity to review and ponder the many pieces selected for this anthology. However, there are several poems I wish to honor with special recognition.

Agnes Guilfoyle Edwards (p. 1) produced an enchantingly euphonic piece of literature overflowing with rhythm and alliteration — she has given life to the desert and in doing so has appropriately named her "Jezebel." Jezebel is referenced in the Webster's Encyclopedic Dictionary as "a wicked, shameless, abandoned woman." Edwards does a convincing job of associating the characteristics of a desert with a Jezebelish woman:

She has her tender moments when she bows her head in prayer,
And breezes soft as cotton wave the sagebrush in her hair,
But like a fickle female with an ever-changing mood,
She calmly counts the cost of each and every interlude.

The slightest touch of anger brings a flush of scorching heat,
To make the pock-marked mountains bend to shade their burning feet,
And when the lady listens to the winds that howl and moan,
A spasm rocks her fickle flesh and quakes her sandy throne.

Because of the outstanding composition and detailed images displayed throughout "Jezebel," Edwards was awarded Grand Prize.

Another prominent poem, "Eating Air," by Charles Bibeault (p. 171), revolves around an emaciated child who was born into a land full of dry air, perhaps a land like that of Ethiopia. Bibeault provides explicit description enabling the reader to envision the suffering child eating air. In this land the "air" is "death":

Sunken cheeks, eyes half open, ribs through skin,
a neck the size of my wrist,
eating death.

He not only reveals the child to us, but brings to view the dryness, the bleakness found in the perpetual death of children born into this land of dry air; *"A stick man handles her package/ with indifference."* The child portrayed in the poem is seen by the stick man as just another log on the fire. The final line of the poem provides justification for the stick man's indifference, *"Air that's too dry/ for blood, is too dry for tears."* The word *"blood"* represents "life." To the stick man, and the other inhabitants of this dry land, there is no life — and therefore, no death. No death; no tears. With innate skill, Bibeault did a fascinating job of piecing together this verse; sympathy is gained for both the child and the stick man.

Paulette A. Burrier (p. 114) presents us with another solemn piece entitled "David McGee." This poem vividly describes how four boys become caught in Hurricane Felix — and how the grasp of the storm causes one boy to drown. The final stanza of this piece is written with a rapid pace causing the reader to feel the urgency the three boys must have felt in trying to save their friend:

Three reached him off-balance, flailing, desperate
Hands grabbed hands holding, cramping, slipping,
Hands weakening, loosening, fingers brushing fingers
Losing the tug of war between them and the ferocious surf
Helpless they scanned the waters, eyes searching pitch black
Agony replaced ecstasy as they heard David's final, hopeless scream
Then silence, in the screaming rage of the wind

Burrier places the reader there — you can see the *hands holding, cramping, slipping ....* And most of all, after David slips away, you can hear the silence.

Also, in the shadowy realm of melancholy, we have Lori Burks' work, "Bitter Memories" (p. 329). Utilizing detailed description, Burks introduces us to a poor woman who is doing her best to provide a happy childhood for her children while she tries to wash away the unhappy memories of her own childhood:

... [she] recalls her own childhood; cold memories,
winters that engulfed her and five siblings, caged animals.
Breeches of burlap sacks, cardboard soles, bundled rags for mittens.
They too built snow people, entire families, as frozen as their own.
Coal, carrots, and buttons, too sparse, blank faces.
She wipes the window with her apron, ancient coal dust, defiled virginity.

The persona's *"defiled virginity"* is her tainted childhood. It could have been a time of carefree happiness with the warmth of home; instead her childhood was cold and harsh. There were no smiles, only blank faces. And, although the persona is still poor, she puts her dark memories out of sight: *"She returns the webs, unties her apron, washes away the blemishes; dullness"* in hopes of creating a happy childhood for her children.

Another poem touching upon the relationship of parent and child is "Retrospect," by Oma Wilcox (p. 319). Through this piece, Wilcox shows how difficult it is to really let go of your child:

It's right, I guess, that she should grow
Away and up— but...
How good it is to own a little girl
Entirely.

Wilcox's verse does an excellent job of expressing how the bond between parent and child may be so great that it's truly a tough task for a parent to relinquish ownership and allow the child to grow up.

Another outstanding poem is "Kwajalein Cemetery" by William Krasner (p. 313). This somber piece is in reference to the deaths which occurred during World War II (February 6, 1944) when the Kwajalein Islands were taken over. The men in the war were to live forever by remembrance:

They said, "These dead can't die -- whose very bones
Now melt to coral in these coral sands;"

Yet, the significance of their sacrifice fades as the vagueness of the following images attest:

They said: "No one forgets. In other lands
Men give them praise. Somewhere a statue stands.
And on days set aside a priest intones."

And, although there may be some thought of the men who fought and died on these special days, this is truly not enough, as the narrator states in the final stanza:

I do not know. Is it enough to cry
Here where the remnants of their bodies are?
How can I know? What does it mean to die
Wet sand in mouth, and the safe trees too far?
I see their wide eyes staring at the sky,
And hear, at cocktails, voices speak of war.

The images that Krasner projects through this poem lead the reader to believe that to cry is not enough. After the deaths caused by World War II and other wars, if people honestly remembered the loss of all these men, *"voices [that] speak of war"* would not be heard at cocktails; only voices that speak of peace.

"How Quietly Do Years Escape from View," by Christopher Carpenter (p. 258), is a well-written verse explaining how time flows by without being noticed:

How slowly Father Time creeps his way in
to fade the memories of days gone by.
How quietly do years escape from view
and change faces before the ignorant eye.

Although time has slipped away and caused memories to fade, the persona finds consolation in her/his photographs which will last beyond time.

Several other choice poems you won't want to miss: "Refugee" by Neal Amaral (p. 231); "Thou Still Unravished Bride of Quietness" by Oscar Gonzales (p. 210); "Forgotten" by Alison Kaufmann (p. 562); and "Spider Haibun (Homage To W.B. Yeats)" by Stuart Zeno (p. 104).

Although I do not have the time or space to individually critique every eminent poem appearing within ***The Voice Within,*** you will notice that each piece of artistry is an admirable contribution. May all of the artists within this anthology be commended for their talents and efforts in creative writing.

I sincerely hope that you enjoy reading ***The Voice Within.***

Cynthia A. Stevens
Senior Editor

Acknowledgments

The Voice Within is a culmination of the efforts of many individuals. The editors are grateful for the contributions of the judges, assistant editors, graphic artists, layout artists, office administrators, and customer service representatives who have all brought their talents to bear on this project.

Managing Editor
Howard Ely

Winners of the North American Open Poetry Contest

Grand Prize

Agnes Guilfoyle Edwards / Mira Loma, CA

Second Prize

Neal Amaral / Atlanta, GA
Charles Bibeault / Providence, RI
Paulette A. Burrier / Ocean City, MD
Lori Burks / Clifton Forge, VA
Christopher Carpenter / Cherry Hill, NJ
Oscar Gonzales / Washington, DC
Alison Kaufmann / Berkeley, CA
William Krasner / Berwyn, PA
Oma Wilcox / Layton, UT
Stuart Zeno / Richmond, VA

Third Prize

Ralph Anderson / Getzville, NY
Marcia Vinson Arnold / Buena Park, CA
Beetle / Washington, DC
Judy A. Belew / Tempe, AZ
Bob Bird / Lindrith, NM
Clayton R. Bishop / Pratt, KS
P. J. Bresee-Haynes / San Diego, CA
Michael J. Browne / Long Beach, CA
John C. Bystra III / Citrus Heights, CA
Lauren Caldarera / Houston, TX
Amanda Carr / Charleston, WV
Edward J. Clark Jr. / Glenside, PA
Robert Clermont / Staten Island, NY
Dao Mary Do / Garden Grove, CA
Jane Dorr / Ann Arbor, MI
Branden Effland / Davenport, IA
Sally Fennell / Culver City, CA
Dodd C. Gengenbach / Memphis, TN
Kenneth Winton Glide / Royal Oak, MI
Shannon Haas / Mead, WA
Holly Hardin / Louisville, KY
Christopher S. Harris / Old Orchard Beach, ME
Richard G. Henriet / Fenton, MI
Nancy B. Hobbs / Dover-Foxcroft, ME
Jim Hoitt / Quincy, MA
Edwin M. Johnson / Albuquerque, NM
Jed Judd / Gunnison, UT
Mark Kearney / Marriottsville, MD
Zeev Kogen / New York, NY
Beth Anne Kuzmic / Kuau Mauie, HI
Kelly A. Matthews / Savannah, GA
Elizabeth McCabe / Easton PA
Lavonne McLean / Knoxville, TN
Cliff Moore / San Gabriel, CA
Rushanna Mukhamedianova / Los Angeles, CA
Laurie Nash / Farmington, MN
Clara Beth Negoro / Gardena, CA
Damaris M. Norman Sutton / Kilgore, TX
Racheal L. Ogrissey / North Canton, OH
Maureen O'Neal Pereira / Austin, TX
Desiree Petersen / Neosho, MO
Tony H. Price / Tacoma, WA
Johanna L. Prince / Ramsey, NJ
Rebecca L. Rapanault / West Haven, CT
Nick Reading / Indianapolis, IN
Gladys Reeve / Houston, TX
Shilpa Mahesh Sarang / Fort Worth, TX
Warren Shellington / Abingdon, VA
Richard J. Shepherd / Reno, NV
Shirley Shepard / Fort Worth, TX
Philip Sherrod / New York, NY
Angela Stover / New Wilmington, PA
David Tewes / Cincinnati, OH
Kimberly Thomson / Florence, KY
Jeffrey Totten / East Peoria, IL
Roslye B. Ultan / Minneapolis, MN
Denny G. Varney / Brooklyn, CT
William E. Young Jr. / Plymouth, MA
Shoshanna Zucker / Bronx, NY

Congratulations also to all semi-finalists.

Grand Prize Winner

Jezebel

The desert is a lady, fickle, coy and lightly clad,
With naked arms extended to a pioneering lad,
She hints of buried treasures and of secrets yet unknown,
That intimately lie within her womb of sand and stone.

She has her tender moments when she bows her head in prayer,
And breezes soft as cotton wave the sagebrush in her hair,
But like a fickle female with an ever-changing mood,
She calmly counts the cost of each and every interlude.

The slightest touch of anger brings a flush of scorching heat,
To make the pock-marked mountains bend to shade their burning feet,
And when the lady listens to the winds that howl and moan,
A spasm rocks her fickle flesh and quakes her sandy throne.

She rakes her icy fingers and a frigid frost is born,
A psychologic punishment to test her face and form,
But when the need arises for the love of man or beast,
She quickly dons a brilliant gown and spreads a tempting feast.

Then, coy, and prone to tease a bit, she strips her bosom bare,
And prostitutes her silver for a casual affair,
Still, lazy, lithe and lovely, with a Jezebelic brand,
The desert is a nymph endowed with virgin contraband.

Agnes Guilfoyle Edwards

Memory Maker

Look up! Up there!
The sky is flashing, sparkling, shimmering...
That's the word! Shimmering!
Shimmering with a fine flashing silver sheen,
Never before, or since, seen.

Stand here...in the shadow of the house.
Look up! Put the sun behind the roof line.
See it? Glittering, dancing, quivering!
Not visible north or east or west,
Only south — in the aura of the sun.

There! There it is. What is it?
The sky is alive with a lustrous light,
a wondrous silver shimmering...
The image flashed into a corner of my mind
And hid there for over fifty years.

A dark blue summer sky the setting
For millions of silky spider webs
(Nature's gossamer wind-blown strands
each with a tiny arachnoid tourist)
But of the shimmering a memory was made.

E. James Pickens Jr.

Death Valley (Dante's View)

We arrived at night far beyond the edge of my world.
The sky opened up for the starlight to flood our eyes.
It had been a long time on roads that wound with the hills and passes,
Lonely down the fields,
Lonely across the sea of scenes wisping by in wavelets echoed
from ripples caused by a stone tossed in deliberation.
The beats of my heart watched, cautious and apprehensive,
As the stillness of unseen motion blanket the pale valley floor.

The searing heat of the sun woke us to the precious, cool morning air.
We took to the canyons and highlands.
The crescent sand dunes writhed in the shape of the wind;
The mountains cradled the wide stretch of desert
within its palms.

The four of us perched at the jagged edges of purgatory
overlooking salt for the tears of millions
And space to give flight to the dreams of countless more.
We stood to feel the power of the wind-torn sky,
And cheered on the wind-born ravens who call us to embrace freedom;
The freedom the rhythm our heartbeat commands, our universe.

B. W. S. Lau

Ecstasy Of Life

It is nighttime as peace settles upon all that prevails
The soft moon rises casting its gentle light over the dale
Revealing the soft contour of the rolling hills and valley below
Peaceful beauty is taken in - behold!

The rolling hills and valley are gently resting at peace
A gentle warm breeze slowly causes calm to cease
The warm breeze caresses the hills and valley - they awake
In the moonlit night - steam rises from the lake.

The landscape, in its magnificence, is stirring to release
Peaceful co-existence, in the still of the night, will cease
The gentle breeze increases in its strength
Causing the tender grass to move its full length.

Glorious is the landscape as the wind caresses all below
Gently bringing forth life-reap what you sow
Blowing not too hard to hurt that which has been created
They sway together in harmony - elated!

The soft moon and warm sun share the day together
In Summer, Winter, Spring or Fall - whatever the weather
The universe is at peace in perfect bliss
Like two lovers - sharing with each - the ecstasy of a kiss!

Robert G. Lewis

Why Hate Over Love?

When darkness comes, and death colors the sky
the stars will fall like tear drops, from the Lord's eyes.
And the children will cry out, and ask why?
Why must people be this way?

As they drop to their knees,
and wrap their little arms around their mothers legs.
If anger burns with life then blood will fall
as a father gives away his last kiss,
to the one he loves. The last one of its kind.
Why most people be so cruel?

Fire burns the homes where love once rose.
Without love the garden shrivels and
The sun runs, and hides behind the mountains.
Never to be seen again.
Why must people fill their hearts with hate and fear?

While the rich man sits in his house and fills his heart with
intolerance, desperate children flood the streets, starving for
love and answers. Their hearts over flowing with love and hope,
to share with anyone who passes by.
I ask you why?

Stacy L. Keller

The Old Man

The old man walks alone, his back is bent, his head held low
The stone of life is around his neck it bends him like a bow
His old bones ache in the morning chill, he shuffles ever so slow
The cane in his hand he pokes at the ground
The voice of it is an eerie tip tap scraping sound
He mutters his blessings and curses so none can hear
Only blessings that matter only curses that cheer.
An old canvas bag holds he at his side
The faithful old fabric, his treasure it hides
Had a good life he mumbles as he passes along
Loved a good woman, my children grew strong
Memories flood through him as he stands at the gate
He shudders and thunders with anger and hate
The light of remembering leaves his face
He turns, he stumbles, he's fallen from grace
Alone, alone he cries and shakes his fist at the sky
Alone I was born, alone let me die.
The old man walks alone, his back is bent, his head held low
The stone of life is around his neck it bends him like a bow

Robert A. Bimson

Untitled

The world is a pedestal to which each of us own
The sun is our blanket that warms our heart mind and soul
The wind is our chime and our protector that blows away the cold
The moon is our soul that hangs ever so proud and bold
To all of those each of us are found drifting and wandering
in our calming sound
Where your mind is cleansed and body freed your calming
world is always in reach
In essence there is a body of water for your mind to bathe
and a refreshing breeze that will never fade.
The anger turmoil and stress that we feel deep down, these
things are always made better by our calming sound.

Robin James

"The Trees of God"

The trees of God stand straight and tall
A mighty fortress old.

They give us shade to keep us cool
And guard us from the cold.

Virginia Beckwith

every day

every day
the sun rises and sets
giving the night to the far away moon
the wind blows from the west
changing the weather's tune
a family says goodbye to a loved one
who has gone on to another life
a family rejoices at the birth of a little one
who will go on to overcome much strife
miracles occur beyond human imagination
bringing happiness across the sea
tragedies bring sadness to many in our nation
testing the faith of those who believe
these things happen without question
i wonder how to survive another day
of the ups and downs of life's many lessons
but, i know i will be okay
because i have you in my life
every day

l. mickie brannom

The Nearest Place To Heaven A Summer Afternoon

A warm breeze wafts through the Birch leaves
The sun slants for afternoon shadows
Hanging plants swing slowly in white pots
A happy child's high pitched voice is heard
On it's bare-footed way home from the sandy beach.

As always the distant lawn mower's hard earned groaning sound is heard.
Island magic far beyond swaying trees
Life is moving on the water, in boats, on the beaches in the shops.
Clerks looking at their watches toward the time to close the doors.

The telephone rings,
"Everyone is home" says my daughter.
How good it all is, I muse.

Margery H. Cory

...burn the flag

burn the flag...Burn the flag ... BURN THE FLAG! "GO AHEAD."
The supreme court of the United States has said, "It is ok to burn the flag."

But wait! is that a voice I hear? Quiet please! Help me listen:
Yes, barely a whisper, "The Boat and crew are on the ocean floor." [But we did not burn the flag]

"Our bomber exploded over Germany, the crew is dead." [But we did not burn the flag]

"How about Normandy or Pelilu or Guam or Flanders Field or Pearl Harbor or Midway or Vicksburg, Bataan and so many more? Military—civilian, all dead because of war...[But we did not burn the flag]

The lone whisper becomes a voice, growing, growing, ever growing
To a tumultuous shout, BUT WE DID NOT BURN THE FLAG!!

WHO THEN DID?

Maury Meister

Starting Over

Lost my job the other day.
Almost 21 years gone by the way.
Don't know how this could happen to me.
When all the time I was busy as a bee.
Gotta find another job to pay all my bills.
Hope none of my family comes down with any ills.
I'm hoping God has a better plan for me.
When it all comes together oh how happy I'll be.

Sy Payne

I Am Seven

I like rolipolies and snails
and dogs and other things with tails.
I like the moon and stars and the sky
and the lake and sea that are all so blue,
and the sunflowers are good too.

Seth Petersen

Summer Into Autumn

The days grow imperceptibly shorter by degrees,
the sweet tendrils of sunset's darkness
beckoning earlier and more colorfully
to the nesting crows of summer's eve,
temporarily resetting Nature's alarm clock.

The staunch sunflowers in the cracked, dusty fields
remain standing upright and slightly wilted,
much akin to dutiful soldiers
having fought and won a losing battle
with the intense rays of the brutal summer sun.

The tall shade trees formerly blossoming
with the essence of new life and hope
sluggishly shed their green overcoats of joy
leaf by solitary leaf
to don the protective brown shades of a new season.

The gentle breeze blows succinctly sharper with each passing day,
turning the air crisp, clear and fragrant
with the sadly unmistakable aroma
exuded solely by the inevitable seasonal exchange
of summer into autumn.

Michelle Chappelone

Wallflower

I cannot dance
the tango; cannot play the horn or even join
the coupling crowd;
I do not know my business on a wooden floor

is one golden man who pins me
down with his regard from over there
and turns me red.

I cannot breathe. He
must be why
I came

to stand along
the wall in the garden
among seedless women on the Eve.

To wear a dress
of lilac lace and taffeta
draped across my breasts and Baby's Breath
woven in the hair around my face
for this:

Man.

Lysa Fisk

"You Are Always There"

You are always there . . . always
The tender moments always caressing my thoughts.
The laughter so fresh and renewed with each remembrance.
You are always here - though you're not.
How can they understand? I grieve but I grieve not.
You are always there . . . always
You never leave me, but you're not here.
How silly they can not understand!
You are always there. Always

Teresa Glackin McCorkle

What's His Name

Mine eyes have seen, what you have spoken of.
The thunder and lightening, that comes from above.
Is it a sign or a symbol, what is it you're trying to say?
I respond to nothing, that is not of your way.
I worship the ground, that only my father walks on.
Not only do I praise him, when blessings have been bought upon.
I thank him every morning, for my life, health and strength.
He's the inspiration of my life, his love keeps me content.
He is the light of my on going tunnel, the key to my locked door.
The joy of my salvation, my heart, where his love, I store.
He is the fist that fights my battles, the sunshine to my dark days.
He died that we may have everlasting life, and we should
thank him in every way.
Sometimes when I am lonely, I ask, Lord what shall I do?
He says, "peace be still my child, your father is here with you."
Must I cry out to you, say Lord help me please.
Take all of the pain away, help me set my soul at ease.
Everyone has an idol, someone to look up to, a hero.
My hero's thee almighty King, Jehovah, His name is Jesus,
did you know?

Tanessa Moten

The Time

The time we have the time we share,
The time to see the time to care,
The time we walk the time we crawl,
The time to talk the time we sprawl,
The time to touch the time to taste,
Time is everything it is nothing to waste.

The time to hear babies cry,
And time to imagine angels sigh.
Memories are a special thing,
They help you remember the important things.

Mary Elizabeth Petit

To Be With You

I walk along this narrow path
The trees are old, the sky is dark
The demons, they lurk at my weary heart
Lightning strikes and thunder rolls
My breath is short as I grow cold
I stand and face that stone so grey
It's been two years ago from this May
The flowers I left are wilted and gone
The ties we tied are now undone
I've tried to face this world all alone
But the pain is too real, I can't go on
I can't call this a life in which I live
How can I love, when I have nothing to give
I feel you everywhere, but you're nowhere to be found
How am I supposed to hold you, when you're six feet underground
To be with you for now and for on
To be with you is what I want
That's why I take this knife upon my chest
To be with you forever, where you rest

Shane Beavers

thoughts of a seed...

Once I saw a meadow and I laid in it
and became one with its flowers and birds
and they called their friends the bunnies and the squirrels
and they played music of laughter and fun
then came the rain and I laid down my roots
sprouted branches to touch the heavens
and gave my fruit like candy to the world I see
for I was lucky enough to be a tree!

Timothy Alan Gettig

Rain

The breeze blows softly,
the trees sway back and forth.
As if to dance in the wind.
The crickets chirp, serenading me and you.
I lean back in your arms and search
the sky for rain. The clouds say
that rain is near. The breeze becomes a sign.
I feel a raindrop on my cheek,
or is that a tear drop?
You wipe it away and it becomes
nothing more than a drop of water.
Nothing more, not a care in the world.
So we lay back and wait for the
rain.

Vanessa Clark

"Rain"

I look up into the sky, what a beautiful day it is.
The warmth of the sun shines on me.
I look away, upon fresh green grass and abundant flowers in the field.
A moment, not too soon, I look back up into the sky.
Yet, to a surprise, a group of grey clouds pass by, covering the sun.
I gaze upon the park next to my house, deciding if I should play.
To test these clouds of grey, should I?
I stroll down the sidewalk, gazing at the sky.
Out of nowhere a flock of birds fly by.
Could this be a sign?
Creaking trees, rustling leaves, strong winds in the air.
Wondering, what's going to happen up there?
These clouds of grey multiply and turn a pale shade of black.
Still, no rain.
A weary silence hits the sky.
Suddenly, a loud noise and flashes of light fly by.
Could it be?
Rain drops fall on me.

Timothy A. Ward Jr.

My Burning Love

The way you made me feel when you held me in your arms at night.
The way my head rested against your chest, your embrace felt
as secure as a newborn in a mothers arms.

You had sweet romantic lines, which made my heart melt.
And he whispered, "You are my sunset along the sea at the end
of the day, and my sunrise at the beginning."

Through the days which follow, you will stay deep within my soul,
Never to return to the life I once had. I set my deep green eyes
upon the blue fire of love you sent burning through my heart.

The days of making sweet love, of helping our love grow ever
stronger, you will stay forever in the heart and soul of the
warrior, which is I.

Why do I love you the way that I do? How did you touch the
heart of a lonely, lonely man such as I? You are my woman,
my whole world. You make my heart soar like an eagle in the sky.

For these words he had said, have been of the past. For I am
old and these words still burn within my heart.

For I can see the grave and remember how he perceived me, though
he is no more, I can still feel the words, the fire and passion
of our burning love.

Shannon M. Hale

Untitled

candle flickering
the wind whispering
my name
breathing
your ears silently
blowing
listening to my
sighing
epitaph written
drifting
onto your mind
ceasing
me, remembering your tears on my grave.

Matt McClure

Me

The full moon arises as the beasts in me rage.
The wolf arises to give me power,
to understand my fears.
The deer then arises to give me love,
to show my compassion.
The final is the bear to give me hunger,
to know what I feel.
Only my heart can feel these animals.
Only my mind can hear their voices.
My soul is but a chamber,
for these animals are me.

Trish Berner

Grandpa's Woodshop

The pathway ends. Fingers untwine.
The wooden latch dangles from leather,
and rusty hinges creak into cluttered darkness.
Warped planks groan. Old wood and new teases my senses.
I follow, wide-eyed, scanning dark recesses.

In the blackness a twin-headed monstrosity stares.
Flared nostrils and menacing long horns;
I smell the scent of Buck and Bright.
Then sudden light through open shutters reveals
the massive oxen yoke hangs empty.

Now, the old man moves with purpose
placing tools and rough-hewn hardwood.
A shaft of brightness washes the workbench.
"What's that, Grandpa?" I climb onto a footstool.
"A vise," he answers. "A brace and bit"..."a plane."
Muscles bulge with each disciplined sweep down grain,
and walnut shavings roll to the floor.

I reach to caress each lovely, fragrant curl
falling through a golden beam of dancing wood dust.
I fill my gingham lap and my heart's desire.

Teresa Radford-Brooks

Time To Share

My journey as a poet has finally begun.
The words and the music do merge into one.
The world that surrounds me is so clear and new.
In all aspects of life I have a different point of view.
The worst is all over; the best yet to come.
God sketches life, draws life and even paints some.
The wind blows. The sun shines. It's cloudy and storms.
Life is very diverse. It can appear in all forms.
Bad things turn to good. Changes occur every hour.
But we must pay attention while we still have the power.
We have not relinquished it presently. There is time to spare.
But it won't last forever. Now's the time to be aware!
Spread out your hearts, poets, painters, artists of all kinds.
Let's share this news, the miracle of expanded minds.

Lisa M. Lindstrom

The Union Man

He goes to work, He works all day
The work is done, before he plays
If a fellow worker is in pain
He will help him onto his feet again
If he can lend a helping hand
He thinks it makes him a better man
He thinks we all can get along
And make right what is wrong
He pays his dues
He tries to be nice
He listens to others advice
The boss is right, he knows he is
The Union's plight is not his biz
But what is fair to all concerns the union man most
As he does his job and stands his post
He thinks we should all unite
Stand our ground and fight the fight
For what we know and feel is right
He thinks if we do we will all sleep better at night.

Sean McKnight

"Winter's Magic"

I find my happiness on a cold winter night.

The wind blows gently through my hair, all
The world seems right.

Standing on the edge of the wood, gazing as
the ice transforms barren trees into sculptures
that glitter like fine crystal, telling me that
will, is all that could.

A full moon shimmers, against a back ground of
a thousand stars, transforming the sky into a
velvety box of jewels money can't buy.

It is here I see the solitude that no one can seem to find.
Distant from the pressures of everyday life.
Where dreams remain possible, and life is without
turmoil or strife.

With an innocence the world will never know my
mind keeps telling me its only a dream.

But a world without hopes and dreams, and images
of the mind, can only lead one to believe that
any other world will never be so kind.

For dreams will always have a special place in time.

J. Frank Hall

Nobody Hears . . .

Where are you going? And where have you been?
The world spinning round...is there never an end?
Running and running, the clock never stops.
Going and coming. Nobody walks.
Nobody listens. Everyone talks....

Nothing's important, yet everything is,
This coming and going - A hit and a miss.
Who's wearing what? How much did it cost?
Who's seeing whom? Another soul lost?
Nobody listens, everyone talks....

A lonely boat, tossed on the waves
A shattered life - no time to save.
Hurry and give. Then take. Then balk.
Nobody listens, everyone talks....

The saints preach religion, the preachers cry "hell"
The world is in turmoil. Some say "all is well."
Faster and faster we spin through the days.
Wondering why, as we climb through the maze.
Pain in your body, the breath of life stopping.
But nobody hears, you! Everyone's talking.

Gaylene V. Kennedy

Green Trees

There were green trees with leaves like hands, stretching out their arms, wiggling their fingers trying to grab each other. They made a roof to our fort and we could lie on our backs and not have to worry about rain. We hated fuzzy caterpillars that held their meetings in the armpits of trees because we never knew where they would congregate next or how long their meetings would last, and we always ended up squishing our fingers right into their bellies when we tried to pull ourselves up. Then we'd have to scream, (just for effect), because slimy green blood would pulse through our fingers and we'd try to wipe it off on each other. That would break up those caterpillar meetings for sure.

Susan E. Sweat

Life's Greatest Treasure

What a beautiful winter season with trees all bending low.
Their leaves a downy blanket that softens the cover of snow.

The clouds all look like frosting piled high on creamy pies,
and birds that stay all winter, have plaintive, urgent cries.

They call for bits of bacon thrown under bushes near.
They want your voice, your gladness, to help them through the year.

And when the spring has wakened, and shoots of green poke through,
their songs will be a token of love and warmth for you.

So, Brooke and Jimmy take notice of the beauty all around.
That joy is there unbounded in the glorious springtime sounds.

You hold life's greatest treasure, as you share each other love,
and smiles of joy and pleasure are blessing from above,

And then you greet the raindrops that fall gently on each flower,
who's leaves are washed and polished through nature's cleansing hour.

And once more sunshine sparkles, and pebbles on the path
are shining bits of color for Brooke and Jimmy to pass.

Each day is filled with laughter, and love grows more and more,
and gifts of life grow greater as you share its glorious store.

To greet each and every morning with your bright and sunny smiles,
And say "I love you' dearly, that will make it all worthwhile.

Mary S. Goodman

Untitled

I love the way of the old ones.
Their way seemed good.
Through the eagle they could let their soul touch the sky.
They could hear secrets in the wind as it whispered through the trees.
In the sun they could watch their dreams.
In nature could be heard the songs of sorrow and joy.
Thankfulness belonged to the living sea and her mother the earth.
She offered gifts, her heart pounding against the sand.
The past could teach in the firelight.
Woman gained joy from giving.
Man gained pleasure from woman.
We are eating the earth with our greed,
Sometimes I like to think of the way of the old ones.

Rhonda Henderson

Christmas Eve

It's Christmas Eve
and the candles are glowing.
It's cold outside
and the wind is blowing.
You stay awake, hoping to see Santa appear.
but you fall asleep again this year.
You wake up Christmas morning wanting to shout.
But look! Over there! The candles have blown out.

Mary C. Wendt

Love And Life

If through the eyes one can see the soul,
then in the heart a story is told.
In the light we see things for what they are,
but in darkness reality seems a far.
As we age with mother nature,
every aspect is caught in nomenclature.
From birth to death there are stages,
For which there are too few gauges.
Time is constant and too fast,
For as we blink the present is the past.
Items of importance always change,
Due to the ease of forgetting which is strange.
Life and Love are an inseparable pair,
The loss of one brings despair.
In a family where ties are strong,
Quality is life and life is long.
If love in life is nonexistent,
A happy life cannot be consistent.

Travis Watkins

"Hopes And Dreams"

For many years these thoughts lay dormant, dead...
Then you came along and filled my head
With beautiful dreams of things that could be...
Of love and laughter and a bright shining sea
Of happiness, hopes and holding hands...
Of secret vows and wedding plans
Of caring and sharing and showing each other...
The depth of our love and growing together.

But, things seldom turn out as we want them to...
And God said; "Son, I have other things you must do!"
And as you turned to walk away, my heart cried out
"LORD, Please let him stay!"
He is tender, sensitive and caring ... your chosen one
A child of God . . . 'thy will be done'

LORD, when he has finished the task you command,
send him to me I'll wear his band...
And together through eternity we will stand
forever and ever ... hand in hand
AMEN.

Sharon L. Bigler

Setting You Free

The hurt is deep but the words are few
There are words I feel I must say to you
I know my words will fall upon deaf ears
Even though they are written in a blur of tears

My love meant nothing, no matter what I did
My love, tears and anger will now from you be hid
You have made your choice where you long to be
From my angry words I will now set you free

Our lives are separate, and that's how it will stay
Things will not change now matter what I might say
Your life is there and mine is down here
I knew this day would come——a day I would fear

The pain and anger in my life, I will not show
For my own peace of mind, I must now let you go
I'm getting tired and can no longer think
The words pass before me as fast as I blink

Your road of happiness may be through the next door
I pray you will find what you've been looking for
I'll love you always in the back of my mind
Peace, love and happiness I hope you will find

Vickie Moore

When You Were Not There

Dear Gabe,
There have been times,
When you were not there,
Times when you didn't even care;
But there have also been times when you helped us a lot,
It's times like that I try to remember.
Mom thought you would change,
But when you came back;
You were the same,
Gabe, you hurt her a lot.
I'm begging you,
Please, hurt her no more.
For it'd break more than her heart,
It'd break ours too.

Racheal Paul

"Without Words"

Without words, he expresses so very much;
There is his laughter, his smile, and his dear touch.
When he gives us a hug, we know where he stands;
We can feel the love and gentleness in his dear hands.
He doesn't show emotion with a smile or a tear;
But, if you listen to his heart; without words, you know he's near.
Even, without words, I know that he cares;
Because, the love that he owns, is the love that he shares.
The love that he gives, we will always receive;
And, the love without words, we will always believe.
We thank him for the love he gives; and wish for only this;
Even without words, He will send a hug and kiss!!

Mandi Stewart

My Love

There is no shapeness to flowers
There is not line to diamonds
My love for you is boundless
My heart and my life are full of love
I'm so glad you are in my life to love me
You lighten my heart when you talk
The touch of your hand held me throughout my life
My life is passing by, but I know you re not
The fear of losing you is the fear of losing myself
Even if die, I know I'll come back for you
You'll be the stone and I'll be the sun who will make you look golden for ever and ever
All I have at the sun, you'll know that's me who is watching over you
When you look at the stars, you'll know that's me who is shining
Without my golden light, you are a silver stone
Without you in every lives, I'm left with tears.

Umangi Shah

Who's There?

I stand here pondering life; and what do I see?
There is someone standing here; who has been watching me.
I ask, "Who's there?", and I wait for a reply.
Yet there is no answer, and I think to myself, why?
He has a face that; from somewhere I have known before.
His face looks kind; and many have come to adore.
The man is not lanky, yet his legs are kind of long.
He's worked very hard; and he has become very strong.
Yet there's a gentleness in his eyes that anyone can see.
He has a heart of gold that men it could fit in; two maybe three.
So, I called out once more; "Who are you, and why are you here?"
Then with a sigh of relief; I found I had nothing to fear.
For when I reached for the stranger, I noticed he reached for me.
Then I came to realize; My God! It's just the mirror image of me!

Lance C. Wood

Untitled

Down by where the weeping Willows Woe
There lives a women of whom I know
This woman who does little all day
Just sits and watches over the way

You may say that this is a bore
However you must know she does more
The one thing that may seem most odd
is that she cannot been seen

You see this old woman of whom I know
Who lives down by where the weeping willows woe
She is the mother of all mother's whose picture
hangs over the hearth
For you see this woman is Mother Earth

Of whom we are killing every day
As she just sits and watches over the way
"Don't worry" is what they say but are we sure of that
Or is it that we are too lazy and fat

Royce Kerley II

Poor Handwriting

My handwriting is in terrible shape
There seems to be no escape
My writing is one sloppy mess
It is readable less and less
I think that a horse could write better
I just scrawl letter after letter
I am so embarrassed that this handwriting is mine
I can barely stay on the line
I take my time and write real slow
It looks like I have written with my toe
I practice and practice but it does no good
The words don't come out the way they should
I bought a special pen to keep my hand steady
For my handwriting the world is not ready
The pen dripped ink all over the place
I am right back to first base
I would write you a letter, but please take heed
Not one word could you read

Winniferd Gilchrest

To Luke And Lawrence

Together, we had such a short, short time.
There was much hope, and then, you were gone. I know
Regret is, still, and sorrow. That is mine
To bear and share, but you two had to go,

Depart for other homes where joy and peace
Will be, and rest. I cannot understand,
But trust the change will bring you both release
From earthly cares and woes. A happier land

Is yours, right now, where you may laugh and cry
As much as each of you may wish. You are
Alive in my heart. I know I sigh and sigh,
But all is well with you and me. So far

You've gone, but not forever. I shall greet
You both, another time: Again, we'll meet.

Ron Taylor

A Prayer Unanswered

I would like to find that place where you keep your humanity,
And lie down beside it and be as "One" with you,
For there is the Glory and the Power and the God.

Peggy Sue Vickers

Living Lessons

In remembrance of my own school room years,
There were many of secret hurting tears,
Of feeling's not being understood, just another face,
Until, a strong teacher came who taught at his pace.
A man, who was a head of his time,
Who taught with eyes filled only of kind.
I vow to tell few teachers who reach,
To honor those special one's who teach.
The one's who try to comfort the misunderstood pain.
The one's who give and give, with nothing to gain.
I remember Mr. Kassak with warm and caring thought.
Impressions run deep from those who taught.
I will never see him again and that is sad.
But, to say thank you would make him so glad.
Gratitude goes to those who taught like he,
With a special understanding only the heart can see.
So thank you special ones that you are,
Your kind of caring will travel far.

Stella Kempisty

Alone

When at last the time has risen, to undo the deeds that were done, there will be much solitude, because you yourself stand alone. There is no one at your side, nor in front of behind. You have created your own destruction; golden sands of time, forgetting your acquaintances, needing no one to abide by, inducing agony to those with an inclination to care, but now being by yourself, you realize the mistake you made, retaining control you did not posses, trying to help those by neglection, but in reality only endeavoring to abet yourself unknowingly, to ease the pain and suffering, but now being unparalleled, you notice the anguish has only spread, and there is no indemnification. To only your beforehand, could have changed the path of life you took and led, then maybe you would not have done the deeds, that you now need to undo.

Leigh Troha

Invisible

I am invisible simply because people choose not to hear me.
Therefore, my thoughts and feelings are in no way released.
I talk and talk to try to be heard,
but no one hears, not one word.

If people don't listen to what I have to say,
I'll explode from frustration, eventually some day.
I'll scream and scream as loud as I can,
to make my words heard by every man.

Whatever is on my mind is important, I'd say,
and if you listen, it'll pay off some day.

Tiffany Mitchell

I Just Like Talkin'

Get up off that couch, a potato you're not
There's room at the spa; come fill the spot
Exercise with machines, they'll keep you arockin'
But as for me... I just like talkin'.

I hear the old pitch to keep physically fit
But before I get started, I'm ready to quit
Exercise machines bore me, I shouldn't be knockin'
But give me a phone and I'll exercise talkin'.

They say you should choose something you like
Jogging or weights, perhaps riding a bike
Do some aerobics? You're kidding of course
In those leotards, I feel like a horse.

Walking someday in heaven, God'll say to me
Come let us sit down, beside the Crystal Sea
"Lord, it's so much fun to be with you walkin'"
But let's do sit down, I just love talkin'

Ruth A. Amato

I Need Help To

I tell you there's a man over there and he ain't got no shoes.
There's a lady sitting next to him shouting about how she's
paid her dues, and all she has to show for it is a bad case
of the blues.

Paid her dues I say, I see that same lady sitting on that same
bench each and every single day.

Now you walk about two blocks down and here's what you might
see, grown men and women with children talking bout what you
got to give me.

Give? Give? I shake my head and throw my hands up and say
God almighty I wish I could put something in your cup.

But my pockets are hanging out, there sure enough on E, I'm
walking down these streets wondering what somebody's gonna
give me.

So I keep on walking real fast now, trying to forget what I've
seen, although I don't know how, I'm not trying to be mean.

It's just so hard to think about how to help you when I'm having
hard times,"hell I need help to."

Valerie Grisby-Hurdle

A Minute Of Life

Have you ever sat and looked around and often wondered why
there's so much beauty in the world, yet people pass it by?
They're too busy from the time they awake until it's time to rest
That they can't take a minute to see a bird's new nest, or
Perhaps the flower that peeked out first of all,
Or the tree nearby that grew another inch tall.
How picturesque the clouds on the waters do reflect
The small or tallest mountains that stand so erect,
It's the peace and quiet of the world that God has made aware
Yet there are so many of us who don't realize it's there
It has been since the beginning of time and don't you know or care
That when your time has come to die, the beauty stays right here?
So take the time to enjoy the things in life that are free,
Whether it be the smallest flower or the tallest of the trees,
And in this great big land of ours so full of history
And all of those who worked and died to keep this country free,
Two hundred years have come and gone, but how many of us
Have neglected the beauty in it? So
Let's do ourselves a very proud thing and take life's precious minute.

P. E. Potter

I Am A Person

This is not a person,
 these figures on a line.
This is not a person,
 letters aren't divine.

A person is...
 beauty, echoed in a flower.
 laughter, ringing from the hill.
 love, growing in kindness.
 tears, falling on a frown.
 time, giving of itself.
 thought, shaping confusion.
 vision, looking ahead.
 music, caressing disaster.
 water, a being that ripples through a world of rocks and lilies,
  supporting each droplet that washes by,
  falling freely in the blink of an eye.

I am a person,
I laugh, I cry, I give of myself, I reach for the sky.

Shawna Klinesteker

Death Beyond Compare

"Dad here's my report card," I said with a sigh.
"These grades aren't good," my dad replied.
"I'm sorry," I said" I tried my best."
"Hold on," he said, "Let me look at the rest."
"They are all good except for the one."
"The 'D+' you mean what have you done."

Sharla Ann Bailey

Untitled

This circle of women
These women who celebrate life,
who celebrate love, who celebrate friendship.

Tenders of homes, lovers of gardens.
Those who sow and those who water,
Those who prune and those who graft.

SINGERS OF THE SONG! HEARTS FULL OF MUSIC AND JOY!

Some old and bone brittle, bent and prayerful,
These tearful women, lovers of children, lovers of grandchildren,
the story readers, the listeners.
Some young, who take up the strength of service,
those who are learning the song.

This circle of women, these Martha's these Mary's.
The ebb and flow of age, passing of wisdom. Gentle encouragement,

These Belles, these Bouquets, these Spirit Fragranced Women,

Women of Will, Women of Grace, WARRIORS OF GOD.

Marcia Wright

The Dance

Tell me... do you see the people dancing?
They are dancing the destruction of the world...
To the beat of the big bass drum.
See the horror of the dancers engulf and captivate the watchers...
Total agony tearing their faces into unrecognizable shreds of flesh.
The watchers try to pull away from this terrifying show of madness...
Yet they are intrigued...
They can't pull away, for they are drawn forward...
Slowly, steadily becoming dancers of destruction... themselves.
This cycle continues... pulsating forth...
Never leaving a sane survivor behind.
All engulfed will soon be mad...
Mad with destruction beating in their hearts...
Waiting to draw more in...
Into the fire that burns with uncontrollable passion...
That causes pain... yet feels so good.

Yvonne Choy

Asking Why

Two little boys, died that sad day.
They are with God, so they are okay.
How could their mother, just let them die.
I am sure, God also asks, why.
They were so small, and trusting I'm sure.
How could their mother, just close the door
She had some problems, in her sad life.
But, killing her sons won't make it alright
Think of the horror those children went through
I couldn't do that to my children, could you.
They sleep on clouds, surrounded by love.
Angels will help them, bloom up above.
God, will help them to love and to trust.
I just hope, he can also help us.
Deep in our hearts, we must learn to forgive.
For, it's up to God, if Susan Smith lives.

Mavis A. Castleberry

The Weeks Before Christmas

'Tis just before Christmas, students' spirits run high.
They are very restless as vacation draws nigh.
We teachers are watching our flocks every day.
Each evening at home, we rest up and pray.
We teach them, we praise them, do all that and more,
Yet find ourselves asking, "What's it all for?"
They enter our classrooms each day of the week,
Personalities vary, and some are not meek.
We try every day to establish rapport,
To make an impression 'fore they go out that door.
It often seems futile, we tend to get down,
But sooner or later most do come around.
Little changes aren't obvious to us day to day,
Sometimes we're too close as we show them the way.
We must try to remember the lives we do touch,
Not all to be sure, but for some we do much.
And so as we gather at this time of year,
May our hearts remind us to lend a kind ear.
Let us smile at each other, as we pass in the hall.
May this season renew us - Merry Christmas to all!

Patricia McPhetres Basden

The Dreamers Alaskan Anthem

Scaredy cat hiding in the woods. Life passes me by always. They flinch. They? Who are they? They are those who believe in nothing.

Cherries. The red color. Maroon maybe? I didn't come here to run away. I came here to take control of my existence.

That thing you call... life?

They treat me like the four letter word adults scorn at. What are adults? Parental units? What is that? They are assigned to us. She didn't fail. Neither did he. I took control of my existence I didn't runaway. I'm starting a new life. In the cold I wait. Wait for what? They thought it was cold down there

wait till they get to the Arctic Circle.

Life. Everyone has the right. Those like me we don't just use that right we are those who make something out of it. We look at opportunities, we take the challenge. We dare to dream. For us tomorrow is another day and then... once again we dare to dream.

Stewart Schuster

The Quest

On their quest for perfection
They hath begetted the edge
In its ever growing steepness
and venomous sledge
It grew till its height, an unbearable peek
With the help of their push would engender
eternal sleep
For their quest of his perfection
Though a might worthy cause
Would surely the boy shatter
Under detrimental claws
And so they pushed on in their almighty quest
Lacking the knowledge to know what was best
And toward the end as their push grew too strong
They heard a cry; but too late, he was gone
For over the edge and down he went
Though anguish and toil his life had been spent

Paul Schafnitz

Take Time

People live day after day.
They pass on the streets, without a word to say.
There always competing to get ahead.
not even knowing what anyone has said.
They don't take time to wave or smile
but will ask for the inch, and take a mile.

Time is the word, cause it's all we've got,
but many don't understand, its the way they've been taught.
So when you go out, Take Time, look around!
Cause who knows, what your looking for
just might be found!

Larry M. Nicholls

Death Upon Us

As family and friends gather to say their last good-byes...
They reminisce, trade stories, and wipe their eyes...

Time spent will be cherished and memories held near...
So we need not worry and live in the fear...

Death is often seen with much despise...
Always having to question the why, why, whys...

Just hold on to the love that has been so dear...
And if need be, shed a tear...

When one does not allow one's self to mourn...
Our lives become empty and held in scorn...

Sharon L. Burleigh

Zoe's Eyes

I saw her eyes
They struck me with awe
They overwhelmed me with amazement
Her eyes were deeper than the color of the waves of
the Caribbean
Brighter than the clear blue sky
More tranquilizing than the blue on the mountains
that seem to touch the heavens
More brilliant than morning glories peaking through
the grass sprinkled with dew before sunrise
Zoe's eyes.

Trinette La Shawn Hicks

Dare to Discover Friendship

A friend is someone you like to be around;
They're always there for you, just to be pals.
Friendship is blind to size, beauty and race.
Friends look for inner beauty, not just what's on
your face.
A friend will cheer you up, when you're down,
Because they care and don't like to see you frown.
A true friend keeps in touch through moves and other
hard situations.
And sends you a postcard from every vacation.
To make a lasting relationship, keep up your end of
the deal, too.
Your friendship won't last long if your partner does
all the work for you.
Friendship is sometimes like seasons of the year;
Winter represents hardship, followed by spring
which brings cheer.
Friendship includes a special kind of love,
A kind that includes 'all of the above'.

Mendi Chappell

Impact of a Dream in a Wandering Mind

I cannot take control of my thoughts anymore.
They're swimming and swarming above me,
just out of my reach.
My highest leap only inches away from
grasping one of the ideas I once possessed.
So they fly above me,
mocking me as they flutter in circles.
I stand.
I stand with my arms shrug
and a lifeless mask covering my face.
I can't think.
My mind is stuck on a single
track on a train of thought.
I know not where it is headed, yet I am anxious
for the next stop, possibly to board a different train.
A train with new opportunities, new ideas.
A train where I will rule my mind,
where I will be the master of my dreams.
Until then, I stand here
waiting for the train to hit me.

Matthew H. Holmes

Brown, Misty Room

There, in a brown, misty room, I sat—
Thinking and wondering
And searching for the answers—
For the truth.
I was pensive, melancholy;
Reveling in the truth and in wisdom to come.
A window was open in this brown, misty room.
One window.
Its curtains gently shifted from within the room
To the cold night air outside.
Everything on the outside
Seemed artificial and deliberately slow.
The street light had become moon,
And, as the curtain continued to drift,
Automobiles whispered, "I am your future."
Unyielding, the curtain swayed,
Taunting me as it did.
In and out, in and out...the curtain swayed...
In and out...

Monique Hazeur

"His Little Lamb"

No time for rehearsal,
This grave day of reversal.
Nearly dead on the day He died,
Justified to take the gentle ride.

Her sweet gentle spirit aglow,
His recipient was absolved to go.
Prayers ceased, released to God,
All wills succumb, He would only nod.

For His "little lamb," He delayed transfer,
For He wished to endow us with His nectar.
His "little lamb" of divine rebirth,
Has been risen by Him on earth.

This ultimate Sacrifice - to heal, to stay,
His "little lamb" - our sweet mama, here today!
She only asks that we should pray,
For she knows He is here today!

Her spirit flowing this deep belief,
She remained through our time of grief.
On His day the Spirit gently came,
and she left us without blame.

Lucille Jacobs

The Night Country

My Mind keeps on going back to it,
This image of us running free under starlight,
Our bodies light as the air which flows over us like water, as we run, naked,
the short grass welcoming to our feet.
It's not the walls of Olduvai Gorge which surround us;
the level plain stretches for miles.
We are in the High Country.

Perhaps we will always run there,
Lions pacing beside us,
Delighting in our company, our laughter,
Joining in our hunger as we, in our hunger, join.

It is always night, there,
Just as we seemed forever night to me,
Not the sun-drenched light, falsely cheerful,
enslaved eyes all unknowing,
We are creatures of the night together,
Where trees sing to us,
And scents drench us, matching their passion to ours.
And the birds' flights across the sky are tracked upon our skin like the stars track their courses through the night.

Steven Wadas

Contrast

I am alone in love, in love with the pain.
This pain knows me well, it's presence keeps me sane.
Without my lover I would not know pleasure in my life.
Without my lover pain I'd have no strength to be his wife.
Good and evil, black and white; apathy the twin to grey.
I fade to black with empathy towards those who are in fact...
In love with the pain.
If only to remind themselves of those times when the ecstasy of life does come. For it is those times:
The love, laughter, joy, birth, elation, creation...
That makes us know..
The pain is soon to follow, soon to linger, soon to pass...
And soon will come again.

K. M. Ruppel

The Stranger

There he stood invading my space
This total stranger with the familiar face
When I was a child he left me alone
Now he returned now that I have grown
What did he possibly think he could gain
After all those years he caused me pain
All those times I yearned for a dad
Now here before me stood this cad
This man saying he was my father
was really nothing more than bother
he knew nothing at all about me
nor had he ever cared far as I could see
If even once he had bothered to call
we may not be in this position at all
Now as he stood before me I wanted to squirm
he was only my father because he donated his sperm
As I turned and walked away I started to smile
I could finally rest after all this while
I had became this great person at my own pace
Without this stranger with the familiar face.

Laura Lambie Swanson

Without Love

Isolated in a world of death and darkness,
This world I'm lost in is void of happiness.
Alone; with only my thoughts to think,
My love for you is the missing link.
To the world I've left behind,
Because of you, I'm left here to find.
My only company are the shadows.
These shadows were once people like me,
Don't you see? Soon like them I'll be!
Alone, forgotten, and left behind,
Without out another of their kind.
Please don't leave me here, apart from you,
I feel them taking over, isn't there something you can do?
The answer is simple and always will be,
The answer is easy, love is the key.
Love is the key to the door of this land
Please tell me that you understand.
Unlock the door, let in the light,
Please end my everlasting fight with the doom of night.
Because without your love my day is night.

Staci Smith

A Golden Life Together

It's been fifty years since your vows were said.
Those sweet words 'I Do' and 'I Thee Wed'.
Today is proof that some loves are true,
One has to look no further than at the two of you.
Golden memories of a life together you share,
Hold them close to your heart for they are so rare.
Your unconditional love has touched so many lives
Your sons, a daughter, grandchildren, are husbands and wives.
We love you both more than words can say,
It can not be expressed fully in any way.
Now continue on with your wonderful life
Just as you promised when you vowed to be 'Husband And Wife'
And always hold the words 'I Love You' dear to your heart,
Just as you don't fifty years ago
When you said to each other 'Til Death Do Us Part'

Ray Helper

What Does It Mean To You?

It's raised every morning, and taken down every night
Those thirteen bars and fifty stars,
What does it mean to you?

Men who fought, men who died and those men who lived
But wished they were among the graves

What about the teenagers who just began to live?
As quick as their adulthood came, it was take away, or ruined forever
Have you ever counted how many times you said "I wanna go home?"

Women who lost their husbands, children who lost their fathers
The country that turned their heads away when the men
representing their country, and who would have died for it,
returned home

When you see the names on the wall, do you see a bunch of
strangers, or do you see their reflection looking back at you?

Do you see the names and think you can't count that high,
or do you realize that these men are special and they died for you?

The next time you see the American flag, know what it means,
why it's there, how it got there, and who died for it

Melissa Saldutti

Love

Love is something hard to describe
Though many have tried and get filled with lies
Some complain it's hard to explain
Due to it being filled with happiness and pain
It's quiet a task, so many ask
Is it the warm of the sun after a cold rainy night
Or watching a bird in it's solitary flight
Is it the touch of a child or a word spoken mild
Is it a meeting of hearts or paths that will part
Is it laughter and teasing and looks that are pleasing
Or is it sorrow and pain and hopes that will wane
Is it only for the young as many have sung
Or can even the older still want to hold her
Is it a holding on tight with all your might waiting for Mr. Right
Or a letting go and watching it flow who can know
Will we know if it's right and pure
Only time will tell for sure

Lisa Leville

Sensations

Many things created by nature have yet to be explained.
Though, somehow they make us smile...taking with them
all sadness and pain.

Birds sing songs like never heard before and you long
for them to continue singing until, suddenly, you cry
no more.

You feel the cool sand as it forms beneath your feet.
Without any warning, tensions are gone as your mind
is swept away for a much needed retreat.

A gentle breeze brushes across your face and your once
anchored spirit soars like a bird, filled with freedom
and grace.

These things are good, without explanation.
They exist, merely, to bring us joy and
wonderful sensations.

Sylvia W. Wilson

Untitled

Rivers full of dreams
Thoughts going down streams
Hopes hit rocked walls
Love goes down waterfalls
I look patiently at the moon
And hoping one day, just one day soon
That as I turn to each star
Believing they are near and not far
That I am getting closer day by day
To a new and yet better way
of living out all my dreams
Instead of sending them down streams
Putting my hopes up high
Then kissing my first true love good-bye.

Mary C. Alley

The New Kid In School

When you're the new kid in school you get some dirty looks, and a lot of new books.

When you're walking down the hall people stop you and ask you questions that are off-the-wall.

Then when I was walking to my first, second and third period classes, bullies stopped me and broke my glasses.

The rest of the day I couldn't see a thing, so I was so relieved when I heard the bell ring.

Lizabeth S. West

Melancholy Lights

Warm, radiant lights of melancholy shine upon my soul, when happy thoughts of childhood days bring memories of school attendance rolls.

The lights illuminate a well remembered smell, of running through warm fields of swaying arms of grain, the schoolhouse cradled in the dell.

Oh sweet remembrance of summer days, the one room school house, the
yearning, for the recess bell to toll and free my spirit, trapped
in those rows of seated learning.

Rays of melancholy display my hearts' desire for friends and play, for childish bantering along the way to home and love, at end of schoolhouse day.

The lights display the passing years, the schools and friends, their happy lives traversing through those final years, to childhood's end.

Higher learning merges with sweethearts and proms, bands and sports and cheers, till baccalaureate and diploma toll the bell, to end those wonderful years.

Though the final bell will someday sound for this poetic soul, the lights will shine forever, it's just a recess toll.

J. D. Hummel

Untitled

A phrase, a word, a note of song; Trembling with questions and
anxiety
Three hundred years of terror is hard to wash away
Out thoughts run deep, our memories long; surrounding subtle
forms of
propriety
In sundry muted shades of grey

We sleep and yet we have no rest, in our minds the questions lie
Eternally replay the past
As we put our freedom to the test, spreading our wings we start to fly
Will peace within be ours at last?

Oh troubled souls with heavy hearts, they slump in needless shame
Stuck yet not sure why
Angry, screaming from the start, stripped of our rightful names
Inside ourselves we cry

Take care, wake up don't ruin yourself (remember but don't dwell)
We change the future not the past
In coming years lies all our wealth which only God can tell
And peace within will come at last

Tina M. Wright

Rich Quick

I made fun of the whole thing
Threw it in the trash
I should have kept it there
Lord, I should have kept it there.

A pox
A plague

And all would turn
On forces found by angry wives
But refuse is no refuge for the vitally misplaced
She picked it up and mailed it off.

If only Prometheus
Had just asked a little less
We'd all be cold today.

If only she'd been shy
More reluctant to comply
I'd be happier this way.

Thomas Haring

"Expected Expectations"

Heaven, Nirvana, Heaven of heavens,
throne of God, inheritants of the saints in light,
Paradise, Eden, heavenly city, Celestial bliss,
eternal bliss, happy hunting grounds, the Highest heaven,
eternal home, resurrection, Bottomless pit,
Habitation of fallen angels, everlasting fire, lake of fire,
worm that never dies, purgatory abyss, Hades,
inferno shades below, rivers of hell, beauty unadorned,
charm, calmness, gentleness, mental calmness,
relaxation, remission, tranquilization, sedative,
soothing syrup, compose, quiet, bliss, pacify,
rock to sleep, subconscious self, provisions,
telephatic Hallucinations, premonitory apparitions,
death lights, crystal vision, speculum, reflector,
mother love, God of love, Karma, bud, blossom,
bloom, flower, Sunshine, Solace,
Salvation.

Levi Green

Your Daddy And I

We've traveled together, your Daddy and I,
Through all kinds of weather, with smile and with sigh.
We've traveled together, your Daddy and I,
When life has grown weary and death has been nigh.

All through the darkness of mist or of wrong,
We've found there was solace in prayer or in song.

There have been bad times and sad times,
But also good times and happy times
We've shared them all together,
In all kinds of weather.

So now, what could part us, your Daddy and I?
Shall disappointment, discouragement, or all things that try?
Oh no, my dear children, we will walk in the light,
Using the Sword of the Spirit to put these things to flight.

And still through life's journey, until our last sigh,
We'll jut stick together - your Daddy and I.

Take courage, dear children, do not stumble,
Though your path be dark as night.
There is a Star to guide the humble,
Just trust in God and do what's right.

Pearlie Dupree

To My Far-Away Friend

If an eye could see could gaze
Through physical limits
And see the soul
The eternal part of me
Which does not breathe yet
Lives forever

It would hear and feel the
Pain possessed heart that
Silently and oft subconsciously
Weeps its bitter agony
And reaches out for a heart that hears that cares
The heart of a friend

Sometimes more and sometimes less
Yet often do I wish you were here
A tear stained heart cannot be healed but by time
The need to wait till time has come
And meanwhile say
I miss you friend

Sabine Munzinger

To The Mirror-Lady In Her Tower-Prison

Now, 'gainst western sky, across the river,
Thy tower, a-sparkle when morning-lit,
Shows somber in night shadow.

Where Heaven comes down to earth
And western hill reaches up to sky,
Thou, with upraised mirror, horizon-outlined.

Thou hast no thought of me
In thy tower retreat from life,
Among thy memory-kept mirror-thoughts.

High hidden in your prison tower,
Thy former glories, bygone images,
Are barely remembered in darkened windows.

Set thyself free! Breathe deep the air!
Look outward from thy refuge
And hurl thy prison-mirror on the rocks below!

But, stay! Decree not thus thy doom!
End not thy life in scattered shards!
No, remain forever in mirror pose, inviolate,

In Prison-Tower, 'gainst western sky,
As I face west, atop my western hill.

Royce W. Miller

"I, The Wind"

Whispering among the forest frees,
Tilting their leaves in rhythmic silence,
Playing nature's melodies on the marsh's tall reeds
As I blow across wetlands with soft spoken reverence...

I bring to your senses sounds of the past,
Fragrances I offer from lands far away,
A merchant I am, my travels are vast,
A wanderer am I, never to stay...

Surrounding and swirling everywhere I am found,
Yet when I steep my name you'll not hear,
I can move with such grace in any direction I'm bound,
I can cause quiet a havoc when my mood is Austere...

I usher in seasons, I escort them out,
The eagle's comparison, the swallow's highway,
I have many callings, there seems no doubt,
Come and go as I please, I do as I may...

I can carry your kiss to the lover you miss,
I can change the array of clouds in the sky,
Should you wonder my name or if I exist,
One answer to both ... the wind, this is I.

Robley B. Hayes

Time

Time holds everything to us so dear.
Time is the water gently flowing down the
Mountain stream.
Time is when you listen to the birds singing
And watch the animals playing in the woods.
Time to me is everything good.
Time is love, sometimes fear.
Time is family going out on their own.
Time is slipping past me as I grow old.
Time is a child's gentle kiss on your face.
Time is sunrise so beautiful spring, summer, and fall.
Winter sunrise can be a cast of purple and pink
In the sky with the snow on the trees a picture to
behold.
Time is sunset with its glow of yellow and red
spread across the sky.
It is something to see and enjoy
The wonders of the earth.
All of these memories we don't want to erase.

Shirley Henze

Changes

Days pass by, time moves on.
'Tis but a short time, and then we are gone.
Summers come, summers go.
Winters chill, winters snow.
Spring is fresh, Fall is crisp.
Always changing, that's the gist.
For change, it changes everything.
Summer, Winter, Fall and Spring.
Change is there, and we must change.
No matter how hard, difficult and or strange.

Sam Fox

Love Is Like A Roller Coaster...

Love has often been compared
to a roller coaster with
its ups and downs,
twist and turns.
Not knowing
which way to go,
which turn
to take.
And, it often leaves us breathless
when we plummet from the pinnacle
then climb again,
zigging and zagging our way around
one curve after another.
But we almost always end up where we belong.
The highs are seldom great as
they seem, but neither are the lows as deep
and depressing as they seem
at the time, in this crazy business
that we proudly refer to as eternal
and undying..... Love

Timothy M. Churchill

Three Score And Six

One year over the traditional three score and five. It is still great to be alive. Ponder, ponder, ponder, what direction should one take? Look backward, look forward, look both ways and what are the stakes.

Look back and the mirror reflects, good times, bad times, good deeds, bad deeds, accomplishments and mistakes, enjoyment and disillusionment.

Look back, inwardly, have you benefited from the experiences? Have you learned the lessons, are you better for having lived? If not, you are subject to pity and perhaps sympathy. If so, the golden years will carry a rich reward.

Look forward, and the eyes grow dimmer, the hearing falters, the steps lose their resiliency, but never you mind, keep the brain alert and the spirit willing.

Look forward, and the forces of society and economics will push you to pasture voluntarily or involuntarily.

Resist, resist, resist, do not let it happen, for if it does, the machinery will rust and corrode and you become an empty shell.

Resolve to stay young in thought, keep working, oiling and honing and life at three score and six will be the best ever. So look backward, look forward, look both ways, but never stop looking until the final curtain comes down.

Sam Posner

I Look Down And My Shoes Are Filled With Feet

What would happen if the word for what you know
To be "apple" was switched with "weasel?"
Would we say "as American as baseball, Mom,
And weasel pie?"
Cortland, Ida Red and Granny Smith weasels.
"Oh dear, let's go for a stroll through the
Weasel orchard."
A weasel a day keeps the doctor away.
Could, in fact, the word "apple" mean "flightless waterfowl" or
"the feeling one gets when lied to," in another literate reality?
Words are meant to mangle-wrangle, twist and bend and do our
Will. Frolic like old sausages and cry like pitchers of hot
Milk. The laws governing them are no more binding than those over
You. They were meant to be broken. That's when they
Sizzle, for like salt it gives them taste. You don't really have
To pay your taxes, and verbs don't have to verb.
Essays explain, books control, pamphlets taunt and billboards
Yodel. Poems are puzzles, they aren't meant to be keys.
Most are lumps of mashed up Wonderbread, unsuitable for turning
The lock.

Peter Kelly

To Be Free.......To Be Me

Is this freedom?
  To be born out of slavery, yet still bound
    by tradition, rules, conscience, and loyalty.
  To be educated, yet restricted by past practices, narrow view,
    inner conflicts, and status quo.
  To be creative, yet stifled by lack of vision, negative
    vibrations, censoring words, and unthinking
    thoughts.
Or is this freedom?
  To be free, unfettered
    to travel and explore,
    to communicate and express,
    to experience and remember,
    to delight and enjoy.
  To be free, unrestricted by people, things, situations,
    and confronting thoughts.
  To be free, creative, visionary, positive, supportive,
    loving and caring.

To be free is to be ME.

Patricia J. Baker

Encourage

I encourage you,
to be... to fly... to soar.
To open wide, what were once closed doors.
I encourage you,
to see... to try... to do,
everything positive, that resides inside of you.
No regrets, no complacent sighs.
I encourage you,
to master all that you touch.
And leave your mark, upon doing such.
To take pride, when your name,
rolls off the tongues, of those impressed,
with a job well done!
I encourage you,
to go, to your land of dreams.
And render them into reality.
Let no force, hinder you,
Now that you're on your way . . .
Seizing the moments, forging like a Smithy, molten steel... the days.
I encourage you, in every way...

LueWana J. Bankston

I Give My Love

To thee whom I give all my love and care,
To betray you my heart never dares.
Please you in every way is what I strive,
One look brings my love for you alive.
Our love is true, that is what I believe.
No beauty but yours, my heart will not deceive.
Passionate can be the love I feel for you,
Our love will last, I hold that true.
Our love is a flame, forever shall it burn.
If love is your lesson may I always learn.
When I look into your eyes, my heart goes a blaze.
Your love fills the empty space during long days.

Pasquale DiMassa Jr.

You

To rage the powers of the fight,
to brighten the darkness of the night,
to heal these wounds and make wrongs right,
this is life.

To pet a purring cat and relax the inner soul,
to help a bleeding poor man become one in whole,
to help someone get their life under control,
this is happiness.

To feel good about yourself and the clothes you wear,
to like the way you walk and talk and how you comb your hair,
to keep your mind healthy, alert, and really very aware,
this is confidence.

To get jitters when a special someone walks by,
to see the world unending as all water and sky,
to promise your heart to someone until you both shall die,
this is love.

When you add this life, love, and happiness your almost half way through, your confidence in yourself and others gives you something true, it brings out a wonderful, healthy, ever so special you!

Ray J. Carter

The Shattered Crystal

You step into a darkened tent, out of the wind and rain,
To catch a glimpse of what the passage of time will bring,
In desperation you have tried to erase your life-long pain,
And find the magic that will make your sore heart and soul sing.
The Gypsy stands across the room, adorned in a cloak of black,
Then a voice sounds forth behind a veil that keeps her hidden.
"Come, sit down," she commands, then slowly turns her back,
Reluctantly, you move forward to do as you were bidden.
The Gypsy turns, and in her hands, she holds a crystal ball,
The colors marble together like valuable masterpieces,
Suddenly the Gypsy screams, and lets the crystal fall!
You watch in horror as it smashes into a thousand pieces.
You start to rise, but she places a weathered hand on your arm,
Her fingers are bonny and crooked; and her voice is suddenly old:
"Do not leave, do not run away, or feel any alarm,
That crystal ball is worthless. Listen to what you are told.
You cannot find any happiness in what you see today,
For your complaints are many, and your heart is full of strife;
You will find joy on the morrow, if you learn to love this day,
And you will find contentment for all the days of your life."

Lisa Post

To Live Well

To live passionately
and bestow upon others much of your spirit.
Something lasting...
far beyond the physical presence.

Mariana Berner

I Wonder

I wonder how it would feel to grow up innocent;
  To discover the troubles of the world slowly.
I wonder how it would feel to have a life of self respect;
  Not a life of constant disrespect.
I wonder how it would feel to love someone, not just a friend;
  A love towards a stranger turned companion for life.
I wonder how it would feel to not be on guard;
  To trust another at word, not think of their past disregard.
I wonder how it would feel to be happy without contemplation;
  I just wonder.

Natalie N. Brooks

Foreboding Splendor

My death is planned — my mind is made up.
To dispose of my life — you'll think it's corrupt.

To self-destruct is my only goal.
Just watch my act. Please pay your toll.

It might be ill you won't forget.
A four star show you won't regret.

A noose on my neck, a gun to my head.
A bomb to my waist for sure I'm dead.

My neck will break, my brains will splatter.
Intestines explode a blood cake batter.

Clean up my mess you've had your fun.
If you get old please tell your son.

That I deserved the Oscar.

Phil Hopkins

Soldier's Private War

They told me to forget the scene,
to erase it from my mind.

But they didn't see the horror or feel the sorrow,
They can't comprehend the death and agony which followed.
My world caved in on me,
Suffocating me before I could react.

Trapped in a lifetime of hate
That can never see the light of day
Never having anything except my silent darkness.

No sense of love or peace, or even life itself
Just my mission to seek and destroy.
An empty hearted killing machine.

My world was made so I could suffer.

And the time had come when I ripped out my heart
You all gasped.
I dropped to my knees in front of a mirror
Then I watched myself die.

Now please let the vultures have me,
Let me rot where I lie.

Michael Paul Sprague

Third Eye/Third Ear

It is thru the dark of night, that all things are seen;
And, thru deafening silence that all things are heard;
The quiet of silence is deafening....
And, it is in fact the loudest sound you will ever hear.
Anyone, can speak loud enough to be heard;
But, it is thru deafening silence that the real
message is given and comes..

Olivia D. Lawe

A Revolution

I dwell alone in complete darkness, trying to reach down from within to find an answer why life can be so cruel.

Initially being optimistic I thought to myself life is too short to let things get me down.

However, I was naive to the tortuous situations that awaited me.

Feeling suicidal frequently, I questioned my sanity before indulging in such matters. Then it came to me. It was God's fault.

How could he let so many things happen if he is such a good understanding, and kind God.

Alas! In the middle of my rage, I looked upwards as lightening scattered across the sky. I saw the figure of an illuminated strong man. It seemed as though all movement around me stopped.

A tingling sensation ran through my body as I feel the presence of someone.

Standing alone in complete silence, tears rolled down my face like never before. I now know the answer to my question. As the figure slowly disappeared, the moon shone as radiantly as the sun.

Suddenly I felt knowledgeable, brave, and ready to take on the world.
A REVOLUTION had taken place and I knew that GOD would always be
with me.

Reginald J. Lipscomb Jr.

A Mother's Prayer

Isn't it wonderful what God can do?
To form a baby sweet as you?
One who smiles, and coos, and cries,
With a bit of Heaven still in his eyes!

God loves us so much He's willing to share
This precious babe, so small and fair,
With folks such as us—to have and love;
This one sent from God from His Throne above.

Help us, our Father, as day by day
We share our love with him and humbly pray
For thy help and guidance to help our baby find
Thy love, Salvation, and Peace of mind!

Phyllis E. Cochran

A Candlelight to Burn

I need no eyes to see my way,
to guide me through the dark of day.
I have a heart that can conceive,
the beauty of life and the soul to believe.
With open arms, I feel love too!
And have compassion, the kind that's true.
My mind is sharp and eager to learn,
for knowledge is my sight,
a candlelight to burn.
Through darken paths, I will climb a road so high,
no matter how far, to succeed, I must try.
So please take the time,
use your eyes and watch me grow.
It may even surprise you, for what I may know.
And remember...
I need no eyes to see my way,
to be all that I can be.
God's precious gifts, I'm sure to use,
will always set me free.

Rebecca S. McNaughton

Tell Me

When the last small bird has flown away
to leave the nest empty at close of day
tell me, do you know? Does the mother bird
sigh, returning to that empty nest or
almost cry?
Does she find a small feather on its floor?
Lift it in her beak, remembering so much more.
The day it grew from naked wings, the love she had
for each small peep, the fine days all summer through.
Does she linger there unable to leave the nest?
With its memories full of happiness.

I've watched her and think I know!
She tucks the small feather in the nest and turns to go.
Her heart is full, she starts to sing, she leaves the nest
on upward wing, rising to meet another spring.

Sue Roberts

The Evening Fire

It seems a simple thing to do,
  To light a match and touch it to.
The bits of kindling wood and stick,
  That has been placed upon the brick.
The fire will crackle steam and spit,
  As flame consumes logs bit by bit.
Then soon a warm and rosy glow,
  Comes forth to spread so nice and slow.
'Tward all who set and feel the heat,
  That warm the soul the hand the feet.
But most of all the pleasure seems,
  The greatest to the one who dreams.
As silently they set and stare, into the flames and know not where.
There fantasies will take them to, a distant place or just to you.
They see the smoke curl up above, dream special memories of love.
A touch a glance or just a walk, it seems as if the fire could talk.
And as the flames diminish slow,
  The dying embers softly glow.
The hour demands we must retire,
  And take us from the evening fire.

Quentin R. Arbo

Inside

In the soul there is a power that abounds...
To make the weak strong without a sound...
To make a light bright when it is dim...
To make a church vibrate with a beautiful hymn...
To make life sweet when it is sour...
To make a loser into the man of the hour...
If you do not believe the things that I say...
To your knees you must drop and the Lord you must pray...
For there is one thing I am certain...
Without a soul any show must close its curtain...
Like the beauty of a flight of a dove...
A soul is not powerful if it is not full of Love...

Stephen Rudenis

The Color Red

Many things of beauty are symbolized with red
A rose blooming fully in a garden bed
An oriole winging in the sky above
A red heart with arrow tells us of love
A bright shiny apple that the fruit tree bears
Is given by a child to a teacher who cares
But remember the one red with great association
It was shed by many to defend our great nation
When offered a veteran poppy wear it with pride
Show you remember those who have died

Marlene A. King

"A Special Lady"

I was just sitting here thinking and wondering what I could say
to make you feel special on your birthday, And I started to think
of all the things that make you the beautiful person that you are.
God must have wanted the world to know what a wonderful person
you are.
He gave you a strong back for the hard times in your life,
A proud walk that is yours alone.
A beautiful face that smiles through tears, then he gave you a
heart so filled with love and caring that it shows in all you do.
One night he plucked the twinkle from a star in the sky and
placed it in your eyes to light the world when you smile.
I do believe he commanded the birds to kiss your lips and leave
the gift of song and expression, enhanced with the ability to dream.
And when the creation was finished, there you stood -
A beautiful black woman,
Proud and strong!!

Ruth Turner

Untitled

The softness of your touch brought life to my soul.
To my eyes it returned the sparkle...
my heart began to beat again.

Your hand on my face made me feel alive once more,
my laughter was awakened and my feet could remember
how to dance.

Your sweet kiss brought the taste of love back to my lips,
my passion came alive and a song returned to my soul.

Your love gently returned life to me...
my heart could sing, my feet could dance.
and I could love again.

Tracie Dye

A Soldiers Last Words

Trained to kill, at only eighteen;
To protect our freedom, and the American dream;
Shipped far from home, while mother cries;
Not knowing whether he will live or die.
He is there to fight, but he doesn't know why;
And neither do the others that are standing by.
In the trenches he lives, which his buddies die;
Scared as hell, he runs, but there is nowhere to hide.
Desperate, on his knees, he cries out to the Lord;
"God, take my spirit to heaven, as my final reward!
I have done my best to live; I have tried not to die,
But I know I will see you soon,
Somewhere beyond that smoky sky!"
And with his final breath he pronounces, "Amen!"
And is hit in the head, with the final sin.
He is to die like the others, from the outside in;
And he will never even know if he ever did win.

Matthew A. Koehler

Affirmative Action

'Twas once a fair maiden of charm and grace
a personnel peach cloistered in black lace.

In cubicle sequestered...demeanor serene
enigma and beauty, aura suggested

To chase or be chaste...such a dilemma

A personnel peach on a maiden voyage-down the
corridor and right to a void...

To view the rear vista, I now understand,
what is meant by affirmative action,
all across the land!!

Thomas Nesbitt

Untitled

Life is a process that all of us must go through
to retain things old and learn things new
it's something similar to a maze
as it takes you through the days
consisting of obstacles and heartaches
some only give as much as it takes

Survival of the fittest is what some people call it
But what can you do when you just don't fit?
It's not fair to let someone else take the blame
When trouble arises, defend your name
it takes stumbling blocks in the road to
force us to obey our intuition
life is one of your toughest missions
that which we fear most surely comes upon us
if you spend your life worrying, your dreams
will turn to dust

Perhaps life's subtleties are what make it so worthwhile
if you're not afraid to make a mistake,
you can walk through life with a smile.

Salena Quinn

What Is Love?

A four letter word, we use at will.
to seduce, to persuade, to conquer, to kill!
The weapons of love are sharp beyond compare: Look, but don't
touch, take caution, beware!!!

What is love?

The piercing of the heart and blinding of the soul. The ageless
consequences of love have never been fully told.
You escape with a scar on your heart this time, love is searching
for more, putting your all on the line!!!

What is love?

For lack of a better word, you see, love is taken for granted
very easily.
Love is being pushed to the side, alone and unwanted, rekindled,
encouraged to love on and then taunted!

What is love?

Love is a four letter word, we use in any content, to keep going
throughout life proclaiming, "I love you, next!!!"

Singleton Tate

Thanksgiving

To be with family
To see bright faces - quizzative grins
Little faces lighting up a room
Older voices guiding and gentling

A mad rush of hugs as we come together
Hugs at knee cap level and a face lifted in shining glory
Hugs at eye level and heart level - exchanging without words
What words are never adequate to deliver

Sitting together - holding hands - giving thanks
Filling plates with the good food we are blessed with
Telling stories, playing games, remembering when
We will pass on our traditions
The greatest tradition being the one of our love and the
ability to share it

We pass on our love
And for this I give thanks.

Lynn Tweedie

Untitled

Although life can be hard sometime it's never just one way.
To see the morning sun break in a brand new day.
To stroll upon a quiet beach and hold someone you love.
To see a little, gentle rain falling from above.

It gives life to the dry-parched ground and causes things to grow.
Yet, life can be a fragile thing as thinking people know.
But there's a life so far above that nothing can compare.
To see a newborn reaching out for its first breath of air.

The misery and hard-hard times that came before this day.
The worry and anxiety have faded all away.
To look upon this brand-new life that starts our family tree.
I just begin to realize how much you mean to me.

Yes life is hard but that's ok, our strength it cannot fade.
The bond we have is tripled by this new life we have made.
So as we work and feed and teach and help this baby grow.
Our morning sun will always shine...because I love you so.

Waco Impson

A Rough Day at the Course

It's now 5 a.m. and time to arise
To see what the day holds for surprise.

We're off to the golf course, to tee off at eight
We're downing our coffee, we best not be late.

The golf course is gleaming with dew on the grass
The pond is so still, it looks just like glass.

We play the first nine holes with barely a hitch.
From ten to eighteen it sure was a switch.

We found a few sand traps, one ball in the pond
On the tenth hole my ball went far beyond.

We ride in a golf cart, "old age" setting in!
We're out for the exercise, who cares if we win.

We break for lunch before the second set started
Some couldn't take it, they've long since departed.

We tee'd off and putted till our arms felt the pain.
That didn't stop us, nor did the rain.

Our spikes are all muddy, there's sweat on our brow.
The sun is now setting - we'll throw in the towel.

The drive home is boring, one foot on the brake
We need to get rested - tomorrows game is at stake!!

Linda Davis

The Only Decent Thing

The scientists put out their eyes
To see what they had done
They caught up in a silver net
The gold heart of the sun

But the girl in the shop doesn't care about that
She's dying on her feet and she's thinking about her cat and
You couldn't say it was fair
I heard those lies everywhere
Like a face in my window, I heard it whispering:
"The only decent thing"

They stood us all in suntanned rows
We counted first to last
We sang until our voices broke
Like bubbles made of glass

But the girl in the shop doesn't care about that
She's dying on her feet and she's thinking about her cat and
You couldn't say it was fair
I heard those lies everywhere
Like a face in my window, I heard it whispering
"The only decent thing"

Tres Smith

Life's a Long Winding River

From the beautiful sunsets that we've seen from time to time,
To the many mountains we've had to climb,
Precious moments and memories etched upon our minds,
Life's trials and tribulations and all the good
and bad times we've seen,
Times of happiness and heartache's that run so very deep,
Minutes turned to hours as our lives went slowly
by like leaves floating gently down a stream,
Without love the river's current would pull us under,

Down into the deep dark lonely water below,
But girl I've got you and your sweet, sweet love,
So "Life's a long winding river" that flows
with lots and lots of love from my heart to yours!

William Soffa

A Penny? A Penny?

The key! the key, I must have the key!
To unlock the door, and see what you see.
To know what you're feeling - know your thoughts,
From your position, what do you really perceive?
A penny? A penny? If the pun could come true,
I would liquidate everything into pennies for you.
I would throw down my robes and tear off my rags,
I would bring to you pennies, in overstuffed bags.
All for the answers I constantly seek.
The feelings and thoughts, we never speak.
Bound by decisions too stubborn to change,
As if, telling the truth would make us more vain.

D. Karl Yost

Dark Beauty

Tonight I paused at my window
To view the beauty of nighttime
To feel the softness of darkness
And marvel at moonlight divine

Tonight I can see all the treetops
Black silhouettes in the sky
Silhouettes of a tower of power
And of beauty you cannot deny

Tonight I can see many houses
With lights of friendly glow
With lights that beckon a welcome
But only to people they know

Tonight I can see all these beauties
Which are lost to people in day
For this softness of moonlight and darkness
Is lost when dawn has sway

Lois F. Fay

The Morning Light

Light through my window sill, the
trees are silent and very still.

Not even a breeze or a chill as I
step from my bed to the window sill.

The world in solemn stillness lay,
but I'm awake by the light of the day.

No creatures are moving not even a
peep, because the world is still very much asleep.

I'm awake by the light of the dawn,
to see a new day come and to see one gone.

Marsha Stine

Only The Strong Survive

Here I sit resting in my thoughts,
Tonight it's cold, not in temperature, But in
my heart and soul, I feel alone, maybe that's
the reason I don't feel warm. I kick back
and relax, I have a sudden brainstorm.
Of things that happened in my life, the reality
of it cut my heart like a knife I fight
back the tears, try not to think about it.
But I only bring more fear, not concerning
me, though my family will they make it through.
This night, will everything be alright. All these
thoughts bring me fright! So please stand up
and don't be scared to fight! All these things
that occur in life. Let me tell you only the
strong survive. I wrote this for my family,
to help them stay strong, think before they
do wrong, and to show them that I care.
In the end the ones who stayed alive,
Those are the Strong who have Survived!

Marco Bazan

Runaway Child

Runaway child lost, confused, abandoned, hurt,
Traumatized and oh, so all alone.
What dear child has driven you from your home,
To walk the dark, treacherous streets, on your own?

I pray to the Lord, that He will surely keep you safe;
As you run, your dangerous, nightmarish race.
I don't know you by name, for to me, you are simply;
A sad, lonely soul with an unclean, nameless, pitiable face.

Hollow, unemotional, vacant eyes;
That mask the most excruciating trauma and pain.
Oh dear child, please go back home, or seek out
A warm shelter, to lessen the stress and the strain.

Healing does ultimately come from within,
But at your age, you need a mature guiding hand;
To lead you to the peace within, on which you will one day,
Confidently and triumphantly, stand.

A peace, that you have probably never known before;
But one that can surely be yours, along with unconditional love.
Just open the door of your heart and be willing to receive;
The help, that can only be obtained, from above.

Michelle Louise Pierre

Remembered Snow

The sky falls soft upon the ground
Trees tower in silent reverie
Sentinels to the quiet beauty of the falling snow

A lake of glass now fogged with winter's breath
And the bouldered shore now balls of cotton
With the silent intensity of nothing, nothing all around

This is where I want to be, lost in distant memories,
To sit and watch the twilight sun sink in pink oblivion
On the downy horizon of snow

A forest caressing the sky as it descends,
Coating each branch, each twig, each finger
As they reach in stark nakedness for the nothing all around

With nature's consistent precipitant
I see myself slowly submerged in the delicate white
I hear not a sound, for there be none in this land of wonder

The frozen gems now glisten above my neck, my head
I'm blind to the world and it to me
Yet there's nowhere else I could exist
Than buried in this nothingness
Of remembered snow

Roy Rasera

ApronStrings

Angels guarding over you when I cannot-
trusting is the most difficult part.
a child, always in my sight, my reach...my control.

Control.
Your life, your destiny- your universe...
am no longer than center of it.
remember...a soul...independent...with choices of its own.

Choices...Responsibility...
no longer there to see you choose wisely....
or rather...
to choose...as I want

...Control...
I relinquish it
I give you the gift of a free thinking spirit
your own choices...
your own intuition...
angels, guard over her..
now that I cannot.

Rebecca Dominguez-Karimi

Morning Glory

Sunlight creeps into my lonely room,
trying to use nature's alarm clock to wake me.
My head rises up, clearing a path to see
a picture of my family.

The wooden frame cannot contain the presence
of my nephews playing on the dusty cement floor,
my nieces posing as glorious models,
my cousins sitting on the bamboo chairs smiling joyfully,
my uncles and aunts standing tall and proud of their family
or my mother, father, and I embracing them.
Time froze to preserve a moment
capturing a deep, heart felt love
that gathers once every decade.

A new flavor of life enters my body
every morning
sparking a never ending joy throughout the day.

Mark T. Rosario

Young Child

Young child, young child
  turn around
  tell me what you see that I've never found.
Young child, young child
  come before me,
  for I am bound to the ground and cannot
  turn around.
  For I am old and weary, and know not
  what's about me.
Young child, young child
  I envy your spirit for I have no more
  that I shall liveth.
Young child, young child you have turned around!
  you've become great 'cause you've learned from
  the old man's mistakes.
Young child, young child
  for I see not what's before me, so kindly
  tell me.. what is it you see?

Winnie Sanders

Sinless

I'd like to walk thru a meadow of purity
Turn back the hands of time
Relinquish thy self in mother earth
To a day when the land was fine
Skies so clear, not black as soot
Seas had been unsailed
Extinction oh so fathomless
When innocence had prevailed

I'd like to walk thru a meadow of brotherhood
Run my hands thru the hands of time
Relinquish myself in moral teachings
Back to a day when man was kind
Skin was protection, not a reflection
The beating heart still warm
Hate not bred, greed unfed
Oblivious, the concept of war
Honor thy mother and father
Respect had not yet failed
Innocent still described the child
When justice had prevailed

H. M. Hungenberg

Infinite Joy

The happiness of knowing that my life gives life to your life...
Two hearts beating for each other...
And after 267 sunrises
all the pain in the world is little
before the infinite joy of holding you.

Yes, infinite joy:
Because there hasn't been a sunset
without my feeling fortunate to have you.
Because for every star that embellishes the heavens
there is a better reason to love you, even when I don't need any.
Because my soul dances listening to your laugh,
and my heart rejoices before your sweet glance.
You are a whirlwind of gentleness and graces.
You are pure tenderness become flesh.
And now it is YOU who gives life to mine.

Maria de los Angeles Ramos de Sotolongo

Odie

I'm drawn to be inferior,
unable to even speak up in my own defense.
You only see me lazily panting in the background,
my fat saturated tongue
living a life of its own,
my ever wagging tail speaking
of oblivious contentment.

Don't you realize I'm doomed
to wander in two dimensional world
in blissful ignorance?
I'm nothing but a roaming target
for an overstuffed feline,
a prisoner of his demented conception,
a world of endless naps and lasagna!

That fat cat's bad attitude and nasty habits
have made him rich,
while I wait in the wings,
silently screaming,
hoping to be noticed,
living for the laugh.

Trina Roberts

A Devoted Description Of Karen's Day

She wakes up in a peaceful valley
unaware she sings Karen's Song
she is a VIOLET blooming in an alley
of my heart where I can hear Karen's Song

She fills her mind and ties on Karen's Mask
prettied up in a DAISY dress she'll be
beautiful through the pearl eyes of Karen's Mask
with WATER LILIES floating by her reflection she'll see
the soft elegance of the colors in Karen's Mask
as she sails off on the open silver sea

She is bending in the wind with Karen's Heart
a WILD FLOWER bouquet woven in her mind
petals from the fall like rain in Karen's Heart
the morning DANDELION in her are lingering onto a kind
of night that can only be seen by Karen's Heart
that shines like a star that is too far to find

She goes to sleep in a peaceful valley
unaware she finishes Karen's Song
the VIOLET has been picked from an alley
of my heart where there's an echo of Karen's Song

R. Emmett Ryan

A Storm At Sea

The wild wind roars over the vast, unfriendly ocean
Under a misty midnight sky.
The sails carry them through the mountainous waters
While the violent, western wind steers the bow
And commands obedience.
They fear for their leader grasping the mast
While the sea floods the galley's little floor.
The flag signals panic as it observes from above.
Jolly Roger isn't so jolly as strands turn to shreds.
The ropes connecting the mass of confusion
Cry in dismay for the captain and crew.
A desolate comrade shivers in the brig's dampness
Fearing his wasted life to be endless nothing...
Drowning in the underworld of Earthliness.

Randall Ingram

Tent

I drive the dozen stakes to grab it down,
unfurl the flimsy fabric on the knockdown poles.
A sleeping bag, and foam to pad the ground
(though little they do to smooth the rocks and holes).
Ah, how a storm might strew my plans asunder;
torrents of rain, dislodge my steadying features-
and tension, quite neatly, could tumble my sense of wonder.
so near in the star bright night to forest creatures!
I'm here to be close to wild life for a time
(with insect protection my principal limitation);
to let the heron's great blue wings be mine,
to squirrel about in a scamper of pure elation.
But here's the nagging itch I can't assuage:
to them, it seems, I sit within a cage!

R. Francis Estes

My Worth

You tell me my worth has no value because I am of
another color.
You tell me my worth has no value because I am of another sex.
You tell me my worth has no value because I am of another religion.
You tell me worth has no value to you because I do
not look like you, talk like you, and act like you.
My worth does have a greater value more than you
think because I am the opposite of everything that you are not.

Michele LeVan

Unable To Touch Bottom

Hot sand and wind
Unrelenting crash of wave after wave
Sea gulls call out loud my terror,
"Fly!...Fly!...Fly!"

Beachgoers carry coolers, blankets and suntan lotion
Expecting a day of lazy fun
Children dip pudgy toes in an ice cube ocean
And giggle and run from the waves,
From the foam,
The deep pull of the ocean's core.

I cannot fly away nor dip my toes so freely.
Strands of greenish-brown seaweed
Wrap around my waist,
Pulling me in under the waves,
Out to the labyrinth of the sea.
Water fills my lungs, one swallow at a time.

And the oatmeal blue sky,
The hot sand and wind
And the circling of sea gulls
Dissolve into a heartbeat of darkness.

Robyn Martinez

A Missionary Departs

I'll miss your sound of laughter all the while
Until your coming home with wink and smile.
Imagine inner beauty you've revealed
If eyes reflect the kind of soul concealed.

I see the ones who look for things to get,
You always gave of self to those you met.
And now we know you'll move across the sea,
I'm sure that you'll befriend a chimpanzee.

Whenever feeling lonely, contemplate
Your angel sent with love from heaven's gate.
For when it's difficult, you should agree,
Assistance comes from God - it's yours for free.

As prayers rise to him from friends, you'll know;
For that's when graces are bestowed to grow.
And now I hope the will of God: to give,
As seen in you inspires each day I live.

So at that time we face to say goodbye,
I'll wish instead to hear your cheery "hi."
And while we keep in touch when far apart,
I'll find a bit of you inside my heart.

Thomas Michael Grebel

My Father's Hill

Such vivid silence covered his hill
upon which I sat, where gale birthed chills
penetrated deeply through woolen threads.
Feathery snowflakes settled on beds
of His dwarfish trees, so weathered and contorted.
He silently watched as I pondered and sorted
through feelings of peace and contentment,
releasing to him all fragments of despair and resentment.
Quietly, me he temporarily tranquilized.
Allowing silver lines cloud to release crystallized
kisses drifting downward and settling within,
cleansing my soul and ensuring me I'm forgiven.

Martine Louise Robbins

Concept Of Life

Recollect yesterdays activities,
Visualize life as tomorrow.
Pinch hard for every minute today,
Live tight and be motivated at your own speed.
Excite as you please,
Adventure into your own instincts.
Seek pleasures of your own enjoyment,
Practicality is at your leisure.
Character traits are yours to conduct;
Secure, unjustly or wisely, softness is collective.
Be harmonizing, loving, and shun discord.
Criticize without malicious intent and at your own risk.
See the unfinished product and accomplish it most efficiently.
Yesterday, tomorrow, and especially today,
Be you.

Nancy M. Bolton

A Time of War

Weary men to tired to fight
Wait and watch in a cold cold night
One by one they stumble and fall
Till only a few stand straight and tall

He fights all day, stand watch at night
Tired and weary, but he has to fight
A soldier who believes it's to make man free
He goes to die across the sea

A shot rings out in the velvet dark
The chilling scream as it finds mark
A silent tear as buddy cries
He knows before it is over many more will die

Few are left, but more will come
Bringing with them the sounds of guns
Our boys and girl who fight for Uncle Sam
They went to die in Viet Nam

A. Marie Welsh

I Sat Here Today And Thought About You

I sat here today and thought about you
waiting for business, what else would I do
I could prepare, but that I always do
so sweet thoughts crept in, sweet thoughts about you

I've had these warm feelings often before
like small quiet waves caressing the shore
many would think me a foolish ole bore
so I filed them away, fondly to store

They come and go, but they always bless me
these innermost thoughts no one else can see
like lovers alone neath an old oak tree
or sailing along on a glass smooth sea

There's no way for me to ever tell you
describing love is impossible, true
like telling the blind, "how pretty the blue"
so, I sat here today and thought about you.

Mac A. Wilson

Couch Potatoes Love Chant

Play soft music
And turn the lights low
All we need is the firelight's glow
Hold me close and speak of romance
While the music soars and the bright flames dance
Here in your arms, love, content to lie
Till song is no more and the embers die.

Frances J. Starr

"Fire And Fear"

In the still of the night I lie wide awake
waiting for you to come and take
my heart and broken soul
for my feelings for you are nothing fake.

In the still of the night
I walk helplessly in the rain
worrying and thinking full of pain
for it is only you that keeps me sane.

Fire and fear in the mist
wait to scorch those who resist
but peace for you and peace for me
that's the way it ought to be.

In the still of the night I lie wide awake
I cannot help but wonder if you feel the same
or if my feelings for you are nothing but a game.

In the still of the night
In pray to God for assurance
that this one way romance
is no cheap performance.

Leona Shimada

Untitled

She sits waiting,
Waiting in the slanting sun of afternoon.
Her ears are pierced by each slamming car door
And she analyzes every passing motor even more
Hoping to recognize his soon.

She stops stirring,
Stirring if there might be a chance he's there.
Her breath is taken, her stomach sinks and pulls
'Til stepping sounds fade upstairs and she joins fools
Who wait in vain; another fallen tear.

She sits listening,
Listening near the window on the street.
Her eyes form a vision of his long lines on the bed.
His smell seems risen and fills her like thoughts
She wished she'd said
When they'd come together and their souls would meet.

Mary P. Seni

I Walk Where You Can Not Possibly Go

I have seen you there; in broad daylight.
Waiting to cross the street; at the checkout counter.
In a room full of people or at the edge of a lake.
You laugh and think that I am unaware,
But you are wrong. Wrong to be so smug.

I am stronger because you are there,
The evil, the misguided, the unfortunate ones.
It is futile to ask why you are there, you are.
You cause pain, suffering, and broken lives.
But only because sometimes it is forgotten that you exist.

You will remind me and others before it's too late.
It is your pleasure; you may not know why.
I no longer ask why, because I am stronger.
I know that as hard as you try to breakdown my heart
My spirit is my own and you'll never get near it.

You will never get near it or break it or seize it.
My spirit can thrive even when you are closest.
I walk in my place of peace and sureness.
I do not try to make you see
I walk where you can not possibly go.

Shirley Kosmerchock

Reminiscence

Thinking of you, with eyes clear and bright,
wanting only you, my heart in endless flight.

Reminiscing with past conversations, thinking of all things said,
my heart skips a beat, my feet leave the floor,
as thoughts of you fill my head.

Walking on air, never touching the ground,
smiling deep inside for the joy I have found.

Times spent together, both few and far between,
such precious memories, with more to be seen.

Your voice in my ear, on a warm summer's night,
you're kissing my lips, as your arms hold me tight.

I'll never leave you, I'm here to stay,
but only if you want it that way.

You're what I want, you're my ideal,
these feelings I have can't be more real.

I hope you realize, I hope you can see,
you're all I want, you mean the world to me.

Michele Holtam

Frederick

He sheltered me under his wings from the moment of my birth.
Was this his first being upon earth?
He must have known that at the tender age of five
I would never again see my mother alive.
He closely guarded my adolescent years.
He calmed all my fears as in later life's complex situations.
No doubt he joined in all our family celebrations.
One dreadful night when I was threatened with a gun
He quickly sent someone to foil the robber's fun.
Oh what plans he carried out for the big moment of my life
When I promised to be that widow's loving and loyal wife.
Then suddenly in the middle of a night,
After many years of pleading and pure rhetoric,
He mystically, majestically revealed his name, "Frederick".

W. Anna Kamas

To Never See You By My Side

I didn't want to say goodbye
Was torn between love and pride

You kissed the child from behind
brought out the women from inside
I thought I'd never leave your side

I left the hands that held me tight
For which I didn't stay and fight

I'm sorry I had to go
and hide the love I didn't show

You meant the world to me
Why was it so hard for me to see

I didn't know my thoughts and ways
Would hurt your caring ways

I cry all day and night to see the morning light

I feel you in my dreams I see you in my thoughts
I cry the tears, I fought

I live each day without you, to wishing you were here
To hear you say the words, I long to hear

The years go by with the hurt inside
To never see you by my side...

Sandra Jane Engler

No Crime

When we first met, experiencing our first kiss,
Watching a lilac sunset, there is so much I miss.

A love that is so strong,
  every time we meet,
Lasting so long,
  knowing my life is complete.

Laying next to you at night,
  watching shooting stars,
Everything feels so right,
  for once, without any scars.

Our love will never die,
  we were always meant to be,
I'm not telling you a lie,
  just you and me.

We will never again be the same,
  while our passion is burning,
Once I start sharing your name,
  our souls will be learning.

Wanting you all the time, I love you,
That's no crime, because you love me too!

Lia Sanders

Aloneliness

The hollow sound of the rain betrays the emptiness in my soul
Watching the drops race in a frenzied anarchy
down my steamy window pane,
reminds me of the frailty
of the threads by which my sanity is hanging -
fraying with each breath that crystallizes in the cold night air.
The rumbling of the thunder
is drowned out by the beating of my own heart,
the relentless sentinel
at the gate between life and death.
The lightning mercifully sears through the veil of pain,
shielding me from the world's indifference.
I turn to the moon in desperation,
but he too has taken cover
behind the malevolent, faceless clouds.
I laugh at the darkness
and it stares back at me with fascination,
then it too turns in disappointment
and walks away.

Meggan Jayne Christman

Illusions

In fanciful places,
We dances and played,
Reality was replaced by true bliss,
But reality always comes back,
As it did for you and I,

Real life,
Full for evils and black lies,
Blacker than death they are,
Cold Cold world,
You damn us to toil in the hell that is being,
But just as reality comes and goes,
So do fanciful places,
And we cling to the unreal,
To survive in the world,
And if you don't,
You soon will not be able to cling to the real,
And the unreal will become hell.

Madeleine Selene

Untitled

We met
We had such good times
Now you're having those good times with
Someone else.
You've cast me out like a filthy rag.
But still, I love you.
I am blind.
I cannot see what you're doing
I tell you I love you
Do you reciprocate?
I care about you,
You are the light keeping darkness away,
The eye of my undying storm of unleashed passion.
Do you feel it?
In my eyes you could do no wrong.
I love you...but
Is this love?
For if it is, I want no part in this
Game.
A game where everyone loses.

Richetta E. Penn

Cyberduction

Peering through the toils of life,
  we hope to look into unseen places.
Routes of escape from daily stress,
  beckon to us to join the fantasy races.
Senses are deluge with electronic frolic,
  with technology too much for most minds to bear.
Detachment making it easy to leave morals behind,
  we've forgotten there is a heart, with which to care.
Shifting life into a cyber world,
  reality has now become the fiction.
Amidst the tides of Pride and Knowledge,
  hacking, surfing a net, cyberspace, becomes an addiction.
Busy being someone we're not,
  has led our minds to reject what is real.
The intrigue of electronic communications,
  became a thief, as love, feelings, it did steal.
"Come join us on our inner-world highways,
  enjoy the freedom and tantalizing surprise.
But you must be warned... what you will experience...
  may be to your characters utmost demise."

Marilyn Fritz

Horizon Of Guidance

We may lose direction in the woods,
We may lose direction in ourselves.
Guidance is the horizon,
Which we constantly move toward,
Yet never seem to reach.
Northward we turn,
Reaching for the now which in turn,
Disappears in our hands,
And freezes us both mentally and physically.
The sun rises from the East.
It opens our minds,
And frees our bodies.
We confide in the wings of the westward winds,
Which vamoose us away from the frozen thoughts of the North,
And the arid minds of the East.
Our feet grind the ground of gravel in the woods.
We are lost,
As much as in the woods as we are in ourselves,
As we seek the horizon.

Reagen Pocsik

To A Technical Proposal

We must hurry, we must scurry, we must flurry, we must worry.
We must get it into typing right away.
We don't know if it's all here, we're not sure the meaning's clear.
But the typing cannot wait another day.

There's no time to read all sections, there's no time to make corrections,
There's no time to check the logic of each thought.
We must hustle, we must bustle, we must show our mental muscle
And ignore the basic grammar we've been taught.

Get the Navy on the wire! Hello, Captain McIntyre?
Can we raise those stresses higher? What? We can?
How will that affect the torsion? What's the maximum proportion
Of propellant weight to jetevator span?

As we're getting near the deadline and they're chopping up the redline
And our eyes and nerves are bloodshot, red and raw,
We get snippy, we get lippy, we get yippy, we go dippy.
It's the most fantastic mess we ever saw!

It is now the morning after, and the tension yields to laughter.
The proposal's sent and all our hearts are gay.
It's not as good as we had planned, and frankly, hard to understand.
BUT IT HAD TO GET TO TYPING RIGHT AWAY!

Walter W. Lehwalt

Sins

Before the heavens come and take us away
We must live like there's not another day.
With a dripping candle, an incense half way burnt
And with the devil we sit and flirt.
Wondering if it's going to hurt.
Wearing he's red mini skirt.

Dancing in his fields of gold
As we start to get old, wondering how old.
Running back to are powerful Lord
Telling him we just got corrode.

Having been told thought we were so bold.
As we start to fold, as we slowly decored.

As our bones start to break
Knowing that I'm to late.
As me and God start to hate
Having no fate, having no state

I want to pass through the gate
and not just sit and wait.

Tia Martinez

First Meeting

Our first meeting was special
We never knew or saw each other
If LOVE at first site is possible,
Well, it is possible for us!
for you see, we were in love the very first time
our blue eyes met and dazzled among us.
He looked so soft and gentle yet his muscles overwhelmed me
along with his skin so tan and dark
we said our hellos with smiles
so big, you just knew it was right.
We were among the moon and stars speaking so gentle and pure
We knew we were never leaving
whether bad or good
we'll never leave
for you see on and on
how our love grows
brighter and brighter
even stronger now than before
because of our first meeting
one on one forever!

Michelle Tercho

Pain

What is this thing called pain
We see it and feel it again and again
There is the heart when a lover leaves
And a death for which we surely grieve

There is the illness which we endure
The birth of children to be sure
The feeling when our house is burnt
And all the lessons we have learned

The cancer eating away the bone
And loved ones feeling all alone
It's hard for them to really know
How much we love them and don't want them to go

Standing by when those who are dear
Are living thru their own kind of fear
How in God's name can we explain
What is this thing called pain.

Violet Zdenek

True Values

In the morning we rise and smile at ourselves,
we stretch and yawn as sunlight pours through the window
and dances off the walls in golden drops.
Then we continue to smile as we witness the birth of a new day.

How empty would be the morning song of the birds,
the cool clean air and the pure warmth of sunshine,
if we had not the faces of friends to look forward to each day?

How quickly would the sun's gold tarnish without the love
of a friend to make it shine?
No birds song could we hope to hear, for loneliness
would pound too loudly in our ears...

The love and respect of a friend is the Elixir of life,
the fountain of youth that man has searched for since the dawn of time.
Our true friends are our immortality,
For we will always live in their hearts. Deep within,
where no weapon devised by man could ever hope to reach.

I will always love and cherish you, my friends, for without you
there would be no dawn and my days would blur together
in an everlasting night...for this, for you, I thank you.

Neil R. Boucher

Gentle Beach

Gentle waves erased our footprints in the sand
We strolled quietly along the beach,
Hands around waists.
Cheeks pressed loving cheeks.
Dreams and memories were high.
Bronze-golden sun setting.
Our shadows stretched long on white-dimming sands.

Kismet, why, how did you miss us?
You guided us wrong for oh, so long.
Help us recapture the missed love,
The embraces, the rapture of experiences lost.

By gentle waves of the beach,
Wash our hearts to a gentle shore.
Let us love and cherish and
Sing forever more.

Marvin H. Glass

Sideshow

Life is just a game, a very realistic act
We take it so seriously
Knowing that heroes never die
They always stay in tact.

Why should part of this play depress us to a point
When we can come in the middle
The rest of the play is irrelevant
Like a long, long riddle

Actors, take your places
Now you must please the crowd
Please don't ever let on that it's ourselves we portray
The protest will be loud.

Verna M. Gulley

Forever Love

We were bound by a love so strong.
We were certain nothing was wrong.
We loved our children and raised them well,
We knew that our lives could never fail.

He woke me one morning with tears in his eyes.
He explained to me that it was his time to die.
He wanted to stay, but he had done his part.
He left me with love but he took my heart.

I carried on with my empty life.
I was no longer my beloved's wife.
I was finally able to sever all ties.
I felt his arms as I closed my eyes.

Laurie W. Howard

Available Space

I spent the day with a special friend,
We work hard, so it will never end.
He does not know me, nor you, his speak mundane,
We see through his basic talk, feel his common pain.
Time to show a life of courage, to show people
a better way, things we love and cherish,
on everyday.
Hurting the people closest to me, maybe
a loner is all I can be.
I want all to care and all to see,
What life offers and what we can be.
It will start with a pair that once was great,
Evil changed them, that was their fate.
Everything to me, has complexity.
We cry because we're happy, our thoughts abound
When we read his writings, our sadness
can't be found.
My face grew red, squeezed real tears,
Finally realizing, my deeper fears.
My fiends was dying.

Paul Alan Jones

Yesterday's Innocence

Yesterday brings a thought of regret.
Unfulfilled dreams, things left unsaid and untouched.
What you once had will never return,
Yesterday's innocence is in the past.
Yesterday makes you look back on memories.
Memories pushed deep into the background,
Not wanted to be seen or known.
Things left behind for a reason.
But yesterday insists on pushing them back into your life.
Thinking of yesterday brings back reality of pain and lost loves.
Yesterday's innocence brings with it guilt and regret.
The innocence of yesterday is lost in tomorrow.

Nicole Giustino

A Little Lasagna

"A Little Lasagna," or so you said,
"We'll bring to your house, cause Anne's in bed."
But when you brought it to our door,
"A Little Lasagna" was much, much more.

A "Four Course" meal is so much more
Than a "Little Lasagna" brought to our door.
It fed us both three meals or more:
That "Little Lasagna" brought to our door.

We thank you so much; we thank you some more
For the "Little Lasagna" brought to our door.
Your pie was great, so was your bread.
You made quite sure we were well fed.

A "Four Course" meal! Lest we forget
To thank you two, and thank you yet
Some more for salad of red hue:
Raspberry! Quite our fav'rite too.

So "Thanks!" dear friends, for your kind deed;
For thinking of us in our need-
For bringing food that hit the spot.
But a "Little Lasagna" it was not.

Reuben Steinbronn

Clutch

Sleep, baby, sleep.
We're safe, for tonight, you know.
Guns on our shadows;
Flames for the cold.
Flattered days; past memories.
Sleep a good dream for tomorrow must rise again.
Battle comes to our door shedding the blood of labor.
Sleep, baby, sleep.
We're safe, for tonight, you know.
The skies gleam bright, for we can see through the night.
Stare in the skies, imagine the days,
For the winds come from the west.
Powder wreaks its breath.
Sleep, baby, sleep.
I know not how much longer.
For soon we may part, forever and ever.
Sleep, baby, sleep.
We're safe, for tonight, you know.
Holding each other.

Michael A. Heintz

Fall Picture

Red, Amber, Yellow, Green
What a beautiful picture
These leaves make
Sunlight hitting just so
gives them a brilliant glow

As I walk along the path
that is lined with the colorful leaves
My soul leaps at the beauty and calmness it gives
with a slight breeze
I can catch sight of
another leaf falling to farther line the path

Soon the colors will be no longer
the trees bare and brown
the path dried up with dead leaves
soon will be colored with white
But now that a beautiful picture
these leaves make
Red, Amber, Yellow, Green

Loretta Feldmann-Garemore

Strengthen Our Country

The United State of America
What a great and powerful name
It once meant strength, integrity, freedom
And to every nation ever sought for fame,
It meant its people pulled together
And served when called to do
Guarded, protected, embraced and loved her with faith again renewed.
A weakness has crept in, not all at once but through the years
The strengths she had in days gone by are fading fast it seems.
So many have put their faith in man
And not in the Lord supreme,
Dear United States of America
I hope that you don't fall
From the weight of the evil deeds of men
The burden of pollution and graffiti on your walls,
Many times she's gone to war,
And felt the sword and its sharpness,
But if her people pull together in
the common goal to save her she'll portray a light
That cannot be hid in darkness.

Oralee Schadler

Pit-Pat, Pit-Pat

Pit-Pat, Pit-Pat
What could it be,
The sound of a kitten walking?
No, too off key,
Perhaps the gentle rain hitting the window?
Couldn't be.
Pit-Pat, Pit-Pat
What could make a sound like so?
It couldn't be me.
Maybe the sound is from scary monsters under my bed!
No, all the monsters live in the closet.
It couldn't be a bumble bee,
Cause they go Buzz-Buzz.
Pit-Pat, Pit-Pat
What goes like that?
Possibly a leaky faucet?
No, that goes Drip-Drip.
Oh, this sound scares me!
Wait, silly me it is only the sound of my heart beat!
Pit-Pat, Pit-Pat

Valerie Ruebusch

Delight In Your Baby's Eyes

Hugs and kisses, cries and sighs,
What delight you'll find in your baby's eyes.
Hours of play and nights of no sleep.
And watching your little one starting to creep.
Creeping and crawling and laughing and bawling,
Standing and jumping and stepping and falling.
And as you step back, and pause for awhile,
Remembering these moments as you sit with a smile.
Along comes a tot who's just turning three,
Tugging at mom cause he's got to go pee.
And off you will run anticipating each day,
As he grows ever faster paving the way.
He'll have school days and friends, and pictures to treasure,
You'll hold in your heart every moment of pleasure.
So with hugs and kisses and cries and sighs,
Always remember the delight you'll find in your baby's eyes.

Paula Vadala

Remorse

My baby
What have I done to you my precious person
Broken in my arms you are limp and cold
Bruised-torn from life by my bare hands
Beloved child who opened up my tender heart
And stepped into my crowded world.
I silenced your bright laugh, unable to
return to gentle ears; -
Dried fragile tears, never to dampen your
delicate cheek, softening willing hearts;
Relinquished your innocent smile for sharp frowns;
Ceased unnoticed achievements you would have reached
Only for my fatal heart in selfish frustration.
My disassembled doll cradled in my guilt
Be free now you are gone
Your spirit left your body and now must I go on
As you find and meet your Heaven
I suffer my new found Hell.

Ruth G. Jeppson

What Is Love?

For centuries man has asked the question,
What is Love?
The answer to this may be best answered by discussing
what love is not.
Love is not something you can see, hear or hold in your hands.
I'm not even sure that love is a feeling.
Feelings are intangible. You hear people say, "I feel good,"
or, I feel bad." Love, therefore, really could not
be described as a feeling.
So, what is Love?
I believe that love is a way of life! Love is an awareness
that grows and deepens over time as you start to realize
how special a certain someone is.
Many people go through life without ever experiencing
the wonders of love.
I fortunately am not one of them. I have met you.
For this I will be forever grateful.
Thanks to you, I can finally answer the question,
What is Love?

Raymond S. Barrosse Jr.

The Way It Used To Be

The way it used to be
when all the world was you and me
nothing at all got in the way
everything was find day after day

Nothing could have changed my mind about you
just like the sky will always be blue
and all the clouds will be happy and light
just like the love we had shinning bright

The way it used to be
will you ever see
it was so true
just me and you
The way it used to be

Tara Johnson

He Runs

She forces him to see himself, he runs.
When conflict appears, he disappears.

Back to the past, to all he runs from.
The days will be long again,
sorrow will be her companion.

He returns,
life is good, time is short.
He brings her uncertainty, tomorrows anxiety
and the child in him.

She will meet the loneliness in his heart,
fight the war raging in his soul.
The battle will leave her with scars.

Then he leaves again, no goodbye.
She wonders...
about abandonment and survival,
what good is compassion,
how long has peace been gone?

Reality has a hard handshake,
he will be difficult to move from,
and impossible to forget.

Virginia Allen

Lament Of An Unwilling Immigrant

It seems like ages ago,
When I left my native country for the Western shores,
In search of the golden fleece.
Little did I realize that a decade and some years later,
Surprise lay in wait for me, like a hunter for his prey.
Little did I realize that in searching for my future,
I will become an unwilling Immigrant.
Why? You ask.
You see, most of the returning natives,
Who went back to the old Country to settle,
Found that the seemingly meager existence of the West,
Is a life of luxury in comparison.
Days become months, months turn into years,
Yet a decent job is still a pipe dream.
In the end, they were forced to return,
To the foreign shores,
To continue their marginal existence,
As an unwilling Immigrant.
Hoping upon fast-fading hope, that someday, maybe someday,
The old Country will become habitable, once again.

Zee L. Oduola

Sent From Heaven

You were sent to me on a wing and a prayer
When I look by my side you are always there
I only have to look in your eyes to see
This love that I feel was always meant to be.

Sent from Heaven out of the blue
On angel's wings a love so true.
Sent from Heaven out of the skies
I only see love when I look in your eyes.

Like an angel sent from above
You give me unconditional love
You let me know I'm the only one for you
You came into my life like a dream come true.

Sent from Heaven out of the blue
On angel's wings a love so true.
Sent from Heaven out of the skies
I only see love when I look in your eyes.

Tina Cormier

Uninspired

My muse makes me mad.
When I want her I am without
Inspiration. I need her help. I sit,
I wait, I worry, but all in vain. She
Will not visit me at my desk tonight.
I give up pen for pillow and she comes to me,
Flirtingly filling my head with volumes of poems
And plays, and a plausible plan for peace on earth...
Once upon a midnight dreary out damned spot I have a dream and then
Without warning
She is gone.

Thomas J. Tedeschi

Untitled

You know who you are; you know what you are
When I was able to see I looked in the sky for a most beautiful star
I took the star in my heart and from a rose garden, selected a beautiful rose
My star and rose became one, a woman I adored
My star disappeared and the rose wilted
I can see stars - but not like the one I chose
I can make roses - but not like the one from this garden
No use for a crystal ball when I cannot see at all - only a gloomy sky
But in my mind I see all the sadness, which is memory
And erase my thoughts to hide my depressed and broken spirit:
The beautiful memory of a love that no longer exists.
What about the beautiful star? The rose? The charm? The fantasy?
I'm a dreamer, an old one and the warmth of my lover has grown cold!
And the chill is a signal which compels me to believe I have lost her
Why did the star choose to disappear and the rose to die?
I ask myself the question and I cannot get an answer, except perhaps,
I am old myself, and perhaps the star did not disappear,
nor the rose wilt.

Thomas H. Greer

At - One With Love - A Sonnet

I am made by Love.
When in fear I hide, Love surrounds, protects me.
When I call out in blind distress, Love responds.
Should I weep alone in self inflicted grief,
Love distills my tears to purge the guilt away.
Only in quiet and in solitude do I notice.
Love is always with me, waiting.
The presence of Love is certain, now.
My layers of imagined woes dissolve.
Love create me like itself.
I'm Christlike thought within Love's mind,
With no posts nor distance set between.
My moments of forgiveness and gratitude,
Are material reflections of Love's mirror.

Oliver McDermott

Little Girl's Loss

I was just a little girl at the tender age of eight
when Momma had to leave me, she was called to Heaven's gate.
Daddy's days were filled with sadness, his grief so hard to bear,
then the year I turned eleven, he slipped away to meet her there.
Why did they have to leave me? I would really like to know!
It was at a time I needed them most to help and watch me grow.
I needed my mother's tender touch throughout my childhood years
to soothe my hurts and heartaches and wipe away my tears.
And I sure did need my Daddy with strong and gentle arms
to hold me close and hug me tight and keep me safe from harm.
I envied all the other kids who had their Mom and Dad,
and if they sassed or lied to them, it really made me mad!
I felt an emptiness as I grew up that nobody else could ever fill.
I felt it then, I feel it now, and I guess I always will.

Lavada Zeek

Tomorrow

Will you still love me tomorrow,
when my hair is white with few strains of brown,
when my mind is more senile than sound,
when my hands are thin-skinned and bony to hold,
and my body shivers constantly from the cold?

Will you be patient and understanding
when I can no longer remember my name,
when the times of yesterday and today
are spoken of the same?

Will you read me stories when I can no longer see?
When I sign my name, will you hold the pen for me?
Will you hold me gently when I can no longer walk?
Help me express myself when I can no longer talk?

Will I always be the only girl you see?
Tomorrow, will you still love only me?

Marilyn Viola Kavanaugh

Veteran's Day

I am a disabled Veteran, you think of me once a year,
When on the 11th of November,
Everyone takes time out to remember.

When in time of hostilities, you think of me so dear,
And all the gallant lads whose
Families have shed many a tear.

I am not bragging you see, for my country has been free.
And I would answer the call,
Before I would let my country fall.

Sometimes it is easy to tell,
What we went through was hell.
Or the others who did not have it so well,
Who were buried, there where they fell.

Having a seeing eye dog is not cute,
And being blasted into a deaf-mute,
By the empty part of my suit,
On the battlefield, my arm has taken root.

But on the other 364 days, no one thinks of the ways,
I spend these miserable, lonely days,
Sitting in the sun's golden rays.

Rex T. Rice Sr.

Cry Forever

The structure of our meaning can only live at best,
when sorrow meets the border of energy and rest.
A subtle wind or look, will increase its priority,
when paupers write a book of Kings in a once lost society.

To arrive on time with virtue is the dream of every man.
But in years of keeping score with mindless metaphors,
a beggar takes what he can.

The internal struggles of sensibility and art
are lost in the fantasy of idle being.
You can cry a little and get what you want
or cry forever and get nothing.
For the most you store in a single moment,
is the plague that sets upon untraveled lands.
And the mystic priest you thought you sent
to carry the sage's reply,
has escaped to the coast with jewels and brides,
to preach of visions that have died.

And finding the route through adversity and pain,
enhances the tales you'll tell.
Your spirit can only be as much as your freedom will allow.

Richard Huffman

"Look With Innocence"

Things are not always as they seem.
When the evening rain falls freely from the sky,
Is not the sun still glistening high above the clouds?
And even though the bitter coldness from the
Harsh winter destroys the beautiful flowers,
Does not the gentle spring renew the
Blossoms to their fullest?
Or when we go to the house of the aged,
Instead of seeing only the sadness, should
We not look beyond their fading features
To find the wisdom and love they still possess?
Let not your judgment be made too hastily.
Always look at things with the innocence of a child.

Liz Nettles

In Autumn Time

I love all the seasons but the Fall is my fare,
When the leaves are all color in the brisk Autumn air.
The fodder is shocked and all standing in line,
Like an array of trim soldiers just waiting on time.
The wild geese are calling while winging their way,
Across the blue heavens and South for their stay.
I stroll through the orchard, the leaves at my feet,
The fruit has been gathered, but the air is still sweet.
A red squirrel is scolding as he flashes around,
To gather the nuts that are there on the ground.
God's purpose and pattern are all in the scene,
Its all so refreshing with beauty serene,
To witness this marvel and smell the crisp air,
I'll always love Autumn with its offering so rare.

Marion L. Klimkoski

Move Into The Night

When the silence within me grows unbearable,
When the thundering of my heart drives sleep away,
When I fear emptiness will finally consume me,
I escape onto a fifth floor fire escape
sit in the fragile web of steel
waiting for the drama to begin.
Embracing the life of the night city around me,
Breathing in the lights and sounds,
Wrapping night air around me,
like my cloak for the evening's performance.
And I sense above me the faintly glowing stars,
spectators to the story unfolding below,
And once again I feel at peace with my world.

Maya Mauch

My Moral Of Our Rainbow

In remembrance of Daddy, as he told.
When we reach the end of our rainbow, all will be gold.
The view for me I now will unfold,
My moral of our rainbow yet untold.
Through faith our Savior will show,
what lies beyond his rainbow.
For he created our beatitude row,
Color as equality for all mortal souls.
As it appears over our eternal home as rebus,
for heavens halo.
Many mortal colors on earth yet his one heaven,
for all our immortal souls.
For throughout he has controlled the road, as when or whom may go.
Behold his counsel guide for his arms
unfailing, uphold and tribute our soul.
I foresee our rainbow as heavens halo,
beyond our eternal home with gates of gold.
For sure one day we all will know,
this heaven without end as one's soul.
As where and what's beyond, our rainbow.

Willie M. Jordan

Friends 'Til the End

Remember the day we met,
When we seemed like two specks
In a crowd of friends,
Chatting like hens.
We were both kind of shy,
And we only really said hi.
We've been together from the start,
And you'll always be in my heart.
We don't see each other much,
But, when we're together we can't be hushed.
You've listened to my troubles,
And reminded me I didn't live in a glass bubble.
I've helped you with yours,
And together we've opened doors.
Now it's come to an end,
And I'll pray we'll see each other again.
And believe me, I'll never forget,
Being your friend was never a regret.

Stephanie Roman

Summer Is Gone

The once golden days of youth
When we would talk and share,
Now hold cluttered shadows
Of unseen terror and fear.

The safe, warm days of summer are gone.

I remember our happy days
And our love so strong and deep,
But memories are shattered as I
Watch dark torment in your sleep.

The soft, gentle days of summer are gone.

I want to lash out at the something
That robs your every thought;
That cruelly takes away your nimbleness,
And fills your hours with naught.

The happy, exuberant days of summer are gone.

The gold has turned to blackness;
Our laughs have turned to pain.
I wait with lonely emptiness
For a time that will not come again.

Our golden days of summer are gone.

Mary Ashley Axtell

Night Time

Black is the night
Where darkness over takes the sky
And dreams filter in like stars.
Evil lurks behind your door
And in the corners where your mind
Can only explore.
Children dreaming scenes
of hatred, love and war, nightmares galore.
Prowlers looking for their pots of gold.
Creeks, bumps, and squeals fill the room.
Where are you?

Blackness, so cold, so gripping
Tears it's way through the sky.
Relentless like agony it lingers on.
When will morning take over this terrifying doom?

Paula L. Mott

Stormy Weather

When life races by and you begin to wonder
where did you loose control.
You try so hard to catch up and keep up,
maybe you're farther along than you know.

Things happen so fast, the wind is in your face,
blowing so... that it's hard to see,
while braving the wind your eyes will open,
to so many realities.

One reality is... If you look back
you wouldn't be where you are today.
You made it this far, you survived past storms,
now you're ready to face another day.

With the wind at your back and the sun in your face,
when it's cold you will stay warm.
So don't be shy even when afraid,
go ahead... Take the world by storm...

Just don't forget your umbrella!

T. J. Pardel

Winds

Where do the winds go as they cross the sky?
Where do the winds go? No one knows, nor do I.
They softly pass in skies of blue.
Where do the winds go? I wish I knew.
Up ward and downwards then disappear,
Only to come back so still, so clear.
Up to the heavens aloft they lift.
Backwards they come again ever so swift.
Like angels with wings they soar to the sky.
Twist and turn and then softly die.
They remain out of sight no one can see.
And dance to a tune unheard to me.
Where do the winds go when they are out of sight?
They dance on forever and into the night.
Into the seasons, all four they travel,
Making their mysteries hard to unravel.
Where do the winds go? Up to heaven that's where,
To return once again to hide in their lair.

Philomena Rossi

Untitled

My angel hides life's secret in her eyes,
Where golden promises shimmer 'neath ebony
And stars of silver mock those of God's skies;
Some proud and silent truth is kept from me.
She taunts and teases to my heart's dismay,
Its rhythm lost, then found, but not for me,
But she controls my bloody current's way,
And but a glance begets a fire in me.
A word of kindness quenches my torment;
No sooner giv'n than changed to mocking jest,
And yet received with pleasure, as a gift
From one, who's pow'r to charm has known no rest.
My mind's a slave of Ariadne's maze,
But helpless, lacking thread of golden fleece.
I speculate until my life is haze,
And all, save love, is lost divinity.
Within her soul's deep windows I have seen
All that God or Satan meant for me.

Robin K. Reed

"A Special Valentine's Day"

Once a year a day comes by, a special one indeed,
Where love is shown by those who care for the one person that they
 need.
You are my one and only love I think about so much,
I hope you know my dear love, I cherish your gentle touch.

This is a special time when hearts will bind as one,
The time of year I'm most thankful for all the good that you have
 done.
The hearts, the candy, the flowers; the ideas, and the time,
Darling, I love you so very much; I'm so thankful that you are mine.

The wine, the candles, the fire light, the romance in the air,
I only hope your heart feels the same as mine, sweetheart;
 I so very much do care.
So on this special Valentine's Day, I hope that I can make you smile,
You're the love of my life that I cherish so much,
 you make my life worthwhile.

Suzanne DeLullo Henry

Love

There's a place that I hold so deep in my heart
Where love-stays forever its never apart.
Where the sun always shines and the
stars always glow
And the love that I have for you
Will never ever go.

You can't replace, and you can't take it away
It's tucked way down deep inside
For each and every day.

You know how much I cared about you
I know you had to know
That I will always love you
No matter where you go.

Majella Reha

"There Is A Place"

There is a place that's known by all,
Where many great things lay upon a wall.
Where many fantasies have taken place,
Something no one can erase.

In this place lies a secret field
Where memories of romances are concealed.
Where many lovers they have come
So their hearts could be as one.

It has been said that one wish will come true
As long as you're with someone who truly loves you.

And in this place at the end of the field
lies a stream a human man did build
where fish swim and children play
while lovers sit and chat all day.

A place where strangers would become friends
And would be lovers in the end.

Kiffany R. Bethel

Friends

Friends are a blessed thing
a joy to life they bring
how miserable we are
when they must travel afar
We must not be sad in their leaving
But rejoice instead of grieving
To have known them is surely a pleasure
A memory that we will always treasure

Roy Collett III

Molasses And Honeysuckle Time

The honeysuckle blossoms scent is in the air,
Where snowfall and blizzards are mighty rare.
The Deep South is where hospitality still reigns,
Where you hardly ever see a lady with varicose veins.
The sky is nearly always the brightest blue,
But it's very hot and sticky in the long summer, it's true.
Relatives greet you with a loving hug and handshake.
People there don't complain over every little ache,
The mockingbird wakes you with it's cheerful song,
The summer days are mellow and long.
Molasses are slowly flowin',
And in the wind the dandelions are gently blowin'.
The bright sunshine only occasionally gets hazy,
The warm summer breeze makes you sleepy and lazy.
It's time to nap and snooze,
And forget all about your trifling blues.
Here comes big ole jolly aunt Jemima, sugar plums,
Jemima's staggering, she must have drunk some rum.
Watermelon is a treat that Southerners eat,
The inside juicy red fruit can't be beat.

Terry Pieszchala

Untitled

Love is a singular emotion
which can be wider than any ocean
It can reach as high as the sky
It can be sweeter than any apple pie;

Love can be deeper than the sea
It can overwhelm you or me
It can affect heart, mind and soul
Love is beautiful, Love is bold;

Love is still a singular emotion
that creates trust, loyalty, devotion
It creates raging, violent, strong reactions
Love of itself has a multitude of factions;

Love an emotion, controlled by you
given to whomever, you five it to
It has nothing to do with sex or greed
Love when shared fulfills the greatest need;

Silly as a goose, somber as a hymn
Solid as an oak, spread out like a limb
repressed, ignored, rejected, bared
LOVE to be Love......must be shared.

S. Gussie Felder

Unconditional Love

I sit in the amber glow from the candle sitting next to me,
while another flame flickers from across the room.
It's brilliant dance brings to mind, the sparkle
 of love I remember in your eyes.
I gently cares the flame next to me, and I
 feel the warmth of your smile in my heart.

I sit and reflect on times gone by and can't
 help but wonder, what happened...
To the love we once shared,
To the time we spend in each other's arms,
To the walks, hand in hand, on warm summer nights,
To the joy and laughter we gave so freely,
To the feeling of oneness we would have forever.

I close my eyes to hold back the tears,
 But the memories within have touched too deep.
You once said to me, that tears wash the windows
 of the soul.
And these tears have helped me to understand,
 The gift you have given to me...
 That I must love, unconditionally.

Ronald E. Longo

Celebration From A Distance

Celebration of an engagement for two,
while Distance makes us have no clue.

Big Brother celebrate and enjoy,
while we Distant remember you when you were a boy.

Congratulations, and the best to you,
words from a distance are only a few.

Promise thou that we'll have fun,
when Distance between us burns in the sun.

The joy we see you all in celebrating,
comes to us in a tape by someone's creating.

Happiness that filled all of your eyes,
from a Distant filled my eyes with cries.

To end this, is like to end,
the Distant feeling, pain to be bend.

Suhair Ramadan

Night

The still and velvet dark around us creeps
While here within our home there is no light,
Yet nature is alive and nothing sleeps
In all the open realm of deepest night.
The friendly moon floats in his cloudy bed
And sheds abroad his silvery day-like gleams.
The playful little creatures have no dead;
They romp and play beneath the yellow beams.
The bony trees stand out in stark relief;
Their fingers like a cradle rock to sleep
The living things that hide beneath each leaf,
Till all is wrapped in silence soft and deep...
No longer 'neath the moon do creatures play;
The dawn's first rays have chased them all away!

Martha J. Ramsey

The Romance Of Night And Day

People call you the sun, the morning, the day,
while I'm called the moon, the evening, the night—astray.
As the day you inspire the children at play,
while I as the night tuck them in—safe and away.
I see you but twice when we are together,
in this relationship that has lasted forever.
The first is the sunset, the second—the sunrise,
these are our kisses and time for good bye's.
The sunset is my way of kissing you good night,
our embrace warms the sky with red and orange light.
The sunrise is your way of telling me good bye,
it now is your time to take over the sky.
I look upon your blue skies, white clouds—and when you are gone,
I give you my stars for you to wish upon.
I hide in my shadows with all of my might,
but by morning you seem to find me with your soft glowing light.
If it were not for you—there would be no tomorrow,
no yesterday, today—I'd be alone and in sorrow.
Together, with our friendship we control the heavens above,
knowing that we share a special kind of love.

Richard Gregory Navarro

Untitled

But gently blow autumnal zephyrs
As time approaches for the vespers
With frozen rains of winter nigh
The land exhales a misty sigh
The field's rich harvest reaped and taken
Await they spring to reawaken

Steven W. Ireton

Untitled

You come like a shadow,
a whisper on the wind.
Something that gently taps at
the door of my heart, and stirs
the consciousness of my brain.
Quietly and gently you fill my soul,
and quickly you depart.

Tammy Lewis

Blue Indigo

Blue is the moon, blue as indigo,
while my heart is in pain.
Will I ever live in happiness,
Will I know love again?
When will my heart be free from turmoil,
And be given a chance to rest?
Only when I find true love,
Then I'll be truly blest.

How I long to see that day, to love and receive love back.
To have security and peace,
A peace that I now lack.
Can I possibly know that joy,
Will anyone share my dance?
Come along my elusive love,
Come and take a chance.
Be my companion, be my friend, be the one I cherish.
Let us live a life of bliss, and never let it perish.
Is this really going to be; finally to be free?
Now the moon is bright as sunlight,
No blue indigo for me!

Sharon Olmos

Life Goes On

It was the summer of 95 she died,
while others were occupied with launching a rocket into space,
blowing up the whole human race, or trying to survive the
temperatures outside.

Her life was a tribute to the service of man-
whether they were cold, hungry or searching for the plan of
salvation from this greedy, heartless land.

Many a day spent in prayer,
even more wondering if others would care about the suffering
everywhere and Do something.

A ripple in the lake.

Ruth J. Davis

Silver

And so he held her in his palm
While she danced against type;
Casting no shadow.
Sharp-edged. Lean-lined. Hollow.
Strung so tautly she vibrated.
The subtle hum visible beneath alabaster perfection.
A mindless marionette.
Controlled by his demands.
Battered by his fists.
Yet, one single, steel strand survived,
Bisecting the suffocating darkness.
A glinting, fragile trace of yesteryear
On which she ultimately gambled.
Bolting headlong and fearless;
Freedom's silent roar deafening.
Months later, her body supine; naked; cooling —
The solitary metallic thread again focused her soul;
Gleaming tinsel in a vacuum of stark light
As blood warmed a crimson pool in the snow.

Vickie Morgan

The Wait

As I wait, death grows near;
Whispers from the crowd are all that I hear.
Sweat runs down my neck and onto my back;
And as I wait, I hear a loud crack.
As I look over, I see a head fall;
I watch it roll down the stairs and strike a brick wall.
As the blindfold is placed over my eyes;
I think of the revolution and of those I despise.
The razor sharp blade rises again;
This time the Monarchy loses and the Revolutionaries win.
As I listened, I hear the people chant their hateful words in French;
And with that my last sound, I do not flinch.
As I walk up the stairs and I breathe my last breath;
The razor sharp blade drops, and I am laid to rest.

Matthew Robertson

I Am My Own Lover

I am my own lover.
Who I am is in the confidence of my stride,
The soul in my laughter, the story in my eyes.
I am my own lover.
Who I am is in the apprehension of my failure,
The longing in my heart,
The questions in my appearance.
I am my own lover.
Who I am is in the softness of my caress,
The overflow of my passion,
The eagerness of my body.
I am my own lover.
Who I am is in the fragility of my certitude,
The hunger in my soul,
The emptiness in my arms.
I am my own lover.
Who I am is in the power of my love,
The strength of my fidelity,
The gentleness of my discernment.
I am my own lover.

Sunny Green

Emotions

I am emotionally involved with someone
who I claim to be all mine, my emotionalist
Quality can break down to nothing if she shows
Any signs, of wanting to abandoned me for any
Essential reasons, my emotions have gotten stronger
From the involvement that's has lasted for four
Seasons, on the contrary my satisfaction longs for
More to come after, only to be granted love,
Tenderness, and appreciation, so God disregard any
Disasters, these just emotional feelings we share
Has to last a life time, she who is my companion
Needs me, I need her so we both can shine, together
Not aloof so we can learn to read each others
Thoughts, ease each others pain that consist of
Altering into shameless faults, even though our
Emotions are pressured by individuals who
Wish they could interfere, but our love for each
Other was not created to tear or wear, those who
Eagerly anticipate that wish to come true,
Will be truly surprised once they hear me say, I do.

Larry Smalls Jr.

Conversation Above

"Stephanie," a voice whispers out, "over here, do not be afraid."
"Who is it?", replies Stephanie, "It is me, remember Dave?"
"Yes, I remember you David, but where am I, why am I here?"
"I have so much to show you Steph, do not worry, do not fear."
"I am not afraid, indeed worried, I do not wish for them to cry."
David says, "Alright then, let's paint a rainbow in the sky!"
"I did this once for mom and dad, for one moment they did smile."
"It is little things like that we can do, to ease their pain awhile."
"Mom, dad, and my sisters, who will see them through?"
"You are their guardian angel now Steph, this help will come from you."
"Your family will be fine, they have memories and lots of love."
"It is up to you and I right now, to comfort from above."
"Let's paint that rainbow David, make it powerful and bright!"
"We must ensure our families, that everything is alright."

Thomas E. Moser Jr.

"It Was Me"

It was me...by your side on your shoulder,
Who made you warm when you were colder,

It was me...in your heart on your mind,
Your guardian angel you did find,

It was me...guiding and protecting,
Always there and never neglecting,

It was me...for every smile and every tear,
Assuring the vanish of any fear,

It was me...who solemnly swore,
To give you all I have I shared,

It was me...throughout the night and day,
Whom expressed myself in this powerful way,

It was me...the one in the world for you,
Who promised my life when I said "I Do."

Robert J. Collins

If I Could Be

If I could be someone else...
Who would I be?
Would I be rich and or famous?
And what color or nationality?
Would I be well-known or obscure?
Would I "MAKE" the news?
Would I be "ON" the radio?
Would I be an author or poet or
Would I be a famous "ROCK STAR?"

Would I be an actor on T.V.?
Would I be a hero or a trader?
Would people "READ" about me and look at me?
Would I "MAKE" Newsweek or Time or...The National Enquirer?
Oh well, after thinking all of this through
From January to December,
I would not want to be -
You or you or you!!!
I know "WHO" exactly I would rather be...
I'm perfectly happy with just being ME!

Terrence Johnson-Cooney

Thankful Power

When there's wind to take away-
be thankful for no flood.
When there's water to flood or none at all-
be thankful for no fire.
When there's fire that burns out-
be thankful for the earth still stands.
When the earthquakes crack the ground that you stand-
be thankful - that you're a witness of all
powerful things.

Rhonda L. Russell

A Prayer

Who'll sing songs in the rain?
Who'll cry out in pain?

Who'll be watched over today?
And who'll be led astray?

And, Lord who will I be today?

Who's child will laugh, with joy unbound?
In which child's eyes, will tears be found?

Who'll begin a feast, with a word of grace?
Who'll stare at another empty plate?

Who'll embrace love with both arms?
And for whom will love only bring harm?

And, Lord who will I be today?

Who will reach for silk, to dry his feet?
Who'll search the alleys, for a place to sleep?

Who'll be chosen to sit, on a palatial throne?
And who will be stripped, of all he owns?

Who'll receive a name, on this day of birth?
Who'll leave a name, to lay beneath the earth?

And Lord, who will I be today?

Vickilynn Harvey

I'm Sorry Dad

As I sit here, grieving the loss of my Grandmother,
Whom I loved very much,
I can't stop thinking of your grief-the loss of your mother.
A grief so similar, yet so different.
A pain I can not even begin to imagine.
Yet somehow, due to the bond between a Father and his Daughter,
I feel your pain, your pain is mine.
I realize that with each passing day, my grieving pain eases,
But the pain I feel for you, my Father, does not!
I worry more about you, and your state of mind, than my own.
I'm letting go—letting go of emotions-not memories.
Emotions bottled up; wound so tight I feel as if I might explode.
Why are we born to love and to do for others,
Just to leave them behind?
But then I realize these people are who make us strong.
These are the people who help mold us into who we are today,
So we carry on the lessons we hold so true and dear to our hearts.
Sighing now, I feel tired-completely drained.
I have said all I can say:
On to my grieving.

Melissa Ellis

She Was, She Is

I came across this woman in the travels of my life,
Who's outlook on the world around her was tainted not with strife.
An apron on a house dress, was what she chose to wear.
Along with a bandanna wrapped around her graying hair.
The English that she spoke was broken, her accent very strong.
Though sometimes words are just not needed to help you get along.
She worked the earth and seeded it with plants she was to grow,
To feed her family and her friends and those she didn't know.
She sold these crops to those who could afford to buy her ware,
And gave for free to those who couldn't all that she could spare.
Her life was not an easy one, the work was hard to do.
Still she gave to those who needed, and managed to get through.
The courage and the strength she was there for all to see
But the kindness that she showed was what most influenced me.
I think about her now and then when I find it hard to cope.
And the light she had comes back to me and gives me renewed hope.
Though she's now among the angels, and we are now apart
Through me her kindness still abounds because she's in my heart.

Shelley Normand

Who Am I?

I look in the mirror and I see someone
whose life lives behind a face of an obscure identity.
I am a prisoner within a body that has no control
over itself.
Who am I? What am I?
Can I be who I want to be? Or be what others expects me to be?
I look in the mirror and I see, an image, a reflection
of what others see...
Tell me.. Who am I? What am I? What should I be?
This world is too confusing, what is my destiny?
I wonder what this world would be like, without me?
A question I've asked for eternity...
I look in the mirror and who do I see?
The person that know me best...that person is Me.

Nerissa Mae Lorenzo

Rape By Fahrenheit

Golden glows the coal from the great stoker
whose molten gaze caresses bare shoulders
sea-caps and banquets whose appearance suggest
they were sewn by a master tailer on a verdant
wedding gown for a final embellishment
Buzzing winged performers dance on a field of blue
burning copper in the spotlight
Crimson fingers move teasingly through the lush
locks of summer trees and flesh melts while flowers
and parasols open to the day
but side-walks and sand hold running feet at bay
This eye of passion
This burning Napoleon that ravages this body this
mother earth
Is it lover rapist or savage
Shall we like a submissive piece of clay yield
or armed with cool waters sword know he cannot lay
waste while we merely observe like Caesar viewing
the carnage

Marcia Vinson Arnold

Summers Of My Childhood

To be a child again in Summer season
Why can't it be so? Give me a reason.
Roaming about with no parent to see.
Too young to have responsibility
From dawn until dusk, the whole world was mine
I explored its vastness in rain and shine.
Butterflies, fireflies, and crickets at night
All played their part in giving delight.
During morning dew and afternoon sun
all times of day were for me to have fun.
Blue skies, yellow flowers, green grass and trees
No playground gave me more pleasure than these.
The wonders of nature awed one and all
My friends and I always answered its call.
Active all day I was tired by night
Was ready again at mornings first light.
But never again will a child I be
And never again will I feel so free.

Thomas Newman

The Daffodil

The golden wings of the daffodil
Before the cold March sun unfold,
As if to tell
That errant orb
Spring is here,
Behold.

William T. Ellison

Name Calling

Dear Brooke:
Why do people call me names?
I do not know
Why do people lie and cheat
And hurt me so?

Sometimes they don't mean it?
Sometimes they do
Sometimes they say things just to
Make me mad.
And sometimes what they say aren't even true.

I'm tired of all the cheating
I'm tired of all the lies
I'm tired of the name calling
When I call him names, he just cries.

Why do people have to be so mean?
They make me so mad
If they move
I'll be glad.

Stephanie Johnson

Threads Of Time

The threads of time have been broken
Will this time ever be repaired and made right
We try to bring back the past by actions,
Places, people and music
These remind us of time long ago lost
The heart and soul feel lighter
The mind remembers old thoughts
Can you get these feelings to remain in your soul
Time is hard to recover once the threads have
Been broken
Think of a love long past and gone
The sound of her voice, the touch of her hand
Yes the threads of time have been repaired
It is up to your heart and soul to keep these memories
For if you forget the thread of time will be broken
But time is only in the mind of the dreamer
For those that can hold a memory are forever
Young in their hearts and soul.

William S. Molster

Trust

If I give you my heart
Will you cherish or neglect it?
If I share my thoughts and keep my morals can you respect it?

If I give you my love can you keep my trust?
Will you show me it's love and not meaningless lust?

Love is not something just given, it's something you must earn
But if you show me your love, you'll have mine in return

If you can love me this way you will find
I will love you with heart, body, and mind

Will you stand by me in good times and when times are rough?
If you hold me real tight your love will be enough

Will you be there for me and love me both day and night?
When I'm scared will you comfort me and erase all my fright?

I want to know just where you stand
Because I'm putting my heart in the palm of your hand

Leilani Carinio

Will You

Will you sing me a song?
Will you make it sweet and long?
Play me a tune that will send me to the moon.

Will you hold me for awhile?
Will you walk with me a mile?
Whisper in my ear, while that we are here.

Will you spend your days with me?
Will you stay with me and see?
For you hold the key, we were meant to be.

Will you think of me in everything you do?
Will you give your heart to me?
We'll walk hand in hand and journey through this land.

Will you say, I love you dear?
I shall have no fear,
As long as you are near to wipe away a tear.

Will you love me tonight?
Will you hold me tight and say good night,
As gentile sounds of slumber over take the night?

Peace fills this place, for tomorrow I can face.
No more will I roam, for I am home.

Marcia Burns

Rocks and Hills

Rocks and hills, grass and pines,
Wind and clouds and you on my mind.
Traveling faster as each day goes by,
So, I won't have time to stop and cry.
You've gone away, God only knows where.
Perhaps to someone else, your new love to share.
The rain falls gently on my window pane.
But, somehow it doesn't sound the same.
When you were here, it was only rain,
Now it's mixed with tears; tears of pain.
Rocks and hills, grass and pines,
Wind and clouds, with you on my mind.
All that's left is a memory
of a precious love that's no longer mine.

Sylvia Nadolney

Your Eyes

Your eyes
Windows to your heart
A passage to your soul

Through your eyes, I know you, I feel you
When I dream, I see your face, your hand reaching out to me
I reach out to take it and you smile, with your eyes

Your breath, soft and distant, yet I can almost feel the warmth
Worlds apart, I can only imagine your eyes
I burn internally, wanting to embrace you, wanting to hold you
Longing, if only, but for now, only through my eyes

I try to run, but there is no escape from my love for you
You are ever present, on my mind, in my heart, and in my soul
I hear your voice whispering in my mind, loving me

The wind brushes my hair, I imagine your touch, your eyes
I'm searching for the answers, but it doesn't matter
Wandering, waiting, knowing, you are always here, in my eyes
And I stop and yearn to feel, and to see, once again, your eyes

Stefanie E. Kerkela

Loving Thoughts

You are always in my every thought.
Wishing we were together,
Wanting you next to me,
To make me feel comfortable and complete.

I long to see your smiling face and hear your sexy voice
I have to replay the times we were near each other
without a choice;
Just to be close to you would be very nice
When it comes to you, I don't ever think twice.

Often fantasizing how would I feel in your arms
Makes my heart beat fast but I remain calm;
I don't know what it is about you that turns me on
But the way I feel, I think I've waited far too long.

I picture us relaxing, playing soft music with a slow groove
Along with thoughts of making love, make me want my whole
body to move;
Slow, sweet and smooth like you never knew I could
Hot, passionate love, I definitely would!

Robert B. Crouch

Meeting Mary

I met a sweet lady not long ago
With a frail withered body
And hair white as snow.

Her eyes were the bluest that anyone's seen,
You couldn't imagine her petty or mean-
The same beautiful Mary of the old silent screen.

Her mother she called blessed-how refreshing to hear!
Her sister so beautiful and father so dear.

How hard to keep her on the right track
And get wanted info from way, way, back-
Fairbanks and Gable, Valentino and Wayne-
Mary entertained many a swain.

She clasped my hands snugly between both her own-
Her hands, like her heart were amazingly warm.

I was glad that I went there
It was out of my way,
To meet Mary McLaren,
A gentle, strong relic
From an earlier day.

Naomi Ruth Burkhardt

Back Then

Look down there comin' from the fish creek,
With a tub full o' brim;
Hair tied down with a wide straw hat,
And a brightly colored scarf at its rim;
Is that you Mama?

I remember Sunday mornins', when we'd awaken from our
slumber,
All my Mama's impish children, eleven of us in number;
We would grope towards the bathroom, staggerin' on our way,
First the younger, then the older, to begin our early day.

I see starched and ironed table clothes, when I look back yonder;
I smell pancakes a sizzlin' on the fire,
Bacon, sausage are a fryin', mmm what a wonder!

Mama... those were difficult days,
You suffered long through every phase;
Nudgin' each child toward his own twinklin' star;
God's love shown through thee, is surely the key,
That has helped us to be, what we are.

Lillie M. Adams

Her Domain

There once was a Scandinavian goddess,
with brazing red hair, a wild vixen without a care.
Bareback she rode, wind everlasting through her hair.

Queen mother to her clan, she ruled with a vengeance.
Man tribes feared this warrior queen,
her dominance was a sight to be seen.

Once upon a time, long, long ago; in a far away land,
a renegade Viking clan over powered her kinsman,
who tried to make a stand.

But the cold brutal steel slashed wildly,
as the riffraff silently fell,
rival blood spilled endlessly, so the warriors tell.

The red haired princess, with soldiers by her side,
finished combat and prepared to ride.
Quickly mounted, they wandered the countryside.

Arriving at their hamlet, nestled deeply in forest green,
full of many song birds, "oh," how sweetly,
murmuring songs, songs they sing.

Blackness followed as the day hastily slipped away,
Her domain was safe, once again, for another day.

Tim Pugh

Untitled

Oh my precious little grandson
With eyes as blue as the sky
And hair that glistens like the sun
With those tiny little hands
And those cute little feet
That are so anxious to explore
Your mind that sees a magical world
Beyond your imagination that can possibly see
For you've only been with us for one short year
Yet you've changed our lives so completely
You have given us back our youth
And our imaginations are at work
Our dreams and our hopes take a new meaning
For you see we can share them with thee
For you come from the seed of Papa and me
Through the love that was shared from
your parents you see
And from that magical love they shared
Brought you to Papa and me

Patricia Marsh

The Prison

Locked in a box
With familiar freaks and lifeless clocks
That clap with coarse, broken fingers
Music and voices are all around
That seem to pull a blanket
Over the life of certainty
The vast, silent, side of morning
Begins a journey that leads to a nightmare
A nightmare of doubt
The unknown future
That lurks behind the stained glass window
I desperately try to see out
Only fog lies before me
I begin to feel the coldness
Of the white tile against my bare skin
My silent screams remain unheard
Yet the echoes are noticed
As they dance on the cellar walls
Only contradicting themselves.

Nikki Browning

Sun

Sun, sun, I look at you,
And I see the universe above you.
What can I see, but something
special to me.

Lauren Elizabeth Summa

Amy-Class of "95"

To my friend named Amy Degrote, the one who doesn't have to fight with her brother for the remote
All of us are going to miss you guys.
Your cheerful smile, loud laughs, and all the eyes. You've touched the hearts of many and enriched their minds, and at times you've kicked the deserving ones in the behind. You've shared and had many memories at Mendon HIGH. And now that you think of it, you realized how the time flew by. When it comes time to walk down the aisle, You'll look around and just smile. At the end, all the hat's will fly, and when you hug all your friends, You can't help but cry. Just be glad you've come this for and through the classes you've stayed alive. We're going to miss you and everyone, Class of "95!"

Natasha Runyon

Soon

Though he lives in his world and I in mine
With him in my life most everything's fine
For when I lay in his arms I feel him gently hold
The key to my heart as my feelings unfold

So why does my heart ache throughout each day?
It must long for those words that I wish he would say
He tells me I'm special and that he cares for me
But to say those words he would no longer be free

At the end of each day as I prepare to sleep
My loneliness sets in so deep
For as we laugh, talk, and murmur on the phone
I know that after "goodnight" I'll be so alone

Yet I know this man can never be replaced
For I see his whole heart in his beautiful face
So as darkness sets in and the clouds hide the moon
I keep telling myself I'll hear them soon

Yes, I believe in my heart, I'll hear them soon.

Rosalie Cappoli

First Love

I never was struck before that hour
With love so sudden and so sweet,
Her face, it bloomed like a sweet flower
And stole my heart away complete.
And my face turned Pale as deadly pale,
My legs refused to walk away, and when she looked, what could I ail?
My life and all seemed turn to clay.
And then my blood rushed to my face
And took my eyesight guilt away.
The trees and bushes round the place
Seemed midnight at noon day.
I could not see a single thing,
Words from my eyes did start
They spoke as chords from a string.
And blood burnt round my heart.
Are flowers the winters choice?
Is loves bed always choice?
She seemed to hear my silent voice, not love's appeals to know,
I never saw so sweet a face as that I stood before
My heart has left its dwelling place, and can return no more.

Matthew B. Bolden

Time Ticking

Clock ticks time in staccato fashion,
With monotonous rhythm, it hammers the
seconds soundly into history;
As if nails, securing their rightful order
in chronology.
It taps and taps until the tapping is no
longer noticed,
Until it must be noted, to declare
this time,
When it too, must take it place along
side the others.
Accompanied by the incessant ticking of time.

Margaret Kist

Ego's Song

I am the core of the rights of man and EGO is my name.
With morals lost and ideals tossed,
Into a fast paced flame.

Stay out of my way if you value your sanity.
I will beat you and defeat you,
There's no end to my vanity.

I'll use ignorance and fears to make you cower.
Close your eyes and look in your mind,
I definitely have massive power.

I am greater than GOD I will vastly proclaim.
I know all and I see all,
False propriety will be my gain.

No kindness appears whenever I'm doing my best.
You'll proud and play GOD,
And not have a moment of rest.

Give me your mind and I'll find a way.
To tune it and prune it,
You will have a miserable day.

Paul J. Toth

I Watched The Children Swimming

Resting on my bike in route to the store
with my feet moving backwards making circles with the pedals

Hands gripped on the chain fence keeps the balance of the bike
I watch the children swimming but only see myself

That's me over by the diving boards
friends pushing and daring me just to jump off the high-board

That's me again over the concession stand
trying to be the joker in order to make the group laugh

That's me once more over by the lifeguard
being scolded for running
after the lifeguard soundly blew his whistle

That's definitely me getting out of the water mad
cursing the other child who just "dunked me"
aqua-phobia ruling my anger

Now look at me tear in my eye from the memories
hidden by dark sunglasses and fogging my vision

I want to steal their age
so I can run up to them
be in their groups
if only for this afternoon

Robert E. Simpson

Courage

When I have a friend, I am Wise.
With my friend, I have no thighs
Or, at least, they do not steal the scene
Or make it so awfully cruel and mean
To have them there.

When I have a friend, I am Tall.
I even venture from the wall when standing
Out in public places, and Thank the Lord
I don't have braces on the off hand chance
My mouth should open.

When I have a friend, I'm Pretty.
Instead of my usual frenzied fits
Over this face that's full of zits,
To mine and everyone else's surprise
Someone will actually notice my eyes.

Just last week, I heard this guy,
"Who's the Babe behind the glasses
Who's got the eyes like warm molasses?"

I almost had the nerve to say,
Which maybe I'll actually do one day

Because I have a friend.

Stephanie Ann Malina

Still Life

The artist, God, develops life
with skill on ever-changing Earth.
Each shadow and expression small
is given constant care from birth.
He paints with several styles and
for each there is a palette gay.
His paintings are alive, but when
they dry and colors turn to grey,
He draws His final masterpiece.
In charcoal He depicts the scene,
as strength-filled strokes create still life,
the rest of death remains unseen.

Susan Elizabeth Wildey

"Going Home"

On the terra where men stood - stood death.
With somber shadow eyes, tall and still.
Its face looked smooth, like burned ashes turned to powder grey.

Onward and forward, soldiers are command to go in war!
despite the threat of death, that engulfs their every step.
Onward and then the boy is dead.

On the terra where men stood-instead, stood death.
I had seen his anguish pleading eyes.
Invoke to mortal man.
Engulfed by death's somber shadow eyes.
And saw him standing tall and still.
His face looked smooth-ash powder grey.
And yes, I saw death standing there.

I commanded! . . . him.
Into the face of death.
"Onward!" I - I, said. "Onward!"
And then. . . and then . . . I cry.

I am "going home" I said. Minus a leg.
Upon the hill of war! The purple-crimson Hill; I waved good-by.
Regretfully to death.

Samuel M. Soto

Autumn Swim

The day is surely an Autumn surprise.
With sultry heat and clear cool splashes mingling
to create sensations so sweet,
they left me gasping with delight.

Autumn always hugs me with snug deliberation,
makes me feel exalted and deliciously cared for,
when the soft breezes and gentle sunshine
caress my skin like familiar lovers...

...and I dream
of waters that are calm and clear
and soft swishing meadows
that gleam in the sun
...and I run
hand in hand with a lover
who's soft eyes meet mine
across a path of acceptance
on the tortuous route we've come.

Tania H. Adendorff

Embrace

She dreams
with the stare of thought and concentration
That which has been created in her heart is still of a seedling,
much to give, as to experience
Lighting the candles which give off radiant energy of Inspiration
Hope and Creativity-glisten-with that stare
What you can see of what gives her sight
tells stories to which children fall asleep
left with expression of security, fulfillment, and peace
awaiting the day to come
To spend time with
thoroughly defines every second that passes
One that thinks now is flooded with questions
stimulating growth
expanding the boundaries of knowing
The words exchanged have more meaning than that man
could ever fathom or bring about
God has only created the mountains and oceans just as beautiful
Another evening ends
Embrace

Michael J. Russamano

Oh, How I

I feel as though I have been left alone to deal
with the unknown. With every step that I take, I
feel uncertain of my life that's known.

For you had always been there for me, and now I
face the long, long road alone. Oh, how I wish that
you were here, to see and watch us grow.

With Joshua now four starting off to school to learn
lots more, and Nicole now thirteen, going to the eighth
grade and middle school once more.

Candice now eleven, heading to the sixth grade, hopping,
jumping all the way, with her feet upon the ground. Oh,
how I wish you were here, to see each one grow.

Oh, how I miss you and long to have a hug and hear you
say, "what are you doing girl?" and I would reply, I'm
home to see you mom and stay with you for a while.

Oh, how I long to hug, smell and hear you and see you again,
but I just don't know when. But until that happy day
please know, that I love you so very much and that we
will hug and smile with each other again someday.

Rose Marie Kessinger

The Run Of Life

Spontaneously, she began through the jagged hills,
With unknown obstacles ahead,
She fled with determination and courage,
Drenched with salty sweat,
Infinite tears streaming down her flushed face
In the cold refreshing winter day
Her breath visible in the misty weather
"Just a little longer" is her incentive
Her aching muscles ready to collapse
like a strand of dominos at the tip of a finger.
Trees branching over her,
Blocking the sunlight and sheltering her.
The feeling of persistence
The want of succeeding
Determination, fear, peace, and question all in one.
The run of life.

Laurie Goble

God's Talk

God's talk is soft and kind
With words from his heart and not from his mind

Thoughts of thanks are sent his way
When people on earth kneel down to pray

We send him prayers and petitions of hope
And know that he is helping us cope

But, we know that we can really resolve
All of the problems we ask God to solve

God's talk is comforting and quieting
And calms us down when we are fighting

To help us realize violence isn't the answer
When some are fighting not wars but cancer

Or abuse or addiction or hatred or aids
or trying to survive unexpected raids

But if you are quiet like a preying hawk
You might just be able to hear God's talk.

Shannon E. Schueller

My Little Girl

Nine years ago, Easter Morning, at 2:32, the Lord saw fit to bless us with you.
You were wrinkled, red and not much to see,
But you were my little girl and everything to me.

As the years pass by, and how quickly they've flown,
it's hard to believe how tall you have grown.
No longer a tot, with a question "where brother go"?
But a little lady with seeds in life that she much sow.

Before my eyes, a lovely young lady I see, that makes me proud I'm
the father of she. Through your youth and innocence in your face
I see, the purity and goodness that God intended there to be.

Your eyes beautifully bright, clear as the quiet sea. Like the
stars in the heavens racing through eternity.
Your mouth is expressive filled with a laughing ring,
that makes your father feel like a youth on the first day of spring.
Your chin is classic like a Grecian art, that among other girls,
it stands you apart.

But the treasure you possess, that I admire the most, is inside
you, put there by the Holy Ghost.

For your radiance, tenderness, compassion, a gift from above;
This is God's definition of the word called LOVE.

J. Leo Bainter

Patti M.

She was young and wild
Without a care in the world
A temper far from mild.
Though she was very honest and pure
Her problems were many -
We didn't see a cure
Thoughts ran dark and deep
Parties; Dancing, drinking
What could she be thinking
Years have gone by
She has grown and become responsible
Although none thought it possible
A job. she'll retire from soon
But - has she fully come out of her cocoon?

Mary K. Goss

Homeless And Alone

A little girl sits lonely and cold.
Without anyone's love for her to behold.
Lonely without the attention of one.
Cold when no love has been shown.
A crystal clear tear drop falls silently down.
It slid down her cheek and fell to the ground.
One single tear drop was all she could cry.
Not even a sound, just a sigh.
She wonders why she is still here today.
She has no guidance to show her the way.
She has no one to love and behold.
She only sits lonely and cold.
A little girl left in despair.
Without anyone to care.
Now she has no fears.
The good Lord took her and wiped away her tears.

Stephanie Slater

The Wolf

The wolf stares with an evil glare.
Without knowing he starts running, but from what?

Only he knows something is out there.
Here, there, and everywhere it is.

Suddenly he stops without notice or care.
He sits on his haunches, and as he howls on all is still.

He looks ahead,
only to see what he knows is already there.

In the ebony darkness,
he looks only to find himself.

He runs and runs to catch up with himself,
but it is not enough.

Try harder! He thinks,
but still it is not enough yet.

The sun is starting to rise. Quick! Return to the start.
When he reaches it, he must lie down and sleep.

He did not succeed tonight,
yet he will try harder and harder each time.

Go to sleep for now, do not think.
Till he succeeds, there will be no end.

Laurentia Ash

No Longer Here

My days are long, my nights are short, my heart is empty without you to start.

You're no longer here to make me smile. You're no longer here to wipe the tears from my eyes.

You're no longer here for the little things I need, for God is supplying all my needs.

You're no longer here for the road I have ahead. For in your children I can see you're not dead.

You're no longer here to make me see the smile I so often see, for I have you in a special place in my heart for there you will never part.

Without your memories I couldn't go on. For I ask God to make me strong.

Phyllis S. Burney

Journey of Mind

Each dawn begins the journey to find
Wonderful thoughts to fill the mind
To follow a path in quest for treasure
Of beauty and love, our fountain of pleasure.

How joyous the thoughts to capture by sight
The majestic trees the sun so bright
To breathe in creations with an awesome sigh
While the birds sing softly as they soar on high.

Life is a mystical journey for sure
A search to keep mind with thoughts that are pure
Because the peace that is sheltered within the heart
The journey of mind becomes a work of art.

Such noble thoughts, a right since birth
For our is the sea, the sky, this earth
Then suddenly a voice within us sings
Thank you "Lord" for all these things.

Marie C. Scarna

When We Shall Meet Again

I sit upon the seashore,
Wondering what is to become of me,
Now that you have gone.
The waves roll in and out again.
I listen for your voice to talk to me.

Why did you have to leave me here,
and fly away without me to the sky?

The evening comes on quickly.
The stars appear like tears upon my face.
I wish that you were here.
Remembering all the good times,
The smiles, the tears, we shared together then.

But now you've gone away from me.
On angel's wings you soar above the clouds.

I think about tomorrow,
I know someday we'll walk along again.
Someday on heaven's land,
Then life will be eternal.
Friend by friend, with God, we'll be together,
Forever.

Miriam Adams

I Made Mommy Do It

Mommy what have I done this time
Won't you explain why you beat me, make me scream and cry
Please don't punch me in mouth I won't say that again.

Mommy I promise I won't do it no more
I'm so tired of being knocked down on the floor
My lips are swollen and my eyes are black
The belt buckle put a hole in my back
Please Mommy your hands they are choking me.

Oh Mommy I love you I'm sorry I made you cry
I'll cover my marks and tell my teacher a lie.

Mommy I told you nobody will take you to the court in town
I told my teacher I fell down and all she did was frown

See Mommy I'll protect you and we will survive
I'm only 5 but I know how to hide and to lie

Mommy why did you push me down the stairs
Ouch Mommy why do you keep hitting me in my head

Oh God what have I done to Mommy, I wish I were dead

Mildred Briscoe

The Voice Within

When silence is greater than spoken thoughts
Words overtake my mouth
Sometimes they hurt then try in mood
To swing, but they don't fool
The sharp old world.

When rivers of doubt cut through my thoughts
Like clouds cut up the sky
Important ideas wavering stand
To lose, but they don't fool
The sharp old world.

When thoughts of mine surprise myself
They shadow beliefs yet hug
Like tough old roots in ground
To bloom, but they don't fool
The sharp old world.

When finally God's thoughts prevail
And dwell within my heart
With joy, faith and love
To give, the sharp old world
Takes note.

Olive Anne Curtis

One More Day

From the day you brought me into this
world as a small human being called
a precious baby girl,
The Lord has stuck by my side from
the day I was able to open my eyes
and rise,
He's been that special little guide
that will protect anything that
stands in my way,
I pray, "Lord Spare Me One More Day"
We all have problems that we must face,
We all are running in life's terrible race,
and must stand together and not apart
and give God our soul and heart,
so take the time from now and then to pray,
Lord if you may,
"Please: Spare Me One More Day."

Veleka Edwards

The Pages Of His Book

Would you like to know how the world began?
Would you like to know how and who made the
animals and man?
It is sweeter than honey, better than money, the
pages of his book.
And all we have to do is open it and look,

If you want to walk and talk to him and keep
your life free from sin;
Take his book and begin you will find how from within.
Are you seeking answers to your prayers?
Then look to the book and ask one who cares.

He tells us our salvation is more precious than gold
And the story of sweet Jesus is the most beautiful
one told.
How he died for our sins and as predicted, he arose.
The pages of God's Book are impossible to close.

Virginia L. Fenner

Untitled

His light pierces through your
yearning for deceiving demise.
He sees all your intrepid disguises,
as is it didn't already appear
like a scribe on your sweet beautiful face.
Oh world, can't you see?
Oh world can't you see yourself anymore?
The world evolves through
time that stops not once for any one thing.
One God moving it all. Guiding
the seconds with His light.
The sun and the stars continuing
and containing endless abounds
of lives content of contentments.

Maxwell Twylight

One

You are nothing, grandmother told me.
You are everything, grandmother said.
You are the child of my child and her children.
You are the mother of our mothers, she said.

You are a hundred thousand million.
And...You-you are...One.

I will come to you only when you call me.
I will walk your visions. We will travel far.
I will go with you only if you want me.
I will be your eyes, you will be my heart.

Then grandmother took me to the shadow of my memory.
The rivers ran together, the paths became a road.
The trees became a cradle for the children of the future.
The leaves whispered secrets of what we've always known.

You are a hundred thousand million
And...You-you are...One.

Cheleque

Ode To The Fly

You wing your way into our home
and aggravate, but yet,
you take off each time you land
just like a boeing jet.
The swatter is your biggest fear.
I see it in your eye.
So you zoom and zoom around the room.
Then splat, so long, goodbye!

Ruth Ann Myers

My House

My house is nice and big and warm
A good place to be in case of a storm
It has a porch and a big upstairs
With lots of tables and lots of chairs

Linda Leisring

Hero

Do you know you are my hero?

You are everything I love.
You are my hero sent from above.

You are what I admire and what I want to be
You are a shimmering diamond in the sky for everyone to see.

You're the highlight of my life and
I cherish the times I'm with you.
My only wish is that you feel the same way too.

You are the wind that soars under my golden wings to help me
fly up in the sky.
You are there to lighten my days when I feel the need to cry.

You are like the crystal that makes the prism when the sun
shines through
And no matter what you are or what you do I will always love you.

I hope I shall be with you always and never part
But if we are separated you will always be in my heart.

You are not alone even if you are far away
In my heart you are here to stay.

Nicole K. Sharpless

A Comet Seen-Dark Of The Morning

You race across the vastness - pursued by the Hounds of Time;
You burn, tear, melt your way through the stygian black of
the universe;
To what rendezvous? With what purpose?

You scream in silent speed through unbelieved emptiness;
Your fiery form cold in the abysmal depths of eternity.

Man sees you and, learnedly, says, "Ah, a comet!"
Or more commonly, "Money, Money, Money."; Earlier, in fear,
"A Sign!"

But, you hurtle your lone, speeding bit of hell,
Enroute to another place, another system, another time;
Probably unknown, un-named, Predestined?

Your end?
A fiery explosive spray ... to microcosms of dust?
A flash out - to a dark hulk?
Tearing on - ever on - in a vacuum of forever-night.

William G. Redel

Halloween

Kids may think on halloween
you can just trick or treat.
Prank, scare and run amuck.
Well, you're wrong and out of luck.

Because ladies when you put on that gown,
the bodies will start coming out of the ground.

And guys, when you put on that fake cut,
they will devour you like sipping tea out of a cup.

So you can go out and play
and stay up all night and day.
But tonight you better watch your back,
for you may be their mid-night snack.

Lulana Calhoun

Untitled

Living and learning and paying your dues
You can't understand 'til it happens to you
What do they mean when they tell you what's right,
It's hard to believe cause it's not in your sight.
Experience is the teacher that serves you the best,
Something new every day puts yourself to the test,
I try so hard to make the right choice,
Which road to take, which opinion to voice
I am still young my whole life ahead,
And I'll strive for success 'til the day I am dead.

William L. Clay

Shadow Drift

As the shadows of past memories drift along in full review,
you come to mind, so often, just as if you planned anew
to open up old doors and set the windows of my heart ajar
and stand and watch the teardrops fall.
As always - from afar.

Don't be afraid to share; we did so in the past and there
are more than memories, if only the net you'll cast.
For the sea is ever changing as it ebbs and flows each day,
making all things fresh and new that wander in it's way.

So, as the shadows of past memories drift along in full
review
come, sit with me awhile and I will share with you.

Mary Lou Lieblong

Not A True Friend

Lord I've failed my friend I didn't understand,
You could reach her through me.
I was so busy with my life, I never took time to say;
"God Loves You"!

Words unspoken time pasted,
Forever gone, it did not last
A true friend I was not,
Three words unspoken...

Now comes the time to say goodbye;
And so few years pasted
I can't look, the casket there, of one who trusted me;
Words unspoken throughout eternity.

Melody Faircloth

Dad

When the world had seemed to give so little,
You gave to it so much,
Whether with your poems, rhymes and riddles,
Or with your gentle loving touch.

Your faith in God was O'so great,
Faith that money can not buy,
Although this sickness claimed your fate,
Your spirit never died.

You taught me everything I know,
On the field or at the school,
You sped me up when I was slow,
And showed me all the rules.

Your smile's the thing I remember best,
It never left your face,
Even when life was such a pest,
Your smile showed such grace.

I talk of you and fill with tears,
I think of you and sigh,
I wish that you could be right here,
Cause it's so hard to say goodbye.

Ryan Johansen

Procrastinator's Confession

My robot hands reach out at down.
You greet me sweetly every morn.
I yearn to soak up all you know,
quietly mesmerized by your glow.
Held captive by you through the years,
you brought me laughter, brought me tears.
There were times, I must say, you made
me sick, I'd walk away.
I've been disgusted by your sight, but
I returned to you each night.
My heart knows for what I'm meant and
you can never pay the rent; I let you separate
my soul, drown noisy fears of this life's goal.
Never letting on you were more than distraction
nor confessing true attraction.
You've been my comfort, ever bliss, on
long and lovely nights as this.
Revived from dreams by your gentle hiss.
It's been forever plain to see you'll always
be right here for me, I'll never leave you dear T.V.!

G. Held

The Street

I see you walking down the street,
You have no shoes on your feet,
The clothes you wear are torn and tattered,
By the bruises you're wearing, I know you've been battered,
I see you walking down the street,
Wondering tonight where you'll sleep,
What's happened for you to live this way,
And why oh why do you choose to stay?
Life's not easy, no one said it would be,
But we have a choice you and me,
Living on the street will drag you down,
Next thing you know you're six feet under the ground,
Life is worth living, someday you'll see,
Then you'll know you're truly free.

Pamela A. Downey

Step-Mother

"I want a baby," I heard her say.
"You know I had two that passed away."

"Two boys and two girls,
A perfect family's what we're striving for."

For better or for worse was commitment enough for me
Until a pleading call to take in Stephanie.

Difficult to love and impossible to manage,
She was flown from Florida for us to fix and to bandage.

Runaway, truancy, drugs, and suicide;
Her only defense was to escape and to hide.

Anger, resentment, abuse, and hatred,
What had this soul of fifteen been fed?

To doctors, judges, and counselors we went
Seeking guidance, support, and a chance just to vent.

No fancy house, expensive clothes, or nifty car-
The best we have to offer is who we are.

I'm different because I can choose to love and nurture-
No natural or legal requirements for this or anything more.

This is my gift to you from me:
To say "I love you, Stephanie."

Nancy Hunt

Wonders Of Wonders

Have you ever watched a tear drop the from the cheek of the one you loved,
Or watch a bird fly from the ground to the sky above?
Have you ever watched the leaves of a willow tree bow slowly to the ground,
or watch a pup at play with a little child?

Have you ever watched a raindrop slide down a window pane,
or seen the sun turn scarlet on an autumn's eve?
Have you ever seen a rainbow after a storm, or seen a rose
bow its' head after its' leaves are torn

Have you ever watched an ant make its' little home, or seen
a child's wonderment of kittens being born?
Wonders of wonders what my eyes cease to see, but the
biggest wonder of all is how God can still love me.

La-Verda F. Andres

Being Perfect

To be acknowledge in our society,
You must be what is considered a perfect ten.

To say and do the right things is cool,
You must be in style and not out.

If you are overweight people gawk at you,
If you are a nerd they laugh.

Every one has a good quality,
Though it may not show on the outside.

You must take the time to get to know a person,
Then you will know the treasure within them.

What really makes someone cool,
Or makes them a nerd?

Are they cool, because they know a lot of people?
Are they nerds because they are really smart
and wear glasses?

How can we win when every day we are judging someone,
Or being judged by someone else?

How are we to judge what is, and what isn't
When no one is really perfect themselves.

Sareena Houmand

These Are The Things I Want

I want to hold you close and never give
you reason for tears.

I want your days and your nights,
your months and your years.

I want to do for you the little things that
will bring a smile to your heart.

I want your nearness, I want your love.

I want to walk with you and talk with you,
to love you and make love with you.

I wanted you before I knew you, I want
you now and I'll always want you.

These are the things

I want.

Larry L. Moore

Don't Kill Yourself

Don't kill yourself, there's no hurry.
You should not make a decision out of sadness and fury.
Life is not as horrible as it seems;
Don't end it all now and give up on your dreams.
You must realize you have your whole life ahead.
You surely can't enjoy it, if you are dead.
Before you know it, it will be your time to pass.
Life is precious, and it goes by too fast.
Lots of people can be cruel, that is definitely true.
But open your self-centered mind and
realize that others have it worse than you.
Suicide is selfish, it destroys the ones who care.
You aren't the only victim, you should be aware.
Instead of being pessimistic, you should think positive.
There are so many reasons you are meant to live.

Natalie Luber

Afraid of My Heart

From long ago there was one untrue to you
You stood in line, yet love never to find
I am here, the line has disappeared for you
Afraid of my heart, I give unto you!

You wondered for years, looking for a love.
Desert heat, northern storms, couldn't yield a love
And yet, you looked for that one true love
Afraid of my heart, I give unto you!

Sometimes, I think you are still looking for a love.
Yet, you don't need to look further than I for love.
For you see, true love is within me for you.
Afraid of my heart, I give unto you!

I'm here for you to love now and for eternity!
Don't look upon a love that lost, set yourself free!
Don't spend days or years looking back to them.
Afraid of my heart, I give unto you!

Lynn Vaughn

"Praise And Love For You"

I have watched you over the years as
you struggle and drag your way through a day...

I have seen you with the weight of the family
and life's cruel ways fast at your back while you
call forth wishful dreams to quiet the tears from your eyes.

I have heard you singing on the edge of a nights dream
as you pass your heart felt feelings to those in need, and as
you recharge us with your smile and soft spoken words.

I have wondered with my eyes open wide and full of glee
as I say on to thee, what a woman my sister must be as she
moves with great strength through earth's fog with such grace
amidst the rain and urge us all to take onto another day.

......and although I can't carry a tune,
I want to sing with you a simple duet with quiet echoes
telling of love and deep emotions that spirit your fears away
and calm the painful nights.

All this I say before you, to let you know dear sister,
you are here on God's Earth for those who love you and need to
hold you near.

Yvonne V. Gray

Farewell My Friend

You came to me from out of the blue
you were lost, you were hungry, yet you knew.
you knew you found a place called home and thus
you became my very own.
You were so very small, but the joy you
brought was best of all.
As time went on we became great friends
we had good times, we had bad times, but we
always made amends.
We grew together almost as one,
boy! all the great times we had together
if I could only pick just one.
I'll miss you buddy, I'll miss you a lot
like in the morning when you tapped your
paw gently on my cheek, or when on a
cold winter's morning you snuggled at my feet.
I'll miss you, more than you will ever know,
but believe me when I say I'll never let
your memory go! So with a tear in my eye,
I must bear the burden of saying goodbye.

Scott E. Scholl

"The Doorway To Your Heart"

You weren't quite back on your feet again
You weren't even wondering when
Someone else would come along
That could fill your heart with a song

Here I am standing at the doorway to your heart....

The one you've almost finished repairing
The one he tore down without caring
But I won't do that to you
I don't want to see you blue

Upon this step I will stay
Please don't push me away

Here I am standing at the doorway to your heart....
Will you let me in?

Robert Lamb

"Reach Out"

As a Toddler, I would cry
you would come running as fast as you can,
You would speak a silent word to me and reach out
And you let me take your hand.
As a baby I would fall down
Or twist my ankle in the sand,
You would lovingly wipe away my tears
And gently reach out your hand.
As a teenager I would feel left out
Without any friends to help me stand,
You'd try your best to make me feel complete
As you willingly reached out your hand.
As a young adult, I would get depressed
When some things didn't turn out as planned,
You would give me your shoulder to lean on
And caringly let me hold your hand.
As an adult, I am now able to balance
Get to my feet at my own command,
Which is why now when you need help
I can confidently reach-out my hand.

D. Travis McWilliams

Cappuccino Lady

Did you know you're her favorite regular?

She's the brunette always behind the counter
You'd think she lives there
Who says her name? (the one everyone forgot)
What do you know from her polite greeting?

Yeah, she's real as real
with a cat, two sinks, burnt toast
A bed to fall into when she finishes her shift
No one greets her
But she's happy just the same
Music fills the silence
No mirrors on he walls
because she's afraid to see the scar
Afraid to remember the pain
No one will see
She protects herself now

Morning breezes through the windows
It's business as usual
Coffee and cake cover everything
Don't they?

Leah Carlson

Cancer

I fighting a war that cares not who you are
Young or old life unfinished, untold
cancer has a hold
and God is waiting for my soul
taking away all my pride this I can not abide
he is fierce and strong
and though I've done no wrong
with the loss of hair I no longer care
the sun doesn't shine
because the day is not mine
from dusk until dawn the fight goes on and on
how can I stand proud when I'm not allowed
I just wanted to be a part of what's here you see
so I leave this rhyme hoping it will survive time
and someone will pleased that there really was a me
but if you can't see the beauty of this day
how can you know me in any way
I can never tell if I'll be remembered well
now the battle must go on
and it's just we three the devil, God and me

Nancy McCombs

You Stand at My Door

Predator, you stand at my door
Your eyes a blaze of evil,
Your greedy jaws with which you kill,
And your appetite for innocence.

But this child is mine,
And you shall not have him.
The cold world beyond this place is yours
To devour and destroy as you wish.

But predator, you stand at my door.

Behind this door is warmth and love.
This child wears the armor of my faith,
Wields the sword of his Fathers love,
Holds high the shield of his family.

If he cannot resist your temptations,
I will rise up against you, and I will defeat you.
Predator, you stand at my door.
Predator, Beware.

Michelle Weninger

Cliff Diving

Rocks press gently on the soles of your feet
Your flesh begins to warm from the suns constant heat
The fall is raging and fills the air
A cool mist rises, do you dare?
Fifty feet down the pool is deep
It's an excellent ride, but it's steep
Extend your arms and close your eyes
For a moment, you think you can fly
Go to the edge and bend your knees
Then throw your body into the breeze
It seems so long till you reach the end
The freedom you feel begins to extend
Water surrounds you, body and spirit,
Your blood is rushing, you know, you hear it
Then out of the freshness you feel no pain
And climb the cliff to do it again

Paula McKinney

The Lord's Flowers

The Angel said to the Lord above
Your flower is here, the one you ordered with love

He looks so nice in our bouquet
We will have to let the family know he's ok

Heaven is in a heavenly bloom
We are truly sorry we had to take him so soon

The Lord needed Cody in heaven with him
Up here a new life with the angels will begin

Sometimes the Lord will order an old fern
Ferns accent our bouquet and help the younger ones learn

Or maybe he'll order a middle aged carnation
He'll set her in the vase and sit back in admiration

At times he'll want a bud or two
I know its sad another one had to come from you

Then the Lord will say
I want some baby's breath today

We will order another flower again
Life is not over - it will just begin

One day you too will be in our vase
Looking again into your baby's face

Tamara S. Sebesta

Guardian Angel

May the angel of goodness watch over you
your guardian angel be.
As you walk through life may your steps be strong,
and no stumbling along the way.
May you ever be humble, watch over those
lest fortunate than you,
And show the love for others that God
bestows on you.
Though the river of life rages beneath you,
show ye no fear have faith in your
guardian angel for she is always near.
Happiness, love, joy are near as long as
you believe in your guardian angel

Shirley Conaway

Mothers' Hands

I remember your hands
Your hands together at rest.
Like the wings of doves
Keeping love and peace within.
I knew their touch well
Since earliest memory.
My small fingers holding on for love and life-
There was safety always
In your arms, mother.
Your cool touch still lingers
On fevered brow remembered,
Soothing away disturbing dreams.
How wonderful it felt at graduation,
Your hands clasping me close
Wishing me joy, wishing me well!
And I remember the last time
I touched your hands in sorrow
-Delicate, veined marbled hands,
Lifetime love in hands at rest.

Olga Blaus

Dear Sister

There were eighty guests at your birthday party, one for each year of your life.
Here are a few happy memories minus the drum corps and fife.
As teenagers: I borrowed your new winter coat although I knew it would give you a rise.
I felt in the groove, which just goes to prove that once I wore your size.
Swimming: You tried to teach me how to dive. On the diving board I'd hop.
You're known for your beautiful "Swan Dive," I'm known for my "Belly Flop."
Ice skating: New years weather was B-zero. Street lights gave off soft beams.
It was so nice being alone on the ice, when we were in our teens.
So gracefully you skated the figure 8. My envy was the color of green
Cool as a cucumber, I doubled your number and skated the figure 16.
One thing, for sure: We will never be "over the hill," you and I, no matter what the climate.
In order for us to be "over the hill", first we'd have to climb it!
It's wonderful having an older sister who can live to be one hundred and three, because no matter how old I get, you will still be older than me.

Ruth Chapman Keith

To The Third Season

Your wind brushes my face as I step out of the door,
Your scent tempts me with fragrance more and more,
Generations upon generations have spoken of thy lore,
Autumn, you thrill my soul to its very core!

Your faithful, ever changing trees,
Are seemingly taunted by the bustling breeze,
Until they shed their colorful leaves,
Falling, wavering to and fro like the waves of the great seas.

Who has not beheld your charm and your grace,
When the dreary heat of summer you replace?
You send a smile of delight O're my face,
You take me away to a heavenly place.

Autumn, who can express your worth,
When your flowers and fruit spring forth?
Of your sweetness there is certainly no dearth,
Rising, rising from the abundant earth!

Shelley Wilson

I Do Like You

Everyday that we are together, we are bound some way forever
Your smile, your touch, and your dark eyes, they are all my sunshines
Talking to you makes me feel comfortable, I'm glad that we're both stable
there are some secrets, but for now they are kept
How do I tell you how I feel, I want you to know that I'm for real
You may think different but that's on you, just letting you know I'm no fool
I've always felt this way, it seems like everyday I pray
I hope you understand, this is something that was unplanned
Do you know what I'm getting at, or are things just out of whack
It's hard for me to tell you this, I guess I'm afraid of getting dissed
Would you do that to me, would you just leave things be
Hopefully you won't, 'cause I know I don't
Is this a shock to you, I'm only giving you a clue
I might as well tell you now, let's just say everything is a big 'wow'
I really like you, I really do, I hope in your heart you like me too

Melisa A. Racho

My Quest

I open Your Word, I long to see,
Your teaching of wisdom, Your perfect decrees;
Prepare my mind and train my ears;
Speak to me, Lord; allow me to hear.

I can't live without You, for my sins are severe;
They've brought You the Cross, they caused You the spear.
Words of forgiveness have set me free;
Act of deliverance restored me to Thee.

Your Grace and Mercy will find no peer,
Your limitless Love is all too clear;
The eternal Hope does dry my tears,
Your Promise of glory sure calms my fears.

My quest to You, Lord, is most sincere,
So, grant me this wish for my remaining years:-
I seek Your presence, I want You near;
Just let me be ready when You appear!!!

Margaret Chan

The Last Moment

On a long and quiet highway road
You're in my car in a freezing night
And it's watching me through the car window
When you leaned on me at a gentle carve
You remained silence and gave me a smile

The bright street lights lead,
The both side of highway road
It seems like forever...
You're still in my car in a freezing night
And it's watching me through the car window

The highway is getting the end of road
The beautiful city-night-lights seem like,
They're shooting stars in the distance
But we are driving on the wrong way...

Please don't say anything right now,
Just by my side
And just hold me,
Just hold me.

Ryuji Iwazaki

Loves' Beacon

It turns me on to see you, you've got to know how much
You're the reason for my heartbeat, I've got to feel your touch

Your voice is like a beacon, to a ship that's lost at sea
When you open up your heart, and take time to talk to me

The way you talk to me, lets me know that you care
Your words fill up my mind, and follow me everywhere

The things we talk about, make me break out in a smile.
It gives me such a good feeling, that I haven't known for quite awhile

I forget all about my worries, I'm so happy to be here
My spirit is floating higher, like I'm walking around on air

There's nothing I wanna do, but to be here by your side
And share my dreams forever, with you throughout our lives

One touch from your hand, sets my soul on fire
My passions start to burn, you light up my desires

Look into my eyes now girl, and you'll know that this is true
There can be no denying, about what our love can do

Our love can free our souls, from the traps of previous love
And make our lives complete, as intended from above

So now I send this message, to let you know it's true
I'll always have this feeling, forever will I love you

Victor J. Arca

Lost Souls Walking In The Mist

When you look don't be blinded.
What you seek is never what you find.
There are always secrets within, that no one sees,
Until the moment you go to far,
The point of no return.
You become a lost soul walking in the mist,
Never letting you real self out again.
You put up a shield that will never fall until you do.
Fall into the sadness forever.
Never to regain what you lost,
Only to hold on to the sadness,
Because you cannot see any other way.

Michelle Schubert

Count The Cost

I sit, I stare, and I wonder...
Has this race truly been worth it?
What has become of the dreams of my youth?
I wait for the answers as my head slowly sinks downward.

Then softly...
So softly there comes a slight whisper.
As if brought by the wind the whisper now answers.
The joy that you seek in these riches today,
Can never fill your inter-most vessel.
To late too many learn the meaning of worth,
The love, the laughter, the hand that we hold,
This is the treasure that never will grow old.

Then the sound turns to sight,
As I raise my head upward.
The sunset appears to late for the running.
It's glow reaches out with it's warming embraces.
Yet it cannot hide the advances of darkness
Life too soon is rapidly fleeting,
And the cost is not measured,
Till the sand is all gone.

Thomas A. Bendler

Without A Name

Today is just another day of hurt and sorrow which passed my way...
To share, to love, to hug and kiss, these are the things I miss..
We fuss, cuss, and use awful names, but in the same breath we want to change.
My heart is sad when he comes near, I know he's not satisfied till I'm in fear...
I cringe and cower from his hatefulness, then wish for only peacefulness
Some days I feel weak and others strong, for all I want is to along
To be in love with love no one should live, it takes two and both must give...
Me to you and you to me, that's the way our marriage should be...
Not fussing, cussing, and calling my mother, but loving, trusting,
 and caring from each other...
There is much to learn from our mistakes, but for now, can't we take a break?
Time apart is the subject at hand, but do you really think we can?...
You claim you don't mean the "words" you say, naturally I believe at
 least for that day...
Then it's "you b*tch! I hate you... get out of my face!! Pack your
 sh*t and get out of my place!!"
I walk away with a heavy heart, and wonder why I simply can't depart
My family and friends wish I would go, but then again they just don't know...
Each day I ask, why do I stay? When it's painfully obvious he wishes me away...
I guess I believe he will change, but he's already said no!, so don't don't complain...

Renee Antonia Robinson

My Mother

As I look back on my childhood days, there are wonderful things to recall;
The Winter that meant so much more to me then, the Spring, the Summer, the Fall.
Excitement of Christmas, the beauty of wild life, curiosity of things yet unlearned;
Gifts that I bought when Mother's Day neared, with great pride from the pennies I earned.
Cakes that were baked when a birthday arrived, stories read every nite
Rushing home from school every day, to a smile so cheerful and bright;
From my mother whose weariness never showed thru, no matter how hard things would get.
A beautiful woman, many people would tell me, and that beauty remains even yet.
For in spite of the worry, the heartache, the struggle, that plagued her until we were grown;
She continued to smile and to keep us amused, greater love will never be known.
Ah yes Mother, how hard you did work, to bring all of your children up well;
If we in our blind youth could only have known, how much you were too proud to tell.
I know I for one had a beautiful childhood, and I know that I speak for the rest,
When I say that when it comes to mothers there's no question that we have the best.
And so Mom, with great pride I write you this poem to express admiration and love;
And to help you to know that all was not in vain, your prayers were heard from above.

Phyllis Knowles LeBlanc

Dawning On The Plains

I awakened as the morning star was flickering its last.
The sky was a gray blue with a blending to light, almost brown at the horizon.
The trees and land were but dark silhouettes as lights from the city flickered about.

Sunrise - a new beginning - a fresh start - a new day with a wonder
 and splendor all its own, never before seen quite as today.
I can see small thin clouds appearing above the eastern horizon,
 making a pathway for her majesty the sun
Would that I could paint these words on canvass to show the beauty and awe I feel within.
I find it difficult to describe the hues of blues, purples, browns
 and shade of yellows and orange beginning to emerge.

The plains - a sunrise on the plains - how many have really seen this
 magnificence; have only stirred and covered and slept until the moment was gone.
I shall not. I shall wait and watch and wonder at what God has given
 me. Another glorious new day, a new beautiful time to love, laugh and be alive.
Above the horizon it's a pale orange now, with a water tower standing
 as a giant monolith guarding the morning from the night before.
The trees are black and jagged against the pale citrus of where they reach.

How quickly God moves his paintbrush to change the colors of dawn.
The sun is up. Awake world. God is alive.

Shirl Stewart

Late at night
I sat at the desk
and stared at indented markings . . .
I had pressed too hard for a poem.

. . . perhaps a sign
would appear
on the sand-pale carpet.

Instead
I saw I had a hangnail
and pulled at it . . .
to make it hurt.

S L Morrow

Eternal Flower Child

Sister mine
Precious sibling
I knew not in my youth.
Had I but taken
A moment,
We could have forged
A shield, you and I
Around the two of us
From the maelstrom
That surrounded.
What seemed to be
A shield of your own
Was only a shell;
And when I pierced it,
discovered the invincible
You that you were
All along,
Eternal flower child,
Sister mine.

Whitney Weinstein

Blind Justice

Stop and think what would it be
If no one on earth could see
If God had just made up his mind
To create a world totally blind
Would there still be hate
And violence and crime
Would we stop seeing the color
And start seeing the mind
Or would we adapt
And find other ways
To segregate like the older days
Problem is what group are you in
The popular group
Or the one condemned
So stop and think
What would you be
Close your eyes
And see

Tammy Pacheco

Daniel, My Love

You touch my heart
so that it hurts
to be away from you.

You give me strength
when I am weak
to go on through my life.

Daniel, my love
how I love you
Can I be your love too?

Rachel Sheldon

Let's Take An Endless Journey

Let's take an endless journey,
Through love's rainbow highway,
And color each other's lives,
With love's hues of priceless gifts.

Together we will taste,
The flavor of love,
And smell the fragrance,
Of a sensual and spicy life.

The love we shall share,
Will shine thru, the crystal rain,
Foretelling us, we'll weather storms,
While helping to ease, our trivial pain.

Taking walks, under the artful display
Of the dancing stars, against the dark sky,
Will serve to remind us, how different,
And important to each other, we will always be.

Thomas W. Halverson

I Am A Book

I am a book who's pages are blank
A book that needs to be written,
I am a book that must have a title
And one that cannot be smitten.

I am a book who's volumes fill the mind
With wonders of thought within,
I am a book of wisdom and hope
To where all good stories must end.

I am a book of laughter
And also a book of sorrow,
Can I be a book to all the people
And still be able to call it moral?

Yes, I am a book who's pages are blank
A book that now needs an ending,
I am a book that's ready to be read
I just hope its not too condescending.

Timothy Mockus

Child Of The Night

Through the night
A child walks
Carefully trying not to stumble
And fall on her face

Through the dark, night sky
She can only see the
Shadow of what awaits her
Praying it is someone to help her

Around every corner
A new worry is waiting
One that if it doesn't kill her
Will only make her stronger

When every hill is a
Challenge of her strength and
A great triumph when complete
Only to be followed by another hill

This child of the night
So fragile, yet strong
Walks slowly, in fright
In the soul of every one of us.

Casey Waswick

LETTING GO OF A MEMORY

A CRAMP OF THE HEART
A CRACK IN THE VISION
A CRASH OF A LIFE
A DECISION OF CLASS
UNIFORMITY OVERCOME AT LAST

A LAST CHANCE
A LEASE ON AN ESCAPE OF
A LESSER MAN
A DECISION OF PRIDE
TAKEN IN STRIDE

A DOSE OF DEPRESSION
A DARKENED DIGRESSION
A DARE FROM DEATH
A DECISION OF FAITH
FRUSTRATED WITH THE WAIT

A CHIME OF LOVE
A CHAIR FOR ONE
A CHOICE TO GO ON
A DECISION OF AGONY
LETTING GO A PIECE OF ME

Paul Kingston

"What Is A Mother"

A mother is love
A devotion that grows,
A from the heart feeling
That she alone shows

She's deep and understanding,
She's friendship that's rare,
She's someone to count on
Who will always be there

She never stop caring
She never stops giving
Her helpful advice
Prepares you for living

Her lasting affection
Will keep you together
A mother is love
That stays with you forever

Nina V. Gonzalez

Many Speak

Many speak of hating wartime.
A docile world they crave the most.
Yet their venom strikes at others,
Waging war within their souls.

Many speak of liking people
And hoping things go well for them.
Yet when the needs of others surface,
They lift no finger; that's no friend.

Many speak of loving children
And wanting them to seek what's good.
Yet do not hug and seldom chide
Then wonder at their selfish ward.

Many speak of being happy
And rightly say it can't be bought.
Yet then they envy other's holdings,
Making wealth their focal thought.

Perhaps we're not so smart a people.
We know what's right yet do what's wrong.
Perhaps, in fact, we're fallen creatures
Who need a Savior after all.

Mark A. Robbins

Come Away and Dream

It's time to go a flying,
A flying in the sky,
To see the clouds of cotton candy,
And watch them all go by.
It may be just a dream to you,
But it's just like heaven to me,
To close my eyes and dream, awhile
of flying in the sky.
And to feel all the stress go away,
Its also like a dream,
So come, please come and fly with me,
Away up in the sky,
So you can dream your dreams awhile,
And wake up with a smile.

Yvonne Williams

Open Bible

Large open Bible on her lap...
A lady stooped and gray
Sat near window reading
At lamplight time of winter day.

My evening bus was crowded;
Each face showed stress and strain;
But as we passed that bright window
All eyes sensed peace again.

Mellow light in picture window;
Wee lady shawled and gray;
Open Bible giving her comfort...
Enriched bus patrons' end of day.

Ree Shaver

Marina

Row upon row, line upon line
a mast forest...
waiting.
Eager in the breeze,
chafing at the waves.
Wind is calling -
"Come fly with me!"
Water is calling -
"come dance with me!"

Bound and lashed - tied.
some struggle. Some, wisely, wait:
No guide for the tiller
no hand on the sheets,
eager for the uncleating touch that says -
"You are free;
let us chase the wind
and catch the waves!
Sun - Salt - Sea
We are free!"
Waiting.

William E. Belli

Flying

What is space?
Between clouds and heaven
As far as you can see
I feel its only me
No sound beyond
only space.

Between land and me
I feel a quite calm
For flying is space
just beyond.

Velda R. Townsend

Sharing Success

We got this note at school today
A note so smooth and kind
It spoke in simple childlike words
But from a grown up mind.

"Thanks a lot for teaching me
Thanks for what I've learned
Thanks for making me speak up
Each time it was my turn.

"Whenever you corrected me
Or put me to the test
I still can hear the things you'd say
You always talked success".

Each teacher who did have that child
Was say'ng "That note's for me
For I recall that student well
So that note's mine, you see".

But after they discussed their claims
They all concluded, thus
That "this great person we had taught
Is thanking ALL OF US".

J. B. Freeman

Gifts

In a hollow, soft and lush
A peasant lived in the brush
He had no money, gold, or such
He often said he didn't need much

The beauty of the countryside
The reverence you feel inside
The puffy white clouds in the sky
The birds chirp a soft lullaby

The fields alive with goldenrod
The bees buzzing from pod to pod
The wheat chaff swaying in the breeze
All these sights to us do please

These things are free to all who seek
The young, the old, the loud, the meek
Our Lord, our God, has surely blessed
"Enjoy these gifts, my child" he said

Molly Kramer

The Front Room

The front room was just for show.
A picture of prosperity, prominence
complete with pleasant faces
adorning ornate furnishings.
No one questioned what lay beyond
the formal facade of this stately manor.
There were no close friends
those who see past paneled walls
into opaque eyes betraying
disinterest, despair, fear
thinly veiled by undying loyalty,
faithful to an unwritten law.
Always pretend, Never tell,
Appearances are everything.

Lynette Lynch

Ode Too...

Kismet was finding you.
Adore you for eons, I will.
Tantalize my heart, and soul, you do.
Habitual is my love for you, still.
Ywis.

Glenn King

No More

Seeking to find
A place in time
Where no war
Will surround me.

Futile efforts
For peace endure.
My mind can hold
No more.

There is no time
In death I'll find
Peace...forevermore.

Teresa Malmberg

May You Find

In your circle of life may you find
A place of hugs and harmony
A place that does not bind
A place to embrace the new
A place to leave the old behind
A place for growth and healing
A place where all is kind
A place to hear the silence
A place to use your mind
A place to gather love and laughter
In your circle, all of these, may you find.

Marilyn Carte

Trees

(With Apologies To Joyce Kilmer)

I think that I shall never see
A poem as ugly as a tree.

A tree that hangs it's head all day
Because its limbs are hacked away;

A tree that can't in summer wear
A robin's nest for lack of hair;

A tree whose roots are damp with tears
From mutilations through the years;

Upon it's bosom snow can't lay
Because its heart's been cut away.

Poems are made by fools like me,
But only man can ruin a tree.

Margaret Owsley

Closest To Her Heart

The pain of a family forever parted.
A precious love forever lost.
Never a thought for the one most dear
The closest to her heart forgotten..

Pushed
The brain
snaps
Saps the
strength
Left to deal
alone
Pushed......

Without the love the heart dies
Leaving a hollow shell
Reaching out for the end
Praying, hoping,
Yet it never comes.

Richard Poindexter-Huseby

What Price Life?

Commentary On The Oklahoma City Bombing

It is impossible to imagine
a price to be levied
for our life.
Nothing
could entice us
to give up our child.
A husband could not barter
for his wife
nor accept a token
when life has been defiled.
Yet now we try
to reason with this carnage.
Our heart convulses
through the whole world's
loss and pain.
We grieve.
The world is drowning in its sorrow.
And we wonder
why the universe
has gone insane.

Nellie L. Mackey

The Ohio

Riverboat churning down stream with
a purpose - what secrets do the
murky waters tell you of?

These river secrets still hidden,
forever hidden, not letting loose
their adventures-

Mighty Ohio, where are the boys who
paddled those rafts and whose
adventures are untold?

Did they discover their treasure of
rubies, diamonds, gold and silver?

Or are their treasures still in their
minds hiding in the immensity of
their dreams still seeking the pirate's
treasure?

River stillness, waters gliding quietly
knowing and not caring,

Your secrets hidden, and in the
vastness of your flowing arms,
never telling the inquisitive mind.

Martha Zackeroff

Stopping Quiet

How do you quiet,
A rippling brook?
Only if the rain,
Quits coming down.

How do you quieten,
An old oak tree?
Only if the wind,
Stands still.

How do you stop,
A flower from growing?
Only if the heat,
Will go away.

How can you quieten,
The forest so loud?
Only if the Lord,
Takes the earth away.

Linda Jolly Hallmark

Past, Present, Future

"Who are we," used to be
a saying for those
who questioned, reasoned, wanted
to know from whence they came
Are we now all playing a different game?

Only a few seem to care, from where
and not in labor, so intense.
Now it's all a pretense.

No thought of then, nor of morrow
or of the possibility of eternal sorrow,
parted from the Giver of life
by a self-sharpened knife

Inherent evil with no attempts
to overcome or to win
urged to inaction by the
unceasing lure of sin

Turn away, run fast
Don't stumble, fall or come in last
Begin again, to Love, to live
Yourself, what a gift to give

Walt Wilkerson

A Penny For The Thought

The darkened night, a howling wind—
a searing pain to feel
The limit of the fear is lost,
among the jumbled graves—
To conflict turn, a time to lose.
A reason we must yearn
The thought of night is day to some,
a place they get to go
The lost they turn around to see,
a far distant place to be
The peace to keep among the rubble there,
a feeling soul is found
To be consumed—a giving up,
the total to be gone
a living light, to turn among,
the fleeting of my life
A soul to bare, a living there,
a witness to my strife
Bound together in this time given to,
this living rhyme.

Roy Collett

Question Of Questions

Come, You must whisper
A secret untold.
Please open to me
The realm you withhold.

For we are the ones
Who inherit the seeds
And are destined to plant
The world with our deeds.

Come, you must show me
The path to the field,
The furrows of grain
That my plantings will yield.

Please, you must share
The vitality of life,
A gift of a song,
The absence of strife.

For you are the one
Of all heavens and earth
Who conceals the key
To life's very worth!

Margaret Anne Knox

Someone To Care For The Children

A little love, a little care.
A sense of being, treated fair
A gentle touch, a friendly smile
Will warm their hearts, for quite awhile

Someone to start them on the way
Someone to guide them right each day
Someone to help them with a task
Someone to care, that's all they ask

If you give them this, you'll discover
A beautiful child beneath that cover
If you give them this, you're done your part
For you're given them a real headstart

H. C. Huie

Love

Love is indescribable
A sense of security
Like a moonlit night
A path in the direction
of happiness
Love is indescribable
Like being touched by angels
A golden warmth glowing within
A strong burning of passion
Warmth by one's presence
Love is indescribable
A waterfall of emotions
Knowing you've got each other
Bringing forth joy
Love is indescribable
The rainbow after a storm
when all else fails,
you've still got love
Love is indescribable.

Tiffany Hall

A False Rose

In a vase, stands
a silk rose
trying to imitate
the delicate original,
and succeeding
at times.
The falseness of plastic and cloth,
the observant notice.
Negligent miss the imitation
and believe.
Silk wishes for vibrance,
and life:
The Natural for
eternal existence

Radhika Sreeraman

Untitled

Words are feelings so she writes
as a hobby as her life

Feelings she expresses
are feelings she can relive

She wants to scream or laugh or cry
this is a way to keep it inside

Her life is a paper
her future's the pen

Sonya Kay Yaw

Untitled

I have a friend,
A special friend,
Who's known by none but me.

We call, we talk,
Enjoying each others company.
We talk of he or of me,
For he thrives on my energy.

Lovers once we might have been
If not for a friendship lost.
Our love is deeper than most by far,
For it's of friendship true and dear.

He's there as friend
To care and to give
He nurtures my every soul.

Few have I know
Who give so much
Than can listened to me
With a love full and free.

Paula Copeland

Journey Though The Night

Everywhere I turn
A tree is falling.

Lost... in this forest of
Thoughts and confusion.

I feel I'm going deaf,
From the thunder.

This storm scrambles my
Thinking...

Blinded by the darkness
For so long...
The rain has stopped.

I see the gentle pink and purple
Dawn light coming over the hills...

Creeping through the forest.
I feel safe now,
The reaper seems distant.

Steven Lail

A Wanderer's Life

In this life I yearn to be
a wanderer lone and ever free;
Free as the wind, free as the tern
that flies from the land to the sea.

The rolling hills beckon to me
to take up the trail soon as can be;
Through pleasant meadows and valleys deep
with spirits a-high, and gentle glee.

I long for lands of distant sight
of old forgotten musty towns;
With paved streets and stone-walled inns
slumbering in peace in the evening light.

Stop I would from time to time
to rest awhile as the sunbeams wane;
But not for long, lest it be too late
to take up the beaten road again.

The endless sky would lure me on
till I take to the final way;
But fear I cannot, since life is a path
which must gently fade some day.

B. Preetham Kumar

These I Have Loved

Large heaps of blankets
A warm, comfortable bed
Some good night's sleep
Without nightmares to dread

Soft reading light
Which glows in the day
The sweet smell of roses
And sound of blue jays

The ripples of troubles
How could I smooth them away?
Those that I loved
Have been betrayed

Cool wind howls
In which the trees sway
Beckoning the trouble
The troubles away

Yet I'm still bitter
Bitter in my soul
Bitter at people
Especially those who destroyed my goals

Samuel Chen

Wishful Thinking

Paint me a rainbow without a storm
A waterfall without a splash
Where hateful winds are not blown
A lightning bolt without a crash.

A tornado without the wind
An argument without a fight
A relationship that will never end
The night without darkness, oh what a sight

A world without hate
Can we all get along
Torment, anger, and frustrate
I guess I was wrong.

Timothy Bickel

Lights

The lights blare glaringly into dusk—
a zillion unblinking, luminescent eyes
that see nothing, but brighten the way
to the Big Cities:
Paris...New York..and Las Vegas
where the asphalt melts under neon signs
that hum...seemingly forever.
Beams weave drunkenly
and dance the Can-Can
Night after night after night
Glass bulbs fluoresce vulgarly
in a spectrum of color and size
Brilliance penetrates the frazzled air
and hangs like a parasite on the dark.
In the name of our country
and at the calling of war
we blackened the windows
and snapped the lines—
but not for else.
We don't believe in stars anymore.

Shilpa Mahesh Sarang

Winds Of Time

The winds of time are blowing
Across the endless sands,
It covers and it moves, all the
Life we understand,

Sometimes the winds will rest,
And life will be serene
Then blow again make life a blur
And put us in a dream,

So while the winds are sleeping
caress the love you feel,

For the winds are cruel,
They'll blow again,
and leave an emptiness that is real

Leonard Sellig

Ships at Sea

I have been one with the sea in ships,
Across the waves and the tide;
I have been once with the sailing ship,
And the gulls along my side.

The waves beat on across the stern,
With spray that's almost rain;
And speak to me of sailing ships,
Lost again and again.

The water slaps upon the hull,
A reminder just for me;
Whose the one to steer the course?
Myself or the violent sea.

Alone are we now, the course is unsure,
A ship far out in the sea;
Where all men go to search
For themselves, and immortality.

There are those who find their peace,
Others, only a notion;
Immortality, is but a fleeting thought,
In the spray, in the fray of the ocean.

Michael Druck

"Without You"

Drops of rain
Against a pane

Clouds of gray
Nothing else to say

Without you
I feel so blue
I hope you feel this way too

Apple of my eye
Makes me wanna fly
The heat from your hand
Makes me feel I can

Silver or Gold
With you, I wanna grow old

Love and happiness
Happiness and love
Neither means nothing without you
my love

Tracey M. Jackson

Burdened Ground

They faced death in single-file,
all damned before their due.
In silence, those peaceful people,
were stolen out of view.

Poisoned thoughts gave birth,
to the poisoning that ensued.
And the fully harbored fears,
fathered the guilt that we elude.

Millions of tear drops fell,
to wash away a blood stained ground.
So many questions still remain,
the answers may never be found.

When the last ash fell,
and the last body was buried.
History was set in stone,
but memories were poorly carried.

Phil Karl Smith

"Wings"

Wings
All I ever wanted
Wings

Every now and then
I'd fly
Up to the moon
And sing with the stars
Sweet dreams
And lullabies
To sleeping babes

No such thing as fear
Nothing
To hear
But the footsteps
Of angels
On the moonbeams

Michelle L. Ault

"Science"

Man alone may create,
All manners of things,
Small and great.

It's come to our aid,
When we're in doubt,
But needs not be repaid.

To our fault we abuse.
The one true gift,
We always use.

It's the good side all know,
But to those more observant,
Be it friend or Foe?

Peter A. Jacob

Dandelion

O, fuzzy dandelion,
As I blow thy seeds away,
They will be,
What thou is today.

Thou art fuzzy,
At thy top,
'Tis nice to blow your seeds away
So this poem will never stop.

Nathan E. Davis

White Roses

When you take a dozen white roses
All of them the same
Their beauty is breathtaking
Yet if you take a red rose
A single red rose
Place it amongst the white
They pale in comparison
In comparison to the red rose
The single red rose
The same is group of women
If you take a group of women
Place them together
They will be breathtaking
You are my red rose
My single red rose
The one to catch my eye
The one to dominate my every thought
To dwell amongst my dreams
To own my heart
My red rose, my single red rose

Michael Vincent Schultz

"Fingernail Grip"

There is a moment in every life when
All that is left is faith and hope
That God will not leave you
to the world,
to circumstance,
to yourself.

In that moment when
there is only you and Him
All of heaven is open
For you to take
as your faith allows
And to move into His presence.

Michael L. Moncayo

The Trees

The wind howled thru the trees
Almost tearing them down.
Their leaves flying in air,
Holding their colors, of red and brown.
The trees bow their heads,
Their boughs almost break.

The storm is severe, the sky black.
Suddenly the wind turns soft, and black,
Suddenly the wind turns out, and slack,
Up in the sky there's a silvery crack,
The trees are smiling, the storms on the run.
There thru the crack, comes the sun.
The storm is over, the trees have won.

Norma Smead

Autumn Fires

In the other gardens,
and all up the vale;
from autumn bonfires,
see the smoke trail.

Pleasant summer over
and all the summer flowers.
The red fire blazers,
the gray smoke towers.

Sing a song of seasons,
something bright in all.
Flowers in the summer,
fires in the fall.

Rebekah Slagter

The Garden Wall

I sat against the garden wall
alone in reverie
and let my mind go wandering
amid the years gone by

There is a special garden
in each and every soul
where flowers planted long ago
bring warmth and afterglow

And so my memories are rich
oft touched by rays of sun
as loving moments catch my breath
of children, one by one

I would have held them close to me
and never let them go
to free upon their own life path
but that was not to be

So now I have my reverie
my mind's great open door
where all of thought is sent to me
and comes from evermore

Nancy Allen Kelly

Drunk Driver

All the signs were there,
although I did not care.

With many traffic tickets received,
this problem I never perceived.

Until one dark night,
I went through a red light.

Striking a car broadside,
throwing the driver to the roadside.

I had taken a life,
a man who had a wife.

I am now in jail,
without any bail.

All those warnings I did ignore,
now my troubles have begun to soar.

Nicholas J. Kayganich

Do You Remember?

You will hardly know who I am
Although I walk next to you day by day,
You saw my face in the crowd
But, again, you were hidden
from reality.
Today I whispered in your ear
But you turned and
went the other way.
I will stand next to you
And you will never know me or see me,
But I am still here
and still...
you hardly know me.
Walk this way,
Listen to my still, small voice
Calling you again and again.
Finally you turn my way,
But it is already too late!
You've been caught and, even now,
you are being pulled from me.

Neal Rogers

American Jade

It's fun to be an Asian girl,
an angless China doll.

Most people ask if I am old
enough to drive a car.

I do get carded every time
when I am in a bar.

You wonder White man sitting there,
you leering from afar,

Obedient, silent, gentle wife.
I'll cook good food for you?

Mail-order bride am I, you ask?
Where can you get one too?

You wonder if I'm nice enough,
approachable and true?

I'm sorry but I'm not like that.
I'm an American like you!

Paula Angeles

White Sails in the Wind

White sails in the wind...
And a blue sea that rocks and rolls.
This is the life I love!
To hear the huge waves beat and break
Against the side of my ship,
To feel sprays of foam splash
In my face...

White sails in the wind...
And a gypsy stir that lures me on
To adventure and romance
Beyond the sky.

Virginia M. Heprian

Dream For Eternity

If I ever fall into a deep sleep,
and am never to awake.
Do not cry, do not ache,
For I have not died, I am
simply in a deep sleep for
all eternity.

Dress me in white satin lace,
lay a single rose up on my face.
Then lay me down on the
soft sandy shore, I ask of
you nothing more.
Do not fear death, it is the
beginning of the end.
I assure you we'll be
together once again!

Melissa Kleinman

Where Angels Fly

Where angels fly,
A way up high,
The Lord does keep,
The rewards we'll reap,
And all good souls from earth,
At the end of life's story,
As we are from birth,
Meant to be in His everlasting glory!

Maureen A. Pabich

Rage

There's a fire blazing in my soul,
And anger serves as fuel.
The flames are dancing beyond control
As I become the Devil's tool.

Yes, evil is the best of games,
Which everyone knows how to start.
Evil is the breeze which fans the flames
And blows away the ashes of my heart.

My mind becomes the inferno of hell,
So there a phoenix will hatch.
My rage becomes my prison cell
Until somebody strikes the match.

Whenever resentment takes root,
Revenge becomes the sweetest fruit.

Thu-Thao Nguyen

Untitled

There was a man who took a stand,
and asked a lady for her hand.

They went out to a dance,
and found some romance.

Then she finally let him know,
I'm not alone, I've left three at home.
So it's about time that they've been shown.

With Big Hunks in hand, they met that man
and invited him into their home.

They spent some time and wined and dined.
Then decided to take a stroll.

He made it clear,
he wanted to be near.
So he got a rose,
then kneeled and proposed,
that seemed so long ago.

Twenty years you see exactly to me,
because I was one of the three.

Pamela DeVe Mitchell

You Are My Friend

You dry my tears
and calm my fears
you are my friend

You're joys in my highs
You console when I'm low
you are my friend

You are the calm
within my storm
and when the tempest subside
you are nigh
you are my friend

There are times when I despair
When I don't know here from there
Some how you know
and then you show
you are my friend

Some have lovers
Some have homies
I have that and then some
Because you are my friend

B. J. Smith

The Willow Tree

Beyond the garden gate,
And deep into the wood,
Blowing gently in the wind,
That is where it weeps.

It weeps in joy,
In happiness,
It weeps in sorrow and mourn.
Quietly and gracefully
In darkness, light,
Dusk, and dawn.

It weeps, it seems, eternally,
Ending only when come the winter snows.
Yet, even then,
It's boughs gracefully arch,
And in the soft spring breeze,
Again it peacefully flows.

Beyond the garden gate,
And deep into the wood,
Blowing gently in the wind,
That is where it weeps.

Nicole Deegan

I Walk the Mountains

I walk the mountains in early Spring,
And feel the silent hush.
The soil is soft beneath my feet,
And the foliage green is lush.

I walk more slowly in heat of Summer,
And smell the mountain flowers.
The gentle breeze sings in the trees,
And quietly moves the boughs.

I tread so softly in Autumn
Upon a colorful carpet of leaves.
The trees stand beautiful in color
And sway with the gentle breeze.

In Winter time I slip and slide
As I step upon the rocks,
But, Oh, the views my eyes behold
Are worth the painful knocks.

I walk the mountains in deep respect
All during every year,
To view the beauty God has made.
I hold each visit dear.

Margaret Carey

Taner...

I went out into the evening
and felt the cool brisk air....
  And I realized you couldn't tonite.

I looked at the moon with all
its beauty and majesty...
  And I realized you couldn't now.

I noticed the majesty of the heavens
and even the "Big Dipper"...
  And tonight you could not.

I saw some colored lights
and the picture all the lights made ...
  But it was not for you.

I prayed to God for understanding
as to what Heaven's splendor is
  And now you know, I'll have to wait.

Loren W. Mosman

Why, Why, Why

I could ask a million questions
and find a million answers.

Why is my hair brown and
why are my eyes blue

I could ask a million questions
and find a million answers

Why why why
am I me?

Why does the rain fall?
Why does the sun shine?

I could ask a million question
and find a million answers

Why does the grass grow green or
Why am I me?

I could ask a million questions
and find a million answers

Why are frogs green or
why are leopards gold?

I could ask a million questions
and find a million answers.

Stephanie Lutz

Carefree

I'd like to be a little bird
  And flit among the trees,
To light upon a branch
  And be blown by the breeze.

I'd give a call to other birds,
  "Come play among the leaves."
Drink the early morning dew
  As it drips from off the leaves.

I'd have no worry about shiny nose,
  No need to comb my hair,
And no toil with dirty clothes
  With feathers of 'wash and wear'.

What fun to fly above the earth
  And look down upon the land;
To find food and other needs
  Provided by God's hand.

Roverta Olinger

Awakening In Time

In time we awaken,
And from our dream emerge
  laughing
Into the light we dance
In wider and wider circles
Our finger tips touching
  as we pass
The fire peaks
  and we stand naked in the ring
Alert
  and ever thankful
  for each other's arms

Terry Weeteling

The Scientist - Challenged

He rushes unafraid into the horns
And grappling with these points of death
Twists life with all his sinews taut
Into a conquered heap.

And deftly rearranges it
By sword and brawn and brain
Into the form of intellect
And masters it again.

Then rising on the carcass of
his brilliant victory
Gives forth a mighty warrior's shout
"Bring yet one more to me!"

Marilyn Zitar

My Love Has A Cold, Wet Nose

My love has warm, brown, gentle eyes,
  and hair of golden hue,
Though no word is ever spoken,
  I know his love is true.

He does my every bidding,
  and never questions why,
No matter how hard the task may be,
  I know he'll always try.

No pirate's treasure trove could buy
  the love that's mine alone.
A truer, more devoted heart
  no one has ever known.

He brought sunshine to my sightless life.
  Patrick brightens up my day.
He shows me how he loves me
  In so many different ways.

As we walk through life together,
  our friendship grows and grows.
Patrick holds my key to freedom.
  My love has a cold, wet nose.

Samantha Hamilton

Ticket

Seems when things don't go just right,
And I can't seem to win
It really helps to take right off
Get goin' with a grin!
Now I don't know why I'm grinnin'
But it doesn't cost a cent
So maybe I can help someone
Before my life is spent.
If I can't leave this world better
By some little thing I do,
Then I really haven't earned my way
Might as well not have passed through,
So I will try in my small way
Some poor soul to cheer,
I want to have my "glory" ticket
When I am leavin' here.

Lottie Hindman Bryant

Me and Thee

Days and nights simplicity
as love is set upon a touch,
to long, to need so very much
and know much more of me.

Eyes beholding beauty fair
a multitude of words to share,
for moments found or moments lost
are all but thoughts of thee.

Marvin Blevins

Another Chance

I thought when we married
And I gave him my heart,
This union was forever
And we never would part.

Five short years later
He looked at me to say,
"I don't love you anymore,"
And he just walked away.

So many years have passed
And no matter how I tried;
I couldn't forget the rejection
I can't believe that he lied.

Today I met a new man
And I knew right from the start,
He is everything I needed
And could surely break my heart.

So I have another chance,
It's up to him to choose.
I've got everything to gain
And I've got nothing to lose.

Susan Zaborsky

Verse from the Ghetto

I seldom see the robin,
  And I never heard the lark.
My thoughts are always kindly
  For the sparrow in the dark.

Country lanes I have not walked
  Babbling brooks I have not seen,
Between our broken sidewalk cracks
  Shoestring grasses turn up green.

And once I saw a butterfly
  So minuscule against the sky,
Exquisite in it's fluttering grace
  It descended low to kiss my face.

Sarah Omanson

This Connection

Foraging more
And into this find,
I leave everything there
To be you.
This one little part
Becomes so much more,
A full soul in sight
Of a wishful daybloom.
Dreams lifting me up
From the low I create
I see you there, waiting,
A grin as we free.
That tiny piece
Of the map we become,
So meaningless there
But everything here.
It gives to me life,
A crystalline mind;
The flight of the moon dweller
In the plight of mankind.

Lindsay Blonquist

Life

  Life unfolds each second
and is swiftly ticking by.
  He cannot hold back
time no matter how hard we try.

  Every thought, every action
forever done - hopefully to our
satisfaction.

  Precious days, special
moments swiftly lead to
yesterday.

  Memories that bring hope
for life we live each and
every day.

Sally Shorter

Untitled

I saw my face today,
  and it looked older,
Without the warmth of wisdom
  or the softness
Born of pain and waiting.

The dreams were gone from my eyes,
  all hope is lost in the hollowness
Of my cheeks,
  A finger of death
Pulling at my days.

So I did my exercises
  and wondered if I'd ever find you again,
To have you see my face
  with friendlier eyes than my own.

Maria N. VanKregten

The Birth Of Friendship

Kind gestures you make
  and kind words that you say
portray an intimate picture
  of yourself everyday.
You're never too young,
  too mean or too old
to pass on warm feelings
  to those that are cold.
Each day you can see
  the changes you inspired
in those who perceived
  friendship was not desired.
A hand wave, a gesture,
  a "Hello" or a smile
gets most people started
  which is always worthwhile.
So keep passing it on
  it will soon find its way
for in all types of people
  friendship's born everyday.

William T. Redden

Ode To Jenny

The bed will be empty
And the feeding dish too
The bark just may echo
In the mind's recesses for you
But memories will last
A whole lifetime through
Of a dear companion
So loyal and true.

Sheila H. Sykora

What Is A Grandmother

As I take the future
and leave the past behind
no memories of old
escape my mind

A grandson I am
your favorite choice
a caring figure
with soft spoken voice

Who let me get away with things
and drive her car
and not just because
that's the way grandmothers are

Who enlightened my childhood
and brought it joy
I may be all grown up
but inside I'm still a little boy
A boy's mind of memories
that of its cheer
as a reminiscence of this
I wish you were here!

Shaun Abrahamsen

Woodland Smoke

Sorrow-filled by evening's call,
And lonely as a homeless child,
A train of smoke steals wearily
Among October's blue-hazed hills.
Hopefully it picks its way,
Drifting by each hovering tree,
Seeking the breasts of quiet fields,
Haunting each hollow, and moving on,
Searching the spot where autumn waits
To cradle it in windless sleep.

W. C. Robocker

"Revelation"

I close my eyes, relax
And look into the past
The years have speeded by
Open my eyes, and begin to cry
Water fills the room
Thoughts reside in lonely gloom
I sit, and dreams of inner peace
Emotions constantly increase
I stand and scream in pain
Hide myself in shame
Romantic thoughts, rarely seen
Enclosed in granite, that must come clean
Sculpting, piece by piece
Unwanted genesis must decease
Into my soul, you tend to stumble
The walls protecting begin to crumble
I feel the love I have yet to find
But I let the darkness cloud my mind
The panic raged into fear
A sea of emotions encaged in a tear.

Thomas McDaniel

Therapy

God gave us a beneficial thing I
call therapy or laughter.
Let's use it more and exercise
our face, here after.
Look in your mirror and smile,
and it will smile back to you, true?

Lenola M. Franks

From The Moon

I sat on the moon
and looked down on my son
holding him close within.
As if we were back
where it started before,
where the mother and child began.

I sat on the moon
and cried to the sun
"Where does it stop and begin,
to free the mother from trapping the soul
over and over again?"

In honor of life
and beyond what I see,
I'll go to the moon again,
removing the chains, I bound to my son,
Free to become his own man.

Sue Anderson

You Have Gone

If only I could explain what I feel
And now I dream of the days of old
When we would walk hand in hand
Just talking of things to be
And of dreams to come true.

But now there's a void in time and space
Sometimes it is so very hard to explain
The loneliness and the sadness
That my heart carries with it
Now that you have gone.

William J. Barss Jr.

A Thing Of Beauty

A jewel is a thing of value
And of exquisite beauty.
It brings pleasure to the eye,
And makes the wearer sparkle

A rose is a think of beauty,
And to some, quiet valuable.
It will smell wonderful
And brings happiness to a woman's heart.

Have you ever seen a jewel
Caring a Rose?
Much value there would be
And ten times the beauty

Every man who loves a woman
Has something, both valuable, and beautiful,
A treasure of the utmost delicacy
How much is she worth?

Every Thing.

Shane Myers

Friends And More

Friends are friends,
And I have many,
So when I finish
I will diminish,
Any enemies of these.

And when I do,
These fools of terror,
Will run away and scream in horror,
And never be seen again.

Stephanie Akins

Patiently I Wait

A patient Soul am I that waits,
And patiently I do.
For the one I love and cannot have,
Still patiently I wait.

Nothing in this world I see,
Means more than having you.
But still I patiently wait,
Until you see its true.

You're committed to the three,
That so, dominates you and me.
But still I patiently wait
For what ever is my fate.

And maybe one day, fate will intervene
To give what I love and need.
Until that day I hope and wait;
So patiently I wait

Maria Benedict

The Phantom

He leaves unspoken
and returns as swift as the wind,
He knows what's happening
As he return my body is his
He knows I can't refuse him
for he is my lover
and for whom I care for

Lost in my thoughts,
he kisses my lips,
he holds me close,
I'm lost in his abyss.

I feel everything small,
as he holds me in his arms
his heat on my body
chills running through my skin

He holds me tightly
My breath is gone -
and so is he staying only for this encounter
and gone with my heart and love
lost for eternity.

Sara Oquendo

You Are Someone Special

When family and friends are far away,
And sadness seems to settle in,
Take heart and be glad to know,
You will always be someone special.

Even when your journey is long and hard,
And life appears to be so unfair,
Let your smile be a ray of sunshine,
To brighten even the darkest of days.

Cast aside those feelings of gloom,
Be thankful for your many blessings,
Cherish the good memories forever,
Anticipate joyful things to come.

Never be afraid to dream,
To climb aboard to rising star.
Go forth with renewed self-confidence,
Happiness is an attainable goal.

Larry N. Michelson

Inner Truth

Burning minds
 and searching souls
Dream of love
 and fight off cold
lonely hearts
 and restless minds
Dream of love
 and often cry
Frightened men
 and greedy lies
rely on gold
 to get them by
righteous men
 of love and truth
Stand strong in end
 there souls will rule.

Michael L. Geiger

"As I Look Out The Window"

As I look out the window,
and see a white night,
I then look at the sky,
See the moon-light.

The branches like hands,
Touch the moon,
But as the wind blows,
I hear the winter tune.

As I watch the snow fall,
There is something I hear,
It is not the winter tune,
But it sounds very queer

The cold brings a gust of wind
Which blows the snow around
As our thoughts are lost,
And may never be found.

Nicole Pugliese

Life's Ups And Downs

Have you ever looked back, one day,
and seen how far you have to go,
to get to that point in your life
where you have reached your goal.
To see how many times you were a quitter or
a loser, an encourager or a winner,
and to see how many times you fell
off your bike and hopped back on again.
You look to the future, there may be
encouragement, promise or regret but
if you look in the past there still
may be confusion and regret yet over all
we lived through it and say,
"How happy I am to..." but you stop in mid-
sentence and remember how many times you
looked at your work and said,
"Not bad but I'll work on it!"

Rebecca J. Frank

Untitled

May your years to come
Be those you will treasure
And each passing day
Be filled to it's measure
With happiness, love
That make life complete
With the bountiful seed
Of the things that you need.

Murle Geal

Jesus Of Galilee

I love to be with Jesus
And sit upon his knee
And have him tell me stories
How he walked upon the sea

And how he raised dear Lazaruz
Raised him from the dead
And how with five loaves and two fishes
The multitude was fed

Jesus healed the sick and
Gave sight to those who could not see
There never was a man so kind
Like Jesus from Galilee

I would love to walk and talk with him
Hug and kiss him too
And tell him that I love him
And tell him why I do

There is no greater happiness
In all this world for me
When I think of precious Jesus
Jesus of Galilee

Mary R. Leason

Tales

I have heard some wild stories
And some I think are true.
Would you believe the tales you tell me
If I told them to you?

Some folks let their speech
Take them to disastrous brink.
Think long at what you want to say
Before saying what you think.

Some folks are so long winded
Telling some wild tales.
If they are sailing the river of life
They had better trim their sails.

It's alright to talk a lot.
But to these thoughts adhere.
If you are going to be a motor mouth,
First get your brain in gear.

Russell B. Frizell

Moma I Remember

Through all the laughter
And sorrow and tears
I remember moma best
In the latter years
She learned to love
In a gentle way
And with kindness
She filled each day
Moma walked in sunshine
And she walked in the rain
Many time as she walked
She walked in pain
And now her life
On earth is complete
And she is resting
At Jesus feet.

Laura R. Jarvis

A Piece of Music

My heart extols in the joy
 and sorrow of your sound
I listen to you and am filled
 with life
I feel life's energy bursting forth
ready to jump from inside me
I look down below and see me smile
I have attained bliss
The beauty of your sound has sent me
 to the utmost depth of my soul

Mary Perifimos

The Feelings Inside

I think of you often
 and still wonder why.
  I've got feelings for you
   still locked up inside.

The things that you said
 you knew weren't true
  You just tried to hide feelings
   locked inside of you.

And now when I see you
 when you see me too
  It brings back those feelings
   for me and for you.

Michael D. Bender

What It Is

What it is, is what it is
and that's what it is.

I guess I never
tried to figure it,
because it never mattered.

What it is that makes
what it is,
what it is.

Because if I figured
out what it is that,
makes it what it is.

A dream would be shattered

Michael T. Ford

The Charioteer

I'm the minister
and the fornicator
I'm the Samaritan
and the criminal
I'm the Lamb
and the liar
I'm the lover
and the hate-monger
I'm somebody
and nobody
I am what man is...

A charioteer
bounded by two horses
going in paradoxical paths

Sean Yoon

Always

The trees are overgrown
and the grass needs
trimmed. I didn't know this
would be the effect of me
loving him.
I haven't done a thing for
at least a week or two. I
can't stand the thought of him
Being so close, and loving
you know who.
The days and years will
pass, and maybe I was
wrong, but I can't help listening
to my heart that says look
to the window and leave the
porch light on.

B. Robinson

The Foundation

I am the prince of darkness
And the Lord of light
Contemporaneous
Beast and man
The lover of spectacles
And the lover of wisdom

I see the footprints
But never the walker
I see the accidents
But never the substance

Shadows...
We live amidst a
Swirl of shadows
We live for an after image
Ephemeral

The heart of life
The changeless ground
Lies unsullied and pure
Forever beyond our reach.

Ralph Aquila

Beyond Death

Beyond death lies eternity
And there you'll find no end
The meaning of your life
You'll finally comprehend

Your time on earth is just a test
Determining how you'll spend it
Decisions you make every day
Will stand undefended

All your days are numbered
Inevitable is your death
And it's too late to change things
After your last breath

On Judgement Day you'll stand alone
No one by your side
Remember your turn's waiting
From Him you can not hide

Lisa Ann Glossup

"Nachtzeit"

Still I have wonders
And wandering children
And green tinsel dangling
In dreams night brings forth.

How long have you waited
To ask me such odd things
In scenes only night brings,
Erupting inside?

How many of these things
Were born fresh and green things
And plucked from the fertile rows
Of your mind's own field?

Or am I the sole guide
To all I burn inside
My own mind's envisioning,
Vivid and real?

If so come be with me,
Traverse these imaginings,
See why my eyes burn
From green dreams that cry.

Leslie Cantrell

Goodbyes

Time flew by,
And we had our fun,
But now the sadness,
Has just begun,

We spoke no words,
We told no lies,
All we said,
Were out goodbyes,

But when I look,
At your handsome face,
My heart starts to beat,
At a different pace,

When you're around,
My happy side shows,
But when you're gone
You will not know,

The time has come,
For us to part,
So always and forever,
Hold my heart...

Michelle L. Payne

Life

I left the house today
around ten o'clock.
I was going to the woods
to have myself a picnic.
When I got there
I was not alone.
All around me there was life
beautiful life.
I sat there just listening
and I was at peace.
I walked through the woods
taking pictures of life.
I was in harmony
with the creatures.
I left the woods today
around four o'clock.
I was going home to sleep
and to dream about the life.

Savonne Bassett

Untitled

The sky is gray,
and will always be
because humans weren't careful
and they couldn't see.
They said hey,
it will go away,
but they were wrong
and now they pay.

The cans in the water,
the smoke in the sky,
why can't they see
we will all soon die.

Soon they will see
but it will be to late,
for they have already made their fate.
Were scared! They say
What can we do? They hesitate!
Just wait,
Just wait,
we will soon pay for are mistakes with fate.

Marisha Richardson

Be My Valentine

Here we are - another year
And yet, another Valentine
Many things have we held dear
Since you said "Will you be mine?"

A paunch you have today, 'tis true
Since I became your bride
But, I must confess to you, too
That my hips also have grown wide

Your hair is white and so is mine
There are wrinkles on my hand
But we remain true Valentines
In spite of what life may demand

Love means taking the good with the bad
And we have had our valleys and hills
And thru the many years we've had
We stand, holding hands and feeling the thrill

I still see the face that shows me love
And hope you still see the same in mine
And so, my dear thru all else above
Please, be my faithful Valentine

Margaret Helbling

The Reason For Storms

When calm azure conspires with nature,
as shadows obscure the sun
and breed formless monsters —
light and color die.
Flashing skyline!
The next bolt alights.
Dark funnel clouds
spin their furious
unearthly forces,
as raindrops sprinkle down —
cold.
Wet.
Teeming.
Blurred rain abound
intricately confined,
as it washes and blows away —
evil all around.

Stephen J. Wacker

My Fair Maiden

I'm sad with myself
and you as you walk away

the forest path leaving
only footprints behind

I sit by our tree
as rain softly falls
upon your folded hands, my face

the sounds of creatures
in the night blanket
my need for you

to return
to help me
to shelter me

for when nightfall breaks
and day begins

you will no longer be with me
and your footprints
will be gone

though the way you touched
my heart will never leave.

Lisa Marie Gilreath

"Reality"

When your life's work is finished
And you lay it all down;
Someone else will pick it up
When you're no longer around.
All living things have their
Own time and place;
Then off to the great beyond
Leaving hardly a trace.
Our children grow older
With each passing day
And before we know it,
Our friends have gone away.
Time moves on like a
Rapid flowing stream.
No one is indispensable
And life is not a dream.
Take time to enjoy your family
And to appreciate your friends.
Realize who and what are important
Before your life comes to an end.

Peggy Hester Ballard

Spirit

Step onto the earth,
and you will see the eagle soar
and hear the lion roar.
Step onto the floor,
and you will hear the music.
Feel the movement of the song.

Step onto the stage,
and your voice will sing
and your feet will dance.
Step onto the mountain,
and your legs will climb
and your body will move to the top.

Step onto the sun,
You will glow
and the wind will blow.
Step into the sky.
Your bones will strengthen.
You are the spirit.
You are dancing!

Marusia Czemerynski

Being Lonely

Did you ever feel lonely,
And you're hungry for bologna?
You were talking to the trees,
Going to pay your library fees,
And afraid of the bee?
Nobody around,
Not that I've found,
I walked by the dog pound.
The dogs will bark,
When it starts to get dark.
Hey, There is a tree in my way,
Right by the bay.
I looked at the sidewalk,
I saw some chalk.
I picked it up,
I put it in a plastic cup.
I still haven't found anybody,
So I'm going to play with my silly putty.
Well, good-bye,
I'm also going to eat a pie.

Lydia Majewski

The Devil's Night

The moon sets at the rising sun
another night is over.
The creature goes to sleep
his day is over
his evil is done.

He doesn't breath the same air
as you or me
but the air of the dead

He sleeps while we play
waiting for another night.
Awake he will,
at the rising moon.

The beautiful pale white creature
flies through the night
scouting for that one special person
in which he'll feed on,
and enjoy the precious red liquid

The vampire makes his move,
The body goes limp
his deed is done.

Lesley Rinna

Untitled

Dear Mom and Dad, I want to go where you are.

Beyond the Moon and the Sun, beyond the Stars.

I want to see all my aunts, uncles and
cousins too, every one who loves you.

All those who have gone away
To laugh and sing and dance and play.

I want to see all the dogs and cats I
ever had.

Romping and laughing as a lad.

The picnics, birthdays, weddings, holidays
together.

All of us like birds of a feather.

It gets lonely when I think of everyone
Enjoying themselves beyond the sun.

I guess I have to wait what more can I do
Except to say I still love you.
Your son Philip

Philip P. Albanese

Medicine Ball

The fine points of life
Are often lost
In this cold and sterile world.

The stainless steel cutting edge
Of a scalpel
Realizes a cold reality.

The sound of the revolving door
That separates life and death
Is the heartbeat here.

Amid the suffering is the joy
Of a newborn child
Who inhales his first breath of fresh air
And screams for all the world to hear
I am alive, I am alive.

Amid the suffering is the relief
Of an old man
Who inhales his last breath of air
And sighs the end of his suffering
I am leaving, I am leaving.

A. Richard DeSandre

Untitled

Sixty-five year old men
are out scaling mountains
while I sit here staring into the space
where the Cheshire cat was
but there's no grin looking back
or croquet pink flamingos
playing on checkerboard lawns
only the suffocating softness
of this sleeping bed
where the pillows are whispering
"Off with her head,
Off with her head."

Susan R. Hicks

One

Are two hearts beat as one
Are two souls are as one
The love we share no one has ever
And someday we will join
And be as one
Forever till we die
And when we die it will be as one
But we will no what it was like
To be as one

Tracey Loper

"My Friend"

Who is my friend, how do I know,
are you absolute,
or are you foe?
I give of myself, as your well aware,
I wonder my dear,
If you really care,
you've shown me concern,
you've answered my prayer,
I love you my friend,
and hold you so dear,
so why should I wonder, why should I fear,
when a friend like you,
is ever so near!

Patricia Sheftz

To Acknowledge Everyone...

To acknowledge everyone...
as a human being...
as a person...
All have different views
of how life should be lived.
All have images of who
they should be or who
they really are!
Who are we really?
But we are all
individual...
Apart from all that is
and all that should be.
The drunk, the beggar, the old
the dying, the lucrative, the disabled
the common person...
We are all in this together,
Why not acknowledge each other
because after all we are all still just an
INDIVIDUAL...

Veronica Segura Rocha

Julie's Day

"She's a beauty," he says
As he smiles down at me
A new Mom, a new Dad,
A new family.

As a young child and teenager
We are right, it is clear
Perfect strangers will tell us
"She's a beauty" my dear.

Through high school and college
Out in the work world
Everyone she touches thinks
"What a beautiful girl."

And now on her Wedding Day
She stands for all to see
"She's a Beauty!" The groom whispers,
And of course, we agree!

Susan Walker Edwards

Sarcasm

Sarcasm is visualized
As tearing flesh like a hound
mostly ironic
Sometimes sardonic
And it's use is to confound

Sarcasm is sometimes
a very helpful speech
But without care
We must be aware
It's sometimes like a hound unleashed

Rudy Minton

"Ryan"

I see you through tears of pride,
as you hit that ball into the sky.
I've watched you grow from cradle to cleats.
From t-ball to baseball.
You are my strength, my todays
and all my tomorrows.
When my pain is great, your
Touch makes it all go away.
You are my life.
You are my "Grandson"

Phyllis J. Pollock

Life ...

Experiencing, knowing, learning
change, knowledge, disease, pain
experiencing, knowing, learning
slower, older
death

Sarah Curtis

Oh! The Mountains Of The Sea

Oh! What wondrous beauty be
As the clouds billowing from the sea.
Not granite, wood nor stone
Only water and gases they may be.
Oh! The mountains of the sea
Raising majestically higher to Thee.
Ever changing for me to see.
Only graces for the birds of flight
Through this time and eternity.
Oh! The mountains of the sea
With flashing colors and hazes be.
There the proof of a God to me.
With fire and thunder amongst their mist
A daylight breaking amongst is grip
Oh! The mountains of the sea.
For only a true God on high
Could create a mountain that flies.
Boundless beauty does exist
In this world of gas and mist.
Oh! The mountains of the sea!

Tom K. Hurlburt

To A Lady In Waiting

You surely must be anxious,
As the days are winding down.
And you probably feel your belly,
Has always been this round.

But, no matter how your labor goes,
All thoughts of pain are gone.
The moment that your eyes behold,
That dear and precious one.

A new baby puts you to the test,
Of that there is no doubt.
Diapers, feedings, cries and grunts,
You have to figure out.

But cherish every moment,
For time will surely fly.
It may seem as though it's been a month,
And a year will have slipped by.

So when you hold your little one,
Think not of sleepless nights.
But rather of the many ways,
She will enrich your life.

Ramona Sardina

Untitled

The tree yelled with pain
as the glowing finger cut
it into pieces.

The twirling slinky
gobbled and twisted its way
like a mad giant.

Falling, twisting to
the ground with the ease and grace
of wind; its master.

Mike Slawinski

Reality Or Insanity

The realms of reality do fade
As thoughts of life press on my mind

I sit here in the shade
Still trying! For it to find

But it hides deep within the glade
The glade of my upper mind

Reality in the shade
Or insanity in my mind

It seems to always be
Here and there

But when I look to see
I find it no where

Will it find me
Or leave me to store

Come set it free
If you really care

Steven Sandusky

Bittersweet

Jumping grasshoppers scratch our bare arms
as we walk through crackling grass
to the woods path where
the Bittersweet vines
twine high in a tree.

Already night frosts have
freed the enclosing petals,
revealing orange-red berries,
bright against beige leaves falling
to form the carpet under our feet.

Bittersweet are our lives, when in youth,
covering petals hold with fierce vigor
the red heart of quiet wisdom
faith and eternal hope.

Only in old age will they spread wide,
releasing the bitter-sweetness of
fading dreams into the peace
of acceptance.

Margaret D. Kirkland

Untitled

I watch
as you walk away
into the wintry night
silent...

still...

Snowflakes
brushing the soul
sound like
...thunder...

Stan Williams

Of Love

A torrent of love
Cascading through
The rivers of life
In search of the ocean
From whence it came
Will find its way
For
God if love.

Lorraine R. Perry

Vanity

We saw a tractor
At M M today,
It was so proud
To be on display.

As slick as a kitten
As neat as a pin,
It begged us humbly
To peak within.

What precision and skill
What infinite care,
Had been taken to make
This tractor so rare.

It smiled to itself
And winked its eye,
As we gave it our praises
As high as the sky.

It purred like a kitten
It sang with delight,
To be so conceited
Just didn't seem right.

Rosalie Willemsen

Good Dog

We have a good dog named Spark.
At squirrels and chipmunks he'll bark.
He comes when you call,
And loves to play ball,
And take you for walks in the park.

His breed is a tri-colored mix.
His parentage we never could fix.
His Papers are nil,
But we love him still.
He's good for a hundred face-licks!

Shirley R. Riddle

Waiting

As little children each of us looked
at the world with open arms.
We embraced life
we expected good
we loved everyone,
but,
Sometime between then and now
somewhere
somehow
someone made us close our arms
to protect ourselves
to stop embracing life and start
fearing it
hating it
waiting it out and hoping
it would get better.
Some of us are still waiting.

Marlo Muraski

For Jack

You are no longer my husband,
But these things you are and will be.

Love and joy of my youth
Good husband of my life
Father of my children
And forever
Best friend.

Lou Ann Townsend

The Last Seduction

Deeper and deeper the needle's thrust,
Auburn are colors turning the sky.
Sunk into water her hands, palms uplifted,
Asking redemption for the last time.
Bluer and bluer the iris brights;
Clearer the surface after the rain.
Droplets of error, salty with thought,
Melting the icicle in her eyes.
Smiling, lazily, with an attempt
To seduce last bitterness
Of the temptation.

Rushanna Mukhamedianova

Morning

Tickle, tickle, tickle....
Awaked!?
Baby tulips!!!
Fondly,
Sun bedew
Poppable bubbles.
Make love to plums,
Make love to do, mi, sol,
Tiny trails of squirrels....
Tiny trails of rabbits....

Mi Arreola

Sports

Play baseball and hit a home run
Basketball is so much fun
Soccer is really cool
But kick the can is for the fool
Tennis is a dedication
Boxing needs medication
'cause you get your brains knocked out
Trip to E. R. every bout
Fishin' is for the lazy
Swimming in ice is for the crazy
But I guess a sport is a sport
I like sports played on ice or courts

Travis Amundsen

Mark's Place

Warming myself by a blue fire
Basking in the afterglow
An evening of chit chat
Proof that the art of conversation
Is alive and well
Carefully scripted words
That danced off your tongue
Harlequin gestures
A command performance
That leaves me in awe
Off you go
To be left alone in my thoughts
Those blue flames
And across the room, in a chair
Dressed in camouflage, sits a bear

Plato Kuvelis

The Eyes of Justice

Are blind to you and me
But for just once
I would like for you
To take the blind off of one eye
To really look at you and me

Norman W. Bohn

The Treasure Chest

A ball of twine, a blue jay feather
beads and bangles strung together
A robin's nest, a shiny stone
buckles
shells
a broken comb.
A child's treasures plain enough
are
dreaming things and magic stuff.

Tattered post cards from far-off places
bottle caps and old boot laces
skeleton keys and rusty locks
hoarded
in
an old shoe box.
A treasure chest can't hold enough
of
dreaming things and magic stuff.

Laura Jacobs

Love Is Silent

I can only say like
Because love is silent.

Don't think it's so easy to say;
If love is only a nest,
The wings of love will never land on you.

Don't think it's too hard to show;
If love is a dead fossil,
The shell of love will never open for you.

I can only say like
Because love is the sound of your heart.

Tommy Chiwen Chang

I Cry

I cry for the world,
because the world sheds no tears.
I hurt for the world,
because the world feels nothing.
I fight for the world,
because the world is unable.
I kill for the world,
because the world has no defense.
I watch over the world,
because without me the world wouldn't
survive.
I love the world,
because the world doesn't care.
I do all this for the world.
WHY?

Rachel McCollough

Who I Am

Why am I afraid to tell you WHO I AM?
Because you won't like me, and
I know it will crush me.
Besides shouldn't you expose
yourself to me, first? No that
isn't the key; the key is vulnerability.
That's something I just don't see in me.

Why am I afraid to tell you WHO I AM?
For it shows all over, I'm not
a shame. You know what I've
learned in this life's journey.
That it is my responsibility to
trust you with my vulnerability.

Marcia Winston

Before

I walked the darkness, of the night.
Before I walked, into the light.
I crawled the streets, where strangers stalk.
Before I found, the strength to walk.
I cried the tears, of hatred and pain.
Before I found, strength to maintain
I hid in shadows, of disgrace.
Before I found courage, to show my face.
I shed my blood, I faced my grave.
Before my heart beat, strong and brave.
I fell like a beggar, on bended knee.
Before I learned, I could be free.
I kissed the hand, of laughing death.
Before I found, life in my breath.

Shannon Shay

Souls Eternal

Once - a long time ago
Before we were a thought
It was fate for us to meet
And become the best of friends.
Moments: loud and vivacious
quiet and sentimental
Have all made it worthwhile.
Long talks and mellow moods
No wonder there is a sense
Of comfort and satisfaction
Sharing everything - tears to smiles.
A special thanks to each of you
For sharing who you are with me
I will forever be enriched by you,
My best friends.

Tsha M. Bilow

Oregon's Pacific

White scallops trim the indigo
Between the sea, the rocks and sand;
High cliffs maintain the status quo
While restless tides assault the land,.

Each panorama stuns the eyes:
An inland lake, a sheltered cove,
A dark green headland's towering size,
A quiet tide pool's treasure trove.

Hear sonic pound of crashing surf,
The gliding gull's harsh-sounding cry
Announcing this is his own turf:
"Intruders better up and fly."

Occasionally the smell of fish
Invades the tang of salty air,
Or bonfire smoke creates the wish
To picnic in the driftwood there.

Often there's no one in view,
Just blue on blue of sky and sea;
Though rugged, wild, with comforts few,
This tranquilizer comes for free.

Naomi Hicks

Life Or Death

As a breath is taken
A thought occurs
Of what if does not matter
As long as it is taken
For granted or for worth
As if it does not matter
If it's never taken
Can it all occur

Michael H. Scheide

Evening To Night

Trees darken as the sun goes down,
Birds return to their nests,
The sky turns from blue to pink,
Then purple to black
Bugs come out to look for food,
Then bats come out for them
They streak dark lines across the sky
The first tiny light, then more
As the sky fills with stars
The huge bright moon
Shines over the world.
I fall asleep.

Madison Lalemand

I Am Black Woman

I am a Black Woman.
Black is my beauty.
Black is my pride.
So I must always
Hold my head high.

Black is my brother.
I loved so dear.
Black is my mother.
Who brought me here.

Black is my father.
Who worked so hard,
To provide for his family,
But we were still poor.

Black is my heaven.
I'll go someday.
When this old world
Has faded away.

Nora L. Steed

You All Along

I asked the winds they even told
Blew whispers in my ears
Of information longed of old
Yet I heard none too clear
So I asked the bird singing in the tree
Of time that I may borrow
Tell of what he'd learned of me
He shook his head with sorrow
I begged the clouds to fill me in
Said back Get off your knees
And painted the direction I should go
He sent me to the seas
I said Dear sea I have to know
Waves roared mountains of blue
I'll tell you where you need to go
She sent me here to you
And now I'm here should have realized
'Twas you I needed all along
For it's now that I see when I look in your eyes
The meaning of every love song

Tommy Cumberland

"Death"

Death is so final,
Death is so real,
Death is so over, you'll never
know how it feels.
You may not think it will
ever happen to you, but someday
soon your time will come too.

Tina G. Towler

Untitled

I can feel my hair...
But my hair can't feel me...

Samantha Rabon

Vampire

Cunning and graceful,
Blood in a faceful,
Environment of death,
Through each whispered breath.

White, pale, power,
With the beauty of a flower,
Sharp, white, Red,
My coffin is bed.

Large glowing eyes,
Nature's laws he defies,
Like a kiss from a Rose,
How much left, heaven knows.

Sweet dark kiss,
Full of somber bliss,
for the Light do I lust,
And all my hopes become dust.

Matt Jamison

At The Seashore

For as far as the eye can see,
Blue waves dance with glee.
Sunlight glistens as the crest breaks,
Each morn when the world awakes.

The sun wings its way
Across heaven to begin the day.
Sunbeams sparkle on the sea,
Beautiful as diamonds can be.

The sea gulls flutter so gently by,
Like brilliant windmills 'cross the sky.
Morning breaks, the gulls seem to say.
Welcome, sojourner, to a glorious day.

The sea has a drama for you today.
Perhaps, sojourner, you would like to stay.
Let the splendor of my shore
Take you places, you've never been before.

Feel the energy that radiates from me.
Ever so gently, whispers the sea.
Let your spirit absorb my love.
It's sent especially to you from heaven
above.

Mary Ann Norton

Hatred

Hatred is a virulent spider,
Boasting obsidian eyes.
Claws of ebony, obscured darkness
Mystical shadows conceal.

In furtive cape of devilish whims
Burning obsession lies.
Vengeance stirs, intensifies as
Filaments smother prey.

The widow pampers her prisoner,
Relishing crimson wine,
Extracting vibrance from vigor,
Hideous smirks prevail.

Ronda Brandt

Glass Lady

lovely is the meat on
bone, so curved and soft and
slightly slung and beneath
that throb are heart and
lungs as blue as eyes that
guide them.

But
though savage as the world
once seemed, yet remains that
simple dream. Amen

Mark Vineyard

Untitled

Surrounded by volumes of knowledge
Books from wall to wall
I realized that I knew nothing
Nothing, nothing at all

My brain was filled by trivial facts
My knapsacks heavy with books
But my heart echoed empty
My eyes cast longing looks

The mind tingled with numbness
Of not ever knowing love
The fingers tapped in silence
Prayers carried to the God above

My whole heart ached in restlessness
My soul caved in from yearning
Eyes closed with openness
Nothing to sooth the burning

Sarah Cook

Inside the Roots

Each flower beginning to bud,
both in firm soil,
begin to look to one another
for light and growth.

The power of each's petal
blooms.

The capacity will ponder
upon each's own strength
and none will change...

Sarah C. Hencsie

Pets

I went to the petshop
Bought me a cat.

When we got home
It hit me with a bat.

I went to the petshop,
Returned the cat and
Bought me a rat.

When we got home it
Bit me, then it hit me.

I went to the petshop
Returned the rat and
Bought me a roach.

When we got home, I
Put it in box and
Fed it to an OX!

Sana Alam

Twilight

When midday sun begins to fade,
Bowing low to evening shade,
The sky aglow with amber light,
Now every mother says goodnight.

Slowly first, then quickening still,
A locust starts her gentle thrill,
And calms the earth with her soft song,
The day is past, the night's begun.

A dove coos soft, the sun sinks low,
A gentle breeze begins to blow,
The leaves, they whisper "Hush-a-bye",
Now every mother says goodnight

An owl hoots, a cricket sings,
There, the rustle of robins' wings,
Children's laughter now wafts dim,
Twilight's soft glow filters in.

A mother hums her child to sleep,
And sweeps fine hair from silky cheek,
Knowing now that all is right,
When every mother says goodnight.

Teri Ashford

Untitled

The sky above is full of love,
Bright blue, white clouds and cheer.
I blink my eyes, now gray the skies,
The clouds begin to tear.
The dark clouds cry, I know not why;
The world is charged with fear.
The storm clouds blow, The skies soon glow,
The sun does reappear.
Our faith in man since time began,
Has gone from high to low;
But then I sigh, from low to high,
Why? Only God does know.

M. J. Fogarty

Listen Up Girl

You cried, as have so many more,
But dry those tears or hide them.
Dark glasses screen the overflow,
And no one sees the hurt you know—
You hide right there inside them.
And smile—the mouth's a give away,
It need not match the eye.
Now hurry. You can make it, friend;
And once inside, no brave pretend,
Just close your door and cry.

May Glenn

Where Oh! Where

I Love my daddy
But, I don't know where he is
Mom said he's gone.
But I don't know where.

I wonder if he is up in the sky
Way up so high
Is he in the wind?
I think I could feel him.

Maybe, just maybe, one day
I may just see him.
Did you see him?

Rosita Smith

The Fall-ing

It was a tithing of my heart
but ended as an ablation of it.
Her tender feet broke scarlet leaves
as she walked away in the morning's mist.
My mourning is unleashed and heaven is
deafened by my inutile cries.
My pain is echoed by the empty willows
by my sides.
Night falls and so do my hopes.
The forest's skeleton stands but bears
no fruit or color.
I had vaunted about my sweet but now
I challenge my emotions.
It's the season I explore but can't find
any other
My breaths decrease and start to slow...
Now, I lay still...
I fell . . .
in Autumn.

Warren Shellington

Grandmama

I loved you,
But God loves you too.
In my mind I'm happy,
But in my heart I'm so sad.
For the life, you have now
is better than what you had.
I can see you now, as we weep;
Singing and Praising at our Father's feet.
I know now you have many things;
Along with your halo and beautiful wings.
I'll never forget how you cared for me;
You're the best, that, anyone can see.
I'm going to miss you my Dear,
For in the heart you're near.
My days with you were as a dream,
Because it's a thing of the past, as though it
seems.
Oh! I'll be on my knees to pray;
Hoping we'll meet again on Judgement Day.

Vanessa K. Miller

The Bystander

My aim is true,
but I missed by a mile.
(The bystanders said a mile and a half.)
I was so close I cried.
(The bystanders were annoyed.)
That's when the bottom dropped
and my emotions were exposed,
before their very eyes.
(The bystanders were properly shocked.)
So they threw at me
shreds of dignity,
closed their eyes and turned away.
But I stood there before them.
Bragging.
I loved it.

Shelley S. Kubitz

First Love

Love can be spoken,
And Love can be broken;
But a true love can
never leave ones heart.

Tricia A. Rittenhouse

Everything In Me

I'm not very special, deep inside.
But I've got feelings,
I've got pride.
And what you have to offer,
Is more than I can give,
But I know I will love you,
For as long as I live.
People never look beneath the
Surface of the skin,
At my mind, my heart and soul,
And the love deep within.
When your hand touches mine,
There's something I can't explain.
Time which subdues the memories,
And eases away the pain.
So here I stand alone, vulnerable for you.
A mythical tale revealed, a dream coming true.
So I'm giving you my secret, something
others don't see.
I'm opening up and giving you, everything
in me!

Michelle L. Guske

Untitled

You had love,
but love hurt you
when you found your love
Was only playing with you.
So you lost your love,
the only one you thought you could love.
You found yourself lonely
looking for somebody, anybody
to hold you;
and make you feel loved,
even if it was just for one night
Then you say to yourself
"Since I hurt, they should too,"
So what I did for one night
Wasn't wrong, It was not a sin
because I'll never love again, I can't;
and now you find yourself
falling in love...
All Over again.

Sara Savalli

Tadpoles

I used to be a tadpole,
But now, I am a frog.
With lumps and bumps all over me
I lounge upon my log.

I sit and watch the fish go by
And think of tadpolehood.
The days without a single care
And living felt so good.

But now, my aches and pains agree
That I am getting old.
My lumps have turned to crevices.
(Or so I have been told!)

However, I won't think of me
But watch the little fish
And fight until the end to live
Upon one golden wish.

Melinda Porter

The Tree

Once I existed proud and free;
but Romans came and severed me
from roots that clung to barren ground
and when I fell, 'twas a leaden sound.

They hauled me away and cut and planed
till only my inner core remained.
Then they placed two pieces, one 'crost one
and lashed them fast; but not yet done

Upon my arms His arms impaled,
upon my foot, his feet were nailed.
I felt His pain amid their sneers.
My sap oozed down as bitter tears.

Naureen Bouchard

Life's Tune

A stately march to some is she
But some from whirling discord flee
To some a somber dirge plays slow
Devoid of melody or glow.

To some, a cheerful happy song
Throbs through the music all day long.
To some discordant syncopation
Deep depression, wild elation

To most of us the song may be
A varied ever changing key
Deep discordant chords as well
More anguish than the soul can tell

Each of us but dimly hear
Each other's tune, so far, so near.
Why can't my deafened ears hear true
The tune that now plays clear for you?

Lyna Goodhue

Time

Time to say goodbye, for now,
but the sorrow will not part.
Until the time we meet again,
I will hold you in my heart.

I know the place is a pleasant one,
it's beauty and peaceful feeling.
Even knowing that,
the sadness is revealing.

For the time to say goodbye...
I thought, would not be so near.
To hold you once more as grandmother,
would be a happy tear.

I think of how strong you are,
and try to place that with me.
Not to speak of you with tears,
but laugh and talk,
as if you are beside us here.

Wendy Sue Bower

Eagles

Between the water so blue,
And the clouds so white.
Soar the eagles,
With there eyes so bright.
When the eagles die out,
All peace is lost,
You might not understand the cost.

Missy Albrets

Just Thoughts

It's not so much the things we do,
But the things we leave un-done,
That gives the greatest heartache,
At night, when day is done.

It's the burdens we might have lifted.
The loving words unsaid.
A prayer for God's direction,
The scripture left unread.

The little acts of kindness,
That we were too busy to do,
A visit to the sick and lonely
the forgotten ones - they need us to.

Too busy to fix a broken toy,
To wipe away a tear.
To hold close the precious hours of youth;
While as yet we have them near.

At night when it still and quiet,
Then suddenly we realize -
That life is too short and too precious,
To waste on a self centered life.

Margaret Nightingale Kraft

Smoking

Smoking might be rather fun,
but to me, I think it's dumb.
It makes you choke and cough and spit,
so why not get rid of it.
Who needs cigarettes anyway?
They're bad for your health,
I've heard doctors say.
It's not just your health at stake,
but think of others, whose hearts
you'll break.
Loved ones seeing you gasp for air,
is a sight that's hard to bear.
Please let Jesus take you by the hand,
and help you break the habit
while you can.
Don't put it off until it's too late.
Just tell yourself that death can wait.

Ruth A. Jackson

Only A Rock

It's only a rock,
But together we built a fortress,
And conquered the world
Of crayons and paste and
Make-believe.
Then we awoke
And realized we had also
Lost.
Then they were my crayons and your paste,
And if I hold a rock,
I may not place it in the fort's wall.
I can do anything,
I am told.
Yet no one fears my
Intentions,
Or guards that world we once ruled,
Until the fort has crumbled.

Suzanne Smith

My Secret Garden

There is a secret garden,
but where I do not know.
I love the secret garden
It's where Love and Flowers grow.

This garden is my refuge
A place where I can rest
There's safety in that garden
that's why I Love it best.

Why can't I find that garden?
I need so much to sleep
My body is so weary
Oh! Please don't let me weep.

I know there is a garden,
if only in my mind.
It's a place that I can go to
and it's Peace that I will find.

P.J.

Untitled

You cannot see or hear them
But you know they are always there.
The memories that you hold and cherish
Make life much easier to bear.

At times you feel their presence.
They are walking there with you.
These times renew your faith in the Lord.
They clarify your view.

His mother's pain when He was gone
Was much the same as when we mourn.
But she knew well that he'd gone home
To share his Father's throne.

So when a loved one passes on
A door is opened there
And we are blessed with memories
That we can ever share.

J. Berg Hansen

To Henry My Beloved Husband (The Traveler)

Each time you traveled far away
  by car, by air or sea
I feared much for your safety
  'til you returned to me

One day you took an unplanned trip
  and I was soon to learn
The trip you took was one from
  which you never would return

For just a little while I thought
  I'd lost all trace of you
But memories and lasting love
  soon changed my point of view

For love, 'tis said, can build a bridge
  from here to eternity
And no matter where you are
  you're never lost to me

So travel on my love, my friend
  I need no longer fear
I know you're safe, and somehow too
  I know you're always near

Mary D. Carnes

Swamp Memories

Long shadows cast on water
By cypress knees awet
Enhance a heron's blueness,
Oft hide a key deer's step.
I love what life now brings me
On this day od dark and gray
With sky and clouds a dripping
To wash old leaves away;
To clear warm air felt heavy,
Refresh the blowing breeze,
Accent soft sounds once muted,
Thus allowing me to see
A world ablur in raindrops;
'N hear the sounds in silence
That filter through the swamps
Oft bathed in hazy sunbeams
O'er mocs upon the moss.

Roger Q. Smith

Wish

I wish you were here,
By my side,
Holding me tight
Through my life,
You see right through me,
Yes, you do.
Because all of my feelings
Relate to you.

I then realize
That you are not
By my side,
Holding me tight
Through my life.
I wish and I wish,
Only for you,
Knowing that
I'll never get through.
Wishing and wishing,
Only for you.

Pamela Johnston

Everyday

Breaths of want, her eyes in sorrow
  carry the lips away
Caress the folds of lonely arms
  within her lacquered grin
Shiny days pass, shadowed textures
  of a wall, the drapes stay as one
Her wants, motions in a breath
Fingertips fall, lines traced, entering as
  a whole, a demand of giving
Break sanity, loss of soul
  creases in a human being
Artificial lust, natural state
  combine the temperatures, heat
Tainted thoughts, caressing minds
  her life a constant circle, a rotation
The past never released, only evolved
  through truth
Everyday lies of her life.

Leslie Sademan

Alone

Candles, candles burning bright
casting shadows here and there
in the darkness of the night
soft, oh softly say a prayer

Creaks and rattles come and go
pounding heartbeat, ringing ears
moaning winds through windows blow
bringing out all hidden fears

Footsteps walking cross the floor
lightning streaks across the sky
something's scratching at the door
looking for a place to die

Do not look out through the curtain
to it nothing you must say
what's outside is not for certain
till the morning stay away

Candles light is softly keeping
as you lay down upon the bed
outside the rain is sadly weeping
mourning something now that's dead.

Regina Letiro

Why Worry

Often we may tend to worry
Cause our hearts to be afraid
Who are we that we should worry
Doubting every promise made.

So wrapped up in our convictions
Unforgiving from within
Who are we that we should ever
Doubt that He forgave the sin

Count the blessings you've been given
Though some you may not recognize
Who are we that we should ever
Seem so small in Father's eyes

Take the very air you're breathing
And the Soul that dwells within
Who are we that we should ever
Doubt that once we walked with Him

Ears to hear that age old story
Unconfused He set us free
Who are we that we should worry
Since He gave our eyes to see.

Sherry Rust

Welcome To My World

Your entrance into my world
comes like the sun in the morning sky,
slowly rising in me
an awareness of your existence.
Your warm gaze upon my face
brings brightness into my life.

Your touch moves my soul
like a pebble in a brook,
sending ripples of sensation
to the farthest edges of my being.
The weight of your presence
settles into my deepest depths.

Your love caresses my heart
like a musician playing the harp,
skillfully stroking emotions
to compose a melody of love.
It echoes through my every chamber
and welcomes you to my world.

Tia-Lyn Vatter

Do List

House to clean, each room special
Clothes to wash, each size sorted

Floors lack wax
Dogs demand groomers
Jelly spots the fridge shelf
Counter crumbs sticking.

This realm of eyes, nose, ears and hands.
There's more - I just can't see...

Hearts to mend,
Feelings splintered
Eyes turned downward
Souls slashed
No pity.

Houses cleaned
Clothes for wearing
Counters glisten as
Floors flash
Smiling dogs.

A world beyond the senses...
Who, pray tell, is cleaning in the super-natural?

Marcia La Reau

What's Inside

Breathing in the cold night air
coats my lungs with sugar
the pure sweet kind
you can lick off your finger.

Thinking of the memories we've had
why can't I change things
why can't I let you see
the truth I know

Oh, how it kills me to see
the suffering that you're in
You've never felt the pain I have
Or heard the screams of rage
I'll scream when I see you
swallowed up inside
of what I thought to be true
You see I never took the time
to look within.

Shauna Hedberg

Paper Weight

Rainbow master
Color my way
Guide me to the place
Of all my dreams, I pray.

My all is what I'd give
All which can't be seen
For each, myself on paper
Written words, I always mean.

Love once tried to kill me
Nearly stole myself inside
But for love, myself on paper
Written words, with truth I do confide.

To the one who's less enchanted
It is my thoughts I'd like to give
Then for me, yourself on paper
Giving breath so the dream may live.

Be kind to me dear future
Father Time please take my hand
My will would like whole happiness
To be the rock on which I stand.

Peter Matthew

Planet Life

Color of sand,
color of sage...
sliding, softly,
stage to stage.
Knots to unsnarl,
webs to reweave,
this ability's mine
(if I believe).
Color of fog,
of wave-driven foam...
shades glide and blend -
my earth, my home.
We all share this gift:
each human may choose.
A soul can mend,
or rend, or lose.
Colors of water,
colorful woods...
winds sending messages;
bend them to good.

L. Marie Brosier

A Love Poem

'Twas few a day, not been apart,
come springtime here at last.
Such long cold winters chilled my heart,
a curse broken, slowly past.

Her yellow sun did thaw my bones,
which brought on heavy rains.
soon jelly weak my heart of stone,
sweet fruits clang to my veins.

My rugged skin, smooth as sand,
to hers, tender as a rose.
Oh, how I longed to grasp her hand,
but no sandy seed she knows.

And in her mind, all beauty bled,
I'd die to make her see.
Behind this shell, in flower bed,
lies a garden, the real me.

Steven Klinshaw

Happiness

Happiness...
Comes from reading a book
sending a card

Comes from a family picnic
helping a friend

Come from taking a walk
having a talk

Comes from hearing a joke
singing a song
Come from giving a hug
playing on the rug

Happiness come from you

Laura Ann Crowder

Love Can't Be Explained

Love can't be explained
Does something funny to your brain
Mickey Mouse, Elijah Wood
I'd go, with him if I could
Love is explained.

Laura Miller

Southern Summer Nights

The day is done and the darkness
Comes gently floating down,
On a sleepy, southern village,
Which we call our town.

A night like rich, black velvet,
Embroidered in choicest gold,
With a million tiny fireflies,
What beauty to behold!

From a nearby drowsy woodland
Comes the call of the whip-poor-will;
The friendly light of a neighbor,
Twinkles on a distant hill.

A mocking bird is singing,
Notes trilling in the breeze,
Comes the smell of honeysuckle,
And fragrant magnolia trees.

To sleep with quiet contentment,
In prayer to God we go
With thanks for peace and beauty,
And may He keep it so.

Ruby White

"Ode To A Vacation"

The plans are O so grand
Complete with all detail
The sojourn off to surf and sand
Will surely cure our pale

On the road cries are heard
Are we there yet
Replied I, how absurd
This van is not a jet

Splashing and frolicking is now begun
Sunning and burning on to a bake
These endeavors may be fun
But mostly for Vacation's sake

Now you've expired and look who's tired
While youth's energy begs for more
Listen, your heavy toll is not required
On my sandy shore

We hear your shouts for a change of pace
And beckon us to play and ingest
But return me to that familiar rat race
So my weary bones can rest

Robert E. Lee

In a Moment

In a moment you can say good-bye
Contain the past in a single sigh
Expelled in cool crisp autumn air
Dispersing sorrow for the world to share

Next moment finds you face to face
A parting kiss seals a last embrace
A turning back; there's no turning back
Fall's colors fade to relentless black

The moment's lost and you are found
In darkness complete without a sound
Wondering how and wondering why
As a tear escapes from a sightless eye

Steven LoCicero

Broken Apart

Confusion is my master
Controlling the unknown
So many questions
Answers left unspoken

A heart torn between
One belonging to another
Where do I go
With whom shall I be

For I am unhappy
Twisted, uncertain emotions
In the arms of one
With thoughts of the other

Difficulty lies ahead
Anguish is guaranteed
I need to be true
Love will not survive

Rachael Cove

My Lost Friend

Days of laughter and smiles
Conversations galore,
Love, longer than infinite miles,
Memories we adore.
My lost friend

Hanging out, just being cool
Chillin' with my friends,
Knowing that we had it all
We were on top of the world.
My lost friend

Taking risks, exploring life
Doing any and everything was fun,
Completing homework at the very last
minute
Then rejoicing, I'm done.
My lost friend

Those days are part of the past,
But, our friendship was quite splendid
It was cherished, loved, but didn't last
It really hurt when it ended.
My lost friend.

Michelle L. Edwards

Surrealism

Watching the sunset
could be fun
yeah...
Silently the colors
fill the sky
the sky at Gay Brilliance
Soo ... Brilliant
Mist over flowing under the ancient cliffs
the majestic hues
melt into
tarot dreams
while sipping on a cup
of
warm electric numbness...
Yeah...

Sue Pettinati

Daddy I Sea You!

The ocean waves
crash on the shore.
Here lies my father
whom I see no more.

It swallowed him up
and swept him away.
Here I visit
on a brisk spring day.

I'm drawn to the sea
though it gave me much strife.
I'm drawn to the ocean
for it brings him back to life.

To swim in his love,
I go to this place.
I stand on the shore
to feel his grace.

The ocean waves
crash on the shore.
Here, I too wish to die
so I can see my father more.

Sierra Junemann

Romance

With just one romantic line,
cupid is going to make you mine.
It would be so divine,
to kiss your ruby lips of wine.
one says that love is blind.

Together we shall be
one heart-
never shall we
be apart-

Forever in love we shall be.
Grow old with me,
the best is yet to be.

Let us caress-
let us kiss-
let us savor every minute of the day,
as though it were our last breath of air.

Be here for me,
and I'll be there for you.

Let us fall asleep in each others arms,
until another day dawns.

Mary Jean Iannuzzi

New Night

Fingers spread across the sky.
Darkness split by light.
The earth beaming all around me
sitting listening to the night.

Silhouettes of trees
against the dark blue-gray sky.
Crickets chirping, creating melody,
against the wind's soft sigh.

Fireflies create a light show
under the sky empty of stars.
Comfort in the quiet
in spite the distant hum of highways cars.

The smell of cool dampness hangs in the air.
Perhaps the morning dew.
Everything around me...so familiar,
yet this night makes it new.

Nichole M. Allchin

One Damn Big Beautiful Buck Caught In The Crosshairs (You)

He's a trophy buck
damn him anyhow,
up to his neck
in antlers and age;
But I saw him—
caught a glimpse
through the scope,
I don't need to hope
the deed's already done—
he'll never run.
For whatever reason
he showed himself to me
let me see
the prize antlers—
his coat the perfect hue
then I knew
he was mine..
make no mistake
he is mine for the asking.

Priscilla Stark

Fleeting Existence

A cloud
dances gracefully by
Twisting, twirling
in the breeze
Spinning imaginary
shapes of fantasy

Temporarily crossing
the sun's path
It casts
a shadow below
And makes
its presence known

Will even
one busy person
Stop momentarily
and take notice
Of its
unique fleeting existence?

R. J. Bowen

Lustrous Night

As the pure white moon
Dapples the blue black lake
Like a jar full of shimmering
fireflies
Till the breaks
scattering across the sky,
black as ebony
Twinkling above
Till morn awakens
Enveloping night
in her yellow white cloak
of reminiscence.

Lindsey Banigan

Let Go And Running

Brown, dry, lifeless
Fallen by Fall
A leaf scampers across the highway
Flying from its home
Running from its mother
To become her nourishment
Earth

Theresa A. Pannesi

To Scare The Crows

He stands in the field,
dark and tall,
as a flight of the birds
comes to call.
He remains still, looking
eerie and grim.
They rapidly descend
and perch on him.
He's a failure of his purpose
but he doesn't mind.
For he's forced to patrol there
all of the time.
He has no opinion,
not even a choice.
He speaks with silence-
his only voice.
He shall not move,
he shall not go.
His objective is
to scare the crows.

Nikki L. Barth

Darkness

There is no light
Darkness is all around
Darkness surrounds you
Trying to suffocate you
You cry for help
But no one hears
You cry lots of tears
But the tears do no good
You hurt so much
And soon the darkness
Settles in
And misery comes
To be your one and
Only friend.

Mary Johnson

My Goodness

You shall not stand in my way,
denying all that I possess,
You may not gain permission,
to destroy my goodness.

I cause you to feel ashamed,
for I have shattered your myths,
Confidence is my constant companion,
as I display my wondrous gifts.

My ancestors are smiling at me,
as I dance through life with finesse,
My love flows in abundance,
as I strive to share my goodness.

How could you want to see
me hurt and downcast?
What moves you to want to kill
my spirit and past?

Though you walk and live in ignorance,
I still do my best
Though you struggle and strike out at me,
I'll still share... my goodness.

Von-Na F. Chism

This Is A Silly Question

This is a silly question:
Did you ever hold my hand?

When I was a little girl,
Did you every hold my hand?

Please help me remember Dad
When my hand was held by you.

Why does this simple question
Make me feel so sad, so blue?

Could it be that important,
A man holding his child's hand?

Do I have enough words now
To hope you will understand?

Watch him gently hold her hand
She is so small by his side.

He smiles, talks and laughs with her.
His heart full of love and pride.

She is standing by his side, this man, her
dad, her father.

She knows that she is special. She is his
precious daughter.

Dad, before you leave this world, as we all
must someday do,

Yes, I will still hold your hand. Remember,
I do love you.

Patti Pearson

"Hypocrisy"

Fortress of the Night.
Disparager of Light.
Quintessential elements used
For the Last Great Fight.

Obsoletist Functions.
Incoherent Rambunctions.
Impossibilities that abound
In continuous compunction.

Destroyer of Faith.
The causative Wraith.
Utter deplorability completely
Left unscathed.

Helplessness smothers.
While Hopelessness covers.
The unchosen path
Along which Nothingness hovers.

Robert DelGiudice

Wishes

Wishes,
Do they ever come true?

People wish all the time,
But do they get what they want?

I wish I still I had you,
I wish she was still alive,
But none of it will happen,
Because what's done,
Is done.

Sandra Wood

Untitled

New comer
  Distant,
  but close by
Pacing,
  up and down
  in and out.
A brief, unsure
  grin
trying to be a
  friend
Awaiting the unexpected
On lookers
  Suspicious, a little
A subtle joke sometimes,
Complex, but composed
  most times
Caring, sincere and
  understanding
Dedicated to his calling.

Terri Simicich

Love

What is Love?
Does anyone know?
Where do we find it?
How does it grow?

This question is ask
Time after time
If you seek the answer
You shall find

Love is a touch
from a gentle hand
Love is the beauty
which comes from the land

Love is a smile
you see on a face
Love comes in all colors
religions and race

Love is a tear
which is shed for another
Love is a power
like no other

Wilma Marcum

Love Died

Don't ever take love for granted.
Don't ever treat your love wrong.
For if you abuse love,
Or if you misuse love;
One day you'll find that it's gone.
One day you'll wake up and be haunted.
You'll realize just how much she tried;
But her heart was breaking,
And so full of aching,
That little by little love died.
So now you're the one who is hurting,
But somehow she just doesn't care.
You'll remember she tried,
And how much she cried,
And how much she wanted to share.
She tried hard to keep love from fleeing.
She tried hard to keep it inside,
But she'd reach out for you;
And what did you do?
You ignored her and slowly love died.

Lila M. Abeyta

Wayside School Is Falling

Wayside school is falling down
Don't you wish you heard that sound
People going round and round
Sayin' how many schools fell down
Schools don't fall down
They are burned down
but this school wasn't burned down
This school didn't fall down
It just went round and round
People want to know if the kids fell down
Some say yes
Some say no
But some people just say they don't know
How could a school fall down
That's what I want to know
Will somebody please tell me that
Cause I'm goin' crazy, and I have a hat
Don't worry I'm not going to throw it at anybody
Cause I'm not mean like that.

LaVetia S. Kea

Untitled

Into the depths I plunge
doubtful I remain unscathed,
Nobody sees me falling
the fear, anxiety and rage.

My grip on the edge is weakening,
but still I don't let anyone know
how the darkness beckons to me
"I will catch you - just let go."

"Let go" it says, "your turmoil will cease,
peace of mind at last."
I close my eyes and pray to God
that this struggle will soon pass.

This battle is making me weary;
between insanity and death
"End it you coward!" the demons scream,
"Put your mind and body to rest."

Where is the light at the end of the tunnel,
the hope-the faith-the cure?
Please take me from this living hell
so I will suffer no more.

Leslie Bliss Lewis

"Destiny"

I walked around, the sunbeams fell down on my face. I started to wonder, "Will I ever find him, the man of my dreams?"

The sun started to go down. It was cold, dark and scary. I leaned up against the wall, staring at the ground thinking; "What's stopping him?"

Then the moon came up. It started to get lighter outside. I looked up to see the moon.

I saw your face smiling at me, knowing that I'm looking for the man of my dreams. You say,

"DESTINY!"

Maureen Olsen

Under the Morrow

I fell
down the stairs
to get rid
of a cold,
but my ribs
refused to go.
They stayed
on the top step
and laughed
that strange laugh
that only ribs know.

Leonard E. Sackett

Downbent Dust

Slime,
Downbent dust,
Drifting, descending into graying pits,
Then plunging seven apparent roots
Downward towards hell,
Look up.
Judean sunlight
Casts a shadow of a wood framed bier
Over you,
Drawing all things to itself while rising
Towards the blue.
Divinized dust,
Loosen earth-fed pseudo roots,
Climb.

Mary D. Griffin

Casey's Eyes

Two distant points of azure blue
Draw me into their realm
Where hope is born and love is new
And peace is life's anointing balm.

What's this? But pain is mirrored there,
Because these eyes have known
The bitter seeds of love and care
That without harvest she has sown.

At times those pools run overflow,
And trickle down in tears
Reflecting sometimes, utmost joy;
Revealing, sadly, inner fears.

The two eyes search, yearn, and cry for
A prince in shining mail.
The eyes can never sleep nor rest
Until she's her own fairy tale.

And will she be? In truth, she is,
I see it in her eyes.
Those eyes, the only two I know,
That in two spheres engulf the skies.

Morgan Ashton

Amidst The Rose

How shall my hand
Create you be
I fear not grand
But you I see

From spinning ideas
I have come to pose
You for all time
Amidst the rose

Rick Schneider

My Muse

Affinity for someone who
Engenders feelings in the soul
Of beauty, truth, of poetry
Reflective images of you.

H. Calvin Cook

Motionless

Whispers rest on the breeze
dreams motionless as the sky
love young but rooted like trees
hope behind her deep brown eyes

Flawless texture of my loves embrace
purity envelops her every breath
strength to behold finally to face
imperfections of love I do accept

Never trivial however she's precious
to he who will rise and stand
natural womanly touch expresses
to him love and yes he does understand

Yet what does he have at all
all is love and simple ways and means
devotion before dishonor but stand tall
motionless as the sky are his dreams.

Walan Womack

A Common Man

Trapped in the soul of thy mind.
Dreams of thee, I do see.
Thy dreams go on, from time to time.
Thy eyes won't open, and let me be free,
Oh please, Oh please, open thy eyes and see,
It really all was just a dream.
To have thee, that is in my dreams,
are but an illusion.
To dream the future, to dream the past,
must thy, want thy dreams to be reality,
must thy eyes, be open to the truth.
Thy eyes open, and thy mind speaks,
It really was, but just a dream.
But in thy dreams,
I have so much love for thee,
for thee is but a common man,
a common man indeed.

Tamilee Sue Moran

Untitled

We spent the night together
Dreams that filled the air
Of what be forever
And feelings that we share.

But now that you are gone
It's only for a while
'Cause your memory lives on
When I think of you and smile.

I look forward to September
When I will see you again
And I ask if you remember
How we made it back then.

Don't want to wait that long
But the days that we will spend
Together as our love grows strong
Will last us until the end.

Paul J. Lennon

"Matter Of Time"

In the early morning light,
During the day,
Throughout the night
I see your face,
Hear your voice,
Searching for your presence...
Screeching tires,
Sirens roar,
I can't protect you anymore.
In my heart
You'll always be,
Even though you were taken
Away from me.
Too young to die
I continue to cry
Will the nightmare ever end?
Bound by something I never knew
There was no stopping you
From the vicious cycles that torment ones mind
With you, it was only a matter of time.

Renee Dipoma

Beautiful Picture

I gaze upon a picture
  Each day at eventide.
The frame is nearly seven feet tall
  And over three feet wide.
It's colors are so many
  Red, yellow, indigo.
A splash of blue here and there
  A touch of gold to glow.
There has never been such beauty
  For everyone to see.
Some have tried to duplicate it
  But that will never be.
It's name is "Sunset Splendor"
  No other name would do.
I bow and thank the Artist
  For this and so much more.
His name of course is God
  The frame? That's my back door.

Violet Hatch

Momma Can't You Hear?

Sweet lil' baby hurting ever so bad
Each expression full of fear,
Momma can't you hear
the cry that is so sad?

Tantalizing memories haunting
in her dreams,
Momma can't you hear
the agonizing screams?

With the drop of many tears
Without near comprehension,
Momma can't you hear
the sweet voice plead for protection?

Growing through the years
Still often wondering why,
Momma can't you hear
Your lil' girl still cry?

Teresa Anne Willard

Snow Flakes

Tiny specks of crystal water
Each uniquely bright
Beauty with the individual
Elegance with the white

Dancing the mezzanine of wind
Gently drifting to Earth
Resting on the landscape
Bringing the promising of new birth

Nomadic in their constitution
Evermore facilely floating by
Wonder and amazement abound
Magnificence descending from the sky

Sandi Cassavant

The Essence Of A Man

The essence of a man can
easily be torn apart, but
it takes time and patience
to develop a potent heart.

And with that time and
patience, wisdom comes about,
taking us to the right path,
and guiding us on the correct route.

This route we're taking leads
us to things that will come
into sight so that we can
walk in the air of eternal light.

And no more man this task
can afford, without the
ever present half of our
Father, the Lord.

Tyris Allen Young

Untitled

The hollow forest
echoed the death
of the lingering
rusted machines,
their lives long since wasted
from their captivity
in the clearing.
forgotten-
disregarded-
lost from the world
they sit there returning
to the earth from
whence they
came.

Phillip C. Dobyns

Of Bubbles And Rainbows

From the child's bubble pipe
Flows a stream of round fragile forms,
Spreading on wafts of air.
Varying in size and direction
Blown about by unseen forces,
Onward, upward.
All to a certain end, some quickly,
some lasting.
Caught in moments of sunlight,
Reflections of rainbow colors,
Beauty simple, beauty magnificent,
Each different, yet all the same.
Like life, yours and mine.

Letha Brunkow

The Children Didn't Cry

That day in Oklahoma City,
Eighteen small children died,
But the bandaged and bloodied
Never whimpered; never cried.

They stared straight before them
With shocked and wounded eyes,
Carried by parents or strangers,
They made no sounds; no cries.

I think the bombed hurt children
With the far staring eyes,
Momentarily saw God that day,
Is why there were no cries.

That cowardly, dastardly bombing deed
Will always haunt those who didn't die,
But the haunting thing to me will be,
The small bombed victims who didn't cry.

That's the picture I'll see always
With closed or opened eyes,
The small children or opened eyes,
Hurt, but uttering no cries.

Louise M. Rice

Bicycle Warrior

Goggles on
elbow and knee pads
torn jeans
black ripped shirt

Helmut strapped
under chin
decorated with
slogans and wants

Between shoulders
slung a sack
filled with letters
and small packs

All bedecked
Bicycle Warrior
racing on an
old Schwinn bike

Legs a pumping
arms taut
tearing by
goes Bicycle Warrior

Peter Amato

Ode To A Daphnid

Water-flea of lakes and ponds,
energy unequalled;
hurriedly "jumping" in random fashion,
what is your great secret?

Does your energy come from what you eat,
bacteria, flagellates and algae;
or is it because you have no mate,
reproducing parthenogenetically?

Reproductive success, you have found
through mitosis, producing daughters;
needing males only in times of stress,
leaving energy for other matters.

So swim on, daphnid mother,
may you rich with offspring team;
living your life without a male,
of which other females can only dream.

J. A. Zuiderveen

Untitled

A universe of stars
extends forever above;
a billion points of light
twinkle endlessly on.

A bright white disc
is absent from the sky,
exposing even more
than I ever imagined possible.

For one brief moment
a bright streak cascades;
part of the celestial beyond
becomes one with the earth.

An illuminated river of light
runs between horizons,
and only affirms the fact
that stars are infinite in number.

One cannot help but wonder
what lies beyond this world,
and if somewhere far out there
stands a believer just like me.

Ryan Kelly

The Walrus

Torrential downpour.
Eyes lonely, pleading
by the side of the road.
Help me I'm lost.

Once a mother's son
now old and achy
dirty and disheveled.
Cars splash him.
Water trickles off his
gray beard.
Hands weak, bony
clenching the buttonless
clothes.
Feet tired, weary
with nowhere to go.

A blink
he's gone
except for the memory.

Nancy K. Byrne

Fall

In the fall, the leaves
fall from the trees like
tears from a young girl's
eyes. The wind blows through
the trees like a ghost pushing
them out of the way. There
are big fluffy clouds that
look like popcorn floating
through the sky. The sky's
the color of a little blue river.

It's so peaceful listening
to the leaves rustling and the
river rushing through the
woods. I wish I could sit in
the woods and listen to the
sounds of the wilderness forever.

Trisha Boewe

The Wonder of Snowflakes

Have you ever watched the snowflakes
Falling gently from the sky...
Have you ever tried to catch one
In your hands as they drift by...
There is magic in their splendor
Twisting, turning as they fall...
And if by chance you happen to catch one
Suddenly its not there at all...
Like a mother placing a blanket
On the child she tucked in bed...
The many snowflakes cover the hillside
Where a child will pull his sled...
I just marvel at the snowflakes
And how similar they seem to be...
To the intricate detail of the lace doily
My dear granny once gave to me...
It's no wonder that the snow flakes
Are of value to young and old...
For the worth of nature's beauty
Is far greater yet than gold.

Virginia L. Jones

The Rain

The rain,
Falling ——— like
Hard,
Steel pellets,
————— As if
To punish
The cold Earth.

The rain,
Falling
From above
————— As if
Remembering
An unheard,
Unknown soul.

Lisa Margaret Tuck

Snowflake

Pure in color
Falls from grace
Shape of its own
Cold Embrace
Icy Crystals
Frozen state
Liquid that solid
Water that can break
Sound, it has none
Tender is its touch
Green it will never be
Destination is the sea

Russell Mayes

Rain Song

Rain, in rhythmic staccato,
Falls on the rock-cradled stream.
The stream becomes a river,
All part of God's great scheme.
Where the gulf enters the ocean,
The rivers cease to flow;
But, through time eternal,
Nature orchestrates the show.
Vapor steams from jungle leaves
And mist from forest floor.
Clouds form o'er sea and mountain,
And the rain begins once more.

Marilyn Collins Hickman

The Races

Hurry up, catch up, pick it up
Faster and faster they go.
Never reaching a destination
That they will ever know.

Fast lane madness
Conspicuous consumption gladness.
Gimme more, gimme more
Give to the rich, take from the poor.

Dogs on hovercraft skirts
Crash into the outfield fence.
Lassie, Rin Tin Tin, Spot, and Bandit:
The chase ends with abrupt realty.

Tom McCreary

Wandering Thoughts

In a sea so deep,
Fathomless depths
Horizonless stretching,
Forever unbound.

Derelict ship
Moved by winds unfelt
On waves of emotion
Of turbulent water
Or lullaby drift.

Steering against
Currents of doubt
And away from
Sweet siren's song,
Only to run aground
Upon reality's abrasive shore.

Stewart E. Carrick

Earthquake

Battering, suffering
Feelings that shocked the nations heart
Scared, mixed up, shaken, shocked
To see the people in the building
I think it killed all of us
Too long, too hard
Every little shake hurt us
I didn't want to go on
I couldn't bear it
I couldn't stand it
That is why we left.

Marianne Styles

To A Tree

Here I stand with my
Feet in the ground,
My arms up-stretched
Long and round.

My body is bent in
Different ways,
My hair is lightened
By the sun's rays.

As I stand here through
Rain and snow,
Feeling the people as
They come and go.

My friend, the wind,
Is always near,
Whether it's cloudy,
Or whether it's clear.

Lynda L. Scaggs

"Limited Freedom"

Walls closing in,
Fences keeping in the desired
And getting rid
Of the undesirables.

Racism, sexism,
Hatred keeping people divided.

Borders marking off what's "mine"
And what's "yours",

People claiming that they are free
Yet still being prejudiced towards others,
Still fighting battles in order to say
That one is better than another.
Is that really freedom?

If but one person can begin
To break down these barriers,
Then can we say
That we are truly free.

Michelle Vincenti

end zone

tripping on a memory blank
filling in the thanks
of gifts gone by
there's a hole
in the end zone
of victory's playing field
and tomorrow
keeps falling in
as yesterday applauds
the center
of every lost day
when the drought
has too much to think
destiny pulls it's chain
one yank of rain
at a time
one drink
for every sign
one stretch
for every bind.

tom bert

To Bridge The Distance

Here you are
Filling my thoughts again, from afar

Feeling further from you
Than the closest star

I know how to reach you
But so I really know

What it takes to be a part
Of where I long to go

Silent hours of the evening
As I am drawn to rest

And lay upon these feelings
I have eagerly addressed

To entertain with dreams
Many scenes, I am shown

With thoughts of you beside me
I am not alone

T. Kevin Steinbrecher

Canyon Weed

Sometimes a searing memory of shame
Finds root in deeds buried in an
Ancient canyon of the soul.

In a bottomless pit—chalk-white
Fossils of regret—they will not die.

Small and green,
Like a canyon weed—
A weed of self-contempt,
They are destined to live again...

And again
And yet,
Again.

Will they ever truly die?
Perhaps fossilized in time,
Billions of years hence.

Or, even as this cinder planet spins
Round its dying star, through some eternal joke,
Life's shameful memories will survive...

Dreams too lonely or afraid to die.

Richard B. Taylor

Heaven Bound

Two hands reaching across the sky
Fingertips touching
The bond, not the tie
Two sets of arms never hold back
Holding up, holding on
The lovers pact,
It's the me in you, the you in me
Two souls united in
Their yearning to be free,
Two bodies entwined, Soft in the moonlight
Two souls are searching
Safe, in the night
Two hearts connected
Never bound
My lover, my friend together we've found
The me in you, the you in me
Two souls united
Have set each other free.

Terri Nierman

Joy

The Joy of the Lord is like Inner peace
Flowing within my soul,
It is the fruit of the Spirit
Bursting forth with gladness untold

The Joy of the Lord is higher
Than the sky,
And deeper than the ocean blue
It is because of God's love
That's flowing through Jesus to you.

The Joy of the Lord is my strength
From whom all blessings flow.
Like a mighty rushing river
From the Father when the Holy Spirit
Takes control.

Scripture:
And these things write we unto you,
That your joy may be full. 1 John 1:4

Mary Phillips Manuel

Never Too Old

Never are humans too old to be bold,
For age alone doesn't quench desire,
The responsibility is ours to light
our own inner fires,
Knowing our own limitations best of all,
Refuse to let others determine your call,
Try something today just for you,
In those years left of only a few,
Don't wait! Don't hesitate!
Set your own goals to light your
own inner fires,
Only then can your secret mountain
be climbed of reachable desires,
Given but one opportunity to contribute
during our time,
Every minute of everyday is precious
of yours or mine,
Those influencing the world in a positive way,
Spread joy to others during their earth stay.

Willie C. Williams

"A Seafarers Widow"

A woman waits
for her husband dear,
Only to learn
what others fear.

Her love falls back
to second in command,
As the sea become s
his first demand.

A part-time Widow
is what you'll be,
As there is no way
to fight the sea.

The hypnotizing waters
Will keep him there,
While you are waiting
for time to share.

Thressa J. Wengland

Love's Hope

The tide leaves the shore
for hours upon hours,
But always returns,
with all of its powers.

A leaf on a tree,
may turn brown and descend,
And all in due time,
there's green once again.

The moon may be hidden,
by clouds from afar,
But on a clear evening
it's as bright as a star.

Misfortune has plagued us.
Our passion it has shunned.
So I live for the day,
when it's work becomes undone.

Michael Vincent

From My Heart

Is it so wrong not to love
for I love no-one
to love means to
get your heart broken
I have loved so much before
that I can not love no more
for my heart has been shattered
into tiny pieces
It can not be broken anymore
for I am so young
that my poor heart needs
time to mend
maybe one day I'll be able
to love again.

Rebecca Davis

Eternal Sigh

I load the gun carefully,
for I make no mistake.
Soon I'll be resting peacefully,
The Lord, my soul to take.
I press the cold, steel object,
hard against my head.
I close my eyes and say a prayer,
for soon I'll join the dead.
Boom! The gun goes off!!
I emit one last cry.
Smiling, I slump to the floor,
lost forever in an eternal sigh.

Polly Miranda Hume

Liberty

Speak the word of liberty
For ourself and our propriety
Fight for our right in every way
Upon the land our father lay

For the land our father fight
For our freedom for our right
Signing the Declaration of Independence
Adding on the Tenth Amendment

We have laws, we have rules
This is no game for only fool
So we must respect the truthful man
Who run our country as strong as he can

Let freedom ring throughout the land
Give support, fulfill it demand
Without this country what will it be
There wouldn't be a place for you and me

So cherish her like your own
As she shelter us with her home
Lets give love, rejoice, and sing
As the liberty bell right, ring, ring

Sarin Van

'Tis A Pity

How sad to die;
for the death of another,
to win a mad game.
There is no winner,
the loser chooses to be.
So close, yet one choice changes all.
The freedom of death takes
others with it.

Leslie Fisher

Searching

I have spent my life searching
For something that was not lost
Something never found, only known
To me in a fleeting dream.
I never knew that I was looking,
For something with no name.
Just a feeling that flirted, with
The back of my naive heart.
It lead me blindly on
Toward an unknown goal.
Then I found you,
In a place quite unexpected.
My vision became much clearer
I thought I understood.
The meaning was hazy,
But the reason was clear
The completeness that filled me.
Full peace from inside.
My search was finally over
It was love I needed to find.

Patrea Lois Scott - The Stone.

Untitled

Today,when I saw you,
for the first time I didn't feel
scared or nervous. I felt secure,
confident, and happy. You've always
been there to see me through
the good and the bad.
And today I realized
you helped me get where I am.
You're a part of whom I've become.
A strong, independent, woman.
I want to thank you for
everything you've done for me.
Everything you've done for us.

Patricia J. Castro

Brick And Stone

Hell on earth is made of stone,
For the man who has no home.
Brick and stone, broken bone

This hell on earth is his home.
Red brick, gray clay

Wash the sands of his life away.
Can he stand it for another day.
Brick and stone, broken bone

This hell on earth is his home.
Black tar, yellow sky

You higher people just walk on by,
Never looking into his eyes.
Brick and stone, and broken bones

This hell on earth is his home.
Green grass, clean air

Tell me people why don't you care.
For your brother who stands out there.
Brick and stone, broken bone

He spends another night alone.

Maurice Turbide

Smile!

It's the perfect treatment,
For whatever ails you,
It's like a God send,
To get you out of the blue.

We do it for different reasons,
At different times and different seasons,
It's an expression,
That's part of our profession.

It's not always seen or shown,
It won't always be,
We don't all get along,
We don't all agree.

It can disappear quick,
Or fade away slow,
Sometimes it will stick,
And never let go.

It's part of a mood swing,
Within us all,
Happiness it will bring,
To get us past that wall.

Rhonda Barringer

The Answer

He wakened me one morning
Form out a slumber deep.
He had me rise from off my bed
Though I sore needed sleep.

He had me rise and bade me meet
A morning damp and dim.
He willed that I should walk and think—

How could I question Him?

He led me to a verdant heath,
My troubles mind to soothe:
When I set out for home again
My soul was calm with Truth.

The price so small! No rest at all
I pray Thou grant to me!
If Thou wilt break my Final Sleep,
—And bid me come to Thee.

Paul Bordman

Untitled

Ideals in me remain
Foul expression runs amuck
Tried and true
The brush paints me blue
A better life
Not one filled with strife
I walk along and see the weeping wounds
Tiresomely I think of ways to heal
Thinking this cannot possibly be real
Racism bruises my heart
Who are they to tear us apart
Certainly joy is a stranger to them
Let us stop all the accusations
Succumb to better persuasions
Emotion flows like an unyielding river
There is a message I must deliver
Let us live in love and respect
For all creatures big and small
Life is short
That is all...

Noni Alvarez

When I Whine

Dear Lord help me when I whine,
From pain that rocks this heart of mine,

Help me to know, in future time,
That I am yours, my soul is thine.
And Lord forgive me when I whine,
I am only human as you can see,
Not always as brave as I should be,
So when I groan from pain of knee.
Dear Lord forgive, and please help me,
And to remember thy Pain on Calvary,
Where you so bravely Died for me,
Help me to bear this pain of mine
And Lord forgive me, when I whine.

Sera L. Smith May

The Beach...

The beach is the tides rummage sale,
from pebbles to sand,
to shells and rocks.
Colored by seaspray and sunlight
washed clean by pounding surf.
Seething with life, nurtured by wind,
fed by sea creatures.

Buy from the sea the shells that show
pounding surf, and winds that blow,
a form of life's retinite,
fluted and colored with delicate hue
some grown old, and some born new.

Showing a glimpse of depth,
when salt and spray,
and time and tide
became the elemental way
to house all living things.

Marian P. Gott

Modernized

Life has modernized.
From record players to C.D. players.
From radios to T.V.s,.
From typing to computers.
From wood stoves to microwaves,
From black and white T.V. to color.
From projectors to V.C.Rs
From the pony express to fax machines.
Life has modernized!

Sarah L. Cordero

Memories And Tears

The sweet spring blossom burst
From the ground.
The birds in the trees, Oh!
That beautiful sound.
The green of the grass,
And the memories as they pass.
Like echoes they come
To haunt my mind.
Memories of happiness past,
Can be so unkind.

Victoria J. Suriano

"Master Memories"

Memories that come
from the Master's mind,
enter my lonely heart
as the long, long day wears on,

In the dark silence of my room
I know I'm not alone,
my Master stands so close to me
unseen, in silence He comes.

My heart recalls the happy days
as my Master calls them back
I close my eyes in blessed sleep
it's tomorrow -, the
lonely day has passed -

Mary Frances Donnell

Memories

So many friends and faces,
From the past.
They never really seem to last.
The days they go so quickly now,
They go by faster than I would allow.
Good times they come,
And then they go.
We turn around and just say, "so."
How can we ever say good-bye?
All I want to know is why,
Oh, how I wish,
That I could again see
All of those who have been friends to me.
But yet,
I do not fret.
I know these things forever live,
They never die,
They'll always give,
Memories can go on and on,
We each have our very own special one.

Rebecca (Becky) Bailey

Untitled

I had a passion for the written word,
From the voice inside my head.
So I wrote them down just in case,
I went crazy or dropped dead.

I kept them to myself a lot,
Thinking no one else would care.
When I would recite for someone else,
A certain spark we seemed to share.

If I did my writing well enough,
Then I really had no fear.
'Cause the one response I wanted most.
Was a sympathetic tear.

If I got the reward I was looking for,
Then my efforts seemed to double.
And profusely words would strike the page,
Sometimes bringing lots of trouble.

'Cause no two ears are quite the same.
And what they hear is true, some.
But sometimes words get in my way,
And what comes out is gruesome.

Robert Lea Lovejoy

Mother's Treasures

I have two little treasures,
From which I cannot part,
For they give all the pleasures
That fill this hungry heart.

For when this weakened spirit calls
And says, "do this and that"-
They do not stop, nor fail, nor fall
But these little feet go "pit-a-pat".

And when I lay this fevered brow,
Upon my bed at night;
Here comes my treasures ready,
To make the dark look bright.

And when the blessed Savior stands,
And says, " 'tis finished, come",
I place my treasures in his hands -
From him I trust they will not roam.

You ask me what my treasures are?
Perhaps you've never entered this gate;
They are greater and grander than gold by far,
'Tis two little girls, one twelve, one eight.

Tulia Watson Jefferies

The Waiting

The void inside cries sit and wait!
Fulfillment lies not in the hands of fate
The urge to run and want to hate
Overwhelm and still I hesitate

The moments pass, to the morrow they send
Untouched chances to heal and mend
Love proved not, I'm quick to offend!
I understand not this need to defend

Doubt, the captor of another day
I wonder when love with find its way
Forever the void threatens to stay
A long lost forever on my heart to lay

I close my eyes to the sun's last ray
A tear falls gently, another token to pay
A gentle remember of a love gone astray
To keep me trying, and not run away.

Pamela Avila Roseboom

Song of the Soulmate

To My Lady,

Mated for life, souls intertwined,
Gateway to heaven, soulmate divine.
In a world that's fragmenting
With the pieces all skewed,
Our spirits are joined,
God's covenant viewed.

I find joy in your beauty,
Joy as a man.
Destiny in caring
For our growing clan.

Your spirit was formed,
To complement mine.
Our union has fire,
A light that's sublime.

Loren D. Anderson

Untitled

As I stand out in the darkness
Gazing at what once was pure
I now see houses rising
And now I know for sure
I don't belong here

The call of someplace better
The call of nature's best
Is what I have been made for
I've made it my life's quest
There's something wrong here

A human is a being which
By rights should always be
In tune with his environment
Like nature; to be free
I want to live here

Someday, when I am able
To have my place to fly
I'll find the place I want to be
And I will tell you why
I want to be here

Lawrence A. Evans

Raindrops

Raindrops, Raindrops, so soft,
Gentle and smooth,
Like my mother's skin.
I can hear the wind whistling
While the raindrops
Keep going, tap, tap, tap.
The winds remind me,
Of Eagles soaring through the sky
Like Angels gliding through the clouds
Looking down on us,
To see how we're doing.
To see how we're feeling.
Raindrops, Raindrops,
How sweet they are to listen to,
Like the music of soft bells,
As I sleep through the night.

Sarah Louise Oduola

Eternal Wings

The wings spread majestically,
Gliding through the sky of sad blue.
Many an obstacle there will be,
But the wings will stay spread.
A storm, a violent thrash,
Anything may come.
But the strength and perseverance
Of the wings refuse to die.
The angels in heaven watch over this soul,
Always amazed at the wisdom
Implanted in the spirit.
Even when all feel the time has come,
Never, never will the wings cave in.
Many ponder at the sight
Of the unclosing wings,
Wondering how it is done- -
Not knowing the true strength
Which keeps the wings apart.

Sara Jane Sternberg

The Beauty of the Rose

The rose of beautiful red,
glowing green, out of the
earth, caressed by rain.

Nurtured in soil, toiled and tilled,
serenaded by the moon and all
the nights past, this is for eternity.

A single stem, leaves fully
flexed, a body slender and
a face as beautiful as the
intended bestowed, I love
you said the card with a
seal by a single tear drop.

Shawn Williams

My Son

At age four
God spoke to Him
At age ten
God spoke to Him again
At age eleven
God has taken Him
In heaven
Only to awaken him
With all the Angels above
To embrace Gods love

Terri L. Ekdahl

A Very Special Person

You're a very special person
God's creation, his design.
No other person's quite like you,
You're exclusive, patterned ever so fine!
So, feel good about yourself today,
Hold your head and shoulders high!
Look and see the beauty 'round you,
You'll find a rainbow in the sky!
He has made you in his image,
So be proud of what you are;
Be the person God has made you,
Be a bright and shining star!
Determine in your heart
To be the best that you can be!
And with God's help you'll make it
For now and for eternity!

Virginia C. Blaich

"Granny"

Just the other day,
Granny passed away.
She kept me when Mom gave birth,
Until it came time to leave the Earth.

I love her like a mother
Never like another.
It seemed like she was Mommy,
Except she was my granny.

I never will forget her,
For everyday she's nearer.
Sometimes I wander to myself, O,
Granny why did you have to go?

Now every night,
I try to sleep tight.
Just like she told me to do,
In case I caught the flu.

Sarah Shown

Cycle

...and tonight the sky is bleeding;

It has been said that all
good things come to an end
but perhaps that is the nature
of a cycle

Designed to swiftly run its course
and then gestate until it can
begin again

Well, tonight I am among the
elephants
the patient
we sit in a field under the
midnight sky
we wait
we laugh
we work nine to five.

It has also been said that
before it all is to begin again
a sword must be taken
to the heavens...

Mike Weltz

Little Things

All the little things done
grow in magnificence,
and as the years go by
they appear as mountains
in memory's eye,
until with remembrance
the heart beats violently
and the blood runs warm,
a fire pulsating constantly
keeps alive a soul which can bless
a wearied world with tenderness.

Peg McKenzie

Unforgettable Love

Unchanged feelings in my heart
Grow stronger everyday.
Anxieties upon my mind
Constantly do play.
Visions of togetherness
Wake me from my sleep.
Yet knowing you are happy
Strengthens me when I'm weak.
My love for you I'll keep forever
Deep within my soul.
Until the day we become as one
And both our loves unfold.

Lee Burton

Christ the Lord

Long long ago, There was a star
Guiding men from near to far
To the savior that was born
In a manger filled with hay and corn

The shepherds heard from an angel
About Christ born in a stable
He was not in fame
But Satan's wrath He will tame

Let us remember Him
His light is not dim
But so very bright
Power and praise at His sight
With an open door
It is Christ the Lord

Richard M. Baker

Invictus Revisited

For some,
growing old is a wasteland,
barren,
devoid of warmth and love,
a no-place to wait
for the inevitable.
For some,
it is a time to re-collect
memories,
fadeless blossoms
that defy the stretch
of time and space,
against that fading day
of lost other senses,
when one can live inside
the mind
and experience the ever-present
past.
And wait.

A. Louise Mays

"Our Son"

Because God knew that John and I -
Had lots of love to spare,
"He" placed you in our "waiting arms" -
To "cherish" and to "care."

Although you were not born to us,
We chose you from the rest,
For every single place we looked -
We loved you far the best.

Your Dad and I agreed one day,
That you should know the truth,
I thought it best to tell you now -
'Fore you became a youth.

To know you is to love you, Phil,
You've filled our hearts with joy.
There's no one else could take your place,
You're such a darling boy.

Our prayers of "praise" are said each day,
For you our "precious one"
That you may someday come to know -
We're proud to call you "SON."

Virginia M. Carroll

"Treasure Mine"

A found of treasure, my telling is true.
Hair glows light o'er eyes brown deep
As stars bright in a moving to cloud sky.
The face glows a weathering hue.
Skin soft as a touch to down feathers.
Life lines smile out a pleasant grace.
Laughing twinkle eyes are a little moist.
On thin drawn lips, love whispers hold.
A voice deeper soft is pleasing meant.
Lyrical rhythm and country south lean.
Flow moving in a quickened pace.
Step walks as the wind through trees.
Knowledge of living only from time.
Life's wisdom is forefront prominent.
The heart dwelling Spirit, God alive within.
Hands stroke smooth a wellness crumpled.
Silver, copper or gold shines better not.
Life treasure locked in a conformance world.
Two into one will the world bond break.
Treasure mine is life love desire possessed.

William J. McNeely

Tattered Petals

You were once a beautiful flower,
Happy, cheerful, and bright.
Your smile would blossom with a radiant glow,
And your eyes were full of light.

Then when life got tougher,
Your petals began to fade.
More problems did soon arise.
What a mess you've made.

Your locked in an endless sadness,
Trapped from joy and life.
I feel the shadow of suicide.
Your only way out is a knife.

Depression is a deadly fate,
Like a dying flower.
Filled with sadness and hate,
You loose all reality and power.

Tristen Alberts

Vile

The sun shines down,
hard on your face.
The clouds are few,
and scattered like lace.
The tulips are fresh,
new with beauty and life.

I too, am special
beyond the day and night,
my body the treasure,
my soul the light.

Special to one,
so I am told.
Bewildered at times,
is our passion too old?

Dread of a desolate future
haunts my heart and my dreams.
Devotion is not
always what it seems.

Shannon Barnette

The Word

The WORD itself, you've noticed yourself
has been in meaning
partly deceiving
it's use perverted
it's beauty inverted
so now it's inelegant
almost irrelevant
to say it now
seems to disavow
what I feel.

The WORD itself, you've noticed yourself
has been neglected
and hardly respected
is sometimes deceiving
to the point of grieving
but in all it's misuse
it's hard to reduce
all that it means
which is more than it seems

I LOVE you.

Theodore A. Ott

Freedom

Freedom is a state of mind,
freedom has nothing to do
with your state of being.
Think happy, think free,
and you will have freedom.

Rhiannon Davis

The Death Of My Friend....

The death of my friend
has brought so many tears
and fears that death is now
here.

The death of my friend has
brought heartaches and pain,
and nobody knows who's even
to blame.

The death of my friend has brought
broken hearts and blame and
no one will forget the goals that
she made.

I say to you
much love my friend.
Rest in Peace. We love
you dee-dee.

Taneesha C. Parks

Winter's Arrival

A transformation of my world
has occurred before my eyes
A different beauty has emerged
with Autumn's last goodbyes.
Sunshine playing in my yard
Shadows sharp and crisp
And even though it's freezing out
I feel a summer's kiss.
Dripping diamonds caught on trees
paralyze my sight
I cannot begin to understand
how this happened overnight.
Everywhere are sparkles
A sea of sanded glass
it's purer than I've ever seen
in all the world a mass.
If I could keep one day
in my heart and in my mind,
This crystal palace undoubtedly
would you forever find.

Lisa Carucci

Love (The Oasis Of Life)

In the beginning, God sculptured the clay.
He beckoned the call for man to appear
And nearer, nearer without a plea,
The dawn of woman unto man drew near.

Now we are three.
Spirit of God.
Male and female.
Orderly fashioned
A creation of Him.

Nurtured in splendor, ordained in Love
Joins the oasis — gestured from above.
Beneath her brow, as nature resounds:
Two hearts in spirit, triumph as one.

Regina E. Simmons-Jones

God's Promise

My Lord died alone, on the cross one day.
He died for you and me.
He suffered the agonies of death
And from sin He set us free.

He taught us through His preaching
Just how we ought to live;
To love and be kind to others
And our tithe to always give.

He was a good example
Of how we ought to be
And He promised to love us always,
And to take care of you and me.

We don't deserve such goodness
But help us to be true.
And we have your wonderful promise
To spend eternity, in Heaven, with you.

Ruth Nelson

Warrior Of The Heart

To fight the beast within his mind,
He had to use his heart.
He had a weapon on his side,
He knew just where to start.

His eyes could see, not only out,
But also inside too.
And his mind, only, could comprehend
The war he would construe.

His weapon was his strong, brave soul.
His shield, it was his heart.
His master-plan was to overcome
Before he fell apart.

His war, it was a short one.
The battles, they were few.
And yet, his victory was great.
Rejoice it was not you.

Todd Kirby

Not Yet Julia

I am his Julia.
He sighs upon my clothes -
Upon my legs -
Upon my breast;
I am young and lovely
To the world that gazes.
My legs and hair are long;
My breast and lips are full;
My face and stomach, unlined -
This is their beauty;
It is not mine.
My beauty will come
When the gangling fawn fades
And the graceful doe emerges.
My legs will be sturdier stout;
My breast fuller filled,
Lines on my face and body,
Will trace the tale of true beauty
As my mother's and grandmother's do.

Nicole Muehleisen

The Battered Child

It was only three years ago
He was unwantingly born
The child in the corner
That's all shattered and torn.

He sees all the world
Through fear-filled eyes
He can't see any truth
Because of the lies.

He couldn't understand why
He had been beaten so
They said he was in the way
They wanted him to go.

Sitting with a dirty, tear-stained face
He tightly clutches small hands.
Trying hard to obey
Their unrealistic demands.

He tries hard to be good
The best that he can.
But whatever he does
The hitting starts over again.

He believes this is the way
Things are meant to be.
That is the really sad thing
About this little boy only three.

Terri Taylor

"No Escape"

All alone in a dark room
Help can't be found.
Lonely feeling that won't suppress.
So confused and bewildered,
Wish a light would appear.
Constantly searching for that way out.
Why can't a door be opened?
No one can hear my out cries.
Nor see the pain devouring my soul.
Why, why must I suffer in this despair.
No escape from this monster within.

Peggy Sue Rankin

Ode To Grandma Upon Reaching Ninety-Seven

Frail yet strong
Her heart beats on

On her own
Yet not alone

Loves and cares
Receives and shares

Old friends are gone
She still carries on

Strong in mind
Keeping ties that bind

Faithful to You
In seeing life through

Lifts thoughts in prayer
Thanks Lord for her being there

A model for me
To be all I'm to be

H. Ann Johnson

The Artist

The artist sits and thinks
Her imagination running wild
Before she goes to work
Her demeanor is calm and mild.

The painter sees the colors
Blending in her mind
Maybe the mountains and trees
All of a different kind.

The purveyor of design
Catches a circle square and line
The mix of hues comes after
Creating something quite divine.

The poet grabs her pen
As the words come tumbling out
Does it rhyme or is it blank
Le bon mot brings forth a shout.

Artists one, artists all
In their hearts they heed the call
Hoping to bring to the world
Beauty, peace and joy so tall.

Rhoda J. Abrams

Lights Darken, Her Presence Known

Lights darken
her presence known
passion burns
love pierces deep
Deep
feelings
lust becomes
deep within
into night
as stars glean bright
her eyes glisten
as I gaze into
night
between
two
hearts
love burns

Mark Evans

"Gibber-Jabber"

Blah, blah, blah
Here you go again
Scribbling down the thoughts
That race throughout your head...
A blessed rhythm
A catchy rhyme
Unpredictable emotions
Escaping from inside...
They come and go
You make it look so easy
Always a message to give
Whether ugly or pretty...
So, write them all down
Don't lose the feel
Keep your concentration
Make it sound real...
I get sick of the poetry
The continuous rhyme
But nothing seems to stop it
I guess it's just an addictive talent of mine!

Renee C. Fasano

Eternal Friend

What a friend we have in Jesus
He's a friend to you and me
and the friendship that he offers
if for all eternity

It doesn't matter where you come from
nor if you're rich or poor
for the wealth of this world
cannot open Heaven's Door

No, the key the Kingdom
God gave to you and me
in the form of Sweet Jesus
who died to set us free

I thank you, God the Father
for giving up your son
to bring us to salvation
and to teach us how to love

I want to love you Jesus
with all my heart and soul
but to praise you in Heaven
is my ultimate goal

Tresa A. Montoya

Buried Treasure

Beneath earth's surface
Hidden from the day
Lays pure and undiscovered
A cave never touched
by a human hand.

Where's no day or a night
Where darkness fills the hole
Where everything seems dead
There is a life and a beauty
blooming from everywhere.

Exotic crystal bushes
climbing up the walls,
Stalagmites extending upword
from the cavern floors,
Flowstones becoming waterfalls
of grace flowing stone.

So many things to see
So much the earth hides
The underground world
The wonderland of stone.

Monika Zagajewska

A Cold Night

Alone, he steps from the curb.
His car like ivory, gleams.
Frost hangs in the air
of his breath.

Black marble skies gloat above.
Burning pink lights over highways of odor.
Dying grass trampled by the thoughts
of people rushing by.

Turning back, his reflection gleams
In the eyes of the car staring ahead,
Paralyzed by beams of light.
Piercing through to the heart.

Reach out to touch the ivory gleam,
A hand frozen in motion.
Roar of the sulphurous beast beneath.
Warm at last.

Stephen E. Latta

Seasons

Oh, the seasons, always changing.
How many seasons has it been?
Oh, the people change like seasons.
The years come and go again.
But you my friend, remain unchanged.
You remain as time goes by.
Your friendship to me, will always be
As endless as the sky.
Though there were times we were apart,
I missed you even then.
But that doesn't mean our friendship
Can't be all it's ever been.
For like the seasons, though they change,
Still, they'll always be.
And like the friend I've always known
You're always there for me.

Laura Janca

Poem

An understanding to which is known
how masters of sight seek out their own
to cherish, yet know, in an unknown tone
that they are here to die all alone.

All alone never to be heard
all alone to reason, reason what is
learned.
I am it, it is my companion.
Once again my hand is held
caressed by the sweet incentive smell
The realm, I see, miracality beheld
to know just why, I hear angels cry
for the desperate understanding
of man.

Marc Martinez

Never Again

How soft the words I used to speak
How tender my commands —
I gently spoke the words of love
And sweetly drank them in.

I followed love here and there
Yet scarcely wore a smile.
I trusted love to take my hand;
It lead me like a child.

I bore the pain it brought my way;
I embraced it like a friend.
I asked for love to comfort me,
Yet I never will again.

I thought that love would bring some peace
And calm my wounded soul.
I thought true love was there some place
For every soul to know.

Yet, I've never found it with my eyes,
Or held it in my hands;
And though I've looked all my life,
I never will again.

Peggy Lorraine Lanier

Enter Slowly

Enter slowly into the warm, dark loam
How thin and sharp is the moon
Hung thin between the dark, and the dark
Light gathers in pool

Old, laughing coyotes,
A cry of defiance
Bridges quake with fear

Wind - wavering
Eagles hie and hover
Bats strumming their teeth
Depths of icy stone
Breezes of an ancient sea

Shannon Haas

Untitled

A traveller once told
How to an inland water slanting come
Slim boats of cane from rivers of Cathay
With trembling mast so slight,
It seemed God made then with a hand of air
To sail upon his light.
And there
Soft they unload a jar of gold and jade
In the cold dawn, when birds are dumb.
And then away
And ask no words and seek no pay
Away they steal
And leave no ripple at the kneel.

Thus the tale is writ.
And now, remembering you
I think of it.

George Gibson

Untitled

Do not stand at my grave and weep.
I am not there, I do not sleep.
I am a thousand winds that blow.
I am the diamond glints on the snow.
I am the sunlight on ripened grain.
I am the gentle autumn rain.
When you awaken in the morning hush,
I am the swift uplifting rush.
Of quiet birds in a circle flight.
I am the soft stars that shine at night.
Do not stand at my grave and cry.
I am not there, I did not die.

Traci L. Carter

Dream Believer

I am she,
I am the dream believer.
It is I who comes
in the dead of night.

I take you to
a world beyond belief!

Through the vine covered walls -
past the narrow sunken streets.
Through the corridor and up
the stairs -

From beyond the depths,
from beyond the soul-

Beyond the window
and out the door-
is where I'll travel to
tonight once more!

Melissa A. Carrillo

Why Do I Love You?

Why do I love you?
I ask myself everyday!!! I come up
with so many reason's, I really don't know
what to say.
I love you because...you are so sweet.
I love you because...I know our love
can't be beat. I love you because...
You let me know your mine, Just by being
yourself and being so kind.
I love you because...you laugh at the
things I say, you also see me at my
worst, but you love me anyway.
I love you because...you are always
there, with a knowing look that tells
me you care.
I love you because...you are true,
but the reason I love you most,
is just because.... YOU ARE YOU!!!

Sherri S. Wilkerson

The Sunshine Of My Life

It seems so very long ago
I brought into this world
what ever mother is hoping for:
A healthy baby girl.

She was the sunshine of my life,
her daddy's pride and joy.
We couldn't have loved her any more,
even if she'd been a boy.

But years have past and she has grown,
from toddling to her teens,
I can't say she's always sweet,
sometimes she's just plain mean.

For all the gray that's in my hair,
and the wrinkles in my face,
believe me when I say,
that child put every one in place.

Times get rough until she sees
some things she just can't win,
she's still the sunshine of my life,
and she's also my best friend.

Wanda Lyons

Why I Love Being Cold-Blooded

I love being cold-blooded
I can live in the mud
Where I can find a best bud
Then we'll run hither-tither
To find a fast food dinner

I love being cold-blooded
I can fall asleep during winter's chill
and awake in spring with a thrill
At times I'm parts of a child's play
but soon let go to scurry away

I love being cold-blooded
If part of me is lost
It's at no great cost
To be able to regenerate
Is truly a wonderful trait

I love being cold-blooded
I'm so very glad
It's not just a fad
Although I'm never hairy and sometimes
it's quite scary

I LOVE BEING COLD-BLOODED!

Shelley Rank

My Love

Beneath the weeping willow tree
I can see you now beneath
The way we lover's used to be
When our love was complete.

If the moon could tell a story
of the lover's who were true
That loved beneath this willow tree
The special way that lover's do.

The wind will blow and blow
Through this weeping willow tree
It will sing of your special love
that you had for me.

In my dreams, I'll meet you
Beneath this willow tree
And we will be together
The way we lover's used to be

God made this beautiful tree
Not only for lovers you see
But he had a purpose in mind
Like love, it grows with time

Laura Durbin

I Can Remember

Across the miles
I can still see your face.

I can feel the touch of your lips
so tender and sweet.

The first time we made love
I can remember my words
"now I'm your wife"

It seems so long ago
or was it just a dream?

I can feel the beating of our hearts
from passion and fear.

I can remember the cool and dreary
summer day.

I can remember the silence between us
Knowing we had to let go.

I can still feel the longing in my heart
and the tears.

Across the miles I can still feel
the love.

Terri Johnson

My Heart Is Caught Upon A Rock

My heart is caught upon a rock,
I cannot get off;
I've washed it with some happiness,
Loosening it is tough.

The rock bears scars of prejudice,
Some malice and some lies;
It hardened, oh, so gradually,
Before my very eyes.

I need good weather and some sun
To break apart this pain,
For if I don't, I fear I won't
See my heart ne'er again.

Lana Bischoff

Untitled

I found a feather today it felt magical.
I didn't know what to do with my find.
It was the only one I saw today.
At home I took my feather to my room,
Soon an answer came to me.
Feathers belong to birds who soar up
High beyond our sight.
I hold my feather and I dream
"I am that bird."
Who takes my spirit with him as he soars
Up, up beyond the cloud, taking me to a
New height renewing my spirit, baring my
Soul to great new wonders, I can still
Find in my life.
My magic little feather now sits over
My bed in a circle with other magical
Feathers. To bring all my dreams alive.

Laura Mae Betts

My Fish

My fish beautiful and suitable.
I feed them once a day, that's it.
They're colorful and playful.
They don't bother me a bit!
When I turn on the light, it helps
me see, all my fish starring right at me!
My fish are crazy and lazy.
They swim around all day.
They eat and sleep in a funny
Kind of way.
One fish, red fish, pearl fish, cat
fish in my tank as happy as can be!

Rayford T. Bacon III

Class Reunion

Wonder why your classmates
Have aged far more than you?
Perhaps its only an outward thing.
I'm sure for me that's true.

Down inside where I live
I'm pretty much the same
It's only on the outside
Where age has staked a claim.

Violet Ross Senn

Untitled

Music is a beautiful thing
Countless moments of pleasure bring
From brass and ivory and strings its heard
Including the song of a happy bird
Its gladdens the hearts of lad and lass
God given talents portrayed in song
Praising the Lord all day long

VirDel B. Parrish

By The Sea

Sitting by the silent sea
Connotations of love, memories
Crashing through upon the shore
Repeating the words, legendary lore
Of love that rose encompassing all
Only to recede at the moon's radiant call.
Rejoice oh voice of the prisoner now free
...left sitting by the silent sea.

Shirley McLaughlin

Nature's Melody

Who wouldn't stop to watch a sunset?
Stand in silence, amazed in its awe.
If we could all just stop to watch a sunset...
Feel the magic as you pause, Shh in a moment
it will be gone.

In the distance a small echo begins to roar.
You can hear the beginnings of a thunderstorm.
As you stand you see the lightning, feel the
breeze, watch the clouds form.

Tiny raindrops fall to wash the world anew.
Look into the horizon as the sunshine pushes through.
Out of nowhere budding in the afterglow, what can be
more magical? Rising up from the misty fog the
glistening colors of a rainbow.

How wonderful our world could be,
if we could stop to watch the sunset,
pause to listen to the breeze, or
reach out — to touch a rainbow.

Patricia K. Wright

Who Am I

I'm tall, proud and exceptionally strong.
I never speak but often roam the countryside with you.
You need me. Your children needs me.
You bring me into your home for the celebration of Baby Jesus.
I shelter you and my beauty is often taken for granted
and I'm abused in numbers. My roots extend
deep with tips that reach
high above to meet
soft blue or occasional
angry, stormy looking
sea. I sway with the
wind and small pieces
of me fall and clutter to paint the ground
below with magnificent shades of bright orange,
fire red, and glorified gold. Who am I?

Tony J. King Burnett

Just Beyond The Mountain

Just beyond the mountain a light shines forever bright.
A beacon of love that glows steady in the night.

The radiance does not diminish, falter, or sway,
But stands as a sentinel all along the way.

Rays of warmth outstretch to the heavens and pierce the sky.
Their expanse betrays all darkness and guides the eye.

Inspiration generates hope to replace dire fears
When strong hands reach out as support to cease tears.

Faith pulls us together in search for eternal rewards.
Just beyond the mountain a light shines brighter
that we all must move towards.

Ron D. Titus

Self Made Men

Sometimes when you see a "self made man"
Do you ever wonder where he got his plan

And do you hope, as I heard one day
The "only mold" was thrown away

Then there are other self made men
It matters not if acquaintance or kin

Who chose for themselves the right mold
And selected materials of finest gold.

Odessa Lockley

Poem For A Friend

Once in a lonely dark shadow, in a dreary shell of a life,
a beautiful ray of sunshine broke through as a glowing light.

The light was unfamiliar in this cold, dark and unforgiving land,
it was light with a smile, that was able to take me by the hand.

Open a mind that had lived in the shadows of pain, that smile
allowed the hurt to pour out as if it were pouring rain.

It was with the gentleness of a child, and the nurturing of a
powerful man, a smile with so much caring that, you were sure it was a
helping hand.

It was on a person that was so wonderful to see, a person that
smiled, and talked, and was in control of everything, but wore a
golden wedding ring.

I am so thankful for that smile, that gave me rest for a little
while. I am so thankful to this special friend, who is indeed a
wonderful man.

Phyllis Prewitt Van Winkle

A Cry to Be Heard

A craving world, a vibrant town;
A blend of people who don't seem to fall down.
Yet, stands a woman on the edge of a curb;
In whose lonely sorrow, no one dares disturb.
An old battered dress, a smudge covered face;
Is sure enough human, yet so out of place.
She owns but one penny;
But, her memories are many.
Her wisdom is much;
Yet, not a soul can she touch.
For many reject her words;
And to many it never occurs;
That a body so despised;
Has a soul that is so wise.
So, they leave her to her wisdom;
They leave her to her curb.
And she remains rejected;
With her sorrow undisturbed.

Tiffany Rayer

The Warmth of Christmas

Are you shopping for a stereo or shiny brand new bike?
A computer or designer clothes in style?
Imagine when asking your kids what they'd like
If they said, "I'd just like to feel warm for a while."

Imagine a father who prays for a way
To give his chilled family some heat.
Imagine the sorrow he feels every day
That he can't buy them coats or put shoes on their feet.

Imagine a mother who's dream is made real,
Who's Christmas wish has come true.
To serve to her family a nutritious hot meal—
That prayer could be answered by you.

Imagine yourself in this season of giving—
The love and the joy you'd impart.
By sharing what you know as everyday living,
You, too, will be warm—in your heart.

Susan Shields

Untitled

Fresh out of school
a diploma all his, yes HIS own
he had earned it.
tall and gawky like all other guys his age
BUT on that day he was different.
Shoulders thrust back and head held high - pride
proud of the uniform he wore
proud of the country it manifested
love of that country
love enough to fight
BUT, for what?
even after he was over there - for what?
his buddies wondered too - for what?
then his death - for what?
BUT you and I know -
or at least we hope we know
BECAUSE
He is my brother and your son and HE couldn't have died in vain,
COULD HE?

Rita A. Ruminski

Untitled

A whole water drop contained
a direct line to my alive pain
formed within these swollen eyes
to flow onto a pink peeled skin.
A rainbow encircles the sun
with shades of blues, blacks and reds.
But tears that have no outlet to the eyes
lie inward to brush the bruised and stay
to darken, grow cancerous, and parched.
Foreign openings of love without pleasant meadows
or plenty of sky to soften with clouds of mist,
cannot free the sun to brighten a clear day.

Thelma T. Rountree

Dancer

I am a flower, a beautiful flower
A fuchsia as you would say
I am vibrant shades of purple and pink.
I know I'm the best flower around
Because I can dance.
I am a ballerina dancing in the wind.
A beautiful sight when all alone in the world.
Someday I will really dance,
On the ground, with legs.
But for now I just spin freely with the wind.

Tracey Nisky

I Wunda If Heaven Got A Ghetto

I wunda if heaven got a Ghetto.
A ghetto that I can go to or something to remind me of home.
And I won't feel so all alone.
I wunda if heaven got a Ghetto.
And does the Ghetto has a phone?
Will my mother be there or will she be here?
Will my friends be there, or will I be able to play with them
Again.
I wunda if heaven got a Ghetto.
Will the shooting stop? Or will everyone drop? Will there be
Any guns? Or will there be any hit and runs?
I wunda if heaven got a Ghetto?
Or just something I can relate to.
I hope when I go, I don't go by myself.
Maybe, there is someone waiting for me!

Tiffiny J. Cobbs

Guilt

Guilt is like a lonesome song,
a hurt within when you've done wrong.

May you be guilty is not what's asked,
it's in your heart where the lonesome song last.

A lonesome song with no words or ballad,
one composed by humility is one that's valid.

Many men live with tone deaf souls,
ruthless deeds and devious goals.

They rip through life and don't look back,
always on guard ready to attack.

Forgive them "O Lord" for they don't know humility,
the lonesome song is beyond their ability.

Some day "I pray" I can stand on a hill,
enlighten the meek for it is not wrong,
to feel the guilt and the lonesome song.

Martin Mitchell

What Is A Kiss?

A kiss is love's warm language...
A journey to the moon...
Capable of turning...
December into June...
It is a sign of fond affection...
That fashions heaven's key...
A kiss is a sweet promise of happiness untold...
Telling those who share it...
To always have and hold...
It is a wondrous narrative...
Told by yearning lips...
Instilling faith and hope in those...
Who sail on dreamy ships...
It is the beginning and the end...
The door to all of this...
That opens into paradise...
A treasure is a kiss.

Nancy J. McGowan

"How To Start Again?"

Young, confused, alienated. No direction.
A laborious, lamentable life, a soul lost amidst the throes of
a nefarious nation's descent into insanity.
Then life happened. Abused, used, refused by all from whom he
would seek friendship and succor.
Dejected. Fortune appeared and vanished, not seized when present.
Time's tumultuous, tortuous testing triumphant.
Failure. Forlorn, fighting only to remain alive.

Birth of his child revived him, new hope, new life.
As fast, the daughter taken deceitfully, unceremoniously.
Recalling life's past journey, apparent he had lost.
A simple story, a similar sadness experienced by many - yet
Different. Oldness had overcome him before he had lived.

Would that he could reach an understanding of what troubled
him, held him back, forced him into docility.
How to start again? Familiar strategies now stale, new
profferings meaningless, impracticable.
Hollow, empty, lifeless shell, emaciated entity - barely existent.
"How to start again?" He mumbled aloud as he turned on one side
and drifted into a delightful, peaceful slumber.

Stanley P. Hershey

A Poem

I want to make love on a bed with satin sheets and rose petals, I want a man to hold me in his arms and tell me he doesn't love me. I want to wake up and dive into a pool and feel clean again, because sometimes I'm soiled and hours of washing won't make me clean. Sometimes I want to wash the thoughts of hatred and killing from my tender, virgin mind, and be new. Sometimes I want to die. Then sometimes I want to hit myself for ever thinking it. I want to beat my head against the wall till all my blood pours out upon the floor, and stains the cleanliness that I no longer possess. I want to kill the maker of my pain and then I want to kiss him good bye and tell him he'll be missed. I want to run in the rain slicken road and laugh at the oncoming traffic as it runs me over with no qualms. Ha ha, we're even. Now I can sleep in peace, and dream in the hopefulness that is only captured by the mind of a child and only destroyed by the hand of a man. Now I can look at foolishness and smile with a feeling of knowledge, while the others are still stumbling around below wondering "What the hell is going on?"

Laura Dreist

The Flowing River

There is a river,
a mighty flowing river,
which leads into the future.
There is uncertainty, fear, hope, peace, sorrows, tenderness,
Understanding, knowledge and wisdom in the turning, winding
waters of flowing fire.
At the beginning of the river lies childhood, first
experiences and innocence.
The boat of understanding, and the cars learning, begin the journey.
Traveling on the river, new faces, ideas, thoughts
Stand on either side, some to be taken aboard, all to be turned,
into memories. The waters pick up speed, life begins new turns.
The boat is nearly overturned.
The waters still. Calmly, quietly, the boat continues on its path.
The knowledge darkens the waters, the oars get lost in the water.
Wonder acts as wind, propelling the waters forward. The destination
nears. Dry land is reached as the water runs out. Arms embrace,
reaching, hugging, holding on. The river answers, crashing as it
runs into the land. Ending as a single drop of water, beginning the
same as it finished.

Robert Trotter

Nighttime

Nighttime is a Dark and Dangerous time; it's also,
a Misty and Scary time.
It's a time to lay down in the soft, green, grass
and gaze up at the mysterious sky, and
all of it's Amazing Wonders.
Nighttime is a time of Peace, a time of Quietness, and
a time of Relaxation.
Most of all, Nighttime is a time of Dreams;
Dreams that can be reached, just as
Dreams impossible to reach.

Michael Ginger

Rainbow Of Love

God painted a wonderful rainbow today,
A multicolored ribbon in a sky of gray.
Magically, as I watched, it became two,
A rainbow for me and another for you.

So, here is my gift from far away,
May it brighten your life, whatever the day,
This message of love for your eyes of blue,
A rainbow for me and another for you.

There seems to be more I want to say,
Perhaps in time and in another way,
To share life where our friendship grew,
A rainbow for me and another for you.

Robert E. Garrett

What Is Black?

Black is beautiful (ugly nigger), African-American (stupid darkie),
a noble race (lazy coon).

Black parents raised me white -
so I'm superior to blacks, but inferior to whites.

I've been confused.

Two minds separate two worlds in one head.
The black-mind fills with false pride:
"I'm better than those darkish", is puffs.
"I'm smarter and prettier than those monkeys", it smirks.
But the white-mind condemns:
"You're dark and ugly, and your hair doesn't swing", it sneers.
"You must prove yourself worthy", it challenges.

How I have wasted so many years and swallowed so many lies.

Now my mind is beginning to clear, the lies are being seen.

I am none of those things they have said,
What I am, what I will be, I don't know.
The One who does will tell me,
In His own time.

My skin is black, but that is all.

Michele Conyers

The Only True Love

An uncertainty overwhelms my heart with promise.
A promise of faith, hope, and contentment.
How did I find someone so gentle? So caring?
The anticipation fills me to my fingertips as his continuous love
warms my lonely heart.
The midnight darkness surrounds us like a protective shield as we
gracefully dance in the street with a sense of freedom.
When time brings us together, we capture the precious minutes that
we desire.
In an instant, we are one with each other.
The love soaks deep within us as we grow into those timeless
moments.

Is he the one?
His elegant face burns on my brain as I long for his gentle touch.
The taste of him as our tender lips meet surges the answer through
my mind.
The confusion has disappeared and it is all so clear to me now.
This is the only true love I desperately long for.
The words are indescribable when I visually see his handsome face as
I am mesmerized by his trusting eyes.
It all seems like a dream somehow.
It's as if I stepped into a fairy tale, but it's real,
And it's happening to me.

Tanya Marie Stefan

Reflection of Me

In your eyes I see myself,
A reflection and not really me.
Am I then, a part of you?
Or are you somehow, a part of me?

I see myself in your eyes,
Reflected (refracted) and returned.
You send me back to myself,
But only the shell of me.

In your eyes I see myself,
As I am to you (as you wish me to be).
With your consent I walk freely, but my soul remains behind.
A prisoner of your heart.

I see myself in your eyes.

Melanie Instefjord

America, In Denial

Is O.J. guilty? Did he commit the crime? Is Mark Fuhrman really
A racist? Is Furhman really ly'in? The world is pointing fingers,
So excited, judgmental, it's news! A terrible crime committed,
Trial of the century, they're all confused!

What do you think of the lawyers, the jury, etc, the judge? What
about the news media, the victims, the families, etcs., oh fudge!

This is like a weird movie, a soap opera, America is completely
removed. "It doesn't touch me", says America, "I'm in denial.
It's that famous black guy, he's the one on trial." Poor Ron, poor
Nicole, her poor children, the pained families, so bold.

Is O.J. guilty? Did he commit the crime? What about Mark Fuhrman,
Is he really ly'in? "It doesn't touch me," says America, "I'm in
Denial. I'm the judge, I'm the jury, I'm not on trial."

O.J.? Fuhrman? Those guys, I can't relate. They're the ones in the
News, they created their own fate.

"It doesn't touch me", says America," I'm in denial". I've never
Accused or abused, I can't possibly be on trial.
I didn't discriminate or promote racism, I'm not on trial.

It doesn't touch me, I'm America, I'm in denial.

Shirley M. Garnett

I stand before the stairs to the sun
A range of mountains without name tags
This one.
The mountain I have chosen stares calmly down upon me.
I stare right back.
Let us begin.
Neither of us taking credit for the echoes resounding between us.
The stone is hard and unyielding beneath my toes and fingers.
I must teach it to yield.
Rocks thrown toward me. Stones disappear from under my grip.
Storms beset me. Winds buffet me.
My feet ache. My arms melt.
Reach. Pull. Reach.. Pull... Reach.... Pull....
Undeviating like a master musician I reach the summit.
We stare at each other as before.
I see his face as if looking into a calm, placid mountain lake.
I cross the gulf between us until we are face to face.
He bows to me and motions me onward.
I step forward, thrusting my hand toward the sky.
I grasp the sun.

Philip Courter

Oh Tutor Time

The teacher time, restorer of strength and healing,
A refuge for morbid memories and wrongs of failed romance,
Time the momentous teacher is reluctant to stand still,
She refuses to out smart death and frowns on foretelling tomorrow,
Bittersweet time is the fondest dream of the younger days.

People people people, reminiscing time and wishing her back,
Most denounce restless angry memories even though a lesson taught,
Yet dare retrieve only the moments sweet as in melancholic brood,
And momentous time hums and passes certainly and often suddenly,
As mystic windblown footsteps of sea or as the bold tramping army.

Bruised fingers hold not life's major themes, this monarch,
For there's realization of character daring not to repeat patterns
And the final let go, the remission to the winds of all hurt,
After much sweat the bales are ginned and a new self apparent,
Knowing the character did it and it was inside all this time,

Oh, phantom time you storehouse of unique genes and rare free bird,
Or imagining's in the mind's window is for some a distant horizon,
Time you're laughter, love, celebration, seasons, and life,
You're a reminder of our omnipotent creator who's coming in time.
I mourn not nor envy, oh Tuto Time.

Sandra Tucker

A Tale Of Goldish Flock And The Tree Pears

Once upon an olden time
A shepherd hailed, "The gold sheep are mine"
When townfolk asked from where they came
Shep boy answered each he same.
One came from summer when it was hot.
One came from winter when it was not.
In spring they gathered and had a lamb
When the weather was 'Just Right' throughout the land."
There was a secret he never mentioned
As to why they were gold and captured attention.
They ate under a tree with golden pears
That shook in the he wind and fell through the air.
And so ends the story thee teller bears
Of the 'Goldish flock and the tree pears'.

Roberta Pank

"A Happy Moment"

That split second of bliss and comfort,
a smile that overcomes your face and you think "life is good."

Yet you don't know why, and you don't really care.
Floating in a lucid pool of nothing, limp, light-headed in a dream.

A situation, a person, a picture or a place can trigger this bliss.
It hits without warning and is always a pleasant surprise.
In your car, at work or at home.
As quick as it evolves it disappears, leaving you wanting more.
To gorge on such a feast would starve the self,
Leaving it to hunger for nothing.
We all need to forget problems at hand and have a happy moment.

Michelle Gamby

The Hunt

A moving shadow, a glittering eye -
A tawny movement in the bush.
I see a sleek figure dashing by -
on and on, I watch it push.
Dusty air beneath the sun -
Prey and predator's burst of speed -
A distant chase that matches none -
The gazelle's last run of life, indeed.
The gap between them is quickly closed -
Merciless predator prepares to leap -
Sparkling jaws and down it goes -
the rest of the pride, nearby, is asleep.
Proud lioness supplies meat for all
Because of the chase, the attack, and the fall.

Sarah Ann Windisch

Waiting

Late one day as I sit and wait,
a terrible thing came to be my fate.
A tall young woman said to me,
What is it that you want to be?

As I sat and wondered what I should be,
she said if you wait it will never be.
So as I wondered she flew away,
never to be seen another day.

Those types of chances only come once,
If you choose to wait then you are the dunce.
So the moral of this story is to get what you need,
for the next time may be gone and you may never succeed.

Lilith Terry

Untitled

It matters not what time of day,
A thousand thoughts of you persist,
Your gentle touch, that brings out much,
In me, unaware it did exist.

I would rather much forget,
Intense feelings for you deep inside of me,
As it engulf my sense of reason,
Leaving me here, disillusioned.

The love and passion that you have brought,
I would rather forget them all,
But how can the mind ever forget
When the heart chooses to recall.

Nancy Diaz

Reflections

Life is as a shadow of the past,
A thread that falls from the shears on the last day,
To plummet into the chasm of darkness to which
all must succumb.
And new threads are woven to replace the old,
Springing up from the dragon's teeth to found a
new world
And in their attempt to discover the new, they
only succeed in uncovering the old,
Reforming the pieces into an image — a mere
reflection of what was.
And with the tools that have long fallen into desuetude
they are given a sole command:
"Redeem the world — for you were left behind to
resist the evils that have doomed us since the beginning;
Refute that which gave voice to the despair of our hearts, 'Sic
transit gloria mundis.'"

Steven Perez

Reflections

The sun is out and it's raining in my soul
A vision of home is created inside my head
Repeating itself at night when I'm alone
Repeating itself at night when I'm alone
Reflections of the past are speaking to me in dreams
Childhood seems like a lifetime ago
Yet, it's right there in my sleep
I am visited by these memories haunting me by day
Broken hopes have split at the seams
A survivor by night through shattered dreams
Broken hopes have split at the seams
A survivor by night through shattered dreams
Broken hopes have split at the seams
A survivor by night through shattered dreams
A child's imagination, in need of inspiration
Reflections of the past are speaking through my dreams
Just a passenger of time, on the outside looking in
Just a passenger of time, on the outside looking in
Just a passenger of time, on the outside looking in
The sun is out and it's raining in my soul

Meg Dahlen

Farewell To The South

Farewell to a place where I used to be
Farewell to a place that I loved to see
Farewell to a place that has blossom and ease.
Farewell to the south, farewell to the trees.

I want to go back to the beauty again.
The first time I went, I was only ten.
Farewell to the walks; farewell to the sea.
Farewell to a place where I used to be.

Leslie Blair

Rocking Horse Memories

Now I am all grown up.

And every now and then when I forget about youth, nostalgia pays me a visit.

Back come the old familiar sounds into my ears, and how the old house in Boston smelled, and how the third step up used to creak, and the boxwood hedges and the dandelion puffs on the lawn.

These are rocking horse memories.

Remember the candy store on the corner where you got a whole bag of salt water taffy for a quarter? And penny candy was always on the house.

Now I am all grown up.

I still have my rocking horse.
Furiously I would ride the twin grey ponies.
I know well the scratches I left on the hard wood floors.

Those are the rocking horse memories.

When cotton candy seemed to go on forever, and the merry-go-round was romance.

now I am all grown up.

And every now and then when I forget about youth, nostalgia comes to pay me a visit.

Back rush those rocking horse memories, and I remember when the world was my playground.

Stacy M. Brooks

Beth

How wonderful it is to see
A wee born baby so newly freed,
Small hands groping at unseen forms,
The new discovery of outstretched arms,
The simple pleasure of kicking feet,
A healthy burp that makes a meal complete.

So new, yet knowing of all the love
That's hers for the asking from that form above,
The one that hovers and seems to await
Her smallest wish or her whims to placate.

These moments for her shall never return,
And yet when she's older - for them she will yearn,
When all things were centered around a small babe
And simple pleasures did not quickly fade.

Marjorie J. Loring

My Summer Love

A tree is beautiful as it can be
A whisper is as soft as a honey bee
My thoughts are as clear as my heart can be
Thinking of you under that old oak tree
The sun shines in my eye, thinking of you when
Time fly's by
I see a rose in front of me
As I pick it for you from me
Think of this as my love for you
When I'm gone listen to the whispers of the
The same old song
Touch the rose with your hand, feel the beat's
That sure are mine, someday you will be mine

Michael R. Danaitis Jr.

Post-Modern Retrospective

In thought, I pondered...
a whisper of insight to our collective soul.

The past as future...
lonely - forever absent of meaning, no love.

A progeny before and yet...
disillusioned, wayward, drifting.

In darkness...
peace is without.

Images wallow in denominations...
rapacity.

The tears of acknowledgement...
console without understanding.

The night wind notes our passing...
cry not, past - present.

Yet an illusion of insufferable hope...
peace - purity - love.

Philip W. Kaso

Seasons

Fierce, proud, fragile
a wildflower is unwillingly faithful, unbearably naive.
Petals flag the wind, idolize the sun,
in fissures of broken earth alien to survival.
Crocuses, jonquils, daffodils,
cloaked in soft armor against the last
slanting sting of ice and snow, gather courage.

Dressed in bright orange, the hunter checks his traps.
A crippled snow fence, crusted with dirt shudders as he passes.
Goldfinches and robins circle the field and grove of fir trees,
searching for food and lodging,
turkey buzzards sway in a dance with the wind,
and a mouse zig-zags his way through the gopher holes.
Two deer, the buck with one drooping antler, and the doe,
wearing a tired brown coat, pant in the aftermath of mating.

Wooden stakes, with their red bows, tied like Christmas presents,
stretch across the horizon,
while the grimy yellow dozer waits for the next thaw.
Freedom is near the brink of extinction.

Sheryl Wilcox

Why Can't There Be Peace?

With a heavy heart I have sat and thought
About the many lives taken in the countless war fought.
I've pondered this hard with every once of my brain,
But there's never an easy answer for the cause of such pain.

From across the land there has arisen a great cry for peace.
A cry to end the hatred and a cry for wars to cease.
But I'm puzzled still why some leaders choose not to hear our
plea. It's a pure and simple statement, but a powerful decree.

So raise your voice and cry out with me a loudly as you can.
Then they will hear the voice of every woman, child, and man.
For the sake of our children we must come together.
We must make the world safer and make the world better.

We must join together and work hard to achieve this simple goal.
Together we can unite the countries and make the world whole.
If everyone comes together and joins me in this endeavor,
Then we will have a long and lasting peace from now until
Forever.

Vernon Lloyd McIntyre Jr.

Christopher

He was born to my brother and his wife,
According to most people, too late in their life.

Oh, how they were wrong,
for he has brought nothing but joy to their home.

He fills his dads heart with pride,
"Little Buddy" is what he calls him by.

His Mom adores him, he's the apple of her eye.
She loves him so much she could cry.

His hair is red, cheeks are rosy and eyes of brown,
They love to show him around.

They are so proud their hearts could burst.
You would think it was their first.

His older sisters and brother love him to pieces,
He was born an uncle with two nieces.

He'll be loved and protected his whole life long,
Growing up in a Christian home.

With the other children now leaving the nest,
They thank GOD for being so blessed.

Sandy Mitchell

I Don't Know What To Say To You

I didn't need you to understand me, recognize me,
acknowledge or know me.
I didn't need you to see me.
I only wanted you to love me.

I'm a prophet you see.
For when I stared out into heaven through candle light,
I could only chant softly to myself in song:
How I long to love you even if my love can only bring me pain
How I long to take you captive even though your love can never be true

Over and over, I foretold the truth
That my love stretches over the land and into the sky,
where it wraps and envelopes you in the air
in the wind, where you may not be able to feel it, but it is the
mourning of my heart that calls to you in the silent earth.

Vicky Lee

Who Am I

We travel the whole world over, looking for who we are
across the oceans wide and to a distant star.
We look into a mirror to see if we can find
a glimpse of ourself in this space and time.
But it's only a reflection of what we want to be,
and a near to nothing image of what we really see,
we read the latest books that give us all the steps
for finding who we are and to give life more depth.
But the books are soon forgotten and we're off to search again
looking for the rainbow and trying to catch the wind.
When the answer is so simple, why did it take so long
to find out who we are, and just where we belong.
Tonight look into a sleeping face, and their peace will fall on you.
Touch the warmth of their body, and it will warm you too.
Reach out a helping hand and give away a smile.
Run through a summer rain while playing with a child.
Get in touch with love and life and you'll soon begin to find
you didn't have to search at all, you were there all the time.

Shirley Rowland

Peace

The music of rustling leaves
Activated by a gentle breeze.

The ripple of clear mountain streams flowing.
The peeps of fluffy little chicks and a roster crowing.

The singing of birds that fills the morning air.
The adornment of flowers and the colors they wear.

The peace generated from the stillness of the night.
The moon and glittering stars that shed their light.

The calming effect of hearing the ocean wash against the shore.
Seeing the beauty in mountains and other scenes that you adore.

The dripping sound heard during a summer rain shower.
The captivating smell of a fragrant flower.

God in his creation has given us much and all so easy to find.
Places and things that are important to our peace of mind.

But none of this can compare to knowing God and his peace.
To know that with him this feeling will never cease.

Make sure that you keep your temple prepared for God to reside,
Or, you will never know the real peace of having him inside.

William J. Mace

Resplendence

Sometimes, I think about the first time I saw you
after all those years...
I can see you sitting in the closeness of that car
with the dusky darkness
almost completely concealing you from my eyes.
How magical and mystical you were sitting there
and you looked up and smiled
and all the loss of twenty years fled my life
standing there looking at you...

Sometimes, even now,
when I want something special in my life for me
for just me
I think about you then
...again.

D. Susan Tanner

Let Me Be The One

Let me be the one you turn to when you decide to love again, and let me be the one to hold you when sadness might settle in.

Let me be the one to greet you at the end of a trying day. With a hug and a kiss, and the words of "tell me about your day."

Let me be the one you turn to when things get hard to bear. I'll shoulder the burden for you, because I really care.

Let me be the one to listen to your troubles that we all go through, and to have the understanding when you don't want anyone to bother you.

Let me be the one to love you when your passion starts to rise, and when you look into my eyes. I hope that you will see that you're the one and only love for me.

Robert Derrick

War

The dull roar of cannon rings in my ear;
All around me bullets and bombshells fly.
My brother falls, lifeless, to the ground.
He begins the journey back
To the dust from where he came,
Shot by another
Of our kind.

The earth is shrouded in mortuary black during war;
Too much is lost for nothing to be gained.
We are all just grains of sand,
Not meant for use in the
Hourglasses of kings and presidents,
But in castles, for the world to see.
Beautiful and serene.

Tim Dalton

"The Hope"

Precious moments, precious memories of yesterday:
All my hopes, all my dreams have slipped away,
I had a dream about a rainbow that was just for me
I guess I'll never see the end of my rainbow.

I have these feelings of emotion deep inside of me
Will I ever understand them, will they set me free?
All the memories of my youth are very dear to me
I guess I'll never see the end of my rainbow.

Jesus said come to me and I will set you free!
Is it possible that thru Him I'll see eternity?
I really do believe that,
HE IS THE END OF MY RAINBOW.

Tommie J. Ortiz

The Mother Of The Bride

A wedding! A wedding! And everyone's aflutter!
All thoughts are of the Bride and none are for her Mother.

"Tis true, of cause, that everyone will want to see the Bride
To ooh and ahh and wish her well as she goes gliding by,
But, is there any one who will think to draw aside
and compliment that someone...
the Mother of the Bride.

That someone, yes, I'm sure you know has sacrificed and planned,
To give her daughter everything that possibly she can,
And on that day she'll place a veil upon her daughter's head
Then speak some private words to her before she's to be wed.

The Father's not forgotten, he'll walk her down the aisle,
Present her hand in marriage, and encourage with a smile,
He'll turn and take his place beside that someone waiting by
That someone who is crying...
the Mother of the Bride.

Lorraine A. Fitzpatrick

I Do Not Love You

I do not love you, love, for beauty's sake
Alone, though after seeing you, the moon
At full reflected in the softest lake
Presents a scene as harsh as desert noon;
I do not love you, love, for amorous words
You send, although your letters ease my plight
I hear your soft voice whispering like birds
That cross the ocean in an endless flight;
I do not love, you love, for passion shared
Though few have reached the Everestian peak
Of thinnest atmosphere that we have dared
To climb, facing a future bright or bleak;
I do not love what others in you see,
Or I'd soon tire of you, and you of me.

Mel Goldberg

Weeds 'R' Us!!: The Urban Weeds' Cry To Civic Volunteers

City people complain, "Weeds are a Menace!"
Along the streets, under the trestles are so many weeds —
They make us Sneeze!!
It's not fair
That rats hide there.
Garbage is thrown
By people now grown.
In them, birds poop,
LIKE THEY'RE OUT OF THE LOOP!!!

But the weeds also shout —————
"CUTS US OUT!!!"
"WE CAN'T STOP GROWING!!!"
ON US BIRDS ARE DROPPING, PEOPLE ARE THROWING
UNCLEAN THINGS!!!
WHAM! BAM! ZING!!!"

To civic volunteers, both people and weeds cry —
"P-L-E-A-S-E COME REAL QUICK!!!!"
"These weedy roots just pick!!"
"We'll then THANK YOU,
For cleaning this messy URBAN ZOO!!!"

Rosalind Pinto

"A Songwriter's Dream"

You'll get there sooner or later
Although now you are a singing waiter
Just keep on writing songs where ever you go
And show them to people who are in the know
The doors in "Tin Pan Alley" can't be lock forever
Just write a good song show the publishers your clever
Put your whole heart in it body and soul
For a song that is good your returns will be gold
Some days may seem black and idea's thin
But Don't give up for that's the time you will win
Your letter will come back and you will be surprised
For those cruel publishers at last opened there eyes
They like your song they says it will be a smash
While your heart is dreaming will it bring in the cash
Though your song don't climb to the top right away
Have faith and hope for "ROME" wasn't built in a day
So if your after songwriting for success
Keep on pulling and good luck and GOD's best.

Sal Consiglo

Shunned

With hope I go from one day to the next.
Always searching.
But always getting shunned.
Burden to always carry the feeling of
loneliness.
Living in a world of solitude.
Never to find the true meaning of happiness.
My soul I would give.
Just to know the true feeling of love.
For I have been teased.
By demons masquerading as spiritual beings
of love.
Only to be ripped apart when I am the most
vulnerable.
A fortress I am.
Constantly searching for cracks in my armor.
I am terrified.
That the demons will get me again.
But without the chance.
I may never know true love.

Phillip Randall

Daddy Ain't No Angel

Daddy ain't no angel,
Ambitions were strangled by the streets
Leaving this middle-aged man gasping for air,
Cherishing forbidden thoughts;
His Mental Ghetto.

Longing for it's bitter taste,
Chasing empty dreams with a face of confusion;
Unknowing that the illusion of life
has escaped his limp brain years ago.
Tears flow for a wake that never happened,
Clothes blackened to mourn the loss.

Life goes on,
with as much direction as a stray bullet,
Praying that his physical will die as well.
His heart colonized by demons,
Living a life equivalent to Hell,
Selling his soul to anyone within reach
with a speech diluted in alcohol;
"Help me be an angel."

Paul Branton

Mother Mary Peragine De Vito

Did you ever lose a diamond
an emerald a pearl?
Encased in gold or silver
Perhaps belonging to your little girl?
Or an opal surrounded by platinum
With begets that shimmered in the sun
Did you ever see the crowned jewels of
Queens and kings?
And marvel at their beauty their
brilliance, their grandeur their vast wealth?
Did you ever see my Mother
Women of great beauty
Who was always a lady
And oh so brave in he dying!
With no crying
Whose sewing was of designer caliber
Whose cooking was truly gourmet
We lost her today
We gave her up to Christ and
His Blessed Mother.

Maryann De Vito Landi

Remain Sitting

Dead, lifeless, empty
an empty box
Once used, now thrown into a corner.
Buried under problems,
dead, not noticed
So I sit and wait to be found.

Unrecognized, unknown
No one knows me, no one cares.
No one see me, I remain unknown
none hear my screams of agony
my cries of silence, suffering is my only answer.
So I sit and wait to be heard.

Falling, flying, failing
Am I falling? Am I flying?
Confused yet alert I whisper
Still unseen, still unheard.
So I sit and wait to be seen.

Michelle Won

Grandma's Song

Together with the birds I shall sing
an endless serenade.
While saplings waver in the breeze
in a seemingly endless parade.

Free at last, of my earthly strains,
floating silently o'er the mountainous range.
My soul unleashed of its confines.

Although sadness fills your hearts,
please don't mourn for me.
Remember how it's always been,
and it shall always be.

For the dead are only those forgotten.
Myself, I am not dead,
I am free.

So, if tomorrow a cloak of warmth envelops you,
or a shadow passes through the corner of your eye,
when a silent breeze wisps through your hair,
you will know, I am there.

Nancy B. Hobbs

Black Lightning

A raven, dark and bewitching, alone against
an ivory sky...
He is...
Black lightning, the beauty of the
night, with a presence far too deep and so
beyond real... it's unmistakable

He walks into a room-the very air shifts
into a surreal dream that is mysterious
and lovely... none can escape it

With an aura of pure gracefulness and strength
it is enchanting.. majestic... and just so powerful...
it is truly of another world

Such a sweet and gentle touch he has...
Like honey and silk...

It is a gift to know him, he has the
essence of midnight all around him,
He is, wholly and completely,

Black lightning
And he is wonderful.

Michelle Whelan

Arizona

Arizona is hot
And a unique place.
Red Rocks are forming
the horizons they trace.
Illusions rise up,
because the heat is so intense.
In August is when the air is so dense.
Jets zoom through the sky
with great speed across the night
The clear Arizona sky
provides no barriers for flight.
Owls overlook the ground for food,
their lonesome calls add to the desert mood.
The stars shine bright in open sky.
The eagles then nest and cease to fly.
The rodents come out at night to play.
Then they go to sleep for the rest of the day.

Nathan Stanfield

Yesterday

It seems like only yesterday that I was eight or nine
and all the problems in my life were easy to define.

I'd brush my teeth and comb my hair then go outside to play
and then sometimes I'd watch the clouds and dream about today.

I could see a great big house with doors that opened wide
I could see the mom and dad and the kids who lived inside.

I could see a lot of love and never any fears
I could see the joy of life but never any tears.

It seems like only yesterday those years just seemed to fly
and all the little dreams I had have vanished in the sky.

I brush my teeth and comb my hair and stumble through the day
and now I watch the rain come down and dream of yesterday.

When I saw the great big house with doors that opened wide
when I saw the mom and dad and the kids who lived inside.

When they were so full of love with never any fears
and when there was such joy in life but never any tears.

Linda Mascetta

"Memories"

It's been along time since we've spent time just laughing.
And although we've gone our separate ways and pretended that
it meant nothing. I felt the need to let you know
I think of you and the fun we had at every chance.
You didn't know, but it meant so much to me at the time.
Now it gives me great memories of a time and place I have since left
behind. (But will never forget)
There are no regrets over what we had and the time we shared,
except that It ended too soon.
Although I am happy with the choices I made in my life,
As time goes on I find that some things bring me back to that time
and place, and I find myself smiling.
I wanted to thank you for all you have helped me learn about life,
and love.
And to let you know that I will never forget that time in my life,
or that place were I left my childhood.
Our lives may never cross again, but you should know that there
will always be a special place for you in my memories, and my heart!

Peter Freymuth

A Lesson Not Heard

I joined nature in praising of the CREATOR,
And applied my heart and followed its lead
As my Maker's Spirit gave the lyrics;
Think about God, trust in Him.
The sea, like an accordion played
By an invisible hand, so enchanting a tune gives;
Think about, God trust in Him. While the breeze
Playing the flute, and lightly touching each plant,
Make them flutter like wings of angels, celestial harps.
The sun plays the lights, bathing everything in gold everything,
getting sighs of contentment and bewitching perfume
From plants and flowers to the LORD the ETERNAL.
The birds drank with light, sounds and sweet perfume,
Sing happy and lovely songs, in perfect harmony.
My heart, like a sweet burning offering, ignited
By love, rose gently to the Lord, guided by faith
In knowledge of his answer. While my tears witnessing
The ever unchangeable answer:
I love you trust in Me.

Viviane M. Hopper

Was Taken Away

A nice, warm day were we informed,
And bawled so hard that day;
Underground would he be doomed,
Cancerous goodbye on his birthday.
I'd do anything to bring back his life,
As any granddaughter would;
But oh, that aneurism took away his life,
If I could have saved him I would.
I will cry for and mourn him
Until I see him in heaven someday.
Too afraid to go visit the bed he lay in,
That I'll bawl again like on the day he died.
He could make anything, his death unfair,
So loving, so gifted, so true;
If only he knew how guilty I feel
For never saying "I love you."

Meghan R. Kiser

April's Song

In springtime flowers of bloom gaze to Heaven,
And birds make their way back home,
In the warmth they soar.
If springtime brings a song to the hearts of lovers,
Why April, do your golden rays of sunshine no longer fall?

The glimmer of hope in your deep blue sky,
Destroyed when you closed your eyes.
The ocean of many colors, that danced upon your face,
When the waves crashed in fury or rolled in delight,
The sea that was never calm is forever still.

If springtime brings happiness, birth and growth,
And the renewal of faith whispers in souls,
Why is icy cold snow your embrace?
April is winter.
What turned the color of your sparkling springtime,
Into shades of gray?

Rochelle Cave

Comes The Dawn

After a while you learn the subtle difference between holding a hand
And charming a soul.
And you learn that love doesn't mean learning
And company doesn't mean security

And you begin to understand that kisses aren't contracts
And presents aren't promises.

And you begin to accept your defeat with your head held high
And your eyes open, with the grace of a women, not the grief a child.
To uncertain for plans,
And future have a way of falling in mid-flight.

After a while you learn that even sunshine burns if you get to much,
So you plant your own garden and decorate your own soil,
Instead of waiting for someone to bring you flowers.
And you learn that you really can endure, that you really are strong
And you really do have worth.

And you learn and learn ....and you learn

With every goodbye you learn.

Rodger Clayton Tabb II

A Love Note

Love is a feathery bird pushing people,
Blinding them with soft feathers of lure;
And, quite often, after being amply fed,
Does excrete prodigiously on its patrons.

Sinkinson Otruba

It Happens Every Sunday

From under center he takes the snap,
And checks the defense as he drops back.
His offensive line stands undaunted;
He could stop and down a coke if he wanted.
He turns to wave to a fan in the stands,
Then spies his receiver covered man-to-man.
He cocks his arm and rifles one out,
And connects with Mark Clayton completing his route.
Into the end zone to secure the win;
Marino to Clayton for six again.

Shawn Palmer

His Spirit Lives

My King is not dead, His Spirit lives
And continues to flow and forgive.

His Spirit beacons come unto me and I will lead you
to a fountain of power overflowing.
Where the pastures of love will never stop growing.

He is mine and I am His forevermore
His everlasting arms surrounds me through an open door.

His love is overflowing through the window of my heart
As I am pressing forward never to depart.

His light guides my spirit through to higher dimensions
in His love
Where I will live and soar like a majestic dove.

Patti Martin

September Serenade

Dedicated to my mother Susan and to my children —
Landen, Lacey, Lindsay, Lisanne, and Lee Jay II.

Within the darkened chamber, my heartbeat echoes strong;
and deeper
still another beats its own eurhythmic song.

The unborn child within me, for whom I live and breathe;
this faceless, nameless wonder
is a miracle indeed!

Together with an unseen force who lends a Divine hand,
this child
conceived in love between a woman and a man.

My constant friend, companion
but only for awhile
will soon be one among us
a sunny, radiant child.

As ageless as the mountains, eternal as the sea,
the sacredness of motherhood
this is my legacy:
to bear this child, help give him life;
to love, to teach, to know;
and all along
one day to find the strength to let him go.

Laura M. Kamalani-Paikai

"Graduation"

It is now time for us to be pushed
from the nest,
And walk in the fog of uncertainty.

Our fears have escalated to their highest point
As we walk in the void.

The world is offering many doors, once locked,
Now opened for us to grasp every dream.

Michael Burke Jacobs

Violence And Gangs

Every day a person dies,
And everyday a family cries.

Because of the violence, and the gangs,
Their lives are gone with the bangs.

And whether they get stabbed, raped, or shot,
People are hurting a whole lot.

A little boy, with his whole life ahead,
Because of a drive by, he is dead.

Here is a girl, waiting for sweet sixteen,
Yet the day before, she lost that dream.

A woman is killed, her unborn baby too,
Because of violence, their lives are through.

There are just so many senseless killings,
Can't we stop them? Is anyone willing?

Tara S. Rivers

Lessons To Learn

Life can have a twist or turn
And from each one a lesson to learn.
The love I'd dreamed would always be mine
Has gone away, but I'll be fine.
The love we had was one time good
And hold onto it, I wish we could.
But sometimes life changes the road we took
And over our shoulders we cannot look.
And so my love, you have gone away
So thought it's hard I must finally say
Even though you have been part of my past
My future is without you, I accept at last.
And so my friend, because that is all we will be
The desire I had for you I now set free.
I wish you the happiness I thought we would share.
It's a concern for you that recently has been rare.
My love for you will no longer burn
Because this lesson I have finally learned.
What I sometimes think cannot be good for me
I know is the very place, I must be.

Yvonne Irwin-Rossenbach

Hopeless

I stood beside a chasm filled with broken, cast-off dreams,
And gazed into a future void of plans and hope-filled schemes.
The rusted, cracking edges of myriad prayers, stored up in sheaves,
Lay scattered across the bottom, like fallen, rotted leaves.

A waterfall of promise, once cascading down the years,
Now slips from up the jutted peaks, like a broken chain of tears.
"No promise here," it seems to cry, as trickling down, it falls,
And fades into the crevices along the chasm walls.

A bridge of golden future things, that feet had never traced,
Was flung against the oblivion of the far-off chasm face.
No birds of brilliant plumage wafted on this gloomy air.
Their nests built high, of downy fluff, no longer flourished there.

No butterfly fluttered, no coyote called — the land lay still
and dead.
And looking on this futile place, my heart was filled with dread.
Here my future. Here my past. Here in this hellish place,
I looked and saw myself as lost, among a host called
"Human Race."

Theda Myatt

Circles

Depression came by for a visit last night
  and greeted me this morning
I'd forgotten how well he knew me
  it's been a while since his last visit
insecurity was in his baggage
  and has settled in for an extended stay
sadness stops by now and again for coffee
  the visits don't usually last too long
insecurity is making noises about moving on
  if he really goes it'll be a short stay
confidence came by for tea this afternoon
  it was a pleasant visit
I've invited him to stay
  and he's considering it
happiness calls occasionally just to say
  he misses me, I miss him too...

Tamozelle Jennings

Spring Love

Spring, the bride has arrived. The flowers have bloomed and her veil is lifted. We gaze upon the beauty of her face. Our's is the joy of the groom as we anticipate seeing more. The candelabra of daffodils and tulips light the sanctuary of seasons while the bird's morning melody entertains us with the wedding song. The flower girl, wind, has tossed petals of Dogwood pink and white along the grassy green carpet, the carpet the bride will walk along as she approaches the altar to unite with the groom summer. He is ravished by her beauty and his smile causes her to blush with roses in response to his warm affection.

Reggie L. Tryon

I Walked in a Beautiful Garden with God

God asked me if I would like to walk with Him,
And I replied, "Yes, it would be my pleasure."
Can you just imagine the joy I felt?
It was beyond anything you can possibly measure!

He asked me if I wanted to hold His hand
And reached over suddenly to grasp mine!
How would you answer that question from God?
I said, "Of course, it will certainly be just fine."

I remarked, "How lovely He made the sky,
And how each day the clouds appear to be
More beautiful than the day before
What an awesome God He is to me!"

We walked side by side down the path and chatted
Like old friends who knew each other well.
This went on for an hour or longer.
I lost track of time. Who can tell?

The path was strewn with magnificent flowers
On either side that seemed to make a part.
I spent the most glorious time of my life,
With God, in the beautiful garden of my heart.

Theresa Fish

Without Demand

The desert sand all plain and tan
Can glisten and glow throughout the land.
it's beauty will grow with each shift in the wind,
The ripples and rows which are created within.
It will tell all its stories of the wind and the sand,
The most beautiful thing not created by man.
The sun, the sand, the moon and wind will continue to
  exist without demand.

Lynette J. Engelhardt

Untimely Passion

I won't try to change you or your outlook on life
and I'm proud to be the one you look up to
Since we were very young I fantasied about us
becoming husband and wife
Now, years has passed and fate has thrown us back
together again
Oh...I know few of our parts have put on a little rust
But, when we're together I still feel the way I did then
I'm not ashamed to let the world know that my heart
will forever belong to you
And from that "Glow" in your "Loving eyes" I see that time
has deepen your love for me too
So, Darling let's cherish what we have for today
A "Love" that's so true.

Phyllis Ann Talbott

To My Son Frank

Oh, Frank, I hope you're all right
And in London town tonight.
Hope you accomplished your travel plans
And will now come home again
To live with us on around.

Hope your flight will be safe and sound
And comfortable all around.
Safe by day and by night and the landing all night.

Now back to work you must go
And perform as usual, you know
May you be rested and refreshed
And looking forward to life with zest.

Were I poet, this would I wish you
A girl, a home, a dream come true.
That you may know life's deepest pleasures
And sum then up as Precious Treasures.

Though tears may come, and hearts shall break
Life will sometimes be hard to take.
Don't give up, smile a while
The clouds shall pass, the sun shall smile!

Stella Lemanska Olbris

The House That Binds

Memory-house with memory stairs,
and memory-walls and memory-floors—
where girlish whispers haunt dark bedrooms
and arguments grow stale from lack of use.

A baby's cries can be heard from the attic
and baseboards sing lullabies from long ago.
Blood dries on the steps of the front porch
while giggles bubbles up from the cellar.

Tears flow from the sink on the second floor
where chiseled initials scar the inside of closet doors;
spiders spin soft webs on forgotten corners
and women's sweat made the wood boards creak.

The red tile fireplace lived once in Spain
and brought here the dreams of Spanish children.
Laughter from Christmas morning hides
in the dust of the curtains closed against sunshine.

Intangible traces of people leave their mark
on the houses that remain behind them on their journey,
seeping into a foundation that assures that they
left behind more than a blue ball buried in the yard.

Lisa Arth

Old Testament Summary

The Old Testament tells us God's creation,
And next began the birth of a nation.
God made a covenant with Abraham then,
And later renewed it again and again.
He delivered his people from Egypt and Pharaoh,
And led them always, though the wanderings were slow.
The law and the statutes to them he did give,
And warned them to keep up as long as they'd live.
To the Promised Land He finally took them,
And in spite of their murmurings He never forsook them
But God did allow sin in the world He had made,
And sin separates from God, and a price must be paid
So wise men of old recorded the story
Of the mighty acts of the King of glory:
How he sent the patriarchs, judges, and kings;
He sent the poets, whose praise the church sings;
He sent the prophets, both minor and major,
Whose warnings were dire enough, I'll wager!
But none of these could bridge sin's separation,
So He'll send His own Son for our soul's salvation.

Mary Hamilton Stephens

The Kiss

As our lips meet before God's altar
And our love is visible from afar,
It marks the time of change of time
When I am yours and you are mine.
A kiss that says more than the words "I do"
Nay, a promise of a lifetime through.
The last kiss of courtship sweet;
The first in marriage we meet;
All the hopes and desires are there;
All the deep love that we share;
All the feelings of happiness and care;
All the wants and needs that we wear;
The last lingering touch of lips in love;
The first of many memories of marriage's dove;
To have and to hold, to love and adore
Your husband my wife forevermore.

William Pierce Clark III

touched

like touched in motion

gray-spreading over in gales, furniture
and outlined glass-
  rippled figures,
smelling everything like touched passing

the fluidity of touched standing, skeleton
bend forward, leaning

  comes terrible,
a smudge in the breathing that carries the
books, the air, the trances, the misformed

nudes and paper kissing-orgies in rows along
the bottom

  i'm merely moving,
touched is standing still by the fan.

Patrick Wagner

Dragons' Jubilee

The Dragons plumed like peacocks in Springtime,
Billowing and flapping their silver-blue wings
Against a powder-blue Eastern sky.
And stretching their crimson talons
Into the pink stone of the mountains
During sunset.

Rachael May Shields

Switching Life

We can only see what is here
But the next life is only a door step away
Our journey in life continues beyond earth
Our resting place can only be eternal bliss
For when our life ends here
We only open our eyes to everlasting care.

Wycliffe E. Tyson

The Pretty Face

She wore a bright red dress
and painted her face with sparkling white powder.
She danced and laughed and enjoyed her night,
but when it was over she was left in an empty house,
alone.
She wept while watching the last of her acquaintances leave.
She took off her fine silk gown
and cleaned the artwork from her face.
She sat and looked in the mirror
and thought of what was in front of her.
There was an image of a beautiful girl
and that was all she could see
and all she could remember being.

Mary Koch

Untitled

He strolled along the corridor
and rapped upon her door.

He walked through the passage way
and approached her in the eve of day.

He looked down upon her lovely face,
stroked her hair, and studied her grace.

He held her eyes in his
forever in sweet bliss.

He touched her cheek lightly and her lips
ever so slightly.

He listened for the rhapsody of her heart, and
they suddenly became one instead of apart.

He waited for so long to share this precious moment.

How precious could it be?
It was gone within an instant.

He longed for her to be by his side.

With each passing day, his loneliness
would not subside.

He lived his life in solitude.

He died knowing she loved him too.

Maria Marta Steward

Summer Ride

There waiting for her, brave and still and strong,
and rein softly laid side of the sleek coat.
She gathered herself then spoke in a song,
setting in the saddle, playing each note.
Rising winds parted her lips to a smile,
it grew till laughter ripped the streaming hair
and tail behind, caught in the strands awhile,
tangled, as the beating hooves of the mare
pushed the gaping ground far behind the two.
The pink, winded face raised then turned aside.
A sudden, hidden burst of power flew,
barring breath back in her mouth. The won pride
was enough for a day, so she said 'slow
to a stop,' pleased, but saving for tomorrow.

Rebecca Lynn Wetzel

Awakening

I awaken to reality's pain
and seek knowledge of the door.
The door sealing me into deep blackness,
where the sun seems to shine no more.

Life as I knew it, has deserted me.
The veil of darkness hangs over my heart.
What is to become of me, this empty shell?
Now that we are so far apart.

"Do not give up," speaks a voice,
"There's light and love coming your way."
My soul cries out in despair and pain,
and I listen, with nothing to say.

My mind sees the light at the tunnel's end.
Arms reaching, I race forward in fright.
Then peace settles over my shattered soul,
as love permeates from the light.

The veil is lifted from over my life.
God's arms enfold me with care.
I know that tragedy can no longer harm me.
God's message is, "Call, I'll be there!"

Marilyn Auen

Broken

When the sky had condensed into nebulas
And the clouds crumbled to ashes and dust
The rain came down like it never had before
Rotton flesh cracked back and tore

There no pain left to comfort or feel
Once you've been burned by life's chemical peel

As the poison leaks apathy across the land
Mesoplasts pour out from the sand
Plastic guilt hides all abominations away
To masquerade the damage of another day

Their endorphins only plague all that's intact
Draining closure out of umbilical sacks
Hidden alone without device
Gathering the significance of the darkest night
Sifting through every feelings branched out vine
Their only thoughts back track up to lesions
That intertwine

Decorated wounds with scar-tissue ends
Unwind the seams that break before they
Bend

Libby Freeman

Christmas Season

It's once again that time of year
And the holiday season is finally here

We remember friends and family, wherever they are
While sending out christmas prayers, to lone ones a far

Forget the gifts, remember how lucky we are to keep in touch
Be thankful for being loved and never forget how much

So now that the year is coming to an end
Be thankful for family, be thankful for friends

We send you our wishes, whether far or near
So have a Merry Christmas and a Happy New Year

Summer Lynn Woodridge

Drifting

Life goes on without stalling,
And the love that drifted away
May one day be calling.

Everyday that goes by someone is recalling
the time they thought it had to be another way.
Life goes on without stalling.

Time seems to lend us time for crawling
into the future to play,
but we are not at all sure when love may one day be calling.

There is no time for applauding the mistakes
that have gone astray. Life goes on without stalling.

Each and everyday someone will be falling.
Listen to the broken hearts from far away,
No one hears the calling.
Life goes on without stalling.

Linda Rolan

Think Of Me

When the shadows have fallen
And the moon shines brightly with the stars,
Think of me.

When the sun beats down its warmth upon you
And there is a light, cool breeze
Blowing through your hair,
Think of me.

When the trees are swaying
And the birds are singing a romantic love song,
Think of me.

When you look up into the sky
And see white, billowy clouds -
Loose yourself in them and
Think of me.

When you are sitting all alone
Thinking of what to do - Stop, and
Think of me.
For I am forever thinking of only you.

Mara L. Vaill

The Temple, The Shrine And The Palace

"What of this thing we call life?" said the apprentice.
And the sage of the age replied:
"The body is like a temple-
strong, comforting, protective-yet vulnerable;
While the mind is like a shrine-
hallowed in examination, execution, evaluation-
yet also vulnerable."
"But what of the soul?" inquired the student.
"Ah yes," continued the aged sage.
"The soul is like a palace,
where the spirit can shine,
bright, infinite and timeless in beauty-
yet, perhaps, the most vulnerable of all.
Hence; as the sun is to the day
as the moon to night-
The pyramid of life bestows question and light.
For each bridge is lit
with paths of decision-bearing toll;
So worship wisely, and honor the domains
of the body, the mind, and the immortal soul."

Stephen J. Alexanian

The Time Of The Healing Wound

When the wind goes
and the stillness listens to itself,
When the waterfalls has reached the river's quiet;
that is the time of the healing wound.
the soul whirls round and round
dropping in exhaustion,
to find sleep at last;
ending in beginning again,
a new feeling regained with the disappearance
of the numbness.

Susan Lenore Calig

When The Tulips Bloom In Spring

When the lilies of the valley expel their sweet perfume,
and the streams of sunlight trickle through the windows in my room,

When the mockingbirds and orioles join robins on the wing,
you'll be with me, when the tulips bloom in spring.

And, each time I pluck a pansie, with it's dainty painted face,
and set it on the table in a pretty China vase,

I will think about the old times, and start remembering,
and, you'll be with me, when the tulips bloom in spring.

For I never see a lilac or a rosebud kissed with dew,
or a sprig of scottish heather, that I do not think of you!

Oh, how pointless would our lives be without those of whom we're fond,
for the memories we treasure last a lifetime and beyond.

So, if by chance I wander in the garden in the morn,
to feast upon the sunlight, as another day is born,

I will listen to the melody the meadow lark will sing,
and you'll be with me when the tulips bloom in spring!

I've no doubt one day the time will come when we will have to part,
but every precious memory is safe within my heart,

And, the love that we have always shared will keep on flourishing,
for you always will be with me, when the tulips bloom in spring!

Susan F. Cook

The Last Day

What does it matter if another day has gone,
And there is but an hour left to crowd my blessings on,
There is a future still, with memories of those who have gone before,
Only she and I remaining - to hold this family generation alive for an hour more.
It may hardly be noticed when our days ends,
The immediate family perhaps - some relatives -a few close friends,
The heart of a family lineage - we've stamped fond memories on,
Only these - hardly another - will be aware that we have gone.
Sadness? There is no need, maybe only for a short while,
For the patriarchal two, the last of who, will leave this world in style
Oh - I may be happy if it is I - that I may say,
That I was chosen from heaven - of these honored seven,
To see my generations - last day.

Patrick Barbato

Dreams

Dreams can take you away from here
Dreams can make your thoughts disappear
Dreams can give you joy and adventure
Dreams can help you defy nature.

I love to dream my dreams of flight
They take me away in the long lonely night
To be in places I'll never see
To be that person I'll never be.

Robert Newhouse

Untitled

Love will always be within our hearts
And to her memory, it shall never part
With the care that she gave and all that she did
Was just an image of the life that she lived
Her strong caring ways
Her everlasting love
Shall be in our hearts and in the stars above
All we can do is think of good times
And all that she did to brighten our lives
Everything she taught us
About how we could survive
It makes us look back now and it brings tears to our eyes
These are no longer tears that always carried pain
These are tears of what a great women she was
And that she will always remain
We will always lover her

Ryan Fimreize

The Real World Kills

She was the little girl who had it all, with the two parent family and two big brothers, too.
She was the one with the giggles and smiles that could melt your heart away
And brighten up an otherwise dull day.
Her long golden curls would blow gently through the wind
And those beautiful blue eyes would radiate and sparkle wherever she went.
She was a beam of sunshine that never got cloudy.
And I say was because she is no longer.
You see, she grew up with an innocence and false sense of security
And when the darker side of life came spiraling toward her, she started to drown.
A couple of times she came up to get air,
But her strength was fast fading and her hope almost gone.
She had to be hospitalized, just to be safe - no knives, blades, or razors, or alcohol either.
No nothing could be near her, not even the inviting screws in the wall.
Soon she was discharged and sent back to her cruel world
To pick up the pieces and start over again.
But the shocking and cutting and drinking still continued
And soon wore down her hurt heart and kept it from beating.
And now the little girl who once had it all, had nothing at all.
It must have been much easier that way to die a short life,
And live longer away from the world she once radiated, but now has erased.

Susan Kristine Svendsen

The Mirror of Time

I looked in the mirror one day,
And wasn't pleased with what I saw
Why, oh why did I look this way.
When day by day I tried my best,
To smooth away the signs of time.
I clean and cream and all the rest
But to no avail - time knows best.

I looked again and what I saw
Stirred my memory - made me think.
And what I felt left me in awe
Of what I really am today.

I got a glimpse in the mirror so clear
Of a sparkle in my eye that brought back to me
The memory of a mother so dear.
Strange I didn't see it before.

Now as I look in the mirror each day,
I see little hints of dear ones now gone
No longer have I a feeling of dismay,
Just a heartfelt warmth in the blending of time.

Ruth Silva

The Anniversary

Remember that day when we pledged our love,
And we stood there together at the Altar of God.
Our family and friends sat witness to,
The wedding rites where we said I do.
It's been many years since that first day,
We're older and wiser in a great many ways.
We've had many ups and even some downs,
Two lives grown together into something profound.
We are closer together now than ever before,
It matters not if we're rich or we're poor.
So when that day comes around every year,
I toast my good fortune for having you near.

Nadine Heaton-Owens

"The Sea"

I looked to the sea for answers but rejected, sat down
And wept; My love was gone, a mere shadow in a watery grave, ne'er to hold me again!

When storms raged, sending their waves to pound the shores,
'Tis then I look seaward and look and seek, but have yet to find, that which was, but ne'er can be again!

Shall I go to the arms of yet another to love and be loved,
That I may chance being e'er reminded of that which was,
And could be again?

Or do I await death's sting, knowing it's cruel bite, and
satisfied I have chosen well, submit myself to a life
Inland, and far away from the sea?

Robert H. Wyatt Sr.

The Baby's Box

This box is empty today
and will be filled on those rainy days.
Looks can be deceiving
because it is for the first hat your baby will be receiving.
This box is for all your child's things
to remember when he spreads his wings.
Take time to fill it with care
because later you and your child can share.
He will enjoy all the memories in it
when he is grown and independent.

Pamela Voyles

Untitled

Sometimes I wake in the night...
And wrapped in dreams of you,
I feel you here still,
Your arms holding me so close
It's as if we were one.

You bring to me the sunlight, the moonlight...
Every smile that's ever brightened my day,
Every song that's been sung,
Every color of the brightest rainbow.

I feel safe when I'm with you...
Secure, totally content...
And even when I'm not with you
You're here,
Because you're always in my thoughts.

When you look at me, something inside me
Turns over...
And I realize that somewhere along the way—
You filtered your way into my heart,
Searched around,
And made yourself a home.

Pam Donovan

Our Love Is Forever Lovely

When your cold hands become wrinkled,
And your golden hair has turned to silver.
My love for you will be the same.
As on the day, you took my name.

Tho' you may quiver in your speech.
I will ever be within your reach.
To take you dear; down to memory lane
Where we shall think and speak of love again

To your eyes may come tears of happiness,
From memories of our youthful days.
And in the silence, our happy hearts will say
That our love was always blest.

Always I'll kiss you so tenderly.
Although be it not, in reverie.
My weeping eyes may envelope your sadden eyes,
Knowing that within us, a deep true love lies

Greatly, I shall embrace you,
As your warm smiles will behold me
To the beats of two happy hearts
Who reveal that our love is forever lovely.

Peter P. Gecevice

Cyclone Crevices

Oh, gentle flowing brook, heal me with thy waters.
Angelic voices of harmony, may thy singing arouse my spirits.
Rustling winds, please enliven my cheeks
Clouds bursting, free my sorrowful being.
Enchanted sun, cover me with thy blessed warmth
Soaring heavenly sky, exalt my heart, even a little.
Tender flower petals, I also am as delicate as thee.
Ascending mountains, oh, that I might climb as you.
Polar regions, must I be frozen with sadness?
Erupting volcanos, may my gloom also be set free.
Cracking earth, I also quake in the depths of my soul.
Speeding light, I await thy quick rescue.
Luminescent stars, enlighten my path.
Dense forest, I am lost and cannot see.
Treasures of the earth, would it be that I were invaluable.
Desert sands, scarce is the essence of life.
Snowy avalanche, may my core be not melted.
Hollow caverns, fill my emptiness.
Thunders of heaven, open mine ears to peace of mind.
Lightning bolts, strike me with brightness of hope.

Shirley Shepard

Patrick

Your smell and your presence, help to calm my mind.
Another love like yours, I could never find.
I love you so much, I could never say,
what it would do if you went away.
All of the problems you've helped me through,
Make me more sure of how much I love you.
Please tell me again that you'll never leave.
Please tell my heart that it won't ever grieve.
I need your love now, more than ever.
Our type of love could out last any weather.
I want so much to start a life with you.
I want to make your every dream true.
Your black hair and loving eyes,
have helped me know and help me realize.
What I've said or written, it's all completely true.
But I'd say it again,because I love you.

Lora Smith

Words Not Spoken

These words can mean more than the words that are heard.
Anyone can say them without uttering a word.
They can bring a tear to your eye, or smile to your face.
They're spoken in every religion, nationality, and race.
They can cut like a knife, and heal wounds too.
They can be a cry for help, or a simple "I love you."
These words are taken in different ways.
Some take it as an insult, others in praise.
You can not hear them, but feel them inside.
You feel different things, like a roller coaster ride.
These are the words that come from the heart.
These are the words not spoken.

Nicci Hosfeld

Pretending

When I wake up in the morning sun, and look next to me, you
are not there; I stare inforth a shadow and pretend that you
have already gotten up.

When I get up, I go cook our breakfast and get two plates and
glasses to set the table; pretending that you are out getting the paper.

When I get ready to go anyplace, I make sure I leave a note,
saying where I am going and what time I'll be home; pretending
that you will be waiting.

When I'm driving in my car and our favorite and special songs
come on the radio, I clench my fist on the steering wheel;
pretending it's your hands.

When I go shopping, I always pick you out something that you
would like; pretending you would wear it the next day.

When I go out to dinner, I always make reservations for two;
pretending that you will come.

When I'm watching our favorite comedy shows on T.V.; I pretend
that you are laughing right along with me.

When I go to bed, I hold your pillow, kiss it good-night;
pretending that you are right beside me.

When I close my eyes to dream inforth the night, I pretend
that I were dead, so I could join my love.

Veronica Rose Perrin

I Love You

These three simple words
are often said
with no real meaning
instead of with true feeling

When said, unto another
looking back one should see
a confidant, best friend and lover

Both should know
that together they'll live,
carrying each other through the pain and temptations,
standing side by side through the laughter and joy
on a daily walk through a lifetime of experiences

No more needs to be heard
when the simple expression is spoken truly
FOR THE FEELINGS EXPRESSED MEAN MORE
THAN THE SOUND OF THE WORDS

Tara Blackburn

Peace On The Streets

Children are playing, when danger
arrives. From rowdy teenagers drinking
and driving, just look in their eyes,
you see tears and fears
throughout the years. From then drinking beers.
A child is killed, and parents
tears are spilled, this shouldn't be
just wait and see.
Too much crime, from people
who are slime, they should do time.
Put them behind bars, where they
belong, not in their cars,
where trouble starts.
Guns, knife, crow bars, bombs, bottles
drugs, alcohol all starts a big brawl,
let's just teach our children right
so they won't start to fight, let this
world, live and not get beat. Just let us have
peace on the streets.

Rosemary Bittner

Why Didn't I Know?

Why didn't I realize how quickly time would go?
As a child's laughter on the warm spring breeze 'twas blown away.
Each day, so precious now, was thrown away.
"Mommy's too tired to play."
Oh, to have one back and say,
"Of course, my darling, I'll show you how."
That childhood of my own did plod
As if with feet of lead it trod
My girlish path. And yet,
Upon hummingbird wings those days
Of sticky fingertips have flown!
Oh, if only I had known...

Tami Blount Darley

Two Hearts Joined

Dearest Sister sent from God above
as a gift for all to love!
Fragile, tenderhearted, beautiful
in sight, may the Lord bring
blessings into your life tonight.
For now your moving on my friend
still a sister, but with a new blend.

Ryan came into your life with no
rhyme or reason, but what a delight!
"No B" they call him and what amazes me he's my new brother in
law and its Ryan without a B.
Tonight lets join our hearts in one
accord and pray for this couple has unto the Lord.
For when God joins hearts he
does it in three Ryan and Denise and Jesus to be.
Sweet little sister I am happy for you for now that you
married my wedding will come to.
Let's join this occasion and make it its best for with Love
its a mystery that's now put to rest.
Again to hearts are joined Ryan and Denise

Sharon R. Aurednik

Resurrection

Passion resurfaces in distant rumbles.
From another place and time it tumbles over untended senses
until they pulse again. And when the throbbing soul tenses,
the touch is all.

Peg Nelson

Adirondack Spring

A drop of dew dances on a spider's web
As a thrush trills softly in the distance.
The odor of wood smoke mingles with hazelnut
As I sip my coffee in front of my camp.
Perched on a log, I watch dawn's frosty veil
Evaporate in the morning sun.

A slight shudder travels down my spine
As the water's stillness is broken by a short "Pop".
With the sound of a cork being eased from champagne,
A trout pierces the surface to devour a fly
Leaving only a ripple in its wake.

A wry smile crosses my face.
Releasing the cup, I quietly, carefully
Reach for my rod.

Nola Royce

Last Melody

Haunting music hung in the air,
as bodies rushed here and there.
I stood watching all of them come;
some walking, some on the run.
From the days that are no more,
through the door that lays on the floor.
Hopeful eyes seeking and finding
the loved ones with whom each heart was binding.
Through the smoke and through the haze,
a miracle arose out of the maze.
With misty eyes I watched the sight,
of the boarding and leaving, by day and night.
when..silently, he touched my outstretched hand...
The passengers were gone...
and so was the band.

Marjorie Bowles

Heavens Above

The horizon dances with beautiful colors of purple, orange, and red.
As darkness sets in, the universe becomes clearer in my head.
Planets race across vast areas of empty space,
But as I watch, they seem to move with me, staying in place.
For a brief moment, I feel I am the center,
Then without warning, visions of reality re-enter.
The stars before me, oh how I admire their twinkle and shine,
Light emitting at this moment won't reach here till 3009.
With the light taking so long to get here at last,
do we not know, but are we actually living in the past?
Earth is just a speck in the heavens abound,
Like looking from a plane at me on the ground.
Was there once life on the planet mars,
Or is what we see there, just reaching for the stars?
I'm sure there is other life out there, somewhere.
I don't know whether they look like us, maybe covered with hair.
I am a mere mortal in this niche in time,
for me now, just watching the heavens is just fine.

Randy L. Goodling

"Love"

Love is a creation, we alone must find
Given to us free to always bear in mind
So open your heart and see for yourself
You may have been hiding it on dark pantry self
So put love in your heart for all races and creed
It's something this old world constantly needs
Such a small thing requested from our God above
Yet, to some of us it takes a long, long, time to
really find love

Mary Louise Farrar

What's In A Name, Little Austin James?

The old man hugged by gold epaulets, cast a stately grey silhouette
As he reviewed black snarled heaps, charred formations on Peach Tree
Street.
"It's all gone, your store, your home", whispered old friends he
chance met,
And strangers stopped for news, to rage, lament-rejoice as gentle
folk greet.
Everything was gone. Even his Yankee wife fled
With Sherman's Army, and her last letter read,
"You did it to yourself!" That's all she said.
The old man went back to his land, in Carolina started over again.
Where Springfield stands on his land, years ago was called
Austinville.
He had two sons, two daughters; one a Judge's son wed, and then
One son, a senator, had a son who commanded as Admiral in still
Another war, whose Secretary of State had read law with the Judge back
when
He was young, and the old taught the young before the last war we'd win
And strong men embraced defeat's invitation to start over again.
"You do it to yourself", in choices, decisions; life's circumstantial
blend will mold.
Honor discards imposed blame or shame, no man owns another's soul.
Loud whispers echo his epitaph, as the old soldier rests where his
gift to the church enfolds.
What's in a name, my month old grandson, my "Peach", Little Austin
James?
A legacy of valor and honor in strong men whose name you now claim.

O. Emily Williams

Love's Penury

I grapple with love,
As I do a curiosity untold,
A mystery unfolded.
With a determination to overcome
But with fear, yet desire to satisfy.
Love, the great conqueror, or will I be conquered?
Warm recollections, cold calculations.
A bitter-sweet suspense unfounded, dumbfounded?
Life goes on amidst this ever increasing turmoil,
Love having no easy or definitive solution.
I writhe in agony of where, how, what if?
I live in firm belief and on limited evidence,
Blissful ignorance tainted with sadness.
The unknown surfaces, rumors rife,
The present uncertain, the past a fading memory,
The future formidable. I know not what to do.
Should I succumb, exist, or resist such temptation?
I look to you for inspiration.
Some day I will know the answer
And my heart will be satisfied.

Rosemary Murphy

Little Child

I see the little child
As I hold her in my arm
And to myself I think,
To this world she can do no harm.
Her tiny little body, as white and pure as snow
She is so young and innocent, no evil does she know.
I stare into her eyes, those light blue lipid pools,
And wipe her chin as she dribbles a tiny bit of drool.
I hope to God this innocence that she owns will last,
But I soon realize this is a hope far too crass.
For I know if this great, big world keeps going on
the way that it is
Her innocence will slowly fade
like carbonated fizz.
But for now, as I hold this little child
within my giant arm
I know, to this world
She can do no harm.

Michael B. Kirwan

Lover's Quarrel

Tonight, my lover sleeps with loneliness,
As I lay next to her in bed;
Tonight her eyes are weary from weeping,
Because of thoughtless things I said.

I wish I had not been so blind and cruel,
To cause my lover so much pain;
I wish I had not been so cold inside,
When I myself was much the blame.

What good can wishing do, to take away,
The bruise that scars my lover's heart?
What good are wishes now, when I have played
So brilliantly, the fool's part.

Tonight my lover sleeps with loneliness,
And dreams of valleys full of fears;
Tonight, she whispers softly, I love you.\,
And fills my eyes with tears.

Terry Don Lee

First Time

The lights are low, and were alone.
As I reach out and touch your face,
The moon lights up our first embrace.
Please don't hesitate, hold my hand.
Don't be afraid of the feelings in your heart.
Just promise me that we'll never part.
No one will mind, if we fall in love.
It's the first time, the first time for love.
There could be so many mountains we could climb.
Together the two of us tonight.
The two of us we're quite a pair.
These lonely nights we both can share.
Always and forever
We can bare,
but only if you care.

Laura JoVon Kelso

To the Future

Today is mine, I will not own defeat
As I stand viewing first red rays of dawn,
That light the pathway for my eager feet
Now restless for new land to tread upon.
The mountain beckons with it's summit place,
And wind whipped waves tempt me to ride their crest,
As NASA signals with the thrill of space,
I anxiously await each new conquest.
My feet can scale the mountain's loftiness,
I'll trust in Christ to make the waves serene,
My flight in space will be crowned with success,
Courage can conquer all the unforeseen.
I'll discipline myself for newer role,
As scientists penetrate the aureole.

Ossie E. Tranbarger

The Wind

The other day I saw a lady
as I was walking down the street.
As sure as I'm writing this
she must of had wings on her feet.

She whizzed by me and up the street.
I followed just to see,
What ever the rush could be.
She was moving so fast, she looked like a pea.

Now just between you and me
No one should hurry like that
but who am I so say?
When it was the wind who had her hat!

Wilma C. Troop

The Director

Her face adorn
As if the girl next door
Girlish but not quite a woman
She's writing the script
Her life long acts
Love ones emotions
Played on harp string cords
Pondering her passion
That cascades through her hands
Using platonic friends to unsettle companions
As twisted knives heart
In friendships lonely fiction
As her beauty fades to oldness
Like a haunted ghost whisper
She may stand alone

Lawrence F. Leaf

Where Am I In Dreams?

I can dream a feeling but I can't dream me.
As long as there is togetherness
Every detail, feature, emotion of you clearly seen
My face shows happiness, sorrow...I weep; you're gone
My heartaches to dream the past...can't see you
Can only visualize a blur of presence
Close eyes, mind wanders, daydreams
Stop! Ponder, seek familiarity
Faint...hints of style, poise, maybe a dimple?
Where has my being hidden without a trace?
Think long, hard...use a mirror... blink, frown, cry
Try harder... thoroughly awake... alert, frustrated, spent
Reality sets in.. clear as glass with you.

Mamie Hines Catlin

She's Gone

Now, when I need her most,
As my father slowly fades,
My best-friend, she is gone,

When I wake,
Before the funeral starts,
I know she won't be there,

When I need her to lean on,
And for her to give support,
She is laying in a coffin,

When the dirt hits the oak,
I start to cry,
As daddy and she are taken from me,

I now know how to start over and learn to live again,
Meet new people and new friends,
But the two I loved the most are now in another world.

Tearie Heilman

Why Not?

Why not create a bomb to destroy mankind?
A bomb such, that would melt the human mind.
No trucks, no planes, no ships, no cars.
No Irish pubs, or western bars.
No pain, no sorrow if I could I'd drop it tomorrow.
No more anger, no more hate.
No more arguing, not one single debate.
I know this sounds crazy, but in my mind, humans
are all to sick and lazy to clean up what has been done.
Killing, polluting, and inventing the gun.
Why not have it all end, and out of the end of a sick race.
The earth will replenish itself and bruce for.....
man to rise again!

Matt Petrovich

Only God

Only God can form the beauty of a Rose
Give fragrance to the flowers that grows;
Or cause to come from the Wren's breast
Precious melodies of many notes and so.

Only God, could fill the world, from brim to brim
With lands, mountains, and lakes, all praising Him.

E. B. McAteer

The Dresser

The dresser stands at dusk
as my unyielding eye stares upon
a picture frame filled with memories of
things long since gone.

I've wanted to throw it out.
I've been meaning to throw it out.
I've tried to throw it out.
To bury the memories for good.

Grasping it above the basket.
Poised, ready I stand.
A teardrop splashes its surface.
No sooner than it's in I take it out and wipe it off.
I shove it in the drawer awaiting the next rainy day.
remembering,
Always remembering...

Todd Phillips

Freedom

Bondage is not always bold and forceful. Sometimes it comes
as quietly as a caterpillar spinning a cocoon. It wraps
you tightly into one identity and robs you of your freedom to fly -
There are many facets to the personality that makes
you unique and with time comes the perfect balance that
makes a butterfly. Many beautiful colors make up the
whole and trust in God is the wind that gives you flight -
Amazing things are happening in this cocoon; away
from prying eyes is the force of nature beginning to
perfect who I am and a sense of urgency to break
free - free to explore all that the world has to offer.
In an explosion of color a butterfly breaks forth. No
longer identifying with the cocoon that held it prisoner
but dancing on the wind, rejoicing in what is to come
Never mourning what used to be -

Patricia Leigh Knorr

The Gift

That day she was feeling lonely
as she would sometimes do
You came to her and touched her
and she was born anew.

I saw the change come over her
as she read the words you wrote
There was a new look of confidence
with a glint of hope.

The happiness overcame her
it was a wish come true
And I knew it would one of those forever moments
she would hang on to.

For music is the gift
that makes her different from the rest
It's all she wants to strive for
so one day soon she can pass the test, and play among the very best

There is so much to live for
there is so much to do
All she needed along the way
were words of encouragement from you.

Mickey Cook

Autumn

The time seems to fly in the late hours of evening
As the early morning tide will roll back across the sea.
So many great wonders my eyes have seen
The power of God cast in colors at evening time.

I have watched the miracle the precious gift of life
I have held your miracle close to my heart,
Enjoyed the many pleasures and treasures of life
I have often been lost on the narrow and rocky road of life

When my shadow must disappear in the last days of autumn
I pray you will grant me this one last request,
May I carry all of the beautiful pictures and memories
Of love and kindness that life has shared with me.

May I understand the pain in the mistakes that I have made
Grant me the strength to share your love and kindness.
Please guide me down the path to my finally request
There I may enjoy your miracle, the closing of my autumn days.

J. J. Staker

All Is Well

The day seems to grow longer,
As the hours float timelessly by,
She runs toward the open arms of the sea,
But stops when she is at the waters edge,
And gazes into the sunset sky,
The wind blows softly though her hair,
And the sweet smell of honeysuckle and roses
Dances in the breeze.
Her mind keeps expressing fantasies,
of far off places and excitement with her love,
Enchanted castles and silver horned horses.
She takes her amulet in her hand,
And she gazes, oh so deeply,
She sees her one true love,
But waves crash and the sun falls,
And he is gone,
Just a memory in her mind.
A tear falls, Her heart is shattered.
But now he has returned,
Taken her in his arms, and all is well.

Rebecca DeRienz

A Sense of Direction (I Have Not)

Flash of white, flash of gray
As the houses go by
Circles on the street fill with light
Showing me a little more of the road
I thought I knew so well
The car is warm and buzzing —
A distracting sound
Turn the station up
So I don't have to think how many times
I've been on this road...I forget
The high-beams aren't helping
No matter, the battery is low
Drive fast enough and maybe
The houses and trees will stop moving so fast
I know this road so well,
Yet suddenly I remember something —
That I'm lost.

Melissa Guillet

September

Gradually independence will end,
as the long harvest moon wanes,
and Indian summers, with cerulean skies,
manifesting the land.
We must revert back to our Spring routines,
back to work, to school, and endless responsibility.
Back in the groove, push and shove, and empty houses.
Yet it all is solidly fixed,
as if etched in stone,
an essential law each person must pursue.

B. J. Whitehurst

The One

Our meeting was sudden chemistry
as these souls of two intertwined
not knowing where the other came from
for some reason it did not matter
as if we knew each other the whole time
maybe we embraced in a past life

We shared a moment of laughter and secret attraction
we held each other on two separate occasions
with feelings I cannot put into words
for it would take an eternity
crazy for two who knew now each other

Realizing the moment was too powerful to last
for she walked this life with another
and problems were hidden behind a shy smile

For we must part for now I pray to be in presence again
and if this moment never comes
with the girl I call the one

She will always be an eternal sunset in my mind
like the sun fades into the sea and is no more
the beauty and the splendor you never forget.

Michael Jones

Love, Happiness, And Peace

Our lives are busy, I know it's true
As this message comes from me to you
Out of sight you may be, but not out of mind
You're a special friend, you're one of a kind
I so often put important things on delay
Because I'm so busy, I happen to say:
Tomorrow will be soon enough
So often I do say
Why put off until tomorrow
What I can do today?
As I kneel to pray to the Lord above
I ask Him to grant you His blessed Love
I ask him not for your success
Instead I ask Him for your Happiness
As I continue to pray with so much ease
Last, but not least, I ask that He will grant you Peace
Tomorrows seldom ever come
When we put them off today
I ask the Lord to give me strength
To do tomorrows right away

Violet M. Diaz

Special Place

I want to take you to a special place
Give to you my love and embrace
Run with you on the oceans shore
Make love to you forevermore
I believe in dreams come true
Reality depends on me and you
True love will stand the test of time
The future holds what's yours and mine.

Lynn S. Raineri

Heroes In Twilight (A Salute To The Men Of The World War II Era)

The echo of your strong voices grows ever dimmer
As twilight, in deep advance, has begun to glimmer

Your once myriad ranks have with each passing year
Been relentlessly cut by Mortality's shear

Your merciless war instruments have long preceded you
Now rust-eaten and forever concealed from view
Enshrouded by tangled brush on some Pacific shore
Or entombed in the mucky ooze of a distant ocean floor

Your once smart battle dress by moths has been consumed
While oft retold victory tales you once more exhumed

Many toasts to your long-past conquests are still drunk
Sadly recalling lost planes and submarines that were sunk

Once sturdy-shouldered, with courage, you fought to a stand
Like eagles, your opponent in some embattled land

Present at again another national commemoration
Now stooped and spent remnants of a warrior generation

Mary V. Groll

The Decision

When we're in bed and everything is quite the alarm goes off.
As we get out of bed we think about our day, the things we must do.
There's a lot going on in our life and on our job to.

We have to decide what kind of day we will have. The choice is
ours we are the only one who can choose. To put a smile upon
our face or wear a frown in its place.

If we decide a smile would surely be great our family would
enjoy our happy state. Our world would be wonderful as we went
about our day. It would make the world a better place to see
a smile upon our face.

But if we chose the other, "a frown to wear", be grumpy and
angry all day and grumble at everything that comes our way.
Everywhere we go everyone we know will try to stay out of our way.

A smile is so much better and makes the world a happier place.
But the decision is ours to wear a smile or a frown upon our face.

Patricia A. Patterson

"Pacifica"

Ocean - I reach out to you
As you reach out to me,
Challenging the rocky edges
With foaming threaten of waves.

My eyes seek the mystery
Of your deep, of your denizens,
Of your endless space. I search
Your edges for your gifts
And treasure every little stone.

I stand in awe of your power
Respect it, and do not challenge it.
I love your ever-changing color;
Like a jewel, you reflect the light of the sky.
You own the clouds, and send them
As you will, to dominate the land.

At your side, I gain peace.
I look and look
And I see, not just water, but,
A lesson on my own infinitesimal self.

Lois L. Conway

The Glimpse

The foot of the Cross,
At a distance I stand;
I see blood drip from two nail pierced
Hands
The thorns in his brow blood flowing
Like tears,
His countenance, so fair, keeps drawing me near.
His eyes so tender, loving and kind,
The agony of death, not his heart, but mine.
His face, O' the love, what sin
Did he see?
The compassion was mine....
He died there for
ME.

Shane Roberson

The Lighthouse

Standing alone on a wind-swept shore,
At its feet, the ocean waves roar,
And, as they beat their restless sound,
The lighthouse vigil will ever be found.

To many seamen, thru countless years,
The lighthouse beam has calmed their fears,
For, knowing the light would be there to guide,
Has kept them safe as their ships they ride.

You don't have to be a seaman seeking light,
As thru life you struggle both day and night,
In need of the security a lighthouse gives,
As you seek shelter from all the life's ills.

The lighthouse for all the lost and afraid,
Is not a tower that man has made,
But, the out-stretched arms of God above,
Who guides each seeker with beckoning love.

The light He gives to all who implore,
Is available now and forevermore,
To show you the peace-filled way to live,
If only your heart to Him you'll give.

Nalda Morris

The Wind

The wind has taken you, your finally
at peace.
So still you lye, leaving your cares behind.
The pain is gone, gone with the spirits in eyes.
Now your wondering around above us looking
downward as we cry.
You've flown into the wind, escaping all the hurt
with in took to the sky.
Leaving the world behind, so young to die.
How could you let life pass you by.
And into the wind go so many dreams that
you're held inside.
Now you're just a memory burning inside my mind,
So young to die, how could you let life pass you by.
And now you'll never know I liked you, and you'll
never know I cared,
I really liked you and I really cared.
And now you'll never know.

You'll just fade into the wind.

Mary Isom

Overlock

You take your threads of belief
Attempt to stitch clean lines through my cloth.
Trying to better-design me.
Though it would make more sense for you to sew
Within and around
Patterns already present
Outlining, defining, what already exists.
Rather than this sad attempt to reinvent
Time's ancient tapestry;
Rather than denying yourself for wanting me as I am:
Garish, velveteen, multi-bright.
I am better displayed when you
Stitch your golden threads
Exactly around my paisley,
Over and under my sunflowers,
Outlining my carousel ponies and
Adding the most delightful pucker to my skipper's wheel!
You, making a curious quilt
Over me,
Warming us both.

Susan Eberly

Love Sleeps

Awake the Love in Thy Heart, of Me
Awake Thy Love, I have put to sleep
Your favor I ask, though do not deserve
I pray Your advance, of just one more chance

I long for the light, the sparkled your eyes
That came from your heart, and reached out to mine
The sound of your laughter, the taste of your kiss
Your loving embrace, these things I miss

Lest my heart burst, with the love that I feel
Might your soul stir, hence knowing it's real

Your love and forgiveness, being all that I need
I'm sorry I've hurt you, and have treated you mean
A stupid mistake, by a worrisome mind,
I'm sorry I've hurt you, that I've been unkind

Together these blossoms, of thirteen and five
Together their magic, to bring Us to life

Awake the love in Thy Heart, for Us
Give me a chance, to regain thy trust
Limitless love everlasting, for Thee
If we can awaken your love, that sleeps

Mark Dwight Trubey

The Bridge

The river flows gently below the bridge
Backed up with noisy cars and traffic,
All in a hurry to get somewhere else.
I wonder if I'm the only one
Who looks over the railings to watch
The river gently go on its way,
Totally oblivious to the bridge and its cars.
Occasionally I'll see a barge
Pushing a loud of lumber down the river,
Making ripples that stretch to touch the banks
In the otherwise peaceful, still waters.
Somewhere far upstream it must have rained
Because the lowest limbs are submerged
Where only last week they brushed the surface,
And still the river runs tranquilly along.
Then suddenly the traffic moves forward
And I am left with the memory of the river
As it flowed on while I was stopped,
And I was thankful for the delay.

Stephanie Swofford

Soulmate

I believe there is one soulmate in our lives
Be it man or woman.
You will know by the love you share
The emotions you feel
And the total commitment to the other.
You are willing to risk all for this ONE
And never being afraid to be who you are.
Love has no boundaries, it encompasses all.
It's in your smile, your eyes, your touch
And surely when you make love.
Making love is not the physical act of love
But instead the holding, the caressing, the kissing.
It's brushing lightly against the other
And feeling the excitement of each others body.
Remember always to be first a friend.
Never walk in front of me, I will not follow
Never walk behind me, I will not lead.
Take my hand and walk beside me
As my friend, my lover, my equal.

Sandra A. Bell

"Powers That Be"

Darlin, please don't fight it, go along with these powers that be.
Be not afraid, just accept the fact, can't you just admit you do love me.
Trust in me, open your eyes, try to understand, and
soon you will be able to see.
Just admit to these things, so we can put a lock on
life's treasures, our love is simply the key.
I beg you to say yes, say you will agree, if you do say
yes, I'll be so happy I'll climb the tallest tree.
I will treat you like a queen, this I truly guarantee.
Darlin' we can have it all, house, new cars, and
we can even raise the perfect family.
True love is all we will ever need, don't you now agree?
It's all there for us, if we only both trust
in the powers that be!

Ronald J. Waversak

The Admiral's Sovereign Fleet

Over choppy waters sails a vessel
bearing the name of the holy city, New Jerusalem,
making a fleet of itself alone;
carrying survivors of a barge sunken by its skipper.

Purged from that wreckage in tyrant seas
we are redeemed aboard an unsinkable ship, a sure foundation.
Our Captain! We humble ourselves unto you
for bestowing your essence for our impotence;
commissioning us to be your officers.

Our Helmsman! You navigate not by compass nor stern wheel,
but by power and comfort from your Commander, our Admiral.
who awaits our final docking
to award us a medal of life
for receiving the hand of his highly decorated liegeman
and not of those pirates that drift blindly to destruction.

Salute the Captain
give honor to the Admiral.
We are delivered from troubled billows
sworn into a perpetual fleet
there being none greater. Amen.

Ronald A. Wallace

Clouds And Me!

Today is a beautiful day of love!
Beautiful clouds, warm sunshine, wetness in the air and soft billowy
"pillow" clouds in a blue, blue sky;
Angel's featherbeds to frolic and sink into and to jump up and down on like a trampoline.
The sunshine is "tall" in the sky; poofy, frothy, wispy, cotton fluffs,
Oh, the joy to experience the world from a new open loving place!
There are no hidden angers, just peaceful floatings and warm yummy yearnings for companionship and love.
Oh, to reach out and hug the softness of the expanse, to squish the stuffin's out of the middle, to touch the moisture to my tongue, to taste the essence of energy and aliveness.
The wind drifts the pleasantness along its way to our destination.
There is love in the air!

Shirley Anne Christian

Time Of Day

Heavy rain clouds over my points of view.
Beautiful gray with black and white shaded scenery.
Mixtures of paints ad textures of color,
blended together to form a lifetime.
Dark pain regrets of old forgotten picturesque landscapes.
Caricature paintings of the long clandestine past,
show the gray days, the black pain, and the white knights
All surrounded by incandescent dreams.
Scenario skits of future mishaps and mistakes
are all too real for me to accept as unadulterated truths.
-I feel the painted moon shining around me.
-it's apologizing for the way it distracts me.
-But it won't give me the time of day.

Shannon Linderman

Mother Rabbit

Thank God I can see,
because I saw, the most
beautiful sight ever seen.
A Mother Rabbit nursing her young,
and keeping them ever-so-clean!

In broad daylight, there she crouched,
as her babies suckled away.
They laid on concrete, more hungary than brave,
with all the elements at bay.

One by one, the little bellies were filled,
and soon the Mother walked away.
The bunnies hopped to a nearby nest,
and the Mother stretched out in grass-like hay.

ALL were content, as the babies slept,
and the Mother Rabbit rested....
AND, I watched it all from my doorway!
What a wonderful sight I ingested!

Mary E. Keller

The Snow Leopard

As the rising sun comes up,
the Snow Leopard also wakes up.
Hiding, sleeping all day and opening his eyes
he climbs to some rocks and stares
at the delicate sun going down.
The moon comes out,
and so does the Snow Leopard.
Running! Running faster and faster he runs.

Nicole Loyet

Untitled

Mother, I travelled the underworld
before I was conscious -
bundle of instinct
grey in the doctor's hand.

Your white world was sterile;
snow kept you isolated
while I lay behind glass.

Always, it was your struggle to keep me here -
spirit-child, one foot in the beyond -
in and out of the hospital,
turning down all food.

You buried your nails in my heart
and dug your heels into the ground.
In spite of my best efforts,
you would not let me die.

Virginia Mohlere

Unconditional Love

Unconditional love must be found in One's self before it can be accepted from another.
On the same hand it must be in one's self before it can be given.
What is it you ask?
It is the willingness to overcome any pain and sorrow a person has afflicted upon you.
To forgive and show your love, concern, and dedication to that person in spite of what's happened.
However, There comes a time when you must accept, in spite of all your efforts, the second party does not have that special love inside of them.
Then it is time to move on. But no matter how painful it gets never forget you gave it your all,
You gave, unconditional love.

Stephen F. Mello

My Son

My son if there is one thing I could leave behind,
before the sun sets and has no memories of things left to find.
Pay attention so you can grasp not with ears for listening,
but with discernment that will last.
Seasons pass like the tides of the sea,
generation come and then quickly flea.
When life leads you to frustration,
and the nights full of anxiety.
Remember never give up your dignity
Remember your piety.
This phrase should be written forever in your heart.
"That it shall pass,"
and in passing become yourself before you part.

Marilyn Oszustowicz

Reason for Ryan

This life we've dreamed, both you and I
Has helped us see, and hear, and cry.

While time must pass, so must life
God gave us love through warmth and strife.

The joy and happiness from deep inside
Has changed to sadness where dreams preside.

A loss to us all...Now we all must try
To put this trial behind, and to our side.

Life is still young and sadness cannot deny
A gift from above: A warm healthy child.

T. D. Younger

Untitled

I stand on the beach and think of you.
Behind me, the rocks jut forth like Scylla's unhappy abode.
Before me the whirling ocean.
I face the ocean and think of you.
Waves advance and retreat, they lap at my feet,
luring away grains of my sandy soul.
I question their intentions and think of you.
My hands build a wall of sand to block them out,
but they tenderly caress it away and retreat.
Again they advance and pound softly at my feet.
I look into the blue infinity and think of you.
The spray against the rocks refreshes my face
bringing with it your fragrance.
I hear the wind sing and think of you.
Does it know my name? Or is it just a siren's song,
and I happen in its path?
The wind whispers my name with your voice,
and my heart assured, it is time to go.
I will return again tomorrow to ponder eternity
and think of you.

Michael Hoppe

True Love...Needs Effort To Bloom

Love is very delicate, very memorable for me.
Being in love is like the petals of a rose
So delicate...and yet so beautiful.
There are happy times, there are sad times too
In both situations, there is pain.
With or without someone there beside you.
The rose is very much perfection
and doesn't lose it's beauty
Until it starts to wilt and die.
Then the love of it fades away into nothing.
Love between two people...
If they don't get along, if they give up
on the relationship
There's no hope to capture the beauty of love again
and soon, like the rose, the relationship wilts and dies
It hurts so much when you lose
the person you love.
It's like the rose that withers and never blooms again
because it never even tried.

Rebecca Groves

One World, One Peace . . . . One Love!

Sometimes I sit and stare, taking a look at the world we share.
Being raised with totally different outlooks,
visions and realities for life.
Raised to hate, taught by the cruelties of the world.
Some how we drifted and learned that different was okay.
Later learning to love one another deeper than we have ever
loved before.
I dabble the thought of what is the purpose of hatred... What goals
can it possibly accomplish?
If we have to share the same air, share the same water,
share the same world...Why not share the same peace,
share the same joys?...Why not share the
same LOVE!!

Nichelle E. Mitchell

Mad

I am so mad right now I could cry. Things never seem to
go my way and I don't know why. I try so hard in every way
to do it right and it always comes out wrong. I try to love
and it's not enough. I try to understand and it's not enough.
I try not to yell but it keeps coming out and I should try to
leave it alone but I always think it needs help. So what do
I do or where do I turn because the life I live now can no longer go on.

Sandra Pires

Bells Of Freedom

Let me hear the ring of the
BELLS OF FREEDOM,
Oh, My Lord.
Let them ring o'er a FREE LAND
We call AMERICA!
The land, our boys fought
and died to keep FREE.
'Tis the land of all Faiths
That can ring their Church Bells of FREEDOM.
From the great Pacific Ocean
To vast Atlantic Shore
Up to the Canadian line
Down to the Mexican Border.
We can hear those BELLS OF FREEDOM RING.
Those chimes, Dear Lord, will remind us
of the sacrifices made for you and me
and be proud to have a right to be Christians
that only we can only be in a FREE Country
We call AMERICA.
Always and Forever let those bells of FREEDOM RING!

Sue Peverly

I Am

I am a unique individual; I am a child of God
Beloved by Him at all times.
I am.

I see, I hear, I comprehend, I love, I laugh, I cry.
My moods range the spectrum of sublime to ridiculous.
I am.

I dream, I conjure, I ponder, I strive, I achieve, I do
I am not so much the sum total of my achievements
As I am the sum total of my trying.
I am.

I garner knowledge, both good and bad.
I learn from my mistakes; I grow from my challenges.
I am.

I give and in giving receive; I love and in loving am loved.
I aspire and dream only to be challenged anew.
I am.

But in all that I am, in all that I feel, in all that I strive for,
I know I am loved because...
I am.

Marilyn Slaght-Griffin

Your Picture

Dearest, the light from the hall's shining in
Beside me, brightens your face in the dim
Duskiness of the night shadows deep
Which laden my eyes with the sweet call of sleep.

I smile and look for you to smile back at me.
I reach out my hand to touch yours tenderly.
I whisper softly, "Goodnight, lover mine,
Pleasant dreams will enfold us, our heartstrings entwine."

No echo, but only a silence replies.
I know the reason, and though it defies
My wish to have you close by me asleep,
Your picture will guard me and tender watch keep.

Margaret Mills Muntz

A Soul

The innermost part of a man. That cries out for solace in a better land.
Longings that cannot be uttered, loss of words that become phrases stuttered.

Seeking for an innate peace, that permeates through the void of the deep.
Tossing when the body toils from restless nights of no sleep.

Desiring comfort for the weary mind, needing healing that would be divine.
Reaching upward for a Heavenly Find

Gives us help through Faith not to Fear it,
the sounds of Destiny as in Judgment we sit.

When the great judge announces the Fate of a SOUL!
I'm laboring daily so Heaven will be my Goal.

Patricia Vernon Adams

East Of The River

It was told, East of the river,
beyond their fires...
stood unholy and black
a funeral pyre.
Three days ride, and no courage left
I needed to see the fault of his death.

My soul feels so empty, my body so cold,
my lover forever, my religion sold.
I saw what took him, he wanted it this way.
This land is strange in oh, so many ways.

My lover would battle
in times when you think it strange battles were needed
in Gods holy name.
To die in battle, was honor its true,
but I am old here, in a land far too new.

It was told, East of the River,
beyond their fires,
stood unholy and black........a funeral pyre.
Three days ride, courage to see,
one funeral pyre, what's left now of me.

Stacy Schiffour

Memories

I remember a little Pomeranian dog
big brown eyes; long, soft fluffy hair - red.
Wet pointy black nose and perky tail
curled like a pig's.

Memories of her warm, small body next to me at night.
Cold evenings curled up and snuggled close.
The sound of her shrill, tiny bark.
Most of all, her loving ways.

I remember good times.
She saw me through bad times -
death, divorce, school, moving.
Where are you now?

I wonder if dogs go to heaven.
I'd like to think so.

Rhonda Weaver

Piggy Back

My Daddy rides me piggy back,
I first have to climb upon his back,
He hoist me up and we go straight and round,
First at a walk, then at a trot,
It's so much fun riding my daddy piggy back!

Otto M. Van Duyn

Summer

Summer is for fun and frolic
Bikes, falls, skinned knees, and scares

Summer is for quarrels with sisters
Brothers with black eyes and broken teeth

Summer is for quietude by the creek
Soaking my toes in the stream, catching crabs

Summer is for fishing poles
Worms wiggling, hooks striking fingers

Summer is for climbing trees
Waving maple leaves in the breeze

Summer is for watching birds
Chirping robins, whistling to the wrens

A summer evening is for hopping toads
June bugs crawling on the beet leaf

Summer is rain drops and puddles
Then the sun comes, or maybe a rainbow

Summer is for spiders building webs
The glistening dew painting a gossamer

Summer is for picking big juicy gooseberries
Busy gophers piling black fertile soil in mounds

Leathia R. Siewert

Sudden Storm

Rain approaches quickly
Birds halt melodies, seeking shelter
beneath upturned leaves.
The sky closes in.
Black blankets cover,
but refuse to warm.
Winds echo whispered warnings
of fast-approaching storms.

Large, slow drops merge into drenching rivers.
Rivers rush down swollen hills.
Lightening cracks its angry whip
with fierce fury.
Thunder follows rumbling low and loud.
The storm declares its fearful majesty,
ruling with threats of watery nightmares.

The storm flees with the same urgent
quickness with which it began.
Now-calm winds blow spent clouds
across the softening sky.

Sara Burke

Morning Dusk

As I gaze out the window I see the horizon,
Birthing a golden disk.
It radiates shafts of light.
The blades of grass that house the morning dew,
Rise to welcome their God above.
Jubilant chirps of early birds,
Coach the deliverance of warmth,
And awaken the world.
The twilight's hue of dominant gray,
Is transformed to a gilded glare.

Susan Mathai

Changing Winds

Scenes of pleasant winds roll across the earth
Black suit funerals and white gown births
Things they don't appear
As they ever were

Sun warmed rivers flow across the earth and stone
Dirty preachers preach as the money flows
How could mankind
Ever sink so low

The blinding elements they have crossed my mind
Polluted rivers and the seventh sign
First amendment rights
On the firing line

Clouds of black and white, days of rain and shine
Peace and civil war another million die
Young men fight the fight
As their mothers cry

Ralph A. Lezoche Jr.

Insight

Vision crucifies me
Blazing across eons, it pinions my limbs
Into mute conciliation.
Powerless I watch as time moves unfettered
Etching pain into walls of flesh
Buried deep within a willing Earth
Poised to serve as Mankind's self-selected crypt.

She is the Mother and the Victim of her own generosity
Repaid by self-absorbed children
With ignorant contempt and careless abandonment.
She is the crumbling core
Her disease terminal
A failed marriage of Nature and Progress.

And yet in all her misery
She still sings lullabies to new generations of children
Despite her knowledge
Helpless as Prometheus to alter a course foreseen
She dares to bring forth life in an age of chaos
As an act of faith.

Terri Wainwright

Rama Micol Aherim

Canopy of warmth engulfing one's spirit...
Bond unfamiliar to most yet desired by many...
State of being that transcends materialism...
Capacity to embrace a non-reciprocal slit or...
Essence of serenity within a dark hollow shell...
Abstract presence that harbors immense trust...
Ability to experience fear while unleashing passion...
Expression of vulnerability unbound by any limits...

An extraordinary love above all others,
this higher love is Rama Micol Aherim

To know loss is to Know this Love
To understand loss is to Live this Love

Lorain C. Prevaux

Daddy

Stop a minute Daddy, before you turn and walk away;
Do you finally feel my feelings, hear the things I couldn't say?
Do you hear me crying for you in the middle of the night?
Do you see my arms are reaching, trying hard to hold you tight?
Couldn't we have had just one more minute,
another chance to set things right.
Would you wait for just one second before you step into the light,
I've one more thing to tell you before you turn around to go,
Oh! Daddy, Daddy, I always loved you so.

Simmone Hofsommer

Under The Deep Blue Sky

Under the deep blue sky, the old tree stood.
Branches reaching out into the everywhere.
The young boy glided across the golden field
and stared at the old tree.
Clouds and memories drifted by the still day.
The boy climbed.
And climbed.
And climbed.
Until he could climb no more.
He was so high he saw the stars through the clouds.
The world below was smaller, but wider.
The boy could see his future. His world.
Brilliant rays from the blazing sun lit his face.
The old tree held the young boy.
And smiled.

Patrick Rodio

Spider Haibun (Homage To W.B. Yeats)

Mechanical mouth spits steaming saliva
breathe in its hot breath,
smell the mildew, see disintegrating walls, watch rotting paint,
become one with the roach colony, and avoid stepping on tattered
carpet.

This shower, hell within hell within hell...

Adam. Dumb Monkey. Has a complex to be touched.
What happened to Adam, paradise lost, needs to touch real fur,
smell real Eve at his side, but what he feels is only a fan
blowing on his sweat soaked body-empty nest.
Adam searches for another...

The only breath you feel is mechanical-Air or steam.
The only face is in the cracks of the shower, it has eight eyes
and mandibles, there only by fate or science.
Adam reaches down and grabs a scattering waterbug and tosses
it into its last jump...

The bug twists, shutters
linear silk embrace of
the weave- spider attacks.

Stuart Zeno

Neighborhood

Summer days are hot, humid and long
Breezes and even sprinkles of rain
Cannot be had for a song.
Birds fly high in the skies
Alit in the treetops that soar above
Squirrels scamper along power lines
And the grounds below and around
As the perennials grow and bloom
Other flowers and plants abound
Lawn mowers drone and hum
Making carpets of the grasses
Children play, sing, run, skip and holler
To teach, train and discipline for their valor
Traffic in the streets roar, bounce.
Squeal, screech, rev and falter to a stop
Near the homes where all who dwell
Find the peace and tranquility to crop-
Into and thru the night
To rise the morning after
Returning to their perennially.

Theresa B. Trapp

Dawn

Early she journeys from a place far away
Breezing through the darkness to embrace the light.
Welcomed by sailors, after the storms of night
A gift she brings, hope for the day.
Like a lioness stalking her prey,
She steals upon you unaware.
So calm, so enchanting is she
Boldly commanding the darkness to flee.
Awake! Arise from thy slumber
Take hold of her hand,
Accept the gift she offers
She'll soon be lost in yesterday land.

Loretta V. Justice

Missing A Loved One...

Smiles in the past,
bring tears to the future.
Memories of her will linger on,
and for no reason will ever be gone.
A big heart always willing to give,
and never expecting to receive.
A very special person,
that meant the world to me.
In my life she played an important part,
but when she left she kept part of my heart.
Though I know we will meet again someday,
at heaven's door.
She will show me heaven,
and I will see it like it's never been seen before.

Nichole Krueger

Wedding Anniversary

They return once again to their home of youth
Bringing experiences they jointly accrued;
Events of the past now appear brand new,
Including the change in a spouse or two.

Sibling discord is tacitly tabooed.
The celebration days will be short and few,
Created to honor the special two
From whom the whole, random family grew.

Grandchildren, cousins (they're all really the same),
Are running; conversing; just playing a game.
Adult intervention is seldom and tame,
Renewing their friendships is why they came.

Too quickly the gathering hours ebb and wane,
Having added new memories to family fame.
Was this choice of people truly the aim
When a man and a woman shared one name?

Sharon R. Nemeth

Turmoil

The sky is dark as the heavy clouds
gather.
The winds increase and swirl as the
storm approaches.
We seek shelter to avoid the
onslaught and turmoil.
Sometimes we escape or the storm abates
but not always.
And another may appear.

Sharon V. Moone

The Climbing Tree

I climbed to the top, and a limb gave me a bop.
I climbed up so high and looked in the sky.
Then I looked at the ground, so brown.
I hoped, I would not fall down.

Ryan Connor

Loose Change

Loose change in my pocket,...
Brother can you spare a dime?
Restlessly hearing the jingles,
That will all add up in time.

A nickel, a quarter or two,
Yes and even a shiny penny.
Lose change to spare,
I'll take all and any...

Whatever money comes my way,
I can put it in my little bank.
And wherever lose change comes from,
Someone is sure to be "thanked".

Thinking over again, day after day,
Thinking what all those coins can do.
With all the lose change that comes my way.
I may end up with more money then you!

Saundra M. Welch-Bey

Love

I met you when my heart was dying, you took me in your arms and brought me back to life, you said I'd be safe and loved with you in my heart. I let you in.
But soon your heart grew separate and far away from mine. Our dreams vanished and our togetherness died. We went our own ways and it's been that way for so long that we many never fine the love we had for each other. I heard today you've married I hope she is what you need, and she makes you very happy, for I knew I'd be replaced that's why I'm gone.

Your memories will live forever in my soul and heart, your face shall always be in the sky above, and your eyes shall shine like the stars above, someday we will walk through time holding each other close but not in this life in another life or maybe in Heaven above who knows what the future holds for each of us.

You shall live within my heart until my mind is released from sufferings of the past and present your voice shall echo from the past and I will listen as you speak my name with great joy and we shall live in each others lives as if there were no death.

Paulette Cain

My Dear

I know this time is hard for you, for an emptiness you feel inside.
But darling child please don't cry.
For although I can not be with you, in your heart is where I am.
I'm there when you are sleeping, and when you are awake,
Or when you're standing in the sun, or when raindrops fall upon your face.

For as you celebrate this time of year, and loved ones gather round.
I am there amongst you all, for in your hearts I am bound.
Touch your hand upon the tree for me, and I will feel it too.
Hold and hug the ones I love, that's like me hugging you.

Though most of all I need a smile and laughter across your lips
Each time you do, I'll smile too, I'll think of it as a kiss,
I'll watch you age, I'll watch you change
From year to timeless year, but remember I am within your heart,
And love you so, my dear.

Lori Lee Monk

I'll Take My Last Breath, With You

I don't no where to start, I guess it will take sometime
But deep down in my heart, I'm really glad your mine.
There's something in your smile, there's something that you do
For it has been awhile, since I met a girl like you.
I know it won't belong, because I always dream of you
And I just want you to know girl, I'll take my last breath with you.
I miss your beautiful smile, and I suddenly realize,
For it has been awhile, since I saw your sparkling eyes.
I miss your tender touch, we know it's just not fair.
For I love you very much, and I know you'll still be there.
Your love is all I want, a love that is so true.
And I just want you to know girl, I'll take my last breath, with you.
The thought of losing you, would really break my heart,
I don't know what I'd do, if we were torn apart.
But when the time has come, and it's down to me and you.
I just want you to know girl, I'll take my last breath with you.

Richard Orozco

Lonely

I pray everyday, in every way, to make it better for me.
But how can that be, when I'm so lonely.
Life is more than work and home, you see.
What about the fun and sun and all the parties?
Yes they exist, I know they're there.
But being lonely has brought a certain fear.
I can't go out, all by myself.
It will be boring, useless I felt.
I work and work, to forget the loneliness in my heart.
But that's how it is, with many people.
So how come I feel so alone?
I guess it has reached down to the bone.
Lonely am I, how can that be.
In such a crazy place,
Like, New York City.

Natasha English

The Carousel

It was there the first time I saw you, that feeling I can't explain.
But I knew I would always love you and I knew love would cause me much pain.

My heart was alive like a carousel spinning and reeling around,
The music box lightly was playing all because you had been found.
Nothing could hold me back - like the wind I was free to run wild
To tell everyone of my new love - but I played the games of a child.
The more my love grew for you the further away you seemed.
But I knew one day you would return you had to - you were my dream.

But the carousel sometimes stops spinning and the laughing children all run away,
The music never has to keep playing and time can just stop for today.
For us there was no tomorrow. Only dreams in my childlike head
I pushed for something I never had until at last your love was dead.

It was there the first time I saw you that feeling I can't explain
But I knew I would always love you and I knew love would cause me much pain.

Ruth Vincent Alexander

Mother

Mother is a word I find, that means a lot to me.
For it brings back lovely memories of what life used to be.

Happy times of love and laughs is what we shared back then.
How I wish, with all my heart, it was like that again.

But as the time goes rushing fast we're sharing more and more.
And adding to those memories, times not there before.

I love you mom and want to say that until the very end,
I want to share my life with you cause you're my one true friend.

Nancy J. Legenhausen

You Told Me

You told me not to look,
but I sneaked a peek.
You told me not to listen,
but I couldn't help but overhear.
You told me not to touch,
but my fingers tingled with each new sensation.
You told me not to love,
but my heart got wrung out just the same.
You told me to never disappoint you,
but to your rules my traitorous self
did not conform.
You told me not to miss you,
but my tears roll silently on.
For how can I not miss you mom?
How can I not?
The tears roll silently on.

Talin Babikian

The Lonely Little Rebel

I was born in Virginia and I'm proud as I can be
But I'm a lonely little rebel in a Yankee family
My mommy hails from Boston and daddy from New York
As for Margie, Linda and Sharon you just have to hear them talk
They have new England accents of which their proud as they can be
I guess that I'm low man on our own family tree
Some folks call me rebel others call me Yank
Everyone kisses my North end what's my South end for to spank
Though I'm just a 4 month old baby some day I'll have to choose
I guess I'd like to be a Yank if I could get used to wearing shoes
On the other hand they tell me all these friends and folks I know
There's lots of fun to be had where the cotton and tobacco grow
I guess I'll concentrate on my Pablum and let the folks decide for me
I'm a lonely little rebel in a Yankee Family

M. M. Keneally

To Vicki Rene,

In Love

We struggle and wrestle through the night.
But is our burning cause just and right,
Or is it only greedy grasping for selfish pleasure;
Seeking the glitter while missing the true treasure?
Do we strive for pure gold or accept mere gilding?
Is this a bridge or a wall we're building?

And as the incandescence of passion explodes;
And the molten lava of climax courses the old roads
Burning through the shackles of the material;
Are we giving the bonds of flesh a temporary burial
To dance spirit to naked spirit in the blinding light?
Or do we hide from this miracle in panic and fright?
Do we fear to gain full knowledge of each other;
Afraid it's a weight that will hinder and smother?

Oh, my love, we are two halves of a whole!
Complete parts, each with its distinctive role.
Never losing our separate identities,
But melding together in transcendent complexities.
Becoming more than can ever be dreamed of
Without the mutual gift of sharing, in love.

G. David Mc Daniel

Growing Night

I love the flowers blooming big and bright.
I love watching the birds in flight.
I love the trees blowing East and West.
but I think the plants are one of the best.
I love the crickets chirping at night
And the still garden in the bright moonlight.
I think it's time to say good night
While sleeping under the bright moonlight.

Suzanne Alaouie

Every Minute Of Every Day

It's beautiful when the sunshine on the bay
But it is not every day
Your beauty is in your every movement
It is never gone, not even for a moment
I am really a very shy guy
But I thought I'll give love a try
For I can't stand for you to be away
Not for a minute, nor a day
I'm lost without your charms
Because it leave's me with empty arm's
When you're gone, I feel so alone
I miss you most, and start to groan
So please won't you stay
And I'll make you so happy, every minute or every day.

Thomas R. Stiglmeier

Surrender...?

I sit here in my quiet reverie
But my mind is filled with misery,
For that which I have done and lost,
All those unlucky paths I've crossed.
Inside, my anger runs too deep,
My pride too strong for me to weep.
As I raise my voice in my defense,
I know the turmoil which will commence.
You see, I've been through all of this before
And I'll fight the whole length of the war.
In war, one side must always lose;
But to lose my pride is what I refuse.

Marisa Marranzini

Stones In The Road

So unpretentious, seemingly benign
But oh how deceptive, these doubts in my mind
Awaiting the moment, to throw me for a loop
When most unexpected, like a hair in my soup

Like a full dress rehearsal, awaiting my cue
To go through the motions of dancing with you
The World fades and softens, like wind in the pines
Then the doubts spring from nowhere, like forgotten lines

We sit in the twilight, with feelings sublime
Our hearts joined forever, suspended in time
Then without warning, the doubts come so soon
Like an ominous storm cloud, that covers the moon

I find myself longing, for your sweet embrace
With eyes closed so tightly, I still see your face
I picture us walking, through grain-fields of gold
Then the doubts cut so deeply, like stones in the road

Robert C. Taylor

The Ghetto

The Ghetto is always thought as a bad place,
but once you take a look you don't realize what was
in your face. You finally realize that you never
knew what you were saying or doing. You never knew
or thought a dream would come true living in the ghetto,
but once you see the light and happiness in people
in the ghetto you never thought it could happen.
People you never expected become movie stars and celebrities,
but nobody can picture or see it happen. They would
never see or understand the happiness or joy in the
ghetto. The walk and the talk you never could understand
was like a different language from a far away land.
No one should judge by the outside no one can.

Natalie Eisman

Untitled

Across a moonlit field, I once saw heaven
but saw it not with my eyes.
For it was too pretty, it was too kind
to fit with the dankness of my lies.
It was there in the midnight meadow
but why did it want me so?
For I'm no hero and I'm no king
and this heaven I do not know.
I found it there that azure night
or it found me I should say.
For every weary and troubled step
has lead me down this way.
The weary traveler, now I lay, in its arms
on this fertile ground.
And at last, I know my journey is over,
because of this heaven that I found.

Scott Dinho

Just Memories

If time were like an ocean, our lives would never end,
But since our time is limited it's just a matter of when.

The people do there duties and accomplish what they can,
Though power and money can't change the fate of man.

Our days have all been numbered and when our number is here
They'll be no more worries and nothing more to fear.

The earth will keep rotating and life will continue on
The sun will go down in the eve and rise again in the dawn.

The joys we've had the tears we've cried, will all be a part of the past
Just memories of a once lived life that only went too fast.

So now is the time to take advantage and do all there is to do,
Before the good intentions become regrets when our life is finally
through.

Stephanie D. Gonzalez

The Power Of Time

We built a friendship so strong during the short spring months
But suddenly time became our enemy,
moving so swiftly, knocking us down,
leaving us little to be hopeful for.
What happened to meeting after class,
and the basketball games we played?
Are the memories of our late night talks for real?
Or did time rush these memories into my heart?
Our time is up and she no longer lives two blocks away,
The pain is like fire, and burns through my heart.
But where are the tears?
I see them now, if I look in her eyes.
They are real tears she is crying.
I do not want her tears to fall,
I fear each tear carries a hug, a smile, or a memory we shared.
So shed no more tears, my friend,
Just hold on to those long talks, victorious basketball games,
and encouraging words that brought us together.
Those memories will keep us alive,
until time allows us to be together again.

Rachel Villareal

On the Occasion of a Wedding Anniversary

Twenty-five years —
Has it been that long?
How time flies when life is a song!

Twenty-five roses —
For each year flown fast
To store in memory the future of the past
Twenty-five years.

Leonardo V. Cortez

"My New Life"

That I should not smoke, I had known for years
but the idea of quitting would reduce me to tears.

The weekly housecleaning had become a strain,
A full day at the office was a horrible drain.

It is hard to smile and pretend to have fun,
when you are extremely short of oxygen.

The dread emphysema was here to stay,
and getting much worse every single day.

It was time to plan for the inevitable,
As nothing else seemed very creditable.

Then I spent twenty long months living day to day
while on the Lung Transplant list at UCLA.

My husband, lover and best friend in life
was my caretaker who carried me through this strife.

At last a generous Donor was found for me,
and now I have a new lung named "Charlie".

Children laughing, birds singing, trees and flowers galore,
Everything in life seems much better than before.

Religion, dawn of a new day and warmth of the sun,
are all fresh and exciting as my new life has begun.

Rosemary J. Currier

Invisible Wall

I want to touch. And to be touched.
But there is a barrier.
Something for which I cannot see. But it is there.
I try - everyday - to chip away at this invisible wall.
But to no avail.
The more I try - the stronger the wall becomes.
Maybe I should give up. I can't.
For my greatest love is on the other side.
I need to touch her. And she to touch me.
So I continue to try, but I fear I am losing myself.
Why is this wall between us?
The wall is her past. It is her pain. It is her sadness.
She is a victim. A victim of those who have used her.
They used her beauty and innocence - And left scars in their place.
But I can see her beauty. And I have felt her love.
But the scars remain. They say in time the scars will fade.
But what about the scars in my heart. My hurt. My pain.
My love for her is stronger - I will break through the wall.
Love will triumph. It must.

Richard Brodt

Pt. 1: The Sensation

I walk home alone tonight as I usually do.
But tonight feels different somehow.
The streets are unnaturally quiet and empty,
And though I walk with no one, I know I am not alone.
My imagination runs wild with thoughts of thieves and worse.
Looking behind I see nothing, and dismiss my unfounded fears.
My eyes see formless shadows and my heart beats faster...
My heart beats louder and louder until it is too much to bear!
The beating of my heart is silenced by another sound...
Someone is calling my name! Once more I turn to find nothing.
I want to run but there is nowhere to run to... nothing to run
From. What is it that makes this night so eerie?
The way the moonlight reflects in the glass on the buildings?
Was it simply the wind that called to me?
Is it the chilly night air that makes my blood run cold?
Or is it simply that I'm walking home on a deserted street?
No...someone is watching...watching me...
The feeling is too strong to shake...
I am being watched...followed...
And there is nothing I can do...

Scott A. McKendry

Where Did The Time Go?

When I was very young, I thought 30 would be fun,
But, too soon, I was there,
And then came 40 with graying hair.
Now 50 is history, along with 60
When I became depress. With old age I was obsessed.
It was the beginning of the end,
With death and retirement of many a friend.
My husband went to be with the Lord at 62,
Something you think will never happen to you.
Now, I am a widow. How can it be
This is really happening to me.?
Now I am 70—well preserved I've been told.
That's because I wish to never grow old,
But wishing won't make it so,
Sooner or later we all have to go.
So I'll go on clear to the end,
knowing in Jesus I have a good friend.
I hope you all know Him in the same way
So we'll all go up together on the resurrection day.

Mary Ann Alexander

A Bold Change

I was a mother of two and gainfully employed,
But wasn't on a job that I fully enjoyed.
Had a deep down ache to do more than just file,
So I quit, "cold turkey", and returned to school for a while.

I was older, wiser, and ready this time,
Knowing I, alone, had to cough up each and every dime!
Never ever knew how I'd pay for each class,
Or how I'd buy my books, my supplies, or even my gas.

Yes, times were tight, but my mind didn't quaver,
So the odds of continuing school stacked in my favor.
Though my state of health and finances turned for the worst,
A desire to finish school and to teach was my constant thirst.

The challenges were there, and I worked hard, you see,
But those rough and tough times paid off for me.
I graduated with honors and got my teaching degree,
And have never doubted that which was meant to be.

Linda M. J. Thornton

A Lonely Checker King

You move each man one square at a time.
But what's His next move?
What's on His mind?
so the game continues on, both of you attacking and
scheming, both seeking, a kingly role,
That feeling of power, the essence of control.
But only one was crowned.
And now You are king.
You go and jump whomever you please,
and go wherever you want
To your subordinates you even seem to intimidate
and taunt, their every move,
until you capture them all.
How viscous! How cruel!
But now there's no one left. There's no one
there.
Except you and your lonely Checker King and
his 32 squares.

Tameka D. McDaniel

And Now...Farewell?

So many ways to say "farewell"...adios, goodbye, so long...
But why do all these words feel wrong?

We've known each other for so many years,
and weathered so many storms.
Are we now to be blown apart by a passing breeze?
Have we mellowed and matured with passing years,
Or merely closed our minds and hearts to all possibilities?

What now, my friend? What now?
How do we go on from here?

With so much distance between us,
do we dare to risk being there for each other?
What investments are we willing to make and what risks take?

Shall we make the conscious effort to nurture our friendship
Or simply yawn and blink, and, dreaming,
let it slip through our fingers,
To drift away like a dream that is forgotten when we wake.

Patricia L. Bouligny

Justin

You can not be my lungs breath, for God keeps all life,
but you are my hearts greatest treasure. If I did not
have such a jewel as you in my heart, my heart wouldn't
be as great. Unlike a queen, who without her crown,
would still be a queen.

You are the finest thing life has to offer, and when you
are gone, the memories will linger like the scent of your
cologne on my pillow. When all the gold and jewels are
tarnished, you will be as beautiful as the first time you
ever entered my mind.

My feeling of love for you is eternal and our time
together here is too short for a love such as ours Eternal love
does not fade with time or with passage, but grows
stronger and deeper.

I can only hope our parting will be a bitter sweet
beginning to the time we have yet to share in another
life. I can't say I won't miss your touch, but when
we are together again, I'll love you just as much.

Lori Warning

To You My Dear

You don't realize what you've done to me,
but you've stolen my heart, and won't set it free.
I pray to God everyday and night,
to get your voice out of my mind.
The feeling of your hand upon mine is gentle to my touch,
now my love for you has grown so very much.
My love for you is never ending,
so, this poem to you I'm sending.
You don't know how much I love you so,
And when you caress me,
I never want to go.
I want to know what I have to do,
to let you know how much I'll always love you.
When you look at me your eyes seem almost hypnotizing,
they make me feel safe like I'm never dying.
But even so you will not take the time of day,
to listen to what I have to say.
So now this is your last chance I'm giving to you,
to show you how much my love is for you.

Vanise Leon

The Flight Of Two

People like sea gulls fly in all directions
By chance, by fate, by luck..two meet
Afraid and tired of the cards life has dealt

Two trusting, caring, sensitive people
Treading ever so softly into a fire raging with passion
Carefully they explore
Talking, listening, learning, holding

Please stay he asks
She does, but is so afraid
Too many times her giving has been tainted
By those she believed were loving and compassionate

She'll stay for a while and take down her wall
The wine he has already given will last a long while
Memories to reflect

Whatever may happen, wherever they go,
Both will have shared tender moments,

Most will never be fortunate enough to ever experience
The high of...the flight of two

Sherry Freitag

Prisoner Of Time

For years I felt imprisoned,
By countless past sufferings.
Never to endanger my inmost thoughts,
For fear of judgement or denial,
Disapproval could weaken my fortress.
Incapable of coping with demeaning remarks,
I guard my heart from attack.
So, 'til I feel the sun's reflection from life's voice,
I resolve myself to blindness.
Within the dwelling of my soul,
To remain secure and gather strength,
Forceful enough to burst forward,
With an intense blaze,
Pungent enough to penetrate,
The citadel of fear.
And allow myself,
The release to freedom.
The freedom of happiness.
An awakening to life.

Susan G. Tinschmidt

A Mother's Prayer

I don't know how to thank, you Lord, for everything you've done
By granting me this miracle that I can call my son.
Such wonder fills his marveling eyes, so soft his silky hair.
His peaceful sighs make song birds thrill as music fills the air.

Love him? Oh yes! I love him, Lord, with every part of me.
I'll do my best to guide him to be all that he should be.
If he should ever falter Lord, as children often do,
Please pilot and direct me with this person sent from you.

Lord, grant to me your wisdom help me understand his ways.
Assure him that within my heart he'll always have his place.
Protect him from this sinful world and help him understand
He must be strong, bold, brave and proud to become his own man.

When my work is completed, Lord, and life on earth is done,
Send angel voices on the wind to say, "I love you Son."
And I will wait by heaven's door to look into his eyes,
For only with my loving child can I have paradise.

J. M. McGee

No Where To Hide

You're always hurt more,
by the ones you love.
This is a law, written in the heavens above!

For them you open
doors to your soul,
When you're without them,
you never seem whole!

And if one should rip
a door from it's hinges,
It sends your heart, straight into twinges!

This is why I tried to let go;
to spare myself,
more sorrow and woe!

But cast you aside, I could not do;
for I am too much,
in love with you!

I'd rather chance suffering more pain,
than to never, hold you,
hug you, kiss you, again!

Terry A. Sauls Sr.

Shadows At Dawn

I am
called have been and will be
many things not all of which
i understand or accept
or can even do well

nonetheless

i am each day reborn
made from the same mold
that has given I birth many times before
and like it or not will do so again

each night

closing my eyes till morning I dream
drifting like the moon until I awake to
if not what I was before then

surely a shadow

of what once was
and hopefully with dawn
will be with the rising of the sun

again

Richard G. Henriet

Unlike Mary on the Halfshell

Pain-Rene-ing tears
Calming fears
and pillowing the steel edges of institution.
Caring delicately,
handling fragily as a Pineland institute child.

In your nesting therapy
My Hermitage as in CRAB speculations
is my need of HOME... at a snail's progress
That will buffet and beach rolled
into new atolls of living ocean.

Tonight inside
I climb into a smoother incoil stairway sea shell
under a pebbled pattern camouflaged disguise
Your beachcombing eyes pocket my patterns
And I feel like a Star
Fishing for compliments -
You, a pearl inside my oyster exterior.

Joan Frazee

The Only Answer I May Know

Who? Who is he?
Can he see that his absence changes me?

What? What was he like?
Did he have a big smile? Was he nice or was he neat or
was he the patient type?

Where? Where is he now?
The only answer I may know gone in heaven I am sure he is up there,
not below.

When? When did he go away?
On the porch when dad was young, I guess, that was the day.

How? How will I learn?
To know about him someday is one of my concerns.

Why? Why don't they barely talk any?
One picture I've seen with him in a group and people many.

Questions go on forever, until answers come to stay.
I never knew him, never will. I love my Grandpa any way!

Patricia C. Keehn

Heaven

If the oceans were green and the skies were blue,
can you tell me, if you know what we would do
in a world with love
that peace would abound.
What would they say if when woke up they found,
nothing to complain,
disarray turned around.

Birds in the skies, fish in the streams,
would they know what it all means?
Unlocked doors, gates torn down,
flowers without pestilence, cover the ground.
Or would they go on, same as before,
not hearing, not seeing, not feeling,
ignore...
...everything that is different,
that is different,
that is same.

If hit in the face, with anything,
anything, with grace.
Would not recognize Heaven, this place.

Marc Lance

Time

The reason our paths have met,
cannot be fully understood.
This crossing we find ourselves at and the things beyond,
will be revealed only as the fullness of time blooms.

So while we wait for the truth to be known,
let our communion be a harmonious one.
Let it be full of love and understanding,
so that our lives might be enriched by the rewards of our meeting.

With our eyes caught up in each other's gaze,
and our arms resting in sweet-warm embrace,
our spirits will cry tears of joy, even
as our hearts sing of the passion that is our love.
We are, one step closer to eternity.

Lawrence A. Young

If You Were Only But A Dream

If you were only but a dream, the thought you would linger, gently caressing my heart with a touch of hope.

If you were only but a dream, each day I'd be your sunshine and sprinkles of morning dew. I'd be a mid-summer's breeze gently stroking your body while whispering tender thoughts of nothing else but me.

If you were only but a dream, each night I'd undress you and place you upon a cloud. Then I'd be the moonlight that envelops your body with a shimmering glow of love.

If you were only but a dream, I'd be the water in which you bathe... warm and soothing to your mind, body, and soul.

If you were only but a dream, I'd be the covers between which you lay each night keeping your body warm until the morning light.

If you were only but a dream...
To You . . . I'd give unconditionally.
For You . . . I'd rearrange the stars to say "I Love You"
With You . . . I'd be forever strong.
Good Night My Love....If You Were Only but A Dream.

Rose E. Webb

Pizza Heaven

The pizza delivery boy had arrived
Carrying lots and lots of pizza pies
He looked around for a man named Mr. Porter
Who had supposedly placed the order
He put the pies down on the table
I was ready to eat, willing and able
Pepperoni and sausage as far as the eye could see
The two went together like perfect harmony
The delivery boy paced around on the floor
Until he gave up and walked out the door
No one picked up the pizza pies
And I don't think I'll ever know why
So let it be known to Mr. Porter
Who never picked up his pizza pie order
That the next time the delivery boy arrives
I'll be taking his pizza pies.

Michael P. Henry

Music In Our Lives Today

We have technology beyond the 'kin of most humans the world over,
Cars, Jets, and even the newest 'Land Rover'...
Our quest for 'More' and 'Bigger' has been answered one way or another,
But what about the spiritual side of 'little sister' or 'big brother'??
If I could give each of you a great gift today,
It would be 'Understanding' and 'Peace' as you go on your way..
But wait a moment, maybe nature has answered before we asked,
What about the human voice, or the gulls overhead as in the sun we basked?
There is music all around us as we hasten along doing life's chores,
Oh yes, Nature put music in the world, we just seem to ignore.
The sound of a brook as it runs on its way so sparkling and clear,
Sh! now, that's really music you hear.
On a busy street, the sirens, horns, and noise galore,
You've heard that sound in "Rhapsody in Blue", it's written in the score.
I've heard the loon as over a lake it took flight,
There's no musical sound that we can copy that sounds so right.
Nature gave us music from the beginning I feel,
And we humans tried to embellish it with noises and corny spiel.
But give me a person who is right with the world and its strife,
And I'll give you a human with "Music" in his or her life...

Marjorie M. Paquette

Food

What I want is apple pie and nice and warm a ham on rye.
I also want a cold cut sub and a big, cold ice cream tub.
I want mashed potatoes and fresh, shiny red tomatoes.
I want a chocolate cake and a large strawberry shake.
I want warm French toast and some fresh turkey roast.
I also want some Spanish rice and some Italian ice.
The final thing is a rocky road.
And on the last bite I'll just explode.

Marie Peters

Phantasm

Alone, between reality and fantasy, I dream of her.
Caught in thoughts of touch, fragrance, and sight.
Far these fain moments, I am there;
among the living, where there is light.

This darkness I see, broken only by fantasy.
We walk together hand in hand, touching, holding,
seeing sights unseen when I walk alone;
feeling, smelling, tasting, Light; Ecstasy.

Her eyes of Caribbean blue, gaze into my soul,
edging ever closer to the center of my heart.
Pulse racing, heart pounding, I await her touch.
On the stove the kettle whistles; Reality, Dark.

Marcy Kennemuth

Relationship

You may never fully understand
Cause it takes two to make
it work, and time.
So when, you find that some
one special, grab a hold of
him or her and don't never let go!

You look and like what is on
the outside, but it's the inside that counts.
If both hearts are willing and ready to accept the
love from one another to love means to give,
share, be honest and most of all to trust.
It's different with different people.

But, as long as you are
willing to share that love,
to accept responsibility
For keep your trust in one another,
and expect a little disagreement from time to time.

Shannon McCarty

Love for My Angel

It may come with the power of a hurricane
Causing helpless hearts to beat as if insane
It may come with a gentle spring breeze
Suddenly putting you on your knees
My love for her has grown over the years
Now that I am away my face flows with tears
Being with her again is my hope as I pray
for her to be my angel this very day

My heart has erupted with total satisfaction
for this woman who sparks such an attraction
Love flows through each and every vain
In this world she is what keeps me sane
She has helped my emotions grow and peak
Without her presence, my heart will grow weak
I looked in her direction and saw such a beautiful sight
Heaven had to be missing an angel that night

Now I could never regret the women I chose
Whose skin is as soft as a pedal from a rose
Love has no boundaries and knows no time
So eternity I will spend loving this angel of mine

Michael Calarco Jr.

Remembered Love

How sorrowful it is when love goes sour,
Causing the whole world to come tumbling down.
Enclosing all the grief with shocking pow'r.
Remorseful tears streaming, yet not a sound.
Illusions first hinder hearts from breaking.
Hearts holding false hopes within, amid dreams
Of wistful thoughts, no fear of forsaking.
The love, imperfect, not all that it seems.
Though unaccepting, the truth emerging,
All is in the past; it's time to move on.
Despite memories, constantly surging
O'er us upon waking, distorted, but fond.
I'll nevermore cling to our special bond,
Bittersweet, fragile and easily gone.

Lindsay Fitzpatrick

Keeping Long Lists

Man forces himself on all that exists
Changing, arranging, keeping long lists
A chromosome here, a chemical there
Girders and rods suspended in air

Hybrid plants with much greater vigor
New firing pins, a much faster trigger
Venom that cures the sting of a bee
Mutating you slowly in ways you can't see

Crack an egg from some incubator
Ride the waves on a great oil freighter
Fly through the o-zone as it gets thinner
Enjoying the taste of a microwave dinner

Slipping through cracks, reaching dimensions
Paving the way for the final ascension
Changing, arranging, keeping long lists
While there's still time and we still exist

Robert N. Wormington

Brothers In The Wind

I hear brothers in the wind
Chanting, praying and singing praises
To him, to them, to the one
The sound is not altered
Nor are the vibrations which are set and bound
Though there are many miles apart
They are of the same tribe
Beating upon a drum with all of their heart
Singing in their native tongues
Asking for the blessings which are given generously
The wind travels from afar
And carries all our words
The sun waits, the moon waits
The great one, the mystery, the invisible one
They hear brothers in the wind

Pedro Torres

Deliverance

From the beating of our slave owner.
God brought us from the cotton and tobacco fields.
God has brought us.

From the filed of chopping cotton and pulling corn
God brought us.

From the hiding under pot and closed doors to pray
God has brought us.

From living in houses where we could look out
and see the moon and stars at night.
God has brought us.

Martha L. Holt

Change

As change looks you in the eyes you fear if it's the devil himself.
If you look past those eyes into the inner sole of that change,
You'll realize it's not the devil, but yourself behind that fear.
Look deeper into the sole, and find the courage to go on.
Once that courage is found it's no longer the fear, but your
hopes and dreams.

Tonia Houttekier

Nature's Cry

Man, Man, can't you see? You take away my
children, the trees, rivers and animals. You replace
them with concrete building, malls, and parking
lots.

You have taken my rainbow of flowers, and
my fruits that I give. That would have sustained
you as long as you live.

You choke me with your chemicals, your
factories, and your smoke. You may become
richer, but soon you will be broke.

My forest are shrinking. My waters are
polluting, and my animals are dying. Man, Man,
can't you see what you've done to me?

I am the one who sustains you. I give you
the materials to build. Remember if it was not for
me you could not live.

My animals, rivers, and trees are dying; and
they need all of your help. I am getting sick by the
minute. Can't you see the tears I have wept?

Shawn D. Johnson

Untitled

A Christmas thought by Lloyd Frederick 1994
Christmas time is here for all to know
Time to count blessings and let our worries go
Celebrate Christ's birthday and spread good cheer
Time to look forward to a happy new year
Let joy ring out it's time to shout
Goodwill to man that's what's it's all about
Spread the good word for all to hear
Thank our Lord for those we hold dear
Leave our troubles, put them aside
Call family and friends and be happy with pride
No matter where you may be thank of happiness not misery
Even though it's been 2000 years
We have our Lord and have no fears.

Lloyd Frederick

Memories Of Our Summer Love

Through the mist of time, I can see your face
Close to mine, in a tender embrace.
Sweet memories of a summer love,
Kissed by moonbeams from heaven above.

Stored in my heart, forever and ever,
Safe from time and tarnish they will never.
Priceless treasures, more precious than gold,
Always there for me to behold.

They grow like flowers, but never wither or die,
They bloom with each year that passes by.
They brighten each sad and somber day,
In my heart they will always stay.

Sometimes when everything seems to go wrong,
I think of the words of our old love song.
Although we are miles and miles apart,
"Goodnight my love," you're still in my heart.

Ruth T. George

The Storms Of Summer

Do you love the misty rain, spraying on the window pane;
Cloudy skies from up above, hiding the warmth of the sun's love;
Fierce wind whirling all around, deeply whistling an eerie sound;
Violent thunder bursting in rage, beating a rhythm like a drummer on stage?

Do you love the passionate storm, spilling on the summer morn;
Relentless sleet pouring fast, startling the animals in the grass;
Large hail falling all around, loudly cracking it's shotgun sound;
Streaks of lightning from miles up high, dancing and flashing across the sky?

Do you love the sunny skies, bringing warmth when storms subside;
Colorful arcs of the rainbow, leading the eye to a place unknown;
Pillows of clouds floating away, dispersing quickly the sky of gray;
Wondrous miracles coming to life? Through God's grace we see these sights!

Pamela Dawn Cottrell

Autumn Leaves

The leaves are tumbling from the sky, to cover up the ground, the colors dazzle all a glow, to grace the "Autumns Crown."

The pumpkins mask now hollow, as it withers on the doorstep, now a pie, a turkey thigh, almost November, don't forget.

The crested moon on crisp cold nights, your breath upon the air, the swishing sound from leaves kicked 'round, as you hurry with your cares.

Natures takes the posture, like signs upon a map, she prepares with daily grandeur, for the long and wintery nap.

We begin the countdown, the year comes to a close, old friends reunited, new ones just a rose.

The season brings a gladness, cause it makes us all reflect, on family ties, soft goodbyes, of loves we shant forget.

Larry W. Moses

Where The Children Play

Before you close your eyes and run away.
Come see where the lost children play.
Look in the cold room where they are dying.
Walls crush their skulls, they are crying.
Piercing screams ripping through the silence.
Terrified eyes praying to stop the violence.
Painful blows knocking you to the floor.
Screams for help behind the locked door.
Fist banging on the wall, needing someone there.
But Mommy wants you dead and Daddy doesn't care.
Smelling the alcohol, feeling the ugly touch.
This is the only time Daddy loves you so much.
Tears turn to ice when they laugh at your sadness.
Swallowing your pain, you join in the madness.
Silent screams still cry behind your empty eyes.
Love turns to hate and you learn to survive.
Shrilling screams scratch out the tears.
You have become what you always feared.
Skulls crushing, your child is crying.
Laughter shrieks on, your child is dying.

Tricia Bruzard

I Will Say This But Once

I am a human being, I am a man, I am an American of African descent.
I help settle America.
I help build America.
I help govern America.
I help defend America.
I help Entertain America.
And I will help destroy America before I give it up or let
Anyone else have it.

Leonard Young

Alone

I sit alone watching for your face, I think I see you coming, but then you disappear into the darkness around me. For an instant I am happy, warm and fulfilled, but then I go back to a cold, sad and unfulfilled state. Why do we have to be apart, when will you return to me? Please don't go away, I'm afraid without you, and for you. For an instant I feel safe and protected, loved and cared for, but then you disappear, leaving me cold. I think I hear your footsteps and then I get all excited and filled with joy, but then you never come. I think I feel your touch on my shoulders, but then I realize it's a dream. I realize I'm alone in a cold...cold, dark room. Waiting to be rescued from the unknown evils that lurk about, I look for you, but alas, you are lost far from me, and can not hear my screams in the night. No one hears them so why should you? I love you and I'll wait for you, forever if I must. meanwhile, I will remain alone with the perils that lurk in darkness, and I will cry your name in hopes that you will one day be close enough to hear me, and will answer my call. I'm alone in a place with darkness and no windows, evil and little good, war and no peace. Please take me from it, listen to my scream, can you hear me yet?

Rebecca A. de Velder

Receive Grace

Our Holy Father authors verses of love
Conducting is the Son with notes from above
As the Holy Spirit gives voice like a dove
Saying grace is what the gospel is made of

That writes new songs onto a heart like a page
Utilizing a working lyrical stage
Upon which God's word acts in every age
Blazing in our souls, wisdom makes it the rage

For Christians to live by the Scriptures' sweet song
Giving thanks and praising the Lord all day long
With pure hearts ringing instruments like a gong
As Holiness and Love keeps right from all wrong

And fills our hearts with joy, causing us to dance,
Quickening our spirits, making all minds prance
For Jesus; the Bridegroom, the Church does romance
Following God's plan we are not here by chance

Christ gives us words to sing in every place
Inspiring music with His shining face
For all the souls of man in this fallen race
Receiving God's gift of Salvation called Grace

Pat Ireland

Untitled

My love is natural as running streams,
Containing the design for perfection
With softest light of heaven her eye beams;
These essentials increase my affection.
She speaks: the gentlest breeze overcomes me,
And with her breathing, I do sigh and moan;
Affected by the Moon as is the sea,
This mercurial love is not alone.
She sings as the lark, and like him flies
Encompassing the world under her wing.
Staring deep into all things with her eyes,
Obed'ance due her, more than to a king.
  And so is my love with nature a part,
  And always it may thrive within my heart.

Paul Woodall

Untitled

This cruel insanity-what perfection. Keeps me coming back, keeps me consuming. To sleep, to write, to run, to illuminate my fault and fight the sun although I'm much a part of him. Hear the pounding in my head. The fever that lies; Waiting for the moment, to pounce upon the thread; To emulate the sweltering passions-the substance of this pod; Its fertility the embroidered: with the lines of my palms, the way of my walk, the hour I became...this motion of silence I've been here before, and I've got one leg up, 'cause I find I'm keeping score. A stranger to this fine shape of human dignity; my iron field of cold ooth rendering. Spotting the ache in my head, thieving for the belly of the swine. Pigs get their fill!...so why can't I? Clasping this precious madness to the stem of my brain (the image in my hands) to place me in the light. This final sensation plaguing me, but I keep smiling. So don't you worry, don't you cry for me. No, you'll know I'll be alright. 'Cause I've got my ear to the ground, the cool wet grass against my cheek; the way the blades that part of my lips. Hear the sound they fight to create. They leak the news into my breath gathered up into my consciousness, no longer able even if I tried, to spit out the fever's crying quest. They tell me my wish will soon arrive; to be held and covered completely. They tell me every thing's going to be alright.

Ruth Flores

The Lovely Gaze

The most beautiful things in the world
Could be seen through this priceless mirror
Glance of inaccessible splendor
Reflect of the dearest gift in whole

What treasure could be so rich and suave?
Promise of sweetness coming in wave
To those whose prayers go beyond eyes
Offering its quintessence in grace

Call of Mother Nature in labor
For her children in crude affliction
Everywhere there is barely ration
In regard to Mercy and Candor

Ray of Sublime Light that transcends Earth!
Souvenir of the Original Peace
We still carry in our deepest dreams
May you bring us all humanity
An everlasting Happiness ...forever in Unity!

Roosevelt Carre

Departure Of Youth

Once puerile mischief ruled this mortal case,
Coursing full its breadth and height in vessels laid.
'Twas youth's yearning set astir, propelled by haste,
To outstrip time's seize of vim 'fore its fade.
For time is the despot that holds full sway
With allotment of self 'twixt young and old -
Filling those fresh, emp'ting those in decay;
Quick'ning new with warmth, slowing aged with cold.
So, if nature's craft deceives the sharp eye
With image foreign to expectation,
Think not that it's flawed vision; it is I
Who survives, but less'd by declination.
Beginning and end, at start, did conspire
To set flame aglow then smolder the fire.

Samuel W. Beasley

In A Hurting World

Born with a disease, may not see another day,
cried blood tears, so they might stay.
Guns, knives and drugs is killing the nation,
call on God, he is our salvation.
Today's society is filled with hatred, prejudice and lust,
just stand on God's word and count on his trust.
Bomb threats, fear and suicide is why we are not succeeding,
we are jewels in God's presence, let us not be defeated.
Leaders, we must be for our children to see, that America
has to be drug free.
One minute your in the crack house, frying your brain,
next your in jail, just look how we fail
Sisters and Brothers are hurting each day
when are we going to stop, stand up
and just pray.

Reginald Holmes

Midsummer Night Songs

Songs of night, listless and blissful,
crying out for reasons, known not to all.
Songs of the night, peaceful and distant,
listen now to the darkness call:
Zidget, hiss, creek, crawl,
bleak yet striving nights echo dost fall.

Songs of a summer night, they hinder the sun.

Light batting moth, tilting his mills,
silk covered wings flutter till still.
June bug jubilee, lasting all night-
soon though, August, shall be stopping their strike.

But alas it's still summer,
and the dew's on the lawn-
and slowly again, the birds beckon dawn.

Lewis I. Chance

David McGee

(Died August 1995 Hurricane Felix)

The boys laughed into the shrieking wind, as surf crashed
Dancing high-stepping, salty seas swirling, spraying
Eyes flashed, riveted to towering white mountains of foam
"Hurricane warnings!" one yelled at the abandoned Atlantic
"Never, in the Emerald Isle!" another joked and they thrust their
Guiness high, clinking
Four lads who had grown together, toasting jigging,
singing Irish songs.
Experiencing bonding exhilaration One with nature and its power

Waves swelled crested surged, tides sneaking, creeping
Unsuspecting, it caught them chest-high, rolling over them,
keeping them down.
Riptiding, pummeling, pounding, pulling, it seemed alive
Survival instinctive, they twisted belly down, grasping digging
holding sand, gasping breaths
One cried out, a primal scream, the undertow sucking him
Churning, wrapping around him, claiming him

Three reached him off-balance, flailing, desperate
Hands grabbed hands holding, cramping, slipping,
Hands weakening, loosening, fingers brushing fingers
Losing the tug of war between them and the ferocious surf
Helpless they scanned the waters, eyes searching pitch black
Agony replaced ecstasy as they heard David's final, hopeless scream
Then silence, in the screaming rage of the wind

Paulette A. Burrier

Show Me How To Fly

Life will take your dreams, and throw them into the sea.
Daring them to rise and soar, to be tamed or to be free!!

Love awakens dreams buried so long ago.
Now I have a reason to chase them, places I never dared to go.

Let me see above the clouds, what great things I can do.
Let me soar with wings of eagles let me live because of you!

You must jump off a mountain to make yourself fly.
It takes courage not to limit yourself, to how low or how high!!

Just let the wind take you, don't look at your past...
...and you will soar through the clouds, to have your dreams at last!!!

Rachel M. Schlosser

Watching From A Distance

If what happens in life could be controlled,
Death would not have come to my door so soon.
You see I wasn't ready to let go of you,
I didn't get to see you grow up.
The first year of your life was so memorable,
But I left to early and missed to much.
I didn't get to teach you to tie your shoes,
To see you reach the first grade and graduate from high school.
I didn't get to show you how to bit a baseball,
and watch you hit your first home run.
I didn't get to watch you leave for your first date,
and I didn't get to see you walk down the aisle.
I didn't get to see you enjoy the experience of fatherhood,
and I didn't get to see my first grandchild.
You see life shut its door on me and left me waiting,
Waiting for the day we'll be together again.

Nathan A. Chiaravalle

Family

The beginning of one's life and existence
Deep beneath the ruins of today
One has no choice, though they have resistance,
But to accept the member and their way.

Keeping within the walls of the future and
Relating to one and others troubles
Staking no claim to mutual things
But living and caring within the family bubble.

Giving the things that one has to give
Helping those who are weak or in need.
Thinking of one another during good times and
Bad, holding hands during sorrow and greed.

Loving and sharing the faith we have
Being a caring and humble host
It's God's will that the family shall
Stand, in the name of the Father, Son
And Holy Ghost. Amen.

Samuel R. Dawson

Crossings

"Don't cross the bridge 'till you come to the river".
I remember, I said that before
But there are so many rivers and so many bridges,
And ahead, I can see even more.

What I must remember 'bout bridges and rivers-
They can only be crossed one by one,
And there's Someone to hold you and Someone to help you
Until after your crossings are done.

Norma Russell

First Impulse

I love you from the still place—the first impulse.
Deep in its one-celled silence,
where the deaf and dumb in anticipates
and the face of all we are to love is forged, you were my thought-trailing stars for seed across the membrane of desire
till I held your face in my aching eyes,
after children and sorrow and years —
the first face.

Our from my want for your tenderness,
to know your hands sculpting the stones of my skull with intent—
fierce urgency—to merge with the breath and bones of me,
I summoned your life with the driving force of my tongueless cry.

Was it your passion, the brilliance of your star shining in me
that awakened my longing from its solitary bed—
that quickened my hope with promise?
As yet, before I felt your form,
your face whose light gives utterance in the still place—
the silent cell where we create,
where we sense the others's star shining to be known,
I loved you.

Victoria M. Oliver

Grandpa

He was a shadow of the man I knew, a face without a name.
Despite what I have learned from books, I'll never know his pain.

He used to be a spry old gent... "What shall I be today"?
A gardener, a carpenter, a fisherman he'd play.

Death has a way of robbing life long before one dies.
He steals the people that we know, right before our eyes.

He called for Grandpa once before, many years ago.
The doves were pulling at his feet, but Grandpa wouldn't go.

But this time when the doves flew down, they found a tired man.
They didn't have to fight so hard, he didn't make a stand.

He said "goodbye" to all he loved, his hammer, and his plow.
He said "goodbye" to all his pain, he smiles always now.

We'll miss you Grandpa, on this earth, more than we can say.
But we're happy that you found a place to garden, fish, and play.

Sheila Goole

Journey Through The Substances

When we began our journey's into life,
different fluxes of force or "substances"
enforce their wills or "influences" on the
pool's mixture of our beginning being.
As children we are but only lumps of clay
unexpectedly being shaped or molded by
alternating auras of growth from the substances
that surround us. Each substance leaving
a minute residue or imprint into our clay
minds and spirits. Through the passage
of growth, the imprints that are left in the
mold began to manifest themselves in our
psyche. Some of the manifestations can
make us cold, hard and unfeeling. While
the others can be warm, soft and full
of life. And finally as time passes, our
forms continue to solidify. Finally the mold
hardens as we burst from our childish
cement cell into a statue of adulthood. So it ends,

The Journey Through The Substances...

Lee K. Wells

Kuala Lumpur

Malasian people
Dim ancient legend
Flows floating on the river

One after another
After the hard labor of a day
The place of promise where they gathered around
The grief of meeting and parting
Feeling tired of
The river flows from two into one

A mosque at this place
The descendants of ancestors
Pilgrims are forming a queue in a procession
Civilization and nature together as well
Kuala Lumpur
The capital is breathing

Still today
The river water
Karma
Fluttering travellers' hearts
May flow

Sung-Hi Lee

Possible?

To rebuild from nothing - is it worth the try?
Disgraced, a drunkard, always living a lie.
All efforts dashed at every turn.
It seems so hopeless, yet still I yearn:
For squandered fortunes and self aplomb,
Atoning for omissions due those from the womb,
Break bread once more with old friends forsaken
And personify success to a love just taken.
But, rationally comes the somber realization,
These quixotic dreams are but a fantasization.
For with a pauper's purse and only a pen,
Is it really possible to rebuild again?

Samuel M. Keck

Parasites

Bloodsucking creatures that live off the efforts of others
Disgusting? Sometimes.
Deserving? Occasionally.
Hardworking? Rarely.
Useful? Never.
What purpose do they serve, these creatures of no value?
Do they get rid of things that others have no use for?
Are they there simply to live, and let others suffer from infection and disease?
Or can these leeches, these mosquitoes, these parasites, evolve into something useful, something strong, something worth respect?

Mark Robertson

"Time"

Time; like a machine, tuned and perfectly suited for its purpose,
Constantly running, constantly changing things,
changing lives, faces and never stopping.
The face of a little girl now is a work of art,
sculpted and designed in such a short time.
The stars, always dropping, always burning;
The earth, always changing, moving, always running...
Until time takes its toll, until time runs the life from everything;
drowning all glory.
Until...only time can tell a story...

Ronald Lewis Williams

Untitled

Letters, cards, bills and junk mail too.
Dishes, laundry, vacuuming and
thinking about you.
Groceries, work, the office and stuff
Makes me see that your voice is not enough.

You are there and I am here.

Daily routines, schedules and plans.
Meetings, classes and recycling cans.
Every minute of every hour, everyday
Makes me proud to be your fiancee.

I've talked about you, and me together
trying to express my love for you, Sweet Heather.
Everyone knows that you're not around,
you're out and about on Tennessee ground.
But that's not stopping me, oh no siree,
I'm talking all about you constantly.

My days are lonely and long, but at
night I dream that you're singing my favorite song.
It's the only thing that pulls me through.
So hurry up and come home, 'cause I miss you.

L. Houle

Secret Love

How do you tell someone how much you care?
Do you risk it all, hoping he'll still be there?
True feelings are hard to show,
Especially when you fear that person will go.
So many things are left unspoken.
Should I take the chance of getting my heart broken?
Should I say my true feelings? Lay them all out to see?
Would he listen, or just turn away from me?
And if I tell him, will his reply
Bring happiness or a tear to my eye?
I don't know if I'm ready for his response.
My heart is still frail, and I couldn't bear the loss.

Why does something so beautiful look so deceiving?
Is it all giving and no receiving?
How many tears will have to fall
Before he will realize I could be his all?
Does he know or does he care?
Should I accept such a dare?
When and if I do decide to speak my mind,
Hopefully a blossoming love is what I'll find.

Stacey Woods

Why?

Why do people have to fight?
Does it make them stronger or make them right?
Daddy yells at Mommy then mommy yells at me.
Don't they know how wrong it is? Dear Jesus can't they see?
I know they love each other and they both love me to.
Can't they stop yelling? Is there something I can do?
Can't they see how bad it is to hurt each other so?
Why don't they stop fighting then their love can start to grow?
Let them learn that fighting wrong before it is too late.
Let me grow up to know their love and not to know their hate.

Sherley J. Smith

Desert Storm

Bullets pelt the ground
In a rain of endless fire.
Steam arises forth
from the dry, cracked, desert sand.
The desert storms have arrived.

Paul S. Kim

Does Thy Bear

Is thy the bear does hunt in the stream?
Does thy come from a beam?
Does thy eat fish shot in the head?
Does thy have a soft quilted bed?
Give me some answers, Please!
Can I have a Kleenex, I'm going to sneeze?
Does thy have a job? Does thy open a door with a knob?
While sleeping, do you snore?
Does thy buy food from a store?
Does thy bear have any fun? Does thy eat when the day is done?
Could you tell me why thy is called a Bear?
Why does thy have so much hair?
It would be nice if thy would respond.
Does thy bear swim in a pond?
Does thy bear eat like a hog? Does thy bear breath smog?
Does thy bear run around? Does thy ever get found?
Answer these questions, I'm getting bored. Do you even have a lord?
"NO I don't," replied the bear, "But I do have a lot of hair."
"You're no good at all," said the boy.
"I'm going home to play with a toy."

Reed A. Day

Clouded Minds

One steps too far, one crosses the line, not knowing what they've done.
Before there were two who stood and fought, now stands only one.
You can't undo what you have done, and you have been so blind.
You finally see violence for what it is, the voice of an ignorant heart and mind.
With hate and prejudice clouding your thoughts, you never can see what is true.
Every man and every woman, the same as me the same as you.
There are no differences in hopes or in dreams,
yet we continue to kill as voices turn to screams.
They say "No", and we say "Yes", can we never agree on what is right.
Can we never live in perfect peace, weather our skin is dark or light.
No, we must carry high pitched whistles, and numerous cans of mace.
I hope someday to live among you my friends, no matter what your race.

Sierra Pollock

Paternal Pride

In Loving Memory Of My Dad

He passed along to me, his son - What, were he here, he would have done
Nostalgia fills my reverie - with all the things he used to be.
Gentle a man with everyone - though sometimes too aloof for fun.
The image lingers ever long - of him decrying right from wrong.
Now often as I reminisce - about the man I sorely miss,
Meticulous, maybe to a fault - yet passing time cannot assault
Embers of memory burning like fire - my mentor was my friend and sire.
Who taught a toddler to behave - and showed his son the way to shave.
Often I try to emulate - his specialties which made him great
And even though I saw him sob - the day he did that perfect job.
Today I'm standing in his place.- and pray that someone has the grace
To view my works and say OUT LOUD,
OF THIS YOUR FATHER WOULD BE PROUD.

Richard D. Fuchs

Simple Pleasures

Clouds caress the reaching fingers of majestic mountain tops,
Hot asphalt kissed by Summer rains fragrant cooling drops,
The distant drone of an airplane brushing across the azure sky,
Birds sweet singing in the dawn, to end your lullaby.
The perfume of new mown hay drifting through a lazy summer afternoon,
Crickets evening chorus set against a silver moon,
They are only simple pleasures yet my heart lifts up in song,
For the things that get forgotten as we rush our lives along.

Roxanne Hale

Children Need Parents

Dedicated to my two daughters, Ellen and Michelle

If you have children, listen to what they say.
Don't tell them you're busy, don't push them away.
Don't shut them out when they need to talk.
If necessary, take their hands in yours and go for a walk.

Children are human and need special care.
They need you to guide them and help them beware.
There are so many ways a child can tell
That with his problems you wish not to dwell.

Try to understand what your children are thinking.
Their thoughts are important, as eyes are of blinking.
Love them and help them through each and every day,
By being there for them in their own special way.

It's not always easy to be the best parent around;
But it is important to our children to have their feet on solid ground.
Pray with them, play with them, your girl or your boy,
For you will find you'll all have an inner joy.

Be there and be strong for them with each and every day
And they'll be strong when it's time for them to go their own way.
Above all, pray and trust God to lead you and guide you
And you'll always have the love of your children right there beside you.

Shirley S. (Farr) Carmell

Disposable Intimacies

It's hard for me to speak my mind as I want so for you to care
Don't worry, I understand the realities of this affair.

God, there is so much I want to know, do you feel the same as I?
No, please don't answer that. I fear another part of me might die.

You see, I'm only held together with a bit of spit and glue
But, you did hold me like you love me...yet I know that can't be true.

So, please be my substance for a time, as long as that time can be
Of course, I understand you must know you can anytime be free.

Oh, am I making you nervous? It is really not my intent.
Just bring me thru this one night, please that is really all that I meant.

Hold me close like you love me and reassure me that I'll be fine.
Oh God, I'm scared! Please acknowledge me with even the slightest sign.

I am fragmented and it has become too much for me to bear.
When morning come's I will not keep you, I swear it, I would not dare
See, I understand, I too have had disposable intimacies...too many for me to share

too many for me to bear.

Bobbi Schevitz

The Beauty of the Rose

As I sit here quietly looking at this rose in bloom,
each petal so perfect it brightens my room.
The stem of the rose is long and slender.
It's strength of the rose upon which sits the bud so tender.

As I look at the leaves it reminds me of the
different paths our lives lead.
The different people I've known and all the love I've shown.
As I see the dew that kisses each rose it reminds me of a love
that has touch my heart which I will never let part.

As I look deeper into my rose I feel the velvety touch of each petal
which caress my skin, it awaken my senses in each part of my body
and limbs. As each petal unfolds the heart of the rose,
so does the beauty of life and its bittersweet
memories of love and strife.

Peggy Frost

Eye Witness

Hear the boom boom? Clear another tomb. Beware prepare the temple of doom.. Death exhumes in all the rooms. Replace the smell of sweet perfumes Gun powder fills the air sirens blare everywhere. Occupants in a trance just stare. She caught a bullet her body is wet leaking freaking fluid like a faucet. Blood's dripping her friends tripping. No since sobbing, she'd be gun pop, pop, pop, popping, boosting and robbing if her heart were throbbing instead, two to the head. Body spread like; a crash dummy yep, def like a mummy caught in a trap now she's taking a dirt nap, at the cemetery when they burry friends cry, why? Tell lies, like how she's missed with teary eye's why they cry in the mist of the storm same mudder didn't utter Gods name once when the body was warm. What a shame who you blame? Erry day girls play this way: Let's get ready to gamble; on this corner you a goner mate if you date these ladies from hades. Hot blazing tricking and raising. "Nobody move no body get hurt, life is round, now you down! Covered with dirt. In hell you yell cuss "Throw us some ice" well you should been nice. Roll the dice pay the price. Hypocrites die twice. Kick the flab as eyes blab square biz their it is. This one down and dirty from the underground in D.C. Lord have Mercy!!

Beetle

Untitled

The Victorian manor, flanked by the poplars like a child's cut out dotted line exists still at the end of a lane of dirt and stone.
A horse from my childhood whinnies like the pealing of the dinner bell which called the farm boys in to dinner.
The broken walls of the stable are like schooners dashed against rocks of an unlit beach.
The aging women on the porch rock in the heat of the day smelling of peach and rose water.
They wait for their final baptism with needles and scissors; potting plants, reading magazines, and making pillow for nieces.
As my car and I travel up the driveway the air vibrates, the boxer dog yelps, and the aunts unlock the gate at the top of the veranda stairs
Then the ladies and I return to the rocking chairs on the porch, the only escape from the humid closeness of the mid-summer heatwave.
They offer iced water, fresh milk, tea and cake.
Declining, I settle into pillows stitched by hands, quite wrinkled, but more able than mine.
The afternoon passes with only the snip of scissors to count the time.

Michelle Phelan

Color/Sound - For Paul

Black and white ivories, sounds impress half-tones.
Double sharps, doubly sharp - white flats, flatted to black.
Xs cancel - unnaturally - chords bind. Then freed - sudden
arpeggio flights - up and down.

Ups and downs - the leit motif.
Time is a one-way street. Space is enclosed.
The world is black and white - or muddied grey,
But you hear reds, purples, yellows -
Petals swaying in the wind.
But white snow sifts, freezing red petals,
Tied notes held too long.

You solve the riddle of the silver key
And storm the dark tower.
Sub-dominated, modulated,
In a green meadow
You silently lay your head on the black, earthen block -
Stretching your hand for the white Pearl.

Teresa R. Amuso

Your Wonderful, Your Living, Beauty

So pleasurable the field scene of these — of God.
Dressed in crispylike clothing
Their flower parts seem to say things of Love.

Tulip blossoms' justlike song
With a sureness withers all of mundane wrong.

Oh radiant blossoms — these tulips
Uttered on my entreating lips,

Happy flower,
Dwell, a part of me, empower
Through your wonderful, your living, beauty
Within my spirit permanently.

Rose Galfano

The Spirit Sadness

Blue-green feathered flowers
drift on a question of why.
Slow motion free-form flying,
through a midnight sky.
And all along the horizon,
a million beams of pinpoint light,
slice in all directions.

Fly up along the fractures
that elude our close detection.
Like a broken pane of window glass, screaming.
Don't you miss the dreamlike cloud?
A pale disguise of focus,
tears upon his faith.

Crawl along the outer shell,
transparent to all dimension
Held up in place by standing waves
and shadow friends with hollow lives.
Layers of sound depression
Don't you wish you could fall through, too?
Can't seem to find the words in this place.

Troy D. Street

Choosing the Peaceful Land

I have been in the United States for twenty years.
During the whole time I have been living here,
I realize that the original settlers
And thereafter the continuous comers
Were coming largely from Northern Europe
And other countries on earth...
These people of different cultures
With a purpose of attaining a beautiful future
Left their homelands and established in the United States...
They were absorbed into American life soon or late,
And created a homogeneous population...
They surely have been very fond
Of America - of the United States,
For they have found here plentiful freedom and happiness.
Even to this day many more people
Are longing to get to America too.
Why? - Because they are not unlike the birds
That choose the peaceful land on earth
So as to settle on the branch.

Vinh Dinh Ngo

Working Together

A FORK and a KNIFE were created one day,
Each to serve in a very special way.

They were equally important. Each was meant to serve.
The KNIFE was strong and straight. The FORK had quite a curve!

The curvy FORK had four large prongs
To jab, to poke, and push food along.

While the KNIFE was flat and was made to cut,
To spread and lift and to do lots of stuff.

It was not by chance. It was not by fate.
These two fell in love over a dinner plate.

When a steak was served that was mighty raw,
The FORK had to hold - while the KNIFE had to saw.

When they realized what they had done,
And that working together could be fun -

That dashing blade - that old cutting KNIFE
Asked the curvy FORK to be his wife.

It wasn't long afterwards - in fact it was soon,
They included in their family a little silver SPOON!!

Loa Lee Nelson

Seven And Eight

Seven and eight, frightened and confused,
eighteen years old and nothing is new.
a death is a death, something I can't understand,
nothing I expected, like nothing I had planned.
Looking down on her, although it's the end,
I know that she's gone, yet I still pretend.
I want her to reach out, and give me hug,
someone please wake me, give a tug.
the rooms illuminations, just pull me in,
the soft colors, low lights, where to begin.
The sound of shaky laughter, fills the room,
deep through the laugher, I feel all their gloom.
Sadness and sorrow, everyone tries to hide,
Although it's easy to see, how bad we're hurting inside.
I want to cry, yet I want to give my support,
I realize now, to live everyday to it's fullest, for life is too short!
Seven and eight, on my tip toes, what's inside the box, I don't know.
Eighteen years old, and I know now,
I try to understand, but I don't know how.

Stacy M. Malson

Untitled

In the beginning
Emptiness; all is void
Thought arises from a pool of possibilities
Giving birth to you.

In your childhood
Creativity; all is formed
You utter the words that give meaning to your life
All things are created by you.

In your maturity
Fertility; all is reborn
I utter the words that give meaning to my life
All things recreated, all things renewed.

Throughout eternity
From one life to the next
For you my spirit searches
Nine are the months it longs to rest

Through you I will be reborn
Through you the work is done
For you are my eternal mother
And I am your eternal son.

William R. Kamenski

"Love"

Seeing is believing, never nothing you hear.
Emptiness between us is something that I fear:
Everlasting love is the way I want it to be.
Inside my heart is a book, I want you to see.
Never miss a page read it line for line.
Give up all your doubts remember it for all times;
Inside the book is a riddle you hold the only key.
Slip the key of love inside and set the riddle free;
Believe in what you are reading it's totally true,
Everyone can see it but it's meant only for you;
Love is in paragraph written with such care.
In between the lines is the love we share.
Eternally together is the way this books is written.
Velvet tender clouds above where we are sittin';
Entwined in each others arms never letting go.
Nothing to guess about the book plainly shows:
Gather all these words and except the love you are receiving!
Never believe what you hear only what you are seeing.

Victor Lafountain

Winter Ice

A clear transparent, cold, dead weight
Encasing branches in a tomb-
An hour - a week -how brief the time,
Until the sun befriends the future blooms.

Along the fence the crystal forms
Sparkling with all colors bright.
The patterns with their diamond shapes
Produce a truly wondrous sight.

The pines form drooping skirts
Providing shelter from the weather
As an old hen clucks her chicks to warmth
So the pine boughs do resemble feathers.

Ice is nature's starch for blades of grass
They stand alone straight, tall and unbending
While sturdy oaks, locust and apple branches fall.
Their groans into the night air sending.

The clearness of the icy ground
Does provide a long white view
Yet this sparkling wonder hides more shapes and buildings
Than green foliage and skies of azure blue.

Marie M. Maggard

To Poetry

Poetry! Dearest and gentlest of muses;
Enchantment flows from your eloquent phrases.
Brimming with imagery, you charm and delight.
and imbue with pleasure all those you invite.

Of heroes in battle you have boldly sung;
Your masterful epics thrill old and young;
Such vivid scenes of history you portray,
Like tales richly woven within a tapestry.

How nobly the tender verses outpour.
Blissful reveries on nature spring forth.
the earth applauds the golden praise -
fields, streams and forests, their voices raise!

Alas, my muse, your closest companion is Love;
Metaphoric expressions take wing like a dove,
Ardently capturing this rapturous emotion -
You render it with endearing affection.

Trudy Julian

Soul Witness

There is a way, that seemeth righteous man, but the end thereof, is a fall from grace. With blindness, He is led, onto a pathway of grief, and stumbling into darkness, he grasps deceit. He knows not the uncertainty, that lies ahead, but, stiff necked and determined, he is surely misled!

Unwise in judgement, and lacking sound wisdom, but still he remains steadfast and strong unknowing of the doom, that lurks beyond, he continues his journey, so unaware, of the dangers he's treading.

Filled with selfishness, and worldly greed, he searches endlessly, seeking to fulfill empty need. Desiring forbidden pleasures, that destroy the soul, and so vain in his ways, it's no wonder, he's so bold!

All puffed up, with envy and pride, he becomes more boastful, in his ungodly ways. As his conscience sleeps, he dares to climb higher using evil to destroy those who are weaker.

So sad, it is, to watch man at work, witnessing his soul as it slowly self destruct!!!

Mary F. Nicholson

One Thought

How do you accept losing someone,
Especially when it is one very young?
How do you face a mother in pain?
What words of wisdom could possibly explain?

We try to accept what we don't understand,
Looking for answers and a helping hand.
The true answer lies with the one we can't see;
One who's existence is a mystery.

"The Lord giveth; and the Lord taketh away..."
The reason He has is not for us to say.
One thought comforts me; perhaps it will you
Our Lord in Heaven needs babies, too.

Vickie L. Scraper

Faith Of Sincerity

Oh mighty one up above
eternally endless for all
and in my mind, attempting to find you—
to touch your thoughts, grab some advice
and milk you for all the goodness
there is left.

Oh mighty one up above
inevitably questionable for all
and in my soul, fighting your strength—
trying to succumb, as to fall into a belief
that may not be sincere
for I seek the truth.

Oh mighty one up above
object of desire for all
and in my heart, wanting to feel your presence
need for loving guidance, longing for security
lending my ear to your silent whispers
won't you raise your voice to me please?

Staci Fischer Laico

I'll Miss You

I'll miss you
I'll miss you on good mornings and bad days.
In happy times and sad times
I'll miss you and your smile
I'll miss you and the caress you always gave.
I'll miss you and the kiss that made my day
I'll miss you when the night is long and dark
I'll miss you when the ache is strong and unyielding
I'll miss you but always I'll love you.

Pam Lewis

To My Children, Magean And Patrick

Wake each morning with delight at whom you see in the mirror
Even if things seem a little fuzzy, blink again, it will get clearer
After all, it's the start of a new day and it's only beginning
A good attitude and a zeal for life will make you come out winning.

There's so many things I need to tell you and you need to learn
There are going to be particular assets only you will be able to earn
Be true to yourself and all else will fall into line
Be aware that there will be times when that line may be very fine.

Honesty, confidence, and selflessness I try and teach
With much love and determination, your being, I hope to reach
Distinct convictions of what is wrong and what is right I have taught
Know that these values are not just commodities that can be bought.

At night when I'm alone and have time to reflect
I search my heart, mind, and soul to find my neglect
I pray, dear God to guide me with tender yet resourceful direction
To help mold you into individuals, not striving for perfection.

I've made so many mistakes and been so overbearing
It wasn't through thoughtlessness, just a mother's caring
I realize you cannot possibly understand right now
You will, I promise, when you become a parent that's how.

Mary R. Dooley

Dear Father

Oh Father, where would I be without you?
Even now, when I talk to you,
You make my problems seem so few.
Remember when I was small?
You took me in your arms,
And there I felt that only you,
Yes, you could protect me from all harms.
As I grew older, with my wild imagination,
It was you who enjoyed me with complete fascination.
And through the mind shattering teen years,
It was you, Father, who helped me understand the tears.
Now, because of your understanding,
I am a woman with a free spirit.
And I want you to know I mean this when you hear it,
"I love you, Father." Thanks for being you.

Rhonda Gilley Young

A Poem About Clover Reed

As the day goes by, I see an
everlasting smile on your small furry face.
I see the rain fade away and the sun begin to shine.

I see my everlasting sorrow and pain that fills my heart start
to fade as you start to look my way, your beautiful eyes
filled with excitement and happiness.
It brings a smile to my face.

You my dear friend are dearer than anyone else in the world
and don't forget I love you so.
You are my best friend forever, in time.

I hope you always stay by my side.
Too many deaths have made my heart fragile and filled with pain.
I don't know what I'd do if I ever lose you.

I hope that you will always be with me for you always make
the pain fade away and bring the sun to shine over me.
I'll love you till the end of time.

For no one can make me as happy as you.
You are the greatest friend in the whole world.
No one could ever replace you.

Rosie K. Boyd

If Only I Could Change The World!

If I could change the world—
Every American would have our flag unfurled;
To show respect to God and country, for ancestors who fought, those fighting still-
Even to those against their will.

If I could change the world—
Every home would have no angry words hurled;
Especially to God's children He gave us to raise,
But instead of shooting, each other would praise.

If ONLY I could change the world—
There would be love and peace in everyone's heart,
Even to those countries grown so far apart.
And the urges of man would change from greed,
To give ALL races a chance to succeed.

Marjorie R. Hathaway

Forever

Every day of my life existing I feel as if you are here beside me.
Every sunny day that dawns reminds me of your warming smile.
As the content and calm rays of sunshine reach to encircle my aching body I remember you.
Every sound that pierces the stillness makes me only too aware that you are but a few hours away from me.
You are my knight in shining armor. Every ugly and unhappy thing that I see day after day never enters into my life when I'm with you my darling.
You are patient and calm so that when I need a body to lean on you are there for me.
Forever, let me be yours.......Forever.

Mary Margaret Barrett Anderson

For A Friend

The trials and tribulations of everyday life
Everyone has them
Some come out on top
Some succumb to the trials
While others let things happen to them.

For one so young, my dear
You've been through a lot
Got married too young
Cost you much more than a ring

Physical and emotional scars you bear well
Time is the only cure for such wounds.

A loving person, always and forever
You bring out the best in others
Life is a journey of faith
Have faith in the ones that are dear
And the ones you hold near.

When the chips are down
And things look bleak
There is a light at the end of the tunnel
As long as you have friends around.

Larry Charest

Ex-Girlfriend

When the moon comes up and the sun goes down
I'm always thinking on how to change my life around
Right now working and sleeping is my life style
It would be perfect if I could see your tantalizing smile
The images of us together do not leave my mind
Without you I'm always lost feeling left behind
Thinking back to the days that were great
Especially that cool spring night, our first date
Happiness has a very expensive cost
Please let me know now if mine is lost

Mark Alan Klein

Shyness

You don't feel normal but aspire to be.
Everything you do feels like a herculean task.
You always feel nervous and awkward.
You wonder what people think of you
And hope they like you.
You want someone to talk to
but you don't know what to say,
so you don't.
You want friends to laugh with
and go out with.
How will you do this?
What will you do
when your heart beats faster,
your hands get sweaty,
your stomach is agitated by butterflies?
Will you walk into the crowd
or turn away and run
and say, "Next time"?

Laura Thornburg

Autobiographical Me

My life is an open book
except for the chapters that have been edited
"YES!"
You all have been reading
the abridged version of my life
it is one of those
Reader's Digest condensed books
in large print
Read the good parts
Read the parts that are there for you
Read between the lines
The rest is there somewhere
I think I'll reveal it
in the form of a flashback
in the sequel
or maybe
when they make the movie
then you will know me
not the fictional me
But the Autobiographical Me

Mike Winner

Grasshopper Hatch In My Green Bean Patch

I planted the seeds early, called contender beans,
Expecting a miracle to equal my dreams.
I worked early and late to be sure they were nourished
Happy with promise as they grew and flourished.

Forgotten were the elements which often oppose
And the insects with appetites like nobody knows.
The hurricanes came in early May.
Those beans, the target! to my dismay.

Battered and beaten, they were left in water;
The winds let up, but the weather got hotter.
Quick and alert, the grasshoppers came;
They soon had me beat at their numbers game.

They laid their eggs on the leaves and vine;
It was on my beans they planned to dine!
"I won't allow it! I'll pick the beans
when the water recedes, to foil the friends."

But it was no use; the crafty leachers!
I was beat by elements and those creatures.
The water stayed high in my green bean patch,
And the feast was savored by the grasshopper hatch.

Lois Dahlberg

Untitled

Warm breath moistens the cheek
eyes cinched in furrows of passion.
Soft rose petal skin,
bodies swirling, sticking.
The point where one ends and the other begins
is
not important.
Sweet smell of sweat permeates the nose
tempting the forbidden senses.
Hands search for answers to questions
never verbalized.
Surroundings are blended into shapes and colors
of a life unlived.
Fire fills the heart until pain is pleasure
and screams are a mixture of fear and fulfillment.
Sensuous sounds twist
into rhythmic concentration.
For a moment
the point where one ends and the other begins
is important.

Melissa M. Blackard

Without A Mirror

How does the pansy know she is purple
—eyes looking inward,
blind to sky, bee, curling of her own leaves
in the early mist mornings.
Her delicate nerves stroke the earth, perceive
organic scraps and slime trails;
at Nature's heart, the blood well
is tapped and vacuoles swell
with the life of their mother, whom they feel
—can't see —but know deeply.
When her China-fan petals spread wide
their bright velvet night brushed with moon,
she won't know that those walking by can
distinguish her from the rose.

Melynn Minson

"Some Day"

I'm forever longing for the day that tears won't
fall and cries won't cry.
And My heart will soon find its way.
Please someone, someone tell me please.
Which way to go, and now to get there, where pain
and fear will not be.
Let the forgotten be remembered and the
controlled one's could learn to lead,
and not forever surrender.
And we could all have what we need.
Let the dying live again,
to add more memories to the one life
that will never end.

Misty Payne

Love Of Oneself

I am falling, falling from the sky
Falling further into the blackness
A hole is beckoning me
The energy of matter is leaving me
Drifting, drifting
I am all alone
The coolness comforts as it wraps its arms around me
Falling, falling, forever
Does the end ever near?
Does the answer ever come?
Love never felt as good as this
Free to be me
Free to be in love

Shanna Mitchell

Like Me

My youngest daughter, gregarious, impetuous and ambiguous like me,
fighting the world most of her life,
searching but not finding herself,
her identity lost to herself and everyone else.
Lost in her rebellious youth for many years.

Her life has changed,
moments of doubt, insecurity and fear
occasionally consume her, however,
she's focused now, her artistic abilities
giving her an outlet, a sense of accomplishment.

She has matured, her life has meaning,
she's happily married, her soul mate, her anchor.
She's accepted who she is, finding herself finally
and liking herself.

She fought being like me,
said she refused to be like anyone else,
she had her identity but grudgingly admits
as she matures, she's surprisingly
more like me but can accept it now.

Mary Tenrreiro

Quarters Past Now?

This was a day,
Filled with play.

Not a thought of tomorrow,
No remembrances of past sorrow.

It was filled with the present,
Only a slight chance of being hesitant?

All the time pieces ticked evenly,
As the day slipped by unseeingly.

No one really thought of the future,
They needed time to heal and apply a suture?

Not caring to see what they could not grasp,
Nor open up time and relive what was last.

They were only happy to be,
Enjoying nature's wonderment was all they could see!

Time continued to tick, click, click, click, click.
Everybody was happy, nobody was sick.

Not a one wondered why or how?
They were just content to live "A Quarter Past Now"?

Ralph C. Rogers

Jef

Bare as air is this white room. Bare as air and dead, I said. Filled with things but utterly empty like the car I left on the side of the road. It could, it should be filled with monumental, magical things like the story you told me yesterday. Or visions of kittens at play all day. Dance, dance and celebrate to Mozart or another famous dead composer anything to lift this room from gloom. Why the great screaming mask, I ask? Take it off and fill this room this corpse of a room. Fill it with your smile, awhile. Open your eyes and fill this room with their glorious green sheen. Oh that wonderful light! And your skin's a sin that adds a distinctive shade of dream. Let the boastful rain come dance and prance on the bathtub filling the desperate hunger with velvet joy. Stay, I pray and awaken this room with crystal moans that beg for eternity.

Racheal L. Ogrissey

Forest Fauna

Twilight reveals twinkling stars sprayed from the hand of God.
Fire-flies illuminate spiral ripples as fish break surface
Forming a miniature ebb tide sliding over ragged rocks
where cricket and cicada perform chirped duets.
Bracken ferns rustle in caressing breezes,
Leaves whisper a forest lullaby
As ebon-masked raccoons listen, furry tails flickering
Ambling near the pond, drink deeply, survey woods for danger
Inspect the pond for a midnight meal of fresh fish
Whose scales once glimmered in waning moonlight.
A spotted fawn approaches as night shadows lengthen
Sips sweet waters as ears twitch,
Detects the harsh scent of fox on the breeze.
As twigs snap, fallen leaves crackle and dislodged pebbles
rattle under the paws of youthful inexperience,
The fawn scurries for safety and rapidly escapes.
The lone fox wails, howling an eerie yowl of defeat
as moon and stars are swallowed in inky black night.
Creator watches His creations.

Linda Darlene Evans

"The Honeybee"

The honeybee gathers nectar from all the flowers.
Floating from flower to flower,
Until it reaches the sweetest one.
The nectar more succulent
And glorious than any flower.
Not wanting to alert others to his prized flower
The honeybee tells no one of this jubilant flower,
Keeping the thought provoking flower to himself.
When I kiss thee,
I am that honeybee.
After the first tender succulence,
My desire is to keep returning for more
Of thy prized nectar.
It is hard to stop,
Because thy tender kiss,
From thy ruby lips
Is sweeter than the finest honey.

Michael L. Lausch

On The Pond

A lone girl in the middle of a pond
Floating in a big black inner tube, floating along
Wondering, dreaming, singing a song

She dreams herself as queen of the sea
Commanding a fleet of dolphins
With the prettiest of fish sitting at her knee

Children yell at the beach, in the waters on the ground
Splashing and yelling
Her safe haven has been found

Wishing, hoping, praying.
She doesn't want to leave
She can't be staying.

But, for now, she just dreams,
about fish and dolphin fleets
about her mermaid queens.

She's floating in the middle of a pond,
floating along, a child dreaming,
dreaming and singing,
singing a song.

Michelle Ann Fleming

Goodbye

The sun shined on stormy nights
flowers grew around christmas time
anything was possible
when we were in love

Forever other people lost
Lonesome valleys other people crossed
We didn't share the tears other people shed
goodbye was what other people said

The sun doesn't shine on stormy nights
flowers freeze around christmas time
nothing seems possible
now that were not in love

Forever was what we lost
Lonesome valleys we crossed
People saw the tears we shed
goodbye was what we said

Nikkie Josie

Autumn Leaves

Autumn leaves like so many butterflies
Fluttering on your shoulders in breaths of wind
Binding our footsteps on empty streets
Amid the tall trees casting broken shadows
You say to me that my love
Is like autumn leaves
Spectacular in so many colors
Red purple and yellow
Brightens your eyes arousing passion
But not ever so lasting
Like autumn leaves dying in splendor
Yes my darling! Our love is like autumn leaves
That follow the cold winter winds
Vanishing into time
Leaving only memories to remember forever
Of the long nights in your arms
Our lips together
In burning passions
But like the dying leaves in an autumn that is ending
Love is never lasting

Vinh Q. Tran

Reflections Of A Summer Day

The air was warm, with a soft gentle breeze
  fluttering the leaves in the tall majestic trees
All of nature was in its own simple way
  carrying out on life's stage
The grandest theatrical play!

Suddenly the curtain rises, and there on the ground
  the woodland creatures appear with their marvelous sound
The symphony of music; a beautiful creation
  fills the air with joy and magic
And every heart with glad anticipation!

All the sounds of the woods; the babbling of the stream
  blend together in chorus, like a heavenly dream!
Listen... quietly... hear the familiar sounds
  they rise, they fall, they rise again
Capturing everything they surround!

Reflections of a summer day
  are recommended; don't delay!
Catch them quickly; hold them tight
  so as the seasons begin to wane
You can reminisce to your delight!

Trudy E. Draves

Is It Better?

Is it better to be loved by millions
for a performance on a stage,
acting out a make-believe life,
one made up on a page?

Or is it better to be loved by one,
for what you are, not what's pretend?
A person whose love is all about you,
only wanting to be your lover, your friend.

If this one loves you with a love that is true,
what wonderful joy it would be.
Finding in each other a soulmate, a friend
sharing a love as big as the sea.

Always knowing what to say,
If the other is sad or scared.
Each living for the other,
dreams and passions shared.

Think of how wonderful life could be,
if all these things became reality.

Scott Trotter

Thank You ISP

I am here to thank you, ISP,
for giving me back the pleasure of writing poetry.

From morning till night my mind is constantly filled,
with thoughts I have to write down until they are all spilled.

But with this renewed passion, I have to let you know,
now with the hours spent writing, I have let my house go!

While my husband dresses, he also says to tell you thanks a lot,
as he searches through his drawers for clean underwear and socks.

I see something growing up the wall I think just waved at me!
How long has it been since I have washed or cleaned?

Later my daughter appears giving me a dramatic display,
of how from lack of food she is slowly wasting away.

As my husband comes home from work, he weakly staggers in.
Is it just me, or are they both looking rather thin?

A sudden pang of conscious I am now starting to feel,
as I can't remember the last time I cooked them a decent meal.

We all turn our heads as our dog begins to dance and moan,
for he hasn't been let out all day and is about to explode!

So with this dose of reality, I will set my pen aside,
but I smile knowing that tomorrow I will once again write.

Theresa Dischinger

To My Wife

September's promised sonnet never came,
For I, in the Springtime bliss of that first reign,
Forgot, o'er whelmed in Love's first flower's year
Which grew in grace and beauty shining near.

Then did the quickening flow of time us turn
To life, details of the world now ours to earn.
Absorbed in building this our lives, new needs
Shaped love, exchanging tenderness for deeds.

New born, the child's miracle burst upon us,
Sounding our love in a key we barely hear.
We listen, her soft young smile growing dear,
Insistent, green with Christmas promise joyous.

In this new work I've found my promise true;
You've blessed to me what I once promised you.

B. Paul Cotter Jr.

Untitled

I hate having died;
I hate knowing the Me who once was,
And the Me who is now,
I hate it.
Yet I accept it.
But I don't like it.
Not one wit!

Lianne E. Hansen

The Light Of The Candle

The light of the candle glows upon his perfect face
for it glows upon the one I love
The light guides us through the dark when the world has gone blind
The candle shines on the face of the one who holds the light
It is now burning with all the love in the world
When it went out the world was dark and quiet and my eyes saw nothing
Until now the match lies upon the candle
The light once again shines upon his perfect face
The light of the candle cannot last a perfect lifetime it will once again die
Will the match again lie upon the candle
It must sometime come down to the end
When it does no other light will be as bright as he the one who holds the candle.

Lindsey Self

The World Exists

The world exists to sustain life
For life should exude love.
But yet, the world exists regardless of
the tragedies of life and love.
The world exists for day and night
For human error and foresight.
The world exists for dreams never realized
And realities never dreamed of.
The world exists to satisfy power and greed
While allowing gross poverty and dire need.
The world exists to cultivate conscience
And reward innocence and truth.
Still, we nurture, mold, protect and sometimes kill our youth.
The world exists even for the unknown.
The world exists.

Simone McKenzie

"A Dead-End Street"

If there is a dead-end street in the town to it I say be gone.
For no matter be it long or short I always wind up there on.
I don't really know why it happens I guess it must be fate.
But I have wound up on more dead-end streets than I care to relate.

One day while traveling through Nashville on the way to a national park.
We were up early and after breakfast, did on our way embark.
My wife watching for road signs said, "You should have turned there!"
You guessed it I missed the turn again, I could almost pull my hair.

"No sweat, I'll swing around the block and pick up the road again."
Once more fate took over and I wound up on a street with a dead end.
Now I know this may sound foolish, but this thing sure has me beat.
No matter where I go or way I turn I wind up on a dead-end street.

I try to not let it get me down, I still travel almost every day.
I've crossed the country many times on the nations great highways.
We have traveled from the east to the west and then back again.
There is always that dread experience of a street with a dead-end.

Now I plan to go to heaven, so I live with that in mind each day.
And when I get there I expect to travel on heaven's great highway.
As I travel from place to place up there I expect to meet a friend.
One of the things I will be thankful for is no streets with a dead-end.

H. Fizgerald Durbin

Alone

Searching, Seeking, Hunting
For someone who cares
Yet, I see no one
ALONE

Screaming, Shouting, Yelling
Trying to get your attention
Your ears are deaf to my cries
ALONE

Hoping, Wishing, Praying
That you could understand the underlying reasons
Behind my actions
ALONE

Sharing, Discussing, Talking
All to no avail
My voice is lost in the wind of Ignorance
ALONE

Crying, Sobbing, Weeping
Because I will never see you again
And I forever shall be
ALONE

Rebecca Soule

God's Gift

For Nikki,
For the day has come ready to give it my all
And my love for you won't let you fall
And I long to feel your warm gentle touch
For the rest of my life I'll love you so much
And you are a new book and I am your cover
Always close always your lover
And I will turn your pages slow
And read you with pride
Cause instilled inside my heart you know
Your love coincides,
With all my love for all of my life
And I found inside of you
What I've always been looking for
And I pray your God's gift to me
forever more

Rex Richardson

Untitled

Impossible, I've always thought,
for us to be together.
But here we are,
Down this street,
Your arm around my shoulder.
Your arm.
How many times, in my dreams,
Have your arms encircled my waist,
holding me,
lifting me up,
up, high,
till the heights we reached equaled that of the gods?
And,
circling round,
We travel the Universe together.
Your strong,
and
my weak,
encompassing all.

Rebecca Hartman

A Greater Existence

I see beyond the stars above some sort of heaven in the night sky
Forever shining brilliantly above the Earth
A place, where I, in my dreams have given birth
Where things are as they seem, because there are no boundaries to the mind
In the soothing aura of the midnight sky

Take my hand and we shall fly above the Earth into the sky
As high as faith can take you where reality is left behind
Beyond the moon and stars below take my hand and we shall go
To a plane... a being... a state of mind
Leaving dreams to the faint of heart to live an existence with hope and faith
Going higher, ever higher, to find more
But what more is there than life itself beyond this mortal being?
Can life on Earth be just a test to know a life worth knowing?

Keep flying higher with faith in mind and soon you'll be rewarded
With knowledge... wisdom, you won't believe
Until you go where we are going

I look back briefly to see the Earth a pinhead to the eye
I realize then to my surprise I was immortal then.

Tammie Harper and Jim Crider

Let There Be Light!

Hi! — I'm Photon, a bundle of energy
Forged by terrific pressure and heat intensity.
I sparked out of nuclear fusion in the sun's core—
A very minute x-ray with a very short wave length.

In fact, I'm invisible yet compressed in a volume of gas
Hard as rock and ten times denser than lead.
So I wiggle, oscillate and radiate to flex out my wave
To surmount the hold on me by density and gravity.

I twist and tumble with granular convection
And pushed out to the photosphere by sound wave action.
From a heavy unseen ray to a light visible light—
Hey! Can I say "I emerge from darkness to see the light — myself?"

But it's no kidding, a million years is too long
To negotiate the sun's radius of 432,500 miles.
I make about 186,000 miles per second through space,
So how far will I be in a million years?

I will be with you in only eight minutes
For you're only 93 million miles away.
I synthesize you foods and compounds for life;
I'm Photon - your strength, your warmth, your light.

Lorenzo S. Camacho

A Winter's Journey

Five horses quench their thirst
from an icy water hole
in the Rocky Mountains
on a cold December morning
as the sun first gleams
on the milk-white, rough-edged mountains.
God lays his head down
next to the mountains,
separating the placid horses
from any danger that may come
from the mountains to cause them harm.
He will lie there, in the shadow of the day,
until they drink their fill
and pass on through in their journey.

R. A. Matthews II

To Sharon

Green crushed black walnuts left dark circles on Bradshaw Road.
Freshly strawed grass encircled sparkling new brick abode.
Corn-baited fields, Remington oiled, hungry doves feasting.
Old Nell eagerly awaiting first day of bird season.
Life is good in sweet anticipation.

Big sister Angela gently rocked by Granny with rhyming folklore.
Bulging tummy, no labor pains on the crisp morn of November 19, '64
Perganol-assisted, might have been four, exhilarated were we
To start the slow drip at Jennie Stuart in rural Christian County.
Life is good in sweet anticipation.

Wailing 'til dark, Aunt Tebby goes home, just the time you'd planned.
Valerie Gayle you'd be, til through the defined name books I scanned.
Quickly, decisively, making your grand entrance at 6:30,
Dark haired, perfect and petite, not Valerie hefty and sturdy.
Little like a flower, Sharon Elaine, life is good in sweet anticipation.

Pleasure, devotion, excitement, laughter and charm, all rolled into a tiny fist,
You were all we'd envisioned, and still are, more cherished than words can list.
All a bright, sensitive, loving daughter could be, could be spoken of you,
Happy, happy birthday, twenty-eight years later this November 1992.
Life is good and sweet.

Patty Primm

Friend Or Foe?

I sense a man is following me.
Friend or foe, which will he be?
I didn't notice him much-
when I was young,
I only paid attention to having fun.
It seems sometimes he's in front
and other times behind
Will he do me harm? - Or will he be kind?
I used to wonder at his very slow pace
Now, to stay ahead of him,
I feel I'm in a race!
And though he has spent all my life with me,
It is I who have aged - but never he!
Here I am now - frail and grey
I'll pass beyond his clutch someday.
But I have a feeling youth will renew
And then another human he will pursue
Will he do them harm - or will he be kind?
Only "time" will tell as we march to this rhyme!

Lois Williams

Suddenly

It seems as only yesterday we departed.
From a world of wonders to the depths of the seas.....

Suddenly.
Suddenly the world has gone and left my lonely thoughts.

The whispers of the leaves and the sun.
The happiness of summer to come.....
Suddenly.

I've asked myself over and over again when will it end?
Or does it keep coming forward until it can't anymore....
Suddenly I've asked myself. From black to white from
red to yellow and gray and purple. What do these colors
represent? I've asked myself........
Suddenly.

Nina Avril Head

Untitled

There once was three pigs who lived in a house across
from the big bad wolf who catches other animals and
eats them all without protection from a farmer or a bigger
animal then the wolf went after the three pigs
who lived in the house across from and the wolf and, over
to their house and said they you three little pigs let me
in said the wolf and the three pigs said not by the hairs
on are chin chin chin and the wolf said then I'll huff
and I'll, puff and I'll blow your house down said the big bad
wolf, and then before the pigs said do it they already left
their house, went to the barn and set a trap for the wolf
which was a net on the ground hidden form the big bad wolf
hung behind the tree, so after the wolf blew their house down
went after the there pigs the wolf was caught in the
trap the pigs set for him, them the pigs burned fire wood under
the pot and the wolf and ate him up.

Ronald Eugene Johnson

"In Your Memory"

WE honor you, we remember you, we miss you;
From the heart of our heart we kiss you.

The war, you have fought,
Whether it was north and south or east and west;
The lesson you have taught,
To win peace, the World At Rest (WAR).

The noble cause, you called upon,
The worthy duty, you performed;
The honest courage, you shown, and
The precious life, you offered.

We promise you, the torch of freedom,
You have passed, we will keep it lighted;
And pass it to the next generation,
With dignity, we will make you delighted.

The next century with no war,
Laying its foundation, is our mission;
Cooperation and compromise,
Will be the winning weapon for resolution.

We admire you, we respect you;
We love you, we salute you.

S. Devendra K. Verma

I Protest

It's not easy, to be humble,
Especially, when your efforts crumble.
And most of all, when you are not sincere,
Because, you really don't feel like,
Your students are peers.
Why do I have to stoop, to a mindless level,
And welcome, the tactics, of the devil.
I open my arms, to embrace, what is wrong,
To bless the sinner, with a humble song.
I can't be part, of the soul saving crowd,
Forgive me God, I protest, clear and loud.

Maurine Fergueson

Night Time

Did you ever watch the whole world fall asleep,
Drift from pleasant drowsiness to slumber deep?
The flushed and golden sun, spent from the day's routine,
Silently rests its head within a great ravine
Of softest sky, pink and golden blue,
Of fluffy treetops, verdant in their hue,
And of river waters lapping in the breeze
A lullaby designed to soothe and please;
And have you seen the world's eyes closed so tight
That everything is wrapped in velvet night?

Mildred S. Cooper

"Wrinkles, Wrinkles, Wrinkles"

Wrinkles...yes...we all have wrinkles...on our Toes...Bold...
Wrinkles...on our knees...oh please, wrinkles on our noses...when we sneeze...
Wrinkles...you've got them...I've got them...large and small...

Wrinkles...when we are Born...but no wrinkles when we are Gone...
Wrinkles...on our Fingers...Front and Back...Bold like God... wrinkles...
Wrinkles...on our Belly Buttons...wrinkles here...wrinkles there... yes...

Wrinkles Everywhere...Beautiful wrinkles...Everybody has wrinkles...
Wrinkles Everywhere...you've got them...I've got them...Large and Small...
Wrinkles Everywhere...what beautiful blessings...that grow and glow with Time...

You have wrinkles...I have wrinkles...all God's people have wrinkles..
Yes...Smiles...Hugs...Laughs...and yes...Tears....Bring wrinkles just when you
Blink...Bold...like Gold...the special stamp of God...wrinkles large and small...

Wrinkled Saints...Don't Leave Home without your wrinkles...on your feet...And
Wrinkled Hands...knees...Arms...Faces...Smiles...Are ONE way God shows his
SPECIAL LOVE TO US IN WRINKLES...HIS STAMP...OF WRINKLES...

Father God...Thanks for the Free Gift of Wrinkles...That show off your Grace
In each of Us...All God's People have wrinkles...large and small...
Thanks more for your Holy Spirit...within us...that we shall not forget our
Wrinkles...Wrinkles...Wrinkles..

Lorene Verdell Hunter

"Talking To The Mirror"

Do you ever stand in front of a mirror and talk to that person you see?
"Why don't you, how could you, when will you?" O, mercy, that culprit is me!

Do you ever watch the acts of a friend that are tho'tful and loving and kind-
And think in your heart, how careless of me—how I wish that those deeds had been mine?

Do you ever think of people you've known, some wonderful, some good, some the best
Who've helped you over some mighty rough spots and asked, "am I failing this test?"

Life's trip is a challenge in so many ways, hills to climb, pavement slick, detours, too,
Some tangles with others, but mostly with self, smooth sailing is seldom for you.

Stop right where you are and take a deep breath, take a look in that mirror again—
Please don't laugh—and don't cry, don't even bat an eye, as you talk again to that friend.

Name your burdens and worries, each care of your heart—be honest, be tho'tful, be true-
Ask HIS care from above, and HIS wisdom and love—and your burdens HE'LL carry for you.

Marian Stewart

Cravings

The mind thought it wanted the experience but after all was said and
done, it realized the craving for the experience did not come from the
heart but from the humanness which surrounds the true self and hides
it from all.

So...unless the mind is trained to be quiet and neutral,
it is forever seeking experiences to bring it fulfillment...
thinking of things to do, places to go, people to see
in hopes of feeling satisfied and whole.

How ironic that the way to wholeness and satisfaction lies not outside
ourselves but at the heart of our awareness.
So simple, so pure, so true.

"Are you sure it's so simple?" the mind asks.
"Yes" the heart answers. "Would you like to dance with me in peace
and joy?"
"I don't know if I can" the mind ponders.
"Yes you can" encourages the heart. "Trust me. Let go of all thought
and expectation and I will show you the place and fulfillment."

The mind thought it wanted the experience but after all was said and
done, it realized that the best experiences come from the stirrings
of the heart set in motion by the direction of the mind.

Marsha Jane von Aschersleben

Your Name

The wind whispers your name.
I am alone, need someone,
In my heart, you are there.
The wind whispers your name.

Your name blows through the trees.
I hurt inside, need comfort,
In my soul, you are there.
Your name blows through the trees.

The rain beats out your name.
I'm confused, need answers,
In my mind, you are there.
The rain beats out your name.

The crashing of the waves say your name.
I am empty, need love,
In my life, you are there.
The crashing of the waves say your name.

Katrina L. Barnett

Untitled

Her eyes are liked diamonds
full of beauty and light
Her arms kept me warm
on some cold winter nights

Her hair is like silk
light and soft to the touch
These are the seasons
I love her so much

Her smile could brighten
the grayest of days
Her body is perfect
in all of its ways

My heart races
whenever she's near
With her passionate kisses
I could never see clear

But now al that's over
and we are apart
But I want (her) to know
(she's) still in my heart

Robert Wicks

Untitled

In my mind
I am dead
It has already begun
The sweet man came
To take my heart
Long before it was done

Beside me in silence
Cold fear fills the hall
There's nowhere for my love to go
Except to forever fall.

I cry in the darkness
That should be my sleep
Light enters my mind
But the pain is too deep.

Cold wind beside me
A wound with no blood
How could he leave me
I just want to run.

Christella Short

The World Today

Is a scary place to live in
Can't trust anyone, not even kin

Everything so computerized & fast
Hurry! Catch it! Before it past

Definitely out of control is life
A man wants a man to be his wife

Little kids badder & tougher than you
Will blow your head off, just say boo

Drugs, disease, & violence infested
Causing early death to be invested

Innocent kids being abused left and right
How can you people sleep at night

Will it get any worse than this
Or will it soon end with a bliss

Frances M. Carter

Untitled

Dear Larry:
Your side of the bed
Ain't full no more without you
I'm in the middle.

Even though I try
I can't squeak them slats alone
Come on back to me.

I tried other men
Nuffin good in Ohio
So, where are you now?

I need to be warm
Want your body close to mine
Sock it to me boy!

Robert C. Boake

Tiny Raindrops

Tiny Raindrops
You've pattered the same sweet song
All day long.
I am glad that you came
Just the same.
You have cooled the heat
With your beat.
You have brought life again
Where you've been.
Up have gone the peoples lips
Like wood chips.
Their eyes are shining bright
There's new light.
You have brought courage and hope
To all folk.
Yes you are welcome here
You're so dear
Tiny raindrops.

Marguerite Tripp

A Dangerous Mind Is...

One that challenges ALL stereotypes, in spite ofs and what could have beens.

Despite outward appearance, and lack of socioeconomic status,
A dangerous mind operates outside its confined and oppressive restrictions.

A Dangerous mind continuously rises to levels that no one would believe
And its power should never be doubted

Stephanie D. DeRios

Did You Ever Wonder

Did you ever wonder why our world is so corrupt with violence?
Why the only way to survive about the streets is with silence.

Did you ever wonder why kids are looking upon the world with fear?
Why our future is becoming so unclear.

Did you ever wonder why more kids re carrying guns?
Why precious lives are being wasted just for fun.

Did you ever wonder why the American Dream seems lost?
Why people are giving up hope at such a devastating cost.

Did you ever wonder why different races are grouping together and dividing?
When we all should really be uniting.

Did you ever wonder why today's education doesn't seem to be doing any good?
Why kids today don't seem to be learning what they should.

Did you ever wonder why there are so many sick and needy?
Why the only people who have the power to help are those who are greedy.

Did you ever wonder about the consequences of no one trusting one another?
Why if we could only get past that barrier, there would finally be peace on
earth, forever.

Linda Russell

Mulberries

There it stood, an old wooden bench, its slivered sear upholstered
with mottled shadows, and I seemed drawn to it by some invisible
beckoning finger.

Perhaps it was the welcome shade of dense mulberry leaves promising
relief from the glaring midday sun that called me there, but as my
weary body sunk to the weathered bench, I felt a kinship to the old
tree standing guard over it.

Closing my eyes and drawing a deep breath, I could smell the nostalgic
scent of fresh green leaves and rich red berries exploding on the
tree down the lane of so long ago.

As my mouth watered in anticipation, I could savor the juicy berries
grabbed from low swinging branches and stuffed into cheeks, faces
grinning like innocent as rich red juice dripped from corners of smiles.

On the wind rustling the branches, I could hear children giggling as
they locked plump fingers with friends, skipping in circles on spindly
legs to the tune of "Here we go round the mulberry bush, mulberry
bush, mulberry bush,.."

And in the glint of sunlight peeking through the treetop, I could see
impish barefoot children gleefully squishing the large berries
between their toes as if to save the world from giant crimson bugs.

Today as I first sat sheltered by the stately mulberry, there had
been a poem in my heart, waiting to be unlocked, waiting to find
voice on the scrap of paper clutched tightly in my calloused
fingers, but no poem found shape or form.

For mulberries beckoned me with the invisible finger of a childhood
long forgotten.

J. Anderson

Untitled

The book of life is hard to read.
The living soul is hard to feed.
There is no street by the name of easy
For every flower has its weed.

There lies a shadow beneath each light.
The touch of a kiss hides a bite.
It's tough to positively think in this world
For every breath holds back a fight.

Goals of perfection are impossible to achieve,
And pains of heartache are impossible to relieve.
Mind games are commonly struggled within,
While more worries and burdens are often received.

If time was only taken to look all around,
In obvious places so often unfound.
Smiles of pleasure actually exist.
The sky can be reached; we're not earth-bound!

Amanda McKinzie

Special Bulletin

Special bulletin have you heard
The Lord is building a kingdom that's almost prepared
Turn away from your sins every woman and man
Because the end of the world is at hand
The king of this world is very busy, telling you there is plenty of time
But don't you dare listen
Tomorrow is not promised to you
Nor the next second
So prepare yourself now
Christ will descend from heaven
He's coming as a thief at night
But to the righteous it will be a glorious sight
The wicked and the unrighteous lost in sin
Will wish they had a chance to start over again
Put on your armor and pick up your sword and shield
Now battle to the end and do God's Holy will
I now turn you back to a little peace of mind
Remember God's children we are living on borrowed time

Eddie R. Robinson

Special Person

Sometime in Life
The Lord sends someone special our way
No matter how low we are feeling
They know the right words to say

They really give our spirit a lift
The Lord with his great wisdom gave them the words to say
He just seems to work through them
We feel better right away

We might have had problems in the past
that were very hard for us to bear
This person had the same problems
so ours they can relate to and share

The more I talk to this person
somehow closer to her I seem to grow
Then I realize God on his throne above
sent her for me to love

God with his great mercy
sees everything we need
First we have to live by Faith
then with other things He will proceed

Claude Carter

"Raining Tears"

She screams at the sight of a dead man.
The man is mutilated and she has done it.
Who is this man who attacked her in her own bed?
There's a storm and it's raining tonight...

Back to the dead.

If he's already dead, what is she so worried about?
She runs outside and yells, but no one can her pain.
The rain tries to wash away the tears but
they're going to there for awhile.
The cops arrive and ask her questions, have they no decency?
All she can do is cry and that's understandable.
One murder makes a villain, but this one hero.

Chris Roach

When I Came To You That Night

You cannot deny the beauty that surrounds you as the fire burns inside
The memory of a passion you try to hide, as you look away from me, I can see it in your eyes
The touch of a new woman, the scent of his cologne
The memory that takes us far from home
The price I paid for someone who was never really mine
the price we pay for passion, one more time
And as the walk away, were you afraid you would want to stay?
You and I both know we can never be set free
You can never be the man she wants you to be
You wrapped yourself around me like a coat for someone cold
The feeling we knew, never once growing old
And as walk far away, we can never be that far, for the burning of a passion, leaves a long and lasting scar
I can't explain the feeling in the darkness of your room, you and I both knowing we would have each other soon
As you touched my body, as I felt you deep inside
the passion that was hidden, it burst and came alive
I can't explain the feeling but I know that it as right
As you stood in front of me, when I came to you that night

Cindy Weinstein

Without A Word

A starry and cloudless sky
The moonlight shining way up high
The sound of thunder as the waves crash
So gently against the sand

When he takes my hand, so suave, yet so nervous
I know this is the man

Without a word, without a touch
All I receive is a glance
To let me know that without me he does not want to stand

The night is warm, the air is calm
He takes my face and gently rests it in his palm

I know he loves me, I know he needs me
But will he be here to stay?

Without a word, without a touch
But with a single look he tells me
That he will never go away.

Alicia Cristina Martinez

Life Of Sacrifice

My best friend is an angel,
the most beautiful one at that.
Her skin is pale,
like freshly fallen snow on Christmas morning.
Her eyes are blue,
like the blue glass sea you dream of in the heat.
Her lips are red,
like the blood drawn from your finger when pricked.
Her hair is black,
like the sky without stars at night.
She has a way about her, that can't be described.
Protecting me is her life,
and I her inspiration, though she is mine.
I dream of being as angelic as she,
though I know it's not possible.
God truly sent me an angel,
when he sent my Mom to me.

Courtney Ashby

Open Country

The prairie runs to the mountains
The mountains run to the sky
The sky sweeps across to the faraway hills
And here in this country am I

Hills crowd down to the streams
Streams run down to the rivers
Rivers run by the trees
The trees shed its shadow on sunburnt grass
And here in the shadow is a person called me

Shadows creep up to the top of the mountains
Mountains grow black against the sky
The sky burst out with a million bright stars
And here by the campfire am I

Doris Earl Ezell

Blue Sherbet Skies

Miracles and magic, fantasies and dreams
The mystique of a child's imagination
Is the reason for his schemes.
Childish observations that are made everyday
Are perceived by little minds in a most unusual way.
Giant sugarcoated mountains tickling blue sherbet skies
With cotton candy clouds quickly floating by
Is the way it is seen through a child's eye.

Curious young people who ask questions galore
Thirsting for answers, craving to learn more.
The miracle of childhood goes by very fast
For a short time, it is the present
Soon after, it is the past.
All the fantasies and dreams that played important parts
Become the cherished memories tucked away in our hearts.
If we can feel the magic of blue sherbet skies,
We will remember our childhood with stars in our eyes.

Carolyn Kessler

Protected

Listening to the rain pour out its melody
In the otherwise quiet night,
I feel safe here, lying beside you in the dark.

Wrapped in your arms, I feel the strength of your love,
And know that nothing can harm me.
The rain and your embrace are my reassurance.

The sound of the rain seems to have washed away
Even my most permanent worries.
I will be able to welcome any dreams tonight.

Lynn M. Green

The Halloween Night

Once there was a witch, a boy, and a ghost,
the nasty ole witch was dressed the most.
They went to houses with their trick or treat bags,
made out of paper and old dust rages.

There was a ghost made from a towel,
and a cat sat on the fence with eyes like an owl.
A big spider web hung off a house,
and a little squirmy thing posed like a mouse.

A big fat pumpkin sat in the window,
full of leaves, fire, and flowers aglow.
And a big stick tree fell with a crash,
and all the kittens ran off in a dash.

Angela Shamell Coleman

The Night Song

Hidden from the ears of occupied, restless man,
The night song plays.
Caressed by the inaudible blowing of the wind,
The night song plays.
Never before has a band been assembled that can
even faintly echo the beauty of the night song.
Starry sky portrays the simplicity sought
By the seekers of the night song.
Simple, quiet, yet resounding with the intensity
of an orchestra.
Tranquility attracts the lonely during the
Production of the night song.
The moon above adds intricate detail to the
Already awe inspiring sound.
On cloudy nights, only those who are without can hear the night
Song play.
For it is they that seek the calm and melodic rhapsody,
To ease and comfort the thoughts that keep them bound.
Artistically, quietly, the night song plays.

Jeremy S. Schwartz

The Wolf's Eyes

I could feel the weight,
the penetrating stare of the wolf's eyes.

I debated for a second, but I couldn't resist.
I looked up, our eyes met, and I knew.

He felt all my sorrows, all my fears,
All my lost hopes, and all my shed tears.

He was relentless. Stripping me of my defenses.
He knew everything without a spoken word.

Every fiber in my body screamed, "Look away!"
"Don't lose the walls you have worked so hard to build!"

But, I couldn't move. Despite my better judgement,
I felt comfort there. An understanding unmatched.

I stayed as long as he would let me.
Relishing that passionate moment, until he was gone.

And in my mind I go back there.
He gave me a silent escape from a chilling world.

I'm able to hide my inner soul from those who look but never see.
But through the wolf's eyes, even I could see the true me.

Elena Ritchhart

He's On Another Line? May We Leave A Message?

Hello God,

We are calling for a friend and a favor.
The phone company said they have changed your
"calls waiting" to "calls piling up." We know how busy
you are. We even noticed your "gone fishing" sign is
collecting dust and your "out to lunch" sign remains
unhung. Like the many calls you receive, ours is important.
We hope that before you break for a moment to rub your
tired eyes, straighten your desk and continue your long
day, you could make just one more visit. To Mimi. You
know her. You have spoken before. She needs your hand,
a little more of your help, your healing and your
prayers. She is in our daily thoughts. You see this call
is from her friends and we love her very much.
Understanding you have many other calls to return, it is
not necessary to call us back.... Beeeeeeep.

Mimi's Friends

Untitled

I do like to hear the rain
The rain does not give me any pain.
When raining stops the sun comes out
That's the best time to stand up and shout.

In the rainy days is fog and blizzard
That makes a man look old and grizzled.
Never more to see the sky.
That's much worse than you and I.

Puddles splash and splash and splash some more.
And I can see them if I look through my front door.
Oh, how I wish I could get wet
Because I'd run and jump in those puddles, you bet!

Alben Slimovitz

Hybrid

The brain pulled tight against the casement
the reins up under the chin
the animals pacing in their cubicles
the view beyond a bracing panorama of refuse
and occasional palm in its birthday suit.
A time of lily pads is idealized
bulletproof tabloids litter the markets
and children are fodder for the sun.
The clues that lay within the heart of the beast
have long since dispersed.
The vaporous moorland, a dragnet for roaming squatters.
The queen shops for hats and handbags
one of the few remaining bits of protocol.
Eyes peering through the seizure dawn at the intrepid castle.
Dozens chew around the radioactivity
picking through the clammy pulp in the evenings
the glare pulled down.
There is still the memory of cool sand
and the joy of rooting the odd hybrid from its asylum
the blossom too stubborn to die.

Jane Carpenter

Realm Of Light

Do you know what I know?
Is your mind alert?
Superstitions come and go
Called back down towards the dirt.
Old beliefs strain under new thought
Visions and ideas strike deep.
Entomb the rumors that were taught
Raising wolves instead of sheep.

Robin Jackson

Mysteries Of The Sea

The crystal clear, sparkling sea waves splash against
the rocky shore, taking in scurrying crabs and pointy sea urchins.
Snow white sea gulls glide across the shimmering sea.
The beach is full of children swimming and building
beautiful tan sand castles.
Under water there are bumpy red hot coral reefs where
turquoise fish dart back and forth from predators.
The lights glimmers off the bodies of sharks, letting their
eyes sparkle.
Grass green sea weeds are beginning to be nibbled away by small fish.
The beach, the sea, the animals, and the plants
The four things the creatures of the sea need: The beach to rest,
The sea to swim, the animals and the plants to eat
They are all connected for beauty and enchantment
of the mysterious but beautiful sea.

Jesse M. Giroux

Rose

Petals wilting brown,
The rose of yesterday cries for water.

Twisting down into an empty glass,
A stem cut to early searches for the reassurance of life.

Leaves worn dull by callused hands slowly crumble into the dust of
Reminiscence.

Bared thorns grown thick with life's misery grate against the glass
Forcing all away.

Dregs of past waters stain the crystalline shroud,
A vague reminder of a painful vanishing past.

Dust and decay mingle with the scent of youth,
Bringing memories of an open glade bright with sunshine.

Petals of hope fall one by one drifting forgotten to the floor,
As dreams are lost upon awakening.

Broken with despair the last petal falls,
Swept away on the winds of life.
Left a tomb holding a husk of a rose,
with no soul of petals to reach for the morning sun.

David A. Kunz

Evening In November

Ah! What reposeful mood — a lovely sky;
The rosiness of sunset tints the west
A silvery pond of ice — the bare, brown fields,
Half-clad with snow — a stack of hay, late mown,
A dog — a boy — a pail of fresh white milk,
And just beyond, a road — a bridge — a wood
With branches high and bare against the sky,
And little bits of blueness in between.

I gaze; the earth grows dark; the azure sky
Submerges into gray and then to black.
I stare at utter darkness. Soon appears
A star — a sparkling, radiant, lumber flame;
A scintilla here, another, and still more
Till all the heavens glow, transplendent, light!
A whippoorwill calls mournfully from the hill;
Then all is still—the world is clothed in night.

Doris Van Owen

No Need For Love

If tears quenched all the pain,
The seas would overflow.
If words could mend the heart,
The stitch would always show.
And if a simple sorry,
Would make it all O.K.
There'd be no need for me,
There'd be no need for You,
There'd be no need for love.

If I could take this lifeless piece of clay
And form You by my hand.
And with a single, solitary kiss,
Breathe life in You again.
If I could take the sunshine
And place it in Your eyes -
There'd be no need for me,
There'd be no need for You,
There'd be no need for love.

Erich Mahnke

"Wistful"

The night's been decorated with magic -
The sky is lined with blue - gray clouds
And silver moonbeams stretch toward forever.

The jagged silhouette of black trees
Accentuates the midnight sky
And my eyes swim in pools of moonlight.

The tranquility is magnificent -
Not a sound disturbs this irreplaceable peace
And the world rests with an air of mystery.

Twinkling lights play hide and seek
As they dodge in and out
Of the sea of continually moving clumps of star dust.

Little yellow night lights brighten up the scene
As they go on their way
Searching for someone to love.

I sit alone in the middle of it all
Remarking the beauty
And all of my thoughts are with you.

Christine Filipowski

Christmas - Once Again

Let us sing-Christmas-is soon to be here-once again,
The snow will glisten-upon our window pane-
We've no chimney for Santa-so-we'll give him a key,
Gifts for all-will be under the tree-
A touch of wonder-to us will belong.
With carolers-going door to door-singing a song-
It's time to reminisce-as it draws near,
of christmas past-we hold so dear.
Outside we'd see-the falling snow,
Children with sleds-their faces aglow-
Grand papa carved the turkey-Grand mama cut the pumpkin pie,
They'd stop-look around at us-a twinkle in their eye-
Our home always filled-with family and friends,
Everyone happy-as we'd all join hands-
Grand papa would lead us-as we gave prayer,
First he'd give our love-to all who couldn't be there-
Ask for peace-thanks for food and shelter-bless friends and family,
Then we'd all join in harmony-
"Let next Christmas-bring us all together-once again-Amen-"

Allene M. Flora

Unforgettable

The twinkling stars on a warm summers night.
The soft moon light on the still waters bright.
The way you feel when your hopelessly in love.
The stars the skies and the heavens above.
Watching the snowflakes gently glide to the ground.
Answers to mysteries wonderful yet still unfound.
The sweet smell of the ocean blue.
The cool evening nights leaving the flowers with dew.
The soothing touch of a dancing stream.
Sitting on the realm of a unawoken dream.
The whispering breeze stirring up the smell of flowers.
The relaxing sounds of the April showers.
These things are all unforgettable.

Erica Thompson

"Purple Death"

Finally it ceases.
The soft pink skin-ashen.
The bright eyes-dulled.
The rose colored lips-chilled.
He kisses,realizes how he let it all slip away.
The silky hair falls limp.
From somewhere the memories swarm, around.
He remembers them all is unable to run away.
The sound of desperate pain makes him turn to his right.
She sits there looking at what once was her life.
Again the memories begin to haunt them.
They stand together looking at what once they had.
Now unreachable.
Their eyes cloud over by tears and cascades of purple.
Everything is so distinctly what she really was.
Silently people stream by.
He stands in front of them all, holds onto the cold, delicate hand.
What once was everything in noticed is now profoundly nothing.
He kisses her once more, steps slowly out the door into
the changing leaves.

Karen Zaremski

Playground

THIS is a new day starting, and the sun has yet to arise
the sound of my alarm clock, is the trigger to open my eyes,
There are pigeons on my rooftop building new homes for their young
traffic moving, horns blowing, several church bells being rung.

As you enter into the playground, each day wondering, what's to gain
while you struggle to keep from falling, being careful of affecting pain,
On the playground in this city, there's lots of people everywhere
you may enter when you want to because nobody shows they care.

What is out there on the playground that may attract you everyday
homeless people, gangster children, beggars asking you for pay,
Women standing on the corner, selling tricks out of the sack
some will sex you for a quarter, even less for a piece of crack.

On the playground, no ones safe now, it don't matter who you are
as you're heading for the playground, jackers come to steal your car.
Once you exit from the playground, and you head on home to stay
consider yourself very lucky cause you've made it through today.

THIS is a new day starting, and maybe the sun will rise real slow
you won't have to open your eye's, because you have no place to go,
There's no noises to awake you, there's just peace and quietness
nothings moving on the playground, everyone's been put to rest

Crickett Rashon Rayne

The Christ-Mas Star

The night was cold, but clear and bright.
The Star shown in the sky like a big ball of light.
The three wisemen followed it for days,
Through cities, towns, over mountains, hills and dales.
Throughout the country as it went, they followed on content.
Knowing that it would lead them to the King,
As to Him their gifts they bring.
It lead them to a hillside, - but surely this can't be,
It should be in that mansion in the distance we can see.
But no! By the hillside cave it stays,
So getting down and going in they find a baby in the hay.
A sleeping baby sweet and mild upon a bed of hay,
Brought hope and love to all the earth on that first Christmas day.
Even the animals stood in awe at the wondrous sight they saw.
The Baby Jesus, Lord and King, came to earth for you and me.
To die upon a cross that you and I may see,
The home in Heaven He's gone to prepare a place for you and me.
So, as we follow the Star that lead the wisemen to his side,
Let's you and I brothers and sisters,
Keep CHRIST in each Christmas Tide.

Alice Tourtellotte

Evenings' Dusk; Daybreaks' Dawn

The silvery light casts celestial shadows into forbidding corners.
The stars appearing one by one, create a wishing canvas.
The serene stillness lulls me to a gentle sleep,
As the soft gentle light of dawn lingers near.

The rising sun projects hope into the hearts of the hopeless.
Its bright rays arousing me from my slumber —
The clouds form mystical figures of illustrious truths,
The silhouettes of dusk are close at hand.

The kaleidoscope colors of eve fade into the blues and black of night.
The cool sensation of faithfulness allows me to be calm.
Rainbows of hidden color slowly fade into the night,
And day's freedom gives in to nights' liberation.

Kate Aronheim

Shades of You

We never would have wasted a night like this
The stars, the breeze, a soft sweet kiss
But your memory is a ghost that haunts my heart
These roses, like the pieces, have fallen apart
But where can I go
What can I do
Will I forever be searching for a girl like you

And I've tried to rid my heart of sinful things
But I can't hide from the thoughts your image brings
Like the streetlights that reveal a sidewalk view
I see nothing in the shadows but shades of you

And when the stars color the sky
Nothing in their light compares with your eyes
For when the moon shines down with its subtle grace
I recall nothing in its beauty but your gentle face
So I sit by my window with my lonely wine
'Cause all that's left are these tears of mine
But crying for me is nothing new
When all I ever see are shades of you

Kevin McCafferty

Hope

Hope, is something so near.
Hope, is something that will stay right
Here!
Hope, is something you can not lose,
Unless you don't believe in
You!

Stamatula Chiotis

Nightmares

No one there to catch me as I fall — the "dreams" again!
The subconscious remembers, what I choose to forget.
Dark shadows abound — a face, a hand — no!
I awake.
Where am I — whoo?
A child with long dark curls, hiding...
Trying not to breathe, not to cry, not to scream!
The face that spoke of love, the hands that desecrated — no!
It's only a dream, but she is there.
She survives and calls to me...
I don't want to hear.
I can't look! ...
Eyes open, sit up!
Breathing hard ...
Sweat trickles down...
It's only a dream — specter of the past.
A child alone — spirit waning.
A woman kept lonely — torment never confessed.
But even now, the dreams!

Cheryl Black

Summer Heat

The summer heat is taking over me
The sun is shining as far as I can see
Raymond seems as if its on fire
And the temp. is going higher and higher
It's days like this that make me wanna wish
That I was a tropical fish
Swimming through the sea
Just as pretty as can be
And playing in the Coral Reef
That would be as perfect day
That may make this heat go away!

Ashley M. Quinn

Love

Moonlight awakens
the sun rushes to hide
and sheets lay open — seeking
a wrestling dawn,
where upon another venture of gesture falls between
the interlude of sleep nestling
before the morn.
Leaves the colour of ecstasy,
its pallor vaguely seen.
And time is unrecounted
lest through a taste of wine be it told
the frequenting caresses and kisses as it unfolds.
From where it is given birth
to when, if it may, ever die,
its face in kaleidoscope,
its nature simple and wise.
Deeply felt, yet so misunderstood,
as all things from above
it is the wonder granted all fools
this precious gift we know as love.

Christine Juska-Smith

Love

What's love people say
Is it only for a day,
Is it forever and ever, holding me tight,
Or is it just fleeting, gone out of sight
What's love people say
Is it only for a day
Or is it in my heart
Where it's never going to part.

Venus Ward

A Tear

I walk along the beach, the wind blowing through my hair
The sun setting to the west, dreaming of things I love best
Talk to me ocean, I understand
The rippling sounds of water
The roar of waves crashing on the shore
You talk of love so warm and tender
The way it really should be
Arms reaching out for me, I walk closer
Ready to surrender myself to you
Suddenly a voice cries out
I understand the ocean too
But the arms reaching out to you are mine
Come, let me show you the love, the ocean talks about
I move closer to the voice
The face I know it, but could it be?
Its you
I look back to the ocean
A tear falls from my eye
Thank you ocean
Good-bye

Janet Stefo

Yearly

A day like any other day except.... you were there.
The sun was out shining so bright as you walked into my life
brightening a new light.

A day like any other day except.... you were there.
Rain, thunder, screamed and stormed; but you passed through it
so kind, calm and warm.

Snow fell heavily as the vision of you grew dim; but you
wiped your eyes still seeing me.
A day like any other day except....you were there.
Leaves piled so high, the day seemed long I wanted to cry,
but you raked the old leaves leaving me happy without a tear
in my eyes.

A day like any other day except.... you were there.
All year round you are my king, I am proud to wear your crown.

Eileen Russell

The Funeral

The gathering of so many sad faces to show respect of a brave soul.
The tears and sorrow the living share of a lost loved one.
"May they rest in peace."
"No more suffering."
The droning of repetitiveness....but....after the ceremonies,
And after the breakdowns,
And after the last rites,

The empty shell reaches its final destination,
And the soul is allowed to show
That death is true peace,
And death is true freedom.

A new journey begins.
Where spirituality is the realm.

Though gone from the physical world
One's spirit survives—
Through friends.
Through family.
Through memories.
And through love.

Dorothy A. Young

Touching

Some people pass through our lives as the breeze that moves through
the trees,
Touching us lightly with moments of love, then turning and setting
us free.
Some come in as a thunderstorm, with brilliant clouds of fire,
To challenge us to turn within, that we might be inspired.

Some souls forge pathways in our hearts,
to guide us through the night,
And then support our heads to rest, within the morning light.
Others touch us as the silver rain, that falls from radiant skies.
To nourish our souls recurringly with familiar loving ties.

And then there are those special souls, who come for only a time,
The beauty they nourish with light and love truly is sublime,
To suggest within the immortal soul, the mystery of the night,
Then with beauty profound, to etch our soul with memories of light.

And thus we pass through light and love, unveiling the source within,
Until transcending from beyond the light, we begin the journey again.

Barbara D. Myrick

Alone

My eyes open to reveal the same sight that caused them to close
The view of emptiness!
Grabbing for the feeling of company
I have all that I want
Who would want all that I have?
I feel the need to touch
Like the feathers of a chick's mother around its soul
But all I feel is the flight towards the ground
Only to have the ground vanish
And to awaken back to the loneliness I just left
Do I put out the light and not put up a fight?
The choice is mine!
I am here for myself.

Edward Colton

Untitled

Gray mountains stood before me on my path,
The walk around them seemed endless and far,
Though blocking me, I felt no sort of wrath,
Instead, I gazed upon a guiding star.

It beckoned me to climb the rocky face
And conquer all the steep and jagged cracks,
The base was rough but soon I found my face
While leaving many disappearing tracks.

I reached the top and eagerly viewed round
Nothing all the places unexplored,
I realized what it was that I had found
And why this long struggle I had endured.

Down, I climbed, much easier than first;
My path made clear and smooth by those before,
Reaching the base I saw the guide-star burst,
But found my path despite my short detour.

Amy Snow

Dreams

Everyone needs dreams
In a world without hope
We need dreams to live
In a time where no one laughs
We need dreams to make us smile

Your dreams may seem impossible to achieve
Nothing is impossible in a dream
If you put your heart into it
If you put your mind to it
Your dreams will always come true

Rebecca McIntyre

As Boundaries Dissolve

Running toward the stream
The water leaps from its boundaries and extends its cold arms
They hold me
The darkness curls its fingertips over my eyes
And I sink into the peace of the unknowing
slowly
slowly
Slowly I dissolve as the water consumes me
Our fingers tangle
Our bodies merge
I am hidden
I rejoice
The fire of music is begging to be released
My mouth opens to let it seek freedom
and I feel the rush of water fill my body
I know where I exist
The fire turns to ash
The music must remain silent
only the marrow of my bones will ever know its song

Cindy Thompson

"Twenty Years Later"

It was a cold, windy sun fall on the night that I was born
The wind blew steady and quick.
While the others gleamed and others screamed
In their mother's arms,
I wallowed in my new given life.
My brother was sad and lonely
A sister was not in his dreams.
My mother was sleeping soundly
Waiting for the years to begin.
My father was steadily drowning
Still another mouth to feed.
The years of growing
And sad days dawning
Still resume twenty years on,
But hour by hour I see new light ahead
And I silently wonder
Where it is taking me.
Alas...it was a warm, breezy sun fall on the night I wrote this verse
Twenty years later
And I'm still on this earth.

Carol Mangner

Seasons

The leaf as it drifts rocks lightly to the ground
The wind like the sea tosses it round.

The winter is chasing the summer away
The sun is turning to a dark dreary gray.

And where am I going?
Do the seasons change me?
The more they go 'round the older I will be.

But the summer will soon come again you will see
The sun will brighten once more.

But we will have to pay a fee because each time it changes
So do we.

And where am I going?
Do the seasons change me?
The more they go round, the older I'll be.

Cheryl K. Coulam

The Beauty Of Winter

I watched the mild winter wake,
The wind stopped by and froze the lake.

The bears rested in their beds,
The trees were bare, weak and dead.

The snow was falling gently, mild
Upon the face of a dreaming child.

I sat beside my window pane
And remembered when the earth was plain,
Though some men would have thought it vain
To sit and watch the frozen rain.

The trees stood tall, like a long parade,
The sun came out from behind the shade,
And I watched the beauty of winter fade
From the lovely earth that our God made.

Aaron McGriff

A Special Anniversary

An anniversary is the way to count the years since you were wed
The years that have come and gone since the day the word
"I do" were said.
A wish for an anniversary that will be the best
For an anniversary more special than all the rest
An anniversary with that number of years not shared by everyone
Only by those who have endured through many many years.
Happiness and sorrows, births and deaths they share
But through it all with each other they care.
Down the pathway of life they hold each other's hand
And with each new day together they will stand
Till one day before their maker they will be
And then together forever in all eternity.

Elizabeth M. Peters

Apathos

They suffer more whose pleading is ignored
Their cries reduced to ink shapes on a page
And folded through the mail slot in my door
Or lit within the TV's glassy cage.
They look at me but cannot see my eyes
I'm safe behind my one-way mirrored wall
To measure out my grief in doses small
The critic viewing art to grant the prize.
Save me, save me! moans the two-year-old
Her image in my face demands I move
But Loving Heart's entrapped in flesh grown cold
From reasoning that she's too far to love.
Save me, save me from this hardening shell
Where embers die till I in grayness dwell.

David O'Connell

A Window

Secrets - so many - yet unexplored.
The romantic fields
Contain the flowers; fall flowers.
In the moments of times
Lives the heart of the soul.
Reflections gallop across
The shadows of tomorrow's dreams;
The voices echoing virgin hopes, like the snows.
Secrets - sometimes the power of imagination;
In a moment, transferred into
The pasture of time's pleasures.

Cynthia J. Schmer

A Little Girl's Sorrow

I lie here while tears roll down my face
Then I sit back and stare in space
Sometimes I feel I want to die
But the only things I do is cry
No one can feel the pain I do
So sad, so down, so blue
Sometimes I start to grab a knife
But the only things that stops me
is the urge for life
No love, no life, nobody for me
People are blind and can not see
No one to hold my hand and say it will be okay
No sunlight when it comes to day
There is only one person I can count
on in this world
And it is me a little girl
So I sit here with a world of sorrow
And think about what will happen tomorrow.

Jennifer Parks

The Panther

The night was silent, as leaves on the trees
There appeared out of inky blackness
Eyes piercing orbs of gold
I can't help but wonder what aged secrets they hold.

I dazzled charmed watch black form
lazily draped across a moss covered log,
Suddenly springs across the green weedy bog.
Witches companion, Lucifers friend, devils own
Slowly approaches, I wish I was home.

Holding me captive with it's powerful emerald gem eyes
unsheathes sharp claws in my full view,
Death was drawing near, about to be ripped clean through
Moonlight bounces off sleek shining pelt
As I prepare to die.

Amazingly changing direction with a miracle whim
Ignores me a poor pitiful human and leaps back into the night
My heart returns to normal daring now
To let me breathe as my mind erases my fright.

Alma Young

Untitled

In this world
there are so many ways to survive, I just wonder what's kept me alive
was it the thought of her holding me, if not just what could it be
was it her smile or her embrace, that kept a smile on my face
was it the dreams that we shared, or the thought that she cared
I just want to break the chains, from all the heartaches and pains
But as I sit and wonder why, the more I want to cry
for what I feel for her will never die.
In this world, which one of these things did I learn
over whom did I always yearn, why do I cry like I do
am I really missing you. In this world
There are good times, and there are bad
what is it that makes me so sad, I just keep wondering
What was it that I said, what was it that I did.
to make you feel the way you do, I guess there is nothing I can say
to make you feel the same way, I guess I'll have to stay alive
to see if our love will survive.
no matter what I say, no matter what I do
I will always love you, so if these words that I say
don't chase you away, then I'll know, then I'll learn, then I find
more than one way to survive, in this world.

Justin Hess

The Way

Do you ever think of yourself as a bee?
There are workers, drones, and queens, you see,
All have certain duties,
Swarming here and there all summer long,
Gathering pollen and nectar with a dance and a song,
The beehive is the source of these activities,
Comfort, shelter, strength and food they'll need,
No time from the busy schedule to be at ease.

We also have a purpose to be liken to these,
We hustle, bustle, and do what we please,
Sometimes forgetting to get on our knees;
Though time occurs when we need to consider our course,
To give thanks, to count our blessings and consult our inner source.

Delores A. Mattox

Nothing

There I was, sitting
There I stood, staring
There I tried, crying
There I went, dying

Here I am, wishing
Here I stand, trying
Here I try, dreaming
Here I go, dying

Sitting, staring out the bare open window
Crying, dying to be in a land full of snow

Wishing, trying to catch the morning sun
Dreaming, dying in the absence of playful fun

But praying to be lifted from this unwanted gloom -
And slip into her arms, not fearing a dismal doom
But still lost in the knot of friendly betray -
I sit, stare, cry, and die along the mourning way

Yet I wish, try, dream, and die once again -
When I greet her as I plead not to offend
Her wandering thoughts as I slowly melt away -
I realize, finally, what holds me at bay

James Alvin Bruce III

The Mounds

When Rumi wrote...
There lived in Pennsylvania
A race of people very, very tall.

They predated the Six Nations.
Who were they? Asian Nomads?

Where they the same people
Who lived in Illinois, Ohio, Mississippi
And Virginia at that time?

They loved black walnut trees
And so do I—

How did they disappear when native American
Tribes flowed so magnificently over our land
When it was ecologically strong before the
White Europeans came?

Will we ever know?

Do secrets lie in China?

Janet Washington

Freedom

Come sit by my side and stay quiet like mice,
There once was a girl with a heart cold as ice.
She had veins of steel, could not be bought for a price,
She knew not that love could be Freedom.

Along came a man with a heart made of gold,
His soft amber eyes could never be cold.
He brought her a promise of dreams yet untold,
He showed her how love could be Freedom.

Like fire and ice they clashed in the night,
With undying spirit he kept up the fight.
He melted her heart with a love that was right,
He gave her a small glimpse of Freedom.

He made her so happy, she could not deny
The future of promise she saw in his eyes.
He spoke to her softly and told her no lies;
She saw how love could be Freedom.

The joy was so endless, their devotion so true
As they weathered each storm, their special love grew.
He held her hand tightly as the cold wind blew
As they soared onward toward Freedom.

Cassandra De Los Santos

The Sun Came Through

I could tell that she was sad
There was an air of really bad
Yes, she was very down and out
Her heavy load was not in doubt

And now turned blacker than before
When never then could bear no more
For sky come dark with rain and storm
It seemed she thought why was I born

Steel blade showed from at her belt
This was the end she must have felt
For nothing more was of concern
The time had come, it was her turn

Then quick it cleared, the sun came through
She turned to me, and then I knew
That a kind look could change her thought
And hopeless mind now could be bought

My face thought tensed, was quick with smile
It did some good, perhaps a pile
For blade appeared on sand to lay
With nod to me she walked away

Jim Pene

As The Fog Grew Thicker

In a dark forest I awoke to find myself.
There you stood over me as I lay on the cold ground.
The fog was thick and my head ached so.
Stare is all you seemed to do.
You came close and kissed my hand;
Next you kissed my lips.
Something ran warm in my eyes.
With my kissed hand I wiped the blood away.
This was a kiss goodbye I would soon discover.
You raised the club;
I was silenced forever as the fog grew thicker.

Christine M. Zentz

There's Hope

My son,
There's always hope.

As long as my love flows, I will try.
I try, you try, we try.

We haven't failed, simply never totally succeeded.
Soon my son we shall achieve
the ultimate closeness and understanding
of mother and son.

Trust me my son, I only wish to reach
the plateau of happiness and fulfillment
you so deserve.
Smiles and laughter, warmth and love
I wish to share with you my son.

There's always hope.
As long as my love flows, I will try.
I try, you try, we try.

I love you my son!
My love for you will always flow!
My love for you will always grow!

Therefore my son, there's always hope!

Judith Clinton

My Love

I wish you were here, my love
There's nothing I want more
But now I see, my love
That you weren't meant for me
You were sent from heaven just to comfort me
Now your time is up, my love
You must move on
No regrets and no lies
Our time together was magical
But someone needs you more than I
So don't you fear I understand
God's sent you to help me and you did
So good-bye, my love
I shall never forget
You were all I had, my love
And now you've gone away
But I'll be fine, my love
For you are here even when you're not
I'll never forget our time together
Because God works in magical ways.

Becca Hoffman

"Freedom"

From blindness I can see, all of
these blessings, I am free
to use, because of His goodness, to me.
Free to share any knowledge or deed
to the many people that is someday
or some way cross my path.
  There is never a loss in giving or
just being there whether in deed or prayer.
  I am rewarded spiritually.

Sometimes I am stricken with illness and pain;
but to revert and meditate
to prevent becoming vain (with vanity).
Then I am told by a very dear friend "Erodeen"
that "I hold you as a role model."
What more can I ask to be held
in esteem as being observed.
As a God given example in this world.

Ada Belle Kimbro

Femme Fatal

'Tis delight to watch them acquiesce
These creatures bequeathed as queens.
Unlike sweet maidens who shy from quest
These maidens sport craftily as libertines.

They coddle for favors to choose the best
Alas; perhaps there is a scheme.
They lure proud suitors with simple jest

These femme fatale - though ladies they do seem.

Artful romance is their game for kings who hunt
And think they calm; provincial dowries of royalty.
But oh, this prey young kings instinctive chase
Spins a snare of strategy.

For kings may beat their chest of might
And glaze their flesh with fertility
While her majesty discreetly beheads her guest
And wraps him for savoring-triumphantly!

Chris Dodson

"You Are Leaving"

You are leaving me and here with an empty love I remain
These feelings will forever be insert, dormant, yet full of strife.
I would prefer even sleeplessness to this emptiness and pain.
I would prefer to die instead of living a lifeless life.

You are leaving me and you take with you this tree's roots
Your farewell reminds me of dryness and death.
I will remain in the forest, dreaming of past flowers and fruits
I know that these dreams will vanish if I again should feel your breath.

Your earnest hands are waving good-byes
Your quiet eyes for new adventures are thirsting
Your deep loneliness yet a deeper anxiety denies
You're leaving me, carrying off my heart bursting.

You are leaving me, while my soul is sobbing
You are leaving me when I long for you so.
It is our very lives you are so calmly robbing
Forcing a smile as away from me you go.

You are leaving me, I lament your parting
You are leaving me, and I long for your tenderness in disbelief
You are leaving me, my sleepy eyes are smarting.
You are leaving me, but you will forever remain locked within my grief.

Elena Genao

Untitled

The wounds of the world can't be healed with Band Aids and smiles.
These gashes need cleansing.
Down on hands and knees, help your brother.
This child must die, this child must die,
while you're dining he's lying in a ditch.
Don't worry he wasn't anyone's.
Close your eyes to all this, yes close the curtains again.
How many more screams do you need to hear.
And in your selfishness I see an image of myself.
Is that why I'm so bitter towards you.
Are you me in fancy clothes?
There is so much division.
Those of us with everything cry for the one thing we lack.
Those with nothing, choking on their hunger.
I hurt so much, why am I so selfish.
I need to let go of many things.
These new dresses could feed so many and yet I still like the fit.

Jennifer Richards

Thoughts On Political Power

From where do they appear,
These men who aspire to mold our lives?
They with the names like some entity
from an alien planet.
What is a Gingrich, a Limbaugh, a Ralph Reed?
Did I ask for them to control my destiny?
I did not cost my ballot for them,
yet suddenly they are there.
Their every word casts a pall over my security.
The oppressive curtain of hatred is rampant.
I wait with dread anticipation for their latest
pronouncements,
And I wonder, is this the McCarthy era revisited?
Are we really doomed to repeat the lessons we
did not learn.

Elma Barclay

Man's Infatuations

Some, are spoken unconsciously...
These words that wander through our thought,
Some, remain guarded, silent declarations.
They speak, in silence, of equality...
The promise of freedom, that has been bought,
Bought with taken blood, beastly insatiations.
The dreams these illusive dreamers see...
Won in furious battles that have been fought,
Have dominated for enslaved generations.
And surfaced in hopeful, woeful prayers that be..
To almighty God, who is continuously sought,
With pleas for some sort of relations.
These prayers as wafts of smoke that we may see,
Are from the burning of sod mixed with rot,
The stench of death that drifts over nations.
Death of expectations of truly being free?
But remaining here the dream still feeds, caught,
Hope remains, in place of truth; Man's infatuations.

Elizabeth Broze

Marriage

When two people fall in love with each other
They are most happy with one another
hardly ever fight
They get married and the groom
carries the bride away into a new life
with her as his wife
but sometimes love doesn't last forever
when two people can't stay together
their relationship was based on love, trust, and respect
now it has turned to lying, cheating, neglect
For those who stay together forever
I envy them, and only hope that people could
stay in love once again
So I could only hope that
people will not keep coming apart because
Sometimes they don't realize
that they needed each other from the start

Jennifer Warren

From A Speeding Train

The landscape flashes by
In a kaleidoscope of sea and sky
Like the images of my mind
As I reminisce and memories unwind.
Some almost forgotten yesterdays.
Then comes the images of my fantasies.
Which are more real - or unreal?
Those already lived that I still feel,
Or future images in my mind
Like the flashing landscape left behind

Loma Jennings

Forbidden!

You and me together. Forbidden!
They call us names that hurt so much,
and the others tell us not to listen,
but can you really block out 3/4 of the word.

Is it possible that you and I might
live in peace if we suffer the hate now?
Will you and I and our relationship
survive through the torment of a man's
prejudice views?
They, the one before, started this fight,
and we can't stop it, because we
have gone too far to turn back now.

Janet Allred

Boys

Boys can be a pain.
They can almost drive you insane.

They can become the meanest devils that they can be.
Then all of a sudden turn into the sweetest, adorable angles you would ever want to see.

Once you get to know them, they are so friendly,
But the way they like to flirt can become almost sinfully.

Sometimes I think boys are better friends than girls.
They're more easier to get along with without curls.

Just all you have to do is pet them up,
And they'll be sweet as a new born pup.

You'll love your friends that are boys to death.
With what little nerves you do have left.

Denesha Day Evans

Angels

The spirit they bring the vibes that
They give,
That touch that surrounds them,
With that halo of a glow over that
Smile and grin,
Giving off the mood that's needed when
Patience is wearin' a little thin,
Giving off that reflection that only God
Could send,
That special feeling they give to you knowing
Beside you stands that invisible twin,
Giving off rays of reason and the glow
Of hope within,
Off them into your soul it spins,
There a lot more than just someone you know
There allot more than just friends,
There allot like your family or allot like
Your kin,
There messengers there angels that God to you
sends,

David Martin Johnson

"Cancer"

It comes as a Thief in the night,
It comes silently, onward,
It comes progressively, tenaciously,
Unannounced, it comes,
To take the greatest treasure,
A life, sometimes,
Cancer comes, unbidden,
Unwanted, unseen and
Unwelcome, it comes.

Mattie M. Stewart

Those Clouds

Watching the clouds roll across the gray sky
They look angry and full simply waiting right now
for the perfect place to unload that which they carry
Their job is nearly complete - they should be happier.

The small children laugh as they splash in the rain,
jumping in puddles making beautiful mud
Their joy is contagious even their mothers can't scold
As they too wish they could let the mud ooze between their toes

The young boys play on not even noticing they are wet
the game they play is the only thing important
The young girls huddle close as they watch the boys
Rain isn't going to chase them away from THEIR game

Two young lovers wander down the damp lane
Hand in hand the water doesn't even slow their pace
what they share together is to perfect for the rain to spoil
No...it simply makes it even more romantic-OH LOVE!!!

Grandma and Grandpa sit on the porch swing together
Smiling as they watch it all happening all over again
Remembering all the love, the joy the laughter the peace
the rain from those Ugly Gray, Beautiful Gray Clouds brings.

Debby Baer

Thank You

I thank you "all" for the gift of trees,
they mean to me what life is meant to be,
A gift to love, nurture, and share,
A daily reminder that friends truly care.

A "thank you" from the life that was,
whose purpose was to teach me love;
A life that was to reach my heart,
A life that was not totally mine from the start.

I'm thankful for the years I've had,
They'll give me strength for the years ahead,
Days pass slowly as I let go,
The physical gone, the spiritual to grow.

As understanding slowly creeps along,
This lessens my sadness as I learn to reach,
The true point of knowing which is to teach,
This comes as I've remembered,
"Not my will"
But "Thy will be done."

Janice Kay Worwood

Elegy

The news got it wrong on that July 4th holiday
They said you turned Lollipop.
Them yuppy white rich folks don't know s**t
About you— about me—
About what it's like to fight your way out of one death trap after another.
But you had a different plan.
I remember in high school—
You wrote a rap with that too-proud-back-man, Aaron Carr—
About the real American experience
And I remember Ms. Kline wouldn't let you enter
The literary contest,
Because she said it wasn't art.
Well, it was art to me
And every other boriquan
Real intelligence
Too smart for all that "para la familia" - mierda
Proud Puerto Rican
But everybody knew Trigga was destined to snap
Just, no body expected him to take you down too.

Jennifer Carlino

If Only Grown-Ups Would Listen

If only grown ups would listen
They would be proud of our dreams.
Not cussing or fussing and not even scream.
If only grown-ups would listen.
They would see that we are the world
No matter if we are a boy or a girl.
If grown-ups would listen they would see
that we are not perfect we are only human beings.
It is a time for grown-ups to see that we
can make a change no matter how hard it may be.
In time the children of the world may
see no matter what race or color you or me may be.
To strive hard to have confidence, courage
and to have responsibility.
If only grown-ups would listen.
They could see that we are shining stars ready to be free.

Demica Thomas

Comfort

It is hard to cope with the lose of a loved one,
Thinking about all you did together and the endless fun.
When you found out they were gone
You felt as if you were all alone.

With a blank feeling deep down inside,
Your heart and mind went
Along with the grief came hurt,
As you see your loved one buried in dirt.

The day when you need it most.
People are there to help you cope.

Donnie Ray Palmer II

Reminiscing About Aging

As I sit in my den all alone,
thinking back fifty odd years,
about when I was a kid with my mother living at home.

I was a young inquisitive girl,
just starting out in the world.
wondering what it would be like to become fifty-two years of age.

Now that I am nearing that great wonderful stage.
It isn't as old as it once appeared to be.
I am eagerly anticipating the year that I reach the lovely
age of sixty-three.

Will I be mobile independent and self-sufficient?
Or living with my only daughter and being solely dependent?

Well only time will tell about this chapter of my life.
Hopefully I will be home with my spouse of forty years and
continuing to be his lovely aging wife.

Albernia G. Clark

O Glorious Light...

O Glorious Light who fashioned quick
This aging temple, yet now indwelling forever -
How can it be that your healing hand is severed
From its mortar and its brick?
Will you not mend that which is broken, and heal that which is sick?
Dare I question your skill? Never,
Except upon viewing these pillars decayed from ill weather
Even then in my doubt my conscience is pricked.

O Sovereign Lord, owner of my soul
And Potter of every clay vessel, make
Only this chipped heart whole.
For to heal every wound and mend every break
Would make heaven less famed and full
And this poisoned earth much easier to take.

Kenneth Cardillo

Untitled

Dearest God
This is a letter from your little girl almost two,
Can You spare me a minute while I read it to You?
Since I was born my parents have chosen to go their separate ways
Do I have a lot of time to right this wrong or is it just a matter of days?
From the very start of my life I couldn't eat or play,
But my Grandma Betty comes to see me every day!
My Mommy Candi, comes when she's not too busy or feeling bad.
My Daddy Randy comes once in a while, but he seems so sad
Why God, am I not like other children on this earth?
I only know I've been this way since birth.
My Grandma Betty and My Grandpa Jack
Love me dearly, no matter what my little body lacks.
Thank You God for the Doctors and Nurses they have been so good
to me,
I was wondering God, will I live to be three?
I just wanted You to know God, I love You, Really I do.
As always, this is Shelby Lynn Collins, Your little girl, almost two.

Joyce F. Collins

Sincere True Love

You see everyday how love in the home, sometimes strays away,
This is usually caused from listening to bickering every single day;
When that special someone is sick, we love to help if we can,
As long as it doesn't interfere with our already made plan;

Love is not to be used as a tool to get your way,
It's should be used to show affection so that a special person will stay,
Love is that special feeling which makes everyone feel happy and good,
And helps each person set new values as every nice person should;

Love you share with your family and friends should always be true,
You can feel and see this when they are being good to you;
Honesty and love between husband and wife is a must,
If you are ever to have what is known as complete trust;

True love between your children can be seen during hard times,
Especially when their problems does not result in crimes;
Kids will always test you to see what makes you mad,
But as long as they trust you and say they love you, that's not so bad;

Share this feeling called "love" with everyone each day,
Don't let hate build up and get in your way;
Be understanding of problems others may have to face,
Especially in a world where love has no boundaries to a specific race;

Clifford F. Simpson

On We Travel

To be with me and I with thee,
this really should be.
To lock up tight like stars with the moon at night.
The rose with the aroma and color so bright.
The fire with air to give it its might.
The phonograph with the record brings sweet music to delight.

The road to the sunset was quite the night.
Thus we have traveled with some fright;
not to give in and yet not flight.

Simple pleasures of life we share, stay in my sight.
For this to be, I say yeh, and yet you say neh.
To love I do still, for you give strength and pleasure
to my life which is not in your sight.

Yet as we might, still travel through another day, to share as we
will, each time a new road as we turn left, or even to the right,
may we find one day you have come to see the sight.

With this my words cease, to you a token of love in these words
I bequeath. We will go on to share company, a smile we will keep.
To be with me and I with thee, dearest of friends always we will be.

Joyce Seymour

"A Broken Heart"

Let it lie dormant, let it just sleep
This way you know & never will weep.
Weep for a lost love, weep for a feeling
That goes down deeply & up to the ceiling.
So keep it inside you, just let it stay
That way it'll always be out of the way.
Out of the way, you'll hurt deep inside
So heed my fair warning, just let it hide.
Don't let him know it, just keep it alone.
This way it's better you'll never atone
No one can hurt you, again like before
If you keep it locked tight behind closed door.
Oh love drives you crazy, it tears you apart
Sick at your stomach & rips out your heart.
For you knows it's gone, it just couldn't stay
I guess you would tell me stay out of your way.
No more will I share, this old heart of mine
It can just lie dormant till end of my time.

Alma L. Albaugh

Dear Bill

Dear Bill:
Tho much of the usual's going on,
we've missed a lot since you've been gone.
We've missed the jokes you used to tell.
Not that they were all that swell.
We might have heard it once before,
but we loved to hear your laughter roar.

And you know in the low down parts of songs,
where your big booming voice belongs,
there doesn't seem any more to be,
that res'nant rumbling sound you see.
Not the one we used to hear,
in all those days when you were here.

But you know here just the other day,
a thunder storm came by our way.
And we heard a low down booming roar,
we thought we might have heard before.
And then the thought just crossed our mind.
We wondered if — naw — never mind.

Allan Voigt

Those Eyes

I look into those eyes and can see his sufferings.
Those eyes,
Blinded by resentment, anger and misunderstanding.
Those eyes.
They are mirrors of thought,
Of a brilliance yet undiscovered.
He can hide behind the composure of his expression,
And all, save one, are fooled by this game.
One look in those eyes tells all I need know.
Those eyes.
They are a pathway to a soul worth seeking,
A thread to the true emotions of the man I love.
I see so much pain in those eyes.
I wish to pluck them out,
As if to banish the torture they represent.
Instead, I love with my whole self: Body, mind, soul.
Love will fight the evil demons that plague those eyes.
Tears shed by he and I will cleanse those eyes.
Those eyes will see again.

Amie Link

The Beach

French fries, ice cream,
those old wooden boards screaming under my feet.
Cool wind, hot sun;
We're back at the beach, and it's time for some fun.

The girls are in suits you can hardly see,
the guys are in shades trying to take a peek.
You got winners and losers; some stranger than others,
But nobody cares, and nobody bothers.

By the end of the day and the sun's going down.
everybody's gone, there's no one around.
They're back getting ready for the second round,
heading out for that big night on the town.

Some friendships will flourish and some will die,
Some lovers are made and some live a lie.
Some ride the waves, Some say good-bye.
And the carousal circles endlessly, under the bright night sky.

Albert Schmidt

A Civil War Poem

Blue against gray,
Those words will never go away.
Just a while ago we stood together proud,
Now families have their heads bowed.
Everyday we know there are cannons being fired,
The brave soldiers are always hungry and tired.
Why do we have to pick sides,
All we do is kill each other's hides.
Innocent people really get hurt,
While soldiers get their faces pushed down in the dirt.
Many women are becoming widows,
Many people are weeping like willows.
Can't they see all the blood being shed,
Can't they see all our countrymen dead?
Many families are split apart,
But they will always be together in the heart.
As the tears of the people fall,
We know we can no longer stand tall.
The people can't take this suffering anymore,
We pray this will be the end of the war.

Katie L. Eberhardy

"A Lost Soul"

The world is black as the claws of depression clinch my heart as though he is trying to rid me of love and passion. My mind runs wild as if she is hungry for happiness. Things look so dull and unwelcome, that I hide my feelings in the deepest, darkest corner of my soul. My body is engulfed with much darkness as my heart cries out for love. See my tears of passion as they slowly drip from my fingers. My sense of sadness withdraws me from the universe and surroundings. The pain of loneliness grows stronger within me. I try to overcome it but its strength is no match for me. My heart is weak and only love can save me. The soul is lost and shall only be found by looking at your inner passion. Only then will love shine through and fill your soul with peacefulness. Look within yourself to find your own soul growing much strength with each new day.

Julia A. Goecke

Untitled

A closeness like ours doesn't flower overnight
It unfolds ever so slowly
Through the sunshine and shadows of time

Nurtured with the summer and winters of shared experience
until at last the seeds of affection we've sewn, mature and blend

Bringing forth a garden of rare beauty
Bright with blossoms of faith and trust, that can never fade

Renay Martin

Forever With Me

It's been hard to go on without you here
Though I know that you are always near
It seems so unfair that you had to leave us this way
Every night we look up to the heavens
and for you we pray
God is a savior we all must believe in
For cursing him would be a greater sin
In time our hearts will grow strong again
Though I can't tell you when
Mine has already begun to heal
Even though this nightmare is real
I now appreciate my life and will to be
And I know that you are forever with me.

Amanda Johnson

Changing Times

How I wish I had lived in another year
Though my life now I hold very dear.
But what a difference time has made
how the same, nothing has stayed,
Oh, had I lived in another age or life
Though in earlier days, there was much strife.

The words and the dress, flamboyant or prim
And the romance that danger could always dim.
Peril and evil would everywhere wait
To escape it, merely a twist of fate.
Surely I'm much safer, I can live it through a book.
So very many lives back then, death claimed or robbed or took
Before they had a chance to live, before they could grow old
And how terrible it must have been that life was bought and sold.

So my blessing I will count, and in this life I'll stay
For life has taught it's lessons, shown man the error of his ways.
Aren't we very fortunate that we've become so wise?
Danger is gone, we've seen the light...or am I telling lies?

Ignorance must be very strong, through time it merrily goes.
The only thing we may have changed appears to be our clothes.

Julie A. Stanford

Gone

He sits alone with his head in his hands,
Thoughts and memories running wild,
Trying to remember the good he's done,
Only bits and pieces come to mind.
Wishing and hoping for a better future to come
Knowing the past he lead will always haunt him.
Wanting to leave it all behind,
But it clings to him like a blood thirsty leech
A tear forms and falls from a sleep deprived eye
Knowing he must start over and forget it.
He feels lonely and like he can't go on,
The memory of her tears at his heart, she's gone.

James Wills

For Just A Moment

I heard your voice,
I saw your face,
For a moment, I felt your touch...

A sudden breeze, came through
the room, was I imagining all too
much?

The scent of your loving presence
For that moment, seemed all too real,

I heard your voice, I saw your face,
If only I could feel.

Madalin Zajko

Untitled

"In the tears of guilt"
Thousands of miles away,
Photos reminding me of you,
Lonely heart which then was so happy.
Those momentous times we had seem now to fade away.
And then there was those downhearted days,
That were sometimes to hurting to take.
All those years we spent together,
Shared our ups and downs,
Helped each other when one of us needed it,
Laughed together and cried.
Then that painful day had come,
When we had to say good-bye,
Leave all those great memories behind
And come to a thought that we might
Never see each other again.
My dear friend I didn't want to do this,
Believe me it was so hard for me
I moved on,
But I still sorrow from the pain.

Kinga Szymoniak

Front Seat Struggle

Six people in a car,
Three in the front
Three in the back
Those in the back can state some facts.

All six waiting for the driver to move,
Buckle-up was said and we all approved.
Those in the front were having a time-
Pulling, pushing, sliding and searching for the seat belt hole
they couldn't find.

Understand, the three in the front DID know the
seat belts were working,
But observing from the back you would never know this
from all the movement and jerking.
Laughter began to soar.
The more we laughed, the louder the roar.

The "Front Seat Struggle" finally ended with a 'click'
Everyone knew exactly what this meant.
They liked the sound-
The laughter continued, the car started moving, all six
were home bound.

Annie Ruth Arrington

Love

Love is long-suffering, strong, courageous, and pure
Through defeats and victories
Tribulations and glories
No matter what, it will always endure
Love is the essence of life and the flame that keeps it burning bright
Without love, there would only be darkness, there would be no light
You are truly blessed if you have a love unconditional
A love that you give with your whole strength, mind, heart, and soul
Love is the unity between every race
For it looks beyond the shape of your face
And the color of your skin
It finds the true person within
To love is to sacrifice, it is whole-souled devotion
For love is more than a feeling, it is more than an emotion
It is what's shared between two people, between friends,
and between man and all living things
Happiness, joy, and peace are what it brings
Love is sweet, caring, and divine, too
Even when there is no hope, love will always shine through
It can cause sorrow and laughter
But it can also lead the way to "happily ever after"

Jamie N. Brazo

Solitaire

Breezes pass through leaves as thoughts pass
Through our minds,
Some as gentle whispers; some at whirlwind
speeds that blind.

Rain hitting rooftops can sound as torrential as
tears to the soul,
At times it lightly drizzles; then at others, it pours
out of control.

A mountain reaching high, it's peak intimately
brushing the clouds,
Can be as our endeavors to overcome a fear which
cowers in shrouds.

An ocean which assuredly plunges to unfathomable
depths and wonders,
Is as our attempts to look inside ourselves and correct
our errant blunders.

The sun setting in the horizon with it's colors
so muted and subdued,
Compare them to the souls which journey through
life solitaire and misconstrued.

Cynthia Vaughn-Thrift

Untitled

Let us begin the journey of pain, it'll take us straight
through the stains left by previous couples, gross touches us
in ways unknown to the young, dance free the spell used
when possessed by the dark spirits of the underworld.
Live by the emotions left from dawns' powerful blow
towards a new dimension of understanding reasons for
erupting into something more cruel than that of the worst holocaust.
Friends welcome your actions to their lairs
of agonized and tortured souls. Fresh adventure peels the
eyes of the awaited. Let the attack of malice be the first
step in the conspiracy created for the end. Confusion is
permanent, evolving into something wished for since the
last "blue moon," eventually it will stain itself to me...
Then! Rebirth is presented, when the time is right I'll exit this
reality, and seep into eternal bliss! That's when it will all
be worth it.
Join me in my hell to achieve what is deserved,
consider it initiation into the celebration.

David Tewes

Autumn Sunrise

See you hill as it mistily rises
Thru a cloak of whispering fog.
As the season for sleep nears,
It is clothed in golden and scarlet hues.
Ah - see the rising sun
Push questing fingers of silver
Thru the welcoming arms of drowsing trees,
Changing quaking droplets to iridescent gems
Of shimmering miniature rainbows.
As the magic brush of creation
Paints an enchanted landscape
That will for all eternity
Enrapture the soul...

Jenifer V. M. Wilcox

Untitled

To gazed upon by millions
Kings, queens they may be
The insignificance of earthly praise
But to be smiled upon by God
Means you have pleased him - don't you see

M. E. Roberts

Untitled

Temerity, like a downward current
thrusts my body into a whirlpool
Sinking, sinking,
plummeting past schools of fish, plankton, and porpoises

My friends perhaps are content to frolic
in the shallow and safe surface, the threshold
of this submerged paradise.

Journeying further into opaque darkness,
I wonder if I am not welcome in
this oceanic realm and have fallen
prey to the invisible guardian of
the deep; its vicelike grip of despair
tightens and silences my screams in soundless space
then slowly loosens as if the Lord's
sovereign hands were prying the tentacles loose

Sapped of strength and gasping for air..thinking of dear friends above
they wait, resuscitate me back into the commonplace of reality.
Away from the illusory paradise, if God had intended me to dwell
among the depths, then I would have fins and gills.

Brandon Der

Passing The Torch

It's your turn now. It's time the torch is passed.
Time for you to take the lead. Your time has come... at last.
Time for you to leave the nest; to spread your wings and fly.
Time to find your own life's quest and carve your piece of pie.
Time to take the world by storm and bend it to your will.
Time to dream a noble dream and make the world ideal.
It is the torch of freedom. It shines the light of truth.
We've borne its burden gladly - almost from our youth.
We've borne it in our triumphs. We've borne it thru our tears;
We've always tried to hold it high. We've borne it well for years.
We had a shining vision of how the world should be;
When we were young and foolish. When we were wild and free.
We thought that we could change things, when we were in our prime;
We knew we'd make a difference - if only given time.
But time is tough to master, as history has shown,
Now the time has fin'ly come to pass our burden on.

It was a lovely vision - to bring a better day
But when we lost our focus we let it slip away.
So keep your dreams close to your heart - learn from our miscue;
It is a sacred trust we give. We pass this torch to you.

Eddie Lee Turner

Prison Walls

Crimes of injustice, of passion, of lawlessness
Time passes away, for we prison mates

Damaged walls
gloomy cells
bars of steel
inlaid with a toilet stall

Men packed together
No room, yet no where to put us

I number the memories with each writing upon these walls
I cling to pictures and hold them close, and hope that I
can touch, smell, and feel their presence

No sunlight to bathe in, no wind presseth against my face
I remember of times gone by, of hopes and dreams that
linger in my head

I strike a deal with the man above, and hope in his mercy,
so that I may hold on

My thoughts in the nightlife are visions that attack me,
of rats of monsters and scary things

I hope to be gone soon, but for now;
my home is my prison walls....

Jacqueline L. Evans

The Brass Ring

Swayed by misconceptions, searching for the truth
Times are constantly changing, and so are points of view
Nothing satisfying, there is no peace of mind
There's no more use in denying, resolutions what I must find

Staring ahead into the distance, running against the wind
Pace is slowing from it's resistance, being pushed back once again

Alternating choices, overwhelming possibilities
Losing sight of what really matters, failing to win against a destiny
Depression slowing motivation, dreams are traded for stability
Overcoming hardships with fading grace, falling through the cracks
of society

Remote to things that are close at hand
Dreaming of travel to a distant land
Trying to follow a desperate plan
While the brass ring slips from my hand

Sometimes it seems so hard to go on, why not quit and play it safe
Striving for an attainable glory, or reaching out to a hopeless fate

Old friends become familiar faces, left behind in the search for fame
Everyday adapting to changes, nothing will ever be the same

David Gillen Jr.

"The Letter "D" Remains As One"

To be the one
To experience the love
To be the one
To experience the sadness
As you are the one
I will deeply miss

My love for you will
never change
It will only better

I say to you
No matter how close
No matter the distance
My internal love will travel to you, with everlasting existence.

Darren Reynolds

Heaven

Heavenly voices of angels sing,
To God on high our heavenly King.

Peace, hope, and love
Dwells in this place above.

Hatred and war does not exist,
Because God won't allow it on His list.

Families are always together,
And life exists forever.

Love will show no color,
Because there will be peace among each other.

Pearly gates and streets of gold.
Treasures that have never been told.

I don't have to say anymore,
Because this is a place everyone should adore.

Heaven is the name of this beautiful place,
Where we always will see His face.

Jenny McClease

"By My Side"

I would bottle the seas and conquer the skies,
To have and hold you here by my side,

My love for you grows stronger with each passing day,
Together until the end, we're here to stay,

You are my dreams I dream every night,
My goddess of love, you are my life,

The love of your touch, the lust of your kiss,
My feelings of you grow, I cannot resist,

Our wings of love grow and together we fly,
Up to heaven with you by my side,

Words do not begin to tell how I feel about you
Actions speak louder, so this I would do,

I would battle the seas and conquer the skies,
To have and hold you here by my side.

Billie Jo Stillwell

On Staying Young

It takes much or than Oil of Olay
To keep those lines and wrinkles away.
You've got to diet and exercise
To stay in shape and protect your eyes.
Stay out of the sun, don't lie on the beach
In case the strong rays are still in reach.
But most of all it's what's in your head
That tells the truth, it must be said.
You still must exercise your brain
To keep your mind in the proper frame.
So think about others, what you can do for them
Will help the most in this youthful game.

Eileen Marquet

In Pursuit...

We must dance the dance of want and wain
to know our desires less guard against the pain
of possible rejection from our souls fulfillment
and our loves gain.

If, in my heart, should I unfold
All that is there to see
would you turn away, in fear
and leave me with this space free?

Where do we meet...this common oasis of love
and shed our cloth of dance
to face each other without a shred
except for who we are?

Look at me and see what gifts I have to give.
They can only be seen by eyes like mine.
Eyes that reflect back the warmth, the want, the same.

Are you there? Are you mine?
The music plays...my heart beats so
the music sets the pace.
Come, be my love
if you feel...if you hear...and greet me face to face.

Debra Doherty

Happy

I'm just a happy girl
living in this world.

I start each day with a positive attitude
even when people treat me rude

I'm just a happy girl
living in this old world.

Patricia Striggles

Impossible

When you play your cards real cleaver.
Lady luck might make it, best hand ever.
So when we go to dine, remember, my horse
Could be "any kind."

Richard L. Willis

When I Leave This World

When I leave this world I hope to be able
to leave something behind to let those know
who I was.
And what I am leaving behind is my poetry
for others to enjoy.

I hope in due time that my poetry will touch
hearts, and helps you, and guides you in your
daily lives.

My poetry is not my whole life.
God, my family, and friends is what I live
for everyday.
I love them with all my heart and I always will.
I hope it will be a long time before I leave
this world.

Danette S. Atkins

Just A Note

Have you not yearned to write some word
To lift the load from weary men-
Some word of hope, of cheer, of strength,
As coming from the savant's pen.

For each such dream, I am most sure
There waits some soul to be thus prod,
And put back on the higher road
That leads, through rock-bound paths, to God

So ponder deep the Spirit's plea,
And think of some you may befriend,
By holding forth a helping hand-
And grasped therein a loving pen.

So write that note of love today
To bring a lift from suff'ring's maze;
And light again a lamp of hope
To guide and keep through coming days.

For strewn along Life's rugged path
Are those half-bent 'neath sorrow's load;
Who need the love of stronger ones
Who walk along the higher road.

Clarence William Jones

Power

Fear causes men to be boys
to lose themselves in panic
sweating out their last breath
it causes men to lie
and causes them to expose the truth
with a storm in their stomach
and a hot coal in their heart
it makes them do what most men never fathom
And above all this,
Fear brings out respect
you must respect this thing that holds your life
which has caused you to see yourself
who you really are
what kind of a man are you?
And he who causes souls to fear his name
and gains the respect of men.
Only then does he have complete power

Eric Laing

See Me Pray

Jesus Christ, this isn't my fight, against the one I love.
To make a decision, I hate this religion,
What choice do I have with this?
Confused, uprooted, demented, unsuited:
How will my argument end? Within myself, dug out and polluted,
Anguish terrorizes my joints and continued. I beg, "Subside", yet
all Satan cries.
'Til death do us part? This won't help my heart. A jealous regression;
A demonic possession, which should I consider? Take over my hell,
Hurt my bell, find my only way to yell. Torture me, reduce my speed,
end my everlasting plea. This cannot contain a purpose.
Please begin my metamorphose. Expel my mind from signs of thought,
Repeat to me, I almost forgot, Good ridden's to you,
Say good-bye, your blue. Remind me never to talk to you.
If it takes to much, don't try to care. Your pulling out all of you hair.
I loath your oppression, you increase my dimension,
Point your anger in the right direction. Hate your fate,
I don't care about your mate. Drop this stupid tackles weight,
Decide your way, Involve me later in the day. But don't talk to me,
I have too much to plow,
I can't handle your constant complaining right now.

Christine Ann Paolini Barnes

I'll Be There

Dear I'll always be there
To run my fingers through your hair
To hold your hand
And to discover the promised land

I'll be there in times of need
And I'll be there to give you a pat on the back when
you've done a good deed

Even if I seem a million miles away
I'll be there on any given day
Through the tears and pain
I'll be there in the sunshine and the rain

Through the thick and thin
I'll be there to laugh and grin

I'll be there when a hug is needed
And I'll be there when the lawn needs to be weeded

Darling I guess what I am trying to say
Is that I'll be there 'til my dying day

Connie B. A. Blaine

Dear Lord How Can I Thank You

Dear Lord how can I thank you for giving me this chance,
To show I can be a mother, although not by normal stance.
I've waited forty years, for this child to be born and all the hurt
and anxiousness will leave with the light on the morning that he is
born.
I can't believe it is happening, although I know it's true.
I'm going to be a mom, very, very soon.

Because she can not care for him, she has given the job to me.
I will make you proud oh Lord, you can count on me.
I know that without you by my side, without your strength to endure
I would of lost it years ago, on this I'm very sure.

You've led my life to this child, and how happy I will be,
When I hear him call Mommy and for once it will directed at me.

A women who can conceive cannot imagine this special joy,
No words can explain how I feel awaiting my baby boy.
I will praise you everyday oh Lord, you have shown me the way.
Whether times are good or tough, I will kneel down and pray.
Dear Lord how can I thank you,
Each and everyday.

Judy Horka

De Profundis

Desperate anger, clinging with fermented glee
To shrinking shreds of rationality
You and I, we search but cannot find
The sacred broken ties that bind
Or choke if the air proves unclean
We will never become what might have been

The only end that justifies these means
Washes this face that is not as it seems

My brothers hands are driving my blood
That flows from my mind in a drowning flood
It runs down and turns the wheel
That turns the world that turns my heel
As I turn to crush your blighted rose
Between the lines of your sickening prose

De Profundis, out of the depths, I weep
You do not hear, for you forever sleep.

Cheryl Anne Ricks

The Price

They come to me in the dead of night. When none but I do stir.
To sing me songs and poems and tales. Of kings and dogs and singing whales.
And fill my head with wondrous words that I have never heard.
The sounds do echo in my soul and fill me just a hollow hole.
Till I bulge with maddened verse an haunted tune or worse.

But oft the stories refuse the page. The melodies will not be caged.

I'll not be charged with setting down the sound and fury all unbound, till I am blinded by the light, burnt and blistered by their might.

They but mock me in my plight.
My near madness their delight.
They like their candles short and bright.

Who asked them here? Who bid them come?
At night. To me. The seductive ones.
When babes, in beds, are sucking thumbs.

To whisper sweetly in my ear, and fill my soul with fear.
At the price I must pay.

Allen Knapstad

Corridors Of Darkness

To walk upon the feather-light softness of love
To sit upon the knees of destiny
To touch finally the velvety essence of dreams:
  One must walk down the Corridors of Darkness.

To be the samaritan instead of the blind man
To become an individual amidst a sea of faces
To awake one morning to the sound of Fate's footsteps:
  One must journey along the Corridors of Darkness.

To clasp hands with those of another culture
To bend down to the wishes of the universe
To forgive when hate is the easier emotion:
  One must stroll among the Corridors of Darkness.

To remember what is most dear to heart
To recall the simplicity and complexity inherent in life
To be lucky enough to wake to another morning:
  One must stumble within the Corridors of Darkness.

But to be all that one imagines
To be the epitome of goodness, to be the savior of one's own soul:
  One must endure the Corridors of Darkness
    And laugh in the face of Agony.

Deverie Lee Halfen

It's My Flag

People have said, "it's a freedom to burn my flag,
To step upon it, spit upon it, try to make it a dirty rag,
But I tell you this, my friends, and not so friendly too,
You'll never burn the spirit out of my precious "red, white and blue"!
New flags can be made of cloth, and cursed
  and dirtied, too,
But in the hearts of all who're fought, died,
  and lived under her; like you,
Will always be able to close their eyes, and
  see "old Glory" my flag, red-white and blue

Al H. Phillips

Shadows Of Man

Money is power in every man's game.
To the top man must brawl.
As death devours, he has no shame.

Time is consuming, so cling to your fame.
Wishes of many to rule over all.
Money is power in every man's game.

Up the mountain man must climb, down the path he does maim.
First you shall crawl.
As death devours, he has no shame.

Heartless and cold, no man shall be tame.
Poor and rich divides by a wall.
Money is power in every man's game.

In the end, we all the same.
Beware, do not fall.
As death devours, he has no shame.

To God there is nothing in a name.
Time slips away while you stall.
Money is power in every man's game.
As death devours, he has no shame.

Jessica Monas

To Those Who....

To those who love you oh, so much,
To those who treasure your every touch.
To those who want to be your friend,
To those who will help you to each day's end.
To those who keep you safe at night,
To those who show you God's own light.
To those who you pray for every day,
To those who see you in a brand new way.
To those who you love with all your heart,
To those who you will never part.
To those who help you laugh when you frown,
To those who lift your spirits when you're down.
To those who taught you wonderful things,
To those who helped you broaden your wings.
To those who will be there when you cry,
To those who will hold your hand when you die.
To all of those people so special and dear,
a warm, little thank you forever to hear.

Ann-Marie Strike

Confession That I Want You Here

The freshness of a dream come true
is what I think when I see you
You walked into my life that way
And it's the same way everyday

When I have you by my side
All my lonely feelings hide
The feelings I have when you are near
Confession that I want you here,
Forever

R. J. Rymshaw Jr.

What Is A Home?

A mansion full of precious things
  to view and impress our neighbors -
If cold, not love resides inside
  we've defeated all our Labors!

A little tent upon a hill
  with warm loving people
Towers above the mansions
  and deserves the highest steeple!

For in this life with it's troubles and strife
  we need someone to share
Our feelings - which helps us challenge things
  - The secret is to CARE!

So give me a home where we congregate
  'round a warm and loving fire
Where we all discuss the events of the day
  - to fulfill my heart's desire!

Catherine M. Cullen

The Sounds Of Morning

The shrill buzzing voice of the alarm clock telling everyone
to wake up.
  Groans all around the house
The clock giving its threatening final warning
A stampede of pounding feet rushing anxiously
to the bathroom
  A racket of voices in the kitchen
    Dishes clanking and crashing
The front door closing with one last BANG!
    Before silence over comes the house

Erika Capalla

If You Were to Leave Me Behind

If you left me behind,
to walk on my own,
Memories are all I would find, of wonderful times we've known.
When the first streak of light crawls upon the day,
And when the moon pierces the night,
You'll see me walking along my way.
When in autumn the first leaves will fall,
and in Spring the flowers bloom.
When summer turns to fall, you'll feel me calling out to you.
Along the path I'll hear, your laughter in the wind,
Reaching out will be your care,
And the hand you'd always lend.
We've shared happiness, and above all, love,
We've had a friendship that will always stay.
Memories are a gift from above,
That death cannot take away.
If you left me behind,
There's one thing I'd ask of you,
Walk slowly with care, and keep in mind,
That someday I'll follow you.

Julia Campbell

To See Infinity

I look up at a jewel-spattered sky
To see the stars
Thousands of faceted diamonds, rubies, sapphires,
Glittering against the black velvet of night.
As I look up, I wonder
Whether there are other worlds,
Other lives
Like ours
Or perhaps not so like ours
Looking into their own night skies
And wondering the same thing.

Cheralyn L. Lambeth

Untitled

Why is it that I feel the way I do
To want you like no one else could
A twinkle in my eye that people say I get
When I talk, see or just think of you

Deep down in my soul is a burning passion
of love that will never be told
I will never whisper these feelings I have
Hidden in my heart it will always remain

Over the years our feelings have changed
You don't like to see me with someone else
So I'm not the only one not to tell how I feel
What's holding us back from being more than friends

I love you with more than my heart and soul
Would it be worth our friendship of gold
To try what our hearts want the most
Or is it best to leave things alone.

Dawn Marie Robidoux

A Real Joy

My mother likes to help, to dry the dishes when I wash.
To watch her small hands with a towel find their way
around and around each cup, dish and silverware.
So proud is she that God grants her strength to do so.
She loves to play cards but too soon tires.
I read to her from books and magazines,
as she used to do when I was small.
She hangs onto every word as I did when she read to me.
To listen to her tell stories of her childhood and later years too.
She loves to go for a ride on sunny days, arriving home,
she always asks, is the ride over already?
She is like a shining star, with twinkles in her eyes.
Bright as a pure gem.
My mother drives a wheelchair, 96 years young, legally blind,
but a real joy. "My Mother."

10:20 p.m. February 18, 1995.
Then the angels came to visit mother, to invite her home.
I'm ready she replied, let's go!

Jeane W. Burnham Jr. (her son)

"The Tale Of The Bomb Shelter"

The town was frenzied I should say; when told to run without delay,
To whichever bomb shelter was the nearest;
  but first to warn all their dearest
Friends and neighbors they could get; and in the process, not to fret!
Slowly they began to calm; trying not to think about the bomb.
The man to my left was a psychiatrist I could tell; by the pin of
  honor he wore on his lapel.
He spoke of many people he had cured; of psychological maladies which
  could not be endured.
In a peculiar tone said he'd been hopin'; that he could somewhere find
  a window he could open.
I do not know the reason for his query; but I do admit he did look
  somewhat weary.
I feel that I should mention just one other; who took both roles of
  housewife and of mother.
She spoke of what her children meant to her; but did not once inquire
  where they were.
She claimed to work until her bones were frail; yet could recall soap
  operas in detail.
She bragged about her car a dozen times; and hoped she gave the meter
  enough dimes.
She could not wait 'till this ordeal was through; to unite again with
  her new Malibou.

Carol A. D'Amato

Life

Life is something you have to deal with; it brings good things to you and also takes them away.
You have to make and shape your own Life; you can gain from the experiences that Life brings you.
Life is not one alone, it is for all.
Life brings two people together, but it can also put them miles apart.
This thing called Life can break your heart if you let it.
Life is dealing with it.
Life is not filled with all good times, because it has bad.
You might shed many tears in your Life time, but oh, wait for the joy Life can bring. It will make you turn right around and sing,
If your Life is a Life.

Carolyn L. Manigo Rose

Time

As I sit here listening, almost straining to hear the tick
tock of time passing me by my mind wander back when
life were simpler and heartaches few. All the things
I once held so dear to me seem now like a speck on a
window pane with just one wipe everything would
disappear without a trace. My soul seen barren with
a solace so great that it takes my breathe away, Time
is a powerful tool, a device that is unstoppable, So as
I sit here I ponder my future, my faith for time marches
on and waits for no one, All of a sudden I felt a tremendous
rush to my head, like tiny particles exploding scattering
my very existence all over the unversed until I disappear
no longer visible to the naked eye. I am afraid of the future
for I do not know what time have in store for me. I can
only hope and pray it will be more Kinder and gentler
to me. I look around the room at the clock and I see
time have move on silently like a thief in the night creeping
without making a sound so I just sit here patiently
waiting for my time.

Alice J. Daniel

Stained Glass

Love is like a piece of a stained glass window,
Together a beautiful masterpiece,
In bits and pieces a painful reminder of reality.
I broke that window long ago with my fist in a fit of rage.
Pieces scattered for miles around.
I've come across many pieces but none seem to fit.
I found a piece today,
So beautiful it surpassed the rest.
But it was already in someone else's window.
I lost it long ago
Now I won't get it back.
Maybe it was never meant to be mine.
Yet, now that I've seen it
I can't get it out of my mind.

Catherine J. Henderson

Autumn Time

Once I was young and carefree.
Indeed, nothing at all bothered me.
I could stay up till the wee hours,
And get up at the dawn to head out to work.
But, that was before autumn.

Once I could drink with the best;
In fact, I'd never shed a tear,
For I had all.
But, that was before autumn.

Oh, but how things have changed,
Now that autumn has come!

Robert Davis

"Awakened By Inspiration"

While it is true that I, myself, created my monsters by sewing together the crosses I have born, no one in the world—this conscious reality—will ever know the private suffering I endured!

Cracking the mirror of my dreams, Demons snatch my life as their own
and token me with a fragmented reflection of what my soul was to be.
Rejoicing in this pain, I comfortably drown in deceit and manipulation
Spinning and spinning, I run from the garden that would save me.

Does this way madness lie? Or enlightenment? Circles must sleep.

A sailboat crosses the seas of mind, and I join the journey.
My soul awakens to hear your voice—my teacher, my Inspiration.
The constraining winds no longer steer; I am the Author of my world.
Inspiration's prophecies teach me to laugh at my sunken, wailing demons, and I begin my life masterpiece without fear of the ending.

My mind stretches past the moon, the stars, into Heaven itself... seeing

My soul—burning tree of life, nature of knowledge and inspiration.
Everyone has their own leaves, their own special gifts.
Mine burn with a fire of emotion so passionate at times, so deadly at others. Inspiration rekindled these leave—these fallen embers
into a blaze that will touch and merge with any star it crosses.
My soul is awakened, and I will never slumber again.

Karen Christine Benninghoff

Untitled

Today is like no other day
Tomorrow will be the same
If there are no changes in my life today
I must change
I must give all of myself equally
To the formulation of my dream of life
I must take control of my life
In its environment I must become involved
With my world, myself and with others
If I should chance to meet someone today
Who feel and think as I
I want to become involved with that some one today
For tomorrow will be the same
If there are no changes in my life today

Earl M. Hill

In Search of Summer's Soul

Giant sphere upon the sea, golden warm and round.
Touching, laughing, hands on lips, we watch it sliding down.
Electric flood through my veins, as I catch your scent.
Eyes closed, my mind is full of days together spent.
Looking again from afar, light is fading fast.
And with it goes lessons learned from days of painful past.
You turn to me, I walk away; still searching for summer's soul.
Waves eat the last of day, and I'm left in night like coal.
Water, rising higher, beats now upon my breast.
Silent shriek from mortal lips, a cry for angels blessed.
In my eyes the blazing salt no longer seems to sting.
and in my chest, a heart like coral no longer cares to beat.
I hear my name from the distant bank, as you call me home
And numbness leaves my body, as returns the brilliant dome.
As the waters thrust me harshly upon the gritty shore
I find you waiting patiently, and my love is lost no more.

Amanda L. Gunter

Transition of Winter Wonderland Imagery

Snow falls softly from the cloud-filled sky,
Touching the grass of green so lightly,
As the hope-filled green of love so lovely,
Becomes the peaceful dove that flies,
And the graceful wing of the dove afar,
Spreads generously its unspoken wings,
As it sweeps the ground of immortality,
Watching with a peaceful eye,
It's gratitude was carefully aware,
Of the widespread fingers of its ancient ancestors,
And as it listens closely, the sound of a white blanket,
It senses the birth and life of its beginning

Elizabeth Dillon

Ghetto Meadow

There's a vacant lot on every other block... In every city and every town there's one small and large. The one I like the most is the urban one. You know the one... just around the block.

This urban plot hides a lot, among its weeds
and wild flowers. Signs of the city abound...
old tires, illegal dumpings, a hefty bag contents unfold.

A thriving plant and insect echo system. Home of field mouse and swallow, a cat prowl. This eyes sore to many, a place to avoid and ignore. Is to me a sign of life a sort of ghetto meadow.

This ghetto meadow lets me know, the harshest
place can give life. Within this field life
abounds, little so we think as we make our rounds.

As I pass on weed choked path, it's planty smell
mixes with my street sense. Earthy colors stand in
shape contrast to sidewalk grays and asphalt blacks.

A ghetto meadow in every block is what I wish, some place for that boy and his grandfather to get worms to fish. Or fulfill a budding biologist scientific wish, an urban farmers green filled dish. A ghetto meadow is much more than a vacant lot stop... and give it a little thought.

Christopher T. Day

An Experience

So go figure:
  Transcending
   Church
How did I rest in patches of Fluorescent Green
playing a genial game of Checkers with God
  Among the clouds (swirls of tinted light)
Like a Renaissance painting by Rafael.
Between heaven and hell
  I can open up my Personal self;
there is nobody here but
  Us.
Red lighting on Black
  Black lighting on Red
Jesus asking me how does it feel
Oh how it does feel.

Eric Wong

Dreamsphere

Come with me, my friend
Let me take you to a mystical place,
That is filled with every possible pleasure:
In the air floats mellow music,
The natural springs flow through soft earth
with happiness,
Fruit can be picked from blue trees of sky,
And on the ground sprout buds of peace,
which blossom into love.

Halima Cassells

The Butterfly

From cocoon to bright wings in the glistening sun
Transformed new creature of God
As you pause in flight, vivid colors one
With the rose and the goldenrod.

Life is beautiful for you as for me
Alas, it won't always be so,
When the storm winds break and the winds blow free
Lovely butterfly, where do you go?

You're content to leave lovely memories behind,
To fulfill God's plan on your path,
Adding joy and beauty to whatever you find
Never mindful of the aftermath.

If I can but leave a bit of beauty behind
Soft and gentle as the butterfly,
Perhaps, I too, God's answers will find
To eternity's unanswerable "why?"

Betty J. Rosness

Little Boy Blues

Muddy feet and dirty faces,
"Treasures" stashed in impossible places,
Holes in his dungarees, scuffed up shoes -
All are a part of the "Little Boy Blues".
He won't keep his hair combed or shoelaces tied;
He won't keep his coat on when playing outside.
There's holes in his sneakers -
He just can't keep clean,
And sometimes he chatters 'til you could just scream!

He never stops going from morning 'til night;
He hates a bath and his bedroom's a sight!
But when you are lowest and think you can't cope,
His little boy smile can bring you new hope.
He always knows when you're feeling bad;
He'll hug you and smile and say, "Please don't be sad".
Then, late at night when he's tucked into bed
You look in and see that small tousled head.
You can't help but smile at your Little Boy Blue
As he sleepily says, "Mommy, I love you".

Bette Lynn Gardner

Your Sister, Your Friend

Sisters are Treasures,
Treasures you see.
But sometimes they aren't what you want them to be.
They might make you cross,
They might make you mad.
But no one can say that sisters are bad.
You'll be lifelong buddies,
Share secrets at night.
So don't get too angry,
If you ever should fight,
For sisters will be there your whole lifetime through.
She'll be there you see
When you don't know what to do.

Ashley Susanne Wollam

"Love"

Love is the creature, the essence of earth.
Love is the one that gave me my birth.
Love is a timeless count of the stars.
Love is poetry of the greatest by far.
Love is a song, the sweet smell of spring.
Love is power of this which I sing.
Love is lightning that can not be stopped.
Love is a masterpiece that can not be burned.
When you are loved you can not be hurt.

Melissa Lyons

Not So Bad

Does everyone thrash around — like I did?
Tryin' to find a way to shine — like I did?

All those flubs ... those desperate dubs ...
That sunk the wheels up to the hubs — like I did?

I hope they didn't stall as long — as I did,
To find a job — to find a wife —

To build a home — without the strife . . .
I nearly missed — the Caboose — of life
Oh yes ... oh yes ... I did!

Grand-children's pictures — are flaunted now,
To me and Grandma — we know not how . . .

How such a change from working years,
Can compensate — 'gainst all our fears.

Life's not so bad ... when all can win . . .
Not so much by cheek and chin . . .

But letting other Ambitious Ones . . .
Pull back the hammers — on all their guns!

Hit or miss . . . away they go . . .
I hope they don't shoot off a toe . . . like I did!

Joe R. McArthur

Untitled

Sitting in my solitude
Trying to compose something of meaning
My mind wanders to an unknown place
A place where words flow easily
Where thoughts form like dew
A place free of any discrimination or prejudices
A place in my inner soul
Crying to be released
Yet wanting to remain untouched
Unchanged by the world.

Amy Ryan Hoover

Save Our Souls

We try to reach beyond the walls of the earth,
Trying to find our place of birth.
Searching and searching through all eternity,
For some kind of sense of sanity.

Oh, True Father, our Holy One,
Help us to find you in the sun.
Beam your light upon our souls,
So we know that you are our goal.

We know that love is the answer to our pain,
Love for you and others is our gain.
Try to help us all to know,
That with you we will grow.

Why must we live in Satan's domain,
To prove our love to you again and again.
We know the answer is "God up above,"
Only with you we have eternal love.

Reach down to us with your glory,
So that we can start a new story.
In a world where there is no sin,
Please come down and let us in.

Cathy Long

Untitled

As our battered eyes met I realized the truth.
Two lost souls in a world of confusion.
Of pain, hurt, agony.
Try to find the light.
Searching, exploring, for a way to survive.
For something, someone to take away the insecurities of the world.

In you I found the soothing of my soul.
The pearl inside my heart.
Can you, will you fill my void?
For deep inside you, hidden but not lost, the capability exists.

An aura love is, so immaculate, so divine.
Yet so tangled and uncertain.
What an oddity it is,
For something that tastes so sweet can bring such pain.

Give to me your heart,
And I will care for it like no other.
It will be my treasure,
And kept golden to me.
For I love you.

John Zajac

Our Valley Bell

For many years your rings been true
Under clouds of darkness
And skies of blue

We give you this our valley pride
A word of thanks from deep inside

Your songs are heard for miles around
O then top of mountains, and in valley towns
So for everyday we hear you chime
It will bring to us a peace of mind

Ring out loud and ring out strong
Bring us safely to our home
For without you, it's hard to tell
Which way to turn...
Our valley bell

Darrell D. Cox

Hope

Live for today, not for tomorrow,
Undo worry brings on sorrow,
Smell the air and feel the rays,
Stop your thinking for just one day,
Pretend your a child with no sense of time,
The beauty of life is worth more than a dime,
Dreams will come true, be patient at heart,
What you can't do today, tomorrow you'll start.
Just give it time, don't run or you'll fall,
When you find the truth it will make you tall,
Reach for the stars.
Dig deep for treasures,
And always remember life's little pleasures,
The sun shines again,
The clouds roll away,
Hope fills your heart for one more day.

Karen Reiss

The Things God Creates

Oh! Sandy, the things God creates are so beautiful,
Look at the trees, look at the flowers, and the sky.
Oh! It is so blue.

They're all so beautiful, but none compare to you.

Reggie Rendon

The Answer

Prayer, intended for one met the needs of two.
unselfish love brought me to you.

Faith, in the Lord our Father to keep her safe
As she journeyed on to another place.

Hope, to share her life with another friend
till the Lord could bring them together again.

Love, for a friend changed the lives of two.
We thank the Lord for her knowing you.

Grace, bestowed upon us from an unselfish love.
Brought one her healing from the Lord above.

Blessed, with a bond that we all will share
that the Lord is our savior and will always be there.

Praise, for the Lord who will always care.
He joined three lives through a loving prayer.

Cathy O'Connell

My Father The Artist

Sentenced to retrieve my own pain...
Unspoken thoughts racing through my head
I hand the artist his brush.

No questions to answer
Only words to listen to
The brush begins to paint...a familiar picture
coupled with the look on his face.

Only fear of myself
Wanting to run
Begging to die
Wishing for love

Hoping for the last stroke...
But the artist continues to paint shades of blue
all over my body.
Certain that no one will see his work.

Joey Mendoza

Observations

I watch you in the late late hours.
Until the morn.
You don't notice my presence
for I am not one to toot my horn.
I hear you as you think your deepest
thoughts
for I hear all.
I hear the rumbling of the waters of the Atlantic Shores.
From coast to coast, from left to right,
I hear you calling in the night.
I hear you call, yet I don't answer, for you have not gone on a path
completely out of sight.

Erica Nurse

A World Of My Own!

I live in a world that only I can see, with pigs that fly
up so high. And dragons that spit fire, and lions that laugh
with glee. With lollipops for trees, and dresses that live
to eat bees. The crocodiles sing, and all hearts ring.
For the wind howls a song all day long. I stay here to listen,
so my heart can glisten. Because the world I actually live
in is not what I like. Everyone around me treats me like
I am a four-year-old tike. So as long as I live in a world
where no one cares, I'll dream all day long that I'm in a
world where everything fair.
Now I'm in ..... A WORLD OF MY OWN!

Dennis Nissen

Perception

What do you see when you see a rose,
Velvety petals, color that glow?
Do you smell the aroma that reaches your nose?
Or do you see only thorns that prick
And sting your fingers as roses you pick?
So in life —
Are you pleased when a friend greets you warmly by name,
No matter what happens he treats you the same,
A hug when you're glad,
A hug when you're sad,
A pat on the back when you've played a good game?
Or do you note words that should not have ben said,
Bits of gossip that should not have been spread,
A snub when you meet
Someone on the street,
White lies or half truths by which you're misled?
If you look for the thorns they're easy to find.
But look for the rosebuds and bear this in mind.
It is well to remember that old well known line,
"To err is human, to forgive is divine."

Bernice Lovekamp

Cupid's Cunning

Spindles of hope silently weave without notice.
  Visions they make
From threads unknown.
  Squint my eyes!
If cannot see, I will not be subdued.

The images linger making me weak.
  Stop configuring the colors I seek!
But celebration they knit.
  The design unique.

I was fine before you began your craft!
  Laughter, hugs, kisses, commitment
And dance they wreathe.
  Denile a useless ally.
Oh the truth! I surrender!

Jody Sue Toerber-Clark

The Dove

I sit here waiting like a Dove patiently waiting for her love,
Waiting for the one who can show me true happiness,
The one who can show me there is more to life than pain and sorrow,
Just waiting, waiting patiently for my one and only love,
As the days go by I wonder is there really love out there or is it
all a mirage,
Do people really fall in love or do they just lust for someone to
fill an empty space in their hearts,
Am I so far from finding love that I do not hear the cries from my
own heart,
Would dying be the answer to ones empty heart or would it just be
the end to all those that have ever loved,
Adam and Eve found a way to create love in this world, has the world
changed so much that love is no longer one's decision but the decision
of the prejudice of the world,
Will there ever be a love so strong that nothing will ever be able to
hold it back,
Will this love show the world that our generation can make it on our
own or will we be trapped in the love our parents want us to have,
Will we ever be able to find a love that will overcome the fear in our
eyes and the pain in our hearts,
Could this love be so powerful that only two could share or could it
take over all those young and lusting,
Until the day my heart is filled with love I'll sit there waiting
like a Dove waiting patiently for her one and only true love.....

Angela V. Lincoln

Bitter Tears

She sits beside the phone alone, waiting for it to ring,
Waiting to hear the voice that, for today, can make her heart sing,

She hasn't seen him for a long time, he's too busy to come around,
So she sit's alone, by the phone, in silence, not a sound,

She sit's there and as the tears begin to fall from her eyes,
Her heart slowly breaks, searching once again for alibis,

She say's I know he's married and has a family of his own,
They're probably out on a picnic, not even close to a phone,

He could be sick, doesn't want me to worry,
Why, I bet I told that boy a hundred times, slow down, don't
be in such a hurry,

She say's he a good boy Lord, not too many better could you find,
He's always treated everybody he knows so gentle and so kind,

So, if he doesn't call today, I bet I know the reason why,
It's just that he loves me so, he doesn't want to hear me cry,

Why, he could be on his way home right now, want's to surprise me,
If he does that, I don't care how big he is, I think I'll put him
over my knee,

So she smiles with that thought in mind and gently goes to sleep,
But before she wake's, her soul God takes...It's his turn,
Bitter Tears to Weep...!

James E. Moses Jr.

Life In The Mountains

Get far away from everyone.
Wake up and see the orangish yellow sun.
Up high independent and free.
Sit and sing near a large beautiful tree.
Have peace and be glad.
No one can put you down or hurt you or make you sad.
Take quiet naps laying on a long comfortable chair.
Never no worries or nothing to fear.
It is a pleasure to get away.
But much longer than a day.
You will always want to stay.
Move away from problems and pain.
So why not gain a lot and stay sane.

Jeanette Sullivan

A Baby Girl's Prayer

Dear God,
Walk with me as I grow up,
Please be by my side when things get tough,

Teach me the meaning of life one step at a time,
Show me the joy in sharing what's mine,

Guide me through that awkward stage,
Keep me healthy and beautiful as I age,

Help me to learn by my every mistake,
Remind me it is better to give than to take.

Catch my tears when I'm feeling sad,
Comfort me when things go bad,

Give me power to always do what is right,
Give me an open mind, and world-wide sight,

God, just one more thing I want to pray,
and I mean this in the biggest way,

I feel that I am lucky and very glad,
That you have sent me a great Mom and Dad!

Kim Horodowicz

Finding True Love

Dedicated to F. Kevin Lee

We journeyed into a new land
Walking together hand-in-hand
Discovering something new
Finding a love - ever so true

I always said "It'll never happen to me"
Those kinds of love are only fantasy
Well I must be living in a make-believe world
Because you're my man and I'm your girl.

You showed me a new life
A love that could cut like a knife
This can't be real, it can't be true
Am I actually falling in love with you?

I always said I'd stay on my own
Even if that meant being alone
I never thought I could feel this way
About anyone, anytime, on any day

I want to "Thank You" for opening my eyes
And showing me "Fantasy Love" is not a lie
I realize the "Make-Believe" is true
And that this love could be for me and you.

Jamie M. Vaden

The Stranger

Unfamiliar, unknown, unto mine own,
Walks into my life—A stranger.

Heart and soul, secrets unfold,
Brought together by pain—A union.

Broken hearts mend, time feels no end,
Strength unfound, yet has no bounds—A Godsend.

Trust deepens, faith renewed, fear and suffering subdued,
Freedom to feel—A love.

Touching souls not amiss, affirmed by a passionate kiss,
Strangeness becomes—A oneness.

Never to lose, only to gain,
A passion for life is what remains—

My stranger, my friend, my angel—
Evermore.

Angela Merrill

Grand Theft

Stolen hours on sunny days with you,
Wandering rosy mazes through the grass
Scented with honeysuckle, rose, and rue;
Not thinking of how quickly they would pass.

Stolen kisses, freely given to you,
Who taught me all of love's sweet secrets, then
With one swift word, the anguish of "adieu",
As hand in hand we walked the shadowed glen.

Sweet stolen dreams I cherish secretly;
Though many years have passed since that lost day,
I still do not regret the larceny
That made one summer beautiful and gay.

Bette V. Levine

In Your Arms

Home, I wan na go home tonite
Wanna lift my wings and take flight
By your side, I'll be me
It's by your side my love will break free
Baby help me break free

Home, home is where I wanna be
In your arms, they comfort me
Home is always in my sight
Baby I wan na make everything alright

Home, I wan na go home tonite
Wanna lift my wings and take flight
Baby would it be alright
If I could have one more nite
It hurts to much to leave the place
All I have to do is close my eyes to see your face

Home, I wan na go home tonite
Home, Just hold me tight
Home

Curtis Leach

For Now

For now, I watch from a distance;
wanting so much to be a part of the dream
I see every day, that's tearing me apart.
For some reason I can't let you go!
I wait in silence, so much wanting you to know.
My emotions are crushed daily,
as I fail to realize my dream.
Of you and I together,
people seeing us as a team.
But for now, I stand on the sidelines,
not able to play my own game,
and wishing over and over for you,
with only myself to blame.

Bethany Sloan

A Warm Little Bundle

A warm little bundle so cuddly and soft; wrapped up in blankets to ward off the frost. A little girl with big brown eyes; weighs in at 9 lbs., 2 ozs. - now that's a surprise. So healthy and pure; must we really search for a "cure"? The first 2 years went by just fine; in fact, it was a wonderful time. The thirst was alarming; and the pale shadowy skin was not real charming. What's that you say?
The diagnosis is diabetes, and it's here to stay? Oh Father, give us strength to handle this; For it sounds like it will be anything but bliss. Needles and test tubes, dips and strips; Insulin and diets, and doctor trips. Low blood sugars — what a nightmare; how would we ever
adjust to such care? Those sad little eyes that could not share all the "normal" things that other kids loved, of sugary delights; for us the holidays and parties had lost some of their flair and sparkly sights. While other kids ran home to wash up for dinner; we learned learned to give needles and prick little fingers. Headaches and dizzy spells were certainly no fairy tales. Balancing insulin with diet; and low sugars and high sugars, it's all such a riot. A "cure" must come, there's no other way; God has put us here to strive each day. To work very hard and to do our best; while He conquers all and does the rest.

Deborah C. Long

Poems

Poems speak of many things
Of childhood dreams remembering
Of Trinkets, Dolls and simple things,
Of music that the church bells bring.
If naught for thoughts in life unfold
There won't be Poems to be told.

Rita J. Hambrick

Tangential Spirits

Eyes and mouth as smiling as the sea around us
Warm my skin and bring me back.
The spray of life hurts my eyes.
To be the idol of one's idol
Love reasons without reason
Ooze your being all over my aura.
Come on over and be my martini
F*** YA MUTHA!
That shows my ignorance, but at least I
know it - S***head!
Nothing's coming to my mind.

Diane Pastore

Silver Linings

Twenty-five years of wing tip laces
Warm relations, smiling faces.
Leadership, a guiding hand
Always able to understand.
A milestone, so time to reflect
Of moments that stand above the rest.
Perhaps they're of work, time on the phone
Or perhaps they are of time spent alone.
We hope they're all happy, ones you'll hold dear
Congratulations on twenty-five years.

David Pearce-Shane

"The Thrill Having A Son"

My first sight of a little Babe
Was beyond all grandeur and delight
Yes, ten little toes so right
As years come nigh-I live night and day
For all his success and manly ways
My first dance with my son
It took my breath when he said
"Mom may I have first dance"
Once again I was reminded of that little son.

Anna M. Stull

Memories Of Mother

Your first sights of your mother, were while she
Was holding you close to her breast to comfort you

As you grew she was there to teach you
The difference between right and wrong
Smiles and words of encouragement were
Heard from her, no matter how old you got

Always there to offer guidance and help you
To choose the right road to travel
The times when you needed to be corrected she
Was there with her strong will and tender voice

Although she has gone to be with Our Lord's Angels
You will always feel her spirit close to you
When you turn to see her, you will see
Her warm caring smile gazing upon you

The memories that you have of your Mother
Will be with you in all that you do, each day of your life
Her love will always be there as she watches over you
Making sure that you are safe from harm

Diane E. Wittig

Untitled

How was it that I died, last May
Was it a time of sorrow, say
Were the old men gathered around the door
Speaking the truth and nothing more
Were the ladies whispering and crying
Were there any angrily sighing
Children playing not understanding
leave them be, no need explaining
Why must you say these kind words now.
While I lived did you not know how
Ask O you people, for peace of mind
that I received in my due time.
Be free of the faults you bring on yourself,
and don't sit my ashes on your marble shelves
Give me back to the wind and earth
So to Ms. Daisy I can give birth.

Weeds

May Your Life Become Richer by the Beauty of Nature

When our active life is done, who really won?
Was it all a game played just for fun,
Or did we add to the pleasures of others?
There may have been sisters and brothers,
But what about those we didn't get to know.
Did we help some of them grow?
Not by caring for their needs
but in their understanding of our deeds.
Is our work in a museum or printed in a book?
Or did we just teach them to look?
To look at their surroundings - to see and ingest
Not only the architecture of man,
Or the paintings of those who can,
But by the real growing and ever changing lives
Of the flowers, the animals, and the birds.
Will they really enjoy and learn from these things?
Will their lives become richer by the beauty of Nature?
Will they see majestic mountains and glorious sunsets?
Let's hope they do - for then we will have won and can spend
Our remaining days enjoying our thoughts in the sun.

Charley Sayre

Andrew the Hurricane

Andrew why did you come?
Was it because of what we haven't done?

Andrew what did you do?
Like a thief in the night you came.
Windows blew out from their frame.
But, our souls still remain.

Andrew oh! Andrew, what stormy weather.
Will we learn ever, no not ever.
Andrew the roof is gone.
But, our souls hang on.

Andrew our homes are flooded.
Full of water are the buckets.
Water we can't drink, the thought drives us to the brink.
Our souls are about to sink.

Andrew you drove us to our knees. To ask forgiveness of our deeds.
In kneeling down in prayer. We found out that God does care.

Look Andrew the trucks are coming. Bringing food, clothes and water. Coming from the east and west, from the north to the south, coming to the rescue. Our faith and souls are renewed. Andrew, Andrew bless you.

Carolyn J. McCall

Rewards

Never
Gentle, winter's coming.
Fierce winds...harsh cold...
Yet...only then...can we hold a
Snowflake.

Patricia R. Stuessy

Our Last Fishing Trip

Jim and I went fishing not long before he died. The fishing wasn't very good, but Lord knows we tried. In the shade of a big oak tree out of the summer sun, Jim caught two nice bream, but I didn't catch a one.

We ate a lunch of chicken while looking over the lake. Jim probably knew it was the last fishing trip he'd take. As we made our way back home, we chatted all the while. Some of the things we said brought a laugh, or just a smile.

Now Jim has gone to Heaven; we can't go fishing any more. One day I'll go to meet him upon that golden shore. We'll have the time to chat again about one thing or another. I'll recall to memory the day I went fishing with my brother.

Albert E. Woodard

Four

See them stretch and yawn in the warm sun, and the cooling rains. Watch the reawakening of the world around us. Colors fill the air: pink, yellow, red, green, orange, and blue. A spectrum of colors and smells swirling together in chaotic harmony.

See the rich, lavish, emerald greens. The sounds of all different types of laughter fill the air. The days stretch out to their full length, and the stars twinkle against their midnight blue backdrop. Look around at all the rich beauty.

A wild array of swirling colors. Reds and yellows, golds and ambers, blending together to form a visual treasure. Busy, busy, busy, everything is constantly working, working, working. The world is laboring to sleep.

A cold and icy world, full of unfeeling crystal covers the land. Blankets and blankets of snow comfort the sleeping life beneath us. Tinkling, shining pieces of ice beatify the dismal land. Now is the time to sleep and to rest beneath their covering for soon the four will begin again.

Kim Blake

Summer's Dream

I have this dream.

Of walking barefoot down a hot city sidewalk
watching poor children feel relief from a gushing fire hydrant
on a humid summer's day.

I think of far away places.
Cool places
icy places
foreign places
of places I've never heard.
I smile as these places come to life
revealing their hidden treasures

Then I stumble on a homeless man.
Weakened from years of living in this neighborhood
pleading for his survival.

And I promise to myself.
One day these places won't just be images in my mind
but my home.

I will walk barefoot down the sidewalks of these places.

Donna Mascho

Alone

A single child walking down the street
Watching the pavement beneath his feet

Nowhere to go nothing to do
Passing the time is all he knew

One young man walking down the road
A heavy heart and a heavy load

Passing the time has long since past
Now he wonders how long will it last

An old man lying in bed
Memories of his childhood dance in his head

Remembering the child with no place to play
With tear filled eyes his time passed away.

Belinda Tibbs

Silence

Silence shrouds over me like the soothing
Waters of a gentle stream, cleansing me of
The noise that spawns madness.
Silence comes to me like a wave of light
Being blown from the sun, and protects me
From the moon and her screams that pierce the
Night.
Silence lets me remember the dreams that
Outside noise makes me forget.
I'm too comfortable with silence, and I'm afraid
To go into the world.
And I'm afraid I may forget everything I've
Ever dreamed of.
It makes me paranoid about the future.
As I crawl deeper inside myself I realize
I can't stay silent forever.

Eric D. Meyer

Borrowed Beaches

We treat the great oceans as our personal property to do with as we will. Not really caring for the creatures therein, we often times harm and kill.

Have you ever stood on a sandy beach and watched the waves come rolling to shore? Is it to you merely salt water? Or do you understand it's those creatures front door?

Have you heard the wave's distinctive howl as they reach their destination? Bringing forth from the ocean's bowels man's refuse as its attestation.

Then you've seen the beauty of a sandy beach as it is swallowed by a crashing tide. And when the water returns, there lies the ugly view of the garbage that came along on the ride.

When was the last time you went to your favorite beach and found a sign "WARNING CONTAMINATION?" I'm sure you felt anger at least in a selfish way. But what about the creatures' habitation?

Will we ever wake up to the truth of our actions? If so, now would be most opportune. For there will come a time when the beaches will appear to have been hit by a toxic monsoon.

Kerry T. Crane

When Love Has Left You Lonely

Where flowers once bloomed,
  weeds have taken their place.
Love in the heart makes it invincible,
  but that same heart did break.
Crying is done in a sorrowful storm,
  for tears can't be seen in the rain.
A hurt like this will never heal,
  for loneliness is the worst kind of pain.

Brad McLawhorn

Walk With Me Forever

Walk with me as you place your hand in mine,
  We'll be together 'til the end of time.
Vow to each other our love so true,
  One life of bliss I promise to you.

Walk with me as our two hearts become one,
  Forever we'll share every rising sun.
As day turns to night and night to day,
  I'll be with you every step of the way.

Walk with me forever, never letting go,
  Not just with your hands, but with your heart and soul—
Sharing each laugh and tear that we cry,
  Joyous hellos and painful goodbyes.

Walk with me as we begin our new life,
  I as your husband and you as my wife.
Best of friends that we will always be,
  Loving each other so tenderly.

Jim Ray Lamb

Siouxblood

He calls me over to him. "Girls-child, tell me more about your life."
Well, me-filled-with-wind, stands toetip, thinking.
"Afternoons, I culture dreams.
My hands, though empty now, are strong.
Restless and reoblind, me ganders among the bulrushes,
collecting the raw works of a loom pattern.
Word generous and mercurial, perhaps overhasty to conjecture.
Was that the color you were looking for?" I pirouette around him.

He regards me at eye level. Much analogy a ruler'd make, if my hands were free to trace the unseen lines.
Still, a life can't be spent collecting minutiae.
He's displaced is tribute and I begin to let is bindings ravel.
It pleases me. I will grow. "You call me a child, but did you ever think other?" My turn: quartzite. He: aqueous. An arch in time.
Both economic and graceful, he turns the corner of his lips in answer.

Dietetic notes play in the rustling air. Tendons to muscle limber, I await what might be said. He does not know how dangerous I am.
Daughter of fishermen, of preachers, watchers of the world, settlers of the central plains and weavers of song, I am ready.

This, too, pleases me.

Brandy Woodard

Solution

Everybody screams, but no one can hear a thing
We're floating around in such misery
Everybody's innocent as long as they're insane
Nobody's guilty but, we're all to blame
Everybody cries but, no one sees the tears
So it just continues on through the years
Looking through a looking glass,
I see the world go bad
We all look a moment,
Then turn away again
No one understands, therefore no one cares
Unless it interferes with their own affairs
The one who tried to help us
No one seems to know
He died for us all
A long time ago

Jennifer H. Titus

Finding The Fountain Of Youth

One of man's oldest dreams is to find the "Fountain of Youth". Were you to go out on a planned expensive quest for the "Fountain of Youth", people would mock you. We have been taught since early childhood that the "Fountain of Youth" is mythical and such men as Ponce de Leon were dreamers. Yet I believe that there is a kernel of truth in this dream. My wife and I and many others have found a limited but real "Fountain of Youth."

My belief is that, as a good marriage develops, a sound pair bonding occurs that makes us see a different reality than outsiders see. For a lifetime, we all see our spouses as the beautiful bride or handsome groom that we married. Some may claim that this is an illusion. I say "Nay. It is a gift from God." A truly wonderful and precious gift that is given freely to those of us who are lucky and persevere in creating a long term, true marriage. Reality is in the eyes of the beholder.

David L. Budd

The Day

Seize the day!
What does that really mean?
To hold on to every minute,
to remember every breath you breathe.

To make a difference in how the world turns,

To open your eyes, ears and mind;
learn, learn, learn.

To see a smile glide across a child's face.

To take in the world and make you place.

To dream every dream there is to dream.

To push life to the limit,
without it falling apart at the seams.

To know when you finally lye that you have nothing left to give.

To know as you go that you have
Lived, Lived, Lived.

Abbie M. Levesque

Hello Mr. Tree

Hello Mr. Tree! How did you grow so tall?
What have you had to endure to be so beautiful?
What challenges did you meet in summer, winter, fall?

How many birds have nestled on each limb?
How many Squirrel's have found shelter from within?

Your roots are planted deep within Mother earth.
The sky's the limit for your growth after birth.

A Tree is a Tree is a Tree, and is free
to bend, to sway and Be.

I too can bend, sway and Be;
As long as I declare I Am Me, I Am Me!
Free to live, love and grow tall like the Tree.

I too am one with the earth, one with the universe,
one with the trees, I am one with all creation!

Now I clearly see...only God can make a Tree...and me...and thee!

Jaqualyn Hope Fries

Liquid Fire

What is it, this thing that makes us go on?
What is it that brings us into this world, as well as takes some of us out? What makes us do the things we do? What are the reasons?
Liquid fire.
It is as rare as life itself, two different forces coming together
to form something that is unique in itself. Life.
The blood that courses through our veins runs hot but is also a liquid
Passion helps to drive that liquid fire that sometimes threatens
to consume us but passion is also a product of it,
it can feed from it and be strengthened by it.
We can become lost in a sea of our passion with the real risk of
drowning. But what happens if we do not tend those fires?
If we let those flames of passion become embers?
The flames dwindle, putting out less and less of the life-giving heat
until finally, the flame flickers and dies.
Even though life is extinguished, its heat is rememberéd and the
liquid fire is absorbed into the surrounding environment to be used by
others who will gain strength from it, to be used by those whose fires
are still burning. As long as the struggle for life is still fought
and the blood of passion still sings through our veins,
then the fire will never truly die.

Barry H. Bloch

Fulfillment

What makes the roar of the ocean?
What makes the roar of the sea?
'Tis the work of the God of nature

That brings that sweet music to me.

Like the turbulence of man's human nature
Is the ebb and flow of the tide.

The small waves that break on the surface
Like laughter ripples on far and wide.

The big waves that build up, then break with a crash and roar
Like the violence in man's human nature
Spread destruction the whole world o'er.

Like the vast peaceful sea of the noontide,
Is the endless wish that we could live on
in peace and contentment and sweet humility.

Edna B. Kenney

"You'll Never Know"

You'll never know....
what nature is, unless you experience it.
You'll never know....
what pain is, unless you feel and see it.
You'll never know....
what the joys and sorrows of what our country lost.
You'll never know....
what happiness is because it was robbed from you in a split second.
But rest assure you know,
what sadness is because you have lost the battle of feeling life.

Amber Beal

The Moon And You

When I saw the moon, I thought of you.
Were you watching me? The moon in all its
beauty, I could not help thinking of you. Were
you thinking of me too?
I felt your mind trying to speak to
mine, did you feel mine also? We are
connected, mentally and physically. We may
not know it but we are. Like the moon
and the stars, suspended in the dark night sky.

Julie Reed

About To Be

Look around and you will see
What the world's about to be
All the hatred, all the lies
All the things seen by innocent eyes
Some start so young and destroy what's pure
Do you really think we can find a cure
So many deaths, so little time
Don't they realize life's divine
Don't they care who they hurt
It's like they're smothering you in the dirt
They keep their fears deep inside
They keep on running and trying to hide
Close you're eyes and you will see
This is what the worlds about to be

Jeni McClanahan

Wishes and Dreams

If the world hadn't a boundary, no limit to your dreams
what would you wish for? Would you plan? Would you scheme?

I'd wish for a world where love would abound.
Where peace and contentment, everywhere could be found.

I would wish joy and laughter, for the world to share.
Not just for a few, but for all who care.
Good health and long life would be my next wish.
I'd serve it up plentiful on everyone's dish.

No sorrow, no sadness, no more tears would flow.
No bitterness or hatred—it really must go.

Our prisons would be empty. We wouldn't need guns.
People wouldn't harm each other because it wouldn't be fun.

Unfortunately, wishes don't always come true and dreams always
come to an end.
So, try my advice like only you can. Greet everyone you meet
just like a friend.

Elyse Freeman

Our Moments

We are all given time, time to listen, time to learn, time to fulfill
whatever we yearn.
Time to smile, when our work day is through. Time to heal the pain
that we sometimes must endure.
MOMENTS but, "moments" are different, for we have had many of
these,
unlike time our moments are special indeed.
We respect each others feelings, we care about life, we enjoy being
together OUR MOMENTS give us a natural high.
When we are together, we laugh, sometimes argue, but never fight,
these are the "moments" of pure delight.
OUR MOMENTS are deep, like within one's soul,
OUR MOMENTS are pure and beautiful, spun like gold.
Passion is within our "moments" for we have big fun.
We make each other laugh, we can be silly and yet be one.
OUR MOMENTS are filled with nostalgia, we remember way back
when.
We can talk for hours about what happened back then.
When we met each other, it was truly meant to be, and I hope we never
question it, and stay friends for eternity.
Even though time seems to last longer, but in reality, time is
fleeting and fast.
It's OUR MOMENTS that are special for they cannot be surpassed.
Good Night, Sweetheart

Deborah Palmer

How?

How can you feel like holding on
when all your faith has come and gone?
How do you make the days get better
when sometimes you can't even write a letter?
How do you fight for happiness everyday
when it always seems to be taken away?
How do you get over - getting so close
to all the people you love the most?
How can all the hurt inside go away
when I feel it getting stronger everyday?
How sometimes can you feel so bad
when there's so much love - but yet some sad?
How do you go on day by day
when the sky above just stays so grey?
How do you get the strength to make things right
and have no more fears especially at night?
How can you deal with so much at a time
work on so much and make it fine?
Well, how can all these feelings change?
Don't quite know yet, it feels so strange!

Christine Gillis

The Way Things Are

When people seem to treat you bad,
When everyone is really mad,
When friends and family turn on you, it really
makes you sad.

But, what can you do?
It all seems strictly up to you.

When hard problems come your way,
It's not easy, the things today.

Oh, no, it's just not right,
When friends and family have to fight.

Oh why, oh why does it have to be that way?
It's just the way things are today.

Crystal McLaughlin

The American Dream

I often wonder how it would be
When I am old enough to have a family
I dream of a two-story brick home
Nothing flashy or fancy, just something to call my own
Of course, I visualize a Prince Charming as my mate
And two kids—that's all I could take
I plan to have pets, indeed
Perhaps several dogs varying in breed
This seems as if it were the "American Dream" and it may be
But this is great compared to the other dreams that
feature what's in store for me
I think of dying with a disease whose pain resembles a torture rack
Or the burden to succeed will outweigh the strength of my back
So I will continue to strive (optimistically, if not foolishly)
for the white picket fence
Because in a world of today it is either focus on the
good ol' days or learn from whence

Jaime Parker

Walking In Fear

Fear you buzzard, let me be,
I've locked you out and thrown away the key.
You thought you were smart,
but smart you'll never be,
for I am real
and you
are but an illusion
I no longer see.

Poetlee Morningstar

Once Again

I was shaking all over
when I came to see you that day.
I was so afraid,
you seemed so far away.
How could you do this to me.
This wasn't how I thought it would be.
When I saw you I knew you didn't care.
I looked into your eyes and saw a mean glare.
You were so proud of what you had done wrong,
not at all ashamed.
Who else could I have blamed after everything you said to me,
I thought you were so real.
I guess to you playing the love games no big deal.
Not one tear has fallen for you,
I will not cry for you.
If I wouldn't have let this happen,
I would still be wondering how it would have been.
Now here I sit,
getting over you.
I'm all alone once again.

Dandi Reaser

No Evil

On a quest for knowledge I wandered cross a barren land.
When I happened upon a ruined city strewn with ashes and sand.
I stumbled through the devastation and came to rest beneath a tree.
In the branches sat three monkeys who looked down and stared at me.
"Excuse me," I said, "could you please tell me what has befallen this place?"
The first monkey looked up abruptly at the sky, turning away his face.
As I began to repeat my question, he refused to hear.
So determined was he to ignore me, he lopped off both his ears.
"Did you see that?" I asked the second. His face filled with fear and surprise.
He quickly broke a stick from the tree and poked out each of his eyes.
To the third I said, "I demand to know what has caused all this upheaval!"
Just before he cut out his tongue he spoke the words, "no evil."
Their indifferent blood had infected me and I no longer cared to stay.
So I turned my back on the monkeys and continued on my way.

Diane M. Wedekind

Being Me

I was walking in the woods
When I saw an oak tree,
a coke can,
a black rock,
and
a milk jug half full of dead fireflies.
Being me, I picked it up.
Being me, I shook it.
They stuck together in a big, wet clump
Shaped like the bottom of the jug.
They were once someone's sideshow.
Being me, I scooped them out
And chewed on them. I chewed until they were paste I
Used the paste to fix a crack in my cup and I
Held it out in the rain. I had not drunk in days.
I replaced the milk jug
And,
Being me,
I left the woods
Glowing.

Adam Ruben

Yesteryear

I wish I could go back in time,
When I was a child of eight or nine.

I would run through the grass so green and tall,
Never having a worry at all.

Climbing ever fence and tree
Running, jumping, and skinning my knee

Running by the creek chasing frogs
Playing tag and jumping logs.

Listening at night to the bullfrogs croak
Laughing at my best friend's jokes

Riding bikes and play with toys
Screaming, hollering and talking about boys.

The childhood memories are still fresh in my mind
I recall them from time to time.

This is now and that is yesteryear
The past is there and I am here.

Kimberly Biddle

Him

Sometimes
when I'm not paying attention
He gets out
He's rude to the girl
who runs out of apple croissants
his vicious phrasing bent on slander
He dissects me like a medieval surgeon
with his sharp words
piercing gaze
and slashing ego

And yet

It is His path that follows a drunken discord
not quite meshing with those around him
(leaving a faded trail in his wake)
His voice is the one which falters
when faced with an emotional Brick Wall
And it is He
that sits alone
and absorbs the darkness
(and ceases to be)

John C. Bystra III

"A Gift To You"

I pray that this poem will bring you sunshine
When it's cold or raining
And the happiness of that you are forever mine.
I also pray this poem will bring you
Joy when you're sad and peace when you're mad.
In the event of you being sad and alone
I hope this poem will take you back home.
I also hope this poem will greet you with a
smile, because I'll be with you until that last mile.
I hope you'll remember that I love you so much,
because my love for you
Will never be out of touch.
And last but not least, there's one special gift
That God has given to us all,
A gift of divine love that will never shift.

Jemal Reams

A Birthday Gift

All my needlework is here and I'm ready to stitch,
When my child turns and says, "Mom,
It's my turn to pitch."
I quickly grab my scissors, my needle, and my floss.
Now stitch a little here, stitch a little there,
Hey! Watch out for that toss.
Needle in, needle out, try to stay awake,
Gee, it's twelve o'clock, I forgot the birthday cake!
The day is here at last, and my picture is complete.
I pleased him I believe, with my cross-stitched athlete.

Connie Riddle

Please Don't Worry

When the days are long, and your money is short.
When only your hopes can up lift your heart
You look for HELP, and it seems far away
PLEASE DON'T WORRY, tomorrow is another day!

When the bills are high, and your filling a little low
Wishing for a little solitude, but there's no place
to go. Keep looking up one day it will pay.
PLEASE DON'T WORRY, tomorrow is another day!

I was told long ago from a wise kind sir, swallow
your pride be strong as a bear. Don't hold on to hate
Don't give no one pain. Don't do half done jobs. Don't
play crooked games. Then he said I've got just one
more thing to say: PLEASE DON'T WORRY, tomorrow is
another day.

Corlida Deshazer

Halloween

Halloween is a time of scares,
When people constantly ask for your dares.
the frightening sky behold a witch,
with a monster a ride you hitch.
Some creaky steps lead to a door,
stunned with fear you can't take any more.
A crack of the door, oh no he's here,
you peek in astonished, body covered with fear.
You can feel his shadow, you know he's near,
in the evil dark a monster leers.
A deathful scream has people lead,
into an old spook house one lies dead.
In astonished fear your eyes a flare,
Halloween is a time for scare.

Christina Perry

A Beautiful Discovery

O' for the joy on a summer evening,
When the breeze is balmy and sweet;
To walk in the park at a leisurely gait,
And explore the blue sky decorated -
With fluffy white clouds looking like sheep,
Meandering along the tops of mountain peaks.
Dancing along with heads held high
Makes one wonder what's on the other side.
Then looking around to the majestic and tall,
Imagine sitting on the highest of all -
Looking down on earth's mantle of green
With ribbons of streams and rivers aglow,
What a picture perfect of earth below.
Who made all this so wondrously fair?
Ah, the one who created you and me,
To enjoy a part of beauties so rare
Only with Heaven could one compare!

Alice R. Mitchell

I Remember

I remember when the sun rose at night,
When the heat was so intense
And the passion felt so right.

I remember when candidly we often spoke.
Our words meeting, a moment of understanding,
Our dreams becoming the messengers of hope.

I remember balancing on the high wire,
Fearing the fall through the exhilaration.
Recalling words that could always inspire.

I remember wondering too when it would end.
Praying it would continue indefinitely
Although it was something you did not intend.

The Evening now dark is an intentional ploy,
But I cherish those moments of closeness
Because I remember them with joy.

Andrea Glauberman

Ode To School's Returning

Again its that time in the season
when the lull in the summer is o'er
When those wonderful days of primarily play
we must trade for the classroom once more.

For life, so our elders have taught us
is more than just freedom and ease,
but demands that our own wills be conquered
and knowledge our minds taught to seize.

Having gained the tools to seek knowledge
our world, once shrunken, gains size,
and scholarship, gem of all ages,
becomes our own personal prize.

For knowledge enables the scholar
the depth of man's wisdom to know,
And partake for himself in the conquest
that ignorance may be dealt a blow.

Barbara Olsen

Water Rondo

When the water comes out to dance,
When the rocks want to prance,
They dance to a lovely sound,
When the water flows over the rocks and
hits the ground,
When this happens you can hear the beat,
Of a babbling stream, a small waterfall,
Of blue birds chirps, a small pitter patter
Of little chipmunks feet.
The trees bob back and forth to the music
Of nature's mighty water rondo.

Jonathan Amadori

Sonnet #2

They come, they go. Fading in, fading out.
What is a name but to add to a list?
Forsake me, I know it well. Run about,
and close your eyes, always avoid the fist.
It hits hard, you went past (and out) my life.
I will come like a dry drum, memory lives,
to tell my tale. Your promises gave strife,
I seek a soul that eternally gives.
Falling through, you sought, but you did not find.
Can I help or hurt? Where is your dark mind?
Shall I admit defeat before I start?
Or shall I end this age-old mystic art?

Kurt E. Gruber

Love

Love is Far Love is near
Love is like a gentle
tear that falls to the
Ground. Love is never
Blind. It is sweet as
Fruit and will never Lie...

Lacie Gallagher

To Harold

I loved you in the morning
When the sun was shining bright,
And all the world seemed gloriously new.

I loved you in the noon time
When the sun was riding high,
And all the world was filled with warmth and light.

I loved you in the evening
When the sun was sinking low,
And all the world was quiet, calm and still.

And I love you now at night time
When the world we knew is gone,
And the time for us to leave life is at hand.

And I'll love you in that other time
A new and wondrous place,
Where we'll surely find each once again.

Arlene Sutton

Beyond

Remember me in the hall of fame
When time has blown out the flame,
The memories I will leave behind
Are that of the unspoken kind,
Dreams undreamt and songs unsung,
Trips untaken, bells unrung
Wishes of mine that never came true,
I'll leave them all here for you,
Reminisce, and when you do, think of me, thinking of you.

I am not scared of what lies beyond
Between here and there, there remains a bond,
Linking us, this life and I, no, I am not afraid to die.

Oh, loved ones, that one I'll leave,
When I am finally gone, don't grieve.
It's best for me, don't think of you,
And always remember, in all you do
God will guide your steps through life
Relieving you of grief and strife,
And when your time like mine has come
You'll have a home beyond the sun.

Jean Cheryl Heppner

The Man Upstairs

Sometimes we don't know why we get sick
when we do
There is a reason for it, weather it is a baby,
child or an adult and we don't understand why
The man upstairs is the only one who's knows why
Once after the shock, we try to put our lives
in some kind of order, but we try to do it
alone.
It doesn't work alone because the only one who
can really help is the man upstairs:
Believe in the man upstairs and miracles
will happen
Sometimes it is hard to get on the
right road, but with his help it makes
a difference.

Diana Roman

Soundlessness

Did you ever feel so alone as if nobody cares?
When words are not spoken and silence surrounds you
You are only left to wonder why.
The only way to heal these tiring,
endless thoughts is to the truth
To hear the words spoken by the ones you love
is the most reassuring aspect of life.
Without the truth of words, why bother to speak?
So does that mean when we are silent we have something
to hide, or do we just feel empty inside?
I hope not.
You need to hear love and honesty through words.
Words are permanent on your heart, mind and soul,
more than any action taken
Words are everlasting,
which are embedded in your heart forever.
To live in silence is being negative
Be open and talk out the truth of what you feel.
There is more to life then pain and sorrow
You just have to find the happiness inside you to reveal to the
world.

Jennifer Agugliaro

Springtime

Oh Sensuous Springtime
When your love is floating gracefully in the air,
No one can seem to explain why you feel so fine.
No one seems to know why people start to care.
In you springtime everything starts to blossom and bloom.
Romance shines in the air for the starting of passion soon.
I feel the heartbeat of your love beating sweetly,
And the sunlight reflects warmness from your smile.
The flowers grow from the sight of your eyes that glisten deeply.
Springtime's touch can make the world's problems disappear for a
long
while.
Oh Springtime you make maturity run around like a carefree child.
Springtime if you died the whole world would mourn for only an
eternity.
Morning herself would not find a reason to rise or even to be.
Summer, autumn and winter themselves would never be the same,
Because only your existence would be their reason to remain.
Oh Springtime I believe when God first had you envisioned,
The mold was created as perfection precision.
But only originality of beauty does Springtime contain.
Maybe that's why you're a reason that defines a love to remain.
And until Springtime that people will feel your presence once more,
Your presence is the time above others that everyone adores.

Darron Henderson

The Knight

There once was a Knight that my soul delighted upon,
whence came he by way of white horses.

His armor was brilliant, his loins girt in white,
the shield he didst bear the "Holy Rite".

He fought with our Father, he fought for the church.
Great strength and honor, "Behold him".

The Knight of my passion.
The Knight of my soul.
The one I am called to,
the chosen.

It is the twenty first hundredth year of our Lord.
The Kingdom is in great distress...

Andrea M. Botich

From A Daughter, Gentle Gifts

It's snowing now—soft, fragile flakes from heaven,
Where all things lovely have celestial source . . .
Mementos of the gentling gifts she gave me,
Of comfort, calm, sweet charm, and purity,
Conceived in heaven, she, then loaned to earth
With love's deep beauty brightening lands and sea . . .
Love brightening lands and sea . . .

She knew that I loved snow; oft I would be
With winter face turned upward to receive
Cool kisses which kind Heaven bestows graciously.
Now, when it snow, I fancy . . . can it be
She's there, and with angelic smiles . . . gathering
Gifts of snowflakes to gentle down on me?
So gentle down on me . . .

Dixie Nicol Black

You Will Always Be Special

Did you know that heaven is a whole other world,
where beautiful angels can see you from their clouds?
They don't want to hurt you but only be your friend,
because someday you'll be visiting them,
someday when it's the end.
Please don't be scared,
because it's a great thing to know,
that when you do have to go,
they will be waiting for you and they really do care.
So whenever you're feeling down,
or if you have any time to spare,
just remember deep in your heart,
that you are special,
to everyone, everywhere.

Allison Kalb

The Road

Here I am standing in the middle of the road,
where I can not see the beginning anymore
where I can not see the end yet.

But I remember the day I made the first step
I saw the one open road to go
and I marched into it
without fear
searching for my fantasies
Nobody stopped me and nobody told me that
it's the road that never brings me back
it's the road that never takes a step back.

But then, I was younger than now
I was a child.

Here I am standing in the middle of the road
It's time to make another first step
It's time to say good-bye to the memories

Here I am taking a new step
to the road

The road
My destiny

Kumna Han

Our Meeting Place

There is a far off place beyond the trees,
Where Dawn and I like to play,
We sing and dance and jump and prance,
All in our secret meeting place,
I tell her secrets and she whispers some back to me,
And that is what my best friend and me do in
"Our Secret Meeting Place"
way beyond the trees.

Ashley Tempel

The Peace Planet

There's a place on a planet
Where I'd like to be,
Where all earths Extinctions
Are there for me to see.
Where pollution is illegal
And stealing is banned,
Where wars are not heard of
And there's freedom in the land.
Where all animals are fed and loved,
Where money's no object
And looks aren't thought of.
Where all are equal not black or white,
Where no boundaries are set,
And there are no fights to fight.
This would be great because the way it looks
the people on this earth will never see this
happen before they die. For one day this earth
will be so terribly bad, God will destroy it
and make a new land where everything will be
perfect and grand.

Amy Fraleigh

The Walk

I went for a walk in the woods today
Where its quiet in a nice way
Where I could really think
About a world lost on the brink

When a Noise came from no where
As if it came from the air
It was a strange noise
Soft not rough of course

"What have you done to our land," it said
Then it told me of a world soon dead.
Pollution and all kinds of waste
Of things we have done in bad taste

I thought I heard a tear fall
As the voice said "for what you have done there is no call"
Then I heard a horse walking ever so slow
And on the back I saw Setting Bull

John R. Dunn Jr.

Men Cry Too

In this new age of life
Where men and women are in constant strife
Is it alright for the male to cry?
They should not feel bad if they do cry
For it is a human emotion
That is found very often in motion
Found occurring both in Female and Male
If men lie about it you can bet they are telling a tale
But, If the female cries it is excepted and understood
If only the male's tears fell close to where the female stood
So let us gather up our tears and fears
And listen to each other through clear ears
Both the Female and Male have much to give
Now we must really try to live.

Johnathan E. Berglund

Surprise

At sixty-three I've found the world has turned and changed a-plenty.
It's not at all the place it was when I was only twenty.
Then, people moved a slower pace and it was plain to see
That girls were girls and boys were boys, and hair was never green!
The coffee was a nickel, a donut ten cents more,
And you could buy a childhood dream at the five and ten cent store.
The world has changed, but in my mirror I've seen a constant me,
Until surprised by window glass, I glanced, and gasped, "who's she?"

Luana Buhler

My Brother's Cabin

There is a little cabin in the corner of Gloryland,
Where my dear brother now resides,
Now he and grandpa walk hand in hand,
Not a shimmer of a tear in his eyes.

There are white roses in his garden,
Mixed with flowers of purple, pink and green.
Creating the most wonderful fragrance in heaven,
They are the most beautiful flowers you have ever seen.

I can see him standing at the cabin's door,
Motioning me to come his way.
Together we will be forever more.
In that little cabin in Gloryland someday.

Danette Gayle Bennett

The Struggle For Significance

Destiny brought me to this place
Where my journey would begin
I had hoped to find God's grace
As I looked for the truth within

My trip took me to a distant shore
After a friends love challenged me to be more
I had to find a deeper meaning to why we live
Then a light from heaven asked me what did you give

Along the beauty of the shore I had hoped to see
God's grace and gentleness reaching out to touch me
I looked for a spirituality that I could see
The fact that I would always be a traveler was key
When I realized the gifts I visioned were in me
And that logic and knowledge alone could not set me free
But that The Way would find me

Sometimes enlightenment seems so near
Now it is all so clear
There is a truth which helped me mend
That He is the beginning and the end

Kenneth Spring

My Battleground

My battleground is the emotional plane,
Where scars are made and forever seen.
Oh time, will pass and they may fade,
But they reappear some other day.
My battleground is the emotional plane.

The wounds I make are deep and dark.
I always aim straight for the heart,
And I never miss my mark.
You may be wise and show no pain,
But then it hurts when you see it rain.

My battleground is the emotional plane,
Where wars are fought and never won.
You may say that you are the victor for today,
But then tomorrow comes and you are done,
Because someone turns you away.

Pleasant things come from time to time,
But I guarantee the scars tow the line.
Try to ignore them and they may hide,
But don't forget they too survive.

Jeremy A. Bessee

Three Days

In a time deep in my memory, I recall past time so inviting
Where the magic overtook all that I knew
My heart felt so wonderful and free
Three days spent with you, so carefully chosen yet forbidden
Bringing such happiness to us both, a time we'll never forget
As the sun faded each day we grew closer, closer to each other
And closer to the end which we knew would come too soon
A time we's have to say goodbye
Forever and ever, never to reveal ourselves again
Never to see each other's face or reflection
Only our thoughts to keep us alive
With our shadows piercing the ground
Separate, but as time went on
Together as we were, bodies and soul
Forgetting all else but what we had
At that moment and forever after
Those three days I'll never forget
The joy you brought to my heart
And the tears that come to my eyes when I come to realize
That I can never see you again

John Gonski

The World that I Dream Of

There's a world that I see, one that I dream of.
Where there's no need for fear, no hatred, just love.
Love sees no color, no religion, no race.
We all stand together, bound by God's grace.

Though it's all just a dream, I can't help but to smile.
I want to be happy, just for a while.
I dream of this world and wonder, "Why not?"
What do they have, that we haven't got?

They all stand together, bound by God's grace.
While love sees no color, no religion, no race.
There's no need for fear, no hatred just love.
It's a world that I see, that I only dream of.

Joy Perreault

"Everyday"

Everyday there's something new,
Whether its good or bad or I've got the blues.
Everything is so confusing, my head starts to spin, I think I'm going crazy, then it all begins...
I'm wondering what will happen next?
Live or die, know one cares,
Knives and guns become a scare.
Gangs are a reality, whose got the juice?
Dreams shattered with traces of abuse,
Racism and hatred become the truth.
Everyday there's something new whether it's good or bad
Or I got the blues.
It's up to us to make the change,
Know one else can say the same.
So while were waiting for your voice,
Hurry up and make the choice.
It's already 1995, we've wasted a lot of time.
What type of world do you want your kids to live in?
!!!EVERYDAY!!!

Anne Jennings

"In The Sky"

In the sky,
Like a bird,
Underneath and forward;
Near a hill as high as the moon,
Will lie a place forever.
Down the hill as low as the ground
There someone cries the tears
Go down . . .

Sarah Kemper

Maxine

Time for school, Maxine.
Oh, Maxine!
Remember, Maxine—-
Walk straight to school.
Straight as an arrow, Maxine!

Patricia Holzappel

"...On The Eve Of Tomorrow..."

We know not what the morrow brings,
Whether twill be a triumph or sorrow;
But keeping the faith while holding fast,
We stand together, on the eve of tomorrow.

I promised you on a cold, wintry day in March,
That we would brave all the storms of life together;
And I hold you now as I did that day,
Ready to face the future, no matter whatever.

We've passed a crossroad in life's plan,
Where no man returns for time to borrow;
And faith is transformed from ideals to reality,
As we pray; on the eve of tomorrow.

The cool, gentle breeze wraps around me,
As if it were the winds of change passing by;
But we hold fast to the merciful hand of God,
Who controls all things, both sea and sky.

We'll face the unknown with caution and prayer,
Knowing not what will unfold on the morrow;
While holding onto each other's love with the Savior,
As we stand; on the eve of tomorrow.

Jeffrey W. Holleman

Strength Is But A Word

I wrapped my life about a thread of straw
Which blew across a fallow field of dust,
A straw which caught the colors of the sun
And tossed them for the morning doves to grasp.
I wonder... do you really think life died
Because the winds did shift as seasons change
To tear from me the love that dwelt within —
And do you really think that if you touched
My hand again someday, I would return?
An answer shall not fall from out my lips
For what fool wants his folly to be known.

Johanna L. Prince

Time For Remembering...

I think back, of long ago;
Which direction did the wind blow?
A small child, alone and scared,
Into a woman whose soul has been bared.
Through all the ups a downs, from smiles to frowns.
Laughter to tears, confidence to fears.
Has it been worth it, all of the worldly bulls**t?
I'd be the first t admit, many times I've wanted to quit!
Never give up, never give in, so many trails I have been.
When the time comes for me to leave,
No mourning, and try not to grieve.
For the most part, I've been content,
A few times — hell bent!
Thinking over it; all and all,
I still would've taken the fall!
To receive love, in it's the truest form,
To be kept safe and receive no harm,
To be kept secluded, one can only conclude,
From what horizon did I come,
And which Plateau shall I leave from????

Candy Arndell

Hopeless Aspirations

All things have purpose and meaning,
Which help define
Myself as a human being.

Grains of sand upon the beach,
Remind of dreams which
Seem so out of reach.

Lost in a world of confusion and bewilderment.
Makes me ponder of days on
Earth I've spent.

Stars in the sky which seem so far away,
Fill my head with wonder
And dismay.

One of many, lost in the race,
Dreaming of a better
Time and place.

Searching for utopia, but never found,
Gives chills of anxiety
In which I drown.

Clint Garner

Midnight Tryst

White velvet slippers, and black satin robes,
Which only half reveal your pink fleshy globes,
Are all that you wear there panting in the mist.
You linger on this corner for a midnight tryst.

He breathes in your hair. His fingers feel your face.
He leans you back with feline grace.
Your skirt's drawn high, you seem quite willing.
To play with fate for just a shilling.

Kisses soft upon your skin,
You do not question where he's been.
Thus the moment's ripe, he strikes
When there's no priest to speak last rites.

He's thrilled you with a sudden flash
And swipes again your ruddy gash.
A playful spray then paints the bed,
And soaks the linen, moist, and red.

You spied a trick. You crossed his path,
The victim of a doctor's wrath.
A tear rolls off a velvet slipper,
Out the back steals Jack... the Ripper.

Daemeon Pratt

Love Is...

Love is something special,
Which you cannot hide;
For it comes from deep inside.

It's your deepest feelings and thoughts for the
One you love;
true love is as pure as a dove.

It awakens your senses and
heightens your joy and contentment.
Love knows no resentment.

Love is freely given;
By the heart it is driven.

Love cannot be seen, heard, or clutched;
for it is a feeling by which one is touched!

Ellen Rebekah Harden

Remembrance Of Night

A dark night covers the sky
while I sit and watch with my head in my hand
The radio is on, playing a tune
while my mind drifts by and by

Things I remember come to mind
While I sit wishing they would go away
I ask myself a question as I done once before
Why, why had I been so blind

Somewhere are those who days are lavished with cheers
And elsewhere those whose hearts are gay and fun
With this I cry, and go aside saying it would not be
Had I not listened to my fears.

Desmond J. Stevens

Think

Listening to your endless talk of machinery
while my thoughts think of metaphors describing you
i am always awaiting your presence,
but you dream at such a slow rate
your continuous stab of silence makes
me wonder if you plan on being
very temporary
i feel childish missing you
right after you've walked out the door
the black depths of your eyes
control my feelings
now you are changing not at my will
you turn my station,
you sing my song,
you play my notes

Julie Smith

Lonely Child, Lonely Woman

For a second fear grips my heart
While searching for new changes to start
Looking deeper inside at a child I once knew
Realizing parts of her never really grew
She held onto the fear of being alone
While outside a lonely woman has grown
Allow the lonely woman to hold your hand
As together you will unite and make a stand
Being alone means finding what's inside
No longer allowing you inner child to hide
No man can give the comfort she is searching for
Only the woman who has grown can open this door
So unite this lonely woman and this lonely child
May this create a peaceful happiness when reconciled
I cry for you, inner child, so I can rid of your pain
This lonely woman can forgive of her past with so much to gain
Lonely child, Lonely woman, to you I want to say
Allow the peace searching within to find its way
This will rid of the fear of being alone
For within each other a friend will have grown.

Barbara Jo Gruel

Vampires

Awaken to darkness on this place we call earth,
One vampire's bite brings another one's birth.
A vampire wakes with bloodthirsty needs,
Oh the warm rich sensation he feels when he feeds.
He stalks in the night like a disastrous beast,
And what once was alive will soon be deceased.
So when the last bit of sunlight disappears from the sky,
You better watch out unless you want to die.

Victoria Boatwright

Untitled

Luminous, white moon
Above rippled sands of time
In a starless sky.

Brigette L. Phillips

Waiting On The Night Incognegroe

I suppose I can go soon
While the curtains are drawn,
And the only trace of light, is from the moon.
Then, no one will notice me
And wonder where I'm from,
Or where I'm suppose to be.
I'll be as swift as a melting stream,
Nonchalantly running;
As if caught up in a dream.
My footsteps will be as light as snow,
Silently flaking the earth.
It's really sad,
I don't know why I'm running
or where in the hell I'm supposed to go.

Glenda Lewis

"Twilight"

The moon casts a romantic light,
While the sun squeezes out the night,
The moon and sun share the day,
Each doing its part in every way.

In many ways our love is the same,
Although we differ, we keep one another sane,
Let's do our part to make things right,
Like the sun and moon that share twilight.

Nature has taught them not to fight,
Even though they are always in one's sight,
To share the day and share the night,
Each must sacrifice for the other's plight.

While others are doomed to search night and day,
They can never find the love we share in every way,
When the sun and moon pull one another each night,
We'll be making love in that special moment they share,
Twilight.

James Thomas

Untitled

Three blind mice sip peotey tea
while watching wheel-of-fortune on a small
TV.
The audience applauded,
and the mice would cheer if there was
any other reason it's no longer clear.
First mouse said with a vacant stare,
the cat's away and you two don't care!
Whose guarding the cheese,
the second mouse chimed, I could starve clean
to death while I'm feeding my mind.
Then both they together to the third mouse then turned.
Opportunity lost was a lesson well learned.
But third mouse said nothing,
nor nodded his head. His blind eyes stared
nowhere, as if he were dead.
What's wrong with you,
said the first of the three?
F*** it said third mouse,
and went back to his tea.

James Gregory

Symphonies

Each shiny drop follows it's guided path downward
Whipped by the ferocious, headstrong winds.
Flashes of radiant white light rip through the darkness
Giving the drops a lit runway.
The luminous clouds etch space
Like a frame covers a picture.
The tiny drops make up a full orchestra that
Entices the ear and sets the stage for climax.
At each climax the stage flashes
And is accompanied by a thunderous, echoing bass.
Each part contributes to a whole, making one of
Nature's finest symphonies of light shows ever.

David Gunn

Abandoned

The chicken's body traced the air
White-blonde feathers flying.
My father's wild-eyed laugh,
Incongruent, creature's wild-eyed terror.
Head alone. The hickory tree.
Body running running running.

White-blonde feathers soaked in blood.
"My Father's dead," flatly stated.
"No, no child," the woman said. It was true. I knew.
My sister and I wide-eyed bewilderment.

White-blonde hair sun glistening.
My Father blasted; thrown in air.
Where was Mother? Broken life.
White-blonde head bent; sobbing.

Did my Father's head lay still;
Staring wild-eye terror; severed?
Body a horror, running running running?
What is funeral? When would he come home?

The hickory nut tree; little girls, alone;
White-blonde hair sun-brushed, tenderly.

Diane E. Dalton

"Mirror Images"

I look in the mirror and wonder.
Who am I?
Does the image before me represent my inner being, my soul?
Or does it merely reflect the torture and brutality of the
world around me?
Am I a member of the blessed or of the damned?
Is the world a place of misery and thoughtlessness?
Or is it a struggle of hope and despair, crime and utopia?
Which side of the mirror am I on?
Does the other side look and see a different image?
Does it ponder the same questions, think the same ideas?
I wonder if the image in front of me lives in a life of bliss
or a life of sadness?
I leave the mirror now - keeping the thoughts in my mind -
and wonder what I will see next time.

Jeremiah Avery

The Glories Of His Majesty

Warmed by His sunlight,
nurtured by His love,
I partake of nectar
streaming from above:
When I cry out, "Father,"
wherever I may be,
I am reminded of His majesty...
the glories of His majesty.

Mary Ingram Stanfill

He Thinks Of Me

You are my friend, my very special friend
Who cares about me and comforts my soul.
You wipe away my tears and protect me
from what you see as evil. My good friend.

I know you want to kiss my lips gently.
I know you want to hold me in your arms.
I know you try to take my pain away -
he who causes it is my one true love.

It is your friend. It is my heart. And when
tomorrow begins, it is I who will
Cry. It is you who will recognize my
Pain and try to make me smile once again.

You constantly try to figure out why
I love him so. There are no answers. There
Are no means of a better way for me.
Sometimes I wish you could stay forever,
But you also belong to another.

Christine M. Florio

The Human Albatross

Some are like the Albatross,
who fly swiftly through the air.

They don't know where they're flying,
and really they don't care.

They just want to prove to all their friends,
who is the best of fliers.

And of course, we all know,
they really are not liars.

They fly for perfection, gracefully,
never getting into a bind.

But, unfortunately the truth comes out,
when they land, on their behinds.

Jeff Strong

My Prayer

Lord grant that I can be eyes to the blind,
Who misses the beauty of all kind.
Let your love so shine through me
Through darkened eyes your love they'll see.

Let me, I pray, be legs to the lame,
Who've lost all hope of walking again.
My little, I agree, may not be much,
But maybe I can be a lame man's crutch.

Let me help to loose all chains that bind,
From heavy laden hearts of our times.
Fear and discouragement are their great enemy;
May they find a source of comfort through Thee.

Jennie Hill

Looking

Feeling without seeing, seeing without knowing
Where can I honestly say am I going
Walking without moving, flying without wings
I knew that it was slowly happening to me
Crying without tears, being scared without fear,
yet still not knowing what is happening to me
Loving without heart, ending without start
Trying to find something hidden in the dark
Falling without tripping
Reaching out to nothing, then finally discovering
I am looking for me

Kimberly Jean Flores

Three Foot Creatures

There's a three foot creature in most every house,
who rules over you, your money and spouse.

They feast on happy meals, candy and cake,
and need every greenback you possibly can make.

Out of their mouths come funny little sounds,
a complete family history and a thorough background.

Of all the gossip you ever did say,
it's repeated from this three footer to the
gossipee today.

These cute little creatures are only programmed
to recall,
anything to send you flying up a wall.

But we couldn't do without them,
they're as loving as can be.
If you're missing one in your house
get one and you'll see.

Kathy Pennigar

Shadow

Who knows what I know and does what I do;
Who talks like I talk and walks like I walk;
Who sees what I see and tries to be me;
The Shadow does all of these.
I can't try to stop him. I couldn't try to run;
The Shadow will find me, and consider this fun;
I'm very afraid of this monstrous guy
He'll follow me till the end
Then die when I die.
He has no logic. He has no reason;
He'll follow me stride for stride
season by season.
He has a mind, but not of his own;
he's his own person, but to me he's a clone.
I think of him and shiver in fear;
for I know that, the shadow is near.
I live my life the best that I can;
the Shadow does too
because he knows that he can!!!!!

Jay Hadfield

Mother of the Night

I am as the moon
Whole and complete
Sometimes you can see me - sometimes not.

I may shine and rule the night.
I may be totally covered up,
Covered by the shadow of your world.

I am the mother of the night.
The stars are my thoughts,
The light I give was given by the Son-Majesty

Rarely you see all of me
But still only half appears.
Even when I appear dark and covered
It is only because your world blocks my light.

I'm still here, still as bright,
Still as real.

But may angels carry me on their backs,
May I fly through the void, the fertile land,
Even when the Son shines and blinds me out,
I am still here waiting patiently.

Julia Hickling

Untitled

There are people from every walk of life,
  Whose lives are so cluttered with hatred and strife.
They see only sadness and feel only pain.
  They can't see the sunshine because of the rain.
Their hearts don't know gladness, their faces don't smile.
  They trudge through the world, stopping once in a while,
To wonder if they'll ever find that good place
  Where sunshine and laughter invades every space.
They've carried their burdens for many a year.
  They don't ask for mercy and shed not a tear.
So let's grant them mercy and shoulder their load.
  They're grateful for any small kindness that's showed.
Let's help them find sunshine and give them a smile
  Somehow we must show them that life is worthwhile.

Barbara J. Maskow

"Here's To Connie"

Here's to Connie, organist extraordinaire-
Whose repertoire of music depends on her hair

When her hair is straight and hanging free,
She chooses music with a li'l melody.

When her hair is set in page-boy style,
Her music has harmony for a little while.

When she ties it back with a pert little ribbon,
She plays music so light, I think I'm in "hebbon."

When her coiffure is fluffy and a little sexy,
Her selections are churchy and very vexy.

When she pulls her hair back into a tight little bun,
My experience tells me she's not having fun,

She's likely to play some ancient selection,
And everyone's glad when she finishes this collection!

In truth there's no question of her great ability,
And for real music critics(a-hem), like me,

Can see she's accomplished in playing music all,
But I wonder what she'd choose if she were bald?

What I'll remember when I forget her hairstyle,
Is that Connie ALWAYS wore the same smile.

Bob Hammill

My Journey

I was in an accident, and have often asked God "Why?"
Why does it hurt so much? Is my frequent cry.

I'm not the way that I once was, it sometimes makes me sad,
When I think of all the things I've lost. Things that I once had.

Sometimes I just fuss, worry, and complain,
Then Jesus says, "Kristi, to make the flowers grow, I send the rain."

Then when I walk and talk with God, He always makes me smile,
Because I know that I will be with Him in just a little while.

When I take my eyes off myself and put them on my King,
I know that I can stand it all! I can take anything!

He tells me that He's using me best just the way I am,
And not try to figure out all that's in His plan.

He tells me that He's still in control of everything concerning me,
And if I have my eyes on Him, I can always see.

My Jesus how wonderful and marvelous He always is,
He takes good care of everyone who's His!

I was in an accident, and often wonder "why?"
Then Jesus says, "So that I might be glorified!"

With Jesus as my Savior, I can't help but win,
And if this is what He wants, I'll do it all again!!

Kristi Stapleton

The World

Why is this world so bewildered?
Why must we all fight?
It is because we are greedy, because we want more.
We do what we want to, we don't listen at all.
We can't get along, for we're all different people,
  at least that's what they say.
Yet we can get along, we just have to try.
If we don't try, what are we?
Are we quilters? Are we losers?
We must try, for if we do not,
  the fire between our worlds will grow, and we will all die.
We can save the world,
  we can give it peace.
Make friends
  and forever be in unity.

Krissy Mickevicius

Love And The Forces Of Nature

Both uncontrollable and unpredictable, like the blizzards of winter will blind you to everything around yourself. Will come out of nowhere like a northern wind. Your life will be turned upside down with the intensity of a tornado sweeping through. Your emotions will run through you like the raging waters of a hurricane. Desire coursing through your veins like molten lava flowing down a volcano. The ferocity of it resounds like the clap of thunder and some times the rain beats against your skin like the sting rejection. Both terrifying and also beautiful to behold. You can't hide from it, because it will always find you. You can run from it but, it will always be there waiting for you. But don't fear, it doesn't always destroy you. Both uncontrollable and unpredictable, the only way it could be.

Connie Berry

One Can Only Dream

When I'm alone I sit and think, how my life will be.
Will I get married, have two kids, or will it be just me?
Will my house be great and bold, with a pool just in the back?
Or will my home be cold and dull, like living in a shack?
Will my spouse be trustworthy, always at my side?
Or with my feelings in the air, will he just run and hide?
Will my name be famous and will I be well known?
Or will I have to watch my kids and always be at home?
As my thoughts gets washed away like water to a stream,
I hope my life is filled with joy, but one can only dream.

Dawn M. Priddy

A New Love

The ocean so deep, dark and blue
will never drown my love for you.
While winter days are cold and long,
my love for you will still be strong.

When springtime brings the warming sun,
our hearts shall beat as if they were one.
A single beating heart in song,
with you is where my love belongs.

Through storms may rage our peaceful dreams
our love will never end it seems.
Even though we may sometimes fight,
we make up by the sun's early light.

As we know our love is young
and so many songs yet unsung.
Nothing you could ever do,
could ever take my love for you.

Ann Reed

Untitled

Will they remember?
Will they care?
Will anyone feel inspired?
Walking along, looking at the passing days around me, I wonder.
Will they know that I was here?
Will it have mattered?
Will I only be another record, unimportant, with only a birth and a death date?
Will my ideas only turn to dust?
Questions I ask whose answers I will never see.
Memories, things I hold dear, will they one day be carelessly cast aside?
Will anyone grieve?
Will anyone miss me?
Questioning my value, my worth.
Will it have mattered that I was alive?
The greatest gift, and sometimes the most wretched curse, is to...

Remember.

Ann-Jeanine Hall

Grandpa

Will it ever be the same?
Will we ever see those days again?
Time must move on, but must it move so quickly?
I know that he hasn't much time left, his health is not as it used to
  be; but while he's here, can't we keep the traditions alive?
Will it all end when he's gone?
Are we only holding on for him?
Is he only holding on for us?
Who will spoil the children?
Who will tell the stories?
If one exception could be made, couldn't it, please, be him?
I can hear his laugh, how can such a simple sound tell your heart
  your home?
Who will win at cards, and make sure everyone knows it?
I love him so, I don't know what I'd do if I were to walk into his
  house and he wasn't there.
Will I cry, will I curl up and hide,
Or will I just... remember?

Kelley Edwards

Reflections

Droplets on a field of green
Wind a'swirling, howling mean
Breathing life's moisture on all flora seldom seen

Sunlight sparkles, shines about
Bringing heat and light throughout
the valleys, plains, and mountaintops
and horizons of amber hue

The ocean's roar is deafening, swishing, splashing on the shore
Waves dance on sandy beaches, then silently slip away once more

Shadows becoming more distinct, blacker shades dark as ink
Are cast upon by a mellow haze
As the moon passes on it's yellow gaze

Design's of geometric marvel, crystalline shapes held tight to form
Make all the living seek shelter by robbing all the heat from the
  warm

Reflecting on all of Nature's delights sends the imagination
Soaring out of sight
Animal, vegetable, mineral be
God smiles down on all for us to see

Jeffrey Totten

Photographer

Thundering, thundering, crash, boom
Windows blown open, angel's wings flapping, riding on the wind
Woke us from sleep, cuddling deep, aroused, loving you
While the lightning flashes, frisky, snatching snapshots in the dark
Like the passionate storm
Our thunderstorm voyeur, touching, tickling, sneezing showers of delight
Sprinkles flown in by the wind, sprinkled on our intertwined love,
Like salt on hot peppers
Iridescent diamond chips of rain sat on your raven chest hairs,
A microscopic view, alien creatures played on your heaving chest
We were like little children running through the rain, laughing, kissing, Dripping
Angel's wings were set free, and wrapped around you and me
While lightning clicked snapshots, the wind stole a kiss
As it blew across our lips
And we'll always remember our thunderstorm . . . photographer.

Diana Dolhancyk

The Homeless Man

He stands there at the corner,
Wishing he were never born.

He examines his life,
Full of struggles and strife.

He has no wife, he has no home,
He lives on the streets all alone.

He walks aimlessly around,
Food no where to be found.

He asks for spare money,
But people just stare at him funny.

He sleeps on the ground freezing to the bone,
His faded pants needing to be sewn.

He's up everyday at the crack of dawn,
Thankful that the previous day is gone.

Finally he realizes that he would rather live than die,
Even if it is a life full of sighs.

Cassandra Ewing

Tribute To Father

He had a gentle face with dancing eyes the color of an azure blue sky with a few lines of character not showing the worst of wear. His smile was not perfect but truly genuine in expression. His caring hands were large with square tipped broad fingers. With his hand, he expressed welcome with a firm hand shake, compassion by gently wiping away a tear, and pride by a heart felt pat on the shoulder. He was a man with a soft, calming voice who loved to tell stories of days gone by. Children adored him and when he approached, they would run to receive his giant bear hug, and they would never go away disappointed. With sounds of glee, they thought their stuffings would be hugged out!

If anyone ever needed anything from a girl friend to a car, he would search to the ends of the earth to find the person's desire. He had many friends for he touched many people. He was a man who knew no strangers. His most valued possessions were his family. He was always there in time of need and always told us he loved us "bushels."

Denise S. Cook

A Modern Adage?

Blond is the color of freedom
of happiness and fulfillment
It is thoughts feather to
which all cares fly away
It is Sun...Light that
only shines on the known.

Scott C. Thompson

Faded Memories

Long past her youth
Now quite frail
She gently caresses
A shirt across her face
Faded scents rekindle
Their love in memories.

Michael Daniel Lopez

The Gift

You ran to my doorstep
with a hand full of wild flowers,
some still clinging to their roots;
the ones you pulled hurriedly
anxiously awaiting my pleased expression.

In a dusty attic you dug
until you found Gibrans' best art,
leafing through its tattered pages
underscoring the knowledge you found
most accurately applied.

I can hear the hollow emptiness
as you shake your coins free,
hurrying to the wine seller just before closing
to purchase a small, but exquisite bottle
of our favorite, domestic wine.

And who in a world of riches
could deny, that yours'
is the richest gift of all?

Diane Harder

Flannel Underware

They sit in their corner booths
With aesthetical countenances
Languidly sipping their black espressos,
And envisioning future works of art.
Their lithe fingers
Wrapped around various pens and pencils
Immaculately marking anything
In their path.
The future is in their ubiquitous minds
Screaming to be unleashed on the world.
It's in these minds that intriguing
Mysteries still remain in these times.
They are the sorcerers of illusion, in which
Love and Death stand in the center of their
Devious plot.
They are the spirit of the Diamond Stars in the sky.

Anda Scafaru

Lake Andrews

It's as still as a mirror, yet in another sense it's lively.
With all its living things, most unknown to us.
The ones that are known and visible are
The friendly ducks that do not move as you pass.
Ducklings follow their mother speaking their language of "Quacks".
A language I do not understand.
Afternoon finds the ducks in the shadowy haven of birch trees.
These astounding trees peer into the gloomy water.

"Help restore nature's balance, Please don't feed the ducks", signs say.
Most of us act unaware and feed the ducks with bread stolen from dinner.
The waddlers follow the breadman fighting for the food,
The little ones unable to get much.
Another is the beautiful loon that's heard slightly past dawn.
He swims silently and loses himself in the peacefulness.
For a few minutes he is enclosed in the water's coolness.

Angel Deschaine

Always There For Me

Angels, take lessons from this story of my best friend.
With all the powers from heaven, I know you are a God send.
The things I see now, I could never see back then
Now that I am hurting, it's easier to know where you have been.
At any time, I would ask for your help; your heart opened up so wide.
You are my best friend, I can truly say from deep down inside.

When God sent you, he left an Angel here on this Earth.
There is not enough gold to compare what your friendship is worth.
You always gave me so much more than I would ever ask for.
Whenever I call your name, it's like knocking on Heaven's door.
There are friends, and then, there is only one friend like you!
Angels, take lessons, for this story is so true.

Kevin R. Bell

To My Grandson, Jeremy

My dear, you came into my world, a babe
With curly hair and eyes as bright as stars
And somehow I knew the moment that we met
One day your destiny was Mars.

Already you have felt the cockpit's lure
The aircraft panel's multi-signalled voice
And I can see you in your captain's garb, all set
To take off on that runway of your choice.

But still you have some growing up to do
My chance for love before you reach the skies
And though I doubt your dreams just won't come true
You'll always be a "captain" in my eyes.

Emily M. Buchner

The Veteran

He came back —-
With death and despair marked upon his face
And a purple heart pinned upon his chest;
In the fight for life, he'd won the race
Still he remembers the deaths of the men he knew best.
Time, they said, would rid him of his strife
And time he had (or so he thought);
He couldn't cope with his 'veteran' life
First Vietnam, now in Beirut he fought.
Death he's seen and death he saw
It was no bizarre sight for him;
It had become a way of life, a new law:
Kill or you'd be killed by them.
Now he lives from day to day,
Knowing he will never be the same again;
"I hope my child will never know...," he prayed
As the gun shot rang out and his life came to an end.
He came back, and he fought 'til the bitter end;
He came back, but now he's gone again.
He came back — God bless his soul, Amen.

Darlene L. Moses

Freedom

Running through the night with the rain against my face
With the villages behind my back
With the gun shots echoing in my ears
Is it worth it? This fear? This sacrifice?
Yes, yes, Freedom, Freedom means everything.
Rocking against the shore, awaits the bamboo canoe
So frail and yet so determined
To take its precious cargo to the awaiting boat.
Goodbye home land, Goodbye Vietnam.
We will meet again.
Is it worth it? This fear? This sacrifice?
Yes, yes, Freedom, Freedom means everything.

Dao Nguyen-Wahlen

Fill My Dreams

From her auburn hair to her pretty face
With her gentle smile that spreads warmth to ones heart
And sparkling blue eyes that shine a loving light to ones soul
Her tender lips speak so softly words so discerning as not to offend
Oh Lord, I pray, fill my dreams, let me pretend

Let me dream of holding her and catching her might she fall
Let me dream that I am her king and she my queen
In my dreams let me be her servant
Serving only the best of love in a silver dish
Oh Lord, I pray, fill my dreams, make this my wish

For on her finger is a golden band
Placed there for the same reasons by another man
My Lord, I know it is a sin, I should be so bold
Be that as it may, I ask you to fill my dreams
With the one I may never hold

Carl J. Darbyshire

Skydiving From The Ground

You took me up in an airplane
  with my feet on the ground.
You took me flying - the wind beneath my arms
  only - in my dreams.
We tumbled through the sky, only to find your arch.
  Your joy - brought tears to my eyes.
The freedom.
  Exhilaration.
    Testing -
      no, knocking down the boundaries of your reality.
The sky's the limit?
  I think not.
The sky is yours and you are the skies.
  You are the skies.
From all of us here - with our feet rooted in the grass,
  we envy you.
    Enjoy for us
      what we can only enjoy.
        In our dreams.

Beth K. Stephens Dulaney

Jezebel

The desert is a lady, fickle, coy and lightly clad,
With naked arms extended to a pioneering lad,
She hints of buried treasures and of secrets yet unknown,
That intimately lie within her womb of sand and stone.

She has her tender moments when she bows her head in prayer,
And breezes soft as cotton wave the sagebrush in her hair,
But like a fickle female with an ever-changing mood,
She calmly counts the cost of each and every interlude.

The slightest touch of anger brings a flush of scorching heat,
To make the pock-marked mountains bend to shade their burning feet,
And when the lady listens to the winds that howl and moan,
A spasm rocks her fickle flesh and quakes her sandy throne.

She rakes her icy fingers and a frigid frost is born,
A psychologic punishment to test her face and form,
But when the need arises for the love of man or beast,
She quickly dons a brilliant gown and spreads a tempting feast.

Then, coy, and prone to tease a bit, she strips her bosom bare,
And prostitutes her silver for a casual affair,
Still, lazy, lithe and lovely, with a Jezebelic brand,
The desert is a nymph endowed with virgin contraband.

Agnes Guilfoyle Edwards

Untitled

Walking across... across the open sea
With only you... you and me

As we hold... hold each other's hand
We can open up... and cry on the golden sand

we look as the waves come and go
just like our lives
the lives we now know

I drop a tear... in the open sea
Hoping it will... wash up for you to see

I have given you... a part of me
For everyone to see... that I will be here
Whenever you're in need
To start out... fresh and new... only between me and you

as we listen to the breeze
and the deep blue sea as it sings
sings us a new song
that will last as long
as long as we live
for I will give you anything
because you mean everything to me.

Jerome Ortiz

The Salmon

The sky is dark, the air is cold,
With rods and reels and gear all set,
The fishing trip begins.

The thumping when you walk,
Across the long wooden dock,
Brings back memories of last season.

Casting short, casting long,
Casting shallow and deep.
Waiting for the sun to peek.

Suddenly the line stops quick,
Jerk it hard, you must be slick,
For what he thought to be a meal was a trick.

Hold on tight, don't give him slack,
Let him run and tire out,
Reel him back, careful now.

Gently guide him to the net,
Scoop him up, bring him in,
Now it's time to cast again.

Janice K. Eisele

Creature of Nature

My heart beats
With the pulse of life from the Earth
The heat in my body
Is from the warmth of the sun
My blood flows down the mountain side
My eyes see
The beauty of life that surrounds me
My ears hear
The soft voices of my forefathers through the trees
My thoughts race
Like the wind over the plains wild and free
My nose smells
The fragrance of flowers and trees in bloom
My senses feel
The same pulse of life in all around me
As I reach out
Shadows recede from my sight
My soul flies free
As I emerge a creature of nature

Debbie-Lyn Wren

Heavy Hints And Subtle Glints

Street cars and funeral bars
with subtle glints of hope
Back alleys and sidewalk stars
with heavy hint of dope

Highways and Byways reaching in the air
Sunlit screams and terrible dreams
While everything good rests in her purple hair
Inside her eyes the light finally gleams

The world is walking away from us again
If we hurry, maybe we can catch it
Stuff it back in our pocket
Before it reaches the end

I sit at the edge of night
I think to myself,
What a place to notice life?
And realize it could use help

Heavy charges and Smelly barges float in the sea
Trying desperately to get even
I see the reflection of me
Looking for her in heaven

Adam Wright

Undeserved Memorials

I see the quilted landscapes
With their professionally manicured stretches
of great lawns and mosaic gardens;

But they are too perfect;
they do not sing;
they inspire only a terrible emptiness.

My ear automatically close
To the ceremonial sounds of the bugle
that punctuate the orchestrated stillness;

But they are too perfect,
they do not sing,
they inspire only sorrow and tears.

My entire being rejects
The many acres of meticulously arranged patterns
of gleaming white symbols.
Woven into a tight tapestry,
Hoping to call attention to some visual delight;

But they are too perfect,
they do not sing;
they inspire only a promise unfulfilled.

And how are we to accept the new, glistening obsidian walls
With names etched into columns as in a commercial directory?
Does it nurse the ache of its searching visitors;
Does it finally seem to make things right with its sleek perfection?

Will we ever know the degree of hurt targeted for the young, the unfortunate?
Who had not yet had their chance to slumber and dream in a bed filled with love?
Would they have designed their own memorials,
Like a road map pointing to a hallowed spot of buried memories?

Our hearts can only reach out like a sea bird soaring
into the indeterminate twilight,
Accompanied by a ghostly sound.

It is not perfect, but it does sing!

Charles E. Rybacki

Eating Air

Eating air, breathing death — a child
with tree branch hands, her eyes half-
open, her mouth sucking on the coarse
nipple of an empty breast. Veins
bulge on her hairless head, her neck
the size of my wrist. She is eighty,
though she never reaches eight.
Sunken cheeks, eyes half open, ribs through skin,
a neck the size of my wrist,
eating death.
A tattered sweater hides her fragile
nothingness. Tomorrow, she is wrapped
in burlap, and stacked on a pile
of logs readied for the fire.

A stick man handles her package
with indifference. Air that's too dry
for blood, is too dry for tears.

Charles Bibeault

Christmas At Our House

At christmas time, excitement grows
With wrapping paper and shiny bows
Then Christmas eve, with lights so bright
The kids are begging "Lets open 'em tonight."
Then Christmas morning, up at daylight
Opening the presents. What a beautiful sight.
Then Christmas dinner, with turkey and dressing,
And Grandpa Fox to ask the blessing.
Then the cleanup, doing the dishes
People are leaving with holiday wishes.
Then comes the part that I like best,
It's just to sit me down and rest.

Juanita Rippe

Untitled

I feel like a giant jigsaw puzzle
  with you as the puzzle master.
Trying to fit the pieces together
  but none seem to for now.
I see you trying to make it fit
  before it is too late.
You love this puzzle.
  It is a challenge and you know that somehow
    the pieces have to fit.

You seem so sure.
  But wait
What if the puzzle is messed up
  and takes longer to put together.
Will you stay as the puzzle master?
  Or give up on the puzzle.
Leaving it unfinished
  as you move on
    to another.

Deborah A. Post

Without A Trace

Trying to find a place in this life
Wondering why things are the way they are
When I know that things aren't sometimes in our
control, but when we can choose the steps we take
we should be for real and not fake! Because with
every passing day you could say there is more at
stake!! Starting to believe in an image, I pray
won't break. Friendship pressure in one spot, but if
it's evenly placed, it can stand a lot!

Jody Swinford

Snow

How long could a person go,
Without such a thing as snow?

It blankets the earth at Christmas tide,
Something that everyone can abide.

Like a fresh coating of paint,
Yours truly, from this earth's saint.

Snow is cold and lovely, yet wet,
Yes, snow is the grand laureate.

Children delight in their warm woolen mitts,
While horses get ready in reins and bits.

So forth, to come to the great conclusion,
That snowflakes are more than an illusion.

They are happiness, enjoyment, pleasure,
Presents, gifts, prizes, riches, and treasures.

Snow means that Christmas must be near,
And snow shall make everyone cheer!
No one that I know does not love snow,

Cold, wet, white soft, chilly,
In the back, all is hilly,
In the back, all is hilly.

Jacquelyn M. Thayer

Necessary Evils

Without censorship, there is no freedom
Without war, there is no peace
Without evil, there is no good
Without hate, there is no love

Without tragedy, there is no comedy
Without stupidity, there is no intelligence
Without ignorance, there is no enlightenment
Without hate, there is no love

Without hell, there is no heaven
Without death, there is no life
Without wrong, there is no right
Without hate, there is no love

Without chaos, there is no tranquility
Without sickness, there is no health
Without pain, there is no pleasure
Without hate, there is no love
Without hate, there is no love
Without hate, there is no love
Without hate, there is no love

Keith Kanderski

Estranged

Surrounded by people,
  yet completely alone.
Surrounded by talking and laughing,
  yet I am silent.
Surrounded by ideas,
  yet alone with my thoughts,
Immersed in a dream world.
I sit bodily on earth,
  but my mind is traveling distant galaxies.
A rocky, winding path lies ahead and I am blindfolded.
With no one to guide me I stumble along,
  running into obstacles head on.
Slowly the blindfold becomes more transparent
  and shapes appear.
Never knowing what could be ahead,
  I go on step by step.

Anna Catesby McGehee

Believe (Side By Side)

I don't know whether we are here to be spirits
wondering alone or if we were brought to this earth
to someday become one together.

I do know that there's too much hate in the world.

People turn to lives of crime and violence out of desperation;
the desperation to achieve power and status; to replace the
love never found at home; to escape their deepest fears; to
escape themselves.

The truth is that you can't escape yourself; you are who you
are, so why fight it?

I believe in the flight of the birds; the eagle displaying pride and
majesty and the dove portraying peace, love, and hope.

I believe that someday we will all fly together-side by side; touching
the tops of snowcapped mountains and brushing our wings across the
flower painted meadows.

I know that somewhere someone shares my same feelings,
my same dreams.
I would like to tell her never to give up; to always believe in
something; and remember what I say....

My pen is my eagle, my words the dove; together we fly-side by side.

Jennifer E. Marvin

My Vacation

Sitting on the beach, watching the waves come in.
Wondering if I should grab my boogie board and go for a swim.

Walking along the pier, watching the gulls fly around.
Seeing all the fishing boats with the fish piled in a mound.

Walking on the sand, letting the surf tickle my toes.
Playing in the lagoon where the calm water from the river flows.

Staying at San Luis Bay Inn overlooking the bay.
I went swimming and made friends in a really big way.

As we ate our dinner on the pier, watching the fishing boats float.
Out of the water comes a seal to sun himself on the back of a boat.

As I return to my school this coming September.
I will always look back on the best vacation to remember.

Eileen Coppula

"Behind The Wall"

I see unhappy faces from all races
Woolly and straight, young and old
Big and bold...behind the wall
Days are all the same, some don't know their name.
Lost and confused wondering what they have to lose...
behind the wall.
Five minutes of phone time - click, click it's over,
fighting for more time to say...from behind the wall.
Official visits, family and friends.
They're not to blame.
You should have sought them out before you played the game.
Now you want all the attention to appear.
Where were you when others cared.
Out there somewhere knowing all the answers.
Instead of listening you were laughing.
Oh, did you forget it was you that brought yourself
'Behind The Wall.'

Doreatha Marshall

Convex

The knife is used to cut, across worlds and
worm holes its serrations like so
many crescent moons slicing through the cooked
night. They find their way into our hands to do
a job: Dismember our dinner, dismember our hands
bypass or triple bypass.
Spoons click and clatter as the criminals in
their box cells attempt to escape. Spoons
the eating utensils make my nose big and hold
my cold medicine which I slurp down anxiously
waiting for the soothing effect to grapple me into
sleep, wonderful sleep, only dreams now, blurred
visions and I view a scene of rotten detail, the
male unit spoon in left hand and spoons that make
me wonder.
Forks aren't very big, the shine lustre gleams.
Four pronged forks in my side stuck through all
the way, can't move tied up tied down with forks
of Damocles hung over the head of some smooth
skinned alien creature, growl retreat and attack.

Jonathan Nuner

If Jesus Came Back Today

If Jesus came back today
Would He like to live and stay
Or would He like it better in older times
When there were no killings, riots or crimes
No drugs dope or drink to muddle their minds
No cigarettes or pills of any kind
The only trip they took was on Camel back
Something to eat and water to drink was all they would pack
I hope he could get use to our ways
The complicated things that fill our days.
The one thing we still have to share
Is the Holy Bible that shows we each still care.

Jean McSwain

The Crystal Heart

A warmth of the fire, from the crystal heart.

Which burns my soul with it's touch, and
yet...
does not burn, but, grows with intensity
from intimacy.

The blaze of the inferno pleases my eyes,
the door-way into my self.

For to burn, would be by your hand,
and yet...

The light of your touch heals my wounds.

Craig Snider

Forever and Ever

Flowers, sparse in assembly,
  Yet full in color.
The petals, narrow in width, lengthy in white.
Their numbers are few,
  But deeply intriguing.
Though subtle and quite plain,
  Their beauty is remarkable.
Their texture compares to the silk of webs,
  And resemble those who walk them.
Their choice was exquisite,
  Like the hand that picked them.
They remind me of forever and ever,
  And shall now replace my eye's.
For I have seen their beauty as you have,
  And I shall see you when I see them.

Christopher A. Torres

78 Degrees And Sunny

Oh, how the iron structure stands amongst the cloudless sky.
Yet it sadly stands alone patiently wondering why?
Now off in the distance comes its saviour, running stride for stride.
Bouncing its favorite friend along the pavement with evident pride.
The time has now come for dreams to be begun,
As the two friends join together, join together as one.
These two work together to develop a child's dream,
The dream of endless wonders set in a primordial scheme.
Now the child has entered the haven for his dream,
The dream that begins under the bright, bright gleam
Of the sun, that is as present as money,
Shining over the court, 78 degrees and sunny.

Kevin Sharp

Oh Son of Mine

So beloved this child of mine
yet only I see the passion in my eye.
I hope this day never ends
for it shall be as I want it, never forget.
See the sun rise and fall
Oh my son
let the world shine upon your glory of eyes
don't cry for it has just started
where it ends no one cares to know it.
But along the way you shall see the light
for which direction to go from this day on.
Stay a while and we shall see,
knowledge me, for I have come to be,
a man of faith and belief to see and seek
for all eternity.
I know not what I do best,
for I shall seek life, just like you
Oh son of mine.

Bijan Eshaghi

"My Special Love"!!

Since we first met I knew this day would come, that
you and I would unit together, together as one.
My love for you is so great and so strong, I hope each
day we spend last forever long. Your eyes I will always cherish,
your hands I will always hold, for me your the only one I'll
ever need in this whole entire world.
My heart is filled with so much joy and love, and when
I see you it's like heaven sent from up above.
The big blue sky, and the great bright sun, don't
compare to your beautiful face, you'll always be my only one. Every
smile I make and every tear I cry, will always be for you, My
sweet cutie pie.
When I kiss your cheek and feel your hair, I feel so
special nothing could ever compare. When I first saw your face, it
was so hard to believe that someone so beautiful was not make believe.
In this world so big my heart has found you, and ever
since then my grey sky's have turn blue.
With you in my life I need no more, all I need is
your heart ye tu amor. I give to you my heart and soul, for I
will never leave, you will never be alone.

Cruz Lucero Jr.

Auntie

Oh dear Auntie of mine,
You are a absolutely truly one of a kind.

Behind your laughing eyes and devilish grin
There's a remarkable woman lying within.

There's just "something" only we share
Seems we're in each others thought even when we're
unaware.

I hope we can be close the rest of our lives
And continue to share these very special ties.

Bonnie Sweeney

Trace You

It took me years to remember
you, beautiful heron, my hero,
and that fateful flight your feathers,
soulless, took into the pain that was my deskside window, now
porthole to the world I haven't known.

What was it
you said—AAACK—feathers and phlegm,
as you reeled,
and what was it, anyway,
that triggered your leap, laser-eyes half-focused,
into space, into the edge of
what was my place?

It comes clear to me now, sitting here,
reaching, pen-for-fingers, to test the strength of the mold of your
imprint,
refractive and defied, how
you saw that day looking into the world as it must
have seemed coming in—
webs, cracks, a thin gleam of light, the end
of which is the end.

Brian Gardner

Nothing

Just as I'd learned to deal with being lonely
you came back into my life.
Wanting just to be friends.
How can you be friends with someone
that you have loved forever?
I don't think that you can.
You don't want to care but I do.
So now what?...Nothing!

Soon you will leave again and I
only wish I knew how to make you stay.
To be your love and your companion
for ever and ever.
But I only get to love you from a
distance and that distance breaks my heart.
Always to have just a part of you
or nothing at all.
So, I take what I can, while I
can and when you leave once again
I'll have...Nothing!

Jeanette Mikeal

Confusion

Everything seems calm, until your head starts to spin.
You don't know where you came from, you don't know where
you've been.

You think it to be crazy. While your mind begins to bend.
When will it be over, when will this horror end.

There's nowhere you can hide, and nowhere you can go.
Your hope is now slim, as the terror starts to grow.

Fear turns your stomach, ripping it in two.
It stares you down with chilling eyes of blue.

Your heart stops beating, your face turns pale.
The fire is burning, as if to be in hell.

The thought enters your mind... Terrified, you scream.
But wait! No!? Could it possibly be?
It all was just a Dream.

Brad Bell

Pain

You and I are part of the same circle, my friend
You exist not separate
But, rather, part of the strength
Silently shouting
Pointing at pitfalls unheeded
Waking an unknown center

At first light, you frightened me
But I have learned to hold your hand
Sauntering down open paths
One with the scent of budding flowers
One with the soft breath of falling leaves
We have come far, you and I

Jane Dorr

The Air That I Breath

You are the air that I breath,
you fill my nostrils, with the sweet promise of the morning dew.
You are the air that I breath,
you fill my throat, with joyful taste of a summer morn.
You are the air that I breath,
you fill my lungs, with the hope of a sunny noon.
You are the air that I breath,
you fill my heart, with the tenderness of a lazy afternoon.
You are the air that I breath,
you fill my mind, with the beauty of the evening sky.
You are the air that I breath,
you fill my soul, with the calmness of the gentle night.
You are the air that I breath,
and without you, I would surely die.

Jeff Draft

Your Tiny Hands Rest In Mine

Your tiny hands rest in mine feeling so delicate yet so powerful.
You grasp my finger with an absolute certainty of trust and security.
Your tiny hands rest in mine with a love that is unconditional,
providing me with the strength and conviction needed to carry on, and
to persevere in the hardest of times.
With you by my side, your tiny hands in mine, I vow to do everything
in my power to guide you through life with all the love I have
to offer as your mother, your friend, and your mentor.
When the time comes for you to let go of my hands and walk alone,
making a life for yourself, remember this:
The hands that once held yours have never withdrawn, and will
always be here to guide you through the hard times.

Jami Stinson Tipton

Untitled

I should have been born at the time of Rodin.
You know, when eccentricity and sensitivity were
understood and perhaps admired.

My Soul belongs in a quiet aesthetically pleasing
place rather than this ugly, ugly world I seem not
easily adapted to.

If I were a sculptor (like Rodin himself or perhaps
even his mistress, Camille, whom he adored, hated, and
eventually betrayed. [Ah! the tragic paradox of yet
another love lost to lost souls]). I would chisel and
hammer and bleed my knuckles a most beautiful pure white
virgin marble box.

In it I would lie down quietly and fall into a peculiarly
most peaceful slumber.

Jai A. Mitchell

Hello Grandma

Hello Grandma, yes it's me, who once was small and sat upon your knee.
You look at us and smile your sweet smile, but in your eyes we see,
the lost and confusion look of "How could this be?"
We know your mind sometimes slips back in time, to a little girl
looking for her daddy.
As the cars race by the highway, you see his horse and buggy.
Oh how we wish we could give you, that ride back to yesteryears
But Grandma all we can do is love and hold you, and try to take
away your fears. You weren't robbed of all memories, you know
we love you
Still,
Sometimes you can't remember why? But we pray someday again
You will.
I have written and dedicated this poem to my Grandma Tura Grisham
who is now 90, And who has for the past five years
had symptoms of Alzheimer's disease.

Karla K. Gan

Forget

Do you think of me?
You looked deep into my
soul and knew me, my
desires, my dreams.
My lifemate.
I lost my soul to you.

Do you see my face?

You exposed my passion, then slipped away. Now
there is only the incessant breathing, speaking,
living.

Are you haunted by my loving eyes?

Why can't I forget your handsome face, your strong
hands caressing my body, your lips fierce, passionate
possessive on mine.
It was paradise you showed me.

Do you long for me?
Do you love me still?

Let me forget.

Kathi Schroemer

The Power Of Love

If I could change the world right now,
You might be wondering why and how.

First of all, I'd like to say,
Bad things are happening every day.

Families and friends, are hurt all the time,
It makes me wonder, will the next ones be mine?

How can we live with all this hate?
What's the world coming to? What is the fate?

Instead of yelling, talk and discuss.
Don't say bad things and scream or cuss.

Instead of anger, show kindness and love.
Take things from the heart, not your mind above.

Take small steps and open your heart.
Things might not be perfect, but at least it's a start.

Janice Pierson

Body Of Conflict

Hate...her body filled with things you'd rather forget
You push her back into the darkest recesses of your mind
Occasionally she escapes from those depths
Finding the key to her small prison... making promises, promises
But she is naughty, filling your head with rubbish
You punish her and try to lock her away
So she takes up gardening, planting seeds of envy
The seeds grow and flower, their blooms stink of death and violence
Each day of neglect makes her stronger
She weeps with loneliness, her tears turn to blood
Pulsating rivers of crimson and black
Rivers that rage through your body, consuming you
Until your last breath is warm and still in her palm
Sending it through the air like so much dandelion fuzz, and it is gone
her laughter shatters glass, and makes grown men cry
The kind of laughter that can be heard in the sound of a gunshot
she will never leave, always be there, a permanent tenant
You grow small, too tired to fight, until she takes over
and locks you up in the darkest recesses of your mind
Hate.

Erika Gentry

False Love

I believed you when you said it was forever,
you said we'd always be together.
Day by day you said our love grew stronger,
but all you did was play me longer.
I used to dream of us walking in the night,
now it's gone...all out of sight.
you had no idea how much I loved you,
you really had no clue.
The whole time, you were so kind,
little did I know, you were playing with my mind.
I remember the day you said it was the last,
you said everything should be kept in the past,
I'll never forget the way you hurt me,
I'm just sorry you had to set me free.

Jenny Sterner

Proud Mary

We've got proud Mary
you say she's through,
remember my family
she was tougher then you!

So don't remember Mary this way!
her proud mind will return again some day,
it will be in heaven, with oceans so blue
she'll be smiling at sea gulls
that are staring at you!

With her bonnet, fishing pole, and so tanned,
we will follow proud Mary to the tide to stand
it will be such a beautiful remembrance,
O' so grand", to talk with proud Mary, hand and hand

With Mary's proud mind we loved so true
together, forever!
we will never be blue
thank you proud Mary for seeing us through.
we will continue to always love you!

Chris V. Curry

Birds In Flight

The smell of morning floats into my room
You see more birds now than you would at noon
They fly so smoothly through the dense air
Turning and diving I can't help but stare.
I wish I was a bird so I could fly far away
But I am not so it's here I must stay
It must be wonderful to fly above the trees
You fly all day and fall asleep in the leaves
It's almost fall so the leaves are turning
This is a beautiful morning.

David M. Famulari

Mother

You did more than just encourage, ten children to be good.
You served as our example and made sure that we could,
See that it took effort, knowledge and confidence,
But most of all, faith in God and prayer with diligence.

Our place was always clean and your strength made it secure,
Which added to our foundation, the expectation to endure,
Against the challenges in life and now we all can see,
That it wasn't things that gave us pride, it was your dignity.

Our backbones were built, from your determination.
"I can't," became "I can," in challenging situations.
It seemed impossible at times, but you always found a way
and gave us the self-assurance that we appreciate today.

We cherish happy memories, of things we use to do,
and each recalls the laughter, that we enjoyed with you.
The stories are even funnier, as we go back through the years,
The many versions of what really happened, still bring us to tears.

All ten of us have made it, and we know from our success,
Your love deserves the credit, because we have been truly blessed.
God shared with us the best, from heaven's storehouse above,
He gave us you, to be our Mother, and He filled you with HIS
LOVE.

Jerry L. Rankin

Things You Think

You sit by the window sill watching the dew,
You think of things that are new,
You think about life, you think about love,
You think of a bird - perhaps a dove.
You think how the dove flies and soars,
You think how a lion meows and roars,
You think of people and what they say,
You think that tomorrow's another day.
You think of the world as it turns round and round,
You think how you're able to stand on the ground.
You think of what
You think of who
and in the end, you think of you.

Julie Ann Tutwiler

To You

What is this I feel about you?
You disturb my peace all the while
You fill my soul with wild desire
You haunt me in the stillness of the night.....

What is this I miss about you?
Your kiss as gentle as the wind
Your embrace that burns my numbness
Your touch that reaches my heart.....

What is this I dream about you?
A place just for you and I
A time where there's no end for us
Ah......but you who could never be mine..........

Enriqueta Laird

Homeless

You see them on the street everyday.
You turn up your nose as you think, "They have
nothing important to say,"
All he wants is a dime.
You refuse, "I'm not buying your wine!"

One foggy night your car brakes down.
You're frightened, you live on the other side of town.
You hear someone coming,
Here they come running.
He draws a knife and begins to curse
You panic and hit him with your purse.
You hear another man coming and he scares the first away.
At first you don't recognize him, he has so much to say.
"The dime I ask is not for wine. I give it to my daughter.
It's ten cents for every glass of water."
You pass that way,
To the man a dollar.
You realize, to have something to say you don't have to be a
scholar.

Crystal A. Whitman

Average Boy

Naughty, naughty little boy, you've got so you can't keep a toy;
You want to see just how they're made
And you don't care where they are laid,
I find them laying on the floor, I can't keep "cleaned up" any more.

In your pocket I find a frog, you say you found him on a log;
In your hands you have a snake
Where did you get him? for goodness sake,
It's dangerous to stay here anymore
They may be crawling on the floor.

When I tuck you into bed, you ask me if the bugs are fed;
You say you collect them just for fun
I think you are a dangerous one,
But when your eyes are closed in sleep
Somehow you look so innocent and sweet.

Maybe, when you are a man
You'll forget these things and change your plan;
And when you have a little boy
You'll know how it is to fall over a toy,
But there's no use to look a fright
Things will probably turn out alright.

Beatrice Pennington

To Shed A Tear

Like an old withered tree in an open field,
Your broken heart will never heal.
As the leaves fall from the old withered tree,
You hope for the love that will never be.
As the rain drops drip from the tree limbs,
So do the tears you shed for him.
The image of the tree slowly fades away,
But your feelings for him will always stay.
Where the tree stood is a reflection of the sun,
Reminding you that he will always be the one.
There the tree sits in the back of your mind,
Thinking of the one you will some day find.

Kristin A. Difilippantonio

This Cleft Between What Was And Is

Serene, at peace, with a wistful smile
Your face appeared in a soft white cloud
That moved with the breeze on an azure sky.
I prayed this vision would endure,
But all too soon, you were no more.

At another time, in a mirth-filled room
That rang with laughs and buzzed with words
I heard your voice. It called my name—
Just once, but oh, so true its tone.
I listened, but you called no more.

In a crowded lift on a building's lee
As it climbed toward the moon and stars that night
I felt a tug on my sleeve and then
Your hand squeezed mine as it used to do—
Just one caress. I felt no more.

Your spirit lingers, that I know;
But time subdues and dims your form.
Please answer, dear, if spirits may—
Will this cleft between what was and is
Ever free my heart to love again?

Elmer J. Mueller

Ode To A Dying Mother Earth

I do not have a memory of the day,
Your great vitality began to go away.
I noticed those aging traces of gray,
I smelled in the breeze the odor of decay,
As I was walking on your beach today,

Perhaps my mind was blurred and slow,
Since your nourishment did not go.
There is ashes on the winds that blow,
And on the sand is garbage people throw,
And now waste is drifting on the flow.

Your green mantle they rend and tear.
The albatross once floated upon the air.
The dolphins used to splash and play there,
And now the water the fish cannot bear.
You die because your children do not care.

All that we have lost, we gave not a sigh.
While you suffered, we did not hear your cry.
When you called in pain, we did not reply.
We could have saved you, but did not try.
Yet, we hasten the day that you will die.

Dennis D. Yeager

Lifeless Needs

Your love takes me places I've never been.
Your heart soars through my body
Like a bird through the sky
And even on this night, we cannot hold each other
I hear your voice fluttering in my mind
As though to try and tell me why you are not here.
Another perhaps, is fatal in my heart
When the sun falls on the earth
When the moon rises to save us
As they are taking me to their sweet place of misery
I cannot bare your loss.
Each day I rise above
Each night I sleep below
I will remember your eyes,
How they made me feel
Your kiss, how I wanted to fly to heaven
Yet now I'm gone, talking through paper
I love you as much as a flower does its seed
I need you as much as a dream needs to live
Goodbye to our love and our lies.

Josette R. Munson

Love

When your heart soars like an eagle,
Your in love.

When butterflies flutter in your stomach,
Your in love.

When your knees shake like an earthquake,
Your in love.

When nothing can make you sad,
Your in love.

And when your in love you should never let go,
For it could fly away like a dove.

Christi Urash

Edges

My friend, laughing, said to me
"Your life is so quiet...you play things too safe - you need to
live more on the edge!" on the edge he says??
as I open my eyes and find myself on an outcropping
the climate around me gloomy and overcast; typhoons expected
with Winds welcomed as they are the breath of my embered rage
Anger my surveillance for danger
and as they blow, the blustering familiar; at peace with isolation,
danger's excitement mistaken for feeling alive;
I reach out to hold onto the edge...
my Edges of
connectionless—a penetrated aura misapplied Love
a sentenced soul foreboding sensations—an unoccupied life weighted
emptiness—a disparaged spirit imprisoned laughter—a denounced
personality-sequestion from the universe
Yes, friend, my life is too quiet; the quiet of endangered sanity
Glancing below, I anxiously listen for the wind's possible whisperings
of Hope
and pray to either the up-currents or the down-drafts...
Please blow hard enough—because I'm tired of living on the Edge

Kelli Cordon

The Knock Of Love

Behold, I stand at the door of your heart,
Your Lord and Savior desires to come in,
With my still, small voice; a gentle knock
to enter forever, to keep you from sin

The knock I give is my spirit of love,
That silent tug you should never ignore,
For it is my plea to come sup with me,
And to share my glory forever more.

Turn not away from my spirit's pull,
But open your heart and welcome me there,
To receive all my blessings of life and love,
In my glorious kingdom forever to share.

The latch of your heart is your stubborn will,
The latch I will never force you to lift,
But the door of your heart, when freely opened,
I will enter and give you my eternal gift.

Billy J. Young

Dear Love

Of all the guys I've ever met, you're the one I can't forget.
Your heart is like a pot of gold, hard to get
and hard to hold. In all my dreams our lips have
met, just wait dream boy I'll get you yet! Some
say kissing is a sin, but if it is where'd it begin?
Adam kissed Eve, Eve kissed others, so why can't
we kiss one another? Kisses spread germs, germs
are hated, but kiss me baby I'm vaccinated! so
I send this letter to you my dear, I could
express it better if you where hear.

Janette Vaughn

Untitled

Mother
Your love has always been.
A strong foundation
of warmth and caring
a Roof to shelter me for storm
a window on the world
opening to dream unlimited
a doorway to life itself!
Thank you, Mother, for the gift of your love
May your day be just as warm
and wonderful as you are!
with love today and always!
Happy Day's ahead

Carol Gipson

Untitled

No, I can't understand your needs,
Your reasons.
I couldn't ask a letter why,
Or scream out how sorry I was that I ruined
Something.
I know it was me, not you, and
When you pressed your gift of life
Across my fevered forehead, I felt the same
Indecision (or fear?) that you
HEARTLESSLY
UNTHINKINGLY
and HORRIBLY
wrote...

Now I am calm, I suppose, and rivers have ceased to swell
From the rain the storm flooded them with.
But, damn it anyway.
I'm the fool in my own court.
Tables turned, and now I have the silence to listen for laughter in.
I'll always love you.

Amanda C. Starcher

Being Sick

Being sick is not fun,
Your temperature makes you feel hot as the sun,
When your sick it means the germ have won.
You have a runny nose,
And you always have freezing toes,
All you want to do is doze.
You're constantly looking for your hanky,
You want to curl up with your blankly,
And most of the time you're cranky.
Sometimes you can't breathe,
Then you start to really wheeze,
Now you're going to sneeze.
You could have a headache for days,
When you are sick you feel many different ways,
Throwing-up is just a phase.
Your medicine makes you say ick,
Because of your sore throat you have a popsicle to lick,
It's no fun being sick.

Bryna Lynn Reiff

Summers Bay

With people on the gray bridge looking over the rails
Onto the calm blue water where nice sail boats
Sail away.

With nice blue fluffy clouds and a nice sunny day
A cool breeze blowing the tall cat tails
And big fluffy trees to and fro.

And nice big two story houses that people can look
Off their back porches.

Ryan Jones

What's In A Name

Fall dear fall, or should I call you Autumn
You're a confusing time of the year
Are you an ending or a new beginning?
Both sides of this I must weigh clear.

Fall is a word for an ending
Summer vacations coming to a close
No more running free and wild outside
Fall ushers in winter cold and snows
Windows and doors getting ready to close us in
No more sitting under night stars with neighbors and kin.

Autumn is a word for a beginning
A new school year off to a new start
Autumn ushers in a new circle of holidays
Labor Day, Halloween, and a day we are thankful from the heart
And winter gives us Christmas, we're not angry that you led it in
This is a busy time of year and autumn let it all begin.

So fall or Autumn, what shall I call you?
I really don't think it's so important the name
Your coloring of leaves makes you a most beautiful season
Fall, Autumn, whichever, I'm so glad that you came.

Eleni Mouzakitis

You Know You're Growing Older When...

They play Beatles music at the Oldies concert.
You're working with people who are 24-32 years old.
Your hairdresser is younger than you are.
You want to play golf.
You're glad your babies are grown up.
It's almost impossible to lose weight.
You want to walk for exercise.
You're invited to your twentieth college reunion.
You attend your twentieth college reunion.
Your joints ache and you think 'arthritis'?
No more refrigerator art comes home.
The last margarine tub for the art teacher is given.
Prunes solve your problem at times.
Kids come to your garage sale and talk about your 'old' bicycles.
You find a grey hair...in your eyebrow.
You use the ladder to get out of the pool.
Younger people offer you a seat.
You're saying "maybe that was before your time" more often.
It's difficult to skip.
You buy a book about menopause.

Edie Delamaide-Winters

An Acrostic Poem

My two uncles came and visited my family.
Yup two uncles, had a crowded house.

Sleeping in my sister's room was okay.
Urging to get out soon!
My 6th grade workbook had to be done.
My old friends from school gave me a ring on the telephone.
Eating at the table was crowded with my uncle's family.
Reading, I had lots of time.

Vacationing at Yellowstone was great!
Animals everywhere.
Camping in the cabins at "Old Faithful" was fabulous.
A deer garden was beautiful
Tiny little cute squirrels scampering around.
Incredible mine canyon!
Open-pit copper mine was marvelous.
Nothing there was dull or boring to me.

I went to Yellowstone for five days.

Having fun at Yellowstone was m goal.
A fun time I had this summer.
Disneyland was great with the new "Indiana Jones ride."

Connie Fang

Gray

Gray is the color of a cloudy day.
Gray is the color where the seal pups lay.
Gray is the color of a puppy's cry.
Gray is the color of a year gone by.
Gray is the color in the eye of the eagle
His tarnished feathers once grand and regal.
Gray is the color of a hawk dying
Remembering days past of endless flying.
Gray is the color of the balcony
As the sun sets low on the endless sea.
Gray is the hue in the morning rays.
Gray is a walk in the woods winter days.
Gray is in the shadows of a huge oak tree.
Gray is in you.
Gray is in me.

Sarah M. Kunkel

Untitled

A pretty rose with lovely hair,
grew taller and taller with the nights warm air.

She would always, always stand up straight,
even when it was very late.

She knew she would die someway, somehow
so that's why she was so perfect now.

She went to a psychic to tell her when,
she would die in her horrible end.

The psychic told her when she would die,
and then the rose said "Oh my!".

The days passed and she still stood,
as proudly and brightly as she could.

And then the day finally came,
when she would have to end her fame.

Everyone cried and cried and sobbed,
even her enemies which she still loved.

And the next day she woke up again,
and saw she was alive in her own bed.

She remembered the days when she was a kid,
and after that she stood as proudly as she always did.

Raquel Gonzalez

From Whence I Came

My mind wonders back searching far distant past
Groping for my ancestors, the lots they were cast
There were hundreds, thousands, all unknown to me
But alive in their time within history

Whoever they were and wherever from
Energetic or lazy, timid or aplomb
Dressed well in satin eating fine cuisine
Or wearing rags and hungry, even unclean

They were all my people, and special they be
And I hope to meet them in eternity
Could they have possibly looked forward to now
As I look back, try to find them somehow

Well, if the truth be admitted, its really a blur
I can't imagine how they lived or where
And its impossible that they had a forward view
Of my life in this space age, electronic milieu

But they all came before me, each life in turn
With its cares, duties, joys and concern
And each contributed to the making of me
Some strength, some weakness, but my heredity.

Maureen O'Neal Pereira

Wrong Way

I took the road less traveled and it led me straight to hell
I chose to stray from the beaten path
Now I find myself so lost I couldn't make my way back to who I was or where I came from
Even if I tried

I dove into the ocean and swam against the tide
But struggling to reach the shore again
To feel wet, cold sand beneath my feet and remember what it was
To stand with confidence on steady ground
Left me only beaten and breathless
So I dragged myself beneath the waves I wanted so badly to make
And drowned as I sank with the weight of my potential chained to me like an anchor
What faith can I be expected to have when I scream my desire into the
wind and it blows right back in my face?
Am I afraid I will choke to death when I swallow my pride and admit to myself
That all I wished for and dreamed about was worth nothing more than the price of a ticket
For a short ride to nowhere on a train that traveled the wrong way
before jumping the tracks and dumping me off
In a lonely, forgotten heap of broken promises
With empty pockets and an even emptier heart
By the side of a road I wish I had never taken?

Robert Shulze

Moment By Moment

Moment by moment I wonder why, why I left my country without saying good-bye.
Moment by moment I try to understand, an alien country an alien land.

Moment by moment I sit and pray, praying to God I never go astray.

Moment by moment I ponder my thought, being interrupted by another gun shot.
Moment by moment I feel the pain, the pain of another soul in the cold rain.
Moment by moment I hear the cry, the cry of an innocent baby about to die.
Moment by moment I see dreams fail, another brother another sister thrown in San
Francisco jail.
Moment by moment I listen to the sounds that ring, the sound of another ambulance siren.
Moment by moment I watch people crave, crave for the substance that leads to their grave.

Moment by moment I wonder why, why we let life cause us all this strife.

Moment by moment the Lord reminds me, this is the world we live in, a world full of sin.
Moment by moment He comforts me, reminding me of His unfailing love deep within.

Nma Uma Eleazu

Mother And Time

With crackle of light, she spoke to the moon and in return the stars
were their witness. The union of mother nature and father time awoke
the world with swirls of wedding dress leaves and moss covered hat.

Oh - lives of endless age and love as old as the mountains, they
create with only a kindness that once upon time's birth flowed like a river.

Excellent clouds float upon womb of earth and four children begin
to play in fields of plenty with names of change;

"They work well together" father notices, and mother nods in satisfaction.

And children grow and children change as often they do change
leaving parents behind and though hard as it be, it is willed.

Time heals mothers wounds. And he too is weathered with worries,
about his children and those animals of knowledge that often act with none.

On bright days you can hear mother laugh as her children have come to
to visit. Sometimes they don't get along and winter likes to give
everyone a hard time but together they eventually create a spectacle,
a magic show hillside of snow and green grass with budding flowers
and radiantly colored leaves.

And then they are off again...

Rainbow smiles will shadow their sleep, hope exists within a bed of
sea and sky and land. It is said that they cannot exist without one
another. The death of mother nature would surely be the end of time.

Nina J. Smith

Two Lost Souls

Two lost souls found one another
the one soul can't live without the other.
Alone, desolate, they searched far and wide,
if they had kept on any longer,
they would have withered and died.
Only, the souls had the will to survive.
They came together as one, never
to be sad again, or ever cry.
This one lost soul was so young
at heart and mind
the other lost soul had a heart
no one ever bothered to find.
But together these two souls are now,
at last never to be apart, forsaking
both their pasts.

Debbie Rozmarynowski

Nothing

I am not the light of the sun and moon,
Illuminating those who would see;
Nor am I the splendor of my gifts.
I am not the life that grows,
Never ending, from the seed of dreams
I've had since youth.
I am not the host of conviction,
Nor even the guest of commitment.
I am not the pain that lovers feel,
The strength of their kiss,
Even the emptiness in their parting.
I am not the mask of my words,
Neither am I the truth.
I am not who you think I am...
Indeed, in the dead of night,
When feelings come quicker and harder,
I am not even who I think I am.
I am nothing.
All of that which life is
Is all that I am not.

Jason Manzatt

Parody of Joyce Kilmer's Trees

I think that I shall never see
A car as lovely as a Z -

A Z whose racing treads are prest (sic)
Against the highways snake like breast.

A Z that sits in the sun all day
And sheds its top to catch each ray.

A Z that may in summer wear
Four wire wheels to give it flair.

Upon whose hood the snow has lain
And turtle wax repels the rain.

Ford made Models A and T,
But it took Nissan to make a Z.

Carol Marsh

Friends

I never knew you,
I never will.
I thought you were my friend,
But still.
Something haunts me,
That tells me your here.
I want you in my arms,
Where you will love me.
As a lover will.

Rebecca Doran

Child Of The Night

Through the night
A child walks
Carefully trying not to stumble
And fall on her face

Through the dark, night sky
She can only see the
Shadow of what awaits her
Praying it is someone to help her

Around every corner
A new worry is waiting
One that if it doesn't kill her
Will only make her stronger

When every hill is a
Challenge of her strength and
A great triumph when complete
Only to be followed by another hill

This child of the night
So fragile, yet strong
Walks slowly, in fright
In the soul of every one of us.

Casey Waswick

Childhood

A bib,
A crib,
A dirty mess

A book,
A doll,
A princess dress

A smile,
A nod,
And there's a start

A rose,
A date,
A broken heart

A pen,
A sigh,
The S.A.T.'s

A joke, a thought,
All A's, two B's

A wave, a tear,
A kiss from Mom...

You don't know childhood, until it's gone.

Amber L. Kernes

"A Dream"

A dream is something you can be,
A dream is something you can't see.
A dream is something when you sleep,
A dream is something when you cry and weep.
A dream is something in the sky!
A dream is what makes you fly.
A dream is something soft and kind,
A dream is something in your mind.
So if you ever have to be
Something you don't seem,
Think of this poem and there will always be
A Dream.

Anna Shea Lucas

The Wild

The Wild is a place I know:
A ferocious stir of emotions,
A shrieking call of need.
Everything's in a commotion;
Everyone's out to feed.

The Wild is a beast, I'm told:
Crushing anything in Its path,
Stalking Its unsuspecting prey.
Beware of Her wrath;
Stay out of His way.

The Wild is within.

Cheryl A. Castro

Lightly

Time without motion
A frozen moment
A capsule of life
Held secure but lightly

River churning
Cutting its path
Deep and wide
Through my heart

Fire burning
White light shines
Too brite yet
Feeling so good

Run with me
Through fire and water
You and I shall be
Held secure but lightly

Douglas Buzby

Doubts

A mind full of questions
A heart burdened with need
Doubt preys on the soul
and uncertainties
waiting to feed
on answers that will
guide you to your destiny
How will you find them?
Where are they hiding?
What corner will they meet?
If you only knew the wisdom
I seek
The scrutiny goes on and on,
but the answers are still unknown...

Carol D. Hand

The Materialist

A gray flannel suit,
a house in Jersey,
a plastic man
with no soul fibre.
Broads loom large
in his shoddy life,
hops in the sack
for free or for cash, mere
lackluster attempts
to make himself felt.
A dyed-in-the wool
insincere sucker
I can't cotton to him
an emotional chintz.

Andrea Giambrone

Alauda Arvensis

From meadow, still and verdant green
a lark arose, singing.
Into the sun till scarce be seen
ever upward, rising, winged.

What have I done o' winged creature
that ye should rise to me
and my heart enrapture
with crystal note and melody.

'Tis I who should but kneel and praise
and in humbleness give hearing
the hymn that ye in heaven raise
to me; an earthly being.

Ah, but there on nature's carpet lies
the meaning of the joyous spate
your pulsing throat with trilling cries;
new-born nestling, and there, your mate.

So sing, sing ye bird of the wing;
sing out, sing loud till the heavens doth ring.
Till man of this earth your song is heeding,
such joy, in my soul, my heart is pleading.

John Anderson

The Real Piece Of Pie

Coming to your table
A little tired
And not as well dressed
But just as good.

The chef's pie has no flaws.
You can't really tell if it's real
Or just good table art.
Imitations are very deceiving.

Unless your looking closely
and confronting it.
You will never know the complete truth.
Try to understand its purpose.

Is it there to temp you?
It makes you dream, it makes you drool.
And eventually sometimes, somehow
It may satisfy you.

The pie will always be there
But the real piece of pie is at your table.
Its always getting the immediate attention
And the glory it deserves.

Angela Murrell

To You And For You

Into your heart I come with love
A love that's sanctioned from above
It's filled with warmth and cheer
It's filled with thoughts of you near
Hold it close to your heart
Just like you did from the start
Say you'll be mine each and every day
Say you'll be mine and never walk away

Kenneth M. Killings

Threes

(With Apologies To Joyce Kilmer)
I think that I shall never see
A man that is as fat as he.

A man whose expanding chest is pressed
Against his snug, tight-fitting vest;

A man that runs about all day,
And lifts his beefy arms in play;

A man that may in summer snare
A Ringling Brother tent to wear;

Upon whose plump and bulky face;
A triple chin has set in place.

Men are made by God you see,
And this one takes the place of three.

Don J. Koz

Help Wanted

Sad, but true
A man was found dead
At my place of employee today.
One of the other men
Standing nearby casually remarked
"Well, there's another job opening."
Another job opening
He lived, He breathed, He died.
Another job opening
Life goes on without us
without any of us
Say the things that you always
meant to say now.
If you can't or you won't, or
If you'd rather do something more
important, I happen to know of
a job opening.

Karen D. Adams

Donna

Remaining yet to be danced
A midst the eons and dreams
Asunder the darksome schemes
Remitting what seeming chanced
Remaining, yet to be danced;
Steps, delicately waken
Spins, sinuously taken,
Yearnings of a life entranced
Surreal but a moment past;
Perchance to share if I may
Your patterns, a life to last;
Ancient, unsullied I lay
A love I no longer chance;
remaining yet, shall we dance.

Kevin G. Hiester

Silent And Violent

You live your life,
a pack of lies.
You do not care,
who lives or dies.
You hide the facts,
though they are violent,
You live each day being silent.
Take a look at life itself,
it is a blessing and nothing else.
So please speak now, don't hold back.
Just get this problem, off your back,
do not hang within that pack.

Please speak, it was murder.

Debbie Smith

Guilty

I sit alone in a chiseled mask,
A pale face, like a broken mime,
A china doll in shattered glass,
Crushed by the throbbing hands of time.

I watch the world pass me by,
In streaks of light and endless dark.
I want to be alone to die,
My destiny has missed its mark.

My heart is sore with the weight of regret,
My soul is drenched in endless pain.
My past lingers and I can't forget
All that I've lost, so little gained.

Like a child without a home,
On the streets of loveless sorrow,
Through the darkness, here I roam,
And wait for the dawn of another tomorrow.

I reflect on my life and all that it's worth,
And ask if life is what it seems...
Wandering aimless upon this earth,
On the boulevard of broken dreams?

Josh Nantais

The Rain Inside

As the clouds cry,
  A sadness sets in,
    Tears then fall
      From my eyes,
        And loneliness begins.

Knew it was over
  Before it was even said.
    To search the entire world
      I would find no friend.
        That fantasy, of love
          Forever, is dead.

To see the old dream today
  And realize it is lost to the wind.
    A special spot and
      Small fraction of love in the heart,
        But, those in-love feelings
          Have all drawn to an end.

Barbara Bernath

Life

Through difference we find similarity
A sameness often painful to view
Fears, as well as fantasies
Dwell inside me, dwell inside you

The paths we follow are sometimes hidden
And confusion reigns supreme
But a common bond we all share
Helps us see that which can not be seen

As we journey along our path
We notice other wanderers with us
We wonder if we fell off track
Would the path dare to miss us

We are connected on unseen levels
Silhouettes on each other's glass
Candles burning each other's oil
More than glances we have to pass

We all dance together as one
Euphoria blinding us from pain
Joined by fear, ambition, and joy
Separate links in a common chain

David A. Jacobson

The Ocean Battle

A wall of foam
A shaft of light,
The eruption of an ocean home
That disrupts the water into flight.

A burst of speed
That carries far,
The wind to the ocean heeds
With the ocean water to spar.

The rocks are battered
By the incessant crash,
Of waters tattered
And gone in a flash.

The wind dances
With the water flow,
The waves take such chances
To dash onto the beach where only the foam
will be left to show.

Brenda M. Starcher

Untitled

I am a voice
  a silent echo over and over

I ride a wind
  that knows not what direction to blow

I am a refrain in a song
  too far behind to be enjoyed

At times a careless whisper
  to ears I'd not request to kiss

I am a blessing
  I am a curse—
    yet an absolute necessity

I'd ask to be listened to
  but for now I'm only asking to be heard

I am love.

Justine M. Meyers

Stranger Inside

There is a stranger in the world somewhere,
A stranger who might be your friend.
You might have seen him many times,
But never felt his grief inside.
He might have been your best of friends,
But never has he shared his grief with you.
For he had only days to live,
But lived them as he always did.
And now you stand upon his grave,
Knowing what you had never known.

Boris Gluzberg

Untitled

A winter night,
  a summer day.
The light quickly fades,
  and shadows reign.

Cold, frosty air,
  a ray of light.
Fierce raven ends
  dove's peaceful flight.

Cold, hard steel,
  the echo of a breath.
The sound of salvation
  is the sound of death.

Jarrel Baldwin

The Awakening

In the night came
A touch,
A gentle whisper,
And I am free
to soar.
Impenetrable walls,
Unspeakable terrors,
Gone.
With hands held
Around my heart
To hug,
All my fears
Disappear.
The child within
Emerges
To be seen once more.
Healed by His touch,
I await the dawn.

Kathleen R. Neville

Mother

A mother like you is hard to find
A treasure from above.
The impression you've placed in my mind
is of goodness and of love.

I know that with the passing years.
you've experienced many things.
Happiness, sadness, smiles and tears.
all the feelings that life brings.

But you've been courageous through it all.
a real champ to me.
In my book you stand real tall
a strength of character, I see.

So, Happy Birthday to you, dear mother.
Be joyous all year through.
On this earth there'll be no other
as special to me as you!

Jeannette Arbogast

"The Tree"

Such beauty I see from my window
a Tree laced with colors of splendor.
Spreading it's branches for all to behold
Leaves of green, red and gold.
It's still trunk in the breeze,
forever present unceasingly.
As time passes leaf colors fade,
branches are dim, there is little shade.
Rain starts, seasons begin,
tree colors are ever so dim.
On another spring day I look for the shade,
my favorite tree brought
during the heat of the day.
No leaves are seen, the tree looks gray,
Smog is present which causes decay.
Branches are drooping, no leaves in sight.
What happened to destroy such delight.
The trunk is present, but looks like a log,
The tree has died from Industries smog.

Juanita J. Crawford

To Death To Undo Death

Bobby McLaughlin lives
Accused of a heinous crime.
The jury thought he was an evil man.

In Bobby's land the law says
Death Cannot Undo Death
Only God has this power.

But, Bobby's father knew the truth,
A terrible mistake had happened.
He spent years trying to convince
Politicians, lawyers, and judges of
The injustice.
Finally, they believed his words.

Bobby is free.
As every human being is born to be.
This could only have happened
For the law is written,
Death Cannot Undo Death...
All because Bobby's father knew-
They would finally see the truth.

Janet Christensen

Untitled

The sheets lay loose
across my flesh
worn and soft by
time and dreams.
You drift, silently
into the edges of consciousness
I always meet you there
my heart it hears you closer still.
Forever hold you
once my flesh
come to me thru
time and dreams
you breathe, gently
God's grace across my writing heart.
He always meets us there
and lets our hearts beat closer still.

Angela Davis Lane

My Fear

The silent darkness of my own room
Adds to the confusing things in my mind.
I'm lost in the shadows of my own bed.
Light is what I need to find.

I'm feeling very dizzy, I need to sit down,
I curl up on the floor,
Trying to clear my mind
So I can find a door.

A door out of the darkness
And into my past, I'd love to go
Where the sun is shining
And the people I know.

Dreaming is all I can do for now
To get away from my fear.
Something I feel towards everything,
Even those that are dear.

Abigail A. Harman

Newport

Mansions lazily sunning themselves
against the backdrop of grey seas.

Lovingly caressing lawns of emeralds
studded with the rubies of azaleas
and tulips.

Ghosts of bygone eras,
patrolling the Cliff Walk —
waiting for sign of sail.

The leftovers of a lost Atlantis.

Elizabeth Walton

Untitled

Beating, pounding
Against the doors of my mind
Thoughts, feelings, regrets
Flood the gates
Suddenly I am on trial
My conscience being
Judge, jury, and executioner
I stand justly accused
Unready to serve fitting punishment
The punishment of a lifetime:
Plagued by guilt
Filled with shame
Being unworthy.

April Reilly

Untitled

Sadness is a depressed man
all alone,
the tears on his face
sticking to his cheeks
from which turn very red.

Happiness is a woman in love,
loving the man she knows
sharing her smiles with him and
knowing he loves her too.
she is often remembering the
puppy love they once experienced
turning into true love.

Then Happiness and sadness meet,
A sudden look covers their face
from seeing the two differences
Sadness starts to cry,
The Tears will never be able to exclaim
his feelings about seeing the joyfulness
she sprouts out.
Then Happiness gets a smile on her
face and starts dancing down the street.

Krissy LaFave

Someone Is No One

I saw someone the other day,
or maybe it was no one,
it is hard to say.

Someone comes as no one goes,
and when you look for no one,
someone shows.

Someone and no one start off the same,
and if you become no one,
who is to blame?

Philip Brown

"My Dad, David Mattera"

Just another day in the E.R.
all day long when everything
seems to go wrong..
Patients need stitches, doctors need help.
Needles are resisted, nurses
need assistance.
Just another day in the E.R.
The whole world is sick today.

David Mattera bed three
needs you, no delay
David Mattera, could you get to bed two
Sometime today?
In-coming ambulance,
they need strong arms
David Mattera puts on his charms.
Bring in the stretcher,
This old lady has no pressure
David Mattera does C.P.R.
this is how things
really are, for David Mattera in the E.R.

Chad Billiris

Untitled

For the man who has touched
all our lives
Who could place love into
any hateful soul
you have filled the emptiness
in many hearts
and made them solid and whole

You lifted spirits with
your strength
when hope had seemed so far
A made who could take the worst
of a promising athlete
and turn him into a star

When life had seemed close to an end
you gave it a brand new start
There's no time like the present
to tell the father who gave us
life laughter and love
you will forever remain
in our hearts.

Kendra L. Rogers

Thinking Beyond

Many years of remembering
All that seemed so dear
The dreams we both so cherished
The love we wouldn't fear
All has passed beyond us
As we have drifted apart
Never to return again
To claim each others' heart.

The path that you have chosen
I'm forever forbidden to cross
Never again as long as I live
May I retrieve my loss
Life alone is more than empty
Without you all is dead
Thinking beyond is out of the question
With loneliness forever ahead.

John J. Pomazal

Mute

I am compelled out of reality,
Alone and happy into silence.
I pull out of what is me,
Alone and happy into silence.

And I cry, and I cry,
For how it's suppose to be;
A world that is more than lies;
An existence outside of misery.

My voice rise, it rises,
Speak? I can't- but never try,
For I am lost within disguises;
Pretty painted wings can not fly.

I am compelled out of reality,
Alone I weep my silence.
Forgotten who once was me,
Alone I weep my silence.

DeAnna Z. Verley

Ember

Again, the sun sets.
Alone, I face the cold wind.
The clouds, red with fire.

The moon, a curved blade,
Cutting through the glacial blaze,
Its reign to transpire.

Dark trees, silent guards,
With iced air, their only voice,
Summon each celestial fire...

...And kindle my heart's desire.

David Felman

Sister

Sister, you are the best to me,
Although I want two or three.
My sister, oh sister, how you treat me
So,
I think it's this you better know.
That I will be there for you, night and day,
Even if you don't come out to play.
I'll be there for you, day and night.
To take away all your fright.
Fright that someday I won't be there
For you,
For one day, it could be true.
But for now, we go to sleep.
Side by side, and never weep.
As we think of what become of us
Two,
For only the future know true.
How we separate or come together,
But we will be sisters, from now until
forever.

Jennifer Smith

Another

Another day dawning
on a weary world,
Another flower dying
unfurled,
Another dream being
cast away,
Another bomb
was made today.

Nancy K. Lundberg

To Be or Not to Be?

To be or not to be? I have
always asked myself. Will he
always be there for me? or will
he leave?
I guess this question has been
answered. I know for a fact that
five months ago it was
answered by a very special person.
He has been there for me through
it all. This person walked to Kalama
and back to see me. He was there
at the hospital every night when
I tried to commit suicide.
And to this very day we are
engaged and nothing can break us apart.
This person is my boyfriend.

Crystal Hearld

True Character

Highly opinionated,
Always right.
Full of conviction,
Sometimes polite.

Can be arrogant,
Maybe even rough.
Willingly sarcastic,
Convincingly tough.

Eternally needed,
Possible to understand.
Permanently there,
Forever a man.

Anita George

The Seasons

I am the seasons. Sometimes I
am white and sometimes I am green.
In the summer Mother Nature uses
green on me. She has a paint box
that she spills on the land.
In the winter I am whiter than
the whitest white. She gently
puts a white blanket on the earth,
And you can not see any green.
As the Winter passes by I can't see any
Jackets, or mittens, or gloves.
While children are jumping and
happily running around.

Kevin Drury

That's Life

A baby cries
an adult cheers
but the joy is lost
among the fears

The world we live in
is all but gone
a world of violence
moves the child on

When the child grows
who is to pay
it's society that
treats him that way.

Andrew Chilkowich

Susan (A Miracle)

A miracle is said to be
An act of the Lord above.
Lucky are those to receive this gift
Of such an immaculate love.

I, for reasons still unknown
Was blessed with this heavenly boon.
I'm graced with every sunrise
And so under every moon.

Susan, you're the miracle
Of which I speak so high.
You've blessed me with your presence
And warm me when you're nigh.

I've breathed your air with every breath,
Consumed you for every meal.
My body now depends on you
To live, to love, to feel.

I promise to make you happy;
I'll vow to you "I do"
Susan, you are the everything.
It's no miracle that I love you!

Chris Cammack

The Wedding

On her father's arm she floats forward,
an angel adorned in white lace.
The once soft fuzz of a tiny child
cascading beneath the fine veil.

The memories of a joyous youth
embraced for a moment in time
like a deep breath on a cool morning
to be remembered later on.

Her ever thoughtful eyes and heart
so deeply trusting of this man
now focused intently on another.

He waiting, grins, young and handsome,
fibers pulsing with expectancy,
eager to unwrap the future.

The graceful step still confident
Young face so full of radiant love
On her father's arm she floats forward
an angel adorned in white lace.

Joyce Byrd

The Waitress

Such a sight beheld my eyes;
An angel in a peasant's guise
Serving coffee, cakes, and tea,
While forced to brave indignity
Daily for a meager pay.

Surely there must be a way
To loose this vision from her chains,
To free, that she may fly away
To find the world she's etched in dreams,
A better place with better means
And ways to play her heart's sweet tune.

But there is nothing I can do,
For I am but a traveller who
Must carry on, just passing through,
Upon my weary, lonely way;
To never pass this way again,
To never even know her name.

Anthony V. Bocchinfuso

Images

A deep nostalgia fills me;
an anguish vibrates in my blood
from all the memories of a place,
and silhouettes covered with the past.

The past of a child of naive desires,
of dreams and great fantasies,
that turned into new ones or flew away
like a doubt searching for an answer.

Oh, how I remember the silent eyes
filled with a bright inner light,
that lit my years of innocence
and embraced in its warmth my anxieties.

The hands, so white and fine,
were the hands of my mother.
What a beautiful image I keep of her,
thinking of her tender, loving fingers!

Everything comes back in stages,
like pages that fall together,
harmonizing in my mind; loving and rebuilding
what is still beating and arising from my yesterday.

Clementina H. Torres

I Could Have Been

I could have been a president,
An astronaut, or mother.
I could have been your aunt, your friend,
Your cousin, or your brother.
I could have been a missionary,
A teacher, chef, or engineer.
I could have learned to love, or hate,
To live, to laugh, to take and share.
I could have been so many things,
But that was not to be.
My mother made the CHOICE instead
To take my life from me.

Carol Morrell

The Forgotten

He lives among a lost dream,
an empty bottle and a stray cat.
Nobody owns him.

He walks by himself, beside
the odorous trash in the alley
where others like him

Linger at night,
and the ground is cold
with the darkness of evil.

He beholds stern glances
without kindness.
No hand reaches for his.

He scrounges until he is tired
or nothing can be found.
He starves quite often.

When he fumbles with his bottle,
he stops suddenly
to hear death's call.

Elizabeth Tepe

Untitled

Sending snow
Hurling hail
Blowing blue
Peace prevails

Riordan Winds

My Sex

My sex is the poison of souls it seems
An object of lust
Once you've had me, that's it
Your tainted
Forever plagued
By MY sex
There's no turning back once it's happened
If I'm conscious, you feel guilt
My sex is the torture of me
And it will become yours
If you don't run away
So run and hide from my sex
And keep yourself safe
Crawl back to your girlfriends and forget
Only remember in your drunken stupors
Or in mine and taste it again and again
Then flee or it will catch you
And drag you to my world
Branding you with the countless others
Who have not run fast enough

Amy DeStefanis

To Be Somebody

Will I always be like this?
An outcast, a nobody?
I want love, I want happiness.
I just want to be somebody.
I am uncertain of what lies ahead,
but I know what I leave behind.
Good-bye to this unhappiness.
I wish to cry no more.
As the stars shine above
in the darkness of night,
I sit alone and realize
only I can make my future bright.
Today is but a step
down a long and winding road.
It is only the beginning
of releasing this heavy load.
I wish to rid myself of this burden,
and lead a normal life.
Eventually, I will be OK,
Soon, I will be alright.

Amy J. Fox

Within

No motion within, only silence.
An unfaced horror, lying dormant.
Only an occasional thought,
releasing a pained realization.
Acceptance played no part,
in this twisted game of pretend.
Reality was hidden in some corner,
that only time, could only find.
The future looms ahead,
unwanted.
Hope becomes escape,
and yet;
No peace within only silence.

Erin M. Espelie

Old Bainbridge

Drawn to its ancient power and strength,
Ancient live oaks out reaching
With stories of five human life times.

Twisting,
Whispering,
Quivering,

Hovering, over the trailing motor
With a haunting delight,
Want to stay,
Meandering through the arms
of Quercus Virginiana.

Judy Newberry

What Peace Means To Me!

To be at Peace remember this,
And always keep it in mind.
There can't be peace without justice,
With honest effort entwined.

Waters on life's sea can be rough,
The Hugh Waves and Heavy Gales,
But if we try with trust enough,
We can then adjust the Sails.

Faith believes that God can bring peace,
By trust we know that He will.
His love for us will never cease.
Stormy oceans he can still.

We seek Peace, Peace is not a dream.
We must work to make peace true,
And fight the good fight as a team.
Peace starts in the heart of you.

God said, "To you my Peace I give."
Which will satisfy your needs.
Strive for His peace as long as you live.
To 'Eternal Peace' it leads.

Joseph J. Blanchfield

No Silver Lining

You can't just state it was Watergate
And blame it all on Nixon
It's true he burst a bubble or two
But there's more to our affliction

So many are so cynical
So willing to believe the worst
A pessimistic pinnacle
Where doubt is like a curse

Suspicion's a tenacious beast
It tears your trust to pieces
Like victims of a vulture's feast
The bleeding never ceases

Those we anoint will see fingers point
And get knocked off their pedestal
Guilty until otherwise proved
The fingers become tentacles

Optimistic isn't realistic anymore
No silver lining on Capitol Hill, no Knight at the White House door
Skeptical is sensible and faith's a dinosaur
No silver lining on Capitol Hill, no Knight at the White House door

Keith Steinbaum

Roses And Candlelight

We once shared roses
And candlelight
Music we danced to
Every night.
You wore dresses
Made of lace,
Every step you
Made was grace.
Your blue eyes
Touched my soul
Your gentle touch
Made me whole.
If only I could
Change your mind,
Give my apologies
One more time.
If only I could
Make things right,
We could share roses
And candlelight.

Chadwick Loyd

The Mirthful Fairy

They called her "The Mirthful Fairy"
And cute was the word they used most.
She danced like a flower blew by the wind
And floated in space like a ghost.

She met with the elves and pixies.
And dived with the frogs and toads,
Her voice was kind and witty
It lightened the ants heavy loads.

She flew with the bees and fireflies,
And rode on the back of a beetle
She studied and read a great deal in bed
And sewed with a pine cone needle.

A robin just whispered he saw her
Sleeping upon a moss bed.
Her golden hair shown in the sunlight,
A pillow of light framed her head.

Her eyes opened wide with excitement,
She darts to the top of a tree,
Cause fairies don't like to be noticed.
Their life is a mystery to me.

Dolores B. Higgins

The Glory Of The Phone

I sit up high upon my throne
And fake the need to be alone
A happy life I've never known
But for the Glory of the Phone!

I dial the phone to help me hide
The feelings that I feel inside
Oh, woe is me, I'm all alone
I NEED that blasted telephone!

The phone helps me to hide my fear
When insecurity is near
I laugh aloud to mask the tears
Because I'm certain no one cares

To hear the tales I need to tell
But those who know me very well
Will listen 'til their eardrums SWELL
To gossip from my life of hell!

I sit up high upon my throne
And fake the need to be alone
A happy life I've never known
But for the Glory of the Phone!

Alethea K. Jennings

I Am Not Your Mother

I fed you a warm lunch today
And fixed your shoes again
But I am not your mother
And cannot take you in.

I tried to talk to your Dad
But he was just to drunk to hear
But I am not your mother
And cannot take away your fear.

He returned the toys I gave you
Found hidden beneath your bed
He said I am not your mother
Don't tell him how to raise his kid.

I've seen you only once since then
Looking dolefully at my door
But I am not your mother
He won't let you play here anymore.

I went to your funeral today
It broke my heart to see your end
I was not your mother
But I should've been your friend.

Charity F. McPherson

The Blue and Gray

They believed with passion
and fought with fury
when it was finally over
No one questioned their courage.

The rain poured down
and the bayonets trusted
the trenches ran red
with the blood of the just.

They revealed raw courage
beyond this feeble praise
scattered wounded lay dying
in the mud-trampled graves.

Peace be given unto
the souls that mourn
Those left with hearts bitter
in a country so torn.

Woe unto this Nation
to forget this day
a better future secured
by the Blue and the Gray.

Christine Roskelley

Friends

Friends are for needing,
and giving, and sharing.

Friends are for keeping,
and loving, and caring.

Friends will not leave you,
and are always the same.

Friends will uphold you,
and build up your name.

Friends are for trusting,
and believing in us.

Friends are from our Father,
and faith from Jesus.

Karen R. Lolkema

Nonsense

If America is a place of freedom
and goodwill, then where am I?
It is nonsense to say that everyone
belongs somewhere.
You can't feel comfortable and at ease
with everybody.
Is it nonsense to say that I don't
live in the "Promise Land"?

Are hopes and dreams subjects of non-
sense?
Am I right or wrong?
But they don't always come true.
They are something to rely on when
you're down
in
the
dumps.
Even if America is nonsense and not
always fair, it's my country.

Keyonna M. Summers

Lisa, Lisa

Yesterday I took a walk
and heard you call my name;
I turned around and who was there?
No one, but a blame.
I kept on walking and still I
heard; that call
which called my name.
So soft and sweet but, there was no one.
Why did I hear my name?
I hoped and hoped it would be you.
How much I hoped that voice
was yours that called my name
Today I took a walk, and
thought I heard my name.
I knew it was my illusions, and
there I heard it still the same
Lisa, Lisa, and on it went
I walked around and turned my
head to see who called my name.
It was truly you, you were the one who
called my name.

Cam Ngo

Our Dear Lord

When the world seems lonely
And I need a friend
I count on Our Dear Lord
Who always has an ear to lend

When I need a little guidance
Because I'm living in a dream
I can hear the whispers of Our Dear Lord
As he watches o'er me

He watches me from above
He gives me a sense of protection
Yes, it's Our Dear Lord
Who guards me with his love and affection

When I think I am all alone
And I'm filled with fear
I can feel the closeness of Our Dear Lord
Who is always hovering near

One whom I feel close to
He is my soul mate
It is Our Dear Lord
In my mind he's God the Great

Anne Stadelman

A Poem?

I'm Not a Poet,
And I show it!
Through Rhyming book,
I search and look.
Lots 'o words finding,
For writing, tantalizing.
But for great thought,
A Poet, I'm Not!

Oh Give me a warm Fire,
Another's poem to inspire.
Someone to cuddle and woo,
Kipling, Service, My Waterloo.
Oh, to read, love, and dream,
But if to write, I Scream!
A Poet, I'm Not 'tis true,
I'll leave that job, to you.

Angela C. Schiller

Love Me Or Not

When I look to the sky
and I think of you
I truly understand
why God made it blue
why did she hurt me?
I ask of the air
but only to find, the answers not there
I've never been great
a face with no name
but the love that I gave you
I did with no shame
if I was in charge
I'd paint the sky red
for when I think of love
it's the pain that I've bled
As I ponder these ideas
my most gruesome thought
is I must keep going on
if you love me or not

Clifford E. Henry Sr.

The Time Has Come

Open up your Bible Folks
And listen to God's words
He promised us a comforter
If we trusted in the Lord.

The time has come to call upon
The Saviors Blessed Grace
To get down on our knees
And pray to him with Faith.

Ask of him to send his Angels
To comfort, oh, the many
Those who lost their loved ones
In Oklahoma City.

And ask Him for deliverance
For this surely is a sign
That Satan has great power,
He has an easy firing line.

But Love will conquer all my friends
Seek and ye shall find.
Keep the word of God upon your heart
And salvation in your mind.

Deborah J. Lewis

The Apology

For the many times I've sat there-
And marveled at your kind.
Your majesty and beauty seems to
Always ease my mind.

Your harmlessness and innocence
Often makes me wonder...
How I could ever hurt you—
You or any other.

So I send you this apology,
Your thoughts and heart are near.
I wish you well and bless you
With these few words—sincere.

Ben Stover

Blueprint For A Brave New World

Build me a God from love and compassion
and men for pain and fear.
So they'll look above for a guiding hand
and a healing presence near.

Build me a world of far away places
and long forgotten faces.
So meeting again, after moments or years,
will flood our joy with tears.

Give us knowledge as our king
so our eyes can see what all should be.
Give us hate as rope to bind ourselves
and love to set us free.

May our minds be ever eased
by pleasant thoughts of home.
And never ruled by jealousy
or fear of being alone.

Our eyes will pierce ever darker nights
and see all things bright and clear.
We'll fly on winds, enlightened,
to places far and near.

John Di Donato

A "Heartfelt Prayer"

God please help me not want him
and miss him night and day,
Keep me from writing letters
or calling him today.
Please God, stop me from crying
to be held in his arms,
Please keep me from desiring him
and his lovemaking charms.
God please dissolve the memory
of the sight and smell of him.
And please God stop this heartache
for the way things might have been.
God help us forgive each other
this destruction is a sin,
Please give me strength and wisdom
to go on with life again.
Amen

Deborah Morgan

Fall Colors

My autumn eyes behold
Orange leaves on a tree
Yellow grass in my backyard
Red flowers in a garden.

Vaneza Dussac

For Your Always In My Heart

In our darkest hour,
and my deepest despair,
Please do care.
Will you be there?
In my trails,
and my tribulations
do our thoughts and frustrations
and my violence and my turbulence,
through my fear and confessions,
and my anguish and my pain,
through my Joy and Sorrow,
and a promise of another tomorrow,
I'll never let you apart,
for you're always in my heart.

Katie Jacobson

My Teacher

When I am late for school
And my excuse is bad
Who is the best friend
I ever had? ...My Teacher.

When I fight with others
And can't get along
Who has to listen
To that same old song? ... My Teacher.

When my problems are great
And my troubles are many
Who asks for my pencil
When I haven't any? ... My Teacher.

When my homework isn't done
And I can't say why
Who looks at me
With that gleam in her eye? ... My
Teacher.

When June is here
And school is at an end
Who is most happy
For summer to begin? ... My Teacher!

Charles Leslie

Forgotten Generation

Our children are crying
And nobody hears.
Violence, gangs, and drugs
It is more than I can bear.
Our children are dying
And nobody seems to care.
Murder, rape, and hate
Is this our children's fate?
Our children stopped trying
And it breaks my heart.
I hope this lost generation
Won't tear our families apart.

Dana Marie Ginther

Serenity

A million tiny raindrops
Or more are falling down
Drifting ever earthward
Until they hit the ground

The peaceful night unbroken
As the clouds do gently weep
Taking us ever onward
Toward the land of sleep

Bullett

Untitled

To write one must be inspired
And not in limbo acting tired
So if I take pen in hand.
I hope what comes out you'll understand
If I say something strange today.
I hope you will love me anyway.

Must all poems rhyme or can they be
Another style that they call free?
If they don't then its called prose
But just as profound, I suppose.

Charles E. Abernethy

Love Is Easy Love Is Light

It grows, blooms
and overflows
Into everyone's life

We start with love
And look for it
Always

God is love,
Light is love
It comes in all sizes
Shapes and forms

Flowers, birds...
Touches - looks
Feelings
And from the heart

Look for love
Find it,
Hold it
Watch it grow!

Dolores Bates

Untitled

Your eyes hold mysteries
and pain
long eyelashes frame
beautiful brown eyes

Smile - so cruel
Real?
Speak of love
TRUE?

Jennifer Joseph

Versentry

My daughter found a contest, neat
and said: "Hey, dad, you should compete.
Dad, it's no gimmick. There's no cost.
So, if you lose, what have you lost?"
It sounded proper and upright —
all poet-geared and not up-tight.
The tug to enter whipped my doubt
except for what to write about!
The rules said twenty lines at max
on any subject (fiction, facts).
A scope so vast intrigues the mind;
a choice from much takes time to find.
While shaping verse a poet knows
some readers wish we'd stick to prose.
It's how they feel but we insist
more fun is rhythm, rhyme and twist!
Down to four lines — not much yet said —
between the lines perhaps you've read?
If you have weathered this and laughed
chalk up an aye for verbal craft.

Arnie Norbert

Friends

People may come
And people may go,
Being with my friends
I am always at home.

They never judge me
They never hurt me
And every once in a while
They support me.

So tell me why
With my graduation so near
I have a new fear:
It's not getting out into the real world
But it's leaving my college world.

I've seen it before
Writing becomes a chore—
And calling "What for ?"

But
I will bet
That my name will live in their hearts
Because it's just so hard to forget.

Darius Karsas

I Love You When

I love you when you come to me
And say just any words
I love you when you come to me
And share with me your world

I love you when you say to me
Our love will never end
I love you when you say to me
I am your greatest friend

I love you when you touch me
And hold me O so tight
I love you when you touch me
On a cool and stormy night

I love you when you share with me
Your hopes and every dream
I love you when you share with me
Each torn from every seam

I love you when I think of you
You're always on my mind
I love you when I think of you
I'm yours 'till end of time

John S. Rice

The Stranger

I look in the mirror,
and see a stranger.
Someone's staring back at me,
yet I don't know who it is.
A face without a name,
staring deeply into my eyes.
I turn away and wonder
who this person is...
I want so much to know her better,
yet I know not where to start.

Kelly Howard

If...

If we could all learn to love
and show that we care and
if anyone ever needed us we
would always be there.

If there weren't any wars, and
no one would ever fight, but they
would sit down and talk and do
what's right.

If love would fill the heart of
each and every man we could all
stand together, hand in hand.

But the world is not like that, people
don't seem to care about how others
feel, that act as if life is a joke
and none of it is real.

If the word could go my way there
would be no bad people or bad
things around, and there would less
and less people being buried into the
ground.

Conesha Hart

Mirror

Sometimes I look up
and smile.
Other times I don't even need to look up
to cry -
my reflection is in your
restless eyes,
sure to wander,
I realize.

When I look up,
I see me.
Another look, I'm not so sure I know
who I am anymore.
Am I the wrinkle
or the visible pores,
am I woman
always dying to be more.

When I look up,
the smile fades from my face.
All is lost when I look in your eyes -
they tell me where beauty lies.

Kim Stinger

Stronger Than I

You are stronger than I,
And so powerful, too.
I need you to be here,
To hold my hand.
Be here when I close my eyes,
And again when I awake.

Lend me your strength.
I am so afraid.
Time is too short,
To have this feeling.
So, stand next to me
While the clock ticks away.

Courtney Goode

While We Wait

The day are fleeting by
And soon, Oh soon
They will vanify
Jesus coming in the sky
For his saints are standing by

So while we wait
A little longer
Each trial will make us
A little stronger
To see Jesus a little fonder

We are listening
For the trumpet sound
And with Jesus shout
We will leave this ground
The Bride and Groom,
Heaven bound

Dorothy Vanyi

"Thoughts Of Desert Storm"

As I lay upon my bed
and stare into the night
I think of the servicemen
in battle
and ponder, oh! that must be a sight.

With weapons and gear weighted
heavily on their backs
They trudge along leaving miles
and miles of desolate tracks.

For Patriotism and Freedom
Oh! what a big price to pay
For some of these Men and Women
Meet such an awful fate!

But on they fight so courageous
and strong
To better their country—AMERICA
To which they belong.

Janice Slaughter

Change

The flowers bloom, the flowers die.
And stars wait in the Eternal sky.
The fruit is ripe, the Seeds appear.
A time of change is coming near.

The wolf she howls, the dove he cries.
And spirits dance before our eyes.
Below red sun, 'neath violet moon,
All know the time is coming soon.

A crystal gleam, a golden tide.
And Secrets wake from deep inside.
The Voice it calls, in angelic tone,
"My Children, My Loves, please come
Home."

Karen Crase

Step By Step

Today is a time
Of hope. For
Mankind knows not
Of what the future holds.
Realizing this, we must
Remember that we
Ought to
Walk each new day, step by step

Lisa Andresen

Why Didn't Someone Hold Me

Why didn't someone hold me
and tell me everything is all right?
So many chances you had
To comfort, to hold tight
So supple, so pliable, a child's heart

Grown, able-unwilling to try
You made a child cry!
Tender, shy, soft
"Someone to care" I cried oft
where were they to show me the way
where to play - to run to have fun?

work hard - don't cry - be still!
They have broken my will
Nowhere to go, there must a place
Someone, please — see this face!

My eyes cry - my soul does weep
Curl up - try to sleep
weary - at age seven! Maybe heaven wants me
"Call me, God. Is there something I can do
for you?
Hear my plea - they don't love me!"

Doris Knowlden

The Broken Promise

You said you would never leave
And that she was just a friend
You kept telling me
That we'd be together until the end

When you told me that you loved me
It was just a lie
I thought I'd never see the say
When I had to tell you good-bye

I guess I was wrong
When I thought this would always last
I just can't believe
That this came to an end so fast

It's still not the same
Since you left me
But I guess
That things just weren't meant to be.

Christina Siebeneicher

Life Line

You are the life line of my soul
and the essence of my being...
I am the strength of your foundation
in the life line of your touch...
You were the light of my awareness
and the warmth of my discomfort...
I am the warmth of your heart
in the darkness of your comfort...
You were the steps to my salvation,
Keep me free from degradation,
Filled my life with contemplation,
Gave me hope when all was lost,
Set my feet in righteousness.
You are the essence of my being
And the life line of my soul...

Bennett Thompson

Goodbye

The sun will set,
And the rain is wet.
These things will always be.

The fall is blood,
And the snow is cold.
These things will always be.

You have changed,
And it's ever so strange.
You will not always be the same.

So I say goodbye, my friend,
And don't forget to send
A letter once in a while.

Kelli Ledford

Whispers

If the wind could only whisper:
and the river raced to tell
how swift my life is fading
how long the rain prevails.

If the wind would only whisper:
and the trees told a tale
the heavens held a picture,
of a ships broken sail.

Sow, would the sun,
reveal in the same,
If the wind would only whisper:
the rain should reap my name.

Reap my name in a downpour,
Reap my name in the sea,
In the smallest little teardrop,
The rain would cry for me.

Connie Vinsant

Eclipse

I once wished the sun forever to shine,
And the stars to turn to dust.
Because the night brought loneliness,
And the dark, I could not trust.

Since then, I've learned to close my eyes,
To lead my life, not by the skies.
I found the moon inside of me.
Without the light, I still can see.

Though there are times, I still can find
A reason to stop believing,
By clearing my mind from any thought,
My heart begins its healing.

The sun still shines; the night still falls.
But the importance I found above it all,
Be a smile, a tear or anything else,
What matters, I'll find, within myself.

Danielle Rae Bird

We Met

We met,
  And I called you stranger.
We laughed.
  And I called you friend.
We loved,
  And I called you husband.
We share children,
  And I call you dad.
As the days turn to years,
  I'll call you grandpa.
And eternity will call us one.

Julia Ann Thomas

Sunlight Love

Each morning when the day begins
  And the warm sunlight shall arise,
Our hearts are filled with love
  As we gaze up to the skies.

We spend these precious hours
  A gift of one more day;
This is a new beginning,
  As we go along our way.

When we see twilight descending
  And the sun sinks out of sight,
We know the sun will shine again
  As darkness turns to light.

Each day is filled with new sunlight
  With a warm and vibrant glow,
Given back to each of us
  A true love we all know.

As time goes drifting slowly by
  And autumn time grows near,
We always hold within our hearts
  The sunlight we love so dear.

Bea Kajut

Waiting

Torn between two emotions I toss
and turn in the night.

Not having the courage to go on,
I sit lonely on the side of the road.

Multi-colored cars whiz by.

I take a ride in some, but only short rides
and then get out again.

I wait patiently for the one car.

The car I've longed for,
the one who will whisk me away for,

The ride of my life.

Angie England

"A Day In Heaven"

I had spend a day in heaven
and was so beautiful and fine.
That I'm back just to tell you.
Don't be ever afraid to die.
I had seen friends and family,
that one day were called to part.
They were happy and enjoying,
so much beauty in the sky.
They had show me hell and heaven
and their difference from life.
That I have to come and tell you
please be always good and kind.
Hell is grief and pains for ever
Heaven is so beautiful and fine
That in heaven I will be waiting
for the day we will reunite.

Angel Ruiz

Untitled

Alone I sit.
Memories of life.
Awaken the mind.
New thoughts.
Dawn of hope.
A vision of beauty.

Raymond C. Jones

Somewhere Inside Me

I weave a web
And wear it
To protect me.

Life
Once so light
Seems heavier now.

I sit in the sun
Listen for my voice
Muted by memories.

Hearing
But not understanding
Words from somewhere inside me.

Ceci Taylor

"Remember Me"

I looked into the window of life
And what did I see
A beautiful picture
A picture of you and me

My life has been bitter
My life has been sweet
But never did I consider
That one heart with mine would meet

Once I was half
But now I am whole
For you were able to reach in
And touch my very soul

Never have I
Met anyone like you
Who came along
And turned my grey skies blue

So to my dearest one
I make this plea
That wherever you go
You always remember me

Edith Catherine Morris

Unborn Child

I could have been a general,
and won the greatest wars.
I could have been a president,
and opened many doors.
I could have been a captain,
and sailed the seven seas.
I could have been an environmentalist,
and saved one thousand trees.
I could have been a superstar,
and played a lot of sports.
I could have been a designer,
and made new types of shorts.
I could have been so many things,
to make the world of different place.
My mother wasn't interested,
to see my little face.
I could have even been a painter,
from the city Paris, France.
My mother never wanted me,
I never had the chance.

Katie McGivern

Open The Door

The songs of time pass slowly by
And won't slow down how hard we try.
People come and stay a while,
Others pass by with a smile.

And as the tunes roll on some more
They open up another door.
And one more next to that one too.
Down the line for me and you.

In each door another face.
Another time another place;
Of losers and lovers and all in between,
A butcher a baker a candlestick queen.

Coming and going all in turn,
Flashing and raging a heart to burn.
Down the hallways all in a row,
Millions of different seeds to sow.

Remember this and hold it tight:
Always keep your door in sight.
It's yours to hold within your care
And find the magic awaiting you there.

Dana Fullmer

The Hatchet

The blade did fly
And you did crow
Back and back, I go, I go,
Hashing, swinging
Chopping fright
You are mad and I in flight

Screaming, swiping
Frothing death
You are felon, I a quest
Hatchet me
Do your wrong
The blade is shining, sharp and long

On my back!
In my head...
Numbing, bleeding
Beheaded
Dead...

John F. Morgan

Untitled

A bit of ivy
and you forget the decay.
I have always constructed myself as
a sacrifice
and have found

When the autopsy of life
is over
When the ambiguity bites
and the reality dies

I am the pall bearer of my soul

And in this corpse of expression
my veil wraps about me
arms of a rose
and drowns my reflection.

BethAnne Kuzmic

The Comforter

When the days are long and dreary;
And your feeling weak and weary;
Lift your eyes to God and pray;
He'll give you strength to face each day.

No matter how alone you feel;
The Father's love for you is real.
Perhaps your heart is filled with grief;
He'll give you everlasting peace.

He knows all your hurts and cares;
So take them to the Lord in prayer.
Though you're burdened with deep sorrow;
He'll give you hope to greet the morrow.

His loving arms are open wide
And longs to bring you to His side.
Under His wings safe and secure;
He'll give you love forever more.

Janet Lee

Ema

Ema, I could write a poem for you
Any day, any week, any year.
I could fantasize, romanticize,
Symbolize your charm and beauty.

Ema, I could write a poem about you
Very short, very long or in between.
I could exaggerate, manipulate
Your wisdom you share so willingly.

Ema, I could write a poem for you
That will last through eternity.
For as long as books exist and man can read
They will grasp an image of you.

But most of all Ema,
I could write a poem
That for once and for all will explain
Why my silence is prevailing, I love you,
But words cannot ease my pain.

Anthony A. Medina

Untitled

The ancient powers
Are unknown
The voices you hear
Destroy you
Your words ageless
Marking the way
The myth is eternal
For the shaman
The spirit of a generation
The only solution
Isn't it amazing!
You found your only friend

Jeffrey C. Bristow

Evergreen

A revered sentinel
Armor wrinkled;
Weathered through millennia
the age old knight
of the round table lost
Warrior in silence
keeping the magical secrets
of the dark forest floor
The evergreen soldier
stands alone.

Wil Carrero

Dedication

To dance, as in a mystic ring,
Around a flame at night,
Bespeaks of gods of which we sing,
Who reign, beyond our sight!
Pray, ask for what that fire is for;
For lasting, healing peace?
Or is it with a rage for war—-
A hell, to never cease?
We dare not bid the Muses, die,
With Bard and Song, destroyed!
Proclaim, with prayer— your torch,
held high!
Cast, Evil, to the Void!

Joseph Krengel

Blind-Huggers (My Family's Hugs)

Suffocatingly blind-huggers wrap
around me and finger my spine.
Their hugs are non-embracing, serpentine.
Not the soothing, nourishing hugs,
nor soft, sweet secure feeling hugs.
No caressing, no neck touching,
nor hair stroking hugs;
blind-huggers are simply
doing their duties.
Blind-huggers cock their lips to kiss,
in their eyes is an obliqueness
that is easy to miss.

Betti Edmonds

A Vague Mistrust

January breeds a vague mistrust
As colder days most often must
For what reason have I to believe
That winter's turning home to leave
When it's warm a day and cold a week
And the chill remains to stir and creak?

When January's bathed in warm
The winter breeze is out of form
In not wailing, cold and bleak
To sound alarm of icy storm.
I cannot help but curse and despise
Frosted somber steel-gray skies
And deceitful tricks that winter plays
With single solitary warmer days.

Chris C. Herrig

I Can't Drive 55

There is no valley as deep,
As deep as the gas pedal.

No hill too wide,
To be covered in fifth.

Why try to catch the wind?
Why not create it?

Freedom:
Is passing on the left,
Of a broken yellow line, in a green valley.

Time has left me,
As I make more of it.

But there must be enders of dreaming,
White hearses flash red and blue,
Badges sting like wasps,
Bringing a painful reality.

Jason Topham

The Dreamer

How sweet are the thoughts, of the dreamer
As he lives in a world all his own
For his is the treasures untold of.
He's a king on a dreamers throne
He drifts with the tide of his fancy
Today he's a rich man's son
Tomorrow a soldier of fortune
Or maybe a hobo or bum.
But he's not alone or unhappy.
For his dreams are of many things
His journeys are far - far reaching
No place is beyond his dreams
To the dreamer we say be undaunted
For your visions may some day come true
But even in dreams you have captured
The things that escaped from you

John A. Melvin

War "Death Of Innocence"

The pain in a young soldier's eyes,
As he sees his best friends die.
And the tear stained face, of a
little orphan girl;
With no one to comfort her as she cries.
The loneliness and sorrow,
When you know there'll be no tomorrow;
And never again a yesterday......

Gabriella A. Plantz

He

He brings forth to us a new day
As he sun shatters the dark of night.
He will help us face the oncoming
By the presence of everlasting light.

He can erase our sins and
Ease our troubles and strife.
He will help us in sickness and health
By turning over to Him our life.

He will not forsake us nor
Turn away at our call.
He is Jesus Christ our Savior,
Lord and Master of all.

Dale Gustin

Balloon Trip

Big blushing red balloons
As high as the sky
Lifting very high
Like a sunset
Over everybody
On the clouds
New colors in the sky
Trying to be beautiful
Riding very slow
In the sky
Please make it fun

Andrew York

Color

Star, dark star
Rose, red rose
Song, deep song
Dream, sweet dream
Star, rose, song and dream
Deep, dark, red and green.

Michael J. Murphy

Launched

His hand, growing steadily
As I hold it in my palm,
Less often, as he matures
Wandering further from my grasp
Toward manhood, drifting on his
Own now, without me pushing him
Becoming his own person,
Looking back occasionally,
To see me, still
Right behind him.

Katherine M. Capano

Behind The Walls

I come to see him most every day
As I look into his pale, thin face
I wonder why this had to happen
To a man I know was sent from heaven
He tended and loved me when I was a child
His greatest joy was to see me smile
Ill health has taken it's toll on him
His heart is heavy, and his eyes are dim
He sits in this place day after day
He worries that he is in my way
It's so hard to tell him how much I care
Each night he's the first one in my prayer
His strength is gone, and his spirit fading
He sits by his door with open heart waiting
Surrounded by people both day and night
He watches and waits for a familiar sight
My heart is sad as the end draws near
He's my friend, my hero, my father, so dear
It seems so cruel to spend his last years
alone
Inside the walls of a nursing home

Judith B. Yow

I Talked To The Angels

I talked to the Angels last night,
As I sat beside your bed.
I asked them for the courage,
To get along without you here.

I watched as you slept peacefully,
Not a care in this world.
A young man with so much to give
Ready to take on whatever came.

I talked to the Angels last night.
There was so much to say.
I asked that my love for you,
Would never fade away.

You were everything to me.
My hope for better tomorrows.
You brought laughter into my life,
When there was only sadness before.

I talked to the Angels last night,
I asked them why this had to be.
I told them to take care of you,
When they came to take you from me.

Cynthia Wiggins

Jowls Of Doom

Jowls of doom
Snapping at my feet;
Talons of steel,
Ripping the ground to pieces,
Trying to catch me.
Soon, they will.

Ryan Randall Cooper

Life

The quiet blackness surrounds me
as I sit in my easy chair blowing
smoke rings contemplating the eternities.
I feel my Marlboro, my only link to
reality slipping through my fingers
as I feel blackness enclosing my heart
and my eyes. The path to the end lies
ahead. My fingers go numb as I fall,
fall into infinity. When I finally stop
I realize it has all got to cease.
As the madness encroaches on my senses.
Must fight my way to the top and back
to reality but I keep falling back.
Finally as I return to reality, the
realization frightens me as I seek
to rise above the muck we call life.

Amanda Bowers

Her Majesty

Have you seen our beautiful Mount Rainier
As it rises from out of a cloud,
Or the sun comes over the highest peak,
While it's clothed in a snowy shroud?

It weathers all season's changes
With arms stretched ever wide.
Majestic she stands as a sentinel,
Guarding our Northwest with pride.

In spring her radiant beauty unfolds,
Exposing the wonder God planned.
There nestled snugly within her skirt
Are flowers, untouched by hand.

Warmed by the sun, kissed by the rain
And caressed by the gentle breeze;
Lending their beauty to nature,
Awaiting the winter's freeze.

Mother Nature spreads a blanket of white.
Flowers wither and die on the slope.
Their seeds have been scattered to await the
spring,
When they will bloom again with new hope.

Betty M. Larson

A Fairy Tale Rose

A rose, is a rose, is a rose
as some may say
but in this fairy tale
a rose is an epitome of beauty.
Its petal is like a thick velvet
surging as a rich lather of cream.
Yet its color is like a scorching flame
burning in the deep darkness of night.
While its enthralling aroma
captures gentle whips of sweetness
unknown to reality.
It's leaves of green
derive the world around it
with an aura of dignity.
While the thorns upon it, seem to warn:
savor but let it be
for in this fairy tale
its left for the beauty of nature.

Joanna Korolyshyn

A Tribute To An Angel

My thoughts are whisper soft and free
As the butterfly dances so gracefully,
You too have taken flight
On translucent wings
Upward and beyond
Yesterday
I wept for you,
My Friend,
Our dreams,
like fallen snow,
Melted into pools,
Of crystal clear memories
Flowing freely as a meadow brook
In spring
I hear the melody of life renewed,
I hear your laughter in the breeze,
I feel your warmth
In rays of sunlight,
Your are forever in my heart,
My Friend.

Kay Mitrzyk

On the Death of My Father's Father

The grandson heard the news,
as the church bells ceased their ring,
on a cold wet rainy day
toward the beginning of the Spring.
A day like any other,
being part of any week,
but the day my father's father,
closed his eyes for final sleep.
This grandson thought, tomorrow,
when the grandsons gathered round,
carried coffin covered soundly,
placed it in the frozen ground.
And buried with the elder,
generations sorted bliss,
with his four sons standing round him,
casting shadows in the mist.
The sons bode well their father,
as their sons stood by their side,
he will not go on forgotten,
nor this rainy day he died.

Edward J. Clark Jr.

Hate Has Blinded Those We Love

Hate has blinded those we love
As the cover has been lifted and
the dye has been cast. We have
loved with our hearts, though
they can not see the past.

Hate has blinded those we love.
With a shadow of doubt, words of
hate flow from their lips, love
ones turn away.

Hate has blinded those we love.
With a sickness of hate, they
poison the weak, but the truth
pulls through the darkness of
greed. Those we love are left
in lies. Let us grieve, but not
for long, for we have grieved
enough for all!

Dorothy Bell

You and Me

We wake to see each other
As the morning light shines bright
Passing each other through the house
With only enough time for a hug and a kiss

We make what we can
Out of what we have
Day after day
Through good and bad times

Sometimes fighting
Sometimes laughing
No matter what happens
Our love comes out on top

Thanks for your love

Carol Osborne

Emerald Morning

Silence is cold in the morning fog
As the pines stand tall on guard
The whippoorwill breaks the midst
As it moves around you
Like a morning kiss
The presence of Gods beauty
Is everywhere for its golden rays
Gives a silver luster
Like diamonds of dew
On a green emerald cluster.

David R. Jones

All Quiet

All quiet
As without the sounds of bombing die away
And we look forward to another day
Given us.
All clear
And without
The first faint ray of sunshine shows
A crocus unmolested
Ours to enjoy
On this miracle of a day
That may never come again.
But now it is ours
And we will take it and run until dark.
We will find more flowers in the ruins
And gather them to us;
Salvage what we can and rejoice, rejoice
That we have this one day
To live.

Jennifer R. Sparlin

Excuses

You can't pass the class
because the teacher.
You don't go to church
because of the preacher.
You've got no money
because of your spouse.
You've got no furniture
because they broke in your house.
You don't have a car
because of an illegal tow.
You did not get promoted
because of a coworker foe.
What you do have is an excuse for
everything in the past.
One for the future probably
if one asks!

Cora Barley Harris

Our Star

I look into the night
at all sorts of art
Many colors each are bright,
our own star, a small part.

Our star seen only at day
Is our every breath.
Without it we will lay
For that day will be our death

Held together with such great force
Giving warmth and energy to nine
At different rates each runs its course
Passing through each of the 12 signs

Although not perfect and clean
Sitting in the photosphere
Spots have been seen
Returning about every eleventh year

Much larger than seen by the eye
When shadowed you can see it grow
Hard to believe it will ever die
Five billion gone, five billion to go.

Kristin Ritley

The Reign Of A Royal Favorite

Oh the lovely Pompadour awaits,
Awaits for the love of her life.

The colors so bold,
Yet so gentle as a flower.

Anticipating but never expecting,
for she's only a mistress and not
his wife.

Makes you feel the love
you want, need and desire.

Almost seems to real.
Is it or is it not.

The love in her eyes the
steadiness in her hands, makes
you wonder what she dreams about.

Her love is much to powerful
for words, and her touch is as
dangerous as a sidewinders bite

She is a lovely as a rose,
but remember this "you may look,
but you may never touch".

Christy L. Jones

My Cup Runs Full

'Twould seem a glass of wine could not
  Be filled past overflowing;
And yet my cup of love for you
  Runs full — but keeps on growing.

Each time I think my love for you
  Is full beyond all measure,
I somehow grow to love you more,
  Increasing thus my treasure.

For in your love I've found my wealth,
  My happiness, my joy;
The beauty you've brought to my life
  No pain could e'er destroy.

I realize these lines are not
  Those of a polished poet.
'Tis just, my cup of love runs full,
  And I want you to know it.

David C. Hadley

Spring Haiku

Dandelions grow
In the very hot grasses,
Waiting to make seeds.

Rob Bever

Two Hearts

Two hearts united
beating as one
each beat a word of love
a love so strong
to last forever
this kind of love
I will give to you
a love strong enough
to last forever
and one more day
on into eternity

Don Beller

Who's Tear

Maybe it's a little girl's tear
Because her doggy didn't stay.
Maybe it's a little boy's tear
Because his kite blew away.

Maybe it's a teenage boy's tear
Because his girlfriend went away.
Maybe it's a teenage girl's tear
Because together her parents didn't stay.

Maybe it's a grown man's tear
Because his wife didn't stay.
Maybe it's a grown woman's tear
Because her daddy passed away.

Maybe it's an old woman's tear
Because her youth slipped away.
Maybe it's an old man's tear
Because his dreams didn't stay.

Or maybe it's God's tear
Because our innocence didn't stay.
Maybe it's God's tear
Because our world is passing away.

Bart Bush

Spirit

I am as well as I will ever be
Because there is nothing wrong with me
I am not my fear, my sadness or shame
I do not need anyone to blame
I am not those who are full of despair
I am a servant of the Lord
With His love to share
I can listen and speak
And quell doubt with a shrug
And for all who need me
I am there with a hug
For I am not just flesh and blood and bone
But spirit
With a straight path to follow
And never alone
When my journey in this life shall cease
That is when I shall truly know peace
I don't know when this time will be
But I know that then
There will be a hug for me.

Karen A. Drum

Before

Before she says you cannot fly,
Before he lays me down to die.
From the mountains to the sea,
Then back to air for you and me.
Men and women, boys and girls,
Toddlers and infants form the world.
While they hide behind their drugs,
They wonder when he'll pull the plug.
As they know that pain will hurt,
One man will sink into the dirt.
And while she seeks with her screaming eye,
A woman will fall into a fight.
They must stop the cold,
Since the darkening evil is getting old.
What they say will come from their heart,
In any way or form of art.
Before the end shall meet you hear,
We all should do nothing supported by fear.
Change before the end is new,
So when God passes heaven won't miss you.

Dawn M. Hammonds

Transition

Twilight's gentle silence
Beguiles the anxious light,
Brushing in nocturnal moods:
A prelude to its flight.

Dying days seek refuge
In the shadows of their friend.
As silhouettes of yesterday
Prepare for journey's end.

Day's weary eyes will slowly close
As twilight slips its bonds.
Night will fall, in layered veil,
Surrendering at dawn.

Morning springs on sober breath
With challenges anew.
History claims its measured wage,
Then vanishes from view.

James O. Kelly

Untitled

I never had a chance to say good bye,
believe me when I say I tried.
Oh, how I tried.
I could not look you in the eyes.
I could not tell you I was leaving.
Again,
Always leaving.
Time is so short,
always leaving
never stopping
years upon years of leaving
too many
good bye's
I have no more left,
save one for you,
Good bye.

Drew Wassel

"Roy" And "Ben"

Take time to walk slowly
beside the crippled boy named "Roy" -
His conversation makes you laugh -
His company is a joy!

He said "his ever faithful friend -
A shepherd dog named Ben
was run over by a car
and had to stay home "in bed"!

My mother is at work -
and Father is away -
So I pretend that walking
might be good for me today!

Some folks say dogs
don't talk but I know differently -
for I understand everything
that "Ben" says to me!

So I must hurry home -
he gets lonely when alone -
and if I did not have him -
I'd be lonely too.

Eleanor B. Hyndman

Peace With Death

He is at peace now.
Beyond this life lies one of peace.
It reaches beyond our thoughts;
beyond our prayers.
"Here I am" he said,
do with me as you see fit."
"For I am your servant,
your faithful follower."
Though I am not with you,
my family and friends,
I will live within your hearts forever.
Beyond today, beyond tomorrow.
For I now share my life with Christ,
the Savior of the world.
Do not morn or feel sadness in my leaving,
for I am with you every hour, every day
for eternity,
within your heart.

Anita D. Burris

Sunrise

Beauty in the morning...
Birds chirping...so happy
a new day is dawning.
Dew damp on the green
blades of grass...
Covering everything with
its misty content.
Animals searching for food
in the quiet of the early
morning hours...
The sun rises to its strength
of the day
Its rays seeping through the
branches of evergreens
Making a red cross of
expanded light and a hope
for a new beginning.

Arlene E. Bjornson

On This Day

On this day...
birds fell from the sky
I know you wanted to cry
all the bells broke
and everyone saw evil's black cloak
the children cried
and all the flowers died
every thing you loved was taken
hearts could be heard breaking
now the bells won't ring
the birds won't sing
the flower beds are cold
and young hearts are no longer bold.

Amanda Burchell

what was that?

that was my
blink of disbelief
bitter no more
watch as I leap yes!
I will dance
that was my tenacious
sigh
gasp
silent and shaken
moistening my amazed
and smiling
hazel-green eyes

that was my joyful relief

JoAnne Totten

Roses and Romance

Between the beauty and its life's
blood, there lies an evil domain of
natures design, through which the
blood flows to create the beauty
the eye beholds.

Within its sweet smell and satiny
velvet touch, the memories it brings
and the horrors it beholds. All within a
single solitary rose.

Through the mind's eye the senses
began to detect, its lovely presence,
waltzing the waltz of memories and
chancing the dance of romance.

Donny Boyles

Twenty-Two

Demons cast out their
bloody sea
I am you and you are me
an angel sits on my shoulder
and whispers her tune
No one follows into the muck
of the inky lagoon.
Hello orange morning
hello black night
Can you see my midnight delight?
It comes from far and goes
too quick.
Chanting in the lagoon, getting very sick.
Grant peace on earth, capture the
demon before birth.
And we all shall become one
under the warm kiss of the sun.

Jerome Burdi

Ava Lynne

The wood-bine twines, prim roses
bloom mid moss on velvet feet.
A distant bird sings "Ava Lynne
so sweet, sweetie sweet."
The wind sighs her name, it echoes
through the hills.
Her ruffled hair is reflected on
the crowns of golden daffodils.
Barefoot she runs, cunning as a vixen
in the glen,
fair and lovely, haunting allusion,
the wood nymph, Ava Lynne.
A brook caressingly sings, "she is mine,
enchanter of rhymes."
In dreams of misty illusions, I roam
the valley where the wood-bine twines.

Doris Hartsell Brewer

A Woman and Her Purse

Perfume, compact, mascara,
blush, lipstick, eyeliner,
We are waiting
wallet, driver's license;
mirror, pen, paper,
address and appointment book,
Can't you hurry up
Keys, brush, breathmints,
pepper spray, hairspray,
sunglasses, eyeglasses,
"PLEASE miss we don't have all day!"
cigarettes, lighter,
aspirin, jewelry,
nail polish, photos, checkbook,
"The store will be closing in ten minutes."
"Aisle five now open."
"Aah, I found the penny."

Kelly Kirstie Hillmantel

Tempus Fugit

Celebrated.
Body deteriorating,
Memories fading,
Mind slipping,
Death approaching,
Presents given,
Birthdays.

Christina Brenneman

Fragile
Breaking
Bumping
Nudging
Slipping
Bobbing
Hissing
Tinkling
Surrounding
Free
March ice on the river

Karen Ann Jonker

Life's Aim

The pensive Earth, encircling Sol,
Breathes forth boreal breath
To make me know with chilling awe
That life's one aim is death!

The barren lands and icy streams
Are proofs of transiency,
While bitter winds in naked trees
Pluck forth Earth's eulogy.

And other signs of dying life
Are seen each ebbing day,
When sunny hours kiss Earth goodnight
And choke their light away.

Diana then encircles Earth,
Still moans boreal breath
To make me even more aware
That life's one aim is death.

Kenneth E. Byrd

The Faithful Stars

Shining, shimmering silver
Brilliance burning bright.
Daytime eyes can't behold
Those distant diamond lights.

Trust - rest well assured
That tho they're out of sight,
They're truly there and constant
Thru the day as well as night

Oh, but what care we of cosmos
as we laugh and work and play?
We're not seeking silver softness
In sun's golden gift of day.

Darkness comes, how comforting
Those dazzling dots can be.
They whisper love and life and light
Thru blackened mystery.

And isn't it the same when we search to
know God's light?
His brilliant presence blinds our eyes
When all seems good and right
It seems to take in finding him, a cold, dark
night.

Bonnie J. Williams

The Unforgettable Fire

The unforgettable fire
Burning inside me as a desire

Feels like missing a part
Leaving a vacuum in my heart

Your breath is so far away
Miss it more and more every day

What a time we had together
Will keep dreaming of it forever

Life is a mystery

or is it what they told me, destiny?

Andreas F. Gmuer

Untitled

Candle whipped and twisted
Burning without flame
Lonely heart is crying
Hollow in its pain

The rose is dead and withered
Its petals black and old
Thorns still sharp do prick
The silence of the soul

The embittered cry of "love, my love"
Rings upon deaf ears
Forlorn and lost, unloved faithful
Pours forth with silent tears

Cruel goddess, love, you mock a man
Throwing him to fate
In the end he turns his heart
To fill with poison hate

Thus the blow is struck
So the mighty fall
To the wanton woman
Who smiles as she calls

Jeffrey Forrest Boyles

Me

My countenance may seem rather harsh,
But, I am gentle deep inside.
Often a city feels like a marsh,
I love an open countryside.

In life I find only work and toil,
So, grime, more often, is on my face.
My clothes are faded by sun and soil,
I wear no skirts of satin and lace.

I try not to show my pain or fears,
God's inner strength is a always there.
I often smile when full of tears,
When in doubt, I kneel in prayer.

People in my life may come and go,
Wondering how this woman came to be.
The truth inside, they will never know,
Hidden well, is who I call me.

Belinda F. Hooper

Daddy

I've been told many things about you,
but I can't believe they're true,
even though I haven't met you,
I know every part of you.

I see you every time I look in the mirror,
we look alike you know,
the saying "Daddy's little girl,"
applies more than you could know.

I've got your eyes , your nose, your mouth,
I've even got your smile.
And just knowing you're a part of me,
makes this search worth while.

I vowed someday I'd find you;
and to this I'll be true.
You don't know you're my daddy,
and how I love you so.

But someday we'll find each other,
then you'll know my love is true.

Cydni Mertens

Not Only You

I hear your scream
But I don't care.
For mine is much louder
Louder then yours will ever be.
My scream is silent
deep within me, with-in my soul.
No one can hear it
No one but me.

I feel the pain you feel
But I don't sympathize,
For you don't feel mine.
The suffering that I live in
is too great to bear,
Yours could never compare.
With no bruises, with no scares,
No one can ever really know
No one but me.

Corinne Sobiegraj

Distant Father

Miles apart we are
But in each others
Hearts we stay
For we weep for
One another's presence
Not seeing each other
Day to day.
Not a face nor a voice
Waiting in agony for
The telephone to ring
You it is not
But it isn't my choice
There is no equality
None to this predicament
It's too much intensity
My love to you as
A daughter which
Will soon consolidate
Afresh.

Denise Steward

The Voice Of A Child

As one who is seen
but not often heard,
a Child can 'speak volumes'
without saying a word...

In the eyes of a 'Little One'
are seen thoughts never spoken -
the revealing of truth,
in silence unbroken.

Acceptance and Guidance,
for these he cries out;
to know he belongs,
to trust without doubt...

These prayers of a child
though quiet and small;
are heard by the One
Who Created us all.

For God lives in fullness
that which we know in part:
The Voice of a Child
is heard with the Heart...

Anna Wayne

Being Young Again

We have a chance to be young again
but only once in our lives;
To be the little child that is hidden
and in all of us strives.
To romp in the grass, play hide and seek
and play with all kinds of toys.
We can play make believe and climb trees
and relive our childhood joys.

We have a chance which spans a few years
but we can't go back in time.
We can become as little children while
yet in our prime.
The prime of life, that of parent hood true,
when we have our children small.
With them we have many things to do
through which we relieve it all.

Joel O. Trevino

A Winter of the Heart

Winter is here,
But only within me.
I do not shed a tear,
Of my sorrow's sea.

I feel the winter deepen,
Becoming bitter cold.
I feel even more forsaken,
As this night grows old.

Even in my sadness,
A spark of hope is still alive.
I dream of next spring's kindness,
But will my heart survive?

Then I feel the cold disappear,
And there is light once more.
Finally spring is here,
And my heart is no longer sore.

For all those who despair,
And walk alone with pain,
Remember that I've been there,
And the rainbow follows the rain.

Amanda C. Bauer

She

I never saw her,
but she opened my eyes to the world.

I never talked with her,
but she inspired my soul.

I never touched her,
but she gave my life meaning.

I never sang with her,
but her song rings throughout my heart.

Who, who is this mysterious women?

She is me and I am she!

Deep brown soulful eyes has she,
eyes that have witnessed many things
racism, hatred, and anger.

Rich, dark, peaceful skin has she,
skin that has felt many things
whips, sticks, and spit.

That skin, those eyes, saw and felt those things
so that now, through me, she can live and be
free.

Claire Jefferson

Requiem

Our tears are not tears of loss
But tears of love
Dew drops of compassion
Keeping sweetly fragrant
The forget-me-nots of remembrance
That we bring prayerfully to God
To our heavenly father
For those of our loved ones
He has called Home.

Blessed Lord, pray with us
That God our Father
Will receive our offering.

When our tears
Reflect the sunshine
Of God's merciful love
A rainbow of hope and forgiveness is born
Spanning the distance
Between Earth and Heaven
Uniting us with our Creator
and those we love...

Charlotte O'Hanley

Mystified Self Images

I try hard to see myself,
but through a misted over mirror
there are many things I over see.
Many masks hide true identity.
False images of myself
stick with me
from days past and hurtful words
which were spoken.
Every morning the mist is different,
weather by shape, size or color.
I try to wipe it dry,
but it still lingers over me,
covering any wanted, true identity.
Yet still, everyday, I make my heart see
the wonderful gifts God has given me.
For I am as blessed as any blessed man to be.
Even though in my heart I know the mist,
some days,
may cover me.

Jamie Dolieslager

A Rainbow and Wonders

I've never touched a rainbow,
but yet I know it's there;
All it's beautiful colors
so very light and fair.
The wind is quite elusive
and yet I feel its breeze.
I watch it move the treetops,
and gently shake the leaves.

Our God up in heaven...
I cannot see his face,
But yet I know that He
creates and loves every type of race.
The wonders of the rosebud
that opens to the sun;
Each miracle of dawning
and stars when days are done.

We needn't see our Savior
to feel His loving care;
Life's wonders still bless us,
each time we kneel in prayer.
So remember the glowing far-off sunset,
untouched by human hands...
And take yourself to the Lord,
that's what I highly recommend.

Chantal Marie Bryant

Lifeless

I have the fruit
But yet no seed
Why would my God have forsaken me?
There can be no more fruit.
And all because of me - the seed
Should the fruit live?
Can the fruit live with no seed?
Shall the seed go on fruitless
Shrivel up
Blow away in the hard cold wind
Down a lonely and long winding road
Into the salty, salty sea?
I wish my God would answer me
And put me on a fruitful tree
For the sun to shine on
And all the world to see
A seed like me
Can become a fruit
Called "we".

Carrie D. Turner

A Stranded Friend

I never asked for anything
but your happiness,
and now that you have found it
I should be glad I guess.

Who needs you every day and night
Who misses their best friend.
I only need to see you once
to know if it's the end.

I tell you that your loneliness
has brought me to this grief
You left me there all alone
Alone walking the streets.

I thought you were the only one
Who said you would not leave.
Now I sit and wonder why
You left me, all lonely, in my dreams

Jessica Boisen

Childhood Friend

Summer's warmth and happy cry,
Came and brought the fourth of July,
Swimming pools and climbing trees,
The summers that you spend with me.

Fall sprung up and pumpkins grew,
Picking and carving them with you,
We'd are yards in the autumn breeze
As leaves fell from the sleeping trees.

Winter came when noons went dark,
Sledding and snowball fights in the park,
Christmas presents under the tree,
Those were the winters you spent with me.

Those fun times we had in spring,
There were so many brand new things,
Flower picking and easter fun,
Picnics and walks under the sun.

Best friend, those were the sweetest days,
Though childhood is just a phase,
And because I know I should
I'll always remember our childhood.

Amber Garby

Anything Real

Is there anything Real today?
Can we believe in anything Real?
How do we know what's Real?
Today's a new start at anything Real
Belief has to be a motivating factor
Are dreams a chance at Real?
IF Dreams keep you striving for Real,
what's the harm in them anyway
I believe dreams can be Real?
I just have to decide what dreams
are Real, How can you tell?
Do Dreams die when Nothing's Real,
or persevere, to believe in anything real.
Any Real Dreamers out
there, Anything Real? Today
belief has to become more Real!
How do I know if there's
anything Real. Anything,
Anything, Anything Real, anything.

Evan Ferneau

Summer Nights

Summer nights are soft and sweet
can you hear the birds.
The stars are shining bright and clear
The moon seems all so near.

The quietness is as the still of dew
The wind Blows lightly Through The Trees
as I am praying on my knees
Thanking God for the summer nights.
As I hug my kids oh so tight
and I lay down in my bed at night.

And listen to the sound outside
safely in my home I do abide
summer nights seems weary I know
But in the air you see the bugs a glow

I love the summer nights you see
The days are long, the butterflies are free
Summer nights, oh summer nights
Never go and stay,
I'll see you again the middle of may.

Berlyn Dean Reese

Going Back

Lost in darkness, eyes adjust
Can't fathom how long it's been
Wandering down this trail of dust
Down the path some would call sin.

Don't remember such darkness
Much easier getting here
Happened so fast, seemed boundless
Took no effort to get here.

Many had traveled with me
But I'm alone coming back
Some journeys ended abruptly
Others still far down the track.

It's so hard, this lonely plight
Too easily fall off track
Determined to make it, keep right
Promise I'll never go back.

Never sure I'll find my way
To the old fork in the road
Where I, one unfortunate day
Turned on this dark, lonely road.

Amanda J. Sharpe

Confused

Is anyone out there
Can't you hear me scream
Is anyone out there
Won't you help me please

My life is in shambles
I just can't understand
Why does this have to happen
Why does it always happen to this woman

My heart beats loud
But there is a tremble in my voice
I'm afraid to let go
For I fear the unknown

What is really out there
Can't you make me see
Don't you know what's out there
Or are you as confused as me

Danielle McCarthy

Poetic Writings

With open fists, you are prepared.
Care, with loving hands,
But with closed eyes one cannot see.

With a loving touch, you are felt.
Feelings are yet, oh so warm,
But a closed door has no entry.

With open thoughts, you may dream.
Including someone else too, is special,
But with closed ears one cannot hear.

With an open mouth, you may share.
Give things to someone special,
But with a closed mind one is not romantic.

Jason Sims

Baby Semper

My sweet little kitty went to
Cat Heaven today -
My eyes are filled with tears
that fail to go away,
Baby developed a disease
that made her very ill -
When I think of the love
we shared I feel a chill -
She brought happiness into
my life for eight short years
everyday - in every way.
It is a sad thing when
you lose your pet -
I still cry when I think
about her yet -
I will never forget her
faithful way with fluffy
white hair and eyes sky blue -
I will always remember her each day
what more can I say.

Jacquelyn Payne

Valley Cleansing

I walk through the valley of cheese
And drink of the finest of wines.
My nostrils do taste the foul breeze
That drifts off the putrid black pines.

The sound that I follow eludes me
And lingers beyond my cold thoughts.
The elements surround and besiege me
And seek to erase my black spots.

Jeremy Dirks

Renunciation

A dewdrop's dazzle
Caught my foot in flight
It lit my brain
And exploded in my heart,
When suddenly
All the world went out.

No,
I am not afraid to stand here
Alone and blind,
Knowing the earth
Will be a shower of white.

Anthony Midili

Moments

Moments, like the cloud
Changing, Fleeting . . .
The moment is all there is
And I am in the moment and
What I do in the moment is
part of that moment
That moment is part of me.
It is changed and I am changed.
Life is only moments and moments.
Each by each our life is spent...
Just this one now
Then like the cloud
It is p a s t
and what I did
For good or ill
Is
Part of the Universe.

Katherine H. Granville

Grandma Rocking

Rocking in my rocking chair
cheek against his downy hair
grandson cuddles, soft and warm,
against my heart, within my arms.

It seems like only yesterday
I rocked his mother just this way.
The same soft warmth within my arms
keeping both so safe from harm.

Baby stirs and stretches, yawns,
dimple flashing but soon gone.
I see my daughter in his face.
I hold them both in my embrace.

Rocking, rocking, I muse content.
This is loving time well-spent
with my grandson, feather-light,
rocking, rocking through the night.

Joan Borrello

Untitled

I think that when you whisper,
caring people hear.
So I will tell my secret,
softly in your ear.
Someone sent an angel,
sent him just for me.
His wings always protect me,
and his spirit sets me free.
So how then do I thank him,
for helping see me through?
I guess I'll whisper gently,
"The angel sent was you."

Jaimee W. Blamire

Remembrance

Legends live - Heroes die
chivalry cannot be denied
embraced by the hand of beauty
of a lady in waiting
never to be forgotten promises made
together watching the sun rise:

Knights of white - Knights of black
in battle sure to fall
tattered armor broken sword
in the name of the Lord
forward marching never to stop
unless the rogue arrow pierces the heart
as roses split the color of the sea
warriors die a poetic dream:

David N. Coleman

Crossroads Behind

Did you see the crossroads behind?
Choices made by the blind?
But the terror is not yet known.
That the choices were our own.
But a new bridge we have found.
A bridge built on solid ground.
It spans the gulf of the past,
Where the foolish of before were cast.
The bridge is open to all,
Yet many still come and fall.
Their eyes too dim to see,
Their crossroads behind set free.
As for me, with wide eyes I cross.
My crossroads behind, I'm no longer lost.
On the other side, a new path I find.
Escaped from the wrath of crossroads behind.
The footing is firm, though the path be small.
The crossroads behind; I answered God's call.

Brian J. Svik

The Path

Upon the path I strive to
climb up toward the Mighty Divine....
a balancing act upon a fine line
walking a tightrope time after time.

Staying focused spares my
mind from the fall in which I
have so well inclined... have
been very lucky as of yet, for
God has put under me his
safety net.

How many distractions
must be endured?... before
my spirit is fully cured.

Dana Ingrahm

Untitled

I held a little hand last night,
So gentle and so neat.
I thought my heart would surely burst,
So wildly did it beat.

No other hand into my life
Could greater happiness bring,
Than the little hand I held last night,
Four Aces and a King!

Robert J. Sward

Coming Home

As our lips combine into a single
Colors mix into shaded blurs of red
Racing a run down my spine, a tingle
Runners exhausted, glee tears to be shed

As our eyes behold a hypnotic spy
Coal resemblance in your viewing eyes
Engulfed amid staring we start to cry
Exultant outpour, weeping to display

As our hands connect among the tall weed
Gaily swinging to and fro on depth ways
Holding reassurances guidance lead
Intuition to ask your hand and stay

As our souls unite, we embrace to pains
Attention flooding brooks of narrow veins

Elizabeth Gunning

Pangs Of January

My day is bleak and dreary
colors run like dogs
away from the suppressed
nucleus of my life

Quickly they are fleeing
escaping burning madness
scrambling into the hills
stuffed maternally with silicone

Ants carrying the dead
pull me along in their current
of muddy waters
entrapment visible in their ripples

I feel naked and alone
my security has sauntered off
leaving my fingers to scald
as they probe the questions of
humanity.

Devon Sprague

Where Does The Sky End?

As the setting sun cast
Colors upon the sea,
I took a walk, sat on a rock
And watched the water ripple away.

The sea calm as a ship
Drifted out of sight.
It felt cool and quiet outside,
But I had this funny feeling inside.

I thought as the ship disappeared
In the night—where does the sky end?
Does it just disappear out of sight?
Like the twinkling stars shining bright?
Does it end at the end of a rainbow?
Maybe we should ask ourselves —

Where does it begin?

Cindy Nunn

The Colors Of My World

Sunshine Sunshine,
shine on me.

Daffodil Daffodil,
be as yellow as can be.

Rainbow Rainbow,
be like me.

Theresa Bergner

Another Dawn

Winter to spring, summer to fall.
Constantly changing, it's our call.
Leaves flying, dancing to the ground.
A different duty they have found.
When beautiful flowers close there eyes.
They're only changing, nothing dies.
Seeds spring up in different places,
Showing there beauty to different faces.
Everything on earth is changing form.
To God's great plan it does conform.
So it is with friends who've gone.
God brings them to another dawn.

Anna Marie Bandimere

The Grounds

Flowing, descending gardens,
Cover two breathtaking acres.
Lush trees and vines,
Arches of greenery.

Plots beautifully laid out,
Variety of exotic plants.
Green beans reaching toward the sun,
Magnificent view of Charlottesville.

Gorgeous tulips reflect,
Fish swim gracefully,
Curving pathway encompasses,
Timeless beauty.

Diana Grace Newsom

Myself

Broken hearts
  Crying eyes
    Frowning lips

SCARRED!!

Abused and sadly used
  I'm no puppet on a string
    I am myself
      No one can hurt me now
        I'm indestructible!!

Immune to pain
  And yet IT knows my weak spots
Pain attacks the weak

BUT DOES THE STRONG ALWAYS
SURVIVE??

Jennifer L. Amorin

Maggie's Song

Birds rise to greet her
Day breaks with a melody
Singing Maggie's song

With flawless beauty
She stands tall in full sunlight
Meeting its measure

No time is enough
To marvel at her wonder
No gaze is too strong

No secrets haunt her
She moves without a shadow
But to cast pleasure

Kimberly A. Corry

"Illusion"

Wandering around nowhere to go
Crying inside but no one knows
I paint myself happy for everyone
to see

Hoping that one day I'll be free
Locked up inside myself
Trapped in a maze
My soul is weakening I'm starting
to leave

God help me this time, please
I look at my friends crying for me

They don't understand I was
so happy

They did not know I was
dying inside

Now they realize it was suicide
Now they all regret that they
let me slip away.

But there's nothing they can do now I'm
buried in my grave!

Jawanna L. Williams

My Problem Is Perception

I mistake
Curiosity for interest
I mistake
Inquiry for inquest
My fault is in perception

I mistake
Lust for love
I mistake
Flesh for soul
My weakness is inn perception

I mistake
Kindness for compassion
I mistake
Criticism for hate
My problem is in perception

Alejandro Rey Gamboa

Deliverance

With dark eyes
Dark hair
Dark hands
Dark longings
He moves across my body
Like a shadow
Like a creature of the night.

Softly he touches me,
Drawing me closer.
Softly he speaks to me,
Warm lips upon my skin.

Then, suddenly, stronger
He urges us onward.

My Moses, my Moses
A stallion of a man.

He lifts me up running
He lifts me up flying
He delivers me home

Jane B. Lofton

"Let Me Go Free"

The Winter skies looms
darkly over head the Wester Mountains
the summer breeze heats
the cooling earth

The pool of sorrow
lies beyond the ridge
The shadow of doubt
reaches from a far

As my tears fall like the
river running below
jealousy knocks at your door
pounding hard and fast

So very cunning you was
as the drifting snow
you caught one in your trap
upon these Wester Mountains

Could you please let me go free
so I can soar like the eagle
with no pain, no sorrow
I just might come back to you, let me go free

Barbara Bouchet

A Child's Eyes

Slipping in your tiny room
Darkness steals our day
Silent shadows sneak away
The sun falls to sleep
I pray to the Lord my son
Nothing shall we keep
Gently sail away, sail away to sleep

Nestled close, twilight finds rest
Deep within your eyes
Crystal blue windows give view
A glint of heaven
Sweet springs season, lit color
A child sleeps in peace
Gently sail away, sail away to sleep

Clouds darken, eclipse the view
Your eyes softly close
Silent angels lose their wings
Spring rains gently weep
Thru your eyes I'm taught to see
The Heaven I seek
Sail away gently, gently my son, sleep

David A. Montgomery

Take Flight

Dylan Thomas lies!
Death is not right,
Rage?, and the light
Never, never dies!

Death lies not in dying!
but in the wrong living
of life; and not giving.
The wise men are lying!

Death is not inevitable!
Wise men?, err!
Life and death are absolute;
and forever!

Life is the gift.
death is a choice.
Love is the answer.
Listen to His voice:

Don't fight!

Bill Thomas

Shadows And Lights

The golden sun rays
deep blue skies
marvelous clouds
scattered like sand bars

Sizes, shapes, colors
of peoples and things
once I could see
to appreciate life

Now, only shadows and lights
reflecting on my eyes
voices, sounds I can hear
touch and hear, my only guard

When the silence of the night
my mind stops wandering
to God Almighty I trust
His loving care surrounds me

Darkness can surround me
defeated I should not be
His everlasting Love to mankind
forever is my Guiding Light...

Jocelyn A. Reyes

"Take Us Into Your Heart"

Take us into your heart, and look
deep into our eyes.
Feel our pain that's torn us apart,
And look for the one who cries.

Look deep into our soul, and look
at the parts that died.
See what they have stole, the innocence
of a child who's only choice was to hide.

Step into our shoes, and live in them
for a while.
Feel what it's like to loose, and is
always the one on trial.

Slip into our dreams as we try to
sleep.
It was as they seemed, and all
you can do is weep.

Hold me in your arms, and don't run from me.
Keep me from life's harms, and
help set me free.

Kathy Cribbett

Oranges

There is a fruit
delicious to eat;
from the top of your head
to the tip of your feet.

This fruit is filled with Vitamin C
very much in fact;
Some people get deficiencies,
this Vitamin they lacked.

If you don't buy sunkist,
you don't know what's inside;
A monster came out and
scared me till I cried.

I guess now you know
what I'm talking about;
Oranges, my dear friend,
not sauer kraut!

Deanna Butler

Mercy

Longing — to lunge into the fire.
Demanding — to be seduced by your desire.
Wanting — to loose all track of time.
Waiting — to feel your heart race with mine.

Is it you... or is it me,
that burns this fire endlessly?
Who's to win? Who's loose?
Neither of us wanting to choose.

In the future... in the past,
who's to say how long it will last.
No matter if it's today or tomorrow,
mercy
we seem to ease each others sorrow.

We know each other all to well,
that's what makes this a living hell.
You have a lover... and so do I.
Yet we both know that our feelings never lie.

We can't control the temptation inside,
too late... there is nowhere to hide.

David Alexander Cano

A Devil's Compromise

This was not our compromise
Didn't you think I would soon realize
What you have done with my heart and soul
Maybe just for tonight
We can pretend it is alright
For all the lies you fed me
Just when I thought I was making sense
You destroyed my self-confidence
All I want now
Is to cry
And say goodbye
I am even more messed up then before
Because you stole
What I once controlled
You make me bleed
And now I need
You to promise me
Your soul.

Emily Chai-I Chang

Untitled

Why, when I hear your voice in the distance
do I rise with expectation
as though you were calling me
to be near you?

Why do I seat myself in the open field
exposed to your tremble
as though some great endeavor
were about to begin?

I place myself deep in your rumbling belly
in the palms of your competent hands
that I might be soothed and shaped
in your laboring strains

I am thrilled by your coming
bereft when you are gone
returned by your absence
to the tune of my own song

And when my voice has lost insistence
I will rise to wander
in the fertile field
that received your thunder

Joan Carol Ross

What About Them?

While we sit in our ivory palaces,
do we seldom wonder what fate befalls
those by chance of a throwing die
have met the poison of the asp.

How often do we see
starving children in search of food,
the plight of the primitive,
or the old woman on the street
that sits beneath our altars.

How much do we know
of their silent screams of agony
and wonder of their destiny.
Where will they take their pleas
and in turn be given solutions?

It takes just one hand
to lift the helpless out of the murky water
and into a land of promise.
And no one will wonder about them
anymore.

Beth Lazzazero Mack

Untitled

Fish swim quickly through the sea,
Do you worry about being caught by me?

Do you worry about larger fish?
Or do you not worry about being caught on their dish?

Are you totally free?
Are you free to roam the sea?

Are you one to swim and explore?
Do you journey around the ocean floor?

Fish so nice, totally free,
You are admired, especially by me.

Jennifer Gannon

I Still Don't Know What To Write

Can you give me some advice?
Does it have twenty lines?
That's it!
Can't be!
Hey, Dad, do we need a period?
Now what do I write?
Okay.
All right!
Now what?
I don't know.
Wait, is this good?
I guess so.
So what do I do next?
All right, I guess that's good enough.
Now what?
What else?
I don't know?

Daniel Rome

Are We Really Real

Are we really real?
do we have matter, or are
we just compressed particles
of nothingness? Are there
really colors? Is there
really matter? Or are we
just a dream of a dream
in a dream of a dreamer?
Are we really real?

Chris Patchett

Changin' Season

School's in, Mom's out
Dog's home, Dad's about
Leaves fallin', furnace runnin'
Feels for sure like winter's comin'
Days r' shorter, geese a yelpin'
Homework's here, Mom's a helpin'
Birds gone south, corn's a poppin'
Pumpkin's ripe, pig's a sloppin'
Apple's red, heads a bobbin'
Sparrow's here, no more robin
Corn's in shocks, pasture's brown
Scarecrow's wearin' frosty crown
Wood's stacked, fireplace waitin'
Day's too cool, no fish baitin'
Deer's a hidin', hunter's frettin'
Cause no quota he's a gettin'
Wind's a blowin' from the north
Winter stands, marches forth
Snow's a comin', hushed and still
Spring's asleep beyond the hill

Joyce E. Rose

Try To Do What Is Right

Stand for what you believe
Don't be taken to either side
For when the worse comes to past
In no one can you confide.

If it takes humiliation
To bring the dark things to light
Be not afraid, take courage
Get in the battle and fight.

Earthly gain is so useless
Many cheat steal and lie
Living on earth in luxury
Believing he will never die.

If man would stop and think
About that great and terrible day,
There would be less confusion
Each would take time out to pray.

Pits and traps would not be set
Instigators all would cease
Instead of turmoil and heartbreak
This would be a world of peace.

Adele Giddins

The Search

Look higher than the mountain
Don't cast your eyes toward ground
Seek to pierce the clouds on high
With gaze toward heaven now be found.

Don't stop at lofty peaks to dwell
Where man can climb and victory tell
But long to soar beyond man's means
To places formed for God's redeemed.

Look higher than the mountain
To where the flowing streams begin
The source is not in snow capped peaks
It has it's starts where all things end.

James E. Morel

Last

I see the light but I
don't know what way to go to find it.
I hear the voices, just
don't know who's the wise one speaking.
I feel the heat, the love they give me,
but I don't know what or who it is
that is giving it to me.
I'm lost in my own little world
were no one can find me
no one can hurt me.
If only their leave me only.
I'll be fine.

Becky Aldridge

The Hourglass

Sand filters slowly
  down the narrow passageway,
Counting down the minutes
  of every passing day.
Second after second;
  the closer we all come
To that final grain of sand
  before we become,
Angels up in Heaven,
  back where we belong,
Walking with our father;
  for this day I long.
I anticipate the moment
  that I finally see,
The very last grain of sand,
  telling only me,
It's now my time to return,
  to the place I yearn to be.

Jennifer Petterson

Destiny

Taking flight
Dreaming drifting
Attempting to Stand alone
  I slowly push you
  away while struggling
    to hold on
    Watching as you
  stumble unable yet
    to glide
    Dipping and
    falling
  Not ready for this flight
    I turn my head
  for one instant and
    It's gone
your insecurity and
  instability have
faded and I watch
amazed as you
soar away

Danielle Wattleton

Mother/Father

Mother
gentle, firm
working, joking, teaching
laughter, hugs, food, farm
feeding, planting, harvesting
beautiful, busy
Father

Ruth Damery Walls

Dream Deferred

The sky once shone bright with hopes and dreams
Each one dulled and faded a
w
a
y
though
Many stolen by rejection or
Run down by ridicule
Leaving the night sky dark and dying
Only one dream remained
Hanging low and
alone
in the night sky
The dream that once shone bright
fell slowly to the ground
The last of its kind now lay crying in the road
Shall the dream cry forever?
Will he ever forgive me for letting him cry so long?

Jacqlyn Schneider

Grandfather

These are hands of life —
each crease
each wrinkle
the mark of a touch —
the folds of creation.

Green thick vines twine the soft brown dirt
in his gentle palm
cupping the years with patience —
thoughtful of time needed
for strong roots to form.

He held my little hand as it grew
nurtured by his knuckles
so big by little fingers —
he didn't rush
blossoms
sprouting from big stalks.

His steady hand coaxed life
of everything he touched —
he grew love
green vines thick in generations.

Jennifer C. O'Kelley

If We Could Relearn The Way

If we could live a thousand years,
Each day wiser than the last,
We might regain an innocence,
Lost along our distant past.

We could relearn forgotten truths,
Known by the ancient sages,
About natural law, simple ways,
The wisdom of the ages.

But we must live a shorter span,
Most learning mere illusion,
Forsaking our rich innocence,
For poor manmade confusion.

When the way is lost we struggle,
With our mortal ups and downs,
As the stars smile on knowingly,
At their microscopic clowns.

Cary L. Graves

Easter

Is a time of fun and colors.
Easter is a time of joy.
The sounds of
children running to
find the colorful easter eggs.
Easter is filled with the
many colors of life.
The pretty blue
bonnets and daisies are
everywhere you see.
The for-get-me-nots
and daffodils tulips and orchids.
Wherever you look
signs of new life
are forming. And
who could miss the
little bunny's hopping
here and there.
Now spring is here . . .
can't you see. Easter

Allison Nooning

Untitled

In moonlit meadows We Stand
Embracing the night
Facing down our fears.
Pushing back the shadows
Warm stone shelters us.

What lies in the Forest?
unbent grass invites:
Step beyond the dusty paths within
Our fences...

Nay, we shall not venture
past the hard clay
past the light.

Serenity, Complacency,
hidden, buried fears.

How warm the hearts?
Not warm enough.
Not one enough
to melt the core.

What Brave faces we show.
What Brave Masks.

Elizabeth Davies

Sparks Of Life

Blue world waters and crystal seas
Emerald green grasses, fields and trees
Dew drops glisten in the sun at dawn
New Born animals made of chiffon

Thunderous lightning crashes the sky
Sparks of life, you and I
Gods finest miracles ever made
For this life, there's nothing I'd trade

Loving children chosen for us
Full of life, faith and endless trust
Singing and dancing in perfect harmony
In their eyes you'll find eternity

Allen James Gourley

Untitled

A sunset-hued sea shell
empty
with echoes of the sea.

The chair beside me
empty
imprinted with your memory.

The sentinel mailbox
empty
without a letter for me.

Another day that I am
lonely.

Dorothy Hamrang

Clouds

Soaring high above the
endless clouds seeing a
whole new world.

It expands further than
the eye can see.

Each fluffy cloud has
a different shape and
size.

What could be hiding
behind those big, white
clouds.

No one knows, but
the clouds itself.

April Jo Hurt

Untitled

The black mountains
Enter the sky
No one to touch them
For they are to high
Darkness is felt
And emotions seen
Remnants of the
Old regime
Souls wait in the
Hovering mist
While tranquility and peace
Is missed
Pinnacles of power
How they have been showered

Kerry Marie Caldera

Farewell to Uncertainty

Entirely yours.
Entirely out of time.
Entirely gone.
Leaving a world
of uncertain destiny...
Shackled by fate
and torn by loss,
I am witness
to the last
of my summer moons...
My autumn twilights.
A lifetime
of pleasant confusion
dies quietly;
muffled in denial
of certainty.

Arch Dixon

Human Tongue

Ere there was bird that cast a nest
Ere owl to prey upon her young
Ere there was cloud or sky above
There once was civil tongue.

Ere there was a flaming sword
Set at Eden's gate
Ere there was paradise or tempter too
Ere there was life upon the earth
There was a tongue most true.

Of generations come and gone
Or blood that had been shed
Of all the world so full of words
The human tongue has said
No book so big can earth contain
Or volume end to end that sprung
Like a river over falls it flows
The life and breath of human tongue.

Betty M. Jensen

The Face Of A Memory

I see a lost image
Etched in my mind
Searching for something
With nothing to find

Eyes cold as Christmas
With small tears of hope
Frightened and fraying
Like the end of a rope

A nose for the pain
It so easily finds
And ears for the harsh words
Heard time after time

Lips and a tongue
That lash harder than chains
And a heart that is shredded
From too many rains

Kristy Pincock

"Without You"

The days are always cloudy now
Even when there's sun:
The rain falls so hard inside
While outside there is none.

Time is just a measure
That means nothing with you gone.
You left me not too recently
But I don't know how long.

I wake up in the morning
And say, I'll be just fine.
I go to sleep at night
With only you on my mind.

Your always on my mind.
My thoughts not of you are few.
I know life must go on
But how "Without You"!

When life seems just too hard to bear
Without you to love and care
I feel so lost and down
But love will someday come around.

Judith Needham

Love

Love is like the wind -
ever changing direction
ever changing its mind
Love is like the ocean -
always beating and moving
forever leaving its mark upon the sand
Love is like the sun -
ever bringing warmth and bearing life
Love is like a mountain -
unsteady and uncertain on the way up
breath-taking at the top
Love is like the rain -
always needed, seldom appreciated
Love is like a rose -
fragile and delicate
yet, able to bring beauty to those who see
it open
Love is like a shooting-star -
rare and special
wish upon it, grasp hold of it, and
never let it go...

Danielle Lewis

Why?

Set beneath
everlasting skies
seeing all the suffering
hearing all the cries
wondering, wondering
ask the question why?
Searching
for an answer
I look toward the sky
experienced by emptiness
for what my heart
is yearning
I know not
for the feeble
things I'm learning
are enabling me to endure.

Donald J. Love

The Afghan

Every threaded inch
Every blackened square
Patterned purple royal
Silver shimmered trim
Every woven angle, every hour given
Thoughts focus within
Creating anew its spirit
Perhaps she wondered, with me on her
mind
As the pieces came together
I was with her all the time
A gift of the only love I know...
Unconditional.
She wraps it around, keeping me always
warm.
I'm sure as the years progress
And as I weaken with cold
I will gather in the warmth she gave
Never truly growing old
For she will always be inside...
I will always be her child

Aaron Weinstein

Retirement

How the time goes by
every day and every year
My eyes get dim
and I shed a tear.

People I've seen every day
come and go their way
their voices I still hear
though they are nowhere near.

Memories will always be with me
as time goes by so very quickly.

Although we shall all be apart
My dear ones will always be in my heart
so I'm not really saying goodbye
just wait until we meet in the
by and by.

Jeanne H. Marks

"Endless Love"

Passion enduring
every moment; tension
not found here. Winds
of love passing through
leaving hearts filled
with joy and laughter.
Love as this only exists
with in two souls of
honesty. When one soul
shall die a miracle
will inhabit to leave
an endless love.

April McFarlin

Mother Nature

She made this world,
Every tree,
Every bee.
She makes snakes to be curled.
She makes people die,
As time goes by.
Now, as factories evolve,
By smoke and paper she is killed,
But soon we will be billed,
At a price that can't be paid.
No more trees,
No more bees.
Listen to the wind,
Listen for the voice pleading,
Help stop pollution.
Can you help Mother Nature?
Please?

Chris Barlow

A Bad Day

When everything ruins your day
Drugs won't show you the way,
When you feel really bad,
Don't use drugs, don't be sad,
When everyone has a beer,
Really, have no fear,
Drugs are the wrong thing to do,
Trust me,
I know people worse than you.

Breana Sheffler

Eyes

Do you have eyes?
Everyone does.
But...
Do you see not only the colors
and shapes but also
the hatred and coldness in the world...
in people's eyes.
If you look hard enough,
you can see
love,
caring,
and humbleness.
In others eyes, you can see hatred...
Ice-cold hatred.
What do you see in other people's eyes?
What do they see in...
your eyes?

Annika M. Fesler

Madness

I wake up I fell so angry with
everyone it scares me.
It scares me to a point where
I feel I can hurt someone.
Madness is something I want out
off my life but won't go anywhere.
It seems to always come back to me
I received my madness from my mother
who I love to death but her madness
is stronger then mine. It seems she
has a demon in side of her which is
red and black with horns. My Demon
is green and orange with fangs.
My Demon is always being let loose
because of my madness. My madness
is very scary to me and I hope I
can get it out of my system before
I really hurt someone

Kisha Johnson

He Touched Me..

I came to the end of my life
Everything seemed negative,
I couldn't turn left or right
Tears flowed like a river
When I lost my brother-in-law
My beloved wife and mother-in-law
he touched me
When I decided to kill myself,
Ignored my kids and began
Drinking, two gallons of Bacardi,
large cokes a day. Yet...
He touched me.
Life was meaningless, I overdosed,
Wanted to die, turned homeless,
No where to go, no one to
Love, no one to care, he
Touched me, he gave me
Strength, hope and power,
He wiped the tears
From my face and made me
"Whole" He whispered:
Be still and know that, I
Am God (Psalm 46/10)
This man who touched
Me was Jesus Christ.

Akwasi Asiedu

you see real

now i'm just trying to cling
everything you see real
grasping oh so desperately
vain attempt to get a feel
everything you see real
i don't want any of it
i don't want my shell
everything you see real
burn it all to hell
don't blame me you made it
solidly forged steel
none of it means anything
none of it is real
i don't want to cling anymore
i don't see the need
everything you see real
means nothing to me

erik johnson

Untitled

I couldn't sleep, my mind raced on.
Excitement! Anticipation!

I wondered just what it might be like.
Wonderment! Imagination!

Making sure things were packed just right.
Sound judgment! Exhilaration!

The smell of the air.

The glow of the sun.
Be dazzlement! Titillation!

Then suddenly, it was time!
Awakening! Jubilation!

Yes! Today for the 1st time in my life!
My daddy is taking me FISHING.

Daniel J. McDonald Sr.

Roman Rituals

As the trumpet
excitement swept over the crowd,
The two contenders entered the arena.
The combat was about to begin.
The weapons were drawn.
The crowd grew silent.
The gladiators jabbed,
at each other.

As the spectators watched in awe
the gruesome battle continued.
The floor was covered in blood.
The injured loser lay on the floor.
The wounds were fatal.
The victor was ecstatic.
The champion ignored
his competitors pain.

As the arena emptied no one
mourned the life that was lost.

Jennifer Volksdorf

Flight

Up wing
Down wing
Bird

Philip Lyman Livingston

Interest Of Point

Extreme studies.
Extinct facts.
When softly combined,
gives guidance towards new knowledge.
Creating strength in the extraordinary.
Gently formed,
developed in experience,
creates a self inflicting creature.
"A Parental Unit".
All beings become one.
For no being is without wounds.
Parental names each as child.
Respectively share a common breath
of death.
As inflicted wounds trip mental surprises
of shock.
Big seas of red part,
as natures tall mountains,
dance with wild motion.
Thus creates the bottom line...

AnnMarie Connie Pedersen

Pages Of Life

Small fingers unfold
Eyelids flicker,
Open, close
Hard bound covered books
Story yet untold
Innocent smile
Blinded
By the binding
Of the untouched pages
Smell of newest
Virgin like
Protected by its' cover
Not yet worn
Unprotected
The pages become torn
As the story begins
Innocence will be gone.

Diane Audoin

Summer Nights

Glowing golden afternoons,
Fading red to purple light,
Katydid choruses ringing in
A sleepy Southern night.

Underneath a sweet gum tree,
Sipping lemonade,
While on the porch the old folks rock
And watch the children play.

Crickets are chirping noisily,
The music of the night,
And the softly glowing lantern,
The fluttering moths invite.

The fan squeaks easily,
As it winds down the day,
A train blows in the distance
And the hounds begin to bay.

The children are all gathered up,
To get their PJ's on,
The lights go out one by one,
A cricket sings alone.

David Ford

Irene

Prettiest of all the Pretty
Fairest of all the fair
O, what a joyful time is had
When she is near to care.

The world is always the prettiest
When she is near each day
For never a frown is noticed
As her heart is light and gay

The sweet sound of her lovely voice
Is always music to me
And always makes my heart rejoice
When otherwise sad I'd be.

She has such wonderful pretty eyes
Nothing could be so keen
and she has become very wise
my beautiful little Irene.

Carl Sunderman

"Come On Gramsy"

Thanksgiving day's around the corner
Fall is in the air.
I guess you know what's coming
Halloween is almost here.

Pumpkins dancing on the square.
Broom stick witches everywhere.
Kids all screaming "Trick or Treat"
Don't you wish gramsy was there.

You could run up the street
Ringing bells...wouldn't that be neat.
Then catch matt, coming down.
Dragging gramsy all around.

Can you eat all that candy?
If it filled your hat
Would you give some to gramsy?
And to me, and Matt.

Come on gramsy, don't you know
One more stop, before we go
We'll tell "Paw" we had so much fun.
Keeping gramsy on the run.

Anthony J. Picou Sr.

An Angel

In September 1994 an angel to our
family came.
A mere little fellow,
with a strong will to be on this earth
Cameron, is his name...
The Lord holds him in the palm of his
hands and helps him to endure,
he is a ray of sunshine when a cloud
gets in the way, a miracle baby for sure!
God knows the power of prayer and
how much this angel is loved,
so he gives strength to Cameron's
parents and blessings from above.
An angel so pure,
a miracle baby, for sure!

Julie Meenagh

In The Depths Of The Sea

In the depths of the sea,
far from the shore
it goes so deep
nothing can touch its floor.
In the depths of the sea,
far from the land.
No creature can swim
not even man.

April Lynch

Life's Poetry

Life's poetry flows in rhythm,
Fearful symmetry with rhyme.
Beat for beat expounding
On our losing war with time.

Life's poetry flows in rhythm,
Though we scare take time to hear,
Our every breath give echo
As the final beat draws near.

Life's poetry flows in rhythm
Even after we are gone.
So add your stanza to the piece,
That your rhythm might live on.

Brandon Woodruff

Beauty of the Day

Let the beauty of the day be told,
feel the ocean beat in your soul.

Glimpse the golden strands of sun,
climb silently on the day to be done.

Mountains seek the heaven's light,
as birds take to morning flight.

Flowers unfold their beauty and charm,
to protect their friends from harm.

Silken breezes cool the air,
as the day's end draws near.

Precious moments are held tight,
with the passing of day to night.

Elaine Monaco

Untitled

finding myself in your arms...
feeling myself in your heart...
seeing myself in your eyes...
knowing we're forever

i realize,

if i never had
a penny
to call my own
for the rest of
my days,

i couldn't be richer!

Brenda Schlegel

Moonlight

God's night light from above,
Shines as a vision of love;
Encasing the earth like a glove,
And is white like a newborn dove.

Michele Renee Sumara

My Love

I was standing on a swing
Feeling the wind on my face
And what I suddenly realized
Brought tears to my eyes.

Up and down, back and forth
The motion of the swing
With the wind whirling round
On that swing going no where.

My life is like standing on a swing
Up and down, back and forth
But my love is like the wind
That blows past my face.

When that swing stops its motion
Will the wind stop its blowing?
I pump that swing with all my might
To keep that wind on my face.

My love for you is undying
Not like the motion of the swing.
My love, built on years of trust and devotion
Like the wind, will blow forever!

Cheryl A. Hoffman

Feelings

So many different ways to feel,
Feelings of hurt and feelings of heal,
Feelings of happy and feelings of sad,
But that feeling worst of all,
The feeling of being so very small.

The feeling of being left out,
The feeling that makes you want to shout,
Shout at your friends who seem to neglect,
Your need for a little self respect.
When you feel you have no one,
You go to them and they say "So what!"
You say to them, "What did I do"
Then continue on, "that so offended you?"
But they ignore you and turn around.

So many different ways to feel,
Feelings of hurt and feelings of heal,
Feelings of happy and feelings of sad,
But worst of all a feeling so bad,
The feeling of being left alone again,
The feeling of not having a friend.

Emily Dail Hottenstein

"My Mother, My Friend"

Needing her the way I do,
Fighting back the tears,
I think of her both day and night,
Remembering all the years.
So painful are the thoughts I have,
I wish they'd make me smile,
And though I know, someday they will,
But, that will take a while.
She was so many things to me,
A friend above the rest.
At times our thoughts were different,
It put our love to test.
But, deep inside, we always knew,
Our love for one another.
So close to me, she'll always be,
She was my friend, my Mother.

Donna M. Harding

Bygones

Walking down a hall,
filled with the scent of memories,
I come to a door
that seems familiar to me.

I open the door
to a room with no light.
Revealed to me is a shadow
to which I hold a spite.

It is not the shadow
that I view with horror,
but what it represents
is what I lay at its door.

I turn off the hall light
just to find,
the shadow will always be
within my mind.

Brooke Meredith

The Chord Of Life

Flowing delicate,
Fingers resonate the tones,
Endows living air.

Soft carvings in wood,
Rolling lines, petals and stem,
The aesthetic harp.

The chords pulled taut,
Tightly tuned melody
Dead cats in back.

Jeffrey Bahr

Cloud

A hovering sunder of flocculent
fleece,
Accumulating in the solitude of the
night.
Dropping crystal pendants which
cling
to the leaves of parched
flora.
Ethereal columns, rising steadily into the
sky.
Then dissipating in the morning
light.

Brandon Takahashi

Untitled

Ten thousand million candles,
Flickering with their light,
Floating in majestic Grace
These bastions of the night

Who placed them in their wondrous paths
Of curves and spiral seas,
Like children of the universe
They are as you and me

Great poets wrote of the night time,
And lovers entranced in their dreams,
Gave birth to the beauty of star light,
And became filled with their magical
dreams.

And if ever you should gaze some night,
Upon this shimmering sea,
Remember, creation wrote, on that first day,
When the last day of destiny shall be.

John La Boda

Mom

Countless souls adrift so high,
Float down.

Each unique as snowflakes in the sky,
Pure, white.

They softly rest upon the earth,
Through mother's womb are given birth.

Protected in her cradled arm,
Kept warm and safe, away from harm.

Implanting values she has know,
A mother teaches 'till we've grown.

A loving life to emulate,
We sever the cord to strike our fate.

New wings ar spread, wobbled legs are tried,
Some flow with, some buck the tide.

But rich or poor, or all alone,
When we're with mom, we're always home.

John E. Avanzato

Love, Peach & Happiness

My thoughts wander as my bored life
floats away
aimlessly.
They go to the happy years, the sad ones
and the ones I don't care about
and the ones that I do.
Thinking of places I've been
and of places I'll never go.
Damn life's funny that way.
Thinking of people I've loved
or have wanted to love. Sometimes
I forget which is which. But
one thing I'll never forget is
that this is my life, I make
the choices and these are
my thoughts.
Mine.
Alone.

Ayrron Lee Comini

The Kiss

Dewdrops on a petal,
Fluffy clouds in the sky,
Rainbows emerging,
Gods on chariots riding by.

Healing waters pass through
But leave no trace
For the Earth drinks eagerly
From the gold embrace.

We must learn
To rejoice in its wonders,
Or we will perish,
Die like thunder.

Kimberly Igo

Rainbow Dance

Petals from flowers follow the wind.
Flowing in the air they spin.
Winding down they fall and sleep,
Till once again the air would creep
Upon their resting souls to chance,
And wake them into rainbow dance;
Breaking up the drear and haze
Of two dear friends forgotten days.

Erika Long

A Child Had Been Lost

Silence fell upon my heart today
For a child had been lost
Stolen by the test of my love
For a man who never sought
So simple to let a little one go
Whose life has become complex
For now our lives have just begun
So another life should end
Seconds pass like hours gone by
I sit and I await
For now the torment is yet to start
As sure as the day is to end
Systematically he eliminates my pain
For the lack of care and understanding
Silence fell upon my heart today
For a child had been lost

***Dejana Cinquepalmi** - Always*

"Put My Little Shoes Away"

Now come bathe my forehead mother
For I'm growing very weak
Let one drop of water
Fall upon my burning cheek

Tell my darling little playmates
That I never more will play
Give them all my toys but mother
Put my little shoes away

You will do this won't you mother
Please remember what I say
Give them all my toys but mother
Put my little shoes away

Soon the baby will grow larger
Then they'll fit his little feet
Won't he look so handsome mother
As he walks out on the street

Santa Claus he brought 'hm to me, with a
lot of other things
And I think he brought an angel with a pair
of golden wings

Mother soon I'll be an angel by perhaps
another day
So you will my dearest mother put my little
shoes away

Anna Artuso

Can't You Hear Me?

I imagine you being there
For me. You say,
"If ever two were one, then
Surely we."
Oh why can't this be,
This love that we brought to thee.
I love you more with nothing told.
You may have a new other,
But this love for you has no dweller.
Look into your heart, my love,
And see our love story that
Has never been told.
My pleaded heart calls out to you.
"Can't you hear me?"

Crissa DeVivo

Friends Forever

We've been friends,
for quite a while.
You make me laugh
and always smile.

Then one day
We were torn apart.
There were tears in my eyes,
and pain in my heart.

But I knew all along
we'd always be friends
friends forever
until the end.

Carrie Williams

Christmas Prayer

Amid the busy preparation
For this Christmas celebration
Take a private moment to pray
About why we have Christmas day.

Remember how the Christmas star
Seen by wise men from afar
Led them to the very place
Infant Jesus, full of grace
Was born to bring to us the love
Of God, our father up above.

As in the quiet church we sit
With all the Christmas candles lit,
Let the peace within us grow
Until it match the candle's glow.
Forgiveness for our sins, we plead,
Rid us of jealousy and greed.

Of hate and envy, set us free
To mold ourselves like unto thee;
To understand our fellow man
And help each other all we can.

Alice M. Lintz Russell

Daughter

She has a million dollar smile
For you, she would walk an extra mile

Always with a helping hand
If you knew her you would understand

With a heart full of gold
As it has always been told

A wife and mother
You wouldn't trade for another

She loves her church
And life's simplest things

Nothing can compare
For the happiness it brings

Listen now, It's no tale
I'm telling you about my daughter, Gail
I love you, Mom

Juanita Hersom

Friend

I call you friend
for you should be nothing less
I call you friend
for you remind me of goodness
I call you friend
for the few words you left with me
said you care
I call you friend
for in spite of obstacles and aches
and frustrations that many may think
a child of God should not have
you said in a few words you understood.
I call you friend
for your special mention to of me
whilst you pray
I call you friend
for you've truly displayed concern
I call you friend
FOR ME, YOU WILL BE NOTHING
LESS!

Chyron Hosten

Untitled

Reaching
for your light
that lights my path
each and every day
you fill my life
with your own life
that you did give
so I could live
and washed my shame
from blood you shed
with hope anew
because of you
you felt my pain
and comfort me
you give me strength
to face the day
for you are my shepherd
who lights my way
and will always love me
each and every day

Deborah Bombich

Homeward Bound Again

How long in life must we refrain
From spreading joy and hope
Latent virtues that have lain
Within our human scope.

To quell the fear of some poor soul
Who wanders in the dark
Without a friend, without a goal,
We must but light the spark.

To fan the flame that lies below
And smolders in despair
The seed of faith we must but sow,
Just take the time to care.

Then all too soon we find that we
Have crossed the bridge and then
Brought from despair eternally
Homeward bound again.

Carol A. Kaup

Dare To Love

Can it be that I am free
From the pain that love can bring
No, here it comes to me again
But can I bear it, share it...
After all my lonely wanderings
Over pathways broad or steep,
Ever alone but for memories
Lying deep...
Within
Oh, surely it's not too late...
Let me love again.

Agnes Gwynne Baker

Lonely Sunrise

Shade on the river.
Frost on the ground.
Everything peaceful
not a sound.

The sun coming up
for its first morning view.
My feet are soaked wet
with the newly found dew.

Incomparable beauty.
Impeccable scene.
And you beside me -
It was all a dream.

Kerry Sileo

When Summer Appears

Rainstorms
Give lusty greetings
When summer appears
When summer appears

Clouds and sky
Billow with whiteness
While blades of grass
Stand film

And only stones
Weep joyful tears
When summer appears
When summer appears

Bridget A. Bonczyk

1995 XC County Meet

Purple and Gold warriors race about.
Gliding back to back and head to head,
We take the Lead. 800 meters to go.
South. Ha. No where to be found.
North Rockland. We wore them down.
  100 meters left now.

Must think Fast.
Nervousness, this can't be:
palms sweating,
  legs dragging,
    heart racing,
      mind boggling.
We're gonna Win. Finish Line:
First...
  Second...
    Third...
      Fourth...
        Fifth...
Clarkstown North County Champions!

Kevin Joseph

Who Am I

Who am I?
God only knows.
A complex individual
With worry and woes
With hurt and pain.
A complex individual
Filled with joy and peace
Filled with hope and love.
A contradiction in terms.

Who am I?
God only knows.
Maybe an important question,
But after the quest -
What is the answer?
In ones quest for self
One finds a deeper quest
For understanding
Whose Am I and Why?

Kermit O. Shrawder Jr.

Here...It Is

Why am I here
Going thru all this torment
Allowing myself to be...Somehow
Amazingly in pain

How do I escape
Not much logic in the heart
My thoughts turn to again...Emotion
It's a wet kinda thing

I want to feel better
Saying goodbye is not supposed to be
Any kind of compromise...Hopefully
There are endless possibilities

Could I be wrong
Consideration must be way up there
Just when you think you know...Maybe
Peace of mind is rare

I know why I'm here, so here...it is

Donna Sievers

Good-Bye

Good-bye again
good-bye I say,
but God I hope.
there'll come a day.

A day when I can
hold your hand,
when I can finally
make my stand.

A day in which
I'll finally know,
there's no where else.
I have to go.

James K. Bristow Jr.

If I Were A Bird

If I were a bird
So pretty and small
I'd fly to the top
Of a tree so tall

I'd spread my wings
And glide through the sky
And call out to God
How free and thankful am I.

Rachel Ann Gilliland Knight

Sunset

I'm sitting on a
grassy plateau
in Flat Iron
Mesa Park,
watching
clouds swim
across the horizon,

Wrapping themselves
around the sky,
suffocating the color.

The sun,
  sinking
past violet mountains.

Unplugged
lamps—darkness

Winding around me,
seeping into my
ears and eyes,
anchored
till dawn.

Adria Barnes

Untitled

The waters
grew
around her throat
and strangled
him
with icy milk
I cried,
but not for
him
for he should
die...
or learn to swim

Ghighua

"A Small Country Town"

A young man in a small country town.
Growing old with friends all around.
Where life is sweet with memories.
Living in a small country town.

Kids laughing and playing in the street.
The simplest things are so neat.
Where life is good, it's understood.
Mom and Dad are always around.

Where time can change things.
Let it be slow.
Tears are hard to be found.
Where life can mean things
Everyone knows.
In a small country town.

Pretty girls in long hair and tails.
With dreams that never seem to end.
Where sweetness grows, the Lord knows.
Living in a small simple town.

Chuck Heffelfinger

The Florist

A snowy flower
grows through the ice.
Quick death by nature
will be its price.

The living plant
derides the cold,
to warm the hearts
of the young and old.

Blossoms wither
as they meet their doom.
Cut from life
to decorate a room.

Allison Dodd

Summer Beauty

The beauty of summer is
hard to explain. Of beautiful
flowers and breezes washed
of rain. The soft sunlight,
beaming down on your face
With the wind blowing
softly against your face.
How beautiful the summertime is
with roses sparkling in the wind.
I love to go outside and see the
beautiful summertime smiling at me.

Julie Collinsworth

Fire

It burns and yet,
Has so many meanings
Love, hate,
Jealously, courage,
Rage, happiness, sadness,
And yet it fades
A fire in you can start those things,
Those meanings,
Those feelings
They build up and fade
Yet if this thing
This fire
Has enough age,
Can burn forever
If it's significance is still in you,
Bad or good
It's there
In the fire
Waiting to be burned.

Carly Drahus

Untitled

How can one decapitate another?
Has thy Mother abandoned or abused you?
Is this madness caused by insomnia,
inhaling toxic waste
or direct contact with the Raven?

Why must the massacre continue!
Stop killing your brothers and sisters;
every death and violent act is another
spear into thy mother's heart.

If you would stop looking at yourself,
you would see the turmoil in her tears.

RJ Harsey

The Sea

The sea breeze
haunts my dreams
In the night air,
the sea calls to me.
The sea woos my heart
with a sweet melody.
The tide whispers my name
in full symphony.
Sometimes in dreams,
I stand beside the sea
and watch the waves,
I hear them calling to me.

Charlotte Burrous

The Many Faces Of God

The many faces of God
Have you seen them?

They are black
They are white
They are tan
They are bright

They are smiling
They are innocent
They are serious
They are thoughtful

They scream for help
They seek respect
They challenge your mind
They cross your heart

The many faces of God
Have you seen them?
Look around you, let them catch you

The many voices of God
Have you heard them?
Close your eyes and dance in their echoes.

Erian Armanios

He

When there was nothing
He gave everything.
When all was dark
He gave light.
When there was hunger
He gave food.
When all was empty
He gave fulfillment.
When there was pain
He gave comfort.
When there was confusion
He gave direction.
When all were lonely
He gave love.
When all were lost
He gave his life.

Kim Taylor

Untitled

I'm delighted in disorder and chaos,
So long as it remains refined.
I'm enlightened by a mind that rots,
So long as it remains defined.

I'm lost in places organized and pure,
Enamored by experience
I'm tossed into spaces left unsecured,
Trapped beneath a spiritual fence.

Mike Anaple

In The End

He thought he was bad,
He thought he was cool,
He left her sad,
feeling like a fool,
He acted as if it didn't bother him none,
He didn't even care,
Her love for him was over and done,
Her feeling he didn't spare,
But in the end its he who lost,
The love he never had,
For her emotions had been tossed,
And he was the one left sad.

Kara Beauchamp

Remembering

He was our uncle,
He was your son.
He was their brother,
With whom they had fun.
He was her husband,
His father,
Her father.

Though he's not here,
To be with us now,
We'll never forget him,
How could we, how?

He was their playmate
He was our friend,
You were his loved one,
On whom he depends.

Whenever his name
Is spoken or heard,
Remember his voice,
Remember his word!

Barbara Peck

Geese

Listen!, and you'll
hear it soon,
Like a hundred trumpets
getting in tune.
From whence does it come forth?
Its the geese flying North.
Buffeted by the wind they fly.
Oh so high in the sky.
They soar at noon
And in the shadow of the moon.
Every fall and every spring,
They get ready and take wing.
Flying in a perfect vee
How on earth can this be?
I must tell you and
This is no ruse,
They are taught
By mother goose!

E. Barbara Jones

Untitled

There once was a boy I knew
So kind
So generous
Always loving, gentle as a lamb
Minding his business one day
Was shot by a crazy man
This once kind, generous
Always loving gentle as a lamb
Is now with the Lamb
The Lamb of God

Sara Wilson

Untitled

Can you hear me through the night
Hear my cries of childish fright

Can you see me in the day
See me tremble and turn away

Can you hold me despite the hour
Hold me fiercely under you power

Can you love me in the rain
Love me forever cause me no pain

Can you touch me over the fear
Touch me tenderly pull me near

Can you feel me between these walls
Feel me breathing restless calls

Can you remember me despite the rest
Remember my name I loved you best

Can you resist me over the years
Resist my temptations console all my fears

Will you please keep me content in your arms
Keep me forever bind me with charms

Kristie Fink

My Life

A reflection off
her Soft clear mirrors
Entices a force filled
calm

To enslave that image
Which cannot be touched
Is to be still, forever
Allowing only hypnotic
Suggestions, the soothing
Ocean tide, to influence
Her sandy shores

I am the passive cause
of this continuous massage
of her skin

A glimpse of my love in
her waters would
overwhelm my solitary confinement
and for that moment I could
stand beside my pale reflections.

Kevin Casad

She Is A Beauty

The ripples on her back are so beautiful.
Her soft salty breath so sweet.
She touches you with foaming waves,
moving you around with a gentle caress.
Upon sight each ripple glistens,
while the sun shines on her back.
Her colors are as an aqua rainbow.
Peaceful is the sound of her roar.
She is a beauty,
she is the sea.

Her ripples can turn into caves.
Her breath can blow you away.
Her touch can be rough,
swallowing anything in her way.
She can be dark and mysterious,
demanding the world's respect.
She has two faces,
the beauty is also a beast.

Joni B. Parrish

Dream Girl

Her's is a gentle beauty,
her stride is full of grace.
There seems a glow about her,
like an angel kissed her face.

Her legs are full but slender,
her hair's a chestnut brown;
Her face is always smiling,
and she never wears a frown.

Her eyes are clear as crystal,
the mirror of her soul;
With a voice as warm as sunshine,
to make her body whole.

In her I see such beauty,
that can't be bought nor sold;
Her lips are a sweet love story,
just waiting to be told.

These words of admiration,
are as far as I dare go.
Because who I am and what I am;
I guess she'll never know.

Ken A. Orso

The Clown

Standing in front of the crowd
Hiding his face behind a mask
He knows if they ever saw his real face
He couldn't be a clown anymore
Because they would see
His true self, not forever happy
Filled with joy and glee
But human
with other feelings
Who is sad, depressed
Tired, frustrated and withdraw
He can't show this to the crowd
Because they expect the spirit
of the clown to be high
Who is the clown
Behind this mask of glee
This man of one face
With no true identity
With only his happy facade
This clown...is me

Erin L. Moore

Potentially But Not

A new days dawning
Hope and inspiration are born

The fog is thick
Each step is uncertain
I walk the straight line
To the edge
Now I stand on a ledge
Do I push the others off
Or do I fall alone

We get caught up with the
petty
Another day passes
I'm still not ready.

NIGHTFALL

Andre Lane

You

I sit in stillness, waiting for you
Hours yet before you come to me
But you are here.

I feel your hair, softly upon my face
Your lips touching mine
Your hands caressing me
Filling me with desire for you.

Our bodies together
Giving love, sharing love
As one
As only true love and lovers can be.

You will always be near me
With me, inside of me
Touching
Loving
All of me.

You are here
In my mind, my heart, my soul
There would be no life
Without you.

Ken R. Lea

Summertime Relief

The earth is shadowed by a
hovering bleakness. The feeling
of refreshment captivates me.

White cow birds are a
flying illusion among
the grey misty clouds.

An invisible force crawls
through the trees
creating a soothing relief.

A violent crack rips
through the placid silence,
followed by distant gentle growls.

For a second the crack
reveals an opening
of blinding light.

All the frustration, irritation,
and sadness in the sky are
released through pelting tears.

Amber Frye

"When Thought Dreams"

Oh
How a thought during the day...
Turns into a dream
As night tucks away, each child
In us who falls asleep...
To a seraphim's psalm, while a
Cherubim keeps.
Even with the awakening sun...
Kisses each and every one's
Somnolent cheek,
Opening eyes wide from their
Waning twilight seek.
This innocent thought that...
Braves to think - yet - dares to dream,
Like roping a cloud come rowing
Down stream.
Be it by day or be it by night?
Oh
How a thought can seem...
Seldom real, when thought dreams.

Kemberly Duckett

Touching

"Keep in touch"
How could three little words
Make me so happy?
He couldn't have known
They would make me so happy
My fantasies had him
Using those words
But I never thought
the dream would come true.
I can write anytime
Not waiting for an answer
But keeping in touch
means mail or phone
Not hands and lips
Now I want more than
Keeping in touch
Hugs instead of hello's
Kisses instead of cards
Loving in person as well as in letters.

Barbara R. DuBois

Pages of My Life

Slowly I gaze back upon the past
How I always searched for a brighter day
The wishing well never worth the toss
Opportunity knocks whenever I'm away
Now I lay here staring at my ceiling
Trying hard to forget the memories
I close my eyes and start to wonder why
The future's bright for everyone but me
I try to think of the good ol' days
Killing time with all my old friends
But then I find those pages missing now
Though I thought those days would never end
And I scream aloud in bitter rage
Against the man who wrote this tragedy
I close my eyes when I realize
That man is me
Then I try to open my eyes again
To stare at the book that's in my hands
A chapter on virtue, two chapters on sin
As I turn the pages of my life

Jason Dozer

A Better Place

If time could stop
How wonderful it would be
All the rest would be at rest
There would be no homeless, no poverty
All problems would disappear
The nations would be at peace
No more fighting, no more tears
All pain would pass away
The world would be a better place
No more disease, no more piper to pay

If time would stop
So would all babies being born
There would be no more joy
No roses or the prick of their thorn
All celebrations and holidays would stop
There would be no more laughter

No warm sun rays or rain drops
It would bring an end to all we hold dear
There would be no future
Nothing to look forward to or to fear

Carrie Brown

"Thou Still Unravished Bride Of Quietness"

A breeze that ushers confidential memories inaugurates the day and from the sea the fog wanders toward the streets coiling its nocturnal body in the copper chronicles of dawn that mysteriously recreate the innumerable morning of the first Eden.

The Great Spirit awakens in the word and Her voice reaches your lips, transformed into verses that shiver like sapphires of silent music that lead to the sea.

The acoustic moss of the submerged coral, the buried time of the Mediterranean, the vast lake of dusk in sudden twilight, is your presence.

You are and always have been the word, the verse in time, the country that receives me and accepts my autumns of exile, and the sensuous allegory of my saddened music, as your snow falls, filling with white bouquets the distant star of my silence.

I imagine you among the Troys replicated in many hearts transformed into a sidereal transparency, wherein rehearse the melancholy odes of Keats.

The mysterious aroma of your sibyl masters me and has become the visage that brings me closer to the motherland, the breathing of the sea and the gilded tomb of timelessness.

Oscar Gonzales

Cereus

Delicate petals lie safely hidden
From the white-hot light of Day
Slumbering, Waiting for
Sunset's chime of days close
To release the fragile jewel
To the Joys of Nights' dew...

Icy Iridescence in the Moon' waning glow
Fading, Wilting with the dance of Dawn's awakening

While Love quickly captured lies
Aching, Groping for Honesty
Betrayed instead to Satin's heat
That cools with the Sun's first caress

Plucked, Her luminescent Beauty
Shimmers but a moment
Like a Heart chained captive prisoner
Yearning to lose her wings
In true Love's embrace

Timothy D. Yost

Queen May

May comes to us in the loveliest gown, a dew jeweled necklace a garland crown.
Her beautiful dress, multi-colored flowers, Especially presented by gay April showers!
Heraldic, triumphant, flashing a smile, She walks resplendent down a rainbow aisle.
Alone she walks a most Regal Queen, Sprinkling bright flowers over hills so green!
May is the month when the heart breaks free, The world stands still for all to see.
Come walk with her each sun-blazed day, She enchants us forever and then steals away!

Louise L. Lentz

Ebbing Night

Ancient orb awake yet not suspends a blue-black sky,
Silence hears it's whispered runes soft against the night.
Winds caress, trees doth wail, prophecy in song,
Owl takes flight amidst the night,
Hung upon the moon.
Shadows fall, silence calls, bright sun is dawning soon.

Sans Cook

Thank You God

I thank God because He first loved me
Gave me life and has set me free.
Once was made blind but now I can see;
Dear God, thank you for letting it be
Your Son, Jesus Christ, who died on the cross at Calvary.
I thank God because He has done it all
Before Him we shall all fall
Our names He will call.
I thank God with Thanksgiving, a time to celebrate
A very special day, a very special date,
Taking time to pray with the dinner we bake
This world we live in, only God could make

Priscilla Cohen

Night Travel

The black of evening rolls toward me-
Gently at first, flowing over me,
Then fiercely changing face to writhe about me,
  through me,
  enveloping and devouring me.
Terror-soaked linen soon creeps around me,
  shackles me,
Makes me prisoner to my bed
  as it rockets me higher and higher
  to some unknown destination,
Then suddenly springs its release
  to plunge me to the netherlands of reality
Where I waken to the echo of my beating heart
And the taste of a half-remembered scream upon my lips.

Lois Baughman

Acadian Rhythm

One rising slightly higher.
Gifted with the infinite view.
A small white peak on the horizon
Melted in tan matting of the distant isle.
Precocious porcupines play with fire.
Scorching and clipping to mold unique virtues.
Glowing tops that no longer spin.
Trustfully grasp the gentle waves.
Baby barnacles bathe in the mist.
Clustered together in tenuous masses.
The force of many shields the strength of one.
Engulfing the wispy locks that flutter out of sync.
Is this a slow waltz or a tantalizing tango?
The crescendo rises.
A white spray hurls onto my fingertips.
Luring me to join the dance.
I step forward then back.
Retreating toward the summit.
I meet the gaze of the tallest pine.

Shoshanna Zucker

Making A Living

Another spring, another long season
Growing tobacco, there's no sane reason
Planting, cutting, stripping and packing
These vital steps you can't be lacking
Working from sun-up till the sun goes down
That's what people do in this small town
An honest day's work for so little pay
Sweating your brow off the whole long day
Out of town buyers will come to see
What they can get for such a small fee
Sometimes they'll give you a decent price
But more times than not it's your sacrifice
We know that smoking isn't good for you
But tobacco farmers need to make a living too!

Nancy E. Hall

Shy Laughter

How do I hide my fear, if I touch you
Give my passion and trust, incinerate barriers
And you are not the One.
The burning, intense intimacies would scar me.

Not incinerate leaving a shadow of twinned souls,
joined at the heart
Etched into the stone of time
For all to see, forever
And our journey would be over.

How do I hide my fear
That I'm not he one for
You.

We seek in solitude, breaking trust
Educated in Foolishness
Eye to Eye, I to I
My fear always make me laugh.

Michael Richard Raziel

Joy Inside You

Joy like the dawn of the day,
Gives life a song on it's way;
Soars to new heights for a stay,
Tells blues good-bye - stay away!

Life holds excitement each day;
Change brings new hope, and a ray!
Love grows in you, and the beauty grows, too,
For the joy inside you - give away!

Don't be afraid when you feel,
Things deep inside you hold dear;
Just let Christ's life dwell within;
Love and hope there as your friend.

Remember, life holds excitement each day;
Change brings new hope here to stay.
Love grows in you, and the beauty grows, too,
For the joy inside you - you've given away!

Charlotte M. Skinner

Eternal Flame

Burning bright, the candle's flame
Giving warmth and love and life
When suddenly the light is taken
To a place where eternal flames burn bright

Here there is no peace within
Only emptiness and pain
Why, dear God, must it be now
The flame must not remain

But God in all His glory
Who cries with you today
Knows your child's bright light has not gone out
But is with Him, guiding your way

For all the bright lights are His children
Shining radiant in the heavenly sky
Their flames have left our mortal soil
To shine with Him on High.

God begs you to remember
"Your child is here with me
And I am with you always
Together we are with you, through all eternity."

Vickie Lane

For Mom

One tiny moment had passed when you became my mother
Gliding through a threshold, in life it's like no other
Mother and child entwined in soul no parting can remove
From the love that's shared between us, hurts in life are soothed
Growing from the smallest of small beside me you were there
Picking up the tiny pieces, you made me so aware
The nights became the days and the days became the years
As the memories behind us both are filled with love and tears
No one owns anybody so wings you gave to me
Rooted in the knowledge some day you'd set me free
The years engraved a map and the world became my own
I know just who to thank, I didn't make here alone
Beside me then and with me now the bond will never part
Through all of life's successes, your love is where it starts
I thank God for who you are and I thank you for having me
I appreciate all you give and all that's meant to be
Thoughts and feelings felt, though words can't say what's there
I love you, I love you, I love you, forever I will care.

Patricia A. Cook

The Vision

The vision I see before me: the light of life, the blaze of love, the glow of peace.
Together, as one, the world is life;
And I am life.

This vision I see before me: creation itself, but destruction as well.
We live a life, the deception of spirit.
Can we learn the truth?

This vision I see before me: entrapment to some, liberty to others, yet death to few.
The flight of freedom, captive in our claws.
Fly high with life.

This vision I see before me: is it but a dream? What do we hold and possess?
What mystic thing do we hold in our hands?
This we do not know.

Samantha Tilanus

God's Plan

Before you knew me, even a thought in your mind,
God had a plan, part of a perfect design.

A seed He did plant, and a baby soon grew.
Covered in love was a feeling I knew.

I grew so quickly and time did pass by,
And before we knew it our tears we did cry.

Just a child, but I was so ill, to my rescue
You came, and my emptiness did fill.

A bond was formed between you and me,
Something so strong like a rare golden key.

In ones life, such love is a treasure,
Beyond all words, above all measure!

Your my comfort and strength, my mother my friend,
The one whom I can always depend.

I'll love you now,
I'll love you forever...
for in our hearts we'll always be together

Lisa Marie Labrecque Allen

A Teardrop And A Song

An angel was right with them, so close by their side, as the watery
 grave became their last ride.
To heaven she took them.
Into the loving arms of Christ, to hold and to comfort them, for the
 children had paid the price.
As we prayed and as we searched for them, we pondered,
 "where did they go?"
Our Lord Jesus was holding them, little did we know.
He will hug and kiss them tender, as we wonder, how could this be?
Why would a mother do this, for all the world to see?
Christ cry's out, "why are my children dying?"
As our teardrops fall, for selfishness and flesh, does
 Satan control us all?
"All my children are precious, be they big or be they small.
Is this the way I have taught you? Love is nothing at all?"
The pain has been so numbing, we all have cried like the river flows.
So try to picture them, holding their teddy with forgiving smiles
 that show...
The angels are singing them lullabies, to all that are now gone.
As our Lord Jesus holds them lovingly, with a teardrop and a song.

Lisa M. Wood

Power Of Love

The power of love can inspirer meek men to greatness and great men to meekness. It can turn hate around and melt prejudice in this vast world of ours.

The power of love can produce a miracle in the form of a child.

The power of love lets a woman experience the magic and joy of a baby at her breast, and lets a small child grow in a family of compassion and caring.

The power of love cares for the aged, the infirmed and the less fortunate of our society.

The power of love can bring nations together to end the fighting and bloodshed, to live in harmony with our fellow man and woman.

The power of love can make this moment we share on earth the way God intended for us to live.

Nicholas Cokinos

Taciturn Love

When we two parted in silence and tears,
Half broken-hearted to sever for years;
Oh, pale grew thy cheek and colder thy kiss,
That hour will bespeak such sorrows as this.

The dew of the morning sunk chill on my brow.
It had been the warning of what I feel now.
They vows are all broken and flight is thy fame.
I hear thy name spoken and share in its shame.

They name thee before me, a knell to mine ear,
A shudder comes o'er me-what have I to fear?
They know not I knew thee; who knew thee so well?
How long shall I rue thee? Too sadly to tell.

In secret I met thee; in silence I grieve
That thy heart could forget; thy spirit deceive.
If but I should meet thee beyond these long years,
How should I greet thee? With silence or tears?

Sarah Kate Huggins

With In

A congenial face, with a painted on grin;
Happiness only skin deep, with out
seeing with in.
A friendly gesture, a smile or two.
But will they ever see what's inside of you?
A losing battle, a lost cause for sure.
A desperate call for help-no one knows
what I endure.
They say time will mend the wounds-when
nothing's left to gain; But they never mentioned
how it will decrease the pain.
Sadness grasps hold, the mirror falls to the floor-
I'm not sure the image is me anymore.
Tears fall slowly, smearing the delicate
paint - The glass shatters, and they
see my real face.
Out in the open, a heart on the mend -
Letting my guard down - they saw the
pain with in.

Robin Kelly Hawkins

My Black King

My black king
has no certain shade of brown,
he certainly isn't the tallest in town.
but he most definitely has to stand tall.
on a level in which I stand. A level of
respect, maturity, and understand it's
not the size, shape, or shade of a man. It's the mentality,
immorality, actuality, authority, and reality of the man,
that makes the man.
He is my shield, by which I stand. He is a callous,
in which I have softened. There is a marriage, not
a mistake. There are babies, in which we make.
He never plans to escape. We are happy at this rate,
because of our education and money that we make.
On this earth he planted his seeds, never will
they ever need. This is my black king.
He understands the lives that he makes. He
educates and never tries to escape the marriage
and vows that we take.
My black king.

Marcinea Pearson

Past Perfect

The cat, scratching at the door
Has spent the night out
Lying on the pine spills in the dark.
Lives so perfectly what he is.

My wife complains; the Yoga class
seeking cosmic peace, tried to take
over their community center time at exercise.

The TV tube transcending glow at each abode,
blasts out a reader's call to celebration
of fifty years time since the myth of world war II.
I channel skip and find a game show piece
where history has died of celebrity name recall.

Phoenix rises, a roman-numeral generation devoid of a past.
We are the people of the cutting edge;
For we have extended life and "DNA'D"
Evolution's fittest, like God is dead.

I open the door, enters the cat in Darwinian selected splendor,
He is what he knows.
What are you and I?

Quentin E. Armstrong

Second Best

Janice is going bald and Phyllis
has the ugliest feet in the world.
"Shall we do lunch?"
Kathy laughs out loud in her steamy library.
Unmussed, sleek Carloyn turns forty-four
While Diane's children hug her unshaven legs.
The Second Best Woman
is best by far and
the New Woman will be
an Old Woman
soon enough.

Talked into being Cinderella
Talked out of it
Talked into Motherhood
Talked out of it
Until the Clock is
Done with her.

Women haven't changed, really,
still they harken to the loudest voice,
answering the question, "for whom do they dress?"

Ronald L. Haun

Orphans Of The Marriage Wars

"It is with great fear that I reawaken the many feelings that have remained locked within me;

To the many friends and children who have felt and lived and suffered the things that will remain forever in our nightmares and our living sorrows, I dedicate this my small attempt at rendering the horrors of the forgotten children to be scrutinized.

May God help us first to forget and if not forget then to forgive those who trespassed against the innocents.

Love does not conquer all, time cannot heal all wounds, there are for some scars that will forever be a part of what we are now; the children.

We could not strike back then, will not strike back now, even that which is the truth cannot salve the wounds of the children wronged, the children wronged.

Orphans; it is for the children, we never got to be and the children that will never get to be, that I pray will be healed Before they are wounded; so help us God."

Michael Anthony Seidler

Satan Is A Snake

The mother in church reached out to take the rattlesnake.
He bit her on the arm, no trip to the hospital did she make.

Mother stayed home and died.
Her five children cried.

Her father-in-law, the preacher believed in handling snakes
to prove his faith in God.
I pray that he repents before he is buried under sod.
His grandchildren has lost their Mother.
We would Love not Harm one another.

Read God's Holy Word and Understand.
Satan Is A Snake to be Killed by Man.
Snake handling preachers Will Learn.
Satan Is A Snake, In Hell he will Burn.

Vivian W. Howard

The Buddha In India

Buddha woke up in his meditating posture
he did not look at the Banyan tree,
but the Banyan tree looked at him, and said,
"My Lord did you meet Mahatma Gandhi?"
Buddha did not give his reply.

He began his walk along the mighty Ganges river.
He did not look at the waiting goat driven cart;
he looked at the Rolls Royce of an Indian Minister.
He did not see the Minister,
he saw himself in the Minister.

He did not open the eyes of the Minister,
the minister opened Buddha's eyes.
He saw the Minister meditating in the temple of Gandhi,
wearing a white innocent Indian cap,
but in his mind there were only dollars in a bank account.

Buddha's heart quivered in NIRVANA,
when he saw the kidneys of his disciples in Arabian market.
His heart broke, and he went to the Ganges to still his burning throat
and suddenly like the Nazi army, the Indian Ocean marched on him,
and swallowed the Banyan Tree and the meditating Buddha.

Vishnu P. Joshi

Memories

I once knew a man who taught me a lot,
He gave me a gun and made me a good shot.

He taught me to load it, and taught me to aim.
As a teacher he could have made the hall-of-fame.

We had a great summer, and had a great fall,
Until one February night my life became dull.

Cancer is bad, living is good.
Now I am the teacher, and my grandpa is not,
My dad is the student, but I'm still a better shot!

My grandpa is gone in the long days since then,
I miss him dearly, he was my best friend.

Sean Moffatt

Look What He Gave Us

He gave us the sun shining so bright,
He hung the moon like a little night-light.

He gave us the forest and the field,
He provides the rain for the crops to yield.

He gave us the ponds and the fish,
He twinkles the stars upon we wish.

He gave us the deep canyons and tall mountains,
His love is unconditional, overflowing like water fountains.

He gave us breath, heart, soul and life,
We create our own stress and strife.

He gave us each other,
His son Jesus teaches us to love one another.

He gave us our families to care for and love,
He gave us peace in the sign of a white dove.

He gave us the Holy Spirit for comfort when we are in pain,
He gave us understanding so that we can learn and gain.

He gave us the Holy Bible to be our guide,
He gave us voices to tell everyone about Him world-wide.

He gave us so much more than we deserve,
He holds for us a place in heaven in reserve.

C. L. Haller

Spring

Flowers are blooming.
The bulbs are growing. Roses are blowing.
New seeds are coming.
Nothing is dying because spring is an outburst of colors.

Michael Sebastian

Midnight's Hero

He is a deadly creature of the night.
He is never heard but, you know he's there.
He is there for justice and to do what's right.
Prepare your soul to take to the air.

He is the judge, jury, and executioner.
His heart is good, his mind, filled with rage.
Those who see him say he's an illusion.
His untouchable soul will never be caged.

His life's purpose is to fight world's cruelty.
His only friends are himself and angels above.
Unlike others he let his soul and body free.
His heart has paid the price, unfeeling to love.

Maybe when his life comes to its long end
his soul will rest and won't be his only friend...
Doubtful.

Nick Pierce

Shadow

A beast roams the darkness of night.
He is unseen and unheard as he stalks the forest shadows.

The ground shakes and rumbles as he races through the woodlands of the wild.
His black coat turns to silver in the moonlight.

As he runs through the night, his muscles twist and turn under his velvet coat.

His mane and tail float gently behind in the midnight air.

His nostrils flare like fire.
As morning draws near, he races against time and then disappears in the darkness of the forest shadows.

Susan Robison

The Master's Hand

I have been touched by the Master's hand,
He lifted me, and now I can stand,
In His dear presence, without disgrace,
For I have looked into Jesus' face.

Once you've been to the throne that's a King's,
And seen the grace and power He brings,
You'll never again be near the same,
Once you've repeated that precious name.

He fills my cup to overflowing,
And oh, the joy that comes from knowing,
That He's always there, both day and night,
To fight my battles with all His might.

He let me see a glimpse of His glory,
Now I must tell the wondrous story,
Of the precious love He is sending,
His love for me is never ending.

He loves me, He loves me,
'Tis the old, old story,
And soon, I'll be with Him,
Up there in glory.

Linda Waltman

I Didn't Know His Name

He was middle aged, or more.
He lived inside a cave.
His coffee brewed in an old tin can.
At night upon the cold ground he lay.

Except for swimming in the river,
His clothes were never cleaned.
From morn 'til night he searched for pearls,
To fill a poor mans dream.

I set beside his camp fire one night,
To rest myself a spell.
Questions flooded my curious mind,
And he had things to tell.

"I left my wife, and kids," he said.
"For work could not be found.
But I'll go home a wealthy man.
I want to make them proud."

I knew that night he'd found his wealth,
By the twinkle in his eye.
I prayed he'd have a safe return.
To the ones he'd left behind.

Laverne Roach

Our Dad

Our Dad is someone special, he's also our best friend,
he never gives up on us, no matter what he'll love us to the end.
When we need him, Our Dad is always there,
He fills our lives with happiness, love, and care.
Each moment we spend with our Dad will always last,
For the time we spend together passes much too fast.
Only one thought comes to mind when we think of him.
"Our Dad's the Best"
That's what makes him different from all the rest.
Our Dad brings us more happiness, than any wealth,
For another year has passed, and he still has his health.
So we want to Say - "Happy Birthday" and many more too,
We're proud to be your Son and Daughter -
But most important Dad,
"We love you"

Pam Crow

Orpheus

There once was a greek musician, orpheus was his name
He played sweet music on his lyre, goes his story book fame
Everybody loved his music, even the winds stopped to hear
A pretty young Grecian maiden, was serenaded by his lyre
They fell in love and was married, goes the Grecian myth
Aris, their only servant fell helplessly in love with
The beautiful young Grecian maiden and wanted to get her along
One day she went out walking, not every far from home
He caught her and tried to love her, but she quickly ran away
A snake bit her as she was running, and she died that very day
Orpheus was so broken hearted, he descended to the lower world
Hades, the king of the dead, had power to hold his girl
He was so charmed by Orpheus and the beautiful music he played
You can take her and return to the light of the day 'he said'
He ordered orpheus not to look back, as he ascended to the light
Soon he forgot and looked back, and she disappeared from his sight
Orpheus vowed he would not give his love to any women on earth
This made the women angry for he had degraded their worth
They killed him and threw him in the river along with his lyre
From that river come a sweet sad music you can always hear.

Martha J. C. Robbins

Father And Child 1910

His toes touch the water's edge.
He remembers the forgotten umbrella.
At 34, his worry makes him laugh.
Even overcast days are Shangri-La.
Her little hands are his luxury.
The dress she wears is waterlogged.
He won't play taskmaster. Not today.
He walks as she scampers in front of him.
The beach without crowds, lends a serene and sanctified silence.
No better way to mark the anniversary.

His life is no sullen routine.
Dullness becomes a virtue when the guns stop shouting.
Carriages not Kurd bandits rule the streets here.
His fingers probe the sand for periwinkles.
These morsels are their feast.
He knows this Saturday spell must break.
His jacket covers all but her resting head.
The effusion of hair now blowing on his neck,
heals 100 ancient wounds.
They wave goodbye to the sea gulls.
For supper is waiting and there is a home to go to.

Lisa Lahr

Heaven's Gate

I dreamt I went to heaven and stood before the Lord,
He said, "My child what concerns you?" as he opened up the door.

Before I enter in the gate there is something I must know.
Why do loved ones have to die and leave the world below?

My son, I know that you are hurt, I feel it in my heart.
Please let me try then to explain, I know just where to start.

Just like Job, in days of old, when you're put to the test,
it strengthens each your heart and soul and brings about your best.

It brings out love and friendship and true comradery,
the hugs and tears are your own will the rest all comes from me.

All the loved ones that have come to join me in this place
will meet you here again one day with tears upon their face.

There won't be sadness in those tears but tears of joy instead.
So, fear no more my precious child, you've much in store ahead.

And as I woke up from my dream, I thanked my God above
for pouring down his blessings, for surrounding me with love.

Though now sadness fills my heart, truly, I can say
There will be a glorious reunion, when we meet in heaven one day!

Michael Baumlein

Salute To A President

There was a man so brave and true
He was the bravest man I knew
He was loved by many in many lands
And this I know is true
Until one day like a nightmare out of the night
The villain played his part
And shot a bullet which hit its mark
And put and end to President Kennedy's Heart
Although this great man is gone from our mist
He still lingers in our memory
And there he will stay like the passing tide
Each second of every day
So let's all stand and give a salute
To a man so brave and true
The ex-president of the United States
Mr. John F. Kennedy

Thomas A. Trojecki

The Moors

Walking along the purple moors
He watches, he waits, he listens.
Walking all day, no place to stay
As a teardrop that falls, glistens.
He watches for the way that loneliness lures
A man out to his death.
To take him slow, let no one know
How he changes with each breath.
He waits for the way solemnness cures
The hassles of the day.
He walks along, but sings no song
For his death is on the way.
He listens to the voices that come over the moors
That cry out in whispery words;
They seem to scream, words obscene
Carried on winds by invisible birds.
The end opens its doors,
He drops down to lie,
Totally lost, paying the cost,
The price is to high...Now he must die.

Leslie Williams

"The Love Of Father"

Every girl should have the love of her father. His gentle eyes the heart to twist round a finger. Quiet times content with each other. Someone to look up to with the deepest admiration. A savior. My valiant knight. For in each soul we've measured our worth on our fathers ruler. With guidance and love, self-confidence given, we seek our mate. With the love of our fathers relationships flourish. For only with this love can we find the daddy in all men. Someone to carry on a legacy of emotions we feel we deserve. Those lost, who've never known this love can forever search and never find the love of a father.

Lori Ray

So Unique

This woman is so unique.
Her brain and her body from the rest are so different.
Thus giving her confidence and making her independent.

This woman is so unique.
Her mind and her muscles are beyond strong,
Giving her the intellectual and physical power
To last more than long.

This woman is so unique.
Her entire self is unbelievably rare.
Go ahead, try to duplicate her if you can... if you dare.

This woman is so unique,
That she is compared to the Queen Bee.
When I look in the mirror, this unique woman is who I see.

LaToria S. Walker

Life

My life is an earring hanging on an ear listening to the world
Hat on a head
Inch on a wall never ending
A cheek red and hot
A hedge that is growing
A neighborhood full of voices
A room full of noises
A paper that is blank
full or
empty
listen, listen to my mind
life can't be put on paper.

Sarah Waldman

Escaping Blindness

Captured in the woods by haunting eyes
her derelict smile
Intoxicated by the shift and rise of leafed limbs and
her deft and silent approach,
weaving through the ragged brush
The burning fluid feel of swelling storm,
eyes marbled as dawn breaks wide open
from in the midst of him
Rushing with arms back in remembrance
She tackles the white hot of his soul
embraces it with her mindbite
The gazelle dance
wringing off the dark tatters that bind the soul
they fall far into the deep waters of alive
Folding, breaking, growing,
beaching on ivory sands
They heave with the earth and meld together
to sleep in a field of lotus buds
Red with the passion of being.

D. C. Mattox

"A Woman"

A woman is stronger inside than out.
Her endurance grows longer with every bout.
She's been covered in dirt, made to look bad;
She's been beaten and hurt through centuries had.
Although the night may be old or new
there's the old days fight, still so much to do.
She glows in her sleep from the moon and the wind,
whispering hopes so she can begin again.
Her nerves are shaken or so it seems.
She must awaken her self esteem.
Give credit woman, where credit is due.
Listen sweet woman, I'm talking to you.

Lynn Parker

"Breezes"

I sat upon my steps and watched
her limbs blow in the wind. So huge
and lush you are. How sweet the
breeze you give
Your shade comforts me from the beaming Sun
I look and See how the birds
flock to you, I do not blame them
for you are our haven.
Even in the fall when you change
your colors and your reflection sets
my living room ablaze with a gold
and crimson flame.
I will await you in the spring.
When you start your new life again

Sonja Tillman

Yes Or No

She stirs in her sleep.
Her mind in a turmoil from her worries and dreams,
Scared of what she wants to be; but unsure if it's right.
Yes or No.
She wonders if the love is really true.

As she rises in the morning, the anxiety is still building.
She paces back and forth, Waiting for his return.
She holds so tightly to what she remembers,
The laughter in his eyes, the way she feels with him.
But she believes she must let go a part of her to be one with him.

Her thoughts and worries subside by the sound of his voice.
And the answer flows from her heart and soul.
She realizes that there will be no goodbye to what she already knows,
Just a new beginning, Where their love will grow.

Tara-Lynn R. Walter

There is a Woman

There is a woman out there who knows not of my love. I try to tell her through the crack in my voice. Letters I try too, but the pen slips from my grip as my hands become moist. It's hard to hold my breath long enough to describe her. My understated description a Phelony, to describe this feminine melody. Natural elegance, she is of the earth. Love resurrection romance rebirth. I see this woman, who sits in her seat, a young woman I dream to desperately meet. I lean forward to the left and with a stretch and a try, I can see the brown pupil from the corner of her eye. And that hair that sits upon her head is shades of brown and roanish red. Those lips make the smile. How I live for that smile! If love were a crime I'd be on trial. I cannot ration this passion. It comes in large doses, as I dream of sweet candy kisses or just rubbing noses. She nibbles and gnaws on her favorite pen, I see from the rear my own private heaven.
Slowly and sensually from tooth to tooth, from lip to lip and tongue to roof. The skin of her apple I want to eat. She quick dries my concrete. And her voice?! Oh, her voice is the sweet trickle of a backwoods brook, like the songs of heaven, sung in whispers that tickle my ear and makes my eyes dizzy. Is it my love you've read? Could you feel the tears I cried and the blood I bled?

Rhoan West Laymon

Beaches

Beaches make up many parts of the earth,
Here and there and everywhere.

With a single sea shell I can hear the ocean roar,
Everyday more and more.
Low tide every speck of it
No one needs an ocean kit.
For all a person needs is a single shell.
As I sit down on a beach, one beautiful evening,
I hear crabs, birds, ships, and boats.
In front of me, I hear sand, water, and people on floats,
I see darkness, some lights, and off course the stars and the moon.
Behind me I see more lights, crab holes, and plants on a sand dune.

Vandna Jerath

Thanks Given Morning

As I awake thanks given morning as I fall on my knee,
here is the prayer that come to me.
Heavenly Father.
You have bless me all my life.
Even tho I haven't done lots of thing right.
I know I fell you in so many way.
But you have never turn and walk a way.
It is no secret what you will do
if we will put our trust in you.
when time one hard and friend are few.
And satin is trying to get the best of you,
fall on your knee you will see
Jesus has the victory.
Lets not let nothing get in our way.
Or stop us for thinking Jesus Christ for
this and every day.

Virginia Dale Williams

On My Mind

The day the sun reflected of the glass with a misconceived caress
He saw a figure float down the isle in a white bridal dress
Her faint laughter and whispered cries, he remembered would shine
In his mind, she would never age nor display a single line.
Familiar with her scent and feel of her touch
He'd lie awake, eyes on the photo of the woman he loved so much.
A touch on his shoulder was a feeling of her left hand
He stole a glimpse of the finger that wore the gold wedding band.
No tears of goodbye, not even a chance
Over in a moment, same as their first glance.

Raquel Bermudez

The Light

Enveloped in the darkness, shadows overcome.
Here lack of light is common, figures dark and fierce,
trample what I've worked for, there is nothing for me here.
I must start over, I must begin again.
There is a long road ahead of me and if I hope to win...
I've got to keep on fighting, look how far I've come.
I see the light ahead of me, the battle's nearly won.
All I need are just two steps, I can almost reach the light.
I'll pull my strength from within, I will win this fight.
I struggled and I pulled, again with all my might,
the war is fought, the battle's won, I'm standing in the light.
I must regain my strength again, time is drawing near.
Circumstances have arose, I must not show I fear.
Life's situations turn and twist the road I face ahead,
with weakness and intimidation constantly a threat.
Many times throughout our lives we turn and walk away.
We give up and leave the fight, to be fought again another day.
All I ask from you dear soul is to double back.
Face your problems one by one, if it's courage that you lack,
say a little prayer to God, let him be your sight.
You'll understand that in the end you'll find eternal light.

Tracey A. Miller

Stone - Henge

At the dawn of time watch the story unfold,
Here's the truth of what happened no longer untold.
When all was still darkness among endless chaos,
Before there was this order or a God who boss.

In the breeding grounds of hell a new form was born,
As the light shined forth the order of chaos was torn.
Then some came to worship while other's turned away,
The light and darkness separated, just like night and day.
So chaos elected someone strong so something could be done.
That they might deal with this bitch and her seemingly
evil glowing son.
So lucifer gathered up some braves so they might make war,
On the bright shining one and the dark - forsaken whore.
But this new God prevailed and those of the dark were kicked out
And a prison of fire was built where God spit them from his mouth
So the chaotic became fiery and twisted and now wish for revenge
And you can hear them howl on witches' eve at Stone Henge
As the moonlight turns to liquid near those unknown aged stones
They'll take your place and you'll feel there pain down in
your souls
While they drink of moonlight and you burn in hell
They'll have a break from damnation and you a story to tell

Steven A. McFarland

Alabama Peach!

Oh, I love my Peach, and I think he's great;
He's from Alabama, a man from a southern state.
I have beautiful memories of the times and things we've shared;
He's done so many thoughtful things to show he really cared.
What stands out in my mind is his concern for me;
Instead of giving "no" for an answer he just says, "we'll see".
I give tribute to his parents because they raised Peaches right;
I reap the benefits of his training, my Peach is so polite.
I love my Peach because of the way he knows how to respect a lady;
I don't have to worry about him doing something shady.
He cooks, he cleans, he irons his clothes, he even does the dishes,
My Alabama peach is nice 'cause he acknowledges my wishes.
And what I think is really nice is my family loves Peaches too;
He's kind and very intelligent and he knows how to talk to you.
And so I think you've guessed by now this Peach is not one you eat;
His name is Larry Joe Jones and I think he is so very sweet.
This peach is not the soft fuzzy kind that one would say is edible;
But let me tell you this one thing "My Peach Larry Jones is
INCREDIBLE!"

Yolanda W. Martin

"If Only"

There's this boy, I can't mention his name.
He's sweet, and understanding.
Handsome as a prince,
looks don't matter, only thing that does is.
I love him.
He's smart funny, and caring
I've never felt this way about anyone, except for him
I guess it's true love
If only he knew how I felt
If only he could understand how I feel about him
If only I had the courage
to go up to him and say I love you!
If only I could tell him how I feel
I guess it's true love.
If only he knew how I felt
If only he could understand how I feel about him
If only I had the courage to go up to him and say I love you!
If only I could tell him now I feel
It would be so easy, if I wasn't so shy
If only I could say, "I Love You!"

Shannon Brown

"Braces"

Braces are metal covering up your teeth.
"Hey, Doc! Got a pain right here in my left cheek!
Braces are a hassle. They make mouths sore.
Sometimes I want to kick them right out the door!
The orthodontist tells you what you can eat.
No candy or sweets? Now that can't be beat!
But 'cha know, if you really look hard braces aren't that bad.
Don't even leave a scar, they're colorful, pretty, and extremely
bright.
But if you wanted you could even just get white!
Dr. Cohen is my orthodontist's name,
All of his co-worker make braces a cool game!
Mom likes the rule, "No candy or sweets."
She's not always nagging "now eat your beets!"
My orthodontist explained to me, what'll be happening
in my mouth, cause I can't see!
Vicki's the one who got me started.
She helped me through until my braces and I parted!
I was pretty glad to see them go.
But I'll miss seeing Dr. Cohen and his workers though.
Braces might be a hassle and might make you mad.
But in the end, they'll really make your teeth glad!

Shelly Mayers

The Wish

A dying wish that soars up alone,
High in the sky, to our creator's reign
It escaped her mouth with barely a moan.
It's asking.

He looks down from His throne on high,
The wish is heard whispering.
The Taker and taken both sigh,
It's ending.

It is confirmed to me with a silent nod,
That here she will live no more.
I look up to heaven and know she's with God,
It's final.

Meaghan Ann Dolan

Untitled

I see a man running down a dark road.
His identity is not clear and he seems
To be running only because the road is there.
As he runs, it gets darker, in his eyes.
Wait, he has stopped.
He stands over a solitary flower.
He stays long enough to appreciate its beauty
And its resilience in this gloom.
As quickly as he stopped, he began to run again.
He ran for a long time, until he got to a dark curve.
He couldn't see what was ahead so he went back the way he came.
As he was running back, it seemed to be darker than before.
As he made his way through the darkness, he came upon that same flower.
As he approached it, he noticed a difference.
There was a dim glow from behind the flower.
He looked closer and saw a field of brilliant flowers and light.
He had remembered that if he opened his eyes he might just see
More than the edge of darkness.
As the light shone upon his face, I shivered.
The face hidden by the darkness was mine and the flower was you.

Zachary Al-Chokhachi

Untitled

The one who took my place.
His name is Jesus, my Savior and Lord,
He came into the World to die upon the Cross.
He died for all who has or will be born,
He now lives upon the throne, where
One day He will call us home.
I met Him many years ago, when my life
was in a tumult and my heart was very low.
In the goodness of His grace, I met Him face to face;
He lifted my heart at the break of dawn,
There He placed a peaceful clam.
As I go through life, knowing not where,
I breathe a prayer, knowing He is there.
He died on the cross to set me free
Shed His blood for you and me.
He came, a life to give and hearts to fill,
He gave His all that we might live.
My Savior, the grave could not hold.
The most Precious Miracle known and told
His wonders and riches to behold
Praise God; Jesus paid the toll.

Wilsalma Anderson

Dream Fire

I am restless spirit...
Hopelessly trapped in the white man's world.
A native warrior, once free
Like the eagle and brave like the grizzly,
Snatched from my land,
My beautiful land...
Once the hunter, I am now the hunted,
And like the proud eagle and the mighty grizzly,
I fade into the dream fire...

From this burning fire of dreams, I shall be reborn!
My quest, to breaks free...
My destiny, to live free...
And in my painful rebirth, I shall emerge from the
Mighty dream fire a Free Spirit!

Tracy McLeod-Brown

Shadow Dancer

A young child was attempting to escape his shadow
Hopping and Jumping, Skipping and Ducking
The shadow was forever stuck.
An elder paused the lad and asked what was wrong?
"It won't leave me alone" the boy cried
Frustration was endowed upon the child's soul.
Replying the old man, with a smiling face
"Your problem, a simple one indeed.
The shadow holds great respect for you.
That is why it mimics you, it is yours.
And until you purposely respect yourself
The shadow will remain your mystery, forever unsolved
And you shall be eternally doomed, never to respect
Your shadow."

Steven Allore

Horses

Horses are pretty.
Horses are nice.
I love horses,
And so should you.

I like it when they run fast.
And so should you.

I love horses,
And so should you.

I like it when they have babies too.
I like it when I ride them too.
I love horses
And so should you.

I would love to own one.
And so should you.

There are Shetland ponies and stallions too.
But most of all I like white stallions best,
And so should you.
I love horses and so should you.

Tiffany Chaffee

Ever Again

How will I?
How can I escape the desolation, the despair, the despondency
that have become my constant companions?

They overwhelm me!
They walk with me as I take aimless steps that lead nowhere.
For where am I to go?
The love, my love has been snatched from what was once my life.

Desolation, despair, despondency, they lay beside me.
We share endlessly dark, bitter, sleepless nights as one.
They are with me when the morning sun has the nerve to rise
Though my love is no longer here to be warmed by it's glow.

My heart is so heavy; my spirit so weak.
God, are you still there? Are you hiding somewhere in the blackness
that surrounds me both day and night?
Will your light ever again penetrate the darkness that has become my existence?

I was riding high; so secure, so wanted, so loved.
Now, I am devastated. My life has been cancelled from prime time.
Will I ever again experience joy, peace, and fulfillment?
I fear not, ever again.

Sandra P. Pointer

The Garden

I remember how you looked at me when I told you of the garden,
How it's flourishing and growing,
At first only a seed, but now steadily spreading.
People always forced themselves to believe
That the weeds in the garden were part of a phase that would pass,
For no one mentioned its immortality, no one dared to see the truth—
That the weeds in the garden would continue to grow
Until the flowers realize that the garden needs the weeds,
They are a part that must live now in order for them to die tomorrow.
But the flowers are too arrogant, too ignorant, to understand.
All they keep on repeating is "not me, not me, not me."
They close in on these weeds, until they suffocate and wither—
No poison from the ground could kill them
As these things of such a sweet scent do kill.
Day by day the weeds grow, until the suffocation cages them in—
They perish, almost destined to die.
I remember how you looked at me with such a dreaded hate
When I told you of this garden—
For the weeds that the garden has created are not weeds, but flowers.
You have become a true weed, and a flower.

Sarabeth Stockmal

"How Fragile Life"

How very fragile life is
How little thought we give it
As we recklessly pursue our way
Without concern to our length of stay

We go along as if it will never end
As if we were immortal
If only we would stop a second
And realize how fleeting it can be

It is but a breath, a heartbeat,
Each so short in duration
Yet without either, life ceases
What then, do we perceive it with longevity?

There are no guarantees
No promises, by anyone
That you will breathe your next breath,
Or that your heart will beat, its next beat

So do not trek through life so unconcerned
With your actions of the moment
For know it or not, this moments actions
May be those for which you are remembered,
YOUR LAST.

Leo C. Wilson

Time Marches On

Did you ever stop for a moment and think
How rapidly time into years could sink,
And years accumulate into an age,
Of disappointments from life's early stage?

And there's your pulse beat tolling your time.
It beats for a special reason in rhyme.
Do you sense the meaning of your pulse beats?
"Think twice, think twice, think twice!" It repeats.

Time can be wisely absorbed, when in use,
Of planning on methods from which to choose,
A deciding factor for a great success,
Assuring a future toward life's happiness.

Apparently we know this to be true,
That there'll always be work for us to do.

And whether, or not, our work is done,
Slowly, but surely, "Time marches on!"

William Shelest

Impenetrable Mysteries

How many stars are shining in the heavens?
How many blades of grass grow on the land?
How many drops of water fill the ocean?
And on the shores, how many grains of sand?

How many bits of earth have formed the mountains?
How much steam erupts when geysers boil?
How many leaves and petals fall each autumn?
How many seeds have lain beneath the soil?

How many birds and beasts and crawling creatures
Have lived and bred and died through all the years?
And do we know when man was first created
And brought to this vale of laughter and of tears?

How many thoughts and dreams remain uncounted
That passed through the hearts and minds of all mankind?
We are so proud of facts and figures we have fathomed,
But how many answers will we never find?

How many can be sure of a tomorrow?
How many know just what the future brings?
And after death, just what shall we encounter?
Only God has knowledge of these things.

Madeleine Matthews

Mother

Mother,
how the days
bled
into each other
masking the true,
time
and beauty of life
and who'll see the struggles within?
And who are
"they",
but unfound sinners?
As a long and glorious upheaval does falter
cascading its many truths
down unto the earth
and so I become a digger
where shall ever I walk,
but to look?
And back again shall I go
'til my eyes do see
let misguidings be in their disguise
for they'll not
beguile
the one who "sees" with her mind
nor shall they ever endure
her will to survive!

Steven Paul Alfrey

Untitled

How sweet does the red rose smell?
How thorny is its stem?
The smell and sting of those weeds lose worth
when you're compared to them.

The night with its billion stars
is outshined by the day's sunrise,
but the lights of both worlds are eclipsed
by the beauty of your eyes.

No one has seen the depths
of the storming raging seas,
but you can more clearly perceived their depths
than see how deeply you've touched me.

Thomas Jonovich

Friend

A friend says: Look how we have changed
How we've gotten older we don't look the same,
How devastating, how insane we think!
We look in that mirror, and looking back -
is someone we lost,
Our youth, our days of dreams
and looking beyond,
When we would make everything clearer

Now we laugh
We look in the mirror,
of our lines in our face,
our hair showing silver
Our girth seems to expand
What seems to be a rapid pace,
Oh, my friend; but we
still are the same,
Our hearts are still there
our feelings unchanged
but oh, the pain!

Nora West

American Indians

Indians lived here first.
Hunted and fished in the untamed forests,
where now modern cities burst.

Their canoes glided quietly along the rivers,
which now are crowded with ships.

They created beautiful arts and crafts,
invented calendars and a system of math.

Their throbbing drums have waned
vast temples fallen into ruin,
but, Americas Indian heritage still remains.

Maureen Carmickle

My Sunflower Goddess

My thoughts are legion, clear, divers unjust,
I allot free rein, full of wanderlust.
My Sunflower Goddess plays her song
for me to cleanse within to stay fresh among
the Pleiades.

My Sunflower Goddess came to me in the mid-year
of my life, to send her song for my cheer,
to refine me, accept me, to raise me to the heights
she implores I can reach, just set my sights
on the Pleiades.

In cloudless skies of blue appears Mirasol, Mirasol,
face of loveliness, golden pedals full,
reaches out, a quest, are you he I seek?
Set out, fly with me, from on high take a peek
at the Pleiades.

I leave this exile land with my Goddess cold
to rise unbounded, her pedaled face behold,
and have no fear of dashing from on high
as I soared and hear the Mirasol song, I sigh
to the Pleiades.

J. J. Hinojosa

Rainbow

Red is a rose on a late afternoon,
Orange is a pumpkin on a bright day too.
Yellow is a very bright sun,
Green is a leaf so bright so young.
Blue is a river on a really stony street,
Violet is a grape so delicious so sweet.

Teari Schnakenberg

"Flea - B - Itis"

While in my reverie, a mischievous flea
posed to bite me on my knee,
Alas, it disappeared mysteriously.

Sylvan Dan Brody

The Rose

I am the rose, not just a rose.
I am a story of sunlight, a tale of gloom.
I am that from which true love grows.
I am dark as in death, a message of doom.

Alas, my thorns have pricked your lonely heart.
You have found joy where there once was none.
Yet, to the grimace of His pain, I took a part;
And bled the soul of the Begotten Son.

You think me the flower of love too oft.
Trust not my stem, but cherish the bud of red.
I should have soothed his wounds with petals soft;
But they used me to prick his mind instead.

So, pass me by in the garden, do not look down.
I can bring you pleasure or pain—only He knows.
Will I be a gift of love, perhaps a bloody crown;
I am a mystery. I am the rose.

Susan J. Rose

Abyss Of The Forgotten

Sometimes love, other times pleasure
"I" am conceived to be a joy
The future looks bright and prosperous
"I" am going to be the president
Successes have all been predetermined
"I" will become whatever "I" wish to be
"I" am now aware and can see all at hand

But, "WAIT!"

The love or pleasure is now mere regret
"I" shall no longer be a joy, "I" have become a burden
There is no longer a future
"I" will cease to exist in a short time
"My" successes have become your failures
"I" will become what you desire, For "I" have no choice
"My" awareness has been your misconception

"I" forgive you
for what was to be
and
for what was not.

Rene Casarez

Storm Madness

Everything is calm and gentle
I am happy and sentimental

A light drizzle begins
My mood darkens

As the thunder roars by
Madness can be seen in my eye

The wind, rain and ground are fighting insane
I am wanting to cause pain

Across the sky lightning is flaring
Bruises, bumps and cuts are appearing

Then the storm suddenly flees
And I am left at ease

Leslie Romano

Remember Me

Surrounded by thoughts
I am left behind.
I am but a memory;
Not more than a recollection
yet so much more than a fleeting thought.
I ache to live; to breathe; to exist,
if only for that moment
you remember me to be.
You want to change me; capture me; create me.
I am your past.
I am who you are today.
REMEMBER ME
and in doing so
REMEMBER YOURSELF
for only by knowing where you've come from
do you find your destination.

Tracy McGee

I Am America

I am america, I am all that is good of america.
I am the native american indian,
I am the irish immigrant and the scottish landowner,
I am the chinese american missionary worker;
For sure I am the african slave...

I am america! I am golden in color with hair and
Features of my indian and european ancestors.
I am all nations of people who have
Gathered here in america for peace, freedom and a better life.

I am america, I am full of hope regardless of
What I have seen of the injustices towards
All humanity. I can not dwell on all of these things
Or I will never be free

I am an indian princess who loves all of nature,
The blue sky, green grass and wild flowers
That seem to sprout up everywhere...
The majesty of the mountains and the
Beauty of a clear water stream.

I am america!

I am full of dreams.

Shirley Ladson

Shades Of Gray

I write the words that you read
I am the poet, I am the seed
I fill the imagination you make real
I make you see I make you feel

Do you know me from what I write?
To you it is black written on white
My words are but expressions from within
Some are happy some are grim

You don't know me, you never will
For I am only words transpired from ink, on the tip of a quill
And when my ink dries up then so shall I
For here I am safe to laugh, safe to cry

These words are my voice you need only hear
My sentences cry out, wanting someone near
My life is more than the black and white you see
Life is not all that clear to me

I am but a mixture of the two
Not one strong color, just a hue
For all my life has been this way
I see, feel and live in SHADES OF GRAY...

Linda Kay (Avramov)

Aimless Wandering

Nothing exists in this frail body I call myself,
I am utterly lost,
unknown to me is this world I inhabit,
I do not know why I feel this way,
I only know that I do,
I await Death,
for I know that this will doubtlessly come,
everyday I live this putrid existence I am brought closer to Him,
I've already surrendered,
all He must do now is claim me,
I shall willingly be His servant,
for it is in His domain that I belong,
my soul is dark just as His,
so I await,
await for the end of what some call life but for me is merely existence.

Roger Emmick

Why Live?

At the crack of dawn, as the sunshine stretches across the land,
I ask myself; Self, why should I live? Why should I live,
when I'm no longer safe in my own neighborhood. Playing in
the yard with no worries...gone. Riding my bike into unknown
areas...gone. But why? Is it because my peoples...my brothers
and sometimes my sisters can only see a gun's length in front
of them? At my young age, I already realize my life is worth
much more than a bag of weed. Still, why live? Why live
amongst a group of intelligent people when only the ignorant
ones shine!
Yesterday, little Johnny played catch with his dad. I wish I
knew mine. I search for role models, but no one rises.
Instead, I hear...Kid do I even resemble your mother or
father?
It is no longer the crack of dawn, but more toward the
beginning of dusk. As I look to both my sides in disbelief
that once again, I've been left alone. I say to
myself...Self; I have not come up with now self ful-filling
reason to live. Except, if there is not someone there to be a
beginning to a solution, then there cannot be an ending to a
problem. To see peace within my people, I then must be the
Alpha and the Omega...The leader that carries them to their
mental freedom.

Terrence King

Who Can You Turn To?

Who can you trust?
I ask the question.
Even when you must need a friend, everyone
seems to pretend they are a friend forever
till the end.

As the days, months, and years continuously
proceed, you began to see that later in life
people become so mean.
And people began to take advantage of you and
you think that you can manage it soon. By
running away and never let go so that no one
will never find what is within your soul.

The many laughters and cries of your old
friendships start running through your mind.
As your trials and tribulations will finally
come to an end. And you began to look around
you again and again thinking how honest
your true friends have been.

Rhianon Bacon

Despondent Hope

When the morning sun begins to dance upon my face,
I awake with a sullen tone and my happiness a trace.
A tranquil torture settles upon the room which surrounds,
Again and again within my brain this emptiness pounds.
I gaze about only to find none who care,
I exhale out a repulsive and destructive air,
It is enveloped in hatred and engrossed with lies,
All innocence and loyalty deeply it does despise.
Does this wretched world possess any of the values that we once cherished,
Has all love and nobility just simply perished?
As an addict deprived of it's constitutional bliss,
I crave for the warmth found only in human tenderness.
But to whom do I turn and where shall I seek?
When I live in a world that constantly preys upon the meek?
Like a blind man in search of light, for love I despondently grope,
But still within my heart remains a shred of hope.

Misty Rhiannon Goff

Paradise Is Brief

As the sun comes up,
I begin my journey through the forest.
The dew glitters on the patches of grass along the trail before me,
And the rays of sunlight sprinkle light between the leaves.
My first steps.

As the fresh air enters my lungs,
A smile appears on my face.
Behind me, I hear the song of a cardinal,
And the heart beats a little faster.
More steps are taken.

As the sky darkens,
A cold breeze blows across my body.
A snake slithers beneath my feet.
With each step, more effort is required.
I stop.

Suddenly, I realize it is too dark to see in front of me.
There is no moon to guide me back.
I fall, and the last breath enters my lungs.
A tear rolls down from my eye.
Paradise is brief.

Thomas Berntsen

A Moment

The very mention of her name sends my heart into a tailspin.
I begin to quiver like a leafless tree.
My mind takes flight along side the most heavenly of hosts.
My eyes twinkle as they look through the darkest of moments.
The memory of her face comes crashing like waves.
My being shines a light on this otherwise condemned futile place.
For one moment all is right in the world.
If only I could choose the moment;
Let God take me now:
For I would sip my last breath of air
With the greatest of smiles upon my face.
And for once the world would see a moment of true love!

Tim Prince

Lost In Love

My love is but a bird way up in the sky
That drifts above us aimlessly and longs sometimes to cry
My love is but a leaf falling from a tree
It shatters as it hits the ground - carelessly
My love is but a song touching peoples hearts
It doesn't matter - near or far - together or apart
My love is but a wave drifting and lost at sea
I wish another wave would crash right into me

Traci Amelsberg

The First Lady

Mother Theresa you have a twin,
I call her, "The First Lady," to begin.
I have known her for nearly half a century,
If I may please, make this entry.
A person who gives herself to others,
Her credits goes even further.
Her wealth doesn't include a lot of money,
Like a queen bee with lots of honey.
To open her home, no matter the number,
In fall, winter, spring, and summer.
Understanding plus love is what she gave,
To everyone who she saved.
No one could come and go, without her smile,
Her kindness stretched for miles and miles.
Regardless, of the difficulties that came her way,
She always said, "The future would be a better day."
As I have illustrated you can see,
Her wealth is unselfish generosity.
Being blessed, as she still is today,
She is richer, than yesterday.

Pearl M. Clemons

Magic In The Sky

Lying silent under endless stars,
I can feel the throbbing thunder beat
Call me back to bare and bloodstained Mars.
Divine lights that lace the sky to treat
Mortals' eyes with glimpses heaven bound
Fail to quench this burning, drum-like sound.

God unfurled an inky blanket whose
Riddled surface covered Earth in bloom.
Years have passed but still angels amuse
Themselves peering through from heaven's womb.
Would that I had such religious views,
Looking up on evening's cheshire moon.

Vistas dry, yet stained with blood, instead
Dominate the landscape of my mind.
Strange adventures, struggles strewn with dead,
Tales that made my life and dreams entwine.
I compose this, Burroughs, just for you
Whose imagination fanned mine too.

W. Jason Peck

Lost

The morning dew hasn't yet left the grass.
I can not know for certain what the road ahead will be.
The fog is thick and dense.
I am trapped. I am lost.
I can not see ahead.
Is there a fatal accident...pain?
Is there a dog running...fear?
Is there a meadow with beautiful flowers blooming...pleasure?
I can not tell.
I watch things drop from sight.
The car in front of me is disappearing from sight.
I can still make out his lights, but soon they too are gone.
Everything is gone.

Michelle Broun

Stolen Moments

I cleaned out all the Canadian coins in my car.
They'd been lying there for years
like lint in my pockets,
My only pair of jeans.
Quick and easy she comes to me
And that's how she leaves.
Believe me that's how she leaves.

Michael P. McCann

Gods Way

Standing on the in side looking out,
I can remember all of the times I was
filled with doubt.
Where did the love of God go?
And where's my life headed, when I get there
will I know?

Growing up never a fear for right or wrong,
now locked away for so very long.
People fading away into the past
I'm searching for a love I know will last.

Places and faces change as I go,
Understanding and knowledge. I reap and grow,
But nothing can replace the loss of
love or mother,
You can look around you and see it
on the faces of your sister or brother.

Miracles do happen and I'm waiting on mine today,
In the meantime I'll live and go Gods way.
No fears for losses lest my soul I do impart
I'm giving God my whole heart!

Sherry Colvin

The Plea

The time has come when you want to say goodbye
I can't even face you, because I am going to cry
You said you want me to let you go and be free
Why are you so blind to our love and can't you see
You are my world and life, and my reason to go on
I'll always love you, even if you are gone
I can't live without your tender love
You are my angel sent from above
Please I beg you for another chance
You have been my greatest romance
In my heart I felt like I never felt before
You took my body, mind and soul
All I ask is for your love in return
Our love together can forever burn
If you would only say, we will give it one more try
Then we won't have to say goodbye.

Tomasita Mary Martinez

I Never Knew

I never knew how much
I cared until you walked away
There's nothing more left to do
Nothing else left to say
I know I can't go on without you by my side
At least I didn't give up
At least I know I tried
I didn't see it coming
I didn't see it there
But you didn't say a word
So I guess you didn't care
I let my heart fall too fast
I gave my heart away
Now my love is gone forever
And there's nothing I can say

Shannon Smith

Freedom's Defenders Rest

They have gone, to a better land,
Over there, across the great, open divide.
Please take care of them, My Lord, Almighty God.

They sacrificed, their lives and loves,
For their country and its freedom loving people.
May they rest, in peace for now, and ever more.

Medford D. Harmon

Children Can Say the Funniest Things

Children can say the funniest things.
They run and shout and laughter rings
Throughout the house and off the walls.
Don't mind the mess. Step over the balls.
Pick up a pencil and write it all down,
Just as they say it, just as it sounds.
So you'll always have it, good or bad,
To cheer you up when you're feeling sad.

Sherry Taylor

The Black Ribbon

All at once I loved the warmth of your room.
I chased my shadow onto the thick red rug
and when you drew the curtain
and the soft lights glowed flesh toned and hot,
the vague imagined promises trembled and rose to my surfaces
under the soft yellow dress
my red heart beat faster than the seconds could ever race.

It was in that flood of heat and warmth
that you took me away,
when you saw me sitting in the old brown chair
and you gave me the black ribbon to hold in my hands
and the flower to wear in my hair
and you stared.

I itched and I flinched and I kept turning my head
but you wanted me still
so you painted —
two black wide open eyes
and a red mouth stunned silent;
somewhere I learned to stop moving and became
a study in color, a chef d'oeuvre, a soul you stole.

Marina Mohr

In February

I arise early in the morning
I conduct the song of the birds
With the baton of a branch
The distilled impatience of the wind
Silently sways the reeds lined against my window
And suddenly I watch clouds align across the sun
The cold blue sky of early February
Becomes colder.
And I sense that although we are not the same
We align in the wind.
As the reeds which silently dance
And the clouds which cling to the sun
In early February

Skip Norfolk

Summer Fun

In the sticky heat of the day,
I cracked on my bubble gum that had lost it's flavor.
The bees buzzed all around me for the sweet strawberry
savor that no longer existed.

I got a popsicle and watched it melt into a
shiny, cherry pool on the dusty earth.
I walked passed the sprinkler which all of a sudden
went wild and soaked me.

"Was this summer fun?"

At supper, I reached back to get a napkin;
over backwards I went with a bang!
Excusing myself from the table, the tablecloth
attached itself to me and came along for the ride.

As I readied myself for bed, the nagging thought
entered my mind again, "Was this summer fun?"

NOT!

Meaghan M. Norman

My True Dad

There is not much I can recall from the day Mom and I left you.
I do remember, though, sitting in the front of the 'big' green car.
I sat there like a lost puppy, found, being told what to do.
I didn't know what to think at the time because I was so confused.
As time progressed, I adjusted to all the changes.
Since I was so young, I thought I was special to have more parents than other kids.
Later, I did not like to leave my new home to visit you.
I was a prize, being fought for at two different sides.
I 'adopted' another dad.

This one was everything you weren't and everything you should have been.
He loved me as I was his own. I dreaded being with you, not him.
The day you decided to give me up forever was one of the happiest for me.
When I left the court room, which freed me from you, I felt two things.
I felt pain - you never again wanted to have anything to do with me.
I was your own flesh and blood and all you could do was rip my heart in two.
I felt joy - I now had someone I could call DAD!
He cherishes that title in his heart, you could careless.
When I needed someone the most, who was always there?
Him, not you.
He is and always will be my only father.

Tasha Reisz

From A Distance

From a distance, I can see you standing there.
I don't know why you are there, but you are.
And, from that distance, I can see you like I have
never seen you before.

From a distance, you are not very clear,
but, I know why you came.
You came one last time
to see the flowers bloom and the trees grow.
But, most of all, you came to see me one last time.

From that distance, you are so very clear
in my eyes.

Nicole C. Zanelotti

Ages Lost

As I look into the dark tomorrow,
I don't see tomorrow but visions of today.
The warm summer sun, shining its golden rays down upon every living pore of my body, and filling my mind with memories thought lost.
Then I see myself young and new, sailing along the winds of time.
The current is strong, but I'm not fighting it, just letting it take me where it may.
When the wind finally ceases and my feet touch the virgin soil,
I look back through the ages and see my own family and friends that died.
They stand before me with their arms outstretched, beckoning for me to follow,
But with every advancing step I take, they get farther and farther away, until finally...they disappear.
And once again I'm left alone in the world,
Left to think and ponder.
My eyes wander down to my old crippled hands,
Withered by years of labor.
And a cool ominous wind begins to blow.
I remember the first time the sun touched my body and lifted me to the heavens,
And the calm sullen night that brought me down.
A tear rolls down my cheek and I realize that even through time.
Tears, always stay ageless.

Mathew C. Holding Eagle

I Dreamt That...

Just like Martin Luther King, I had a dream.
I dreamt that no one would starve and no one would
have a belly that was swollen and ached with pain.

I dreamt that racism would be a word that would not exist
and peace would be the word to describe the world.

I dreamt that love would flood our hearts and there would
be no room for hated to live there.

I dreamt that if my dream came true, the world would be a
better place to live for all.

Just like Martin Luther King, I had a dream.

Samuel Gutierrez Jr.

I Dreamt That Night

One night, as I laid to rest, I dared to dream a dream.
I dreamt the world was at its best, crystal clear were the streams.
The flowers grew in hundreds, the animals were wild and free.
All the world was humbled, and they canceled all decrees.

They chose to lay their weapons down, they loved their fellow men.
They let a smile replace a frown, they all walked hand in hand.
For the world was at peace, no more reason to fight.
In my blanket of fleece, that's what I dreamt that night.

And when I awoke, when the dream was done.
Someone spoke of a new war begun.
And I thought to myself, 'Will it ever end?
Will they ever think of others? Will they ever become friends?'

I have reasons to believe and reasons to doubt
That people don't see what friendship is about.
And maybe someday my dream will come true.
When all people are safe from each other on through.

Nicole Arbuckle

Dreams Untold

At night I drift into a somber sleep,
I fall into another world so deep.
No one, but me has seen this other side,
I can get away from reality, just hide.
These thoughts and feelings collide in my mind,
I try to sort things out and deal with all I
find.
Sometimes in this world it's either laugh or
cry.
I don't understand, I'm always wondering why?
when I awake the memories unfold,
to all of my dreams untold.

Tessa Murphy

"Woven Reflections"

I see the loneliness that lives in your eyes,
I feel the longing, time has denied,
The pattern of our lives are woven in
this unreadable design.

Why time has chosen to weave this pattern thus,
or is it the angels that has made this time us?
Are we supposed to question this gift from God above?

The why we cannot unravel, the pattern so designed?
By some fate or master hand we don't know in this time,
Are reflections of my life mirrored in your eyes?
In this crazy pattern, do I see me in your design?

Rebecca Gail Mathews

Rain

As I walk out into tonight,
I feel the rain falling as gentle as the touch of dawn's first light.
Rain, rain don't ever go away.
Rain all night and day.
As it falls on the ground and upon my face,
I feel the tears of past memories fall into place.
It will wash away everything that has gone bad.
It can bring life to all as well as take all that we had.
Rain, please give us peace among this troubled world.
What most can't understand is that people have to live together.
Through life, death, hate, love, and all kinds of weather.
As the tears fall from one more persons own rain;
We must help each other to help everybody.
The rain of life flows through all of us.
We may not have much longer to complain or fuss.
As the rain falls down this pallid and lonely face;
I feel the pain followed by tears of past memories fall into place.

Trissi Hineman

Escape

When I close my eyes and pull the covers over my head,
I go to my dream world, I go to bed.
I wish I could live there, instead of living here,
I would always be happy, I'd never shed a tear.
I am grateful for what I have, what I've got isn't bad,
But I still like to go there sometimes, like when I'm sad.
It is my escape, my special dreamland,
I wish you had one so you would understand.
When I get mad or even a little sad, I run upstairs and just cry,
And cry and cry until, at last, both my eyes are dry.
This is when I make my trip, this is when I sleep,
And let out all my secrets, for my soul to keep.
Even now, when I get sad,
I like to go there, once in awhile,
Just to make me happy,
Just to make me smile.

Rachael Smith Caldwell

Crissy Saylor

I had an incurable disease.
I had the courage of a lion,
And the compassion of a lamb.
But that didn't matter.
Because all the courage in the world
Couldn't save me.
Not even the angel of death
Could blame me for trying.
I was only sixteen, so
It really didn't seem fair.
I never got to marry or have a family.
I hope my friends whom I sadly left behind
Get to have all the wonderful things I didn't.
Thank you everyone, thanks for believing in me.

Susan Blanchard

When Will It End

Children crying because their stomachs
hurt from hunger; when will it end
Children crying because there is no
shelter from the cold or blazing sun;
when will it end
Children crying from physical and mental abuse;
When will it end
Children dying from lack of food, shelter and medical
care; when, when, will it end

Louise Padgett Sutton

Visions From The Heart

In the sunrise's wakening smile with bright new promises of
morning,
I have witnessed a spectacular view
Eyes of opulent browns
Smiles of equal brilliance
Profiles of seductive measure.
In the music of mid-day, in the tender soaring vibrancy of love
songs,
I have heard your voice
Sensuous soloist united in Spirit
Virtuosic sword of humanity
Majestic Phoenix conquering all barriers.
In the evening's tender caress, sheltering the warmth of sunsets,
I have felt your serene touch
Boundaries of no exits
Pompous excitement within
Interludes of breathless ecstasy.
All things beautiful in my world have whispered a breath of
sensitivity, magic, and the miracle of you
I love you today and forever more.

Michelle Marano

Great Temptation

Will it ever be the same my friend when I watch you sing?
I hear the tension in your voice, I wonder what it will bring.

Is it easy for you to sing those songs, does something play your part?
It's not the one you love right now, but the one whose in your heart.

Should I cast my spell of love on you or would it waste my time?
I've watched you so patiently, oh why is love so blind?
Will it ever be the same my friend, the way we used to be?
The kiss hello, the kiss goodbye, it's just not enough for me.

Will it ever be the same again, the hours on the phone?
Reciting poetry and love songs - when we're all alone.

Will it ever be okay for you to walk back toward my life?
Are you happier now than then - in your eyes I read advice.

Sometimes I pray at night for you to watch me dance.
The fire on the floor - so wanting your romance.

You gave me the most memorable times,
I could dance with a great sensation.
Remember all the songs I wrote
While our love was the Great Temptation.

Nancylynn Laauwe

All

We trapped the morning in our own disbelief.
I knew we did when the sun prevailed a kinder light,
There is nothing definite to explain, and I know nothing more.
The colors of heart are sweet when the screaming is a song.
You are an instrumental reason, you give me the control.
There is a valley of creams. Angels seem to enjoy-
Riding the stars that pall into our hearts.
On and on we'll go, one in all, the world is ours
The candle is soft and glowing now.
The morning is night but will always be new and fresh,
Like a newborns smile at a simple pleasure.
And the extreme of pain and pleasure is simplicity.
We both know it but won't breathe a word.
When we're together-something takes over, memories to
Come we make each day-and the feeling is love.

Nicole Egletes

Untitled

You are my guardian angel - always
I know that you are here
Watching over my shoulder
Guiding me, helping me, protecting me
You are such a big part of today, even though you are so far
I hope it is beautiful where you are, and that you are happy
Not a day goes by that I do not think of you
Please know that even though you cannot physically be here
You are no less loved, nor forgotten
If you only knew the emptiness inside me
Especially on this special day, because you are gone
But now someone wants to fill part of that void
He has promised to take care of me
He wants to love me forever, please be proud
I ask that you be with us, and be happy for us
Welcome him into your heart as I have
Guide us down a lifetime of love and happiness
I thank you for all you have done, and I know you love me
Will you now love us and, daddy, remember that no matter what
I still am and always will be your "little girl"

Victoria Marie Knotts

Lack-Of-Sleep Poem

You snored last night.
I laid beside you,
hating you in a flourishing, festering passion
for keeping me awake
as my eyes
stuck
with grape jelly to re-runs of the ten o'clock news
and angels in army boots rode the subway to heaven
packed in so tightly their wings were smashed and broken
and their feet squished the guts
from caterpillars and chameleons on the floor
as they ran from the mushrooms
to the kitchen
where I would make you
breakfast
and you would hold your
milk
and your sausage
would try to find my
eggs.

Laurie Nash

Best Friends

I know I have a chance, but I made a mistake
I let other peoples feelings influence the decision I made
Now five years later, and years of being friends
I realize what I have done, and the pain will never end

Sometimes I see you, and wish you were with me
But lately, every time we talk you seem to retrieve
I don't know what I have done, or what I will do
But I can honestly say, I want to be with you

We're the same age, yet you seem to be younger
You go out for fun, love, pain, or is it a hunger
Life is more serious, I wish I could make you understand
You need someone, and I am holding out my hand

We're getting older and there is still love for you
There is part of me hanging on, to see what you will do
But I will try to start my own life, instead of sitting hear waiting
Before our friendship turns my love into hating

Best friends, why does it have to be this way
Once you wanted me and now I want you
Why is best friends the best that we can do
Best friends!

Michael Shane Carr

Under the Sun

As I sit under the sun closing my eyes.
I let the warm sun warm my face.
I am carried off to a distant beach I can hear
a light breeze flowing through the trees and it
reminds me of waves dancing and playing in the
water. As a helicopter flies over head I wonder
[??] where is he going and what is he doing.
As a strong wind carries me of to a giant
Sea where the waves are ripping back and forth,
Like a whip cracking at a horse drawn carriage,
as the boat rocks back and forth I am carried
back to my towel where I slowly open my eyes and
let the sun's brilliance slowly creep in then I'm
flooded by the sun's light and discover once
again God's wonderful creation.

Natalie Jacobson

My Choir

Some Days I seem to find myself, outside of heaven's door,
I look about and say, I couldn't hope for any more.
In delightful contentment, I just stand there so meek,
While these scholars of lyric, hit a choralistic peak.
As my eyes travel quickly, through the aggregate of sound,
The array of the participants, would make many head turn round.
The knack of the director, and the message she conveys,
To achieve such uniformity, dedication is what pays.
I'm ever proud to be there, entwined amongst the rest,
An apprentice, I can only hope, to do my very best.
I take note of many faces, appreciate the blend,
It's instilled in us, articulate down to the very end.
As the voices close, the mighty organ moans with pleasing tone,
The multitude is speechless, they detect we stand alone.

William Driscoll Jr.

Upon Leaving This Universe

I heard a far-away scream, a sound of dying departure.
I looked to the sky and saw a new hole among the stars.
Gaping dark and ominous, this pit of unending black
seemed to draw the heavenly lights into it,
to gobble them up like a lean lion, never to be seen again.

That last scream of forever farewell
announced the death of a star.
That light has left our universe
and entered the realms of
unknown darkness.
The karmic wheel must be mighty indeed
To have turned on this ancient helium god.

When I die I too may scream
but not as loudly as that distant brother:
For I know now, by that star's cry of anguish,
that I am part of a vast and inescapable nature-
That I am not alone.

I share my destiny with every living being,
even the screaming stars.

Richard G. Moll

Fairy Tale

Cool, bare feet light on twilight's clear blue stream
Tip-toe silently to rest on mossy green
Transparent eyes with hues of blue and flecks of gold reflecting
Flaxen locks of braided flowers, the agile stems connecting
Trembling fingers delicate and reaching, touching starlight
Laughter tinkling rhapsody with moonbeams dancing so bright
Twirling 'round arms raised high, the petals fall on dewdrop ground
Secret smile for dawn's first light
Sweet rapture not to be earthbound

Marcel Cornett

In Mysterious Ways

As I walked my dog, with a buck in my pocket,
I looked up to God in the sky,
when an enormous white cloud in the perfect formation of a feather floated by.
I marveled and wondered and stood in great awe,
Then off I ran to the Lottery store.
With dreambook number in mind,
I plunked down my buck, and thought
"God, please let me score!"
At the day's end, and the Lottery's evening broadcast for sure,
I watched the Lottery drawing and smiled when I saw,
I could say "Thank you, God!, You've given me $500 more!"

Michael A. Harrison

Untitled

My dearest love,
I love you more and more,
As the sun rises and sets,
Rises and sets over and over,
Over and over like an earthquake or taxes.
It seems as though my love is diminishing,
Like the clean, clear air and water which we struggle to intake,
However it won't ever die.
It won't ever die.
I shall keep it inside of me, like so many things,
I will have it even when I don't show it.
Why are things so confusing here?
Death, Life, Girls, people in general!
What can you do to satisfy any of it?
Who knows? Who cares?
The end of Life is near.

B. J. Kirschmann

My Eternal Cap

I once bought a cap to cover my head
I loved that ole cap, even wore it to bed
At first when new it was proud of its shape
As it belittled the world from the top of my pate.
It was proud and aloof as each shape I would primp
Alas the years took its toll and the cap soon went limp.
The sweat from my brow soon loosened the thread
It settled closer and closer round the top of my head
'Tis sad to see that the cap had to age
And face obscurity like the end of a page
Yet 'tis not the end—as an idea was born
Let youth carry on with the tattered and torn
Once more the cap would be lifted up high
With steps that are youthful and spry.
So as I come to the end of my story
I bequeath my cap to my good friend Lori.

Marcus Oladell

Thinking Of Jesus

When my life ends and my savior I meet;
I hope my work here has been complete!
Down on my knees I want to go,
And rivers of tears shall overflow
Then washing his feet, I'll dry with my hair;
And hope that my savior will welcome me there!
And smile and remind me why he died on the tree
And how the ones who obey him forever are free
And how the ones who obey him forever are free
There to sing with the angels so wondrous and sweet;
And loved ones shall gather, each other to greet.

Laura E. McPherson

The Wall

I always try to show my happiness,
I may show that I am not sad,
I may show that I don't care,
I really do care,
I am hiding behind a wall,
This wall protects me,
Makes it so I don' have to show who I really am,
This makes me feel safe,
No one can hurt me when I am behind this wall,
For behind this wall shows my true self,
I don't think I will be glad to get rid of this wall,
It has hidden my deepest feelings my entire life,
This wall is a part of me now,
For when I come out from behind this wall it will be like saying,
Watch out world here comes the new me.
I don't think anybody wants to know the new
me just yet,
I won't totally forget this wall,
I may some day go behind it again, as for now,
The world is going to see a new me.

Tracy Tracy

We Go On! In Spite Of

I welcomed you in my world and my heart was never the same.
I met you when I was a girl laughing and running with the wind.
I loved you as a woman, and now I keep you safe in my heart, with respect and dignity, even in your death as a lady.
I am standing in front of the mirror but I see you.
I wash the Leien again, again Today but your scent is engraved much too deep.
I turn the page of my calendar guess what?
It would have been our forty ninth Wedding Anniversary. So instead
I celebrate you in death.
I know now that no one can quiet me if I lose control.
So I go on.

Marilyn Hayes Jackson

Memories

Could I but rid my mind of mem'ries from the past.
I might awake and find myself at peace at last.
But oh! What should I do - with memories all lost?
For in them there is you - I could not bear that cost.

Those youthful happy days when our whole world was so young
Your sweet and gentle ways, loves sweetest songs we sung.
Our happy carefree times, sweet blissful hours we shared,
Days and nights like vintage wines-soft words that said we cared.

Our wedding day so fine, on a lovely day in May.
I was yours and you were mine on our perfect holiday.
Then the children came along as time slipped quickly by.
Each was like a lovely song and made twinkles in our eye.

We watched them as they grew, and loved them every day.
Each day was something new as they moved along life's way.
The everyday routine the love all through our life
Gave the darkest day a sheen with joy you were my wife.

Now, you're with me no more, yet precious thoughts I keep.
My heart is deathly sore with dreams of you so deep.
But I do not despair, for we will be one again
And I know exactly where but the Lord won't say just when.

Robert J. Simmons

Life Stories

Now that you've finished the chapters of your life.
I miss you, but know in some small way your here
showing me the purpose for your strife.

When memories of your story move me to shed tears
I know your teaching me to embrace living
and cast away all my fears

It seems my eyes were clouded by unimportant things
Now because of you, I appreciate health, happiness,
and the simple joy that love brings

As the last pages turn, I see your fight to
hold onto life was a valiant one
you taught me to stand my own ground,
not to turn around and run

The story you wrote served to teach
myself as well as others
that love and understanding can uplift us
while hate and indifference only smothers

So, I hope wherever you may be
you realize just how much
you have opened my eyes to see.

Lisa Dugan

Debbie's

As I look into the midnight sky and see God's beautiful creation
I often wonder "What more could be out there"
Only if God would let me see his wonderful universe
Beyond what we have here on earth

There are universes to see And galaxies to explore
There are stars to study And planets to view
We have many things here But what do we have out there

Who knows there might be a cure for cancer
Or a solution for world peace
There could be higher technology
Or a way to rid pollution

Then I think of what I have here A beautiful lady who loves me
And whom I give all my love And couldn't think of straying from

It's someone I give my every thought to
Someone I love to spend my every moment with
The love I have for her can't compare To the wonders out there

When God created you he created the greatest wonder in the universe
There is no substitute out there for the love we have for each other.

Michael J. Manuel

For It's His Will

It breaks my heart, to see you like this,
I only pray, I could heal it with a kiss.
But kisses can't heal, what's going on inside,
And that we must face, we can not hide.

For hiding won't fix, this terrible mess,
All we can do, is do our best.
To hold back the tears, and sorrow we feel,
And give it to the Lord, its his to heal.

The Lord has His reasons, this we've been told,
It's in His hands, we must be bold.
Bold enough to except, what's to come,
And not loose the faith, and where it comes from.

Faith is what, will carry us through,
We must believe, He won't fail you.
Trust in Him, as He wants you too,
And you'll find out, there's nothing He won't do.

"Me"Linda L. Maynard

Face of the Night

As I walk the empty roads at night,
I pass many flickering street lights....

Just when I think I'm walking alone,
I see a shadow in the lights dome...

Just when I think it's the face of darkness
meaning me harm...

I realize it's my savior,
with wide open arms...

Now, as I walk the crowded streets
in daylight...

I'm no longer in fear...
....of the empty nights....

Beverly Cady Rowe

Distant Friend

I sit and gaze at the setting sun as it bids a fond ado;
  I peer at the glistening rise far away, and often think of you.
The morning comes with the spirited light and dances across my face;
  And my mind turns to thinking of you, in a gentle and distant place.
The hands of time will not retreat, nor sacrifice one hour;
  It will not delay one moment for us, for it has not the power.
But time past is a kinder friend, who allows us an embrace.
  A moment to peer at the sun with joy, and view your loving face.

Ronald I. Gould

A Gift Of Heart

As I touch this heart to my warm skin
I pray it shall encompass my deep love within
Angels etched in picture perfect gold
for you to touch each day, for you to hold.

The passion of two souls we so admire
one touch, hug or kiss adds fuel to the fire
Though we agree two hearts needing one another
two different worlds cant live within the other.

Eyes of feelings, so many sacrifices we make
Young promises made in marriage now left to fate.
The vows early spoken, the cards already dealt
we uphold our commitments in pain of what our hearts felt.
When your spirit wanders and forms memories of two —
Touch upon this heart, it is me missing you...

Susan Kuckowicz

If I Could Be Anything...

If I could be anything, I'd want to be...
I rock all alone sitting under a tree.
Maybe I'd be the air all around,
of else a raindrop sent to the ground.
Maybe a waterfall so peaceful and clear.
Or at least a person who has only one fear

If I could be anything I'd want to be...
A little fish swimming deep in the sea.
I'd like to be a person who cannot hear,
sitting in a corner shedding only one single tear.
Maybe I'd be a person who has a need,
to kill and see others bleed.

If I could be anything I'd want to be...
A blind person who cannot see.
I wouldn't mind to be a lion so brave and bold,
or ancient writings with a story yet to be told.
Maybe a bullet made of lead.
To tell you the truth I'd rather be dead.

Sherrie Bakke

You're Still In My Dreams

I had a dream the other night, perhaps you'll think it's strange.
I saw a herd of horses grazing up on heaven's range.

And yes, there she stood! A black Thercheron.
Oh, so graceful, as she was when she was down here on Earth.

This majestic horse, I knew her well. I once owned her, you see.
No, perhaps I have wronged, I think that she owned me.

For years she had served her friends on Earth.
But then, oh too soon, came that final day.
From which she left me and did depart;
I left there standing with tears and my broken heart.

So, if horses go to Heaven, and I'm sure they do.
Then this Christmas wish I make,
Some how, some way, in my prayers I pray.
She knows I loved her most of all.
And this message I send along to my dearest Friend, Kahlu,
For old times sake.

Mary W. Dobrin

The Sailing Stone

Clad in suit, with eyes of mahogany,
I saw you then, dressed in black, weeping there.
I watched as you shed one tear upon me
And kissed thee the Stone with thy lips so fair.
Cast away was the tear, sorrow set sail.
A rose, a relic of love unfurling,
You had taken as you hid in your veil.
In my mind, your mien shone like sterling.
As we parted, I glanced at you once more,
In the chaste white of angels you appeared.
I now would have the heavens to explore
And to go alone is a fate much feared.
But mem'ries still remain, I'm not alone
As you bend to the earth and kiss the Stone.

Mark Lomanno

Untitled

As I sit in a daze under a big oak tree
  I see a beautiful warmth of fur sitting next
  to me full of sweetness.
Little creations of someone's imagination flying
  around me.
There's a soft quiet humming sound flowing
  with the wind.
A gentle life-like creation growing deep
  beneath the grass - its full of color and
  innocence, peaks up from the grass for air
  and never makes it back down before it dies.
I start wondering are we fit to be in a place
  as gentle and wonderful as this?

Lauren Stauffer

I Am Your Friend

I am your friend; I seek no gain.
I value your needs; I feel your pain.
If you should call, I will be right there.
And if you don't, I will not despair.

I simply will wait, and be ready for you.
I believe that is what a good friend would do.
There may come a time when I can do more,
And when you will share like you did before,

But first I give space, from deep in my heart.
We can't start anew, but again we can start.
I ask for no favors; true love is my end.
I will be here! I am your friend!

Paul A. Blechner

Wings Of Talent

Beyond the bliss of where the fowls fly,
I see reflections of life in the depths of the sky;
a natural peace so comforting warm,
but along the way I'm brought before storm.
I'll struggle strong to sore straight
with the wings of the living;
every moment giving thanks, to he,
by whom wings are given;
for without him I'd fall
to the dust of the floor,
suffer life and be no more.
I say no! instead, I'll take those wings
above clouds and vain dreams,
past the blackest rain and rough wind streams,
go as high as I can in all good things
where I can see the clouds dance
as the starlight sings.
I'll chase my dreams as a sparrow, free,
'til the heavens make known my purpose to me.

Richard Faraino

"I Miss The Man I Fell In Love With"

I talk but, you don't listen.
I see you but, you don't notice me.
I cry but, you don't comfort me.
I yearn for your touch but, you don't hold me.
I hurt but, you show no emotions toward me.
I feel down but, you are not there to lift me.
I want to be appreciated but, I am not!
I want to be allowed to be myself, but, I am not.
I want the old you and I back but, they're gone.
I miss the good times we had,
  The bad not out weigh the good.
All the reasons why I fell in love with you,
  Seem to constantly fade away.
I miss the man I fell in love with.
The man I fell in love with, I ask myself
  was he real or someone I hoped for?

Linda Hunter

For My Father

When I look in your gentle eyes
I see your strength and wisdom inside
A man full of love for his children and wife
A man who has given so much all his life

My childhood days are precious to me
Our Sundays together are sweet memories
I keep them treasured in a special place
Thinking of them brings a smile to my face
Listen to the words I have to say
Your father's presence is with us today

His voice is strong, yet soft with care
He spoke of his son and the love that you share
Stories of him you tell with pride
With the deep devotion you carry inside

I wish I could have known this man
To share in his laughter and sit on his knee though
I believe, I have felt his love, through the love you give to me

The ring you wear is a symbol of his love
He looks down on you from the heavens above
Some words from your father he has longed to say
He is proud of the son that he sees today.

Susan Elizabeth Olsen

Redeemed Soul

I lived for myself and just how I pleased
I served not God because He knew not me
The blood Jesus shed was so long ago
I have lived my life with nothing to show
Now I lay on my bed, that leads me to death
My heart is not strong as I take my last breath
As my spirit departs I walk on toward hell
Suddenly, I am stopped by a very sweet smell
As I turned my head, my legs could not stand
Jesus before me stretched out His hand
He forgive my sins and held me so near
My life was just starting, I had nothing to fear
My spirit He returned to my body that day
I'm a new creation with something to say
Now I cry, Jesus is Lord!
I am His soldier, righteousness my sword
He died for me so I might live
Eternally, my praise I will give
Though my whole life I stumbled and fell
He saved me from going through the gates of hell

Pam Mantooth

Song Of Myself

I stand not alone,
I stand upon a world of war and peace,
I stand among family and friends, who accept me until the very end.

I live a life working for success,
I live a life of harmony,
I live a life of ignorance, but through education that
will all come to an end.

I wish for the abolishment of the still existing inequality.
I wish for the opportunity to share my love to all.
I wish for the sufferings of all to come to an end.

I will love humanity unconditionally,
I will love the simplicity of life.
I will love honesty, loyalty, and respect until the very end.

As I look into my inner self I find a little girl,
Ready to emerge from her cocoon,
And enter into the unsheltered world with ken intentions,
To make a difference to all of mankind.

I do not stand alone,
I stand united,
Until the very end!

Linh Hue Ly

"Lonely Walls"

Here I sit, in this lonely room.
I stare at the walls, and think of my groom.

For he's up in heaven, he's climbed the stairs,
And soon I'll go up, and meet him there.

You see, I am sick, and in a nursing home.
I have no family, to whom I belong.

I'm losing my eye-sight, and my teeth have fallen out.
But that's no reason, to sit here and pout.

I'll just have to wait, for when the Good Lord calls.
And then I'll no longer, be staring at these walls.

So I'll just sit here, and wait my turn.
For there's still so much, that he wants me to learn.

Someday you, too, may be in a "home."
And I just pray, that you're not all alone.

For there is no joy, hidden in these walls.
You'll just have to wait, for when the
Good Lord calls!!

Tammy Benson-Ross

Somewhere Over New Mexico

As I am floating across this grand heaven,
I start to realize how secluded my life is.
Through one small opening is a window to the world.
No walls, no boundaries,
Just miles upon miles of vast planes.
I would love to explore these unknown lands,
for it seems that in my life I am trapped:
Every new day brings forth another ending,
and with every new ending I become terrified.
Are the walls of life closing in around me?
Am I just letting them take control of my desires?
Can I just stop for one minute and say to myself, I am alive.
I can!
I can push these barriers down, expanding my horizons,
because as I look out this small port hole,
I realize that life isn't what is right in front of my eyes.
Life is anything I do or anywhere I go.
The adventure is what stops the seclusion.
The thrill is what makes me look forward to the unexpected,
And the love is what holds it all together.

Margaret Bello

Untitled

With each and every passing day
I thank God for the blessing he's brought my way

I thank him for the roof I have over my head
the clothes on my back and a nice warm bed

I thank him for the food I have to eat,
and the shoes without holes that cover my feet

I thank him for the health of my family and friends
and for giving me a love that has no end

I thank him each day for a new chance at life,
but I thank him most of all for making you my wife

Though life can be hard and filled with adversity
I look at what I have and realize God has smiled upon me

For he has given me the greatest gift any man could receive
You as my wife and the new life we conceived.

Scott R. Turrentine

My Love,

Each night whilst I'm drifting off to sleep
  I think of thee
Thou art so real in my mind's eye
  I truly see thee
Thou art here
I touch thee
I smell thy fragrance and taste thy sweetness
Whenst thou art gone from me
  I feel no loss
Thou art ever in my mind
Thou art the maker of the beats of my heart
Thou art so deeply ingrained in my soul
  There is no thee
  There is no me
  But only the oneness of us
  The oneness of we

Laura Strauss

Grain Of Sand

He gave to me a small grain of sand;
I took the grain and held it tightly in my hand.

He gave to me a love so true;
I took the love and divided it by two.

He gave to me months of joy and fun;
I took the months and counted the year as one.

He gave to me memories of two years;
I took the memories and shared with him my tears.

He gave to me a new life of eternal love;
I took the life and thanked the Lord above.

He gave to me a ring of gold, to last forever;
I took the ring and promised we'd part never,

He gave to me a star to wish upon;
I took the star but he was soon gone.

He gave to me his blessings, before the angels took him away;
I took the blessings and love him more every day.

Rebecca J. Wilde

Beau Soleil

Beau soleil
I understand how others came to worship your mighty energy...
Your gentle tentacles of springtime joy
Caress my cheeks seductively, leaving them blushed.
Even the leaves follow your movements, with avid anticipation.
How do you make the sky appear such a joyous blue,
When I know it is an empty void, bleakness beyond imagination?
The moon even turns her face
To shine in your radiance
Kissed in your warming embrace.
You must be more than burning gases
And tugging gravity.
Do you compel us to do things we should not
Or help us to do those that we should?
What mighty force are you
Ever present star of the day?

Linda C. Books

4th Of July 1995

Just let me die on the 4th of July
I want to die on the 4th of July
I don't have any motivation
'cuz I'm in a state of depression
My life seems like a lie
Makes me want to die
I have nowhere to turn
No way out that I can discern
No one that cares or is concerned
I'm all alone in a black hole
With a broken heart and a sad soul.
Everyday I face a brick wall.
No hope, no way out of it all
Everyday I constantly cry
That's why I'm giving up and I just want to die.

Theresa Mrozowski

Champion

To be a champion is a dream.
To be the best at just one game.
To do something no one has done.
To go forward, to stride to be the best.
To improve as you go on.
Bringing out the champion in us,
takes a little confidence, and commitment.
if this is in you, you are a true champion.

Scott Marut

Changing The True Colors

Your words used to comfort me with their softness and truth
I was naive then.
I did not know the unconscious lies resting under your tongue
But my heart was on my sleeve and the deceit slithered underneath it,
squirmed and squeezed until my heart slid off landing flat on the hard
floor covered with your wild kats.
Your ears grew pointed, your teeth grew sharp, and flesh to fur
you roared your coldest roar and devoured my loyal heart.
I walked alone, a sad mouse living in a hole in the wall we
built together.
I formed furniture from your banished leftovers.
And I became a leftover, frozen in the icy cooler, trapped
in Tupperware, pushed to the back, ignored for something new.
And I became something new.
I became the glass in the window pane and I still held your careless
pane.
I saw all ways, your ways and the unknown.
And I became unknown, transparent to the foolish eye, as well as my
own.
Then you returned, knocked on my pane, and invited yourself in.
So you and your kats nestled in my pane but you got wet and it didn't
come from the rain it came from my pulsing pane.
You and your kats left me behind for a drayer place but left you my
withered heart on my solid wooden pane.

Tricia L. Sebes

True Sorrow

At the moment I saw thee,
I was quietly sobbing with an indescribable pain:

It was because thine immaculate face made me aware
Of my ugly stained one with dust and sweat.

It was because the subtle perfume
Of thine vivid vitality made me aware
Of my fading youth which I can not hold.

It was because thine fresh and crisp firmness
In delicate beauty made me aware
Of my weakness and timidity in roughness.

It was because thine intangible lofty grace
Made me bow to thee quietly
As if thee was an Immaculate Goddess.

It was because I became to know
What the true sorrow is - living with the memory
Of my own lost and forgotten fragrant crown
Long ago.

Ok-Gyung Kim

Refugee

Under the sun's golden syringes I knew
I was in the middle of some rite of acupuncture
I knew goddamn well there was more fluoride
Soap on the giving end of the scythe
Deciding though on barbed justice,
And the highways on my hand, convinced
Seas are but tears of the martyr
Wearing poor sneakers, I divided
The wind with pure adrenaline
Courage and fear are equally fast
Causing rifts and shards of breeze

When I reached the other side
My hands were no longer hands but squid
The reason was simple
My poor sneakers
my jacket made of night.

Neal Amaral

Who Am I?

I was thrown against a rock near the sea,
I was shattered and broken to pieces.
I tossed and tumbled endlessly, being roughed up all the while.

I was washed up against the sand repeatedly and my once
Sharp and jagged edges have now smoothed over.
If I remain in this turmoilous and shifting existence, I
Will dwindle away to nothing.
There are moments that I am in the dark and am submerged in
Water, and other moments that I can lay on the beach and
sparkle in the sun.
Things feel so repetitious, a change would be welcome.

I've drifted back momentarily to that peaceful,
sandy spot on the beach
Oh look, a little girl! Oh, please notice me shining here
in the sun. Wait, I think she sees me, she's coming right
toward me - Yes! - She picks me up, looks me over - turning
me this way and that. Please take me with you - use me,
exhibit me, add me to your collection, so that I may find
another part of me - or some of my sea glass friends!

Sharlene K. Perry

Life

What were you?
I was the ink of the pen
I was the silken paper that received it's flowing script.

I was the string of a harp
I was the golden tones that combined to form melodies.

I was the spark of a light
I was the wax dripping and melting from the ignited blaze.

I was the cloud in the sky
I was the wind that blew the tree tops and all were under my power.

Who are you?
I am the vision
I am the bright green eyes that beheld the wonder.

I am the idea
I am the lips that formed the words of the thought.

I am the love
I am the heart that danced wildly with excitement.

I am the soul
I am the body that acts as a shell for life.

I am the muscle
I am the arms thrust out for affection from around me.

Patricia Anne Reeder

"Rainbow Colored Houses"

Rainbow colored houses on cobblestone streets,
Pride and heritage run within them deep.

They speak of a time gone by
When men were stoic and women cried.

Representing a way of life
Torn apart by war and strife.

Children's laughter echoes the sound
Of cannon shots heard the country round.

Seeing them you are drawn to say
They were left to enjoy another day.

Terri L. K. Wiggins

She Cried...Tonite

She cried on my shoulder tonite
I wept on the inside for her pain

When I saw her full lips and hair that night...
When I saw the sensual caress of her hips
Against her dress.
I knew that tonite she'd let me
Touch her. Kiss her. Feel her. Adore her.
I knew that we'd be one as lovers should be.

This was all that I'd dreamed of

What she needed though
Was understanding enough to ease her pain
So I listened and tried to hear
I even said the right words.

In return I received the joy of seeing...
Seeing what a lover really should be.
Seeing what a relationship really should mean.

Well...
Everything's alright
Because she cried on my shoulder tonite.

Pershaun Reynolds

Untitled

With sunset shadows creeping,
I woke a woman I found sleeping,
And when she spoke her eyes turned dark and cold.

She said— "All I'm doing is learning how to cope with the constant
burning of unfulfillment trapped within my soul."

I could sense that she was tired of trying,
And in the dark I thought I heard her crying,
Condemning unknown actions in the rain.

She said— "Little acts of kindness mean nothing if they don't
remind us that sunlight never reaches those in pain."

I followed her to where the waves were tall,
And I saw her raise her first and call,
A challenge to the demons in her mind.

She said—"Trace the path that I have worn, beneath this coat my
heart is torn. Would I miss these things had I been born
in another place and time?

Then she fell upon her knees,
Where she was promptly swept to sea,
And as she went she turned her head to speak.

She said—"The Earth will always turn, but the world will never learn
That the only rest you'll ever get is Rest in Peace."

Steve David Stewart

The Breath of God

The breath of God hung low across the land.
I woke from a restful sleep
and the world was surrounded
in the light white mist
that escaped His lips.

I got up that morning happy to be the first awake.
I packed my bags and entered into my Lord's breath.
I was excited, walking along, seeing no one.
Being in the breath of God.
His arms surrounding, everlasting, and ever-loving.

This, this is my God
and He,
He is Good.

Margaret Rose Gouveia

"Life Is A Great Sport"

I played great tonite
I won the game to my delight
Sometimes you have to give it your all
Push it to your limit, have a ball
Never give up
Never stop trying
Get over your mistakes
Get over your crying
Life is really so good
Enjoy every moment you see
Sometimes have fun just like you were three
When you think about the end
It shall come to all of us someday
So just enjoy your life and play, play, play.

Russell Symmes

I Am

I am a gentle animal looking for a home.
I wonder if there ever was a unicorn roaming the world.
I hear the cries of the animals crying for their lives.
I see a beautiful world in the future.
I want love and peace for the world.
I am a gentle animal looking for a home.

I pretend I'm a princess watching over the world.
I feel the life of the world fading away.
I touch the hearts of every human who wants to be free.
I worry that the future will be different.
I cry when I hear the cries of the world becoming louder.
I am a gentle animal looking for a home.

I understand that we all look and act differently.
I say that everyone should love one another.
I dream that I will have a wonderful life.
I try to be nice to everyone I meet.
I hope everyone will be kind and loving.
I am a gentle animal looking for a home.

Michelle Cordova

Heirloom

If I had the world on the edge of a string,
I would put all the demons inside a ring.
They could never escape they would never be free
No one in my world will create misery.
  I'd get rid of pollution, no drugs will there be.
I'd destroy all the weapons and clean out the sea.
No one is hungry, homeless, or scared.
No one is lonely so much love being shared.
  Now all the pain is gone, disease obsolete
Now my world is almost complete.
  If I had the world on the edge of a string,
I'd give it to you, now it's your turn to sing.

J. R. Mata

"All You Want"

To keep you near
I'd give you all one man could possess
Anything you'd ask, would just be but a thought away
I'll add joy to your thoughts
And a touch of love to your dreams
And when you feel a cool breeze tingle your
Spine on a hot day, it would be my touch
I'll be your shadow, so you'd never be alone
The softness of the ground to comfort your steps
I'll be the shade of a tree, on a bright day,
To relax your eyes
I'll be all you ever asked for,
And all you ever dreamed of
Just to spend a moment near you.

Ray Ramirez

If I Had A Hammer

If I had a hammer, a carpenter I'd be.
I'd hit a nail on the head and build a house for you and me.
One, two, three, four, five, six, seven.
One, two, three, four, five, six, seven.
One, two, three, four, five, six, seven.
I'll build a house for you and me.
An adorable house, a beautiful house, a charming house, a
darling house, an enormous house, a fabulous house.
If I had a hammer, how happy I would be.
I would work all night long, on that house, so we could have a family.
One, two, three, four, five, six, seven.
One, two, three, four, five, six, seven.
One, two, three, four, five, six, seven. Oh, what a family!
I'll build a fence around the house for our family haven.
Swings and slides, a dog and cat, for our little kin.
If I had a hammer, betcha I'd wear a great big grin,
Cause I'd focus on where I'm going, not on where I've been.
One, two, three, four, five, six, seven.
One, two, three, four, five, six, seven.
One, two, three, four, five, six, seven. Yes, that's our house.

L. A. Glick

If I Could

If I could wrap my arms around the world and hold it tight
I'd shade it from the noonday sun; I'd sing to it at night.
I'd feed the hungry multitudes; I'd bless the world with peace.
I'd spread God's mighty love around and make the fighting cease.
I'd sweeten bitter waters, climb mountains soaring high.
I'd sing the song of all mankind - the world would never cry.
I'd water thirsty deserts with quenching drops of rain.
I'd visit all the lonely - the world would know no pain.
I'd mother all its children and sing sweet lullabies.
I'd fill the world with flowers, blue skies and butterflies.
I'd try to conquer all the wrongs and strive to make them right
If I could wrap my arms around the world and hold it tight.

Patty Callahan

Pots Of Gold

How would it feel
if a cool wind never blew,
with clouds floating by,
and the sun shining through?

The soft fur of a cat,
contentedly purring at a quick steady pace...
Wrestling in the grass with a puppy,
trying to keep him from licking your face,

A strong hug from a small child -
shamelessly needing to be touched,
I wonder if they realize
we need them just as much.?

Someone special close beside you,
the beat of her heart makes your skin tingle with joy.
In ecstasy, you realize she loves you,
the same comfort your mother gave you when you were a little boy.

Life is too short!
Pain makes you heart grow cold!
So valuable is the warmth
in these little Pots of Gold!

Ronald Boatner

My Son

The world steps aside to let any man pass
If he knows where he's going, my Son.
There are principles to be upheld,
There are battles to be won.

Do not be content to stay where you are
But start your climb from the bottom rung.
There are many steps 'ere you reach your goal.
There are many songs to be sung.

Never be satisfied with less than the best
But reach for that highest star,
Although it may seem beyond your grasp
Almost impossibly far.

Keep a dream in your eyes built of star dust
And a song in your heart as you go.
For it lightens the load you must carry
To give a hand to others bent low.

Let that Lorelie star keep your head in the clouds,
Your eyes fixed on its glittering fire.
Let the world hear the shout from the top of your voice,
"Onward, Upward, Excelsior, higher, ever higher."

LaVey Adams Alexander

Love

Love,
If it is like a rose,
Then it shall whither and die,
One day.
If it is like a fire,
Then it shall engulf itself and die,
One day.
If it is like a beautiful sunset,
Then later hours shall come, and it will die,
One day.
Even our lives,
Though they be filled with
Roses, Fires, and beautiful sunsets will die,
One day.
But our Love,
Is forever entombed
In our Spirit and Soul,
And that shall not die,
One day.

J. Kyle Gray

I'll Always Remember You

I'll always remember you as the one who always listened to my dreams.
I'll always remember you as the one who
always knew how to make me laugh.
I'll always remember you as the one who
let me cry, but stayed to wipe my tears.
I'll always remember you as the one who
believed in what I wanted in life.
I'll always remember you as the one who
let me be myself, never wanting to change a thing.
I'll always remember you as the one who
taught me to listen to my heart.
I'll always remember you as the one who
said remember yesterday but go on to tomorrow.
I'll always remember you as the one who shared my pain with me.
I'll always remember you as the one who
showed me that the stars can be a guiding light if you let them.
I'll always remember you as the one who
kept me strong, you never let me fall.
I'll always remember you as the one who
was always my only true friend in life.

Natalie Cynkar

Please Save Me

I'm leaving this earth piece by piece.
I'm ironing my heaven clothes for that special crease.
Really I think I'm falling in love.
There's nothing else to think of.
I'm falling from a very high tree;
please save me.

I've been struck with an arrow, hit with a stick,
all these different emotions are just making me sick.
I've been cut with a knife, stabbed in the heart,
pushed away from somebody, just torn slap apart.
It's plain and simple for you to see,
please somebody save me.

I've jumped off boats, swam the ocean,
put on clothes made mainly of lotion.
I've driven a nine (929), taken apart a six (626),
broken so many things that just can't be fixed.
I've loved a man who was shot dead; one bullet to the head.
I really hope this isn't my destiny,
but if so somebody please save me.

Luschenia Nicole Phillips

Mind Shadows

I feel scared as I'm walking at night.
I'm not looking for trouble, nor for a fight.
There are shadows lurking 'round every corner and light,
I don't want to run, but I feel that I might.

Suddenly a figure appears from the dark,
My heart skips a beat, I'm too scared to dart.
It is a black man; I think that I'm through.
But then he offers his hand and I don't know what to do.

He escorts me to my home, all safe and sound.
And then it hits me, a realization I've found.
It isn't his color that scared me the most,
But all of the stereotypes that follow me like a ghost.

I apologize and thank him
And then in the end,
I find that I've made
A truly good friend.

Michelle Jelen

The Friend

I'm the friend every girl has,
I'm the friend without a face,
I'm the friend no one cares about enough to hate,
No one knows me,
No one cares,
For I am just the friend,
You'll never know my name,
You'll never care to ask,
I'll never ever tell you,
Because I'll never have the chance,
You'll fall in love with all the rest,
The curvier, prettier bunch
And because of this
I've never had a boyfriend,
And I doubt I ever will,
Because to all you guys everywhere,
I'm destined to be the friend,
The girl you never knew.

Mei-Ling Eng

Imagine That

Dear Dr. King,
Imagine peace...Well, what is peace?
It isn't innocent children getting shot in the streets.
Peace is the sound of childhood and cheer,
not the sound of gunshots, breaking the silence, causing the fear!
Peace is the sound of racial unity undisturbed,
not the sound of dying crack addicts lying on the curb.
Peace is the sound of black and white, hand in hand,
not the sound of racial riots plaguing the land.
Peace is the sound of love in the air,
not the sound of struggling families living on welfare.
Peace is the sound of racial barriers falling,
not the sound of prejudiced name calling.
And, yes, peace is the sound of Martin Luther King,
it's a sound of change, not a dangerous thing.
But, peace is a sound that we struggle to hear,
instead, we listen to the sound of hate and fear.
And if we listen to peace, then the dream will come true,
the dream once imagined, imagined by you.

Michael Rudnick

Untitled

You give your love so freely to me
in a world where everything has a price
You treasure what you have with me
in a world that takes love for granted

You're always there when I need you
ready to pick up the pieces
ready to give until it hurts
and then give some more

I wake up every morning feeling safe and secure
because I have you next to me
I can face the world each day
because I know you're with me

How do I show you how much you mean to me?
How do I return what you have given to me?
All I have to give are a few lines
to tell you that you're
the only one I need
the only one I trust
the only one I Love

I Love You

Sherri MacCheyne

"A Tear"

To shed a tear though some may say is a sign of weakness
In actuality — humanity's gentle sweetness
To shed a tear — beneath the shadow of your brow —
They help you to grow though no one can explain how
A tear — so fragile yet strong
Helps us to love — the strong bond
If tears should flow from your face
Please don't hide them — there is no disgrace
Allow the tears to fall beneath your eyes —
Heaven knows — there is no disguise
Tears no longer hide —
Tears are love-locked deep inside

Ronald Pease

Love Versus Hate

If the world was put to a test,
To see which would prevail,
Love versus hate,
One shall presume, if optimistic,
That love is the overpowering emotion,
But one shall suppose, if pessimistic,
That it is preterhuman for all to love.

RaeLynn Van Ornum

H.I.V.

Hunger, as it cries out across the distance, passion,
In addiction of merciless fate, the violent storm.
Sweeping us off of our feet and coursing through our veins!
What is it?
To speak of in gasping breath on our death bed,
The passing of sentence, in death, in a heart beat,
A newborn, children beaten black and blue by the very blood
That courses through their veins.
To live for the day, a moment, we kneel and pray.
What have we done?
When life in all is sucked by the very marrow that sustains us.
Lonely it leaves us in our pains to endure the numbers of which
We became.
Justification in the eyes of God?
The rotted seeds we have sewn across the distance, in
A jungle called man.
Let us starve and let blow the winds of change to calm this storm.

Humanities Innocent Vision
H.I.V.

Michael S. Groseclose

Treasure Island

Our tragic story did begin
In Admiral Benbow's lonely inn,
Where Captain Bill Bones did stay
(Who never a red cent would pay).
He preferred Capt'n to Billy Bones
And sang his songs in very gruff tones.

But now steps in the beggar Pew,
Who with his card caused much ado.
Upon seeing this card, the Capt'n died
And left a chest with a map inside!
Later this chest young Hawkins found,
With money and map, in oilskin bound.

The map now started a treasure guest,
In which the doctor and squire did their best,
With a strong and mutinous cook aboard,
Bring back the gold in one large hoard.

But wait, now I have changed my mind.
So pick up the book with story true,
For now the rest is up to you!

William Robert Vanderslice

In An Instant

A month ago today, again I saw your face.
In an instant:
With eyes of fire and hands of stone, you burned old
bridges and smashed through brick walls.
On a blanket on the floor, through my patio door.
In an instant:
With a heart of silk and lips of velvet, you caressed
my heart and comforted my mind.
In an instant:
With endless passion and perfect honesty, you captured
my sole and harnessed my loyalty.
While talking about the years that have passed by us, you
peaked my curiosity.
Over a home cooked meal and a football game, you touched
the deepest part of me.
In an instant:
Every instant your near;
My love light shines brighter then I ever believed it could.
In an instant: Destiny has brought us back together.
Now I believe it intends to keep us forever!

Maria Lynn Mull

Because I Didn't Call James Merrill

There were no earthquakes frogs or floods because I didn't call
in fact I challenge anyone to notice it at all

A man that shaped a part of me just never really knew
he wondered if he had a cult of people with a clue

A quarter of a century I carried The Mad Scene
and used it like a touchstone when earth cares seemed obscene

When madness gripped the world then me he didn't know my dreams
he couldn't see the laundry there that softened others schemes

Wanderlust and Weltschmertz tugged and warred and no one won
at least one tree burst into grief 'til that dark day was done

But when I finally found that "my" poet was nearby
did I call to thank that healer that had shared so much grey sky?

I'm sorry that the courage needed simply wasn't there
he died before I had the guts to try to make things fair

So now I write this tearfully and use his poem once more
because I never called and yet we knew the same dark shore

It could have been a high point stumbled thank you on the phone
somehow I hope he hears me now and shares this clumsy poem.

C. G. Weaver

Forever Friends

I miss you now, for you are no longer here.
In morning your loss, I shed many a tear.

Why the Lord chose to take you away,
I honestly do not know.

You survived such a long time with your deadly disease,
And through it all you were ever so strong.
You were a fighter,
You were an inspiration to all who met you.
We all love you Jeralyn,
And I for one will remember you always.
For happy memories are all we have left.

I treasure the memories from days at Cedar Point,
The countless days at recess and from the skating parties too.
I will always remember all of the wonderful days that I have spent
with you.

You always watched over me just like a mother would have done.
You always shared your love with me...you made my heart overflow
with glee.

Now that you are up high in the heavens,
I am sure you are watching over me the way you used to do.

Wait for me up in Heaven and someday we will meet once again.
I love you Jeralyn and I know that you love me too!

Megan M. Glinka

Beloved

Last night you came to me.
In the stillness of the midnight hour you came to my room.
Quietly you slipped beneath the covers and with
strong arms you gathered me close

Hands searching and finding
Eyes and lips - drinking - drinking.

And hour after hour in rapt wonderment we loved
sinking into waves of ecstasy.

Hearts and souls trembling with joy - holding
and enfolding.

Fiery passion - icy tears falling from my eyes

How I missed you- Oh, how I miss you.

Sigrid Castaldo

Misery

In this green meadow stands a lonely sad tree
In reality this tree symbolizes me
Without the right proper care this tree may die
But if you'd only understand it,
believe it and hold a place for it inside

Situations for this tree are very enigmatic
It needs something in its life to
make it ecstatic
It belongs in the forest where it's
dark and cold
It needs the love back it once
did hold

This prudent young tree just wants to live
And project all the love it can give
It can promise a love that's for eternity
And that's the love it wants you to see

If you really care about this tree
Release if from all of its misery
Treat it nice and special too
And it will return its love to you!

Missy Heller

Somewhere, Somehow, Someone

Somewhere,
In that misty world between consciousness and sleep,
the journey began.

A maze created by lies, covered with thorns of discontent.
Mists that clouded judgement, under skies that brought a monsoon of
tears.
Swamps fed by private fears, surrounded by vines that strangle the
mind.

Somehow,
Vast gray hollows of emptiness shattered,
chased away by a light more intense than the sun.

A dark world, erased with the sweep of a hand.
Choking haze, swept away with a gentle breath.
Icy air, dispelled by an inner warmth.

Someone,
Granted exodus from this world of throwaway souls,
and silenced the deafening echoes of the past.

Stripped away dismal shades of black, unearthing a kaleidoscope of
vibrant colors. Replaced a hollow chest, with an accepting heart.
Exchanged a shuttering soul, for an unwavering spirit.

Revealing flowers of hope on the horizon.

Lisa Keeney

In My Heart

Lies a space where only a few were allowed to come
In that space God has placed one special friend
This time when it was filled
He put someone
I would become close to
The closeness due not so much as
The quantity of our time
But what we did in the time we had
In my heart he put you
I wished we had more time
But our closeness was cut short
In time I hope the sadness will cease
But everything we shared
Will be
In my mind
And forever
In my heart

Shirley Ann Flowers

Feather And Stone

There is,
in the hollows of my childhood, a memory
to which I now am recalled:

A rook flew over me. I was five.
I stood in a field of corn, submerged
in the tall sea-green silkstalks,
holding high my pellet gun
like a breathing tube,

but swiveling it, lining up sight with the bird.
A heartbeat's space passed (a fancy
passed there, too)

The onyx wings of the rook froze, in shock-motion;
the bird fell like a stone to the earth,
a black swan-dive,
a quick silence into the rocking stalks.

The rook never had an idea of what hit him.
Neither did I.

Michael T. Williams

The Tiny Twig

One sunny summers day
In the merry month of May
My father bought for me
A tiny little tree
I dug me a hole
Just like a crazy busy mole
I went forth and planted the tiny twig;
Hoping soon it would be big.
Than there came one day to my surprise to find that in
Disbelief somehow my little tree had shrunk in size
For my brother Steve as I could see had stomped
Upon my little tree; when for some silly unknown reason
he was angry with me. So.....
Once again my father bought for me
A tiny little tree.
I planted him in the front yard but that little tree is now
Full grown in the flowers garden as you can surely see!

William Hurt

"After The War"

The young lady sat on the bench each day—-
In the park, (as she'd done many times before.)
Puzzling over her lonely life?
It seemed like some parts were "missing", for sure!

But this one day, as she quietly pondered—-
A middle-age man, up the pathway wandered.

He'd spent many lonely weeks of his life—-
In Hospitals—after the War...
(Some didn't think he would "survive,")...
The wounds were so deep and sore.

When he said, "Hello, little Ellie,"—-
(She couldn't believe what she heard!)
How could a stranger know her name?
For a moment, she never said a word:—-

Then she gazed up at the gentleman,
—And smiled, and said "Hello,"—-
It seemed she'd known him " All Her Life!"
—But she knew that wasn't so!

She gazed intently at the man—-
—And said, "Then you are my — "father Dan!"

Pauline Myers Howell

"Life Is Like Ice Cream"

Life is like ice cream.
In the Rocky Road of Life
There are many choices to be made.
One decision after another;
Each with their own risks.
Which flavor? Single or double scoop?
Cone or dish? Soda, shake or float?
Toppings? And which toppings!?
For here, or to go?
... Tempting fate...
Insatiable satisfaction.
Now and then, you come across a few nuts!
But that doesn't diminish the pleasure.
In fact, it gets better with every spoon or lick.
But... before you know it... it's all gone.
Over too quick; and we're left wanting more.
Looking back at an empty dish,
Wondering how different it might have been...
Overcoming sweet addictions,
But grateful for the experience.

Robert J. Feldman

Candle In The Wind

In the darkness of my life
In the stillness that surrounds
You are the flame.
You are slowly setting me on fire each moment that I live.
And now, there is not much left of me to burn.
So I must blow you out and try to survive
without your warmth and light
Or I must allow myself to be burned
while clutching tightly to my pride
which will diminish in the fire anyway.
Either way I'm losing
Myself or you, my fire.
And not since the moment you touched me
Will I ever be the way I was before

Sarah Delaney

Inside Of Me

Inside of me,
In the very depths of my soul,
Runs a great, thrashing river—
Endless, unyielding,
Compassion for nothing in its path,
Along side a thick, impenetrable forest,
Where no one is welcome,
And those who trespass will be lost forever,
From which one single light glows—
A small dim candle,
Burning on and on,
Defying expected death,
And lighting the way
For the brave, brilliantly colored snake,
Heartlessly coiling tighter and tighter
Around the silver dagger
Plunged deeply into my helpless, innocent heart,
To be removed by only one.

Sarah E. Crawford

Listen

Carrying the burden further
to the destination "unfound,"
with sparks of laughter, and purity
of children we once knew

And losing something we can't see
and playing with something we can't feel
the cry you hear and the buried fate
encases your fears and betrays your soul.

Stuart Card

A Beautiful Rainbow

We walked out of the building and looked up in the sky;
In the West the sun was shining, in the East clouds passing by.
The storm had come and gone within less than an hour;
And there we saw a rainbow, exhibiting God's mighty power.
It wasn't just a single rainbow, but two and full and bright
From end to end what colors! Oh, what a glorious sight!
It seemed to be right in our reach as we stood there amazed
Though we've seen rainbows before, still we stood and gazed.
The lower bow was strong and bright with rainbow colored hue;
The upper one, though not so clear was fully in our view.
God promised man through Noah, many long years ago
That He'd not flood the earth again, and created the rainbow.

Margaret Good

Autumn

The muted clangor of the calling geese
In wedge-formation winging high above
The city streets—so high to almost cease
From sight of wondering knowing eyes that love
The signs of wild things wherever they occur—
Gives sad desirings to flee from here
To woods that mark that final, frenzied stir
That rounding of the season's bend where sere
And shushing autumn leaves are carpeting
The ground in gold and scarlet colored hues
And stag and doe from dawn to star-setting
Make feverish court until when all subdues,
The winter's snows enshroud the dying year
And I am left to linger, lonely here.

Robert Clermont

The Lowest Form of Wit

How kind of you to demonstrate my unconquerable
inadequacies
lest I waste a lifetime searching
the fellows of this world
for solace
I am so glad that you convinced me of my affection
lest looking shyly inward I should hold my feelings true
and find in me some
love
Indebted I remain for the long years of disinformation
that I can't challenge the improprieties of those angels
(introduced to me by you) and battle them
Demons
of the night full of fingers
My Congratulations for your intellect
applied with vigor like a cat's tongue
lest seeing at last that the filth is on the outside
I cleanse myself of you and
take flight.

Sarah Bramley

From Loneliness To Love

An angel must have looked down at me
Inside my heart only she could see
The loneliness I did feel inside
No place on earth I could ever hide

You came to me one day in June
You are now my stars, my sun, my moon
My life will never be the same
For I can banish the loneliness with just your name

You show me how deep love can be
Now I know you are the one for me
To make you as happy is now my goal
To this I strive with my life, my love, my soul.

Susan J. Klein

Affairs

What most people consider an affair is not my own-self interpretation...I feel it's real happening in your lifetime to be remembered, not imagination.

Affairs can be acquaintances, loved ones, or a memorial experience that sticks in one's mind. It wraps and enfolds you closely and when it's over or disappeared, it's difficult to define.

An affair can be holding your first and the knowledge that perfection was made; and you were the fortunate one, for in your arms perfection laid.

Or one you loved, whether for a brief or longtime, could have left such an impression that you couldn't forget the impact and you used no discretion.

You might have gave your all, or might have wished you had gave more. Only you would know how much happiness or sorrow your soul can endure.

For others, an affair could be a splash in the silvery water on a hot humid day in July. At that time it eased all their sorrow and pain and on that water they relied.

But to explain to another, just how deliciously cold and refreshing it was - would be impossible for others to understand; they don't realize that it was merely because...

Because you were down, because you were there, because it was what you needed that particular day. And to get you through at that time, it was the only way.

Speaking of my life, as I pass over and through each December; I can truthfully say I've had affairs to remember.

Margie Dusel

An Ancient Home

Midnight, I listen to Brazilian Music.
Intimate, the words the tones, I come home.
Late at night, their voices sound thick
Melodic sounds take me to places where I can roam.

In my soul there is music, Brazilian a feeling.
This music to me is differently the same.
These sounds to exotic, leave me reeling.
Familiar it heals, I have known these sounds before I came.

Shapes and sounds excite - I recognize heartfelt some.
Smells, images I travel back a long time come.
Brazilian song I step into my heart's tome.
The essence brings me back to an ancient home.

Teresa A. G. McQuone

Gardens Of Three Women

Everything in my garden
is green and fierce.
Even at night I can hear
the greedy thrust and twist
toward hidden water,
hidden light.

My mother's garden is exultant.
The corn stalks groan with tasseled weight.
The trees and vines shout with gladness.
And yet shadows have begun to form
In the corners where the herbs are cloistered.

The garden of my grandmother
grows down, not up.
Sometimes, on mild days,
she digs a little in the soil
for old bones and arrowheads -
a layered harvest of ghosts.

Sharon L. Martin

The Midnight Clock Just Won't Stop

In wee hours of the darken nights. Crossing over,
into the early hours of the dawn. The stroke of twelve, midnight.
The vision of darkness. Darken by the continuous and countless
strokes of the clock. The time persists to never insist to stop.

As the clock, keeps going on ticking and clicking by.
The seconds continuously and gradually unwinds down. Only to
be found. The sounds of the bells, from the stroke of twelve.
All is well to proceed. Indeed, into the start of just another
day!

The midnight clock awaits to come again and again.
Just to begin. To the start of another days, count down.
As the seconds slowly surpasses us by. Gradually proceeding on,
toward the stroke of twelve, midnight.

What a fright! To feel the threaten theory of the clock.
Surpassing us by. Each night after night. Such a magnificent
precision. Inside the decision of a clock. That continuously
moves on. To gradually approach, into the drifts of tomorrow.

By the stroke of twelve, midnight! It's surely to come.
For those who will awaken just to another day.
THE STROKE OF TWELVE, MIDNIGHT!

Tyrone Nixon Sr.

Reunion

Like the heart that has been plunged out of me
Is gone
It still beats a listless and weak song
For my love
That is temporarily gone
Seems so long
The song sounds the alarm of my eyes
They water to fill
Fall
I cry
Quietly
As the running tears of salt stream down my face
I swallow them
The warm breath and moist lips of the man
My love.
Caress truly
The taste of tears is with us both
For this reunited kiss is only the first

Shannon Atkinson

Where Is The Dream?

Where is the dream that He envisioned?
Is it evident in the lives we're living?
Of all the marches which came to pass,
are those people "free at last?"

Where is the dream which gave us our voice?
The freedom to vote, the freedom of choice?
Do we today, treat one another
as we would our own sisters and brothers?

Where is the dream that He did see?
A glorious land as yet to be.
A nation of people living in peace.
Where is the dream or when did it cease?

Where is the dream of our dear King?
Does freedom from every mountain sing?
Where homelessness abundant and children cry,
where is the dream or when did it die?

The dream so envisioned can only be made clearer
by the people we face each day in the mirror.
To make the dream a reality
it must begin with you and with me.

Wendy V. Burgh

It Rhymes

Where a poet learns to speak
Is just beyond my wild imagination.
What he writes is tongue-in-cheek;
It gives the reader some small indication.

A poet should be charged with crimes;
He violates our Language as we know it.
He'll butcher words to make them rhyme.
It's legal. He's got license. He's a poet.

We've seen him do it oft' enough,
To change a word for timing so it fits.
A custom alteration's rough,
When words with many syllables sudden quits.

They'll read it and acclaim it,
So all responsibit' he can dodge.
They'll give rewards and frame it,
And list him in a critics antholog'.

I'd like to test his mall I.Q.
To see just what it is that's on his mind.
But I'll never be a party to
The writing of adulterated rhyme.

Paul Vandermeer

Black Warrior Or The Warriors Call

Listen old warrior why do you hold your head so low - your strength
is spent your hope is gone
You feel lost, hopeless in this place you call home, this place of
concrete and stone
Are you dreaming of days long gone, when you were a warrior in
your long ago home

Listen young warrior I see you standing there, I see your hurt
your total despair

Stand up old warrior you have never known defeat, stand up young
warrior you must answer the sound
The battle cry of the drum beat the call to all warriors to gather round
Let the memory of a thousand nights fill your soul, you cannot
forsake the warriors goal
You are a warrior never forget, your fate and destiny must be met

Come with me into the night, black as velvet dark as ebony
running feet pounding out the sounds to the drum beat
swaying to the rhythm of a thousand nights
strong black bodies sweating in the jungle heat.

Minnie G. Brown

Mister Redbird

A flash of scarlet—what's that I see?
Is that Mister Redbird out there in my tree?
I thought I heard his cheerful song
When I first stepped outdoors this morn.
I couldn't seem to spot him, tho'
The snow made walking rather slow.
He knows my cats just "live to eat"
And would enjoy a tasty redbird treat.
He wears his colors with quite a flair
Is there just one or several there?
Oh look! There he is, and some lady friends.
I hope they nest here when winter ends!
I'd love to watch them, there in my tree
Raising their little ones, wild and free.
There they go, rushing off again.
Good-bye and come back, my beautiful friend.

Mary F. Herndon

The Picture

The Rhodesian Coast scene upon my wall
Is the painting I treasure most of all
Painted by a doctor long ago
For the nurse he loved
She told me so

I admired this picture
As I visited one day
This dear old lady, who would soon pass away

The love story she told was a beautiful thing
Trips to Paris, boat rides in the spring
Shopping for gowns to dance in at night
In the arms of her lover
Who held her tight.

The Boer War ended
He sailed away
She never forgot him
Until her dying day.

Mabel E. Lodge

The Pledge To Life

What, I ask of you,
Is the true definition of that
Taste?
Such foul matter emanating from Nature;
Externally magnanimous,
Internally bitter.

Now, I ask of you,
Why do you resemble such fruit of acidity?

To be forgiving is to be in love;
To trust is to enjoy the sweetness of life.
Lamentations and despise,
Oblivion is where they reside.

Embellishment lies
In the winds of humility and giving.

Sandra Weber

"Construction Of Life"

To change the poison to medicine in our life,
is to change the war to peace and end the strife.
The power of cause and effect must be respected
or life's benefits may be rejected.
Seeking the spirit of hope and harmony,
we are like a conductor without a symphony.
Education, is a necessity for youth to grow
and we, as leaders, teachers and parents need to show
our participation in building a stronger foundation
consisting of faith, encouragement and appreciation.
Embracing the energy of the Universal Law,
Will bring forth wisdom and understanding of the Mystic law.
Positive dialogue and discussions is the key
to support humanity with equality and unity.
So take action world-wide
listen to the voices inside and outside
with sincere determination to put into action
to save the future from destruction
so we can keep on living
and never stop believing.

Susan Godsey

The Ways of Us All

Some say the only way to beat the gunmen
is to pull a gun just as fast.

Others say the only way to live
is to make the good things last.

He says the only way to survive the hate
is to quench it with violence.

She says the only way to be heard
is to break the oppressive silence.

You say the only way to earn the respect of others
is to kill your enemies and ignore their cries.

We say the only way to achieve the peace we dream of
is to put down our guns and open our eyes.

I say the only way to survive anything
is to do what is right.

But deep down all of us know the only way at all
is to be strong and when need be, fight.

Stacey Cline

What I Want In Life

What I want most of all in my life,
is to still the everyday living strife
I want to feel a strong and binding love,
that protects from life's push and shove

You my dear to wake with a smile
have breakfast together and linger a while
Then off to work we go today,
in the evening - we'll call it a day
we've had a good meal,
LOVING you is good deal.

I love you my dear,
the sound is sweet and brings to my eye a tear
I'll love you as long we both shall live
my whole life for you, I willingly give
Come summer we'll be together for many years
There's been much happiness for me my dear

Just love me true 'til the day I die,
never make me lonely, and never make me cry
I will share with you in many ways
and try to add happiness and love in the coming days

Pat Crockett

Whimsy

Whimsy is a fun way to think
It comes and goes in hues of pink
It's merry, gay, joyful, and light
It's easy to visualize and keep into sight.

It's over and under, and all around
It can be high or low, or fall to the ground
It's full of smiles, and laughter delight
It's young at heart with lots of insight.

It's imagination grown up, and gone wild
It's crazy, and lazy with a silly ole smile
It's projection, reflection, fast beams of light
It's giddy, and witty, way out of sight.

I love to relax in this light hearted way
It keeps me afloat day unto day
It's easy to manage my mind into flight
It's whimsy, whimsy, whimsy away!

Laura J. Deacon

It's so Hard to Leave You

When the baby came so early, so quick,
It didn't take long to see she was sick.

With alarms, tubes and needles, and those tiny little hands,
To leave her there alone was more than I could stand.

"It's so hard to leave you. I know you'll be fine.
Be strong, God is with you, dear daughter of mine."

So I knelt down beside her and prayed with my might,
"Dear Lord, I can't be here. Will You hold her tonight?"

But soon we could see, with blessings unfurled,
We finally took home our dear little girl.

The night time medicines, the feedings at dawn,
It took only a day and my energy was gone.

Then came mother, to help us get through.
She hugged and kissed her as only Grandma can do.

But when she got ready to head for home,
With tears in her eyes she found me alone.

"It's so hard to leave you. I know you'll be fine.
Be strong, God is with you, dear daughter of mine."

She knelt down beside me and prayed with her might,
"Dear Lord, I can't be here. Will You hold her tonight?"

Kim Davis

The Colors and Ways of a Road

I saw a picture the other day
It had many colors in many different ways
The picture was of a winding road
It had many burdens of a load

The road had barriers thick and thin
Full of goodness and of sin
There were mountains to climb and rivers to cross
And people along the way trying to be your boss

The people were of many colors
Some were bright others more mellow
Some thought good some thought less
But we all must do are best

No matter what color no matter what race
We all have the same goals to face
The road had many curves and many bends
But in the end we all are friends.

Leah Harman

Perks

"How ya doing"
It has it's perks to be a star,
But only if your happy with who you are.
There are many stars of stage and screen,
But a star of life is seldom seen.
For we all suffer from the same sorrow,
The uncertainty of each tomorrow.
But with the advent of growth maturity,
Comes the realization, there is no security.
We all meet the same fate,
A thing called death is everyone's date.
Lives are spent concerned with the mystery.
But unsolved, we move, into the pages of history.
For we come to realize if we're not too dense,
That in the end,it's all Abbey rents.
So take some time to enjoy and go slow,
And work on your growth and reducing ego.
And as we move on the teach ourselves how,
To be grateful for the past,
But live in the now.

Read Morgan

Ode To My Dreamcatcher

Like a guardian angle
It hovers over my bed
To protect me while I'm asleep.

Through its maze no bad dreams may pass
Only the happy ones
That will make me smile and laugh

Its white feathers are suspended in Courage
And its web in the middle
Forms its shield.
While, its long strips of brown leather
Hang from it like
Bronze hair.
The blue beads that hold onto its feathers and web
Are its light to see all throughout the night.
And a black feather
Sits atop its head like a
Crown of glory.

This is my protector.
My very own bodyguard.
It watches over me when I'm most vulnerable when I'm asleep.

Samantha Ragan

Untitled

This poem is for my brother
it is about hope
and moment of despair that often enter our lives
it is about past promise that gave hope to future prosperity
it is about set backs that should not be allowed to deter us
this poem is about fulfillment
it is not about meeting the expectations or standards others have set
it is about being true to ourselves and our talents
it is about not letting present hardship discourage us
it is about learning
and using those experiences good and bad for the better
this poem is for my brother and all other people
it attempts to illustrate some of life's difficulties
it is a lesson that this life we live is never easy
it is a reminder that nothing is promised to us
it is a messages that the journey will not always be free of obstacles
it is a promise that the destination - if we work for it- can be rewarding

Oneal Allydice

Mom

Mom, I want to thank you for all the love you've shown
It is by far the sweetest love that I've known
Oh mother, how you reach out to me although you're not here
I long to hold you in my arms and say "thank you, mother dear."
Thanks for all those times you did without so you could lighten my load
Thanks for holding my hand and walking me down life's road.
There are times I feel your presence in little things I say and do
Things that are a part of me, that I get from you.
You've given me a mother's love that no one can take away
It fills my heart and that's where it will stay.
A love so pure it lifts me up and makes me whole
A love that reaches down inside me and touches my very soul.
Somewhere "beyond the sunset" at the rainbows end
waits that glad reunion of my mother and my friend.
And because you're not here to listen to me say
I send this request to Jesus, and this is what I pray.
That he would hold you in his arms and say,
"From your daughter happy mother's day."

Rebecca T. Fisher

God Specializes

It is he who made us in his own image.
It is he who molded and shaped us to what we are to be.
It was the "Master" himself who created you and me.

To some with Knowledge and understanding and the vision of what we
are to be.
To other's the uniqueness to complete every goal and face reality.
To some the gift to speak, teach or lead.
To other's the possibility of having the gift of all three.
To some the personality to withstand the trials and tribulations at
hand.
To other's the skills to listen and understand.
To some to witness as Job did when things seem out of hand.

We all are unique in every way After all, We're God's creation, molded
shaped
as God saw fit. We're the "Master's" creation which we'll never
forget.

It is he who made us in his own image.
It is he who molded and shaped us to what we are to be.
It was the "Master" himself who created you and me.

Robin D. Owens

The Road To Grandma's

It is 54 miles to Brighton, but that was 3 years ago.
It is much further now, but I went there anyway.
I went to visit Grandma.

I passed places vaguely familiar or forgotten in 3 years.
Billboards taken down; mile markers faded.
The road slowly less traveled.

I remember Grandma differently 3 years ago.
Pictures lost; memories faded.
Grandma, slowly less familiar.

I opened the letters never sent, filled with things unsaid.
Like maps to places of feelings once felt.
Once felt, 3 years ago.

Her life didn't pass me by, I passed by her life.
Like missed exits of places never visited,
Where people I'll never know life.

It is 54 miles to Brighton; 54 miles and 3 years,
And it keeps getting further every time,
Every time I try to visit Grandma.

Paul Schultz

Untitled

Dedicated to A.K.

It knows no boundaries, limits, nor ends...
it is my love for you.
When put through the trials of ev'ry day life,
it remains strong enough to pull through.
When I am with you it is visibly extant,
and felt when we hold each other tight.
It is a warmth, a softness, a comfort, a force,
whose mem'ry pulls me through lonesome nights.
My absence from you increases its strength,
always and each day ever more.
And my undying love for you reveals
that each other is who we were made for.

TEMALI '95

Water

Our life and our treasure.
It is our liquid gold it is as shiny and as clear as a
clearly cut diamond sparkling in the light.
As the gargantuan white caps dwindle by the
scolding heat of the sun. It melts into our life as
it will always be needed for existence . Water
may always stay as our only source for life.
It surrounds us every where and guards to be
relieved during the peak times of the prickling heat.
Water, clear, and cool.

Pascual Castillo

What Makes A People Free

What makes a people free?
It is said to be, responsibility
The taking charge of one's destiny.

What makes a people free?
Discipline, could it really be
The proper balance of liberty.

What makes a people free?
To choose to serve his brothern
Rather than selfishly serving just me

What makes a people free?
Maybe its just believing, with positive energy
That they are free.

What makes a people free?
The knowledge of God and self you see
Responsibility, hard work, discipline
Truth, believing and unity.

Margaret Echols

What Is Death?

It is an empty chair, an open space,
It is silent room.
It is a lonely house.
Solitary belongings that no longer have an owner.
A quiet restiveness hanging above the World.
It is a faded picture.
A lost reminder.
It is a candle without a flame.
Plants that must be watered by other hands.
Such a stillness.
As if things are frozen in a Moment.
A Moment where human hands never touched
these things.
As if Life had never once been.
It is an empty chair.

Lisa Preziosi

Finding Innocence

Wisdom is not age,
It is simply the knowledge of the more experienced.
Experience that provides courage to the few.
The few who will have the greatness to bend history itself.
But...It's easter not to be great,
It's easier to be a follower...than to be a leader.
But why follow the road.
When you can create your own?
Don't drown in this sea of oppression and ignorance.
Fight...swim to the land of innocence.
Never forget the power of the young minded.
Listen...you can hear them.
These are the words of my generation.

Oldwen Adriano

My Earthly Home

Home is such a beautiful, lovely word
It is soft, elegant, easy to say: Home Sweet Home.
Home where we can let down our hair, or get in a favorite chair.
Here we can relax, even let our feet go bare.

Some people like to be on the go, and I have done my share.
The mountains, the beach, the cities and towns
Lakes and streams, their beauty abounds
But they are nothing to compare with Home Sweet Home.

A lot of folks think home is just a place to hang their hats
Get a quick meal, or take a short nap.
But I love the friendly walls, and the floor so firm
Even the water faucets that are hard to turn.

There's the door where the children were measured
And their pictures around, that I'll always treasure.
The same old chair where I kneeled to pray
When things were needed, or skies looked gray.

Home is where I have put my roots down
So deep that I think they have become entwined
With the love I have for home and God who so designed
This place for me t reside, and love, Home Sweet Home.

Lillian A. Scoggins

Polka Time

Yo! They don't do the polka in Poland.
It is very dated and tres passé.
The best place to hear a good polka band
Is right here in the good old U.S.A.

One-two! One-two! Dance a fast double beat!
We can get some frenetic dancing done.
Loose and earthy, watch out for flying feet!
It's twirling, swirling, fast and bouncy fun.

Oompah! Milwaukee does the tuba things.
Chicago is accordion and drums.
Pittsburgh zings to some elaborate flings.
Down South you get guitar and banjo strums.

Don't judge it as hopelessly déclassé.
It's widely embraced in the great Southwest.
Las Vegas tunes it in to those who play.
Tex-Mex dip polkas are among the best.

You don't have to hanker for rural roots.
American polka is well defined.
You can skip or canter in shoes or boots.
It's there to please and tease your state of mind.

Frank Ducat

Paid In Full

I heard a song just yesterday, it touched my heart and soul.
It made me feel so warm inside, like that of burning coal.

This young boy had charged his Mom, for chores that he had done.
She looked at him with loving eyes, even though she felt quite stunned

She loved her son so dearly, but had no cash to spare.
So, she paid her son with these few words, to let him know she cared.

She told him of the months she spent, his soul within her womb.
Happy that she had this gift, that ended much too soon.

She reminded him of all the nights, his tiny body ill.
Holding him so closely, to take away his chill.

The love that she had given him, over all the years he grew.
She told him that's what life's about, her view he never knew.

When his Mother finished talking, there was an awesome lull.
Then he said so proudly...Mom your bill is "Paid in Full".

Susan L. Kline

Mammas' Hands

Mamma, I saw you hide your hands today
It made me sad you were embarrassed that way

It's true they are not hands for fancy jewelry or painted nails
But, they possess loving comfort that never fails

I've heard about your childhood on the farm picking cotton
Stories of a difficult life I've not forgotten

Never afraid of hard work, I've seen them with blisters
Yet they always felt soft and tender to myself and my sisters

I remember how they would pat the backs of my infants with colic
And years later try to guide them as teenagers when away they would frolic

They have gently touched many a shoulder
Especially at the church among those who were older

I've held them tightly during prayer
I felt your squeeze just to let me know how much you care

Your hands have been gloriously dutiful
Though you may not think they are physically beautiful

Yes, I'd say from this daughter's point of view
Recognition of the love in your hands is long overdue

Rebecca Johnson

Turn Back The Clock

When I think about the clock of life;
It makes me happy that your my wife;
We've had good times and we've had bad;
I'm so very sorry for making you sad;
I want to spend my life making you happy;
I hope this poem isn't to sappy;
Life is short and life is great;
A number 10 is how you rate;
Life stinks and is so very gory;
For the pain I've caused I'm so very sorry;
Broken in two is what I've done to your heart;
That's how I feel whenever we're apart;
The sky is blue and the water is too;
I promise again to never make you blue;
There's nothing as high as my love;
Like the wings of a snow white dove;
There's a ship that just come into dock;
For the pain I've caused I wish I could turn back the clock.

Jerry Nancy Erwin Sr.

In Remembrance Of Mary Frances Stewart

It seems like only yesterday that you were here with me
It only took a laugh, a smile to fill my heart with glee
But then one day you went away, I thought I'd never see
a happy reflection in the mirror looking back at me
But Jesus came down the road to carry my heavy load
He told of a place far away where we would reunite one day
He talked of how happy we would be, of all the joy and tranquility
that we would share as never before
If only I'd open my heart's door, the glee would return forevermore.

Rita M. Stewart

Dear Santa

I've been a good boy. As good as a boy can be;
So I'm quite sure, dear Santa, that you'll be visiting me.
But Santa Dear, when you've listing each Christmas
sweet and toy. Won't you please be sure to remember
every hungry girl and boy.

I am sure I can't be happy this bright and day
Christmas morn if any one's best trousers are badly
Patched or torn, or if anyone lacks some Christmas joy.
So Santa, I send my thanks and love from a little boy.

Mary Bleier

When I Look at Your Complexion

When I look at your complexion,
it puts a tingle down my
spine. Your skin smells so soft it reminds
me of a soft pillow. Your lips
are so moist they're like a branch over
a cool running, breezy brook. The dew
from the morning, that lay on the leaves of
the olive branch. Your hair shines so
bright, it looks like a black stallion
running through an open field, longing
to be stroked by a gentle rider.
Your light in your eyes reveal the
warmth, of your heart. Your height
is like a little teddy bear that I
can cuddle to. Your voice, sounds
so sweet, yet stern it shows you have
direction and purpose. You are a bright
large beautiful star that stands out in
the milky-way, and universe of LIFE!!!

Santy Salernitano

"Lead Me"

Oh great master planner, what's in the cards for me
It really matters not too much, if the plan is made by thee
All I must do, is to accept, what your will is to be
And work to carry your will out, as you make it known to me
Yes, I have wishes and desires I cling to selfishly
But through the past, I have learned at last
I know not what's good for me
So on you I now depend, my life is in your hands
From my will I must be free.
What's to be is what's to be, I say with confidence today
I must trust in your plan faithfully

Scott Mueller

"Realization"

Sometimes along life's path, I fall into a bottomless pit.
It seems as though I'm all alone and suffer quite a bit.
I yearn for hope and dream of a day when all the pain will cease.
I peer into my heart of hearts and see a dreaded disease:
A disease of doubt, of guilt, of hurt; a disease that's full of me,
A disease that's hidden by the flashy smile I allow the world to see.
My trials I claim as my own and know not where to turn,
Then I remember my Lord who died and waits for my return.
He walks one step behind me for I've chosen the faster route.
He quietly walks behind and cries, for it is I who's shut Him out.
I hear a soft pitter—pat of a gait that's smoother than mine.
I hear a hurrying, breathless step and realize that it's time
To turn around and wait for Him to calm my sightless flurry.
He embraces my sobbing, aching heart and says, "My child, don't hurry.
My path is a simpler, more peaceful one than this one that you're on.
Our Father is waiting patiently for you to come back home.
I know your pain. I know you ache. I've heard your every cry.
I'm standing here beside you, feeling your weighted sigh.
Please let Me love you and heal your wounds, dear sweet child of Mine
And let Me give you strength to move a little more calm this time."

Leah L. Hollis

Nature's Calling

Billowy white clouds against the blue sky,
Trees reaching upward ever so high.
Sun kissed leaves, a carpet spreading green,
A more beautiful painting never to be seen.

Cool breezes flow through the tall grass,
The aroma of flowers fill me as I pass.
Everything sways as the wind blows by,
Leaving me alone, just the mountains and I.

Rachel Mousseau

My Last Thoughts

At night when the day has met it's end and
it seems only darkness is my friend
This hour as I drift off to sleep,
is the only real time that's mine to keep
I may dream of the days to come, or simply what I should have done

My thoughts may drift to an autumn night,
walking on the beach holding on so tight
I wonder if what I am about to try will make life happy,
or make me cry
Then I, like so many before, wonder what lies beyond death's door

Thinking about my family and home then just like you,
wondering why I roam
I think about my since gone friends,
wondering if they were just passing trends
Everyday I try to learn one thing, for wisdom should be like a ball of
string

Tomorrow the sun will bring a beautiful day and I wonder if my feet
will stray
In this world of mine I wear no mask and nothing seems to great a task
Often like a child I dream, of peace of mind in a world supreme

Perhaps tomorrow I'll meet my end, or maybe meet a new close friend
And just as sleep comes reaching through,
my last thoughts are always of you.

M. F. McGann

A Thought About You

Thinking of you right this moment
It sends the laughter to my head
Remembering that warm smile of yours and the funny things you
always said.
The times together, they are priceless
Just thinking of you puts my mind to rest.
I can see the sun, but not the light.
I can see the birds, a pretty sight, but fail to hear their music.
But when I see you, my mind floats free
Oh, the wondrous times we had,
just you and me.

Santwana Barik

Darkness

Of the night I ask: Should my heart fear you?
It speaks through the stars: Fear you shall have not.
The peace that darkness brings me comes to few
With it I reach, what for long has been sought
The darkness creeps to the depths of my soul
And with unknown key, sets my spirit free
To be my own, never must I pay toll
The night sounds fill my head and release me
In the dark I am at peace with myself
I dance among the shadows of the night
Material things such as fame and wealth
Seem non-existent in the moon's cool light
Never in the darkness shall I feel fear
For I trust whatever god hath brought me here.

Vida Long

Endless Footsteps In The Sand

Endless footsteps in the sand.
Signs of people hand in hand.
Where do those footsteps go?
What are they trying to show?
They are trying to show the meaning of sharing,
And, the meaning of caring.
Endless footsteps in the sand.
Many lovers walking this land.

Lisa M. Cole

The Traveler

The road-
It stretches out before me,
seemingly endless in the distance.
Who knows what perils await me
on that rocky, uncertain path?
True, others have trodden it before me,
on smooth and even highways,
with comfortable shoes to pad their steps
and lush trees to shade their way.
And others have trudged along barefoot,
on rocky, harsh, deserted roads,
suffering and burning, beneath the scorching sun.
Some have given up wearily,
and others have ran along,
at a fast and ever-quickening pace.
But, alas, life is not a race.
I must go on, steadily and bravely,
never giving up, until I have reached the end;
As a traveler on this, the road of life.

Mia Iwama

Make It Be Eternally

My beautiful love, stand tall and respect yourself with dignity.
It takes strength and support of a knowing man to restore my respect in thee.
I'm struggling but striving to show the world that I'll stand by my man.
Our love in the struggle will be easier if we walked hand in hand.
Why do I have to be just an object of sex, sport and play
Can't you see the true beauty in me I'm trying to display.
An innocent love inside me that's pure tender and real.
Above the uttermost passionate love a woman cannot conceal.
Open your eyes and see my love the beauty reflecting in me.
No, it's not that disrespect for self your trying to make me be.
I am a precious emerald so delicate and fine.
The very essence of my nature is a gift from God the divine.
It is love and joy combined that heals the heart, the soul and mind.
A divine melody, sung without words, a harmony expressed in understanding.
Be strong, knowledgeable and wise that I won't despise.
Love me and understand me with the truth behind that disguise.
And melt away those graven images of falsehood and lies.
Nurture our love with the things that will last.
While healing the hurt and pains of the past.
Let's share our love like God from above and make it be eternally.

Lonnie A. Person

Fishing

I love to fish; I've always been that way.
It teaches patience is what they say.
But all I know it's just a lot of fun
To bait my hook and cast it out, and wait to see it run.

A boat or two sits way out there
The sky is blue, a bird sings, too
And all along the shore
folks are fishing just like you.

It all seems sort of friendly —
Like the shore of Galilee.
Men were fishing from a boat
And Jesus came to see.

It's kind of nice to know
That he's still right here with me,
And might say "Cast your hook out there",
Then I'd catch two or three.

But guess it's not my day,
I've put my fishing gear away.
Once again I'll have to tell them that
"The big fish got away!"

Lula E. Payne

Poetry

Poetry to me is an expression
It tells what's on my mind
It's an extensive collection
Of words that sometimes rhyme

Poetry can differ greatly in content
It can be of joy or sorrow
It lives in my heart to a great extent
And will be with me all the days after tomorrow.

William A. Higdon

It Used To Be Me

It used to be me you turned to
It used to be me you came to in your times of need

When you were sad, when you were mad
I didn't seem to matter

But suddenly she, has taken my place
We used to be so close, you used to tell me everything

You've taken a turn and left me standing
at the crossroads
Here by myself I stand in the rain
Looking into the puddles of my own tears

In those puddles I watch the times we shared
The times we laughed, the times we cried
The times we fought and the times we tried

I used to be your best friend
But now, she has taken my place

Stephanie Tetreault

A Time Never To Forget

It was a time for caring when I first heard your voice
It was a time of pain and sorrow for me when I felt your touch.
It was a time when I searched for someone and you came to my rescue.
It was a time when laughter meant so much to me, and you laughed with me.

It was a time for learning when you shared your wisdom with me, and those who came after me.

My heart was full, my mind knew you well, and I could not forget.
I could see the deep meaning of your love for people, and I saw nothing else.

For every time there was a need for you at a time, your love flourished from your heart like waves of the sea, and blossomed like a flower that had just bloomed.

Walk close beside me, hold me close to your heart because my soul has been shaken and inside my mind will always be a time I will not forget.

Laverne Farmer

Broken Bird

She flies along on handicapped wings.
(It was cut missing line)
Some would see her and say,
"See how free she seems."
Gliding along, carefree, above it all.
They couldn't possibly know,
this bird with a broken wing doesn't fly at all
Just drifts from here to there
tired, listless eyes begging someone
to end her misery.
Clip her wings for good.
So she can rest on a safe spot of ground somewhere.
And finally sleep; dreamless.
Undisturbed by hauntings of freer flights.

Peggy Morrison

Gone But Not Forgotten

August 25, 1937
It was five years ago to-day that the dark cloud passed our way, bringing with it in pain and sorrow which becomes brighter, with each thought of to-morrow.

It was God's will that he should go happy, peaceful, and unafraid and well we all know that when the time comes, we too must go.

Go to this beautiful place called Heaven far above earth where you can see the pains and sorrows of each poor person as he carries them along happy and free.

And that was the way of our loved one he was happy and carefree then we hope and pray that he still is for he is gone but not forgotten.

Ruth E. Dyche

Quiet Morn

We rented a cabin among the trees,
It was peaceful and serene.
I walked to the lake, fishing pole in hand,
The water was quiet, almost pristine.
I looked across the lake and saw a deer watching bold,
As if to say, "What are you doing in my part of the world?"
I set down my pole and took off my shoes
To dangle my feet in the water.
Fishes were swimming free and loose,
Catching them did not matter.
I had the most pleasant time
Watching them swim thru the sun rippling in the water.
And when my friends came back too show me their catch,
They found me browsing thru the blueberry patch,
Remembering the deer, with the knowing eyes.

Marie E. Martinez

"Something About You"

From the first time I saw you, I knew you were the one.
It was something about my love, I knew could not be undone.
There was something about your eyes that made them sparkle when you smiled,
And there was something about your appearance, that gave you lots of style.

There was something about your walk, that gave me chills down my spine,
And that's when I knew all I wanted was for you to be mine.
There was something about your laugh, that made me feel warm all over,
And there was something about your personality that made me become bolder.

There was something about your kiss that was oh, so sweet,
There was something about your touch that made my heart skip a beat.
All this and more are my love of you so true,
I don't know what it is; there's just something about you!

Leigh Ann Paige

For Van Gogh

Insanity brews slow and strange

Calm and quiet, self destructive
unexplained imbecility

And she said nothing to entertain

As I lay trapped inside a feeling
with only a hope of receiving
my God's blessing

William E. Young Jr.

Happiness

Happiness is difficult to define,
It's a certain mood, a state of mind.
It's sharing everyday affairs
With one who understands and cares.

It's tender look or a gentle touch
That says, "I love you very much."
It's a smile of encouragement when you're blue,
A dream that shared, a dream for two.

And happiness — it's even more than this
It's a warm embrace, a magic kiss.
It's a special blessing from above;
It's what you have when you're in love.

Lori Page

What's It All About

It's about mud and grime; it's about water and smell.
It's about dirt and slime.
It's about the feelings you have that are bad all the time.

Dirty clothes you know that will never come clean.
Pots and dishes that have lost their sheen.
Pictures and papers; you can't make out the faces.
The writing's all blurred.
How could this have ever occurred?

No one knew; no one cared.
We needed the rain, but why couldn't we have been spared?
From this mess that makes fire run through your blood.
We didn't really need all that rain that caused such a flood.

It hurts to the bone; water up to the top.
It took our home.
Little things that you have saved that mean a lot;
Little baby shoes and toys.
You hold them in your hands and stare through the tears,
and remember the joys.
The water might destroy, but it will never find.
No; it can never take the memories in my mind.

They say it will never happen again.
O, God; I pray that's what we can believe in!

Mary Anne Davis

If You Know How To Lie

I don't hurt anymore you cry to the world
It's all over, its done, let it die
And your gay, you can laugh
You can do it so well
It's easy, just learn how to lie

You go dancing and playing to parties and shows
You can prove it so well if you try
Just pretend that your happy
And having such fun
Oh it's easy. Just learn how to lie

But your bluffing you know
As the tears start to fall
And you lift up your eyes to the sky
Oh Dear God please forgive and please grant this one prayer
Make it true. I don't want to lie

But the love that was kindled
Still lives in your heart
It still hurts, you still want to cry
And you know, no one knows that I'll love him forever
Yes it's true. I've learned how to lie.

Sharon Blackwood

"Sadly"

My happiness is my world
It's beauty given to me by my Lord
His ever-abounding creation unfurls
Threatened soon to become no more

So sad am I, when I realize
My children will never see
Life as it should be, only as it will be
Without cattails, dogwoods, and hickory trees

I miss the spectacle of dogwood in bloom
While watching squirrels gathering hickory nuts
The cattails bow to the wind, while losing my shoes
Crossing a stream of blue mud

Now our streams flow with pollution
Fewer and fewer parks are kept alive
Soon only cities will clutter our earth
There'll no longer be a peaceful countryside

Sadly, my life is only a memory
Trapped in a heartless city of crime
My children will never know the peace
Recorded deep in my heart and mind

Louise Aldrich

An Appeal To The Babe

Its been 77 years since we heard the cheers,
Its been 77 years that have ended in tears.
When you left that bitter cold night,
Nothing at Fenway has since been right.

In '46 Pesky held the ball,
While Enos Slaughter touched them all.
In '67 we had a great team,
But in the last game Lonborg ran out of steam.
In '75 though Fisk won the THE game,
In the end the story remained the same.
In '86 with one strike to go,
The Buckner Boot ended the show.

Since 1919 other heartbreaks came and went,
Like the play off lost to the Cleveland...
...and the homer by Bucky Dent.

There have been other close calls too many to mention.
What we need now is your undivided attention.
Winning it all this year would be great.
Please don't let the curse turn 78.

Paul Borsari

Dream Fantasy

When twilight falls and night comes stealing...
It's then I missed you from the start.
I do not wish for fame nor fortune,
It cannot ease a broken heart.
Through tears of joy, I thought I found you,
Then woke to find it but a dream.
I'll keep on dreaming dear about you.
The ecstasy of days gone by;
Sometimes I wonder why I try.

Your loving smile lives on forever.
It seems like only yesterday;
You touched my hand and said, "I love you",
Then all my cares would fade away.
Now your gone and I'm so lonely,
But love like ours will never part;
So please come back and in the meanwhile,
I've locked a treasure in my heart,
The memory of you sweetheart.

Ruth E. Moran

Mind and Memory

When I close my eyes, images and memories suddenly appear;
It's hard enough, to live my life, now that you're not here.
I'm remembering you when we were together;
I'll be thinkin' of you forever and ever.
What ever happens, happens, but my feelings will always stay true;
I've met a lot of girls, but none have compared to you.
As my mind clears, my thoughts start to unravel;
Help me God, I'm not sure if this is good or evil.
Of all my memories, only one shall last;
The memory of you and I, together in the past.
As hard as I try, you will never leave my mind;
Even when I'm lost, that memory I still find.
What good does it do when It's stuck in my head;
I'll never see you again, so maybe I'm better off dead.
As ridiculous as it sounds, you will never know;
The pain I went through, starin' out my window.
You would invade my mind, like some kind of plague;
What I knew for sure, was still quite vague.
Why am I so confused, about what I knew; every damn memory was always
about you.
Never will my memories, start to subside; because my love for you I just can't hide.

Michael A. Isles

A Cowboy's Life

A cowboy's life is kinda hard to explain
Its more than any fortune or fame.
To him its a way of life
The saddles, ropes, and his wife.

The woman has to be strong
Cause the road ahead is gonna be long.
The cowboy lives, breathes and sleeps rodeo
But to him its more than a show.

Of course, a cowboy needs his lovin'
But he'll be right there if push comes to shovin'
Whether he's out feeding or fixin' fence his work is never done
But no matter what, he'll get his share of fun.

For the younger one he has hopes and dreams of the NFR
Standing up there and being the star
For the older one a ranch, some cattle and a good time
Is all he needs to stay in his prime.

But just remember that a cowboys life would never be
Without his woman, his rodeo and being free.

Michelle Kennington

Here's To Texas

Here's to Texas, the Lone Star State,
It's time to party and cut the birthday cake,
It's time to remember her remarkable past,
When the Cowboys were legends,
Who could ride hard and shoot fast.

When longhorns and buffalo roamed wild and free,
And the land belonged to Indians, called Sioux and Cherokee,
When the brave men at the Alamo, fought to the death,
To free all of Texas from Santa Anna's wrath.

When immigrants came, looking for freedom and land,
And laid the foundation on which we now stand.
Here's to all Texans, no matter where you are,
Let's sing the song that says it all,
In only a couple of bars.

"When I die, I may not go to heaven,
Cause I don't know if they let Cowboys in,
So when I die just let me go to Texas,
Cause Texas is as close as I've been."

Maxine De Troy

The Voice Of Love

The voice of Love cries on high,
It's unending sound is always nigh.
From the depths of the sea
To the highest of hills
The voice of Love is never still.

From the cries of the babe in it's
mother's arms at night,
To the pitter patter of Little feet in flight.
The voice of Love is always there.
For all to grasp, for all to share.

Love Lifts us up to a higher plane
Above Life's toils and wretched pain.
The voice of Love shall unending be.
Always there for you and me.

Wanda J. Brown-Smith

Changing Horizons

The sinking sun slowly etches
its way below the purple
shadows of mountains standing
unconquered on the far away horizon.

Those majestic mountains remain
strong and bold, being whipped and
battered by the various conditions of nature;
yet like you, they stand
stalwart and unconquerable.

And I, like the sun, must
meekly lower myself into the
shadows of yesterday in your mind.

I must try to go my own way and
rise again in the morning
on a different horizon and
continue to live and love
because of differences.

Paula Warner Jorgensen

Poetry

Poetry is as beautiful as the rain in the forest; and
It's words are as soft as the greenish waters of flowing rivers,
and the wild flowers in the dense pasture valley,
covered with the fresh morning dew.

Poetry sounds like the serenade of new lovers, the Waltz
of weddings danced by young couples, showing off their fashions
made of French Lace, and matching hair pieces of pastel
color feathers.

Poetry can have you change moods, content or sad. It's an
inspiration that comes from the heart, sometimes makes you laugh,
other times makes you cry.

Poetry is sincere, honest, truthful. It never lies.
It has no limits when combined with expressions of love;
It's the endless Universal Sung, cause what Poetry is all about;
It's the story of our lives.

Olga E. Ramirez

Wisdom

Go ask the Mona Lisa
What the weeping willows taught
"Just listen to the wind," said she
"listen to the whispering silence of being"
then she smiled.

Victoria Lynn Santi

A Lonely City

I now sit as a lonely city once full of life.
I've become like a widow who weeps bitterly in the night.
None to comfort me; I have no vibe; I'm one amid no other.

In the midst of distress, I'm oft overtaken by grief.
All roads to freedom are blocked by hills of my enemies.
All pathways to happiness are cut short by rivers of my adversaries.

The closer I get to the wings of the eagles of the sky,
the more they seek my life. Our dance is that of anger; one
I particularly care not to step to. Why do I feel discouraged?
The dance has been stepped for generations.

Is there but one who can save me? The joy of my heart has
ceased. It seems that the delight of the laws rest only in
individual hands; they are not just. I meditate and give all
my cares to the One who dwells within me.

He hears my woes, and answers me in His righteousness.
My refuge, and my strength is in Him; for no other can spare
me the pain. I look to Him to save my life.

Theresa Mack

The Sands Of Time

I've walked the valleys and felt her despair
I've climbed the mountains to breathe the fresh air
I've sunk to the ocean's bottom and bathed in her filth and scorn
I cursed my mother for the day I was born
I picked a beautiful and fragrant rose and
Was bitten by her thorn
I've known lust and her jealousy
I've known hate and her anger
I've known love and her beauty...but never
Have I seen beauty like the beauty that I
See in you.
I know my emotions and these I try to hide
Like the ocean hides her shore with her ebb tide
My love is the ocean
My emotions are the shore
And each and every grain of sand is the
Time I shall spend with the one I adore

Oly Wolden

Let Him Go

Since the day you left me,
I've never been the same.
The tears just won't stop falling,
but I know I'm the one to blame.
The words you said so sweetly,
I still ponder in my mind,
the question, if I'll ever get over you,
haunts me all the time.

But now that I'm living without you,
well, life can't get much worse.
Even though you've been gone for a while,
my heart still really hurts.
I'm slowly getting better,
though you already found someone new.
And now... it's over...
but I just can't let go of you.

You have gone on with your life,
I guess now I should see,
that even though it was good while it lasted,
we just weren't meant to be.

Shawna Peters

Time-Wise

Time marches on in measured steps - sunrise, sunset, sunrise.
Join in the march, but set your pace and do not compromise.
Time is a rare and precious gift that must be shared or spent.
We occupy a space in time and we must pay the rent.
Remember, when we're spending time - we can't recall one minute.
Be sure each purchase that you make has something worth-while in it.

Consider time when counting out the cost against the gain.
Just moments spent unwisely may bring you hours of pain.
Hold close the precious moments, and live life every day.
You cannot stay the hands of time, they quickly move away.

We all share time with loved ones, to show them that we care.
But when it's peace of mind you need, then spend some time in prayer.

Madelyn L. McGinley

Cancer

The call came the week before Thanksgiving. The news wasn't good.
Junior had just returned from Rochester. There was nothing that could be done.
Go home and enjoy the quality of life you have left.
They mentioned chemo only as a pain reliever later on.

Death. Imminent death for my young brother.
I recalled instances of people with pancreatic cancer and knew they didn't live long.
What must he be going through at this moment with that awful knowledge?
Or his wife Or the three children, an eleven year old son and two teenage daughters?
They were going to lose their dad. Had he told them?

The trip back to Bismarck from Rochester must have been just awful.
How could their minds not whirl with this knowledge?
How could they possibly think of anything else?
Will he make it to Christmas?
What an awful season this will be. Everybody will be cheery.
How can this be a merry time when all the Christmas glitz means absolutely nothing,
When every moment Junior knows he's going to die?
When his family must be asking, "Will this be our last Christmas with him?"
But how can they even think Christmas?
This will not be a Christmas they will want to remember.
I wish Christmas could just be obliterated.

Margaret Bitz

"A Face In Crowd"

Lost will I ever be found
Just a face in the crowd
In a crowd where no one knows your name
Are we all here just the same
Quantities of laughter supplies the air
Others crying and speaking aloud
Who is wearing the smile
While disguising the frown
Change the seasons of your hair
Notice the inspections of dissimilar stares
For variety inhabits near extinction
Glance up to the North star in the circle where you stand
In guidance toward the direction to the freedom that is grand
Differences that possess each other
Represents the marked beauty that is discovered
Lost will I ever be found
Just a face in the crowd

Stacy DelCastillo

Jesus My Lord

Jesus this is a personal letter I write to thee,
just because I wonder if you really care for me.
For if you truly did why would you give me this pain
but then again you gave me the beautiful rain.
Oh!! the beautiful rain to wash my tears
with yours to let me know that as I cry.
You silently stand by.
Hold me dear God in your loving hand,
and guide me through your lovely land.
Oh God! How great thou can be!
That you suffered so much and gave your life for me!
Teach me your beautiful ways so I can believe once again in me,
And so I can truly love all that I see.
Whether one has hurt me or not, Let them not rot.
Show them the way, for from you no one can stray.
So in this closing Lord my beautiful light,
Keep my faith in all burning bright.

Melissa Barrera

Home, Sweet, Home

Home's not just a place to come home to
Just to eat and to sleep and to be
Home is a place where you're loved a whole lot
And that's what's important to me

Home is a place full of sunshine
A place to be happy and free,
Home is a place where you just can let go
A place where you're V.I.P.

A home is a place full of laughter and fun
Where everyone's all full of glee,
A home is a family together.
Where it's not lots of "I's" it's a "we".

So now that you understand the meaning of family and home
You probably think your family is great
Well, I'm sure that it is, but you'd better give up
Because mine's already won for first rate!!

Sarah Sydlowski

Give Me A Sign

I wish I could speak to him in a dream,
Just to know that he's all right.

He may not be alive anymore,
But he's with me day and night.

In my heart he memories will stay,
To help me grieve in my own way.

I will remember him forever,
His smiles and his laughter,
The good times and the bad,
The happy and the sad.

I wish he could watch my child grow,
But he's watching somewhere, this I know.

There are things in life we just don't understand,
Like the things that happened to this good man.

For whatever reason it had to be,
He suffers no more, that I see.

I love him with all my heart's content,
Please God, let him have a sign sent.

Tami Poulin

The Universal Day

Searched high upon its rest,
keeping our strings taut,
She supports the master's festering hand
rips at our hearts,
tears at our souls,
the strong prevail,
the weak fail;
And they will be puppets,
not only to the hooded plague,
but to the helpless mortal as well,
It is the people that challenge death's strings,
who shall truly live
it is those people who still die,
yet it is they
that won't be controlled,
but who control.
They break the mold,
They seize the throne and thieve the mace,
and so replacing the cloaked one on it's roast,
Relieving the puppet master of it's strings,
until,
fate takes their last breath.

Robin Dzvonik

Gods Child

Kiss me beautiful child of God
kiss me with lips of wine
kiss me oh! child with kisses of your soul
kiss me with mouth of time
kiss me beautiful child of God
kiss me for your love is delightful than time

Kiss me are your fragrance of your soul intone
kiss me with your name as mine
kiss me the perfume of passion of first
kiss is like forever in times last
kiss me beautiful bride of God

Zeke

Golden Place

The soft summer rain trickles onto my hair, as I walk into the golden lair.

I feel a welcoming presence in this mystical place, as it gently wraps me in it's warm embrace.

The sounds all around are like a mother's heartfelt voice, and the ground beneath is cool and moist.

I feel so peaceful, so welcome, so at home, hearing the birds' quiet chirps I know I will never be alone.

The quiet reminds me of the people who love me, and I start to cry, thinking of the people who never again I will see.

As my teardrops hit the stream below, I start to see the faces of people I knew long ago.

As my tears take me back in time, from the tree next to me falls a leaf of some kind.

While I look at the leaf I count the people who have died, and the endless number of tears I've cried.

As I'm leaving this golden place I see a stream of light, and the wind carries my pain back into the night.

Lauren Romestan

Dreamscape

Years of miles and miles and miles of years
Lay spent, upon my doorstep.
While the child inside, all this traveling fears,
wanting only to be safely kept.

Amidst the shadows, dreams are born, dying ever
in my morning wake.
Yet the dreams still succor the child it seems;
For dreams, they give, what all else takes.

The world it grows so small, so small,
and I so large, it seems.
There is no place - to hide at all,
except, perhaps, within my dreams.

C. R. Wohlford

When The Next Battle Comes

Pearl Harbor Spirit,
Will make us realize.
Our glorious flag,
Still waves in the sky.
With its red, white and blue,
It will always be viewed.
We defend this great nation.
We don't have to prove,
That Iwo Jima still lives in our minds.
With blood no retreat, we don't have to teach
That freedom prevails.
Every star is a state, that we know are all dates
Of the men who all died.
What we challenge is fate.
When the next battle comes,
We will fight till we've won.
Nationalities we are,
Let it live in our hearts.
When we salute that proud flag,
With its red white and blue

Peter F. Barrow

In Memory Of Samuel Evans Sr.

As I heard the news my throat tightened and I prayed
"Let it not be true" as I fell to my knees - I heard a quiet inner
voice say ever so sweetly "Be still"

Pain seething through my soul like a molten rod of steel - all joy in my heart overcome by the shadow of death - my thoughts raced of past memories and happier times as the tears trailed down my face. Again the inner voice "Be still"

I thought "What manner of God has removed this man is his prime when
so many people cherished the essence of his life. Is it the same God who changed him from a wild-spirited troubled youth into a gentle loving man. The same Lord that brought him safely home from Desert Storm.

Would I choose that Samuel had never breathed life that I could escape the agony of his death. Can I elect to praise God for the sweet and not be willing to praise him for the bitter. I choose to be thankful that by the death of one man others are wiser, more compassionate and closer to the will of God.

Thankful that the colors of spring appear more vibrant knowing that they too shall fade. Thankful that melodies are sweeter as they release the buried emotions. And thankful that the aroma of life is more precious, because I will never forget the taste of death.

A new joy and peace has entered my heart knowing that death has no dominion over Samuel. He now rests in the house of the Lord. Again, louder and clearer I heard the inner voice "Be still and know that I am GOD!"

Michelle E. McKinney

Demiurge

Oh Demiurge! Let me dream with the winged Golden Dragon
Let me ride on it, watch the earth from high above,
the totality
You that rendered to us the alchemy, and we untied wars
Never knowing how to handle it with harmony

Oh Demiurge! Let me dream that I can be a dreamer
That I can run with the wind and surf it
That time does not have being
That I have found eternal love

Oh Demiurge! Let me dream with the revealing epiphany
That I decipher the arcane essence of life
That the fantasy become real
That I behold the concealed reality lying behind
appearances

Alas Demiurge! Who knows the fate of our hopes?
If not you.....Am I dreaming my ontology?

Paulo A. Oemig

God's Day Well Spent

Oh Lord, on this beautiful day you have made,
Let my use it to the glory of you.
Let me walk, let me talk, let me yield to your will,
In all that you desire me to do.

On this day dear Lord, let me testify,
Be an example of your love,
Let me preach your gospel, your sacrifice,
Of sending Jesus from above.

I want to lead some lost soul, to the cross today.
I want to help a backslider to again find the way
And for your faithful servants who have been tossed in the wind.
I'll be an anchor for strength, I will befriend.

And as for me dear Lord, as the day passes by,
I will take time in your word, so I too can survive.
And at the end of the day, as I kneel down to pray,
Let me feel your sweet spirit, let me hear you Lord say.
My servant, my servant, I am pleased with you task,
And now I give you sweet rest.

Victoria Logan

Untitled

Tucked within my own imaginings,
Lies and breathes a sacramental creature.
Could I but loose and yet control its nature;
Its all enveloping passion;
What glorious wonders it contains.

Yet time — the kindly enemy,
Brings more layers of cover.
I hide it — to protect me.
I hide it — they expect me to.
And when it does sneak out — out of control,
They say "too bad".

I need enriching fellows who will say,
"LOOSE IT!"
"We reveal in such passion," "How alive!"
Passionate companions,
Let us find each in the other.
Sacrament for sacrament.

Patricia Dickson

"Life"

Life is precious, simple and sweet
Life begins when two people meet
Life is love, and love must start
Life is when it comes from the heart
Life journeys forward when two people make love
Life for three starts with a gift from above
Life is the son that grows big and strong
Life for him should be pleasant and long
Life goes on with his thoughts in a whirl
Life continues, he's met that special girl
Life is the ceremony that makes her his wife
And continues in this precious, simple and sweet circle called life.

Scott E. Wilson

Freedom's Flag

100,000 voices echoing from the past
Like 100,000 trumpets
Shaking the heavens with a mighty blast

Veterans marching in review
Brave men and women who gave all for the red white and blue

Heroes with silver stars and blood-red bars
Who bore the battle scars

They paid the price for you and me
That we may continue to be free

From battle fields with names we have forgotten
Come honored dead who can not be forgotten

I hear their voices calling out

I hear the mighty shout

I hear the message clearly

Don't let them desecrate our flag
The flag that we love dearly

Clearly the flag is more than just a symbol
It's the soul of freedom.

It's the heart of this great land- may it forever stand.

God Bless America!

Uriel E. Glidewell

You

Independent and strong
Like a beautiful written song.
It rings through the night air
Restless and wild like a child so fair.

Determined to fight until the battle is won
For you are the only son.
Tenderness and passion overtake the storm
To be lost in only a form.

Lost yet, directed to find the way
Like the sun as it rises over the bay.
Discover the fields of golden brass
And gently enjoy the aroma of cut grass.

You are a man
So spread your wings like a fan.
And fly- fly to the clouds of heather blue
And rest while watching from where you once few.

T. Strieter-Mandrik

Wife To Mother

Like a son,
Like a mother,
They are all the same.

So I weep and cry for the sadness in your eyes,
So I say to you in thanks of having him,
You used to be a wife,
But now you are a mother.

Now I say from the bottom of my heart,
He used to be a little egg in your womb,
Now he has everlasting life,
So I weep and now I say good-bye,
To you and say the same.

J. Blyn MacLaughlin

D

Piercing
like an owl scoping its prey.

Mesmerizing
as his sharpened eyes focus upon your soul.

Enticing
with his cunning grin
shearing through your most private fantasies.

Seducing
your will from a racing heart of desires.

Seizing
innocent flesh with charm and wit.

Swallowing
the life spirit; left to soak
in uncontrollable passion.

Quenching
his thirst, you are held in ecstasy.

Relinquishing
the torpid phantom of him mortal kiss...

Odessa Petty

Strained Ego

With great pomp I was mounted on a pedestal
Like I was gold, diamonds, pearls or crystal.
But all was powder and a lot of dust;
And all was fitting for trash and destined to rust.

My soaring ego really got a strong hold on me;
And I rushed to invite friends in to see
All the awards, plaques, books and pins
Until the source did wear so thin.

Before you become so swollen and great,
You better think for you might be a plate.
Sometimes having others improve your pride
Might be better for all brag left inside.

We are all princes, kings and queens
If our lives are pure and our bodies fed beans.
Everything light is better than kings' meat;
And bowing the knees and praying is best treat.

Then our proper ego will come out pure gold;
For there's nothing new and nothing old.
We need to spread the Good News to all
Before we see "in that day" and miss His call.

Lillian M. Donahoe

Rock

The beauty of a rock - what of that?
Like pieces to a world long gone,
Like a passage to another time and place,
Breathtaking statuaries "chased and scored",
Similar to the design of mother earth,
Pieces to a great mystery not yet answered,
Little remembrances of a time cherished,
Marble, obsidian, evidence of our planets' great beauty,
A clue to the creation of the universe,
A doorway to understanding,
Long after the extinction of man will remain
These little treasures of a time gone by,
All different yet alike,
The key to knowledge.

Melissa Danielle Loggins

Friends

A ship at sea, carried by all which surrounds you
Like wind, they direct you to new uncertainties
  Some dangerous, some not
Like fish, they roam troubleless only meaning well
You only wish to jump ship and be so free.
On the horizon, your kin await with open arms
Hoping that in the end they show the way home,
Each hour you drift is a heart breaking eternity of doubt
Because they know....
  They know, they were all once adrift.

Sammy Miller

First Love

A baby lay in the cradle, he walks in the door and now the little baby cries no more.

The little girl breaks her arm, he holds her tight and now everything is alright.

The young woman hurts from a love gone bad, he holds her and her world is no longer so sad.

The aging man gasps for air, she holds him tight and says a prayer he is now breathing fair.

His head is down, the angels hold him tight and he can no longer fight.

Daddy come back she begs, but he can no more his wings are there and he has given his share.

Now he is free, but what about me.

Sally Davis

The Brother

There he sat, that small nephew of mine
looking sad and glum but extremely kind

What could make those huge, beautiful brown eyes sad,

You only have to look around him to see the
circumstances and understand why he would be so mad

For this little brother of his would pester, pinch,
and fight with him only to get his own way again

So there's never a moments peace he can share alone
therefore, he must pull into a world of his own
for his little bother to have all the attention it seems,
just irks him and I know he wants to scream!

Please help him someone, he needs to excel
with his brother he can't, he'll be in hell!
For in his heart he wants a bond with his brother
but he can't do it if there's no help from others!

So he trudges along this painful, silent path
hoping that his brother grows up fast
so they can have a friendship that will last.

Maybe someday!

Paulette Blackburn

A Daughter's Lament

She often dreams of what it would have been like to be daddy's
little girl,
To have a daddy on whose lap she could curl.
One with whom she could talk about things, only they could
understand,
A daddy who would try his very best to teach her all the things
that would make her life grand.

When it's time for father's day, she is left feeling dismal and grey,
Hoping that if she could have given him a gift he would have liked it.
How she wished that when someone asks, how is your daddy?
She could say "He is just fine, thank you, he's at home waiting for me,
We're going to the mall on a shopping spree.

Unable to answer the question, she is left to reflect,
That God has never made a mistake yet.
A daughter is God's perfect gift given to special people down below,
People who are expected to watch over his gift and help it to grow.

Two are entrusted with a daughter's care,
Mother is one, Father is the other who completes the pair.
It was never meant that in his desire to make us three,
that daddy would leave, making the circle incomplete.
Her wish will always, always be, that her family was made up of
Mommy,
Daddy and Me.

Marcia Prince

Air Force Wife

She is often left alone,
lonely, single parenting.
No candlelight dinners, no movies,
no sex, no communication.
Just empty walls, cluttered closets,
boxes and memories from station to station.

She is often mistaken, no identity,
no rank, no pay, no promotions.
She is often forgotten when her man goes to war,
she copes, she tries, she fights to keep
her family together.

She's loving, supportive, a warrior and a jewel.
When the last assignment comes, she's retired!

Nicola Brown

"This And More"

Her face is lined with memories;
long hours spent in thought and laughter,
hope and despair.

Her smile projects a rhapsody
that grasps the beating heart
and suspends the moment there.

Treasure chests of precious glimpses past
I view and touch and fold to myself
and long for the endurance.

Fair maiden when young, now the contrast;
she teaches still the babes she cradles,
unknowingly, and with gentle perseverance.

Our mother's hands do not deny
the labor of her love, tilling years away;
nor the justice of her court.

They sculpted character - and I-
I have bore witness to the artist's masterpiece
set upon life's easel, so short.

We are her dreams fulfilled, entwined
from a love grander than others purport.

Mary Blanchard

Inspiration

A panther looms inside of me....
Longing; lapping; panting; crouching.
I wait. I wait...
I pounce and the idea escapes me
with music I don't understand;
a cage bars my effort to spring,
though I observe the pinnacle.
So, I eye the eagle,
never able to steal its' wings;
as it scars teasingly,
I remain
forever black, forever lonely...
searching for my mate,
while the blood trickles scarlet from my fang.
I purr....I growl....
I purr for the day my nature shines,
as my heart beats with the sun;
to give me life....
or to kill the eagle.

Grace Adoms

A Lifetime of Dreams

A beautiful young woman I see,
Looking in the mirror Back at Me -
A person so pure, sweet, and shy,
Make up streaking my face as I begin to cry.
My white dress falls down to the floor -
I straighten my veil and head out the door.
And with my father I walk down the isle
Through my tears, at my mother, I try to smile.
I glance at my husband-to-be
While he is looking down the rows of people at me
A lifetime together we started that day
With the two little words that we did say
A world of promises, hopes, and dreams
Never to be broken - or so it seems
We try our best to succeed
Only to find out to live our dreams -
Each other is all we need.

Vicki Backman

"A Curious Thing, Love"

A curious thing,
love -
personified by
a soft smile
twinkling eye
radiating touch
in these we may see it clearly
but do we pay attention
to its diversity
like a pansy bursting with its spectrum of colors
pain
joy
sorrow
contentedness
even in these forms
it has always been there
ever changing, blooming
like the progression of a close friendship
a curious thing,
love.

Laura Harrison

Treasures - Tears Of Time

Whenever someone special dies, you swear that you'll never love again.
But then someone new comes into your life, and becomes your closest friend.
That friend may help you soothe the pain, to help you again appreciate sun, wind, and when it rains.
You will soon realize everyone that is important to you has given something memorable, a sweet memory or two.

Grandma's cardigan blanket, your brother's bronzed baby shoe,
Momma's beautiful stuffed rabbit, Dad's autographed football, too.

Some people have riches, some people have jewels, but everyone has memories of young, old and new.
Make the most of your life, enjoy it in its prime, before you reach the Tears of Time.

Sarah Grenleski

Love

Love is a thing you cannot hide,
love is a feeling you can't set aside.
When you love someone you can't let him go,
cause you know you love him so.
When you look in his eyes all you see is love,
just like a bird a lonesome dove.
Love is like a wish flying in the sky,
cause love passes by and by.
Love sometimes makes you sad,
but sometimes it makes you a little mad.
So go learn to love,
and find your lonesome dove.

Stacey Maynigo

Death

Accept me for who I am,
Love me because you want to,
Care about me,
These things I need.

Love is universal.
Everyone needs love.
Because care is a style of love,
It is expected by most.

Why do I ask for these?
Because, maybe they will make me feel better.
Why do I ask for these things?
Even though I know I cannot get them from his world.

Death, hate, and excitement,
This is all in this life.
Death is the answer to all my needs.
(Why do we have needs?)

Even though no one can feel your needs,
Maybe Death can relieve your needs.
Is Death the answer?

Sarah Williams

The Live Within

The rainforest with its beautiful tones of green,
Is no longer to them cold and mean,
As they walk the path they come to life,
And forget of their world of pain and strife,
They started lifeless and dead, but now they have seen.

They will go back to their jobs and lives,
And some will forget, while others will remember and strive,
To never let go of the happiness found,
In this great land where none are bound,
And the life within is found and revived.

Roy Lee Hartman

Storm Clouds

In life, time and time again my heart seems to get broken,
Love shouldn't come from the outside beauty only, but
from with in.
How do I get the respect that I deserve,
instead of always getting kicked to the curb.
Why do I get treated bad for the things I have yet to do,
always being considered an outcast treated like I should be in a zoo.
Life has gotten me down to the point where I can't
take it any longer,
with trials and tribulations I have yet to get stronger.
If there was a chance to take my own life would I?
I don't even have enough respect for myself to break
down and cry.
What I need is silence in a time where the world is
roaring and loud,
I can tell that it's going to rain because here come the
storm clouds.

Michael T. H. Reed

"A Wish"

I once knew a person who loved to be alive.
Loved everyday of her life.
Then, one day darkness fell upon this person.
A person who used to laugh, smile, and joke
Was now taken over by crying and loneliness.
Deep down I knew that the person I once knew
Was in that lonely soul.
If only somehow that person could be released.
This person is so near and dear to me.
She is my grandmother.
If somehow she could be the same.
Then all the pain would go away;
And everything would be the same.

Patricia Ferraiuolo

Dreams

Sleeping so soundly by the moonlight,
loving dreams come softly at night.
The cuddly cute kitten warming your feet,
dreaming kitty thoughts that to them are so sweet.
The world is so peaceful not a sound to be heard,
but a faint baby cry in the night will be heard.
Life is so peaceful calm and serene,
but its so fragile it remains to be unseen.
God gave us a gift so take it to heart,
it won't be here if we take it apart.
So count your blessings everyday,
give life a chance and live day by day.
The future generations are here to stay,
for the world won't be here if we throw it away.
Dreams we all know can surely come true,
only if we work hard and watch what we do.
So when you lay down to dream and rest,
know that God loves you and your truly blest.

Margaret Beilfuss

The Vision

Walking alone through hills and meadows,
knowing not what lies beyond the fields of green clover,
but still going on,
hoping to find that enchanted dream that has followed me since
childhood.
It's a part of life that comes only once.
Looking forward to each day and not being afraid of tomorrow.
It's a child's world of dreams, hopes and love —
not to be forgotten, but held deep within sweet memories of time.

Trina D. Moore

Epiphany

Yes ma'am, no ma'am, thank you, and please.
Lower your eyes, don't be a tease.
Shoulders back, stand-up straight.
Praise the Lord whatever your fate.
The rules were hard but life was simple.
Your conscience was clear, your body a temple.
Your colors were quiet, your manners were too.
You walked a straight line and never said "Boo."
What really happened who's to know.
On your sixtieth birthday you started to glow.
Your hair turned gray, your face turned a wrinkle.
Your heart felt full, your eyes felt a twinkle.
Your hat was red, your dress was mauve.
People said you didn't look suave.
You traipsed downtown to ogle some men.
You sat on a curb and sang "Amen."
You cooed at the birds and sniffed the flowers.
You swayed "tai chi" and danced for an hour.
People stared and started winking.
Someone asked, "What changed her thinking?"

Stephanie Wolicki

The Sparrow

I saw a sparrow fall this morning
Lying so still upon the ground
I touched it gently with my toe
It didn't move, nor make a sound

I'm sure God was looking down from heaven
For he saw that sparrow fall
I believe his heart ached, a little
For it's mate will never hear its call

I guess it's just the way of nature
As its cycle turns once more
And the little sparrow that fell this morning
Is singing sweetly on another shore.

Ruth Woods

Candles

Candles of many colors large and small
made of wax, a flame flickers tall.

A candle is lit when the sun dips low,
it flickers through the night with it's illuminating glow.

Candles used in churches to show the way,
used on birthday cakes to make a brighter day.

As the candle wick burns, the wax melts down,
small candles form many colors found.

The sun rises in the morning and brings the early light,
a candles flame will be extinguished until the day turns night.

Robert R. Rogers

All The While

All the while I was away,
I thought about you every day.
I thought about our moments together,
Of how I'll always remember,
Your warmth, your touch, your gentle smile,
They stay with me all the while.
And every mile that distance made,
I knew my love would never fade.
An eternal flame it will always be,
That has brightened the path you've made for me.
So from this day forth, wherever I go,
My love for you will forever grow.

Lois Ann Witmer

I Wish

I wish I could change things,
Make new things old again.
Engage little children in play time.
Make them proud to give
All that love brings.

I wish there was a recipe
To mix the good and the better,
Stir minds and hearts together.
That is the way it ought to be.

I wish I could make all things smooth
For children who can be moved
In this world of hate and deceit,
Keep the away from harm and grief.

I wish this world could blossom
With buds of brighter thoughts and intelligent minds
And guide us all in a Godly way
To be respectful, honest, loving and kind.

Wilma J. Washington

The Shadow Of Fear

Shadow that lies on one's soul,
Makes life a terrifying show,
Yet without it you will never be whole.
Why it gives chills you might never know.
In a dark alley on a dark night.
Is a place where one might encounter with fright
This shadow,
Ashamed you might be, wanting to flee,
But this shadow will not easily let you go.
Always know that the shadow has more to show.

Seth Fishman

Modern Man?

Society is evolving downward day by day
Man killing man in the worst way
People these days simply don't care
Most times it's like too much to bear
Trouble amongst acquaintances and family alike
Cynicism, pessimism, racism - "nigger, spic, kyke"
Almost no job security
Water lacking purity
Racial tension on the rise
With hate groups spreading their lies
Women having children with out being wed
People jumping from bed to bed
Drugs, gangs, and drive by shooting
Unpopular verdicts - rioting and looting
Homelessness severe
Politicians don't hear
Aids - killing millions
Debt in the trillions
The tragedies go on and on
And so too will our faith with each dawn...

Laura L. Poll

By The Hand

Can I take you by the hand and lead you to a mountain top
Up beyond the clouds
Can I take you by the hand and walk on the sand so white by
The water so crystal clear

Can I take you by hand and lead you to a place where we
Can never be separated

A place where no one can reach us
Can I take you by the hand and lead you to my dreams

Sheila Holwell

A Cry For Help

You always know how something seems
Later on that day I suddenly screamed
I woke up hot and I lay again
Words go through my mind that were once spoken
Thoughts erupt in my poetic brain
The sting of his response caused such pain
Light of mourn cracked my eyes
Further and further they open wide
I softly speak but words don't appear
In my painless voice you can hear the fear
Deep inside lies still my soul
Torn and broken from young to old
Another bruise, the tear trickles down my face
Another nightmare, I'm being chased
Stabbed with a question, I wonder why
The truth is hiding, I tell another lie
The life I live is truly a bind
Does it get better or fade in time
Unlock my mystery and see what's inside
For deeply in pain is where I hide

Courtney Croll

"Decision"

I hear their caring whispers call,
Leading me further into the night.

I'm so ashamed that I hear them at all.
For my soul's been born into the light.

I sit at the edge of my own existence.
The voices they call me with loving persistence.

The darkness beckons, it's so mysterious.
The voices hail me, God help me, I'm curious.

I stand at the edge of my own eternity,
Pondering my fate, deciding in my soul.

The light, so bright, begins to comfort me,
Giving me strength, making me whole.

I hear their caring whispers call,
Moving away into the night.

The light embraces me, I can't hear them at all
As I walk further into the light.

Demetrius McCormick

As the River Runs

An urban second grader,
Learned of mother nature's true graces,
As they were meant to be,
For the first time.

The inexperienced innocent,
Learned to smile,
For friendships for all,
Accelerated on these waters.

Around the corner from white whispering foam,
Glittering water opened new passage ways through the mind.
And plush green trees passed,
Near newly befriended woodland creatures playing on a slowly eroding path.

An old memory,
To one who has seen a seven year drought spread the disease of the future.
For half the plush green trees are now brownish-red,
And the waters paths erosion slows down the water.

To restore an original is too costly,
Yet fire will come if left this way.
The earths youth has passed,
And it took my innocent smile.

Jennifer Roizen

Oklahoma Bombing

Once in the city, the sun went down;
Leaving a quiet and peaceful town.
There are some men who just arrived;
Planning evil deeds quietly inside.

Now in the morning, after the rising sun;
Their evil plan will soon be done.
Now the sun is very high,
A shattering boom flies through the sky.
But soon after the smoke has cleared;
A devastating site will appear:
A Federal Building down town has been bombed.

The entire world is now alarmed
This incident has harmed;
Many people physically and mentally too.
Now the question arose, "What shall we do?"

As evil provoked, good increased
And soon there was helping everywhere
Then the ashes of the tragedy arose a caring and kinder world.
The ray of light people looked for;
Was finally here.

Aaron Paul Beatty Broxterman

A Child's Pain

Creature in the night so cold and mean
Left me feeling dirty and obscene
Mommy dearest hear my cries
The worm is eating out my mind

Lover for you, fear for I
His words of deceit to you I cry
Those shrieks of lies are not true
Mommy, please believe these words I speak to you

His reign of power must be seized
Mind erosion, inner corruption,
he wants you to conceive

Pain and destruction from him is all I've felt
Upon his grave I would've gladly knelt

But now I know, the bars he will rot behind
Are the one's from which
my soul has died
To see him suffer in my young minds cell
Satisfaction!
and to him, Welcome to Hell!

Danielle Matarazzo

Seasons By The Month

January brings a turn for the better with
Lengthening days and a hope for warm weather
February is ground hog, a myth of old
When spring will arrive is supposed to be told
March winds and April showers
Bring Mayflowers and June roses
And fireworks on the fourth of July
August and September means country fairs
October we store summers goods with care
November we gratefully thank Him above
For all He has given us, especially His love
December is the month we look forward to
For January is next and soon another summer.

Elizabeth Marston

O Tree

O tree!
Let me touch your highest leaf and taste the sweeter air
which makes your leaves so red.

The branches, the twigs, your frail bones. So many
like a spiders web of lace no royal gown could imitate.
You stand tall yet not at all proud, your elegance
is far greater than pride. The rains from God above
must have fed you nothing but liquid heaven.

Seduce me and let me hear the songs you've
heard from birds whose lives have gone.
May I express my love, and the passion you've snuck
into my heart?
O tree! O beauty! O strength, wisdom and elegance
of age you are!
May I love you? May I just in one dream live in that
web of lace which kisses the beginning of heaven and
can see from above your roots?

Jennifer Jimerson

First Fantasy

Listen softly as I speak
Let my fingers touch you deep, as I am laying against your side-
I'll make love to you all night
Misty shadows on the walls- dancing wildly, as passions calm
I run my fingers through your hair
Caressing your body, Ahh" I'll love you all night
I'm over you, I am under you. I touch your back, I am on top of you-
My tongue slides feeling you. I am in you deeply, as we feel one
Another, caressing you-touch me softly.
Up and down in and out around and round over and over almost
Spontaneously we explode...
Passions running deep running wild
We lay arrest-our bodies tremble- I kiss you.
I made love to you all night.

Anne T. Hall

The Welcome Burden

In a corner sits someone who has experienced the potholes in
life's road.
Potholes formed by life's never ending trials.
Some are wide and deep, others are small and insignificant.
In their eyes you can see the love which has caused their pain.
As you look into their eyes you can see the tears rising to the
surface waiting to break free.

As the tears of frustration roll down their strained, worn-out face,
they wish there was more they could do.
The individual slowly rises to their feet, breathes a sigh, wipes
away the tears, and begins to walk away.
You see, the pain they bear is not their own but yet,an
overwhelming sense of care and concern.
They bear this burden with delight for it is caused by the
suffering of a friend.

Someone they love is hurting and they want so much to take the
pain away.
They want to be able to give their friend the magic answers to make
everything all right
again, but they cannot for they don't have them.
Their pain is the pain of a friend;
A friend who cares, worries, listens, and loves.

Amanda Foust

My Perfect Angel

As a perfect angel you came to me,
lifted and led me, when I was too blind to see.
When I felt like giving up, you said "Give it one
more try",
always lending your shoulder when I needed
a good cry,
your special smiles and encouragement sometimes
got me through a week,
your pushed me to continue, even when the finish
line looked bleak,
I have shared so much laughter and love with you,
I always admired all the things you do,
All the memories in my heart could never be replaced,
All the memories of you and your pretty, smiling
face.

Julie Grotto

The Storm

The night was dark and stormy.
Lighting flashed and thunder boomed.
Rain lightly pattered against the window.
As the shutter banged against the window pane
a distant dog let out a eerie howl.

Lighting and thunder locked in a fierce battle.
The noise of the battle grew louder.
As quickly as it began the battle ended and the
tired soldiers laid to rest.
As the green earth drank in the rain.

Keilah Frank

The Load That We Carry

Insurmountable! Is the cry we bellow as we confront our existence;
Like a donkey, a mule, we should marvel at our resilience.

Instead of claiming, exulting in victory, all we hear is confusion
and noise;
As though our birth, our demise, were predicated, by choice.

Like a rat caught by a trap,
Whose sense of direction, is confounded, without the aid of a map.

Refusing to let go or give up hope;
Choosing to fight, not mope:

Because he holds life so dear, so precious,
So certain that, he will not find another one, analogous.

As the executioner, one cannot, but feel, respect and pride,
To see how mightily he struggles to surmount his expected fate,
and turn the tide.

The load we carry, the burden we shoulder is not only for ourselves;
The battle we wage so valiantly, is for our offsprings, our better
selves.

Like Sisyphus, we are condemned to push the boulder up the hill,
But, only in that endeavor, do we experience life's thrill.

Like a colony of ants, passing sugary food down the chain link, to
ensure survival,
We should similarly take charge and responsibility for each other,
to bring forth, revival.
Acceptance of our condition, should be our modus-vivendi, our
predicament;
For in this life alone, will we find satisfaction, as there won't be
another installment.

Alain J. Vielot

Thoughts Of Life

Have you ever loved someone that turned you away?
Like a flower that grows, then fades to gray.

Children learn when they play.
When they grow don't let them stray.

Life goes on with hurt and pain.
Like the soft wind blowing in the west rain.

Love ad hate as we know.
Is like autumn turning to winter then there's snow.

Listen to your heart beating so strong.
but always remember it's only for so long.

Darlene Westerman

How He Makes Me Feel

Spring forth like a child engaged deep in play
Like a ray of sunshine on a mid-summer's day,
An autumn leaf rich with color and crispness.
Winter night sky silently crackling with newness.
Fresh as wild daisy shadowing a gentle breeze
Intense heat, whereas, I crumble to my knees,
Harvest, a time in which I gather my senses
Snowflakes that penetrate all of my defenses.
Whispering raindrops cleansing forest depths
High noon, life's summit, ascending steps.
Whirling winds bringing chaos then order
This is how my man makes me feel.

Karen Lee Levesque

How Quietly Do Years Escape from View

My youth opens and closes before me
like a textbook longing to be read,
scattered amidst air-tight pages
of lives being lived and those already dead.

How slowly Father Time creeps his way in
to fade the memories of days gone by.
How quietly do years escape from view
and change faces before the ignorant eye.

All the actions of lives already lived
blend into shadows like an artist's pen
that traces over pictures a thousand times
hopeless to revive their beauty once again.

How my age cuddles up beside me
and changes my face and dulls my hands.
How quietly do years escape from view
and turn mountains into grains of sand.

A hundred billion lifetimes lost before me
lie forgotten and absent of names,
but hidden quietly closed in places well hid
their faces smile behind dusty picture frames.

Christopher Carpenter

Women Are Nice

Any Culture, that is around.
Where, the society puts women down.
You will find war, and trouble.
When, the men's testosterone begins to bubble.
Women play, a large part,
in giving people, joy, compassion, and heart.
When they are not allowed to have their say,
men with men, fight all the day.

Richard A. Granholm

Olympia

Rain forest saplings from toppled trees spring
Like bonsai of behemoths they tenuously cling
To the cycles of living with which the woods ring.

Ferns line the glacier-fed, pumice-laced stream
While nestlings of eagles return mothers scream
In the rhythms of feeding beneath the moon's beams.

Falls tumble and roar with last winter's snow
O'er the misted, worn rocks awash in the glow
Of the days broken sunlight on the meadow below.

Everywhere, all the while, the pulsations continue
Through moments and decades in all the world's venues
The life-making dying is out there, within you.

Measured in seconds and counted in ages
The hum of the galaxy steadfastly rages
With infinite music on all of life's pages.

We think we began but we feel we can't end
Just what is the message of the senderless send
From the universe inside us that forever wends.

Clifford Mark

"Snow Flakes"

Delicate snow flakes wafting from the skies,
Like gentle petals caressing my eyes.
Dazzling me with their prisms of light,
While they dance around in the night.

Softly falling to the ground,
Like fluffy white eiderdown.
Covering Mother Nature's breast,
And the robins in their nest.

Slowly melting in the morning sun,
Like lovers when they join as one.
Flowing together in a union of love,
Giving life to the earth and creatures above.

Dorothy Riggs McTague

Breaking The Barrier Of Love

Love will always come and go,
like that of day and night.
But a true love is one that will stay with you forever,
even through all of the fights.
The real thing is what most are in search of,
like that of a new life.
People must learn love should be cherished because one
day it could be taken without a second thought.
Love between two is such a
special thing and it breaks my heart to
think I still stand alone.
I yearn to feel one's tender touch caressing my
body in the late hours of the night.
I have gone so long, without love,
I no longer know what it actually feels like to be loved.
Alone in solitude,
waiting for a new love to come break
the unwanted barrier around me a
supplement of the entity of my forgotten desire for true love.

Alma E. Klingle

Untitled

If we are just yet specks of mass
upon this air filled ball,
Then why do we exist while it seems
we should just fall?

Melanie E. McGriff

The January Puddle

This dirty cold water freezing in the cold of January.
Reflecting the faces of passing citizens.
Flowing with the force of the strong wind.
Muddy, drab, slowly forming frost on the top.
A single dime has been caught in this muddy pit of despair.
Lively and moving, reflecting the sun's rays, pleading not to freeze.
Shimmering with innocence of a newborn child.

Shannon Ray Shepherd

Cavalier Nights

Humid air hangs
like wet linen from the sky
as the wheels of my Cavalier
spin upon highway 17.
In the horizon
sits the red August moon
reddened ripe for the harvest
while false lights acne the broad
back of the Binghamton night,
105.7 love songs
snake their way through the
maze of space biting my
memory to remember, remember the memory
of that idiosyncratic deer sauntering from shadows
of suburban lawns to stop my Cavalier way
to speak with a non-blink of earthy brown,
the goosebumps shivered,
I tingled then.
I tingle now.

Dodd C. Gengenbach

Modern Politics

Today's tomorrow
lingers in its bewildered grasp of truths
exhausted cleft of utter lies.
As times spent past is in credence,
with its grateful ongoing.
Crushed in worn paths of deceit
are the promised.
Coerced in leadership,
without an embattled conquer of faith or confidence.
Its struggle moves on.
As tomorrows yesterday,
has decided its future enhancement,
the lies have again begun.

Jeremy R. Edwards

I Will Never Know

I will never know what it feels like to be you,
Living within your own little womb of integrity.
Groveling to the upper class
like a lowly peon.
Never knowing what its like
to be your own individual
Your unwillingness to be
unseparated overwhelms me,
unleashing in me all the
disgust toward things I abhor
I will never know what it
feels like to be you
Actually I never could endure
Your way of thinking,
So shallow a soul I could
never adhere to my own
So live your life out with
your lowly beliefs
As for me I will stay
safe and secure within my truths.

Della Taraska

Beyond the Horizon

Dense are the shadow's we are among,
Long are the day's - yet they be young
Silent are our dream's of hope's to be,
Beyond the horizon - our destiny
Only the brave shall walk thy land,
With one desire - to be a man
Surrender our heart's to the will of our Lord,
For beyond the horizon lie's our reward
The gift of life we treasure so dear,
Beyond the horizon - far and near.

Gone are the year's of fear and strife,
For, they too, were a part of our life
Silent are our dream's of hope's to be,
Beyond the horizon - our destiny
Treasured are the smile's that hold back our tear's,
For the love we've shared throughout the year's
Look upon the bright side of life we must,
And watch our troublesome care's, turn to dust
For, silent are our dream's of hope's to be,
Beyond the horizon - our destiny.

Donald Reamy

Untitled

Go ahead, keep on running, maybe it will go away. Just don't look back for fear of everything. Maybe you'll see us staring back at you, knowing you were wrong. She doesn't even know you, maybe she never will, but she won't ever go away. I wonder if she'll love you without ever knowing. I wonder if she'll hate you for being gone. I wonder if I'm enough, if my love will help her survive without the pain she shouldn't have to know. But will she, because you see no one but yourself, nothing but your own little world? Are you inconvenienced somehow by her presence? To you she's nothing, to me she's everything. All the things you destroyed, the love you took so thoughtlessly she restores each and every day. Although you don't know it you're giving them all back to me, not by choice, but through our daughter. She's so beautiful. She smiles at me like you would. In her eyes, I'm wonderful, always. She looks at me with trust in her eyes, like you did. She reminds me of you sometimes, all the good things. Sometimes I think she's an angel, what I've always wished for, just like I thought you were. But unlike you her love is true and pure, undefiled. In her eyes are my dreams, In her smiles are my future.

Kristen Smith

Love's Second Chance

We are the masters of our fate, the keys to the future
Look beyond the horizon and unfold the many mysteries of life
We are the ones who can shape our future and control our destiny
Our pasts hold untrodden paths-unspoken words- unfulfilled
Dreams and desires
Today is the now of "Another Time another place"
Take each tomorrow-embrace and delight each enchanting moment
Add to the joys of yesteryear- revel in the glory of the
Adventure and cherish the feeling with every fiber of our being
Reach in and touch the very depths of our souls an unleash
Our emotions as we stand on the threshold of a beautiful, deep
And abiding relationship
Our paths have crossed again so let us embark on another
Journey into the vast unknown
You alone can make the difference - to enchant - to delight-
Make the most of it as we may never again know the beauty,
The magic and magnitude of togetherness

Evelyn Hughes Jordan

Just For Us

Look to him in time of need
Look to him for a friend indeed
To love him is to love his father
Ask anything of him, it's no bother
He'll be there through the trouble and strife
He's in your corner throughout the fight
He'll never turn his back, no sir indeed
Because he's a good friend just believe
So go ahead and ask, it's no bother
He is our God, our father.

John Tidwell

Healer, Heal Me

Oh, Holy God who from your Holy Hill,
Looked down from heaven into the hearts of men.

And saw within their battered shells,
Their wounded and damaged souls.

Bound in scars like braided bands of rope.
You willingly stepped down.

You took the crown of piercing thorns to wear upon Your brow.
You bore the cat-o'-nine-tails for thirty-nine stripes,

You poured Your blood upon earth's alter,
So that with Your blood stained finger,

You could gently touch each wounded heart.
And Heal each bruised and buried hurt—

Let loose each cord that bound.
You set free the captive from his chains in body, soul and spirit,

To live as You have Willed.
Healer from on High, I pray—

Come nigh—
That I might know Your healing work in me.

Healer from on High,
Come nigh—touch me.

Cathleen S. Mize

"The Lady Is Eighty"

At the mirror I stare
Looking back at me there
Is a stranger I do not know
Her arms are flabby; Her house-coat is shabby
Her slippers flap on the floor
Her hair is silver, not golden like mine
How could this have happened in so short a time?
Memories haunt me - come back to taunt me
As I nap on the sofa or chair
Through struggle and strife
As I journeyed through life, often daring to dare
There were good times and bad times
Glad times and sad times; Which friends were willing to share
Promises broken - words left unspoken; too late - now needless to say.
There were men who adored me; and told me they loved me
Who could not rec-og-nize me today
Would I have changed it? in truth, I don't know
The Bible says you reap what you sow
Still I wonder; But who is to say
That it may have been better some other way.

Josie L. Wilson

Village Of Souls

He rides into town on a pitch black horse.
Looking for an answer, he screams for fear nobody has heard his cry.
There is no answer from the town that had housed many.
The priests, the ministers, the rabbis, the loved ones.
Again he screams.
Again nobody answers.
Finally there is a sound.
It comes from the faintest part of the city left in shambles.
"What?" whispers a lone survivor hobbling in the shadows.
"HELLO!" the rider bellows again.
The shadow steps out from the burning wasteland of a long forgotten town.
Then another and yet another.
Finally the town center is filled with an overwhelming joy that the devastation has ended.
These people. Victims of a holocaust.
Never again.
Never again.
Hell is better.

Jonathan C. Marden

Moon's Melody

She sat in the sand
  looking out to the sea,
As the waves rolled in hurriedly
  to gently kiss her hand.

The stars peeped out to say hello
  and the gulls asked the man in the moon,
If we sing a sweet song, will you play the tune
  for our friend who listens below?

The moon bid the wind to be his violins
  and the twinkling stars, his harpsichord.
The most beautiful song in all of the world
  was composed just for her by the heavens.

Brenda C. Mazy

"Request Denied"

I know it cannot be the time for the
"Lord" to take you away; The doctors
must find your answers and it is this to
The "Lord" I pray.
You must grow stranger and keep up your will,
for I know you have dreams which are
not yet fulfilled. You are my heart,
you are my song; it is from you I've
learned to be strong. I admire you more
than any one woman in this world;
You stand far above the rest and if
the Lord is strengthening you through all
this, he will touch you with his light
because you've done more than pass
his test you've won the fight.
So gather now all the strength and
courage you have left in your soul,
for the "Lord" is giving us "you"
And your love more time to behold.

Deborah Sterling

Three Aphorisms

Chaucer's space means opportunity.
Today opportunity rarely means space.

Courtly gesture: Court Jester
Court Jester; Courtly gesture.

Emily Dickinson's search for God:
Twice sought,
Once bought.

Maria M. Links

To Cut

The women's emotion on birth or
Loss of birth can only be known by her.
To grab the pain, expel the joy,
To cut the cord.

When is the umbilical cord cut,
At birth or loss of birth when the cut is made
Do we carry the "bond cord" to our grave?
Why must the cord be such a struggle to cut?

To cut the cord of dependency,
To make a clean slice of the sticky spaghetti cords of ambivalence.
To be in a women's arms must be like it was before the cutting of the cord.
O to be again before the cut.

Douglas M. Dayhuff

Where

She runs through the forests, and screams at the night. She's lost the will, she lost the fight. Her environment is bringing her down. The wide open space makes her frown. While he sits on the roof tops and breaths the exhaust pipe air, and wishes he was somewhere else, he doesn't care. She longs for the neon horizon, but he wishes the smog didn't block the sun. The grass is always going to be greener when there's somewhere else you're rather being. The truth is that you're never happy anywhere, it's like a sappy ending that seems unfair. The hustle and bustle of the city, the sound of the cars turn her on, but the sound of the cricket in the silence of the night has a certain charm.

Douglas Howard Proschaska

Now I Lay Thee Down To Sleep

Now I lay thee down to sleep
Lost to dreams so very deep
Never to wake, never to rise
Never to open your beautiful eyes
No more to speak, no more to breathe
From my life so quickly you leave

A beacon in my heart so bright
Killing dark notions with cleansing light
Loving me, and painting me a smile
Lingering in my life for just a little while
A joyous presence untouched by rain
And now that happiness is yours again

My memory has put you close to my heart
So from my mind you rarely part
Creating from remembrance the light
That chases the darkness from everyday life
An angel now in skies so blue
Flying with the love given to you

Katherine R. Porter

Life

Life is breathing, talking, laughing,
Life is loving, trusting, forgiving,
Life is hoping, finding, adjusting,
Life is understanding, thoughtful, giving,
Life is helping, caring and sharing
Life is befriending, belonging and respecting.
Life is believing, praying and rejoicing
Life is enjoying, resting and retiring
Life is living as we are preparing
.... to be leaving.

Bonnie L. Davis

Love

Love is more than just a word,
Love comes from the heart.
Love is something in which to take part.
Love is the most beautiful thing that
has ever been heard.

Love is something which has no end.
It is what you give your Mom and Dad.
It is the most precious thing, that has ever been had.
Love is like an old best friend.

If you have love, no time passes by.
Love is more precious than anything you'll see.
It is more precious than a bird a tree.
Love is so great, you feel you could fly

Love is more precious than silver and gold,
It is the best, you see, as I have been told.

Kathryn Gilmer

Love Life

Lovely she fell, into my heart
Loved her always, from the start
Love to her, always I cared
But love we couldn't, we never dared

This love it would seem, a shadow's been cast
But of course love is prevailing, it shall last
Love we all, our neighbors and friends
Love it shares, borrows, and lends

As love has, such simple rhythm, and rhyme
Let each partake deeply, while we yet have time
To be amiss, to truly have lost out
Surely life is a meal, nay a feast
And yet love, merely, nectar there of

A short while, and we're gone
So toast, and drink, and inhale of it
To the sweetness of love's glowing embrace
A song, maybe some cheer, or simply a tear on a face

John Boylson

The Dawning of Devastation

A midwest city filled with devastation,
Loved one missing and families crying,
People sent to an ultimate destination.
These are the things that a nation is trying to forget.

Ribbons being tied
For the citizens that died.
These are the ways
We show that we care.

Babies are dead,
Shrapnel in head.
These are the sights
That the rescuers see.

How much wonder?
How much fear?
How many lost
The ones they love dear?

Who did it and why?
Do they want so many to die?
These are the questions
We ask our God.

Jennifer Fugal

Sometimes I Wonder If It's Real

The streets are made of asphalt, the cars are
made from steel, and the buildings hide the sunshine
from my eyes.
There are no trees or flowers to bloom with April
showers; sometimes I wonder if it's real.

The stores are lit with neon, the fronts are made
from glass, and the screeching of the city ring in
my ears.
There are no smiles on faces, just people going
places; sometimes I wonder if it's real.

The kids are lost and lonely, there's no place to
play; the sidewalks and the alleys shape their
minds.

There is no sense of beauty or even love of duty.
Sometimes I wonder if it's real.

James T. Bennett Jr.

The Greatest Loss

You brought a sparkle to my eye
made me glow with such delight

Your love was special to me
more than you could ever see

When your love was taken away
I didn't know what to say

I couldn't say anything, only cry
and only hope that I would die

Nothing meant more than your love
it was like a sweet gentle dove

I hurt inside, hurt deep down
I can only give a simple frown

That smile you created has gone away
shattered and faded to yesterday

I can only hope that once again it will be mine
your love so sweet and so divine

Your love lost and taken from me
is the greatest loss there will ever be

Kristine Valdez

Separation

Paint me a picture that captures my love
Make the sky blue like the color of your eyes
Give me a moon that shines your warm smile
Let the shooting stars go round and round,
Like the curls on your crown...
Sprinkle the heavens with amethyst stones.
Sing me a song as sweet as red wine.
Draw me two Mountains, one for
Your World and One for mine
Fill the ocean between them with my tears
Send the birds to make me smile
Now close your eyes and breathe a deep sigh
Feel - the calm of the sea
Hear the waves splash against the rocks
And roll into the sounds of the night...
Build me a lighthouse upon the shore
May its beacon shine across the ocean
So there may be safe passage from
Your World to Mine.

Dorothea Alexander Adamo

My Midnight Ghost

Raindrops on my windshield, glistening in the night,
Making me lonely, I don't know why.
A tear for me have you shed?
I doubt this but wonder yet.
Driving through the night,
I wish you were by my side.
As you were long ago,
When I would take you home.
Buried kisses and boxed up promises,
Have you forgotten?

Moonlight shining through my window,
Perplexing shadows of the ghost,
In the passenger's seat you are by me now.
I have you here, why do you frown?
Moonlight and rain: a curious combination,
Numbing my mind of continual pain.
You are with me, and I won't let it end.
Pouring rain blanketing the bridge ahead.
I am for the end and my love declare.
We will go together, together in the rain.

Jill Christine Bradley

A Hand

It occurred to me, perhaps by demand,
Man's worst weapon must be his hand;
That forges steel to pierce the skin,
That directs armies to begin -
Which holds the handle to release the bombs,
That crushes the children of heart-torn mom's.
And then by subtle observation
I saw the hand assist creation;
To build machines that fly like birds
To paint on canvas and write these words
And it dawned on me through deep expand
That man's greatest tool must be his hand.

Jeffrey Manresa

Those Were the Days...

I see life in a different point of view,
Many are dying, and those who survive are few.
There is so much going on in the world today,
People don't care what they do or say.
Many things have changed throughout our lives,
Guns weren't so frequent and neither were knives.

Back into the times where life was easy,
Men weren't always drunk and sleazy.
Women were appreciated for who they were,
And children cared about the things that occurred.
Those were the days where we could have some fun,
And when you didn't need to threaten any one.
And the riots, what were they?
Those were the days...

Jennifer Sneed

A Song To Sing

Who can tell what tomorrow will bring,
Maybe I'll cry, maybe I'll sing;
Maybe a storm will level my home,
Maybe I'll be left all alone?

Maybe there's gold all over my land,
Maybe I'll feel God's judgement hand?
Maybe I'll grow to be eight feet tall,
Maybe I'll suddenly know it all?

I'll never know what tomorrow will bring,
I'll never know if I'll cry or I'll sing,
But if He's on my side, then I don't have a care,
I'll win that last battle, everywhere!

Andy Marshall

Parents

There are strange things in this world
Many of which nobody can understand
So much happens that can change things
All the people that try for us deserve a hand

These very special people are always there
They make it possible for us to fly
We have already destroyed so much
But these special people make us able to cry

They are very special people to us
Everything they do is for me and you
They work hard to buy us certain things
Everything we receive is especially new

There is no mistaking the fact they work too hard
In the beginning it was all new to them
Their lives are put on hold as our parents
Everything they do they go out on a limb

Keli Larae O'Loughlin

One's Name

What's in a name
Maybe not much
But it was mine if only for a short while
And I had grown to love it
As if it had been mine to keep forever

That's the hardest part
Letting go of something you've loved
Giving up a part of yourself
Your hopes, your dreams
Closing a door where all these once lived
Never to reopen again

Now as you slip from my grasp forever
I will think of you from time to time
When memories steal from their hiding places to remind me
That once you were mine
On those times I will remember you only in love and gratitude
For the time we shared
Time that stole away only too quickly
To become a memory

Barbara M. Thomas

The Mind

Ideas come and go
Memories are lost and found
Dreams are kept alive by the hope that is in the mind.

The world is seen in many different ways
Some experiences are kept stored away while others are being shared
The opinions that you hold dear are developed in the mind.

It causes you to judge
It tells you right from wrong
So can the problems of this world be blamed upon the mind?

Because our minds do not always agree
Is it right to punish those who think differently?
Do we know how we really feel or are we just prisoners of the mind?

Can we learn to listen to our hearts?
Can we learn to trust our instincts more than we do?
Or is it best to continue along blindly following the mind?

The mind is a treasure that everyone can have
It is an unexplored place that no one can truly understand
So we use it the best that we know how
Never knowing the truths the mind is hiding from us.

Kevin W. Coons

Beneath the Wings of an Angel

For Angles:
men have sought hither and thither,
from mount Sion to the deepest depth of the Red sea,
thus the administering of angels unveil what Shepherds seek,
having me adjourn to a journey beyond the river Euphrates.

Where for art thou, Oh Suriyel and Salathiel,
Thus a bewilderness becomes those which behold your beauty,
your eyes beheld the before time of Adam in the garden, as did
Gabrael, soon the angel Raphael will appear before nightfall
draws near.

Weighted in the balance
is a purity of purpose, a protection which preserves ones path,
thus heavenly host provide sanctuary until the storms aftermath,
in a whirlwind of flames, cherubims are our compass as the northern
star in the sky, noting how way leads on to way, we venture forward
by and by.

Thus patience is a virtue as my thoughts do collide,
focusing upon a celestial chorus, though they subside,
heavenly shades of splendor permeate the higher heavens found,
as sweet as amazing grace, how sweet the sound.

Kevin Fisher

Untitled

CHILLY, Chill. Frozen thoughts surface as she shakes helplessly,
mentally burned by the FEAR that is so very cold. Is it because she
is naked that she is so cold? But she has all of her cloths on and
it is very warm in the room in which she lies. His body heat alone
supplies her with a temperature that is definitely comfortable.
It was a new beginning, or January, yet her face was on fire before
she had even arrived. It was a happy time or at least it was suppose
to be. A time of rejoice and celebration, until...
SIN set in.
To abuse one's own temple, (and YES, the Lord did punish me), is
forbidden.
Yet to have another decide that choice for you is another story.
Her own Guardian Angel had to reveal the trouble it was witnessing to
its
Highest Source and from there the GLOW turned to... BLACK.
When the Spell had lifted, so did her eyes as well as his body.
HORRIFIED, running, wiping, driving, crying...there was no where to
run, no one to help.
"She" felt guilty, at fault, dirty. IT'S NOT MY FAULT! HE is the
criminal, the sinner, the one I will forever fear. "HE" is the one I
want to HATE...but won't because I am better than that. So I move
on...
with a black spot tattooed on my soul.

Danielle Kathleen Sawyer

Vortex Under An Essene Cranium

Going down the whole, with darkness, to fissure
mercurial amour.
Shout up a furnace, a jagged path, an oracle
to cover siren scintillations
cast up in foundry; cast off limbs and writhe
in molten crux; no time, no face
inscrutable amour.
Split the armor, the chord and sorrows-
possess me as a god, consume me in eruption
ravage me through evolution
compulsive amour.
Whirling word, weaving lip a maelstrom
rip the spark, soar off center
cast me down in a crimson well
sacrifice my pain
tear it apart, piece by stringy peace...amour.
Torque thief, cinder slut
shatter the bone, enigma the fragments
release dust out of starry dust
torrential amour.

Al Zaruba

We're All Pawns In One Big Game Of Chess

"Occupation?" asked the first.
"Mercy killer." Answered the other.
"Were they sick?"
"No, to put them out of theirs, and my, misery."
"It says here that you.."
"Yes." "You don't deny it?"
"They deserved it."
"No remorse?"
"No." "They were living beings."
"The Lord gave me divine inspiration."
"To spread the word?"
"To spread the word."
"Would you do it again?"
"Yes." "To whom?"
"Everyone."
"That includes yourself."
"i've solved the problem."
"How?"
"Come back tomorrow."
He was found in his bed, wrists open.

Christopher Alves

Miniature Hands

I've seen the masses of small starving mouths...tiny toes and miniature hands.
No tenderness nor safety seen,,, in garbage dumps and suction hose,,,
Lost in this world,,, these little souls.
Politicians promise, groups protest, the insurmountable facade of
Social workers goals,,,and lost in the balance are these little souls.
In depth of blood and senseless violence victims mount,,, while
Pedophile, murderers and rapists taunt.
The judges hold high the scales of justice by bribe,,, as the highest price paid are by these little souls I describe.
The smallest of the weak in violence are locked...
By the powerful and rich,,, as innocents they mock.
Through ghettos, cities and war torn lands,,,
Lay crushed little souls, with miniature hands.

Damaris M. Norman Sutton

Dusk

The crisp air of early night hangs,
  misted over scattered rows of cottonwood trees.
Deep shades of crimson, magenta, tangerine
  bleed into an indigo sky.
The sky, so vast and intense it seems to be an ocean,
  dancing with the cotton clouds.
The clear glass lake gently laps
  onto the darkly tanned cheeks of the shore,
  singing soft lullabies as dusk lingers on.
Far in the distance, the golden hills roll into mountains,
  their darkened silhouettes fading into the empty horizon.
The winds slowly waltz amongst the clouds,
  and softly lift the wrinkled leaves,
  rescuing them from the solitude of the cold ground.
The rocks, in their weathered shades of rose and lime,
  look up through tainted eyes at the darkening sky above them.
The dark bronze sun, with his tired belly,
  slips slowly under the mountain's shoulders.
The few colors left in this ocean of sky welcome the new moon,
  who is now but a silver of her whole self...

Anna Tyler

Love Lost?

Time is of the essence. The hands, they slowly past.
Moments shared are cherished. The little time we had.

We part, goodbye forever. At least that's what we thought.
Life isn't fair, it's selfish. Life's bargains can't be bought.

Embarking on life's highways. Detours that never end.
Yellow is the road sign. Caution our only friend.

Was it love we found together? Left behind, was it the end?
Blind confusion. Anger building. Caution thrown unto the wind.

Hearts are broken, cast aside. Brushed off, put back together.
Lessons learned, wounded pride. Trusting others, maybe never.

Fate unyielding; no control. Embracing lives; entwining.
Interceding subtly. The ties we had were binding.

From the past a distant voice fearing new horizons.
We don't forget. We don't regret. New hope eternal rising.

Hearts unclothed. Naked souls. Apparel is none finer.
The scent is passion unabashed. Love is our designer.

Dymphna Sharpe

The Way That I Feel

If I could express the way that I feel,
more friends I would have, the happier I would be

I could talk to a stranger without a big deal,
If I could express the way that I feel

There would be no misunderstanding, time would just fly,
no one would care if a whole day went by

Just to talk or to chat, just to be with someone,
is a magic feeling that's second to none

No insecurity, no coldness, no tenseness nor fear,
just the sound of joyful laughter for all to hear

The world at my fingertips, all hearts I could steal,
If I could express the way that I feel.

Danny Lee

The General's Cried

The earth was scarred for what they did
Mothers held their babies close to their breast
As guns roared into the night, they hid
The weary and crippled know no rest

One armed boy must slay another
Orders he must follow
If not he than maybe his brother
This is thus the cycle of sorrow

Eventually thunderous noises cease
The soft weeping of orphaned children begin
The hollow victory should bring peace
To see two foot corpses is such a sin

Those with the stars hung on their chest
The one's so tested and tried
Now see armless babies with the rest
And the generals cried.

Brian Mooney

Fabric of Life

Family is the thread
    which sows our mere existence
into a bright, wonderful fabric
    for an ever enduring future.

Monica Rowland

Choice

What of suffering and sorrow
Must I learn its lessons grim
When my dearest has been taken
And I struggle without him.

What of joy may I retain now
From the endless source we knew so well
I will garner every crumb and eat with relish
And will wrap up in its bounty - and there dwell!

What of hope is left to me now
Since I know he cannot come again
I will lift my eyes to heaven and see sunshine
And will gladly shout "It always follows rain!"

What of peace could I dare hope to find now
While my tortured spirit writhes and yearns for calm
I'll remember all the good and all the beauty
And will let it wash my spirit with its balm.

With my joy and hope and peace I will go forth now
I must choose to look ahead to vistas faint
And with colors of my CHOICE and brush of laughter
I will burst upon life's canvas - and will paint!

JoAnne M. Baucom

Married To A Farmer

The farmer rises at the rooster's crow, as there are many fields he must sow.
With hopes his crop will prosper and grow, he prays mother nature will be friend not foe.

The farmer flows from dawn 'til dusk, upon a tractor red with rust,
and once the seeds are covered with dirt, he hopes for rain, it's a must.

With herbs to tend and fences to mend, the farmer's chores are without end.
His pastures of green roll and bend, it's a labor of love without end.

The farmer's life is not princely and financial profit is small to none,
but without question there's no better trade, you see, I married one!

Jennifer Brown

Awakening

I wish to awaken
My back upon Scottish soil
My eyes upon the heavens and God;
beyond glen and dale.
The Highlands and my history,
under my nails and on my palms.
Identity embedded in soil where blood runs deep and warm.
My history in ground cold, foreboding and life giving.
My essence passed from generations gone;
in the soil: Proud, Hearty and Strong.
The Highland soil blending in hand with my blood.
The nails digging deep and deeper;
into the ground, into my palms. I regain my kindred.
Unknown progenitors coursing through my veins;
though stilled and bound to rocky soil.
I feel their presence, awakening corporeal memory of:
My Clan, My History, Me.
My back upon Scottish soil.
My eyes upon the heavens and God,
beyond glen and dale.

Dean Wallace

My Eyes

My eyes blaze with fire and ice
My eyes glow with love and desire of affection
My eyes look away in time of despair
My eyes die when you cry
My eyes capture the radiance of the sunset
My eyes shine with glory
My eyes burn with thee eternal flame
that will never go out
My eyes see right through you
My eyes cry out in pain, blurred and shattered
My eyes show the sun when it is raining
My eyes mesmerize you
My eyes sparkle like the moonlight
shining down on a glass ocean
My eyes petrify you
My eyes never lie
My eyes never want to see you say goodbye

Derek S. Hatch

Dreams Of The Ancients

This waking dream I hope not to end
My eyre beyond the Great Wall
To witness the tragic rise and fall
of Carcosa, founding city of all men.

The name echoes within my mind
A forgotten instinct reveals it so
Dust before the great Pharaoh-Kings rose
Glory lost by waking mankind.

It sweet fountains and silvered walkways
Embraced by lordly arches and observatories
Their pagodas extending to the Hyades
Carcosa, dimmed beauty beneath old time's haze.

Slowly now, the splendor crumbles to its carcass
The shimmering minarets start to fall
My heart wrenched away, I cross the Great Wall
No longer I remember lovely Carcosa.

Joshua Perkins

Remember Me

Remember me
My hands are attached to the plow but I labor in darkness
Far into the oppressive night
Do I seek my crown—the healing light
An affirmation of my goal
To heal my spirit—to cleanse my soul

Remember me
I kneel beneath the healing tree
The rugged Cross of Calvary
The warmth, the blood that covers me

Remember me
Grant me clemency—lily of the valley, bright shining star
Lover of my soul wherever you are

Remember me
Cooling waters of Grace that washes away the sin, the pain
Oh heavenly Dove, shower me with love—rain, please rain

Remember me
I stand convicted and in need—Lord do you see
When you have come into your Kingdom—please
Remember me

Andrea L. Jackson

Broken Tortured Heart

This broken tortured heart of mine —
My heart is forever broken by the pain,
My life is forever sprained,
This tortured heart of mine.

My love is forever behind lock and key —
This tortured heart yells why, why me? Everything grows dead,
Everything bleeds from the wound,
Everything that is true and beautiful is hidden behind thee

These dear blue eyes of mine are actually stone —
Why can't my love sit on thy throne?
If I shall die thee will ask why.

This broken tortured heart pleads to be set free,
But the key to the lock is invisible to thee;
It is lost in a world that is lost,
Lost from love but knows only of the hatred and cruelty of
this meaningless world.

People don't know how much I cry, but still I try —
I feel so much like an outcast, only to outlast
And forever be a tortured heart not worthy of thee.

This broken tortured heart of mine.

Carolyn Joan Prenger

A Lesson Learned

I heard you were getting married just the other day,
My heart was broken, what could I say.

Not long ago we were the best of friends,
I swore our friendship wouldn't ever end.

I always thought you would be by my side,
For you were like my shadow, from nothing would I hide.

No matter what, you were always there,
Always reassuring me how much you cared.

But how long can you be there for me, with your broken heart,
Always giving, but being torn apart.

Unfortunately love is blind, for I could not see,
I surely hope you don't make the same mistake as me.

The moral of my story is sad but true,
The chance of a lifetime is what I blew.

What I suggest to all, with great nerve,
Do not settle for less than you deserve.

Sometimes we search too far, instead of looking near,
Often what is good for us is already here.

We overlook close friendships for strangers we think are a better
match,
But in the long run, we lose the better catch!

Cara Dyson

Writer's Block

My imagination and creativity are blocked,
My talent to write has stopped,
I've got a disease, not a cough, nor a wheeze,
I'm diagnosed with writer's block.

I can't think of a thing to write,
It keeps me awake at night,
I'm racking my brain and going insane,
I'm caught with writer's block.

The topics are flying through my head,
I think of things people have said,
I put them together to see what I've got,
but I'm stuck with writer's block.

Erin McCabe

No One

No one can love you as much as I do.
With all of my heart, I believe this is true.
I never want to be with anyone but you.
My only wish is that we'll always be together.
But, even if we're not, I'll still love you forever.

Missy Maceyko

The Twentieth Century Idiosyncracies

The gale, named The Twentieth Century Idiosyncracies, hit my flesh.
My humble desire to live in peace shattered into pieces.
The bell in the belfry knelled to bury my ancient pride.
The threnody of traditions and norms was played without mourners.

The hail of contempts and chastisement pricked my very bare skins.
I consumed embarrassment with a broad smile.
The ritual of a masquerade followed a birth to a charlatan.
Donned in pretense, I concealed myself thoroughly.

No one knows my agony that breathes beneath the blithe.
No one smells toxic fumes that emit from the stabbed heart.
No one fathoms the excruciating pain that tortures me.
No one hears my wail that is repressed by a hearty laughter

But only a twinge of conscience still grabs a string of my lineage.
Contrary to my ancestor's teaching,
I feed love on hatred and nurture goodness on evil.
Suffering from the consequences of my blunder.
I vomit the scarlet from the bottom of my heart.

The gale, named the Twentieth Century Idiosyncracies, swallowed me,
But still I stagger to erect myself up.

Jane K. Lee

My Wish

I sit on the porch on a cold, cold wet day
"My life has no surprises", that's what I say
I wish I had an adventure or two in my life
Like ghosts, and getting lost, or finding some old knife
Or solving a mystery or solving a case
Or going into a haunted house filled with satin and lace
Or meeting a queen or meeting a king
I'm getting so desperate I'd do anything!
To go on a cruise would be very nice
Like candy and sugar plums, and sugar and spice
Oh, to fly like a bird or swim like a fish
All of these things are just one wish!

Kelli Thalman

Alone

Alone I sit with my thought;
My mind begins to rot.
They reach inside me and take my soul;
My warm, lifeless eyes slowly turn to coal.
My morals are erased;
My beliefs piece by little piece away are chased.

Alone am I;
Yet I still do not know why.
The world will continue to turn;
As my memories will continue to burn.

Alone I sit with my thought;
My mind beings to rot.
They sway the watch until I am hypnotized;
My deeply, buried chaos has now arised.
Life is all a dream;
Nothing's what it seems;
It's just one huge scheme.

Andrea Black

A Love

He moves me in so many deep ways
My soul aches when he walks away

Yet, when he is near I feel deep comfort and free
To express my heart and soul

I love ... I ache to say
Yet, I fear for my safety that he might run away

So, I will not push or prey
Simply enjoy the moments I have with him

Every ... other day

My body yearns to be connected and pure
A strong union of trust and passion

However, the chance may not arise
So, I reside in my dreams and look from the inside

"I love you"!
I long to say...
However simple in so many ways

I love and always will
Please allow us the chance ... to be still

Jennifer Deputy

Pain

The air is still the night is cold, my heart is heavy and my soul is worn. No comforting words for my weary days, my heart is aching in so many ways. There's not much happiness in my life anymore everywhere I look there's always a closed door.

A storm is coming I can feel it in the breeze, the leaves have turned brown and have fallen from the trees. I can't help but think where did I go wrong, I must have strayed off course I hadn't been strong. I'm tired now and its hard to think, my spirits hang low and my heart starts to sink. I lay in my bed and cry myself to sleep. I get no rest for a constant pain I keep.

Daylight brings no comfort and evening gives no break, I have no peace in slumber for I'm constantly awake. I have but one enemy and my friends are oh so few, the fire and the rage of pain can burn and consume you. My heart is hurting and there is no escape, my life hangs in the balance and pain is my fate. So let this serve as a lesson and a warning to the few, don't let the pain of this life get to you too.

Erika Sharae Coffee

Unsuccessful Dreamer

Looking at the sky today,
My thoughts were many miles away.
I dreamed I had a perfect life,
With money, happiness, and a beautiful wife.

A great big house and a couple children too,
Nothing in the world could make me blue.
But then in the distance I hear a scream,
Suddenly I'm awaken from my dream.

Reality sets in as I reflect on my life,
No money, no happiness, no beautiful wife.
I close my eyes as a tear drips down,
Realizing nothing can erase my frown.

Reaching in my pocket for my final fate,
I pull out my gun because I can't wait.
Shouting "Oh how my dream was such a great ride,"
I point the gun at my head and commit suicide.

Donald J. Dressman

Expectations

In the night of my burlap sack
My tools float in darkness.
A shovel balancing in my ghost hand.
A pick, resting on nothing.
Over the cemetery wall -
An obstacle conquered.
Cursing the guilty moon
For shining revealing light
I plot, dig.
Quickly.
Day an unwelcome curfew.
My shovel plunges - the Earth penetrated.
Thrusts of dirt through air - to ground.
Heavy breathing, deeper in the soil.
Pausing, lighting the cigarette of reward.
Sweaty hair, hands. Nervous success.
Shovel slides, clockwork.
Anticipation a rousing stench.
I open the coffin.
Empty.

Daniel E. Gray

Is That How You Picture Me?

Is that how you picture me to be—
Naked, Vulnerable, Exposed,
Straddled across you, or reclined, on your snow-white beach?
The beach of endless impossibilities, desires, and dreams.

Porcelain skin bronzing,
My sculpted, oiled flesh,
Beads of dew trickling down the crease of my inner thigh,
My flesh, aching for your kisses and caress—
Is that how you want me?

Did you imagine me crying out for you,
Reaching for you to satisfy me,
to quench my frustration, my hunger?

Is that what you want—
To touch the razor exterior,
To taste the delicate, moist interior?
To connect with me, to be part of me?

Maybe you can,
Maybe I would permit it.
If only you would let me.
If only you would kiss me.

Joliene L. Dexter

"White Violets"

Growing around the Woodland Spring,
'Neath the black-gray rock -
Where it gushes forth,
Grows the velvety, fresh, white violets,
So dainty and pure, with their
heart-shaped leaves.

The Dutchman's Breeches are growing
there too,
Beside the Ferns and the Beautiful Spring,
Waxy white, and perfectly formed,
and the Indian Pipe, gleaming here and there
Adds to the woodland scene.

Deer pause to drink here,
Eyes searching for danger,
Poised in an instant, ready for flight,
And the spotted fawn,
lying hid in the bushes
So still - for its Mother it quietly waits.

Juanita Lavender

My Garden

My garden has been my life. At times I have let it go, how I have neglected it with bad thoughts and blame. I felt the shame. My special spot of once carefully tended soil has gone to seed.
Thank heavens I have finally dug deep within my garden, so deep that Thistle no longer grows and Itchweed screams as I approach knowing it will be yanked straight out and not allowed to fester.
Joyous is my garden now, the birds are heard their song majestic praising. "Open hearts, keen minds, clear vision."
Happy are the pheasants roosting by my creek. They have come to stay, make a nest, and raise their young. They know they will be fed because my garden is bountiful, full of love, food, and beauty.
I hope weary souls will come and rest and partake of heaven's air — to calm the soul's unrest and send them on their way.

Katharine Kivett

"Life Is A Job . . . Make It A Career"

Allow a dream to fade - You give in to reality
Never give in, out, or up -

A Mother's Love - circles, infinity . . . see the connection?
Connect the ... dots ...

Policies
Politically correct . . .
Correct politics?
Ranking success 1. Woman, 2. Black, 3. Man, 4. White
Out of sequence?
Use your mind - not your fist -
Love, honor, obey ... obey ... listen

Hold your head and heart high
For that is where you will find your goals,
Your true friends,
And your success in life -

Kimberly Dawn Anderson

The Pipe Man

The pipe man sits on his rocking chair in his corner of the dark room
Never moving, never listening
Holding his pipe in the shape of a bird in one hand, blowing
Creating sounds that only he could hear in ways only he could imagine,
Never caring, never worrying
About the child next door.
A child's crying is not heard in the corner of the dark room
Where an old man is making magic from a pipe
Chaos wheeling, chaos kneeling
And lighting it underneath the flame-light.
The pipe man adds a log to the fireplace but does not light a match
Chaos dreaming, chaos screaming.
The flame lights and the corner is still dark, creating abnormal
Shadows on the behind wall. The old man stops playing and
For the first time hears the crying from the other room,
And sheds a tear,
Fire lighting, fire burning,
But picks up the pipe once more and plays once more,
This time never stopping, never continuing
Until the cries stop and the fire is long burned out.

Daniel P. Eiras

My Destiny:

Why does my heart ache
wishing for things that only love could make
deep inside I burn in desire
dreaming of a beautiful empire
day and night become longer and longer
as my feelings and needs suffer of a deep hunger
missing that darling part of me that only you and I can see
through yours and my own eyes you are my destiny.

Loreta Ramos

Insomnia

Insomnia, you rascal, stealing into my inner sanctum like a thief at night, robbing me of my most priceless possession, SLEEP!
Ah, too often I feel your penetrating eye entering the recesses of my mind, lulling me into the anticipation of a refreshing sleep.
But you, Cupidic Monster, shrewdly clothed in shadowy dream-like nightmares drenched in sweat, haunt my reverie.

I do not want to review the day's activities... I have lived them already!
I don't need to set the plans for tomorrow! Simply put...
I want to rest, sleep, and be done with you!

Ah-h... again my flickering eyelids close and I am drifting into a beautiful blissful sleep; I shall be ready for a tireless day tomorrow. Sweet, sweet dreams at last... I am in control.

And then, you fiend, whisper ever so softly, "Did you lock the door? I hear someone on the doorstep."
My subconscious reacts, saying it is only the wind and nothing more.
Insomnia says, "Are you sure-sure-sure?"
And I get up, turn on the lights, check the door, get a drink; better go to the potty... and on and on and on.

You stealer of peaceful rest, rascal extraordinary; finally I get some rest at 4 A.M.
Insomnia, I abhor you! Please, please pretty please... darken my mind nevermore!

John G. Meeks

Ode To Past Black Olympians

They Trained to compete in these games,
No colors, no races
all one in the same.
They went to foreign shores
and won the gold.
While at home, stories of praise and glory
were told.
But when their feet returned to this shore,
The songs once sang, were sung no more.

Back of the bus, don't sit here.
Mocked and spat on as they walked near.
Couldn't even go to a nice place to eat,
Unless they ate in the kitchen
and stood on their feet.
Men and women, once heroes to all,
Reduced to nothing,
without a baton, or a ball.
It's amazing what these people went through —
All for the glory of the Red, White, and Blue.

Benevolent Allah

My Nickname

Patricia is my real name, but no one calls me that.
No one calls me Tricia, Patty, Trish, or even Pat.

I'm a very pretty little girl - smart and sweet and good.
I don't deserve the nickname they gave me and if I could
I'd give them names that sound like snakes or spiders
or bugs,
Even though they love me and give me lots of hugs.

Can you guess my nickname?
It's clever, so I'm told.
Not many people are baby frogs,
But me.
I'm one.
I'm Tadpole.

Kay Harvin

Annabelle Bees

Annabelle Bees calling deafly to the trees.
No one hears their cry for help, they just
Go on praying upon their knees.

Those Annabelle Bees of life.
Who are they calling to, those creative
Creatures of God?

How they long to light upon the lovely flowers.
Annabelle Bees, where shall they start? If only
They knew where the race began!

In their silent rage, they buzz around deaf souls
Who bumble about in life's deadly hole!

If Annabelle Bees could only see the wonders above
That hole!

Oh, the sweet fragrance we long to quench our
Thirst upon!

Wait! What's this?

Annabelle Bees have flown away to conquer new
gardens,

As Annabelle Bees now can see the loveliness of their
souls!

Janet D. Everhart

Alone, Not Lonely

I closed the door to my first home.
No one to bother me - but no one to care.
Loneliness flooded my being
It seemed too much to bear.

So many empty hours to fill.
A world of things to do and see.
A hundred thing to learn.
No one to hinder me.

I learned to love myself,
It was so hard to live with me.
So many short comings
As any one could see.

"How can you stand being alone," I'm asked.
"I'm not alone, Jesus is with me," I say
Every hour, every step, every word, every deed
He lives in me and leads the way.

My companion, my helper, my savior is He.
He taught me to be alone, not lonely
For I'm never alone while he holds me.
Enveloped by His love, how can I lonely be?

Dorothy M. Jefferson

My All

No story ever written, no movie old or new
No song ever sung can explain my love for you
No prize is as greater, no dream ever dreamed of
No one is as beautiful as my one true love
There is nothing on this earth, the sky, or in space
That can match your features, beauty and grace
I wish that we could journey to a world of our own
The both of us hand in hand, far away, and alone
Free from every trouble, every pain and every fear
Together forever always, together forever near
I long to see your face, hear your voice, feel your touch
Anything you do would mean so very much
I would climb the tallest mountain or swim the deepest sea
Anything and everything just to be with thee
If we were to part then the music would be through
My life, my world, my dreams become lost without you
Of all living creatures whether great or small
None are as lovely as my heart, my love, my all.

David A. Watkins

Jigsaw 305

Dusk begins to rust the steel blue sky
No t.v., or music, comes from 305
shaking fingers search and stumble
for the corner pieces of the puzzle
the jigsaw is a way of passing time
every ridged piece, one day, one life
colors once so bright, fitting in just right
but the second the piece is made
the colors start to fade
a whole existence creeping closer to gray

The night has forced the lamp to be the sun
in gloom the silence seems to be at home
squinted eyes, through glasses, on the prowl
each piece the prey, each hand another owl
the puzzle almost full and near complete
the easier it seems to find each Piece
and the final Piece falls gently into place
the sun rises, colors paint the gray
a puzzle now a portrait on a wall
an artist's view is from above it all

Jim Hoitt

Salute To Chief Beverly J. Harvard

Some said you'd never make it; some told you to your face, that
no woman could ever hold this job, this is a man's' world and race.

You held your tongue, but kept up your pace; secure in the knowledge
of your dreams, and hopes and the reality of God's power and his love.

And when the Mayor called your name for all the world to hear, your
dream came true, your hopes realized, nothing left for you to fear.

And now you are at the top, Beverly J. Harvard, Chief of Police,
a shinning example to all mankind, a shinning torch for peace.

The administrator, the manager, the negotiator too
these are just some of the attributes that God has given you,
to lead us into the future with the right amount of class,
you have done it—and will continue to kick the criminal's a....

And just a word of encouragement, to send you on your way,
keep working hard, keep love alive, you'll never regret these days.

Thanks for all you've done, and for all you do,
for our children and this city. Oh never lose sight of your vision
or goals, if you do, that would be a pity.

Chief of Police! Chief of Police, this salute is just for you.
You have our pledge of support and respect, as we travel this road
with you.

DeLois K. L. Brown

Alexia - 1995

I don't need a picture to remember your face.
No...your image is burned into my brain.
Even now, I can close my eyes, and there you are.
Has it been thirteen years since that letter arrived,
Since a terrified twelve year old girl demanded answers?
Terrified and angry...oh, so angry!
But with who...you or me?
There were so many things I never told you,
So many things left unsaid.
We never got to laugh together, like we planned.
Did you know how much I loved you, Alexia?
They tell me you do now, but sometimes,
That's not enough.
So I'll say it now.
I loved you, Alexia...so very much.

Debra L. Taylor

Where I Should Have Been

Together they walked on silver sand,
No words spoken hand in hand.

I watched in silence from a place up shore,
The only sound, waves whispering "no more, no more".

A touch by a lover's hand,
Passion's flame was soon fanned.

But there I was alone again,
Wishing it was me, not her, with him.

From my position on the sandy dune,
I watched the love play inside the room.

I laid down on my sandy hill
My body, my mind, quiet and still.

I let the waves wash over me,
They emptied my mind and set me free.

My soul floated over those sandy dunes,
It silently stilled into the lover's room.

It was me touching him, his hair, his skin.
I was finally there where I should have been.

Brandi Rachelle Fox

Free Spirit

I want to go to Tibet.
No you don't he said, this man I wed.
I am going to let the dog in, she is all wet.
No you're not he said, this man I wed.
You need to go to the store and get some tea.
Who me? I don't even drink tea.
Well get some for me, so said the man I wed.
This verse was becoming very terse
So I said get out of my bed.
We are no longer wed.
It's like I finally got it into my head,
I didn't always have to do what the man I wed said.
Now I live alone and let my dog in and out at will.
I also have a cat who rolls around and gets hair all over the mat.
She never would have been allowed to do that.
I even drink tea and go to the store and buy it just for me.
Now I am free, the man I wed and me are friends,
Though I haven't been to Tibet — yet.

Barbara J. Walls

Resurgent Delusions

I sleep in want for what I ask
None of left but all to cometh
It frightens me, the Delphic horrors of the night
Yet I search in circles chasing the shadows of dawn
And when I awaketh one day to see true beauty
None is there to be found...
The great abyss has seen me whole
and there is nothing to stare back to me
I am but a lonely face in the torturous minds of twisted men
I am but seen as a toy for which to be played by the hunter
A focus for which to tease as he dances
in his wanton debaucherous call around the fire
Eyes aflame with fiery glazes and a glassy eye,
haunted—fainting with the deep glimmer
which one falls upon through the thick darkness of the past
...The wistful pensive progression of harrowing
distortions of envy and with the inevitable thickness to choke
Can I or he be similar yet so disparate in our kind
For is man more than his shadow
or is it essence that acquiesces the mind and admits the soul

Aton E. Magill

Sun Dance

Summer.
Not a whisper of air.
The sky is silver, cloudless.
It ripples from the stillness.
And the heat.

Inside, the children lay coated with sweat.
Silent, staring sightlessly into the fan.
But there is no coolness.
Only the heat pushed into eddies and currents.

A hiss from outside.
The children move to the window.
A timer has set off the sprinklers.
Now the sidewalk is soaked by the liquid coolness.

With a shout the lethargy slides from the children.
They are out the door, down the stairs.
Shrieking they leap into the
Shimmery, rainbow arc of water..,
Dancing.

Dona Westbrook

"Separation"

As the cord was severed and the newborn infant began to cry, probably
not from physical pain, but from "The Pain of Separation"
As the young mother released the small hand and walked slowly away,
on the first day of school-again "The Pain of Separation"
Off to college or maybe to military service, sometimes temporary,
sometimes for a lifetime. Again "The Pain of Separation"
As they go their separate ways, "Irreconcilable differences",
"drifting apart", or whatever the reason "The Pain of Separation"
As the frail elderly one walked slowly away from the nursing home,
heart broken, overwhelmed by loneliness; together for maybe 50 or 60
years, again - "The Pain of Separation"
And then comes "Death" sometimes as a blessing from God, sometimes as
a terrible enemy, but always "The Pain of Separation"
Even God himself, as the Savior hung on the cross crying out - "Why
has thou forsaken me?" felt "The Pain of Separation"
When this life is over and we enter through the "Gates of Pearl" and
walk the "Streets of Gold" reunited with our loved ones, secure
forever in the arms of God. The greatest blessing of all will be -
never again to suffer "The Pain of Separation"

James E. Young

The Lesson

I spoke to the Wind, but the Wind did
not hear me.
It was busy cooling the forest and blowing
new seedlings across the prairie.
So I spoke to the Brook, but the Brook
did not answer.
Tumbling over the rocks, it was rushing
to water the valley below.

Then I hear a Voice that answered:
Hear the lesson I would teach you.
As the wind blows through the forest,
By its breath the land refreshing
And the Brook pours out its blessing,
Freely giving of its waters,
So a life that's lived for others,
Ever giving, soul refreshing,
Finds a joy not found in getting
Learn the lessons that they teach.

Carolyn Shafer

Peaceful Fillings

I was a secret for a while though.
Not knowing how the bodies were here,
But if at close look happened, fillings.
A chance for peaceful fillings

Just walking through the tatterdemalion
Even when thought they were standing on
But no one really looked down to see...
The mission was one of purpose.

With a secret mist did water here.
How could one of these stand on one of those?
Who was it, never could stand before!
But has the baby child changed any at all?

And there is no secret anymore.
Even in the place of filling, having no pressure,
Nothing with strength enough to destroy the day
Neither pull the Victory from the hand.
But when he lay right, and right he will be...
ON PEACEFUL FILLINGS.

Jimmy Williams

The Crumbling Curb

Tearfully he sat on the crumbled curb
Not knowing what he did that was so absurd
Day in-day out, and into the night
His mother a whore, his father a tight

Anger, hatred, the order of the day
Thought it through, wished it not, even tried to pray
Love is firm, but stronger is the guilt
"Amo te", "Confiteor", "Must my family wilt"

The houses was filthy, the rations were moot
His siblings too, with the scars of a boot
They came, they went, and only stared
The "Red Tape" was deep and nobody cared

Mamma's dead now, via the AIDS
Daddy imprisoned in a permanent craze
They live in different places, miles away
With his brother and sister he could not stay

The house is fresh, a bird bath in the yard
His fosters are gentle, his love is hard
The curb on the street is in total repair
But the crumble in his heart will always be there

Dennis J. Dopkins

My Child Is Gone!

My child is gone! She no longer exist.
Not laid at death's door, but somehow consumed.
A viper feasts upon her as she barters her life away.
Her spirit and lustrous colors of youth are fading fast
And pictures are all I have of a happy past. A happy past.

My child is gone! Fate has deceived a master of deception and
The web of untruth has hooked its own weaver. I detest her hard
And brittle surface and I'm sickened by her dark side. Still,
I'm tempted to reach out for my woman-child and draw her near,
But being hurt again remains a constant fear. A constant fear.

My child is gone! Now my thirst will have to be satisfied by
The glorious nectar that fell from her branches; her children.
They say you can never lose something you never had.
Somehow, this distant child was never mine. Never mine.

My child is gone! My adopted daughter; my only daughter is gone!
But shadow not my days with pity or feelings of sadness
For she'll remain the fruit of my life, my hopes, my dreams,
My labor, and my harvest, though chemistry has proved to be
More compelling than my love. So be it! So be it!

Beverly J. Sweeney

Unknown Love

While asleep in my dreams you came to me.

You from my past so long ago.
Nothing but a young girl I was then but you were there.

You buried so deep beneath my
first love, my best love and my forever loves
Not knowing that you were there.

Your arms were around me
holding me safely and securely.
Your kiss has left me longing for you.

You are my soul mate is what was spoken to me and this is where you are supposed to be. How can this be?

There have been so many years
between us since I've seen your face
Marriage is between us miles separates
us and time and age are against us.

I did not know that a dance
so long ago would come back and haunt me so.
If only I knew I should have kissed you then.

Awakened!!! I wonder does he know that I'm there.

Where did you come from the love that I have never known?

Beverly Jackson

Thanksgiving Bells Ring

On this very special occasion,
Nothing like Christmas cheers.
It's a soft time that brings
Sweet music to our ears.
Lift up your voices and sing
Thoughts of love, peace, and joy.
It means more than just fancy trimmings,
Not wrapping paper, ribbons, bows and toys.
But the true meaning of Thanksgiving.
The love we receive from a father and mother a sister or brother.
A world filled with peace and we hold so dear not to live in fear.
The joy that spread from coast to coast.
Let's take a stand and have a toast.
I'd just like to say THANKS for instilling those old fashioned values,
Which included independence, education,
Self-respect and self-determination.
Let's continue to empower our youth,
Remember the smiles of hope amend.
Love, Peace and Joy is our best friends.
But Thanksgiving is everlasting, thank God it never ends.

Barbara Cross

The Black Hole

The gravity grabs a gargantuous hold
nought is the nature of a bleak black hole
space and time bend, break, and fold
until reality itself is no longer whole
light turns black in a negative pole
the universes do turn and reality rolls
matter shrinks and shrinks to a little node
and completely changes its normal mode
a black bold hole bears an infinite load
and space and the time are locked in a deep hyper cold
the galaxies swirl around this celestial soul
and the matter of gods shall soon be told

Allan H. Lambert

Untitled

Our relationship has come to an end
Now I can only call you my friend

It's time to let go and move on
Although it hurts I'm glad you're gone

Here's my chance to be free
To be the best that I can be

No mourning now no tears to cry
My big question would have to be why

Things will get better I know that they will
But it's going to take time for my heart to heal

I shall start this life and then
I will love and be loved again

Janette Aguilera

A Girl I Know

A girl I know drives me mad.
Now my life has gone from solid to plad.
It's not about her appearance, but what's inside.
But all these emotions I'm forced to hide.
When I think of her my mind is a haze.
Walking a straight line becomes a maze.
The warmth of her touch, the twinkle in her eye.
Is she the truth or is she a lie.
I'm a ship at sea and she is my forever of light.
My world is black, but she is a streak of white.
She has another, but should be with me.
From her spell someday she will set me free.
She is my song, my heart is he beat.
But getting her to see me is no small feat.
Bottled up emotions to her I'll someday show.
Because I think I'm in love with a girl that I know.

Jay Peterson

Leaving

Autumn comes, the leaves they change; new color they wear;
Now the leaves will travel by dancing here and there.

Adding beauty, casting shade, is part of their call;
Leaves fulfill their purpose when they break off and fall.

The wind sings the song of life; leaves take off and prance;
Time, it marches on as it calls them to the dance.

Leaves dance as they each are tossed by the autumn breeze,
Taken from their summer home there among the trees.

Though the leaves are seemingly snatched against their will,
They leave naked all the trees to face winter's chill.

As the wind allows the dance and the leaves to pause,
Now, while still, they find new roles and another cause.

Leaves received their nourishment; now they give it back;
Through the ground they can restore what the trees now lack.

Trees are bare, the leaves decay, but the songs ne'er ends;
What the winter seems to tear, springtime always mends.

Life continues even when broken from life's source;
Life will have its seasons as life will take its course.

Barbara Veeder Lamb

Alone

Stay with me till I must go,
What lies ahead no one may know.
I am afraid to be alone,
Just hold me fast till I have gone.

Ginger Purdum

Blind Faith

With all the horrors and atrocities
occurring in the Middle East and throughout
the rest of the world it makes you wonder
what happened to the virtue of religion.

Ascertaining religious convictions
In modern times of Holy War
Two words that render contradiction
Excusing death and needless gore
A conflict over power and land
Guised by a divine crusade
Seems to tolerate a gun in hand
Though all the more the faith does fade
Battles waged on false desires
Children forced to take a stand
To fuel prevaricated fires
To seize the precious promised land
My God does not kill for land
Nor force upon unwelcomed will
Though he has just one command
Quite simply put, he does not kill.

Jason Stein

A Child's Prayer

As evening cast its shadow the moon shown on the head
of a child as he knelt to pray before climbing into bed.

I thank thee God my Father for my home on a peaceful shore
sat back among the trees far from the throes of war.

I thank Thee that my folks and I need not take shelter from the fight.
I thank Thee for my home where bombs don't drop at night.

A home when coming back from school I find it clean and neat,
a home where Mother's waiting with a meal that can't be beat.

A home where I was taught to pray and to learn a memory verse,
a home where we can worship you free from a tyrant's curse.

This is the home that I have loved and have lived in since my birth
and I thank You God my Father that its on this side of earth.

Charlene Idoux

Remembrance

You remind me when I look at you
Of a love that I have felt before
For one who loved me no more than do you
Yet your eyes, so dark, probe deep into my memories
And my emotions overwhelm me
As I remember...
How he took my breath away with his every touch
Electrified my senses with musical ecstasy
My body as a harp, his fingers running upon the wires
Lifting me in the rhythm of the melody he played
And still it lingers in my soul
The notes of which vibrate my very being
When my eyes catch sight of you
And though I know you not at all
As I knew him so well
Still I almost love you, too
When with that same strong essence, that rare and painful beauty
You remind me...

Erin Miller

Mother Earth

World of many what secrets do you behold
Of ancient civilizations and cultures long lost ago.
You were there when the sun first rose and the moon came into glow,
Your nurturing hands gave us land to live upon
And water to drink from.
In times of old the ancients took care of you and caressed you with love
But somewhere through the years greed turned us from you.
Your hands that gave us land to live upon
And water to drink from,
Have slowly withered with our ungrateful abuse.
Your waters now flow with disease
And your lands weep with the pain human hands have caused.
'O' Mother Earth, will our suffering ever end?
I long for the day when I can stand in your meadows
And no longer hear your sorrowful cries echoed upon the wind.

Jennifer R. Terrill

My Silver Silky Threads

GOD gave to me, my silky, silver threads,
of hair.
I did not earn them, could not, would not,
It's not possible.
He wanted to give them to me, at age 26.
I said, "No, thank's."

I colored my beautiful auburn locks, jet black,
for many years.
I became a grandmother and had,
two granddaughters.
When they were 13 and 11 years of age,
A baby brother was born.

I decided to let my silky threads,
be natural.
I'd style my mixed threads in different ways,
and spray silver.
I wore many interesting wigs and hats.
Had great fun!

Connie James

Love Interrupted By Economics

In a society that rushes every second
of its own existence to climb the corporate
ladder, you sit and ponder, "What ever
happened to the love that was here?"
Was that love some how tossed aside?
Accidentally mistaken for a missing step,
in the ladder that should have been replaced?
So very often, love has been tossed aside, in our
society, to be replaced by monetary lust.
Even though, that very same dollar will still
be there tomorrow, that last little emotion
called love that has been replaced by those
fat greenbacks, will not be.

Jeremy King

I Would Not Write A Sad Poem

I wish to write no poems of children dying young.
Of lovers and betrayals, of a mothers only son.
I offer no sad images of ladies wasting away.
I have no need to use them, at least not for today.

I would not write a sad poem, just to make you cry.
At times life is a sad poem I often wonder why.
Why do such things happen to people kind and true?
Such things as death and illness from somewhere out of the blue.

Could be perhaps a lesson, sent from up above.
A lesson for His children of forgiveness, peace, or love.
For everything that happens to His children good and bad.
If we each could learn our lesson, it wouldn't be so sad.

Carol Grubbs

Thoughts In Winter

I sit beside the fire and think of all that I have seen
Of meadow flowers and butterflies in summers that have been
Of golden leaves that fill the trees in autumns that there were
With morning mist and silver sun and wind upon my hair.

I sit beside the fire and think of how the world will be
When winter comes without a spring that I shall ever see
For still there are so many things that I have never seen
In every wood, in every spring, there is a different green.

I sit beside the fire and think of people long ago
And people who will see a world that I shall never know
But all the while I sit and think of times there were before
I listen for approaching feet and voices at the door.

Joseph Wayne Fox

Creator

Your sunsets are sketched into the depths
Of my imagination
Your mountains in all of their majestic
Beauty will forever keep my soul at peace
Your giant deep blue waters are the
Essence of my being
Your trees are endlessly beautiful
Your flowers make me stand fast in
My tracks
Your entire creation quickens my heartbeat
Creator, your creation is an extension of yourself
From your soul to mine

Cari Bryan

Silhouette Jewel

Dawn breaks capturing the huge silhouette
of the bluish-grey mountains,
cloaked in mist and morning clouds.
As the sun rises, mist disappears as if magic
Unveiling beautiful mountains adorned
with snow-capped peaks gleaming like
jewels in the sun.
The soft wind makes ripples in the lazy
streams as it passes its' base
Water from the melting snow makes its' way
to the bottom of the mountain gently finding
way to the stream.
Mid-way, full sun increasing flow of melting snow.
The stream below pulsating with energy created
by extra flow caresses the banks.
Sunset spreads an orange glow, the cooling
air reduces the water to a trickle. By nightfall
the stream flow is normal and mother nature
ready for another day.

Cleone M. Ward

To My Sister

We survived some of the battles
of the traditional dysfunctional family, barely.
We wouldn't or couldn't communicate about it
until we had families of our own.
Still, all the truth has yet to be mentioned.
I suppose, sometimes maybe it's better not to-
be shocked by memory all at once.
Ironically mother denied our memories,
as if they hadn't existed.
I guess it's easier to phase them out-
The fears that plague us won't disappear.
We have to be certain we won't disfunctionalize our children.
Aren't we already with the excess baggage?

Debi Kottke

The Hardened Soul

My eyes are open wide with the twirl
of the volcano, ready to burst within side.
The boiling lava that takes all that
stands in her way.
The harden rock with time, it turns
so bitter sweet.
Cursing all who touches its serenity.
Will time heal such fury
Or will time just kill the mountain of beauty.

Diane Holdaway

"The Plaque Of Nations"

"We face problems today among the world's nations
of very hard times and perilous situations. Men
loosing their lives, beaten by police and thrown into prisons
by corrupt men in power and the leaders of their
systems. As we watch television everyday we are shown
pictures of sex, hatred, violence, and men doing wrong.
As we watch these things we may wonder inside, "are these
the things men try to hide?" We search for answers
but they seem hard to find and somewhere they are hidden
in a very good mind. If we would just take the time
to sit down and study, God's word, The Holy Bible, somewhere
with a buddy. Maybe then we will find in some
divine way, the answers to the problems we face today.
Men and women of the world, a cry comes forth
from this holy book, "Please! Open me up and take a
look!" and maybe then we will find salvation and
The answers to...The plague of nations."

DeLaney E. Holly

Oh Grandmother....

Oh Grandmother, the little girl said...What is Life?
Oh darling, Life is what God has given all of us.
Each one of us serves a purpose in Life. Life should be free of a
Troubled mind and soul, and internal conflict should be resolved as an
Aid to mental health.
Life is....Always.

Oh Grandmother, the young girl said....What is Marriage?

Marriage is a bond that you make to that person you really love and
Cherish in Life.
Love him cherish him and most of all be equal with him, as he shall do
for you.
Be happy in Marriage, for you are best friends, buddies and soul mates
Marriage is....sacred.

Oh Grandmother, the woman said....What is Death?

Death is only the beginning of an experience that the living cannot
understand.
When you die, God will cradle you in His palm, and you shall live
eternally in the hearts and minds of those who love you.
Death is...forever.

Oh Grandmother...What is Love?
Love is Life, Marriage and Death all intertwined together.
Most of all, when you say those words....I Love you-it means forever.
Love is...everything.

Oh Grandmother...I Love You!

Kimberly S. Hobson

Untitled

Used to buy things for someday
well, someday has passed
and it's not as much fun to dream
anymore.

Pauline V. Iwao

A Father Grieves

What sorrow, sir, to lose your only son!
On blood-soaked fields of rice 'neath hostile gun

This painful message briefly came to say
his soul and body went their separate ways

Deceitful death knocked twice at thy abode;
the sun withdrew and left a darkened road

Sharp steel was driven deeply through your heart;
it buried there with grief and cannot part

Thine eyes are cast with shadows strangely sad—
how much you loved that brave, courageous lad

Strange warrior he who felt war gravely ill
poor weapon to perform the soldier's will

When twilight falls I see thy downcast head
recalling nights your child was safe in bed

I hear a sigh of woe escape thee now—
behold a look of strain across thy brow

For as you hug and kiss a tattered toy
you think he was a man though still a boy

Deep sorrow fades with passage of the years
yet wish that I could stop thy falling tears.

Zvelyn Olson

Vagabond Soul

I have flown on spirit winds
on lengthy voyages of the mind;
And seen the visions that send
my soul to heights to find
adventure as my inner self pretends
to follow heroes of many kinds.

I credit printed words that bend
to knowledge all that goes behind,
for what we read will always blend
to form what we call "the mind".

We learn that imagination will transcend
what limited experience can find.
I have dreamt the dreams from ideas not my own
from fantasies by some one else's pages sown.
So come sail with me on seas of pages
that we might glean from all of history's ages.

Clyde Flanigan

Leaving Home

Too young to be old but too old to be young —
On memories of the past my mind gets hung.
Times I can't remember, others I can't forget —
Looking through pictures my eyes become wet.
No longer a child, not yet an adult —
Of adolescent choices here sits the result.
Years I took for granted that cannot return
Make-up the foundation of the future I must earn.
Days I spent praying for time to quickly pass
I now spend praying and hoping it will last.
I feel the fear of the bird that has to leave the nest,
Go out into the world and find another place to rest.
I wish I could recall the day this little girl was changed
Into a scared young woman whose life's been rearranged.
In the land of make believe you never have to cry,
But age fades the pixy dust and you have to say good-bye.

Ashlee Gardner

Hours After

Hours after he's left me to go and be with her, I can still smell him.
On my hands, and my clothes, and even the pillows and sheets of my bed.

But no, it is not only his scent lingering there.
It is ours — not completely him, not completely me — but we.
A warm, sweet smell.
The smell of the candy department at Sears when I was a little girl, years before I met him.
Of popcorn, and chocolate, and taffy.
Of shopping trips with my mother.
Of warmth, and safety, and security — of love.

Sometimes, hours after, I press my hands to my nose and am reminded of our mingling.
And I feel warm, and safe, and secure — I feel loved.

But, too often now, hours after he is gone, mingling with not me but her,
I press my hands to my nose and am reminded that the candy department at Sears has long since been closed.
It's popcorn, and chocolate, and taffy gone.
It's warmth and sweetness gone.
Just as he is gone — to her.
And I am alone.

Elizabeth Corcoran

The Next Trail Of Tears

The Americans that walked
On that Trail of Tears,
Their cheeks still damp
After all these years.

Stripped of their land,
Stripped of their pride.
No place to run,
No place to hide.

They see sprawling cities on old hunting grounds,
Condominiums on burial mounds.
That trail of Tears is still making them pay,
And what the future holds, only God can say.

Let the white man build.
Let the white man destroy.
On the next Trail of Tears,
You'll see a little white boy.

But maybe he'll learn
What the natives know.
You have to love this earth,
So your soul will grow.

Richard Don Breedlove

Colors Of Dust

A stained glass window falls.
Once - a picture of collected thoughts,
Now - shattered pieces of carefully composed light.

Trying to gather scattered feelings.
Seeing itself - a million uncollected pieces.

A broom...
Swept into the sea,
A million uncollected pieces.

Seeing itself as never before.
thoughts
  floating
colors
  released
to go on forever.
colors
  of dust
    in the sea.

Julia Froemke

My Someone

Single white male seeks woman who likes reading, music, and long walks on the beach. Must have strength, individuality, and be cool under pressure. A person whose laughter can brighten my mood when I'm happy or sad. A person who can solve their own problems but is not afraid to ask for help. A person whose beliefs are open, but firm and unwavering in the face of opposition. A person who can engage in open debate without being malicious or ruthless. A person who can defy those who will try to slow or stop her.

Do you lie awake at night dreaming of me, even though you don't know who I am? Do you sometimes feel as if you have no complement? Are you alone in a crowd, but secretly look into the eyes of strangers to see if I'm there? Do you know that you have no limits? Can gently cradle the universe in your hand? Do you feel the power of life in your soul, ever reaching, ever progressing, ever expanding? Does some art and music become your body, mind and soul? Do you feel the pulse of gardens both real and secret? And do you know that there is more?

Are you a person who needs nobody but want me to complete you, as I want you? Then I am here for you, and together we shall find us. Because we have found ourselves to be extraordinary people, but somehow incomplete.

Anthony Giannetti

Mother's Day

Mother may I take this time
On your very special Day;
To say some things to you
In a very special way.

Mother may you always feel
Welcome to forever call on me;
To share a funny line
Or to request a certain need.

Mother may we always speak
And speak kindly when we do;
And may our misunderstandings be far between and few.

Mother may your days get brighter
With sunlight to warm your shoulders;
And may the burdens of this world get lighter as you grow older.

Mother may I thank you sincerely
For all you have done for me;
For rocking my cradle gently to turning me over your knee.

In the "Hall of Fame" for mothers
Your name will surely appear;
And in my heart you will always be very precious and dear.

Jacqueline Molena Andrews

A Fountain Of Tears

In my garden is a crystal fountain,
One day a mother bird and her fledgling came into my garden.
They tarried awhile eating the seeds the flowers brought forth.
I tried to get closer to them to be a friend but they flew away.
Each time they flew away I was sad and dropped a tear into the fountain.
One day the mother bird did not come back and I wondered her fate.
Had she been killed by a cat, a fox, a hawk, or a car or had she tired of being a mother?
Each day the little bird came back, I wondered, and dropped another tear in the fountain.
For years my little bird grew and became beautiful but she refused my friendship.
Each time she left, my heart lost a bit of itself and I dropped a tear into the fountain.
One spring the little bird did not come back and I wondered her fate.
I would have shed ten thousand tears for my little bird who refused my friendship,
But both my heart and eyes were empty now, though the fountain was full of tears!

Alfred A. Mann

Roses Two

Two roses sit side by side
One dead, the others pedal's open wide
One in vase and nurtured to bloom
The other still in it's plastic tomb
Our love is much like these roses two
Your love for me, and my love for you
Your love for me was kept wrapped and never allowed to grow
It's beauty it could never show
My love for you was allowed to flourish
With kind word and deed it was nourished
Take heed these roses side by side
Open your heart, let the pedals grow wide
Yet alas, love you will never know
For it's beauty you will not let grow
Now look the second wilts away
For where love is not given, love cannot stay

Ashley T. Michaels

Faithfully Yours

Nature has the answers
One for me and you
To every question conjured
The keys of life and death too
Nature can cure, nature can cleanse
Nature is the beauty of life
Nature can replenish, nature can kill
Nature is the "if" in life

If we can figure it out
"If", 'cuz it's all there
If we blend our colors
"If", 'cuz only nature will bare

So look, look to nature
Everyone must try to help each other find the answers
So no one has to cry

Nature is involved with love, nature is our life
Love this world and all within
And treat her like your wife
In sickness and in health, for better or for worse,
I do.

Joseph Negrete

Creation Sonnet What Is The Truth?

If one ever contemplates creation
One may come to a revelation
Of love in purest thought and harmony

Love's fleeting pleasures
Vanish after one's treasures
Have been ruptured and revealed

Passion illuminates the fine contours
Two glistening bodies intertwined
Intoxicating scents seeping through pores
Simultaneous ecstasy released from love confined

A momentary act of exertion or
A game of perversion?

Deborah Patora

Starlight Awe

It was just another starlit night that night. Then my soul surged suddenly to the Heavens. Far beyond human heights. Yet the bond of all people...A common bond, lingered in my throat like a taste of sweet honey. And you.

Something gentle almost Holy filled the Holiday air with light beyond the stars as understanding flashed like a bolt to give simple prayer purpose. The taste of sweetness lingered like a wraith with love of God's works. And you.

M. Stuart Blattner

God's Proud

God's proud of a child in the plain
one who has the heart of a 110 angels
yes, God gave him the talent and the
creative songs that he sings
than he turns him lose to dance and dream
doing what he was born to do, entertaining
fans and pleasing God too
He is a friend who lends out a
helping hand, to all our farm friends across this land
yes, God is proud of his child who
sometimes dresses and acts a little silly
but we all know him he's our friend Willie

Carole Martin

"My Mother"

One who's sacrificed for my needs
One who loves me endlessly
One who spent time with me each day
One who was there to help me find my way
One who cradled me when I was sick
One spent hours helping with arithmetic
One who could soothe all my fears
One who gave me continuous support throughout
  the years
One who is now far away in miles, but not in
  thought
One whose value could never be bought
One who could never be replaced by another
There's only one that defines all of these:
  My Mother

Erika Ledbetter

Cornbread And Buttermilk

With this thing I do all right
Only if I manage to stay on my diet.

One thing I know is true
Cornbread and buttermilk will not do.

Of the things I love to eat
Cornbread and buttermilk are hard to beat.

Sitting at the table and all the duration
I just wonder what happened to determination.

As I then consider this situation
Up pops my wonder determination.

Where have you been I then inquire?
I need your help for abstinence to inspire.

If you just eat in moderation
But I have a problem with determination.

Desperately I turned to my wife for help
Just leave it alone she did yelp.

So if I continue with my health in tack
On cornbread and buttermilk I must turn my back.

Saying goodby to my dearest friend
Our relationship is at an end?

John L. Williams

Why Not Me

Why is a flower, a flower and not me?
Why am I not a flower, why not me?
Why am I me, and not you?
What makes you, you and not me?
How do I know I'm not you, and you're not me?
Who said you were you, anyway. Not me?
What if I am you, and you are not me?
Who are you, if you are not me?

Sharon Michaels

Reflection

The taste of youth is like fine wine
Only in remembrance; at the time
You went rocketing down the obstacle-cluttered
Corridors of adolescence

Hot and sweaty to achieve
Then loins bulged with promise
One cruised the beaches in chauvinistic splendor
Or suited up for war and barely escaped oblivion

Or maybe the politico would show up
Beckoning you from your flat
With golden oratory and a crooked finger
To stir up the stew of your idealism

So you pollchecked in the dingy garages of democracy
And found it made no difference
—but wait: Just dip a toothpick of truth
Into my tears and I'll write you a secret message,

baby: it never changes—now as old men we
Sit in our studies the atlas of our lives in our laps
Turning the heavy telescope of time
Still seeking incandescence

James L. Sharp

What Is It About You That I Love So Much?

As one would remember a mountain top that touched the feet of heaven, or an umber sun melting into a tranquil sea, so too is the vision of your beauty embraced in my mind. What is it about that I love you so much? Perhaps it's the way you make me feel when I'm near you, as if God, after creating the world and all that is perfect himself placed you by my side in answer to all my prayers. Perhaps it's the way I can feel your love for me without you having to say the words. Or is it that when the world turns against me and all is in upheaval, you're still there to tame the inner beast inside me, and yet you ask nothing in return? Perhaps it's because my heart that used to be empty and lifeless now beats for two, or maybe it's that when I'm with you I feel as if there's nothing I cannot do. I don't know what it is about you that I love you so much, all I know is that I do!

Joseph G. Petronella

She

There is a piercing stab in the silent dark.
Or is it a silent stab in the piercing dark.
The Wound is deep, deeper than any knife.
Pain, horror, guilt shoot through her.
But it lodges.
Right in the corner of her beautiful eye.
It is only when she turns to the side
That her wound is revealed.

Now the only memory of that fateful morning
Lies in the yellow love letters
Tucked away in the drawer.
Yet she is reminded each time she looks around,
For she cannot lead a life straight on.

Mothers stroll by her,
With their exasperated, yet proud expressions.
Her eye stings,
Tears stream down her face,
Until she is all alone,
In a flood of Guilt.

Amy Retsinas

What Color Are The Colors In Your Life?

When you see blue, is it the blue of depression and sadness,
Or is it the brilliant blue of the sky,
Or maybe the deep rich blue of the sea?

When you see green, is it the green of envy,
Or is it the green of new growth and life,
Or maybe the green that is forever?

Is your yellow cowardly and afraid,
Or is it the warm glow of the sun on your skin,
Or maybe the glittering riches of gold?

Is your red hundreds of flashing stop lights,
Or is it a beautiful, fragrant red rose,
Or maybe a blazing sunset?

Tell me, what color are the colors in your life?

Judy Rae Beier

Passaway

We live in a world where all things pass away,
Or is it we that pass and they, that seem to stay.
If I could stop my heart from breaking,
I could relieve my existence from aching.
I seem to breed an aura of sadness.
I take it as my individual and only happiness.
Your voice all I remember, your vision all I see,
When I'm gone will you even remember me.
My pain I project is forgotten only by you,
In this time nothing ever comes true.
As I lay on my bed, satin and silk darkness,
I only ask for one thing, forgiveness.
My time is now over as the sun arise
And cast an orient over your eyes.

Joshua Potter

The Weather

The weather can be sunny and bright
or it can rain both day and night.

It can be cloudy, windy or still,
or it can snow, sleet, or hail.

There are thunder, lightning, and windstorms galore,
hurricanes, tornados, and tidal waves ashore.

There can be heat waves and sand storms in places,
or snow storms and blizzards that freeze our faces.

The weather is constantly changing our land,
with flooding, erosion, and loss of sand.

Lightning strikes trees that burn up our woods,
causing a shortage of lumber goods.

Hurricanes and tornados leave death and destruction,
causing great sorrow, repairs, and construction.

If the weather is nice, be joyful and sing,
for we never know what tomorrow will bring.

Barbara J. Mixon

The Desert

(Bunni)

I will stand Immortal!
When the mighty Sphinx' have crumbled,
And statues of Marble, Granite and Bronze-
Erected by men seeking to haunt the Mind of Eternity-
Have decayed and molded to dust;
I will stand...
The Wind is my sculptor;
Eternity my accomplice.

Mel Scott

The Innocence of a Child

Have you ever stopped to watch a child play,
Or listen to the things they have to say.
The games they have they make themselves,
Not even bothering to use the toys on their shelves.
They don't know about crime or pollution.
Even though when they grow up they will have to be
the solution.
A child's innocence may be the key,
To end all war and poverty,
If they can keep that special tool,
To stay calm and keep their cool.
Their world will be better, all problems will decease,
And their lives will be full of love, happiness, and peace.

Jenilee Grabenhorst

Time

Should TIME be judged by those who wait
or should it be "It's simply fate."
Should we count the moments 'till the moments disappear
or do we wait until it's forgotten and no longer clear?

If too much TIME is what's expected,
does it rob the future of what we've reflected
In our hearts and minds, or is TIME
what's necessary to make you mine?

Time is such a worldly invention
to have it rule me is not my intention.
I want to have it all...right now!
What lessons to learn from knowing how
to wait for TIME to flow somehow...

So, for now I simply live
and room for TIME is what I'll give.
But, to wait too long may take away
the TIME we need for love to stay.

Kamille Kae Beebe

Others

Others built the ancient empires.
Others fought the fierce battles.
Others made the important discoveries.
Others solved the curious scientific questions.

Others played beautiful music.
Others wrote the masterpieces of literature.
Others explored the wondrous unknown.
I sit alone, writing my poems.

Jeff Meyers

Mythological Fiends

Suffocating babble - clove scent wrapping around
our bare throats.
Dim lights the place
Jumping candles illuminate the stoic faces of the patrons
Some humbly drink their flavor fill
others vaccinate their fix with caffeine
Idle bulls**t erupts from an X'er table
Meaningful attempts at understanding and life
float through the smoke filled air
At chess people show their strategies
Others read fast to show their intellect
We all gather together,
a community of espresso beans
Filling the jar
Waiting to feed the machine
In the mean time we'll sit, have a smoke and a good cup of
coffee.

Brain Hillman

Rain

Teardrops are dropping from the sky;
Our evil deeds make the angels cry
Some people say that Heaven is a place on earth.
If that's so, then heaven is a place in hell.
I'm sick of this life.
I'm sick of this world.
I don't know why I feel this way.
I don't know what I'm supposed to say.
Don't you know that I'm so confused,
I don't know what to do?
Teardrops are running down my face.
There are no angels, just open space.
If our deeds are evil, then it's the human way.
I'm sure no one will listen to what I say.
Teardrops are dropping from the sky.
They're not tears of joy,
They're not tears of pain,
They're not tears at all,
It's just the falling rain.

Chad Murphy

The Beach Of Love

We walked along the beach of life together.
Our hands grasping each other tightly.
With the waves of pain and frustration gripping our feet,
We continue on with the warm sun caressing our faces.
With you at my side, giving me the courage and strength to carry on,
I was able to have faith in life and never to loose hope.
The winds fierce power trying to stop us,
While the powdered, soft hands cushion our feet as we proceed on our
journey.
Through all this, your eyes were reassuring and strong,
And your smile was warm and comforting.
Our love, like life itself is powerful, yet contain beauty and grace.
It has been fifty years now, since we began this great journey together.
Throughout our time together, you have taught me how to understand,
To forgive,
to trust,
and most of all,
how to love.
And for this I will always love you.

Kendra Dion

My Sanctuary

It's our little secret.
Our private retreat.
It make's me feel better almost complete.
Riding my horse with the wind in my hair.
I feel free with nature without a care.
We run threw the meadows, and cross the field.
Cool our feet with a splash in the creek.
Right up the mountain straight to the peek.
Glide between the two large pine trees.
Stop for a minute to feel the cool breeze.
Our destination is very near.
We are both excited were glad to be here.
Down the side of the mountain until
you see a cliff with a big fountain.
Mountain spring water a crystal clean spray.
That's why we come back day after day.
A certain time the sun's just right.
The spray turns to a rainbow a wonderment sight.

Deborah A. Derliunas

The Fog

The thick mist blew beneath the trees
Out of the forest it swoops through the reeds
Over the water toward the parallel coast
Twisting and turning like a hideous ghost
The city now, its humble abode
Caught in the clutches of the fog's icy cold

A battle now is about to begin
For the fog does not want the bright sun to get in
But the sun is persistent and the ghost bows in shame
'Cause the sun is the victor again and again

David D. Ealy

Unsettled

Why does sleep elude me so? I'm so tired and have such anxiety
over such images that flash through my mind.
How I wish my mind could rest.

If it should rest the thought of sleep would become a reality.
Why does it trouble me so?
Why do these strange scenes constantly flash through my mind?

These images of faceless people constantly invade my most
intimate thoughts.
They cause me to be fearful and confused.
How I wish they would leave and let the blackness of sleep
overtake me.

But, when sleep does come.
It is but only for a minute and once again the faceless things
appear and begin their relentless and systematic invasion of my
most private dreams.

What can I do?
Remain awake so these scenes do not return?
That only proves to be even more tiresome and unsettling.
Lord, help me to someday confront and conquer this crime
of Rape of the mind.

Garrett W. Brooks

Mountains

In my youth, I loved to wander
Over the mountains, so I could ponder
About a future I could see
That lies ahead, awaiting me.

I marveled at all of nature's wonders
Surrounding the view like rising thunders
That follow when the lightening showers
Its grand display of God's great powers.

The woods above the mountains creep
Over the hills that rise so steep;
And after walking all day 'til the sun goes down,
I cherish these memories that I have found.

I look forward to coming back again
And reviewing these scenes where I have been
And discovering new wonders on display
That I might have missed on a previous day.

Jack A. Feldman

Rex

Rex, oh Rex, you eat so much by day,
Your stomach is so big, I can barely say.
Your teeth are really big, your mouth is really wide,
If you had been around, people would have died.
You have eatin' everything from a palm tree to a moss,
You didn't even brush your teeth, or use your dental floss.
You're nasty to the bone, you're even nasty more,
you're so very nasty, cause you're a dinosaur!

Sean Hreha

Checkmate

Utterly confused and distraught;
Over what, I have no thought.
Been raging blindly through my fear.
Mornings fade and disappear.

Every day same as the last.
Moving quickly; tearing past.
Times too tangled in twisted speed,
Unused chances used by greed.

Not guaranteed to come but surely goes.
Flies away swiftly as a mean river flows.
Insanity! Inanity! A salty lack of clarity.
Donating funds for my meager mental charity.

Stumbling and tortured, I'm totally lost.
Unable to make decisions; afraid of the cost.
My mind snaps this way; my heart leaps that.
Now mad as a Hatter, I'm Cat in the Hat.

Sometimes there's more, but too often there's less;
In this never ending, mind-bending, wretched game of chess.
But the match must end, at any rate.
And the last word from my lips will be "CHECKMATE!"

Chad Christopher Smith

Pictures

Drawing pictures in the light, images of life.
Pain and sadness, joy and happiness.
Life experiences, life trials,
Life's anguishes, life's denials.
Moments of despair, times when you don't care,
Jolts of pain too hard to bear.
Life's struggles, life's burdens, difficulties mounting.
Decisions pending, choices to make, pressures and stress.
People envy-spurn-lessen-hate-hurt.
Lack of compassion, feelings of loss, loneliness.

But dark covers not all

Sunshine sparkles, lakes reflect.
Birds sing, and flowers bloom.
People laugh-grow-change-live-love.
The magic of hope, the joy of accomplishment.
Dappled leaves, clouds drift, lazy warmth.
Embraces gold, kiss of innocence, hands held.
Good friends enveloped in night, entranced by day.
Blue sky, green trees, bright sun, dazzling stars, satin moon.

Beauty abounds.

Joseph A. Dennemann

Blanket Of Faith

All of my life, I've been around
People who weren't looking, but were found.

I've always felt warm and loved and safe
Because of the blanket they wrapped around me,
called faith.

In good times and in bad, when troubled or sad
I covered my soul with the blanket of faith
and my heart was once again glad.

I can never repay the love that's been shown,
Except to say that when I am grown,

I will give each girl and boy of my own,
the feeling of love and of being safe,
and cover them with the blanket of faith.

Kay L. Forbes

Abortion

Women imagine the hurt on our God's face
Pained in agony instead of grace.
A baby, held in his hand the future of this earth
Aborted without choice, instead of birth.
Made in His image this precious little life
To be born in happiness to husband and wife.
Instead to be thrown out like so much waste
Without thinking or planning-just done in haste.
God in your wisdom, please help them to survive
Help us Lord to keep them alive.
God created heaven and this world too
To follow in his plan, both me and you
To give us life and create birth
To fill with babies upon this earth.
To love and care for them, not to abort
Life and death is God's, not The Supreme Court's.
So, think you women with abortion in mind;
For peace on earth, you'll never find.
Bring forth that life and give it a face
Take the agony from God and put back the Grace.

Joyce Cates Hoffman

Musical Memories

Gossamer wisps of music dart through their memories
Painting pictures in their minds of days that used to be.

It's the "old songs," "their songs," embedded in their souls
They hear them played, and words unfold as if upon a scroll.

One word comes, then two or three
The lyrics fill their memories.

Gossamer wisps of music, thank you for being there
To fill their minds and bless their souls with something they can share.

Joan A. Gerber

"Our Family Tree"

Our family tree grew in Brooklyn, NY, after Mom and Dad said "I do",
Parenting three daughters and four sons was not an easy task for two.
Coping with seven different personalities required a lot of patience with their clan,
Striving and doing their level best for each child was their plan.
We may not have been as close as some kin folk seem to be,
But, when one needed the other, support was given to their plea.
Parents feel it's unfortunate to loose a child before they have passed on,
They lived and lost two young sons before they were gone.
After our parents passed on, five children tried to view their lives with some hope,
In six and a half years four more departed, leaving their family members to cope.
A once full tree has dwindled down to just one branch,
That's me,
The life span of this branch is a mystery, that no one can foresee.

Anne Devine

Union

The stars envy us our beauty,
we shame them with our brilliance.

We breath light into dawn.

We are two hands on one body
caressing the newly formed vase
full with tears and joys;
Holding a single rosebud
just beginning to bloom.

Saundra T. Woods

Parental Misguidance

Parents are to be good, warm, and kind
Parents are to sooth all our troubles inside
Parents should discipline, when necessary with care
not because they are angered by some other affair

To be disciplined when at fault, is easily understood
but to be yelled at for convenience is never comprehended.
She is trapped in her house with her parents shrills and their screams
And longs for the day she is free and can leave.

When she is older, and has moved on
She can live a new life, because the pain is now gone
Her only regret is about the child inside
it has long since been buried, because it has died.

Her eyes are red from the tears she has shed,
there are so many troubles within this girl's head.
She comes to you now, and her soul has one question
please can you love her, and help heal her depression.

Cindy Dawn Lester

Marionette

Life was being mapped by a book of directions:
Parents prepared dos and don'ts like a creed.
Whispering instructions with no interruptions
Hoping their decisions would plant the seed.

And against my better judgment, I agreed.

I became a doctor after perpetual schooling,
Losing my celibacy, but made a bad team.
The war inside my soul continuously dueling,
Yet everyone was telling me my life was a dream.

And against my better judgment, I agreed.

A lapidifying statue I changed overnight,
An irruption of thoughts in my mind arousing.
Arriving at an answer, and packing very light, I
Went guiltless to the door and slammed it closing.

And against my better judgment, I agreed.

Into the wild I went without a coat of armor-
The world was much colder than I could believe.
A hulk I was becoming instead of a charmer,
Those people I left I now realize I need.

And using my better judgment, I WILL succeed.

Christina Lynn Price

Dreams In Time

The time is short and time goes fast, before we know, the year is past.
And this year's dreams like thoughts well meant, are lost for now and like a dream,
They join the past, how dead they seem and time waits not, for time moves on,
A piece of life, our dreams are gone, a memory how we've lost and won.
Without a goal to stir your soul and guide your every tread,
You're dead as dust, with naught to trust, you'll never lead, but always led.
So look up high at star and sky and grasp a dream so bold,
A vision true, just made for you and turn your dreams to gold.
Now is the time and it's your life, don't waste it, have some trust,
Success is earned, with no help spurned and work you surely must.
So make your choice, decide your fate, you cannot pass the blame.
Remember for both rich and poor, the truth remains the same,
It's really not the time you have, it's how you play the game!

John Kust

Patchwork

We cross this patchwork of time
pausing occasionally to
measure the days with rulers and weights and spoons,
to measure the soul by its own certain fullness,
by its sincerity of giving and receiving

What are we anyway but foils of one another?
Flesh, Blood, Soul:
Tired, fallen rain in stagnant piles
yet delicate edges of a crystal puzzle
fitting without fail,
the bright spot
in darkened tunnels
between hand-shaped mountains
under the pleasing skylight of need

In ancient days
we will remember friends as those
who could reach through the outer shell
and touch the quick, those
who could stir your insides
as if with a spoon
and then join the eternal search for
that polished hour of worth

Benjamin Ayres

Mr. Job

There was a man in the Land of UZ,
Perfect, upright, and righteous, he surely was;
The greatest of all the men of the East,
His household was great, He owned many beast.

Satan going to and fro, in the earth,
The Lord said have you considered what Job is worth?
Satan said does Job fear God for aught?
If you take away His riches, He will serve you not.

The hedge was removed, soon Job found,
Riches, children, and houses brought to the ground.
Three men came to comfort, they as a friend,
They each had their say many words with out end.

Job was afflicted, His wife did reply,
Why don't you curse God and die?
You talk like a foolish one, Job did say,
The Lord giveth, and the Lord taketh away.

Job was healed, his riches restored,
Seven sons, three daughters replaced by Lord;
He lived many years, many full days,
He trusted in God, that really pays.

Dorothy M. Fannon

Plastic Tablecloth That Looked Like White Lace

The snap dated 1961 brings many memories
Playing cards after dinner
At a table covered with a plastic cloth that looked like white lace.
George, the father, died the next year
Only 38, but years of hard work had taken their toll.
Glenn, the oldest son, than 30 years later,
Has two children in college,
Harvey, the youngest son, now a doctor with a small girl.
And I, the fourth player in the game
Stopped a moment in time
When I took the snap
Sitting at a table were the three players
And the plastic tablecloth that looked like white lace.

Clara Beth Negoro

Communion

Speak to me when I call your name.
Please, impose upon me your
hidden agenda so that I may understand the
longings of myself.

Whisper in the chamber of my secret room
I won't betray the pact made between us and
It's sound will live anthem in my thoughts.

Listen, when I say to you,
few in words, abundant in expression.
Delight in my passion and bathe in our rapture.

Make melodies with me my lover. Lyrical
notes that only you and I hear.

Your breath upon my cheek, my heart against your
chest, your flesh against my flesh.
Dance with me my lover, pull me close
and again engulf yourself in my overture.

Put your lips to my lips, speak and I shall hear.

Edith H. Conner

Free Your Mind

Please take me from this confusion.
Please save my heart from this contusion.
Must we love a person with blonde hair and blue eyes?
Must we love a dark-skinned brother with African ties?
Rid your eyes of color.
We should love one another.
Rid your mind of old fashioned ways.
We have more to worry about now-a-days.
We need to stop this hate.
Take your mind on the great escape.
Escape from the vengeance.
To hold on to such a rage would just be your arrogance.
Forget what my ancestors did to yours.
It's about time to close those doors.
A person's true self is what we chose to adore.
Race and religion is not a factor.
Many years ago we were said to have been set free.
But many people still hold a strong animosity.

Janet Nees

The Crossing

A dead deer of at least a day's decay on the highway,
Probably hit by a car while crossing,
is red must against the road's shoulder.

I can see the thumb print the car made
when it smashed into Her bosom like water,
  and they had to scrape Her dripping
  insides off the windshield, and
  clean raw meat out of the grooves
  of their tire with a shovel.
She's all here, and some over there,
getting nothing more than a child's curiosity or a
sympathetic second look from a tourist's wife.

She probably suffered for an eternity of a second
then decided the flies were better company.
But her eyes are still open - maybe Her last revenge.

It was Her own fault for coming down.
With Her safe mountains only miles away,
and the highway with the cars whizzing by,
SHE should have realized it wasn't safe.

Courtney Morris

Estuaries - The Liquid Lands

Our coastal bays and coastal wetlands, our estuaries.

They form a system of liquid-lands with the highest productivities.
What is land today, may, tomorrow, become open water.

The magic is in the wetlands, the stream flow, and the tidal waves altogether.

The fresh water stream delivers nutrients and deposits sediments in the lower bay.

Where the salt water sneaks up with the tidal waves and wash them away.

This dynamic interplay of heterogeneous environments offer something for everyone.

Our estuaries support the national economy through wildlife production, fisheries, or just recreational fun.

Ann E. Castaldi

To Protect Always!

Protect your heart as a priceless diamond
Protect your body as a precious Jem
Protect your dreams as shiny pieces of gold.
Trust your heart to lead you to love
Trust your body to lead you a long-life
Trust your dreams to always guide you.
Your heart cannot be bought
Your body cannot be placed
Your dreams cannot be stolen.
Your heart may break
Your body may hurt
Your dreams may shatter.
If you protect these 3 important, priceless things...
Your heart will lead you to love
Your body will lead you a long-life
Your dreams will always guide you.
If you protect these 3 important, priceless
unreplaceable things, your heart, your body and dreams
will always be yours, always!

Kiki Wilson

Who Am I?

Who am I?
Put on this earth but why?
Was it to be someone great?
What is my fate?
Doctor, Lawyer, A.I.D.S. or Cancer?
These questions I wish I could answer
Confusion, laughter, pain and tears
All that I have gone through my teenage years
At times I feel trapped, as if in a cage
Insides overcome with rage
I wonder, will I ever have a true friend?
When will peer pressure end?
If my life were a book it would have no plot
For interesting and talented I am not
A good person or so I am told
Some might say strong and bold
To be honest I am still trying to figure out
What it is I am all about
While my "friends" are out getting high
I am sitting home wondering — Who am I?

Brenda Cruz

Cursed By the Early Eighties: My Youth

Carter in a stuper
Reagan considered "super"
12 years of Hell
a bulls**t sell.

Everyone conservative with short hair
Reagan strategy: Red Scare!

Military aid goes up
More homeless begging holding cups

President Stupid
Death of Cupid

Reagan crushed the poor
more aid to Nazi government in El Salvador!

Reagan gave aid to Contras and broke law,
in his warped mind there was no flaw.

Dark ages for thinking
The poor were sinking

The early eighties
For young leftists
like life in Haiti!

Bill Frizlen

Filled Unfulfillingly

I was a man like all the rest, with my green browned and my eyes reasoned shut
I stood against the Earth's sigh as it blew me
I fought against the tides as they turned me
I cursed the skies as their overfilled bellies waterfalled against my barren chest
I stared relentlessly into that golden medallion as its rays as arrows reigned down upon my body
I hailed those sprinkles of the night sky with taunts returned only in twinkle
I plunged myself against the raging mistress of the river's bed
I put my shoulder into the moving of those staunch inhabitants of the ranges
I raged so fire as only a step behind reason
I brawled so clenched as only a rung below betterment
I lived so ordinary as only a desert between fulfillment

Keith Cox

Remember Me...

Remember me with a smile and a thought,
Remember me ... forget me not!
For I think of you, each and every day,
Of all the talks, the moments, the way
You changed every life you touched ... So know
Oh how I'll miss you Carlos, but please go
And find what you're looking for: You KNOW it's there —
That dream that lives in your eyes and heart! Dare
To be who you are, to care, to live
The life you want. For all you give
You deserve to have the best and more
The happiness you've been looking for ...

Maybe once in a while, WHEN you are THERE,
You'll remember me with a smile and a thought?
For time is no issue ... and no matter when,
I'll remember you always, I'll forget you not!

Anahita Hashemi

I Already Loved You

I have loved you for so long, it is no longer important to remember when my loving you began.

I loved you as a friend, the one person I could feel safe with and open up my feelings and fears.

I loved you as a person, with all your imperfections, moods, and unexpected changes of life.

I loved you when your heart was inaccessible to mine, and you created distance between us.

I loved you as a lover, with all the beauty of discovery and enhancement of love.

You are no longer in love with love; You are in love with me.

Can my heart dare to trust your passion?

The little sparrow cannot hear her own heart beating within her breast.

Yet she flies into the darkness of the night.

I already loved you;
Now I must fly into the light of my own desiring.

You are my Sanctuary.
You are my beloved.

Jan Atchley Bevan

Letting Go

He raced around the many paths
Remembering once and once again, the past;
The heartbeats, the smile on the lips, the
smile in the eyes,
The laughter,
The tenderness and the carefree moments.
But then again, the careless times;
The tears
Streaming under the stars,
And the wishes upon the moon's craters
For the crooked paths to end,
For the seas to cease rolling
And the rivers to flow back.
He watched ambivalence careen off shadowed pathways
And finally, wasted, found indifference beckoning
in the grinding gloom
on a road to nowhere.
Ah!...But each mind has a natural way of letting go
So the heart can start anew.

David E. Weber

Spring

Spring is a tease, a taunter
Seducing us with a warming breeze
Only to turn her back and deliver a cold shoulder
Sending the sweet song of robins
And the howling wind with its icy embrace
What a wicked mistress, what a wanted child
For what other season is looked forward to with such longing
And yet is despised so much for its deliverance

For spring never promises summer
Though that is what we wish.
Spring is grey and yet it is also the end of grey
It is cold and damp and yet it is the end of cold and damp
It is light and shadow illuminating bare trees
And adding depth to our world.

Kathy Marcinek

Retiring Gent

Pushed and shoved by swooshing and smashing,
Repetitive, relentless, corroborative clashing.

Carried to brimming, barbaric brinks,
Brutal, beguiling biting links.

Zapped with sinister, snapping pleas,
Growling, goading, grinding sleaze.

Torched from turbulent, twisting turns,
Vicious, venomous, voracious burns.

Angered by arctic, abrasive attacks,
Whining, whipping, whirling whacks.

Scooped the scum from scandalous sources,
Frothing, fuming, filthy forces.

Restrained in quicksand from June to June,
Greedy disciples delight in the ruin.

Tell-tale footprint left en-masse,
From furtive centipedes stalking grass.

Served with alleges and forced to succumb,
The coveted goal is "Two for One."

Pushed and shoved by swooshing and smashing,
Repetitive, relentless, corroborative clashing.

Annabelle M. Sherba

The Chaplain

The Rev. Mr. X stood still and straight
Robed in black, his sermon great

His pulpit high was empty now.
The organ moaned its final tone.

And the good earth piled full and round,
Looked splendid there with a flower on.

His congregation uttered no sigh,
Those few at hand, those long gone by.

While all around the lightning played
Midst the ghastly bomb blasts, not far away.

And the souls that came, came from hell and more, hell to be at his grave side and wish him well.

It was here in a land not worth fighting for,
That the Rev. Mr. X came back from war.

Hastily covered in one little heap,
He was tenderly settled for eternal sleep.

Some blamed the Devil, some said Fate,
While others thought called, to a better state.

But for those who could hear his sermon great,
They saw him standing still and straight.

Arthur T. Jack

You

When I rise up and when I lie down — you are there,
When I'm happy or sad — you are there,
When I hear a romantic song or one that's sad — still you are there,
And when I see two lovers kiss — always, you are there.
So why can't I reach out to you?
Why can't I touch you?
Why aren't you here beside me?

Roberta S. Hoffman

Harvest Moon

Fire in the dark, night sky, burning away the stars.
Roots of licorice falling from your mouth.
That blanket is no longer ours.
Now I walk with blood in my shoes,
My skin is no longer my own,
Tasting of fruit and tobacco but no one will ever know.
Did anyone see me when I fell?
You were too busy watching her change.
Now I cover my bruises well,
Along with the truth lying under my name.
I give and give,
Then gave it away.
I don't mind if you take it all.
It's not of any great importance,
Just bits and pieces of my soul.

Emily Bernhagen

After the Tears

Will I have the ability to finally,
Run free, play, and be carefree, those times that were missed in childhood?
Will I be able to make up for all those lost years,
After the tears?

Will I be able to stop and ignore the pain of words that led me to feelings of worthlessness,
And come out on top, even at this late age,
After the tears?

Have I learned how to love my children right, or will the cycle continue,
After the long battles within myself to grow past the dysfunction of long ago,
After the tears?

Yes, most of the dysfunction I have conquered,
But loneliness and abandonment still haunt me,
Leading me to believe is their really a phase of...
After the tears?

Joy Hill

Untitled

My mind is lost in a maze of chaotic confusion;
running feverishly, scurrying unconsciously.
The dizzying pace at which it runs blinds me from other alleyways.
The searing stares and impure thoughts of others
frighten me.
Because of fear, logic has no place to reserve itself.
It is lost.
Fear quickly transforms into paranoia.
which swells grossly, painfully,
like an overfilled dam - it breaks.
The frustration forces itself
from my vocal cords, strongly, dangerously,
shattering anyone's security and peace.
They know I will never be silenced.
They know my anger will become violent,
kicking and slashing its way out of me,
to the point where it consumes
all reason, logic, and faith.

Aneesah Jarrett

And The River Flows

A gentle flow down a river bank. A silence in the rushing leaves. Frogs jumping to lily pad to lily pad.
A heron cleaning its wet body of feathers. And the river flows.

A deer running from morning forest. A owl closing its wearily eyes. A turtle sunbathing on a smooth rock.
Flowers dancing with the calm breeze. And the river flows.

Gulls in the morning glide. Children building sand castles. The waves pounding against the sanded beach. It travels far and it travels near, and now the river ends.

Jennifer Feldmann

Untitled

Traces of past loves, someone's comb, another's chap stick.
Scars from other times and travels.
The dog who won the race.
The spoke that finally broke in the Bad Curve.
All lessons hard learned and imprinted on my memory.
Also the times memory failed from the embrace of liquid courage.
The so sweet nectar of my every waking breath.
Until age, wisdom, and the reality of my true destiny
opened my eyes to a new self; a sober self;
a self that I'd never met before.
Was she always there, waiting?
Or did the knight create her for himself?
Whatever answer, I think I like her.
Maybe we can be friends.

Jessica Denise Sawyer

Scattered In The Sand

Every mere mortal is a grain of sand
scattered across the beach
a small child, a young man, a grown man - out of reach

If we look into another eyes, what we may find
is a cascade of lies forming in ones mind
travelling with time into another dimension
some will never understand a shattered life scattered in the sand

I know the time will come when we will face our maker
that time is growing near
but as you look around at others dying, inside all you see is fear
a small child, a young man, a grown woman - out of reach

In your heart you feel the knife turn
but after the ones you lost, you still yearn
why can't life be easy, as you separate the untold truth of lies
where everything counts, out what's important you must realize
everyone's entitled to their opinion, just open you mind and listen

A small child, a young man, a grown woman - out of reach
Scattered in the sand, along the beach
out of grasp, out of reach
scattered in the sand

Kimberly M. A. Ellis

Rainbows In The Water

I watch the rainbows in the water,
You tell me of something called fish
I do not understand your sadness—
Or this loss
What could be more beautiful
Than these colors on this black glass?

Graham Jackson

Easter

The pain He went through His hands and His feet.
You should be thankful, He hung there for you.

Then on the third day He rose from the dead.
So you could join Him. In His home Heaven.

Robert Bedgood

Sunrise

The sun rose.
Scattered pieces of color shattered against a pale, grey tarp.
Muted tones of a watercolor painting,
Dripping, running, meeting, joining,
One, entirely new.
A newborn baby,
Reaching out, tiny fingers to touch the pulsating grey sky,
Eager, yearning, waiting for new life to grab hold of,
And bless.
The birds burst open with melody, as he struggles to lift his head,
And the leaves rustle and dance with expectant joy.
The wind whispers softly to him, and then, gently,
Oh, ever so gently,
Lifts him into the sky.
He breathes softly, quiet colors surround him,
Run together, washing away they grey,
Leaving streaks of white on the painter's easel.
The sun rose.

Kimberly R. Purdy

God's Many Miracles

At twilight as the winter weaves its way through the trees
scattering what's left of the summer leaves
I can hear the melting snow gently dripping from the eaves.
I watch and listen in awe and wonderment at God's miracles
which never cease, he seems to do them with so much ease.
Soon the moon's soft glow will shine on the snow
making the world beautiful and bright.
Then, like the night, it will be gone and in early morn
somewhere a little child will be born.
Then, as the sun turns the night into day,
someone will take their last breath and slip quietly away.
Each night I get on my knees and thank Him for His miracles
and for the beautiful world he gave us to live, work and play in.

James Monroe Story

Getting To There

Crawling under fields
screaming into her catching breeze

By the fetch
we run back and fifth
craving to grasp

Drains that lay under our walk
words that flow through the rock she saw shine

Keeping a shaky speech
everything comes to scare
like knives in the backs of flesh

To grade our day
the week
and month
well spent into fun

Challenging
the grueling pain that bleeds
my knees
stepping forward on
the grounds rocky voice

Anel Flores

Gifts

Surrounded by names of people unknown
Searching for one in cold marbled stone
Petals are scattered from winds once blown
Needing a friend but standing alone

Eyes now misting from finding the place
Reading the name, remembering the face
Placing some flowers in an old copper vase
Visions rush in that time won't erase

Some precious moments remembered in tears
Thinking of good times, a smile soon appears
Sharing words of love, faithful he hears
Knowing the gifts he gave will last through the years

The gift of a family who is always there
The gift of laughter for others to share
Courage and strength for times tough to bear
The most special gift, how to love and to care

Keep these gifts inside, alive and new
Bring them out in the open, when feelings get blue
And always remember, for this so true
The love he held, was special for you

Amy Prenatt

Digging

I dig down deep, bludgeoning my soul,
Searching for the pieces which once made me whole,
My shovel is your words, they cut me to the bone,
I throw away my own self, until I'm all alone.
I discard thoughts and feelings, which you said get in the way,
I throw them to the side in hopes of a better day.
I'm overwhelmed by the image, of what the others see,
And I'm afraid to allow myself to just become me.
I keep digging, digging, digging, And throwing to the side,
Everything you said was wrong, everything I was trying to hide.
I threw so much away that I just can't regain,
Now I'm left alone in a deep, dark pit, wriggling around in pain.

Anne Luck

Spring

I love the sights, sounds and feelings of Spring, to see a flower blooming, to hear a bird sing. To see a newborn fawn try to walk, to hear the crickets start to talk. To feel the warm sun upon my face, to see the green grass all over the place. To see a squirrel play among the branches, to see a butterfly do her magical dances. To see a bud on a tree, to hear the calls of a buzzing bee, to see a rabbit hoping along the ground so slowly and quietly trying not to make a sound. To see the ice cold snow melt away and to feel the weather get warmer everyday.

If you look with your eyes, listen, and feel with your heart, you will learn that you and nature are not very far apart.

Kristina Murdock

One

One - alone
Seems so small
And there's not much one can do.
But add one more
And you'll be surprised
At what two can have in store!
One finger can't snap; it needs a friend,
So God gave us five on each hand.
And one person so small can't do the big job
Of changing this whole land.
Come, friend, take my hand,
We'll show them what two can do!

Jo Jaimeson

Our Dear Old Flag

I hear firecrackers from the west
See the sky filled with rockets, the very best
The noise is loud to we older ones
but the youngsters are having so much fun
It's a national event celebrated each year
Thanks for our freedom, a prayer so dear
On this special day when fireworks are so plain
"AMERICA THE BEAUTIFUL" comes to mind "fields of grain"
We love our flag and seeing it wave
On the flag pole which our children gave
It's colors of white, red and navy blue
Stars in the corner, it flies for me and you
So hats off to OLD GLORY: this 4th of July
May it always be honored and continue to fly

Carolyn Boss

Through A Child's Eyes

Nothing seen clearer than through the eyes of a child
seeing it all for the very first time.
An innocence to everything.
That age has made us blind
a rainbow, a snowflake
though trivial we may find.
Can open worlds of wonder
in this tiny little mind.
For with each new discovery
a priceless gift they earn.
A chance to grow inside
with each lesson that they learn.
so patience we must offer
when they linger for awhile.
For there's much to see and do
Through the beautiful eyes of a child.

Brenna Prosser

I, Burnt Umber Mud: An Uprooting

I, burnt umber mud
seething up through toes, and over the nails.
I, bubbling up, covering.
I, taking root.
I, inhaling nutrients in.
You, grass greening.
I...I am local.
I...I am content,
until I am hungry.
I, panicking,
I, trying to evolve.
You, grass browning.
I, struggling to break my roots.
I, pulling.
You, pulling,
but I'm only breaking my femur stem.
I realizing I will never leave.
Dying here in the very place you picked.

Angela Stover

Southern Belle

Like a solitary flower in a vast, lonely field,
she brings beauty and solace without any yield.
Sparkling sunsets in her eyes, she'll show...
and that smile which outbrightens all stars and rainbows.
Compassion, affection, love, and that laugh
will be remembered, almost as her epitaph.
Thinking of her I lose hours of sleep;
the moments with her are treasures to reap.
I find myself smiling for no reason at all,
because of a woman with a soft, southern drawl.

Anthony Michael Avanzo

life as i know it

i need intensive care to get it i know not where
self-help books laced with your t.v. shows
my antique anger grows and grows
well i write as i die far too callous to cry
watching my livelihood shrivel from this world so uncivil
i've eaten from churches and dumpsters i hate to starve
with internal rage my arms i carve
i've painted pictures with my own precious blood
if hate were water my reality i'd flood
and drown in the feelings i'm ashamed to hold
to prove once again your world is thoughtless and cold
but why should i die for this carnival of disease?
When i'm one of the mannered few who still says "please"
don't rape or kill me i'm not ready to die
cause drugs help if you'll accept that shaky reply
it's a paradox i know my writings will show
and fear is the reason i dare not leave
so myself has the function to the world deceive
so i'll suffer stay and get worse every day
till violence and despair break my last impulse to care

Abe Masek

Conflict

Your life is your life; my life is mine,
separated but joined, bound together by time.
You don't rule my life, I don't rule yours;
although you sometimes wish I would;
but I think no matter how much I tried, I don't think I could.

With my head bowed I take the strikes and blows,
I feel no pain but when you cry my anger shows.
I can clench my fist, if needs be I can fight;
although usually meek I'll stand up for what's right.

How long has it been since you've laughed?
How long ago was your last smile?
No matter what you tell me - it's been quite a while.
I will not take this anymore,
I will not turn my face and close my eyes;
I will not shut my ears and be deaf,
I will change things - or at least be the one who tries.

Karin Brown

Untitled

The moon arose at dusk and the meaningless
shadow of a man had entered this twisted world,
Through a bolt of lightning and an eagles cry.
Overhead was a raging sky a sky of blue.
red & fiery orange, for the horizon is
nor the beginning nor the end of eternity in
which those sunset riders of the West
the killing beast of man who cannot understand
the essence of himself but only greed
and when you have achieved to tall knowledge
of yourself your life is gone but in a
flash of light it's over and then a new
time, a new struggle, a new beginning, or
just a continuance of life in a new form,
or perhaps just a different point of view.

Donnie R. Wilson Jr.

Untitled

The candle inside me has lost it's flame.
That's why I feel so cold, empty and unhappy.
The only time the candle light's up is when I see you.
The flame grows so bright, so warm, so enlightening.
At this time I feel hope that we shall return to the couple we once were.
This flame shows me that there's a promising future for us.
How I wish this candle would never blow out inside me.

Elda Irizarry

Overture

Suddenly, a willful wind that flies in early spring
Shatters all those quiet places where the shifting hazes cling
Raising rowdy ripples amid the greenish seas
Of slender blades and greens around the trees
Driving startled birds from place to airy place
Till all that's light submits it its embrace

Then passes, leaving earth and air released
Now free to mourn and miss and to await a wind that's ceased

Sudden too, a newborn mood that hints of first romance
Breaks what was a lonely peace that's banished by a single glance
Stirring racing heartbeats while hoping to conceal
Confusing thoughts now shared by two who feel
Nameless visions, dreams they know not why or how
Most love-wise lovers weave into a vow

It passes, leaving echoes to resound
For in this love that's lost the heart for lasting love is found

Joan Mitchell Blumenthal

Unrequited Love

Pain and pleasure, pleasure and pain;
She brings one but the other remains...
Pleasure at a smile, or a touch, or a word;
Pain because that phrase will never be heard—
"I love you" the phrase from her to me,
I know that this scene will never be...
For she loves another, I am not the one—
I am not her stars, nor am I her sun...
Life without her I must learn to live,
For her love to me she cannot give.
For now to be her friend is all I pray;
However, there is much to her I'd like to say.
Some things are better left unsaid;
These thoughts are best left hidden in my head.
But when all is left, said and done,
She is my stars, she is my sun...

Allen Hood

Remembering You

I remember the night when she called.
She called to say you were no longer here
I remember my mothers screams and cries that night.
When she told us she said you were gone.
She told us it was alright to cry, and she held us tight.
I remember the night before
I wish I could have been with you longer
I remember when we were kids.
We'd run and play in the rain.
We'd cover our selves in mud.
I didn't want to believe
you were no longer here.
It all felt like a dream.
But now I realize it's real.
I feel the pain every day and night.
I feel the burning tears on my face at night when
I cry because I miss you.
I never got to say good by or how I felt about you.
And now I say to you Aaron,
I love you and why did you have to die?

Jessica Rogers

Armature

The poet in my soul is in no rush, no hurry, at all;
She could sit content at word play for hours, even days undisturbed
Romancing the English Language, turning words over and around-
Thinking, all is at peace with the world; all is well with the universe.
The artist in my heart is not worried, not concerned at all;
Resting surrounded by brushes and pencils, exploring all the while
Painting with broad strokes, etching in fine lines
Dabbling with colour, until discovering one never before seen-
Believing, all is tranquil with the moon; all abide by the stars.
The dancer in my head is not burdened, not sorrowed at all;
Spinning and leaping like a white feather in the wind
Feeling all flight of fancy, freedom of expression-
Assured, all is warmed by the sun; all is comforted by the lazy breeze.
The vocalist of my spirit is not restless, not silenced at all;
Her voice trills across the meadow like an endless chorus of birds
Beckoning rainbows and soft light, banishing bleak shadows-
Promising all shall be blessed by a new dawn,
All shall be kissed by an awakening day
At last, the trials of the long night are over.

Debrah Sterling

Untitled

You—you are so beautiful. You're so beautiful to me.
She cries out you are beautiful, so wonderful.
Her eyes appear before me, her head a dream center of lust.
You're beautiful, she screams to me.
If only we had more time, if only she hadn't died.
If only she hadn't screamed you're beautiful.

She wanted me—she told me so.
She would give anything, give anything to be back.
She screamed in frustration, "Oh so beautiful"!
But she's not there, she wasn't there.
But I keep hearing those words, you're—no!
No, she won't let go, she's not in my room.
She's standing in front of me, she's telling me I'm beautiful.

The glamours repossessed as she cries out my name and disappears
Only to reappear and haunt me until I am forced to sacrifice all
And join her so she too can be beautiful.

Jim O'Malley

For Mary Molly M.

I tried to show my feeling for Molly, yet I failed.
She does not want me?

I can't tell Molly, how much I love her,
so I tried to block her from my mind.

But fate is so unkind.

The more I covered and buried my love for her,
the greater it came exposed to me.

The tighter I closed my eyes to my feeling and love for Molly,
the clearer I saw.

The harder I tried to ignore the whispers and sensations of love for her,
the louder I heard loves song.

The father I ran away from the passion, the yearning, and anticipation
that burned in my heart in hope that we would be together,
the closer these feelings approached me.

From now and forever, I will have these feelings for Mary Molly,
from the first time I saw her, I knew that I would love no other.

John Raymond Sheldon

A Stepmom

A stepmom is a special person who I am glad to know.
She is someone with whom I can grow.

It will take some getting use to.
Just remember she will adjust too.

If you think she's just a little sour...
wait, because she will bloom just like a flower.

She will always take the time to talk to you
although she has other things to do.

She is there to lend a helping hand,
when there is something you just don't understand.

A stepmom always seems to go out of her way
just to put a smile in your day.

So I say, a stepmother is just a mother.

Jennifer Samples

My Plain Brown Guitar

My plain brown guitar is all that I have in my life,
She is there for me like a husbands wife.

When I am depressed she is there for me,
And she gives me blue music
From the touch of my fingers.

And when I am happy, joyous and glad
she gives me music that won't make me sad.

Her voice sings to me in a soft sweet tone,
And the melody echoes through my ears,
And stays in my mind wherever I go.

Her body is smooth and curvy,
That which reminds me of a beautiful lady
Like Marilyn Monroe.

I am glad she belongs to me and not some rock star,
Who would smash her on stage,
Because he thought it was a cheap guitar.

That's why I love my plain brown guitar.

Damian Bramlett

Youth's Exile

I stand at my window, my eyes are damp
She is waving good-bye and never returning

Her white ribbon
Blows in the wind
Her rosy cheeks
Catch the mark of youth

Her voice is light
And her songs homemade
The chords linger
And fill the air

Her footfalls are slight
And leave little trace
On the long road
I have not trekked

And I catch the last glimpse of the wide smile
The echoing voice
The pattering feet
And the white ribbon

And as she waves good-bye,
she takes with her her youthful dreams and ways
And I am left alone at my window now only remembering

Joy Jansen

[he is indeed amused at her tenderest transports]

he is indeed amused at her tenderest transports
she must long to be cruel, yet cannot legally kill her nemesis

for one with feminine pride
it is quite difficult to recognize and assuage
for the high-spirited one
it is but a new way to show power
for the ultra-delicate
it shocks the modesty

thus subsides the state of naturalness
and pique is but omnipresent,
a mania of absurdity

he is smug, content
(these mad fools! lost
in one of life's greatest upheavals)
who can save them?

she knows of no remedy
for this terrible affliction
but the death
of either the person who inspires it
or of the one who experiences it

Dao Mary Do

Her Sheep Knew Her Voice

"Good morning, girls," I heard her say and with her sense of humor
she rolled her clouds away.
She needed no rod nor staff for them for her sheep knew her voice,
then.
She had come far up her mountain, tho' her path was rocky and steep
She loved the wild flowers around her and her bleating, friendly
sheep.
"The Blue Velvet," she said, "that you see is a Violet that was
named after me"
She quipped with a twinkle in her eye, "else why the curtsey as I go
by?"

She finished her education and kept right on growing as she started
clubs for the youth of her mountain and recreation for
their families.
But something kept calling to her from the green lush valley below
"Somebody down there needs me," she said, "and I know now I
must go."

The Seniors found a friend indeed with youthful ways and
a yen for fun.
She was right there, wherever there was need
And still will be till her day is done.

Bessie Arnold

Brave Heart

A blizzard has started, my life is at stake.
Show has covered everything, the mountains, the lake.
Through this weather, I cannot see,
No place to hide, no place to flee.
But a ray of sunshine appears ahead of me,
A beautiful dog that sets my heart free.

The brave-hearted dog knows just where to go,
As he leads my sled in the cold Alaskan snow.
His heart is determined and as free as a bird,
And he is ready to go at just one word.
I will always love my brave-hearted dog,
As he leads me through the ice and the fog.

Ann Tabor

Times Are Bad

I was watching the news on T. V., when my mom called to talk with me. She said, "Things are bad, don't you see? This is it—World War Three (III)!" I listened closely to the pain in her voice, saying, "Things must change, the world has no choice."

People are dying day by day, who'll be next? No one can say. A mother died, and then her son; the father couldn't stand the pain, so he loaded a gun. It's all so rough, the pain is mean; where's that doc, with his death machine?

We need more funds, don't you know—we could have it now—and it wouldn't show. The nurse was careful, when she felt a prick—and got infected, just that quick! HIV is the virus ' name, and it's killing babies, which is a real bad shame. I can't appeal to all your tastes, but if somebody heard, then my words weren't a waste. After a while, she went on to say, "I could get it too, and I'm not gay.".

They say it's a new disease, transmitted through sex, but it's in the Bible, just read the text. It's not just about who's getting laid; kids are dying of this disease called AIDS. A killer virus, named HIV, who's stricken next? Just wait and see. The rich, the poor, it has it's pick. The young, the old, they all get sick. Oh, it's a sad, sad thing to watch them die; she was trying to be brave, but I could hear her cry.

Eleanor Henderson White "Sissy"

Catching The Wind

He opened his eyes to a new day
She was there...
An image more real than yesterday
Reality blossoms into today

If you're so lucky, if you're so frank
Love comes your way and you don't need chance
Just open your heart and love shines through
A perfect flower with the sweetest perfume

To see certain things, you have to lie on your back
With tears in your eyes and ache in your heart
It's possible, I think, that you have to have hurt
To see anything at all, to make a new start

Hold on to what's precious, to what's dear
Forget empty spaces, embrace what is clear
Throw out your hands, catch the wind
Don't fear gathering storms
For she will be there

Jane Olmstead

It's The Turn Of The Century

And I Still Don't Have A Name

I look at my mother holding that molded bread
She won't give me any.
So, I watch the smoke rise from the mill across the street.
I wonder if the layer of dirt on my skin
will protect me from death.
I look down the alley (that I call home)
and see many children who look like me.
We're probably all related like the stray cats.

They call home-"The Land of Opportunity"
I call it-"The corner of E. Jackson and 2nd Street"

I look at my mother holding that molded bread
She won't give me any.
So, I pretend that she's dead.
I want to see the locomotives
that are making all the noise.
I tap my foot in a make-shift stream
of urine, tears, and blood.
the fleas are on my back, but I do not move.

I look at my mother holding that molded bread
I take it from her because she is dead.

Katy Young

Dedicated To The Children

Precious children, where are you?
Sheltered in the arms of God, sheltered safe from harm and fear.

Your voices are singing with Jesus who loves you so much.
Heaven is brighter now that you are there.

America, we need to turn back to God and be a Christian Nation.
God is our Creator: He gives life and He takes life.

America, wake up to the happenings in our Country.
Precious children, where are you? Sheltered in the arms of God.

There will be no more suffering, no more heartaches, and no sadness.
God bless the loved ones who lost precious loved ones in the bombing

In Oklahoma City, Oklahoma on April 19, 1995.
God be with you and strengthen you at such a sad time.

My prayer is that our love for each other will take the place of hate,
Which is so strong in our Country, and the whole world.

May we be drawn closer together Americans, and show love for each other.
Fellow Americans, God will heal broken hearts, as sure as the sun rises.

Put your trust in Him, obey Him, and let the whole world know we are
A strong Nation when it comes to loving our enemies.

Precious children, where are you? Safe in the arms of Jesus.

Bertha Turner

Soaring

Soaring...
Shiny black dreams fade into terracotta oblivion
Carried on azure wings of the imagination
A flight of the mind
Or a fury of the ubiquitous unknown
Where is the end Where is the final seat
To prop up my feet and let the pleasant scent of all tomorrows rush
over me in two seconds

He touched my leg—
I unfolded myself
he reached of inside of me and felt around for himself
It was only me tucked away in a corner, hiding in the frightening
chasm of His world
He recoiled, not the baby-soft skin, the flesh of the innocent he
thought he had seen
I was alone again, acid tears cutting rivets in my now-hardened skin
black and green, pus and pain, anger
and sadness, eyes swollen red shut.

I stood and stretched, face still sore but beautiful
Triumphant in its newly discovered me
Once in a while I dance, pointing and flexing my legs sore from years
of cramping
Elongated they kick extended to the heavens, lowered to my source of
Earthly strength

Terracotta spears of light dance on my upturned face
Smiling for a new son

Ayanna Andito Cage

Silence

The doors shut, the windows closed,
silence floats in from the distance.
Blackness fills the house.
The mourners have gone.
Sympathizers shook their heads and walked away.
Silence lays thick, like a midwinter's snow,
colder though.
The great equalizer has been.

Darcy Elgart-McKeon

Journey to Your Soul

Reflect the sadness of sorrowed eyes
shrouded in a watery disguise
Every tear in a timeless fall
sends gentle ripples-a silent call

End over end, the final shard
tumbles from the frame of a shattered heart
Piercing the image of a lonely face;
echoing needs through time and space.

The tears are drawn into the air,
leaving my heart exposed and bare;
Drying in the arid weather,
paper thin, light as feather

Swept up in the winds above,
guided towards a heart of love
A magic journey to your soul,
pieces assemble to make me whole.

Entwined together we are strong, harmonizing to love's sweet song
You fill my life, you make me sing, lift me to an Angel's wing
Union of immaterial essence,
finally in each other's presence.

Amy Shepard

That Is Right And Good

Young and innocent, sharp as a tack,
silly as can be, that's my son!
He's all himself, with bits of me, bits of his dad.
Those bits are physical only.
He's all himself and that is right and good.
I see his father's features in his face,
those dark thick eyebrows,
that unusual nose and his dad's ears too.
So a bit of his dad lives on.
Lives on his features.
Lives on his heart.
Lives on in my heart.
And that is right and good.
He didn't die in vain.
He left a legacy in his son.
A legacy of love, caring and companionship.
A legacy of unique humor and laughter.
Those are the gifts he left his son.
And his legacy lives on.
And that is right and good.

Janet A. Havery

The Meaning Of Life

Life was made to Glorify itself
Simply, Beautifully and Wonderfully True

The creator? Don't cross 'em, He's
totally awesome (and there's no need
for insurance 'cuz we weren't made to suit)

Life is too the individual's gift
to pursuit, make new, be true in
whatever God would have you do.
The Creator, Did we cross Him?
You bet we do!
Too simple for you? Need a clue?
Anti-Agnostics help to fill the fountain for few
(Christians truly serving, not pointing fingers at you)
Are you thirsty?
Warn the arrogant puffed up people perishing.
Sing for the Shepherd whose sheep He's been nourishing.
The Flesh shall pass away
but we will never die in Jesus Christ Our Lord
Amen

John Aragon

The Pathways Of Light

I came across a man one day,
Sitting atop the canyon in a peaceful way.

I asked, "Do you often meditate here?"
He replied, "Why surely, but it's praying, my dear."

He spoke of the Lord with such wondrous awe.
I said to him, "Ohhh, you must mean The Law."

He explained, "No, my Savior, who looks over these pastures."
I nodded, "I see. That's who I call The Master."

He said, "My sweet child, you must worship the Christ!"
And I asked, "Wouldn't praying for guidance be just as nice?"

"Oh, young child... you are not born again."
I replied, "Yes, I am, many times I have been!"

"My friend," he wearily stated, "When I say it is black, you just say
it is white!"
While I said, "I do not wish to offend you, I just see different light."

"You see, I believe that what you wish to attain,
Is truly a goal that I hold of the same."

"Your path is not wrong and neither s mine
It's convincing who's right that wastes so much time."

"One thing we will share on the paths that we trod,
Is that glorious day at-one-meant with God!"

Kelly Kunz

Six Good Kids

Thru the bumps and the bruises, the joy and the laughter;
SIX GOOD KIDS, that's all you were after.

And now we are grown, living miles from home;
A home we've all known, a welcome you've shown.

But now looking back, on all the years past;
One thing comes to mind, it's a gift often asked.

"SIX GOOD KIDS, That's all we want";
"SIX GOOD KIDS, That's all we need".

So once again the question is asked;
And once again the answer is matched.

"SIX GOOD KIDS, That's all we want";
"SIX GOOD KIDS, That's all we need".

So when the question arises, just stop and remember;
There's not only six now, but three times the number.

Well whatever the number, the same answer is heeded;
"SIX GOOD KIDS, That's all we've ever needed!"

Jodi Kathleen Collins

"My Parakeet"

White as snow, white as milk
Smooth as glass, smooth as silk
Not a chirp, not a tweet
Nothing from my parakeet

Cocks his head, to stare and see
He's got to keep his eye on me
Not a chirp, not a tweet
Nothing from my parakeet

He pecks and pecks his feathers clean
But stops the minute he thinks he's been seen
Not a chirp, not a tweet
Nothing from my parakeet

On his swing, trying not to move
"I'm not having fun", he's straining to prove
Not a chirp, not a tweet
He can't pull that one over on me

Anna Grady

Locations

SKIN - Opaque, stern, hard, red skin
SKIN - soft, blank, bland, white skin
SKIN - Deep , almond, nubian, brown skin
Union, coming TOGETHER, Blending

Creation, a soul, a being named Ancestry
Three precious appendages flow from my body of Ancestry;
Three different pasts come together to make one present - me.

The Great Smoky Mountains; The plantations of times gone by"
The African Countryside

- I WAS THERE -

The woodlands and waterways; the vast fields and elaborate mansions; The Savannas and Oasis

- I WAS THERE -

The war paint and harvest celebration; The battle field and the courtroom; The great tribes and the slave auction

- I WAS THERE-

The Cherokee, The Caucasian, The African

- I AM HERE -

Jason R. Greenfield

On A Hot Summer Day

On a hot summer day, some toddler left shoes under my swing set;
Small and white, I put them on the top of my slide.
Kids come and go; for six days, the shoes still sit there softly.
Maybe she was swinging in my neighbor's yard;
Maybe she left another pair under some other slide;
"You can have my shoes; I don't need them."
"The grass is soft; swing set is fun; what do I need shoes for?"
The wind whispers on the rustling grass.

On a hot summer day, China dropped a missile in front of Taiwan;
Big and fierce, Taiwanese cannot push away the blast;
Swung high and low; for six days, belly-up fish floated stiffly on the turbulent sea;
One launch a day, the gusty flame swung toward the Island;
The missiles darted from the Mainland kept snarling;
"Taiwan is part of China; return to the motherland!"
"You are mine; Don't you dare leave me!"
The wind blusters over the quaked Island.

Somewhere that little girl swings high in my neighborhood,
"I want to have fun; I don't want to stay inside!"

Some kissing-ers are sniffing the pits under the yellow-brownish Mao-suit.

Kuang-Chung Huang

Living In A Scene From A Movie On A Friday Night, Toward Home After...

At dust the sky is
smoke-glass, the
world is
blacklit surreal. The
silvery jet traces the
freeway in descent. Its
redflashing winglights leave a
neonesque streak above the
red-ribbon of taillights painting a
mood on the
highway, while
Sting sings in
stereo a
medley on
smooth-jazz
radio.

John W. Howell

If Only For A Moment

Awaiting your presence, looking before me, there were the
Snowy trees reflecting my memories of when they were
covered with leaves which seemed to protect and keep us
Away from the rest of the world.

Back in this moment, I wondered what we might encounter,
And there you were sitting beside me. After exchanging a few
Words, neither one of us knew what to say or do next.
Knowing deep within my soul I was burning with passionate
Desire to hold you, if only for a moment, as close as your
Heart would allow us. Then I realized how many times
Before, I have felt this wonderful feeling of pleasure with
You—When you held my hand and rubbed your thumb on my
Palm, I would feel a warm tingling sensation through out
My whole body. When our cheeks touched from one side to
Another, every part of my being would be aroused. Then,
Our lips met, and I knew I have discovered, once again, how
Much I wanted to be exploring, loving, sharing, and playing
with you, my darling.

This my friend, is a co-creation of one of my man desires, if
Only for a moment. I love you.

Irene L. Hoyt

Petal of Life

A petal on a flower so delicate, so new
So beautiful, and yet so few
A tiny life form, on which many can live
the bee with it's power, swerves in and out
between these petals, but never once hurts it
with it's mighty wings

The breeze is so cool it blows and blows,
and knocks the petal round, but never once
does it push a petal to the ground

The butterfly with its elegant wings, beats
around these wonderful prizes, but never once
does it fly right by in harmful demise

Why can't life with it's quarrels, be like a
petal on a flower, so beautiful and yet so
untouched? Wouldn't life be so much easier
if we were a petal upon a flower...

Katrin L. Adkins

We Three And One More

It's just we three and you make one more,
so come on and open the door.
There's a lot to see and a lot to explore,
for we three and one more.

There are the clouds in the sky,
we'll teach you to fly to the stars at night.
Oh! What a sight.
The sunken ships on the ocean floor,
the fish underwater to adore.
There's plenty to do for we three and one more.

In the rain and in the sun,
we won't stop until we finish our fun.
So much to do, so much to be tried,
run, jump and laugh till your dreams are satisfied.

We three and you make one more,
together we'll take on the world, just us four.
We three and one more, we'll see the world below and above,
with the eyes of; we three and one more, we'll see love.

Chanin White

Unity

As the sun shines thru the skies of blue,
so shall the Son shine thru our hearts as true
loves seen with the eyes of Christ like clear,
open our hearts that we wight hear. The sound
of your voice so quiet and still, united together
our hope to fulfill. Blessed by the Spirit, healed
by the Son, once we were separate, now we are
one. The vows that we speak, the words we
confess, bring closeness and nearness, in God
we are blessed. So grateful, so thankful, your
grace has enhanced; the lives of two people
you've granted a chance. To share, commit, be
faithful, and true, we give our lives unselfish
to you. Mold us, and shape us to bend with your
plans, use us and help us extend open hands.
Make us a blessing so others may see,
God's work in our lives was intended to be.
Ordained from beginning, complete to the end,
Grant us a mission, your spirit to send. Word of wisdom,
truth of light, wings in motion, spirit in flight.

Cynthia Pumnea

Whispers in the Wind

It seems like only yesterday I heard a whisper in the wind.
So soft and sweet and gentle saying, "You are welcome to come in."
When lost in the desert I was blinded by the sand,
I heard a whisper saying, "Come and take my hand."
Not knowing which way to turn and without shelter from the wind,
Only hearing a soft whisper saying, "I'm coming." once again.
My face was dry and burning and I was still astray,
Again this whisper said, "I will lead the way.
You only hear my whispers and my face you cannot see,
I will never harm you but you must follow me."
My throat so dry I could not swallow and now finding it hard to think,
This whisper was so soft and gentle saying, "I have plenty for you to drink."
My feet were blistered and my legs were weak, there was nothing I could do.
Then I heard the whisper saying, "Now I'll carry you."
I reached out in desperation for this whisper I could not touch,
Realizing I was taken care of which meant so very much.
As time goes by and life goes on our paths may cross again.
Listen to the whisper, the whisper in the wind.
So soft and sweet and gentle saying, "You are welcome to come in."

James McGahan

"Just Another Midnight Lust"

Could it be, should it be, would it be forever
Softly spoken hearts in vain late night promises
Tell me lies of pain given souls for lust.
Could it be, should it be,would it be love
Time will tell its tale feel me close to you
In lust and love warmly
As the night grows long
We together will be one tell me you want me
For yourself and forever
I will stay another night
To feel you again Hot, sweaty, sinful.
When I leave your side
Could it be, should it be,
Would it be our last good-bye
Yesterday is forever and tomorrow remains today
I will see you again
Lovely, beautiful, wantingly
Would it be, should it be,
could it be just another midnight lust
Only if that's what you wish.

Jeremy Prudic

Paths

In my lifetime I have traveled many paths
Some have been straight; some have twisted in funny ways
Some have been lined with flowers
Other have been burnt by the desert sun
Some have led to beds of Roses
Yet others have led to arid ground
On many the sun has shone; the skies been blue
On a few the storm clouds never cleared
Some have been endless; others so short
Many have been exhilarating; yet others filled with despair
Some have filled my body; others my mind
The sights and sounds have filled my life
No matter how winding or straight
They have filled my being and lifted my soul
They have given all of which I asked
I cannot want for more.

Albert C. Jackalous

Untitled

Have you seen this guy who has invaded our lives?
Some of us love him...others would rather have hives.
His teachings are fun and FULL OF LOVE,
How could anyone want to give him a shove?
One of the kindest sort of guys,
Always looking for bright and shiny skis.
He says things like "hip, hip, hurray" and "super dee dooper,"
He is all purple and green...quite the trooper.
Certain children for him yearn,
He knows he is there for them to learn.
I know at my house when the music starts,
Children come running, he has captured their hearts.
We love him, we really do,
We are his fans and real true blue.
With him...learning is so much fun,
Bareny! Barney!
He's the one...#1

Annette Schreckengost

A Christmas Remnant

I think that I shall never see
Something sadder than a Christmas tree.
Stripped of its trimmings and tossed on the lawn,
Its days of glory so swiftly gone.
All through December it was a beautiful thing,
And oh, what happiness it did bring!
Every family member making a bet
That this year's tree was the prettiest yet.
Christmas morn found the girls and boys
Searching its branches for gifts and toys.
And now, cast aside and forlorn,
It waits to be picked up early some morn
And hauled away to a landfill somewhere
To share a mass grave with the other trees there.
Or be recycled — it well may be,
But it can never return as a Christmas tree.

Arlene Sena

Untitled

Like a thunderstorm up in the sky
Sometimes my eyes just want to cry.

Blue skies and sunshine are what I desire
Instead it's more tears to quench the fire.

I live in two worlds far apart
The things I have and the desires of my heart.

As I walk the straight road of doing right
I cry myself to sleep another night........

Janice Martens

My True Feelings

We've been friends for a long time
Sooner or later hoping you'd be mine
I wish we had some time alone
So that my true feelings could be shown
So I'm just letting you know
I hope our friendship will continue to grow
I know that sometimes I don't show that
I care, but I really do
But one thing that will never disappear
Are my true feelings for you
I wanted to say this from the start
But I didn't know how to put it in words from
My heart.

Christopher W. Martin

Moonlight Seduction

As the moon hovers above the sea
soothing her roar with his glittery
yet distant gaze
I hear the ocean serenades the cool and remote
sand into submission

and as the waves
Tantalize the shore with sweet caresses
t feel the breeze
it penetrates the innermost part of my soul.

Katherine R. Hughes

Sleep In Shadows

The pain I feel, it must cease, the look of
sorrow on my brow, if ever the hurt
decrease, I pray that it be now.

the emptiness into which I hold, I can't take
the pity or the treason. I must be bold.
For the one who does, I will never know his reason

To hold hurt, but one day let it go, free as a
butterfly, as I would like to be. Only he who hurts
can ever know. Loser of good fortune it is me.

I missed the day of a shooting star, I hurt for
my love whose gone I'll search forever near
or far. I'll sing to him my lonesome song.

Strength can bewilder intelligence, pain can
over power happiness, my love and I haven't
spoken since. As days go by I think of him less.

I look at darkness, and as I stare, you are pain,
you are absent, but are you there? No,
alone I am with the truth only to lie in Sadness

Jessica Johnson

Mademoiselle Mephistopheles

Blushing beauty of truly darkest night.
Soul of Satan with an Angel's face.
The Helen of hate, a beau at first sight.
Her sweet voice of honey that makes hearts race,
Hides a demented mind of coal intent.
Winding men around her talons of greed,
Stealing their spirits and leaving hearts rent.
Hades incarnate, a femme fatal of need,
Her dichotomous tongue warping truth
With her deviously malignant lies.
Beautifully elegant, always couth,
She'll twist her knife 'till her victim dies.
Beware the Janus-faced love dealer,
Don't fall prey to this rash heart stealer.

Eric Giles

To Be A Child

Bygone days of backyards and dandelions-
speaking a now forgotten language with the lizards.
Misty-eyed reflections and shaded memories
of a time that slowly fades in my existence.
Echoes of my laughter in the days of youth,
coupled with my innocence and imagination.
Reason and reality played no role in my life
when the sun rose and set just for me.
Countless plans made in my own little world,
plans that held no real meaning in time.
Mommy and Daddy were my everything;
my end all, be all to each little situation.
Where have you gone, my days of daydreaming,
of mudpie making and ladybug chasing?
I planned my future on a swing with my dog,
humming songs that played only in my mind;
seeking my fortune in the grains of sand
that slipped through my fingers like childhood.

Kelly A. Matthews

..Special Little Angel..

Special... Special Angel .. clearly now I see....
Special ... Little Angel truly I believe ... that ...
Miracles can happen ... For ... God surely has blessed me ...
From up above ... he sent down an Angel's Love ...
My precious gift ... I now believe ...
Brave ... Brave Little Newborn I never will forget, the Brilliance of the Halo that shined above your head ...
Still ... my tears ... they kept on falling ... and I was so scared of losing you
... but ... then I felt his presence ... and watched ... as God's Love surrounded you ...
Special Little Angel... clearly now I see now I see it took your pain and suffering to somehow strengthen me ...
Yes ... Miracles do happen ... For ... God surely has blessed me ...
From up above ... he sent down am Angel's Love ...

My precious gift ... I now believe ...

Kathleen A. Badaracco

My Friend, My Dad, My Pal

I feel like I am losing my whole will to survive because of someone special who is about to die. Sometimes I feel so selfish, I just can't seem to let go. If only God could help me and tell me what to do, I know that I could hide my fears and dry some of these tears.

My heart is oh so heavy and hurting all the time because of his pain and suffering that has taken so much time.

My family tells me to let go, and maybe soon I will, but you know he isn't just a daddy, he is my best friend and pal.

The love I have for daddy is deep and oh so strong but I know God will have a good friend in this one.

God, all I ask of you is please be kind and give us all the strength we need to say good-bye to our dad - friend and pal.

Dad, although I will miss you more than you will ever know, I also know it's time that I let go. I will always love you more than life itself, but God will take care of you and I'm sure He'll make me tough.

Just one thing before I close this note, that I say it from my heart, is that I thank the Lord above for giving me my dad. I only want to remember you just the way you were the love of life, your corny jokes and the love you had for all of us. We will treasure you forever and thank you with all our hearts for just being there when we needed you, and I think we did our part. I made you laugh, I made you cry, but dad, you are the apple of my eye.

Today's the day we say good-bye, but God is by our side to give us strength and lead the way to your final resting place.

Good-bye my friend, my dad, my pal.

Darlene M. Trujillo

Our Savior

Jesus is our Savior, acknowledge it today,
Spread His word to others you meet along the way.
Always be forgiving, never hold a grudge,
Be loyal to your neighbor and never-never judge.

Read the Bible daily, spend some time in prayer,
Be concerned in helping others, show people that you care,
Visit those who are ill, remember the struggling poor.
This is to His liking and adding credits to your score.

Watch over the widow and orphan, be considerate to the old.
This is the path to follow that leads to the streets of gold.
Keep the ten commandments, try—with all your might.
And if you slip a little trust Him to make it right.

You're going to make mistakes the best that you can do.
Just keep striving for improvement and His presence will bless you.
Be attentive to your church, keen to do your part.
He loves a faithful worker with an energetic heart.

Be liberal with your giving and generous with your love,
Remember-he expects this as He reigns from up above.
Just follow these instructions and maintain your best behavior.
The prize will be eternal life, in heaven—with our Savior.

James F. McCabe

God Bless The Child

God bless the child, in this world today..
Starving for love, and a place to stay...
God bless the child, surrounded by drugs...
And different territorial gangs, hanging on curbs..
God bless the child, hungry to be embraced...
By parents who left, without a trace...
God bless the child, confused in a world...
With strangers that hurt, little boys and little girls...
God bless the child, who can rise above...
And make a future, in spite of the crud...
God bless the child, who makes the world change...
By their individual existence, and desire to remain...
God bless the child, a beautiful small frame...
As he grows and grows, with strength, like Abel and Cain...
God bless the child, true in heart....
With a bliss of innocence, ready from the start...
God bless the child, created everywhere...
By God, who's most powerful...So you better beware!

Chandra V. Mosley

Inspiration

Passion fills my soul and
stirs me from my soundest sleep
evoking deepest thoughts that
come rushing forth like
torrents breaking through the dam
flooding every channel, gorge, nook and cranny,
the words gushing out as I
jump to my desk with pen in hand
searching for that notepad I can never find,
scratching letters hastily onto the page;
forming them like a mother bear licking her
new-born cubs into shape
until the ink stops flowing
and I behold the Poem.

Edward Nuzzo III

September

There's one thing that all of us must remember;
Summer is dying when we reach september.
People desert the beach, or a cool swimming pool;
While millions of students go back to school.

It's a time to eat some home made pie;
As formations of wild geese bid us good-bye.
The crisp fall season will arrive very soon;
Our landscape is bathed by a full harvest moon.

Billions of grapes are plucked from the vine;
Marble sized fruit that is almost divine.
A frenzy of footballs blurs saturday's sky;
When the gridiron wars hit an "All-time" high.

Occasional rain washes each window pane;
But beware of the horrible hurricane.
Thank God we're alive, as September's still here;
It won't come again for another full year!

Austin F. Stebor

An Angel's Gift

She lies on her back on a stark white
table
Tiny and delicate, like a porcelain
doll.
Her perfectly proportioned naked milky white
body is certainly a miracle for all to see.
Her perfect little arms and legs flail about
in total incoordination as if to say,
"You wished me here! Well here I am!"
She stares at me with round blue eyes
the color of the sea.
Deep eyes and wise with the secrets of
creation.
She knows me instantly!
In one long soft gaze we bond
together for a lifetime.

She's my granddaughter.

Deborah J. Redding

Joni

Come to me,
take my hand
and we will float
to never-never land.

Me on cloud nine
and you just shy of heaven.
The warmth is so abundant
like the seven wonders times seven.

Happiness will fill every corner.
The love multiplies so fast;
Grasping, touching, feeling of the heart.
Hand in hand, our lives in the water of love cast.

So glad to have you, woman of charm.
Come to me, lets float, arm in arm.

Dale McCombs

A Christmas Reminder

A christmas
Star shines in
The heaven's above
To remind us that
Long ago a star shone
Ever so brightly over
A crude manger in Bethlehem
To guide the shepherds and wise men to
The place where the prince of peace lay sleeping.

Jean Ewing Kuhn

"Corrections"

The sun sets quietly on a prison's day
taking with it unjust trials and
tribulations of the guilty and innocent alike -
Merciless pleas once wailed upon uncaring ears
Voices bemoaning their fate
Outstretched arms receiving no embrace
The sun hides away for a time a
moment, bitter agonies
It's strength not known to man
to endure such pain
Only to rise again to radiate hope
amongst bondage
The sunrise brings freedom
One must only stand still
and wait.

Kathy MarGarette Miller

A Child's Unspoken Prayer

Teach me, Lord.
Teach me tenderness and love,
to always seek the truth.
And Lord, please teach me
kindness of the heart, and peacefulness within.

Teach me, Lord,
Patience with myself, and to trust in your will.
And that you'll guide my steps
throughout my life on earth:
A journey without fear.

Lift me up when I fall down.
Strengthen my body, mind and heart.
I know there will be times, in darkness, I'll feel alone.
But, my God, you will be there; you will always be there.

Teach me, Lord. This is my prayer.
A baby in all things.
Always growing, learning, finding ways to love while
resting in your arms.

Reaching out and walking humbly. Hand in hand with each other.
Hand in hand with my God.

Carolyn Sue Ingram

Nature's Anger

It emanated anger as it rushed down the canyon of colorful rock, tearing out handfuls of dirt and throwing them into itself until its color was no longer crystal, green, but thick, cloudy brown. The dark stone wall was not afraid of it's raving, nor was the cascade of wildflowers that decorated it's face, absorbing its protection; shivering with fear. They stood with proud splendor resisting the urge to banish their poised serenity to further the emotion below. The fist of the water pounded against it's bed trying to reach out and of grab the space it wanted; tearing out the life that was heedless of it's warning roar. Herds of gray clouds swarmed to see, sprinkling their encouragement on the show of anger and strength. Fireworks of lightning shot through the forbidding sky, not to be left out of the rebellion. Straight shouldered thunder bounced off the barrier of the stone walls and was sucked down the canyon gaining more depth as it traveled along for all life to fear. The clouds piped up gaining excitement at the success; heavy rain rushed away from the sky to join the rage; one last show of beauty as it bubbled down the red cliffs in the graceful fall of water to be engulfed by the thick brown torrent the river had become. It carried tired trees and animals too weak to resist it's boisterous pull.

Amie Ader

Reflections

Hearts were crushed and crying eyes very sore.
Tears and prayers were the order of that memorable day.
Many were hard hit by the chaotic destruction
of such a picturesque demolition,
For the duration of this horrendous disaster
Summed up in rubble and plaster.
"Can you imagine the anxiety of loved ones,
Who stood by and watched in awe, with teary eyes
For days on end, none daring to leave, or otherwise
Trying to find a solution to this complex sight?"
"Horrible!" they scream, staring at crumbling walls, and floors,
Balconies, seats, shelves, frames, pictures coming into view,
While firemen, volunteers and workmen searched for victims
Hourly, daily, more or less, from nine to eleven,
The dead accounted for, so far, numbered one sixty seven.
"What is the excuse for such a dynamic deed?"
This action will teach one and all to take heed.
Finally, the task ended revealing bodies, three more,
Trial, then judgement for punishment, open the door!

Josephine M. Cox

Farewell To Love

Regrets surface and open the way to sorrow.
Tears form, sealing the blinds on a bright tomorrow.
Forever was only a word we used when young.
Our love is just another song, never to be sung.
I find letting go the hardest of things to do.
Even now, when it's over, I'm still in love with you.
You feel only your pain, I'm wrapped in my own.
Never can one miss something, unless it's gone.
So go ahead and walk right out that door.
You just can't hide the fact you don't love me anymore.
Find your path to happiness, no matter where it leads.
You might even find that someday- it leads right back to me.

Donna Johnson

Lost

A raging storm within the mind
Temptress of fate eyes that are blind
Tears that fall to ease the pain
The ebb of tide the fallen rain

Life goes on and so it seems
We live our lives through broken dreams
Time is lost behind the hours
Beneath the sands amidst the flowers

Love remains through it all, the warmth of summer the peak of fall

Peace in mind a restless soul
A found love to make me whole
A heart of passion that longs to be free
A passage in time a song to sing

The song's the same with different words
Life's tragic comedy, love absurd
Oneness in mind divided by the heart
An unknown future casts us apart

My love for you a presence sublime
Voices say to me disappointment to find disappointment
not in love, but in the wait, my foolish heart... Love too late...

Joanne M. Carozza

Robert

The baby lies in my arms
  tense crying uncomfortable.
I hold him closer - he pushes further away.
I prepare food and offer rest
  he wants neither.
I set him on the floor, and he begins to comfort himself,
Cuddling the blanket that I give him - that smells of me.
I sit
  watching wondering waiting.
He turns to look at me - almost asking if it is okay to be this far away from me.
Away from my protective love.
In answer
  I nod and smile.

And he smiles Back.

Kathryn Maisonville

Love Is Pain

Love is just like faith in God, it is often
Tested with pain, without the pain,
You truly will not know what love is.

Some of the greatest things achieved by man
Have been results of the struggle with pain.

"Be glad about the trials you suffer
Their purpose is to prove your faith is genuine.
Even gold is tested by fire and so your faith
Must be tested so that it may endure."

The same thing can be said about love.
When you are having love problems
And don't know what to do, don't give up on love,
Because that's the worst thing you can do.

Look through the problems for the light
At the end of the tunnel, for better
Things are hidden there and it is a reward
For all your pain and troubles.

Christina Lavergne

Wedding Day Exhortations

Surely such mutual affection deserves nothing less
Than a mutual commitment to give married life your BEST

Nurture the friendship you have and treasure it to no end
Don't settle for just being spouses, always remain BEST FRIENDS

Be creative in the ways that you express your emotions
Be spontaneous in the ways that you display your devotion

Open communication is absolutely a must
As well as genuine integrity, supportiveness, and trust

For this is your cherished partner to share life's joys and tears
This is your beloved companion to stand by you through the years

So build each other up and sweetly comfort too
Extending to each other the love that God extends to you

For God's love is tenderhearted, it's patient and it's kind
The most enduring and unselfish love that anyone can find

It's neither jealous nor demanding, neither is it rude
And it's not displayed half-heartedly or with an attitude

Above all else it's CRUCIAL that your focus remain on Christ
Allowing Him to shape and mold your marriage and your lives

For the only way to ensure success (though these hints may help, I'm sure)
is to keep God at the CENTER, both now and ever more

Angela Eleazer

Abija (Beloved)

Abija, my fallen angel straighten up your wings. It is for you that blue birds sing, the bells of Heaven ring.
Oh, Abija, I have called you, I've brought you to this place.
Where the evil's abhorred in my eyes and you I can see it in your face.
Abba you've cried all the day long it's not that I can't hear you.
Proving your love that grows ever strong, oh, beam of light, your love is true.
Though pestilence surrounds you, you hold on to your faith. Many have been the times of doubt, encumbering you your space.

But, you understand with the trust of a child, the truth that
it will come. As we join in Heavenly bliss, forever we are one.
Abija, my fallen angel you've turned your smile up side down.
There'll be rivers of living water at your feet as you stand your ground
The deeds that bring on the coming age. Life as we know it must turn the page. So wipe your tears get back on the rampage my son, my dear sweet sage.
Oh, Abandon, I have called you now. The keys of hell are in your hand.
It's time to meet up with your destiny, stop playing in the sand.
Beloved, my fallen angel, now is the time to awaken from within.
To go where eagles soar above the clouds, to fly you must spread your wings.

Charlene A. Moore

Sunrise On The Beach

We stood in prayer holding hands.
That early a.m. on the beach.
The ocean roared quietly not fully awake
The sun cast a glow in the sky.
And on the water
A single gull flew into the sun
Reflecting its shadow on the sand
Our song was joyous, full of love and hope.
A new beginning in the early moments before dawn.

Elaine M. Murphy

The Star

God took a star and shined it bright
That first Christmas night
So bright I say, night looked like day

Joseph and Mary were in flight used
That star for their light
Alone and cold without any friends
All they could hear "No room in our inn"
Had they know who their guest would be
The Inn-keeper would have offered hospitality

With the star as their guide and light
A stable was brought into their sight
Joseph and Mary entered, Mary was placed on the ground
As she laid on the fresh hay, a light showed around

To the animals surprise and delight
Baby JESUS was born that wonderful night
Three kings with great insight followed
That star and to their delight found
Baby Jesus the first Christmas night

I wonder as I lay down my pen, what shape the world would be in
If JESUS CHRIST had been born twin?

Dorothy Stanfield

The Mirror

As I stand facing the mirror, I see silver threads of hair
that have replaced the once-ebony black:
the lines on the face that seem to mock,
the once silky skin, and the cheek bones
that have withstood the test of time.

I stare, and I wonder, is this life:
Is this the reality of it all?
Do we live just to face the uncertainty of death?

Death... What is it?
Is it some unknown presence we will never be certain about,
some harrow, or is it the return of a long lost friend,
and will we welcome it with a full embrace?
Do we understand it when it will pick us up,
and sweep us into eternity?

I turn from the mirror... and weep.

Once more, I slowly turn to the mirror, a silent tear falls
from the once high cheek-bone of my indian heritage...no more to be.
Such sorrow...such emptiness, Will it remain forever?
I cannot say, I can only dream of yesterday,
and dread the unknown of tomorrow...of eternity.

Edna Frampton

A Glimmer Of Light

In this dark and lonely tunnel
That I walk through everyday,
Oh, how I wish that A Glimmer Of Light
Would somehow come my way;

24-7 it's darkness
No light anywhere in sight,
The world would seem so much better
If I had just A Glimmer Of Light;

All hopes and dreams have vanished
Still I fight with all my might,
What I need to get out of this deep dark hole
Is the smallest Glimmer Of Light;

So I pray to God up above
For only He can understand my plight,
And before my prayers come to an end
I see it: A Glimmer Of Light;

As I thank God for answering my prayers
The Light shines brightly through,
And that's when I began to realize
That the Glimmer Of Light is YOU!!!

Bernard LaVaan Martin

You're Not The One

All my life, I've looked for that special someone,
That I would be able to spend my eternity with.
Then you came along and my quest was won,
Thinking that you were only part of a myth.

Knowing that you were Heaven sent and all mine,
My hearts desire burned like a flame.
But yet, there was something seen, so small, so fine,
And my love for you was not to blame.

If your love is unable to touch me,
Then turn away so I am able again to start looking.
And so my passion for you can be set free,
Knowing I evaded your desire and love at first sting.

As I move on, I know you'll cast your spell on some fool,
Who's mind and heart is weak, yet strong only in desire.
Thinking he has acquired the most precious jewel,
When only he is placed within your ring of fire.

Bill Jordan

Good Over Bad

There is so much bad in the world today
that it over shadows the good,
people don't take the time to see
the good things around them they should.

People who help in times of need,
that lend a helping hand,
should be commended for the time
they give to our great land.

The volunteers who give their all,
for the hungry, the sick, and the old
their's is a story which should be stressed
one to treasure and hold.

So before you give up on the world of ours,
before you say there's no hope,
remember the one's who are there for us
the one's that can help us cope.

Karen Semrau

The Lost Soul

The lost soul
that lives at night
Forever searching the dark
haunting the streets and alley ways
Pity the souls that wander at night
For he is sure to find
the look of desperate passion in your eyes
The taste of blood in his mouth
the coldness of his skin
He does his dirty deeds behind the cloak of darkness
living for the thrill of the night
To lie his days away
He is the vampire of the night

Becky Lyn Tegze

Leaning On The Savior

Let the light of Jesus shine within my soul,
That other souls might hunger for His great love untold
Through living for my Savior in all I do and say
Perhaps I might lead others to follow in His way...
It isn't always easy to live the Christian life
But God is always there to help in times of strife.
So often we ignore Him and on ourselves depend
But through much toil and anguish we turn to Him again.
If we would only do this, from the very start
Much lighter would our burdens be that lay upon our heart.
So always lean on Jesus in everything you do
Because He is always there with open arms for you.

Judy Livingston

Old Masters

With hands that can eye unmolded clay and miracles
that place precision at play.
This thought so easy for those that are blessed,
can give the world a gift that will last.
An ear that hears what I can not hear, that blesses
the wave of music so dear.
To sculpture a bust that will last through the years
that gives delight in a world through an age,
for time will pass and years will fade.
But the talent that's given to those that will share.
Paint on a brush that swirls with ease, that
leaves this master for eyes to see.
But where does the thought that minds our
hands and see's cast bronze with figures of man?
Through out the world we stop and see that
the talents of man were given by thee.

Dickie Bowes

To Remember

Time passes ever so fast
That the plans we had made
Seem so far in the past

Your illness had put everything on hold
While we wished and prayed for your health to unfold

I can never ever forget the courage you displayed
During all the procedures that the Doctors outlaid

When everything was tried and nothing did succeed
Even through those that were unusual indeed

It was then that you chose
That your Book of Life should be closed

God picked that day for you to take leave
That special day that I started to bereave

I'm so grateful for all that we shared
in the past
And I thank you for all the memories
that I know will last and last

Arthur Wiland

Someone Special

There's no one in the world
that was as great a man as he,
I was his special girl,
and he was always there for me.

I was always there for him,
we've done so much together,
now that I am feeling so grim,
why couldn't you live forever?

We've gone to many places, almost everywhere,
I loved you with all my heart,
deep down, I know you really cared,
why did we have to part?

Even though we're not together,
you'll always be there in my mind,
precious memories will last forever,
and I'll just take one day at a time.

I know I'll always have your love,
now, today, and forever,
and you'll be watching me from up above,
one day we'll be together!

Jaclyn Trezza

Footsteps In The Snow

I can give you time—and male sensitiveness
That was often denied me back when I
Was a boy—and I can give you the joy of my
Worldly wisdom—like how to fly a kite—
Put a worm on a hook—and capture golden
Fireflies at twilight...

We'll hike in the mountains—swim in the sea—
Pitch baseball and go fishing—just you and me—
We'll take the time for nature walks—and
Man-to-man quiet talks...I'll teach you how to
Cope when there's little hope of having things
Your way...we'll sip hot chocolate and play
Canasta on a rainy winter's day...

And when you're big enough to see the
Making of your own footsteps in the snow—
In future years that are yet to be—please
Take the time to think of me, your grandpa—
Not just an old guy—but a man with a young heart—
Who loves you so—especially when we're apart...

Judith M. Durnbaugh

A Walk In The Dark

As I fall through the clouds of realization, I am faced with the fact
that you, my friend and companion, are dead.
I am also faced with the fact that someone killed you mindlessly for
no reason I can see.
The fun, the pleasure, I do not know what would have possessed someone
to kill you.
You were nice and thoughtful with a future that was so wide spread.
Now, after you have passed, I sit here and remember your smile, your
laughter, and most of all your friendship.
I sometimes wish I knew who killed you so I could in turn shatter
their lives just as easy and regretfully.
Yet, as I think to myself, I know that will not bring your spirit,
soul, or friendship back.
You, though once my friend, are now gone and I would not want anyone
to suffer as I, no matter what the cost.
Some do not realize that we are all human and that we can die just as
easily as the next.
But then, who would want to be faced with the fact that
next time you see or talk to your friend, might be the last.
Yes, my life has changed and I understand it will never be the same,
but in turn I know the murderer's will not either.
The guilt is there and the damage has been done, but I must move on
and continue to live with the setting sun.

Avangelina Maree Parsons

My Prayer

Dear God in Heaven, to Thee I pray,
That You'll guide my life each passing day.

And as I walk down life's rocky road,
May Your loving arms help carry my load.

While upon this path with You, I tread,
By Your helping hands, I will be led.

And then, if I should stumble and fall,
Please help me, God, when for You I call.

When on this journey throughout my life,
May You travel with me through sorrow and strife.

My many sins You have forgiven,
Please save a place for me in Heaven.

And as I walk my last long mile,
May I cross the finish line with a smile.

Dear God, for this I pray.

Amen

Betty J. Bond

Death Watch

I heard you say, "I'll try to make him comfortable.
That's all I can do."
Can't you try harder, Doc?
I can't even talk.
Just listening doesn't make me comfortable, either.
All that "when you get home" crap—
I'm not ever going home, and I know it.
I want to tell Flora our thirty-five years together were great.
God! I can't even cry.
Just fight to breathe,
Hold hands,
Love.

Janice L. Briggs

The Wild Girls

Wild child, wild girl
That's what they say you are
Wild child, wild girl
Are you very far?

Wild girls, always get what they want
Wild girls, wild thing
Our motto - you made
Wild child, wild thing
Where are you today?

are you living a good life or girl, Is it bad?
The last time I saw you
your life was so sad.

Wild thing, wild girl a teenage mother you were
Wild thing, wild girl
Now everyone knows that for sure

Wild thing, wild girl
I sure do miss you wild thing, wild girl
Do you remember me too?

Wild thing, wild child
We don't always get what we want.

Carrie A. Johnson

The Pain And Sorrow That Is Deep Inside

I wish, I hope, people could see
The anger that's inside of me.
I act all happy, and full of joy
But sometimes, my life, I could destroy.
I try to be smart, helpful, and witty
But, those other girls are far more pretty.
I force a smile, fake a laugh
People are proud, on my behalf.
Girls spend their nights with their favorite guy
Me, I cuddle up in bed and cry.
"Studying?" Dad asks.
"Yes", I lie.
When really I'm wishing I could just die.
Sometimes it's really hard to hide
The pain and sorrow that's deep inside.

Dessiree Lynette Turnbough

Life Cycle

As it soaks up the rain and collects the snow,
the bare bush is quietly bursting.
Through the fall and winter, we know;
the bare living bush is quietly thirsting.

As the wind blows, the musically bare bush
dances to the wind whining.
And when the wind dies, the bare
living bush quietly mosaics the path winding.

As the sun rotates, the bare bush bursts
with the morning dew gleaming.
And then the rain, the roar, the bare
living bush is quietly greening.

As the earth moves, the bare living bush,
is quietly awakening.
And then the deafening, sweet smelling,
rose blooming bare bush is quaking.

As the heat rises, the rose blooming bush
scatters its' color over the soil tempting.
And then revels, again, the bees' attentions
to the bare living bush quietly trembling.

Bonnie J. Bourn

Inspiration

Poetry for the sake of poetry is a Sin.
The brazen altar of literature chants,
And calls for words to be sacrificed,
While in the dark recesses of the heart,
From far within,
Comes a cry,
A cry when inspiration longs to feed you,
Yet you have closed your mouth,
And already gluttoned yourself on uninspired words.

Writing for the sake of writing is Blasphemy.
Did God create man simply to create man,
Or did He have a purpose that you and I fulfill?
...Instead of wandering as only beings being
For the sake of only being.
It is not an issue of morality —
It is one of mortality —
For your words are alive and powerful,
If you use them when they are in their highest state —
The state of inspiration.
Otherwise, they are dead.

Elizabeth Lundquist

The Hidden Message

The rays of the sun envelop me,
the breeze gently touches my face,
it beckons me to gaze upon the heavens.

Above, the cloud of wisdom and knowledge dusts the atmosphere.
Above, the cloud of kindness and love caresses the sky.
Above, the cloud of peace and harmony floats among a background
of blue.
Above, the cloud of dreams come true and hope sweeps the heavens.
Above, the cloud of truth and justice sails through the celestial bodies.
I rejoice with a vision of the beauty this world holds.

Suddenly, the dark cloud of fear and despair looms against the sky,
Thundering its fearsome roar,
it challenges me to seek shelter from its threat,
its jagged swords of light descend mercilessly,
it anticipates my retreat with its powerful drench.

The message it sends is clear,
or is it?
At a backward glance, the gentle rainbow triumphantly shines through.

Cyndi Hoffman-Porter

I'm Reminded Of My Love For You

When on the darkest night I look up and view
The brightest star, miles and miles afar
Or look down into the still blue
Water of the deepest sea
I'm reminded of my love for you

There are times when duty causes us to be apart
And your very absence pierces my heart
My days become longer my nights seem endless
Finally comes the dawn with its morning dew
And I'm reminded of my love for you

When I think of all the hurdles we jumped, mountains
We climbed yesterday seemed so tough now when
Looked back on bring a smile to our face and we just say
It was rough, but as we remember and as we touch
I'm reminded of my love for you

When I think of all the obstacles we faced though
Hard on both of us, you comforted me your smile said
Don't worry your embrace so strong, trusted, and true
Tells me I'm here, come near 'tis then
I'm reminded of my love for you

Betty Davis

"The City"

I saw the City from my window today, the City so cold and yet so gay,
The concrete and iron structures in gloom,
The vehicles and humans seeming to gasp for more room.
I ask myself what is this strange attraction that casts a spell?
Where life seems absorbed in this Canyon of Hell.
The mechanical monsters crawling on wheels.
The Human machines following on their heels,
Then dusk approaches and the tempo increases,
The people swarm madly, it never ceases,
'Til the hour of seven and quiet reigns,
But this is only a false lull, the city feigns,
Whithin the hour, the whirl of activity begins again,
And slows down only at the hour of eleven.
Then quiet and loneliness engulf every city block,
'Til the hour of seven A.M. strikes on the clock,
For the City is nothing but an empty shell,
Only showing its character and personality when the people dwell,
It has its different moods just as you or I,
Without the people flowing thru its veins this manmade marvel
would surely die.

Julius C. Mladinich

"Dreaded Twenty-Second"

An important man was shot one day
The country said not J-F-K ?
There was a cloud of gray smoke
Over by the book place and the fence
Where a number of footprints were made in mud,
And his suit now red surprised everyone.

The sharp sound of the powerful rifle
Made a dog bark a while.
The air was cool, but everyone seemed
To sweat. These moments dry up my
Throat but for some put tears in their eyes,
And his son needed a gentle hug.

The thrashing bullets had just cut
Straight through the tough skin and bones of two men,
President Kennedy and the unlucky Governor
of Texas. Minds seemed in the sky
As Lyndon took over to govern the nation,
And everyone just kissed John's life Good-bye.

David M. Truxillo Jr.

Pagan Delight

Worshipfully he walks among the trees.
The darkness before dawn is his only wrap.
In this place his mind is at ease;
The dew on his crown in his cap.

Down by the river he greets the Sunrise.
The water runs deep and slow.
He watches intently for the fish as they rise
To breakfast on silver minnows.

Orange and yellow Touch-Me-Nots
Lend themselves to the morning.
The meadow echoes with starts and stops
Of the busy woodpeckers boring.

Daisies, Buttercups and Goldenrod
Add their gift to the day.
Queen Ann's Lace gives a nod,
Gently the breeze has its way.

Worshipfully he takes in the scene.
He is one with the pine and the birch.
Earth, Wind and Water a team;
What more could you ask of a church?

Barry L. Lyons

Darkness

All is still; All is quiet;
The darkness shall kill and all live recessively by it.
No one stirs; The skyscrapers ghostly stand;
The darkness shall always lurk when life hides in hard sand.
The bitter coldness; The silent loneliness;
The darkness laughs at all future assurance.
The bare lands; The naked waters;
The darkness bands together all man colors.
No more troubles; No more racism and war;
The darkness plays, for that's what time is for.
Warm sunny days swept away with the tide;
The darkness is the princess of death, sister
coldness creeping by her side.
The oceans pound against lands of ice;
The darkness is the future children call nice.
But then one day light shall give a call,
And darkness's reign shall surely fall.

Kim Moorehead

In My Heart

He was always there for me,
the day I was born,
the day I came home,
the day I was baptized,
the day I took my first steps,
the day I tried to ride a bike.
He was always there to pick me up when I fell,
or to hold me when I needed comforting.
He was there for me even when we found out he was dying,
until one day he said, "Take care of your Mother."
That was two days before he died.
Since then, he hasn't been there.
And he won't be there,
for my confirmation,
or my graduation,
or my wedding.
He won't be there to pick me up when I fall,
or to hold me when I need comforting.
But he'll never leave me here,
In my heart.

Jodi Neumann

The City

"Chomp, Smack, Gag, Gasp,"
the decayed mouth troubles over its food.

The window travels beyond a cemetery of stone slabs and shrines,
the young hand honors yellow daffodils to the dead.
Shut them out

Long, warn faces peer out from the water logged bus shelter.
Red 'Class War' is sprayed on the culture.
The almost neon sign calls to "Pray for peace in Northern Ireland."
Shut them out.

A boy wears a scar across his untouched (?) face!
Flowers for a price!
A road sign where the elderly will cross - some won't notice anyway!

The setting sun drenches the gray billowing death that rises to the
sky...
I cry for those who shut them out and do not notice!

The decayed mouth troubles over its food
Don't you see the resemblance?
The Misery Could Choke Us All.

Katherine M. Parker

Arizona Holiday

I retrace our steps along the path where friendship took us:
The desert high in bloom,
Pueblos steeped in reverence of lives long gone.
The Apache Trail, whose expectations we did not dream of
Bobcat revealed,
Great Blue Heron soaring downward upon
the green Salt River.
The existential beauty of the moment!
A tapestry of canyon walls in sage and ochre,
black stripes impressed by raging floods.
Saguaro cactus standing regal, as sentry of time passing.
A perfect synergy of people, place and spirit,
A magical effervescent memory engraved upon my heart.

Edith David Sundermann

Untitled

Two doors stand before me.
The door on my right is a door filled with light.
The door on my left is a door filled with darkness.
My mind is clouded with images...
Images of inadequacies of my life.
Images of achievements I have accomplished.
The inadequacies outweighing my achievements.
I stand between the two doors, looking at each with wonder.
I wonder which one to choose.
The door of darkness draws me near , as my body is inundated with feelings of
sadness, depression, and self-doubt.
I step toward the door of darkness, but then the door of light
summons
me.
As I look at the door of light, my body is overwhelmed with the feelings of
happiness and hope and things yet to come.
My mind goes blank and I stand between both doors.
Which shall I choose?

Kyle Clark Imbimbo

"Apathy"

Images rippling from blistering heat
The earth is withering beneath his feet.
Through parched lips he cries as he drops to the sand.
"Where are the blue skies and the flourishing land?"
Foreboding hippies warned them of their fate.
They were too busy and now it's too late.
They knew what they were doing.
They didn't seem to care.
The hole just kept growing as smog filled the air.
Now it's all over, with the ozone depleted.
His eyes rolled starward for one last fatal glimpse
To see the result of mankinds' ignorance.
His head hits the ground with a dull dry thud.
He leaves the world without a sound, without tears, without blood.

Chris King

The Rose

As the sun rises over the misty skies
The clouds roll back, as the rain subsides
There's something far away, alone in the clear
I can see it now as I slowly come near
I was awed at its beauty, as it slowly arose
It was the soft pink petals and green stem of a rose
Sitting there watching it, I see a rain drop roll off
I reach out to pick it up, but it's too beautiful, too soft
So I'll just leave it there, I'll leave it there right where
It is, for someone else to share

Jerry Young

To Alter Life

Without the sun's warm-light; to shine upon us,
the earth would be dark and cold.
To whom will a wolf cry out to,
without a full-moon's fluorescent glow.
Our eyes would be blind of bright colors.
if flowers were not to exist.
Life would not be the same,
if it just isn't the way it is.

Without faith to rely on,
our dreams hopelessly disappear.
our feelings are to be confused,
with no-one caring; from far or near
Our hearts would be endured by sorrow,
if love we would not miss.
Life would not be the same,
if it just isn't the way it is.

Like an endless river;
life doesn't change, the way it flows.
To live in a shadow, is to die in the light,
for there is nowhere else to go.

Alexander Castillo

The Surprise #4

The yard this early time has a new look.
The fallen leaves rest damp upon
Rain-soaked sand.
Clear skies allow bright fall sunshine,
And reveal what was before hidden.

Shafts of light cut through thinning foliage:
Stunning red triangles are heightened
By the rippled rows of black and grey.
Bibs of charcoal rest above whitish gray,
Accented with dark splotches.

One winged visitor glides to a feed-box,
Flashing white back under wing-cover.
And busily feeds upon its insect residents,
While flock-mates hop to feast on grass-dwellers;
Distant yellow breasts gleam from fence-row wire.

This time set apart for recall:
The busy flock gleaning choice bits in
Elegant formality, careless knowing of its beauty.
The yard this early time has a new look,
Revealing what was before hidden.

Della N. Carson

Untitled

I'm alone in my house, my parents have gone out
the family has left they're out and about
now is the time to make my decision
between life's dreaded chances and death's bulls eye precision
I slip into the bathroom locking the door behind
with many different questions, running through my troubled mind
life or death? a coffin or a bed?
even I don't know the answers to these questions that I've said
I move over to the cabinet - my walking it is hesitant
I creep like this because I know that inside me fear is resident
grabbing the pills from the cabinet, I pour some from the container
I choose out ten, then carelessly I throw away the remainder
I regard the pills I hold shaking, bouncing in my quivering hand
the question now is not if I should but even if I can
I finally raise the pills to my mouth but then I hesitate
this life I've had for a few years, is this what I want to desecrate?
I shake my head and tip the pills so they spiral down the sink drain
now the questions that plagued me lie dormant in my brain
this was like the world's biggest game of chanceful hit or miss
but this is part of living life and would you die for this?

Justin Hutson

"Running Spirit"

Souls locked and lost over the days,
The free spirit runs forever away.
Hurt and pain are all it has ever known
Frightened as a fawn; mature, and yet never grown.
Free floats the soul in a boundless love,
Running spirit, flying as the dove...

Hair of wind, and eyes of the deepest emeralds,
My love soars with thee, in a meeting that builds;
A crescendo of an ultimate pleasure in freedom
Love, sex, affection, compassion, all within our kingdom.
As our souls believe in the union of body,
Who dares challenge our journey: Nay, nobody...

Mile after mile, and journey to journey - in a soul,
Brings the definition of the mate whom with you'll grow,
The majesty of your aura, and the person you shall be,
Determines life's advantages; made you and me,
And within this realm of a couple's love in it,
You are my most precious; "Running Spirit".

Brian Carmichael

Favor

Do the world a favor and bless us with your smile.
The greatest tragedy humankind could ever know would be
not knowing who you are. You can stop the flow of a river
with a simple gesture, and bring us all to our knees with a tear.

Where you walk, flowers reach to bloom to you.
But don't trip on the stairs when you're climbing
up on the pedestal. You can climb as high
as you'd like (please bring us a star as you pass one)
but don't forget us in the end.

Do yourself a favor and give yourself a smile.
The greatest tragedy you'll ever know is not forgiving
yourself for your own imperfections. You can stop the beat
of a heart by entering a room, and bring the world to your
feet with one call.

When you sing angels gather to join you.
But don't drown them out, since they only enhance
all the beauty. In order to find beauty, first
look within yourself, and then become a window
so the world can share.

Do me a favor and bless me with a smile.

Jason Price

The Lake

The gentle lapping of the crystal lake,
The leaves in the trees exchanging whispers,
The sweet bird songs, together make,
Tranquil music like distant vespers.

Now and again a louder sound
Will pervade my peaceful mood,
And leisurely I look around,
A leaping fish in search of food.

A galaxy of color I behold,
The blues and greens of the dragonfly,
The deep-toned lake does her art unfold,
To rival the glory of the sky.

If only my tongue could find the words,
To tell of this beauty before my eyes,
But my eyes have seen, and my ears have heard,
And my soul has stored, to immortalize.

Edith Congdon

She Is

She is the rainstorm in the desert of my dreams
the life giving moisture of all things
She is the lightning and the thunder,
the wind that moves the clouds through
the sky of my soul.
She is the blossom that unfolds in spring
the shade beneath a tree in summer.
She is the turning of the colors of the
leaves of my heart, to red and gold,
falling to the ground giving back life
to the very source of their beginning.
She is the glimmering stars of a frozen
winter nights sky, the snow that
blankets the meadows of my being,
that one day in spring will find it's way,
melting, to the lakes of our love.
And as that water finds it's way back
to the clouds once more
she is the rainstorm in the
desert of my dreams.

Joseph P. Spada

Sounds

When I reflect upon my life, it all comes down to sounds,
The little words like I love you, brought joy to all around.
And when I heard my children laugh, or when I heard them cry,
It'd make the difference of a smile, or a tear drop in my eye.

Many sounds are without joy, like the breaking of a bone,
Or the sound that silence makes, when you've been left alone.
And have you heard the look you get, from one who doesn't care,
Or heard the sound of emptiness, when loved ones were not there.

And the sound when stress becomes, like thunder when it rolls,
And finally breaks and causes pain, it's such a costly toll.
The sound of rage when reason stops, a gun its hammer cocked,
A shot flies out it's now too late, the sound cannot be stopped.

And the sound a gavel makes, when the judge will hear no more,
Or the sound when freedoms gone, when they close that iron door.
And have you ever hear the sound, of a soul filled with regret?
Or heard the silence from the ones, who can't or won't forget.

Of all the sounds that hurt the most, is when you finally see,
That those you love will not forgive, or accept your humble plea.
They've let this silence of their love, turn their hearts to stone.
And one day too, they'll know the sound, of being all alone.

Charles T. Johnson

Unbelievable Suffering

People are so careless, thoughtless. How can someone cause so much
pain, suffering, crying? What could drive anyone to such great
lengths of insanity? I don't believe our nightmare of reality.

Nothing is resolved by fighting, or causing many deaths.
Nothing would allow you to kill hundreds, no amount of beating as a
child, or insanity.

Many who do these terrible things plead insanity, go to rehab, become
free, while we have to live in this nightmare they sent us into,
forever. For our family doesn't come back to life when they say that
are sorry. My anger toward people such as these, who blow up someone
for fun, Or for a grudge or revenge is indescribable. People like
this make our world the way it is today - sad. This sadness is deep
down at the bottom of our hearts. Good, kind, caring, generous people
suffer because of great, unnecessary losses. The generous help the
unfortunate victims, if the people who committed these crimes were
sensible, we wouldn't need to send aid to all of the misfortunate. At
night many kids dream their pleasant, peaceful dreams. If we let
these people start to take over our lives by bombing or shooting,
these dreams shall be taken away, from children, from all.

Jason Matway

Shasta Late-Show

On a no-moon night I lay by a lake
man may have made but nature amplified
and watch Orion hide at times behind
patches of the day's heat-haze that linger
but are rearranged by September winds
that spiral down through the tops of the trees
then along the shale shore where they fairly
race across my face to keep me awake.

I can hear the rhythmic squeak of the dock
rubbing against bobbing hulls and gunwales
distinctly syncopated with the calls
of pygmy owls perched high in distant pines
that look black against the cerulean sky
like the shadows of peaks surrounding me
that seem so close but move farther away
as morning glows rosy and climbs on stage.

Linda Ray Ferro

Growth - Lessons Learned

Young, naive, and eager to please,
Married a man with children of ease,
I can do it, no problem, a family we'll be,
Little did I know what the future would see.

Anger, resentment, and cold,
Why wasn't I told?
Step-motherhood wasn't the bill of goods I was sold,
It was hard.

Lessons in life are not made of comfort,
Pain and tears and regret,
I was not who I thought I would be,
Cinderella was right!

Step-mothers can be gruel,
Children of others think they rule,
In the end we all survived,
Growing older, growing wise.

Pam Schultz

Faith In Me

The sky brightened, then appeared the
Master of the universe!
There is a look of sadness, and tears
Streaming down his cheeks.
With outstretched arms and dressed in white,
He focused on the sight below.
"What is happening?" he asked in a quivering voice.
"So much pain caused by the evil of many
The innocent, in the wrong place, taken hold of
by the more dominant persons.
I send tears of rain to cleanse
And sunshine to heat and dry, but it
accomplishes nothing!
So I anger and send storms, but still
no response!
The young need guidance from the adult!
The aged must be released of helplessness!
Faith in me, form is of no importance,
For religious or not, faith will have strength to conquer!
Please follow, I am near and here!"

Mary Rubino Andreatta

Untitled

Come down to where the sea meets the land
Match the stars with the grains of sand.
Look at the moonlight coming down in streams
Welcome to one of nights little dreams.
Run down the beach feeling free
Build a sand castle next to the sea.
Relax, enjoy life's as good as it seems
Live your dreams.
Watch a wave lift in its graceful curl
See the love between a boy and girl.
Gaze at he gulls going by in flight
Continue now to the next dream of the night.

Paul Bartley Boroughs

To Karyn Beth

Welcome Karyn Beth to a great life
May you enjoy it even with some strife.
Living on this earth may be rewarding
But not determined by only hoarding.

What you do for others may be the key
For the enjoyable life ahead of thee.
The good Lord will prosper the life of all
Who choose to live big - instead of small.

The small person thinks of only herself
While the big one forgets the personal pelf.
So Karyn Beth as you develop and grow
What you want to reap, you'll have to sow!

Milt Kvikstad

Friends At Their Best

Friends at their best is really true, for they were close by let me tell you.
When we were going through life's troubled storm, they were all there
and their wonders to perform.
When we were down and out and had many needs
Through Gods good graces, our friends worked their good deeds.
Each of them did their part and most of all it was done from the heart.
If I were rich or even well to do
I would repay them, it would be wonderful and true.
I have not a lot of things but something I could surely do, is give
them a hand when needed if they asked me to.
In the meantime I can pray for them each and every day, that God
would grant them love, peace, and prosperity today.
I know that God will lead, guide and direct their paths with each
passing day, these friends of mine are all wonderful, may God bless
them all in a very big way.

Ethel E. Beyer

Tama

Slip on a set of comfortable sound;
Melodic, cathartic sky and ground.
Rhythmically, lyrically purge the soul,
Musical strength puts the weak in control.

Circular shine and sable shell,
Brassy crash and stinging splash, pounding plastic,
plated parts, metallic kick, a solid stick.

Wooden hands channel my emotions free;
Strenuous, tenuous land and sea.
Playing through times of heartache and of fears,
Three intense minutes will re-live three years.

Circular shine and sable shell,
Brassy crash and stinging splash, pounding plastic,
plated parts, metallic kick, a solid stick.

With gripping hands and fluid feet;
Erotic, chaotic sweat and heat.
Each piece of her is a piece of me,
Wandering through time, corporally free.

Randall J.

The Picture Not On The Wall

Looking at our family photos framed upon the wall,
Memories of your life, I sit and try to recall.

I feel your presence in my soul, but your body I no longer hold.
Heaven is your new home now, where you are walking the streets of gold

There is no pain or sorrow there.
You are now healthy in God's loving care.

Although I miss you so very much,
I would not change your new residence for that last physical touch.

I loved you as only a mother could,
With kindness and patience, as a parent should.

The final picture I see of you is not hanging on the wall.
It's the vision of you greeting the savior, Jesus Christ, Lord of all.

I see the two of you embracing, then walking in through Heaven's door.
Son, your new life is in Heaven; what more could a mother ask for.

Linda J. Breithaupt

Eulogy To Criten

I douse the cigarette amid the dark
Memories tug at my aching heart

I feel his presence, but cannot touch
Tears fall silent, I miss him so much

His quiet dignity and determined grace
Complimented completely to his feline race

My big grey beauty winks at me from safe distance
Arches his great body, stretches for an instant

He purposely concedes his every movement
I see him now, sitting noble, yet so innocent

I must let go, and find retreat in happier days
Before life introduced death, turning the final page

Glance my way just once more, my Criten
So I can hold our moment, and forever let it sweeten

Lana Dee Barnes

Sewing

You have come to me a cloth of space with frayed ends of sanity.
Mine is the stitch of time - mine is the bind, the communion.
With each loving pierce I do wound you for your eyes have begged me so.
Through deepening pains of impropriety I thread the rainbow colors,
Somehow crimson falls most common.

The stitch falls quickly, as do I - dripping, I make hate of haste.
With rhythm of hand I do my worship of divinity.
Your quivering voice, near unheard, you beg me to gather all loose ends,
then my tainted blade to lay rest.

With each prickly thrust I do evoke, with frenzy, your howling.
I hurt and then close the wound with a tailors draw
and only when you lay there motionless, and I pursue my work,
beyond my beaded brow, my heightened pulse, only then I see
my needle threaded from the cloth I have sewn to.

Richard J. Shepherd

By The Power Of Our Difference We Made America

By the power of our differences America was made.
And by our differences we are unique. By being
unique brings us strength to realize. That we all have
the same origin of the heart. By the heart we all strive to make
a better place on the land which we live on, and by the
power of our differences we give the cause that united
we stand and divided we fall.

Eric Jon Tanner

If I Had Never Met You

Dedicated to R. P.

If I had never seen your eyes, what beauteous enchanted
Moments I would have missed. Your lips have made me realize
I would have never known such sweetness when I kissed.
If I had never given toast to you. So shallow are the thoughts
I would have bared if I never held you close.
No warmth of real exotic passion would I have shared
If I never had known your love.
I never would have known true happiness of the heart.
I thank fate that wrote above.
Give me the trip to heaven, that you alone can start.
I love you very much I cannot write to you, sweetheart
and passions lines delete for like a throbbing from the start.
They constantly complete. I cannot speak a word of you,
In ordinary strain. And those from me heard of you.
Recall my sweet refrain.
Though solitude may blaze afire.
Where pleasures were immense the least of thoughts that you inspire.
Brings fire more intense. No line or sound that speaks your name
Can pass without the touch that prompts me to again exclaim.
I Love You Very Much.

Yolanda I. Conklin Scalzitti

A Pocket Full Of Sunbeams

When I was a little child at home on a cold winter
morning, I looked out the window to see the panes were
painted white with Jack Frost's magical designs, and
streaming through it I saw a beam of sparkling sunbeams
from the top of the window to the floor. I followed it
trying to catch some of the beams in the palm of my hands
and put them quickly in my pocket. I then ran to my mother
to give her my prize. I dug my hand into my pocket and to
my dismay when I opened my hand there was nothing there.
I burst into tears. To console my disappointment my
mother told me that it was Mother Nature's way to give a
little child a ray of sunbeams on a cold winter morning so
they can catch a pocket full of sunbeams.

Ruth I. Kuchko

Untitled

The soft glow of the moon peeked over the
mountaintop,
Then seemed to hesitate, as if afraid to embark
alone over this wide expanse of sky.
Understanding her hesitancy to journey alone
over this vast dark earth,
He reached up and embraced her; then gently
he released her.
For he had to stay, and she had to go.
As he is a monarch of the land and she
of the sky.
But as all true lovers know;
She will always return to him;
For that soft sweet kiss, that fleeting
tender embrace, and that silent farewell.
For this is their destiny.

Raeona Marsing

The Rose

The rose is like a lovely lady
All decked out in pink chiffon
She sparkles and glitters with happiness
And tucks her tiny feet within the lawn

The rose's teardrops in the morning
Tell of fear, death or maybe a broken heart
But as the petals come softly open
Her teardrops break apart

Catherine Fritz

Reality

Perched in heaven sits I
A sorrowed man with an angry cry
Yelling down do or die
So you can end up in heaven just like I

David Brumley

Your Gift

(For Mom)

As I grow older and wiser I hope,
much more do I see
I understand that all the gifts are not
beneath the tree
For sure the candy canes and mistletoe make the
season bright
Packages gaily wrapped, family, carols in the night.

The gift you give throughout the year
Serves to keep me strong and allay my fear

Hope when I despair and the future seems so bleak
Faith to stand and be there when I am weak
Charity when I am ill and need a hand to hold
Your love unconditional keeps me from the cold
Gifts as these have no season
Love is truly the only reason

These things I could never repay
But this poem is yours
On Christmas Day

Robert Carr

The Phantom

As a soft and sweet sound of
music fills the air,
somewhere in the darkness,
a loved-one lights a candle with
a mystical dancing flame.

Slowly as the music fills,
and builds to a soft sound of warm love,
the small dancing flame strives to live
in the mysterious atmosphere once created.

For the sweet sound of music brings the
flame to a new height,
for one day this flame may only live
in the silent memory of light.

For this silent memory of light will
live by the flame and die
by the wind of life.

This is the mystery of the Bright
Red Flame!

Nonie M. Pietrzak

The Bumpy Road I Travel

As I see the others try and fail, I
must drive on.

When the people around me lose
confidence, I must drive on.

I see my fellow man laugh and make
fun of me, but still I must drive on.

It wounds my heart to see people
hurting other people, but I still must drive on.

My journey will never end, but
my only oasis from the big, hot
sun we call life, is a friend.

Melissa D. Harper

Loneliness

...erodes the joy once my calling card,
Muting the gladness did illumine my soul, glowing so with life.
Desecrates a peace reflecting the touch of the Master's hand;
Paralyzing the courage — the strength to go on...face it again.

Secluded by life's harsh circumstance, heartsick in solitude.
Disappointments, discouragements, disenchantments — these I can
endure.
But what of betrayal? Of abandonment? Being forsaken in times of need?
Under these cruel treatments I can not stand — I quickly succumb.

What grand design shall I engage, when overwhelmed — when
trodden down;
Anesthetize the pain inside, 'till I feel nothing...only numb?
It may eclipse my barren heart, make the emptiness desist;
Tho' I know the hollowness will penetrate through.

Is there hope, any saving grace, can resurrect my soul again?
Where do I look, or turn my face, tear streaked and anguishing?
Is there one who understands, who's walked this path before?
Oh touch me then, let me know love...once more.

Susan Lee Hughes

Beautiful, Dead Rose

My friend, she can see the bitter end,
My beautiful, dead rose,

I no longer think of my fragrant,
flower, the pain draws close within the hour,

I remember her favorite things:
The beautiful sky, with the brilliant array of colors,
But, the sky is gray now and rain falls down like
the tears of a clown.

My beautiful dead rose, why did you have to go? I cannot
stand to see your petals fall, I do not understand it at all.

My beautiful, dead rose
I will wait till spring, I will bypass everything, until you
come back. I will listen to your cries for sunlight, I will wait
in the dark at night.

Sandra M. Johnson

Diary of an Alcoholic

The days grew shorter and the nights grew longer,
My body felt cold and empty.
I began to ask myself "Why?"

The drinks grew stronger and the nights grew longer,
My mind was filled with unsure memories.
No one and everyone was my friend.
Loneliness was closing in on me.

Life grew shorter and death drew closer,
My body became a mound of lifeless tissue,
My mind, it never became.

Death was the last drink in the bottle,
Which I took blindly, never knowing how it all would end.

Monica Howell

A Friend

Is someone you can talk to
Always there when you're in need
When selfishness is absent
You have found a friend indeed
If two people give more than take
And trust each other to the end
That is when you will realize
That you have found "A Friend".

Bruce Levens

"Pigskin"

Now I am kicked, and I am punched with glee;
My body is squeezed, I get dirty as can be;
But when I was an "oink" and mother protected,
I was well fed and never rejected.
I was her piglet and ate all the slop
Along by her side, with never a stop.

Then one day came a stranger and said, "That one,"
And I was taken for my final run;
My body was mutilated; they filled me with air
No more four legs and pretty pink hair.
I sat on a counter in a sporting goods store,
With other unusual surroundings galore,
'Till a little boy's daddy came in and touched me;
Then he grabbed my tummy and shouted, "Whee!"

Now I belong to his little son, Freddy,
Who gives me a pillow in his little "beddy"
He calls me his football and squeezes me hard,
Which makes me remember I used to be lard!
Sometimes my head aches from the punching I take,
But - I'm thankful he loves me, and I'm not pork steak!

Marguerite Popovich

Untitled

I remember my mother's saying to me,
"My child, I have no recipe;
I did just as my mother said
With the "makings" in the back of my head.
If you will do just as I do,
Your lemon meringue pie will be perfect, too."
Later on, in my big chef's hat,
I mixed a dab of this, and a pinch of that,
A blob of butter, eggs (I think it was three),
About so much sugar - simple, you see;
Next I added the lemon juice
Which I didn't measure (what's the use?)
Now I know you can very well guess
My perfect pie was a perfect mess;
And I wondered with a perplexing frown,
"Dear Mom, why didn't you write it down."

Mary O. Rude

My Faith

My God is King of everywhere;
  My Christ is always very near;
I hold them Both so very dear;
  Life's ups and downs They help me bear!

To the brink of fear They go with me
  and share the burden of things to be.
They give me vision some future to see,
  Perspective to judge; commitment is free!

My faith tells me that They are there
  with lasting love my life to share,
In promises made of - for Loving care;
  I may not fail; I would not dare!

"Fear not!" They said; "Just follow through.
  Trust the Word; We'll be with you."
To me, They've proved it oft times too;
  My life-time lived proves that so True.

God the Father; Christ the Son!
  Belief and Trust is Victory Won!
With Love and Faith, both true and strong,
  In triumphant voice my heart rings out in song!

Nathan Hale Snider

"Daddy"

I wish upon a star so bright
My daddy could come home tonight.
You see he's in the Army And
very far Away.
Defending the United States I am proud
to say.
Soon he'll return to my family and I
But only to go T.D.Y.
He's a wonderful dad and lots of fun
And I just can't wait until his job is done.

Presley Mitchell

With You

My heart beats faster when I'm in your embrace.
My day grows brighter when I see your smiling face
Every time I see you I grow a little more
And my feelings for you I can't ignore.
When I see you every single day
I just want to hold you and beside you, I'll lay.
Let me caress you and touch you.
Let me kiss you everywhere old and new
I need to show you my feelings are real
Touch me, kiss me, hold me I want you to feel
Together we are one, and one we are together
When my heart is close to yours I feel better.
Don't let this feeling between us ever end.
For you more than my lover-your my friend.

Lyn Sanders

Untitled

I stood high on a hill.
My eyes were filled
With the beauty of life,
If not for living.
I looked first up, then down.
Above me were faceless eyes that sparkled,
Watching and waiting impatiently for me
To make my decision.
Below me was the blue-green covering of the earth
Daring me to take the path that would
Abate my burden.
The burden of life,
Heavy on my no - longer broad shoulders.
I thought, and then it came to me.
The battle was no more.
In the end the sea had won.

Sandra Lee Russ

Immortality

Immortality is the seed of my faith that form my belief in
my Father: Immortality is the need that form my will to yield
to my Father will: For his guidance and love and protection
within his joy and peace and his security as I live the
will that his will ordain for mines to be immortality is
my Father in I immortality is I in my Father: Immortality is
the treasure that my Father have granted to me, immortality is
the life that my faith in my Father have form I to be
the immortality of his love, the immortality of his image,
the immortality of his glory, the immortality of his wisdom
the immortality of his peace within his forgiveness cover
in his patient even when eternity is gone, my Father and I
will still be for we have no beginning and we know no
ending: Immortality is my Father for I am his first love,
his first treasure, his first heaven, his first image, I am one
of his first chosen one to be apart of his light of immortality
that will shine away the darkness that seeks to put out the light
of my Father in I and I in my Father and his children that
seeks to return to the light of my Father that form immortality
to be the keeper of you and I us; and we the children of GOD

Willie May Smith

Palms

As I gently ascend my palms
my folded hands reach for a dream
They slowly open into the air
seeing clouds, a sun, gentle birds of flight
animals and creatures, all of the earth
nature's beauty in a single moment
My heart skips a beat and I open my mouth
but it is breathtaking
Then as I slowly descend my hands
through the clouds as folded in prayer
I realize now that God was with me
he was there in all his glory to let me know
that no matter what wrongs we commit
He will always be with us...

Patricia Calcagno

Jeff

From the moment our eyes met and our lips embraced
My heart has been running a never ending race.
When I am in your arms
I know that I'm safe from all harms.
I just wish you knew
that when I'm with you
I could never be blue.
Every time we're together
I wish it was forever!
I know your leaving me someday
and you don't feel the same way.
I just want you to know
before you pack up and go.
You'll never find someone as true
because no one can care for you as I do.

Summer Gorrell

To Mamma

Oh Mother Dear
my heart still cries, please hold
me close and dry my eyes.

This pain that hurts so deep inside, it hurts so
much I can't describe.

You always knew just what to do, please help me
mother to see this through.

They say that time
will ease the pain, How can they know that's true?

They didn't know
your special grace, or see the
beauty in your face, or feel your
warm and loving hands, What
I would give to hold them now.

Her hands that held me as a child,
her voice so sweet, so soft so mild.

To God in Heaven how I pray, to grant my wish
for one more day, to hold her
closely to my heart, and
keep her there and never part.

Linda L. Taylor

Pelicans

He's certainly not elegant, that old pelican. He sits on posts and takes his stance. But when in flight, how gracefully he glides across the water, wing tips touching, leaving little ringlets on the surface. Then with all his might, soaring, diving ....with such a purpose. A little pirouette to end his dance.

Jacqueline J. Wakely

My Hope

I have no hope, only fear.
My life gives me pain, I wish someone could
wash away my tears.
I feel so alone, is there no one that can hear
my moan?
There's no one that knows how I feel, though
many say they do, but there only lies to comfort
my fear.
I lie to people about my pain, I cover it up
with a smile or silly game.
I used to have hope, more than anyone ever
knew, but it faded away,
Just like the dew.
Maybe it will come back someday, and change
my outlook on life and my attitude.
But for now all I can do is take life day
by day, and one step at a time.

Tia LaFollette

Loving and Murdering

Cradled deep within yourself you became of shade of gray,
"My life is full of hurt. It's full of shattered dreams and
piercing words."
Lost like a child in a playground full of strangers,
"Hope is gone as I walk on the broken glass that was once
my heart."
You flickered as the wind kissed your flame,
"Depression is a disease and love is the virus."
Too blind were you to see that you were a rose on a stem of
thorns,
"I am a grain of sand in a pile of diamonds."
Too deaf were you to hear the love my soul desperately cried,
"To love without being loved back is murder."
I was too late,
"You murdered me."
All I have left to say is good-bye.
"Good-bye."

Veronica McCoy

"Good-Bye"

When the time came to say good-bye
My mind was filled with thoughts of you.
I knew this moment would come
But I hoped it would not come this soon.
And yet it seems like only yesterday when first we met
Remembering the moments we shared
Even though we had our differences
your memories will be with me forever.
Good-byes can be hard, but we must be strong and
remember the good times we shared.
Now we shall go our separate ways and
try to put the past behind us.

Patrick Hastings

My Mother

My mother is gone,
My mother is gone,
So why do I often feel her along?
Can she really be gone?
Can she really be dead?
Oh no, I don't think so, not at least in my head.
She'll be with me always, where ever I go....
I can tell, I can FEEL her, she's here, I know.
She loves me and told me that she'd never leave,
And I love her too, so in this I believe.
For the rest of my days, never alone shall I be,
Cause my mother is here, she will never leave me!

Sue Kelvington

The Bird

When I was a very young and artless boy,
My only sibling, my little brother, passed away.
My elders said he was with the angels, a place of joy,
And I, of course, believed the words of such as they.

I was with my aunt as she drove Model T,
Just the two of us, toward the burial site,
When suddenly a bird, a wren perhaps, or a chickadee
Came to rest on the door beside me, and cocked an eye so bright.

My aunt reached over me and clasped the bird,
And gently placed it in a pocket of her clothes.
The she said the words in many dreams I've heard.
"Did Billy come to say his last goodbye, do you suppose?"

Since, the better part of a century gone by,
I have had my doubts as dark as night.
A hereafter, an anthropomorphic God on high?
How can believers really know they're right?

Then I think about the little bird anew,
That propitious happening; when it was later freed
From my aunt's hand, it winged up, up into the blue.
It makes me wonder; it gives me hope; it fills a need.

C. E. Fitzpatrick

Lily of the Valley

As I awoke, early one fall morning, a certain persona came within my presents. As the hurt and pain on my inside were still present, the Lord cometh to mind it seems like a sign, a sign of life. As the day turned to gloom. I started to ask why? Why? For I take a deep breath. I exhale. I looked up. And asked the Lord. Lord
what is going on? As I started to walk I stopped I looked skyward once again the Lord cometh to mind, I heard within the mist my child take my hand. Those words pierced my soul. I turnith, I look around. My heart takes on a warm feeling I felt the presents of God. For I hear deep within the valley, my child open your eyes. I feel a warm affection through out my body. I open my eyes. I find myself in the Sea of the plushest most greens, for I am in the Lord's valley the Valley of the Lily. The Lord sayith my child I do not fear, for I am the Lord Jesus Christ, my child you have called upon my name for now I am here, walk with me. As we began, we walked into the
vast plains of life. For I feel the warm precious glow of the full spectrum of sun for life. The Lord says: I know you hurt at times everyone hurts. Continue on the righteous path and I will always be here for you. For the next time you feel down look skyward and you will find yourself in the "Lily of the Valley"

Robert H. Mather, Jr.

Awakening

A man catches my eye; I stop seeing
my world becomes smaller; my friends become fewer
dreams and goals grow dim, like fading stars
a sunset goes unnoticed; a letter is unwritten
my inner self cries for attention
where am I?
I crawl into his backpocket; forgetting my own legs
he now carries me, while I complain I have no direction
my life waits for me with bowed head
my gifts go ungiven
I now drift through life, like a leaf in the wind
until
I almost cease to exist
finally
my strong sense of self bursts forth from its sleep
like anxious tulips in early spring
I am awake
I leap back into my own life; and with great excitement
I see, I feel, I do, I love, I know,
I am

Patricia Artichoker

"A Charge To Youth"

"My Babies", "My Babies, how can I reach thee?
My quest is to search for that long lost key.

Society refers to you as the generation, lost;
How quickly we forget, our share of this cost.

For life has dealt you, some horrible blows;
The outcome of this, you alone will know.

Rid yourselves of the "garbage" and in life you will abound;
The rewards of your efforts, will most assuredly astound.

Live each day to the fullest, to be all that you can be;
To all your "Successes", only "You" hold the key.

Do not ignore the past, as some scars it will leave;
But use it as a stepping stone; as a basis to achieve.

To unlock the hurt, pain, and anger is the challenge that I take;
In hopes through all your endeavors, a better person you'll make.

My purpose in life is not to alter your path;
But to share in your growth, anger, sadness or an occasional laugh.

A bended ear, a strong shoulder, or a reprimand or two;
These are a few of the options that I offer you.

For your presence in my life, has made a better me.
This charge to Youth, I return to thee.

Michele Denise Glover

An Old Cowboy

I'm just an old cowboy down at the ranch
My shirt is wrinkled and I got holes in my pants

My hat is soiled with sweat and dust
My spurs are old and covered with rust

My boots are worn down to my socks
I have a helluva time walking on the rocks

The old shack is about to fall down
But I know I'll never move to town

My old dog comes and sits by my side
I look down and stroke his hide

My faithful friend all thru the years
I look up and shed some tears

And when he starts to wander and roam
He knows he'll always have a home

I look out and see the cows grazing in the morning sun
The calves are playing and having a lot of fun

It's a beautiful sight to see
This is the only place I want to be

At the ranch I'm going to stay in this old shack
Until the good Lord calls and wants me back

Terrill E. Staples

Same

The dark alleys, with black cats,
and no lights.

The crowded night clubs, with loud noise,
and strange people.

The lonely bedroom, where I lie
without you.

It's all the same, the music
still plays.

Kelly Crisp

The Kindness Of Your Kiss

The first time I saw you, the emotions you stirred within me consumed my soul.
Like a wildfire burning out of control, your passion engulfed me.
The gentleness of your touch, the moistness of your kisses, bathed my senses like newborn silk.
The comfort of your smile and the reward of your eyes, brought assurance that my life was complete,
And life was complete until....
The pains of immaturity and jealousy overshadowed our love.
The mortal sin of pride took hold of my senses and blinded my eyes.
But still we tried, we tried to overcome what neither of us could comprehend.
That our love was stronger than any family bond or defect of character.
That true love happens but once and is never ending no matter what temptation may bring.
But still we hate, because of what we both are, never realizing what we both could be.
Because growth only comes out of conflict, and with forgiveness love begins anew.
New and refreshing like an early morning rain, soft and sweet like the kindness of your kiss.

Mike Smith

Ode To A Lost One

When you left me, my world fell apart
My soul and body crushed and so was my heart.
I loved you, darling, oh, so much,
Your caring, you concern, your gentle touch.

No one ever could be quite so true
As you to me and I to you.
Ours was truly a bonding made in heaven.
That only became richer when "we" became "seven".

"I love you" seems so trite, but oh,
How wonderful to hear it and really know
That special someone really meant it
And not just anyone could have said it.

What's left for me now, I really don't know
I long for your loving arms and face all aglow,
Wishing we'd be together forever and so
All would be well as eternity looms
In God's House with its numberless rooms.

Louisa T. Griswold

Dreams

I dream of starlight dust and moonbeams in my hair. My twilight wonder years are made of rainbow stars, chasing colors around a lighted sky. Beyond the clouds are gold and silver wishes of my childhood fantasies, untouched by father time.

Cream puffs filled with little hearts, dancing to a lullaby. Tricolor ribbons and bright colored ponies made of coral bells and wishing wells. Sand castles made of gingerbread cookies and lollipop flags, forever loved, forever mine.

Ice cream clouds passing by my window with clown like faces and sugar plum smiles. Candy kisses sailing upon a midnight moon. Gumdrops pouring down from the havens to lay at my feet. Cupcake balloons and jelly bean dresses are all apart of a simple place in time, that is with me still.

Sunshine flowers with picture mirror faces, pink lemonade ponds and teddy bear crayons. Baby dolls dressed in yellow daisy dresses and buttercup shoes, polka dot bubble gum and marshmallow ducks. Jumping jack snowballs, butterfly biscuits, purple daffodils and, I am a dreamer of dreams.

Shirley Shuler

Off the Beaten Path

I come to a clearing in the fields.
My weary body tells me it's time to relax,
but on this sun-drenched day
it is time to keep going.
This worn-out path has many footprints
of tired men just like myself.
Soon the path narrows
and fades into the grass
and I notice
that only few have traveled as far as myself.
Miles away from where I started
but I am not even close to the end.
I will blaze new trails
and be followed years down the road
by pioneers like me,
and maybe someday
someone will travel further.

Norb Aikin III

Reflection 4

Shall I but know the
  mystery of a life so
blended bittersweet with memory
  of yearning for lost love
while catching rapturous dancing streams
  or throwing balls over roofs to
open hands lives connect with mine?

Shall I now taste again the
  ecstasy of love so deep
my mouth goes dry and loins grow damp
  at yes, the very thought of facing you once more?

Shall I yet sense the comfort
  of a hand touched softly by a magic woman reaching deep
  into the spirit of a wounded, broken child
bringing pounding peace into a cold, moist palm?

Shall I still know that
  all is possible and all is coming yet
to me...sweet peace, lost love the tender union with God
whose spirit makes me ache with joy
  whose passion catapults me into life again.

Sally Fennell

"Pieces Of The Hard Earth"

Rocks. . . Just stones . . .
Mystical colors, strange designs ... unique ...
Pieces of the hard earth . . .
Cracks, crevices, glitters, fades, crystals,
and shades . . .
Telling of journeys, truths, folklore,
Rolls, life, death, and the worlds bare . . .
Thought provoking, question risers . . .
Something to hold, commanding a long stare . . .
Pick up,, 'Feel! . . .
Listen,, Hear! . . .
Twist 'n' turn in thy palm . . .
The mind wanders, and wonders . . .
'Take a 'grip! . . .
'of lore . . .
of roles, of ships . . .
on death,, on life . . .
'take a grip,, 'on . . .
a part, of
the 'wo-r-l-d . . .

Mike Porinsky

After..(2*Shots)of..Vodka-

-Smirnoff..on(The*Rocks)Pain-Shot..
N'(Mye*Gut)..from(Your*Carping/Complaining)-
*Captions/of-Bone*Spur/Calloused*Corn/or-Hammer
..(Head)*Toe(?)-of Why(Didn't*You)Wear-Your..*
Reboks(Soft*White(Bunny*Shoes)?-So(You*Could)Hobble
-(??)-at(Art*Exhibition)?)-Between the(Arti*Facts)-

(SomeWhat*(Your)*Senior)?..(I)*Thought..
-What(Fault*Findings)-Got(To*Do)*Real-or*Evident(?)-
Among(The*Pictures)of-American (Academy of Arts & Letters)
-Grown(Insipid*Without)*Intellectual*Assertion..
-of(Individual*Genius)Gone*Public(?)-You(Picking)*..
The*(Bones)..from(Private(Images)*Gone*Rampant!!(?))

&..(Labeled*)YourSelf..As(Conscientious*Objector)
-Objecting to..the(New*Damsels)in..*Distress!!(?)
-Is(Nothing*Compared)to..(*Envelope*with(Lips!!)?)-
Stuck(or*Stick)(Stuck*(in-Red)..&in(Ink*)Drawn..
Technique(*Tongue)..Stuck(Out*Like)*Devil..or(Evil)-

*Illusion(of*NymphoManiac)..Having(48-to*52)Climaxes..
in*An(*hour)&(15*Minutes)Leaving(Me*DumbFounded)(?)(?)
"But-(Hell(Haft(No*Fury)??))Like..A(Woman*Scorned!!)(?)".

Philip Sherrod

Untitled

I'd like to take this time to say,
Nelle, how I feel, if I may,
I thank the Lord for you my dear,
So listen closely and you will hear.

How to God, you're a special being,
By receiving his love, and therefore seeing,
That bearing a child is a gift from God,
Of which we should cherish and hold dear to our heart.

Not everyone is as fortunate as you,
So of this wonderful calling, make sure to be true,
May you admonish this child and nurture him in love,
With the same joy, peace, and strength that comes from above.

This precious thing that we refer to as a child,
Is entrusted into our hands for such a little while.
So just love him, cherish him and raise him to be,
A seed of God, that grows into a flourishing tree.

That can give us shade from the hot burning sun,
And a place of comfort to which we can run.
So this gift from God, as a priceless pearl,
Already has his purpose from the foundation of the world!

Lydia Cooper

Teenagers

Baggy sweats and baggy jeans hanging down below the hips
Never looking quite just right without their share of rips

With clothes and tapes all over, their rooms won't pass inspection
But they are at the stage of life, their goal is not perfection

It's trying to find a place just where they will fit in
When kids and parents daily chore, is who will finally win

They're trying hard to find a way to make their road in life
When the presence of a single zit will cause a day of strife

But time has a way of passing and making all things right
When kids who just were in the dark will finally see the light

And evolve into a person who will someday rule the world
And caterpillars will disappear, and butterflies unfurl.

Linda C. Corkery

The Girl in the Mirror

Until we met, I never knew the girl in the mirror...
Never thought she was pretty enough,
strong enough,
smart enough...

Then for a very brief time you came into my life...
And you gave me the hope and courage,
to live,
to love,
to trust...

No one has ever touched my soul the way you did...
Even through your sickness and pain, you
were strong,
and gentle,
and knowing...

You accepted me for who I was, no questions asked...
And you forced me to do the same,
with love,
with grace,
with regard...

Dad...I wish you Godspeed, till we meet again, so long.

Melody Smith

Never Speak If You Should Listen

Never speak if you should listen.
Never walk if you should run.
Never leave if you need to stay.
Never love if it's not returned your way.
Never laugh when you feel like tears.
Never linger days that turn into years.
Never stop before you begin.
Never close your hand if another extends.
Never give in when you still feel like a fight.
Never go in when it doesn't feel right.
Never touch a beast if there is fear of bite.
Never sit in the dark when you can have light.
Never eat alone when you have friends.
Never be straight if you know you should bend.
Never give up today for tomorrows come our way.

Linda L. Lee

Instant Replay

A door is closed, gently but firmly.
New interests claim attention, fresh ideas emerge,
other joys bring pleasure to living. An aura of
freedom lends jauntiness to step, sparkle to eye.
But occasionally nostalgia, as a great fierce wind,
blows open the door, tumbling in disarray the neatly
labeled contents: Camaraderie, common purpose,
anger, hurt, joy, tears, love. The myriad components
of a block of one's life, building day upon day,
exciting or mundane, joyous or painful, emerging
in retrospect as halcyon days.
One examines each spilled-out content lovingly,
wistfully, sometimes sorrowfully,
Then carefully replaces them and quietly closes the door.

Rolena Ingram

Untitled

Though chains and ropes can bind my hands
and trap my mortal body here,
None can move my spirit.
None can restrain my being.
None can make me lose hope
for my dreams are always near.

Cecile F. Lim

Gift

A woman carries a plush animal that towers
next to her head and whispers in her ear.
Patches of fluff are proud upon its ears and paws
and between is a satiny smoothness, pure white and gleaming.
Ears and feet the color of turquoise
that the Aztecs use for
bracelets, necklaces, rings.
Its nose and eyes, black as a cave, beneath
the Earth and deep,
to lose oneself and come out blinded by the swirling stars.
A smile of black thread stitched with infinite care
from ear to flapping ear. Inscribed across
the summer sky of paws: "I love you."

Rachel Lund

To Nurse

From the Daughters of Charity through the times of
Nightingale to the professionalism of nursing today
the definition has remained; to nurse is to nourish
Unconditionally we entwine ourselves with the ill
of body/soul. Our oath we hold secure. Scrapes to
cardiac arrests we give all our knowledge and skill
to each patient encountered. We aid patients with
their war against Death. Battles won we pray for
many, battles lost are grief felt from within by
the unspoken law of constant composure. We gently
cover the lost; assured Death was not allowed to
cheat. With each breath taken we are hand holders
to bedpan cleaners each task as important as the
next. From backache to heartache our dedication
never falters, as we strive for the success of
healing. The awards we ask are small; for the
patients to go home at last one and all.

Rebecca J. Vance

Why Me?

The quietness the child fears before his
nightly abuse starts, leaves us to ask,
why me?

The continue screams and shouts coming
from the inside of their room where they
dwell, ring in her ear where music should always
be plenty but the only lyrics she hear is,
why me?

A man and woman find fortune in a bed
Where love is suppose to be shared only,
but only body and lust is found and a
little girl sweats when their door is
closed because where he didn't find pleasure
before, she knows as the door closes in
her room she will be asking, Why me?

Life deals us a lot of problems where we hope
we can find some of the solutions but one
questions that can never be answered
by the one asking, only by the one looking
in her window at night saying, "I am glad it ain't me!"

Shewanda Williams

The Fall Of Nature

The tall, brown branches sway back and forth,
As the golden leaves carry north.
The dandelions and daisies dance in the wind,
While the rotten, crackling wood is forced to bend.
The creek gurgles and flows,
While the grey eyed owl knows
Nature is slowly being destroyed.

Kendall Blair McGhee

I Long To Live

Only death lives in the tomb of flesh.
No earthen strength can loose the bands of iniquity.
From weakness and bondage of flesh erupt power and liberty.

O, One Who Is Able, consider my groan and to me true life — do give.
Yes, I pray death to my flesh, for my spirit lusts to live.

O, Jealous Breath rend me from my defiled nest built up with
rushes of sin;
That there may be cause for Your righteous threads to mend me once
again.

O, Precious Lamb be not dumb, but roar against my vicious way.
Lift from my tongue words that are my own and place thereon
Yours to say.

O, Glorious Light blind my eyes that I may clearly see;
the straight and narrow path which stows Your holy intent toward me.

O, Bounty Of Mercy I bless You for the decay of self which has begun;
From which now flows the fragrant odor of life willed in Your Son.

O, God Most High, grant the blessing which is only Yours to give.
Salvation abides not in flesh.
Father, slay me, I long to live.

Makesha C. Reynolds

Sunshine By Day, Moonlight By Night

Oh precious is she who stands by my side
no glare can compare to the brightness she provides.
Eternity is not long enough whenever I'm with
you. Time is unlimited there is no curfew
Sunshine by day Moonlight by light she has
touched my soul and launched it into flight. Soaring
so freely, so obviously by sight look there goes my
heart, it has forsaken me tonight.

Her smile, her walk, her eyes roam free, it's all
good, she's so sexy.

Oh precious is she who stands by my side, no
glare? Can compare to the brightness she provides.
A touch of perfection with a presence of
love. If there was any better our creator.
must have kept it up above

Sunshine by Day, Moonlight by Night she has
touched my soul and rendered it to flight.
Soaring so freely, so obvious by sight, zoom
there goes my heart it has abandoned
me tonight.

Ronald Lavel Jarrett Sr.

He's Special, He's My Brother

From the time we were just little kids, I followed him around.
No matter what chores he had to do, that's where I could be found.
I helped him feed the chickens, and give the cow some hay,
I helped him fill the wood in bin when he called me from my play.

"Come sister, help me build a kite, and I'll let you hold the string.
I'll even let you make a tail, and we'll fly it in the wind."
When he was sent into the bogs to find berries ripe and sweet,
I too must go along to fill our pails with tasty treats.

When he grew up and brought a car, (an old black Model T),
when first he took it for a spin; there by his side was me!
Then one day he joined the service, and left our little home,
he looked so splendid in his dress blues; a sailor boy all grown.

Thoughts of time wander through my mind, as memories re-echo again,
steps we climbed as years fled by, pages of a book in life's frame.
Through sorrows or happiness, whatever befell, we remembered each
other,
God bless and keep him in His care for, he's special, he's my
brother!

Ruth V. Shillito

God Plucked The Rose

A rose struggled among the weeds to start it's on earth.
No one noticed it's simple beauty or it's gentle birth.

It spread it's roots into the dust, it grasped as best it could.
Small, but strong, this humble bud did what no other would.

It fought the pain and the jeers from the teasing weeds, the more
they teased the stronger it grew and withstood their wicked deeds.

The weeds spread their jealous pollen to choke the blooming rose.
They failed to see, with blinded eyes, the way the pollen blows.

The rose blossomed and grew with pride, it was sweet among the
weeds. It flowered the earth with grace and love it's struggling seeds.

The rose spread it's seeds of love and only asked to live with peace
and joy among the weeds and wanted to forgive.

They did their best to rid the dust of their gentle foe, they saw it's
strength and flowering beauty and so the story goes...

Above the clouds God saw it's pain, the weeds like greedy crows,
with anger threw it to the earth...
And God plucked the rose.

LaVanda Meyer

Dreamland

Elusive, mystifying, soft wind sighing
No stomachs bloating, no children wailing
No souls sailing
No fathers beating, no mothers screaming
Ever dreaming
Perfect world
Dreamland.

Satisfying, clear water flowing, clean air blowing
No tainted blood, no children missing
No killers hissing
No hate-torn lands, no bombs blasting
Peace everlasting
Perfect world
Dreamland.

Death defying, careless breeders, self-serving leaders
Power plays, strategic dancing
All life chancing
Ultimate pact, malevolent mushroom clouds
Vaporized crowds
Perfect world...

Sharon Hawkins

The Lost Traveler

To be a child sometime means to be alone.
Nobody wants me, nobody cares for me.
I made enemies everywhere I went.
I burn many bridges, but I haven't yet cross over one.
Sometime I think I'm better off dead.
I can't overcome the images of a child
that many people think I am.
I am grown, but still not wise enough.
I am strong, but at the same time not healthy.
I am a child alone that nobody cares.
I am a bum, I am a loser cause that
what people me made to be.
I am a fighter, I am a thief
but these people really don't see.
I am a child alone, that's what I must
be, till one day I could just be me.
To be me I will give it my all.
To shake the shadows that created me as I fraud.
See me as me, not as the image you created for me.

Tomasina Pitts

To Comfort Those Facing Extinction

The Prosecution:
  Not enough courage.
  Not enough will.
  Out of style.
  Introspective.

The Defense:
  But intelligent.
  but kind-hearted.
  Different.
  Fresh.

Will the species on trial please stand.
Madam Jury, what is your verdict?

We the jury find the defendant unable to survive.
The induced form is not for this time.
What is the jury's recommendation?
We recommend this kind to extinction.
The hammer fell...
  Thus I left the world without progeny.

T. David

A Prayer For Pastor

Lord, from my deepest heart, I pray Thee now;
Not for myself — though I gain somewhat too
But for that gentle soul Thou sent to us
Not long ago, to guide and teach us through
The works and deeds he does in Thy dear name,
The while he shares with us his daily bread
Of family, of hopes, and dreams to be
As one with Thee where'er Thy path be tread.

He is not well now, Lord, but yet the yoke
Is not one jot the lesser than when he
First took it from Thee with great joy of heart,
And visions of Thy kingdom still to be.
I pray Thee, then, make light the yoke for him.
Do make him whole, for joy of wife and kin,
And we, the flock Thou sent him to attend
Here on this earth, be safely gathered in.

Robert D. Hanks

College Greets

Young men and women leave high schools
Not having a sense of the right tools
Choose college, not a job
Society doesn't need another mob.

Day after day you come the streets
Wondering when your mission will be complete
Here is a treat,
Arise! my friend, college greets.

It might be four years, sometimes six,
Don't be frustrated, this is better than a fix
So get in the mood
Young people, college is food.

There will be sleepless nights,
But books are all right.
Aching feet, sometimes you can't even eat
But look over into the horizon
Alas! the strides are over
Education is your cover
Under its wings you shall hide
Now reap, my friend, reap.

Una Smalls

A Rose By Comparison

I am hidden in a blanket of protection,
  Not ready for the world to see me
The sun wants to shine upon my face,
  So I give a small peek shyly
I am small in size, delicate to the touch,
  And fragile as glass
I can change gradually or I can die,
  But either way time will pass
If I survive I can become almost anything,
Sweet sorrow and joy, even tears I bring
I am always your symbol of love
As you would think of peace when you see a dove
I can be shared or given on a special day
Or maybe it doesn't matter you might say
I am picked amongst the best, chosen just for you
I wake up and stretch my arms at morning's first dew
I am cut off from the rest, put in complete solitaire
Gleaming with a pretty face and sweet scents for you and I to share
I am what you want me to be, whatever you have chose
I am all I am able to be, I am a single rose

Michelle L. Hoon

Love For Love

Why is there so many who can't love another,
Not speaking about family - father and mother.

A love that can be received and also given,
By those who know its a love brought from heaven.

When do you know when your love is to be shown,
To the person you want to stay unknown.

In your thoughts and dreams he's all time adored,
But as you know dreams are secretly kept stored.

Can a persons love for another become broken,
Or does love always act happily when spoken.

Does love feel like it would never come to an end,
Or maybe it can be mistaken by a love for a friend.

How can you tell when a love is so true,
By the smile on his face or the lips that say "I Love You"

Does every love come with a touching hand,
Or does love become unbearable to understand.

If only we had our someone right now,
Then perhaps we'll know for sure what loves all about

As I've been growing up I know this for sure,
That love can hurt another or be that common cure!

Regan Ponce de Leon

Complexion

I never knew dark brown could be so black
Not 'till the blackness of my skin was shone so bright
In my face
It nearly burnt out my eyes
Not even the rush of tears could nourish my sight
All I could feel was the salt
On my open, wounded soul
That was left to die
In a dark brown body
That never knew dark brown could be so black
Not 'til the pills of shame were regurgitated and
The scars of self-hatred on my wrists began healing
Only when this dark brown soul in a
Dark brown body
Mocked blackness with its life
Did I know dark brown could be so
Beautiful.

Wanda Swiggett

A Lover's Heart

Listen...
Not with your ears,
Listen...
Not with your eyes,
Listen and hear the swarming of the heart's fire flies.
The hunter who seeks to capture the flies
will forever be on a lost journey and sorrow's tears he will cry.
Behold the meek... who least expects to see the glow
for sorely they are the ones the fire flies will show.
No wealth, no fame, nor the deepest of veins
will grant you this glow.
Even a lover's heart blues can truly shine through,
If the lovers are strong and true.

Romeo King

"Starboard Lookout"

Ten miles out to sea
Nothing bothers me
But ten miles into shore
They fight a raging war

They make me watch it every night
Sometimes they make me watch all night
I pretend that I don't care
Children crying, mommies dying
Hatred and vengeance, sadness and despair
Fill the air, bombs bursting ten miles away
Turning the night into day

Ten miles out to sea
Nothing bothers me
You cant scream and shout
On starboard lookout
Or they'll lock you up
And throw away the key
And claim that you have insanity
Bittersweet serenity
Walking through the fire of my own destiny.

Steven T. Albert

What I Thought

I thought you would love me until the end,
now it turns out you can't even be my friend.

I thought you would be there through bad times and good,
to hold me, reassure me, as my true love would.

I thought you would be the one upon whom I could always rely,
but it seems as if I can only cry.

I thought and I thought but thinking was not good,
to realize my true love to be, you never would.

Renee Marie Garbitt

Kwajalein Cemetery

They said, "These dead can't die"—whose very bones
Now melt to coral in these coral sands;
Whose foxholes, dug with jerking, clawing hands,
A single tide washed smooth; whose dying groans
Were lost in rushing surf between black stones...
They said: "No one forgets. In other lands
Men give them praise. Somewhere a statue stands.
And on days set aside a priest intones."

I do not know. Is it enough to cry
Here where the remnants of their bodies are?
How can I know? What does it mean to die
Wet sand in mouth, and the safe trees too far?
I see their wide eyes staring at the sky,
And hear, at cocktails, voices speak of war.

William Krasner

Uh, So Was I

My name is Tommy and I just hates, that feeler of my sister Kates.
O he's older and might fly, but he's a kid;
Uh, so was I. One night he came down by the gate, I guess it-must-of-been awful late. And Katie she was there, and everything was nice as pie; cause he was there, Uh, so was I.

But they didn't see me cause I slid, down under the bushes and hid.
And he was talking all the while about her sweet and loving smile, saying his love was greater then all the stars above in the glorious heavens place, then his arm dropped round her waist. Then he hugged her closer some, I heard a kiss, "Yumm, Yum-m". Katie blushed an grew
and sort aside and sort-of-coughed, "Uh"; and so did I.

When that feller looked around, and see'd me there down on the ground, was he mad you bet your boots, I gets up from there and scoots, cause I see'd blood was in his eye. I ran very best I could, but he couched up, as'I afeard he would. Then he said he would teach me my manner's he'd allow. Then he shack me awful gee, he just thrashed the ground with me. By and by he stopped cause he was tired, Uh, so was I.

He went back around the gate, but he couldn't find my sister Kate, cause she'd gone in to bed while he was running round thumping my head. I got back in the shadows dim made a face and gufed at him, and the moon laughed in the sky, cause he was there; Uh, so was I.

Shirley Brand

"Life"

Life; So Precious, So Naive, Gentle as the flow
of a mid summer night breeze. Showering in grace,
guided by faith leads any to eternity through the
swiftness of a sneeze.

Life; So Intensified, So Indefinite, and so very
Indecisive. The fullness of the heart and the
heaviness of the mind. Be not estranged to the
cries that one hears, When the soul is trudged,
but tiring near.

Life; So Full of Hope, So abundantly enriched with
Wonderment of any yesterday and today. Little does
anyone know as one grows strong, but yet weary, all
must be accountable for all paths of life along the way.

Life; So Compound, So complicated, So filled with a
huge multitude of bountiful space. A treasure given
to any fiber of the state of all being. Surely knowing
a time will come when all must gather and find
one's own place.

P. D. Slaughter

where does it end?

Walking through the echoing halls
of a nameless mall
I feel at the bottom of the crimson stomach
of the capitalistic society I live in,
where registers ring to celebrate the victors,
while the vanquished stay on the shelves
losers in the latest slogan joust;
and where retailers do battle for the right
to gut the undiscerning consumer,
to digest the dollars given them
in a flurry of spending by sheep
who are trying to keep up with television advertising,
and keep up with children
who want to at least look like they can play
the games their heroes play.

Michael Werling

Our House

The rooms in our house, one by one, tell a story
Of a young family who's world had just begun.

From within its walls could be heard hearty sounds
Of laughters, mingled with every angry and kind word.

Its speckled walls that have been painted many times
Still fill the rooms with memories our hearts
Cannot leave behind.

The quietly remembered sounds or footsteps, in our
Hearts still remain, over the worn floor coverings
That seldom had been changed.

Its leaking basement, over the years, had been
The source of frustrated tears.

Our children's antics, from these windows we have
Watched, were full of laughter and pain as they learned
About life and friendship here on Saint Boniface lane.

Through our laughter and our tears, in our own
Special way, our family grew in this house day by day.

Our house faced many changes in thirty three years
But was full of the love and happiness that always
Overshadowed our fears.

Mary A. Kozel

That Damn Cheeseburger

At a gathering with friends
Of course there is food,
Of course there is fun,
I'm amongst friends,
I felt a bit of an appetite,
I had a cheeseburger.
As the night went on my friends...
Oh... my friends had nothing but drink.
By nightfall, hunger approaches all but me.
They, without thought nor consideration, chose
to go out and get a bite.
I was not hungry.
They were gone, I was alone.
Later that night, I was at attacked by a
mule. It was in my own home.
That damn cheeseburger.

Rich Yost

Reflections On My Fiftieth Wedding Anniversary

I came across a picture
Of myself the other day
Taken when I was a child
And long since tucked away

It was the strangest feeling
To look at it and know
The thoughts and hopes that lived within
That child of long ago.

"What ever happened to you?", I cried.
"Why did you go away?
You were a better person than
The woman I am today".

I felt that I had betrayed her
By the promise of things undone.
God, in your mercy, grant me
The chance to fulfill just one.

Sara Parker

Dreams

I am full-commander of my ship
As the wind is caught within the grip
Of sails hoisted so high
They nearly reach the sky.
So, in dreams, far out on the ocean
I join the waves in rolling motion.

Jim Arlen Record

Downtown, Morning March

Time will pass, though fade not thoughts,
Of protected marches, through rain or sun,
Past darkened glass of storefront doors,
Halting at corners with "don't walk" flashing,
Then continue briskly on concrete path,
Mid starring eyes from thin, dark men,
In knots of two or three, sometimes thirty in all,
Awaiting hope of a day of work -
Detained among them, a street lamp parting,
Them from her, keys jut through finger slots,
In token self defense, in readiness, a warning,
Before "walk" signals, she crosses beneath
The major artery of the city,
Nearer safety and a day of work.

Patricia Howay Walsh

Going Home

The narrow gravel road meanders to the top
Of the wooded hill. In the distance Thunderhead
Rises to the crest of the Appalachian Chain.
From the fence row the fragrance of honey suckle
Bursts forth like a spring shower while new mown hay triggers
Visions of a hot, dust filled barn loft. In the woods
Squirrels bark as they scamper up a white oak tree.

The house is filled with the clanging of pots and pans;
Cornbread baking in her favorite black iron skillet,
Blackberry cobbler cooling on the kitchen table,
Cold buttermilk ready to pour into the glass goblets.

Distant but not forgotten are those sights, sounds, smells;
Resting in a squeaky rocker by a warm log fire,
Accepted by those who seek nothing in return,
Deep wounds are healed; an anxious spirit is calmed;
That familiar place, home, that succor for one's soul.

Terry L. Simpson

My Christmas List

My kids asked me to make a long list
Of things that they could choose from
When time came around that they needed a gift
That each of them could pick some.

Well, I studied and studied and studied some more.
I made a long list, but threw it out the door.
For I realized you can't settle a score
By buying gifts - like three or four.

So I said to them "This may sound funny
But all I want - won't cost any money.
But it will affect the way you live
If from your heart these things you give.

To top the list is love and respect
Consideration and a hug around the neck.
Obedience and kindness, too.
I know it's much to ask from you.

I'd like appreciation, too
And help with household chores from you.
But most of all for you to feel
Salvation free and know it's real."

Lena Mae Lott

True Loves Ghost's

True love is like seeing ghosts. We all talk about it, but very few of us have ever seen one.

And being alone is like a shadow. We hear a constant voice in our heads, only to turn around to our shadows.

And saying "I'm sorry" is like admitting we lied. Why be sorry when we are speaking the truth.

So in this I say to you. "I will be your true love, your constant shadow". "And I'll never again have to say to you "I'm sorry",.

So when you think of that other person in your life, or talk to him on the phone, or slip around the corner to see them, remember this:

I'm sorry will be your shadow through life, not your True loves ghost.

Tommy Steele

Reality

My fairly young friend had so much to
offer and so much to give, but now only
time will say how much longer he'll live.
He let one cheap thrill take away all that
was real. Now there's no way he can ever
heal. It's scary to think it's really like
this. I wish it was like a fairytale and
could be healed with a kiss. But in reality
it's all too near, usually it's something
a lot of people don't fear. They say it won't
happen to them. Well it's possible because
it happened to him. Soon one day he'll
be far away. I really wish forever he'd
stay. But now he'll never be the same
because he thought that sex and aids
was just a game!!

Sarah Sullivan

Sweetest Smell of All

I stopped and smelled the lilacs,
Oh what a sweet aroma.
I stopped and smelled the roses,
Oh how wonderful they smelled.
I stopped and smelled the desert when it was in full bloom,
Oh what a wonderful aroma.
I thought I would never smell anything sweeter than that.
One night in a dream,
GOD spoke to me.
He opened the doors to heaven,
what a wonderful aroma.
THAT WAS THE SWEETEST OF ALL!

William Dowling

Untitled

Individuality and the uniqueness of one
Only exploits thru time and patience
A personal goal of acceptance of another
Remarkable being
Reserves all ability to explore
To find and educate the desires and needs
Of which people can not restrain from
Frightened by disappointments and withering
Through the process of pain
Allows not the strengths of the wind
Nor the powerful waves of the ocean
But forge the successful and bearable to endure
The ultimate force
Then and only then will one rise to domain
And recover the virtue of commitment
As well as the reality of the
Hourglass and sufferance

Maya Suraj

Nature's Show

When Autumn leaves are falling
Old Jack Frost soon comes calling
The leaves of brown, yellow and gold
Give lasting memories to the young and old

Soon old man winter makes his show
And covers the land with blankets of snow
You can hear the laughter and children's delight
As they slide and skate in winter's moonlight

Seasons come and go quickly throughout the year
Old man winter will then slowly, disappear
Spring budded out with all its glory on hand
And spread its beauty throughout the land

We can't forget summer which some think is best
It is better for children than all the rest
They give laughter and joy all through the land
No one gets lonely with children on hand

Fall, winter, spring and summer
Each differs from the other
There is always beauty from night to day
It's nature's way to keep us gay

Leota Todd

Final Irony

The shadows fall. The sun goes down. The shades are drawn
on senior seniors who writhe in pain.
While oral saints from pulpit wide bugle their pious hymns
on ethereal wings from south to Maine.

To put to sleep a cancerous sheep, terminate the agony of
a pet— a dog, a cat—that's humane.
To help a similar folk find eternal peace and bliss is
wrought with guilt and shame.

The soul of our religious belief is "love your neighbor.
All men are brothers. Prolong life and multiply."
These broadcast our hopes and highest goals.
For them we live and sometimes die.

But bottled in this finite world
our noblest beliefs fill up our space.
Our food is gone. Our air is foul.
Our streams run urine yellow.

No evil force outside ourselves
brings on our Armageddon.
Indulgence of our high beliefs
brings famine, war and sunburn.

Volney Faw

Tis Frore . . .

True emptiness prevails,
Only the dark days and nights still linger on.
Ah! Tis Frore.

Hence with poignant grace, a slow hand shivers, clinging
As rose to finger and warmth to cold the smell of a daisy
wilts rapidly amidst the deadly smile that still glows.

While patiently waiting for the final fold ..
Ashes to ashes and dust to dust ...
Hasten onward and wait no more my tiny frore.

Humbly the shiny light of day reflecting off the solid,
Enormous ground, bends to tenderly kiss our tiny bundle of joy,
And upon arising silently whispers, Never, Never, Never,
Wilt excruciating pain haunt this wee frore.

Past memories most people tend to leave behind,
While reality is but of a different kind. Shh!
Tis the void, impalpable presence of frore.

Lorraine Arrol

The Calla Lily And The Rose

They stand among the wildflowers
On that common beach.
One from the West,
One from the East.

The Lily standing tall, strong, sturdy;
Yet gentle and delicate.
The Rose soft, fragile, fragrant;
Much as a steel magnolia.

Together in the center of their world,
Comfortable, not saying a word.
Surrounded by beauty, free to bask, give, take.

The mist refreshes, livens, energizes.
The glow of the fire shines through to the soul.
They complement each other,
By their simple presence.

They stand alone and radiate,
Together, they mystify.
They laugh with the wildflowers,
And cry with the wolf.
They are friends; The Calla Lily and the Rose.

Winola Swinks

Nearing Grace

Here I am, with madness inside, so here I stay
On this cold and lonely—empty day
I feel the reality begin to drive home
Realizing what I've done, with terror inside—
Of what I have become.

With God-like grace I can destroy!

Your blood, like wine—it stains my name
The book of life has been closed again
My nails—they shred, while fire—it burns
Through your heart I tear, yet for release I yearn.

With God-like grace I have destroyed!

What I've become or what I have always been
Not even a man, perhaps a false king
I've raped the day—I've made her mine
And now I'm walking the edge of time.

Too late to stop and soon I'll fall
No! I am not the God of all.

Timothy M. Schwartz

Untitled

If I give you the sun will you promise to wear it often in your eyes,
on your lips, and forever in your heart

If I give you the moon will you swallow it so that when you talk to me
I'll bathe in the light of your words.

If I give you the stars will you keep them in your hands so that
when
you touch my body I'll tingle with electricity from head to toe -
inside out?

If I give you the clouds will you lay me down, kiss me all over and
while searching out the source of my love take me floating into
tomorrow?

If I give you a rainbow will you allow me to ride it with you into
ecstasy?

I'll give you my all. Every part. Kiss my lips so I can start.

Staci D. Wright

The Beast

See here the mighty lion, the king of beasts,
On zebra, elan, and gazelle he did feast.

This domineering ruler, each lioness his bride
To service his needs and hunt for the pride.

'Twas he who was sovereign, was respected and feared;
Whose subjects would shudder whene'er he neared.

'Twas his puissant body and maned head so massive,
At rest neath a tree 'twould appear to be passive.

Befall his realm to threat 'twould spring to do battle
Baring saberlike claws, though omitting any rattle;

'Twould rouse like a shadow and maneuver in silence,
Such a stealthy approach, to dispense regal violence.

Omnipotence to kill, nobly tempered with wisdom,
To uphold the species inhabiting his kingdom;

'Twas he, the lawful monarch o'er all his domain;
Absolute majestic presence o'er the African plain.

Now "How" ask you, "came he to this end?"
A lion skin rug on the floor of this den.

'Twas a royal mistake. 'Twas imperialistic vanity.
He grossly misjudged a BEAST known as humanity.

Thomas J. Bembenek

The Lost Comb

Miss Sassy lost her comb, you see,
One day when she went out;
She could not think where it had gone,
And she began to pout.
O, she searched for it high, O, she searched for it low,
And all, it seemed, in vain;
She could not bear to think it gone,
It caused her too much pain.

One afternoon she went, you see,
Along a well-worn path;
She had been there before, you see,
This was an aftermath.
And there it was, staring up at her,
All pristine, white and whole;
It was a treasure dear to her
As eating guacamole.

Mary Prince

"Porcelain Doll"

O, how I have been hypnotized...
one look .. one breath ... one face.

Eyes, nose, ears, mouth, hands . . .
so perfectly placed as if you were,
- An Angel -

Your eyes, O so beautiful as if they were gemstones.
So perfectly placed they were,
but . . . you can't see.

Your hands look as soft as silk,
but . . . you can't feel.

Your lips so perfectly shaped and parted,
but . . . you can't kiss.

Your hair long with a sweet smell of flowers,
but . . . you can't smell.

I make a wish, as I look at you ...
- my Porcelain Doll -

Louis H. Everett Jr.

Money Matters

We're born into this world with just
one thing, that the breath of life and
the hope it brings. We grow with time and
our hope are never shattered, but we soon
find out that money matters. How can
the human race be bed such astray, And
for a small piece of paper we act that
way. Is it the valuables, the possessions
or the power it brings, it's just something
about money that makes it king of
kings. It make us steal, lie and kill
one another, for the almighty dollar
we would turn on our brother. Some say
it's call survival, and many say it's for
the finer things, but all have yet to
realize the pain and hurt it sometime
brings. Happiness and hope is what
this should bring, so despite all you been
taught to believe, just remember money
doesn't matter.

Larry Johnson

An Angel

Softly she steals into my nightly dreams
Only to leave me when the morning comes.
Descending from the sky on moonlit beams,
Each step thundering like African drums.
A set of lips made of the finest silk -
Meant to encase pearls of the purest white -
Drain my spirit as if it was sweet milk.
Yet I yearn for her to be in my sight.
She works her magic to make my mind clear
And to mend the wounds where my soul is shot.
She whispers "pamoja" in my brown ear,
Only to awake and realize we're not.
An angel I love with bitter-sweet hate
Is gone when the sun warns her it's too late.

Monica Williams

If I Wake Up And See You Are Gone

If I wake up and see you are gone,
Only warmth of the crumpled bedclothes is left,
I shall cry and curse the heaven
For the sake of the yesterday's hopes undone today.

And the scent that you left behind
I shall breath into my empty chest,
Peace with myself I shall break,
I won't be able to sleep any more.

A downcast look that yesterday
You brought into bed concealed,
I shall re-create with paint,
And the current of despair will flood it all.

In self-vindication the heavens
Will send forth a host of mute lightnings,
And my heart will quiet down
As soon as torrents of oblivion start pouring.

But, keeping the covenant we had made,
A vision of me you will conjure up on your way,
Without chiding me for my desires
Once again you will set your heart on coming to me.

Zeev Kogen

Untitled

Are you there
Or am I lost in wishful thought
Does it matter if I care if your real
or is it over rated, reality, is it subtle, understated
I understand if it does
Do you know do you have the time for me
because if I'm afraid if I don't believe
If I need do you exist for me
is it time to stop the time and look backwards on the time
Sometimes I think I know you
And your thirteen separate faces on the flip side of a coin
or are you just a thought
or just a clock I know I've never seen
but it goes on anyway making moments just the same
If you had the time would you take the time
To turn your face on me
To define a day for my deliverance

Matthew Caucci

Do You Go To Church On Sunday?

Do you go to church on Sunday?
Or are you the type that goes once a year?
Maybe you're the type that goes at your own convenience
To worship Him all hold dear

The door of His house is always open
To rich and poor alike
He knows all creeds and colors
And bars no one from His sight

He must be kind and considerate
To welcome us to His home
And greet us not as strangers
But one of His very own

He listens to our trials and tribulations
Every day through out the year
Waiting and hoping for a friendly visit
So He can quell our doubts, and worldly fears

If one would visit Him on a Sunday
I'm sure they would hear Him say
Welcome home my children
I've missed you since you've been away

Tracy Mulvey

Great Ones

Was Elvis one of the kings,
Or just one of society's hot flings?
Was Marilyn Monroe the hottest woman ever alive,
Or just a good reason to go out and jive?
Was JFK the best president,
Or did we need a clue or a hint?
Was Babe Ruth truly the greatest,
Or were we looking for a hero to give our minds a rest?
Was Martin Luther King Jr. a great leader,
Or was he just a sacrificial dreamer?
Was Henry Ford's car a good invention,
Or just a murder of our population?
Was Adolf Hitler a true bad guy,
Or did we just need someone to fry?
Were they people to look up to,
Or are we just waiting for you?

Seth Hoover

Of Youth And Freedom

Have you skimmed across the water in a boat with a sail,
Or run like the wind on the shore by the sea?
Have you hiked for days along an endless trail?
Then you know what it's like to be young and free.

Can you soar through the clouds on a moon-lit night,
Or ride 'cross the plains on a horse with me?
Will you ski down slopes of powdery white?
Yes, my friend, you are young and free.

With not a care in the world or a troubling thought,
I throw back my head and laugh with glee.
I'm just like a bird that can't be caught;
How I do love being young and free.

Wendy Kraus

Millennium

So we are generation x,
  or that is what they say
And who would you be
  if you grew up today!
There are more choices
  than cognition can comprehend
Technology growing in all directions
  with an exponential fever.
So many demons have been exposed
  a cancer crouching behind every corner
  and that B.L.T will clog your circulation,
  by the way.
Sometimes we get some news
  mixed with the nightly death and tragedy report,
but even with entropy abound,
  make no mistake
for us to enter this new era
  love and compassion is what it will take.

Mark J. Byron

Despair

Does it matter whether I weep with my eyes
or with my heart?
No one hears me,
Or sees my tears,
Or offers me a word of comfort.
I, like the watcher,
Looking in upon a world
Of warmth and light,
While the tears come like rain.
I smile and laugh while my heart is breaking,
And no one thinks twice.

Shangrila Willy

A War On The Infant

There's a war going on, our own mothers are in charge, she gives the order to kill us for a crime we have no control of. Why do we have to pay? We are just miniature copies of your self that you don't want to face.

The reason why you want us to die is because you don't have the time. There's no place in your life for us. You say you are too young to raise a child; now you give the order for the infant to die. Mothers, did you for once ever stop to think before you said yes. Which one of us would pay for the choice that you made.

There's a war going on, our mothers are in charge. Why do we have to
die for the crime she made? Kill this infant so I won't have to pay. Kill it before it even breathes or has a brain to think for it self. Why should it live? When I'm the one who will pay. Destroy this infant today.

Toni Lee Dillard

Great Men

Who are the Great Men?

— They are those who work while others sleep, those who die that
others may live
Those whose souls can't be bought except by God
Who not only look beyond the horizon but further beyond
Those who show us that life is worth living
They are never behind themselves, but with themselves and
more often ahead of themselves
When in our darkest moment, they appear and give us light
and when in our happy moments prepare us for the storms to come
They never think to benefit themselves but in the things they do,
they are indirectly benefited and others as well
They may be unsung or renown but not matter what,
They are the force that accelerates progress,
the firm hands that check evil, and
the souls that thank God for all of us for His goodness and grace
Their works, their words, their deeds, or their dreams maybe
unknown
to us but in whatever they think, they feel, or they do, it is for
mankind, for us weaklings who are ungrateful, for us who would eat
or kill our fellow men to live or to satisfy our desire
They are the kind of people, when you have fully understood,
you would respect, praise, thank, and salute
They are the giants among us. Because they care, without them, the
world is no more.

Nestor Cruz

Patrick

So long, it has been since first I saw this man;
Appreciative eye I cast, and the pulsating began!!
Precisely fine was his form, 'twas beauteous to see;

And so desire grew, as each day slowly passed;
When near this magnetic man, in visionary elixir I basked.
One day he looked my way, so stunned I almost dropped;
With perfect mouth he spoke, and bodily function stopped!!

Friendship has since formed with this exquisite work of art;
Each talk sends pulse racing, just as from the start.
Yet should he ever know, my feelings, so very deep;
And that his image remains, even within my sleep?

A certain lure, I believe to me he does feel;
He acts not; is he afraid it's his heart I will steal?
Does his heart belong to another, this I do not know;
I wish only the precious chance, his affection for me to grow.

If never we should love, my heart's pain will be felt;
A joker's card to us both, will certainly have been dealt.
And yet, I treasure the bond, that clearly has been made;
Richly may it endure, unless destiny, shall it fade.

Valerie Straughn

Womankind

The Book of man says;
Perplexing temptation, a seducer
of destructional delight.
For it was her who had cost them Eden.
Apples - nothing but rotten to the core.
Punished because of thy fruits, now labor.
She had born the wicked garden, from which
murderous seeds did grow.
And the effigy of the Almighty, the mortal god
cast her kind into voiceless, stirring souls,
to bear the weight of the world mercifully
upon her back.
'Tis a dubious, perennial existence,
to be eternally buried alive.
Forever, trapped inside this womb.

Lisa Ward-Morales

The Fear To Achieve

What is it that prevents us from achieving
our ultimate goals?
Fear of failure?
Fear of others knowing our weaknesses?
Fear of others seeing our real self?
Fear of not having the ability to seek
out the resources we need to propel us forward?
OR
Is it the incredible amount of time and
effort we must lend to our own development -
The development of our families,
our friends, our country,
our business?
What do you think GOD meant for us —
To achieve?
To accomplish?
To aid or CREATE?
Millions of questions are flowing in my head!
But,
No answer comes — It still remains unsaid.

Nora Belle Bynum

Retrospect

She was ours. Ours alone.
Ours to love. Ours to possess.
Nobody asked for a share of her
Until the years began to march past our door.

And some voracious years nibbled like acid
At the chains which held us close:
Others brought demands: "The law
Requires your attendance,"
And behind the brick walls
They borrowed pieces of her heart.

Some years were subtle and seductive.
"Please join," they said those clever years,
Coming and going, each carrying off
A part of her.
Then one bold year, albeit softly, said
"Be mine!"

It's right, I guess, that she should grow
Away and up— but...
How good it is to own a little girl
Entirely.

Oma Wilcox

untitled

Out of the shadows stepped i
Out of the binding darkness I came;
To feel the warmth of the sun on my face;
To bask in it's rays;
To run along the beach and feel the sand between my toes;
To revel in saltwater kisses;
To glow pink and peach and plum along with the sun
As it hovers over the horizon,
Minutes away from its rendezvous with the sea.

Then...a darkness
Swept in without a warning
And the beauty of the day forgotten,
In the cover of the night.
The once placid sea,
Illuminated now by a sliver of silver moon,
Tossed and turned in its bed
Unable to sleep.
And Somewhere in the distance a winter wind whistled its sad song.
And into the shadows stepped I,
To wait the long wait for the dawning of a new day.

Sally-Ann D'Amato

Crystal Memory

From the old farmhouse,
painted gray by passing years
and not a painter's brush,
find the path well-worn,
made crooked by generations
of barefoot kids.

Continue to the spring-fed pond.
"Watch the prickles. Don't slip on the mossy rocks."
Take the plunge!

Let the jade-green coolness
make you silly.
Ignore the water gnats and tree frogs
for they intrude on perfect moments
and sun-glanced settings.

Images of childhood
come like light through crystal.
Bent and changed,
technicolored to perfection,
so unlike reality, but in the mind,
so true.

Robert A. King

The Unicorn

Golden sunlight glistens in a magnificent spiral
Patterned from the massive horn atop his perfect head.
His voice rings through the trees like grand golden bells
Chiming in a new day.
Thunder seems to erupt from beneath the ground when he gallops,
Yet it sweetly calms the soul.
Standing erect in the brilliant sunlight he arches his neck
To graze on the lush greenery below him.
His muscles twitch and his ear twists
Straining to hear even the most minute of sounds.
Quickly, as if startled, he races through the meadow
Allowing his silvery mane to silently flow behind him.
The petite pond catches his eye and he veers toward it,
Looking down, his reflection is painted flawlessly
On the crystal surface.
Slowly he drifts away from the pond,
Only to find the cooling shade of a majestic pine tree.
Gracefully, he allows himself to relax
And soon he is asleep.

Sheri McClure

Beachcomber

He walks along the beach,
Patterned soles crunching coarse feldspar sand,
Brown leather feet kicking shell pieces and barnacled driftwood.
He walks,
Eyes sifting sand through mental sieves,
Eyes sorting fragments, caressing wave-polished stones.

He walks along the beach,
His back to the north, his path crosswise to the wind.
As gulls scream and waves roar.
He walks,
Through rows of tangled seaweed,
Through treasures from other shores.

He bends down,
Reaches out,
Places one round white stone in his pocket.

Sandra L. Powers

A Love Note

Love is a feathery bird pushing people,
Blinding them with soft feathers of lure;
And, quite often, after being amply fed,
Does excrete prodigiously on its patrons.

J. Sinkinson Otruba

Sonnet When Tartuffa Left

The quake jolted our family one day.
People arrived, their faces ghostly glassed,
To see our shatter'd lives in disarray,
And hear of the horrors recently passed.
Her tremors still shake the ground that we walk.
Her presence makes daylight turn into dark.
The princess of darkness haunts those who talk.
Even the dog, sensing perils, does bark!
Her wrath coerced us to servitude
We suffer endless torment she deserved.
Now what I do is pray for latitude
Craving her soul will descend unpreserved.
  Devils you will never see; 'til too late.
  Unbeknownst good friendships can grow to hate.

Lauren Caldarera

A Tall Tree

If I was a tall, tall tree,
People driving by could see me.
My branches would be so high,
They would reach up and touch the sky.

Birds could sit and sing with glee,
Dogs would come and rest by me.
Families could gather to picnic and cook,
While children climb my branches to take a good look.

In the summer I'd have green leaves,
But then with winter I'd be bare and freeze,
In autumn I'd give a splendid show,
And soon all my leaves would fall and blow.

My special job is giving oxygen for free,
So people can stay healthy.
What would the world be without a tree?
They all depend on me.

Mariann Catanzaro

The Traffic Curse

As the day grew worn, twilight was reborn,
People prepared to end their work and leave their jobs,
Driving off in cars headed for the traffic mobs,
In order to pass the time while waiting in the congestion,
Some switched on music others turned to the news, watching
nearby roads, get indigestion,
It practically became a contest, to see who would win,
That chance to grab the space, in the lane that started to thin,
Patience began to wear out, some folks would even yell and shout,
Exasperated drivers having a rough time,
Blew their horns making angry gestures in pantomime,
Engines idled as the pressure mounted,
With stress and strain the seconds they counted,
Slowly, finally the lines broke through,
One by one increased their speed and destinations could continue,
Action took over the place of suspension,
Which gradually dissolved the stress and the tension,
Awhile ago the sun had set and a great wave of relief had
passed through the air, but tomorrow, is waiting to bring yet another
traffic curse which all must face if they dare.

Maureen Purcell Hassoun

Cloud Nine

Oh say 50 years ago, one quiet morn,
People saw the black bird, forlorn.
In 45 sec. so many a ton,
For 2 weeks later #2 was done.
Oh say 50 years ago that sound was so loud,
As went high as that gray mushroom cloud,
Most were sick and dying,
As the blackened babies were crying.
Oh say 50 years ago the world was shocked,
As Hiroshima buildings swayed and rocked,
Huge was that loud din,
As the people went out with black skin.
Oh say 50 years ago I see that erie expression,
Only came out was anger and aggression,
As debris and glass flew shattered,
Humans lay beaten and battered.
Oh say present age from this what have we learned,
For out of war what have we earned,
Now at ground zero that faming site,
To see the city a shivering fright.

Levy Cohn-Lerner

Woodstock

In the year of 1969,
people waited on line,
to see a concert of a different kind,
that was on a farm near a great-uncle of mine.

It was called Woodstock,
and the music went around the clock.
It was wetter than a dock,
but people still listened to the rock.

Then in the year of 1994,
the people still wanted more.
Some people thought it was a bore,
but others are waiting for Woodstock three and four.

Tracey Dowd

Dream Of Life

Tears sewn into a pillow; laced with silk thread.
Placed upon the dying angel's bed.
Flower's drink up the earth growing.
Still in that never-ending lake, rowing.

Bare feet pulse through man made sands.
Cursed sayings drying up our lands.
Reality lost to the stars again.
Who's to trust: Where are the friend's?

Lost in a world of noise and song.
Can't decide: Where do I belong?
With the good in purple skies;
Lying below amongst the lies.

Smell out love running through.
Sea gulls crying: Reminded me of you.
Eyes staring back, full of wonder.
Into dreams I deeply plunder.

See the light that guides us along.
Life is just another question answered wrong.

Falling forever more
into the dreams of life.

Megan Alix Fishmann

To Becky, My Birthday Wish

On this special day,
Please take me away.
Take me away to a May, before all of his sick days.
If I could go back to those days,
I don't know what I would say.
I know what he would say, "Happy Birthday!"
I want to go back to when everything was O.K.
But I can't go back not even on this day.
I thought I would never love another.
I was wrong because I love you more than any other.
I wish you could take me away.
But you can't, not even today. This is why I try.
I try because if you leave me I want to know...
If you cried, if you lied, and how you died.
If you leave me, I will begin to cry, I will lie,
And I will feel like I died.
I will want to go back too.
So I can say, "I love you."
But if I say it now and keep saying it maybe I want
Need to come back to you.

Matthew Miller

I Am

a bamboo;
pliant, supple, strong
forever swaying - bending;
erectly tall, yet springing back even
from the ground.

an orchid:
naturedly alone
amidst blooms in desert sky;
crafted HANDWORK in solitude, though
ne'er lonely.

a lion:
Fierce ... calculating
lording over dominions, but
tamingly tender to faces of
innocence.

an eagle:
ever watchful with
claws posed to clench - reshape - thrust
innocent preys; freely I soar 'cross
space and time.

luz g. albarracin-nwoke

Song Of Life

A droplet ... a mere drop of water
Plops to Earth and rejoices.
Joining with the multitude
It's caught in the current of life.
Racing, chasing, whirling, dancing to a tune of its own
It sings the Song of Life.

Roaring defiance, rushing blindly, dodging, skipping,
Tumbling, plunging, it challenges the flow
And chases headlong after the adventure called, "Life".
Splashes and sparkles, it croons the Song of Life.

Cascading over stones, it bruises and batters
the borders of its world
Questioning, seeking the meaning of Life.
And all the while, sings the Song of Life.

Slowly it tires, slows its pace
and wearies of the chase.
Seeking a more quiet tide
It comes to rest in a tranquil pool
Softly humming
Humming the last strains of the Song of Life.

N. E. Layden

Awakening

These hosts that we have picked to live in
problems many problems
the choices were far and in between
we push on further and further
feelings rise between you and I
looking at each other through eyes that seem to not be our own
our hearts beating faster than ever before
my head drops to look at my feet
they do not feel like running anymore
when we first met I felt old, tired, and weak
my mind wasted from this tyranny
you took me in and loved me and held me
taught me, taught me to leave this run down body
you found a younger me and pulled me out
the whole world could feel me again
I screamed - LOUD, LOUD, LOUDER
screamed I AM ALIVE
now I live for you
and would die for you
I owe this to you for teaching me again how to live.

Todd Koebke

Discouragement

I built my doubt upon a rock
put it in a room and slapped on a lock.
I forget about that room every day
unlocking it release the music it may play.
The song is dirty and rotten
everyday it is still forgotten.
Inside is a beast that preys on my soul,
It buries my confidence in a big deep hole.
I found out how this can come true
It sees the gap, the difference between me and you.

Mike Workman

T.B.I. (Traumatic Brain Injured)

I am lost, still looking for answers in my mind,
Questions still haunt me, the answers I cannot find.
I am smart, can't you see?
All you do is look and declare my mind empty.
And so I am lost, please won't you give me a break?
I've lost so much and still I cry,
How much more must I take?
Don't shut me away and please don't point your finger at me
Does it really matter, but only to me?

Why is life so unfair-
I lost my friend and my sound
I'm lost within myself, with no answers around.
Please give me the answers, all of those I'm looking for,
Help me rest my mind, please don't shut your door.

Teresa E. Mynhier

Daydream of the Seashore

Come with ya for a walk
quietly across the sandy beach.
do not let you to be alone,
and share with me there.
there are some white cumulus clouds in the sky,
that move slowly through the air by the windy day.
and also there is only one sea gull, that soars with its wings
through the air in a quiet moment over the ocean.
there is an arch of the mountain over the ocean along the sandy beach,
Nevertheless, we can wade wildly with our feet through.
There are some shells that lie all over the sandy beach.
Finally, look at the lighthouse that establishes on this mountain there.

Lu Ann Fancher

Prejudice

Poor judgement on
Racial conflicts. Always
Ending in
Jealousy. People
Underestimating others because they are different
Discrimination is complete
Ignorance.
Culturally biased people creating stressful
Environments all around.

C. Marie Burse

Beams Of The Future Lurk Ahead, But I Run Blind Against Them

Rain pounds on the roof, my heart beats,
Rain hastily tries to gather its children as
they scatter from her grasp.
My heart beats,
I dread the moment that is near; I fear for it is
finally here,
Although I won't, Although I'll cry, they'll make
me say but I can't say goodbye,
Rain cries, on the roof, her children are gone.
I cry below the roof, my friends are gone,
I seek no further I cannot find that sorrow and
remorse I have inside,
Although I have done nothing wrong, I feel remorse
my friends are gone,
I see no face I feel no hands, I say no words, no body stands,
But souls still live they never die, for now I know I cannot cry.
Because I know, I never fear, even though not present my
friends are still H E R E.

Michelle Metallidis

The Woods Were Silent

The woods were silent.
Reaching out to the warming sun,
Nestling bird between its branches,
Protecting squirrel in its hollow body,
Ants crawl up and down its trunk,
While woman lies beneath its shade.
The woods were silent.
Night crept up like cat on mouse,
Wind howling through it,
It standing guard like a warrior.
The woods were silent.
Dawn had come,
But there was no bird, no squirrel, no ants, no woman,
Just men with a beast in their clutches.
The beast came alive with a gut-wrenching roar
Cutting through its life,
It was gone.
The woods were silent.

Rebecca L. Rapanault

Who Knew?

Waking from a sleep, a haze, a
phase of your life to discover what
you've done and what's left to do.
Who knew? Only you, self-reflection
Through inspection and serious dissection
of your likes and dislikes, emotions, and
emotions, and views of worthwhile events. Opinions
are formulated and further developed,
enveloping your persona or character.
Previously the actor, now a solid soul
with no holes in your theories or stances;
only celebrated dances of joy because
you've become one with you, who knew?

Matt Pedicini

Filling - A Lesson

And when you turn the next hallowed page
Read it, or fill it. Learn a game, or Father, teach a game.
For your sake alone, when you cross a barren land,
leave your mark. You never know which one the tracker will
pick up, which one he'll adopt.
It's a jungle out there and one can't be too many places.
So fill your tablet with wisdom. Travel, swim, walk, fly to
a new place. Take a friend.
After all, here, on this page, is where our education is.
Not only in the confines of a cloned room, but also in the
vast plains of individual minds, along the cruel, rewarding
and unyielding path of a troubadour named Life.
This is one of the things I have learned.
So regret nothing, just learn. Your professor is Past.
Treasure all the places you've played, all those you've made,
all those you've slept, all those you've wept.
So go, start on your way. You teach me, I'll teach you.
It is born, when you turn the page.

Nick Reading

Cry a Tear of Pain

Tiny drops of melted glass
Reflect the pain inside.
The tear will leave its salty mark
When memories have died.

For every tear that's wiped away
There's more that didn't fall.
When tears are pain, the feeling stays,
You can't release it all.

A kind of blessing, yet a curse.
The sore is dulled, but still gets worse.
Your heart is patched 'till when a verse
Turns back the hands of time.

Sara Vance

Silence

There's a silence between us, a chill in the air. Our eyes
reflect tired souls. Eyes are windows to the soul, I am told.
A distance exists, it's foreign, not welcome, it's new. A wall
being created needing communication to tear down and break
through. Words can be weapons, leaving no outward scars to see
yet the hurt is buried deep within strangling ones spirit,
grounding its flight, not free to be all it should be. Emotions
all consuming, the mind filled with confusion, you feel separate
from the one you love, with whom you chose this union. Thoughts
of the past, when did love begin to slip away? Memories held
dear in the heart and mind. You pray the chill will pass, hoping
it will in time. Conversations dance around the obvious,
laughter less frequent, eye contact is virtually nil. Yet when
you winnow through the present and remember days gone by, you
know the depth of your love, you feel it still. Touching ceases,
loving words thought of, go unsaid, romance not nurtured, silence
increases. Passion put on hold, a strange hesitation surrounds
your desires, lightheartedness is amiss. Still embers are
glowing, desperately crying out in need. Take time for each
other, rekindle the flame. Create the fire once felt, be aware,
pay heed.

Linda Toland Vogel

"Peace"

There is a peace within your walls
A special quiet all its own,
A person to whom one bares his soul
Awaits to have your thoughts well known,
He cares in such a special way
And gives you comfort to ease pain,
His sensitivity to all
Shows us that life is not in vain.

Eleanor-Ruth Stevens

Life And Death

Looking back at when we first got our start.
Remembering the feelings blooming in the heart.
Over the years and with time the feelings did grow
What the final outcome would be we didn't know.
We learned so much about ourselves and each other,
So many things never to be shared with another.
We became real close and the best of friends,
Talking and listening for hours on end.
The magical friendship grew into Real Love
With blessings from our Guardian Angels above.
We shared the emotions and passion inside
That we both had mastered so well to hide.
A Special Love - unconditional, deep and true
Filling us with life and making our spirits new.
I cherish those sweet memories now that you're gone
And every night I look to the Star we use to dream upon.

Terri Stoddard

A Chance Encounter With An Old Lover (At Jury Duty)

I touched my fire with my healed hand,
remnants of its heat teased my memory
but why it could hurt
I no longer understand

I know it burned once with obsession
fueled by an energy of lost rage
but why it was so necessary
I no longer have reason

I remember flames destroyed my defenses
burning through my structures of survival
but why it was worshipped
I no longer can make sense

I touched my fire with my healed hand,
and the fire was only a man

Margie Deck

Celebration for a Homecoming

Candles of lightening guiding the way.
Rending the clouds.
Loud peels of thunder clapping.
Deaths standing ovation.
Miracles in raindrops, tears of joy.
A soul leaving this earth.
Tired and ready, to journey beyond the clouds.
The celebrity enters, flashes light the sky.
Far into the distance, echoes of safe passage.
A body grown weak, a soul strengthened.
So vast, so alive, and yet so final.
Now at peace, leaving rainbows of memories.
Fear not the storm, for it's only a celebration for a homecoming.

Maureen A. Winberg

Whimsical

A can of soup in the middle of the table
Sad and alone helplessly wandering
Across unknown limits of life's boundaries
Fright and fear surrounds every corner
Dark and humongous demons
Blue and purple spotted flying pigs
Hovering and screeching over a helpless little one
What a sad, alone and frightened creature
Ever curious of what these demons are doing
Picking him up and rolling him down
Oh, how it hurts!

Maria Erlinda Santiago

Loving You Is:

Watching sunset's glow at eventide
Rich, golden hues, and shimmering silver sheens,
glimmering and gleaming on ocean and wet sand

Sand-pipers running to and fro, searching
evening meal at water's edge.
Sea gull's homeward bound, silhouettes of graceful
movement against a purple sky
Colors ever changing, bursting into great panorama of beauty
Pounding heart and far-away thoughts encompass all of being
Love is there and you are there and nothing else exists

Autumn leaves, in gentle breeze,
falling softly —red and yellow
And golden brown, drifting down in varied shapes
upon the ground
Dreams are there and you are there and
Nothing else exists

The warm and friendly glow of
burning wood upon the hearth
Flickering candles on the mantle-piece
You and love and peace are there and nothing else exists——

Robert F. Taylor

Feelings

Feelings are what help you do the
right things
Without those feelings, you can't be
someone or something
They help you express your emotional side
Your happy, sad, angry, joyful, or otherwise
There not just there to help us in our ways
But everyday, every minute... always
Sometimes they can get hurt and sometimes
they can't
But to avoid that, you have to be strong
and not bent
Because feelings are hard to vent
Open your mind and express your feelings
free yourself and everything
Free yourself like a bird and mother nature
Don't think your stupid or a failure
Be yourself and have an open mind
Search for your goals and others to find

Victoria George

July At The Beach

We were all there together sitting in the sand,
right where the water swallows the land.
Piled up on the beach and searching up high,
for the first firework to light up the sky.
We waited and waited, and then with a crack,
the sky filled with color, an explosive attack.
One then another shot up and slid down,
overlapping each other, spinning around.
Like colorful stars all jumping about,
turning the night sky inside-out.
I looked all around me at wide open eyes,
watching in wonder at a display of such size.
Suddenly there was clapping along with loud cheers,
then sounds like thunder ran through my ears.
Again more amusement surprised all the crowds.
The blasts were like bottles that smashed in the clouds,
and the colorful fragments gave off a glow
that lit up the faces of the people below.
Then the lights slowly dimmed and we all walked away.
We brushed off the sand and ended our day.

William J. Merrell

Paper Messages

Open the mailbox
Rip open the fragile white paper
fringed in red and blue,
decorated with the exotic portrait of a hero.
Unfold and release captured sighs and deep shadows
into the light.

Uncork the bottle lying there in the sand,
Let the escaping warm and salty sea smell
fill your head with fancies.
Carry the treasure to a private place, then
unfold and release captured sighs and deep shadows
into the light.

Uncork the bottle, open the box,
All arrested time
standing heavy on your soul escapes
and trampolines around the room.
All of the hope of a window thrown open is yours.

Uncork the bottle, open the box,
Unfold the message and let the written words
wash upon your shore, again and again and again.

Pence Revington

Her Gypsy Heart

Brown eyes flashing, gorge arising,
Rivals bring forth blades with clashing.
Spanish señorita shaking tambourine and quaking.
"Will they kill each other heedless
that she dallies, nothing serious
in her make up, only memory,
lost friends dying painful suffering.
No, she will not let her guard down
to admit she has no heart left
after Holocaust of Hitler,
after ovens, gassing, torture.
Only Hungarian gypsy blood can save her,
if she let it raise her courage
meeting life head on — she won't perish.
Only friendship she once did cherish
leave old scars where hatred claimed them.
Epilogue: Is she having attacks of asthma?
or is it just the old miasma
of a lost lover, tragic, binding?
Her heart trembles, thawing, loving!!

Veda N. Steadman

Take A Walk

Inward and throughout
root hairs seek out
a flower grows.

Unpainted canvas unneeded
unbeautiful unknown
skinned over wet, oil paint, rainbowed.

enfolded in pure admiration undeserving love
gentle child peering into flowers
in a field of yellow daffodils.

Childlike love so blind, so forgiving,
blemishes, chosen to be unseen,
and I so full of these.

Muscle entwined fingers tenderly drawing
my heart to You strings detaching
a tug-of-war between want-and-need.

Fear of the forsaken road begging to be tread
'walk with me' a whispering plea
alas, I hesitate.
Take my hand and leaf, dear Friend this last time I give
for, oh, forbid I should turn again.

Shannon Dow

Contemplation

Death of sun
Birth of moon
While silence reigns supreme
In an empty room———-

Jim Brogan

Colors Like The Wind

Colors like the wind, blowing through the breeze.
Ruffling through the grass, and sliding through the trees.
Hurt and pain blowing away, with every single step it takes.
I'd do anything for the love it brings.

All your sorrow, all your pain,
Throw them away in the winds of change.
Let them blow all through the air.
All your sorrows, all your cares.

Hurt can last forever,
But love gives you only one chance.
So do your best, to beat the rest,
And you will live on, forever.

Colors like the wind, blowing through the breeze.
Ruffling through the grass, and sliding through the trees.
It whispers through the wind and rain, to take away all your pain.
I'd do anything for the love it brings.

Lisa Wolk

The Golden Comb

A little girl runs from the store carrying a golden comb,
Running, running quickly with excitement to her humble home.
The door opens wide, her hat is off; she shyly stares at her face.
Then lovingly, she combs her hair with poise and gentle grace.
Her eyes close, she feels the bristles dancing through her strands
As the weight of the golden comb is upon her delicate hands.
The reflection from the battered mirror casts a subtle glow
Of her locks, so rich like chocolate, along her back they flow.
The soft caress of the golden comb makes her hair bounce so free
Like a touch upon the waters of a calm and sleeping sea.
With each movement, her brilliant locks awaken from their rest
To show a maiden of beauty as they sweep along her chest.
She lays the comb by her side to reflect upon her day:
The mirror shows a girl of strength, lovely, warm, and gay.

Teresa G. McDill

Without Consequence

"Be a good lamb lest your soul go to hell,"
Said the reverend to his flock one day.
They cringed in fear at the power of his words
And bowed their heads quickly to pray.

"Be a good man, or you'll go straight to jail,"
Said the judge to the handcuffed teen.
They let him go, thinking he had reformed,
And he had... when he could be seen.

"Be a good girl, or you'll get whipped bad,"
Said the mom to her ten-year-old Sue.
Sue nodded and smiled and six years later
She told her own daughter that, too.

"Be a good player, or you're not my son,"
Said the coach to his basketball star.
They lost in state and next morning at eight
That boy was found dead in his car.

"Live your life well. Try not to hurt others,"
Was the lesson a man taught to me.
I grew up watching him, and turned into a part
Of the goodness he showed life to be.

Shana Smith

The Golden Rose

There's a golden rose that climbs along the
scented summertime that used to be.
Only silken petals fall as showers lace the
hours hiding love from me.
Barefoot through the sand of dreams my love came
running and her hands reached out to me.
And by the sea of ecstasy I knew a moment destiny
had saved for me.

Now the golden days are gone
Fame and fortune I've not won
and my love has gone away
But the golden rose of love I held one day.

Somewhere there is bound to be another
garden and a dream beside the sea.
A golden rose is waiting there and yes, a day
beyond compare in memory.
Just have the heart to find the way through all the
shattered yesterdays and you will see,
The sands of time have left behind the path that
one day led my love to me.

Wayne Brazeal

Yesterday

When I think back on my younger years,
Search my heart for the loves and fears
The memory of you is like a warm embrace
And all sense of time escapes.
The years lapse into yesterday
As if you never went away.
Once more we're together and I can see your face,
Feel your touch and taste your taste.
Feel your heartbeat next to mine
Hear your voice inside my mind.
Hold your laughter in my soul
And never let the dream grow old.
For although we're apart
We're forever as one,
And I'll be your friend
Until time is done.

Susan Villines

Autumn

Listen to the hush of silence,
Search the dark skies for a stillborn sun;
Smell the frayed petals of wilted rosebuds,
Feel the kiss of earth's icy breath.

Wind and rain no longer whisper
Of life and love but sigh and moan.
Trees blackly weeping cry
Brittle tears of dry brown leaves.

Birds chirp no more.
(Will you fly with them to some distant shore?)
Hold me close, give me warmth.
Speak to me in the language of summer.

Banish the doubts and fears;
Their coldness chills.

F. L. Agas

Untitled

There are no more broken men
Beyond the dream of life
There are no more crying children
And no more lonely wives.

Don Olweean

Someday...

Someday I'll be the person I want to be,
Secure in my knowledge of God and content to be me.
In the meantime I have a goal to always strive for
And try each day to get closer to the mark than the day before.
I always knew that there was a piece missing from my life,
But until recently all I really knew was conflict and strife.
Now things have improved and peace is starting to fill the void.
I realize I was wrong to turn and run myself trying to avoid;
For if you do not face yourself you cannot improve or grow
And you miss out on all the wonderful blessings
God wants to bestow.
It is not easy to depend on God but that's the only
way to be independent.
One must deal with the past but live in the present.
Learn to lean on God and let Him show the way.
Though things may not be great today contentment can be ours
today.

Rachael Merchant

Story Time

I fondly remember story time on the farm
secure in the warmth of my great grandfather's arms
he would ease his long, weary self into that big, old rockin' chair
then he would pull out his faithful pipe and tobacco
ever so slowly he packed his pipe
after he puffed a minute, he put me on his warm, oversized lap
in my tiny hands I carried a book
grandpa held the book in his giant hands
after reading two or three pages he would puff on that pipe,
filling the air with a sweet aroma
I loved grandpa's pipe, although I could never make it work
back to the story, two or three lines more
he puffed on his pipe again
the aroma taking over the room
I heard the creak, creak of the rockin' chair
the story is almost over, my eyes are almost closed
no more words, creak creak, smell of his pipe
tired little eyes close, secure in the warmth of my great
grandfather's arms

Renee Susanne Poynter

Isn't It Amazing What A Smile Can Do?!

Smiles! Smiles! Smiles, oh, how plentiful they ought to be.

Please God! Let everybody wear a smile for all the world to see!!

They will cure so many ills, imaginary, and real.
They will always make you happy no matter how low you feel!!

They are good for melancholy, and all other grievous things that be.
They fill your heart with gladness, and your joyful soul with glee!!

For some it's oh, so natural to put on a beautiful smile, but
for others they need to practice to acquire one after awhile.

Everybody loves to see a smile, no matter who's face they adorn!!
Even if the face is homely, it becomes lovely when a smile is worn!!

Of course our inner-feelings are reflected by our smile, and
God will bless us dearly if we wear one all the while!!

A lovely smile can perform miracles, and will energize a
failing will!!
It can rejuvenate the feeble, that are almost over the hill!!

Praise God, above all others, and let your smile reflect it.
You could be awarded Life Everlasting, and Paradise earth
perfected!!

If there were smiles on faces all over the world, not one
could possibly do, the godly things that please me like the smile
that is worn by YOU!!

Vollie R. Russell

Seasons

Autumn is the summer's end,
seems as if it follows a trend.

Leaves will shrivel and trees will die,
Bears will huddle and birds will fly.

Autumn is the beauty's bend,
something we just cannot mend.

Red, yellow, orange, colors galore,
for green, is no more.

Winter is here to stay,
Autumn has gone away.

Winter with it's slender ice and gentle snow,
seems to stop the path in which things grow.

Winter's calmness brings a sudden sadness,
But great white beauty and holiday madness.

Not to worry, all too soon, the slender ice
will turn to streams, as the white snow to greens.

Once again spring will strive,
to bring back all of the bright life.

Samia Naseem

Dreaming

In the sky I see a cloud that seems to me to be a lonely one, separated from the rest, just floating as clouds so often do in the winter or spring or whenever you please. And as I watch it seems to form a shape. Not a shape like some other clouds where you look into them and see a dog or an ice cream cone but something very different, something abstract and not at all easy to describe. It's as if this cloud could look into my soul and become whatever it is I most want to see, be it a dog or an ice cream cone or something abstract and not at all easy to describe like joy or peace or love. So we sit together for a while, this cloud and I, as I dream my dreams of joy and peace and love and the cloud floats as clouds so often do in the winter or spring or whenever you please with nothing better to do than make my dreams real.

Tony Dalessio

Alone

I feel so alone, left out, by myself, it's like I'm put upon a shelf
Set aside awaiting my turn, I sit and watch, while they all learn

Nobody cares, if I live or die, they tell me they do but I know it's a
lie should I go to them and ask them how come? Or will they look at
as though I'm stupid and dumb

I do need love, but where do I go, I try and find it, but they don't
know my world around me, all tattered and torn
I dread the day that I was born

I'll look inside my empty heart, and try to find where it all came
apart I'm so alone all by myself
Just sitting here upon this shelf

Patricia A. Wassil

22 October 1994

I searched all over, long and hard, down
many roads.

But only when I took a look deep inside
did I realize, that somewhere on my quest, I
had passed you by.

In an odd quirk of fate, my road turned to
lead me to the path that you had chosen.

And now, I pray that we will journey life's
byways, together.

Lisa LeAnn Loendorf

The Greeting

The air thick from morning fire smoke
settles in mid air as the pines quietly choke;
A young indian dresses in skins of deer,
entering freezing waters that rush along clear
The hands of a growing boy grasp a canoe paddle
in water of constant change he travels the middle
In the cross of rivers he chooses the hardest,
never knowing when will be his last
The sky is lightened by a winter sun
further down stream the slower river runs
Before opening to massive lake water flies an eagle,
screeching like a morning beagle
In that moment the young indian has made a life friend
whose spirit will be his own in the end.

Natalie Worley

A Voice In The Dark

As I wait for the coming of night,
Shadows trick my mind in the diminishing light.

They tell a tale of sorrow and strife,
A tale of love between a man and wife.

The spirits of night with phantom faces,
Twirl and dance with ghostly graces.

Such spectral visions awaken my mind,
And I have dreams of a remarkable kind:

A man whose eyes shone
With a luminous light,
Wonders at what had befallen his love
As he looks out upon the stormy night.

She was stolen away,
By one he called friend.
One who'd sworn his devotion,
Yet deceived in the end.

Is this man speaking directly to me?
Is his story meant for the world to see?

A man from another world, from another time,
Spelling out his legacy in the form of my rhyme.

Meghan James

Suzy's Special Stars

One night, a little girl looked up toward the heavens.
She asked, "When I grow up, I wonder what I could be?"
Her mother said, "You can be anything in this world. No . . ."
She stopped. "anything in this universe you want to be."

The little girl seemed surprised and turned back to the sky.
She gazed in wonder. Green eyes shinning like the stars above.
She didn't have to think long and then in strong voice said,
"I think I'll be an astronomer and study the stars I love."

School started soon. Her teacher helped her with her goal.
He told her that she must start early to do an organized plan.
High school came next and the dream grew so big and real
That she knew the direction was right and quite near at hand.

College was hard. Few women in her field who had gone before.
Times changed. New avenues appeared. She would pay the toll.
She would build the cameras instead of studying the stars.
A change from astronomer to physicist would satisfy her goal.

Life's a wonder for twenty plus realized years of her dream.
She is making her contribution to history's scheme of things.
We are blessed with dreams and if sincerely followed through,
Each day would be exhilarating like a fresh breath of spring.

Rita M. Smith

The Gift

She didn't understand, she was so very young.
She didn't know what the words meant that came from her mother's tongue.
She's always been so quiet, the one who's never spoken out.
She had a low self esteem, she didn't know how to shout.
Then someone showed her who she was, and what she could really be,
All the things people did that she could never see.
She couldn't see herself and what she really was,
All the sweet things she always says and does.
Now she doesn't mean to do this, they just all come out,
And she only speaks the truth in what she's talking about.
And now today she understand about the one thing she always did,
Even when she was young, she also did it as a kid.
The one true gift God gave to her from heaven up above,
She never gave up on anyone and she always knew how to love.

Megan Duran

An Ode To My Mother's 100th Birthday

To my mother, who shed's no tears
She gave of herself, for many years.
She struggled and saved thru out the depression,
To rear her children, without any concession.
A classy lady, in her time,
and now she's in love with father time.
One hundred years, of toil and strife,
and now she's just beginning her life.
So heres to your good health as before,
I wish you now, one hundred more.

William E. Hales

Her Life Has Gotten Way Out Of Hand

Her life has gotten way out of hand,
She has scrapped the bottom of the pan.
She is a young woman, but you can't tell,
She's had to endure her own living Hell.
What made her start alcohol and drugs?
What makes her hang on to life with that thug?
She came from a family who gave her all that she needed.
Now, they can't understand the awful way they've been treated.
She only calls her family when she is in trouble,
They pack her up and bring her home, then she burst their bubble.
She runs back to the same scum,
She doesn't even remember, that she has a son.
The drugs and her husband have more pull,
I don't understand this, to me it is bull.
I wish that I could pluck her up, and put her in a cell,
I'd dry the alcohol and drugs from her body and brings her back from Hell.
I wouldn't let her out no matter how much she cried,
'Til the poison was drained from her body, and that evil demon died!
But I understand that the healing has to come from her,
And until she admits there is a problem, there cannot be a cure.

Susan Purcella

Gifts Of Hell

Fairest gifts of hell, which only the devil posses
Such a horned, brutal, beast stands
only one whom cursed the sweet scented earth
to such a fatal dark doom,
dreadfully overcoming life, called death.
One who discovers death,
will close her eyes never to reopen.
Your sinful soul will silently sink into the earth's surface.
Down, Down, Deep into the ground.
The Boundless world of the devil,
whom captures souls filled with evil.

A. F. A. Alexakos

The Lady of the Sea

The Lady of the Sea
She is so beautiful and powerful.
The peaceful sound of her waves, as the tide moves in
Moving oh so so slowly a pace.

The Lady of the Sea
Can act so much like you or me.
She has her "good days".
The beautiful reflections of the glowing sun makes her dress glisten.
The Lady feels so warm and loving,
And oh how sexy and glamorous is she.

Just like you or me, the Lady of the Sea has those "other days".
When her anger needs to roar.
Her waves come violently rushing into the shore.
Such strength and such height, causing havoc does she.
The Lady of the Sea acts so unsettled and frustrated on those "other days".
Not as glamorous not as sexy is she.

However, the tide comes in again.
A new beginning for the Lady of the Sea.
Another day, another beginning.

Mary Carroll Ingamells

"A New Baby"

You have a new baby, so cuddly soft and cute too!
She is your first and as perfect as can
be. You knew the moment you seen her
you'd love her forever.
You bonded with her that very first
moment, you held her too! Now you'll both
see just how much joy your baby Ashley will be.
The sound of your voice will calm her when
she's scared.
Your touch will sooth her when she falls
and feels pain.
You know have a lot to loose but even more to gain.
Her smiling face and loving touch will let
you know just how much each of you mean to her.
In a while she'll be saying momma and dadda
and your hearts will leap.
But you'll calm down and that is when you'll
see how much joy your baby Ashley can really be.
The day she say "I Love You" will make
you so proud you'll sing out loud!

Michelle Denner Burns

Gretel Grown

The wizened old witch in her candy cane house,
She knows me better than I know myself.
I see her eyes,
They almost smile at me.
But this is serious
Her face is still, and dark, and wise:
she waits.

These fourteen years have left me wandering,
She knows I've lost the path
She sees my eyes,
The path is overgrown.
The crumbs I've left along the way
are gone.

The wizened old witch in the candy cane house,
My only hostel on this lonely road.
I enter now,
Her eyes are smiling.
But this is serious —
My face is still, and dark, and wise:
I weep.

Sharon Hauselt

A Loss Greater Than Gold...

He stood on the winner's platform, the world sprint champion.
She lay in a nearby hospital bed, dying of leukemia,
They had raced as children: these two and a brother.
Now there was just him.

Today was his big day, the call came early they say.
She had indicated he should race, her confidence in him deserved first place.
'His skates felt different,' he said.
You wonder what went through his head.

He took his place. 'REDeee.'
False start...now hesitant he had to be.
Gun up, he tried again.
But halfway through the bend,
he fell, sliding into the wall:
tripped Kuroiwa, and ended it all.

He held his arms high, and looked to the sky.
A loss greater than gold...
There's no more to be told.

Trevor Starnes

A Helping Hand

Can I help Grandpa?
She startled me,
Spying me in the garden
on bended knee.
Measuring out rows for crops to be.
Tina left her play and hurried up to me,
to say.
Mercy me! You surely care
I would love your helping hand
You've dressed for work you're in your jeans
Suppose we plant these row's in beans?
I drilled the holes, as we went along. She
dropped in the beans, with such good help
it didn't take long.
Can you think of a more pleasant way
to start a garden on "any old day" with
a little granddaughter who'd leave her play
to lend you a hand?
It made my day.

Robert Shepard

My Mother's Mother

My Mother's Mother has passed away, a generation gone today.
She took her last breath when we left the room,
Too proud to have us watch the gloom.
The life she led was short but full,
We stood strong and proud under her rule.

She has gone away from us now, as our heads take a silent bow.
We are left here now without her voice,
to carry on with our lives, we have no choice.

So into the ocean her remnants will lie.
as we stand in this cold water saying goodbye...
I am stricken with grief as the tide takes her away,
for I have said farewell to my Grandmother today.

I miss her severely and hope she is well,
as I look out over this place where her ashes will dwell...
She was tough in this life, always did her best,
and I hope in her death she can finally rest.

My Mother's Mother has passed away,
I guess there is nothing more to say.

Shawna Ellsworth

Suspicion

One rainy night, on August and three
She walked in, as beautiful as could be.

Fifteen years eleven wed
She accused me one night, of defiling our bed

Pink stuff on my shorts, pink stuff on my socks.
I don't know, it was a terrible shock.

Three months of yelling, three months of cussing
Every day full of nothing but fussing.

Our hearts were broken, our lives were shattered
Nothing more seemed to matter.

Harsh words flying, she said I was lying
I am completely faithful, so stop your crying.

The suspicion was gone, the trust is there
I promised to her, I will always care.

On May 20 '95, We repeated our wedding vows
With tears in our eyes.

Friends among us, God looking over
I gave her a kiss, and began to hold her.

Thank you God, each and every day
So Rhonda and I, can grow old and gray.
Your loving husband,

Randy

"Donna Amore"

I saw a lovely lady with beautiful soft eyes,
She was full of beauty and I was aflame with love.
A strange delight awakened in my soul such longing,
I was moved to tears and uncertain gentle sighs.

Tormented with happiness she bewitched my heart with pleasure,
I said to her: "If this is love how my heart aches."
On a white marble balcony filled with colored flowers,
She offered me her heart underneath the silent stars.

The wind soared over the earth and the heavens rested,
She burned the flame of love in my heart and my life.
Hand in hand we entered heaven softly opening its door,
She said to me: "You give me great love and a joyful heart."

I was a captive of her love in this holy place of joy,
My heart was carried to paradise as she had taken my love.
Overcome with passion our bodies trembled in embrace,
We kissed and became one spirit that melted the sun.

The burning passions of love are determined by the heart,
And the echo of a kiss can endure for all eternity.
Drowning in her beauty I looked into her loving eyes,
Then I said: "I will love you as long as forever and no less."

Marcia Schwartz

Nebraska

If Nebraska were a child
she would be spontaneous,
yet laid back.
The eyebrows of a few
would be cocked wondering about her.
With her sun-kissed skin and eyes of the palest blue
she would win the hearts of many,
but keep the heart of only one.
If Nebraska were a child
she would have long, flowing, golden hair
that shimmered beneath the harvest moon,
dancing in the crisp autumn wind.
Never wanting it tied back
for the fear of her spirit being trapped.

Nicky Haworth

Untitled

All the colors of the rainbow
All the magic of the sea
All the pureness of the flames
Are inside you and me

Katie Burmeister

Bitter Memories

Withered hands busily knit the sweater that will enfold him,
sheep's clothing, trap skin against wool against bitter cold.
Outside, the children build Frosty, three layers tall,
each mound proportioned slightly smaller; coal for eyes,
the last fuel for baking — she'll chop wood before bedtime,
cool steel wooden slivers; a huge carrot resembles
Aunt Bertie's nose; angled Italian style, Irish descent;
buttons from Granny's tea tin imitate a crooked smile;
Pa's pipe stabs the corner — corn husk from last season's crop.
She lays aside the yarn and needles, pulls the lace from the window,
spider webs, and recalls her own childhood; cold memories,
winters that engulfed her and five siblings, caged animals.
Breeches of burlap sacks, cardboard soles, bundled rags for mittens.
They too built snow people, entire families, as frozen as their own.
Coal, carrots, and buttons, too sparse, blank faces.
She wipes the window with her apron, ancient coal dust, defiled
virginity.
She looks beyond snow caps, a white sea of trees, smoke stacks,
village ghosts.
She envisions the cities beyond, blinding glitter, her childhood dream,
swan's dance: silk and taffeta, twirls of red and blue; winter's
bitter breath, tainted.
She returns the webs, unties her apron, washes away the blemishes;
dullness.

Lori Burks

Hungry Harlot

Like a clever jaguar awaiting in the shadows.
She's poised seductively in the moonless dark,
Clothed in masses of coifed midnight hair.
Prowling her territories searching for prey, the feline's
Tainted face and emerald eyes scan the quarry.
After she spots her victim like that base cat, she entices
The tender yearling to venture near her den.
The time is right — Pounce!
Like the weighted struggle between the cat and deer,
Her consorting inferior moans for a bit,
Until eternal sleep succumbs. Then as a huntress,
Her share she takes with belly full
And abandons the carcass for other's profit.

Sarah Ganiere

Nature's Babies

The apartment cast a shadow over the front lawn,
shielding the morning dew from the rising sun.
He glides by on silent steady feet,
never missing a single beat.
Most of he time no one
knows when he's around,
For no verbal sound can he make.
When human eyes have him in sight, he's
quite a delight for a toddler to behold.
He can blaze a trail all alone, unlike the
toddler who has to be guided home.
We both stop in our tracks looking the other over.
Was that laughter we heard as he crawled
over the dry grass left from the weekend mowing?
He's a baby we can tell by he's feet and
that small shell.
Turtle or tortoise to the naive it's hard to tell.

Melva Bryant

Time Out-Principles

Alive, human, problems, decisions and skill
Shows the great value of a person, if you will.

Remember the importance of human beings
Practice the principles you are learning.

Show an interest in your relationships
The good that comes will be evident.

Give people the space that they need.
That will allow you to follow or to lead.

Don't impose on others your expectations
It will improve your relations,

Life may not always be like Apple Pie
It can be bitter or better depending on the "I".

Peggy L. Bogle

memorabilia

torn pages of life,
shredded into the leaves of time,
being blown back to where they were first created
by the voices of the past.
running to catch one last glimpse,
as the fire arises from hearts
and burns the memories.
generations pass to pick
the flowers of your tomorrow,
their yesterday.
watch for the start of the circle,
around and around until
boredom strikes the souls of the young
with a mighty knife,
and the circle bleeds,
opening until all pieces are unrecognizable
by the first who started the long walk,
passing by the same troubled minds every time,
finally a page is turned.

Naomi Tarle

"The Other Side"

Where am I going, into or out of this seemingly endless pit? The sides, there are no sides, no top, no bottom. Where am I? I am constantly being drawn to the "OTHER SIDE"by something, but that can't be, there are no sides. As quickly as I was drawn to this "OTHER SIDE," I was thrown into a different direction, never reaching my goal.

I turn here, nothing, I turn there, nothing. What's going on? Who am I? Could it be that I was not meant to be, or that I'm just in the wrong place at the wrong time? Or, could it be, is it possible, that maybe, just maybe, I'm not at all?

Ron Derby

Love I Seek

One Time, I thought, it was unyielding.
Sleep, I must, to warm my heart...
I was not whole, I knew too dearly,
...the stars did rise, the dawn did break.

Love, I learned, was not for reaching.
Of those I watched, I felt ashamed...
To have someone, this was not for me,
...the hope they shared, was not to blame.

One night did pass, as like another.
A stir amidst, I had no clue...
A flicker of light, beamed through the darkness.
...awake, I did -that light was you.

Steven F. Roth

The Winds Of Time

A restless wind cries through the trees on an Indian summer day,
Sighing with nostalgia for time that's flown away,
Searching through the tree tops and underneath the trees,
Scourging every maple shaking autumn leaves.

Where's the children I recall playing in the brook?
The barefoot boy in old blue jeans with a healthy country look.
And where's the gal with the gingham frock skipping up the lane?
The one with pigtails laughing in the rain.
It must have been just yesterday or just a few days past,
Or maybe many years have flown since I have seen them last.

Oh, where have all the summers gone
And where's the shady nook, where's the flowered path
Leading to the brook?
Why, here's the girl, a mother now with children of her own.
And there's the boy behind a plow toiling in the fields of corn.
And there's another gingham gal laughing in the rain,
And there's a little barefoot boy;
Life circles 'round again.

Orva Lee McCarson Warren

Black Ice

I hear laughter and see happiness within his home, a sound and sight I have not heard in my house in such a long time that it seems to have been forever ago.

In his home I feel happiness, love, safety and comfort. When, in my house love is only shown by being yelled, pretended, or it is just cold and empty.

Within my home, having him by my side is like a drop of the love, the happiness and the virtues of his home, making my house a true home.

Until the coldness comes back, then we might as well have the Black Ice standing all around my house.

Still being with him I am happy. He has showed me love, he has showed me how to laugh and trust. I return to him my love and respect, that others have yet to earn.

Because Black Ice turns and pumps through their veins, around their stone hearts.

Ice cold are their thoughts, but mine are surviving, my thoughts are still pure, as my memories are being replaced with the memories of him.

Sarah E. Jordan

The Song Unheard

It's been summer and autumn, and almost winter
Since those beautiful creatures sang
Both their voices blended into one
Producing beautiful music that only they enjoy.
O, how lovely it was that wonderfully pleasant day
When beautiful music was made,
That echoed no sound or voice, but was displayed.
Beautiful creatures, pray ye, sing again!
Springtime will be here soon
And for you, together, new compositions make.

Those beautiful creatures will again engage
In the springtime, when all flowers bloom
There will be no restraint; but total surrender
For tickling fancies will be their domain.
How glad those beautiful creatures will be to again engage
In what echoes no sound or voice, but is displayed.

Sherilyn J. Savery

Cityscape

A cop sits in his patrol car
Sipping luke-warm coffee from a plastic cup.
A scrawny cat slinks across the dimly-lit street.
A neon bar sign makes a red gash in the night.

"Why am I here?
"Well, it's a job.
"It hurts when people call me `pig'.
"But then, I've always wanted to be a cop.

"It's awfully quiet — maybe too quiet,
"Like the other night.
"Dear God, please God, I pray
"I won't have to use my gun tonight."

Robert Kenneth Moorhead

Thunderhead at Sundown

It boils—as I fiddle,
sister picks her dulcimer and brother his banjo,
father strums the guitar and mother at her harp,
little Shara flutes along
with cousin Ian's sweet highland pipes.
Its steeples takes on gold—as the heather breeze
fills the air with happy Celtic quick notes
sending our wee people to dance about the green.
Its tower shades red—like wild roses spreading
within the lavender and blue bells upon the glen,
as food is gathered by Grandmother and Aunt Evelen.
It mirthfully lets down—amethyst legs
and fulgent flickering feet races to join us
with bass voice unites a trio to quartet.
It drums our shelter's roof—as we play on
enjoying its refreshing gift to the lea
and brook where the sprites dwell.
It bids us a farewell—as the last of the sun's rays
colors its song of good omen
with our musical rhymes.

Lillian F. Winks

These Dreams

Strange Dreams...In life it seems a major distraction;
Sleepy nightmares with odd people roaming about.

Friends and lovers take on an unrealistic air
And dreams go where the wakeful mind wouldn't dare.

Do you believe dreams to be of some meaning to our life?
Perhaps a premonition...a tale yet too be told;

Or could they be only memories mingling, converging and confused;
Our thoughts of yesteryears; A merging of our laughter and our tears?

Well, to me they seem to be the strangest fantasies
Of things gone by and things that I have yet to see.

Or maybe it's just entertainment that my mind creates
To keep my soul half asleep and half awake!

Martha Diane Ballard

I Am A River

My life is like a river: smooth at points, rough at others
but I still keep up with all my brothers.

Sometimes I move through life with the greatest of ease
and it makes me feel really pleased.

When it is rough, I say "Oh, no"
I feel like I will overflow.

Drifting, changing, growing...
Still never knowing where I'm going.

Aaron R. Ensinger

The Awakening Of An Orchestra

The sun begins to peak over the horizon,
slowly you begin to see his smile.
Then out of no where you begin to hear pretty song,
song by an orchestra of birds.
The smile becomes brighter and the songs become louder.
In the background you hear an instrumental,
the sounds of a crystal clear stream flowing down the rocks into a
enchanted pond where the fish wait to be served, listening.
Rocks begin to fall down the mountain sides,
drums, begin, to end the beautiful sounds of the orchestra.
The wind and leaves begin to clap, as the sun beginning to curl up
under the horizon to dream of what beautiful songs that will
be heard when he awakes.
It was truly the awakening of an orchestra.

Ron Weaver

First Day

Doors opening...
Small fry milling...hustle bustle...the beginning!
A delicate lad, diffident...
Potential caricature of the man yet to be.
(Poet, God called, sensitive, tender, caring)
Now hesitant, shy...the fledgling wanting its Mother.
Pushed from the tree.
Unknowledgeable of veritable treasures...
Not yet questing environs, unknown friends, or sharing.
"Good Morning, Children."
Authoritative voice...order demanding...instant silence.
Overwhelming a small tremoring body, searing it to the soul.
(The grown man remembers the trauma still-time cannot erase)
Being scrutinized...
Name pronounced...Theodore...teacher ogre, calling roll.
At last, bells ringing, yellow buses lining close...home bound.
Longed for Mother,
At the door, familiar eyes warm and steady.
"How was school?" Loving voice...bosom found...
"I only cried," Abashed he sobbed, "Because my name is Teddy."

Mary Bernice Plummer

Small Talk

It all started out as just a little
small talk,
Two people sitting together, passing
the time away.
But as they kept on talking,
She noticed how intense his eyes grew.
When he was deep in thought, and his
voice made her feel all shivery and alive.
And he realized that her laugh sounded a
little like bells, calling him closer,
and that her hair caught the sunlight
like a painting he'd seen once in a
museum.
It all started out as just a little small
talk to pass the time away, but
below the spoken words two hearts
were already whispering in a
language all of their own!

Teddy De Vore

Untitled

There was a rattle at the window,
but it was a tree branch rapping
against the window. Then there
was a thump thump on the floor, but
it was only my dog wagging his tail.
Then the door creaked, but it
was only my mom coming in to
kiss me goodnight.

Jez Kirkpatrick

A Little Extra

Throw a kiss... Catch another in your hand.
Smile that smile... he will understand.
You didn't forget... the message tucked into the
pocket of his coat.
Your brightest lipstick print...
and the enticing words you wrote.
You grin knowing... that packed
into his brown sack lunch.
Is a little something extra...
that will pack a little punch.

In your mind you see him
... a slow grin on his face.
When he finds his sandwich
...is wrapped in a bikini made of lace.

"I'll be working late" he had said
... as he was walking out the door.
So why aren't you surprised
... he's home at three minutes after four.

Sharon Freise

Lonely

I am so alone
so alone
it is not fair

When I look around all I can see is bare
I feel so sad
so sad
that no one's aware

Why can't I be glad
Is it because I'm scared

Help me make it thru today
Help me to remain completely sane
Help me understand why everything isn't okay

He knows what is in his heart
If he loves me then let him say it
Let him say it with graces

Lisa Clancy

Leap Of Faith

The young girl we met today
So full of anger and scorn
Is now opening her hand in a gesture
Her emotional state forlorn

Her revenge has a special purpose
Occluded only by a secret obsession
While the end of the sate, is driven by hate
Girl, you need to be taught this next lesson

Many before you survived
To evolve while keeping you alive
They grasp at the good, and discard the evil
The restoration of our family revived

So child take my hand when you're ready
And we'll help you take that hard leap of faith
It's your turn to be the successor
And carry on in your own special grace

Lynn Carmichael

"Dream Journey"

At night in my dreams, I have visions of you,
so soft and warm, so exciting and new;
I gaze at the water, as the moon shines down,
reflections of you, rise up from the ground;
The sun in the sky, as I look through your eyes,
beams through your hair, as my soul starts to rise;
As I reach out to hold you, I notice with a glance,
that you have fallen into a trance;
So as I pointed ahead at our destiny, I said,
"as we fly through the skies our souls must stay alive,
and wait for the master of our journey to guide".
Over looking the sky was the setting sun,
as a spectrum of rainbows, all spun into one;
molding and forming to the shape of a lamb
its thundering voice echoed, "here I am"!
so hand and hand, our journey began,
on a glowing frontier to forever land;
Our spirits became one as we escaped the night,
as our hearts united rising into the light...

Paul Dempsey

Heaven Is A Short Distance Away

Let me walk in thy shoes my friend,
So thy can rest thine weary feet.
The journey has become too much for thee.
I will carry thee on my back,
For heaven is a short distance away.

If thou should faint because of thirst,
I will give thee the last of my water to drink.
Should thou hunger for a bite of food, the rations
I have should sustain thee,
For heaven is a short distance away.

It is a long walk my friend,
Yet, heaven is a short distance away.
I will watch for stones in our pathway,
For these will be thy trials and tribulations.
Hold on tight, lay on my shoulder and rest now,
my friend,
For heaven is a short distance away.

Ray M. McKenzie-Martin

"Friendship Or Love"

I thought we were just friends.
So, what are these feelings I'm having inside?
When we're not together, I wish he was near.
I know I want him in my life.
He makes me feel so warm,
And no one has done that before.
I know we should only be friends,
But it's not that simple anymore.
Is it right to have feelings for someone older?
But how can it be wrong,
When these feelings come from the heart.
I know I have to do what's right.
But these feelings are true.
So, what do I do?
Should I go with what my heart says
Or toss these feelings aside?
What do I want?
Friendship or love?
With these feelings, I can't decide.

Shelly Kay Miller

Voice?

Crying death of the individual
Society blushes in glory

Enjoying tortured slavery?
Proud of bravery?
War crimes and immature death worth savoring?
How about tasty flesh flavoring
To garnish loved decay?

Have you ever gone on a guilt trip
All expenses paid by an optimistic enemy?
Felt jolts of fear-induced energy?

Have you ever confronted embarrassment?
Abandoned abandonment?
Gazed hypnotically through the soul of sentiment?

Do you weep, creep, and keep what you've found?
Do you bellow and yell without creating a sound?

Have you met yourself?

"'Tis what this chaotic sphere of military existence?
Ominous vibes of mass resistance?"
Curiosity lurks . . . and smirks . . . garbage pail perks
Garbage pail perks such finding
"Such findings."

Steve Flanning

Friends

Friends are like a thought.
Some are staying, some are floating by,
some stay, although should not.

Friends can benefit from you.
You can benefit from them,
or just simple love can bind you two.

Sharing is a friend like thing,
kindness is included.
Friendship is crucial, when hard times do seem.

Only with a friend may you tell a secret,
talk to them personally,
tell them your regrets.

A good friend, is to the end,
no secret can you keep.
For a true friend will always have his hand to lend.

Paul Garrett

Moon

You are much like the moon on countless nights.
Some nights you are bold and show your full self.
You look powerful, ready for the fight.
You beam so bright showing your inner wealth.
You fight to push back the darkness around.
You may not succeed but inside you're proud.
Some nights you hide and fight without a sound.
You shrink to a sliver hiding in clouds.
You are small and I search the sky for you,
And I know that you have lost to the dark.
Your pride is gone, you shrink away to new.
And now I wonder, ponder and then hark,
Why oh why, oh moon, do you come and go,
And why do you remind me of me so?

Terry Ryan

Gemini - The Twins

Bold brilliance of Sunday afternoon
Some novel award for not going insane after forty days and nights of violent skies.
Nothing really to show for it,
save a field of mushy ground and a group of water-smudged windows.
As in life, the reward comes later
hills turn green and scads of flowers bloom
to pollute the breezes with wishes and perfume.
The prize for a moment: a rainbow.
For a lucky few,the spectrum of colored light presents a kind of hope;
a momentary twitch that falsifies the belief that there is a pot of gold.
On a rare day when sun shines through misty breezes
a double phenomenon - somehow less awesome,
One rainbow more radiant than the other.
One downcast by its twin.
Her dazzling beauty pales in comparison.
Tends to distort the idea of hope - even though both know the same sun and moon.
Just as the faded rainbow, the down shodden twin must strive to be noticed.
She continues to reach for bluer skies, stretching the hope for her own pot of gold.

Nicole Eccles

There are many ways to face the world.
Some stroll blindly
denying anything they cannot explain
others fear what they do not understand
thus hide in what is comfortable.
Some bang there head against a blunt wall
leaving no visible dint.
Others sneak, subvert, or tunnel.
Anything to save themselves which in the
process loses any value they once had.
Others follow the crowd rather than their conscience
because the first always speaks loud and
the second only speaks the truth.

Better to be a Howard Roark
than a Holden Caulfield
both have a shared vision
one is overwhelmed
the other takes responsibility
for self and than lives accordingly.

Robert D. Longo

Wishes

A wish is like the weather;
Some turn out and some don't.
Some wishes turn out hopeless,
But others prob'ly won't.

'Cause when you set your mind to something,
You know that you won't fail;
Though wind and rain might block your way,
And sometimes even hail.

But someday all your work pays off;
You may be young, you may be old.
But after the storm, at the end of the rainbow,
Your wish is a pot of gold.

Sarah A. Bennett

Weeping

It seems almost as if it's crying,
As the wind blows through its branches,
Like a lonely widow
Crying for companionship.

Kelly A. Simmons

Love

Love is like a river, or like a waterfall.
Sometimes it's high, sometimes it's low,
And sometimes it's not there at all.
It's something you can dream about and often fantasize.
A hope for a companion with passion in their eyes.
Of course, it has its negative, side, when love does not appear.
It sometimes will upset you, you might even shed a tear.
When love becomes desire and your heart ignites a fire,
You know that you're in love and your heart sings like a dove.
But when that dream or that desire becomes an empty lie,
It tears your self esteem in two, it causes your hope to die.
When you're in love you know that you want someone's love returned.
It raises your love into something new
Towards the love for which you have yearned.
Your heart knows when you have love and attraction to another.
You know that they're the love, and that there is no other.
It comes and goes unexpectedly, it fades away so easily.
It will ever be a mystery.
No matter where you go or what you do,
Love will be there...always.

Pamela Morris

The Search

Along the way paths you'll find
Sometimes the journey seems so unkind
You make your way or you follow the plan
You search for freedom in a barren land

There's a mountain top just out of reach
If you happen to touch it you'll see a higher peak
And climbing upward it's doubtless you'll fall
Don't let it stop you it's just part of it all

Without the mountains there would be no peaks
Without the challenge there'd be nothing to seek
Without the search we'd never find
Sanctuary or peace of mind

Nina S. Lyne

Racism

The names people are calling each other
Sometimes we forget we're all sisters and brothers
My friends and I don't think it's fair
You an hear those names anywhere
Killing because of other races
Or just because they don't like their faces
Hitler and the Ku Klux Klan
Get rid of others that's their plan
Playing these foolish games calling people racist names
Martin Luther King Jr.'s I have a dream speech
Sadly some people it didn't reach
Most people now feel racism is very real
Not many people love to hate
But those who do think it's great
some of the victims come to a horrible end
Just because they were trying to be a good friend
It shouldn't matter the race, religion
color, or culture of your friends
Civil rights activists won't be able to
exist peacefully 'till this hatred finally ends

Lauren Maxwell

Friendly People

Thank God for friendly people we see from day to day,
sometimes we meet them in the market as we stand in line to pay.
Thank God for the cashiers who very often will say,
Thank you very much and have a nice day.
Often when I am shopping as I go into a store,
some nice young man will step a side to let me in the door.
I thank God for the fathers who must have had a hand,
In teaching such a nice young guy what its like to be a man.

Let's not forget the mothers whose work is never done,
Think how proud she must be to have him for a son.
And some times one may pause a while and have a word to say,
These little chit chat now and then will often make my day.

Thank God for friendly faces who will often lend a smile,
It really lifts my spirit if only for a while.
I feel very fortunate to live in such a place,
where I can often look around and see a friendly face.
Lets thank God for our blessings whether they are large or small,
To learn the art of friendliness is a lesson for us all;

Marie Gresham

"A Shadow Of Heart"

There are times I'm lonely and blue
Sometimes when I'm thinking of you
You have always been my shadow
Giving me love and lots of care
When I am in need of your help
You make yourself available and there
When I am sad you make me smile
You talk sweet things for a long while
When times come that I seek your advice
Where my decisions would be rolling the dice
You listen with open ears and a heart
And help me know my options part
At other times there is no shadow or sun
I stand in the cold, I am the only one
These are the times I am lonely and blue
The times I am thinking of only you
Thinking of you, because you are not with me
My shadow is missing, I'm blind and can't see...

Michele M. Barks

World Of Sadness

There is this world I can not find,
Somewhere in it there is a life that once was mine.
The world I'm in is a place of sadness,
Everyone in it has a time of madness.
I searched and searched, yet nothing was to be found,
All that was in sight was that cold damp ground.
It seems as if there is no right door,
And my hope is lost and exists no more.
Every path I took led the wrong way,
Failure passing by my face every single day.
No more can I bare this life,
I give it up, don't I have the right?
I guess it doesn't matter anymore,
For now I'm standing at the foot of the shore.
And as I looked out into the sky,
I realized the only way out was to fly.
So I let my soul escape from me,
And beyond this world I was able to see.

Lisa Ann Comiskey

Never Changes

Within the temple of God
Space exist within itself
Where is god? Where is God?

Within the temple of space
God exist within himself
Where is space? Where is space?

Within the temple of God and space
God exist in space and space exist in God
Where is God in space and where is space in god?

Within the temple of God, space and matter
God and space exist in matter and matter exist in God and space
Where is God and space in matter?
Where is matter in God and space?

Within the temple of God, space, matter and light
God, space, and matter exist in light
Light exist in God, space and matter.

Light changes to matter, seen and unseen
And matter changes to light, seen and unseen.

As space never changes, neither does God.

B. H. Marcroft

Untitled

You are one, of a delectable spirit; you are seasoned with sweet spices and bitter herbs. The aroma is often strong yet pleasant. The taste is spicy never bland. You have a hint Of being overbearing, which in you is a state of being masterfully aggressive. There's a Shade of insolence that peeks out every now and then, not giving the quality of rude Disrespect but rather the presence of too strong a will. You have the quality of being Mentally overpowering, and yet seemly, can be mentally overpowered. Your presence is Delicious to the eyes, you are flavored with an atmosphere of sweet charm. Yet, dare to come close every now and then, you might get a sting of stagnation, a raw view of truth. You appear to be capricious, I say your whims are no more than the (God-given) four seasons, Each having
their own aura of wonder! You are quite august, a noble statesman, a Chivalrous creature, spirited, valiant, intriguing man, and behold, every now and then Peeks out a timorous, mischievous nature of mother's little boy. You appear to have Stepped out of the century of gallantry, perhaps a swash-buckler. You have been seasoned By the ancient of days. Dare not to let the rain of common men spoil the delectable work of The potter's hands. For such is sought out (desiring) to be destroyed.

Michelle Hayes

To Poem-Forest In The Yin-Chuen Botanic Garden

Under the immense northern sky, solemnly,
standing the Great Wall.

The City of Yin-Chuen, surrounding by
serene rivers and mountains tall.

Fur goods are gathering, piling and selling
all over the steaming markets,

While in the National Botanic Garden,
beautiful flowers and trees sprawl.

Numerous rock tablets are elaborately engraved
with rhythmic lively poems and songs,

Cheered up with the laureate friendships, the
grasses are puffing fragrance and call.

The faraway moonshine of Tung-Ting Lake,
shines over the Silk Way too;

Even the heart-beatings of cross-the-ocean,
sounds like from next door.

Richard S. E. Den

Beauty In Christ

Your personal possessions may not make you rich according to the
standards of this nation,
Nor bring you into the limelight with the social and the elite.
But what God has given to His children since creation
Is the only riches you will ever need to be complete.

The salvation of Jesus Christ that shines through and through
From the crown of your head to the soles of your feet,
Crying out in praise with a song of victory so true
Making you want to shout His name up and down the street.

I can see Jesus in your eyes. I can see Jesus in your heart.
What a vision God shows me of your joy: Thank you, Lord!
Oh, how I pray that from Him, you would never depart,
But allow to be sufficient, that love within you that He has stored.

So when those trials and valleys, they do appear
You may cast your eyes to the heavens so high
And with confidence, know there is no need to fear,
For it is Jesus you can see, coming through the Rye.

So continue with this beauty, which, to you He has given.
Believe in it, both inside an out.
Let it shine forth through all your livin'.
Shout it to the world, "Jesus is alive! There is no doubt."

Walt Parry

"Blowin' In The Wind"

Waitin' on a train that never comes.
Standin' on my feet that never run.

Driftin' all alone, I sit and stare...
Livin' on my own without a care.

Never walked a mile I couldn't bear.
Always took the chances no one dared!

When I saw your face, I knew it then...
You could taste the wind like this old friend.

Couldn't stand to watch you walk on by...
Had to toss that look into your eye!

Madness feel ore me when you just stared...
Blowin' in the wind, parting the air.

Must have been a vision in the night...
Night owl took to flight beneath the light.

Moon was shinin' brighter than a star...
Just like the cold steel of my guitar.

Played a little tune for you and me...
Midnight riders lone upon the sea!

Glidin' through this universe alone...
Like a King and Queen without a throne.

Robyn Murray

Hurricane Notes

Oh little candle glow
Steam from the coffee below
Spiraling, transparent ribbons flow
Winding, reaching, meeting smoke of the cigarette aglow.

Oh little steeple, cone
Dark against the great, blue dome
Opposite, contrasting tones
On this night so hurricane owned.

Oh thrusting wind, blow
With raging tantrums, throw
Calm, quiet and silent night known
Into the morning, after the mighty storm's gone.

Reba Wauford

Prejudice

She said, "ain't nobody gonna
stare at them, when they walk
into General Store."

He said, "you ain't gonna see them
going to the back of the city bus,
just because they're different from
everybody.

She said, "ain't nobody gonna call them names,
and obscenities. Because of the color of their skin.

He said, "They ain't never gonna
know of words such as: BIGOTRY
SLAVERY, and HATE. Because those are
their words of hatred and ignorance.

I'll always remember what he said,
what she said, what they said.
Because they're my parents, George
and Olga Welch.

Taja M. Welch

Maker Of The Stone

Often in the evening, sitting all alone.
Staring at the mountains, majestic castles made of stone.

Constructed by the Creator, the Maker of the Stone.
The castles so majestic hold secrets untold.

Why the Maker calls some to Him and leaves others all alone,
I was left alone to challenge the wisdom of the Maker of the Stone.

Shared her love for me, then answered up his call
Her love for me never faltered, like the stone castles that never
fall.

Often my mind drifts back over the misty years of time
Of how another set beside me, her gentle hands entwined in mine.

The early years, the happy years, a full life sublime.
For forty years her memory still not faded, by slowly passing time.

Sitting here without her-alone. Asking questions, seeking
answers,
from the Maker of the Stone.

Robert L. de Timmerman

Lovers

She was a woman dreaming awake
stars were shining in her eyes
Always wishing, like an infant
to be cradled
in embrace of many arms

He was a man with a lot's of courage
living for nothing, but happy days
He thought he could both eat and keep his cake
and burn the candle on both ends

TOGETHER-
and it was than "now or newer"
they slipped out of their body
and left it look like one who dies
But their spirits
alive forever
were sailing to freedom
on the sea of stars ....

Marta A. Prochazka

Ode to the Ladies of the I. C. U.

In this modern world of ours
Steeped in physical and emotional scars,
Stands an army of angels, tried and true.
Steadfast ladies of the I. C. U.
They heed not fashion or gems so rare.
Only compassion for the soul in their care
Ever alert to the cry in the night.
Their primary purpose always in sight.

God created this special breed.
For he saw in this world, a desperate need
Man should be aware, of the tasks that you do
All the more he would appreciate you.
So hold your heads high, be proud of your profession.
From your dedication, we could all learn a lesson.

William N. White

Cowboys Future

A tumble-weed moves over the plains powered by the wind,
steered by the rocks and land.
Where it is headed no one knows;
When will it stop tumbling who can say.
In it's early life, it was green with spirit reaching for the sun.
Today, it has no future and is just in the way.

A Cowboy is much like a tumble-weed.
He is driven to his life-style by a unseen force.
He is steered by the land and the fences.
A cowboy doesn't known if he has a future
And is not sure where his future is headed.
He was once the back bone of a growing nation;
Today he has no future and is just in the way.

Tomorrow's cowboys will be men on steel horses with rubber
hoofs.
Cowboys will be replaced by men in laboratories with white coats.
The pastures and steams the cowboys called home
will turn into concrete, grass, and steel trees.
A life style of the past has no place in the present.
Today is the future and the past is in the way.

Travis A. Martin

Striker, A Friend

His coat the color of cinnamon toast over a lean frame,
Striker's Jeep was his registered Appaloosa name.
With chipmunk cheeks and liquid brown, intelligent eyes,
He gazed on his new world under cold January skies.
He was green as I, and just as scared: neither of us knew if riding
could be fun.
We broke the rule that intoned, "Never place a novice on an untrained
stallion!"
Trust we built as piney woods we explored, with Ray on Chief as our
lead
Stepping over logs, sniffing flowers, crossing creeks when there was a
need.
With daily grooming and exercise and practice rides in the show ring
Striker learned and improved and soon was Windy Hill Stables' king.
He grew quite adept and when show time drew near
We were the bareback riding champions that year.
One hot Georgia summer, on a two day wagon train, I felt the most pride
When unsuspecting people asked, "He's a stallion?" at the end of the
ride.
As fifteen years rolled by, his manners grew ever more exemplary
Twelve foals called him their sire; most of his traits they carry.
Striker became one of my best friends, his sudden death a sad blow.
Now my gentle companion waits in heaven; together we'll ride
again, I
know.

Libby Torbush

Untitled

Feel you in my gaze,
study moves, unnoticed reactions, touch
skin, soft, tender velvet, eyes invite,
smile consents, afraid. Say its ok. Do I
dare. Not this day, now or never, have to
walk away...

Endless conversation.
Time slips bye never can keep track.
Dream make love, waterfall backdrop, endless
treasure, bodies twist, water steams in
our mindless bliss.

Real world hear again
stiff, hard reality. Can't get out of bed.
Fight off phone calls, rock on my brain
(Rock meaning pimple just encase you
wondered)

J. C. Reinhardt

Love's Chisel

To wait and still to wait.
Such a loud silence it makes!
I'd like to scream aloud with blaring haste into
This silence through which I wait.

How can I tell you I was once where you are?
Locked in silence and fear, yet wanting to share.
Someday it will come like thunder cracks!
Never again to be held back.

My chisel is sharp with love's edge.
Slowly whacking, chipping, endless beating.
Eventually to knock a hole through
To let the sunshine of sharing come in.

Let go and Love Again!

Mary K. Thuresson

Time

When I feel like crying but I don't know why
Such a meaningless life, just passing me by
I'm starting to feel lost I have no where to go
My troubles are coming down like a blizzard of snow
My heart is beating like it's going to explode
My mind keeps reminding me, I'm all alone
No one can see me, I'm not really here
My hands are all shaking trembling with fear
Exhausted, I am but not can I sleep
For my brain is the playground for my problems to creep
Leave me alone, I wish they would
But deep inside it's understood
Memories once had can never be erased
We are all victims of that one endless chase
TIME

Teresa Sharp

Away But I Love You

Once again away from you,
but in the stars the sky stays blue.

The thoughts of love will hit my mind,
thoughts of a sweet girl I left behind.

Though once again I'll be away,
since in your heart I couldn't stay.

I promise though my love is true,
cause in the heart I'll always love you.

Jimmy Quiroz

Dreamlike Sleep

Pouring over the black; wheels constantly spinning.
Sun creeping up the windshield.
Head contacting vinyl, unintentionally snared,
eyes now disclosed to world.
Verdant hills robed in green,
not on a long car trip.
Signs I once would've noticed are not there now.
A mountain capped in snow.
All I can see
is the beauty of the surroundings cavorting through my head,
captivating me wholly.
Startlingly awoken, as if to a shocking jolt.
Dusky grey shadows overcome dull buildings
now composing our surroundings.
Building after building like a funeral procession.
My happy dream has vanished completely.
No longer a part of me,
it is gone forever.
I know I will doze again.
I ignore your warnings and let my eyes slowly close.

Scott Miller

April In The Country

The white, billowy clouds above, with backdrop of azure blue sky;
Sun playing peek-a-boo behind fluffy boats sailing high.

New life bursting forth; the warming earth beginning to green;
The persistent drone of tractors dicing; seeding: A familiar scene.

Stark gray and black outline of trees, breaking forth into bud and leaf;
Coats and jackets shed, barefoot children bounding in gay relief.

The frolicking of baby calves in the pastures no longer brown;
New born pigs, frisking colts, gentle lambs, and leaping goat kids, abound.

The call from the geese formation above, flying north from wintering land:
Their uniform flapping and gliding a part of their Maker's plan.

Birds happily warbling and chirping, giving forth to God their praise,
Adding their notes of cheeriness to brighten our busy days.

Ruth Stimson

She

There She stood gowned in Virginal White.
Sunlight glistening like a million diamonds on her breast.
Poised, regal, shy and yet
There is more to see.

Like a young nymph in shades of green.
Flowers adorn her head like a royal crown,
Free of spirit, innocent, pure
But the future holds more.

Spirit high, dressed in red, red rose.
Garlands of flowers stream down her breast.
Feet unshod walk in meadows green.
Who could know the rest.

Abandoned blithe in hues of orange and brown.
Tattered dress about the knees
Gypsy lady who would be queen,
Stand proud to the end.
Giah, Goddess, Mother Earth
You will start once again.

Patricia Anne Melville

The Soft Silence In The City

There is a soft silence in the city.
Sure the cars are racing,
the people are talking, laughing,
the music is blaring from the cafe'.
It is all so beautiful so beautiful.
And beneath that is the tip toe sounds of feet disguised by
gutter noises and car horns beeping at one another rhythmically.
No one heard the bang,
Maybe a few, but no one turned a head.
Then there was that soft silence...
and no one mourned the death of the young boy.
Whispers disguised behind newspaper and coffee cups daunted and gasped
"He must have been a drug dealer."
"He must have been one of them."
No one bothered to find out his name,
and the music still blared from cafe'.
People still laughed and murmured on.
That night I walked home in silence,
and listened to my own footsteps on the pavement.

Melissa Lantz

Hopeful

Lost as a youth with nowhere to go, I learned to
survive the game; with no emotions left inside me an
no remorse, I looked all around me trying to find away.
Away out to release myself from all this DYING RAGE.
Turning away for the first time everyone seemed
mystified by my actions, leaving them with nothing left
to say. Making me to wonder, if this is how the world
should really stay. Still I feel somewhat helpless knowing
that it can all be changed if we all just came
together and spent a little time to pray.
Things would change, they would have to change leaving
all the misery and pain to be washed away with the tears
in the foreseen rain. Sin after sin washing away, the
feeling of belonging is here to stay. The last cry that
everyone will hear today will be happiness; for the pain
will all to soon be forgotten with the past of the DYING
RAGE.

Ramon Essex Garcia

Fallen: To The Lost Angels

With the sickness: Loss of immunity, of spirit,
sweating night blackness dripping from the ceiling,
groping in the dark, blind hands seeking,
they discover time and the ultimate wall,
feeling terror of alone,
crying in the arms of the mattress-

Hospitals with sterile gauze glances,
bodies decayed, sunken into their own depths,
terrible smell of rotting life,
visitors are frightened by the shadows,
and never return-

Falling through dreams of disturbed color,
screaming brains cannot bear the burden of realization,
alone at night, the darkness vast and incomprehensible,
dying memories of sunrises-

They cling desperately to the dissonant light,
children needing their mother,
the fading leaves a tormented emptiness,
that neither prayers nor screams will purge.

Empty eyes of pain are their reality.

Scott Bennett

Languishing

Oh! the pains of age.
Sweet, sweet youth,
how I long for thee.
You once embraced me with your strength
and drugged me with your scent.
How I long for thee, you once befriended me.
I know not when,
but now I miss you once again.
Come! and sit by me, here, by my side,
whisper in my ear of times gone by,
tell me thine secrets of life everlasting.
Whilst I long sleeping your love ever wanting.
Give thou me thine breasts to suck,
sweet vanity's elixir of life.
Come my fair maiden, enter my dreams,
escort me to heaven's home of the King
Bring all of your wonder
and precious moments a fleeting;
that I grow not somber
Eternally sleeping!

Leopoldo Dorantes

Take Me When You Go

Fancy drifting to the past and hear the rooster crow.
Take a trip to yester-year but take me when you go.
We'll sit under the apple tree like we did when we were young,
pick up a fallen apple that fell from where it hung.

Lie in the grass beside the brook and watch the honey-bee,
then bite the apple sweet and warm...but give a bite to me!
Travel back to long ago when we ran in naked feet,
and heard the song of the whippoorwill...but take me too my sweet!

We'll catch the blinking firefly when the moon is hanging low,
My simple soul is singing....Take me when you go!
Dream away the loneliness thru the pathway of the mind,
fly my love to the furthest star....but don't leave me behind.

I'll wear a diamond dewdrop, and flowers in my hair,
and the smile of an angel-dreamer....for that's what dreamers wear.
We'll sing all the songs of Venus as we lay where ripples flow,
'neath the pattern of the apple leaves,....oh, take me when you go!

Lavonne McLean

The Mystery Of Oneness

Come
Take my hand and allow me to softly subdue your personal space
(the mystery of oneness)
Lost inside a dream of you belonging to me and I belonging to you
(the mystery of oneness)
Eclipsing each others Energetic Silhouette
(the mystery of oneness)
Exclusive Completeness Penetrating every fiber of your form
(the mystery of oneness)
Arousing Passions to a MAGNITUDE of
TRAN-SCEN-DEN-TAL MET-A-BOL-IC MAGIC

MET-A-MOR-PHIC
Falling like stars from the Sky
EMBRACING
THE MYSTERY OF ONENESS

Miriam Renee Smith

Wish

Chase a star my friend,
Chase it's fire and chase it's light.

Chase a star my friend.

Please make a wish for me.

Christopher Knight

Discrimination

When you think you are better than others you see
Take the time to ask yourself, "Can this really be?"
Why do I feel I can look down on you?
For reasons in my heart I have accepted as truth.
Maybe it's your looks or the way you walk
And I really can't understand it, when you talk.
Maybe it's your size; 'cause you aren't very thin.
And I surely don't like the color of your skin.
So maybe if I deny you the opportunities you seek
You'll abandon your dreams and you will grow weak.
For instead of embracing your life with dignity
You'll be stripped of your resources and any financial liberty.
If discrimination is allowed to exist in this life
We have nothing to look forward to but pain and strife
I would rather extend a helping hand to another
And walk by your side; we are sisters and brothers.
For together we stand and divided we fall!
And what's on the outside doesn't really matter at all.
For the content of my heart and character, you see
Is my real contribution to all humanity!

Michelle Maria Perkins-Heard

The Robbing Of My Grandpa

So unfair, so unkind
Taking a great man before his time
I wasn't asked if I was ready
Even though I was carrying the first great grandbaby
Angry because there was nothing I could do
As he died before me, I didn't have a clue
Not understanding why this took place
Failing to recognize heavens grace
Traumatized by it all I finally saw
How fortunate are we
That God is not as selfish as me
Because without the death of his son
Salvation for us all would be none

Melissa Walker Neal

Angel's Cry

Why must I awake to the sound of sobbing angels,
  Tears falling from the heavens above,

They know the love that lies deep within her heart,
  They go mad with that knowledge,

I ask thee dear Angels, show me the lovely lady you cry for,
  Reveal to me what lies behind her most sacred door,

I beg you, share with me a glimpse of her soul,
  Blinding light, a touch of sorrow,
    So much love and hope for tomorrow,

Eternal bliss, a poet's sigh, a lady's kiss, an angel's cry,

Forever haunting me throughout my days,
  Oh lonesome-lonely shadowed heart,
    Cry out with me this winter night,

Show me the lovely lady you weep for,
  For her love to death I'll fight,

Reveal to me her radiant beauty,

Eternal bliss, a poet's sigh, a lady's kiss, an Angel's cry,

The sound of sobbing angels rings out through the morning air,
  They know the love that lies deep within her heart,

  They go mad with that knowledge.

Weldon Largen

"40th"

Cheers its been 40 years,
Tears no one hears.
Tears for happiness, may
God bless this class of M.H.S.
We've had our ups, and we've had our downs,
We live in other states and other towns.
We have came far, and we have came near,
and some of us live right here,
to celebrate this 40th year.
Soon we will depart and go our separate ways
remembering the good old days,
and before too long down the ways,
there will be another countdown to the days.
It's that time again, grin and pack,
we are on our way back.
Class of 52, I love you.

Phillip D. Keele

Baby

I want to have a baby,
Ten fingers and ten toes,
Wherever I lead my baby will be sure to go.

If I have a girl she will be so fine,
With the biggest bow,
The prettiest dress,
They'll all know she's mine.

If I have a boy,
So handsome he will be,
He will not only be sporty, but sensitive,
Just like me.

To have a baby this is what I pray,
May my baby be strong, healthy, and beautiful,
God please send my baby right away.

Stacie Meadows

My Friend

I have a friend worth more to me,
  Than pearls that lie beneath the sea.
She's never said an unkind word,
  And often praise of her I've heard.
She's always there whene'er she's needed,
  And never a call she hasn't heeded.
This friend of mine is really a honey,
  She turns my gloomy days to sunny.
This friend grows dearer every day,
  Enough about her I cannot say.
A friend like her, I'd never find another,
  You see, this friend happens to be my Mother.

Ruth L. McAfee

Betrayal

I would that love had died of sheer neglect
  Than see it strangled like a frightened child;
The trees are tall around us and the starless night.
  Howls on its sightless journey shrill and wild.

Despair beyond all grief, a grief beyond all pain
  strips back the tattered curtains, whistles at the door
Breath in the nostrils is a senseless, screaming thing,
  And human dignity a heap upon the floor.

This is the echo of a shattered dream,
  A whirling spiral in the center of a cloud.
The empty world without and silent core within
  Look on with staring eyes and shrunken heads
unbowed.

Thelma G. Nunley

I Thank God

Thank you my Father for being there
Thank you for a mother who cares
Thank you for sunny days and rainy nights
Thank you for all togetherness, blacks and whites
Thank you for the summer breezes and the water that freezes
Thank you for my sisters and brothers
Thank you for all good mothers
Thank you for the children who can't hear
Thank you for others who love them and find them dear
Thank you for the birds that fly
Thank you for the blueness of the sky
Thank you for allowing me to be me
Thank you for the silence of the trees
And thank you Father for the ability to see all things around me

LaMara W. Hicks

Thank You Jesus

Thank you Jesus for your love that you've given to me
Thank you Jesus for your mercy that is always so free
Thank you Jesus for dying in calvary's tree
Thank you Jesus for what you've done for me.

Thank you Jesus for your grace that you've given to me
Thank you Jesus for your love that is always so free
Thank you Jesus for your blessings I see every day
Thank you Jesus for what you've done for me.

Thank you Jesus for your life that you've given to me
Thank you Jesus for the cross that has set me so free
Thank you Jesus for your caring for all of my sin
Thank you Jesus for what you've done for me.

Thank you Jesus for the mansion you've built there for me
Thank you Jesus for heaven where I'll always be free
Thank you Jesus for making my life full of joy
Thank you Jesus for what you've done for me.

Lee Stuck

To Mom...A Special Mother

Written for my mother, Liz Clark

I once met a woman, so beautiful and kind
That cared deeply for her children, and let her love shine.

She opened up her arms with the purest of love,
even when her grief-angered children just pushed and just shoved.

Through tough times and heartache, through happiness and praise, her love for them never lessening, it was more love that she gave.

No matter what might happen, she always makes it clear,
her love she'll always give us, and our hearts she'll hold so dear.

No one that I know, has experienced a true unconditional love like this. They don't know what they're missing, an overwhelming, emotional gift.

The woman that I cherish, no other can compare,
her life filled with many challengers, even the hardest were done with care.

The reason she so special and for her I deeply care,
she's my one and only mother, and one as great as her is rare! HAPPY MOTHERS DAY

Marie Katzenberger

Still

I was crying so loud
That I couldn't hear you say
"Be still"

My eyes could only see the darkness
I couldn't see your light

My pain was so strong,
That I could not feel your gentle, loving touch

But
Still you stayed
Still you held open the door
Still your love enfolded me
And you carried me

You held on to me until
I finally heard your voice
"Be still and know that I am God"

Mary A. Ambrose

I Wish...

I wish I hadn't been told that warm day last June,
that I had the big "C"-what an unhappy tune.

I wish that my children numbered more than two,
when I had my second baby, it was my last-but who knew.

I wish the Cancer, the chemo, the radiation and such,
had treated me more gently, and not made another baby too much.

I wish the last time I held my second newborn in hand,
I would have known then another baby could not be planned.

I wish I had cherished each second that they cried and we snuggled,
I wish my first child was a newborn-as a new Mom I was puzzled.

I wish the clock could be turned back and again I could have,
the feeling we all lack until a baby is had.

I wish Vinnie was new, and Micaela yet to be,
I wish my children could number at a minimum three.

The Cancer's about gone now, but giving birth-it won't be,
I wish I had hurried 'cause now I'd have three.

Two beautiful babies I have to watch grow,
but if you're a Mom, then my feelings you know.
To be told "no more babies," it just breaks my heart,
I wish one more babe I could have from the start.

Tina Famiglietti

Death

Death is when a loved one, friend, or someone
that is close to you is shot and killed or
died from a disease or just natural causes.
Why does death hurt so much? Why do
people have to kill another person just out of
jealousy or revenge or because of a jacket they
can't pay for?
Hundreds of thousands of people die each year
because of drugs, drive-by shootings, and or gang
related activities but some of them are from
STD's, sharing dirty drug needles and sex.
Death is the saddest and worst thing that
could happen to a family. Sometimes death happens
for a good reason, like someone who has cancer real
bad.
But whatever the condition is it leaves the
person's family with pain, anger, emptiness and
a lot of suffering.

Melissa Motylinski

Girl-Friend

I'm writing this with a lot of faith,
that it will bring a smile to your beautiful face,
Remember all the times, some good and
some bad. Remember how we laughed,
and were sometimes sad.
Remember all the troubled times, I thought
we were through. But, most of all remember
that I love you,
You've been here girl-friend through thick
and through thin. But most of all you've been
my best friend.
I know right now you are lost and
confused. I guess in my own way,
I am too.
I'll be here girl-friend through thick and
through thin. I won't walk behind you,
for you may not end. But I'll proudly
walk beside you and be your best friend.

Tami Hawkins

Heartbreak

At times I know she makes you cry
That lost, painful feeling you carry inside.
No matter what she says or does
You insist you're still in love.

What kind of love could this be when one can not stay or flee?
With iron chains around your heart your guilt won't let you depart.

And when she takes you to that place
Where emotions and passions often race
You know the next day you have to face
That lonely feeling saying it's all a waste.

And when she's cold and cruel she knows all she has to do
Is hold you tight to her delight making you believe it's alright.

You carry such heart felt pain willing to give in for her gain
Turning your back on the way you feel
Believing in things you know are not real.

It pains me to see your endeavor not knowing if this will go on forever.
Such a fear I hold wondering if you will ever know.

I pray someday you will see the treasure inside you are the keys
And love is not only what you believe
It's a gift from above and can't be deceived.

Sherry Jo Amyotte

If Trees Could Talk

If trees could talk, I wonder what they'd say?
That Oak that hovers tall in my front yard
Was there before Columbus sailed away.
It's stood the test of time, its strength unmarred.

So, Tree, within whose shade I've often played,
What have you witnessed of our history?
You ruled when only creatures sought your shade.
It's rustling leaves then spoke their soul to me.

"I've known," it said, "a time when nature reigned,
When those that lived revered the ground I love,
I've watched the ground below me paved and stained,
And breathed the poisonous fumes that float above.

"There was a day when only creatures sang,
When only crickets hailed the evening light.
The birds now sing beside a deafening bang -
A rumble, rumble, morning, noon and night.

"I've watched the boy who grows too old to live,
But stays alive in those he left behind.
I'm in this cycle, living life to give
Your children's child a life of peace of mind."

Natalie Stewart

For Adriana: Love In Fourteen Lines

Was it by chance? By luck? By charmed twist of fate
That opened up our eyes and our hearts?
Is it a divinely planned destiny, both mystical and great,
or a haphazard Cupid tossing his darts?
Can we find the needed answers in our palms,
or the necessary clues in our horoscopes?
Will the Tarot guide through storms and calms,
alternately raising and dashing our hopes?
No astrology controls my emotions.
My love is so strong; my love is so real
Like unceasing tides in the deepest of oceans,
Right or wrong, 'tis the way I feel.
My love for you is constant, never to be lost
And unlike less determined lovers, we shalln't be star-crossed.

Stu Blandford

Our Three Children

Our first born is a girl named Nydia
that rhymes with the name Lydia.
She was born in London on July 23rd, 1986
the same month as her dad but the year 1956.
She has brown hair and big brown eyes;
by age one, she was biting on her dad's neckties.
her hobbies are playing bowling and collecting bears;
if she lose her bear named Pinky, she will be in tears.

Our second child is also a girl named Natalie
who was born in Pensacola on September 12, 1991
the same month as her Aunty Maria but the year 1951.
She is a smart girl who loves to read books and sings
along with the movies that has songs, actions and flings
but wonders why do birds have wings?

Our third child is a boy named Nicholas who was born
in Pensacola on March 18, 1993 and loves to eat corn.
He is a typical boy who loves to collect cars and balls
when he runs after his sisters very fast, he falls.
he loves to go swimming with his dad in a pool and gets a tan
and when he gets home, he reads a book by a fan.

Sylvia C. Yanis

Missing

MISSING: (A pain that no one should have to feel)
That word, the most dreaded that I've ever heard.
MISSING: Not wanting to believe, trying hard to be at ease.
Saying; it must be a mistake, for this pain
I cannot take.
MISSING: That word playing over and over in your head,
while you're praying to God, Please don't let him be dead.
Days later, Still no trace, and you constantly Pray;
GOD let him be SAFE.
Your mind start searching for some type of clue,
feeling helpless, not sure what to do.
Your heart is aching by the minute,
while your body's feeling like its reached its limit.
For every ring that comes through the phone,
You hope and pray to hear; he's coming home.
Another Day, Still not Found..
you wish the perpetrator could hear that sound,
then perhaps he'll set him FREE, and
Bring my MISSING CHILD Back to ME.

Yvette Edwards

My Parents

There are moments each day when I think of you and all
that you mean to me, like love that filled a room that went
beyond your smile.

Mom and Dad, you could have just left me to wonder hopelessly
to what life had to offer, but instead you taught me
to listen, to question, you gave me wisdom that goes beyond
words and the strength to choose my own destiny.

When I felt life giving up you stood by my side and dried
my tears like no one else could, simply understood all my fears
just because you love me.

I'd like to thank you for a lifetime of gifts too precious
to wrap, the ones that come from within, in each dream you dreamed
with me and encouraged.

My love and respect for you is beyond any words. My life is
more meaningful now, my memories more cherished and so much
brighter
because you shared your life with me.
Mom and Dad, I LOVE YOU, I MISS YOU, My friends.

Lorraine L. Chrone, "Lady Blue"

The Saddest Day

There was this chimpanzee and her baby living high in their nest in the
forest. The happy playful little chimp, and his loving and patient
mother. One day the little chimp awoke to find his mother gone.
They had never been separated: the bewildered little baby cried
out for his mother, but there was no reply. Only the echo of his
mournful cries.

Hesitantly, the brave little chimp made his way down from the nest
to search for his mother. After many long and weary hours, he
came to a stream, and there he found his mother lying at the waters
edge. The little baby jumped with joy at the sight of his mother.
He ran to her, hugging and tugging at her fur, pulling at her
lifeless body trying to wake her, but to no avail.

Exhausted, he lay down beside her, and holding her tight, fell into
a deep sleep. The next day he awoke and again he tried to wake his
silent mother. He tugged, he pulled, but no sound came forth.
Finally, alone, tired and hungry, the little chimp made his way back
to the nest he shared with his mother. He covered himself with
twigs and leaves, curled up, and never came down again.

He died there of a broken heart!

The saddest day is when...a... mother dies.

Margaret Lane

Hail To The Chief

Hail to the Chief!
The battle's over; the chief is done,
How brief the lives of those who fought.
Young men — now lost to all the world;
Now gone, now dead — what have we wrought.

Hail to the Chief!
Who now can tell what he has done?
To change the world — so dearly bought,
What payment gained — the flag unfurled?
What treasures lost — what have we sought?

Hail to the Chief!
One day the world must learn
To count the loss — the gain for naught.
For there they lie — on fields of blood
Young, vibrant lives — who glory sought.

Hail to the Chief!
God give him strength to find a way
to keep the world at peace.
"Love one another" must be taught
And war and conflict cease.

Miriam Kassekert

Vision

As I trepidatiously stagger through the covered bridge,
the bitter blackness confuses my wayward path,
while the aging timbers, decrepit and decaying, warn of what
lies ahead.
Belligerently ignoring the danger, I continue,
for my incredible journey has just begun.

The sage voice of the river below guides me,
for I am rendered blind by the ominous black habitat,
Still I march forward, fearing equally the past and the future,
but as I lift my sagging eyelids, a refreshing light restores
my precious vision,
and I scamper, relieved, from the jailing darkness.

Standing restfully, with the haunting bridge at my back,
I'm suddenly enraptured by the delicious aroma of blooming
poppies.
The scent, so blissful and lively, awakens my entire body
as I gaily frolic through the lavish garden,
Every luscious breath of life is held sacred, and celebrated.

While gathering a regal bouquet to accompany my flight,
the solemn river whispers an imperative message,
but the language is foreign; I cannot understand.
I plead mercifully for a meaningful translation,
but the engaging stream is once again mute.

Thomas Tyson Pulliam

One Luminary Clock Against The Sky

I sit upon the rocky shore
The breakers fill my ears
I turn my eyes upward
And see the moon smiling down at me
For it is now the hour

The wind grows cold against my cheek
I will not leave this place
For the moon has promised me a crown of stars
Like the one he himself wears
For it is now the hour

His deep blue robe surrounds me
A soft velvet with white sequins
He sends a walkway upon the water
And beckons me to his side
For it is now the hour

The wind howls as if to call me away
I try to look away from the moon
But, alas, it is too late
And I have become one with the night
For it is now the hour

Rebecca R. Thomas

The Chains Of Chastity

You have made me put on the chains again —
The Chains of Chastity.
From your cold, cruel and mocking heart,
You have utterly blotted me out.

You have damned me to wear again
The Chains of Chastity.
With your cold, cruel and mocking eyes,
You have even put an ocean between us.

Do you think that I must bear again
The Chains of Chastity?
For a time, half a time, and many times besides
I will be ensnared...

Until the dull red bulb shall
Burn itself out.

Michael W. Veronin

The Fairy Of Spring

Spring is said to be the time of young love,
The bringing of baby animals, the call of a dove.
Well, you may be wondering just how does this occur?
I think it happens when the leaves begin to stir.

I think that out of the leaves a magic fairy appears,
Who breaks the spell of winter and casts away fears.
She can fly above high or walk on the ground,
But wherever she goes, she spreads wonder around.

She warms up the air, she graces the trees,
She blossoms the flowers she hums with the bees.
She makes people smile, she softens old pain,
She gives people humor, she takes away strain.

But there's something even more special that this fairy can do,
She gives things second chances and lets opportunities renew.
She surprises people with that unexpected new friend,
And assures the doubting that true love will not end.

And when the warm months begin to turn cold,
Don't worry, this fairy never grows old.
She simply goes back to her home in the trees,
To return the next year with the stirring of leaves.

Lauren Melissa Nowenstein

Lake Moraine

Spring waxes to early Summer. The glacier lake turns a milky green.
The canoe tips up then back and settles quietly as we step in.
We pause, then push off and slowly pull away.

Encircled by ten peaks, the mountains still tower above us.
We are part of the sky here. Clouds move quickly, silently;
changing our outlook, softening our perspective, bringing us into focus.

There is no wind for a time.
The sunlight spreads its arms of fire across barren rock.
It moves stealthy down to touch the lake
and sculpts the water's surface like jade
crafted to a smoother finish.

We watch for awhile, then let go.

Paddles dip and send ripples to every shore,
then glide; the canoe licks the water.
No noise, no breath.

Eyes closed, we think of home.
The water's coldness stuns, stings,
reminds us that this place is far and away.
But it will whisper, gently coax and we will slip easily into its embrace
holding our lives in that one moment of perfect balance.

It is so still. Its' majesty is kingdom come.

Martha Fetter

Prisoner Of Love

The walls which surround me stand solid and tall
The cell which I reside, sees through to the other side
The chains that restrict me, bear heavy in weight
For the court o love has given no date
My plea for release from within my heart
I've counted the days from the very start
The bars that confine me from moving
pass, are keys to freedom here at last
For scaling the walls solid and tall
In hopes to escape from where I reside
My only escape now through acquittal you see.....
For life in this prison is not for me

Margie D. Smith

Stormset

The crack of lightning, a sound of thunder.
The chimes ringing as the wind blows them around.
Creaking of trees, and houses and cars.
We as people, to the earth are bound.
The rain pitter-pattering onto the rooftop.
The glow of the fire.
A man and a woman.
He to she admires.
The radio is silent.
No TV on at all.
Just the storm to remind us,
that we are still very small.

Rebecca Bundy

Reflections Of Haunting Memories

Memories of a lost love haunts me. His ghost floats through
the cobwebs of my mind. I guess I will bury his memory and
in time I will move on and leave his ghost behind.
I stare at the wall and I try to escape his haunting eyes as
they follow me around the room. I feel like I am being
pulled into a vortex and my spirit he threatens to consume.
As I avert my eyes, the projection of the images of our
lifetime upon the blank wall unfold. I feel a shivery,
eerie feeling come over me and I am very cold. I
finally convince myself I must put the past behind me;
so I bury his memory in a tomb. And just when I think I am
successful; His likeness kicks me in my womb.

Sylvia LaVerne Wilson

Colors

As you look out the window,
The colors blend,
But know that their boundaries exist.

The colors may confuse you,
And even push you back,
But don't forget that you are one of the colors.

Find your shade and know it well,
Learn it's most intricate details,
Never conceal it, color the world with it,
Let your color show.

Luis Sandoval

Oleander

I went wandering today about the country green,
The country of my childhood days,
The old Harrell place and the
Railroad that lies between
My friend's house and where
We used to stay.

Beside the tracks the white dirt road
Winds its way to obscure places
Shaded by the Live Oak tree and
Bumpy with its roots that here and there
Laces its careless path.

If I close my eyes I can see the tender green
Of the new grass
And the Palm tree's darker frond,
And hear its rustling in the gentle breeze
And feel the summer sun.

And press my ear to the harsh grass
And listen to the summer Oleander afternoon,
Silent, save for the buzzing of bees and the
Crashing sky of blue.

Myrna Kanekkeberg

Quiet Music Plays

Quiet music played -
The day sweet and bright as marmalade -
The bay a bowl of jade.

Quiet music played -
A moody man turned up a ten of spades -
In the game, he wished, he'd faded.

Soft music played -
Children in pig tailed and braids -
An old man with heavy-lidded eyes watches from his chase.

The foam creamy-white as dabs of mayonnaise -
On and on the music monotonously plays -
The children endlessly fill a cup cracked and crazed.

Pierritz

What Does Love Look Like?

What does love look like?
The description of love is complex and intriguing.
Love is deep like the caves and caverns far below the earth's surface,
growing precious crystals and diamonds.
Love is powerful like the ocean's crashing waves.
Love is beautiful like a red rose,
with the fresh morning dew upon its petals.
Love is moving like that of a gentle spring breeze,
dancing among delicate water lilies.
Love is soft as a small kitten nestled in its mother's fur,
looking for warmth and protection.
Love is as strong as an age old tree, deep within the forest,
who has taken all Mother Nature has thrown his way.
Love is love.
It has no particular shape, no certain size.
Love is deep, powerful, beautiful, moving, soft, and strong.
Love, is love.

Sarah Cathleen Gresham

"Run Away"

I run away from the pain that boils up inside,
The desire to get out of that box that sits deep down and hides.
Wanting to stop and wanting to run.
When the pin point is leashed and the rage begins.
Temper and anger burst from every limb,
And runs in all directions.
Pain antagonizing the temper to rage and flare of fire,
Running away from the pain,
That's driving me insane.
Running fast and free,
From the pain that no one can see.
Its killing me by the mile,
But all I can do is put on a fake smile.

Shannon Marie Becker

On Growing Old!

The stairs get steeper with each passing year
The doors get heavier, too, my dear;
You can't remember the day of the week
You can't always hear when some people speak!
One spin on the dance floor,
Your head's in a whirl,
You just can't perform
Like when you were a girl;
Your mind goes fast and your legs go slow
This modern world your really don't know,
Don't try to keep up, just go your own pace
Keep a song in your heart
And a smile on your face;
"It'll all come out in the wash", so they say
Chin up, tummy in, and HAVE A GOOD DAY!

Lynn Jordan

Serenity's

I slowly awoke as the warmth of the sun shown gently upon my face,
The droplets of dew falling to the ground were glistening all over the place.
I tilted my head and stared over the fields of the golden grains that grew,
The winds slicing through them with the strangest sounds, for all to listen to.
The sky above like a vast open sea, birds soaring through the blueness of space,
Staring into the never ending hue, it all seeming like a mystical place.
Babbling of waters in a nearby brook, soothing like music to the ear.
Small animals running and chattering along, so free and ever so near.
Together these things as one idea, like a picture for all to see,
Would be the greatest thing that one could share, his thoughts of Serenity.

Michael S. Jeter

"When Mirrors Speak The Truth"

Peering through unknown space, I witness the end of a Mind: Slowly, the drums have beat silence into chaos; wisdom into pain. The pictures of the rainbow are brilliantly dull, blurry blues and violets reign over the crowded abyss; while Fortune smiles it's toothless grin: I am sentenced to an unspecified length of time in this world of meekness and unfamiliarity; the conqueror, now the conquered, the loser now the winner.

Hopes eternity has come to rest on this dimensions grays and whites; there are no smells, Only the constant ringing of the bells, drowns out the roaring silence. Beckoning to the weary, he quickly appears to be laughing: but at what? The face is not known and suddenly drifts from the front of consciousness; However tall one may be, the height of wretchedness humbles all who sup it's bitter draft!

Violently the plane spins counterclockwise; it's unusually intoxicating, yet innerly revolting. Above there are no clouds or rain, yet neither is there sun and warmth; Looking past the haze, skeletons reach out their hands: "Come back to us dear," they slur and hiss; Jumping off at one point into clear obscurity, A feeling of warmth and comfort pricks the senses, while placidly the pupils shut: Looking down one finds the grave.

P.S. Niemand

The Golden Ray

The early air begins to rise.
The early bird gets a prize.
A fading darkness gives way,
To bright sun beginning the day.
The first golden rays of morning
Fall upon the autumn leaves so bright.
For the moment all is still;
Except the cascading water at the mill.
The covered bridge filled with a light of gold.
The quaint village never seemed so old;
. . . and yet, so alive . . .
The golden rays move on to the west,
Leaving behind memories that are the best.

Matthew Edward Whitman

Uncertain

Gentle breeze swaying the leaves of a tree to and fro.
But no one knows when gentle becomes rough.

The motion of the waves, so subtle, so calm.
But no one knows when the tide will come.

Springtime blossoms. Will they grow? No drops from the sky.
Seasonal warmth turn cold.

Life abundant. Sorrow Joy Choices Decisions
Death inevitable. Years unknown.

Donna Rose Wilson

The Graveyard

In memory of my father

Pain is buried within a casket built of memories
The earth around the grave has grown sour and hard
The graveyard releases a groan
and the dusty mounds among the headstones
tremble
The pickax of truth digs into the grave
and rips out the coffin from among the roots of death
Creatures of evil and pain lurk within the darkness
and feast upon the memories
Denial is the misted cobwebs
which veil the stone inscribed names
from our visual sight
Apparitions creep in and out of their burial sites
and leave us feeling haunted and condemned
A vulture whispers to the dead that it is hungry,
which memory shall it devour now?

Mandi Marie

The Crystal Child

The stirring starts,
The emotions flow,
Love absorbs the total soul.

Liquids of silver,
Meshed with liquids of gold,
Entwined together,
For the eyes to behold.

Brilliance streams across the heavens gates,
Down below,
The earth she doth quake.

Eaten up by the dragon's fire,
The flames rise higher and higher.

To melt the gold and silver lining,
The new birth of the Crystal Child,
God's immortal is eternally shining.

Patricia Diane Hill

The Full Human Being

It costs so much to be a full human that there are very few who have the enlightenment or the courage to pay the price. One has to abandon altogether the search for security and reach out to the risk of living with both arms, one has to embrace the world like a lover.

One has to accept pain as a condition of existence, one has to court doubt and darkness as the cost of knowing.

One needs a will stubborn in conflict but apt always to total acceptance of every consequence of living and dying.

It is a law as certain as gravity, to live fully we must learn to use things and love people, not to use people and love things.

The behavior of the full human is always unpredictable, simply because it is free!!

Lois Redford

Orange Street

Brick Road shaded by sprawling greens
  that tumble from sturdy old oak trees
Underneath an azalea little pieces of a chipped paint
With an eye roll and strength of length
  the weathered houses are easily seen
Bleeding rust is left from nails
  that were once tight against these decrepit iron boards
Boards which left the distinct smell of sawdust
  for the first year
One hundred thirty-two years ago

Robert Wayne Still

"Blessings"

What can be more blessed than the gift to see
The faces of the ones you love
The sky with the stars, the moon the heavens above
What can be more beautiful than the flowers and
Trees and every living thing you see
The sun, the moon, the rain and the snow
And the wonderful things of nature wherever you go
What is more beautiful than to hear
A loving voice, the singing of the birds,
The music that is made up of every sound on earth
What is it worth to touch someone you love
To touch the petals of a rose
And every living thing that grows
What does it mean that we can say
I love you, I love you every day
What does it mean to walk and talk and see
To read and write and sing
To me these blessings mean everything

Wilma B. Flynn

Autumn's Elegance

Step in from the Autumn chill.
The fire is warming and the baking apples
fill the room with an aroma of spice.
Isn't' it nice to relax in the peace and
easing silence of Autumn.
Outside the frost tinted window,
with a grace of their own, bronzed leaves fall.
Crisp, conceiving all beauty of this season's elegance.
A couple walks hand in hand,
dressed in sweaters the color of nature.
They laugh.
What memories this time of year brings-
hot cocoa and pie, wool blankets and classic books.
There is no reason to not enjoy the pleasures of Autumn.
It is within my soul-
The mysteries of our changing Earth.
My senses are struck.
The sights, feeling, smells and tastes of a season so intimate
bring me joy.

Monica Lynn Perry

Spring Rain And The Snow

The snow has fallen all around, there's no blemish in the white.
The forest is still, not ere a bird wings past in silent flight.
The giant moon shines high above and stars glimmer every where.
You gently take me by the hand and lead me up the stairs.
A fire glows warm upon the hearth and that soft rug upon the floor
gently beckons us, there, you gently, tenderly,
lay me down and caress me with your hands, your lips
so warm find my own and all of time stands still.
There's a fire in my heart that time cannot quench as you love me
o'er and o'er
There's something there that belongs just to you as you whisper
your love in my ear. My body, my mind, my heart and my soul respond
to you anywhere.
Just speak my name and my heart takes wings and sores to the eagles
heights.
All that is mine I would willingly give for one of our fabulous
nights.

G. J. Ferguson-Adkins

"The Brighter Outlook"

Come one and all, I have a message to share,
The future may look gloomy but do not despair.
Look not at the past with its failures and fears,
Naught can be gained by fretting lost years.
Look to the future with faith and with zeal,
Take God into your life, He will make Himself real.
Don't go it alone, He knows what's before you,
All wisdom is His and He is faithful and true.
When burdens are heavy, added strength He will give,
And His peace can be yours as long as you live.
These blessings you will experience, if you give Him control,
He is offering His salvation to every living soul.
Our country is in turmoil and our problems are great,
Crime is rampant and minds are filled with hate.
Much effort has been made to eliminate God,
What a treacherous path we have knowingly trod.
Let us turn back to our God, He is waiting to bless,
He will exalt our nation with His righteousness.

Vera E. Andersen

Glasgo

The tranquility that abounds from Glasgo amazes me
The glistening of the water, the rustling of each proud tree.
My fondest memories like the waters reflect from this place.
The overpowering blue skies, the vastness of this alluring open space.
Even as a child I never took this beauty for granted
Like a seed the love of this place has forever in my heart
and soul been planted.
Many weekends were shared here with family and friends
Times like these you truly never want to see end.
I've drifted along in my canoe many times thru-out my life as a child,
a mother, and as a wife.
Escaping occasionally from a certain amount of turmoil and
drudgery of
every day life.
But this place seems to restore your outlook on life's many ups and
downs.
It's like a cure for all your mental and physical problems - so I have
found.
So many years have been spent here boating and swimming and having
picnics together
We've enjoyed a vast variety of both good and bad weather.
This place will be here after all of us are gone
We unlike the waters will exist just so long.
But for now I will savor this place
For I know God has lent us a piece of heaven for our own tranquil
space.

Nancy Simpson Childers

A Key That Opens A Reflection

The farther away... The more forgotten.
The harder it is, to tell the tales . . .
That make up the life, that we live . . .
For you are a key . . .
That can open it's own door.
Revealing all that it is, and more . . .
For you are the joy that tomorrow will bring.
Just as yesterday has done the same thing . . .
By looking hard at that certain place . . .
A mirror set in front of the human race . . .
And every now and then, a smiling face . . .
Will notice the puzzle, standing in their place . . .
Every piece forgotten, yet still . . .
Ever so quietly lingering about . . .
Barely whispering a forgotten sound . . .
Hoping you'll realize, the life placed behind you . . .
Is the key that has opened the door of life to you . . .
Just as you will someday too . . .
And you will someday become the past . . .
But yet in a way, the past has always been, you . . .

Melissa K. Cardamon

Rustic Voyager

I looked toward the barren lands grey soil that had once been brown
The homestead did no longer stand for wind and rain had brought
it down
The smokehouse that was built with care of granite stone and
earthen clay
Appeared it was no worse for wear preserved through many yesterdays

I grasped a poker near the hearth that once gave warmth from
fire flame
I speared the flue to make depart the blackened soot that had remained
In silence I did hear the wind wailing through the cracks of boards
Crying out the ancient sins of those who walked upon these floors

My heart stood still as I approached a desk against one wall in tack
Its drawers held fast the farmers ghost in rusted tin type photographs
The literary works contained a diary in journal style
The story of their lives remained an honorary history file

I camped the night 'til daylight broke studying the things I'd seen
They touched my heart with what they wrote about their lives and
hopeless dreams
I left without a second glance upon the place once called a home
The sky looked on with arrogance while fields of barley danced alone

Matthew A. Page

"To Heal A Broken Rose"

I wonder, how does one heal a broken Rose?
The hurt that you've felt, there's no need to disclose.
I mean this with respect, I don't wish to impose...
Your smile is so kind, please don't let your heart close.

Potential from unborn, joyous tears in your eyes...
Can help ease the pain, of past false promises and lies.
Your essence is good, and your dreams they will fly...
With your feet on the ground, keep your head to the sky.

What kindness does it take, to help rid your pain?
Your glance touches the soul, and soft voice clears the brain.
With time as a key, then your heart will unchain...
And great chances of Love, will be there to obtain.

Life's peaks and valleys have lessons, with which we transcend...
And give rare bright chances for us to befriend.
You are someone special, and this I intend...
The most positive thoughts, to you I will send.

Now, I must state, and the truth does expose...
I mean this with respect, I don't wish to impose...
Your smile is so kind, please don't let your heart close.
I'd sure like to help, and Heal this broken Rose!

Michael J. Chassion

To A B-29

I wonder where your lofty wings will go,
The clouds above what nations touch.
Weather what storms of wind, hail and snow?
What nations, British, French or Dutch
Will hear your mighty motors roar
And pause to glance into the sky,
To see what monster dares to soar
Up there, where only birds should fly.
Perhaps this very plane I see
May shelter from the canon's blast
The one I hold dearest to me
And bring him safely home at last.
With hopeful eyes and fervent prayer,
I watch you skim across the field.
May all your missions over there
When in true glory are revealed,
Some day proclaim throughout the lands
Our pride in you, our work of art.
The masterpiece of willing hands,
The pride of each true American heart!

Ruth Scofield

Depths

Rising from the unfathomable depths below, it swells as
clear as the morning sky, reaching tremendous heights, only
to come crashing down pu**y and white. Blending back into those
depths again it gives rise to even clearer and more wondrous
things, until they too crash, and give rise to those that may
one day surpass those equally unfathomable depths of our minds.

Kevin Murphy

Freedom

I'm so tired of listening to the murmur of stronger voices.
The irritating squeal for attention when they know they can't have it.
I'm bored with the idea and Now I'm wasting time
being chained to this chair and the key is just out of reach.

I don't want to go home either. I don't want to know why
I'm sick from what's being fed to me
Maybe I want more... too much... not enough
too late but just a little early.

She screams in my ear but doesn't listen to either one of us.
I'm eighteen and I know it all—perhaps, maybe—NO
They say the world is yours and then say in fifteen years it's not.
You know everything and nothing confident, Cocky, Convinced!
Yes—exactly, absolutely... ...Maybe—Not—it could happen!!

I know at forty, you don't know— So you look and you're rash to act,
so in spring you learn? Can you forget what you teach?
Where's the example?—You don't know? Didn't think so...
I'm eighteen and I don't know—but I do.

I despise being restricted. I want to feel more
Deeper places to explore, foreign shores, new doors
Hard floors scores and Scores of people who haven't given up yet.

Shelley Rohm

The Seasons

The air smells sweet, the grass does too,
The leaves are green, the sky is blue.
The sun is warm, the breeze is light,
The flowers are tinted - yellow, pink and white. (Spring)

The sun is hot, the air is too,
The trees are green, the sky azure blue.
The breeze is warm, the grass is green,
Flowers - yellow, pink, white - are seen. (Summer)

The trees have shed their leaves of green,
The flowers have hid - no more to be seen.
The air is now cool, the breeze - still here,
The sky is pale white ' "winter" is near! (Autumn)

The snow falls gently on the quiet ground,
Winter is here for a cold season bound.
The air is still - the sky signals "snow",
The trees are quite bare and the wind - it does blow! (Winter)

Mary Miller

The Music

The authority of trumpets, the silken-tone of flutes,
The liltings of the stringed harps, the musings of the lutes,
The rise and fall of voices, a symphony of stars,
The diamonds of the universe, celestial feldspars.

The softness of the reverence, crescendos loud with praise
Resound throughout the Heavens as the souls of men shall gaze
Upon the scene no eyes have seen, no mortal ears have heard,
The orchestra of angels with anthem psalms that stirred

New hearts to greater heights than they've ever been before,
The euphonies, fantasia, all harmonize to soar
Forever through the cosmos and we'll join in joy to sing,
To let majestic music waft on boundless, choral wing.

D. G. Cox

The TURn

We call ourselves human, how often do we show our humanity?
The lives that we touch, the lives that we see,
the live that we live, what does it all mean.
We mean well and do nothing, we just don't have time.
Caught up in our own lives.

Have we done with our lives what we've wanted to?
We've made or decisions and we've laid our path;
never calling them destiny nor fate.
Reflections of wants that were compromised.
Realization lies around the corner, change is apparent.

Do we compose change or lie in the past, always realizing and
dwelling?
Our newly found dreams and potentials are around the corner,
however yet pursued.
The unknown consequences awaiting us, always with question of
uncharted paths.
We need to take the chance, we need to make The TURn.

Phillip A. Michon

Untitled

It's spring, and now the earth begins to yawn
The long and silent winter's sleep is done
The sound of birds returning greets the dawn
And warmth arrives with rising of the sun.

The still cool breeze has lost its frigid bite
And neighbors missing since the autumn's end
Emerge as if from one extended night
For there are lawns trim and shrubs to tend.

It's time like these that make one feel alive
And ready for the tasks that lie ahead
It's fragrant air of spring on which we thrive
Rememb'ring ev'ry springtime poem we've read.

But boundless joy I really can't express
Because my mind dwells on the IRS.

Lester Fox

Untimely November Sun

I was out raking leaves yesterday,
the mailman came my way...
He stopped and had some friendly words to say;
Handed the mail to me, smiled and drove away.

soon a neighbor strolled across his yard
Looked about and patted a dog on her
head-
"Beautiful day, isn't it?" he nodded and said.

We can bask in the untimely November
sun and chat with friends today.
But what about tomorrow?
Will it continue to be this way?

As the days fade into darkness,
and the cold winds begin to blow-
The mailman and,maybe, the dog will show,
but I will draw away from them to watch the fire glow;
Will the warmth of November linger or will it go?

Pat Turlington

Unidentified Flying Object

A feisty old lady from Mars
Decided to fly to the stars.
When her UFO landed
She was soon reprimanded
For illegally entering ours.

Alice Lu Cornelius

The Meaning Of My Life

Thank you Lord for my wife,
The meaning of my life.
For she will always truly be,
The greatest gift you have given me.

I thank you and praise you Lord from my heart.
When you gave her to me, my life did start.
Now Father fill her whole,
The way you have my soul.

My Love, you are as fragile or so it seems,
As a shimmering bubble in the moon beams.
Yet you are continually without a doubt,
My source of endless strength, for which my soul cries out.

I love you, Melly, more than words could ever say.
If only I could please you, but just once each day.
My love for you grows constantly without bounds.
If you but like me, my life would have no downs.

Your servant forever I will be.
All you need do, is just stand by me.
Your love in return, is more than I deserve.
Both you, Lord and my wife, shall I always serve.

Terry L. Clark

Untitled

Caged
the mighty lion is restless,
pacing in quiet alertness.

Waiting,
watching,
his majestic form awaits the moment of freedom.

It has arrived. He feels it, senses it.

Grabs the chance, runs and runs until he can no longer breathe.

And dies

In the arms of freedom.

Teresa Stephenson

Oh What A Beautiful World

The stars shine down the light of years gone past and ask, "Why?"
The moon turns a sad and humorless smile our way.
The sun rises, and even with all it's burning intensity,
cannot take hold.
And the uncertain planet that we call Earth looks
back...questioning.
Oh, what a beautiful world, where children jump and play next to a pond with foam on it's shores. A world where trees no longer stand proud and strong, but, instead, lie silent, side by side. Where rain forests are destroyed, barren, only machinery visible. Terrible, steel, shadowed creatures that seem to rise straight from hell, The Devils Lair. For what could take such beauty away, but a devil? A devil that walks and talks in the form of a man.
Oh, what a beautiful world, where our once blue and green seas are now
black with oil, the blood of ships. Seas which before had carried life and beauty, now carry death, and images of birds, sticky and coated with oil, fighting to be free of it's grip. Or fish, no longer jetting effortlessly through the water, but instead...floating, in their not so graceful acceptance of death.
Mother Earth holds such beauty, such love, and she is so willing to share, but we rape her again and again, never satisfying our selfish needs. Every raindrop, every drop of dew, it's not as simple as it seems. These are the tears of our planet. Tears that have fallen silently, sadly, and with regret. Tears that go unseen.
Oh, what a beautiful world, what a beautiful f***ing world...

Steve Meadows

... of God's Will

A Breeze through the Air... is the Breath of the Lord
The Ocean is the drink that fill His Cup

The Salt of the Earth... is the Sand's Ocean Floor
And the Moon and the Stars are for Love

Great Fields of Harvest-gold give grain, corn and wheat
And the fruits from the Trees... are Abundant and Sweet

Miles of green Rolling Hills... border a Wondrous blue Sky
As Clouds of white fluff... take their time drifting by

Flowers in every color... fragrant the Wind
So natural a Potpourri... of... aromatic blend

Rivers and Streams... keeping steady with sound
In continuous motion... ever moving round

Snow-capped Mountain Tops... cool the Land down below
While each Heavenly Sunset... kisses all things aglow

A tranquil Lake... a serene Pond... so peaceful and so still
As reflections dance...

From Stars above...
And show the Beauty... OF GOD'S WILL

Linda C. Burns

Domina

I AM the one who watches from her cage.
The one who steals visions and weaves them into colors,
Hues of green, fire orange, night sapphire.
I AM the old one weaving the color,
The one who drapes night's sapphire over the bars,
Tying each into knots with strings of fire.
I AM the one who watches from her cage,
The one who waits for the color inferno,
Exploding from inside.
I AM the wind who rips the cage from its hoary roots.
The wind who watches it rupture,
Discarding pieces to the vortex.
I AM the one who rips the colors apart,
The one who hurls invisible threads
Freeing the colors from confinement.
I AM the one who catches mystical threads,
The one who dances over the earth,
Watching the path of colored threads flow to open arms.
I AM THE ONE FREE.

Sandra H. Staley

Creatures Of Extremes

To the ones who could never sit still,
The ones who come late, that leave early,
Who never fit in anywhere.
To all of you creatures of extremes,
You rule breakers, devil chasers—
This is one for you.

To the ones who don't know what "enough" means,
That live with a hunger, exists on the outskirts of everything.
Where nothing is sacred, where there is nowhere safe.
To you renegades who find yourselves always
Making the exact same mistakes—
I pray you find some peace.

To the ones still out there, the ones that know
What the fire feels like or how cruel the wind can be.
To you thunder makers, promise breakers
Who've watched too many bridges burn.
This is for all lost children
Who learned young how to run.
I hope that somehow, someday,
You find a way ... home.

Michael J. Browne

In A World Of My Own

In a world of my own
The pain I feel is not known
Nobody listens to a thing I say
So I just shrug and walk away
In my head, I wish I could jump back into bed
Sometimes I feel as if I don't exist
As if I were lost in some kind of mist
If only I had a clue of something I could do
A way to make people see
That only they hold the key
If they choose to give it out
There would be one less person in doubt
One less person to hold the thought
That others will never be taught
They can't always turn their back
And hide behind a veil of black
What I have to say may be useful to them one day
It's their choice if they decide to hear the voice

Malaina Hodess

The Quiet Man!

In his quiet sea, the quiet man who . . .
The quiet man in his quiet rage.
The quiet man what a war to wage!
The quiet man what do you feel inside?
The quiet man what do you have to hide?
The quiet man...
Why do you hate me???
The quiet man how could this be?
The quiet man you are becoming loud, please, I have already bowed.
The quiet man do not come near.
The quiet man is already here!
The quiet man listens to... Quietness.

Manish Pandya

Spring Rain

Today we can't go outside and play.
The rain has been falling from the sky all day.

We wanted to run and jump and hop.
We were wishing real hard the rain would stop.

Our mom said now that spring has come,
The flowers need the rain as much as they need sun.

Our smiles appear as we see the light.
The rain has stopped, the sky is bright.

We all gather 'round and go into a huddle.
Do you see what I see?
IT'S A GREAT BIG PUDDLE!

Oh what fun we'll have, we can hardly wait.
We'll hop and we'll jump. It's going to be great!

Patricia A. Fleishman

Embers

Embers are the remnant of a glowing fire;
The remembrance of something radiant and warm,
With it's bright orange fingers reaching out higher
As if to embrace you from all harm.
Ultimately, the embers will die,
Relinquishing all their warmth and peace
All that is left are the ashes that lie,
Bringing back memories that will not cease.
Could embers yet be an analogy
Of our lives when one day they expire?
The memory that's left for eternity
Depends on what was put into the fire.

Susan Blackwell

The Sea and I

As I walk beside the sea
The sea and I are lonely
The waves break upon the shore
Rushed on by the angry winds -
The turmoil which seethes within
My heart is like the sea.
As the waves beat the sands in
Futile desperation - so I try to
Maintain a sensitive love
Can he understand my need, does he
want to!!
Or shall I spend the remainder of my life -
Lonely as the sea, ever searching -
Never a final resting place, just a constant
And futile wandering of my soul.
The sea and I.......

P. Kelemen

Old Memories

Some things just seem made to rub up against old memories. They fill the shadowed corners of a heart and mind with feelings and faces from times thought long forgotten.

A clear, full moon, or the sound of rain on the roof swiftly draws images of the past from the deepest well of ones soul.

The faint melody of an old song whose words are still remembered, or yellowed letters tied with ribbon, unfold tender images that were neatly tucked away in a closet of abandoned dreams.

As memories flood the mind, fleeting youth steals its way along bright corridors and the sweet sadness of its passing clouds aging eyes whose color and clarity have faded with the passage of time.

The scent of burning leaves or the cold stillness of a winter night become the thread that binds old memories to the tattered fabric of an aging heart.

Sandra Heffington

Wedding Of The Vampires

They were married on a cloudless midnight.
The silver moon their witness;
the stars their congregation.
A lush mountain meadow their sacred altar.

They danced to the world's most ancient rhythm
in time to the crickets' song.
The coyote stared and howled
In harmony with their cries of consummation.

Their flesh afire — their love spent — they rested,
awaiting the morning sun
to erase the deep blue night,
to raze their ceremonial refuge.

As the eastern sky began to pale,
they went their separate ways
to avoid the hunters' eyes;
to prevent discovery of their Eden.

Their memories the only evidence
of the pagan union
before the silver moon
in a meadow on a cloudless midnight.

Luciano L. Medeiros

Volumes

In the volume
I browse,
Gently thumbing
The pages,

Searching,
Scanning,
Listening.

Uncovering
The source.

Looking for
Words,
That speak
To my spirit

Finding a
Glimmer
Of hope,
And joy.

I discover,
That which
Was within.

In the end, I know and
Am known.

Kathy J. Barclay

"I Wish"

I wish...
I could have met you
I wish...
I could have saw you
I wish...
I could have told you
I wish...
I only had a chance,
Then I wouldn't be,
alone.
Alone,
without a love,
of my own.

Anthony Berzoza

Angel In The Sky

There's nothing in the world
I can't give to you,
nothing on earth
if asked, I won't do.

The feelings you give me
that hit me inside,
are better than any
roller coaster ride.

You make me realize
what life's all about,
and why there's no reason
to cry, fuss or pout.

I will give you this world
and all of my love,
because you are my Angel
sent from above.

Eternally linked
are you and I,
my wish has been answered
my wish from the sky.

Chris Danley

The Sun Is On The Horizon

The sun is on the horizon for those who have labored here
Letters of reduction were issued ten weeks ago with six to go more 'till we clear
We knew they were coming, they've told us all year of cuts coming down the line
"Will it be me?" Each of us asks, "Will I stay or go this time?"

I had a feeling when they had the last one that I was missed by the skin of my teeth
That I'd better get ready, better make a plan to vacate the roar of this city
"This is my chance," I tell my friends, "don't you want to do something else?"
"I've done my time in this line, there's a life out there and I'm gonna go find it."

But I've been preparing for a few years now, been taking classes since "88
Because the time would come when the non-vets would go, And I could move to a quieter part of the state
Now they'll hand me a check as I exit the gate, seven quarters of tuition they'll pay
After several years of my multiple duties I can see a graduation day.

There won't be many left when they get through whittling from the cuts that the law imposed
Given a choice I would rather go now than stay and wait for the gates to be closed
So I would love to sit a watch your sun go down, maybe tomorrow you'll see
But I've to go, got chores to do, because the sun's just comin' up for me.

William Bart Parslow

"Counting My Blessings"

I've counted my blessings from day to day, adding, multiplying, never taking away.

One for my life, another for my senses. So far God's covered all my expenses.

The privilege of being one of His creations and knowing He's there during my tribulations.

I'm always provided with food, shelter and clothes. Never worrying over problems, for each one He knows.

As I think on, many others come to mind. Gods gifts are so pure, so loving, so kind.

Each night He keeps me while in peace I slumber, another blessing to increase my number.

The ability to express what He's done for me, is a blessing for which I thank Him dearly.

While adjusting the figures, not quite right yet, I found a mistake that I cannot forget.

Excuse me, I must make one small subtraction! Minus satin, from me he gets no satisfaction!

So my book remains open, and the number continues to grow.
Every blessing is precious and I want the whole world to know.

Claudia T. Jones

Woman At The Well

Meet me at the well. Draw near with me to this deepening place—This
mysterious place whose source is unseen.

Help me to allow your healing grace to flow through me, to wash away
the shame, of my wounding—I have not valued myself. I have not valued you.

Forgive me for my shallowness, forgive me my inability to love.

Oh how my soul thirsts for you.

How my body aches to draw deeply from your water.

To nourish myself with your compassion and forgiveness. I desire to
bathe my self in your waters—to cleanse my body of it's wounds. To feel your purity.

My tears fall, blessed relief seeping into the ground, oh let them be
added to the waters of your well. The ground takes these hot tears of
pain, grief, sorrow and shame and purifies them into cool soothing water for my
burning soul.

My soul cries out for you,—I have not valued myself, I have not valued you.

Your compassion, love and forgiveness brings hope anew. Life here at
the well. A second chance. A new dawn.

Every second of every hour I draw from you. There is no shame here.

I drink freely from your cool water and satisfy myself. I lower the
bucket and draw back my refreshment.

Your supply is always ready, replenished from unseen underground
streams. There really is enough here. Enough to satisfy my hurt.
Enough to satisfy my heart. Enough to satisfy my soul.

Jean N. Hair

Shadow of Age

The tide has turned over and the season gone away. A sad and lonely shadow is still sitting by the bay waiting for that miracle—for time to stand still—for everything to about-face, even against God's will. That shadow isn't loneliness or even the deepest pain; and it isn't the wishful farmer waiting for fall rains.

Again the times have come and gone but the shadow still sits there. A little less, a little greyer is the description of its hair. The outline of the face has changed—a wrinkle by the brow, and yet the shadow sit s and wonders, "Will time stand still now?"— too foolish not to see that some wishes won't come true, not for anyone—not even for me, and no, shadow, not for you.

The lonely shadow is still sitting there—down by the bay, tears rolling down wrinkled cheeks and a dim mind wandering astray. The children are gone away now and were years ago, out and about in the world with their own seeds to sow. How many years gone by now? Who knows the exact amount? Only that lonely shadow has tried to keep a count of hours spent wishing and praying and trying to arrange that if one thing stayed the same—the human wouldn't change. Time would turn around or at least stand still, and the signs of time would be gone without the shadow footing the bill.

Angelia R. Hawkins

Alone

Sometimes I wonder why I feel so alone. Always feeling I don't belong One of a kind, that is me, someone special, but know own can see. That loving, giving person inside of me. Everyone or everything I love always seems to leave. I can't help but believe somehow it's me. That they could be so blind never caring enough to see, that very special someone inside of me. I try to stay alone, for everything I love, soon is gone. I hope someday I can find a place to belong, for I know it is no fun, to be alone.

Elizabeth L. Wangberg

Beautiful And Rare

Oh! Unicorn of midsummer's night.
How bold and beautiful you are! Blue as the velvet sky.
Gleaming in the light of night with your shimmering horn of gold.
Passionate and proud. Your fiery spirit is the very essence of summer love.

Desiree Dawn Petersen

The Cloak Of Silence

Frustration...sitting in this room feeling like somehow you were suppose to be in control and I forgot to let you.

Feeling ashamed, we once again argued only to hear our voices rise one above the other like echoing thunder.

Sadness...Realizing, I would have to make things right by again saying I was sorry, even though I felt once again that I had done nothing to deserve this outburst.

Stumbling upon ways I could right the wrong, knowing deep down inside that I did not like this dark side of you.

Embarrassed that once again I would have to explain to the neighbors that everything was alright and you were just having a bad day.

Guilt...Trying to reason to myself that you seemed to feel better after each major outburst, but I felt like a deflated balloon.

Looking to guidance under the night stars as I walked to ease my pain, which I somehow felt I deserved.

Rejection...Wishing you would return soon and knowing that you were safe and secure and home where you belonged.

Warming as I began to think of the nice things you had done and the good times we had shared.

Dreading the initial confrontation when the door handle would turn and the dog would run to greet you like nothing had happened...Comfort?

Tony A. Sutphin

Home

As I wander alone
I am hit by a stone
as I fall to my knees
I wish I were at home
As I fall into the darkness
that now surrounds me
I wonder is anyone there
does anyone care
As I look up to a throne
A man sits alone
For there he sits and waits for me
but am I worthy did I
live righteously do I
deserve to sit by him
for I am man with flaws to bare.
As he speaks to me I must hear
Come my child and sit with me
You lived your life righteously
and now I sit there by the throne; and
wish no more that I was home

Brandi Burningham

Juggernaut

I am the rain on your parade
I am the splinter in your hand
I am the fester in your sore
I am the virus in your blood
I am the bullet in your skull

I am the wolf at your heels
I am the fear in your heart
I am the darkness of your dreams
I am the shadow on your conscience

I am the thorns pricking your brow
I am the spear thrust in your side
I am the nails through your hands
And the hammer that drove them in

I stand in conflict with the Gods
I stand in conflict with the Earth
I stand in conflict with all that is beautiful
I stand in conflict with your Sons
I stand in conflict with You.

Josh Kienitz

"I Walk In Dreams"

This is dedicated to Bert Fonté,
With one heart, one spirit, and one love.

As I lay in bed, in the dead of night.
I can feel you here, holding me tight.

When I close my eyes, your always here.
Bringing me happiness beyond compare.

For in dreams we laugh, we live, we cry.
It's a place where love never dies.

But in the day I'm lost and confused,
And feel so lonely because of you.

You cannot lose someone you never had.
I realize this and it makes me sad.

But you my love, you'll always be near.
For I walk in dreams, you are always here.

Joan C. Causey

A Perspective Check

There's a fly on the ceiling,
(I can tell as I'm standing on the floor,)
He seems to be walking,
to me his life is a bore.
Now were I that fly,
would I be standing on the floor?
And would that human,
be walking on the ceiling?
Were I to fly,
over to a wall,
would I then be standing on the floor?
And that human, on a wall?
My sister could walk in,
(my human sister,)
and solve it once and for all.
Or I could go and ask her,
(in human form,)
but I'm afraid I might fall...

Daniel Whitehead

No More Excuses

Mystery man, what's in your eyes?
I can't see through your disguise
Isn't this just one fine day
You're gonna waste it all away

Well I've driven my friends all away
Maybe they'll come back some day
One thing's for sure, it's in my plan
No more excuses for the way I am

Are you happy, are you sad?
Come on now, It's not that bad
We're all trying to like you
But we don't know what to do

Now I'm all alone where I belong
Moving to a different song
The people who cared don't give a damn
No more excuses for the way I am

There'll be no more excuses for the way I am
No more excuses for the way I am

Dennis A. Eschrich

Love Secure

Blues in a smoke saturated chamber,
I contemplate life's significance
Sunset light flickers in amber
I reflect any unfulfilled chance

Dreams are met with such eminence
Failures linger and extend
Hopes spark the fire, hence
True love is foremost, I contend

Once cherished completely, you discern
Acceptance surrounds and impends
All doubts and wisdom's unlearned
Lapse from memory and quandary descends

Christine Shoukri

Untitled

Webbed words
  clogged in mouth
As spider leg pen hogties brain
  Warm venom binds
the creative paralyzed figure
  in the net of apathy

Dave Graham

Mr. Lonely

Being alone is a simple disease
I could do everything
Women will never be please
Candy and flowers hardly work
It's most likely me
To then I'm considered a jerk
I give them all the love I possibly can
It's just not enough
They still holdout their hand
It doesn't matter what I do
After at least week
They always say were through
So from now on I know for sure
I'll never stop searching
For a heart so pure
Though I maybe on the journey of ny life
Someday soon
I'll find the perfect women to be my wife
So let them call me Mr. Homley
Cause I know the truth I'm just Mr. Lonely

Edward A. Clark

The Storm

I knew the storm was coming
I could feel it in the air
The clouds-dark and foreboding
I could feel the current there.

I turned and gazed and saw
the swirling, far above my head
And then I longed to be a part
of a strength some people dread.

My need was just to be at one
with the forces in the sky
For just one moment some inner part
of me fought, I know not why

To reach that place of power and force
and tho I really tried
It simply was not meant to be
and in my heart I cried.
"It is that I'm not to be allowed to be that free?
Or is it that, perhaps, I should just be at one
with me?

Jennifer Freerksen

Betrayed

The door was closed
I did not see who closed it
Or when
Or why

I tried to open it
But it would not open
Part of my world was on the other side

I felt a fear I did not understand
But why and who
And yet I did know and why

I said goodbye
To a broken trust
And turned slowly away.

Dorothy Manning Sarto

September Moon

The moon sits in the sky,
Trying hard not to cry.
The stars try to help,
By eating up the kelp
But that did not work,
So the moon has a smirk!

Sarah McQuate

The Suns (Sons) Poem

There was a time, I was so innocent
I didn't know the pain I'd caused.
There was a girl I was close to,
No longer here.
And,...I am because!
The way I am.
There was a man though he loved,
Gave pain as plain as the sun (son).
But, he didn't understand the sons love,
For he only saw her.
So...
He tried to hide his guilt.
But the shadow of the sun (son)
Was the girl, and pain...
And it remained...
To control the outcome of the way I am.
I knew a girl...

Jeff Koutsogianis

My Feelings For You

When I hear your name
I don't feel the same.
We used to be friends but
I don't know anymore.
My feelings for you.

A song reminds me of you and me.
But I'm not sure about
my feelings for you.

But I'm sure about this,
loves a funny game people play.
Good things happen
and people get hurt.
Why we play, I'll never know.
My feelings for you.

Amanda Osborne

What's That?

There's something in the schoolhouse.
I don't know what it is.
There's something in the schoolhouse.
It says it likes to "niz"?
There's something in the schoolhouse.
It is colored green.
There's something in the schoolhouse.
It came with gasoline.

There's an alien in the schoolhouse!
Oh! My gosh!
Aliens! Aliens!
Ate my cousin Josh!
Aliens! Aliens!
They are colored green!
Aliens! Aliens!
They look like some machines!

Aliens! Aliens!
Oh! My gosh!
Aliens! Aliens!
Ate my cousin Josh!

Benjamin James Mann

Reassurance

Soon enough I realize.
I don't really need you all that much.
You led me through your tricks
Your traps.
But why I ask you?
This lifetime of charades
of lies.
Tell me this
Will you?
Do you enjoy these...
games?
I'm not quite sure I understand.
You know.
All that I've been through.
No, not at all.
I am quite sure that I don't need you.
That is what...
is all that I understand
Now.

Adam Weber

Birds

Their wings run through the heavens above
I fall to the ground below

Oh how I wish I could feel their freedom
But the sky trips me back

I run to follow them
Oh how I crave for the sky

Where the streets are nameless
And the boundaries are unknown

Take my arms and give me wings
Take my flesh and give me feathers

Take my life and give me new
I want to feel sunlight below me

I want to wrestle with the wind
To rest myself upon a cloud

To sing songs of unknown grace
Oh how I wish to feel their freedom

Jason Isaacs

In Our Setting Sun

When I watch the sun set
I feel a warm closeness to you.
I can just close my eyes
and see the things we do.
The wind on the bluffs
blowing your hair back for me.
To show me your shining face,
It's so beautiful to see.
I can see your lips,
glistening in my mind.
And your twinkling eyes,
just smiling in the sun.
I can almost feel
your hand in mine,
talking about silly things,
Laughing and Loving as we go.
Walking Hand in Hand,
In our setting sun...

Dennis Clark

Dreams

As I sit beside a stream,
I feel I will begin to dream.
It may be good or even bad,
some can be very sad.

The dreams are here,
they're always here.
They take me away
as I sit here today

Dreams flow like streams,
streams flow like dreams.
Coming all at one time,
these dreams are all mine.

My thoughts, my fears,
and sometimes my tears.
Nobody can share
my thoughts that are there.

I have a dream
beside this stream
when something I hear
makes my dream disappear.

Amanda D. Smith

The Bump On My Rump Villanelle

Yesterday I got a large bump.
I fell down at Point Defiance Park.
The bump is right on my rump.

I hit the ground with a pretty loud thump...
So loud a deaf man yelled "What, hark!"
Yesterday I got a large bump.

I felt like a major league chump,
And my mood grew incredibly dark.
The bump is right on my rump.

My friends told me to quit being a grump.
Then they threw a big piece of bark.
Yesterday I got a large bump.

I tried to dodge the incoming clump.
But it landed right on its mark.
The bump is right on my rump.

I made an incredible jump.
I swear I looked eye to eye with a lark.
Yesterday I got a large bump.
The bump is right on my rump.

Aaron Paker

Shut

"Behind a blackened steel door is where
I find peace,
One being with myself.
To leave would mean to vision all
the dreams to crush and to imagine
all the destinations end.
Is that the pain we see but don't
think about?
I want to seek the mysteries of
shadows of the deepest darkest part
of the Earth,
but am I afraid of my surroundings.
Will I get up and walk or will I
sit and listen to the gossip that
kills us each and every day.
We all need help.
Help to find ourselves within one another.
I see new horizons appearing in my soul."
The gloomy door opens.

Aimee Martinez

Untitled

Standing on these Brazen Shores,
I flip my Hair back
Watching Scores of legions cross the Beach.
Their final words
of Doom and Death
They've lost their Breath
They cannot see.
I am the One who has Come,
to Save them from their Misery.

Vision of the Spotted Mind,
I close my Fist
inside it I find a Flower,
It jumps in my head
Rattles itself and Eats the Breath
that fills my Hallowed Frame.
Besides,
What little chance does it have to live in
there.
It only wants to speak.
It only wants to see
It only wants to think.

David Schneider

Mothermilk

In pre-dawn grog
I gather my wee clutching,
clambering, already suckling bundle.
After the first frenzied greed of
latching on,
The satisfying burn of milk flow
soothes us both.
Your laborious task leaves a moist
film twixt skins.
I marvel at the perfect sea shell
earmark embedded on my arm.
As you gaze intently, I ponder the
tiny newness of you and dream
our possible tomorrows.
Even as you grow old enough to ask
Nay, demand - a "nuss,"
our special time feels so right.
Can my love possibly mature to
greater heights as you do?

Denise Brace

Untitled

For a long time,
I have been wishing
You could be mine
In my heart
I know
It could never be so
Even though we feel
We belong
To one another
We know it is wrong
For us to be together
Let's remember the
Love
We share
Forget the tears
We shall cry,
To turn away,
To say,
"Good-bye"

Connie M. Johns

Sleep

Sleep my son, for tonight
I have many words to write,
of hopes, and dreams, and fears,
and prospects for the coming years.

Sleep my son, while I contemplate
of what's to come, what's our fate?
Of how to teach you what I've seen of life,
of love and sorrow, joy and strife.

Sleep my son, watched from above,
while I write to you of your father's love,
and how I will carry any load,
to help you down life's gravel road.

Alexander J. Hicks

Down By The Sea

I feel God's presence by my side,
I hear the tide rushing by.
I see the waves high and low,
I feel the sand between the toes,
I see the sun setting low,
I see the moon coming up
with a glow,
My friend its time we must go,
For God has shown us the way
To make the best of each passing day.

Carolyn M. Barton

Love

I see you walking,
I hear your sweet voice talking.
I wonder if there could ever be,
A magical LOVE between you and me?
And BABY I know it's there,
And things could go wrong!
But in my heart,
It's a magical LOVE song!
And I know in the end,
Things will be better!
Cause' Baby, oh, Baby,
We'll be together, Forever!!

Crystal A. Hamrick

Maggie's Poem

In my memory
I hold in my heart this
two year old girl who was so
special to me
I knew that no one could
take her from me
she was looking for a bone marrow
transplant one day
I hoped that God wouldn't
take her away
I knew in my heart she was
a sick little girl
I prayed for her each day
In hopes that God would
let her stay
she was such an angel to me
waiting for her little wings
I know she's in heaven in
my heart
and nothing can tear us
two apart.

Brandi Brecheisen

The Dark Gift

How I pity my mortal prey!
I hunt at night and never at day
For the suns rays would scorch my
pale white skin,
Some call me evil but I say to
them how would you like to live
in immortal sin?
I bite the throat soft, but firm
I like to see them wiggle and squirm
The stake through the heart is an
old wives tale!
And a vampire almost never fails!
I drink until the heart stops,
For the dark gift is all I've got.

Kim Hill

Why Do You Affect Me So?

I had a lovely thought today
I knew exactly the words to say
then I saw you standing there
and my voice faded in the air.
Tongue-tied and shy,
I felt I could cry.

Oh, why do you affect me so?

When I'm alone
my thoughts, how they roam.
You would never believe I could say so much
about how I love you and such.
Your eyes, oh yes, and your smile
keep my head in the clouds quite a while.

Oh, why do you affect me so?

In my dreams we dance
and talk of love
then I awake and blow the chance
to overcome shyness
with soft words of love.

Oh, why do you affect me so?

Jaunita Wallace

The Mountains

As I lay here under the big pine trees,
I look and see the honey bees.
I see a bunny, and then I spy a snake
that slowly slithers by.

I listen and hear a blue-jay cry.
I watch how the stream flows,
a chirp came from a near-by nest.

I looked and guessed, a baby crow.
I glanced and saw a butterfly,
and then I wondered, I wondered why,

Man destroys all of this being,
When GOD made it for you and me.

Amanda Lea Leibee

"Sacrifice"

Racking lamb
beneath the blade;
The torsion eases
and sheep is staid.
Sweet evening breezes
sweep the yard.
Sun has set.
Meat is charred.

Kristin Bergantz

I Wait For You

There's a picture that I have of you
I look at it from time to time
and just to touch the stained past
helps me to wait for you.

You are standing at the top of the stairs
in black and white, I still love you
and I stare at you and you at me
I still wait for you.

I will always be in your reach
your troubled times are mine to keep
and all my time I will give
to stay here always and wait for you.

Elsa Martinez

The Flight

A cold October afternoon,
I look down from way up high.
I let go.
Wind whipping my body.
Looking down,
Spotting a place to land.
Turn left,
Left again,
Flip,
Glide,
Gently,
Not too fast.
Look at me!
I'm flying!
Turn right, almost there
Another left,
One more flip,
and...
I land safely on the ground with the other
leaves.

Kevin McDaniels

Faith

Feeling the heat of frustration
I looked toward the sun
  to lite my way.
With a cool breeze on my neck, I noticed
the moon and stars and saw it was nite.
  and not day.
Looking around trying to find my way
  trying to find solid ground.
Looking for warmth, feeling for faith and
digging for strength,
  but none was to be found.
With two eyes to see,
  but going blind.
With a world of possessions,
  but losing my mind.
I fell to my knees lost in a hope
  of finding a way.
Sensing another knowing of all my troubles
asking me to pray.
Wondering if I was too late. A kind voice
spoke have faith, believe
and love me and you shall enter through my
gate.

Chuck Akins

Basic Need

Please love me.
I need for you to love me.
I need for you to want me to love you.

But I do not need to love you
Unless you love me.

I fear you will withdraw —
You will pretend —
You will push me away.

Each has its own hurt.

And so I do not say, "Please love me."
I pretend —
I say I do not need your love.

Yet — I am in pain.

Christine Baker Welton

Let the Night Come

I know the words,
I need the words,
but there's nobody to hear the words.

If only we shall meet
never to part again,
no sorrow would come upon me,
no power could overcome,
never gain will loneliness set in.

Tonight I shall let the night come
and the gentle breeze rock me to sleep.
Tomorrow when a new day is dawning
the sun will open my eyes,
the clouds will kiss my lips
and I shall hear those words.

Jennifer Baker

Our Love

I need your love
I need your touch
To hold one closed, so very much

Where did it go
The love we once had
It was there far us so long ago
Somehow it all turned had

He had our love
But it burst like a dark cloud from above
Its there for us to share again someday
The rain can't wash it all away

A growing pain within me aches
To start our life together again someday
To try hard for both our sakes
For I believe its never too late
To keep the vows that we once made

Let's share our life that we once had
and he together till death do us part
I will pray to our Lord for a new start

Janice E. Dirkes

Colors Of Life

White supplication
Blue destination
Red anger
Black stranger
Yellow gold
Grey hold
Silver blade
Midnight spade.

B.J. Scott

Mother's Day

When Mother's Day rolls around,
I never know what to do.
I think about the money I should spend,
Then I think about you.
There will never be a price tag
on my love for you Mom; As
there should never be.
Through all my ups and downs, you
were the only one that could see
the real me.
Thank you, for your love so true;
You know I'll always care about you.

Karen K. Estep

Thoughtful Feelings

In the seat in the heat
I no you are very neat

In the morning in the noon
I hope I see you very soon

In the sun in the cloud
I hope you speak very loud

In the front at the back
you surely look like a sack

If your short if your tall
I hope you don't hit the wall

Barbara Bell

Your Dreams

Last night while you were sleeping
I plugged into your dreams
Stealing the secrets you've been keeping
Lost and lonely footsteps creeping
An echoing tunnel of screams.

Last night while you were snoring
I understood your pain
Out of the river infection was pouring
The secret of sin in your eyes so alluring
The heavens have nothing to gain.

Last night while you were breathing
I found myself lost in your mind
All of the characters lonely and grieving
I have nothing left to believe in
As I slip back wards into time.

Last night while you were drifting
I captured your wandering thoughts
Your mind surrendered shaking shifting
Into dawn your eyelids were lifting
From the dream in which you'd been
caught.

Carrie Antel

How Many

The times to sit
Alone or together
In gentle quiet or
Laughter

Somehow there's always the time,
Hopes and dreams
How many
I don't know

Aren't you glad
We don't

Jim Schmidt

Unanswered Questions

To those days gone by, to my stepson
I replied...
Would I go back and begin again?
Those little hearts try to mend?
Return to the days with gloves on hands?
Making dad a big snowman?
To be a Taxi, were those days well spent?
And sit inside a rainfilled tent?
Redo those one day fishing trips, to
catch tad poles you thought were fish?
The bathroom cleaned; and laundry done?
A hug for each and every son?
With each unanswered question,
would come the same reply...
"In A Heartbeat"
to those days gone by.

Bobbie Thomas

Time

Where is yesterday...
I saw it a moment ago
Time is far away...
Can't seem to hold on, melts like snow
I'll put tomorrow in a bottle
on my shelf - safe and secure...
to open when I need
to borrow.

Kay Gregg

I See the Snow Fall

As I look out my window I see snow
I see, the snow fall
I see it cover the ground
The snow clouds make the world look
white and gray
I see the snow come down light and
hard, as if it disappears and
reappears right before my eyes
When the world is snowy every
one stays and people talk with there
family's in front of a crackling fire
I realize that the snow can be good
and can be bad as I look
I see the snow fall.

Alina Fowler

When I Close My Eyes

When I close my eyes
I see your smiling face.
That's when the tear drops
fall everywhere for you.
I spend most of my time now
just thinking about you and
The times we had shared.
All I had to do was close
my eyes and you were there,
Not only in my mind, but
in my heart as well.
I felt so much better when the
memories flooded my head.
I hope to see you very soon.
So when I close my eyes again
I will be in your arms
Loving you.

Jennifer Groszewski

Dancing In The Wind

Dancing in the wind
I sing to myself,
a song that only I can sing.
Pictures stained from vanished words
stream before my eye.
The melody lilts within.
My arms embrace the wind.
My hips sway in easy tones.
I close my eyes
so I can see.

Kathleen O'Connell

Look Upon Thee

Look upon thee. Remember every word
I speak. You will always be in a
wrong patch, but you will find the golden
key to the lock that will match.

Look upon thee.
Sit under a tree.
Stare at the sky. Listen
to the man above. He never lies.

Look upon thee.
Open up and talk within your soul.
Never stand next to a demon himself
who pretends that he is bold.

Look upon thee
Every word I wrote I never lie
Never trust or believe one who spies.
Just look upon thee and see.

Amy R. Hawkins

Untitled

Into the brownest eyes I've ever seen
I stared with all my might
Into the cutest face upon my dreams
Befell the look of de-light.

One month we have together passed
Nine more we have known
Who would have thought to know it then
That we would sit upon the lover's throne.

Imperial happiness, yet the greatest fear
As black and dark as night
Holds us in a state of wonder
Not knowing it wrong or right.

Desire awakens, passion grows
Within our hearts so deep
Love is stirred within our hearts
Forever for us to keep.

Lay down upon your pillow
And close your eyes to sleep
Lay down upon your pillow
And there in your dreams we will be.

Darcy Niedowicz

Patience

I crawl, but not too fast....
I see a closed door.

I walk, But not too fast...
Once more the door is closed.

I run, a little too fast-
Slam! The door is locked!

I lay and wait
Where is the door?

Lisa Anne Kennedy

Love Once Held

Love once held in your heart
Can never be erased
It is only set aside
Like a rose in a vase
Only to be admired from afar

Brenda Clopper Lewis

A Special Place

As I walk so quietly all alone.
I think of something that's unknown.
A fantasy land for you and me.
A distant place, I wish I could see.
My only reach are in my dreams.

Now I sit in my special place.
With the late night moon beams in my face.
I sit and wish of more happiness.
Wondering of my peacefulness.
All my thoughts flow out in a stream.
Only so that I may dream.

So I close my eyes to fall asleep.
As I lay back, I begin to count sheep.
Only so I may fall to sleep.
Asleep I dream of my special place,
Where I'm with a friend, we sit by a river
bend.

As we bid farewell to the day.
While the day comes to an end.
We both go our way to dream of our,
Special place once again.

Adrian C. Martinez

Life Beyond The Horizon

One beautiful morning
I was walking on the beach
and I was thinking,
"Is there any life beyond the Horizon!"
Just about that time
I saw a dolphin jumping
out and in the water.
Then I said,
"Yes, there is life beyond the Horizon."
It may not be human life
but it is a Glory life..
God's gift of life."

Brittany Lauryn-Michele Winters

For Captain

Not only do I pine;
  I waste away.
Time has never been
  An enemy.
But what have I to do.
  No plans for love,
  No future gain;
Promises fall flat.
  The prospect of never
  Seeing him again;
I guess the plans we made
  Are no more.
Why kiss, why make love?
Is it the sex;
  Or does it make a difference?
We were one;
  No longer do I know
  He will be there for me.
I wish we had talked.

Joanna A. Price

On Being Shy...

I am a wall flower,
I watch and listen
and say
nothing.
No one notices me
even when I am
right under their nose.
I notice them,
my tongue aches to speak,
but nothing comes out.
I am afraid.
I wish I could say, "Hello"
to someone I know,
but would they see me
and say, "Hello?"
I don't know.
So I will say
nothing,
nothing at all.

Ann Shaw

The Dawn

Sitting on a bench outside,
I watch the day awaken.
I see the sun with golden light,
Shining down upon me.
I hear the birds start to chirp,
I see the squirrels run wild.
As all of God's creatures arise,
They look toward the sun.
They see at that moment,
The dawn.

Andrea M. Deline

When He Left

  He turned his head and walked away
I watched, and felt afraid
  I pleaded, but he wouldn't stay
I watched and felt afraid
  Before this, our love fell apart
I watched, and felt afraid
  He cruelly trampled on my heart
I watched and felt afraid
  Helpless when he crushed my soul
I watched, and felt afraid
  I stopped him not, my life he stole
I watched and felt afraid
  And while he did all he could do
I watched and felt afraid
  My life he took, and my love, too
I watched, and felt afraid
  But still I begged him not to go
How he could leave I'll never know
  I couldn't believe he'd leave me, so
I watched and felt afraid

Catrina M. Johnson

Storm

Thunder cannonade
Grey rioting sky
Hurls hail
Wild
Soothing wild

Rain slashed mountain
Wind wrenched wood
Drips
Jewels

Karen D. Zurawski

Untitled

Smile once for me,
for I am smiling too.
I haven't really gone
you see
I've left my heart with you.

Jennifer Meyers

Untitled

I think of you often
I wonder if it's because of the rain
Drops of water making their way
down the windows pane
Seemingly painting your portrait
within my mind
I wonder if you see as much as I
when our eyes meet
It's as though we could have an affair
in that brief moments time

I knew you were warm and sensitive
from the beginning
I knew it when our eyes met
and our lips touched

I wonder if it will ever stop raining.

Ken Kennedy

Heart's Desire

If you could have your heart's desire
I wonder what it would be
A spacious house expensive car or
Maybe a money tree?

Perhaps a never ending trip
To places, like the Taj Mahal
Or be the 'Chairman of the Board'
Or maybe do nothing at all.

Would you like to sit upon a throne
With servants at your feet?
And jewels and gold and silver and
Exotic foods to eat.

Or would you choose to be at peace.
With everyone you meet.
And wish that all would have enough
To make their life complete.

And share with all with what you had
And be content with life
With love, good health, good friend and joy
In a world that was free from strife.

Eleanor Kurtz

All These Thoughts Inside My Head

All these thoughts inside my head,
I wonder where it ever ends
All I can do is dream of you;
Your lips so sweet your touch so fine,
Oh how I wish that you were mine
I dream of you every night,
And all about your kiss so light
I want to touch your skin so soft,
To hold you close and never stop
I want to kiss your lips so fine,
And with your touch so genuine
I want to look into your eyes;
And know you will be mine forever,
I hope we'll always be together
With all these thoughts inside my head.

Kimberly Jackson

I Am

I am a fly
I wonder why
I hear so much
I see that
I am a freak of nature
I fear the thing called a fly swatter
I feel the power of the human hand
I touch my wings for comfort
I worry for my life
I cry out in horror that
I am afraid
I understand that I am not like humans
I dream of eternal life
I hope I survive this cruel world
I am a fly

Joseph Winstead

When I Hear Your Voice

When I hear your voice
I would
just like to be
with you forever.
When I hear your
voice I start to
melt because your
voice is so sweet.
When I hear your
voice I feel like
I will never get tired
of saying "I love you"
When I hear your voice
I want to love you to the
end to time. When I
hear you talk I feel
like I am the luckiest
man in the universe.

Chris Gonzales

Do They Know?

If I could do it again, I wouldn't,
If I could live again I would.
I had some dreams, ambitions,
Yet no one told me that I could.
They said that I was worthless
They called me crazy, mad.
They said that I was nothing,
And now I wonder if they're sad,
To know that I am under ground
I wonder if they cried,
When they found out what they said to me,
Led up to how I died.
I felt the razor cut me,
I felt life drain away.
I know just how they found me,
In a pool of blood I lay.
Do they know just how they hurt me?
Do they know how much I cried?
Do they know I couldn't take it?
So I committed suicide.

Emilie Ann Fabiny

Humpback

Graceful
Gentle giant
Communicates with songs
Beautiful nice gigantic slow
Lovely

Christopher Lee

Dreams

D is for dying, time goes so fast
If we don't start caring
Our world just won't last

R is for rainforests
They grow oh so green
But as we speak
Most are diminishing

E is for endangered
Most species are
The elephant, the lions,
The whales and the gaur

A is for acknowledge
It's what we need to do
To make this world a better place
For me and for you

M is for mother nature
She's dying at the moment
The world will be real dumb without her,
won't it

S is for savior, that's what we need to be
We all have the power to help her,
both you and me

Josh A. Dilegame

What Good Is Fame And Fortune?

What good is fame and fortune,
If you do not have a friend?
If you do not have someone,
Who will be with you in the end.
Your riches can not buy you,
A Heavenly Home and Golden Crown,
And all your earthly treasures,
Can not comfort you, when you are down.
All your fame and fortune,
Will not buy you happiness and love,
Or your name written in,
God's book up above.
It is true on this earth,
You may buy the world things,
But when your life is over,
You won't see anything it brings.
You may buy a nice car,
And a big fancy home,
But what good are they,
When you are left all alone?
On earth you may have,
A lot of it's worldly gold,
But it can not buy love of a friend,
When your heart has turned cold.
So give a little of yourself,
And some of your earthly worth,
And ask God for His forgiveness,
Before you leave this old earth.
Then you will have more riches,
Than you could possibly ever dream,
And a home up in Glory,
Beyond the Peaceful Stream.

Elouise Collins Mason

Untitled

A love so true is so rare
But it is the love I hold for you
Love is sweet
Love is kind
The love we share is so divine
One that other's dream of
But may never find

Jody B. Miller

Three Score And Seven

When I'm three score and seven
I'll have a house up on a hill,
With two cars in the driveway
And flowers on each sill.

When I'm three score and seven
The children will be raised,
My husband will retire
'Mid accolades and praise.

When I'm three score and seven
We'll travel far and wide,
Enjoy our country's beauty
With grandkids by our side.

Now I'm three score and seven.
My dreams have all come true.
The "express train" of life has passed me
And there's still so much to do.

Three score and seven years are gone.
We wonder where and how.
But I'm content to stay right here
And enjoy my dreams for now.

Emilie L. Schmauch

Football

Football is my lifelong dream.
I'm built like a truck,
I'm a fighting machine.
Down the sideline to the goal,
I'll block and tackle, here we go.
Spin one left, spin one right
Hit those guys with all my might.
I'd try to punt, maybe a pass,
Holy Cow! A touch down at last!
Yelling, screaming could this mean,
A lifelong contract to my dream?
Maybe yes, Maybe no.
Let's just see how far I'll go.
Dear Mom and Dad, so you can see
Just how important this is to me
If you would please just sign right here,
I could start my dream right now this year.

Chris Kuhar

Relic

I feel like I don't belong;
I'm not one of your kind.
My heart, my soul, my way of life
are lost in another time.

I have always been the nomad
who doesn't have a home.
Wounded, restless, tired, searching,
in this I am alone.

I am a relic of the past,
clinging to what I can.
Wanting things that are no longer,
failing to understand.

Saddened by every centuries' passage
and wishing to stop the clock,
to turn back its thieving hands
as I, upon the door of the ages, knock.

Alas! I wander through the years,
solitary in my quest
to find my place, my destiny,
before I take my rest.

Christina Bowman

Nothing

Nothing
didn't do anything
at any time
anywhere
for any reason.

Andy Cobble

Ode to Joe

I used to be a "we" and now
I'm only "me"
You were part of my life
the day I became your wife.
You wanted to live life your way
and sometimes you didn't hear
what I had to say.
But just being with you made my day.
My so-called friends are few
and most of them relatively new.
My heart is heavy and my
life is empty.
Every day I desperately miss you
and some days, I really don't
know what to do.
You promised you would
always be here for me.
You are now gone and I'm
forlorn because I used to
be a "we" and now it's only "me"

Beatrice Fierstein

New Day

The sun is up.
I'm ready to go.
A new day has begun.

On with my clothes,
And a bite to eat,
Now out the door I run.

The morning's good.
I work very hard.
Soon will be time for lunch.

In afternoon,
Problems do arise;
But I give them the "punch".

Wow! On to home,
My abode of rest.
My supper's soon. Hooray!

Now night is here.
Lay me down in bed.
And wait for a New Day!

Daniel R. Nazelrod, Jr.

Coming of the Light

With misery sitting at my side
In a blackened world alone I cried
The darkness kept consuming me
I knew to live I must get free
I searched my soul for the will to fight
I kicked the darkness and saw a light
Then through that light I quickly flew
To find the source led right to you
With darkness gone I've got the sun
To walk our path together as one
We'll take that path through eternity
Just us two my love-you and me

James A. Wiskochil

Archipelago

Sitting here
in a chair
breathing air
without care

Scattered thoughts-
battles fought
lessons taught
order sought

Fractured soul
hopeful goal
Paid the toll
make me whole

Existence
make some sense
living's tense
death immense

Sitting here
in a chair
breathing air
I do care

Brian Trusiewicz

Untitled

Oh see the maiden standing aloft
In a gown of molten gold
Light catches the sparkle in her eye
The shimmer in every fold

A figure appears at the stair top
Tailored from head to toe
Shyness seems to overcome him
Anxiety is his foe

The two proceed descending to meet
Smiling at one another
Gracefully bowing he folds one arm
Then offers her the other

The enchantment of the music
Carries them off into the night
The first cautious steps that are taken
Are suddenly performed right

This love, this perfection, this feeling
Is strong to say the least
They never thought it would happen to them
Beauty and the Beast

Jill Chamberlain

Trying

Did you see me
in a tree
on a branch
doing a dance
jumping down
on the ground
in the air
going there
laughing out loud
on top of a cloud
starting to cry
because I can't fly.
But if you've seen me try
You'd wonder why
I really want to fly.

Catherine Robidoux

Dear Friends

I am pleased, exhilarated
In all that you have
Examined, and recognized
Chosen from my life
Of love, is worthy
And without a doubt
All, that I have received
In recognition of this fact
Is, encouragingly stimulating.

"EAST OF THE SUNRISE"
I did receive it's beautiful!
Cost, via heritage
As no comparison
All other associated
Memorable, optional articles
I feel, somewhat
The very same
No-less do I rate
My poets corner.
I kindly thank you.

Jean G. Daniel

The Etch Of Crimson

The land is red and green shoots up
in bushes and trees and skulls
of the graveyard archaic gods
left to burn in the sol of sound.
Caverns run deep into the blistering
bosom of the earth,
and the blood is blue amidst the red
of sharp shreds of crushed
rocks kissing the etch of virgin land.
The horse bends his majestic mane,
gallantly sweeping cracked hooves
into the blood of caverns older than
the beating brawn of running rapids
rusting the fair red of an oncoming
tomorrow.

Denys D. Thede

Dark Child

I am the dark child in the fire
In Her is my passion, my sexuality
my arrogance, my power
In Her soul is my devil, my destroyer

She can taste the blood,
revel in their deaths
She is not afraid
not even of Her strength

She is beauty
She is woman

With Her I can be whole
With Her I have expression

She is the voice of my silent child
the embodiment of my shadow

She is grace
She is will
She is fury
And She never forgets

She is the dark child
And She is Me

Elizabeth Claire Celli

Alone

Trapped
in her own little world,
all by herself.
Dreaming
of someone breaking in,
rescuing her.
Wanting
to live her own life,
to be free.
Thinking
of how it would be,
on her own.
Knowing
someday her chance will come,
pass her by.
Trapped
in her own little world,
all by herself. Dreaming...

Alison Sgroi

My Meadow's Elfin Maid

I pondered 'pon her, briefly napping,
In measure, whilst I spun my dream;
A'fore the 'morrow's knock was tapping,
'bout an elfin, bonny maid.

A tiny maid of golden-face,
With locks of honey-golden dew;
And dainty fingers, gently wrapping,
Wild flowers and other meadow stuff.
Blithe she was, with pale-grey eyes,
And dressed in dand'lion fluff.

Kobi L. Johnson

Success At F.L.I.

I'm just a struggling student,
In Mrs. Creamer's class,
I work my old typewriter
to get some speed, to pass.

My "A's" turn out as "S's",
The "L's" type out as "K",
The darned old "F's" look just like "G's",
But I'll never show dismay.

Because,—I'm going to be successful,
Typing is my pride and joy,
I'll write adventure stories,
About great girls and boys.

But, arthritis is my problem
As I'm sixty five years old,
My fingers will not bend at all,
And I'm a failure with my toes.

But, —if I'm going to be successful
I cannot be morose,
I'll find a better way to type
If I have to do it with my nose.

John R. P. Northage

Heaven

A place where you never worry
A place where you never die
A place where God keeps your soul
Safely up in the sky
A place as beautiful as ever
A place full of friends
A place that is unlimited
A place that never ends

Kristy Richardson

Until Today

I see your reflection
in my mind
Your touch is so gentle
your words are kind
When you pass your smile brings
sunshine to me
Like petals from a rosebud
a beauty to see
If only for a moment
our lips could meet
So soft and delicate
warm and sweet
Never before
have I felt this way
Never before
...until today

Kimberly Carmona

The Library Shelf

Silently, I wait —-
In such a
Crowded, small space.

Suddenly, I hear:
Standing near
A child in place.

Nothing more...

There: a soft sound,
A movement —-
A book is gone!

A remarkably, precious sight:

A child and a book,
Alone.

Carolyn Kight

For Justine

Green winds began
in sunshine with blue sky

The ritual of shoes unlacing begins

In bare feet
the skin of the tree
is rough and warm
newly hatched leaves
tickle and rove the wind
we have learned to conquer
our learned fears
deep breaths and unsure footing
we haven't fallen.

We become like children, unafraid.

Branches hold hands
stretch where we sit
this tree an old friend
a warm lap embracing us
shiny leaves rustle a lullaby
this place where the world escapes us

tree, as warm as your hand in mind.

Carin Abria Steger

Untitled

It's hard to see
In the blinding light
through the cloudy haze
Of bright midnight
Where the moon don't shine
Flowers blossom
Silently watching
And the trees whisper their secrets
To any who will hear
But the darkness demands silence
So all may be revealed
The surf pounds out a message
Saying to point
Some things shouldn't be known
And time refuses to stop
So the planet spins on

Christopher James Westervelt

The Question

What secrets are buried away
  In the dark crevices of the mind
There are passions and sins and crimes
  For all - they say in time.
But passions are considered a
  Sin to some.
And both are considered a crime
  So how do we differentiate
When we are in our prime.

Dorothy M. Krueger

"My Grandma's Shawl"

A dear one strong of faith;
In the darkness I remembered
As I sat upon the sofa,
Though in time suspended.

As I came to kneel beside her:
She whispered, as if joking,
"Come place your hand upon my knee
And feel the old bones croaking!"

A rub she used to ease the pain;
How strong the musty smell.
It would penetrate through every room:
Winter Green Alcohol!

The words of wisdom spoken
Etched deep into my memory:
"Drop a knife and kiss a stranger
Before you're twenty three.

Although the years have passed,
All the love I still recall,
Of that sweet and great, great lady
Wrapped in my Grandma's shawl.

Connie M. McDonald

Untitled

I awake to the dawning day
Only to re-enter
My dreams of alabaster

Footfalls
Upon the ivory path
Leading to the ebony touch
I've been searching for

The white desire
That will forever
Taint me.

Matthew C. Furey

Good Friday In Church

I dropped on my knees
in the engulfing silence
of sorrow;

I collected my thoughts
in solemn contemplation
of the reason for my Lord's
dying on the cross. . .

I reached deep
into the bottom
of my heart
for undiluted sincerity
as I recalled (in pained repentance)
The transgressions perpetrated
against my Saviour;

And raising supplicating eyes
to the shrouded form
of my Lord on the cross
at the altar
I implored forgiveness
for being a sinner.

Diomedes C. Gonzales

Self Termination

Now is the time to make a change
In the lives we lead.
We must try to rearrange
And learn to take heed.

Look at all the things we have done
To endanger our world.
While we were out having fun,
Our futures began to whirl.

Danger is right in front of our faces
But we are too blind to see
That we are destroying the human race,
And there will be nothing left but pleas.

Pleas for release
From such a cruel existence.
Where pain will never cease
And there is no use for resistance

Maybe with a little help,
And lots of determination
We will help the people who wept
And stop our self termination.

Kawanna Michelle Bright

New Tomorrow

A lost bird sings alone
  In the night
He doesn't know where he's going
  As he takes off in flight
To the mighty crash of the waves
  He will follow
In his long desperate search
  Hoping to find tomorrow
As he flies he follow the brightness
  Of the moon light
Before it disappears in the darkness
  Of the cold night
As his wings grow tired and his
  Eyes become weak
He keeps flying finds his mother again
  And falls asleep on her warm breast
The sun rises at dawn
  And he sees the dew sparkle
He take off again
  In search of a new tomorrow

Clark Adams

If I Should Fall

If I should fall, my head I'd bump
down to the ground I'd go.
With a sudden crash, my head I'd bash
on the hard hard bricks below.

James Kirby

Woman

I thought of you
In the silence of shadows
Yet born-immaculate
I thought of you
The earth
A cradle of fire-pure
I thought of you
Of life and death
I thought of you and me
Disguised as a dream-real
An ancient lore
A secret doctrine
I thought of you
The light of the world...

Arly P. Denis

Perspective

Different people have different views,
In their search for understanding,
They have come across different clues,

Some have incredible fortune,
They may be sheltered and naive,
But receive life's beauteous portion,

Many don't have such pleasant luck,
They've no hope for a better world,
Because they are hopelessly stuck,

People ask which God gets to choose
Which people are blessed with success
And which people constantly lose,

With those whose lives are sugar sweet,
Communication often fails
With those who are hopelessly beat,

Society's optimism
Relentlessly battles against
Society's cynicism.

Kevin Wiatrowski

This And Other Beds

How often we have lain Love
in this and other beds in
this and other lands
Lain loved and dreamed such dreams
as then seemed apt
regretting only what had been
and what was yet to be.

Or was it only I who in
those fractioned ages before sleep
dwelt again in rue Lamarck?
Who lured by warming ozone smells
and urging screech of steel on steel
descended to the Flore to seek
what was not there?

And was it all in vain because
there was so much we could not know?
(Or did you know?
I wonder still.)

Karl Zimmer

America The Beautiful?

"Why do we have such dirty air?
In this country of rockets red glare,

I know all the children care,
We want to grow up with the
old grey mare.

Are we insane?
Wanting freshness of home on
the range,

I find this air issue strange,
That most of us refuse to change.

With a long heavy sigh,
I smell the tainted apple pie,

Because we continue to
pollute the sky,

Someday, prematurely, we all
may die!

So today I urge you to do your share,
No more smoking it ruins the air,

Don't drive one in five,
It just may keep us all alive."

Ashley Harper

But A Child

I am but a child,
in this vast world.
I am not a man,
not a stubborn independent man.
I am but a child,
a blameless, innocent child.
Life yawns before me,
like a dark bottomless pit.
I know nothing of it,
of the journey I am to take.
I am but a child.
I am but a child.

Jennifer F. Null

Dreams

There are many people,
In this world,
The good and best,
The bad and worst.

All with different dreams,
Kept in mind,
Until the day they first walk
'Till the end of time.

When they achieve their goal,
They feel special inside,
A feeling of hope,
It's a feeling of pride.

Like they have climbed,
The highest mountain,
Or have searched and found,
The youthful fountain.

Dreams are not always,
To be famous singers,
It could be a hero,
It depends on the dreamer!

Alexis Koskan

Seat Of Wisdom

Liquid loving eyes
in touching true gaze.
I see into Her heart
as few words fill a page.

The voice of Holy Love,
clear, gentle, ringing
through. Confident wisdom
of what must come true.

A persisting question
within my brain is broken
up and goes up in flame.

How lucky Her own to be.
To cross over, on eagles
wings, with one lovely
as She. Eternal and free.

David W. Domansky

Blue

Blue is an ocean,
in your dream.
Blue is a street,
in a stream.

Blue is a shirt,
worn by Bret.
Blue is a ribbon,
I won in a bet.

Blue is a sapphire,
that gives a sparkle.
Blue is bright,
unlike charcoal.

Blue is a cool,
refreshing drink.
Blue is a color,
just like pink!

Jason King

Untitled

Girl
innocent face
full of life
energy knows no bounds
discovering and testing new experiences
questioning all that is
dreaming of future
growing, changing
Woman
mature beauty
awakening of self
new life is born
Core of being, forever changed
realization of childhood dreams
continuity of life
forever young
Mother

Jennifer Solomon

Tulips

Tulips in the twilight
Fading in the light
Do stop and wonder
If magic is in the dusk
Seeping into the tulips
As they fade away
Into the darkness.

Juliette Wigley

Wild Horses

Wonderfully Beautiful Creatures
Intelligent
Lovable
Daring

Happily living in the wild
Outside is where they should be
Running is their game
Stalls are not their thing
Eat lots of hay
Sly, wild horses

Amy Christine Ellsworth

Brotherhood Fabric Of Man

Multi-colored fabric of life.
Interwoven by the Master's hand,
While holding fast together,
See how tall we all stand!

But let the fabric be torn,
And the threads we do no mend,
The fabric of life unravels,
And sorry we are at the end.

So each must look to his labor,
Let peace and kindness abide,
And face our communal future,
Woven in love side by side.

So we as daily weavers,
Need heed the work of our hands,
For each of us are threads of life,
In the brotherhood-fabric of man.

Joe E. Barrett

Untitled

When I look
Into the future
And all that I
Hope to be.....
A wish is that
My children
Have a
Father.....
Like the one
You are
To me

Audra Sigan

Missing Lover

A silent hum entered deep
into the mind a widows weep
all has failed her last request
return the soul allow eyes rest
sorrow deepens another night
all alone held pillows tight
a bird chirps but not one stir
death it seems has become of her
allow not the soul to rest
again and still life exists
into the black your mind may go
but let his soul be free

Karen Schaedel

A New Day

Rays of brightness
Invade the sky,
Whispering to nature
Night is passing by.

Each moment is new
And no one can say,
What may happen
On any given day.

As the rooster crows
And dreams fade with awaking,
Another day begins
with history in the making!

Christine Hammer

Dreams

I am the nightbird
invisible during daylight
invisible by the night
I perch alone
I am the nightbird
my flight is smooth and silent
my dagger sharp and swift
my work is never done
I am the nightbird
I soar just beyond your threshold
I play just past your pain
I know your every fear
I am the nightbird

Bob Gossett

Color Of Peace

Around about our blinded eyes
is a world where color lies.
But we as people have learned to look
only at similarly written books.
We fail to look past a cover,
and thus we fail to discover,
that other books are bright and cheery;
scaring us and make us leery.
Scared of something yet unknown,
never thought or never shown.
So, we stay ignorant fools
never seeking to change the rules.
In a world of black and white,
we fail to see where colors fight;
to change a world where they can use
all their shades of tints and hues.
Oh, what a world it would be
if all our eyes the colors see.
Of all the color our eyes would feast
I wonder what the color is...of peace?

Brian T. Cross

Light To Darkness

My friend
is breaking a heart
my heart
our friendship
was like a willow tree blowing
in the soft sweet wind
Now the wind has stopped between us
the sun use to shine so brightly
now the light
has turned to
darkness

Judith Ann Jones

Endless Love

My love for you
Is as the sands of the sea,
My precious one.
It has no boundaries;
You are more precious than
The finest rubies, and
Until the end of time
I will love you with
Endless love!

My love for you
Is as the stars of heaven,
My lovely one.
It is as far reaching as
The vast infinity of space.
You are more desirable
Than purest gold, and
Until the end of time
I will love you with
Endless love!

Donald M. Kappel

The Rose

The precious story of our lives together
Is beautiful like a rose—
Each year is more vibrant and cherished
As every petal unfolds.

Nothing else in this world could compare—
So strong and yet so sweet.
In it's gentle, kind, compassionate way,
It it's faith I can believe.

Just as one cannot appreciate
A rose by sight alone,
We could not know the joy we have
Had we not touched the thorns.

The delicate rose will fade and wilt
As time passes by, but
We will grow stronger and closer to-
gether—
Our love will never die.

Carolyn Michelle Slemp

Life

What is the meaning of living
Is it to be kind and giving
To share our lives with others
To love our sisters and brothers
Often people ask why
How come we live, how come we die
Why do we keep going on
Why do we always wake up at dawn
Is it because we have a goal
A special feeling in our soul
I believe it is because of the love,
that we get in our heart from up above
The Lord is the one
who gave us his son
So let me ask you
and have you wonder why
What is the meaning of our lives

Kelsey Samuelson

Inquisition

What is Osculation?
Is it war within a nation?
The word itself is rare
But if defined, the fact is there
That it happens every second
practically, or almost, I reckon.

It isn't a menace
Is happens in Venice
No: it isn't contagious,
Though handed down thru the ages.

It's just a name
But it would be a shame
For one person to miss
the delights of a "Kiss."

Eileen Shea

Candle Dancer

The burning candle's flame
Is like a dancer.
It leaps and pirouettes through
The air.

Quietly it performs,
Dancing to an unheard tune.

As it dances on,
Its stage is lowered slowly
To the ground.

When it gets to the bottom,
The flame stops.

Done with dancing,
It goes to sleep;
Waiting for someone
To light a match.

So it may dance again.

Kristine M. Roof

Culmination

The past, no matter what it be
is like the breeze that stirs the sea;
You cannot change the wind's wide sweep
Nor alter the past—why mourn and weep?

The future with its winsome ways
And all the allure that it displays
Lies always just beyond the hill
Which scaled, reveals one farther still.

Only the present is yours to hold,
To shape, to fold, to press and mold;
In the present lie the why and when
Of all that shall be, or ever has been.

Edwin M. Johnson

Childhood Lost

Little brownie bear
with dust on your paws
Peaking out secretly
to a world of flaws

Little brownie bear
with tears in your eyes
Yes, I will hold and rock away
all your tender cries

Sandra Barker

The Bitter Sweetness

The bitter sweetness of our lives,
Is like the Sun's last fading rays.
The beauty lingers just so long,
Until it's one more yesterday.
A newborn dream awakes inside,
Of every heart that holds the key.
But as each moment passes by,
So very few will set it free.
Determination plays a song,
That reaches far beyond the skies.
But when our hope has turned to tears,
It's only our defeat that cries.
We could find the rainbow's end
Whose measured worth cannot be told.
But we're too busy searching life,
To find that shining pot of gold.
The bitter sweetness of our lives
Can be no less, yet nothing more.
Cause harmony still waits beyond,
The perfect world we're looking for.

Katie Bayer

Death Raw X Twa

Somewhere - someone
is the mother of the murderer
And deep inside, she bears the pressing guilt
failure
grief...

He, created in and of herself, and by her issued into the world -
Warm, tender, soft, dear - perfect
full of promise...

Convicted now - condemned
for the ultimate ugly act of
Squelching the breath of his
earthly brother
Silent no remorse....

But as the switch is set in its finality,
She screams!
At the tearing loss
of her flesh
And soul...

Ann C. Butler

The Sword And Plowshare

The plow of my friend
is the sword of my brother,
we are here till the end
born into war.

The babies cry restless
without their fathers,
the babies won't guess
he's gone off to war.

They don't have a clue
even while they fight,
they never ask - they only do
never asking, why war?

When will it end?
When will there be war no more?

Jonathan J. Miner

Untitled

Am I dying?
Is this real?
Seeing, hearing.
I can't feel.
Foolish acts.
Wrong undoing.
Stuck together,
And still gluing.
What has happened?
I can't see.
Whose is this grave,
Here next to me?
Can I help?
How do you do?
Will you give up,
Or start a new?

Crystal Villegas

A Cloudy Night

The moon on a cloudy night,
Is very dark with specks of light,
Filtering through the clouds on high,
While I upon my bed do lie.

While the clouds upon the moon dance,
I watch as if in a trance.
My eyes never weary on my face,
Looking at the moon in space.

Erin Little

The Cry Of A Whale

Out where the sun shines bright,
Is where the wild one's wander free.
Together as a complete family,
One gets more attention, Yes!, it is she.

And when one gets caught,
There's nothing we can do.
Yes we have fought
We always cry, too.

The whales are not happy now,
It's just not the same.
If only the whale was here
And there would be no more games.

The cry of a whale
Still lasts today.
Please stop the pain-
Make it go away.

Jessica Cervenka

Belong

I didn't do nothin' wrong.
It was you who decided I didn't belong

So, my skin ain't so white
That don't mean that I bite.

I'm just doin' my best
While tryin' to fit in with the rest.

So I don't dress the same
And maybe my hair ain't so tame.

But as I live my life,
I wish you'd look at me and my strife

And look back and say:
I wish I'd have said 'Hi' that day

I didn't do nothin' wrong
It was you who decided I didn't belong.

Jocelyn Estes

Time Spent Expecting

A night of love and passion
is where this all began
A feeling of apprehension
which I didn't understand

A week of constant waiting
for the result to be known
A feeling of pure elation
when would I start to show
A month of genuine confusion
anxiety, sadness, joy
A feeling of motherly intuition
will it be a girl or a boy

A partial year of growing
both outer and from within
A feeling of utter desperation
was this ever going to end

A lifetime of celebration
The waiting is now complete
A feeling of fulfillment
as I tickle his little feet.

Brenda Walid

I Have Known Love

I have known love.
It came to me on silken wings,
And lifted me high above velvety clouds;
It carried me across infinite space—
Into overwhelming ecstasy!

I have known love.

It seared my heart into blacken ash,
And tore my soul asunder;
It plunged me into the abyss of despair,
And buried me in a pit of hell!

I have known love.

James C. Crawford

Love

Love, love it can make you feel sad,
It can make you feel glad
It can even make you mad.
Love, love it can make you feel happy,
It can make you feel glum
It can even make you feel like a bum.
Love, love it can make you feel stupid,
It can make you feel dumb
But then again it can be fun.

Christopher Lee Bohanan

Untitled

The adrenalin rushes
Through my veins.
It gives me a high that
Won't get me killed.
It sends an energy through
My body that is unlike any
Drug. It gives me the strength
To do the impossible. It does
What it can do and nothing
Else.

Sean P. Bakersky

"One For Mark"

In a day or stormy night,
  it falls on you or me.
It doesn't matter if you're rich
  or if you disagree.
It sits you by a fireside,
  to warm your hands and think.
It is a curse to work in,
  it makes your eyelids blink.
It fills a raging river,
  or falls and makes a plink:
It's caught by men and purified,
  to fill the kitchen sink.
Sometimes you think it nasty
  or wish that it would stop:
Farmers always pray for it,
  to help to raise a crop.
I know you know this item,
  sometimes it is a pain:
But where would you and I be
  if God hadn't made it....?

Arthur W. Clausen II

Vampire

Have you seen a vampire?
It hovers in the night.
He'll come into your window
And fill your face with fright

As you faint slowly
Your pillow turns to mud
He bites your neck firmly
And sucks out all your blood

His eyes start glowing
He's got a new mate
You feel your strength returning
And your eyes to illuminate

You sit up in the silence
There's nothing left to do
But go along with the vampire
And start killing too...

Brandon Joseph Cranmer

Happiness Is...

Happiness is knowing you are being loved,
It is a good feeling from above.

Happiness is a perfect time,
You cherish it as if it were a dime.

Happiness is not jewels or money,
It is not a name like dear or honey.

It is what you feel inside,
A feeling you should not hide.

Johannah E. Zabal

Today

Today Lord, may we be
  glad,
For this day that thou
  made.
That the wonderfulness
  of thy creations,
Will be seen in all of
  our situations.

Judy D. Lang

The Birds

I see a bird,
It is a swan,
It is so beautiful,
Like sweet words from a song.

I see a bird
It is a blue jay
It can run very fast,
And surely it will get out of your way.

I see a bird,
It is a parrot,
What lovely colors!
For they make noise like a tot.

I see a bird
It is an eagle,
It is very brave,
Mighty strong - not feeble.

For I love birds,
They can fly high like a jet,
They are soaring in the sky,
How I wish I had one for a pet!

David Tidwell

A Little Wish

I wished upon a star today
It seemed so far away.

My heart was light, eyes bright
for a spectacular sight.

Gazing at the sky above
a path above approach.

I search to find that special one
Giving off beams that dance in the night,
The performance is a sheer delight.
Be patient and you will see
It's not always easy as it may be.
With spirits soaring
Tonight could be the night
Believe in yourself.
This could be the day
To take you far away.

So wish upon your star
And don't give in to time
After all is said and done
The world is yours and mine.

Dee Krouppa

Rain

Spatter, spatter comes the rain
It trickles down the window pane
Bringing moisture to the grain
Flowers, trees and everything

Some magic clouds up in the sky
The blowing wind goes swiftly by
Thunder roaring a fury cry
Bring the rain to you and I

At last the clouds all roll away
A rainbow can be seen at day
Without the essential appearing of the rain
Life on earth could not remain

Doris Beams

The Feeling

The feeling come in a mood
It was like a dark blood
a heavy wind swept by my face
and closed in on me like a web of lace
I knew it meant I had last
It felt as if I were touched by first
a quickening night, and beginning bright
I faced a moon that was quite bright
Where was God's magical light?
The clouds came class, and touched the earth
a spark of lightening revealed the Devil's
mirth.

Bunny C. Porter

My Worlds

I heard the demons wail in hell -
  It was me.
I heard the angels sing in heaven -
  It was me.

The weight of the world was upon me -
  Then was gone.
My feet walked upon the clouds -
  Then I fell.

No need to fear hell -
No need to anticipate heaven -
  I am there.

Barbara A. Barnes

The Battery

I got a new battery.
It worked just great.
It got better and better.
I gave it a high rate.

I guess I did something wrong.
It started to get low.
I loved my battery a lot
I said, "Please, don't go."

I said, "You don't understand.
You know you're the best."
I needed my battery more than it knew.
It just said, "I need a rest."

I should have never used it all at once.
I'll never see it again.
Now I miss my battery.
Should I try to rebegin?

Julie Anne Rodak

Old Friend

How are you my friend
it's been too long
This message I send
even though you're gone

I thought of you today
as so often I do
There's so much to say
a world so new

I whisper through tears
with each passing verse
it's been four years
since you've left this earth

But not a day goes by
until the end
that I don't question why
God took you old friend.

Kris McCaie

Broken Hearted Venture

Burned by Love's fire.
It's destruction leaves no desire.
Someone pays for someone else's mistake.
No forgiving. No giving now.
Just all take.
Blinded by pain.
Oh God, another day.
Pray.
Nothing ventured nothing gained.
Bad attitude with no clues of what to do.
Direction.
Wrong way on a one way street.
Collision with Reality.
A vision.
Light. No more fight.
Give in to open arms...
To warmth. Love's charm.
Chances. Take them.
With love's emotional dances...
Again.

Kristina Marie Helphenstine

The Old Clock

The old clock sets on the mantel
Its face looking out over the room
Its brown with pretty curves and bends
and golden trims
This old clock once was Mothers
but doesn't work at all
And neither does mother
But with out this old clock on the mantel
Time just wouldn't matter
You couldn't know what mother remembers
When she ask if it could be fixed
And you say oh mother! its old and of no use
But mother remembers when it was bright
And shiny and was a piece of beauty
And it was always used
You should remember
that old clock on the mantel
May not mean much to you
But you could remember mother

Judy E. Skinner

Volunteerism

It's a way of life for many people,
It's foreign to some.
To be a volunteer
Is how many things get done.

A variety of skills are used
In many areas of life
To help make life better
And end the pains of strife.

Volunteers are found in churches
Hospitals, schools and such
To make life a bit better
For those who need so much.

A volunteer is one who gives
Both time and energy
To friends and strangers in our midst.
All are treated equally.

Volunteers are found across our land.
They come in every shape and size,
All races, religions, and ages
Without compromise.

Elizabeth Anne Hemberger

Love

Love is a beautiful thing
Its like a permanent smile on your face
Its love and laughter, joy and happiness
all mixed together in one special place

Its the twinkle in your eyes
and the love from your heart
The feeling of togetherness
Right from the very start

Its taking the time
No matter when or where
Its sharing your feelings
and showing your care

There's nothing more precious
Then having love in your life
Spending all your time together
possibly becoming husband and wife

There's nothing more special
Then flying high like a dove
There's nothing in this world
Like being in Love

Beth Compton

The Wishing Well

The wishing well weeps alone
It's murky bottom full of coins
From wishes that never came true
It stands alone
And hears silent cries
The pleas of mother
Wishing for lost sons
Of lovers wishing for a loved one
I went today to make a wish
And heard the cries
The cries of the wishing well
Weeping all alone.

Jacqueline A. Dauzy

My Head's Room

My head rents out a certain room,
its name is brain- or mind
and whatever thought lives in it,
that virtue you will find.

Dreams used to live in here.
but now they all have gone.
Don't fret, they haven't died,
but in fact, they've just moved on.

Reality lives here now.
A difference has overcome.
The games are packed away,
And all my dreaming's done.

Although dreams were kinder
Reality is true,
And it does not consume all space,
As often my dreams do.

Someday I might have room for both
I hope they could be friends
But I guess it all depends on
How much space my brain decides to lend!

Erica James

No Time for Time

Time is of the essence.
It's never here when you need it.
There's not enough when you have it.

You can't slow it down,
And you can't speed it up.
It's continuous.

You may make time,
And you can take it away.
You can watch it go by,
But you can't break it.

It seems to repeat itself.
When it's gone, it's gone.
Then there's no time for time.

Jon Curtis

Little Lost Child

Alone, so alone. Is anybody there?
It's so dark in here.
Does somebody have a light to share?
It's so lonely, dark and empty.

Sir? Ma'am? Can you help me,
To find my way;
Listen to my pleas,
And lead me to the light of day?

NO! My soul is shattered.
Hope has passed me by.
Seeds of friendship gone unwatered,
Leaves a black void behind.

At Last! A pinprick of light
Shines in the wasted plains of my soul.
Closer, closer - it strengthens in might
While warmth begins to fill my heart's
gaping hole.

Slowly, the light suffuses my soul,
Like unto the sunrise o'er the mountain
range whole.
Seeds of friendship since replanted,
Now companions are no longer doubted.

Jessica C. Richards

It's That Thing

It's that that can't be bought,
It's something hat can't be sold;
It's that that you have touched,
but something you can't hold;
It's that which I will give
It's something that you can take;
It can be hard as stone,
yet something which you may break;
It's that which can be precious,
It's something which some would steal;
It's that that can be yours,
It's something which you can feel;
It's that that has a mind,
but I isn't always, too smart;
It's that which gives me life,
It's something that's called my hear.

Jay C. Swalley

"The Visitor"

Hello again, it's me!
I've come to drink the dew!
I've come to hear the robin sing,
Come to slay the rose of spring,
Come to tear away the wings
Of butterflies, or lesser things!

Hello again, it's me!
I've come to steal the eggs!
Come to climb the hosting tree
For speckled eggs that shall only
Be tears awaiting in the nest
For gentle mother's reddened breast.
I'll laugh to hear her sad decree!

Hello again, it's me!
Skulking on my bungling feet!
With fingers evil, sharp, and swift,
Wretchedness, I humbly give
To honey bees, and wiser trees,
and those who in kinder things believe,
a thicket goblin they'll never meet!

Alison Mann Beach

Last Will

Fare thee well now,
I've lived
And so should you.
Go to sleep now,
I've dreamt
And you can too.
Face the world now,
I've learned
And so will you.
Stop your crying now,
It's done
There's nothing you can do.
Go on with your life now,
But know-
I'll be there with you.
Fare thee well now,
I've lived
Now go live too.

Catherine Carroll

Memories

All of my life
I've lived without lying,
Or tried to
I've tried to abide
Each season anew
With a springtime resolve
"To thine own self be true"
But now that I'm nearing
That awesome December
My only truth is
"I just can't remember"

Katharine Brown

Friends

Friends are like branches
that swirl through
raging waters
At times touching
Other times drifting
Sometimes entangled and
holding back floods
BUT NEVER ALONE

Lauren Caffrey

The Sun

Where does the sun go at night?
Does it go and hide from fright?
From the wind, or
From the skies?
From the child's watching eyes?
Where does it go, oh
Where does it go?

Kari Prigge

Through My Eyes

Since my birth
I've seen much beauty on this earth

The sky is gray.
There are fields of hay.

The mountains are steep.
The oceans are deep.

There's no doubt.
The trees are strong and stout

There's pebbles and big rocks,
And ocean docks.

There's lots of people
And churches with big tall steeples.

The grass is green.
I know there's a lot I haven't seen.

There's beauty to behold.
It can't be bought or sold.

Big, tall, short and small.
The sky is a blanket for us all.

Bonnie Marie Adkins

A Cry For Help

Just a little pathway,
Just a little road,
Winding down to nowhere
With my own abode.
Trampled many, many times,
With worn and weary feet,
Yet, holding up a wagon,
And a horse hoof's beat.
No one to comfort me and I sigh,
Think of years to come and years gone by.

Clydess Hill

The Stream

Runs quietly in spring,
just so that it sprinkles a
bird's wing.
The stream
rushes fast in the summer,
where kids young and old, wade,
fall, and say "bummer."
The stream
runs gently in autumn
too cold for a bunny's bottom.
The stream
barely runs in winter
slightly frozen, cracks as
thin as splinters.
The stream
the stream never ends
no matter to the turns,
curves, and bends.
A stream is always there
as long as you treat it with love and care.

Kiersten Mathieu

The Thoughts of Yesterday

Time passes by
Just where am I
Years connect with life
Moments share the strife
Hours signify the destiny
Seconds control our agony.
"Thoughts of yesterday"
Will they wilt away?
Or do they just drift on day by day
To help us have faith along the way.

Eleanor Cahill

Wanting To Grow

Have you ever counted the stars above,
kissed life on the cheek or were afraid
to love?
Have you ever dreamt of happiness yet
lived in pain, prayed for forgiveness or
gave someone else the blame?
Have you ever felt the hand of a stranger
that you really knew, walked backwards
through yesterdays or discovered the image
in the mirror wasn't actually you?
Have you ever given everything up only
to loose, been given two wishes but then
had to choose?
Have you ever felt the rain upon your
soul, wanted to learn but never had the
chance to grow?

Hannah J. Koleszar-Ours

Together

Restless moments spent together;
Knowing it will last forever.
Thinking of what tomorrow brings;
Dreaming on its golden wings.
Soaring high above the earth;
Giving us a brand new birth.
Walking on tomorrows edge;
Hanging from its narrow ledge.
Reaching out to shows care;
Just hang on we're almost there.
Today I'll hold you close to me-
Tomorrow, for eternity.

Carol Heath

The Last Person in the World

The stage lights shut off
Like a record player
Its cord yanked from the wall
Music distorted
Lower and lower to
Nothing
I walked out on that black stage
With a black set, black floor
After the show
I addressed the black seats
And their black audience
Words that made no sound
They started taunting
Throwing balled-up programs
With other people's names
Why can't you hear me?
They got up taking their seats
And the set, and the floor

Then someone lit a candle
And I knew it was God

Julie Anne Schroeder

Hope Had Died

A buried man with a deadly heartbeat
lay within his coffin;
no longer standing on his feet.

One by one he hears dirt piles fall
sunshine soon would vanish;
human voices never to call.

"How did I end up here?" he cried
as he felt the panic;
"I only said my hope had died."

The light began to fade away
reality sunk in deeper;
the paler of his life was turning grey.

His wife and loving children prayed
one last stabbing prayer;
but hope was gone and so he stayed.

Deeper seemed to be his grave than just 6 feet
the darkened walls closed in;
he breathed Freedom's last breath and
claimed defeat.

"Why does daddy stare-off so?" the boy
would beg his mom;
"Oh, he's just tired, dear...there's a lot that
we don't know".

Kimberly Tetsell

Never Goodbye

Goodbye is always the hardest to say,
Leaving that special someone someday.
It's going away to a new time and day,
I guess that's the price you have to pay.

Leaving behind the memories and dreams,
Feeling all alone or so it seems.
Venturing out to a new dawn and day,
This is the price you have to pay.

Crying inside pains takingly so,
For wanting so much but letting it go.
Leaving your family and friends far away,
That's the sacrifice you must pay.

Goodbyes are never easy,
Their the hardest words to say,
The longest to forget,
That's the price you pay.

Now I won't say goodbye,
For reasons I've explained,
So I guess that I will say,
"Until we meet again".

Dustin L. Schappell

Time

Life's been a cruel opponent,
left silver in her hair,
The wealth and joy of living
have passed her and left her there.
Her eyes are veil with sadness,
hands tremble now and then
The silhouette has thickened
from the willowy form that had been.
the quick pace now is lessened
as the years increase
the once proud voice of triumph
is now a whisper, weak.
Oh time you youth destroyer
why wont you let us be?
You have consumed the others
You're now consuming me.

June Edwards

Let's Love One Another

Come on everyone
Let's Love One Another
From the beginning of time
We were all each other's Brother
As time went on
Which is plain to see
We went from Loving each Other
to Loving plain little you or me.
An Eye for an Eye
A Tooth for a Tooth
We seldom go around
Telling the truth.
If we love one another
one by one
Our progress toward love
Will have begun.
One love
Two loves
Three loves more
One more love will make four.

Earnestine Reed

Spring in the Air

Once the lily bloom
Life will flow like
Sunshine in my heart.

Never give up Spring
Because love will bring
Sunshine to us all.

Walk along the ocean
To see your face
In the blue water.

The sun will shine
Through your hair
To let you know
Spring is in the air.

Cathy Goodwin

Duncan

Seclusion
  like a frost
 no warmth reaching his life

Anger
  like a storm
 brewing forever inside his heart

Sadness
  like a mist
 distancing his tormented soul

Love
  like a rose
 long dead, never to bloom again

Jacob Brabbs

The Essence

Your scent still lingers on my pillow
like a powerful drug assaulting all my
senses.
Until at last my resolve weakens and my
mind relents and memories of our last
union quickly flash.
We appear as soft, muted auras of pastel,
caressing and blending into each other,
creating an essence of one!

Joyce A. Mahoney

Sorceress

Exotic, erotic, feeling free
Like a traditional princess
Won't you worship me?
Possession, sensation, a
Sacrificial selection -
A powerful Goddess with
Brilliance, you are to me.
Forgiveness, stillness, the
Sensibility of a European Queen -
A sweet caress, out of blackness,
in my consciousness dream -
The magical beauty of
Perfumed fragrance, provoking
Lustful, ecstasy, a sorceress,
With the stars n' the moon
as her destiny -

Edward Torres

Angelkist

Her beauty shines into my eyes
Like sunshine on her hair
The angels gave her kisses
To freckle skin so fair
My love for her unspoken
I cannot let her know
I love her oh so deeply
But now must let her go
I cannot ever reach for her
And express my love so strong
For my love for her is secret
It is as secret as it is wrong

Allen L. Columbus

Sunrise

Scarlet blue
  like the red of my robe
Tears the sight from my eyes
Cool and burning
In the night of the morning

(Shhsh, I am sleeping)

Taking my hands
  my arms, my legs
You melt them into yours
Taking me over
Like nothingness awoken

(violently silent)

My flesh slips
  from these twisted links
As it is pulled endlessly
Through my soul
Unraveled, but still a chain

(Shhsh, you are sleeping
On the face of the sun)

Jennifer B. Kim

Destination

Upon foot's destination
From childhood's embarkation
Tugging at our sinless sleeves
Ever growing stronger

Onto fate's resignation
To make just, one hesitation
Find another that believes
Walk alone no longer

Deric T. Olschner

Trying to Survive

I hurried along the train platform
Like the wind
Whirling round about me.
I was trying
To get out
The way of every big
And small foot.
Lucky for me, I
Was not in anyone's path.
I was once full
Of life; I
Have since changed with the season.
And now, I
Have only a little
Life left. I,
A weary dry brown leaf
Am trying to avoid
Being crushed.

Anne B. Harris

"I Love You"

I have heard love is a blessing from a bird
Like wise I see in your eyes,
Lilian dear,
That blessed tear
Mixed with the spirit of love.
What can I say? What can I do?
But to love you, to love you,
to love you more and thru.
You will know all you mean to me
when you see
That tender dove
Warming your heart with my love,
Whispering low,
Darling, "I love you so."
A deep and longing look... a kiss...
Ah dear... She sighs...dear Carlos, "I love you too.
O yes, deep from my heart I do."
Now I know how is to be loved...
Thanks to the message of the dove.

Carlos Colon

Mother

My father, arms
limp, stands
in shorts and
undershirt staring
at my mother,
wet droplets
resting on the brim
of his lashes,
his eyes lifeless,
as her voice echoing
through the room,
continues to murder
his soul and I
stand clinging
to the door case
just behind her.

Jennifer Fischer

Awaiting On The Quay

Awaiting on the quay
Listening to the chimes
Lovingly, she breaths another day

Abandoning their pasts
Sailing through her gaze
Ships swallow wind in their masts
Floating through the evening haze

Awaiting to be a worthy sailor's quest
Patiently, here she'll abide
Praying 'tis here that one will rest

Abandoning his pride
Lovingly, he'll vow her as bride
Swearing that his sheen will not fade
For 'tis a queen he has made

Barbara McCain

Until Next Time

As you turn to leave,
loneliness begins to overwhelm me,
I stare into your eyes,
Smiling bravely, I say goodbye.
Never showing the agony of the moment.

Then you turn to disappear
from my world,
You smile one last smile.
Blowing me a kiss, I capture it.
With an unspoken promise,
you will return.

As you fade from my sight,
emptiness begins to fill my soul,
As quickly as you came,
you are gone.
I realize, again...I am alone.

I bravely wave goodbye once more,
but you cannot see me,
You are gone....

...until next time.

Diane Frederick

Nowhere

Lonesome death,
Lonesome cry,
Weeping sorrow,
Heart so shallow.

Soul-to-die
Of unwilling death,
Wake my soul,
Won't you go.

It's hard to stay,
But, why won't you,
Aren't you free,
Why won't you leave me.

Is it possible,
For tears to drop,
Weeping soul,
Please, don't let go.

Wake me up,
Please wake me up,
This life of mine,
Saddens my soul to blind.

John Gaines

Chains

Retrace the footsteps of yesterday,
Look at all that's new.
Hear the footsteps of the gone,
Hear the chains they took too.

Look at the young at play,
Remember how you were.
See how they will be someday,
Hear the chains we give them.

Close your eyes and open your mind;
All that died for what they love,
All that cared for others
Still walk with chains above.

They hold captive the soul.
Listen: Another heart is tore,
And that sound will drive you mad.
Chains - forever more.

Kimberly Riggs

Love Loves No One

Step out into the moonlight,
look into my eyes.
I see the face of an angel,
the love of my life.
You eyes are so determined
to hide your breaking heart.
I just can't seem to hide my
own,
instead I fall apart.
A one last look goodbye
before you go away,
I've got to explain how much
you mean to me,
Somehow I'll make you stay.
But going with your crowd,
you leave me all alone.
You've made me realize
love simply loves no one.

Angela M. Haycraft

Expressions Of Friendship

Eyes as spring green as the grass,
looking around everywhere.

Lips, as pink as watermelon,
smiling and being happy.

Hair as beautiful as the sun,
hanging in a pony-tail.

Arms as pearly white,
as pearls hanging on your neck.

A favorite shirt,
as a dandelion,
as a lemon in the fridge.

Friendship is like a rose,
putting more love in our lives.

Kendra Chatel Hyland

Untitled

I'm watching the time going by,
Hoping my lunch is a pizza pie.
Went to school my lunch I bring,
I like to eat most everything,
The thing that makes me want to gag,
Is finding tuna fish in my bag.
The most special thing I can pack,
Is a great big bag of cracker jacks.

Katie Blair

Sand Dollars

I was treading through the water,
looking for a sand dollar.
I came across a mermaid,
swimming through the water.
She found a handful,
of sand dollars.
She swam over to me,
like a swan in the sea.
With a handful,
of sand dollars to give to me.
Then after that,
she gave to me an eskimo kiss.
Then the mermaid said,
where do you live?
I had said to the mermaid,
in the city.
Then we both said goodbye,
to each other, and I thanked her for the sand
dollars.

Christopher Berg

Survive

Afraid,
Lost,
Lonely.
No where to turn,
No one to talk to.
Please let me make it through another day,
Without dying
Under the knife
Held in my own willing hand.
Listening to the voices
Inside my head.
Hoping I can keep from
Constantly thinking about ones
Already free from this torture.

Wondering,
About the ones I may hurt.
What will I do?
Live?
Maybe.

Die?

Jennifer Sorensen

Lost, But Not Forgotten

Are you there,
lost one,
Are you there,

Are you the wings of an eagle,
Are you the cries of a loon,
Are you the stars,
the moon,

The wind touches my soul,
Are you there,
Your presence is known,
Are you there,

Your voice,
Your footsteps,
Still Heard,

Are you there,
lost one,
Are you there.

Cindy Lichtsinn

Where Is Love

Love is everywhere.
Love is found in your mother's heart.
Love is found in your father's eyes.
It is found in your grandparents stories of
when they were your age.
The doves flying by, on their way to their
nest. That is love in the sky.
People saying I love you, that is love in
the air. Love is found in songs and in
other people. You can find love in poems.
Love is expressed by you.

Becky Barnes

The Dream

I once had a dream
love was all around
the beauty of its sight
was a sweet sweet sound

The dream was about a love
unlike any other
you the princess of light
me your knight in shining armor

Sidetracked by time
we walked our separate paths
searching for a love
one that would last

In the dream you were searching
never losing faith
I was walking aimlessly
on a road called fate

The winds of change stirred
the day you came into view
it was then I realized
the dream was you

Daniel Niemchak

Sister And Brother

When I was growin' up the world
loved one another
Just like sister and brother;

People used to all be friends, makes
you wonder if the world is comin'
to its end;

Sister and brother at play
Now it just ain't that way:

The violence and the cryin'
The wars and the dyin':

Life used to be so simple and sweet
but now we're afraid to cross
the street.

'Cause everyone hates each other
Husbands and wives with separate lovers.

It just ain't no kind of world,
Just boy and girl, sister and brother
hating each other.

Jennifer Tallant

Ebony And Ivory

Black as the night
Lovely as the moon
With radiant spark of light
Thou guide me to the path
of pleasure

To behold thee, even thy crown
The ebony of thy locks with
streaks of ivory flows
To lay between thy towers
and watch in awe as the
Heavens descent into shadows
of blackness, deck with orbs
of silver
So are thine eyes in there sockets

Image of black and white are thy
smile
Contrast of ivory set in ebony
Oh! Vision of blackness compatible
with silvery asymptote

Black as the night
Lovely as the moon
So is my "Belove to Me"

John Paul Wong

Death's Shadow

Death creeps quietly
Lurking in the shadows
Waiting.....

Silently closing in to
catch me unaware
if only for a moment.

Taking slowly bits and
pieces until one day
it's grip is strong.

Then I greet it
with open arms like
a long lost friend.

Finally succumbing to it's
force only to find that
I am not the one.

Now here I sit quietly
in the shadows
waiting.....

Karen L. Michel

A Millionaire???

I do not own a house,
Made with brick and clay;
I own an open doorway
To greet each bright new day.

I own a piece of God's earth
Where pine trees grow and sway,
And toss their shiny nettles
About in seeming play.

I own a thousand sunsets
In myriad colors gay,
A stream of shimmering water
Beside an old roadway.

Could I but count my millions
Totalled in coins of gold,
I'd be the riches person
The world has ever known.

Katie Treadwell Barnett

The World Is My...

The world is my shadow
lying beneath the Universe. My
soul is spinning thousands of
miles an hour. My brain is just
growing as I grow each second.
The life of me shall no longer
exist. I shall not fight for my life.
The world is my life and it is
dying every minute. The world is my
future I will try my very best
not to destroy it. The world is
my freedom I will cherish it
with all my heart. The world is
my heart beating faster and
faster and the world turns.
The world is my friend I shall
treat it as respectful as possible.
The world is my love I shall
love the world so that the
world will possible try to
love me. I love the world.

Brad Chapman

1796 Canvas By An Unknown Artist

Who lit the eye
Made come alive.
Whispered care
On threads of hair.
Paled a dawn,
A smile so drawn.
Glowed a light,
In candled night.
Warmed a season
Sweet with reason.
Touched a force
Through nature's Chorus.
Gently over canvas poured
A genius hand? "My Lord."

Doris Denton Carr

Belief In Life

My children in my life, have
made me realize, how lucky
I really am.
It's all in God's hands.
We put the belief there.
Some people never care.
Some never realize, the
preciousness of life.
The love that's really there.
All they have to do is care.
Just put out your
hand, and let God
lead you through his land.

Alice T. White

Untitled

I step into
the July sun,
momentarily blinded
by white-blue sky.
The hot wind smells of
dying grass.
It dries my lips and face.
Chicken-fried day.

Teresa O'Mara

Untitled

Thoughts and fears
make up the tears
of a love that's been apart

You cannot find
the needed time
to control the longing heart

Words of encouragement
we need to share,
it's the assurance
that our hearts will hear

The honest truth
I'll tell you again
there's no one else I love
but my sweet princess.

John Null

Dream Weavers

Like a knitting needle,
Making blankets of warmth.
Through trial by fire,
And dealings with ghosts;
And romantic tragedies
That are cherished the most.
With diamonds of sunlight,
And all the different kinds of
happiness
We see our books of yesterday.
And when the curtain is lifted,
We find ourselves as weavers of
dreams...
Each one of us special gifted.

Corey Hutchins

Built

Lifting my eyes to the insane
making you look back again
infectious streams outrageous denials
broken again bathroom tiles
draped over a broken heart
pierced blue finish to start

Couldn't have gone any farther
lasting true beaten harder
sick of it long to be searching deep
never as strong as you, as you

Collapsed on the ground
relapsed by the sound
of a voice never by choice
resurrected feeling subjected

Longing to feel your hand on my face
stricken smiles through
a clenched fist with a trace
of disgust reflection of me I must have been
here before
a body with a mind too disconnected to see
too built to be free

Jennifer DaRe

A Dynamite Surprise

A basket case named Egore,
His master sent Him to the store,
He smiled at the cashier, and went to get
A cart,
Then he let one of those rippers,
A stinkbomb explosive fart.

Donna Borton

Untitled

Panda Bears, Polar Bears
Manattees, Dolphins
Cheetahs, Tigers and Lions
Animals all over the world are crying
Some of them are even dying
Don't let extinction get out of hand
By not moving in on animals land
Don't make them go with hungers or thirst.
After all, who was here first?

Amie Fox

The Heart Of A Poet

Many have written
Many have seen
The life they lived
Once in a dream
Fiction, fact and opinions of life
The study of love, joy and strife
We soon write and faintly forget;
No one can know the heart of a poet.

Daniel Terence Bol-le's

Vacant

Emptiness surrounds
me....
When once, your
essence embraced
me.
How different these
four walls enclose
me.
The silence is even
different now that
your belongings are no
longer here.

Carolina Montufar

Reflection

I'm still in the same
Mental spot as years ago
Only now it's much
More complicated
How such simple corrosion and
Waste of mind can change
Such blackened soul and
Dented heart ferment
And from it arises new and
Uglier illnesses.
One aspect of which is truly
Horrifying and sick
The one where you go back
And do everything the same,
Differently.

Denise Murphy

Could You Love Me Like That?

Could you love me like that if
I weren't a queen, could you
love me like that if I weren't
Supreme, could you love me like
that to heaven and back,
through a lover's spat, could
you love me like that?

Jemalia Renee Akpele

Andante

Sounds,
merging into words
assembling into thoughts
yielding to wavering moments
of distractibility,
choreographed and captured on a page.
Words that breathe
words that ache
words with a pulse—
creating a dance of images
they glide along
to find their own rhythm,
their own dance.

Katharine Blaker

Midnight

Midnight, the clock ticks away;
Midnight, I hold my breath;
The clock ticks away.

We can't look back;
We wait.

It was just like yesterday,
When we thought about tomorrow,
But tomorrow is today,
And today will be tomorrow,
And again we will have yesterday.

The clock ticks away,
And a new day begins.

Edith Astrid Yeager

Francie's Last Words

"Hours from life
minutes from death
I think of the time
that I might have left
My breathing is faint
My pain makes me weak
I think of the place that
I am forced to greet.

There in the distance
I see a light
A light all so bright
It never sees night
yet here in this glow
I am filled with such fright
But I know where I am going
And I'll be alright... (Silence)

Bobbianne Worthing

Best Friend

Miss your smiling eyes
mischief ways
your Big Bear hugs
that seen to say
"everything's ok"

Your sweet voice
that said I love you
most everyday.
Until we meet again
I'll miss you Dearest Brother
(my friend).

Doris Timberlake

For Caitlin Mary

Sweet
  Misconceived baby
We hardly knew you
  but we loved you so.

Sweet
  misconceived baby
We opened our hearts to you
  but you had to go away.

Sweet
  misconceived baby
We opened our home to you
  but knew you could not stay.

Sweet
  misconceived baby
We breathed for you
  and you became a living soul.

Sweet
  misconceived baby
We asked you to stay
  but knew you had to go.

Jack M. Stack

Hidden Fear

The water crashes to the
moonlight shore
As her weak body
falls to the floor
The sound of distant ringing
pounds in her thoughts
As she crawls to the door
to pick the lock
She looks out the window
and all she sees is the
smoke stacks swaying
violently
She imagines the smoke to
be souls escaping to freedom
but is distraught when they
fade into oblivion
She cries, sobs, moans in horror
as she hears the footsteps
getting louder and louder.

Chava Weller

Come With Me

Come live with me and you will see
Morning peeking through a windswept tree.
Come live with me and you will hear
The scampering sound of a little deer.
Come live with me and you will see
A big green forest and a bumble bee.
Come live with me and you will feel
The plaintive cry of a whippoorwill.
Come live with me and you will see
Fluffy white clouds over a forest free.
Come live with me and you will hear
A flock of birds with which to cheer.
Come live with me and you will see
A little white cottage with a lock and key.
Come live with me and I'll give to you
The sunkissed softness of a bunny's nose,
And the hushed repose of a red red rose.
Come live with me and I'll give you
A blushing flower all covered with dew,
A magnificent love that you never knew.

Dixie J. Murray

Insectisuicide

I cause my mind to transgress
mosquitoes riddle my conscientiousness
where are they headed?
  And why?
Going nowhere knowingly like us
flittering by flame and lust
  again like us?
With no reason we can discuss
flying in airs of content and wonder
our dead carcass they plunder
draining the blood of vampires
  again like us?
Taking time only to rest
swarming for the love of a partner
clipping my wings would be smarter
  and why?
A mosquito has no reason to die
they are content to feed and fly
while I'm content to bleed and die.

Daniel M. Thurber

"Black And Shining"

Black and Shining,
Most Divine,
Apple of Mine...
I dare not blink, or look away
What? And miss out on this?
I'm not crazy, just in love
with the Mystic, Dark Mr. Black.
yes him, who's converting?
to conform means to deny.
I dream of Ebony Hands
like Warm Winds
from Oceans of Onyx...
Holding me,
Completing me,
Bliss...
Do you think I'd think
twice about this?
God has placed the Black before me,
and I approach,
softly.

Kara L. Lewis

Somber Mother?

Somber
Mother?
Ahh, your fat hand
  That rubbed my smooth
  Baby bald skull
With a smile,
A loving joyous thank you smile.
  Could you ever have been true?
  In all your weight,
Your vulgar mouth,
Your smoking and belching?
  Gentle
  A dawn
When the sun spoke his tongue twisting
Moist dew language,
  You
  would smile,
Somber
Mother?

Jack E. Wright

Cowboy

He sits high on his horse
Moving the cattle to the ranch
To slaughter and cut
for food and mush
His life has been long and hard
To finally come to the end
When the cattle reach the ranch

Jennifer A. Vieira

Everyday Struggles

Everyday struggles
Multiple jobs get juggled
Heat just Adds to the trouble
Drugs still get smuggled

Unwanted births
Sperm donors wit no worth
Babies found blue like li'l smurfs
Two foot graves all laid in the dirt

Men can't control
Women eyes get swoll
Time behind bars the toll
Children see'n fathers as trolls

Money's a thought in a bubble
It also causes trouble
Politicians often smuggle
Greed is a disease to all these everyday struggles

Antoine Feltha

Call Of The Portrait

My mouth can not say;
My body can not sway.
I have said,
And I have swayed
With my eyes
And your eyes.

My soul wants to fly;
My heart wants to cry.
I can not fly,
And I can not cry
Out of my frame,
Or your frame?

Alicia Hsuing

What I Was Afraid Of

The Boogyman at night
My brother beating me up in a fight
Doing something that is not right
I hate being scared.
A man throwing a shoe
An old guy saying boo!
Not knowing what to do
I hate being scared.
Getting hit by a tool
Breaking a really bad rule
Being kicked by a mule
I hate being scared.
Turning out to be a bum
People thinking that I'm dumb
Being sick to my tum
I hate being scared.

Jamie Gruber

My Dad

Rough and tough cowboy
My Dad

Texas Born
My Dad

His friends
Old pickup truck, Mom, Queenie and buck
My Dad

His companion morning sunbeams and God
My Dad

His whistle
Brings the horses to their knees
My Dad

His cattle
Know him by name, by sight
My Dad

His hands
warm, brown, worn by the wind
My Dad

He prays for rain and for me
My Dad

Bonnie Patterson

Trucker's Grandson

My poppa was a trucker,
My dad is a trucker
I'm a little boy trucker,
Just like my kin.
I wanna do what the big
boys can.

I'll tell you a tale of
that big blue rig, throbbing,
and bouncing about as they do.
Waiting for that day that I will too.

I'll steer that rig with all my
might right on into broad daylight.

The radio blasting his favorite
song. Let everyone hear and sing along.

I'll wave my hand in gratitude.
Sound my jake brake noisily to.
Holding the count till I am
through. I'll honk that horn in
memory of you. Grandpa this one's
for you. Love Branden

Eileen Mason

Though We Have Never Met

Though we have never met eye to eye
My feelings for you have been true
Through the letters and the calls
I have gotten to know the one as you
I feel an emptiness in my heart
Because there is a space reserved for you
The future holds a place for us
May it be forever true

Is there a place for me in your heart?
I know you have the key to mine
So please take care of it as I have done
For you have two and I have none
No matter what the future brings
You'll always be a part of me.

Kevin Dodson

A Dream So Real

A dream so real that I could feel
my heart begin to race.
I look at her,
She looks at me,
We stare off into space.
Our eyes are windows to our souls,
and our loving past.
The love we feel for each other
will forever last.
I listen to her loving words
about a different realm.
I hear of all she's seen and done
and I am overwhelmed.
But now alas we must part,
she must return to heaven above
but I know someday I'll be with her
and experience eternity with love.

Erin Rebecca Fadgen

"Trying"

I've tried so hard to live
my life right. But no matter
how hard I try. I can't figure
out why I even try to live
my life right. I just screw
up real bad and everyone gets
mad. The pressure sometimes is
so hard to bear I often wonder
if anyone cares. I even cry my
self to sleep at night wondering
what I'm still doing a
live. I don't wanna try any
more. So please hear me when
I say I love all of you and
I'll miss all of you when I'm
gone. Please understand what
I'm trying to say. I'm
trying to say, I can't
handle living my life
this crazy way.

Edwina Koen

Every Time I Say A Prayer

My body chilled with uncertainty,
my lips quivered in fear.
The news I heard cut through me,
my eyes fought back a tear.

For a while I didn't believe it,
it was just too much to bear.
My years ahead seemed pointless,
thoughts of you not being there.

It's been almost a year now,
and time has come and gone.
Your smile will last forever,
and my love for you lives on.

Sometimes I get discouraged,
there was so much for us to share.
But I know that you can hear me
every time I say a prayer.

Kimberly Rye Treece

Untitled

My respect for you, unceasing
My love for you, eternal
My belief for you, undying
Your trust in me, fraternal

My partiality to you, irreversible
My faith in you, immense
My gratitude in you, unending
Your piety, intense.

My need for wisdom, infinite
My deity, timeless
My benevolence, demanding
Your encouragement, limitless.

Cyndi Gardner

Morning

I walked
my mind bogged
by the smog
of everyday things.

I suffocate,
non-communicate,
my mind bogged by smog.
I cannot breathe,
my soul wreathed with fog.

My eye caught,
gleaned, kept tears wept
in early morning airs.....

There, serene
embraced in green,
tiny liquid rainbows beamed...

DEW!
God said: For You!

I walk
clear, sun and pure,
alive with breath and depth.

Joan M. Bastress

Summer Stars

Summer stars
my only light
Guiding me forward
into the night
Deep blue waves
lining the shore
Beating the sand
like never before
My mind up above
my body below
My mind with the stars
and their twinkling glow

Kelly Brigman Tickner

The Gentle Bear

If I had a gentle bear,
I would take him everywhere.
Up the stairs and down the street
Even to grandma's,
Wouldn't that be neat?
I'd feed him pretzels and gingerbread boys,
And let him play with all my toys.
Yes, If I had a gentle bear
I would take him everywhere.

Alisa Aubrey

Here And Now

If a life would be a thousand years
My portion would be small
Why just one century on this earth
Would hardly be a life at all.

But if a life would be a day
Why then how rich am I
10,000 lives have come to me
10,000 more before I die

Then do we measure life with time,
With hours and days and years,
And would it ever be enough
If we lived 10,000 years?

For even then the clock would win
And bring it to an end.
And the truth is all we ever have
Is here and now my friend.

Janet Marie Poole

You Are Strong

I used to feel badly for
My sorry little life,
With all its woes and agony,
The problems, pains and strife.

I used to wonder, "God, why me?"
And cursed the fates above.
Why was there so much misery
When I just wanted love.

I used to turn away from things
I didn't want to see.
I even thought to end it all
In order to be free.

I used to cry and carry on
When no one was around.
I hid from life in loneliness
Not making any sound.

But then like magic something touched
A place inside my heart.
I heard a voice say, "You are strong,
Let's try a brand new start."

Kimberly D. York

My Night

Hot summer night
My sunroof up
And the wind is rushing through my hair
Faster
Speed along open roads
I feel so free
Alive
My music surrounds me
With life
Not a care to deal with
All is forgotten
On the long stretch of
Road.

Karen Bernardini

The Trade

Alone inside
my thoughts collide.
I loose my stride
and try to hide.

But God resides
I must abide,
And loose my pride
as I confide.

He takes no side
over this tide.
Confess the slide
and span the divide.

Ask Him to guide
and smooth the ride.
He'll stay not wide
if you have cried.

D. W. Brooks

Bottle Of Thoughts

Though years have passed, consumed by time,
My thoughts of you have aged like wine;
A wine that sips so sweet, my friend,
I've come to taste it once again.
But this time, unlike those before,
I hesitate before I pour;
For, I've just realized that I
Should, one day, find the bottle dry.
Afraid of what I know will be,
I set it down quite carefully;
Then, curious to see what I'd
Used up so far, I look inside.
What I found next can't be explained;
That all the contents still remained;
As if to say, the thoughts that I
Still have of you, shall not run dry.
In seeing this, I draw two sips,
Then take the vessel from my lips;
For, too much thought, if given time,
Is harmful; just like too much wine.

James Allen Kreitzer

A Midnight Walk

As we trudged through the snow,
my two grandchildren and I.
We were awed by the beauty
of the night.

The silent cold,
the muted stillness.
The stars that showered
us with light.

The snow caressed our cheeks,
it sparkled in our hair.
The darkness of the midnight sky
was a joy given us to share.

We held each others hands
and laughed with pure delight.
For we were a part of a memory
of a truly, magical night.

Bobetta Keller

A Way Out

Wanting to escape
Needing to be free
Walking on glass
Trying to see past
Get to the light
That's all i need
Maybe he won't notice
Maybe he won't see
Can't turn to anyone
They don't listen to my plea
The only one to believe
The only one to trust
The only one
Who understands
Is the one and only me.

Jaime Florian

"Sunrise"

Darkness enlightens and slowly clears,
Needles of light cut through the sky,
The moon fades and disappears,
And stars whisper goodbye.

A blush of rainbows paint animation,
A pool of gold ascends,
Each daybreak the sun alights upon blue,
Releasing its splendor and ardence.

Andrea Hsue

Untitled

I watch you through unseen walls, you
never knew it's me who calls

You touched my heart in your special
way, but yours was always to far away

I felt you, you felt me
We touched and loved in ecstasy

Then one day I knew something was
wrong, when we touched there was no
song

No rhythm, no heat, no pumping, no beat

It was just, so long, farewell, and go
to hell

When the time came, to say goodbye
I was the only one I heard cry....

Alyette M. Keldie

Panoramic View

The night was crisp and cold.
No clouds hung in the sky.
Moonlight softly fell on the
snow covered mountain tops and
the fir trees that were nodding
in the breeze. The stars looked
like five carat diamonds
sparkling in a black velvet sky.
The beauty of this quiet night
could not be denied.

Alyce M. Nielson

You Never Can Catch Your Shadow

You never can catch your shadow,
No matter what you do.
You run and run,
And your shadow runs,
It does the same as you!
You never can catch your shadow
If you work the whole day through.
For you're in back of your shadow,
And your shadow's in front of you.

Carolyn Bowman Parent

A World of Violence Change to Silence

If I could change the world today;
No one would have hate.
If I could change the world today;
There wouldn't be debate.
No gangs, no war, no violence;
The world would spin in peaceful silence.
Everything would be all right;
Through the day, and through the night.
Pressure would be history;
Drugs would be unknown.
No one drunk from alcohol;
Which is best just left alone.
But things might not get better;
And only get much worse.
Pollution, drugs and violence;
Is this just a curse;
But even through the war and hate;
And with all of the debate;
I'm glad I live here where I'm free;
And I can share my liberty.

Jessica Shellum

Needs

O, my soul to rest with Thee,
No other place I need to be,
And keep my life within His hands.
His the strength I need to stand.

In his love He shows me light.
Gives me the power of His might,
To bring me out of my own sin,
Then the fold He leads me in.

With a strength I had not known,
Out of the darkness I am shown,
Tho I am not spared all the fight.
I see the candle through the night.

My needs are met by Thee.
My life I give willingly.
With Thy love I continue,
And walk beside Him too.

Amanda Eaker

Untitled

She who first upon whose vision
this image lies

Possesses in her eyes

The understanding of that
full truth

Known only to those who see

Beyond the obvious

Thomas I. McArthy

Most Precious Gift

Give to me not walls of marble
Nor tons of polished gold,
But give the me a child
A child I can hold.

Give to me not praise of title that
From my child makes me roam,
But give to me the MOTHER name
And more children in my home.

Give to me not earthy pleasures
Of body or worldly wiles,
That would surely steal from me
All of my childrens smiles.

For my child is my very life
My youth when I grow old,
And when I'm gone my legacy
The warmth in this world of cold.

Most precious in this world of gifts
All its wonders on me that's smiled,
I am blessed and I thank God most
For my precious, precious child.

Beth M. Miller

Untitled

It was midnite on the ocean
Not a street car was in sight
The sun was shining brightly
And it rained all day that night.

That evening as the rising sun
Was setting in the west
Little fishes in the trees
Were huddled in their nest

Rain was pouring steadily down
The moon was shining bright
And everything that could be seen
Was hidden out of sight

As the organ peeled potatoes
Lard was rendered by the choir
While the Sexton rang the dishrag
Someone set the church on fire

"Holy smoke" the preacher shouted
In the rain he lost his hair
Now his head resembles heaven
For there is no parting there.

Dan S. Kerpan

There Is A Time...

There is a time for love
-Not a time for hate
There is a time for peace,
-Not a time for war
There is a time for sharing
-Not a time for taking away
There is a time to live
-Not a time to die
If we all take the time for love, peace,
sharing and life;
there would not be a time for anything else.
So lets remember....
there is a time for everything.

Elizabeth Craigg

Memories

Even though you can
not feel their tender
touch, or do things
you enjoyed so much.
Just remember God
has taken them up
above, you are still
showered with their
love.
The memories that
are placed in your
heart, will be there
forever and never part.

Ann Butchor

The Free-Spirits Kiss

I travel and wander
Not knowing which way to go.
I am lost deep inside my soul,
And yet I am whole.
Let me kiss you for a moment
And then fly free from your arms.
Let me run
Naked on the flat sand into the horizon
And then spin until
I fall.
Let me dance,
My darling,
With you,
Until you cease to tickle my heart.
And then I am alone,
Again
In the shadow of your love,
That I will break through
With the confidence of my soul.

Alexandra Blantyre

Our Rage to Kill

Earthquakes explode, hurricanes roar.
Nuclear proliferation woe abhor,
We've famines, floods, and fires galore.
Aren't these enough? Why faster war?

Our rage to kill, and copulate,
Was stamped when nature held the reins,
Emotions surged in primal state,
But now, man rules and nature wanes.

Two world wars our seniors knew.
Millions killed. We pay and pay,
Win or lose, we're never through.
Iraq and Korea. There we stay.

God and country media extols
War justice comes through barred of gun.
To kill wild life is hunters goal.
Sportsmen assure: "Killing is fun."

Meadow lark is singing a mating song.
Her plaintive lilts enter my door.
Retort from powerful scatter "gun,
Sweet bird, and melody, no more.

John Adams

Dear God

Awakening to a new birth,
of a dawning day,
Casting my eyes upon the,
sky to hungrily pray.
Life is a game we all have
to face.
Pride is something that highly,
takes place.
Love is spread deeply even,
harshly by so many.
Only given in a right way
it'll gain plenty.
By the blood of Jesus I'm trying
To obey what you say to do,
Because the greatest happiness
in my life
Depends on honoring loving,
praising you.

Darlene N. Coffee

Untitled

I remember the days
Of being carefree
Playing with thing
Only imagination can see

Falling deep in the
Wells of my mind
Away from everyone
Where no one can find

Many day I spent there
Playing without worry
Running through golden fields
Or dancing in a snow flurry

Those days are gone
Like whispers on the wind
Still...every now and then...
I run through those same fields
Or dance in the snow

Blaine C. Rabel

One, I am Music

One, I am music
of captivating passion
and beauty understood.
Timeless boundaries
of mist, of dawn
and moon of night.
Endless universe
of cosmos colliding
bursting
becoming one
certainty is found.

Carin G. Salonia

The Patient's Dilemma

I can be a pincushion and
and never mind the hurt,

And I can play it cool when
the blood begins to spurt,

But conniptions I go through
and my belly all but gyrates,

When I am asked to strip
to investigate my privates.

Cecilia Robinson

Dark Days

The deepest days
of darkness flow
in my past as on
dire fears.

I knew not then
A life without
fears.

No hope, just dope
The hollow ring
of empty things
No life but an
empty shell.

Never, Ever
Dever Trevor
shall I call
a chemical
my god ever again

John B. Wechselberger

Memory Of A Friend

A picture of you is etched in my mind
of four padded paws and a happy whine.

Your pointed ears and your short tail
forever my friend without fail.

I know in my heart you will always be
placed in a part for no one to see.

I will go to my memories whenever I am sad
and one thought of you will make me glad.

I will cherish you as long as I live
good-bye to you my dear little friend.

Kimberly Waller

Salt Lake City My Pages

Unfolded Salk Lake City her summer-book
Of green-leafed pages turning
Sunshine spilled on silver sidewalks
Flower-blossom perfumed air—
Wisdom's white-haired mountains holding
Golden slippered grasses children there.

Doorway to prophetic vision
Hope's child on the threshold peeking
Into painted portraits of tomorrow's
Dream mirrored future in her heart.

Look not to Camelot nor Eden
Read today alive in story
Book-bound knowledge fountains pure.
Find again the sea gull's statued glory
Miracle awaiting prophets' entrance door.
Angel-touched her Temple love dressed white
Granite spires rise heavenward her prayer.
At asphalt feet the treasure-book falls open
evermore.

Kathryn T. Gainey

Her...

Her eyes, as deep as an abyss.
Her hair, flowing like a gentle stream.
Her lips, redder than any rose.
Her legs, long as the Nile.
Her face, as one of a goddess.
Her mind, as one of a scholar.
Her heart, warm as a morning sun.
Her, as beautiful as heaven itself.

Adam Hickey

To My Unborn Grandchild

You've become an untold source
of joy,
Though I don't yet know you as
girl or boy.
I love you, and I'm glad you
are there,
It matters not your sex or
color of hair.
I don't care if your eyes are
brown or blue,
I just know you are special
because you are you.
You'll inherit many traits
down the family line,
and somewhere inside you will
be something of mine.
So while inside your mother you
peacefully grow,
I patiently await you, most
anxious to know my "First Grandchild".

Erma H. Hudson

Woodstock Nation

Once there was a gathering; a gathering
of kindred spirit.
Where love and music filled the air, and
we were all there to hear it.
And just for a moment the world had
to listen to the message that we
carried,
And see where Spirit and Soul go to
the cosmos where they meet and are
married.
The song and dance they did was of
God's freedom and peace;
With a prayer that the love they
felt for their brethren would
never, ever cease.

Bonnie Heil

The Gift

Wrapped in the package
of life, living
Comes many wondrous gifts
Sometimes the packages
Are so small
the gifts go unnoticed
By the naked eye
guided by beauty, size, association
Often small gifts
Are left last to open
Some never unwrapped
These gifts seldom
Hold grand things
Instead when
torn open by a surprised find
Unleash joy, happiness, love, content
But are often unappreciated, stepped over
By the one they're meant to please
Who is
Overly eager to open the prettier packages

Debbie A. Davidson

A Special Place "Heaven"

Please help me Lord to bear the grief
of losing my dear son.
The joy you once gave to me
Somehow it is all done.
Please fill this empty space he left
on returning to your side.
Please fill this space with your love
and come in and reside.
Reside deep in my heart and soul
and fill that empty space.
That you and he filled so full
Don't let the love decrease.
Fill the part that he left
With more of your sweet gifts.
And we will know that there is
and eternal resting place.

Thank you Jesus for inspiring me
to write a Special Place in memory of my
son Jerry.

Carol Ann Lemerise

Untitled

From a distance she reminds me,
of someone I used to know

From a distance I sit,
and think of old times

From a distance I wish that,
I could have her back

From a distance I think,
of how it may have turned out

From a distance I think,
of how lucky I was to have her

From a distance I am jealous,
of my friend and his relationship

From a distance I watch.
couples and their love blossom

From a distance I wonder.
could this be the one

Kevin K. Haberman

Because I Am One

Because I am one
of ten trillion more,
I am the sand on a surf-ridden shore.

Because I am one
among many to be,
I am a wave rising up from the sea.

Because I am one
part of a few,
I am an ocean's magnificent view.

Because I am one
never standing alone,
I am the Earth with a plentiful moon.

Because I am one
child of God,
I am the sun... I am a star.

Jeffrey Aaron Schmidt

God In Heaven

There is a God in Heaven,
Of that you can be sure,
And his Son is there beside him
Where they both shall long endure.

Now, Jesus had a mission
So with love He came to earth.
He gave us faith and happiness
To dwell with peace and mirth.

He traveled many miles
To spread the word of God.
He made our lives worth living
With comfort of "Staff and Rod".

Yes, there is a God in Heaven
Far away, up in the sky.
And He's willing to help you all ways
With His blessings, as was 'I'.

Emily Marsh Kline

My Job

I'm standing behind the counter
of the local convenient store
Acting my given role as clerk
But really being much more.
Advisor to the lonely hearts
Friend to friendless souls,
Counselor to the ones that fail
To meet their daily goals.
Directory of the city
For those who lost their way
Referee of the couple
Who had a fight this day.
I never knew the skills I had
They're way beyond my age;
It seems to me I'm worth much more
Than this check for minimum wage.

Diane L. Neiderheide

Feel, See, Hear, Honor

Feel the beat,
Of the one lone drum.
Feel the beat,
From the heart of one.

See the smoke rise,
From the burning sage.
See the lovely bird,
Free from its cage.

Hear the voices of the elders,
As they sing the ancient chants.
Hear the voices of the elders,
As they sing for the spring plants.

Honor the circle as you live,
Live with the earth that breathes.
Honor the circle as you die,
Die with the earth that grieves.

Courtney N. Wear

Friends

Friends come,
and friends leave,
but when they
leave you have to
believe that you'll
never part because
there always in
your heart.

Brandy Delaunay

Black (A Halloween Poem)

Can you feel the cold unfeeling presence
of the phantom,
There in the silvery night?
While you stand on the devil's fiery tomb,
And stare at the ebony statues in the light?
Can you taste the horrible sadness of death,
While you stand in the graveyard and
take your last breath.

Elizabeth Bremser

Untitled

I'll weep for you, as I weep for me,
Of things that weren't, and could not be,
Of a long past love, and pony-tails,
Of cotton skirts, and school-yard rails,
Of an August day much like this,
Of golden sun-light in your lips.

I'll grieve for you, as I grieve for me,
Of things unsaid, that used to be,
What were you thinking for all those years?
You never shared your thought or fears
But, perhaps you did, and I didn't hear.

I'll mourn for you, as I mourn for me,
Of the many things we didn't see,
How could we have known there was no time?
You're gone, and I'm alone,
I'll never be able to hold you again,
Nor rekindle that brilliant glow.

But, maybe, when I get there too,
We can erase life's middle part, and once
again, as long ago.
Be soul-mates of the heart.

Judy Covey

Untitled

The warm memories
of where we have been
lingers
Each place I wander
you are there
to remember
Memories of you
won't leave
Stillness
The memories are what count
They comfort at times
and keep you close.

Nancy Murray

Untitled

Over the wind swept waist land
Old Washington D.C. is the spot
Battling the storm's that Congress forgot.
They know not what to do so soon
The people they're present have forgot

At night the wind keeps blowing
On we who are forgot

We are Americans so they tell us
But we hear no baw or bones

Someday we will send them
Home to live on the land they
Forgot to represent.

James E. Boulware

Resting Place

I picture you in an open field
of yellow daisies
With the sun shinning warmth
upon your face.

"Strange" is your reaction
Not at all my type of place.
But where else would "GOD"
lay you for your final Resting Place.

You may say a ditch where
no one knows your name.
In a far away country where
everything looks the same.
Where bombs blast from
morn till night
Where the people are but
a pitiful sight.

No, I can't leave you
there in my mind
I'll bring you home where you will find
your final resting place.

Donna King

Honey You've Got So Much Time

Honey you've got so much time.
Oh, how I wish it were mine.

I wish that you could be free
to spend your time with me.

While you're far away in prison,
I think of you and listen

to what my heart may say
and wish you were here today.

Jean Christensen

Impossible Without Jesus

Each day I live my life
oh Lord, I surely write
my story.
For what is life without love
and the vision of walking
in your glory.

For when I walk with you Lord,
my days are truly blessed.
You lift me up and make me
whole my sins I do confess.

Sometimes I stumble,
Sometimes I fall, but you
help me to see the light.
I don't rejoice in doing what's wrong,
Lord help me do what's right.

Jeffrey T. Jones

Living Death

Dying inside
And
No one can know.

Dying inside
And
It does not show.

Who else is there
To share these words?

Elli M. Vaughn

Untitled

Oh silly girl
Oh lost little girl—
Where have you been?
Frolicking among the wildflowers?
'NO'
Wandering throughout the cherry orchards?
'NO'
Pretending you are a fairy princess?
'NO'
Practicing jump-rope with your friends?
'NO'
Tell me then,
How you spent the day—
I was hiding, hiding all day,
And waiting for someone to notice that
'I was gone'.

Elizabeth Zambito

Banana Peels On The Road Downhill

I'm up and facing my today
Oh what, what to do
Decisions are being taken away
Avoid battles I've been through

Don't ever reach for that pen
Don't ever, ever sign
I'm now protected from myself
My future, no longer mine

Environmentally, soon I am extinct
But all that must be changed
Speed up the process, youth can't wait
Waiting is a foolish, foolish game

I can't choose for myself
No more I ever will
Youth now rules my today
There are banana peels on the road
downhill

Daphene Cody Reid

Ever

Have you ever cried for the moon
on an overcast night?
Have you ever run for the bus
when the ticket's at home?
Have you ever been swallowed by the eyes
of a beast at the zoo?

Have you ever tried talking
to God?

Have you ever planted a tree
on a construction site?
Have you ever fallen in love
with your best of friends?
Have you ever cried for the moon
on an overcast night?

Ben Levine

The Problems Of The World

Stop the violence, or, peace not war,
feed the hungry at our door!
Give money to the poor, for the homeless
a home, help the needy wherever they roam.
Help the sick, strangers or friends,
make sure the peace never ends!
Everyone should help even kids too,
because, remember, this could be you!!!

Danielle Tornabene

Fire And Thunder

The fire I see
on distant hills
is a flaming sunset
crimson
with the glory
of creation.
The thunder I hear
in my heart
is the echo
of exultation.
God reigns!

Jane Huelster Hanson

Right or Wrong

Night sky ... tears dully thud
on earth bone dry and cracking.
The People mourn.

It rains.
The drops mix in dust
blood red and dying.

The heavens aren't disturbed.
This is old stuff.
It will pass.

Black rain.
Blood red tears.
Phantom people, watching.

Skeletons, wrapped in steamy blankets
of evaporating souls.
Following the Fathers home.

Bones of our Fathers
or yours?
What difference?

Bones, white bones.
What color right or wrong?

Joan E. Menter

Wild Wild

Wild, wild, the fortunate man.
On fierce winds, on desert sands
With free will to give or choose
Wild, wild, you'll never lose.

Wild crowd, wild flower,
No need for help
You've got the power.

Wild, wild, wild life
Got no time to think
Or take advice

Wild, wild on the wings of doom
In shallow brooks, a shadow, a tomb.
Always has, always will be
Wild child ... that is me.

Eric C. Paxson

"Hourglass Of Life"

As the hourglass slowly loses its sand,
I try to hold time in my hands,
All though no mater what I do,
Each grain of life slowly passes on through,
sliding on through the last of the sands
I now know my mistake...
...holding time in my hands

Craig W. Daley

Death Of The Soul

Soft rain falls
on my broken shadow
Spread in the gutter
rain washing away my tears
Flowing away
mingling with the blood
draining in the street.
There's no one left to
clear away the pain
Alone but not forgotten
dying in the rain!

April Johnson

The Storm

I see the raindrops tumble,
On my window sill.
I hear the thunder rumble,
As the troublesome clouds seized our hill.

Finally the turbulent storm subsided,
I want to go out and play I decided.
And when my Mom said "yes,"
I was so excited.

As I went outside
I saw my friend Emily from next-door,
And thought oh good she's no bore.
We played until we could play no more.

Elizabeth Ehlers

There You Lay

There you lay
On the deserted bay

You feel so cold
And you weren't that old

From the decision you made
You soon began to fade

You left me here
For I shall no longer be near

The time we spent
Was forever meant

The words spoken
Were a cherished token

What words are left to say
Are only felt in such dismay

I sat under the sleeping willow
And dreamt of you under my satin pillow

Now that you are gone
The sun has reached dawn

The tears that I have once cried

Now 'tis the time to set aside

Jill S. Kenosian

Friends

Giving a part of yourself
leaves a mark to shape the person
you are
there for the Good
the Bad
from the Birth
to Death
yours to choose.

Amy Pierzchala

The Slam Of The Door

The slam of the door
Is the firm final word
Of the impatient youth
Or the quarrel not heard

Candice Kelly

Christmas Love

As I walk through our home
on this eve of Christmas Eve
I live and feel the love and happiness
that only you could bring.

The Christmas cards on the fireplace
the table dressed in green and red.
The warmth of my true love
beside me in our Winters' bed.

Over the next two days
only one goal will be my quest.
A promise to give to you
a very loving and Merry Christmas.

K.D. Villines

Courage

The rock
On which people lean,
Your guide
Who remains unseen.
A partner
To whom you confide,
A feeling
A sense of pride.
Your guard
Who helps you face your fears,
The dream
Undying through all the years.
The path
On which always remain,
A savior
Always humble, never vain.
The light
That guides you until the end,
An untiring hope
Your ever faithful friend.

Allison Ottino

To My Dearest Brett

If I had to choose
one place
where I could live
forever,
I would not pack
a suitcase
or drive to an airport,
Because I would choose
to live inside
your heart.
There I would have
many places
to go, like,
your arms
your life
your soul.
Being in your heart
would be like
a trip around the world.
Our world.

Barbara Blaho

Life

Life is a precious gift from God
one that should not be taken
or left wandering abroad.
A gift so precious
a gift so kind
for one to take it
he must be out of his mind.
Open your heart, your mind and your soul
look unto him
and make living your number one goal.
No one can save you
except God and yourself
so put your life in His hands
he'll provide you with riches and wealth.
Maybe not rewards of power or money
but laughter and kindness and days that are sunny
let the gloomy days pass
like storm clouds in the sky
remember you are His
until the day that you die.

Anne Allbritton

My Love Lasts Forever

My love lasts forever,
Open my heart and pull that lever.
I know you want my love,
I hear it in the song of the dove.

People say love is just a hoax,
My love you don't have to coax.
There's only one true love for me,
You're the one it should be.

I love you girl,
Your love gives my life a whirl.
I see it now,
Our love will survive somehow.

I need your love so bad,
It's driving me mad.
I must be with you,
Start something new.

Your love drives me crazy,
My days of loneliness are becoming hazy.
I'll love you until the day I die,
We both know why.

Kevin Holmes

A Joyful Servant

If it is at home to stay
Or be a missionary far away
Seeking and doing God's will each day
A joyful servant I'll always stay.

If it's to lend someone a helping hand
Or following order and heeding commands
Seeking and doing God's will each day
A joyful servant I'll always stay.

If my tasks be great or small
I'll be listening to hear God's call.
Seeking and doing God's will each day
A joyful servant I'll always stay.

JoAnn Sawyer

The Man Inside

Don't worry about mistakes you've made
or tears you may have cried.
When life's burdens start to get you down,
just turn to the man inside.

Believe in your heart there's a better way
to fulfill your destiny.
Search your soul to find the truth,
it's there for those who believe.

There's only been one perfect man.
He loved us all the same.
So in the search of finding glory,
we must also feel some pain.

We all were given different lives;
different roads to travel on.
Some burdened with more trials
than others dealt upon.

But in the end, who really knows
how hard each one has tried?
Perhaps the hardest thing in life
is to make peace with the man inside.

Cheryl Mallory Vice

New Generation

Its not that ... we don't care
Or that life ... makes us unfair
If handed damn, damn is handed

We'll be quick and too precise
Or maybe slumber and small like mice
If banded arms, then arms banded

Of shimmering shade
and shallow shrine
To bickering blades
of the beckoned blind

Maker of windows ... of tinted glass
The winded listeners came falling fast
To be apart, not apart so from

Thrasher of dreams ... of waken sorrows
Echoing days upon hallowed hours
Sunrise, sunshine, moonlight run.

Jason Mark Stych

"Night Vision"

Yet the sky was pure gold,
ornate in its eternity. A
unification of inadequate,
fictitiously spiritual and
emotional elements. These elements,
these looming clouds bruise easily.
Insomniatic interludes placate
not the continents in this dream.
Atonement is absorbed, bleeding
through the fluorescent and
insatiable air. Slipping, slipping
away towards the violet dripping dawn.

Ken Quass

My Kitchen

I love my little kitchen Lord,
I love its every nook
It's where I spend a lot of time
It's where I bake and cook.

Caroline Black

Why

Why do we like to destroy
Other creatures' environment
We tear down trees to make paper
But did we forget that squirrels live here
Or that the trees turn our carbon dioxide into oxygen for us.
We also pour toxic waste into the waters.
Don't we know that it kills the fish
And other living creatures down there
Do we do that because we don't care
Or because we are selfish?
Who knows why we do the things we do
They just happen.
But what we can do is to
Not always think of ourselves
But to consider other creatures.

Danielle R. Allen

Aging

Some accept it gracefully
Others find it hard to see
Day by day
the aging body
moving towards eternity

Eyes once bright grow dim with haste
Slower steps now set the pace
Ears that used to catch each sound
must strain to hear those gathered round

Fading memories
lost with time
mix with present scenes and signs
New confusion in the mind
keep past and present intertwined

Slowly now
those things I see
One by one intruding me
Should I just accept the fact
or vainly try to turn time back?

Eleanor Hughes

My Friend?

Can you remember this of me?
Our dreams were never meant to be;
'Twas better so — you did forget
but now I find — I love you yet!

Can you remember this of me?
I asked no promise, made no plea;
For all I could not share — or know,
I cared enough — to let you go!

While 'twas my lot — to ever roam
God gave you family — and a home:
And though I've never been a wife
Two great loves — have filled my life!

My love for God — and love for you
have always held me steadfast, true
I know -until my dying day
my two loves shall ne'er go -'way!

You tell me now, my friend you'll be
I'm glad! for that's enough for me!

Dorsie G. Davis

For Donald Lydic Miller

Peace

We walk along the beach.
Our footprints in the sand.
The smell of the ocean.
The salt in the air.

We sit quietly and listen,
to the sounds of the sea.
They are so amazingly beautiful to me.

We holds hands and chat.
Our voices echo in the wind.
The tide comes up as the sun dims.

Time goes by so slowly.
The water explores every inch of my skin.
The sand between our toes.
I feel it within.

We sit on a rock.
The waves crash at its point.
We look up and see a dolphin in flight.

We lie on the beach and look up at the stars.
The sky is so peaceful.
Reality so far.

Emily Argis

Untitled

Richard - Dear Friend,
Our Friendship Is A
Wonderful Feeling That I Will
Always Carry In My Heart

Because you are the wonderful
man you are, were friends.
Whether it was your smile
or your laugh
that caught my eye,
it was definitely you
that captured my heart.
When we first met, I felt like
I had known you all my life.
I can talk to you so easily;
I can trust you with my
inner most thoughts;
I can laugh with you on the spur of the moment.
Richard, my friend,thank-you.
I will always cherish our friendship more than words can ever say.
I love you always.

Beth Riley

Reaching Out Beyond The Stars

Reaching out beyond the stars
Out of the limits of the sky.
Forever it had seemed so far,
Because perhaps no one had tried.

But what if I could be the first,
To try to make my dreams come true?
To find the best, to conquer the worst,
And to do things I never dreamed I'd do.

And if I fail, I'll try again,
For I know patience is the key,
To unlock all locked doors and then,
Unlock our dreams and set them free.

Debra L. Siegel

The One Room School House

Walking along that old beaten path, with a dinner pail in my hands. On my way to that one room school house up on that land. When I reached on the top of that land, I heard that old school bell ring, and the children came from miles around, to hear the school teacher sing. At our seats, we sat listening to her teach, our eyes gleamed with interest, at math, and reading.

When she asked us to get wood from the shed, we obeyed her orders, and leading ahead was there no room for it on top of that land, so we fled down the hill to the bed.

JoAnna Holt

My Little One

Like a little angel
Peacefully you sleep;
In a soft little slumber
You dream so sweet.

My precious little son
With a head full of hair;
And a soft little body
Cuddly as a teddy bear.

Your eyes twinkle
So vivid and blue;
Happiness from your heart
Makes way for your coos.

Uttering not a single word,
Your little fingers grasp my hand;
Passing forth the love
We both understand.

So much joy we have in holding
Our first newborn son;
So much love we want to give
To you, our new little one.

Joan Case

Untitled

I sit alone in a crowded room.
People are all around me
Every one is talking at once
No one is talking to me.
The season suck
Every year nothing changes.
Every day the hours stay the same.
It is always Indifferent
I feel lost in a world that has no place
no time
no meaning for me.
The word friends is just a word
love
happiness
delight
They are all just emotions that can cause a smile
I have forgotten how.

Amanda Turner

Reunion

Why do we seek roots of our family tree,
Perhaps to find the purpose of you and me
To study the secrets of the past
And know how we have come to last
Above all the trouble and strife
Contributing something to this life.
You, John, have given us a fine start,
What of our life, are we willing to part,
And so, John, you have left us a quest,
Oh may we be proud to do our best
And work together like a hive of bees,
Let our country know of the family Lees

Doris Y. McNamara

Self-Titled I

I tattoo myself to feel some pain,
physical wounds exorcising the emotional.
But the positive message gives me strength.
You tried to rape me, invaded me.
So-called friend, used me at your whim,
shamed into secrecy.
But no more...
I speak out against you
and what you've done to me.
It's not my fault.
I finally understand
you've left me scared,
permanent wounds on my soul,
anger in my heart.
No longer little girl, carefree
but no longer woman cowering in fear
from men who think they own the world.

Bonnie Bowell

Yesterday

As I lay my head down on my
pillow and close my eyes,
Thoughts of yesterday fill my
mind. Yesterday you were mine
and I was yours. Yesterday we were
so much in love. Yesterday you
and I were walking hand in hand,
Talking and laughing about yesterday.

Amy C. Crow

"Storm"

Pitter, patter,
Pitter, patter.
Clouds darkening the lightly bright sky,
Confusion clatters the sight for reason.
Raindrops opposing the strong winds,
Tears forming into a deep hole.
Thunder crackles from miles away,
Anger violently bursts in rage.
Wind wrestles the trees,
Hands move into violent motions.
Lightning blinds the darkness,
Action truly speaks louder than words.
Pitter, patter,
Pitter, patter.

Chris Koenig

Alpine Beauty

Bounding high amongst steep stones
Placed precisely for my path
By mountain forces now unknown
Who before me came.

Did they live within this beauty?
Severe cliffs of brown and gray
Softened by the flowers bonny,
Covering fields in which they lay.

Stopping now to watch a daisy,
Swaying with a tune
Wind blows through pipes of branches high
Bending stem and bloom.

In but a week I say adieu
Leave this nature's sanctuary.
A reflective thought will bring me to
This alpine's heavenly beauty.

Joetta Swift

Off Stage Finale

I spoke the lifeless words
placing them carefully below feeling
like subtitles on the late show.

My decision posed moments of
planned sounds
emptying into
your cold and watchful
silence.

You took the cue
smoothly averting the clumsy course
of polite protest
and it was over.

Each life practices small endings
to rehearse the final act
Scenes played with the light touch
forgive the beginning.

Betty J. Wells

God Bless My Daddy

God Bless my daddy who flies in the sky
Please guide him and love him and
don't let him die

First it was grandpa called off to war
To cover invasions and end war of wars
Peace was declared and grandpa came
home

But soon Uncle Robert to Korea was flown
He fought long and valiant
But never came home

Then there was daddy to Vietnam called
Decorated with medals
But in the dark of the night
Death came and called him
On his very last flight

Now I am grown, to the Gulf I was called
Little Kuwait was being destroyed

I hear my little son now praying
God bless my daddy who flies in the sky
Please guide him, and love him and
Don't let him die

And to all the presidents, kings and emirs
Please do something to stop
A small child's fears

Dottie Egan

Stormy Existence

Rain falls from the clouds
plop, splat, kerplunk
each an individual with force
hitting the ground and then
diminishing invisibly
into the air again.

The clouds darken and rain
falls harder as thunder
crashes and lightening illuminates
the sky but for one second
such as we do for moments on stage
in the limelight of life.

Puddles form, eventually floods
covering the earth
where did Noah and the ark sail
but there's no one to save us
from ourselves from who we are
which is a storm in itself.

Katherine McQuitty

You're

Waking up the thunder,
Pouring down the rain,
Melting ice caps with a smile,
Showering sunshine on the sand.

The middle of the day,
The middle of the night,
You're everything that is,
You're everything that's right.

The magic of the morning,
The magic of the moonlight,
You're the dawning of the day,
You're the dawning of a dream.

You're not young, you're not old,
You're the Princess in every story told.
You're the lightning in my life.

Waking up the thunder,
Pouring down the rain,
Melting ice caps with a smile,
Showering sunshine on the sand.

Kevin D. Barrowclough

Hats Off To June

Lovely June is here
Pretty roses bloom
Blue skies seem to loom
Cameras click and zoom

A time for grads
And also dads
Romance and brides
Splashing high tides

Cook outs and pop
Picnics, no stop
Boating, camp outs
Water gun bouts

Our ace in a hole
Strawberries in a bowl
Refreshments and fun
Smiles out in the sun!

Kathleen Spencer

"Jewels"

Cracker Jack boxes, dime store baubles,
prize machines at the grocery-junk!

Rhinestones, faux pearls, cubic zirconium -
my life, my love.

Simply costume jewelry while you search for
sunken treasures.

Only a substitute, a meaningless stone,
filling the setting until you find your
rare and precious jewel.

Garnets, sapphires, rubies sparkle in
store windows while I wait encased in
a cheap plastic box.

Will I too one day be a gift of love?
Will someone see me as shimmering and
stunning?

Will you?

Kimberly Thomson

First Words

Lined up like soldiers
protecting their claim
trees surrounding serene blue waters.

Her reflection of sadness
mingling with the
calm sapphire sky.

Pen and paper
her only friends
clutching them closely to her chest.

Snapping turtles groaning her misery.

A duck sounding his horn
waking from her trance.

Slowly, brightly she writes
though
with a heart full of gloom.

Telling of their's son's
first words
with trembling hands.

Her tears rippling in the water.

Jo Anne Mitchum

Struggle Within

Struggling within I find myself
Pushing and pulling my will
Complaining to God, oh poor me
Stop it Lord just let me be free
he says; to me you were bought for
a price
But, I replied oh Lord I can't bear
the pain.
This struggle within is pulling me down
My son, He said with love and grace
Pick up your cross and finish the race.
The victory is yours when you cross that
line
Leaving those struggles within, all far
behind.

David Miles

She Sews

All day long she sews
Putting the small pieces together.
Piecing a quilt she says
Little bright colored pieces.

This one is for you, and this one for her
And maybe for her child
Tiny little pieces for a coverlet
to keep a child warm.

The Mother makes things for her children
And her children's children.
She sews all day and into the night.

It makes her happy the colors are bright.
Little flowered pieces warm a
Mother's heart.

Blanche Griffin

"The Gift Of A Sunset"

The vastness of the valley
reaches out
to an almost infinite stillness
A mass of blue sky
touches the living
and non living
bringing a glow of life
to all its surroundings
But more than ever now
a warm yet chilling quietness
embraces all the world
casting an array of beautiful
yet blinding colors
for our eyes
to behold
a captured moment that whispers
another day
is done
another tomorrow
to come.....

Cheryl A. Tate

One Soul

Together hand in hand,
Ready to take the final stand.

Pledging to each other and to God,
Their betrothal and the new road
they will trod.
Life now begins it's toll.
as they become one soul.

Dave Kochensparger

Untitled

The bottomless pool
Reflects more than I see
But only for a moment
The fleeting image fades
Submerged in darkness
and the empty face
Stares back at me
the eyes no longer see
Feelings in a shell
Hidden by a mask
Forever in these black waters.

Arianna Swink

Carnival Rides

Spinning folks in steel gray chairs,
Riding, gliding
Swallowed hearts in dizzy brains,
Shattered, battered
Feet crouched up in turning cages,
Frigid, rigid
Eyes locked tight in lashy shutters,
Blotted, spotted
Fingers cased in wired walls,
Stabbing, grabbing
Bowels freed and lodged in breasts,
Crashing, smashing
Frightened souls in laughing mouths
Reaching, screeching.

Fantasy people in fantastic boxes,
Willing, thrilling
Living high in unknown bodies,
Feeling, reeling
Spending seconds on a dare,
Fleeing life in shouts of fear.

Antoinette Michocki

Liars

Two lovers on the verge
Riding on the wings of a bird
Both denying what is to come
Turn their backs and begin to run
Noticing what went wrong
Always loving each other all along

Jaclyn Jones

"Quiet Place"

Far away is a quiet place,
Right now, just somewhere in a dream.
In the distance there is a face,
And to me how real it can seem.

Holding out, in welcome, a hand,
Large enough to hold me steady,
Take my burdens, and help me stand.
He's always prepared and ready.

Here I fear, wonder, and stumble,
Unsure, life is a constant fight.
See lonely world start to crumble,
But still, the face shines on so bright.

Wherever this far away place,
It will remain back in my mind,
While the time runs on for this race,
'Til in time, quiet place I'll find.

Corinne L. Hacker

Chyenne

Chyenne, the indian,
Roamed the land,
Through rocks and sand,
All across the lands.

They fought with pride,
Side by side,
One by one,
They would all die.

But,
They knew if they gave up,
It was only because they didn't have
enough.
Chyenne!

Candi Baber

Things That Might Have Been

It does not seem so long ago
I found a seed one day
I thought that I would plant it so
It might start on it's way

I gave it all I had to give
And watched it grow because
Although I knew that it did live
I wondered what it was

I had hope that it would flower
Into a beauty thing
Growing nobel like a tower
And make it always spring

One day I heard the thunder plain
Like that we have in May
And with it came the pouring rain
And washed my flower away

So though it never had a bloom
That I could smell and touch
At least I knew that it had been
And I shall love that much

Mary C. Henson

No Time

What has happened to me?
I have changed and grown older.
My grasp on life seems to weaken,
even though my will to live gets bolder.

I have no hold on time.
It slows not for me.
Days go on and nights fall,
with sunrise and sunset for all to see.

There is so much to do in just one day,
in these rapid paced times I live.
There is work to provide my existence,
which leaves little time to give.

It was once so very simple,
before time had me in it's grasp.
The days were filled with time,
and the nights would seem to last.

In those days I was in love
and loved in return.
I think that it is this
that time does not concern.

Steven G. McGrorty Jr.

Sweet Dreams

Go, go unto a happy place,
I have to stay until my calling
day.
Know you're free enjoy this
place.
I'll meet you, I'll see you again
some day.
I cried at first but I know
now,
It's better there than here.
I'll miss you.
I love you.
Sweet dreams.

Venus Nirelli Bortz

The night is still
I hear my thoughts
run through my mind
is thinking quietly
walking slowly down
the road I walk
into the silence of
the night is still.

Rachel F. Lewis

Whispers

I hear whispers
I hear whispers coming from the dark
What do they say
What do they want
I do not have a clue
Why are they here
Why have they come
I do not have a clue
What do they want with me
What will they do with me
I do not have a clue
I wish they would go
I do not want to know what they want
Wait...They are gone
Everything is silent
It's dark...No sound
The door opens
What do they want

Lucianna Savage

They Came To Visit

When our child died
I heard them say,
"We know just how you feel."

They had read the stories
Of love and loss,
And it had seemed so real.

They had even shed tears
As they wiped their eyes
And kept on reading still.

But they had never felt:

The retching in the heart
And the sharpness of it's pain;
The anger of the pulse
Or the suffering in vain.

They never knew the longing,
The ache of the despair;
The crying deep inside
Or the disbelief that's there.

But I knew they came to visit
Just because they cared.

Nina Lois Carrico

Reunion

In the gloried lights of dawn,
I knew you;
In the ever reaching stars,
I held you;
In the quiet of my dreams,
I see you;
In the kindness of the day,
I find you;
In the souls eternal span,
I love you...

Noelette Prestwich

For Her

From the time I saw you,
I knew you were the one
For love with you
My heart has won.
My days and nights are filled with pleasure
My love for you I cannot measure.
Your eyes are like windows into your soul
Reaching it is my ultimate goal
Whenever we part, it cuts me like a knife
For with you, I want to spend the
rest of my life.

Robert Thomas Baer

Lonely Tree

O little lonely tree
I know how you feel.
To be so fake
In a world so real.

I pass you by near
The setting sun.
I live in your world
And it's no fun.

I know what it's like
To be left by yourself.
Hidden from the world
Put away on a shelf.

We have a lot in common
You and me.
I know how you feel
Little lonely tree.

Scott Clanton

When I

When I saw him,
I liked him.
When I liked him.
I kiss him,
When I kissed him.
I loved him.
When I loved him,
I let him
When I let him
"I lost him."

Viona Jasmin

A Canadian Love Song

I love the rain...
I love it as I love your eyes.
As I love the memory of your touch,

I love the cold...
I love it as I love your smile,
As I love the gentleness of your voice

I love the wind . . .
I love it as I love your body
As I love the echoes of your words

I love this city...
I love it's walls, it's gardens,
it's monuments.

Because it brought me to you.

I love the rain as I love you eyes.

Sandra C. LaPlante

Our Holy Father

Heavenly Father
I love you so much
Feeling you hold me
The sensation of your touch.

I say a prayer
And I know you are there
Feeling your arms around me
In the thinness of the air

My Holy father
Blessed be forever
A God so divine
I will always endeavor.

Glory to God
Jesus, our host
The bread of life
Father, son and holy ghost.

MaryGrace Esposito

BETRAYAL!

Pain floods in like an ocean tide.
I loved and trusted you
only to discover that you'd lied.

So go on, off with your so-called friends
and have a laugh at my expense.
You have no conscience —
you don't know the meaning of repentance.

I'll get along fine without you
and see that you never know
the hell I went through because of you
I refuse to let it show.

Stacey Perkins

Untitled

As I walk through timeless lands,
I meet a strange, but familiar face.
One I know not, yet know so well
That neither time nor change can hide.

Time, because of love so deep inlaid,
Can never hide your soul away.
The face may change, as well as time,
But love remains to make you mine.

I knew when first I held your hand.
That somehow you would understand,
The depth of love so deep, my dear,
Drawing from life far and near.

In this life, though we may part,
Carry with you in your heart,
My undying love for you, my dear,
To bridge the miles, both far and near.

We'll walk through life hand in hand,
Touching not... yet, I feel your hand.
I'll always cherish you, my dear,
Dreaming each night I hold you near.

Sue Tidwell

Seeds For Growth

There is a garden, I am told,
In every heart, both young and old.
The flowers there are thoughts and deeds,
And when they die where go the seeds?
To our children they must go,
Be careful of the seeds you sow.

Adelaide Berends

Dying for Love

In a park, where I did dwell,
I met a guy I knew so well,
He took my heart away from me.
and now he wants to set it free.
He met a girl he did not know,
and told her that he loved her so.
He sat her down on his knees,
and told her things he never told me.
I went home to cry on my bed.
Not a word to my mother I said.
Father came home late that night.
He searched for me from left to right.
and through my bedroom door he broke,
To find me hanging from a rope.
He got a knife to cut me down,
and on my dresser this letter was found.
"Dig my grave, and dig it deep.
Marble stone from head to feet,
and on my grave place a dove,
To show the world I died for love".

Yanci Rodriguez

Today

Blonde hair, blue eyes,
I miss my boy today.

Freckled face and silly grin,
My eyes don't "smile" today.

Small hands, making prints,
Are absent from my walls today.

Mommy tackles and breathless hugs
Won't disrupt my stance today.

"I love you" in a deep silly voice,
Is silent from my ears today.

Spilled food and gooey mess
Don't grace my floor today.

No soap in sinks,
Or towels that missed the "bar" today.

The house is empty and sedate;
It's "life" is gone today.

Nanette Metskas McCarthy

Dedicated to my wonderful son, Collin.

"Thank You"

For the first time in my life
I needed a shoulder to cry upon
But the tears in my eyes
Turned the brightest of days
Into the darkest of nights
So I was left in the dark
With no light to guide my way
And for the first time in my life
I felt alone
But then in the darkness
I saw alight (and it was moving toward me)
And the closer it got to me
The brighter it got
Until finally when the light got to me
I found that it was no light at all
It was you
Lending a shoulder for me to cry upon
So now I thank you
For being there for me
During my darkest hour

Timothy "Teague" Collum

Spleen

I was put in an x-ray machine.
It was found I had no spleen.
When I got up, I gave 'em a buck.
And that was the end of the scene.

James Karl Wurster

"Madonna Of The Street"

Alas! I cry!
I passed a Madonna by.

There on pavement
Crouched and cold,
Clutched she her babe,
Doll-like yet old.

In the midst of hawking passersby
She sat stoic and forlorn.

Are you the Mary of Him?
Or the Magdalene?
Why chained to street of stone?
Why for coins sit you so alone?

May God in his heaven
Bless thee thrice!

I passed a Madonna by.
Alas! I cry!

Marion A. Hoeman

A Daughter's Prayer

Before I sleep at night
I pray to God above
That one day I may see
My mother's face in the sunlight
We may live worlds apart
But I just want to let you know
I love you very much
Wishing you were here from the start
I know I will see you someday
Hoping and praying for the moment
I can give you a hug
And never feel far and away.

Tricia L. Sahgal

Divorce

When I close my eyes
I see a loving family
But when I open them
it seems to disappear

Why can't things be perfect
Why don't people care
Can't we just love one-another
Is life really that unfair?

Divorce is very difficult
Although some may not see
People try to understand
But you can't, unless your me

I try not to blame myself
I do the best I can
But no matter how hard I try
The hurt comes back again

I'm often torn in two directions
Never knowing what to do
If only I could close my eyes
And make my dream come true.

Robin Antonelli

When I Look At You

When I look at you
I see your loving eyes
I see the crystal blue seas
I see the beautiful skies.

When I look at you
I see your heart-warming smile
I look at your long, curly hair
I remember my inner child.

When I look at you
I see your beautiful face
I know that you belong
In this wonderful place.

I want you to come away
Come away and travel with me
And if you do
Together we will always be.

Virginia Elaine Logan

Untitled

I am a man of honor
I serve when called upon
Within a moments notice
My life here could be gone

I guard uncertain borders
I hold my head up high
For without such acts of courage
My daughter would never fly

Her wings may thus be bounded
Her mouth a silent tongue
Her hands and feet not happy
Her face no smile found

Some say we have no purpose
That we should not be here
Yet without my stance of honor
We all would live in fear

Richard M. Louth

Life's Mysteries

Life is a mystery
I should know.
Why do the days go slow?
Why do people come and go?
And why do I feel bad,
When I should be feeling glad?

Life is a mystery,
I should know.
I have so many questions,
But there's never time to ask them.
When will there be time?
Time goes fast.
Time goes slow.
There are so many answers,
I don't know.

Tami Berg

island

the biggest sh*t I am
like Marlon Brando
who watched his public
from an island
strip him
like pieces of bacon.

Bohdan Kot

"A Summer Dream"

While resting beside a mountain brook
I spied a little Elf,
Sitting on a mossy stone
Enjoying himself.

To my surprise, he winked at me
Then in a flash was gone,
I think he must have disappeared
Into the bubbling foam.

I never saw him afterward
Though I lingered by the stream,
Perhaps he wasn't there at all
and it was just a summer dream.

Ona E. Mustaine

This Shouldn't Be

As I sit in this world of darkness,
I start to cry, thinking of my life
and how I want to die. I wish I could
fly and spread my wings out like
a dove, or walk to the light of the
world of happiness and love. As I
start to walk I become weak and I
can't hold my body up, so I try
to fly, but as I start to fall I feel
the need to die. I wish I could pick
myself up and keep on, but now
the sun is up, and it is now dawn.
As I wake up from this dream, I
try to see that this is not how my
life should be.

Monique Flagg

Crossing Paths

On this day,
I think back and remember.
It was five years ago,
My heart fell like timber.

Three words Mom told me,
I'll never forget.
The said, "Baby, he's gone,"
I begged? "Please, not yet."

The day had come,
The battle was lost.
Kenny had met God,
Their paths had crossed.

It doesn't seem fair,
In a world so cruel.
But who are we to say,
And what are we to do.

So each day we go on,
Remembering the past.
Until we meet again,
The day we cross paths.

Nyla Rae Sage

Diamonte

Cold,
Icy, biting,
Freezing, snowing, sleeting,
Jacket, snowmobile, sun lake,
Burning, sizzling, tanning,
Sweaty, sultry,
Hot.

Grant Olson

Seeker of the Light

Since my first awareness,
I think I've always asked myself, why am I?
Am I only what I seem to perceive,
in the reflection of my eye?

Is there more to me than what I know?
A brain, a heart, some flesh and bone,
is God the creator of my soul?
Define soul, and who is God?
Am I his to own?

Why is my brain so large?
And yet we use much less then ten percent?
Is it to retain the things of life,
so that after life has passed
we still retain the things of life
and what they meant?

Why does God, if there is a God,
leave us to our own demise?
Surely he must know our flesh is weak,
and we will seek the way our ego lies.

Maybe that's the way of God,
for maybe he too was weak,
and all the lessons that he learned
are there for us to seek.

Rob Roy

Gone Is The Friend

Gone is the friend
I thought would always be there
Gone is the friend
With anything I thought I could share
Gone is the little one
Who brought sunshine and smiles
Gone is the little one
Who is no longer close yet so few miles
Gone is my friend
Who I though would always care
Gone is my friend
Now I must wonder was he ever there?

Norma Aeschbacher

Too Late To Get Acquainted

I passed by a church the other day
I wanted to go in and pray
But I had so many things to do
I didn't have time to talk to you.

I wanted to get acquainted Lord
and learn more about your holy word.
But I was so busy every day
I just couldn't find the time to pray.

And now that times no longer mine
I find that I have lots of time
as I stand before you in my shame
Lord, you don't even know my name.

Marjorie Swyers

Untitled

While you were sleeping,
I was peeping,
at the morning sky,
wondering why,
the sun had chased all the stars away.
Only to be reminded,
of the dawn of your smile,
and wanting to be near you
all the while.

C. Wagoner

Until The End

So young, so frail
I was just a child;
Growing up, getting smarter
A little bit wild.
I took your hand
And placed it in mine
To hold there forever
And see your face shine.
I'm older now-
My hand has let go.
I don't need you as much
But my love I still show.
You're there for me always-
That never will fail.
You're always beside me
To help my ship sail.
I love you now
As I loved you then,
Perhaps more than ever
Until the end.

Rebbecca Woods

To Nan.

I was old till you were born,
I was sad and full of pain,
Creaking bones, sinews, nerves,
Life a loveless journey's end.

You were born and I was reborn,
You gave me a reason to live.
New life surged through every bone,
The creaking stopped, the nerves
renewed,
And Winter turned to Spring.

You brought me youth
You brought me joy
You brought me health
and happiness, my little Nan.

Meher Albara

Fog

The fog drifts slowly down the lane.
I watch it through the windowpane.
It quiets every noisy sound
As it creeps along the ground.

Its slender fingers search the trees
And stills the night birds melodies.
It dims the moon and hides a star
And swirls around a passing car.

I love the fog, as you can guess.
It soothes and calms, relieves much stress.
It hides the scars upon the land
And makes the common look quite grand.

It floats and swirls and drifts along
And muffles noise and din and song
Until a breeze springs from the sea
And sends the fog away from me.

Sally S. Price

What A Day!

When my journeys end,
I will be with Jesus my friend.
I will be free from pain,
Never to have pain again.

I will see Jesus's face,
Live forever in his holy place.
I will see Jesus's throne.
Will be so glad to be home.

Yes, it will be a happy day,
Never again a cloudy day.
Jesus light will shine bright,
Never ever again a dark night.

Never ever again a tear.
Will be happiness everywhere.
The Angels and Saints will all sing,
Praises to our Lord Jesus our king.

This is what we all live for,
To able to go through heavens door.
Never to worry about being harmed,
Be safe and secure in Jesus arms.

Raymond Wiesenmayer

Thinking Of You - Thinking Of Me

Do you think of me as I do you?
I wonder if you're happy or blue.

How do you spend your days
Out there in that L.A. haze?

Sometimes I talk to you as I did when,
You were here and we were friends.

I tell you all my dreams and fears,
Just as I did through all the years.

Now your gone; I know not where
And I wonder if you know or care.

I'm here for you, I'll always be,
Thinking of you, thinking of me.

Stella L. Ashby

I Am

I am shy and gentle in nature.
I wonder what tomorrow will bring
I hear a beckoning call
I see a classroom that I can call my own
I want to become a teacher
I am shy and gentle in nature.

I pretend it is my first day as a teacher
I feel the fear in the children's faces
I touch my desk
I worry how I will make it through the day
I sigh when I see the children leave
I am shy and gentle in nature.

I understand that I can make a difference
I say that I will become a good teacher
I dream of how it will be
I try to prepare myself for that day
I hope that I will become a great teacher
I am shy and gentle in nature.

Laura Sexton

"If I Won The Lottery"

If I won the lottery
I'd buy a wheel and make pottery
At the very start
I'd invest in art.
I'd buy a farm of course,
And have dogs and a horse.
I'd lotion my skin.
Join a spa and get thin.
Then I could look cute.
In a short skirted suit.
With high boots of leather
And splash on fresh heather
And I'd shop and shop.
'Til from exhaustion I'd drop,
My soul I would search
And give to my church.
And I could do more.
To help all the poor
But in the grandest of schemes
'Tis only in my dreams.

Ruth Ann Jones

A Friend To Be

A friend to be, a friend to be,
I'D LIKE A FRIEND JUST FOR ME.

We would laugh and play
every day,
and be good friends
forever.

We'd go through good times
and the bad,
and sometimes even be
very sad,

But as long as
you are there,
I will find time to spare.

A friend to be, a friend to be.

Mark D. Wells II

Untitled

When I was a child,
I'd wake up before dawn
Just to watch him go fishing
On our little gold pond.
He'd turn 'round and look,
Holding tight to his line.
And I'd turn away and blush
As his glittering eyes met mine.
He'd nod-that's the signal.
I'd crawl on his lap.
Just as warm as a puppy
In a midsummer's day nap.
I'd have stayed there all day
All night if I could.
I loved him so dearly.
Any normal child would.
The time came to grow up.
I had to leave my little pond.
But, in my heart forever,
Thoughts of Grandpa stay fond.

Rebecca Rae Devig

Confusion

I wonder if I would
If I thought I could
Maybe that I should
I decided that I would
When I found out I could
And told myself I should
I can't remember what I would
That I found out I could
And really thought I should
Indecision that I would
Caused me to forget what I could
Now I don't know if I should
Was I to knit a hood
Make a carving out of wood
Paint a picture form where I stood
I wish I remembered what I would
When I found out I could
And thought I really should. . .

Wilfred L. Deyo

He's All Boy

My little boy is at the age
If I try and kiss him he'll
Rant and rage.
He'll duck his head and
Turn away to avoid my touch.
Then look's at me as if to
Say, "Mom, you're just too much."
When bedtime comes
I anxiously tuck Him in
And hug him tight so
He just can't win
And this is when I'm
Able to sneak one
Of my kisses in.

Maureen Wickham

The Title Is In Bold Print

How will we know what the main point is
If you cannot clearly
Present your thesis

If you do not follow it
With well rounded sentences
We will get bored

Poor sentence structure
Is enough
To turn off any reader

If you cannot
Make your purpose
Plainly understood

Then how will we know
If your ideas are
Right

For that is what we must decide

Tina Valdez

Love

Love is deep,
Love is strong,
No one knows
how love belongs.

Belong to you
I know I'm bound
For in you, love I found.

Katrina C. Oliver

Why

Why be born
If you will die

Why walk
If you might fall

Why try
If you might fail

Why ask why
You may not get an answer

Why
Why Not

Why not be born
You could have a wonderful life

Why not walk
Great athletes had to start somewhere

Why not try
You only fail by not trying

Why not ask why
Someday you might meet someone with
all the answers.

Tammy Gross

Forever True

Please give me what you want to keep
I'll guard it in my peaceful sleep
Surrounding it with lovely dreams
of twinkling stars and bright moonbeams.
I'll nurture it with love and care,
protect it from this world's nightmares;
I'll give it all I have to give
I'll breath for it and help it live;
I'll cry it's tears when it is sad,
take the blame when it's been bad;
and, if it ever does feel pain,
then I'm the one that you can blame;
I want your heart to join with mine,
to be together for all time;
and in return I'll give to you
a love that is, forever true.

Patricia Strattman

Let Earth Be

The leaves are blowing
  I'm happy it's not snowing
people are caring
  and I am sharing.

There's something in the breeze
  that made me sneeze
going outside wasn't fun
  'cause the wind weighed a ton.

When the wind went away
  it was time to pay
for a cup of tea
  and let earth be!

Maureen Rabbitt

Granddaughter Dear

Katy Beth, granddaughter new,
I'm very glad to welcome you!
With curly hair and eyes of blue,
You're precious as the morning dew!

Katy Beth, granddaughter sweet,
I pray your active little feet
Will go on steps where you will meet
Fantastic folks who are so neat.

Katy Beth, granddaughter smart,
I hope you're always pure in heart.
If I could I'd do my part
To keep you from all evils dark.

Katy Beth, granddaughter dear,
As you mature from year to year
It would be great to always hear
That you know love instead of fear.

Katy Beth, I'd like to know
As up life's garden path you go
You will definitely show
That you'll always "hoe your own row".
God Bless!

E. Kathryn Lavy

Waiting On Love

Waiting On Love
I'm Waiting On Love
To help Me make it through the night
Waiting, waiting, waiting
On Love
When things go wrong
Love keeps me strong
I'm just holding on
I feel free, every time love satisfy me
Waiting On Love
day and night
Love makes it right
Waiting On Love
To fulfill my hopes and
dreams, the joy that love
brings to me
Waiting On Love
Waiting, waiting, waiting
Waiting On Love

Willie McKinney Jr.

Rain Water

Collecting falling rain drops
in an empty coffee can,
he declares his love for her
to the gods.

Rain drops fall down his cheeks
like tears
as if his love,
swollen beneath his chest,
hurts.

Then, his can is full.
He smiles,
walking towards his lover
with the world in his hands.

Traci Delores Anderson

There's This Little Thing Called Life

There's this little thing called life
in between here and there
It winds around streams that flow
fast and slow at times
It brings rain and snow
with icy spots
It brings sun that warm you throughout
It brings you nights that give you peace
and others that do not
It will bring you friends
It will bring you happiness
It will also bring you sorrow
But in between the here and there
Let's have fun living life

Maureen Bahre

Grandpa

I saw the many years of experience,
  in his wrinkled face of old.
I saw the thoughtful art of teaching,
  in the life long stories he told.
I saw the wisdom and knowledge,
  covered by his fading gray hair.
I saw in his eyes the times of happiness,
  and also the times of despair.
I saw the concern for his family,
  that he always had in his heart.
I saw the tears he shed for loved ones,
  when death came to play its part.
I saw the many scars and callouses,
  that years of work had put on his hands.
I saw when I looked at my Grandpa,
  a picture of an unforgettable man.

Roger A. Sager

My Greatest Love

My greatest love is the love of my dreams.
In life, there was not one
for me, it seems.
The passion, the anguish,
the glory, the depths all
elude me as I travel life's steps.
Would I have adored as no
one before, the wrappings of love
had it entered my door.
The tears in my eyes mark
an end to the lies;
My greatest love, herein dies.

Marcia Collette

Dream

Do not call my name.
In my dream there is evil.
The dark shadow of a man.
He knows not my name.

The dark man follows me.
Everywhere I go,
I glimpse his lurking, shadowy form.
And in the dream I tremble.

Yet he can not harm me,
He knows not my name.
That only saves me
From his grasping clutch.

And in my dream I wake up,
trembling. My father calls out
____, are you all right?
And the dark man laughs.

Laura Ketcham

"Democracy"

As I gaze across the distant sea,
in my mind, I hear the sounds of war.
I hear the cries of anguish and pain,
as in many wars before.

These desolate cries of lost souls,
work increasingly upon my mind.
I think of those brace men,
who died and left loved ones behind.

These men have offered their services,
and gone to fight in a faraway place.
So that Americans could live their lives
as a free and democratic race.

All throughout our history,
man have fought and died.
Because the heart of every man
is filled with American pride.

And as time continues upon it's course,
many more Americans will die in glory.
So that freedom and democracy can live
and so America can tell it's story.

Patrick M. Riley

"Back On Back"

Here I sit
In my prime,
Just doing quite
A bit of time.
This time, was not,
Written in the stars.
So, I certainly didn't plan,
To spend it behind bars.
At count time I find,
Myself on my rack.
Wondering if, when I'm free,
I'll be on the right track?
I'm seriously working to,
Change the direction of my life.
Maybe, one day, I'll even
Make a good wife?
There is one thing though, I know
For sure and will shout out loud!
Before the end of my days,
I will make my family proud!

Virginia Clark

"Thank You Lord"

Lord You are the one,
In my time of need,
That listens to my problems,
Every word You heed.

When I feel discouraged,
You're there to guide my way,
And when I'm feeling lonely,
You're by my side to stay.

You never try to change me,
You know just who I am,
You know my limitations,
And when I need to try again.

Thank you Lord for Your support,
And never letting me down,
Thank you Lord for Your love,
It's peace in You I've found.

Renee Gibson

Weaving The Legacy Of Friends

The common threads
in our friendship are memories
Most are not so grand
but then most are not so bad
They are the vigor
of our childhood
For where else is love so pure

So as we age
the vigor fades
One picks satin
ad one picks crepe
Which causes the thread to break

Life goes on
and in our hearts remain
the legacy of memories
in friends now grown apart

The day may come
when the friends
can weave new memories
and rejoin the old cloth with new

Liz Stickney

You Were There

You were there
In sadness, when I cried;
You cheered me when my dreams had died.

You were there
To light dark pathways of my life;
To encourage me in times of strife.

You were there
To hold my hand;
When I faltered, you helped me stand.

You were there
When the shadows did dispel;
To smile with me when things were well.

You were there
When I needed a friend -
True and loyal with no pretend.

And you were there
When I fell in love.

Virginia L. Anderson

The Fearsome Black Cat

The black cat roams,
in the dark of night.
His hearing so keen,
his eyes so bright.
His look so fearsome,
and yet, so mean.
Of all I've told,
of this cat of mine.
The most fearsome part,
is that ear piercing whine.

Lauren Ashley

The Door

Why did you close the door,
many years were left behind,
Another house,
another door
Please don't let we close
the door.

Erica A. Moreno

Alone

Alone
in the dark world
everyone searching
for hatred and rumors, me
searching for warmth
and comfort
only finding someone
full of black
and dreary blues
to satisfy my comforts
wishing to have
the one thing I cannot
I dream but, there's no time
for sleepy dreaming
I miss the red
of what I never had
I feel it but it is lost
in the purple mist
as it melts away
and I'm left alone, again

Summer Litherland

A Mother's Love

A flower blossoming
in the morning mist —
. . . is beautiful.

Clouds caressing the peak
of a snow covered mountain —
. . . is beautiful.

The sun setting on the endless scene
of an ocean —
. . . is beautiful.

The gracefulness of a swimming swans
on a lovely summer day —
. . . is beautiful.

The bond between
Mothers and Daughters —
. . . is beautiful.

The love and care they show
makes a Mother's love
so precious to hold.

That is so beautiful!

Tracy Gand

Melissa

I arrive to find you slumbering
in your father's arms, your bottle
firmly in place.

Your small hand tangled in
your fine golden hair twirls
and twirls, pacifying.

I gently stroke your fleece
covered leg, careful not to
awaken you.

Suddenly you stir,
with a loving smile you reach for me
and I for you.

We gaze at one another;
a mirror image,
we are enthralled.

Susane L. Nelson

"God's Gifts To Me"

God gave me two gifts
in the past few years

My two baby girls
full of laughter and tears

He sent them down
from the heavens above

Knowing that they'd be
taken care of and loved

I have watched them grow
one twelve and one four

I couldn't ask for
anything I'd want more

Each day they amaze me
of things that they do

The caring and sharing
and love of the two

They have blessed me with more joy
than I could ever imagine

My two precious girls
My Kristin and Kathryn

Laura Payton

Crimson Glacier

Sweet red roses
In the rear-view mirror.
Moving in reverse,
They appear much clearer.
I left them behind
And must go ahead,
But there's one thing
I truly dread -
No matter how far
I travel ahead,
In the rear-view mirror,
There's a frozen rose bed.

Natasha Stewart

Untitled

Needles shining
in the slanting gold
of the afternoon,
dancing in her hands,
in a pattern she has decided.
She smiles at me
and my tangled chaos,
needles lying idle.
I don't have that gift fully
that necessary grace
of creating peace,
of making order,
but I have begun to learn.
She listens to the thrilling of my voice
as if it were music.
I watch the dancing of her hands
as if it were a waltz.
Both of us shining
in the slanting gold
of the afternoon.

Melissa A. Messner

16 Weeks

I feel so warm and cozy,
In this world that's all my own.
I can feel my toes and fingers,
It's funny how I've grown.

I started out so little,
Invisible to the naked eye.
But day by day, I've blossomed,
Like a sunflower growing toward the sky.

However, to many I am insignificant,
Just a "lifeless lump of clay"
I wish they would somehow realize,
That they too began this way.

I love my peaceful and secure existence,
But there is one thing I don't understand.
Why - just when my life is beginning,
Are there those who want it to end?

God created me on purpose,
Paving many roads for me to endeavor.
But SELFISHNESS will soon end my short life,
I'll be 16 weeks old forever.

Margaret M. Davies

Life As We Know

The life we know
in time we will grow,
To everyone on earth
We can see tomorrow,
To shed our tears of sorrow.
What can people do.
To help one another grow
People of all ages can see,
Tomorrow till we come together,
So life will be
Life as we know.

Susan Steepy

The Watcher

Day by day a tough world goes by
Indifferent, without alibi
To justify why I can't fly
How long will I believe the lie
When I'm afraid to even try?

I watch I wait, don't know what for
Held down by something in my core
It spikes me sharply to the floor
No guts, no glory, just a bore
A witness to beyond my door.

Decisions are for me too great
My mind can only hesitate
Can't bear to see just what my fate
I think, I fear, it's much too late
Now all I do is watch, and wait.

My life is not my own, you see
But freedom is so easily
Taken from those who will not see.
I've paid the price; this ghost is me
Forever a facsimile.

Laura J. Aldana-Garratt

Two Shall Be One

Surround me,
Inhale me,
Consume me -
And I in thee
Will fatten thee
With shapes and scents of flowers,
With shades and hues of peacock plumes,
With music both intense and sweet,
With magic,
With LOVE!

Martha T. Fugate

Seeing It Through

I b**ch because its hamburger
instead of steal
But, at least its hamburger
and not a cup of rice.

I gripe because its a small place
to live.
But, there's carpet and a furnace
not a mud floor and chilling cold.

I'm sad because the little ones
can't have dancing lessons
And big wheel bikes.
But a least they have a - future.

I scream because there is to much
noise, to much crime, to much pollution
But at least there's not a war
outside my - front door.

Pamela Border

The Eyes Speak

What do you see when you look
into my eyes?
Are they clear as the sky?
Or do you see them cry?
Are they as brown, as a tree?
Or do you see inside of me?
What do you see when you look
into my eyes?
Do you see the glitter of the rain?
Or do you see all my hidden pain?
Could you see inside my heart?
Could you even tell them apart?
What do you see when you look
into my eyes?
Do you see the abundance of joy?
Or do you see the little boy?
Do you see the woman I am to be
Or do you see just plain
oh me!

Norma Knowles

Chi Chi

Chi Chi the pot bellied pig
Made head lines over a
Harley, without a wig

The owner, disowned the
A mours pig

But Chi Chi still loves
The Harley with no wig

Connie L. Rose

Eye of the Beholder

Locked in on the windows of thought
Intrusting the freedom of expression
within a stare
Catching words of instinct
written in the passion of knowledge
From the core of the heart
thoughts extend
Transmitting common
conspiracies
of life's meaning
Touching a new sense
within the body's realm
Hand invisible through the air
Touching the eyes of another's mind
Color that holds comfort
Within the pool of thought beyond it
Putting a power in the eye of the beholder
Giving our eyes a
whole
other sense

Travis McIver

Growing Up

The little boy I use to be
Is hidden deep within.
The man that I still hope to be
Has yet to begin.

I'm living in my teenage years,
Facing many hopes and trials,
With the fear of moving forward
Thru unknown, uncertain miles.

But with my family and my friends,
The deep love they give to me,
The strength I need to overcome
Will be a certainty.

May I make the right decisions,
Make them proud of who I am,
To see the love in my parents eyes
When they say; "My son's a man".

Monte W. Moore

My College Bound Friend

What Is a Friend, I sometimes ask?
Is it a person who wears a mask?
Or is it someone who unfolds,
And lets me into the untold?

Am I a friend or just another,
A mother, father, sister or brother?
Do I do my part in life or am I
Just a lonely fife?

Who is my friend?
I think I already know!
Someone who cares and has
Watched me grow.

My companion, hero, and closest friend,
Is starting a new beginning, which,
I hope will never end!

Although I am here, and she is there,
Our feelings are without wear.
For until my life is near the end,
I will always be her closest friend!

Tiffany Bowers

Is Love This Way?

I often wonder if love is this way,
is it me or my bad day? When your
love is always cold, stand up and show
him you're bold! He'll say he loves you
once in a blue-moon, then you'll treat
him with a long-handed spoon. You
try your best to succeed, but end
up doing the wrong deed. I like the way
it makes me feel, then I wonder if it's
the real deal! Well that's all for now
I say, I often wonder if love's this way?

Miranjani Swiggett

Thoughts Of The Aged

Death at Eighty
Is much in my thoughts.
Will I be aware of the process
Or will my mind shut down?
Will death be sudden?
Some say that is best.
But would I regret
That which might have been?
Will I welcome the end
Relieving the long hours of pain?
Or will I struggle
To draw one last breath?
Will I leave the tunnel of light?
Or will it be the darkness
Of nothingness?

Mary Lee Sabre

A Friend Like You

Dedicated to Patricia A. Harper

A friend like you
Is so special to me
A friend like you
Is as the smell of sea
A friend like you
Means true honesty
A friend like you
Means it all to me
A friend like you
Is what I need
A friend like you
For I shall always cherish
In days and nights to come
For you my friend have taught
me the true meaning of a friend
so you my friend I thank
for being my friend.

Lisandra Santiago

Open Up

To open your mind ...
is to follow a pathway of thoughts.
To open your ears...
is to unlock the door of understanding.
To open your eyes...
is to see through the window of light.
To open your feelings...
is to give for a world of caring.
To open your heart...
is to awaken the universe of love.
To open the universe of love.
is to open your soul...

Steve Messa

Memories

Watching the roads all go by
It brings memories that causes
tears to roll down my eyes.
My box of memories has strongly indulged
It's more likely a spectral.
Thinking of it all depends on time
Because wholesome thoughts
are forever to climb.

When I see that road I stare in wonder
Leaving my problems I become a riser.
Just like the hills and mountains
all so high
Memories articulately keeps my soul alive.

Memories send an important message,
it never lacks
Either happy and clear
or sad and black.
Truly what memories are
It depends on you for it to be
a short distance or far.

Maricar Bulan

Friends

Friendship never questions you,
It doesn't have to ask.
It shows in what you say and do,
No matter what the task.

You cannot see it with your eyes
or hold it with your hands.
Together we must work and try,
to keep God's simple plan.

Our God named Jesus shows us the way
He teaches us what to do,
"Love one another everyday
as much as "I love you"

When trials and troubles challenge you,
and life seems so unfair,
hand in hand we'll see them through
together we can bear.

Over the years as we grow,
It may be put to the test.
It's truly up to us you know,
As friends we are the best.

Marisela E. Ornelas

Girlfriend

Girlfriend, hold your head up high!
It doesn't matter what they think,
Get on your own two feet.
So what, your gonna be a single mom.
It doesn't matter.
Concentrate on life.
And on which road to take.
Go ahead and finish college.
It maybe harder and may even take longer
But you can make it.

Get on with your life.
The world won't come to an end.
Complete your goals you've set before.
Teach your child right.
Set an example.
Show your child that no matter what
obstacles life puts in your way.
You can overcome them.

Girlfriend, hold your head up high!.
Because Girlfriend, your gonna make it!

Valorie Kaye Anderson-Branch

A Little While

I'm waiting for your call son
it has been a little while.
You being out there in the world
let loose and on your own
makes me wonder a little while.
I know you're going to make it just fine
cause you see son, you were kept in line
but I still wonder a little while.
So call me to let me know
then God Bless you, you can go
but that wont stop me form wondering
a little while.

Terri Schumann

The Flame Of Love

Love is like a candle
It has but one true flame
Be careful how it's handled
If it goes out who's to blame

It can burn brightly
If the love is strong
And will bring you light
For so very long

If the winds of trouble come
It may flicker or go out
But it can be saved by some
Who love without a doubt

If the love is untrue
The wick can be crushed
By the unfaithful two
And the love is hushed

Laura Kretschmer

To the One I Love Most

Every time I look at you
it hurts a bunch
Cause your the one I love so much
I wish I knew the truth about you
weather or not you love me too
I love you, but do you love me?
that is what I need to know
so I know if I should stop loving you so
You were my first love
or do you even care
or even when you dumped me out of
nowhere.
It seems like forever since you left me
yet it's only been 3 years
But until we get back together
I will always be in tears.

Nina Penney

Many

My family is immense.
It is made up of my many
brothers and sisters.
They are my family of God.
So when you ask me how many
in my family have been baptized
or if I stand alone.
I say unto you,
that under my father's kingdom
there have been many.

Stephanie O'Neal

The Essence Of Freedom

Freedom is bondage
It leads to confusion,
Lack of direction,
Amusing delusion

No boundaries made,
No boundaries known!
No orders to follow,
Condemn, or condone

Do what you want!
But what do you do?
There still are some limits
Some things are taboo

No lines can be crossed if
No lines have been drawn!
The truth is a lie
So my freedom is gone

Maya Khalilah Kennard

Untitled

Loneliness engulfs.
It overpowers the joy of life
Forbids laughter,
Blackens happy thoughts.
It's dark arms imprison,
Hold tight,
Paralyze the body.

Until love enters...
And comforts the broken heart,
Forbids tears.
It's caressing hand guides,
Softly protects,
Wakens the soul!

Yes, the loneliness adjourns
In the mighty face of love.
And the love lasts forever...
And the loved rejoice...
And all is well.

But this love...
Does it ever come?

Patricia Clark Imbimbo

Kali Maw

Bride of Kali bride of Kong
It seems to me that something's wrong
No handsome prince no gown of white
Just prince of darkness endless night
To have and hold in life and death
A kiss of blood a vampire's breath
To pierce the veil and then press on
Eternal life from dusk to dawn
I cannot change this path I trod
So near to hell so far from God
But if I could I'd dare to pray
And feel the sun for one last day.

M. Karen Shannon

His Love For Her

Written in the snow so pure
is his hearts love for her.
As it melts in the Spring's sun
Winter's fond memories live on.
Slowly permeating the earth
quenching creations thirsts.
Bringing beauty beyond compare
unequalled to his love for her.

Robyn Behling-Flanagan

The Song That God Wrote

I heard the song wrote by God,
it was light and bright and grand,
the singer, he was quite odd,
he wasn't in a choir or a band,
he was alone and singing,
he was flying in the sky,
he was alone and winging,
he was a dove on the fly.

I heard the song that God wrote.
God made it clear to me.
it said be humble, don't gloat,
it said open your eyes and see,
be your best and a friend,
the song was of love for me,
and it said, 'love all' till the end.

C. S. Bennett

Memories

He reached out and touched her
It was time to say goodbye
He was married
She knew why

He really did love her
She touched his soul
She was sunshine and laughter
A part of his all

They both loved their families
Husbands and wives
They had seen the worst
They had to let go...no more lies

They could do it...
Each had memories to last
Every precious bit
Unforgettable moments...now in the past

Goodbye...sounds like forever
Not a see you later
Or see you tomorrow
Not even once...not ever

Patrica A. See

I Saw Today

I've seen the day
It's always here
The sunshine in the morning
The glisten on the hay.
Oh the people you see
People filled with happiness
Others with concern
People who have everything
Some that only yearn
Don't be so hurried
Our time is not long
Stop and say Hey!
Guess what I saw today
I noticed a sunset
A bird and a flower
The smile of a child
The wind and its power.
I saw all of this
And didn't go far.
I just sat and I looked
Then wished on a star

Nancy Broskey

The Ship

The ship lies sunken
its cannons silent.
It will sail no more,
now a home for fish galore

Its crew is dead,
their carcasses lie trapped.
No one can find them
their souls free to leave,
and never to return.

Nicholas S. Dicken

Heart And Soul

Love emotion feeds the soul
It's purpose felt to make us whole
Empowering the heart to open wide
And let the World view what's inside
One Souls then free to express itself
Rekindling its own emotional health
A transformations taking place
In this brief time and this small space
Expressing Love when it is felt
Can in Amazement make ice melt
Around a Heart as cold as stone
A precious treasure rarely known.

Tina Shragal

The Broadest Shoulders

In all these troubled times
It's really hard to see
That He who has the Broadest Shoulders
Is watching over me.

Although he can't be seen
His presence can be felt
And when my troubles get to me
Broad Shoulders bear the weight
For if they were not there
Then I would surely break.

Although He bears the weight
Of all the evil in the world
Not a person has He failed
For when all around begins to fall
The Broadest Shoulders hold them all.

Linda D. Holmes

"Memories"

Memories are truly special
It's true what people say
And no one can take away
the memories we make each day.
And when I go on to make a
brand new start
The memories of you will
always be in my heart.
I'll remember the good times,
as well as the bad
The happy smiling faces,
and even the sad.
I'll love you always, even until
the end
All because you're very special to me
You're my best friend.
If it's true what they say
that friendships never die
Then I know we'll be together,
forever; You and I.

Tracey S. Sulser

Love

Love what does it really mean
I've heard all the definitions
They all see so simple
Could it be that's my problem
Am I looking for a road sign
to tell me I'm in love
Will I over look the sweet,
tender gentleness
And lose the ultimate prize
the one thing no man really
deserves
The true but simple love of
a good woman!

Sam Clark

The Grasp Of Love

I've walked the beach of many shore
I've seen the eagle from a mountain soar.
I've heard the cry's of unknown fear
I've felt the pain of danger near.

Ah yes, my friend, I've traveled far
And wished upon many a star.
I've dreamt of things that cannot be
I've watched illusions the eye can't see.

Yet, through this soul from which I remain
The universe still stays the same.
It gives no clue, nor do I
The mind will always ponder why?

Alas, my friend I say to you
Seek that which you never knew.
Follow near to passions heart
From love's grasp you shall never part.

Renee Price

Reminiscings

I am a full moon on a warm
June night
And the fragrance of lilacs
in the spring
I am the beauty of wild geese
in flight
and a soft melody that
you sing
I am the wonderment in a
young child's eyes
and the tinkling sound
of laughter
I am the reason for his
whispering sighs
and the mystery of life
hereafter.

Nina Richards

April Once Again

I met you in April
Kissed you in May
Lost you in June
Rekindled in July
Said goodbye in August
Parted in September
Met again in April, in a whole new life
With your same eyes.

Martha A. Montelongo

The Dance

She steps onto the stage,
just as the night before,
and the audience begins to fade,
as the music starts once more.

Stepping, stopping,
gliding, turning,

her toes touch the floor,
then silently leaping into the air,
the audience becomes no more,

Now it's just her and the music,
or rather the rhythm it creates,
and from every part of her body,
the moves emanate.

And as the moves she has rehearsed,
begin to come undone,
and the rhythm takes control,
she and the music become one.

Ruth Ann Shallenberg

The Master's Hand

There is a glow the sun emits
just before it gently sits.
Behind the corn it hides away,
until it greets another day.

The sky's alit in lovely hues
of purple, red, gold, and blue.
A painting done, but not by man
a Master Artist drew this plan.

Imagination could not create,
but only try to imitate
the one who paints the sky and sea
and also plans for you and me.

An artist's brush can duplicate,
his canvas also radiate.
But not until he's seen the view,
could even dream of what to do.

If beauty God originates
and nature He coordinates,
should we not trust the Master's hand
to paint the life for us He planned?

Laura Fitzgerald

The Spider and the Mice

The spider on the window sill
Just couldn't stand the chill
He was getting a little old
and was afraid to catch a cold.

To two mice passing near
he said: Brr it's cold up here.
Would you know of a spot
where it is nice and hot?

The mice said: stay where you are
the trip there is dangerous and far
the spider thought: who needs advice
from two silly little mice?

So, off he went, across the room
When, suddenly, there came a broom
It swept him up amid the dirt
and the spider felt really hurt.

There he was on the dustpan
From there, into the garbage can
And just as the lid came down
He thought he saw the little mice frown.

Veronique Maes-Macdonald

Together As One

We existed as separate entities,
Just miles apart.
Living separate lives and separate dreams,
each, thru' one heart.

We experienced the freedoms of life -
social spills and athletic thrills,
academic strife and family life.
But still, thru' just one heart.

The days we've been together,
not all filled with glee,
are extremely profound,
since they're no longer as I, but We.

Our love will grow stronger,
each morning we wake.
Our history longer.
with every breathe we take.
For Stacey, I Love You,
with all my heart.
But the love we feel for each other,
is what makes this a wonderful start.

Michael Peterson

Unpaved

He said to take my baby and go
Just take the baby and go
How can this be
I'm so afraid
Who knows what's made
This road unpaved
Ahead of me

He said to turn and walk away
Just turn and walk away
Red sky I see
A night too bright
I'll be alright
Please take my sight
Away from me

Sunburned holes in the eastern skies
Sad cracked earth spits dust in my eyes
Try to smile while my baby cries
Must not look back as yonder lies
My destiny

Misa Marks

Untitled

Linda - Alan and I went to Las Vegas
Just to see what we could see
So taking a plane, away we flew
To Vegas immediately.

People and lights were everywhere
It was crowded, but we didn't care
The slot machines caught an eye
And we decided to give them a try.

Oh yes, we stayed there all the night
And couldn't be torn away
Until we saw the morning light
And noticed the time of day

But we went to our room eventually
And began counting to sleep
It wasn't done normally,
We counted coins not sheep.

Mary J. Couhson

On Daylight's Rim

The butterfly within
Kept his still house of sleep,
Till light of spring grew deep,
His winter door thin.

Then strange and weak he woke,
Winds damp, remembrance dim;
Wine-dark on daylight's rim,
We named him Mourning Cloak.

And laid him out to dry.
Wings, unacquainted, swayed,
Folded, on high grass blade—
And then we saw him fly!

Eyes and imagining
Followed his May-wild flight,

Marveled at sudden light
Flooding him, brain and wing.

And half surmised that start
Of sun-strength pouring in
Where wine-dark must begin
Each spangled heart.

Roberta M. Grahame

Pannin' For Tomorrow

Hands knotted
Knees locked
Boots wet
Nothin' yet...maybe tomorrow.

Eyes glazed
Lips cracked
Mind a'wonderin'
Nothin' yet...maybe tomorrow.

Farm gone
Traveled far
Skies grey
Nothin' yet...maybe tomorrow.

Injuns close
Belly growlin'
Missus sobbin'
Nothin' yet...maybe tomorrow.

Maybe tomorrow.

R. Marshall Lloyd

You're Leaving

Sadness, Sadness in my heart,
Knowing that we soon will part.
All the secrets I must keep.
As I cry myself to sleep.

Pain so deep that you'll be far,
Sorrow swells and leaves a scar.
I pretend that I am fine,
Loneliness will soon be mine.

Tears that fall, slide down my cheek,
They make me feel so cold and weak.
Heartache that will never mend,
Letters I can only send.

All the times we shared go by,
Now it's time to say goodbye.
And as I watch your plane depart,
These endless tears will once more start.

Sadness, sadness in my heart,
Knowing that we soon will part.
All the secrets I must keep,
As I cry myself to sleep.

Stephanie Williams

Haiku Poem

Look in the mirror,
Have a little laugh,
Consider the matter closed.

Amaryllis Edwards

Watery Laughs

Water moves forward the shore
Laughing in your face.
Sea gulls squawking,
Sand pipers gawking.
All for nothing, yet, for everything!
Sitting on a slippery rock
  Ka-Boom
  Spray!
And another Ka-Boom!
Deafening in your ears.
A whale leaps and
  Splash!
Into the laughing water.
You leap up,
Sand grabbing your feet.
The wind warns you,
"Go in, a storm's a-brewing."
Listen, Listen, it talks to you;
It laughs, Giggles, Chortles, Cackles,
Guffaws!
Elation everywhere!

Margaret Maher

Life

Life is like a tiny
leaf blowing from a tree
at time's you fly high, as
the winds blow good luck
your way then
the leaf hits the ground
troubles abound. You wilt
as the sun hits you and
the rain of life
pours down, you want to
fly away, but there you
lay. You think of the good
times, but you must
accept the bad times and
when the end is near look
to God for comfort and
cheer.

Susie Preller

Family Plot

Let me leave my dead with you,
Leave them to your practiced care.
From me they take no comfort,
Warm blood gives them no solace.

Don't think me void of pity,
I love my poor dead darlings,
Let me slide their broken bodies
into your fixed cold embrace.

I have hid them from the living,
Clutched them close against my breast.
And now I have to leave them -
Add this to my disgrace.

Lori A. Boulanger

Fall In Ohio

The prettiest time of year
leaves of all colors
falling every where
trees left bare
here and there
cloudy windy nights
and lots of rain
without rainbows
fallen dreams
another year went by
with some things gained
and some things lost
taken by
an early frost.

Tammy Robinson

One Night

One night - incredible!
Left to suffer,
Don't understand.
Left alone,
With their child.

One night - pain!
Left to suffer,
Don't understand.
Left alone,
No one wants them.

One night - poverty!
Left to suffer,
Don't understand.
Left alone,
Living on the streets.

One night - dead!
Left to suffer,
Don't understand.
Left alone,
With no mother.

Misty Jones

Song For Madeline

Were it that her name had been,
Less romantic than Madeline,
My voice would not exalt her,
This heart would hardly falter.

But with the dawn's demand,
Her presence did then command,
A praise to last much longer,
Than that of the morning songbird.

Smaller than I, upward she glanced,
Younger than I, my heart romanced,
Innocent eyes and rounded cheeks,
Her cherub's voice sounding as sweet.

When with the dawn's demand,
Her presence did then command,
A praise to last much longer,
Than that of the morning songbird.

Matthew R. Dow

Untitled

Feelings are like leaves trickling
off a branch, they grow, they
produce, and they flutter
to a lower place with no
protection to get trampled
by careless limbs.

Diana Richards

Untitled

Cushioned seats
of make-believe
rattled brains and
mended jeans of
yester year

Erma Watson

Contradiction

Push off the burdens of all mankind
Let every man himself to find
That in this world of ours so small
Heed not your brothers desolate call.

See every man plowing deep in sin
While God still saves the souls of tin
But judges he not twice nor thrice
Just only once in life's short strife

All tho' much is taken, much abides
All evil men shall stand aside
While holy members fly abreast.
See ye the knowing God, not less.

Rebecca Sibson

The Bench

Hello, are you there?
Let me tell you about my day.
I walked over to the park,
you know, where the children often play.

I did not see laughter,
nor did I see joy.
What I saw was disaster,
a boy playing with a gun like a toy.

Hello, please don't hang up.
Because I saw much more.
A girl forced to be a woman,
baby in her arms and her face worn.

I can't help but wonder,
do these characters exists?
For this can't be real,
how could you allow all of this?

Hello? Just one more thing.
Please watch over me,
as I wander in the cold,
....waiting for the Spring.

Marcia M. Damiano

Star Angels

So many stars I see tonight
Lighting up this beautiful land
each with its own special light
made by God's creative hand

Little angels looking down
or sleeping in the sky
carefully making not the littlest sound
But, watching us as days go by.

Love and mercy is what they feel
They love us enough to never move
a love so great, a love so real
They have nothing else to prove.

Some are with us in our dreams
Some stay in the sky,
watching over us with a beam
as the years go by.

Lisa Cliburn

Cold Winds

People drift in
like a cold wind.
Don't be afraid,
the wind is warm.

Know them once or
forever,
then they drift out
leaving you cold.

Call and beg them
back from the grave,
never they come.
The wind can't hear.

So stand outside,
open yourself.
Another cold
wind always comes.

Luke Kelly

On The Verge Of Madness

Red hot boiling blood
Like a dam breaking into a flood
Is pulsating in my heart
Ripping it all apart
Like an erupted volcano exploding
Waves of anger are controlling
Throwing books, hitting walls
Making sure everything falls
Taking deep breaths calming down
In the room looking around
Now laughing at the mess
But only on the verge of madness

Trina Baclig

Sabotage

Marching through life
like a grim, tight-
lipped soldier to
reenlist Wounded
each breath a hoarse scream
I forge on
Viewing myself through
the cold impersonal eyes
of the Enemy
I find my reaction
to War interesting
Engaged in heavy combat
under direct fire
I do exactly as
I've been told I
blindly obey orders
I kill myself in battle
I miss myself in action

Sheri M'Ladka

No Trees, No Earth

No trees,
No air,
No earth,
No solid ground around you.
No snakes to hiss,
No you,
No me,
Just space,
Black, empty space,
No place,
Polluted earth.

Nicole Rae Michael

A Ride on a Sleigh

Time goes fast
Like a ride on a sleigh,
You're down the hill before you know it
So make the most of each day.

It use to be all tomorrow's
But will soon be yesterday,
Time goes by so quickly
Like a ride on a sleigh.

Let God be your partner
And ride by your side,
He'll be with you at the bottom
And with him you will abide.

Your life will be over
Your time will stands still,
Yes, life passes so quickly
Like a sleigh ride on a hill.

So when you reach the bottom
And your life has reached its end,
Make sure its filled with happy moments
So your partner can pass them to a friend.

Sarah K. Weymoult

Champ

His nose is wet,
Like an ocean; a sea.
His eyes are sad,
Like a honeyless bee.

His ears are as long,
As a magic rainbow.
His face shows "alert"
Like a brown, prancing, doe.

His forehead wrinkles,
In time of deep thought.
He lies in the shade,
When it becomes hot.

My dog is colored,
Like a chunk of gold.
He keeps me warm,
When I am cold.

His tail is a motor,
That moves day and night.
My friends think he's cute....
And I think they're right!

Lauren Russell

The Maze

Thoughts, dreams,
Like candle, twinkle...
Seeds are planted,
nurtured...
Some then forgotten.

Patches of blue, dark shadows...
become reality...
The joys and the fears,
Tinkle of bells...
Sounds of yesterday...
Music in our memories...
Becomes tomorrow's hopes,
tomorrow's joys.

Images dancing...
Flittering neither here...
nor there...
Thus is the labyrinth
of our minds.

Lily-Michele Alexis

Grocery Shopping

People drive their shopping carts
Like their cars in the super marts.
Some zip up and down the aisles;
Some just seem to rack up miles.
Some block the way; one can't get by
While choosing what they want to try.
Some stop to chat, won't pull aside.
Some chase their kids who try to hide.
Other people are in such a hurry
That one really needs to worry.
We need mirrors on our carts
To see ones turning fast as darts.
Carts need signals; carts need brakes.
"Cart-alarms" for one's mistakes!
Carts need lights and steering wheels.
Calculators for finding the best deals.
Steps people use to reach the top
Of the items that otherwise would drop.
Now is the time to pave the way
For easier shopping a future day.

Pam Gershkoff

The Chesapeake Bay

The moody Chesapeake
Lined with stately homes
to the North,
Gentle saltmarshes to the South
Flanked and inbred with history
Some remembered,
Some forgot!

Sunset awashes her face
Reflecting God's peace as
She gently rocks the naval fleet
Their great shadows
Silhouetted against the sky
As the wild geese fly overhead,
Singing her praises.

Sea gulls call out her name
As shorelights twinkle
Good night!

Mary L. Borgstrom

Listen

Listen Darling;
Listen Dear;
I love you so,
I want you here;
By my side,
Everyday;
Because I'll love you,
All the way.
Until the end,
I'll love you so.
More than you,
Could ever know.
And someday,
I hope you'll be;
The one who'll love
and care for me.

Teresa Gail Hollomon

Ashes

Whenever I see snow
lively flakes falling gracefully,
swirling, landing and rejoining...

I'll think of ashes
falling, swirling, piling unjoined.

Whenever I see snow
innocently covering
the trees, ground, cars, graves...

I'll think of the innocents' ashes
falling reluctantly,
landing tentatively
Never melding, melting like snow.
Sinister gray leftovers, dry as dust.
THE PRESENCE OF ABSENCE.

Vicky Nathanson

I Live In Laziness

I live in laziness
long abed, rising slow
like a thin vapor trail,
the atoms of my body
ethereal, not wishing
to become too solid too soon
I tell myself
to give myself time
for spirit to
catch up with body
but the indulgences
of lagging behind
with my soul
are too strong...
a weirdly gleaming cast of light
a city bird's alarm cry...
the sound of a friend's voice...
one more kiss...
one more piece of toast...
I live in laziness

Maureen Connolly

Changing Seasons

So used to walking in beautiful gardens
Looking at blooming flowers
Finding no weeds
Except for the occasional dandelion.
Listening to the wind
And watching
As it makes the flowers dance gracefully.

But now that grace is gone
Why has winter come?
The days are harsh
The wind no longer sings
It only howls and screams
And scares
All the flowers until they wilt

And die.

Samantha Armstrong

Come To Me

Come to me with your smooth, meek,
mahogany body. Let me wrap and enslave
you with my mind.

Come to me and let me resight old
love poetry to you. As we go up and
down and around the membranes of
knowledge.

Come to me so we can share this
sacred love we have for one another.
Touch my body as I lie on
top of you feeling your heart beating
all through me.

Come to me for I know not of
true love but only what I hear of it.

Come to me for one day I can
feel you inside me until I burst
out and say oh you are so knowledgeable.

Come to me

Tamara Milling

Summer Rain

Rain in summer
Making music
Like tinkling bells
As it falls
In valleys hills and dells
Creating rainbows
Red blue yellow green
An umbrella of colors
Emitting a sheen
to a once parched earth
Of thirsty brown
Its moisture providing
Relief to the ground
Jumping joyfully
Blustery mean
Dancing lightly
cool and clean
Ah! Summer rain.

Leondra Howard

The Color of Peace

Though fierce winds
  may blow hard
Against my soul;

While waves rise
  high in aquatic contest
To beat me low.

When sea weeds
  threaten to bind
My weary bones;

Tis' then that the strong hands
  of my Saviour
Brings the gale to harmony,
  and all nature stills to witness
His signature in the glory
  of a rainbow.

Pamela L. Whittington

Grandmother

Myrtle Beatrice Manigo
middle name says it all in Latin,
"She who makes others happy,"
see my smile.

She gave up her body
December 6, 1993, casket fold.
Now she lives through me
Mind, body, heart, and soul.

Birth: June 1, 1918
Union, South Carolina
Was blessed with a little more
sunshine and a little more kindness.

By the time that final date
came around in 1993
the world lost a model
citizen dear to me,

On that day it seems
we lost a whole empire in Myrtle B.
Maybe the next legacy is
hidden somewhere in me.

Michael Armelin Jr.

Wisdom

Her eyes are blue
misty with age
her hair is white
like falling snow
Do not ask of her
what you do not want
to know
but if you do,
listen! listen close

Crows feet
are roadmaps
of places she's been
of the Narrow Path
the way she went
she knows...
  she knows...

Stefani Keever

"Love"

I love you so very much
more than words can say
more and more each moment
of every passing day.

I often sit and wonder
why I love you so
there are so many reasons
only I could know.

The way you understand me
and all the things I do
the way you sense my sadness
and soothe me till I coo.

The way you take my problems
and add them to your own
the way you're so attentive
and listen to my poem.

How can I help but love you
when these and more I see
that I have never ever had
and you give all to me.

Mary Ann Heller

The Traveler

I am in my element
moving over earth ...
Flying with the hawks
doves and sea gulls
fluttering with butterflies
running with zebra, coyote
and gazelle ...
Touching noses with rabbits
kittens and skunk
I am rustling through tree
and bush ...
Over mountains and oceans
I am the wind

Sheila Siemer

Harrow Up The Soul

It takes you to the quivering night
Moving slowly into your throbbing heart.
It haunts you with the moaning wind
As you hear it shuddering, fluttering.
Like a voice stricken with terror
Turning you restless and petrified
Making your torrid blood slowly run cold
Darkness of shadows surrounds you.
Leaving you cold, alone, and astound
With a trembling, sinking heart.
As the dawn of fear enters your mind.

Pauline Fernandez

The Drunkard's Path

This patchwork is The Drunkard's Path
Much like snakes in the hollow.
It makes a very pretty quilt
Not wise for men to follow.

It is a very crooked path
Only pain and horror.
The devil waits at every turn
To lead you into sorrow.

My friend, there is another way
It's called the Straight and Narrow.
So get on this path today
Don't wait until tomorrow.

Now on this path where Jesus waits
You'll never walk alone.
He walks beside you all the way
And will lead you safely home.

Sarah E. Bowley

Lonesome Me

In the morning I can't get up,
My alarm clocks have gone away.
Without them I can't look forward
To the beginning of the day.

The house is very quiet,
The children are all gone.
I hope you know, we miss them,
The playing, and their songs.

For two years, we did raise them,
And very glad we did.
A house is oh - so - lonesome,
With no noises from a kid!

Penelope O. Ewing

The Struggle Within

My body, my life
My heartbeat, my strife
Lost battles, lost tears
My memories, my fears
The demon lies within,
Slowly taking what's not his.
Go away! Leave me alone!
Don't come into my happy home!
These breasts are mine to keep
"I will fight," I say as I weep.
The war is done, but have I won?
Maybe for now, but my time will come.
My heart soars, as I look to the sky
I've won for now, and I will not cry.
My body, my heart,
My struggles, a new start.

Rika Cullen

To Whom It May Concern

To whom it may concern
My life is no grand
Will it keep going or will it stand

To whom it may concern
I cry at night
Then I wake up and fight
I fight because the way I look
They judge the cover instead of the book
Will I ever be at the top
Will this fight ever stop

To whom it may concern
I know my life will bring something
to this broken and loosen wing
I know I'm going to do my best
I'll try harder than the rest
These are my thoughts and what I want to learn
To whom it may concern

Sarah Cochran

My Love

My love is wonderful,
My love is kind,
My love keeps me from loosing my mind.

My love is strong,
My love is cool,
My love will never make me a fool.

My love is happiness,
My love is pure,
My love 'till the end will endure

My love is blest,
My love is true,
My love forever, will be you.

Lorraine M. Klinge

Untitled

Another forgotten rose
Speckled - wilted - bug bitten
A beauty decaying
losing life from lack of care
Only friend a spider
dangling from thorny web
Beautiful web veiling the dead.

Nancy Nassoura

I Thank Thee God, I Love My Mother

I thank thee God, for granting me,
My Mother's love, a part of Thee.
Through all the years, of love and strife,
She leads me ever, to a Christian life.
When from Thee, I go astray,
Her righteous words, show Thy way.
Thy Son, my Savior, she brought to me,
And taught me of, His work for Thee.
Her hopes, her prayers, her faith above,
Led me, and others, to know Thy love.
Whenever darkness, clouds my way,
Her loving kindness, lights the day.
And that light, will forever shine,
Even when, her life is Thine.
Until with Thee, I shall abide,
Her light shall be, my path, my guide.
Of all things mine, I'm proudest of,
Thy one great gift, my Mother's love.
And as Thou taught us, to love one another,
I thank Thee God, I love my Mother.

Willard H. Andrews Jr.

I'll Always Love You, Grams

You were my inspiration,
my motivation, my drive
Through you I've learned selflessness
Through you I've learned to strive

Remembering Saturday trips to the market
Eating as much as we'd buy
Watching TV 'til you'd put me out
I'd sneak back in your room and hide

I don't have any negative thoughts of you
You've always been there for us all
Opening your home and your heart with love
GOD thank-you for hearing Grams call

Sincerely Me

Strange And Eerie Midnight

Darkness had crept into
my room, around my
body and held me tight.
The sound only heard
was the rap of my
heart, frenzied with fright
and teary-eyed, I shivered
inside this night.
With all my soul, I wished
for might to conquer and fight
this fear of strange and
eerie midnight.
Before the scream hissed
out, I noticed dancing
in the corner, a sliver
of magical moonlight.
My savor, the bearer of
my sight.

Sabrina C. Kraus

"A Blind Man's Dream"

To feel you in a day
Takes my breath away
The touch of your skin
Brings my joy within
I just hope and pray
That you'll never go away
It would be a dream come true
If I could have just one look at you.

Shawn M. Brooks

May Apple

You are the companion of my spring,
my shield from the rain,
my parasol in the sun.
And when the wind blows,
you reach down as if to listen—
and pull me closer.
I am a young bud
put in your care;
but when the spring departs,
you must leave me to grow
on my own.
To smile as you have smiled,
to cry as you have cried.
And soon you will leave me—
not because you want to,
but because you must.
Though another spring
will bring you another bud,
as for me,
I will only have one May apple.

Melissa LaRose

Thank You!

When I thought
my world
was crumbling
on top of me,

Nothing made sense.

You came into my life
and showed me how to pick up the pieces,
rearrange them a little, and put
them back together again.

Now I am content, happy within my heart.
You showed me sunshine
where I could only see rain.
Thank you!

Mary A. Carter

The Guards Of Matilde

Hold fast your weapons of blood
neither can you puncture
nor pierce
for now the Christ has rise
once and for all
the Guards of Matilde shall openly stand
as the last lost statues of stone

Your children assembly defend your land
and wolf your starkened patch
upon your stinking wars
iron cast mankind

Michelle Suzette Patente

Budding Rose

Budding Rose
New to the world
Changing to blooms
Opening up for all to see.
Then, too soon
Petal by petal
They fade and fall away.
Behold the budding people
Changing sometimes too quickly —
They change, they go
away.

Susan Cargal

Like - A Winning Hand

When I got married at twenty,
Never dream such busy life-
Along come seven children -
I was more than a firemen's wife!

They bring their families and visit,
Sometimes complain I'm not home-
But they fail to ever mention.
They are prone to freely room!

We leave notes on kitchen table
Where I am a tea bag and cup,
So no one feels neglected.
Go home and just give up!

Of times I call on the phone
Even those who live close by.
The answering machine I get.
But I never will fail to try!

We all seem to get together,
For an occasion or a meal.
Especially for all our 65 anniversaries,
And that's a winners deal!

Rose Marie Wilkin

A Vision Of Violence

All was quiet, all was still.
Night had fallen; an ebony chill.
Moonlight danced across the floor,
To a serenade of the days of yore.
All of a sudden, I heard a sound
Of footsteps falling from a bend around.
I heard angry voices, seething with hate,
Each syllable sealing a disastrous fate.
Without warning, they came into view,
The magical silence now abruptly askew.
An aura of anger filled the room,
Heating the air with eventual doom.
I could hear their angry, hate-filled words
Flying into my mind like corrupted birds.
The wild rage mounted, mounted.
The seconds ticked by, I counted, counted.
The feeling of fury they created
Moved me forward, motivated.
I stood quickly, yet steadily.
I stood and turned off the t.v.

Rene Lassourreille

Eternity

Infinity
no beginning...no ending
seemingly amidst of nothing
without comprehension of the idea.
Past
time elapsed...time obsolete
never to regained
striving for experience of the idea.
Present
time existing...time absolute
a continual change
forever a melioration of the idea.
Future
time uncertain...time precarious
trying for preparation of the idea.
Infinity
no life...no death
forever in presence
without comprehension of the idea.

Peggy L. Nuckols

Omniscient

Have I seen the wind?
No, but I have felt it.

Have I felt the clouds,
or sky, or stars?
No, but I have seen them.

The sun, I can feel and see.
The moon, I can see
but not feel.

The rain and snow,
I can see and feel.
The colorful rainbow,
I can see, but not feel.

The most important thing, of all;
I cannot see,
But can feel so well,
Is God's love
and His arms, enfolding me!

Viola M. Browning

Untitled

There's not one night when there is
no crying.
There is not one night when no
feelings are hurt.
People say stop the violence.
But now can we.
With no love and with no sympathy.
They say love one another, not fight
one another.
These rules should be obeyed, with
the thought of what could happen
tomorrow.

Lindsey Fossett

First Person, Singular

Everyone has gone,
No one is here,
Only I am here,
Alone,
Hurting,
Remembering.

"I", first person singular,
Can be a very sad word,
A dreadful sound.
Listen:
First person, singular,
Singular, singular,
Single!

It used to be "we",
But now it is "I".

Oh God, what will this "I" become without
him?

Ruth Wernersbach Shreve

Lucy

So sick
she was turned within herself.
Hurt my mother so.
Offers of sweet sliced carrots
golden corn,
Won't talk to us.
She slipped away in one year's time.
Mother wept.

Virginia Kinsey Christisen

Untitled

You're all alone in the hall.
No one knows your name.
For all they care, you're not there.
You don't even exist.
Welcome to my world,
The world of solitude.
Never noticed, never bothered,
Never given a thought.
But being alone isn't that bad,
You never have a fight,
Or a breakup, or any of that,
For it takes two to do so.
Besides, I don't mind it,
Not that I matter much.
Not really...

Stephanie Wood

The Fire Is Out

the fire dies down
no one left to tend it
i slowly fall asleep
with the cold air to my back
i dream and dream
unable to remain conscious
places i'd rather be
people i want to see
they always leave me
they promise to write
i cry and learn to be alone
until i fall in love again
the fire is out
my heart is frozen
breath is cold
growing old

K. Michael Spencer

She Looked For Fairies

She was an only child
No siblings with whom to play,
So she went out looking for fairies
At the dawn of each new day.

Tiptoe through the backyard
Dew on little feet;
Stop, and look, and listen,
For the fairies she hoped to meet.

She kept a little shoe box house
Underneath her bed,
And listened to Mr. Stevensons' poems
That her mother read.

The years went by, her hair turned gray,
No fairies were ever seen,
No fairies lived beneath her bed,
But they lived within her dreams.

Now she's in her twilight years
And fairy songs she still sings,
I think when it's time for her journey to
heaven,
She'll fly on a fairies' wings.

Tracy D. Kemp

A Halt At Spurs Of Any Peak

There are no spark,
No sinner's souls below;
Above the pass, as th'welcome sign,
A starlet beams by green,
Around Quite is reigning over...
The best of any place is here.

It seems to me the time has come
To have a rest for tired legs,
In th'low Dark to kindle the Light,
To build the hearth,
To boil some tea;

And to prolong with Ghost of Fire
A friendly talk about endless Living
Above,
Among the stars,
And fleeting joys of th'Earth's Being.

Sergey Kulakov

The Road Home

When ones we love have left us
No words that others say
Can help to ease the sorrow
that fills our hearts each day.

Though you may try to hide it
by saying you are not sad,
The fire you lit between you
won't burn like it had.

When you are feeling lonely
or having a bad day,
Then look up to the heavens
and repeat what I say.
Don't think that they have left you
just look into your heart,
And know that they still love you
and never will depart...

Lora Baker

Someone To Believe In

So many trials and tribulations
Not enough smiles or jubilation

But if we take His hand
And walk through His land

Bad feelings are soon to ease

Good feelings are sure to please

In a world that's sad and lonely
The presence of His love only

Can ease the hurting pain
And help us feel once again

Jesus walks with me
Jesus talks with me

So I'm never alone

He'll be there for thee
When we need Him to be

So we'll never be lonely...
...again

Michael J. Barker

The Wrong Way Out

Sitting alone in silence
Not one feeling inside
Longing for the love
That you just can not find

You sit and you wonder
Of how it would be
In bigger better places
Did you think you would be free

Did you think about your family
How everyone would feel
Did you think that we would miss you
You know this pain is real

I hope you do feel better
Since you've said goodbye
When you pulled that gun out
Did you think that you would die.

Mandy Forest

The Beast

He's down, ma, and nothing fits
not shoes or wit, but he'll come 'round
till then he stands with tin in hand
as blind as any pencil man
hoping for a precious pound
to buy his girl a birthday gown
a worldly gift, his price to pay
to keep her faith in him.

Don't cry, ma, be strong somehow
why, even now he shuffles home
the beast in chains, your weary swain
returns to waltz with you again
still, as you dance the price goes up
next time he'll need a larger cup
remind him, too, no gowns for you-
the faith comes from within.

T. M. Fowler

The Charmer

A cold woman I would be
Not to feel the sting of flattery.
Warm smile,
Lips cold as ice.
Charm exuding every pore
  penetrating poison upon its victim.
Success walks in their heels.
Life submits to the charmer,
  one victim at a time.
Abuse of mind and spirit are the tools
  Wielded by the master.
Step aside
Or be tread upon.
To follow is sure sorrow
  if disfavor exists.
Where is the next victim?

Susan Travis

Guns

Times have changed, guns remain. Nothing ever stays the same. One on one against each other. Killing they have no right. I often hear "You'll be dead tonight." Can someone save us from this violent rage? Great leaders like Malcolm X were shot on stage. For all you people who don't understand. Guns are killing the race of man.

Shannon Donehoo

Christine's Angel Of Music

The violin, once played so sweetly,
Now silent.
Alone and scared, I sing on an empty stage,
Dreaming of joy and happiness.
He peers through the mask and listens.
An angel, a father, a guide, a friend,
He teaches as I eagerly learn.
The power, fury, love and pain
All one, in his voice.
I hear and love,
The longing for love,
I give him gently and smile at that face;
The test of love.
The torment, hurt and anguish inside
Disappear as we sing love's song
And he is whole.
The dark, mist and gloominess
Leave, afraid and ashamed
As light enters, into a world of darkness,
With his song.

Stephanie M. Huish

Crossroads!

You are at the crossroads of life
Now you must choose...
Which way to go,
Whether you win or you lose.

Remember my friend,
I'll always be there
To share all your burdens
And remind you I care.

In the dark days ahead,
When the sun stays away
Remember our friendship
And let hope guide the way!

Willi Bradburn

Tomorrow

Always anxious for TOMORROW,
  Obsessed with wonder and thoughts,
Before us a better existence,
  If only TOMORROW will come.

Will TOMORROW ever come
  To fulfill the wanted needs,
Dazed with the hopeful feelings,
  If only TOMORROW would come.

TOMORROW is the strength of what
  Will be,
    Could be, and
      Might be.
  An important arrival since
TOMORROW becomes TODAY'S
YESTERDAYS.

What do we have
  If we do not have TOMORROW?

Patricia A. Perras

Oceans

Oceans are a magic place
I feel the breeze upon my face
The sun shines across the sea
And it seems it looks straight down on me
As I walk, the sand sifts through my toes
How it got there no body knows.

Abbey Rae Smith

Winter Thaw

Through velvet setting of darkness
Of a cold, damp, and cloudy night.
A gray day darkening into evening,
Shadows falling through the light.

A chilling wind sweeping down
Upon the valleys and fields.
Pulling a cold blast of snow
Covering the trees and hills.

Cold, so cold, the air that blows,
The winter snow over the ground.
Drifts piling higher and higher,
White flakes falling with no sound.

Winter is here for a time, then gone,
Snow soon to melt and run free.
Into the brooks, the streams, the rivers,
Then eventually into the sea.

Sarah Aylitta Hoover

Midwinter Fire

I stand again in the purity
of a midwinter Michigan night
on a rounding hill in the fresh
trackless snow,
frostiness in my nostrils,
coldness bathing my skin.

As I make friends again
with the deep blue velvet of the
watchful winking sky,

you
silently join me,
and I lift up my face to catch the stars,
wet and twinkling,
tiny points melting into our kiss.

How long stood we there
turning the snow into rivulets,
clearing a circle around us?

Long enough for me to know:
the fires of love can warm long after
the night and the winter and you are past.

E. June Rudd

Awakening

I've heard your call in the pulse
of a song.
Seen your glory in the dark eyes
of a tree.
Felt your soothing warmth in the arms
of the sun.
Touched your soft glowing light in the
smiles of my friends.
Sensed your presence in the chilling
fingers of the wind.

Life holds me, love fills me, truth
haunts me.

Silent and persistent you sit on my porch.
And as I lye sleeping in my
cradle of time; you watch
Rippling around me as I open
tender wings; to fly.
Bound by my illusive dreams of
pain and imperfection.
I await your motion to rock me gently
awake.

Teresa M. West

Black

Black is the color
of a stormy day,
Black is the pupil
of the eye.

Black is the night
with glittering stars,
Black is the space
that stretches past Mars.

Black is the slate
you write on with chalk,
Black is the emptiness
before you walk.

Stephanie M. Edison

Golden Dream

At night as I dream I dream
of a time when sunshine and
laughter bring back golden
times. I wake up delighted
still savoring my dream then
look all around me and
sorrow seeps in for I am all
alone the sunshine is gone
the laughter has left me
a cry of alarm then sorrow
wraps round me a blanket of
tears. I look to my window with
out any fear and there in the
moonlight shimmering like gold is
my dream long past dreamt a
spider web spun of sunshine
and gold!

Shauna Benns Walker

Dare To Look Inside

I am dressed in the raiment
of anger to cover the gaping
wound of my pain

I designed these garments to push you
far enough away, that my needs
would be concealed

My vulnerable yolk; beneath this
hardened shell.

My hostility, like a second skin repels you
without question and your intolerance
lends alliance in my mission to
separate us

Never to see my silent tears or hear
my eternal plea for a greater
compassion; one that reaches close
enough to touch my needs

Help me find my way to the door of freedom
on which is written love and trust
And with the eyes of patience,
Please dare to look inside

Mildred L. Williams

Color of Tears

Can you hear the rhapsody
of another Autumn dream?
Enjoy the rites of Autumn.
Reach down and throw a
handful of fallen leaves into
a playful gust of wind.
Pause and ponder its sighs.
Innocent laughter reaches
your ears as if a child was
trying to capture each falling
leaf before it touched the
ground.

It threatens to soften the
hardened edges of a heart
grown callused.

Yes, we are a product of the
world at large that is harsh
and all so slow to forgive.
If I am not willing to
reconcile then a rift shall
threaten the rainbow.

Stephen Moy

My Mystery

Should I bear the mystery
Of life and death in ecstasy?
Should I take sincerity
When faced upon my enemy?
Should I keep my heart you see
The world is all so plain to me
Should I take solidarity?
Never a soul is let to see
The part that is my mystery
Of shattered dreams of ecstasy
Of love and hate for all to see
And bitter dreams that yet to be
A part that is monstrosity
Of love for life will ever be
Should I keep the mystery
Of all that follow and wish to see
Of my life a tapestry
Woven from hands that did make me
Given the blood of a father to be
I am I too a destiny

Shalaina A. Pinkney

Query To Erato

Why do poets sing
of love in Spring?
Spring love is but
evanescent fluff.
Spring knows not enough
of life and love;
has not probed the regions
of Heaven and Hell.
We know this well
who love in life's Fall.

Shall we then, fellow poets,
salute those who know its
highest joys, deepest sorrows -
the Autumn lovers?

Nancy E. George

A Fool's Folly

The exquisite agony
of love suspended
between heaven and hell
floods my soul
awash in flames
of bittersweet tears
as you scream
goodbye
in stony silence.
Wretched
glorious despair
my kindred spirit
in ecstatic misery
forever
and a day...
Oh thou woman
whom my soul loveth
more than life itself...
why?

Wolfandre Wanka

My Love

My love is like the quiet flow
Of sunlight into evening glow
The warmth of a cheery fireplace
The tenderness of a fond embrace
Like lips that kiss and express so much
Or the comfort of a gentle touch
The shining eyes that cannot hide
The wealth of feeling deep inside
A heart that will always ache and yearn
With love that can never be returned
Except by one God chose for me
My soul-mate for eternity.

Mary Ann E. Holmes

Untitled

People seem to grow older sooner,
old yet young in age,
Pressures are immense,
it makes no sense,
yet we hide internal rage,
Minds cluttered and confused,
logic distraught, ego's bruised.
Life continues we remain
a little frustrated,
a little insane?
There is hope,
and time to try.
There is hope
for the heart, soul and mind
and in time one may
learn to find,
just what heals the
heart soul and mind.

Mary L. Rose

Time

His mind has time
She was with him
Happiness was touching them
Together is alright
Their eyes look over and around
They saw a lemon-yellow hummingbird
Under dark grey clouds
The peaches are outside
Also paler

Saundra Kuckie

Once In A Lifetime

I can remember it like yesterday,
On that hot summer day.

We were standing in that long
amusement line.
I looked so bad I could have cried.

I had sweat dripping down my face,
And as for my hair not a single thing
was in place.

But, for some reason you didn't mind.
I could tell by the way you starred into
my eyes.

The next thing I had spoken to fast,
And we were put in a different class.

By the time I got off the ride,
You were gone with the passing tide.

As we were leaving the park I had to let
out a sigh,
'Cause I knew that we might never meet
again, at least not in this lifetime!

Shirnetha Brisbon

Senior Citizen

She basked in the sun,
On the bench
When nite was done.
Dressed and fed,
With trivia in hand
She noted time as it sped.
What to do today?
Watch children play,
On the way to school?
Or people scurry
To work today?
Like a leaf fallen dead,
Unnoticed, ignored,
Anointy rears its head.
A grey shadow melting,
At this point bored.
Ready to leave
With halting steps
Walk -on Home
Or a facsimile thereof.

Mary Goodman

A Garden In Time

In grandmother's garden, time stood still
On the day she left us.
Day lilies blazed beneath the oak
Their ruby-throated, orange splendor
Standing at attention
As her gaze wandered over them
To the passion purple iris
Woven, wildly, into fence rows

The China rose, infant in her garden
Given more care by her loving hands,
A needy child, it seemed to weep today.

Sunlight touched the bridal wreath
How long had it taken her
To coax the spray of foam white petals
Into perfect symmetry
Rising a little in her bed,
Looking long at her garden, lovingly,
She said, "It is more beautiful today!"
Then she was gone.

Leota M. Tucker

The Love String

Love is a thin string.
On which we grasp to strongly,
or try to cut.
The sensitive.
Caring,
romantics
grasp it with a dyer need,
to be loved and held.
The heartless,
cold,
overbearing,
avoid love;
cutting the string,
on which others hang.

A thin string,
that once held,
The very souls of all who lived,
now separates us into groups.

Majkin Peters

God

This that I Am,
Once a fallen star,
Out of a dormant and darkened Breast
Moved through aeons afar —-
And lo, the ecstasy of the Light
Unveils the Being we are!

This that I Am,
A bright and morning star,
Rose in ascendancy,
To Heaven's Glorious Bar,
And face to face with Him
Knows this we are!

Subie Childress

Illusion

The world
One big masquerade
My costume
Hides my pain well

The painted smile embodies my sorrow
My laughter replaces my screams
The sparkle in my eye
Not from joy but from tears

We hide behind everything
Sadness is not aloud
Loneliness, forbidden
Depression is unacceptable

Only joy and
Happiness is permitted
Smile be happy
Walks out of every mouth

But darkness and
Despair
Pours out of my once pure heart
Now blackened by a sadistic society

Sarina Kemp

Untitled

In darkness there lingers
One unspoken word,
Where fear remains imminent,
Where shadows are long,
Were life is never ending,
Yet death not so far,
Madness is possible,
Yet sanity is a friend,
There falls a fine line . . .
Between knowing happiness
And being alive,
Between knowing sadness
And needing to die.
With labored breathing
And one first step,
The walk of time
We each shall tread...

Melissa M. Curran

Prejudice

The insulting lyrics you throw
Open a window deep inside me
They tear me apart
As my emotions become extinct

Your venomous hate fills you electrically
Giving power to your drill
As its salty bit grinds
Mixing poison in my veins

You take me in the spotlight
And continue to crucify me
Killing an innocent soul
As I take up your worldly desires

Am I so different from you
That you would do anything
In your dominion power
To destroy my individuality

Scott T. Pietruszka

I Can Never Let You Go

I can't say its been easy
or always even fun,
but the years I've had with you
have been very special ones.

You've given my life balance
by all the things you do.
You've picked me up when I was down
and always got me through.

If I could have one wish in life
I'd know exactly what I'd do,
I'd wish for every day to be
like the ones I've had with you.

I love you in ways I can't express
and in ways I'll never show.
You're so much a part of me now
I Can Never Let You Go!

Margaret M. Dunn

Abyss Of Misery

Drowning in a sea of despair,
or an ocean of tears,
sadness encircles around me,
like the sky wraps Mother Earth.
Fear, hatred, depression, follows every
step I make, creeping as a shadow would.
Happiness and joy are deprived from me,
littered away in a far off place that
can't be reached.
Closing my eyes, trying to void this place
of misery,
I attempt to think of enjoying moments.
But as I open my eyes, a shark of
terror and evil is ready to devour me.
Nowhere to go or turn, I let the vicious
animal tear at my body as I scream
my silent pleas for help,
which no one but God himself and I
knows who calls out.

Vanessa Franada

Friends

Mending a saddened heart,
Or just sharing a simple tear.
These are a few things
That make a friend so dear.
Having a word or two
Or making a dream come true.
Perhaps a token gesture
To see a good friend through.

A mountain of gold is bountiful,
I dare not contend!
Yet will ne'er best the feeling
Of having a good friend.
For friends are to care
If life be ours to share!

Michael J. Riley

"Time Of Harvest"

Sometimes do it for the money,
or maybe for touch, don't
you feel empty, does it all
seem too much.....

Splintered wings, come alive,
give it time, fly everything,
Down the path to the gateway,
run, run, go away.....

She was the object of my obsession,
angel painted portrait of perfection,
giving all that could allow,
bend to the stars, make them bow.....

Out there, somewhere gasping in
thinner most air, backlash of night flash,
Across American Skyline, out thru the
desert, where the seas have ran dry.....

Life on the road, was all too
cold, after awhile it got old,
I will not let my harvest get sold.

Ryan M. Hall

Stay or Leave

You can't judge a book by its cover
Or so the saying goes.
You take a chance to get to know
Someone with an evil past.
Maybe he's nicer than people say
Or maybe he's changed.
He's raped someone. Why does that
Not scare me like it does everyone else?
Do I think I'm immune, that nothing
Bad can ever happen to me?
I don't think that is true.
I should get away people shout.
But if I go, will I miss out?

Mary Timothy

The Sin

Now that I can't hear you talk
  or touch you
I wish I didn't know you existed.
A flagrant energy of faith
  and feeling
Chokes my breath and makes my
  eyes ache -
All that's in me responds too ardently.

I have impressions for you to
  recognize
And power to spend against you.
I want to fill your deep consciousness
Exhaust your strong body and
  confirm
The inclinations of your heart.

I have tried to live here and
  suppressed myself
Because there is no place.
I could have waited for Heaven
Had you not enlivened me!

Sally O'Brien

Poem For Louretta

Hush! Was that a butterfly fluttered by
Or was it the wings of a bird
Or the wish of an angel's wings
That I just heard?

As I stood there in silence
A gentle breeze I felt go by.
It must have been an angel
I know, and I'll tell you why.

My loved one left this earth today
The angel came to take her away.
God promised He'd never leave us alone
Even when He called us home.

The angel took my loved one's hand
And guided her safely to that blessed land.
He told her, I can just hear him say,
"God is waiting for you today.

Take my hand and don't be afraid.
The way is smooth from here to there.
Your Father waits for you
At the top of the golden stair."

Naomi Slater

What I know

I don't know what the future holds,
Or what tomorrow will bring.
But what I do know is,
Every time I'm around you,
My heart begins to sing.

I don't know if I'm a wise man or fool,
For thinking the way I do.
But what I do know is,
Everyday that we are apart,
Is another day I miss you.

I don't know why I live and breathe,
Or how I came to be.
But what I do know is,
You have brought my soul into the light,
And I never want to leave.

I don't know why I have only known love
as a dream,
Or why I feel the way that I do.
But what I do know is,
That it is a dream,
I want to share with you.

Scott Crook

"Remember Me"

No matter where I am,
Or where I will be,
I'll always remember,
The love you showed me.

I hope you remember,
The time we shared,
Because nothing in this,
World can be compared.

The love I showed you,
And my loyal Devotion,
Is all to you and,
Your loving emotion.

And in the end,
Time will be,
And I am just,
Asking you to,
Remember me!

Ralph Leon Williams

Night Before The Auction

Black limousines creep from shadows deep
Pale street lights on beaded dresses sweep
Ladies... lustrous in their style
Gliding past the doorman's wooden smile
Doffing coats and hats... they haste
To view the artists' work displayed
For one last time before the sale.
Enthusiastic students stayed...
Another round of drinks they made.
Standing still... contemplating...
Pointing, chatting... conversating...
Here comes the waiter with hors d'oerves.
That man in cowboy hat... what nerve!
"Shrimp?" "Yes, believe I will..."
"Dip it?" "Yes, and drop the shell."
"Champagne.....try it, or tequila"?
"Orange and vodka.....marguerita?
Such a crowd of upper class...the
Artists if they are here... are masked...

Tobi Kumar

The Awakening

How do I begin?
Papers blowing in the wind.
Cars flashing by.
A stranger...dark hair, blue eyes.

How do I begin,
To let the feelings start to flow.
To let my heart open
and my soul find words.

It's been so long.
Afraid to look into my heart.
Afraid of what I might see.
It's been closed so very very long.

LaVon Koenig

Socialism

One of the main
parts of life,
is socialism.

It may consist of pain,
or even a future wife.
That good ol' socialism.

It just wouldn't be fun,
to sit there alone.
Kicking back in the sun,
getting burnt to the bone.

Without a friend,
to accompany you.
Having no one to send,
a beautiful flower or two.

Where would we be,
without a friend?
Not very happy,
but, sad till the end.
Without that good ol' socialism.

Steven D. L. Hardin

Patterns On The Land

Airborne, I look at
Patterns on the land
Patterns made by God,
Patterns made by man.

It took a Mighty Hand,
To make the mountains,
The rocks, the sand,
And the rivers that run
In this great land.

And, looking down,
I think that God can scan
The patterns
In the mind of Man.

Rilla Black

"Autumn"

Autumn leaves begin to fall,
Summer's breeze no longer calls,
Days gone by so soon for all,
Summer's gone...Now it's fall.

Autumn leaves blanket the ground,
Brilliant colors all around,
Season's change is abound,
Fall has fallen...Without a sound.

Trisha Worley

At Christmas Time God Gives A Gift

His gift is wrapped in music,
Perfumed with spice and evergreens
The package is so beautiful
It dazzles us it seems.

At Christmas time God gives new light.
Known as Illumination—-
A new understanding for our delight
To each in his own generation.
Sometimes the understanding
  Of a carol heard for years;
Sometimes the understanding
  Of serenity through tears;
Sometimes the understanding
  Of the stars—so universal;
Sometimes a thought is given
  For one's honest, calm perusal.

Let us love the wrappings
Thankful for the artistry;
And when we know our Father's gift
We'll drop upon our knee.

Maravene Barnett

My Blessing

The maker of this Universe
Planned things so carefully
That man has searches their lifetime
To fill the needs of humanity

But he was thinking of me
And answered my secret prayer
When he sent me a little secret
With eyes so dark and cheeks so fair

Through experiences in anxiety and
pleasure
Mingles with sorrow and love
We've built a bond of companionship
But receive faith and hope from above

God proclaimed his existence
In everything on earth
But the greatest blessing I received
Was with my sister's birth

Lora M. Lockhart

My Calico Friend

Laughing softly, I sit and watch my cat
Playfully leaping around the old hat.
Suddenly she stops; and sniffs, and
Nudges, and bats; Backs up
Wiggling this way and that.
Before the pounce, I wonder what she
thinks,
Stalking this hat.
A giant mouse perhaps?

Brought from the ranch three years ago,
Scrawny and sick, and quite flea-bitten.
Our vet saved the life of this tiny kitten.

Healthy now - she plays hide and seek,
And attacks when I peek.
In play she romps and pounces and rolls,
Thunders upstairs and down.
Day by day, quicker and quicker,
This ranch cat has become
A City Slicker!!

S. Marlene Sheppard

Untitled

Living in a world where pleasure is sin
Playing a game, doing anything to win.
Tangled up in a web of lies.
No one willing to compromise,
all for nothing or nothing for all.
One will win and one will fall,
and as the game is played.
Both friends and enemies are made.
But friends at this time are no longer true,
everyone, is plotting against you,
never knowing what to believe,
master of ways to deceive,
never love and never care,
never learning to play fair,
a hard gone without any rules,
no second chance if you lose,
always hiding the pain.
The hurt isn't always worth the gain,
but this is the life I choose to live.
Nothing chances and nothing gives.

Lara Saltarelli

Song Of The Sea

Sailing on the bosom of the sea,
Playmate of the sea gulls, wild and free,
Skimming o'er the billows heaving high,
Again I hear that old familiar cry.
'Tis the song of the sea
'Tis the song of the sea,
'Tis the song of the sea gulls,
wild and free,
'Tis the deep-throated roar
Of the waves on the shore.
'Tis a song I'll remember forevermore.

Raymond J. Shuster

Domestication

My gentle giant, gray and white,
pleads to go out into the night.

Sitting on the kitchen floor,
he begs me to open the back door.

He'll guard our house with claws and fangs —
until he feels his hunger pangs.

Gleaming eyes see through the dark.
Keen ears tune to a possible bark.

But glimpsing his shadow on the wall,
he suddenly feels so very small.

So now he's scratching at the door,
asking to come in once more.

His bowl of food becomes his prey,
He wouldn't have it any other way.

Then, finding comfort in my lap,
He purrs and settles in for a long nap.

Stephanie Brown

Untitled

There was a young man named Perry
He rode and rode 'till he came to a ferry
His traveling was slow
And days and days did he go
'Cause he left Pennsylvania in a surrey

Cleo R. Dalby

When My Ship Comes In

When I go to sleep for the last time
Please friends and loved ones
Let their be no grief

I have always tried to keep
My ship on a straight and
narrow course
I will not end up on the reef

Thou I have been through
rough waters and a serve storm
I will dock in heaven on
that bright and happy morn.

There I'll meet all my loved ones
On what rejoicing there will be
There face to face, I'll see
My master who died for you and me

Orris Hosler

Abuse

Riddled with guilt, filled with shame,
Point the finger, who's to blame?
The soul is thirsty, starting to die.
There's too much pain, I ask why?

Running scared no place to go,
The heart is trapped, no one can know.
People around, but totally alone.
Broken spirit, brittle bones.

Where is the light? I cannot see
There's too much darkness inside of me.
Scream for help...no sound will come out!
No one hears, no ones about.

Go away nightmares! I don't want you
here!
Go away Satan...God is near.

Find the power. Find the light.
Angels are here...I'm alright.
Let the peace come over me.
God please let my soul be free.

Lori J. Storer

Priceless Time

Stolen moments...
Precious time.
Stolen moments...
Priceless time.

No words to express
the deepest emotions
No time to steal...
priceless time.

Too little time
when we're together.
Too much time
when we're apart.

Sitting on the front porch
gazing at stars...
Talking, thinking...flying time...
priceless time.

Time.
Too little.
Too much.
Priceless time.

Verla Martin

R. D. S.

Throw on your mask
Protect your hidden past
Constantly build the walls
Hide yourself from all
Hurt the ones who love you
To keep your illusion of control
Subconscious rearrangement
Fend off friends and foes
Contain your feelings
Condense yourself
A special person wasted
To afraid to give of yourself
Patience and persistence
I wait outside the walls
A continual tapping
Until one day they fall.

Michael Baxter

Hidden Haiku

Archie has a haiku hidden in his heart
put there by Mr. Bogartus
who caught Miss Flouts by the
hand, the lonely art teacher
with a platinum wig
off center. She spoke
Spanish on the first day
and Archie, in love with the raisin
brown seam on the back
of her shimmering legs
as they whispered by him,
has forgotten this scene
so many years in the past
but not the haiku
centered in his heart.
It reads simply:
humble heart
region of the stars
wig off center

Stephen Edward Nicolini

On Telling Whether God Is Female Or Male

It is as
Putting your gentlest hand
On a warm womb
Of a warm belly
of a warm woman
And you know someone is there!
As you listen
And try to guess
Whether they are a boy or a girl

Ronen Murad

Life

Life is
really cool.

Don't just sit there
and act like a fool.

Make life useful
while it lasts.

'Cause if you
don't watch out

Life can go by
really fast.

Meredith Brewer

End Of The Draught

To look at the
rain
through my dusty
window.
To see the world
outside
being transformed.
To hurt myself
changing.
To follow a storm,
a woman making love
to the rain,
to heaven
to hell.

Norman Nichols

Bound By The Beast

Cold, tired, and confused.
Raindrops are falling.
Tears from heaven.
His souls in bondage.
Chained down by sin.
When will the madness end?
Thrusting his fist into the air.
Restrained by the chains.
It's so clear.
The key lies before him,
Well in his reach.
In order for him to
obtain it he must practice
What he preach's
When will the madness end?
When will he just give in?
Humbly reach his hands
Forward, and unlock the
Chains bound by the beast.

Samuel E. Fraijo IV

Truth

Look at your life,
reflect on it.
Look, into your eyes.
Do you see?
Are you with me?
Can you see your disguise?

Do you look with contempt,
despair, in reproach?
Can you see all of your fatal lies?
Now sit with me.
Tell me.
If you want to know,
what's in me I greatly despise.

I wanted to know what goes on in my head.
I needed to know the real me.
Now that I've opened that pathway to sight
I'm afraid of the things that I see.

Rafael Carlotto

Love Is

Love is nothing less than a beautiful feeling,
Love is nothing more than our entire being,
Love is something nothing can replace,
Love is something we all must face,
Love is the one true thing you cannot hide,
Love is the only feeling you want to confide,
Love is the most beautiful thing to share,
Love is the only way to show you care.

Emily Johnson

Reflecting On Sunset Highway 29

Here I am again
Reflecting on Sunset Highway 29
My newborn mood just happens ...

... Threaded, translucent clouds ...
... Sunlight sliding through ...

... Guides me toward a feeling
Where concerns no longer hold me
An inner warmth directs the way

It's happen before
The sky panorama
Pushing my dark mood away

It's February
Known for clear, azure sky
Brown trees turn golden

Feeling its warmth
My new focus flows
Blends into Highway 29

Transforms my winter brown
Into textured insight
Where my path belongs

Ralph Anderson

To My Brother Arnie

All of our lives we've been
related by blood
A few, years ago a friendship
began to bud!

I'll never let you forget
how special you are
In my life you will
always be a star!

You will always have a
place in my heart
With Elton's help we'll
never have to part!

As long as I'm able, I will
be here for you,
You are my brother and friend
I love you, that is true!

Trudy L. Colucci

Do You Think Of Me?

Do you think of me?
I think about you every night
Cause loving and thinking about
you feel so right
Do you think of me every day?
I think about you even when
your away
Do you think of me?
I think about you
At night I stare out at the stars...
And wonder do you think
of me where you are?
Do you think of me?
I think about you

Nicole Matthews

Dreams Of A Trailer Park Debutante

Handsome knights without their armor
Ride out with sundown light
To chase the night-wind lure of love
No ancient dragons, left to right.

So slowly on, they seem to come
Their crowns just barely glowing.
From side to side, dark gazes fixed
Their weapons not yet showing.

From star to star, the hunters ride
To find the sweetest bloom
As fair maidens sound the age old call
And beckon from their castle room.

The warrior comes, his weapon drawn
No man-made steel can better
And her maiden rush, matched his thrust;
What else in life can matter?

Night-time dreamers, dream alone
And no-one hears their sigh.
Trailer Park Debutantes, always gone
To their lovers in the sky.

Ray Padgett

Summer

Hurls a blue green haze over the
Rockies.
Sagebrush,
Sharply scented, dots the brown
slopes of the mountain.
Rose - red Western soil covered
with moss-green brush
Touches mounds of white hail -
stones,
Caught in the corner of stone steps.
A chapel, yellow, tinted. Voices
raise in prayer to
the heavens flung above the
mountains.
Benedictine monks
stroll leisurely to prayer.

Marie Cox

Is This What It Comes To?

Run from the hate
Run to the sun
Spread my wings
Soar over fields
Look down on a picture
That I was once in.

But now I am out.

Free my mind
Free my body
Free my soul
Let go of the hurt
Which was everything.

So I am falling...

Louisa Trackman

French Wine

French wine
saturating
goblets fine
rich blood
seasoned spine
dark grapes
caressing and fine
insane emeralds
sacrificing vine
molded to birth
within time
slipping slavishly
as steeples chime
beneath the hand
of wicked divine

T. R. Winters

Never Listen

Never listen
Screams the youth
Hear the cries, see the truth!

Never listen
Screams the native
My land is dying, bloody save it!

Never listen
Screams the preacher
Love and hate will be your teacher!

Never listen
Scream the Gods
Worship, defy the odds!

Never listen
Screams the fly
Hallucinate and never die!

Never listen
Screams the mother
Now I know you love another!

All together is the voice
My world is full, disturbing noise.

N. Littman

Save the Children

Listen closely to the children,
See their faces streaked with tears.
Listen closely to the children,
Hundreds of them die each year.

In a far off distant country,
Hunger strikes the very young.
Hear the little children crying,
Will their battle soon be won?

Listen closely to the children,
Pain and hunger rule their dreams.
Let us save the little children,
We can do it you and me.

In our hearts we have the power,
Make a child's dream come true.
Set them free from pain and hunger,
Give them just a little part of you.

Listen closely to the children,
Can you hear their painful cries?
Let us save these little children,
Before another has to die.

Ricky J. Nash

Written Among The Alps

A prince among the clouds am I
Set rough upon a granite throne;
My sight is filled with open sky,
My castle made of ancient stone.

I pay homage to the Eiger:
Dawned with a white mantle of snow
His lordly peak does not falter
Though tempests break upon his brow.

I've been moved by higher powers,
Traveling to lonely mountains,
Garnered and blessed with wild flowers,
Purified by icy fountains.

Long lasting is this high domain
Of virgin pines, of hoary slopes;
Through ages of man it will remain
While mankind for nobleness gropes.

Michael Goldberg

"Through The Storm"

Sometimes I feel like a tiny ship
Set sail on a great rough sea.
The wind blows boldly 'gainst my sails
And the waves they buffet me.
The darkness falls, an awful mist
rises from the sea,
For my very life I now am fearful
because of the roaring sea.
But I recall through this awful time
the purpose being worked out here for me.
And I am comforted through the night
upon the great dark sea.
At last night ends and morning breaks
forth on sparkling waters.
A gentle wind blows my little ship,
Safely home on quiet waters.

Ruby Reeves

Motherhood

Motherhood is the happiness of
  sharing your love,
with the man that
  won your affection.
And brought your life to
  the pinnacle of perfection.
In a short time it is revealed,
And can no longer
  be concealed,
You can happily
  share your joy,
While you wait for your
  little girl or boy,
Each day now has a
  meaning so deep
You will forever this
  feeling keep,
you remember the first
  sensation of life
Knowing the meaning of being a wife.

Margaret Block

Faithless

Sounds of the growing seed
shattered his ears
and emerging tiny tendrils
squeezed his heart
till tears streamed from his eyes,
dripping to fingertips
still wet with Christ's blood.
Forsaking the spark of life
for love's brilliant flame
he now hovers on the outside
like Paolo, trapped forever
in a swirling universe of moaning souls
straining vainly to affect
the flower's bloom.

Thomas B. Kelly

Slowly My Dear

Slowly slowly slowly my dear
She chants in clam belief
Orbits align in timeless space
We waltz in calm relief

Slowly slowly slowly my dear
And brings me to her side
Her wisdom has captured me
I pace to match her stride

Slowly slowly slowly my dear
I recognize her volition
Jupiter -n- Mercury conjunct
A most harmonious position

Slowly slowly slowly my dear
No rush no haste no hurry
The longer it takes, the longer it lasts
No schedule no pressure no worry

Slowly slowly slowly my dear
Spread circles of devotion
Waves and ripples travel warm
Relaxing in deep emotion

Michael LeClaire

Fancy

Fancy is my little pup
She really is a poodle
And when I go to pick her up
She wiggles like a noodle

Small and black, she's quite a pill
She keeps me in a muddle
Especially when I take a spill
Stepping in a puppy puddle

She chews up everything I own
My socks, my shoes, my ear
But dear friends, I cannot moan
Because I love the little dear!

Linda C. Rich-Lindner

Northern Lights

Incandescent sprays of light
Rolling in slowly on a misty night.
Winding, twisting, curving,
Snakelike, so undeserving.
Looking up at nature's milky glow
Her beauty secret we'll never know.
Standing in awe of all her radiance
It's a privilege to be in nature's presence
One last look into the sky,
Reminds us, don't let life pass you by.

Theresa Anderson

Silence is the Echo

Miles away from the calm
She sleeps
Slowly, reluctantly, drowning
In her dreams

Tossing and turning like the ocean waves
Her soul crashes to depth unseen

Crumbling memories seep from inside
Tears and faith lost to the tide

As her mind explores the darkness...

Rushing through are thoughts and dreams
Her fears she comes to face

Within herself
She pleads

But silence is the echo
The echo of her needs...

Miles away from the storm
She wakes

By the sound of sea gulls
Gently touching heaven with their wings

Michelle Lynn Falcone

Send Me An Angel

Bent on her knees
She started to pray.
"Please send me an angel
To show me the way"

She prayed this request
Night after right
Yet no angel came
To show her the light

She struggled along
Day after day
Her goals her dreams
Slowly slipping away

She had lost all hope
No one seemed to care
She cried and screamed out
Into the still air

A strong, warm embrace
Full of unconditional love
Tightly wrapped around her very soul
An angel from above

Zarine Andolino

Waiting For Croesus

The mistress is the whore's Prometheus.
She steals the fires of their youth
for the perversity of men.

On a city boulevard stands a late teen
enchantress
strung out on coca since thirteen.
Skirt cut mid-thigh;
blouse reveals more than cleavage.
Waiting for Croesus.

Five minutes of a garbage strewn alley
she is ready to escape.
Her souls own Judas she earns silver
to buy a moment of freedom
from her procuress.

The trollop gnashes her teeth,
cries out from the abyss,
seeking harmony in evil, white power.

Tony H. Price

A Moonbeam

I see a moonbeam in the air
She wears a ribbon in her hair
Her aura pervades my very being
She brings my life special meaning
Her beauty is so much more than skin deep
From within, it takes my soul to keep
I am no longer my own person
I am hers, with ample reason
She is naught but a work of art
Who has found a place deep within my
heart
There is no place for her to hide
For she is love personified
I would that mine she'll always be
My dearest, sweetest Rosalie.

William E. Selzer

Another Day

Silently she cries herself to sleep.
She wonders if she'll survive.
He taught her to laugh,
to play,
to love,
to cry.
Cry...taught...made is a better word.
She thinks over and over
What did I do?
How can I get him back?
Then the crying stops as fast as it started.
She knows.
She knows he's not the one,
Not the man of her dreams.
The one never makes you cry,
Never breaks your heart.
He holds, cares, laughs, loves,
And cures the long cries.
He's not the one, she'll survive,
And another day goes by.

Maribeth Grattan

Sky

Clouds
Shifting, changing, ever reminding,
change is good
Sunlight
beaming, streaming, warmly dreaming,
ever bright
Wind
blowing, flowing, ever going
on its way
I'll go with you
one day.

Lisa Dyess

i am

barefoot
pouring rain
my hair streaked
against my forehead
i run to nowhere
just to run
breathe deep the air
of fading summer
the wet smell of
grass strong
my face tilted back
and i am Free

Meredith Hutcheson

A Present

A present for you
should arrive any day
A present I sent
from miles away.

This present should bring
a smile to your face
A smile of happiness
that I want to always stay.

This present has no bows
or paper to rip apart
This present I gave
straight from my heart.

This present is a kiss
I sent from me to you
A present that has no stamps
It is a present that I blew.

Teresa Dollries Jostworth

A Time To Sorrow

Please don't despair for me
Should I pass away before you do
For I will be among the heavenly
Solace will come, dear one, to you
In this sorrowed time of life
Remember the good, and the blessed
When our young family was our glory
For we gave them our very best
And, now their love is returned to us
So, take heart, my love
Continue in my behest
Keep looking to above
Where I will be at perfect rest
Nevertheless
You have remained behind for a reason
So give the world your very best
Our time was all too short
Remember me, but don't chagrin
Goodby for now, my darling
Until we shall meet again.

Mr. Rolland H. Schaller

Masked Mayhem

He descended on us in the night
Shouting his demands.
His face was covered with a mask.
Our lives were in his hands.

As daylight dawned, we realized
His plan was not to leave,
But to stick around and case the joint,
Deciding what to seize.

He'd been abandoned as a babe.
Like fools we bought the act.
We'd seen his type so many times;
But he was no stray cat.

He hit the bottle way too much,
Though vigilant and alert.
For months he feasted on our best
Insisting on dessert.

We fought a fight we couldn't win.
Hindsight wisdom oft imparts.
He fled with treasures we couldn't protect.
That pesky raccoon had stolen our hearts.

Sally Seidling

Fortunes And Misfortunes

Echoes quite annoying
Shouting people act insane,
To the deaf it wouldn't matter
To hear someone call their name

Many complain of imperfections
There are ways to make them right,
The blind man would say "That's perfect"
For his dark is also light

Fancy houses built like mansions
Lacy linens for every bed,
It's out of reach for the homeless man
No place to lay his head

What determines a tomorrow
Is it today or yesterday,
No future for the dying man
His tomorrows just fades away

Remember those less fortunate
By lending a helping hand,
Misfortune has no boundaries
Quite different for every man

Lynda Baker

These Hands

These hands, so undaunted,
shrouded once in flesh of youth,
many a hurt did soothe;
they wiped away tears,
calmed troubled fears
and guided the way to truth.

These hands, so venerable,
now shaky and gnarled with wear
from honest work and loving care;
whose daily physical deeds
submit to spiritual needs
when clasped in humble prayer.

Linnea Ward

Captives Of Dark Blues

Three orange and golden dragonflies,
Silent and still, within, a blacken frame,
Their tears, are square, encircling them -
As, they await, my pen, to give them wing.
Anxious, to hum, "Dark Blues".

When, there was, forget-me-not's—
To sow, you left!
I wandered, lonely-searching—-
far and wide,
Finding only, those imitation—-
Blossoms, without root.
You, couldn't know, I needed—
Real, forget-me-not's,
Had you known—
You might have tried, for-
One more moon, to sow them!

Lilia S. Huston

Trapped Soul

Our souls are trapped
underneath the ground
forced to face the torture
of the inferno
punishment for a life full of sin
while we live in a sleep
over the camp called earth
that eat away at dying lost souls
we mourn the living and celebrate the dead

Artemis Agadakos

Speaking Of...

It's been so long
Since we last spoke
You and I...

Too much happens
In our daily lives,
Making constant contact
A lightly held dream...

When will I remember
How good it feels to talk...
Of things and times and fancy schemes
To make the world a better place,
Can it really happen?

Perhaps it will stick,
Please stay with me!
This wondrous, elusive way of words...
Until such time, I bide my breath
and wait with pen in hand.

Hold onto your dreams no matter what your
strength may be...
For life is only as full and good
As the words we share for free.

Steve Synnestvedt

In The Garden

I'm in the garden of my dreams
Sitting on a bench
The table of life giving objects
before me.
My plate is empty,
The food is all gone,
I have eaten the last of my
Life-giving love.
There is no more,
For you or anyone
and no one is to blame.

Natosha A. Zimardo

Ghetto Child

Ghetto child of manner mild
Sitting on the upper stoop,
Viewing all the pained and wild
Furor of an angered group.

Do you dream? Do you conceal
Gentled thoughts long deemed taboo
Among the strict and sullen zeal
Of those residing close to you?

Yes, there are reasons - histories
Creating rages smoldering long;
So many voices tough to please
That blur the shades of right from wrong.

Of that you hear, of that you see,
What process weighs to separate
The fiction from reality?
And what's too soon, and when too's late?

Will you in time desert in bold
Strides the blocks so long defiled,
And then become of mankind's hope,
Oh ghetto child of manner mild.

Marcy Magnus

I'm Not Alone

As I gaze upon the
sky tonight
I pretend it's you
who's holding me tight
I pretend the stars
are your reaching arms
The moon's your face
spilling forth your charms
I listen to the waves
gently slapping the sand
And I know it's you
reaching out to touch my hand
This night's not lonely
here all alone
Because the wind is your breath
that's guiding me home

Suzanne M. Hodges

Silent Death

As she lies there silent as if to be
sleeping without a breath
shivered up and dead under
the night sky, he sits
next to her bearing the sight
of which he has committed
and still wanting urgently to pull
the knife out instead of driving
it in further and deeper
into her heart but yet she still
lies there helpless and silently
under the night sky.

Randi Finkey

Eclipse: To My Underachieving Nephew

Sun shadow blackens moonlight
Slowly shutting out silver—then
Slowly uncovering light.
Night time sky above Albany.

It seems such a sun shadow
Shades your light or a moon shadow
Blocks the sun of your talents
Somehow I know change is coming.

Slowly, steadily, shadows
Softly slip away—like watching
An eclipse, lunar, solar.
Change is coming. Change is coming.
I know.

Soon, soon...
Your light will brightly shine!

Soon, soon...watch out!
I see the edge of your light emerging...
Shining bright!

Rosarita Annussek

Presence/Presents Of The Past:

Washington, D.C.

The 1970 the city council
repealed the laws forbidding
panhandling
They thought the mendicants to be
all Georgetown
pseudo-hippies
Lily white
rational and
orderly

Mark Kearney

Never Enough

I man go through life free
smart-but let's see.

I man find someone I love
committed too-become one

I man see another ooo but
What of my true love —-
"Never enough"

I man tell my true love for-
give me—together forever—-
"Let's" see

I man envision another —-
O' dear "Never Enough"!!

Paulla Jackson

Life Is So Precious

Life is so precious
so be strong,
Live your life in the right way
things won't go wrong.
You see my life almost be
came shorten, but with the grace
of "God!" I'm here and "Happy!"
Enjoy life to the fullest the right
way, accomplish your goals
the best that you can, "God" will
be there every step of the way.

Rhonda Pennington

Wonder Of Life

This Life is placed in my hands...
So delicate, So beautiful...
Exquisite lack of cognition...
The treasure in my hands...

What the life brings...
What is taught...
That of what I forget...
The still deep waters within...

Respect...
Let it be...
Don't disturb...
Don't move...
Only think...
What it all means...

Trust in yourself...
Trust in life.

Lynne M. Suddeby

"Generations Of Drops"

Silver drops of tears
pooling, coalescing
testaments to generations
of eyes
leaving me with the ability
to release this silent sob
did they know I would be here
hurting
over you? Did they think of me
as they, too, cried?
An ocean weight of tears went
into this one drop
and all I ask is do you care...

Lauren Martin

Darkness

There is a side of me,
So evil, but so much fun.

As if in a trance,
All I feel is hate and anger.
A desire for revenge.

Something powerful and lasting
That fills you with fear.
Takes you all the way to the top
And drops you all the way down.

Down into a deep, dark pit
of horror and misery.
Without light, without hope.

But there is a way out.
They say it leads to death.
It's dark and scary.
But it's one awesome ride.

So dangerous, scary and unknown.
So evil, but so much fun.

Susan Renee English

The Dance

Oh how the bitter dance begins
So fast, agitated, full of hope and pain.
It moves with quick, changing steps
Like a million disconnected rhythms.

Soon the dance slows.
It slows to a frightening halt,
And each dancer finds new ways
To move and laugh and survive.

The music renews its deafening call.
The dancers struggle to push its tones away.
Yet their bodies speak to follow sound,
And the dance begins again.

Again the dancers form and flee.
Each time the hope falls away,
And yet the steps become smoother,
And the chaos finds shape.

Finally, the dance winds down,
And one dancer softly reaches up to kiss
The skeleton she was dancing with,
And with that gentle freeing kiss, the dance
of grief is ended.

Lori Lee

Inescapable

Attraction unnatural
Such a simple request
Piece out my meaning
My death will do the rest

Tied up in the words
Hidden in the pretense
Sleeps the secret of my heart
In which I make sense

You can never find
What I won't allow you
Driven by an obsession
Shadowed by truth

In my greatest victory
I find unrest renewed
Now ends the story
The person you once knew

Sean Medigovich

Visions Within

The masses call out.
So few are heard.
Darkness from the depths
of your deepest nightmare.
And then came the light,
almost as if to purge
the evil that dwells in the
furthest recesses of the
darkest minds. Scream if you
wish. Call upon the angels.
No one can save you now.
For true salvation comes
from within. Like the star you
Saw last night, an ember
glowing, still flickering, in the
heart of humankind. There
will be a judgement day! But
not for me to judge you, for
you see, the soul is the
mirror of all that ever has
been, and everything yet to be.
So when searching for that
truth look ye not too far!

Terry DeVere

A Tribute

She's neat and petite,
so kind and so sweet.
She's cute and she's pretty
and, at times quite witty.
Oh yes, and she's smart
with a very big heart.
And talents a-plenty
you'd think she was twenty.
But surprise, surprise
she is now eighty-four
And too, thank God,
she is going for more.
And who could this be
you're asking me?
It's none other than Sadie
that delightful, remarkable Lady.

Lucille Petry

Things Unsaid

I left in such a hurry
so many things unsaid.
I never got a chance
to tell you what you meant to me.
You never, ever listened
to what I had to say.
I tried so hard to tell you
I never wanted it to end that way.
You didn't understand me
or what I had to do.
I told you that I loved you
but I also loved him too.
In my eyes I did what
I thought I had to do.
Now the things that were unsaid
are as plain as day.
The story that was in my heart
was bursting out to say
I still care for you
in every little way.

Melissa Hazlett

Again

So often the laughter masquerades the pain,
so often your smile is in my heart again,
too often we fight about the stress
of life, giving us so much less.

We deserve the feelings that we share,
but they somehow overwhelm this pair.
Two souls unleashed unto this place,
the laughter now evades my face,

For with you I have found so much,
I've treasured the pleasure of your touch,
but now the reality has settled in
My heart ripped apart—again.

Sidney S. Hataway

Nature's Beauty

A sunset's delight
soaring through the orange sky
bird's flight at sunset

Pink sweet smelling blooms
drooping branches hanging down
The Weeping Cherry

Lilly-pads, algae
slimy fish and frogs of green,
Ponds of living things

Yellow strands of fuzz
weeds, but in a way, pretty
The Dandelions

All different kinds,
Mother Nature's many leaves,
surround us falling

Lindsay Zahradka

Dream Weaver

Sitting in the cool of early morning.
Soft fog rolling about.

Trees growing all around.
Little clothes pin birds resting on the line.

Old boat sitting in a sea of grass.
Sunbeams poking around and about.

The first day of the new year is here.

Everywhere has a lived in look.
Great God its good to be alive...

Tim Stephenson

Untitled

Red was angry,
Pink was trying to be pleasant,
White never took sides,
While Black was full of resentment.
Yellow wanted to run and hide,
Green was so jealous,
Than blue lied.
Purple just cried and cried.
Swirling brushes combined them together,
Controlled by the hand,
From the mind of a man...
Forever.

Wendy V. Kimbal

Cloudy Day

As I watch the clouds go by
Softly sailing across the sky,
I wonder of the many places
They have shown their changing faces;

Have they travelled a mile or two
Or from a far off place called Timbuktu,
From mountain slope to plains of green
Sometimes violent, other times serene;

Many will pass silently and slow
Others will drop their rain and snow,
And a tempestuous one may prevail
With thunder, wind and even hail;

Even when they block the stars at night
With their dark and stealthy flight,
Or cover the blue of the beautiful sky
From many a dreamy and gazing eye;

They will eventually fade away
To the beauty of a bright new day,
And to those of you who truly believe
These endless dawns you will receive.

Roland K. Swanson

Untitled

Everything is twisted
Sole to sole we walk.
Our paths shifted
Side to side, no longer to meet
Lids to be remained uplifted
Darkness only perceived
Our 'ship has drifted
Into the horizon faded

All we have wrought,
gone awry.

Is it conceivable
A venture back
May this be believable
A regaining of the past
Am I truly unreasonable
To ask for that I've wronged
A stay to the retrievable
To a 'ship that has lost itself

Look aside and reach
See the warmth become again

Michael Fox

I've Hurt My Loved One

I've hurt my loved one today,
Some things I shouldn't say
But my old cantankerous self,
Had to say them,
Without thinking how they'd sound
Oh, they came out pear-shaped round,
Criticizing my lot in life,
Not taking time to see the blessings
Just words that could stir up strife
But they didn't do that at all.
He just felt so dwarfed small,
Agreeing with me, my lot was hard
And how patient and sacrificing
I have been.
Then I realized how sad he looked,
My words had saddened him,
And yet, I am the loser,
For sadder yet am I!

Margaret Gamber

Somewhere Up There

High above the clouds,
Someone waits for me,
High above those fleecy clouds,
The face of God I'll see.

He holds out his hands so kindly,
He asks me to come in,
I hesitate... for many times I've sinned,

He says "My child come closer,
And look into my eyes,"
The light that I see shinning there,
Made me realize......

That he said to me this day,
"When I died on Calvary,
Your sins were washed away.."

Marian Ferch

Bicycle Rodeo

Evolution of the bicycle rodeo
sparked building burning flames
in the makeshift neighborhood.
No paper dolls. No slingshots.
Only cracker jack houses filled
with marathon noses
spill out to the block.
Sidewinder spokes of back talk
graze the grass as
we leap to the ground to fly.

Sheryne Lyon

I Wish

I wish upon the brightest
star and still you won't be mine.
I wish on a four leaf clover, still
you won't love me. I wish as much
as I can and still the same as
always you won't talk to me,
I wish always and still your not
here. Why, why won't you be mine,
love me, talk to me, be here with
me. And then, one day, I wish as
always, but there's something different,
your here, with me, loving me,
talking to me. So, as they say
wishes do come true.

Shaye Shadwick

Images of You

My images of you-
such good company

Close my eyes-
You suddenly appear

Your smile-
caressing my heart

Your eyes-
touching my soul

Your touch-
satisfying my senses

My images of you-
Oh-how they comfort me-

Caroleann

New Life

We
Started -
And so far
From us you came,
Here - we're one.

Yes, very familiar -
So wanted,
Through fever, through
Impulse, through plan.
And here,
Fortunate just now,
To gather,
And to confirm you.

A heartbeat away,
A soul's
Breath at
Hand.

You wonder,
You gift -

New life.

Steve Russell

Evolution

It's so sad how many of us
stay static, scared to
change, afraid...to move
into the new and unknown
we take chances with everything
but our own personal growth
we become intellectually stagnant
the mind becomes rusty
from nonuse, we do only
what is required, think only
enough to keep our jobs
spiritually we accept what is
fed to us . . . never
questioning, never finding
the truths for ourselves
like the diamond process
evolving is a painful
and rewarding experience
but if we don't allow it to
happen, we'll never know what might have
been...

Sandi Moody

Kid Thief

Abused a child made of gold
Struck a diamond four years old
Sold him for all he's worth
Made sure he would never know
He's a penny saver
Saves up in his piggy bank
The blood and some
of a child's identity
No regret, no guilt
Doesn't care about what he felt
He'll forget, I'll feel guilt
Doesn't care about what he left
Behind .... Inside

Michael Duarte

Untitled

Fallen, I check for bruises
Stunned at the brutality of my belief
below the self-supporting platitudes
lives the hidden fear and shame
to be moved through before freedom
and I are one.

I face the shame in my path head on
shaking as its prickly tentacles coil round
the filaments of my soul undermining
my conviction, my right to be who I am.
Calling upon all the strength I can
I hold myself together until
awareness breaks upon my horizon, balance
turns in its dance and I recover from the
encounter with my hidden demon, pain.
Shaken in my core, I move on now
knowing how to survive.

Mary Anne Blaszczak

The Storm

Ominous cloud cover
Submerging the peaks of the city
In eerie darkness.

Monotony of raindrops
Meeting glass
Merging into a liquid landscape.
Hypnotic music
Lulling the senses into submission.

Grey fading to silver
As a stray beam finds its way
To earth.
The cacophony subsiding,
Transforming into soft harmony.

The nimbus lifts
Leaving behind prisms of light-
A gift from the gods,
A rainbow.

Meredith Reno

Hats Off!

In the church Bill sang with gusto
Such that neighbors turned around;
And Bill's voice kept rising, rising,
With that voice his church had found.

So he kept on adding volume,
What with tremolo and trill,
Even awe-inspired rafters
Needs must vibrate with our Bill.

Still the neighbors went on staring;
Still his sounds fortissimo-ed
-Then a doubt was born and lingered
And the tones pianissimo-ed.

"Was his singing real attraction?"
He deflated in the lurch,-
When it dawned he had forgotten
to remove his hat in church.

Yvonne Nobert

Ink Tears

Does the Ball-point cathartic-device
suck passions soul-born,
Splattering white sheets
with esoteric grins
Speak truly of passions,
anxiety, despair-ridden,
Moments of need
escaping to the mind's ear
Of fellow others,
sweet fleeting-moments,
Saying, AH YES!
SHARE, we see
Truly, Brothers of the Cloth.

Michael Scott

Created All By Thee

Lo and Behold,
Sunrises, Sunsets
Arising, Falling
Amid deep blue waters in breathtaking hue's

Mountains, Plains
Sweeping, Rolling hills
Sunny green meadows in awe-inspiring views

O'Creator, Great Author
Full of Mystery, Unfathomable Majesty
'Tis True, Thou hath made it all

At Thy Commands, Mere whispers
All that Thee Beckons
Responds to Thy Mighty Calls

The Foolish, The Blind
Grope they in Obscurity
These, chosen not to see

Thy Wondrous, glorious Works
A Vast greatness, Thee Created All
O'God, All Created only by Thee.

Lucy A. Aguilar

Bellwethers

How often even our loveliest things
Suspend their accustomed roles
Appearing unlike ever they seemed before.

Beleaguered . . . Stands of Asters
Tossing their haughty heads
In tangled disarray . . .

Becoming . . . Fall's lingering brigade
Bright buttons on the gray coat
Of early winter . . .

Beguiling . . . As the lone vestige
Of the snow queen's mantle
Lining muddy, hidden hollows . . .

Bejeweled . . . with the crocuses of spring
Heralding the tender season
When the world is new again . . .

And to God
We are
Beholden.

Patricia Gallagher Gibbs

Civil Defense

In the event you opt
Take a scissors to my heart,
Be gentle with your genius
and artful with your art.

Strum me with your song
Please me with your paint
Texture me with your tongue
Draw me, near and faint—

But see me with your soul,
For I'm wily to your ways.
Protect me, peaceless passion
Fashion me, fevered forays—

And when I shift into neutral,
the hum sure feels good.
Simple strokes, and tender, knew
of a wet, greenish wood.

So, just who's the brave one
Now, she asks?
The answers come, my friend
In time, and in tasks...

Sandy Hackerson

If Love Is Senseless

Silence song birds;
take lovers' voice,
by sight I make
my heart's true choice.

If love is blind,
then take my sight.
I'll feel my love
in private night.

If love is numb
remove my fingers,
the soft, warm scent
of her doth linger.

If taken back
her loves sweet smell,
God cast me in
the blackest Hell.

If love were senseless,
dreams I'd chase.
Her night's sweet kiss;
my lips, I taste.

Mozar Dianoboe

Walking

Come walk with me awhile.
Take my hand as we traipse
the cutting cotton of yesterday.
Ride the turbulent
waves of the future.
Voice your fire-fueled dreams,
and tease me with creativity.
Fear nothing!
Your safety comes from
what your shadow lacks.
Listen, the haunting laugh
dances on the wind.
It calls you, but grow
a deaf ear.
Hear only the orchestras
of your own mind.
They play your own
soothing songs of support.
So come walk with me awhile,
as we grow into our young selves.

C. Nicole Detwiler

Home Sick

If you must speak to me of home
Tell me of the whip-poor-will,
And tell me of the shy red bud
That blushes on the hill.

Remind me of the lazy creeks
That quench my native clay,
And talk of green tobacco fields
A thousand miles away.

But do not speak of loves ones there
Lest sleeping pain awake,
And say no messages of love
Or else, my heart might break.

Rosemary Muntz Yasparro

Tell Me What You See

Look into my eyes my friend
Tell me what you see
Do you see the one who longs to cry
"You were meant for me!"
Let me take your hand my friend
I'll follow you anywhere
Time with you is magical
Can't you see I care
Listen to my words my friend
The silent ones that pray
"Please don't ever let me go,
I love you more each day!"
Someday I'll be brave my friend
We'll stand face to face
Then I'll sing these aloud
And melt in your embrace!

Nicole Farley

Odyssey

Whispering winds
Telling tales of old
Chasing the future
Carrying the message
Of the living kingdom

Of the forgotten odyssey
From whence we came
The power given and taken
The magnificence of existence
The enchanted moments

Of the honored odyssey
The grateful past
The unexpected gifts
The introduction of fellow travelers
The fact of just having lived

Of the uncertain odyssey
The unknown prime mover
The extent of illusion
The unclear reality
The fickleness of whispering winds

Philip N. Papaccio

No Song To Sing

There's no song left in that tiny form
  that lays so still on the neighbor's lawn.
There's no song left in the small lad's heart
  for he threw the stone that ended the song
Of a small chickadee with a fine black cap
  and tuxedo of grey with a vest of white.
Please God, let this a lesson be
  on how quickly a life can be snuffed out
If only it is but a small chickadee.

Norma Bobbitt

A Daddy's Love

There's a certain kind of love
that a daddy can provide.
This love we have is always there
even though it's so deep inside.
I show my love to you in my own
certain ways, it may come out
through my eyes or something I
might say.
If there ever is a problem
which I could only solve
I'd hope you'd come to me,
no matter if its big or small.
I always feel so specials
so wanted and so loved
this way you always make me feel
can never be rose above.

Paul Bellmer

Goodbye

Wipe away the tears,
That are slowly falling from your eyes,
I'm not sure I can find a way,
To easily say goodbye.

You will go on without me,
I will go on without you,
But always remember how close we were,
When we were a pair of two.

All of the times,
We have spent together,
Will remain in my heart,
And my mind forever.

So now as we are slowly drifting apart,
Always remember you're still in my heart.
So wipe your tears and dry your eyes,
For the time has come to say goodbye.

Lisa Scattolini

Joy's Song

Majestically rising from my past
That cloak of fear my heart doth cast
I climb without; past life lies damned,
And begin to seek just who I am.
This road I travel is long and hard
Yet hold my trials in high regard.
As long as this hard road may be
I know inside I walk it free.
Released am I from chains of doubt
Insides safe from fear without.
I've finally found a better way.
I smile in the mirror of my today.

Michael A. Reihl

Dream Days

I seem to dream a lot,
Some days.
Blue sky's with white puffs.
The wind with dust
From the country air.
The lazy cat occupies my chair.
A tractor in the barn begins to rust.
Dark clouds raining rough.
Some days,
I sleep a lot.

Moiria E. Seiber

Cross Country Running

CROSS COUNTRY RUNNING

Muscles in my legs tighten to the shot.
Faces strained and to each other unknown.
Eyes focused on each others backs a lot.
Breaths deafening, all else is muddled tones.

LET THEM NOT PASS!!!

Hearts like animals fatigued with fighting;
Beating, trying to escape from prison.
Legs always stretched, the whole body striving.
Wet fingers of salt drips on my vision.

LET THEM NOT PASS!!

Rain the Last mile; feet blistered in leather.
All breasts yearning for the ribbon to come!
I have the lead, try a little harder!
Sustained by a force known only to some.

Let Them Not Pass!

Endless moves, slowing time, journey of miles.
The last leg of the race, its almost kind.
Quick and dark a dream breaking image smiles.
The ribbon reached his breast first; LOST from mine!
Let Them Pass.

Carvel Lee Jonas Sr.

Untitled

Have you ever felt like you would fall a sleep
Fall asleep while standing upon your two feet
Have you ever had that kind of look on your face
Although you couldn't see it, that look of disgrace
Have you ever had that kind of look that caused a stir
That kind of look that screamed you love her
Have you ever fell to your knees and confessed your love
Have you ever fell to your knees and prayed high above
Have you ever dropped to your knees like me
Probably not, because you're not me
Did you ever feel like you could steer a cloud
Did you ever wake in the dark and scream out-loud
Did you ever see into a persons soul
Did you ever see a black bird call from upon a pole
How do you learn from all these things
Should you simply accept what the future brings
How do you learn to see without your eyes
How do you absorb the truth without the lies
How do you learn to be the real you
How do I learn to be the real me, too

Eric J. Walper

Daydream

There are some days when I'd rather be
fishing 'n camping 'n hiking and free,
Days when my heart really says "of course!
we'd rather ridin' a horse."

Oh to be on the beach and runnin' wild,
Jumping and playing as when a child,
Kicking the water up high in the air,
Splashing and wetting a pretty girl's hair.

Or to be in a pasture, in grass, just so green,
flat on my back and enjoying each scene
made by the clouds as they form way up high,
as they boil, change, and tumble and move right on by.

The bubble is burst, the daydream subsides,
the work all around me is growing like tides.
I must get back at it, to do and complete
This ne'er ending jumble, so we can compete.

Jerry Earl

Summer's Storms

Set aside in my mind are memories of summer evenings in our old farmhouse. I used to sit in the deep sill of the living room window and gaze up at the hazy sky. Chilled, misty air filtered through the screen as I inhaled a scent of rain so pungent I could taste it. And, far away, the thunder hinted that a storm was nearing. Slowly, one drop on a leaf, one drop on the roof, one drop on the ground, it began.. The thunder would mumble to me, It's getting closer," and I knew that it was true. My dog would jump up on the white bench outside the window, press her nose to the glass and stare at me with those milky eyes until I'd let her in.
Together, my dog and I would wait with anticipation for the storm to arrive. For me the wait was like waking up too early on Christmas morning; when I knew I had to abide another hour before I could open the gifts I had been longing for, and a slight chill in the air mingled with the thrill of anticipation.
Finally, the clouds would cry out for warmth and needles of lightning would begin to embroider a quilt in the night sky, Rain tap danced on the sidewalk and currents snaked around pebbles in the driveway. I would stare in admiration at the beauty in the chaos, the renewal in the destruction, yet more quickly than it had appeared, the storm would go.

Carrie L. Holbert

Dreaming

To step out on the vast terrain, gazing at the mountains of our dreams
Fearing nothing but the failure of our so called shallow schemes.
We call ourselves fragile dreamers. They call us dreaming fools.
We leave the ground to walk the wire or delve the deep dark pools.
Alone by choice, they tell us, but how can we agree?
We search not for whose we are, but for who we are to be.
They romanticize the dreamer, while romantics dream on.
Take heart. As fools we dreamed alone, but as dreamers we belong.
And in belonging we're made free to live as we should be
Not lives of idle dreamers, but the dreams.

Daphne Johnson

Reactions

I would like to feel myself fall back to earth,
Feel Mother Earth gravity pushing back upon me.
Falling victim to the laws of equilibrium:
For every action, an equal reaction.

Ascending upon my spiraling descent;
A consciousness gained through physical amnesia.
As the vacuum gives something for nothing;
And for every action, an equal reaction.

Yet, when I jump up, the earth jumps away,
And when I come back, it comes back at me,
Hell-bent on revenge for defying its force.
But for every action, an equal reaction.

For the rain forests are gone, and the air is polluted.
The factories close, and houses get shot at.
The prized go private, and public scores drop.
They advertise more, but we vote less.
Though we've beaten Iraq, Colombia beats us,
So we go back to church, but he's back in space;
Lord have mercy, Christ have mercy,
Because for every action there is an equal and opposite reaction.

Anthony S. Dodge

Seeing

Amber color lights fill my eyes with such delight
My heart sings with joy as I watch the graceful birds in flight
My eyes tear at the sight of a tiny child in sleep
My eyes sparkle as I watch the wild rabbits dance and leap
I feel alive and vibrant from the very center of my being
God how can I thank you for the wonder of just seeing

Kathleen Lowry

Colors

With so many colors in the world,
How can I pick which one to use.
The purple, the green, the aquamarine.
Oh, how many beautiful colors can be seen.

Alicia A. Roemer

Spirituality

He who enters into this path of light, Follow with me.
Feet instilling into soil Beneath...
Earth grabbing up
Pulling inner soul down.
Steady...
Keep small steps down this journey into discovery.
Glancing into the colors of light that flash around the sky.
Jump, Spin around...
Swirling movement Screaming deep from inside.
Move, Stomp...
Getting closer
Closer and slow it down.
Is this where it ends?
When the beat of the drum comes back into view
Begin again.
Feel the pounding, Yearning to be expressed.
Turn and go the other way-
Do not be afraid.
Go where you've never gone.
Learn to accept.

Debi Rugg

Grayish Eyes

Myriad love,
Firebugs, imprisoned within a sheet of black night
King's blood draped over the moon's glow
Cries of a raven,
Lost within the fierce wind's blow
Endless roses,
Scattered across endless beaches
Youth against the tides
Angels scattered naked across the city's inner lines
Faith dies in the arms of the believer
She remains alone with him,
As he takes religion from her
A cross dangles around the dove's neck
Night ends in a TV blue sky.

David Reiff

"No Words Were Ever Spoken"

The old man remembered his days ...
First only a pup sucking it's mothers milk.
Crushes then sweetheart then fiancee then a wife ...
Growing up the pup learned obedience and trust.
In healthy days he fished, played football and danced ...
Side by side the dog ran then walked.
Now the man's eyes were growing dim, seeing less ...
Time for the old dog to feel weary grew near.
Smooth skin now wrinkled and dark hair now snow white ...
Fading bright eyes looked lovingly up to the old man.
His heart hurt and his chest heaved ...
Silently understanding the old dog laid down to wait.
Memories of a pet always near, always there ...
Water and food were no longer needed.
A drifting fragile arm fell down to the side ...
With lifted head and ears erect the time had come.
The old man's fingers stroked his life long companions head with love...
Gently the night cradled both young man and pup, old man and dog in it's arms for their final sleep.

Becky Ann Brinn

Dummy Defense

Wham!
Flash of light like 2000 suns

Safe falling from ten stories up
steamroller going ninety
mad elephant charging like no tomorrow
cement truck barreling through town
freight train rumbling through like the load was due two days ago...

Flying like an eagle, floating like a cloud, hanging in suspended animation

Landing like a ton of bricks
bouncing like a rubber ball in the middle of June
Lying peaceful like a man dead ten years
No pain, just grateful knowing that I was alive
never turn your head from a senior.

Chris Andreasen

In The Stars

Prisms of life,
Flourished in your soul.
Love flowed in and through you,
As does a rushing river to the sea.

A husband, who was there 'til the end,
A father, who knew no limitations,
A grandfather, who always had advice and open arms,
A man... one of few, who was always there when needed.

Quick with his wit,
A smart alec no one will ever hear again.
One who enjoyed the finer things in life,
Drink champagne and eat caviar or a beer and peanuts,
There wasn't a class he couldn't fit.

You will be missed but never forgotten,
Our love for you will always burn like an inferno.
Now that you are in heaven hold your wife close,
And watch us, your family, protect us from harm,
And guide us as always from your place in the stars.

Eric Corbitt

Spring, Fall, Winter (Birth, Aging, Death)

The beginning of life for many of things;
Flowers, trees, the sweet song birds sing.
The birth of a child so fresh and so new;
Raindrops on petals, grass with it's dew.
It's the season that brings us such wonderful things,
March, April, May are all part of Spring.

The passing of time that has turned old men gray;
The sweet smell of life has disappeared from the hay.
The aging parent whose saddened child tries to cope;
The green leaves on trees have changed with one last breath of hope.
The twigs that once were, have become giants so tall,
The changes we see tell us it's Fall.

The birds that once sang have moved on their way;
Hope still remains to see them again some day.
The relatives and friends who we've buried below;
Have gone to a much more majestic place, away from the snow.
The still of Winter and the wind that's so cold,
Takes breath away and until Spring, it will hold.

Jennifer L. Bentheimer

Perception

Tread upon the memories of time
Flowing as a melodious rhyme
Through the miles and the years
Phoney smiles and bittersweet tears
People are like leaves on some trees
Changing with the seasons' filigrees
Visibility obstructed...unclear inner sights
Reacting instinctively by rights
Obstacles unfurling upon a clear path
Take it lightly...buffer...nurture that wrath
Always questioning— why? What reasons?
Not all will endure life's ominous treasons
Anticipating...Where is the next step?
Direction unknown... perceived by PERCEP...
...TION!??!

Betty Lesny

Angel On Earth

Listen to the music of your Soul and tune with it. That's you!
Fly in the clouds of freedom above the seas and the mountains,
carry with you the wind of Love and spread joy wherever you go.
You will collect many fruits in the garden of friendship
and there will be always a gift for you behind the corner.
Pray for the Sun to shine in everybody's life, everyday and forever,
and you will always be the one who catch the first ray at dawn.
Talk with the birds in the blue sky and show the limits of sadness
so no one will cross those borders anymore.
Take the hands of misery and fill them with Light of prosperity.
Don't cry anymore. Tears do not belong to you, they were meant to
to become the jewels of your secret treasure.
You got enough to live happy from now on.
I am here to listen to you when you need help,
but I know you will not.
Bless is with you in the path of your life.
Flowers and the song of a black bird will remind you that
I am with you forever.
I do care.

Dominique Frausin

To Be An Eagle

I would feel unworthy to be such a majestic creature flying on the gentle breeze of a warm summers day. I could only begin to imagine what it would feel like to have such freedom from the pressures of everyday life. To soar above all my problems would elevate my soul to the highest level of joy.

To be capable of clenching a gleaming trout or scurrying mouse in a pair of razor sharp talons in a single dive. Being a natural survivor in harsh country and a father to young eaglets. I would go to unmeasurable lengths to provide for my children and me. I would use the talents I have to further my kind.

To be an eagle and to glide through the clouds with little effort would blow my mind, and to have the view of the land through the eye of the eagle would be the most ultimate thing I ever did, yet I am not an eagle so the only thing I can do for now is imagine.

Benji Dean

Fairy Tale

Once upon a time lived a beautiful fairy princess.
One day she meets a handsome prince.
They fall madly in love and live happily ever after-a familiar tale.

But fairy tale romances are an illusion and reality a disappointment.
You meet your knight in shining armor and are swept off your feet.
Only later you discover that his castle is his retreat, his armor is
his defenses and the dragons to be slain are his own fears.

Dana F. Sullivan

"He That Stands So Tall"

I looked in the library to find a poem to cover it all,
For a man that stands so tall.

I looked up and down from poem to poem,
I just could not find one to fit a man that stands so tall.

I looked to a great poet to say,
She had something for president Clinton's inauguration, but I could
not find one to fit a man that stands so tall.

So I said good bye to her and look to another,
But I just could not find one to fit a man who stands so tall.

So I moved on my way.

Then something inside me said right about the man inside that
stands
So tall.

For Dr. Rorie.

You are a man that stands so tall, is for us all,
For that's the man that stands so tall.

For the man inside you, he guides you, he keeps you, and he leads you,
For that's the man that stands so tall.

So I'm glad to say, I to am glad to know the God inside you,
For that's the man that stands so tall.

Carolyn Udell Allen

My Special Love

At night I think of you with wonder knowing you're mine if only
for a time,
Those fleeting moments between dark and light into which you and I
can climb.
I hurry to your side, time is short and soon it will be light.
When we must go our separate ways until the coming of the night.
We are safe for now cradled in the shadows of each others embrace,
Leaving the cold world outside and disappearing without a trace.
To a magical place filled with the warmth of flickering candle light,
Where anything is possible if we just dream and hold on tight.
I treasure our time together no matter how measured it has to be,
Because a precious moment in time will be etched in my memory.
When fate brought us together I found someone to love and hold
tight,
A sympathetic soul to guide me through the darkened night.
As daylight dawns and time has come for us to part,
I won't be leaving alone you see, I'll have you inside my heart.

Joyce A. Coker

When Do You Say Rape?

The day I met him was the best day of my life.
For he said I was his love and soon to be wife.
I cared for him much but we still took it slow.
When things started to get heated all
I thought I had to say was no.
When he said he loved me that's when I knew it was time.
For that night I thought would be something
Special and I could say he was all mine.
When that night had arrived on his face was a big smile.
I backed away from him and thought for awhile.
For while I was thinking my mind I had changed.
For when he approached me my body rearranged.
For no I repeated many times.
When he said yes he was committing a crime.
I said no and meant it.
He said yes and expected.
Now a year later he is nowhere to be found
I am standing alone a baby my arms are around.

Alisa Heisen

The Rain In May

My grandma used to say "Rain can wash anything away."
For a time I felt that way The sorrows of winter
washed gone by May

One rainy day in Maine, I was walking through the Park of Alfred Caine, I was letting the rain wash my sadness away

Walking on I found someone sitting there on a bench
"Hello," I said
"Hello," she said
"May I stay?"

After that day, in May, in Maine, in the Park of Alfred Caine
I became close friends with Fay, and we set a wedding day

After the wedding, we would walk in the rain to let our sadness wash away and enjoy the happiness after the rain

We loved each other day to day, May to May
and we always walked in the rain, in the Park of Alfred Caine

As time went on we were happy together, but one rainy day in May
Fay faded away

And now I sit here in the rain, in the Park of Alfred Caine
and tell myself grandma wasn't always right... Rain can't wash everything away.

Jonathan L. Sutton

Shorty's Canyon

I know of a beautiful place God has made out of stone, it is a place for everyone to see, not just his own.

You won't find any trash here, the only litter you will find here is acorns and pine cones, that is why it is so dear.

The air is crystal clear and so is the water, maybe it was put there by mother nature's daughter.

The snow is melting, the water is starting to run, filling a pond that is being warmed up by the sun.

The birds are singing, the frogs are chirping back and forth; the sounds are bouncing off the canyons south to north.

Rocks shuffle when you step on them, the grass crackles and smashes; the snow melting nearby will make a limb fly and you will think that something is in the bushes.

This is the only place you will find a beetle swimming under the water and long-legged bugs skating on the surface, tadpoles become frogs, they all have a purpose.

If you look up real high where no ladder can reach, you can spot an ancient petroglyph just waiting to teach.

The cliffs reach the sky, like skyscrapers, from one end to the other; when you cross the snow you can see the ground come to life as the tiny black spiders make for cover.

Kate Ferguson

Night

The night is quiet and cool
Fireflies are all around the meadow
The call of the whippoorwill breaks the silence.
The sky is filled with shimmering stars
And the moon is rising above the mountain.

Somewhere I hear a dog barking.
I could get lost in this night forever.
The serenity of it clears my head of all the stress.
Let me stay in this moment of time for awhile
And I will return at dawn.

Betty H. Wagner

Hold On To The Dream

Hold on the dream you have so dear
for its chance at reality may soon be near.

Hold on to the dream and don't think twice
for if you do you may soon pay a price.

Hold on the dream you have today
for somewhere in life it will pave your way.

Hold on to the dream you have in sight
for it will be useful when the time is right.

Hold on to the dream you keep in your heart
because if you don't it will tear you apart.

Hold on the dream you keep as a token
but whatever you do don't let it be broken.

Erica Bland

Christmas

Christmas. It's a nice word, but what does it really mean?
For little kids, it means presents and candy
and little bitty hoof prints on the roof top,
with the sound of a jolly "Ho, Ho, Ho!" behind it.
But what does it really mean?
It means the birth of a little one,
who brought many joyous events to our lives.
So on this day, Christmas, we celebrate the birth of a joyous one.
He really is the reason for the season.

Kira Cusano

Light The Way

The wait of the world lies on the shoulders of a blind man,
For only he can write that which he sees
And what he sees...Insanity is reality
Wear do you live
Only in my mind...I know no other home
Do the men in the sky laugh at you like they laugh at me
Do I believe that they are there
What else can I believe the book says so, and books never lie
Do you believe darkness holds truth
The seeing ones are light
I like being darkness
Protect your mind from the ones in the field
The sun has set on my field of grass
And darkness has prevailed
My heart pumps rainbow-colored gray life through my vanes
She is of the light
And she makes me want to cry
Step into my reality and live a lie
Step into my insanity and live

Darrin Jacobs

Dragon Fly

The dragonfly darts about the trickling brook
For only those who stop to look.

Today he's blue with violet tones;
He seeks his mate on sun-dried stones.

She is blended with the shore;
Hoping that he'll come once more.

Then tandum they fly about the brook this sunny day;
Reflecting over still pools as they play.

The carefree life of a dragonfly
Is yours to share for passing by.

Kathy Marshall

My Solitude

No One is more deserving of my love, than you;
for Only with you would I share
this
Single
moment.
I see the sun come off the ocean in fragments,
a billion shining diamonds of time, each birthing, each living
it's
Single
passion,
each yearning for One—
frozen moment...
and seeing your faraway eyes in every crystalline flash,
I turn to my shore and ponder,
this freeing or stilling of water;
for I am this One moment flowing—
allowing—
your diamond wave to crash—
to end—
in cold, One-hearted sand.

Joseph Neuville

Who Am I?

Some try to speculate on my return
for shows have proven so.
No one plays me better than I.
The audience flutters when I materialize.
My presence is met with a gentle roar,
like the shutting of a door.

Crevices open to feast on it's prey,
not being picky, just what's in its way.
An array of edifices quality,
and lemons satisfy.
Levees don't do their job,
so rivers begin to bob.

Rick Tor-rents is the judge that supplies the evidence.
His scale starts level and goes to intense.
The drum doesn't beat,
but it keeps track of the heat.
The needle won't cut,
like a scalpel would.

The vote is in, and I win,
with a ride down a landslide!

Denise Jacques

Love Hunger

Have you ever desired?
For something you want,
For something you need,
For something that makes your blood boil and your heart bleed.

I have desired so many men,
Desired so much it felt like a sin, (but I know it is not)
It is just an emotional lusting within.

But desires and pleasures,
Tear the heart in two,
One to love,
One to lust,
Unfortunately there is a choice that is a must.

I never want to give my heart away again,
Because I will lose,
And the universe all will win...

Cheran Schick

For A Blessing's Going To Come

The life I live-not to be ashamed
For the life I live is all of pain
Too deep to share and too far to hide
This pain I have lies deep down inside
Often it fades, but it's still there
I know I'm loved, but my knowledge and my feelings aren't the same
If so why this pain
there are many questions of why I feel this way
But answers aren't found not even today
But as life continues, hours pass
I wonder how long will this pain last
For another minute, for another day, for
another week, or the next month of may
Whether the amount of how long it'll last
I'll still thank the Lord for my future and my past
All tribulations that I may going through
I know the Lord will turn all new
It may not be today and it may not be tomorrow
But mark my words when the time comes, he'll be good and ready
So until then I'll hold steady
For a blessing's going to come and it's coming just for me
So that I might see why these/those things happen to me

Critesha L. Thrash

April Thoughts

Face on the mirror, don't turn from me-
for through your eyes I write
the lies that live with me.

How fondly I solicit to hallowed thoughts
that become an eyesore,
when my eyes are fixed on a love that is no more.

But this same sad reflection cannot move me to action;
for I am one who hates labels and titles
and runaway lovers!

-Would you have me in your memory,
after I have put an armor to bosom's truth?
will you come and lie and plot affection
because I choose to love and not reason?

I'll drink with you and embrace;
and perhaps get a taste
of that which craves to be remembered
a warmth that seldom flows
but always grows.

Evangeline Gee Sison

From The Untold Lover

To her beauty only muses can be invoked,
For valor, our Valkyrie's are sent,
But love-passion's fire yields no smoke,
It burns blue and bright like her eyes I've dreamt.
Her figure, an hourglass whose sands run slow,
Her name may well be etched in the stars,
For only heaven has words for such glory refined,
My love's affliction towards her all cures does bar.
How young hearts do quickly kneel,
To feel the tender skin of her hand.
The reason for their love is past care,
Through her fingers they fall as grains of sand.
Since foolish men with this are content,
Give them your whispers — one kiss is heaven sent.

Armen Ryan Panossian

In Memory

You are now a star, burning bright
forever you will light up our nights.

While you glow and keep steadfast in the sky,
you will watch us grow and help us fly.

Your flame will pulse strong; and
through it thoughts will pass of right and wrong.

Your wishes of hope, love and life,
your teachings of work, disappointment and strife.

These will be lessons for all to hear.
forever you will always be near.

Elaine Brignola

Forget

Forget his friendly smiles
forget the lovely things he said
Forget the good times you had with him.
Remember he's not yours anymore.

Forget the big heart candies he gave you.
Forget his way he showed his love.
Forget the times you had with him.
Remember, he left you for her.

Forget the red roses
Forget the way he said, "We will always
be together,"
Forget the friendly, lovely hugs he gave you.
Remember, he's not yours anymore

Forget that friendly house where you went
Forget the warm kisses
Forget the way he smiled, with those puppy eyes
Remember, he left you for her.

Angela Karapetyan

My Destiny

I wonder if I may ever be,
Free of the constraints that haunt me.
The tethers which ground me to New Jersey,
While I long for the tranquility
of the Colorado Rockies.

The Western air, how clean and pure,
While the East blusters pollen and spore.
I long for that sky of azure hue,
with its whisper of crisp morning dew.

I long for the day of the slower pace,
when I can relax, with nothing to race;
to live with increasing . . . open . . . space!

My days living in the East grow small,
although I shall miss the Autumnal Fall.
To leave, no worry, after all.

I dream for the day to flee this place,
so I may glance at the mountains' Face.

Colorado, I can hardly Wait....
My Home, and yes, alas.... My fate!

Donna Piccone Marthins

Mind Block

The thunder has done its job,
paralyzing us with its blanket of rolling sounds.
As it leaves us pondering its true duty,
Why its left us so suddenly, so quietly.
Abrupt.
Mind block.

Erin L. Facciolo

Dreams And Reality

As a child's balloon is let go
Free to drift skyward
Lazily at first
Higher and higher it climbs, until it is out of sight

So must some dreams be let go
One must realize that the dream was not meant to be
Knowing deep inside maybe it could have been
Letting go stirs feelings from the very core of one's soul

A dream long held onto is like the treasured balloon
It is reluctantly released to drift away
Having let go knowing it won't be there again
Leaving no trace behind it is as if it were never there

As in most things there is an end
Or a point where what was once so important
Has become impractical and unattainable
The dream becomes like the balloon set free without destiny

Leaving one to ponder
What is important to hang onto
Some things are but passing whims held for a while then released
Other dreams need be tied securely and kept close by

Kris Frost

semanteme

scathing accusations ride unbridled...through my head...
frenzy...fury...phobic fears...depositing their dread...
rapids...raging rivers...rushing 'round my wretched brain...
pleading...bleeding...needing you...to touch...to feel...my pain...
scalpels...scaffolds...scandals...fill the hollow of my soul...
androgynous encomia...encore and take control...
Rebel Child of Darkness whispering... "I don't have a name" ...
toxins that intoxicate...erode the fleshly frame...
deluded by Delusion...extricating the extremes...
fatal fascinations...fragments floating from my seams...
extemporize extensively...I slice and dice, once more...
behold the body in the blood...it's mine, there on the floor!...
an oozing orifice that offers...opiate, at last...
sequestering the schism...shards that once composed my past...
juxtapositions jumbling...disjointed imagery...
surrealistic surcease...supersedes insanity...

Catherine Patrick-Newman

My Grandma

As the spring appeared and the tulips started to show,
fresh at the break of dawn; off to Grandma's we'd go.

The relation eventually gathered, as we took turns
plowing the field, looking forward to the day when we
would share our yield.

As our brows would begin to moisten, still we worked
till the sun would settle, thankful for the moment when
we could give thanks, and smell Grandma's kettle.

Soon the dusk would turn to dark, and the folks would
order us to the car, though Grandma would stop them
and say "Not till they raid my cookie jar".

As father time takes over, and the families begin to
dwindle, my love for Grandma on Mother's Day will
always be rekindled.

Jay Allen Schramm

I'd Be A Vegetarian, If....

I shot an arrow into the air...

Actually, it was a rock.
From a homemade slingshot.
Not up, but on a flat trajectory.
And accurate, striking its feathery target.
The sparrow never had a chance against the Great White Hunter.
I felt a moment of elation, perhaps an ancestral echo from millennia
of hunter-gathers. Followed by...

My neighbor had been a witness
And imparted to her son—my hunting companion—and me, her
feelings of
my unnecessary act.
My elation soured.
I had nought against the bird, did not wish him dead. I had no
interest in his ounce of flesh, nor
taxonomic designs on his tiny carcass.
Just a kid with a new toy.
And now a new outlook.

We gathered up the lifeless remains, still warm, and buried them in
the woods across the street.
Gone, but not forgotten.

Kenton Chauncey

Mars

The swirling icy winds of Mars tell a story.
From chasm deep comes the cry of civilized glory.
Now the haunting storms hush the cry,
That cry that wants to know why.
Was there a day such as today on that distant ball,
When birds could sing and the red leaves fall?
Did some being have feelings such as I?
Did he ever look up at some night sky?
Was he troubled about nuclear wars?
Did he wonder who made all of the stars?
What dug that canyon deep?
What caused that icy wind?
Was there some red button connected to a deadly heap,
With an eager finger connected to an angry mind?
Did such a union cause a holocaust?
Is this the cry that is now lost?
If we could hear that distant story
Would we change our civilized glory?

Dean Albritton

Some Things Aren't What They Seem

Come join me, sit, feast upon my grapes of wrath, drink
from my golden goblets until you overflow!
Take from me, take from me, I have so much to give, to
your advantage the pendulum swings, tick, tock, tick, tock.
My how times flies when your having fun!
Here let me show you to your dungeon, oh, um, I mean your
guest chamber.
I'll make sure your comfortable before at last I tuck myself
safely into my bed!
Oh, and when you awake don't bother to draw the drapes
to gaze at the morning light, the windows, sealed shut, are
painted black.
You should find some candles on your night stand.
Ah! Good morning, did you sleep well?
No interruptions I hope, no strange noises in the night?
I myself suffer from a bit of insomnia.
I tell you what (you're such good company) how about staying
a few days, weeks, years, eternities longer, it would be
an especially tasty treat.
What do you say?

Annie Mae Raus

But What About Me!

Eyes so full of joy and wonder,
from seeing the fantastic things that One could do.
A Heart pounding, with great, great thunder,
because it was all so exciting and new.
Lips that spoke of these wonderful things,
thinking that all who heard would feel the same.
Only to experience through the Ears
words that gradually made a Heart cry in great pain.

The Eyes no longer see with joy and wonder,
all has been replaced with blackened tears.
The Lips that once spoke such wonderful things,
resentment now is there.

Why is it that no one could hear or see this beauty
in the rough?
Why could no one take the time to Love, to Care....
was food, clothing and shelter ever enough???
Yet, what about me?!

Earlyn W. Martin

God Invented Basketball

God invented basketball just look around.
From the blue brothers faith up town,
To grey kids expectations in hick towns.

Halo to me rhymes with hoop,
On golden, glistening, elevating wings; angels love to swoop.
Light'ning! fast.

The creative spirit abounds, peach baskets, old bike rims and
New spheres.
The circle round' life sound balls bouncing in time.

Asymmetric game, seeking symmetry similar to life's plane,
Played on a ecclesiastical vector complete with angles, God ordained.

Players pray for strength to escape gravity's pain.
Evolved champion with chiseled frame, an aureola form, fluvial fluxion
is the norm.

Rebound for past sins.
Players leap high to ascend to him but God is in the stands.
Delivering last minute finishes and touching fans.

I seer God in his playing days, with vengeful ups, almighty handle,
and forgiving touch, an omniscient point guard in the clutch.
Now he's retired coach of infinity three years running, God loves
the game.

Anthony Brent Chappelle

Take Me Away

Take me away
From this cruel world.
Bring me to a better place,
A place where knowledge isn't one's self-demise,
Where one need not wear a mask to be merry,
Where one can dream without being mocked,
Where the truth can never hurt
As a kick from an ass hurts,
A place where one can be free.
So, please, if you have the heart
To take pity on a poor, lost soul,
I beseech you a thousandfold,
Take me away.

jill olivier

Frustration Be Gone

When in the middle of the day
Frustration abounds in the greatest way
Look for relief in the least expected places
By casting an eye on your neighbors' faces.

A smile, a nod or even the quirk of an eyebrow
Will relieve that tension and you'll say wow!
At the turn of events this magic has wrought
And frustration disappears without a thought.

Perhaps on those days when frustration lingers
And one has the desire to count one's fingers
Put a smile on that face and lift up those shoulders
And the frustration leaves as though buoyed by boulders.

You say what is the purpose of this rhyme
As we all deal with frustration at any given time
To overrule that frustration is the key
This makes for a happier you and me!

Jean B. Hall

The Decision

Standing on the edge of forever,
gazing into that neverending, black abyss.

Warm, wet tears running down my face,
glistening in the starlit night.

Do I begin that long trek back through the desert,
Or plunge head-on into the unknown?

Hopelessly lost in a rush of confusion,
and drowning in a flood of tears.

Someone help me-!!!

Jennifer D. Wendt

Get Over It

What is all the hatred and anger about?
Get over it!!!!

Is it worth all the hardship?
Is it worth doing without the friendship?

Not truthfully.
I want to share this world with you peacefully.

Let's all get over the color thing,
and start letting freedom ring...

RING, RING, RING for our "one nation under God",
for we are all one nation and of one origin,
whether you like it or not. Get over it and accept it.

Please be my friend, love me for who I am.
And I will be your friend, loving you for who you are.

We all come in different makes and models,
but when it comes to feelings and needs,
We all want to be cuddled.

Please get over the hatred and anger
because we all have to share this small space.
Let's all work toward happiness and
work even harder at living in peace.

Arlene Joy Pickett

A Common Sight

I saw her loneliness clearly as she wandered along.
Shriveled and frail, she came cautiously toward me,
Holding back ever so slightly.
Her pale skin and deep-set sapphire eyes
Pleaded with my heart.
I heard her speak softly, no louder than a whisper.
I felt sorry for her.

Jennifer Gill

The Beauty Of It All

The magnetic beauty of a Sun Rise,
gives promise of the day to be.
Viewed from a point of vantage
stretching outward over the sea;
reveals majestic beauty,
nature has prepared for you and me.

Drops of moisture, kissing the tender breath of a leaf;
pearls of water linger, an bring innocent relief.
The dewy eyes of an awakened child,
views it's mother's face and timidly, conveys a smile.

Long stemmed roses - red -
received in tasteful grace,
are scented, caressed and softly embraced.
A lover's kiss, sweet gentle and kind,
is rendered over and over in a sleepless mind;
as one inebriated in a tie that binds.

Nature closes the fruitful day,
chores are reviewed and put away.
The sun will set slowly in the West;
and all life's beauty, will temporarily, be stilled in rest.

Elva B. D'Antoni

Stepping Stones

O Heavenly Father, reigning in splendor above
Giving us graces, our lives and your love,
Those mysterious wonders magnificent You perform;
That carry us through all strife and all storm

The days of my life should give praise to Your name,
Instead it's foolish needs that I beg for in shame!
The glory and honor You deserve when I pray,
Is somehow lost by my cares of the day.

When everything's wrong, filled with suffering and strife,
And stumbling blocks hamper my pathways of life,
My doubts and my fears running out of control,
I'm helpless, I'm down, and I've lost sight of my goal;

If, from behind the events of life I could gaze,
I'd see You providing my needs everyday
So, why should I worry, be unhappy or sad?
You take care of my life, I'll give thanks and be glad.

Then I realize O Father in heaven above
You know all my needs, You give me Your love!
The praise You deserve from all creatures down here,
I'll give you that glory, every trouble and fear.

It's then that you come wash away foolish fears;
You give me Your grace and dry all my tears;
You come to my rescue; Your light shining through!
Those obstacles of life? They're stepping stones - to YOU.

John J. Drew

Life In The Fast Lane

Climb the ladder, Strive to succeed,
Grab the brass ring, Always be the one to lead.
Call all the shots, Fight all the way,
Pull no punches, You'll have it all some day.
Don't give up your dreams, You have what it takes.
Don't settle for second, Be the best for God's sakes.
Others may fall short, Don't stop along the way.
Someone will help them, for their weakness, you shan't pay.
Don't forget about those dreams,
You can make them all come true,
As long as you remember
The strength to do it, can only come from you.

Khristine L. Carroll

"And Now They Are One"

They were brought together by a true act of fate.
God only knew Dave would be Debra's mate.

October 22 - A day long awaited
Much preparation, everything appreciated.

A long and happy life together they will live.
By asking God to watch and always help them give

Affection, Grace, Understanding and Love
All under the direction of God from above.

Today is the beginning of their "Life as One"
The greatest of moments under the sun.

How grateful we are that you came to share
The coming together of such a devoted pair.

Love eternal for all to adore,
Here on the threshold of love evermore.

Judith M. Haynes

What Is Life Like?

What is life like?
Going nowhere and pedaling the bike?
Or is it a road that you can't see because you're blind?
No, it sometimes comes with troubles that you don't need to find.
Life is like a planet that's unknown,
And there's no map for it drawn.
Life is like a chair you're nailed to and cannot move,
It's like millions and trillions of debts you owe.
It's like trying with little hope,
And there comes the question: "Did you do It?" Nope.
Life is like a little flower on the grave,
That shows that the person was brave.
Life is like a day with a bit of sunshine,
That says that today the happiness is mine.
Life is sometimes good to you they say,
But not each and everyday.
Then what is life like?
Cynthia says, "Why don't you ask Mike?"

Beatrix Kaldor

Down On Our Little Farm

Horses, Cow, and Little pigs,
Grandma doing the Irish jig,
Turkey, Ducks, Geese and Chicken's.
Our cat had baby kittens.
Daddy's working in the barn,
Oh those were the day's,
Down on our little farm.
Ten little kids and, a dog at play.
When their chores are done, at the end of the day.
Momma called us into eat, should have heard the sound
of our little feet.
Grampa smoking his corn cob pipe, and we're all lined up,
to kiss him good night.
Looking back thru the years.
dream a lot, shed tears.
After our bath, We said our prayer's,
Off to bed, we climbed the stairs.
God only know's we did no harm,
While we were living,
Down on our little farm.

Elma L. Gabel

Color of Humanity

I used to love colors, the shade, the hue,
Grass that is green, a sky of blue.

I've used colors to describe emotion and feeling,
Yellow was happy, red sent me reeling.

There are two certain colors I have grown to hate,
It seems their difference have sealed my fate.

If we could just dispose of black and white,
Maybe the people of the world would see the light.

I like the idea of a world free of color,
Where people are free to love one another,

Without all the pressure from those who judge,
The narrow minded whose opinions won't budge.

God please stop the world from all this insanity,
Help everyone see the beautiful color of humanity.

Cindy Bradley

'Perspective'

With a voice loud as thunder to creatures crawling below, a god spoke great truths it was indeed a fine show.

"Your world only survives by my breath of grace, with a blink of my eye your universe I could erase. So remember this well, dare not to forget. My wrath is unforgiving, I love you as my pets!"

Then the little boy smiled looking down on summer grass. He lifted a few souls from the dark swarming mass. "Grow big and grow strong," he demanded of his flock. After all, he owned the only ant hill on the block.

Christopher J. Raso

A New Beginning

Morning mist upon the horizon
Greets me as I am arising
It signals the start of a brand - new day
Leading me to wonder what the world holds for me today
The birds awaken, as if on cue
Their sounds add to the misty morning hue
Some of the sounds and colors one cannot see
But can only be felt through the heart tenderly
To me these are times of quiet reflection
Which add to one's soul and give it direction
This is when I also think fondly of a special friend
and a loved one so true
Who have enriched the grass of my life like the misty morning dew
They add to my life so much wonderful bliss
Much as the mist gives nature her misty morning kiss.

Amy B. Schulz

A Flower...A Child

A flower planted by seed / Just as a brand new life
Grows according to natures clock without toil or strife

Bursting into the sun with strength extraordinaire
becoming stronger with passing time just give love and care

The stem how straight and strong / The leaves shiny and bright
With steadfast roots and radiant sun its life brings joy and delight

Tho' just a bud the time is soon to open up and flower
So will a child become more beautiful with love as it's growing
power

Carol L. Short

Between A Father And A Son

The bond between a father and his son
Grows stronger when they grow together

All the time spent together
Building a home
All the time together in the workshop

Looking back there couldn't have been
Enough time for a father and his son

There was so little time, but he gave it so
Generously and selflessly

He taught me everything I know and was
So patient about everything he tried to
Teach me, even when I was distracted by
Sports and friendships

Why didn't we tell each other that we
Loved each other more often, I wonder

Maybe its because of that unspoken
Loving bond
Between a father and his Son
I'll miss you Dad

Carmen Bird

The Gift Of Garcia (Aug. 1, 1942 - Aug. 9, 1995)

That plant in the great room never flowered before
Gyoto Monks filled the air last shows that I saw
'Fore the passing of such a friend
Who heavy hearts could always mend
From Heaven, the lesson, it's time to change
Into the unknown, destiny un-named.

Recall that first night, August the ninth
Cried to a full moon upon waters bright
The owl spoke from standing people so tall
Alone in Big Sur, now Jerry is gone.

As I walk fields of fennel fear of losing a piece
Of the best part of me where playfulness will never cease
Yes He's Gone, but the Music must Never Stop

So Thank you Creator
For The Gift of Garcia in my life...
He's Standing On The Moon with friends
And we'll miss him so...
Bye Jerry

Anita Tavernier

To Be A Friend

You have an art to be quite petite
Habit to show people you care and you are complete;
You take friendship like business, and
Never definite;
You think you know what friendship
Should be.
You think you are tops on earth, and
You shall be...
But it takes sacrifice, with feelings
Within thee.
It takes more than just words,
To bring friendship and happiness to me.

Dolores L. Garilli

One Year Forever Dear

THEY spent more of their lives together than apart,
had their troubles but shared the same heart.

THEY had souls that seemed so in touch
at other times not so much.

THEY were married and had a family
not a fairy tale but a close facsimile.

THEY shared forty years plus
they share their time with us.

THEY spent their retirement on many a so journey
fulfilling a life time of yearning.

THEY shared everything it seemed
as if it was just one dream.

THEY became ONE on a horrible afternoon
too fast-no, no, it's to soon.

THEY no longer share their life in this earth
one alone-first since birth.

THEY can no longer walk hand and hand
nor see their footprints in the sand.

THEY were apart for just ONE YEAR
now together cloud walking forever dear.

Deborah Simmons

Anne Bonny

Anne Bonny with her fire green eyes and her red-gold
hair that shone in the sun was a ravishing beauty.

Yet this was no lady for court or Kings.

But Anne Bonny was the mistress of the sea.

The ocean became her home for this green eyed woman who
whose passion was wild and free.

Stormy and reckless to men's desires yet her only
loyalty was for the freedom of the sea.

With a sword in one hand, and the other clenching a
pistol, Anne Bonny was a fierce warrior of the high
seas

Anne Bonny was not born to be a lady, but a
legendary pirate queen.

Keri Fry

Zero

10... you enter my vision for the first time, my eyes go ablaze my hands tremble, my heart goes off, start thinking of the different ways. 9...do I dare approach you, do I turn and walk away making excuses while I punch the walls, or scrawl from day to day 8...my hand reaches out...like in a cloudy dream, I can't comprehend but you don't run exchanging glances, some words, then a kiss, the romance has begun 7...please excuse me if I pull your arm, but I'd really like to try denying all physics, challenging the universe, to fly before I die ten seconds at a time 6...baby, it's magic, you don't even have to say a word, I don't even have to know your name. maybe for once we'll feel something, maybe what we feel will be the same 5...I can see how quickly the seconds pass, I want each to be special to be mine because I know the only way to fall in love, is ten seconds at a time 4...maybe I'll break down a barrier, show you a secret place in my heart give you something to hold inside, while in this world we carry on 3...what would you do if I clung to you, and our love carried us to the stars making love in the nothingness of space, finding out who you are 2...the words come now, oh, too difficult, I think the rain is washing them away but I remember a beautiful princess, and how she loved me for 10 seconds one day 1... and so my love is over, another dreamer has awoke think I'll go play my red guitar, star out to the sun, and just let go.

David Gomlak

A Time In Place

Sitting alone on a green carpet of grass, I imagined I could fly away.

I tried to think of a place that I could go, a place where I would be happiest.

When suddenly, I was swept up by a great gust of autumn leaves. They carried me to a place called Memories. There I found time. As each leaf floated to the ground, I recalled a specific time when I was truly alone.

As this time rushed to my mind, I saw myself weeping. Surrounding me were the people that I loved. My mother reached out her hand and asked, "Why are you weeping?" I answered, "I love you all but, I do not love me?" Her hand disappeared instantly. Frightened, I fumbled to sort each leaf, when I noticed one glowing green leaf hanging from a branch. It was heart shaped. As I looked closer, I saw my three year old son Daniel.

At last, I was finally freed from all of my bad memories. And I would never have to go back to that place where I found time.

Jaye C. Brown

Ode to a Pet

To those who give us the trust of love, and we never have to ask.

Those who stand by us rain or shine, through the happy times and the sad.

They give us bright, sunny days and warm snugly nights. They worry when we're gone too long, but always greet us happy and bright.

A truer friend has never been placed by God on this green earth. No one can begin to understand how much their love is worth.
So when the time comes to say goodbye, our pain is deep within. As God reclaims what He has given us, the simplest and truest of friends.

But they continue to warm a heart and share their love you see. For these friends of ours they move along to lay around God's feet.

So even though it's very hard for us to let them go, just remember the meaning God gave to their lives, truer friends shall never be known.

Edie A. Monlux

Wild Women Have the Blues Too!

Wild women have the blues too! You see my life is filled with the Harlem nights, the Vagas lights, the t**ty shakers, the BIG money makers, the law breakers, but I got the blues. This man I once knew said he loved me too, well h*ll I can't tell I wish he'd go to h*ll 'cuz he's the cause of all my down falls in life. My life is filled with the Harlem nights, the Vagas lights, the New Orlands funk, but I've got the blues. I got 9" nails, a long ponytail, my sexy looks, short skirts and high heels. I L-O-V-E to party and all the men I know are some low
down
shames I won't call no names, but they know who they are. They're the ones in the white trimmed brims or the hat to the back but they never look back no matter how good you look, 'cuz it's all about that game. You see, I lost a child which really gave me the blues I was young and loved the sun and fun, but I got caught up in the hustle and bustle now I am huffling and scuffling trying to get things right. I never understood why they said wild women couldn't have the blues too! Now I am old as h*ll and I've been to jail mo than once. And 1/2 those low down shames don't even remember my name 'cuz I can't wear them 9" heels no mo and I threw that ponytail out the door. Now as I sit back and look at the life I once lived I never understood why they said wild women couldn't have the blues too!

Ericka J. Myles

Dear Soul

Dear Soul your voice screams loudly throughout me. Your harsh thoughts terrify me. I am in a constant tremble. You are the core of my very being. You are the foundation to which the rest of me builds and feeds on. I admit, I have ignored you, I have left you to stand alone. I have locked you away years ago. I am embarrassed of you, if I allow you to be seen, what will that do to me? You have been solemn for months at a time, but then you awake and I am shaken once again. Even the closest people in my life have not seen or heard of you. They deny your existence, but I know it's only a matter of time before you take control.

You have been patient, and understanding, your love for me has been unconditional. You have never abandoned me, but I have made you hide, can you forgive me?

I believe it's time, It's time for you to be unchained. Together we will break the calluses that cover you. I must let you breath. I believe the Lord has blessed me with you, So intense, So loving, so many of emotions. I will not compromise to amongst the rest; I will wait patiently until my mate, my soul mate, appears.

This is a new beginning for me, I will no longer reflect on the years that have passed, but I will focus on the years to come.

Dear Soul, never let me shelter you again. You must continue to scream loudly throughout me. You must grow stronger than the impostor that once occupied your space.

I believe in you Dear Soul, I believe in Me!

Jo Ann Meyer

Who Gives This Woman

Who gives this woman, did you say?
Has the time already come to give her away?
It seems only yesterday that God gave her to me;
And though she was given, she wasn't free.
I paid for her with worry, care and love.
I earned his gift with all of the above.
The effort was worth it, and I'll never scold;
For everything I gave, she gave back threefold.
I've gathered my memories year after year;
And with those I'll hold her near.
I now give her to you on this your wedding day;
And for this gift, the price you must pay
Will be your worry, care and love.
You must earn my gift with all of the above.
She is now hours to have and to hold -
And remember, everything you give
You will get back threefold.
Who gives this woman, did you say?
I, the Mother.

JoAnn Burton

My True Love

He gives me beauty for ashes, joy instead of mourning.
He gives me a song in the night, and gladness of heart with sweet sleep and safety.
He is my refuge in trouble - help when needed.
He is my food and drink - my highest joy.
He counsels me and gives me wisdom.
He gives me the exquisite pleasure of His Eternal Presence.
He is my contentment.
He rescues me and keeps me from falling.
He gave his lifeblood for me.
In HIM alone can I depend and lean on, and find no disappointment.
He is the strength, the security, the tenderness I need.
He is my True Love.
He is my ALL in ALL...He is my Jesus, the LOVER OF MY SOUL!

Jo Ann Wibberley

We, Who Are Not As Others

We believe faith is a given, but never given out. If you believe you have it, there's no such thing as doubt. We believe equality's all, and if you don't agree with us, we don't need you at all. Imbalance is nothing without small or great. Scales of equality exist without Weight.

We believe that you receive only if you give, but without expectation Is the proper way to live. We believe if you expect more than you Should get, your time for want's completely gone; your time for need Is met. We believe necessity is all you'll ever need, but never grab the extra bonus out of simple greed.

We believe in the natural course of how all things should go. To Push things way too fast in turn will cause things to go slow. We Believe there is no end to any time at all; there's just one minute Before the next, no matter big or small.

We believe we think you can, so you should think so too, and if you Don't agree again, we'll try until you do.

We believe if you believe you can believe us too, you'll live a life Of understanding common sense and truth.

If you wonder who we are and what we're all about, just think to Yourself "I am my own and like nobody else."

Clark Layman

What Have You Done For Me Lately?

What have you done for me lately?
Have you lent me money, bought me a car,
made me feel like a rising star?
Have you boosted my ego, given me praise,
Told me you'll love me all of your days?
Have you treated me to dinner, mowed my lawn
rented me a movie, walked my dog?
Have you sent me love letters, bought me
something gold, defended my honor in front of my foes?
Have you paid for my vacation, bought me new
clothes, listened to my problems, sent me a rose?
Have you thrown me a party, gone the extra
mile to lift my spirits and make me smile?
Have you made me soup when I was ill,
Brought me water to lake my pills?
Have you fluffed my pillows, sat by my bed,
kept me company, rubbed my head?
Have you soothed my heartbreak,
helped me forget my past? Do more for
me, please. What you have done won't last.

Kathleen A. Kolar

Untitled

We have been going out for awhile,
He always said he loved me.
He moved away and left me here.
After he left, I heard a bunch
of bad things he has done with my best friend.
I confronted him about it,
and he said he had nothing to do with it.
I caught him in a lie,
then he told me the truth,
I was crying and very angry,
I asked him why.
He said whatever happens between
us I'll still love you.
I told him I love you too.
I didn't want to tell him but I did.
I don't want to care or love him
anymore for what he did.
But I know I still do.
What happened between us is
over and I want it to be over forever.

Amanda Dee Wilson

Bizarre Responses

So strange! Insane!
He changed TV station.

The honey face
on screen resembled his back-knifing coworker.
He turned off the smooth-silk singer.

A trying day.
Tomorrow would be better.
He discarded a half tube of tooth paste
and a once used bar of soap.

Pajama time.
But not those fancy three times slept in pair.
He was wearing them while reading a letter
telling him one of his life's plans died.

Next days work clothes. Not that shirt.
He was wearing it when blamed for an error not his.

A call from tips saying that the game was off for him
because bumpy was going, making five in the car; and
a friend of his was killed in a wreck with five in the car.

Quickly returning the phone to its cradle,
he said, "That Guy's Weird!"

Dorothy Randle Clinton

"You Don't Have To Be Alone"

I watch as he walks down the street,
He is lost in his own little world.
He thinks of his problems and this makes him shudder.
Alone and scared, like never before.
And as I watch, I think to myself
"You don't have to be alone and scared, for I am here to be with you."
I know he can not hear me as my feelings run wild inside.
I can't even prove them, to do so would hurt us both.
But sometime soon my feelings will hit him.
How hard? I can not tell.
I know he'll either run or confess.
So as I look into his eyes, I get a feeling of loneliness
I cannot help him, he will not let me.
All I can do is pray.
Pray that he will be safe as he wonders down the path of time.

Kailee L. Morrison

The Lord Is

The Lord is my hope in times of trouble
He is my joy in times of sorrow
He is my strength and my salvation
For without Him, there would be no tomorrow

He promised never to leave me nor forsake me
He'll be there right down until the end
For throughout this world of searching
I come to know, no greater a friend

He healed the sick and raised the dead
He's full of tender mercy, joy and love
So whatever problem you'll face in this world
Come boldly before the altar and give them to the Lord above

He'll carry you through many trials and tribulations
It's during those times that our heart sometimes seems to tear
But keep on praying, trusting, and believing
Because God won't put no more on you than you can bear

Love, patience, peace, joy, and happiness
He will supply your every need
If only when you hear Him knocking
Open the door of your heart and do take heed

Deborah E. Williams

My Soldier Buddy

He fought in Vietnam many years ago,
He left behind the people he loved.
He hardly wrote or even gave me a call,
He always had to hide in the mud.

He shot machine guns and threw hand grenades,
He saw the deaths of all his friends.
They killed and fought a senseless war,
What did they all have to gain?

I got a letter one day from my soldier buddy,
But he didn't have a whole lot to say.
He said he was fine and he would be home soon,
The next day he was shot in the head.

Six months later my buddy came home,
The bullet was still in his head.
He was never the same, always running and hiding,
Like he was fighting the war again.

One day we were talking, sitting in the hot sun,
My buddy started feeling kind've bad.
His head began to ache, he fell over on his back.
I cried because my buddy was dead. I cried because my buddy was dead.

Darlene L. Harvey

Violated Woman

Some strange person came stalking me,
He lurks in the darkness...I could not see

With each footstep, it draws him nearer
I begin to run though my legs get wearier

My heart is pounding in my chest as he grabs me close and tears my dress
I begin to scream in such distress, "Someone please help me out of this mess"

It seemed as though nobody heard my cry
As he strips me of ..."My body"..."My pride"...

God, help me to start all over again
God, help that sick and bewildered man, but let him remember with each passing day, this "Violated woman" on which he preyed

The woman who resisted with such force, the same woman he raped with no "Remorse"

Though I know in time my wounds may heal

But the memory of this day is in my mind like the words that are etched in steel.

Denise A. Holmes

The Man

A man was walking along the street, his clothes were worn and old,
He shivered as he walked along, because of the bitter cold.

I thought to myself as the man walked on, when did he get this way?
Weak and homeless, hungry and cold, could he name the day?

I looked down at myself in my big warm coat, my clothes were pressed and clean,
I thought to myself how lucky I was, and my eyes began to gleam.

I wondered how I would be if put into that circumstance,
Weak and homeless, hungry and cold, I wouldn't stand a chance.

Now when things aren't going well, and times are hard and rough,
I think of the man on the street that day, and things aren't quite so tough.

Jennifer Smith

The Love of Jesus

Oh what a friend I have in Jesus; He will never leave me alone.
He walks with me thru life; He tells me I am His own.

He comes to me when I need Him; He listens when I cry.
He shows me the light of His love; He's always by my side.

He shares with me my laughter, and wipes away my tears.
He gives me the strength I need to turn away my fears.

He picks me up and carries me when life's waters run deep.
He gently lays me down when it's time for me to sleep.

He whispers in my ear the sweet sounds of His love.
He encourages me to go on instead of giving up.

He calms me when I'm angry, and soothes me when I'm tense.
He gives me understanding when things don't make sense.

He comforts me in sorrow; And picks me up when I fall.
He allows me to make mistakes and still stand up tall.

He shows me I am special no matter what He does.
He gives me so many things, but most of all....
He gives His love.

Barbara Lilley

Rev. Dr. Martin Luther King, Jr.

Dr. King taught love, he was a peaceful man.
He wanted equality for all, he had a peaceful plan.
In Chicago he moved into a West Side slum.
When they heard about it, the press did come.
He pointed out the poor living condition
And tried to end slums which was his tradition.
On December tenth nineteen hundred and sixty four
He was given a great honor - that's for sure!
He won the Nobel Peace Prize that day.
He and his family went to Oslo, Norway.
He helped to make civil rights legislation,
That helped the people throughout this nation.
He fought social injustice everywhere.
To show all people that he did care.
He suffered pain and inhuman treatment,
To further the cause of the Civil Rights movement.
Always avoid violence he said as he spoke from town to town.
But show hate to no man, that only pulls YOU down!
His eyes were on the final prize, he never would turn back.
He taught dignity, self-respect and pride in being Black!

Alyce Pearl Smith

A Daddy's Girl

Was spiffy the word for my daddy?
He was so great.
He talced his face and polished his shoes
And carried chocolate drops in his pocket.

Was rich the word for my daddy?
He was so great.
He earned twenty five dollars a week
And taught his family of six respect for self and others

Was caring the word for my daddy?
He was so great.
He spread his overcoat on my quilted winter bed
Coal was short and sparingly used for the fireplace.

Was gifted the word for my daddy?
He was so great.
By example he made me a reader and conversationist
His listening ears were big to what I told him.

Was aging the word for my daddy?
He was so great.
Many years go by - my daddy is now a memory
His cloak of kindness is still spread over me for warmth.

Annie Ruth Luna

Christmas Day

No daily paper, delivered on this Holiday but I
hear the chimes as they ring,

Silent music fills the chilly air, children playing
with gifts and even a little squirrel seems to sing,

Rays of sunshine brightens the early morn, no daily paper
could capture this story,

Good news fill the hearts of men, women and children
all over the world sent by the Almighty in His Glory,

Gifts of love shared by His children brings peace
to us and today most forget their fears,

Some love ones have passed away and in silent
moments we share our tears,

No daily paper today to report the news but
the "Book of Life" tells the story of Jesus, God's only Son,

All should read to understand, all we own given to us
by God above and without our love of Him and His
only Son we could have no fun.

Joseph Armstrong

Sometimes I Dream

Sometimes I stretch and fight and yearn,
heart - felt efforts, begging to earn;
to reach the highest summit.

Sometimes I sit in thought and prayer,
my heart wondering if I should dare,
to leap towards the sky.

Sometimes I sit, as a thoughtful child,
wondering, in years to be, will I be outgoing or mild?
Who will I be, and what will I have done?

Sometimes I try hard to be me, ignoring the passing craze.
I'm looking inside as I work, not towards praise;
I want to do good.

Sometimes I look at things today, and I ponder on my life,
will I make a difference, can I ease the strife?
Will my deeds as an adult touch a human soul?

Sometimes I realize there are wicked, deadly problems now;
I am growing older, and I vow,
"I will try to make things better, patch the seams,
for I am a thoughtful child, and I dream!"

Christie Harner

The Pang's And Joy's Of Loneliness

Satan said unto himself, I'll make man slay God's son,
He'll turn his wrath on man, once this I have done.
but at your baptism, God's spirit did descend,
Which let you preach in hell, then to heaven you did ascend.

Your out of sight in heaven, but in my memory,
The one thing keeps me happy, is your love for me.
Sometimes my heart stumbles, as if it were blind,
And a hurting overtakes me at that time.

Christ I won't forget you, cherish your memory,
You died to save me from sin, on the cross at calvary.
I still have assurance, of your will is for me.
Ye there's still a lonely feeling, deep inside of me.

The greed an cruelty in the world, folk's heart's so cold,
I still surrender, my heart to you to hold.
You can't come too quickly, an say come unto me,
an free from this loneliness, down inside of me.

I know angel's keep my sleep you know my dreaming too,
Christ, the word's you give me, you know before I do.
Your will is to heal my hurt, so my tear's never start,
The words that I now write of you, nearly break my heart.

Joseph Lewis

Untitled

Cradled precariously in uncaring arms
Helpless and vulnerable
Isolated from those who may intervene
Lonely and tired
Dependent on those who are selfishly taking from me
Hoping in vain for safety
Overwhelmed with the grief
Of powerlessness
Despair is all that is left

Christian Siler

Beach Girl

She stands looking out into the giant gray waves,
her blue eyes half-closed in the wild wind.
Blond hair blows back, whipped by the wind.
Waves crash and roar, throwing foam and spray up
and out onto the sand,
Chasing one after the other they touch bare toes
with their cold wet bubbling foam.

Laughing wildly now, she turns to look at me.
Eyes dancing, giggling madly, she turns
once again toward the wild ocean.
Squatting onto the sand she pats it and says
"Happy, happy" with all the joy and
Abandon there is.

Christine Fluet

The Question And The Prophecy

When Mother Earth has lived
her final day among the stars,
and when the mighty fire that gave her warmth
itself becomes a darkened ember,
will there be in all the vastness of the skies
one solitary thing that still remembers
once there was a thing called love?

When all the creatures of the earth are dust,
and even time itself
deserts the dark and silent chill,
in some distant eon there will come
a wandering, godlike, alien thing,
and he will stand upon some barren hill
and, viewing what is left, he will indeed perceive
that...yes, out there within the ancient atoms
of our lifeless dust there once was love
and tenderness...
and even beautiful little things called kisses
passed between.
And he will smile through tears.

Bill Harrell

Young Love

Rain dances on the edge of the window.
His scent fills the air.
I grasp for the lingering fragrance of the soul.
I see his eyes of wisdom and courage, filled with compassion
of which I desire.
I stare as if he were the only sight,
Longing for his tender touch that will caress my soul.
I say nothing, nothing of my desires deep within me.
Quick glances,
Sweet smiles.
The feelings way deep can only be expressed in matters being.
The craving for his lust builds within.
Feeling his presence electrifies my body.
He settles inside, where he will remain

Beatrice Lemoine

Old Mrs. Reinhold

Mrs. Reinhold has been dead now for many years.
Her memory remains, though, as my own passing nears.
When we were young all the neighbors played in her yard.
It was a kind place...long before life became so hard.
There was Bobby, Brian, Betsy, Gracy and more.
We climbed trees and counted dandelions.
Nothing seemed a bore.

I have images in my dreams of walking through her house.
It is a welcome stay, guarded from the other haunting rouse.
She appears as gentle and fragile as a freshly spun silk.
She'd offer me cookies or cake and a warmed glass of milk.

She was always so careful to speak in proper tongue
Whilst all the while she trembled and scared the other young.
But I knew she was real with a heart that was pure.
She only wanted company as her husband died long before.

I wish I could go back and swing in her hammock
If only for a moment or two to escape from the panic.
But I was eight then and that is how life was to be.
Soon I'll be in her shoes with someone looking after me.

Anthony J. Dodds

Daughter

I touched a miracle today...
Her name is Love, or Beauty, or Joy—
(It doesn't matter anyway.)

Bright brown eyes looking out, yet hidden;
Gentle, soft smile—lips parted to speak;
(Relaxed; at peace; waiting; away.)

She is my heart—my soul,
Laughing; hoping; reaching;
(Embracing my spirit tenderly.)

Present to me, but apart;
Soothing voice stilled—yet constant.
(Far away, but with me always.)

Settled in quiet repose, she gathers me in;
Basking in afterglow, my heart sings.
....I touched a miracle today.

Joan M. Sherwood

To Those Back Home

How many times I've missed my wife
Her tender touch, her love is my life
My oldest son, my pride and joy
My hope for him, is a field of dreams
My youngest son, I love him so much
I miss him so, a tear in my eye I touch
My little girl, so full of life
I love and miss her, she shines so bright
I love and miss them, so very much
I pray to God, to keep them free of harm's clutch
I'm so proud of them all, if I could touch and kiss
But duty calls, in a distant hostile land
As war and peace, tee-totters in an uncertain breeze
How do I explain, to those I've left behind across the seas
That I really care, I know I've hurt them so much
So young, I hope they understand and are aware
For their freedom, is why this uniform I wear
And hope that one day, this cross, an airman will no longer bear.

Dennis P. Bevenour

By Our Side

The Lord God never leaves us
He's always by our side
Although you may not think so
You're perfect in his eyes
He straightens our paths
And leads us from temptation
He created everything
Every land-every nation
He loves us just the way we are
And catches us when we fall far
He's a rock we can lean on all the time
Because He's always near us-He's always by your side

Kristin Herrick

Child Support

Congratulations you have a child
  He's nine years old
So I'm told

I hired an attorney but, wished I had a jury
  Because now I owe for a child I'll never know

I ask where he's at but, they can't release that
  They can't help me find my child
Because they don't have his file.

I begin my journey to find him in a hurry
  Because he's mine and I don't have much time
Only to find he isn't mine

The courts have taken him since he was two
  because he was severally abused

They say he belongs to me
  But since he was three
They put him in a foster home
  Without asking me

They took my rights before I could fight
  But, yet I'm told I still owe
How is this so?

Brenda Morris

The Raphael Sapphire

There, but not there,
Hidden in the heart of Genesis,
Lies the answer to the greatest mystery of all time;
The identity of the forbidden fruit.
Its name is Dominion;
"I give unto you, Dominion
Over the birds of the heavens,
The beasts of the fields,
And the creatures of the seas."
Conspicuous by its absence,
I do not give you Dominion over man.
Embrace this law,
That thou mayest live
And know mercy unto your third generation.
That never from your own lips
The most haunting question of all time;
"Father, why have you forsaken me?"
The infinite mind is not cruel,
But of necessity is unforgiving
Toward those who ignore its law.

Edmund Ralph Wright

Eagle's Call

Circling
High above I see him

Soaring
Effortlessly on sturdy wings

Calling
Together Brother Eagles and the Bear People.

Feasting,
Before long winter's chill sets in, can begin.

Swimming
Up rivers and streams, the Salmon People return from the sea.

Keith J. Rogers

Success

I am the last hope of man.
His desire, his happiness, his life's work.
His greatest agonies are of my creation.
I am the strife of every soul.
and the sweat on the brow of all who seek me.
Everyone wishes my company
but I greet only the best.
I am known to each by a different name
and I lurk in the shadow of your mind.

Dannielle Heid

The Redman

He sits upon a sandy hill lost within his pain,
His land is gone, nothing for him to gain.
The wind carries his life story,
His people fought: there was no glory.
No one sees his tears or hears his cries.
The white man has hidden them with lies.

The wolf carries a song of sorrow,
Will the Redman's day be the better in the 'morrow?
The eagle the Redman will soon become,
No longer living a life that's numb.
His spirit with the hawk will soar,
This life will be a closed door.

He stands upon that sandy hill,
The white man he vowed to kill.
He takes the steps to end this vow,
"It is over," he yells, "forever and now!"
His anger has been laid to rest,
Sorrow is all that remains in his chest.
The time has come to end this war,
Fighting is over, The Redman is no more.

Dianna Norman

Pure Heart

Sometimes I feel all alone,
Never glad to see someone home.
Because I know the truth of things
and I know how it is and how it's been.
Punctuate clear, all pure heart.
Taking care of what is not
I, a child and she an old lady.
Never sleeping, crying nights.
Holding tight with all my might,
Hoping she'll be all right..
Purest of heart I fight with all my might.

Tulani Gonzalez

Liar

Ugly man struts around pretending.
His life is a farce.
And he plays me for a fool.
liar-

He is an ingenious inventor.
dictating to his faithful foot lickers
"follow me, do as I say, or suffer".
liar-

Dancing around like swans on a lake
They sorrowfully surrender to demeaning demands
Supporting his propaganda loyally
liar-

He savers the power the way a lion does the hunt.
The fabrications are unraveling like a pulled
strand of yarn from a sweater
He no longer orchestrates my every thought.
liar-

Jaclyn S. Taylor

Broken Hearted

The little blonde haired boy stood before me
His little dark haired brother by his side
Trying so hard to look strong and brave
Swallowing quickly as tears they tried to hide

My heart was breaking with the sadness
I witnessed deep within their eyes
Dear God I know not what to tell them
There's so much heartache in their lives

Daddy's gone he doesn't love us
With labored speech the older said
I tried to find some words of comfort
But broken sobs came forth instead

I gently put my arms around them
And closely to me drew each one
This was more than I could bear
Because their "Daddy" was my son

Beatrice Plourde

Sebastian

Sebastian was a rebel in the French Civil War,
His mother was an angel and his father was a whore,
Sebastian never tried to hide his ugly past,
And of all the men to die that year, Sebastian was the last
He held no love in his heart for anyone but himself
Although he fought the civil war he cared for no one else
Many feared Sebastian's wrath his anger knew no bounds
He went to trial for murder and rape, he could not escape the hounds
He stood before the guillotine, the last day of December
I was not there yet I could swear, it seems like I remember
Right before his head came off, he looked me in the eyes
I saw no fear nor a single tear this man was truly wise,
He chose the path he walked in life his destiny misplaced,
He probably could have been a king, oh God what a waste,
This was all a dream my friend and it seemed so strange to me,
But now that its about to end, I think I truly see,
The moral of Sebastian's tale,
will put your mind on pause,
Don't go through this living hell
Being a rebel without a cause

James V. Halliburton Jr.

Self Destruction

Bathe me in affections;
Hold me in your arms;
Kiss me on the mouth;
Save me from the false alarms.
Close my eyes and shut out the sounds
Of the passing afflictions of the world around.
Love me and hate me,
Hurt me, and infatuate me,
Use me, abuse me, waste me away.
This is how you will get me to stay.
Slip inside my dreams and make them all come true.
Shatter all my aspirations, make me want to despise you.
Whisper sweet promises into my ears;
Break them without a second thought;
Laugh at my innocent tears.
Send me boxes of candies and vases of flowers;
Love me and kiss me and hold me for hours.
Pretend to understand;
Say you know how I feel.
Make it seem real.

Angela Gries

New Direction

Full cyclical vacuum
Hovering life's precious exuberance
Just makes me hate the treasury even more.
Once,
Happily,
I sifted temptation hands
Through the boss man's chest
And pulled crisp green from dark.
Oblivious
Oblivious because I did not know how it tainted my hands
And gangrened its wa to my heart.
So I now cleanse myself with pumiced uncertainty
(the very well-stocked junkie that insured my greedy fixes)
I'm searching for the good life
Elsewhere
With soul-fulfilling specs
Which make objects seem closer than they appear.

Kenneth Winton Glide

Thinking of You

Here is a rose that comes from my heart
Hoping that last for you a long, long time.

Within this time, I'll be thinking only of you
And I hope to be in your mind,
Because darling I love you.

Now that I pinned it on you
It is hard to tell you apart.
It looks so beautiful on you
Right beside your heart.

If I miss seeing you one day,
My heart will cry for you.
I'd just like to tell you if I may
If you ever go away,
My soul will be lost for you.

And within this time, I'll be thinking only of you.

and I hope to be in your mind, because darling I love you.

Jesse Govea

A Dead Sleep

Each eve you close your eyes,
hoping you'll wake by morn.
But the mystery of sleep survives,
not to be solved at dawn.
Confusing dreams of the recent past
or maybe the present soon.
Scenes of your life come in a flash,
they can only tell your doom.
You're body's resting, your mind's awake,
always seeming to control.
You shake yourself, make no mistake,
your mind's in a fiction role.
Falling, falling, in a never ending dream,
your death is just below.
It comes to you in a rushing stream,
you're being starts to flow.
A dream is born, a dream can kill,
faces all around.
You're soul is resting, you're mind is filled,
you're body's on the ground.

Kathleen L. Ford

A Separation Of Love

From across the room, I look at you and wonder.
How can anyone separate us from each other.
How can they say that we should not fall in love.
When all I feel is your goodness, instilled in my blood.

How can they tell us what time we should spend.
And how each other should be feeling within.
How can they say that it's just not right.
When you make me aware, of the beauty, in the night.

How can it be, that life brought you to me.
And now everyone thinks I should set you free.
Do they not understand, that time has taken it's toll,
On all that I once cherished and could hold.

How can it be that God built us a love, which is strong,
And now they say it isn't beautiful, but is wrong?
Do they not realize that "He" doesn't give love lightly,
To anyone who would cast it off, ever so slightly.

How can they tell us how to lead our lives,
When their beauty, is seen only with their eyes.
They have forgotten that love, that is kept apart,
Would only bring pain and agony to any man's heart.

Beverly Massingill

The Betrayal

Frustration and confusion all pass my mind
How could she do it when she knew he was mine
She took away my one true love
Took him away flew like a dove
All the words I care to say
They can't escape this mind of gray
I'd like to run just run forever
Escape this anguish ending never
My heart is burning eternal pain
What can a fatal life possibly gain
I hope someday that the right one will come
Oh how I yearn to live again
Without the pain of shame and sin
I'm tired of living this life of ruin
Betrayal, Betrayal the words of my life
I hope this doesn't end with the slit of a knife.

Kristen Seay

Lockeport

The fishing village is so old and quaint,
How I love to walk down by the wharves
And watch the fog roll in.
It nestles 'round the buildings 'til they're quite faint,
It envelopes the ships and their bright colored scarves.
Overhead the loud screech of a sea gull is heard
So lonely, plaintive, and melancholy.
From a distance a foghorn bellows,
"To launch out now is naught but folly."
What's that in the distance? A vision? A saint?
Perhaps 'tis St. Andrew who left all for Jesus,
Come to bless the ships, the sea air so pleases.
The white fire of the sun is seen
Burning away the clouds of dark,
Now the sunlight dances on the waters
Gleams from every hull,
Cheers each lonely gull,
Glistens on each moistened edifice,
Outlines every rocky precipice,
Bids the longing soul, "Embark!"

Beverly A. Johnson

Reflections

Click click goes the camera... I see all your lovely souls and how I miss you, so, deeply and for so many different reasons.

Click click... Season to season, old and new enter into my life.

Click click... How fortunate am I? My memory goes back to all the various rooms we all have shared. All I can say to myself, "What great fortunes have been bestowed on me. What more do I want out of life"?

Click click... I stand here at the crossroads. We all stand here at the crossroads together. Where do we go from here?

Click click...

Katherine Anne Lewis

To My Friend

How long does friendship last? Forever I hope.
How long do you keep a friend? Eternity I hope.
How far can you carry a friend? To the end I hope.
Is your friendship just in your eyes,
Or do you carry your friends in your mind.
My friends go wherever I go.
The time I spend being a friend is everlasting,
The time I am kept as a friend is up to you my friend.
I do not forget my friends, my friends forget me.
To go away and leave a friend is only in your eyes,
To go away and keep a friend, is to keep them in your mind.
Flowers, Kisses, Making Love is not what makes a friend,
Its the thought of just being a friend, that makes a friend.

Judy Wright

Eyes

Emerald green, brilliant blue, and brown
  Hazel, grey, and midnight black
Some with specks of brown and some with gold
  Ones that have no color yet are still beautiful
Some full of passion and love
  Some clouded over with pain
Some downcast with shame and despair
  And a few burning with hate
Eyes: they are the windows to your soul
  So don't shutter them, always keep them open!

Kaitlin Schwartzel

"Shoe"

I'm soooooo sick and tired of hearing about it
how your size seven just doesn't seem to fit
tangled with who knows what
gnawed on by the family's mutt
collecting dust on your tongue and blue sole
hiding in a closet next to skates that can't roll
you used to win every race
but nowadays that sure ain't the case.
taken to the nearest junk yard
yeah, you think you've had it so hard
don't tell me about your childhood
I'd much rather be the right if I could
man I've bathed in the muddiest puddles
ached real bad on the way back to huddles
I've been scarred for life by permanent markers
shoved into the smelliest gym lockers
my laces are untied and frayed
the once bright colors are starting to fade
I was sold at a yard sale for half of a dime
so who do you think has had a rougher time.

Chris Miller

Cutting

A dandelion swayed
Humming to herself.
She stretched her leaves in the October sunshine
Teasing the sweet crisp air.
Dreamily, she closed her eyes
Remembering the smell of summer grass.
She was naive
Born long after the last frost had melted into dewy teardrops.

A small hand reached out in wonder and innocent desire
And plucked her slender stem.
She had been asleep, sunning herself.

Jessica Nusbaum

My Mother Nature Feelings

I am a dove fluttering in the snow.
I am an eagle soaring high and wide.

I am a running river in the Spring run-off.
I am a raindrop slowly falling down.

I am a cougar hunting for its prey.
I am a horse running wild and free.

I am a rock hard, round, and smooth.
I am a soft white snowflake on the ground.

I am a wolf howling for the call.
I am a coyote calling at the moon.

I am a mountain higher than the others.
I am a hill not higher than a bump.

I am a desert, hot and dry.
I am a prairie rolling lakes of green grass.

I am a lion in a pride of many.
I am a dog searching for a friend.

I am a thunderstorm pounding down rain.
I am a drum sounding the beat.

I am an owl sitting on my perch.
I am an Indian protecting my tribe.

Janelle George

Pain

Bewilderment! Anger! Hurt! Frustration! Overwhelming sadness! I am consumed with grief. A part of me has shriveled and died, died from loneliness and grief. What happened to the man I met all those months ago? The beautiful letters he left for me to read. Did they mean nothing to him, were they all make-believe? Such confusion! How could he forget everything he wrote, everything he said? How can you forget love, how can he? I'm so cold, so lost so lonely. Do I not deserve to be loved, to be able to love? The man says he doesn't know what he wants. Why? What do I do now? Guilt! Such an ugly word. I have so much for my children. What have I done to them? I took them away from all they loved and held dear for "love." It was supposed to be a new start, a new beginning, for them, for us, for the man but something has gone awry. What went wrong? So tired, so tired of always being wrong of always failing myself, my children. So much pain, so much suffering. The pain is consuming me. I need to heal, to feel joy, to feel happiness again. I want the man to heal with me, beside me. Man...I love you.

Kathleen Taylor

Thoughts of a Mourning

Somewhere in the lost eyes of memories
I am drifting into nothing
The stare is never forgotten
Not for as long as I'll live
I remember the days when we sat by the fires
In the dead of winter
The land was silent will bleakness
Calm, serene, quiet.
Peaceful is the rain of leaves that may fall
Your empire no longer stands so tall...
In the mazes, I will search for destruction
In your gardens, I will grieve
Bereavement is upon us;
Now we shall weep.
When they're here, we take their presence for granted
When they're gone, we're encumbered by sadness
Veils cover the lines on the roads to nowhere
Tempestuous winds moan and whimper...

Blade Cody

Potentitude

When the coast is clear across this still morning door,
  I am here.
In the funk of your body's bedly smells.
In the film of oil and salt on your face
  which makes you feel pretty when you wake up.
In the lattice work of your folds,
  when others cannot see your sprawl.

You're so happily alone that you flatulate into
  your own hand.
Yet I too there am caught.
With you, in you, in the unity of your, yes,
  perverse sickness, too normal to interest your peers.
In the naive, self-preserving creatureliness
  which makes you mine,
is the all of my potential.

Despite rampant oblivion
  interrupted briefly
A handful of times throughout the years.
When the coast is clear
  it is I who Am your solitude.

Christa Mogan

"I Am Lonely 2 - I Know"

I am lonely: When the sun comes up in the morning
I am lonely: When, I can't see your face or your smile
I am lonely: When we are not together
I am lonely: Most when I can't touch you in every way
I am lonely: For you day and night
I am lonely: For a love that's true and most of all pure
I am lonely: For a love that's for me today
I am lonely: 2 for you, I love you, I am lonely
I am lonely: More than ever before, for you
I am lonely: I will be lonely forever more, without you

I know: Your love should be with me always
I know: "2" you are lonely for me "2"
I know: I will be lonely until I get you back into my arms
I know: You are what I need in my life always
I know: We must keep the faith and the feeling of love
I know: My love for you just won't go away
I know: God knows we are lonely 2. I know
I know: Love brought us together, and love will bring us back
I know: Love is a key of everlasting life
I know: I love you now and forever more, and ever more.

Johnson D. A. Sr.

In My Dreams

In my dreams,
I am not who I seem.
In my dreams,
I have changed.
In my dreams,
I am different.
In my dreams,
I am free.
In my dreams,
There is peace,
The world is peaceful.
In my dreams,
I am one with the earth,
I am one with the true keepers of the earth.
In my dreams,
man has changed.

Jessica Irene Long

A Father's Words Left Behind

Don't stand at my grave and weep—for I am at peace
I am with the Lord my God now that I am deceased.

Don't mourn my death because I am no longer in pain
I'm finally in comfort now that I'm in God's domain.

Don't think of me as gone because I am watching you today
I see you when you sleep at night-when you wake and when you pray.

Don't pray for me at that time because I am just fine so far
When you gaze at night into the clear blue sky
I'm your own sparkling star.

Don't let my death interfere with plans you have for your life
I didn't mean to ever hurt you or cause you any strife.

Don't stop moving forward—you can definitely survive
Don't think of me as dead but remember be alive.

You're still daddy's little girls and I hold you close to my heart
Even though I can't be there our souls will never part.

I am with your mother now for we are finally reunited
don't mourn this day-but celebrate
for we are peacefully delighted.

Christine Coleman

Missing You

A dawn of another day,
I awaken as I slept,
Alone

I picture your face
In a moment of sharing:
The depth of your eyes,
The slight parting of your lips,
The shadow of your soul
Joining with mine.

Background noise destroys my image.
Once again I'm at the kitchen table
Staring at printed words on a page
Lonely

When will we be at peace in each others arms again?
Sharing our love
through glimpses and touches.

When can I stop missing you
And hold you close
Heart to heart,
Soul to Soul?

Deborah Tassinari

"Four Days Of Rain And The Wing"

A steady downpour from the skies above, keeps falling,
I can hear the noisy birds, from tree to tree calling.

How sad to watch and see them search for dry shelter,
They fly in flock and in frenzy, a helter and skelter.

I watch them closely from my window, what a pitiful sight,
To see those water-soaked feathered-friends in their troublesome plight.

They land here and land there, looking for something to nourish,
I see nothing in sight but wetness, with which they cannot flourish.

Two large handful of bread bits, to them, I quickly throw,
They swarm down instantly to feed, the sparrow, strange ones and the crow.

Now with full bellies, maybe the rest they could bear,
And as I look around, I see no shelter for them to share.

With the trees so heavily drenched, how could they possibly find,
Some branches or clumps of leaves that they could hide behind.

I know, the hot sun will break through, if my prayers are heard,
Then these poor shivering soaked creatures, can once again be birds.

Francis P. Piccola

Ode To The Road

Traveling by car, mile after mile,
I can not do it with a smile!

Speed and large trucks don't seem to mix,
Miniature cars go by with a whisk.

The enjoyment comes through in the landscape
I spy,
While the sunshine burst forth out of the sky.

Pit stops are many and food needed too,
Grumpy the words espoused for the time lost,
by you.

What to eat, you asked for the hundredth time,
Make up your mind, it isn't a crime.

New friends we meet on our travels so long,
Joys to carry home with love and song.

When our destination has finally been found,
How happy am I, my feet on the ground.

Judy Christman Cottle

The Lake Is Frozen

The lake is frozen now.
I can still remember the days of summer
when the sun cast its warmth upon it;
the little waves lapped at the sandy shore;
the clouds drifted lazily across the sky;
the leaves rustled softly in the trees over my head.
Days were peaceful;
days were carefree;
days were warm.
Now the shores are hidden under a crust of snow;
the trees point barren branches toward an empty sky;
and the lake is frozen.

John B. Cowgill

For Some Reason

I can't believe I never told you,
I can't believe I never said;
What burned and ached in my heart,
What was hidden in every letter you read.
I dreamed and screamed when I was alone.
I cried and nearly died and now you are gone.
But what you really meant to me
Is what I can't believe.
And the fact that you wouldn't either
Made me really grieve.
I cared for and loved you when we were alone.
I hated and despised you once you were gone.
And even now I can't believe
That I have never said-
What I will never be able to say,
But it's written in every letter you've read.

Christa Midcap

Solitary

I sit here by myself, my thoughts are dull and few,
I can't figure out who I am, or what I should do,
Times have changed, friends have gone, yet I'm still here,
It's just me with my hopeless dreams, and my constant fear,
I sit here by myself, full of self-pity and sorrow,
I can't figure where I went wrong or if there will be a tomorrow,
Times have changed, enemies have gone, yet I'm still here,
It's just me with my wandering eyes, which are now filled with tears

Joseph Myers

"Special People"

The tears are falling in this dark, gloomy place.
I can't stop them from running down my face.
I wanna be free from this prison I'm in, and I can't seem to leave, its too dim.
The pain and misery are too much to bare, the people we mostly what I fear. If there was a place to go, I know I would do so. But the problems of life that are oh so common just seem to stay with me, and their not stoppin'.
But I won't give up hope or kill my dreams, cause there's something beautiful waiting for me.
There has to be, and I know there is I just don't know what or when. But when the time comes, it's gonna be nice, and I'm gonna look back and say, "the pain and misery that I once had, now are gone away, and I deserve the beautiful treasures that I have today. Cause I'm special, and the most important thing to me, and I'm never gonna be the way I used to be."

Deborah E. Powell

Climbing the Walls

While searching those puzzling eyes,
I catch a glimpse
Of something familiar about them.
But it is so vague - I cannot recall
The recognition which I see.
A longing for companionship
Is hidden behind those walls
Which keep me out.
I can't help but wonder -
Who were the builders of those walls?
Possibly the desire to hide feelings of fear and guilt -
Or the hope that someone cares enough
To climb the steep walls with a willing heart
And conquer the withstanding structure with love and friendship!
A desire grows deep inside my heart -
The desire to enter into the world behind the wall.
The eyes come to life.
They begin to twinkle like stars.
Now I realize that I have found -
A lost friend.

Janene C. Larsen

No Sleep Tonight

Hi, Lord! It's late and I can't sleep.
I close my eyes to count the sheep,
But all too soon my mind's off track-
And I'm still lying here on my back -
Stare at the ceiling, then toss and turn
Next time it's offered, the coffee I'll spurn.
Now up I get to check the "John" -
Oh, hurry up, Lord, bring the dawn! -
Shut my eyes, let sleep prevail,
And off to dream land let me sail.
It's sleepy time, and half past "Late,"
Still I lie in a wide awake state.
I listen to all the night time sounds -
That in my mind, all make the rounds.
The quiet sound as "Hubby" snores -
Which in my mind resounds the more.
The cats that run across my roof,
That sound like elephant on giant hoof.
The night bird calls as dawn draws near,
No sleep tonight, my dear, my dear.

Deanna J. Schelske

Closer Than A Heartbeat

I am so lonely for myself
I could cry a million stars
But I shall wake up from this dream
And realize I am the star I cry
For sinners and saints are golden girls and boys
Without self love there is no poise
And sacred is a meaningless phrase
Without self love there is no raise
In consciousness as victim and victimizer
Are one and the same
When you play the game
Of me versus you
Fear not, the angels are preparing
A bundle of joy
And even my toes are smiling
As I walk across the planets
Like they are pebbles in a brook
Closer than a heartbeat

Jackie Starr

Always A Child

As an infant I found myself helpless and small,
I could move and cry, but that's about all.
Though unknown to me my mind and body were growing,
Through the love and care my parents were showing.

Then came my toddler days, when I could finally walk.
I could run, play, and even try to talk.
Independence is what I thought I had,
But, when in trouble, I would run to mom and dad.

Then came the milestone of becoming a teen.
I thought all life had to offer I had already seen.
I didn't think I needed help from anyone.
The job of my parents was complete and well done.

Now I am an adult with children of my own,
Who are dependent today, but will soon be grown.
I want them to experience the childhood I had,
So I am constantly seeking help from mom and dad.

I sometimes apologize for not doing it all on my own,
But they have a unique way of making their love known.
They explain that their child I will always be,
Because I could NEVER outgrow the family tree.

Debra L. Yager

Elucidate

As I watched him sleeping
I could not help but fall in love
With the peacefulness that pervaded his face

I became forgetful of the thoughts, maybe misgivings,
Of what I have feared would keep us in isolation
Of the possibilities that may exist

And, for that moment,
I felt the tranquility
That I have so consistently desired and sought
Amidst this storm of emotions full of question and uncertainty

I long to escape to a world
Where I would be sheltered from the reality that I cannot change

...A place where I could drop my defenses and be secure
In the comfort that I felt during that single fleeting moment;
A place where I could grasp a vision of the outcome

...But the outcome
Can only beckon me
To reach for it with the faith of my heart

And to face the consequences,
Or to bask in the glory of its reward

Kristi Krautwurst

Blue Eyes

I could see it in her blue eyes.
  I could see it in the way she cries.
We were taken away faster and faster,
  and were beaten and tortured by our master.
They kept our possessions, all that we had,
  which made her, not upset, but mad.
We were sent in two lines to face our doom,
  the weaker were sent into a gas-filled room.
We walked to see where fate would take us,
  we learned and saw that many would hate us.
The bodies were piled clear up to the sky,
  and many were asking, "Why, Lord, why?"
We lived our lives united until,
  they took her away and gave her a pill.
No one could see through their many lies,
  but I could see pain in her blue eyes.

Jennifer Ford

Free And Strong

I proclaim my freedom to be a strong woman.
I don't use pseudonyms; I wear my name proudly.
Free and Strong.
I don't function as a cyborg; I have independent thought
and purpose.
Free and strong.
I don't wander this land aimlessly; I have a nisus to succeed.
Free and strong.
As I revel in the quietude of my inner self, I am proud, for the
cauldron of my soul never boils over.
I proclaim my freedom to be a strong woman, with a thirst for life
that can never be quenched.
Free and strong.

Denise Curry

We Are Not Alone

The darkness of Depression engulfs, encompasses me.
I fall deeply into the void.
If only I were a chrysalis,
Could spread my wings like a butterfly and float
Up toward the sun, toward hope.
But I am wingless, a creature grounded.
Unless the heart has wings...
But I have ears finely tuned
And from somewhere nearby I hear a tune,
No, a song,
Strong, valid, uprising
From the cocoon of my home, a song completely
My own! Then,
A thousand songs, voices singing in unison
"We Are Not Alone".
The song is mine, yet shared, and finally known!
Depression is not a silent illness.
If you listen carefully, can you hear us crying?
Come closer still, hear how hard we are trying
To blend into the community with you...

Christina M. Johanneck

Untitled

You ask me what I am afraid of:
I fear playing the fool -
For I do that often
I fear staying the fool -
For that is what I see before me.

You ask me what I am holding back:
I hesitate to bare my soul -
For I cannot trust others
I hesitate to become what I know you need -
For all I see in myself is a smiling idiot.

You ask what in me feels wrong:
But I feel nothing - and Nothing is the problem
And I could not tell you anyway -
I can say only Nothing
And I would ask for help -
But then others would see my incompetence.

So I hold back, because I see myself
Smiling and hiding.
And dying inside, hurting.
AND I WILL NOT PLAY THE FOOL.

Allyson L. Williams

Ballerina Of Destruction

I stand at the window watching.
I feel a combination of fear and awe.
Fear that she will turn my way and see me.
But so much awe that I can not tear myself away.

She is like a magnet
Drawing my attention to her.
In her awesome destruction
She is almost beautiful.

Her ballet demonstrates her gracefulness
She moves with little effort.
Her toe barely touches the ground
As she twirls and spins clockwise.

She bows and dips, embracing everything in her path.
Then casts it all aside as if she no longer needs it.

If she didn't perform for you, you don't know her.
If she danced your way, you learned to hate her performance.

I still stand in awe at her beauty
As well as her destruction.
She doesn't see me staring;
And I watch her glide pass and beyond.

Diane Greer

Little Bird Of Love

As the sun shines down on my little spread wings
I feel all its warmth which reminds me of things.

The touch of your hand so gentle, calm and kind
Caressing - soothing spirit, peace and tranquility come to mind.

The bright heated sunrays represent your precious smile
Enlightening my world each time warming my heart all the while.

As I soar above the trees landing briefly to look below
The beautiful miracles of nature, tiny green clover and the river flow

And like the wind under my wings I feel strongly about our love,
Supporting and lifting me up so I can soar high in the sky above.

One little bird among many but a greater love you'll never know;
And with each passing day my love only strengthens and grows.

I may be a wee little bird but let me lift you as your love has lifted me;
Forever to fly through this world and beyond loving you unconditional
and whole heartily.

Jennifer DeLann Beller

All the Time

The way you look at me,
I feel it all the time.
The way you hold me,
I need it all the time.
The way you kiss me,
I love it all the time.
When I'm with you there is a smile
on my face,
The void in my heart you've seemed to replace.
I see your figure in the clouds,
I see it all the time.
I only wish you were mine,
Mine and no one else's,
All the time.

Chris Day

Being Alone In My Room

When I'm alone in my room
I feel like I'm away
From the rest of the world -
The land, the trees, and the bay.

When I'm tired I go to my room
Because I feel the world is just too noisy
But when I step inside my room I feel like
I've traveled someplace far away like Boise!

When I'm mad I go to my room
My eyes turn fiery red
But when I get inside my room I calm down
Lying atop my comfy bed.

I don't like my room when I'm energetic
It's just not a very good place
To be running and jumping around
(There's just not enough space).

I also don't like to be in my room
That's when I'm happy and gay
But then I open my door and
Run outside and play!

Kedar Kanitkar

Laughing On The Rock

Laughing on the rocky mountainside
I felt like a newborn baby
It was as if I was born into a world of beauty
It was the kind of beauty you couldn't buy or sell
I stood on the highest rock I could find
The higher I was, the closer to God I felt
Laughing on the rocky mountainside
I wondered how the mountain could stand so firm
No matter who or what wanted to tear down the mountain, the mountain
stood strong
It was as if God was holding it near the heart of heaven
It was that special way that God holds all of the children
Laughing on the rocky mountainside
I could see a stream that was as perfect as a sunrise on a summer dawn
The stream was so pure
It seemed as though the water was a stream of holy water
Laughing on the rocky mountainside
I heard the sweetest, most comforting sounds
Laughing on the rocky mountainside
A bit of peace entered my mind and heart

Kirsten Ellis

Separated

Is this true or tale? Are you gone or are you real? I feel the scream for help, but don't know where it's coming from. Two close friends are now separated by the darkness between life and death. Two worlds that will never meet.

My heart does not stop narrow. The world becomes colder and lonelier, but the light of heaven shines the warmth of your heart down on me. I wish for your death to become the far future instead of the distant past. No fear of death fills me, like an old war novelty. But I still wonder how it feels to look down from heaven at the people who still grieve for you. Perhaps, they are the ones that love you most. Or, perhaps, they are the ones that don't realize where you are now. They remember you as your last days imprisoned you with fear. Your freedom of the complications of life are what they have yet to realize. Some only saw your outside. But some also new your inside. I am one that understood you. Never forget. The best friend that I remember may be gone. The memories may now be the distant past that can never reoccur. But one thing that will never leave me...

Your spirit and your love. One day, I will see you again.

Jennifer Cowan

The Bluebird

When I was just a child of four
I gazed with envy through the door
At older kids en route to school,
Who played fun games and swam the pool.
But — once in school — when I reached twelve,
My dream became that I might delve
Into high school, where there unfurls
The world of cars and sports and girls.
Alas! In high school I was shy —
Afraid to date, or even try.
My college days were bittersweet,
Where fun and knowledge did compete;
I yearned to find my special niche —
Career and marriage — maybe rich!
Career success was not my course;
My marriage ended in divorce.
Through spring, then summer, as fall concludes,
Bluebird of happiness eludes
My hopeful grasp; oh, do you nest
In winter's chill, or heaven's rest?

Charles N. Hooper Sr.

Sifted Sand

On the rocks, beneath the sand,
I feel the warm touch of your hand.
The midnight sky beneath the stars,
there's no other love quite like ours.

The ocean air given off the waves,
I sit and count the passing days.
As sea gulls fly overhead,
washed up on the shore, all the fish are dead.

As sea shells lay upon sifted sand,
there's no other one who really can,
love me for what I am,
except for myself, and that I can...

Cherie Bochenek

My Lost Love

I am here. He is there. The love of my life
I had to spare. Only for her, her love
not fare. For she is his only care.
I cry and wondered why not me, for he
is my only I wish he could see.
I loved once, I cry twice, for his
love is worth any price. I begged and
pleaded then let it go, but his love
he did not show. I never knew how
he thought, I only wish his heart could talk!
You only love once, but I cry twice. why does this feel
like a stabbing knife? If my heart could talk
it would say, I wish my love would come back someday.
The pain of my life I will bare but, did he ever care?

Carla Harvey

Untitled

On the factory walls, stacked on their
sides, lie the conformists, boxed and
awaiting shipment to the U.S.

Bradford Carlson Locklear

To My Daughter Paula

Paula, here's a poem for you, I hope it turns out right.
I haven't written one for years, but will try with all my might.

I did enjoy the time we spent alone this summer night, looking
through my great big trunk, and laughing at the sight of
You claiming all the things I've gathered year by year,
because you feel they should be yours, and want to keep them near.

I hope you will enjoy yourself someday when I am gone, as you get
together with Your child and pass the memories on.

Kathleen M. Dale

I Took A Step Backward Today...

I took a step backward today...
I hear your quiet breathing
Feel the warm glow of sunrise.
A dove coos, and the sparrows chirp

I took a step backward today...
Along the garden path, through the woods
to the orchard.
A blue jay screams with joy

Along the stone wall
the sun warms our backs.
Our fingers touch.

Around the orchard, circling back
the sun now warms our faces.
We watch a hawk in flight; our spirits soar!

A dark cloud passes over,
enveloping us in its chill.
The cloud has passed, and I am alone

Now, I must step forward...
to a life filled with changes.

Dorothy M. Clauss

"Miracles Above"

I felt so cold and empty, and I wanted life no more.
I hoped that death would walk with me when I stepped out the door.
Not being worth his company, alone I pushed ahead
Into the dark world waiting that had pulled me from my bed.

I thought that even mercy stayed away from that black place
When over me it just appeared, to cover me in grace.
Was I surprised when I glanced up and something stirred in me.
I looked again, then froze in awe, at what my eyes could see.

The moon in silver splendor watched the dancing stars at play.
The sun in golden glory woke and chased them all away.
The clouds in bright white wonder crawled across the blushing sky.
The day in brilliant blue reached out to wave the night good-bye.

I saw these things behave in ways I knew they couldn't do.
I wasn't sure what caused the change that altered all my view.
Was heart or soul or spirit moved to place into my mind
Those images that on their own my thoughts would never find?

I'm still not sure which part of me was touched by joy so rare.
I only know my life transformed by God, who put it there.
Perhaps He kept me on this earth protected by His love
So I could be a witness to His miracles above.

Diane Skvorc

I Can't Fall Asleep

I've laid here for hours I can't fall asleep
I keep hearing every spider, cricket, and mouse as they creep

I hear the faucet each little drip
I hear the people upstairs each toe and each tip

I've tried counting sheep, pigs, and cars
I've tried counting elephants, giraffes, and stars

I pulled the blankets and pillow up over my head
I even put my head at the other end of the bed

I turned on some music relaxing and soothing
Reminds me of some years that I'm losing

I move to the couch and lay down with a book
Then I smell food someone is starting to cook

I turn on the television that always works
I start to doze and the coffee pot perks

Up and at 'em some kind of night
Up comes the sun it's getting light

I get to the office I put down my head
I fall asleep like I should have when I was in bed

Dennis Michael Craft

Living On

I've lost a special person - so very dear to me.
I know it's only natural and death must surely be.
I wonder why we couldn't of had - just a little longer,
to share our lives, gather thoughts, and make the bonds stronger.
I ask myself; 'who do I morn for?'
Me, for I only wanted to know him more.
I wanted my children to grow like him, and him to watch and see.
I wanted to share our memories with him, a part of "we".
I know I won't hear him speak or see his friendly smile.
I shall often think of him and linger for a while.
So memories and loving thoughts will keep loved ones living on
I shall keep him in my heart and his grandchildren will be his song.

Donna S. Cooper

A Simple Pair Of Shoes

I danced awhile and laughed awhile in someone else's shoes.
I know not where that person lived, I know not even whose.
But all the while, I felt compelled by some nostalgic force,
to actually relive their past, their existence to endorse.

I once was told, when I was young, an aura does abide
in shoes once worn by someone else whose past has lived and died.
Now I find, I feel it's true, and my own thoughts peruse
The history and long lost past in a simple pair of shoes.

The cut, the style, the way they fit says so much indeed,
About the times, the way folks lived, their hopes and fears and needs.
But what of them? What of their life? What pathway did they choose?
Who would have thought I'd wonder at a simple pair of shoes?

I'll never know the answers to those questions most pronounced.
I only know my life is changed by the aura that surrounds
Those artifacts of life least noticed but most widely used.
A step back into time I took in a simple pair of shoes.

Connie P. Brinkley

Ageless

Oh, how ageless are our thoughts.
Retaining the beauty that they once brought.
It doesn't matter if we're three or eighty-three,
Our thoughts again can make us feel and see
The same excitement of our many firsts,
The innocence we had and of which we now thirst.
Isn't it grand that inside our heads,
The hunger for youth can be eternally fed?

Jackie Smith-Thrasher

Shadow

I see the world as a shadow of everything.
I know that sense of death in a grave,
I feel the sun growing hotter and hotter,
I hear everyone's screams for help, but yet that is not enough.
I am that burning match that starts a fire
I hear that bird, do I care?
Does it care about me, I feel for it.
I am that sky above me,
I am that ground below me,
I hear the water around my boat
I see those rocks, do they see me.
I see that tree, I am that leaf.
I hear that twig snap!
I feel its pain.
I am on top of the mountain
I feel that snow, it's white, but what happens when it melts!
I know why the world spins.
I'm the shadow that no one sees.
I hear you, I feel you, I see you, I am you.
I am a great celebration!

Craig Nicholas Bennett

Ain't No Thang

As I sit in the dark
I listen to that music
They say "now I gotta wet "cha"
I just lay there on my back.

Some more I listen, but do I really?
They say "ain't nothin' wrong with slangin ' rock"
But hey, them lyrics don't effect me
Cause words is just words, I ain't no statistic for you to mock

And here goes something you don't know
I think, I breathe, I can die just like you
Maybe I know just a little more than I show
'Cause I ain't three, no monkey see monkey do

As I lay here on my back
My mama's tears just hit me on the cheek
I know I should a moved when I heard that nine crack
Now I just lay here with this lead in my spine

Aja Vasquez

Vivo - I Live

Vivo - I live.
I live in a room that holds many sounds of laughter and tears of joys and sorrows that once was my life. Vivo.
I live in a house where ends never meet, and silence is only a word. Vivo.
I live in a city that fills daily with the words of cold minds and rash hearts. Vivo.
I live in a state that is big, but filled with little dreams of wise fools. Vivo.
I live in a country that harbors the minds of the fortunate and drowns the helpless kittens. Vivo.
I live on a continent where clouds can be bribed to lose their silver lining. Vivo.
I live on a planet where green paper rules the people and the people know not the value of lives. Vivo.
I live in a solar system that is charted by ways of numbers and not by sight. Vivo.
I live in a galaxy that is ignorant of it's surroundings and place in time. Vivo.
I live in a universe that is a reflection in a mirror of what it wants itself to look like, a happy place. Vivo.
Now the mirror is broken.
Vivo - I live.

Brandy Ashcraft

Untitled

I see you so often,
I look into your eyes,
They ask me so many questions.
When am I going? Where will I go?
Will it be a long journey?
Will I hurt any more?

Look into my eyes and I will tell you what I know,
soon you will leave,
you will go to a safe place,
it is but a short trip,
you will feel no pain.

I wish you God's speed, remember me well,
I will see you again.

Joan H. Moses

Untitled

The first rays of sunlight break the darkness of the sky
I look towards the Heavens and tears form in my eyes
A cold breeze blows behind me and a chill runs down my spine
But for some reason all I feel is the sun shining in my eyes
I look at the valley below and smile at the beauty of the scene
Tears fall from my eyes as I walk alongside a beautiful crystal stream
A simple familiar tune strikes a sweet chord and any soul it seems to call
I follow the sound and soon I've found a magnificent waterfall
Orange and red color the sky is the suns last rays descend
I gaze in wonder at he beauty that brings me peace within
The day is almost finished, and as I leave one again I feel the sorrow
I say good-bye for the day knowing I'll return tomorrow
Knowing that one day soon we'll once again embrace
Fills my heart with happiness as I leave your memories in this place.

Adrian M. Neal

Philosophical Debate With The Cat

Pondering Nothing and Everything, upon the couch I sat
I looked at the cat and asked, "Hey, what is that...?"
"What is what?", asked the cat, and again I asked
"That-...Which-Everything-Is?"
"And what is Everything-That-Is?", inquired the cat
"Nothing," I replied
and to that says the cat...
"Well if Nothing is Everything...and Everything is that,
then which that is it, Man, this that...or that?"

"Alright Already! Enough!", I said
"We've both been fed, cat, let's off to bed
all of these that have gone to my head!!"
to which cat replied
in perfect B-flat

"meow"
and that...
...was that.

Jason E. Hill

Ageless Beauty

Rain is perfume for an elegant mistress.
She applies it sparingly yet,
Its freshness lingers for days.
The sweet, delicious aroma disguises any foul stench.
And draws any man, young or old, to her beauty.
When the fragrance is gone and all hope seems lost,
Once more the mist is sprayed onto her aging skin
To be made young again.

Autumn Cossi

Two Faced Heart

I can't understand this two faced heart of mine
I love, but love with hate.
I am a liar and a bigot one minute,
the next a patriot to all man kind.
Who am I? I do not know.
I look up to see hopes and dreams,
but look down to find nothing but my failures.
I can't understand this two faced heart of mine.
Am I being punished? I do not know.
God let's me feel,
but feel only hurt and pain.
The hands of time are closing on me.
What to do? I may never know.
I try to speak,
but the air chokes me when I try to speak against
what I truly believe.
But ultimately,
I know I will be left here standing by myself,
figuring out the game of life.

Andrea Vu-Nguyen

Alison

I love you babe your not around to hold.
I love you baby yours arms are cold.
I long to squeeze you and hold you tight
I always need to hold you in my arms at night.
That may not be the case right now.
But I'll always hold you in my arms some way somehow.
Even if its in my dreams my love and space precludes our touch
I will hug and kiss and love you ever so much.
I know you stand among the clouds and look down upon us here.
And even with all that space we feel that you are near.
I hold my hand up to the sky and feel your hand in mine.
And we will walk thru heaven gate together in another time.
I know that time will come to pass when you and I will join.
But till that time you and I will be hands across the sky.
I peered outside and saw two clouds who touched so gently.
And saw you and I upon the beach sharing so lovingly.
We shared our hearts, our souls, our dreams.
And also our angers, our fears, our screams,
I am going to miss your earthly being babe, And am feeling sad and blue.
But I know you will hold my hand, And I love you thru and thru.

Edward J. Morrissey

"Til Death Do Us Part"

I love you now
I loved you then
I just can't understand how a love like ours could ever end

I search my heart and soul for a reason
but life has many changes, just like the seasons

Some changes are for the better
but you gave me no clues, not even a letter

The one thing that will never change
is the love I feel for you, even though you and I are apart.

One can never replace you in my heart
for that bond we had, can never tear us apart.

You and I grew as friends and then lovers
our friendship grew into love, which I'll
never find with any other.

We are the living, not the dead,
so get this through your head, "My love for you will never end."

With all my heart and soul,
I just can't seem to let you go.

With all my heart and soul,
I just can't and don't ever want to say, "Good-bye".

Jacqueline Paz

Please Listen

Please listen to me, before I walk away,
I may have something of interest to say.
I intently listen to all the stories you tell,
And, through these, I feel that I know you quite well.

PLEASE, listen to me, I desire communication,
Just a little kindness, with a touch of compassion.
LISTEN, PLEASE LISTEN!!!
And hear what I have to say,
To dominate conversation is simply not my way.

PLEASE LISTEN TO ME!
I'm not requesting much of your time,
It's just that your attention is needed, from time to time.
when my heart becomes heavy burdened, and I face distress,
A strong shoulder to cry on, brings me a little rest.
And, when I am bubbling with joyful gaiety,
Someone to share thoughts with, fills me full of ecstasy.

Please listen to me, that is all I ask,
I don't think that is such a tre-mendous task.
Besides, you may just discover, some similarity,
In our psychological, intellectual, or emotional, reality.

Darlene Schnackenberg

The Empty Place

For anyone who has lost a loved one.

Whenever I see that Empty Place,
I miss that smiling, happy face.
I miss the warmth that flowed from there,
the laughter and joy from one who cared.
Though these things all have fled,
Memories - beautiful memories - linger on.

Thoughts of the one I loved bring me
both deep joy and searing pain.
Amidst all these commingled feelings,
Memories - bittersweet memories - still remain.

The suffering, pain, and all
have disappeared behind a wall;
a wall of love from God to man;
a place that's part of His holy plan.
Through life that brings not an end, but change,
Memories - precious memories - linger on.

On my face, I know there is a trace
of sadness caused by the Empty Place.
Through lonely days and watchful nights,
Memories - sweet memories - forever burn bright.

Doris H. Torosian

Until You

I never listened to the sounds of a rushing stream...until you.
I never would allow myself the chance to dream...until you.
I never heard the beautiful music of a songbird...until you.
Poetry was nothing more than pages of words...until you.

Until you, there was no heaven, only hell.
Until you, myself I did not know so well,
Until you.

The days meant so little, nothing but time...until you.
The brilliant sun would set on eyes so blind...until you.
The waves crashed against a body that was a mere shell...until you.
My life, it seemed, was spent in hell...until you.

Until you, days and nights seemed to blend.
Until you, my old wounds would not mend,
Until you.

But now you are gone, and all seems lost.
My broken heart is the most expensive cost,
When it comes to you.

Corrina Fisher

The Pawn

Today because poverty had me in a choke-hold,
I pawned my mother's wedding ring.
A ring I had asked for 2 weeks earlier because she said she was throwing it out.
Finally after 20 years she was tossing the memory
of a bad marriage, a terrible husband, and an even worse father.
As the product of what that ring first symbolized
I took it; saving it from the trash thinking this was my parents
after the bar they met in and before they hated each other;
A circle of love with no beginning, no end.
But that's not quite right because here is where the ring's bent,
and there the diamond has lost its sparkle.
Mom was right, about the man then and the ring now,
It's not worth keeping.
So with my pocket full of memories, a backward glance or two,
I hauled what was left of my parent's marriage to the pawnbroker.
And after 6 years of marriage,
2 kids, 1 divorce,
and 20 years apart,
that marriage was worth 35 bucks.

Ashley P. Finley

My Fair Fruit

I planted a garden so fair and so fine
I planted hatefulness for selfish design
I watered it daily, I trimmed back the shade
I sang it my love songs in the heat of the day.

The ground was so fertile, it grew healthy and strong
"My beautiful hatefulness, you'll do me no wrong.
Oh, when I display you showing what I have grown
I will be envied with you who I've sown."

"Yes, you are ready, the harvest is now
My beautiful hatefulness, my craved upon crown.
I'll taste you my workmanship, you'll be wonderfully sweet
Satisfactory meal, you'll be my good treat."

"But oh, you taste bitter, no bliss but shear pain
My dear perfect hatefulness, you were planted for gain.
My hands, they have withered; my lips, they are cold
I thought you would save me, you've become my fool's gold."

Sown in anticipation with magnificent dreams
I thought I'd be honored, I deceived myself, it seems
Now I am dying, a wretch I've become
The thing I thought could save me, has my life undone.

Brenda Kristine Lundquist

It's Never Easy To Say Good-Bye

It's said that time will ease all your pain.
I say to myself as I sit out in the rain.
These tears that I cry, will never bring you back.
It seems the power of controlling life I some how lack.
I think back to all the times I shared with you.
The colors were vibrant and the sky was always blue.
Now all colors have turned a dull black and white.
The colors I once knew are now out of sight.
As I walk alone on this wet pavement street.
I dream of a time when we will once again meet.
I could make that time come sooner then we think.
All I have to do is just take a drink.
But what would happen if my life came to an end?
What would become of all my close friends?
I don't want them to cry as I cry for you.
I want their colors to be vibrant and their skies to stay blue.
So as my life now continues on.
I still remember the life that now is gone.
It's said that time will ease all your pain.
I say to myself as I sit out in the rain.

Jennifer Joseph

Finals Week Prayer

Now I lay me down to rest,
I pray "Dear Lord" I pass my test.
As I blink my eyes at a quarter to three,
I know Professor Jones will remember me.
For all those times I snoozed in his class,
Telling him it's from studying night before last.
When we all know and we mean well,
Just couldn't pass up that party,
Over in east hell.
Closing those books at 5:56,
Knowing you got a class,
Before you can get a wink.
And right after class,
At a quarter past twelve.
Late for work, oh! what the hell.
Come in the house half dead on your feet.
Only parents and grades,
Your eyes seem to greet.
You tell them you'll try harder,
And do better next time.
But they shake their heads,
At that twelve grade old line.
So they throw their hands up,
And swear to be through.
But the very next night,
They'll join prayer time with you.

Oh heavenly Father, let me pass this test.
Help me see this kid through,
Then let me lay down and rest.

The Midnight Writer

My Gentle Prayer

Lord I am here by Thy blessing. All my seeing is with Thy eyes.
I pray for Your ear and say MY GENTLE PRAYER.
Oh Father, in my life all I seek is Thy wisdom, first your forgiveness.
May I find Thy path and go it's way. Seeking Your blessed knowledge
help me know my life's' script written by Your merciful hand.
Assign me to be Thy first lieutenant as I surrender all control.
Bless what I do in Thy name Lord. May I find myself always in Your grace.
Searching, I only seek Thee in me. Come forth Lord, become Thyself again.
You are my Alpha and Omega having brought this dust to life. It is not me
but in body that I am even here, So as I walk in Your way may I be a righteous
man and be blessed by You every day.

David A. Heard

Shangri-La

I said to myself, "What a beautiful day."
I reached for a book from the shelf-
Went out on my porch and swung on my two-seater swing
As I read, the sounds in the yard fill my ears-
My thoughts of reading the book disappear—
In my garden I hear the sound of the babbling fountain-
The chirping of the birds around the feeder.
I look at the trees swaying from the breeze-
I hear the pleasant sound of my chimes when the wind softly blows -
I look at the clouds in the sky moving ever so slowly-
I have discovered the imaginary land in "Lost Horizon" by James Hilton
My Shangri-la

Doris Lambertson

A Lasting Impression

As I sit here in the audience watching you graduate, my best friend,
I realize there is a bond we share between us that will never end.
A friend is someone who comes in when the whole world has gone out.
I look at you and realize what true friendship is about.

You have taught me it is what is inside a person that counts.
I can think of no better lesson I have learned in a greater amount.
Together we have shared laughter, disappointment and tears,
Through your strength and courage I have learned to overcome my fears.

When things seemed most tough you were always there,
To lend me your time and also your ear.
I think you are a person who is very precise.
I thank you for giving me your often used advise.

As the ceremony comes to an end
There is one thing more I must mention.
You are my best friend,
You touched my life and made a lasting impression.

Gwen M. Squire

"The Essence Of Me"

My soul was scared by what life offered
I refused to play the game
as a result I escape in myself
and found a empty soul

My soul desired love from images
I search for love that can not be seen
as a result attempts at perfection are made
but never attained

My soul is made full by art
I own an invincible impulse of expression through art
as a result that impulse to create provides solace
but its this urgency that keeps me breathing

Living through the art is my salivation
it is the essence of me

Daniel Lugo

Sunshine

I remember my Mamas' garden.
I remember the warm sunshine.
I remember looking up and feeling
the suns' rays kiss my skin.
I remember the smell of green things growing.
I remember popping a cherry tomato
into my mouth, biting down.
I remember sunshine bursting forth onto my tongue,
floating down my throat.
I remember my mamas' garden.

Celia B. Anderson

"Life"

Life is sometimes Stubborn.
People think they can run from it.

But it stays with you until you die.

In life you go through things that you do not
want to go through.

Well, that's how things are.

Life is a part of you and it will stick with you
forever.

Sheree A. Jacobs

Judy's Tomorrows

Say good-bye to me, don't cry for me
I said good-bye to my old tomorrows.
For I must go to another place!
Leave this place called life!
I shall continue on to find my new tomorrows.
I shall be watching over you, do not feel sad.
For I shall reach my new tomorrows.

I say good-bye to my pain and tears
But, I live on in your heart and souls.
For I am by your side.
Cry for me, as I reach my new tomorrows.
Feel my joy, as I leave this earth.
For I cry no longer for my old tomorrows.
I say good-bye and farewell as
you say hello to all of your
new tomorrows!

Afton C. Scroggins

Inner Madness

When I looked into his eyes,
I saw a sadness to my surprise.
Crying out from the madness,
there is a man looking for gladness.
Sinking deep from within,
there is a pain you can't pretend.
From the shadows there lurks about
the reasons why he is in doubt.
Seek and find the answers from deep inside your soul,
take the emptiness and make it whole.
Each and every answer is in us all
sometimes we stumble, sometimes we fall.
But through it all, if he believes,
he can unlock the inner madness and set it free.

Kami Fryberger

"Rainbow"

Blue sky and blue ocean
I saw many yachts, blue, red and yellow
And also I could see big ship, back and forth
Yes, here is in Hawaii

Suddenly, I was terrible wet
as taking as the bath.
I am feeling so refreshly.

Urgently, I came under the palm tree
where I met a young handsome man.

"Hi!!" We said each other.
Little while we are nothing to say.
Just we saw eye to eye.

All of a sudden, he said so loudly,
"Look at the rainbow"
Big rainbow was right front of us.
"Wow!!" I screamed.
He said "beautiful".
I said "yes, it is".
He said "you",
I thought he is typical american.

By the way, I am typical Japanese woman.

Junko Kuroda

Wish

One night I sat and looked above and wandered why
I saw only one star in the sky above I realized it was
The brightest star yet standing all alone.
I made a wish that night my wish came true it was you.
The next night I sat with your arms around me.
We looked up to the sky above.
We saw two stars standing all alone.
They were two stars yet together they shone
As one bright star in a sky of darkness.

Jenny L. Benson

When I Went Out Walking

When I went out walking
I saw the skies cry for rain.
I saw the fields in flight of laughter
And the heavens groan in pain.

When I went out walking
I saw a woman in a summer dress,
Flowing in the moonlight,
Soft with each caress.

When I went out walking
I saw a naked tree reach up to the sky.
I saw a thousand pilgrims asking, "Why?"
"Why is there a Jesus, and will He let us die?"

When I went out walking
I saw an army in the west,
A soldier boy in uniform
Telling the storm clouds he'll do his best.

When I went out walking I saw the blood pour from the sky,
It once was in the body of an angel who's
Simple heart always made me cry,
To fill a tear in every heart and a terror in every eye.

David M. Brickey

Prism of Life

As I look through the prism of life
I see a world of pain and strife;
The cruelties of this world, how can we bear?
What happened to the gentleness that used to be there?
I think back to my younger days
When I used to sit and read Shakespeare's plays.
The days when I would just lie in the sun
When we would walk through the woods to have fun.
Now all I see and hear is how people are killing each other
When we are all supposed to be sister and brother!
Then you hear of people dying from taking dope
Soon this world will have no hope.
We are the only ones who can change our way
So our children will be able to live in a new day.
Or there will be no world left for them to live in
Surely this would be a sin!
Why can we not learn to live in peace
Before the world that we now know begins to cease?
God did not intend for us to tear this world apart
For surely it would tear open His heart!

David C. Jenkins

Untitled

In my mirror I see someone I've never seen before.
I see someone who has a reason to smile every morning.
The image before me now has goals for the future-
Instead of taking each day as it comes, I now make each day.
In my mirror I see someone I've never seen before.
The looking glass shows an older, wiser reflection-
One that now knows what life's all about-FAMILY and LOVE.
For this I thank you, Benjie, my husband and Levi, my son.
In my mirror I see someone I've never I seen before.

Angie Bayne

I Love Life

I'm alive and I love life.
I see beauty in the simplest things,
The song of a bird is a symphony,
Magic flutters on butterfly wings.
Roses, daffodils, lilies of the field
A bouquet of fragrances lift through the trees.
The sun swells a spirit of warmth on my face,
Clouds wisp like angel wings in a warm breeze.
The dancing and sparkling of water falls,
The babbling brook, the buzz of the bee,
When I no longer walk this earth,
Share these pleasures, don't cry for me
For I am the magic, the symphony
I am the bouquet and the angel wings.
I babble and buzz, sparkle and dance.
I love life, I am all these things.

Kathy Lovell

Part Of Me

As I look into the window,
I see only half of me staring back.
Knowing I can not find it,
I keep searching for that missing piece.
With desperation I search my soul for a beginning
The need for life pushes me step by step.
Suddenly I stop and realize
The way back has disappeared.
Choked by the tears of hopelessness,
I bury my head in the leaves.
Reality seems to be so distant
When part of me can't be found.

John Michael Taylor

Dream Of Love

Night falls
I see the image of your face across the moon
Stars of love sparkle deep within your loving eyes

Drifting into sleep
I enter a world where true love exists
Our troubles vanish like the mist of a waterfall

Moonlight shines
We lie on a bed of rose pedals as we hold each other through the night
A touch of light embraces your velvet skin

Waking up
Your sensuous eyes set my heart aflame...

Jessie Song

Fall In Love Again

Why do you torture me so
I see you again and I fall in love
But you always leave me torn apart
In a hell searching for paradise
And deceived thinking it's you
Can I ever get off this merry-go-round of
love and pain.
Of joys and tears
I wish I could say I love you no more
But my heart denies me the words
Even though my mind knows you could never truly love me
My soul wants to hold you tight and never let you go.

Joy Strang

Forever Friend

The sun is setting; the stars are in the sky.
I sit alone and make another wish tonight.
I know in my heart it won't ever come true,
But that's when you're there to pull me through
Too many times. I don't realize all you have done,
And how, when we're together nothing seems dumb.
I love you, friend, with all my heart
And I promise to you we'll never part.
Even if, for any reason, I have to go away,
I swear in my heart you will remain.
I'm sorry when I hurt you; I don't mean to make you cry.
I don't always make things better; all I can do is try.
I want nothing more then to be your best friend;
Promise our friendship will never end.
If you ever have a problem or something you don't understand,
Just reach out for me, and I'll lend a helping hand.
I want you to know how much, for you, I care,
And if you ever need me, I'll always be there.
So I'll say it one more time, just in case you forgot.
I love you, dear friend, and you're always in my heart.

Carmen Walker

Border Dream

I had a dream that I spent the night inside the River.
I stepped in late last night and saw women with their children on their backs.
Keeping them dry, I saw this while the water touched my toes.
I stepped in the River late last night and saw the straw sombreros, dirty hands and dirty fingernails.
The water rose and touched my heels then soaked into my clothes.
I shivered, I dried my eyes while I stepped into the river, feeling its greatness.
It was open for them to enter.
Through the mouth of the river they would dream without awakening.
In the mouth of the river, the water touched my waist.
The water grabbed me by my hands, guiding my dream.
The water touched my neck as I felt what they feel, freezing.
Screaming, wading without direction.
I had a dream that I spent the night inside the River.
And he swallowed me up that night.
I drank the water from the river that night and opened my eyes.

Elizabeth Arvizu

Peace

As I sit beside my window and look out across the way,
I thank the Lord for all his beauty and don't know what to say.

The birds are in the feeder, the doves, the finches, sparrows, all,
Squirrels chasing each other to a maple big and tall.

And now and then a dog or two with someone close behind;
The flowers, they are beautiful with colors you'd never find.

Now tell me Lord why can't we be as wonderful as these?
Maybe, if we took the time to give you thanks and say please,
The world would be a better place to watch and see all these;
And we could talk and love our brothers across the calm and gentle seas.

The world would be at peace and we'd hold each others hands,
And there would be love around the world in all the different lands.

Jean E. Richardson-Oliver

My Favorite Toy

Of all the cat toys to the test,
I think I like my tail the best.
My balls roll away and hide under a chair,
But my 12-inch appendage is always right there.
It flips and it flaps and sometimes does wiggle,
And when I pursue it,
It makes my mom giggle.
It's constant companion,
Just ready for fun,
And I tuck it right under me
When I am done.
I wake up from my nap
And it's there without fall,
Don't you wish that you had a tail?

Adele Hackenson

Country Living Is The Best For Me

As I travel through the streets of city strife,
I think of warm and gay festivities of country life.
Though there be times of hard work and pain,
the country still fills my heart with joy just the same.
Because the streets of the city are hard and cold,
but to me the country is filled with sunshine and gold.

Through the hustle and bustle of crowded city streets,
everyone is afraid to speak.
But through the dusty roads and glamorous lakes,
everyone is trying a friend to make.
In the country, the fresh smell of pine and honey fill the air,
but in the city only soot and smog is everywhere.

In the city and ghetto the buildings are a terrible sight
This makes me feel that this is not right.
So I must leave the city because I clearly see,
Country living is best for me.

John Terry Woods

What We Really Need

After a hard day that sometimes takes me away
I think on the better things and what they have to say

The way to desire can set a Soul on fire
with True Love the heart becomes inspired

With our present being our future we are seeing
a new form taking shape on the past we are keying

So, that we can look back and tip our hats
and see where we were and where we're at

What we really need is to destroy all greed
and find a way to plant a new seed

So, that love will grow and that we may know
all of the secrets love has to show

Sometimes life seems long and for others life seems wrong
but, Life is a Melody we have to learn its song

Sing of Love's Praise in all the many ways
that is needed in these times and in these days

What we really need is to destroy all greed
and find a way to plant a new seed

So, that love will grow and that we may know
all of the secrets love has to show

Clarence M. Tucker Jr.

Father Dear Father

Your struggles through life were not easy
I think you did the best that you could
Some of the things we did not understand
I think now are well understood

You came to our rescue so many times
When our lives were too much to bare
If we were broke or our kids needed you
Somehow you were always there

You worked very hard for those that you loved
You asked nothing from us in return
Except to do the best that we could
And we all continue to learn

Father you are connected to us
In our hearts, bodies and mind
You were the strength that guided our paths
When our world would start to unwind

So father dear father I hope you're at peace
and I hope that you knew that we loved you
I can't say farewell, so long or good by
I can only say adieu.

Karen Kinses

Untitled

Why won't anyone understand what I'm feeling right now?
I try and tell them but I can't make them understand somehow.

Am I not making it clear
Or do they just not hear?

I'm yet to find
That kind

That will tell me
What I want to hear, gee

If someone tells me what I need
No more will I heed.

Only if someone understood
Then I could

Understand why
I want to die.

Angel Brodsky

I'm Doing My Very Best God

I rise up early each morning and toil the whole day away,
I try as hard as I can Lord, but always fail anyway;

No matter which way I turn, it never comes out quite right,
I'm sure I'll die of frustration, I feel like a kid's lost kite;

Other people mock and spite me, and tell me what to do,
But little do they know me, all shoulds are like the flu;

Each day I try to find, the path that's right for me,
These woods are dark and lonely, mere humans just can't see;

The agony and the ecstasy, every forlorn artist's strife,
To hurt, break, and suffer, it's not our chosen life;

I endeavor to be noble, I endeavor to be true,
I trod the broken cobblestones, to mend my heart's adieu;

Life's river twists and turns, I care not where it flows,
At last I've come to trust, a future no one knows;

My eleventh hour is nigh, I'll walk the extra mile,
A writer's strength your will, persistence is my style,

So forgive me and love me God, and please help me too,
Cause I'm doing my very best, for me and for you.

Douglas E. Wight

Sacrifice

I push the window open, and her light fell thru the ground,
I try to dig to catch her breath, but she never made a sound.
I pull the window softly, don't disturb the secret rain,
That attempts to touch the undulating ripple of her pain.

I push, I pull, I bang my head,
I nail my foot, It's what you said ,
"Don't look at me, but know my fear."
You shovel down
I disappear.

I knock the window wildly, so that it bangs against the brick
there never was a witness to this death abiding trick.
So I close the window easy, her light filters thru the moon,
I watch her lift, I crack the glass, sitting quiet in my room.

I push, I pull, I bang your casque,
I nail my hand, It's what you ask,
"Don't come too close, but stay right near."
I shovel down
you disappear

Kelly H'Doubler

I Used To

I used to but now I....
I used to be scared of the dark but now I'm not.
I used to sleep with a light but now I sleep in the dark.
I used to be eleven but now I'm twelve.
I used to pee in the bed but now I don't.
I used to play with Barbie dolls but now I don't.
I used to play the recorder but now I play the flute.
I used to be short but now I'm five foot four.
I used to think Santa was real but now I know he's fake.
I used to think that there was a boogie monster but now I don't.
I used to have little feet but now I don't.

Candice Alexis Anderson

Protection From Our World

My little girl so innocent and pure,
I want to protect you from the violence of our world,
but this I cannot do.

My little girl so loving and caring,
I want to protect you from the hatred of our world,
but this I cannot do.

My little girl so happy and carefree,
I want to protect you from the depression of our world,
but this I cannot do.

My little girl so honest and uninhibited,
I want to protect you from the corruption of our world,
but this I cannot do.

This is the world you were born into,
and protect you from it I cannot do;
Teach you to help change it is something I can do,
while always providing a safe haven for you.

Karen Mae Weber

Awakenings

The earth,
now drenched with mother earth's morning cry
joyously welcomes the warmth of the dawn's light.
As the clouds separated, brilliant colors of red, orange, and yellow
sprang out through the openings
mad puddles began to dry and the grass greened
birds sang their glorious songs
the awakening sounds of animals echoed through the mountains
A new day had begun.

Dawn Tenney

One Small Life

When I was but a small child
I was meek and my head was bowed
I was poor, and I was so cold
I was five, but I was so old.
My Mother worked hard; I owe her a lot,
but there were so many things that couldn't be bought.
Our neighbors gave us knowing stares
Our "friends" gave us hurtful cares.
Sometimes I was angry—we were so poor,
Especially when bill collectors came to the door.
I was confused, Mom was always working,
Yet we had nothing, poverty was always lurking.
You can be poor, but you can be clean.
Hide those tears, don't let them be seen.
Work hard, be stubborn and hold that head high
And dream those dreams, don't let them die.

Diana Kauffman

Longing

I wish I were young and beautiful
I was never beautiful
But I was young.

Young men stared at me lustfully
Old men stared at me thus
Middle-aged men actually

I wish I were young and beautiful
But now it's all gone
Now there's only the memory of a poem and a song.

Young men stared at me longingly
Old men stared at me so.
A middle aged man became a beau.

I wish I were young and beautiful
The face has aged; the body is gone,
But the heart is still there.

Why does no one want a heart to share?

Kathryn Smith

Ferret Zoo

Here's something so very true
I was once alone and blue.

Until I decided to get a pet
And wouldn't you know it was a ferret.

I saw him in a pet shop one lazy afternoon.
He was so cute I knew he'd be my friend really soon.

I took him home just to let him run fast as he could go.
Before I knew it I let him down- he had hold of my toe.

He's mischievous, he runs, hides, and even dances
To this family and to others only enhances.

We thought one ferret exciting and now we have two.
Seeing them play together is fun and something new.

There is one more thing to say about your little ferret
Please keep your valuables up and place this tip on merit.

So don't ever seem to feel alone and blue
Remember the story of the ferret zoo.

Dawn M. Nowak

Why Have I Come?

Why do I live in your midst?
I who have never spoken a word;
Never taken a step? Have I come
to make demands? What mission could
I possibly have? Have I come as the
Least to expect the most of others?

Could my mission be to teach acceptance,
Patience and tolerance? By accepting me
Will you accept all mankind, regardless of
Appearance or ability? By accepting me will
You free yourself of bigotry and prejudice;
Harboring malice toward none?

Will I succeed? Will your hands and heart
Reach out? Will you reach out knowing that
I can give nothing in return? Will you love
Me for me just as I love you for you? Maybe
Then, for a fleeting moment, you and I can
Reach beyond time and know eternal truth.

Judy A. Akin

The Princess

I must teach the children of things unknown
I will hold up a finger and say,
'This is the one' then on with the lessons
Until he knows of these handy things
Called fires - although curling a little,
  with these he tries.
What are the things fires may not do?
Do not bite your brother lest he bite you too.
Thus learning in light until his father
Takes up the tune and teaches of
Wisdom that makes men....Men!

Elisabeth B. Constable

In Excelsios Deo

Look deep in my kaleidoscopic eyes
I will show you places off the beaten path
Green places that you have never seen
Take my hand
Follow me
Down the spiral staircase into the hallucinatory underwater world

A crown of thorns floats on the piercing whiteness of the lily pond
Bite into the fruit
The free-falling juice dribbles down your chin
And fall into the valley below
Apple blossoms in the dark night
You see everything from your blue-eyed sky

I burn for you Eve

Diane Ritch

Words That Hurt

"You were a mistake!
I wish you were never born!
It's your own damn fault,
Don't sit around and mourn!"

Words can hurt allot
When they're said by people you love.
Why people say such unkind words
Can only be answered by God above.

Sure enemies may say they hate you
But that doesn't seem to hurt one bit.
It's when said by the one's you love the most
Sometimes it wouldn't hurt less to get hit.

Erin Styczen

The Letter Carrier

When the Postman or Postwoman arrives at your door
I wonder if he or she could guess,
That in delivering the daily mail to your home
What message brings grief or happiness?

How could the Mailman know at the end of the day
What letters would undo your stress,
A friend could send a gift in an envelope or box
that would help to heal you and bless!

The Letter Carrier be it man or woman
Has a difficult career to do,
They walk in the rain, the snow and the heat
To deliver your mail to you!

So let us be grateful to the Postman and Postwoman
Their job is successfully done,
Some work in the office and some walk the street
Some trudge in the cold weather and grueling sun.

Whether the mail is delivered by air, land or sea,
Lets think of the purpose and place
Then when the Letter Carrier travels to your door,
Greet the person with a smiling face!

Jeannette F. Adams

White Knight

My mind is in the long-term struggle.
I wonder if its worth the fight.
In the still of the night the echoes of turmoil are there;
awaiting the morning light.
But I poor soul "The Tarnished Knight,"
wishing to be illuminated white.
Must face the day,
forbid the night.
With head held high,
with eyes that are bright.

James L. Neu Sr.

I Am

I am a friendly guy who likes to write stories.
I wonder what I'll be doing in 20 years.
I hear the calmness during the night.
I see my life is full of promise
I want to be happy forever and ever
I am a friendly guy who likes to write stories.

I pretend I'm a best-selling author
I feel the pressure of overcoming problems I have.
I worry about losing my loved ones someday.
I cry for all the violence on this earth.
I am a friendly guy who likes to write stories.

I understand that life has its peaks and valleys.
I say respect others as you respect yourself.
I dream about the life that's ahead of me.
I try to do my best in everything I do.
I hope I'm successful in fulfilling my goals.
I am a friendly guy who likes to write stories.

Eliot Parker

Breezes

Blowing
Randomly coming and going
Enveloping us with life, movement
Escaping to a far away land
Zipping along a course unknown
Easily moving to and fro
Sadly the breezes go

Brian Gates

For I Am Dying

For I am dying
I wondered what it would be like to be dead,
Now I hear angels calling me toward the light ahead.
I see millions of other dying people in this place,
I want to go to the light for it is as peaceful as a pretty face,
For I am dying.

I sometimes used to pretend I was dead,
I could almost feel my spirit leave my head,
I could touch the sky and stars as they fall behind,
I worry how my family feels, their spirits are all so kind,
I cry for my parents whose wounds cannot heal,
For I am dying.

I understand how my parents feel,
I believe they know where I am is real.
I dreamt of this day for a long time before I died.
So I tried to make my life mean something: oh how I tried.
I hope my parents will stop crying,
For I am dying.

Joshua B. Q. Lewis

Tell Papa I Cried

In memory of "Papa" Joseph Dassinger

He died... and I did not cry.
I would not... and people thought I was strong.
Those people thought wrong —
they did not know that I cried every night since
they did not know how hard I took it.
His death — I was not ready for.
Ten days — I watched him lay with eyes closed
I listened to him unanswer my questions.
I begged God not to make him suffer.
On the final day, I sat next to him.
I held his hand.
I told him I loved him.
I said good-bye.
The phone rang... and I knew.
But I did not know it would be so final.
So, God, please... tell Papa I love him
and God... tell Papa I cried.

Jeanette M. Brandt

"If It's Love"

If it's love, you automatically know
If it's love, it takes time to grow
He'll love you no matter what you do
And when times are rough, he'll help you through
If it's love, then he'll always stay
He would never leave or just go away
If it's love, it couldn't be replaced
Not by a great body or a beautiful face
If it's love, it was love from the start
And it's easy to tell by the beat in your heart
So if one day your heart rapidly beats
As you scream for joy as you run in the streets
When you sit by the phone waiting for it to ring
And it's only love songs you seem to sing
Then take hold of him and love him true
Make him happy and never blue
'Cuz if it's love, you'll be happier than ever
And if it's love, he'll leave you never

Kimberly M. Lagsdin

"If Only"

"If only" I had done this thing a year ago 'tis true,
If only I had loved them more, this makes me very blue.
We cannot change the past, no matter how we try,
We'll never change our outlook then, it will not help to cry.

"If only" make us quite depressed, they do not help at all,
Forget the past, as God has done and stand up straight and tall.
Bury the past and think about the love you'll give this minute,
For if you dwell on yesteryears God is never in it.

But we can work on how we act and re-act for today,
We can work to be a kinder person, and have no regrets along the way.
With the help of God, you can become a person you'd be proud of;
No tears of regret tomorrow, for control comes from above.

Next year you can look back and say, regrets I have not one;
The Holy Spirit guided me; what he wanted I have done.
I can look back on yesteryears and bear a well earned smile;
For I know the past and present for me will always be worthwhile.

Catherine I. White

Is My World On Track?

How do I know if my world's on track?
If the path that I'm choosing's the one?
What if I make a big mistake,
And have to start from where I begun?

What if my dreams don't come true,
After years of planning and work?
How about those treasures from a hidden past,
That only get covered in dirt?

What if I'm confused and I need help,
How do I know what is right?
If I'm lonely and scared and don't know my way,
Who's going to shine the light?

What if I fall and skin my knee
On one of life's broken roads?
Or if I have to stop and pick up more,
When I can't even carry my load?

But there must be someone watching over me,
'Cuz all has gone well, looking back...
Now that I stop and think about it,
Does that mean my world is on track?

Karen Vigil

Lord Help Me

Lord please help me I'm falling again,
I'm so afraid he will cause more pain.
I've been hurt many times before,
I've kept my heart locked behind closed doors.

Do I let him in do I give him the key?
Lord only you know what's meant to be
Can you show me, just give me a sign?
Is this one more obstacle I have to climb?

I know love comes and goes in time,
I need to know, Lord, will this love be mine?
How long will it take before I see —
Is his love meant just for me?

Is he the answer to all my prayers?
Is this the man who truly cares?
These questions keep coming back time after time.
Am I out of his sight, and out of his mind?

When will these doubts be erased?
Will true love take its place?
Lord only you know what's meant to be,
Oh Lord is this the man for me?

Karen Beeken

Prelude

There's a story in every one of us, way down deep inside,
I'm willing to share my experience, there's nothing I wish to hide.
When everything else has left you, you still can have your pride.
So listen to my narrative, I have much I need to confide.

From my cramped jet window seat, I looked down from the sky,
It all seemed so insignificant, I thought to myself with a sigh.
I'd been persecuted by the 'man' and it was all I could do not to cry,
From crib to corporation, I had climbed the ladder high.

My life isn't yet over, I can begin it again!
With a brand new perspective, my face cracked a grin.
But below me, the war rages, as the earth does it's spin,
My problems seem so petty, compared to all the world's sin.

As I gaze down I keep thinking, it's all part of THE PLAN,
Hold steadfastly to his love, place your life is His hand.
When injustice surrounds us, remain as firm as you can,
Only God has the answers, don't trust your fate to mortal man.

Joyce M. Hardeman

"Drama Of An Alcoholic"

Young women seated upon a stool,
in a bar wondering where her future lies,
open headed and clear minded,
shocked because faith always wears a disguise,
she knows she will be someone, somewhere, somehow,
how one day she will look into the mirror and see the image
of someone who will make her proud,
the only problem in that her future lies in her hands, you see,
not exactly what she had in mind,
she tries to take any opportunity that comes along her way,
but not one single one of them have led her to succeed,
she fears this will become a pattern along her years of strife,
she can not accept how this is the real image of life,
while she meditates on that thought,
and takes another sip from that beer,
she realizes that all humans really fear is fear,
and once she overcomes that phase of her unimportant life,
all she really has to fear,
would be another sip from that fatal beer.

Caroline Cortezia

"That's Life"

On the day that I was born -
In a strange place I came to be
On a blustery, wintery, snowy morn.
Became another addition to the "Family Tree"???

The first five years, I was able to learn
All my body motions and sounds so loud
Found out how much energy I could burn
And "Boy, oh Boy, was I ever proud!!!

Then another surprise was in store -
Was introduced to a thing called "School"
First grade, Second grade and there were more
Believe me, I did learn about the "Golden Rule"

I became a very Important Person in my field -
Married and bought a house in the lane
Raised a family and now my life I do yield
"Lord, please don't put me through this again"

Betty Jean Knight

I'm Gonna Make It Someday

A lost child destine to succeed,
In a world that could be cruel indeed.
Where there's a will there's a way, that's
what he says, as he wakes with despair everyday.

He will keep trying, despite rejection,
Because in his heart, he knows perfection,
In all his dreams, and plotted schemes
he keeps trying, without hope, at times it seems.

When success comes, will he be happy?
He's not quite sure, for he's been so bored
Wondering how it would be, but until
that day, I keep hearing him say...
I'm gonna make it someday.

John Andrew Cline

Voices

Throughout the course of a life many voices are heard
In childhood, usually it's parents and teachers
Young adulthood, the voice of friends, enemies or ego
Adulthood brings the voice of necessity - work to do
Later adulthood brings the voice of introspection

A time of relative freedom - the rage of youth is over
Time to view life and think about all you see and know
This is when deeper and more insightful thoughts occur
Listen - is that your own, quiet, knowing, inner voice
Living has taught you much, maybe even a little wisdom.

Carol A. Rebmann

A Shattered Spirit

Captured in a frosted maze, lays a shattered spirit.
In functions, it knows not where to go.
For many times it found the darkened path,
and damaged it along the way.
As it glides down those hazed paths,
it may pause along the way.
Finding a little sparkle dust,
that sends it on its way.
What will become of this godlike spirit?
For it carries a deep treasured bond
with the golden spirit.
So it must find its way,
but the frosted maze
keeps getting in the way.
How can this shattered spirit
break from its maze?
Only by capturing
the golden spirit's sparkle dust
can it break the frosted maze.

Elizabeth R. Johnson

Recurrence To The Middle Ages

Before the town's gate, among the fussy crowd
I'll sigh when tell goodbye
The river under th'Moon,
My lone fire,
The Dawn,
Aroma of the fields at Noon;
And all my dreams
Which have been left behind those pine
And hills.

Fellow Carp, I'll see you soon!

Georgii Nikolaev

The Little White Lie

Yes, I am little and I am white.
In pockets and purses you will find me.
To some I am old, to some I am new.
Come on, let me into your pocket, too.

I am really very popular.
You can find me almost anywhere.
Look for me on the corner and also in the store.
Pick me up and try me—you'll come back for more.

I don't cost so much
Just a couple bucks a pack.
Cheaper than most things you can get.
I'm just a poor, helpless, little cigarette.

I do so many good things
For those who use me or give me a try.
I stain their fingers, I bite their tongue,
I yellow their teeth and give them cancer of the lung.

I am your refuge and your fortress.
In me, you can find much comfort and peace.
When you are on your deathbed, ready to depart,
I'll be with you in your pocket, close to your heart.

Betty M. Gunn

Eternal Life

That I should sit for an hour,
In the company of a flower,
To feel the completion of it's bloom,
The intoxication of it's perfume!

That I should sit still for an entire year,
And know the flower sheds no tear,
Throughout it's winter under cold snow,
No pain or effort to grow does it know.

Under the sun's fiery heat,
It's miraculous sprouting will repeat,
With brilliant green finery to adorn,
The glorious celebration of being reborn!

Cycling again it withers and dries,
Yet still no sadness as it 'dies,'
The flower knows a permanent place on earth,
It knows eternity enfolds both death and birth.

Jeanna Voit

Goon Elf They Sand

The revellers took pride
in their ways of guile
said there would forever be riches on the side
massaging fat tummies full of bile
they poured scorn on victims cast aside
left alone to suffer with a smile

Iron in the rough they are, said lucky crowd
they lack a hint of sparkle beneath
and they dare not cry out loud
for that could hasten their well-earned death

Soon the party was over
daybreak exposed the fouling of the nest
revellers sought help, seeking rejects for cover
over a blow to one of their best
sorry, said the wretched, nothing to offer
but your man had better pass the test.

Josh Arinze

Untitled

The sky's the limit
in this world of dreams
The dance of dreamers
The song of birds
The clouds in the sky
is where our dance takes place
The moon and the stars light the night
for the groovy little shindig we have in
the sky.

Denise Grover

Innocence Stolen

Oh, lamb of purity
In this worldly state,
Let not thy fleece be soiled
Let thee not tempt fate.

May thee never go astray
Upon this mother earth
For thou art a prism of innocence
And by that, truly blessed.

Oh, lamb of curiosity
Be not caught in the storm
For if thee wanders into the forest,
Thine virgin eyes and ears shall surely be poisoned.

Oh, sweet and weak lamb
Thou hast been confronted by temptation
And thy spotless fleece has been stained
Opened wounds now are thine eyes and ears;
A whip now is thy tongue
Thou hast now become a thief among thieves.

June L. Nesby

"Dreams Snatched Away"

Hope's gone, yet loving memories linger on.
Inspired by his Big Brother, a doctor he had hoped to be.
Can't hear his laughter anymore or see his smiling face.
The sound of the basketball no longer awakens me.
"Dreams Snatched Away".

His golf clubs stand in the corner,
I'm not ready to give them away.
He was going to be an Uncle soon; work in construction in the afternoon,
Shoot hoops, design the deck, help his friends, finish reading a book,
Tell jokes, and tell me, "Mom, I love you."
So many things he had planned to do.
"Dreams Snatched Away."

In a speeding car on the highway;
Forty-five miles per hour;
A few seconds it took!
No! I can't be, he was only sixteen.
I am old; he was young; dear Lord, why didn't death take me?
His dreams, my dreams, what more can I say?
"Dreams Snatched Away."

Doris Stedmire-Pitts

Grass

The grass is growing and it needs mowing,
Oh, I'd rather lie in the sun.
But the grass keeps growing and it does need mowing,
I'd rather go swimming for fun.
The grass is growing and it needs mowing.
It does it all night and day.
If it keeps growing and I don't go mowing,
I'll have to bale it as hay.

Candace McClure

The Dorm Room

The summer breeze blows lightly o'er the Frisco Bay
Into an empty dorm room.
The semester's over, the students home,
The dorm room stands empty.

The laughter and cries of sorrow it heard,
The joy and failure it felt,
It feels no more this Spring,
The dorm room stands empty.

The parties and celebrations that thundered the walls,
The quiet and solitude of all nighters that whispered the walls,
Have all departed, ready to return in Fall,
The dorm room stands empty.

New students will arrive
Full of hope and determination to succeed,
Once again the room will feel the full range of emotion; but for now
The dorm room stands empty.

James K. Barnes

Desire

To want something so bad and not be able to have it
is a dangerous ground, somehow, though, there is a
force. Physical? Perhaps. Emotional? Definitely.
This force keeps you from it. It is enough to make a
man kill another man in cold blood and not think twice
about it. You may say you think this sounds foolish,
but, perhaps it isn't. Then, maybe it is. Is love
involved? Maybe. You be the judge. Be independent.
Stand up and know what you want. Do not let a "want"
control your life. Pray, and if it is meant to be, it
will happen. If not, set new goals. Be yourself and try
to control how bad you want something.

Jennifer Clontz

"A Fight"

A fight with you,
Is a fight that never ends.
It may have started out small,
But it turns into an ugly brawl.
Things are said, feelings are hurt,
Why are the innocent, the ones to always get burnt?
You sit and think, you sit and cry,
You realize it started out over a little white lie.
You sit and pout,
When you know you should be working it out.
Your consciences tells you to make it right,
But your pride soars out of sight.
A voice is heard from up ahead,
The words "I'm sorry" creep into your head.
Smiles and hugs are given,
So you think you were forgiven.
But remember that next time you're in a fight,
Forgetting and forgiving are the things that are right.

Kristy Denise Lear

Autumn Day

An autumn breeze gently blows by,
Impelling, vivid leaves from the deep brown earth.
A whirlwind, twirling round and round
Multicolored kites swiftly gliding higher and higher.
The skies, pink as a rose,
The sun on the western horizon, thin blankets
of clouds all around.
Sketching the majestic mountains,
Rough and jagged.
All is still.

Erica Dawn Underwood

Mom

My mother told me, she would always be there.
Is a great lady, for that she really cared.
At my side she stood, and helping when she can.
Mean nothing but good, to be her only plan.
She is the greatest, tops at everything.
For she is the best, with the good she will bring.
I love her so much, giving her all my heart.
My feelings to touch, because she is a part.
The love that she gives, better than any more.
For her my heart lives, and do anything for.
Anything at all, I am willing to try.
Is her name I call, and for her I would die.
Not saying so mild, I love like no other.
For I am her child, and she is my mother.

Jason E. Lee

Breezeway

The world wind breeze...
Is flowing..
Through my hair...Once again...
This flight has been exhausting...
And yet...Exhilarating...
The wind..
Has taken me up high..has turned...
And abandoned me...
In places unimaginable to a conceivable plight...
I raise my wings...
In order to be uplifted..and consumed...
By the breeze...
The anticipation...of the next unperceived plan
Escorts me..to the newly illuminated delusion...
My life's breath is taken away...
And again..restored..by a single force..we know
So little about...Life's blood flows freely...
Through my existence...until...
The world winds breeze..ceases to have an entity...
I am that and it is mine...

Catherine M. Bishop

War

My heart is all tattered like flags from the fray
Is it morning or nighttime? You'd better not say.
And are there two stars or one that darken the day?

The bread, it is scarce; for rats were the hosts.
Their tails curl like butter off hot, dripping toast.
And there's only one thing that I long for the most.

With faith-smashing terror they come in our sleep,
"Enemy" attacks even now as we speak.
And we've been wrapped in the same bloody sheets for a week.

The heavens are bleeding, my comrades are gore
To stretch themselves out 'neath Mother Earth's floor
Where the cursed and slain lay scattered galore.

The stench of the bodies; empty shells at our knees,
Makes breathing a trial in the hot, salty breeze.
And the moans of the dying will add to these.

I'm ready to go for the things that I've seen;
My headless companions and all my friends spleens;
Have deepened my longing to help the earth green.

Kendra Webb

Untitled

So now is the love lost -
Is it now gone?

He was our leader -
Can we now carry on?

Some people may say "He is better off dead"
Who's going to help us keep the love in
our heads?

Can I explain what it was like to be there?
Ten thousand or more - you felt like they
cared.

Dancing and swaying and singing the songs -
It was a place we could go to feel like
we belonged.

Maybe I needed to write this - to fill that
empty part -
JERRY GARCIA will live FOREVER IN MY HEART.

Kimberly Giaimo

Love

Do we even know what love is?
Is love the kind you receive from family?
Or is it the kind when you really like a person?
Do we know what love is?
Can love make us feel lonely, happy, sad, or glad?
Do we know what love is?
Do we have it within us.
But
We just don't know it's there?
Can love break our minds, our hearts, our souls?
Do we really know what love is?

Amabelle Valdellon

Woman

The woman I stare at in the mirror every morning
Is not the woman I was.
The woman who loved him couldn't have been me.
I wouldn't have let myself suffer or be taken advantage of...
Who was the woman I used to be?

Did I leave her when I left him,
Or was I there all that time?
My identity must have been her's,
And I guess her's was mine.

I had dreams and hopes
But I shoved them all aside...
To be with him, to settle down,
And become his wife.

He loved the woman I once was.
How could he ever love me?
The woman in the mirror...
The only woman I can be.

Abigail Hosford-Mathis

"River Of Size"

River of size.
Knows no end.
Time her only compromise.
Gently, but inevitably, eroding away the earth , exposing the
very roots of my affection for her.
Will I drown in a sea of loneliness.
Never to drift on her loneliness.
Never to bath in her waters warm caress.
Or will I sail the beautiful river of size to an endless ocean
of love.

David E. Hickman

Everyday

The carcass that holds my thoughts and ambitions
is quickly getting tired and confused

The carcass looks for the branches that will lead it to that one
most desired point. It pulls on one and it slaps it in the face

No longer can it trust its own intuition
for every time it gets caught up in the roots of its past
and can't move on

Wanting to let go of the things that have
bound it to the past the carcass gets sick
and falls apart.

Relentlessly trying to pull its self back together
it misplaces the bones and is thrown into a deeper state of
confusion.

Now that the marrow and flesh has no direction
it is left to decay and evolve into something else.

James P. Bailey

Love

I sometime think, this little word
is so widely, misunderstood!
The meaning is no secret, really it quite clear
It's trust and honestly, respect and faith:
all that heaven and earth, all that pure and good.
It does not last, just for a little while.
For real love, never truly ends!
It sometimes changes slightly rearranges,
But you always end up at very least friends.
Love is not blind, for it sees inside,
Deep enough to find your very soul!
That fragile place, we try to deny then to
to hide it away, with our lies and anger
our jealousy and our stupid pride!
So please don't run when I say I love you
nor worry for our love is rare and special.
What I'm trying to say, is really clear to see
That I love you
for who you are, then please
just love me for me

Kathy Jean Baughman

My Mother

The most beautiful woman in the world to me,
Is the only one my eyes can see,
She is my mother, I love her with all my heart,
And nothing in this world could tear us apart.

She's my pride and joy, I love her to death,
I'd give my life for her my every last breath,
She's there to listen to most of my problems,
The ones she understands she tries to solve them.

She's always there when I cry over silly things,
A smile of happiness she then brings,
She's one of a kind, no one has her face,
I only have one real mother, and no one could take
Her place...

Karen Newcomb

Sins Of An Angel

Though her beauty is soft like the palm of an
infant, though her voice hypnotizes like a grandfather
pendulum, though her eyes bear the innocence of a child
at play and her touch is as calming as a thousand
fairy-tales, with a heart as pure as poetry, she steals
my love. These are the sins of an angel.

Darick Parrish

Making My Dreams Come True

Making my dreams come true
is to take matter into my owns hands,
this world is cast upon evil
suicide thoughts, and white faces on my back I am
looking for a way out
making dreams a reality coming true
life is forever if you make it
looking in to your soul to bring dreams and imagination
aspirations being a writer
of mind body and soul
and opening up doors about real life
and how I will achieve them
by looking at life for it really is
as I take my mind around the world in 80 dreams
I see greed and lost souls looking for life
but there is no life.

Would I achieve them
yes, because my mind is like a BOMB!!!

Corey L. Robinson

Consider the Answer

"The common question we often hear...
Is where do we go after death from here???
One theologian will say to heaven, and another to a burning hell,
Still another says to purgatory, if we don't do too bad or too well."

"Ec. 9:5-10 (KJ) says we go to the grave at the end of our time.
That's why all our activities, when alive, we should do very fine.
But that just refers to the body you say?
We have a soul that goes a different way?"

"This is the general belief I know, but, is it true?
Genesis Chapter 2 verse 7 is plain to me, and I think you.
It says God breathed into the nostrils of the form that He made,
And man became a living soul and not that He gave."

"The soul, then, is you and to make it more clear,
Read Ezekiel Chapter 18 verses 4 and 20a, dear.
It tells us here with emphasis that it's the very soul that dies.
Then the dead soul is put into a grave where it unconsciously lies."

"Now don't become angry and think badly of me!1
These are Jehovah God's words (Ps. 83:18), please try to see,
That this death isn't the end for those of His selection.
Because John 5:25, 28 and 29 tells of the resurrection!"

Artista J. Dobis

Proverbial Woman

To go deep into your inner soul
  is where I want to be
To find your mysteries
  to understand who is the man to know
  and I the woman who shall be
I am but a small speck
  wanting to grow in the realms of your existence
Knowing it to be so
  when trust is the factoring key
You are a man to your own beliefs
  and I a woman to my own
Our binding of each other
  is not a want in wanting
  but a shared purpose to grow
I will follow as I should
  and lead when it is needed
What is settled let it be
  what is open, will come to terms
In this a man and a woman would know
  what it is to be united in unity

Dawn A. Jackson

My Mind's Eye

There are times when my Mind's Eye
isn't scanning the Past
or contemplating the Future
and it turns
to observe Me in the Present
Like, a gigantic Cyclops
it peers and squints
blinking wildly as it records and calculates my data
Having evaluated from infancy to pre-senility
It's expression changes
from nonchalance
to a questioning frown
then surprise
and merriment
I can now boast
"I have witnessed a Cyclop laugh aloud"

Jo Anne Carson

Untitled

Although christmas comes but once a year
It brings with it great warmth and cheer

A time for friends and family too
A time to make your dreams come true

There's Santa, and toys, and the holiday season
But let's not forget that most special of reasons

For this is the day that Christ was born
He was wrapped in a blanket all tattered and torn

He died on the cross for the sins that we made
But how easy, we forget the price that he paid

So enjoy all the gifts that Santa Claus brings
But just don't forget this most precious of things

And tonight before bed take the times just to say
Merry Christmas Dear Lord and Happy Birthday

James E. Oliver Sr.

The Thread Of Life

This thread of life is a question, so precious, so thin.
It connects us to life and to our journey within.

For a child, it is a boundary, meant to guide...
That is stretched beyond limits. How far can it glide?

As we grow, we continue our journey, we roam.
The thread gives some more, but always leads home.

As we mature, our journey takes a new turn.
It's inward, now searching, it's peace that we yearn.

We soar to the ends of the earth for our clues.
Out of body, into the soul, our private recluse.

Not until we achieve peace is the picture in place.
What our thread has weaved is the answer. But of course, it's God's face!

It was there all along. Why couldn't I see?
This thread of life connects God with me.

If only I'd known, I could have saved a lifetime.
But I would have missed the journey and the lessons that were mine.

Kassie Kiernan Nowak

A Stolen Angel

Postmaster, the destiny of this letter, is so very far away, but
it contains an urgent matter, you must express it right away!
It has to go to heaven, far, far, above. And then it will go
to Jesus, requesting his help and love...He will know it's
contents are urgent, when he reads the first few lines...
DEAR JESUS,
You know, and see all...
Someone has taken an angel, an angel, so very, very small!

His eyes will fill with tears, as he attends this urgent matter.
At once he will call all spirits and angels good and kind!
Their instructions, find this angel, this angel so very small.
The smallest are the greatest, I love them most of all!

And should any harm come to them, there will be a price to pay.
So make hast, go find this angel, take it back to it's home today.
There is no time to waste now, go be on your way!

Tell the one who took the angel, I have, but one thing to say!
They had best start, to make amends, before their judgement day!!!

Julie Ann Lelievre

Ten Million Stars

It flew through the night
It crashed the earth!
That lonely star who once was bright.
Then try I might I thought of that night and heard how-
Ten million stars inside me swim.

Ten million stars within me dwell
They come from far, they come from wide
Each one big and each one small.

Singing, shouting, shining waiting in me.

Only the fringe of the universe knows
Where winds blow strong
and ten million stars stand as one.

Each have I counted wanting to be free
Each have I named these stars in me.

Ten million stars inside me swim
only one spirit holds them within.

So when on a clear summer's night you look to the sky
Fall on your knees before the sight and know that
God's in the heavens and all is right.

Joan M. Mandato

Untitled

I don't think that it really matters anymore.
It does not matter what you say or what you do.
It's the damage that has already been done.
You can not go back and turn the clock,
time can't ever be erased.
It does not matter if you say "I love you,"
because you don't mean it.
Saying and doing are two different things.
Love is something that grows and stays
and does not go away.
A feeling which is strong.
Saying it to me everyday wasn't what
I had anticipated.
I had hoped for a long stemmed rose.
All I ever got from you was an
artificial flower.

Bronwyn Stuart

Race

Does my race offend you?
It does. Well, I'm glad.
It should,
It offends me too. But don't worry,
So does yours, and his and hers.
Race in general offends me.

It doesn't matter what race you are,
There is someone out there who hates you.
It doesn't matter what race you are,
Someone thinks you are inferior.
It doesn't matter what race you are,
There is something in your history to be ashamed of.
It doesn't matter what race you are,
Cause I don't see your color anyway.

So please, If I myself have somehow wronged you,
Let me apologize now,
For I would hate to offend you.

Christina Price

Jilted

Life is not a board game.
It ends and cannot be replayed.
Events leave impressions, not mere lose a turns.
Skin is more susceptible than cold hard shells of symbols.

A sickness is real, not a minor set-back.
Diseased, Regression, Alzheimers.
Shrinking 7ft giants to cowering infants.
It steals the breath from the living.

A child, impressionable. Watches the dying.
Loses a playmate, love and support.
The eyes of a child behold more than can retell.
Grown to adolescence the outward scars run deep sores within.

We are actors in God's play.
Our roles are written in ink unseen.
His fancy is our path.
Exploding continuity ends his dull day.

We are the colored pieces on God's two toned board.
Hasn't anyone told him? Doesn't he know?
Once all the pieces are gone,
He won't be able to play anymore?

Jeani Barchalk

Dusty Rose

Dusty Rose is a gentle color like a soft wind blowing -
It fades into the background but is never outspoken.
Like an old pair of ballet slippers hung up for a mature life...
...It's the flush on a little girl's cheeks that later becomes a blush as the girl ages.
Yet dusty rose is not just a pastel - it has deep volume.
It is able to comprehend, and love you like a friend at the same time.
Dusty rose can be a bush, a tree, or a rose bud,
hoping to blossom before it's time.
Dusty rose is the symbol for love, peace, and compassion.

Clare Ettensohn

Poetic Justification

As a petal falls and oneness deepens
So is a man poised in his thoughts
To catch a phrase
Passed from the flower of his dreams

Bob Perdue

Ode To Dad

Dad's majestic old willow tree was a welcome sight
It guarded our home both day and night
Its branches grew tall for so many years
But when Dad was ill it seemed to shed tears
A large cancer had attacked poor Dad
But his pale blue eyes seemed to say "Don't be sad."
He fought for his life until his last sigh
As the old willow tree seemed to shout please don't die.
Dad's heart couldn't take it but his spirit lives on
Sometimes the old tree seems to be singing Dad's song
The wind brings his message both loud and clear
When you get to heaven there is nothing to fear.

Janie Smith Vega

A Thousand Years

There is a piece of my heart that cannot be mended
It happen the day your life ended.
It seems a thousand years have gone by.
Since you closed your eyes and breathed your last sigh
I miss your smile, your hug, your love.
An angel you are from above my dear precious mom, my best friend
You are always with me now and forever again.
I will teach my children all the good you taught me,
the caring, sharing, ending love as deep as the sea
You are an angel with God way up high
With all of his children in the beautiful blue sky
Not even a year since you said goodbye
A thousand years it seems, and that's no lie
Only ten months that you went to rest
When God took you, He took the best.
I love you so.

Barbara M. Brennan

Destiny

From the down of creation
it has been destiny
for us to find each other

and now that time has gone by
and experiences have occurred
we've arrived at this place called "together"

how do we know
how long will together last
and how do we make use
of the time that we have

do we use it to know
do we use it to do
do we use it as one
do we use it as two.

Brian A. Williamson

My Jesus

My Jesus died for my sin.
It is He that I put my trust in.
My Jesus is always by my side.
Through thick and thin or when a friend has died.
My Jesus is always there for me to pray.
Every single year, month, week, and day.
My Jesus loves everyone.
Even those whose faith is none.
My Jesus will come back someday.
And on that day I will say.
My Jesus Thank You!

Bill Blundell

The Highest Freedom

Skateboarding is my soul
It is my freedom

The highest freedom attainable, that is one thousand freedoms in itself

Together we are one
And our movements express the varying thoughts and songs of my life

A single flash in time, a trick gone by so suddenly, leaving only one of the many memories imprinted in my book

The style of which, explaining in full, my unyielding passion

The bond made of indescribable feelings that shall never be forgotten nor lost on my vast journey of life

For I have been battered many a time

And I have also felt glory, a peak which can go no higher

When from my grave of sufferings I have risen with the knowledge of victory

And the understanding of my being

So it may continue through the years and past my time of death

That these words remain true as my soul shall to this love

And may they be the description of my simple, wonderful joy

My life's foundation that shall never, ever be crushed.

Jasun Botiller

Confusion

I am home, or so I believe;
It is not as I expected-things have changed.
Everyone is in such a hurry-it has all grown
Even the river-with water as blue as the sky,
Once flowing through a field of green
Now flows, hidden, between towering glass buildings.

A woman I do not recognize is looking at me.
Why is she coming this way?
I squint to see what she is holding:
Black letters scream,
"Will work for food"
I am scared. Why? I do not know.
I turn away.
I won't have any part.
This woman is dirty, rejected, scared.

I cannot help but look back.
The sunny day is over-shadowed by the tears on her cheeks.
I am confused. Why should I care? What can I do?
I have to leave. The air is getting too stale.
I wonder how long she will stay here.

Aaron Kay Sales

Goodbye

One time a thing had occurred to me,
it is not you or me, it is the things
for which we cannot see. Going blind,
out of reach, If I could I would have
saved you from that deadly beast.
So Uncle Jim don't die down on me,
I need you oh for so many many things.
You were always there when I needed you most,
and I know you'll be watching over me with
all of the heavenly hosts.
Uncle Jim I kept my promise from my loving heart,
to be by your side when you had to depart.

Kyle Casey

A Blind Man's Miracle

To see, I saw, was not at all, what it was said to be.
It made me think, to know, to feel, to care for things that now were real.
There was a time, when I did not understand,
What treasures I held in my hand.
But now I see, as well as hear, and smell, and taste, and touch.
It's like a storm cloud in the sky, never raining, but always near by.
You learn to live under that shadow,
Always secretly, wishing it would pass.
Then, one day it really happens, the storm cloud goes away.
You rejoice, and thank the Lord, for this better day.
But... still, somewhere in the back of my mind,
I wonder about this miracle.
It is so much like a fairy tale, that I think...
Maybe it's all a dream, it won't last,
It will never... ever... last.
But then I slowly look around, from the sky down to the ground.
And I realized, that all of this is not a dream.
It never was! It never will be!
It's real.
It's all so wonderful... and real.

Jennifer Salee Bubela

Turn Back The Clock

When I think about the clock of life;
It makes me happy that your my wife;
We've had good times and we've had bad;
I'm so very sorry for making you sad;
I want to spend my life making you happy;
I hope this poem isn't to sappy;
Life is short and life is great;
A number 10 is how you rate;
Life stinks and is so very gory;
For the pain I've caused I'm so very sorry;
Broken in two is what I've done to your heart;
That's how I feel whenever we're apart;
The sky is blue and the water is too;
I promise again to never make you blue;
There's nothing as high as my love;
Like the wings of a snow white dove;
There's a ship that just come into dock;
For the pain I've caused I wish I could turn back the clock.

Jerry Nancy Erwin Sr.

A Little White Lie

A broken promise and a broken heart.
It makes you wonder... How did it all start?
The first "little white lie" I forgave with such ease.
Did it give the wrong impression: this lying's a breeze?
Then the lies came more often, each a little bigger than the last.
Always the same reply to the truth, "I'm sorry, can't we put it in the past?"
As the days went by more slowly, I found doubt with your every word.
Each time I brought up the subject, I wondered if you heard.
So tired of excuses and exhausted from the fight,
When you told me "good morning," I'd have to make sure it wasn't night.
I started to doubt the world, and myself as well;
Waiting for the next lie someone had to tell.
I put up my defenses and my heart started to grow cold,
All from a "little white lie" that was long ago told.

Alan Gibbons

"The Magic Of The Moment"

There is such a quickness as it's arrival, then,
it quickly goes away,
Oh, where does the best time of our life go, why
can't we make it stay,
Our whole song is playing, but we hear only one note,
And, though it's a wonderful sound,
Why must it come and go so fast, and then always be
Lost, so soon after it's found,
Such a beautiful gift is this time, too good to happen so
seldom, to nice to be so rare,
We should be allowed to savor the event, and share it
With others, showing how much we care,
It's our instant of self-worth, and a great thing to cherish,
A joyful feeling, if only it would last,
For all too soon it is gone, having left its mark, it
becomes one more memory of our past,
We experienced the "Magic of the moment", though it
was our's for only just a little while,
It made us better than we were before, and we will
never forget it, and each time we remember, we will smile!

James Roy Hartmangruber

You And I

As the gentle night air caresses my face,
It reminds me of you, your charm, your grace.
Hot summer evenings and cool autumn nights,
reminds me of you and I dining by warm candlelight.
Sipping champagne on a starry moonlight eve,
praying and hoping that you will never leave.
Our love for each other will last forever;
eternity will pass and we'll still be together.
Taking each day one day at a time,
makes me happy knowing you are mine.
Gold and silver line you heart,
and your love goes through me even when we're apart.
Day after day I love you more,
knowing I'm the only one you adore.
The misty mornings and the mystical evenings,
makes me know what our togetherness has its meanings.
Our love will never fade nor will it die,
as long as we're together,
together, you and I.

Eileen Schaefer

The Silence

How blessed the silence
It renders the mind peaceful
Allowing it to appreciate a trueness of thought
How un-complicated life is here in the silence
None but that which the Creator intended to
fill the soul,
The breeze, rustling leaves, coo's and bird song,
dancing waters,
How peaceful this place silence
Here one can appreciate how all the
raucousness of human-kind must
Fill the air of the Creator's domain, his air,
and if we render ourselves a disability
with our noise and boisterous ways
Surely he too, lives with an irritancy
from the constant drone of it
Listen - you too can hear the silence
You too can have trueness of thought,
Peace of mind
The silence, how peaceful it is here.

Joan A. Shonk

My God Mothers Prayer

Beautiful skies above we see
It shined the day you were chosen for me
The clouds together, flow just so
I'm glad you'll be there to watch me grow

We'll read and dance enjoy sun at play
You'll tuck me in after a wonderful day
To tell are future, its hard to say
We'll learn from each other along the way

Afraid of shadows, late in the night
I'll laugh again when you hug me tight

Your love I will feel and I'll know you care
Girl talk and secrets I'm sure we'll shave
Even when I choose most devilish dare
Things we'll turn out right, for I know your there

Song's of joy we'll sing together
Friends we'll be forever and ever

Charlotte Briggs

Life

It's hard to understand, but every time something dies,
It then lives.
God chose us,
And we're here, never to end.
The body may expire
And be left behind,
But that life is unremitting.
The spirit rises,
Now uninhibited, freed.
This is not a choice of the living,
For life is unending.
Never again born,
As life is deathless.
We're not disputing death's door,
But rather the cessation of life.
Nor the reality of the grime-reaper;
But the subject of being immortal,
For life is God's choice.
And we will live on through all of the ages.

Jennifer Smith

My Son

There is a void in my life that cannot be filled,
It was put there the night my son was killed.
Just to hear him say, "I love you mom", one more time.
He was taken away before his prime.
I never heard my son sing.

I laid yellow mums on his eternal rest,
Yellow mums were the flowers he loved best,
Every time I see a bouquet of yellow mums,
I think of the sad loss of my son.
I never heard my son sing.

I'm so sorry for the things I didn't do or say,
That could of brought more happiness his way.
Rest now my son, you are in God's care,
You cannot find better love anywhere,
Did you know I never heard my son sing.

Jacquelyn Brown

Late For New Years

I bump into the door, flinging
it wide as I scramble in,
undressing as I go, I snap
my Wonder bra across the room and it splats
like a huge malformed rubber band
against the cement dorm wall over my bed.
I shimmy backwards into nylons, jamming
my feet through two pair with reinforced toes before
I snatch up tights, instead.
Juggling clothes, breasts, and hair,
I grind myself
down into a little black dress with just enough
spandex to keep me perky and shapely
well into the next year.

Christina Aldridge

Scorpio Curse

How can I be in love with someone I barely know?
It's a Scorpio curse -
falling for someone at first sight.
Is it her twinkling eyes, her shapely figure
or her mysterious yet charming personality?
Maybe it's all of those.
At times lasting friendship are built, yet at others
love
falls
apart
before it even has a chance.
Does it happen to anyone else?

Or am I alone in my Scorpio curse?

I can love passionately and fully.
I want to prove to her that my love really means something.
She'd be treated like the proverbial fairy tale princess -
maybe I'm no knight in shining armor
but I could still be her hero.
That time may one day come

- if she only knew how I felt.

Cary S. Ashby

New Beat Bible

GATHER, It just does not matter
It's a tea party and I'm the mad hatter
A prophet for profit is what I see
Said the Lord of the beat said he
Let me just mention, before I forget
Through divine intervention I bring on this set no regret
Headlong into this song
Baptized by the rhymes as they come full on
se the gifts you have been given
Step out of the boat, walk across the rhythm
Try again you've been fooled my friend
You thought we'd never get together again
But we did, disciples were sent
Check the text it's a brand new testament
So congregate till the cathedrals full
It's the mission YOU've been given so unite in the ritual
So blessed is the Strength of the Strong
They shall inherit the beats that go on
And Blessed are all Reborn People
Who are following the word of the New Beat Bible

Brett Bryan

County Fair

The county fair's held once a year - sometime in July
It's always hot an' you sweat a lot - that I can't deny!
But there's somethin' about being out that makes me feel so neat
Eatin' cotton candy an' elephant ears an' all those things so sweet.

I like to see farm animals-the horses, goats, and sheep
An' pigs that sleep in little pens with hay built in a heap.
The horses are gettin' washed, the sheep are gettin' sheared,
An' the goats, they pay no never mind that we're a-standin' here.

Roller coaster, carrousels, double ferris wheels
There's just so many rides, that one could have a thrill.
I like to ride some and others I really don't,
Especially the one's that tend to leave my stomach in my throat!

Now that the fair is over, I'm really, really sad
But I'm lookin' back and rememberin' the fun times that I had.
So when the school bell rings, and blasts into the air
I know it won't be too long 'fore the next county fair!

Emily E. Freeman

Think

The universe is big yet so small,
Its amazing to think we're a part of it all.
So vast yet moving very fast...I think....I think,
Why were we put here?
Were we some sort of genetic experiment from another planet?
And were we so hideous we were banished?
Or are were aliens ourselves trying to find out who we really are?
And as we go through life wondering what's it all about,
We should ask ourselves a question, why?...
Why should we want to know what its all about?
It's all there in front of us, so why worry?
We have all these opportunities laid out in front of us, so why should
we worry?
Sometimes when I'm lying in bed trying to go to sleep, I wonder why.
What's it all for?...Every day, every year, every hour, minute, second
Why bother to do anything at all?..
So many questions, just so many.....
So as I think, well, that's really all I have is to think...and to
hope...wish...and pray.
And so, this is what I think or want to know, or whatever,
So in the meantime, I just keep thinking.

Jonathan Embry

The Visit

It's cold in here.
It's been like this for the past fifteen years
Close the door...It's already closed.
Shut the window...That's closed too.
Turn up the heat...It's as high as it goes.
Then why is it so cold..? Surely you know.
I'm not dead am I..? No you're alive and well.
Are you sure I'm not in .....?
No, you're not in hell.
But, I see angry faces...That much is true.
And look! Over there, isn't that Jealousy?
Yes, I see him too.
Envy just winked at me...Maybe you should wave.
But he's standing next to Hatred! Come, you must be brave.
What's Lust doing in here...? You tell me.
I don't like this place...Soon we'll see.
Who are you...come let's depart.
You know I can't leave...I'm the landlord of your heart.
But it's much too cold in here.
It's been like this for the past fifteen years.

Calvin Gorrell

Her Picture

Her Picture graces my bedside
It's been there always
The black and white of her photograph
makes her seem ethereal

Her sad yet beautiful eyes reflect
the heartache she must have felt
knowing she would never see her precious boy... become a man

A frightful, deadly disease stole her away
so very long ago

Though I never met Her
heard her voice touched her hand

She is the one that I
talk to when I am sad
long for when I am alone
love more than anything

I know she is watching me
from somewhere up above

I know she loves me
helps me and that I am never

Truly alone

Julie Rae Barnett

The Surprise

Mommy, mommy! What's that noise?
It's coming from my room and it's not my toys!

The sound is coming from my room, in there!
It's grumbling and growling like a grizzly bear!

Mommy, come with me and take a peak,
Maybe we'll catch him if we sneak.

So I opened the door and in we crept,
And we heard him breathing as he slept.

What could it be under my bed?
And we heard him moving as mommy lead.

"Don't be afraid," mommy said with a grin,
"Lift up the ruffles and take a look in."

So over I walked and lifted the sheet,
And crouched right down to my stocking feet.

And when I looked into that space,
OUT came a puppy licking my face!

Jennifer D. Santoro

Life

Life is a river that flows to the sea
Its current and eddies carry you and me
To our destination, where 'ere that may be
As we travel the journey of life

Life is a poem in a beautiful book
With fine illustrations; we're too scared to look
To see what's ahead, what paths that we took
As we read the story of life

Life is a beautiful symphony
Where violins and trombones play
Life is just a merry go round
Round and round; night and day

Life is a garden of beautiful flowers
We tend and we nurture the love that is ours
Come close and hold me; we'll share all our hours
As we drink a toast to love and to life

Bernhard Gordon

The Cabin

There is a cabin that sits among the pines,
it's exterior old and weathered, it's windows circled in vines

In an earlier day it was a happy place
a home full of memories, to many to erase

It was built for shelter and furnished with love,
it was shared by the family, with their God up above

It warmed those inside and weathered many a storm,
but each year took it's toll and each season changed it's form

And with each passing season things began to change
as the family inside aged the cabin was rearranged

And as the years passed the young ones moved away,
leaving only the original two, with a limited time to stay

Then the original two were both called away
and the cabin was left alone to let nature have her way

Even to this day, as the cabin gives way to rot,
the love and warmth it once housed, will never be forgot

Jeffrey A. Jackson

The Master

The colors surround me and my head starts to spin,
it's hard to describe this place I am in.
It's very complex and also quite fragile,
It can be limber and also quite agile.
It locks away a secret no one has uncovered,
and up till this day I haven't been discovered.
I live here and play all day,
others visit but they can't stay.
I'm the only one who can go where I go,
and what I see I mustn't show,
For I am the Master of the Rainbow

Kendra Keel

Boxes Twenty-Four

Undo each day,
its hours strip away them in the sun
till gladdened heart smiles phosphorescently in joy
forevermore to claim rich parcels for itself,
primeval time's inheritor.
The ribboned shred of gay decor,
grand covers for my boxes twenty-four.
Hide treasures which though shadowed be,
are all that fate provides for me.
So they are mine, my thence unbound;
no nothing sought, know nothing found.

James C. Little

Remembrance

Fifteen years ago we met on a crisp September day.
It's love, he said, with a gleam in his eye. I didn't believe, I shied away.

My first love, my endless love.
What did he see in me?
I was awkward and plain, but to him I was the most graceful beauty.

Those long ago days were magic.
Now I wonder how that could be?
The stars were brighter, the moon was whiter,
The laughter was lighter, when he was with me.

Love was a promise then— A promise I learned to accept,
An acceptance I would never regret.

For fifteen years I've held a memory in my heart.
It's way down in a corner—I haven't looked at it in awhile.
But today, I did.

Caren Nelson

The Gift Of Love

Under the tree is a gift of love, this gift is given from above
It's not a toy or a simple pleasure it's the gift of love for
us to treasure.

So open up your heart and receive it, pass it on and just believe it
As it's given full and free the gift of love will always be

Christmas day, a time of giving, let us change our ways of living
For it's not the present that surround us, but God's love that has
bound us

So moms and dad's and little children, remember what christmas
Is all about, it's not the toys that bring us together it's
God's love, and that's what life's about.

So open up your heart and receive it, pass it on and just
believe it. As it's given full and free, it's God's love
for you and me.

Dave A. Ward

Just a Moment

Infinity scares the s**t out of me.
It's not death, really,
It's the ugly knowledge of death.
The bloated waxen bodies of children
and the Grandparents we've all seen
pumped full of preservatives and made-up like mannequins.
We pass through life in lines
of awkward smiles and careful mourning.
We touch death.
I don't mean the abstract death,
the death of a soul, or a relationship.
I mean this:
These hands scribbling words
the sinewy joints that shake hands and wave goodbye,
these will stiffen and stop.
We know this with peculiar rage,
yet we see the grace in a skein of bluebirds
rhythmic and ragged slicing the sky.
For a moment we forget,
and we live.

Jeffery C. Milligan

Don't Have Time

The hourglass is pressed against my mind.
It's sand just keeps on falling, seems I've got no time.
Time, that elusive thing, it's never right at hand.
When you look at your watch, see how still time stands.
My watch can't keep it, time's always on the fly.
I can't stand still too long, or time will pass me by.
Hourglass, yeah pressed against my mind.
There's something I have to do, but seems I've got no time.
I cannot buy or borrow it, to whom do I go?
Fore who has bottled time, to sell or just to show?
I've come to know a truth, that was not so hard to find.
No one can own this thing, because we belong to time.
Even brick and mortar shall crumble in its hand.
Time will still be flying, when no trace is left of man.
I've often heard the phrase, that one's time must have been up.
But, perhaps it is time, that has poured us from it's cup.
The hourglass no more, shall press against my mind.
One day it shall not pass me by, fore I will walk with time.

Donnie F. Hailes

Love

Love is a feeling that you feel.
It's something that should be taken for real.
To be in love is to be there,
Not to let down the one that you care.
If you find someone that you're able to talk to,
Is nice and caring and you know it could be true
Then that person just might be the one for you.
Hope nothing goes wrong,
And love will last long.
If ever there's misunderstanding and
Things are settled within the heart,
Love will not be part.
So if there's anything wrong whatever it's about
To make it last and not worry just work it out.

Drusila Rodriguez

Untitled

My Lord said softly to me, "Come!
It's time to leave, your job is done."
My eyes grow dim, my body slack
My heart beats fade, then flicker back
Then STILLED; as breath deserts the frame
As moths will leave a dying flame
The wisp of an Eternal Soul escapes!
Wait - !! STILLED no more - Unfettered — Free!!
My Soul released — Unleashed to flee
To leave this place of pain and grief
This place of woes beyond belief.
I'll not look back
My onward rush
To meet the light
Cannot be thrust backward
Slowed
Or forced to halt!
My free and floating Spirit cries
Touch me not - don't weep for me -
My home is here — Eternity!

Barbara Hass

Miss Her

Today is Sunday, the most special of days;
I've been thinking about her, like I do always.
She's far away and I'm here caught in a bind;
Yet she stays, she stays always on my mind.
I wish she were here, I wish she were near;
Three days apart is far too much I fear.

Does she know how much I care?
Does she know that I'll always be there?
Does she now that she's everything to me?
Does she know that by her side is where I want to be?
And do I, do I tell her often enough...
that I love her, I love her.

Words can't express these new feeling in my heart;
It's as if my life has been given a new start.
And yes she cares and loves me abundantly;
I feel a certain sweetness each time she touches me.
What I'm trying to tell her with this...
is that I miss her and yearn for the warmth of her kiss.

Chip Haddock

Ocean

As I walk along the shore
The mist sprays in my face
With each step my foot touches the cool sand
The waves ripple in one by one
The wind whispers a song in my ear
and there is constant peace

Jessica Geesaman

Meeting a Deadline

Since I was a teen I've been writing verse
I've been told that I have a real flare.
At a moment's notice, at the drop of a hat,
I can write a great poem on a dare.

It's a talent from God, a gift I've been given
I use it whenever I'm able.
I can jot in a cab, a boat or my bed
But I'd rather sit up at a table.

All the topics are chosen for special needs
at the time when I sit down to compose.
I write poems for birthdays, for comings and goings,
and for my own pleasure, God knows!

I thought about sending some poem I hold dear
But it had just one line too many.
You might not agree that this one's as good
But it's better than not sending any.

Betty Jane Day

Life's Mystery's Cup

After eighty, eight years I've summed it up
I've drank the bitter and the sweet out of life's mystery's cup
I've had my up and downs, spent time just clown 'n 'round
I've skimmed and saved and tried to pre-tend
I'm practical and logical right to the end
I hang to keep-sakes and even old dolls, save old cloths
Sew and re-model, un-till goodness knows
I buy old dolls that are for-lorn and un-wanted
Re-dress them caress them and give them a home
People wonder what makes me tick
I just look for-ward to what comes next
My life has been a wonder I've made it so
Ex-citing things happen where ever I go
I live for the minute, I've spent the past
It's up to my maker how long I will last

Alice L. Hartley

Maturity

Old! How did it happen so soon?
I've just caught my breath from
the race to keep ahead of teenagers.
Grandchildren are living proof that
Old is here. So are the lines on my face,
the spots on my hands and the gray in my hair.
Old doesn't reach inside unless one lets it in.
Inside are young dreams not yet
fulfilled—time is running out;
Old is trailing me,
hoping to catch me not paying attention.
Old shows in my failing eyesight, my shaking hand;
yet my Young heart sees still the majesty of mountains,
the contrast of gray and yellow days and hears
songs of birds and feels the crispness in the air.
Old needn't take away the appreciation of
beautiful things; it should be ever
more conscious of a world of beauties
Young is too busy to see.

Karen S. Talbot

Softly And Gently

I will stand tall and strong like a giant redwood tree
I will be as gentle as a feather blowing in a gentle wind
I will be as loyal as a dog is to his master
I will be as soft as a kitten's fur
I will love you always as you will me
I will show you with my eyes or gently whisper in your ear
Only then, and only then will you know my feelings for you
are pure as the white snow

Anita Makkos

You're The Only One For Me

I'm wild about you girl
I've loved you oh so long
I know we'd get along
Just one look and I fell in love
I looked at you every single day
I'd like to get my loving arms around you
My heart is overflowing with love
No other face can quite compare with you
This time I feel that we belong
Oh girl, you're the only one for me

We come so close to perfect love
What in the world am I so shy of
Then you came along and mended my broken heart
You know I'll love you every day
We'll share each other's happiness for now and ever
You are the dream that saved my life
I'd thought I'd never find a better love
That made my heart set on fire
I'm telling you that you are my kind of girl
Oh girl, you're the only one for me

David Hennessey

Kimberly

Being with her is a new adventure,
I've never had a girl quite like her.

When I look into her eyes,
I get lost forever in the skies.

When I see her or know she's coming,
My heart starts racing and ears hear humming

Of glorious music from Christmas time,
The time when she became mine.

I love her and respect her dear
And feel pleasure without fear, when we are near.

But when we kiss and depart,
I can feel my beating heart

Crumble to the idle seas;
The longing drops me to my knees.

And I wonder if she'll stay mine
Because her beauty is so fine,

Or if she shall leave me, I know I'll freeze,
And I'll die mumbling, "Stay Kimberly, please!"

Jason Antczak

Untitled

Today I feel such rage inside
I've said things today that I just couldn't hide
It's just that they get me so mad
And when I react, it just makes things bad
I know we're all supposed to love one another
And there's bound to be arguments between a sister and a brother
But today there was something different about this dispute
Everything around me was all mute
All the yelling was burning my ears
I was listening but I didn't really hear
All I could think about was the come back
The bull in me was about to attack
I said so much garbage that I would never mean
Now I wish I had a chance to make the air clean
I know that today I used words of hate
I just hope the time to make amends doesn't come too late

Christine Davis

Bliss

All through my life
I've seen pieces of a puzzle
That come together
Like the flash of an ember
As it becomes a flame

Glimpse of Heaven
Subtly shared with me
As I rest in Him
Whose Word abides in me

Bliss reaches to my soul
Nothing compares to this heaven I feel
Deep in my heart, yet right on my sleeve,
My heart lies open, open to receive

Taking me to heights only known to Him
His hints and wisdom continually abound to me
Standing in awe, basking in His glory
Feeling His love, His life dwelling in me

Dawn Akers

The Cross and the Nails

The soldiers nailed Jesus to the cross
Jesus let them do this to pay our cost
He died for our sins
So we should praise Him by singing songs and hymns
As the nails went through his hands
His blood dripped to the sand
He did this so we can have everlasting life
So go out and be a light
We know we can never repay Him
So don't let your light go dim
He calls us all to be Disciples
So don't be like Adam and Eve who ate those forbidden apples
We all should be a living sacrifice
For it is God who saved our lives
And the Lord thy God never fails
So remember it's been all paid by the cross and the nails.

Chad Watkins

The Cup

Come share the cup with me.
  Joy, wealth, good times you will see.

Fill Grandma's old crazed cup that she had to use,
  rekindle memories and thoughts that amuse.
Cherish a collector's cup held once, not more,
  it's value too high for a daily chore.
Share the cup of communion wine,
  outpoured for us by One divine.

Each cup a story to be told,
  to consider, and to hold.

Moments quiet, sip tea from a sweetheart's cup, a gift,
  romantic daydreams lift.
Drink coffee from a friend's prayer cup, once his own,
  send his heart's desires before God's throne.
Stack twelve fancy cups in a row,
  await holiday company you know.

Our cup runs over with love,
  blessed by the cupbearer above.

Carolyn Sanford

Untitled

Jane goes to the beach
She always eats a peach
She goes in the water
And fights with an otter
The sea gulls above will screech

Ashley Schainuck

Morning Prayer

Put me in your window sill, perhaps
just by your bed.

Be sure I'm in a busy place so
daily I'll be read.

Hush now, quiet, be so ever still.

Cocooned up in my presence, listening to my will.

Feel my Father's spirit as it's
poured upon your head.

Bowed in morning prayer, your soul is daily fed.

His love drips in your eyes, his grace
just kissed your cheeks.

Your lips embraced with kindness to
others as you speak.

Give me all your worries, let fears and
doubt depart.

In prayer, you held my hand. In love,
I'll hold your heart.

Peace and joy are yours today. Serene,
so calm you'll be...

Because in morning prayer, each other we did see.

Anne Hartwig

Human

Human, made through no will of my own,
  Just like any other flesh and bone,
Dreams and desires that are different
  some just like everyone.

Live and love, treating everyone the same,
  others wish to hurt me, call me out my name.
Reasons they have are only one,
  I am different, not a "Regular" son.

Get to know me, see how I exist,
  There's one thing you can never miss
I'm human, made through no will of my own
  Gay man of flesh and bone.

John Ed Lowery

"Time Waits For No One"

Time waits for no one, so let it be known
Just one final time I step down from my throne.

Trapped in a jail cell with no room to fight
What else can go wrong, now that nothing is right.

Lost in a daydream where all I could see
was the rays of the sun, as they were shining on me.

Lost in a nightmare that must have come true,
I wake up to bars that keep me from you.

At war with my conscience; a duel with my pride.
With nothing to gain and nothing to hide.

As time waits for no one, the Lord knows it's so true.
There's nothing to stop me from dreaming of you.

Billy Koonce

Albatross

Southern latitudes, the sun rising
sextant out, what's the angle
Company ! an albatross!
motionless, but gliding
just off the bridge wing, watching
Staring majestically.

I ask. " what are you thinking"
he only stares.
how can we communicate, I ask.
he only stares.
blink, if you're a seaman's soul
He blinks , I think.

Are you lost, I wave the sextant.
he stares, balefully
Are you lonely ? I ask
He stares, a tear ?? mine or his?
A slight movement of the wing
he soars, away to sea and sky

Edwin E. Davies

Joy

Joy,
She does not allow herself to be
intimidated by others.
Joy,
She may unintentionally be
insensitive to the feelings of others.
Joy,
She can be a tyrant at home and
difficult to live with.
Joy,
She is bright and witty.
But most of all, Joy is my loving
mother.

Jamie Johnson

A Worthy Jewel

Peggy Rachel is "Autistic"
she is a cherished dear.

She goes around and asks for hugs
when anyone is near.

Our Lord knows why she does not talk
in a normal way.

Yet when she does go to speak
we heed what she will say.

All love her quite deeply
body, mind and soul.

And trust that someday very soon
she'll reach her well earned goal.

Beverly Higgs Both

The Messenger Has Been Sent

The dove has flown home
She is free
Free to go home
Free to be with him.

She has but one course
And a promise to be
She is going home this day
Where she can be free for eternity.

Antoinette Owens Watson

A Friend

One who knows you through and through, knows the very things you do
Keeps on pulling just for you, that's a friend.

One who loves you all the while, grips your hand and shares a
Smile, bears no thought that's not worthwhile that's a friend.

One who's troubles trouble you wandering, thinking how you'll come
Through, prayerfully taking your burdens to god, that's a friend.

One who loves you when you've treated them wrong, smiles amid
Trials and tribulations of home, keeps the secret you've confessed
To them, that's a friend.

Often as I sit and wait, I sometimes wonder if I mistake, the true
Loyal friend I should be, where troubles knock and you call on me.

But, when mothers, and fathers friends are gone, this old world is
Desolate and you're alone, you think of the presence of God above,
God's friend Jesus for his is love.

Ada Marche

No More Tomorrows

We once said we would grow old together, our marriage vows would be forever.
The years passed swiftly one by one, we worked hard, took pride in our children.
They grew older, so did we, we had no worries, the best was yet to be.
One cloudy day, that threatened rain, our hopes and dreams came to an end.
With a burst of pain, and a soft cry scream, all our tomorrows crashed to the earth.
I never had a chance to say goodbye, and now I can only cry, "If only"
So to those couples out there with their lives intact, I can only offer this advice,
Fulfill your dreams now, give that hug and kiss, do all that you've dreamed of,
For tomorrow will come, don't look back in regret, wrap yourselves in love,
Let your memories be filled with what you've done, the two of you made one.
Gone is gone, never more to be, the saddest thought is "Why didn't we"
So do it now, give all your love, never look back and say "Why didn't we?"

Janice Jackson

"...If I Should Die Before I Wake..."

The innocence of childhood is over, such a spirit is now free.
The love of the heavens overcame it, yet not of the earth,
which its memories preserved. Time has yet not cradled those
hearts who mourn. A face not seen, a voice not heard, laughter
only known of God. A small step upon this earth not taken,
cradled by a mother's arms it was not, But only in a dream
does it remain.

Cheryl Butler

Images

As I stood looking out the window, watching the sun beaming bright,
I saw Images of you and I loving till dawn's early light.
It reminded me of happy times and all our sunny days,
Images of how our love was a giant bonfire set ablaze.

As I stood looking out the window, watching the rain fall down,
I saw Images of sad times, but still our love would not drown.
The thunder and lighting brought Images of love's stormy nights,
Images of how love sometimes was scary and offered us some frights,
Images of how love sometimes will bite and cause some occasional fights
But through understanding and forgiveness, love set straight our sights.

As I stared out the window, watching the snow fall outside.
I saw Images of our special times; felt so fondly, I shed a tear and cried.
It reminded me of drinking wine inside by the fireplace,
All those quiet and peaceful times I looked into your eyes and touched your face.
How the wine in the crystal glasses glistened by the fire's dimming glow.
Like diamonds sparkle in a jewelry store when first put in the case for show.

I looked out the window one last time,
Watching a million stars sparkle and a full moon shine,
I saw endless Images, reminding me that our love is special as 200 year old wine,
But most of all I see Images of us together; memories that will last
a happy lifetime.

Pat Kastler

Instead Blue

Blue - filled sky,
rounded over my head.
Don't tell me,
accept me instead.

Crystal - clear glass,
sliding over top the sand.
Don't push me down low.
instead take my hand.

Exploding - bright sun,
painting red my skin.
Are you really who you think?
Instead I'm letting you in.

Instead make it blue,
please do not let it remain.
If I can't find it by myself,
I'm afraid of what I'll gain.

Jennifer Curtis

"Rush"

Rush.
Rush.
We rush into things.
We dive in head first.
We think we're in love.

Rush.
Rush.
Why do we have to rush?
We can take it slowly.
If we wait it will be better.

Rush.
Rush.
Rushing isn't as good as waiting.
Please let's wait.
I promise it will be better later.

Rush.
Rush.
Let's wait.
Wait.

Angel Kay Fowler

Inside Outside

Sat in myself
Sat inside too long
My eyes tend to wander
My heart not as strong
As my mid dims
My fingers tend to twitch
I find myself sad
For calling my love a bitch
Life is too short
This can't happen to me
I only did the coke
So my soul could be free
Free it is now
Floating above my body
There will be no more beer
There will be no more hot toddy
I hope I am forgiven
I hope I go to heaven
I can't go to hell
Emotionally, I'm only eleven

Jon K. Davis

A Single Wedding Rose

A single wedding rose,
saved from old times.
Once as fresh as new love,
now as bitter as wine.
Brown around the edges,
Wilted and dry.
still it brings back memories,
of a day now gone by...
Filled with love and joy,
they pledged their love for always.
Arm in arm they'd walk,
no matter what others may say...
Life was never easy,
and they fell along the way;
but they faced it together,
and they made it any ways...
A testament that true love,
forever shall endure.
A rose may wilt and fade in time,
but true love, is for ever more...

Jacqueline Wittman

Insanity

Voices inside my head
Screaming, Yelling
This tearing of my heart
Ripping, Bleeding
Trying to find a way out
Escaping in my dreams
I hear beauty calling me
Standing with freedom
Upon the mountain
I am here in the valley
I am entwined
With fear and hate
Screaming inside
For the words have no strength
To escape my lips

Karen Kelly

Untitled

Cloud horses septuple
seriatim sequacious
in fields azure,
from the west
agallop
chasing the east

unbridled unridden
wind driven
manes sericeous
writhen
by gusts boreal

Jim Shawver

Awakening

Too long
she slept
beneath the cold,
white
winter blanket
of doubt.

In glory,
she has burst forth
to laugh
and love
and say....
I am!

Katherine R. Mule

Envy

As she looked up at the light,
She wonders again, 'It this right?'
The feeling she feels is so strong,
Turning away others, to do no wrong.
Is this love like it should be?
To him its still a mystery.
He loves someone - I know its true.
But tell me Allie, me or you?
She sat down there in the light,
All night wondering, 'Is that right?'

Apryl Bozarth

Sunshine

The sun knowingly
shines
down upon us.
The sunbeam
feels
sorry for our poor, lost
stranded souls.
Radiating,
it's warmth.
Glowing
through our cold, selfish
black hearts.
Softening,
the hard lumps within our chests.
Giving us
one more chance to experience
true love

Cristina Ng

Doors

Open them
Shut them
Slam them in their face
To let them in
Or show them out
Or keep them in their place
Behind the barriers of race

Be a door opener
Look a little closer
Tex-Mex, Soul, or Kosher
With life we have to cope-ner
Welcome all who knock
With a little bit of grace

Greet them when they're coming
Mourn each one when they're gone
Whatever color, race, or creed
We all belong.

Bonnie W. Milks

My Century

My century
Shy twenty five,
An endless arena
In a moment of time,
I know it well,
A piece of heaven
Tempered with hell.

My century
If still alive,
No longer
Shy twenty five.

Arthur Vines

Untitled

Lavishly vivid
sighting hundreds of trees
squirming branches
dropping their seeds
to the floor near the flowers
where petals fall too
next to the water
running on through
dodging the boulders
creating a stream
under the bridges
travel the leaves

Karen Yoo Allegrini

Wishes Unheard

Wishes unheard, visions unseen.
Simple world, but what does it mean.
Torture my soul, I really don't care.
I've lost my faith, but I'm not sure where.
Prayers to God, lost in the clouds.
They have gone silent, but once where loud.
Christen my blood, abandon my dreams.
Thoughts are nothing, but silent screams.
Supernova shall form in the sun.
Day is over; night has eternally begun.
Wishes still stand, prayers still fly.
Answer them all, God, and tell me why.
Unheard they are and they are wishes too,
Made by people maybe much like you.
The prayers are silent; no one hears.
Their unheard wishes tell our unseen fears.

Jennifer Lynn Johnson

Untitled

Whisper sweet nothings in my ear.
Sing me a song no one can hear.
Kiss me when the time is right.
Watch the sunset go into the night.
Romantic settings,
Or stars in the sky.
Sharing dreams,
Or dancing slow dances.
A moonlight walk,
Or a sunlight stroll.
These are the things that untame my heart.
These are the romantic things that
Make me love someone.

Alexandra F. Melius

Untitled

Old man
  sitting on the dock
the paths you've walked
  have sketched their map upon your face.

Wise man
  what do you see
as you watch the tides
  run the moonstar's race?

There you serenely sit
  silently talking,
yet so few will hear
  or understand.

Here, I curiously wait
  for a glimpse of acceptance in your eye,
a grasp of friendship
  from your hand.

Barbara Smithson

Untitled

Sitting here wondering if this is real,
Sitting through all the emotions I feel.
So many people die everyday,
Each one dying in their own special way.
Some by nature, some by another man,
But sadly there are some that die by
  their own hand.
How wrong of a mistake can someone
make,
To feel that the only solution is their own
  life to take.
Pulling a trigger, or popping a pill,
Is a way of expressing how some people
feel.
The pain that they felt may have gone
  away,
But the pain in the hearts of their loved
  one's will forever stay.
It's a scary feeling to think that a friend's
Life could one day soon come to an end.
So I do all I can, and try in every way,
To be able to stay with the one's I loved
  for just another day.

Jodi Miller

Snow

As I sit outside the window
Snowflakes fall about my face,
  a glow inside - inviting.
I check the scathed face
  of my grandfather's pocket watch,
  three o'clock and no sign.
I stroll down the way,
  quietly singing
  hoping to hear her refrain.
Snow dances lightly.
I sit and sigh.
The appointment was for two,
  I think I was lat
  she knew I was.
I sang as she walked by,
  her eyes
  never looking back.

Alex Dalton

Snowflakes

Snowflakes on my window,
Snowflakes on the ground.
Snowflakes on the house and
Everywhere around.

Gracefully they fall
Leaving nothing more in sight.
They lie down to rest and
Gently say, "good night".

Amy Thorne

Mental Illness

Terrifying voices
Stampeding raising clouds
shouting out responses
from persecuting crowds

Magpies cackle daily
Even if eyes are closed
reality drifts by vaguely
nowhere is where you've froze

Craig Rich

The Rosebush

Once there was a rosebush
So beautiful and blooming,
it stood out among all others.
Once there was a gardener
who took very special care
of these roses all year long.
They bloomed every summer.
No matter what the winter was like.
Every day their gardener went out
and checked on his very special bush.
Rain or shine he was always there.
Then the gardener became ill.
only once in a while he made it out.
The roses became less and less.
Finally one day the gardener died,
and the roses wept.
They knew they had lost their best friend.
One day the last rose bloomed,
it was placed on the gardener grave,
where they, once again, would be together
forever more.

Barbara Roberts-Franco

Clover

Clover growing in the fields
So beautiful to view
Needing nothing but the sun and rain
To nature thru and thru

All summer long it will stay put
And then the winter comes
Somewhere it finds a place to hide
As all the flowers do subside

Then the spring is back again
Again the clover blooms
More lavishly blooming all the time
Never needing to spend a dime

Dorothy S. Zelenak

Guinea Pig

Guinea pig, guinea pig,
so faithful and true.
How lucky I am,
to have a friend like you.
Sleeping all night,
at the foot of my bed.
Your noise makes me happy,
while thoughts fill my head.
Guinea pig, guinea pig,
so faithful and true.
How could I ever,
re-pay you.
I feed you and groom you,
this is true.
Your friendship is more,
than a comb and a cage.
You are my good friend,
throughout all the days.

Brenda Hartwick

The Well

A well is like your mind,
The water, your soul,
Each drop a dream or thought.
Never empty, never full.
You draw up your bucket,
And pour your thoughts onto paper.
So others, may as yet, try to understand you.

Erin Ricketts

Priority

Moving
So fast
All coming all going
No time
No past
Keep on!
Remember no slowing.

Remember...

Only a ride.
Look around.
Behold.
Sights. And the,
Sound...

On this red, blue, green
Earth
Terminal velocity
Is not
What it's worth.

Eric M. Mikkelson

You See

Intimate corruption inside
so harsh to hide
you saw my face
convicted my place
you only see
a shadow of me
a shadow is a mystery
when it is full totally
when it melts into night
all at once, no shadows to fight
think of me as an eclipse
only admit to ignorant lips
sticks and stones
break bones
calling names
wicked games
now you've done it - taken the bait
found yourself in the hell of hate
if what you see is what you get
you haven't seen me yet

Jenna Hoffman

Isolation

I just lost a friend
so I isolated myself from
life and I said I would
never love again.

I was mad so I got
into drugs really bad
I didn't know what to
do with my life sometimes
I wish I had a knife.

One day I almost died
because I came close to
committing suicide I would
have been dead if my brother
didn't find me.

Then one day to my surprise
I saw a girl with blue eyes
and blonde hair that looked like silk.

She was so beautiful but I had a doubt and I was scared to ask her out because if she turned me down my life would go back to isolation.

David Dillenbeck

April 28, 1993

'Twas on this day our child was born
so precious and so loved.
This child was such a blessed gift
sent to us from above.
God made our baby with such care
and you and I can see
How special and how cherished
that this child will always be.
We valued every moment
of our tiny child's short presence.
And we'll think of this as a special time
for every moment hence.
For God could see as well as we
the treasure we were given.
And He chose to take our baby
to his special place in heaven.
So now we keep our child with us
embedded in our heart.
He's just our little angel since we now must live apart.
With deepest love, Mom and Dad.

Bonnie Hess

Moonlight Dancer

Moonlight dancer
So smooth upon her feet
Gliding through the shadows
So quiet
So discreet
Feeling eyes upon her
But not turning around
She leaps and lands
Over and over
Without making a sound
She spins around and raises her hands
With one last pirouette
And gently falls
Into the arms
Of the stranger she has met.

Kristin K. Robel

Untitled

A cobweb, life; spider spun line
So strong and safe for all the strife
Of troubled fate there to entwine
A cobweb, life.

Yet cut so clean, nor with a knife,
It's broken off just with a sign
Of wind or breath, torn when it's rife
With strength and light, order Divine
Can flick it through. Be man or wife
Its slender silk slips, incarnadine
A cobweb, life.

Barbara Drummond Gilman

Mommy

She is nice, she is sweet
She is mannerly and very neat.
She is kind and what
a nice Mother I wouldn't
even want another, why is
she nice? Why is she neat?
Why don't I want another?
Because she's my Mother.

Justinna Porcelli

The Poet

He speaks to me in rhyming words
So sweet rolling from his tongue
The meanings are all to close
And the memories unsung

He says the words in my ear
I can feel them all throughout me
He knows what exactly to sat
He knows how to make me believe

He talks of worlds I get lost in
With an emotion in every phrase
Flowing with rhythm
Filling my mind with haze

He sings to a song only I can hear
I know that he want me there
His poetry takes me far away
And into his ever-so-timeless stare

Angela Rooke

Untitled

If I were a sea gull
Soaring through the air,
I would be way up there!
Without a care!
Out over the ocean,
and back to the sand!
The ocean water is the color
of the sky!
Sometimes gray, sometimes blue,
always, always, a beautiful hue!
Then I got the thinking,
I'd rather be me,
Watching the sea gull,
Over the big, big sea!

Florence Brush Magnuson

One Simple Prayer

A caress across my silken shoulder,
Softly as a sweet gentle breeze.
Increasingly his touch grows bolder,
A storm on the raging seas.

I knew him forever, I thought.
But these rush of feelings are new.
In a world of emotion I am caught.
I know not what each day will do.

When I am sad with sorrow,
He looks at me with those fathomless eyes
And says wait for tomorrow
And I will wash away those thundering skies.

He is wondrous, gentle, rare.
Together we are destined to grow.
And so I have one simple prayer:
O God, — Do not ever make him go.

Kristin D. Milot

Alone

Touch has a memory
Sight and words do too
Remembrance of you in lonely hours.
Satisfies my need for you.

If visions spoke,
And I could live my dreams
Enough, it is enough for me.

Carol Doolittle

The Burning Fire

Smoke lifted above the field.
Soldiers lie in bleeding pain.
Many lives for a crying soul.
The echo of battle can still be heard.
The smell of war is in the air.
The wind blows the fire down;
It shall always burn forever.
Even after peace is made,
The fire burns within us.
Through the smoke, comes a light.
Shining brightly on our souls.
Even though we feel the fire,
That simple light blocks it out.
When tears are shed for each other,
That's when our doors open,
To peace and togetherness.
The wind carries the smoke away.
The smoke shall always lurk,
As long as the fire keeps burning,
Deeply inside of us.

Christopher N. Loudon

Mask

Some people think I'm happy
Some people think I'm glad
Some people think I'm outgoing
But in reality - I'm really sad

Some people think I'm independent
Some people think I'm homely
Some people think I'm a brat
But in reality - I'm really lonely

Some people think I'm bold
Some people think I'm brave
Some people think I'm strong
But in reality - I'm really afraid

No one knows who I really am
Because no one ever asks
No one will ever know who I am
Because I'll continue to wear this "Mask"

Belinda Handy

Unfinished Collections

I wonder if
some will receive
the time of day
they deserve
—once precious moments
now forgotten
and buried in a pile of paper
waiting for the return
of inspiration—
open to frustration,
small victories
and who knows what else

I cannot find them places
of their own
in my book of dreams
and so they remain
unfinished collections
in my folder of hopes.

Alice Chin

An Instrument

Somewhere,
Someone plays for me.
An instrument,
I hear the tunes and give the world
melodies.

Somewhere,
Someone speaks to me.
An instrument,
I hear the words and give the world
poetry.

Somewhere,
Someone plays for me.
An instrument,
I hear the tunes and give the world
melodies.

JoAnn Hilton

Stranger?

Have you ever known someone,
Someone you can't forget?
Why, do you ask yourself
Could this be someone I've met?
Maybe in the pre-existence
Yet someone they met it's true,
Perhaps that spirit came to earth
For the purpose of tempting you!

Duane H. Jensen

On The Other Side

Life is sweet and all to strange,
Sometimes I feel kind of deranged.
I can't wait until the day,
That we can run, sing, and always play,
On the other side.

Sometimes I don't know what to do,
You know when your down and feelin'
blue,
Then I start thinking of you,
And I can't wait until the time,
When we don't have to deal with time,
Or fuss and fight the daily grind,
When we can visit again, on the other side.

Who knows when it will be that hour,
When we are surrounded by His mighty
power.
When we complete the triangle of life,
I surely will miss my wife.

All things must eventually come to an end,
When we are surrounded by family and
friends,
Far off in ever land, when we all meet
again,
On the other side.

Barry Kempf

Alas, My Love

Alas, my love, our days draw nigh
Soon we part to set sail in the
celestial sky.
We know not what the journey may
bring. Will it bring joy? Will it
'cause pain?
God, I trust, will grant me grace
to continue our love in his heavenly place.

Charles W. Baston

Untitled

Bits and pieces
souls joined - forever entwined
spiraling toward
a heavenly infinity
words never spoken
though the thoughts
reflected are received
as we but need gaze
dreamily into forever
our destiny held
wondrous in each others eyes.
All is Beauty
never once to deceive
and love said, Beauty
at once rightly cherished
ever changing - yet remaining
constant from the start
how much to love you - my soul - my heart.

Kathleen Therese Reeves

Vivus

I am, the breath of birds, and
sound, of rustling leaves.

Passion's kiss, is the wind, and
sweet fragrance of man.

A part of massive vistas, and
unbounded oceans.

The total essence of all earth,
in a sparkle of dew.

Distinct, yet joined, in the
one, of all creation.

WE ARE!

Barbara A. Pietraszak

Mountain Pool

Spirit of the mountain
Spirit of the air
Spirit of green leaves,
Dark earth, crystal water
Spirit of cool wet stones-
Oh spirit - I hear you,
As I sit here in
Your fragrance,
I hear you
And my spirit answers,
Dances, in joy,
With yours.

Jennifer Akers

Love By Proxy

I'm a surrogate lover
Substitute for another
No, they're not my lips he's kissing
It's not my hand he's holding
Not my face he's seeing
Only hers.
He can't forget her.

But I'm standing in her place
Pretending it's me he really loves;
For being loved by proxy
Is better than not being loved
At all.

Katherine Rowland

Dislocated

Fullness abounds in yuletide gladness,
spoiled girl, bringing on madness.
As composed and self-contained.
I rode the horse through the village,
near the cottage, I boarded a train.
Abound and aloud, "How sound!" I found,
aboard, discreet, though temple ablaze,
unbridled passion hath found the grave,
Of youth and squire, alive, on fire.

In a ride out of town, to be let down,
time dislocates, and selfishness abounds.
Pioneered through abstract sadness,
lying awake in morning's gladness,
a scent of rose in the wind doth blow,
despair has arrived, I raise a toast.
Looking away, over sunbeam's wings,
seeing dreams, I thought I dreamed.
Alive, away, in the air of morning's fare,
through rivers of ice and fields of yore,
I awoke, only to find myself there.

Kenneth Hartsoe

Sunset Of The West

A broken wagon wheel lies in the dust,
Spurs alongside full of rust.
Morning dew drips from the metal
As if tears falling from a rose petal.

Empty forts now silent, no bugles ring,
Blue columns of long ago no longer sing.
Ghosts of the past file slowly by
Only to march off to a cold gray sky.

A wisp of smoke from a mesa near,
Drums now quiet leaving no fear.
Call of a wolf in a lonely night
No longer bays in the moonlight.

Tepees gone, feathers on the ground,
Never a chant or dances sound.
Warriors so gallant in their paint,
Now only a memory so very faint.

Cattle drive fires now lie cold,
Cowboys and herders grown sadly old.
Alas, flights of war arrows bend
Leaving a crimson sunset in the end.

Jack Rex

The Guardians

They are most visible at night
Standing two by my side
My soul is washed in comfort
Inner thoughts do I confide.

Warding off unseen dangers
Winged warriors take flight
Fighting battles unknown to man
Swords entwined they face the night.

In the morning when I wake
Unaware of my guardians plight
Selfishly I face another day
Shielded by my guardians in white.

Donna Roberts

Our Country

The glory of its flag
stands out like a star in
the middle of darkness
Its an interesting concept
very idealistic, very pretty
Men fighting for it, cast upon
shores or castaways upon our shores
we fight under our flag for this
our country.
Our country stands for freedom
against prime evil, dangerous
for the bad
Protection for the good under
the blue hem of justice, red for
the blood which was shed for us the free
the white for the stars that glow
above us - for we set our dreams
upon this - our country.

Joseph T. LaLonde

The Moment

I sit mesmerized
Staring into the deep tranquility
Which others call your eyes.

Haunted by your beauty
As fire light dances
Across your supple skin.

Loose tresses of silky hair
Fall across seductive shoulders
Enchanting me into dreams

Longing sated by mere vision
Of perfect curves
Restlessness eased by soothing song
Of your sweetened breath.

Engulfed in rapture, heart aflame
I caress your cheek with loving hand
Softly now, without word spoke
I lean to you and gently kiss.

Bradly Cozby

Mother

You gave me life one
summer's day,
and cared for me
in your gentle way.

You taught me it all,
from A to Z,
but best of all,
you believed in me.

You said I'm special,
one of a kind.
I seldom thanked you,
but you didn't mind.

You opened me up and
tore down my wall.
You're the only one who
knew me at all.

You've been there for me
my whole life through.
So in my own way,
I'm saying thank you.

Carrie Brummett

Dancing Sunlight

As I write;
Sunlight dances on my bedroom wall.
Such a pleasant winter sight,
Like little children playing with a ball.

It warms my being,
Uplifts my very soul.
More of a feeling, than seeing;
It caresses my spirit so.

It brings me promise of a power;
Greater than common man.
A glimpse at an eternal hour;
Mankind can't understand.

It seems brighter now than summer,
Much more Holy somehow.
It's like a distant drummer,
Or a lonely bugle call.

Dance on, dear sunlight,
Let my spirit grow.
For soon it will be night;
And I'll be left with just a candle glow....

Bill Fleming

"Sedai"

There she stands;
Sunlight radiates through
the slightly jumbled mass
of titian hair.

Eyes kind and inviting
holding friendship warm.
She winks at you playfully,
and smiles her smile, so enticing.

Tiny hands dance over flower petals;
You can almost see her euphoria
as she breathes in
the honied air.

Watch her dance,
Watch her play,
But know
that you are
The one who
Stole the stars
and put them in her eyes...

Anathea Carrick

Grief

Please don't tell me how to grieve
support me in my sorrow
don't tell me to get over it
or time will heal my wounds
allow me my tears
listen to my heart with understanding
but spare me any judgement
for it is not opinion that I seek
My Grief, is not so Universal
it's rather personal
and it belongs to me
Don't tell me how I've changed
or expect me to be my former self
because in my grief
I am forever changed
say a prayer for me
But... Please, don't tell me how to grieve

Cheryl G. Carson

Birthday Present

Again you gave to me the gift
Surpassing all by far,
That shows me more than any act
How wonderful you are.

Such sacrifice for loves own sake
Inspires my heart to swell
The culmination of our love
Shines from that baby girl.

Not with all of eternity
Could I begin to give,
The smallest part of selflessness
Which every day you live.

Time flees away from our light grasp
We know not where it goes,
But giving birth, that surely is
Something that lasts and shows.

I have in you the best of life
and still you've given more,
Yourself, a boy and now two girls
To cherish and adore.

James E. Grant

"Urban Dreamscape"

If you can't win, don't play the game.
Survival ain't about fortune and fame.
Shot dead for the clothes you wear,
A Mac-10 and an icy stare.
Prison bound for teen-age homicide,
A one-way paddy wagon ride.

Livin' on the streets, got no choice
Heroin is your Mama's voice.
You want to change, there's no escape
From the land of murder and rape.

You'll end up dead, in a sewer.
You're only crime was being poor.
Obituaries on page six,
No one cares, Mom's turning tricks.
Buried in a box, lying cold,
Died in a city where twenty is old.

Keith Jalbert

Childhood Album

A little pair of
Swedish shoes

Golden glazed with
Summer hues

Little tots with
Bows and ties

Little dolls
And apple pies

Raindrops falling
On little noses

Little girls with
Button noses

Apple butter
In the churn

Wash is done
And years to learn

Come and come
My little dumpkin

Life is young
Let's bake some pumpkin!

Kristy A. Gilberto

Beelzebub

Dusty dry swirling sand
Sweep the dirt into her hand

Shut it out cry aloud
See her now standing proud

She let it go she walked away
But her mind alas had gone astray

The clouds above the darkened sky
Let go of its tears and let out a sigh

She tried to run to escape its eyes
But then she died and here she lies

Her time was up her hair was grey
But before she died she began to pray

"Forgive me Lord, for I did sin,
I locked you out and let the devil in

But I regret my choice with all my heart
Let me be in heaven let me be a part,

Don't leave me here don't leave me alone"
She begged and cried until our dear Lord
turned her to stone

She sits alone, by herself still in that lonely
place
Her sorrow still lingers in her tears that
streak her cold stone face

Kara Ramsden

Wonders Of Life

You thank God, for the
Sweet baby child
At two you pray for God's
Help for five to come soon.
At sixteen to eighteen you pray for the
Right directions.
Than comes marriage and
Another sweet baby, that now
Makes you a proud. Grandparent.
These are God's wonders of life.

Kathy L. McGuigon

The Crow

Black as night
Swift as sight.
Back from the dead
Oh, dread, the fright.
Have mercy, you say polite.
What is this terrible sight?
The crow, they say.
He's black as night.
He can really fight.
Oh, dread. The terrible sight!

Chris Caballero

Dreams

A world of truth and unreality,
Swirled together with a touch of dark.
Withdrawing sharply at the break of day
Till it lurks again in its dark domain,
Unremembered but as dim shadows
And faded memories.
Disturbing remnants of forgotten times
Too pale to be seen,
Too distinct to be ignored.
Obstructive clues to an inner self
That few will ever find.

Annaka Kalton

Dear Dad

Thank you. I can carry a tune,
tap my feet with the beat,
swing a racquet, write a skit,
flex my calves, show my wit,
stand up straight, walk the line,
choose my gait anytime,
play some golf, dance all night,
see beyond, win the fight,
laugh or cry, reach my dreams,
realize it's in the genes.

Amy Ackley

Once More

Once More
tears fall from her eyes.
Once more
blind faith is her demise.
Once more
sorrow fills her chest.
Once more
loneliness causes her unrest.
Once more
love escapes her grasp.
Once more
forgetting is her task.
Once more
questions burn her mind.
Once more
her lover was unkind.

Amanda Barnes

My Baby

Ten little fingers
Ten little toes
Mothers love growing
The more that you grow

Today and tomorrow
Lots of thoughts filled with you
Not knowing your name yet
But Mommy loves you

What color's your eyes
How long is your hair
Someday you will know
How you've answered my prayer

Denise M. Ammons Wright

Why? Goodbye?

Paths which were open before
tend to gradually grow over
God why? Why was it you?
that had to confide in what I do

It is over, what does it mean?
Is it what I have done?,
or what you have seen?
Not what I perceive it to be
Just a little jolt of reality

It is dead, thankful for that debt
Why? Still my eyes are wet
Can it be my morality?
After all, it is my sanity

Had it all and did not care
Looking at me in a hollow stare
What have you done?, Why to me?
All that I know now is curiosity.

James P. Joyce

Do You Dare Touch The Fire?

Do you dare touch the fire
That burns inside?
The passion that you keep to yourself
The desires that no one knows.
Are you brave enough to touch the fire
Or are you afraid of being burned?
Is it the fear of overwhelming passion
That keeps you at bay?
Are you afraid of losing yourself
To your desires?

Now a new fire burns
It is the flame of my passion
You come closer, like a moth to the flame
Do you dare touch the fire?

Alan P. West

Friends

Everyone should have friends that could be there when you need them. Friends always care about you. Friends are there when you are hurt. Friends are people who you can share secrets with, friends are the most important people to have. Without friends you will be alone and sad. Friends can help you with your home work. Having a lot of friends really makes a difference.

Jenny Magno

Leaves In The Night

Leaves in the night,
that exit like a soul
Escaping the trees and passing slow
Cracking and crumbling when they fall
to the ground
w/the lingering days that have long
since turned them brown
The grassy shades of another yesterday,
that show tonight under the moonlight
where they lay
Retiring to an after-life,
when the wind blows them away
A silence in the air
and the empty conscience of nature's
change

Joe Wolfe

Dear Sister

This is just to say,
that I used all the bubble bath
that was in the bathroom.

You probably
wanted to use it today,
while you read my diary.

I'm sorry,
but it was so comfortable,
while I read your diary.

Elysa Wan

A Happier Goodbye

I've decided when I leave here
That I'm never coming back.
My journey I'll embark upon
As soon as I can pack.
I'm saving my last smile
For when I lastly get away.
Armies couldn't keep me here,
Or anything you say.
See, it's places just like this one
Where the people make it worse.
So my feet are facing eastward
And are never to reverse.
Then I'll walk and never stumble -
I'll wave and never cry.
And I'll never know, or ever say,
A happier goodbye.

Kathy Fondacaro

The Meaning Of Hatred

Hate is a monster
that lurks in the dark
tears you apart
leaving its mark.

Hate is an illness
for which there's no cure
overcoming your body
taking all pure.

Hate is a killer
stalking your mind
defeating your senses
leaving you blind.

Hate is a demon
that swallows you whole
eats you alive
devours your soul.

Hate is an evil
that lurks in us all
don't let it find you
you'll stumble and fall.

Amy Morris

What Is A Memory

A memory is yours and mine,
That returns from time to time,
It resides inside your head,
Often silent something said,
Sometimes happy, sometimes sad
Former good - latter bad
It can't be touched, as it's out of reach
Reflected upon, it will often teach
Sometimes buried, deep for years
And it's return can bring your tears
Once it's found, it's your's for sure
To remember always and forever more
It's something you alone chose to share
With someone dear, who will surely care
Sharing it brings joy or pain
Remember that in sharing, you will gain
Never allow it to be distorted
One among many that must be sorted
Reflected upon when they are true
Will surely help and benefit you

Kenneth A. Calu

The Wind

There is a strong invisible Force
That ripples through the trees
It moves with fierce and powerful strength
Or makes a summer breeze

It blows the clouds across the sky
On an afternoon in June
In January It scatters snow flakes
As It whistles a mournful tune

It rocks the mighty ships at sea
And lashes the great white waves
It cools a hot and humid day
Above the dim lit caves

It flies a kite with the greatest of ease
And carries it far away
It comes mysteriously in the night
On a dark and stormy day

It has neither shape or color
Or a place from which it came
The cunning, powerful, playful way
Has always been the same!

Coco Proud

My Angel

My Grandmom is a pearl
That shines across the sea's,
She is just like an angel,
That comes with the ocean breeze.

She feeds me when I'm hungry,
She warms me when I'm cold,
That's why she is an angel,
Or so I have been told.

Some days we may be angry,
But only for a day,
I thank God for every moment,
For right now she's here to stay!

So you see my Grandmom's an angel
Sent to me from up above,
And even if she wasn't,
She is still the one I love!

Kimberly Anne Williams

My Winter Song

I look upon the city lights
that sparkle far below
I turn my face toward the wind
and listen to it blow

A rustle comes from atop the hill
the whispering of the cane
the soft patter upon the sill
the falling of winter rain

I sit alone in my winter world
and consume the sights and sounds
at the break of dawn, the echo of a shot
the baying of the hounds

The dismal clouds tread their way
across the cold, gray sky
a flock of geese honk their song
as to the south they fly

The air is crisp and nippy now
the leaves perform their dance
I sit and stare at all of this
as if in hypnotic trance

Judy A. Belew

World Within

I cannot feel the light of day
That touches every blade of grass.
It cannot reach me in my world
Encircled by a sphere of glass.

People say they understand me;
They could help me if they tried.
But I don't see how they can
For they can't reach me here inside.

Here inside my sanctuary,
In my prison I abide.
Scared of what the real world offers
Here is where I come to hide.

I'm beginning to feel lonely,
Dwelling in my world within.
Now that I've learned to live inside
Can I get back out again?

Alicia Quillen

Untitled

No one will see
That which makes up me
They have not the time
Such a brutal crime
The ocean, she sees
And speaks amidst the sweetest breeze
Her power makes my soul glisten
As I feel, watch and listen
She cradles ne in all her might
I see through her my own love light
My loyalties lie with her divine love
Through her I am able to rise above
Without her I would cease to be
With her I am finally free

Candace Elaine Proctor

"Love"

Love is a feeling
That you and I share
When I look into your eyes
Your heart is in your stare

As I go to sleep
In the midnight blue
You're in my dreams
I dream of you

When you hold my hand
I am in complete bliss
When you're not near
It's your kiss I miss

I want you to know
That you are in my heart
I want us to last forever
And never to part

Cereida Rivera

Untitled

God's love is simple,
The love is pure.
It is Jesus we adore.

You can see it in the flowers,
You can see it in the sun.
Jesus is the one to turn to.

That love is every where.

Elizabeth J. Sicurella

The One

In your arms is the right place
to be.
A right place.
A very righteous place.

The only home for me.

Daniel V. Fitzgerald

Goodbye

Once I saw you, then I knew,
That you would be the one.
My heart was racing over you,
This all had just begun...

Then I saw her next to you,
Just then my heart had broke.
I wanted to scream out " I loved you!"
But it came out as just a croak.

To even try to make you see,
That I had loves you so,
all that you had meant to me,
And then to see you go.

Christy Warren

But...

I used to firmly believe,
That you'd never leave,
But now I'm not too sure.
I always saw you by my side,
the most beautiful bride!
But maybe I was wrong.
We laughed together,
Said it was forever.
But did we really know?
I told you that I loved you,
And you said you loved you me too.
But was it really love?
There were more good times than bad,
I thought the best we had had.
But weren't there other times too?
I always said I would never cry
If you were to say good-bye...
...But I was mistaken.

Christopher R. Soltys

This Child Has Many Faces

She's fooling all with smiling eyes
  that's hiding mental anguish
and only talks to teddy bear
  about the things she wishes

There's sadness in her little eyes
  as round the house she races
avoiding questions, feeling fear
  This child has many faces

She sees and hears much violence
  and tightens up inside
growing fast with no real pals
  and no safe place to hide

Exuding toughness, hiding shame
  wishing someone would trade places
sometimes hard and sometimes soft
  this child of many faces

And so the cycle goes and goes
  putting others through its paces
cause no one ever noticed that
  this child has many faces.

Bertha Gaskill Hrynyk

Untitled

There is a tree
That's not too far
It's falling down
Right where you are
If you don't move
There will be gloom
Cause where your standing
There's not much room.

Dominick DelVecchio

The Song Of The World

Can you hear it?
The angelic words,
Of nature all around.
The song of the world.

Can you see it,
Through the seasons?
The changes all over.
The song of the world.

Can you smell it?
The flowers aroma,
In the spring.
The song of the world.

Can you taste it,
Pollution?
It is the cry of pain.
The song of the world.

Can you feel it,
In your heart?
The love for the earth.
The song of the world.

Amber Watkins

Think About It

Imagine life
the beginning
entering a complicated realm
innocent
unaware of good and evil
only knowing the touch and scent
of mother -
just imagine

Imagine death
the end of living
Yet entering another complicated realm
innocent
unaware of heaven and hell
only knowing life -
think about it

Jannita D. Lands

Feelings

  Twinkle Ring Sing,
The Bells of Laughter Twang,
  Drip Drop Splash,
The Pints of Teardrops fall,
  Stomp Crash Bang,
The Footfalls of Anger sound,
  Jitter Jingle Jangle,
The Shakiness of Excitement goes,
Feelings that Rise, Jump, Fall, And Shake.

Chelsea Baldwin

Hay, Sunlight, Barn

The smell of sweet hay,
The sunlight; shining bright,
The barn filled with life.

Emma Howes

This is Dedicated to Chuck from Brenda:

Well Dear, It's been a year today
The best year of my life
They say the first one's hardest
For a husband and a wife

If the past year was the hardest
Then all the ones to come
Will be filled with love and happiness
As was year number one

I don't understand that saying
It wasn't hard at all
I'm there for you, you're there for me
When one of us should fall

So on this first anniversary
I hope you understand
I meant the vows I said that day
When exchanging wedding bands

I'm saying this to you today
Because as this love grows stronger
Words won't be able to express
My feelings any longer

Brenda Roberto

This Old Barn

There's an old barn along the highway
The cars and trucks go passing by
And no one seems to even notice
That in this spot once stood a farm

But the highway it cuts right through it
Where the crops once used to grow
And the people who used to farm it
Have gone so long ago

But this old barn it is still standing
Though the years have took there toll
And the memories that it once held onto
Are lost and never told

But this old barn lives on forever
In a time that we can't see
On a long stretch of highway
Where a farm once used to be

Dan DiNicola

Trees

Trees, O trees,
The chipmunks hide there nuts,
The kids climb and play,
And get their kites stuck in May,
The munks play and dig,
They give a home to the honey-makin'
bees,
The kids also play Hide-and seek,
The birds hide there beaks,
Trees oh trees what a wonderful thing.

Anjana Ravi

Try

Up or down
The choice is yours
To be

Shall you succeed
Shall you even try
To fly

Or will you stay
Safe and sound
On the ground

Not knowing what the future holds
Will you risk your dreams
For others to criticize

Do you hide from them
Do you make believe everything is fine

Will you risk yourself and your dreams
To be what you should

Or will you be one to stay
Safe and sound on the ground
Not daring to try to fly

Becky Foust

Epitaph

The sweet smell of
The city burning:
The final pollution
The dying screams
The smoldering dreams
The love
The hate
The secrecy
The fools
The fights for something
The fights about nothing
The birth
The life
The death
The package thrown into the fire
The orderly laws of man
Destroyed by chaotic laws of nature
The scar and the memories
Will never disappear.

Damion Drover

Rain

I'm wet and cold from the weather outside.
The clouds have strength to only mist,
But not to cry in torrents.
Clouds get tired - too tired to rain.

Dampness seems to penetrate me.
Saturated earth waits for the sun
Waiting for the warmth and the light.
Cold and dark, the light does not come.

I want to fade.
The gray landscape is showcased
Against gray skies and clouds.
Each shade overlaps and blends.

Where is the day's joy?
Red tulips wait for spring,
For warm gentle breezes to come.
But what of the chill that is now?

Joy Isabelle Ammond

"Love Through All The Seasons"

'Tis spring
The Daisies, Daffodils,
Tulips, Roses and Orchids
Will soon bloom once more
To compete with each other
Their beauty enhancing the world
Once Again.

Their riot of colors
Will last until Fall
When they would be forced
To retreat
Because of Winter
But you, you, my sweet
Your beauty will
Shine forth and
Light up My Heart with Love
Come Spring, Summer,
Autumn or Winter.

Aziz A. Rashid

Losing A Friend

Black and cold is the day
the day they withheld you away.
The car was found upside down.
blood was every where they
pulled you twisted from it
and it was too late you
were gone, and with you
went my heart.
I never though I could ever
be so blue.
I have gone to all the places
we use to go.
Our special place that wonderful
waterfall, remembering
the day you held me there.
Our own world no
worries no cares.

Diseree Barr

Freedom

Longing for freedom
The dreamer prayed
Hoping for space
Time uncaged
Wanting the day
With freedom to choose
Unbinding the chains
Escaping the noose
Freedom comes quick
A blink of the eye
The Dreamer is free
Gulls sail by
Air is so clear
Sky so bright
Freedom a taste
Wind with a bite
No need to look back
New life ahead
The Dreamer walks on
Freedom is said

John M. Dakan

Just For A Moment

A silent whisper in my ear
The earths sky could be my eyes
And its rain my tears
The winds, my emotions
And lightening my fears
If my lips could trace
Across a thousand words
I could speak the warmth of the sun
Just for a moment
A prayer answered
I could then turn fear into stone
Make all the lonely
Not afraid to be alone
But if I only had one moment
I'd wipe that small boys tears
Replace them with happiness
To guide him through the years
And with my last breath
I'd blow dust from my palm
Watch it turn to gold
To send warm thoughts
Into all hearts that are cold.

Juli L. Leonard

Theories Of The Dream State

Once there I felt the calm
The feeling of floating
Drifting through the vast void
The darkness is all

I was there
The life, the breath
The all of life
Solid and real
Unyielding and unmoving

Then I felt the calm slip away
Out from underneath my body
Unsolid and unreal, terror grips me
And I scream, but no one hears

Then I awaken to the total darkness
To the horrible realization
It is but a dream
And now I am free
And once again I feel the calm
Until again it slips away

Judy McPherson

Through The Eyes

Watching as the sun rises
The flash of light is sublime
The warmth of the rays dries
up the morning dew.

Looking into the field of yellow
The grass stands proudly
The strands blow tentatively
reaching for the sky of blue.

Glaring above to the clouds so high
The puffs begin to thicken
The big white blankets
move slowly across the horizon.

Staring into the bright light
The hues are brilliant
The afterglow flickers
into a reality.

Sighting a shadow
Unknown to the conscience
The vision of hope
slowly fades away.

Kristy Lynn Parlato

Destiny

Destiny is our future
The Future is our destiny
Peace within is peace indeed
To rise above all else
To sing the joy of all things good
and to surpass all things not.
The future is bright and full of light
To be filled with what we will become
Your destiny is your future
Like your future is your destiny.
Look forward to better times
and all that life has to share
Hopefully our future is together
and to fill our destiny as one.
If our paths should fade away
Please remember that our love is there
So the chances of two for one again
Could still be our future, to be one
So be still, be calm for our Destiny is our
Future
The Future is our Destiny.

Barbara A. Pierce

Mary

Oh pretty girl inside I know you're there
the girl with the pins I know you're there
sweet girl with your eyes shut
I know your thoughts
I can see into your holes
an empty void oh what a shame Mary Mary
the one with the eyes
you know if I could see you through this
I'd just let you drift
I can hear you giggle how was I to know?
Oh Mary Mary the girl with the pins
I will bring you in
I want to be your ugly secret
I want to hide in your closet
see eye to eye if only I could
my baby girl give me a smile your pearly
whites
raise your empty sockets to me
oh pretty girl inside you can't fool me
I know you gouged them out how you hated
to see
yourself, when they told you you were ugly

Kellie Miller

Across the Room

Sitting off into the distance,
The glint of her moistened baby blues,
Grab my sight.
Her uncontrollable weeping and sadness,
Biting into my consciousness.
Feelings of obligatory guilt rush,
Into my heart.
Surges of compassion bellow,
In the deepest partitions of,
My mind.
I sit there watching her suffer,
Never knowing,
What pain or horror,
Could so shadow a soul.
At only six feet of standard distance,
And measure,
I hold witness,
to the birth of a tragedy,
Named GRIEF.

Donald L. Edwards

The Eagle

I watch the eagle fly
The glisten of his eye
Golden wings
Move like puppet strings
A SNOW white head
Deserves a soft bed

Oh what you know I've got to go
Good-bye eagle good-bye
Go on fly on by
With a glisten in your eye.

Carrie Slater

To Follow The Last Free Mind

Like a gently flowing trickle of Grace,
The glow of beauty upon her face.
Created by the King of Kings,
For her, in heaven, all angels sing.
Upon this earth, she came one day,
To dwell amongst us, if she may.
To live a life, of a simple fate,
To love one man, and be his mate.
To bear a child for God above,
To him a gracious gift of love.
But this life was never meant,
For a lovely mind, from heaven sent.
Because this earth, is full of greed,
God will harvest this lovely seed.
To dwell with Him, the Holy name,
Towards God's home, goes Germaine.

Carmine L. Colarossi

Graveyard

Protected by the trees that resemble
the gnarled hand, ready to steal the
passer by into the night.
Graveyards are protected by the
thoughts we put into them.
The fear that we build around
them.
Where the dead sleep.
Where one is put to rest.
Seeing the markers and wondering
what that persons was about.
Are they in heaven?
Can they feel the cold?
Are they lonely?
We spend our time wondering
about the graveyard. For what?
We will all have our answers
in time.

Angela Sawle

Valentines!

Valentines, Valentines comes from
the heart. Make a wish and blow it out.
Write some cards and letters too,
Don't forget the lovely tune.
Sing a song or play a game,
it doesn't matter because it's all the same.
Smile, smile, make a blush on your
face, don't dust it off. Because it's
love and love will do anything you can do.
Don't forget it, it's too soon to
forget that lovely tune!

Juliann A. Cardenas

As For Myself

Spring passes I haven't gathered
the herbs I love.
A garden goes unplanted another summer
The perfect lover has no intention
of nesting
A riper woman this year
Alive alone looking for the perfect
pairs of ears.
As exultatious ideas go unspoken
So many plans to make
So many not to occur
Wear lavender of surrender
Lavender of unrequited love

Denise Whitestone

Dreams

In the misty meadow beyond
the high grown grass,
There is a place that you
should see.
It was build for our family.

Not too big, but not too small,
Oh! it looks so great in the fall.
Just enough room for the
youngings, you and I,
to live for ever in America's
apple pie.

Joyce Nirelli Dudziak

Reflection

I keep trying to repair it:
the image I had of you,
of a kind and thoughtful person,
the friend I thought I knew...
I can't piece the glass together,
it's just too hard to do;
the shards are sharp and splintered,
the image splintered, too.
I hardly recognize you.

I look away from the mirror,
and turn to gaze at you;
but your face reflects the image,
your face is fractured, too.
How strange that before you smashed it
it gave a different view;
the odd face now reflected
is the image that is true.
At last I see the real you.

Doris K. Wall

Puzzle Piece

A puzzle piece could be anything.
The jewel on a crown of a king
Or a strand of straw in a nest
Or the button on a maiden laid to rest.

Maybe the glint in a baby's eye
Or a piece of apple pie.
Could be a pedal of a rose
Or the end of a garden hose.

Bet it's a raindrop in a storm
Or a ballerina in perfect form.
Maybe a lock without a key.
Yes, you never know what it will be!

Elizabeth Leigh Kenney

About Writing

It has been awhile and I miss
the joy.
Sometimes you have to put the
pen away.
With the changes that each
new day will bring, ideas
and thoughts are renewed.
That is the beauty of our mind.
That is the pleasure of writing.

James Nichols

Hope

Lying in the Darkened Myth
The last piece of hope you swallow
And blindly I follow unable to see.

I can feel them
Laughing and pointing at you
You cry, you cry in the still dark
Night.

You gave your love and happiness to
them.
They run their fingers through your
silky hair.

A blanket of depression drapes
Over you, slowly, you wait for a light of
hope, you look, looking over me, you see
the light.

Lying in a brightful myth you find
The last piece of hope, and blindly
I follow unable to see.

Amanda Carr

The Worlds

The thunder claps, so loud, so clear,
The lightning strikes, so bright, so near.
The rain falls pouring to the ground.
Yet in the new world I have found,
The sun shines brightly everyday,
The birdies chase the clouds away,
The sky's the bluest ever seen,
And everything that's here is clean.

Cheri LaFlamme

Celtic Brother

The plight of our people
The loss of our land
We have been pushed
To a subverted level
Democracy has done nothing
We are still inferior
The languages we speak
Disappear like rain in the desert
Return to our heritage
Or soon we will have none
Then the past will become
No more than a history
Listen, do not simply hear me
The Manx, Cornish, and Gauls
Are no more
The rest will soon follow
Arise from your sleep
See where you're going
Refuse to fall

Clayton R. Bishop

Why

The heart will love
The mind will think
The body will grow
The water will flow
The sun will shine
The world will end
The stars will twinkle
The diseases will spread
One day we will all be dead,
But our souls and spirits
Will always be free
For that we'll never know
Why, was this meant to be

Elycia Andreotti

Oklahoma City

My happy heartland home was well.
The morning sun. The coffee smell.
My friends all ready to start the day.
Knowing not what was on the way.
We heard the roar of a hundred trains.
Glass came flying from a thousand panes.
Concrete fell from the sky like rain.
We saw the blood and felt the pain.
The floor gave way and down we fell.
Descending to the depths of hell.
The blast had ended the children's voices.
Who would make such horrible choices?
That day we died, my friends, and I,
Along with her, Miss Liberty.

Jim Eicholz

Under The Crescent Moon

Who is frolicking in my yard?
The new moon's sliver of crescent light
Showed me shadowy elfin forms,
Two tiny figures playing games
Or, perchance, performing a dance.
Under the Crescent moon.

The two darted and leaped and pounced,
Then tumbled and rolled down the bank,
And crept like a mist up again.
They tip-toed like ballet dancers,
Then took sudden flight from the light
Under the crescent moon.

The yard looked like an empty stage.
Was the scene a will-o'-the-wisp?
Was it just a mystical dream?
No! Pansy-faced Kittens appeared
And, perchance, they may always dance
Under the Crescent moon.

Elizabeth Curral

Love And Roses

The only one I'd ever love
The only one I'd ever need
Love has made a rose
Of what was once a tiny seed

With the sun the rose will grow
But it also needs the rain
Like the love we share
It has its pleasures and its pain

But if we know our love is real
And that it's not a lie
Our love will go on growing
Long after the roses die.

JoAnn Fearon

Lest I Feel

Decay...
the painted window sill
in the shower
sheds its blue paint
and rust
becomes the wood...
(Does wood rust?)

Chaos...
the grass grows thin
as spiny weeds invade
its uniformity
and too many blades
are of unequal height...
(Is all lost?)

Vision...
clouds gather as emotions
condense for droplets
of tears
Pain has entered
my life... Like a storm

Cory Cook

Future

At times the present goes sadly by
The past has gone to rest
If future was observed by many
Success might be their guest

But would you look so far ahead
And think of things so dear
Or would you hold in mind one thought
The future call not hear

Some say there's a time for every thing
Tho' good or bad are they
Just take them all with a smile
And let future have it's way

Alexander C. Jones

The Road "Goodbye"

I walked along the road, "Goodbye",
The path looked strange, I wondered why?
A strangers hand I felt in mine,
I walked along and paid no mind.

All the friends I once knew,
Took the road named "Goodbye" too.
There were no two roads quite the same,
Only called "Goodbye" by name.

A friend of mine I did see,
She didn't choose the same path as me.
I looked around and I grew scared,
I asked myself, what am I doing here?

Again the strangers hand, I felt in mine,
I had to turn and look this time.
When I looked, what did I see?
That the stranger was actually me.

My task is done, some left to do,
I only know I'll make it through.
Because in the stranger, I did see,
Something special inside of me.

Kristine'a M. Loiselle

Beautiful Black Woman

Beautiful Black woman,
The Queen of her domain.
Who can smile on the outside,
Though inside her it rains.

Beautiful Black woman,
Sacrificing for her children.
Because she knows,
They've been doomed since the pilgrims.

Beautiful Black woman,
An overflow of pride.
With a meaningful stomp,
In her every stride.

Beautiful Black woman,
So determined is she.
Taking and defining the world,
With inherent originality.

Keziah Osborne

A Love Poem

The moon cried
The stars shined
From the sky fell a lonely leaf
Your kisses were airy and brief
Our minds meshed becoming one
The trapped feelings I felt came
loose and undone
In your arms I wanted to always bask
With my terrors my fears all unmasked.
These memories strong are
in the past
Our love it sprinkled away,
it didn't last
Like the morning dew our love melted away
Only to come back with someone
new another day
Perhaps someday in a purer
way? I cannot say
It seems all love is trivial play.

Kristy Boucher

Wrong

For Alan

The earth is square
The sun is black
This can't be right
I want you back.

The grass is brown
There is no moon
What can this be
The month is June

The brooks don't flow
My tears won't dry
What's going on
I need my guy.

The stars don't shine
The birds can't sing
What's happening here
The bells won't ring

Near is far and
Far is near
Of course they are
You're not here.

June Boivin

Optimism

The days are getting longer,
The sun is shining bright.
It's amazing how things seem clearer,
When seen in brilliant light

The long old row to hoe
Seems shorter now somehow,
When one can see the end in site
Knowing soon you'll take a bow.

For a job well done—complete—
In spite of all the spills.
Just to know that you can do it
Gives one an inner thrill.

If I wake up tomorrow
With mountains yet to climb,
I'll know that I can manage
If I just make up my mind.

Judy Bolton

Untouched Love

The shallow heart lost without reason
The untouched love not given
Lovers come and go like seasons
Wounded souls are not mending

A single beat of one lonely heart
The love that was never shared
The truth that was never told
The lonely heart never seen

The hidden secret of the pain for love
Wanting to be touched; to be held
To feel the feelings that are never felt
To feel the heart beat once again

The secluded love never having
The tears that keep falling
The heart that has endless aching
The shallow heart lost without reason

The distance you feel between everyone
The laugh you laughed because you forgot
Forgetting the pain you truly feel
The loneliness no one understands contin-
ues

Jamie Stevens

The Traveler

Along the lonely crimson sea
The wanderer has come.
He wonders at its beauty
that reflects the morning sun.
Then he pauses to look skyward
to the freedom that it holds.
And to gaze upon a bird in flight
as its lovely wings unfold
He pauses by the water
to ponder on its shore.
And think about the future
and what it has in store.
He stops upon the hillside
in the shadow of the trees
To look upon the majesty
of all the things he sees.
He walks upon the rolling plains
and through the valleys deep
And when the shadows fall on him
he lays his head to sleep.

Judith E. Bailey

Song Of A Warrior

Deep within my patient heart
The Warrior...whom I've become
Sees the journey...brave and strong
Sees no other way to go

Sees the child I once was
See the woman I've become
See the challenges I've melt
Thinks of those which still might be

Honor, courage, love, respect
These are goals I've known as mine
Centered in my peaceful core
No one can disturb me there...

One with nature...One with God
One with all that is Divine
Crystal vision is for those
Who regard the World as I

Go in peace, my earthly friends
Let discipline become your key
Then health and happiness shall yield
The warrior you, too, can be...

Erin O'Connor

Sudden

Swish, Swash
The water rushing by,

Like rush hour in big cities
Moving fast and loud.

Rushing over boulders
Flowing by the banks,

Moving swifter than a deer
Yet it is peaceful.

Then, CRASH!
Up against big rocks,

Caught up in the rapids
Moving faster than the eye can see!

Then down, down, down
Down a waterfall,

Then, all is quiet
And the water slips away.

Courtney A. McCann

Untitled

Take me where
The waters flow
And the pussy willows grow
Forever.

Take me on
The road that never ends
And goes on and on again
Forever.

Take me to
The forest that is still green
Where everything lies unseen
Forever.

Take me up
Where others can't be heard
To fly with the birds
Forever.

Take me to my dreams
Where I will always live in peace
Forever.

Katrina Anderson

Reincarnation

Death isn't the bitter end
The way we thought it to be
But a brand new start
With family and loved ones
We once knew
Who are waiting for you and I to come
And when we approach them from afar
We will recognize them one by one
And amongst them there will be many more
Waiting for their own to come
Then, we'll all be reunited once again

So do not fret when you see that bridge
Just pass on over and be glad you did
For in the beginning it was God's choice
And, this is the way He set it down:
Reincarnation for Everyone.

Belva K. Makinnen

The Ocean Bay

The clouds, the rain,
the wind, the sky
How powerful it is - I dare not lie.

The moon, the sun
the dark, the light
How hard it is to know what is right.

The small, the big
the short, the tall
Did you see the colored ball fall?

The sea, the sand,
the night, the day
That is what's on the ocean bay.

Jessica Black

Good Bye

The summer sun is said and done
The winter moon is full.
Blue water lays with an icy glaze
As the air brings forth a chill.

No longer does the evening hold
A quiet whispering breeze,
And now instead the leaves are dead
As the plants drop to their knees.

So now I say
"Good Bye summer days,
I'll see you once again;

Until that time,
I'll remember the rhyme,
Of when the birds sing summer again."

Alexis Ziarnowski

Trees

Trees are graceful against
The winter sky
With branches tangling together
In grotesque patterns
And buds hanging like dark jewels
Waiting to burst into color, and
Eager to spread their delicate fragrance
Through the wind - cooled air
Of Spring.

Josephine M. Sharitz

"Never Again" the Holocaust

A million children died today
Their bones burn all alone
A man so mean,
A heart so weak
The children had to go.

The gas chambers await the men
Their hearts are filled with joy
But then they're crushed,
A promise broke,
To every girl and boy...

Brittany Longdon

The Mess

There are prisons, without bars,
Their products are life. In the
desert the sun i shining. The
sea is calm. In the jungle the
foliage penetrates the million
it is like a Caesar salad, a normal
conversation. It is like a pack of
lies, a des of money changes,
The king sends out tidings
The die is cast, it is the
Ideas of March. We cross the
Rubicon. All is quiet on the
Western Front, nobody is
moving. We are all alone with
it and our super egos. All
is lost, at what a cost.
"Ah, Battleby, Ah humanity," C from
Melville's
Barthley the savena.

James R. Aronson

Rumors

I started to wonder, then I wondered

What I was wondering about.

I thought maybe it might be true
then again it might not be.

I can't imagine who would know if
it's true.

I know I don't know.
Do you know or think you know?

It seems strange how your thoughts
can seem so thoughtless, even though
you thought they were good thoughts,
as long as you kept them to yourself.

All this confusion, was caused by
a rumor.

Dorothy J. Rozgowski

Merri Sunshine

You're the frosting on the cake,
The extra fruit upon the vine;
Oh, little Merri Angelie,
I'm so glad that you are mine!

When all my other sunbeams
Have scampered far away,
My little "Merri Sunshine"
Will brighten up each day!

Bettie Alder Turngren

Loving A Friend

If loving you is so hard to do
Then I just want to be free
Because sometimes all you do

Is just stand there hurting me

Sometimes you say that you really care
And that you never want to loose me
But then again I turn around
And all you do is use me

Just let me leave and say good-bye
Then that would be the end
And if we would ever meet sometime
I hope we could be friends

Please don't be mad or angry
I just want you to understand
When we were loving each other
We were just loving a friend

Edith M. Miller

Ten And Seven Years

If I were older and having in my
then 'infinitely wise possession'
the advantage of many years,
then perhaps I would find within myself
those 'jewels of wisdom' so often
beguiled by youth,
for they say, 'You haven't yet gained such
experience to be permitted to understand
that knowledge, child.'
Perhaps in your youth, but I'd rather
not in mine!

Joseph Cortegerone

Alone

I am alone,
there for I am lonely.
When I cry,
no one hears.
When I hurt,
no one feels
When I am sick,
no one cares.
When I smile,
no one sees.
When I am scared,
no one knows.
And when I write,
no one reads.
I am alone,
there for I am lonely.

Kristina Kennedy

A Hidden Message

In many stories, songs, and poems
There is a hidden message.
Many people miss it.
By reading it aloud
or even slowing down.
You may be a lucky person
because now you can find
a secretly hidden message.

Jerri Jo Kinzie

There Is Love

In a twisted world of unjust,
there is passion
there is lust

In the abhorrent society
we are living,
there is sequester
there is giving.

In this lurid berth I lay,
there is lull
there is stray.

In this untimely rise
of pain,
there is droll
there is sane.

In a perfect place
from above,
there is immortal
there is love.

Dannielle Tiffany Sabito

Feathers

It's been so long since we began anew
There is so much left for us to do
So many places we have not been
Dancing like feathers in the wind
Won't you even let it try
To soar throughout the midnight sky
I only ask for just one chance
To be alive, to sing and dance
How can you tell it no
Deprive it of its' right to grow
Who gave you the right
To kill its' dreams out of spite
Even though it's not real clear
In your heart you hold it dear
Why then are you afraid
Defeat the demons that you have made
Only then will you see
Until then you'll never be free
Running from the evil at night, loving
darkness
Afraid of the light, never knowing the truth.

Beth Templeman

Bush Soul

Separate from me
There she flies
Upward, toward the skyline.
A free spirit unleashed.
Rare in her madcap flight.
Scattering among us
Meaningful illusions
To seek and find.
And, the frosty clouds part
Allowing her to soar
Higher and higher,
Beyond my recognition.

Jannice Brooks

The Dream

I had a dream, late one night
There was no sound only sight
Walking on a beach of pure white sand
Watching the waves sweep the land
The sea gulls graceful as they fly
The puffy clouds race across the sky
Sitting in the sand, I notice with despair
Oil not only in the water, but everywhere
The gulls no longer gracefully fly
Only able to struggle as they die
To the top of the water float the fish
If I could only have one wish
To stop pollution of every kind
Is the thing I have in mind
I know to well it will never be true
What can only wishing do?
I look at the mess that causes my fears
Frown upon my face, eyes full of tears
Then I awoke with a tear stained face
Hoping this would never really take place.

Don Peters

Friends

Much more than smiles and laughter...
There's a special touch,
A helping hand,
A reassuring word.

So much more...

The memories to keep you going,
A picture to wash your worries away,
Someone to lean on,
And someone to need me.

Friends...
Such a beautiful word,
With so many definitions.

Be a friend,
And have a friend for life!

Kelly Jackson

The Revolution

DOES NOBODY SPEAK MY LANGUAGE
There's been REVOLUTION in my family
With REVOLUTION there's pain and tears
Hanging on
DOES NOBODY SPEAK MY LANGUAGE

DOES NOBODY SPEAK MY LANGUAGE
Seventeen in just one month
Tears masked by anger
I love you, I love you too
DOES NOBODY SPEAK MY LANGUAGE

DOES NOBODY SPEAK MY LANGUAGE
Together twenty-one years
Unable to shed tears
Fear and anger a cancer within
DOES NOBODY SPEAK MY LANGUAGE

DOES NOBODY SPEAK MY LANGUAGE
Oh how's my little sweetheart
Just fine mom just fine
Any rain your way
DOES NOBODY SPEAK MY LANGUAGE

Cynthia A. Fowler

Enter The Doorway

There are white walls,
they come in four.
If you know there's release,
there is also a door.

Entry allows,
not only what's to come.
There is present and future,
and where you come from.

Life is what you make it,
it's what you see beyond.
You can make it what you've hated,
or what you have become fond.

Enter the doorway,
with hope in your heart.
Things will fall together,
and you will become a part.

Believe the threshold,
will only bring something new.
Not only life,
but a new beginning for you.

Carol Stutchman

'Til Their Day Is Done

The fire bells ring...
They rush ahead.
We seem so calm, but scared.
We never know
That the work they begin
Immediately might come to an end.
Think about their families...
Think about their friends...
Think about their neighbors...
There is no end.
We pray, they'll come home
when it's over.
We pray they'll come home,
Because we love them so.

Cherrie Fuller Belcher

The Beast

I can remember the nights-
They were many by number;
The nights I could dream,
And sleep in spite of thunder.

Troubles never existed
In my dreamland of peace-
Until something broke those dreams;
I call that something The Beast.

I hear his scratchy voice.
I see his evil eyes,
I vow I will be the winner,
But he overpowers me in size.

The night has come once more,
Routinely, I get into bed.
I try hard to forget
The Beast that's in my head.

I toss and turn
And remember when I was younger,
I was carefree and happy-
And I slept in spite of thunder.

Karen Warren

There Is Peace

If you want joy and peace of mind
Think of Jesus Christ today.
A closer relationship with him brings
true happiness your way

Keep your mind on Jesus
He will always carry you through
No matter what the trial or test
He knows what is best for you

The Lord our God is wonderful
He loves us one and all
I love the Lord, he heard my cry
And answered when I called

Oh Savior of mine I worship you
In word, in thought and deed
In you I have a friend oh Lord
I know you supply every need

I'm saved today by God's grace
I've turned my back on sin
I've made up my mind to serve the Lord
Through him I have peace within

Jennie V. Harris

Thirteen Box Turtles

Watching
Thirteen box turtles
Spend a whole sunny summer day
On the old railroad tie
Just off a point of
This pond
I feel a connectedness.

Knowing some bird songs
Playing Irish guitar CDs
From them (for me)
Offering sunflower seeds
A participation
In the rituals.

Even as a micro-grain of sand
In a universe of
Imploding gaseous dust
And nuclear furnaces,
A connectedness.

Hearing shots in the distance,
I wonder about the origin of species.

Denny G. Varney

With Honor

They stepped into the fray with eyes closed
Those that live will never be free
Nightmares will haunt
Flashbacks will torment
Fields o green splashed with crimson
Embittered soldiers weeping
O'er the bodies of friend and foe alike
Now with eyes open wide they return home
No honor received for their destroyed lives
Lion hearts hesitant to appear
Marching to ridicule feeling only pain
They served their country in homage
Win or lose they've lost the game
Respect they deserve
Dignity is theirs to claim
They are our history and our future
For keeping us free
I humbly thank you.

Christina Anderson

My Gift

Such a special gift we all possess,
This capacity to love.
It can lead you to the lowest place
Or to the skies above.

It can run you down a danger path,
With troubles high and low.
It can lead you into happiness
With all the beauty it can show.

Many times I've often wondered
Now I know that it can be,
Of all the gifts from God on high,
He gave this one to me.

It must have been to show His love,
That yes, He truly cares.
With all the problems of this world,
He is there to share.

Alone, you say, oh no I'm not,
For He can never leave
This human spirit, a piece of Him,
On this, I do believe.

Kimberly Claunch

Unkept Emotions

Two hearts collide on a ravaging sea
Thrashed about in search of a dream.
Waves wash over unkept emotions.
Are they mine?
Are they yours?
Can they weather the storm?
Can love survive the past?

Elizabeth Angsten

Spring

I took a walk one clear Spring Day
Through a fresh green country side
The sun was shining bright above
The sky was blue and wide.

A gentle breeze brushed past my face
as I picked daffodils
The grass was like green velvet
Spread across the rolling hills

I walked along an old rock fence
That had stood for years in style
It had dressed its self for spring
With roses blooming wild

I heard a bluebird singing
Its song seemed just for me
I listened to its concert
'neath a weeping willow tree

I wandered on and found a brook, so quietly
it did run
The water rippled gently, like silver in the sun

I sat beside the little brook, just filled with
perfect bliss
I'm sure if God lived here on Earth, it
would be in a place like this

Flossie Shackelford

Enduring Sable

A teal breeze
Through a half open window:
I have inhaled nothing
But deep thoughtful breaths.
My cotton blanket
Against comfortable nakedness,
His gentle hand
Slides into mine.
Lashes close.

My isolation and thoughts have been
broken.
Do I dare lie longer?
What time, day, month,
Year will be right?

That selfish urge
To keep my life mine.
Like enduring sable —
It is me.

There is no such thing
As "never too late."
I quickly let go.

Branden Effland

Poetic Fancy

Innocent thoughts
through my mind
ride as fast as the wind
coming to a stop.

As the water crashes
against the rocks
a warm breeze runs deep
inside me
a cool shiver I feel

A bonsai sits
majestically
atop a barren hillside
Waiting for someone to notice it's power

AND THE CHILD STEPS OUT OF HER
CRADLE
FOR HER FIRST TIME!?

Dilip Lahiri

Life

A walk, through his eyes.
Through years and years of distant lore
I've walked through many a different door
I've climbed a mountain high on high
I've seen the sun melt in the sky
I've learned true love is hard to find
and love and hate get so entwined.
I knew a man throughout the years
he lived in vain and died in tears.
I knew a child that grew up in horror
and ended up in deep, deep sorrow.
I've heard of men that die in war
have known a few, maybe more.
So behold this world before you now
and do not bend or do not bow
For in this world for you my friend
is life with grief that never ends.

Jon R. Travis

Overdue Love

My love, my love I give to you
Through years of sorrow your love was due.
You took each day with hopes and dreams
Happiness, for you, it did not seem.

You had a love, which did not sail
You thought another would surely fail
And many nights would end in tear,
Never knowing if love was near.

Then fate stepped in to lend a hand
One special day you met a man,
Whose life had been the same as yours
You felt then, your heart was cured

The two of you were meant to be
His love for you, and you for he.
With all his love he vowed to you
On the day you said I do.

Since the day it's been sweet bliss
Your heart found love that it had missed
Together you've found a greater love
Other couples will always dream of.

James A. McDaniel

Thundering Silence

Weighty tones
thunder
through corridors of
cogitation.
Inflections
are drowned
in a sea
of loquacious
retrospection.
The aggregate is beyond
audibility.
The edifice
palpitates.

Carol Dorsey

Terra

Terra,
thundered the voices
of the majestic trees
in the forests
of the dark continents

Terra,
echoed the rocks in the hills
and mountains of the great rockies

Terra,
wept the mammals
in unison and in tears
from the vast lands and seas

Terra,
roared the waters
surging through the
channels in the soil

Terra,
whispered the clouds
in the sky as the earth stood still
Then softly upon the earth fell the rain.

Antoine Delgado

The Onrushing Tide

The onrushing tide
Thunders toward shore
Caught up in its design
It heeds not the solitary wind
opposing its path
But swells up even further
in wild fury
Blindly hurtling itself forward
To its inevitable prostration
On the shore below -
It's fate long sealed

Jared J. Gardner

Written To Thee

Two hearts
tied together
in hope for eternity
in reality, soon thereafter
unsure destinations
but lost in
silent prayers
future of dust
long gone; ahead
devastation, misfortune, tears
present joy
strangely content lamenting:
accepted turmoil
sweet, thou Woeful Weeper
thwarted, in love
yet at thy side
and love thee.

Caroline Dazet

Awaiting

Keeping watch for you, I am,
tilling through my thoughtful land,
with eyes perplexed
and gaping hands-
keeping watch since nigh'.

Peering fast for you, I will,
with boiling eyes that have not fill
while take steely, in your stride,
I catch a glimmer, full with pride
peering fast, as morn' arrives.

Stealing time for you, I have,
in tending all that wants your still,
discarding each and every rhyme
that without you, can have no thrill.

Kimberly K. Russell

Storm

Aggravating with a scream,
Time, but passes by,
Torrents knocking on the sill,
Heave a heavy sigh,

Forgotten altogether
Leaving, but alone,
Longing for some comfort
For sins not yet atoned.

Bonnie Ratzloff

Frustration

Ringing phones, a lonely sound.
Tinny voices on answer machines,
Heard over and over and over.
A poor substitute for needed love

Vain attempts to win a smile,
To achieve that fleeting moment.
Please last longer and longer and longer.
Any substitute for needed love.

Are all good things so hard to hold?
Do all cost so high a price?
Frustration over and over and over,
There is no substitute for love.

Bruce P. Fontana

Untitled

'Tis not what I have seen,
'Tis not what I have read.
'Tis not the thoughts and figures
Which dance upon my head - I dread.

I see the waters rising
Upon of which I float.
Eyes strain across the Scottish mires -
The thick, and flooded moat.

It closes you in without a thought,
To fight it, you face it - carry the load.
Inside it, you mold it,
Extract what's been lost; leave it untold.

From the heavens above,
To the earth at your feet;
What were thy chances,
Lest, you defeat?

Yet, what's brought to thy mind,
And held close to thy heart;
'Tis fate, that adheres us -
'Til death, thy, do part.

Carol Marie Meister

Going Away

Packing up and going away,
To a new place - I'll come back some day.
For my turn has come
To go back to the slum.
There is nothing for me here
I shall not shed any tears.
They have treated me well
So inside I do not swell,
But it is time to go.

Good-bye, so long, have a nice life!
Now I shall ride away on my bike
And not be a bore
To anyone, any more.

Jane Daniels

Winter

The birds fly south as if
they know winters coming,
The deer go down to try to
get there last drink, even
though the river is frozen
but still running fast
below. Then snow comes
some trees get snow
some look bare that's the
scene of winters care

Jessica Kampa

Untitled

Though it seem so hard
to bare
I close my eyes though you're
away you always seems to
be near
The tone of your voice
seems so clear I can
even see your face appear
I seem to feel your lips
against mine kissing me
so passionately
And the soft touch of your
hand that caress my
body so gently
Now if your sitting along
with nothing to do just
think it seems I am their
with you.

Donnie R. Wilson

Care Free And Smiles

As I sit here by my Self, Trying
To be Happy, like we use to be,
Care free, and smiles, looking
Over the River, A fishing pole
In my hand, I remember the good
Times, with you as you laugh
At the ants, and flying bugs,
And so upset, when the big
One got away, all the sun
Sets, we looked at, and your
special star, you always liked
So well, as you are far, away
now, I will always remember
The things we shared were
So special and warm.

Barbara Simmons

"Lonely Heart"

An empty room in a broken man
To be, it seems as such
He does but only as he can
For a lonely heart to touch

Could it be as once was sought
To ask can't be too much
To touch a dream, to feel a thought
Just a lonely heart to touch

A broken heart in a lonely man
He longs to find a crutch
If he could have just once, just once
That lonely heart to touch

His mind rewound his thoughts expound
He gave his all 'twas known
He once was lost but now he's found
That lonely heart to touch...his own

Clyde L. Diggs Jr.

The Versifier

Poetry is the gift of man
to express himself in the rhythm of words,
to caress a reader in a foreign wind,
to make time go and come again,
to be sometimes out and sometimes in
the thoughts of which he gives
to the life in which he lives.

Debra Goodrich

Past, Present Or Future

Life needs love
To be seen from above.
A heart needs a spirit,
Where heaven awaits for it.
Joy is in giving
To the needy for living,
Peace is a day
When all wars fade away,
Hope is a home
Of a place yet to come,
And faith is the key
That will set us all free.

Judith P. Dowell

Free To Be "Me"

I'm trying so hard
To be the person I need to be.
I'm trying so hard
To be me and only me.
So many times I try,
To be a person I'm not.
Knowing inside...
One day I'll get caught.
Why can't I be
Me and only me.
Why don't I see
What others see in me.
I see my failures,
Imperfections and faults.
That's someone I'm not.
But, I'm only human
As anyone can see
So instead of being someone I'm not,
I'll try to be me,

Emily Clark

New Beginnings

Farewell, farewell
to candy coated dreams,
mysteries of fairies
and things unseen.

To tales of darkness
suddenly brought to light.
Amongst the strange
newly discovered life.

Farewell, farewell
to dandelion rose,
hours of play and nap time.
And awaken to this
newly discovered life.
Amongst the strange... Adulthood!

Daniel Robert Corkery

Help Me

Help me O Lord
to get through this day,
To meet your requirements
and do things your way,
To keep me active
in whatever you deem,
Through thick and through thin
no matter your scheme,
I feel I can't make it
you know this I'm sure,
So help me and guide me
and open your door.

Eileen M. Staines

Drowned

Wispy Journey
to forgotten faces;
Wandering in the darkness,
Lost amongst all normality.

Trapped
Beneath the industrial waters;
Reaching for the surface;
Finding comfort in the silence.

Past the muffled cries;
Beyond the restless eyes;
Searching for utter deception.

The paranoid,
Helpless mind,
Confused,
Plotting pointless escapes.

Final arrival,
Enveloped in peace and
Drowned.

Jessica Garcia Lewis

Desire

Everything needs, it is a necessity
to gain subsistence, it doves us
to our objectives, it creates, it
obliterates, it fosters our push
through existence. Without
aspiration, without hunger, we
linger inertly and still orb.
It being a blinding light, which
we must project to gain affluence.
Proper...

Ken Christensen

Rain

It's music to my ears
to hear the rain,
falling on my roof
and window pane.

I don't like the lightening,
it's too frightening.

I want to hide,
and stay inside.

Karen Dobson

One Wish

One Wish
To hope for peace worldwide.
One Wish
To dry all crying eyes.
One Wish
For the hungry we must feed,
One Wish
To satisfy all needs.
One Wish
To cool the global warming,
One Wish
To quell the violence storming.
You have but one wish
To make everything right,
Draw on your pains
And all your hindsights.
Love them, protect them,
Nurture them, teach them.
For the only wish that will further men,
Is the wish for true happiness for all
children.

Joyce M. Fuller

Desperate

Too many decisions. Too much
to loose. Too many choices. I
just don't know what to do.
Too many feelings I shouldn't have
to feel. Too many wounds left
yet to heal. So much pressure
brought upon me. To many decisions
then I'd rather there be. I
just can't do it. Not now. Not
ever. When will it stop.
It seems like never. I wish
it would stop. Just come to
a halt. Please somebody help
me. It's not all my fault!

Kristen McMann

To Be Of One

To know you is to love you,
to love you is to grow on you.

To have you is to honor you,
To be on one is to combine.

Love is within you must use the light
Of commitment to guide us through the
Pain as well as the glory of love.

It is to feel the desire of each other,
Never having the yearning for another.

The love two can give to each other is
Undying if two hearts can become of one.

To be of one is the one thing we all
Truly desire at some point in life.?

Carlene M. Whitman

Such A Birth

Such a birth is this-
to my hands it extends.
My heart it laments,
and my ears it pervades.
My tongue it stifles
as I gawk
at its azure berth,
overtly experiencing
with my eyes
its tears tumbling
from the ethers
as droplets of dew
upon the verdant sea.

All bloodshed shall be doused
by such a birth as this, this so-called...

LAUGHTER.

Brennan M. Thomas

Autumn

The falling leaves of autumn sway
to the rhythm of the wind,
whispering mellow sighs of a long
summer's end.
Soon the colors of golden and rust,
will become nothing but nature's
own dust.
The winds carry scents of hickory
and spice,
while the cattails chant their last
songs into the night.

Kimberly Enas

Women

A son you had, and up you brought
To raise the seat, was what you
Taught
So women! If you stand like a man
Please raise the seat if you can

Come on women! Lets be neat
Come on women! You better heed
I might be the one you meet
That says,"upon the seat she peed"

Ladies! You really make me blush
Pads in the toilet, do not flush
The companies give you, bags of pink
To hide the red and rid, the stink

There's receptacles, for your pads to
Hide
Come on women! Where's all your pride

Joyce Jensen

Daimon

So many have come and tried before,
to stand the threshold of the door.
Pulled by the wind
Pushed by the fire
Holding on to let go
of all we desire.
Grasping at both worlds
yet neither are gained,
for all of our pushing
just pushes us away.
Struggling within fear
of the demon we are,
so divided from ourselves
we dream - oh so far.

Bradford E.

I'm Scared!

I'm scared! I'm scared!
To start at my new school!
I'm scared! I'm scared!
I'll be a big fat fool!

I'm scared! I'm scared!
Those kids, look really mean!
I'm scared! I'm scared!
I'm as skinny as a string bean!

I'm scared! I'm scared!
I'll really stick out!
I'm scared! I'm scared!
I'll probably pout!

I'm scared! I'm scared!
I'll be a klutz in gym!
I'm scared! I'm scared!
They'll think I'm really dim!
I'm just really SCARED!

Ashley Bouder

Thunder Clouds

Raven black clouds rumbled... rumbled
The pale sickly sun vanished
Round drops darted down... down
Rain glistened... glistened like jewels
The clouds cleared
The sun brilliantly shone
A rainbow touched from tree to tree

Elizabeth Hays

This Hour Is Mine

Sun streams through my window
To start each mystic day.
I know not what it holds for me
Now how well my hand will play.

Yesterday is memory,
Tomorrow, but a dream.
This hour is all that matters now
In life's grand unfolding scheme.

I must not waste a moment
Of this gift I have received.
It's mine to work great wonders
Or to wantonly deceive.

The sands of Time rush fleeting by,
We know not for how long.
With faith, we know each moment
Can be antidote for wrong.

I humbly ask forgiveness
For dark errors of the past;
For grace to fill my heart with love,
And to ever be steadfast.

Aimee T. Hester

Alcohol Addiction

It is indeed a fight,
to stop the liquor.
An unending plight,
to get back to who you were.

You were re-born,
and things were dandy.
Soon your good intentions became torn,
and it was back to the Brandy.

Usually you feel nauseous and upchuck,
and then you sit and cry.
Realizing that life sucks,
and you will certainly die.

Cut the bull s**t,
you can't live forever.
Resolve to quit,
for it is now or never.

DB Johnson

Fetal Kick

To Becca

Beauty breathes inside and kicks softly
to tell you Hello, I'm doing fine.
Thanks for the food and the fresh breath
of second-hand smoke, at least you
care, for rubbing my back and keeping
me calm while I hold myself and keep
myself warm.
Please just hold me and sleep try
not to think, don't worry I float in
space and the stars inside watch me
closely thinking of a strange new.
I wave in slow motion and they know
I mean no harm, only a new existence
in there world for a short while.
nine months to be precise.

Jason McMillion

Eve Of July 4th, 1995

"I pledge allegiance
To the flag
Of the United States of America"
Which gives us unbound freedom.
Freedom to speed on back roads
Freedom to buy, under-aged.
Freedom to curse, demean, and spit
Freedom to hop the White House fence.
Freedom to steal our neighbor's cat
Freedom to batter our pregnant wives.
Freedom to conceal deadly weapons
Freedom to sell crack to the fourth-graders.
Freedom to get away with L.A. murder.

Freedom
To burn our nation's flag.

"God, bless America."

Debra Schowalter

Untitled

Drip down
to the pool of flavored life.
Soak in the sweetener,
feel the energy.
Touch the wax walls,
scrape through to escape.

Go flat,
lose the chill.

Evaporate.

Erica Leipheimer

Christmas Day

As the snow drifts down
to the soft cold ground
and the bright lights
give off the final glow of the night
and the children dream things
about what Santa will bring
the soft glow of Christmas Eve fades
and in the night comes Christmas Day

Ashley Paige Cutchin

Micheled

The softness of dawn cannot compare
To the softness of your eyes;
There is a kindness there
That is far too comforting for words.
A time ago, I would dream of a place
As serene as a summer's day,
As bright and poetic as the stars,
And as wistful and innocent
As a child's imagination.
The time for dreaming had passed
Yet I am not saddened.
Reality paints a more beautiful picture
And has chosen as her canvas,
Your face, your smile and your eyes.

Verna

Woman

Woman is like the virgin mary
to the world,
Sacred, hallowed, and eminent.
She is illustrious, delightful,
Wonderful, and magnificent.
She is feminine power,
Sensuously different;
Individually virtuous,
Uniquely exquisite.
She is love, life, warmth, and
affection.
She is like a precious jewel,
To be appreciated, cherished,
and treasured.
She is the object of perfection.
The most beautiful entity in
the world.

Cornelious Reynolds

Tonight

As I lay in bed at night
To think of the events of the day
Sometimes it gives me a fright
So I decide to pray
I wait until I can see
The heavens and stars above
Then I get down on my knees
And pray for peace and love
For all the people far and near
The victims of a crime
The criminal did not shed a tear
Children dying before their time
Then I sit back on my bed
And I turn out the light
And I erase the horrors from my head
But still I toss and turn all night.

Casey Tenniswood

Empty — Now The Crosses Stand

A mute reminder
To weakened man.
Stark and lonely,
Testimony in pain.
How can we
In comfort here - complain?
Within my heart
I confess my sins
And to the Savior, - say...
Come, welcome in,
But still in twilight,
Life's refute.
The crosses stand,
Reminders in mute.

Barbara E. Stratton

One And Only

So I sit here with my
true love before me.
How shall I tell him my
tales of glory. How shall
I cry to my one and only,
I don't want to let
him go. I don't want to
see him leave, because
when he does he will
brake my heart like
bridle leaves.

Delores Jimenez

Untitled

I discovered your eyes again
today...clear, focused, soft and
warm...promising everything and
compromising nothing.
I discovered your lips again last
night...full, expressive and perfect
in every way...and never more
beautiful than when they say
"I love you."
I discovered my heart again
today...just like every day around
this time when I think of you.

Happy Valentine's Day.

Keith A. Tisdale

Untitled

Anger and frustration on mixing
together to form a distinct fist of
rage.

Thoughts floating like bubble of
Heat.

Hot tears miserably falling down
an icy face.

Swelling so much ready to burst
Why? It hurts! No!

Suddenly a loving arm is placed
across a shuddering shoulder,

Anger turns to sadness and
Calms frustration.
ceasing as the years go by but
never leaving completely.

Emi Carbone

A Child's Love For The American Flag

A child's love for the American flag,
too young to understand the trials
and tribulations of war, but old
enough to understand the love
and courage Old Glory bore.

For she stood in a sand pile and
she seemed to whisper freedom with ease.

Yes, she is tired but not tired of
standing all day in the hot sun,
but tired of war and sorrow.

And we know that Old Glory soon will
see a bright and better tomorrow.

Judith Oster

Live Life

Live life, the best way you can
to fulfill your ability of wants and needs.
Live life, of joy and happiness of man
for all power of God shall exceed.
Live life, helping one another
to get better or well.
Live life, our sisters and brothers
of the society, need someone to tell.

Cynthia Howard

The Sun Will Rise

The wind blows through my hair
Tossing it gently in the air.
I wait, burdened by grief and pain
Weak with sadness, no hope to gain.
I stand shivering in the dark,
When suddenly I see a spark.
Though just a glint it quickly grows
Until a sliver proudly glows
In the darkness of the night,
Into my soul, that ray of light.
It chips away the hurt and fears.
It comforts me and dries my tears.
It tenderly strips away my sorrow,
Bringing in another tomorrow.
Promising one more day.
Reminding me the pain won't stay.
The sun will rise.

Jill M. Gambill

Death

Death is such a
tragic thing, people
come and people go

But some people are
still living, in this
world we call home

But dead or alive were
still the same, walking
through the streets
of doom

Saying we will be
back some day soon

Amanda Garske

Spanked

Monday: I got spanked.
Tuesday: I was spanked.
Wednesday,
  Thursday, and
Friday: I got spanked, spanked, and
  spanked.
Saturday: We talked and talked, and
  talked
Sunday: I went to church.

Jordan L. Oseguera

Life

Life, a perilous journey.
Turning corners blindly.
We write in the pages of our existence,
Day by day, minute by minute.

Casually we forget,
Pages are not crafted from iron,
But of delicate paper,
Torn from our grasp with ease.

Everything is taken for granted,
Until it is gone...forever.

Kyle Murphy and Kevin Murphy

Untitled

Call of ancient fate above
turns my heart towards men to love.
Some call this wrong, perverted, bad —
For those who do I feel quite sad.

They will never see the cheer
that can be when one is queer
The strength of heart in one so bold
who will not let a lie be told.

Blind themselves to something great
crying 'choice' not quirk of fate...
screaming faggot in my ear
but I just choose not to hear.

I live my life as I see fit.
For me, not them, each tiny bit
And if they truly wish me dead —
For all those truths that I have said

They may try, I will still fight
for all the things I think are right
And should I die this very day
Despite their hate I'll still be gay.

Ashavan Whitman Doyon

What A Pair - On The Stair

Furry faces with glowing eyes
  Twice the mischief for their size
Found that red-ball thing
  Down the stairs - one long string
Through the rail
  Round a tail
Poor mistress now ensnared
  From table leg to arm of chair
Braided round and round
  And knots, up and down
Fanged and dragged upstairs again
  And there, between steps, hangs
    the end

Too bad, taking place at night
  Would love to see in day bright
Weary, bed beckons - I cannot stay
  And intrude upon this nocturnal play

  What a pair, on the stair.

Colleen Lydon

Light

At first Light,
  Two hands meet under
satin sheets,
  Deep in sleep.

One large
One small.
One calloused.
One smooth.
One black.
One white.

Each caresses the Forbidden
  and savors the nectar of
  an unknown fruit.

Eyes opened to the Light
Anguished,
In the wake of this rare sight.

Courtney M. Burton

One Dozen

One rose to say I'm sorry,
Two to say I care.

Three roses to say I'm with you,
Four to say I'll be there.

Five roses to say I like you,
Six to say I'll share.

Seven roses to say I've stared at you,
Eight to say whenever I can bare.

Nine roses to say I'll pay,
Ten to say whatever the fare.

Eleven roses to say I love you,
Twelve to say we're the greatest pair.

Jolene Monson

Untitled

Darling toddler
  Two years old
Sometimes bashful
  Sometimes bold.
Cuddling upon my lap
  Hopefully will take a nap.

  Looking at the world with you
Everything seems fresh and new.
  Watching, listening and learning
Fast
  Your baby days are nearly past.

Let's read some stories and
  nursery rhymes
And let me hold you
  a few more times
Before new interests lure you
  away
New friends, then school
  and work some day.

Anne Dietrich

Bang! Bang! Bang!

Bang! Bang! Bang!
Unconscious of the banging,
Undaunted by the pounding,
This lovable object just sits there.

Bang! Bang! Bang!
Unconscious of the hanging,
Undaunted by the hounding,
This lovable object does not care.

Bang! Bang! Bang!
Not the cause,
Not wondering why,
This lovable object has to bear.

Bang! Bang! Bang!

Kenneth Hines

"This Soft Place"

Penetrate the skin
Touch explores
Familiarity within
Sanctity ignored
Realization of the past
From pleasure we are born
A comfort not meant to last
Ripped from bliss, life learns to scorn.

Keith Murphy

Fields Of Glory

Another weary morning
Under bruised clouds on solemn fields
Solitude fills the atmosphere
And stones veiled in weathered day
Obscure the names of yesteryear's

The presence finds no relief
Bound to the realm of its cause
Like some fate sealed in time
Our anger and confusion
Inherent to the same that forbade life

Among columns of gray
Looms a sense of resented wealth
Glory that clings to only a memory
As steeped in time and distance
As the price they paid for being free

Generations have kept their groom,
And their purpose evermore content
Our pride at their cost
Where no glory is spent
And no freedom is lost

Blake Gray

Vault

I keep my emotions
Under lock and key
The only trespassing done
Is done by me

I want of a burglar
Proficient in the greatest art
Who'll cherish the precious gold
Who's skilled at taking vaults apart

A vandal who need not
Be strong nor brave
To steal from within me
The Love I save

To separate the pieces strewn
The vault does dearly hold
And take from me
That stored and precious gold

Diane Dyer

Free To Be

The world was so magnificent
Until you came along
You held my hand so gently
And then you sang your song

This is how I see it now
The day when all is gone
The day you let me live my life
Will live forever on

I used to think I'd go somewhere
Now it just seem all wrong
You told me things were special
And then you sang your song

This is when I fly away
Without my wings I'll soar
With my soul I will leave you now
It is time that I sing my song

Becky Venuti

"My Smile"

  My smile is a very special gift
unwrapped and always working
  My smile may imply hope, faith, or love
but it doesn't mean that I'm easy
  My smile is yours to keep
tucked away in your memories
  My smile is not a sign of weakness
but it does imply strength
  My smile is not a point of denial
but more to say you're welcome
  My smile is not of hate
but more to say I love
  My smile is an investment and
thru you do I see my returns
  My smile is free and never ending
and that too is true of my blessings
  My smile is one of my many gifts
My smiles says I'm happy
and none of worries does it bare
  My smile say's that God has been good to
me!

Dwayne L. Wilbert

Wings

Your life is a sorrowful stain
Upon the fabric of this place.
And how can you truly explain
The sorrow upon my face?

Neither time nor joy can erase
The tears of loss I have shed.
Neither age nor length can deface
The memorial of my fallen ken.

I have walked in the Goddess'
Holy Light,
I have stood among the depressed,
And prayed for Her to lift our sight

To gaze upon Her glorious form,
So filled with loving peace,
That cannot be broken by any storm,
Nor ruined by our touch.

What I must ask is not much,
Just a tiny thing among many things.
I ask for Her beneficent touch
To relieve me of my broken wings.

Christopher S. Harris

Winds Of Prayer

We cast our worries
  upon the winds of prayer,
  they twist and turn,
  as they flow upwards
  to the Lord's hands,

The Lord takes
  the winds of our prayers,
  and turns them into breezes,
  then he gently blows them
  to where they'll land,

And all is done,
  as to his will,
  to all his good works,
  to what he needs,
  and wants of us
    who believe.....

Catherine P. Griffin

"Golden"

Golden is a word
Used in many ways
It's fun in the sun
With its golden rays
Golden is magic,
Golden's my boss
Golden is Jesus, And the sign of the cross
Golden is flowers when they bloom
Golden is home with lots of room
Golden is summer, sunny and warm
Golden is dewdrops clinging till morn
Golden is mystery
Golden is here
Golden's the white, On the tail of a deer
Golden is time
As long as an hour
Golden is petals
on a golden sunflower
Golden is our friendship, strong and true
Golden's the love I have for you.

James Trainis

I Love You

Alone I sit
Waiting for the sound
Of your voice.
Please call me.
I cannot stand
Being without you.

No one is more interesting to me.
I hang on every word you speak.
I prize every moment I am with you.
I'm devastated whenever I cannot see you.
What is this power you hold over me?

Every time we meet
It is like the first time.
One kiss from you
And my world turns upside down.
I would climb any mountain,
Storm any castle,
And slay any dragon
For your love.
Can't you understand, that I love you?

John Mann

The World

World wide death
War and hell fire
Nobody gets rest
Old men retire

People seeking love
Love running away
Flightless is the dove
That tries to go astray

Help us God we are men
Walking crooked roads
Caught up in our sin
Reaping what we sow

We all think we see
How can we tell
If we will be set free
Or fall into the well

David Michael Meehan

Used To Be

Used to be you gave me flowers
Used to be you gave me candy...
but that was long ago.

Used to be you promised me
stars from the sky
water from the moon
sand from the sea
but that was long ago.

Used to be you gave me diamonds
Used to be you gave me pearls
but that was long ago.

Used to be you gave me
anything I wanted
but that was long ago.

Now you give me love
and I find - that's all
I ever really needed.

Debby Maksymiw

A Warm Friend

Here I sit upon the bed
Waiting to have some fun,
Trying to remember words unsaid
Thinking of things left undone

Reminiscing about the past
Of happy carefree days,
We have been together for so long
And know each other's ways

My fur is bare
My clothes are torn
Could it be she doesn't care
I feel so old and worn.

Shh, I think I hear a noise
She has come back for me!
She left all the other toys
But could not go on without Ted D!

Cindy Campbell

The Prettiest Sight

The prettiest sight I've ever seen
Was a mountain covered with snow,
What's the prettiest sight you've ever seen
I'd really like to know.

It may be a field of flowers
Or a deer that's eating grass,
A rainbow after a rainfall
That never seems to last.

A sunny day with a bird flying high
That will chirp till the bright days end
A mother father sister or brother
A pet or even a friend.

You can make it whatever you like
Just tell me oh please oh please
I have to hear what it is.
I'm down on my hands & knees.

You'll tell me what it is
Oh me oh me oh my,
It's a newborn baby you hold in your arms
With a smile and a tear in his eye.

Christen Bell

"Grandparents"

A gift from yesterday,
Very near to the heart,
Gentle we like to say,
Right from the start,
Full of memories from the past,
Sharing them with you,
To make them last,
Along with fear inside,
Helpless they seem,
With nothing more to hide.
Showing a new gleam,
With the young at their side,
Helping them through,
Having God as a guide,
With nothing left to do.
Peace in their hearts,
As a new life they start,
Holding hands with God,
For their journey to start.

Debra M. Vanderwood

Taken For A Stroll

Amongst the strange calm
Walking with long shadows
Leaves rustle with the wind
The moist air settles on my brow
Thinking of what lurks in the dark
The scent of a damp evening
Soothes even the lone spirits
And makes me forget my feelings
A touch of dawn in the air
Makes me miss the night
I'm the only person here
And I can only see the light
Soon will appear the sun
but now is the collection of the dew
Springing life from every puddle
Drip after drip it's something new
Now I'm awakened from my dream, stole
Knowing I was taken for a stroll

Jeramiah D. Harris

Sergeant

Talking with you once again
Was just like coming home
From far-off, foreign places
Where things are alien, unknown.

Knowing you protect us
Is like sweetbreads oven-browned
With delicious, sweet security
And quiet all around.

Feeling you may suffer
Is like tolling bells' alarms,
With dirges, prayers, and helplessness,
And dust held in our arms.

So please, don't ever leave us,
And stay covered, close, secure,
So that all those you make feel like this
May be inspired to endure.

Aimee Kent Ballantyne

Untitled

if tomorrow
was my last day
i would have lived
to the fullest
for i have loved
and been loved

not an ordinary love
but one - more beautiful.
a love that fills
my life with joy

but most importantly
a love returned and shared.
during heights of happiness
or depths of despair
He is there

with a love
that fills my soul - completely
a love...His love
a love i'll feel
forever -

Ellen M. Peterson

"Always Leaving"

Yesterday I took a walk out in the rain.
Water washed down my cheek
As rain melted into tears.
So many people crowd onto
a page from my life.
So many people...
So close...
Yet so far...

Yesterday I took a walk out in the rain.
I practiced all the things
I had to say to you.
...Forgotten to say!
I walked away, but you
were always leaving!
The rose you gave me was
already dead!
I walked away, but you
were always leaving!
...Always leaving!
...So I took a walk out in the rain.

Josh K. Burchette

Think Earth

Sea's oceans, shells and sands.
Waterfalls and big badlands.
Canyons, streams and mountains high.
Devils tower touching sky.
Stop and think if it was not there.
If trash and dump had better care.
If vanishing creatures could come back.
And rain forest trees grew by the pack.
Meadows, flowers, reefs and air.
If we all pitched in and did our share.
Think of how the world would be.
For animals, lands, and even me.
I know somewhere, there is a key.
To unlock that door for us to see.

Becky Vanden Boogaard

Poppy

A field of flowery blood
waves methodically under a westward sun,
and whilst the dwindling breeze yet dies,
is born a winter's eve.
And statued in that midnight snow,
a petal drops,
shattering fragments of darkest red,
Upon the whitest ground.
In my field of silent poppies.

Angela Colvin

Crossroads

There are many crossroads
We all come to in life;
Some filled with happiness
Others filled with strife.

Which road do we take?
How do we know
Which road to travel,
Or how far to go?

But God with his infinite wisdom
Is always standing near by;
Waiting to hear us call out
Oh Lord, how weary am I.

So whenever I come to a crossroad
I stop and whisper a prayer;
And ask the Lord to guide me
To keep me in his care.

Then I travel where He leads me
Taking one step at a time;
On the right path and knowing
I'm doing His will, not mine.

Carol Goff Williams

Passages Of Time

Through the passages of time
we learn to follow
the inner tunnel
which seems so hollow.

And we search for the seed of love
to plant in our empty room,
Hoping for the distant tomorrow
to see its flower in full bloom.

Ana Darias-Natali

"Moonlight Lovers"

We met along the moonlit tides;
we walked the beach alone.

We talked and sang a soft love song;
which we both once knew.

The tide swelled up, as did our love;
and washed all other thoughts away.

Our love was clean and beautiful;
as was the wave washed sand.

Our love was smooth and rhythmic;
like waters beyond the reef.

We both knew, as all things do;
our love would fade away.
As did the receding tide of day.

Bonnie Younger-Scott

My Friend Jesus

Jesus is a friend of mine
We talk most every day.
He shows me where I'm going wrong
For he doesn't want me to stray.

He came to me when I was lost
And could not find my way.
He touched my heart and changed my life
When I knelt down to pray.

My friend, Jesus, is your friend too,
If only you will call.
He will help you solve your problems,
The big ones and the small.

If you are lost, out in this world
And you don't know what to do.
You call on my friend, Jesus
And he will come to you.

My Lord Jesus loves us all
There's nothing he can't do.
All the things he did for me,
He will do the same for you.

Joe Dunning

America

I am so proud to be an American
wearing red, white, and blue.
Standing beneath the stars at night
I know that it must be true.
The senator who makes the laws,
the soldiers who fight to keep us free,
I knew that night this country
was definitely for me.
The teachers who teach us everything we
know,
our moms and dads who help us to grow.
Come to America and you will see,
it is the best place you could ever be.

Kim Drevalas

Sister To Sister

Sister to sister,
We'll always be
Love twixt friends
you and me.
We've shared our childhood,
together not apart.
If we aren't near physically,
We are by soul, we are by heart.
I'll love you until this world ends,
You are my sister, we are great friends.

Jessica Ricciardi

My Dad and I

My Dad and I,
went down to France
To see the little women dance.
we go inside, turn out the light
we look around, we get a fright,
I know that I, would like to
stay, But tomorrow is another
day, Good night for now,
I'll see you soon, If you'll
remember me, just look at the moon.

Katharine S. Long

If Every Day Was Like Christmas

If every day was like Christmas
What a wonderful world this would be.
Then Peace on Earth (for all it's worth)
would be there for all to see.

It would be a time for giving presents,
but finding that giving is much more fun
and the joy they bring
make your heart sing
with love for everyone.

Sharing with the needy,
helping your fellow man
all these things you bestow
bring a soft warm glow
and a touch of a friendly hand.

So, every morning when you awake
and start along your way,
lift your eyes above
and fill your heart with love
and make them all like Christmas Day.

Bob Hayden

Irony

That last breath
What is on it?
One you had,
or one you wanted?
Do you reach for it,
or cry of loss
of it all.
Helpless pain and tears
Serpent Age
each day stealing a day
to the last.
Fear it or laugh,
rush it or wait.
You can't take it,
but you take it.

Adam Lewis Wiener

Life's Paradox

Hello Life - What is your purpose
  what is your job
  what is your line
In the Lords game of time
  your born
  you grow
  you work
   you grow old
you wrinkle and slow, but your
  Brain see's no snow
Your body them Die's
  Lifeless you go!
  Still what was
   your purpose
  Where do you go
After millions of years
  still nobody knows!

Donovan Ray Von Lindern Sr.

If Air Had Colors

If air had colors
What shades would they be
Pastel pink, green, and blues.
Oh! What a sight to see.
If air had colors
A beauty to behold.
Breeze of blue
Gales of green.
And giant gust of gold.
The colors whizzing by our eyes.
They sometimes take us by surprise.
But even when the wind seems dead
Light breezy colors fill your head.
I'd really like to see a swarm
And all those colors in a storm.
Mixing with the clouds above
Making new colors for all to love.

Amanda Leger

Promises

I wonder so much,
What there really is,
I begin to ponder,
What good are promises?

They can be broken,
Some don't even care,
They just say it's because,
The world is unfair.

"I'll love you forever,"
Is a common one heard,
But how long is it until
Divorce is the word?

You long for something,
And make a wish,
In an ocean of promise,
You are the lone fish.

So a true promise
Can only be found,
If those who promise it,
Can make you safe and sound.

Julia Ogg

Blind Eyes Can't See Nothing

If people only judge people on
what they see the judgement is
wrongly accused on the innocent,
and the guilty runs or gets sheltered.
If murderous hands murder again,
then an innocent mind is persecuted
by a blind jury when blind eyes can't
see nothing. The blind Jury will soon
see again, and the innocent mind
will be paranoid by the rings on
the murderous hands ringing.
Both the jury and the hands will
be wearing hand caps and the mind
will be locked up for insanity.
Blind eyes can't see nothing.

Elinor Collotta

The Love You Throw Away

Don't put off tomorrow.
What you can do today,
For someone will pick up
The love, you throw away

They will nourish it and cherish it,
As if it's silver or gold,
And the fortune of this love.
Will never go untold.

Jean Adams

All The Way

Explain all the way

Is all the way realistic?

What is all the way?
What's all, is that endless.
Is that possible?
Which way, where are we
going, do we know which way
is the right way?
Does all the way mean forever,
Or until we don't want to travel
That path anymore?
Is all the way too idealistic
For today/tomorrow?
Is all the way a possibility
or even just?

Daniel Jones

Infinity

When time stops,
When babies no longer cry,
When yesterday seems so far away,
When tomorrow takes forever...
this is when my heartbeat starts to slow
and my freedom is yet to come.

The moon will seem brighter,
the stars within my grasp,
a silent song will sing on forever,
with a peaceful stream babbling along.

My life will then find peace,
  and I will go,
with nothing else in tow.

Forgotten dreams will come true,
Along with ever pleasant thought.
My body will be left behind,
my soul set free;
one journey will come to an end
and another will just begin.

Denise Scherschel

Elizabeth Rose

Your petals of pink have bloomed again.
When from a solitary broken branch,
You were propagated, regenerated,
To mesmerize my eyes.
You were salvaged from the bruising winds,
To live, and not to die.

The growth was slow, but steady,
In a jar of water clear.
I gaze upon an open blossom,
Your beauty has no peer.

A finer Rose Elizabeth,
I believe will never be.
A Queen you are, a fragrant flower;
This summer's lovely memory.

Jack De Young

Take A Friend A Flower

'Tis a sad day, he said to me
When he returned from the cemetery:
I took my friend a flower.
Would you believe some low-life bum
Took the gift I took my chum:
I took my friend a flower.
Fret not, said I, the thought was pure;
He knew you'd come, of that I'm sure:
You took your friend a flower.
If some poor soul who had no job
Loved, as you, his dear friend, robbed,
He'd take his friend a flower.
Four souls were cheered, if you but pause,
Synergistic bliss because...

David Redden

Dreams Do Come True

'Twas at the English club one night
When "He" walked in the room,
He looked at me and then I knew
that I had met my doom!

We seemed to "go steady" I guess
from the very start
And new year's eve of '49 was the night
cupid's arrow hit the mark!

We've had loads of fun together
And our little problems too
But in the end it always seems,
our gray skies turn to blue!

And oh the happiness we've found
since that October day,
Knowing we'll be together always
Travelling along life's way!

Betty Kugelman

Poem To Brendon

From Grandma Inez

Brendon is my grandson
when he's around, he's lots of FUN
I love to see his smiling face
and watch him, around the house, race

He likes to bake and play ball
and we both like to sing when I call
my favorite grandson on the phone
With him, I'll never be alone

He loves parties, helicopters and hats
and knows how to swing a baseball bat
But most of all I love it when he says
He loves his Grandma INEZ

Bebe Santry

Untitled

Seems like the rain was wetter
when I just let it fall,
Rather than coaxing it down from the sky.
Seems like the time passed slower
when I prayed for it to go
rushing quickly by.
These two lines were written many years
apart.
I set 'em down
And passed 'em round
And now they call it art.

Jay Lee Joslin

My Miracle

You were sent to me at a point
when I needed you the most. I was
blessed with you my miracle from
the Father, Son and Holy Ghost.

You are my miracle sent from up
above. I am truly blessed because you
have an undying love.

You are my miracle who shines so
bright in the sky, they say we should
not question as to who or where or why.

But at times I look at you and
truly wonder why, my sun hasn't fallen
and left me here to die.

They say God created us in his own
image. And gave us all his own unique
trait. For him to send you to me I
guess is what they call fate.

Jamie Sue Scott

I See

I see nothing but blue skies
when I think of you
I see so many wonderful things in you
I see a beautiful sunset
when I look in your eyes'
I see a bundle of roses
when I see your smile
I see my heaven with in my grasp
when I found your embrace
I see so many wonderful things
when I see you
but I don't see any of them with out you

Daniel Aaron Vernon

Age

long time ago
when I was small
lived in this house
crazy things on my fingers
olives, bugles
silly leaves
from that "peter pan" bush
pretending to be
woman they say I am today
with gloves and pocketbooks
millions I spent
with a checkbook from a closed account
everything has consequence
like swinging too high
breaking a bone
and growing up.

Ashli E. Foshee

I'll Always Love You!

I'll love you
When the Rain Falls
When it's hard to love
I'll love you
When your fast asleep
When we're together
Every second we're alive
I'll always love you!

Jenelle Henry

Reap The Harvest

Lord, never let us worry or fret
When the sowing has been done.
Of who will reap the harvest
As long as souls are won.

For time is drawing nearer
No more sowing or reaping will be
There's something here we all can do
To be working here for thee.

May we stand before you boldly
Knowing we worked hard for you.
May it be counted worthy
As souls stand saved before you.

Dottie Childers

Beauty Is Beauty

How can I write of Beauty
When the tears of the ancient Saints
still burn on my pillow?

The closeness of your body;
gone, into the Abyss forever,
and I manage a smile.

Beauty is never phony;
Like a smile holding back the tears
of all that never was.

When Life becomes beautiful
I'll pour my spirit in it's cup
and watch it overflow.

Jenny Lea Gregory

Faith In God

Sometimes I get discouraged
when things start falling apart.
The storms begin to rage
and torment my troubled heart.
When I start looking at my problems
instead of at my Lord,
I become doubtful and impatient,
and fear becomes my reward.

You see, it's really simple,
faith in God is the key.
If in all things we can trust Him,
with Him we'll spend eternity.
Since He'll never leave or forsake us,
He'll work all things for our best.
Don't fear the clouds and storms of life,
Have faith in God ... and in Him rest!

Cheryl Diane Meyer

Reflections

Blood red are the roses
which grow
From the garden in which
I keep.
Deep are the emotions
which bind,
The very thoughts
of one's own heart.
Weary am I!
When the cold winds
of December blow.
For these are very much,
The reflections of my soul!

Karen Kenyatta Moody

Life Has a Way

Life has a way of laughing at us
when we least expect it.
Not laughing with us, but at us.

For not doing the things that would
make us happy,
or that we have a talent for.
And for not trying hard enough,
to make our dreams come true.

Life has a way of really pushing us
to succeed,
but won't push us in the direction
that we really and truly should be going.

I should laugh back loudly,
and push back hard and say
"This is not what I wanted and
this is not what I dreamed about.
Don't laugh at me and don't push me.
I know what I was meant to do and
I will.
Just stand back, be quiet, and watch me!"

Kathryn T. Oliver

Missing A Friend

I look at her old house every single day.
When will this pain that I have go away?
I had a friend who once lived there,
but then she moved away.
I figured that she would
come back to stay with me one day.
We aren't as close as we used to be,
but I still feel that she is to me.
This pain, I think, will never go away.
Although at least we'll have
our memories in our hearts to stay.
I miss you, Jill.

Janelle Susko

The Book

I was a volume unexplored
When you approached the stalls
That half-concealed my pattern
Against the dingy walls.

Invited by my meekness
You chose me. From my place
You drew me, turned my cover
And scrutinized my face.

I spoke my lines, you listened.
Each word I formed with care
Remindful that your presence
Disclosed me to the air.

And as you read, you ventured
More faith, and I, more free,
Pronounced the requisition
That turned your thoughts from me.

You left the best of me unread,
And should you ever think
To study me a second time
You'll find my pages blank.

Alma Gramita Reinecke

The Moon

The moon is in the starry sea
Whenever I look up it stares at me
I saw the moon all silver and gold
Just like, a story that's been told
The moon is just like a rhyme
It takes you forward and back in time
The moon has a silvery glow
Just like freshly fallen snow
Sometimes late at night
The moon looks just right
Just like a bird in the sky
It seems to be so very high
If you decide to climb a ladder to the moon
Be careful or you fall to your doom
Sometimes the moon looks so bright
You could read a book outside at night
Just like a owl at night
It seems to rest until no light
Just like a feather in the sky
It seems to float just as high

Kathy Gardner

Homecoming

Soaring through auburn locks,
where a lonely shack smokes rain
under pathways traversed by foes and hues,
intimate flies swoon remains-
an idle breeze of sycamore
clings to the stagnant river
flourished by a single flower
dripping blood from a fallen leaf
chilled by the hate of peace.

Dawn M. Morrill

In Memory of Quinton Wright

I saw a portrait in a field,
where corn grew green in ribbon rows.
And, there I saw a Cracker Boy,
from fifty years ago.

The wind and sun caressed his face,
and sweat dropped from his brow.
He walked a deep, cool furrow,
behind a mule and plow.

He wore a pair of overalls,
patched about the knees.
A hat of straw cocked on his head,
no shoes upon is feet.

As the sun warms up the earth,
He's in a field of white.
Whistling songs, picking cotton,
'till the long day greets the night.

This portrait that I saw today,
was just a vision in a field.
But, years ago when I was young,
the picture, it was real.

John Shadix

Life's Lesson

All of tomorrows are too short,
To worry about yesterdays.
For yesterdays are all long gone,
But the memories linger on.
Now is the time to live for today,
For tomorrow may be your last day.

Dorothy M. Kane

Reality

Dark, lonely faces surround me.
"Where could I be?" Maybe in
an abrasive land, where I cannot
see an alternative way out. To
all eternity, reality shouts.
"Let me find light!" Let my
spirit reach the ultimate height!
Only is it reality. Reality is
pain and uncertain futures, new
broken hearts by windows of power.
You can find a light in the darkness
more intense than a light-tower.
Believe in the creator, Jesus Christ.
He is the way out of this harsh,
bitter, iniquity - stricken world.
Trust and believe down to the very
depths of your soul, even when satan's
darts at you are hurled. Therefore,
this is the way to live a life where
reality is not so hard.

Gail House

Why Did You Leave Me?

Why did you leave?
Where did you go?
Where are you now?
That is what I want to know.

Will you come back?
I wish I could say.
All I do now,
Is hope and pray.

Will I ever see you again?
Or should I just put down my pen?
Tell me what I want to know,
That is, where did you go?

I met you when I was just a tot,
That is why I miss you a lot.
Lots of fun is what was had,
When I was just a lil lad.

Why did you leave?
Where did you go?
Where are you now?
That is what I want to know.

Charles McDonough

"Indecision"

Indecision —
    where is life taking me?
Indecision —
    who is life making me?

I'm traveling down a city street,
    sidewalk empty beside me.
In the distance I see a light —
    my goal, my dream, clear but hazy,
    dissipating in the sunrise.

Clock is ticking, life's blood is flowing.
Hair is growing and hits the ground.
Anxiety is a constant
    as young leaves are blown off the trees.

Indecision —
    what am I looking for?
Indecision —
    who am I looking for?

Catherine Corrigan

Calvary

I caught a glimpse of Calvary
Where Jesus died alone,
Where on the Cross He shed his blood
For my sin to atone.

I caught a glimpse of Calvary
And knew He died for me,
I asked Him to come in my heart
And now my soul is free.

I bowed my knees at Calvary
Where Christ my Savior died,
I asked Him to forgive my sins
And in my heart abide.

Lift up your eyes to Calvary
Where Jesus died for you,
He'll cleanse your heart, forgive your sin
And make your life anew.

Bertha Shoudel

Untitled

I's come from a place...
Where not many have went.
me mind looketh over.....
me heart be's so bent.....

Mine eyes overlook em....
What troubles they've seen....
No-where am I going....
No-where have I been....

My momma don't be here....
Though really her should....
My poppa don't mean much...
Him really no good...

I be a loner forever...
Me have piece of mind....
I the girl of the ghetto...
Me one of a kind...

Elizabeth Bell

Take Me To The Mountains

Take me to the mountains
Where the air is fresh and clean,
And the waters of the valley
Meet with trees of evergreen.
I'll walk beneath the trees arranged
In Autumn's red and gold;
And rest beside a mountain stream
With waters clear and cold.
I'll climb the rugged mountain trails,
Ascending to the sky;
And pause to watch the graceful flight
Of eagles soaring by.
Oh, take me to the mountains—
I long to feel the peace;
Away from city's struggles
Where troubles never cease.
I'll wile away the hours
Where lofty breeze Blow,
And gaze in silent wonder
Upon the world below.

Bonita S. McDonald

That's Where You'll Find Me

Where the ocean meets the land,
where the mountain meets the sea,
where the rivers meet the lakes,
that's where you'll find me.

When the questions in life are
"Isn't this GREAT?" and
"Dad, can I have another worm for bait?"
Where a boy and his dog roam far and free,
where happiness is all you can see,
that's where you'll find me.

Where Moms relax and read all day
and Dad's have time to talk and play
and we kids go on running
even after we get stung by a bumble bee,
that's where you'll find me.

In summer times and wet bathing suits,
where every so often a boat horn toots,
where kids sit in the shade of a tree
and find safety in its roots,
that's where you'll find me.

Ashley D. Yost

I Am Searching for Someone...

I am researching my "Tucker" clan,
Which has become quite a chore,
Is there anyone out there,
That can help me find out more?

I am searching for someone,
And yes... it is a man,
His name was Andrew,
And his wife's name was Ann.

I do not know if Andrew
Found another mate,
After the death of Ann,
Who died in 1868.

This is who I'm searching for,
I need to know the truth,
Could his father be David?
What I need is proof!

I'm not searching for fortune,
I'm not searching for fame,
I just need to know...
WHAT WAS HIS FATHER'S NAME?

Darlenea M. Tucker

The Last Mile

I watch the minutes slowly pass
While each one strikes my heart anew
There is no peace for me — alas!
I've killed a man — ah yes, 'tis true!

Now I must pay the sinner's price
And walk "that mile" on this fair night
So when the clock has struck but thrice
God, pity me in this my plight!

Joy E. Heidemann

A Navy Wife's Prayer

Please Dear Lord watch over my husband
While he's out at sea,
Keep him safe and healthy until
You return him back to me.
The kids and I will be just fine
At home on our own,
I'll play my part as Mom and Dad
Until you bring him home.
Assure him that we'll be alright
And that our love won't die,
We'll keep the letters coming
To help the time go by.
Lord please hear my special prayer
Six months is a long time to be apart,
Guide him through this and let him know
That he's here with me in my heart!

Denise Schmink

My Sunshine

Unseen...Arising with a yellow glow
While surreal knights still duel.
Warming unseen seeds to sprout
And start with life anew.
While cobwebbed eyes begin to stir
And open with an inner smile
At beams across the room.
The thoughtless loss in daily bustle;
Taken for granted,
In spite of iridescent wings of gulls
And rainbows round the world
Until it nears a distant curve
Of clouds along the sea
Then shimmerings of orange and green
And at the last curved beam,
A tremble, and a sudden chill.
The long cold night begins.
Will I see it rise again

Edward A. Brozyna

Portly Piggies

There was a lady down the street
Who, a piglet she did buy...
She extolled her fondness on this pig
Adorations to the sky!

She took it on her daily walks
To the bank and to the store...
She tried to enter the doctor's office
And nearly started a war!

This mini-pig was so well-fed
Corn, eggs, and buttered toast...
She treated it to candies
Like any kindly host!

Soon, this pig took on tendencies
Of swollen legs and girth...
The neighbors raised their eyes a bit
At this porcine, beefy mirth!

Soon, it could barely climb
The steps to her abode...
This stoutly pig, so adipose
Now had to drag it's load!

John G. Ritchings Jr.

Because

Tommy was a little boy
Who always walked alone;
He never played with other boys
His toys were all his own.

One day he saw a little girl
Come running down the street;
She beckoned with a cheery word
To all she chanced to meet.

Down the street she skipped and sang
Without a single care;
Tommy marvelled at her laugh
And watched her golden hair.

Nearer came the laughing child
And soon would have passed beyond
Had she not tripped on Tommy's foot
And tumbled to the ground.

The startled boy reached out his hand,
"Why do you have to run?"
The child stood up and turned to go,
"Because it's lots of fun!"

Kenneth Carter

The Grave

They closed the grave, I can't see
Who entered the grave to eternity
My eyes have searched all around
The first or second cannot be found.

The grave is closed once again
Makes one wonder what is the end
Another closure in chapter of life,
Time continues with more strife.

Some years and more have passed
The space between growing vast
Touches once felt are drifting away
They closed the grave, he couldn't stay.

I've searched for entry to no avail
My heart's in there, I often wail
They closed the grave, took life from me
But my heart and soul went to eternity.

Annie McClure

"Where Did The Love Go"

Where did the love go
Who has it now
Does she feel the same

Where did the laughter go
Who hears it now
Does she laugh the same

Where did the happiness go
Who takes care of you now
Does she care the same

You took the love
You took the laughter
You took the happiness
I took the pain

Charlotte Hartman

Wonderful Man

There's a wonderful man
who lives on our street.
Who is strong and cheery
and nice and neat.
He's special to me
he's special to you,
When something is wrong
he knows what to do.
I've lived with him
for 11 years,
He's always been there to
wipe away my tears.
He always makes me
fill better when I'm sad,
That wonderful man
is my dad.

Brandy McKinney

Untitled

There is a man
Who took a stand
To better his being and mind
He rid his life of terror and strife
And
Left the muscle and bulls—t behind
Materialistic need and monetary greed
No longer plague his brains
He found kindness and warmth
Love and tenderness came forth

Now only frustration remains.

Andrew Arrigali

Burdens

Why do we not love one another?
Why do we not care?
I care about the world around me
And I will be there.

You can cry on my shoulder
I won't pull it away
Who cares about my crying
Oh, that's okay
I'll just push it away.

I'm ready to take on the worlds burdens
But I cannot carry my own
I'm not strong enough to carry two
So I'll just carry one.

I just have one last question
When I set the worlds burdens down
Will it learn to carry its own?

Christina Modlin

Life

A mouth that has no words to speak,
Will be forever silent.

A house that you cannot call your home,
Will never feel love.

A piano without sound,
Is only heard by the deaf man.

A tree without roots,
Can never experience feeling.

And an unlived life,
A waits death.

But the meaning of living life itself,
Has no comparison.

Karla Bowsher

November's Pain

O my God, why
Why does it have to be this way?
Our souls where once as one
Now they're come so undone

All I can do is cry
Just wondering why you didn't tell me why
You tried to blame and yell at me
Just to cover up your lies

I did so much for you and us
You did so much for us too and me
We promised forever and always
Praying that's the way it would be

What do you see in her?
That you didn't already make of me
I can't even begin to imagine
You told me I was everything
You wanted me to be

The overwhelming feeling that comes
With just the memories of your touch
Makes me realize, I miss you so much!

Jessica Hinckley

Untitled

Mindless thought thoughtless mind.
Why should some be so blind.
Saw a star misconceived;
did they really believe "If you believe"?
Saw a dream watched it pass
Long been forgot, but it's not the last.
Saw a dream kept it true
Thought shattered in color across
The Universe...
Violet, red, silver, purple
all dim shadow compared to you!

James Ray Howard

We Will Fight (The Civil Rights Movement)

We don't understand,
Why they can't hear,
Our moans and cries.

We don't understand,
Why they can't see,
Our faces with tears.

Why does it have to be this way?
We ask ourselves.
We don't know.

We are all the same,
The human race.
Why can't they see that?

Do they wish us dead,
Gone forever.
We don't understand.

But we will never die,
For them.
Nor will we ever be gone.

We will fight forever,
We will, we will, we understand.

Kendal Smith

2-Morrow

2-Morrow,
will come, but not to some.
2-Morrow,
will be another day, but that's
only if you stay.
2-Morrow,
will then pass, just like the
dead grass.
2-Morrow,
Has now gone, just like an
old song.
2-Morrow,
is now a memory, that is
written in your diary.

Dena M. McCollum

Shining Star

Oh shining star up above
Will you ever go away?
Please tell me now
There's no one here to hear you
Yell it out
Blurt it out
Tell it out.
Or even whisper it
Over the hillside I stand
Please tell me now shining star
Don't wait too long
Before it's too late!
Oh thank you shining star
For telling me
The things I need to know
Thank you
For saying yes!
That you will always stay

Dianna Bastien

Arise Tempest

The warm touch of eyes,
windows of quiet skies.

Holding and waiting
for the Tempest to arise.

To break free from
the chains.

Wash off the pain,
and feel life rushing
through her veins.

Only one can set
her free.

He alone holds
the key.

Holding and waiting
to spark the fire
she can be.

Jennifer Moskal

Life

I have wept in the night
What for I don't know

Perhaps at how swiftly
We come and go

With never a firm grasp
Of the why.

Doris Burkart

Searching Warmth

Since you are gone,
Winter is the season;
feeling cold and empty,
lacking you is the reason.

The frigid wind howls,
sounding faintly of your name;
shivering from the core,
the brutal chill must be tamed.

Longing for warmth,
and to follow behind;
for the lone lost wanderer,
winter is lifeless and unkind.

Hold on to hope,
refuse the urge to run;
Hold on dear life,
another season will come.

The experience of knowing,
the ardor and desire;
the warmth will return again,
love is the eternal fire.

Janet Wood

Tears

I sit here and watch you cry,
Wishing I could dry your eyes.
But that is not allowed to be,
For you love her, and not me.
She cause pain, and tears, and grief,
And yet through all the misery,
You love her still,
And always will.

You say someday,
When she is gone,
(But for those days,
You do not long.)
You say someday you'll give me love.
And so I stay, and watch you Dove.
The day may come when she is gone,
But watch out carefully or our time will be
gone.
Don't risk it all on untrue love,
But come home first to your own true love.

Alyssa Renee Brown

Chain Events

Laying on green wet grass
With a tint of blue
My hands feel freedom
As the fingers weave
Thru the blades
Swords, daggers, knives
Stream thru society
Feeling no remorse as they
Corrupt and promote
Destruction of mind and soul
Thought, concept, realms
Diminishing to nothing
Yet should be a part of life
As they give knowledge
Meaning, wisdom, depth
Not yet fully discovered
Until the beginning of life
Death.

Anjanette Garcia

The Presence

The rushing waters speak to me
with a voice so calm and clear
I can feel His awesome presence
coming quite near.

It grows stronger and stronger
as each wave rolls in
The Presence is felt coming closer
to wash away all sin.

It tells me of life
and how I should live it
It tells me of peace
and how to give it.

It guides and directs me
to all that is right
From the early morning
to the silent night.

The rushing waters grow calmer
as The Presence starts to leave
All things start to make sense now
and all I had to do was believe.

Karrie Park

"Our Woodlot"

In the spring the trees are covered
with buds so new and green.
And for miles within our woodlot,
newborn beauty can be seen.
Then comes Summer with bright blossoms,
new designs and shades of green.
And again within our woodlot,
a different beauty can be seen.
Now it's Autumn and new colors
dress our treetops all around.
And the leaves so softly falling
makes a carpet on the ground.
Then winter brings a beauty to,
as an angel waves her wand.
Dropping star dust on our tree tops
as the sun comes up at dawn.
No brush or paint or canvas,
can make beauty quite so dear.
As the beauty in our woodlot
all four seasons of the year.

Claire Euber

My Mother

She was soft, she was warm.
With caring eyes of blue.
Her voice was sweet as honey.
And a heart so loving and true.

She was mine, but not mine alone
I had to share her with the others.
You see, I'm not her only one
I have sisters and brothers.

"I love you all the same" she said
And I thought "that cannot be."
We are all so very different
She would have to love us differently.

As years went by, I understood
Being blessed with children of my own.
With "All your heart" you love your kids.
My mother's love, I'm so thankful to have
known.

Betty L. Smith

Echo

On the edge of a canyon,
"What am I?" inquires the man.
And after a moment of thought,
"What am I?" replies the valley.

Amar Lohana

My Son

My son, just born...
with eyes alight and searching
What events shall you witness as you
grow....
as your little arms become strong
and one day cradle your own son...

With your eyes I will see beyond my years
and reach into the future...
and with your spirit and will
may you accomplish the things
which I have not...

Small bundle of flesh and bone,
my flesh and bone...
with the potential of eternities
in your little soul...
Welcome to Earth, My Son.

Ken Matthews

"Wish"

Little Miss Mouse went to Town
With her ears upon her crown.
A small little smirk of a smile
on her face,
And a bounce about her quick
little pace.
She had no worries or disturbances
as such,
And was always happy without
the use of a crutch!
If only I were a mouse.

Judy E. Townley

Lethal Weapon

The human mind
With its many
Wonders,
Is a gift from
God, that is needed
To succeed, and
Yes-deal with others.

Some people use it,
Others may abuse it,
But how can we
Obliterate the negative
Bondage that surrounds
The human mind,
And locks out the much needed
Knowledge.

This mind of ours that we
Use so freely everyday,
Brings joy to some who have truly
Paved the way.

Our mind is a wonderful matter
That is imperative for some,
And to others it is considered
to be their "lethal weapon".

Alysia B. Scott

Love

Love is a sacred thing,
With joy and care,
Love is not very rare,
It could be puppy love,
Or with turtle doves,
Love could be joy,
Or playing with a favorite toy,
Love could be sharing,
I think it's caring,
Love is thinking of someone everyday,
Or saying they care in every way,
Love is love,
No matter what they think,
So share,
And care,
Every day.

DeLaura McVey

"Life's Meaning"

Life was given to us,
With much to learn of -
Only a short time we have,
Destiny in the heavens above.

It has something for everyone,
More than one may need -
Instead, crime and violence,
A world full of greed.

For we all run too fast,
In a hurry and haste -
Not enjoying life's wonders,
Polluting with toxins and waste.

This gift we were given,
For some don't really know -
From the mountains to the ocean,
A fresh fallen snow.

Let's stop, my friend, to look,
Together we should be -
Taking care of what abounds us,
God has given us for free.

Gary Scott

They Call Me A Dreamer

They call me a dreamer,
With my head in the sky,
They call me a baby,
When I feel I could cry,
They say I'm a loner,
I stay by myself,
They call me a thinker,
With books on my shelf,
They say that I'm different,
I'm not like the rest,
They say I'm no good,
I'm just second best,
But I'll whistle a tune,
And look at the sky,
I'll keep my hopes,
And my head up high,
And just as I've done,
For all these long years,
I'll continue to smile,
Right through my tears.

Emily Jean Wemmer

"Little Girl No More"

March was cold and marked
with rain,
in a childhood filled
with hurt and pain.

Tears were shed
of guilt and shame
nothing would ever
be the same.

Alone in the house
Scared and unsure,
wanting to forget and
remember no more,

But it's hard to forget
when I look in your eyes,
seeing no love,
only hate and despise.

Christina Brennan

"A Patriot"

'Twas cold and crisp on this fine morn,
with the brilliance of rays from the late
autumn sun.

Nearly a whisper or a sound,
except for some spades,
moving the ground.

Bold and strong, these few men worked,
moving the earth, although, it hurt.

Why were they there, on this day so new,
many wondered, but each really knew.

'Twas a day of mourning, yet so bright,
for a man with vigor, who found life a
delight.

so young was he, yet wise indeed,
he brought a smile to all, in need.

Eyes were in tears as he passed by,
yet you could hear him say, "keep your
head up high."

"MOVE ON, MOVE ON, to the New
Frontier,
MY FELLOW< MY FELLOW, do not
despair.

Kenneth D. Michaud

Ode to Grandpa

He stands tall and wise,
with the silhouette of Santa Clause.
His eyes have seen war and
his nostrils have smelled fear.
His hands are proof of hard
work and his arms are laden with
the profited strength.

But, low, what is this?
Why has sullenness glazed his
jolly eyes? What has made the
friendly giant fall?

Within his white surroundings he
breathes one of his limited breaths.
His loved ones gather at his sides as
the glorious sunlight hugs the last
breath from him.

Jennifer Mertz

"The Way Love Begins"

Love always begins
with the thoughts
of never ending.

A Romantic affair
with fantasies pending.

With desire of being
there, In times
of need or not.

To offer comfort
and caring, is
the basics of this plot.

The dream of starting
a family and
walking down the aisle.

THE WAY LOVE BEGINS

With a hand shake
and a smile.

Ken Lowery

Forever With You

Forever is so long,
With you time passes on.
There isn't a moment that goes by,
I don't wish to say more than "HI."

As long as there is forever,
I'll be by your side whenever,
I'll be your moon and sun,
For you're the only one.

Until the sun fades away,
And the moon lights the day.
'Till heaven falls to the ground,
You are my world turning 'round.

I'll be loving you,
As long as you love me too.
I'll be there beside you,
As long as you're there beside me too.

I wish you all the best,
Up to the final rest.

Jhonna Petrancosta

Open Your Eyes And Believe

Young Black children
With your courageous ambitions
and wonderful dreams,
In time of pain and suffering
There is hope,
JUST LOOK UP!

Young Black children,
Descendants of Kings and Queens,
In time of drugs and violence
There is hope,
JUST LOOK UP!

Young Black children
With your talented ideas and gifted skills,
In time of sorrow I death,
There is hope,
JUST LOOK UP....
and PRAY!!

Donald Crumby

Within My Heart

All I see is part of me
Within my heart
My hopes and dreams
But in my heart
There is a space
Where only you can fill the fate
That space is filled with love and joy
Kind and true...a lullaby
That chimes deep within that space
To carry my worries to a faraway place.

Julie M. Borovicka

"Bob"

He walks the streets all day
Without a destination
He talks continuously on
But there's never a conversation

As we pass by him each day
No one bothers to even speak
And if Bob should venture too close
We shamelessly cross the street

We then continue on our way
And force him from our minds
After all we tell ourselves
He's really not our kind

But the belongings he didn't possess
As he walked the streets alone
Like our acceptance, he didn't need
You see this homeless man was going home

So as I walk to catch my bus
I pray to God one day we'll meet
For Bob has reached his destination
He now walks God's Golden Streets

Anita Faye Crenshaw-Osborne

Where Self Is Anonymous

Thou trojan beauty,
Won't you accept this wreath I bring?
My offerings to thee, deity of love,
Thy devotee's life fulfillment!
Light those inviting eyes emit
Fight gloom in the world beneath
Brooks vie with rivers and oceans
To carve a girdle for thee.

Stars and waves of the skies
Space, sun hence time even
Glance, see and stand transfixed
Encircling the magical spell.
Why is it that cosmos refuse
To revolve, then evolve?
Could be to sip and drink to lease
Thy metaphysical, celestial, divine charm.

I'll swim and sink or sink or swim
In the fathomless deep seas seven
Dissolve, di-sso-lve, di-ss-ol-ve
Into that freedom of wisdom.

Alex Abraham Odikandathil

Binding Wisdom

Knowledge is a treasure
Worth more than all the money
In the world
All packed into our minds

Now, here is the beginning
Of the quest for knowledge
The quest that drives my life

The quest for knowledge is a passion
That burns inside of me
Giving meaning to all that I do

"Curiosity killed the cat" they say
But I don't really care
So get ready, go!
Onward, the quest begins!

David Wilson

Snow

I wish someone, somehow,
Would let me know,
How to get by in this world.
When I am trapped inside,
By all the snow
Of my thoughts; I'm always so
Alone.
By Myself.
No one to stop my thoughts.
They just go.
And go.
Forever in my thoughts
Of snow.

Jackie Hilderbrand

Untitled

Death
wraps her arms
around your body
sucking
on your tongue
to taste
the sweetness
of
Life.

Alisa Fiddes

My Father's History Book

An open book lies before me
written by men who expect us to
read with closed eyes.
We see.
We read.
We know.
For the authors of our brittle knowledge
taught us how.
Their strife to teach us what they
wanted us to know has only let
them down and pulled out the
pedestal of idealism set before them
by the children whom they wanted
so dearly to grow up just like them
betrayed by their own damn lies.

Christopher Chester

The Birthing Of A Dream

Labor was long -
Years - decades -
Nearly a lifetime -
Breathing exercises
manifested as the peaks and valleys
of everyday living -
with joys and sorrows,
hope and despair,
fears and faith clinging...
Some imagining's climbed clear
off the reality chart -
Some times my soul sank
deep into shoal
seeking spiritual rebirth.

Now personae flower petals
have opened to the sun
exposing full emotional expression -
And a child's dream
is emerging as
poetry for publication.

Carol M. Reed

"So Close, Yet Still So Far"

I can see you there,
Yet I cannot reach you.
I can feel you beside me,
Yet I cannot touch you.

Your face seems distant
Your eyes are cold,
You hide behind them
With stories untold.

Come go with me
Take my hand
I'll lead you away
To a faraway land,
Where no one can hurt you
And time will stand still
Where the past is forgotten
And the future is ours to build.

You can't have what you want
That's what they've always told me.
But I won't give up
'Til you're lying here beside me.

Keri Ann Amedeo

Alone

I feel all alone,
yet my friends are here.

I feel like crying,
yet I am laughing,

I feel confused,
yet I know what I am saying.

I am worried,
yet I don't know why.

I feel weak,
yet I know I am strong.

I feel like I am freezing,
yet I am burning with a fever.

I feel alone,
yet here you are.

Kim Keding

"Unheard Voices"

You talk I listen
You ask I do
You want I give
Your voice is heard

I talk you don't listen
I ask you don't do
I want you don't give
I'm the unheard voice

We live in harmony
But I'm still unheard
I hear but do not respond
And I'm the one to blame

To hear each other
Is the communication of our feelings
To be heard is to care
That is not to be the unheard voice

Jackie Scholting

What Happened

You came as an angel,
you came as my hope.
The perfect guy,
for poor little me.

The way you felt,
made me melt.
The words you said,
to ease my head.

Then it stopped,
for why I can't tell.
No more calls,
just more cry's.

I'd like to know what happened,
between you and I.
For was it me or you,
Only you can say.

You just left me here,
just tearing apart.
Because why,
it didn't feel right?

Elizabeth Mason

Colored

It has been like this forever
you can't been together,
people judge on what they see
never to stop and think can that be?
people see the world in black/white
none of us are right.
past the skin inside,
to see the color that lies
It is not black
It is not white
it is a color we all should see in
the light.
Every one has feelings,
Every one has blood,
just like
Every one should be loved.

Chelsea Sparks

Those Few Lost Thoughts

Sometimes in thinking
You decide it's not worth it.

Sometimes talking
You begin to speak your mind
Then stop.

Why these mixed thoughts?
Your conclusion is to sit still.

When it's safe, you open your mouth
But where are the words?
Shortly, the thought is gone.

Now you feel dumb.
After you feel dumb.
After the humiliation has set in
You write the thoughts down.

When the moment of truth arrives,
The room is dark
No One's around
You cannot see the paper.

The final thought you have:
sleep on it

Christy Tressler

Fears of Wanting

The first time I saw you
You definitely caught my eye.
But my life was in turmoil
and I had lost my pride.
My emotions can run deep
because of who I am.
I cannot change that
not for any man.

For me the attraction was there
right from the start.
Because of a betrayal
I have harden my heart.
Never again do I want to lose
my self esteem, confidence or my pride.
Not in the terms of human abuse.

Now I have gone back to
the old fashion ways.
Guarding my heart so
it won't be betrayed.

Christine Doucette

If God Did Not Answer Your Prayer......

If God did not answer your prayer
you don't have to fear,
that the God did not hear
what you ask for in your prayer....

If God did not answer your prayer
you don't have to be discouraged,
for His answer maybe "later"
teaching you to be patient, my dear.....

If God did not answer your prayer
maybe you asked amiss,
maybe His answer is "never"
because He knows it is not the best.....

If God did not answer your prayer
you always have to remember,
that God will leave you never
and surely, He has something better.....

Elizabeth G. Grindulo

"To Me"

Some people say
you don't know what you got
till it's gone,
Well I don't think it's true
See I have already realized
I could never live without you.

It does not take a rainy night
or a darkened sky
All it takes is an open mind
and the right guy.

I have found all I've dreamed of
Directly in your eyes,
The way you hold me
oh so tight
The way you make me sigh

No one has ever made me feel
Quite the way you do,
You are very special to me
No one else will ever do.

Christine Newman

Emotions

Riding the sea of emotions
You don't know where to turn
God is your captain
He's standing at the stern
He takes you where He wants
To do your highest good
That's why be on good behavior
And do only as you should
Though the sea may be rough at times
And you make it through the night
God is there beside you
Holding on to you tight
And when you feel the calm
Still the waters deep
You know on the sea of emotions
You can safely sleep

Doris J. Alvis

Note Pad (The Loaned Child)

Dear Lord I thank you for this child
You gave him to me for a little while
I heard him laugh and seen him smile
I never will forget it all the while
I had him only for a short time but,
Lord he taught us all. His rhymes and
talks and love he gave to every one
The walks we took together no matter
what the weather were always
enjoyed by all. The times we read and
learned so many things, they all seemed
so small since he is gone
I know he stands with you to hear my
prayers, so Lord I thank you for the
loan, even though I am sad since he
went home.

Eleanor Hoagland

Runaway

Star of love, burning bright,
You guide me through the empty night.
Upon my brow you shine your light.

My shadow's cast upon the ground;
My beating heart, the only sound;
My destiny, now nearly found.

The fire of dawn is drawing near
Upon my bosom, full of fear,
And down my cheek, one lonely tear.

All my bags already packed,
Slung o'er my shoulder, a bulging sack,
I've gone so far I can't turn back.

Life's passages I'll tread alone,
Through streets now bare I'll always roam.
A runaway, I'll not go home.

Elisa Keck

Do You Know How It Feels

Do you know how it feels when you feel
you have no one? Do you know how it
feels when you feel you are the only one?
Do you know how it feels to cry
yourself to sleep at night and hope
when you wake everything will be all
right. Do you know how it feels to
have your heart broken? Do you know
how it feels to miss someone bad
that it just makes you mad? Do you
know how it feels to want to disappear
and never ever ever be found? Do you
know how it feels when your not wanted
around? Do you know how it feels to have
your feelings hurt? Do you know how it
feels to do wrong though your intentions
were
on doing right? Do you know how it feels
to have
to say bye and always wanted to say hi? All
I
want to know is do you feel like me or
am I the only one.

Katrina T. Kelsey

Untitled

You said it wouldn't last
you left me in the rain
Now I don't know how
to let past this pain
You walked into my life
I could have charged you with theft
you stole my heart away
and now you have left
I want you back
because I miss you so
And I never ever
will let you go
All I want
for you to do and see
Is to give one more chance
back to me
I can't live without you
and I came here to stay
Without you my life
is like that rainy day

Kevin Wood

Mirage

You glanced, I smiled.
You requested, I gave.
You called, I answered.
You invited, I accepted.
You spoke, I listened.
You promised, I believed.
You laughed, I cheered.
You cried, I cared.
You touched, I felt.
You led, I followed.
I spoke, you listened
I requested, you denied
I was free, you were busy
I waited, you never came.
I called, you never answered
I needed, you weren't there.
I pushed, you pulled
I held tight ... you let go.

Aliseia Colt

Untitled

On the day that you left me,
You said you had no regrets,
There's a bond between us,
That hasn't been broken yet,
And the feelings between us,
Will never disappear,
How can you be so far away,
When your spirits here.

Our love will last forever,
Nothing can change it,
And the seasons of our love,
Will change, I know,
Maybe that's the reason,
You felt you had to go,
But soon you'll be missing me,
Darling, I know you well.
There's a magic we share together,
And no one can break that spell.

Jo Hill

An Orange and Blue Bird

I'm calling on this bird to send
you this message, you'll understand what
it is and you must accept it. A one time
offer so catch it quick, without you I
feel real sick. Wanting to taste your
very soft skin, and if it's a battle of
wills I must always win. Struggling with
my own desires and mental power, wanting
to be close to you every minute of every
hour. Listen to me and listen close, as
much as I can say it you mean the most.
Wanting to look into your eyes and
tell you what I feel, this is something
no one can ever steal. After it's
all been heard, it all started with
this letter delivered by an orange and
blue bird.

Aaron Harbin

Confusion and Pain

Just when life seems to be alright
you wake up late one night
The footsteps in the hall
make you wonder about it all
Just when did it all begin
and will it ever end
Anger, pain and frustration build up
everyone seems about to blow up
What is the answer
it seems as if there's a cancer
Plaguing this family
it is hard for me
To understand why
they can't see eye to eye
Communication is a vital part
you've got to express what's in your heart
You'll never guess
how the others feel about the whole mess
The result is confusion and pain
someday the answer will become plain

Jessica Clegg

If I Were A Gateway

If I were a gateway
you would be a star
To shine into my dwelling
no matter who you are.

You could be a stranger
who had knocked at my door
My portals would be open
to welcome you ashore.

When you're ready to leave
I'd give you a smile
To beacon your way
for every single mile.

Edith F. Bondi, Ph.D.

Lost Love Found

If you could only read my mind
you would know my secret thoughts
of how much I truly love you.

You cannot begin to imagine
how long I have waited for the time
to come, it is here and I am afraid.

Afraid of being hurt and
afraid I could never trust you
again with my heart.

Once you've loved someone as
I loved you that love never
dies, it just grows stronger.

Please... don't leave me again

Jen Landures

Vacation

Vacation can be nice,
Yet it can be like spice;

Take your pick,
But don't get sick;

Don't take your house,
Just bring your spouse;

Remember this tip:
Tan your hip!

Kaylan S. Baxter

A Sister's Love

Dedicated to my sister

A sister's love is great to have
You'll know it's always there
She knows how to make you laugh
You'll know she'll always care

You may play with dolls and crowns
And pretend that you are mothers
The both of you have ups and downs
But you're always there for each other

That very special time will come
It's time for you to marry
You know that you will both have fun
Even if it's scary

You might not see each other much
And miss each other dearly
But you can still feel her touch
And love each other sincerely

A sister's love is great to have
In no way is it a game
Even if you don't always laugh
I'll love you just the same

Amanda Boroff

I'm Home

You stand before me worn and warm,
your candles burning bright:
A gracious glow of family
that illuminates the night.

Familiar faces, sights and sounds
renew the ties that bind,
Replaying scenes I've seen before
with mirrors in my mind.

The winds that may have parted us
like chaff from hearty grain
Have sown my seeds in distant lands
then blown me home again.

Your roots run deep as ancient trees
with leaves of finest jade.
You purge my pain and soothe my soul
beneath your loving shade.

I'm home to where my heart is free.
This home is still a part of me.
I'm home to lay my weary head
upon my mother's knee.

Karen Harper Sweeden

Untitled

You're, all that I have ever wanted,
You're, what everyone wants to keep from me.
You're, all that I have ever needed.
You're, what rescues me and sets me free,
You're, all my happiness and all my joy.
You're, the only person in my heart.
You're, the smartest and sexiest boy,
Why, does everyone try to keep us apart?
Why, do they treat us like kids?
Why, don't they just let us love?
Why, do they just want us to be friends?
Why, can't we be set free like a dove?
Why, are they keeping you from me?
Why, won't they just let us live?
Why, can't they see?
Why, don't they understand the love we give?

Jessica A. Harper

If I Could Make...

As I hold your hand, you look on me.
Your child, your daughter, your friend.
You cannot speak, but oh your eyes,
What am I, in them?

Your muscles have forsaken you
But strength and will survive.
If I could make your arms to fold
I don't think I would ever leave them.

I know you must feel terror
Trapped the way you are.
If I could make you wings to fly.
but mother, what will I do without you?

If I could make these last few days
Be changed in any way
I would take the fear and pain I see
And gladly beer them for you.

I would give my lungs to see you breathe
A deep and healthy breath
If I could make you well again...
My mother, my love, my friend.

Brenda White

Him And I

You shine so bright
Your such a beautiful sight
Your around
When I'm feeling up, and feeling down
I can feel your presence
And there isn't a sound
Your in the Heavens
And the earth you made round
I can feel you speak to me
through my heart.
Through you O'Lord
I found a new and better start.
I keep prayin'
Day after day
To thank you God for saving me
And putting me on my way
I can hear you speak to me
In all different ways
And I know... I'm on my way
To a lot of brighter days.

Joel Joaquine Baptista

Gone!

On a quiet day you left me
Your voice I no longer hear.
The face looking out from the portrait
Is dimmed by a falling tear.

All that is left are the memories,
Which cannot erase the pain
Nor stop the grief and sorrow
And tears that are all in vain.

I don't know why you had to go
And leave me here alone.
To wander through an empty house
That was once a loving home.

Time will help, they tell me.
And I suppose it must be true
'Tho it is hard to build a life
That can never be shared by you.

So you are gone and I am here,
Alone with a life to live,
To face each day as best I can
Accepting what fate will give.

Beverly M. Hickok

Untitled

Ah, says the public,
You're a venerable age.
You've reached sixty-five,
So we'll deduct your wage.
Your face is all wrinkled,
There's a slowing of gait,
You therefore are senile
We must leave you to fate.
Work in the market place?
We can't use you old fool.
Our young brains are churning,
We're just out of school.
Your talents have flown
With the passing of years,
Your mind's become rancid
It brings us to tears.
We can't have you near us,
You remind us of death.
So sit on your porch steps
Till you draw your last breath.

Beverly E. Gerstein

"Reincarnation"

Once in the realm, you can't turn back.
You're at the point...of no...returning.
Casted away, like wind in a breeze.
Gentile as clouds, lighter than air.
Your all alone, nothing is felt anymore.
The world that is theirs, once was yours.
You try to scream, you utter no word,
the living world cannot be heard.
Spinning in another dimension,
Tearing at the walls of retention,
What seemed like eternity seriously split,
you find yourself in an empty pit.
Then in a flash of exasperating pain,
your eyes open slowly, you're born again.
So the cycle repeats, you soon forget.
That this life is yours, it's not over yet.

Burrell L. Robertson

The Cream of Hearts

Life dealt the hand and said:
"You're not from these here parts."
"No," I replied and almost cried —
He'd dealt me the Cream of Hearts!

"I'm from the Old Dominion of Virginia,"
I said, playing my cards in a dream;
"The home of Jefferson and John-Boy" —
I vowed never to discard the Cream.

Dear, when I first met you
On the campus of Ol' Mizzou,
I knew I'd drawn the Cream of Hearts;
It's what drew me close to you.

Cream always rises, they say,
To the top it's a lover's rule;
The goodness in your cream of hearts
Reeled me in like the string on a spool.

They call the game "Once in a Lifetime" —
No need to hail from "these here parts" —
Just recognize your good-luck draw
When Life deals you the Cream of Hearts.

Charles Hedrick

True Love

I've had my times, times so sweet just being with you as we walked down the street. Hand in hand face to face, I have never thought of a better place. To be with you till the sun goes down, to make you laugh when you're down. The places we go, the things we do, there's no use in living if I have to live without you. Your smile is so pretty, your face is so cute, the hair of an angel, the voice of a flute.

The mountains we climb that are higher than all the rest, nothing comes this close to beating the best. We dance into the night on a narrow rocky cliff, I hold you real close as you give me a kiss. With your delicate head lay down on my chest, we both fall asleep into a deep rest.

We awake the next morning still holding each other tight, I wonder to myself why there was a word such as Like. Love is the only feeling that one could ever miss. The most powerful feeling that's sealed with a kiss. From our late walks in the park, to our games in the dark, there's no telling what I'd do if we ever grew apart.

Maybe I'd climb a tall tree and never come down, or roam the streets with an empty frown. Please don't ever leave me, your the hand and I'm the glove, stick with me forever and we'll explore the boundaries of love.

Brad Peterson

His Going

"How like a Winter Is His Going From Us!"
How the sunshine in our lives faded away! The heaviness of sadness
entered our hearts and forever changed our beings. As the months
passed by the cold of winter remained. We moved about - searching.
We fed our bodies and went about our daily tasks - with no joy!
We looked about us and saw no light - felt no warmth - and wondered
why and how long this could be. For still the cold of winter remained.

Then gradually there came a glimmer of light in a small part of our hearts.
God's healing was taking place! The peace that only He can give -
began to seep into our lives. The cold of winter in our hearts slowly began to crack.
The light became brighter and we began to see that his going from us
was in God's plan for him.

Forever we will miss him!! But he is where he wants to be - in
a bright shiny place with his Lord. So we know one day the summer
will come and we will sing again and the cold of winter will be
lessened with each passing day.
Lessened - but not completely gone from our hearts!!

"How Like A Winter Is His Going From Us!"
In Memory of
Lieutenant Colonel David Allen Douthit
Killed in Saudi Arabia May 3, 1991

Charlene Douthit

A Prayer for the Planet

Lord please save the earth from chaos and destruction, turn us around and set us aright...
Bring to us many divine teachers and beings to train us and to teach
us in the correct use of the light.

Make us aware of how important it is to maintain an undefiled temple so
that reception is always at it's peak...
I pray that that inborn desire to be in harmony is the foremost goal that all of us constantly seek...
...Teach us to pray...to send to the very throne of God requests which are for the good of all mankind...
Give to us sacred tones which balance and soothe and heal the body and the soul and the mind...
In willing surrender may each of us release all hindrances to the
manifestation of this ultimate good...make us all aware of that
force, that life and death power...by us may it be clearly
and reverently understood... May this planet no longer be under the
threat of annihilation and subject to the uncertainty of darkness
and of night.. Hold us in your favor, give us the insatiable and
desire to be lifted forevermore into the consciousness of love and of light...
...With sincerity I pray that adoration, thanksgiving and praise
rise from earth as vapors of sweet perfume,... The fragrance of
devotion to God emitting into the universe our desire and willingness
to be harmoniously attuned... And at one with God forever.....
Amen

Katherine O. Warren

Called to Witness

As Christians, we are all called to witness...
To preach the "Good News", spread it far and wide
But my heart's concern is the emphasis
We place on our words and not what's inside

There are too many sorry examples
Of loud voices without any substance
Bombastic and proud, they lure disciples
On the strength of their powerless pretense
I know we are called to give an answer
To those who sincerely ask of our creed
But wise hearts will weigh our word's caliber
On scales that balance our motives and deeds

The tangible traits of all witnesses
Glare throughout lifestyles in a clear language
With words preceded by appearances,
Our actions will carry the real message

So witness my friend, but remember this...
Words can't shield motives, they're clearly in view
What starts out covert, insight will undress
Because though you speak, they'll hear what you do

Bob G. Martinez

Instill

When we lose a loved one
we feel our lives have been turned up-side down.
We can't believe what's happened,
and wish we could turn it around.
Then we sit and think of all the things we did
and cry for all the things we didn't,
Simple things like just saying I love you
or hugging someone good-bye,
Remembering them on their birthday or just calling to say "Hi!"
We really must remember just how short life really is
and hope to God we can all instill it in our kids.

Cheryl Walkup

The Window

Standing in stony silence, lost innocence of a child
fills the void..

...light splashes through the window pane
it's tendrils snake toward me and call my name
I heed the summons and peer into the blaze
as it engulfs me
a form leaps into view, feral and lupine
inviting me to follow
through the window the cool white light fingers my soul
and I go
drifting in a place without pain
I'm different here
colors are muted now, to dark shades of green
the scent of everything is in my head
as I adjust to cruising speed, wet leaves
scrunch and loam cushions damp pads...

..."What do you see in the window?" My mother asks
"the Wolf",
I reply and turn away,

She looks, but doesn't see.

Julie Anne Wagner

Untitled

What have we to celebrate in 88
200 years of white lies
what have we done to a whole sacred race
destroyed, confused and put to disgrace
"Their subservience and humor is very charming"
we have stolen their freedom and captured their harmony.
Their knowledge and wisdom of the earth to its core
is something we should have learnt before
and still we send them to degradation
for we only accept sophistication
we will not associate with anything less
you see, we lack the wisdom they possess.

Angela Murphy

Twenty Years

Listen honey they're playing our song,
25 years, has it really been that long?
We've grown together in so many ways
And stuck together thru the roughest of days
Between the week long trips, and sleeping alone
Saying " Goodnight honey, I love you" by telephone.
The kids, the house, and trying hard to make ends meet,
We barely had time to sit and rest our tired feet.
Hardly having time alone to hold each other tight,
We gave it all we had to raise our family right
No matter what came about our love held us together
Because 25 years ago we made a vow, we vowed forever
Our love is still so deep and true
But so much stronger now then when we said I do.

Jodie M. Wiegand

Rebirth of an Author

Fragments of thoughts...like reviving bones...
A blink, shake the head, then blink again.
It swells within and tries to rise,
Throbbing through stiff fingers.

It must be like resurrecting the dead.
All these half-thoughts before me,
Broken shards on fly-away paper,
When will they go on?

Like a well-spring within,
Still semi-capped decadent and rusted,
It creaks, groans, and flows for awhile,
A small trickle of crystal water.

Moisture tries to reach the bones,
To raise the hardened, shriveled heart,
Encased in a self-made wasteland,
An eternity of years....

Joints are brittle — dry, leather heart expands...
Flesh forms, fingers flex, blood flows sluggishly.
Frame sways, falters, falls — rises again.
The trickle becomes a stream.

Diedre J. Holland

Jealous Sea

The sea is pounding hard tonight —
A booming slap of bass upon the rocks
And symbol crash of spray into the air...
Hello, my Ancient Friend,
Are you angry that I've stayed away so long...
Or jealous that I've come tonight
To visit with my new found friend
Instead of spending time with you?

Johathan Robert Jamison

Seasons

She came to be born in the depth of a valley
a child of the earth
untouched by the storm.
Happy the child in the shade of the willow
the sun as her playmate
the wind sang her songs.
Sheltered she grew to the music,
caressed by a life
in a valley of dreams.
Too soon came the day when the fortress was shattered,
for time came along
and brought with it age.
The child was now gone to the memories of a woman
who had no time to play
or sing songs in the shade.
The sun slowly faded
the wind died away.
The only sound heard
was the weeping of the willow.

Kim Rucinski

The Chord Unplayed

You have touched a chord in me as yet unplayed;
A chord by which sweet melody is made.
I hear the harmony inside my head.
I am aware of words as yet unsaid.
In unison with yours my heart sings out.
Your heart beats in response, it seems to shout.
The notes are written down at your command.
The music in my soul makes no demand.
It plays as if by some strange bond;
A rhythmic sound that reaches far beyond.
It leaves me with a chord as yet unplayed;
A chord in me too loud to ever fade.

Dolores DeLoach

Next Tenant?

I sit in front of the tube watching
A clean up crew fish out more death from the oil slick.
Sometime earlier I heard a reporter do
A story about our ozone shield, in our atmosphere.
Mother earth has been a patient landlord.
Everywhere you turn man is destroying his living
Space, like a bad tenant that demolishes his rented room.
Nuclear waste flows into our everyday lives from poor
power plants or nations still doing atomic testing.
Greedy business merchants destroy the rain forests
Our largest source of life giving oxygen.
Chemical companies foul our drinking waters with
Their poisonous refuge. While no one stops these offenders.
We are not the first tenants to lease
This terrain surface over the eons.
For countless millennia, she had not opened
Her doors for any vacancy.
Then she left life in to her portals, and it
Grew and expanded thinking their time was eternal.
They are long gone and if were not careful there could be a next
tenant.

Kevin Badillo

Untitled

It's so easy to be passed
We're all going way too fast
Trying to get to that final destination
We're only asking for that big frustration
How will I know that my work is done
Can someone tell me how long I still have to go on?

Dee Rank

A Child's Cry

I hear a child's cry in the night
A cry for help, and a plea for peace

I hear a child's scream to stop the fighting
A child who has lost it's innocence to this violence

I think to myself why can't this stop
Stop this torture of war

Bombings and shootings which fill the streets,
where the foolish child inside everyone is released

I ask myself why they can't see, see it through the eyes of the
children
Eyes that see it as only stupidity and pointlessness

Why can't they hear that great voice of knowledge
Stop the wars and the fighting!

Chie Saito

Lament of Love

In the shadows of the night you come to me,
A figment of my imagination - maybe

But, regardless, you take away my loneliness, hold me in your
strong arms,
And make me feel safe once more.

Why can't I realize that in the light of the day when all is said
and done,
The only one I can depend on is me.

And the needs that I have to love and be loved
Are within my thoughts and perception of myself.

What then is love, can it be found? I think not - for me at least.

For, when I think I have found love, it's gone like yesterday.
Yet parts remain, the fragments - oh so painful -
like shrapnel in a wound.

And... after the wound, the scars... To harden and wall up the heart.

What then of love - its purpose.
Is it to soothe and stroke before the hurt begins, as the calm
before the storm?

I have no need for this falsehood, this masquerade.
For laughter suits me better, and pain is not my friend.

Carol Barto

"Discovery"

They said love happened like a shooting star
A flash, a dazzling light, bright, all at once;
They said that it would come with deafening sound
To shake the heart, as if a million drums
Were beating madly all across the earth!
They told me love rushed in, like urgent waves
That dash and pound against the open shore.
They made me think love flamed like mid-October,
To set one's world ablaze with dancing fire!
They told me love would rock the earth, and fling
A storm of rainbows across the waiting shy.
But now I find love comes a different way
No sudden tumbling rush of light and sound;
My love is sweet and warm, like April sun,
It softly came on pussy-willow feet.

June Parker Goldman

More Than Just An Image

I knew from the beginning that you were just
A flirt, and I fell in love with you knowing I'd get
hurt,
I thought I could tie you down and make you love
Just one but how could I do something no one else
has ever done,

I used to love you, cause I thought you loved me,
But now I can see, I was as blind as can be,
I know you'll never love me, and I'm trying
not to cry, for I must find me strength to say goodbye,
When you ask for me again, you'll find I
Wont be there because I want a love to call
my own, not one I'll have to share,
So I'll hide my broken heart, beneath a laughing
face, and though you'll think I never cared,
no one can ever take your place?

Darlene Diaz

The End of Pity

Cruelly placed upon this earth,
a flower struggles polluted turf.
The petals fall onto the ground,
near traffic lights and chaotic sound.
Its sense of beauty will conquer all,
even though its petals fall.
One by one the onlookers see,
the flower glowing intensely.
Its head rises against the wind,
Like a virgin who has never sinned.
Its moment of glory the flower is proud,
for all of its beauty is not a shroud.
This flower still stands in its part of the city,
and no onlooker since has looked with pity.

April Volak

A Rose In Need

A soft tap on my shoulder, and I turned to see,
A frail, middle aged woman, looking back at me.

In her timid hand, she bore a short stemmed rose,
taken from someone's yard, I'd supposed.

"Would you like to buy a rose" she said,
"I need the money to put a roof over my children's head".

I politely said "no", and then went on my way,
thinking of her simply, as a beggar on prey.

But as I journeyed home, her presence remained,
and suddenly I felt, deeply ashamed.

For I had let down my fellow man, in the moment
most, when she had needed a hand.

Denise D'Addario

Love

Love is the beauty of the night
It shows the way to the light of happiness
Like a stream, it flows into the depths of the future
Forever it lights the way to joy, happiness,
and never ending thoughts
Showing the way, it completes the future, and never ends
Everything ends sooner or later,
but love, true love, goes on forever...
even after death.

Andrea L. Brewer

Friends

A friend is a friend through thick and thin
A friend is the one who knows the way in
A friend is true when the going gets tough
A friend sticks with you when the road gets rough

A friend comes running when beckoned to action
A friend is selfless, it's their natural reaction
A friend knows no pity, they provide only strength
A friend is the one who can go the whole length

A friend is honest and true to the core
A friend brings their love and wants nothing more
A friend is so special, 'cuz they love you for you
A friend is a friend, 'cuz pure feelings come through

A friend knows giving as well as taking
A friend is genuine, there is no faking
A friend knows serious, or when to play
A friend will not leave you 'cuz friends do not sway

A friend is a person with no agenda in mind
A friend just listens and then talks when it's time
A friend is a friend 'cuz they want nothing other
Than a friend whose a friend, 'cuz there's love for each other

Bill Rance

Master's Touch

A master's touch is one of love,
a gift bestowed from the one above;
he holds his power deep inside
with a heart of gold which he cannot hide.
He loves the world with his heart and soul
and would give his life for those he does not know.
People come to feel his touch,
to heal their hearts; sometimes they ask for too much.
The master though he does not care
He will give it all without despair
until his body can give no more
he will ask the universe for just one more
and in his final attempt to heal,
the mater will die.
This is the way he would want to go
for love and healing is all he knows.

David A. Blunk

Indulgence

Brown leaves float on green water;
A green fog jumps into the stagnant pool.
Water engulfs the shapeless body:
No one can identify the fool
That slithered into the depths of the soil.

An unknown face peers back from the idle water
With eyes not of a monster, but of an entity
Trying to protect the future of his genre:
Setting up the basis for the upcoming society
Who shall safe guard this child from infirmity.

Scientists of the future mingle truth and fiction
So civilization can find answers to
Questions beyond their comprehension.
Seeking to find explanation into
The last great mysteries of their impression.

Who will be next to look
Into the youthful fountain
To find himself amongst all the world:
Conquer himself and not be a minion,
But to himself do an investigation.

Jed Judd

"Another Day"

Another day another gun was sold
A gun shot another body lies cold
A person stabbed from a knife
Another day another life
Who sees the pain who sees the tears
When will the violence end or will it last for years
Whether it's murder or if it's suicide
Either way another persons dies
No one can help not even a cop
Tell me when will the killing stop
People afraid to walk alone
Violence is the reason it's very well known
People live with this horrible fear
Violence must end, it must end here.

Danielle McFall

"She"

She crawls into his arms
a heavy sigh escapes her lips
He gently rubs her arm and whispers into her ear,
asking what's wrong.
"I can't talk about it," is her reply.
"Can I just lie here for a while?"
A tear drops from her overfilled eyes
and lands upon his arm.
She tries to restrain it,
tries not to cry,
but her tears flow as rain from the stormy clouds above.
She silently cries.
She knows these arms are hers whenever she wants-
but she doesn't want them.
The ones she wants are closed to her.
He just lies there and holds her, doing a better job of restraining
his tears than she did.
But he knows why she's crying,
and the cruelty of their situation is too apparent.

Kate Kozeniewski

Memo To Death

Autumn morn awakened, bathed in golden sun.
A joyous refrain from feathered friends.
Bushy-tails gather the bounty,
Gifts from the oak and hickory.

Equine friends rest in warm sunlight,
Guarded by the stallion, head erect, ever watchful.

Then you came, Old Man Death.
Flaunting authority, casting gray shadows on golden morn.

Fluids of grief cloud mortal eyes,
Ears now deaf to joyous refrain,
The black cloak absorbing golden rays.

Casting gray light into our eyes,
You strike your victim to his knees.
Man begs for mercy, there is no reply;
The breath of life siphoned to your accord.
Then you took my friend. Death is victorious.

Oh death, could you not see?
Eyes blinded by victory, His spirit rose and
galloped free beside a son.
Head erect, ever watchful!

Carlton E. Odell

A Christmas Wish

No candy canes or dolls and trains,
A little girl crying, her father far away.
She asks her mother, "Will Daddy be home for Christmas?"
Her mother sighs, "No, Dear. He's going to fight
For the fuel we need to live warm and in peace."
What a joke, she sneers, fighting for peace.
The little girl looks up at the mantle,
An empty stocking, a half-burnt candle,
A hole in a sweater, and one lowly glove.
She wishes that Santa will give Daddy her love.
The night that he left, she put one of her gloves
In his pocket to remember her by.
"Bring him home safe from the war."
She promised she would not ask for more.
Dad's sweater that's torn and a little lost glove,
"Bring Daddy home soon and give him my love."

Joseph Ballay

"Sleepy Man"

Goodnight my little angels, it's time for sleep.
A little tuck here so your blankets don't creep.
The sun has gone down on this fun, loving day,
tomorrow you'll rise and once again play.

Mister sleepy man comes and closes your eyes,
roll over, my child, and try not to rise.
It's time to sleep now, so, to sleep you will go,
And dream of the dreams where the sleepy man goes.
Of candy and popcorn and play toys and more,
with birthdays and sunshine and rainbows galore.

The Stars shine above now to light up your way,
to go to the place where the sleepy man plays.

April Casparriello

Pops

My dad remembers the day I was born
A long journey ahead with no end in sight
Left alone by his wife and society, left alone with a baby in his arms
Just a baby himself in so many ways, 20 was the age
He and his son would grow up together

Down the road they traveled on his Harley
A biker, a rogue, now a father
Zooming down the road of fatherhood-many twists and turns-
unchartered
territory
Accompanied only by his son riding on the gas tank
Fueling his father's will to keep going

My dad remembers the day I was born, that was the day he became a
father
New responsibilities, new worries, no one else to help him
"Give him up for adoption-how could you take care of the child-
You can't take care of yourself?"
Society's gavel already passing judgement

My father beat the odds
He cared for me, he was there for me, he loved me
There were tough times, always on the move, in search of work
But I was always with him, riding on the gas tank, zooming down the
road

My dad remembers the day I was born-it was the day he became a
man

John Outen

Hunger

By the moon of a hot summer night
a lowly growl emerged from the dark.

It hungered for the first taste
of its prey.

Teeth flashed,
Eyes glared.
Sweat emerged.

The pounding beat of the beast grew stronger
as her breathing deepened into the
rhythm of a chase.

'Tis not by love that binds the hunt,
but by the thirst of its nectar.
Sweet as honey.
Thick as molasses.

In one swift motion, the beast pounced upon her feast
and the sweet nectar of life was clutched
within her jaws.

The air was filled with symphonies of cries
and the praise of longing for more
echoed throughout the stars.

As the lowly growl subsided,
the darkness fades with only
the light of the moon
shining through a hot
summer night.

Joanne Quan

The Heart Of My Rose

I dwell within the heart of my rose
A mind without form, intoxicated or enchanted,
I do not know.
Deadly thorns fashion the emerald bars of my prison
Placed around me to keep me from the deadly pluck.
So, Sire, you taste your finger in hurt surprise.
Now come, see what you have done.
A drop of blood anoints my brow,
And something now
Reaches beyond my will toward you.
If you come into the heart of my rose
You will be forever bound.
Already you are feeling the sweet death within my arms.
My love, is ecstasy found?

Elizabeth K. Riley

Untitled

A boy's dream shattered like glass.
A nightmare scream.
In the dead night crickets chirp in the grass.
Their little fiddles they play.
All night long the blade flashes and the family figures clay.
In their beds while asleep it happened, almost silent for the crickets chirp.
While no one watched a whistle blew, only one scream away.
The glass broke as a frightened boy mustered courage to stay.
Stay he told himself, while the midnight owls joined the wolves in a howl.
Helpless was he to help those the knife slashed. Frightened was he to prevent the last victim's crash.
But bold was he to await the creeper in the midnight hour.
With eyes in the dark he took aim and blew him away.
The silent scream lasted forever that day and in that place the boy's family will forever lay.

Donny Bruce Peace

The Rose

He holds it in his lonely hands,
A perfect bud of flowing glass,
Clear and delicate and beautiful,
Who's depth is unsurpassed.

He lays it down carefully
And turns away his forsaken eyes.
Tears of the lonely flood his sight,
Melting crystal from his view like a lie.

But through the night bursts the sunrise
And he finds that his heart is another's soul.
He's found someone to light the dark,
Found his diamond in the coal.

He sees that crystal petals have opened to his love,
And only then does he realize the rose is his soul.
It is his blood and his breath,
And the rose bloomed eternal with beauty untold.

April Buchberger

Alone Full Of Souls

Emptiness inside of me, difficult to explain
a product of all I've read and seen, never truly me
seeing life through countless eyes, reacting ne'er the same
a host for souls of innumerable years, prisoner over time
overridden by many minds and lives, never solely me
crying out for who I am, mourning my stolen soul
too many lives to live for, no room left for me
watching from a corner, broken over time
somehow afraid to let go, and be left with only me
a husk bereft of lives forsaken, lives never to unfold
or possibly what haunts me, the question that keeps me still
is when it comes down to who remains, will it ultimately be them or me?

Jennifer Elise Diviney

The Prince of Darkness

Pitter patter on the rooftop tin
A ragged old day and I watch it begin
Haziness rests like the inside cocoon
Without sunlight grey and thoughts to be soon
The whispers are laughing to start the descent
The pathways are mismarked, twisted and bent
Goodbye wings of reason, no match sparks a light
The scarred one eyed jackal, a-prowling the night
The emptiness whistles like unhappy wind
Gaping black caverns, no voices have been
The monarch of darkness has abandoned the throne
And darkness itself lays claim to its own
The angry black oceans have smothered the fire
With shapeless tornadoes that swirl ever higher
A creeping black hand stretches forth o'er the sky
While cities will crumble, in ruins they lie
Pitter patter, my minds wretched eye
On the rooftop I must die
So evil will come and retake its domain
A shapeless nothing to emerge and reclaim

Arthur Whitman

Untitled

Baby blue heavens of Amsterdam
Hover the flesh colored mansion
In the enchanted garden
Swaying leafy elm trees
Shelter violet, lavender and ivory Irises.
Brush covers the earth like a mother to her newborn child
Rough soil nurtures sprouting roots and vivacious florets
Whispering wind creates whispers of mystery.

Jennifer Monson

Red Headed Stranger

I look in the mirror and what do I see?
A red headed stranger looking at me.
Who's view of the world is tainted and stained.
Terrors of childhood in her head still remain
The child within her she can no longer find.
The part that was innocent, trusting and kind.

Her skin has grown older;
Her Heart has grown colder.
Where is the child that knew how to love?
Without fighting and hating when push come to shove?
I look in the mirror and what did I see?
A red headed stranger looking at me.

Kelly Wise

Images

I look in the mirror and what do I see,
a reflection of a man who looks like me.
A blink of an eye or a move of a limb,
I know there's something different about him.
Is it because he stands there with nothing to say,
or is it this thin wall of glass that stands in his way?
If only he could speak out through the land,
if only I could reach out and touch his hand.
He glares back at me with a blank look on his face,
as if he's wondering should it be me in his place.
If I could switch with him I probably would,
for all I know it would do the world good.
He holds his head high all true and proud,
as for me, I'm just another face in the crowd.

Carl W. Ragland

Untitled

A director's meeting is called, and a quorum is declared
A secret major project, is to be aired

Should it have the Lips, of a Chinese Chicken?
Whoever suggested that, needed a likken

What about the Feathers, from a Lizard?
She suggested that, as though a wizard

Perhaps the Feet, should be those of a Fish
All agreed the Fish, would be best on a dish

It certainly needs Ears, but from a Snail?
To that suggestion, he turned tail

Next on the list, does it need Eyes?
Someone said "A Bat!", to everyone's surprise

Think of some legs, to walk about
The idiot stated "A Snake", without any doubt

Of course it needed, an agile Neck
How about a worm, he shouted "By Heck!"

Then come the Legs, that are truly basic
But from an Eel?, that would be tragic

The eventual results, that were decided
We've discovered "THE GLOB", all chided

Clyde Wilson

Graceful Art

At first it seems so lifeless and cold,
Then there is movement graceful then bold.
The figure brings with her both beauty and skill,
All spectator become awestruck and still.

Her routine so full of funful precision,
Is more a careful dance of decision.
The hours of practice not seen by most,
makes this skater worthy of boast.

Dawnmarie Brigidi

The Dance of the Oaks

The oaks encircle me,
a slow dance as their fingers lazily sway
to catch the voice of the Wind.

They look down at me,
as the luxuriant rhythm
of their movements
catches me, spellbound.

I am a small child in their protection
at the center of their circle;
They are the parents of my dreams.
Beneath their branches I sleep
in the depths of Nature's singing,
which keeps the rhythm of their dance.

The dance of the Oaks is like the circle of Life;
and I am but the child
who is always in need of protection
no matter how well I may imitate that dance.

Dorothy C. Pfaff

A Man Is Made

An announcement, an invitation, a cap and gown,
A solemn procession to organ strains.
A bobbing tassel, a diploma, a handshake,
And in a blink a child is a man.

The years of preparation fade in a blur,
As I crane my neck to pick out mine.
In a line of rippling fabric, posture erect,
My eyes meet his with blinding love.

Ceremony over, mingling crowds, kisses and hugs,
Pride is palpable on a breezy May day.
Congratulations abound from one and all,
As I look into the eyes of a child, now man.

Leaving a campus once called home, images ingrained,
A myriad of feelings spill over like sand.
A future, a past, now seem as one,
When did my child become a man?

Dog days of summer now, is he really gone?
This house is his home, changed, yet the same.
A mother, now redefined, but still a Mom,
My baby, my child, has become a man.

Delia M. McGrath

In Ja

A whisper on the wind,
A song yet unsung,
A breath so gentle
It seems to drift alone
Except for the notes that hold it aloft.
Subtle rhythms seem to float her along
To a place where she can rest on angel wings
And ponder the hidden place where her heart lives.
Then with a wisp she rustles
Past her meaningless milieu
To touch so softly the being that waits.

Catherine M. Dixon

Gratitude

Drinking in the fragrance of Nicotiana's
White Stars,
Seeing a glittering lace coverlet of fire-flies
Lift toward the pale blue cloud-veiled full moon
This was God's gift to me of June.

Elizabeth Price Heinsohn

To The Place Where The Memories Lie

All it takes is a thought, a word, an object,
a sound, a smell, a name, a place, a face
To take us where the memories lie.

A place not far, so very near,
deep in the backs of our minds,
where cobwebs spin and dust gathers thick,
and time no longer ticks.

To get there you may whirl and twirl,
spin and leap, jump from thought to thought,
or you may simply get there quick, not a second lost!

It never takes long to reach it,
your desired destination is always prepared,
to take you back to places known, or where you've
grown, or people you love best.

The place where the memories lie
is open all the time (Even longer than 24-hour shifts),
to anybody, anywhere - all year long!!!

So close your eyes, dream a bit, think a bit, relax a bit,
and take a non time-consuming trip
to the place where the memories lie.

Joanna M. Crump

Avery

The call woke my slumber, and few words mentioned shattered a comfort. A thing I'd never fathom true; a bond since childhood-lost. Within a night's fury. Rage of hurt, anger, loneliness. A decision acted upon, finally made, fore pondered. As I'm told, breath tainted with liquor, diseased mind; she fled. Into the dark aline away from the house full. A singular swing sat, seen the years, caressed by children's grasp, joy turned to weapon. Upon this sight she was pulled, as the wind blew it's whisper. Trapped her in this idea. Her concoction did right, and she hanged from this... struggle not seen; alone I remind you. Did she fight? Did her suffocated screams cry" let me go!....I'm not ready!"? Minutes past and near the hour she was found. Silence cast and crowd a shiver, and my heart could be heard falling with the thunder of others. Together we gathered. All connected by her. Lurid crowd, we crept to the flower blanketed coffin. Words chanted, sweat mixed with the muffled tears, and upon the ask of prayer I listened. The man's voice drowned out, locusts screamed, and the trees rustled with the wind. She was there. Free. No longer would these boundaries of flesh trap her in a jail of inescapable mind power. Higher than any of her powders, and pills could ever peak, she was finally alive.

Antonia Light

What Is Freedom?

I remember a time not so long ago,
a time many have given their lives to make so.
I remember walking down the street, feeling the cool air,
trying that now, no one would even dare.
The distant memories of those times, makes me feel low.

I remember when the flag meant pride, honor, and love,
and we prayed to our Father who lives up above.
The country stood together, it was a must,
and we all lived by the motto "in God we trust."
All the while the spirit of God descended on us like a dove.

Now our country is in shambles, and no one cares,
because everyone is out to get their own share.
Now our country means power, money, and fear,
the cries of justice no one seems to hear.
It seems we now live in a Dragons Lair.

We must turn our hearts to God, if only people would see,
turning away from God, this is not the way to be.
When our Founding Fathers came here, it was God they sought,
to turn from righteousness they knew they must not.
Only when we rediscover this can we truly be free

Darran J Allridge

Crossing The Channel

As we cross the channel
a translucent sea gull flies on true above me.

Her still wings span invisible air currents
as she nestles effortlessly into the changing turbulence.

Sunlight filters through symmetric feathers,
makes illuminated soft-wing lanterns.

Moving crescent mirrors are carried on the water,
swing in bright pendulums at the ocean's rise and fall.

Encircling clouds fill with cold white light,
race forward, keeping pace with the gulls and wind.

The wings, the clouds, the reflecting water
make a holy place for flight without flying.

Beyond the continuous flapping of the community of earthbound gulls,
she sails alone, centered on the wind.

She closes her eyes, breathes slowly, knows the wind's ways.
She replenishes the spirits that make her...soars.

Kate Moran

Carrie

My joints are stiff, oh! how they ache,
A trip to the garden, I have to make,
It's morning already, the hours just flew,
Did I really sleep the whole night through.

Is someone calling?, do I hear a sound?
Why don't they speak up, it's hard to get around,
Quiet at last, finally alone,
All day to snooze, no one home.

Another day over, another day gone,
The evening's are peaceful, the TV is on,
They read their papers, I go to sleep,
I'm a 15 year old spaniel and life's one big treat.

Cheryl O'Keefe

The Mauve Of Dawn

The mauve of dawn foretells a new day coming;
A unknown pulse, an unknown shade in time
For one golden moment, yet at dusk succumbing
To the reach of eternity. But fleetingly prime
It precious is, as a new-born child
Or the tender love of a friend—
Intangible — but real, yet reconciled
To its passing and its end.

The mauve of dawn obscures a new day coming
Nor marks it to be fair or overcast,
But lifts and leaves it to a world, succumbing
To the day's brightness. And when the day is past
Its deeds may echo down the following years
And bring a truth to light
Or hide a sin, or wipe away some anguished tears
Or sweeten some long night.

Jim Patton Jr.

The Storm

The sky is unyielding the constant desire to become free.
A scream from the Heavens.
The wicked lasers from the eyes of jealousy.
The angels envy someone with the perfect love.
A heartbeat from God.
The raging anger of sins.
An echo from the shrieks of the sinners in Hell.
A shuddering chill.
The tears of the damned.

Amanda Oberhouse

Adam's Eyes

Adam, a boy unable to walk
A young child that will never learn to talk.

I wonder what thoughts lie behind those brown eyes
And if you know the questions they rise.
Can you feel the warmth in the early spring breeze?
Do you hear the sound of the wind through the trees?
Can you smell the scent of flowers in the air?
Do you yearn to leave your cold wheelchair?

I wonder if you see the drops of morning dew
Resting on blades of grass on this day dawning a new.
I wish you could tell me what you think
We could store it forever - written in ink.
I try to find answers but don't see a trace
I cannot read the expressions on your face.

All I see is the reflections of the skies
And wonder what thoughts lie behind Adam's eyes.

Cheri Lynn Sawyer

The Strength of One

Loneliness and silence
accompany me on my walk into oblivion.
No one else around,
No one cares to walk this way.
Except me.

It is my choice,
and I welcome the silence.
Silent are the voices
that once surrounded me,
and silent are the incessant whispers in my head.

The darkness is almost overwhelming,
and my loneliness aches.
But the pain feels good,
like hunger pangs in my soul,
numbing it.

I welcome it.
My choice.
My walk.
Alone.
It makes me strong.

Amanda Nawman

Aging

Let me tell you 'bout this body I have
Aches and pains that sure do cry for the salve.

A back that's tired of always standing erect
Someday knees will fail, or so I suspect.

Fingers swell up tight, and do pain me some
Hips don't want to, when I tell them to come.

Feet have callouses, go deep and they crack
Lungs that bellow, when I cough and I hack.

Teeth that now can only chew on one side
A belly to here, that I can no longer hide.

Ears have tuned way down, so volume must rise
Words just disappear, forcing me to revise.

Mem'ry went somewhere, I do not know where
Energy's lax, comes and goes with it's flair.

Elbows puckered up, and loose flabby arms
Earlobes are taut, though: one remaining charm.

Inside parts are quiet, with all their squirts
It's good to thank God, when not a thing hurts.

Just a bit of a wreck, is this body I have -
But, I'm still inside.

Jowan C. Freshwater

Wandering Spirits

They walked, hypnotized
across the wide, blue ocean
not even realizing they were dead.

In life, they existed in a similar state
living day to day in a fog of dreams
living for the future
and always attempting to undo the past.

A large oceanliner passed right through them,
sending chills up the spines of only the sensitive passengers
who could sense the restless vibration of death.

But the wandering dead, caught up in their mental chaos
did not notice the oceanliner, or the reddish-orange moon
that hung above them like a lantern, nor where they aware that they
were walking on water.

They passes on, to solid ground now, oblivious to their environment
and their damned fate. A young girl sitting under a tree shuttered as
they passed.

But just as she could not see them, they could not see her
because they were so lost
in the superficial of their minds.

Annette Jackson

Metamorphosis Of Obesity

So very delicate am I, depressed and dreaming, of better days to come.
Afraid to be consumed by the unfriendly ones.
I long for happiness and the freedom to sore.
Always longing and looking for more.
I am must crawling along so slowly.
Round and out of shape and lonely.
I am so desperate and fragile, I don't know who I am.
Timidly I search for a place to find peace,
a hide away were I can sleep. Then in time I am "Born Again"!
To fly, and sore, with spirit free, and totally full of beauty.
I am free of hiding for my sanity.
Who am I? I know, I am a Beautiful Butterfly!
Now I can fly, here and there, or up or down,
and no one can make me unhappy. For I have found my spirit inside.
And people will love my beauty.
But they will be sad because I am just flying along, and won't be
here long but they should remember, when I was just crawling along
so slowly. They forgot to see my inner beauty.
Now they're sad and lonely. I have gained, but they have lost,
but we most always realize there's a cost.

Alberta M. Cornell

The Caterpillar And The Butterfly

I was a caterpillar all fuzzy and brown
All I ever did was crawl all around

You were a butterfly with eyes in your wings
Each time you flew you saw everything
I met you one day as I crawled up a branch
You asked me to fly and I told you "I can't"

You thought for a moment and then you replied
"All you have to do is look into my eyes"

So I looked and I gazed will all of my might
And then I saw the most beautiful light

So I spun a cocoon and you know real soon
I was flying so high with my sweet butterfly

And needless to say
I fell in love
With the most beautiful butterfly
Whom showed me the way

Charlie Recotta

Pain

Pain has became a part of my life.
After I submitted to a surgeon's knife.

My common bile duct was just a fixture
which became diseased by staph and caused a stricture.

Because of uncleanliness and dirt
I am the victim of this hurt.

I lost my job and it destroyed my career,
which became another fear.

It caused me a lot of strife
but I did not lose my position as a wife.

Because of my family's and husband's love
I have a foundation to rise above.

In addition, I cannot eat,
so daily living is not a treat.

Pain and diarrhea add to my grief
to this end there is no relief.

If only cleanliness had not been neglected,
my health would not have been affected.

A doctor's skill should not maim,
but to me it has another name... PAIN.

Barbara Heskett Luthi

Vermont

The matronly bosoms outlined
against the sky,
Smug is the surety of these old dames
that hill-tops, nor sand dunes,
can make no claims,
cannot in posture, nor maturity vie
the outline of bosom
they project to the sky.

The cities below, on a more level slope
light their night torches in beauty to cope
'til the Lake reflects their iridescent gleam
on the Four Brother Islands bearded in green,
who cozen their outline in smug self-esteem.

Anna L. Steeg

Our Heaven

Come with me to the meadow where the grass is green and the
air is clean,
There we will find no sadness, anger or pain.
This is the place where the sun will warm our backs and
our hearts.
The birds will sing their songs to us and we will feel
their love.
We can lay in the grasses and watch the white clouds float
slowly across the sky,
The warm breezes will make the green leaves sparkle like
emeralds as they flutter.
Small things scamper through the grasses where there is no danger,
Little rabbits scamper across in the meadow happily while
the squirrels jump from limb to limb chattering.
We can watch the mighty eagle glide gracefully across the sky,
Song birds will sing their melody to us,
We will know only peace and happiness...
For this will be our heaven.

Joseph D. Ceriani Sr.

Coming Of Dawn

From the great silence of the night lull
All creatures roll down for slumbers call
Having their dreams realized with fantasy
At brink of day nothing left but memory.

The barns and yards where flocks are herding
Calmness get disturbed screaming and growling
While younger calves and sheep are feeding
And the other stocks remains loud snoring.

The aroma of flowers and fresh air we're breathing
Giving pleasures and charities for all serving
Leaving vigor and vitality very fascinating
Making us great and sturdy humane being.

Rushing waters and whirling of currents chanting
Running rivers and streams to Susquehana flowing
Turbulent waves of Chesapeake's shores crumbling
Composes the silent melodies of evening's luring.

The fisherman paddles to a distance his canoe
The farmers wait and pray as their fields grow
And the faithful bless with pity by the Almighty
Hum a tune, "The Coming of Dawn" what a wonderful day.

Aureliano C. Evardo

She Sat Alone

And then she sat alone
All happiness of the past, forgotten
The agony before forgotten, unwanted
Dismal agony before unwanted, dismembered
And still she sat alone
Left to drown in her miserable sorrows, ignored
To be forgotten like her happiness had been before
Left to survive the problems she thought burdened her
Left there to sit alone
All her walls crumbled down around her soul
Leaving blackness lurking in her life, not whole
Suffocated by pain in her heart, a hole
Dying from sitting alone
Abandoned by friends pushed away, unknown
Rotting in her forgotten joys, unknown
Walking around, not herself, a clone
Of death left sitting alone.

Catherine Gross

Memories Of You

The years have come and gone.
All I have are memories of you,
Gone are the days of laughter,
For you are not here anymore.

Sometimes I wish and wish, if only
Wishes could come true.
I would wish only one wish, a wish
that I could be with you.

For when you were here, it was
by your hands I was fed.
For when you were here, you led
and encouraged me.
For when you were here, you
Comforted me with your sweet and loving care.

Memories of you still linger.
An idle wish has had me on a vain journey,
A journey of emptiness.
For a wish is nothing more than
language of the heart,
With an indelible seal of memories of you.

Billy Lambert

Walls

I feel so wanted I feel so loved
All I need from Him are kisses and hugs
The warmth He gives me is taking control
Of my every emotion as so I'm told
My walls came down my defenses are gone
I've got to build them back up before too long
This is too good to be true too quick to be real
Yet there's something there deep inside I feel
The way he looks at me the way he touches
His strong embrace makes me yearn so much
The want and desire is definitely there
Yet at the same time I feel so scared
Of how it will happen then how it will end
Then there go those walls all around me again

Jacqueline Marie Husbands

The Seasons of Life

The spring of life;
all is lovely and free,
Rich green fields
as far as the eye can see.

As Summer sets in,
and time travels on,
part of your youth
is already gone

Turn your face to the setting sun,
Youth is over, Autumn has begun.

Winter engulfs you, the bitter winds blow.
the seasons have ended, prepare for the snow.

This is not an ending of life and all things;
because after the winter begins a new spring.

Amesha Kendrick

Untitled

Sleep baby sleep
  all night long,
  never to wake up,
  till the dawn.
Sleep baby sleep
  dream those dreams,
  think of those that will cherish those things.
Dream of the stars that twinkle that night.
Think of those happy things that day brought.
Wake up to a refreshing morning light.
Bring a smile of delight.

Jamie Webster

Untitled

Everything about her is perfect, she's so pretty, nice and neat,
All of the guys flock around her, and bow down to kiss her feet,
I stand in her shadow, watching her shine,
Envying her life, and wishing it were mine,
A guy will walk passed, and she'll get that look in her eye,
She'll win every last one of them, and that you can't deny,
When I'm around her, I feel like I'm not alive,
On a scale of one to ten, she's a ten and I'm a five,
I try to tell her, the way that I feel,
but my efforts don't work, so it doesn't seem real,
Why she acts like this, I can not comprehend,
but regardless of her perfectness, she'll always be my friend.

Brittany Rugotska

The Gang

Together again. Oh it's so great to be with
all of you my friends!
It's lonely so when I'm without you.
But I'm comforted when I'm around you.

The laughter, the pain,
the tears, and the shame.
We share it all together
and because of this we'll last forever.

More than just family, more than friends.
We stand by each other; and will to the end.
Sticking together through thick and thin,
the GANG hangs together forever friends!

Debby Lindsey

an animal

i was an animal made of rose pedals and ponds
all that was around me was black and blue
then I would hear a noise call my name
and I answer

i was an animal wandering thru a forest
the leaves on the trees were orange
the leaves on the floor were white and dried
i took a glass of water and
poured it onto the roots of a tree
then left the scene

i am an animal sleeping with blankets
i'll furnish my room with chairs
then find a window to stare thru

and I don't forget that night
is just a dark representation
of day

jason vogelpohl

Giving Back

Looking out before me I can only see
All the beauty and the glory God has given me
By the people in my life and wee ones by my side
The home in which I live and the guidance he provides

The beauty of the flowers and whistling of the leaves
Friends that I can trust and myself in which I believe
I know I owe a debt that I can never pay
But I can share with others by how I live each day

Take the time to listen and think before I speak
Share of what I have not expecting to receive
Go an extra mile or helping those in need
Giving back to others what I have received

Kim Hopkins

When The Clock Struck Midnight

When the clock struck midnight, and the children were in bed,
All the dolls and toys started to move their little heads.
Then secretly and quietly they jumped down to the floor.
Then to the playroom they all romped through the open door!
The Teddy Bear climbed on the stool and said, "Let the fun begin!"
The dolls came to the floor and danced with the Nut-cracker Men.
And when their feet got tired, they all stopped to talk,
Then on the rocking horse they rocked, and rocked, and rocked.
Then Molly, the doll, noticed the coming of the sun,
"Back to the shelves!" She yelled, "Dawn has ended all our fun!"
The toys ran quickly back through the bedroom door,
And took their places on the shelves just like the night before.
The little girl woke up and said "Toys, it's time to play!"
But she never quite understood why they looked so tired that day.

Kari McClelland

No Birthday Cake

Christmas day is over and I know that it was great.
All the toys and games were played until real late.

The tree is glowing brightly and I sit and look at it.
Yes, Christmas is all over, it was really quite a hit.

But we forgot one thing-it was Jesus' birthday too
There was no birthday cake and suddenly I feel so blue.

How could we forget him? It was a beautiful day.
When Christ came down from heaven and was born in a special way

So I offer up a prayer or two, to the King whose day it is.
I resolve that next year my family will show him bliss.

I look out my window at the stars so bright,
And I wonder if the Star of Bethlehem is shining in the night.
And so the day is over and tomorrow I will bake,
Although it is a little late, Jesus will have his birthday cake!

Anne Marie Morris

"What's Expected"

What's expected of a man who understands it
all? What's expected of a man who'd save you
from a fall?
Knowing eyes, he seems so wise. Who could
ever care so much; who comforts with his
touch?
What's expected of a man who never tries to
change the ways of a youthful, troubled
mind? What's expected of a man who'd take you
in if you were sick and nurse you back to
health?
No one even talks to him; no one even cares.
The only thing they think to do is walk by
him and stare.
What's expected of him, but to sit among the
streets. Filthy on the outside, but clean
beneath the sheets.

Jordan Pitts

Perspective

When you first see a rose posing gracefully on its stem, You think almost instantly of the beauty it holds within. Of the delicate, silky petals it grasps securely like a puzzle... Of the perfectly-shaped leaves that surround the pedestal on which it reigns.

There is one thing we fail to see because it is hidden. The thorns that rip away the flash, the adoration, the essence of its innocence. The thorns resemble guardian angels...in deep sleep until called upon by an unsuspecting admirer. How could perfection made by God's hands have such a cruel destination?

If a rose could love, would it love us like God love His little children? If a rose could laugh, would it laugh with us or at us? If a rose could learn, would it learn to care for those less fortunate and encourage those who are hurting? If a rose could listen, would it listen to our most secret hopes... fears...dreams?

If a rose could hate, would it treat us like enemies? If a rose could cry, would it cry because of the loss of love in the world? If a rose could feel the pain of others, would it apathetically go on with its life or stop to help? If only a rose could see, would it pass judgment immediately or wait to sense our inner beauty?

God blesses roses because they are His creation. How much greater God
must care for us whom He made in His own image! We try so desperately to please God knowing we are full of imperfections. But God, he Creator of this universe, sees, all, forgives all, and loves all in spite of our thorns.

Brooke Gary

"The Clock"

My face belongs to your fleeting glances
Along my hands and numbered chances
I am the harbinger of your dreams
your past romances
And the shadows of sun and moon;
Enduring your sighs I go too slow
too soon
Yours looks to heavens for truth on Earth
While I measure your soul, your worth.

I am your joy, your longing, your sorrow
I am the day, the yore, the morrow;
Listener of hearts tic in tune with my own
Knowing that yours must mend alone.
I am the maker of fate, and the taste of fine wine
The minutes, the hours, the mountains you climb —
I am the holder of planets, the stars fiery shine
I am The Clock — the messenger — the symbol of Time.

Donald Wayne Bement

My Christmas Gift To All

Christmas is a time that we share our love for one another.
Although we share that love throughout the year;
It is simply a special time that all can set other things aside so we can reflect upon all the reasons why we love those who mean so much to us.

It is a chance for all to remember the greatest gift of all that God has freely given to us.
It was not diamonds or rubies, it was not little toy trains or curly headed baby dolls.
No, the gift that God gave to us all was simply the gift of life.
It was His desire to come to earth and share His very own life with us.
That gift is the Lord Jesus Christ.

It was His demonstration that said the greatest gift one could give to another,
Is sharing their time, their love, and their life with each other.
This gift requires no money, no hustle and bustle, no holiday stress.
It simply requires one to believe that they really do have something worth giving,
That gift is themselves.

So during this time I pray that all of you will come closer to experiencing the true meaning of Christmas.
And believe in your heart that all of us have something to give.
And that all of us have been given the greatest gift of all,
The gift of love through our Lord Jesus Christ.
Have a very Merry Christmas and a Happy New Year!

Cheryl Ann Reimer

The Void

It always feels that something's missing.
Always hoping, always wishing.

No one just right to take the place.
No one quite perfectly fitting the space.

Who is this new father figure going to be?
Someone who will tenderly love and protect me.

Always strong, gentle, and wise,
Who gazes at me with loving eyes.

Whom my family can rightfully trust.
Whose eyes aren't blinded only with lust.

So much love are we willing to share.
Not to be wasted on one who won't care.

Someone who's not looking to use,
Or our kindness to abuse.

Oh great father from up above,
Send us this worthy person to love.

Brooke Renzullo

Speculum

Staring at her, and she stares back...The same face I always see when I sit here. Sometimes angry, sometimes sad, and sometimes smiling back at me.

Often she could look better, but often she doesn't care. "Do you care?" She says, holding her head the same way I hold mine. Without an answer we both shrug our shoulders and continue to polish the glass between us...

With one last look, one last wondering gaze into her eyes wishing I knew who she was, I flick off the light and leave her once again...

Maybe the next time I see her, she can tell me who I am.

Desiree Petersen

Searching

Subtle turns in the river like path of time:
An endless unfolding disappears into ancient forgotten pasts
and still invisible, infinite futures, only imagines and waiting.
Freedom is the space within nature's cosmic womb
giving us to this valley of dry white bones
to break our death-grip on the superstitious illusions
of our father's blood and brain.
We have come as the mind of God, consciousness stalking like
a quick, muscled wildcat bounding from a dead, leafless branch
to the edge of a gorge fashioned by floods of countless red summer
moons, searching open fields of memory and dreams for the
threshold
of a paradise lost in the unrepressed primal scream.
Our eyes are the hungry black-winged eagle
gliding fitfully against brutal winter winds in search of meat
below an orange-stroked blue purple sky.
Our bodies are the centaur's arrow reaching for a distant star.
We are flesh, heart and blue fire — anew generation of Gods,
the murdered children of heaven's holy womb, reborn:
the prophet's vindication and the last coming of Christ.

John Foster

Leaving

What madness lies skulking in the corners of our minds?
An evil purveyor sucking out feelings, hopes, and dreams.
Leaving a desolate vacuum in the place of the yesterdays.
Something we both have to live with,
In different parts of the world.
Would it make any difference if we were in the same city,
the same frame of mind?
We would still be tempered by our indifferences and refusal
to believe the inane and illogical.
In essence we could be side by side and alone.
Must we go through life questioning the reason we chose different
ways?
The only answer offered is the loneliness that pervades our every atom
and with the passing of time still lingers on like a slow,
immutable death.

Crystal D. Adami

Happiness

Happiness can't be defined. It's a certain mood, a state of mind. It's sharing everyday affairs with one who understands and one who cares.

It's a tender look, a gentle touch that says - "I love you very much". It's a smile of welcome when you are blue, a dream that's shared, a dream of two.

Happiness is even more than this. It's a warm embrace, a tender kiss. It's a special blessing from above. It's what you have when you're in love.

Addie P. Curry

Wilted

Roses and love are two of a kind.
There beautiful and graceful that someday you'll find.
So enjoy it's beauty because nothing last forever
Rose and love will soon die together.

Janet Strehle

Untitled

I replaced
an injured black sprinter
Holding their hands,
Where, O faith, is your victory - they prayed
Dividing the sound of gun
and smell of black powder
I ran the curve marked out for me

I raised my baton and stretch out my hand over his black hand
Moses came back alive - they praised
Our steps were perfect, so perfect that
I thought we were a part of high-speed photography
His black vibration trembled my flesh
Through the yellow baton,

After the race
Coach said,
The relay team with unimproved records
never never drops their baton.
Was I running or had run their race in vain or is it just their sigh

Jeffrey J. Kim

Calella De Palafrugell

Perched gloriously just above horizon's divide,
An orange moon reflects on the Mediterranean.
Her swirling aura of blackened red heat
Reminds me of flaming sisterhood with the sun.

Sol y Luna
Each with their own siesta:

Sol overlooks the breeze and the blue,
As they lap the shore
Dissolving into crystallized sand.

Luna illuminates the rolling peaks
Controlling their reach,
Melting in Spanish darkness.

Amy Norton

Black And White

Think about it: what good would
An Oreo be without the chocolate
Cookie and vanilla cream?
Variety is a privilege.

In a world where no one's exactly the same,
There is one thing we all do share.
We share a world full of wrongful hate,
We share a world which is very unfair.

This country says we have our rights,
Why then do we continue to fight?
Why can't we just all get along and realize,
We must stop being proud and we must apologize?

But who is courageous enough to make the first step?
Who is bravest enough to speak out?
Who will become the first to call a truce?
Are we finally willing to listen and not shout?

Black needs white and white needs black,
We all need each other,
We are all the same in God's eyes,
We are all each other's brother.

Ebony Joy Christopher

The Clown

The clown's red nose was big and bright
An up-turned smile cheery—a true delight.
Red hair and rosy cheeks made her face complete
But sad, blue eyes said it all—defeat.

The laughter, the antics, the jokes, what fun
Her appearance is the happiest under the sun
She laughs on the outside, she's a happy clown
But cries on the inside—her world turned upside down.

One day he loved her, her life was euphoric
Then he was gone, their love was historic.
A clown she became to hide her tears
Laughter she brings to quell others fears.

How many people are clowns this day?
What tears and hurts beneath surfaces lay?
How many smiles, whose laughter is fake?
How much more hurt can a broken heart take?

Judy Backman

Card Board Boxes

Lived a life in an old broken down house,
And a corner that was devoted to the family mouse.

A bed broken down and springs worn,
Ragged shoes and a shirt that's torn.

Remember the times you fought and they rung the bell,
And the babies that was born and then you sell.

The people don't remember when your so lame
And the babies that are born with silver spoons think it's a game.

It's a particular thing when you hear them sing
Of the problems that attack them, of their lives,
Their homes and their families grim.

Need a place to live!
Need a place to sleep!
To shelter us from the,
Creatures that creep!

Need a place of protection
Free from rejection
And full of affection we seek.

James Bobik Jr.

A New Beginning

The song of the sparrow floats softly through my window,
And a new day begins.
A day filled with promise and hope,
A new beginning.
Whether there be sunshine and laughter,
Whether there be sorrow and pain,
I greet this day with joy in my heart,
For I have been given another chance to find love.
If I do not reach out and grasp the glimmer of promise,
The hope of what may be,
Then the promise that shimmers on the horizon
May vanish before I can claim it as my own.
I must strive to caress and nurture this day,
For today is the hope of tomorrow: It must not die.
I will use this day wisely,
For no one knows what the future shall bring.
Guard it jealously,
For each precious moment is truly a gift,
And as those seconds move swiftly by,
They are gone forever, part of what might have been.

Claudia Patton

Heaven

As I sit and wonder, what is heaven?
White horses with wings, marshmallows,
golden gowns, or just fluffy clouds?
Who do I ask, when will I find out?
It's all just a mystery fluttering
through my head, like a restless
butterfly.

Ashley Candy

The Smoke Poem

Will smoke rise from my grave and find its way around
and as it wipes away the words, hear the sadly happy sounds.

Will someone walk alone in good and realize her dark reason
and read from scrolls of hate and smoke that ponder holy treason.

And as it wraps around you, will the tears of smoke reach high.
And when you float away with words, something whispers its a lie.

Will you look for something to hold onto, but fall into yr grave.
In the ground there are no tears so smile like a slave.

Will you see them floating upward and laugh from too much life.
And sedated from a time within you, feel the kiss of a blade
of a knife.

When will they realize its in the air and stop running from
the ground.
And now I know I should have left, and now I cant be found.

Elizabeth Rodio

Night Sky

As I sit here on my front porch,
and as the sun has a light like a torch.

I look up at the changing sky,
and I watch the last sign of day go by.

Soon the sky turns a blackish gray,
I imagine I hear the moon say...

"I'm up, I'm up it's finally right,
stars, stars come into my sight!
Get into all of your places,
and shine down on all those smiling faces."

The sky looks like a blue lagoon,
and now, "Here! Here!" says the moon...
He gives a great big huge yawn,
and says, "Go away stars, it's almost dawn."

As the last stars go away,
it starts the beginning of another day.

Amanda Cockerham

What He Caught

The fisherman woke up before the sun began to shine
and astute hands did knowingly begin to knot the line.
He cut the bait, prepared his rigs, and sharpened every hook.
A waste of skill, thought he, is to return with none to cook.

About him as about his lines, a quiet, forceful sea,
and gull's calls spoke to him than his mind's industry.
A sea wind blew right to his soul, and warmed him to the bone,
and so did he begin to see, for every sense does nature hone.

He felt a tug upon his line and gave his rod a pull,
and thought its run did then become extremely powerful
he had it tight with all his might so not to loose his prize
until at last his line did snap. A dreadful compromise?

I and he, for repartee, do now propose to answer thee:
to loose a fish but win the sea is truly a grand victory.

Jason Libsch

The Butterfly

In dark, secluded space she spun the shroud
And crept inside entombed in living death.
To solitary sacrifice she bowed;
Essential to God's plan, she proffered breath.

The long night passed; the sun reclaimed its day.
The Pupa stirs within the brown cocoon
And breaks the bonds, emerging into May.
She rests and dries her wings and knows her boon.

A golden garden waits neath sapphire sky,
And ruby roses dwell midst emerald lawn.
She sips the diamond nectar with a sigh,
Then turns to make a new life of her own.

The others flock and kiss her searching soul;
The memories fade, and life becomes a whole.

Barbara Deer

Memories

Now and then I go to sleep
And dream about the friends I'll keep
For years to come. I've always be blessed
With wonderful people - they're surely the best.
I'm sorry to say that some have died.
More than once, I've sat and cried
Contemplating my feelings of loss.
But I won't let sorrow be my boss.
I remember all the fun we had
And know in my heart, I'll always be glad
That I have such memories to hold so dear,
Even if my friends aren't near:

Annie Beckerle

The Wall

My friends name is on the wall,
And each night, my tortured dreams hear his memory call.

For I watched as the bullets pierced his breast,
And I held him while he died,
I remember burying the body,
And just how hard I cried.

He saved my life, and I owe him.
As time goes by, the memory just won't dim.
Finally, the country calls him "HERO",
But his body's still not home,
Lying out there in an unmarked grave,
To all but God, unknown.

I walk past a cemetery,
And hear the bugle call,
Reminding me of all those heroes,
Whose name are on the wall.

James M. Rudy

Innocence

I want to run through the fields,
and feel the sun's heat kissing my gentle face.
I want to talk to the birds and the flowers.
I want to look up at the moon,
and feel that I can put my tiny fingers around it.
No worries,
No pressures.
Not knowing what hate is.
I want to feel the innocence of being a child again.

Daniella Levin

"Forever Lasting Love"

For years that's passed, for present time,
And for years ahead, we cannot see,
You know I'm yours, I know you're mine,
A love so strong, it reaches to eternity.

A love that came, from out of nowhere,
And caught us in, its clinging grasp,
A love that has stretched, across the miles of time,
And held our hearts, together fast.

Time apart, has separated us in years,
But our love so strong would now allow us to forget,
Then like the wind our love came bounding back again and brushed away our tears,
Now our love is stronger, deeper, than when we first met.

Forever lasting love, so true so strong
Kept our memories alive, with the things that used to be,
And just when I thought, all hope for us was gone,
You reach out your heart upon the wind, and send it back to me.

Now at last, our love is secure, and will last for all, eternity,
For what its worth, my love is yours,
And all of your love, belongs to me.

Andrea Blizzard

Eagerly As A Child

Eagerly as a child I reached into a large bag filled with surprises
and groped around the wrapped up shapes and sizes.
Finally caressing a small soft thing, I lifted it out with care....
then hurriedly ripped off the paper with a flare.
Oh how I laughed and chuckled as I held my prize close to me——
A tiny rubber Indian lass was chuckling back at me.
I felt love and was loved in return by that dear little laughing rubber face saying thanks.....you made your heart my Place.
How is it God always knows when I need a special joy like a little laughing toy?

And so it goes— whoever knows the meaning of such events?
Are they sunshine paying rent or simply me being me——
Grateful for a smile and holding it a—while?

Betty Lou Hinckley

Havoc In The Garden

Tur nipped the snapdragons
And his friends, the dandy lions,
Won't lettuce alone.
The tiger, Lily, was on our side, But she was squashed,
And her blood leeks out of dozens of wounds.
She may survive,
But she'll be forever blighted from this encounter.
Pump can maybe egg our plant on
But that pickle doesn't relish his chances.
It's true that they'll beet him up if he's caught,
But Lima said
She'll bean them if they try it.

Ashley Wickell

Reflections

Looking through a mirrored glass
Wondering what is and what shall be
Not knowing the right move to make
Never knowing what is right for me.
I have stumbled down the road of life
Never sure which road I should take
Will there be but pain and sorrow
Or will life give me a break.
I look ever deeper into my heart
To find the strength of soul
To carry on each night and day
Until my heart is full.

David Oakes

Don't Cry Anymore

Somebody snatched my soul
 and I don't know where it went to.
Somebody causes me pain
 but I don't know why I feel so numb.
Do you see me?
 Do you see me crying in the open rain?
Do you feel it?
 Do you feel the pain I try but cannot show?
Somebody loved me, yes,
 but again love hurts more then it does good.
What can I do when I know
 the one I loved is not here anymore.
People say I like to live in pain,
 I say my love likes that for me.
But I don't complain though I died from loneliness
 the day you ran away from me.
When I walk through these forgotten roads I see me as I am.
If I cry tonight, Would you hold me?
If I cry tonight, will it rain? Yes, it will drown the world.
I won't cry tonight, Cause I won't have your hands anymore to stop me;
 It will drown the world.

Biag Jameel Mirza

To Dad With Love

Dad, I know that you and I don't always get along,
And I know that I am sometimes in the wrong.
I really want to get to know you, and you to get to know me.
Those fourteen years were missed, when at night we could have kissed.
I know now that you are here to stay, and hopefully you will never stray.
I look to you for guidance and care, and now I know you'll always be there. I thank you now for I can sleep, knowing that you will always keep
That promise to mom you once did make,
Her body you'll hold, her hand you'll take.
When dads I see at sporting events, pulling their hair and getting real tense,
I think to myself how strange it is to see dads caring about their kids.
I know that by you I was not wanted, now I am glad that I have confronted
The feelings for you that I do have, for maybe someday I will be free of this pain I carry in me.
You and mom I love so much,
You're in my heart that special touch.

Kristie Wichman

Believe

Believe in yourself
And I will believe in you too
That is really all you have to do

If you don't believe in yourself
How can you expect anyone else

Never give up on your goals you see
Never give up on what you want to be

Keep reaching high for the sky
Never stop to question yourself why

You must believe in your heart, mind and soul
Never listen to the negative things you are told

Believe you can do it in your heart
And my friend, that is the first start

Believe in yourself that's all you need to do
And I guarantee you others will believe in you too

Be determined and keep your goal on your mind
After that, it's only a matter of time

Love what you are doing with all of your soul
And you will reach your ultimate goal.

Angela R. Scott

I Won't Forget....

I won't forget you lived
And I'll never say you died
And it will always be pulling at something very deep inside
I won't go to your grave and weep
Or stand by it and cry
I will never go to it and say my very last good-bye
You are not what is in the box laying in the ground
You are the air, the wind, the stars the clouds
I know I won't see you physically again, but I will in my heart
Because you hold a piece of my life that is a very special part
I won't forget the happy times and I will remember the sad
But I will never ever say they were bad
I'll think of you always and I know that I will cry
I'll stop and ask over and over again just tell me "Why?"
In my memories, thoughts and dreams you will be there
And I know your tender spirit will be everywhere
I won't forget you lived
And I'll never say you died
Because you will always be with me somewhere very deep inside

Diana Messer

A Kid's Point Of View On Life

Life is both good and bad,
and in between you will feel sad.
But no matter how little you try,
you will always get by.

To help you succeed you have your friends,
they shall help you get through until the end.
Then there is your family who gives it their best,
even if they do yell when your room gets messed.

And of course there is school,
which really is cool!
There is so much to do,
if you hate it, you are a fool!
They have so many choices for you to choose,
it will help your future, so you can't ever lose!

I hope my poem shows how life is for a kid,
now my thoughts are out, and I am checking what I did.
These are just some things that all kids know,
I might be wrong, but usually that is how things go.

Candace Neybert

Mother Has Gone Home

There was an angel in our midst, her sweet smile now is gone.
and in our hearts she's sorely missed since Jesus called her home

The peace that she had waited for has settled in her heart.
She walks now on His shining shore, they never will part.

The hand that guided her through life has lifted her away,
to never know of pain and strife, in His eternal day.

The lips that spoke so sweet to us, now speak to Him above.
She's sitting there at Jesus' feet and basking in His love.

And somewhere in the sky tonite a star began to shine,
with a soothing and a gentle light for us she left behind.

She lived her life within His love, so she had love for all.
Now she rests with Him above, she lived, but for His call.

She walks no more with us on earth, but she gave all she had.
She's living now in her new birth, let not your heart's be sad.

She went away with Him in peace, her heart at last is free.
Her joy will never, ever cease through all eternity.

Try to walk within His light and cry for her no more.
He'll guide you through the lonely night, to her at Heaven's door

So trouble not your heart, but live as best you can,
then you and she will never part, that's God's eternal plan.

Carolyn Kissinger Mann

Untitled

You are the one who appears so elusive,
And it certainly seems quite conclusive.
That you find me not on your list,
Of those you care for and kiss.
In years gone by,
It's possible that I.
Would have felt much chagrin.
But now, I can only shrug and grin.
Do I really need a significant other?
Perhaps, it's best, I love you like a brother.
But, please be patient and kind,
When you look into my eyes and find,
That what you see,
Can only be,
A lovely reflection of you and me.

Jean Clark Deremo

Memories

You crossed my path of life,
And left it as you came,
Silently,
But if it was a barred and empty road before,
It now is filled with memories.

The rock which blocked my way before,
You moved it as to open a door,
To let through love and happiness,
And I, with eagerness,
Followed you.

You turned the rain into sun,
And the sound of a cricket to beautiful music,
And following you,
My heart discovered the beauty as you knew it.

Was our meeting only short on the path of life,
I always remember the former,
As each time I stumble over a rock on the road,
I halt and recall how you helped to move it over.

Britta Von Rothe Hansen

"A Cry To Heaven: Meredith's Vilanelle"

O pity! My Dark angel, nurse thy wounded wings,
and let my love distract thy torn pain.
It is of thee, my broken one, that I forever sing

of how silvery bells, for thy virgin soul, loudly ring
and cry bitter tears to God in bloody vain,
"O, pity our Dark Angel, and nurse her wounded wings!

From Hades he came, Lord of Lies. His lust did bring
him to her, to leave on her breast his bile stain.
It is of her, our broken one, that we forever sing

of how he waits still on Earth, in silence, lying
to rape her again and again with his poison kiss profane.
O, pity our Dark angel, and nurse her wounded wings!

and of how you crawl back, nightly, to return, broken and bleeding
to his embrace - Why? We beg thee, our Dark Angel, refrain!
It is of you, our broken one, that we forever sing

of how, even now, in wicked malice, black skin, kneeling
over you, the grinning demon ties his leathery reign—"
O, pity my Dark Angel, and nurse her wounded wings!
It is for her, my broken one, that I'll forever sing.

Adrian Feliciano

Love Is Not Love Till You Share It

No man can have friends if he won't be a friend,
and lift someone's load who can't bear it.
And folks are not right who the right won't defend,
and a heart found that's broke, won't repair it.

A face doesn't smile with the lips downward turned,
and a deed can't be done till you dare it.
And blessings don't come when the blesser is spurned,
and to energize faith, you declare it.

The gift of God's grace is the gift above all,
for there's nothing with which to compare it.
And one can't love like Christ till he learns to love all,
and seeks for God's realm to inherit.

Well, flowers won't bloom without showers in spring,
and a life without hope has no merit.
So, to give your life goal, whether pauper or king,
pursue every dream till you snare it

A song has no worth if there's no one to sing,
and a robe gives no warmth till you wear it.
Birds are not birds if they never take wing,
and love is not love till you share it.

Charles E. Mieir

The Sun

I love to sit in an open field
And look at the sun that will never yield.
I watch the great sun go down behind the horizon
Hoping tomorrow there'll be a great supriz'en.
For tomorrow I'll see the sun again
In hopes that my journey will never end.
I couldn't imagine the world without the sun
And every day know that sunshine won't come.
The world would be full of darkness and despair.
I think the sun is the answer and none other could quite compare.
We should thank The One who made the sun
And know the sun shall always come.

Chae Carlson

Romanticize, Idealize, Logic's Eyes

I tried to smile, but this was serious
And my eyes lay dejected, staining the concrete
Love is not logical
Therefore, there is only logical separation
It is not uncommon for humans to completely destroy themselves
The floor of the sea was exposed
Rock sculptures led to the heavens
Every color of my life was firmly embedded in the rock
Meanwhile, the sand ached to breathed
Then, in my book of dreams, truth starred
As reality hit heavy and hard, words were hastily chose
untimed and not properly exposed - to logic
And I vent anger on those who had spent
their life smoothing out my dents, thus I went
Alone, without family or peers, and soaked in the years
Speaking to no one, I spoke my fears
Then someone, grabbed my heart and choked the tears
After a smoky sunset, I rode out of Eden
And the following morning, I woke up sad
missing that which I never had

Daniel Rucker

Don't Just Do Something; Sit There

When you've mainly written prose,
Why would you be writing a poem?
Because when life is coming toward its close,
You want to spend more time quietly at home.

Joann L. Busteed

I'll Remind Myself... "I Can"!

Please let my mind be blessed with pride
and my heart with compassion.
Give me the strength and courage to greet each day
with a "smile", "optimism" and "passion".

Please don't let my rainy days
overwhelm me and take over my control.
Please don't let me become depressed with life,
because it will takes its toll.

Please remind me of the children's laughter
and the beauty of our mountains and our shores.
So I don't dwell on the sadness of the rain,
and instead...open "sunny" doors.

Please remind me to stop and smell the fragrance of the flowers
and how after "rain" they stand still strong, and bloom beautifully again and again.
So I can smile at the challenges of "my" rainy days
then, I will do my job God, and.....REMIND MYSELF.....I CAN!

Darlene (Swanhart) Fragale

Sunshine Rays

A warmth permeates her soul,
And once again her broken heart becomes whole.
Love rises like the sun's golden rays,
Showering light on darker days.
It fills her soul with hope and penetrating bliss,
Only Venus could have invented this.

She had known great love in her life,
As a mother, a friend and a faithful wife.
As she sat letting the sun warm her face,
She remembered love's comforting embrace.

She sat all alone,
On the porch of her ocean-side home.
She watched the waves crash against the shore,
And all of a sudden wanted nothing more,
Than to be sitting in that place,
Golden sunshine upon her face,
Remembering the happy days,
When love had warmed her like sunshine rays.

Jennifer White

Until We Meet Again

Our paths have crossed the road of life,
and our hearts have touched;
even if only for a brief moment.
Although we may separate and go our own direction,
we continue to traverse our path.
Whether or not the path comes to meet at the crossroad ahead;
always cherish the good memories, and remember what
we have learned from the bad.
Living today for tomorrow - with no regrets.
My friend, I wish for you love, luck, happiness, and most of all
peace within yourself...
...until we meet again!

Deborah "Sunny" Harvat

Untitled

A sound so precious, full of life and energy...
Silence of innocence, silence of life...
The soul longs for sound, for life
The heart enjoys innocence and silence
To feel with the motions of sound
To listen with the love of silence
How exciting it is to enjoy the
Silence...

David L. Watson

Do Not Cry

If I should fall, from a mountain of stone.
And perish at the bottom, lost and alone.
Tell all the people that I did for once embrace the sky.
Do not cry, for this is how I wanted to die.

If I should crash, in a race in bad weather.
Entombed all in mental and the sweet smell of leather.
Tell all my good friends, who knew my life's love
was the drive.
Do not cry, for this is how I wanted to die.
If in the arena, I receive the bull's stab.
For remnants of life my soul will not grab.
Tell all my family who knew I must try.
Do not cry, for this is how I wanted to die.

But if I should die, asleep in a bed.
Entrapped by the tubes that kept me fed.
And if it is true by dreams our life is sustained.
If they're still within reach the let me remain.
But if they're out of my grasp, then let me die then.
My dreams will lie waiting 'til they're dreamed up again.

Jason Adelore Rodd

But The Hours Grew Short

I called her Mommy
and she took my hand and we chased butterflies in the clover fields, and we laughed and sang, she showed me the wonderment of a new born kitten and taught me to recite John 3:16.
BUT THE HOURS GREW SHORT AND I GREW TALL

I called her Mama

And we climbed the hills, played baseball and croquet, drove the tractor, pitched hay and cooled off in the pond. She showed me how to garden, sew, and cook and taught me to read the Bible.
BUT THE HOURS GREW SHORT AND I GREW AWAY

I called her Mom

And we differed on hair styles and what clothes to wear, what time to be home, and driving privileges. We couldn't see eye to eye on make-up or T.V. shows or the necessity of keeping my room clean but she showed me how to think on my own and taught me to go to church.
BUT THE HOURS GREW SHORT AND I GREW UP

I called her Mother

And we went shopping together and made baby clothes
and talked for hours on the phone reminiscing about
the good old days. She showed me the art of patience
and inner strength and taught me how to pray.
BUT THE HOURS GREW SHORT AND I GREW OUT

Before I knew it I had a daughter who called me Mommy, Mama, Mom and Mother.

BUT THE HOURS GREW SHORT AND I GREW WISER
AND NOW I CALL MY MOTHER — FRIEND!

Jan Kuhlman

Colors

The blue sky doesn't fight the green grass.
The black sheep shares pasture with the white.
I bleed red, just like you.
We all live in one home...mother earth.
Put down your weapons of hate.
Pick up your hearts...tools of love.
Let's live in peace,
The way it should be.

Joe Price

Independence

The compass pointed east
and so she went west.

The guide said follow the current,
so she paddled upstream.

A dead tree was on the scavenger hunt,
so she found a tree, blossoming vigorously.
And she plucked one of the blossoms
to mingle with her hair.

The card catalogue said fiction,
she found a book in biography.

Everyone cried at the funeral.
She chose to remember her Great Aunt
with laughter instead; recalling the good times.

The letter called for 35 cents worth of stamps.
She dropped the letter in the slot,
70 cents worth of stamps licked into place,
the sweet taste of the backing still lingering in her mouth.

The map said "X" marks the spot.
Why? she thought. Why leads to the answers.
Oh, what treasure will she find with independence on her side?

Chad Callaghan

I See

I see that some people are bad,
And sometimes that makes me so very sad.
I see that it is wrong to hate,
Just because one race is different in a way.

I see all the people dying,
And know the world will end up crying.
I see outside the clear, bright sun,
I wish the war would someday be done.

I see the whole world watching,
Their tears fall silently, unheard.
I see the blue, beautiful sky,
I wish we could get up and fly.

I see the bombs bursting,
As we all pray in fear.
I see that some people have no heart,
But maybe by saving some of us, it is a start.

I see the war is about to end,
But the millions they've killed they cannot mend.
I see a clear, bright light,
And pass away without any fright.

Jeffrey Scott Drew

The Road

The road leads somewhere,
And somewhere is where I'll go,
But who knows all the hardships the road shall bestow.
Who knows all the sufferings and problems I'll face,
And who knows all the happy times I will embrace,
Who knows how far on the road I shall roam,
Who knows all the times I'll be on my own,
Who knows how long on the road I will strive,
Who knows how long, the road keeps me alive,
To these questions only God has the key,
As I travel the road of uncertainty.

Ellen Stathopoulos

Mark of the Cross's

The crosses stand with reaching arms,
And span the fields that once were farms,
Enfolding all and guarding all,
The remains of those who once stood tall.

The crosses with their arms out reaching,
Lessons to us all they're teaching,
They stood their guard o'er the dust below,
How our comrades suffered we'll never know.

Now years have passed through miles of grief,
And loved ones found from tears relief;
But there in rows in a distant land,
The crosses ever remaining stand.

In memory to our brothers all,
Who paid a price beyond recall;
We bow our heads, in peace we pray,
While crosses guard where comrades lay.

Ernie E. Buss

The Rose

Burns said his 'luve's like a red, red rose'
  and sweetly praised her so,
But to liken love to that certain flower
  simply does not flow.

Though silky smooth are its petals
  to the finger's touch,
The path to love is often crooked,
  and never smooth enough.

Varied,
are the hues of the simple rose
Complex,
are the emotions induced by love.
Raging red anger, trembling with yellow fear,
Blushing pink cheeks, and lonely white tears.

At criticisms of love, many lovers do scorn,
But even lovers must remember, that every rose
  must have its thorn.

Archana Patwardhan

Troubles

Troubles come in every shape
  and tend to make one frown,
But just cheer up, and never let
  your troubles get you down.

For if you stop to think of it,
  more often so than not,
Your troubles don't seem quite like the ones
  that others folks have got.

If only magic spectacles
  could really help one see
That troubles are but stepping stones,
  and not catastrophes;

For on this journey we call life,
  when troubles bring dismay,
There's always hope and promise of
  A clearer, brighter day!

Kellie R. Stueve

A Crying Heart

I gave you my heart to do what you want
and that decision will forever haunt
My heart, my soul, and my mind too
because your one action made me feel blue
You made me laugh but then you made me cry
but then you could just look and I can't deny
The feelings that you make me feel
sometimes I wonder if they are real
Your so shy and you never have time to talk
but I can't find the strength to get up and walk
Away from you and away from the lies
that I tell myself about you being my guy
So just one last look, for one last touch
just one last kiss before my heart bust.
So good-bye forever there will be no more for me
So good-bye my first love it was never meant to be

Christina Alcala

The Hourglass

When twilight creeps across the garden wall
and the dark fingers of night fall
silently across the trees,
the moon awakens to find her sister Sun
retiring for the night.

It's a time for musing and recollecting
on how you spent your life.
Did you stand for something,
or for nothing?
Did you invest, or waste your days?

The tides of time roll in and out,
and your hourglass is sifting away slowly.
Reach out your hand and feel
the softness of the night!

Diane B. Merceron

Herald Of Spring

The Blue Ridge was veiled in a misty blue haze
And the March sky that morning was gray.
In the air, I could feel a piercing chill
And for miles snow covered the way.
The Countryside lay so quiet and still
For no sound of wildlife was heard.
Then, from the woodland brushed with white
Came the soul stirring sound of a bird.
A Thrush, so enthralling and rapturous its song
I stood at the door and listened long.
The tune seemed to swell from the balsam nearby,
This beautiful music from a creature, so shy
From its threat came a crystalline sweet melody
And I stood there enchanted as its song came to me
Spring had arrived amid snow and skies of gray,
Its only Herald was the song of a bird that day.

Adele Lee Martin

Creation Glories

Words cannot convey the spectacular beauties of the Earth
And the materials of galaxies beyond comprehension.
The composition, colors, and spiral shapes, patterns of worth
Found in galaxy and genetic codes of life, to mention
The creation of living souls, blending body and spirit.

And words cannot convey the glorious sounds of great music.
Music, with the power to lift our spirits and enlighten
Our minds with the glories of all creation and to fuse it
With light and give us joy within and our earthly lives brighten,
If we are willing to look up beyond ourselves and hear it.

Kay Thoreson

Little Church at Taiban

The plains of fair New Mexico, where tumbleweeds are blown,
And the muddy Pecos River has the only water known;
Where upon a lonesome hill, within De Baca county lines,
Stands an aging testimony in a simple country shrine.

The little church at Taiban holds the history of all,
Hidden deep inside the weathered cracks of ninety-year old walls.
Winter snows or summer thunders, welcomed by the hands
Of the little congregation carving livings off the land.

Simple folks from miles around, no matter what their views,
Came to pray and sing in chorus, as they sat upon the pews
Of that little church at Taiban, where the Lord would come to call,
In birth and death and in between, his message was for all.

From cowboys on the ranges to the folks who tended stores,
The strongest men were humbled when they entered through its doors.
When loved ones got their calling, and the last respects were paid,
The bell would toll remembrance, and perhaps an organ played.

Blessed be the ones who gather, for to them whose trails directed;
Just a solitary tribute from a house that faith erected.
For among the waving gramma grass, a sentinel remains;
The little church that watches over Taiban on the plains.

Bob Bird

"Dawn"

When it's early in the morning,
and the sun is coming out
The peacefulness, quiet and beauty
let you know what life is all about.

The stillness of this time of day
is always so special to me.
When I look out over the mountains,
the great imagination of God is so easy to see.

There's the pinks, the blues, the violets
together they beautifully contrast.
But as the sun moves on, their like life in itself,
they fade and are gone way to fast.

But the stillness of those few moments
when the world slowly starts to wake
Is one great and incredible pleasure
that God was so careful and considerate to make.

Aynnett Booth

Guiding Light

For it is written, that seasons of the weather will always change,
And the World will forever spin;
For God will forgive us of our sins.

For it is also written;
With each day that goes by,
The love I have for you will never die.
Always growing, burning bright,
Like the stars of the night.
For in these stars you can see,
The story of my love for thee.

For Destiny has come to pass,
And my prayers have been answered at last.
The future is so bright,
For in your heart resides, my guiding light.

So when there is no hope to be found,
And darkness is all around;
You need not look far for insight.
Just close your eyes and hold me tight,
For inside you rests my heart, my GUIDING LIGHT.

Keith Phillips

"... And When I Dream"

My heart trembles as I touch your lips,
 and trace your features with fingertips
Your warm breath upon my hand...
 your every wish is my command!
Behind closed eyes your image is clear,
 through memory, I find you, and hold you near
And dare not open - not even for a tear...
 for fear you should vanish, and disappear
And should I wake and find you gone...
 find I have dreamed, and dreamed alone
Pray let me sleep and wake me not!
 ...lest you be a mirage, and soon forgot
But should I wake and find it true...
 that I have not dreamed, and it is you
Pray let me wake and never sleep...
 ...lest you be immortal, and mine to keep!

Debra Evans

Mixture Of Life

You took my life—mixed it with laughter.
And, turned into love.
You took my fears, sprinkled it with strength
And, turned it into faith.
You took my tears, added an ounce of Joy
And, turned them into hope.
You took my doubts, added a dash of courage
And turned it into trust.
So, with love, faith, hope and trust.
You took me, added yourself.
And, it became—US!

Jeanette Bancroft

The Unborn Poem

As if blood or tears were to touch the air
And twine in midsummers fresh non care...

Why have you not set yourself down
And in nimble eagerness brought forth a truce
In which once has settled mind in yours
Will from this time forever more
Touch each soul that dawdles near.

Not ever shall this come about
But still breathing in your soul doth rot
Never seeing light
Nor touching lips to breathe to conscious minds
But alas
Endlessly plaguing you in time
Of eternal forgetful moments of remorse.

Many a day you slip in time
To a collectors place where treasures are stored
You seek to grasp one line, one phrase
Of the ever forgotten phantom
That strips away your guilt of delay.

Karla Chrisman

Longing

What can I say, what can I do
When everyday I live, I'm lost without you

I miss your touch, I miss your kiss
And all I have are memories of yesterday's bliss

Not long ago you were holding me tight
It was just us two on that beautiful night

How can I say, how much I want you back

So I'll say I love you and hope you love me too
And we can be together just me and you.

Bonnie Hardy

It's Time to Let Go

God gave you to us but a moment ago
And we welcomed you with open arms
We nurtured you, cared for you, loved you so
And were enraptured by all your charms.

You learned to crawl, and walk and run
It was a joy to see
Like the blossoming of a beautiful bud
Happening so beautifully.

Your flower of youth is open now
Your colors are vibrant and pure
We see you for the truth you are
Honest, sincere and sure.

And if we could count just one special thing
That made us so proud of you
It was that you loved every single human being
With all the whole heart of you.

It's time to let go - to let you move on
There's much to explore and to see
And no one wishes you greater success
Than your daddy and Little Old Me....

Kathryn Trnian Koler

Friends

Some people are treated differently
and yet nobody knows;
That they are equal in quality
but sometimes fail to show.

The hurt and pain they're going through is very hard to bare;
but many people look at them, and fail to even care.

Even though they may look different, or attitude quite rude;
we should give a friendly smile and help to ease the mood.

Sometimes others just need a friend to help them feel much better;
or sometimes it would be as kind just to send a letter.

So be a friend to someone special and go that extra mile;
you'll feel much better when you turn and look to see
them smile.

Erin Plemons

Time Be Done, Start Anew

Nights of unrest, horrors and pangs,
And yet she wept.
Brutalized, mentally physically.
Made a choice.
Released herself from guilt, unjust guilt.
Long nights of helplessness, thought a change
But disillusionment and ignorance claimed another tear.
Correspondence a blessing a wanting.
To receive to fulfill, all emotions subsided for brief words.
Unsettled, reward a small compensation for ones sanity.
Start anew, forget past pain, come to terms with failure.
Content metaphysical endurance to prevail.
Show of arms in defiance of all previous oppressors.
Thine has come to prosper.
Be real in a material world.

Daniel Stokes

Untitled

My husband, my love,
You are everything anyone could hope for,
Everything a woman could dream about,
And you are mine, my husband, my love.

Jill S. Cushing

Tears

You have to strain your ears,
To hear the sounds of silent tears.
Doesn't anyone want to hear my fears.

Amanda Merrow

The Comforter

When the days are long and dreary;
And your feeling weak and weary;
Lift your eyes to God and pray;
He'll give you strength to face each day.

No matter how alone you feel;
The Father's love for you is real.
Perhaps your heart is filled with grief;
He'll give you everlasting peace.

He knows all your hurts and cares;
So take them to the Lord in prayer.
Though you're burdened with deep sorrow;
He'll give you hope to greet the morrow.

His loving arms are open wide
And longs to bring you to His side.
Under His wings safe and secure;
He'll give you love forever more.

Janet Lee

"Epitah"

Tomorrow would have been your 75th Birthday
And your passing last September 13, left me
feeling lonely, for you're my true love!
Even though, we have nine grandchildren
I feel, as nobody lives in our home,
and hope your eternity is more peaceful
than loneliness I feel without you.
We had a good life, together, poor, but
honest, as our six children graduated
from College with their degrees, and married.
I hope the parents around the world
could have done the same.
The world would be enjoying, its population,
instead of families; worrying against one another.
Rest in Peace, until I, your husband,
will came, and rest beside you, Again!!!

Joseph S. Kish

Why Die In War

I see happiness, sadness delight,
anguish, bliss, anger, and more.
I wish I could not see the corpses we make
the death of family and of friends.
Hearing the death of those none can see.
The fright in the child's eyes when
the thunder claps.

The anger that glints in one's eye.
We see, hear, and experience
all in one lifetime
The news tells us of all the war and death.
Why do we fight those who can be
our friends and take one's treasure: FREEDOM

Why do we isolate ourselves from others?
They are of mankind, God's creation.
We wish not to see the corpses we leave.
They say they do not care.
They are too frightened and seek
refuge from the truth
Shall we die in war or peace. You decide.

Ellen Clark

The Artist's Perfect Touch

Nature awakes with a determined decree
Announcing spring with her dynamic glory;
She has broken free from the blast
Of winter's dismal prison clasp!

Spring periodically evolves a treacherous scene
When billows of black angry clouds convene;
They pour forth flood which clasp
The earth with a torrential grasp!

But as the furies of the sky become peaceful and quiet
A cloak of solitude reunites;
Soft, clean breezes whistle tunes of delight
Rustling young, tender leaves as through with foresight.

Nature's ultimate gift can now be fully seen
In trees and grasses with shades of green;
She has painted these with her artistic hand
Leaving the earth with a new fresh carpet,
colorful and grand!

Katherine Gant Maxwell

Life Goes On

Another child,
Another past

Another gone,
The pain will last

Today in this world too many lives are at stake,
Tomorrow another heart will break

Growing changing never the same,
In our hearts children they will remain

Another dream shattered by carelessness.
Then we open our eyes and see a new light as we realize
Life goes on.

Amy Keller

Soul Mates

To each of us God gives to us a soul mate
Another person who to us we are joined
By a silver thread that stretches between us
To join us at our very souls

So many people spend their whole life looking
For their soul mate pulling on that silver string
Yet never finding the very thing they seek the most
So they give up and take what ever comes along

Most stop trying because they don't believe anymore
It's just a story someone made up it can't really be true
But in there souls is an emptiness they can not fill
They feel half not whole yet they don't know why

Then one day when all seems lost and they feel life is over
They may just get to meet their soul mates
Most just go on though because they think this can't be true
Some of the few lucky ones, like me, recognize there mate like I did you.

Jacqueline L. Fegley

Friendship

Like the sun, it will rise and set
Wisp away into the wind, if you let.
It can provide some light in to the darkest days
Changing your life in good or bad ways.
Like a boat, it can crash and sink,
Or be rescued in a way you would never think.
But I think that it is more like the ocean waves
Mostly calm, but choppy on certain days.

Julia Marcella

"Reflection"

I cannot let the autumn pass without remembering by-gone things;
Apostrophes in English class..stars with midnight wings,
Neighbors in the living room...dropped by to "sit a spell",
A thresher spewing golden grain—the cattles' steamy smell.
A lamb, too weak to trust its' legs—a bon-fire (outdoor fun),
A stove-cooked meal at supper time and "haying" almost done.
A handle on a back-yard pump, a rooster's daybreak crowing;
A school bell's ring— a clarion sound, and cattle softly lowing.

The rain on roof—the frantic wind, the snow as high as fences,
Mittened hands, a heated brick...scarved heads (a child's defenses)
Where are they now, life's token joys? Possessions of the years
Or were they fragments of reality, buried too deep for tears?
NOT LOST...I often bring them back, and view them one by one.
The haze of forgetting...the sting of remembering!
And the ebb of life's tide...Mostly done.

Elaine Dekker Bryant

The Restored

The words that are spoken in truth by a slave,
Are more powerful than lies spoken by those who have gold,
For God can make his servants be brave,
But the greedy, alone, can never be bold.

Those who have faith are restored by His might,
But those who lack it are left incomplete and unwhole,
For the trusting in heart are given their sight,
But the hearts of the impure are angry and cold.

So we who are restored by His love,
Shall live our lives as slaves to His grace,
Then someday we'll move on to heaven above,
And see the glory of His beautiful face.

Erin Denham

Conscience

Thoughts scurry in my mind.
Are they the same? Or of a different kind.
Pieces of people that go right to the soul.
Those are the pieces that make me whole.
Happiness is always deep in my heart.
Sadness is what takes up a very large part.
Laughter is what helps me stay sane.
Knowledge is what I need to gain.
I'm a leader. I am one.
Then there's followers, there are some.
There is beauty hidden inside.
Some can't see it, but I don't mind.
There are things I tend to hide.
Then there's guilt when I had lied.
Life is often a game.
If you mess up, things won't be the same.
I'll try to do my best!
Is God giving me a test?
The answer must be YES.
Then the conclusion is to confess...

Bethany R. Dornberger

A Family Is...

A family is a group of people who care for one another
They need not be related, to love just like a brother.

Through thick and thin, good and bad, they always stick it through
No matter what the problem is, they all know what to do.

A simple pat, a loving hug, and then a chance to say
"I know what you are going through", makes the problem go away.

And then a bond begins to form, as strong as it can be
And that, my friend, is what it takes, to be a family.

Janet M. Cash

Ghost Lover

You aura of presence is upon me, day and night;
I yearn for your touch and sweet smile;
Visions of your strength embracing me until I can no longer resist;
Your delectable kisses are ever so powerful;
I have reached an unspeakable height.
Where are you, ghost lover?
Who are you, ghost lover?

Kitty Allen

My Bunny Rabbit, Squirrel And Butterfly

They scamper, run and all but fly the breeze and sun
are with them as one. Shouts of joy, peels of laughter an
occasional harsh word float in the air, fleet feet running
jumping, bike peddles racing, faces sweating. One minute
power rangers the next basketball superstars nothing seems
to them unreachable or too far, best of all by far is they are
mine. Rhymes and hand games that boggle my mind, double
dutch, wall ball oh how easy to remember them small, one
like a bunny rabbit so shy but ever so sly, one like a squirrel
always in a whirl, the other my butterfly so very free much
like me, very best of all they belong to me. Comrades in play
as only 2 brothers and a younger sister can be through my eyes
only love can be, they belong to me. Mom Mom, Mom Mom
overwhelmed by three each lovingly saying look at me
look at me, how lucky I am they belong to me.

Carol Miller

Life's Struggle

Your struggle may start some early morn
As a baby you struggle to be born
You struggle for air to stay alive
You struggle daily just to survive
You struggle to grow and try to talk
You struggle to crawl and eventually walk
You struggle to win when you compete
You struggle to cope when the answer's defeat
You struggle with ideas and emotions you feel
You struggle with what to tell or conceal
You struggle with trials of strife and sorrow
You struggle with worries of the outcome tomorrow
You struggle with memories out of the past
You struggle with time - it flies by fast
You struggle as you take your last breath
You struggle to escape the angel of death
Your struggle is over in this life to keep
Your struggle ends now in Eternal sleep

Elaine Slaight

"This Pain In My Heart"

This pain in my heart goes along way back.
As a child dealing with fears and insecurities
and all the things I lack.
As an adult this pain grew stronger and stronger
But I chose to survive, this cannot continue any longer!
I've always been a trusting soul, looking for love,
acceptance, and respect I felt I deserved.
My husband and children, are what I'm about.
And failure of any kind in this area, leaves me empty,
and full of doubt.
I wish I had more to give to the people I love,
For at times, with all that I give, it seems its just not
enough.
And now, as I grow old, and try to go on.
This pain in my heart, won't leave me alone.

This pain in my heart is like an old friend
It reminds me always, there will be no end.
So when you see me smiling or telling a joke
Just remember deep down inside, this pain in
my heart is keeping me a float.

Debra Babins

Seaview

On the waterfront the cool breeze breathes a spirit of tranquility,
As a rippling wave lazily caresses the sparkling sands.
Only to recede again and be overtaken by another,
To lose its identity in that entirety of blue
Which meets the morning sky in a giant panorama of wonder.
The fearless flight of a tern is detected as he dips low,
The call of a gull pierces the calm of the early waters.

As the setting sun suggests the closing of day,
Another scene is set on the stage of the sea.
The flaming red globe is enhanced by wispy clouds
Cluttering, en masse, all the powder blue background.
Then the first star peeks and prepares for the next act.

As the curtain of night envelopes all the principal characters,
Myriads of shimmering stars beam and dance on the waters.
As the breaking of each wave, splashing the slippery rocks,
Alone echoes this tale of life!
Intermittent flashes of light signal to all the crossing vessels,
While the glistening moon chuckles during this magnificent scene.
The solitary spectator enjoys the enriching performance,
While the Producer is applauding the result!

June F. Banfe

Confessions Of True Identity

Months willfully wander through me,
As do visions of a mythical man never seen.
He spoke from afar hesitating softly,
Bearing confessions of true identity.

Concealed within immortal decades,
His emotions indecisively cascade.
An innocent child resigned at infancy,
Now desires him without illusive irony.

Turbulent years brought no remorse,
Experiencing him is a steadfast force.
A little girl's imagination perpetually ages,
Inquisitive she speaks, no answers, empty pages.

What thoughts does his mind possess?
Passions rage seeping through my pale flesh.
Seconds pass as years, throbbing hearts quiver,
Graciously gliding eyes blend together.

His intense face a mirror image of mine,
Silence is bliss, a rendezvous in time.
Destiny's one gift, a longed for wish,
My father he is, our fears vanquish.

Janice W. Schramm

Blessed As You Are

You are not alone,
As God awaits by the moon to comfort your thoughts.
Heal your soul,
before you mend the pain of a lost heart.
Those astray will again return by the light of the stars,
and guidance of our lord.
He will return.
Do you see?
Can you feel it?
A star appears in your name,
as God holds you in his arms.
He lifts his head slowly,
as if to say,
in his name he has blessed you.
Blessed with so much, yet still so little.
Return it to him, as he will to you.

Annie Parr

Race For The Sunrise

I made it!
As I turn the corner
In my pleasant rush
It blinds me with its ethereal beauty

Climbing up over the horizon
A magnificent sight it is
An orange ball ascending
Spewing a collage of blues, pinks and purples

Waking the world with its power
The blinding beauty forces its way
Into my sleepy eyes
What a gift our sight is to see such a spectacle

As if to tease my watchful gaze
It playfully seeks partial refuge
Under the cover of clouds
But it cannot hide completely

Even the water takes its colors
Like a pallet of brilliance now in corals and yellows
Majestically spilling over a waking landscape
It fills my senses with hope for all new days

Diane Lynne Stewart

One Rose For My Casket Spray

I'm here alone most of the day,
As I watch the trees as they swing and sway.
There's not much to do, and I've only one thing to say.
Just give me one rose for my casket spray.

Most people would want a dozen roses,
But it takes only one, to brighten my day.
So grant me this one wish,
And give me one rose for my casket spray.

Roses of many colors,
That we see along the way,
But one red rose will do for me.
So just give me one rose for my casket spray.

As I go on through life,
Walking down God's lighted pathway.
Remember when He calls me home,
Just give me one rose for my casket spray.

Bessie Lucille Medlock Cockfield

"How Can We Live"

We live in a world where everything seems bad.
As if people can't come out of always being sad.
We live in a society where everyone says they're right.
We live in a society where everyone has to fight.
We live in a place where kids don't know right from wrong.
A place where you can't even hear the church bells dong.
We live in a world where the thing is to keep killing.
And we can barely hear all the children crying.
We live in a world where everyone is so blue.
We live in a world where you never hear thank you.
We live in a world where you never hear about all the good.
We live in a world where it seems the bad is a should.
We live in a way that no one can understand.
We live in a way that when people look around all they can
see is land.
We are living in a place where people are starting to lose hope.
We are living in a place where people are starting to
disbelieve in the pope.
But if there is a hope we cannot lose then that has to be
our faith.

Chantel Boucher

The Price We Pay

The price of wisdom is death
As is the price of love
For every day we love, we die
Our souls given in whimsical fancy
Our hearts thrown to the wind
A return for that which we have given?
Never, and yet, perhaps
Another's soul to replace ours gone
Another's heart blown to us on that same wind
With the strength and courage to catch and hold it,
I believe the return too precious to know
And death and wisdom become worth the price we pay for love

Cassandra Wright

The Final Act

The day arrived when you came on stage and became an actor.
As mom held you in her proud arms looking at you with an unforgettable smile.
Years have come by and you've encountered many difficulties, yet you were strong enough to let them pass.
You never gave your role to any other human being, instead you brought yourself to a stage where no man had ever accomplished such many treasured moments.
But one day you were struck by a thunder from heaven which ended your career.
The lights turned off, the camera stopped rolling, and the action came to an end.
You stood on stage while making your mark, as the audience sat filled with awe.
We knew a production will never again show such talent and inspiration in our lives, but the memory of your presence will always be real in our healing hearts.
We are all still here cheering you on and keeping you alive in our heart, mind, and soul, as the curtains have come down on your final act.

Janina J. Panganiban

Helping Hand

"What's the fussing 'bout" said Annie Lee
as she opened her eyes, but she couldn't ask it.
She was lying stiff and the crying scared her
as she sat up slowly in her wooden casket.

The preacher's mouth turned to sulphur, he dropped
his bible and ran; most of us just withdrew.
But Lucille had felt half dead before; it was
not the first resurrected corpse she knew.

"I thoughts you was dead?" Lucille said as she helped
Annie out. Her hand was the last touch Annie felt.
From that day on she was shunned like a sinner,
for playing the cards in the hand that was give her.

The ship can't go back through the mouth
of the bottle, it's not the way through.
We can't unmarry or unbury a love; unburn the fire;
unyearn the desire; unwear the glove; or unwalk the shoe.

Is Annie alive? Well as far as we know.
And Lucille's still reaching to help those below.
We cannot cheat death, we can just make it kinder;
Next time we leave Annie Lee just like we find her.

David J. Berndt

Vulnerabilities Of A Child

As silent as the tear, she speaks, without saying a word
As sullen as a latent fear, she weeps, but her cries cannot be heard
Alone at night, she slumbers, encumbered with her thoughts
While her hope is non obtainable, and the trust inside her rots
He stares around the darkness, but not a light is shown
He waits for known security, but the doubt inside has grown
Safety is a fantasy, and love?
Its make believe.
The unreal thoughts of innocence, are all that he may need.
With claims of consciences, we tend to be aware
Our bodies absorb shock, and our jaws drop as we stare
The past remembers them, as the future may occur
It is to be certain, they are children we once were.

Jamie Wuthrich

Rumors

Like blood flowing through veins
As swiftly as a raindrop
Rumors can spread as heat through flames
There's no telling where they'll stop

Sometimes we hear what should not be heard
And at times see optical illusions
With just a hint of information
We perfect come wild conclusions

Rumors once started are hard to shake
They sure can rattle the roof
But they quietly disappear
When a listener asks for proof

If we overhear conversations
And depend on what we hear
We best insure we have facts
Before we put our mouths in gear

This is a rumor story
Please remember what it said
Lets get facts before we speak
Don't let a rumor spread

Clyde Sanders

Survival

Time is of the universe,
As that of man,
A distinguish element that will soon come to pass,
and that which shall be remembered is that which has passed.

Now try to remember a time in the past,
When we were as one, with one common goal and one common thought — that of SURVIVAL.
How could we have grown so blind and still hold so tight to our Holy Bible!
Even to one who doesn't hold so tight, to even Him, there is rendered day and night.

Now if this time could pass when we have grown so far apart,
Maybe then we could realize we hold the key to the world's SURVIVAL somewhere in our hearts.

Daniel L. Pounds

Coriolis Affect: K-Nine (K-Trey Perhaps)

Around and around she goes
The same direction the toilet flows
I often ask her but get some dumb response,
"If we move South of the Equator
Would the counter clock-wise pull be greater?"
How many curs, after adoption
Are given the option
To have a reversal of their universal?

Barbara Streeter

Shadows

Riding across the plain
As the late afternoon sun fall behind the Tetons,
I find myself in a constant shadow.
It is cool there. No sun in my eyes.
Seeing straight and clear my campsite to be -
off in the distance.

Out of the blue, "The Man" comes to pull me over.
Galloping along I say: "You are of no use here. Go away!"
He has vanished - into the shadows of his wanton mind.
Riding along with shadows behind me.

No water needed, my destination upon me.
I'll lick my lips when my goal is reached.
Lying before me are the swaying evergreens
and ample wood to warm me.
Antagonize me now and you'll be seeing -
my shadow behind thee.

James P. Sunderman Jr.

The Wild Hunt

I can almost feel the hounds, nipping at my heels
As they try to chase me down with supernatural zeal
In the chill night air, I can see my labored breath
I hear the master of the hunt screaming for my death
His voice instilling horror, terror within my breast
I must continue fleeing, there is no time for rest
The hounds continue howling, a chilling chorus of the night
Then the hunter adds his growl, adding incentive to my flight
I dare not turn around to see what I might find
I don't think I'd like to what is close behind
I wish this wasn't real, just a nightmare in my head
Just a dream from a fever, I'm still sleeping in my bed
But this is really happening the silver moon
Perhaps I'll get away if I don't get tired soon
Is the hunter having fun, I can almost feel his toy
Like some vicious little child and I'm his brand new joy
I wish to see the dawn, but its many hours still
But with the wild hunt at my back, I don't know if I will
In the hours before that dawn I know what it is fear
That the hunter will finally catch me and split my heart with his spear.

John O'Bryan

The Angels' Song

The Angels sing a song of sorrow
  As we live our lives of lies,
Marching off into tomorrow,
  Throwing blaspheme in God's eyes

The Dragon wakes from eternal slumber,
  Imprisoned in the hearts of men,
Raising its head to burn and plunder
  The cage that it is in.

Lord, who should I say has sent me?
Lord, who should I say has given me Life?
Lord, who should I say has sent me?
Lord, who should I say you are?

I AM!

What's right is wrong, what's wrong is right.
  Why do we even try?
I'm ready you meet my Maker,
  Are you ready to die?

Josh Morris

Life's Illusions

Life's Illusions pass me by
As winds of change and sands of time

Shift and blow, swirl and blind,
Take my sight and steal my mind.

The hearts a fire have turned to ice;
The roads of life are no longer nice.

Confusion rips by like a bat a night,
Wings all a flutter as you start with fright.

You don't know how, you don't know why,
But suddenly, you want to die.

Attitudes taken, insults received
Friends try to protect, only to deceive.

Love may blossom but pick the flower
And will it wilt or keep its power.

I stand alone, dreaming a dream
That passes me by through conscious stream.

Over the falls, into thin air
To cloud the mind, then fall like rain.

Erica Lynn Webel

Passage Of Time

My precious little baby, what did you dream
as you lay sleeping softly in a moonlight beam.

My sweet little child, where did you go,
when you took your first steps up on tipped-toe.

My dear little girl, how far did you run,
as you play with your friends in the summer sun.
With the passage of time, will my memories fade
to black and white photos and pictures you made.

I'll hold your hand now, I'll dry all your tears
I'll watch you grow up, all through the years.

My beautiful daughter, dancing away
you'll always be with me, my hearts where you'll stay.

Amy McSpadden

The Eagle

Oh beautiful eagle, so wild and free,
  as you soar through time, and space;
You thrill the hearts, of folks like me,
  with your majesty, and grace.....

You spread your wings, to cover the land,
  as you glide through the endless sky;
Protected by God's loving hand,
  while you rest, in your mountains, high.....

Oh wonderful eagle, so proud and strong,
  may you always fly free from care;
For, this world of ours, would seem so wrong,
  if we looked, and you weren't there.....

You're one of God's creatures, sent from above,
  to give beauty, where there is pain;
And fill our hearts, with joy and love,
  like the sunshine, after the rain.....

Oh majestic eagle, so brave and true,
  could we ask for anything more;
Than to see our symbol, against the blue,
  so close, to Heaven's door.....

Dorothy Howard Lamp

Peace And Harmony

Peace rules with the crown of harmony,
at his side, to guide him.
For the blind,
can see with love,
and the deaf,
can hear with joy.
If there's no way home,
you can still be happy.
The poor survive and to the rich a message,
Peace rules with the crown of harmony,
at his side to guide him.
The people of this wondrous place,
all deserve it, if you don't, don't feel the need,
to help.
Help itself needs time,
but time can work itself.
Caring is one thing, love is another,
so you know,
all the people deserve it.

Emily Locey

Whispering Wind

As I walk along and look above,
at that Colorado Sky.
That brightest blue I really love,
and watching the birds flying by.

Out to the west majestic and bold,
the Rocky Mountains crested with snow.
With Evergreens and Aspen with leaves of gold,
and places where Columbines and Tundra can grow.

The wind blows softly whispering to me,
as it gently touches my face.
Please open your eyes I would like you to see,
what people can do to this place.

Look down below where you walked on the path,
you will wake up immediately.
Paper and boxes and pieces of glass,
dropped by your people so carelessly.

Go back to your people tell them to change,
restore the beauty I helped make.
Pick up the trash from my mountain range,
and leave it intact for our children's sake.

Jacob Dutch Groothof

The Rivers Rage

The river travels down its well worn trail,
attacking its captivating walls, swallowing everything
in its path, swirling in a great tumult
towards a cascading fall, running down the face of the cliff,
swallowing its seething frothy fuel.

Sediment once stirred, now settles on the
water worn sandstone bottom,
effaced and covered by time.
Etchings of a trickling stream
ever widened by the ongoing battle against the bank,
its weapons, the captured.
Finally released from the tyrant current,
calming, no longer agitated by the serpent
full of rage, settling into an Estuary.
Once again rolling in a rhythm out to sea.

David Nemet

October Days

Now the season changes,
Autumn, is in our mist,
Now, the leaves are falling, fall, will now persist.

The leaves in all their rapture,
Their hues, of brown and gold,
All picturesque, in their beauty, now, that fall unfolds.

Memories will linger,
Of the fun, that has past,
Joy is in the making, for the days, yet to grasp.

The world, in all its beauty,
The season, now at hand,
Unfolds gradually before us, subduing, all of man.

The days, they are gentle,
So tranquil in their way,
Make note, of their passing, take heed in their display.

And time, as it does pass,
Appreciate what you do see,
October in all its splendor, displayed so beautifully...

Charles H. Jones

My Solitude

Entering the cool, dim woods
Awaiting time like a vigilant creature
The hush descends with anticipation
Of opening night on stage.

Creeping forward cautiously
The leaves crackle like popcorn
The low drone of forest sounds
Like air conditioners on a hot day.

Scintillating light flitting and flickering
As fireflies on a summer's evening
A stream, gently tumbles along
Like a curious, wandering explorer.

Venturing on, a radiant
Cathedral shaft of light
Shatters the stained glass foliage
Illuminating a clearing in the woods.

Swirling like the great Milky Way
In this sun-centered universe
Transported beyond time and space
In my retreat, my solitude.

Julie L. Sudler

The Fawn And Its Mother

As morning dawned gently upon the green forest,
Baby birds were soon to be heard from their cozy little nest.
As they chirped a fawn awoke from her peaceful rest.
She lay quietly beside her mother, as she felt
The sun's warm glow and the gentle breeze that had began to blow.
Suddenly her mother stirred, then her
Mother's loving voice was heard, "It is dawn,
So come, my fawn, and eat in the meadows
With me. Come for I shall lead the way,
So you shall not stray."
With these words the fawn arose, and
Followed her mother leaving behind the
Chirping of the baby birds.
So the mother deer led her fawn like a
Shepherd without fear.
And the little fawn trotted along knowing
That her mother was quite near.
So a mother is with her beloved child,
Making sure that all is secure as
They walk along their way.

Carey Lynette Bahr

To See

Swing, Swing
back and forth, back and forth, back and...
lonely eyes stare out
at naked hands groping blue silk sleeves.
the closeness of your breath is comforting.
soft earth envelops our bodies as
private lives become obscene thoughts.
back and forth...
the wind blows and seeds are planted,
petals fall and the sky's color
becomes that of the silk shirt,
and it rains on her.

Eyes close in disgust at
how she used to be,
and the swing blows...back and forth.

Abby Hoffmann

I Would If I Could

I would love to have climbed to the stars
Be alone and look down on the earth,
But that right is reserved for people so few.
For those of great wisdom and more noted birth.

I would love to have written great poems;
Express inner-most feelings and thought;
But those must be written by bards of repute
And words from an unknown's not sought.

A book with a theme of great depth and thought
I would write for great minds to peruse;
But reading the words I've put down on pages,
The thought uppermost, "What's the use?"

A beautiful painting, piano concerto,
Stories bringing tears to the eyes,
But none of these things am I able to do;
So I'll settle for, "Hey, that is nice."

Kathy Kendall

La Quinceanera

Leave your childhood behind they say,
Be more mature they say,
Act 35 they say
No way! I say:

Live life to the fullest and thank God every day
for giving me choices to live by each day.
To know when to say Yes!
and when to say No!
and know in my heart right from wrong.

To love and to give, to live and let live.
To look at the sky and the beauty all around,
and for my Dear Ones to feel oh so proud.

To accomplish all of my goals.
What more could I ask for?
And that's how it goes.

I still have a long way to go, to get where I'm going,
but I know where it's at and that's a fact.

So with God at my side and not losing faith.
I will continue my journey and He will determine my fate.

So give me a break!

Elvira Lugo Gonzalez

East Of Your Sunrise

I am happy here east of your sunrise,
Because I travel much to the north, south, west, and east.
I want to read your newest book of poems at sunrise,
And like an ancient religious believer,
I will turn my body facing east.

After all my travels I have stopped briefly east of your sunrise,
I feel content,
I smile at sunrise,
Maybe...I will remain here although it was not definitely my clear intent.

All my happiness comes from writing poetry,
(perhaps) you have the geniality for publishing poems,
Others really enjoy the pleasure of reading poetry,
All of us somehow love, work, and avoid the death of poems.

Jairo H. Nemocon

"The Cries Of A Woman"

I sit listening to the cries of a woman
Because she feels inside that she deserves
nothing but pain
Hopeless, full of pain, full of despair,
she cries
She cries out to a man, who is not listening
He has his own pain
He beats her, she cries, he leaves her,
she cries
Hooked on drugs, feeling useless, no self esteem,
she cries
Love for someone should not be greater than the love
you have for yourself
Bills are due, baby is gone, phone is off and
she cries
Terrorized, tortured, begging for mercy from her
perpetrator, she cries
I sit here wondering how could she take that pain and
my answer is this...

Kathy Cook

Best Friends

My friends and I travel by pack,
Because we do not lack,
You see,
We're best friends Meghan, Nicole, and me.
We go together better than ever,
Because no one can sever,
Or pull us apart.
We've been like that from the start.
We know to be forever loyal,
To each other, because if we're not it will spoil,
Our friendship you see,
The friendship between Meghan, Nicole, and me.
Together we have laughed and cried,
And even laid,
On the floor,
Talking about what's in store.
And that's the way we'll always be.
Best friends. Meghan, Nicole, and me.

Courtney E. Nelson

In Remembrance

Some little flowers aren't meant to bloom
With petals too soft, and fade too soon
And why the most beautiful flower of all
Will sometimes be, the first to fall
Just a shadow away, neath an angel's wing
A small flower waits, till God can bring
The face of an angel, truly God's work of art
For now just a tear, that lives in the heart

Della Noll

Just A Speck

There was two youngsters in a stew,
behind a bush just out of view.

On his porch an old hermit sat,
swatting at flies, all he could get.

"I saw him slay forty the other day!"
Our dads would slay us if they knew where we play.

They saw their dads heading their way,
and began to scream, "Go Away!"

Just then the old hermit saw them too,
and with one swat killed them through and through.

The youngsters began to cry, "Were Orphans,
hurry let's fly!"

They did not see the frog who hid,
under the bush where he lived.

"Not anymore," he replied as he rolled
in his tongue with a sigh.

Barbara Markel

My Scar

My Scar is not one you can see,
Believe it or not it's inside of me.
It's not the kind you make with a knife,
Not the kind that scars your physical life.
The scar is deep in my heart and soul,
I try to heal it, To console,
But all that's left is a big wide hole.
Inside me is the tear
That leaves me in great despair.
For help is what it asks for, For love, For hope
I help it, Love it, and fill it with hope,
I bandage it with a true love rope.
It grows smaller and smaller and smaller still,
To leave an opening for love to fill.
My pain and anguish are almost gone,
The thing I have been waiting for so long.
But low and behold
There it still may be,
Because my emotions will
Always be a part of me.

Kristina M. Parker

Come In From The Cold

Come in, my friend, come warm beside the fire.
Bequeath the world to the wanton frenzied hoard.
Forget the cold, and hold to something higher.

What games we play! We, servants of desire!
O'er things of sand our thoughts and souls outpoured!
Come in, my friend, come heal beside the fire.

You hear the sound? So sings the earthly choir.
They cadence on a distant, dissonant chord.
Forget their song, and hold to something higher.

To what grand end do fellow men conspire?
I speak the truth: They have their just reward.
Leave off, my friend, come warm beside the fire.

Be still with me. I have what you require.
Put down your weight, and touch the two-edged sword.
Forget the cold, and hold to something higher.

Come. Look upon my Strength and my Supplier.
The way, the truth, the life: The worthy Lord.
Be close, my friend; come warm beside His fire.
And treasure with me the hold of something higher.

Elliott A. F. Marchand

Sunset

When the sun has finally set
Beyond the shadowed horizon,
You may feel that the darkness has encaptured you
And the night has cast you in.
But know that the sun will soon rise again.
And with it, the heavens will be radiant
with the most vibrant hues that illuminate the dawn.

Though the dew may form, and the fog may settle deep within the valleys,
Do not dwell long here.
Cast the night away and look upon me.
Though I may not be by your side -
I am there in your heart.
And I will live again in your memories and in your laughter.

So look now at the glow on the horizon and remember me.
Not through sadness and tears,
But through the colors in the sky
That light upon your face -
Like a smile, a touch, or an embrace;
And know that I am with you.

Christi Leigh Robbins

The Definition Of Black

The Color of Me
Black: The darkest of all colors.
Yet my mind shines as brilliant as
the sun when captivating words flee from my lips
And when elegant written passages
drip from my pen

Black: Gloomy, depressing
Nay!
I am uplifting and courageous in the
sight of suppression
All because the color of me

Black: Evil, wicked
To the contrary, black is beautiful
and compassionate when hatred stomps
equality
All because the color of me

Justice is blind
But it sees the color of me all to well

Black is simply what it appears to be
The opposite of white

Kendall Ivy

Escape

Lights by the millions high above the trees,
Blend into the wood pile, roll up your sleeves.
Where is time? Nowhere to be found!
Just the lovely meadows which beauty surrounds.
The glow of a campfire late at night,
quite unlike the glare of dirty street lights.
There is no pain, no worry or despair,
Only peace and tranquility everywhere.
Up in the morning, coffee in hand.
Off to the job to meet the demand.
Up here the coffee tastes so sweet.
No errands to run, no dead lines to meet
So after a vigorous week on the job,
Come up here with me, but please, leave the mob.

Clarence Innocci

Let The Thistles Grow

Daisies wave in the field nudged by a gentle breeze
Bluebells shyly nod their heads, pansies shiver in mossy beds
Roses bloom and hide their thorns, a mother cries when her child is born
Her tears soon turn to joy, as she holds her baby boy
But not all seeds get to know the warmth of a sunny day
Before they're barely in the ground, they are tossed away
Torn from God's bouquet

Let the thistles grow
They're worth more than we'll ever know
Let them grow, let them thrive, they hold great beauty deep inside
They need love, they need time, for their flowers to unfold
Let the thistles grow
They're worth more than we'll ever know

It may not have been your plan to reap the seeds you sow
Life hangs on by the whim of man, stay the willful hand
Life hangs on by the whim of man
Let the thistles grow

Anne Penna

And Like A Flower

The flower is born in the springtime when everything is new,
Born under the comfort and warmth of the dew.
It takes a long while before it can really grow,
Long after the winter, long after the snow.

The flower too will live through summer breeze,
With shade from buildings, rocks and trees.
The flower still will continue to grow,
It waits until it has something to show.

Finally one day it will come into bloom,
With colors and smells to rid you of gloom.
It stays pretty and sweet until one day,
The petals will end on the ground where they lay.

Soon things will change to be much colder,
The flower by then will look so much older.
Soon the magnificent plant will wilt,
Its stem with all its glory becomes tarnished by silt.

The days become shorter and cooler are things,
It seems that nature holds the flower's life by strings.
And like a flower will say good-bye,
and like a flower you too will die.

Jannell Colton

Two Candles

Two candles burning in the night.
Both identical, orbiting, tied together in flight.
Indistinguishable one from the other,
Known only by feel. They are love and hate.
Equal in practice, equal in zeal.

I know them well and both flames burn white hot.
One lights, the other is lit.
Tell me if you can, from the description given,
which is which, and the sins unforgiven.

Kevin Conard

Graduation Good-Byes

We've learned a lot, and some we've known
Yet in these years, we've truly grown
Good times with friends, we often shared
It's great to know, they always cared

This is good-bye, but wait I'll see you later
It may not be here, but somewhere greater
But take with you faith, hope, and love
And shine like the bright stars above.

Charlette Peterke

Untitled

Four little bunnies under a mound of dried grass
Bounded out of a hole as my Lawn Mover passed.
They ran a short way and looked for each other.
How they all wished they could find their mother!
I caught one little bunny - for she was too slow.
I don't mean to keep her - I then let her go.
As soon as the four feet touched the ground
She took off with a great big bound.
I said "Now little bunny I'll grant you a pardon —
But please from now on stay out of my garden!"

June M. Lokenvitz

Marcus

You came in
borne on angel's wings
so sudden yet quiescent
like moonlight flooding a dark room
through gossamer curtains

It's kismet
as the sun would rise and set
when you took your first breath
thirty and two summers ago
so your heartbeat would syncopate with mine

You've walked through fire
like a wounded soldier you survived
the tears you shed I catch with my hands
and turn them to rain
to quench your weary soul

Among the bluegrass of spring
we'll share the secrets the cardinals sing
and canoe the white waters of every stream
as a leaf ever sailing smooth
silently running over deep

Apple V. Acebes

Teddy Bear

{I used to have one of those (sigh)}
I watch him squiggle and squirm (squirm wormies)
brainfreezed eyes glazing into my
I watch him (watch) laugh (ha ha ha ha)
maniacal laughter, his - at me, me!
my folded (folded) hands (hands) behind my back (back; backed, backing, backwards)
folded behind my back
with a razor
(which, am I correct in saying, that very razor attempted to serve you so long ago?)
yes, yes, I am...GUILTY OF THAT CHARGE!
a razor grasped in my piggy fingers
slice him down his fuzzy-wuzzy
tummy-wummy
bloody cotton balls spill onto me like
infected sperm (do you know where babies come from?)
POP! POP!
out go his eyes like buttons (buttons...pop pop)
no more staring, the teddy bear is dead (DEAD).

Amy M. Braden

Believe

You must reach to touch a rainbow;
You must climb to catch a star.
Go out on a limb to follow your heart-
If you stretch, you'll fly far.
You must put yourself at risk
If e'er you are to gain.
Let obstacles not slow you
As you strive toward your dream.

Erin Donelan

Mama Ain't Tired

Mama may we have a longer
breakfast, with toast and jam and
may we have fresh squeezed juice
MAMA AIN'T TIRED.

Mama may you take us all
to the shopping mall for
our new school clothes and
may we stop at the video store
MAMA AIN'T TIRED.

Mama may you read us a
bed story that never ends
and may you tuck us in
before we go to sleep
MAMA AIN'T TIRED.

Mama you are asleep and we can not wake you.
Your face is so pale and gloomy and friends
and relatives are all around you.
People are crying and sad mama, as
they see you lying so still. Wake up mama....
MAMA AIN'T TIRED.

Angela M. Williams

Voices from Yesterday

Surely! The divine plow of life
breaks ground here in my bosom
the deep trace of joy;
furrow watered a thousand times
with the fresh water of illusion
that flows from the soul

How many seeds of gaiety I sowed!
Singing to the fair morning and singing
to the dark night, while my song uncombed
the wind and my voice got tangled in the stars

Over there, in the valley, the music of the river
sang its tenderness with gentle voice
and the earth smiled with the breeze of love.
Oh yes! How much love there was in its womb!
And how much music in the river's mouth!

Today time has emptied the sand of oblivion,
and in my soul, while joy blossomed yesterday
today; only the flower of reminiscence grows
stirred by the hidden song of a voice
that disappears in the distance of long ago

Jaime Martinez-Salguero

Helen Keller

Helen,
Bright, strong, confused, intelligent,
Friend of Anne Sullivan and Louis Braille,
Lover of writing, spelling, and to be able to hear,
Who felt disturbed, alone, and once in a while she would feel happy
that she accomplished something very important,
Who needed a person to understand her point of view, a teacher to help
her succeed with her goals to live as a normal person, and someone
to love her as she was,
Who gave Anne Sullivan by teaching Helen what she needed to
know for
her own good and in every day life, her own time during the
war, and also gave her time to speak in presentations,
Who feared not to understand, to be trapped in her own world that was
full of darkness, not to be able to help other people like her,
Who would of liked to see words, to see with her eyes instead of
having to picture things, and to be like everyone else,
Resident of Tuscumbia Alabama,
Keller,

Adrienne Casto

The Precious Present

We are allowed small pleasures throughout our lives
Brilliant sunsets, naps on rainy days,
unexpected compliments, new found friends,
truth in a world of make-believe.

We are also allowed desolate times
moments of question, misunderstandings,
trying with no support, struggling to no avail,
seeking and not finding.

We are given three special places to go
a past- to remember, to retreat to, to learn from
a future- to strive for, to wish for, to hope for
a present- to live in, to love in, to share in.

We search for a lifetime to find the one who can share
these things with us
only to find that we've known "the one" all along
we are given the chance to enmesh two lives, two families.

And once upon a lifetime,
we experience a love that grows with each passing day.
And we become aware that we truly have been given
The Most Precious Present

Amy Christine Carson

Faith

Dedicated to Margaret Tarter

A streak of red seen from the flash of an eye
Brings laughter and wonder along with a sigh.
The heavens have smiled upon this troubled soul
Gracing my life and making it whole
With the sweet sound of singing, enraptured delight,
Of a beautiful cardinal about to take flight.
When everything seems to be falling apart,
When answers are wrought with fears of the heart,
This beautiful spirit flies down from the sky
And tells me that God in His heaven will try
To make all the pain and questioning cease
And bring back the love that true faith can increase.
So I cherish the bird as it spreads bright red wings,
And with its sweet song, my heart also sings.
We all need some guidance and help from on high.
When life is confusing, we still have to fly
Away to the future to see what life holds
And hope that an angel our lives will enfold.
The cardinal's my conscience, it guides me back home.
With him on my side, I'm never alone.

Beverly Schilling

The Search

"Yo! Sleepyhead! Have you seen my
brother or sister?" Asked the pen.
"Huh? Are you talking to me?"
"Yeh, I'm talking to you!
Did you hear me?
Have you seen my brother or sister?
"Who are you anyway?"
"Well, dah, I'm a pen. You didn't know that?"
"No, I didn't know that. You're a pen?
How could a pen be talking to me?"
"I don't know. Man, you got some bad breath.
Would you like some ink to refresh your breath?"
"No, no thank you."
"Well, I've got to go tell my
Mechanical Pencil Dad and my felt tip point
Mom that I can't find my brother or sister."

Ashley Raines

Dost Thou Hear Me?

I reach for life with an anxious hand,
But all I hear is a discordant band -
Blatant trumpets and throbbing drums -
I wait for music which never comes.

O where are the sweet notes of the lilting flute,
The melodic tenderness of the sensuous lute?
The rapturous lift of the violin,
Oh dear God! When will life for me begin?

Life, with its pieces all in place-
Someone with love written o'er his face.
A home of laughter, love, repose -
Of quiet strength - as twilight grows.

Lord, is this too much for me to ask?
Must constant turmoil be my task?
I've vied so long with sorrow and strife -
Please lord - make a symphony out of my life!

Doris Quaglio

Aura

Oh,
but do you not know what it is to get lost in the beat,
The silent time...?
I am a mime in this ever-so-deep one-dimensional world
To see seems a crime
like garish happy music
"I got lost I didn't know I'm not too pretty but I ain't slow"
Sluggish getting lost,
and loving saturation
inverted maturation
"first and foremost," my English teacher said,
"poets play with language."
And sometimes birthright names are a mistake;
I watch her fry phrase in a dry, raw wok
and there is nothing playful in her unfluid struggle,
there is not a smile teasing the overused skin of her face.
Who has the monopoly?
There is none. Not for tears, nor cooking oil.
And be I, somehow, the happiest to walk this place,
it wouldn't matter what's writ on my face.

Jenny Johnson

Look Deeper

You see me and I see you,
but do you really?

Do you really see me or do you only see your impression of me?

Look deeper,
Do you see my mind, my brain, and my intellect or do you just see what you want to see?

Look deeper,
Do you see my personality, my hopes, my dreams, or do you just see something that is strange and unfamiliar that you can in no way relate to or understand?

In other words can you see yourself?

Anthony J. Dennis

Sister Of Praise

Behold my Sisters of Praise
Chanting with a heart of love
Full of beauty and grace
The apple of my eye
Guiding their children before the savior's face
Giving and Sharing a measurement unseen
Full of laughter
These Sisters I have Redeemed

Joyce P. Bolton

A Dream

Forget about the days when it's been cloudy.
But, don't forget your hours in the sun.
Forget about the times you've been defeated.
But, don't forget all the victories you've won.
Forget about the mistakes that you can't change now,
But, don't forget all the lessons you've learned.
Forget about the misfortunes that you've encountered.
But, don't forget all the times your luck has turned.
Forget about the times when you've been lonely,
But, don't forget all the friendly smiles you've seen.
Forget about the plans that don't seem to work out right.
But, don't forge to always have a dream.

Antonie Martin

Sadness

I am crying
But each of my tears
is a drop of nectar
Offered to that group of poor people
Buzzing in the hive of inequality.

I am ringing the bell
But each stanza of my oration
is a cry of justice hurled for all those people
locked by the jailer.

I am singing without harmony, without cadences
I am the poet of sadness, but my sadness is the spring
Where all the escapes from the prison of inequality
Will come to quench their thirst
In the days of torrid heat.

Enock Guillaume

After Death

We are no longer nature's children
but her masters.
What else when chaos
draws all forces inward
to shape a single leaf.
Let no one say we did not fight until the last.
Of course I'm not a spy!
The enemy has spies.
I am a scout!
"Never surrender."

No sheath shall hold what finds its
home in flesh.
"Where is it written that beasts must
cause pain?"

Donnie Dunn

Good-Night Mama

I will close my eyes and try to sleep
but I am so cold.
Will you hold me, mama?
Will you please just hold me while I shiver?
Will you hold me tight?
Will you hold me long?
Will you hold me 'til I stop?
You always said God don't like ugly.
I bet God won't like a cold hearted sinner like me either.
God Mama,
I am so cold.
Hold me.
Please just hold me while I shiver.
Just hold me 'til I sleep.

Christal Dawn Henderson

Confession

You know darling, I never thought I'd say this,
But I need to relieve my pain.
I want you to know that I love you.
No, I am not going insane.

My love is like a rosebud
Blooming for infinite years.
It grows and grows forevermore
Watered by my tears.

I cry because of you, my love;
Because you are not mine.
Another heart has stolen you,
But still my love will shine.

Will shine for all the world to see,
Like a candle in the night;
Pushing out the darkness,
Bringing in the light.

And so I say goodbye my dear.
Of this I am quite sure,
That my love for you my sweetest one
For eternity will endure

April Mornings

Untitled

Some say life is happy, some say life is true
But I'll tell it from the words of me and not the words of you
I always seemed to talk, but my words seemed to be dead
Meaningless and unheard thoughts were all I ever said
My life began to get lonely, my life began to get sad
So I turned my thoughts into words to keep from getting mad
Now people read these words and say that they are good
But all they seem to see are "words" and
still I'm not understood
I tell them to go beyond the words, then they
think it's some kind of mystery
Go beyond the words and thoughts and you'll
find it's only me
Not all will understand, not all will see me more
For I am just one grain of sand on an endless
sandy shore
Some say life is happy, Some don't know what to do
Some think I am strange or odd but it's not
me it's only you

Candace Lorraine

Love And Loneliness

She thought she was doing the right thing, giving herself away,
But in the end all it gave her was sadness and pain.

He said he would never leave her and always be by her side,
She quickly found out she was living in a lie.

He was so sweet, she couldn't say no,
There was a special place where they wanted to go.

It was a wonderful night for her, but in his eyes it just didn't look
true, For in the morning was only a rose by her pillow, she knew that
they were through.

She does not know where he is now, and she doesn't really care,
Her life has now moved on slowly, to love again she only dares.

But now and then, she can't help wonder if he's still using his lies,
But she will never forget him, no matter how hard she tries.

Amy Barker

My Loved

There is a line, between you and I
But it is a line that only love cannot see
Between your life and mine
Our lives could be one
But you see the line
If only you could see how much I loved you
But you have hurt me, torn my heart in two,
Because you all too clearly saw the line
and you have made it stronger, on your own will

Why should it matter?
Who really cares?

I would rejoice if you broke the line
if you listened to your heart
if you heard the song, ever so sweet, that my soul was singing
then your soul would be one with mine.

But, alas, you didn't listen
you laughed and mocked along with others,
etching an echo of love and a permanent mark,
a line,
in my heart

Christy Smith

This Is What I Think

I think about the good times...
but my thoughts are growing sad.
I think about the smiles, the tears;
I think about the minutes, the years.
This is what I think.
I think about the pictures you weren't in;
I think about the wrongs, the sin.
I think of the words that were never meant;
I think about the pain we were sent.
This is what I think.
I thought about visiting, day after day.
I wasn't sure if you'd hug me or turn me away.
What would it be like if we would have stayed?
Tearing apart, we wouldn't have paid.
This is what I think.
I prayed each day with my heart,
that our torn family could be one heart's part.
I think we can start from the bottom and rise to the top,
I just want all this bickering to stop.
I can honestly say, this is what I think.

Jeanine Patricia Dubois

The Promised Land

Many a kingdom have I seen,
But not a kingdom as great as this,
Different faces, places and cultures,
That blossom and keep it above the rest.

All her life, she has been raised on freedom,
Has embraced all that accept her laws and values,
A freedom that I dare not take for granted,
But one that I shall admire and cherish.

Mother Nature has blessed this land, our land,
Has given us great things and great places,
Has given us breath taking views and spectacular sights,
As she trusts that we will protect her gifts.

Many have come to be part of that dream,
A dream for all those who take a chance,
A once in a lifetime chance,
A chance that never comes again.

My father in heaven, I thank thee,
In bringing me to this promises land,
Across seas and skies and great plains,
A simple pleasant in such a great land.

Cyrus Noronha

Brokenhearted

I knew what would happen before it started
But now it's too late, I'm brokenhearted.
When I first saw you, I knew you were too fine
To ever in a million years think of becoming mine.
When our eyes first met, naturally, you smiled.
You may not have known this but it made my heart go wild.
Since then I've said "I love you" so many times
That it echoes in my head like door chimes.
How else can I say "It's you that I adore"
You must be used to it by now;
You must have heard so many times before.
But to do you wrong, I would not dare
I'd only treat you with the utmost care.
As sensitive as a mother, I'd wipe away all of your tears.
As protective as a father, I'd rid you of all your fears.
But with your permission, I'd like to be your friend
And once it starts, that friendship will never end.
Well, maybe we'll meet somewhere else in life
Where I can be your man and you can be my wife.

Akin Aina

Growing Old

I used to think that growing old was very frightful;
But now that I am 85, I think it's very delightful.
No longer need I get involved
With silly things that bore me
It's quite alright for me to say,
"Late parties simply floor me"
I dress the way I want to and my diet doesn't matter
Nobody will notice now if I am thinner or fatter.
I can sleep late in the morning
and catch up with my reading
while other people shovel snow
or wrestle with the weeding
I have medicare for doctor bills as well as many tax deductions
Plus many discounts without any sort of compunction.
But best of all I've settled for
This peaceful contemplation
Content to watch the watch the world go by
With quiet resignation
I think when father time creeps up to tap us on the shoulder
He leaves us with the peaceful skills we need for growing older

Christine Kearne

The Promise Of Success

I thought I'd buy a nightie to use the whole year through
But on second thought this little plant would be the best for you.
The green is for prosperity sent from heaven above
The basket represents the abundance of God's unfailing love.
As you pour the water on this plant each day
Remember he's your husband so don't forget to pray
If one day you look and a leaf or two is brown
It's just to let you know turn that frown upside down
As it begins to grow and flourish day by day
Let it be a witness of a love that's here to stay
If there is a time or two when it seems like shaky ground
Keep in mind that those who endure shall surely wear a crown
All the marriages that succeed can let their praises ring
Because the ones that stand the test are founded on the king

Carolyn Blackley

The Sunshine Maiden And Mr. Night

Sunshine streams down on the grass. It is like a bright yellow dress. It is the dress of the Sunshine Maiden. She plays in the sky and sleeps under the clouds, in a big black bed. Her brother is Mr. Night. He wears a long white suit, while she plays,
He
rests.

Jennifer Cuatt

Untitled

It's hard to say from where you stand, exactly when it all began.
But some place there's a point you cross the line.
You see the tears that stain your face, and you know it's time to leave this place behind.
It's a long way from home.
Trying to retrace your steps, all too easy to forget just which way to go. Outside the sky is threatening. You slowly gather up your things and you wonder how you'll ever explain. Walking out so self-assured. Yeah, you've going to change the world.
Though walking back a child in the rain.
It's a long way from home.
How can you retrace the steps you've been trying to forget?
Still it's time to go.
And if you lose your way, just keep your eyes on that endless broken line. Throw your bag under the bus and sit among the curious. It happens to the best of us, you know. Starting to retrace your steps you learn to live with your regrets. Next stop, heaven knows.
But you know it's time to go. To go such a long way from home.

Brandy Cravens

More Than Friends

Beauty may lie in the eyes of the beholder
But the real beauty lies within
Should we live to be one hundred or even older
You shall always be more than just a friend

There's an automatic bond between us
A companionship that warms the innermost fibers of the heart
There's mutual respect, a love, a trust
Though in separate places, we are never apart

So here's a toast to you my dear
May our relationship never end
And may our thoughts remain forever near
Because you're more than just a friend

Bernard Hatcher

Untitled

He begs for their attention
but they don't understand
At night he sits alone listening to his favorite band
He dreams of being far away
He makes his plan
Mom and Dad, they don't seem to care
They don't even notice
if he's ever there
Days go by and the distance seems to grow
He tries to reach out
No one even knows
The pain is too much, he can't seem to cope
He's given up on life
He's given up on hope
Taking his last breath, he reaches in his drawer
he pulls out a gun
They'll ignore him no more

Jeffrey C. Burton

Nature

Hear a bird sing songs of love
Hear the snap of a crisp oak twig
Hear the swish of a chill autumn wind wisping through the branches
Hear the wail of a majestic eagle screaming victory as it glides away with a trout Impaled on its talons.
Hear the babble of a brook flowing elegantly over the stone bed.
Hear nature
The eternal bliss of sound

David Joseph Rose

Unfamiliar Newness

The days are long, the days are short...
But they're all the same.

Some things work out, most things don't...
There's no one else to blame.

The monotony is comforting, the monotony is unending...
The familiar seems strange.

Ambitions run high, ambitions run low...
I can't make a change.

The things that I should do, the things that I shouldn't...
I can't differentiate the two.

My life feels tired, my mind feels old...
But what scares me is the new.

Erica Luongo

Cancer

We are not here to possess one another
But to learn from and live with each other.
Life is but a blink and then it is gone (as we know it)
But what we know is this reality
Of jealously, of hate,
Spite, terror, war and fate...
Hey maybe it's not so bad after all to go on to something else.
But then you find those special times
A child's love, a husband's kiss
The artist's fulfillment in achieving his best;
Somehow it's all worthwhile.
I always thought I'd be here
For 30, 40 years or more
But to think the end's tomorrow
How can I possibly borrow
That extra time I might be cheated
When there's so much more to live.
It isn't fair;
I'm not ready to leave my children...

Alice J. B. Fitzwater

"Planning"

So many plans...we have for our life.
But we forget that God made the sacrifice.
Through His Son Jesus...Who died for our sins,
And soon...He will be coming back again.

True, life is a struggle...with pain and grief.
And we all wonder why we cannot find relief.
But we can, if we could only see...
What Jesus did when He died on the tree.

Jesus gave His life not only for me,
But in pain...He died to set all men free.
So when we plan a utopian life...
Let us not forget Who made the sacrifice.

The Word of God...the "World" may have read; however,
Some still think that God is dead.
But, He is still living...He is in my heart.
And there He will stay...He will never depart.

So, here it is true and straight.
Each man predicts his own fate.
We must know Jesus...steeped in His love.
And He is the One...Who will lead us above.

Joshua B. Mungo

Make The Children Small Again

You asked me several times before to make the children small again,
But yesterday was yesterday and you can't go back to then.

Today is now, and we do our best to believe the futures bright,
Though there's times I know when we reflect on whether the past
was handled right.

But tomorrow is another day and tho we know not what it brings,
We can sit back and remember good, bad and many happy things.

As youth grows up and they are kids no more, just who are we to say,
That what they do or who they chose, will ever make them lose their
way.

As the years go by and we grow old, lets hope the kids grow tall,
Cause we know too well, no matter how we hope, there's just no
way
to make them small.

Edward F. Fiorina

Will She Smile For Me?

I have a friend named ____, who is smart and pretty and talented.
But ____ does not smile any more.
She is very sad and that makes me sad too.
I wonder — if I bought her a present, would she smile for me?
If I went to work for her, would she be happy?
If I helped her with her homework, would she be glad?
If I told her a joke, would she laugh?
When she laughs, the room is filled with merriment;
Her eyes twinkle, her friends are thrilled at this rare surprise...
But she does not truly laugh now;
There is naught but a brief and cynical cry for love.
So young and, yet, so bereft of hope!
If I told her she is special, would she listen?
Someone: Hand me the key to her laughter and smiles.
Is it love? I will give it.
Is it patience? I will listen.
Is it laughter? I will share mine.
Is it peace? I will supply some.
If I tell her she's my friend and I think she's special,
Will she smile for me?

Cynthia Montalvo

Save It For A Rainy Day

I was told quite often
by friends that were supposed to know better,
SAVE YOUR MONEY FOR A RAINY DAY
And
while they squandered theirs away on
trivial pursuits...I spend mine on life
but I find life has become what
other people pronounce it to be...
an arena caked with disillusionment,
and irresponsible liars...that take no prisoners,
and craft a world filled with iron bars
that lock us into desperation ...
and our despair maims and mutilates us,
as our crippled bodies retreat into the corner
of the cell...
succumbing to the barrage
of tentacles,
as they slash and rip flesh...with
their vile and gloomy
divulgences

Jon Swier

Mediocrity

Mediocrity is measured by the man
By the man who accepts the challenge to make a difference
Who accepts the challenge to make a change
Mediocrity is measured by the man

By the man who accepts the challenge to make a stand
To make a stand to be all that he can be
Act as a role model for one of you and for me
Mediocrity is measured by the man

By the man who has a drive
We all have it - it comes from inside
It's an innate feeling we have within
It's the drive that makes you want to
Run life's race and win
Mediocrity is measured by the man

By the man who accepts the challenge to make a difference
By the man who accepts the challenge to make a change
By the man who accepts the challenge to be different
By the man who accepts the challenge to make a stand
By the man who has a drive within - to run life's race and win
Mediocrity is measured by the man... you

Djuan Perry

"Concord Grapes"

Our purple grapes along the chain link fence here in
California bring back memories of a time long ago.

When as a child of seven I stood at our Minnesota farm
home and was fascinated by the grapes in row after row.

I helped pick those luscious grapes entwined in the small
wood trellis houses of slats of white.

Mom made dozens of jars of jam and jelly and some days
she worked long hours far into the summer night.

The grocery stores were eight miles away, a long drive from
our farm, so we grew what we need to eat and keep us warm.

Our gardens yielded vegetables and the orchards bushels of
apples red and green and the fields acres of the alfalfa bean.

The pastures were filled with trees to supply wood for warmth
all winter long, and in spring we heard the wildbird song.

I now see concord grapes along my California fence beside the
old plum tree, I hope they hold memories for my grandchildren and me.

Here in sunny California far from the Minnesota snow, I have
a row of grapes where I didn't think Concord Grapes would grow.

Doris June Winkelman

Sitting, Wondering and Waiting

I sat, I wondered and I waited, but you never came nor
called on the phone.

It would have been better had I never loved than to
constantly love all alone.

But your loving caress, your sweet tender kiss at the
times when we did chance to meet; set me afire with
flaming desire, then like ashes I lay at your feet.

But, no longer have I the heart or desire to let you
scrape up the ashes and rebuild the fire.

The north wind will come and blow them away, and tomorrow
I'm sure will be happier than today.

Jacqueline H. Russell

True Love...

True Love; When you're in it, you think it's unreal. You
can only tell if it's true by the way that you feel.
It doesn't just take a nice body or face; It takes loving and
caring, anytime, anyplace.
It takes someone who'll hold you and tell you he cares. Not
just flowers, and gifts, and cute teddy bears.
Someone who will look you straight in the eyes and say to you
he'll never tell you any lies.
Someone who won't force you into anything at all; who'll
understand you and carry you when you fall.
Someone who you've known for quite a while, who's simple
thoughts make you want to smile.
Someone who you know won't ever break your heart and who
gives you the assurance that you'll never ever part.
With him and only him, should you think of making love, so
save it for that special one you're always thinking of.

Janet Rocio Hernandez

Angels Of Light

They whisper quietly to you, telling what you should do.
Carefully, they guide, standing by your side.
They are with you all the time, and never let you down.
As you journey through life, they guide you all around.
To help you to come home, so you will never be alone.
They protect you, direct you, and help you see the light.
They lead you, believe in you, and help choose wrong from right.
They love you and know what it is you need.
They keep you safe from harm, through every little deed.
With understanding and care, they guide you through your test.
Standing close they share special secrets
to help you achieve your best.
When Satan tugs you down, they come
to lift you off the ground.
By showing you their light, they guide you through the night.
To Heavenly Father's arms you will fly
as they take you to the sky.
To Heavenly Father's throne you will go
with familiar friends you know.
For they help you to achieve, Heaven's Kingdom for eternity.

Deborah A. Davis

The Child, I

Who is the child? Why does he live?
Cast him down, down to the depths,
never to be seen or remembered.
It is but a single soul, no one cares or wants it.
Cast it over the rail, for it will never be missed.

Wait!, it is a life, it must live.
We care not, it is but one of millions.
Please, it is a child, a lovely child,
it may never return again.
Cry not human, We grant your wish.

This child is Ours, and shall forever be Ours.
Roam the land, drink in the view and live.
Your life is Ours, you must obey Us,
but feel free to enjoy time, it is short.

Create in your life, create life, so be it.
It is commanded, you must obey.
Be as one with the Cosmic Forces, they are your friends and love you.
Call on them, they will protect you through this life,
as they have done in the many other lives before this day.
Go, be loved, be a child of the Universe.

Alfred H. Berger

Nectar Of Thundershower Splash

Kitten sojourned in a spool's avalanche serene paste!
Child swarmed in a toy's fiction praline taste!
Grass volleyed in a wind's review sordine haste
Grizzly larking latent smiles transforms
amputating claws crushing paws
cotton caress architectural finesse of cubs rumpus!
Hazy arms of handles beams parry through a barricade of leaves to the
wrinkling
glass, spreading like a fan tracery. A marriage with the wind!
Prompt intimacy, instant
conception TWINS BURST in a miraculous creation of being!
Then-one/simpers a mesmerizing

Glitter and-its/sibling winks a glare harvesting pirouettes
boundless, a pond not uttered.

Into dulcet eyes silence fury's immense - to anyone who's focused.
Evidence of things unseen, in a vault of real perceptions considered
that is to conquer mundane facades.

Dexterous SPLASH REFULGENT mountains, of the Ancient of Days' radiant
ornamentation dainty slopes gestural gardens ADORNED
in the dictum of sweetness!

Carmine Sauchelli

Only A Child

Click, Click, Click, Click -
Child why are you perched on my counter for cooking?
Put away that bottle of vitamins, dear.

But, mommy I've tried and tried my hardest -
Why won't this lid come off of this bottle?

The bewildered blue eyes wait for a good answer -
Her grip on the bottle never slackens.

The wrinkle between the woman's brow fades -
Her lips curl up and she chuckles aloud -
I buy it what way, only adults get it open -
Child-proof is what the store would call it.

Click, Click, Click, Click -
But, mommy I've tried, I just don't understand -
How does this bottle know how old I am?

Catherine R. Adair

Circle Of Wonder

Circle of wonder
Circle of life
I look to the heavens in search of my life.
The face of my father
The stories of past
What are the answers
Which is the path?
I look for his eyes in the stars that shine
The wisdom of the ages to guide me through time.

Circle of wonder
Circle of life
What is my story
Show me the light.
Give me the wisdom
To make the right choices
Give me the courage
To listen for the voices.
The eyes of my father in the sky above
Look down on me
With not judgement...but love.

Dana M. Ulmer

Untouched

Rain falls dank and cold.
Claps of thunder
echo
through darkened clouds.

Bright-white flashes of lightning
cast shadows on the wall.

The wind thrusts driving rain upon my dwelling place.

Ravaged by the storm,
I remain serene,
untouched, calm.

Slowly, it fades.
The storm has passed.

Tomorrow,
sun-yellowed clouds
will drift aimlessly
upon blue skies.
Warm southerly winds
will push gently
upon my back.

Daniel L. Angeski

Cold Air #1

I think I skinned my knee
climbing up onto the structure outside your house.
I guess it was the way you
carved a heart around our initials with my car key
that made me think twice about ever
really walking away from you.
You're so incredible... to me.
Not just the way you growl at me,
it's your hands that I hold to keep from falling
off the earth.
I guess you were right when you implied
that I'd sink without you.
I needed you there to keep me from
puking my life away
Just like I needed you there to catch me
from falling at my mother's punch
Just like I needed you to be
my sweat shirt
when I was cold.

Bethann Mangel

Prayer Of Desperation

Lay down your head,
Close your eyes,
Fall asleep and dream my child;
Dream of beauty, life and innocence,
For while you are asleep,
You are safe;
I will pray for you and me,
I will pray the next breath we draw will be our last,
Never to see the next horror filled day;
Murder, Guns, Drugs, and Rape,
All lead our fragile existence to hate;
How I wish for death,
To take us away into her arms;
To travel places beyond the norm to become incorporeal,
But a ghost on the winds of time;
Such prayers are for fools,
And I'm their king;

Christopher L. Ritt

Shadows Running To A Setting Son

Underneath clear blue skies
Clouds seemingly so close
You can touch them if you tried

Running with the crowd
Friends and family all around
It seemed like any other day
Yet different in a funny way

Up the hill we ran, as fast as we can
We were separated by a man
Then there was only he
Separated from friends and family

I heard a mother cry, with a tear in her eye
By a fence they stood, a mother and her son
Standing so close they looked like one

Then the thunder came, without any rain
Where two did stand, stood only one
A mother without her son

Have you ever seen a cow cry?
I'll tell you of the time
When a mother saw her son die.

Kirk Nakakihara

Untitled

Tempted, under pressure.
Cold fury in eyes lost in the longing,
trapped in foreign lust so strong...

Such as rush, so hard to touch;
Hell's fire in hair so red!
Blood, spit, pain; a mutter...

Eyes so black I cry...

Hate takes death by throat!
Passion smites evil with outstretched fists.
Pummel! Maul! Kill the ice like fire...

Forward Flow!
Hush, sweet baby don't cry.
You won't burn...

Mother! I come, come, COME, COME!

Awash in semen, blood, and fury
mother's seed must die!
Black mouthed serpent speaks to me;
Where's your fang?

Place at the temple and SCREAM...

Christopher L. Carson

On Alzheimers

You are here!
But are you really?
Is it you?
I see your face
But you have changed;
You are slowly slipping away.
I knew you so well
But now you're becoming a stranger
And I'm becoming a stranger to you.
My heart is full of love for you
But my heart is breaking.
Now I can only cling to cherished memories,
Memories of happier times when all was well.
These thoughts will always be with me
And keep you alive in my heart forever.

Barbara Ann Gajda

Insight

The shock of disillusion drives my body's interior insane.
Colors become fugitive in my sight - and pain is of no time.
Seeing you lying there, thinking I know what I'm doing...but I don't.
Fear trembles throughout your body as I near to wipe the sweat from your brows.
You don't love me anymore for the pain and inconvenience I've caused.
Need I tell you I couldn't help it?
An arched brow forms on your forehead

— As a crease of deceptiveness forms across your face.
You're laughing at me with no sound penetrating your lips.
I turn quickly so you won't see the stupidity I feel...as I begin to cry.
I turn to say words more than apologies, but you are crying too.
I reach gently for you-
Feeling something pierce my hand, I look at your face trying to find an answer for my pain.
The tears you have cried turn red...
blood...

My awareness is taken aback after finding I broke the mirror in my outrage.

Annalyn Gill

Realization

I've marvelled at a sunrise of radiant, rosy hue,
Combed strands of crystal beaches and gazed upon the view
Of aspen-dotted mountain peaks in shades of red and teal,
And counted sun-drenched waves of grain in countless Kansas fields.
I've crouched atop a boxcar and watched the firefly's dance
And worshiped endless seas of stars and known omniscient hand
In each and every wonder, in every tree and flower,
Yet pondered what my place was within this awesome power.
I read of Native folklore - their fetishes and rites,
Did seek in vain, enlightenment, within the astral lights.
The Eastern Mystics offered hope - Arjuna's quest was mine
- To find the "truth" within the self, the link with all mankind.
The more I read, the more I probed, the more it came to seem,
No matter what the path I chose, they had a common theme.
The parables of Jesus, the tales of Krishna fame,
The reverence for rock and tree - the paths came out the same.
Within each heart there lives a place that never, ever dies.
It belongs unto the universe - the planets, trees and skies.
The world I view with new-born eyes - with new respect perceive
The universal truth I sought resided within me.

Elizabeth Elliott

The 54th

The 54th of Massachusetts the 1st black regiment
Commanded by Robert Gould Shaw as he was content
To command them
to fight the south for the U.S.A. in the Civil War
To fight to die for one's ideals
To fight to be heard
And the 54th through all the prejudice, spite, and hate
Pulled through
And soon became great
They fought well against the south
Willing to fight willing to die
Which some undoubtedly would
And after a few battles Colonel Robert Shaw
Asked if his regiment might be in the front
In the front of the disaster at Fort Wagner
And so they went into the fray some were condemned to die
And this included Robert Shaw
Who fought and would die and to this day we still remember them
For their bravery and say
"They fought well"

Aaron Krygier

Delicate Reflections

Whispers of the silence penetrate the truthful heart,
Confessing the love which envelopes the essence of becoming one.
Intended souls capture that silence and challenge each day,
With the strength from one, then the other, uniting both,
justifying all.

Shadows of desperation rise then disappear,
Sighs of decadent warmth radiate with each pulse.
Every nuance of light engulfs the twilight,
Serenity is now delivered from the silence.

Cheryl Chapman Guilford

One Evening At Cocoa Beach

The horizon is endless builded by the waters
Constantly troubled by the tireless waves
The waters came in fine folds
Washing the overlooking sandy shores.

The waters littered by surf boards
As well as man of both sexes settled on sands
Lovers cuddling and entangling under the blissful cool breeze
Intermittently pestered by the onrushing waves.

A number of birds fly and perch
Gliding atop the men and women on sand
Like the waves cresting along the beachline
Complimenting the life on the shore.

God is marvelous, He is wonderful
With unquantifiable guts, He created them all
The man, the seas, the waves and the birds
All act dependently to bless the wit behind creation.

And as the cool breeze adds glamour to the pervading freshness
It is continuously reasserted that the Almighty is great
As the boundless sky continues to change color
The whole phenomena cannot but compliment the Creator.

Ayodeji Awe

Message In The Wind

Did U know who I was when U first saw me?
Could U sense my motives for wanting to help U?

I am the change in the wind that blows by every once in a while to make U think.
I am the breeze that clears the air so that U may witness the blue skies your dreams are made of.

I am the warm summer day that brings back memories of a childhood
past that passed into a future of what U were, wanted to be, and are,
but still think U could be more.

I have come and gone, but will always remain to see just how U R doing.

U R doing a little better than the last time I saw U
But U R still trapped by your blindness.
Your failure to see your true perfection.

U seek the unnatural and cheat yourself of true vision,
to look into your past and learn, and to see into your future and dream.

All that U see now is false, U have programmed yourself into believing that U can control your destiny through unreal motives and desires.
All that is real is that which was here before us.
Seek the reality of your surroundings.

Cameron Bowers

Persian Silhouette

Spindly minarets pierce the horizon...
creating a mysterious silhouette which defies the fiery tempest
of sunset.
Hazy heat waves cling heavily to shadowy images as dusk approaches.
Ancient bastions of faith await the last call to prayer.
Once a soft, melodious wail intoned with humble emotion,
the message screams forth — amplified.
Exotic trills accent the syncopated chant enticing the faithful soul
to worship.
Shivers of romantic delight ripple through unbelievers.
An interlude of silence...the caller rests. People pray.
Night falls.
August monuments of religion guard the sleeping city until dawn bursts
forth seeking a new horizon.
Mosques re-emerge as silhouettes suspended before dawn's
illumination.
The muezzin awakens and greets the inspiring vision.
Beholden to Allah, he summons his people to pray.
As the azan rings out from its pinnacle,
the emboldened silhouettes fade in the brilliant sunlight...
silently receding from the reality of an inimitable day.

Elizabeth A. Albright

Wind

I am sailing, flying on the back of the wind,
Dancing with the birds of the air.
Light as a feather, I ride on the back of the wind.
My heart carries no weight, I am burden-free.
There, in the sky, a rainbow smiles down at me.
I will ride with the wind, ride up and catch
that rainbow in my hand.
I sail higher and higher.
Soon I will crash into the sun.
Now, I can run with the creatures of the earth.
I will run for an eternity.
My heart feels light, for I have been sheltered from the
world and it's woes.
I gaze in wonder at the simple beauty that surrounds me.
I run with the deer, forever and forever.
Running, running, running

Jessica Smelser

Dandelion, Sweet Dandelion

A green outstretched field, within the center of which, a solitary dandelion stands. Beaten by the storm and trampled by the feet of humankind, her head is bent in sorrow. Her eyes are cast downward toward the earth. Dew drips from her and rain falls from the sky as heaven, earth, and dandelion weep.

She does not yet truly know herself, therefore, does not yet know true love. But like a warm spring breeze, I shall dry her tears and lift her head skyward, that she may see the beauty of heaven and earth, rather than her damp, desolate field. She has not yet seen the beauties and greatness of life. I shall show her the world beyond the boundaries of pain, despair, and loneliness.

The sharp, spinning, loveless, life-taking blades commit their acts of execution. Blade by blade the fearful grass meets, with tragedy, the end. But the grass does not die in vain. With the presence of God in the field, the blades of grass, standing straight up, hold their heads up high and die with honor.

What of sweet dandelion, whose loveliness is reminiscent of God's perfection? Like a rock I stand before her, shielding her from the mighty, hellish machine. No harm to her shall I let occur. Between God and I, no power can conquer us, I and my sweet dandelion. I am the rock that shall shield her from the mowing machines of life and the world. And God is my strength and my courage, but dandelion, sweet dandelion, she is my love.

Aaron J. Lawreszuk

Pop! Pop!

Pop! Pop!
Death exits the chamber and enters the still air
It cuts through like the doctor's scalpel to follow
Pop! Pop!
It's the echo heard by the mother whose child
 death has struck
She has no idea why she was chosen to carry
 such grief
Pop! Pop!
A sound heard when playing war
War was fun to him
Pop! Pop!
A seven year old with the only worry of losing
 his tooth
But today he's losing life.
Pop! Pop!
Why?

Brian Wyckorf

Untitled

There are grasshoppers screaming ecstasy
 Deep within my brain
And dancing wolves who swear to clouds that
 The sky's are insane
There are helicopters drawing straws to
 See whose side I'm on
And I'm only happy when I'm raking
 Babies off the lawn

There are garage door openers laughing
 At the sight of green
And bilingual monkeys who don't know what it means
There are tractors counting sheep to
 Make it way past dawn
And I'm only happy when I'm raking babies off the lawn

There are coat hangers hanging deep within my soul
And skipping horses who talk to frogs
 That are drowning in a bowl
There are liquid telescopes playing chess
 Without the needed pawn
And I'm only happy when I'm raking babies off the lawn

Jim O'Malley

Friends

Friends are people who are always there;
Dependable like a cozy bear;
Sharing and caring — always lending a hand;
Reliable as the hourglass sand

Friends give a strong shoulder to cry on;
Thoughtful advice you can rely on;
There to support and to help you get through;
A special trust only gained from a few

Friends console — try to help ease the pain;
Talk, listen, give a chance to explain;
Through the smiles and tears; the laughter and fear;
Friends are forever year after year

Kathy A. Morris

Empathy

My eyes full, limbs trembling, the pain splits.
The jagged pieces are caught with your fingertips
and are slowly drawn to your chest.
I see your eyes full.

My heart begins to pump with breaths of hope
and a sigh of relief expands and lets go of my lungs.
The tension cracks and shears off my body.
Your eyes carry my weight.

Kate L. Hawkins

Soul Search

Calmly, cautiously, I walk the night
Desperately seeking to conquer the fright.
I walk and walk in shadows dim
Searching the strength from deep within.

My eyes are closed but yet I see
What this strength has done for me
I shed my fears upon the ground
And left my body soft and sound.

Into the hills so fluttered with trees
I galloped and bounced on a bellowing breeze.
I motioned above to mountain range
I swayed, I danced, and then I changed.

The star-lit night was dimming so
And I realized it was time to go.
Back to the streets I enter in
The body that now has strength within.

Destined toward my home I see
The strength which conquered reality.
The soul search is over-as I lay to rest
Where tomorrow's dreams shall be the best.

Cecilia Ann Doetschmann

Reflections

Have you ever been in a crowd, yet felt all alone?
Did you ever sit in your house not feeling at home?
Have you ever had a problem that no one could solve?
Did you ever fall in love, yet fear to be involved?
Have you ever entered a room feeling like you have
been there before?
Did you ever feel the cold spot on an otherwise warm
floor?
Have you ever had a question, but been afraid to ask?
Did you ever have real feelings, but choose to hide
behind a mask?
Have you ever had such fear that you body would
tremble:
Did you ever open your eyes to find there are others
you resemble?

Ernesto Pinoffio

Best Friend

Hello again my long time best friend
Didn't I tell you there would be no end
To the storm clouds and the pouring rain
To the silence of loneliness and the pain

I once thought I saw a rainbow or two
But the only rainbow I found has been in you
I always keep coming back again and again
I found my pot of gold in you my best friend

In good times and in bad you've always been there
You never asked questions or said it wasn't fair
You've never let me down or turned your back on me
You've been a true friend and you always will be

So I give a toast to you my best friend
You're the words on paper; the ink in my pen
So I bow my head and turn away
I know you'll be there like you were today

Anita McBroom

You Alone

Walking in the unknown, may sometimes require a sense of direction that may stir you on a lonely road, to new heights beyond your safety zone. Giving up the familiar in search for the unseen dream that has been deposited in you heart and soul alone.

It is a pathway that is leased traveled, for fear of the unforeseen, this path will reveal and carry forth the dream. Determining if this is the road you really want to take. Creates circumstances you never though you would have to face. Being questioned by those who doubt your ability, who can only see a hopeless end to your fate. Can make you want to give up, become weary and want to faint.

Thought contrary to popular belief, you won't be held in high esteem simply because you dared to dream. You must depart from the popular and be acquainted with the peculiar. For other's cannot see what has been entrusted unto thee.

Take courage and do not fear, what you've ventured into will cause many to depart and separate from you. Move out and take hold of the dream, you have a purpose and a plan, along with wisdom it's fulfillment will be grand.

Anita Merritt

Day in the Park

Lincoln seemed to be pondering the flag while Washington and Gandhi
discussed the political correctness of the world.
Children played with their parents among the human wreckage which
was made up of soul takers, skin givers and substance worshippers.
Trees, flowers, grass and other foliage did indeed have life here,
but under close examination, the grimy filth of the concrete
jungle show through.
Like a kaleidoscope, the colors and hues of different individuals
blended together, causing a harmony of sorts.
I'm startled by the sound of a police officer roosting a
man lying on a bench, his crime...using the front page of
the times as a blanket.
A melting pot? Maybe not. But this place, it sure gets hot.
Laughter in one corner is mocked by muffled cries in another.
I walk away, always returning.
this is my park and this has been a day in it.

John Patrick Lynch

Homeless

Look at that figure, alone on the street
disheveled confused and so full of defeat,
No - -don't look away - look right in their face
for it could be you, standing there in their place.

That lonely figure, once might have been
a once happy person - a leader of men,
Or perhaps someone's mother, so precious and dear
before fate dealt it's hand, and brought them here...
to stand alone ... hungry and cold, with no one to
love them and no where to go.

So the next time you see them, just give them a smile,
It could make their step lighter, on their next lonely mile.
Say a prayer for that stranger and perhaps in some way
They too will find comfort at the end of their day.

It's a very fine line between heaven and hell
And each lonely figure has a story to tell,
So... walk softly my friend, count your blessings too -
For the figure you see standing out there today
Tomorrow could be YOU!

Jan Edner

Priorities

As we sift life through our questing souls
Dissecting each grain to understand
Where in the fabric its smudge is intended
Caution must remain intact
Against the piping call of self centered intellect
Make sure we hear the joy of a newborn cry
Rejoice the rains tapping call
Remember the spring season of all things
Release our tears of happiness at each sunrise
And also each returning moon
Forget not the gifts of our mother earth
And her mysteries
Wonder at the power of the spark of life
That glows within all
Embrace the call of love
Of passionate lust
Dream the dreams of hope, of gaiety
Hear all sounds, inhale wondrous perfumes
But above all else
Celebrate the joyous miracle of our existence

Don Johnson

Dichotomy

My winter window is a wondrous thing,
Dividing outer cold from heat within.
So strong! — and yet, a spinning stone
Could shatter into shards a wall so thin.

Inside I reign in velvet pillowed warmth,
While through the pane, a bird with jewel eyes
Accepts his frozen realm without complaint,
And sits, cold-puffed and winterweatherwise.

We rule our winter worlds, the bird and I,
Until the summer sun, with yellow smile,
Usurps the power of dividing glass —
And makes our kingdoms equal for a while.

Barbara R. Sands

Footprints In The Sand

How busy is "busy" or "busy as can be"
Do we leave footprints for the world to see?
Do we flitter from here to there so fast
We don't see what we have passed?
Are our greetings and conversations so short
We miss the message or good-news report?

If you went to the well and it was dry
The dipper was empty - would you sit and cry?
Or would you dig deeper into your soul
Then pull the rope till you were filled up with hope?
Now say to family and friends
"No, I'm not too busy to leave
Footprints in the sand."

Diana K. Leising

Divine Lovers

Lovers in another life
discovered how to do it right
Came back to enhance each others light
in the midst of a world so full of strife;

Reconnected joyous souls
embraced the light they now behold
In each others arms they are consoled
as their spiritual journeys continue to unfold;

Time and space does not exist
in the realms they now assist
They've accepted their eternal youth
and live to serve their highest truth.

Kay Vonne Cason

A Child With No Name

How does it feel to be a child with no name.
Do you ever get over the pain or the shame?
You ask yourself was my mother just someone to bed,
And did the man care if I even got fed?
Was I the result of lust in the night?
Did he leave my mother before morning light?
Would abortion have been the right thing to do?
Will Mom ask this question, her whole life thru?
Will I keep on searching only to find,
That he does not care if his eyes are like mine.
Is he now married, or maybe was then,
And am I just someone who should not have been?
No one cares that I even exist,
It hurts very much knowing something like this,
So my life is spent mostly alone,
Searching and seeking, 'til I finally find home.
When it's time for me to wed,
Will I be afraid of our marriage bed?
Can I forget that I was born in shame?
Yes, I am the child who has no name.

Janice Elliott

"A Little Voice"

I love you Grandma, her little voice would say
Do you have a cookie, some candy, do you wanna play?
You can see a twinkle in her little eyes of blue
Her hair glistens in the sunlight her checks a rosy hue
Oh what a wonder a little one can be
They love to come and visit to see what they can see
I love you grandma her little voice would say
I'm hungry, can I stay for supper, call mom see if its OK
The day is slowly ending she must be on her way
She heads through the doorway turns and gives a wave
I love you Grandma, her little voice would say
Don't be sad, don't you worry, I be back another day.

Darlene C. Szala

Taking A Minute With The Lord

Hello Lord, it's me again.
Do you have a minute for a friend?
Satan's been busy making life rough.
I've tried to ignore him, but the going got tough.
He's disrupting my life, I'm lonely and sad.
Things will get better, right Lord...
and this too shall pass?
Rebuking him is hard, he's busy all the time.
Lord, give me strength so he won't control my mind
Just one more thing Lord, before I go...
Is there anything you think I should know?
Thanks for listening, I know there's no one greater.
I've got to go now Lord and I'll talk with you later.

Denise Stewart

The Stars

Look up to the stars and tell me what you see.
Do you see your destiny or just the black of night?
Do you see you guardian angel watching over you?
Do you see loved ones of the past hoping to share
in your joys and comfort your fears?
Or is it all just a blur in your mind?
That stars hold the key to the future and also to the past.
You must decide what you see an whether to move on
or stay were you are.
It's all up to you.

Misti Jo Painter

The Dare

He calls me and calls me and I just refuse,
Doesn't he realized that he's being used.
I ask him do you love me and he says want to see,
Before I know it he's kissing me.
While we kiss I just forget,
I shouldn't be doing this and I let.
But it's all just the same,
And its only a game.
I just can't refuse,
So what do I do I use.
And I don't really care,
Because, I know it's only a dare.

Karen Peterson

To A Grandchild

It doesn't matter, if: Your eyes are blue, green, or brown...
doesn't matter..... I'll still love you!

It doesn't matter, if: You're a tough little guy or a dainty little girl...
doesn't matter..... I'll still love you!

It doesn't matter, if: Your hair is blonde, red or brown...
doesn't matter..... I'll still love you!

It doesn't matter, if: You have dimples, but usually frown...
doesn't matter..... I'll still love you!

It doesn't matter, if: When I change your diapers, you're a total mess...
doesn't matter..... I'll still love you!

It doesn't matter, if: You burp-up all over me while being fed...
doesn't matter..... I'll still love you!

It doesn't matter, if: Your busy little hands break a few things...
doesn't matter..... I'll still love you!

It doesn't matter, if: Your questions are never-ending and you can't sit still...
doesn't matter..... I'll still love you!

It doesn't matter, if: At the end of your stay, I'm worn-out...
doesn't matter..... I'll send you home... but I'll always love you!

Beverly Greeson

Just Because I Kiss You

Just because I let you kiss me,
doesn't mean I love you
just because I hug you,
doesn't mean I want to be held
Just because I lay in your arms,
doesn't mean I desire you
For when I do, you will tell
for the mountain will roar with laughter,
the sea will whisper your name
passion will surround you, nothing will seem the same
Oh, when I love you, you will
surely know, for the stars will guide you
the moon will lead the way,
the earth you stand upon will up and float away,
Oh, the day you enter me,
I will set your soul on fire
Hell will feel the passion,
Heaven will envy my desire,
So just because I kiss you,
doesn't mean were in love

Constance Harris Keemer

In Her Garden

As I see her in her garden
Doing things she loves so dear
Working at flowers. Trimming at trees
Moving in her own sure way doing it with care

She loves the fields the sloping hills
The paths along the way
The simple things of hill and dale
The flowers along the way

There is such beauty I can say
As she moves along her way
Her golden hair and skin so fair
Her love of life as it passes there

In her garden life passes there
No cares no worries follow her
In peace and love they bloom with care
The lady with the golden hair

At times I watch at times I share
In her garden her garden so fair
Of this speak as I see her there
Her toil of love in Garden share

John D. Steinbroner

Heaven

I had entered a state of oblivion, and I was no longer pain's dominion.
Now peace fills my soul, since life took it's toll, and my time on earth has came to an end.
But where am I now?
In this place that's somehow, so distant but yet so relaxing.
And the people that are here, I've seen them somewhere...in a picture, on the street, or in my youth.
And I know in my heart, that they played a part, of a time in my life days before.
They welcomed me in with a hug and a grin as they directed me to a path I must follow.
As I walked down a way.
I could see through the gray, a light just too bright to be stared at.
I had to hold back the tears as a form did appear to take my hand from my side, it slightly trembling.
The memories rushed through my head, as I realized...I was dead... and this place that I'm in is called Heaven.

Debra L. Conner

Life at HLCV

When I got old, happiness went.
Don't worry about happy, try for content.
The most happiness had in my life
Were the years when I was a mother and wife.

I realize those years are gone
And I'll do my best from now on.
Some days I think all around me are mad
And other days are not so bad.

The food is all canned or dehydrated
And believe me, that's over-rated.
All the cooks must have been good lookin'
They sure weren't hired for their cookin'.

No onion or garlic, and course, no spice.
Just a little salt and pepper would be nice.

I am here by own consent
Not very happy, but mostly content.
And I know when I pass death's door
They will be cheering me on from the other shore.
I'll be forgiven the sins of my past
And find happiness again at last.

Betty Hanners

The Zoo Shed

"Take this out to the zoo shed, Son," said his dear old Dad.
"Don't you mean the tool shed, Pa?" said the smart young lad.
"What do ya think's in there, son? Well, I'll tell ya, of course.
We have a snake for plumbers and a big ole saw horse.
And we got a hammer that has claws over there on that bench.
Here we got another kind of animal-it's a monkey wrench!
Now son take this parrot pliers out to the zoo shed.
And no more arguments, boy or I'll have your head!"
"But Pa, it's not a parrot pliers. Don't you mean `a pair'?"
"Well, son, you might be right so I'll try to be fair.
But explain one thing, boy-what am I gonna do?
Where will I keep this weasel if I got no zoo!"

Cheryl Quickle

Weeping Willow

Weeping Willow please don't look so sad,
Don't you remember all the great times we've had?
The days in the sun, me on your swing,
When with the birds I would sing.
On your swing I could fly,
I would coast through the sky.
I always felt so great, so free,
Without you Weeping Willow, I could not be.
In your shade I would bask,
Your friendship and protection was all I could ever ask.
I always knew no matter the time,
The reach of your branches was mine.
But now I am lost, I just don't know,
I feel betrayed Weeping Willow, do you have to go?

David Griffin

Choices

I chose to take the easy road. It's easy to run downhill.
down... down...

The easy road in my youth. down... down... It's very easy.
The easy road in life. Down faster and faster. It's easy.

I chose the easy road in love. Down again. Now I'm sliding.
It's fun. It's easy.

The easy road. It's painful when you crash at the bottom of
the hill. Agony... despair... at the bottom.

I will never again choose to take the easy road. It's too
easy to run downhill... and far too painful to hit bottom.
Total destruction.

I chose to rise from the rubble of a broken life, from the
easy road. It's very hard. Help... hope... I can heal.

I finally rose up and began to climb again. It's not easy
to begin climbing the hill. Courage... faith... I will make it.

I've finally found a beautiful path leading up the hill,
taking me higher and higher to the summit, where I have chosen
to be. Strength... endurance... My life is becoming whole again.

Kani Forman

"Love, Unearthly"

Love, like renewing showers of spring rain ...
Converts inevitable death into a gain ...
Thrice majestic as an odorous flower ...
Bestows thee blessings every hour ...
Fairer than the most beauteous maid ...
Eternally soothes our fears to fade ...
Costlier compared to gold in any form ...
Succors our hearts in the storm ...
Love, nobler than all other loves imaginable ...
Astounds our finite minds because it is unfathomable ...

Andre Edwards

Spiral

Spinning
Down, down
Into black oblivion.

The inky black envelopes me like a thick, warm blanket.
Hard to move
Hard to think
So comfortable
Here
Suspended in the depths of my inner thoughts.

Must go back
A voice calls to me
Slowly the warm blanket unwraps
As I spin upward
Never stopping
Again rejoining the present.

Kate Hamilton

Unconscious Reality

Slipping, slipping,
down into a deep, dark well.
Peacefulness, happiness,
await you there;
away from the worries and troubles of the world.
You don't see or hear conscious reality, or any such thing.
Your only companions being
the angels or demons of subconsciousness,
flitting or flying around your head,
running or dancing around your feet,
making your dreams come true or
your fears come alive right before your eyes.
Then conscious reality starts
to fade in and out,
and your peaceful haven
is shattered,
only to come back again
the next night.

Brandie King

Remember

My basement door creaks open and I move blindly
Down the steps, into a place that holds unused memories
and unwanted emotions
Cobwebs block out the bright interior walls,
My feet grow numb as I walk across the cement floor toward
the mildew encased trunk covered with dirt.
As I reach for the top of the large black box
I find a lock as tight as a chastity belt.
Why can't I unlock this trunk, and retrieve
the forgotten items inside?
What is hidden inside of there?
Please allow my memories to attack my mind,
like killer bees swarming a body.
Why can't I remember - who am I?

Kathy Olp

My Family

People probably think I dwell on the past too much,
Dream about my childhood and such.
But of one thing you can be sure,
We had love-and so much more.
We had each other when we were down and out.
We were all we had, and without a doubt,
We were all we needed.
Maybe I was just young and didn't realize
How the real world was in other's eyes.
But even now, after we're all grown,
I hope there's a chance we can go on
Needing each other, never letting go of the love we had

Betty

Dreams

Listless are my clouds that fall where roads will end in broken dreams,
the sun and moon, the stars and skies, the right to self-redeem;

My life has been a travesty of illusions that I hold,
while living in the past is bad, my dreams are made of gold;

If only when I fall into some dreams that feel so blue,
something whispers in my head, and I think of only you;

It must stop someday this is clear, my mind is only cast,
with dreams of you that seem so blue and visions of the past;

Where can I go to save my soul from harm that wreaks awake,
for in my mind, I often find, dreams I seldom make;

They come from within while lingering, and stay for quite some time,
with cuts so deep and nothing reaped, dreams colliding on the side;

It's time to bid farewell again and choose a different path,
for anger, fear, and loneliness, make dreams of bitter wrath;

The dreams of you will be remembered, your eyes I'll not forget,
you saved my soul from darken days, for this I will admit;

Time will pass and days will drift, new love will appear on the rise,
but the dreams I had for you that year,will open up my eyes.

James Byron Waits

Untitled

Beyond closed eyes, down the winding hidden paths of your mind,
drifts a valley that nighttime holds in a blanket of slumber.
As you sleep, it awakens.
The creatures of the meadows and the forests stir;
the whispery morning ruffles their fur and feathers.
The crystal mountain glints in the newly born sunlight
which, in turn, paints the emerald mists surrounding the stream
the river
the waterfall
colors and hues that shine in a magical, fluttering way.
The waterfall, raining dreams and wishes, pours far beyond
tomorrow,
and your imagination watches and ripples in the water.
You cannot clearly see your reflection.
The image flows softly, and one hundred thousand voices sigh,
their sapphire song dancing in the air as a lullaby.
lulling
soaring
Near nothing at all,
in a world of spirit footsteps and dimming dew drops,
you escape into harmony and pure imagination.

Brandy Ball

The Sounds Of Harassment

A word from our language came here to play.
Driving all in the house in complete disarray.
Congress flittered and fluttered in utter vexation
Convincing constituencies over the nation.
The meaning, once clear, was now being obstructed
In five minute speeches artfully constructed.
It intimidates, exasperates, and irritates persistently.
When it titillates and animates it must do so consistently.
Scholars traced "harass" to "harer" with roots in old french
"to set the dogs on" made good sense to the bench.
But the meaning's not changed however you say it.
To pronounce it "Hares" a smooth sound we hear.
To pronounce it "harass is sharp to the ear.
In spite of its harshness it's a practical choice
With guidance for spelling placed in the voice,
The accent on "ASS" reveals a device
To remember, when spelling, to write the "S" twice

Catheryn Eisenhardt

Time And A Garden

A garden full of roses
Each dream waiting to bloom
The caress of sunshine and rain
Giving each blossom strength
Strength to tolerate the wind
That threatens the delicate petals of life
You, my child, that fragile rose
Shimmering in royal crimson
You, my child, now face the wind
That will toss you to and fro
Your fragile stem bending with each breath of a cloud
Yet, your garden of dreams will still await you
Concealing both beauty and thorns within
Stems will be broken and stolen by the wind
While others stand strong in their defense
Holding on for yet, one more dream to bloom
You, my child, will see another dream blossom
For time will endure your painful scars
The scars inflicted by each severing thorn
And your garden will bloom once again.

Beth Ellen Dunlap

I Will Lift Up My Eyes

I will lift up my eyes toward heaven,
each glorious passing day. Because God is
my saviour and the compass for my way.
When times get hard and the road of life
seems so rough, in you and only you Lord will I
put my trust.
I'll hold my head up high, for no matter what
I'm going through, this battle that I thought was
mines, I know now belongs to you.
I will lift up my eyes and thank you Lord
for what you've done for me. Being near
to guide me and loving me unconditionally.
I will lift up my eyes late in the midnight
hour when my pillow is wet with tears. Because
I know with God on my side, I have nothing,
nothing to fear.
Yes, I will lift up my eyes to Jesus,
the one that died for me.
The man that died for all our sins,
that day on calvary.

Donita Davis

Brookshire, Texas

My Big Chance

The men were gathered in the camp; 'twas sure a sight to see,
Each one of them could be "The Champ", and one of them was me.
Good friends are we - like Brothers all; each year we make this trek
To meet and walk with Nature's Call, and 'bag' our deer - by heck!
November's air was crisp and clear, The 'Seven' were all set,
Each knew his path, with sunrise near, then with the Woods we met.
So silently we crept along and found our way to where
The whippoorwill will sing his song (but we will first be there).
As sunlight filters tiny rays through limbs and boughs of trees,
In shadows that were blues and grays a 'point' or two I sees!
Oh my! I thought, the time has come for me to show my mettle,
My heart's a-pounding, feet so numb, oh stomach, won't you settle?
I wait what seems a hundred years for this moment to be past
And after weighing doubts and fears my target's there at last!
What a doll! An eight-point-buck; he'll fill the freezer sure,
With steady aim and a little luck, I'm sure to win his fur.
My rifle weighs a thousand pounds - won't raise above waist-high,
My pounding heart drowns out the sounds and all I do is sigh.....
And as my 'prize' strolls proud off I become a sure believer,
Never, Never will I ever scoff at them who claim "BUCK FEVER"!

Jim Renforth

Untitled

Tears lie on my cheeks dew from the morn
Each painful memory lies one by one
Petals of truth fall forth
Crying out to be noticed

Feeling my life slip down my cheek
A bitter smile spreads across
Remembering how things had once been
Trying hard not to think how they've become

Delicate buds that never bloomed
Our time together wasn't enough
Now the starting emotion runs forth
Like a chalice overrun with wine

The hardest part though is accepting
That I now crave for your hand of mercy
To gently wipe the pain from my eyes
But yet they fall untouched

Alison Colwell

Today

The sun falls and every shade of the pastel colors flood the
Earth, filling the desolate desert with a once a day beauty.

The clouds flow overhead like flocks of geese heading south
For the winter.

Another day falls by a 21st Day of July in the year of
1994, a day that will never exist again.

The look of anguish on a man's face passes by.
A man of experience in the game of life.
A man I will never see again as long as I live.

The roads buildings and people cut through the natural
Desert in a day that will never again exist as...

"TODAY"

Josh May

Embroider the Psalms

Embroider the psalms on your heart
Embroider all the lovely things in the
  Bible within your soul
Braided and zigzagged and stitched for God
With His lovely designs each being
The floss is the loveliness
The stitching is the soul-touching
Teaching and admonishing in our homes
Loving and guarding ourselves and God's flock
From sin's harm or others
Flossing and Stitching-teaching and guiding
Embroidering up the soul and all the life within it
Finished and shining with beauty
With life in every part
Because God is the great designer and finisher of our hearts

Judy Mallory

Do Something

Get up, do something
Don't let the river of life pass you by.
Make a friend
Make an enemy
For goodness sakes do something before you die,
Life is full of adventures for the takers
Reach out for one, take it with your hands
Hold it, cherish it, use it the best you can.
Be a leader
Be a follower
But don't you dare be the watcher
For all you'll get if you watch
is a pocket full of lint and an empty heart.

Christine Dill

Prism Of Love

My love for you is like glittering lights shinning through a prism.
Enchanting lights spread vibrant colors only lovers can see.
The passion of red when our hearts ignite warms my smile.
The vitality of yellow when your words of love caress me keeps me comforted.
Sensual blues as endless as the sky and our love ensures my trust in our future.
I savor the greens for it brings new life to each day.
The prism lights in our hearts can take your breath away.
They sparkle in my eyes when I speak your name.
They shine all day and are lasting unlike a firework display.
Even though they sleep, they faithfully return with glistening charm in the morning light.
In storming days they stay intact and solid and hold true for a new day.
Our prism of love will radiate with each day, pure and timeless.

Ann Marie Stein

Early Spring

As I gazed across the lake watching the foaming white caps
encouraged by the gusty wind,
Twittering birds anxiously singing in flight, heard over the
the rumble of the blustery wind.
Overhead, perfectly blue sky, not a wisp of cloud,
across the horizon streamed a hazy gray azure.

Yesterday the lake was glass smooth, no ripple from a breeze,
So peaceful compared to the invigorating feel today.
Tulips, daffodils, newly budded tree branches, all swaying in the
brisk wind sweeping across the black colored water.

Soon summer sultry heat flecked only by the slightest breeze
will replace this wonderful expression of spring.

Eleanor Luke

True Beauty

To look at the picturesque visage, the sculpted body
even the glistening eyes
Is to miss the true beauty of him.
Given by God is the face of an angel
Blessed by Him is he molded in perfection
and seen only through forever are the heavens in his eyes
and the reflection of his soul.
But go on
for if you do not, you miss the reason
the reason to love.
A soul given to few deserving
so rare and fragile
to see it, to feel it, to know its touch
is to know his true beauty of life.
This soul
a gift from God to one
shared with another
is love
The beauty of him
forever.

Kimberly A. Orofino

"Wonders Of The Waterfall"

A gentle rush of water
Caressed the majestic heart-rending pain
Flowing like a cloudburst of tears
The fall beckoned the great shadow of depression
Approaching the surface the moisture weld up
Releasing the sorrow and welcoming peacefulness
The mountainous pain escaped
As the water cascaded over her,
She experienced the wonders of the waterfall

Jennifer Sutton

Untitled

Warmth like the sunlight,
even though it has set,
this isn't the first,
we have met.
Your face shimmers in the light,
your tears, soft as the blanket of my comfort,
My soul cries out at your sight,
there are things we most sort.
Our love was lost in the mist,
the rain falls softly,
I shudder under your light kiss,
though things still seem haughty.
I cry in the sight of your hurt,
I look to the imaginary candle for light,
I feel like dirt,
and it all gives flight.

Jodie Lea Higby

"Our Gift"

Beauty that surrounds me, why did it take so long to see
ever there and always has been, not just there for me

In the Winter as the snow falls and the sun reflects each flake
diamond-like reflections as we extend our hand to take

Springtime welcomes blossoms, appearing on branches bare
anticipation filled with wonderment, an array of color everywhere

Balmy nights of Summertime, so quiet so serene, the birds, the
bees and butterflies, give each day an Artists scene

Autumn in all its splendor, the golds and rusty reds, awesome
in its solitude, a single word need not be said

Can't place a monetary value for the cost is simply free
this Beauty that surrounds us, God gave to you and me.

Doree' Du Teau

Bound . . . But Free . . .

When the world turns against you, and
every friend is foe. You sit back and
wonder will there be more. You give
it your best. All you do is fret.
Tears start to flow. Your mind
goes blank. You don't stop to think
asking yourself why is this happening
to me. All I want is to be free
Like a summers breeze...Unchained
swirling in unknown directions
no where in particular. Just part of everyday life.

Katherine Eldyne Evans Starling

The Circle Never Ends

It all starts when you fall in love,
Every obstacle you'll rise above.

As days go by, they ask where's the ring?
So much persistence for such a small thing.

When the ring is received no one can wait,
Time to get busy; you must set a date.

When you finally make it to marital bliss,
Opportunities to ask for kids they won't miss.

Just like the farmer with a garden to tend,
The work doesn't stop when the sun descends.

As time goes by, intentions you'll defend,
Love is like a ring: a circle with no end.

Kelly Newsome

Insomnia

The vast kingdom Night consumes with infinite darkness
Every still house abandoned by the fleeting Day.
Sleep governs the citizens with the cool repose of dreams,
To acquiesce them from the belaboring Sun.
But I, awake, plead to the coupled throne of Silence and Seclusion
For some sympathetic sigh, that would crumble the lonely monarchy.
Fervently restless, hungry, irrational - I toss, tremble and stare.
Sleep! Dutiful governor! Can you pass so indifferently over my bed?
Oh careless lover! Betray me, abandon me, madden me!
But by darkened Morning's first hours, slip intoxicatingly upon me,
That I forget the shackles of reality and welcome you gratefully.
Deep, deep Sleep - too short for dreams or peace,
Then militant Morning's mistress lures you away
And I am awake, a prisoner to the Day.

Elaine C. Fajardo

Captured

So amazing, your beauty, your grace,
every time you look at me my heart begins to race.

Your smile so passionate as we dance beneath the rain,
you brought happiness to my life,
pushing out all the pain.

The wind blows your fragrance and my love falls true,
you have turned my darkest of skies so perfectly blue.

The forest whispers your name in my ear,
just trust in my love and you will never shed a tear.

Kiss my lips for tonight forever will start,
there is no turning back, you have your hands around my heart.

Anthony Marafioti

Why Did I Have To Be Me?

Everywhere I go trouble seems to follow,
everyday of my life is filled with sorrow.
Nothing I do seems to be right,
I spend hours at a time, crying myself to sleep at night.

Love is a stranger that I've never met before,
I'm just a speck of life that it seems to ignore.
The pain is too heavy, it's making me weak,
understanding and compassion is all that I seek.

Can't you see all the pain, I'm dying inside,
slowly fading away, I have nowhere to hide.
Soon there'll be nothing, I don't want to live anymore,
life is something I don't seem to adore.

They say what doesn't kill you will make you stronger,
I've tried to be strong, I can't do it any longer.
Some of you might not feel this way,
but what I feel is just something I have to say.

Saying this is hard because its all true,
hearing all this has probably made you blue.
I'm hurting inside, can't you see.
please tell me truthful, why did I have to be me?

Kim Thai

The Park

O beautiful park, so wondrous and vast,
Your trees tall and majestic, like ages long past.
You're so full of trees, so big and so wide;
All animals live within, with places to hide.
All peoples come see you, so marvelous, so great;
Your beauty shows out, which no one can hate.
You resemble other parks, but you're named specially.
You're so warm and so caring, and there just for me.

Kurt Buhr

My Life

When I was a baby
Everyone said just maybe
She can be president someday.

Then when I became a little girl
Everyone said she is as pretty as a pearl
Out of the deep ocean blue.

Now as I am a teen
Everyone says there's a lot you haven't seen
So don't try to grow up too fast.

When I grow older
They'll probably say that I've grown colder
To the world around me.

And as I lay on my death bed
They'll just might say the life I've led
Was not my own, cause with everyone telling
Me what to do, I never found it for myself.

Deseree Strack

Reflections

He sat in the chair. He could not feel anything except for the warmth of the sun. He looked at his hands. They did not move on their own anymore. He looked at his feet. He smiled. He had always liked his feet. He tried to wiggle them, but they would not wiggle. He tried harder. They would not wiggle. His vision became blurred. A tear or two trickled down his cheek. Why did it have to happen to him? He did not deserve this! Nobody deserved this. He let the tears fall from his eyes. He thought of what it had been like before. How wonderful it was to run and be free. But then he stopped and thought about back then. He took everything for granted. He did not say thank you to God for anything. Then he came back to reality and let the tears just role down his pink hot cheeks. He looked up at the sky and smiled. He looked at his toes and smiled. He looked down at his hands and smiled. Then quietly, so that almost no one could hear, he said "Thank you God, thank you."

Breigh McKinney

Windows

A tan box contained my thoughts,
expressed by ivory keys
and exhibited garishly on the screen.
Beyond the monitor
the window was muted by lace curtains
separating life into a honeycomb.

My eyes rested on the hummingbird
hovering above the fuschia in the back garden.
Dumpster, my black and white cat sat poised
intent as a child at a video game
waiting for the high-intensity bird to light
on the delicate flower
a fast-food nugget for his pleasure.

I rejoiced for the predator.
I grieved for the prey.

The screen offered me a choice
to Delete, Search, Escape
But the window offered me
no such options.

Kate Wallace

"Man Of Stone"

Your brown eyes are expressionless and cold and your
Face holds many lines for your age.

A multitude of women have passed through your life
And your affairs could fill many a page.

You have scornfully replied that you have never known
Love - forbidden has been its birth.

And as a conqueror you somehow rule and you gaze on
Your subjects with mirth.

Yours seems to be a world apart which no tender words
Can caress.

You appear to be a man of stone - no heart do you possess.

Many are the times I have tried in vain to look into
your soul -

Only to find your arms outstretched - my presence to withhold.

When age plays its role in life and your cold brown
Eyes are not sure;

And your now graying hair bears the color of snow,
I wonder "can you endure?"
Will you always be your own world? Will you continue
As a man of stone?
Or will you at long last learn to love so that in your
World you won't be alone?

Carolyn Dawne Conner Flora

My Day in the Sun

Like the sun I wait for her to rise.
Large, beautiful and powerful I am compelled to stare into her.
Basking in her love if only for the day and her
Memory enough to warm me throughout the night.

Like the sun she comes without warning.
Giving without taking.
Sharing with no need of compensation.

How can I not love her.
How can I hide in the darkness when her
brilliance makes me feel so alive.

David E. Hickman

This Woman Known Only As Arow

There I sat, sipping lemonade with eyes closed and mind slightly cluttered by thoughts of times past. And as casually as I sipped, she appeared. She appeared like a cool breeze that caresses the coast just before sundown on a calm summer day. And there I stared at this woman; this beautiful woman; and in every sense a woman as she aroused the most erotic of feelings in me with just a mere glance from behind her angelic eyes.

She was breathtaking. She was sexy; no, exotic and quite seductive. She was beautiful, bold, vivacious, radiant, majestic, and devastatingly hypnotic.

And on my word she was desired. Desired, like a sleek bed on a steamy night in a scantily lit room filled with the exotic scent of female attraction.

And as I rose for a second glance, I was reminded; reminded of what it felt like to be in love. This feeling, this incredible feeling which brought to mind days reminiscent of bold discovery and beauty often dreamed but rarely seen

She walked toward me gliding with every step, and with every step illuminating sunlight and divine grace. This vision who stood before me with heavenly beauty and brought to me meaning of my mere existence, and bliss to my once saddened heart. And my mind and my heart danced in blissful glee as I stood before perfection.
This Arow, this beautiful and wonderful woman known only as Arow

Kendrick LaKeith Barnes

WLM : URNS - MCMLXXVI - 2A

My friends were sitting around the fire
roasting a frog who had croaked too loud
joking among themselves
over the language-linked relationship
of pure silence
to the bit of meat
spread-eagled on the grille

Perhaps in his wee animal mind he too like a god
expected to make effects without suffering causes

Perhaps a training in philosophy instead of poetry
might have left his hauteur unsinged in the purple air

Well before him one history after him another

Perhaps he had within him saving thoughts
had he sung with less éclat
his strange unfathomable happiness

We frogs tho have never been known
for clarity of thought

But then what are friends for

wlm
08-21-95

Spring Violets

Her scent came in and wrapped itself
around me. It came from the spring
air, in through the window like an old
friend. The day before she died.
She's here, I can feel her. *Hello Grammy.*

Hi Dollface.

For me, objects that she owned don't
hold her memory, it's the springtime,
the church bells, and my mother.
All remind me of her and how much
she meant to me. *What's it like in heaven?*

It's beautiful.

I would ask her questions about my life
and what it's worth but I already know,
she already told me. With Him by her
side she told me. *Tell Papa I said hello.*

I will.

Kimberly A. Harring

A Perfect Pet

Darling little dogs to have as
A friend to cheer you up when you're down; with their
Cute and innocent faces, these small
Hound dogs are
Smart and intelligent; they
Have long bodies and short legs; they look rather
Unusual, but they're
Nice, sweet dogs; no
Doubt about it.

Monique Miyashiro

Sara

Sunday morning
About ten-thirty
She sits crosslegged on the floor.
Wide-eyed and winsome,
Lost in luminous thought,
She sips her cinnamon tea
And reads a tattered copy of *Anna Karenina.*
The sunlight dances across her face
Playing tag with the soft outline of her features
While corkscrew curls fall in perfect proximity
To a half-crooked smile,
And all the while
She never knows how I silently study her
And decide that she is ultimately more intriguing
Than even the heroine about whom she reads.

Kim A. Goss

Birth Defect

O, cursėd birth defect that tears my heart with anguish
And gives me up to scorn from men of less estate.
What matters wealth? For though I'd countless millions
As long as I am thus cursed is my fate.

And so pronounced in form e'en though not too uncomely,
But hated with such passion is my evil bane
That I, like to the leper of time olden,
Would cry out when approached, "Unclean, unclean."

Repulsed, oppressed and scorned I turn to that above me
Harassing Heaven for some surcease of my lack.
Who answering my prayer aborts hope unborn;
No cure has this cursed birth defect, Born Black!

Alfred T. Mitchell

Halloween Night

Hearken to the chilling howls of werewolves on the moor.
Are you safe inside your house, with crosses on the door?
Listen to the fearsome wind that blows down from the mount.
Look to God to save you from dread creatures beyond count.
Over blasted countrysides fly demons on the wing,
While witches pay black homage to Lucifer, their king.
Enchanting music tempts you now to come forth from your bed.
Everyone who heeds its call shall join the walking dead.
Netherworld horrors seize their chance to go where man doth dwell;
Now the world shall know the vengeful denizens of Hell.
If you wish to see another dawn, you must be brave;
Ghouls are gathering in the moonlight, envoys from the grave.
Hold your pistol at the ready, keep your dagger near.
They're coming to devour your soul — God help you — now they're here.

Matthew Spaeth

Intraflection

Reflection - - - - - - - - Scrutinization
Contemplation - - - - - - - - - Meditation
Dedication - - - - - - - - - - - Vocation
Commitment - - - - - - - - - - - Expectations
Responsibilities - - - - - - - - - Obligations
Consideration - - - - - - - - - - - - Promises
Indignation - - - - - - - - - - - - Retaliation
Contemptible - - - - - - - - - - - Reparation
Negotiation - - - - - - - - - - - - Resolution
Intelligence - - - - - - - - - - - - Prudence
Supplication - - - - - - - - - - Restitution
Resignation - - - - - - - - - - Quiescence
Participation - - - - - - - - Fulfillment

Patrice

Another Decade

It's hard to believe the 80's have gone,
As well as a musician, a "Beatle" named John.

"Yuppies" and cabbage patch, and Cher's derrière,
While AIDS and abortion made us socially aware.

A rebellion was crushed in Tiennamen Square,
And "cough potatoes" said, "they didn't care."

Crude oil devastated an Alaskan bay,
While recycling trash became the new way.

There were Olympic boycotts, and a Chernobyl disaster,
While in the N.H.L., Gretzky was master.

With a "Phantom" on Broadway, an E.T. on screen,
To a 'quake in the Series and Life Magazine.

A new leader in Russia changed the face of our world,
The Nobel Peace Prize would be Gorbachev's herald.

Norman and Strange were driving the ball,
While Pink Floyd and Berlin were destroying a wall.

So let's celebrate the end of a decade,
The memories we have and the friends that we've made.

In the coming years a century will leave,
And once again we will say, "It's hard to believe!"

Jay Warren Downs

Behind the Mask

I try to smile, but it's no use.
How can I smile when taking abuse?

Day after day, night after night
I run in terror, scream in fright.

The pain, the hurt — will it ever be gone?
Is this torture a result of my doing wrong?

Why does he do this? He is my *dad*
So why does he treat me so cruelly, so *bad?*
- It hurts -

Lisa Martin

We Toasted Friendship

From the sky, a floor of Aztec puzzle pieces,
Land gave leaves of sea-grape trees saved for a memory;
we dined on sandwiches of smoked pork, garlic, and Cuban bread
and spent the day shelling with the sandpipers-pelicans swooping,
sea gulls eating, bathers baking in the ocean sun.

Lizards, hurons, red-headed ducks at home in the sawgrass,
we, sipping wine, exchanged our recipes
for spinach dill rice and caramel cake.

Early, after coffee, muffins, and cream cheese,
we drove through the Everglades to Sanibel Island,
the mangrove trees' giant roots exposed and sucking up the water
alligators lazed in on the way.

At "Ding" Darling Refuge, double-crested cormorants, anhingas,
egrets, roseate spoonbills, moorhens, and osprey thrive;
we preferred the shopping, piña coladas, and the sun.
And so, we bought our souvenirs and shelled again and read awhile.

Portofino's served the best scampi and Delfini salad, brass-railed
elegance, grand-piano ambiance; we laughed and toasted friendship.

Susan Diane Bidwell

I Often Walk Among The Noble

Hidd e n i n strange recesses of my mind
She's always the r e a n d I'm blinded
By the brilliance of h e r s u mmer dress
Thrown haphazard l y o n a nearby stone
I find refu g e i n her arms
Nourish e d a s if a child
Giving all I a m f r eely
Gaini n g t h e respect of my people
Blowing the du s t f r om my tainted treasures
Never before divulging are the s e g o verned lips
Beseeching th e e M y Queen
Bear my cro w n m a nifesting this jester's dream

Mending the hollows of my fragile soul.

Erich W. Maas

In Loving Memory Of Andre Deyampert

Young man, young man,
what do you say?
"Trust in God"!
He made me this way
To bring strength and love
to all my kin,
to challenge the world
again and again,
To be the pride
in my mother's eye,
to know the meaning
behind her sigh
To spend time with you
for a little while,
and go home to him
while still a child.

Virginia G. Farmer

In These Times

It seems at times the world is on my shoulders
When I seek for love and comfort I cannot find it
I cannot find the answers no matter where I turn
Those who love me try to help but cannot overcome my tears
These are the times I must turn to God in all His glory
The times I face that cause me anguish
That sometimes make me crazy; that make me someone else
When I looked for love and love was not there
The times I needed someone yet I was left alone
These are the times I must turn to God in all His glory
The times I needed tranquility but got noise
When I needed loving arms but the arms were tired
The times I'm weary yet I'm faced with responsibility
When all these times fall together and break me down
These are the times I must turn to God in all His glory

Magdalena Menné

Music of the Spheres

Pulsing in cold brilliance, whirling in mystic stillness,
Fires in filled voids, are ancient yet ageless.

Infinite from its birth, is such majestic pageantry.
In deep seated splendor, rites of ancient court are gently performed.
In dimensions above and of their own sing stars of eons.

In changeless changing paths, in orbits deep and clear,
travel stars forever
To the music of the spheres.

Christy Bond

Do I Exist?

I am walking down this road
You can hear nothing, see nothing, feel nothing,
Therefore I am nothing. — Or am I?
Even if you can't see me, or see what I do,
Does that means that I do not exist?
I play music
And dance for the stars at night.
They know who I am
Just as I know who they are.
I may not exist in your world,
But I do in mine!
And I will exist until the dawn of time.
Dancing around you in circles,
Teasing you, tempting you,
Even when you can not feel me.
But, When you feel me
You will be hit by all the stars in the night.
Then, I will not be quiet!
You will feel me with each beat of your pulse,
And the dreams of your heart.

Aimée C. Russell

'Albert'

A world renown face, while most never knew,
Your legend recognized, perhaps in notorious view
Remembered for your ideas, maybe more so by I.Q.,
Forget the rumors, let's try to understand you

It's been said you ushered in the atomic age,
Loving freedom, you understood appeasement's wage
While opposing violence, you were aware of course,
There was no reasoning, counter Adolf with force

Your engagement in conflicts, were mentally fought,
Simple talk of life, while yourself in deep thought
Dreams of the future and the prospects of peace,
Knowing if only one side negotiates, peace will cease

Teaching yourself science, foreign to most of us,
All types of physics, even the formidable calculus
Oh Einstein, you were certainly no man's fool,
The first to split the atom, would surely rule

As a Swiss patent officer, you so naturally excelled,
Respecting the Fatherland, against Hitler rebelled
A generous mathematician, your work gladly shared,
The world still upholds the victory of: $E=mc^2$.

Dane S. Jester

Dessy Belle

Dessy Belle floats
down the canal
peacefully
Gently
caressing the final destination
with her voice.

Sometimes she has s>h>a>t>t<e<r<e<d me like
the beating, **beating, beating** of my "tympani"
in the wild drum-song of life.

She can be cruel sometimes with **great number**
or she can be kind and pacific as the
ocean wave...(evaw naeco).

My beautiful Dessy Belle
I love you dearly, for without
you
Praise
would fall on deaf ears.

Decibel, can you hear me, my love?

Barbara E. Riley

Why Do I Have A Garden?

I love to smell the scent of green, of growing things around:
sweet basil fragrance, sharp tomato leaves, the clean green odors of the ground.
I cherish the aroma of rich and loving earth,
newly dampened by sprinkler or rain releasing the essence of nature, of birth

I love to see the yellow-green humps of beanstems push through rich, brown soil;
the mouse-ear leaves breaking out of the seeds springing from the stem's tight coil.
And I love to see the yearning vine reach high to find a pole to climb;
and to watch the vines grow taller each day as higher and higher they wend their way.

I love to see the proud, new corn shoots point impudently up through broken earth,
then fling blades on either side as arms in praise of their own birth.
And I love to watch them thicken and grow like the strongest of soldiers in a row,
yet cradling ears, papoose-like corn with golden flowing hair, turn brown.

I love to see tomato plants, tiny and tender, straggly and frail
grow full-leafed, thick-stemmed and bushy high, wafting their spirit as I brush them by.
I love to see the baby tomato expand and change from green to yellow to orange to red.
And how my chest swells up with pride at the largest, smoothest and roundest of them all.

I love to smell the scents of green, of growing things around:
sweet basil fragrance, sharp tomato leaves, the clean green odors of the ground.
I cherish the aroma of rich and loving earth,
newly dampened by sprinkler or rain releasing the essence of nature, of birth.

Lani Keetch Pappano

Keep Believing

The Blessings of the Lord happens everyday it helps you in good ways.
Even if you do not believe in Him He does things for you.
And if you do He does things for us.
So we just have to keep on believing in His name.

Janine N. Johnson

Mom

My Mom is dying this I know but how can I accept it and just let her go?

God is coming, He is near, but how can I let Him take her and swallow my fear?

I never told her, does she know? How much I love her so. Will I ever be happy like she
wanted me to be? That is the only thing my mother ever wanted for me.

Two beautiful granddaughters will never fully know the grandmother who loved them so.

Who will ever hold me and make me feel safe, and now who will wipe the tears from my face?

We will try to be strong, we will have to go on, but how can we dot this, our best friend
is gone. My mother will be gone soon, taken away from my sister and me.
Will we make her proud the way she deserved to be?

My worry is for my father, how will he go on when his wife, lover, and best friend is gone?

We will be there for him, we will be his rocks to cry one. We will carry him
through the rough times and make him push on. Someday the pain will ease
although never be gone, and my daddy will find happiness and a way to move on.

Cancer is ugly. Cancer is mean. How many loved ones will it take before we find a vaccine?

Cancer can take away my mother and take away my dream. But cancer will
never beat me or make me mean, because someday we will find a cure and the
suffering will end. No more chemotherapy, no radiation, we can say goodbye to them.
And I hope I live to see that day because cancer took my precious mother away.

Goodbye for now Mom. They tell me I have to let you go. But we'll be together again . . . this
I know. The place you are going is so beautiful I've heard
And it's free from all the pain and suffering you have endured.

Go on your journey, go Mom in peace knowing we'll all be together
again in a place free from this disease.

Your loving daughter,

Kimberley Zublena

So often this poet takes pen in hand
when loneliness surrounds.

Failing to create an effect
in the material world,
it's an attempt to leave and try
from outside its bounds.

Taking my message with all its thoughts
I convert them into words and sounds.

Hoping and trying again
to cause any impact,
I'll be happy even if
my poem only astounds.

The listener's reactions thrill me
and I come alive as I realize
this evidence of success is grounds
for me being in this shared universe
where life - after all - abounds.

(December 23, 1994)

Carisa Marion

Smash the Hash

Smoking on a butt
Feeling kind of high
Your body is relaxed
With your bloody red eyes

Now you're smoking more
You're starting to see things
You're looking over your shoulders
You're hearing bells ring

You lost support of your family
You lost your friends too
You want to get help
But you don't know what to do

You're at the treatment center
Getting the help you need
You now lost your appetite
And you cannot sleep

6 months have gone by
Since you last smoked a joint
You got your friends and family back
Did you get the point?

Keisha LáToi Singleton

Each Day I Still Can

Thank the Lord I can talk.
I'd be quite upset if not.
For you see I can't walk.

Thou not perfect I can see.
Sun, sky, my family, also trees.
This is wonderful, I'm so pleased.

When spoken to, I can hear,
Outside sounds, friend, family dear.
Thunder, rain, music, voices even tears.

I'll smile at all with ease
So: Make my day you'll see.
Just smile at me, yes please.

All above is quite a treat.
Typing this would make it neat.
Now I'm going right to sleep.

Mildred V. Schall

Peace Be Unto You

Be at peace within
Understanding can begin
Be at peace without
Teach and don't shout
Be at peace with others
Treat people as your brothers
Be at peace with yourself
For peace receives knowledge.

Jonathon S. Jacobs

The Silence Of God

God is silent to all our cries
And in silence hears our prayers.
He bears in silence our demise,
And silently shows He cares.

He stands in silence by the grave
And silently wipes our tears.
He heals in silent, soul to save,
And in silent grief, He hears.

He stood in silence at the cross,
And in silence gave His Son,
In silence, He conquered Death,
And in silence, the victory won.

He speaks to us in silent ways,
In silence only is He heard.
He whispers to our silent hearts,
And silently reveals His word.

He stands in silent benevolence;
In silence His love is shown.
He forgives our sins in silence,
And in silence, claims His own.

Gerald E. Hood Sr.

My Son

How can I explain
A gift sent from above
A wonder to behold
The meaning of your love

How I do convey
A happiness so rare
The kind that floods my heart
Completely uncompared

How shall I express
To this precious baby boy
Who is my only child
That he fills my soul with joy
Jesse is your name
You are my inspiration
These last two years have proved
You are God's rare creation

With love so unconditional
Let wisdom be my guide
To raise our precious son
Who is my greatest pride

Gerrie Harrison

Knowing Now

In motion
Going nowhere
I see
I am
Now here.

Helene M. Cross

The Red Carriage

Solemn faced Moscowitz stand as still as statues along the stone wall of the railroad station
Huddled close together in the sweeping massive space, but over there a solitary one.

It's winter and Chantal's camera catches touches of color on scarves 'round shoulders and necks
guarding against the bitter gusts of wind from the approaching trains.

Silently, they, the people wait and watch today, like yesterday, and tomorrow
So *matter-of-factly*
They are in a place that has no time, in a space of infinite dimension.

The camera moves slowly from the crowd to the individual sitting on an isolated bench.
Methodically the sequence unfolds countless anonymous faces
People on line, in line, in a circle *patiently waiting*.

Subtle gradations of light reveal undercurrents of life flowing past
Then, unexpected pleasure reconstructs the monotony of the repetitious pattern
A bright, *ruby red carriage* interrupts the weary crowd and, all too quickly, moves on.

Once again, we are left with the tolerant passengers - baggage close at hand
Waiting, waiting for that flashing light that will signal the train to *somewhere*.

Roslye B. Ultan

What Does It Take?

Does it take a man, to be homeless?
Does it take a woman, to be harmed?
Does it take a child, to be parentless?
Does it take a family, to be destroyed?
No, I think not....
It takes a man to stand tall and to be proud of his accomplishment
and dreams, that becomes a reality.
It takes a woman to care and save the world from immortal values.
and know her being is important to us all.
It takes a child to grow and increase our knowledge and wisdom
but, not allow us to be weak.
It takes a family of all race, sex and creed to be as one.
To use our backbones as people, to unite us in life and tradition of
moral values.
And no matter what we do, and how we do it. It takes God who sees
our souls and spirits alike, to revive our living and help us to be,
as people, black and white, good and bad, young and old. To put
aside negative thoughts, but lift up the good that will always defeat
the bad. Now, that's what it takes for us, as people, to be, as **human beings.**

Paula F. Cooper

Day Ghost

In the neon lit room you were no more than breath, just a glimmer of translucent thought,
Yet you can called to my heart, iridescence alive, immortality in whispered word,
And the deep of my mind that gossamer thread was from thence inescapably caught,
And I longed from that hour for the glimpse of a movement that heralded your faint return,
But the rest of that day and its cold empty night were bereft of the gift that I sought

On the following morn as I poured over books in the beam of the same neon light,
Came a shimmer of gold in the corner beside me that formed once again into you,
I was wrapped in the tendrils of warm glowing mists, and the sea of your jade colored eyes,
Set me free as I'd never known freedom before, independent of all winds that blew
On the surface of earth, yet my joy was short lived, for you vanished with oncoming night

In the gathering darkness I grieved, for my loss was unnaturally painful to bear,
And the chill of the evening bit deeper than flesh, reached the hollow gray vault of my soul,
And I prayed to the stars for the warmth of your smile, for the soft, pale wisps of your hair
For the calm, melting green of your large-irised eyes, for the vision that might make me whole,
But the black night lived on an eternity more, only dawn brought the end of despair

It has followed consistently, days turned to years, and my nights remain hopeless and bleak,
Would that I could be blessed with enraptured embrace of your arms in the moon brightened dark,
But as I watch you climb in your car once again, unaware of the chaos you wreak
In my soul, I hope vainly you might let him know, set me free of the miserable stark
Lonely nights without you, leave his ring and take mine, my beloved, at last, stay with me!

A. Muir

Birds Eat

From far away I watch the birds eat;
A dove, a cardinal, a jay, a tweet.
They dip and peck and scratch and dip
Until the sun says, for this day I quit.

Henry Langston

The Waterfall

Pouring the precipice over,
All day and into the night,
Caressing rocks projecting,
Descending its Olympian height.

The cataract's tons of water,
Plunging to the depths below,
Translucent mists upsurging,
Creating a spectral bow.

Roaring! Foaming into the crucible,
Exploding! Into white water spray,
Swelling, tossing, heaving, churning,
An unkaleidoscopic display.

Harold L. Sampson

Untitled

Birthed from pleasure
And born unto need,
Your life arose
From a single seed.

In this bustling world
How will you grow?
Who will be your teacher?
And what will you know?

You could learn the lyrics of life
From tales of the old,
Or live by songs of strife
Sung by the youthful and bold.

No matter, your path,
Golden or green,
Age will have its wrath
Quietly gentle or boisterously mean.

Regardless of the many voices
Who seems to make you prone,
Remember the gifts of personal choices
For your life is your own.

Frank Hartley

Dew On The Early Morning Rose

The rose awaits for the dawn to break
and dry up the moisture from her
delicate petals.

She quivers with anticipation for the
rebirth of her strength.

Moon's last glint of light has faded
into the western sky.

The awakening of the sun radiates
warmth onto the rose and gently kisses
away the dew.

Gina Thomas

"I'm Your Mother"

I have to kiss your face
And invade your space.
I'm your mother.
I can do that.

I wash off some dirt
With some spit and my shirt.
I'm your mother.
I can do that.

I see you playing hard and free.
I'm sorry when you skin your knee;
If you want to, bleed on me.
I'm your mother.
You can do that.

I love to watch you grow;
But someday I'll let you go.
I'm your mother.
I love you.
I can do that.

Genevieve Armstrong

"Unity"

May peace become our aim in life
And love become our goal.
May dreams become reality
And people be made whole.

Let joy be lasting in each heart
And friendships deeper be.
May Earth grow smaller everyday
With dialogue the key.

We'll turn our spears to pruning hooks
And all the wars shall cease.
We'll live fore'er in utter bliss
In harmony and peace.

The greatest gift that we can give
Is joy and peace and love.
For this my friend is unity
Descending like a dove.

May joy live now within you heart
And faith remain your stay,
And love become your light and hope
For living day by day.

Helen C. Nowlan

Untitled

I looked into your eyes
And my soul disappeared
Behind them
I followed to search
To search
To search
In our moments and minutes
Until its found
Or with fortune
Look forever

Gary Ferree

Her

Sweet and anxious.
Naughty and carefree.
A warm bundle
A memory that defied more then a year.
Little words to say so much.
A look of happiness just because I am here.
A little person, a heart so big.
Her name is Voya, she is my dog

Anghel Tchividjian

Waiting

If you're not sure what you want yet,
And need some time to decide,
I'll give that time to you,
But hold my pain inside.
You should be come to me sooner,
But instead, you just lied.
I tried to avoid the possibilities,
Those thoughts I just denied.
My feelings for you are strong,
That fact I cannot hide.
This love is the kind that
I've been searching for, far and wide.
But I will not beg and plead,
I know how to keep my pride.
I'll just wait for your decision,
But I'll be right by your side.

Holly Townsend

Just A Phone Call

If I could just pick up the phone
And talk for just a minute-
I'd tell you of my love for you
And every dream, you're in it.

I'd tell you how I've missed you
Since the Lord took you away
And how I say a prayer for you
Most every day.

I'd tell you how I miss your calls
And the funny things you say,
I'd love to hear your voice once more
But the Lord took you away.

We were only granted fifty years
And then your work was done,
An angel took you to a place
Beyond the setting sun.

I'm not supposed to grieve for you
You're in a better place
But I wish that God would just once more
Let me see your smiling face.

Frances M. Rader

A Tribute To Edward

Edward was my husband
And your father too.
He left us for a better world
When he was only 72.

His last days were peaceful
And he just drifted away.
We all tried to help him
But these was just no way.

So when he left us
All of our family was there.
It made it a little easier
For all of us to bear.

But we'll always remember
That in our hearts he'll always be.
We know he's keeping watch
Over all of you and me.

But life must go on;
That's the way it has to be.
We'll keep him in our prayers
And in our memories.

Helen D. Hardon

Destruction

Nature keeps going and going
As we keep destroying
Everything goes in a circle
And it is changing to a square
We need some conservation
So stop and make a notation
The trees and animals are crying
Losing their homes and dying
The rain forest might have a cure
For something we are unsure
Oil spillage in the sea
Does nothing but harm to me
Air pollutants make acid rain
That is a threat and hard to maintain
Everyone needs to look out for each other
Instead of hurting one another
This is all I have to say
Lets start working on it today

Heather Julian

A Cry From The Heart

Justice mocks a sultry smile
as you approach
the crowded aisle.

All those awaiting judgement fear
their deep dark ride
on evil's rear.

The DA and attorney's mannerly approach
is just a "show"
of human touch.

When all along their plea has been
to keep the client
kept within.

How ironic when justice rebounds
and it is found
that they too
have also sinned.

Grace Barral

The Miracle

A sweet angelic voice calls to my heart
beckoning to let my spirit run free
to believe, to trust, to love.

A beautiful vision appears before me
revealing wonders yet to come
unfulfilled dreams yet to live.

A fiery warmth overwhelms me
kindled by passion and desire
aglow with tenderness and care.

I now understand...
The beauty of the songs of the angels.
The colors of the rainbow,
bursting forth,
to reveal wonders hidden for so long.
The power of love,
not only for one another, but life itself.

For it is now that my beautiful angel has
appeared
to lift me from the cold dark depths, to lead
me to the warmth of the
light, to listen to me, to care for me, to
simply love me...
To simply accept my love.

Gregory Minardo

Forgotten Soul

Don't wander too far
Beyond the depths of night.
Whether only it be your soul,
Or your thoughts
In aimless plight.

Don't lend yourself to weariness,
For endless it may be.
Your journey to the other world,
Where evil preys on thee.

Instead remain lighthearted,
Those who will to hold the key.
Shall gain eternal happiness,
In His arms will always be.

Gale Naquin Leblanc

Tchye

The earth is breathing
Blue smoke dances slowly towards
my window
Then away
Like it is teasing the fireflies that lay
Just out of reach
Kissing the night air
It hesitates
Then whisks out
Unable to
Restrain itself any longer
The Mother opens her eyes
and waits for that next hit here
the earth is breathing

Inga Joy Cantley

Snow

Snowflakes,
Born in heaven, individual,
Fall, float, arms outstretched,
Their crystalline beauty
Hidden by macroscopic view
And countless numbers.
Each with countless facets white,
Radiating in harmonious symmetry,
Radiates all wavelengths of light.

All fall softly on dark earth,
Alone at first,
Untouched by others,
Populating the sleeping grass.

Silently two touch, then four,
Synchronous with so many more,
All soon softly surrounded
Then covered.
The dark earth becomes brilliant
In the silence of touching.
In the reflection of light.

Howard Jones

Tomorrow

Seeds await their planting
the chosen path of the heart
Life beckons in the distance
promising struggle
but also hope
Love offered returned
knowledge to be sought
Truth and justice to be found

Eva Kaye

59 Lives Gone

A Romanian Airline
Bucharest to Brussels
Sleet, storm
Exploded, crashed
Bomb threat earlier
NO SURVIVORS
49 Passengers, 10 Crew
All 59 People died
Not known, not identified
Body parts, blood
Frozen ground
Soldiers carrying body parts
Investigation
59 Lives gone.

Heather Messmer

A Revelation

We all know that the world is tough
But the world can also be very kind
So when things appear to be quite rough
Let pleasant thoughts enter your mind

As we get older and our skills rise
The complexities of life seem to increase
In these times we are now more wise
Enough to put our minds at ease

We can see a child's innocence
They are protected from most trouble
Let us too have some common sense
To not allow ourselves to tumble

As we make it through each day
The puzzles of life abound
Remember that we can enjoy it as play
And spread happiness around

Gregg Batary

Christmas Is The Magic Holiday

X'mas is the magic holiday,
Celebrated the world over in their own way.
It puts joy in peoples' hearts,
With children it plays a big part.

It brings to all ages lots of gladness,
It helps do away with sadness.
With cheerful cards and greetings,
Joyful get together's and meetings.

Beautiful trees with sparkling lights,
With many decorations and charming sights.
Christmas music in the air,
Helps make us forget our cares.

Christmas is the magic holiday,
It's traditions are here to stay.
Let's all remember the kings of kings.
In honor of the Blessed Jesus Birthday,
With tribute and praises sing.

Grace Lucille Sullivan

My Loving Mom

I remember the fun we had
Playing with mom and my dad

Even though my mom's not here
The memories of her I hold so dear

From my heart these thoughts go out
I love you mother without a doubt

Fred Knoppel II

"Mauii"

Seven pools
Enormous lush soft fronds
Contrasts of sharp colorful rocks
And earth,
Sweep across the tunneled
View of the island.
Imagine graceful movement,
Laughter, softness of bare feet
Running joyously,
Singing birds and people
Recreating what they
Learned from those
Before them.
Does the circle of life
Continue or disappear
Into desolation
Of soul.

Ilene Ann Evans

Shadow In The Corner

I can care about you, hold you,
Even love you, in a way.
I can think of you, console you,
But there's a price that I must pay.
Because you touch upon my feelings
And it hurts to let you in.
I don't want to fall for anyone.
I don't want to love again.

There's a shadow in the corner,
Of what use to be my heart,
And it covers all emotions
That could tear my world apart.
It also holds a memory
That I just can't let die
Of a love that still possesses me
That I cannot deny.

So, I can't offer anything
But friendship, and that's all.
Because what isn't shadowed
Is surrounded by a wall.

Geri Nelson English

Ending To Begin

Desire for safety
fights
the gypsy Desire.

Wanting to move on
when
finding life Wanting.

Growth is completed.
Now,
seeking more Growth.

Always seeming to say
farewell.
Parting Always.

Heart restless.
Search
to fill an empty Heart.

Helen E. Prien

Untitled

She rises in the morning,
Filling the world with light.
Slowly, she moves
But with a grace possessed
Only by natives of the celestial sky.

She opens up her arms;
The glory of her heart revealed.
And all around her
Reaches out to feel
Her warm gentle touch.

My lovely Sara,
Some say it's dawn,
But I know it's you.

Gregory Monson

O, Dove! O, Dove

O, Dove! O, Dove! My beautiful Dove!
Flying so high above.
How pretty you do look
with your wings spread out so wide,
as if to have no care at all.
O, my pretty Dove!
Won't you please light upon this ground?
So I can see you,
as you light upon this ground.
I would not hurt you,
as you light upon the ground.
For you are much to pretty
in the sight of my eyes.
But I know you are
frightened from that cat roaming around.
But never fear! I won't let them
hurt you as you light upon this ground.
I'll scare them all away,
as you spread pure your pretty wings
to light upon the ground.

Eunice Arnold

"Very Good Friend"

Today was a special day for me
For you handed me a pearl.
If fell from the sweetest lips I know-
From yours, my darling girl.

I'll always remember those special words
From now until time's end.
For of the many things you could call me-
You called me "very good friend".

I wonder if you'll ever know
How you thrilled a grandmom like me.
And how very touching from one so small-
My love, you are only three.

I'll try to always be with you
For each and every special day-
As you grow up and older
And travel along life's way.

But when I am no longer here
And have reached my journey's end-
I'd like to think you'll remember me
As always - your "very good friend".

Ida May Podolsky

The Gentle Breeze

The soft evening breeze
Gently caresses my skin.
How hot the day has been!
Oh, little breeze,
Don't tease.
Come my way,
And, awhile, stay.
Cool my parched epidermis.
I won't make a fuss.
Little gentle wind,
Come and be my friend.
Send some cool air,
So, these hot days,
I can bear.

Glenna Weber

I Am

Her white and grey
hair let down to show
her worn and wrinkled
face.

Her eyes, old and blue,
her smile, yet perfect
as ever.

Her tattered and worked
hands, grey and wrinkled
from the hard work she has
dealt with all her life.

I am, the old lady in
the mirror.

Heather Johnson

Russells Russells Russells

The James Russell Family on this earth
have given life a lot of mirth

Their humor sees them through the strife
that causes problems during life

Whatever they do they do it well
and then they sit and rest a spell

They think back on their lives so far
and know that they're a shining star

The children of these Russell folks
are filled with love and lots of jokes

Each generation that arrives
will add more love to all our lives

The James Russell folks will always be
living here on earth making family

And those in heaven look down and smile
and know their lives were all worth while

Florence Jordan Russell

The Birth Of Witchazel

Today is the birth of Witchazel.
"Who is she?"
A wise old woman.
Two years in her birthing.
Eighty years in prenatal growth.
"What is her sign?"
The Rainbow.
"Did anyone believe in her coming?"
Yes, one - a granddaughter.
"What is her name?"
Julia Marie Cook

Hazel Marie Cook

A Little Bird...

A little bird flew into my house
He did not say a word,
I looked at him
He looked at me
Grandma and this bird.
Then a great big bunch of pretty red
hearts came flowing through his beak
That was his way of reminding me that
Valentine's Day is coming next week!!!
And as those red hearts floated and
danced around my head,
What loving thoughts they did convey,
And this is what they said...
I love you, love you, love you
On this Valentine's Day
I miss you, miss you, miss you
today and every day!!!

Greta Rosenberg

Survivor

Always laughter and
his certain satin skin
laughter being
the other thing
we do well
for the millionth time
I think the same thing (mine) but
does he miss the bruised girl
he used to
ease into
does he want to examine
how much of this passion
is rooted in pain, in children
does he know the healing
is him
I say his name
to remember who I am
then
spontaneous, simultaneous
yes, I can

Greta Sue Messner

The Awakening Of Love

Why I love you the way that I do dear,
I do not know.
I only know that the thought of you,
sets my soul alive and aglow.
The realization of your being sweeps
over me so gently, so sweet,
THE AWAKENING OF LOVE flows
through
my veins to every part of me,
from my head to my feet.
Emotion caressing my body like a soft
gentle breeze on a July's summer night.
Here the fountains rise.
Your presence thrills me beyond my
ability to speak.
My very soul keeps saying, love me.
Love me again and again.
Then let me love you in return,
My Adored One.

Helen Daily

After the Death of My Mother

In agony too deep to voice,
I saw the red and yellow tulips
Sway gently in the wan sunshine
And watched a playful pup
Pull happily at the leash
Held in his masters hand
And watched a couple walking
With arms around each other
Together in the spring time
And saw my Mothers face,
Smile gently in the wan sunshine
And wished that I might die; to end
The agony too deep to voice.
After the death of my Mother.

Evangeline H. Fredric

Awakening

The air flows around me
I scan the waters of the sea
My feathers touch air
ruffling like a humans hair
My screams echo across the peaks
I do not know what my soul seeks
I dive low, my stomach skimming the water
I return to the sky with ne'er a falter
The trees fly below, quietly yearning
Snow scattered, silently burning
My eyes, green, hard, and seeking
My consciousness rapidly depleting
No longer the frightened child
But the hawk, born free and wild.

Holly Rigby

A Special Friend

I had a special friend
I told her everything
She never moved her mouth
Never said a thing

I didn't mind at all
Her not uttering a word
She'd sit, and listen to things
No one else has ever heard

She understood me perfectly
Knew all that I'd been through
She'd seen other kids
Go through them too
My special friend is gone
Yes, she's gone for good
When I look back now
I remember all she understood

All we ever shared
is now a memory
I wish I could have a time again
for just Sarah and me.

Georgia Barreiro

Saigon Rose

So pure was my little red rose,
So sharp were her thorns,
So fragrant was her personality,
A drop of rain, a ray of sun,
And a blossom for tomorrow,
Only to look, smell, and be beautiful,
To what it has been for eternity,
To prick the finger with her thorns
And to laugh at the sight of my blood.

Garland S. Springs

A Father's Wish

If I controlled the universe
I'd make all time stand still
And keep you at this tender age
Your destiny my will.

This wish is just a fantasy
And selfish though it be
I want to keep this time we share
Not just the memory.

Each passing day brings closer
The time you'll leave my care
Then all I'll have are memories
Of the times we used to share.

So off with you my child
I'll help you find your way
The world is yours tomorrow
But you are mine today.

Gerald Salustri

Evening Garden

Chains locked in tight
if only to free
from my mind, from my stomach
exploding out in a sigh
of reason upon realizing
the life of it all;
the fruit relaxes
ripened to perfection
ready to take a bite
but my gut—
my aching, repressed soul...
Eve in the garden
in the evening
rain falls in the garden
washes her hands
taste the fruit
take a big bite!
Today is no tomorrow
today is no perfect world
the garden is dead.

Trib

Untitled

"Something for you, Ma'am?
"If you'll be so kind...
"I'll need some white pine boards.
"Planed smooth at the mill.

"We'll fit them together
"To make me a box,
"Six feet by three feet,
"Fresh-smelling and new."

For years the tree grew there,
High on the hill,
Soaking up sunshine,
Rain and sweet dew.

In the box I'll diminish,
A day at a time;
Soon there'll be only
A white, grinning mime.

But six feet above me,
With green grass my cover,
Bright flowers are dancing
The gift of myself.

Genevieve O. Miller

Granny

Does your memory go to the past.
In the middle of the night?
And time seems to go to fast.
The things I want to do are out of sight.
I am to old. My day is gone.
I look at the wall.
As I lie all alone.
And wonder why I'm here at all.
Then on the wall I see.
My grandchildren's pictures.
Looking back at me.
And I know no one could be richer.
For they seem to say.
Without you we would have no day
Then I forget my sorrow,
Go to sleep happy for the morrow.

Frances Hensley

Serenade

Love came on the wings of grace,
In the warmth of the sun's embrace.
With fluid change it entered night,
And made my spirit light, so light.
The dipper dripped wine,
Our fates entwined,
As the wind sang a serenade,
Of the love we had made,
On a warm summer's day,
Beneath the willow's quieting sway.
It came on the soft, green slopes of spring,
In all of the hope that autumn brings.
With gentle care from heaven above,
My heart was filled with a grand new love.
The sky melted in cool array,
Our fates were bound to forever stay,
As the wind whispered through the trees,
With sweet peace that frees,
The soul from all fear,
And brings my love near, so near.

Heather L. Miltimore

Dreams

As I gaze out
into the sunset
I dream. I dream of
a world where true
lovers may be reunited
by some higher being.

As I gaze out into
the sunrise I
dream. I dream of the
One who can understand
the meaning of
unity. The one who
will always know what
it means to look out
to the ocean and think
of eternal peace.

As I gaze out
into darkness
I dream...

Gretchen E. Morris

Our Dog Prissy

Our dog, Prissy, quaint and small
Just went away and left us all
Perplexed and sad, lonely without
Warm, cheery feelings pets all tout.

Two dogs greeted us at our house.
Rass lived outside, Prissy with us,
They were dog friends who liked to bark
And chase around till it was dark.

Rass got sick, eventually died.
Prissy was empty, but she tired
To be happy, but thirteen years
Turned out too much to dry her tears.

Now, we come to an empty house;
Jump at whispers soft as a mouse;
Check out Prissy's favorite chair,
But never find our Prissy there.

Hazel Buckley

Beyond My Past Into Your Future

Twisting turning kicking
My scarred past tissue you
With the weight of
My conscience
Centered at my hips
A child waits and grows
In my past I hurt my body
Now balancing on the edge
Of life immortal with a life
Created born in
A world of disease
I wish I could spare you
From my body you
Come tiny infant
Feel the sunlight on your face
Feel the fresh air fill your lungs
Feel my hands tremble
Nervously anxiously anticipating
Never before conceiving
Of becoming a mother

Gregory F. Woods

Name At Last

I took my son to the S.P.C.A.,
My son picked out a cute stray.
It's been wormed, has its shots,
On license they want a name.

I bright "Idea" just hit me,
A brand new name it will be,
It's not in any dictionary,
Nor comes up and computer machine.

His name shall be Comhere
Comhere is the name we gave him,
It's the name he will keep.

Everyone laughs at it,
They think, it's funny, we agree,
We called him lots of names,
He will not pay attention.

Now we all call him Comhere
He knows now it's his name
Comhere is King in our town,
In the good ole U.S.A.

Gladys E. Walker

That Feeling

Here comes that feeling again...
No! No, go away, please!
But it keeps coming back to me.
Over and over.
Each time it cuts a little deeper.
It stings a little longer.
This last time...
It was different.
Oh, it was real all right.
The worst ever.
I cried until my tears
Made a little pool under my feet
And then
I stopped...and it was over...
Forever.

Irene B.

Leetza

This poem's a little late
No time to celebrate
But you're "cookies on a plate", to me.

The wind's blowing cold
And the bread's getting old
But you're precious solid gold, to me

So smile your shining smile
And we'll chat a little while
In your ritzy domicile, you and me.

Happy Birthday to my girl
She can set your heart a whirl
She's a diamond, she's a pearl, to me.

For my Leetza from her Mama
And from her Papa, too.

Gene G. Beyer

Diann

This is just to let you know,
Of memories long ago,
Of a young and lovely face,
From another time, another place.

Frozen in the memory cells,
That recall simply tells,
Of a moment that will always be,
As long as there is a me.

For all your thoughts and your care,
During the time you were there,
Have always lingered within my mind,
Of that other place, other time.

The alternate pathways of this world,
Can leave ones mind in a whirl,
But each has to fill their destiny,
And their future not theirs to see.

Now my future looks very bleak,
To prolong, I do not seek.
Just wanted you to know,
That I remembered long ago!

Franklin J. Warren

St. Hilarion Castle

Along the wooden heights of Kyrenia
On a harsh, enormous cliff,
A crown of stone and mortar
The skill of man had built.

A symbol of omnipotent life,
St. Hilarion Castle stands eternal.
Its prominence is long past
Yet, one feels its power still.

With bible, sword and flame,
Barbarosa, the red bearded crusader came
Into its vast expanse, but
Man's transcendence could not escape.

Today, covered with riotous greenery
Quivering, poignant and unyielding,
St. Hilarion Castle stands
Majestic, silent and serene.

Helen Chromy

Untitled

While spring time through my
open curtain sang,
wasp, upsidedown to my window
clang.
What must he think of me,
oh noble fly,
so sleek of wing so keen of eyes
for while I flit 'tween Yen and Yang,
wasp, upsidedown to my window clang.

Greg Eastridge

Goodbye

To my family and friends
please try to understand;
why I left the way I did.
This is my beginning,
while others may think it's the end.
I know I didn't say goodbye,
for I knew you might cry.
Please don't be sad and blue
for it was the Lord who made
my wish come true.
He loaned me to you for just a short time.
Don't weep, be strong,
for I will see you again,
another time, another place.
Just remember that I will be with you
always... in your memories.

Estevan I. Torres

Untitled

I know where the Lilies grow
Quiet places, fragrant green
Flowing water murmuring
Champagne air in my dream
Exultation, sheer delight.
Longing memories of the sight
of where the lilies grow.
Everything within me pleads
Return, return to all of these
Lilies, places and the dreams

Hazel Chipman

Life Is Beautiful

Come, live with me
See the trees bend and sway,
Green leaves frolicking And dancing
to their own symphony,
Against the beautiful blue
of the summer sky
See the humming bird
Caressing, the blooms of the Coral Bells,
See the brilliant butterfly
pausing in the sun,
Hear the birds serenade with song,
Watch the splendor of the summer sunset
The flowers in the garden are
Nodding and softly saying
Look at me "Look at me"
Life is beautiful
Come, live with me

Helen A. Hessney

I Forget

You would think I'd learn
So many times burned
That
Goodbyes are forever
And see ya's come never

Why my hopes mount
Like a mall fount
For times that count
I'll never know
I turn and go
Some where
I'll find one who cares

I'll forget
All regrets
Time not spent
No matter how well meant

I'll forget
When they leave
They won't come back
Once they start to pack

Inger Maria Avant

Falling Raindrops

Remember the sound of
Soft running water.
Remember the sound of
Raindrops hitting the ground.
Each drop is different and unique.

Like the children we teach
Are different and unique.
Each one going their own direction
Each one striving to a different level.

For you are special.
Because you are a teacher.
For you are special,
Because you treat each child
Like a falling raindrop.

Esther Summers

Miracles Of Love

May your heart rejoice with Love,
Starting from our Savior above.
From the cradle to the table
Mother's love guides you thru,
She'll teach you right from wrong-
As life passes in review.
Then the love of your life
That moment when she becomes your
wife.
Loves Cycle starts again at baby"s birth.
Life's "Love Miracles" here on earth.

Genevieve Detweiler

A Plea of Love

Troubled, wounded spirit
Stubborn, wayward heart
Hear me when I call-I've called so long!
Is the bitterness and anger harbored
In your soul so sweet?
Does rebellion blind your eyes so
That you cannot see?
Poor, foolish one; you go
Your way. not mine!
My whispered Name, in faith,
Can calm the storm that
You endure; so tossed about.
I'm here for you, I wait for you,
I yearn to meet your needs;
Yet you refuse. My rest, My peace
Elude your plans.
And still you hold, always closer
To those things that do destroy.
And I am grieved, poured out
For you; I am God.

Gwen Case

Peace

An unknown feeling of comfort
the air of tranquility
Smiles of friendly faces
When old friends meet.

Everyone is seeking
let there be peace.
Those whose paths are crooked
the way of peace only seems right.

There is one kind
that truly is peace,
Peace with God,
Which only he can give,
not as the world gives
but as God.

Frankie K. Richardson

Plumb Tree

All winter through my window pain
Through cold and sleet and wind and rain
I see your long branches reaching high
So lonely looking toward the sky

But now! What miracle is this?
Has spring revived you with her kiss?
All dressed up in brides array
How beautiful you are today

Of all the things that grow
All blossomy bright in feathery white
It seems plumb tree I learn from you
Forget the past and build anew.

Geraldine Jackson Porchia

Nowhere

The scorching beams of sunlight
The pillows in the sky
The gentle breezes blowing
Trees swaying by and by

The glisten on the water
The birds up in the air
The soft sweet sounds of nature
Don't question if you dare

The lush green carpet on the ground
The blue ceiling up above
The shining of the lamplight
Where am I thinking of?

I tell myself it's nowhere
As I look around my room
I tell myself it's nowhere
As I sighed, "It's just my room"

Heather Thompson

Full Sail

Streamline bow, and shiny brass,
the teak wood smooth and bright.
Rope line cast and coiled,
it starts its graceful flight.

A crisp point sail, a hearty gale,
cuts through the placid sea.
I think of as an ocean swan,
glides on majestically.

The blue horizon holds white clouds,
the vessel pulls full sail.
The captain bellows orders,
as white knuckles clench the rail.

With hand arched on my forehead,
to block the blinding rays.
This solitary seabird,
rides off into the haze.

Gregory Loupos

In Love

If I had made the universe
Then you would be the sun.
I'd watch you glow from day to day
And dark would never come,

Unless, of course, you needed rest,
Then I, to you would race,
I'd lay your head upon my chest
And caress your loving face.

You would not burn nor scorch me,
'Tho you'd light me with your fire.
Your soothing touch would tingle,
While it filled me with desire.

Ah, I did not make the universe.
And you, you're not the sun.
But my world revolves around you,
For with you life has begun.

Gwendolyn Hamilton Tucker

Love

Love is grand
There is no sand
  under the foundation
  of my love for Judith

Love is grand
Give a hand
  for those who
  developed Judith

Love is grand
Looking to the land
  you'll find no other
  better than Judith

Love is grand
All should stand
  and give applause
  for my love Judith

Greg Burns

A Question Of Beauty

Though many may say,
there is nothing as beautiful as a tree.
I must correct them that, that it
is you see.
For I know that God has made the
beautiful tree
but he has also made you and me.
Now the tree may shade us for
a part,
but only beautiful people can
shade the heart.

Gowens Williams

I Quit!

Cigarettes!
This is WAR!
I'll fight you harder
Than before!

I've got the power
Now to win.
Nevermore,
Will I give in—-

To your noxious,
Curling smoke,
That burns my eyes,
And makes me choke.

Death or illness
Is your name,
And I'll not play
Your deadly game.

So burn yourselves
Right into HELL!
That's it! I QUIT!
Good riddance! Farewell!

Ghayle Y. Kilgore

The Unknown

The unknown wonders
The unknown hovers over
The unknown sinks behind the known
The unknown is inside
The unknown is sacred
Some people are scared
Some people are unaware
That the unknown are us.

Eve Lucero

Jennifer

So peaceful she lays there
this sleeping beauty
When was barley into her teens
the angels they came
in the still of the night
and carried her spirit away
God in his wisdom
he only knows why
her short life came to an end
She will miss all the hardships
that growing up bring
Jennifer sweet Jennifer
Goodby.

Gladys Ellison

For Better Things In Life

Where shall I send my thoughts
This young fine day
To the highest peak
Climbing all the way

I'm leaving the valley far behind
And passing the shadows too
For better things in life
And on to what's new

As the day begins to end
And I'm slowing down in stride
The challenge in climbing upward
Leaves me with joy and pride

I know tomorrow will bring
Another longing in my soul
I know of nothing better
Than moving toward my goal.

Frank White

Perspective

Love is unknown.
To me, it is unreal.
Love is unfounded.
To me, it is hopeless.
Love is not mine.
To me, it is untrue.

But I met another
Who changed my views.
Love is now known, real, and true.
It's foundation strong,
A love with no limitations.

But I found another
Who changed my perspectives.
Love is found once more, tender and sweet.
A love of protection and nurturing ,
A love like no other.
A love that knows pain and suffering
But also a love I could never abandon.
A love filled with hope.

Ivy S. Rayle

"A New World"

I looked around the world
today and thought its getting
bad. It isn't how it used
to be and it makes me kind
of sad. Life used to be so
young and gay and people were
so kind, but that was
oh so long ago, like in
another time. Perhaps
someday someone will
come along and turn the
tide. It would be nice to
have a plan that would
be nation wide and then
the wars would ever
cease and men would not
be called and all the world
would live in peace
with love for one and all.

Evelyn Daniel

Green Mountains Of Vermont

In the Green Mountains of Vermont
Were the bubbling brook's run free.
In the valley, where the lovely Laurel
grows.
No lovelier Flower ever grew,
it grow's so wild and free.
Along it's bubbling brook's
where the red wing Black Bird's sings.
The meadow-lark signs there sweetest
melodies in every field and stream.
And the morning doves are resting
in the whispering pines.
At the closing of the day you
can hear the night birds crying,
and the wind is sighing,
And the shadows fall,
No prettier place on Earth,
them the Green Mountains of Vermont.

Frank J. Jameson

"Shadows"

What darkness lies beyond reality,
What's afraid to let it show.
The kind will be rewarded but,
The scar remains on the soul.

I've gone through life unsure,
Of what I'm looking for.
Who I am and
What I stand for.

Shadows seem to linger,
And hang around my door.
Harassing and threatening,
Is very hard to ignore.

I'm not sure why I'm crying,
Or why they are at my door.
I guess if I stop crying,
They won't bother me anymore.

Heather A. Foulke

Stories

My father told stories,
While my brother and I
And my mother
Waited in the car.

"Mom, when's he coming?"
We agonized, in turns, from the rear,
Squirming, it seemed, for hours.
But she never answered.

When Dad did return,
His face faintly flushed,
None of us ever said a word.
Nor did he.

Harry L. Tindall

Advice To A Bird

Little bird resting alone, on the trestle
Why are you here now?
It's ten O'clock in the morning
And all your friends have flown
To scenes distant and unknown.
Why are you here alone!

Are you hungry and in search of food
Or just a late starter enroute?
There's been only one plaintive call
Echoing shrill out there, somewhere,
Can you find that perch
And interpret, solve and cheer?

You must have heard me,
You have vacated the trestle!
Now where did you go?
I'm sure you'll make your day.
Keep on moving, join others as you go.
There's safety in numbers! You know!

Hildred Marjorie Schloss

The Glory Train

All aboard the glory train,
With eyes fixed heaven bound,
We know Jesus is coming again,
A great day when trumpets sound

We wait at the great station.
For a grand tour of life,
It starts from time of birth
With the good and the strife.

Don't give up your journey,
For the best is yet to come,
Walking with God at your side,
You can't loose for you have won.

Stay on the straight and narrow track.
Where God is at every bend,
No need to run to and fro.
With God life will never end.

Evelyn Carrera

Why?

Fish, simple minds, no time
Wishing well, oh well spare the dime
A soda pop disney jerk kid
Bladin' down the sidewalk
Dustin' out the body chalk
Evidence of last nights crime
Thirty-eight nickel plate
Momma's gotta work late
Now bloods spillin' from the heart
I'm askin' why did it start.

Gordon Strunk

The Mute Bell

How mute the bell
Without a clapper!
It is reduced to
An utter indignity
For a bell - silence.
No more pealing forth.
No more the giving of tone.
The bell must be bitter,
Not able to sound the Angelus
And such for the
People all around.
Most certainly the
People miss its call
That cannot now come.
I sympathize with the bell.
There are tones, perhaps,
Waiting within me
To be bursted forth.
But, alas, I am a
Bell without a clapper!

Harris W. Hollis

Untitled

Yesterday was gray and dark
without hope, without a spark
clouds and thunder in the air
feeding on your heart's despair
then morning came, with sweet surprise
the warming sun was on the rise
promising your troubled heart
a new beginning, a fresh start
take heed, yesterday has gone forever
only today does count, and never
dwell upon what could have been
only be glad that you have seen
another day, another hour, to live
to breath, to love and give!

Helen S. Gowen

The New Webster Dictionary

Hey Mr. Webster!
You with your two inch solid spine
and 1,532 intimidating pages of words.
I don't know how to spell
those quizzing words like
methylphenidate or quinquennial!
So I've decided to flip through
your narrow crisp pages and
and find these needless in your
haystack of words.
After I'm done finding out what
methylphenidate and quinquennial
mean I'll go put you back on the
shelf with all of your
boring relatives and there
you will sit until someone
else doesn't know what exquisite
means or how to spell sauerkraut.
Then you can have another adventure
in your world of words.

Harold Joseph Haskins

Enclosed Porch

You walk out protected.
Your head surrounded as fog-filled tears
roll, pause, and end in new form

on the screen,

a built-up moisture
seemingly created on its own—
a random start to finish,

all back dropped

by thick white and gray.
For them, a long life each will have...
even with a risen sun.

Heather A. J. Kennedy

Life's Prayer

I love you Lord and sing your praise.
You've blessed me in so many ways.
Forgave me if I changed to sin,
reach out your arms and drew me in.

And when I've called to you in prayer,
I've felt your love and comfort there.
You've guided me in truth and light,
and helped to keep life's pathway bright.

But when life's joys are small and few,
I pray you'll call me home to you.
And let me kneel there at your feet
when life on earths no longer sweet.

Ila Christiansen

Flame Fatale

A
man
stands
watching
a flame
that
is

burning across the way;
seemingly unattached
to the candle beneath
it. He consciously takes
shallow breaths, allowing
the flame to burn undisturbed.
The flame, oblivious to her
spellbound admirer, rages on.
Others also pass and are
struck by the intensity and
passion of the fire. Some,
like over-aggressive, mating
moths, blindly race to the flame
only to be instantly incinerated.
Their ashes pile at the candle's
base becoming buried underneath her red
wax that slowly drips down the taper's sides.
The flame continually dismisses expired wax
until she is wading in it's pool. Flickering,
suffocating, she struggles vainly to burn,
only to drown in her own blood. The man awaits
the candle's resurrection, alone in the dark.

John J. Connelly IV

Guitar

I will
hold
you
and
love
you
I will wrap myself
around you and pour
my feelings
into you as
I sigh and stroke the
silvery slickness of your strings
and hope the music can be as beautiful
as you will always be

Larry Cody

Eyes Like Mine

In my eyes, I have seen
A baby's cry
In my eyes, I have seen
A Mother's sigh.

In my eyes, I have seen
A father's sin
In my eyes, I have seen
A sister's end.
In my eyes, I have seen
A brother's pain.
In my eyes, I have seen
Life in vain.

In my eyes, I have seen
Hatred rise, Endless lies.
In my eyes, I have seen
Promises broken, wishes' token.
In my eyes, I have seen
A people's strive to stay alive...

Evelyn Dean

Loving You

When I awoke this morning,
and reached for you,
forgetting you were gone,
I felt only pain there is your place.

Sleepily I wondered:
if loving you brings this much pain,
brought on by simply waking up alone,
Can loving you be worth it?

I slipped gratefully once more
to sleep's waiting arms instead,
and there I dreamed of all those things,
The things that make me love you so.

And on remembering these,
I knew that I could handle pain,
And let happiness wait,
For just a few more days.

Mary Ann McMillian

Untitled

The colors are going West,
Following the sun
To be born a new.
Already they are receding,
To black and white.
And grayish hue.

Penelope Jeche

I'll Never Let You Leave Me

I'm telling you today, baby
And you may even think I'm crazy
I'll never let you leave me!

Come what may!
I'll do anything to make you stay!
I'll never let you leave me!

You can kick, scream, and cry!
Honey, I'll tell you no lies
I'll never let you leave me!

And if your heart tries to wander,
I'll put you six feet under
Before I let you leave me!

Sylesia A. Gethers

Known To God

Faces were somber voices muffled,
as we trudged along in the
brilliant glow and warmth
of a summer day - To a
destination try beyond.

White marble sharp against the
summer sky
Laminating and reflecting a warmth
Uniting all as one.

The sounds of drums and marching feet
Men, sincere meeting face to face
a brief encounter in a common bond
To watch over the unknown
Only to God.

Jean H. Barringer

Was I?

I thought I was sleeping
Because the trees were so tall and green
And the sky was so blue it cooled my
mind thoughts.
Then suddenly the wind went through
Me, like ice melting
My every thought became heavy
I felt like I was carrying the imperfection
of mankind on my shoulders
But then a light of hope from a bad dream
letting me know I had left behind the
pain of other me sins.
I look at the light again only to
Realized I wasn't sleeping I was dying

Mark Goss

Child Of Innocence

Oh Child of Innocence,
Frozen image of my youth
Ever staring from your stop in time
You've seen the lies, and known the truth.
Vestige of my carefree days
Father to this man;
If only your smile could now speak,
And be here to hold my hand.
Return me to your simpler times
Remembered child of play,
Before I'm caught in fading age
And your times have slipped away.
Was I really you so very long ago?
Are you but a pictured memory?
I knew you then, please stay awhile
And free the child in me.

James J. Murray

My Fisherman

My husband is a fisherman.
But he is not the only one
He's taught all our sons very well;
All the secrets... never to tell.

How to rise up before the sun.
So the fish can't see any one.
How to freeze in ice cold water,
'Cause fish won't bite when it's any hotter.

How to get real soaked to the skin,
Sneeze.. dry out... and go back again.
He's taught them to fish in ice,
And fish at night with little mice.

To fish from shore and from a boat.
(If they had one, they'd fish a moat!)
Yes, they are all really good,
But, I have never understood...

Why they go out and freeze and all...
And bring in a great big haul...
And when Mom prepares this great dish...
They all look up and say... UGH! FISH!

Allene Wolfe

A Poem Of Pure Lust

As the midnight
changed the colors of
the room, confucius might have said,
"Woman who waits
alone is bound to long"
I thought as I
sat at the edge
of my bed and looked
into the tale-less
mirror hanging at the
foot of the bed.

No longer confused
As I stare at the
vanishing red colors,
the subduing sounds,
and the
empty glasses,
along with the
movement of
St. Augustine moons.

Gale Madyun

A Christmas Story

Dasher has a broken leg
Dancer has the blues
The elves all have the whooping cough
And santa has the flu

And what of poor old Rudolph
With his big red nose?
He's turned up with hay fever
From sniffing at a rose

There won't be any presents
There won't be any joys
Christmas has been cancelled
For lack of any toys

So we'll have to do without it
To me there is no doubt
Christmas has been cancelled
Santa's not about.

Sarah J. Camp

Untitled

Dearest Mom And Dad,
Do not weep for me
Because I'm not here
I live in your hearts
Where there is no fear.

My spirit is free
My wings are set
To soar on a journey
Where there are no regrets.

So do not weep for me
Because we're apart,
I live in your soul
Forever in your heart.

Your loving son,
Christian

K. M. Rajpathak

Sleep Walkers

The soul's of the dead
existing in the living

Taking control in their sleep
so as not to disturb
the host

No one to hear their forgotten cries,
just sayin' hello to lost good byes,
sunsets in the skies

What goes bump in the night
maybe more then just your fright,
it could be the light
sent hear to ignite
your fire

On all the dimensional planes
there's an eternity that remains
you may not want a soul stalker
yet it's inevitable that you'll become
a sleep walker.

Josh Gorrell

The Imaginarium

There is a special place I know
Far beyond the grasp of time,
It is a place of mystery,
A place of rhythm and rhyme.

It's more vast than the universe,
More amazing than the stars,
A place free of corruption,
Free of protective bars.

In it lurk fairies and wizards
Dragons and goblins too,
There are also enchanted castles
Just to name a few.

You can fly high in the sky
Free as any bird,
And you're sure to meet someone
And exchange a friendly word.

So what and where is this place
Full of adventure of every kind?
It is called the imaginarium
And it is all in the mind.

Reynda King

Fear Is...

Fear is the shadows within the dark.
Fear is a huge dog with menacing eyes.
Fear is dying within your soul.
Fear is loved ones departing from Earth.
Fear is being left alone at night.
Fear is being in a nuclear war and
surviving only to die slowly.
Fear is another World War.
Fear is being around until the end of
the world, brought down by the wrath
of God.

Tanya P. Riley

Soaring Sea-Gull

Oh, how full of wonders
Fly through my mind
Close my eyes
Fly high, fly high
Oh, soaring sea-gull
Don't look back
Dream on, dream on
For eyes are closed for eternity
Of wondrous places
Fly on, fly on
Oh, soaring sea-gull a tear of dreams fall
Oh, please, fly higher, fly higher
Tears of life, fly like a bird
Dream on, dream on
A single dream, from a young heart
Opens, like the wings of a bird
Fly higher, fly higher
Oh, soaring sea-gull
Good-bye, good-bye
Oh dear, dream on

Fiona J. Keown

Old Magnolia Tree

God, why does the Magnolia tree
Grow so high in the sky?
To the very top I'd flee,
If I like a bird could fly.
God, if my love were one of her
Flowers, so snowy, so stately,
with grace,
With wings of ease, I'd hover
Close and kiss him on the face.
But if he wasn't a Magnolia flower,
But he, like me a bird......
We could fly together by the hour,
And be so content without even a word.
We'd fly over streams and view
The reefs of the sea,
We'd pick berries together and
Then retreat
In the top of the biggest and
The tallest old
Magnolia tree.

Patsy Harvey Brady

"Summer Rains"

The sky was dark and cloudy
Again and I knew we
been gonna get some rain
No one didn't really cane
Cause it always cleanse
the air - and oh what a
pleasure is that fresh air

David Adams

Untitled

Lead me to a rock that's
Higher than I.

Take me to a place
Where I can fly.

Show me a face
that has a sigh.

Winter of discontent
By and
By.

Reason with no doubt
I can't cry.

But as hard as it is
Every times a lie.

Person deep in a corner
is just too shy.

Wisdom of truth
only to try.

Claudia Saenz

Mind Scan

I lost my glasses.
I can't read the trees
On the horizon.
I can just barely make out
How few there are.
And there's just no way
I can see how the mirrors
Of the world
Turn the magic of spring
Into autumn
A hemisphere away.
You might say I'm near sighted.
But that's all the more reason
To help me find my glasses.
If I don't find them
How will I ever see the world
When the peach blossoms
A hemisphere away
Are falling
On your hair?

Michael Ridenour

Untitled

The sparrows fly high above the sky
I look up sadly and begin to cry.
The wind is wild, the wind is free,
Oh Lord give me freedom and let me be.

The sparrows fly hastily through the trees
No one knows no one sees,
Oh tell me your secret for I will not tell
Then there will be no reason to rebel.

Rickey Lee Singleton

Roses

Two souls built this home
And it was all their own

Today they become one
Tomorrow they are alone

Roses will bloom
Carrying its deadly thorns

As two hearts bleed
With endings torn

Cheryl A. Crowe

Oh, S**t!

Five years ago, my mother died
I tho't that I'd die, too.
So, I tho't I'd spend
All that she'd left
But, that's pure hard to do.

When your face and voice
When your mind and choice
Say, "Look, baby, I'm here, too."

Oh, yes, I tho't
Some peace could be bought
So, that's what I tired to do.

But, with will out
And go 'round about
When you have no dough to give.

And, you finally come
To the one true sum:
Oh, s**t! I guess I lived!

Joyce Williams

Sea Of Sight

With all the appearances
In every which way

The life that you live
The one that's all say

It's forever changing
It's one unique kind

In all that you use it
It's always all times

So incomprehensible
Too vast and ahead

Too often mistaken
It's missed when it's said

Whenever it's true and all words can say
The how of what is in unending ways.

Kymberky Barton

Together Again

You were the wind
in my hair
You were my soul, my body,
and my mind
You were the ground that
I walked on and the grass where
I lay
As I gaze upon the seas
beyond, I dream of the day where
we will be together again drinking
in each others souls

Louise Wilkins

John F. Kennedy

John F. Kennedy I will always
remember was killed on the
22nd of November.

He rode down the street so
Happy and gay as Lee Harvey
Oswald fired away.

We will always remember
his smile and wave and
his ended life in an
Arlington grave.

Patrick Pickering

Bless The Special Children

A special child in the home
is a gift of love that only few know
it makes you wonder how one copes,
but the courageous child knows the ropes.

The pain and discomfort they must bear
puts a mother in a distant stare.
But when the procedure is over and done
they hug their doctor and go off and run.

Yes they are strong and so full of love
and peaceful as a morning dove.
They're full of laughter and sassiness too,
and the future for them will be brand new.

So when a special child passes your way
pray for them so they may stay.
For life is so short and they are so pure
And some out there shall find them a cure.

Nanci S. Wollinger

My Friend

I've heard it said a true friend
Is a treasure sent from heaven,
Than what a wealth I must possess
For the friendship you have given,
Has been a comfort and a joy,
A place where sorrows melt away,
A secret garden for my thoughts,
And a shelter for my rainy days.

Even when the trials of life
Seem to be too much,
You the clear small voice inside
My head that tells me I am loved.
The heart that knows my heart,
Even when I try to hide,
The eyes that see the beauty of me,
The soul that touches mine.

Yes, there is no greater treasure,
Nothing greater that heaven could send,
And I'd like you to know, always,
I am thankful for you - My Friend.

Nanette J. Justice

I Can't Seem To Live Without You

When I look into eyes, what do I see?
Is it our fate-our destiny?
All I know is what were feeling
Really can't be.
Still, we go on through time.

Each day passes, we live lives
of separate roads-then
We will connect all over again,
Well we ever be as one
And let our love mend?
In our hearts and our minds.

I can't seem to live with you
Or live without you,
Is our love ending?
Is our love through?
Maybe we can work it out
For my love is true.
I cant seem to live with you
Or live without you.

Maria A. Hines

A Magic Secret

Sawing a woman in half is common,
It's the trick in many magic show,
But how is it done?

The audience is anxious to know.
The secret is the table,
On which the magician puts a box,
It is built to hide a second person inside,
He showed the audience all the locks.

When his first assistant climbs in the box,
She stick her head out one end,
And brings her knees up to her chest,
While the hidden person gets amend.

The audience believes only one in the box,
The Magician saw through the middle,
He disconnect two halves,
And dance with a waddle.

When the box is put back,
The hidden person puts her feet in place,
The Magician unlocks the box,
She steps out unharmed with a relief on
her face.

Gennevive Bailey

"Looking Up"

I'm trying to hid all my aches and tears,
Knowing no laughter, nor any cheers.
I clasp my hands;
my knuckles are white.
My heart is pounding with a
frightening might.
I feel like running,
but stay in one spot.
God is watching from the very top.
"There is no need to run," I say.
"God's given me the strength to stay."

Arvella Wallace

Untitled

Expectations
lie
in relationships
winter flies
on window lips
half live
half dead
stirred by
false winter's warm
of wants
unsaid

Gail R. Morris

Breathing Death

Standing on the side of reality
looking through the porthole
made by idle curiosity
I don't see the aluminum dawn
But scenes it's warmth and
shiny hatred
Blistered popularity screams at
the open night
And I, being both empty hearted
and stupid in a delicious combination,
laugh at the complete idiocy of
the idea
Apparently, tears fall somewhere
in the realm of existence that I
call breathing death

Timothy James Swanson

My Best Friend

On a warm spring day on
May 21st you told me
something that defiantly hurt.
You told me you were moving
far, far away but all I wanted
was for you to stay.
I felt so lonely and empty
inside that I thought I would
cry all the time.
Though I know you will
always be my "Best Friend" it
is always sad to think of
again. We've been through
those times, the good and
the bad, the happy and
funny and even the sad.
I remember those as the
happiest years of my life but
no matter what, we'll be
"Best Friends" for life.

Victoria Rachel Vanlandingham

"My Little Angel Buddy"

Hey my little Buddy
My Angel in the sky
I know you're up in Heaven
I see your Star so bright and high
I catch that little Starlight
Out of the corner of my eye
It twinkles out to tell me
I love you and not Good-Bye

Gerard J. Hagardorn

The Gift Of Love

Of all the gifts one can give or receive
None is greater than the "gift of love"
For love can always find a special way
To bring us blessings from God above

Love gives life to our body and spirit
Helps us to learn flourish, and grow
Nourishes our hearts with happiness
As we give, receive, increase its flow

Love brings us peace and fulfillment
Makes every experience very special
When love becomes a part of all we do
It makes life much more meaningful

Love is the gift that'll be remembered
Truly cherished until the end of time
When it comes from within the heart
It's the greatest gift - yours and mine

Bill Feole

No Secret

My love for you is further than
the eye can see
Simply because I care for you
so fervently
But as time goes by each day. You
fill my life with happiness and joy
But why am I telling you this?
Especially when you can feel
my compassion and gentleness just
in a simple kiss.
What I'm trying to say is that
as long as your with me
Whether in my arms or faraway
I will love you more and more each day.

Asrean Brown III

The Colors Of The Seven Festivals

Red and Green make up the Joy
of the Christmas Spirit.
Orange and Black make up the fright
of the Halloween scare-it.
Green and White make up the Luck
St. Patrick day brings.
Red and White make up the Love
St. Valentine's day rings.
Brown and Gold make up the peace
Thanksgiving day shouts.
Pink and White make up the celebration
Easter sings out Loud.
Red, White and Blue make up the freedom
The Fourth of July is about.

Doreen Ruiz

Duke Ellington

Edward Kennedy Ellington was his name
Often decisive, naive, and sophisticated.

Born to middle class parents who valued
A strong sense of family and home

Had a special bond with his mother
that was all remarkable on its own

His musical talent got him known
when he played party after party and
usually had a girl leaning on the piano

But listening was his great asset
His long time associate Tom Whaky would
Say, that too, was how he would become
A great composer and orchestrator one day.

Kandis Jamison

On My Front Porch

On my front porch I can see many things
On my front porch I can see the faces
Of different people.
On my front porch I've seen my
Neighbor mood change to riches to rages
On my front porch I can see those
Sweet little faces that use to make me smile
Bring tears to my eyes.
On my front porch I've seen many
Lives change from good to bad.
But on my front porch today their
Is something special. A grandbabe
God's greatest creation of all
On my front porch I can see the being.

Lineda Irone Davis

Power

Power
only you
can tap
into
to feel
my burning compassion -
feeling of ecstasy
revolutionary
in form
more superb
than perfection
outweighing
lust
in action

Patricia E. Holloway

Tenderness

Touch - only a finger or two
Searching - given truly
Eyes aglow and shining - I am me

Touch - share a kiss
Love - take freely
Fighting back the fears - I am me

Touch - lost in embrace
Nestled close, held safely
Shivering subsiding - I am me

Touch - freeing trappings
Accept each other openly
Smiling tenderness - I am me

Touch - gentle motion
Thought is racing ceaselessly
Destroying any barriers - I am me

Touch - held closely
Resting peacefully
In each other's arms and floating
Whispering and emoting
I am me

Mark Parker

Satellites

Dawn becomes...
swiftly fleeing breeze
supple willow branches graciously bend.

You keep me enticed.

Dusk arrives...
rain beating cadence
flickering fire answers.

I cry watching you.

Gibbous moon beckons...
milky clouds lie awaiting
calm sea submits.

I sleep in your eyes.

Jared Gruber

Running With Time

It was just not yesterday or today
That I first heard the wind blow,
Or felt the sunlight warm my brow
And heard rainfall on a rainy day.

Time is a factor in all of life,
I refuse to exceed it or ignore it.
It will not hinder, but it can blight
Time demands that one must fight;

To meet demands and make new plans,
To work and accomplish each set goal
To shrink from neither hot or cold,
But stand and face defeat

And struggle and dare to rise again
To feel warm sunlight on my face,
Caressed by sweet refreshing rain,
Regain my stance and win my race.

Rubye D. Peach

"God's Hand"

Have you ever listened to the wind
that whispers in the trees,
Or marveled at the beauty of the
ever changing seas?
Have you listened to the innocence
of children at their play
Or the lovely strains of music
drifting quietly away?
Have you noticed the perfection of
a tiny baby's hand as it reaches out
for someone who will love and understand.
Have you seen a peaceful valley
nestled softly in the hills,
or sunlight on a meadow, or a field
of daffodils!
Have you watched the twilight shadows
stealing softly o'er the land?
If you have witnessed ONE of these,
then you have held, GOD'S Hand!

Alene P. Cummins

Sssssssssss

I ask you what is a lie?
the answer, a snake!!
Surprised at my
response? They
slither across your
life and creep
into your backyard.
They appear harmless
but are deadly to
the touch. They are
quick to ruin your
life and there are
not many things you
can do to prevent
yourself from
being bitten,
and when you are
bitten the sting lasts
a very long time!

Eva Maynard

Discouraging

You never did appreciate
The joy of being young
Your body in a healthy state
Hale in heart and lung
Then you found as years went by
Some parts began to wear
Now doctors look you in the eye
And say you need repair
They looked in every aperture
Prodded, poked and pried
They didn't miss a thing for sure
On surface or inside
They say they'll fix you up like new
You'll regain your endurance
With all the things they want to do
You'd better have insurance
So savor every hour of youth
And exercise restraint
For growing old to tell the truth
A barrel of fun it ain't.

Holt Andrews

Instant Wake

These thoughts did impassion
The winds own breathe
Gently passed the face of desire
In forces around the world.

Who's absents, couldn't be replaced
So much a part of all that is,
The strength that holds us together
Admiration meanings express

For their life sense of character,
That comes alive in your existence
I celebrate the present on every hour
This instant now has been proclaimed

When beauty did empower
By an image left upon the moment
In the wake of emotion own touch of heart
Of my days, impart to me,

A love alone that will always be,
To wonder around eternity's influence
In search of just one more hour,
Among the one's I call memories.

Robert A. Davis

Greatest Grandma

Gone in a blink of an eye
There was nothing anyone could do
All we could do is sit and cry
Why did God chose you?

How hard it is to say goodbye
I couldn't be pulled away
Why did you have to die?
With us you should have stayed

You I will always remember
Forget you I cannot do
The memories of you
I will always treasure

Because grandma I love you
I accept that God has chosen you
His power I can not test
But now I know I finally realize
God only takes the best

Lynn Answeeney

The Guardians

Those from prairie spaces say
They hem them in,
They smother them,
And even make them fear.

How can such thoughts and feelings
Be provoked by friends
I long have held
So dear?

So many moods to match my own;
Serene in peaceful slumber,
Or as smiles upon a summer face,
Or spring-time frown.

Such wealth of dressings do I see,
A winter ermine cloak,
A fluffy cloudy necklace,
A russet printed gown.

But more than this, a sturdy mein,
A guardian army
They. My mountains! How I look to them
To take my breath away.

Yvonne F. Rasmussen

My Castle - My Throne - My Old Country Home

You are not even pretty to look at
through the years,
I have not had funds to keep you
up with the times.
But the memories I had with you,
I would not trade with a millionaire.

You have weathered over a hundred
years, now your wood is beginning
to fall to the ground.
But the wood you were built from
was real wood -
So part of you will be standing
when I am no longer around.

I would be happy to see you restored
But the carpenters price will
have to come down.

But the memories of you, my old
country home are still very real
So why should my castle -
my throne have to fall to the ground.

Lola Dunn

Life's Grand Intangibles

I want very much
To be in touch
And to be in tune
Morning, night and noon
With Life's Grand Intangibles,
which interrelate
with the small and the great
Tangibles of the world
And deftly create
Goodness and beauty and peace.

Could God, perhaps, be
THE
Totality
Of Life's Grand Intangibles?

Ken Holmes

Under White Wing

Show me crow
where my spirit flies
when my heart lies
open to the wind
when my eyes bleed
lonely seeds
show me crow with your caws
teach me to see with my jaws
Oedipus or Sampson slept with his mother
pick a legend fly in the sky
soar like love pray up
under the white wing
sunlight lashes the hawk to heaven
look up see a prayer
say a prayer let the love
like the light lift you higher
under the white wing
show me crow where the circle starts
the secret of all life love like light
under the white wing

Mic Woicek

High School Ring

He paid for it from savings
While in the Senior Class
His symbol of young manhood
A reminder of the past
He volunteered for service
His country was at war
Was trained and sent to fight the foe
In battlefields afar.
He landed with his buddies
On England's fabled coast
For final live fire training
"The Best" - his outfits boast.
They were called for the invasion
D-Day - a living hell
A mortar shall exploded
Hurt mortally he fell.
There wasn't much left of him
To make identify
But the ring still on his finger
Read "The Class Of Forty Three."

George F. Johnson

Who Fifteen Times

Who was that
Who just passed by
Who glanced at me
Who made three beings be
Who frowned one million times
Who cried ten thousand times
Who laughed one thousand times
Who sighed one hundred times
Who lived once
Who died once
Who denied a soul
Who turned to ash
Who could not be
Who can never be
Who may never have been

Robert G. Combs

"I Ask You Why?"

I ask you why? Did you stop loving me
Why did you love me alone
Why did you never come home.

I'm crying, "why?"
Were your eyes searching mine
For answers you never could find
Secretly, I loved you all of that time.

The problems grew and grew
And I was ever so blue
Communicating was hard to do
But I'm so sorry we're through

Are you afraid (it was cut missing words)
The intelligence to tell me the reason why
Please help me as I cry: "Why, why, why?"

Fran Sapser

Ultimate Victory

In a field of rubble rained by warfare
Pushing upward mid crumbled-stone air
A rose gently blossoms in spring.

Straight into a valley infested with mines
In bold defiance of "Forbidden Zone" signs
A lark dares to fly and sing.

Dorothy Hubbard Roth

True Meaning

Love is a word of true meaning,
As one to one, A love of a mother talking
to our God whom only shares unbinding
love. A love that has no limit to whom
or who we share true meaning.

Betty Jean Dorr

In Memory

She crossed her last bridge
without any fear.
God was holding her hand,
and she knew he was near.
for her we must not weep,
She left so quietly
in her sleep.
The Old Rugged Cross at last
She lay down.
With loved ones she meets
She'll be wearing a crown.
The friendship and love we shared
will remain in my heart
until the day I am called
to be with her once again.

Ardale Millard

With You

When I am with you nothing in the
world matters. Looking into your eyes
makes me feel safe. Knowing your arms
are always out to reach for me
makes me feel secure.
With you my world knows only
joy and laughter, although we've
shared many a tears. With you
there is nothing I can fear because
I know your always there. With
you there is always a shoulder
to cry on, a smile to comfort
me. With you my world is so
full of love. I cannot see my
world without you because with
you I have all I ever wanted.
With you my life is complete
for only you have given me
the joy to be with you always.

Lourdes Arroyo Cintron

Black Cat

Oh look at you,
you filthy thing!
Claws and tail covered in mud,
Tangled in a piece of string!

Your back and ears,
Covered in bloody-mud,
On the street, in a fight, for a fish?
You reek!

Don't cry to me
For my pity,
Dishonorable kitty!

My house is clean,
You filthy thing!

Out of it now,
Or my shoe will find you!
OUT!!!

Marissa Lynn Moulta

Momma Patterson

Momma Patterson
A beautiful black woman
Small in stature
Slightly bent at the waist
But solid as a rock
The corner stone of the family

Momma Patterson
The carrier of the seed
The bearer of many a beautiful flower
Flowers that grew, seeded and bore many flowers more
Which makes this family continue to grow

Momma Patterson
We love you
We need you
We thank you for being the soil, water and sunshine for this
Family of flowers, which continues to grow

Happy 90th Birthday!

Grady A. Patterson

Thoughtless Thoughts....

Standing on the edge looking for forever
A glimpse of eternity is a shooting star

Midnight arises across my foreign sky
As the thunder rains when the unborn child cries

Blackness hangs over a darkened heart
As I watch the world fall apart

Broken eyes watch the ocean floor
The human beings are wanting more

Deep within my oak tree grows grabbing hold of an empty soul
Thrusting forward but falling down; no looking back... just fall

As relaxed as the earths motion I grab to reach a star

Moon beams cast a spell on a lake while curious gestures are heard
The trees bend back trying to catch the song in the wind

A white horse jets across an open plain
As radiant as the knight upon it

Far off in a forest the wolves feast on the full moons curse
Hypnotized by their calling I follow

Spread across the skies are the clouds of Venus

Thoughtless thoughts surround me although nothing is around me
But yet in the distance there is something venturing right behind me.

Heather Raigosa

Jellybeans And Buttercups

Jellybeans and Buttercups
A good reward, for sweeping the yard
Our mom and dad taught us to share
Walk the railroad tracks, turn a stone to fine a horse's hair
We played jacks, and never talked back.
Hopscotch figures carved in the dirt
Jumping rope would flip our skirts
Shooting marbles was good fun
Fishing for crawdads in the pond.
Lightning bugs, we'd catch at night
Put them in jars, and watch them light
Watch that snake, he surely will bite
Look up to the sky, and count the stars
Jupiter, the big dipper, and then there's mars,
Makes you wonder just how far.
Bubble gum to chew all day, put on bed post then throw away
"It's time for bed; our mother would say"
We all kneeled down and then we'd pray,
"Close your eyes you've had a good day."
Jellybeans and buttercups, we played these games while growing up.

Geraldlyn Scott

"My Secret Love Portion"

I'm going to cast a spell, to win someone's affections
A little bit of magic, tossed in the right direction
A secret recipe, a secret potion
To win me love and true devotion

I'll start with a dash of kindness, mix in a compliment or two
No special kind required, I'll just tell the truth
A dash of generosity, stirred in nice and smooth
In the form of flowers and candy, and presents like perfume

I'll blend in a little tenderness, like everybody needs
In the form of gentle hugs, and kisses on the cheek
And the one main ingredient, so my potion won't be weak
Is lots and lots of love, to sweep her off her feet

Yes this is my secret love potion, feel free to make it strong
Follow these directions, and there's no way you'll go wrong.

Gary L. Edwards

Memories

A piece of paper, a scrap of cloth, a trinket here and there,
A small gadget, a button, a thought, all somehow marked with wear,
The thoughts of children, playing, laughing, growing up one by one,
Pictures of children, giggling, smiling, their faces marked with fun-
Save all your trinkets, gadgets, and pictures for when they're grown and gone.
Then, get them out, see the fun you had and all the things you've done.
If you feel gloomy, sad or depressed, think on when you were not,
And remember other memories—another happy thought.
Don't forget the good times you have known—the fun that you have had.
Remember all those good times, and you can learn from all the bad.
Memories are treasures in our lives—the riches from our past.
So, cherish all the precious moments, and make good times last.

Holly Hardin

On Becoming My Mother

A month ago, or maybe three,
A sudden thought stole over me.
Where once I looked for guidance strong
To keep my feet from staying wrong,
No more that someone else can guide
Nor evermore to me confide.

Long years have passed since last we met
And still I know I'll not forget
The values taught so patiently;
Her values now are mine, you see.
Those self-same words have often flown
From my mouth to my child, half-grown.

And from my child the circle grows.
To her own precious child she shows
The lessons learned so long ago.
They'll be passed on, this much we know.
My mother lives; she lives through me,
And I through my child,
And her child,
Eternally.

P. J. Bresee-Haynes

Feelings Of The Air

Crushed and damned from the world's door;
Eyes that see and quickly look away.
A heart that melts in deep sorrow
Shaky footsteps are grasped and pulled down.
The sweet smell of life turns to dust.
Dreams that glow are slowly hushed with time.
The feelings that once burned with
greatness fray and the wind carries
them away.

Brenda J. Flannery

Love

Love is like a fresh rose.
A thing of beauty, tender and sweet.
It is delicate and slender as are the petal's
curves which gently flow.

It is to be handled lightly and with care,
not a thing to be tread upon as the ground
beneath your feet.

But, as are all things, love is not perfect.
It too has its thorns and fallen petals.
The hand that picks a rose or tries at love
must be one that is kind and delicate.

Or it will cut and tear at your heart,
as skin and flesh is torn by the thorn of a rose,
even though it looks so elegant.

But, as the rose, love can not mature and blossom
unless it has roots firmly planted.

So do not pick love off the stem of life; you
must leave it if you want it to grow.

Greg Lee

Constancy

You are-A lone white wispy cloud
Afloat in the vast expanse of sky

And The seas' foam crested waves curling swiftly
To crash panting upon the shore

You are-A hot, still summer days' errant breeze
Lifting the hair from my nape

And The dazzling blue-white fiery flashings
Of a raging sweeping storm

You are-The soft tremulous harmonics Of a violins' sweet eerie voice

And The brash smashing cymbals of a symphony
Heroic, exciting, sensuous

You are-The first crocus of Spring pushing upward through
cold-still frozen earth

And The last sad violet-Silent-hidden
Brushed aside by Summers' urgency

You are-The perfume of a rose-velvet-petalled, full-blown

And The smell of fertilizer in a garden Circled with humming bees.

You are the myriad parts of all that is

I see you in the brief flicker of the morning star

And I know you are here with me — Constant and forever.

Helen V. Urbanski

Snow

There's nothing so beautiful as morn,
After a winter nights snow storm.
To see the green pine trees,
As the snow falls with the breeze;
The children all look forward with delight
When they see the ground covered white.
They like to make snowmen
And get out the sled, and then
Down the hills they will ride
And pull their friends over country side.
When its warmer and snow melts away.
All say its been good, but glad to see warmer days.

Helen J. Knoblett

Untitled

Why would I bring you to another land with only a voice:
an essence really?

Do you remember the promise of meeting another of your kind;
to quench the thirst of a loneliness known only by the few?

No matter how old the spirit, nor their accompanying guides,
we are still subject to the same human frailties of loss, rejection,
and longing.

I see so much more than I reveal to all, but those I recognize aware
of the Elysium realities; and yet,
I laugh and dance as a visitor far from the home I can't recall.

For one as sensitive as you, choose wisely those in whose eyes reflect
how exquisite you really are.

And teach me in this moment, however brief, the embrace of one who
longs to be touched in sacred places with open sky.

Gregory Thrower

Forgotten

We peeled the shadows off the wall
And flung them to the dusty night
They raced into the murky town
They danced and sung in candlelight

They clambered up the stony wall
And slithered down the other side
They rustled and crackled like burning leaves
They wailed the wail of souls who'd died

They tumbled toward the center Halls
They crept about the wrinkled streets
They scratched and tore at ragged weeds
Their figures lost their arms and feet

The faceless, formless shapes ran on,
The terrors of our haunted dreams,
They wrapped themselves around our necks
They squeezed out cries and tortured screams

Then on they marched, the Nameless Ones
The idols of the twisted lands
They laced the ocean with their tears
And dove into the flaming sands.

Alison Kaufmann

Pulse

A breeze flirted with the mercury but it was still hot
and Grace and I contemplated a stirring inside us
as a butterfly also enjoyed July.
We spoke and said more than we intended
not really knowing
but knowing all along about hope.
So we smiled a political smile,
honestly.
This that we harnessed, the unharnessable, we let go
like you're supposed to goes the old saying
and we intrusted our futures in the words of a cynic.
I held my breathe as I passed her.
She looked up and I hoped she walked fast
and was holding hers too.
She nodded ballet-like
when I knew then her parent's premonition
and realized
as our paths crossed nine oh two, monday
that even a breeze has a pulse.

Cliff Moore

"Love Is..."

Love is always telling the truth,
And it don't matter if you're weak or a brute,
Then the others will then think you're cute,
Cause you tell the truth.

Love is always being together.
And it will be strong, not weak like a feather,
Then our love will be better,
Cause we'll always be together.

Love is showing how much you care,
And no matter what the dare,
Your feelings you have to share,
Cause you have to show her how much you care.
And that's the way love is.

Frank Beekman

My Father Kissed Me

My father kissed me last night,
And it was for the very first time.
So what is so extraordinary when a father kisses his daughter?
To me it was absolutely sublime.

I touch my cheek and still feel that kiss,
That helped to put me in a state of bliss.
For he never did kiss me when he was alive,
Altho' of nothing I was ever deprived.

The closest he came to showing affection,
Was to put his cheek against mine.
I was always under his loving protection
Which never ended with the passage of time.

Last night he came to me in my dream,
Leaned over and kissed me
As if to redeem,
The kisses not given when he was here,
But his kiss in my dream, I'll forever hold dear.

Helen Fay Sobel

My Mom

With grace she waltzed across the kitchen floor
And sang some ditties I hear no more.
Her face was lovely without a line.
She was beautiful, young and sublime.
Her hair was never out of place,
Dark and curly, it framed her face.
Her eyes twinkled when she'd smile
As she willingly went the extra mile.
Her love encompassed all of us
No matter if we made a fuss.
Her lessons taught us right from wrong
With words, her deeds and her song.
She loved her Lord with all her heart
And taught us his word from the start.
She has now gone to her great reward
Where she's at peace with her dear Lord.
Some day I'll see her waltz once more
Across the Lord's kitchen floor.

Frances M. Dornan

Waterfall

Swirling waters in frothy attire
Daringly frolic in jagged terrain,
Leaping boldly off a cliff
Plummeting with a deafening roar.

Displaying its power in grand finale
With turbulent, churning white foam,
Forcibly splashing in masterful tone
Flows away babbling a language its own.

Gladys Reeve

Each night I awaken from salvation in a dream
And wait until the dawn, listening for the screams
Thousands of souls about me, spirits screaming falsity
Once when I was younger
I walked among them
And sang a simple melody
Then one stopped screaming, stopped and looked at me
And then screamed the same
I was told to let it be
In my search for beauty
I once thought that I only must try
Now I only wonder
Do their dreams lie

Hans Hammond

A Tribute To Grandma

Many a day we sat in your porch and watched your red roses bloom. And we marvelled at God's handiwork as their fragrance filled the room. We watched the birds as they flew back and forth to feast from your red feeder. And we would comment how God took care of us all, even His smallest creatures. The hummingbirds were faithful, too as they would come to drink the red nectar. We could tell by the joy in your eyes and smile on your face, they brought you a great deal of pleasure. On hot summer days the wooden duck would spin his wings with just the greatest of ease. And we would wonder why setting in your porch, we didn't feel that grand breeze. It was the simple things of life that meant the most to you, Flowers, birds, your home and porch and lots of family love mixed in there too. We'll cherish the talks and all of the love you gave so freely to each one of us. For you set the example and showed us how to live and continued to worry so about us. You could quote the Bible and often said how you knew we all we were in His care. And we know there's rejoicing in heaven today because God has you there. We love you, Grandma and we will miss you here on this earth. You were such an important part of our life right from our birth. But we must let you go to do your heavenly duty, because your work here on earth is through. For we must keep the faith and cling to each other so one day we will be in heaven with you.

Gloria C. Conley

The Journey Of A Night's Echo

TUNE IN the night's lively sound
  As an enchanting echo rides the ground
WATCH his timeless journey take
  Like a mellow, soft, and downy flake
O BEAMING mists of crystal crowns
  Who form glistening patterns all around
FEEL the echo's journey awake
  Like the mellow, soft, and downy flake
O HEAR his yearning for yesteryears
  As that weary echo comes to tears
LOOKING BACK to days gone past
  For a brief remembrance of his task!

Gene Larrimore

When Red Roses Bloomed

I met you when red roses bloomed
'Twas in the Month of May.
I fell in love when roses bloomed, in love with you that day.
I love you when the skies are blue,
I love you when they're gray, I love you when red roses bloom and when they fade away.
I love you when skies are blue,
I love you when they're gray,
I love you when red roses bloom and when they fade away.

Hazel Whitlock

"Our Swing"

I sit at my window and watch the stars
As I pray to God for the healing of some scars.

Then my thoughts turn to just you and I,
Sitting on our swing under the awesome sky.

We could hear nature singing a love song or two,
And I could reach those stars just by being with you.

Some days were very busy, confusing and long,
Calmed by those twinkling wonders...
Soothed by nature's song.

As we drifted in peace on that old wooden swing,
We shared a love that only God could bring.

Now alone, as I watch those gems above,
my prayers include thanks for having that love,

And a hopeful wish that sometime close by,
We'll be together again under that lovely sky.

I know that God will answer and soon will bring,
Once again that peace and love we shared...
On our "old wooden swing".

George Burkhardt

The Yellow Rose

The sun is up and I am at my window.
As I sit looking out of my window into the garden,
I see a pretty yellow rose.

As it reaches up towards the sunshine,
I can see the early morning dew has gently kissed;
Each and every small petal.

Nothing I have ever seen before is quite as beautiful.
Then, as I reach to pick it, I feel a stick, and I realize;
Even the yellow rose with all it's beauty,
Has it's own kind of protection;
So it can keep it's beauty as long as possible.

And so, the rose remains in the garden outside my window,
To display all it's beauty from there.
Still the small thorns will protect the beauty of
The Yellow Rose through the ages.

Ferdinand Buendia

Humanity, Humor, And Humility: The Realities Of Golf

Is the game of golf like a mirror of modern mankind?
As one partakes of golf, the varying perspectives of
Glory and failure are found contrasting on a continuous basis.

In life, these viewpoints are more tightly wound into the
Dynamics of one's daily trek through a lifetime.
Life and golf are both games, filled not with winners and losers,

But of survivors who must confront reality on its own terms.
Preparation, performance, and the pursuit of perfection are
Critical driving forces if one desires success in either endeavor.

To gauge these factors we must use distinct measurements:
Shot by shot, hole by hole, round by round, or
Minute by minute, day by day, year by year.

Whether we journey through life or a round of golf,
Our emotional state will waver between humor and humility.
Like a roller coaster with a diversity of twists and turns,

Our frail psyche will have to endure the range of human feelings.
The knowledge of today's golfer must be available to the next
generation because
Ultimately, this gift will help define the true nature of life
itself.

Gregory R. Bruss

Hurricane

Storm clouds gathering in the darkened sky,
Ashen, grey clouds spawning their dreaded threat,
Shrouding the earth with ebony hued mantle,
Massive, ominous regiments with open bayonet.

Coal black mists opening their portals of doom,
Cascading mountainous curtains of water below,
Drenching the earth with torrential outbursts,
Angry, thrashing winds pulsating the seas aflow.

Hours pass and relentlessly attack the wind and the rain,
The ground falls saturated beyond all repair,
Families begin to scurry, seeking higher terrain,
Hearts wrenched with anguish and aching despair.

Trees uprooted, mangled masses of decay,
Buildings demolished, vehicles crushed by debris,
Woeful tableau of wasteful ruination,
Devastation wrought by nature's savagery.

Finally, the rain ceases, the winds subside,
Merciless onslaught is terminated, over and done,
Damage and destruction rampant on all sides,
Surveying the chaos and havoc, the emerging sun.

George Chrissos

The Plea Of An Addict

Oh Lord please hear my plea
At the gates of hell I've ended
When I strayed away from thee
I chose to use drugs and stay in a rage
But you're the only one who can free me
From this glass cage
I've been doing things my way
For Oh such a long time
That in my mind I will always be confined
My struggle to come back to you
Seems my God so strange
To not be after a drug to me is such a big change
I know if I'm able to just touch your hand
You'll pull me in and help me stand
Oh my Lord please hear my plea
Besides your other children
Don't forget the addict that's Me

George Liverman

Time Bomb Of Temper

There is a time bomb called temper set to explode,
At the slightest friction around any turn of the road.
The temperament holds it with every blink of the eye,
The heart must control it or tempers will fly.
If the heart is controlled the temper is too,
But the time bomb is ticking all of life through.
It stands within reason in a second or more,
An explosion can happen to settle some score.

It goes like an avalanche once its begun,
Wracking its fury till its evil is done.
There's no time for praying when tempers are fed,
It's time for the saying "they're all seeing red".

At inflicting our fury and around us we've looked,
Where temper has taken us: Our goose is cooked.
No one could tell us as our tempers flew,
That these were the things we'd be driven to do.

When you realize you have this time bomb of the heart,
With love reduce friction before evil can start.
The heart strings are fragile that carry the load,
But tough as we are we're not built to explode.

Gracie Hay Arnott

In Autumn.....

Grey cloud-veil rent, the sunlit hillsides flame
The ancient hills a miracle proclaim,
Transforming miracle of leaf and vine,
Like Cana's water deepening into wine;
My spirit kneels, her sandal strings to free,
For God in every burning bush I see!

Helena W. Cullen

Strange Yearnings, Of These I Miss

Wired baskets, commissioned to hold one's clothes,
at the village pool the simplest things, of these I miss,
tears corner my eyes, strange yearnings I can't believe, of these I miss.

To see my mother in the distance, bathing cap in hand, knowing in
just moments I could be near her, water trickling down her legs,
puddle at her feet, hot sun creasing her eyes, as I look up, silently
to get her attention, she is talking to another wet friend, ignores me.

I don't remember her look of annoyance, and the little patience
she had for her youngest, most needy one.
I knew soon we'd be walking up the lawn, cooler in our hands,
lunch on the hot, red lacquered picnic bench,
more sharp tongue laced with reprimand,
towels wet from our bottoms, children's lips red from Italian ices,
running with Popsicle sticks, told to slow down.

It doesn't seem to matter now, the hot car, steamy seats, quiet
distance between us, structured talk, instructions for our "wet things,"
I miss the makings in the kitchen, cool plums before dinner, table
settings, feeling apart of her life, never knowing any more than this...
strange yearnings I can't believe, of these I miss.

Heather J. de Lannoy

Do I Dare?

I evaluate, incorporate, integrate, instill, and enrich their lives,
Bathing in the inspiring ideas of others.

They turn to me and question their beliefs,
Am I knowledgeable enough to quell their greatest fears?
Do I dwell unnecessarily on a topic so mundane
That I lose but half my audience to the more inspiring,
intriguing virtues of nature?

Am I beset so with the paper mounds of cryptic answers
That I do not search deep enough to find the essence within?

For each learner is but yet another individual
Redefined every year in a new form of self-indulgence
Seeking hidden clues to undiscovered escapades.

Can I meet the challenge?
I must try.

Ilene Cooperman

Red Passion

I dreamt in color I dreamt in red, I dreamt we walked along a river
bed, with thoughts of beauty in my head, with thoughts of you, love
and red.

Then I awoke in my bed, and thought to myself, what a wonderful dream
I'd had, to be walking along a river bed, with thoughts of you, love
and red.

I tried but could not clear my head, so I searched to find the river
bed, I walked along with the girl I had, with thoughts of beauty in my
head, with thoughts if you, love and red.

And when I was almost dead, at last I found the river bed, I dreamt in
color I dreamt in red, the one I walked along with the girl I had,
with thoughts of beauty in my head, with thoughts of you, love and red.

And there you stood by the bed, my man at last you've come she said,
with thoughts of beauty in her head, with thoughts of you and me and red.

Gifford Z. Decker

Between Friends

Feel the breeze
Behold the seas
It's beauty and its peace
Both lead toward the land
As to assure its increase

In all there are moments calm and still
Yielding only to the command of natures will

Together they will all take a stand
Challenging the power of the man
Only to resolve in the end
It's challenged its only friend

Then back to its peaceful state
It resumes a sense of wait
For the appearance of its friend
Challenging the land, sea and wind.

Gwendolyn Y. Rose

Untitled

Bessie Mae was grandpa's mule
Bessie Mae was nobody's fool
Work started early, way before dawn
Mae pulled the plow, Pa followed along

And there was a bond between those two
Never heard a command, Mae just knew
She'd step over the rows at the end of the fence
Pa turned the plow and a new row commenced
And so they worked, the hours would go
Heart to heart, row by row

At dinner time there was no bell
Mae kept the time, she knew it well
She'd stop at eleven, turn her head and look back
Pa would look at his watch, bow at Mae with his hat
Unhook Mae with rough loving hand
Walk Mae to the shade tree, put feed in her pan

Now if a mule could love, Mae sure loved Pa
And sometimes I believe Pa loved Mae more than Ma

Florence E. Poe

Thou Art God!

LORD, traces of your goodness flood our view.
Blankets of your considerations cover all
we behold — there, are you.
Magnificent your creation... your touch
upon the tiniest work of life, fresh daily;
care given to perpetuate: it's life,
it's growth, maturity and reproductivity.
Your splendid handiwork... nothing spared, we see.

LORD, great is Your Mind, Your Soul, Your Image!
Explosive! yes, explosive!...
producing, protecting, preserving... on and on,
knowing only what our minds can take in.
How great thou art beyond comprehension:
plentiful, abundant - saturating again
and again, our planet's need and beauty.
Help us, our God, to be endued with capacity
to take in the mammoth visible and invisible
practice of your doing;
your creativity continually moving forward...
never ceasing!... THOU ART GOD!

Harriet Trehus Kvingedal

The Old Man And The Dog

There was an old man who had a dog, a dog as old as he.
Both of them said in their old age, "The end is close for me!"

The two of them, though so alike, prepared in different ways.
The dog rejoiced; the old man cried, "We've not so many days."

The dog began to give away his bones and treats and balls,
And every time he met someone, he'd bless them with his paws.

The man he cried and prayed all day; he could not face this fact.
He counted all his worldly goods and bought the things he lacked.

The day of death had finally come, as both knew that it would.
The man had lived a selfish life, the dog's had been for good.

The dog had lived a life beyond the goals his master kept.
The man however fell so short, his Master only wept.

Grace Pate

The School Custodian

Scrapping, scrapping, scrapping...washing, washing, washing...
Buffing, buffing, buffing...waxing, waxing, waxing...
Mopping, mopping, mopping...
A serene smile.

T.P. on lavatory ceilings, candy wrappers in corners,
Empty, squished milk cartons tucked in hideaway places.

Half-eaten peanut-butter sandwiches, half-filled juice packs, strewn
Haphazardly across school yards.

Traces of name-brand Hi-top skid marks embedded in once shinny, neat,
Well-maintained gym floors...
A friendly 'nod.'

Gum wrappers, sticky gummy bears, pasted secretly under benches,
Crushed-up forbidden notes concealed in stairwells.

A silent room filled with tidy brooms, mops, buckets, cleaners,
Waxers, disinfectants, light bulbs, ladders, snow shovels....
Pavarotti in the distance humming out the mundane...
A gentle man rests.

Gerry Sajetowski

The Weeping Willow

The willow is blown through the wild wind
But do you really hear it weeping from deep within
The pain it feels, the love it needs
Do you hear the willow weeping upon the breeze
The wind passes it from place to place
But never to find a caring face, or a place to be loved
Do you hear the willow weeping, weeping from above
All it wants, all it needs
Is a loving smile or a caring deed
To the weeping willow it would mean a great deal
To be held, to be touched
To feel the love it missed so much
So when you hear the weeping willow cry, do not pass it by
Take it in your home, and in your heart
Give it the love it desires, and it needs
And you will no longer hear the willow weep or cry
Because to its friend loneliness it said goodbye

Heather Nicholl

Past

What happens to yesterday when today rolls around?
Does it get lost in our memories, to never be found?
Do little green monsters follow behind,
To eat up the past we must store in our minds?
Maybe there's a key or a magical door
that would take us back to yesterday for a little bit more.
But after our visit we couldn't stay late,
Because we're in yesterday and today might not wait.

Isabel Stock

Untitled

The Fiery Dragon is out on the moor
Calling the Knights and Chivalry Bold.
To protect the Fair Damsel in Distress
To Heralde the Standard of Days of Olde.

Dragons arise from Everywhere,
And Knights have Standards to uphold
But Damsels must learn to protect themselves
And start our own cars on days of cold.

For Dragons do arise Everywhere
And Knights are not always around
So Damsels must amend themselves
To fend off those Dragons that do abound.

The fluffy skirts and little shoes
Get only in our way
But Knights in awkward armor
Can hardly more or sway.

So deck yourself in comfort
Prepare yourself for flight
And when it's time to snuggle down
Then call in your Knight.

Flo Ginsburg

Fifty Year Reflections

Things have changed in fifty years, we called them "Good Old Days,"
Comparing things of then and now, has made us change our ways.
When dating, just a dollar bought gas, burger, and a show.
A pleasant good night hug or kiss made our spirits glow.
We didn't think of moving in 'till after we were married,
A crush on either he or she was everything we carried.
There were no credit cards to use, nor digital face clocks
Dishwashers were the human kind, no polyester frocks.
No contact lenses for our eyes to make our vision strong,
And polio vaccine, as such, was yet to come along.
We had no penicillin to take when we were ill,
We helped supply the baby boom cause we didn't have the pill.
We weren't brought up with stereos, TV's or VCR's
Who thought we'd ever live to see computers run our cars?
Our terminology has changed, some of it, quite profound.
Being "gay" meant happiness, not turning sex around.
In our day, grass was mowed, not smoked, and "coke" was just a drink,
And "pot" was just a cooking pan we kept beneath the sink.
There's lots of major changes that's happened on the way,
But a greeting that still says it best is "Have A Happy Day".

Harry T. Fern

Ballerina Thoughts While Waltzing

Dear Partner,
Dancing with you is so divine,
Plus listening to Chopin's genius sublime.
In thrill I waltz to every measure -
The melody lines are such dear treasure.

To your lithe structure I gently cling,
While my whole being desires to sing!
Proudly do I point the toe - quite prettily in the footlights glow.

You are the author of my salvation.
Waltzing with you is a revelation.
Your sensitivity so extreme,
Evolves into an enchanting dream.

Then when the curtain calls resound,
My ecstasy becomes profound.
The patrons declare their love of my Art,
Of which you play so great a part.

You are God's mighty masterpiece
Your strength and courage never cease.
The Ballet Scene "you so enhance!
Truly we PRAISE THE LORD IN THE DANCE!!!

Grace K. Smith

A Persistent Turtle

I am a persistent turtle,
plodding along an unknown path.
Confronting each looming hurdle.
Finding comfort in a mountain-air bath.

Dorothy Louise Strang

The Prize Winning Day

As I looked forward to the up-coming
Day, I came to the conclusion, that it would be
A long and tiring one, so I put on my ring
With the magical powers, in that it would
Hurry the day along, to a faster pace,
And, have my mind glide on to other items,
Of more importance, within the space
Of this day, and, it really worked the stems
Off, of what I had imagined
Earlier, about it being, a long
And tiring one. I than took a projected
Move, and just let it sing its song,
As I knew, it had wanted to, right from the beginning.
My, this day, is now the number one, shortest, and the
prize winning!

Eva M. Roy

A Pipe Dream In Welkin

The stellate white dabs, resplendent as is,
deeply shone down with orison,
giving her a special sky escape of endless refulgent sights.
Below and surrounding her lie each matter of nature by substance.
Steel grey is what the sight had dreamed her in.
Thoughts lay in tier spoke prurient to herself.
She feels of time to embolden her knowledge,
unbosoming the bothers that had overwhelmed her conscious,
she screams of throe and pang inside and outside,
which for now flows in a groundless hope for all troubling be gone
by a vanished sea.
Solacium comfort begins as the glimmering night skies subtle
away her symphony.
Onto it lies one toast for the launch of ten agonizing pounds
behind,
piteous meant gone.
She glances in welkin,
and time seems still.
Soon sunrise meets her,
and the stars, goodbye.

Helen Courtney

Awakening

Yesterday brings tomorrow,
Despair with me no more.
I will leave all my sorrow
And all that I adore.

Love is the answer, but also the question.
Death is the end, but also the beginning.
The mighty axe has risen, but when will it fall?
I hear trumpets blowing, but what do they mean?

Time to love or time to die?
Are angels whispering, or is it my love?
I control my soul, but nothing more.
Ten thousand tears, that will not fall.

Hold back tomorrow, until the dawn.
For tomorrow brings the fall.
My soul will rise again
If my name you would call.
Then let today begin!

Irene Church

All Alone

All alone and wondering why,
Feeling sad and wanting to cry;

For never expressing how I feel,
Keeping within me, my thoughts are so real;

Opening up to the one above,
Knowing inside he's the one to love;

For life is short, and always running out of time,
If only for a moment his thought were of mine;

Searching inside for that special love,
Turning to friends, and the one above;

In the still quiet night I just sit and think.
Wondering were in life is that missing link;

I need answers, I have questions and why,
For sometimes I want to be free like a bird and fly:
Free spirit.

Geralynn Niederlander

Uncle Bob

When the sun makes a new day its soft rays
filtering through misty morning pines

I'll think you

When the hounds in a distance I hear symphony
to the sportsman's ear

I'll think of you

When by the springs edge, a cold sip I'll
take, crystal, and pure

I'll think of you

When the north winds blow hard, and
cold, doves dart in fast, and low

I'll think of you

When in the hardwood lot the flitting
of a squirrels tail I spy

I'll think of you

When on a four count, a crappie I pull
from a pool dark, and deep, I'll think of you

When in the autumn of my life, when the sun retires an
old day, when it's soft rays filtering through the
pines, warming my old and worn bones, Uncle Bob, I'll think of you.

Hubert Ladner Jr.

Growing Friends

F inding a friendship seed is hard to find. But when you
find it, make sure you place it in a very special place.
Like your Heart.
R eading all the instructions is very important, because it
tells you how to keep it alive.
I mportant thing to do is give it lots of "T. L. C." Please
don't forget that.
E nrich it by sharing "God's" Love.
N ever be unkind.
D on't forget to pray for it everyday.
S hare some of your time and sunshine to make it grow faster.
H andle it with very special care, and
I n times of need, then you will get back what you gave to
that seed.
P raise the Lord how wonderful your friend has blossomed.

Ginger Tucker

8/28/67 DMZ Vietnam

Young boys off to war at a time when ideals soar.
From far away it's not so real, at nineteen, it's no big deal.
Vietnam is our destination, I went without hesitation.

On that first night, as I cruised on station with eyes wide open,
a pounding chest and the glow of napalm chilling my breast, my
fantasies of war were laid to rest.

I did not know him, say by chance. We argued over duties called
in the gangways darken hall.
The after hatch watch, my turn had come. But I out ranked him
after all, so Frank Leroy Bellant would stand my call!

It's now 28 years to the day, since my shipmate has passed away.
Be it fate, or by chance, I walk this earth not Frank Bellant.
The events of that day are painful still. The guns were roaring,
the ships at high speed, shrapnel spraying, glory to one,
posthumously!

Now for me, one more call to see his name upon the wall. To touch
the stone where his name resigns. I can't pull rank here, I'm not
number one, I'm just lucky to bask in the sun.

Frank P. McDonough

The Staten Island Ferry

I arrived at the station just in time to hear the thunderous blast
from the horn of the departing ferry as it glides out of the slip.
With twenty minutes to kill, I make my way through the remnants of the
arriving passengers and into the snack bar for a Heidi cake and a
coffee, light and sweet.
Minutes later, back on the street, I stroll over the One NEW YORK
Plaza for a seat on the cool marble to indulge my obsession.
There is nothing quite like a piece of crumb cake with a strange name
and a hot cup of unknown pedigree when you're waiting for the best
ride in NEW YORK City; The Staten Island Ferry.

Henry Winston Brown

Fallen

Blundering through time's maze-like corridors;
Groping blindly 'long life's broken relief;
Lost amidst litters of autumn's dead leaves;
Forgotten among dusty tomes of lore:
Unread and read pages alike flutter,
as leaves of life swirl in the winds of time,
scud across sessile relief, and leave rhymes
behind, riddles really, senseless mutters
that echo long through labyrinthine halls.
From across an endless void a voice calls,
lisping past hunkered wrecks of those in thrall,
sidestepping havens dimensions contain
to spiral down time's crowded domains,
there to be heard only by dead remains.

Hans Buus Gangwar

The Secret

No one knows it true
I don't know what to do
Its hard for even me to believe its true it true
If I told someone they would say its not true
But I know its true its true
If someone would know it would be few
But I know its true, its true
Even when my age was very few
I knew it was true, it was true.
Oh no one knows its true its true
It is true

Glendoria File

Echoes... In Sweet Silence

That's O.K., I'd rather be alone tonight - to touch
hands with my Love, without Fright - the moon, not
Full, but ever so bright - I invite - myself tonight.

Tonight - the clouds rush silently by, cold
hands - and warm the vestiges from my glance
I am nocturnal by day, and night - I am the
shining star - so bright.

Kisses wrapped in secrets, petals soft
and crumble at death - I can not chance-
the moment at last - to forget - this
endless romance.

I bow down, with amber eyes - only
to - Fire Skies - and mingle with the echoing
scent - A lovers touch, so hard to forget -
and yet-

I wonder, sometimes, outside myself
and wish to fondle, another....

Eve MacDonald

Forget

Does the woman and her ravaged face
Have to be all that is seen
No one ever thinks about the paper she's printed on
The paper and its wrinkled edges - The paper and its yellowed
corners

Too often we forget
The time the wearies have put in

We forget about the paper tree
And the paper men who milled it

We forget the farmer's dog who has to wait for food
While his master plants the seeds
For the paper trees the men will mill
Next year

We forget about the printer's wife who sat by her bed
And prayed that her husband would soon come home
It's hard to sleep when no one's there to tuck you in

We forget the delivery boy whose mother worries
When he's not home in time for dinner

No, it's just easier
To sit and enjoy the pretty picture
Mrs. Gomez put on the wall

Isaac M. Alexander

Tethered Heart

A restrained heart is feeble,
having known no desired joy.
Chained to past adversity,
it ventures not into loving,
but remains in fear
daring not to appear vulnerable.
Constantly woeful,
the heart makes vain attempts
to steel itself for the next blow;
as though the tattered sinews lingering
could withstand yet another battle.
What will release this haunted soul
from its meager existence of love once-been?
Can it be made anew, to start again?
To pound and feel and be made real?
Consider this the next time you feel frustrated with love --
at least your heart is still beating.

Heather Kitsis

"The Unforgettable Lesson"

When there are no voices left to teach the last man given birth,
he will not need a history book to learn about his earth.
The lesson will be plain to him through things that he can see like
the carelessness of all mankind with past ecology.

The air that he must breath will be lesson number one, He'll find
what there is left for him will cover up the sun and it will burn
into his mind a lasting impression he'll curse those who have left
for him the unforgettable lesson.

Alone he'll sit on a river bank in wonder of the time when if he'd
tried man could have left a much more pleasant shrine, the rusting
cans are the artifacts left in memory there for those who follow
after to show they didn't care.

The water he must drink will be lesson number two he'll find what
there is left for him is of a poisonous brew and it will burn into
his mind a lasting impression he'll curse those who have left for
him the unforgettable lesson.

What meaning has the life of man if destruction is his fate when
his strongest plea cannot be heard the lesson is too late when there
are no voices left to teach the last man given birth he will not
need a history book to learn about his earth. So let it burn into
your mind a lasting impression and let it not be you to leave the
unforgettable lesson.

Franklin A. Moe

Pope

I am there, where discretion has no reason.
I am at where relation has no weight.
"I am at the end of a rope,"
said a pope,
To a room of disciples,
Who doubled a rivals,
As he stepped off the ladder,
And left gravity the matter.

"I am a juggler,"
The artist decreed.
"Juggling your thoughts,
With my cold memories.
And just as the thief,
Who takes without asking,
I shoot what I aim for,
But cling to my masking."

Howard Andron

Heart Song

When I gaze into the eyes of children
I am lost in the reverie:
Swilling down the innocence
Lapping up the joy
Like an orphaned kitten come in from the rain.
Their wonder at the world
Is ambrosia unimaginable;
And it seems to me
Their energy
Is what set the stars in motion.
Ebony and ivory—
Tiny fingers entwined,
The lattice wok of wisdom,
The hope for humankind.
No contrivance in their laughter,
No dishonor in their tears,
And when they raise their Voice in song,
(Of this I am quite sure)
The music travels from their hearts
To the smiling ears of God!

Georgia Hartley

Say Yes

The time I spend around you
I cherish with all my heart.
The way you smile, look at me
and call my name is like an art.

You paralyze me with your eyes
Leave me speechless with your voice.
You have a spell cast over me
With you I have no choice.

I'm a puppet on a string
and you are my master.
With a thought of your or hearing your name
I can feel my heart beat faster.

My fragile heart I can't control
It's like putty in your hand.
Anything that you need or desire,
Your wish is my command.

For you I will do anything
Buy you flowers and open doors.
All you have to do is say the word
One word and I will be yours.

George Rose

Whirlwind

Standing here on the shore
I contemplate jumping in the waves and totally immersing myself
Letting go of all things that hold me back
When diving in as in the past
There seems to be something holding me back
Forbidding me from seeing where the tide could take me
As I swim back to shore
The winds of change pick back up
Life's events return to the whirlwind pace
It is so hard to make progress alone, or so it seems
When I try to slow down to reach out to you
I feel as though I am losing ground
At times I have felt as though I should risk it
But I always end up having to try even harder to fight the whirlwind
I wish I knew the answer
But I'm not even sure of all the questions
At times I would settle for a clue.

Gary Pohl

"On Being Thankful!"

"My Lord has been so good to me,
I give him thanks each day,
Because I know that by His grace,
So many blessings came my way!
We cannot expect only good things to be,
Each one has many trials to bear,
But if we put our trust in the good Lord above,
He'll help us with all our cares!
So, call on the Lord to give you strength,
When the going is hard to endure,
He'll comfort and guide you
And walk right beside you,
His love is everlasting and pure!"

Hazel S. Fulmer

Restless Night

We are sleepwalkers passing through an everlasting dream.
Going day to day, month to month.
Always wondering if wake is near.
Will we ever wake from our dream.

Does anyone know?
Does anyone care?

Ernie Swan

The Rose

I've been around for thousands of years
I have been picked and put behind ears
I have been passed from lover to lover
A flower like me they'll be no other
I am the one that shows love's attention
the flower that brings out your full hearts affection
A flower, the rose, that's so full of love
You couldn't fail with me and a hug
If you're looking for soft loving romance
The gift of a red velvet rose would bring
you that chance
I have made enemies turn back into friends
Then my jobs done and my stem starts to bend
My pedals will crumble and full to the floor
The Rose's presence is needed no more
But I'll be around as long as there's lovers
Because a flower like me there is no other

Gerardo F. Gonzalez

Pilgrimage To The Dump

As I turned the corner, there they stood,
I honked on the horn, but to no avail.
They hopped on the truck as I knew they would,
The two young bare-foot lads.
Sweat pouring down from the sweltering heat,
Gripping my steering because of the load,
I maneuvered the truck up that dusty road.

Scenes flashed along the way,
Shanties knocked together with wood,
Yards strewn with old bottles and clothes.
Barking dogs upon the wheels of the truck,
Screaming children pursuing a ball,
Youths lounging, no care at all.

I braced myself for that awful stench,
Winding my way to the journey's end.
Into full view they finally came.
Searching out their livelihood,
Human beings littered that place.
Bending, stooping, covered in grime,
Digging, searching, one spot at a time.

Gemma St. Cyr

"Summer"

It's like a blank page.
I rage for even a drop of ink to hit the sheet
Boredom turns to anger, and anger
eventually becomes disbelieving laughter
I've become a joke to you and myself.
Watching T.V. becomes a wearisome hobby.
The walk to the fridge has become a job, and
the walk back becomes a sacrifice.

The days become a blur, my good memories
are fading. And I've realized that the
things I thought happened weeks ago happened
just yesterday.
The months have become an infinite, uninterrupted,
everlasting, hot day.
The days' routine is ceaselessly repeating.

Like restless oceans
I await for "it" - yearn for "it".
Impatient, like walloping waves, whipping violently
against each other.
I don't know what "it" is but I long for "it".

Evelie Navar

Through The Looking Glass Within My Hand

Through the looking glass, within my hand,
I search for true reality but come to no real end.
Although I find no answers, my expanding thoughts proceed,
to covet others' insights, with an unquenchable need.
Devouring the pages of endless discourse,
torturing my psyche, for better or for worse.
Through the looking glass, which has no single color,
the forms are everchanging to create as I discover.
It's far from black and white and void of real dimension,
complete in its existence, far too complex to mention.
The looking glass is powerful and full of inspiration.
It draws my mind to consciousness and hand to perspiration.
It guides my soul with purity, relieving me of pressure.
It brings me true tranquility and peace too strong to measure.

Gloria L. Trevino-Davila

Simple Lesson

Hi babbling brook, how are you today?
I sit down to observe and to learn what lessons I can from you.
I see that you originate from this Mother Earth.
You seem unaffected by what debris collects in your path.
Under, over, around these obstacles you seem to flow, only
to reunite on your original path.
Where you have been damned you seem to build up strength and
onward you once more flow.
Even great falls from considerable heights seems not to
dwindle your purpose.
You gather yourself up and onward you march until you reach
your destination.
Maybe there is some lesson you can share.
Thank you for this simple lesson.
I bid you farewell.

Eugene Blake

My Basic Mission

With God in front of me to guide me along His chosen way,
I want to be a guiding light to those I see EACH day.

I want to motivate those I can, and inspire those I can't,
Be a mentor to those who need my help with wisdom that God will
grant.

To truly be an effective force I must live my goals every hour,
For if I am not true to me, my soul will be devoured.

It will be eaten by the beast, of time and false illusions,
And be locked inside jaws of regret, clamped shut by mass confusion.

I'll push to go the extra mile to do the things I should,
For these are traits that separate the great ones from the good.

I'll be innovative in my efforts to create situations of WIN-WIN,
Spreading these efforts to my family, friends acquaintances, and
extended kin.

I'll share love, compassion, and communication with my spouse of many
years,
I'll strive to be more sensitive to things that he holds dear.

I'll practice honesty and integrity in all that I say and do,
And work at balancing all four dimensions in order to effectively
renew.

I'll motorcycle ride and scuba dive, while taking leisure time to laugh,
And try to positively touch the hearts of all who cross my path.

For when I'm gone it doesn't matter whatever else they say,
My actions in life will attest to the fact that a positive force
passed this way.

Harriette M. Grant

Struggle And Victory

This girl was born into a loving family, but she grew up in a cruel town. At home her confidence was brought up, but at school they brought it down.

For seven years she thought she was ugly, because of the words they all said. She lost strength to fight because she begun to wish she was dead.

Yet someone heard her cries for help and begun to change her life. Her strength and courage was given to her, and in one word went all her strife.

With every step she grew stronger, while her life was filled with love. Everyday that went by she kept changing, while blessings poured upon her from above.

The one who changed her saddened life, is the one who would be there forever. The growing love that they both share is the kind that can't ever be severed.

Jesus is her savior from their words of hate, he took away the knife. No more hiding from their sticks and stones, he showed her the way to Eternal Life.

Gina M. Barton

"One Known Night"

And he held my kiss
In such sinful touch
A mellow warp of destiny
and desire
To concur in a harmony
so deep
Though a shallow grape
The taste of poison
that did sour
Swiftly uplifted by tears
We are forever apart.

Elizabeth McCabe

Our Sweet Memories

Sometimes we feel that fall and winter is
in the air. In truth it's Summer everywhere!
Sometimes things seem to be in shades of
grays. In truth sun rays can begin to play
in our memories of yesterday! And when
we let our memories soar we find things
brighter than before. Its true we all have
our ups and downs! But our memories
can shine rays of love and light that can
brighten up our darkest night and heal
our hearts! And pit a rainbow there!
Just knowing that our love ones care. Lets
keep our memories neat at hand to
vanquish all that gray away! And
brighten up our everyday!

Evie V. Britton

She

The knife I hold high, it glimmers in the glare.
It called me to it, "COME" it dared.
I picked it up, on this dark night.
It is demanding a ... sacrifice.
Up the stairs without a sound, I tiptoe slowly on the ground.
At her door all is still. I listen ....nothing.
All is well.
I open the door. Careful yet.
Her breathing is the only sound,
around the open door I bound.
I slip to her bed, knife held high,
As it plunges, I hear her cry.
That is all, she has died.

Gail Mackey

As Life Ticks By...

Life never stops for a heartache or lost loved one.
It's a road of many miles,
A clock of many minutes,
A never-ending song with many beats.
A constant cycle for the human spirit,
To endure.
A road with many fears to face;
With many tears to shed.
Not knowing what the next day will bring,
Or
What the next night may take away.

Hope Simmons

Mother's Day Gift

The greatest gift that I can recall,
It's not a material thing at all.
The sound so sweet from down the hall
As, "Moma, moma", my sweet babies did call.
Half asleep I'd hurry to save you from a fall,
Smiling so contently as I saw that first crawl.

It seems that only yesterday you were so small.
Today I look and you've grown so strong and tall.
I'm so proud of you when you stop and call.
Yes, sons and daughters are the greatest gift of all.

Gayle Greenlee

Cherished Love

Upon a shelf was a book, old and gray.
Its pages were all yellowed, tattered and fray.
Inside the pages was a letter written so neat from a fellow to his girl, in words oh, so sweet.

Inside the letter was a picture of the two
with a pledge to love and to always be true.
A single rose was pressed farther over in the book, a symbol of the love that they gave... and the love that they took.

Though it is yellow and frail, and tattered with ages gone by,
you could tell theirs was a love that was never to die.

I dusted it gently and placed it back on the shelf,
and prayed, "Someday, Lord, let me find that kind of love for myself."

Ilona J. Napier

Maria

She received her crown of righteousness, and wore it with a smile,
knowing she made memories of moments worthwhile.

She was loved, cherished, and adorned,
She was the center of New Home's joy.

Trouble didn't seems to last always,
Because she turned gray skies into bright and sunny days.

Her praises of God was going up, and her blessings was coming down,
A child of God like her, you rarely found.

The storm was anchored in her life,
But she was faithful until the Lord, a good provider and wife.

She put her trust in God and can always depend on him,
She will be missed and always be cherished as a long life never ending friend.

Helen Rene Byrd

The Older Years

I am going into the older years;
Leaving behind my worries and fears.

God has been so good to me;
Leaving me here to reach sixty three.

All of my children are grown and out on their own.
Leaving Dad and me home all alone.

The grandchildren, they too are growing older
and have life's of their own;
I thank God for the inventor of the telephone.

I don't fear growing older, you see;
As I know God is watching over me.

Helen Gordon

Affirmation?

In the purest and sweetest of all sensing
Lies the greatest depth of understanding.
Nothing from the outside—
Completely from the inside, completely from the inside,
And speaking ever so clearly,
Is a marvelously comforting strength
That assures, and protects, and guides, and teaches.......

Let No One Person, Let No One Thing
Serve to Reduce—
Yea subtract from YOU
All that CREATION gave us
Equally.

Likewise choose Not
To give away Power.

Then finally, with Vigor,
Revel in your own Being;
For there is Nothing
More important than Life;
And all YOU will ever need for Importance
Is simply: TO BE!

Ethel A. Harrell

Sorrow, Despair And Pain

Man and Woman, look at them
Look at Woman, so beautiful and wise,
So fresh, no disguise.
Full of scorn and yet so dark.
Who was she, who is she?
Do we really know her? Or know him?
Who are they, the Man, the Woman?
Standing there,
once more full of sorrow and full of despair.
Here, now and there,
They saw they do it to themselves.
Why? How?
Who are they to say what's wrong?
What's Right?
The Man all by himself,
They turn ad walk away.
Each in a different direction.
Help them, know them, see them.
They are us.

Ingrid Tucker

The Gouty Clout

In about with the gout,
Manly tears may appear - with stoicism in a rout!
Even a feather's flick can pin-point pains
In joints, muscles and veins!
Once, the curse of nobility —
'Twas "loud and clear" when it barred mobility!
Yet, many a peasant lout
Became gimpy from the gout!
Did they feign their humble humility?
Knowing a clandestine tryst was lost nobility!
Truly, about with the gout,
Can make one cry out,
Like a catamount,
With it's amount,
Getting cut out!
"Gout's got he clout!", shout the super stout!

Hugh Wallace

Untitled

A young man, one day, I chanced to
meet, on a job so hard, so hot with
heat. A friendship formed it grew and
grew. So many good times and fun we knew
with time of years and a few shed tears,
A bond was formed between two men.
like brothers, tho were only friends.
Their lives criss-crossed down through
the years. They haunted, played and talked
sincere. Their rigs they drove or the
miles of time. Until one day upon
their lives, God looked down and spoke
to one. It's time my son so come on
home. A friend in life I'll meet again
to talk and laugh and reminisce. Pave the way
my friend Joe, until it's time for me to go.

Georgia Lea Ott

"Painfully Aware..."

Wounded, at the dark interface of my dream, I lie,
My bleeding ambition wishfully trying to defy,
A fading motivation, ready to give up and die,
Painfully aware of my obvious shortcoming,
My inability to resurrect my soul, my inability to simplify.

Like the young sparrow who learned how to blindly fly,
I flapped away happily at the thought of summer as a warm, friendly ally,
Denying my instinct for the love I thought I could truly rely,
Painfully aware of my end forthcoming,
Now that the foe stabs cold knives I can no longer deny.

Why is it that I hope against all odds when the land is barren and dry,
To hope for the outpour when there are no clouds in the scorching sky,
When all it leads to mental torture and to miserably amplify,
The painfully aware reality of my own doing,
The desperate search for idealistic wishes to solidify.

Is it the carcass of mediocrity from which I shy,
Is it the single ray or spirituality which encourages me to vie,
Or is it the rewards of mental and material satisfaction for which
  I dare retry,
Painfully aware of the unknown reasons and consequences I'm facing,
I still insulate myself from reality and aim high.

Farrukh A. Chishtie

My Prison Cell

From my prison cell I sit,
no longer afraid of being killed
or of killing my brothers
over senselessness, and unclaimed turf.

From my prison cell I sit,
warm and dry, with clothes on my back;
no more worries of a place to lay my head
at the end of yet another unproductive day.

From my prison cell I sit,
contemplating reading the books that Ma sent
in hopes of providing me with guidance
when I leave this place, and return home to her.

From my prison cell I sit, trying to escape
the reality of the unsafe world
that I've helped to create,
yet am afraid to face.

From my prison cell I sit, and I cry.
In my lonely prison room I want and I sleep.
I sleep, a troubled sleep, until I finally realize
that my prison cell is in my mind.

Ethel H. Guinyard

Sight

True beauty can never be sought
no piercing through black strikes her white
refusing to ever be caught
she eludes and remains in pure night

But upon yielding to the fight
he learns fast of his foolish blind shots
his eyes clear and prepare for sight
to capture what before they could not

Soon the vision forever sought
emerges to its radiant height
defeated he joyously disrobes
and bathes in Her whole heavenly light

Geoffrey W. Vaughn

Birth Of A Soul

My dear friend sleep

He sleeps his eternal sleep with only a Crown
of Glory this does complete

With him does my love He keep in his eternal sleep?

For his friendship and love I shall treasure whilst his
essence shall linger in the depths of my of Soul forever

Fair well O'Friend so dear

May you walk on Rainbow bridges and sleep amongst the
stars so bright to rest in warm embrace of the most
gracious creator of us all

His

Jesus Christ.

Glen Roster

Childhood, Before And After

Illusions, dreams, a rose-colored glimpse of tomorrow
Smiles, promises, the future is mine
Plans, castles in the air, all within reach

Reality — burdensome, crushing, filled with pain
Impossible to form a dream
Where are my comforting illusions?
The future is mine, but not the one I envisioned

Ida L. Rinkenberger

Always

Sadness has taken the sweetness out
of my juice and filled the glass with bitter
loneliness.
The enchanting smile is the ready to quench
my thirst and replace the invisible kiss

Love surrounds the shattered heart that
tried sincerely to reconcile
Immediately tears confused laughter and chastised
the soul like a small child

Forever is so far away, but yet so close
and there, your spirit will eternally dwell
I will inevitably join you to share our
special moments, until then, farewell

Ivory Wilson

Untitled

THRU ambitions, life's entanglements, and moods of daily plight—how
often do we know ourselves—to the degree of being right—When
subconsciously we gather—all the twigs of life's great tree—can
we look at our reflections—and mould a perfect me!—What
hidden segments of our mind——what arteries of heart——control
the fibers of our dreams—to stop or make them start——What makes
our wants so many—and in instances so few——what possessions
make a person—a name—and not just 'you'——What guides our
fingers to delight—to know their satisfaction—what tells our
eyes—compels our ears—to stir—and guide reaction—-
WHAT makes a kiss an act of love——a smile—an act of glad-
ness—what
fills our being with forlorn grief——when we are turned to sadness——
IS it true—that we can reason——add, and make a score—to
comprehend, and know—to take so much—and then no more——
CAN you spare me all these answers—then can you spare me two——
Is it futile? Can I keep on? Forever loving you——
For from all the webs and problems—you're part of what I know—
to be deep, within, inside me—for Always—there to grow——

Harry Tankus

Ode To Oksana

An Olympic Angel she was,
One for all to see,
Not like the others,
And one special to me,

Oksana, they call, "Are you ready to fly?"
I hear that name, and I want to cry!
She takes to the ice, my tears start to flow,
Miles and miles from me,
Oh how I wish I could go!

Oh, Oksana, can you hear my voice?
You are the one, the one of my choice,
She springs from the ice, Lutz, Axel or Flip,
Then once again, how my tears start to drip,

Then at the end, it's over again,
Until next skate, what a show it's been,
Finally now, I dry my eye,
Oh Oksana, it's hard to say bye,
Hurry, oh time, oh don't be so cruel,
Until the next time I see Oksana Baiul!

Gregory Alan Graham

The Presence Of Life

I awoke one drifty morningtide
only to the fresh aroma of the arrival
of an immature day. It felt as if
if the presence of youth, or the
first breath of life was filling
up the entire room. But not only that,
my soul. Although there was only
one human, myself in the room
it felt as if something had blossomed.
I knew there was a kindred spirit abound.
I thought that kindred spirit would be with
me forever. But then, that aroma, that presence,
that feeling all just disappeared,
and a drift of abandonment spread through
the room. At that moment I knew that
kindred spirit was taken away by the
angel of death. Then I realized,
That was my life.

Heather L. Roberts

New Awakening

Hear the birds sing,
See trees stretch their arms to the sky,
Feel the warmth of the sun
Winter, we bid thee good-bye-
Spring is natures awakening, it's a
special time. It's Gods time again to show
his miracle of creation. The trees blooming
Forth, their brand new leaves glistening
in the sun, after being so bare and forbading all winter.
The flowers blossoming in an awesome
array of colors, their scents filling the
air with a sweet bouquet.
The cold cracked earth once again
Turning into a carpet of green velvet.
It's like the beginning of a new life. Spring
brings new hopes and new dreams. It seems to
reach even the coldest of man, for like
Nature man should give his spirit a
chance for a new awakening, give his
soul a new lift & bring more beauty to this world.

Grace Gangi

"Dreams"

Dreams... a wonderful thing
set up in your mind past all the rules,
all the blues, and human things.
Down the street, around the corner
and past the little of man on a bench...
in your own little world
where there's no corruption or crime,
hurt or pain, hate or war
That's where your dreams are.
Just peace and happiness and sweet lollipops;
gumballs, tootsie rolls,and colorful balloons.
Singing and song; dancing with the one you love.
Love so sweet and gentle like a soft feather
Love is all around.
All you need is one single wish
and you can dream through sun or moon
And in your dreams,
You know; all wishes come true.

Holly C. Kling

A God Sent Little Child

There is a little girl, I don't know her name
She has curly hair and sometimes wears bangs

She's the most precious little girl
you could ever meet
she has twinkles in her eyes
and a dimple in one cheek

Whenever you see her
she has a smile
most people say
she's a God sent little child

She reminds you of an Angel
sent straight from above
filled with gladness
overflowing with love

She never hesitate to
give her time
Oh how I wish
this little girl was mine

Whenever I think of her, I have to smile
for I too believe she's a God sent little child

Gladys Lee Henry

"Sophia"

I have a daughter,
She is a gift from "the Lord."
She shows me her love with a sweet smile,
And her laughter fills me joy.

I am very lucky,
For I have a daughter named Sophia.
She is a sweet little girl, that is always by my side.
She offers me her friendship and rewards me with her love.

She is a beautiful girl,
That I admire with all my heart.
"Will you always love me?" I ask.
She assures me that her love is forever.
And forever is a very long time.

There is no need to fear,
Because she is here to stay.
For she will never leave me.
I am once more reassured.
"I love you, Sophia."

Isabel H. Deno

My Best Friend

Where has my best friend gone?
She left me so alone when we had such a bond.
For a women her age, she was healthy and fit,
Who would have thought that she would ever get sick.

We were like sisters through laughter and pain
And from her wisdom I still had so much to gain.
Who will listen to all my problems and fears
When I think of all I will miss, I just fill up with tears.

Never a day goes by that I don't mention her name,
Wherever she is, I hope she's found her "Hall of Fame".
All I have left is the memories we shared.
I wish I had told her before she left, how much I cared.

I loved my best friend who was like a sister,
And God knows how much I miss her.
It's not my father nor my brothers,
Surely, the one I miss is My Mother!

Honey Martin

Ode From An Unassuming Man

Oh to be the rainbow
Shine so bright, admired by all
To hold the gaze of all that look upon you;
You get to dance upon raindrops.

But what of the unassuming man?
I shall peek at you from behind the tree
I shall steal a glance from the distance
Never will your eyes meet mine;
I shall only show you an unassuming man.

I will notice that which all else have missed
I shall remain when all others have left;
Yet never will you notice this unassuming man.

The clouds are now coming to obscure my view
The raindrops beckon your farewell
This encounter shall soon fade away;
I can no longer be an unassuming man.

I shall approach that which has held my gaze
The wind shall whisper my arrival
The rainbow will no longer be alone atop the sky;
Oh, pity, you can only see an unassuming man.

Gerald W. DeWolfe

In Honor Of My Parents Golden Wedding Anniversary

There once was a guy who liked pretty girls
So he got hitched up to one with red waves and curls.

They worked hard together building a life
and soon there were 5 besides husband and wife.

Now these 5, all red heads you see,
are scattered about, 3 married, 2 free.

But not one will forget their Dad or their Mom,
making life great, out on the farm.

That was all awhile back,
50 years to be exact!

Now some folks will say, 50 years! That's pretty long!
But we'll all agree, they've got it all wrong.

Cause workin' it out to the great Golden 50,
Is a job well done and Hey! Pretty Nifty!
Love You Two!

Ina K. Barnes

Why?

This woman I knew,
So strong and so wise.
Spread laughter and joy,
To everyone alive.

She raised two children,
Through hard work and much pride.
There wasn't a day in my life,
I felt unloved, alone or deprived.

One day the news came,
She was stricken with a disease.
She doesn't deserve this,
Oh God don't let this happen, please!

The pain and suffering that she endured,
There were no answers, there was no cure.
The thoughts we shared and memories of past,
The closeness we felt, we knew our love would last.

The time grew closer,
For her to close her eyes.
You see, this woman, my Mom,
In my heart will never die.

Gloria Gioia

Christmas

Christmas is a time of year,
That lets everyone be in good cheer,
We may have fun and admire lights,
But we should all remember that first Christmas night.

That first Christmas night so long ago when a wee little
Babe made his first little cry.
It was so wonderful- that no one could deny.

The angelic mother, Mary, laid the child in his first place to rest,
Many people came from near and far to pay their respects.

Some poor lonely shepherds now looked to the sky,
Some beautiful angels did not tell a lie.
They proclaimed his birth and called him king,
Then the angels began to sing.

The little baby never riled,
As the wise man rode their camels to see the child.,
The wise men gave gifts of frankincense and myrrh,
Mary and Joseph knew how lucky they were,
To have the Lord Jesus as their son.
He is the Savior, He is the one.
I wish today it was the same as the day the wise men came.

Heather Cole

Grandma Said...

I often think of Grandma and the things that she would say,
the counsel she gave in her own unusual way.
"Child..." was the beginning of a lesson to be learned,
her parables drew life pictures from which I never turned.

The topics that she chose seemed more than a hundred plus three
Then, all at once, I realized the wisdom she passed on to me.
She spoke of good values, good friends, family and love,
making sure I understood HIS kindness from above.

These parables became the guidelines of my life...
as I began to see what Grandma had in sight.
Her goal was to be the best that she herself could be,
not just for show or others but especially for me.

So, anyone who knows me, knows my Grandma too.
For they frequently hear the parables, some old and some new.
I think of Grandma often... tho' she's gone on ahead...
when I begin my parables with
"You know, my Grandma said...."

Gwen Robinson

Destiny

Their cry is silent, but heard throughout the earth,
The killers ignore it, as they all disperse.
Don't worry my babies it will soon end,
for the life you have once lived will no longer extend.
Dive deep and never come up, because if you do the killers will erupt.
I warned you my baby, and that's all I can do, you are in my heart,
and my soul too.
The spear pierces into the beast, harming but not killing,
soon the life of the great whale will no longer live.
Good night my baby you're almost gone,
the legend of you though will always live on.
The crystal blue water is covered with red,
the lifeless body of the whale, floats on a bed.
It's over my baby and you are now dead,
we will endure the pain for life's never end.
The heavens will welcome you into their arms,
and once again you will be sheltered from the evil and the harm.
Be grateful that you left, and don't shed a tear,
because once again you are in the crystal blue air.

Isidoro Fattore

A Young Man

A young man would be kissed good-bye as he gathered up his gear
The loved ones left would heave a sigh and many shed a tear
A young man would be on his way to do his very best
On distant shores so far away, he'd be put to quite a test

The young men of our precious land, when sent to fight a war
For home and country they will stand great hardship and much more
The agonies of war so real, we've still not realized
The fear and pain our young men feel, to come home paralyzed

It's more than losing leg or arm or dreams turned into cries
The memories also cause them harm, you can see it in their eyes
For all their bravery I will rave, they all do what need be
To make this their's, home of the brave, for us, land of the free

Ida Marie Dillon

Orange Magic Martyr

Limp and airless at this vertical throne,
The podium.
Such is the lost cause of the orange magic martyr.
Too worn to speak clearly,
He has lead sheep to the slaughter.
He may be the wolf, disguised as a shepherd.
An interested third party stands unaware of all the changes
That have kept things the same.
It was the popping of such an inflation
A drying of the martyr that caused panic in the streets
And recognition of relief in the sane parts of the mob.
A sudden release of that single icon's potency left
Everyone with a tearful of power
And stomachs craving more.
This was a statement of a much grander sort.
This is not a man,
But a martyr now;
And he knew no existence,
Until he ceased existing.

Evan J. Roskos

Three Little Angels

Three little angels waiting on
the stairs, two so dark and one so fair.
They are my everlasting pride and joy.
My two little girls and one little boy.

They look to me for everything,
for this I'm truly glad.
With all the cares that life might bring,
life really doesn't get too bad.
They are mine to love, God's gifts from above.
My Three Little Angels

Now, that they've matured and grown,
with husband and wife and with families
of their own, I hear their voices
raised in praise of all their *Little Angels*.

Helen Stabler

Coming Attractions

Here in valley mountain shades of green
The great Spirit resides closer than anywhere it seems.
These are the last years for those who seek refuge from death and birth.
Many people believe a great change is going to occur very soon right here on earth.
And then there are those who predict nothing more than doom.
The Jews believe that their Messiah is coming at last.
So much is going on it is very hard to grasp.
So be ye Buddhist, Hindu, Christian of Jew;
Let it be good for the masses as well the few.

Gordon Lester

The Colors Of Gray

Wildflowers swayed freely in the song filled air.
The tune of the content birds lay gentle in the breeze.
The grass grew tall and green; color bright and beautiful.
Empty of industry, full of love and solace.
A field of imagination and release.
In a place such as Germany beauty could be found.
The babbling river ran cool and refreshing over moss coated rocks.
Trees pointed in peace toward the Heavenly blue sky.
Home to a wondrous array of sweet scented blossoms.

Workman's heavy treaded soles sank deep into the virgin earth.
Flowers cried when ripped from their roots.
Wire, stiff and barbed, surrounded the once free land.
Trees lay silent, worshiping the master of construction and destruction.
Buildings grew where wildflowers lay.
All things once beautiful turned dark and gray.
Undressed feet began to stand at attention, the earth cringed with each step.
The smell of flowers died when the stench of burning dead became alive.
The screaming river ran cold over human remains of the once beautiful Jews.
Even in a place such as Germany beauty could be lost.
Full of industry, empty of love and solace.

Heidi Nicole Miller

Shattered

The stately sentinels embrace the misty morning's gray ceiling.
Their cold arms cling to the warmth of still falling wet tears.
The ground beneath their feet, reaches up to kiss the dew,
Siphoning the moisture to the table under their toes.
Silver threads and white chords form in each wrinkle on their aging faces.

Tired and weary from years of keeping watch over the city,
The sentinels drop their arms, their hands, and
Thunderously crash to the marshy carpet below,
Lighting the sky with odd shades of green and blue
Lightning as they rip transformers and power lines from their homes.

Even the men who flock into the city to restore the luxuries of heat and light,
Marvel at the beauty of the sentinels.
The glistening silver threads entwining nature's bravest state simply

Even in destruction there is beauty.

Ivas Frost

Pastoral Eloquence

Ambiguous? Ubiquitous? Prevenient? Status Quo?
Their meanings - do you know?
These interesting words I hear.
And now with dictionary near,
Your words, Lloyd Ogilvie, are coming clear!

A new word is like a tasty morsel,
Just roll it around,
And enjoyment is found.
Never let it confound!

Then there's audacity, pertinacity,
esoteric, and vicissitude.
That's quite enough to change your attitude...
And give new latitude, As well as gratitude.

You've "stretched the tissues of our brains",
And the same we can't remain.
For new vocabulary we have gained!

Oh, our ubiquitous God,
Come with Your prevenient grace,
To us Your pilgrims who run life's race.
Give us pertinacity, *and* audacity, *and* sagacity! Amen!

Helen Mitchell Smith

Everyone Needs An Anchor

As long as there's breath in your body storms will come your way.
They have no respect of person, they have no special day.
Sometimes the storms come fierce and fast, before you can prepare.
Other times a distant rumble tells of a storm brewing somewhere.

All storms are not due to the thunder, the lightening or the rain.
Some storms are due to mental anguish, afflictions or bodily pain.
It pays to be secured to an anchor while the seas of life are still.
It pays to be secured to an anchor that is able to support, and will.

That anchor I recommend is Jesus, the one who stands supreme.
The one who can hear you above the thunder,
Even if you whisper, even if you scream.
Whatever betides, cling to that anchor, keep your grip good and tight,
Never doubt that anchor's stability, never doubt it's power and might.

I've had many reasons to cling to this anchor, and it has never failed me yet.
I'm determined to be steadfast, for storms still approach, lest I forget.
If you have not secured this anchor,
Because your storms have not been severe.
You are in for a rude awakening, and subject to perish, I fear.
Don't let it be said too late for you, not when the anchor is free,
The price was paid by Jesus, when he died on calvary.

Eunice L. James

Absence Of Reason

There is a realm in which reason dwells,
  though limits may vary within the masses.
Each of us dictate the by-laws ordained.
  Such a life unexamined, slowly it passes.

So what is the product in the absence of reason?
  Surely, it's chaos reigning King for the Day.
It's heartache, disappointment rooting in your soul.
  A home it would seek, so don't ask it to sway.

Don't look for order, nor logic or balance.
  That fruit it won't bear, since they haven't been planted.
For no seeds were laid, it's fields left barren.
  No fruit was gathered, much as taken for granted.

Left in it's place is a hole and a vacuum,
  with aching and yearning claiming pain as its' young.
Frozen in time immobility sets in,
  bearing the weight much like a soul which was hung.

You think I need a cause to welcome this despair,
  that my gloom in itself is way out of season?
That is only proof, the lack of understanding.
  You see its' only need is the absence of reason.

Gwen Peck

Hourglass Of Time

As a grain of sand falls, singly,
  through the hourglass;
Just so I count the hours 'till the repast
  we planned. I'll not forget, but cannot yet
  take in the pain of knowing
    I will dine alone...

Time has ultimately shown
  my helplessness before the storm
Of Life. (I ever thought that imposter
  would one day call me to repay
  for joys I'd known
Since first it granted me the sight
  of your dazzling smile,
  —eyes reflecting starlight.)

The blue dress you loved is what I'll wear;
  arrive at the appointed hour,
  the designated time and place—
Drink in the haunting sounds and sights
  Pan's everglade could n'er surpass;
See the vision of your face —in my empty glass.

Gloria Plath

Spiritual Connection, Spiritual Direction

Like a shadow in the night, he passed along as they both travel
Through their individual lives, quite unaware!
Suddenly, a casual look would begin a mystery to unravel.
She cannot explain the attraction, must proceed with care!

Her heart beats faster, Her mind races ahead-
There is a small void that resides in a corner of Her heart, but only to God she will confide.
Deep in the soul, a spiritual bond is forming, but yet distance seems to linger instead.
Her instincts suggest express yourself, but like a paradox a voice of reason whispers caution inside.

She needs to explain to Him this spiritual connection, the silver thread that binds-
A thread so fine, quite invisible, but ever so strong!
A last she feels there is a connection, a direction between two souls, but what will He say and what will She find?
It feels so right, how could it be all wrong!

How will this unusual story unfold?
Fact or fiction a mystery slowly unraveling, ready to be told!

Gail Pedescleaux

Why Does The Man Lie There In The Snow

Why does the man lie there in the snow, is it just he had no place to go, was he a man with no family or friend or was this meant to be his just end?

Why does he lie there so totally alone, in the snow like a statue made out of stone, was there no person who cared for this man, a creature of G-D, a part of his plan?

Did you see and keep walking on by, did the thought of his death bring a tear to your eye, did any one person bother to see, if by chance there was life still in he?

For who is the man who lies there in the snow, was he placed there by G-D to see if you know, the meaning of life as it is meant to be, do you care for all men, do you not care for me?

Is there a giving of love in your life or are you too filled with your personal strife, are you aware that you are not alone, do you not know we are not made of stone?

We each have a heart to share with all other, we must live our life as brother to brother, for we must give love and live love for all, for those who may rise and those who may fall, for this is G-Ds way, how he wants us to be, there is no other way for you or for me.

Hal Edwards

Old Ghosts of the Prairie

Twilights steals over the prairie and, oh, how good it seems
To sit here alone in my cabin, but I guess I'm just dreaming dreams!
For it seems I can hear — out of some yesteryear
Voices that once were so merry
I look all around - no ones to be found.
So I know they're "Old Ghosts of the Prairie"

Old buffalo feet - how they used to beat
To the hair raising wild Indian yells;
The campfires, the herders, the long cattle drives,
Have all passed to old ghostly trails.
The old covered wagons-just rumbling along
With a baby a crying, and somewhere a song
But they're all gone now, and no more will they be.
For they've all become. "Old Ghosts of the Prairie"

Seem I will "go west" where the ones I love best,
Seem to be calling to me, and I'll hear them say,
When they see me that day
Why, you're just an "Old Ghost of the Prairie."

Fern King

Faded Horizons

In the calm distant reaches of an early sunset...
Under a brilliant sky splashed by the sincerity of red...
An echoing of desire stirs in the wake of passion,
Whispering promises of devotion and love that is sure to spread.

To walk the fading line leading into the treasures of dreams...
To wander forever in the shaded mist of inspiration...
We turn to the pure and solid source of our feelings,
And surrender to the soul binding revelation.

Severe affections sprout within us, shrouded by rivers of rain
Flowing in each current of life tainted by common fears;
We merge our souls together deleting any sense of pain,
And notice a gentle smile, warmed by caressing tear.

Now as the hours pass, our thoughts safely lashed together,
The sifting of sand is over...
Revealing the emotional ties that are sure to last forever.

Freddy Holman

Under The Shade Of The Family Tree

Sharing memories of our generation
Under the tree that's God's creation.

Where dad expressed for all to hear
the family would gather every year.

A gathering we would not dread
Meeting at the "Old Homestead"
Under the shade of the family tree.

"Independence Day" was dad's birthday
Made all the festivities joyful and gay.

A great celebration for mom and dad
With friends, kin, and the children that they had.

Horseshoes, marbles, basketball
Provided entertainment for us all
Under the shade of the family tree.

There's peace and tranquility
In sharing our love and loyalty.

God's presence protects our tree
As we abide with thee.

Irene Harris Hasty

Ritual

A sleeping generation
  Virgin minds awake
  Black as raven claws
  They come to have wings
Flying through the doors of the mind
  Soaring in a blazon unknown world
  A shining moment to explore
  Unexplained reaches of minds reality
  Knowledge sears the blackened flesh
  Exposed beneath, revealing pure glistening dreams
  Silver arrows tearing through the ageless heart
  Of a reality based upon destruction
Rediscovering exposed truths long forgotten
  In a quest to achieve others dreams
  They will come together, one by one
    Time and again
Different surroundings, changing seasons
  A ritual formed
One used to remember
  How to live.

Greg Larson

Autumn Sonnet

Welcoming arms reach out for autumn days,
We say good-bye to summer with no grief,
The brilliant sun is dimmed by pleasant haze,
And nights, now cool, are bringing sweet relief.
Enjoy the loveliness that now abounds,
This dazzling season will not linger long,
Breathe deeply of the color that surrounds,
And gives birth to a cheery autumn song,
Before frost comes to glaze each window pane,
To steal away the splendor of this time,
The pleasantness that's offered by this reign,
With all that it now holds of the sublime,
  Too soon its red ad gold will turn to brown,
  And we in gaudy beauty will not drown.

Gwyndolyn Smith

Autumn

Autumn is a time of year,
When God seems especially near,
He seems to be shaking colored leaves to the ground
As neighbors rake them into one huge mound.

The dew is sparkling on the grass,
I admire it's beauty as I pass.
Squirrels are storing nuts in the trees,
As their bushy tails blow in the breeze.

The summer flowers have hid for awhile,
Their pale faces are not in style.
They'll return again when the snow is gone,
Arrayed in a splendor all their own.

The dog howls softly as the moon floats high,
While the chilly wind whistles, "Winter is nigh."
The cat sleeps peacefully curled up in a chair,
Seems everything knows that God is near.

As I stand midst autumn's glory, I marvel as I think,
What a wonderful cup of beauty God offers us to drink.
I bow my head and thank him for all these lovely things,
Especially for the colorful magic the autumn season brings.

Irene Nichols

"Life Goes Too Quickly"

It was the third month, I believe,
When I first felt your life stir inside of me.

As the months went by, I talked to this life.
Yes, before you were born we both shared your life.

On that cold day of March twenty-seven,
You alerted me that you were coming, around the hour of eleven.

Oh my, I was really blessed,
A nurse showed you to me and you were all dressed.

Your skin was so soft, and your hair was so red.
I thought, what a beautiful baby as I tucked you into bed.

I read books to you until you fail asleep,
About Little Bo Peep and All Her Sheep.

Now time has gone swiftly by,
The years have gone too quickly for my baby and I.

Today I watched as my baby received,
A diploma he had worked so hard to achieve.

My baby doesn't realize that, consequently,
Life for he and I has gone too quickly.

Some day though, my baby will hold his own baby,
Then and only then, will he know that life goes too quickly.

Frances Pryor Hill

When I Think

When I think about how it used to be.
When I think about how close we were.
When I think about how I was then.
When I think about how I wanted things to be.
When I think how much we have drifted.
When I think about you.
When I think about now it should be.
When I think about the future.
When I will be on my own.
When I will need you most of all.
I want you to be my best friend again.
Again I will need you in my life.
These are the best years now.
When I think how much I love you.
When I think about you.

Heather Mohr

"Why Do We Fall In Love?"

Why do we fall in love?
When we go our separate ways,
it hurts so much.
Why do you care for this man,
who hurt you,
and took advantage of your love.
Why do you still have feelings for him,
after everything that happened.
How come you say you've fallen in love with another,
when you still love the man from the past.
The man in the present,
wants more then your willing to give.
And pushes you farther then what's expected.
How come boys think they can toss us around,
play with our feelings and then forget,
move on,
and Never,
never return.
Only in a memory.

Faith Davis

High Grass

There's certain loneliness - twenty eight years-
When you think of it, it's lonely.
The house we lived in, I pass there
Sometimes and it looks a little strange.
I sold it a while back; the yard's there
Like it was; there's a bench
And the grass is pretty high;
The house is old now, needs paint.

Twenty eight years is a time
For living, and we lived there.
Now it's not the same. I walk
Around and look at things.
Twenty eight years there, and then
She left me, more than half of me gone,
I loved her and she satisfied me.

Now I'm waiting here a little longer.
I know there's justice in things;
Everything's good and fits together right.
It's just this little longer that
I'm waiting is kind of hard. It's lonely.

George M. Pace

Where The Paved Road Ends

Take me back to where the paved road ends
Where dust swirls free in the passing winds;
To walk again where the power lines sing
Along winding trails in the early spring.

I want to wade barefoot in cool, clear streams,
Hunt for wild blueberries, rekindle old dreams,
Hear the frogs' throaty tunes down by the pond
Where fireflies flicker through leaf and frond;

Watch frolicking rabbits from woodland appear
See grazing afield a small herd of deer
With a full moon rising lighting the night
Transforming the landscape to silvery bright.

Those were simpler times when summers seemed longer
Bygone days when the whole world was younger
When a child had time for childhood's pleasures
And recalling old times are lifelong treasures.

Helen Stewart Webb

The Childless Teddy Bear

Where are the arms that once held me tight?
Where is my friend who kissed me goodnight?

Why are you sad when you look in our room?
Where is my friend?
Won't he be home soon?

I lie in our bed gazing at the stars
somehow I know my friend is not far.

My friend used to hold me to make his fears depart
If you like, hold me now and know our friend is in our hearts.

Heather M. Campos

A Dyslexic Is As A Dyslexic Does

I am word blind,
Which means I am behind.
To heck with total recall,
I don't see a word at all.
They may say I'll grow out of it.
The letters keep turning around,
Shoot, I don't know up from down.
Who can subtract.
Math to me is an abstract.
His talents we should appreciate
Even if he can't recapitulate.
I can't spell
I sure hope that don't mean I am going to h—-
We must remember the essence that is he,
If he is to be the best that he can be.

Georgia Anne Smith

Wasted Seeds

Wasted seeds is not the words for a man who
wishes to be happy.
Happiness is what you feel, everybody knows
what it is.
You said, you are the wasted seed - I think
you are the best of seeds.
You are the wind that carries your shout. You
have spread them like pollen.
You are the wind that lifted your banners, but
mother nature scattered the seeds.
Don't think you're a wasted seed, in your heart
you're the best of all the seeds.

George T. Gaviola

Small World

Ah, my miniature railroad wonderland,
With tiny townspeople and matching abodes,
Nestled among sponge-like bushes and trees,
Shining and reflecting from the mirrored lake.

And from my omnipotent lofty perch,
Was run the small world of boy dreams;
Soot blackened smokestacks, a myriad of
Ties and trestled steel rails all pointing
Towards that Utopia that only the
Society of model railroaders can envision.

You can almost hear the banging and clanging
Of hammer and spike that the Lilliputian
Laborers seem to be working tirelessly with.
The B and O, the Santa Fe, and the others;
What an aesthetic display of railfan fantasy!

The lights become extinguished now;
Darkness overwhelms the small-scale display
Of plastered mountains and plastic passengers;
Undersized urban Utopia has finally gone to sleep.

Gregory W. Brentlinger

A Request Not To Alter The State Flag Of Georgia

Removing all the stars and bars,
Would not erase the many scars.
It doesn't condone slavery.
It stands for unmatched bravery.
In case your memory is jaded,
We're the ones who were invaded.
It represents the fallen bones
Of those who fought with sticks and stones.
The number that are wrapped in shrouds,
They met the foe above the clouds.
Antietam, Vicksburg, Shiloh, too.
They gave their all against the blue.
Where our gray ranks were torn asunder.
And all who heard the cannon's thunder.
The smoke has cleared, our cause was lost,
But we cannot forget the cost.
It's over now, the quarrels should cease,
Please pray that we may live in peace.
Display it high, for all to see.
And neighbors, let our state flag be.

Floyd Jackson Mizell

"My Green Cathedral"

I am a mere man, just a simple man,
Yet sometimes tears roll down my cheeks.

Tears of regret, sadness, and happiness,
When my mind strays into the past.

I have prayed in marble halls,
And within those granite walls.

Still I search for that place of still waters,
Where peace of mind and tranquility lies.

Where problems are no more,
And green hills sooth the eyes.

And on God's mountain with tall green trees,
Nature's Cathedral brings peace to my soul.

George Smillie

Desire And Immortality

Women on pedestals are, mortals too,
Yet, when they go,
And go they must,
They leave a trail of longing...
A fire in men who cannot face the mundaneness of life...
Who want to go where She has gone, because
There, they can fulfill
The worship of Godesses...
Who will not remind them constantly of their own
Immortality.

Ah...if only dreams could fit into everyday life.

Gina Sanchez

"Brave Soldier's All"

Mother, you're the bravest soldier of all;
You fight a battle without even a call.
Your battle starts with parting sons;
The giving up of your loved ones.
Though tears you shed, you weaken not;
Less your sons might be forgot.
Your battle is hard, your battle is long;
You're victorious, as mothers all, are strong.
Dad, you're quite a gallant soldier too;
Perhaps the one who's most forgotten too.
Your battle starts when we depart;
One you fight, within your heart.
It's your battle to cheer those behind;
A hard one, yet one that is fine.
One that is right, in any test;
For you have feelings like the rest.
So, I salute you both, as a soldier lad;
The greatest of all, Mother and Dad.

Fred R. Schmidt

Until We Meet Again!

O Dear Father in the Heavens above,
 You have called one of your special Angels, whom we truly loved
You blessed my Mother with this Special Angel in mind
 And together they became both one of a kind
We all live our lives and await from You our special call
 TERESA had the greatest, to spread Love to us all
With only a short time on earth, she had a big job to do
 And she succeeded in her mission, even more than we knew
She greeted each one of us with a hug and a kiss
 Even to those she met once, She will truly be missed
When YOU gave us TERESA to touch all of our hearts
 Never did we think so soon would she part
Her time on earth was short, but so sweet
 And now we must wait, before we shall again meet
TERESA, you will be in our hearts forever, and we will never let go
 Until we meet again, My Beloved Sister, WE ALL LOVE YOU SO!!!

Frank Pisani

Two In Love

Two in love can walk the shore,
Cast stones out over the sea,
Watch them skip and dance 'til momentum is no more,
Then sink for an eternity.
Holding hands, they kiss.

But I walk the shore, I scuff the sand,
Sit down and look at a stone.
The stone is not cast, to skip and dance,
The stone is not cast, for I am alone.

Herbert C. Link

Drinking and Driving

Close by the door he paused to stand,
as he slipped his class ring off her hand.

All who watched did not care to speak,
as a single tear rolled down his cheek.

All through his mind memories ran,
of all the times they once had had.

He held his class ring and started to cry,
he kissed her cheek and wanted to die.

As the wind began to blow,
they lowered her casket down below.

This is what happens to many alive,
when friends let friends drink and drive.

Jessica L. Sweger

Untitled

I am so unhappy, I do not know why.
I seem to have it all.
Inside I feel like a piece of myself is missing.
It's been so long I've had this feeling.
Is it loneliness, confusion, regret or pain?
I wish I could let these feelings known.
I do not know what to do.
I feel like a child, lost, wandering, crying,
Screaming - help! help!
Where am I?
I can no longer breathe.
Mommy? Daddy?
Where are you? I need you! Hurry! Come for me!
Inhaling, I am back to the present.
Where are they? I need them so.
Please, I have so many problems, so many questions.
Mommy, Daddy...
I love you, I need you.
Run. Come for me!
Show me, help me... love me.

Toni Marie Greco

Nostalgia - On Approaching Age 60

Nostalgia - a sentimental subjective placement of one's self in the passage of
years.... trying to glimpse, hold on-to, relate, and find the fleeting mental picture
of Toddler, child, daughter, sister, wife, mother, and the elusive essence of
being.... Me.... Spirit.... Soul.... Self.... Endless questions ----- questions
of reality.... Questions of Sanity.... Questions of reason.... unanswered, unable
to grasp or even do more than look back on one's self, seen fleetingly from
the mind's eye and the heart's pain.
Toddler — Free.... yet fearful and tied to an unseen umbilical cord....
Child — Happy.... unaware of life's awaiting tragedies.... brimming with love ----
Filial, sibling, with threads of Celtic Pride of Clan.... beginnings of mystical,
Yet cognitive premonitions and the dark emptiness of hidden hurt....
Unreasonable guilt and a whisper -- No, an eerie wailing of black emptiness....
A black hole where self and doubt become a separate entity.
Mother -- teaching moralistically, yet striving to allow independent development of
character.... to promote idealism, realism, spiritualism, and a familiar bonding....
All a psychological pattern -- and, like an ink splatter, developing its own boundaries.
Me.... Myself.... I — ageless spirit in an ageing body.... spiritually strong,
Yet battered by negativity and futility. Nostalgia.... in the end, an imperfect
human in an imperfect world, hearing the inexorable drum-beat of Death and
Mortality. Nostalgia.... an ending.... or a beginning?

Grace W. Carlson

'You Sure Know How To Turn A Phrase'

I was walking down the street;
You turned your head and smiled at me.
I looked into those coal - black eyes,
The ones that never told me lies.

And thought you didn't say a word,
The world stood by, and they all heard.
Darling, you sure know how to turn a phrase.

I remember those dark eyes that pierced like daggers,
And lights that sparkled like the stars above,
Against the black, velvet skies,
I stood and gazed into those eyes.
Darling, you sure know how to turn a phrase.

Our arms reached out and we embraced.
I saw the love upon your face,
I hold you tight against my heart;
This time we'd never, ever part.

That was thirty years ago
Yet Darling, I still love you so,
And words could never take the place,
Of that first look upon your face.

Esther M. Thomas

When Every Sunset Counts

Sunset glow, how well I know
your warming rays upon my face.
It was not always so,
that I adored your glow.
In youth and haste, it was a terrible waste.

But as the autumns passed,
and seasons rushed so fast,
I prayed to ease the pace,
I long for sunshine on my face.

Each spring I wait, behind the iron gate
to hear a robin's song, and knew it wont be long
before I dance again along the sandy shore.
And feel the sunset glow,
and wished it was forever so.

Ingeborg Von Finsterwalde

Time Grows Life Breath's

"People Pods"

I was a weed one day
My tears water'd my wild way
Often time friends would come to play
Wind rain washed my fear away
As I lay here in my pasture
  Hungry like a lion
    and
  Starving like a lamb
Who shall I be, who, who, shall I be.

Holli Sue Corbo

Dreams

The dreams we shared, the plans we'd made,
My debt to loneliness had long been paid.

A touch, a smile and security just from you,
I saw our world with a clear and focused view.

But dreams get shattered and promises are broken.
Love vows soon fade and harsh words are spoken.

I hold yesterday's memories as a reason to cry,
but I keep tomorrow's faith as the courage to get by.

Geri Hampton

Weed

Often in life, it is death that will lead,
A flower is born with the death of a weed.

Killed is the old to make room for the seed,
In with the new, out with the weed.

The seedling grows quickly, spreading with greed,
More space is obtained by pulling a weed.

All garden plants struggle for the light that they need,
But competition is removed with elimination of weed.

Now the blooms have all faded, done is the deed,
And soon it is the flower that will be replaced by a weed.

Barbara A. Bennett

A Thing Of Beauty

A jewel is a thing of value
And of exquisite beauty.
It brings pleasure to the eye,
And makes the wearer sparkle

A rose is a think of beauty,
And to some, quiet valuable.
It will smell wonderful
And brings happiness to a woman's heart.

Have you ever seen a jewel
Caring a Rose?
Much value there would be
And ten times the beauty

Every man who loves a woman
Has something, both valuable, and beautiful,
A treasure of the utmost delicacy
How much is she worth?

Every Thing.

Shane Myers

Lilly

Lilly she is my wife, and the joy of my life,

Just like the flower she stands so straight,
And there's nothing about her I hate.

Her eye's are baby blue, and I know to me she's true.

When she hold's me in her arms, I feel safe from all harm.

I plan to love her all of my life, I'm so glad I made her my wife.
And though her, hair may all turn Grey, I promise with her I'll stay.
So Lilly in the valley, or on a mountain high,
I truly will love you, till the day I die.

Hughie Bryant

Snow

I saw something white fall from the sky today.
It was such an odd thing,
As it came floating down as if it were but a feather.
And when it landed on the ground or in my hand
When I reached out for it,
It melted and turned into water.
For a long time this substance from the heavens
fell, landed, and melted. But eventually
the substance ceased to melt as it landed,
but rather collected, thus covering the ground
with a white beauty that only poets think about.
A substance called snow.

Robert Shaffer

A Mother's Achievement

Living in a community in which people think is so poor and under
As I sit here and write, I find that I sometimes wonder.
About the day in which I finally get out of here
Will I jump up and down, will I scream with joy and cheer?

Having been here so long has helped me be real strong
I have mental strength and a will to survive.
If not for me, I need to accomplish for my children
Remaining focused and very much alive.

I need to show them morals and values
That will carry them in life once I'm gone.
I have to instill in them the need of self reliance
That they can count on each other, but really trust no one.

The poverty that they now encounter
May it be a stepping stone.
To study harder, work ardently
So that someday they can have their very own.

So, just as I have tried to set a good example for them
By going back to college and obtaining a rewarding career.
May this give them incentive, may they reflect back again
To this experience and ordeal, may it last them for years.

Gloria C. Beltran

Love Is A Miracle Of Life

Gazing at the stars in the night,
As many that glows
Is the thoughts in my heart.
that overwhelms me within.
Love is like the highest mountain,
Deeper than the deepest blue sea,
So beautiful as the rainbow
across the skies after the rain,
So beautiful as diamonds
glittering in the light.
Love is more precious than Silver or Gold,
Sweeter than honey mixed with God's Goodness.
Love is like than sun that shines
Through a rainy day,
the clouds disappear
leaving the smell of freshness
for a brighter day.
Love is a miracle of life
that will always lead you through,
Love will never fail you,
It is something good that with everything in life.

Natalie R. Begay

Looking Out My Window

Looking out my window my eyes behold God's glory
As nature plays before me I watch a great love story
The story starts as the morning breaks brand new
The sun is brightly shining the ground shimmering with dew.

Looking out my window I'm relishing the sight
Soft white clouds, the bluest sky and then a bird takes flight
Thick green grass, and rustling trees
The vivid color of the leaves.

Looking out my window the day turns dark it's night
The sky is black like velvet, the stars turn on their light
Looking out life's window I see another view
So many unique people, red, yellow, black and white
Just to name a few.

Looking out my window I'm truly amazed at all I see
I know I'm loved and cared for
Thru heavens open window
God watches over me.

Gail Peterson

The Soldiers

The soldiers went into battle
As the skies of blue turned gray
Can't remember if it was in April
Or was it in the month of May

The soldiers where fighting for something
For a cause they did not know
Some were saying it was for the hill of glory
As the skies of the nite begun to glow

The soldiers heard some distant cries
As some them heard loud screaming
All they could do is fight for their life
And hoping that they were only dreaming

The soldiers lost a lot that day
As the battle of war went on
And after the war was over
There were only memories to be shown

Terry Allred

Our Very First Snow Thanksgiving Day 1971

It was Thanksgiving day, when I awoke quite late,
Because of the night before, I refused to go to bed and sleep.
But, oh to my surprise, came falling from out of grey skies
a blanket soft and white, this year our very first snow!
It fell so silently everywhere, the barking of dogs pierced the air
and dulled the sound of cars on the road, for they had places to go.
And as I sit here at my desk, I thought of the night before
when I sang a Christmas carol or two, did I rush the season now?
I was with friends of old and dear, who were more lonely than myself
because of affliction they were bound in bed and had no where to go.
When I am in sorrow, I wish to be alone, and remember these words of a poem,
"I cried because I had no shoes, till I met a man without any feet."
Yes, these words with comfort me filled, for I had my feet still and
pretty new, red shiny boots, which I shall put on and go
walking through the softly falling, very first snow.

Heidi Weber

Alone

You are not around,
but have loved me at night,
in my mind,
you are reality.
Memories of you,
keep me alive,
in lust and desire,
for in the twilight hours,
I am lonely.
Visions of you,
dance through my mind,
as your distinguished scent embraces my body.
I am smothered and aroused by this sensual cloth,
wishing you could hold me.
The morning sun will shortly arrive,
so I must somehow travel back to reality.
Be quiet my love,
for this evening is ours,
although only in fantasy.

Doris Ruiz

If I Knew How

If I knew how to fly a plane I would fly right to Spain
If I knew how to play the piano, I would play "O Susana!"
If I knew how to play the violin, I would play it again and again
If I knew how to be a writer, I might write about apple cider
If I knew how to build a building, I would build it to the ceiling

Jaynae Okon

Life Through The Eyes Of A Strong Woman Who Is Still A Weak Child

I am now a woman living the life of an adult,
But inside I'm still the child
That never had the chance to grow up.
As a woman I have to be strong
With children of my own
But the child within me is afraid,
Hurt and all alone.
The woman in me deals with life
Trying not to fall apart
But the child in me tries to find
A way to mend her broken heart
The body we share tries too hard
To be strong and to reassure
That we can go on and hand all the
Things that life will endure.
One thing that we both have in common
The one thing that we share
When one of us gets too lovely
The other one is always there.

Francis Bolden

Sometimes....

You are so distant with me, that I can't help
but wonder if I am still that someone special
within your heart....

You act as if I'm intruding on you, when all
I really want is to be a part of you.

Sometimes, I feel as though I talk too much and
ask too many questions, when all I want is
answers to understand you better.

Sometimes, when I'm alone and you're gone,
I find myself missing you, remembering
our last moments that we shared.

Sometimes, I just want to be me and you be you,
and sometimes I want us to be together.

Sometimes, I just sit and wonder, sometimes
somehow, all of this will come true.

W. Renee Jones

When The Night Falls...

Stars shine in the midnight sky,
Comets and clouds go sailing by,
The man in the moon winks his eye,
When the night falls...

The entire world is at peace with a smile,
Time and space seem to go on for miles,
I sit and stare out my window for awhile,
When the night falls...

Shadows of trees have fallen to the ground,
The children that were outside are no longer around,
Perk an ear: There's hardly a sound,
When the night falls...

Reminiscing about the whole day through,
Still awake at a quarter past two,
Every thought in my mind is of you,
When the night falls.

Annika J. Swainson

Destination Rainbow

Carry me away with the wind
Encompassed in a raindrop
That I might travel my journey
On the majestic arc of a rainbow

And when I reach my destination; it's end;
That I might be just as glad
That there is wind and rain
As I am that there is sun.

For it is the conversion of all that create one;
One such wonder as the rainbow I travel.

Stacey Seaton

Blue

Blue can be - The color of the sky,
Encompassing everything, yet holding nothing.

Blue can be - The river,
Running towards forever,
Aimlessly, endlessly, with no destination or goal,

Blue can be - A person,
With a hurt heart and no place left to turn,
In this case destroying or damaging the soul.

Blue can be - The saddest color I know.

Rebekah M. Nicholson

Hate Me Not

Why hate me, simply because of my pigmentation.
Even though I have caused you no pain,
My mere presence brings you aggravation.

Hate me not, for I hate, you not.
Hate plus hate equals hate,
It seems many hearts have forgot

To hate me, is to hate the Creator above.
For He is the one that created me,
Mind, body, and soul, out of pure love.

Darren Bernard Bryant

The Unemployed Teacher

I never felt this bad. I was wrongfully accused, and terminated just five days before Christmas in 1993.

Oh how cruel, the anxieties and frustrations I have to endure daily.

I wake up each morning, anxiously at 5:30 a.m., thinking I need to be out there pounding the pavement on my way to work.

It's very frustrating, as I am not used to idleness. These past thirty months had been unbearable, solitude experiences.

I have my ups and downs. When I get depressed, "I think of the wondrous teaching experiences I enjoyed with my ambitious students." What are they doing now?

I try not to waste my time being non-productive. I used to get phone calls, letters, and notes from fellow former co-workers who sympathized, and coached my concerns to return.

But these dreams are now a reality, that line of communication had stopped.

"Oh how cruel, the anxieties, and frustrations, I have to endure.
Another day, in yester year.

Frank T. Brown

Thanks

Thanks for this day with its beauty,
  for every second, minute and hour
Filled with thoughts, deeds and actions
  that makes life interesting, exciting and great.

Thanks for friends along the way,
  the joy their presence and conservation brings
Their tender-loving care and prayers
  add strength and happiness to our life.

Thanks for family that love us
  not for what we have
  nor for what we do.
They just love us, for being ourself.

Thanks most of all Lord,
  for your patience, love and guidance
and knowing that you are with us
  today and everyday.

Yes as I pause a few brief moments
  amidst a busy busy day.
I have much oh! So! Much to be thankful for
  and truly I am.

Billie Ruth Furr

Do Not Be Afraid, Just Be

Go on now...
I know you said you would wait for me but, it is time for change. I need peace and happiness here, now. My children need peace in our home. We must stay and live. Don't be afraid to let go; we will find one another again soon.

Remember our talks of how the universe expands?
I said, perhaps our spiritual self, when it passes upon our physical death, becomes a new star, expanding the universe as it metamorphosed. Go now to become your star. I shall find you, for always there will be a thread of light between you and I. Once again, I shall caress your face and you shall hold my tiny hands within your gentle, gigantic ones. Perhaps we can be twin stars!

I must complete my life here. Never shall I forget, nor shall I cease to love you. But others need me now; and I need them, also Love encompasses much in our fragile lifetimes.

Just a few more moments, a few more words...before you go I must thank you for bringing to my remembrance the essence of strength, my inner strength, which you always stirred you within my go breast. I'll not forget. Be not afraid for me, or for you.

And, know I love you. Now, go on...

Carol Copeland Eidahl

Bless The Child

As I put the bible in my sight,
I must continue each and every night.
Father what can I say,
But I love you in another way.
I thank you for the things you've done for me,
Your generous as you can be.
The life you gave me I'm glad of it,
With you my life is a big hit.
As your my creator and I'm your creation,
I'm glad this had to begin.
Loving the one who made me,
How can that be.
There come times when you have to think,
I must lift my head high and give a wink.
Drop to one knee and pray,
Tell my father what I want to say.
Some might not believe in where they come from.
That's why they live the life of a hum drum.
That's what makes love so wild,
Father please continue to bless our child.

Terrance Hamlin

Falling Leaves

From my third floor window,
I see the falling leaves.
They detach themselves
And fall down to the ground.

From my third floor window
I see the falling leaves.
I do not know if they hit the ground
I am too high up to see.

From my third floor window
I think the leaves are like that dream.
Where something is falling
But that something never hits the bottom.

From my third floor window
I notice one leaf that is fighting against the wind.
It won't come off the branch, it refuses to let go.
Hold on little leaf, fight don't let... it is falling.

Helen E. Jackson

Fun In Church

I went to a wedding last Sunday, it was a gala occasion and very gay!
I took a seat in a back row pew, a splinter entered, the seats weren't new!
I was early but, had brought a book, it was playboy mag. so I took a look!
A priest was walking down the aisle, I must confess it brought a smile!
His robe a few threads did lack, as his bright red jockey shorts
stared back!
I'm sure that this is blasphemy, but it was funny as, I hope you see!
I forgot what I had come here for, until that bride walked through the
door!
You can't believe this sight I saw, this gorgeous blonde without a
flaw!
And as this comely bride walked by, she seemed familiar to my eye!
It seemed I'd seen her recently, and not clad, so-demurely!
I thought and thought where had I seen, the likeness of this beauty
queen!
And then my book dropped from my knee, exposed the center page
to me!
You won't believe, lo and behold, this sweet bride was the centerfold!
I've heard poets are a rhyme dozen!

Gene E. Thompson

Love Blanket

I just want to get comfortable
I want to clean up—wash dishes—whatever
but there you are
just like a comfortable blanket—soft, cuddly, sweet smelling
No matter where I go, there you are also
not smothering, but all over me
pulling me away from things I need to do
I try to put you back on the chair - on the wall - in my drawer -
anywhere, but —
you just hang on, refusing to be folded up and put away
why why why?
I can't get anything done
Not with you hanging around but
it's not you or is it
I can't seem to do anything not even wash my face
You do confuse me even without being here
I don't mind I just can't get anything
and I do mean NOTHING done
But now I don't want to
I think I'll just wrap you all around me and
RELAX and curl-up in your love

Rose Green

Challenge To My Wonderful Son

If you can trust your God with each tomorrow,
if you can lean on Him whate'er your fate,
if you can pray in joy or deepest sorrow,
if you in faith His perfect will await,

If you can serve Christ with your time and talent,
if you can love all men in spite of race,
if you can help to lift that erring neighbor,
if you can point him to the Master's grace,

If you forgive each purposed imposition,
each deft deception, each intended slight,
and still show forth a lovely disposition,
but let the world know sin is never right,

If you in true humility can suffer
and flinch not, ever, heartbreak's crushing pain,
if you prove faithful with what Christ has offered,
triumphantly expect with Him to reign,

If you have given your all to serve the Ris'n One,
have made to count for Christ each fleeting minute,
here in this life you'll be a man, my son!
What's more, heaven will be yours and all that's in it!

Elma Clark Norwood

The Blue Field

Siamese blood sings
in a chariot of gold and silver tones
as we throw soft imaginary kittens
to the tantalizing embrace
of a deep blue sky
fragile melodies brush against our lips
and push us on our backs
these chemical monsters make love to us like ravenous animals
with the sent of violent roses
dashed upon their silken throats
a garden of wicker men
stretch their velvet faces
to the shivering stars
the glitter of trees
wrapped in leather
still hold me up
the appetites of flickering children
dancing in the rain
more beautiful than the sky could ever know

Jason Matisko

Love

Love is a complicated four letter word
It can bring one happiness and sorrow
It's an experience that all have heard
Love can be here today and have gone tomorrow

Love should not make you miserable and sad
It should not treat you like a yo-yo
Love was not meant to come and go as a fad
It's a feeling in your heart you shall know

True love will blossom and stay
You will have ups and downs
It will not stand in your way
True love will make you smile without a frown

Dorothy Nell Starks

At War With The Devil

The Devil's touch.
It feels like a never ending blade, piercing they flesh.
At war with its victim, never leaving them to rest.

Those cold, fewer eyes staring.
The flames so swiftly spreading, the mind slowly melting.
But, as long as the tears are flowing,
thy will not be defeated.

You dragged thee down those darkened halls, inflicting rose thorns of pain.
But soon, my Devil, all you have taken will be mine.

Fear, yes fear your weapon great.
For as long as thy can feel the pain, for as long as thy still suffers,
The war remains.

Fear, no fear, but why?
For me, a weapon more powerful, than any pain, or suffering.
My weapon is life.

Try hard, dear Devil, try hard.
Those tears are tears of joy, once frightened eyes show glory.
Farewell, farewell.
You lose, I win, I live, I stand.

Maria K. LaForge

The Key To The Door

The key of the door is a number
It meant something to me.
The fine lady lives there all the time
They keep the door painted green.

She keeps the apartment neat and clean.
She told me her name was Mary Ann
She is one hundred and sweet sixteen
She looks fine and dandy
With earrings in her ears.

She didn't bat her eyes to me
But stood healthy and clean.
In the night she slept broadly over the bed
The air-condition didn't work very well
The rain fell and beat upon the bed.

In the silent of the night, with hope and dreams
With search dreams she live alone
Calling out for me,
The apartment is so small and sweet.

The phone rang and the voice was loud
She kept singing along with me.

Clyde C. Seaton

Sensitivity

Sensitivity is an important part of me,

It opens my eyes so I can see,
It sparks my creativity,

It opens my mind so I can be me,
It helps me communicate with rhythmic poetry,

Sense, sensitivity, sensuality, a sensuous, mind is a powerful mind,
It can make you strong and ever so kind,
If someone give's you that weak man line,
Just listen to my words as I define,
Our minds are gigantuous sense organs,
The more sensitive you are, the more sense you have,
As I end this poem, that's the bottom line,

Be insensitive and you shall be weak of mind.

Lewis L. Harris III

The Breaking Point

It's been a long time since I wrote anything down.
It's been a long time since my world stopped spinning around.
It's been a long time since happiness I tried to find.
It's been such a long time since I searched for peace of mind.

I have so many things on my mind now-a-days.
I have things to figure out, but cannot find the ways.
I have a son with a father that is never here for him nor I.
I have frustrations of the relationship that I know will never work, but why?

I've grown so much anger, so far I've been able to suppress.
I've learned to be so insecure to know, I'll never be a success.
I've felt for so long, peace to myself, I never get but I've had to accept.
I've known for so long, when it comes to me, my son's father has no respect.

But now here comes my fury and frustrations
Here also comes my pain and my temptations.
Here also comes my thoughts and my feelings.
And hopefully my happy life that so far my son's father has been stealing.

I just hope and pray that one day I will be, all I can be.
I just hope and pray that I can change what my son's father has make me.
I just hope and pray that one day I will once again feel free.
I just hope and pray that I can show my son's father what he has done to me.

Cindy Renee Kurtz

Chosen

When I think of you and all the things that make you you, it makes me glad.
I take joy in the experiences we share and the great dreams that we have had.
When you dwell on your sorrow and pain and what could have been, it makes me sad.

I love you for who you are even in those times you fail and do less than your best.
When you are weak or distressed, I will encourage you to be your best and help you pass every test.
I will be there when you experience loneliness and fear.
I will be ready to kiss away each tear.
You need not fear the future nor feel rejected.
For I have plans for your good and you will always be very much accepted.
I will never hurt you nor do you harm for you are my precious treasure.
I desire that you be with me always and I miss you when we are not together.
When you long to be with me and your heart turns toward my heart;
Then you may desire as I that we may never be apart.

I will believe the best of you. Let others say what they will.
I will cherish and honor you and continue faithful still.
I will always stand by you and promise true devotion until the end;
Because I have chosen you to be my friend.

George L. Guillaume

Love

Love is caring and sharing
Love is togetherness and foreverness
Love is trueness and happiness
Love is not hurting one another
Love is sweet just like candy but sweeter
Love isn't buying gifts day after day
Love is hugging not tugging
Love is a great thing or it can be a fate thing
Love is hoping and praying for one another
Love is saying sweet words
LOVE IS A WONDERFUL THING

Kristen M. Ritsema

Supervision

Searching for the apples of the sun,
me ponder over grapes and biscuits instead.
Underneath the abstract veneer of the slick
red coca, lies a worm with opposite heads.
When people could fly and peer into the
infinite blue heavens, they were not
satisfied, so they reached as far as the
intellect could and grabbed for a spot

just to the right of the left star,
As the star floated non-comprehendingly
in its celestial navigation west, people
stocked their fuel and dreamed unconditionally

about never surpassing their own limitations.
Meanwhile underneath the star, the apples
carried on in their seasonal pattern and
dropped before the doorstep of tabernacles.

Rick Hopping

Phenomenal Evolution

Marvelous transformation, the miracle of life, of existence, from
microscopic seedling to the essence of beauty
Growing thru trials and tribulations, obstacles and always heavy
laden, lost and alone I can not see the forest or the trees, meek;
afraid of every man, all hope is gone, my heart torn, my soul worn,
my head is weary and all I do is pray, praying thru tears and anger
with all consuming guilt and shame, going on but never knowing why,
I'm looking back; only one way to say how
Expanding the mysterious wonders of the world, spiritual
metamorphosis, I am creation at its finest
In awe of the intimacy of my master and me; never knowing true love
until this, fabulous change, strength beyond measure, the ultimate
treasure: Finding my purpose, to sow seeds of love nurturing
mankind, exalting his name
Beauty is in the eye of the beholder and he's made me beautiful, not
like a movie star but fine with myself, ever changing, each cocoon
unleashing something more priceless, magnifying passionate desires
for knowledge, knowledge empowers and I know him
He teaches me, holds me, holds me and rocks me gently, my soul
evolving and exploring until peace, until serenity until all is

Latisha Denise Reeves

The Move

The move is and was as simple as could be,
moving from one place to another, one space to another...
It will and would be an adventure one cannot and could not pass by...
To move from one experience to another there is always,
and was always someone who will or would get broken,
so is and was the case with the move...
Memories will and were packed away tightly and labeled...
to find and would be found stashed away in the dark closets years
from now,
or to be left hidden away never to be found... or to find...
One move would never be enough, one place would never be big
enough
to have... there will be and always was a never and better place to
experience having... thus the move continues and continued...
Someone will and would be lost in the move and moving,
but such is and was the hazards of the move...
never knowing or knew what the next move is and was to be like,
yet needing and needed to move all the same...

Robert T. Ricketson

"Sleep"

Color cubes as I fall asleep, followed by a twitch.
My breath slows, and my conscious minds switch.

Sometimes I free fall, and sometimes I fly.
Instances where I over see all, and in others I die.

Situations that have made me laugh, and in others I've cried.
Limitations abolished, reality set aside.

Fear fills my body, rings in my ears and replaces my blood.
Being chased, I'm in a hurry to get out of here, gotta run.

But escape from who or from what? I run from fears I cannot see.
Maybe from the past or future, or personal demons eager to feed on
me.

Once in a while though, my future is clear.
So concise, with sounds that I can hear.

As my soul wanders aimlessly through the night,
my body heals, and my mind records my plight

Morning comes soon, the sun will rise, and I'll awake.
My soul returns, mind revised, and I awake.

Chris Cunningham

Soul Road

A road less traveled, off the beaten path.
My heart goes there often.
It is a long, dusty stretch, and a lonely wind
is my only companion.
As the tears of the midnight blue evening touch
my cheeks,
I watch the last leaf fall from a tallow tree nearby.
It beckons me to come and sit beneath its boughs,
But I say, "No, I must keep walking." Walking.
Walking to eternity.
Dust devils swirl at my feet.
I close my eyes and feel the sensual peace float
down from the clouds.
I am alone, but content. I am safe here.
I will continue walking, walking...
Maybe, one day, I will return to that tree, and
it will be leafy and green.
And I will lay under it and rest, peacefully,
and my soul will hitchhike its way to heaven.

Andy Keys

You Wear Two Masks Don't You?

The light does not dapple my face.
My smiles locked behind cold alabaster.
The ticking gnawing at the back of my mind does not make me wince,
For the clown's face is glued too tight.
The black tears are frozen on my cheeks.
When was my last act?
When did I paint this mask that endures the frown?
You did not find my performance enjoyable
So you left before the finale.
The flowers up my sleeve fell to the stage
With the sound of silent thunder.
The crowd roared!
They all wear masks.
They don't know when to remove them,
But I can hear the jeers closeted behind the porcelain cheers.
Once you threw a smile without a mask.
Mine slipped off.
Now I can barely breathe from the new one.
You left your smile where you were watching.
You wear two masks don't you?

Gordon Stock

Memories Unbound

Looking out a window,
my thoughts high on sparrows wings.
Bringing memories to focus,
remembering her beautiful face.
There's a light touch on my shoulder,
a soft tickle in my ear.
Wonderful memories pulse within my chest,
jarring the feelings inside.
Tearing through the past I'm reminded of a breast
accepting me without hesitation.
A heart swelling with the fears I gave it,
but never with holding its unyielding love and hope for me.
Looking out this window,
I tremble.
Not tears streaking down my cheeks,
fogging the panes of glass.
All I can think of is saying thank you.
Thank you Lord for my beautiful Mother.

Barbara J. A. Sheldon

Untitled

Suffering neglect with little intellect,
needless abuse, there's no excuse.
Pain and anguish without a smile;
Don't take it out on an innocent child.

Spirits live in the souls last flight;
darkness follows those with fright.
Always respect your child's plight,
send them some love and give them might.

Needless neglect, I'll advise respect,
Don't stop to wait 'til it's too late.
Try to become something for the future son.

Somewhere out there is a world that cares,
live with love and not despair.
False accusations, lots of distrust.
Need I say more. It's life's way of saying children
need love and not mistrust.

Bruce E. Dittrich

In My Sister's Shadow

Never could she say he loves me
Never could she tell of all their horrible living hell
How could I never speak of the pain within my sister's shadow
Should love be the ruler of my sister's shadow
Now all we have are precious memories of all the marks that
were visible to see if only we knew
"I ate something that broke me out
The pride is where I hid the pain
The true pain of my love was the love that was never there, how
could I love in denial for so long, it happened
The price I paid for the freedom of my children by being locked
in the wall of hell
Can anyone see their pain, did anyone hear my cry
Does anyone care, who will sit my children free from the wall of hell"

Gena Williams

Change

The change in newness is the key to our youth,
the first of our days are the best of your ways.
The first ray of sun
warming the dew.
And the first breaths of air for a flower
from you.
The first of a dance, a touch, or a kiss...
The feel of the innocence in the midst of this.
And all from there this too we my find...
Desire for change broadens our mind.

T. Lynn Bedgood

Will Our Love Last?

I vowed to myself not so long ago
Never to let love hurt me so
I told myself the pain would go away
But at the start of each new day; those words fade away
There are times when I want you near me
Yet you are so far away...
Deep inside my heart I pray we'll never part
But if you really don't love me just tell me it's the end
It hurts me worse not to know and pretend...
There is a pain deep inside my heart,
a confusion I cannot stop
I tell myself these feelings are foolish;
and that you love me just the same.
At times I feel your hiding; hiding something from me
Something you wish I not Know
and if that is true; then please say so,
and let me go, be on my own...

Audrey Richards

Walls

Welcome to my universe, a place of walls.
No one lies in my world but me,
I'm all alone.
My space is small, my feelings grand.
This work of walls is a coffin to me.
Smells and fears of death engulfing me.
Ask me the number of cracks, lines and folds,
I know them all by heart.
A prisoner of walls has little to
hope and dream,
Growth null and void.
You're invited inside but you never come.
My best friends are my paper and pen.
Maybe one day you'll read the pages within.
Walls make you think, make you
realize the black hole in
which you live,
It's the smallest universe of all.
Welcome to my walls.

Linda Glaude

Emotions

Reflecting on all the feelings that I ever shared
Or experienced - loving you is
Surely the best
Exciting, enticing
And enlightening you make my love for you stronger
Nowhere else could I encounter the love that we share - Although
Death and other inevitable consequences of life places limits on our love
Forever I will pray to the Lord for us to be together this generation
and forever after
Rational or not - this love is too good to end
Even if I am a Bee and you are a flower - I will make my home on your
petals
Dedicated and devoted I will be - if anyone tries to make you wither
I will sting them a thousand times over
Never would I leave your side for
Loving you is my duty and my pleasure
Overbearing I will not be - for I will flutter my wings to make you
feel Vivacious and rejuvenated in my
Everlasting love for you

Frederick Sutherland

Untitled

What's happened to the world today
People killing people - children born unwanted
Drugs and alcohol available as newspapers at
the corner store
Dulling minds and turning people into fools
that no one wants to know.
The world is too full of guilt, remorse and
hate and fear,
And on "I couldn't care less" attitude.

Now, there's a thing to always keep in mind.
your attitude determines every mood
and thought.
No matter how you feel and act, get a
good attitude!
It won't be easy but try hard and think
positively.
You'll find that people will like you better
you will like yourself better!
Because your attitude is better!
Smile

Eleanor Braden Krost

"Life"

Open your eyes look out to the world
see the pleasures and disasters
from where ever they have come

build on your thoughts from whatever dreams you've had
some of them are good a lot of them are bad

"LIFE" itself can be very cruel

there are those on top who make the rules
and those on the bottom they are the fools

it's unfortunate but you have no choice
we're all dealt a hand and most with no voice
all in one word it's called destiny
that's how "LIFE" is that's how it will be

then at the end will come one very special day
for some it will be joyous though some they will pay

so, open your eyes look out to the world
let the best things prevail- reach out to each other
reach out with your heart during this very lifetime
before you depart....

John Amoratis

The Truth About Ms. Irony

What is this demon you reflect?
She dreams through every sleepless night.
It's insecurity's unending defense and
Mr. Aggression's boundless fury.
It's the uncompromising stench of misunderstanding.
Her tears feed the gargantuan pride.
There's a shadow beyond the mirrored face.
It's the vulgar scene that clings to memory,
While you're forced to regurgitate every attempt.
It's the child you've kept in slaved in cellars;
The surgeon sickened by his own suicide.
This skinny sage of sickly sadness
Gives ignorance the election in retaliation.
She takes a match to the flammable affections.
In a pit of sweltering stain it's you,
Left for doubt in your own reflections.
To keep in chains the inconceivable desires,
It's your choice to sleep with faithful confusion.
Yet somehow a prayer for obvious adultery.
And she said, how long have you carried this demon.

Brian Mills

Life Without Her Goes On

She was 5 feet 2 inches tall...100 lbs all wet
She had see all Brown eyes, Silver thinning hair and all
Her fragrance of "White Linen" still lingers everywhere
Life without her........Where do I start?

We strolled through many years together holding hands
In her arms she fixed my toys, dried my tears, soothed my pain
She always knew when I needed that special kiss and warm hug
Because...She was my MOM
Life without her......Now, must go on

She's the wind in my hair on a breezy day
The wet cool ooze round my feet, when in the mud I play
The strength that holds me daily tall and upright
She's still there.....somehow....near me, when I slumber at night
Life without her......my restless sleep quite

I smell her perfumes, the scent in her hair
Our connection is stronger....for truly she's there
No matter where I travel or how far I will go
She will always be..
For LIFE WITHOUT HER......GOES WITHIN ME
I LOVE YOU MOMMA

Cynthia Rose Crayton

Awake At Last

One at a time and all at once,
Ships of all sorts sail our spheres,
To cure the unknown.
To destroy the cure.
The voyaging glow upon are ships are becoming
Dim and yet too bright to realize.
Like a child born with fear.
The child dreams are real.
The child dreams are dear.
have our ships sailed past our dreams
When our dreams are feared.
One at a time put our reality to sleep
And all at one board our ships.
A child dream should be preserved.
To be closed, to be opened only at will.
Open as the sails when catch the wind.
Closed as the inherent reality within.

Michael Romero

Untitled

Anybody else who wants a little pain grief and misery
Simply open your eyes and follow me
We'll go to a world filled with sorrow
And we won't be coming back tomorrow
We'll visit a man who lives in a room inside his head
A place where everything is dead
In this place there is no light there is only darkness and fright
Darkness surrounds him, it is all he can see
And the darkness that surrounds him is me
I am what is killing him some say
I hurt him more each and everyday
I do not care about the pain I make him feel
I only care that he does not heal
But I know that you do not understand
Not only am the darkness in this land
I am also he who is trapped within
Dying for his greatest sin the sin of love and trust
But ah! I see his golden heart has begun to rust
I bid you all a fond farewell
Come again another time and we'll chat for a spell

Brad Boyko

Look And See

The road of life is long, with many stops along the way,
Some days the stops are many, other days there hardly seem to be any,
The memories of yesterday are of times obscure-
The way seems desolate-devoid of meaning—should we go on?
Look back, yesterday lies back there up the road—empty
Look forward, another cloud of dust,
Someone has gone on before you—go, too
But look hard as you go-
For all look, but see differently.
Look with your heart, look with your mind, look with your soul
Then you may see love—see God
And when you feel that outstretched hand that says,
"I care about you-not as a lover
Not because I need you for what you can give
For what you do or have
But simply as a good friend of mine, because you need me for what I
Can do for you through friendship.
Let me help you then you will know that you have seen all there is to see
For in that outstretched hand you have seen God.
Go forth along the way for you may meet a friend and God today.

Miriam Soltz Roth

Desert Showers

Clouds:
Some white
Some black
Some gray
Textures and designs hanging above the Catalina Mountains.

Pearly-gray salt bushes sparkle-dripping on pebbles.
Washes ripple filling with fresh rain.
Mesquite smoke singes the humid air.

Suddenly-
Sun shafts hit the Tucson Mountains
Lighting the snow from a backdrop of slate-gray sky.

Mountains:
Some white
Some black
Some gray
Textured designs woven on the desert hills.

Cathy Ayers

Little Girl

Little girl, little girl, who becomes a beautiful young lady
standing over yonder please come and talk to me
please come and talk to me
I am standing in your shadow, looking in your eyes
Wondering what you are thinking, let it out,
Let it out please let me help you
But by keeping it inside you will realize many years later
Why you did not say more, didn't say more
So I asked you what is wrong
knowing there is something wrong
but you just say that there is nothing wrong and
that you wish for silences
just want silences
so I respected your wish for silences
what more can I say, little girl, little girl
many a thing gets worked out just by sitting and talking
and understanding the problem, understanding the problem
not to mention how much closer two people can become
just by talking, just by sitting and talking
little girl; little girl.

Frederick Filip

Point Blank

I was trapped in truth.
Surrounded by a prickly maze of bushes.
The distance between start and finish was at
least three times as far as one should not want to imagine.
It was soon, very soon, too soon and now, never.
The use of a bond was not worth depositing for life.
The trapped truth lingered and lingered among
the prickly maze of bushes until the soldier was shot.
It oozed and oozed, not of blood and tear,
but of truth, hard times, never being,
faith of a different being, self caring, and other sharing.
I was trapped in truth and now blinded by its consequences.

Alan J. Joynes

Untitled

God is the warmest color of purple
swallowing blue
I saw her early this morning as I
awoke into a forgotten dream of calm intensity
and security
escaping the hung dark void
of America's poisoned night.
we danced an ancient dance, one
I had never danced before
and fell spine first into
a musical trance
helplessly inebriated
and frozen to immaculate
statue.

Hutch Hill

My Woman

I want a woman that can teach because I'm a man that loves to be taught.
I want a woman that is strong and isn't afraid to admit she's wrong.
I want a woman that knows the meaning of commitment, Someone I
can talk to and chill with.
I want a woman that will make hot love during summer, And
just chill during the winter, Someone that will relax and let me
cook her favorite dinner.
I want a woman that can give a dying man life, A woman I can give
a ring and claim my wife.
I want a woman that will take my cold heart and turn it to fire,
Whispering in my ear only words of love and sweet desire.
I want a woman that is all mine, I want a woman that understand
love takes time.
A woman that will be there when I'm half the man I used to be.

Shanta Reynolds

Let Me Be Free

Months of misery troubled my mind, one day as I was walking, that left me feeling mopey.
After being in this state for some time what I wouldn't do to be happy.
I noticed, out of the corner of my eye, a lonely leafless tree
I admired the branches for they were grand and lofty
If I reached the top what would I see?
But a man coming out of the sea
His face full of glee
While holding a key
For a fee he'd
set me free
to be
me.

Sandra B. Deemer

Eternal

Falling to earth at an alarming rate
The ground coming at me at with intending speed
Fear is all I have to keep me warm
the scare providing a nightmarish need.

Doing this will give me hate
from all those around I have a tear
when it ends I will loose all form
Suffocating in a drowning lear.

If I am to die on this very date
Let it be without regret and pain
My love and prays not to be torn
For those are the things that can't be slain.

Jerome Morton

Over Wyoming

Penchant Locks of Cutzoo curls, gallant winds dust and dirt swirls.
The ground thundered cracks show signs of rage.
The ground there opens is this it's age?

Seasons roll abound without regard
Aged even further, nothing to retard.
The days that roll and mix into years,
further evidence of something unclear.

Pondered without sight never knowing to see.
I crossed a path once traveled by me.

Torrid rays.
The sun there beaks.
The lines in the dirt,
a smell here wreaks.

To the side a puddle,
Reflections of me.
Thundered cracks to the side of my eyes I see.
Turn back to the earth
green goes to brown
back to the puddle
now a frown.

Daniel C. Beeler

Lover of the Wind

The sun moves away making way for the moon, softly changing colors
The trees leaves softly shuffling
The stream running ever so gently
Just the beginning of the wind

Ah, so beautiful to feel the softness of the wind
The sweat no longer on my brow
The coolness of the wind brushing my wet back, ever so gentle
Just the coolness of the wind

The blinds moving gently against the windows
The plants and flowers closing
The birds no longer singing but flying
Just the life of the wind

As I lay across my bed, I can feel the warm air, slowly
taking my mind with it.
I look out the window to see darkness appearing
The lights of the streets coming on
No talking, no music, no movement
Just the quietness of the wind

This is where I find my peace

Denise Adams

"I've Found A Friend In My Lover"

To wake up in your arms, to know that you care.
The understanding look in your eyes,
dreams and secrets we share.

To walk arm and arm,
to have a strong shoulder to lean on.
To laugh and to joke,
to know that love is there when you're gone.

When there's exciting news to tell,
you're always there with a smile.
And you hold me tight, when I feel scared like a child.

You love me, you make me feel like a lady,
You don't laugh, when I cry like a baby.

You talk to me, you love me,
sometimes your like a big brother.
But the real truth is,
I've found a friend in my lover.

Deborah A. Gentile

Turf War

"Lay it down right there, you know what it's about".
Then a couple seconds later the shots rang out
A shotgun to the back, a magnum to the head
It's two in the morning and another kid is dead

Now the sweltering begins in the summer heat
As the drug lords murder so they control the street
They say it's for their turf, they say it's for their pride
And if you don't like it, you better stay inside

The "gangstas" got the money and the fancy cars
So the kids look up to them like they're superstars
The cost to do their business is in human lives
And the trick of the trade is somehow to survive

The thing about a circle is it never ends
The teen who was killed, well you know he's got some friends
The gang will get together and find themselves a gun
It's all about revenge, and the war's just begun

W. Scott Brown

There Was A Road

There was a road that led us Africans here
there was a road. This Road was not of pebbles, gravel
or dirt. It did not wind or bend or guide with signs
pointing north, south, east or west but there was
a Road. We didn't need a ticket to get aboard this
road yet we were forced on with the rest of the
load. I can still feel us being packline like
cattle rounded up in a pen. With us all trying to
breath fresh air with. Oh yes there was a road.
This liquid road with ripples of wars with no direction
unless charted by ink. Cursed with blood and bodies tired
and hungry and full of fear. This road with deep waters
of wave that knocked upon our wooden beds
closed in upon us this road had a salty taste of
home but yet we could not see the form that
rolled on to the sands on to the shores
The was a road that seem to never end. This
was a road to a new world. This is the
beginning to the End of the Road!

Semaj Ramel

Passed Me By

Considering the greatest joys of living was I a day or two ago
Thought of all good things to live before I die and discovered to my woe,
All life's real treasures now held so high
Sadly, but surely, somehow, they'd all passed me by

The time of my youth came to mind, came with a sigh
wasted mine on countless frills
Why can't I live it again, sadly I cry I'd be wiser, my heart feels
To have knowledge and youth on which to rely
Alas, just a dream, it's already passed me by

Thought about my children, aging quickly as days pass by
time with them so precious
What better gift to give them than time, but why over lesser matters I made a fuss
Being with them and loving them was my greatest high
Wish I'd seen then more, but somehow the time passed me by

I think now of my God, all his blessings from on high
should have had more time for Him
Never neglected was I, on his love I could rely
through heartaches and eyes dim
Yes I could have done more, why didn't I try
Sadly I bow in shame, my chance has passed me by.

Eddie Allen

"Birthday Child"

Happy Birthday to you how time passing
through, it seems like only yesterday you
were young and full of play. Now as the years
go by, you realize more and more that it's time
you came to grip that there's so much more in
store. Time out for little pig tails and ribbons
laced with curls, you're living the life of a
teenager in a crazy mixed up world. Oh my how
you have grown although you must realize your body
is not your own. It belongs to Father God the maker
of heaven and earth to which he gave you two
parents to start you off at birth. Even though
sometimes it's hard, they continue in their job. They
only want the best for you. You must admit it's
true for without such loving parents what on
earth would you do? So listen up birthday
girl the best is yet to come, enjoy life now
for soon it...

Kim Johnson

Caged

Have you ever wondered how it would feel,
To have everything changed to something unreal?
To be thrown behind bars for the rest of your years
While bitterness replaces all of your fears
To never be able to talk to a friend
To reach for what life had left to lend

Sitting and staring at a cold gray wall
With nothing to care about, ever at all
Your only last hope when your time comes
Is that all of your past will fall into crumbs
That maybe in your "next world", life will be true
And make your new living better for you.

Debra Escamilla

He Comes

He comes like a whisper on the wind
to save my soul, my sadness end.
No grand entrance, for One who is King,
but humbly and softly, as a dove on the wing.
I call out His name, and lo, He is there
to lift me up from the depths of despair.

In dreams, He comes, like a gentle guide.
I know my Savior's by my side.
My heart, with joy, His praises sings;
His tender voice sweet comfort brings.
"Tho' by your sins, I was defiled,
I love you still, my child, my child."

Candy Gruman

Departure

I watched you dance.

You obtained no rhythm as though your soul
was taken from you and you were left lifeless.

I cried.
You were my laughter,
my answers, my shoulder,
And now, standing from afar,
you are my tears.

Alone...you dance.
Yet, not alone, I saw
your lifeless body in motion with the others.

For a moment you paused, and looked my way.
I saw your soul evaporate
and blend with the air.

Your body was still visible
but you were empty and frail

It was your time to go, so I began to say Good-bye,
but you had already gone.
Rid of anger and at peace with yourself.

I watched her dance.

Lorna Chang

Untitled

We sit and talk or even laugh or not a word we say
We carried on like we'd be here forever and a day,
You were my partner, you were my wife
You were everything I had in life,
We had no fear the day would come when we would have to part,
Not a thought we ever gave of life with a broken heart,
As I relive the days of the past,
So clear in my mind the picture will last,
To walk each step in life today,
Without you here I lose the way,
No one knows the emptiness I bear,
The sadness, the pain, total despair,
As the days go on, the stronger the pain,
The grief so bad all seems in vain,
I try to tell myself that's how it has to be,
Life on earth is very short and has no guarantee,
So I'll try my best to carry on and let no one see me cry,
The toughest thing in my life to do,
Was to kiss you and say goodbye,

Joseph Giuliano

It's Crying Shame

Its a crying shame that
We hate and kill each other.

It's a crying shame that we can't live as brothers.

Its a crying shame that the world has gone wrong
and the children are growing up alone.

It's a crying shame hatred and racism run
rampant in the street and poor people are left
out on the street.

This world must seek love in order
to find peace only then will man find
what he truly seeks.

Theodore Noble

Joy Love And Happiness

When a child's at play laughter fills the air
When a robin sings you know that spring is everywhere
That's the joy you've brought me
and sweet things you've taught me
My world has truly changed
Since the day you came into my life
You made it oh so sweet
You gave a lonely lady
the kind of love that she needs
I'm so thankful that you found me
Keep your loving arms around me
and don't you hesitate
to let me feel your lips upon my face
If I should cry
Don't worry
Its because of what I feel inside

Frances Dew

When I Grow Up

When I grow up, I'll go to school to learn my ABC's
When I grow up, I'll sail the Seven Seas.
When I grow up, I think I'll practice law
When I grow up, I want to be a star.
When I grow up - When I get older
I'll give the world a portion of my abilities and strengths
it will be poetry in motion.
When I grow up - When I get out
The world will hear my laughter, the world will hear me shout!
When I grow up, I want to be someone's mother or father;
but as of right now, inside this package of water,
I have no idea if I'm someone's son or daughter.
When I grow up... well as far as I can see
The gift of life might be taken away from me.
I'll loose the chance to be a star or practice law.
I'll loose the chance to learn my ABC's or sail the Seven Seas.
I'll loose the chance to be poetry in motion.
I may never be grown...if my parents have this abortion.

Tamyka T. Sanford

Reflections Of Life

The ocean was calm
And the sun was a bright and glowing star.

I could feel its rays pushing...
Pushing me into the water.

I knew I could not swim,
But I could not keep away from it.

The whispers of the ocean waves were calling...
Calling my name.

Alice Scott

The Place That Never Left Me

As a child of war I understand
When I see your head on your hands;
You're reminding me of an old war,
Down my head to the ground
My eyes closed, my ears plugged,
'Till fearsome whistles ceased from the sky.

The place and the home I have known
War had claimed for its own;
Even my friend, I have heard no more,
What was war all about after all?

As we walk on and on
I saw strangers came along,
Here and there were smoking drums,
Wounded men and horses dying me left behind.

As we walk on and on
Until my eyes saw the place no more;
Yet such a place has never left me,
Such a home I call my own;
Why o' why should we be in war?
When the enemy you call can be my friend.

Fatima Bantegui

To Wealth And The Sycophant

To be blessed is what they call it.
Yet the spark of envy burns near.
How successful (they say), how accomplished,
But a backward glance (undetected) speaks the truth.
Some praise here, some flattery there;
Do you think we'll be invited?
If not, just simple snobbery;
They always act that way anyhow.

We must have this. We must have that.
Can't have "so and so" out do us.
How do they do it? (humph!) How can they lead?
Such impeccable social standing...
But wait—here they come! Best smiles. Act intimate.
Be sure to show (of course) they are your "friends."

To be blessed is what they call it.
They, the Sycophant, and the Upstart.
To be sure, someday they'll "make it."
Some day they'll finally have made it.
But what will they have then, one must ask?
Friends?—To be blessed is what they call it.

Desirae Brown

"Little Big Sister"

You fought so very hard for so very long
You loved life as it was,
You were a child looking out a window
Seeing other children throw their lives away...
With drug and other harmful things
I wish other children could see
How precious life could be...
Some kinds take life for granted
Thinking tomorrow is a guarantee
But how little they know, with
Drugs on alcohol no matter what the case maybe.
Your only guarantee will be...
There won't be a tomorrow
If you know what I mean...
Little big sister I remember
Your words so clear
Drug and such things have
No part in my life for me...

Theresa R. Briones

The Sun And You

The sky is bright and colorful.
The clouds are puffs of blue.
The sun is warm and plentiful.
The sun shines down on you.
You once asked if I cared,
And I told you that I do;
But I never once showed to you,
My feelings that are so true.
It is the sun that beats down.
It is the sun that heats the cold.
And it is the sun that warms the ground.
But it is my heart that is growing old.
The time has come, I must wait no longer,
I will show you what I must do.
Each second my heart grows stronger.
I will show you that I care for you.
Where the sun meets the sky,
Is where I will wait for you.
When you are ready to fly,
I will show you what you must do.

Patricia Cadman

Untitled

Around the ancient tree of disaster
the accident happened, outside
the ashen maiden cried
her pure white dress was
stained with the wretched blood
she was no longer loved

Would she again see the seed
of what she once was
pale reflections of the moon
silhouetted the once white dove
she was no longer worthy
of anyone's love, below, or above

Now night arrives once again
and divinely tormented she will begin
once again, to enact her ancient sin
but now the sparrows call her name
what once was, is now, not the same
and so is, and was, the end of the game

Mike Cole

Subconscious Reality

Frequently I visit a place
That's dark and scared and lonely
Sometimes I scare myself
With the pictures I create
Subconsciously I'm running from reality
Not too far behind
And if I don't stop running
I know I'll always be fine
Sure I know that I must go
And fight this evil foe
Although I know he's only made of fears
And as I turn and wipe the tears
To face my dreaded doom
I'm suddenly real again
And I have escaped the fears once more
And once again I'm relieved until
Night bestows the land anew
As it does every day and joins with time
To persuade me to try the journey over once
again

Nicholas Fuller

Tones

Blackness is represented through all shades
Our tan might diminish but our color never fades
Because I am darker, my beauty is sometimes overlooked
"Light skinnedness" is the bait to which the Negro nation has been
hooked

The deep hue of my skin does not make me blacker than he or she
That is found through your individuality in which knowledge is the key
Lighter does not always mean whiter, so do not use that to base your
judgment remember to love thy neighbor as thy self as conveyed in the
tenth commandment

The famous three I's: Light skin, light eyes and light hair I did not
obtain unfortunately some acquire these features, unnaturally, because
they fallen into the convincing warp of vain brother. If you look at
me and my ebony sisters through narrow eyes keep your words to
yourself because you have been brainwashed with lies

From Naomi to Vanessa there is equal black radiance I know that my dark
skin, black, nose, full lips and kinky hair was bestowed upon me from
the finest of mahogany elegance the world is cruel but to each other
we need not be vicious remember, brown sugar is sweet but milk
chocolate is delicious

Dion Short

My Mother

Such a strong black woman, she bares the earth with just one short breath
She reaches the earth's soul with just one fingertip, she inspires and
changes peoples live with just one word
She loves a greater love than anyone could love, her heart is as big
and warm as the earth's bare ground, she as is powerful in the heart,
body, mind and soul as mother nature is in weather, she is as
loveable as a big soft teddy bear, she is a queen in body and soul
When she dances her heart glides across the dance floor and it builds
up and your body moves, she laughs thru the good times and tried her
best to smile thru the hard times; no matter how hard the time
She always stands on her own two feet, no matter how rough your day
was she could always make you laugh and if you didn't laugh you would always put on a smile
When you would cry millions of tears she would always share those millions of tears with you,
If she was an island she would be paradise, her land would be softer and flutter than a cloud
Her love inspire everyone she is the perfect mother
She gives the perfect love, she never lets her pain hurt others when others hurt her
She is always the strongest, that is why she is so special, she will
always be remembered in my heart, I love her with my soul
The Lord has really been good to me, I was able to have such a good mother

Shavada Denise Dragg

Lonely Love

This lonely ache I feel as I lie here grows inside me.
As the days stretch into weeks, the need increases; to hold and be held.
I so much need a look, a caress, a hug; the feeling of loving and being loved.
The memories of times together haunt me day and night, so precious;
my sustenance in my lonely world.
Today I should feel joyous and fulfilled, but my day is somber and empty.
Such joy I felt. My heart beat swiftly, my stomach full of butterflies.
How I love the desire in his eyes, the feel of his hands, the sound of his voice.
I love him so much. I have missed him so much.
But he has missed me too and fulfillment is his not mine.
My need is always so great; it is easy to fly swiftly with him on our journey.
But, today I started the journey and was left in the clouds.
There I floated all day, and slowly drifted back into my loneliness.
Today's loneliness is worse than yesterday's.
Yesterday's loneliness was a memory of times past; today's a dream of what could have been.
I'm so very, very sad... Now, I begin again.
The days once more will drift into weeks and my loneliness continues to grow.
And I wait... until once again I can be held in his arms, see the desire in his eyes
and feel the love we share.
Good-night my love; may your dreams be of me as mine are of you.

Gale A. Girard

The Gilded Cage An Acknowledgement Of Battered Women

Come into my space
You will never have to worry again
Come into my space
Decisions are not options within

Come into my space
No one can touch you
Come into my space
The world from the inside out will be your only view

Come into my space
All that you need is here
Come into my space
Bring all that you hold dear

Come into my space
I'll be the most important person in your life
Come into my space
I'll be your only source of happiness, joy, pain and strife

Come into my space
Hurry, come in just for me
Come into my space
I'll make you what I want you to be

Amelia Gibbon

With Him

In his eyes, I see the darkest of nights.
In his heart the wildest of dreams.
In his arms I find the greatest of sins.
From his lips I receive the comforts no other can give.
Being with I am safe from the world that cruelly exist.
Without him I am only half of an existence.
Only with him can I ever be whole.
Only with him can my love ever grow.

Zenaida E. Heslop

How Wonderful You Are

The world is full of surprises, but the surprise that is
deep down in the earth is how wonderful you are.

Sad times, happy times-the one thing that makes the world
sing is how wonderful you are.
What makes the ocean rise, what makes the bird sing?
You...because how wonderful you are!

Suzanne Feda

Mentality

As the grass and I lie,
Admiring the beauty of the sky.
As the exquisite puff passes by,
The motion is slow to impress I.
"Come on FulASoul, it's time to go."
Not moving an inch, but hanging around like an lynch.
Beauty and I were communicating,
Actually, I was just mentally escaping.

Bryant M. Edmondson

Woman's Sacred Touch

Soft as the swell of a gentle wave is the
sweet liquid flowering of the vertical lips of
Heaven. Softest universe of eternity where
two can become one.

Steve Jacobs

James

There is a place for you that no one can see
It lies in the shadows of your memory
It may seem really far away
But places like these will always stay
I love you my child and I want you to know
That this place will be here as the years grow old
Some day you might find it
Although we're apart
But it's here forever
Your place in my heart

Cynthia A. Cox

Feelings

Oh aching heart what would you say if you could speak?
What would you seek?
Would you want the power of infinite love?
Would you seek to find the end of the rain-bow?
A sweet song,
A verse of encouragement,
A lonely soul to cheer,
Would you bring happiness to the sad?
Would you wish for a better tomorrow?

Eva S. Lambert

Trash Or Treasure

I'm sure that Heloise would hint
  That I should buy one of her books
And read even the finest print
  If she saw how my "store-room" looks —
How my nomadic "store-room" looks:
  Things seem to wander here and there
  In bags and boxes, drawers and tins,
  Yes, even in some plastic bins
  Each time I neaten up my lair.

I am a pack-rat, this I know;
  But some strange malady kicks in
When I set out to "sort and throw"
  That makes my head begin to spin —
Mere thought of tossing makes it spin!
  A magazine, a floppy hat,
  Old Christmas cards, a rusty tray
  I put each back and firmly say,
  "You don't know when you might need that!"

Loraine O. Funk

"A Halloween Scare"

Have you ever gone walking on Halloween
The branches reach out to grab your hand
You run until you reach a dead end
The thunder roars like drums in a band

The rain it pours with a thundering pound
Through the rain you hear a howl
You wish you never heard that sound
Now you wish you'd brought a towel

You hear some footsteps coming closer
You wonder who it is
But what if it's not a who at all
You hear your stomach fizz

You wish you hadn't left your house
On this cold Halloween night
You run home and scream your worst
As you were given this Halloween fright.

Mary Kubik

The Storm

I walk on tiptoe through the rapid waters
That drench me clear to the bone
I shelter beneath tall pines
Watchful of the dark thunder

Grey skies stretch out their teeth
to nip at my exposed skin.
Lightning flares along my spine
Searing me with feral flames

I am drowning in the rapid waters
Black rain falling from my eyes
I wait in silence-
For the passing of the storm

Patricia Hopper

Life's A Mighty Ocean

Life is a mighty ocean
that each of us must ford,
And every man's a sailing ship
That has his soul aboard.

Oh, ship that has my soul aboard
What have i done to thee?
Deceitful wind that mourns in sin
Sets you adrift at sea.

The stifling of the silence
The ship's confusing flight,
Oh, cheeks are wet with grave regret
The anguish of the night.

No stars to give direction
The breakers black the sun.
In cloak of grey, the soul will pay
For what the ship has done.

Too late, oh ship, to turn you
Back to the charted sea.
Oh, ship that has my soul aboard,
What have I done to thee?

Parnell Pierce

My God Is Real

A rose, a butterfly, a snowflake
that fall's all say that God is
in charge of it all.
Yes, only God can make
such beautiful thing's as
Snowflakes in the winter and
flower's in the Spring.
So how, can we say that he
is not real when, in all of
this beauty he is revealed.

Susan Brown

Untitled

An aching heart,
A lost soul
That's what you
gave me
When you left
You didn't realize
Just how much
I cared for you
Now you'll never
know
But I guess
That's the price
we pay
For being blind

Felicia Anastasio

What Happened...

What happened? How as it
That I came to forget you...
Do you recall how I loved you
How your nearness
Was my hope and my desire
And now...
I see you from afar
And this loving, gentle heart of mine
Sleeps in the quietude
Of its own celestial sky
Never more to dream the dreams
Of you and I
Being together in a paradise

What happened... how was it
That I came to forget you...
Let me think... oh, yes!
You couldn't love me
You were too busy
You didn't have time
I guess that's why...

Roma

My Rat

I have a rat,
that is fat,
he has a tattoo of a cat.

He likes to eat,
things that are sweet,
but moldy cheese is not a treat.

His friends are fun,
but make him run,
his fur is delicate in the sun.

His eyes glow red,
when he's in bed,
he has a lazy friend,
named Ed.

He has a wife named,
Erla Krife,
she has a very interesting life.

She vacuums, sweeps, mops, and keeps,
The cage in running order.
That is all now, we are done,
telling of my rat that's fun.

Rachel Tilton

"My Desert Home"

Arizona your so Lovely, your
the apple of my eye;

With your mountain and your
Lo-Lands, for they nearly
touch the sky.

Now when I go dawn to
Phoenix and it Happens to
be night and I know I'm
getting closer, when I see
familiar lights.

Oh - I have been so lonely;
for my desert Home

I vow to never leave again
and never more to roam
from my Desert Home.

Violet Howard

God's Skyscraper

I've never seen a tree so tall;
That makes me feel so tiny small;

As I stand here on the ground;
Looking up the tree I've found;

Towering taller and taller, as it grows;
Where it will stop, only God knows;

With it's branches lifted high;
Stretching out into the sky;

Dusting clouds as they go by;
Up where the eagles, sour and cry;

High above the ground below;
Where the nesting eagles go;

To their penthouse up on high;
From where they teach their young to fly;

Souring and gliding to the ground;
To where it's mighty roots, are firmly bound;

Silently stretching out you see;
As they anchor down God's tree;

Reaching deep into the earth;
From where God gave, this tree it's birth!

Robert E. Filip

Lion

King of the jungle
that may be
Lazy and full of curiosity

Scavenger for life
is the way of living
Not known for kindness and giving

Bold and fearless
is the lion way
But hyenas surround its next prey

Lucilla Brugnoletti

Life And Death

Oh by the wicked rules of life,
That our destiny is shaped.
The cancer has come.
The body is screaming for help.
The heart grows weaker.
It is but a lonely life.
But my heart grows fonder.
The rage, the hostility.
I want, I seek happiness.
But then, only uncertainty.
I cry by the fireside.
No one hears - No one cares.
Why do they not help.
They don't understand.
They don't understand.
The heart grows weaker.

Peter J. Belluci

Untitled

Life, as a puzzle, is dignified
to find the pieces to strive
to be better than the next,
good competition life's complex.

And so the puzzle grows as cold as ice.
And nothing is left to sacrifice
Needs are met but won't suffice
our need to be above the ice.

Zach Swan

My Man

In my dreams you appear,
you haunt my every thought;
You chase away my every fear,
a man like this I've sought;
You hold me close when you are near,
Even times we don't agree;
Though seldom times you are here,
you always say you love me.

Rachel Diane Jackson

Untitled

Upon the boundaries edge I stand
That overshadows my own land
Today, I leave my love behind
But where I go he's on my mind
The time we spent, some good, some bad
The memories of him I had
And now I take a giant step
And there I sat, and there I wept

Upon the boundaries edge he stands
That overshadows his own land
I hope his life and love goes on
And prays for me as days grow long
From where he is, he's looking on
And though he's gone, my love grows strong
The memories of him I'll keep
Until one day we both shall meet

Therese Nadeau

Essential Emotion

Love is such a beautiful space
That so many people share
Love is feeling all of the joy
The pain comes when it's not there.
Love is two becoming one
to never ever part,
Love is two who find a three,
A little one to push in a cart.
Love can be so many things
But to each it is thought
Love has one true similarity
It comes straight from the heart.

Ramona Y. Holloway

Everyone's Friend

Sometimes I wish
that time would pause
or that the world
would have no flaws.

When people cheer,
and then shake hands,
with peace spread all
throughout the lands.

With crystal streams
that run for miles,
and a bright orange sun
that always smiles.

White with black,
and black with white;
and no one has
a reason to fight.

A kind of world
that never ends,
and everyone is
everyone's friend.

Rachel Wittenmyer

Untitled

Like a candle blowing in the wind,
That will forever burn,

And the memories we gather,
As life's pages turn -

Our love that we share
Will bring our worlds together,

And the trust in ourselves,
Shall bond us forever.

Michelle Storlazzi

Untitled

I thank you for all your faith,
That you put in me,
And for reminding me once again,
How exciting life can be.

In return, please take this rose,
That within me grew,
For I know it wouldn't have been there,
If it had not been for you.

Nathaniel Bruchey

Separate Lives

Separate lives
that's what we live,
There was no more love
for either to give.

So many things done
so many things said,
But one heart was broken
and left there for dead.

One left alone
one headed for the door,
So many shattered dreams
left scattered on the floor.

So now we're living
separate lives,
Which means no more secrets
no more lies.

Michelle McLauchlan

Remember

In memory
The colors of the day remain.

The field of snow
A palette of white
The shadow of a tree
Bare limbs lifted
In penitence to
A moonlit sky.

Etched across the
Landscape
A curved black shadow.

A murmuring
In the tree tops
Vietnam. . . Vietnam . . . .
Vietnam . . . .

From higher still
Whispers unending
Remember me . . . .remember me . . .
Rememberrrrrrrrr

Myrene Scott Dewolfe

Untitled

Faces brightly painted
The crowd begins to roar
The spotlight hits the center ring
As the clowns march through the door

Such anticipation
From children young and old
Who come to see the circus
And so the story goes

It happens every season
In big and little towns
People see the circus
When it comes around

So, am I a little dreamer
I love the center ring
I'm the voice of the ring master
I'm in charge of everything

Faces in the shadows
Eyes wide with wonderment
Everyone loves the circus
Under the big top tent

Lena M. Wilson

My God And I

We walked the lonely, silent, beach
The dark gray sky hung low and still
The dark gray sky hung low and still
It's right there! Touch it, if you will
We pondered the gulls on the white caps
And the night about to fall
And then I paused to question
The meaning of it all
We walked alone in silence
and a tear fell from the sky
We've scheduled another round of talks
By the sea
My God and I.

Richard Williams

Exile

On one day, somewhere in the past,
The dawn awoke, without me.
Strange there, in my own bed
Lost to myself.
I prayed my pulse would still
Before they noticed I had left.
With deft fingers I rearranged my hair
Into its old disguise,
Drew the eye to proper unconsciousness
And stepped out through the thick wall
Of my complacent womb.
The dawn and I were born
Unobserved.
I ran to find who had fathered me,
To tell him!
But himself had been devoured
Leaving me alone in that exiled realm
of awareness;
Where I knew nothing,
And sensed all.

Marilyn Bray

Midnight

When at first, for a second,
The day again is done
There is no time to reckon,
For the next one has begun.
There's no neutral state of time,
Today is now yesterday.
With the former in its prime,
Tomorrow is on its way.
Endlessly recurring,
The latter slips away
And just becomes a matter
Of Night becoming Day...

Marcus J. Wierzbowski

The Night

As the sun sets, my eyes awaken
The evening is about to unfold

My desire can not be mistaken
My story will now be told

The bedroom seems so lonely
The T.V. is getting old

My inspiration, best friend and lover
Is somewhere miles from home
Musette, I'm lost without you
I can't express that over the phone

Just a few more days to get thru
Until then I must bare it alone

Len Falcone

A Night's Tender Embrace

Leaving behind
The events of last day
I surrender
To the night's tender embrace

Thoughts become dreams
Mingled with reality
Dreams without names
Out of control
About adventures
I wish would never end
Strange faces and places
I never have know before

Finally daytime breaks
With it's shine striking my face
Sweet dreams start fading away
So I do escape
Last night's tender embrace

Sebastian

A Step Outside

I take a deep breath,
The fresh airs enters me,
I am one with the clouds,
I am one with the sky.
I feel my feet lifting,
My body sways with ease.
I dance with the wind,
I sing with its colors.
I am caught in the creation,
For one brilliant second,
Of the coming of life,
The warmth of dawn,
In the birth of the morning sun.

Laura Owings

The End Of Everything

Deep dark eyes.
The eyes tell all.
But nothing is to be told.
The secrets of life.
The misery and pain.
The pain engulfs them, a tear is formed.
The eyes weep.
The pain is lost in the mind.
The feeling of death binds you.
Day by day it over powers your life.
The tears fall down.
When will it ever stop.
It stopped.
The day I died.
Deep dark eyes.
The eyes tell all.
But my life is over and there is nothing to be to be told.

Mandy R. Cockrell

"Little Girl"

Screaming inside myself
The ghost is everlasting
Racing thru my veins
Hate, fear, darkness
Moving like a virus
Shame, guilt, pain
The ugliness is huge
Remembering him
Rage, anger, fury
Why me; Why me
I was much too small
My flesh crawling with the cold
The cold is an awakening
The awakening is remembering
The remembering is the unspoken pain
The pain is everlasting and deep
So cold as a corpse
And dead as one too
Is the little girl laying
Alone

Nicole D. Getchell

A Gift

If I found buried in a box
the gift of clear expression
and with it the key to unlock
the answer to every question...
To see a tear in someone's eye
and wipe it quite away
not by Kleenex or handkerchief
but by the words I'd say.
To be able to, by look or word,
impart some age-old wisdom
that would by its true simplicity
help someone else envision.

If I could hear a little bird
and recognize its song
perhaps the sweetness of the tune
would keep me from all wrong.
If someone could by listening
realize their thoughts in mine,
perhaps a long sought understanding
would come to all mankind.

Rebecca Smith

I Bought A Flying Saucer

I bought a flying saucer from
The Green man down the street
For the low, low price of 50 cents
And a bright blue parakeet
It has some minor scrapes and dings
But basically it's fine
I'll hit it with a coat of wax
And buff it to a shine
Right now it's parked in my back yard
Right beside the apple tree
Because I haven't figured out
How to make it fly for me
But certainly I got a deal
That no-one else could beat
When I bought the flying saucer from
The Green man down the street

Scott "Spider" Ferguson

Simply Existing

Skies are ashen - days are long,
The joyless drone of an endless song,
The mindless motion of daily living,
A tender heart - no longer giving.

Nights are barren - pointless filler,
The restless hours of a tireless killer,
The fruitless fervor of a maddened mind,
A giving spirit - no longer kind.

Years trudge onward - dismal, numbing,
The witness waste of a countless coming,
The faceless finish of pride persisting,
Once full of life - simply existing.

Sheri French

Regrets of the Past

Endless roads unfolding to nowhere,
the landscape a redundant monotony.
Wanting to go somewhere.
Fumbling for a map.
No plans, nothing —
just a road ahead.
Constantly traveling to anywhere
with a head full of dreams. . .
But nothing.
Realizations crash over me like angry waves.
They rush me into the reality of moments
that I had denied.
Frantic, impulsive thoughts
stagnate and dying.
Casualties of a fickle mind
fall by the wayside.
And suddenly I am dead.

Michelle R. Ryan

God's Handiwork!

The sea - exhilarating,
The landscape - mountainous;
The water - crashing with power
against the rocks.

The sunset in the distance -
colors so brilliant.
Water, in rippling motion,
covering pebbles on the beach.

All - God's Handiwork! How Lovely.

Ruth N. Hample

Dreams

I stare at your picture of paper and glass,
the memories flowing from your smile.
I close my eyes and I'm with you,
this place and time I leave a while.

Suddenly I'm by your side,
your arms hold me near.
With distance now erased,
I wonder am I really here?

Gone is the photo and reflecting glass,
replaced with the one I love.
The love that now surrounds me,
was it sent from heaven above?

You pull my lips towards you,
our passion begins to unlash.
Just as I start to return your kiss,
I awaken to coldness of glass.

Here I lie alone once more,
the glass next to my race.
I try to drift off once again,
to a different time and place.

Rosanna M. Jessop

What Is Plaid?

Plaid is the weaving of time,
the oldness of age,
the comfort of a comforter.

Plaid is
the hollow in a pillow,
the straw in a scarecrow,
the knowing look in an old man's eye.

Plaid is the sheen on the apple,
the underside of a leaf.
It is found in the fossils of time
and
in the newness of birth.

Plaid is the knowledge of knowing
and
the smell of the Earth.

It is the tail of a Star
and
the fingers entwined.

What is your Plaid?...

Sue Cesare

The Future

The baby is born
The house should be safe
Who knows which path
Fate will take?

The child grows older
The parent's blows strike colder
Strangers touch, feel, kidnap
Not even safe to nap.

Can we molest, abuse, addict, enslave
The future leaders today
And Still hope the world
Will not Decay?

As times go by
The meek will not inherit
But
Will die.

Stephen D. Lang

My Friend

What shall I give to my Master,
The One great and holy to me,
He gave me the gift of salvation,
The path of redemption to see.

What shall I give to my Master,
The One source of wisdom and right,
He gave me the vision of living,
To keep him forever in sight.

What shall I give to my Master,
The One King of Kings in my life,
He gave me the books of the Bible,
To help me in times of great strife.

What shall I give to my Master,
The One who protects me from fear,
What could I possibly give him,
It seems I have naught but a tear.

What shall I give to my Master,
The One who is willing to send,
All the traits I must faithfully pray for,
To serve you better and humbly - My
Friend!

N. Christine Toney

Untitled

All that's here to comfort me
The only things from home
Are photographs and memories
Of those I left alone

I live the days in constant fear
And lie awake at night
Wishing for another day
And praying for the light

Every day I'm here is Hell
But, the day will come
When dressed in plastic or dress blues
My duty here is done

Sarah Margulies

Untitled

I sit down to write,
the paper stares back.
I twiddle my thumbs,
then look-garbage sack;
it's filled to the top
each paper-four to five words
I throw in another,
Hey, it looks like a bird.

The war of the paper
against little me;
blank paper and full cans
is that all I'll see?
My pens and my paper
they giggle and grin,
we'll see who is laughing,
in the recycling bin!

Marie Ledford

Dark Lovers

The sky catches fire,
the river runs black.
Darkness is coming, Love.
It's time we were gone.

The land fades to black.
The Earth is asleep.
The Darkness is coming, Love
to carry us away.

The world is ours,
until the Dawn.
Fly with me, Love;
the Darkness is here.

Melissa Spellman

Until The Next Storm...

I hear the rushing waters
The song of rapid currents
The whirlwind of Mother Nature
Swishing and Whooshing
The wind is strong - like my thoughts
The river is confused with turbulence
Like I am...
My emotional screams
Are like the rivers temperament
Not sure where the water is going
But is leaving the place it was once at
Twigs gliding above the surface
Like tears streaming down my face
They fall to my lap - my lip - my neck
No direction...
The brush on the water
Soon accumulates to the side of a bank
There to sit
Until the next storm...

Rachael Cox-Rodriguez

To Night

The sky is so high,
the stars are so bright.
There must be a million
stars out tonight.
I dream that one day,
sometime in the night
my heart will ill with joy,
with no midnight fright.
It is so bright tonight,
it is so dark tonight.
Well, I'm getting sleepy...
...so.... Good Night!

Rochelle A. Lee

The Sun Rise

The morning is a beautiful time.
The sun comes up.
Across a deep blue sky,
With a violet streak across the horizon.
Everything is a silhouette.
Against the sky so high above,
With the shadow of the moon,
In the far corner
And maybe a single star left.
There are a few birds twittering.
And some crickets singing,
A sweet lullaby.
Everything is peaceful and calm.
This beauty only lasts a few minutes,
Then it's gone.

Patricia Shea

Letting Go...

The word can go on turning
the sun continues burning
there is nothing without the yearning.
the desire to be free.

the stars wink down on earth
eyes twinkling, full of secrets
I gaze up and he smiles
"I miss you..."

The fires go on burning
the crystal sphere is turning
and somehow we still are yearning
to escape from thee.

The ocean laps the seashore
hungry mouth, full of pain
I look down and he grimaces
"I miss you..."

Michelle M. Salch

The Sun

The sky is gone,
the sun dreams farther away.
Sad whispers ripple through the garden,
like music from a rain.

The wind is moaning,
urging you to scream.
Worship me, my friend,
but never love me.
Live not for the moment
but for the next light.

Shirley Paedae

Clear-Cutting

The silence surrounds me,
The trees, so full of life,
Inspire me to grow.

But one day, the trees are gone.
The scattered stumps, like skeletons,
And the tracks of the trucks,
That drive into the "future"
Tell the story of what happened.

There is still silence,
Only different now.

Meg Tomany

The Show

Playing in the snow
the two of us on a team
sliding down the hill
Racing everyone

We never won
But you still stayed on my team
I always slowed you down
But we had fun

We fell in the snow
So many times
Our toes and fingers
Were red and cold

We went inside
to warm up by the five
and when the not chocolate was ready
I had to go home

Kathryn Heslop

Lament

I cry tonight for you, My Friend
The voice I knew was always there
together we out-reached the stars
We stretched our minds
Our knowledge grew

Today you move beyond my mortal reach
The earthly help you gave
Is now completely gone
The burden here is mine alone

Your voice is added to the help
That comes to me from Heaven
Guiding my heart and hand
In all I do
Each day I live

Victoria Schmidt

Memories

A chill came in off the ocean,
The waves were rising high,
The sea gulls flying low,
The white caps stretched for miles.

My soul was heavy laden,
My heart filled with fear.
My mind was fastly racing,
My eyes filled with tears.

I thought of new and old loves
Of the ones I hold so dear.
I remembered my, childhood,
And my troubled adult years.

I thought of my dear parents,
The pain that I caused them,
I thought again of my adulthood,
Then my head bent low with shame.

If I could just go back now,
And capture the fleeting years.
The pain I caused my loved ones
I'd replace with joy, not tears.

Wanda F. Wade

The Runaway

Along the winding highways
the wind blowing through my hair
Going whenever it leads me
without a burden or a care.

This feeling of freedom excites me
and it gives me a kind of thrill
No one can take it from me
for this feeling of freedom is real.

Everyday's a new experience
always bringing something new
Never letting life pass me by
because there's so much in life to do.

Meeting people along the way
reaching out, touching their lives
sometimes for only a moment
but the feeling never dies.

Being free to be myself
being free to just be free
Living my life my own way
that's what's important to me.

Linda Pisonero

The Evil

Walking through the woods,
The wind ruffles the trees,
The sky is as gray as slate,
The leaves are brown,
The ground is cold,
But you are strong,
You carry on
You have come to the perilous evil.

You race through the leaf like shadows,
Which are from the dark and dreary evil.
An evil so great,
An evil so strong,
You have come to the perilous evil.

You must move on,
To brave the quest,
You must be true,
and fight the perilous evil.

Michael McBride

God's Way

The times we've shared
The words we've said
Can never compare
For what lies ahead.

The things you taught me
Were oh, so true
And they were always
Such a blessing, too.

When it was time for me to go
I wanted to stay,
But you told me
I had to go God's Way.

Now it's your time
And you may want to stay,
But remember what you told me
You have to go God's Way.

Tonya Kimbhal

Good Morning!

The robin sings before the dawn
The world lies sleeping
A haze surrounds the hills
As if it were a shroud
Within, a new day keeping!

There's a hush, that echoes
On and on
The sky has a bright "blush"
All it's own!

A gentle shower begins
Softly kissing the earth
What a greeting, for rising souls
A feeling of rebirth!

The sun slowly rises
The haze lifts
A lovely, clear day unfolds
God's "Love Gift" —
Good Morning!

Nancy Weaver

Flower Greetings

I rose early and went out one morning
The world slumbered in its bed,
And as I passed a daffodil,
It nodded its pretty head
I walked by the lilies,
They moved their stalk-like hands
I smiled at the violets
And they waved their leafy fans
Each rose gave me a sweet look,
Which I returned
A very pretty curtsey
Was given by the fern
I bowed to the grasses as they had me
And went to shake hands with an apple
tree.

Rachel Lewis

Silent He

Silent he, draped eyes within
then carefully at me he looks
forgotten moments end with him?
Written down in my history books

captured seconds now memorized
reality enlarged to dreams
our silence never compromised
but emotions grow it seems.

Not ready for the want to be
best this stillness stay?
Hurt by comfort's silent we
but safely ends that way.

Such fantasy to reality
will never dare be shown
stay worshipping triviality
with true feelings left unknown.

Ruth Elaine Sambor

Silent Night

The pond is silent,
there are no noises around for miles,
not a drip or a chirp of a bird,
the most peaceful moment of the night,
not a breeze or a soul around,
making the atmosphere calm at last,
the fish swimming gaily underneath,
underneath the shimmery, blue waters,
with only me as a lone outsider,
witnessing the act of nature.

Shannon R. Patel

Deep

There is no limit to the mind
There isn't anything that you can't find
Far deeper than the basics
You'll find the principles of life
Searching very deep within
The puzzle pieces of life
Slowly get put together
With just the knowledge that you have
When put to use
Can tell you everything you want to know
Things complicated
Start to make sense
Only if you go deep

Veronica Poster

Love Within

Within the deepness of mine heart,
There my loves grows just for thee.
Yet it is a thing so very tart,
You doth not suffer my love to be.
And to another I can't not send it,
For it beckons only unto thee.
No other can ever befriend it,
From her my love will only flee.
And if thou who art most fair,
Shalt not loose it with thy key,
In mine heart shall it stay there,
And live within for all eternity.

Larry W. Grant

Rainbow Of Souls

Black White Yellow Brown
These are only colors
Souls are transparent
That's what's inside
The body
a shell
that gives a soul life
It matters not
the color of skin
What matters most
Is what comes from within

Melinda J. Hanlon

Puppies

Puppies are wonderful creatures
They are fun and enjoy
Everything
I wonder if they worry about
Meals
And pats
Perhaps not if they live where they
Are always nourished in both ways
Then they are probably just
Carefree, loving puppies
Secure in their food.

J. Marcus Stephenson

Dreams

Dreams dreams,
they are more then they seem,
It's like we're living two lives.
But we're only passing on time,
Though sometimes we have
to wonder what goes on in
our dreams,
We often sit and wonder if
it's all make believe,
Or is it part of our future
that will be.
The world may never known
Or will we?

Tina J. Eldridge

His Eyes, His Soul

His eyes are so gentle,
They bring out the light.
His heart is so warm,
It makes me want to stay and fight.
His arms are so strong,
They can hold me forever.
His soul is so loving,
It draws me near.
In his world,
I am secure.
This love of ours will never die,
It stays strong as time goes by
I can feel him,
I know he is there.
My true love forever,
My soul is here.
Everything I know is in his eyes,
He touches me so deep, so deep down inside.
I hold him, I love him, I will never let him go.
The two of us together, HE will always know.

Linda Kean

Friend Or Foe

In the tall green grass
they crouch and sneak so low
Halt is what I say
be your friend or for

I look into their face
not a thing does it show
Now who could it be
are they friend or foe

I hope some day to be going
back home to my dear wide
And I'll be flying there
from all this war and strife

But then a shot rings out
now I will never know
Who did this awful thing
was it a friend or foe

Sammy S. Lee

Same As You

People make you angry
They don't treat you right
But you must remember
We're not all alike.
You can judge us all
But that is not your place
Just because you dislike one
Do not judge the race.
Is it fair to say
We act like each other?
Does the color really matter
To call him my brother?
Think as if you're us
We'll think of us as you
Same as us?
Same as you.

Marie Day

Untitled

Well, I wonder if in passing by
they even caught my name?
Or do the remains of our bloody bodies
all appear the same...
We were standing there strong
a thousand in number
I alone it seemed
heard that crushing thunder.

My spirit now restless, still in flight,
endlessly questioning the right to fight
Will they remember just what did I gain?

The progress we made
is not so plain
Finished it's not,
the pain and the gloom
When you're an unknown
soldier
in an unmarked
tomb..

Susan Lynn Keller

Regina's Cries

You Sicko!
They scream at me,
even in my dreams,
my glorious dreams.
What's wrong with you?
Why do you want to do that?
Don't tell me that's biological!
You are all right.
I am sick, I need help,
and yes, I CHOSE this way.
I CHOSE to
love men.
live a life
of humiliation,
intimidation and struggle.
I wonder..
If I didn't have a penis,
would you still find
my dress so repulsive?
What makes your judgement so harsh?

Minette Stewart

Maria's Hands Are Moving...

...Coming together, moving apart
they tell her stories
with each stop and start.

While you laugh and listen,
her hands help you see
her joy and sorrow,
her passion and energy.

Her hands fold in prayer
then reach to assist,
and move to her face
as her eyes fill with mist.

Her hands grasp in wonder,
and raise in victory,
they clap in applause
and touch the weary.

If Maria's hands are moving,
Watch each stop and start,
See the grace that moves,
these wings of her heart.

Patricia Calvo

Mother's Love

The fruit of the womb is children
They're a blessing from the start
everything they do and say
Can touch a mother's heart.

A little boy? A little girl?
Before one even knows
The heart begins to fill with love
And that love over flows.

It flows to all her children
How ever many be
It grows with them, it comforts them
And remains forever free.

They need but call, it answers
It's not governed by time or day
Even distance has no hold
God made Mother's Love that way.

Mickie Slotterbeck

Darkness

Colors fade from dark to light
Things unseen are now in sight
Fluffy billows from grey to white
Rays and beams burn big and bright
Behold, the day has dawned.

Solid blue to points of light
Once warm now cool this autumn night
We begin our journey without fright
To fight the evil with heavens might
Beware the demon spawned.

Mike McClung

Always

When you feel the wind,
Think of me...
When you smell the rain,
Think of me...
When you see the flowers,
Think of me...
When you hear the crying,
Think of me...
When you touch the laughter,
Think of me...
When you feel the warmth,
Think of me...
When you see the sun...
When you wish on a star...
When you feel the moon...
When you breathe... Think of me.
If you are ever alone,
Just Call... My name...
And I will hear you...
Always.

C. Ross Hilliard III

Untitled

Think of me as a flower
Touch me with gentle care

Do not neglect me for hours
Nor pick my petals till bare

If rain must fall upon me,
in every season you'll see
I'll bloom again and survive
beneath your loving warmth
of sunshine.

Patricia Faulcon

In the Company of Ghosts

Take tea with me... all alone
This fine day
All around is windy
While here
It is still
Or the other way around
And although you say... nothing
And only look
I feel you within me
Like my lifeblood

Have lunch with me... I beg you
This foul day
All around is raining
And here
We are wet
And we know we are alive
Even if you say... nothing
And only touch
I hold you within me
In my lifeblood

Richard Zachmann

Your Song Of Love

This is your song of love
This is your song
This is your destiny
So string along

I came into your life
It was a sudden strife
This is your song of love
So sing along

This is your very reason to exist
You are number one on my mist
I could not hope for anything more
And to look at you I adore

This is your song of love
This is your song
Remember your soul-mate me
Your true love and bee

It will earn your respect forever
That's all I can expect together
This is your song of love
So sing along

Michael A. Martin

Early Call

Must I wake up
this morning!
Why?

To suffer all alone
the beauty
of a sungold sky
that neons boldly over peaks
still dressed in goblin robes?

"Hi!" Did he
say "Hi"?
But that was yesterday
and days before
he found another scene,
forever closed a door.

Must I rise up and
push a circuit "ON"
to forage out for board and bed?
"Wake up! You are alive
and labor is your antidote,"
my own voice said.

Margaret Davis

Hidden

I see someone no one else can
This someone is a part of me
A part that likes to play
A part that likes to climb trees
What is so different about her
She lives inside of me
Now she likes to keep
A tight hold on my heart
She only lets out
The love I once had
Now all I can do
Is share that love with you

Michelle D. Piontek

Though We're Not Together

Even though we're not together
This special day is still ours
So I'm sending you all my love
Instead of candies and flowers.

My heart always skips a beat
Every time I think of you
You'll always be my sweetheart
For our love is strong and true.

Your sweet kisses I do miss
I want to hold you in my arms
I'm the luckiest man in all the world
To be captured by your charm.

Like flowers, our love keeps blooming
So this is but a delay
Smile and know I Love You
This and everyday!!

Mark E. Outen

Broken

A break..
though small..
in a granite stone..
starts the chain of destruction.
this stone...
though large...
becomes...
separate...
smaller...
pieces.
It's once great defenses..
are broken down..
separating..
forever.

Samantha Helfrich

Magic Wand

If I had a magic wand
To make a wish come true
I would wish that you would get
Exactly what is due.

I know you will, in time you see
As will all - especially me
But what I will most regret,
Is missing what you're bound to get.

All who live will pay the price,
For things we do that aren't so nice.

And when the book of life comes due,
I'll be glad that I'm not you.
But maybe when this comes to be,
I'll also wish that I weren't me!

Robin Carson

Gypsy

Gypsy man with wandering heart.
Thought you'd stay,
but instead you part.
Be gone, gypsy,
Be gone.

Gypsy man with worn out shoes.
Tried to settle,
but found only the blues.
Be gone, gypsy,
Be gone.

Gypsy man you like to roam.
Poor gypsy man,
without a home.
Be gone, gypsy,
Be gone.

Gypsy man you must explore.
Within yourself
there's so much more.
Stay, gypsy,
Stay.

Timothy P. Bush

Sky

Beyond the skies and the seas
Through the clouds with glee
Your soul flies high into the light.

Though many wonder
why your not six feet under
In the pit and flames of wonder.

But you repent
so God sent
a blessing upon your soul.

So now you fly high
along the sky
To the gate of love and wonder.

Greeted by a light
that hugs you with delight.

So now your home
in heavens splendor!

Michael Layne

Time In Flight

As the tide ebbs and flows
through the day and the night
And the sand on the beaches
is shiny and bright

As the sun and the moon
take their turns in the sky
And the stars and the clouds
all go passing by

As the Winter so cold
then turns into Spring
And the meadows are green
we hear the birds sing

As the seconds and minutes
become hours and days
And the months fly by
in a bit of a haze

As our lives dip and bend
like the twigs on a tree
We should cherish each moment
given you, given me.

Ruth L. Mazur

Did I Touch His Face?

A soft stream of sunbeams filtered
Through the stained glass windows,
Mingling with the candle light
Flooding the altar with a golden hue.
It was the morning of my Franciscan
Renewal, and I waited joyfully
For the ceremony to begin.
With confidence my voice rose
Beyond the vaulted ceiling, but
Suddenly the sacredness of the
Moment touched me, trembling
I could scarcely breathe,
Till a feeling of warmth and peace
Descended, I sensed God's love.
Too soon the ceremony ended, but
In that moment of grace I felt
The warmth of God's love.
Did I touch His face . . . or
Was it his hand on me?

Maude Ponticello

Go Along The Shady Stream

Go along the shady stream
To a wild oak tree
And there be shown, a baby deer born
Me to you, a little nip and up
Stammering along then down
Up and try it again

Go along the shady stream
To a wild oak tree
And there be heard, a busy bee a working
Buzzin' around a patch a daisies,
Collecting nectar then flying away
Come back again, he does

Go along the shady stream
To a wild oak tree
And there be felt, a wild wind blows
A coolin' the air, and rustling the leaves
Taking the fragrance of flower, rushing by
Whisking away the seed

Go along the shady stream to a wild oak tree
And there be shown, felt, and heard in whispered word

Stephanie Calhoun

Slate

A void will exist
To always persist
A curse in life to bare
A heart with a hole
But so much soul
A curse in life to share

But in this world
That does uncurl
The twisted knots of fate
As time goes by
The tears we cry
Can bring a mirror from slate

In this desert land
There comes a hand
Not often to be found
Sometimes a smile
Can cross a mile
Without a single sound

Richard Fries

don't pretend

don't pretend
to be my friend
while walking down the halls.
even though i knew you once
you are gone for now, for long.

don't pretend
to be as great as something or one.
don't pretend
to be like THEM,
to say good things
about everything THEY do.

don't pretend to patronize to a zoo.
you're the animal about
to go inside
in your mind....
so, don't patronize,
don't think. don't rhyme.
get a life, friend?

Lauren Agliata

Life Or Death

To live is to die.
To die is to live.
Being in another world,
My spirit is free at last.
Depression in my mind,
Need some way to get it out,
I love the thought of death,
That's what' my life is all about,
There's nothing in this world,
To satisfy my needs.
I knew long ago,
This was not the place for you to go,
You do not belong there,
There's no reason for me to live.
I'm living a useless life.
There's nothing more for me to give.

Star McGee

A Child's Dream

She fell asleep late that night,
To dream of something out of sight.
She had a dream,
That only she could dream.
She dreamt she was an angel,
Peaking through the stars.
She dreamt she was a tiger,
Driving a car.
She dreamt she was an apple,
Hanging from a tree.
She dreamt she was an elephant,
Who could count to three.
She dreamt she was a bird,
And could fly away up high.
And when she woke,
She said they were mine, mine, mine!!

Sally Goodell

"If Jesus Came"

If Jesus came to your house
To spend the day with you,
Would you rush around in panic
With many things to do?
Or would you greet him gladly
And enjoy him from the start,
With your home all neat and tidy -
A model of your heart.

Robert E. Shonyo

Whispers Of Yesterday

Today I drove out to the Country
To find time I had lost
And with me came the memories
Of the one I had loved the most

We had such a short time
But it seemed to fill my life
Now I'm lonely, but not alone
Because I had you as my wife

As the wind blows through the trees
It says "I'll love you always"
But the angels took you from me
And it's just whispers of yesterday

Now I know that someday soon
The sun will kiss the dew
And my life will be complete
When the angels bring me to you

Pat Woolsey

My Flower

I was given the unique power,
to grow a special flower.
a special flower, like a rose
But with a finer elegant pose.
You were my flowers name,
you put all other flowers to shame.
I nurtured it with love,
Giving it petals soft as a dove.
I gave it special light,
so it's colors would shine bright.
I watered it with CARE,
To neglect it, never did I dare.
To this flower, I gave a vital part.
To my flower, I gave to it my heart.
To my surprise, what do you know
Together as one we started to grow,
United as one we've blossomed together,
You and I, growing stronger, now and forever.

Larry Wilson

The Exchange

I inherited an un-natural order.
to have a sense of things,
requires order.

To gather a worthy understanding
of the flow of life,

To make sense of things...
order begins with me.

I must know right from wrong.
I must know, how far to go.
to make sense of things,

I must think.
I must become knowledgeable of the process,
knowledgeable of the order of change,

I must feel.
I must know how far to safely go.
In search of comfort,

To make sense of things...
I reclaim my individuality.

De Grice

"Never Had The Chance"

I never had the chance
to hold her hand in the rain
to feel her embrace just because.
To look at the sun
and look at her
and see the same thing
I never had the chance

I never had the chance
to really show her that I care
to get the same in return
to not have to say a word
to look her in the eye
and feel good inside
I never had the chance.

Wright B. Seneres

Home

They say it takes a lot of living,
To make a house a home,
A lot of love and giving,
So no matter how we roam,

Or how nature's beauty thrills us,
The moon and stars above,
Our hearts seek a home at Christmas,
A place of warmth and love!

So let my heart be home for Christmas,
When music fills the air,
When hope and joy come naturally,
With lots of love to spare!

For Love came home at Christmas,
Love came down from above,
So when our hearts find home at Christmas,
Our hearts reflect that love!

Max B. Kilbourn

Crossing The Stream

I crossed over the stream
To my love waiting there
With arms opened wide
Entering there to be by his side.

The clouds tho they gather
And tear within eye
I looked up to heaven
Where a rainbow of colors do lie.

Suddenly an awaking moment;
Gave my heart a stirring heap
We too would cross another great divide.

Loreda Kasemeyer

Love At The Laundromat

I watch the colors
toss and tumble
like the seasons—
my long-johns playing leap-frog
in the dryer.

While in the corner,
two young lovers
trade kisses
like candy bars,
and black boys race
screaming
through the smoke-filled air.

Teresa Ferner Stamm

The Autumn

The autumn came once again
to paint the Earth with colors
from red to yellow and all shades
and even with soft browns.
The autumn came once again
with air that is crispy clear;
and the sunshine brilliant
the best of all the year,
walking through up state New York
or through the Nation's Parks
the scene resembles Paradise
all painted by God.
One wonders as he walks
through Autumn's picture real
why dream of Paradise,
when god placed it all here.
Is He really surrealist,
abstractionist or painted in real
depends what scene you want to
view, to form your idea.

Sophia Demas

Million Years

It took a million years
to paint this world
with all that it contains
but often all these years
our love remain

It took a million years
to paint the sky
with each and every star
so we could sit and watch
them from a far.

Love never will die
when you and I
make it at home
your Heavenly Bless
is what you miss when you are alone.

The world may change it's
course the sun may dim
but darling have no fear.
For we can sit and watch
another million years.

Robert Byers

A Withered Rose

I know I've waited too late in life
To seek out all my deepest needs,
For now it's become too late for me
To stop this aching heart that bleeds.

For just as I try to guide this pen,
With glasses propped upon my nose,
When reflecting on my years in time
I'm but a single withered rose.

I sink my head into the pillow
My mind seeking escape in sleep,
Even as my mind grows heavier
I can still hear my spirit weep.

Yet I know the day will soon arrive
These petals will blow in the wind,
And some will soar where the eagles fly
And you will breathe the fragrance in.

I hope that you will always inhale
The scent of roses in your day,
It won't be long before you'll forget
A withered rose that slipped away.

Lucy M. Rhea

God Bless

"God bless his footsteps on this day;
To teach him what to do and say.

Please bless his eyes that he might see
All he was sent forth to be.

And bless his heart so he may know
Just how far you'd have him go.

God bless his hands that he may use;
So he will write to send us news.

God bless his footsteps on this day,
So we may know that he's okay."

Lori S. Dunne

Fortaleza, Brazil, 1974

How'd you like to come
  To the beach and
Climb toward the sun
  Up cliffs of sand
With me?

You can listen to the sound of
  The waves
Below, and the silent sky above
  With nothing to mar
The noisy quiet.

Red, rough, the hard clay
  Yields to the blow
Of the steady, constant grey
  Of the sea below
And wind above;

Weather-filed at places
  To fine points of
Delicate strength, with bases
  Massive, carved, caved-in statues of
The sea. Come, climb with me.

Lois Irene Broughton

Celestial Advice

Spine to the Earth, chest
to the Heavens - I feel
the euphoric waves of space.
Their immaculate sparkle,
their, miraculous disorder
Entropy wants to begin
settling down their tremendous beauty.

You sit beside me under
this performance, appearance
shows unilateral neglect.
All of a sudden, while the Heavens
adore us, apologies fly -
we envelope each other.
Cold air solidifies our tears.

To the Heavens I say -
your disheveled appearance
is good to observe from afar.
But disarray for myself
leads me to neglect the man
whom I've faithfully loved.

Tara S. Baney

Friends

Friends will stick
To you like glue
And help you
When you're blue.

They'll keep your secrets
That you tell them
And they won't
Talk behind your back.

They'll never let
you down
And they'll lend
A helping hand.

So don't be shy
To say your name
And they will
Do the same.

Stephanie Henderson

The Naked Truth

Ignorance, Drugs, Alcohol,
Total strangers, becoming lovers;
And those few mindless moments -
Affecting the lives, of innocent others;

Feverish sexual fantasies,
A craving for warm flesh,
Folks shedding morals just like clothing -
Undressing quickly - for slow Death...

For naked - We all enter,
And, Naked - We're gonna leave;
Naked Minds - Naked Bodies -
Exposing our souls, to that fatal Disease;

You must cloth your minds with knowl-
edge,
Then, share it - with our youth;
Please listen carefully, now -
For, this is, THE NAKED TRUTH...

Today, millions carry the aids virus,
And most don't know, so you can't ask it;
Be wise, and abstain from unsafe sex...
USE A CONDOM, OR, CHOOSE YOUR
OWN CASKET!

Sandra Turner-Barnes

The Journey

As the bear from winter slumber wakes
touched by the breeze of spring.
My soul from silent slumber wakes
and stirs my heart to sing.

From dreams to actuality,
I'm born into reality.
To sing a song of finer things,
I know by faith that this life brings.

A traveler from the land of nod,
I grasp the masters staff and rod,
To journey through hot fines of old,
and end at last as finer gold.

Lisa Kay Cunningham

The Search

I can see where the hands of God
traced symbols in the earth
Where He took His Crayola's
and let His imagination roam
Thousands of miles away from the familiar
I fly
drifting closer to the Eden God created
with crayons and wishes
In the life I was living
beauty was sought after
The search was often in vain
In the Land of the Midnight Sun
beauty is
and the search is forgotten

Maureen Muccio

A Man's Lost Youth

Darkened
traces, they
hideaway a promise, fastasleep

dreams turn into nightmares
they hid the truth
nightmares soon reality
they hide their stolen youth
reality is but a game
they hide from all they had
the game cannot be played
what they hide makes them sad

they cannot make dreams go away
the game, it can be mastered
dreams are the wants, the wants will stay
the game will shape reality
if all they cling to are the dreams
reality's nightmares hide under the bed
than they're flying on broken wings
and dreams will stay their youth

Shannon C. Rushing

Forward

Let me close this chapter of life,
turn the corner, end the strife.
Let me go on to live a better life.

The pain will go and peace accrue.
The sun will shine even with out you.
The world will turn, the seasons too.

Memory will fade, faith renew.
Love will come with someone who,
can return truth for truth, loves due.

My love and I will grow nearer,
when she speaks my heart will hear her.
We will live in harmony in love's bier.

Thomas E. O'Quinn

Fade

The sun now sets
turns all we see to black
Yet my tears
still fall in drops of red
For this life
keeps me chained
To a reality
I do not wish to see
I block off my mind
to stand all alone
With just a memory of you
to keep me warm

Shawn Smith

Love Is New.... Woman

Mammoth ivory ——-
twenty six thousand years old
Why do I know you

Why am I drawn into you
your ancient gaze
Looks into my soul

I am new again ——
mammoth ivory
Portrait from the heart

Your scraping tool
etches the cipher-mind
the stroke of a comb through hair

Your hair, her hair, my hair
the flint caresses a cheek
turns up the nose just so—-

Sculpture of the Ages
Ice Age - Space Age
Freezing wind howls, cuts a knife
In the Nuclear Shadow Woman gives me
Life

G. Robert MacIntosh

For Erato, Muse of Love Poetry

They're still in bed, those two, shivering
under a thin brown blanket
on this wind swept morning.

The windows speak of sparrows
nested in a dying cottonwood and
of grass mowed late the night before.

An early stalking dog shouts to her
but makes no sound
that ever would awaken him.

She stirs, then softly scuds
beneath his outstretched arm
to hide the light from eye and ear.

He stirs and holds her close
while holding closer still
a dream she can and will not know.

She's more than half his reveries,
but he cannot speak of dreams
now lost in mindful truth.

Robert Foster

Imprints Of The Soul

The warmth, the warmth
Under the light,
The light is true, within;
Yes, it is deep within
Life begins with a flicker
Spreading into a great conflagration,
Only with true wisdom does it come,
And only with great meaning of the soul;
Heat burning ahh...
Yet,...it is beyond the shell
Why, Sometimes we wonder;
What happens, that is
After the shell has Deteriorated...
The soul is not left in the dust

Nicole Hunt

The Swing

You bade me come closer
under the shade of the branches.
Pushed by his and her arms,
I embraced the heavens.
The first thing done,
the last before parting—
in the day I met the sun,
in the night I grabbed the stars.
With the Milky Way above,
we talked about life
and we loved.

Lori Kraft

The Jungle

Thick canopy above,
Undergrowth below,
The jungle lives.
Toucans glide,
Snakes slither,
The jungle lives.
Coconuts grow,
Plants flourish,
The jungle lives.
Fire of man,
Smoke of Man,
The jungle lives not!

Matthew L. Vestal

Nothing Tangible

I don't want anything tangible
Unless certain feelings
Happen to be packaged
In the human form.
Then I would consider
Some gift
That I could see
Smell or lift
With its contents
Containing no notion
Of physicality
Only emotions
And sensuality.

Nancy Bradshaw

"Memories"

Memories are here to stay,
Unlike dreams that fade away.
Rainbows reach across the sky
Paving the way until we die.

Flowers blossom, and soon are gone
Their sweet perfume still lingers on.
Our lives, like flowers blossom bright,
Never given thought of the coming night.

We live, we love, we travel on,
Never more to be alone;
Our eyes fixed on heaven above,
A land forever filled with love.

Neoma Peters

Nothing

Parched ground, blackened sky.
Unmotivated wind stands still.
Nothing crawls...
Nothing flies...
Nothing lives...
So Nothing dies...

Insipid wood, leather rough skin.
Outlined forms of long fallen clouds.
Hear no cries...
Hear no calls...
Hear Nothing...
Nothing at all..

Crumbling rock, solidified sea.
Faceless faint pale moon.
See no stars...
See no light...
See our creation...
See Nothing in sight.

Norman L. Bolex

Her Eternity

She whispers to her Lord at night
Until she's steadfast and asleep;
Departing from her world of fright
As she journeys into the deep.

She finds herself on foreign grounds,
A place that's vivid to her soul;
Unleashed by striking scenes and sounds
Her vibes begin to play their role.

She doesn't want to leave this place
Because she fears she may not find
This kind of beauty when she wakes
Tempted to leave her world behind.

Interrupted by the morning light,
She rises to reality;
Spends all day longing for the night
To enter her eternity.

Linda Hanson

Remembering

Summer day reflections
upon a quiet sea,
the waves roll up and down the beach
I remember how it used to be.
The sand was warm and golden,
the sun was high and bright,
and how I loved to sit there
in the darkness of the night.
The silence was its own reward,
nothing else did I ever ask;
but to hear the waves beat on
the beach, like a small and yet
powerful blast.
To hear the sea gulls calling;
and sometimes a seal or two,
and someday I'll return again
to the sea, the beach and you.

Terri L. Creed

House

Please enter me
upon entering, a mist moves.
Surrounding me,
time stops.
I spin back, back in time
to another era.

Oh house! How beautiful,
how peaceful you are.
Void of personality now.
I feel at peace.
I follow you thru a time
long ago.

House, I love you.
The mist again surrounds me
back, back, in time
to an era long ago
I then become a part
of the house.

Marguerite Treon

The Soldier

Ah, how I long to lay my head
Upon her snowy breast;
To end my lonely journey there,
This dully hopeless quest.

The autumn wind is harsh and cold,
The sun gives little warmth;
Trees standing grey beside the road
Seem silently to mourn.

I slowly walk around a bend
To find the same before;
I've passed this way a thousand times
And will a thousand more.

Tomorrow will be as today,
I know what lies ahead.
Tonight the sky will be my roof,
A patch of grass by bed.

And dreams will drift within my mind
Of home and love and rest.
Ah, how I long to lay my head
Upon her snowy breast.

Thomas L. Cotter

It Is He

Little child rest your weary head,
upon the white and silken thread.
Angel dust and heaven praise,
brings the sun to release its rays.
A child from a mortal mother brings,
to present him forth unto queens
and kings.
Ridiculed and taught not to hate,
to designate his eternal fate.
One nation under one boss,
strung him up upon the cross.
Among the people his death begins,
three days later he walks again.
Now realized not to be a fraud,
he is Jesus Christ, the son of God.

Starla Finnegan

My Yard

Squirrels, bunnies, birds and bees
Use my yard as they please!
Playing tag from tree to tree
The squirrels make me laugh with glee!

Bees love all my flowers.
They're doing well, thanks to showers.
If left alone the bees won't sting;
Gathering pollen is their thing.

Birds singing in early morn
Makes me glad I was born!
They have quite a lot of foes.
Why do they? Who knows!

Bunnies live a life of strife.
Darn that cat! He's after their life!
Quick! Run! Scamper Away!
Live to enjoy another day.

I'm glad they use my yard.
In God's plan they play a part.
Watch, they'll steal away your heart!

Rubie Hickman

"Golden"

Golden is a word
Used in many ways
It's fun in the sun
With its golden rays
Golden is magic,
Golden's my boss
Golden is Jesus, And the sign of the cross
Golden is flowers when they bloom
Golden is home with lots of room
Golden is summer, sunny and warm
Golden is dewdrops clinging till morn
Golden is mystery
Golden is here
Golden's the white, On the tail of a deer
Golden is time
As long as an hour
Golden is petals
on a golden sunflower
Golden is our friendship, strong and true
Golden's the love I have for you.

James Trainis

Bitterness

Sitting in the courtroom
waiting
for the
final verdict.
I turn my head and see
the animal who
raped me
the man who
shattered my sense of
Security
he overpowered me
I could not do anything
he would've killed me.
How could he do this to me?
What did I ever do to him?
I hope he rots in jail
the jury is back
they have reached a verdict...
Guilty.
Thank you God!

Marta Trujillo

A Vision at Sunset

I saw him there in the setting sun
Walking away toward the sky,
Parting the heavy underbrush
Walking through flowers knee high.

And there he lingered and looking back
He seemed so young and fair,
Well again, and strong again,
As the sun shown on his hair.

My mom once told me years before,
From death you need not run,
God reaches down, turns out the light
Because the dawn has come.

He waived, then turned and walked away,
I called, I sang, I cried,
For this was the day — the very day,
Mom called and said he'd died!

Pauline Alwes

gone

a lone bullet
wandered through your head
and you were
gone
and I will never know more
than your memory
which haunts my thoughts
I do not have the strength
within my heart
to get past the despair of
a .45 caliber bullet
which took you
away

Sarah Hayes

Suffer The Children

Another young life
Was taken today
Another mother's child
No longer to play
On the porch where he sat
With family and friends
In tears they watched
As his life came to an end
Oh why must there be
So much violence I say
Why can't the children
Go out to play
Why can't the people
Put away their guns
And live in peace
And love everyone

Rodney J. Mercadel

"The Heart"

The heart is not a play thing,
The heart is not a toy,
But if you want it broken,
Just give it to a boy.

They love to mess around,
and see what makes things run,
But when it comes to girls,
They'll do it just for fun.

Leslie Lane

Our Planet

As dewdrops glisten on morning glory,
We can recall the earth's long story.
A cloud, the sun, a blade of grass,
A memory of ages past.

Can earth renew itself forever?
Are we so really very clever?
If we destroy what God has given,
Will there be a place in Heaven?

Wars are fought and lives are lost,
Can anyone repay the cost?
As morning light fades into dark,
Will each new dawn renew a spark?

God has blessed us with so much.
Will we destroy it with out touch?

Wanda S. McDevitt

America In The Eyes Of A Child

People starving in this land,
We don't have a good health plan,
People are put in nursing homes,
We make fun of those who are alone,
Children and grown ups, I'm sorry to say,
But you're killing each other day by day,
I think the bombing was a revenging acted,
Now America is being attacked,
Guns on the street, and drugs at home,
I wish there was no more violence at home,
I hear about murders everyday,
Every night I hope and pray,
That death will not come my way.

Lauren McCormick

Death Of Dignity

We don't throw rocks
We hurl obscenities
Spew spit-filled slurs
Slap venomous whispers
Into the ear

With puffed up heritage
Tear down self
Enslave rights
Hold captive
Feelings

We don't throw rocks.
Swallowed up by the insanity
We justify
Worse
We ignore

Patricia Bell

God Gifts Love

From ever day of life on earth,
We learn to find miracle happen.
We find smile, laugher, tear and
sing song praise of God.

We find grief's, hate from day's
of passing throw.
A gift of peace and grace and
renew are faith.

We need to learn to love God
And yourself, so we can release
gift of faith and hope,
to bear, what we must do.

Sandra Larkin

Untitled

We laughed until we had to cry
We loved right down to the last
Goodbye. We were the best I think
We'll ever be - just you and me.

We chased a dream we never found
And sometimes we let each other
down. But the love we made
made everything alright.

Time goes on, people touch and then
they're gone. And you and I will
never love again, like we did
back then.

Someday when we're reminiscing
we'll both say there wasn't too
much we missed. Through the
tears we'll smile when we
recall - we had had it all.

Renee Swanson

Time...

Time is such a precious thing
We often take for granted.
It brings to bloom the flowers of life
From all the seeds we've planted.
No one from here or there can know
When it will ever end.
So perfect was the makers wisdom
To keep the secret from all men.
We must not tarry in our space
With this great entity.
For life is short and will not
Wait for us...or you...or me.

Lawrence David Johnson

"Wishful Thinking"

I walked with you down yesterday
we stumbled into tomorrow
on the other side of sometime
with only time to borrow.

I heard you in the corridors
of somewhere past my mind.
You shouted out a street name
of some distant place and time.

Oh, to go back to tomorrow
with yesterday's same face,
and build our dreams on emptiness
between the open space.

To glide along forever
on an ever coiling swirl
of a wave whose crest might never ebb,
whose dream would not unfurl.

And walk again down yesterday
and bump into tomorrow
on the other side of sometime
with only dreams to borrow.

Margaret M. Abel-Quintero

Liberty Deceased

Lady Liberty,
We the people of the United States
With the right to do anything we please,
Have raped, robbed, and plundered
Till sterile womb produces nothing
except
Festering sexual scabs,
corruption, greed, and
lust for cankered gold!

Because we have nothing better to do
We want to kick you
And spit in your face;
Shoot you with our guns
Stab you with our knives
and laugh
While the last of your blood
trickles
into the bay!

Tedi Tuttle Wixom

Waltz

When winter wrought wicked winds,
we waltzed while willows waved.
Weather's wings whisked worn-out
wrinkled worms.

We were wild women wearing
white, wispy wigs. We whirled
within woodlands, whispering
witty words while water washed
winged willows.
We waded within writhing
waves when winding waters
wrestled with winds.

Wandering wet walk-ways,
we wielded waking wisdoms,
while watching widows whose
wishes were wasted within wells.

Tammy L. Williams-Ankcorn

A Battered Wife

"A battered wife knows all too
well, how a boxer feels after
each round."
Rounds (1-5) he's enraged with
anger. Rounds (6-10) he's got
the upper hand. Rounds (11-15)
Is the ultimate knock out!
"And what belt shall he win
the belt of courage, or the
ultimate belt of control?"

Yulanda Tisdale

Alone

She waits and wonders
what will become of her.
All she can do is pray
to a person she does not know.
She has no one to care.
for her and her sister.
And all she can do is wait
and wonder...
What will become of her.

Lynn Kozack

New Love

All the ones who came before,
Were good when they had needs,
I took the time to give some more,
Never getting any return for my deeds.

You make me feel,
When all had been numb,
By all the selfish souls, so unreal,
I had always been stung.

Your sweet loving way,
So arousing and real,
I think about it all day,
What I've always needed to feel.

Am I just in a dream?
Or created you in my mind?
How scary it does seem,
Something this good for me to find.

I've only just begun to live,
In this love that I have found,
Sweeter than anything I've ever tasted,
A love that's good to have around.

Tomi N. Heyl

The Last Sunrise

Broken hearts
We've both been terrified
I am not ever losing you
You and I shall never be apart.

Jealousy
We've fought for one another
It's caused us pain
But it brought us closer together.

Promise me
As I promise you
That we shall not stand there
In the shadows of someone new.

Hold me there in your arms
Keep me warm and secure
Until eternity passes
And our sun shines no more.

Rachel Spier

Nevermore

We've looked up at the stars above,
we've lain upon the shore.
We've let our feet touch the mist,
we've heard the ocean roar.

We've seen the sun set on the line -
a russet reddish - gold.
We've felt the rain tell tomorrow's tale -
a long -lasting story of old.

We've heard the birds sing a glorious tune,
and the wind howl a miraculous melody.
We've felt the malicious bite of the ant,
and the sting of the dwindling bee.

However one could never portray -
the loss of one's very own core.
Yet we continue living our term -
one that will be NEVERMORE.

Meredith C. Yeomans

If Instead...

I wonder, the old man said,
What all these people
- rushing to and fro
would do
if instead
a hundred years ago,
they rose up from the bed
on early morning, cold and bleak
and before one to the other one
could speak,
must at once a fire
from it's slumber spell
and water draw
from a garden well
and while still dark
venture forth 'neath starry sky
and work long hours
for well nigh
a small part of one hour's pay
- today.

Piers Wiggett Sr.

"Lordy Lordy"

Lordy Lordy I'm so sad
What did I do that was so bad
I raised my children the best I could
But things don't seem to go the way
they should

I'm so proud of the kids I've
raised
But I'm not looking for any praise
What's become of people these days
Don't they realize there's dues to pay
I'll always wonder what I could
have done

To make things better than what
they've become

Lillie Green

Waiting To Exhale

Waiting to exhale.
What has become is now the foundation
for what will be.
Breathe slowly now with the even tempo
of the day to day.
Monotony, in and out, there is no rush
of blood or baited breath.
Youthfulness is the quickening, panting,
hold your breath, whisper and shout.
The Ancient moves slow and raspingly,
until it pauses and then is no more.

Roxanne Smathers

Untitled

You have brown hair
You have green eyes
Something tells me
You are wise
You told me something
False or True
But still I said
I love you

Tracy Passmore

Life

Life,
What is life,
You tell me,
What is our purpose in life,
To make money,
To help people,
But what if we do that,
What comes next,
Did we do this all for a reason,
Maybe we live life to prove to God,
Prove that we are worthy to go to heaven,
What is life,
You tell me,
The sun, the moon,
The snow, the rain,
They all have a meaning,
What is life,
I'll tell you,
Life is whatever you make it out to be.

Stephanie Brown

Heartland

Laughter.

Explosion.

Silence.

Where am I?
What is this cave of black I am in?
I can't see a thing.
Where is humanity?
This world has gone crazy.
Children scream.
Their parents can't help them.
They call this Heartland

Heart land.

Fire and smoke.

Tears and blood.

Life and death.

Death is predominant.
I, myself, am dying.
Help me God!

Wait-
What is this light I see?

Lindsey English

Christmas Time Is Here Again

It's a special time of year.
To the people in the world. The
lighting of the Christmas Trees,
the ringing of the bells. The
singing of the song that we all
love so well. The family's brought
together far and near. The smells
from the kitchen rise in the air.
The children making wishes, they
hope will come true. All those things
bring back so many memories about
times we spent through out our
growing years. So let us keep
Christmas in a old fashion way,
with the spirited of our love
on this holiday.

Nicholas Ranalli

Teach Me

Father, I need to know
What thou has me to do
My only purpose in life
Is to please only you.

I try to live accordingly
As the Bible say.
To study deeply in your word
And grow along the way.

Help me to understand, my Lord
Exactly what it means
To live and learn a better way
A perfect way it seems.

I open my heart, my eyes
To see what's in store.
The more I give, the better it gets
I'm destined to know more.

About this God, who lives on high
He watches from Heaven above,
He sent his son to shed his blood
In hopes that we would love.

Rosalind Yancy

Tomorrow's Dream

Have You ever stopped to wonder,
What will tomorrow bring.
What say we take a moment,
And think about these things.

We must stand and back and take a look,
At situation's now,
And try to give it some deep thought,
And turn some things around.

Every day we pray for peace,
And want an end to war.
And cure some awful sicknesses,
Now that's worth fighting for.

To love your neighbor as a friend,
And put an end to crime.
And all the starving little ones,
They do deserve our time.

And what of faith and mercy,
Compassion let us see,
And we will live in happiness,
When all the world is free..

William K. Sherman

Auto-Biography

Youngest in my class was I
When I left my Senior High.
Then from college, 'twas the same,
Off to try to teach, I came.
There were times when thing went wrong,
Some were sad, but not for long.
Forty happy years I taught
Then retirement was my lot,
Family needs made me a nurse,
(But it could have been much worse.)
One by one they left my care.
I kept busy, with time to spare
Happy, healthy, am I today
Having lived the Christian Way,
The Golden Rule has worked for me.
(I plan to live to one hundred three!)

Marjorie B. Carlson

If Just For A Moment

If just for a moment...

You could change the world
what would you do
for others and you?

Would you stop hunger?
Would you end all pain?

Would we all get along
But remain the same?

If just for a moment...

Would sex be safe?
Would there be no abuse?

Would there be enough money
for everyone's use?

If just for a moment...

Would all people have homes?
Would you shelter all animals
and leave them alone?

If just for a moment...

Time could stand still and start
all over to begin God's will.

JDenise

"A Different View"

Reflections Winner

Looking at the world above and wonder
what you see, lovely skies and
butterflies looking down at me. The
beautiful mother nature as big as she
may seem, is made up of the little things
that fantasize you and me. But when you
gaze up in the sky from grasses grown
so tall, just wonder what it would be
like if you weren't here at all, and after
you have done that be glad of who you
are and thankful that your imagination
can ride upon a star!

Michelle Lynn Hansen

The Jazz Singer

Al smiled and his black - face cracked
When he sang, "Kiss me Tootie
And then, do it over again,"
And she did not answer.
He frowned and his black - face peeled
When he danced
And she did not smile.
Al cried and his black - face fell
When he got down on his knees
To kiss her hand
And she did not look.
The rain pounded down and thunder like
Fire swallowed the music at the Palace.
(it was mourned like the end of the world)
Where did she go?
Come back for the show,
Please come back.
You ain't seen nothing yet -

Michelle d'Amico

All About Feelings

I get a special feeling,
When I hear "Amazing Grace".
It's hard to define that feeling,
It's hard to remember the place.

It seems I've always had it,
It's a miracle I know.
But when I get to feeling down,
I know just where to go.

I bend my knee, I bow my head,
I ask Him straight from the heart.
To take my life and use me each day,
From Him I cannot depart.

Norma Jean Jones

Rocking Chair Memories

I remember my mother rocking me
When I wasn't much more than three
Rocking back and forth
With me upon her knee

As I grew up, I never forgot
The rocking chair, mother and me
When I had children of my own
I vowed I'd always be
A mother with a rocking chair
With a child upon my knee

Blessed with children and grandchildren
What a pleasure it has been to me
To sit in my rocking chair
And rock with a child upon my knee

I'm now a Senior Citizen
With hair that is pure white
I still enjoy my rocking chair
As I sit and rock each night.

Wilma Wilson

"Tell Me"

Can you tell me where the dreamers go
when it's time for them to dream?
Can you tell me what the poets know
when their words flow like a stream?
Can you tell me why two lovers glow
when their eyes first meet, agleam?

I can tell you why the dreamers die
when their dreams turn into dust.
I can tell you why the poets cry
when their iron words start to rust.
But I can't tell you why two lovers glow
when their eyes first meet, agleam.
I've never had the chance to know
and I never will it seems.

Matt Himlin

Abuse

Late at night
When stinging questions come
Anger runs free
Indifferent to salt-water pleas.
Swollen
Broken dreams
Hidden behind walls
Need only whisper
To pale the moon
In the eyes of the sky.

Marshall King

My Dearest Darling

How can you love me?
When I've been so untrue
I've caused you many heartaches
And probably tear drops too.

How can you love me?
When I have been unfair
I left you Dear, for others
I thought I didn't care.

How can you love me?
And be so thoughtful too
You always have remembered
By lovely things you do.

How can you love me?
And still call me your own
I realize now I love you
Just you, Dear, you alone.

How can I love you?
Dear, you surprise me so!
How can I hate you?
When love is all I know.

Mary K. Allen

Anticipation

I am always overwhelmed in March
When signs of Spring appear
When I can't bear one more winter day
and I long for Summer's cheer
The sign of an early spring flower
Sweeps all winter thoughts away
and then I hear the geese return
and I know Spring is here to stay
I have seen a lot of Springs arrive
The feelings are always the same
I find the child in me returns
Along with the warm Spring rain.

Nancy Rosensweig

Bright Beauty

I love it so
when spring comes round,
since summer
is not far away.

I love it so
when summer arrives,
one can count on
the sun's mighty rays.

It's warm and it's light
and it maintains life,
and it makes people
smile every day.

Bright beauty is here,
cause summer is here,
enjoy and delight in it,
jump, run, and play.

Valerie L. Sanders

"Can't You See?"

Can't you see
When you look at me?
Can't you see
Every time you kiss me?
Can't you see
Whenever you pass me?
Can't you see
That I love thee?

Miranda Rice

How I Want For Yesterday

How I want for yesterday
When the leaves were green,
And my heart was light.
There is nothing that can ever
Bring that moment back to us again,
But how I wish you here tonight.

When we whisper I'm your's forever,
It is nothing but a wishful dream.
Time escapes like sand through our fingers,
Running like a mountain stream.

How I want for yesterday
Now the leaves are brown
And falling with the snow.
My love is just as it was when we met.
How I wish for you to know.

Richard F. Gossett

"Boiling Pot"

How can you say it is no big deal
  When we all know that it is
It is chopping up the earth
  Before burning it to a fizz.

The pot is boiling
  Can't you feel it on your skin?
The lid is disintegrating
  It is really wearing thin.

Let's call the lid the ozone layer
  And the pot the fate to come,
If everyone leaves responsibility
  To hang on the shoulders of one.

Therese Proctor

"Friends, Special Friends"

There were many years between us
when we met a year ago
But nothing back then told me
we could not be friends, and so-

I came to care about you
You cared about me too.
We gave each other something
That was missing this is true.

The odds, they were against us
becoming close, I know.
But the friendship had some merit
And is time began to grow.

With these words I'll tell a secret
It's the only thing to do.
I'll be hoping for the chance again
To spend some time with you.

Mary Lamb

Untitled

I hear your laughter
When you don't know I'm listening.
I watch when you sleep
And lose myself in your dreams.
I feel your love, always
Even when we're apart.
I owe all that's good to you.
Whatever we may wish for
Could never be as precious
As what we already have.

Polly A. Belsenich

The Stream

There's a little stream,
Where the children play,
Swimming and fishing,
And skipping rocks all day.
While I stand there,
So quiet at night,
The water is still,
As it reflects the moon's light.
For some people,
It's hard to see,
Just how different,
Something can be.
During the day,
It's lively and cheery.
During the night,
It's still and a little eerie.

Tiffany Rogers

The Land That We Have Left

On the land and on the sea
Where the Jews have all once seen
All the mighty, all the glory,
All the victory and praise
of their God and their Amoraim
In the light and of their days.

From the sea and from the glory
We came out in to the world
That began heroic story -
Peaceful plough and fighting sword.

With believes and disbelieves
Our victory and peace
Lead us to disperse as leaves
To Australia and Greece.
Russia, Germany and France
World excepted us once.
Our Temporary homes
We'll change to or motherland
To return on ancient stones
And to find our god's command.

Michael Kuznetsov

Dreams At Twilight

On the other side of the mountain
Where the lake is cool and still,
There comes the scent of the lotus flower
The birds calls clear and shrill.

Only calm and sweetness surrounds me,
All the earth should be as serene.
The carpet is dotted with crimson.
The background's an emerald green.

And now as the sun sinks to rest
I gaze at drifting clouds above,
And here in this beautiful setting
I dream about my love.

He wants peace and love just as I do
But pictures them in some distant place.
Why doesn't he know the love that I feel
When I look at his dear face?

Pale shadows now fall on the waters.
In it I picture his face.
I wonder would he, here beside me, find
love
In this beautiful garden of peace.

Marion Hamilla

Moms Are Priceless Gifts

Moms are priceless gifts no matter
where they are oh moms are priceless
gifts no matter tall or small.
They give you love and hope
and care in everything you do.
Their there for you in every
way when things are on so blue.
If you are happy then so are
they, because they love you in
every way. If you are excited
about something you do then
they support you the whole way
through. So on this, special
day in may mom I'd like to
say to you, I love you and
thank you for everything you do.

Melany A. Peters

Untitled

She dances to silent music,
Which only he can hear.
He places her gently in his heart,
She wipes away a tear.
She whispers softly into the wind,
Only he can understand.
She hears him in the distant thunder,
Crying for her hand.
She dreams of them together,
He knows it cannot be.
He dares to contradict her,
When she refuses to believe.
She feels the distance between them,
It's tearing her apart.
The most important piece of him,
He left safely in her heart.
They said "goodbye,"
Yet neither of them knew . . .
That this would be their last chance,
To ever say "I love you."

Megan Esser

Sign, Please Tell Me

Sign please tell me
Which way I should go,
Don't say whose ahead of me
Cause I don't want to know.

Arrows please point to me
Which way I should turn,
Don't try to teach me short cuts
Cause I don't want to learn.

Don't know where I'm going
I'm just heading for my life,
No one to help me make it
But my knowledge and my knife.

Flashing lights please tell me
When to stop and go,
Don't whisper words of caution
Cause I don't want to know.

Sign please tell me
When I should slow down,
Please don't show me U turns,
Cause I don't want to turn around.

Wendy Diane Sayers

Friends

They help you out when you are down;
which you thank them very much for.

They give you hope to try again in this
big world of troubles.

Now you know and you see they don't
let you give up on anything.

You can't believe how you are; when they
try to help you out more.

You can't forget, the things you say;
and you wish you never said them.

Now you know and you see how much
they really mean to you,

They are your friends, it's not the end,
you'd like to be their friend to the end.

You want to show them how much you
care about them.

Now you know and you see, they are
the friends you thought they'd be.

Tara Cook

O Pelican Bay!

O Pelican Bay! O Pelican Bay!
Who art thou that turneth
Man's heart to stone?

Whose day is as black as the night,
That shutteth out the light of day.

Never to see the blue sky
With the big fluffy clouds,
As lambs upon a hillside.

Never to see the changing of the sky
With dark clouds heavy with rain.

O Pelican Bay! O Pelican Bay!
Know you not that God lighteth every man
That cometh into the world?

Know you not that the Lord God said,
It is not good that man should be alone?

Throw down your great stone walls
Let there be light.

O Pelican Bay! O Pelican Bay!
Hear the word of the Lord,
Let man communicate.

Pearline Taylor

A Dying Love

If I weep wearily into the night
Will it change the result of
A dying love?

If I swear on a grave
Could it possibly save
A dying love?

And what if I curse until dawn's light
Will it make right
A dying love?

Should I take away the very breath
That I hold within my chest
And take with me forever
A dying love?

Penny Hathaway

Failure

There are songs enough for the hero
  Who dwells on the heights of fame;
I sing of the disappointed and
  For those who have missed their aim.

I sing of the breathless runner
  The eager, anxious soul,
Who falls with his breath exhausted
  Almost in sight of his goal.

For hearts that break in silence,
  With sorrow all alone,
For those who need companions
  Yet walk their way alone.

There are songs enough for lovers
  Who share loves tender pain.
I sing for the one whose passion
  Is given all in vain.

For the pain would be imperfect
  Unless it held some sphere,
That paid for the toil and talent,
  And love that is wasted here.

William H. Lamkin

The Rose

Look at the beauty of a rose
who else but God could make
Anything as simple as one of those
whose beauty we all love to partake.

Feel the soft petals with your hand
Touch the thorn and feel the pain
The rose is all part of God's plan
which is quite simple and very plain.

Plant it deep and watch it grow
towards heaven, going back to God,
along its stems thorns grow with a woe
To show life's not as smooth as rod.

Yet on the end of the stem
He's put the promise of eternal life
The universe's greatest precious gem
For each petal was part of Jesus' strife.

Just as God will nurture the garden
His son Jesus will nurture His children.

E. J. Faubert

Bob!

Here sits Bob the frog,
Who lives inside an old log.
He has an empty life,
As he has no wife.
It's cold in his bog.

Among the lily pads catching flies,
Looking over, a girl, oh surprise.
She heard the noise, sudden fright
Folded her legs, took to flight.
"There's glamour in her eyes."

Her he turned to follow,
Into a deep and wide hollow.
To her he gave a grasshopper,
She took it, a heart stopper
Crunch, crunch, a big swallow

Here sits Bob the frog,
Who lives inside an old log.
His heart's in a whirl,
'Cause he's got the girl.
Now they've got a polliwog.

Stephenie F.

Blake

No finer man I'll ever know
Who loves our precious Savior so
You do indeed let your light shine
I'm blessed that you're a friend of mine
A truly faithful saint you are
So say friends form near and far
You're sweet, gentle, kind and true
The blessing's our's from knowing you
Our plan for life we question some
But when it's over gone and done
We will be joyful in the place
Where now you're gazing at God's face
So sing out loud with the angels, Blake
Sing on key, for Heaven's sake.
For I hear the angels singing
And I know you're singing too.

Nancy J. Burch

Only Witness

Love is the wolf
Who never sleeps
Tracing the prints
Of his weakened lover
In the pale of the murderess moon
Shadows are food
And the gypsy women is witness
To the distant sound
Of love being torn to pieces

Love is the shark
Black beads for eyes
Stalk of shiver
The devil's deep
Blue sea on Sunday
Is suddenly striped with blood
Where no one hears the thrash
As the devour of love
Takes place below
Where no one is witness
But love

Mark Patrick Acuna

Pain

  If pain is good,
Why does it hurt so much?
  If no one wants it,
How come everyone has it?

I want this pain to go away,
I wish it would leave me alone.
I have no more strength,
  I am in pain

I can usually stand pain,
But my poor heart can not.
It is that time once again,
For my heart to be broken.

I have no love,
No love is near.
I wouldn't want it any ways,
  Who can trust love?

The pain of being used is too much,
There is too much all at once.
There is no way I can take it,
  I am in pain.

Theresa Kuhl

Patty

Patty died at the age of two.
Why? She never did anything to me or you.
She fought and bled and prayed to live
But still her life she had to give.
My girlfriend, her nurse, did also try
To help Patty, that she might not die.
But life is life, and it will be
To everyone, including you and me.
A charm with which we all are blessed,
Until we start our eternal rest.
So Patty dear, if you be near,
Then you my lowly voice may hear.
I do not know how, when, where, or why,
But all of us must sometime die.
So Patty dear, I say, "goodnight",
Hoping sometime soon I might
Meet you in your home above,
Where all do go whom the Lord doth love.
  "Goodnight Patty"
Patty, daughter of a sailor's wife, who
At the age of two had to give her life.

Samuel G. Geiss Jr.

Cat Dreams

Creatures of terror
Will you never stop
Haunting and taunting me?
My fever is high and
That must be why your
Eyes of green are flashing fire.
Hundreds of you with black
Tails swishing keep pushing
This screen door that must not give.
For miles I see you, ceaseless surging,
Each of you with long sharp fangs
Show white against
Jet black faces.
I pray I'll awake
And my fever will break.

Patricia Gibbs Scoggin

Earth Station

River and sun, sand and sea
Wind and rain, trail and tree
Corn and cactus, honey and milk
Cave and castle, steel and silk

Peak and pinnacle, valley and vale
Kitten and kite, giant and snail
Night and day, century and second
Reap and sow, fathom and reckon

Emerald and eternal, sapphire and space
Earth and shadow, galaxy and grace
Arrow and circle, mystery and way
Sing and sail, whisper and pray

Violet Long

"Desire"

I think of you and my heart expands
to the fullest capacity.
Filled with passion and desire.
I quiver with the very thought of
you kissing me, touching me,
caressing my breasts, and I find
myself longing to be in your arms
again if only for one brief
moment.

Laurie Konczyk

Spring Storm

Dry winter leaves scurry at my feet,
wind pushing me down the street.

Tiny pools of water on the sidewalk stand,
a game of hop-scotch I play unplanned.

Bare tree limbs bending low,
with every increasing gusty blow.

Lighting crash and thunder roar,
raindrops tapping, tapping at my door.

After the storm has gone away,
the children can go outside and play.

Luke Neil Keilman

The Winter

Winter is white
Winter is cold
Winter is snow forts
Winter is Christmas
Winter is white

Winter is snow fights
Winter is sledding
Winter is snowsuits
Winter is snowmobiles
Winter is white

Winter is snowmen
Winter is snow angels
Winter is ice-skating
Winter is fun
Winter is white

Steven Smith

Flower In My Garden Of Weeds

Gasping for air
Wishing to be living
Elsewhere
With someone who cares
Anyone
Anyone who can help me.

Trying to grow
And become something
To someone
Anyone
Anyone who can help me.

Spreading my pathetic roots
My dying roots
To go somewhere
And be with someone
Anyone
Anyone who can help me.

Michele Goodman

"Loved So"

There is a train from
Wells Fargo, and it carries a
special cargo, for its mission
is to let you know, that you
are loved so.
When you're feeling down
and out, emotions soaring
all about. (Listen carefully) there
can be no doubt that you are loved so.

Lois Jones

Dream Land

Upstairs dog
With a peg
Old oak wood and jewels
Juice fallen juice
Slumbers in the cold
As the caned man strolls
The violin keeps me close
To the ticker
That painted nose is thrust
Up towards the heat
As I scurry about far
Below the tall ceiling
Picking strands of old material
From my upper arm
The faded bean slides
Down my throat
An unrealistic beast leaps
Amongst the beautiful plastic
Shallow souls

Nancy Bender

You Think

You think you fly
with all the ladies
but all you do is
help make the babies

After that you're gone
do you understand
when they ask for help
you should open your hands

You think you fly
but you just walk
when a woman needs help
you should have their back

Nine months ago
I should have used my head
I should have stopped myself
before I got in that bed

Rachel Aminah Williams

Spring

It is spring, beautiful spring
With buds bursting forth
And streams rippling by
Jonquils and tulips are opening
their sleepy yellow eyes
Cowbells tinkling in the woodland
Sheep in the meadow
Basking in the sun
Brings to our minds memories
and stirs our hearts like a song.

Lois Neal Phipps

My Brother's Room

This is my death-room
with crimson walls
and a shattered ceiling.
The mirrored doors
of a forbidden closet
look me in the eye.
The wooden hooks
that held the
demon of despair
shred my mind
in utter torment.
And the saturated carpet
haunts my soul.

Sarah M. Evans

Being Born

I'm sure we were meant to be
with each other before we met,

And that some measure
of what I am and want to be
will come from you.

You gave me honesty
I gave you laughter

You gave me humility
I gave you strength.

You gave me courage
I gave you hope.

We decided to take a risk,
a chance, a gamble.

We hitched a ride home
on the same comet,

but we touched earth and separate times.
And like electricity giving up sparks,
we grew in character until we approach
being born.

Tony Lashea

Wilderness

The young man looks
with his wild fiery eyes,
out into the wilderness
as if in a trance
"And someday"
he foresees to his companion
"Someday I'll be a part
of all that.
I'll disappear into the trees
I'll float up into the sky
The clouds will eat me
The birds will carry me away.
So kiss me now —
While I'm still yours."

Noah Beauman

Keeper Of My Heart

Are you in love
with me he said
I looked at him
and shook my head
I can not give
my heart away
Because it still
belongs to Ray
He is in my
dreams at night
He is the one
that holds me tight
And one day soon
I don't know when
I will be with
him once again

Shirley Richard

Tranquillity

We stroll the stream at night.
With snow on the ground,
It looks awfully bright.
As the moon rises up above
Its reflection in the water is glistening.
We stop for a second.......... listening.
Hearing not a sound.
Where is everything?
Nothing to be found.
It's as peaceful as can be,
Very close to tranquillity.

Thomas K. Walker

Wrapped in Sunshine

Let your day be wrapped in sunshine
With testing things to do.
Let there be friends to help when needed
And when called are there for you.

Let your day be filled with music
The great songs, both old and new
Let your heart be filled with wonder
When you hear one dear to you.

Let your day be filled with pride
That only new grandmothers know.
Let there be the love of fulfillment
That keeps pace as Blake does grow.

Let your day be splashed with memories
Gathered from along the way
Let this be a beautiful day to gather
Tomorrow's memories, that start today.

Marley Lafferty

August In The West

It is hot
With the accumulated, tired
Heat that festers in
The sump of summer

Drawing up those final shreds
of water that soaked the ground
Last springtime,
Looking to the sky for
Succor for the wilting fields,
Seeing either none or violent plenty

For August in the west
Is generous or cruel,
And he who would be master
Is instead a captive,
A pawn of nature, living, dying
On whatever alms are kept or given,
Survival but a whim,
And we mendicants are weak

Tom Steven

The Dark And The Light

The dark and the light,
the wrong and right.
the truth is love and the hate has night.
But there are two things we need to
see, that we are all in human condition
and that's what's to be, and we are
all judged in Gods sight and that's
what's soon to see.

Terry Joe Smith

Bookends

You are a mystery to me
with the solution hidden
somewhere in the final chapter.
An exciting adventure story
with clues interwoven from
one chapter to the next.
Obvious and not so obvious.

Just when I think I have the answer
I read something new between the lines
and start all over again.

Chapter one.
Same characters,
same lines,
new plot,
new conflicts.

I don't know you any more.
Did I ever?

I am an open book,
transparent to a fault.
Take me away and read me.

Melody Reem Kruckenberg

All My Dreams

In all my dreams
with the thought of you
with the thought of me
could I dream so incredibly
of the stars and the moon

I miss you now
oh - I miss you how
but the stars and the moon
oh - what a dream it is
in all my dreams
such terrific dreams it is

I close my eyes and there you are
the dream of you floods my sight
I lie there helplessly
waiting to recover from my dreams

If only had I known
I would be riding the stars and the moon
I would never ever have woken
from all my dreams
now I really miss you.

Shalirita Singh

Heaven's Gate

He walked along the silent road,
With winter's breath upon him,
The trees were shining silver,
That Jack Frost painted on them.

His heart quickened with wonder,
For over yonder,
The moon lighted a path,
To heaven's gate.

He stumbled and fell,
And there rested a spell,
There was no more cold,
And no more pain.

He knew then,
That he was home again,
For he had passed through,
heaven's gate.

Rosalie Cartwright

Final Good-Bye

Smile down at me
with wise old eyes.
You understood it all..
the joy and yes, the pain

Now you're gone,
my light has dimmed.
It will brighten again, for
in my memory you still live.

I see you there
with smiling gray eyes.
As I reach out you disappear,
left with echoing words.

I'll always love you,
I'll miss you,
good-bye...
I will always remember.

Tears roll slowly down
a smiling child's face.
I love you too Grandpa...
Good-bye.

Valerie Johnson

Last Battle

an aged leaf
withered, brittle
Proudly wearing the scars
of that bold red tongue
that licked it slowly
Until death.
Singed black edges
sharply pointed,
yellowed skin
where the burning flame
could not reach.
Cold veins
the blood which once flowed...freely...
Halted Forever.

Stripped of life
Cloaked in red.

Meisha Hunter

The Last Time I Would See His Face

The last time I
  Would see his face
Or stroke his hair.

The Essence of his life
  His Energy
  His rushing in
  And filling up a room
These would not be
  Put underground.
They are not here
They'll stay at home with me
Forever frozen in this time.
He'll be
Forever strong
Forever young.

Lavone Ferguson

Grey Day

What a nicer day today was
yesterday was grey was
yesterday as grey as I could say
But as grey as yesterday was
today was just as grey was
but a nicer grey today was
yesterday was as grey as I could say-how-
yesterday was, grey as yesterday was
but a nicer day today
Yesterday was as grey as I could say

L. Jay Mozdy

Who

Who can weep like a child,
yet be full grown.
Who can be with family,
Yet not at home.
Who can sit with friends,
and not be known.
Who can be in a crowd,
yet all alone.
Who is lavished by life's warmth,
and death's cold moan.
A person's life that has been blown,
on rocks of strife unbeknown.

Michael Wise

"I Am Not Alone"

I sit here in the woods,
yet I am not alone.
I see no people around
but I do not feel lonesome.

The moon's illumination soaks
into my skin and makes me great.
The delicate wind whispers enchanting
proverbs in my ear.
Shadows frolic in the brilliant
moonlight
The grass is like a soft blanket
underneath me.

Vicious wolves howl far away
and I am scared but the
trees comfort me.
I know I am not alone.

Vanessa McDaniel

My America

I come up for a breath
yet the air is not the same
I come up to see the land
yet my eyes burn from the sight
I come up to hear the peace
yet the only sound is pain
I come up to speak my mind
yet my voice goes unheard

Where is the air once so fresh
all I smell is destitution
Where is the land of beauty
all I see is its destruction
Where is the sound of contentment
all I hear is depression
Where is the voice of freedom
all I know is poverty and despair

This is the place to which I was born
this is my America

Patsy Jo Pollack-Morris

Untitled

Flowers for my lover
Yet they smell not sweet
A rainbow of colors
Yet I see none as bright
Let these mere flowers be a gift
A gift of love from my heart to yours
May they bring some joy to thee
For they do nothing to me
I already have the sweetest rose of all
My wife.

Travis C. Fiveash

Santa Cruz

We sat on the edge of the world,
you and I,
our faces wet by
Mother Earth's salty tears.
We questioned,
and we coaxed,
and we stared
into the changing sky.
We walked,
and sighed,
alone together,
with Socrates's blood,
and we listened
to the voices of
our Mother's messengers.

Rachel Weber

We Two

We are two of a kind,
You and I.
Giving our love,
To all the wrong guys.

What ever happened,
To the happiness for us?
It always seems,
The right guys we never trust.

The ones we
Give in and do.
Are the ones who always
Leaves us Heartbroken and blue.

Yeah! You and I
We're so much alike.
We never seem to find
Any of the things that are right.

One things for sure
It's friends we'll always be
Otherwise, who would we have?
If it weren't for you and me.

Valerie Spehar

Untitled

When you are a child it's a
wonderful world
of lollipops, mud pies, little boys
and little girls,
You play all day in a carefree way
you climb trees, chase bumble bees
you argue, you spat with a
neighborhood brat,
you might even play cowboys and
indians,
but just as it starts it seems to end
and you are older looking back with
just odds and ends.

Santina Benedetti Turner

"Autumn Afternoons"

Darting gold shadows
Beneath floating maple leaves —
Autumn afternoons.

Nona Ann Dasmann

Frozen

I am the Sun
You are the frozen ice cap.
I beat down my warmth
but it barely penetrates you.

I have tried for eons
to thaw your frozen mass.
But you resist and add
another frozen layer.

While I generate much life
you sustain very little.
Perhaps you need that hard shell
to protect a vulnerable core underneath.

I will continue to shed
my light on the world,
It is my nature.
But you will never know
how wonderful my warmth can feel.

Sharon Greenwell

Mindbend

I am your victim and
you are the venom that
seeps into every crevasse of my soul
infesting my emotions
I become static
non moving
non feeling
another day another chance
another glitter another fire another
tear
alone once more
anger wells up inside me yet fades away
as you do
it never stops
never gets better
never goes away...it remains
Only a reminder
of what will never
be again.

Megan Tatham

Taking The Wheel

You were never of this earth
You only visited briefly
Blessing us for a few decades
And even then
You were racing among the clouds
Letting me take the wheel
Amongst puffs of powder
And winged creatures
No, you were never ours
You belonged to the sky
And the sky has reclaimed you
Flying now on angels' wings
And I know one day
Our souls will meet
And once again
You'll let me take the wheel.

Tanya R. Vandergrift

Streets Mixed With Happiness

Streets are weird places.
You see so many faces
Young old, big small
Guys look at girls
Girls look at guys
People with packages
People doing jobs
Or just people doing nothing.

Some streets are dirty,
Some are clean
Some are crowded
Some deserted.
Some have houses
Some have stores
Others just nothing

Streets are weird
But when you're crying in a window
This is all smeared.

Laurie Mather Longchamps

"A Mother's Son"

The Angels sang, the day you were born.
You walked with your mother,
through any storm.
No one can come and take your place
You are impossible ever to replace.
You always shall be your mothers son.
On heavenly earth it shall be done
Sadness comes and haunts me so
From deep within a shadow flows
You might have died and gone away
But you are always here to stay

Virginia Cullen

Goodbye My Love

You left me today
You went into the loving arms of Jesus
You couldn't stay,
you needed to go

You left me today
Without a goodbye,
without a gentle kiss
you left me today,
but still I feel your gentleness.

You left me today
You needed to go
You mission was done
So he called you home

Goodbye my love- 'till I see you again.

Sally L. Tillman

Alone

Searching, wandering—alone.
  You found me.
You came so gently!

Rejected, despised—alone.
  I found you.
You came so gently!

Renewed, uplifted—replenished.
  We are alone.
You came so gently!

Richard L. Merila

"Daddy"

From the moment of birth,
  You were there.

Thru the years your face
  Cheered me on.

Pushing me to work harder,
  For my own benefit.

Having a soft shoulder,
  For my head to rest.

Wiping away the tears,
  Of my heartaches.

Circle of love in the hugs,
  That sheltered me from pain.

Molding me into,
  The adult I am.

A life time of Thanks,
  For a job well done.

Robyn J. Anderson

Thinking of You

You dried my tears
You wiped my nose
and said big girls
don't cry.

You were always there
when i needed you
to pray.
Oh how I missed you
Father dear.

High on the mountain
Low in the valley.
I had a father
that cared.
we shared.

To God be the glory
for fathers because
you are special to me.
You light up my life.

P. S. Fishburne

Recruited Rainbows

Pseudo soldier on our hill
You'll see a rainbow and grow still.
Remembering the strange, sad dream
How rainbows changed to jungle green.

Who plucks these colors from our sky?
Sends them across the sea to die?
Transplanted hues cannot grow
In a jungle full of foe.

Am I but a misfit snob?
To feel rainbows belong to God?
Must we be mute, silent mothers?
Are we not all rainbow lovers?

Who dreamt the dream?
Who gave them birth?
Who buries rainbows
In the earth?

Rainbows were many-splendored things.
To be savored after rains.
Now, I'll look up in the sky
Think of frightened boys and cry.

Sylvia A. Lambert

My Sunshine

Your smile is my sunshine
Your eyes are a glitter,
Your hair is so fine,
You give me the jitters.

To find a gem in the sand,
Is a dream come true.
You make me feel like a man
I'll never be blue,

I think of all kinds of things,
But the moments are fleeting,
But when I dream of you,
those memories I'm keeping.

My cheeks haven't hurt so much as when
Your smile makes my sunshine come to light,
Your face beams back my reflections,
You're why my sunshine is so bright,

Terry Bradshaw

Oh Sweet One

Slumbering at last,
your face so sweet.
Your golden brown hair
and soft rosy cheeks.

I stand there watching,
my heart full of love.
With the glow from the stars
and the moon from above.

Silently you sleep,
I can't stay away.
Knowing you'll need me
with each waking day.

Covering you slowly,
I duck out of sight.
I blow you a kiss
and whisper... Goodnight.

Rita Hensel

To My Best Friend

You don't realize just how much
Your friendship means to me.
You are there when I need you
No matter how small or big
The problem may be.
You can always make me laugh,
When times seem so sad.
You make me smile,
And forget that I'm so mad.
You have always listened to me,
Through all of my problems
And that means a lot to me.
We've got so many more years to go
through
As I'm sure many more tears.
And I know I can always count on you,
As you can count on me.
That's what I consider a true friend
And I know in my heart that
We will be best friends till the very end!!

Melissa Collar

The Rose

The rose is something special, one gives t another
It symbolizes their love and devotion
It shows how much one is cared for
And it expresses true emotions
The rose can take away ones fears
The rose can take away ones tears
The rose can be a special gift
From someone who is very sincere
It could be like your hopes and dreams
And make you feel your loved ones are near
The rose can take away ones pain
The rose can set ones heart aflame
The rose is such a beautiful thing
It can explain things one cannot say
And if can make you feel better
In a loving sort of way
It can make you feel such happiness
And it can say things no one knows
It can make you feel such passion
The rose.

Jessie Burroughs

My Other Mother

There just aren't enough words to express
your kindness and unselfishness
In such a short time you have grown to be
my friend and my teacher
a mother to me
Through my good times and bad
you are always there
Showing caring and guidance
none to compare
Passing no judgement
on who I should be
Only encouragement
you accept me for me
You give me a gift
that cannot be measured
Unconditional love
that will always be treasured

Valerie A. Geiger

The Dispossessed

The sulfuric morning light cast roaming shadow particles
Onto the cellar floor diagonally from the broken door,
Over oozing mason jars of jam and winter apples. Shattered.

Temp Fugitas

Towns, cities, continents.
Changed with kaleidoscopic rhythm.
Things clung to victors, and those who stayed behind,
Round-mouthed admonitions kept them in their place.
Things. Not people.

For many years strangers passed, unsanctioned
In and out our common rooms.

Benevolent memories splattered across our despair
With brilliant light, slowly gathering the dust of decades.
And one day imploded into graceless shards of jam jars,
Of winter apples diagonal to the cellar door.

Krista G. Nash

Cheep, Squawk

I clean my house on Mondays, I finally now can rest;
Phone rings, in-laws coming, must pass the white glove test.
I gather up my soap and rags, put Rover out to play;
Let Tweety free, whilst I clean his cage, what a grueling day.
I've dusted, mopped, and made the windows shine;
I hauled out HULK the sweeper, to finish up on time.
There's something I've forgotten, but have no time to dwell;
HULK is raring to go; he does his job real well.
He looks a little suspicious, but must focus on getting done;
When I hear cheep, cheep; QUICK, Call 911.
SQUAWK. Is it too late? Hurry, please;
Tweety bird is missing, I fear he is deceased.
How could I have forgotten my little feathered friend;
I open up the vacuum bag, I fear it is the end.
No. Wait. Tweety staggers out, a little worse for wear;
As HULK grimaces, foiled again, but beware.
Tweety jets quickly, toward his cage's open door;
So the moral of this story is for now and evermore —
Before you start to clean, let Rover out to play;
Put Tweety in his cage, for the entire cleaning day.

Sharon J. Boan

Handiwork

He was a man, young and strong, who made music
Golden bronzed music and formed words into patterns
And found canvas for his words.
Then, a part of him, younger and small...her...and he saw
Music and words and canvas in bones and blood.
He gave her letters and notes and brushes showed her books
About little jungle boys. "Read this", he implores
Strong and capable little jungle boys.
Flowers grow and bees make honey, smart people know this.
"Watch this show", he says...atoms, ions and supply-side economics
Look what people know. Pulitzer prizes, cures for diseases
and moon walks.
Look what people do! You can too!
She read, heard, looked and grew thinking thoughts while he nodded
And she grew reaching out from her thoughts and he nodded and nodded.
But one day he....."don't be like them"
And she.....because of you I am.

Vicki L. Desmuke

Dreams

Dreams are created by us: We are created by dreams.
Reality is the process of erudition.
Illusion in the erroneous perception of reality.
Most times we exist in the hapless void of this continuum,
Never to discover if we or our dreams dream.

Tracey Rice

BIOGRAPHIES

ABRAHAMSEN, SHAUN
[b.] September 7, 1971, Alaska; [p.] Karlyn and Laurence Ransom; [m.] Nicole Abrahamsen, March 11, 1995; [ed.] Santa Rosa High School, Gene Jaurez School of Cosmetology; [occ.] Cosmetologist; [hon.] The honor of reading my poems at several acclaimed functions.; [oth. writ.] Over 100 poems disbursed in 9 states. A finished book of poetry stored on computer disc for later publication.; [pers.] the art of creativity comes from within, one must be born with such a gift to use what God has given them to its fullest potential.; [a.] Seattle, WA

ACUNA, MARK PATRICK
[b.] March 18, 1959, Silver City, NM; [p.] Edward Acuna; [m.] Yvonne Acuna, October 1955; [ch.] Jim, Terry, Mark, Gina; [ed.] St. Mary's Inter Parocial, Birmingham High School Van Nuys, CA; [occ.] Drafts person, Singer, Songwriter, Poet; [oth. writ.] "All things are become new" original song for Christmas production "Cafe Anderson" Pasadena "Android" 12 single - CA, singer, musician on 1989 release. Other poems published "Evanescent" local magazine "Moon Magazine."; [pers.] I write from my heart beauty and anger. I am a reflection. Only love is obvious - only pain is pain.; [a.] Silverlake, CA

ADAIR, CATHERINE A.
[pen.] Cara "Cara"; [b.] October 1, 1951, Austin, TX; [p.] Dr. and Mrs. B.C. Richards; [m.] Ronnie Adair, January 19, 1974; [ch.] Amanda and Natalie; [ed.] Bachelor of Liberal Studies from St. Edwards Univ. major: Psychology; [occ.] Office Supervisor; [hon.] National Honor Society in Psychology - Psi Chi Chapter, National Catholic College Graduate Honor Society - Kappa Gamma Pi Honorable Mention Dean's List; [oth. writ.] Numerous short stories and poems.; [pers.] Life events drive my desire to use paper and pin to formally catch the moments of life time memories.; [a.] Austin, TX

ADAMS, DAVID
[b.] August 18, 1920, Ashland, KY; [p.] Deceased; [m.] Hazel L. Adams, August 1, 1942; [ch.] Two sons - Scott and Lana; [ed.] High School; [occ.] Retired from Hughes Helicopters - 1975; [hon.] Instructor of Aircraft Engines U.S. Navy I was the youngest employee. To receive a 30 year service Pin and Ring at Hughes Helicopter 1973; [oth. writ.] "Answered Prayers," "Outlaws," "Days to Remember," "Mothers," "Thoughts," "Memories of Yester years."; [pers.] I enjoy writing poetry and cooking - have had some of my recipes printed in books.; [a.] Los Angeles, CA

ADAMS, DENISE
[b.] October 20, 1952, New York, NY; [p.] Ethel and Floyd Milburn; [ch.] Jamal, Frantz Jr.; [ed.] Springfield Gardens High School, Manhattan Community College, York College; [occ.] Sr. Financial Analyst; [memb.] Dean's List, College; [hon.] Scholarship - from N.A.A.C.P.; [pers.] My writing is through my inside feelings. I love life, I love softness I love peace. If I could reach someone's heart then I know that I have accomplished peace.; [a.] Flushing, NY

ADAMS, JEANNETTE
[b.] New York City, NY; [p.] Frances Booker (mother), Father Deceased; [m.] James Adams; [ed.] R.N. Glendale Medical Center, Glendale, California and BS Degree Nursing - Columbia Union College, Takoma Park, Maryland; [occ.] I'm retired a taking care of elderly mother in Laura Mra. Roxie Adams; [hon.] Outstanding Performance Award in Nursing, Walter Reed Army Medical Center, Wash. D.C., Certificate of Appreciation in Church and Community Work, Appreciation for Excellence in Vacation Bible School; [oth. writ.] Poetry and readings on Presidents, history and humor compiled in my personal files and sharing with others.; [pers.] Thank you for the opportunity of presenting my poetry and talent. My philosophical statement is "my joy in work and hope refills, as I help others use their skills."; [a.] Takoma Park, MD

ADAMS, LILLIE
[b.] May 22, 1943, Orlando, FL; [p.] Iris and Leola Washington; [m.] Randall R. E. Adams, March 12, 1966; [ch.] Randall D.'Uane and Ayesa Sonji; [ed.] Jones High, Albany State, Johnson Jr. College, Seton Medical Center Histotecthnician Course, Institute of Children's Literature Writers Course - Awana Commanders Course; [occ.] Histotechnician; [memb.] American Society of Clinical Pathologists Fourth Austin Baptist Church Choir; [hon.] Highest Average in Humanities and Biology, Daughters of the American Revolution, Outstanding Performance in Choir - Johnson Jr. College (Miss JJC); [oth. writ.] Not published poems and short stories.; [pers.] I love to see twinkling in the eyes of the young and old, by writing about the simple things in life.; [a.] Austin, TX

ADENDORFF, TANIA H.
[b.] March 3, 1967, South Africa; [p.] Jupiter Adendorff, Mary Adendorff; [ed.] University of Cape Town, University of South Africa, University of Pittsburgh; [occ.] Graduate Student in Public Health (Masters), Registered Nurse; [memb.] American Public Health Association; [hon.] Psychiatric Nursing Award as Undergraduate Student; [oth. writ.] Several other unpublished poems and short stories.; [pers.] My inspirations are varied, but essentially I focus on areas where human beings can find comfort and solace, such as friendships and nature.; [a.] Pittsburgh, PA

ADKINS, BONNIE MARIE
[b.] December 28, 1958, Mine Fork, KY; [p.] Wilbur Cantrell, Eulah Williams Cantrell; [m.] Bennie Adkins Jr., August 12, 1977; [ch.] Brian Wilbur Adkins; [ed.] Johnson Central High School; [occ.] Housewife; [memb.] New Bethel Freewill Baptist Church - Swamp Branch - KY; [oth. writ.] Poem - the bad side won honorable mention in the world of poetry contest - 1991.; [pers.] I am very proud to be from the beautiful mountains of Eastern Kentucky. I strive to reflect my love for the great outdoors in my writing. I enjoy hiking, golf and gardening.; [a.] Paintsville, KY

ADKINS, GLORIA J. FERGUSON
[pen.] G. J. Ferguson Adkins; [b.] November 29, 1929, Buda, NE; [p.] Rose and Lawrence Ferguson; [m.] James Morris Adkins Sr., October 5, 1947; [ch.] Jeanne, Jim Jr., Jan, Jeff, John, Jodie, Jacque (seven); [ed.] High School Grad. Semester, Jr. College - many many Extra Courses; [occ.] Singer/Writer; [memb.] Does-DAR-Eagles-Pine Drive Baptist Church; [hon.] Community Service Award - NP - 1950's - Episton Sigma, Alpha - State Comm. Ser. Award - Nebr. - Press Women Awards - 10 - For Column and Women's Section; [oth. writ.] Coffee with Gloria - Karamie children's books - Dinosaur sky - misha goes Swisha - banana boat sea - large the left dog - that first with you - poem - fantasy in my mind - winter - peace - gypsy the cowboy - christmas is for children come on in my dear friend - show on the roof many more.; [pers.] Singing and writing are my joys in life I love putting my feelings to paper. Poetry has for a good many years been important to me. To read as well as write. My poems are dedicated to marion.; [a.] North Clotte, NE

AESCHBACHER, NORMA
[b.] August 4, 1958, New Castle, PA; [p.] Harlin and Nellie Aeschbacher; [ch.] Carrie Beth; [ed.] Beaver Falls High School, Community College Beaver County; [occ.] LPN Ellwood City Hospital Ellwood City PA; [pers.] Strength comes from within but love only comes to those who share it.; [a.] Ellwood City, PA

AGLIATA, LAUREN
[pen.] Pyr, Spot; [b.] December 28, 1978, White Plains, NY; [p.] Gerald L. Agliata, Jo Ann Agliata; [ed.] William B. Ward Elementary School, Albert Leonard Middle School, New Rochelle High School, Windward High School; [occ.] Student; [memb.] Tri-M Music Honor Society, OPUS, New Rochelle High School BBS, Chess Club; [hon.] Rising Star Award, Soccer Trophies, Good Fellowship Award; [oth. writ.] "Meow" published in OPUS.; [pers.] Be cultured, listen to others around you, and keep your mind open for anything. Any cue?; [a.] New Rochelle, NY

AHOLT, MARY M.
[pen.] M - Mayme; [b.] March 24, 1917, Boonville, MO; [p.] Mr. and Mrs. Ernest Barlow; [m.] Ralph C. Aholt, May 7, 1941; [ch.] Seven - Living, 22 grandchildren, 5 great grand children; [ed.] I completed 12 Grades Graduated from S.S. Peters and Pauls Catholic High School, Boonville, MO May 1935; [occ.] Homemaker; [memb.] C.C.W. of St. Mary's Catholic Church and Daughters of Isabell; [hon.] A few Certificate Ates of an Assortment of Poems, none have ever been Published in Books, a few in Local Newspapers, or to School Teachers; [oth. writ.] I remember my kin on Anniversaries in poetry. A bunch of poems, my first was when I was in 8th grade in a county school, it was about the school and named for it. Some of them relate to my parents and family.; [pers.] I love doing this, but have never been lucky. Mostly all are more than 21 lines. My deceased twin wrote also and years back I had an aunt who wrote poetry, she had a book published.; [a.] Glasgow, MO

AIKIN III, NORB
[b.] July 31, 1975, Buffalo, NY; [p.] Norb and Audi Aikin; [ed.] Cheektowaga Central High School '93; [occ.] Arby's, Assistant Manager, West Senera, NY; [oth. writ.] Several notebooks of poems, mainly for the purpose of personal release. Nothing published to date, but still dreaming.; [pers.] My objective is to make people think. I try to stay away from the obvious, if you hide your point behind words then it is all the more rewarding when someone truly says they understand you. Thank you Chrissy (my sister) for helping me select this piece, and for encouraging me.; [a.] Depew, NY

AINA, AKIN
[b.] June 30, 1974, Nigeria; [p.] Johnson Aina, Tina Aina; [ed.] M. Eng/BS Electrical Engineering Massachussetts, Institute of Technology; [occ.] Student; [pers.] Life is a poem, how well you succeed depends on how you interpret it.; [a.] Philadelphia, PA

AKIN, JUDY A.
[b.] December 15, 1941, Detroit, MI; [p.] H. Clifford and Ruth Lanier Palmer; [m.] Clayton W. Akin (Deceased), February 14, 1979; [ch.] Adam Tracy Lukity; [ed.] East Detroit High School, East Detroit, Michigan, Class of 1959, Attended Wayne State University; [occ.] Retired, Formerly Interior Designer; [memb.] United Leukodystrophy Foundation, Family Support Network, Children's Special Health Care Service, Michigan Public Health, Research Trust for Metabolic Diseases in Children; [pers.] I am currently writing a book about this marvelous little girl. In her short time on this earth she has taught so many so much about life, love, happiness, tenacity, and most important priorities. Everybody has a mission.; [a.] Southfield, MI

AL-CHOKHACHI, ZACHARY AKIL
[b.] August 13, 1976, Memphis, TN; [p.] Ann and Akil Al-Chokhachi; [ed.] High School degree from White Station High School, Attend the University of Memphis; [memb.] Member of St. Luke's United Methodist Church, Member of Delta Chi Fraternity; [oth. writ.] Poems yet to be published.; [pers.] My poems come straight from the heart, expressing my true feelings. My motivation comes from my best friends Josh and Shannon, who I owe my life to.; [a.] Memphis, TN

ALBANESE, PHILIP P.
[b.] July 6, 1929, New York, NY; [p.] Joseph and Jean; [m.] Rose Albanese, February 27, 1954; [ch.] Camille, Philip and Charles; [grndch.] Christopher, Jeffrey, Janelle; [ed.] Masters Degree - Psychology; [occ.] Fire Safety Director, Retired Police Officer, Fingerprint Expert; [oth. writ.] Thesis "Accultration of Italians in American Society"; [pers.] Life is more than working, sleeping, eating and playing. It's loving, it's respect, it's dignity, it's morals, it's humility.; [a.] Brooklyn, NY

ALBRETS, MISSY
[b.] March 23, 1981, Birmingham, AL; [p.] Dwane and Peggy Albrets; [ed.] Prattville Junior High School, Covenant Academy; [occ.] Student; [hon.] A-B Honor Roll, 4-H Club Awards, Girl Scout Awards; [a.] Prattville, AB

ALBRITTON, DEAN
[b.] June 4, 1932, Wallsboro, AB; [p.] James David and Sarah Brown; [m.] Walter M. Albritton Jr., June 1, 1952; [ch.] Four Sons; [ed.] High School and Art Classes; [occ.] Homemaker; [memb.] The Mentor Club, Wesley Terrace Auxiliary, United Methodist Women; [hon.] Life Membership of United Methodist Women, President of the Mentor Club (1993-1994), 1st Vice President Wesley Terrace Auxiliary; [oth. writ.] Poetry, articles; [pers.] My deep commitment to the missionary outreach of Christ was inspired by my visits to missions in 26 nations around the world. It has been my joy to express my insights about life in poetry.

ALDRICH, THANDA LOUISE
[b.] July 13, 1952, Salem, IL; [p.] Verne and Kathleen Schoonover; [m.] Randy G. Aldrich, August 29, 1970; [ch.] Theresa Lynn (Adams), Tracie Dawn, and Angela Louise; [ed.] Kinmundy/Alma High School - College: Intro. to Business Data Processing, Accounting 101 and 102; [occ.] Housewife - Volunteer Environmentalist; [memb.] Alma Christian Church - Country Connection Country Dance, Windstar, National and International Wildlife Federation; [oth. writ.] Certificate of achievement for outstanding song from billboard music publication.; [pers.] My love for life, humankind, and the environment that surrounds me inspires me to write poetry and lyrics for country songs.; [a.] Decatus, IL

ALEXIS, LILY-MICHELE
[b.] Kapus Kasing, Ontario, Canada; [occ.] Registered Nurse Theater Arts Major, French Minor, University of Louisville; [hon.] Golden Key National Honor Society, Theta Zeta Honor Society Phi Delta Phi Chapter; [oth. writ.] Tales of the Vipissing (short stories).; [pers.] My greatest influence is the people in my daily life.; [a.] Louisville, KY

ALLBRITTON, ANNE
[b.] July 14, 1968, Prineville, OR; [p.] Karen Kellogg; [m.] Henry Allbritton, November 24, 1990; [ch.] Jordan Christian Michael Allbritton, Anthony Deveraux Dee Allbritton; [ed.] Culver High School, Culver Oregon, Central Oregon Community College, Bend Oregon; [occ.] Homemaker and Telemarketer; [hon.] Many different Honors and Awards in High School and College; [oth. writ.] Several poems written-none published.; [pers.] My ultimate goal is to write poetic greeting cards that are humerus yet touching. My writings are all from the heart.; [a.] Bend, OR

ALLBRITTON, ANNE
[b.] July 14, 1968, Prineville, OR; [p.] Karen Kellogg; [m.] Henry Allbritton, November 24, 1990; [ch.] Jordan Christian Michael Allbritton, Anthony Deveraux Dee Allbritton; [ed.] Culver High School, Culver OR, Central Oregon Community College Bend Oregon; [occ.] Homemaker and Telemarketer; [oth. writ.] Several poems written none published.; [pers.] My ultimate goal is to write poetic greeting cards that are humerus yet touching. My writings are all from the heart.; [a.] Bend, OR

ALLEN, EDDIE
[pen.] Perritt Bonner; [b.] May 28, 1949, Kilbourne, LA; [p.] Huey P. and Katie R. Allen; [m.] Deborah Wylie Allen, April 7, 1979; [ch.] Heath, Holly; [ed.] Specialist in Education (Northeast LA University - Monroe, LA), (Kilbourne High School - Kilbourne, LA); [occ.] Mathematics Teacher; [oth. writ.] About 15 non published poems.; [pers.] When I feel strongly about some idea or some event, I write what I feel.; [a.] Kilbourne, LA

ALLEN, LISA MARIE
[pen.] Lisa M. Labrecque Allen; [b.] February 24, 1964, Maine; [p.] Arthur and Constance Labrecque; [m.] Joseph Allen, July 28, 1983; [ch.] Brandon Joseph and Trever Scott; [ed.] Westbrook High, University of Southern Maine; [occ.] Mother, wife and student; [memb.] Windham Assembly of God; [pers.] Most of my poetry has been written to my mother, the greatest women I've ever known. We share a deep faith in Jesus Christ, who has blessed us both immeasurably. My mother now resides in heaven, and I am left behind to unlock all the hidden treasures in my heart, and transcribe them into words upon a whitened page.; [a.] Gorham, ME

ALLRED, TERRY MICHAEL
[b.] February 3, 1961, Aberdeen, MS; [p.] Peggy Lombardo and Jimmy Allred; [m.] Susan Allred, July 21, 1993; [ch.] Jessica and Tony Allred; [occ.] Construction; [memb.] America's Song Writers Association; [pers.] I strive to write songs and poetry from te heart as I see it threw my eyes to reach out to people with both honest and truth. Hoping that one day I might be discovered.; [a.] Smyrna, GA

ALVES, CHRISTOPHER
[ed.] Currently a Student at the University of California at Berkeley; [oth. writ.] Except for this, nothing else published as of now.; [a.] San Leandro, CA

ALVIS, DORIS JONELL
[pen.] DJA; [b.] June 9, 1946, Charlotte, NC; [p.] Joe and Betty Alvis; [ed.] West Mecklenbury High 1964, Southeastern Cosmetology School 1966, New Life Bible School, Cleveland TN, Cleveland State College 1993; [occ.] Foster Caretaker for Mentally Handicapped Adult - Ceramic Artist is Life's Work; [memb.] Revival Tabernacle Church in Stanley, NC; [hon.] Counselling Certificate in a Substance Abuse, BA from Cleveland State Community College 1993; [pers.] My poems are a result of crying out to God and being delivered through the blood of Jesus. I am born again Christian.; [a.] Cleveland, TN

AMADORI, JONATHAN PAUL
[b.] August 11, 1982, Buffalo, NY; [p.] Roger J. and Mary Jane Amadori; [ed.] Currently attending our Lady of Pompeii School, 129 Laverack Ave, Lancaster, NY 14086; [occ.] Student - 8th Grade; [memb.] Boy Scouts Troop 601, Our Lady of Pompeii Church; [hon.] Order of the Arrow Honor Society; [a.] Depew, NY

AMARAL, NEAL
[ed.] Boston College Graduate Philosophy Degree BA '91; [oth. writ.] Author, innkeeper (Pauline Press, 1996), non fiction - remembering Africa's forgotten refugees and a single pricat who takes the time to remember and remind.; [pers.] The Nevada's and the Soyinka's, they were exiles not for weapons they wielded but for one simple reason, poetry. When you can shuffle the masses with words to the point you're sought after with brass, you've achieved something very very special. That, reader, is my goal.

AMATO, RUTH A.
[pen.] Ruth A. Amato; [b.] December 28, 1941, Lorain County, OH; [p.] Howard and Genevieve (Beck) Riffee; [m.] Larry J. Amato, July 2, 1971; [ch.] One Daughter; [ed.] Harding High School-1959, Marion Business College; [occ.] Secretary at United Transportation Union; [hon.] Special religious study, no big awards nothing significant; [oth. writ.] Poems locally; [pers.] Christian - involved in church praise and worship band. I play guitar and sing. Daughter and I sing together.

AMELSBERG, TRACI
[pen.] Alexus Crane; [b.] May 10, 1976, Litchfield; [ed.] Melrose Senior High - Graduated 1994, Currently Attending St. Cloud State University; [hon.] Honor Student; [oth. writ.] Several poems, this is the first publication.; [pers.] Getting my poems published has always been my dream. Rober Frost and Kahil Gibran "The Prophet," given to me by a great friend inspire me to keep writing.; [a.] Saint Cloud, MN

AMMOND, JOY ISABELLE
[b.] January 13, 1974, West Branch, MI; [ed.] Ogemaw Heights High School, Currently: Michigan State University; [occ.] Studying for a BS in Civil and Environmental Engineering; [hon.] Chi Epsilan, Tau Beta Phi; [pers.] There is beauty and poetry in all things from crystal structures to the ever changing blue prints of the galaxies, one has only to look.

AMORATIS, JOHN
[pen.] "AMO"; [b.] March 5, 1955, Philadelphia; [p.] John and Sabina, (sadly deceased); [ch.] John Jr., Jamie Lynn, Stacy Ann (twins); [ed.] North East Catholic and Frankford High Schools; [occ.] Self Proclaimed Philosopher, Poet, Songwriter; [memb.] Prior Local Civic Member, Ambulance Corp. Volunteer, Driver with CPR by American Heart Association, Served Enlisted stint in U.S. Coast Guard, 1972-1978 as Bos'n Mate/Boat Cox'n then Honorably Discharged; [hon.] National Defense Medal, Outstanding Meritorious Unit Commendation Awards for two catastrophic maritime explosions in 1974 and 1975 on the Delaware River near Philadelphia; [oth. writ.] "God and the F.B.I." located in a prior book called Tomorrows Dream. Along with several other poems, yet to be published and of diverse and some what political themes.; [pers.] You must sometimes sail into the wind at times you must buck the tide our life it seems short - and not always sweet. I hope you enjoy your ride.... what really happened to Jim Morrison?; [a.] Bridesburg, PA

AMUSO, TERESA R.
[ed.] Ph.D in English with an Interdisciplinary Focus in Philosophy, Psychology, and English; [occ.] Associate Professor of English and Philosophy at University of Maine at Machias; [a.] Machiasport, ME

ANASTASIO, FELICIA
[pen.] Felicia Anastasio; [b.] March 13, 1980, Brooklyn, NY; [p.] Carmine J. Anastasio, Rosemary Anastasio; [ed.] Tottenville High School; [occ.] Student, Tottenville High School; [oth. writ.] Unpublished poems; [pers.] Not everything has to be understood to be beautiful.; [a.] Staten Island, NY

ANDERSEN, SUSAN D.
[pen.] Shaden Son; [b.] October 9, 1955, Lebanon, OR; [p.] Richard Egan and Judy Rentz; [ch.] Jessica (20), Derek (18), Caleb (13), Ayla (2); [ed.] High School, 20 Yr. Codependency, 24 Years Writing, Continuing in Rapid Eye Therapy and Healing Arts; [occ.] Candle and Card Maker; [memb.] Women in Crisis; [oth. writ.] Star child, man with a plan, old soul.; [pers.] As the light shines on through us all "from the moon" has been given wings, and as the spirits guide the hand and pen, and the angels heal the wounds within, "from the moon cards and candles," and custom designs is now in production for the children who will not be forgotten.; [a.] Salem, OR

ANDERSON, CANDICE ALEXIS
[b.] January 22, 1983, Indiana; [p.] Rodney and Yolanda Anderson; [ed.] Holy Cross Elementary School; [occ.] 7th Grade Student; [memb.] Community Missionary Baptist Church; [pers.] I strive to reflect things in my life in my writing. My 6th grade teacher, Pat Hubler, has greatly influenced me in writing poetry.; [a.] South Bend, IN

ANDERSON, KIMBERLY DAWN
[b.] July 15, 1970, Louisville, KY; [p.] Thomas E. and Geraldine M. Anderson; [ed.] Fern Creek High, Eastern Ky University B.A. - Art, Minor - Interior Design; [occ.] Interior Designer - Jenkins Eliason Interiors, and Visual Merchandiser - Bacons; [memb.] Kappa Alpha Theta, National (Alumni Panhellenic Scholarship Officer), Historic Preservation Society, Habitat for Humanity, St. Agnes Parish; [hon.] High School Dance Coach Honorable Mention, Principals List; [pers.] Truly believe in yourself. I always push myself to the limit, and then take one more step forward. If you believe you can, then you will succeed.; [a.] Louisville, KY

ANDERSON, RALPH HAROLD
[pen.] Ra Harold; [b.] September 5, 1942, Cleveland, OH; [p.] Harold John, Grace; [m.] Shirley Marie, August 19, 1972; [ch.] Sean, Carissa-Lynn; [ed.] Bee (Electrical) from GMI, MSEA (MBA) from Case; [occ.] Principal Engineer - Product Marketing, Harris; [memb.] SHE, SMA, EX (Sigma Chi); [hon.] Winning Entry in Loveby's "Trends in Power Transmission"; [oth. writ.] Poems: Semi finalist/entry only Local Publications 24 Technical papers, short stories: "Day of the Interrupt," "restructured," Novelette: "Damnation Corridor," anthology, "Six Roads to Somewhere."; [pers.] To observe, express and practice the inner truths (of the child) within us all, to avoid the trappings of the interface and mores that man has built (the pyramid of life) in triangular layers over time.; [a.] Getzville, NY

ANDERSON, TRACI D.
[pen.] Traci-Delores Anderson; [b.] July 28, 1971, Spring Valley, NY; [p.] Grady and Jacqueline Anderson; [ed.] MA, Columbia University, BA, Howard University; [occ.] Professor of English, College, Freelance Writing Consultant; [memb.] Kappa Delta Pi, National Council of Negro Women; [hon.] Magna Cum Laude, Howard University, Kappa Delta Pi, Teachers College, Columbia University; [oth. writ.] Poem published in Merlynspen, Nationwide student magazine.; [pers.] There's no such thing as failure - unless you stop trying. Without the patience and support of my family, I never would have realized this. Family is everything.; [a.] New York, NY

ANDOLINO, ZARINE
[b.] September 21, 1964, Munising, MI; [p.] Moshir and Carol Havewala; [m.] Joseph Andolino, February 15, 1986; [ch.] Thomas Joseph, Chaylen Jade; [ed.] Corning East High School, A.A.S. in Chemical Technology, Corning Community College; [occ.] Homemaker - Volunteer Work; [memb.] Corning - Painted Post Roman Catholic Community, Corning - Elmira Area Writers Group; [hon.] Dean's List, several Certificates in various areas; [oth. writ.] Enjoy writing children's literature.; [pers.] The most rewarding part of writing is when you realize you have touched someone else's life with your words.; [a.] Big Flats, NY

ANDREATTA, MARY RUBINO
[pen.] Mary Rubino Andreatta; [b.] April 19, 1924, Omaha, NE; [p.] Alfio and Ninfa Rubino; [m.] Alfredo Andreatta, July 10, 1949; [ch.] Steven, David, Lawrence, Dennis, Gina Marie; [memb.] International Society of Poetry - Verdiettes of Verde Club; [oth. writ.] Wrote the school song (lyrics) for Portola Jr. High School in 1948-49. Write poem for family, relatives and many dear friends on special occasions.; [pers.] I feel I have been gifted with a heart full of love for everyone and a talent for words that make expression come easily!; [a.] San Francisco, CA

ANDREWS, HOLT
[pen.] Peter; [b.] February 9, 1916, New York; [p.] Claude Andrews, Gertrude Holt; [m.] Kathryn Owens (Deceased), August 30, 1941; [ch.] Patricia A. Spade, Sally A. Achey; [ed.] B.S. Food Tech - Cornell; [occ.] Retired; [memb.] Methodist Church Inter of Food Tech.; [hon.] None of note; [oth. writ.] Lyrics to 2 songs paradise to 10 others songs. A number of poems in local publications. I have given away over 700 copies of "the poems of Peter."; [pers.] I have always had a love affair in the words. If they rhyme, I love them both and use them the most.; [a.] Palmyra, VA

ANDREWS, JACQUELINE
[pen.] Jacqueline Molena Andrews; [b.] September 6, 1948, Defuniak Springs, FL; [p.] Molena Strickland Jones (mother); [ed.] Associate of Arts - OWJC, Bachelor of Arts - University of West Florida; [occ.] Director of Environmental Services; [oth. writ.] Several other poems printed in News Letters at my employment, at Delta Health Care Centre.; [pers.] There is a little poetry in all of us - we simply must take the time to find it and put into verse. We must write what we think not sit down and think what to write. Poetry is one of the most compassionate forms of communication.; [a.] Defuniak Springs, FL

ANGELES, PAULA R.
[b.] January 11, 1973, Manila, Philippines; [p.] J. Raul Angeles, Rebecca Angeles; [ed.] Belmont HS, Los Angeles, Temple Univ., Philadelphia; [memb.] Temple University Philippine - American Council; [hon.] 1994 National Third Prize Winner: First Annual Margaret Alexander Walker Creative Writing Contest; [oth. writ.] "Metropolitan Manila" third prize winner in Margaret Alexander Walker creative writing contest (1994).; [pers.] My Filipino heritage, family and people close to me inspire me to write all that I see around me.; [a.] Philadelphia, PA

ANGESKI, DANIEL L.
[b.] August 5, 1955, Altoona, PA; [p.] M. Theresa Angeski, Joseph P. Angeski; [m.] Mary Kathryn Angeski, October 29, 1977; [ch.] Lauren Elizabeth, Michelle Kathryn; [ed.] Gateway High School, PA, Waynesburg College, PA, Central Michigan University, MI; [occ.] CAD Supervisor, Ford Motor Company; [memb.] V.O.C.A.A. Member; [hon.] Ford Corporate Suggestion Award; [pers.] I strongly believe in the words of Oliver Wendell Holmes: "What lies behind us and what lies before us are tiny matters compared to what lies within us."; [a.] Novi, MI

ANGSTEN, ELIZABETH
[b.] November 2, 1962, Bamberg, SC; [p.] Dorothy C. Tatum, Clark B. Tatum; [ch.] Christina Elizabeth and Robert Cooper Angsten; [ed.] Bamberg - Ehrhard and High School Newberry College; [occ.] Sales Rep for Cutco; [memb.] St. George Catholic Church, Alumni Alpha Xi Delta; [oth. writ.] This is my first publication.; [pers.] My children, my fiance and my family will always be my inspiration, because I write from my heart. Dr. Steen Spove, I owe for my style. He thought me everything I know about words.; [a.] Newnan, GA

ANKCORN, TAMMY LEANN WILLIAMS
[b.] February 18, 1971, Stockton, CA; [p.] Jim and Pam Williams; [m.] Timothy S. Ankcorn, July 8, 1995; [ed.] Randolph-Macon Woman's College, English Major with a Concentration in Creative Writing, Cum Laude; [occ.] Elementary Teacher, Lakeside Christian Elementary School; [hon.] Graduated Cum Laude, Dean's List; [oth. writ.] Several poems published in Hail Muse, a college literary publication.; [pers.] I enjoy writing about the beauty of nature and about God's presence in our world.; [a.] Stockton, CA

ANSWEENEY, LYNN
[pen.] Lynn Answeeney; [b.] July 21, 1977, Buffalo, NY; [p.] Yvonne Answeeney; [ch.] South Park High School, Brockport College; [occ.] Our Lady of Help

Church; [pers.] I would like the poem to be in memory of my grand mother (Patricia Answeeney).; [a.] Buffalo, NY

ANTONELLI, ROBIN A.
[b.] May 12, 1967, Providence, RI; [p.] Barbara Antonelli and Robert Antonelli; [m.] Marc A. Neve, June 9, 1996; [ed.] Cranston High; [occ.] Dental Assistant; [pers.] I write what I feel from in my heart.; [a.] Cranston, RI

ARAGON, JOHN JOSEPH
[pen.] Johnny Aragon; [b.] September 28, 1966, Suffern, NY; [p.] Oscar and Josephine; [ed.] Currently enrolled at NYACK College of NYACK, NY, majoring in Musical Performance; [occ.] Salesman (flooring), (Carpet, Floor Tiles, Area Rugs); [memb.] The kingdom of the father of our Lord Jesus Christ... Holy Spirit, pray that you hear it pray that all you know is from the all knowing; [hon.] At this time only the Athletic Presidential Award when I was 12 yrs old (1978) Pine Lake Elementary, Miami, Fla. 6th grade (77-78 school year); [oth. writ.] Many, many lyrics/poems and music. (Copyrighted) I am truly a musical poet. I play classical guitar and I am also studying the violin. I anticipate the composition of fresh, original material from within and of God's Bounty.; [pers.] I only hope to glorify our Lord and Savior Jesus Christ with the talents our Father in Heaven has generously given.; [a.] Suffern, NY

ARBO, QUENTIN RYDER
[pen.] Ken Arbo; [b.] April 18, 1925, Brownville Junction, ME; [p.] Carroll S. and Persis W. Arbo; [m.] Marquerite Hunt Arbo, December 17, 1979; [ch.] Judith and Marsha; [ed.] Mampden Academy ME, Wentworth Institute Mass., San Diego Jr. College, Extension Cal-Western University; [occ.] Business Owner; [oth. writ.] Many poems also songs 4 of which are on the market.

ARINZE, JOSH
[b.] November 14, 1962, Lafia, Nigeria; [p.] Eric Arinze, Bertha Arinze; [m.] Zainab Na'Anzem Arinze, February 16, 1991; [ch.] Onyinye Sylvia, Chekwube Olivia; [ed.] Saint Mary's High School, Ifite-Dunu, Anambra State, Nigeria, University of Lagos, Lagos, Nigeria, University of Maryland; [occ.] Journalist and Humphrey Fellow, University of Maryland; [memb.] National Press Club Washington DC, Committee to Protect Journalists, NY, Nigeria Union of Journalists; [hon.] Hubert H. Humphrey Fellowship, 1995/96; [oth. writ.] Many unpublished poems, several published short stories, articles for the Richmond times - dispatch, Richmond, VA; [pers.] My childhood was greatly influenced by the Nigeria - Biafra war (1967-70) and its aftermath. People of honor need to be ever-vigilant in the fight against hatred and bigotry - for everyone's sake.; [a.] College Park, MD

ARMELIN JR., MICHAEL
[pen.] Michael; [b.] August 7, 1978, New Iberia, LA; [p.] Carolyn Lynn Rose (mother); [ed.] Seaside High; [occ.] Student in High School; [memb.] Demolay, Jayteens, and Youth Commission; [hon.] Master Counsilor, Vice President; [oth. writ.] Two other poems were published in the local newspaper.; [pers.] I hate being the same as everyone else, I love being an outcast. My writing is influenced by E.E. cummings. I also would like to give thanks to God, my mother, and my beautiful girl friend.; [a.] Seaside, CA

ARMSTRONG, JOSEPH
[pen.] Joe Armstrong; [b.] January 17, 1931,; [m.] Dianne R. Armstrong, November 21, 1993; [ch.] Tammy Ann Lamkin and Joseph L. Armstrong Jr. - Jeffrey and Robert Uthe; [ed.] Catholic High - Donald Sonville, LA 1948; [occ.] Retired and Notary Commission - since March of 1982; [memb.] American Legion - Wife (Auxiliary Legion Aire); [hon.] Medal for Marksmanship - Carbine and 45 Pistol; [oth. writ.] About 100 poems and three songs - (all unpublished) poem for president Clinton received letter from him also story poem about ok.; [pers.] My wife says I have the talent for capturing the warmth and life of my subject matter.; [a.] Baton Rouge, LA

ARNDELL, PHYLLIS
[pen.] Candy Foster or C.A. Foster; [b.] March 22, 1962, Evansville, IN; [p.] Linda Wilhite, Harold Byers (Deceased); [m.] Tracy Lee Arndell, May 10, 1986; [ch.] Candice, Billy, Zachary; [ed.] Ged - in 1981 quit 10th 1978; [occ.] Worker at a State Mental Hospital - Pshyc Att 4; [memb.] Women's Aux. of V.F.W.; [oth. writ.] I have a collection of other writings through out the years, that have never been viewed other than myself.; [pers.] I strongly believe in "do unto others." One can beat any odds, if wanted strongly enough. Take no one, or anything for granted, it can change so suddenly always strive to do our best.; [a.] Tennyson, IN

ARNOTT, GRACIE HAY
[b.] March 11, 1924, East Tenn; [p.] Mr. and Mrs. Jess Lindsey; [m.] Samuel M. Arnott; [occ.] Retired after 30 years in a Major Elec. Corp.; [memb.] I enjoy bible course work with the Local Church of Christ, growing Flowers and doing Sentimental Art in Oils; [pers.] I found at Pittman Center much about my Scottish ancestors - one Sir David of the mount was a celebrated poet - our Lindseys settled near Boston, Mass in 1798 my father sold our land for the great smoky Mt. Nat. Park.

ARRIGALI, ANDY
[pen.] F.S.T.; [b.] September 24, 1941, Brooklyn, NY; [p.] Roger and Madilina; [ed.] G.E.D. USMC; [occ.] General Contractor; [memb.] D.A.V., Elks; [pers.] Seek the pleasures of life.; [a.] San Pedro, CA

ARVIZU, ELIZABETH
[b.] June 9, 1976, Los Angeles; [p.] Servando and Elvira Arvizu; [ed.] Sophomore, University of New Mexico; [occ.] Student (full-time); [hon.] Recipient of Regents Scholarship at the University of New Mexico; [a.] Albuquerque, NM

ASHBY, CARY
[pen.] Cary S. Ashby; [b.] November 13, 1969; [p.] Jack and Mary Charles Ashby; [ed.] Fauquier High School, James Madison University; [occ.] Tutor, Adult Learning Center, Warrenton VA, Supervisor, Uptons Department Store; [memb.] Warrenton Presbyterian Church, JMU Marching Royal Dukes and Basketball Pep Band (1988-1990); [hon.] Dean's List, Uptons Associate of the Month February 1995; [oth. writ.] "Bearing the Cross," a short story published in a Warrenton Presbyterian Church Newsletter.; [pers.] I hope my writing reflects my Christian walk of faith as well as my love for life and people.

ASHFORD, TERI
[b.] May 26, 1959, Davenport, IA; [p.] Don and Joan King; [m.] Mark Ashford; [ch.] Trevor and Jesse; [ed.] Davenport West High School, Stewarts School of Cosmetology; [occ.] Daycare Provider; [memb.] American Cancer Society, Home Child Care Association, PTA; [pers.] Writing touched me long ago - certain works gave clarity to my emotions, which in turn gave me the focus to write. I hope that my work does the same for someone else.; [a.] Davenport, IA

ASIEDU, KWASI
[pen.] Kwasi Asiedu; [b.] July 22, 1930, Ghana; [p.] Mr. and Mrs. Boatema; [m.] Mrs. Donna Asiedu, May 27, 1995; [ch.] Ten; [ed.] Graduate Student of the School of Law (USC), BA, MA, JD, Ph.D, Dr. in Criminology; [occ.] Attorney at Law Beverly Hills - PA; [memb.] Member at Cal bar Assoc. Alumni (USC); [hon.] Alpha Sigma Awards, Donations of Blood for the Needy, Member of Ehana Bar Assoc.; [oth. writ.] 1st Time; [pers.] "Nothing can be done without the help of God."; [a.] Sytmar, CA

ATKINS, DANETTE S.
[b.] July 13, 1964, Union County; [p.] Mr. and Mrs. Arnold D. Sanders; [m.] James A. Atkins, June 25, 1988; [ed.] A Graduate of Jonesville High School; [occ.] Housewife; [hon.] Award of Merit Certificate (World of Poetry), Honorable Mention December 12, 1990 (World of Poetry), Golden Poet Award 1991 (World of Poetry); [oth. writ.] Editor's choice award 1995 love is like a rose published in the coming of down 1993. Beauty is the eye published in the East of the sunrise 1995. I'm happy when published best poems 1996.; [pers.] I write poems because it is something I enjoy doing. And hope others can read what I write, and be able to get something from it.; [a.] Pacolet, SC

ATKINSON, SHANNON M.
[pen.] Ashen Lace; [b.] August 19, 1969, Cupertino, CA; [p.] Vaughn and Yvonne Marshall; [m.] Todd Atkinson, May 25, 1991; [ch.] Chantelle and Tenielle; [ed.] Monta Visa High, DeAnza College; [occ.] Housewife and Computer Programming Analyst at times; [hon.] I received the pride in Excellence Award for working on the 777 at the Boeing Company; [pers.] I have had many inspirations, but my father has been my quiet influence of writing, as my mother's influence has been drawing and classical music.; [a.] South Lake City, UT

AULT, MICHELLE
[pen.] Michelle Ault; [b.] October 2, 1972, Loma Linda, CA; [p.] David and Jeralyn Banta; [m.] Jonathan Ault, January 1, 1995; [ch.] Savannah Grace; [ed.] Loma Linda Academy, San Bernardino Valley College; [occ.] Mom, part-time Elementary School Substitute Teacher; [memb.] Vocalist for "Shepherd's Heart" worship team, and vocalist/keyboardist for "Impact" worship team at Celebration Center Church, Redlands, California; [oth. writ.] Mostly personal journals, reflective, poems, and songs.; [pers.] "Every good and perfect gift comes to us from God, the father of lights, who shines forever without change or shadow."; [a.] Loma Linda, CA

AVANT, INGER MARIA
[b.] January 20, 1965, Tallahassee, FL; [p.] George Davis Avant and Gayle Christensen Avant; [ed.] B.F.A., in Studio Art, from School of Visual Arts, at Florida State University, Godby High School; [occ.] Artist; [memb.] U.S.T.A., T.T.A., T.W.A., D.A.R., U.D.C., E.E.E., Faith Presbyterian Church; [hon.] 1st Place Nature Photography Contest 1984 Yattlahassee Jr. Museum, 2 Art Works Travel with Fl. State Fair - Youth Fine Art Exhibit many Honor Rolls/Dean's List,

Girl Scout - 1st Class, Student Athletic and Year, won Tennis Tournaments; [oth. writ.] High School chapbooks, Tallahassee democrat as a child and adult, 1st place D.A.R. essay writing contest, poetry in Penumbra 1994.; [pers.] God is great and God is good, so we better thank him for our food.; [a.] Tallahassee, FL

AVANZATO, JOHN EARL
[pen.] John Earl; [b.] August 2, 1948, Allentown, NJ; [p.] Joseph V. and Elizabeth J.; [m.] Michele K. Avanzato, April 25, 1971; [ch.] John J. and Nicholas S.; [ed.] St. Anthony High School class "67," 77 College Credits Mercer Co. Comm. College; [occ.] Police Officer Trenton Police Dept. (26 yrs.); [memb.]; [hon.]; [oth. writ.] Other poems - "not published" but available upon request.; [pers.] Poetry should reflect the mood or view of the author or his times.; [a.] Mercerville, NJ

AVRAMOR, LINDA
[pen.] Linda Kay; [b.] May 10, 1965, MI; [p.] Richard, Phyllis Kozlowski; [m.] Sam Avramor, May 17, 1991; [ed.] Andover High, Macomb College; [occ.] Interior Designer; [hon.] Equestrian Championships, Young Authors Award; [oth. writ.] Private collection of poems.; [pers.] I write from the heart hoping to express my true feelings through my words. I hope I can make someone feel or think from the words I write.; [a.] Armada, MI

AWE, AYODEJI
[pen.] Easy; [b.] July 8, 1955, Erijiyan-Ekiti, Nigeria; [p.] Rev. and Mrs. J.A. Awe; [m.] Deborah Oluseun Awe, August 1, 1992; [ch.] Tolu Tim Awe, Elizabeth Olajumoke Awe; [ed.] Christ's School, Ado-Ekiti University of Nigeria - Bsc. Estate Mgt., Obafemi Awolowo University, Ile-Efe-Msc. Est. Mgt., International Seminary, Plymouth, Fl - Th.M and Ph.D Theology; [occ.] Pastor - our Savior's Church, Houston, TX, Realtor with Federal Realty, Houston; [memb.] Member, Florida Association of Poets (Former); [hon.] Doctor of Divinity - United (Honors), Christian Bible School, Cleveland, TN; [oth. writ.] 1. A wreath for the victors, 2. Another one bites the dust, 3. Men on transit, 4. Perhaps... God will change his mind, 5. Easier for a camel, 6. Seventy songs of the fatherless (Poetry).; [pers.] "I can do all things through Christ Jesus who strengthens me."; [a.] Houston, TX

AYERS, CATHERINE
[pen.] Cathy Ayers; [b.] March 7, 1942, New York, NY; [p.] Carolyn C. and Walter J. Pringle; [m.] David C. Ayers, June 27, 1964; [ch.] Sarah Christine Ayers; [ed.] Midwood High School, Brooklyn NY (1960), State University of New York BS (1963), Un. of Wisconsin - Stout MS (1991); [occ.] Ella Lewis School, Steuben ME - Kindergarten and Chapter I; [memb.] Early Childhood Ass. (NAEYC), NAST National Ass. of Science Teachers, St. Dunstan's Episcopal Church, Acadia Choral Society; [hon.] Dean's List - Un. of Wis. - Stout; [oth. writ.] Sunrise and sunset - poems april - poem.; [pers.] I try to combine my love of words and my love of nature together for refining my experiences in Maine, Tucson or New York.; [a.] Steuben, ME

BABER, CANDI LYNN
[b.] September 3, 1980, Charlottsville; [p.] Douglas and Judy Baber; [ed.] Huvanna County High School; [oth. writ.] Depression/Suicide published in Seasons to Come, a whole new world published in the Rainbows end. Others that have not been published.; [pers.] I wrote this because I love Native American history, I guess it's because my Great Great Grandfather was a Cherokely Indian. I chose Cheyenne because I've always wanted to do some things about them, the name just kind of drew me to it. And, my uncles ex-wife's son's name is Cheyenne and last year we were really close, I miss him alot and I wrote it because of him.; [a.] Kents Store, VA

BABINS, DEBRA
[pen.] Debra Babins; [b.] December 15, 1956, Philadelphia, PA; [p.] Robert and Sarah Leukring; [m.] Harris Babins, August 27, 1982; [ch.] Summer, Blair, Phillip; [ed.] Frank Ford High McCarrie Tech; [occ.] Housewife; [oth. writ.] Beauty and her beast a twist to the story. And a snowflake. Both published in an Anthology titled Tomorrow's Dream.; [pers.] I have no philosophical statement to give, other than, to and make someone smile today. It takes hardly any effort, and it's a pleasant distraction, to another wise madding world.; [a.] Philadelphia, PA

BACON III, RAYFORD THERNELL
[pen.] Ray T.; [b.] November 16, 1986, Atlanta, GA; [p.] Dorothy E. Bacon; [occ.] 3rd Grade student at Sarah Cobb Elementary; [memb.] National Fraternity of Student Musicians; [hon.] Resa Writing Contest 1993, 1st Place, Resa Writing Contest 1994, 2nd Place, Olympic Reader Bronze and Silver Medal 1995, Honor Student of the Month 1995; [oth. writ.] Snake and Eggs Don't Mix How to Brush A Dinosaur's Teeth; [pers.] I believe in myself and my abilities.; [a.] Americus, GA

BACON, RHIANON
[b.] March 19, 1979, Indianapolis, IN; [p.] Patricia and Terry Bacon; [ed.] I currently go to school at Arlington High School, I am a Junior there also; [memb.] I am a member of my schools Letter Men's Club and I am a member of church name Greater Gethsemane Baptist Church; [hon.] I have received many awards in volleyball, cheerleading, track, band/choir and other clubs etc. (Perfect attendance); [oth. writ.] I plan to go to college and become a successful musician and teach music.; [pers.] I will hope my poem will reflect on the youth to help them realize that everyone is not trust worthy.; [a.] Indianapolis, IN

BADARACCO, KATHLEEN A.
[b.] March 16, 1956, Cleveland, OH; [p.] John and Joan Badaracco; [ch.] Kevin James and Michael Anthony; [occ.] The Plain Dealer Publishing Co.; [pers.] I strive to spread faith, hope and love to all of mankind with the words that flow from my heart...through the years I have been greatly influenced by Phillip Collins and the great love he continues to spread worldwide through his music and songs.; [a.] Cleveland, OH

BAHRE, MAUREEN M.
[b.] January 28, 1948, Hartford, CT; [p.] Herbert A. Bahre and Marjorie C. Bahre; [ch.] Jason, Tom, John; [ed.] Canton High School; [occ.] Disabled; [oth. writ.] I have over 100 poems written but no published, compiled in a book called the Roads Through Life; [pers.] I don't sit to write, I write my thoughts and feelings; [a.] Easthampton, MA

BAILEY, GENNEVIVE
[pen.] Jarrett; [b.] March 8, 1956, Kingston, Jamaica, WI; [p.] Stephana and George Jarrett; [m.] Divorced [ch.] Marcia and Donovan Bailey; [ed.] Windsor High, Durham College; [occ.] Student nursing, Teaching and cashier; [memb.] Baptist Church; [oth. writ.] Short story writings, published in the local newspaper.; [pers.] I like reading, writing short stories and poems.; [a.] Miami, FL

BAILEY, JUDITH E.
[b.] August 7, 1956, Wichita, KS; [m.] Merle W. Bailey; [occ.] Legal Secretary; [memb.] U.S. Coast Guard Auxiliary Charter Member Rock and Roll Hall of Fame and Museum; [oth. writ.] Several article published in local and regional area.; [a.] Wichita, KS

BAKER, LYNDA
[b.] September 5, Flint, MI; [p.] Robert and Mary Commons; [m.] Reginald L. Baker, February 10, 1990; [ch.] Combination of five children.; [ed.] Northwestern High, C.S. Mott College, Bakers College Undergrad; [occ.] GM - Flint Assembly Plant, truck and bus; [hon.] Dean's list; [oth. writ.] Honorable mention for poem "New Beginnings"; [pers.] "Showing is better than telling if you want to be believed." I am inspired by Maya Angelo, poet.; [a.] Flint, MI

BAKERSKY, SEAN PATRICK
[b.] February 21, 1983, Aurora, CO; [p.] Sherry and Peter Bakersky; [ed.] Currently a 7th grade student at Aurora Hills Middle School; [memb.] Boy Scouts of America, Aurora Youth League (Sports); [pers.] Poetry comes from the heart. You don't have to be old to write good poetry.; [a.] Aurora, CO

BANEY, TARA S.
[b.] February 11, 1972, Ephrata, PA; [m.] Charles E. Baney, October 8, 1994; [ed.] Cocalico Senior High, Cedar Crest College; [hon.] American Chemical Society Award, Dean's List; [a.] Reading, PA

BANFE, JUNE F.
[pen.] June F. Banfe; [b.] Ansonia, CT; [p.] Ambrose and Vicenza Banfe; [ed.] Southern Ct. State University, New Haven, University of Hartford, Saint Joseph College, West Hartford, Santa Clara University, California; [occ.] 5th grade teacher Doolittle Elementary School - Cheshire, Ct; [memb.] E.A.C., C.E.A, N.E.A., Education Assoc., Teachers Assoc. - Delta Kappa Gamma - National Science Teacher's Assoc. - Cheshire Kiwanis Club; [hon.] Dean's List College, Past President Kiwanis Club of Cheshire (1992-1993). Delegate and Elections Committee Member at Kiwanis International Convention, Nice, France - June, 1993; [oth. writ.] Numerous poems. The Wedding Gift - Reflections Of Light.; [pers.] Poetry is the written reflection of the true emotions of the heart! I have been greatly influenced by the poets and writers of the Romantic Period in American Literature.; [a.] Cheshire, CT

BANKSTON, LUEWANA J.
[pen.] Luewana Shah; [b.] June 24, 1961, Dayton, OH; [p.] William and Virginia A. Shaw; [m.] Daniel Bankston, December 31, 1980; [ch.] Aviance, Teia, Tristan; [ed.] G.E.D. LeCordon Bleu, Sullivan College; [occ.] Chef; [memb.] Volunteers of America; [oth. writ.] By lines on several local Newsletters, a volume of complete works, submitted to several different publishing houses.; [pers.] From every negative, a positive can be extracted, I believe, that believing, is worth believing in. Therefore, I believe that mankind is on a great quest, striving... understand, accept, looking for that universal 'something' that makes one feel worthy, valued, and unconditionally... loved I believe we will find all that we seek, once we look inside ourselves.; [a.] Huber Heights, OH

BANTEGUI, MIRAL C.
[pen.] Fatima Bantegui; [b.] July 13, 1937, Sta. Cruz Manila, Philippines; [p.] Anastacio T. Caedo, Florencia B. Caedo; [m.] Rafael J. Bantegui, June 19, 1969; [ch.] Abraham, Benjamin, Melissa and James; [ed.] B.S. H.E.; [occ.] Wildwood Inn Housekeeper; [memb.] National Geographic Society, Arbor Day Club, World Wildlife Fund, Columbia Music Club, Book Clubs, Fatima Crusader, Herbal Academy Inc., I.T., Flower of the Month Club; [hon.] Certificate of Merit (Talent and Associated Companies), "Honorable" and "Editor's Choice" received for my published poems; [oth. writ.] Various poems published by Quill Books and Song poems records by Hilltop Records; [pers.] I have always endeavored to bring across messages of what is still true and good and beautiful... just so to rekindle in man's heart a tiny glow of love.; [a.] Florence, KY

BARANSKI, DAWN
[b.] January 19, 1964, Port Huron, MI; [p.] Larry Sylvester; [ch.] Sarah Ashley Anne; [ed.] High School; [occ.] Waitress; [hon.] Being chosen as a semi-finalist in your poetry contest! Just having my work published is an honor! It's the first time I've ever entered one of my works.; [oth. writ.] Only my personal book of poems, which I've titled "Songs of the Soul."; [pers.] All of my writing has come from my heart, based upon experiences i have had during my life. This is all so new and exciting to me. I am truly honored by your acceptance.; [a.] Fort Gratiot, MI

BARCHALK, JEANI
[b.] August 27, 1971, Amherst, OH; [p.] Robert and Joanne Davenport; [m.] William Barchalk, September 5, 1992; [ch.] Nathan and Shannon; [ed.] Will receive Bachelor's degree of Business from Kent State University in Spring of 1997; [occ.] Payroll Clerk, OEM/ Miller Corp; [hon.] Muskingum Alumni Scholarship; [oth. writ.] Articles for college newspapers and company newsletter; [pers.] I choose subjects to write about that are close to my heart, which allows me to put emotion in my words. My goal is to arouse thoughts and feelings in my reader. I want them to be able to relate to my writing.; [a.] Akron, OH

BARCLAY, ELMA
[b.] December 27, 1928, Silverton, OR; [p.] Elmer White, Margaret White; [m.] Leo Barclay (Deceased), August 15, 1947; [ch.] Leona Jean, Nancy Faye, William Steven; [ed.] Waldport High School; [occ.] Retired; [memb.] AARP, NARFE, Dallas Area Seniors, Past President - VFW Auxiliary; [hon.] American Legion Scholarship Award; [oth. writ.] Poems published in local newspaper, Editor, Senior Newsletter; [pers.] Make an effort to enrich your life, and if you are lucky enough to have good fortune, share it with others. This brings true happiness.; [a.] Dallas, OR

BARKS, MICHELE MARIE
[b.] May 22, 1965, Pontiac, MI; [p.] Ken and Jeanette Barks; [ed.] Clarkston High School; [occ.] Paint Operating Technician for the Saturn/GM Car Company in Spring Hill Tennessee; [pers.] "The real beauty of a poem is seen by the writer. And like a photograph, the beauty is shared by its viewers." Early influences by Edgar A. Guest

BARNES, BECKY
[b.] February 4, 1983, Point Pleasant, NJ; [p.] Catherine and David Barnes; [ed.] A student in 7th Grade at Northern Burlington Regional Junior High School, Columbus, NJ; [pers.] This is my first published poem, but I have been writing "all my life".

BARNES, KENDRICK LAKEITH
[pen.] Ken Barnes; [b.] July 17, 1970, Detroit, MI; [p.] LaVerne Daniel, Lunnie Barnes; [ed.] B.S. in Managerial Economics and Political Science from the University of California at Davis; [pers.] Writing is a collection of one's thoughts put on paper. Thank you Arrow, Thank you for all of your love and support.; [a.] Davis, CA

BARNES, LANA LEE
[b.] December 3, 1950, Indianapolis, IN; [p.] Henry C. and Ida A. McCarty; [m.] Joseph, August 31, 1975; [ed.] Graduate of Thomas Carr Howe High School; [occ.] Office Manager at NCH Corp; [oth. writ.] Published author of a book entitled "Fluffy," a cat biography. Published poem in "The American Poetry Anthology," America poetry Association.; [pers.] Writing poetry is my channel for self expression. When inspiration strikes, I take pen to paper.; [a.] Greenfield, IN

BARNES, SANDRA TURNER
[pen.] "Cadillac Lady"; [b.] July 11, 1947, Camden, NJ; [m.] Robert "Bootsie Barnes, Jazz Musician, August 31, 1991; [ch.] Richelle, Renelle, Grandson Reggie; [ed.] B.S. Communications Management - 1989, Peirce College, Phila., PA., 3.85 GPA, Poet-in-Residence - Serengetti Jazz Cafe; [occ.] Performance Poet, Lyricist, Free-Lance Writer, Business Administrator; [memb.] African-American Women's Network, New Jersey Women's Summit, President/Founder - Ebonette Productions Unlimited - Non-Profit Organization Formulated for the purpose of uplifting women and the arts, International Toastmistresses, Inc.; [hon.] 1995 Ebony Magazine Literary Competition - Honorable Mention, 1994 Recipient - George Washington - Carver Humanitarian Award, 1994 - Featured Writer, African American Collection of Temple University, featured poet Walt Whitman Poetry Centre; [oth. writ.] 1st Book of Poetry - "Always a Lady" originally Pub. 1986 - 3rd printing March of 1995, "Cadillac Lady" signature poem, Published in various magazines and anthologies, along with various other poems published short stores - "Burnt Bacon" "Last Out"; [pers.] Sandra Turner-Barnes vividly writes, and speaks of life and love, from the heart, and with the voice, of a "Jazzy" Black Women, as a performance poet, with live jazz, she has the opportunity to bring her poems directly to her audience.; [a.] Palmyra, NJ

BARNES, TONY D.
[b.] April 29, 1962, Fort Worth, TX; [p.] Gordon and Annette Barnes; [m.] Kary K. Barnes, April 23, 1982; [ch.] Robison D. and Scott N.; [ed.] Associates in Applied Science in Disaster Preparedness through the Community College of the Air Force; [occ.] Air Force Instructor, Assistant News Director WDNG Radio; [memb.] Christian Military Fellowship Air Force Association, Air Force Sergeants Association; [hon.] 1992 Disaster Preparedness Non-Commissioned Officer of the year for US Air Forces in Europe, Three USAF Commendation Medals; [oth. writ.] For Garland Publishing World War II Encyclopedia, "Book Burning", "Paris Air Agreement of 1927", "Donald Bennett"; [pers.] I have discovered that without a personal relationship with Jesus Christ, peace and fulfillment can never be truly achieved.; [a.] Anniston, AL

BARR, DISEREE D.
[pen.] Diseree Barr; [b.] May 21, 1970, Jefferson County, Birmingham, AL; [p.] Mrs. Peggy Ferrell and Mr. Curtis Ferrell; [m.] Mr. Charles Blake Barr, September 26, 1990; [ch.] Emily D., Brittany., Thomas B.; [ed.] Pinson Valley High School, Winonah, Int'l School of Cosmetology; [occ.] Housewife; [oth. writ.] None published.; [pers.] Writing comes from the soul. Go inside yourself to know the warmth of your own soul.; [a.] Birmingham, AL

BARRINGER, JEAN H.
[pen.] Jean H. Barringer; [b.] February 20, 1919, Akron, OH; [p.] C. Raymond, Pearle Schmidt; [m.] N. N. Hemenway, June 27, 1938 and Gene Barringer, November 29, 1983; [ch.] Three by first husband.; [ed.] High school-4 years, graduate Pract. nurse -LPN 1961- course in nor PCC rhyme poetry-general-credit; [occ.] Retired LPN-27 years in local Saint Josephs hospital; [memb.] Post-Brownie Leader, Cub Scout Leader-Band Mother PTA Sun School Teacher presently - Church Organizations-PTA. Foste grand parent program; [hon.] Service award for 27 years working out Saint Josephs, 3 years Foster Grandparent Award-Band Booster. My greatest award seeing my children grown and successful ed in no great trouble.; [oth. writ.] Stories-poems, for class work-for my own satisfaction-or grand children-never to be published.; [pers.] I have yet to meet any one I can't see good in-I enjoy life, I love people, especially the someones I have under my care in the Parkersburgh Day nursery five A.M's a week as a foster grandparent.; [a.] Parkersburgh, WV

BARTON, GINA M.
[b.] August 16, 1974, Illinois; [p.] Jerome and Patricia Barton; [ed.] Graduated from North Gwinnett High School in Georgia. Attends Gwinnett Tech. College in Georgia; [hon.] Received Award from Best Creative Writing; [oth. writ.] Has written over sixty poems since her freshman year in high school. Struggle and victory is her first to be published.; [pers.] "The heart is stronger than the mind. To it, please listen, and happiness you shall find."; [a.] Suwanee, GA

BARTON, KYMBERLY
[b.] July 3, 1960, Canton, OH; [p.] Gerald P. Barton, Kathleen E. Hendrix; [ch.] Tara Janel Zernechel; [ed.] McKinley Senior High; [occ.] Housewife, Mother; [oth. writ.] Several other poems and short children's stories; [pers.] All my writings are from my own life experiences they reflect different times and ways I've felt at any given time.; [a.] Canton, OH

BASTRESS, JOAN M.
[b.] April 22, 1934, Baltimore, MD; [p.] Arthur M. and Frances S. Bastress; [ed.] Institute of Notre Dame, Marywood College, Saint Bonaventure's University, M.A. in Theology; [occ.] Pastoral Associates at St. Jerome's Church, Balto.; [memb.] Pastoral Associates Association, Member of Immaculate Heart Sisters, Scranton, PA, Baltimore Assoc. of Catechetical Directors; [hon.] Delta Epsilon Sigma, Czachor Medal for Distinction in Religious studies; [oth. writ.] Magazine Article in Religion Teacher Journal; [pers.] Reflecting on daily events and their meaning, cultivates wisdom and depth of character.; [a.] Baltimore, MD

BATARY, GREGG
[pen.] Steven Wilson; [b.] May 9, 1961, Brooklyn, NY; [p.] Ted and Lorraine Batary; [m.] Suzanne Batary, May 1, 1988; [ed.] B.S. Petroleum, Engineering from

Oklahoma State University; [occ.] Systems Engineer; [memb.] Society of Petroleum Engineers, OSU Alumni; [hon.] Deans List Four Semesters, Scholarship from Sohio Oil Company; [oth. writ.] 1 children's book, various articles for the local newspaper, and technical writing assignments for my company; [pers.] My writings will always be grammatically correct.; [a.] East Berlin, PA

BATES, DOLORES W.
[b.] July 29, 1961, Farmville, VA; [p.] Herbert L. Warner Sr. and Betty M. Dake; [m.] Kenneth S. Bates, July 1, 1980; [ch.] Casey W. and Timothy S.; [ed.] Amelia Co. High School; [occ.] Office Service Specialist, VA Dept of Health, Amelia, VA; [pers.] I try to see the "up" side of situations; [a.] Amelia, VA

BAUMLEIN, MICHAEL P.
[b.] February 22, 1967, Findlay, OH; [p.] Sheila H. and Robert J.; [m.] Melissa M.; [ch.] Jerrica, Chris, Casandra; [ed.] Riverdale Schools; [occ.] Asst. Parts Mgr. Findlay, International; [oth. writ.] Several poems, memorials Christian themes; [pers.] The inner piece knowing that God is, has been, and always will be in charge; [a.] Findlay, OH

BAXTER, MICHAEL
[b.] May 5, 1978, Amarillo, TX; [p.] Kenneth and Cynthia Baxter; [ed.] Senior Vernon High School; [occ.] Student; [memb.] VHS Choir; [hon.] Honorable mention in Midwestern state poetry contest, finalist in the National Library of Poetry contest; [pers.] My writings are a release for my emotions. Most are dark and morbid, but that is what comes out. Let the poems speak to you. Whatever it says to you is what it means. Don't let anyone tell you you're wrong.; [a.] Vernon, TX

BAZAN, MARCO
[b.] April 25, 1976, Mission, TX; [p.] Rosemarie Avalos, Leonel Bazan; [occ.] Student; [oth. writ.] Several poems for family members and friends.; [pers.] I am inspired by my inner feelings and my experiences in life.; [a.] Lodi, CA

BEACH, ALISON MANN
[b.] September 20, 1972, Bluefield, WV; [p.] Lewis Mann and Cherry Belchor Mann; [m.] Mark Gordon Beach, September 11, 1992; [ed.] Currently a Psychology Major at Mary Baldwin College, planning to attend graduate school at the University of Virginia; [occ.] Optical Assistant; [memb.] Volunteer instructor for the American Red Cross Roanoke Valley Chapter, First Baptist Church of Roanoke, VA; [hon.] Academic Art Award 1985, 1987, Barbizon Modeling School Look Book Award 1985; [pers.] I desire my inspiration for living and writing from nature, including the rich tapestry that is our human race.; [a.] Roanoke, VA

BEAUCHAMP, KARA
[pen.] Kara Beauchamp; [b.] December 30, 1980, Mount Pleasant, IA; [p.] Ann Noel, Hal Beauchamp; [ed.] Mt. Pleasant Junior and Senior High; [memb.] Mt. Pleasant Methodist Church; [hon.] I attended the Iowa writers conference for short stories; [oth. writ.] 9 additional poem entitled - Angel, Golden Guy, Steven, What he thinks, True Love, Away, Love, It's so Hard, and If Pigs Could Fly; [pers.] I enjoy writing so much I someday hope to make a career of it. I am influenced by the works of many early poets.; [a.] Mount Pleasant, IA

BECKWITH, VIRGINIA
[b.] June 13, 1934, Trilby, OH; [p.] Ruth Smith and Leroy Beckwith; [ed.] Finished 8th grade; [memb.] Kiwanis Club, President of Resident Council; [hon.] Kiwanis Club Award for Letter Writing (16 years), Volunteer Certificate at Nursing Home, Certificate of Completion of Therapy; [oth. writ.] Has written poetry for several years.; [pers.] thank you for looking at my work. I appreciate it very much!; [a.] Toledo, OH

BEDGOOD, ROBERT DEE
[b.] July 29, 1982, Fremont, CA; [p.] Calvin and Debra Bedgood; [ed.] Hopkins Jr. High Weibel Elementary; [occ.] Student, enjoy soccer, youth group singing just being a teenager; [pers.] I'm a Christian and in my works I try to influence others to become Christians; [a.] Fremont, CA

BEDGOOD, TERRI
[pen.] Terri Lynn; [b.] June 1, 1970, South Carolina; [p.] James Bedgood, Kay Bedgood; [occ.] Creating a ranch, where the young and old grow together.; [pers.] My greatest aspiration in life is too spend everyday of my life learning to grow.; [a.] Boulder, CO

BEEBE, KAMILLE KAE
[b.] October 6, 1968, Pocatello, ID; [p.] Melvin and Barbara Beebe; [ed.] Hillsboro High School, Ricks Jr. College, Portland Community College; [occ.] Administrative Assistant, Sales - Coffee Bean International; [oth. writ.] Other poem published in "Echoes from the Silence"; [pers.] "What Lies behind us and what lies ahead is nothing compared to what lies within" - a quote I live by every day of my life. This poem is dedicated to the one who urged me to share my work - Darrin.; [a.] Portland, OR

BEEKMAN, FRANK
[b.] August 22, 1979, Tiffin, OH; [p.] Flora Sellers, Ben Beekman; [ed.] Tiff in Columbian High School; [occ.] Wendys Old Fashioned Hamburgers; [pers.] When some people are down and sad, they need an escape. And that's why I write poems. It's the best way for me to say how I feel and what's on my mind at the time.; [a.] Tiffin, OH

BEELER, DANIEL C.
[pen.] Daniel C. Beeler; [b.] July 2, 1958, Oyster Bay, NY; [p.] Carl and Kathyrn Beeler; [m.] Sharon Marie, January 7, 1989; [ch.] Kara Nichole; [ed.] Devry Institute of Technology; [occ.] Engineer; [memb.] Society of MFG Engrs.; [oth. writ.] Short Stories, other poetry; [a.] Coatesville, PA

BEELER, DONALD
[b.] March 6, 1927, Wyoming; [p.] Virginia, Clarence Beeler; [m.] Pat, April 1955; [ch.] Ginger, Jack, Sharon, Don, Mike; [occ.] Custodian; [oth. writ.] Church - Prayer; [pers.] Pat has been my inspiration in all my writings, and I will lover her till the day I die and one day more into eternity; [a.] Apple Valley, CA

BEGAY, NATALIE R.
[b.] September 18, 1963, Shiprock, NM; [p.] Nettie and Nelson Begay; [ed.] Rehoboth H.S., NM. State, San Juan College, Phoenix Community; [occ.] Clerical; [memb.] Holy Ghost Filled Baptist Church of Miracles, Inc.; [hon.] Merit Award for another poem; [oth. writ.] Each day published in: Great poems of the Western World Vol. II; [pers.] In my writings I try to let people know life is beautiful.; [a.] Shiprock, NM

BELL, COLLEEN
[pen.] Madeleine Selene; [b.] June 17, 1982, Quebec City; [p.] Steve and Jane; [ed.] Still in high school; [occ.] Student; [memb.] USA Hockey, Centre for Talented Youth of Johns Hopkins University; [hon.] Wooning worth mentioning; [oth. writ.] Some other unpublished work.; [pers.] There's nothing you can do, but you can learn to play the game John Lennon. "All you need is love" the Beatles.; [a.] Akron, OH

BELL, KEVIN ROBERT
[b.] June 22, 1959, Witcata Falls, TX; [p.] Roland and Lavand Bell; [ch.] Jennifer Lynn Bell, Justin Robert Bell; [ed.] Littlefield High, Texas State Technical Institute, South Plains College; [occ.] Letter Carrier, Midwest, Sta. Lubbock, Texas; [memb.] NALC, BSA; [hon.] Eaglescout, Brotherhood Of O.A.; [oth. writ.] An unpublished book of poems dedicating my life to God.; [pers.] My writing is influenced by Robert Frost, and Edgar Allen Poe. Many times I try to exault God or give an uplifting message to drug addicts and alcoholics.; [a.] Lubbock, TX

BELL, PATRICIA
[b.] July 18, 1951, Mount Pleasant, PA; [p.] Rex and Molly Christner; [m.] Eric Joel Bell, December 7, 1985; [ch.] Rachael Kathryn, David K. Monsour; [ed.] Secondary Ed - English, Gordon College, Wenham, Mass; [occ.] English Teacher, Karns City High School, Karns City, PA; [memb.] '95 Fellow Western PA, Writing Project at University of Pittsburgh, Past-President Butler Co. Chamber of Commerce; [oth. writ.] Many Writings, no other published (of course none have ever been submitted!); [pers.] We write and write and write and from the chaos comes a jewel-word, a pearl-statement and that is where the story is. Teaching and hearing through discovery.; [a.] Butler, PA

BELTRAN, GLORIA C.
[pen.] Glo; [b.] December 29, 1961, New York City, NY; [p.] Inocencia Beltran; [ch.] Natasha - 9, Matthew - 5, Veronica - 4; [ed.] A.S. in Broadcast Communication working on B.S currently; [occ.] Receptionist for Medical Health Plan; [pers.] Ever since I can remember, I took a liking to writing at a very young age. As years passed by I put it to the side never knowing when I would pick it up again. Well, my time has come, stronger and positively.; [a.] Portland, CT

BENDER, MICHAEL
[b.] August 22, 1960, Baltimore, MD; [p.] George and Jean; [m.] Tina, May 26, 1984; [ch.] Michael Scott, Jordan Alexander,; [ed.] MS - Loyola, BS - Johns Hopkins; [occ.] Electronics Engineer; [pers.] Thanks to God, my family and my friends for their support, encouragement and inspiration for my writing.; [a.] Sykesville, MD

BENEDICT, MARILYN
[b.] August 18, 1956, Oak Park, IL; [p.] John R. Brown, Catharine C. Brown; [ch.] Jason Brown, Melinda Lorente, Cherie Henderson, John Courtney; [ed.] BFA Arizona State University; [occ.] Senior Graphic Designer, Arizona State University; [pers.] Everything to this end: Life, beauty, love and truth; [a.] Gilbert, AZ

BENNETT, BARBARA
[p.] Raymond Bennett; [ch.] 3 year old, Ian Wesley; [ed.] Bachelor of Science in Early Childhood Education; [occ.] Beginning Writer and "Stay-at-Home Mom"; [oth. writ.] Currently working on my first novel en-

titled, "Endangered Species"; [pers.] My writing reflects my deep appreciation of nature.; [a.] Stockbridge, GA

BENNETT, CHRISTOPHER
[pen.] C. S. Bennett; [b.] August 2, 1967, Flint, MI; [p.] O. Roy and Beverly Bennett; [ed.] Romeo High School; [pers.] A day where you have learned nothing is a day you have wasted.; [a.] Washington, MI

BENNETT, DANETTE G.
[b.] September 25, 1958, Barberton, OH; [p.] Dannie and Dorothy Dickerson; [m.] Bruce A. Bennett, October 8, 1983; [ch.] William, Angela, Benjamin; [ed.] Manchester High School, W. Howard Nicol School of Practical Nursing; [pers.] This poem was written in memory of someone whom I loved very much and who will live in my heart forever. My brother, Eric, Scott Dickerson; [a.] Clinton, OH

BENNETT, SARAH ALEXANDRA
[b.] September 5, 1983, Fargo, ND; [p.] John and Mavis Bennett; [occ.] Student of Agassiz Middle School - 6th grade; [hon.] First place in Fifth grade at Cass County Spelling Bee; [oth. writ.] I have a poem published in a greeting card made by a local art studio; [pers.] With a few strokes of a pen, I can change a mind's outlook on life forever. I can explore big places. I can climb big mountains. I can make big dreams come true.; [a.] Fargo, ND

BENNETT, SCOTT MICHAEL
[b.] February 5, 1978, Denver; [p.] Bruce Bennett, Kathy Bennett; [ed.] Mountain Pointe High School; [occ.] Student; [memb.] National Honor Society; [hon.] National Merit Scholar; [oth. writ.] Poems for school paper, Literary Magazine.; [pers.] In our lust for money and success, we have forgotten that compassion is the highest virtue. I only want to serve as a reminder that humanity has a higher purpose.; [a.] Phoenix, AZ

BENNETT, VELMA J.
[pen.] Joyce Williams; [b.] March 25, 1941, Chicago, IL; [p.] Belle and Floyd Bennett; [m.] Divorced; [ed.] Bachelor's - Western Michigan Univ., Kalamazoo, Michigan, Master's - Loyola University of Chicago, Chicago, Illinois; [occ.] Writer; [hon.] Gold Key Art Award, Quill, and Scroll Award, National Honor Society, Dean's List; [oth. writ.] Book published, Everybody's Poetry, Vol. I; [pers.] My focus is to make the literature I write understandable to all who read, because much is lost when it is not. And, as I revise and revise my work, toward this end, I define, refine, and hone myself and my skills.; [a.] Allegan, MI

BERENDS, ADELAIDE SCHOTT
[pen.] Adelaide Berends; [b.] December 25, 1926, Overlea, MD; [p.] Charles J. Schott and Emma Kahl; [m.] Raymond E. Berends I, November, 1945; [ch.] Cheryl R. Deborah A., Raymond II; [ed.] Elementary 7 years; [occ.] Dietary Aide, Franklin Squares Hospital Center; [memb.] A.A.R.P - N.C.P.S.S.M.; [hon.] Awards from Franklin Square Hospital for a poem used in a Fund Raising Mailing; [oth. Writ.] Waterfall, My Endless Day, Winter, etc.; [pers.] I was inspired by the love of my family and friends and the beauty of nature.; [a.] Baltimore, MD

BERGLUND, JOHNATHAN E.
[b.] May 5, 1970, Devils Lake, ND; [p.] Erland and Aileen Berglund; [ed.] Sheyenne High, University of North Dakota - Lake Region; [occ.] Farmer and Rancher; [memb.] Grace Lutheran Church, Agricultural Advisory Committee, Farm Bureau of Eddy Co., Farmers Union; [hon.] 4-H 10 yr. Achievement, Dean's List; [pers.] My poetry is based on my thoughts and emotions.; [a.] Sheyenne, ND

BERNER, MARIANA
[b.] May 26, 1942, Argentina; [p.] Dora Schenkelman and Raul Berner; [ch.] Alexander, Daniela; [ed.] English teacher - working towards Social Work Degree at Northeastern University and hoping to also became a C.A.D.C. Counselor on alcohol substance abuse; [occ.] Student; [oth. writ.] Several poems never published before.; [pers.] Reverence honor each and every living things... embrace the intrinsic gift of humanity... you'll experience the Divine, give of yourself joyfully... you'll celebrate abundance, join with compassion in the inevitable awe of the dying... you'll find ETERNITY.; [a.] Niles, IL

BERNTSEN, THOMAS
[b.] August 6, 1965, Rockville Centre, NY; [p.] Joanne and Reginald Berntsen; [ed.] B.A. Utica College of Syracuse University '88 (Mathematics), M.S. Indiana University '91, and currently working on doctorate at the University of Massachusetts; [occ.] Math and Physics High School Teacher; [oth. writ.] Article, "Let it Snow, Let it Snow", in the Physics Teacher Nov. 95), other poems "America, the Great Pine", "Come with me to a Distant Star, a Distant Land", "A passage of Time" and "Pineconia"; [pers.] Dreams become reality through hard work, keeping the faith, and staying the course.; [a.] Brattleboro, VT

BETHEL, KIFFANY RENEE
[b.] May 22, Germany; [p.] John and Betty Bethel; [ed.] 10th Grade Georgiana High School; [occ.] Currently searching for a job; [memb.] FBLA, Deliverance Temple Church, Junior National Honor Society, Math Team, Georgiana Marching Band and Symphonic Band; [hon.] National Honor Roll, Who's Who among American Student, Algebra Competition Honorable Mention; [oth. writ.] Several unpublished poems and short stories.; [pers.] I'd like to thank my Mom and Sisters Tinecha and Tuwanna for their support. Also my Aunt Patricia Simms for her encouragement. They're one reason I think that the best people to have in your corner are your family members.; [a.] Georgiana, AL

BEVAN, JAN
[pen.] Jan Atchley Bevan; [b.] January 19, 1947, Jacksonville, FL; [ed.] Earned a B.S. degree in Psychology from Berry College Rome, Georgia 1972. Also earned a Masters Degree and Pastoral studies from Loyola University, New Orleans, L.A. 1992; [occ.] Freelance Writer; [memb.] Florida Freelance Writers Association, on the reading Staff of Kalliope a journal of Women's Art. Published by Florida Community College, Jacksonville, FL.; [oth. writ.] Completed 2 children's books. Published an article in Florida Lions Club Magazine; [pers.] Literature should be the flame that sparks the moral good for mankind.; [a.] Jacksonville, FL

BIDWELL, SUSAN D.
[b.] May 25, 1949, Watertown, WI; [p.] Robert Bidwell, Audrey Bidwell; [m.] Divorced; [ch.] Jesse Schworck - 15; [ed.] Madison West High School, U.W. - Madison, Madison Area Technical College; [occ.] Legal Secretary; [memb.] United Amateur Press MATC Alumnae; [hon.] Fossils Award for Outstanding Service as Editor of United Amateur for UAP, Laureat Awards for publishing Suzy's Journal Editing United Amateur Art Award for UAP, Dean's list MATC; [oth. writ.] Former editor of United Amateur Press, publisher of Suzy's Journal Newsletter for United Amateur Press.; [pers.] I am currently working on two children's book and a chapbook of my poetry.; [a.] Madison, WI

BILLIRIS, CHAD ANDREW
[b.] July 7, 1981, Cape May Court House, NJ; [p.] Marilyn and David Mattera, Charles Billiris; [ed.] At present a Freshman at Middle Township High School Cape May Court House, NJ; [occ.] School student; [memb.] Middle Township, Football and Basketball Teams; [hon.] North Wildwood Art, Exhibit, Third Place, Second Place, various Football and Basketball and Honor Roll; [oth. writ.] First writing, but several art works displayed at Art Shows and art contest.; [pers.] Special thanks to Mrs. Ross who first took interest in my poem and to Aunt Teen who took the time to expose my poem.; [a.] Goshen, NJ

BILOW, TSHA M.
[b.] June 25, 1973; [ed.] SUNY Brockport - Marketing, Communications and Economics; [pers.] I believe that feelings often distinguish one person from another, yet they also form a common bond among us. The emotions we experience are often the most exciting part of life.

BIRD, BOB
[b.] February 14, 1951, Roswell, NM; [p.] Russell and Jerry Bird; [m.] Claudia Sturdevant Bird, August 4, 1985; [ch.] James, Kaitlin, and Shawn Marie; [ed.] High School Diploma, 1969 - from Goddard High, Roswell, NM, B.S. degree in Range Management, 1973, New Mexico State University; [occ.] Part-time Rancher, Cowboy Poet, and full time Gas and Oil Production Specialist; [hon.] Featured poet in Elko Cowboy Poetry Gathering, New Mexico Cowboy Poetry Gathering, Wyoming Cowboy Poetry Gathering, Lincoln County Cowboy Symposium, and many others in Western US and in Canada; [oth. writ.] Poems published in American Cowboy Poets Magazine, Dry Crik Review, Cowboy Magazine and numerous local publications; [pers.] Coming from a third generation ranching family in Lincoln County, New Mexico, my poetry is a method of preserving family stories handed down, and the heritage of the American cowboy.; [a.] Lindrith, NM

BITTNER, ROSEMARY BERNADETTE
[pen.] Rose King; [b.] January 28, 1961, Philadelphia, PA; [p.] Arthur King and Mary Louise King; [m.] William Joseph Bittner, August 21, 1982; [ch.] Courtney Michelle and William Joseph Bittner; [ed.] Upper Darby Senior High School, DCCC - Delaware, County Community College; [occ.] Student, homemaker; [memb.] American Legion Post 204; [hon.] Avon honor society computer-micro-soft word and windows "95" certificate - DCCC new choices certificate; [oth. writ.] Several poems, journals personal greeting cards to family and friends.; [pers.] I love to write poems - romantic, and also what is going on in the word - when things pop in my head, I keep writing and writing, I have a very creative mind.; [a.] Drexel Hill, PA

BLACK, CAROLINE
[b.] December 16, 1912, Hungary; [p.] John and Elizabeth Sack; [m.] Edward (Deceased), April 21, 1932; [ch.] James, Thomas, Suzanne, Karen; [ed.] 10 yrs., 10th grade; [occ.] Housewife; [memb.] Calvary Baptist

Church Missionary Lights; [hon.] 1. Walking Bible Club, 2. "Official Certificate of Registration" - The American Immigrant Wall of Honor Ellis Island, NY, 3. Mother of the Year '93, The News - a weekly publication; [oth. writ.] My Little Kitchen March, Wen Ma Drove The Model T (Short Story); [pers.] I write about the simple things of life that I love and the wonders of God.; [a.] Monaca, PA

BLACKBURN, PAULETTE
[b.] April 22, 1948, Hartford, CO; [p.] Raymond and Julie Bonczek; [m.] Thomas Blackburn, June 7, 1969; [ch.] Tylee Robert, Benjamin Ames; [ed.] Henry James Memorial H.S., Simsbury, Ct., Chandler School for Women, Boston, Mass.; [occ.] Sales Associate for CFH Associates; [pers.] Poetry brings me great joy, and allows me to express myself and my feelings.; [a.] Mechanic Falls, ME

BLACKWOOD, SHARON WEIGHALL
[pen.] Sherry; [b.] October 29, 1939, Twinfalls, ID; [p.] Orville Weighall Roberta Arment; [m.] Arthur E. Blackwood, August 20, 1979; [ch.] Rick, Tina, Laura, Randy, Mike, Sharon; [ed.] High School - some college, Hansen, ID Houston Community College; [occ.] Housewife former payroll Acct. for Gulf Oil Co.; [oth. writ.] Several poems never published. But I am the proud mother of 3 boys and 3 girls and grandmother of 19 and great grandmother of 1.

BLAINE, CONNIE B. A.
[pen.] Connie B. A. Blaine; [b.] October 7, 1969, Stuttgart; [p.] Sharon and Ricks Simas; [m.] Joseph W. Blaine, February 14, 1990; [ch.] Marcus D. R. Blaine - 4, Ryan S. L. Blaine - 7; [ed.] Graduated from Washoe High, am currently taking a course from the Institute of Children's Literature and applying for a Nursing Scholarship; [occ.] I am a warehouse worker; [memb.] United Blood Service, South Hills Christians Assembly Desert Heights Elem. PTA; [hon.] In high school I was placed in honors's English and I won several trophy's in JROTC.; [pers.] I wish to reflect on our romantic side in times of trouble side in times of fun. I was intrigued by a nameless poet in high school.; [a.] Reno, NV

BLANCHARD, SUSAN
[b.] May 17, 1978, York, PA; [p.] Mary Lou Blanchard and Gerald Blanchard; [ed.] Red Lion Area High School; [pers.] I am going to go the college in the fall of 1996. I hope to major in fashion marketing with a minor in writing. I hope my friend Crissy is well and safe in heaven.; [a.] Red Lion, PA

BLAND, ERICA
[b.] May 15, 1980, Alliance, OH; [p.] Victoria Bland; [occ.] Student, Alliance High School; [hon.] 1993-94 Ira G. Turpin Award; [pers.] I never give less than my best in any situation, big or small.; [a.] Alliance, OH

BLANDFORD, STU
[b.] August 16, 1968, Atlanta, GA; [p.] Stuart and Vicki; [ed.] B.A. Emory University '90, MBA Vanderbilt University '92; [occ.] Writer; [oth. writ.] Forest Fire: A love story?; [a.] Atlanta, GA

BLOCH, BARRY H.
[b.] December 22, 1968, Lincoln, NE; [ed.] Associates of Arts, Bachelors in Elementary Education from Washington State University; [occ.] Elementary Educator, Teacher; [pers.] I believe that all children have the right and the capabilities to learn. I also believe that with faith (in yourself) you can achieve anything!; [a.] Bonney Lake, WA

BLONQUIST, LINDSAY
[b.] January 14, 1977, Salt Lake, UT; [p.] James L. and Peggy Blonquist; [ed.] Cottonwood High School, currently at Westminster College; [occ.] Promotion Assistant at Richard Paul Evans Publishing; [hon.] Academics Award at Cottonwood High, Trustee and Faculty Entrance Scholarships at Westminster College; [oth. writ.] Poetry published in Annual student publication at Cottonwood High - Senior year.; [pers.] My highest form of expression comes with my artwork - in which I open up and magnify the wonders.; [a.] Salt Lake City, UT

BLUNDELL, WILLIAM MAJOR
[pen.] William Paul; [b.] October 15, 1976, Peoria, IL; [p.] Mary-Lou and Gary Wayne Ehringer; [ed.] Dunlop High School, Illinois Central College, Illinois State University, I'm still at Illinois Central College; [oth. writ.] This is my first to be published; [pers.] Through my poems I like to show my love and dedication to my Lord and Savior Jesus Christ, my greatest influence is Jesus Christ. My greatest influence is Jesus Christ and a wonderful friend Joel Dryden.; [a.] Dunlop, IL

BLUNK, DAVID ALLEN
[b.] November 7, 1965, Portland, OR; [p.] Shari Whitlock and Jack Blunk; [m.] Divorced; [ch.] Kelci Darlene, Alaisa John, Megan Ann, Dari Shanae; [ed.] Curtis High Seattle Massage School; [occ.] Massage Therapist at Olympic Massage and Teacher; [memb.] A.M.T.A.; [hon.] Honors Seattle Massage School; [pers.] It's not your destination, it is the journey in which you travel to get there that matters.; [a.] Gig Harbor, WA

BOAKE, ROBERT
[b.] November 3, 1935, Chicago, IL; [p.] Challen Fillmore and Josephine Catherine; [m.] Divorced, September 1963; [ch.] Peggy Ann, Robert; [ed.] BA Northwestern University 1958; [occ.] Antiquarian Book Dealer; [memb.] Amer Book Assn, Chicago Milwart Bookfinders Group, Antiquarians of Illinois; [hon.] Various office held while in College and ask fraternity but that was so long ago - not to really mention; [oth. writ.] Many other poems of varying lengths for the most part set in the Souther States for which I have a great affinity bears of this local languages vocabulary and way of speaking; [pers.] Don't really have specific statement but I can tell you of the things and people which and who influenced me on the past 40 years, started with the Beatrice Dylon, Janis Joplin, Southern writers Flammery O'Connor, Richard Ford, various forms or lyrics in C.W. music all coming down to the inherit freedom.; [a.] Evanston, IL

BOATNER JR., RONALD
[b.] September 30, 1968, Montgomery, AL; [p.] Peggy and Richard Snell; [ed.] John Jay High, Palo Alto college, Troy State University, Montgomery Kutztown University; [occ.] Telesales, Full Time Student at Kutztown; [hon.] Made President's Honors List (full time and part time) at Palo Alto College; [oth. writ.] Short stories and satire on an amateur level; [pers.] I write, mostly, to share with my friends and family, feedback reflecting enjoyment motivates me.; [a.] Breinigsville, PA

BOATWRIGHT, VICTORIA
[b.] September 28, 1981, Arlington, VA; [p.] Diane Boatwright; [ed.] 9th grade student in Garfield High School; [occ.] Student; [pers.] When I graduate from High School I want to get into acting and singing. I also would like to continue writing. I live with my mother and two sisters, Michelle and Jessica.; [a.] Dale City, VA

BOBBITT, NORMA
[b.] September 12, 1925, Randolph County, MO; [p.] Fred Jones and Nellie Jones; [m.] Bill Bobbitt, June 6, 1948; [ch.] Stephen, Sharon, Laurie, Lisa; [ed.] Cairo High School, Cairo, MO; [occ.] Retired Church Secretary, Westminster Presbyterian Church, Elgin, IL; [memb.] International Society of Poets; [hon.] High School Valedictorian; [oth. writ.] "If Porches Could Talk" in Where Dreams Begin, "Their Chores Are Done" Outstanding Poets of 1994, "The Silent Schoolyard" Best Poems of 1995, "On Going Home Again" Shadows and Light; [pers.] I like to capture memories of the past in my poetry. My poem, "No Song to Sing" is for my grandson, Zachary. The rest of my poems will be a legacy to my children/grandchildren to help them understand me and remember me as one who valued the past but looked forward to the future.; [a.] Elgin, IL

BOCCHINFUSO, ANTHONY V.
[b.] April 8, 1964, Philadelphia, PA; [p.] Carmine and Sandra Bocchinfuso; [ed.] Frankford High, Penn State, Community College of Phila.; [occ.] Check Processing, Frankford Bank; [oth. writ.] New author, working on short stories, screenplays and poetry; [a.] Philadelphia, PA

BOEWE, TRISHA
[b.] May 3, 1982, Concord, NH; [p.] Joyce and Chris Boewe; [pers.] I'm inspired by nature and often go out to sit by the river in the woods I love life and all its sights and sounds.; [a.] Silver Lake, NH

BOGLE, PEGGY
[b.] November 22, 1935, Columbus, KS; [p.] Fred and Anna Buergin; [m.] Billy Wayne Bogle, August 23, 1986; [ch.] Deanna Warner, Leatha Bolinger, Gayle Garner, Karen Queen; [ed.] Cherokee County Community High School, Columbus, Kansas; [occ.] Assembly Worker, Owen Oil Tools, Inc., Godley, Texas; [memb.] First Baptist Church, Godley, Texas attend Church of God, 7th Day, Venus, Texas; [oth. writ.] Several poems given to family and friends for special occasion in their lives.; [pers.] The inspiration of my writing comes from my relationship of family and friends and the experiences that occur in my life.; [a.] Godley, TX

BOHANAN, CHRISTOPHER LEE
[b.] February 15, 1985, Corpus Christy, TX; [p.] Leann Adkins and William C. Bohanan; [ed.] Student at Walter Noble School in Arkansas Pass, Texas; [occ.] Student; [memb.] 11th Street Christian Church Three years on the Soccer Team, One Year Youth Football; [hon.] In 1994 and 1995 I won 1st place in Science environment project. Best show of over three hundred students. I am now in gifted and talented class for reading; [oth. writ.] Love Flies Like A Dove And Dobber And Tiger, all unpublished.; [pers.] I have been influenced by my grandma Ivalee Bohanan to express my self in poetry. I want to express my gratitude to my Aunt Jaynette and Uncle Charles Bishop for all the support and encouragement they have gave me.; [a.] Aransas Pass, TX

BOLDEN, FRANCIS
[pen.] Sparkle Green; [b.] October 24, 1969, Chicago, IL; [p.] Dorothy and Melvin Craft; [m.] Separated; [ch.] Marcus Craft, Allen Craft, Francesca Bolden, Asia Hardman, Aquan Green; [ed.] Hughe Manley High - Chicago Nebraska College of Business; [occ.] Home Maker, Mother; [memb.] Christ Temple Mission Church; [hon.] Having a poem admitted into the semi-finalist in "The Voice Within" North American 1995 Open Poetry Contest, my First Honor ever, thank you; [oth. writ.] I also write songs so far I have written 10 songs.; [pers.] I hope to make a positive difference in my children's life and in the life of others, I come in contact within my life time and all the time thereafter.; [a.] Lincoln, NE

BOND, BETTY J.
[b.] December 3, 1929, Wellington, TX; [p.] L.D. Allen, Golda M. Allen; [m.] Kenneth, December 11, 1971; [ch.] Michael J., Pamela J., Tricia A.; [ed.] High School, Mesa, AZ; [occ.] Retired from U.S. West, Inc., Phoenix, Arizona; [oth. writ.] Poems in local publications; [a.] Lamar, AR

BONDI, EDITH F.
[b.] September 26, 1919, Berlin, Germany; [m.] Arnold A. Bondi; [ch.] Ardith, Eugene; [ed.] Certification for: Classroom Teacher, Training Elementary School Teachers, Teaching Reading and Language Development, Friedrich Froebel Institute, B.S., M.A. Columbia University, Ph.D. Texas A&M; [occ.] Professor of English Language and Classroom Reacher at Kossuth University Teacher Training School, Debrecen, Hungary, Director, Museum of Children's Books and Museum Zum Chorlesen Der Bucher Fur Kinder, Houston, Texas and Hungry; [memb.] International, Texas, German, and Hungarian Reading Associations, Assoc. for Childhood Education, Soc. of Children's Book Writers and Illustrators, American Translators Assoc., Goethe Institut, German-Texan Heritage Soc., Camp Morasha, Gimmel Foundation of Israel, Harp Soc. Awards for: Raising Reading and Language Development Achievement Levels with Nature Study in Elementary Public Schools and U.S. Dept. of Agriculture Districts, Teaching, Writing, Translation, Lectures, Children's Books, Songs, Poetry, and Elementary School Courses of Study.; [pers.] Kids Are Special People; [a.] Houston, TX

BOTH, BEVERLY JANE
[pen.] Beverly Higgs Both; [b.] October 5, 1927, Chicago, IL; [p.] Harold and Margaret Higgs; [m.] Joseph Richard Both, May 22, 1948; [ch.] Eight wonderful children; [ed.] Proviso High School graduate and Business school. I continue my education by intense reading; [occ.] Homemaker, Mother, Grandmother, (Former Secretary); [memb.] Our Redeemer Lutheran Church, Tri-State Newcomers Club, Lutheran Woman's Missionary League; [oth. writ.] I have written several poems before but never entered one in a contest I enjoy writing to my children one grandchildren who live all over the United States. I keep a journal; [pers.] My "autistic" daughter Peg takes priority in my life. Also my husband and children and grandchildren. In other words I am a contented and fulfilled "homemaker."; [a.] Huntington, WV

BOTILLER, JASUN
[pers.] The power of choice makes us what we choose to be. In choosing to be me, I have made the choice to be free...; [a.] CA

BOUCHER, CHANTEL
[b.] June 30, 1981, Lowell, MA; [p.] Beverly and Robert Boucher; [ed.] Freshman at Lowell Catholic High School; [memb.] Member of the School Newspaper, Member of the paper counseling group; [hon.] Honor student, awards in Literature, grammar, and science; [oth. writ.] Articles for school newspaper and other poems; [pers.] A person that I look up to in the writing field is Maya Angelou; [a.] Dracut, MA

BOUCHER, KRISTY
[pen.] Ebony Black; [b.] April 8, 1981, Colorado Springs, CO; [p.] Sharon and Joseph; [ed.] I go to Colorado Springs Christian School; [occ.] Student; [hon.] I have won several speech meet awards; [pers.] In the fourteen years I've lived on this planet I've come to terms with the fact that life really is a box of chocolates, because you never know what you will get. This publication is proof of that.; [a.] Colorado Springs, CO

BOULIGNY, PATRICIA LORENE
[b.] October 14, 1939, Corpus Christi, TX; [p.] Robert Morris Coffman, Ollie Orene Hardin Coffman; [m.] J. E. Bouligny Jr. (Deceased); [ch.] R. Michael Wynhoff, Renee M. Tantillo; [ed.] BS Univ. of Houston, 1966; [occ.] Administrative Secretary, Bethany Christian Church, Houston, TX; [memb.] Phi Mu Fraternity, Order of the Eastern Star; [oth. writ.] "Letter from the Editor" in monthly newsletter for Christ the King Episcopal Church, Houston, TX; [a.] Houston, TX

BOULWARE, JAMES E.
[b.] February 14, 1924, Cordele, GA; [p.] Mr. and Mrs. R.C. Boulware Sr.; [m.] Vanita Holmes Boulware; [ch.] December 16, 1945, Jeb, Van, Brock and Vanita Mae; [ed.] 4 yrs. College, Georgia State University; [occ.] Retired, Atlanta Journal and Constitution Newspapers; [memb.] GA State Aluminous Disabled American Veterans, American Legion, Veteran of Foreign Wars, Memorial Drive Presbyterian Church; [oth. writ.] Several poems; [pers.] No drinking or smoking for over 6 yrs. I am a better person and grateful to my maker.; [a.] Pine Mountain, GA

BOWLES, MARJORIE
[b.] Minnesota; [m.] John, October 9, 1965; [ch.] Christine; [ed.] Registered Nurse, Master Social Work; [occ.] Psychotherapist, for Harmony - Private Practice; [oth. writ.] Currently writing poetry to present with floral photographs for use on calendars.; [pers.] In order to understand human nature, I feel we just stay in touch with the creative and imaginative side of our personalities. Poetry is an exhibit of this belief.; [a.] Niles, MI

BOWLEY, SARAH E.
[b.] July 31, 1912, White Plains, KY; [p.] Bob and Lizzie Woodward; [m.] Rev. Albert Bowley (Deceased), Jan 4, 1930; [ch.] Wada, Alberta, Loyce, Patsy, Becky; [ed.] Finished Freshman year of High School, later attended adult educ. classes for High School; [occ.] Retired; [memb.] Church Membership only, Mercer Baptist; [oth. writ.] Poems: A Quilters Dream, Flying Geese, ugly blocks, My Log Cabin, Thirty Pieces of Silver, all unpublished; [pers.] I am a Senior Lady from Rural KY. My husband was a Baptist Minister who pastored Rural churches in KY. I am crazy about quilts. I love to make them as well as write poems about them.; [a.] Powderly, KY

BOWLING, KERBY W.
[pen.] W. Kerby Bowling; [b.] May 2, 1927, Memphis, TN; [p.] Winston Bowling - Irma Bowling; [m.] Kathryn Bowling, April 18, 1953; [ch.] Kerby II, Cary; [ed.] Central High, Memphis, Tenn, Rhodes College, Loyola Univ., Univ. of Mississippi J.D. degree; [occ.] Attorney; [memb.] Miss Tenn American Bar Asso., Trial Attys Asso., Military Order World Wars, Sons American Revolution Rotary, IAA (Phi Alpha Delta), Sigma Alpha Epsilon; [hon.] Military Hall Fame Univ. Miss; [oth. writ.] Management Fumbles - Union Recoveries, Interviewing Prospective Employees, numerous poems, "Illusions" - Love Knocked on An Empty Door" etc.; [pers.] I like to write about people - and how some have a misguided conception of their own importance - like "Ode to A Big Shot - From the Mouth of An Ass"; [a.] Memphis, TN

BOWMAN, CHRISTINA
[b.] January 13, Pittsburgh, PA; [p.] Kathy Bowman; [ed.] Trinity Christian, Plum Senior High, Community College of Allegheny County CCAC; [occ.] Network Marketing and distribution, Retailing and Sales Associate; [memb.] Native American Culture Club, Landmark Baptist Church, Junior and National Honor Society; [hon.] Creative Arts Awards, Junior and National Honor Society, Quill and Scroll Award, Magazine Award, Academic Honors Award; [oth. writ.] Poem published in Harvard Poetry Book, several poems and stories published in Creative Writing, books - two years consecutively, wrote for high school and college newspapers.; [pers.] Poetry is not just words on paper, it is an expression of one's heart and soul. I have been very heavily influenced by the simplicity and beauty of the Native American Cultures and their writing, as well as that of Anne Rice and her view of humanity and the spiritual.; [a.] Pittsburgh, PA

BOYD, ROSIE K.
[b.] July 9, 1980, Tacoma, WA; [p.] James and Linda; [ed.] 9th grade Homeschooled; [pers.] I love to read and I love to take care of my rabbit "Clover." I of course love to write, I write mostly poems and stories. Sometimes I write songs. I write whatever comes to mind or whatever touched my heart.; [a.] Spanaway, WA

BOYKO, BRAD
[b.] November 28, 1977, Allentown; [p.] Pamela and Richard Boyko; [ed.] Parkland High, Lehigh County Vocational Technical School, currently enrolled at Thaddeus Stevens State School of Technology; [occ.] Student; [oth. writ.] I have written several short stories and poems none of which have been published... yet.; [pers.] We have all been born with pain. But pain does not make us anymore "Special" than anyone else.; [a.] Orefield, PA

BOYLES, DONNY W.
[b.] September 6, 1970, Winona, MS; [p.] Tommy and Rosetta Boyles; [ch.] Donny Wayne Boyles Jr.; [ed.] Kilmichael High; [occ.] Shipping Supervisor, Stofurnco IAX, Winona; [a.] Winona, MS

BRADSHAW, TERRY
[b.] August 17, 1954, Wilmington, OH; [p.] Allen and Betty Bradshaw; [ed.] Wilmington High School, Ohio State University - years Engineering; [occ.] Self-employed - Bulk Water Hauling - Wells, Cisterns, Pools; [hon.] Private Pilot; [oth. writ.] 'Untitled', Tomorrow Never Knows, "The Hippie and the Flower Child", The Best Poems of 1996; [pers.] Have the confidence, To spread your wings and fly, Let your words, Make a difference, To all passing by.; [a.] Blanchester, OH

BRADY, PATSY

[pen.] Patsy Harvey Brady; [b.] December 11, 1937, Chicago, IL; [p.] Alice Marie Haught; [m.] Paul E. Brady, February 1, 1986; [ch.] I have 1 son by a prior marriage, he has 4 sons by a former marriage; [ed.] Graduated from Seminole High School; [occ.] I own and operate a Beauty Shop; [memb.] Osteen Baptist Church; [hon.] Outstanding Senior of Seminole High School Band 1955; [oth. writ.] I've written approximately 200 other poems, and am working towards the publication of one of two books.; [pers.] I find a wonderful satisfaction in writing, a release and an aim to please the readers.; [a.] Osteen, FL

BRAMLETT, DAMIAN

[pen.] Damian Bramlett; [b.] July 30, 1976, Walnut Creek, CA; [p.] Michelle Bramlett; [ed.] Del Amigo High School, DVC Junior College; [occ.] Student; [memb.] Various Fans Clubs; [hon.] Co-Valedictorian in High School; [pers.] It is time for people to wake-up and see what's happening around them. The planet is falling apart and we need to out it back together again for ourselves and for our children.; [a.] Diablo, CA

BRANCH, VALORIE KAYE ANDERSON

[b.] November 11, 1969, Compton, CA; [p.] Booker and Velma Anderson; [m.] Gary McKinley Branch, August 27, 1994; [ed.] Lynwood High, University of California, San Diego, ITT Technical Institute, Carson; [occ.] Engineering Documentation Coordinator, Watlow-Anafaze; [memb.] Institute of Electrical and Electronics Engineers and New Morning Star Missionary Baptist Church; [pers.] There's nothing wrong with being respectful, sensitive and caring to everybody in everyway. Believe and respect yourself always and be truthful to yourself, you will never go wrong.; [a.] Santa Cruz, CA

BRAZEAL, WAYNE

[b.] February 5, 1933, Oklahoma City, OK; [p.] Orville and Vilma Brazeal; [ch.] Kim Renee, Keith Lynn, Kris Alan, Jeffrey Wayne, Jason Wade; [ed.] Northeast High-Oklahoma City, University of Oklahoma; [occ.] Customer Service Associate, Newport Inc., Hampton, VA; [memb.] The Peninsula Vineyard, Newport News, VA (Kinship Leader), Lay Minister, International Student Fellowships; [hon.] I worked professionally in musical entertainment as a singer-guitarist in Orange County, California from the mid - 60's to the late '70s under the professional name of Wayne Gabriel, with credits in television, night clubs and recordings; [oth. writ.] Several song lyrics individually and in collaboration. A wedding song recently written will soon be published.; [pers.] The Golden Rose was inspired by the writing of singer-song writer Bob Lind. A man called Jesus has become the true golden rose of love in my life and inspires me in everything that I do.; [a.] Newport News, VA

BRAZO, JAMIE N.

[b.] September 30, 1980, Lakeview, OR; [p.] Mark and Judy Brazo; [ed.] Currently a student of American School, High School; [occ.] Babysitter; [memb.] Kingdom Hall of Jehovah's Witnesses, Poets' Guild, Quill Books; [hon.] Presidential Academic Fitness Award, President's Award for Educational Excellence; [oth. writ.] "We Can Save Tomorrow," poem published by Poets' Guild, "My Inspirations."; [a.] Anderson, CA

BREITHAUPT, LINDA J.

[b.] November 20, 1955, Clark AFB, Philippines; [p.] Russell and Edith Geldmacher; [m.] Joel C. Breithaupt, February 29, 1992; [ch.] Aaron Lee (deceased), Angela Lee; [occ.] Mortgage Loan Processor; [oth. writ.] The poem presented in this anthology is the second poem I have written in memory of my only son, Aaron Paul Lee. In June of 1995, at age 14, Aaron died of cancer. His life and subsequent death, along with my faith in God, have been my source and inspiration for my writings.; [a.] Lubbock, TX

BRENTLINGER, GREGORY W.

[pen.] Brent; [b.] March 16, 1948, Salem, IL; [m.] Dorothy Brentlinger, May 20, 1972; [ch.] Brian; [ed.] Bond County Community Unit No. 2 Lamar University; [occ.] Maintenance Supervisor; [oth. writ.] "Compassionate Friends" a local publication designed to comfort those who have "lost" a spouse, relative, or friend to death.; [pers.] The poet is a storyteller, sometimes set to meter, sometimes not. Poetry is spanning the gap between a lyric and a writing.; [a.] Beaumont, TX

BREWER, ANDREA LORAINE

[pen.] Andrea L. Brewer; [b.] November 21, 1980, Cincinnati, OH; [p.] Kenneth D. and Pattie A. Brewer Jr.; [ed.] Currently a Freshman in High School at Christian Center Academy, Mr. Carmel, Ohio, previously was home schooled and attended Western Brown Elementary in Mt. Crab, Ohio; [occ.] Student; [memb.] 1. Piano student, under the instruction of Mrs. Wilma Marugg, 2. 4-H member and treasurer, 3. Member of Christian Center Academy Girls Basketball Team "The Flames"; [hon.] Andrea has always been an honor roll student throughout school, she has received ribbons for performing on her horse "Jacob Star" at the County Fair and open shows; [oth. writ.] This is my first writing to be published; [pers.] I would like to thank God for this accomplishment and allowing my poem to be published. Also thanks mom and dad. My favorite bible verse is Isaiah 40:31, "yet those who wait for the Lord will gain new strength, they will mount up with wings like eagles, they will run and not get tired, they will walk and not become weary."; [a.] Williamsburg, OH

BRICKEY, DAVID M.

[pen.] David Bricquet; [b.] September 1, 1975, Wiesbaden, Germany; [p.] Joseph and Shirley Brickey; [ed.] R. L. Paschal High Fort worth, TX, Sophomore at University of Florida; [occ.] Student, Financial Investor; [memb.] First Presbyterian of Fort Worth; [hon.] I was born; [pers.] "A man of genius makes no mistakes. His errors are volitional and are portals of discovery" - Janen Joyce (1922); [a.] Fort Worth, TX

BRIGGS, ALISON DODD

[b.] February 21, 1971, Des Moines, IA; [p.] Mr. and Mrs. F. Towers Dodds; [m.] Mr. Michael Kyle Briggs, November 18, 1995; [ed.] Lexington Senior High School, Vanderbilt University; [occ.] Artist; [hon.] Arts and Science Academic Scholarship, Dean's List; [oth. writ.] In process romantic novel, and self-illustrated children's books in process also.; [a.] Pisgah Forest, NC

BRIGIDI, DAWNMARIE

[b.] July 28, 1982, Horsham, PA; [p.] Michael and Peggy Brigidi; [ed.] 8th Grade; [occ.] Student; [hon.] Honor Student at Keith Valley Middle School.

BRIGNOLA, ELAINE

[p.] Gloria and Emil Jr. Brignola; [ed.] Cresskill High School, Fairleigh Dickinson University, Wroxton College, Oxfordshire England School of Visual Arts; [occ.] Marketing Consultant; [oth. writ.] Yet to be published: Children's book "Stephen Says Goodbye".; [pers.] Words from father: "What goes around, comes and around, treat others as you would to be treated."; [a.] Fort Lee, NJ

BRIONES, THERESA R.

[b.] October 1, 1961, Houston, TX; [p.] Patricia Speer and Johnny T. Rivera; [m.] Domingo S. Briones, October 10, 1977; [ch.] Alicia, Mingo II, Monique; [ed.] McReynalds Jr. High; [occ.] Home-maker; [pers.] Today is not a day to waste. Today is a day to love, have laughter, strength and most of all faith, if not where will tomorrow be...; [a.] Houston, TX

BRISBON, SHIRNETHA E.

[b.] December 3, 1981, Torrejon AFB, Spain; [p.] Mr. and Mrs. John L. Brisbon; [m.] Single; [ed.] High School Student, (Hampton High); [occ.] Baby Sitting; [memb.] CHROME CLub, Bayview Chapel (Youth), Acolyte Group. Johns Hopkins University Talent Search, HHS Citizen of the month, Presidential and National Academic Awards; [hon.] Johns Hopkins Talent Search; [oth. writ.] Several poems for family and friends.; [pers.] When I want something, I go out and achieve it.; [a.] Hampton, VA

BRITTON, EVIE VIOLA

[b.] May 23, 1923, Mobile, AL; [p.] William and Mattie Britton; [m.] August 16, 1938, January 18, 1952; [ch.] Lynda, Leon (Deceased), Victor; [ed.] Hearing impaired; [occ.] Retired; [oth. writ.] The lovely summer rains of Texas, forever spring, come get to know me, truly care. Morning glory mist, along my road in life, sweet little Barbara Joe, all things revealed, beans on my Balco, NY.; [pers.] Be true to yourself, try to see the good in others, don't dwell on what might of been, live up to what you expect pf others, do every thing you can to better yourself!; [a.] Santa Maria, CA

BROOKS, SHAWN M.

[b.] May 26, 1973, Williamsport, PA; [p.] Terrie A. Brooks; [ed.] Mifflinburg Elementary School, Mifflinburg Middle School (PA), SweetHome High School (NY), I never graduated from High School but got my G.E.D. I also got a trade in construction; [occ.] Manager Trainee at McDonalds in Red Bank, TN; [oth. writ.] I have 22 writing and more to go. This will be the first published poem. And I hope for more publishing; [pers.] I dedicate this poem to my mother the one who made it possible, always believing in me fulfilling my childhood dreams and now the biggest and best dream comes true thanks to her. Thanks Mom I love you. I would also like to thank my brother and sister for just being my big brother and big sister. I love you all.; [a.] Chattanooga, TN

BROOKS, TERESA RADFORD

[b.] June 30, 1937, Washington, DC; [p.] Elbert L. and Nylic Radford; [ch.] James, Randall, Scott; [ed.] Blacksburg High School, Radford University; [occ.] Customer Sales Associate; [memb.] National Geographic Soc., Presbyterian Church; [pers.] Enjoy sharing my love of the natural world and childhood Blue Ridge Mountain experience.; [a.] Norcross, GA

BROWN, ASREAN C.

[pen.] Cary Brown; [b.] November 17, 1976, Canton, OH; [p.] Henry and Mary Walker Sr.; [m.] Cary Brown III, September 16, 1995; [ed.] Canton South High

School, West Liberty State College; [occ.] Customer Service Youth Leader II

BROWN, DESIRAE
[pen.] Desirae Brown; [b.] January 26, 1979, Houston, TX; [p.] Keith and Lisa Brown; [ed.] Still in high school. I'm a Junior.; [occ.] I teach a few piano students.; [hon.] I am mainly a musician and have played the piano for 13 years (since I was 3). On March 6, 1996 my sister Deondra and I will perform the United States premier of Malcolm Arnold's Piano duet Concerto with the International Chamber Orchestra, I have won first prize in the Utah, Summer Arts Piano Competition, the Utah Music Teachers Association Competition, and the Utah State Fair Musicians Competition. I have performed piano concerti with the Wisconsin Symphony the Utah Valleys Symphony, and the American Fork Symphony. I've also won many other top awards in California, Utah, and Colorado. My most recent prize has been first prize in the International Silver Lake Piano Competition. I was also a finalist in the 1995 International Stravinsky Awards being one of only 3 Americans chosen. I was top Utah Composer in the National Composers Guild three years in a row.; [pers.] I love poetry that makes you sit up and think, that hits you hard.; [a.] Alpine, UT

BROWN, FRANK THOMAS
[b.] January 20, 1936, Cape Town, South Africa; [p.] Deceased; [m.] Sylvia Martha Brown, February 12, 1973; [ch.] Alleamore, Sharrone, Mercia; [ed.] BS Art Education, Honors, M.A. Art History from Morgan State Univ. (1976-78 respectively; [occ.] Teacher, Artist, Sculptor, Graphic Artist; [memb.] Alpha Kappa Mu, Honor Society, M.S.U. (1976); [hon.] Sir Ernest Oppenheimer, Mem - Scholarship, Shell, SA Scholarship, Raymond Ackerman Bursary, SA Woolworth S.A. Bursary to further studies in U.S. all awarded in 1973, Alpha Kappa Mu, Hon Society Morgan State Univ. 1976; [pers.] "To be physical, mental and spiritual. The one cannot do without the other." We are all accountable for our deeds. Hobbies, swimming, gardening, reading, philately writing, blowing my harmonica to load off steam.; [a.] Baltimore, MD

BROWN, HENRY
[pen.] Paul David Jordan; [b.] June 25, 1948, New York City, NY; [ed.] Rice High School, Mercy College; [occ.] Corporate Paralegal; [memb.] Sierra Club; [hon.] Dean's List; [a.] Ozone Park, NY

BROWN, JACQUELYN JOYCE
[b.] December 15, 1933, Newton, KS; [p.] Anna Helen Kluge, Henry Alonzo Palmer; [m.] Calvin Brown - died October 1992, August 8, 1958; [ch.] 1st marriage 2 sons and 1 daughter, 2nd marriage 1 son, 1 daughter; [ed.] High School, L.A. Calif.; [occ.] Retired - I earned every minute of it.; [memb.] I have a membership in the human race, and I am a member of God's children; [hon.] The only award I have is the love of my children, that is enough; [oth. writ.] A poem published in Sunday newspaper, a special section, in Las Vegas, NV one poem was used for words to a religious song in a song book.; [pers.] My feelings come through in my poems, whatever I am experiencing at the time. The poem "My Son", was written two months after he was killed by a teenager who was drinking and lost control of his car and struck my son walking to his friends house. He was singing at the time he was killed.; [a.] Belle Plaine, KS

BROWN, NICOLA JAMIE
[b.] October 15, 1962, Hampton, SC; [p.] James W. Brown, Mary Jo Brown; [m.] Capt. Michael A. Brown, December 22, 1984; [ch.] Maikel-Diane, Nicolette Amber; [ed.] Wade Hampton High, South Carolina State College, Bowling Green State University, Troy State University in Montgomery; [occ.] Management Representative for Excel Telecommunications, Inc., Counselor; [memb.] American Heart Association, Mother's Against Drunk Drivers, Pine Grove Elementary PTO, USAA Member; [hon.] Psi Chi National Honor Society in Psychology; [oth. writ.] Several poems unpublished; [pers.] To each his own is my philosophy. I strive to be good and do well. I have been motivated to write by reading the works of Maya Angelou, Langton Hughes, Terry McMillan and Toni Morrison; [a.] Valdosta, GA

BROWN, WM. SCOTT
[b.] September 3, 1957, MI; [ed.] B.A.C. Bowling Green State Univ.; [occ.] D.J.; [oth. writ.] Numerous poems, lyrics, and radio commercials; [pers.] I write for pleasure and or profit. I am always looking for work.; [a.] Fort Wright, KY

BROWNE, MICHAEL J.
[pen.] Michael J. Browne; [b.] May 7, 1964, Decatur, IL; [p.] John R. Browne and Jean P. Browne; [ed.] Santa Monica High School; [occ.] I Currently Volunteer for A Couple of Local Social Service Agencies; [oth. writ.] I have quite a few other poems, and continue to work on my writing.; [pers.] In my life I have definitely had my share of challenges I find that I am happiest and most fulfilled, when I am creating and helping others, I think that the most important thing we can do, in each of our own personal ways, is to endeavor to make the world a better place.; [a.] Long Beach, CA

BROWNING, VIOLA M.
[b.] July 10, 1924, Toledo, OH; [p.] Mr. and Mrs. Eugene Keck; [m.] Robert E. Browning, May 31, 1946; [ch.] 2 daughters, Janet and Catherine; [ed.] High School Graduate-Burnhan High, Sylvania, Ohio; [occ.] Wife, Mother, Grandmother and Great-Grandmother; [hon.] The only awards and honors I've received is my beloved husband and family; [pers.] I'm a caring person, emotional, deep thinking, avid reader of mysteries, work crossword puzzles and try to write poems.; [a.] Toledo, OH

BRUCE III, JAMES A.
[b.] April 3, 1975, Memphis, TN; [p.] Dr. James Bruce, Judy Bruce; [ed.] Jackson Preparatory School, Mississippi State University; [occ.] Student at MSU; [oth. writ.] Nothing else submitted or shown, just this contest; [pers.] I just write whatever spills out. Influences - Tom Marshall, lyricist for Phish. Nothing caught something, but something was lost, when something found nothing, the nothing was boss.; [a.] Starkville, MS

BRYAN, CARI E.
[b.] April 12, 1973, Morgantown, WV; [p.] Mary Carole Howard; [ed.] Senior at Indiana University in Bloomington, studying for my Bachelor of Education (Elementary); [occ.] Full-time Student, 2 part-time jobs waiting tables and babysitting; [hon.] 1st place for ceramic project in High School, lettered in Varsity Softball in High School; [oth. writ.] I wrote some other poetry in a poetry class I took my sophomore year of college and my professor said I should publish one of them for the poetry book at I.U. I did but don't know if it was ever published; [pers.] I find that whenever I write a poem that I don't like it and very well at first. Latter I look at it and I pleasantly surprise myself. It's nice to be recognized for something that comes quite naturally to be awarded for a talent.; [a.] Indianapolis, IN

BRYANT, DARREN
[b.] June 4, 1968, Bainbridge, GA; [p.] Silas Bryant, Brenda Bryant; [hon.] An award of merit from World of Poetry; [pers.] I never sugar coat my writings. I'm a realist, therefore my writings reflect reality. Some are created from personal experiences, and some are based on society, but all are factual. My profound influence is Maya Angelou.; [a.] Attapulgus, GA

BRYANT, ELAINE DEBBER
[b.] January 26, 1916, Hinckley, UT; [p.] Wm. J. and Lida Webb; [m.] Arjaan Debber (Deceased), Wayne Bryant, October 8, 1993; [ch.] 5, 2 boys and 3 girls (2 deceased); [ed.] 2 1/2 years college, taught school before accreditation required Private Secretary; [occ.] Retired still busy; [memb.] Good Sam Club, L.V.S. Church, Sr. Citizens; [hon.] Many but none of note, thanks for this chance, it means so much to me as I am nearly so and still love to write.; [oth. writ.] Many but mostly tributes and musings or church mostly time for family etc.; [pers.] "Do unto all as I want done unto me." "God is always near"; [a.] Delta, UT

BRYANT, HUGHIE
[b.] Logan, WV; [p.] Calvery Bryant and Betty Adams; [m.] Lilly Bell Bryant, June 13, 1972; [ch.] Betty Louise Bryant; [ed.] 6th grade; [occ.] Retired truck driver; [oth. writ.] Songs, Country Love Songs, and Gospel Songs.; [pers.] I believed I have several songs, that could reach the top of the charts in country, but I've never tried too hard to do anything with them.; [a.] Chapmanville, WV

BRYANT, MELVA
[b.] Poteau, OK; [p.] Othella Hughes and Odell Hughes; [ch.] Yasmin A. Bryant, Asaju O.T.M. Walker; [ed.] Muscatine Sr. Hi; [occ.] Student; [hon.] To have been selected as one of the semi-finalist in the 1995 North American Open Poetry Competition and have a blue ribbon winning sweet potato pie; [oth. writ.] Several unpublished poems rough draft of auto biography and a short story.; [pers.] The flowers appear on the earth and the time of the singing of bird is come, and the voice of the turtle is heard in our land.; [a.] Tuskegee, AL

BUBELA, JENNIFER SALEE
[b.] October 6, 1981, Wharton, TX; [p.] Debbie and Eugene Bubela, Jr.; [ed.] Freshman at El Campo High School; [occ.] Student; [memb.] Methodist Youth Fellowship, Baptist Youth Fellowship, Fellowship of Christian Athletes, Christian Club, Yearbook, Student Council, News Paper, Band, Speech and Debate, Drama, Lady Ricebirds, Tennis Team, Swim Team, Red Wave Swim Team; [hon.] D.A.R. Award, Citizenship Award, Superintendent Award of Excellence, Highest G.P.A. Eight Grades. The United States National Science Merit Award, The United States Achievement, Academy's All American Scholar State recognition for Sat., score on the 7th grade.; [oth. writ.] Poem published in the Anthology of Poetry by young Americans.; [pers.] If you dream, you will be prosperous, if you take action, you will be engulfed, if you do neither, life will pass you by.; [a.] El Campo, TX

BULAN, MARIA CAROLINA A.
[pen.] Animal L. Rights; [b.] May 30, 1981, Manila, Philippines; [p.] Whilhelmino Bulan and Carolina Bulan; [ed.] Canoga Park High School, Sutter Middle School, currently in 9th grade - class of 1999; [memb.] Canoga Park FFA Chapter Member, World Wild Life Fund, last chance for Animals, The Humane Society of the United States, American Society for the Prevention of Cruelty to Animals, Paralyzed Veterans of American; [hon.] Honor Roll, Certificate of Merit for Outstanding Achievement in Mathematics President's Education Award Program, Citizenship Award, Certificate of Merit of Outstanding Achievement in Athenians, Certificate of Merit of Outstanding Achievement in Scholarship with High Honors; [pers.] I attempt to show my deepest concern for animals and people through my writings. I encourage the use of helping hands from everyone toward every living beings. I sincerely hope my writings give true meanings to the words "Humane Attitude" and become our No. 1 priority standard in life.; [a.] Reseda, CA

BUNDY, REBECCA
[b.] December 23, 1980, Torrance, CA; [p.] Ann Marie and Roger Bundy; [ed.] Now Freshman at Woodbridge High; [occ.] Student; [memb.] National Honor Society; [hon.] 4.0 throughout Jr. High, 1st place in American Girls Softball; [oth. writ.] This is my first writing published; [pers.] Classical music and nature sounds are the key to unlocking true poems from the heart. Listen, learn and write, what you feel. My parents, Joyce Barlouto, and Sara Hogg have influenced my writing greatly. Thanks.; [a.] Irvine, CA

BURKS, LORETTA ANNE
[pen.] Lori Burks, Lorianna Burkes; [b.] June 20, 1966, Covington, VA; [p.] William E. Burks and Sandra Kay Burks; [ed.] Clifton Forge High, Associates Degree, Dabney S. Lancaster Community, College, BA, Hollins College, Working on MALS Degree, Holins College; [occ.] Full-time Master's Student; [memb.] Pinnacle, Hollins Alumni Association; [hon.] Honor Student, Hollins College, Golden Poets Award, Pinnacle Honors Society; [oth. writ.] Several poems published in Womanzine and The Album, publications at Hollins College.; [pers.] My writing reflects my inner struggle to find "self". I strife to recall those memories of my childhood which directly my current life. My writing is influenced by Gertrude Stein, Margaret Gibson, and Zsuzsanna E. Budapest.; [a.] Clifton Forge, VA

BURNS, GREG
[b.] January 9, 1966, Oklahoma City, OK; [p.] Jason and Darla Burns; [m.] Judith Burns, October 17, 1992; [occ.] Self employed as an audio engineer/designer for live Theatrical performances; [pers.] Society today has lost its respect for God. A key result is the degradation of the family unit. We would better ourselves and out society by focusing our attentions on improving our family relationships and our individual relationship with God.; [a.] Newbury Park, CA

BURRIS, ANITA D.
[b.] March 11, 1959, New Albany, IN; [p.] Ruby R. Burris; [ed.] Spencerian College, Spalding University; [occ.] LPN; [memb.] American Heart Association, National Safety Council, in Firefighters Association; [hon.] Dean's list: Spalding University; [oth. writ.] "Dawn" 3rd place winner contest spalding university.; [pers.] This was written in memory of Marvin Patton Jr. A young man who died much too soon.; [a.] Georgetown, IN

BUSH, TIMOTHY P.
[b.] July 31, 1962, Evans Mills, NY; [p.] Ernest and Joan Hilperts Hauser; [m.] Susan M. Bush, April 6, 1991; [ch.] Rebecca Elizabeth, Lauren Nicole; [occ.] Asst. Manager, Ron Jon Surf Shop, Cocoa Beach, Fl.; [a.] Rockledge, FL

BUSS, ERNIE E.
[b.] October 16, 1918, Winnipeg Manitoba, Canada; [p.] Manitoba farmers; [m.] Delma Buss, September 13, 1947; [ch.] Calvin and Robert; [ed.] Country school near Morris Manitoba Canada; [occ.] Retired; volunteer worker mostly at the Evergreen Care Home, also at various private homes; [hon.] Various war medals and awards showing areas of operation of four years service, two years were in the front lines of Sicily and Italy and Holland; [oth. writ.] Many poems also some short writings; [pers.] "May there be peace in the valley and among my many friends."; [a.] White Rock, BC Canada

BUSSE, RONALD A.
[pen.] Tiger; [b.] April 3, 1967; [p.] Ronald and Marylou Busse; [ed.] Massapequa High School, Nassau Community College; [occ.] Insurance Rater, Musician; [memb.] International Society of Poets; [oth. writ.] I have had other poems published by the National Library of Poetry and I am currently working on writing and publishing my first book of poetry. I also enjoy writing songs and playing keyboards.; [pers.] This poem, Prism Life, gives a perspective of life as one might see it while looking through a prism. I used an actual prism to aid in the writing of this poem. Use your imagination!; [a.] Lindenhurst, NY

BUSTEED, JOANN L.
[pen.] Joan Buspeev; [b.] July 28, 1928, Defiance, OH; [p.] Helen and Jesse Lourash; [m.] William S. Busteed, December 26, 1948; [ch.] William Stewart, David Curtis, Alan Douglas, Elizabeth Ann; [ed.] Defiance High, Defiance College (B.S. in Educ.), Continuing Education in Speech Correction, Bowling Green State University, Private Voice Lessons; [occ.] Housewife and Philanthropic donations and setting up music scholarship at Defiance College and plans for one in Europe.; [memb.] American Association of University Women, Board Member of Schomburg Series (performance individuals and groups), St. Paul's Methodist Church in Defiance (contributor toward funds for music and funds and materials for church - sponsored Boy Scouts and Cub Scouts); [hon.] Academic Scholarship to Defiance College for B.S. degree, recognition as President of League of Women Voters (in Defiance and NW Ohio area); [oth. writ.] Early years Scholastic Magazine contests, Lyrics for musicians compositions; [pers.] I draw on life experience and that of many people I have known, often also from historical material. Life is an adventure.; [a.] Defiance, OH

BUZBY, PEGGY J.
[b.] September 1, 1963, Sellersville, PA; [p.] Edmund and Jeanne Buzby; [pers.] I write to my Lord the glory and survive of Jesus Christ poem inspired by a great woman of prayer, Aunt Jessie, who at the age of 101 shows God's love, power, patience and creativity.

BYRD, HELEN RENA
[pen.] Wall, Wall; [b.] September 2, 1957, Toledo, OH; [p.] Mr. Robert and Claudia Byrd; [ch.] Vanisshia, Butchie, Johnathan, Maria; [ed.] Scott High School; [occ.] Retail sales person; [memb.] New Home Baptist Church Choir Member; [hon.] Never received any honors up to now; [oth. writ.] I write several poems but, never have they been acknowledge. All occasion poem I write. To fit the need of people who ask me to write them one.; [pers.] When I'm writing my poems, I'm putting my heart into, how would I feel if I was in that person shoes how I would feel to help heal and to feel good about themselves or other.; [a.] Toledo, OH

BYRD, KENNETH E.
[pen.] Kenneth E. Byrd; [b.] April 24, 1931, NC; [p.] Roy K. and Glady Price Byrd; [m.] Zoe Messer Byrd, July 18, 1953; [ch.] Susan Leigh Byrd Daughter, Tara Elizabeth Gardner, Granddaughter; [ed.] BS Degree in Mathematics from Wake Forest University, 1953, Minors: English, Education; [occ.] Vice President of Willis Corroon Admin Services, Nashville, TN; [memb.] Various Insurance Industry Associations, Theta Chi Fraternity, North Carolina Collegiate Press Association (while at Wake Forest) Earlier, in National Honor Society, Quill and Scroll, etc.; [hon.] Simultaneously president of Scriberlius Honor Club, Kappa Mu Epsilon Math Honor Society, and Theta Chi Social Fraternity in Senior year; [oth. writ.] A number of poems of various styles and lengths. Hopefully will publish my own collection after I retire from the insurance industry in 1996. They portray the gamut of emotions and beliefs.; [pers.] I strive to use words as an artist uses paint, selecting the appropriate shades and textures to reveal the picture I want to present. Influences include many American poets from Frost to McKuen. I'm a mixture of realism and idealism.; [a.] Franklin, TN

BYRNE, NANCY K.
[b.] December 8, 1946, Erie, PA; [p.] Walter Lee Kauffman II, Elizabeth W. Kauffman; [m.] Joseph J. Byrne, October 18, 1969; [ch.] Laura, Joyce, Suzanne; [ed.] Mercyhurst Prep, Mount Vernon College, University of Kentucky BA-Ed, Fordham University MS-Ed; [occ.] Teacher, Immaculate Conception School, Irvington, NY; [memb.] Conqueror Hook and Ladder Ladies Auxiliary, Federation Catholic Teachers, Univ. Kentucky Alumnae, Association for Supervision and Curriculum Development; [hon.] Fordham - Dean's List; [pers.] I would like to make people aware of their innermost feelings about the society in which we live.; [a.] Irvington, NY

BYSTRA, JOHN
[b.] January 2, 1972, Roseville, CA; [p.] Mary Crespillo, Norbert Bystra; [ed.] Mesa Verde High, American River College; [occ.] Office Supply Store Manager; [hon.] National Hispanic Scholarship Holder; [oth. writ.] None published, but over 150 other poems written.; [pers.] I believe "no pain, no gain," for only through adversity have I fully appreciated life and love.; [a.] Citrus Heights, CA

CADIGAN, DARCY
[b.] July 13, 1965, Eugene, OR; [ch.] Devin, Dillon, Kaitlyn; [ed.] Washington High; [occ.] Management Automotive Towing Management Dry Clearing; [a.] Portland, OR

CADMAN, PATRICIA LEE
[b.] June 30, 1978, Garden Grove; [p.] James Cadman, Marylin Cadman; [ed.] Excelsior Elementary, Jordan Jr. High, and Bolsa Granole High School; [occ.] Student at Bolsa; [memb.] Drama club, choir; [hon.]

Principal's list, eight trophies in bowling, several awards for English.; [pers.] When writing poetry, or anything for that matter, I try to convey the emotions I experience at that time I have read many poems from all different time periods, and have learned a lot from them.; [a.] Garden Grove, CA

CALCAGNO, PATRICIA-ANNE DUGGAN
[pen.] Patricia Duggan-Calcagno; [b.] March 7, 1931, Reading, PA; [p.] Mr. and Mrs. James Duggar Sr.; [m.] Anthony J. Calcagno, November 27, 1948; [ch.] Carol-Anne, Anthony Philip, Angela; [ed.] High-School - Manager of two clothing Dept Stores; [occ.] Great Grand Mother - Retired; [memb.] Holy Guardian Angels Church; [oth. writ.] Short Poems - of People - friends - relatives they - seem to enjoy the gift of them.; [pers.] I want to "Thank God" for this gift. I also want to thank my Granddaughter - "Melanie Calcagno" - for her computer work. And assistance and my Daughter Angela and Granddaughter Heather for the encouragement.; [a.] PA

CALL, GABRIELLE K.
[b.] July 9, 1970, Cleveland, OH; [p.] Michael and Sandra Keefer; [m.] Geoffrey Call, May 21, 1994; [ch.] 2 dogs, Mooch and Louise; [ed.] Shaker Heights High School, Virginia Polytechnic Institute and State University; [occ.] Conservation Projects Manager, The Nature Conservancy; [memb.] The Wildlife Society, WMOT Public Radio; [hon.] Freshman Merit Scholarship, Dean's List, National Audubon Ecology Camp Scholarship; [oth. writ.] Short fiction published in Silhouette, Virginia Tech's literary magazine, conservation updates for the Tennessee Conservationist, Tenn Notes, The Nature Conservancy's Tennessee Newsletter.; [pers.] Have you hugged your pets today?; [a.] Antioch, TN

CAMACHO, LORENZO S.
[b.] August 10, 1922, Philippines; [m.] Leonila A. Camacho, March 20, 1958; [ch.] Dyna; [ed.] Central Luzon Agricultural School, Nueva Ecija, Philippines, B.A., Arellano University, Manila, Philippines; [occ.] Retired Federal Employee; [memb.] American Association of Retired Persons; [hon.] Military: Distinguished Unit Badge with 2 Oakleaves, Philippines and American Defense Ribbons, Asiatic-Pacific Medal, Victory Medal, Purple Heart, Civil Service: Employee of the Year Awards, The National Library of Poetry 1995 Editor's Choice Award; [pers.] I wish to reflect in poetry my hopes for the advancement of mankind.; [a.] San Jose, CA

CAMP, SARAH J.
[b.] December 9, 1936, Ann Arbor, MI; [p.] Dean B. McLaughlin, Laura H. McLaughlin; [m.] Albert Camp (Deceased), August, 1977; [ch.] Thomas A. Burton, Bonniel L. Brooks, Sandra J. Marshall, Veronica L. Deskins, Tami S. Medema; [ed.] Grad: Ann Arbor Pioneer High School 1954 Grad: United Health Careers Institute, 1976; [occ.] Licensed Vocational Nurse Specializing in Pediatric Home Care; [oth. writ.] Several Poems, all non-published.; [pers.] I have a Tendency to reflect the negative side of life it's circumstances in my writing, but look to the brighter, or positive side.; [a.] Hemet, CA

CAMPBELL, JULIA
[b.] January 22, 1975, Lowell, MA; [p.] Robert and Linda Campbell; [ed.] Pelham High, Rivier College; [occ.] Student; [hon.] Peer Outreach, Honor Roll, Dean's List; [pers.] Poetry is an invitation into one's deepest thoughts, emotions, and desires, the end result of a long journey between the heart and the mind.; [a.] Pelham, NH

CANDY, ASHLEY RENEE
[pen.] Ashley Candy; [b.] November 18, 1983, Wichita, KS; [p.] Robert Candy and Kellye Simons; [ed.] Graduated Elementary School, to date, would like to graduate college.; [occ.] Student, El Dorado Middle School, El Dorado, KS; [hon.] D.A.R.E. graduate; [oth. writ.] None at present, published.; [pers.] I enjoy writing because it allows me to express my feelings.; [a.] Wichita, KS

CANNIN, PATRICIA
[pen.] Patrice; [b.] 1952, MA; [ch.] Michelle and A.J.; [ed.] Notre Dame High, Fall River Sch of Nursing; [occ.] RN; [pers.] I view my writing as a form of managed mania that allows me to make some use of the ultimate human solitude that exists in all of us.; [a.] Toms River, NJ

CANONIGO, BARBARA
[pen.] Barbara Sheldon; [b.] August 23, 1975, Dubuque, IA; [p.] Barbara Fisher, Thomas Sheldon; [m.] Daryl Canonigo, October 30, 1995; [hon.] Creative Writings Award; [oth. writ.] Several poems, short stories, a children's book.; [pers.] Reading can bring a certain amount of pleasure. It allows you to add life to whatever thoughts are evoked inside your mind.; [a.] Rockford, IL

CARDENAS, JULIANNE A.
[b.] May 13, 1983, Tamuning, Guam; [p.] William and Catherine Cardenas; [ed.] M.U. Lujan Elem.; [occ.] Student, Agueda I. Johnston Middle School (7th); [memb.] Close-Up, Adopt-A-Beach, Yearbook, Peer Tutoring; [hon.] "A" Honor Roll Student, President's Award for Academic Excellence, 1st. Plave Science Fair Poster Contest, 3rd Place Science Fair, Island-Wide Spelling Bee Participant; [a.] Agona, Guam

CAREY, MARGARET MATTHEWS
[b.] May 21, 1918, Somerville, TN; [p.] Burrus Matthews, Jewel J. Matthews; [m.] Jewel R. Carey, April 6, 1946; [ch.] Benson Owen and Susan Carey,; [ed.] Adamsville, TN High School, Middle TN State University, Cumberland University Law School, Graduated LLB Degree in 1939, one year toward LLM Degree; [occ.] Retired Attorney; [memb.] Iota Tau Tau Legal Sorority, Jackson, TN Bar Ass'n, Lifetime Member in TN PTA, Business and Professional Women's Club; [hon.] Miss Adamsville, TN High School, Life history in Tennessee Room of Jackson - Madison Co. Library (1st woman to practice Law in Jackson, TN), Life history and picture in book - A bicentennial tribute to Tennessee Women - 1796 - 1996; [oth. writ.] Poems and articles in various local publications, wrote and published a book on over all plan of the Bible, told like it is, wrote Church newspaper for soldiers helping with book to be written about my great, great grandmother, Ann Calhoun Matthews, who was first cousin to John C. Calhoun and David Crockett.; [pers.] My Dad was a College Professor (Ph.D) and talking with me about going to college, made a statement I have found to be true. "There are only two things no one can take away from you - Salvation in Christ and a good education.; [a.] Pigeon Forge, TN

CARINIO, LEILANI JANE
[b.] November 5, 1979, Sacramento, CA; [ed.] High School Junior year at Bonita H.S.; [occ.] Pursuing an acting and performing arts career.; [memb.] B.H.S. Drama and Dance clubs. Polynesian Dance Troup: "Halau Keala Lani" enrolled in Equity and Thespian Theatre Programs.; [hon.] Lead and supporting rolls in several Civic Light Opera Productions, Leilani has choreographed musical productions in past.; [oth. writ.] Unpublished book of personal poetry. Also wrote previous published poem. "Pressures of Virginity".; [pers.] The human heart see's things the eyes cannot see and the mind cannot begin to comprehend.

CARLSON, GRACE WILLIAMS
[b.] May 31, 1935, Rural Delmar, MD; [p.] Dan E. and Louise Taylor Williams; [m.] Gilmore Carlson (Deceased), March 1, 1957; [ch.] Gil Lee, Kristina, Karen; [ed.] Masters Degree in English, taught English Grammar, Poetry, and Creative Writing for 15 years in Wicomico County Public School System.; [occ.] Retired widow; [memb.] AARP, NRA; [oth. writ.] I wrote a researched historical/fictional novel over a 3 year period, which has never been accepted nor published.; [pers.] I am a voracious reader, lively debater on politics, religion, ethics and any thing in which this "Gemini" can engage another objective, intellectual being in "debating" philosophy. A sense of Humor of life and one's self.; [a.] Salisbury, MD

CAROZZA, JOANE M.
[b.] June 16, 1964, Waterbury, CT; [p.] Mr. and Mrs. Patrick Carozza; [ed.] Sacred Heart High School MCSSS, Camp Lejeunne, NC; [pers.] 'Create Your Own Destiny'.; [a.] Coventry, CT

CARR, MICHAEL SHANE
[b.] October 17, 1969, Phoenix, AZ; [p.] Glen Carr and Sheila Easley; [m.] Jinae Carr, May 29, 1993; [ed.] College Junior, Arizona State University; [occ.] Security Guard; [oth. writ.] No other writings published.; [pers.] When you give up on your dreams, you give up on life.; [a.] Phoenix, AZ

CARRE, ROOSEVELT
[pen.] Richard Dickson; [b.] December 7, 1951, WI; [occ.] Researcher in Psychosociology (Group behavior), Cryptopsychology (Human and Animal: Dreams, ESP). Actually preparing an 'Amazing Science Tour' Program for enhancing any Celebration!; [oth. writ.] (Forthcoming) Honeymoon Nectar, Nativity, In Quest of the Glowing Birds. Songs of the Morning Stars. How to explore our Hidden World with Music. God and Dog (A look at the other side of the Universe).; [pers.] My daily thing go along resolutely with the humanistic spring which flows merrily in our inner being my desire: Making the world a delightful place for the entire Human Family!; [a.] Philadelphia, PA

CARRERO, WIL
[b.] June 5, 1972; [p.] Maggie Stiffler; [ed.] Washington High; [occ.] United States Air Force, Nellis AFB, NV; [pers.] Inner peace comes with outer purpose, one outer purpose which man should always strive for is the purpose of love. Without love, we can never truly achieve our heartfelt purpose.

CARRERRA, EVELYN
[b.] May 4, 1922, San Jose, CA; [p.] John and Ignacia Silva; [m.] Stanley Carrera, September 29, 1949; [ch.] Five Children; [ed.] Graduate Santa Clara High June

10, 1940, Dry Cleaning School of Clothing Technology; [occ.] Retired; [memb.] Chamber of Commerce AARP; [oth. writ.] Spiritual songs; [pers.] Depend on your God. He is your creator. His promise to us: He loves us, cares for us, and keeps us from harm.; [a.] Montague, CA

CARRICK, STEWART EDWARD
[b.] October 11, 1970, Baldwin Memorial; [p.] Donald and Shirley Carrick; [m.] Wendy L. Carrick, May 1, 1993; [ch.] Malachi Morgan; [ed.] St. Croix Central High School and Wisconsin Indian head Technical College; [occ.] Factory Laborer; [pers.] I grew up listening to strangers tell me my worth was little. My family and friends who knew me, knew better. They have waited... now I shine. Thank you.; [a.] Hammond, WI

CARROLL, KHRISTINE LEE
[b.] September 8, 1972, New York; [p.] Kevin J. and Karen E. Ferrand-Carroll; [ed.] Currently pursuing a degree in finance, pre-law concentration at Quinnipiac College, Hamden, CT; [occ.] Supervisory position in the financial industry.; [memb.] Volunteer at the High Hopes Therapeutic Riding Center, Old Lyme, CT, Volunteer - Homeless Shelters of Milford and New Haven, CT, Diabetes Association; [pers.] I strive to through my writings and my daily existence live everyday as if it were the first, holding steadfastly to the magical wonderment of youth and pursuing the recognition of each lesson the journey of life has to offer.; [a.] Chester, CT

CARSON, CHRISTOPHER L.
[b.] January 28, 1972, Billings, MT; [p.] Joanne S. Holt, George L. Carson; [ed.] Casa Roble Fundamental High School, American River College, City Colleges of Chicago, and University of Maryland; [occ.] United States Air Force Radio and Television Broadcast Specialist; [memb.] Combined federal campaign; [hon.] USAF Basic training honor graduate; [oth. writ.] Assorted radio and television spots, and various poems.; [pers.] My approach to writing has always been to provoke thoughts and feelings not readily experienced, whether love or fear or a simple response such as "oh, yeah!"; [a.] Riverside, CA

CARSON, JO ANNE
[b.] December 28, 1934, CA; [p.] Mrs. Frances Barr; [m.] Eugene Carson, May 2, 1953; [ch.] Two sons, two daughters; [ed.] Grad. Santa Barbara High, California Home Courses in: Art, writing; [occ.] (Blinky) to 14 grandchildren; [memb.] International Society of Poets; [hon.] In poetry and art; [oth. writ.] Stories in Fate Magazine, coming out this year, (Heaven West) a children's book, Carlton Press, Publisher, poems in several Anthologies.; [pers.] "You are never too young or too old, to try something new".; [a.] Central Point, OR

CARSON, ROBIN
[p.] Robert Carson, Pamela Bennett; [ed.] Ellensburg High School, Central Washington University Graduated Cum Laude, BA in Psychology - American Institute of Hypnotherapy - Doctorate in Clinical Hypnotherapy; [memb.] National Honors Society in Psychology; [oth. writ.] Several poems, some personalized for special occasions.; [pers.] "We are spiritual beings experiencing a human existence".; [a.] Ellensburg, WA

CARTER, JAMES
[pen.] James Thomas; [occ.] Airline Transport and Certified Flight Instructor; [oth. writ.] Completed his novel titled Stiletto, Operation: Deepcover and A Twist of Fate and other works include Christmas in the Snow and a Message from Santa.; [pers.] Sand under my feet, sun on my back, clear water.; [a.] Fort Lauderdale, FL

CARTER, KENNETH
[b.] New Haven, CT; [m.] Minette Carter; [ed.] Yale University, Yale Graduate School; [occ.] Professor of French, Long Beach City College, California; [hon.] Phi Beta Kappa, Fellowships; [oth. writ.] Radio Scripts for children's programs, TV Columns, various articles in magazines and newspapers, documentaries for educational videos.; [pers.] Poetry should not only be inspiring and beautiful but also accessible and meaningful.; [a.] Laguna Beach, CA

CASAREZ, RENE
[b.] October 9, 1977, Lamesa, TX; [p.] Juan Casarez, Candida Casarez; [ed.] Currently a senior at Seminole High School; [memb.] Future Teachers of America, National Honor Society, Science Club, Debate; [hon.] Golden Arrow of Seminole High, Honor Student; [oth. writ.] A few unfinished poems and others to come.; [pers.] Opportunity has two basic outlooks: Aspirations of yesterday, dreams of today, and regrets of tomorrow. Aspirations of yesterday, reality of today, and rejoicement of tomorrow. Always believe in the second choice.; [a.] Seminole, TX

CASE, GWEN
[b.] May 11, 1925, Dallas, TX; [p.] Geo. L. and Posie L. Thomas; [m.] Bill D. Case, November 9, 1953; [ch.] Diana and Teri; [ed.] Ninth Grade and GED. Also, business school.; [occ.] Homemaker; [oth. writ.] None. Short poems published in home-town newspaper many years ago.; [pers.] My hope and prayer is that God will touch hearts and that many will come to know Him through this poem. Many are hurting and desperate, God is the answer.; [a.] Houston, TX

CASH, JANET MARIE
[b.] April 17, 1977, North Highlands, CA; [p.] John R. Cash and Genie B. Cash; [ed.] Currently a senior in High School. Graduation in June 1996; [occ.] Student; [memb.] Member of French Club CSF (California Scholarship Federation), Adelanto Community Church, Victor Valley H.S. Jackrabbit Regiment, Fishers of Men (Christian Club); [hon.] Top 5% of class, CSF membership award, 4th place at county history day, outstanding handsman, Academic letter for 3.9 or above G.P.A. for 2 years, Member of All-Southers California Honor Band 1996, Numerous Church awards; [oth. writ.] Poem called The Sacrifice, printed in a Teen Bulletin.; [pers.] Poetry is like a window to the mind. When one writes poetry he is allowing others to step into the intricate thoughts of his mind.; [a.] Victorville, CA

CASTALDI, ANN E.
[pen.] Ann; [b.] August 3, 1982, Austin, TX; [p.] Frank Castaldi, Kee Castaldi; [ed.] 8th Grade, Hill Country Middle School, E.I.S.D. Texas; [occ.] Student; [memb.] National Junior Honor Soc., Symphonic Band (HCMS), Ice Skating Institute of America; [hon.] Special Award - Model Span, HCMS Outstanding Effort Award (1993), Distinguished Honor Roll (1994, 1995), 1995 ISIA Worlds; [oth. writ.] Love 1 (1989), Cute Bengal Tiger 2 (1990), Valentine Letter 1 (1990), He Came Out Of A Dream 1 (1990), I Love The Little Dog 1 (1991), Clouds 2-mentioned (1995), A poem for Texas Independence Day 3 (1995) Austin American Statesman, Westlake Picayune, West Austin News; [pers.] In my poem, nature beautifies the world and science explains the secret of nature.; [a.] Austin, TX

CASTILLO, PASCUAL
[b.] December 15, 1976, Upland, CA; [p.] Pascual Castillo, Maria Castillo; [ed.] Etiwanda High, California Polytechnic University of Pomona; [memb.] To the Interdisciplinary General Education Program, at the California State Polytechnic University of Pomona; [hon.] Most Improved in school Yearbook committee, I have received college credit in my Junior year in Spanish.; [oth. writ.] Written stories for school yearbook.; [pers.] I write from my internal self. From what I learn, see and experience. My writings are how I perceive today's society.; [a.] Altahoma, CA

CASTLEBERRY, MAVIS A.
[b.] January 16, 1954, Augusta, ME; [p.] Lafayette and Edith Hatch; [m.] Jerry Dean Castleberry, October 20, 1986; [ch.] Sherry Freeman, Robin Freeman James Robert Freeman Jr.; [pers.] It's important to remember never give up.; [a.] Cumming, GA

CASTO, ADRIENNE
[b.] June 21, 1980, Guam; [p.] Laura Casto; [ed.] I am currently a freshman at the Ark City High School.; [occ.] Student; [memb.] Fellowship of Christian Athletes. Varsity Tennis team. American Baptist Church.; [hon.] I have a 4.0 grade average, I was a candidate for outstanding student, I received a best sportsmanship in basketball.; [oth. writ.] I write short stories and poetry. I have a port folio of my writings. I write of things that are examples of reality.; [pers.] When I'm writing my poems they all have a piece of me within them that is only expressed by poetry. I also feel it is a good characteristic to let your feelings out.; [a.] Arkansas City, KS

CASTRO, PATRICIA J.
[pen.] Patricia Castro; [b.] February 7, 1974, Los Angeles, CA; [p.] Manuel and Vicki Castro; [ed.] Morningside High School Graduate Southern Regional Occupational Center California (SCROC); [occ.] Rm Service Attendant; [hon.] Slater Award Chavez Award; [oth. writ.] School newspaper; [pers.] I want to let people know they are never alone. I want readers to feel they can live their dreams and challenge fate. Die trying to succeed.; [a.] Inglewood, CA

CATLIN, MAMIE L.
[pen.] Mamie Hines Catlin; [b.] September 1, 1940, LaPine, AL; [p.] Rufus and Eula Mae Hines; [m.] Divorced; [ch.] Vernon L. Catlin and Kimberly L. Catlin; [ed.] B.S. - Edinboro U. - 1962, High School - Aliquappa High - 1958, Masters Equivalency - Graduate classes - Slippery Rock U., Penn State, Clarion Univ.; [occ.] Teacher - Elementary, New Castle Area School Dist.; [memb.] NAACP, American Federation of Teachers, American Business Women Association, Delta Kappa Gamma, Edinboro U. of PA Alumni Association, Advisory Boards of Lawrence Co. Big Brother/Big Sister and Westminster College Minority Recruitment Boards; [hon.] 1992 - Outstanding Female Educator of Lawrence County 1994 - Thanks to Teachers honoree for a partnership for the NAACP African - American History Poster and Essay Contest 1994 - Thomas A. Farrow Community Service Award; [oth. writ.] Original greeting cards, two unpublished books

(Children's book and a novel) unpublished poems.; [pers.] Being the best person that you can be means having a good feeling about yourself through your relationship with Jesus Christ.; [a.] New Castle, PA

CHANG, EMILY CHAI-I
[b.] June 21, 1979, San Diego, CA; [p.] Mr. Yih-Ruey and Mrs. Chan-Yung; [ed.] Junior at La Jolla High School; [occ.] Student; [hon.] Semi-Finalists in 1995 Miss Southern California Jr. Teen Competition. 1st runner-up for speech. (1995); [oth. writ.] (Not Published): Eyes, Prince Charming, Blame, Read Me! A Power Trip, Pain, Choosing A Soul, In Need Of An Apology, A Devil's Compromise, Little Boy's Nightmare, Sweet Sixteen, God's Second Flood.; [pers.] Someday will be your day to persevere and of course... a day to smile.; [a.] San Diego, CA

CHANG, LORNA
[pen.] Lorna Chang; [b.] February 1, 1978, Houston, TX; [p.] Roberta and Jonathan Chang; [ed.] Curtis Senior High School; [occ.] Student; [hon.] Registry Scholarship, Who's Who Among American High School Students; [oth. writ.] Poetry, short stories; [pers.] I have nothing new to learn the world, truth and non violence are as old as the hills -Gandhi; [a.] Tacoma, WA

CHILDERS, DORTHA KAY
[pen.] Dottie; [b.] April 26, 1947, Gary, IN; [p.] Helen Tobey Hall; [m.] Divorced; [ch.] Genola Led Better, Randy Childers, Trisha Shackleford, Melody Childers (Roberts); [ed.] Edison Jr. High; [occ.] Disabled; [oth. writ.] Only poems when God inspires! Would love to see - several published and turned into songs - or left or poems, to touch Hearts of other people.; [pers.] Only writes poems with I feel God inspires me. Then my pastors wife.; [a.] Piedmont, SC

CHIN, ALICE
[ed.] U.C. Berkeley (B.A.) and Hastings College of the Law (J.D. Degree); [occ.] Attorney at Law; [memb.] Commonwealth Club of California, State Bar of California, Asian American Bar Association, Alameda County Bar Association, Queen's Bench, Women Lawyers of Alameda County (Board of Directors, 1990-1995 and President, 1996), California Women Lawyers, Lions Club, Chinese American Citizens Alliance Wa Sung Service Club, University of California at Berkeley Alumni Association, Hastings College of the Law Alumni Association, City of San Leandro Planning Commissioner; [hon.] California Scholarship Federation, Wa Sung Service Club Merit Award (1979), Who's Who Among Rising Young Americans (1992), Women of the Year (1992); [a.] San Leandro, CA

CHISM, VON-NA F.
[b.] October 29, 1969, Madison, WI; [p.] Loretta Chism; [ed.] Webster Groves Senior H.S., Riverside City College, The Art Institute of Seattle, currently enrolled at the Art Institute of Seattle; [occ.] Entrepreneur, Resident Assistant, and Student Financial Services Assistant; [memb.] (Voting Delegate) Delta Epsilon Chi (for Marketing Students, Business Organization) Minority Student Organization (appointed as Secretary); [hon.] Honor Roll student in the past, received the Merit Scholarship; [oth. writ.] Stories (personal for myself), and poems (personal for myself, my friends, and my family).; [pers.] I create strong motivation, strength, and emotion in my writing. I have been greatly influenced by my mother and all of the great poets and writers before me.; [a.] Seattle, WA

CHRISMAN, KARLA RUTH
[b.] February 14, 1953, Lexington, KY; [p.] Richard and Virginia Chrisman; [m.] Divorced; [ch.] Erika Chrisman, Mortyn; [ed.] Masters in Counseling Psychology! (United States International/University), Bible Diploma and Evangelical Teacher's (Bible Institute); [occ.] Training Certificated licensed minister, church dance director; [memb.] Elim Gospel Church and Elim Fellowship, Evangelical Teacher's Training Association; [hon.] Bible School - graduated with honors; [oth. writ.] Primarily Christian poetry (unpublished).; [pers.] I primarily write poetry with Christian themes reflecting the life and work of christ in my life.; [a.] Lima, NY

CHRISTENSEN, KENNETH W.
[b.] November 21, 1973, El Paso, TX; [p.] Alan and Maria Christensen; [ed.] East Carolina University, Environmental Sciences; [occ.] Scholar; [memb.] Sierra Club, Sigma Oh, Epsilon; [oth. writ.] I currently have four books filled, but none yet published.; [pers.] I grow wiser, breath, live, less than tomorrow, but more than yesterday.; [a.] Springfield, VA

CHRISTIAN, SHIRLEY I.
[b.] April 18, 1927, Spirit Lake, ID; [p.] Elbert and Vesta Lewis; [m.] R. H. (Dago) Christian, November 10, 1945; [ch.] Shirleen and Harold; [ed.] Graduated 12th Grade College Credits in nutrition PJC Pensacola, FL Graduation 12 grade at Bremerton, Wn 1945; [occ.] Housewife, crippled just a bit I occupy myself with friends. Growing house plants and some writing.; [memb.] Girl Scouts, as Leader. Sunday School Teacher, Methodist Church. Bagdad, FL. School Lunchroom manager Bagdad Elementary School; [hon.] Volunteer, as reading coach in Bagdad Elementary school certification of appreciation; [oth. writ.] Truth, Sunday's Birds "Friend - My Cane"; [pers.] The one that matters is the one that knows the truth.; [a.] Bagdad, FL

CHRISTISEN, VIRGINIA KINSEY
[b.] February 21, 1924, Carrollton, MO; [p.] Philip and Maggie Kinsey (Deceased); [m.] Donald Christisen, August 30, 1946; [ch.] Rosa Margaret and Laura Jane; [ed.] Sketchy; [occ.] Retired from many years with University of Missouri Stenographic Service, and 7 years Rusk Rehabilitation Ctr.; [memb.] National Museum of Women in The Arts, Swatch Watch Club, Steiff Collector Club, Muffy Bear Club, North Shore Animal League; [oth. writ.] Only some (alas) unpublished poems.; [pers.] My sister was a poet and had many of her works published in a Kansas City paper. My poems are always quickly written, very spontaneous, but always from a true experience or relationship.; [a.] Columbia, MO

CHRISTOPHER, EBONY JOY
[b.] March 20, 1980, Philadelphia, PA; [p.] Bernice and Gregory Christopher; [ed.] Holy Light Christian Academy (Kindergarten - first grds.) Cambridge Elementary (2nd-3rd) Central Elementary School (4th-5th); [occ.] Student at Pennsauken High School (6-8), Pennsauken High current; [memb.] Track Team; [hon.] Awards in spelling bees, reading, writing, running races, dancing and modeling awards.; [pers.] I've always liked writing as a way at expressing my feelings, but I never seemed to finish what I've started, except for now. I'm proud of my poem and hope that others can understand what meaning lies behind it. I thank my mother for encouraging me to send my poem to your contest and especially thank my friend justin Yampolsky for the inspiration and reason for writing the poem in the first place.; [a.] Pennsauken, NJ

CHROMY, HELEN
[b.] February 10, 1918, Chicago, IL; [p.] Deceased; [m.] Anthony J. Chromy, August 24, 1940; [ch.] Conrad and Ronald; [ed.] Schurz Highschool, Chicago, Illinois Two Semesters: Northwestern University Chicago, Illinois; [occ.] Retired; [oth. writ.] Article published in the Foreign Service Journal Entitled: Post Card From Abroad Based on an incident in a Pakistan assignment. Also, several newspaper articles in the Star Free Press, Ventura, California.; [pers.] I have had the enriching experiences of living in several foreign countries, mostly in the Middle East. This gave me the exposure to different cultures, customs and traditions which has shaped my philosophy towards our increasingly global environment.; [a.] Westlake Village, CA

CINTRON, LOURDES ARROYO
[pen.] Lu-Lu; [b.] July 9, 1962, New York; [p.] Rafael and Zoe Arroyo; [m.] Ramon Cintron, July 25, 1989; [ch.] Godchild Lourdes Segarra; [occ.] House wife, Bake Cakes for birthdays or other occasions; [oth. writ.] I enjoy writing poems just for fun. I find it very relaxing and comforting when I am feeling down or feel very happy.; [pers.] No matter how bad a day is or how terrible things have been, there is always tomorrow to give you another chance to make it better.; [a.] Bronx, NY

CLARK, EDWARD A.
[pen.] Eddie Clark; [b.] October 23, 1970, Lewisburg, PA; [p.] Joseph and Geraldine Clark; [ed.] Shikellamy High School Graduate, United States Army; [occ.] Line Operator at Paulsen Wire and Rope; [memb.] Rescue Fire Company, U.S. Army Reserve; [hon.] Just the one that the National Library of Poetry has given me.; [pers.] My writing has been inspired by my family and friends. Also by my girlfriend Jennifer in which I'm able to write with passion and romance. The earlier poets gave me the true feeling that poetry can give to the people of the world.; [a.] Sunbury, PA

CLARK, JODY TOERBER
[b.] September 19, 1972, Iowa; [p.] Larry and Zelma Toerber; [m.] Michael L. Clark, May 13, 1995; [ed.] Bachelors science in Nursing, Fart Hays State University, Hays, Kansas; [occ.] Registered Nurse, White house country manor, own my own business; [memb.] Sigma Theta Tau International; [oth. writ.] A Candlelight Ceremony; [pers.] My works are influenced by my lack of understanding of my emotions. I can he so irrational at times. Which I finish a poem or short story I reach a greater understanding and respect for my complexities as well as others.; [a.] Bowling Green, OH

CLARK, MRS. ALBERNIA GARY
[pen.] Albernia Gary Clark; [b.] April 21, Newport News, VA; [p.] Jamesette S. Gary, Albert (Deceased); [m.] William E. Clark III, August 9, 1968; [ch.] La Tonya M. Clark; [ed.] Booker T. Washington Elem Huntington High, Newport News, VA, Norfolk State - BS Old Domion MS Norfolk in Administration; [occ.] Elem. School Teacher - Bryan Hot, VA, 2nd Grade - grade Chairperson; [memb.] HEA, VEA, NEA, NBDCI, Pres of Lambda Kapps Mu Sorority Board of Directors - Project Reachable of St. James U. Methodist/Peninsula District Bd. of Directors the Potters House International Reading Association; [hon.] Teacher of the Year in '93 at Bryan Elem School, Mother of the year at St. James U.Methodist church having my poem published

by you is an honor.; [oth. writ.] Many - but I have not published any other.; [pers.] My goal is to write poetry that people can relate too, and feel a warm relationship to the words or implication. I look for the positive characteristic on everyone.; [a.] Hampton, VA

CLARK, TERRY L.
[b.] November 12, 1955, Tecumseh, MI; [p.] Lavern and Viola Clark; [m.] Amelia, October 4, 1986; [ch.] Kimberly, Jennifer, Joshua, Kristiana; [ed.] Dundee High School, University of Michigan, Foothill Community College; [occ.] Entrepreneur; [hon.] National Honor Society; [pers.] I simply pen the words that God puts in my heart. As could all mankind if they but listen.; [a.] Toledo, OH

CLAUSS, DOROTHY M
[b.] September 7, 1922, Ridgewood, NJ; [p.] Ethel Mae Clendenny and Walter Seaman; [m.] Henry A. Clauss, October 13, 1940; [ch.] Charles Clauss, Barbara Manning; [ed.] Ridgewood High School, Bergen Community College, R.R.A. classes; [occ.] Retired - busy designing and painting, personal greeting cards; [memb.] Former Ridgewood Art Association, Children's Book Writers Society, Bergen Poets, and Bergen County Historical Society, Ariel Puppet Troupe and Bam Puppet Troupe - Old Paramus Church on going membership Women's Guild; [hon.] Ribbon for 16x20 oil painting "Darryl", published poems, Poetry published in Bergen Poets, "Grandma's Fetish" and "In Retrospect"; [oth. writ.] 1st children's book for my grandson, 23 years ago - today he is an Aerospace Engineer, others since not published, short stories: "Barbara", and short stories, of my childhood growing up in B. City and still living on.; [pers.] The street where I was born, and my mother, and my grandmother all born within a mile on the same street. There's such a joy in seeing the response to my stories in the children's faces and hearing my four grandchildren reminisce about grandma... and her fetishes the oldest - a graduate of Mount Holyoke, life has been good to me with all its ups and downs. My next project is a "story" of my family." "Verbose - perhaps... I will confess... My pride in my family is boundless!; [a.] Paramus, NJ

CLINTON, JUDITH
[b.] May 10, 1955, Queens, NY; [p.] Isaiah Clinton, Norma Clinton; [ch.] Art, Jason; [ed.] John Bowne, H.S.; [occ.] Customer Service Manager, Account Manager; [pers.] I hope my writings help others seek kindness, hope and love. We must first look within our hearts, then to the world around us. We must not stop striving or smiling.; [a.] Freemansburg, PA

COBBLE, ANDY
[b.] August 6, 1981, Knoxville, TN; [p.] Jan and Steve Cobble; [ed.] 8th grade; [occ.] Student, Webb, School of Knoxville; [memb.] USTA, Sequoyah Presbyterian Church; [a.] Knoxville, TN

COKINOS, NICHOLAS
[pen.] Nicholas Cokinos; [b.] July 10, 1944, Paterson, NJ; [p.] Nicholas and Teresa Cokinos; [m.] Kathleen, May 17, 1969; [ch.] Kelly and Kimberly; [ed.] N.J Equiv Diploma; [occ.] Tractor Trailer Driver; [memb.] Milton First Aid Squad-American Legion, St. Thomas the Apostle R.C. Church; [oth. writ.] A Mother's Love, A Special Gift, A Greek Blessing-The Lawnan, The Firefighter - Earth Angels, A Christmas Prayer - a Thanksgiving prayer - The Teacher, The First Aid Volunteer - The Wife Of The Carpet Maker.; [pers.] My life revolves around my loving wife and two beautiful daughters.; [a.] Milton, NJ

COLE, LISA M.
[b.] February 4, 1967, Tucson, AZ; [p.] Carole R. Neubauer and Charles J. Cole; [ed.] Leonia High, night Courses of Banking, Accounting, Psychology and Journalism/Short story writing from International Correspondence Schools John Robert Powers Modeling School; [occ.] Author; [memb.] Holy Spirit Lutheran Church - Leonia, NJ; [hon.] Regional Modeling Competition for DECA - 1985; [oth. writ.] Poetry, short stories, articles nothing published.; [pers.] You need to keep your head up in order to see the blue skies. Always be yourself.; [a.] Mahwah, NJ

COLEMAN, ANGELA S.
[b.] August 23, 1985, Vicksburg, MS; [p.] Michael and Dana Coleman; [ed.] 5th Grade Student at Thomastown Elementary School; [memb.] I am a member of the 4-H agricultural group of Madison Parish; [hon.] A trophy for honor roll 4 awards for being best in school.; [pers.] I have set a path to follow other great poets cause I know one day I could be a great poet too.; [a.] Tallulah, LA

COLLINS, JODI K.
[b.] January 8, 1966, Grangeville, ID; [p.] James and Barbara Frei; [m.] James R. Collins, October 31, 1987; [pers.] A family is a wondrous gift that should never be taken for granted. I dedicate my poem to my family, Mom, Dad, Brenda, Vickie, Laurie, Andy and Teresa, I love you all very much!; [a.] Graham, WA

COLLINS, ROBERT
[b.] June 30, 1975, Kenmore, NY; [p.] Curtis Collins, Mary Lou Collins; [ed.] Kenmore West Senior High, Erie Community College; [pers.] I specialize in romantic poetry. My poem is dedicated to the enduring love of Jennifer Zubek.; [a.] Tonawanda, NY

COLVIN, SHERRY
[b.] August 17, 1961, New Orleans, LA; [p.] Albert Bradford; [ch.] Dale Colvin Jr. and Candace Baas; [ed.] Lakeview High - Central Texas College and Texas A and M; [memb.] Texas Council of Family Violence and Habitat for Humanity; [pers.] I dedicate this poem to my children for they are my world. And for Drew - My inspiration.; [a.] Fort Worth, TX

COMBS, MD. ROBERT G.
[b.] January 3, 1918, Indiana; [p.] Wm. H. and Elizabeth Combs; [m.] Mary Tichenor, June 19, 1943; [ch.] Wm. Robt, James Christopher, Cheryl; [ed.] Bach. Arts, Cincinnati 1940, MD - Cincinnati February, 1943; [occ.] Retired (1987) surgeon; [memb.] Am. Med. Association, Am. College of Surgery, Am. Board of Surgery, Ingham Co. Med. Society, Michigan State Med Soc.; [oth. writ.] None published.; [pers.] After my wife died and I retired I started writing verses for my own entertainment. So since friends enjoyed some of the versed I tried to published.; [a.] East Lansing, MI

CONLEY, GLORIA C.
[b.] April 29, 1948, Lancaster County, VA; [m.] Robert B. Conley, July 2, 1966; [ch.] Amy Marie Conley; [pers.] This poem is dedicated to my grandmother, Mrs. Winnie B. George who was born April 4, 1895 and who departed from this life at the age of 97 years on August 24, 1992.

CONNER, EDITH H.
[pen.] Edie Conner; [b.] October 10, 1960, Norfolk, VA; [p.] Edward and Ella Gaines; [ch.] Elisha Nicole Rivers; [ed.] Deep creek High School, Mary Baldwin College English Literature/Journalism; [occ.] Consultant, Norfolk, Virginia; [memb.] City of Va Beach Recreation Clubs; [hon.] Recognized by Poet Laureate Rita Dove for writings and contributions Received notoriety Mary Baldwin as editor of campus anthology contributor to Elssenoe Magazine; [pers.] "I believe that everyone can learn and grow from each other and the circle that we complete in this life is completed only if we pass on the knowledge within ourselves."; [a.] Virginia Beach, VA

CONNOR, RYAN
[pen.] Ryan Connor; [b.] November 24, 1985, Alabama; [p.] Dr. and Mrs. Walter E. Connor; [ed.] Presently in 4th grade now.; [occ.] Student; [memb.] Boy scouts; [a.] Orangeburg, SC

CONVERSE, CLETIS H.
[pen.] Cletis H. Converse; [b.] November 24, 1926, At home; [p.] Naomi Van Tries-Revey, Edward Revey; [m.] Divorced; [ch.] Debra Guy; [ed.] High School - Diploma from The Institute of Children's Literature, West Redding, Connecticut; [occ.] Retired; [memb.] Ladies auxiliary (Fraternal order of eagles). American Lung Association.; [hon.] Writing for children and teenagers course; [oth. writ.] Other poems published in newspapers. Poem (my miracle Mom). When I was in grade school, I wrote the poems for our school newspaper each month.; [pers.] I have written many children's short stories due to my childhood days. Growing up on the farm, was a very exciting time for me. Many new experiences came up each day. I grew up being outside with my Dad.; [a.] Lawrence, KS

CONWAY, LOIS L.
[pen.] Lois L. Conway; [b.] October 20, 1913, Caldwell, ID; [p.] Auttie and Will Crawford; [m.] Edward Owen Conway, June 23, 1934; [ch.] Two sons and two daughters; [ed.] Caldwell High School, Albertson College of Idaho, Chicago School of Music; [occ.] Retired from 40 years of Piano Teaching currently - Adjudicator National guild Piano Teachers 20 years Austin, TX; [memb.] American College of Musicians, Marquis Who's Who, Community Concerts Assn. Christian Science Church; [hon.] Distinguished Service National guild of Piano Teacher, Who's Who of Music and Musicians, Who's Who of American Women; [oth. writ.] Music Reviews 30 other poems: especially "To a Giant Redwood Tree", "Spring", "Ode to a Waterbird", "The Last Rose", "This Heart" "September in Oregon"; [pers.] Besides family, my loves have been music, and children, and seeing them grow into what became thru my confidence and help their best.; [a.] Hemet, CA

COOK, HAZEL M.
[pen.] "Witchazel"; [b.] January 3, 1914, Udell, IA; [m.] Glenn J. Cook; [ch.] John T., Susan M.; [oth. writ.] "Letters to a young Witch".; [pers.] Witchazel was born November 23, 1994 because of two letters. First, July 13, 1994, Gronma, in 1600, we would have been witches. We are independent women, free thinkers, mix herbal teas, talk to animals and live alone. "The second letter November 23, 1994, Gronma, life is like a Rainbow. You have lived through all the bright and dark colors - and every shade in between. I love you. Julia Marie P.S. Write to me about your early morning thoughts."; [a.] Saint Petersburg, FL

COOK JR., HOMER CALVIN
[pen.] H. C. Cook; [b.] March 31, 1936, Steubenville, OH; [p.] H. Calvin Cook and Ruth Transue Cook; [m.] Annette M. Cook, July 11, 1964; [ch.] Harrison Christopher Cook; [ed.] The Choate School, Bishop's Stortford College, Herts, England, Clark University (AB), Yale University (MCP); [occ.] Town and Country Planning; [memb.] American Planning Association, American Institute of Certified Planners, The Kittansett Club, Marion MA, The First Unitarian Church of New Bedford, MA; [hon.] English-Speaking Union schoolboy fellowship Kittansett Club Champion elected member local planning board; [oth. writ.] Published poem "Journeys".; [pers.] I like to write.; [a.] South Dartmouth, MA

COOK, PATRICIA A.
[pen.] Patricia A. Cook; [b.] December 29, 1960, Cincinnati; [p.] Shirley and Eugene Sunderhaus; [m.] Robert Cook, February 16, 1995; [ch.] Tyler and MacKenzie Cook; [ed.] Cincinnati Technical College, University of Cinti; [occ.] Technical Support Specialist; [oth. writ.] "My Giving Well", mother and me publication.

COOK, SUSAN F.
[b.] December 29, 1947, Salt Lake City, UT; [p.] Dewey J. Fillis and Marjorie C. Fillis; [m.] Divorced; [ch.] G. David Cook, Cheryl A. Gallo, Lora C. Clegg; [ed.] Stevens Henager Business College; [occ.] Accountant for Auto Dealship; [memb.] National multiple sclerosis society; [oth. writ.] The Mouse Of Grandma's House, Gifford The Gurple, The Cow On The Carousel, Wickety Witch, and numerous other children stories which, as yet, remain unpublished.; [pers.] When the tulips bloom in spring was written for my beloved grandmother who passed away at age 98 in January 1995.; [a.] Salt Lake City, UT

COOPER, MILDRED S.
[b.] July 6, 1921, Rescue, VA; [p.] Augustus Young Cooper and Evelyn Rosebud Tennis Cooper; [m.] Single; [ed.] Newport News H. School Peabody College, Nashville, A.B. English Scarritt College, Nashville, TN, M.A. - Christian Education; [occ.] Retired since 1984 after serving as a Christian Educator and Diaconal Minister in Methodist Churches and the Va Annual Conference of the United Methodist Church for 30 plus years my last position (1968-84) was coordinator of the united ministries for the United Methodist Church in the working Virginia Conference - With Youth and youth Leaders at Peabody; [hon.] I was honored when elected to Kappa Delta Pl and to Pl Gamma MU my greatest award was completing work for two degrees in seven years and supporting myself fully by working full time and going to school at the same time! At 26 I was a Freshman - at 33 I earned my M.A. degree; [oth. writ.] Articles which have been published in various United Methodist Magazines, news letters, youth curriculum, etc.; [pers.] I enjoy writing for fun (simple rhymes to surprise a friend on his or her Birthday, for example) but when I contemplate the beauty of the world or am deeply moved (sorrow, joy or love) poetry speaks to me and for me.; [a.] Newport News, VA

CORKERY, LINDA C.
[b.] Bronx, NY; [p.] Otto and Agnes Schween; [m.] Terrence M. Corkery; [ch.] Holly and Robert; [ed.] Evander Child's High School, Bronx, NY and Monroe Business School, Bronx, NY; [occ.] Court Reporter, Dutchess County Grand Jury, Poughkeepsie, NY; [memb.] The International Society of Poets; [oth. writ.] I recently wrote a poem on Oklahoma City that was published in our local newspaper and one for our H.S. crew team that will be used on a poster.; [pers.] I enjoy writing poems for friends and family on special occasions. I enjoy the challenge of being given an idea and then writing about it.; [a.] Staatsburg, NY

CORNELL, ALBERTA MARIE SHOEMAKER
[pen.] Bert Shoemaker; [b.] March 3, 1958, New Brunswick, NJ; [p.] Edward L. Shoemaker, Rita E. Willcox; [m.] Kenneth Gene Cornell, April 1976; [ch.] Heather Gene, Kenneth Edward; [ed.] G.E.D. Allentown Business School - Medical Office Management; [occ.] Medical Training, Allentown, PA; [hon.] Grandson - William David Cornell, Allentown Business School Honors in Insurance Plans; [oth. writ.] Several poems never published used for personal use.; [pers.] Be who you are, don't be someone you're not, to please others. Beauty is within the heart it doesn't matter what... you look like I try to reflect what people are feeling. Feelings are fragile and should be taken serious.; [a.] Bangor, PA

CORTEZ, LEONARDO V.
[b.] July 3, 1928, Del Carmen, Florida Blanca, Pampanga, Philippines; [p.] Francisco M. Cortez, Carmen N. Vistan; [m.] Alice H. C. Cortez, April 20, 1970; [ed.] A.B., M.A. (Philosophy) B.S.C. (Accounting) M.B.A., D.B.A.; [occ.] Special projects accountant; [memb.] Saint Thomas The Apostle Church, Knights of Columbus, Government Finance Officers, Association of South Carolina; [hon.] College Valedictorian; [oth. writ.] A feasibility study of establishing another filled milk industry. Origin of political authority. Pampanga: Yesterday and today a dance drama.; [pers.] In Christ humanity and divinity are United. To know Christ therefore is to know man and God.; [a.] Charleston, SC

CORY, MARGERY H.
[b.] October 13, 1910, Fall River, MA; [p.] William and Ann Hart; [m.] Chappell Cory, December 19, 1931; [ch.] Chappell III, Suzanne, Stephen; [ed.] Abbot Academy, Andover, Mass, Wheelock College, Boston, MA, to teach Private Schools, Dalton School, N.Y. City 45 yrs.; [occ.] Retired; [oth. writ.] Children's Stories, Odes for all occasions.; [pers.] Life is beautiful if you take time to see it.; [a.] Oak Bluffs, MA

COSSI, AUTUMN
[b.] March 1, 1975, Orangeburg, SC; [p.] Donald and Bonnie Cossi; [ed.] Leigh High School, Santa Clara University; [memb.] Compassion International, Santa Clara Community Action Program, Christian Outreach International; [hon.] Phi Theta Kappa, The National Dean's List '94, Santa Clara Dean's List '95, pending Phi Beta Kappa; [pers.] The earth resounds with the Lord's majesty. I will sing to the Lord all my life, I will sing praise to my God as long as I live.

COULAM, CHERYL
[ed.] Skyline High School Weber State College; [occ.] Registered Nurse; [a.] Salt Lake City, UT

COURTNEY, HELEN R.
[b.] August 6, 1980, Springfield, IL; [p.] Harry Jr. and Mary Courtney; [ed.] High School Student; [memb.] Poetry writing, hiking, arts and crafts, I also enjoy working with animals; [hon.] Middle School honor roll and Outstanding Achievement medal - Tae Kwan Do; [pers.] Writing is a way to keep in touch. In this fast pace world so many people have forgotten the true meaning of fellowship, peace of mind, and pursue of life. Poetry is one way to recognize how little things make us give and appreciate, and simple as gazing at the night stars.; [a.] Aurora, CO

COVEY, JUDITH ANN
[b.] November 22, 1942, Flint, MI; [p.] Charles and Daphine Hutchinson; [m.] Glenn Morgan Covey (Deceased), June 25, 1960; [ch.] Kelly Anne, Glenn Morgan, Shannon Dee; [ed.] Linden High, Mott Community College; [occ.] Para Professional For severely mentally imparted/retired; [memb.] Halsey Methodist Church; [hon.] Dean's List in 1998 and 1989; [oth. writ.] Numerous poems as yet unpublished. A poem published in "Stars and Stripes."; [pers.] I write to share my unrestrained joy, and, at other times, to purge myself of despair. My hope is to create a bond, if only for a moment, between author and reader, so no-one feel alone in their emotions.; [a.] Fenton, MI

COWAN, JENNIFER C.
[b.] February 28, 1980, Ventura, CA; [p.] Peggy and Thomas; [ed.] I'm a Sophomore at Bethel High School; [memb.] I have been a participant in band since 6th grade; [hon.] I have gotten many citizenship awards, but I have not let many people read my poems and stories.; [oth. writ.] I have written many poems and stories. This is the first poem I have gotten published.; [pers.] Write what fills your mind.; [a.] Graham, WA

COX, CYNTHIA A.
[b.] February 27, 1972, Bluffton, IN; [p.] John Kashner, Orren Cox; [ch.] Trevor John Goodin; [ed.] North Side High School; [occ.] Business Owner; [oth. writ.] I am currently writing a book of poetry.; [pers.] All things are possible through Jesus Christ.; [a.] Fort Wayne, IN

COX, KEITH
[b.] September 20, 1977, Mobile, AL; [p.] Judith and Warren Cox; [ed.] Finished through eleventh grade in high school; [occ.] Student; [oth. writ.] Poems, short stories, and columnist for Georgia State University newspaper.; [pers.] I am a Christian, and in my writing I strive to proclaim honest thinking and self-evaluation. Any talent or ability I have is wholly due to God's grace.; [a.] Decatur, GA

COZBY, BRADLY EDWARD
[b.] February 28, 1972, Stephenville, TX; [p.] Jerry and Gail Cozby; [ed.] Graduated Stephenville High School, 2 years at Tarleton State University; [occ.] Heavy duty and Automotive Parts Manager; [oth. writ.] Many other poems and songs none of which have ever been published.; [pers.] Love and respect nature and all things in it and believe in a higher power, by whatever name or names you choose to call it. Merry meet, Merry part, Merry may we meet again.; [a.] Stephenville, TX

CRAYTON, CYNTHIA ROSE
[pen.] Taylor Abron; [b.] September 15, 1951, Los Angeles, CA; [p.] James A. and Judy Crayton; [ch.] Roland, Synthea and Delania; [ed.] Perris Union High School, Riverside City College; [occ.] Freelance Artist, Writer; [oth. writ.] Many poems and short stories presently working on two books. All writings inspired by my Mom.; [pers.] My parents taught me I could achieve anything with patience and perseverance. I thank God for them my children, my friends and loved ones I love you Dad... We did it Mom!

CROUCH, ROBERT B.
[b.] June 22, 1973, Brooklyn, NY; [p.] Gwendolyn Crouch and Robert B. Murphy; [ch.] Meleka J. Miller and Brandon T. Stoney; [ed.] College student, (College of New Rochelle); [occ.] College student; [memb.] NAACP, Mason-King James Lodge #1; [hon.] An Editors choice from the National Library of Poetry ("Thank You"); [oth. writ.] An untitled poem for the National Library of Poetry.; [pers.] First, I would like to thank N.L.O.P. for the acknowledgement and I love reading as well as writing. The literature I write comes from my heart the world should listen and express their feelings from the heart.; [a.] Brooklyn, NY

CROWE, CHERYL
[pen.] Cher; [b.] October 29, 1955, Lockport, NY; [p.] Ray and Nora Crowe; [ed.] Business Associates Degree Alfred Stare CNA Certified Nursing Assistant; [occ.] Sales, Production Bakery; [memb.] American Heart Association Cancer Society Volunteer United Way; [oth. writ.] World of poetry in Orlando 1986 poem published Vincent Pike Awarded.; [pers.] Grateful for life graduating by death only.; [a.] Saint Augustine, FL

CRUMP, JOANNA M.
[b.] September 14, 1980, Los Alamitos, CA; [p.] James and Pat Crump; [ed.] Holy Trinity School and Mary Star of The Sea High School; [hon.] CJSF California Junior Scholastic Federation in 7th and 8th grade, Gold Seal Bearer, Bronze Medal (GPA in 8the grade, Honor roll, and CSF, California Scholastic Federation); [oth. writ.] None so far.; [pers.] It doesn't take much to make a feeling of mine blossom into poetry - whether it be a broken heart or the joy seeing the sunset. I believe in writing from the soul.; [a.] San Pedro, CA

CUATT, JENNIFER
[b.] March 13, 1984, Mount Kisco, NY; [p.] John and Joyce Cuatt; [ed.] Currently in 6th grade at Arlington Middle School, Poughkeepsie, NY; [memb.] Arlington Middle School Band, Altar Server at St. Denis Church

CULLEN, HELENA W.
[b.] Shelton, CT; [p.] Mary McEvoy Cullen, James J. Cullen; [ed.] New Haven State Normal School, Southern Connecticut State University - B.S. Fairfield University Graduate School - MS; [occ.] Retired (former Teacher and Principal); [memb.] AARP S.C.S. University, Alumni Assoc., Fairsfield Un. Alumni Assoc., St. Vincent de Paul Society; [oth. writ.] Avon House, Publisher The Year Book of Contemporary Poetry - 1937, Anthology edited by margaret Nelson - two poems: Nocturne, Sonnet

CUMBERLAND, TOMMY KEITH
[pen.] Bo Cumberland; [b.] December 26, 1974, Jackson, MS; [p.] Keith and Hazel Cumberland; [ed.] High School graduate and two semesters at a Junior College; [occ.] Customer Service Agent at U.S. Air Express; [hon.] High School Journalism and Creative Writing Award; [oth. writ.] I have written two songs in which I performed in a country music contest. I have written close to one hundred poems. Several were published in a school newspaper and in my High School Annual.; [pers.] I try, through my poetry to express the importance of love in our society. Maybe you can't live off love but it's a start.; [a.] Jackson, MS

CUMMINS, ALENE P.
[b.] March 3, 1925, New Pastle, PA; [p.] Mary Ann Rigby, Russell B. Proctor; [m.] Thes L. Cummins (Deceased), January 29, 1942; [ch.] Russell C, Sandra Lee (Deceased), Thes L. Jr.; [ed.] Arthur McGill - Geo. Wash, Jr High, New Pastle Sr. High; [occ.] Retired; [memb.] AARP - Amvets Auxiliary and President of Multi Sr. Citizens Center Head Craft at "Center"; [hon.] Golden Poet Award for Poem "Everywhere"; [oth. writ.] Have published, poems and short story (David's Christmas) in local news); [pers.] Have written many poems and articles someday hope to publish a boom. I believe there is good and beauty in all walks of life!; [a.] New Castle, PA

CUNNINGHAM, CHRIS
[b.] October 12, 1972, Lemoore, CA; [p.] Barbara Cheever, Hal and Gladys Reed; [m.] Michelle Giunta; [ch.] Alexis Nicole Cunningham; [ed.] Studying business law at Oxnard College; [occ.] Construction Worker; [oth. writ.] Lots of poems and short stories, kept in journals.; [pers.] I like to write, as a way to express my feelings. The poems are a medium through which I can express those feelings. Thanks to Michelle, Jo Anne, Tom (agent), Mom, Grandparents, my daughter for being born, and God for my abilities.; [a.] Agoura Hills, CA

CUNNINGHAM, LISA K.
[b.] January 19, 1956, Baltimore, MD; [m.] Gary L. Cunningham; [ch.] Sarah, Evon, Justin, Leah; [occ.] Full time - Mom, part time - poet; [oth. writ.] "Hello my name is Adho" Solace, The Return, Autumn, My Secret Place, Battle War, Cleansing Hearts, Taver Tall.; [pers.] We journey through life with a choice. We can travel with eyes closed, deaf ears and a hard heart or with eyes that see, ears that hear and a heart colored with the gift of grace.; [a.] Sykesville, MD

CURRY, ADDIE POSTON
[pen.] Addie Poston; [b.] November 4, 1937, Cleveland County; [p.] Hoyle and Genie L. Poston; [ch.] Melrose P. Webster; [ed.] High School - Green Bethel; [occ.] Cook - House keeper; [memb.] Green Bethel Young Adult Missionary Direction Ebenezer Youth Director; [hon.] Woodman of the world; [oth. writ.] None published.; [pers.] I have written several plays, essays, and poems but have never submitted in to be never submitted in to be published. I enjoy writing and working with young people.; [a.] Greensboro, NC

CURRY, CHRIS VERNON
[pen.] Chris V. Curry; [b.] January 18, 1951, San Antonio; [p.] Charles V. "Buddy" Curry, Mary Ann Curry; [m.] Paula Ann Splichal, March 21, 1981; [ch.] Krystle Dee Curry, Chadwick Vernon Curry; [ed.] G.E.D.; [occ.] Lead Grounds Keeper 17 years; [oth. writ.] I wrote a poem for a co-worker that died. It got copied in main falcon news letter. Also his family contacted me personally, extremely touched!; [pers.] "Proud Mary" This poem was written to give Billy, Chris, Lynn, Joe, Susie, Tommy, Danny Lou Ann, Lela and Sally Jane strength to carry on Life! After the death of our beloved mother on July 12, 1992. "Proud Mary" loved the ocean, fishing and crabbing, especially following the weather about tropical storms and hurricanes. Mary loved the song "Que Sera Sera, and country music's Hank Williams' "Tear in my Beer."; [a.] San Antonio, TX

CURTIS, SARAH DIANE
[b.] November 15, 1980, Anniston, AL; [p.] David Curtis, Dennise Curtis; [ed.] Johnston Elementary, Anniston Middle School, Pleasent Valley High; [occ.] Student; [memb.] Pleasent Valley Marching Band, United States Tae Kwon Do Alliance, Future Homemakers of America, New Liberty Baptist Church; [hon.] Young Author's Conference; [oth. writ.] Our father God, published in Anthology of Poetry by Young Americans 1992 Edition One Snowy Morning; [a.] Wellington, AL

CUSHING, JILL SUZANNE
[b.] April 3, 1971, Somerset, NJ; [p.] Robert and Joanne Mercier; [m.] Edward Burton Cushing, September 25, 1993; [ed.] Aquinas College, Bay State College, Duxbury High; [occ.] Production Assistant, Griffin Publishing Company, Rockland, MA; [a.] Plymouth, MA

CYNKAR, NATALIE
[b.] December 15, 1978, Pittsburgh, PA; [p.] Louis and Patricia Cynkar; [ed.] Bishop McCort High School - Junior Planning to go to college; [memb.] American Diabetes Association; [a.] Johnstown, PA

D'AMATO, CAROL ANNE
[b.] August 11, 1966, Suffern, NY; [p.] John Joseph D'Amato, Susan Marie D'Amato; [ed.] Albertus Magnus H.S., Dominican College I.O.N.A. College: MS in Education; [occ.] Teacher, Margetts Elementary School, Chestnut Ridge, N.Y.; [oth. writ.] A compilation of copyrighted songs entitled "Songs of Joy"; [pers.] All creation shouts this truth: Creativity is a gift from God, the ultimate creator of the universe! (See Relations 4:11).; [a.] Monsey, NY

DAHLBERG, LOIS
[pen.] Loid Dahl, Lewis Dahl; [b.] ND; [p.] Ernest and Pearl Posey Harris (Both Deceased); [m.] R. Russell Dahlberg (Deceased); [ch.] Ralph, Gordon, Lyle Dahlberg, Annette Dahlberg Curran; [ed.] High School, 2 years College, became certified Dental Assistant Studied creature writing History, Geography and others; [occ.] Serving a history mission for LDS, Church; [memb.] International Society of Authors and Artists", National Authors Registry", I was President of Tacoma Writer's Club for a term of 1 year.; [hon.] Accomplishment of merit for "Intermezzo" by Creative Arts and Science Enterprises. "Fulfillment" Amateur Writers Journal "Shaping Up for Poetry" "Am Writers Journal" Silver Poet Award and Gold Poet Award 1986 - by World of poetry for. 1992 "Dear Lord, we thank you for our Nation"; [oth. writ.] Articles and poetry in newspapers and school and church publications, some reporting for the "Parkland, Spanaway Post" and the "Seniors Scene".; [pers.] It is my desire that my writings might inspire troubled youth and the discouraged, to have faith in themselves and to realize that writing can be a satisfying and stimulating outlet for creativity and expression of thought, even recreation now.; [a.] Salt Lake City, UT

DAKEN, JOHN MARSHALL
[b.] January 11, 1973, San Jose, CA; [p.] Kathy Evans, Robin Daken; [ed.] US Navy, currently attending College in Sacramento, CA; [occ.] Bartender; [pers.] You will never succeed if you never try. Take a chance.; [a.] Sacramento, CA

DALESSIO, ANTHONY
[pen.] Tony Dalessio; [b.] April 28, 1977, Stratford, NJ; [p.] Joseph and Charleen Dalessio; [ed.] Triton Regional High School, Pennco Tech (Computer Programming); [occ.] Customer Service at Shop Rite of

Laurel Hill; [memb.] National Honor Society, Smithsonian Air and Space Society; [hon.] Honor roll, Principal's List, Full $16,000 scholarship to Pennco Tech award for excellence in Italian, graduated with honors (top 5% of class); [oth. writ.] Several poems (3 published in literary magazines), 1 published short story.; [pers.] Give yourself a chance. Write for yourself, not for others.; [a.] Magnolia, NJ

DALTON, TIM
[b.] October 31, 1979, Burlington, VT; [p.] Kevin and Susan Dalton; [ed.] Acton-Boxborough Regional High School (Sophomore); [occ.] Student; [memb.] Band - Clarinet, Newspaper - Sports Editor, Amnesty International, Spring Track, Literary Magazine (The writing express) submitted a play for proscenium circus (Drama Club); [oth. writ.] Nothing published.; [pers.] Influence: Winnie The Pogh (and other Bears of Very Little Brain), Calvin and Hobbes, "Philosophical Statement": LIVE!!! Oh yeah, Hi to everyone in Action!!!!!; [a.] Acron, MA

DANIEL, EVELYN
[pen.] Eve; [b.] February 24, 1934, Philadelphia, PA; [p.] Evelyn and Charlie Emanuel; [ch.] Robert, Karen, John and Lisa; [ed.] John Hallahan High School for Girls; [occ.] Home Maker; [memb.] National Assoc. of Astrologers; [oth. writ.] Several poems and songs.; [a.] Philadelphia, PA

DANIELS, JANE
[b.] February 28, 1982, Independence, IA; [p.] Denver Daniels, Sheryl Daniels; [ed.] Whitson Elementary School; [occ.] Student at London Middle School; [memb.] Topeka Youth Symphony, First Presbyterian Church; [hon.] 4.0 honor student, London student of the month, music/arts Institute Honors, Recitalist (Kansas City, MO), Cellist-Ottawa Suzuki Summer Institute (Ottawa, Kansas); [a.] Topeka, KS

DANLEY, CHRIS
[b.] October 10, 1977, Fullerton, CA; [p.] Rick and Mitzi Danley; [ed.] Graduated Ontario H.S. current student at Riverside Community College Majoring in journalism; [occ.] Girls Basketball coach; [oth. writ.] Various poems and journalism articles.; [a.] Ontario, CA

DARE, JENNIFER AURIANNE
[pen.] Sinise Colbran; [b.] January 1, 1970, Visalia, CA; [p.] Louie and Susan Dare; [ed.] The Dolphian School High School only, in Oregon. Graduated.; [occ.] Lead vocalist in "The Extinct". Folk funk-rock band-new album released 4 months ago.; [oth. writ.] Many, but none ever published; [pers.] "There's a first time for everything." In regards to being a semi-finalist in a poetry contest. Never even showed my poetry to anyone before this.; [a.] North Hollywood, CA

DARLEY, TAMI D.
[b.] May 9, 1965, Columbus, MS; [p.] Charles Blount, Betty McCullough Woodham; [m.] Benjamin L. Darley, June 18, 1982; [ch.] Windy Nicole, Benjamin Ryan, Cady Noelle and Lindsey Brianne; [ed.] Behobeth High School, Carroll High School, Dothan High School, Wallace College; [occ.] Homemaker; [memb.] Church of Jesus Christ of Latter - Day Saints; [oth. writ.] Several poems. Children's stories. This is the first published work.; [pers.] I often use pen and paper to express the emotions that are so difficult to express verbally. I need this outlet for my active imagination.; [a.] Ozark, AL

DAVIES, MARGARET M.
[b.] February 25, 1962, Cleveland, OH; [p.] Thomas Davies, Donna Davies and (foster parents) James Torrence and Alice Torrence; [ed.] Saint Joseph Academy, Currently: Davis College; [occ.] Home Health Aide; [hon.] Dean's List at Davis College; [oth. writ.] Several poems published in high school poetry magazine. (Caravelle).; [pers.] My writings most generally reflect my deep faith and great love for the Lord. He has given me the gift of life... and I want to share the gifts he has given me. I find that I can do the best through writing.; [a.] Maumee, OH

DAVIS, BETTY J.
[b.] October 1, 1936, Handsboro, MS; [p.] Florence McGowan and James McGowan; [m.] Ted Davis, May 3, 1975; [ch.] Marion, Karl, Adrian; [ed.] Turkey Creek High School; [occ.] Flower maker, arranger cake decorator; [memb.] Bells Lane Baptist Church Choir and Prayer Band; [hon.] 1978 Volunteer Service Award Jane Byod Community House Softball Program which I did for many years.; [oth. writ.] Family birthdays and anniversary cards several poems none published before.; [pers.] I try to express my tree and personal feelings in my poems.; [a.] Cincinnati, OH

DAVIS, DEAN
[pen.] Benevozent Allan; [b.] October 17, 1969, Seattle, WA; [p.] Oscar and Martha Davis; [ed.] BA Communication/Advertising Garfield High School, Seattle; [occ.] Merchandise Manager JC Penney; [memb.] Board of Directors African American Heritage Museum and Cultural Center Youth Commits CO-Chair; [oth. writ.] "The key" self Published book, Poetry(Due Feb 96) "Love Line" self Published Book Poetry (Due July '96) short stories "Games Show Love," "Penny for your Thought," Novel untitled (All Stories Unpublished).; [pers.] Knowledge is the foundation of all things.; [a.] Seattle, WA

DAVIS, DONITA L.
[b.] December 11, 1954, Vallejo, CA; [p.] Mr. and Mrs. Freddie Lee Davis Sr.; [ch.] Marcus Robinson, (Twins) Joseph and Jeanine Davis; [ed.] Royal High School Brookshire, TX, Licensing, accreditation and certification for child day care management; [occ.] Home day care provider; [oth. writ.] Personal poems for me to read when I am in despair. Poetry for my church look and sometimes for the church food for thought.; [pers.] I can only express myself, through poetry. I am so single parent and the things that happens to me in my everyday life strengthen me, when I think about God's goodness and what He's done for me, through my poetry, I can give him all the honor and all the praise and all the glory!; [a.] Brookshire, TX

DAVIS JR., R. J.
[pen.] Beetle; [b.] Washington, DC; [p.] Dr. R. J. Davis Sr. and Mrs. J. T. Davis; [m.] Mrs. Bonita A. Davis; [ch.] Ryan Jamal Davis and Russell Ahanu Davis; [ed.] Grad. Calvin Coolidge H.S. Attn. U.D.C. City Col. of Chicago and St. Leo Universities, passed EMT course and National Regitra (CCC); [occ.] Fire Fighter - EMT, student; [memb.] Metropolitan B.C. International ASs. of Fire Fighters, Amateur Boxing Federation, and Midtown Youth Academy N.W. DC; [hon.] U.S.A.F. boxing champion 1988-1922, Golden Glove Champ San An. TX 1988, 1991, Continental Sports Champion 1987, U.S.A.F.E. Boxing Champion 1987, Golden Gloves Champion VA. 1993; [oth. writ.] Written and performed at Comedy Cafe, NW. DC, Boston Comedy Club, Village N.Y. Manute Bol's Spot Light Club NW. DC and Pecaso's Night Club, Va. Beach. Also have appeared at Mr. Henry's Night Club. NW. Washington, DC.; [pers.] I think of my works as: Pastoral Poetry, I.E. "A poet takes his pen then forms warm words again, that all in hell have sin... a not her beetle creation. What a revelation?"

DAVIS, KIM E.
[b.] July 30, 1969, Price, UT; [p.] Vernon W. "Bill" and Virginia Slane; [m.] Todd H. Davis, June 14, 1990; [ch.] Jade - 4, Logan - 2, Ashlyn - 1; [ed.] Carbon High School, Snow College; [occ.] Wife and Mother; [memb.] The Church of Jesus Christ of Latter Day Saints.; [hon.] Vocalist of the Year 1987 at Carbon High School, Young Womens Medalion-Church Youth Program; [oth. writ.] I only write poems for personal means and am thrilled to finally have one published.; [pers.] This poem was written about my daughter after her birth. Amazingly enough, she was born on the hospital bathroom floor and was in NICU for 5 days.; [a.] Roy, UT

DAVIS, LINDA IRENE
[b.] March 4, 1967, Memphis; [p.] Jessica and Willie Dockery; [m.] Leo Davis, May 28, 1988; [ch.] Jessica Donise Davis; [ed.] Med Student at Shelby State, Grad from Whitehaven High School major in RN.; [occ.] Lab Tech at Dr. Kelley, office, Memphis, TN; [memb.] MANA Outreach program for the homeless thru MBC church.; [hon.] 2nd honor roll student in 10th grade, most talented student in art, outstanding 4-H leader etc.; [oth. writ.] Small wonders in my hand like little tiny crumbs that lie in the palm of my hands for safe keeping. Small wonders that possess thru time without any warning small wonders that capture every child's life. Small wonders that keep us a float on bad and good occasion thank you God for small wonders.; [pers.] I found that writing is the greatest way of expression yourself. It's my greatest love. Thank you so much National Library of Poetry for making me a semi finalist.; [a.] Memphis, TN

DAVIS, ROBERT ADALE
[pen.] Robert A. Davis; [b.] July 27, 1954, Cleburne, TX; [p.] F.E. Davis II and Betty; [m.] Betty L. Davis/ Johnston, Diane Cekonsky/Davis, August 7, 1992; [ed.] Yes 4 years of College Pichland and Mountain View, Self Taugh in Music, Acting and Poetry/Artist/ Drama; [occ.] Artist/Sculpture, Painting, and Drafting; [memb.] Tesla Society National Geographic Society; [hon.] Acting Position in Oliver Stone's, Movie JFK, Directing David Rintels Play Clarence Darron; [oth. writ.] Language of the Imagined: Written and I'll by Robert A. Davis, Blue Chip Karma: Play: Written by R.A. Davis; [pers.] Statement of expression of this Artist: "An Active Product of Thought", R. A. Davis.; [a.] Colorado Springs, CO

DAY, BETTY JANE
[b.] December 23, 1934, Saint Louis, MO; [p.] Edward J. and Florence A. Freimuth; [m.] Divorced; [ch.] Three sons, Paul M. Day, John E. Day and Michael J. Day; [ed.] Graduated Ursuline Academy, Arcadia, MO June '54 Studied English, Educational Psych. at Fontbonne College, Studied course in Religion at Lael University, both Saint Louis; [occ.] Transcriptionist in Child Abuse/Neglect Unit, for Dept. of Family Service, State of MO. I have been employed by DFS since Oct. 1, 1973.; [hon.] English Pin Award in High School at

Graduation; [oth. writ.] I have written prose and poetry and short stories since I was first encouraged to do so by my English teacher back in high school, beginning with my freshman year in 1950.; [pers.] I guess I would have never known my potential had it not been for my high school English teacher at Ursuline. She was a teacher who took time to tap the hidden recesses of my ability and to uncover the otherwise buried gift-within. Mother Loyola Power, OSU, introduced me to the benefits of participating on the Debate team, of being on staff of the school newspaper, and an active member of the Drama Club, all of which prepared me to write and recite my work in public with ease and confidence.; [a.] Saint Louis, MO

DAY, REED ALAN

[b.] February 21, 1982, Mount Pleasant, MI; [p.] John W. And Wilma L. Day; [ed.] 7th Grader at Earle E. Williams, Middle School; [occ.] Full Time Student; [memb.] Boy Scouts of America, Troop 505-Tracy, CA, National Geographic Society; [hon.] 2nd place Waukeen District Pine Wood Derby, 2-1st place and 2-2nd Place Awards in Tracy Science; [a.] Tracy, CA

DAYHUFF, DOUGLAS MITCHELL

[pen.] Elias Jack; [b.] May 27, 1965, Chattanoga, TN; [p.] Richard Joseph Dayhuff, Ada Sue Dayhuff; [ed.] Terre Haute Baptist School, Liberty University, Indian State University; [occ.] Rental Car Agent, House Painter; [memb.] Indiana National Guard - Honorable Discharge; [oth. writ.] O sweet Leane, Dragonsplot, has always been, other non titled writings the terror, people just happen.; [pers.] Writing to me is a reflection of the self that when touching someone else truly touches me.; [a.] Terre Haute, IN

DAYTON, MANDI MARIE

[pen.] Mardi Marie; [b.] March 10, 1979, Llano; [p.] Gene and Catherine Dayton; [ed.] Currently a junior in highschool; [occ.] Student; [memb.] Youngest accepted nominee in Texas for the Daughters of the confederacy; [hon.] Academic awards, nominee for NHS, National honor society, many other pieces published in school literary magazine, finalist in South Texas National Teen-ager Scholarship Program; [oth. writ.] Portfolio of many other poems and short stories. I am currently writing my first novel entitled Embracing The Dark, involves The Fallen Angels. I am also exploring comic strips, writing one myself titled Prune Face involving an elderly, sarcastic couple.; [pers.] After extensive trips to Liberty Hill memorial and the viewing of my deceased father's head stone, I was inspired to create the Graveyard, I wrote it about 6 years ago. Iwas 2 at the time of his death.; [a.] Round Rock, TX

DE LOACH, DOLORES

[b.] February 4, 1935, New Philadelphia, PA; [p.] Mary Stessalavage and the late Joseph Stessalavage; [m.] Richard E. De Loach, August 27, 1960; [ch.] Donna De Loach Grace, Diane, Katherine and Carl De Loach; [ed.] Saint Clair High School, Episcopal Hospital School of Nursing; [occ.] Semi-Retired Registered Nurse, Primary Caregiver for Husband with Multiple Sclerosis, Homemaker; [memb.] Episcopal Hospital Nurses Alumni Association, Vice Chairperson of Parish Pastoral Council at Maternity BVM Church, Head of Bereavement Ministry Group at Church, Singer in Music Ministry at Church, Volunteer Pastoral Care Visitor at Frankford Hospital; [oth. writ.] Poems written for personal pleasure and to share with others.; [pers.] I like to share my thoughts, feelings and life experiences with others. I am inspired by faith in my God, in my family and in myself, by hope that there is good to be found in even the most adverse situation and by my love for human kind.; [a.] Philadelphia, PA

DE TIMMERMAN, R. H.

[b.] August 12, 1931, Oelwein, IA; [p.] (George) - Maxine; [m.] Janet, February 25, 1956; [ch.] Cheryl, Gallagher, Dibbie Miles, Mike De Timmerman; [ed.] Undergraduate at University of Minnesota, Refresher Studies after Service in Korea at Iowa State teachers College, LLB from University of Iowa; [occ.] Retired April 15, 1994 from U.S. Dept. of Energy as Deputy Chief Counsel; [memb.] Hall Monitor Oelwein High School; [hon.] High School Valedictorian, National Math Society, Jr. Law Arguments Several Superior Performance Awards from U.S Dept. of Energy; [pers.] I was fortunate to discover early in life that there is no greater gift than family. I can't visualize my life without my loving wife, children and grandchildren.; [a.] Albuquerque, NM

DEACON, LAURA J.

[b.] May 29, 1947, New Jersey; [p.] Bill and Laura Deacon; [ch.] Sonia Marie; [ed.] Bucks High School, Mercer County School Nursing; [occ.] Artist, Writer, Owner of the College Collection - Longest in Nation; [memb.] National Assoc. Female Executives, Hugh and Yu Characters Assoc. the Stevenson Foundation, The Salvation Army, Christian Destiny News; [hon.] The Honor of Life, The Awards of Living; [oth. writ.] Other poems and articles, Published. Horizon's News. Published Articles Trenton Times. Goal-Children's Books.; [pers.] Life is what you make it. I've learned to enjoy all the comes my way and grows with it!; [a.] Mercer County, NJ

DEAN, BENJI

[b.] July 26, 1983, Findlay, OH; [p.] Janet Dean and David Dean; [ed.] Sixth grade; [occ.] Student; [hon.] Presidential Academic Fitness Award in 1994 in the Fourth grade, All A's Student; [a.] McComb, OH

DEAN, EVELYN

[b.] October 10, 1966, Cleveland, OH; [p.] Ida Efford Ingram, William Ingram; [m.] Leachuin Dean Sr., January 9, 1987; [ch.] Leachuin Genesis O'Neil, Ricardo Maurice, K'Omari Denise and Kimera Denise; [ed.] John Adams, Ohio University; [occ.] Americorps and Substitute Teaching; [memb.] National Assoc. for Ed of Young Children, Democracy In Education, Project Learning Tree (Wildlife and Aquatic), Gospel Voices of Faith. Institute or children's Literature, Student Government, Americorps; [hon.] National Honor Society Project Learning Tree, 40 BRCH's Chemical Dependency, First Aid and Adult CPR.; [oth. writ.] Several articles published in the Athens News and Campus Newspaper, Children's books "Talking Walking Shoes", and "More Than Just Expecting Twins" not yet published.; [pers.] I am deeply committed to the pursuit of excellence in every area of my lie. I am because, I know I can. I can because, I know I am.; [a.] Athens, OH

DECK, MARGIE

[b.] October 31, 1959, Abilene, TX; [m.] Hank Deck; [ch.] Jeremy and Rachel; [occ.] Community Service Coordinator in Adult probation; [pers.] My written work is always a reflection on a moment in my life of personal significance.; [a.] Andrews, TX

DECKER, GIFFORD

[pen.] Wolfgang Bleached Kiwi; [b.] May 22, 1978, Snowflake; [p.] David and Sandra Decker; [ed.] Junior in High School; [memb.] SMAK, SCIP, NPDA; [hon.] Eagle Scout; [oth. writ.] Many other poems, "Something Special" "Dreaming Nightmares" "From Where Comes This Frail Existence" "Ode, To Question From Where Comes Love"; [pers.] Life is wonderful it plenishes us with good things, and no one is real unless in the minds of others.

DECKER, JENNIFER LYNN MONICA

[pen.] Bethany Murrelli; [b.] November 2, 1972, Sayre, PA; [p.] Late Lewis W. Decker and Marion J. Parks Decker; [ed.] Sayre Area High School, Pennsylvania College of Technology; [occ.] College Student pursuing a Degree in Teaching; [memb.] Phi Beta Lambda, Annunciation Roman Catholic Church, Bacchus, Student Govt. Association; [hon.] Perfect Attendance 3-12 Grade, Honor Roll, Varisty Letter Track and Cross-Country; [pers.] I would like to thank my aunt and uncle for all they have done to see me reach my goals successfully.; [a.] Williamsport, PA

DEEMER, SANDRA B.

[pen.] Jewels D. Meer; [b.] March 12, 1971, Plainwell, MI; [p.] Vicki T. Deemer, Blair Deemer; [ed.] Plainwell High School, Central Michigan University; [occ.] Retail Sales - Currently Searching for a Position in the Publishing Industry; [oth. writ.] Let me be free will be is my first published work of art.; [pers.] Our lives last for only a moment of eternity so we must open our hearts, minds and souls and let love reside there!; [a.] Lynnwood, WA

DELCASTILLO, STACY

[b.] July 7, 1970, Tampa, FL; [p.] George and Sylvia DelCastillo; [m.] Single; [ed.] Hillview High School, currently attending Rancho Santiago College, Computer Science and additional courses of interest.; [occ.] Guest service Rep. at major hotel.; [pers.] Having been greatly influenced by various artist and songwriters. Also poetry and the environment within my surroundings. I am in hopes of pursuing a career in writing and musical instrumental in percussions.; [a.] Tustin, CA

DELMENDO, TINA M.

[b.] December 21, 1960, Danville, IL; [p.] Daniel and Wilma Shelato; [m.] (Fiance) Michael Thompson, December 15, 1995; [ch.] Cody Daniel Delmendo; [ed.] Moweaqua High School in Moweaqua, IL Decatur Area Vocational Center in Decatur, IL; [occ.] Intake Coordinator for Madison County Juvenile Court Serv., in Jackson, TN.

DEN, RICHARD S. E.

[pen.] Zemin (Den); [b.] February 12, 1925, Hunan, China; [ed.] (1) B.S. Hwakiu College of Eng. and Commerce. (2) M.S. Ed, University of Pennsylvania. (3) B.D. Lutheran Theological Seminary. Phila, PA; [occ.] President, Chinese Academy in Phila., PA; [memb.] 1) Pa. Society of Public Accountants, 2) National Society of the Professionals; [hon.] Over 20 Championships of Contests in Essay, Public Speech, and Calligraphy. Honored in "Who is Who in Delaware Valley (89, 90) and in "Who is Who of Overseas Chines" (1993, Beijing China); [oth. writ.] 1) Christian Economic thoughts and the world peace (1956, Hongkong), 2) Den's Poems and Essay Collection (in process of Publication, China).; [pers.] The truth of love is mutual help in peace for progress, personally, socially and internationally.; [a.] Philadelphia, PA

DENHAM, ERIN MICHELLE
[b.] April 24, 1981, Wichita, KS; [p.] James and Debbie Denham; [ed.] Currently in the ninth grade at Campus High School; [occ.] Student; [memb.] First Baptist Church of Haysville, Campus Life (Christian Organization) at School, Concert Choir at Church; [hon.] Honor Roll, 2nd place in District Spelling Contest, 12th place in County Spelling Contest; [oth. writ.] "Love" placed in the Anthology of Poetry by young American, poem published in the Snyder, Oklahoma newspaper.; [pers.] I give all the credit for my poems and stories to the Lord God almighty. He gave me the gift of writing and I then write things to glorify him, giving Him the gift which he gave me.; [a.] Haysville, KS

DENIS, ARLY P.
[b.] 10-18-71, Haiti; [occ.] Student at Brooklyn College; [oth. writ.] Venus, Life Universe of Bridges; [pers.] Life: How sweet it's fruit that grows in the depths of in the ocean of life.; [a.] Brooklyn, NY

DENISE, J.
[b.] 1948, California; [pers.] I want to teach others to live a fullness of life. To create peace within the souls of others through my words.

DENNIS, ANTHONY J.
[b.] Hell; [p.] Two: One of each gender; [ed.] Life and my Personal Studies has been my best Instructions and have truly molded my Artistic Development; [occ.] Student; [hon.] The one I am receiving for being chosen for this Book is most Prominent; [oth. writ.] Numerous poems spanning the full gambit of human introspective, Social-Political Social Humor, Tragedy, and Paradoxes.; [pers.] Perfection is the impossible quest, but I dare it. It keep life interesting. Life is a voyage ridden with unforeseen contingencies. You either reign over them or they will surely reign over you.; [a.] Purgatory, Hell

DENO, ISABEL H.
[b.] July 30, 1966, Dominican Republic; [p.] Eleodoro and Altagracia Hernandez; [m.] Divorced, May 8, 1987; [ch.] Sophia I. Deno, S. Jonathan Deno; [ed.] Nashua High School, Rivier College University of Mass at Lowell; [occ.] UMASS at Lowell Student; [memb.] School Site Council, PTO Pawtucketville Memorial School, Handicapped Service Hiring Committee; [hon.] Honor Society, Dean's List; [oth. writ.] "Mi Querida Mama," worship your life, Jonathan, deceit without compassion, these were published in the UMASS Offering, and in UMASS insights.; [pers.] "My Life," was almost taken away from me, therefore, I try to express my gratitude to "The Lord," in my writing. Life is too short, worship your life.; [a.] Lowell, MA

DENO, ISABEL H.
[b.] July 30, 1966, Dominican Republic; [p.] Eleadoro and Altagracia Hernandez; [m.] Divorced; [ch.] Sophia and Jonathan Deno; [ed.] U Mass at Lowell, MA; [occ.] N/A U Mass Lowell Student; [memb.] School Site Council, Parent Teacher Organization; [hon.] Dean's List, Certificate of Commendation for School Cite Council; [oth. writ.] "Mi Querida Mama," "Worship Your life", "Main Streaming Head Injured Adults"; [pers.] I look at life with a different perspective, for I almost died in a car accident. I give thanks to my "Lord" forgiving me life again. I am an autobiographical writer.; [a.] Lowell, MA

DEPUTY, JENNIFER
[pen.] Jennifer Deputy; [b.] November 5, 1971, Elkhant, MD; [p.] Lawrence and Sherrod Deputy; [ed.] Elkhant Central High, Pepperdine University; [occ.] Equinox International and Lanciani of Beverly Hills, CA; [hon.] Dean's List, President of my Class High School; [oth. writ.] Several other poems, lyrics, scripts and eventually children's stories.; [pers.] I strive to reflect truth, love and empathy in a somewhat mystical manner in my writings. I have been greatly inflounced by men positive healthy romance relationships as well as platonic friendships that have influenced my life.; [a.] Malibu, CA

DER, BRANDON
[b.] November 5, 1973, Los Angeles; [p.] Scott, Christina; [ed.] Marshall High, UCLA; [memb.] First Evangelical Church of San Gabriel Valley Fellowship, Inter Varsity Bruin Christian, Fellowship; [pers.] I find much of the inspiration for my writing from the Psalms and they reflect God's character. In my poem I Try to illustrate now he lifts us out of despair.; [a.] Los Angeles, CA

DESCHAINE, ANGEL B. C.
[b.] November 14, 1978, Edmunston, New Brunswick, Canada; [p.] Real and Anne Deschaine; [ed.] Madawaska High School; [occ.] Student; [memb.] American Legion Auxiliary; [hon.] Aroostook Teen Leadership Camp and MID-Crew (Madawaska Interactive Drama); [pers.] I would like to thank Steve Bunnell and everyone who helped me with my writing at Bates College in Lewiston, Maine. Without the preservation of nature, including Lake Andrews this piece would not have been successful.; [a.] Saint David, ME

DESTEFANIS, AMY
[b.] April 16, 1976, Fussa, Japan; [p.] Genevieve and Robert DeStefanis; [ed.] Cactus High, University of Arizona Glendale Community College; [occ.] Student; [oth. writ.] Personal poems, nothing published.; [pers.] My poems are an expression of my life and soul.; [a.] Peoria, AZ

DEVINE, ANNE
[b.] February 27, 1930, Brooklyn, NY; [p.] Bernard J. Smith, Delia C. Smith; [m.] Henry D. Devine, February 16, 1963; [ch.] William Daniel; [ed.] Bay Ridge High, South Shore Business School; [occ.] Retired; [memb.] The National Society of Poetry, Disabled American Veterans Auxiliary; [hon.] World of Poetry Awards of Merit 1989-1991, Golden Poet 1989-1990, Who's Who In Poetry 1990 National Society of Poetry Editor's Choice Award 1994.; [oth. writ.] Articles and poems published in the Babylon Beacon a local newspaper.; [pers.] The responses I get from individual writings are very gratifying. When a request is made I reply "You supply the data and I'll take care of the matter."; [a.] West Islip, NY

DEVONIK, ROBIN
[pen.] Robin Devonik; [b.] December 12, 1980, Santa Monica; [p.] Marian Sabety, Mike Devonik; [ed.] 9th grade, Mountain Lakes High School; [occ.] Student; [memb.] President YMCA, Youth Group; [hon.] YMCA Counselor in Training Commendation; [pers.] Robin's father passed away in October '94, causing him to have to restart his life. Robin balances his traditional High School sports enthusiasm with his interests in YMCA leadership and school work excellence. He is greatly influenced by the enchanted course of life.

DEW, FRANCES
[pen.] Danke; [b.] November 25, 1948, Preston, GA; [p.] James and Amanda Dew; [m.] Single; [ed.] Ida S. Lowery Jr. High, Preston, GA, North Salinas High School, Salinas, CA, Pasadena City College, Pasadena, CA.; [occ.] Telemarketing and Data Entry Operator; [memb.] Speakers Club of America, Business Professional Women, Los Angeles CA, Bread of Life Christian Center, Columbus, GA.; [oth. writ.] Several poems written for local churches and schools.; [pers.] I strive to write poetry that expresses my inner mind and that which retro-acts both my feelings and emotions. I have been greatly influenced by the writings of Maya Angelou and Nikki Giovanni.; [a.] Columbus, GA

DEXTER, JOLIENE
[b.] June 18, 1974, Los Angeles, CA; [p.] Val Rhodes and Greogory Dexter; [ed.] Incline High School (Class of 1992), University of Nevada at Reno; [occ.] An Undergraduate Student and a Student Library Staff Member at Univ. of NV, Reno; [memb.] A two year Member on the Sierra Guard (a color Guard and Honor Guard for the Governor of Nevada); [hon.] A one year Military Scholarship Recipient, Dean's List, Recipient of Plaques for being a dedicated and Outstanding Participant and Member on the Sierra Guard (the Honor Guard for the Governor of Nevada); [oth. writ.] One other poem published in a poetry anthology, currently working on a compilation of my poems to have them published as my first hard back work.; [pers.] The primary reason why I write is to have an impact on readers both emotionally and psychologically. I want people to connect with me and understand they are not alone after they read my poetry. If people don't feel as a writer I'm or think after reading my poetry not doing my job.; [a.] Reno, NV

DIAZ, VIOLET
[b.] August 26, 1940, Walsenburge, CO; [p.] Cornellio and Amanda Quintana; [m.] Manuel Diaz, February 17, 1958; [ch.] Rick, John, Linda, and Julie; [ed.] Silt Union High; [occ.] Para Professional, Roy Moore Elementary; [memb.] Sacred Heart Catholic Church; [hon.] Outstanding Employee 1993; [oth. writ.] Several poems just for family and friends. I wrote a journal as a memento for our children and grandchildren as a remembrance of their father and grandfather.; [pers.] My writings are a reflection of my faith. In the Lord and what he does for us and what he expect us to do for each other. In our faith we will find love happiness and peace.; [a.] Silt, CO

DICKEN, NICHOLAS S.
[b.] September 13, 1980, Ironton, OH; [p.] Ron, Rotha Brown; [ed.] Shawnee High School; [memb.] Aviation, N.J.R.O.T.C., Color Guard, Drill Team, Riffle Team, Young Eagles; [oth. writ.] Bomb Shelter, Disaster Striker, The Time Warp Triology, and many other short stories and poems.; [pers.] A calm sea never made a skillful senior.; [a.] Louisville, KY

DIGGS JR., CLYDE L.
[pen.] C. Beniel Sharpe; [b.] September 26, 1959, Wilmington, DE; [p.] Clyde L. Diggs, Rosa Lee Diggs; [ch.] Janel L. Martin, Brian Jabree Martin (grandson); [ed.] Howard High School, Wilm. High School, Virginia State Univ.; [occ.] Composer, musician, carpenter and building maintenance mech.; [memb.] Int'l. Brotherhood of Teamsters, former Pres./Vice Pres. Neighbor-

hood Youth Corps. (NYC II); [oth. writ.] None published.; [pers.] I've seen a lot of hurt and pain in our society, both past and present, and I want us to remember that there is only one race on this planet. And its a race that we all are losing!; [a.] Wilmington, DE

DILEGAME, JOSH A.
[pen.] Joshua A. Dilegame; [b.] November 7, 1981, Oroville, CA; [p.] Mark and Teri Dilegame; [ed.] South Tahoe Middle School; [occ.] Student; [hon.] Honor roll student, received letter from President Clinton in regards to a letter I wrote to him about concerns for the environment.

DINHO, SCOTT
[b.] October 15, 1975, New Fairfield, CT; [p.] Arestides and Elaine Dinho; [ed.] Currently attending Florida State University; [oth. writ.] This is my first attempt at publication.; [pers.] I don't write poetry, I just write it down.; [a.] Tallahassee, FL

DIPOMA, RENEE
[b.] October 14, 1970, Albany, NY; [p.] Carol Dipoma, John Dipoma; [pers.] I encourage the expression of one's creative mind, so as to explore the depths of the heart and soul.; [a.] Castaic, CA

DITTRICH, BRUCE E.
[pen.] Bruce E. Dittrich; [b.] August 18, 1961, Hinsdale, NH; [p.] David and Joan Dittrich; [ed.] Keene High School, Keene, NH; [occ.] Chef, poet inspired lyricist; [memb.] ILG, The Literary Guild, NY; [oth. writ.] Lyrics for songs, children's poetry and songs.; [pers.] All my writing shows great positivity I've something important to tell the world. I'll let it begin here.; [a.] Hinsdale, NH

DO, DAO MARY
[b.] October 27, 1959, Saigon, Vietnam; [p.] Mr. and Mrs. Yen N. and Loan L. Do; [ed.] La Quinta High School, University of California, Irvine (UCI), Southwestern University School of Law in Los Angeles; [occ.] Attorney, Poet, Writer; [hon.] Graduated from college in 3 years, Graduated from Law School in 2 years, Published gubernatorial speech writer intern; [pers.] In my struggle to become, I write. Writing is in my blood, I am deeply inspired by the work of my father and sister. My heroes have always been writers and poets. I especially admire George Herbert, Walt Whitman, E.E. Cummings, and Sylvia Plath. To this extent, my journals reflect a journey into the religious, philosophical, artistic, and self-confessional being that I am — that I could never communicate with the world. For the most intimate feelings and experiences are so often understood only by the soul. Thus, as long as I journey towards an end, I find myself continually in a process — a driven, destined process that, at times, can be frightening. But I must go on... for myself is not yet: For myself is not yet.; [a.] Garden Grove, CA

DODDS, ANTHONY JAMES
[pen.] Tony; [b.] June 25, 1965, Pittsburgh, PA; [p.] Mr. and Mrs. Robert James Dodds Jr.; [ed.] U. of Vermont - B.S. in Business Admin., currently pursuing an MBA at Duquesne Univ. in Pittsburgh, PA; [occ.] Corporate Auditor/CPA - H.J., Heinz Company; [memb.] Member - New leadership Board of the Pittsburgh Symphony Orchestra; [hon.] Music Award - Pomfret High School; [oth. writ.] Nothing published, but lots to write about.; [pers.] I have some serious autobiographical statements that are purely non-fictional. If anyone is interested in helping me bring these to the public, please contract me. They are chock full of ironies romances tragedies astonishment and inspirations. All at once.; [a.] Pittsburgh, PA

DODGE, ANTHONY S.
[b.] December 19, 1964, Toledo, OH; [p.] Oliver H. And Roxie Anne Dodge; [m.] Joyce Ellen (Redding) Dodge, June 27, 1987; [ch.] Laurelyn Marie, Elizabeth Ellen, A.J.; [ed.] University of Toledo - English BA, B. Ed. German Minor.; [occ.] English and Foreign Language teacher - Leverette Jr. High Toledo; [memb.] Audubon Society, National Geographic Society.; [hon.] Cum Laude graduate - University of Toledo. Former West Point Cadet.; [oth. writ.] Two books: "A Place To Call Home - the theory of Inertial Entropy in Middle America" and "Quantum Metaphysics: The answer's here somewhere."; [pers.] My writings reflect the very subjective view of growing up very working class in a society that increasingly pulls away from us, and then trying to survive in that world.; [a.] Toledo, OH

DODSON, CHRIS
[b.] March 2, 1957, Kansas City, MO; [p.] Dan Dodson, Hazel Dodson; [m.] Ebtisam Dodson, March 5, 1983; [ch.] Jared Dodson, Johnathon Dodson; [ed.] Fullerton High School, Riverside City College; [occ.] Postal Letter Carrier; [memb.] Boy Scout of America, Moreno Valley Christian Church; [pers.] To use poetry as a language and communicate more intensely than any other way. Robert Frost and Emily Dickinson were great wasters in the pursuit.; [a.] Moreno Valley, CA

DODSON, KEVIN L.
[b.] June 7, 1968, Houston, TX; [p.] Calvin L. Lallenta Dodson; [ed.] Humble High School, Sam Houston, State Univ.; [occ.] Boilermaker, Gonzales Manufacturing Co., Gonzales, TX; [memb.] Army Reserves, Yoakum, TX; [hon.] (2) Army Commendation Medal, (3) Army Achievement Medal, Kuwait Liberation Medal, South East Asia Medal, National Defense Medal, Overseas Ribbon, Army Service Ribbon; [oth. writ.] Several forms published in different Army papers: One published in a book. "All My Tomorrows."; [pers.] Pride, dedication, sacrifice, and hard work are the marks of success.; [a.] Hardwood, TX

DOETSCHMANN, CECILIA ANN
[pen.] Sass, Cecile; [b.] March 18, 1955, Windsor, Ontario, Canada; [p.] Elias and Marie Boutros; [m.] Willy Doetschmann, October 21, 1980; [ch.] Andrea Chantal; [ed.] St. Alphonsus, Saint Mary's Academy, Patterson High; [occ.] Housewife; [hon.] Honesty Award in High School; [oth. writ.] My personal collection of poetry since 1982.; [pers.] I wish to acknowledge that 5th grade Irish school teacher of mine - Mr. Johnson for getting me to appreciate poetry and literature so well, and too I acknowledge here, L. Ron Hubbard, a philosopher, for his teachings on the spirit of man.; [a.] New Port Richey, FL

DONAHUE, PEGGY
[pen.] PJ; [b.] June 19, 1941, Flint, MI; [p.] James and Marie Combs; [m.] Ronald R. Donahue, December 16, 1961; [ch.] Kimberly and Karon; [ed.] Flushing High School; [occ.] HW; [oth. writ.] Lifescape of poems.; [pers.] When I write I look inside my heart and leave a part of me in each poem.; [a.] Palm Harbor, FL

DONELAN, ERIN MARIE
[b.] April 7, 1977, Clovis, NM; [p.] William and Cynthia Donelan; [ed.] At present, home study.; [pers.] If the goals we desire are the same as those God has for us, we can strive for them all reach for them, knowing with certainty that we can achieve them.; [a.] Grand Forks, ND

DONOHO, KATHERINE EVON
[pen.] Katherine Donoho; [b.] December 19, 1941, Dos Palice, CA; [p.] Norman and Betty Porter; [m.] W. Ray Donoho, July 27, 1961; [ch.] Zina K. King, Lisa R. Young, Tara L. Donoho; [ed.] Shasta High Guadalupe, a lifetime of degrees in life itself.; [occ.] Retired mother, grandmother, co/owner of a Gold Smithing Shop.; [memb.] Two Cadillac/LaSalle Clubs; [hon.] My wonderful husband, my children, and my Grandchildren are my honors and awards, they fill my life with love and joy. I would like to inspire encouragement and hope to those who read my poems.; [oth. writ.] A birth announcement in poetry from written for my granddaughter Mariah, published in local newspaper. Many poems in local newspaper. Many poems about mine and my family's life, eagerly waiting to be published for the enjoyment of others to read.; [pers.] My inspirations have always been triggered by my children, grandchildren, and life's comedies and sorrows. Many have come to me in the wee early hours, and I must get up and put them to pen and paper. I've always enjoyed poetry of all styles.; [a.] Carson City, NV

DOPKINS, DENNIS J.
[b.] April 24, 1944, Janesville, WI; [p.] Henry E. and Sylvia R. Dopkins; [m.] Sandra R. Dopkins, January 18, 1975; [ch.] Kevin J., Shannon L., Scott R.; [memb.] Janesville Little Theatre; [pers.] "Proofread your heart before you say your part".; [a.] Janesville, WI

DORANTES, LEOPOLDO
[b.] May 11, 1956, Matamoros, Mexico; [p.] Leopoldo C. Dorantes, Maria Dorantes; [m.] Lucero Dorantes, April 1, 1989; [ch.] Andres Dorantes, Leopoldo E. Dorantes; [ed.] Don Bosco Tech. University of Texas at Brownsville, Liberal Arts, Modern Languages; [occ.] Certified Translator/Interpreter, Chemical Manufacturer Rep.; [memb.] Spirit of Grace Church; [hon.] National Dean's List 93-94, 94-95, UTB President's List, UTB Dean's List, UTB Continuing Excellence Scholarship, A.S. Metallurgy, Naturalized Citizen of the U.S. (5-11-90); [oth. writ.] Poem published in the UTB Learning Assistance Student Newsletter. 9/93 edition.; [pers.] The indomitable human spirit, the greatness instilled it by The Creator and man's eternal struggle to discover who he really is. This is who I am, this is what I write.; [a.] Brownsville, TX

DORR, BETTY
[pen.] Betty Dorr (J); [b.] January 14, 1933, Berlin, MD; [p.] Howard and Edith Richardson; [m.] Lawrence Earl Dorr, Marsh 1, 1969; [ch.] Eight; [ed.] High School and College Course; [occ.] Home Maker; [memb.] VFW Auxiliary, George I'm back Richmond, CA; [oth. writ.] Unfortunately None as yet. Have taken a course in children writing in Conn.; [pers.] If you don't take time and submit how will ones self know what thou can be. A few minutes in a believe may make a wider door.; [a.] San Pablo, CA

DORR, JANE
[b.] September 2, 1937, Cincinnati, OH; [m.] Richard, June 20, 1959; [ch.] Rick, Mark, Sue Goold; [ed.] BA - Univ. of Michigan; [occ.] Freelance Writer; [memb.] Detroit Women Writers; [oth. writ.] Ann Arbor News

and Detroit Free Press since 1980, articles in the Ford Times, successful living Magazine, U of M School Business Administration, Yoga News and Note, countless in published poetry.; [pers.] I believe that one's writing tools are her ears and eyes. True understanding comes from being aware of yourself and others.; [a.] Ann Arbor, MI

DORSEY, CAROL U.
[pen.] Clue; [b.] January 10, 1963, Fort Lauderdale, FL; [p.] Charles and Patricia Ulrey; [m.] Vernon E. Dorsey II, December 17, 1988; [ch.] Vernon Elwin Dorsey III; [ed.] Deerfield Beach High School, University of South Florida; [occ.] Assistant Mgr., World Savings; [oth. writ.] Treasures Within; [pers.] The words which I write are an expression of my soul when it has something to say.; [a.] Pompano Beach, FL

DOWELL, JUDITH P.
[b.] September 3, 1958, Camden, NJ; [m.] David F. Dowell, February 16, 1980; [ch.] Joshua David, Laura Beth; [memb.] Atco Presbyterian Church Board of Deacons, Handbell Choir and Senior Choir; [a.] Atco, NJ

DOWLING, WILLIAM R.
[pen.] William R. Dowling; [b.] November 7, 1933, Brown City, MI; [p.] Frances and Murl Dowling; [m.] Janet A. Dowling, January 7, 1956; [ch.] Wilma, Wilda, Wanda, Will; [ed.] High School; [occ.] Retired General Motor Assembly Worker of 28 Years; [memb.] American Legion, Clifford Baptist Church; [hon.] Served in U.S. Navy 1952-1954, upon his Death (7-27-94) his Organs were Donated to the "Gift of Life" Program; [pers.] This poem came from a dream he had during a time of failing health. It became a great comfort to him to know his greatest trip was yet to come.; [a.] Silverwood, MI

DOWNS, JAY WARREN
[pen.] Matthew Lovell Downarian, Sterling S. Silverpeace; [b.] September 6, 1936, Reading, PA; [p.] Paul S. and Ethel A. Downs; [m.] Divorced, January 25, 1959; [ch.] Patrick Jay, Brian Scott, Michael Allen, Kevin Glenn, Denise Ann, Kathleen Lynn; [ed.] Reading Sr. High, Univ. of Wisconsin; [occ.] Commercial Transportation Director ARCO Industries Inc., Milwaukee, WI; [memb.] International Brotherhood of Teamsters, American Trucking Assoc., WI Trucking Assoc., National Safety Council, National Assoc. on Transportation Safety, American Fellowship, Minister, Alliance Church, Milwaukee, WI; [hon.] National Safety Council, American Trucking, Assoc., Teamster Union/Local 200, State of Pennsylvania Carnagie Hero Award, Univ. of Wisconsin-Literature, Milwaukee Writers Club; [oth. writ.] Published/Associate Editor of Christian Light, Reaching out Words from within, Numerous, Articles Essays, Poems and Short Stories Pub.; [pers.] I am committed to making a worldwide contribution in literature one poem and one person at a time. As a youth I was influenced by the great classics, they are responsible for the accomplishment I enjoy today - Thanks, Dad!; [a.] Milwaukee, WI

DOWNS, JAY WARREN
[pen.] Matthew Lovell Downarian, Sterling S. Silverpeace; [b.] September 6, 1936, Reading, PA; [p.] Paul S. and Ethel A. Downs; [m.] Divorced - Single, January 25, 1959; [ch.] Patrick Jay, Brian Scott, Michael Allen, Kevin Glenn, Denise Ann, Kathleen Lynn; [ed.] Reading Sr. High, Univ. of Wisconsin; [occ.] Commercial Transportation Director ARCO Industries Inc., Milwaukee, WI; [memb.] International Brotherhood of Teamsters, American Trucking Assoc., WI Trucking Assoc., National Safety Council, National Assoc. on Transportation Safety, American Fellowship Ministries, Alliance Church, Milwaukee, WI; [hon.] National Safety Council, American Trucking Assoc., Teamsters Union/Local 200, State of Pennsylvania, Carnagie Hero Award, Univ. of Wisconsin-Literature, Milwaukee Writers Club.; [oth. writ.] Publisher/Associate Editor of Christian Light, Reaching Out, Words From Within, Numerous Articles, Essays, Poems and Short Stories Pub.; [pers.] I am committed to making a worldwide contribution in literature one poem and one person at a time. As a youth I was influenced by the great classics, they are responsible for the accomplishments I enjoy today - Thanks, Dad!; [a.] Milwaukee, WI

DOZER, JASON ROBERT
[b.] March 14, 1975, Central City, KY; [p.] Terry and Mary Dozer; [ed.] Muhlenberg North High School; [occ.] Machinist, premium allied tool, Philpot, KY; [memb.] Mt. Zion, Presbyterian Church; [oth. writ.] Several songs, some of which have been played on local radio.; [pers.] I choose to take a step back and look at life in an analytical sense. Many of my poems/songs deal with the value and parity of integrity. Probably my greatest influence is the rock band savatage.; [a.] Philpot, KY

DRAFT, JEFFREY A.
[pen.] Jeff Draft; [b.] July 3, 1959, Dearborn, MI; [m.] James and Janice Draft; [ch.] Joseph, Matthew and Amanda; [ed.] Grad. of Taylor Center High School; [occ.] U.A.W. Worker; [memb.] Knights of Columbus; [pers.] This poem was written as a gift to C.J. Dugan on Valentine day in 95 who has agreed to marry me in June of 96. I continue to dedicate my love and poetry to her.; [a.] Defiance, OH

DRAGG, SHAVADA
[b.] August 15, 1984, Knoxville; [p.] Latisha Reeves, Charles Dragg; [ed.] Green Math and Science Academy; [occ.] Student; [memb.] Member of Mt. Olive Baptist Church Youth Choir; [pers.] You can be anything you want to be if you think highly of yourself.; [a.] Knoxville, TN

DRESSMAN, DONALD J.
[b.] August 31, 1972, Memphis, TN; [p.] Richard I. and Doris Dressman; [ed.] Maryvale High; [occ.] Frozen Food Manager, Albertson's Grocery Store; [pers.] Never let others influence what you what you want to do in your life.; [a.] Phoenix, AZ

DRISCOLL JR., WILLIAM
[b.] August 31, 1937, Everett, MA; [p.] William Driscoll, Velma Driscoll; [m.] Mary Anne (Dennis) Driscoll, April 24, 1965; [ch.] William D. Driscoll, Jennifer Driscoll; [ed.] Everett High, Bunker Hill Community College, Emergency Medical Technician, Massachusetts Military Academy; [occ.] Custodian; [memb.] Charter Member East Cork Choral Society, Ireland Sacred Hearts Church Choir, Malden, MA; [hon.] Dean's List; [pers.] When writing my objective is to create a scene of encouragement to achievement or reflect upon something which helps someone something which helps feel good about themselves.; [a.] Everett, MA

DRUM, KAREN ANN
[b.] May 14, 1961, California; [ch.] Dale and Robert Drum (Twins); [ed.] Lakewood High, Long Beach City College; [occ.] Church Volunteer; [oth. writ.] Several poems not yet submitted for publication.; [pers.] Life's experiences have tough me many things, and poetry is how I reflect on those lessons.; [a.] Lakewood, CA

DU TEAU, DOROTHY
[pen.] Doree' Du Teau; [b.] March 6, 1929, OH; [p.] Charles P. and Ida M. Gastereier; [m.] Dwight Du Teau, September 20, 1958; [ch.] Gregory Dwight Du Teau and Sherilyn Draper; [ed.] Sandusky High (Ohio) and Inglewood High (CA); [pers.] It is my desire to acknowledge the Inspiration and Love I have for the Natural Beauty and Wonders of our land. Through my writing I will attempt to share this reflection.; [a.] Mission Viejo, CA

DUGAN, LISA
[b.] March 12, 1965, Tinley Park, IL; [p.] Laurence and Anna Hovey, Theodore and Mary Dugan; [m.] Michael Dugan, July 22, 1988; [ch.] Sarah, Maryann, Michael; [ed.] Tinley Park High School, South Suburban College; [occ.] Certified Occupational Therapy Assistant; [memb.] American Occupational Therapy Assoc.; [pers.] The poem "Life Stories" was inspired by my father's fight with cancer and his unwillingness to give up hopes.; [a.] Crown Point, IN

DUNAWAY, MARIA PAZ VERA ACEBES
[pen.] Apple V. Acebes; [b.] February 15, 1968, Manila, Philippines; [p.] Jess N. Acebes and Fe V. Acebes; [m.] Marcus S. Dunaway, November 25, 1995; [ed.] Primary and High School - Saint Scholastica's Academy College, Ateneo de Manila University; [occ.] Front Desk Clerk, Wildwood INN; [oth. writ.] Chill - published in walk through Paradise Anthology.; [pers.] The subject of my poetry is my muse and this muse moves me to put into verse emotions that could have otherwise remain unexpressed.; [a.] Newport, KY

DUNN JR., WILLIE FRANK
[pen.] Houston-Dunn; [b.] September 8, 1961, Kinston, NC; [p.] Mrs. Essie M. Dunn, Late Thomas F. Dunn Sr.; [ed.] Kinston High, Coastal Comm. College, Naval School of Health Sciences, Great Lakes Ill., Field Medical Training School, Camp Johnson NC; [occ.] Hospital Corpsman 2nd Class, Naval Medical Clinic, Philadelphia PA; [memb.] American Heart Association, Prudence Lodge #23 Afam, Fleet Reserve Association; [oth. writ.] Several poems and essay published in local newspapers.; [pers.] Those of us who can read is truly blessed, they said knowledge is power, but a man that can read and comprehend has the dimension, living out their dreams and fantasies.; [a.] Kinston, NC

DUNN, LOLA M.
[b.] June 20, 1922, Pike Co, AL; [p.] Clem and Mary Frances Morgan; [m.] Issac Shelby Dunn, February 21, 1942; [ch.] Lynda Maytrice, David Shelby, Deborah Lynn; [ed.] Coffee Co, Pike Co; [occ.] Housewife, retired; [hon.] Offered at scholarship.; [oth. writ.] I hope to write more poems in the future.; [pers.] I was born in Pike County, AL. I have lived in my old home since I was 17 yrs. old. I am now 73. This is my first poem I've written. It is a very real poem. It saddens me to think this old landmark has to fall down. I want to thank you for considering my poem.; [a.] Troy, AL

DUNNE, LORI SUE
[pen.] Lori Sue Palmer; [b.] November 15, 1973, Provo, UT; [p.] Lee and Susan Palmer; [m.] Jareth Taylor Dunne, June 15, 1995; [ed.] Springville High, Utah Valley State College, Wardley Real Estate; [occ.] Escrow Secretary at Backman Stewart Title; [memb.] Church of Jesus Christ of Latter-Day Saints, Scottish Days Athletic Committee; [hon.] Young Womanhood medallion, Graduate with honors, Lambda Delta Sigma; [oth. writ.] Various lyrics and other poetry written for family, friends, and other acquaintances.; [pers.] To succeed is to believe you can.; [a.] Payson, UT

DURBIN, ANNA LAURA
[pen.] Laura Durbin; [b.] February 4, 1931, Savannah, TN; [p.] James-Beulah Clement; [m.] Floyd G. Durbin, February 19, 1947; [ch.] Dianna Bowers; [ed.] Hardin Co, High School Cosmetologist, Certificate in Millinery Beauty Consultant; [occ.] Housekeeping Bus. Writing Poems; [memb.] First United methodist Church, Hardin Co. Democratic club Woodmen of The World member Ladies Auxiliary to Veterans VFW american Legion and D. Veterans Dav Business and Prof. Women Club; [hon.] Outstanding Citizen for Woodmen of The World Sav. BPW Club American Hearts Ass. Woman of The Year - B.P.W.; [oth. writ.] Wrote poems at early age. But did nothing about them ISP has given me the courage to start writing again, and it is a joy to write for them.; [pers.] I try to do a good deed each day for someone. I am a romantic person and try to see good in everyone. Love my family dearly.; [a.] Savannah, TN

DURBIN, H. FITZGERALD
[pen.] H. Fitzgerald; [b.] February 18, 1915, Todd, OK; [p.] W. R. Durbin and Bertha Romines; [m.] Nolda Juanita Walker, August 15, 1933; [ch.] Seven; [ed.] 8 Public, 4 Bible; [occ.] Minister Retired; [memb.] General Council Assemblies of God, OK District Council Ass. of God, Rutherford Institute, A.F.A., C.W.A., C.A.N., A.L.L., International Society of Poets; [hon.] Gold pen and award for fifty years ministry; [oth. writ.] The Man, Last True Love, After The Storm, five unpublished books of poems.; [pers.] My desire is that my life and writings will exalt the Lord of all creation.; [a.] Wyandotte, OK

EASTERLY II, JAMES CHAPPELL
[b.] October 29, 1962, Knoxville, TN; [p.] Sandra Kathleen and James Chappell Easterly Sr.; [ed.] Robert Louis Stevenson, HS, U.C. San Diego, BS, Cognitive Science, San Diego State, MBA Program; [occ.] Computer Scientist; [memb.] Human Factors Society, Netware Users International Sierra Club.; [hon.] Dean's List; [pers.] Emotions should be shared in all forms of media I choose poetry; [a.] Cardiff By The Sea, CA

EASTRIDGE, GREG
[b.] October 14, 1966, Martinsville, VA; [p.] Ann Beachum; [ed.] Graduate of Art Institute of Ft. Lauderdale Fl. and 3 years at Averett College Danville VA; [occ.] Am-Fibe; [memb.] If I had known how to name them, I should then have signed off in detail from all the societies which I never signed on to, but I did not know where to find a complete list. (Thoreau); [pers.] The Tao that can be told is not the eternal Tao:; [a.] Martinsville, VA

EBERLY, SUSAN
[ed.] BFA Creative Writing, Stephens College, (Favorite teacher: Fred Pfeil, creative writing.); [occ.] Small Business Owner/Manager.; [oth. writ.] Currently writing biography for a private investigator. Will be travelling into southern Russia for exclusive interview with Muslim tribal leaders. Other work in progress: Bio/ Story about travelling in Egypt.; [pers.] Influences: John Irving, Salman Rushdie, Naguib Mahfonz, Quentin Tarantino, Mark Knoppfler, Axl Rose, Rita Mae Brown, Marguerite Henry, Mary O'Hara, A.A. Milne, Mary Renault, and John Irving some more. Can alphabetize or do men/ (or women/man women... but do put John Irving in twice!; [a.] Carmel Valley, CA

ECCLES, NICOLE
[b.] October 31, 1973, San Diego; [p.] Dennis and Jessica Eccles; [ed.] Independence High School, San Diego State U., San Jose State U.; [occ.] Student pre-med; [memb.] Alpha Epsilon Delta, Pre-Med Honor Society, Golden Key Honor Society; [oth. writ.] An entry published in Educational Homicide, Up Against the Wall, an SDSU Student Project; [pers.] Mother Nature provides the best of inspiration for artist. Just when we think that everything has been uncovered, we may look up to discover the awesome beauty of life.; [a.] San Jose, CA

ECHOLS, MARGARET
[b.] December 2, 1943, Memphis, TN; [p.] George Becton, Mattie Becton; [m.] Nick, March 4, 1983; [ch.] Ben, Sherry, Cheryl, Von; [ed.] Lester High, State Tech of Memphis, Lemoyne Owens, Bachelor of Arts Degree; [occ.] Teacher Horten Gardens, Special Summer Prog.; [memb.] Lemoyne Scholastic, All American 1989, African Institute; [hon.] Who's Who 1986,-87, Dean's List; [oth. writ.] Imagine Love (song), Concepts of Love in the Reality of Life, Essential for the Black Man and Woman, prose and poetry (Book); [pers.] The ultimate contribution to yourself and to your community should be achieving a neighborhood of of brotherhood and sisterhood in peace. Heaven here on earth.; [a.] Memphis, TN

EDMONDSON, BRYANT M.
[pen.] (YT)=Yung Tung, FulASoul; [b.] August 20, 1976, Willingboro; [p.] Pat Edmondson; [ed.] Currently a student at Pennsauken High School; [occ.] Full time student; [memb.] 3 Feet High and Risen; [oth. writ.] Wake Up, Thanks for Feeding my Kids, I am I Be, Home; [pers.] The installment that I give to your ear is positive, hoping to make my stand conducive.; [a.] Merchantville, NJ

EDWARDS, ANDRE
[b.] October 14, 1963, Virginia; [p.] Jean and Lloyd Edwards; [ed.] Benjamin Franklin High; [occ.] Odd jobs; [oth. writ.] "The Gift", "Mengazer", "Blackness" and "To Bravely Walk"; [pers.] I believe that writings which helps, encourages and inspires the reader is the best writing of all.; [a.] Philadelphia, PA

EDWARDS, DONALD LEE
[b.] June 8, 1972, Washington, DC; [p.] James Edgar and Donna Ann Edwards; [ed.] Graduate of Randolph - Henry High; [occ.] Illustrator for Family -, Orientated Children's Books.; [oth. writ.] A few poems published in the high-school publications, a winning essay for the American Legion Auxiliary... a long time ago!; [pers.] My poems and other writings take their own voice, giving the reader a chance to experience things in a different point of view and direction than their own. It's more than just words on paper, it's an open door to the imagination.; [a.] Keysville, VA

EDWARDS, JEREMY
[pen.] Jeremy R. Edwards; [b.] April 5, 1973, Saint Paul, MN; [p.] Jack Edwards, Peggy Edwards; [m.] Hilary L. Edwards, February 10, 1995; [ch.] Future plan for.....; [ed.] Westwood High, Northlake Community College; [occ.] Self Employed - Janitorial Business; [memb.] Great Hills Baptist Church and a right winged member of Gods Army.; [hon.] Radio Broadcaster of the year, Jr. High; [oth. writ.] Several published in High School newspaper; [pers.] Live instinctively, without regret and always be who you are, not who you sometimes feel you "should" be.; [a.] Austin, TX

EDWARDS, JUNE
[b.] June 23, 1927, Kansas City, MO; [p.] Herbert Cole, Anna Mae; [m.] Joseph Edwards (Deceased) November 18, 1951; [ch.] Gary, Terrance, Debbie, Joanne, Odessa, Jeffry; [ed.] Took Cosmetology "Training to work c Teachable retarded teens; [occ.] Retired; [memb.] Active Religiously Chaired, Organized, and Worked on many Clubs and Organizations; [hon.] Has background in singing, Performed on stage and radio, Has appeared with the LaForest Dents Band, And Ike Witts Band to name a few, Has received a number of Honors, and Awards for singing.; [oth. writ.] Had poems published in local paper.; [pers.] I have always loved reading, especially poetry. From my early teens I have written poetry. Now as a widow, mother of six, grandmother and great grandmother, retired - I have time to think, dream, meditate on life and put it in writing.; [a.] Denver, CO

EGAN, DOTTIE
[pen.] Dottie Egan; [b.] November 16, 1925, Middlesex, NJ; [p.] Patrick and Helen Egan; [m.] Divorced; [ch.] Kathleen Mary Gargiulo, Maureen Mary Roschel, grandson Sean P. Aziz; [ed.] Graduated Bound Brook High New Jersey 1943, Member of New Jersey Honor Society, Night Classes Rutgers University; [occ.] Semi Retired Banker; [memb.] New Jersey Honor Society, Sales Awards in Banking; [oth. writ.] Nothing published; [pers.] We all need God in our lives, that and enriched family love brings our life full circle.; [a.] Lighthouse Point, FL

EICHOLZ, JAMES
[pen.] Eicholz, Jim; [b.] November 24, 1979, Cleveland, OH; [p.] James Eicholz, Linda Doran; [ed.] I'm currently in the Tenth grade; [occ.] Stock boy at Heinen's; [hon.] Honors in English The Daimler - Benz Award Honor Roll 3rd Place in the American mathematics competitions; [pers.] "Feelings" their very important so follow them and write with them.; [a.] Lakewood, OH

EIDAHL, CAROL C.
[b.] June 27, 1953, Nashville, TN; [p.] Dawson and Bettye Copeland; [m.] Dr. Kyle O. Eidahl, January 9, 1993; [ch.] Daniel, Jessica and Cara Mann; [ed.] BA in Psychology at FSU, MS in Communications at FSU; [occ.] Freelance writer and photographer; [memb.] Golden Key Honors Society; [hon.] Dean's List, President's List, NBWA Scholarships, Psychology Honors Society; [oth. writ.] Local newspaper articles, photographic/literary work in progress.; [pers.] Inside each of us a spring flows. I strive to reach others, touch with words originating from that common source.; [a.] Tallahassee, FL

EIRAS, DANIEL P.
[b.] May 16, 1980, New Rochelle, NY; [p.] Jose Carlos Eiras, Alzira Eiras; [ed.] New Rochelle High School; [occ.] Student; [memb.] The Human Race; [hon.] Honor Roll-, Gloria L. Shimberg Memorial Award; [oth. writ.] Almost 100 other poems, though none published.; [pers.] There is only so much that words can say, the rest of their meaning comes from the imagination of the reader.; [a.] Scarsdale, NY

EISENHARDT, CATHERYN T.
[pen.] Catheryn T. Eisenhardt; [b.] April 9, 1911, Pennsylvania; [p.] Roy and Sophia Thompson; [m.] Emil H. Eisenhardt, September 2, 1936; [ch.] E. Roy, Von Stephen and Carol Baldwin; [ed.] Coughlin High-Wilkes Barre, PA, N.Y.U. Wash Sq BA-, NYU, Main Creative Ed-, and Doctorate '61, Dissertation 1961, Application of Linguistics in Classroom - published (Merrill); [occ.] Retired but active, Sr. Center - Memo Writing Class; [memb.] National Council of Teachers of English, AARP, Nat'l Reading Teachers; [hon.] Granted Prof. Emeritus 1976, NYU distinguished alum, United Nations scholarship, Visiting professorships, Navajo College, Creservation - U of Monrovice Libena, College of William and Mary - Univ. of Flagstaff, AZ - U. of Nevada, Las Vegas, International 95, Camp (Faculty-Music and Drama); [oth. writ.] High School Class Song '29, Original Scripts For Children's Programs, Nat'l Reading Teachers, Nat'l Council Teachers of Eng- (Individualizing Teaching, Educ- JNL of Linguistics - Teaching, Structured of English - Film Strip - How You Say What You Mean - Tinkling Bell and Sounding Cymbals, Conference Speeches, An Ode To Communication Sciences.; [pers.] Basic relief that language is a phenomenal powers within each one of us to be discovered and shaped. As a teacher I must provide an atmosphere of vitality, a curiosity to observe, to share and ask questions. A freedom to make mistakes knowing that correcting them is what counts. Most of all knowing the joy of success is guaranteed; [a.] Cupertino, CA

ELEAZU, NMA UMA
[pen.] Ni-mi-ah Jones; [b.] April 3, 1976, Enugu, Nigeria; [p.] Dr. and Mrs. U.O. Eleazu; [ed.] Corona primary, Queen's College Lagos, San Francisco State University; [occ.] Student; [memb.] Presbyterian Church of Nigeria, Conerstone Christian Fellowship, Intervarsity Christian Fellowship; [hon.] Dean's List, National Residence Hall Honorary Award for service to Black Residents Association of SFSU, S.F.S.U. Housing and Residential Services Award for service to San Francisco State University (S.F.S.U.) residence life.; [oth. writ.] Other poems that were performed at San Francisco State University, Analysis and explanation of my poems.; [pers.] My inspiration stems from a desire to share my experiences of God's faithfulness and sustenance.; [a.] San Francisco, CA

ELLISON, GLADYS
[pen.] Jenny Gale; [b.] February 11, 1929, Tenn; [p.] Fred - Nancy Ellison; [ed.] My education continues there's a lot still to be learned in this Life.; [occ.] Caretaker of God's Gift's; [hon.] No earthly Honors or Awards. Just the love and respect of Family and Friends.; [oth. writ.] Song poems, poetry, article of local interest for newspaper. Memorials For Friends And Loved Ones.; [pers.] I strive to see good in other's when little can be seen. And give words of hope and cheer to those seeking life's, truth's, someone has said I've pass through this life only once "Leave only Good behind; [a.] Hephzibak, CA

ELLSWORTH, SHAWNA J.
[pen.] Shawna Jean Larson; [b.] January 27, 1972, Grand Rapids, MI; [p.] Kathy Romer, Dean Larson; [m.] Divorced since 1995; [ch.] Joshua David Ellsworth; [ed.] High School, currently a part time student at Salt Lake Community College.; [occ.] PBX Operator for FHP, and Mother.; [hon.] My writings have been complimented by friends and teachers over the years, but this is the first time I have ever submitted anything for publication. Thank you.; [oth. writ.] I've never been published before now, but I have a large collection of writings. I write about experiences that change and transform us, and help us to grow personally or spiritually.; [pers.] People tell me I am a very sensitive and deep thinking person. I am into living, loving, and learning, change and growth. Experience is our greatest teacher.; [a.] Salt Lake, UT

EMMICK JR., ROGER
[b.] January 28, 1977, Olean, NY; [p.] Roger Emmick, Paula Green; [ed.] Worth County High, Currently enrolled at ABAC (Community College); [occ.] Student; [hon.] Presidential Academic Award, Kiwanas Scholarship; [oth. writ.] Have never had anything published, first contest I have ever entered which has bad anything to due with writing, I love to write; [pers.] I love the dark aspects of life. I love life, don't get me wrong. I wouldn't give up my life for anything. However, the mystery which surrounds death simply enthralls me. - And ye harm none, do as ye will.; [a.] Tifton, GA

ENGLAND, ANGELA MARIE
[b.] January 7, 1973, Marion, OH; [p.] John and Linda England; [ed.] Pleasant High School, Ohio University, Ohio State University, Kent State University; [occ.] Page at the Columbus Metropolitan Library; [oth. writ.] An article published in Focus, Teaching English Language Arts; [pers.] I feel that my writings are a way for me to escape into my inner-most thoughts and encourage others to do the same.; [a.] Columbus, OH

ENGLER, SANDRA
[b.] July 25, 1962, Astoria, NY; [p.] Peter and Marga Engler; [ch.] Steven, Jeffrey, Jason and Alison; [ed.] Bryant High; [occ.] Freelance Artist and writer of poems and Childrens Books.; [memb.] "National Humane Education Society", "Wild-life Conservation Society."; [oth. writ.] Several poems published for Greeting Card Company, Red Farm Studio.; [pers.] I strive to reach the hearts and minds of mankind, through my writing, and write for all the children who's imaginations are new and growing.; [a.] College Point, NY

ENGLISH, GERALDINE MARIE NELSON
[pen.] Geri Nelson English; [b.] February 21, 1959, Baltimore, MD; [p.] Leo J. Nelson, Berha Mae McElwee Nelson; [m.] Divorced; [ch.] Linda Carol English and Michael Bennett English (deceased); [ed.] Perry Hall Sr. High School 1977; [occ.] Computer operator MMI, Timonium, MD; [hon.] English Honor through Advanced Independent Study Program 1977, Perry Hall High School; [oth. writ.] Several poems published 1993-94 Dignity News Letter, Balto. MD.; [pers.] I have been writing poems since I was about 12 yrs old, but only on a personal level. I enjoy writing as a hobby more than anything and publishing has only been a passing dream. "I have no heart, no soul, no mind. I'm just a mist, a vapor. I bleed blue ink and when it hearts. I just erase the paper."; [a.] Baltimore, MD

ENSINGER, AARON R.
[b.] January 28, 1982, New York, NY; [occ.] I am currently an 8th grade student.; [hon.] School Honor Roll; [pers.] I like poems that make me think and I like poems that make me laugh. Perhaps my poetry will reach someone else, too.

ESCAMILLA, DEBRA K.
[b.] March 26, 1953, Pekin, IL; [p.] Kay A. McCollam and Fred R. Nolte; [m.] Jack A. Escamilla, October 31, 1974; [ch.] Anthony and Troy; [ed.] Associates Degree in Business Administration/Management.; [occ.] Accounts Receivable/Data Entry Clerk at Standard Bearings Co. in Davenport, IA.; [hon.] I was Valedictorian of my class when I graduated from College. I was 39 years old when I delivered the farewell oration. I was very proud, but it was very hard work at my age. I carried A 4.0 G.P.A. for 5 quarters!; [oth. writ.] An unpublished poem entitled "All Alone"; [pers.] I wrote the poems "Caged" and "All Alone" when I was in Junior High School. Everyone said they were real good, so, I saved them. I am glad I did!; [a.] Davenport, IA

ESCHRICH, DENNIS A.
[b.] April 30, 1957, Johnstown, PA; [m.] Catherine; [ch.] Erin (daughter); [occ.] Meteorologist; [oth. writ.] Small collection of unpublished lyric-oriented poems.; [pers.] I always hope for something fresh, new, and different when I write. Will collaborate with serious musicians.; [a.] White Sands, NM

ESPOSITO, MARY GRACE
[pen.] Mary Grace Esposito; [b.] May 15, 1956, Hollis Queen, NYC; [p.] Marilyn Foutz Phillips; [m.] Ralph Esposito, Divorced; [ed.] West Babylon on High School; [occ.] Art Model; [memb.] Sacred Heart Church, also Member (Friends of Sacred Heart Ass.); [hon.] Certificate Awards from other contests from National Library of Poetry; [oth. writ.] 3 poems in methodist poems write Children's Poems, Have Written Romantic, Poems But Not Lately.; [pers.] What goes around comes around, the Lord helps those who help themselves; [a.] Tampa, FL

EVANS, DEBRA
[pen.] Debra Evans; [b.] June 25, 1952, Huntington, VA; [p.] Jack and Marie Frye; [m.] James Evans, July 23, 1983; [ch.] Scott A. Johnson; [ed.] Vinson High School, Huntington, W. VA; [occ.] Environmental Service Dept., Walls Regional Hospital; [memb.] Nolan River Baptist Church; [oth. writ.] Several poems published in local newspapers.; [pers.] M.B.D. - I am the poet... you are the poem.; [a.] Cleburne, TX

EVANS, DENESHA DAY
[b.] April 1, 1981, Jackson, MS; [p.] Clark Evans, Deon Evans; [ed.] Student of Forest High School; [memb.] Beta Club, Wings, FHA; [hon.] Bach and MMTA Piano Competitions, FRA National Americanism Essay Contest, Superintendent and principal honor roll; [oth. writ.] Short stories and poems published in school's newspaper.; [pers.] Express your opinions when you write.; [a.] Forest, MS

EVANS, ILENE ANN
[pen.] Ilene A. Evans; [b.] July 28, 1942, Portland, OR; [p.] James Leroy Evans, Lily Osterback Alford Snr.; [m.] None Divorced, September 29, 1961 to May 1976; [ch.] Gina M. Gerking, Allan L. Gerking; [ed.] Lincoln H.S. and Roosevelt H.S., Seattle, WA. Highline Comm. College, Des Moines, WA. A.A. Degree, Writing inst

Lonny Kaneko, a published poet, who influenced me., University of Puget Sound, Tacoma, WA., B.A. in Soc./ Art, Kappa Delta.; [occ.] Security Officer at SeaTac Airport; [memb.] Pacific N.W. Writers Conference, Pacific N.W. Aleut Council as member and Board Member, Child Abuse Prevention Service in Federal Way, WA. CAPS Group who holds Awareness and Prevention of Child Abuse Workshops.; [hon.] Semi-finalist for poem Re: Seven pools Enormous lush soft... in North American Open Poetry Contest '95 To be published in The Voice Within Summer 1996. Called MAUII; [oth. writ.] Article in Tacoma News Tribune on: Join the Tacoma Art Museum. Which is Delta. Used by Art teacher to inform students. 2 self published booklets on "Toxicity How Personal is is?" 1988 and "The Toxicity of Schizophrenia Victims and Psychosis" 1990. 400 pub. 370 sold.; [pers.] "To be a good writer you must experience life, as we add years, experiences, we have more to write about! I admire Ernest Hemingway, Anton Chekhov, Robert Frost, Alexandre Dumas; [a.] Federal Way, WA

EVANS, JACQUELINE L.
[pen.] Jackie Evans; [b.] July 2, 1963, Baltimore; [p.] Ruth Delores Stanley (deceased), Herman Stanley; [ch.] Terrance Hachim, Shayla Jacquetta Ruth; [ed.] Mergenthaler Vocational Technical High, Catonsville Community College; [occ.] Unit Secretary, University of Maryland Hospital; [memb.] WEB Women's Entrepreneurial Business; [oth. writ.] Short story a poem published in the PYX arts magazine at Catonsville Community College; [pers.] I create from spiritual, mental and physical emotions and attitudes expressed internally and externally. I am greatly influenced by the social unity and upheaval of peoples world wide.; [a.] Baltimore, MD

EVANS, LINDA DARLENE
[b.] January 3, 1957, Fort Smith, AR; [p.] Lois Welch Evans and the late Charles Edgar Evans; [ed.] Westark Community College in Fort Smith, Arkansas, Arkansas Tech University in Russellville, Arkansas, Northside Senior High School in Fort Smith, ARK.; [occ.] Medical Transcriptionist for Cooper Clinic in Fort Smith, AR; [memb.] Arkansas Association of Medical Transcriptionists, Society of Collegiate Journalist - 1979-1980.; [hon.] Dean's List for Outstanding Scholarship, Arkansas Tech University, Soprano with Westark Community College Choir that performed in Washington, D.C. for the Arkansas Day Celebration in 1976.; [oth. writ.] Human Interest Stories and Lifestyle Features for the Southwest Times Record Newspaper, Fort Smith, AR. Poetry in the "Pentecostal Evangel" Poetry in "The Five Cent Cigar", ATU Literary Magazine. Features for "Arka-Tech" newspaper. Poem in East of the Sunrise anthology 1995.; [pers.] I endeavor to live by I corinthians 10:31, "...Whatever ye do, do all to the glory of God," and that includes my poetry. Thanks to Jodii, Evelyn, Michael, Carolyn, Polly Oliver, and my parents for encouragement and help.; [a.] Van Buren, AR

EVANS, SARAH M.
[b.] September 22, 1976, Macon, GA; [p.] Debbie Lefevers and Louis Evans; [ed.] Graduated from Mary Persons High in June of 1994. Continued education at Mercer University - Macon, GA presently 2nd year.; [occ.] Student; [memb.] Alpha Gamma Delta, Mercer University-Gamma, Iota Chapter.; [hon.] Poems published in ETC. - A literary magazine. In high school I won various vocal competitions and wan on Honor Roll.; [oth. writ.] Desolate, Gone, Letting Go, Thoughts of the Dying, For the Body, Beginnings of Insanity, Revelation, Memories, Lies of Love, The Make of Child, and Forgotten; [pers.] All of my poetry comes from my thoughts, feeling, memories, and dreams. I express myself through my poetry. It enables me to let go and feel free to be who I want to be.; [a.] Macon, GA

EVERETT JR., LOUIS H.
[pen.] Clovis Morrison; [b.] March 31, 1974, San Francisco, CA; [p.] Lou and Doreen Everett; [m.] Doreen Everett, July 23, 1994; [ed.] Lawrence Central High in Indpls., In, Southington High in Southington, CT.; [occ.] Interpreter for the Deaf; [oth. writ.] Looking to publish a compilation of poems and short stories in the near future.; [pers.] I'm thankful everyday for a wonderful wife and family who gave me the love in which I write about, and with.; [a.] Penn Hills, PA

EZELL, DORIS EARL
[pen.] Doris Earl Ezell; [b.] July 24, 1923, Kirksey, KY; [p.] Autumn Ezell-Hansel Ezell; [m.] Elizabeth Ezell, June 14, 1941; [ch.] Phyllis Ann Pamela Kaye; [ed.] Kirksey High School graduate; [occ.] Retired - from 32 years of (Industrial-Manager), Manager of Arabian Horse Farm; [memb.] Kirksey United Methodist Church - Methodist Men Club, Chairman of Board of Trustees, Member of Pastor - Parrish Relations Ct.; [hon.] Salutatorian of my High School Senior Class and, received the Award for the "Best-All-Around" Athlete" for four years."; [oth. writ.] Five (5) poems; [pers.] I am a "lover" of Nature, and "Enjoy My Country Home and Farm."; [a.] Murray, KY

FARLEY, NICOLE
[pen.] Nicole Farley; [b.] June 15, 1981, Mid-Jefferson, Nederland, TX; [p.] Mary Farley, William Farley; [ed.] In High School (9th grade), Orangefield High; [pers.] I would hope my poems inspire people to write or fall in love; [a.] Orange, TX

FARMER, VIRGINIA G.
[b.] November 5, 1950, McConchie, MD; [p.] George and Marguerite Spriggs; [m.] William E. Farmer; [ed.] MSA, BSN; [occ.] Registered Nurse; [memb.] NAFE, GSCH Auxiliary; [hon.] Editor's choice Award, 1995 national Library of Poetry; [oth. writ.] What value is life published by Sparrow grass Poetry Forum 1996; [a.] Indian Head, MD

FASANO, RENEE C.
[pen.] Damaris Shobi, Jessie; [b.] July 29, 1976, Harbor City, CA; [p.] Anthony Fasano Jr., Graciela Fasano; [ed.] Carson High; [occ.] Air Traffic Controller, United States Navy, Adak, AK; [oth. writ.] Many poems written, none published; [pers.] I am defined the same as a poem... "A composition in verse, especially a highly developed, imaginative one." For everything I have to say, is always written, and speaks for itself.; [a.] Adak, AK

FAW, VOLNEY
[pen.] Volney Faw; [b.] October 21, 1912, Yakima, WA; [p.] Robert and Birdie Faw; [m.] Maurine H. Faw, June 7, 1936; [ch.] Terry and Rex Faw, Penny Barrett; [ed.] PhD University of Chicago, M.A. University of Chicago, B.A. Laverne College, Calif., A.A. Comptom Junior College; [occ.] Professor Emeritus, Lewis and Clark College, Portland, OR; [memb.] Amer. Psych., Assoc., Oregon Psych., Assoc., Portland Academy of Hypnosis, Internat., Soc., of Clin., and Exp., Hypnosis, Amer., Assoc., of University Professors; [hon.] Ford Foundation Grant, 1952, National Science Foundation Grant, Smith Foundation Grant, Diplomate Amer. Psych Assoc., Diplomate, OR Psych., Assoc., ABEPH - National Society of Clinical and Exp., Hypnosis; [oth. writ.] 16 research articles in Professional Journals: Amer Psychologist, J. of Ed. Psychology, J. of Clin and Exp. Hypnosis, J. of Social and Cons. Psychology etc.; [pers.] I write poetry for fun and pleasure.; [a.] Portland, OR

FAY, LOIS F.
[b.] March 21, 1927, Newport, NE; [p.] W. E. Farr and Vesta M. Farr; [ch.] Gay Negley, Rena Negey, Crystal Fay; [ed.] One yr., Univ., Nebr., Night School at Long Beach City College, one Sem., at West Coast Univ., L.A.; [occ.] Sr. Material Planner at McDonnell Douglas Aircraft Corp.; [memb.] New Life Community Church, Amelia Farhart Society, Ladies Golf Club; [hon.] Plaque at Univ., of Nebr for "Most Perfect and Fastest Gregg Shorthand and Translation - 1945; [pers.] Raised in Nebr., by Rancher and wife, overcome poverty and have enjoyed wonderful life in California since 1950. My philosophy: "Where there's a will there's a way" thanks to my parents.; [a.] Long Beach, CA

FEDA, SUZANNE
[b.] June 27, 1960, Lafayette, GA; [p.] Pete and Fay Granger; [m.] Michael Feda, September 24, 1993; [ch.] Jennifer, Jessica, Joseph, Stephanie, Stephen; [ed.] The Andrews School for Girls, Willoughby, Ohio; [occ.] AR/AP Manager, Air Terminal Support, Inc.; [pers.] My son, Joe, is the artist of this poem, from him, with love - it is dedicated to me.; [a.] Tallahassee, FL

FELDMAN, JACK ALLISON
[pen.] Jack A. Feldman; [b.] December 19, 1923, Amsterdam, NY; [p.] Leon Feldman and Anna Esther, Olender Feldman; [m.] Margaret Waldman Feldman (Deceased), July 19, 1946; [ch.] Robert Louis and Dione Lynn; [ed.] High School and Valedictorian of Electronics, Naval Air Apprentice School 1948-1952 (7588 hours), also taught Math in school of study; [occ.] Retired from 35 1/2 years with Novel Air Station: Electrical Engineering Tech., set-4P Electrical Standard (World Wide); [memb.] "Senior Engineering Technician" with "Institute for Certification of Engineering Technicians" by "National Society of Professional Engineers", Member of "Jewish War Veterans of America" Medic in World War II Platoon 7, Battalion D.; [hon.] World War II: Two Battle Stars Asiatic Pacific Ribbon, American Area Ribbon, Philippine Liberation Ribbon, "Honorable Discharge" (Navy), while working in "Electronic Standard Laboratory, I won several money awards for Inventions in Calibrating Standards in Electronics all over the world as well as the United States.; [oth. writ.] As Senior in Wilbur No Lynch High School, Amsterdam, New York, I won first prize in city and Honorable Mention for State of New York and a certification for essay titled: "How the Spanich American War Helped to Influence Our Present Latin American Policy".; [pers.] I was inspired in Poetry by Robert Frost, Bliss Carmen, Henry Wadsworth Longfellow, William Shakespear, Virgil and Homer (Greek Poetry) (Inspired by Nature, God and Good Deeds). I was also inspired by my deceased wife Margaret Alice Waldman Feldman, by my present fiancee, Shirley Elaine, Gray Wachtler and her friends.; [a.] Norfolk, VA

FELDMAN, ROBERT J.
[b.] October 25, 1952, Buffalo, NY; [p.] Marleen and Herb Feldman; [ed.] Santa Monica College; [occ.] Full Time Receptionist/Office Manager for United Way of Greater Los Angeles and Part-Time Poet/Writer/and Actor; [memb.] I am a member of the Los Angeles Chapter of the American Federation of Television and Radio Artists; [hon.] Recently won the Editors Choice Award for Outstanding Achievement in Poetry, presented by the National Library of Poetry in 1995 for the poem entitled "A Fond Farewell," dedicated to my mother after she had passed away. Received and won other Numerous Acting and Directing Awards for Theatrical Productions.; [a.] Culver City, CA

FELICIANO, ADRIAN
[b.] September 20, 1973, Queens, NY; [ed.] N. Andover High School, Univ. of Mass/Amherst, Life; [pers.] Poetry without feeling just should not be. True passion lies beneath the mind, raging and laughing. I adore, with all my being, the romantics, and heavy-metal. (Hail Trey Azagthoth, of Morbid Angel You are a true God.) Funny how certain people said that this style of poetry would "never be published".

FELMAN, DAVID
[b.] May 1, 1971, Baltimore City; [ed.] B.A. in Psychology from University of Maryland. Enrolled in Post - Baccalaureate Teacher Education Program (High School Physics); [memb.] Golden Key National Honor Society, The University of Maryland Baltimore Country Symphony Orchestra; [pers.] Every mind has boundless potential, dormant for the few precious years of a lifetime.; [a.] Glen Burnie, MD

FENNER, VIRGINIA MEEK MANN
[pen.] Virginia Fenner; [b.] January 22, 1927, Neartiro, OH; [p.] Clearnce R. Meek and Edna M. Leapley; [m.] Carroll V. Mann, November 23, 1946, and Frank Fenner, June 15, 1990; [ch.] Phyllis I. Mann, Gay Lord Mann, Randoll Mann; [ed.] Graduated in 1946 from Iberia High School in Ohio; [occ.] None-retired; [memb.] Grace Brethern Church Galion, Ohio; [hon.] This is the first acknowledgement I have received; [oth. writ.] Yes lots of poems; [pers.] God work wonders in ones life. I am so honored to be chosen for my attempt to write the poems that I have.; [a.] Galion, OH

FEOLE, WILLIAM A.
[pen.] William A. Feole; [b.] June 8, 1956, Providence, RI; [p.] Louis and Marie Feole; [ed.] Cranston West High School (1974), Associates degree in Human Services from the Community College of RI (1993); [memb.] Yawgoog Alumni Association, The Patients for Progress, Consumers Advisory Council; [hon.] Eagle Scout, Dean's List, Special Achievement Award - RIARC; [oth. writ.] "From The Heart," and "Gift of Love," two books of poetry self-published in 1996; [pers.] Paralyzed from the neck down, my writing is based upon personal experience and my desire to help people to learn and grow.; [a.] Pascoag, RI

FERCH, MARIAN L.
[b.] August 15, 1922, Detroit MI; [p.] John and Stella Weatherbee; [m.] Russell E. Ferch, May 29, 1965; [ch.] Irene, Frank, Robert; [ed.] Holy Redeemer High School, Various Grade Schools; [occ.] Retired Cashier from Allied Super Markets; [memb.] Apostle Ship-of The-Sea, Ministry St Andrews Alter, Society. Religious Education, Teacher - all in Detroit, Mich, Retired Seniors Voluntary Program of Inkster Mi. (RSVP); [hon.] Ship dispatcher of year for A.O.S. 1991, Outstanding Volunteer Award for R.S.V.P. 1990, Cashier of the year award five years running; [oth. writ.] Among others. "My Mother" "Things I Love", both non-published; [pers.] I write when I am inspired by the Holy Spirit; [a.] Inskster, MI

FERGUESON, MAURINE
[b.] February 9, 1938, Park City, UT; [p.] Oren J., and Marie Anderson; [m.] Ernest R. Fergueson, December 19, 1967; [ch.] 6; [ed.] 11th Grade; [occ.] Owner/ Manager of Mobile Homes Rentals; [memb.] Layton Area Chamber, Military Affairs, Hill Air Force Base, Northern Utah Apartment Association, Neighborhood Watch Leader C.O.P., Domestic Violence Volunteer for Davis Country; [hon.] 3 Editors Choice from NSP, ISP Poet of Merit 1995, Layton Chamber (Congratulations Award); [oth. writ.] Two Monthly Newsletters for Cedarwood Park and Community Policing. The American Literary Press, Noble House has Accepted to publish my book of Poetry. "My Additude", 7 poems published by NSP including "Best Poets of 1996" Lakeside Review, Utah Highway Patrol Magazine and NAALL profile in Park Record, Park City, Utah; [pers.] I try not to wander so far from myself that when I return, there is someday else, from the day I was born, I knew I was me no matter how much I change, their inside I will be. If anyone else, ever knows me that well, I hope they will use discretion, and never tell.; [a.] Layton, UT

FERREE, GARY A.
[b.] March 14, 1947, Tiffin, OH; [ed.] BA in Psychology from Bowling Green State University, MPA (Masters in Public Administration) from University of Toledo; [occ.] Director of Residential Services at Compass (Chemical Dependency Program); [hon.] Pi Gamma Mu; [pers.] I write for my own enjoyment and release, but hope others may find enjoyment or something of value in it as well.; [a.] Toledo, OH

FILE, GLENDORIA
[b.] February 15, 1972, Thomasville; [p.] Alexander and Emma File; [ed.] Jackson High School, Leroy High School, Fulton Elementary and Texas Meades Elementary School; [occ.] CNA, Certified Nursing Assistant and Seamtres; [pers.] Do not live your life in vain, slow yourself down to enjoy life for yourself not for other people.; [a.] Jackson, AL

FILIP, FREDERICK
[pen.] Smiley; [b.] November 27, 1960, Los Alamos, NM; [p.] Henry and Marie Filip; [ed.] Los Alamos School, University of New Mexico, Technical - Vocational Institute; [occ.] Machinist; [hon.] I lettered in track and field and football; [oth. writ.] Places In The Sun, Dearly I Held You; [pers.] There are a number of people I need to be thankful for.; [a.] Palisade, CO

FINLEY, ASHLEY P.
[b.] January 27, 1973, Lincoln, NE; [p.] Bety Finley; [ed.] BA - Univ., of Ne., Lincoln (In English and Sociology), currently pursuing MA at the Univ., of Iowa (in Sociology); [occ.] Student; [oth. writ.] Poems published in the Univ. of Nebraska's Literary Magazine and in a local literary magazine.; [a.] Iowa City, IA

FISHER, CORRINA M.
[pen.] Cori; [b.] July 9, 1970, Mountaintop, PA; [p.] Karen and Harold Fisher; [ed.] Crestwood High School, Bloomsburg University; [pers.] Life is short and we should all take time out for the things we enjoy, as long as it's positive. That's why I try to write something every day, whether it be poetry or thoughts, I love to write.; [a.] Mountaintop, PA

FISHMAN, SETH
[b.] October 2, 1980, Midland, TX; [p.] Noah Fishman, Sherry Carron; [ed.] Midland Freshman High School; [occ.] Student Writer, Soccer Player; [memb.] B.B.Y.O. Youth Organization, D.FY. RT (Drug Free Youth in Texas), Student Council, Peer Mediation of Midland Freshman High School; [hon.] Ranked City Level in P.T.A. writing competition. Outstanding Student of the year in Physical Education; [oth. writ.] Two short stories just completed. A novel in process.; [pers.] I attempt to get people to understand some basic things about life in my writings, and to face them with their own knowledge.; [a.] Midland, TX

FITZGERALD, DANIEL
[b.] February 9, 1971, Binghamton, NY; [p.] Mary Carol and Ed Fitzgerald; [ed.] University of Maine, B.S. Political Science, Concentration in Environmental Science; [occ.] Fundraising/Development Manager; [memb.] Common Cause, Eagle Scout of the Boy Scouts of America; [oth. writ.] Several other poems all dedicated to my one true love, Vilma; [a.] Fall River, MA

FLEISHMAN, PATRICIA
[b.] October 30, 1955, Norristown, PA; [p.] George M. and Helen Ososkie; [m.] Sid Fleishman; [ch.] Michael; [oth. writ.] I am writing poems about the seasons for young children. I hope to, one day, have them published in my own book.; [pers.] I write poems that are easy for young children to read. That way they enjoy them and will have an appreciation for writing and reading poetry and books.; [a.] Strongsville, OH

FLORA, ALLENE
[b.] June 8, 1923, Superior, NE; [p.] Emma, Joseph Phillips; [m.] Warren Flora, February 19, 1942; [ch.] Sharon Barger-Donnale, Stein Kuller; [ed.] Valley High, Graduate 1942; [occ.] Retired Police Matron, Nursing Assistant - Pediatrics; [memb.] IOWA State Police Association Auxiliary - Past President, American Diabetus Association, Chapel of Faith Church; [oth. writ.] Several - never tried to publish before; [pers.] I wish for peace and love—all over this world. Love - brings happiness — Let's fill our world with Love; [a.] Des Moines, IA

FLUET, CHRISTINE
[b.] September 13, 1960, Manchester, CT; [p.] Melvin Hellstrom, Sylvia Hellstrom; [m.] Scott Fluet, September 25, 1985; [ch.] Alexander and Geneva; [ed.] Verplank Elementary, Manchester High, Western CT, State University, Trinity College; [occ.] Secretary, Ebnezer Lutheran Church; [hon.] Dean's List; [pers.] I try to create emotions and pictures through my words.; [a.] Columbia, CT

FONDACARO, KATHY
[b.] January 15, 1971, Cincinnati, OH; [p.] Joe and Helene Fondacaro; [ed.] Henderson High School, West Chester, P.A. and Northeast Missouri State University, Kirksville, MO; [occ.] Journalist/Photographer, Wilmington News-Journal; [memb.] Society of Professional Journalists, St. Cecilia Catholic Church; [hon.] Young Authors Award, 1986 and First Place Editorial Excellence, 1995; [oth. writ.] News, sports and feature articles for newspapers, training manuals for corporations; [pers.] My writing is influenced by strong moral

beliefs and emotions, my creativity, inspired by my mother - the artisan.; [a.] Wilmington, OH

FONTANA, BRUCE P.
[pen.] Sargent Scar; [b.] December 2, 1950, New Orleans; [p.] Eola and Jake Fontana; [ch.] Jeaneau, Tonya, Nina; [occ.] Fire Fighter-Paramedic; [pers.] I write what I feel.

FORMAN, SHERRY
[pen.] Kani Forman; [b.] Frankfurt, Germany; [p.] Claudia and Jacob Forman; [ed.] B.A. - Psychology (Cum Laude), M.B.A. - Management, currently pursuing M.S. - Psychology, to prepare for PhD.; [occ.] Psychology Student (graduate) at Auburn University - Montgomery; [memb.] Psi Chi, Phi Kappa Phi, Phi Theta Kappa, Blue Key, Golden Key, NAFE, NCMA; [hon.] Mortar Board Scholarship Award (78), Community Scholar Award - Matawan Regional School System (N.J.) ('74); [oth. writ.] Currently working on my biography about my experiences as an Air Force officer. Published information booklet for the International Officer School, Maxwell Air Force Base, AL; [pers.] I strive to reflect a part of myself in my work, and hopefully those who read my writings will benefit from my experiences, both good and bad.; [a.] Montgomery, AL

FOSHEE, ASHLI E.
[b.] May 3, 1971, Quincy, FL; [p.] James and Elise Foshee; [ed.] Mt. Juliet High School, Florida State University; [occ.] Elementary School Teacher; [hon.] Golden Key Honor Society, Womens Club (of Wakulla County) Poetry Awards: First place for 2 consecutive years (1986 and 1987); [oth. writ.] Articles for "I'll Take Romance!" magazine; [pers.] I'm pretty much a realist on the pessimistic side. Most of my poetry reveals a tendency to be bound by the past. Like many poets I reveal in tragedy. I Love Longfellow, Millay, and Twain.; [a.] Quincy, FL

FOSTER, JACQUELINE ELAINE
[pen.] Jackye; [b.] August 23, 1958, New Haven, CT; [p.] Richard and Veronica Foster; [ch.] Quiana and Julian; [ed.] Wilbur Cross High, New Haven, Tuskegee Institute, Alabama, New Hampshire College (College Graduate); [occ.] Community Resource Associate - Department of Social Work; [hon.] English, Science, Dean's List, Most School Spirit; [oth. writ.] Several poems; [pers.] "What Goes On In The Park, Comes Out In The Light - Because The Truth Is Too Big Too Hide"; [a.] New Haven, CT

FOWLER, ANGEL
[b.] August 12, 1980, Bakersfield, CA; [p.] Deborah and Charles Fowler; [ed.] I am a 10th grader at First Coast High School; [occ.] Babysitter; [memb.] Rainbow Girls; [hon.] CPA, Graduation from Jr. High, Dare Program, Science Fair Award, Fair entries, Two First Place Ribbon on Cake and Cookies; [oth. writ.] I wrote the poem "Alone" in Journey of the Mind published by the National Library of Poetry; [pers.] I love writing and I dedicate all of my poetry to my mom, Grandparent, Earl and Mary Moye, and my father who died when I was 7 years old.; [a.] Jacksonville, FL

FRAGALE, DARLENE M.
[pen.] Darlene (Swanhart) Fragale; [b.] November 6, 1952, Princeton, NJ; [p.] William and Marge Swanhart; [ed.] Kelly Fragale (18), Tony Fragale (16), Nick Fragale (13); [pers.] Although this is my first poem in publication, I have authored many. (i.e, Veil of Rain, That Inner Strength, I Hope That Day will Come, My Friend If You Only Knew, To The soldiers In The Persian Gulf #1, To The Soldiers In The Persian Gulf #2, etc. etc). All of my poetry is written from the heart with sincerity and feeling. I began writing poetry many years ago, initially to vent anger and frustrations. As years passed, I learned poetry need not always portray and hurt and that poetry can also be humerous and uplifting. Along with writing poetry, I love to write stories and intend on writing a book in the near future. I dedicate all past, present and future writings to my three children - Kelly, TOny and Nick.; [a.] Ewing Township, NJ

FRAIJO IV, SAMUEL E.
[pen.] Fraijo IV; [b.] April 21, 1972, Covina, CA; [p.] Samuel E. Fraijo III, Gloria Moronez; [ch.] Ashleigh Krystyne Fraijo; [ed.] Valle View High; [occ.] Stater Bro's super Market; [oth. writ.] Several other poems; [pers.] Freeing my mind with papper and pen. Searching for peace of mind from within.; [a.] Alta Loma, CA

FRAMPTON, EDNA
[b.] June 27, 1935, Carlisle, KY; [p.] Ruth Curtis, Wade Bishop; [ch.] Mary Gulley "Daughter"; [ed.] Carlisle, KY, High School, Hazet Green, ACAD; [occ.] Work for Charity Organization for Care of foster Children; [oth. writ.] I have written many poems, but only for friends and family; [pers.] I have always tried to share my most inner thoughts and deepest regard's for the American Indians. I admire their love for the land on which they live.; [a.] Ontario, CA

FRANADA, VANESSA LEE
[b.] August, 5, 1981, Chicago, IL; [p.] Villamor Franada, Esperanza Franada; [ed.] Currently freshman at Larkin High School, Elgin, IL; [memb.] Staff writer - Larkin HS., Newspaper, "Royal Herald", American Kyuki-do Federation (Tae Kwon Do, red belt); [hon.] Honor student at Abbott MS, Elgin, IL, "Those Who Excel," Clinton Elementary School, South Elgin, IL, Expect to be honor student at Larkin HS; [oth. writ.] Submitted writings to "Young Authors," keep own personal journal of writings; [pers.] As time goes by, you are left to accomplish what your soul yet desires.; [a.] Elgin, IL

FRAVEL, KEVIN D.
[pen.] D. W. Brooks; [b.] April 29, 1968, Waverly, NY; [p.] Kenneth D. Fravel, Bonnie M. Fravel; [ed.] Pennsbury High School, Temple University; [occ.] Office Worker, Village Thrift Stores, Inc., Bensalem, PA; [hon.] Who's Who Among Student in American University and Colleges, Norman and Ruth Sun Memorial Award in Economics, Eagle Scout; [pers.] I am influenced mainly by the people and events in my life and surrounding environment.; [a.] Bristol, PA

FREDERICK, DIANE M.
[pen.] Diane Frederick; [b.] November 16, 1956, Detroit; [p.] Daniel Frederick, Ernestine Frederick; [ch.] Anthony David Frederick; [ed.] High School Graduate of Garden City East High; [occ.] Analyst, U.S., Treasury Department; [memb.] United Foundation; [oth. writ.] Personal poems, to perhaps publish one day in a book. Future plans to write. Books and become a well known Author.; [pers.] I strive to express my deepest inner feelings of life, its surroundings, and its emotions, of experiences, and dreams, I was influenced greater by my mother who loved my poems.; [a.] Riverview, MI

FREEMAN, ELYSE JEAN
[pen.] E. J. Freeman; [b.] November 21, 1947, Mason City, IA; [p.] Mrs. Elsie A. Merritt; [m.] Earl E. Freeman, December 2, 1967; [ch.] (2) Michael E. Freeman and Melissa D. Freeman; [ed.] U.S. Grant School, Porterville Junior College, Pontotoc County Skills Development Center; [occ.] Licensed Practical Nurse; [oth. writ.] I have written a few short stories and several poems. This is the first one to get published.; [pers.] I strive to write poetry that is straight forward without hidden meanings. I have always enjoyed the writings of Emily Dickenson.; [a.] Elmore City, OK

FREEMAN, J. B.
[pen.] J. B. Freeman; [b.] July 18, 1948, Abington, PA; [p.] Katherine N. Riley, Joseph A. Freeman (D); [m.] Sharman Taylor Freeman; [ch.] 5 Children; [ed.] St. Joseph's Prep (HS), Phila., PA., B.S. Engineering, U.S. Naval Academy, MS Human Relations, Golden GAte Univ.; [occ.] Entrepreneur, President of T.A.L.K., Associates Consistent Positive Direction Experts, Leadership Development Specialist; [memb.] American Society for Training and Development, The Impact Consortium; [hon.] 1972 U.S. National Fencing Champion, 1972 U.S. Olympic Team, Delaware Board of Education, Goals 2000 Planning Council, created the skills of "Verbal Positive Approach" (Delivered in Workshops Nationwide); [oth. writ.] Workshop Guides on the Skills and Techniques of Verbal Positive Approach. Newspaper Community. Newspaper Article on Community Customer Service. Poems written while overseas 1n 1977.; [pers.] You can always pull allies in the direction of success. Many times it is simple as telling people where you are going, or what you want to accomplish.; [a.] Delaware City, DE

FREITAG, SHERRY
[pen.] Sherry Freitag; [b.] June 1, 1952, San Antonio, TX; [ch.] Matt and Chad Freitag; [ed.] McColluin High School, SA, TX, Howard Payne College, Brownwood, TX, Del Mar College, Corpus Christi, TX; [occ.] Secretary with a Major Chemical Company; [pers.] As my poetry leaves my heart, I hope it enters others, with all the love enveloped.; [a.] Corpus Christi, TX

FRESHWATER, JOWAN CELANIA
[b.] March 13, 1930, Ottumwa, IA; [p.] Frederick J., and Elizabeth Celania; [ch.] J. Gus Freshwater and Annette J. Freshwater; [educ.] Registered Nurse, St. Joseph Hospital, Ottumwa, Iowa, Attended Southwest Missouri Sch., of Anesthesia Springfield, Mo.; [occ.] Retired Director of St. Mary's Medical Center, Surgical Services, Evansville, In.; [memb.] Assoc., Operating Room Nurses; [hon.] Who's Who in American Nursing 1986-1989; [oth. writ.] Other poems, Job-Related Papers (none published); [pers.] My first poem was titled "War Christmas - 1944"; [a.] Evansville, IN

FREY, BRYAN
[b.] November 12, 1982, Atlanta, GA; [p.] Ken and Sally Frey; [ed.] Barnwell Elementary and currently in the 7th Grade at Holcomb Bridge Middle School; [hon.] Honor Roll; [pers.] Imagination is the key to my writings. I enjoy writing stories and poems.; [a.] Roswell, GA

FRIES, JAQUALYN HOPE
[pen.] Jaqua-Lynn, Lynn Taylor, Benna Bard, Jackie Lynn Taylor, Hope Frees; [b.] June 29, 1925, Compton, CA; [p.] Chester and Ethel Taylor; [m.] Jack Fries, August 6, 1966; [ch.] Six beloved step children by two

previous marriages: Brandi Bryan and Bartley Bard, Cheryl Valencia Icard and Jerry, and Anthony Valencia; [ed.] Film Studies and Private Schools (1-12), Child Actress, Began films in Legendary Little Rascals of Our Gang; [occ.] Spokeswoman for "Ultra Life" Natural Health Products. Motivational speaker-teacher; [memb.] Screen Actors Guild (SAG), American Fed. Television, Radio Artists (AFTRA), Sacramento Assoc. for the retarded (SAR); [hon.] San Francisco TV Woman of Year (1954), Honored 1991 for Pioneer Broadcasting since 1951 by Nat'l Academy of TV Arts and Sciences, and San Diego Nat'l Press Club; [oth. writ.] Co-authored book with husband "Jackie Remembers Our Gang" currently updating book in verse and writing "Cat Tails" in verse; [pers.] In America all things are possible to achieve. I have lived the American dream -- it's never too young to begin and you are never too young to begin. Mary Baker Ebby, Religious Pioneer and Elizabeth Barrett Browning have been my inspiration to write. I portrayed E.B. Browning as a young actress at the Ben Bard Playhouse in Hollywood; [a.] Citrus Heights, CA

FRISBY, F. E.
[pen.] Cheleque; [b.] July 7, 1936, Texas; [p.] James and Ona Sprouse; [m.] Raymond W. Frisby, September 1, 1966; [ch.] Mark, Liz, Bob, John, Stephen and Paris; [ed.] Allan Hancock Jr. College, Bakersfield Comm. College; [occ.] Real Estate Broker; [memb.] Sisters of the Sacred Hoop; [oth. writ.] Songbook and tape "Sweet Grass and Poppies" self published; [pers.] I believe in the magic of the universe. We are all pure potential of the unified field. Inspired by Dr. Dee-Pack Chopra.; [a.] Grover Beach, CA

FRITZ, MARILYN S.
[b.] June 11, 1951, Delta, CO; [p.] Geneva Stoens, Paul Stoens; [m.] Michael Fritz, December 7, 1983; [ch.] Robert Paul, Anthony Louis, Brian R., Patrick M., Tina Lee; [ed.] Western High School, International Art Correspondence School, A.C.E, Teachers Training; [occ.] Junior High and High School Teacher Home School, Manager of my Fathers House Church Bookstore; [memb.] My Fathers House Church Leadership; [hon.] Desert Daubers Art Guild, International Art Correspondence School; [oth. writ.] Articles for the Review Journal Local Newspaper, an article for Faith Corner published in True Story Magazine. Poems written for private individuals for reading at a social dinners.; [pers.] Poetry is an expression of Life in motion. To be a part of that expression is not just an honor, but a privilege given by the Creator.; [a.] Las Vegas, NV

FRIZLEN JR., BILL
[b.] October 29, 1960, Philadelphia; [p.] William O. Frizlen Sr., Rita V. Frizlen; [ed.] Mt. Lebanon High School and Duquesne University; [occ.] Counselor in Children's Aid Group Home, Pittsburgh, PA; [memb.] Animal Rights Organizations such as "Animal Passion" - Pittsburgh, PA and P.E.T.A. (People for the Ethical Treatment of Animals) Washington, D.C.; [oth. writ.] Several poems published in local magazines; [pers.] I strive to improve the world of both people and animals by any means that is available such as Protest, Political Activism and/or Poetry.; [a.] Pittsburgh, PA

FROST, KRIS
[b.] December 26, 1963, Burley, ID; [p.] Warner and Tamara Weber Frost; [ed.] Degree in Health Science; [occ.] Registered Respiratory Therapist, Primary Children's Medical Center; [pers.] Through the expression of thoughts on paper, I seek to give back some of what has been given to me. If through my writings I can touch one person, I have succeeded.; [a.] Farmington, UT

FUGATE, MARTHA T.
[b.] September 23, 1920, Idmon, Clark Co., ID; [p.] Dr. R. D. Tucker and Sarah Merrell McDonald; [m.] Ralph G. Fugate (Deceased), March 8, 1945; [ch.] Sarah, Rebecca, Ralph D.; [ed.] Midway High School (Idaho), Brigham Young University; [occ.] Retired except Board of Directors Fugate Industrial Sales; [memb.] Daughters of American Revolution, Daughters of Utah Pioneers, Veteran of WAVES, WWII; [hon.] 1st place poem, B.Y.U. 1944, 1st place short story, B.Y.U., 1940 publication of two poems for Utah Centennial Poetry edition; [oth. writ.] Main author, with sister, of Biographical/Historical Novel: "Your Move, Dr. Tucker", 1986; [pers.] After years of raising three children and helping with family business, I am being more productive—feel I have another book in me and am working on a novel set in rural area during the "great depression."; [a.] Midway, UT

FUNKE, THERESA
[pen.] Theresa Anderson; [b.] August 16, 1969, Cedar Falls, IA; [p.] Kay S. Anderson: Ed See; [ed.] Degree in Acctg., Certified Tax Preparer; [occ.] Accountant; [memb.] National Association for Female Executives; [pers.] I like to write a lot and always put my feelings into everything I'm working on.; [a.] Rock Island, IL

FURR, BILLIE RUTH
[b.] September 29, 1919, Charlotte, NC; [p.] William R., and Lealer H. Perry; [m.] Floyd C. Furr, December 21, 1935; [ch.] Son: Joe A. Furr; [ed.] High School; [occ.] Retired; [memb.] Pineville Church of the Nazarene, Sunday School Teacher 60 years, December 21, 1995 will celebrate my 60th Wedding Anniversary; [hon.] Enjoy sharing my poems and songs within our church family - Joy Club and Nursing Homes. The Reward - adding joy and happiness to others.; [pers.] Have a special love for people. Sharing the joys and sorrows life brings. Have a wonderful Sunday School Class of Senior Adults. 30 active 10 members of home dept. Write personal cards and poems to members often.; [a.] Pineville, NC

GAGNON, JAYE C. BROWN
[pen.] Jaye C. Brown; [b.] June 24, 1968, Somerville, MA; [p.] Joan A. Brown, William T. Brown (Deceased), stepfather: Roger G. Freeman; [m.] James F. Gagnon; [ch.] 1, Daniel J. Gagnon; [ed.] Currently attending Oakland Community College, MI; [occ.] Housewife/Mother; [memb.] PADI (Scuba Diving Assoc.); [hon.] Dean's List at O.C.C.; [pers.] The Clouds are always above your head. You can either sit on them, or lie under them.; [a.] Clarkston, MI

GAINES, JOHN
[b.] November 10, 1979, Whittier, CA; [p.] John Gaines, Margie Gaines; [ed.] Don Bosco Technical Institute; [occ.] Student; [memb.] Boy Scouts of America, Order of the Arrow. National Rifle Association, National Honor Society, Junior Kiwanis Club; [hon.] Dean's list, Principal's list, Eagle Scout award for Boy Scouts of America; [oth. writ.] Articles for the WHittier Daily News, also for the NOAC (National Order of the Arrow Conference) Times, and the National Jamboree News, articles for my high school newspaper, the Tech Times; [pers.] I strive to create a variety of views by being creative and also by being an individual among those who aren't, especially in poetry.; [a.] Whittier, CA

GAMBILL, JILL
[b.] July 15, 1976, Indianapolis, IN; [p.] Rosemary and Ted Gambill; [ed.] Carmel High School, Rochester Adams High School, University of Colorado, University of London; [occ.] Student - Completing One Year Abroad at the University of London; [a.] Rochester Hills, MI

GAMBOA, ALEJANDRO REY
[b.] August 12, 1977, Santa Maria, CA; [p.] Josefina Gamboa, Reymundo Gamboa; [ed.] Ernest Righetti High School - Class of 1995, California State Summer School of the Arts - Class of 1994; [occ.] Full-time student, bus boy; [hon.] 1994 California Arts Scholar, American Legion Certificate of School Award in 1995; [oth. writ.] Supernatural, a three issue graphic novel, several poems published in Bound and Gagged, short screenplay in C.S.S.S.A.'S screenplay anthology, several poems in school newspapers; [pers.] I would like to dedicate this poem to all of those who made me feel, be it happiness or sadness. Especially to Melissa K., Laura-Marie, Meleah, Nicole W., and Leah for believing in me. Also, to my Mother for the Heart, my Father for the Gift, and God for the Chance.; [a.] Santa Maria, CA

GAMBY, MICHELLE LEE ANNE
[b.] March 22, 1974, Bowling Green, OH; [p.] Don and Eileen Gamby; [ed.] Graduated from Perrysburg High School 1992, currently senior at Bowling Green State University, majoring in Marine Biology; [pers.] This poem is dedicated to all the important people in my life: Mom, Dad, Brian, Aunt Sue, Grandma Smith, Cathy, Karin, Amy, Becky, James and Michael.

GANGWAR, HANS BUUS
[b.] January 18, 1977, Point Pleasant, NJ; [p.] Inger Buus Gangwar, Anshumali Gangwar; [ed.] Toms River High School East, 1995 graduate; [occ.] Freshman, Dept. of Mechanical Engineering, New Jersey Institute of Technology - Albert Dorman Honors College; [hon.] Advanced Placement Scholar with Distinction, August 1995, New Jersey Institute of Technology Mechanical Engineering Department Freshman Achievement Award, May 1995, N.J.I.T. - Albert Dorman Honors College Faculty Scholar, March 1995, National Merit Scholarship Corp. Special Scholarship Award supported by Asarco Foundation, May 1995, Edward J. Bloustein Distinguished Scholar, State of New Jersey, Nov. 1994, Represented in 91-92, 92-93, 93-94, 94-95 editions of Who's Who Among American High School Students; [oth. writ.] Two poems ("Let cool winds blow", and "A ship's sullage") published in reflections, a journal of Toms River High School East published annually, Spring 1995, volume 16; [pers.] Each of us sees the world through a different set of eyes. Words can go only so far in bridging the gap between others' perspectives. No one truly knows what another thinks, nor what the world looks like to him, only he knows that. It is an inherent part of the sheer aloneness of being human, of being alive.; [a.] Toms River, NJ

GARCIA, RAMON
[pen.] Ramon Essex Garcia; [b.] August 22, 1970, Los A., CA; [p.] Elvira Garcia and Rosendo P. Romero; [ed.] 1. Sunny Hills High School Fullerton Calif., 2. Cypress College/Cypress Calif.; [occ.] Counselor/Working with handicap kids; [oth. Writ.] Title: Poetry in

Motion/The Realities of Life with No Optical Illusions at Hand. Seen to be released in the fall of "97"; [pers.] I believe that everyone has some control to a certain extent of their destiny. Meaning that what you get out of life, is what you put into it.; [a.] Buena Park, CA

GARCIA, REBECCA K.
[pen.] Rebecca K. Garcia; [b.] November 11, 1979, Randolph County; [p.] Rebecca and Carlos Garcia; [ed.] Currently in the 10th grade at Southwest High School in High Point; [pers.] I have always believed that what you write should always reflect what you feel.; [a.] Pleasant Garden, NC

GARILLI, DOLORES
[b.] September 26, 1905, Rotondi, Italy; [p.] Rotondi, Italy (Deceased); [m.] Silvio Garilli, September 26, 1938; [ed.] Italy then attended Washington College, New York graduated in Chemistry 1934; [occ.] Real Estate Management; [memb.] ABWA (American Business Womens Assoc.) Dante Aligheiri, (Art Organization from Italy) Federal Womans Club (4 million) American Heart Ass. and several country clubs etc.; [hon.] Woman of the year 1975 Western Carolina University Alumni Asso., American Physicians Fellowship Inc. for Medicine in Israel, 25 years ABWA; [oth. writ.] "The Girl from Italy", "What a Shame" (song for Kennedy in Kennedy Library in Boston) donated; [pers.] Be kind to everyone, share your thoughts with others, say "I love you" often. These are the things I live by. Actions speak loudly.; [a.] Surfside, FL

GEESAMAN, JESSICA
[b.] August 16, 1982, Brunswick, ME; [p.] Krystin Geesaman; [ed.] I am in 8th grade; [occ.] Student; [a.] Cedar City, UT

GEISS JR., SAMUEL G.
[pen.] Samuel G. Geiss Jr.; [b.] February 6, 1930, West Reading, PA; [p.] Samuel G. Geiss Sr., and Elsa S. Geiss; [m.] Mary G. Geiss, March 21, 1964; [ch.] Anthony Joseph (A.J.); [ed.] High School Graduate West Reading High School Class of 1947; [occ.] Retired Bell Telephone Co. of Pa.; [memb.] Various Volunteer Fire Companies, Berks Co. Fire Chiefs Assn.; [pers.] "You are what you are, when you aren't thinking what you are"; [a.] Sinking Spring, PA

GENTILE, DEBORAH A.
[b.] August 14, 1964, Williamstown, NJ; [p.] Earle and Peggyann Kubat; [m.] Mark J. Gentile, October 18, 1986; [ch.] Justin M. Gentile; [ed.] High School Diploma, Delsea Regional High School; [occ.] Pre-school teacher; [memb.] Glassboro order of the eastern star of N.J.; [oth. writ.] This is the first of my writings I have ever shared with anyone. All the rest are tucked away in my books.; [pers.] Anyone can write, just relax and let your thoughts drift to paper.; [a.] Newfield, NJ

GETHERS, SYLESIA ANN
[b.] January 26, 1972, Eutawville, SC; [p.] Mrs. Annie Bell Ravenell; [ed.] Graduated East Orange High School - 1990, graduated Winifred B. Baldwin School of Nursing - 1994 and presently a B.S.N. student at Jersey City State College, N.J.; [occ.] Registered Nurse at the Veterans Administration Hosp. E. Orange, NJ; [memb.] American Heart Association, American Lung Association, and National League of Nursing; [hon.] High School Honor Roll; [oth. writ.] Several poems published in high school newspapers and employer's newspapers; [pers.] I strive to reflect the real everyday living of men, women and children in society as I know it. I have been influenced by great poets, Maya Angelou, Rita Dove, and Langston Hughes. I have also been influenced by Ophah Winfrey, whose talk show topics are so provocative that I have been inspired to create poetry from them.; [a.] East Orange, NJ

GETTIG, TIMOTHY ALAN
[pen.] g i.e. tg; [b.] October 27, 1959, Panama City, FL; [p.] Ronald Emerson Gettig, Jo Anne Greene; [m.] Janice Marie Gettig, March 9, 1979; [ed.] Graduated H.S. 1978 at Perrysburg High School in Perrysburg, Oh., graduated with an Associates Degree in Business Admin. with a Major in Computer Prog. in Jan. 1984 from Michael J. Owens Technical College in Perrysburg Oh.; [occ.] Run my own computer consulting business, freelance "self-employed and consultant" computer; [hon.] My poem, "Thoughts of a Seed"... will appear or be presented on the nationally syndicated radio show, "Poetry Today" with Florence Henderson. January 1996 heard throughout the U.S., Canada and the Caribbean.; [oth. writ.] Too many to mention here. One I was published in High School in a book called "words, wisdom, and wit", which featured two of my other poems, "Why Are We Here, Where Are We Going?" and "What's A Poem" in 1975-76, my sophomore year.; [pers.] In writing my poems, I try to provide alternative perspectives of life and mans spiritual purpose.; [a.] Margate, FL

GIANNETTI, ANTHONY
[b.] July 11, 1976, Salt Lake City, UT; [p.] Dr. Ronald and Carolyn Giannetti; [ed.] University of California at Santa Barbara, Biochemistry and Biophysics; [occ.] Research assistant; [memb.] American Association for the Advancement of Science; [hon.] Golden State High Honors Award in Chemistry. UCSB Award for Outstanding Achievement in Chemistry. Winner, Santa Barbara Youth Symphony Coneerto Competition, 1994; [oth. writ.] Cristallization and Determination of the Molecular Structure of the R1-R2 IR Domain of TAU Protein; [pers.] You are the only one who is always there for yourself. Feel on ground, heart in hand, facing forward be yourself. -"John Arden". Imagination is more important than knowledge. -"Albert Einstein". I am inspired by today's talented song writers.; [a.] Santa Barbara, CA

GIBBON, AMELIA
[pen.] Amelia Gibbon; [b.] March 23, 1963, Decatur, AL; [p.] Anna Smith; [ch.] Charles and Sharmeta Gibbon; [ed.] DeVilbiss H.S. Toledo, OH, Stautzenberger Business College Toledo, OH; [occ.] Jury Manager; [pers.] My talent is a gift from God. It is my desire to use it so that others will be encouraged to think about our world and the part(s) we play in it as individuals; [a.] Toledo, OH

GIBSON, GEORGE
[b.] January 22, 1925, Pittsburgh, PA; [p.] Charles and Ruth Bowers Gibson; [m.] Mary Stroock Gibson, October 26, 1963; [ch.] Geoff, Claudia, Pamela and William; [ed.] Graduate: U.S. Merchant Marine Academy, Kings Point New York; [occ.] Retired: Ex Airline Pilot; [memb.] AARP: Institute of Navigation: American Legion; [oth. writ.] Articles published in Local Papers and Trade Journals

GIDDINS, ADELE F.
[pen.] "A" Giddins; [b.] November 9, 1928, Baltimore, MD; [p.] Herman Ford, Sarah Lipscomb Ford Pastor and Founder of Victory Temple C.O.G.I.C.; [m.] Rev. Charles E. Giddins Sr., February 14, 1946; [ch.] Brenda, Charlette, Charles Jr. II; [ed.] Camden County College, Deans List B.S. Glassboro State College B.A. Deans List also Nursery School Degree, Jameson Bible Inst. of Gramling Univ.; [occ.] Teaching a Youth Bible Course at Church, Retired 18 year Public School Teacher. LMI Homework Hotline; [memb.] Church Clerk, Child Evang. Inst. Pres. Vacation Bible School, 40 years Sun. School Teacher, 4-H Club Pres. Manager James Household Plastics, Dir. Victory Temple Day Care Center, Dir. Youth Bible Study Class V.T.C.; [hon.] Chapel of Four Chaplins Camden City Board of Education Delaware Valley Teen Conference Award Victory Temple Youth Pres. Award Trophy "Drill Team" Atlanta Ga. Public Speaking Certificate; [oth. writ.] Editor of Monthly Newsletter Editor of Annual Scholarship Fund Raising Book; [pers.] After reading the poetry Phyllis Wheatly, I was inspired to become a writer and to enrich the lives of both young an old through words of compassion and love. To God be the glory for the knowledge and wisdom came from Him the Author and Finisher of my life.; [a.] Camden, NJ

GILES, ERIC
[pen.] Amfortas; [b.] November 17, 1974, Bartlesville, OK; [ed.] University of Delaware - Bachelor of Arts in History; [occ.] Artist; [pers.] My poetry in general has no real sense of origin, it comes and goes as my subconscious dictates.; [a.] Wilmington, DE

GILL, JENNIFER
[b.] November 6, 1979, Toledo, OH; [p.] Teresa Gill; [ed.] Sophomore at Maumee High School in Maumee, Ohio; [memb.] 4-H Club Member, Member of Marching Band; [hon.] Received the presidential academic fitness award twice, Attended the University of Toledo's, College of Engineering Saturday, Academy for Gifted and Talented Students; [pers.] I write about things I feel, experience, or believe. I have been influenced and inspired only by my own self-motivation.; [a.] Maumee, OH

GILLIS, CHRISTINE
[b.] August 24, 1970, Brooklyn, NY; [p.] Pam Ferolano; [ed.] Tottenville High School, College of Staten Island; [memb.] American Red Cross Search and Rescue Team; [hon.] Spelling Bee Champion, Tract 1st place, Honor Student, Registered Author Award and Certificate of Publication Award also Certificate of Achievement from P.H.P.; [oth. writ.] Several poems published in other an anthologies and magazines; [pers.] I write to express my feelings and emotions and I am striving to be the best I can in everything I do. I am thankful for the influence to write from my Mom, family and all of P.H.P. and friends.; [a.] Staten Island, NY

GILMAN, BARBARA DRUMMOND
[pen.] Barbara Drummond; [b.] May 31, Portland, ME; [p.] K. R. Drummond and J. B. Drummond, M.D.; [m.] E. Jeffrey Gilman, April 26, 1941; [ch.] Jeffrey D. Gilman and Gayle D. Gilman (M. Michalec); [ed.] Class of 1937 Pine Manor College; [memb.] High School, National Honor Society; [hon.] Above, One of 3 book prizes when printed in the triad Anthology of New England Verse - 1938; [oth. writ.] Several poems in the Junior League Magazine and other small magazines before WW II; [pers.] Believing "The bottom like" to be love one another, I seek God's guidance.; [a.] South Portland, ME

GIOIA, GLORIA
[b.] October 30, 1950, Hackensack, NJ; [p.] Bertha and Louis Sedlmeir; [m.] Joseph Gioia Jr., July 27, 1968; [ch.] Michael Gioia, Gina Gioia; [ed.] Ridgefield Park High School; [occ.] Data Entry; [memb.] Ladies Auxiliary to the Veterans of Foreign Wars Post #8867, Trustee and Publicity Chairperson; [oth. Writ.] Co-editor By-lines Vet-lines, Articles for the Ocean County Reporter, Observer, Bricktown News; [pers.] I've always had a hidden love for writing. My poetry is a reflection of "My voice within."; [a.] Brick, NJ

GIRARD, GALE A.
[b.] August 23, 1947, Liberty, NY; [p.] Warren and Iola Myers; [m.] Divorced; [ch.] Michele 25, Kelly 20, Andy 17; [ed.] High School; [occ.] Banking; [pers.] I have never submitted anything to be printed or published. This poem is only one of many entries I have made in my private journal.; [a.] Jeffersonville, NY

GIROUX, JESSE MICHAEL
[b.] July 13, 1984, Bradford, ME; [ed.] I am now in 6th grade at The Central Middle School in East Corinth, Maine; [occ.] Student; [memb.] Olympia Sales Club; [hon.] Cross Country Track Team Award 1995, top scholar 1993, M.E. A's 95% Writing Award, 1995 Most Creative School Writings, grades k, 1,2,4 and 5; [a.] Bradford, ME

GIULIANO, JOSEPH
[pen.] J. A. Julian; [b.] May 20, 1926, Providence, RI; [p.] Antonio Giuliano, Elizabeth; [m.] Anna M. Giuliano (Izzo), October 28, 1950; [ch.] Dianne C., Carol A.; [ed.] Mt. Pleasant High, U.R.I. Extension; [occ.] Real Estate Broker and property management; [memb.] Life member, Veterans of Foreign Wars; [hon.] Commander, V.F.W. Post 10011; [oth. writ.] "Power of the Brain", "Pedal of Beauty"; [pers.] To personally feel and realize the meaning of the entire poem.; [a.] North Providence, RI

GLASS JR., MARVIN H.
[b.] February 10, 1929, Tampa, FL; [p.] Marvin H. and Lenela C. Glass; [m.] Gwendolyn P. Glass, August 29, 1954; [ed.] Tallassee H.S., Auburn University; [occ.] Retired; [memb.] First United Methodist Church, Tallassee, AL, Montgomery Photo Club (I.A.), Alabama Music Federation (I.A.), Alabama Ornithological Society (I.A.); [hon.] Christmas Card Design Winner - George Jensen Inc., N.Y., N.Y., 1st Place Candid Photos, Military Awards, Art Guild — Auburn University; [oth. writ.] Glass Technology, other poems, Newspaper editorial, currently writing a book; [pers.] I loathe wars and their perpetrators.; [a.] Tallassee, AL

GLAUDE, LINDA
[pen.] Nikki; [b.] March 2, 1954, San F., CA; [ch.] Sean, Schuyler, Stephan; [ed.] El Camino City College, Jordan High School, Commercial Art-Major; [occ.] Artist, Crafter; [hon.] President Award for 4.0 g.p.a., Mensa Organization; [oth. writ.] 100's, none published until now. Having M.P.D. all my alters write their feelings in poetry form.; [pers.] Until man learns to look into the heart of man, and ignore what he sees on the outside of man, we will never be able to say we truly want a peaceful planet.; [a.] Houston, TX

GLENN, MAY
[pen.] Mai Glenn; [b.] February 28, 1927, Bedford, WY; [p.] Alma Perkins, Ethel Perkins; [m.] Gerald Glenn, April 6, 1947; [ch.] Bart Glenn, Celeste Glenn Sommers; [ed.] High School and Business College; [occ.] Accountant, Secretary; [memb.] Member of Church of Jesus Christ of Latter-Day Saints (Mormon), Honorary member of Optimists Club, A-1 Grandmothers (of which I am the only member). I am not much of a joiner but I do a lot of community service.; [oth. writ.] Articles published in our local newspaper. Songs and skits used and performed locally. Have written many verses on request for births, birthdays and deaths.; [pers.] I like words. I like the taste and the feel of them. I like short, precise, sometimes powerful and often loving words—words which evoke immediate understanding to the reader.; [a.] Salt Lake City, UT

GLIDEWELL, URIEL E.
[pen.] Uriel E. Glidewell; [b.] December 6, 1931, Springfield, MO; [p.] Ben Glidewell, Pauline Glidewell; [m.] Twylla D. Mitten, March 19, 1955; [ch.] Darrell Lee, Gina Gale; [ed.] Central High, Drury College; [occ.] Retired, Advertising Manager; [memb.] Centurion Flying Club, (U.S. Navy Veteran); [hon.] Outstanding Layout and Design for a Colored Advertisement from the Stokely Van Camp Sales Staff; [oth. writ.] Several other "Cowboy Poetry" writings as yet, unpublished; [pers.] Several years ago I saw an Flay Burned on TV (in Dallas) I also saw Haze for our country and the values we hold so dear. I was so moved - I wrote "Freedom's Flag".; [a.] Fort Worth, TX

GLOSSUP, LISA ANN
[b.] July 22, 1970; [p.] Joe Misek, Patti Misek; [m.] Danny Glossup, September 10, 1994; [ed.] Prairiland High School; [occ.] Manager, Bealls Department Store Sulphur Springs, TX; [pers.] I try to express my thoughts in a way that's direct and easy to understand. Writing poetry lets me share my emotions and opinions about various topics. It can also be a powerful source of persuation; [a.] Paris, TX

GLUZBERG, BORIS L.
[pen.] B.G.; [b.] November 10, 1970, Odessa, Russia; [p.] Leonid and Sretlana Gluzberg; [m.] Natasha Gluzberg, October 31, 1993; [ed.] FDR H.S. Regents Honors Diploma Brooklyn College; [occ.] Account Executive Dean Witter; [hon.] Student Model Congress Member Arts Poetica Journal Daily News "Freedom" award winner; [oth. writ.] Eagle, Winter, Tumb of Glass; [pers.] "Life is like a cool drink on a hot summer day" - enjoy it, live it once its finished its gone forever; [a.] Brooklyn, NY

GODSEY, SUSAN
[pen.] Susan Godsey; [b.] August 22, 1963, Ginowan City, Okinawa; [p.] Shigeko Godsey, Robert H. Thompson; [m.] Lawrence Valencia (Fiancee); [ed.] Garden Grove High School; [occ.] Tom's Bar-B-Que/ Cashier; [memb.] Sokka Gakkai Int'l - U.S.A., Cactus Chorus, Boy and Girls Study Group; [pers.] My wish in this life is to chant for Kosen-Rufu (world peace) my writing have been greatly influenced by S.G.I.'s President Daisaku Ikeda.; [a.] Chandler, AZ

GOECKE, JULIA A.
[b.] April 28, 1973, Columbus, OH; [p.] Barbara and Kenneth; [ed.] Corpus Christi Grade Sch. and Chaminade-Julienne HS; [occ.] Receptionist, The Window and Door Factory; [memb.] Knights of Lithuanian - Council #96; [pers.] Poetry reflects my feelings and deepest my feelings and deepest emotions. When reading my poem you are actually looking deep into my soul.; [a.] Vandalia, OH

GONSKI, JOHN
[b.] June 2, 1972, Waterbury, CT; [p.] Joseph and Sally Gonski; [ed.] Holy Cross High School Southern CT State University; [occ.] Operation, Supervise Central Transport, Cheshire, CT; [oth. writ.] Some poem published in local magazines; [pers.] My poetry reflects my own personal experiences I try to be as true to my feeling in my writing as possible; [a.] Prospect, CT

GONZALEZ, GERARDO F.
[b.] July 8, 1973, Sacramento; [p.] Ana Gonzalez, Humberto G.; [m.] Tina Marie; [ch.] Vincent, Marissa Gonzalez; [ed.] Grant High School; [pers.] I enjoy hiking. It helps clear my mind from living in the city and the everyday stress. While I'm hiking I find a nice place to sit and write a poem. I wish everyone could experience this peacefullness.

GONZALEZ, RAQUEL
[b.] April 19, 1984, Perth Amboy, NJ; [p.] Rick and Diana Velasquez; [pers.] I really like writing poems and I love to read. At eleven years of age, I like my life. It's a life to enjoy. I also like my friends Kayla, Erika and Kristy

GONZALEZ, STEPHANIE D.
[b.] September 21, 1964, San Gabriel, CA; [p.] Gil and Linda Gutierrez; [m.] Oscar Gonzalez, November 19, 1988; [ed.] California State Polytechnic University, Pomona; [occ.] Import Traffic Coordinator. President of Good People, Inc. (Personal Business); [oth. writ.] Journey to Enlightenment Newsletter; [pers.] I enjoy writing about matters of the spirit. My intentions are to expose the great treasures of life and its good people.; [a.] Chino Hills, CA

GOOD, MARGARET
[b.] February 4, 1933, Torrance County, NM; [p.] Claude and Bertha (Crider) Brown; [m.] Paul W. Good; [ch.] Dena Sue Roberts, Edward F. and Steven W.; [ed.] Ewing School, Torrance County, NM, Estancia High School, Torrance Co. NM, Harding University, Searcy, Ark (2 yrs); [occ.] Retired Secretary; [memb.] Church of Christ International Society of poets; [hon.] New Mexico Girls State 1950, High School Salutatorian Scholarship to Harding College; [oth. writ.] Published in Anthologies: High School 2 Years, Plus Sermons in Poetry college 1 year, Famous Poets Society, Hollywood, CA: Today's Great Poems, Famous Poems of Today, National Library of Poetry: Best Poems of 1995, Best Poems of 1996, Plus 9 other anthologies, Vessels: (A Christian Paper for women, by women), several poems; [pers.] I credit my 6, 7, 8th grade teacher, Eulah Watson, now deceased, for getting me started writing poetry. My writings generally consist of things with which I am familiar, specific events, people and religion.; [a.] Stephenville, TX

GOODHUE, MRS. LYNA
[b.] August 14, 1918, Waltham, MA; [p.] Merton Franklin Gray, Alice Alberta (Bezzanson); [m.] William Melvin Goodhue, March 28, 1941; [ch.] William Jr. Steven, Beth; [ed.] Girl's English High, Boston Mass. New York Institute of Technology; [occ.] Housewife; [memb.] Dean's Street Chapel, Northwest Civic Ass, Freeport Historical Society, Old House Society; [hon.] Dean's list I attended college in my late fifties, Medal for a essay; [oth. writ.] Several stories published in High School paper (Magazine) "The Distaff"; [pers.] I have 5 grandchildren. My oldest grandchild served with the 101st Airborne in the Gulf War, then the Army

sent him to West Point. My husband taught at both Harvard and Yale; [a.] Freeport, NY

GOODLING, RANDY L.
[b.] July 8, 1959, York, PA; [p.] George Goodling, Alverta Goodling Henry; [m.] Dianna J. Goodling, September 3, 1987; [ch.] Autumn Jayne, Alexander David, Justin Kile; [ed.] Dallastown High, Dallastown, PA; [occ.] Hershey Chocolate USA; [memb.] North American Hunting Club; [pers.] Until you've tried and failed or succeeded, you won't know your limitations.; [a.] York Haven, PA

GOODMAN, MARY
[b.] November 9, 1903, Ephraim; [p.] Laura and Joseph Steven; [m.] Deceased, 1927; [ch.] Boy and girl; [ed.] College grad.; [occ.] Home maker 92 years old

GORRELL, CALVIN
[b.] June 24, 1959, NY; [p.] Charles Gorrell, Thelma Gorrell; [m.] Ruthie Gorrell, April 23, 1994; [ch.] Shannon C. Gorrell; [ed.] Corning Community College Houghton College, Bachelor's in Psychology; [pers.] The discarding of a previous held belief does not happen because the belief is no longer truthful, but rather, the truth is no longer helpful. This represents both the strength and weakness of man.; [a.] Goose Creek, SC

GORRELL, JOSH
[b.] February 21, 1974, Tuscon, AZ; [p.] Steve and Judi; [ed.] Through reading and living; [occ.] (Sales) Art Gallery - Bradford Art Gallery; [memb.] Member of Humanity, a loving humanity; [hon.] Honored to still be alive. I award great teachers.; [oth. writ.] Had poems published in, 'The Weekly Synthesis', a weekly paper for Cal. State Chico, CA; [pers.] Never become a slave to material objects, rather, have material objects serve you.; [a.] Newport Beach, CA

GOSS, MARK ANTHONY
[b.] May 25, 1965, Kansas City, MO; [p.] Eddie and Dolores Goss; [m.] April Scott-Goss, August 25, 1989; [ch.] Baby Goss; [ed.] Pomona Adult Mt. San Antonio College "Marketing Student"

GOSSETT SR., RICHARD F.
[pen.] Richard F. Gossett Sr.; [b.] January 22, 1925, Chattanooga, TN; [p.] Jesse F. Gossett, Mary J. Rudd-Gossett; [m.] Betty J. Morrison-Gossett, August 28, 1948; [ch.] Richard F. Gossett Jr., Almeda J. F. Shockey, Stephen D., Don A., J. L., Elaine, J. Mary; [occ.] Retired; [hon.] Minor; [oth. writ.] I have written about 3 thousand poems in my 52 years with the pen.; [pers.] I love having the gift of being able to put down on paper something that someone will read and maybe get some happiness later down the road.; [a.] Harrison, TN

GOURLEY, ALLEN JAMES
[b.] February 1, 1958, Brookville, PA; [p.] Fern Gourley and James Parks Gourley; [m.] Faith Kimiko Gourley, July 16, 1983; [ch.] Domino Kimiko, Tiffany Lyne, Talon James; [ed.] Redbank Valley H.S., V.H.H. (University of Hawaii at Hilo); [occ.] Self employed, Helicopter Pilot, purchaser of Natural Resources; [memb.] AOPA, Leatherwood Church; [hon.] It is my honor to be a child of God, and He rewards me daily.; [oth. writ.] Story of my life - sealed for my children; [pers.] God is alive and well on planet earth!; [a.] New Bethlehem, PA

GOWEN, HELEN
[b.] 1928, Salzburg, Austria; [ed.] Formal Education Salzburg Austria; [occ.] Retired Bank Mgr; [memb.] Past Board of Directors Chamber of Commerce, past City Council Member; [hon.] Woman of the year 1968 Business and Prof. Woman's Club; [oth. writ.] Tomi O'Malley, Cat Extraordinary, published 1991 vantage press, NY, ISBN 0-533-09596-4, Variety of columns published by newspapers in Arizona; [pers.] Helen Gowen, a native of salzburg, Austria has lived in the American Southwest since 1955. "Always interested in writing, my poems reflect generally the sentiment of my moods.; [a.] Sierra Vista, AZ

GRABENHORST, JENILEE
[b.] March 27, 1982, Texas; [p.] Patricia Grabenhorst; [ed.] Eight Grade; [occ.] Student; [memb.] Sadd, O.M., and Mensa; [hon.] Young Authors Jr. National Honor Society, State Champs in Odyssey of the Mind; [oth. writ.] Poems published in papers; [pers.] If you reach for the stars with all your might one day you might just touch one.; [a.] Norton, OH

GRADY, ANNA DAWN
[b.] November 21, 1976, Morganton, NC; [p.] Sylvia and Vernon Grady; [occ.] Student at Western Piedmont Community College; [pers.] "To dream of the person you would like to be is to waste the person you are." - Anonymous

GRAHAM, GREGORY A.
[b.] November 23, 1953, Rockville Center, NY; [p.] Robert P. and Georgiana F. Rotschi; [ed.] St. Christopher's Baldwin N.Y., South Side High School R.V.C., N.Y., American Institute of Banking; [occ.] Musician; [memb.] Blessed Sacrament Catholic Church; [hon.] Veterin - United States Navy; [oth. writ.] Unpublished works: "The Living End", "If You Knew How Much", "I Loved You"!; [pers.] My Poetry is sparked by the Love of God and my fellow man. I am intensely motivated by the Love, Passion, and Artistry of others.; [a.] Oakland Park, FL

GRAHAME, ROBERTA M.
[b.] October 11, 1908, Saint Paul, MN; [p.] Frederick W. Grahame, Margaret Caldwell Grahame; [ed.] BA, MA, Ph.D. in English, University of Minnesota; [occ.] Retired English professor and teacher; [memb.] Phi Beta Kappa, Guides at Emily Dickinson House, International, Emily Dickinson Society, Huguenot Society (New Pattz), National League of American Pennoman (until local chapter dishandes); [oth. writ.] 3 books of poems, co-author: Women of Springfield's Past, poems in National Magazined, translations from the French, memoirs and genealogical publications. Radio series and addresses on springfield women (at on time).; [a.] Amherst, MA

GRANT, HARRIETTE M.
[b.] October 27, 1944, Long Branch, NJ; [m.] George Ed. Grant, July 7, 1963; [ch.] Tanya Monique and George Ed III; [ed.] B.S. in Information Management with a minor Business Management from Carlow College, Certificate in Human Resource Management from University of Pittsburgh, Certificate in Sign Language from Western Pennsylvania School for the Deaf; [occ.] Warehouse Manager of Nabisco Inc. Pittsburgh Bakery, Owner of H. Grant Custom Cards of Export, Pa.; [memb.] Greater Works Outreach Church, Monroeville Pa, Womens Business Network, East Chapter, Carlow College Alumna Group, Team Leader for the Nabisco Pgh Newsletter, Deacons Motorcycle Club; [hon.] Deans List - Graduated Magna Cum Laude, Nabisco Commendation Award for Excellence 1991, Nabisco Commendation Award for Excellence 1993, Nabisco Commendation Award for Excellence 1995; [oth. writ.] Various poetry for fellow workers retirement parties, various poems for friends, all of the poetry found in the cards Created by H. Grant Custom Cards; [pers.] My Life is so special because God is my Savior, and he has given me a special spouse, along with two wonderful children.; [a.] Murrysville, PA

GRANT, REV. LARRY WAYNE
[b.] July 12, 1959, Pensacola, FL; [p.] Marvin and Joan Wheat; [m.] Esthen Marina, October 7, 1995; [ch.] Stephane Marie; [occ.] Natural Gas Controller, City of Richmond Utilities; [pers.] I try to reflect my thoughts and emotions into my work. With the belief that we all have common experiences. If I have felt a certain way, someone else has also.; [a.] Richmond, VA

GRAVES, CARY L.
[b.] August 10, 1939, Fort Worth, TX; [p.] Jack and Marjorie; [ch.] Candice and Teresa; [ed.] Graduated from TCU in 1963; [occ.] Financial Analyst; [pers.] Our fate as individuals, and as a specie, depends on how well we walk the path of virtue.; [a.] Sandy, UT

GRAY, DANIEL
[b.] August 6, 1972, Miami, FL; [p.] Paula and Eric Gray; [ed.] Miami Sunset Senior High, (Miami, FL) Miami-DADE Community College (Miami, FL) Florida International University; [memb.] Mu Alpha Theta, Key Club Honor Society, Thespian; [hon.] Top ten mathematics students in the nation - 1990. All-star cast award - 1987, (DADE County Fair), Various local writing awards, Graduated top 2% of class which was 14th in class of 1991, Presidential Academic Award; [oth. writ.] Poems Published in local and school literary magazines. Current projects: Writings a fantasy novel and developing a screen play; [pers.] Mostly, my poetry has been inspired by three things: Literature my first poetry professor Ricardo Pau-Llosa, and my friends and family who never let me give up on myself.; [a.] Miami, FL

GRAY, J. K.
[b.] April 3, 1967, Cape Hatteras, NC; [p.] Donnie and Linda Gray; [m.] Jennie Gray, March 27, 1993; [ed.] Petaluma High School, California State University - Sacramento; [memb.] Sigma Chi Fraternity; [a.] Santa Rosa, CA

GREEN, LEVI ADAM
[pen.] Levi Green; [b.] January 26, 1979, Hamilton, MT; [p.] John Timmons, Gayle Timmons, Jared Green; [ed.] Currently a Junior in Stevensville High School; [occ.] Holding a minimum wage job at "Subway"; [oth. writ.] Several poems published in School Newspaper; [pers.] The Poet is the priest of the invisible (Jim Morrison). I am influenced by the writings of Jim Morrison and Jim himself. I also try to reflect the style of Ancient Chinese Romanticism in my writing.; [a.] Stevensville, MT

GREEN, LYNN M.
[b.] August 7, 1965, Worcester, MA; [m.] Dave Green; [ch.] Laurin, David, Nathan, Erica, Taryn; [occ.] Own and operate small business with husband; [oth. writ.] Published poetry in The Maine Campus Magazine; [pers.] My husband is my inspiration, with all his love

and support, and the amazing train rides together.; [a.] Bangor, ME

GREEN, ROSE
[b.] July 18, 1939; [p.] Both Deceased; [ch.] 4 children; [ed.] Graduated Duq. High - McRey School of Nursing; [occ.] Nursing Asst.; [pers.] I write about the feelings inside me and the way women look at love.; [a.] West Mifflin, PA

GREENWELL, SHARON E.
[pen.] Sharon E. Greenwell; [b.] April 5, 1945, Covina, CA; [p.] Roberta A. and Lawrence B. Gould; [ed.] Covina High School, Calif. State Univ. at Northridge, San Diego St. Univ.; [occ.] Health Care Consultant; [memb.] Employee Assistance Professionals Assoc., National Assoc. of Social Workers, Arthritis Foundation, National Organization for Women; [hon.] SDSU's Dean's List '76-77, Service Improvement Award '88-Kaiser, Community Service Award '90 - Kaiser, Poet of the Month '90 - Cal. Writers Club; [oth. writ.] 3 poems in Finding Our Voices, Speaking Out Against the Violence, "Team Work at Its' Best" - article in OT Week, National Occupational Therapy Magazine. Various local organization newsletters - poems and articles.; [pers.] As a therapist and clinical social worker, I have seen repeatedly the therapeutic effects of the creative process of writing, especially poetry and journal writing. It leads to self discovery and personal validation, for the writer, as well as, the reader. Writing is the perfect blend of the right, creative side of the brain and the left, analytical side. Writing is a freeing, spiritual experience.; [a.] Reseda, CA

GRESHAM, MARIE
[b.] September 19, 1927, Miss.; [p.] Nevers and Roxie Barnes; [m.] Woodrow Gresham, July 1942; [ch.] Annette, Babara, Caroline, Richard, Jackie, Fredna, Yvonne and Ted; [ed.] Eureka High School CA School of Nursing; [occ.] I am now retired I volunteering my service in day care; [memb.] Brokens, Community Church Los Angeles, CA; [oth. writ.] I write birth day cards to friends and family; [pers.] I strive for truth, and finding true poems is easy to write, my first poem was written when I was nine years old I hope I never out grow my love of reading and writing poems.; [a.] Inglewood, CA

GRIFFIN, MARILYN K. SLAGHT
[b.] November 8, 1943, Hollywood, CA; [p.] Chauncey and Stella Slaght; [m.] Lawrence E. Griffin, April 23, 1966; [ch.] Wayne, Devin, and Yvonne; [ed.] A.A. Degree from Fullerton College, 1963; [occ.] Owner of "The Wordsmith"; [memb.] A.A.M.T. American Association for Medical Transcription; [hon.] Finalist Woman of the Year, Fullerton College - 1963; [oth. writ.] Co-Authored - "Mormons and Women" - 1980; [pers.] I draw from personal experiences and relationships in my writing.; [a.] Chino Hills, CA

GRINDULO, ELIZABETH G.
[pen.] Beche; [b.] October 14, Philippines; [p.] Gregorio and Rosita Grindulo; [ed.] Doctor of Medicine De La Salle College of Medicine, Philippines; [oth. writ.] 'Be Prepared', published in Aglow Magazine 1990, Manila, Philippines; [pers.] To whatever success I have and I will have - to God be all the glory!; [a.] Pomona, CA

GRISWOLD, LOUISA T.
[pen.] Louisa; [b.] May 28, 1917, Birmingham, AL; [p.] Mr./Mrs. W. A. Thomas; [m.] George H. Griswold (Deceased), November 2, 1938; [ch.] George Jr., Anne Martin, Jane Kerr, Tom and Elis and 12 grandchildren; [ed.] High School and Business College; [occ.] Retired, School Registrar/Secretary, Elem. and Secondary High; [memb.] Bluff Park V.M. Church, Choir, Melodia Music Club, Melodia Music Club, Wesleyan Night Circle UNW, ARTA, Smithsonian, AARP, AEA NEA, Hoover Historical Society, Teacher - Fellowship Class, Amer Heart Assn. Home Prayer Band, Civitan; [hon.] I receive much pleasure from helping older people in our community from being lonely. I have had retirement awards and president's awards: Civitan President, United Methodist Women, Music Club, Job Retirements; [oth. writ.] School Papers Club, articles and other poems; [pers.] I try to set an example by thought, word and deed to my decendants and those I come in contact with. My husband's passing almost destroyed me but it wouldn't want me to be a quitter.; [a.] Birmingham, AL

GROLL, MARY V.
[b.] December 21, 1931, Allentown, PA; [p.] Mr. and Mrs. Philip Groll (Father Deceased); [ed.] 4 yrs. High School (LaSalle - Peru Township High School, LaSalle, Illinois), Cedar Crest College - B.S. ('53) B.A. ('81), Lehigh University - M. A. (1984); [occ.] Retired; [memb.] Phi Alpha Theta - Honorary National Historical Society; [hon.] Del Phi - Cedar Crest College Sorority for High Academic Average, Graduated Cum Laude from Cedar Crest 1981; [pers.] Having lived through World War II during very aware years of my childhood (10-13), the entire event was vaccinated into my memory, I shall never forget it!; [a.] Allentown, PA

GROSECLOSE, MICHAEL SHAWN
[b.] May 16, 1970, Phoenix, AZ; [p.] Richard W. Groseclose and Anna L. Fahy, step parents: Michael P. Fahy and Pat A. Groseclose; [m.] Kimberly A. Warren, (will be) October 22, 1996; [ed.] Elementary: Madison #1, High School: North High, College: Phoenix College; [occ.] Artist; [oth. writ.] Our Darkest Hour, Lonsome Dove, Shattered Dreams, and many others that are yet unpublished; [pers.] If limitation was put on creativity the universe would not be as great as it is! MIchael Shawn Groseclose "On Sensorship" God Bless; [a.] Saint Paul, MN

GRUBER, JARED
[b.] December 25, 1975, Kingston, Ontario, Canada; [p.] Neal and Cara Gruber; [ed.] Cicero-North Syracuse High School, NY, Univ. of New Mexico for 1 yr; [memb.] Tidewater Scottish Society; [a.] Virginia Beach, VA

GRUBER, KURT E.
[b.] July 16, 1977, Clarence, NY; [ed.] Clarence Central High, accepted to Suny Potsdam; [occ.] Cook; [oth. writ.] A short story published in Young Writers and Artists at Work: The student anthology of the western, New York writing project, 1995. Currently working on a novel.; [pers.] Why settle while the extreme is still an option?; [a.] Akron, NY

GRUMAN, CANDACE JOY
[pen.] Candy Gruman, C. G. Gruman; [b.] February 20, 1948, Wisconsin Rapids, WI; [p.] Howard and Geraldine Gerken; [m.] Roger David Gruman, June 25, 1983; [ch.] 2 daughters: Misty Joy and Laura Lee, 4 step-daughters: Diana, Amy, Julie, and Lynn; [ed.] Wisconsin Dells High School, Wisconsin Dells, Wi.; [occ.] Sales and Marketing Manager, Loch Ness Golf Club, Port Clinton, Oh.; [oth. writ.] I have never before submitted anything for publication, however, I have written many poems, both humorous and serious, as well as several songs. During my years as an entertainer, I performed some of my songs on stage.; [pers.] I hope to touch someone's life in a special way every day, and if, in that touch, I make them smile or feel happy, I have done something worthwhile.; [a.] Port Clinton, OH

GUILLAUME, ENOCK
[b.] July 14, 1945, Gracette, Artibonite; [p.] Emile and Rosila Guillaume; [m.] Altenaise T. Guillaume, October 17, 1967; [ch.] Chantale, Malika et Ader Guillaume; [ed.] Stenio Vincent High, Commerce School, Julien Craan, Federated Tax Service; [occ.] Tax Consultant; [memb.] Highlander Club, Habitat for Humanity, The Colonial Williamsburg Foundation; [oth. writ.] Several other poems unpublished based on loneliness; [pers.] I have tried hard to show my nostalgic face. I have been influenced by Alfred de Vigny and Coriolan Ardouin.; [a.] Westbury, NY

GUILLAUME, GEORGE L.
[b.] 1954; [occ.] Self-employed; [pers.] God Almighty created all things to give Him worship and praise. God's love reconciled us by His divine Son Jesus' vicarious and atoning death (Jn. 3). Sin (disobeying God's will) brings strife, hurt, and death and is cleansed only by turning from all that displeases God, asking forgiveness, and faith in the precious blood of Jesus. Jesus is the only way to the Father and a full life (Jn. 10). Every person needs a personal relationship with God through prayer, fellowship with believers, and the Bible which is our Guidebook for life. We are to imitate Jesus and good and give God praise in everything. We must seek and put God first and love our neighbor as ourself (Mt 6 Icor. 13).

GUINYARD, ETHEL HENDERSON
[b.] September 9, 1952, Island Grove, FL; [p.] Warren an Evelyn Henderson; [m.] Willie Guinyard Jr., May 1, 1976; [ch.] Abebi (16 yrs), Bamidele (14), Shaka (11); [ed.] Hawthorne High School, Hawthorne Florida, BS in Mathematics Education, FAMU, (Dec. 1973), Currently working on Masters in Math, Ed, Florida A&M Univ. Tallahassee, Florida (FAMU); [occ.] Teacher of College Preparatory Math, Tallahassee Community College; [oth. writ.] "Innocence Lost," published Fall, 1994, an anthology of Modern Day Poets. Currently working on completing a collection of poems with the central theme focusing on social concerns that we face today and visions of hope found in nature, dreams of experiences.; [pers.] Education, be it formal or informal, shapes the quality of ones life. Life's experience often time dictate the extent to which we put that education to positive use.; [a.] Tallahassee, FL

GULLEY, VERNA M.
[b.] August 16, 1960, Augsburg, West Germany; [p.] Virgil L. and Loyce A. Williams; [ch.] Miechia Loyce Gulley; [ed.] Associate - Business Management; [occ.] Employee Benefits Administration, Harrison School District #2; [oth. writ.] None Published; [pers.] My poetry is a reflection of my life and a collection of actual moments in time.; [a.] Colorado Springs, CO

GUSTIN, WARREN DALE
[pen.] Dale Gustin; [b.] November 30, 1931, Lander, WY; [p.] Margaret E. and Babe Gustin; [m.] Patsy R. Gustin, August 28, 1973; [ch.] Billy, Vicki, Peggy;

[ed.] East High School Salt Lake City, Utah. Then went into Korean War 1949 - 1953 - U.S.N.; [occ.] Semi retired and oil field work; [memb.] V.F.W. and Calvary Baptist Church; [hon.] Award of Proficiency Professional Investigator; [oth. writ.] I have written many poems for the church and some that were used at funerals.; [pers.] I just enjoy writing poetry or songs.; [a.] Big Spring, TX

GUTIERREZ JR., SAMUEL
[b.] October 24, 1983, Silvis, IL; [p.] Samuel Gutierrez, Sylvia Gutierrez; [ed.] Went to Temple Christian Academy and attending Eugene Field Elementary School; [hon.] Academic Awards; [oth. writ.] Unpublished stories and poems; [pers.] I use my writing to express my thoughts and feelings.; [a.] Rock Island, IL

HACKENSON, ADELE A.
[b.] July 19, 1930, Lawrence, MA; [p.] Anthony and Theresa Atkins; [m.] Oscar E. Hackenson, September 18, 1955; [ed.] Framingham High School, Newton-Wellesley Hospital, School of Nursing; [occ.] Retired R.N.; [memb.] Framingham Animal Humane Society, M.S.P.C.A., Boston, MA; [oth. writ.] Poem published in CAT Fancy Magazine poem published in local animal humane society newsletter; [pers.] My love for animals (especially cats) inspire me to pen animal poems. My cat, "Pepsi" was the inspiration for this poem.; [a.] Framingham, MA

HAGARDORN, GERARD J.
[b.] New Orleans, LA; [pers.] This poem was written in memory of my son, Gerard Tyler Hagardorn, born 8/6/90, died 4/19/93; [a.] Metairie, LA

HAILES, DONNIE FELIX
[pen.] Don Felix Baptista; [b.] February 28, 1953, Norfolk Co., VA; [p.] Joseph and Virginia Hailes; [m.] Divorced; [ch.] Shauna, Demetria and Daimenia; [ed.] 12 yrs Public Ed, 1 yr College, Norfolk St. Univ. 16 yrs 29 month Military Ed/Service; [occ.] Surveyor; [memb.] Christian Brother to Mankind; [hon.] Blessed by God and just being a plain ordinary human being; [oth. writ.] Eye to Eye, in Shades of Blue, Rewrite of America, Persian Gulf, Red White and Blue; [pers.] The struggle should not be, behold mankind floudering in life's flow and ebb, struggling like the spider, that's tangled in its own web.; [a.] Portsmouth, VA

HALES, WILLIAM E.
[pen.] William E. Hales; [b.] September 25, 1917, Collingswood, NJ; [p.] May Hales Mahaffie; [m.] Yolanda E. Hales, September 5, 1959; [ch.] Donna Lynn (age 34), Warren Arthur (32); [ed.] Patton Masonic Trade School 1936, Drexel Institute, Lafayette College, Class 45A Pilot U.S. Aircorps 1943-1945; [occ.] Retired, Tool and Diemaker and Machinist; [memb.] Masonic Lodge, Scottish Rite, Shriners of North America and Royal Order of Jesters, Past President of Phila Tool and Die Assn., Past Commodore of Crescent Temple Shrine Yacht Club, Past Commodore Mid Atlantic Assn. of Shrine Yacht Clubs; [hon.] Pilot WW2 (2nd Lt.); [pers.] If I were 40 years younger and had my health, I'd be dangerous!; [a.] Cherry Hill, NJ

HALL, ANNE THRIFT
[pen.] Anne T. Hall; [b.] August 3, 1956, Atlanta, GA; [p.] William Thrift and Mary Hanie Leos; [ch.] Chassie Elaine, James David; [ed.] High School, Trade Schools, continued education, self taught through books available in our libraries; [occ.] Emergency Medical Technician; [hon.] Honored at early age for poem donated to American Cancer Soc., Atlanta Branch poem titled: "The Last Ten Steps of a Smokers Life"; [oth. writ.] Poem published in local paper, and work related newspaper have written children's stories as well as adult fiction; [pers.] I write with pencil in hand, spreading charcoal effects of my imagination.; [a.] Jonesboro, GA

HALL, JOSEPH FRANKLIN
[pen.] J. Frank Hall; [b.] March 11, 1955, Richmond, VA; [p.] James F. and Nettie M. Hall; [ch.] Joseph Franklin Hall II; [ed.] Hermitage High School Class of '74; [occ.] Materials Handler, Philip Morris, USA; [oth. writ.] A collection of poems, unpublished at this time; [pers.] Writing for me is therapy for the mind. It is my way of expressing and dealing with my inner most thoughts and emotions.; [a.] Mechanicsville, VA

HALL, RYAN M.
[b.] July 24, 1974, Baltimore, MD; [pers.] The Author's writing and poetry reflect his views and opinions on cultural and social events, as well as personal feelings.; [a.] Baltimore, MA

HALLIBURTON JR., JAMES VERNON
[pen.] Tony Lord, Paris Blue; [b.] Detroit, MI; [p.] James V. Halliburton Sr., Alois C. Halliburton; [ed.] Edwin Denby High, Wayne State University; [occ.] Graphic Artist; [memb.] United States Naval Reserve, Founding Member Of The Original P.B.I.; [hon.] Military Combat Action Ribbon, Armed Forces Expeditionary — service Medal; [oth. writ.] Several poems published in various newspapers; [pers.] I am a lover of nature and a lover by nature. I am merely an aspiring creative student of life experience seeking the purpose of my existence; [a.] Detroit, MI

HALLMARK, LINDA JOLLY
[b.] October 3, 1946, Birmingham, AL; [p.] Hosie and Elizabeth Jolly; [m.] Ronald L. Hallmark, May 8, 1964; [ch.] Ron Jr., Christie, Devon and Jason; [ed.] Hayden High School Hayden, Alabama; [occ.] Homemaker; [memb.] Blount County, Historical Society; [oth. writ.] West Blount Community Column in The North Jefferson News, Gardendale Alabama; [pers.] I just enjoy writing.; [a.] Warrior, AL

HAMLIN, TERRANEE
[pen.] Legend; [b.] July 28, 1973, Washington, DC; [p.] Laura Hamlin, Cornelius Hamlin; [ed.] Crossand and High School; [occ.] Crew Member at Popeyes; [oth. writ.] I wrote to jails to help people to keep their minds going in the right way.; [pers.] When people reach my work I want it to touch them about life and them to ray his poems really mean something and that he know what he's talking about.; [a.] Temple Hills, MD

HAMMILL, ROBERT J.
[b.] June 11, 1932, Cedartown, GA; [p.] Charles and Pearl Hammill; [m.] Mariola Stegall Hammill, March 14, 1954; [ch.] Mary Belinda, Karen Lea, Aprille Estella Rogers, Kenna Johnson, Robert J. Hammill Jr.; [ed.] Cedartown High School, BS Chemical Engineering, Auburn University, Auburn, Al.; [occ.] Retired from Law Engineering Corp.; [memb.] Summerville Presbyterian Church, Rotary Club, Tappi (Technical Assoc. of Pulp and Paper Ind.; [hon.] Elder - Summerville Presbyterian Church - American Cancer Society; [a.] Summerville, SC

HAMMOND, HANS TALBOT
[b.] November 3, 1975, Easton, MD; [p.] Arthur and Ritva Hammond; [ed.] Tomah Senior High, currently studying at the University of Wisconsin at Madison; [memb.] Phi Eta Sigma Honor Society; [hon.] High School Valedictorian, National Science Scholar, High School Mathematician of the Year, Second Place in Wisconsin State Art Competition, Honors Research Grant in Space Physics at the University of Wisconsin at Madison, Wisconsin Space Grant Consortium Scholarship, Badger Boys State Participant; [oth. writ.] Voice of Democracy American Legion First Place District Essay, a winner in the Promising Young Writers Program by the National Council of Teachers of English; [a.] Madison, WI

HAMMONDS, DAWN
[b.] October 18, 1980, Concord, MA; [p.] Arlene Hammonds, Elbert Snead; [ed.] Gladys Wood Elementary, Mears Jr. High, Dimond High School Anchorage, AK; [memb.] Brownies, Boys and Girls Club, Honor Society; [hon.] Honor Society; [oth. writ.] Poems I wright when I have the time. Also enjoyed by my family.; [pers.] The way I wright poem comes from the way I look at life compared to what I see in my dreams at night. Everyone looks at life in a different way, and I've tried to put my version of life into poetry just like the greatest poet ever. Edgar Allan Poe!; [a.] Anchorage, AK

HAMPLE, RUTH N.
[b.] June 29, 1923, Philadelphia, PA; [p.] Francis and Mary Wurgley; [m.] George T. Hample, June 21, 1952; [ch.] Linda Ruth and Susan Gwen; [ed.] Kensington High; [occ.] Missionary; [memb.] Rhawnhurst Baptist Church; [hon.] Diploma for "The Shefte Course" of music; [oth. writ.] Editor and one of the writers for "The Encourager" booklet to 500 readers; [pers.] In sharing my writings with others, I hope to bring them encouragement and joy, as well as a desire to praise God with me for His goodness and beauty.; [a.] Philadelphia, PA

HAN, KUMNA
[pen.] Jenny Han; [b.] May 5, 1962, Pusan, Korea; [ed.] Han-Yang Women's Junior College Major English; [pers.] 12 years ago, I came to America all by myself to find my little dream. And I'm still looking for it. It must be a big country...; [a.] Hackensack, NJ

HANKS, ROBERT D.
[b.] July 31, 1930; [p.] Boyd Hanks, Sarah Hanks; [m.] Lore (Nee: Pfeiffer), December 27, 1963; [ch.] Randolph, Rebecca, Evelyn, Roland; [ed.] BA w/Honors - Univ. of Md., MA Boston Univ., Consider McNeese State Univ., Lake Charles, La as Alma Mater, (Special French Student); [occ.] Retired Intelligence Analyst/Linguist; [oth. writ.] The Newest Dunciad, Book-Length poem concerning the conflict between Dr. Velikovsky and Harvard Univ., 6800 and lines in rhymed couplets. Many smaller poems.; [pers.] Mercerville, NJ

HANSEN, MICHELLE LYNN
[pen.] Michelle Lynn Hansen; [b.] March 8, 1983, Everett, WA; [p.] Michael and Victoria Hansen; [ed.] Kenmore Jr. High, Sheltton View Elementary School; [hon.] Reflections District Finals/Poem read at Funeral; [pers.] Many of my poems, like this one, take a different view at the world. I hope that someday my poems can be heard and help to influence people to do more.; [a.] Bothell, WA

HARDEMAN, JOYCE M.
[pen.] Joyce Louise; [b.] November 22, 1950, Greenwood, SC; [ed.] Tallulah Falls, HS, Clayton State, Morrow, Ga., Waubonsie, Aurora, Il.; [pers.] My compassion and empathy for people who have experienced injustice, and my faith in my religion, are reflected in my writing. I've been writing since my teens.; [a.] Between, GA

HARDER, DIANE
[b.] May 26, 1955, Upstate, NY; [p.] William and Jeanne Harder; [ch.] Cats, Ariel and Jasmine; [ed.] Empire State College - Suny; [occ.] Meeting Planner, Johnson, Bassin and Shaw, Inc.; [memb.] Defenders of Wildlife, World Wildlife Fund, National Association for Female Executives, Physicians Committee for Responsible Medicine; [pers.] My writing was greatly encouraged by two special women in my life, Lynn Sanborn, 7th Grade English Teacher and Catherine Redding, High School English Teacher.; [a.] Laurel, MD

HARMON, MEDFORD DELANO
[b.] October 7, 1933, Frankfort, IN; [p.] Arthur and Ola Harmon; [m.] Divorced, July 3, 1954; [ch.] Debra, Cheri, and Cindy; [ed.] High School Graduate, 1 Semester College; [occ.] Factory Laborer; [memb.] AARP, Cutler Presbyterian Church, NRA, UAW; [hon.] Graduated First, in class of 1952, Cutler High School Cutler, In., Tuition Scholarship to IU at Kokomo, In. extension; [oth. writ.] Some poems not published yet; [pers.] I like country and western and other traditional music and classics, I am retiring at the end of 1995, I can write poems.; [a.] Monticello, IN

HARPER, JESSICA ARMINDA
[b.] October 30, 1981, Ellijay, GA; [p.] Lee Roy and Wanda Harper; [ed.] I am currently enrolled in the 8th grade at Gilmer Middle School in Ellijay Ga. At the foot of the blue ridge mts.; [hon.] Honor Roll Student 7 years; [pers.] Before love you party and have a wonderful time, in love your higher than you can ever get, but broken hearted, the worst is all that can come your way.; [a.] Ellijay, GA

HARRELL, ETHEL A.
[pen.] Ethel A. Harrell; [b.] June 1, 1948, Little Rock, AR; [p.] Mr. and Mrs. Henry LaMar Sr., Floyd Harrell; [ed.] Horace Mann High School, University of Arkansas - B.S. degree, University of Central Arkansas - M.S. degree. Additional Graduate Work, University of Central Arkansas; [occ.] Account Manager, Health Sciences Division, Eastman Kodak Co.; [hon.] Phi Kappa Phi; [oth. writ.] Several essays, short stories, short story published in university's literary magazine; [pers.] My writings (and readings) center around positive self-esteem, and personal triumph.; [a.] Ventura, CA

HARRIS, CLARENCE J.
[b.] November 4, 1963, Neptune, NJ; [p.] Clarence F. Harris, Frances P. Harris; [m.] Judith A. Harris, June 7, 1992; [ch.] Samantha Rose Harris; [ed.] Red Bank Catholic High School, I.C.S. Scranton Pennsylvania; [occ.] Operating Engineer; [memb.] New Jersey Society of Asphalt Technologists, Weichart Referral Associates; [hon.] ASB Business Management with Honors from ICS

HARRIS, CORA BARLEY
[pen.] Cora Barley Harris; [b.] April 26, 1939, Huntsville; [p.] Daniel, Orell Barley; [m.] William Anderson Harris, January 1, 1957; [ch.] William J. Harris, Carol Harris; [ed.] BA Master Science Universities of Memphis Cosmotologist - Neologist Cosmetician, Certified in Bio-Chem-General Science; [occ.] Biology Teacher, Shelby State College, owner Jarvis Via Corals Cosmetic; [memb.] Delta Sigma Treta Sorority, Phi Delta Kappa Sorority, National Council Negro Women, Coo - of 100 Black Women, Woman of Achievement Memphis Saint Monitial Society, St. Augustine Catholic Church; [hon.] Teacher of the Year, Curry School, 10 Best Dress Hall of Famers, South Center Bell, Girl Club of America, many, many others; [oth. writ.] "Bending Over Boekland", Tenn - Teacher Magazine, "Inquiry Teaching", TIP by Cora Harris; [pers.] Work to enrich my life, my family-life, and the lives of the community.; [a.] Memphis, TN

HARRIS III, LEWIS L.
[b.] October 9, 1956, Pontiac, MI; [p.] Lewis L. Harris Jr., Betty J. Harris; [ed.] Pontiac Central High, The University of Michigan, Wayne State University. Two credit hours short B.A. in Psychology; [occ.] Student; [oth. writ.] Several poems published in a hospital news letter. I have written forty poems.; [pers.] I attempt to deliver a positive message in my poetry. My writings are of a philosophical nature. I have studied both Psychology and Art.; [a.] Pontiac, MI

HARRIS, JENNIE V.
[b.] February 11, 1955, Memphis, TN; [p.] James Harris, Minnie L. Harris; [ed.] South Side High Health Care Institute; [occ.] Certified Nurse Technician (C.N.T.); [oth. writ.] Several poems of inspiration, written from my own personal insight. This will be the first one ever published.; [pers.] Jesus Christ has been the greatest influence in my life. I strive to let His goodness and mercy reflect in my poems.; [a.] Memphis, TN

HARRISON, GERRIE
[b.] Highland Park, MI; [p.] Milton Abraham, Helen Abraham; [m.] Timothy Joel Harrison, September 27, 1986; [ch.] Jesse Joel Harrison; [ed.] Bentley High School Detroit Barber College; [occ.] Barber/Stylist; [memb.] Epilepsy Foundation of America; [oth. writ.] They have always been personal and written to people I know; [pers.] Most of my poems are written to lift peoples spirits and hopefully leave a smile on their face. Writing, has always been, the only way, I can express my true feelings and emotions.; [a.] Livonia, MI

HARRISON, MICHAEL
[b.] New York, NY; [p.] Rudolph and Thelma Harrison; [ed.] James Monroe H.S., College of New Rochelle; [occ.] Administrative Asst; [memb.] Veteran's Bedside Network; [hon.] 5 years volunteer service award for Veteran's Bedside Network; [oth. Writ.] "The Adventures Of Wings And The Rainbow" as yet unpublished children's book; [pers.] Like the rainbow with God's light, when the human spirit retains its faith and beauty it is. Unsinkable. I try to impart upliftment in my writings.; [a.] Bronx, NY

HARTMAN, CHARLOTTE
[pen.] Charlotte Hartman; [b.] Manchester, TN; [p.] Leon and Verda Bryan; [m.] Divorced; [ch.] 2, Brian T. and Melissa D. Hartman; [ed.] H.S. Grad. - Assoc. Degree in Business; [occ.] Exec. Asst. to G. Mgr. Radisson Hotel Indianapolis; [memb.] National Assoc. for Female Executives; [pers.] I dedicate this poem to Gerard A. Goodbold, Sr.the love of my life. The most influential person in my life.; [a.] Indianapolis, IN

HARTMAN, JUNE
[b.] March 23, 1929, Saint Paul, MN; [p.] Dick and Claire James; [m.] Lee Hartman, March 14, 1948; [ch.] Van J. and Val Dean; [ed.] Edison High Minneapolis Chapman Court Reporter College St. Augustine Technical College; [occ.] Retired; [memb.] Sweet Adelines Salvation Army Organist PADI Scuba Diver Since 1973; [hon.] Recognition for 12 years as water instructor, at the Florida School for Deaf and Blind; [oth. writ.] Gospel songs which I've recorded and asked to sing in area churches; [pers.] I've been diving since 1959. I experience such sheering joy exploring God's gardens. Pearl Buck once wrote an article after discovering the underwater beauty "Heaven Below" I share her excitement!; [a.] Saint Augustine, FL

HARTSOE, KENNETH D.
[pen.] Kenneth D. Hartsoe; [b.] March 5, 1966, San Jose, CA; [p.] Wiley Junior and Rilla Jean; [ed.] San Jose State University; [occ.] Research Assistant/Writer; [memb.] National Civil War Association; [oth. writ.] "Ode to Ashe County" 8/93 fiction, High Point During the Civil was 7/94 (non-fiction manuscript), "BArgain to Ballarag-the birth of American-English" 10/94 non-fiction article, Balcony (can ode to the city of Belfast).

HARVIN, KAY
[b.] March 9, 1947, Arcadia, FL; [p.] Billie and Lum Kerce; [m.] Wes Harvin Sr., August 22, 1964; [ch.] Wes Harvin II; [ed.] B.A. - Fla. State U., M.A. Univ of South Fla.; [occ.] Teacher, Martin County Schools; [memb.] First United Methodist Church, 1978-present; [hon.] Delta Kappa Gamma 1972-1984, Who's Who Among American Education - 1955; [oth. writ.] A poem pub. in "Treasured Anthology of Poems - Fall 1995."; [pers.] "I touch the future. I teach." I'd like to further extend this statement by touching our children through my poetry.; [a.] Palm City, FL

HASHEMI, ANAHITA
[b.] April 17, 1966, Shiraz, Iran; [p.] Parvin Safavi; [ed.] Westhill High, University of Connecticut; [occ.] Advisory Accountant, IBM; [hon.] Dean's List; [oth. writ.] Several short stories and poems; [pers.] My inspiration comes from my family and the people I have had the honor to meet during my unusual life. I am who I am because of them.; [a.] Ossining, NY

HASKINS, HAROLD JOSEPH
[b.] April 27, 1977, Kalamazoo, MI; [p.] Harold and Wilda Haskins; [ed.] Graduate of Centreville High School. Am a freshman at Kalamazoo Valley Community College; [occ.] Student; [hon.] High School - recognized by Creative Writing Teacher for this poem. Also received Drama Award for leading role in school play.; [pers.] I think writing should be fun and not a chore. I have a good sense of humor and enjoy comedy. I find it hard to be too serious about myself or what I write; [a.] Mendon, MI

HASTY, IRENE H.
[pen.] Irene H. Hasty; [b.] September 18, 1939, Tangerine, FL; [p.] Charlie Harris, Ellen Harris (Both Deceased); [m.] T. J. Hasty Jr.; [ch.] Vickie H. Robinson, Ronald, T. J. III and Bradley Hasty; [ed.] B.S. Degree, Fla A and M University in Mathematics; [occ.] Retired from Bell South as outside Plant Facility Engineer Jacksonville, Fla., now co-owner of Arlington Custom Printing Inc.; [memb.] Bethel Baptist Institutional

Church; [hon.] Printing Company Chosen "Manufacturing Firm of the Year" 1994 by the Jacksonville Chamber of Commerce, Company appeared in "The Pubic Work Secor" 1995-96 Magazine - An Ongoing Commitment; [oth. writ.] 1) "A Gathering of the Generations" Souvenir Book for the Harris Family. Article in Local paper, 2) Submitted article to "We the People"; [pers.] I enjoy sewing, shopping, writing and researching family history; [a.] Jacksonville, FL

HAWKINS, ANGELIA R.
[b.] June 8, 1976, Hardin Memorial Hospital; [p.] Owen C. and M. June Hawkins; [ed.] Grayson Co. High, Elizabethtown Community College; [occ.] Office Manager, The Record Newspaper, Leitchfield, KY; [memb.] Clarkson Baptist Church (Youth Ensemble, Youth Group, Adult Choir), 4-H Council Treasurer; [hon.] Just Say No, National Honor Society, Beta, Enoch Grehan Journalism Award, other journalism awards, various academic and sports awards too numerous to name; [oth. writ.] Many articles for The Record, various other poems that have not been published; [pers.] I could not have achieved what I have without the many people who have been great motivators in my life, to them, I am eternally grateful.; [a.] Leitchfield, KY

HAYES, MICHELLE
[pen.] Shelle Stevenson; [b.] February 20, 1960, Newark, NJ; [p.] Milton W. Hayes Sr., and Bertha Hayes; [ch.] Michelle Antonio and Collan Kahle; [ed.] Vailsburg High, Lyons Medical Institute; [occ.] Administrator Bread of Life Ministries Lake City SC; [a.] Lake City, SC

HEARLD, CRYSTAL
[b.] June 30, 1978, Tacoma, WA; [p.] Pat and Verra Bohna; [ed.] Last grade completed is 9th, currently a sophomore in High School; [memb.] St. Paul Luthren FBLA - Future Business Leaders of America. I have also volunteered, time to Rose Vista Nursing Center.; [hon.] Graduation from Jason Lee Middle School, Vancouver, WA; [oth. writ.] So Afraid and others poems. Also to be in the family.; [pers.] I owe the encouragement to write by several friends. I owe them several thanks. One main person is my fiance John Phelps.; [a.] Castle Rock, WA

HEIDEMANN, JOY E.
[b.] July 24, 1928, Dodgeville, WI; [p.] Mr. and Mrs. C. J. Holman; [m.] Donald W. Heidemann, August 27, 1949; [ch.] Arlyn, Christine, Donald, Erwin and Alan; [ed.] Dodgeville - W.I. grades and high school, 3 yrs. University of WI at Milwaukee, major — Music Education; [occ.] Retired; [memb.] Member of various dance bands playing Supper Clubs mainly Martinique (Drury Lane Theatre) for 10 years as member of the "House Band."; [hon.] Honors and Awards in various musical competitions, was Professional Musician in the Chicago Area.

HEIL, BONNIE
[b.] September 19, 1958, Wheeling, WV; [p.] Marvin and Betty Heil; [ch.] Misty Sunshine Gray; [occ.] Waitress/Aspiring Novelist; [a.] Massilon, OH

HELFF, JOHNNY C.
[pen.] The Midnight Writer; [b.] September 12, 1954, Cleve, OH; [p.] George, Melvena, Richard Matta; [m.] Gayle D., November 17, 1985; [ch.] Chentudal and Shabakala; [ed.] C.W. Eliot Voc Jr., H. School, Max s. Hayes Voc. H. School, 3 yrs. O.J.T. and apprentice courses, Graduated Electronic Sys. Mech.; [occ.] Electrical, Electronic Maintenance Mechanic; [memb.] Spiritual Temples, Miracle Church of Religious Science and Science of Mind Center; [hon.] Employed by M.A.S.A. Lewis Research center 13 yrs. Received 17 Technical, Personal and Suggestion Awards; [oth. writ.] Writings of the Mind Master, The K.D.O. Collection - Writings of the Spiritual Temples = Ripe Dream of the Glass Gods and many more; [pers.] Practitioner of Science of Mind-Student of, Metu Neter and African casmag Army. Searching for ancient grate musician and publisher to assist in bring work to full circle.; [a.] Orrville, OH

HELLER, MARY ANN
[p.] Charles and Josephine Apap; [m.] Andrew Heller, August 5, 1971; [ch.] Lawrence Paton and Steven Heller; [ed.] Carmel High School, Pace University; [occ.] CFO - heller Assoc and Hell'er Highwater Ranch, choir and teach sunday school; [memb.] Lakeway Catholic Church, Cattle Woman's Assoc., The Hills Country Club, The Austin Club, International Graploanalysis Society; [oth. writ.] I have numerous other poems that have been privately distributed or given to family and friends.; [pers.] I use poetry as a mirror that reflects my inner heart and soul to the outside world.; [a.] Austin, TX

HELPER, RAY
[pen.] Winston Edward Brooks; [b.] June 26, 1969, Charleston, WV; [p.] Alan Helper, Wanda Helper; [m.] Tonya Helper, August 11, 1990; [ed.] St. Albans High School, Ohio Valley College, Career College of the Airforce, Northwestern Oklahoma State University; [occ.] United States Airforce, Pharmacy Journeyman; [memb.] Airforce Aid Society, Airforce Ass.; [hon.] Distinguished graduate Pharmacy Training School, Distinguished graduate, Airman Leadership school; [oth. writ.] No other published works; [pers.] This work was inspired by the unconditional love that has kept my grandparents married for fifty years. This is for you, "Chuck and Lenora", I know them as mamaw and papaw.; [a.] Enid, OK

HENCSIE, SARAH CATHERINE
[b.] October 9, 1974, Grosse Point, MI; [p.] James and Christine Hencsie; [ed.] Henry Ford II High School, graduated 1992, Baker College, Kalamazoo Valley College; [occ.] Musician, Poet, Writer; [memb.] American Red Cross Volunteers, Sigma Pi Sweethearts, Detroit Zoological Society, Midnight Poet's Club; [hon.] Academic Scholarship-Baker College, Editor's Choice Award, 1995; [oth. writ.] Several poems in college chapbooks, published in 1995 The Garden of Life, to poets with love and 3 times in writer's World Magazine; [pers.] I combine the 'avant-garde' and the 'normal', fuse them together and the birth of my poetry appears.; [a.] Kalamazoo, MI

HENDERSON, CATHERINE
[pen.] "Cat" Henderson; [b.] July 28, 1980, New Rochelle, NY; [ed.] Sophomore - Mount Vernon High School; [occ.] Student; [hon.] 1st Prize Winner in Black History Essay Contest 1992, City of Mount Vernon, Writer of the Month, October 1944, Convent of the Sacred Heart, Greenwich; [oth. writ.] Several poems, plays, published in school and local newspapers; [a.] Mount Vernon, NY

HENRY, GLADYS LEE
[b.] November 9, 1951, Jacksonville, FL; [p.] Charles A. Hughes, Corine E. B. Hughes; [m.] Braxton James Henry Sr., July 20, 1974; [ch.] Nekeasha Denease, Braxton James, Yalonda Nicole; [ed.] Andrew Jackson Senior High, Royal Keypunch Academy, Life Office Management Association I (LOMA) IWC Written Communications; [occ.] Administrative Clerk V/Secretary, Independent Life and Accident Insurance Company; [memb.] Professional Secretaries International, Shiloh Metropolitan Baptist Church; [hon.] Quality PEP'er Award, Cost Cutter Award, Time Saver Award; [oth. writ.] I have written several poems, short stories, etc. But have not had them published.; [pers.] I strive to reflect the wonders of God, the beauty in Nature and the goodness in everyone in my writing.; [a.] Jacksonville, FL

HERNANDEZ, JANET ROCIO
[pen.] Janet Rocio; [b.] April 23, 1976, Long Island, NY; [p.] Elvia Navas and Fabio Hernandez; [ed.] Prospect High School; [pers.] Love is what inspires me to write and to live. Our lives are one long poem of love, yet only those events which are capable of capturing our emotions and of touching our hearts in ways we could never have imagined are magical enough to be written into Poetry.; [a.] San Jose, CA

HERNDON, MARY FRANCES
[b.] May 26, 1930, Sedalia, MO; [p.] Lawson and Josephine McCurdy; [m.] Jack D. Herndon, July 30, 1948; [ch.] Jack D. Herndon Jr., Meladee Bay; [ed.] Smith Cotton High School; [occ.] Housewife; [memb.] D.A.R. - International Whistler's Association - Helen D. Steele Music Club - Sedalia Chorale - Honorary Member Rackensack Society - State Fair and Eldorado Saddle Clubs - 1st Christian Church C.W.F. and Choir - Cushman Club; [oth. writ.] Various poems published in local newspaper and Ozarks Mountaineer Magazine; [pers.] I like to write poems about things I see around me and that I love.; [a.] Sedalia, MO

HESLOP, ZENAIDA E.
[pen.] Zenaida E. Heslop; [b.] August 24, 1975, Down State Medical Center; [p.] Hulda E. Heslop, Winston P. Heslop; [ed.] Meyer Levin Junior High School in New York State, Westview High and currently attending University of Tennessee at Martin; [occ.] Student; [hon.] Dr. Martin Luther King Junior Poetry - Essay Contest Principal's Award, Two Certificates of Achievements in Music, 2 Superior, and one Excellent in the Tennessee Music Association, Solo - Ensemble Festival, Dr. Martin Luther King Humanitarian Award, Merit Award, and Martin Westview High School Senior Band Award; [pers.] I have been influenced by my parents and teachers but the most influential were Mrs. Cheryl Boyte, and English Professor Dr. Miriam Page. I would especially like to thank my sister Zelinka O. Heslop for having me send in one of my poems. I strive as high as you can and you can achieve anything.; [a.] Martin, TN

HICKLING, JULIA
[b.] May 27, 1980, Waco, TX; [p.] Dan and Barbara Hickling; [ed.] Home School; [occ.] Student; [memb.] Music Ministries Calvary Chapel Church, 4-14; [oth. writ.] Several unpublished poems and songs; [pers.] I write because God has given me a gift. I only hope that I use it to His glory. I pray that my writing touches peoples lives, or just the way they look at things.; [a.] Royal Oak, MI

HICKMAN, DAVID ERIC
[b.] June 7, 1964, South Jersey; [p.] Bill and Regina Hickman; [ed.] High School Graduate; [occ.] Auto

Body Mechanic; [pers.] Don't let your thoughts escape you, share them with the masses and receive immortality in Black and White.; [a.] Mayslanding, NJ

HICKMAN, MARILYN COLLINS
[b.] February 10, 1935, Terre Haute, IN; [p.] Roy L. and Josephine Collins; [m.] James L. (Jim) Hickman; [ch.] Lance L. Hickman; [ed.] LIncoln High, Vincennes IN, Vincennes Univ., (Junior College), Indiana University, B.S. 1956, Grad. work - Indiana State U.; [occ.] Retired Elementary School Teacher (35 years); [memb.] Alpha Gamma Delta, Women of the Moose, BPO Elks Aux., American Legion Aux., Church at Litchfield Park, Ladies Auxiliary of Eagles; [hon.] Bachelor of Science with Distinction, National Honor Society, National Thespian Society; [oth. writ.] Honorable Mention for a poem I wrote in "American Girl" magazine. I write poetry mostly for friends and relatives on special occasions.; [a.] Youngtown, AZ

HICKS, LAMARA W.
[b.] November 13, 1958, Newport News, VA; [p.] Casper and Vertia Whitaker; [m.] Benjamin Hicks Jr., February 15, 1985; [ch.] 3; [ed.] Hampton Institute; [occ.] Middle School Teacher at John Yeates Middle in Suffolk, VA

HICKS, NAOMI R.
[pen.] Naomi Ruth; [b.] September 20, 1920, Camden, IN; [p.] Roy and Esther Knight; [m.] Marion C. Smith (Died '77) June 15, 1941, Gaylord M. Hicks May 27, 1978; [ch.] Steve Smith, Vickie Williams; [ed.] Upland (Ind) H.S., Taylor University, (Ind), Pacific Univ., (OR) Bach., Music Ed., and Masters Equiv.; [occ.] Retired Teacher from Public School, Music Elementary Level; [memb.] First Evangelical Free Church, Fullerton, CA, Family Motorcoach Assoc., Northwest Execs, Crisis Pregnancy Center, Portland Rose Soc., Oregon Christian Writer's Assoc.; [hon.] Grey Gowns (Pacific Univ.); [oth. writ.] Am at present publishing two books of poetry. Also published in First Ev., Fullerton church paper and local church poetry book.; [pers.] I am trying to minister of those who hurt, either physically, emotionally or spiritually.; [a.] West Linn, OR

HICKS, TRINETTE L.
[pen.] Trinette; [b.] July 16, 1981, Richmond, VA; [p.] Janet Wooldridge-Hicks and Thomas L. Hicks; [ed.] Freshman - John Randolph Tucker High; [occ.] Student; [memb.] St. Paul's Baptist Church - music ministry; [hon.] People to People Student Ambassador Program to Italy, Austria, and Hungary - summer '95; [oth. writ.] I write many poems in my spare time; [pers.] In my poetry, I enjoy expressing my deep appreciation for the beauty of nature. I also enjoy metaphorically expressing the similarities of the beauty of nature to that of mankind.; [a.] Richmond, VA

HIGBY, JODIE LEA
[pen.] Leigh Van Voren; [b.] August 11, 1979, Mission Hills; [p.] Sharon Lea Neill, Jim E. Higby; [ed.] High School Junior; [memb.] Order of the Rainbow for Girls, Saugus High Band; [hon.] 2 poems published in Anthology's; [oth. writ.] Many many poems, several short stories and 3 novels; [pers.] In my writing I try to show my feelings so that people can understand things. It is my soul that writes, not my brain.; [a.] Valencia, CA

HIGDON, WILLIAM ANTHONY
[b.] August 10, 1977, Rushville, IN; [p.] Dale Higdon, Diane Higdon; [ed.] Rushville Consolidated High School; [occ.] Cabinet Finisher, Corsi Cabinetry; [pers.] Chaos is the essence of life.; [a.] Manilla, IN

HIGGINS, DOLORES
[pen.] Granny Gumdrops; [b.] January 24, 1927, Kansas City, KS; [p.] Francis and Valinda McDonald; [m.] Charles L. Higgins, October 2, 1948; [ch.] Kathleen, Michael, Sean, Maurice, Ann; [ed.] Ward High School - Kansas City Jr. College; [occ.] Homemaker; [memb.] Federated Women's Club of Prince George, The Virginia Writers Club Inc. of Waverly, VA., Fort Lee Catholic Women's Club, Senior Citizens; [oth. writ.] Grace's Cats, published in Hitchcock County News, Hitchcock County, Ne.; [pers.] I write to arouse the imagination of children for their enjoyment.; [a.] Prince George, VA

HILL, CLYDESS
[b.] Bald Knob Ark; [p.] Maynard Miller and Leola Miller; [m.] Clarence Hill (Deceased), February 26, 1939; [ch.] Clarence Jr., Charles, Patricia, Kenneth; [ed.] Decatur High, Decatur Illinois Benton Harbor High, Benton Harbor Michigan, Wayne State, University Detroit, Michigan, BA, Psychology; [occ.] Employment Service Manager, State Government; [memb.] Wayne State Alumni, International Association of Personal Employees, Detroit Women's Economic Club, Greater New Mount Moriah Baptist Church; [a.] Detroit, MI

HILL, EARL M.
[pen.] Marcus; [b.] December 30, 1938, Saint Louis, MO; [p.] Jake Hill, Goldie Hill; [ch.] Sharon, Gail, Dindi, Brandon; [occ.] Commerical Artist; [oth. writ.] Listen to the Soul, Moment by Moment, Loving, Caring, Sharing, Be my Valentine, (the above writing have not been published); [pers.] It is my hope that my written messages are clear enough for any and all humans in search of peace, love and happiness. In the Romantic Poetry of their lives. Thanks for sharing my life, remember "the only thing you can change is your mind."; [a.] Los Angeles, CA

HILL, HUTCH
[b.] May 29, 1978, Richmond, VA; [oth. writ.] Various poems and articles in local publications; [pers.] I am heavily influenced by the beats and the music of blind melon. I hope to one day associate with other writers who also write in "extemporaneous pen" and eventually live a life that is nothing. Short of extraordinary.; [a.] Richmond, VA

HILL, JASON E.
[b.] January 15, 1969, Roanoke, VA; [p.] Kate and Stanley Hill; [ed.] Franklin Co. HS, Radford University -- B.S. Biology, Minor --chemistry, near-minor - English; [memb.] Academic Competition for Excellence Team -- Literature Team Captain (FCHS), LBSC; Cofounder and dubious participant, AXP Fraternity - CEO; [occ.] Of the 28 jobs in the past 12 years, I'm currently employed as an Auditor of Quality Assurance in a Toxicological Research Facility, pursuing a career as a wilderness instructor / college level creative writing professor. [oth. writ.] Various poems, journey journals, some prose and dream logs -- all as yet unpublished.; [pers.] Bicycle Grits Delivery!; [a.] Ashland, OH

HILL, JENNIE V.
[b.] August 5, 1922, Columbia, SC; [p.] Robert and Mady C. Hill; [ed.] 1 yr. college - Lee College Cleveland, TN; [occ.] Retired from Gigna Ins. Co. 1986; [memb.] Certified Lauback Trainer - Tutor; [oth. writ.] Have a book "Reflections and Affections" about people that have influenced or encouraged my life; [pers.] Have been a Christian since age nine. Have taught Sunday School and Children's Church since age 15 until now.

HILL, JODELL
[pen.] Jo Hill, Jodell Smith; [b.] April 3, 1970, Medina, OH; [p.] Linda Anderson and Andy Anderson; [ed.] Graduated Highland High School - 1988, currently enrolled at Tri-C Science Major; [occ.] Lab Tech.; [memb.] Rain Forest Rescue, International Society of Poets; [hon.] Nominated for Poet of the year 6 poetry of Merit Awards; [oth. writ.] Published the following anthologies, The Rainbows End, Beyond The Stars, Best Poems of 1996, In the Garden of Life, East of the Sunrise, and Journey of the Mind; [pers.] Those for refuse forgetting the past are forever condemned to relive it.; [a.] Medina, OH

HIMLIN, MATT
[b.] August 15, 1978, Wilkes Barre; [p.] Matt Himlin, Ellyn Himlin; [ed.] Coughlin High Class of '96; [occ.] Student; [memb.] Primitive Methodist Church, National Space Society, National Honor Society, Young Scholars Program, Wilkes University; [hon.] William Preach Academic Award, Who's Who Among American High School Students, Commercial - National Merit Scholar; [oth. writ.] Several unpublished poems, articles - school newspaper; [pers.] I write sad poems because I think there are too many happy ones. After all, life can be as sad as it is happy.; [a.] Wilkes Barre, PA

HINCKLEY, BETTY
[pen.] Betty Lou Hinckley; [b.] October 30, 1923, Struthers, OH; [p.] John and Eleanor Risheberger; [m.] Deceased, June 14; [ch.] Adair McKinney (Adopted); [ed.] Art Education I.S.T. College, NYU, Millersville College, Pian di Sco, Italy Art Group; [occ.] Teacher of Art Aliquippe, Grove City, Gettysburg, Pa. Hershey, Pa.; [memb.] Poetry Club Hershey, Chautauqua NY, Boy Club and Girls Club, Chautauqua, NY, Art Teacher; [hon.] Poetry in World Treasury of Great Poems Vol. II, John Campbell, Editor and Publisher, Where did the Sunshine Go! Betty Lou Hinckley; [oth. writ.] The Seasons of My Mind, Book of Poetry and Drawings, To Create is to Speak with the Heart and the Soul, Am I I? Or Am I She Who Will We Be, I'm A Twin; [pers.] To be an artist and poet one has only to look at the world around me and treasure it's rhythm and let it touch my soul and theirs.; [a.] Hershey, PA

HINCKLEY, JESSICA
[pen.] Zecca; [b.] May 30, 1980, Boston; [p.] Paula, David Hinckley; [ed.] Sophmore in High School; [occ.] Student of Westford Academy, second degree blk blt. in Taekwondo; [hon.] Local smoke free day; [oth. writ.] Some poems have been in local school and town newspapers; [pers.] I want to thank all the people who have been involved in my life and inspired any of my writings.; [a.] Westford, MA

HINEMAN, PATRISSA CLAIRE
[pen.] Trissi Hineman, Trust; [b.] July 27, 1978, Indianapolis; [p.] Ruthelene V. Hineman, Harry E. Hineman; [ed.] Junior at Pike High School in Indpls.; [occ.] Student; [memb.] Zionsville Presbyterian Church, Spanish Club at Pike High, Chamber Singer at Pike High; [pers.] The joy of living and the wonder of life are two of the things we have going for us today.; [a.] Indianapo-

lis, IN

HINES, KENNETH
[pen.] Monty; [b.] January 10, 1972, Norfolk, VA; [p.] Mary Hines, John L. Bagley; [ed.] B.S. General Business (Management) Norfolk State University - AASCB School of Business; [occ.] Manager: Thomas Market; [oth. writ.] I have many personal writings, however, Bang! Bang! Bang! is my first published; [pers.] If a conflict arises between two people, then those two people should settle that conflict, without the intervention of other people or inanimate objects.; [a.] Hampton, VA

HINES, MARIA A.
[b.] April 24, 1965, Dayton, OH; [p.] Mr. and Mrs. Thomas L. Hines Sr.; [ed.] B.S. Degree in Industrial Engineering, Univ. of Cincinnati, OH, 1989; [occ.] Research Engineer at Armco, Inc. Research; [memb.] 1. Facilitator of Armco Research's Work-Force Issues Team, 2. Managing Diversity Team, 3. National Society of Black Engineers; [oth. writ.] 1. The Tennessee Ten, 2. Stop Aids; [pers.] Writing is my first love. It is the ultimate expression of who I am. I have known this since third grade.; [a.] Dayton, OH

HOBBS, NANCY B.
[b.] August 16, 1967, Brooklyn, NY; [p.] James and Barbara Moonlight; [m.] Craig Hobbs, September 8, 1990; [ch.] Paige and Savannah; [pers.] Grandma's Song was written for my great grandmother Martha McMorland Moonlight who passed away Jan. 11, 1995. She was a woman of great strength who gave a lifetime of laughter and love. I love you Gram.

HOBSON, KIMBERLY
[pen.] K. Hobson; [b.] August 8, 1973, Wheatridge, CO; [p.] David W., Barbara S.; [ed.] Lakewood High School, Colorado State University, currently obtaining dual masters from Denver University; [occ.] Computer Analyst, MCI Telecommunications Corp.; [memb.] American Red Cross, Alpha Chi Omega Sorority; [hon.] Alpha Chi Omega, outstanding Senior - 1995, Alpha Chi Omega - Carol Newton Memorial Award; [oth. writ.] Extensive writing throughout my major in college, also several stories publish in the Rocky Mountain Collegian, Colorado State University Newspaper; [pers.] Oh Grandmother, is a poem written about the four most important things my Grandmother taught me about life. She taught me to always cherish those people around me, and remember to tell them everyday that I love them. This poem is in memory of Virginia Hobson, mother and best friend.; [a.] Denver, CO

HOLDAWAY, DIANE
[b.] June 20, 1948, Salinas, CA; [p.] Widow (Richard Speiser); [ch.] Christine, Kevin, Charnell; [ed.] San Juan Bautista, Gilroy High; [occ.] Waitress, Longhouse, Gilroy, Calif.; [oth. writ.] Books of 100's of personally owned self writings (poems) - nothing published; [pers.] I write poems of feelings and Nature for self healing.; [a.] Gilroy, CA

HOLLEMAN, JEFFREY W.
[b.] December 26, 1969, Winston Salem, NC; [p.] Jack M. Holleman Sr. and Helen R. Rose; [m.] Misty P. Holleman, March 13, 1993; [ed.] Nicholas County High School, WV; [occ.] University Police Officer, Wake Forest University; [memb.] Civil War Reenactor (49th North Carolina, 86th IL, National Historical Society, N.C. Christian Coalition; [pers.] Easter Monday, 1995 the doctor confirmed we lost our baby through a miscarriage. The evening before I was inspired to write a poem for my wife Misty Katherine as we turned together to the Lord Jesus for comfort and strength "On the eve of tomorrow."; [a.] Walkertown, NC

HOLLIS, HARRIS WHITTON
[b.] June 25, Richburg, SC; [p.] William Gill Hollis, Gertha Hollis; [m.] Anna Aitheart Hollis, June 25, 1946; [ch.] Harris W. Hollis Jr., William Alexander Hollis; [ed.] B.S. Clemson University, J.D. University of South Carolina School of Law, United States Naval War College; [occ.] Retired Lieutenant General, United States Army, retired lawyer; [memb.] Association of the United States Army 25th Infanty Division Society; [hon.] Commanding General 9th, and 25th Infantry Divisions Distinguished Service Medal with Oakleaf Clush, Distinguished Flying Cross, Legion of Ment Bronze Star, Republic of Vietnam Service Ribbons Distinguished Alumni Award Clemson University; [oth. writ.] Miscalculation: A probable cause of World War III (Thesis Naval War College) 100 poems by Harris Hollis; [pers.] Despite suffering from Alzheimer's disease at the present, poetry, literature and history have been my most precious hobbies for five decades.; [a.] Aurora, CO

HOLLOWAY, PATRICIA ELIZABETH
[pen.] "Shamika"; [b.] May 7, 1995, Pittsburgh, PA; [p.] Uylssess and Katheleen Holloway; [ed.] Bachelor's Degree in Psychology, Associate's Degree in Pedology, presently attending the Pittsburgh Theological Seminary; [occ.] Prevention/Intervention Specialist in the Drug and Alcohol; [oth. writ.] Published poetry in colleges' newsletters and in church bulletins, published work in local newspapers; [pers.] My poetry is inspired and reflected on the goodness, greatness and love of the Creator, the Supreme Being.; [a.] Pittsburgh, PA

HOLLOWAY, RAMONA Y.
[pen.] Evonne; [b.] June 27, 1960, Norfolk, VA; [p.] Shirley and Roland Holloway; [ch.] Oliver T. Johnson Jr.; [ed.] Oscar F. Smith High Chesapeake VA 1974-1978 Norfolk State University 1979-1980; [occ.] Shipping and Receiving Hampton, Virginia; [memb.] U.S. Army 1981-1984 Served in Ft. Jackson, SC, Ft. Benning, GA, Ft. Hood, Tx., Frankfurt, Germany; [hon.] Marksman M-16 Rifle, Good Conduct Medal, Army Service Ribbon, Letters of Commendation, Care Award 1992 VA Medical Center, Hampton VA; [oth. writ.] Several poems created out of free and pleasant space. Submission of an original idea to the National Idea Center in Washington DC in 1989.; [pers.] If a fairytale can make one happy at heart there is no room for doubt what so ever.; [a.] Hampton, VA

HOLMES, KEN
[b.] October 22, 1917, Chanute, KS; [p.] Reuben and Frances Holmes; [m.] Dorothy Jackson Holmes, September 5, 1943; [ch.] Two sons: Terry and Tim; [ed.] AB and BD; [occ.] Retired; [memb.] Greater KS, Scandinavian Ass'n, Kansas Author's Club; [oth. writ.] Several poems published in periodicals. Lyrics for several hymns and Christmas carols. The last four years prepared and presented annually an original sermon in verse at Colonial United Church of Christ: Prairie Village, KS; [pers.] I use poetry to express my philosophy of life and ideas that are specially meaningful to me. My poetry rhymes simply because I love rhyming.; [a.] Prairie Village, KS

HOLMES, REGINALD L.
[pen.] Reginald Holmes; [b.] October 25, 1982, Charleston, SC; [p.] Kenneth Holmes and Jacqueline Holmes; [ed.] Wilmot J. Fraser Elementary, Rivers Middle High School; [occ.] Still Attending school; [memb.] Nehemiah Lodge Counsel #51 Knights of Pythagoras; [hon.] Good citizenship award, good attendance award, math and reading certificate award, student of the week awarded for one month; [oth. writ.] A poem published in local newspaper; [pers.] I wish that more people would believe in God and stop the violence and crimes.; [a.] Charleston, SC

HOLMGREN, CHRISTINE R.
[pen.] A. J. Morrison; [b.] June 19, 1971, Ishpeming, MT; [p.] Paul and Lorrie Holmgren; [ed.] Ispheming High, Northern Michigan Univ., Children's Institute Literature; [occ.] Medical Records Clk, Marquette Gen. Hosp.; [hon.] A special Publishing Degree from Inst. Children's Lit.; [oth. writ.] Currently trying to get into print: Short Stories. This is the first poem I submitted.; [pers.] I believe you need to write of the feeling(s) inside of yourself in order to make a strong, meaningful piece - and any feeling is worth a line of writing, because somewhere, someone else is going to feel what you did and find comfort in your words. To me, that is the most important meaning in writing - sharing a thought, idea, feeling, on action.; [a.] Marquette, MI

HOLTAM, MICHELE
[b.] February 12, 1968, Evergreen Park, IL; [p.] Carole E. Hampton, Robert E. Holtam; [ed.] Rangview High School, Aurora, CO, NASD Securities Licenses 6 and 63; [occ.] Customer Service Representative for an Investment Company, Englewood, CO; [pers.] This Poem was written and is dedicated to a special person in my life who taught me to believe, "If you want something bad enough, you'll get it." I did! I love you Thomas G. Perito.; [a.] Aurora, CO

HOOPER, BELINDA F.
[pen.] Beau; [b.] February 26, 1957, Bakersfield, CA; [p.] Beverly S. Price, Donald K. Hooper; [ch.] Cheyenne Sherri Golaz, Sheyleana Laura Golaz, William Donald Golaz; [ed.] New Mexico High, Roswell, N. Mexico; [occ.] Truck Driver; [memb.] Disabled American Veterans; [hon.] Graduation from Armory School for United States Marine Corps, Honorable Discharge - United States Marine Corps; [oth. writ.] Several poems, writings, and songs as yet unpublished. Letter sent by friend to Hustler Magazine under pen name Beau for September 1995 issue.; [pers.] I derive great pleasure from my writings, and enjoy sharing them with others. Having been Mother, Trucker, Marine, Waitress, Housewife, and single woman, I have many experiences to draw upon when I write.; [a.] Azle, TX

HOOPER SR., CHARLES N.
[b.] June 14, 1933, Atlanta, GA; [p.] Judge Frank A. Hooper Jr., Carolyn Hooper; [ch.] Charles Jr., Hamilton Corey; [ed.] North Fulton High, Davidson College, Emory University School of Law; [occ.] Retired (from Appellate Courts of Georgia); [memb.] Phi Delta Theta Social Fraternity, Second - Ponce de Leon Baptist Church; [hon.] Sigma Delta Pi (Honorary Spanish Fraternity); [oth. writ.] "The Bluebird", poem published in "The Voice Within"; [pers.] I try to write about subjects which are either personal to me, or about which I have firsthand knowledge.; [a.] Atlanta, GA

HOOVER, AMY R.
[b.] July 5, 1977, Birmingham, AL; [p.] Pam and Ronnie Eades, Vanee and Debbie Hoover; [ed.] Graceland High School, Indiana University (currently attending); [occ.] Student (typesetter, conway enterprises, New Albany, IN); [memb.] National Honor Society; [hon.] Dean's lists (Several Academic and Athletic Awards in High School), Presidential Scholar Award; [oth. writ.] Several poems and songs unpublished; [a.] Jeffersonville, IN

HOOVER, SARAH AYLITTA
[b.] July 19, 1922, Honaker, VA; [m.] Donald Emerson Hoover; [ch.] Larry, Sheila, Janet; [ed.] Various art instruction including courses at Old Dominion University, Norfolk, VA; [occ.] Professional Artist, Carver, and Poet; [memb.] Alexander Baptist Church, Portsmouth, Va., Backbay Wildlife Guild Inc.; [hon.] 1976-Blue Ribbon on Patriotic Painting, Williamsburg Expo, James City County, Jamestown, VA 1985-Mid-Atlantic WIldfowl Festival, Va Beach, VA-Honorable Mention, carved mallard. 1986 - Honorable Mention, carved miniatures. 1986 - Third Place, carved shorebird.; [oth. writ.] Soon to be released poem book, Thoughts In Verse, Spring 1996; [pers.] Through my poetry, I try to bring to the reader a sense of wonder, pleasurable moments, and the awe of nature.; [a.] Chesapeake, VA

HOOVER, SETH
[b.] March 30, 1979, Gallup, NM; [p.] Diane Spade, Stephen Hoover; [ed.] Attending 11th grade at Highland High in Albuquerque New Mexico; [occ.] Student; [memb.] Band (SAX), Speech And Debut, Track and Field, Literary Magazine, Jazz Band; [oth. writ.] "Night at the pops" in collections by The National Poetry Society; [pers.] I dedicate this poem to my 10th grade English teacher at Highland with much love thank you Mrs. Deattman.; [a.] Albuquerque, NM

HOPKINS, KIMBERLY J.
[pen.] Kim; [b.] May 21, 1963, Coffee County; [p.] Ernest and Leona Meeks; [m.] Roy Allen Hopkins, September 6, 1986; [ch.] Zachary Lawrence and Jordan Allen; [ed.] A.S. Degree in B.A. (Business Admn.), B.B.A. in Finance Minors: Info Systems and Bus Admin.; [occ.] Homemaker; [memb.] Sunday School Teacher at Providence United Methodist Church, Alumni of MTSU where I was a member of Data Processing Mgmt. Assoc., and Financial Mgmt. Assoc.; [hon.] Miss Motlow At Motlow, Southern Belle for Kappa Alpha, Student Government Member at Motlow College, Military Science II Queen at MISU and Who's Among American College Students; [oth. writ.] I have recently had poetry published by standard publishing who purchased the poetry from me.; [pers.] I feel very blessed to be able to write poetry that touches others in a special way.; [a.] Winchester, TN

HOPPER, VIVIANE M.
[b.] Guadeloupe, F.W.I.; [ed.] High School; [occ.] Housewife; [pers.] The knowledge of God is the source of poetry, and life is a wonderful poem given to men by God.; [a.] Ottsville, PA

HOPPING, RICK
[b.] December 24, 1955, Galesburg, IL; [p.] Gene and Inelda Hopping; [m.] Beth Hopping, June 11, 1988; [ch.] Cecilia Marie, Aidan Eugene, Aubrey Elizabeth (twins); [ed.] Bach. of Arts from Western Ill., Univ. - Masters of Arts from Western Ill. Univ.; [occ.] Eng. teacher at Gaffney H.S. in Gaffney, S.C.; [oth. writ.] I have nothing else published because I'm still growing into my poetry.; [pers.] I have visions of the goodness of all people buried within but hiding behind a rock for fear of the unknown.; [a.] Gaffney, SC

HORODOWICZ, KIMBERLY
[b.] February 25, 1968, Baltimore, MD; [p.] Fred and Marie Betz; [m.] Andrew Horodowicz, November 24, 1993; [ed.] Villa Julie College, Baltimore Lutheran High School; [occ.] Graphics Designer, Baltimore, MD; [a.] Baltimore, MD

HOUTTEKIER, TONIA SUE
[b.] September 6, 1974, Adrian, MI; [p.] Ken and Donna Houttekier; [ed.] Blissfield High; [occ.] Teller, Adrian State Bank; [hon.] Who's Aho Among American High School Students 1990/1991, 1991/1993 - Bobby Williams, Scholarship; [pers.] Poetry should come from the heart and your true being.; [a.] Adrian, MI

HOWARD, LAURIE WASHINGTON
[pen.] Laurie W. Howard; [b.] August 8, 1975, La Grange, GA; [p.] Larry and Brenda Washington; [m.] Jeffrey Kyle Howard, October 17, 1994; [ed.] Valley High School; [occ.] Convince store clerk, ametuar writer; [pers.] I always try to incorporate truth in my writing, weather it may be sadness or gladness.; [a.] Lanett, AL

HOWARD, VIOLET M.
[b.] November 23, 1933, Cleveland, OK; [p.] Dave and Ina Honeycutt; [ch.] Jerry and David Stock; [ed.] Highschool and Collage Courses Bookkeeping and Typing, Lit - Nursing; [occ.] Retired; [hon.] Art awards, painting; [oth. writ.] Poetry, short stories; [pers.] I try to show forth reality in stories and poetry, of the at most, a sence of nature and beauty. It comes from the heart.; [a.] Kenai, AK

HOWELL, MONICA
[b.] January 21, 1973, Palestine, TX; [p.] Charles and Shirley Howell; [occ.] Student at Sam Houston State University; [pers.] Thanks to my father who has made a big step in changing all of our lives. I love you.; [a.] Mansfield, TX

HSUE, ANDREA
[b.] December 6, 1982, Madison, WI; [p.] Eugene Y. Hsue, Jane C. Hsue; [ed.] Vestal Hills Elementary, Vestal Middle School; [hon.] National Physical Fitness Award, Presidential Academic Fitness Award, State Award (State of New York, (1995), CTY, the Johns Hopkins University, Vestal Middle School Poetry Contest - 1st Place; [pers.] I thank my mom and dad for their support, and my older brother for always being there for me. I especially thank the Lord God for all the blessings he has given me.; [a.] Vestal, NY

HSUING, ALICIA
[b.] August 31, 1959, Taiwan; [ch.] Danny Men; [ed.] Major in Multi-media and TV Production; [occ.] Film Maker, Graphic Design and Poet; [oth. writ.] 15 Poems on various topics; [pers.] I really feel alive when I am writing poetry. I feel every segment of my body "talking".; [a.] Pleasant Hill, CA

HUANG, KUANG-CHUNG
[b.] 1951, Hwa-lien, Taiwan; [m.] Lilan; [ch.] Angel and Andrew; [ed.] SIU/ETSU; [occ.] Computer programmer; [pers.] I love poetry and I firmly believe that "pens are sharper than swords." I admire Da-Lai Lama for his courage against the tyranny of China in Tibet. Taiwan is my motherland, I will always pray for her freedom and independence against the barbarity of Chinese chauvinism. May the Muses help us speak for the truth.; [a.] Novi, MI

HUDSON, ERMA H.
[b.] November 11, 1942, Richmond, VA; [p.] Thelma T. and Albert L. Huband; [m.] Joseph Garland Hudson, Sr., July 1, 1960; [ch.] Kathy H. Campbell and Joseph Garland Hudson Jr., and 5 grandchildren; [ed.] Thomas Dale High School, Chester VA; [occ.] Inventory Manager, Defense Supply Center Richmond; [hon.] 1st prize federal women's poetry contest 1992; [oth. writ.] Numerous unpublished poems written for family and friends and for my own pleasure; [pers.] There is no greater inspiration than the love of family and friends; [a.] Chesterfield, VA

HUFFMAN, RICHARD
[b.] May 24, 1958, Atron, OH; [ch.] Daniel Richard, Wesley Marchese; [ed.] University of Florida; [occ.] Customer Service Business Analyst; [memb.] Writers Build of America, Florida Freelance writers Assoc., National Safety Council Board Member; [hon.] Finalist, Ann White Playwright Theatre Contest; [oth. writ.] Screenplay - "Infidels", Plays - "Lunatic Wind", "The Sanibel Stcop", Novel - "Wasted Time", Over 300 poems/lyrics; [pers.] Risk taking will always allow an opportunity at some point in life. It is our responsibility to identify and act upon it.; [a.] Coral Springs, FL

HUGHES, ELEANOR
[b.] June 26, 1926, Newark, NJ; [p.] William and Sarah Dean; [ed.] 12 years Newark, School System, returned to two year Essex County College; [occ.] Retired from Newark Board of Ed., 1991; [hon.] Seven Golden Poet Awards, 12 Award of Merit Certificates, 1 Who's in Poetry, World of Poetry, Sacramento, Ca.; [oth. writ.] The Verse of Life as I See It, self published 1096; [pers.] Everything in the Universe is poetry one simply has to tune in.; [a.] Newark, NJ

HUGHES, SUSAN LEE
[pen.] Suzzi Lee; [b.] December 16, 1946, White Bear Lake, MN; [p.] Edward M. Lee and Eleanor Trudeau Lee; [m.] October 1, 1966, Divorced October 22, 1992; [ch.] Randall Eric, Corey Garrett, Tanya Suzann, Nichole Lee; [ed.] White Bear High School - Class of '64, student - Lakewood College, University of Minnesota; [occ.] Writer, Volunteer for "Crisis Counsel", single Mom; [memb.] Open "U" (University of Minn.), CFS Association of MN, Courage Center of St. Croix, Sister Kenny Institute; [hon.] Editor's Choice Award, National Library of Poetry; [oth. writ.] Poems published in Nat. Library of Poetry's "East of the Sunrise", 1995. Poetry used in school curriculum, at White Bear High School, Numerous poems, essays, short story, and a novel - yet unpublished. Newspaper pieces, magazine articles.; [pers.] Much of my writing mirrors the "unique" path I've been called to travel. My heart's conviction is to share the undying and resolute love of my living Savior, and very closest friend, Jesus Christ.; [a.] White Bear Lake, MN

HUNT, NANCY
[b.] November 1, 1963, Garner, NC; [p.] Mallory and Rebecca Hunt; [m.] Charles Pearson, April 10, 1993; [ch.] C.J. (8), Stephanie (16) (step children); [ed.] North Carolina State University, BA degrees, Business Management Economics; [occ.] Office Manager for

Podiatry Practice; [pers.] First hand, I've discovered how hungry our children are for love, stability, and discipline. I'm grateful God is using me to heal and nurture, and I pray more adults will reach out and give of themselves to their children.; [a.] Durham, NC

HUNTER, LORENE VERDELL
[pen.] Fuz "Doc"; [b.] July 23, 1937, Ala. Bam.; [p.] Susie Ada Thomas/Cleveland Williams; [m.] Richard F. Hunter, March 23, 1956; [ch.] Rick, Michael, Deborah, Lori, Ralph; [ed.] Withrow High School/ Montessori Xavier/Early childhood Training UC Mercy Montessori Training; [occ.] Civil Service with Cincinnati Public Schools, Instructor Assistant; [memb.] PTA-Allen Temple A.M.E. Church, Great Rivers Girl Scouts Bed. Member... Leader for Brownies and cadets scouts, community groups etc. Ken-Sil Cheer Leader; [hon.] Woman of the Year, Girl Scouts Awards Etc... Drill Team-ADvisor Walnut Hills H.S., Girl and her Government - Cinti. Rec. Richard Allen Award, Allen Templea M.C. Church. Labor of Love Award 1992; [oth. writ.] Friends and Family Children in schools, Just for fun; [pers.] "Let go and let God"; [a.] Silverton, OH

HURDLE, VALERIE GRISBY
[pen.] Valerie Grisby-Hurdle; [b.] August 30, 1961, Newark, NY; [p.] Venicious and Doris Grisby; [m.] Norma Hurdle, December 30, 1991; [ed.] 1979 Graduate of Scotehplains Fanwood High School, attended William Patterson College in Wayne NJ; [oth. writ.] Several other poems and short stories, currently working on a book with hopes of publishing; [pers.] If by my writing I can take you to a place you have never been, or some familiar haunt, or hurt, or smile. If, I can make you feel you are visiting with a new friend, or just sitting with an old one for a while, then I have indeed communicated with you my Kindred Spirits.; [a.] North Plainfield, NJ

HUSTON, LELIA S.
[pen.] Lilia Huston; [b.] December 8, 1919, PA; [m.] Joseph W. Huston, July 6, 1941; [ch.] Leilani, Cynthia, Barbara, Joseph Boyd and Huston; [ed.] Grammer School Centerfield School 8 grades; [occ.] Homemaker, (widow); [memb.] I.S.P. and N.L.P., Midway Manor Seniors, W.R.A.P. Society, Widowed of Reading, Allentown and Pottsville; [hon.] August 4-6 1995, "Poet of Merit Award", Editor's Choice Award, Published poetry in (Anthologies), Sea of Treasures, A Delicate Balance and (current) - A Voice Within; [oth. writ.] A prolific fall season - resulting in my accomplishing an additional twenty five poems plus, a few - comedy poetry - also dabbling to learn to do - "Haiku Poetry" - better.; [pers.] I am bound in my writing, to reflect, beauty, strength of nature - in blossom, song, wind, sea and sky. To reflect the challenge that life requires to stress also adherence to good values - in oneself - always to fly loves banner.; [a.] Bethlehem, PA

HYLAND, KENDRA CHATEL
[pen.] Kendra Chatel Hyland; [b.] January 25, 1985, Santa Rosa, CA; [p.] Robert Hyland, Lisa Hyland; [ed.] Lucerne Elementary 5th Grade; [occ.] Full-time, Fifth Grade Student; [oth. writ.] Quiet Things; [a.] Lucerne, CA

IANNUZZI, MARY JEAN
[b.] March 6, 1960, Neptune City; [p.] William and Mary Iannuzzi, married 52 yrs.; [ed.] Ocean Township High School; [occ.] Day Head of Sales, Stern's Department Store; [memb.] United Way, Unity School of Christianity, The Association of the Miraculous Medal, Member of a bowling club; [hon.] 8th Grade Honor Roll, Honor Roll High School, 2 yrs., Grammer school Home Economics Award, Most Improved Bowler Award, Stern's 52 Club charge Account Awards - 12 yrs.; [pers.] I dedicate my poem to my mother, Mary, who taught me the meaning of tenderness with her gentle hands and sweet kisses upon my cheek and her loving voice of encouragement to guide me onto the right paths. My mother's love for Jesus, her family and I has inspired my soul with faith, hope and love for the future. I am a child of God.; [a.] Ocean, NJ

INGRAM, RANDALL E.
[b.] December 5, 1957, Fort Thomas, KY; [p.] Geo W. and Katherine Ingram; [ed.] 3 1/2 yrs at Northern KY University Major in English; [oth. writ.] Stories and poems; [pers.] Influenced by Victorian Literature, I try to reflection basic aspects of life that are inherent to the human existence.; [a.] Newport, KY

ISLES, MICHAEL ADRIAN
[b.] March 3, 1979, Vancouver, British Columbia, Canada; [p.] Delfin Isles, Teresita Isles; [ed.] Currently High School Student at Bishop Montgomery; [occ.] Student; [oth. writ.] Unpublished songs and poems; [a.] Torrance, CA

ISOKE, JOIYA
[b.] April 20, Seattle, WA; [ed.] Student of Creative Writing Philosophy and Psychology; [occ.] Writer - in Waiting and Student, Barber by Trade; [oth. writ.] Currently working on a book of poetry and prose titled "Desert Soul" which embodies my life experience in New Mexico.; [pers.] Writing is my way of expressing my soul. My goal is to be a voice for those souls whose voice has been stifled and unheard.; [a.] Albuquerque, NM

ISOM, MARY ANN
[pen.] Mary Isom; [b.] April 5, 1982, Nashville, TN; [p.] Mebla T. and Danny Isom; [ed.] I am in the 7th grade at Nashville Christian School, Nashville, TN; [occ.] Student; [memb.] Nashville Christian Jr. High girls basketball team, Craggie Hope United Methodist Church; [hon.] First girl to ever play football for Nashville Christian, Most Improved player, 1995, softball team; [oth. writ.] Poems: My Heart's Crying, The Wind, What Will I Do, Just For You, The feel, The Pain, My Grandmothers Grace, Why Not Me, Dreams A Mother's Way, My Daddy's Love, Dear Sister, No More; [pers.] I think that life's to serious to be taken seriously and that cobat goes around will came around eventually. The person that inspires me to write poems is Vicki Lawrence, my Idol.; [a.] White Bluff, TN

JACK, ARTHUR T.
[pen.] Ajax; [b.] May 27, 1908, Keyport, NJ; [p.] Wallace A. Jack and Ethel Templeton; [m.] Ruby Sinclair, June 29, 1939; [ch.] Robert Jack, Natalie Bevans, Lucille Hutchins Priscilla Bowdoin; [ed.] High School, Two Private Military Schools, Vof me, Chemical Department three years; [occ.] Retired; [memb.] St. David's Episcopal Church, Sigma Chi, Rho Rho Chapter U. of Maine, Life Member; [oth. writ.] I am not a professional however, I have toyed with poems over the years, and recently collected 44 of the best, of which the Chaplain is one, and your contest is the first effort toward publishing. I would like you to read the other 44.; [pers.] If so my philosophical statement in several poems will be clear. I have had the local printer print. Some books, and I can send you one, titled "Thoughts Along The Way".; [a.] Kennebunk, ME

JACKSON, DAWN A.
[pen.] The Duster; [b.] April 10, 1962, Ypsilanti, MI; [p.] M. Roserra Jackson and Charles E. Thomas Sr.; [ch.] Lamarr J. Jackson, Renee Lynn Jackson and Devrenn I. Chrisp; [pers.] I thank God for the creativity he has instilled in me. I believe in the human race and with love of any level we can over come any obstacle. Peace and most of all love always happiness.; [a.] Decatur, GA

JACKSON, HELEN E.
[b.] March 12, 1972, Richmond, VA; [p.] Daisy Jackson; [ed.] Brunswick Senior High School, Virginia State University; [occ.] Substitute Teacher; [memb.] Mount Olive Church Disciples of Christ; [hon.] Who's Who Among College and Universities 1994; [oth. writ.] Numerous poems and short essays; [pers.] My writing is only as good as I am a person, because it all comes from within.; [a.] Lawrenceville, VA

JACKSON, PAULLA M.
[pen.] P. J.; [b.] November 9, 1951, McMinnville, TN; [p.] Mr. and Mrs. Paul L. Ramsey; [ed.] Warren County High School, McMinnville, TN; [occ.] Customer Service Operator Wal-Mart, McMinnville, TN; [memb.] East End Drive Church of Christ for-26-years; [pers.] Dedicated to my family and close friends, to be the best that I can be in my new found talent. I must-not waste the gift of God has given me.; [a.] McMinnville, TN

JACKSON, RUTH ANNETTE
[b.] September 17, 1950, Parkersburg, WV; [p.] Otha C. Arthur, Donnie M. Arthur; [m.] Jackie L. Jackson, October 1, 1971; [ch.] Curtis Lee, William Louis, Nathan Andrew; [ed.] Parkersburg South High School Graduated with Class of 1970; [occ.] Sales Representative; [oth. writ.] I have written a few other poems which has not been published.; [pers.] I was inspired by my mother who passed away on August 9, 1990, from lung cancer.; [a.] Parkersburg, WV

JACKSON, TRACEY MICHELLE
[b.] September 4, 1969, Charlotte, NC; [p.] Edna R. Lattimore, David Jackson Jr.; [ed.] Myers Park High, Central Piedmont Community College; [occ.] Parking/ Traffic Attendant; [memb.] Cystic Fibrosis Foundation, Mothers Against Drunk Drivers (MADD), Cancer Foundation; [oth. writ.] Romantic Novel yet to be published "Windows of Life"; [pers.] More is learned by open ears than open mouths or lips.; [a.] Charlotte, NC

JACOBS, STEPHEN J.
[pen.] Steven or Stephen; [b.] October 7, 1947, San Francisco; [p.] Martin and Madeline Jacobs; [ed.] W.H. Taft High School, Pierce College, College of the Desert, Monterrey Peninsula College, CSU Northridge; [occ.] Musician/Composer/Arranger/Writer/Lyricist. CEO, Chui Productions and Recording Company; [memb.] Amer. Fred Musicians, Loc 47 voting member: NARAS (National Academy Recoding Arts and Sciences), Song Writers Guild of America, ASCAP (American Society Composers, Authors and Publishers); [hon.] Dean's List, College of the Desert; [oth. writ.] 1. Macrotruth and Micropoetry 1984, 2. "This World": A solo album of music and environmental messages on CD and Cassette 1992; [pers.] I wish my compositions to encourage and help humans rebalance themselves to earth's eco-

logical and environmental systems.; [a.] Los Angeles, CA

JALBERT, KEITH A.
[b.] October 20, 1974, Waterville, IA; [p.] Jacqueline and Gerard Jalbert; [ed.] Current Writing Major at University of Maine at Farmington; [occ.] College Student; [memb.] Save the Tiger project at Hornocker Research Institute, College Radio; [oth. writ.] Local newspaper; [pers.] Death is a door which we all must open. Do it with an open mind and a clear heart.; [a.] Lewiston, ME

JAMES, EUNICE LOCKETT
[b.] February 1, 1927, Newport News, VA; [p.] Carrie and Jesse Lockett; [m.] Harry Lee James, September 7, 1946; [ch.] Helen Turner - Sandra Cary, Jacqueline Dinking J. Thomas James and Harry James, Jr.; [ed.] 12th grade; [occ.] Retired; [memb.] Fashion Elegante's, Church choirs, toastmasters and other church Auxiliaries; [hon.] Awarded several trophies for poetry and one for Mother of the Year; [pers.] I thank God for the talent He's given me, and I appreciate any and every opportunity to share it. Praying I will always remain humble before Him.; [a.] Newport News, VA

JAMES, ROBIN
[b.] February 20, 1970, Huntington, WV; [p.] Gloria Browning and Skip James; [pers.] Life is a learning experience from the womb to the grave never be to bold to swallow your pride, or to week to see the right. My words come from growing with life, my advice to you is feel what you write.; [a.] Buckhannon, WV

JAMISON, KANDIS
[b.] July 17, 1980, Washington, DC; [p.] Virginia Heard, Herbert Jamison; [ed.] Ballou Senior High School; [occ.] High School Student; [hon.] Dennis Chandler Scholarship Recipient, Awarded for Academic Excellence in Spanish, Drama, Science through the upward bound Pre-College Program in Washington, DC; [a.] Washington, DC

JAMISON, MATTHEW T.
[b.] November 27, 1995, Maryville, TN; [p.] Cathy H. Crawford and Greg Jamison; [ed.] Freshman at Maryville High School; [occ.] Student; [memb.] MHS Wrestling team, TTJC Karate School, Children of the American Revolution, Fellowship of Christian Athletes, Young Life, Showchoir, Randy King Drama Team; [hon.] First place Karate tournament in form and sparing skills; [pers.] He who would be wise speaks his heart.; [a.] Maryville, TN

JARRETT SR., RONALD LAVEL
[b.] March 17, 1955, Montgomery, AL; [p.] Eddie and Helen Jarrett Sr.; [m.] Patsy James Jarrett, January 19, 1974; [ch.] Ronald Jr.-19 and Brittiany Santa-5; [ed.] 12th Grade (1973) Robert E. Lee High School; [occ.] Contractor; [memb.] Life; [hon.] Being recognized by this prestigous organization is the only honor and award I have registrated to this date. Thank God!!; [oth. writ.] The Lion's Share Don't Destroy Me, Make Me Better A Care In The World, Life's Legacy, Reflect, For What Do I Seek (etc..); [pers.] First seek spiritually and all things will become visible. The more you give the more you'll receive, not money, yourself. Only when you find yourself will you begin to reap the most bountiful and fruitful rewards which life has to offer. The tree of life blossoms.; [a.] Montgomery, AL

JASMIN, VIONA
[pen.] Sincere; [b.] October 11, 1979, Haiti; [p.] Celita Jasmin; [ed.] 10th grade; [memb.] Liberty partnership reflection is a group a kids that write poem and petition the school paper; [oth. writ.] Some poem I have at home and couple in reflection; [pers.] I love writing and story. I like to rhyme, all my poem rhyme. I always wanted to be a writer or teacher and a dancer. I have been influenced by Marya Anglou and for that I love to write.; [a.] Westbury, NY

JECHE, PENELOPE
[pen.] Elaine Luke; [b.] November 5, 1978, Los Angeles; [p.] Harlon and Elaine Jeche; [ed.] Currently a High School Senior; [occ.] Student; [oth. writ.] Several Poems published in the School Newspaper; [pers.] In my poems I try to show the other side of common views. Just to try to put a different slant on things.; [a.] Los Angeles, CA

JENKINS, DAVID CHARLES
[b.] May 28, 1965, Tecumseh, MI; [p.] Charles Jenkins, Marian Hooper; [m.] Joy Jenkins, November 30, 1991; [ch.] Drake Sinclair, Mara Chantal, Foster Caleb; [ed.] Meadowdale High School currently attending Sinclair Community and Community College of Air Force; [occ.] Research Associate - Proctor and Gamble Co. and Engineer Assistant - Ohio Air National Guard; [memb.] Boy Scouts Of America Ohio Jaycee's; [hon.] Airman of the Quarter and Airman of the year 178th Fighter Group. Springfield, OH - for 1994; [oth. writ.] None published at this time. However a poem titled in remembrance of the crew of the challenger was sent to the president when the challenger blew up; [pers.] All my writing comes from the heart.; [a.] Goshen, OH

JENNINGS, ALETHEA K.
[b.] Mount Clemens, MI; [p.] Thomas C. Jennings, Lugusta H. Jennings; [ed.] Mt. Clemens High School, Michigan State University, Washington Saturday College, Averett College; [occ.] Operations Research Analyst; [hon.] As a student of Public Speaking, selected to compete in academic Public Speaking Contests. Awarded First Place (in 1992) and second place (in 1993); [oth. writ.] Copyrighted works include poetry published locally, personal tributes, memorial tributes, "Collection of Works."; [pers.] I am grateful to God for the gift of expression and rely upon divine help for inspiration. In working to promote individual growth, I believe that the honest expression of truth allows us to examine ourselves and promotes our spiritual and emotional well-being.; [a.] Alexandria, VA

JENNINGS, ANNE M.
[b.] December 26, 1978, Minneapolis; [p.] Gayle Davis, Kathy Pershina (Mothers), Thomas J. Jennings (Father); [ed.] Como Park Senior High School (still attending); [hon.] School Mascot; [oth. writ.] I've been writing poems since I was little, but I've always kept them to myself.; [pers.] Everyday was written to open the eyes up of other kids all over, no matter if they live in the city or not, I just want them to realize this is now reality and something needs to be done.; [a.] Saint Paul, MN

JENSEN, DUANE H.
[b.] July 12, 1942, Glendale, CA; [p.] Edward J. Jensen, Mae H. Jensen; [m.] Ruth Jensen, September 11, 1975; [ch.] Paul, Camille, and Michael; [ed.] Logan High Utah State University, Utah Tech. College; [occ.] Custodian; [memb.] Utah State Poetry society; [hon.] Poetry Published in 'Millenniel Star' and 'Crucible'; [pers.] I write how I feel and a fan I Wordsworth, Emily Dickerson and Longfellow.; [a.] Logan, UT

JESSOP, ROSANNA M.
[b.] April 5, 1962, Bagley, MN; [p.] Rufus and Virginia McAllister; [m.] David L. Jessop, May 4, 1990; [ch.] Tiffany Dezirae and Johnathan David; [ed.] AGS Degree Pikes Peak CC, Col. Spgs, Co La Porte H.S La Porte MN; [occ.] Asst. Crew Leader, Next Day Air Hub, UPS, Louisville KY; [hon.] Numerous Military Honors and Awards; [oth. writ.] I write only when emotions are hard to contain the release through pen and paper is ever so soothing.; [pers.] All my writings are inspired by my past. They reflect love, pain, good - and bad. I feel if more people could write how they feel it would relieve the of responsibility these powerful emotions hold on your life.; [a.] Fort Knox, KY

JETER, MICHAEL STEVEN
[b.] January 27, 1953, Houston, TX; [p.] Billie Louise, Otis J. Jeter; [m.] Divorced; [ch.] Jennifer Lynn Jeter, Michael Steven Jeter II; [ed.] Sam Houston High School (Graduate), International Association of Sheetmetal Workers Apprenticeship, Local #54 Houston, Texas (Graduate four years appreticeship at Arney Sheet metal: Special thanks to Truman and Robert, R.T. Arney R.T. passed away at 35 years old. God bless us all!; [occ.] Writer of poetry and short stories. Retired now as of 1995, age 42 due Cirrhosis of the liver and other major complications due to this affliction. Our Lord has bless me with talent to write for the peoples enjoyment as well as the beauty of life, (As I see it), however long or short I may live, I am at peace.; [memb.] Member of Local #54 Houston, Texas Retired 1995, age 42; [hon.] Semi Finalist in the 1995 North American Open poetry contest. International Sheetmetal Association of Sheetmetal workers apprenticeship Award for Grading the four year course.; [oth. writ.] I am currently writing a fantasy, comedy farse entitled "Tales of the Clansmen": 'The Toby Hick Adventure' about true life of inmates. Their only escape is taught to them by the Dutchman. Dutch is myself and the only means of keeping the Clans sanity is to pass through the bars and concrete walls on an imaginary, voyage in time, past, present, or future, anywhere in their universe. The first tale, which there'll be others, as set up in this story is in the past, pirates and the good guys, the clansmen. My first attempt at short stories. Many poems to come.; [pers.] Talented as I was, I could never see through the empty bottom of a whiskey bottle. I constantly wrote poems, good ones as I was told by family and friends but the past office was right after the liquor store, so they never got mailed. I feel Lord blessed me with this 5 month jail time, which I've released in to more months and my Cirrhosis for without this time to clear my head and finally realize I would die if I ever drink again. Thus began my attempt at writing my 1st short story which I'm sure you'll enjoy. I thank the Lord for this talent and for me never hurting anyone in my stupor. I'm now a recovering alcoholic. My dream come true for life.; [a.] Houston, TX

JIMERSON, JENNIFER A.
[b.] May 24, 1974, Long Beach, CA; [p.] Christine Welte and Arthur McNerney; [occ.] Bartender; [hon.] Various Theatrical Awards; [pers.] As an artist I strive to convey what moves me. In hope that I will be able to move the evidence. Weather it be my passion, pain or joy, and this fulfills me.; [a.] Los Angeles, CA

JOHNSON, CATRINA MCTYERE
[b.] August 13, 1968, Niagara Falls, NY; [p.] Polley Page, Father Deceased; [m.] Dexter A. Johnson (Rev), April 28, 1995; [ch.] Rose Page; [ed.] Sharpstown High School, 1987 Graduate. Attended University of Houston and Computer Learning Center of Houston; [occ.] Secretary, Internal Revenue Service, Houston, TX; [pers.] I would like to give God thanks for inspiring me and providing the words to express my heart. I would also like to thank my mother and my husband for always believing in me.; [a.] Houston, TX

JOHNSON, CHARLES THOMAS
[pen.] Charles T. Johnson; [b.] October 31, 1939, Jerome, AZ; [p.] William A. and Willie Ann Johnson; [m.] Catherine B. Johnson, May 9, 1965; [ch.] Kell, Ann and Christopher Thomas Johnson; [ed.] BS Electronics ASU; [occ.] Retired; [memb.] Polio Echo - Ariz Bluegrass Assoc. Scottsdale Bible Church; [oth. writ.] Over 50 other poems none published; [pers.] My writings and poetry reflect the emotions common to everyone and offer a biblical or spiritual resolution to their situation. I have found that if I do the kind thing, I will have done the right thing.; [a.] Phoenix, AZ

JOHNSON, DAPHNE MARLENE
[b.] September 1, 1976, Boone, NC; [p.] Merle Johnson, Marlene Johnson; [ed.] Whiteville High, Campbell Univ.; [occ.] Student of Campbell Univ.; [hon.] 1st Place - A.R. Ammons Poetry Contest - 4th Division 1994; [a.] Whiteville, NC

JOHNSON, DON
[b.] August 1950, Alberta, Canada; [ed.] Bachelor of Applied Arts (Jewelry Design), Goldsmith Apprenticeship; [occ.] Master Jewelry Goldsmith, Designer, Artist; [pers.] My poems reflect the contemplative and emotional aspect of being human and how we interact with our world, thought I try always to show the positive goodness that life offers us all.; [a.] Boca Raton, FL

JOHNSON, DONNA
[b.] February 7, 1969, NC; [p.] Ruth and Roy Porter; [ed.] RS Central High, McDowell Tech, Isothermal Comm. College; [occ.] Adaptive Behavior Trainer, Disabled Children; [oth. writ.] Several poems in newspapers, magazines; [pers.] Bright Blessings!; [a.] Old Fort, NC

JOHNSON, GEORGE F.
[pen.] Formerly - "Garfield" Now "The World Merchant." (R.); [b.] June 11, 1919, Pittsburgh, PA; [p.] Samuel F. and Estella K. Johnson; [m.] Carmen Asch Johnson, September 30, 1950; [ch.] Estella (July 4, 1951) Killed auto accident November 1, 1969; [ed.] Haverford Twp (PA) (1987) Feb '13 Univ of Penna Class of 1954 BA Econ.; [occ.] Observer of the panoply of our existence with its predictable menage of action, reaction, joy, sorrow and perplexity; [memb.] American Legion, VFW (Past Commander) HHS Alumni Assn, Artisans, Del. Co. SPCA, St Cyril of Alexander Catholic Church, 1st Btn 155th Inf Reg 31st Inf Division Veterans Lodge, Richard Vaux Ivanhoe Lodge F. and A.M. of Penna. I arab-American Anti Discrimination League, ACLU U of PA Alumni Assoc.; [hon.] Bronze Star US Army for service in Philippines as Infantry Medic.; [oth. writ.] Hundreds of verses - (Muses of Garfield..) Editor of Creole Petroleum co Senior Staff publication in Venezuela (1949/50) "Brisas of Paraguana" with a poem each issue. On staff of Temple Univ Night School Magazine (1937/8) and U of PA Night School Magazine (1939/40.) Had poems featured in Real Estate Board Monthly and HHS Alumni publication.; [pers.] I write poems free of bias and/or controversial themes. I like injecting humor in otherwise static situations. I would enjoy more travel. I enjoy writing, family, friends, DOGS, cats, birds, fish, BOOKS, 30s and 40s dance and swing music, tapes of same, same period films, LAUREL and HARDY, Cary Grand and other luminaries of that period. One of the best eras of our time.; [a.] Upper Darby, PA

JOHNSON, JAMIE
[b.] November 13, 1983, Roseburg, OR; [p.] Joy and John Johnson; [ed.] 6th Grade; [occ.] Student; [pers.] I am inspired by my family and friends to write. I write about my feelings and the goodness of my heart.; [a.] Medford, OR

JOHNSON, JENNIFER LYNN
[pen.] Laura Lynn Daniels; [b.] November 4, 1981, New Orleans; [p.] Lynn L. Johnson and the late Daniel D. Johnson, Jr.; [ed.] I attended five years at Woodridge Academy. At it's close, I went to Jr. High at Lake Castle. Now, I attend High School at Pope John Paul II; [occ.] I am a freshman at Pope John Paul II; [memb.] Recently, I became a member of Slidell Teen Fashion Board, a division of four - H; [hon.] During my eighth grade year at Lake Castle, I won an essay contest at the St. Tammany Parish Chapter of Daughters of the American Revolution; [pers.] Don't focus on what everyone else see's as right follow you heart and let your morals be your guide. If everyone did what they saw as night, no one would be wrong.; [a.] Slidell, LA

JOHNSON, JENNY
[pen.] Jenny Johnson; [b.] May 7, 1978, Santa Monica, CA; [p.] William and Cyndy Johnson; [ed.] High School (now in senior year) with several College courses; [occ.] High School Senior, aspiring pediatric surgeon, attends Idyllwild Arts Academy in Idyllwild, CA; [memb.] California Scholarship Federation Percussive Arts Society; [hon.] Dean's List at the Idyllwild School of Music and the Arts, Award for Excellence in English and Music during Junior Year, Award for Lifetime Membership in the California Scholarship federation; [oth. writ.] Several pieces published in school literary magazines, a novel in progress; [pers.] Writing is an art not to learn, but to grow into feeling. Each and every word I write is a drop of the passionate stew perpetually warm within me, and I can only hope anyone else who writes for the art also writes for themselves.; [a.] Idyllwild, CA

JOHNSON, KIM THORPE
[pen.] Kim Thorpe; [b.] February 5, 1965, Washington, DC; [p.] Paul Thorpe, Christine E. Thorpe; [m.] Thomas Johnson, September 5, 1993; [ch.] Tamara Thorpe, Lolita Thorpe, Faith Johnson; [ed.] Theodore Roosevelt High, Woodland Job Corps; [occ.] Home maker, Missionary, Sunday School Teacher; [memb.] American Heart Association, Missions for Humanity and Jesus Christ the Rock, Evangelistic Church Ministries; [hon.] Captain of Junior R.O.T.C., National Rifle Association, Missionary Achievement Award; [oth. writ.] 10 poems published in Jesus Christ the Rock Bulletin; [pers.] I enjoy writing poems that others may be blessed in the riches of God. I am inspired by the Holy Spirit of God.; [a.] New Orleans, LA

JOHNSON, KOBI L.
[b.] November 15, 1968, Milford, DE; [p.] Joseph and Bernice Johnson; [ed.] Atlantic Veterinary College, Prince Edward Island, Canada; [occ.] Practicing Veterinarian; [memb.] American Veterinary Medical Association, Canada Veterinary Medical Association, Alpha Gamma Rho, Alpha Zeta; [hon.] Alpha Lambda Delta, Phi Eta Sigma; [oth. writ.] Private collection of verse and short stories, unpublished; [pers.] Able are the ones who can afix a pile of feathers to wings, but extraordinary are they that then soar.; [a.] Gaithersburg, MD

JOHNSON, LAWRENCE DAVID
[pen.] Destiny Cummings; [b.] March 10, 1950, Greensboro, NC; [p.] Octavia E. Johnson; [m.] Patsy M. Johnson, August 14, 1971; [ch.] Lewanna, Tamika, Shavonne, Michael; [ed.] BA Psychology - Sociology 1972 Morehouse College - Atlanta Georgia; [occ.] Concierge - Hilton and Marriott Hotels; [memb.] Omega Psy Phi Fraternity, American Asso. of Social Workers; [oth. writ.] Article in Atlanta - Journal and Constitution, poems and other short stories; [pers.] We must climb over the barriers that keep us from a fuller, more rewarding life. For our lives are not guaranteed from one day to the next, and to take for granted the simplest of God-given freedoms is to inevitably lose.; [a.] College Park, GA

JOHNSON, SHAWN D.
[b.] August 26, 1971, Madisonville, TX; [p.] Bertha And DeFarris Johnson; [m.] Lyndrice M. Johnson, June 10, 1992; [ed.] Lee High School Midland, TX, I.T.T.; [occ.] L.V.A. Tutor of Adult Basic Education; [memb.] Southern Baptist Minister's Alliance; [hon.] U.S. Navy Honorable Discharge, 1993, National Defense Medal; [pers.] I would like to dedicate this poem to my late daughter Alicia R. Johnson. In memory of the six months of love that she gave us. You will live on forever in our heart's (November 9, 1992, May 02, 1993); [a.] Arlington, TX

JOHNSON, STEPHANIE
[pen.] Cheyenne Golden; [b.] July 28, 1981, Rolla, MO; [p.] Curtis and Sherrie Johnson; [ed.] John F. Hodge High School; [hon.] American Citizenship Award; [pers.] Writing can be hard but if you set your mind to it you can accomplish anything.; [a.] Saint James, MO

JOHNSON, VALEREI
[pen.] Hope Ann Lovelace; [b.] July 27, 1979, Peoria, IL; [p.] Beverly and Bradly Johnson; [ed.] Pekin Community High School - Presently a Junior; [occ.] Figure Skating Instructor; [memb.] United States Figure Skating Association, Pekin High Rifle Line/Color Guard; [pers.] The boundaries of the actual are no more fixed and rigid than the elasticity of our imaginations - Henry David Thoreau.; [a.] Pekin, IL

JONAS SR., CARVEL LEE
[b.] October 18, 1954, Salt Lake City, UT; [p.] Carvel T. Jonas, Beverly Clayton; [m.] Shirleen, August 10, 1977; [ch.] Amy, Roger, Celeste, Carvel Lee Jr. and Kiersten; [ed.] Hillcrest High B.A. University of Utah Masters of Education, University of Phoenix; [occ.] English and Music Teacher at Bingham Middle School; [oth. writ.] Several unpublished poems and short stories. Author of "The Joseph Jonas Clan of Utah."; [pers.] As captain of a high school cross country team I gained deep emotions and memories for life. Years later

I still dream of racing. In my dreams my limbs are still unable to keep up with the demands I ask.; [a.] West Jordan, UT

JONES, CLARENCE WILLIAM
[b.] June 7, 1907, Philadelphia, PA; [p.] Clarence W. and Bella; [m.] Deceased, January 13, 1934; [ch.] David, Ann, Diana, Ruth Faith; [ed.] Germatown High - Philadelphia, Eastern Baptist - College, Univ. of Pennsylvania; [occ.] Retired Industrial Engineering; [memb.] International Approved Basketball Official, Collegiate Basket Ball Off. Ass., American Professional League Official, Founder/Life Member Group Naismith Basketball Hall Of Fame, First Baptist Church Hackensack, NJ, Board of Deacons, Bible Adult Teacher, Church Musician Violin - Choir; [hon.] Appointed Observer and Adviser N.C.A.A. Basketball Officials Chairman: Common Education - Hackensack Christian School; [oth. writ.] Christian Gospel Tracts American Tract Society. Compilation of Poetry for publication and encouragement to others.; [pers.] Hold the bible as the word of God for learning, teaching, practice.; [a.] Ridgewood, NJ

JONES, CLAUDIO T.
[pen.] Claudia T. Jones; [b.] February 5, 1962, Coatesville, PA; [p.] Marguerita and Brady Treadwell; [m.] Brian M. Jones (Divorced); [ch.] Chanell M. Jones; [ed.] Millersville 2 yrs. and Self Educated Graduated - Coatesville Area Senior High; [occ.] Family Health Advocate; [memb.] National Chaplains Association Mt. Carmel Church - Deaconess sanctuary Choir - Chaplain; [hon.] Millersville Univ. - Certificate - Intensive Summer Program, Excellent Assistance as President Assistant. Military 2 awards - Spouse Day, Dept of Public Welfare Certificate of Service Award Maternal and Child Health Consortium - for completion of training - certificate; [oth. writ.] Poems, short stories; [pers.] Do good, it will always come back to you.; [a.] Coatesville, PA

JONES, HOWARD E.
[b.] April 9, 1951, Baltimore, MD; [p.] M. Edwin Jones, Ellen P. Jones; [m.] Judi L. Jones, October 15, 1994; [ed.] Loyola High, Loyola College, Essra Community College; [occ.] Respiratory Therapist; [memb.] American Association of Respiratory Care; [hon.] Dean's List - Essex Com. Col.; [oth. writ.] Several poems - none published; [pers.] Like the snowflakes in my poem, our lives touch so many others. Each one of us can make difference. Love, the spiritual side or this universe, is the main source of my inspiration. We are first and foremost spiritual beings learning how to love and this earth is our classroom. Let's pay attention.; [a.] Baltimore, MD

JONES, JEFFREY T.
[b.] May 28, 1958; [p.] Bobby and Edith Jones; [ch.] God Bless my children; [ed.] Crescent High Okla. Central State Univ.; [occ.] Boeing Air Craft Quality Consultant; [hon.] I am honored to be loved by Marsha, Barbara and Randy Jones, my siblings; [oth. writ.] I have written many poems that I share with friends and family.; [pers.] God's word inspires me to think and from those thoughts I dictate true feelings. My heart is filled with love, poetry allows me to share it.; [a.] Wichita, KS

JONES, LOIS
[pen.] Dieatra; [b.] March 25, 1943, Alabama; [p.] Will Thomas, Lucille Thomas; [m.] John O. Jones (deceased), date of marriage February 21, 1963; [ch.] John, Dieatra, Denetra, Durane; [ed.] B.A. from University of Detroit -- Major Art / English minor; [occ.] Detroit Board of Education Teacher (3rd and 4th grade) at DOW Elementary School since 1979-1996; [memb.] Active member 1993-1996 "FFAA" Fraser Fine Arts Assoc., member of the NAACP, member of Detroit Federation of Teachers; [hon.] 1959 Honorable mention from the "Art Institute of Illinois, Deans List 1978-1979 from the University of Detroit; [pers.] You can't make all the money, and you can't take any of it with you!; [a.] Detroit, MI

JONES, PAUL ALLAN
[pen.] P. J.; [b.] May 16, 1959, Walla Walla, WA; [p.] Donald M. Jones (Deceased, April 15, 1959), Marianna Grabhorn; [ed.] B.A. of Fine Arts, 1981, concentration, Sculptural furniture design and drawing. Central Washington University; [occ.] Artist - Designer; [hon.] Eagle Scout, Blue Mountain Council Outstanding Father and Son Award. Furniture Design. Costume Design. Metal Sculpture. Drawing 3-D photography.; [oth. writ.] Film Scripts, Songs, News Articles; [pers.] My poem is dedicated to my loving father, who died April 15, 1995. Life is sharing, wake up happy, do a good deed daily, and strive for truthful communication. Live by Observation, Self analysis, and Empathy.; [a.] Loveland, CO

JONES, W. RENEE
[b.] July 18, 1964, Washington, DC; [m.] Thomas W. Jones, January 8, 1986; [ch.] Thomas ("TJ") and Tyrrel; [ed.] 1982 High School Graduate Halifax County Senior High Attens Norfolk State University 1982-1985 Office Admin Business; [occ.] Military Personel Clerk, Assistant Mgr with it's in the nail; [pers.] If only the little things that I write touches only one than I have touches the lives of many.; [a.] Virginia Beach, VA

JONKER, KAREN ANN
[b.] January 29, 1943, Detroit, MI; [p.] Carl Stuendel, Eleanor Stuendel; [m.] Robert Jonker, October 15, 1977; [ed.] Edwin Denby High, Wayne State University; [occ.] Principal Purchases Agent City of Detroit; [memb.] Soka Gakkai International; [pers.] Writing enhances freedom, Japanese Haiku has been a Major influence.; [a.] Detroit, MI

JONZA, JOHN
[pen.] John August; [b.] November 27, 1978, Long Island; [ed.] Senior in High School; [occ.] Sales Associate at Geoffrey Beene; [hon.] President of my Elementary School, Little Britain; [oth. writ.] I've always enjoyed writing short fiction, and macabre narrations; [pers.] I've been influenced by Nietzsche, Jim Morrison, Williams Blake, H.P. Lovecraft, and Dante. "Describing the world around me is an unaccomplishable task"; [a.] New Windsor, NY

JORDAN JR., WILLIAM M.
[b.] April 30, 1968, Fort Worth, TX; [p.] Dr. William M. and Rebecca G. Jordan; [ed.] Aledo High School (May, 1986), Texas Tech University (1986-87) Texas Wesleyan University (Sept. 1993-Graduation May, 1996); [occ.] Pharmacy I.V. Technician Student; [memb.] Texas Parks and Wildlife Association, The Wolf Education and Research Center, National Parks and Conservation Association, American Psychological Association; [hon.] Who's Who Among American High School Students; [pers.] I believe that in order for mankind to change, he/she must accept the necessity of change. I write what ever I am feeling or experiencing at that time.; [a.] Benbrook, TX

JORDON, EDDIE LEE
[pen.] Toni Lee Dillard; [b.] December 15, 1945, Chicago; [p.] Both Deceased; [m.] Robert Dillard (Separated), October 23, 1985; [ch.] Rossa Grant-30, Erick-25, Sean-16; [ed.] Finish High School - 1yr Jr. College and Arglinton Loop Jr College child Development Beauty School Black History - 1 yr.; [occ.] Special Education Classroom Assistant; [memb.] Mt. Zion Choir - P.T.O. of Zion Benton High School; [hon.] Central Jr. High School a poem! Children will play; [oth. writ.] "Where Is My Child Tonight" "Fly Little Bird", Life Is Forever Changing - The Sand 10c Store. My Broken Doll, When God Brought Forth Man, My Child Will Not Join Your Gangs, etc.; [pers.] There are so much hurt and danger for the children of today, I hope that the poems I write will help someone to make a different choice. My poems are inspired by God, and what life has shown me.; [a.] Zion, IL

JOYNES, ALLAN J.
[pen.] Maatu; [b.] December 12, 1970, Philadelphia, PA; [p.] Sonia Morrow; [m.] Bridget Major-Joynes, May 19, 1996; [ed.] Bok A.V.T. School, University of Pittsburgh, Community College of Philadelphia, Temple University. (Masters of Social work 5/95); [occ.] Social worker; [memb.] NASW, NABSW, 2nd Vice President of Student Association of Black Social workers; [hon.] Member of National Honor Society Member of Educators round table; [oth. writ.] Several poem about my life unpublished; [pers.] Our greatest enemy is ignorance and inertia. I must Motivate All Africans to Unite.; [a.] Philadelphia, PA

JULIAN, HEATHER
[b.] August 7, 1981, Sandy, UT; [p.] Jan Holland, Jim Holland; [ed.] Willow Canyon, Eastmont Jr. High Kaysville Jr. High; [occ.] Student; [pers.] I am really concerned about the earth. I think it's very important to make people aware of how we are destroying the world and what we can do to help it.; [a.] Fruit Heights, UT

JUSTICE, NANETTE
[pen.] Nanette Sordelet; [b.] February 24, 1971, Delaware; [m.] Timothy S. Justice; [ch.] T. Shane and Alex Justice; [occ.] Struggling writer; [oth. writ.] Several poems and children's stories which I am trying to have published; [a.] Bear, DE

KARAPETYAN, ANGELA
[b.] February 23, 1981, Armenia; [p.] Sirvard and Oganes Karapetyan; [ed.] 9th Grade in Hoover High School; [hon.] I Achievement Awards 2 Cope 4 Life Awards, Doggers Diamond Geography, 2 Awards from We Care... for Youth, Dare, a Top Raisin Readers Award; [oth. writ.] Several poems published in school newspaper.; [a.] Glendale, CA

KARIMI, REBECCA
[pen.] Rebecca Dominguez-Karimi; [b.] January 12, 1953, San Antonio, TX; [p.] Anacleto and Rebecca Dominguez; [m.] Rahman Karimi, M.D., May 25, 1980; [ch.] Jennifer, Tiffany, and Yvonne (twins); [ed.] Degree in Creative Writing/Literary Criticism, University of California, Irvine; [occ.] Professional Sales Glaxo Welcome Pharmaceuticals; [memb.] American Cancer Society, Mexican American, National Women's Assoc. Alliance for the mentally ill; [hon.] Dean's List, President's Club Glaxo, Inc.; [oth. writ.] Several short stories published in University newspapers; [pers.] Latin

American authors have had a profound effect on my writing. I like magical realism as it reflects my hispanic roots and I believe the culture and traditions are reflected in my writing.; [a.] Laguna Hills, CA

KASEMEYER, LOREDA
[pen.] Lori; [b.] November 1, 1932, Poteau, OK; [p.] Lonnie and Lee Ann Dorse; [m.] Theadore Kasemeyer, March 31, 1975; [ch.] Martin Gregory, Sharon Humphrey Alice Day; [ed.] Marysville High; [occ.] Retired - and beginning a new line for babies; [memb.] AARP member; [oth. writ.] The Vineyard: By John Frost and poems for hobby not published; [pers.] I enjoy reading poetry this poem was written in memory of my loved ones passing on to another world.

KASSEKERT, MIRIAM E.
[pen.] Emmy Kay; [b.] February 20, 1914, Quincy, MA; [p.] Brita and August Kaipainen; [m.] James A. Kassekert, June 20, 1942; [ch.] David and Jeanne; [ed.] High School, American Institute of Banking, special courses Univ. of Pittsburgh, Univ. of Ohio, Univ. of Wisconsin, Marquette Univ.; [occ.] Homemaker; [memb.] Woman's Club of Mt. Lebanon, Lutheran Church member for 80 years at various locations and in many membership capacities; [hon.] Honor graduate of grade school and high school, trainer - girl scouts of America. Have reviewed over 100 books on many subjects to many groups.; [pers.] Started writing poetry just 5 years ago. My poems are on contemporary subjects.; [a.] Pittsburgh, PA

KASTLER, PATRICK
[pen.] Pat Kastler or Patrick Joe; [b.] January 15, 1960, Raton, NM; [p.] Paul and Marianne Kastler; [m.] Divorced; [ed.] B.S. Civil Engineering Technology and Minor - Computer Science - May 1985 (NAV) Norther Arizona Univ., Flagstaff, Arizona; [occ.] Self employed doing CAD Design Services; [hon.] Residence Hall Council, Treasurer and Vice President NAV; [oth. writ.] Approximately 30 other unpublished poems; [pers.] Mostly always write about Love, Friendship or Positive things: Try not to write about negative things. My writing style is such that I almost always include the title in the last line of the poem.; [a.] Phoenix, AZ

KEELE, PHILLIP DEAN
[pen.] Pine Top; [b.] April 6, 1932, Manhattan, KS; [p.] Geraldine F. Keele; [m.] Soon J. A. Keele, September 11, 1973; [ch.] James, Geraldine, David; [ed.] Manhattan Senior High School Douglas Elementary School; [occ.] Retired U.S. Army American Lake but I work part time VA Hosp.; [hon.] Served 24 years in the U.S. army good conduct meddle, Manhattan high school honors Phillip Keele the class of 52 at its 40th class reunion; [oth. writ.] The National Library of Poetry has published voyage well done, me the bee and the tree, 40th to be publish next (is it possible to have my poems above put in the same the book of poetry that I am buying?; [pers.] I wrote poetry and threw junior high and senior high school in Manhattan K.S. my pens were put in the school paper each week

KEEMER, CONSTANCE HARRIS
[pen.] Isabella Constance; [b.] September 10, 1961, Calvert County, MD; [p.] Nettie Constance Harris; [ed.] Northern High, P.G. Community College, UDC College; [oth. writ.] Currently working on a selection of Poetry entitled, Hedonic Relume, A book entitled Grown Folks Business; [pers.] I write what's in my heart, what stirs my soul. What makes me laugh, cry and think.; [a.] Forestville, MD

KELLER, STACY
[b.] May 10, 1980, CA; [p.] Mary and Chris Keller; [ed.] Freshman Trim of the World High School; [memb.] Cross Country, Band, Church; [hon.] Writing Celebration, 5 grade; [pers.] My poems are not just writing they are how I feel.; [a.] Crestline, CA

KELLY, NANCY ALLEN
[b.] November 7, 1941, Toronto, Canada; [p.] Evelyn and Harold Allen; [m.] Dennis Kelly, April 18, 1964; [ch.] Lisa, Niki, Sean; [ed.] Wheaton Academy, St. Petersburg Jr. College, Univ. of South Florida (majored in business and psychology); [occ.] Office Administrator, Spencer International Advisors, Clearwater, FL; [memb.] Florida Gulf Coast Art Center; [oth. writ.] Poetry included in other NLP publications during 1995/96, including "The Best of 1996"; [pers.] Words are a wonderful way to share our humanity and common concerns and messages, to be reread over and over, gaining new insights to ourselves and our world.; [a.] Belleair, FL

KELLY, RYAN
[b.] August 2, 1978, Ames, IA; [p.] Robert Kelly, Suzanne Kelly; [ed.] Ames Senior High School Class of 1997; [occ.] Part time Checker/Stocker, save-v-more foods, Ames, IA; [memb.] Ames High Band, The Web (Ames High School Paper), Ames High Student Senate, Collegiate United Methodist Church/Wesley Foundation; [hon.] Ames high school honor roll, 1995 Letter of Academic; [oth. writ.] Several poems, short stories and five amateur science-fiction novels: Interstellar War, Interstellar Quest, Interstellar Summit, Interstellar Alliance and The Haze; [pers.] My writing is one of the most cherished aspects of my life. I hope to continue writing for many years to come and find constant joy in the expression of feelings, characters, and images.; [a.] Ames, IA

KELVINGTON, SUE
[b.] July 22, 1951, Salt Lake City, UT; [p.] Glen Wayman, Donna Wayman; [m.] Bernie Kelvington, September 1, 1978; [ch.] Richard Sier, Kristy Sue; [ed.] Hillcrest High, various training seminars; [occ.] Rental Manager for a Heavy Construction Equipment Dealer; [oth. writ.] Personal poems - not publishes yet this is the first - I have a personal collection. Working on a book.; [pers.] I love to read - I hope others enjoy reading what I write.; [a.] Sandy, UT

KEMP, TRACY D.
[b.] August 2, 1963, Middletown, CT; [p.] Evelyn Kemp of Connecticut and John Kemp of Florida; [ed.] East Hampton High; [occ.] Small town factory worker; [pers.] My poem was written for my Mom, whose belief in fairies and in me has always been an inspiration.; [a.] East Hampton, CT

KEMPISTY, STELLA
[b.] October 3, 1957, Detroit; [p.] Frank and Alma Jakutch; [ch.] Walter, Kent, Dayna, Brad, Kendra and Peewee (Ken Jr.); [ed.] 1972-8th grade drop out, 1986-GED graduate - June 12, 1994, Baker college graduate; [occ.] Full time homemaker, freelance writer; [oth. writ.] Currently writing a book, short stories, and poems, along with daily list; [pers.] Everything does happen for a reason, sometimes you may not see the why for years, but we will learn the lessons someday, and will grow from what happens!; [a.] LeRoy, MI

KEOWN, FIONA JANETTE
[b.] June 3, 1982, Woodland, CA; [p.] Frank and Frances Keown; [ed.] 8th grade at Manheim Township Middle School in Lancaster, PA; [occ.] Student; [oth. writ.] Several poems that have not been published; [pers.] I like to let people see life through poems as heart felt emotions, how it's really felt. I greatfully crave emotional poems.; [a.] Lancaster, PA

KERKELA, STEFANIE E.
[pen.] Stefanie Kerkela; [b.] March 31, 1968, Minneapolis, MN; [p.] Wayne and Janet Hanson; [ed.] BA in English, Minor is Psychology at Augsburg College in Mpls. graduated from Marshal High School in Marshall, MN - attended Silver Lake Elementary School in Columbia Heights, MN; [occ.] Marketing Associate it American Express Financial Advisors in Mpls. MN; [memb.] Music Group at Catholic Church in Marshall, Marching Band Member, Choir Concert Member, Soloist, Vocal Jazz Ensemble, and Orchestra Member at Marshall High School. Was in a local rock band as lead vocalist in band called Menagerie in College.; [hon.] Premiere Performer Awards and VIP Awards at American Express Financial Advisors, my current place of employment. Several excellence awards in gymnastic in high school.; [oth. writ.] Articles published in corporate newsletter, several poems and short stories both unpublished and printed in college, student literary books. I also write songs about love and life on the guitar or piano.; [pers.] My inspiration for writing comes from within me. I am an extremely emotional person and express myself through writing. I write about love and horror. My influencers are Stephen King and Shakespeare.; [a.] Saint Paul, MN

KEYS, ANDY
[pen.] Hatch Picard; [b.] December 31, 1978, McComb, MS; [p.] Charles and Gloria Keys; [ed.] Columbia High School; [memb.] National Junior Beta Club; [pers.] I think passion is the key to writing well.; [a.] Columbia, MS

KIENITZ, JOSH
[pen.] Josh Kienitz; [b.] May 23, 1980, Columbus, OH; [p.] David Kienitz, Susan Schamp; [ed.] Shawnee High School; [occ.] High School Student; [hon.] Honor Roll, Varsity Cross-Country Letterman; [pers.] The human race cannot survive without clean air and water, yet we still pollute carelessly, we must fight furiously any attempt to sacrifice environment health for financial gains. We all live in the same world, and none of us have the right to ruin for someone else.; [a.] Lima, OH

KIM, JEFFREY J.
[b.] December 24, 1977, Seoul, Korea; [p.] Ki Soo Kim, Eun Sook Kim; [ed.] Diamond Bar High School (Current); [occ.] High School Student (Class of '96); [memb.] Ephphatha Mission Church English Ministry Activity Committee; [hon.] National Youth Leadership Award. Track Athletic Award; [pers.] My family immigrated to U.S., when I was fourteen years old. That was year of 92. We went through a lot of frustration and ordeal together.; [a.] Diamond Bar, CA

KIMBAL, WENDY V.
[pen.] Wendy Vie; [b.] July 21, 1971, Smithtown, Long Island, NY; [p.] Barry ad Doris Kimbal; [ed.] K-10th, General; [occ.] Secretary; [oth. writ.] I've wrote many others poems just not published, yet; [pers.] Poetry a form of art. A true poet writes what they see, feel, think and believe.; [a.] Jacksonville, FL

KIMBRO, ADA
[pen.] Dr. Ada Kimbro; [b.] April 18, Birmingham, AL; [p.] Earnest and Minnie Lamar; [m.] Widowed, April 18, 1938; [ch.] Lillian, Mary Theresa, Tommy, Earnestine, Anita Louise, Karen Lenore; [ed.] Council Elem. Industrial High Case Western Subjects - I.C. Schools Adult Tutor - Ass. Doc. Cosme. Human Relations - Fitness and Nutrition; [occ.] Cosmetologist (retired) 2nd V. Pres. chapter #1. Adult Tutor 6 children - 16 grandchildren - 6 greats; [memb.] New light B.C. Nurses Guild KVO Karamu Theatre - O.A B. Inc. #1 Alpha Theta Sorority State National Bty Culturists League Inc. Youth for Beauty Artist Guild; [hon.] Published poetry: B.A. - M.A. various certificates in all phase of Cosmetology life - Membership - Distinguished Poets Community Work Street Club Pres.; [oth. writ.] Poem "Awakened One Morn at the age of 4" Life's Entity of Beauty and Love, "Nudged" "Love" and "Freedom"; [pers.] "You are never too old to learn" - the joy of spiritually living and giving of God given talents, having been endowed to us, on this planet.; [a.] Cleveland, OH

KING, DONNA G.
[b.] November 8, 1956, Baltimore, MD; [p.] Robert Schlott, Nancy Schlott; [m.] Divorced; [ch.] Sarah LeAnn and Charity Elain; [ed.] GED 1990, Bible College Tech., Graphic and Freelance Art; [occ.] I enjoy writing; [memb.] The National Authors registry 1995; [hon.] Honorable mention's in the Fall 1995, Iliad Literary Awards Program; [oth. writ.] "Love", Sparrow grass poetry forum, Inc. - "This Year", "A tear", Iliad Press, Cader Publishing, - this year; [pers.] I search deep within, and what comes out in my writing has been my own awareness of my experiences. I hope it helps people to "be still" so they will be aware of "their" emotions.; [a.] Post Falls, ID

KING, JEREMY O.
[b.] January 31, 1974, Dyersburg, TN; [p.] Muriel and Junior King; [m.] Marcia Lee King, May 5, 1994; [ed.] Dyer Country High School, University of TN at Martin (UTM); [occ.] Rubber compounding Technician, Colonial Rubber works; [memb.] National Audubon Society, American Cancer Association; [oth. writ.] Local Newspapers; [pers.] I strive to write the most thought provoking literature that my readers have ever read.; [a.] Newbern, TN

KING, MARLENE A.
[b.] May 18, 1937, Saginaw, MI; [pen.] Orlen and Mary Margaret Brooks; [m.] Thomas E. King, October 22, 1955; [ch.] Lawrence T. King and Patricia A. Perry; [ed.] Saginaw High School Lansing Community College; [occ.] Branch Manager/Baking Officer - Citizens Bank Corp; [memb.] Christmas in April (Treasured American Legion Auxiliary); [hon.] Community action to reach the elderly - Leadership Award; [oth. writ.] Several verses for family greeting cards; [a.] Bath, MI

KING, REYNDA
[b.] December 10, 1979, Torrance, CA; [p.] Bernita King, Robert King; [ed.] St. Joseph's Elementary, St. Mary's Academy; [occ.] Student; [memb.] National Honor Society, California Scholarship Federation; [pers.] Aspire to be your best and you will be.; [a.] Hawthorne, CA

KIRSCHMANN JR., ROBERT C.
[pen.] B. J. Kirschmann; [b.] December 6, 1979, Pittsburgh, PA; [p.] Karen Kirschmann; [ed.] Currently 10th grader, Poly High School Riverside, CA; [occ.] Student; [memb.] B.S.A. 1987-1996, Splash Bash 1992-1994, #1 Club 1992-1994, Jesters Club 1995-1996; [hon.] All A's Award 1993, All A's and one B 1994, Perfect attendance 1992-1994, Honor's society 1992-1995, Presidential Academic Fitness 110% award 1994 award Phy Ed 1994, Concert and Marching Band 1992-1995, 1st place reflections contest for photography 1994 gage middle school

KISER, MEGHAN R.
[pen.] Iso Reiff, Kis; [b.] September 25, 1975; [p.] Gary and Peggy (Fawbush) Kiser; [ed.] Attending Ball State, University, am now sophomore, Winchester Community High School; [occ.] Sales Clerk at Elder Beerman Muncie, IN; [hon.] National Honors Society, Youth Salute; [pers.] I strive to diffuse my true inner feelings through sublimation in my writing.; [a.] Muncie, IN

KITSIS, HEATHER CHRISTINE
[pen.] Heather Christine Kitsis; [b.] August 17, 1978, Norfolk, VA; [p.] Nick and Robin Kitsis; [ed.] Norfolk Christian Schools; [memb.] Youth Group, Band, Forensics; [oth. writ.] Book: Open Windows and Empty Hallways, "A short stories" a Tale of two Brothers," Is There Love?." Other numerous poems.; [pers.] In all the endeavors of your life: make sure you are a whole person before you try to be half of something else.; [a.] Norfolk, VA

KLEIN, MARK
[b.] November 20, 1973, Toledo, OH; [p.] Patty and David Klein; [ed.] Waite High School, Owens Community College; [occ.] Customer Service Representative; [hon.] Who's Who among American High School Students 1988-11989, 1989-1990; [oth. writ.] I have other poems, but nothing that has had the chance to be published.; [pers.] I don't take anything for granted, that way I'm not assuming the unassumable.; [a.] Toledo, OH

KNIGHT, RACHEL A. GILLILAND
[b.] July 31, 1956, Oak Hill, OH; [p.] Calvin and Mary Ellen Bright Gilliland; [m.] Terry L. Knight, July, 1987; [ch.] Tina - 23, Robert - 21, Aaron - 17; [ed.] Jackson High School, Jackson, OH, class of 1974; [occ.] Housewife, Homemaker; [hon.] This poem was published in our local newspaper "The Journal Herald", in the summer of 1995; [pers.] During the Vietnam war, nothing seemed simple. So as a young girl during this war, I wrote this simple piece.

KNOBLETT, HELEN JANE
[pen.] Jane John; [b.] August 27, 1918, Robinson, IL; [p.] Pearl and Phoebe White; [m.] Charles John Knoblett, November 12, 1938; [ch.] Norma Mae Thompson, Charles Wayne, Knoblett, Bernice Jane Boyd, Betty Ellen Boyd, Richard Finley Knoblett (Deceased); [ed.] 8th grade graduate Valedictorian (Mann School - Robinson, IL; [occ.] Housewife; [memb.] Home Extension - Crawford Co., Pandora Club of Women's Club, CB Radio club, Camera Club, Grand Prairie Christian Church, Daughters of the American revolution (DAR); [hon.] Award of Merit by Hollywood's Famous Poet Society, 3rd place in Crawford County District of the Women's Club for poetry; [a.] Robinson, IL

KNOPPEL II, FRED W.
[b.] June 16, 1952, Vallejo, CA; [p.] Fred and Jean Knoppel; [m.] Karen Knoppel (Deceased), July 1, 1978; [ch.] David (1-16-86); [ed.] High School Industrial Electronics Control Apprenticeship; [occ.] Industrial electronics Control Mech.; [pers.] On behalf of my son and myself we dedicate our poem in this book to his mother and my wife Karen Knoppel who passed away July 19, 1993. We love you Mom!; [a.] Fairfield, CA

KNOWLDEN, DORIS
[b.] June 7, 1927, Canton, OH; [p.] Joseph and Helen Geyer; [m.] Deceased, 1947; [ch.] Six sons, three daughters; [ed.] One room grade school in Battlesburg, OH, H.S. graduate at New Concord, Ohio - now John Glenn High; [occ.] Retired Homemaker; [oth. writ.] "Lady in the woods" published in local newspaper, "My love - my husband" refused because it might offend the modern woman!; [pers.] Bless and Love your children. Our children are our reflections!; [a.] Zanesville, OH

KOEN, EDWINA
[b.] February 22, Pueblo; [p.] Jane and Robert Koen; [ed.] Freshman in High School; [a.] Pueblo, CO

KOGEN, ZEEV
[b.] March 30, 1971, Moscow, Russia; [p.] Boris Kogen, Zhanna Kogen; [m.] Eva Kogen; [ch.] Zelda Kogen; [ed.] Yeshiva University, NY, BA, AA, New York University School of Medicine, MD expected in May, 1997; [occ.] Medical Student; [memb.] American Medical Association, Medial Society of the State of NY, American Medical Political Achon Committee; [hon.] Lemler Memorial Award for excellence in Pre-Health Studies, Pekarsky Award for Excellence in Tewish Studies, NIAS Scholarship Award, Who is Who Among Student in American Univ. and Colleges, National Dean's List, Stanley Foundation Scholarship for research in Psychiatry; [pers.] Incessantly new images are being created and old ones are being broken to be laid on the top of an ever growing heap. And only love, like divine emanation, stays upon the earth and imbues human soul with agonizing passion and profound longing.; [a.] New York, NY

KOROLYSHYN, JOANNA
[b.] August 30, 1995, Vallejo, CA; [p.] Bohdan and Ruth Korolyshyn; [ed.] Grafton Bethel Elementary Curundu Jr. High, and currently in 10th grade at York High School; [memb.] National Jr. Honor Society; [pers.] Where would the world be without the chastity of nature, with all its aesthetic power which fills us all with an inenarrable inspiration? For surely God put us here ot to ruinate it, but to preserve it, till the end of time, as we know it.; [a.] Yorktown, VA

KOZ, DONALD J.
[pen.] Don Koz; [b.] February 18, 1924, South Bend; [p.] Joseph and Hariet Koz; [m.] Deane Koz, July 24, 1948; [ch.] Five; [ed.] In State BS Notre Dame - MA; [occ.] Retired; [pers.] "I wish all people would open up their hearts ad let in some fresh care"

KRAFT, MARGARET J.
[pen.] Margaret "Nightingale" Kraft; [b.] June 25, 1923, Fairfield, OH; [p.] The late, Alfred and Lillian Nightingale; [ch.] Linda M. Brown, Raymond A. Kraft; [ed.] High School - employed by U.S.D.A. thru Ohio St. University as county. Nutrition Aide - 15 yrs.; [occ.] Retired; [memb.] United Meth. Woman; [oth. writ.] Personal collection none published; [pers.] I have tried to put into words, the things I feel in my heart, my only desire is that they might inspire or bring hope to others who read them.; [a.] Wellsville, OH

KRASNER, WILLIAM
[pen.] William Krasner; [b.] June 8, 1917, Saint Louis, MO; [p.] Sam and Bryna Krasner; [m.] J. Frances Frazier Krasner, October 13, 1956; [ch.] David E. Daniel A., Lawrence S., James N.; [ed.] AAF Meteorology Schools, Washington U., St. Louis, '35-'36, BS Columbia U., 1948; [occ.] Semi-retired novelist; [hon.] News week's "Top Ten Mysteries," '49 National Inst. Arts and Letters, special grant, '55, 4 weeks on NY Times "And Bear in Mind" list. '54, fellowship, PA Council on the Arts, '81, "Scribner Classic" (republication) '85, "Harper Perennial" (republication) '87, "Krasner Archive" in "20th Century Archives" Boston University, 1989, Amer. Soc. Journalists and Authors, grant for non-fiction, '92, Mary Ross Finn Prize, fiction, '94; [oth. writ.] Novels (published): Walk the Dark Streets, The gambler, North of Welfare, The Stag Party, Death of a Minor Poet, Francis Parkman, Look for the Dancer (German tr.), Resort to Murder, (unpublished as yet): Look for the Dancer (in English), Who is Sylvia?, Carthage Must be Destroyed (unfinished): The Vortex Theorem, (Non-fiction book): Drug-Trip Abroad. Short stories, many popular and technical articles, documentary films, radio and TV, verse.; [pers.] Heart of fiction is characterization, trying for real people. Introduce readers to backgrounds and times they might otherwise not know. Tried, at least most of the time, to be honest.; [a.] Berwyn, PA

KRAUS, WENDELYN BONNIE
[pen.] Wendy Kraus; [b.] August 3, 1973, Abington, PA; [p.] Robert Kraus, Pauline Kraus; [ed.] B.S. in Chemistry, College of William and Mary; [occ.] Research Associate, Edison Plastics; [hon.] Gamma Sigma Epsilon National Chemistry Honor Society; [pers.] I believe life is a beautiful gift, and it is meant to be enjoyed. My writings are an attempt to capture the thoughts, feelings, and emotions that make life enjoyable.; [a.] Williamsburg, VA

KREITZER, JAMES ALLEN
[b.] January 4, 1960, Canton, OH; [p.] James Albert Kreitzer, Wauleka Faye Kreitzer; [ed.] Canton South High School; [occ.] Truck Driver; [oth. writ.] Several unpublished poems and songs; [pers.] Life is a grand teacher, requiring only your daily attendance.; [a.] Canton, OH

KRENGEL, JOSEPH PHILIP
[pen.] Joseph Krengel; [b.] June 22, 1915, NYC; [p.] Samuel Krengel, Celia Krengel; [ed.] Public School, High School, Pratt Institute (Art) 1933-1936; [occ.] Retired, was a Tech. Illust. and artist; [memb.] ASCAP-1963 as member one, Instrumental: "Tokyo taxi", on Captain Kangaroo: used, for several years as background music personal note: Polio-Victim, Life-Long, Fond of Opera.; [hon.] One painting: (Revelation: John: 1, court of heaven), over 30 years, at Chapel, of St. John's Hospital, Santa Monica, Calif.; [oth. writ.] Many light verses in the late, Matt Weinstock's Column, L.A. Times. Prolific letter-writer, life-long to newspapers; [pers.] I am, Pro-Hindu and Chinese, philosophically-speaking. I admire, words worth and tagore. I am, an idealist. Fond of buddhism.; [a.] Santa Monica, CA

KROST, ELEANOR BRADEN
[b.] May 3, 1910, Cleveland, OH; [p.] James and Helen Braden; [m.] Deceased, May 29, 1935; [ch.] James B. Leem-Bruces and William L. Krost; [ed.] Laurel School Grad. High Cleveland 2 yrs. Southern College Petersburg VA; [occ.] Writing Flen Markets Piano Bridge; [memb.] First Church of Christ Scientist; [hon.] No awards ever but "A" for effort; [oth. writ.] Westcherter CC Rye NY. Short stories Bronxville (Amateur) "The Cat that Loved Travelling" sent to 21 publishers (McMillan-Random House-Natl. Geog. - Western etc. not appropriate for them maybe it would be right for you! Geographical Philosophical - fun and educational; [pers.] "Just keep rolling along"; [a.] Virginia Beach, VA

KRUCKENBERG, MELODY
[pen.] Melody Reem Kruckenberg; [b.] May 7, 1958, Aitkin, MN; [p.] Ben and Martha Reem; [m.] Kevin Kruckenberg, July 16, 1987; [ch.] Nate - 15, Keith - 6, Scott - 4; [ed.] 1976 graduate Mandan Sr. High Attended Bismarck State College/Liberal Arts Sept. 1993 Graduate of the Institute of Children's literature, West Redding, CT; [occ.] Office Mgr. - ND Rural Water Systems Assn and Freelance writer; [memb.] V7W Post #1326 - Lladies Auxiliary National Entrepreneur Assn., American Entrepreneur Assn.; [hon.] Dean's List - Bismouck State College, 1993 Rookie Office Mgr. of the year-Ntl. Rural water Assn., 1992 Excellence in Accounting - Ntl. Rural Water Assn.; [oth. writ.] Short story sold to EPB Publishers, Singapore sold 2 articles to Falcon for kids magazine; [a.] Mandon, ND

KRYGIER, AARON J.
[b.] May 30, 1982, Buffalo, NY; [p.] Joseph and Deborah Krygier; [ed.] Campus East, Elementary (Pre-k-6) Home Schooled (Grades 7-8); [occ.] Student; [memb.] National Junior Honor Society; [hon.] Lucinda Yang Memorial Scholarship, Spelling Champion Campus East School 1994, New York State Olympiada of Spoken Russian - High Honors; [a.] Buffalo, NY

KUBITZ, SHELLEY S.
[b.] July 24, 1978, Iowa City, IA; [p.] Doug and Sharon Kubitz; [ed.] Waukon High School; [occ.] CNA at Good Samaritan Center; [memb.] Student Council, Who's Who in American High School Students; [hon.] Published in 1995 "Lyrical Iowa", student editor of "Different Drummers a high school literary paper; [pers.] I'd like to thank God for giving me the gift of expression and to quote a teacher "One day at a time".; [a.] Monona, IA

KUHLMAN, JAN
[b.] April 22, 1952, Oakley, KS; [p.] Clarence and Marthanell Turley; [ch.] Chandler, Corbin, Cristalyn, Chayston and Curtis Stevens; [ed.] B.S. in human resource Management from friends University, Wichita, KS; [occ.] Scott County Clerk; [memb.] Kansas County Clerk's Assoc., Kiwanis, 1st Christian Church, H.E.L.P Domestic violence director, selective service, Kansas Mapper's Assoc.; [hon.] Vice Chairman of Church Board, past Pres. of S.W. KS. Assoc. of counties, 16 yrs. pin for public servant, 10 yrs. for selective service; [oth. writ.] Poetry and short stories written to commemorate special events in my life; [pers.] With God as my guide, there is a reason for everything. I like for my writing to portray the little things that mean so much.; [a.] Scott City, KS

KUHN, JEAN EWING
[b.] June 17, 1917, Philadelphia, PA; [p.] Dr. and Mrs. C. Agnew Ewing; [m.] William C. Kuhn, October 18, 1941; [ch.] William C. Kuhn II, Heathers K. Somers; [ed.] Graduate of Westminster Choir College, Princeton, N.J. '40 as a professional Choir Direct soloist and organist; [occ.] Housewife; [memb.] Alumni Assoc. of W.C.C. Volunteer Assoc. at Hoag Hospital Newport Beach, Cal. Elder and choir member at Presbyterian Church of the Covenant, C.M., Cal.; [hon.] Past President of Mile Square Woman's Golf Club A Plaque from Westminster Rotary Club for being pianist at their meeting. (5 years); [oth. writ.] This is the first writing I have ever submitted. I am so thrilled and most grateful. I published an anthem but I composed the music not the words!; [pers.] You have made my day! If a thing is worth doing, it's worth doing well.; [a.] Costa Mesa, CA

KULAKOV, GEORGII
[pen.] Georgii Nikolaev; [b.] June 23, 1924, Sochi, Russia; [p.] Nikolai Kulakov, Helena Kulakov; [ch.] Sergey; [ed.] Moscow Economic Institute; [occ.] A babysitter of my granddaughter and a poet; [hon.] Only USSRs battle decorations for the participation in the Second World War; [oth. writ.] A manuscript of the poem collection; [pers.] Maybe the verses are the best way to pass thoughts and feelings from one human being to another, to pass them as unexpected presents and useful knowledges.; [a.] Chicago, IL

KUNZ, KELLY
[pen.] Kelly J. Bushnell; [b.] September 20, 1959, Racine, WI; [p.] Robert and Miriam Bushnell; [m.] James Kunz, November 5, 1993; [occ.] Interior Decorator; [oth. writ] Several poems, children's books; [pers.] I hope to, someday, see Emily's beautiful words in print. She's just starting, like I did, at age 12, and someone has to hold on to these kids for dear life...they are still out there!; [a.] Clearwater, FL

KURTZ, CINDY RENEE
[b.] July 20, 1972, Ephrata, PA; [p.] Joyce Kurtz, Paul Kurtz; [ch.] Timothy Vincent Jr.; [ed.] Ephrata High School, Brownstown Vo-Tech; [occ.] Certified Nursing Assistant, Pocopson Home; [pers.] My poems are born out of relationships and the hard decisions in life, the solutions being neither right nor wrong. I'd like to pass on my philosophy for people who are having bad times. I honestly believe God doesn't give you more than you can handle. Be content with what you have today because it may be gone tomorrow.; [a.] Nottingham, PA

KUST, JOHN
[b.] September 30, 1921, Cleveland, OH; [p.] Anna Pospisil and John Kust; [m.] (Current) Darlene, August 7, 1943 and October 17, 1981; [ch.] Valorie H. Kust, Adrienne L. (May) Port; [ed.] East Tech. H. Sch., Arch. Engl, Westorne Res. Univ., Tool Die I fixt Design, Fenn College - 4 yrs. (cert.) Commerce Art and Adlts. (Cooper) Misc. MTM and space Technology; [occ.] Self employed - network marketing (honor Int'l) formerly the Mec. Magoot - Q.C. Engineering; [memb.] Riverview Church, Co Fonder and Chairman Stoorme,, Committee/Grace Evangelical Bible Church; [hon.] Mess Sgt., Mechanized Calv./WW II; [oth. writ.] Approximately (75) unpublished poems/monthly desires letter (circle cream everest) Researched and Company Quality Assurance Manual Fuhet Dw/TRW Corp.; [pers.] Enjoy Architectural designs landscape design and Interior Decorating, enjoy writing - religious and human graces poetry for special Occasions and greeting cards.; [a.] Richmond Heights, OH

KUZNETSOV, MIKHAIL G.
[b.] November 2, 1985, Moscow, Russia; [p.] Mariya A. Kuznetsova, Grigoriy M. Fish; [m.] June 20, 1984;

[ed.] Dziscoll School, Brookline, MA - 4th grade, New England Hebrew Academy Brookline, MA (1-3 grades); [occ.] Student; [memb.] New England Aquarium; [a.] Brookline, MA

KVIKSTAD, MILTON E.
[pen.] Milt Kvikstad; [b.] February 27, 1910, Argyle, MN; [p.] Per and Karen Kvikstad; [m.] Blanche Salverson, June 21, 1937; [ch.] Becky Kvikstad, Betty Ann Johnson, Grandchildren - Christopher and Karyn Beth; [ed.] N.D. University Masters Degree 1940; [occ.] Retired Chm. of Board Northern School Supply Co. Fargo, N.D., retired 1975; [memb.] First Lutheran Church, Fargo Rotary Club, Fargo Country Club, C-400 Club Concordia College, many years on Board Directors, Fargo National Bank, Served on many Fargo Boards to raise money. Masonic bodies including Shrine Editor, Concordian, Campus Newspaper, Concordia Sr. Yr.; [hon.] District Governor, Rotary, National Chairman, School Supply Industry, Awarded N.D. State Volunteer Worker of the year, Served as President and Ch. of Board., Served 5 years as State Chairman of Score of Small Bus. Assoc. of North Dakota; [oth. writ.] Before joining Northern School Supply Co., I wa a school administrator and spent my summers writing farm news and taking farm picture for the N.D. Extension Service in Fargo. I took special lessons in short writing and wrote 10 stories. I have done considerable wood carving and oil and water color painting and have several one man shows.; [pers.] All that you do for others comes back to you.; [a.] Fargo, ND

LA SALA, CAROLANN MARIE
[b.] April 25, 1957, New York; [ed.] B.A., Adelphi, University M.S. Ed. Long Island University C.W. Post Campus, P.D. Long Island University C.W. Post Campus; [occ.] Supervisor of Student Teachers, Professor of Education, Ad. Long Island University C.W. Post Campus Brookville, NY; [memb.] Phi Delta Kappa, AAUW, NCTM, ASCD; [hon.] Dean's List, Presenter - American Dental Society Convention, 1995, Who's Who of American Women 1996; [oth. writ.] "Prisms", Adelphi University (Poetry Anthology); [pers.] Our words must be used wisely, for they can not be retrieved. Make them instruments of peace and progress, rather than serving as impediments to the preservation of humankind.; [a.] Westbury, NY

LAAUWE, NANCYLYNN
[b.] December 2, 1965, Paterson, NJ; [p.] Harold and Linda Laauwe; [m.] David Pera, May 25, 1996; [ed.] Wayne Hills High, The Berkeley School on the Garret Mountain Campus; [occ.] Commitment Processor, NIA Lawyers Title Agency, Paramus, NJ; [memb.] Christ Church in Pompton Lakes, NJ; [hon.] Dean's List, Music; [oth. writ.] A few other poems are: "Don't Forget the Flame", "Love and Loss", "Man Behind the Mask", "Moonlight Feathers"; [pers.] To write anything I can't just sit down and write. It's something you simply have to live, feel and experience within your life.; [a.] Maywood, NJ

LADNER JR., HUBERT
[pen.] Hubert Ladner Jr.; [b.] October 31, 1955, Poplarville, MS; [p.] Hubert and Gladys Ladner; [m.] Connie S. Ladner, July 28, 1979; [ch.] Frank and Seth Ladner; [ed.] Pearl River Comm. College Drafting, MS. Gulf Coast Comm. College Horticule, MS State Univ. Horticultural Continuing Education; [occ.] Landscaping, and Landscaping Design; [memb.] MS Nurseryman's Assn. serve on MNA. BD of Directors, Assoc. of Builders and Contractors, various local boards; [oth. writ.] The Rivers Edge, and The Rose; [pers.] To look out into natures wonderful palette taking in all that you behold, then transcribe that into print for whatever the occasion, is truly a divine gift, weather perceived as good, bad, or indifferent.; [a.] Lumberton, MS

LAFORGE, MARIA K.
[pen.] Mia; [b.] November 24, 1954, Providence, RI; [p.] Marshall Cantone, Marie Cantone; [m.] Jeff LaForge, October 9, 1993; [ch.] Michael Paul, Mario Antonio; [ed.] Cramston High School East Tunxis Technical Community College; [occ.] Tutor/Education Consultant, Writer; [hon.] Human Service Award, "Mom's" Program (Local Hospital); [oth. writ.] Several poems published in college publication. Social Services Outreach Material for Local Hospital, Job manual guide specified for disabled worker; [pers.] Taken from my lifetime of suffering, I hope to share the ultimate pain with those individuals who haven't lived it and I like to share the ultimate joy of life for those individuals who need to overcome it.; [a.] Southington, CT

LAHR, LISA L.
[b.] September 25, 1963, Newport, RI; [p.] Marvin P. Lahr and Lorraine Lahr; [ed.] 3 yrs. Simmons College Boston; [occ.] Nursing Assistant; [memb.] Newport Congregational Church; [pers.] This poems is dedicated to Tex memory of Edith Boyzan.; [a.] Middletown, RI

LAMBERT, BILLIE CARMEN MALONE
[pen.] Billy Lambert; [b.] June 8, 1943, Chapelville, MI; [p.] Mahlon and Evelyn (Magers) Malone; [m.] Robert Lambert, September 2, 1967; [ed.] Associate in Arts Bachelor of Science, College of Education Santa Monica College Cosmetology; [occ.] Homemaker; [memb.] Westwood Hills Women's Group Charles Dicken's Greater Los Angeles Fellowship; [hon.] Zeta Tau Alpha Dean's List; [oth. writ.] Poems "Peekin", "Tuplip and Blueberry", Local Newspaper Articles; [pers.] Sharing someone as a major impact, my writings reflect the love, comfort, security and completion of the effect of my father and mother of my childhood.; [a.] Los Angeles, CA

LANCE, MARCH
[b.] October 29, 1968, San Jose, CA; [p.] Larry Lance, Kit Biehn; [ch.] Joseph Eugene Lance; [ed.] Phoenix High School; [occ.] Sales representative sharp sales, Reno, NV; [hon.] 2nd Place Jr. Heavy Weight Div. United Fighting Arts Foundation 1984; [oth. writ.] Many other poems, none of which has been published to date; [pers.] My poems are very important to me. I write from my heart. I'd just like to thank God for the gift he has given me.; [a.] Reno, NV

LANDI, MARYANN
[pen.] Maryann DeVito Landi; [b.] March 21, 1945, Jersey City, NJ; [p.] Michael and Mary DeVito; [m.] Former Husband Dr. E. F. Landi, January 25, 1964; [ch.] Twin sons, Adam E. and Christian Alexander Landi, Christian is deceased; [ed.] St. Aedan's School, Lincoln High Jersey City. Rockland Comm. College Saffern, NY, JS GPA, American Academy of Dramatic Arts, NY, NY; [occ.] Disabled Manic Depressive and Diabetic; [memb.] 15 years as Third Order Carmelite, Renew Spiritual Strength for Sacred Heart Parish, Suffer, N.Y. Elmwood Club, Mental health Program; [hon.] Basketball merit of Achievement, Highest Honor of Lincoln High, and Varsity Lehers for Cheer leading, President of Cheerleaders Club, Captain of Cheerleaders, Student Gov't Rep. 4 yrs. Gold Key for Extra Curricular Activities. Champion Cheerleader; [oth. writ.] Splinters, Women at The Window, Eulogy For My Father Grandma Peragine, Lost Immigrant, To A Priest, Love Hurts, 4 songs: The Annunciation, I Saw My Son Die On Across, Empty Vessel, John My Beloved; [pers.] My Soa Adam is a graduate of the fashion Institute of Technology and Freelance prop buyer. He also manages a store. He is also an award winning artist and a delight to my soul. We must look to Christ for everything.; [a.] Hillburn, NY

LANG, STEPHEN
[b.] December 14, 1968, Indianapolis, IN; [p.] Dean and Rita Lang; [m.] Christine, June 2, 1990; [ed.] Perry Meridian H.S., Ball State University; [occ.] Machine Set-up Person, CTP Corp. Indpls. IN; [memb.] Phi Sigma Kappa; [oth. writ.] Articles for the Tube Flier; [a.] Indianapolis, IN

LARGEN, MICHAEL
[pen.] Weldon Largen; [b.] November 9, 1970, Hillsville, VA; [m.] Angela Largen, September 12, 1993; [pers.] A generation X poet.; [a.] Stuart, VI

LARKIN, SANDRA
[pen.] Sandra Lee; [b.] June 10, 1950, Elgin, IL; [p.] Art Henschel; [m.] Earl Larkin, April 22, 1977; [ch.] Susan Larkin; [ed.] Helix High School, North American School of Accounting, Basic Computer Corporation; [occ.] Checker; [memb.] Arthritis Foundation, the Susan G. Komen Breast Cancer Foundation, Doris Day Animal League, Cystic Fibrosis Foundation, Unity School of Christianity; [hon.] Volunteer School Aide Award, Benefactors Awards; [oth. writ.] I have written a few article on Oregon Citizens Alliance, about the Commissioner, Wendy Roberts, in a local newspapers in Oregon.; [pers.] Writing my poems was influence by my faith in God, and my daily word by Unty School, a read every day.; [a.] Hillsboro, OR

LASHEA, TONY
[pen.] Shea; [b.] November 16, 1954, South Bend, IN; [p.] Henry Lawshea, Aleatha Lawshea; [m.] Betty Compton Lashea, January 7, 1993; [ch.] Marie Antonette, Toni Louise, Anthony Lewis, Mark Anthony; [ed.] Washington High School, White Bear Lake Vo. Tech National College of Culinary Arts; [occ.] Master Chef Petersburg, NA; [memb.] Elks Club, Jaycee's Jaycees; [hon.] 1st in class 1982 at National College of Culinary Arts. Mid West Business Man of the Year 1986; [oth. writ.] Two poems published in newspapers. I short story readers digest.; [pers.] I have been influenced by my wife Betty. Who continues to make each day more than life its self. This poem is for you Betty. You are my inspiration for all my thoughts. I love you!; [a.] Petersburg, VA

LAVENDER, JUANITA
[b.] May 14, 1907, North-Western Pennsylvania; [hon.] Picture-Paintings: Blue Ribbons, Band: Piano: Player; [pers.] I am very concerned with our endangered species, also the ones, that are not. Our beautiful wild life.; [a.] Ridgway, PA

LAWRESZUK, AARON JASON
[b.] October 20, 1977, Cleveland, OH; [p.] Paul and Sara Lawreszuk; [oth. writ.] Several poems and short stories; [pers.] Some of the most beautiful things in the

world can not be seen, or even touched, but can only be felt by the heart.; [a.] Cleveland, OH

LAYMAN, CLARK BARRY

[b.] December 17, 1917, Escanaba, MI; [p.] Barry Layman, Betty Layman; [ed.] Horizon High School East - Las Vegas, NV, Cataling High School Tucson, AZ; [occ.] Merchandise Delivery for Sears, Roebuck and Company; [hon.] I have a poem published in the National High School Poetry Anthology, from the National Poetry Society.; [oth. writ.] Several writings in my school newspaper; [pers.] I like to reflect in my readers possibilities which have never been open to them before, like their own mind and potentials. I know I can't change the world in one shot, so I do the best I can, the only way I can, one reader at a time.; [a.] Las Vegas, NV

LEACH, CURTIS

[pen.] Curt Leach; [b.] March 5, 1975, Lewistown, PA; [p.] Horry, Glenda Leach Jr.; [ch.] Curtis Lassiter; [ed.] High School; [occ.] Dock Worker; [pers.] Thanks, sue a listen with your heart, as well as your ears.; [a.] Middletown, PA

LEDFORD, KELLI ELIZABETH

[pen.] Kelli Ledford; [b.] March 30, 1983, Catawba County; [p.] Libby and Bill Ledford; [ed.] Mountain View Elementary, Jacobs Fork Middle 7th Grade; [memb.] Youth Advisory Counsel; [hon.] Semi finalist in a Beauty Pageant. Cheer Leading Dance, AB Honor Roll Reading Award; [oth. writ.] I'm just starting out; [pers.] I hope that someday I will be a professional writer or poetrist. VC Andrews (My Fan-Author) has mostly some more on back influenced me.; [a.] Hickory, NC

LEE JR., GREGORY

[b.] November 25, 1971, Fort Worth; [p.] Mike and Vina Wesley; [ed.] Central Texas Taxiderny School; [occ.] Taxidermy; [memb.] Texas Taxiderma Association National Taxidermy Assoc.; [oth. writ.] No published Works; [pers.] Having cystic Fibrosis I have had a lot of time in the hospitals to think. Life can be a terrible thing if you allow it, I don't.; [a.] Fort Worth, TX

LEE, VICKY CHIA-LIN

[b.] November 12, 1974, Duren, NJ; [p.] Mary Lee, Kuen Chen Lee; [ed.] B.A. from U.C. Berkeley in Rhetoric and Asian American Studies; [occ.] Community Organizer, Waitress, Barley Green Distributor; [pers.] This poem was a letter to a boy named John Kim.; [a.] Berkeley, CA

LEMAR, JAMES

[pen.] Semaj Ramel; [b.] July 22, 1955, Philadelphia, PA; [p.] Jeanette and Herbert; [m.] Josephine Brown (LeMar); [ch.] Ebony Niki, Dena, Quadir Cherita Semaj; [ed.] Ben Franklin High (Studied) Cleprical Buss.; [occ.] Combination Welder; [memb.] Mainterie Church of God in Christ.; [oth. writ.] The Roadi was published once I do have more writings of poems. To young, Strength In A Women, It's Your Children, It's Your Children It's My Child, Hey Young Black man Children and Violence. I Cried To The Lord; [pers.] I'm striving to be a good creative writer by putting my heart fill feeling one paper. Vision from within my soul gives me inspiration to write. I try to put my heart and soul in every thing. I feel.; [a.] North Philadelphia, PA

LEMLEY, ANGELA

[pen.] Ang; [b.] November 13, 1974, Norfolk, VA; [p.] David A. and Christine M. Lemley; [ed.] Coventry High School University of Akron; [occ.] Arlington Apples, Delicatessen Employee; [memb.] PRSSA University Democrats; [hon.] Dean's List; [oth. writ.] Voice of Democracy - VFW Scholarship. Poems and Short Stories (Unpublished), Articles in the Buchtellite; [pers.] I am inspired by my life and experiences - it's like poetry in motion. I owe my family and friends a special thanks for their support, without their love my dreams would have never been possible.; [a.] Barberton, OH

LENNON, PAUL J.

[pen.] Pinkman; [b.] September 19, 1970, Manhattan, NY; [p.] Janice Lennon, Bernard Lennon; [ed.] Carle Place High; [occ.] Dispatcher, Sky Courier, Reston VA; [oth. writ.] Many, but have not been published; [pers.] The greatest thing in life is life itself. So it is my mother and father that I owe everything to.; [a.] Centreville, VA

LENTZ, LOUISE L.

[b.] December 31, 1925, Cabarrus, CO; [p.] John Lloyd Long, Mary "Aloe" Harwood Long; [m.] Charles G. Lentz Jr. (Deceased), July 26, 1945; [ch.] Charles G. Lentz III - Helen L. Knapp, Margaret L. Page, Joseph A. Lentz; [ed.] Mount Pleasant High School Graduate; [occ.] Housewife; [oth. writ.] Several poems published in local newspaper - one published in Wildlife Magazine; [pers.] My poems usually reflect my personal feelings and the Greatness of God.; [a.] Mount Pleasant, NC

LEONARD, JULI L.

[pen.] Juli; [b.] November 29, 1972, Port Angeles, WA; [p.] Allan and Dixie Leonard; [ed.] Port Angeles High School, School of Cosmetology; [occ.] Cosmetologist, Cosmetology Instructor, Product Educator; [oth. writ.] I've written for myself since I was a child but this is my first poem to be exposed and published.; [pers.] For each second of emotion there are a thousand words unspoken.; [a.] Port Angeles, WA

LESSER, VIRGINIA PURDUM

[pen.] Ginger Purdum; [b.] August 23, 1946, Culver City, CA; [p.] William Farley, Janice Arkill; [m.] Dennis Lesser, November 12, 1988; [ch.] Gina Romero, Tracy Alfino; [ed.] Culver City High School Los Angeles Valley College; [occ.] Own jewelry business with husband, also employed at Ralph's Markets; [hon.] Graduated Summa Cum Laude from College; [oth. writ.] Co-authored articles on astronomy and literature for Griffith Observer (A publication of the Griffith Observatory) with Robert S. Richardson, a former staff member at mount Wilson and Palomar Observatories.; [pers.] The journey of life is filled with many surprise. Sometimes it takes quite a while to realize that the struggle is the prize and that friendships we make during this struggle truly make the journey worthwhile. I am a child of my times for I agree with those who say that love is the answer.; [a.] West Hills, CA

LEVENS, BRUCE C.

[b.] November 21, 1955, Troy, NY; [p.] Chester Levens, Rita Levens (Higgins); [m.] Catherine L. Levens (Komertz), November 24, 1985; [ch.] Amber, Creig, and Britleigh Levens; [ed.] Graduate of Waterford-Halfmoon High School, Class of 1974, and several Vocational and Trade Schools, Drafting and Legal Researcher's Classes; [occ.] Contractor; [memb.] St. Mary's Church, Waterford, N.Y. Holy Name Society and Boy Scouts of America; [hon.] Numerous trophies, medals, certificates; [oth. writ.] Numerous unpublished poems and songs, Articles to Local Newspapers and to Magazines; [pers.] Through my pen flows a river of thought's that come to life and reflect the inner me. What is brought out in my writings are reflections relative to my: Morals and Standards, philosophical views, and political belief's. I always strive to speak the truth and bring out the goodness in everything I see, for this is what Bruce is all about.; [a.] Waterford, NY

LEVESQUE, ABBIE MARIE

[pen.] Abbs; [b.] January 15, 1969, Valporasio, IN; [p.] Priscilla Ponader; [m.] Kevin S. Levesque, July 25, 1987; [ch.] Jason, Justin, Alex; [ed.] On going; [occ.] Writer and Mother; [memb.] The Poet's Guild and The International Society of Poets; [oth. writ.] Best New Poems, East of Sunrise, Best Poems of 1996, Tomorrow's Dream; [pers.] Never stop reaching, never stop striving to fulfill your dreams. Dreams are the wishes of your soul. A reflection of the person you wish to become.; [a.] Bloomington, IN

LEWIS, BRENDA CLOPPER

[pen.] BCL; [b.] May 4, 1963, Easton, MD; [p.] Howard and Grace Clopper; [m.] John K. Lewis Jr., January 20, 1990; [ch.] Shelby Hannah Lewis; [ed.] Summerville High School; [occ.] A full time Mother and Housewife; [oth. writ.] A private personal collection of poems including my wedding vows, special poem inscribed in stone for a dearly departed friend.; [pers.] I express my true most inner feelings in my poetry. My experiences in life, give me my inspiration. To interpret someone's poetry, can give you knowledge of their self being.; [a.] Summerville, SC

LEWIS, DANIELLE

[b.] June 9, 1980; [p.] James Lewis, Lena Lewis; [ed.] Current Sophomore of Saratoga Springs Senior High School; [occ.] Student (High School); [memb.] Honor Society National Volleyball Association AIDS Advisory Council of Saratoga SADD; [hon.] Varsity Volleyball Letter, High Honor Roll, '95 Saratoga High School English Award Winner, Certificate of Commendation, '95 Institute for Science and Math at Syracuse University, placed with distinction '93 John Hopkins University Mathematics and Verbal Talent Search; [oth. writ.] School newspapers, essay '94 Science Essay Awards Program (The Dupont Challenge), School Essay Contests; [pers.] In life, we meet many people. Each person, no matter who, has some impact on our lives. Those whom we cannot imagine life without and the few that become part of who we are - are the ones who give life to the word - friend.; [a.] Saratoga Springs, NY

LEWIS, TAMMY

[b.] January 22, 1968, San Antonio, TX; [p.] Mr. and Mrs. Wayne Lewis; [ed.] B.S. in Biochemistry from Juniata College (Huntingdon, PA); [occ.] Biological Science Laboratory Technician; [memb.] American Society of Tropical Medicine and Hygiene; [pers.] Most of my friends are surprised that I can write poetry. I think that people should always try to expand their horizons.; [a.] Frederick, MD

LILLEY, BARBARA

[b.] September 4, 1995, NM; [p.] Dudley and Sylvia Brown; [m.] Jerry Lilley, December 29, 1972; [ch.] Lora Leigh and Jerry Magavin; [ed.] Eunice New Mex. High and Eastern New Mexico Univ.; [occ.] Housewife; [oth. writ.] One poem published in "Tomorrow's Dream" no other poems made public; [pers.] All of my poems are messages to help mankind find that Ray of Hope.; [a.] Alamogordon, NM

LIM, CECILE M.
[pen.] Cecile; [b.] March 5, 1981, Manila, Philippines; [p.] Ben Lim, Sally Lim; [ed.] 9th Grade Notre Dame Academy Overland, LA, California; [occ.] Student; [memb.] Student council, California Junior, Scholarship Federation, Drama and Journalism Notre Dame Academy - Los Angeles, CA; [hon.] Highest Academic Achievement, Leadership Award, (Both 8th Grade); [oth. writ.] Several articles and first publisher of newspaper BB Times - Saint Brendan School, Los Angeles, CA - a school newspaper, Contributor of Editor of "The queens" Notre Dame Academy Newspaper; [pers.] When you do something do the best.; [a.] Los Angeles, CA

LINDSTROM, LISA M.
[pen.] Leo; [b.] August 8, 1961, Minneapolis, MN; [p.] Ward and Mari Jane Engebrit; [m.] Jeffrey Rollin Lindstrom, July 25, 1992; [ed.] 1 year college and prior I took 3 (three) grammar classes. I know Copyright Law.; [occ.] Poet, Housewife, Insurance Adjuster, News Publisher; [memb.] Distinguished Member of the International Society of Poetry; [hon.] Editor's Choice Award for poem "Unfantasy" in AT Water's Edge, 1995; [oth. writ.] Anthologies published or publishing "At Water's Edge", Best Poems of 1996 and The Voice Within; [pers.] My brothers, Shawn and Scott have encouraged my endeavors and Dr. Marvin Gladstone, M.D. is a very special Doctor. I also will publish my own works.; [a.] Yorba Linda, CA

LINDSTROM, TERRI
[pen.] Temali; [b.] January 10, 1980, Manchester, CT; [p.] Keith and Vicki Lindstrom; [ed.] Manchester (CT) High School; [occ.] I'm still in high school (Sophomore); [memb.] Manchester Ballet Company (I'm in my 11th Season), People to People Student Ambassador (I went to Australia and New Zealand, July 1994) High School Wind Ensemble (an elite winter/spring group) and Marching Band (football season); [hon.] Ranked #1 in my class for the 94-95 school year (4.0 gpa) Presidential Academic Fitness Award; [oth. writ.] In my leisure I write all of the time. Never been published before, though.; [pers.] I write upon inspiration only, which is why you'll find dedications on my work. I can't just make it happen"....it happens for itself. I'm just the translator. A lot of my work is stream of consciousness so there are no capital letters or paragraphs. (Poetry is usually not my forte'. I excel in short stories and descriptive monologues.); [a.] Manchester, CT

LINK, HERBERT C.
[b.] January 10, 1912, Baltimore, MD; [p.] John and Dorothy Link; [m.] Myrtle (Deceased February 21, 1994), October 29, 1939; [ch.] John A., and Gerald F. (Jerry) Link

LITTMAN, NICOLE
[b.] July 2, 1979, Los Angles, CA; [p.] Richard and Noreen Littman; [occ.] Student; [oth. writ.] None published 3 plays, many poems, various stories; [pers.] Man was created a little lower than the angels and has been getting a little lower ever since.; [a.] Hacienda Heights, CA

LIVERMAN, GEORGE
[b.] July 9, 1960, Elizabeth City, NC; [p.] Junius Liverman, Estella Brothers; [m.] Darlene Liverman, December 29, 1989; [ch.] Dremoine, Preston, Sharisha; [ed.] Northeastern High School U.S. Marine Corp.; [occ.] Disabled Vet.; [memb.] Eliz. City Housins Authority Resident Council Performing Arts Group called New Horizon out of the V.A. Hospital in Hampton VA; [oth. writ.] Several poems written for myself and family and friends; [pers.] I strive to express the pain of addiction and the joy of recovery in the human soul.; [a.] Elizabeth City, NC

LIVINGSTON, JUDY
[pen.] Judy (Dunning) Livingston; [b.] April 9, 1942, Carters Creek, TN; [p.] Fred Dunning, Eleanor Jones Dunning (Both Deceased); [m.] Charles Livingston, February 14, 1958; [ch.] Betty Ann, Charles Michelle, Clay; [ed.] Northeast High, St. Petersburg, FL, Institute of Children's Literature; [occ.] Homemaker; [memb.] Capital City Christian Church; [oth. writ.] Several poems published in other anthologies; [pers.] I tend to let my feelings show through my poems and hope that they will be an inspiration to others. My writing is a gift from God of which I am truly thankful. I want to show my love and praise for Him in my writing as well as my life.; [a.] Puincy, FL

LOCKHART, LORA M.
[b.] June 15, 1903, Farm Dekalb Co, MO; [p.] Hugh and Julia Redman; [m.] Laureno Leonard Lockhart, June 2, 1928; [ed.] BS from Marriville State University; [occ.] Retired Teacher; [memb.] President of Dekalb County Historical Society, Taught over 40 years in Missouri; [hon.] Lora Redman Lockhart a descendant of Nathanial Redman and Jacob Taylor who lived in Dekalb Co. by 1845 or Earlier, Pioneer Family in Missouri Award; [oth. writ.] Writings in Historical Society of Dekalb County, MO.; [pers.] Do all the good I can and as long as I can.; [a.] Maysville, MO

LOCKLEY, ODESSA
[b.] Greenville, NC; [p.] Eli and Jennie G. Savage; [m.] Aaron L. Lockley, August 21, 1955; [ch.] Aaron Ray and Alan Jerry Lockley; [ed.] Pitt County Training School, Oakwood College, Walker Business and Vocational College, University of FL., FCCJ and UNF; [occ.] Retired; [memb.] Ephesus Church Southeastern Conference of SDA Master Guide; [hon.] SLC Society (Scholarship, Leadership and Character), Gamma Sigma Kappa; [oth. writ.] Poetic Oasis several poems published in weekly bulletins, Southeastern Sketches, 1987 American Anthology of Southern Poetry; [pers.] To inspire to excellence.; [a.] Jacksonville, FL

LOGAN, VIRGINIA ELAINE
[b.] January 23, 1984, Salt Lake City, UT; [p.] Jim and Karen Logan; [ed.] Currently a sixth grade student at Desert Valley Elementary; [pers.] I love to write - it just comes naturally.; [a.] Glendale, AR

LOGGINS, MELISSA DANIELLE
[b.] November 23, 1977, Scotland; [p.] Larry and Elaine Loggins; [ed.] High School Senior at Ocean Lakes; [memb.] Student Athletic Trainer at Ocean Lakes High School; [pers.] Never loose sight of the real you.; [a.] Virginia Beach, VA

LOISELLE, KRISTINEA
[pen.] Stine'a, Kris; [b.] February 12, 1966, Southbridge, MA; [p.] Sam and Anne Ricci; [m.] Paul R. Loiselle, May 28, 1994; [ch.] Aaron Loiselle, Brittany; [ed.] Tantasqua Reg. High School, Sturbridge, MA; [occ.] Disabilities, Cancer Prior Hyde Man; [memb.] Massichets Adult Student of the Year 1993 Mace Award; [oth. writ.] "Silence" published in the Quinsiga Mond Collage Adult Student Poem Book Many at Hyde Man. Comp for different events and Mary to my husband Paul; [pers.] Doc to my health problems I've learned that life is what you make it, and is often to short. So look for the good in everyone, and that you can leave your mark in many ways.; [a.] Danielson, CT

LONG, JESSICA
[b.] March 18, 1984, Howell; [p.] Cindy and Jim Long; [ed.] McPherson Middle School; [occ.] I'm a kid; [memb.] 6th grad. band; [hon.] DARE Award, Honor Role at School; [a.] Howell, MI

LONG, KATHERINE SARAH
[pen.] "Kt", Katie; [b.] April 23, 1986, Milford, CT; [p.] William and Marilyn; [ed.] 4th Grade Student Mary Snow School Bangor, ME; [occ.] 4th Grade Honor Student; [memb.] Girl Scouts, Little League Baseball, Dance: Tap and Jazz, YWCA: Swimming Music: Violin, Keyboard; [hon.] "A" Student all City Art: 1st Place Reading and Writing; [oth. writ.] Owl's Moon, Give Me, Don't Give Me; [pers.] KT is a petite, blue-eye, blonde hair nine year old girl. Her talent, wit, and personality is abounding and charming. She love's animals, art, music, reading and poetry.; [a.] Naugatuck, CT

LONGO, ROBERT O.
[b.] December 22, 1960, Wilmington; [p.] Mr. and Mrs. Louis A. Longo; [ed.] Salesianum H.S., King's College; [memb.] English Teacher; [pers.] If it is a true belief, live for it do not die for it.; [a.] Wilmington, DE

LOTT, LENA MAE
[b.] December 27, 1922, Pell City, AL; [p.] Leilus and Ruby Walker; [m.] Richard Lott, March 16, 1961; [ch.] Twins - Janice and Joan, Vicki; [ed.] Graduate of Pell City High School A Alverson Business College; [occ.] Retired from State of Alabama Employment Service; [memb.] Calvary Baptist Church 6th place winner of International Essay contest in high school sponsored by Lions Club; [hon.] Salutatorian of High School Graduation Class of 1941; [oth. writ.] Have written many poems but never had them published; [pers.] My seventh grade teacher, Iola Roberts inspired me to write when she realized my love for poetry.; [a.] Montgomery, AL

LOVELL, KATHY
[b.] March 24, 1949, Cleveland, OH; [ch.] Music Major at Santa Monica College Graduate of Institute of Children's Literature, Conn., Extension Institute/American Management Associations, NY; [ed.] Insurance Investigations; [oth. writ.] Music, Children's Literature, Poetry; [pers.] Today's children will make tomorrow's decisions. I try to instill the necessity for global ecology and world wide peace.; [a.] Los Angeles, CA

LOWERY, JOHN ED
[b.] July 16, 1964, Charlotte, NC; [p.] John and Pearline Smith; [occ.] Coin Area Supervisor Wells Fargo; [pers.] We all as humans should realize no owe has a choice in their genetic make-up. Black or white, male or female, gay or straight, we all need to accept each other for who we are.; [a.] Gastonia, NC

LUCERO, EVE
[b.] December 19, 1984, Albuquerque, NM; [p.] Gene Lucero, Vickie Lucero; [pers.] I believe that poetry is one of my many gifts from God. I use my poetry and other writings to express what I feel as I strive to fulfill God's perfect will for my life through Christ Jesus.; [a.] Arvada, CO

LUCK, ANNE
[b.] March 8, 1978, Princeton, NJ; [p.] Marie and David Luck; [ed.] Hamilton High North; [occ.] Student; [memb.] National Honor Society, Kingston Presbyterian Church, Editor for School Literary Magazine; [hon.] National Merit Commended Scholar, Varsity Scholar - Athlete; [pers.] Jesus Christ is the reason behind everything I do and to Him I give the glory.; [a.] Hamilton, NJ

LUGO, DANIEL
[b.] July 3, 1976, New York City, NY; [p.] Hexan and Olga Lugo; [ed.] I attended Cathedral Prep. High School and spent one year at Suny Morrisville. I am currently at the New York Film Academy.; [occ.] Student Film maker; [hon.] Dean List at Suny Morrisville, National Dean's List, Phi Theta Kappa Member; [oth. writ.] I have never had any of my writings published before.; [pers.] I don't write to change other peoples lives. I write to change my own life. I don't write poetry to win contests. I write poetry because I have to. It is the only thing that brings me so lace.; [a.] New York City, NY

LYNCH, APRIL DAWN
[pen.] April Dawn Lynch; [b.] February 5, 1982, Roanoke, VA; [p.] Mr. and Mrs. A. Curtis Lynch; [ed.] Presently in the 8th grade; [occ.] Junior High School; [memb.] Church Handbell Choir, School Band, Church Basketball Team, Piano Lessons; [hon.] I am an honor roll student. I am a member of the Partners for success scholarship program at my school. I have received several recognition awards for my music ability. I received a sports award last year in basketball.; [oth. writ.] Poems; [pers.] I love music and poetry. I am a perfectionist. I am very academic. I have a Christian personality. I am efficient and professional in all my work. I always strive to be the best that I can be at all times.; [a.] Roanoke, VI

LYONS, MELISSA
[pen.] Mel; [b.] June 15, 1983, Passaic, NJ; [p.] Leslie Ramella and William Lyons; [ed.] Attending Memorial Middle School; [occ.] Student, and Acting; [memb.] A Models Agency; [a.] Elmwood Park, NJ

MACCALL, CAROLYN J.
[b.] April 30, 1941, Pompano Beach, FL; [p.] Eugene and Nora Scruggs McCall; [m.] Robert Adams, Jr., October 25, 1986; [ch.] Howard D. McCall, Randolph W. McCall; [ed.] Graduate of Ely High School, Class of 1959. Graduate of Pompano Business College.; [occ.] Secretary, Allstate Insurance Claims Office; [memb.] Mt. Calvary Missionary Baptist Church. The progressive club and the women's ministry.; [hon.] Dean's List at Broward Community College; [oth. writ.] Several poems published in local newspaper, the Westside Gazette; [pers.] I strive to reflect the goodness of "God" and His blessings to mankind. I have been greatly influenced by other writers of poetry.; [a.] Deerfield Beach, FL

MACK, WALTRAUD I.
[pen.] Ingeborg von Finsterwalde; [b.] September 18, 1938, Germany; [p.] Alfred and Frieda Mueller; [m.] Alfred Mack, May 4, 1959; [ch.] Dennis Mack; [ed.] In Germany; [occ.] Homemaker and Part time Collectible Dealer; [hon.] Editor's Choice Award, The National Library of Poetry 1995; [oth. writ.] Poem published in Anthology "Between The Raindrops", National Library of Poetry and poem published in "The Best Poems of the 90s", National Library of Poetry; [pers.] Life is a very harsh, but fair teacher. If we adhere to its lesson, the after can be very rewarding. Open your heart and listen, learn and convey the message. My wish for the world.; [a.] Poughkeepsie, NY

MACKEY, GAIL R.
[b.] December 16, 1984, Santa Cruz; [p.] Russ Mackey, Dawn Mackey; [ed.] Bonny Doon Elementary School and Mission Hill (Santa Cruz) Jr. High School; [hon.] John Sousa Music Award; [oth. writ.] Through Jaguars Eyes published in The Write Stuff, Mom published in a Student Anthology; [pers.] Life and death are part of the same picture. Some people surround their eyes in life so they don't see death. But the two are a pair and will never be separated.; [a.] Santa Cruz, CA

MADYUN, GALE
[b.] January 28, 1947, Los Angeles, CA; [ed.] Univ. of Montana, School of Geology, B.A., Cal. State Univ. Los Angeles Sociology, B.A.; [occ.] Geologist with State of California; [oth. writ.] Soon to be published: I Danced With the Wind, an autobiography from child of the sixties, Dancing in Guyana - a novel of political intrigue; [pers.] I've grown through this journey we call life from an angry college student of the 60's to a woman of spiritual substance for the 90's. Time calms the turbulent waters.; [a.] Ontario, CA

MAES-MACDONALD, VERONIQUE
[b.] November 10, 1961, Belgium; [p.] Rene and Blanche Maes; [m.] Bill Macdonald, May 7, 1988; [ch.] Kelly Jayne, Michelle; [ed.] Royal Athenaeum Wetteren (Belgium), Regent College New York; [occ.] mother, student, co-owner of Fotomac (scenic photography); [pers.] I believe that poetry can be a wonderful tool to reach and teach children. We can all remember a poem or two from our childhood and the lessons they contained.; [a.] Santa Barbara, CA

MAGILL, ATON
[b.] February 21, 1975, Israel; [p.] Dr. Alfred Magill, Loretta Magill; [ed.] Anderson High School; [occ.] College Student; [pers.] Before one can truly see, one must first fully understand.; [a.] Austin, TX

MAGNUS, MARCY
[b.] January 19, San Francisco, CA; [p.] Birgit Dundas Magnus and Lawrence Theodore Magnus; [ed.] San Jose State University; [occ.] Poet, Writer; [memb.] ISP Distinguished Member, CALI (Cal. Assoc. Lic. Investigators); [hon.] Best Actress A-Cat-Emmy in Los Gatos, CA 1970, 1st Runner Up Youth Poet, Santa Clara 1961, Editor "The Portland Pioneer" Special Edition Newspaper, Finalist 1995 ISP Convention with "Heartbeats Like A Drum"; [oth. writ.] Various poems published in local newspapers, numerous song lyrics (Music by Douglas D. Allshouse), Wkg. on "The Coming Of Age Of Warren McGregor" - Children's Book, Working On Book of Poetry, Pub. Circa 6/96; [pers.] Anticipate the unanticipated, and know your cat knows more than you do.; [a.] Portland, OR

MAKINNEN, BELVA K.
[b.] Edmonton, Alberta, Canada; [p.] Bronell George and Estelle; [m.] Robb H. Makinnen, September 11, 1948; [ed.] High School; [pers.] I came from a Poetry loving family so I can't remember not having poetry around, at age 14 I won first prize for reciting the poem "IF". At age 18 I wrote my first poem but due to being secret of writing it, I destroyed it, but I kept writing and destroying them until the day my husband Robb accidently found one which I had forgotten to destory. After he found out that I had written it he encouraged me to write and save them that he was my witness so for the number of years I have saved them as I write them.

MALMBERG, TERESA
[b.] October 3, 1958, Marianna, FL; [p.] Daniel H. and Charlene Royals; [m.] Robin D. Malmberg, February 21, 1981; [ch.] Joshua Scott, Jeremiah Robin; [ed.] Pensacola High School Pensacola Jr. College; [occ.] Administrative Assistant, ACPMT, City of Alexandria; [hon.] PJC Honor Graduate, Dean's List, President List, USAF Outstanding Unit, Longevity Awards; [oth. writ.] Several poems printed in P.J.C. Treasure Chest, 2nd Edition; [pers.] Never say never and have faith in one's self.; [a.] Alexandria, VA

MALSON, STACY MICHELLE
[pen.] Stacy Malson; [b.] April 19, 1975, Casper, WY; [p.] Russell D. and Shelley M. Malson; [m.] Mark E. Norton, February 11, 1996; [ch.] Sabrina Shay Norton; [ed.] Graduated with my G.E.D., May 14, 1994 at Sheridan College; [occ.] Housewife and mother; [pers.] Seven and eight is dedicated with love to my grandmother Marcelline Foote, who past away November 10, 1994.; [a.] Evansville, WY

MANN, BENJAMIN JAMES
[pen.] BenJ. Mann; [b.] May 8, 1986, Indiana, PA; [p.] Donald P. and Elizabeth Locke Mann; [ed.] 4th grader at Brush Creek Elementary School; [occ.] Full time boy; [memb.] Boy Scouts of America - 4 yrs., Assembly of God Royal Ranger, Jennings County Youth Baseball; [hon.] Perfect Attendance, Star Student, Honor Roll, PTA Reflections Contest District Winner: Graphic Arts, Spelling Bee Finalist, PTA Photography District Winner; [oth. writ.] The Cursed Hotel 5: A Murder Mystery, TEBS (The Electric Bug Series): Cartoons, Comics and Maddening Mazes, Nightmares, Silly Songs for Country Roads; [pers.] I began writing when I needed to stop a recurring scary dream. I wrote the dream as it happened and then made up a good, unscary ending for it. It worked! Nintendo was my inspiration for TEBS, from Silly Songs.; [a.] Butlerville, IN

MANN, CAROLYN KISSINGER
[b.] January 29, 1941, Fort Smith, AR; [p.] Lucy Marie Dye, Leonard Kissinger; [m.] Divorced; [ch.] William Issac Welch, Jr.; [ed.] 8th grade, no formal education. Being an avid reader has given me a lot of help in my writing.; [occ.] Disabled; [oth. writ.] This is my first attempt at being published. I have many poems that I have written over the years that I am working on currently. Humanity in general has been a great influence in my writing.; [pers.] I like to write about innermost feelings and deep emotional tragedies that affect most of us at one time or another.; [a.] Truth or Consequences, NM

MANUEL, MARY PHILLIPS
[b.] Nashville, TN; [m.] Robert F. Manuel; [ch.] Cornelia Manuel, Cordelia Manuel Payne, Frank F. Manuel and Elizabeth Manuel Jenkins; [ed.] B.S. Degree, Tennessee A and I State College, M.V.A. Georgia State University; [occ.] Retired Teacher; [memb.] The Cornerstone of the Living Faith; [hon.] Distinguished Teaching Performance 1984, 1990 Academic Hall of Fame 1990, Dedicated Service Atlanta Public Schools. Honor Recognition as Organizer and Director of the Children's Chapel, Ebenezer Baptist Church - 25th Anniversary, and Children's Day 29th Anniversary, Enenezer Baptist Church, Atlanta, GA. 15 Yr Pin as Girl Scout Leader; [oth. writ.] First Book "Porms of Spiritual Reflections and Restoration". A Book for the Whole Family, Father, Mother, and Children Based on Scriptures from the Bible.; [pers.] I believe that the joy of the Lord is my strength from whom all blessings flow. If I can share these blessings along life's way, it might help to brighten someone's day.; [a.] Atlanta, GA

MANUEL, MICHAEL J.
[pen.] PIM and PIM Hawk; [b.] July 8, 1973, Lake Charles, LA; [p.] Leonard and Theresa Manuel; [ed.] High School - LaGrange Senior High School, Few College Courses, Hawaiian Pacific University; [occ.] Corporal - United States Marine Corps; [memb.] America Online - Hawks; [hon.] 1988 Who's Who Among American High School Students, Navy/Marine Corps Achievement Medal; [oth. writ.] Various personal writings; [pers.] Live life to your fullest potential. But remember to have fun 'cause it's too short not to.; [a.] Kaneohe Bay, HI

MARAFIOTI, ANTHONY JOSEPH
[b.] February 14, 1975, Peekskill, NY; [ed.] Graduated from North High School in Phoenix, Arizona, in 1993. Now I take some college classes of Community Colleges.; [oth. writ.] I have written over two hundred poems plus a few songs, but I have never attempted to publish anything until now.; [pers.] When I am not writing, I devote the majority of my time to the study of Marshal Arts, Jeet Kune Do, and it's philosophy's.; [a.] Las Vegas, NV

MARANO, MICHELLE
[pen.] Marisa Bellotti; [b.] New Jersey; [p.] Michael and Frances Marano; [ed.] B.A. - Elem. Ed., M.A. - Reading Specialist, M.A. - Admin., Superv. and Curr.; [occ.] L.A. and Creative Wr., Teacher; [hon.] Dean's List, Kappa Delta Pi, (Honor Society in Education), Trophy - Young Authors - Creative Writing; [oth. writ.] Poetry and Short Stories; [pers.] I strive to produce a classroom atmosphere, where children lose their fear and gain the confidence to write. I have been greatly influence by two wonderful teachers in my life, my parents!; [a.] Southeast Coast, FL

MARCHE, ADA LUCILLE
[b.] February 28, 1905, Columbus, GA; [p.] James B. Johnson, Lizzie Johnson (Deceased); [m.] Robert Marche (Deceased), July 10, 1927; [ch.] Elizabeth Marche Slater; [ed.] Spencer High School, Spellman College, Albany State College; [occ.] Retired Kindergarten Teacher of Muscogee County; [memb.] Retired Senior Volunteer Person, AARP; [hon.] "1984" Alex Haley Opening, Awarded For The Poem "My Prayer" at Columbus College; [oth. writ.] Several Poems, One Playlet Short Stories used in Schools and Churches. Poems: A Dream, My Prayer, Understanding, Guilty or Not Guilty, Father, A Friend, Lizzie Birthday Party. Stories: The Adventures of Little White Flower, Christendom, Barco Frogs, Peters Turkey Feather Hats. Book: The Four Balls and The Red and Gold Cat (1960); [pers.] It was not until after the death of my mother 1941 that I started doling in poetry. Trying to make amends to my mother or a promise I didn't keep, promoted me to write. My first effort was "Just A Dream."; [a.] Columbus, GA

MARCROFT, B. H.
[b.] California; [ch.] Four; [ed.] BA Degree; [occ.] Retired; [pers.] Life is life a flower, but like a flower, soon wilts and dies.; [a.] San Diego, CA

MARION, CARISA
[b.] November 13, 1961, Flint, MI; [p.] Barry Hollenbeck, Sharron Hollenbeck; [ch.] Brittay and Jeffrey Marion; [memb.] International Association of Scientologists; [pers.] I began writing poetry after reading L. Ron Hubbard's book entitled "Art", a must-read for all artists. I believe all beings are art and creative life and are life and create art. My favorite poet is Edgar Allen Poe.; [a.] Clearwater, FL

MARKS, MISA
[b.] June 18, 1971, Winchester, TN; [p.] James and Emma Jo Morris; [m.] Danny Marks, July 18, 1992; [ch.] Elizabeth Sloane; [ed.] Franklin County High, personal experiences and observations; [occ.] Homemaker, mother; [oth. writ.] Several unpublished poems; [pers.] We are all the same in one way or another. Many times it is easier to recognize only our differences. I feel we should learn to accept and admire but that which sets us apart and that which unites us.; [a.] Murfreesboro, TN

MARRANZINI, MARISA
[b.] July 15, 1980, Bridgeport, CT; [p.] Carol and Robert Marranzini; [ed.] Norwalk High, Sophomore; [hon.] National LAOH (Ladies Ancient Order of Hibernians), Irish History Essay Contest Honorable Mention, DAR (Daughter of the American Revolution), American History Essay Contest Honorable Mention; [oth. writ.] Several poems published in newsletters; [pers.] Out of persecution comes pain, but out of pride comes strength.; [a.] Norwark, CT

MARSH, CAROL S.
[b.] February 12, 1940, Columbus, IN; [p.] Walter and Martha Bush; [m.] Blaine E. Marsh, July 11, 1964; [ch.] Michelle Marsh Kohlenberger; [ed.] B.S. Indiana University '62, M.S. Butler University '75; [occ.] Speech Pathologist Indpls Public Schools; [a.] Indianapolis, IN

MARTIN, ANN BODENHAMER
[b.] October 24, 1927, El Dorado, AR; [p.] R. C. and Vera Bodenhamer; [m.] Kendall D. Elliott, Divorced, July 25, 1953; [ch.] Richard C. Elliott, Mark A. Elliott; [ed.] El Dorado High School, Lindenwood College, U of Arkansas; [occ.] Minister; [memb.] Palm Springs Writer Guild, American Pen Women, IABC, AARP, Clergy Ass'n, Coachella; [hon.] Sports Illustrator, "First Female Voice in Racing", Writers Digest, Short Story Competition 1973, IABC Photography, Newsletter Competition; [oth. writ.] "Calico Families" (poetry), Pelican Publishing, 1979 — "Metabionics - Mystic Power of the Mind" (self help), Prentice Hall, 1980 — "Build A Better You" Showcase Publishing, 1980, Assoc. Editor "Money Tree Magazine" 1976-1981; [pers.] "The only truth we really leave behind us is what we write on the heart of others —".; [A.] Palm Springs, CA

MARTIN, EARLYN WILSON
[pen.] Richard Edward Stokes; [b.] Philadelphia; [p.] Edward Earl Wilson, Virginia Stokes Wilson; [ed.] Philadelphia College of Art; [occ.] Banker; [memb.] Barnes Foundation; [pers.] I believe that death, pain, hunger and tears from all reasons will soon be a thing of the past, but until then, I'd like to thank, Margarita Hauser Gardiner, MD for her gentle smile and warm touch they pulled me through more than a few painful days. Thank you! I love you Mom!; [a.] Philadelphia, PA

MARTIN, HONEY
[b.] September 13, 1941, Halifax; [p.] Ceasar and Alice Martin (Dec.); [m.] February 5, 1972 (Divorced); [ch.] Ronald Gourdin; [ed.] S.L.R.H.S. '60, attended Massasoit CC, Newbury Jr. Coll., Bunker Hill CC, Curry Coll.; [occ.] Assembler for Electronics; [pers.] As a writing assignment for Literature class at Newbury Jr College, I wrote this poem. Having recently lost my Mom within the last few years, as you can see, this was written from the heart as I truly lost my "Best Friend."; [a.] Halifax, MA

MARTIN, LAUREN LYMAN
[pen.] eL, eLM, Larn Mardin; [b.] January 20, 1976, Houston, TX; [p.] Richard Martin, Leslie J. Martin; [ed.] LIFE!! Academically, Trinity Episcopal in Natchez, MS, Millsaps College, University of Mississippi; [occ.] Typist/Operator and Student; [memb.] Amnesty International; [hon.] Spectrum Awards, first place fiction award - Yaknapotawpha Society; [oth. writ.] Published in Echoes from the Silence, short stories for different zines, poetry for friends and loved ones...; [pers.] I write my poetry to get out before me what's bouncing around in my head, which means it doesn't always make much sense, or read out loud well... but, I hope you enjoy nonetheless!; [a.] Oxford, MS

MARTIN, RENAY
[pen.] SA, Raye Martin; [b.] March 23, 1953, Poughkeepsie, NY; [p.] Mary Wilson, Ernest Gervais; [m.] Kevin Martin, May 31, 1992; [ch.] Darlene Michaels and Thomas De Moro; [ed.] HS - Cornwall Central High; [occ.] Office Manager; [memb.] Smithsonian Institute; [hon.] Good Citizenship of USA, The National Library of Poetry, Wife, Mother of 2 and grandmother of 3 Matthew, Katerina and Nicholas; [oth. writ.] This is my first publication. there are other poems. If you would care to review them, please feel free to send a request. Thank you; [pers.] I see so much anger and pain in the world. Writing poetry has helped make it better for myself. If one person gets some pleasure from reading what I've written. I will feel that strength to write more.; [a.] Boca Raton, FL

MARTIN, TRAVIS
[b.] June 7, 1963, Coffeeville, MS; [p.] Dorothy D. Lancaster, W. B. Martin; [ed.] Coffeeville High, Northwest Community College, Hind Community College; [occ.] Meat Cutter Jitney Jungle; [memb.] Life Member, Veterans of Foreign Wars; [hon.] Southwest Asia Ribbon, Kuwait Liberation Metal, Second Place, Photography MJCPA; [oth. writ.] Editor-in-chief Northwest Community College Yearbook; [pers.] What we get out of life is what we put into life.; [a.] Jackson, MS

MARTIN, YOLANDA W.
[b.] December 18, 1959, Dallas, TX; [p.] Welton and Muriel Martin; [ed.] O. D. Wyatt High, Ft. Worth, Tx (Summa Cum Laude graduate), UTA (Arlington, TX) BBA-Acctg (Cum Laude graduate) UTA (Arlington,

TX) MBA - Mgt.; [occ.] Internal Review Specialist (Company Closes 12/31/95) Resolution Trust Corporation (RTC); [memb.] Mountain View Church of Christ, National Association of Black Accountants, National Association of Black MBAs, Toastmasters International; [hon.] Certified Public Accountant (CPA) Sustained Superior Performance at RTC, 1994 National EEO Awar at RTC, Atlantic Richfield Oil Company Scholarship Dean's List at UTA; [oth. writ.] I have written a few poems for "special days" at church and I wrote a poem about my deceased aunt Cecil English, who was a very sweet person.; [pers.] God is so good! I love the 23rd Psalms because it tells me that "The Lord is my shepherd..." and I know He will take care of me. My favorite scriptures are Romans 8:28"...all things work together for good", and Matthew 6:33"...all things shall be added unto you".; [a.] Dallas, TX

MARTINEZ, AIMEE'

[b.] August 5, 1977, Fresno, CA; [p.] Robert and Carmen Martinez; [ed.] San Joaquin Memorial (junior); [oth. writ.] Several poems; [pers.] I strive to write lyrics to escape reality.; [a.] Fresno, CA

MARTINEZ, BOB G.

[pen.] Bob G. Martinez; [b.] June 7, 1949, Las Vegas, NM; [p.] Mrs. Mary Jane Martinez; [m.] Annette E. Martinez, February 10, 1973; [ch.] Lita Renee Martinez - 18; [ed.] Graduated with honors from Denver North High School in '68; [occ.] Security Guard at the Denver Merchandise Mart; [memb.] Distinguished Member I.S.P., Published in 8 Anthologies (including Best of '96); [hon.] Awarded "Husband of the Decade" by my friend and wife, Annette. Honored as "Father of Decade" by my friend and daughter, Lita.; [oth. writ.] "My Time to Rhyme", single unbroken poem (over 300 pgs) as I saw life from childhood today I became grandfather; [pers.] In the same way, words carry deep feelings... so tongues, like sharp swords maim or bring healings.; [a.] Denver, CO

MARVIN, JENNIFER ELIZABETH

[b.] September 7, 1976, Jeannette, PA; [ed.] Hempfield Senior High School; [occ.] Attractions for Walt Disney World; [oth. writ.] I've had one other poem published. I write children's stories also.; [pers.] Always keep love and hope in your heart. Believe in yourself and your dreams. Never give up and strive to do your best each day.; [a.] Poinciana, FL

MASON, EILEEN

[b.] August 11, 1970, Healdsburg, CA; [p.] Lonnie Yandell, Judy Yandell; [m.] Michael Mason; [ch.] Melissa Kay, Branden Michael; [ed.] Anderson Valley High School graduate; [pers.] A very special thanks to all my family and friends for all their encouraging support. Dedicated: In loving memory of Ira Mason.

MASON, ELOUISE COLLINS

[pen.] Mary Louise McCoy; [b.] December 17, 1945, Giles Co, VA; [p.] Morrison Arthur and Hazel McCoy Collins; [m.] Jerry David Mason, June 19, 1979; [ch.] Dennis-Waynelove, Laura-Ann-Hilton; [ed.] Giles High School Classes at New River Com. College; [occ.] Disable; [memb.] Ephesus Free Will Baptist Church, Ladies Aux., at Choir Amherst Society; [hon.] Poetry achievement awards for many of my poems; [oth. writ.] Many poems published in other of National Library of Poetry Books. Many poems publish in magazines and books and paper; [pers.] The words I write are God's I only write them down. If you give God a chance He will lead you where you need to go.; [a.] Blounts Creek, NC

MATHAI, SUSAN

[pen.] Susan Mathai; [b.] September 9, 1983, Dallas, TX; [p.] Drs. Paul and Nirmala Mathai; [ed.] 7th grade: The Hockaday School Dallas Texas; [occ.] Student; [hon.] 1st place: Poetry "The Sound of Symphony", Poetry Society of Texas, (1995 - published in The Society Book). Designed Cover of Piano Independent School District Literary Magazine 1994 - first price winner for the painting.; [oth. writ.] Write short stories - and other projects - not published yet; [pers.] Play piano 5 yrs., Martial Arts 2 yrs.; [a.] Dallas, TX

MATHIEU, KIERSTEN

[b.] September 5, 1982, Boston, MA; [p.] Jeffrey and Karen Mathieu; [ed.] Currently in 8th grade at North Brandywine Middle School, Coatesville, PA; [occ.] Student 8th grade; [memb.] Secretary/Treasurer of Drama Club, East Brandywine Soccer Team, No. Brandywine Field Hockey and Lacrosse Team, Mixed Chorus; [hon.] Best Actress Award for Cinderella, Honor Roll Student, Champions of Soccer Team; [oth. writ.] Wrote poem for Cobblestone Magazine; [a.] Coatesville, PA

MATISKO, JASON

[pen.] Jonathan Forest; [b.] January 2, 1975; [occ.] Wanderer; [pers.] All these faces, all these voices come to me, not together, but as one face, one voice and now that I remember I could never forget and will always forget because I understand that every time it's a little something more to become. Charlotte was right sometimes I do dream, but only sometimes.; [a.] Great Meadows, NJ

MATTHEW, PETER

[b.] February 14, 1970, Des Moines, IA; [p.] Peter Johnson, Elaine Johnson; [ed.] New Hampton High; [occ.] Musician, Writer; [oth. writ.] A book of poetry currently to be published. Lyrics to several recorded songs.; [pers.] I write from personal experience, as well as experiences around me. I find that people generally relate to that which is real.; [a.] Des Moines, IA

MATTHEWS JR., REID

[pen.] R.A. Matthews II; [b.] February 16, 1976, Hartford; [p.] Reid and Patricia Matthews; [ed.] Ellington High, currently a sophomore at the University of Connecticut, majoring in English and Journalism; [occ.] Part-time manager at local movie theater, hope to be fiction writer/poet after college; [memb.] Member of the Keebler Adopt-A-Penguin Program; [oth. writ.] Editorialist for college newspaper, Daily Campus, trying to sell first manuscript; [pers.] I strive to reflect solitude and death along with humor in my writing. I have been influenced by McMurtry, Whitman, Salinger, and Frost.; [a.] Ellington, CT

MATTHEWS, KEN

[b.] August 11, 1959, Montpelier, ID; [p.] Al and Carol Matthews; [m.] Lezli Matthews, September 18, 1992; [ch.] 5 Daughters, 1 Son; [ed.] Green River High, Weber State Univ.; [occ.] Flight Nurse, Emergency Room Nurse, University of Utah Medical Center; [memb.] National Flight Nurses Association, Emergency Nurses Association; [oth. writ.] Article for the Journal of Emergency Nursing; [a.] Sandy, UT

MAY, JOSHUA

[b.] February 29, 1976, Apple Valley, CA; [p.] Chip and Karen May; [ed.] Currently attending San Diego State University graduated from Hesperia High; [occ.] Student at San Diego State University; [oth. writ.] Many unpublished poems, sayings; [a.] Victorville, CA

MAY, SERA LOUIZA SMITH

[pen.] Sera May; [b.] December 7, 1922, Sugar Grove, WV; [p.] Douglas Smith, Maude Smith; [m.] Clement May, April 4, 1953; [ch.] Michael Anderson, Bonnie Rosemary and Douglas Albert; [occ.] Domestic Engineer; [pers.] I had two sisters and four brothers. Mary Smith inspired me to write this poem.; [a.] Cranberry Township, PA

MAYES, RUSSELL

[b.] January 21, 1958, Elmira, NY; [p.] Russell Mayes, Marguerite Mayes; [ed.] Canisted Central High - NY Wildwood Career Center - NY Pima Community College - AZ USAF - Electronics; [occ.] Actor, Writer, Producer; [memb.] Toastmasters, Screen Actors Guild American Federation of Television Artists; [hon.] Arizona Associated Press Citation Hands Across America Daughter of American Revolution Citizenship Award; [oth. writ.] Screen plays "The Shroud", "The Cabin", "Battle Board", "Order of the Wolf"; [pers.] The limitation of the human spirit is only limited to the limits that you limit it to.; [a.] Northridge, CA

MAYNARD, EVA L.

[b.] April 28, 1976, Boston; [p.] Shirley and Edward Maynard; [ed.] Boston English High School, Boston College; [occ.] Student - junior year; [memb.] National Honor Society - English High Chapter President; [hon.] Class of 1993 Valedictorian Boston Herald Writing to Win - 1st Prize; [pers.] My joy comes with the happiness of others.; [a.] Roslindale, MA

MAYNARD, LINDA

[pen.] "Me"; [b.] July 13, 1955, Middletown, CT; [p.] Gordon W. Maynard, Mary Camozzi; [ch.] Scott Borhen, Michelle Capps, Michael Capps; [ed.] Orange Park High, Orange Park, FL; [occ.] Shuttle Bus Driver Foxwoods Casino, Ledyard, CT; [oth. writ.] I have written other poems. For friends and families. I tend, I write when I'm troubled. I always carry a note pad where ever I go.; [pers.] I am the first born of twins. Both my sister and I have a talent for writing.; [a.] Jewett City, CT

MAYS, AMANDA LOUISE POTTS

[pen.] Louise Mays; [b.] June 2, 1914, Atlanta, GA; [p.] George, Carrie Potts (Deceased); [m.] Everett Mays (Deceased), July 29, 1960; [ch.] E. Mays, Jr., Evanette Luton; [ed.] Tuskegee, Univ of Chicago, MA; [occ.] Retired - A Variety of Volunteer activities centered around Iowa Methodist Hospital; [memb.] Many in the past. Currently, I serve on the Advisory Bd of the IA. Meth. Home Care Agency as a consumer representative.; [hon.] Many in the past; [oth. writ.] Letters to the Editor (DM Register) on a variety of topics, 1987-1994. As a Board member I have written position papers outlining my views on particular issues; [pers.] Live each day as though it is your last day on earth. Do a "deed of random kindness" whenever you have the opportunity to do so.; [a.] Des Moines, IA

MCARTHUR, JOE R.
[b.] May 4, 1915, Marlow, OK; [p.] Joseph R. McArthur, Maude Falk McArthur; [m.] Lea Reese McArthur, April 9, 1949; [ch.] 1 foster daughter - aged 15 - 1956 (Jeanne), 3 adopted - 2 girls and 1 boy: Phillip, Maria and Lila; [ed.] Univ. Okla: 1934-38 — A.B. (Eng. major) S.M.U. (Dallas): 1938-41: B.D. — 1941, M.A. - 1941. Graduate Work: Univ. of Chicago ('41-'44), no degree: Social Ethics in Phil. of Religion; [occ.] Retired Teacher: Tulsa Public Schools (U.S. History — World History); [memb.] National Retired Teachers Assn., Tulsa Classroom T's Assn. (Amer. Fed. Teachers); [hon.] Full-bright Scholarship to India 8-wks — Poona University (June-Aug. 1961); [oth. writ.] Personal Letter: The White House, Nov. 1961 — Pres. J. F. Kennedy, Essay: "India, Speak To Me" — 1961, Essay: "Even Thine Altar" — 3/11/81, Essay: "Endurance" — 2/12/90, Essay: "Stature" — 8/31/95; [pers.] I have been given more than I gave in 8 - years teaching Negro-students in North Tulsa: 1966-1974.; [a.] Tulsa, OK

MCCABE, JAMES F.
[b.] June 26, 1921, Bishop, MD; [p.] John E. and Lillie McCabe; [m.] Eunice L. McCabe, January 30, 1947; [ch.] Jay and Ray McCabe; [ed.] High School graduate; [occ.] Retired; [memb.] Showell United Methodist Church, Masonic Lodge - Evergreen No. 153, Retired Director of Home Bank; [oth. writ.] Only a few humorous poems used at parties; [pers.] The death of my mother-in-law, (Margie Lewis) inspired me to write the poem. She was a great lady.; [a.] Berlin, MD

MCCAIE, KRISTINA
[b.] December 25, 1971, Wilmington, DE; [p.] Linda Stiner, John Stiner; [m.] Michael McCaie, July 31, 1994; [ed.] Current Criminal Justice, major at Delaware Technical and Community College; [occ.] Writer at Heart Retail Management for Finances; [pers.] Writing has always been an outlet for me. My pen is my voice screaming for clarity, justice and understanding.; [a.] Dover, DE

MCCAIN, BARBARA
[pen.] Barbara McCain; [b.] April 10, 1968, Monterey; [ed.] Bachelor Degree in Foreign Language Santa Cruz, University of California; [pers.] As an artist in poetry and in painting, I simply release visions of my hopes and dreams, coming from within and released unto paper.; [a.] Santa Cruz, CA

MCCARTHY, NANETTE METSKAS
[b.] August 18, 1949, Illinois; [p.] George and Della Metskas; [m.] Gary Olson, 1992; [ch.] Sean, Lauren and Collin McCarthy; [ed.] Riverside - Brookfield H.S. - Honors English, Univ of Illinois, BA - Honors LAS, Northwestern Univ - M.D., Michael Reese Hosp in Chicago and Medical College of Wisconsin - Residency in Psychiatry; [occ.] Psychiatrist - emphasis on psychotherapy; [oth. writ.] "Custody" poem in the Garden of Life. "To The Mothers Who Have Lost Their Children" in Best Poems of 1996.; [pers.] This poem is dedicated to my wonderful son Collin. He fills my life with sunshine.; [a.] WI

MCCARTY, SHANNON
[b.] June 26, 1978, Philadelphia, PA; [p.] Dennis and June McCarty; [ed.] High School Student

MCCLURE, WARREN L.
[pen.] WLM, wlm; [b.] October 12, 1929, Ozark Hills near Stover, MO; [p.] George and Berniece McClure (Deceased); [m.] Toni (Singer, Actress, Fellow Poet, Lover and very much alive), Christmas Eve, 1952; [ch.] Four (and 11 grandchildren); [ed.] Auto didactic mostly — tho I did hang out for about ten years around the University of Missouri at Kansas City, Missouri, in the fifties and sixties, majoring, at times, in journalism (editor of The University News), political science, history, and semantics. I'm an avid reader (4 hours/day) of non-fiction, especially language studies, and critical essays on the works of the world's major writers, past and present.; [occ.] Poet; [memb.] I'm a loner who likes people — as long as they don't come at you in bunches.; [hon.] From one of my poems — Were Paradise enow Omar a cup, I'd turn it up without a scowl and be content, to wend my way into oblivion thus with only this, sardonic smile upon my lips, and the remembrance of my Love's last kiss, not caring one draught more to quench my thirst, from the fetid Well of Knowledge, nor from wealth, another grubby, penny's-worth. Nor Everlasting Life. Nor caring to leave in the Shifting Sands of fame, one footprint more or less.; [oth. writ.] I have 14 chapbooks (approx. 30 poems in each), and 3 collections (approx. 120 poems in each), of original poetry, from which I desk-top publish, free to my friends, and give public readings in the Detroit, Michigan area. I also post a sampling of my poems (from each chapbook) in the Saturday Review Forum (under the 'The Poets' file) in America Online.; [pers.] I try to look at the world humorously. My pet peeve is wanna-be proselytizers who take themselves seriously. My mottos are: Doubt everything, believe in nothing, not even this. And — Don't ever let anybody pin a label on you. Or your works.; [a.] Huntington Woods, MI

MCCOLLOUGH, RACHEL
[b.] April 14, 1983, California; [p.] James and Martha McCollough; [ed.] Graduated from Foothill Elementary School 1995. Now attending Wells Intermediate; [occ.] Full time student; [memb.] Girl Scout Troop #252, EAOP (Early Academic Outreach Program), GATE (Gifted And Talented Education) Club-Live (Drug-Free Club); [hon.] Principal's Honor Roll (3.9 GPA), Student of the Week (4 times), Student of the Month; [pers.] "There will be no rose if there weren't any thorns." I choose this to describe my poem because it is a burst of reality when you escape to dreams.; [a.] Newport Beach, CA

MCCOMBS, DALE
[b.] May 29, 1958, Cleveland, OH; [p.] Dave and Gloria McCombs; [m.] Joni McCombs, August 8, 1992; [ch.] Matthew McCombs; [ed.] Greenbrier West School High School Graduate. Lakeland Community College - Diploma for Radiologic Technologist; [occ.] Radiologic Technologist; [memb.] American Registry of Radiologic Technologists; [oth. writ.] Book "Thoughts" 1981 published; [pers.] My writing attempts to take every day occurances and relate them to life's larger themes. I also try to point out life's many paradoxes. I believe nature teaches us many lessons.; [a.] Powhatan, VA

MCCONNELL, JOHN BRANDON
[pen.] Warren Shellington; [b.] April 23, 1982, Fredericksburg, VA; [p.] Marie E. McConnell, John L. McConnell; [ed.] St. Anne's Elementary School, Wallace Middle School; [occ.] Eight (8th) Grade Student; [memb.] EPIC (Gifted and Talented Program); [oth. writ.] (I write poetry and songs and stories.) I have been doing this since age 7.; [pers.] I believe age is irrelative when expressing ones feelings. I encourage all young writers, such as myself, to never give up.; [a.] Abingdon, VA

MCDONOUGH, CHARLES
[b.] December 12, 1981, Framingham, MA; [p.] Catherine McDonough, Joe Hudson; [ed.] Eight Grade at Catholic Memorial, West Roxbury Mass; [memb.] CM Forensic Club, Norwood Hockey, Baseball,; [hon.] Brother Edmund Rice Scholarship 1st Honors Roll; [a.] Norwood, MA

MCFARLAND, STEVEN A.
[pen.] Steven A. McFarland; [b.] August 30, 1968, Tacoma General Hospital; [p.] William D. McFarland, Jaye M. Allen; [m.] Mary J. McFarland, July 1, 1995; [ch.] Brian Anthony McFarland, January, 1996; [ed.] Stadium H.S. graduate, some college, presently attending Business Computer Training Institute of Tacoma through 3/96; [occ.] Full-time student; [memb.] Ordo Templi Orientis (O.T.O.), Horizon Oasis; [hon.] 2 Army Achievement Metals, Army Service Ribbon and Overseas, Army Inf. Graduate; [oth. writ.] Several unpublished poems and short stories; [pers.] The social structure must change at its base. Society is ran and based on the ideas of the horde and we are not always allowed to be individuals. Individuals must be allowed to express themselves and the horde must be open to listen. Can any 1 man touch the multitude?; [a.] Tacoma, WA

MCFARLIN, APRIL DAWN
[b.] November 9, 1981, Fort Leonardwood; [p.] Rey and Deborah Rocha; [ed.] Doddridge Middle School at West Union, West Virginia; [occ.] School; [memb.] School Newspaper; [hon.] Presidential Physical Award, United States Academic Award; [oth. writ.] I write for my school newspaper; [pers.] I write for my enjoyment and to express my feelings. My writings are inspired by my boyfriend, friends, and family.; [a.] West Union, WV

MCGEE, STAR A.
[pen.] Star; [b.] August 19, 1977, Colorado; [p.] Toni A. McGee; [ed.] High School, Ultima College of Cosmetology; [occ.] Nail Tech.; [oth. writ.] Two other publishing, one in Famous Poets Society (1995), one in Sparrow Grass Poetry Firm (1996); [pers.] I find writing is a way to let go of things in the past, also take on things from the future.; [a.] Commerce City, CO

MCGHEE, KENDALL BLAIR
[pen.] Kendall McGhee; [b.] October 13, 1982, Greensboro, NC; [p.] Seward M. and Ann D. McGhee; [ed.] Currently in 8th grade at Chickahominy Middle School, Mechanicsville, Virginia; [memb.] FBLA, POP, Cool Springs Baptist Church; [hon.] Reflections, PALS, Honor Roll, Good Citizenship Award, All County Chorus; [pers.] I am influenced by the beauty of nature.; [a.] Mechanicsville, VA

MCGIVERN, KATIE
[pen.] K. Mac; [b.] April 12, 1982, Bettendorf; [p.] Sean and Mary McGivern; [ed.] Bettendorf Middle School, and Elementary Mark Twain. I'm not in high school yet.; [hon.] Just school based. Certificates, etc.; [oth. writ.] None have been published except in the Middle School News Paper. Although I am just 13, I find writing is good for all ages.; [pers.] I usually tend to relate my writings to real life or what I believe. Writing gives me a chance to share my feelings in a clear

perspective.; [a.] Bettendorf, IA

MCGRIFF, AARON
[pen.] Aaron McGriff; [b.] January 12, 1984, Ancon Hill, Panama, Central America; [p.] Chaplain Major (P) Clarke McGriff, Susan J. McGriff; [ed.] Christian Heritage Academy (7th) Westminster Christian School 6th grade at time poem was written; [occ.] Student Jr. High School; [memb.] Kelley Hill Chapel, Usher Board, Praise Puppets, Puppet Team, United States Taekwondo Union, Christian Heritage Academy, Leadership Club, Ft. Benning, Youth Services Center; [hon.] Taekwondo, Yellow Belt with green tip, Honor Roll, Association of Christian Schools International (ACSI), Creative Writing - Superior, Salisbury Fair, Art Contest; [a.] Fort Benning, GA

MCGRIFF, MELANIE ELLICE
[b.] November 21, 1978, Oklahoma City, OK; [p.] Monty McGriff, Gerrie Hibbard-McGriff; [ed.] La Paz Intermediate, Mira Monte High School; [occ.] Nanny; [oth. writ.] Many unpublished poems; [pers.] In my poems I hope to reflect to others my view of life and the simplicity of the things around us.; [a.] Laguna Hills, CA

MCGRORTY JR., STEVEN G.
[pen.] Steve McGrorty; [b.] March 14, 1957, San Bernardino; [p.] Steven McGrorty, Carolynn McGrorty; [m.] Divorced; [ch.] Brittany McGrorty; [ed.] Warrenton High; [occ.] Electrical Contractor; [pers.] True feelings from within are seldom expressed.; [a.] Twentynine Palms, CA

MCINTYRE, REBECCA L.
[b.] March 4, 1979, Albuquerque, NM; [p.] John and Carey McIntyre; [ed.] Currently a Junior at Highlands Ranch High School, Highlands Ranch, CO; [occ.] Student; [memb.] National Spanish Honor Society, Spanish Club, Multi-Cultural Alliance, Students Taking A New Direction (STAND), Choral Group, Arapahoe Road Baptist Church - Active Member; [hon.] Lettered in Music at Highlands Ranch High School, Honor Roll Student, Continental League Honor Choir; [pers.] But those who hope in the Lord will renew their strength. They will soar on wings like eagles, they will run and not grow weary, they will walk and not be faint. Isiah 40:31; [a.] Highlands Ranch, CO

MCKENDRY, SCOTT
[pen.] SM; [b.] February 8, 1977, Cincinnati; [p.] Edwin and Pamela McKendry; [ed.] Sycamore High School; [oth. writ.] None that have been published; [pers.] What is reality? That which we perceive, or the way in which we perceive it? How does one distinguish between the two? After all... every man's fantasy is another man's life.; [a.] Blue Ash, OH

MCKINNEY, BREIGH
[pen.] Breigh McKinney; [b.] September 23, 1979, Brookline, MA; [p.] Rosemary and Thomas McKinney; [ed.] I'm a Junior, and an honor student, at Courtland High School; [hon.] Academic Letter, Forensics, Partnership for Academic Excellence; [oth. writ.] "Revival Season", "Beautiful Women", "The Field", "Church"; [pers.] "Do as you like as long as what you do does not have a negative effect on you or anyone else."; [a.] Spotslyvania, VA

MCKNIGHT, SEAN
[b.] September 21, 1955; [p.] Florence; [m.] Denise; [occ.] Multi-media Artist and Designer; [hon.] Certified EMT-D, American Red Cross CPR Instructor; [pers.] Many things have inspired me to create the poems I have written, mostly it has been the love of all living things, the Arts, and what I have seen, heard and felt throughout my life.; [a.] Linden, NJ

MCKOWN, EMILY
[pen.] "Sunny"; [b.] October 23, 1927, Saint Louis, MO; [p.] Nettie Bell, J. R. Guest Sr.; [ch.] Ray Jr., Bab Watsen, Charlotte; [ed.] Emily Jeanne, Guest Moodys Library - Columbia USC. Music - Julliard USC LaVanne Valentine T.V. Radio; [occ.] Jack of all Trades, Master of some!; [memb.] Baptin Hosp., Silver Spoon TEC, Made and Mowers, LCB etc.; [hon.] Varied "On Request"; [oth. writ.] "1001 Tapes", Poems by the Doggers, "Holiday Membrances", Songs Falling Snow, Music Loves Tranchant USA, Red Cheeriest; [pers.] If we're not doing it over, we are doing it again, and the time still comes, when we need a friend the blind lead the blind, but not as well. And the truth is the best until time foretells!; [a.] Santa Cruz, CA

MCMILLIAN, MARY ANN
[b.] September 2, 1953, Buford, GA; [p.] Lorena E. and Garnet C. Akins; [m.] Michael McMillian, February 14, 1994; [ch.] Katie N. Colvin (11 YO); [ed.] Buford High and Univ. of Georgia; [occ.] Self-employed as bookkeeper and advertising manager for husband's business; [memb.] Buford First Baptist Church; [oth. writ.] Several poems published in local "hometown magazine", and short stories published in student publication in college; [pers.] I have been particularly influenced by contemporary Souther writers, and am cur-own collection of poems around a Southern small-town life theme.; [a.] Buford, GA

MCNAMARA, DORIS Y.
[pen.] Doris Y. McNamara; [b.] November 29, 1923, Abbottsford, NSW, Australia; [p.] Hilton and Hannah Gates; [m.] James S. McNamara, August 28, 1943; [ch.] Carol, Dawn and James McNamara; [ed.] Parramatta domestic Science; [occ.] Network Repros; [oth. writ.] Various unpublished poems, some unfinished; [pers.] I feel that an inspiration from within has to be exposed at times.

MCNAUGHTON, REBECCA S.
[pen.] Rebecca; [b.] January 21, 1951, New Albany, IN; [p.] James W. King, Norma J. King; [ch.] Cynthia King, James Smothers; [ed.] Chadsey High, Mary Grove College, Auto Billing and Accounting; [occ.] Auto Biller, Ray Whitfield Ford, Inc.; [oth. writ.] Flight 255, American Am I, A Will To Survive, My Lord, What Matters, Snow, Mirage, My Gift, Mom; [pers.] My writings reveal human compassion, love of life through time, trials, despair, loneliness, experience, and faith. I am thankful there are such people in this world, given the talent to open others hearts with their words. A blessing, the world itself cannot change. For we feel with our souls and reveal with our minds what and who we are.; [a.] Taylor, MI

MCPHERSON, CHARITY F.
[b.] March 17, 1970, Roanoke, VA; [p.] Leo and Shirley McPherson; [ed.] Lloyd C. Bird High School, John Tyler Community College; [hon.] Optimist's Club Award for Essay, poems published in Community College Literary publications; [pers.] I feel poetry gives a heart to events in our lives that we usually take for granted.; [a.] Chesterfield, VA

MCPHERSON, MRS. LAURA E.
[pen.] Honey; [b.] January 22, 1908, Huntsville, AL; [p.] John H. and Alice A. Minton; [m.] Douglas McPherson (Deceased), August 25, 1925; [ch.] Frances Crane, Joe D. McPherson, John R. McPherson, Zula Kurtz, Mary Oats Vall, Robert M. McPherson, Carolyn Tuba, Kathryn McPherson, Edwin McPherson; [ed.] High school - 10th, Draughns Bus, College Piano, Voice, Elocution, Bible School had recital, sang in four languages; [occ.] I sang in many programs when taking voice. Also for funerals.; [hon.] I am an artist. My picture named the London Bridge. I think is my best. I hope to get copies made.; [oth. writ.] I sent in a poem before won for poet Lauret. I think in 1992. But I couldn't go, so they sent a golden poet certificate instead, I had a reweaving shop, now I'm retired.; [pers.] I try to be as nice to others as I wish them to be to me.; [a.] Nashville, TN

MCQUONE, TERESA ANN GULLIHUR
[b.] January 9, 1955, Las Vegas, NV; [p.] Paul Stanton Gullihur, Gwendolyn Clark; [m.] Richard Lane McQuone, October 29, 1994; [ch.] Kristen McQuone, Lauren McQuone; [ed.] South High, CA State U at Dominguez; [occ.] Artist, Drawings and Water Colours; [hon.] Dean's List, Talents: Sailing, Flying, Delta Kappa Gamma, Art being sold in Galleries!; [oth. writ.] Short stories and other poetry; [pers.] I try to use words as I see my world from an artistic perspective. Humor is my religion for Health.; [a.] Fresno, CA

MCSWAIN, JEAN
[pen.] Jenna Martin; [b.] July 28, 1923, Clover; [p.] Ben and Sadie Beamguard; [m.] Jason D. McSwain, January 8, 1950; [ch.] Three; [occ.] Housewife; [oth. writ.] Poetry I have written for my own pleasure, have a small collection of poems.; [pers.] I love to write poems when I am sad or happy. I lost someone I loved very much, writing about it helped me so much.; [a.] Clover, SC

MCTAGUE, DOROTHY
[pen.] DRM - (Dorothy Riggs McTague); [b.] December 2, Pittsburgh, PA; [p.] Rose Lendl Riggs, Marshall Riggs; [m.] James Vincent McTague (Deceased, December 25, 1982), November 22, 1950; [ch.] Dorothy-Jean and Sylvia-Rose; [ed.] Allegheny High, Community College; [occ.] Retired, Restaurant Owner - now active in Civic and Social affairs doing volunteer work for the Community; [memb.] PA State and Pgh. Lodge, Fraternal Order of Police Auxiliary, Pittsburgh Symphony Association, Allison Park Assembly of God, Regina Elena Social Club, Law Enforcement Officers Memorial; [hon.] Former: Pres. PA State and Local F.O.P. Auxiliary, Girl Scouts of America, Sr. Leader United Fund of Allegheny Co. Ch.M. L.E.O.M. Pgh. "Dunk-A-Cop" Pgh., Annual Regatta; [oth. writ.] Several Poems and articles for local papers, church and civic publications, also song and poem, re: Volcano and "Madam Pele" for Kona Coast, Hawaii, Paper; [pers.] When I was a child, my Grandmother gave me my first book of poems. I was raised in a family of 8 children during the "Great Depression" and quite a luxury, but became my inspiration, I like to write of the beauties of nature, and being a romantic at heart, have written many love songs and poems for my family and friends and my own enjoyment.; [a.] Pittsburgh, PA

MCVEY, DELAURA
[pen.] Laura McVey; [b.] September 24, 1982; [p.] Dennis James McVey, Diana McVey; [ed.] Just finished 6th grade going to 7th; [occ.] Student, Steven Decatur, Clinton, MD; [hon.] All A's, Principal Honor Roll (3 quarters), Presidential Award for Academics, Citizenship; [oth. writ.] A poem printed in school newspaper; [pers.] In my poems I try to think of how a person's feelings would reflect on something that happened. I also like to write about how someone feels about nature or how nature itself, is like.; [a.] Clinton, MD

MEEHAN, DAVID MICHAEL
[pen.] Michael Meehan; [b.] May 28, 1957, Montgomery, AL; [p.] Weyman E. Meehan, Margie J. Meehan; [m.] Melinda Meehan, December 18, 1992; [ch.] Lauren Elizabeth, John Bryant; [ed.] Jefferson Davis, High, Huntingdon College; [occ.] Grocery Warehouse Foreman Winn Dixie Stores Inc.; [oth. writ.] I have many writings that have never been published; [pers.] It would be an injustice not to mention my brothers and sisters, Weyman Jr., Pat, Sharon Chris and Margie Jr. and my nephew Eric. I know that I have been blessed with a mother, Daddy and family that are the best a man could ask for. I thank God for this blessing and I love them all. I wrote about life death, good, bad, and believe one is meaningless without this other.; [a.] Montgomery, AL

MEISTER, CAROL MARIE
[pen.] C. Marie Carol Marie; [b.] May 19, 1970, Reno, NV; [p.] Marjorie Claire and William August; [ed.] Graduated from Newtown High in Newtown, CT, received 24 credits at TMCC in Reno as a Journalist; [occ.] Right now I am currently learning a trade in Carpentry which involves building staircases/balustrades; [hon.] Gymnastics Safety Course, 1994 City of Reno Co-Ed Softball Tournament C1E 1st Place; [oth. writ.] I have written many other poems and have high hopes to write a book in poetry form. This is my first poem to be sent out, so I am proud to say, my first published.; [pers.] The Tree: A symbol of beauty, grounded, yet it hooks the sky. Its roots are like the paths we take, twisting around, but coming together to give comfort, solidity. And when the rains come, the shelter you seek is always found within yourself.; [a.] Reno, NV

MEISTER, MAURY
[b.] August 20, 1917, Tomawanda, NY; [p.] Elizabeth and Wallace Meister; [m.] Meister, Midge, May 13, 1945; [ch.] Toni, Mauria, Donna, Terri, Cathy, Danny; [ed.] School of Life and Living, two years of college; [occ.] Retired US Navy, US Civil Service; [memb.] Fleet Reserve Association, Arlington Independent School District "Mentor" Program Tarrant County Baptist Men's Association; [hon.] US Navy-Honorable Discharge, Good Conduct Medal - Pearl Harbour Medal WW II Victory Medal American Defense Medal Pacific Combat Medal; [oth. writ.] Contributor "Long Day's Journey Into War", University of North Texas, Oral History #836, Baptist Standard "Prayer" Newspapers, Editors...Letters, navy recruiter news releases to local papers, Naval items of interest; [pers.] What I can do to help others will assist in paying the rent for the time and space I have occupied on this planet earth.; [a.] Arlington, TX

MENDOZA, JOEY
[b.] January 30, 1973, Los Angeles, CA; [p.] Robert and Barbara Price; [ed.] University of California, Riverside; [occ.] Student; [memb.] American Red Cross, Kappa Alpha Order; [hon.] Dean's List, Intramural Supervisor of the year 94-95, Junior Honor Guard, Homecoming King 1991, All-League - Football and Wrestling; [pers.] Live your life with honor, with truth, and with love.; [a.] Riverside, CA

MENTER, JOAN E.
[pen.] Elena Fox-Watching; [b.] November 19, 1942, Baltimore, MD; [p.] Deceased; [m.] Divorced long time; [ch.] Two sons, living; [ed.] Some College, adult ed. classes on assorted topics: Jewelry, Statistics, Tax prep.,; [occ.] Quality Assurance Tech. in a factory; [memb.] ASQC; [oth. writ.] Sci. Fi., short stories and a few "dog" stories, some high school poetry; [pers.] I am strongly affected by oppressed people's fight for freedom, fight for basic human rights. I'm 1/8 Cherokee on my mothers side and 1/4 on my fathers side.; [a.] Aurora, CO

MERRELL, WILLIAM J.
[b.] January 7, 1982, Saint Louis, MO; [p.] Duane Merrell, Cathy Lloyd; [ed.] Currently attending London Middle School in the eighth grade; [occ.] National Junior Honor Society; [memb.] Editor of School Newspaper, Scholar Bowl; [oth. writ.] Articles and poetry published in school newspaper and yearbook. Report published in writing textbook.; [pers.] I enjoy writing and hope to have a successful career in journalism.; [a.] Jacksonville, FL

MERROW, AMANDA
[b.] August 4, 1981, Akron; [p.] Debbie and Doug Merrow; [pers.] Read with your heart. Thanks to Jesse and Maryann, couldn't have done it without you.; [a.] Akron, OH

MERTZ, JENNIFER J.
[b.] June 3, 1979, Olivia, MN; [p.] Randall and June Mertz; [ed.] BOLD High School; [occ.] Student; [memb.] Member of the National Honor Society, the 212 BOLD FFA Chapter, and Cross of Calvary Lutheran Church, also Students Against Driving Drunk; [pers.] I was influenced to write by my tenth grade English teacher, Ms. Lipke. And have continued to write under the direction of Ms. Becky Amsden.; [a.] Olivia, MN

MEYER, LAVANDA ROSE
[b.] March 20, 1949, Decorah, IA; [p.] Rosina and Lawrence Guyer; [m.] James A. Meyer Sr., June 26, 1971; [ch.] James Jr. and Elizabeth; [ed.] North High, West Union, IA., North East Iowa Community College; [occ.] Licensed Practical Nurse; [memb.] Member Immaculate Conception Church, Fairbank, IA; [pers.] In memory of my daughter, Elizabeth, who died in a car accident, May 24, 1992.; [a.] Fairbank, IA

MEYERS, JUSTINE M.
[b.] January 21, 1976, Freeport, IL; [p.] Georgina Tucker; [ed.] Freeport Sr. High School, Freeport, IL; [occ.] Taxi Cab Driver, Monroe Cab Co., Monroe, WI; [pers.] To my Mom: I love you and I'm sorry for all the times I hurt you - thank you for being there when I needed you.; [a.] Monticello, WI

MIDCAP, CHRISTA
[b.] August 17, 1978, Jacksonville, FL; [p.] Allen and Sonja Midcap; [ed.] I am currently a senior at Capital High School and planning to go on to Mount Vernon Nazarene College; [occ.] Student; [memb.] National Honor Society 11th and 2nd grade, Church of the Nazarene, Junior Civitan; [hon.] Honorable Mention in Iliad Press Summer 1995 Awards Program. 4th place in SCORES Spanish III Exam.; [oth. writ.] Have been published in two other anthologies; [pers.] "Many waters cannot quench love, neither can the floods drown it." Solomon's Song 8:7a.; [a.] Charleston, WV

MIDILI, ANTHONY
[b.] June 15, 1931, Sicily, Italy; [p.] Salvatore and Josephine; [m.] Helen, August 11, 1974; [ed.] Iona College, BA, Catholic U MA. Eng.; [occ.] Retired High School, now teaching at Monroe College - Eng. Taught at A.E. Stevenson (25 yrs) H.S. in the Bronx - have been an adjunct at Monroe College - about 17 yrs. retired from Stevenson Summer '95; [hon.] N.E.H. Grant-Seminar at Fordham U on Augustine, Hildegarde of Bingen and St. Bonaventure; [oth. writ.] A few poems and an essay on Doestyvsky published in the Iona Quarterly; [pers.] A deep belief that only goodness and love can make us human and happy.; [a.] Hackensack, NJ

MIEIR, CHARLES E.
[b.] January 5, 1929, Perry, OK; [p.] William H. and Constance L. Mieir; [m.] Helen B. Mieir, November 30, 1951; [ch.] Robert, Steven, Pamela Jones and Sharon Beck; [ed.] B.S. University of West Florida (1970), Southeastern Baptist Seminary 1974-1976; [occ.] Retired (Minister of Gospel); [oth. writ.] I Choose To Give the Light (Poetry Volume), Author of Weekly Newspaper Column, "Sunday School Lesson" in Oxford Pubic Ledger (9 years) and Chatham (Virginia) Tribune (4 years); [pers.] Christ is the source of all purposeful existence.; [a.] Oxford, NC

MILES, HELEN
[b.] December 17, 1936, Pittsburgh, PA; [p.] Deceased; [m.] Divorced; [ch.] Ron, David, Kevin, Susan, Tina; [ed.] St. Mary's High, Allegheny, Community College, Connelly Vocational School of Nursing; [occ.] Nurse, Naples Community Hospital, Oncoldgy Unit; [memb.] Natural Resources Defense Council, The Conservancy, World Wildlife Fund, ASCPA, National Audubon Society. International Society of Poets. SCS, AARP; [hon.] Clinical Excellence Award, Special Recognition Award, Excellence for Oncoldgy Patient Care, Certificate of Appreciation for Service - Project Hot line. International Poet of Merit Award, Editor's Choice Award; [oth. writ.] Published poems by Library of Poetry; [pers.] Love is like a garden rose cultivating makes it grow.; [a.] Naples, FL

MILLARD, ARDALE
[pen.] Ardale Millard; [b.] 1897, Lyons, NY; [p.] Elizabeth and Dennis Shaw; [m.] Lee W. Millard Sr., January 20, 1917; [ch.] Doris, Lucille, Mabel, Murray, Lee Jr.; [ed.] High School Author's Deceased December 7, 1994 my mothers poem was written for daughter in law, my wife deceased September 5, 1992; [pers.] Love Church.

MILLER, CAROL M.
[b.] August 27, 1943, Minneapolis, MN; [p.] Gilbert, Margaret Larson; [m.] Robert F. Miller, Jr., Divorced; [ch.] Cynthia, Sarah, Sally, grandchild Troy, Travis, Aunya; [ed.] Stillwater Senior High Columbia, Stephens College MO, U of Minn, Mpls; [occ.] Head of Security Free Library of Phila.; [memb.] ASIS, Womens Way, NFPA, Trinity Luthern Church; [hon.] Co-Chair Library Session Smithsonian's Nat'l Conf on Cultural Property Protection, Library Security Presentation, The

Hermitage, St. Petersburg Russia - numerous Certificates of Achievement; [oth. writ.] Write for myself, friends and family, special interests, American Indian Culture, particularly the Sioux, saving Wildlife, reading, music and golf.; [pers.] Follow the path you choose, not the one others want you to follow. Every person and creature is here for a purpose, respect and encourage these. Always be willing to love, learn and dream.; [a.] Philadelphia, PA

MILLER, EDITH
[pen.] Edie; [b.] November 16, 1965; [p.] William and Carroll Pence; [ch.] Ashli Nicole, Chad William; [occ.] Honda of America, East Liberty; [a.] Lakeview, OH

MILLER, GENEVIEVE O.
[b.] May 4, 1919, Hansford Co, TX; [p.] Gustav and Helene (Jensen) Olsen; [m.] Herbert H. Miller (Deceased), March 10, 1943; [ch.] Audni, Jon, Dion; [ed.] Gruver High, West Texas State University; [occ.] Farming - Retired Teacher, Red Cross Executive, Postmaster; [memb.] American Red Cross, Family Support Services, Evangelical Lutheran Church of America, Amnesty International; [hon.] Academic Scholarships Red Cross Recognitions; [oth. writ.] Poems published in The Southern Lutheran, Images from the High Plains (anthology edited by Craven), A Collection of Poems by the Idaho and Texas Society of Poets, edited by Lawrence I. Thuotte; [pers.] Subjects of poems reflect life experiences, issues of our times, personal tributes to friends, and protest against injustice, war, and exploitation of the environment.; [a.] Dawn, TX

MILLER, LAURA MICHELLE
[b.] August 16, 1982, Floyd County; [p.] Bruce A. Miller and Frankie L. Miller; [ed.] Presently in 8th grade at Armuchee High, Middle School; [occ.] School at Armuchee; [hon.] $50 in cash for "Save the Earth" drawing (grand prize); [oth. writ.] Unpublished, House of Love, Nature, A Pleasant Walk, I Don't Have To Go, Hiking; [pers.] You don't have to be so pretty to win or achieve. Just follow after Jesus and you'll be on the Sid that's already won. You don't have to be pretty to win or achieve anything. Just follow after Jesus and you'll be on the side that's already won.; [a.] Rome, GA

MILLER, MATTHEW
[b.] July 8, 1978, Charlotte, NC; [p.] Thomas Miller, Beverly Miller; [ed.] East Gorton High School, attending Gardner - Webb University; [oth. writ.] Several unpublished poems; [pers.] I wrote this poem on my birthday because I wanted my girlfriend to take away some of the pain I felt for my late grandpa.; [a.] Mount Holly, NC

MILLER, ROYCE W.
[pen.] Royce; [b.] December 26, 1927, Liberty, ME; [p.] Barclay Miller, Susie Miller; [m.] Gertrude Miller, June 28, 1958; [ch.] Marijean Miller, Royce Miller II; [ed.] Ph.D, the George Washington University, MA, Middleburg College Spanish School; [occ.] Retired Teacher of Modern Languages, Gordon College; [memb.] Several Foreign Language Associations, several Genealogical Association, Non-Denom. Church, several Musical Groups (bass singer, violinist); [hon.] These Foreign Lang. Honor Societies (Sigma Delta Pi, Phi Sigma Iota, Alpha Mu Gamma); [oth. writ.] A book and several articles in learned journals on Judalo - Spanish language, literature and culture. Several foreign language texts (literature and grammar), several genealogical and historical articles and books. Several poems.; [pers.] I have been greatly influenced by the lyric beauty of the Poetry of Garcia Horca, by the soarlogical messages, tersely given, of Jacques Pre'vert, and I yearn for a perfect expression of beauty and harmony expressed in few words.; [a.] Gloucester, MA

MILLER, TRACEY A.
[b.] November 2, 1972; [p.] Albert and May Miller; [pers.] Written in honor of my grandmother, Dorothy Herbert, while she was hospitalized and undergoing surgery. She has since recovered. Hopefully this will pay tribute to the trying life she led and for her strength and perseverance. Two traits I admire greatly.

MILLER, VANESSA K.
[b.] April 27, 1968, Crockett, MI; [p.] Mildred L. Taylor and Mack Allen; [m.] Victor M. Miller, October 11, 1986; [ch.] Cherisse C. Miller, Carlos D. Miller; [ed.] Crocket County High School, Jackson State Community College, Union University; [occ.] Insurance Agent for Life Investors (part-time) full-time student at Union University; [memb.] Phi Beta Lambda, Saint Luke Church of God in Christ in Bells, MI; [oth. writ.] I have written many poems but I have not tried to publish them. I hope to be able to get this one published.; [pers.] My work comes from my deep inward emotions. Many times when I'm at my lowest point in life, I get relief by expressing myself to others on paper.; [a.] Cradsden, MI

MILLS, BRIAN L.
[b.] February 14, 1975; [pers.] And the Psalmist wrote: "For troubles without number surround me, my sins have overtaken me, and I cannot see. They are more than the hairs of my head, and my heart fails within me." Psalm 40:12; [a.] Baxley, GA

MILLS, GAIL L.
[b.] September 7, 1976, Tampa, FL; [p.] Linda M. Cooper, Lyle E. Mills; [ed.] Northwestern Senior High School, Houghton College; [memb.] Tri-M Music Honor Society (Modern Music Masters), International Thespian Society; [pers.] "Not that I have already obtained all this, or have already been made perfect, but I press on to take hold of that for which Christ Jesus took hold of me." Phil. 3:12

MINARDO, GREGORY
[b.] January 30, 1961, Allentown, PA; [p.] James Minardo and Helen Minardo, JoAnne Scaghelli; [ed.] Liberty High, Columbus State Community College; [occ.] Carpenter; [pers.] To Debbie Clark who inspired me to write from my heart, and my father who taught me how to love.; [a.] Grove City, OH

MINCEY, ZEKE
[pen.] Zeke; [b.] December 21, 1947, Candler, GA; [p.] Mr. and Mrs. Theo Mincey; [ed.] Albany State College, Psychology Major, University of Illinois; [occ.] Systems Engineer for ROTHR; [memb.] Holy Family Parish (Catholic Church); [oth. writ.] First Pangs of Loves Kiss, My Beloved, Why Ask Love To You, The Plastic Smell of Pleasure, Hello Again Fallen Sky, local publication (Military Paper); [pers.] I try to reflect on the lost souls and loves of young men who fought in Vietnam that the world has grown silent about. Young men who were never young men, but became silent and old.; [a.] Virginia Beach, VA

MINER, JONATHAN J.
[b.] September 13, 1977, Madison, WI; [p.] Donald and Kathleen Miner; [ed.] Madison West High School; [occ.] Student; [memb.] Madison AIDS Support Network and Red Cross HIV/AIDS educator; [hon.] Golden Rule Award for Outstanding Volunteer Service in Education; [pers.] Silence = Death — never turn your head to injustice.; [a.] Madison, WI

MINSON, MELYNN
[b.] April 4, 1975, Salt Lake City, UT; [p.] Stanley H. and Kathryn P. Minson; [ed.] Hillcrest High School, Brigham Young University; [memb.] Golden Key National Honors Society, BYU's English Society; [hon.] Co-editor of Hillcrest's "Expressions" Literary Magazine, Top Freshman Paper at BYU 1993, Dean's List; [oth. writ.] Several pieces published in "Expressions", poem selected by Holt, Rheinhart, and Winston to be published in new textbook series Elements of Literature 12th grade vol.; [pers.] My whole goal in writing has been to proclaim myself to the world — to celebrate the significance of my existence as a unique miracle of the life I have lived.; [a.] Salt Lake City, UT

MITCHELL, JAI A.
[pen.] Jai A. Mitchell; [b.] September 19, 1961, Illinois; [p.] Robert Brehm Sr., Suzanne Brehm; [ed.] Fisher Grade School, Fisher, IL. Oakwood High School, Oakwood, FL. St. Ambrose College, Davenport, Iowa, San Diego City College, S.D. CA; [occ.] Writer; [oth. writ.] Several poems and observations; [pers.] I write what I know and try to write with honesty. I ask myself often what is my motive behind my words? To ease pain? To escape? To relieve my own? To diminish? To Love? Words are powerful. We must honestly look at our motivation behind them and then choose them. Carefully.; [a.] San Diego, CA

MITCHELL, LAVEY ADAMS ALEXANDER
[pen.] LaVey Adams Alexander; [b.] July 21, 1924, Yuma, AZ; [p.] David Adams, Ella Adams; [m.] Palo Alto Mitchell, December 21, 1985; [ch.] William K. Alexander; [ed.] San Jacinto High Sch., Mt. San Jacinto College. I have a lovely daughter-in-law and 2 grandsons; [occ.] Retired; [memb.] 1st So. Bapt. Church of Hemet, CA, Associate of Smithsonian, Associate Civil War Battlefields Pres., Society Auxiliary of DAV.; [hon.] College Honors graduate; [oth. writ.] Wrote Cantata narrative for college in poetry form. Did history finals in poetry form. Poems in poetry form. Poems to make and point in Church efforts.; [pers.] I wrote to express what I find it difficult to say - to bring comfort and encouragement to other. Sometimes I write just for fun.; [a.] San Jacinto, CA

MITCHELL, MARTIN
[b.] May 10, 1956, Shreveport, LA; [p.] Elza and Lyn Mitchell; [m.] Mischell, July 22, 1988; [ch.] Ora Martin and Gretchen

MITCHELL, NICHELLE E.
[b.] August 25, 1970, Bellflower, CA; [p.] Ernest Jr. and Donnise Mitchell; [ed.] Graduate of Cerritos High attending Citrus College in Glendora CA; [occ.] Account Clerk in Finance Dept of City of Monrovia; [memb.] American Heart Association, Save the Animals Association, First Christian Church; [hon.] High School Honor Student, Graduate of Rockwell International Aerospace Honor Program. 1988 Orange County Chapter of Links Miss Debutante; [oth. writ.] Several personal poems, articles for City of Monrovia Em-

ployee Newsletter; [pers.] I strive to make people happy through the goodness of my heart, carry God forever and do my best to have peace spread through friendship.; [a.] Monrovia, CA

MITRZYK, KAY
[pen.] Kay Louise Mitrzyk; [b.] March 2, 1955, Tawas City, MI; [p.] Doris and Ed Rose; [m.] Ron Mitrzyk, June 3, 1995; [ch.] Ryan Fannin; [ed.] Oscoda High School, Bayshire Beauty Academy, Bay Arenac Skill Center; [occ.] Agent for Fairfield Manor Mobile Home Park Bay City, MI; [pers.] I am ruled by my emotions which are often misplaced in the world of reality, so I write my feelings down and share them with only those that truly care.; [a.] Bay City, MI

MIZE, CATHLEEN S.
[b.] April 10, 1959, Indianapolis; [p.] Richard and Viola Mize; [ed.] M.A. 82, Western Illinois University, B.S. 81, Ball State University; [occ.] Speech Language Pathologist - self employed; [memb.] American Speech - Language - Hearing Association, Indiana Speech and Hearing Association. Suburban Bible Church, Highland, IN; [oth. writ.] Poems published in other anthologies; [pers.] I usually write from life experiences. This poem was written in memory of my brother Richard R. Mize (July 24, 1954 - January 21, 1995) during my own healing process.; [a.] Griffith, IN

MOCKUS, TIMOTHY
[b.] December 15, 1965, Menominee, MI; [p.] Edward Mockus, Lorraine Mockus; [ed.] Menominee High, Michigan State University; [occ.] Graphic Illustrator, Walt Disney Studios, Scottsdale, AZ; [memb.] On Board of Scottsdale City Council; [hon.] Athletic Scholarship to Michigan State University; [pers.] My writing is a symphony of words flowing from the pen, from my heart to my mind and from all thoughts within.; [a.] Scottsdale, AZ

MODRZEJEWSKI, CAROLEANN
[pen.] Caroleann; [b.] January 31, 1945, Detroit, MI; [p.] Virginia Modrzejewski; [ch.] Steven, Susan, Julie; [ed.] St. Thomas Apostle Macomb Community College; [occ.] U.S. Postal Service Clerk; [pers.] Love all my poems reflect this most important ingredient your heart must hold love to live life to it's fullest. It really is necessary to "make the world go round".; [a.] Waterford, MI

MOE SR., FRANKLIN A.
[b.] July 11, 1934, Macon, MO; [p.] Dean G. and Edith K. Moe; [m.] Shirley R. (Cochran) Moe, February 27, 1954; [ch.] Micheal, Sherry, James, Frank Jr. and Robert; [ed.] Georgetown High, Cincinnati College, Conservatory of Music, Ohio State U., Wright State U.; [occ.] Teacher; [memb.] American Society of Composers Authors and Publishers (ASCAP) and Ohio Education Association/National Education Association OEA/NEA; [hon.] 1991 Hopewell Regional Exceptional Achievement Award For Work with Special Needs Students, 1982 Honorable Mention Music City Song Festival 1989 Top 25 Finalist Music City Song Festival - 1975 Executive Award for Outstanding Achievement AMG Records; [oth. writ.] Several songs recorded and published by major and small recording companies

MOLSTER, WILLIAM STEVEN
[b.] February 11, 1960, Heartford, WI; [p.] Larry and Jean Molster; [m.] Elizabeth S. Molster (soon); [ch.] William Jr. - 14, Monica N. - 11, Michael G. - 9,; [ed.] Provo High School - GED; [occ.] United Status Army Senior Computer Instructor; [memb.] American Legion Post 16 of Lewistown, MT; [oth. writ.] Lots of poems written but have never tried to get them published; [pers.] My writings come from my inner heart. I try to got people to see the beauty around them they over look every day.; [a.] Geronimo, OK

MONACO, ELAINE
[b.] April 21, 1958, Winthrop, MA; [p.] Marie and Daniel Monaco; [ed.] North Reading High School, Michigan State University; [occ.] V.P. Operations, Centurion Counsel, Inc.; [a.] San Diego, CA

MONK, LORI LEE
[b.] June 9, 1958, Bryn Mawr; [p.] Robert and Shirlee Michel; [m.] Donald N. Monk, Jr., June 22, 1985; [ch.] Michel Lee Finneran - 15, David Nelson Monk - 9; [ed.] 1976 Graduated of Great Valley High School; [occ.] Bookkeeper for Gabriele Library, Immaculate College; [pers.] My poems are all about my personal experiences, and are truly from the heart.; [a.] Malvern, PA

MONLUX, EDIE ANNE
[b.] August 11, 1962, San Jose, CA; [p.] Ralph Reichhold, Lynn Peck Reichhold; [m.] Eric Monlux, August 20, 1994; [ed.] Adrian C. Wilcox High School California State University Chico; [occ.] Emergency Room Adm. Rep. Chico Community Hospital; [memb.] St. John's Episcopal Church, Episcopal Church Women, Butte County Search and Rescue; [oth. writ.] Several poems published in school and local literary magazines; [pers.] I wish to acknowledge the lifetime of love and support my parents have given me. And, to especially thank my mother, my friend, for always encouraging my creativity.; [a.] Chico, CA

MONSON, JENNIFER
[pen.] Jennifer Monson; [b.] February 12, 1979, Barron, WI; [p.] James Monson and Darlene Monson; [ed.] Still attending high school; [occ.] Student; [pers.] I dedicate the success of this poem to my brother Joshua James Monson, who lost his battle to cancer in 1992.; [a.] Chetek, WI

MONSON, JOLENE
[b.] November 15, 1995, Idaho Falls, ID; [p.] Brenda and Robert Monson; [ed.] Currently in the 8th grade as of 1995; [occ.] School; [pers.] I enjoy writing. I might be anywhere when something comes to me. I enjoy everything from reading to horseback riding. I have always been taught to follow your dreams.; [a.] Rigby, ID

MONTUFAR, M. CAROLINA
[b.] March 12, 1971, El Salvador; [p.] Pedro and Carmen Montufar; [ed.] B. A. University of CA at Davis, Native American Studies; [oth. writ.] Poems included in Student's Anthologies and Readers Theatre; [pers.] I dedicate my poem to my grandmother Mama Santos.; [a.] Davis, CA

MOONEY, BRIAN JOSEPH
[b.] March 26, 1955, Jersey City, NJ; [p.] Andrew Mooney, Eleanor Mooney; [m.] Janet Marie Mooney, November 30, 1974; [ch.] Matthew Brian; [pers.] It is every societies responsibility to protect and nurture its children.; [a.] Virginia Beach, VA

MOORE, ERIN L.
[b.] August 2, 1965, Cincinnati, OH; [p.] Mary K. Charrier and Richard Boyle; [m.] Michael E. Moore Jr., October 16, 1993; [occ.] Sole proprietor - Erin's Gifts and Moore!; [a.] Cincinnati, OH

MOORE, GEORGE
[b.] April 8, 1976, Harlock, NC; [ed.] Goose Creek High School; [oth. writ.] Poems published in High School Literary Magazine The Magic Muse; [pers.] If you believe in yourself, even when no one else does, then your spirit as a witness, you can and will go far.; [a.] Atoka, TN

MOORE, MONTE W.
[b.] May 23, 1941, Fair Oaks, CA; [p.] Howard L. and Mabel McCullough; [m.] Divorced; [ch.] Daniel and Amy Moore; [ed.] Clarksburg and San Juan High Schools, Sacramento, CA; [occ.] Courier for United International Investigative Service; [memb.] Gold Prospect Association of America, and the Church of Jesus Christ of Latterday Saints; [hon.] Having two of the best children a man could have; [oth. writ.] Numerous poems yet unpublished; [pers.] I enjoy being able to write poetry that others can relate to and enjoy.; [a.] Sacramento, CA

MOORE, SARAH
[b.] April 6, 1983, Houston, TX; [p.] Marty and Barry Moore and Chuck Lovejoy; [ed.] DeMotte Elementary Greensburg Junior High School; [memb.] Academic Team, Basketball Team, Presbyterian Children's Choir; [hon.] 1st and 3rd in Academic Team, 7 - 1st place finished in swimming, 2 - 2nd place finishes in swimming, 2nd, 3rd and forth in Field Day, 1st place in baseball (1990 and 1991) Most Valuable Defense in Basketball in 1995; [pers.] At my young age I find it a priority to introduce the youth of America to poetry.; [a.] Greensburg, IN

MORALES, PATTY
[b.] December 23, 1953; [p.] Robert and Mary Sapp; [m.] Divorced; [ch.] Shana, Rick; [ed.] Attended University of Indianapolis and IUPUI; [occ.] Warehouse Inventory Specialist; [memb.] "Big Sister" Program and volunteer occasionally at "Guardian Home" for children Secretary on Board of Directors at Genesis II, Inc.; [oth. writ.] My poem "Give Me A Reason" is currently being published in "Inspirations"; [pers.] I'd like to convey, through my poetry, that we all share many of the same emotional ups and downs.; [a.] New Palestine, IN

MORAN, KATE TAYLOR
[b.] February 14, 1949, Evanston, IL; [p.] Gil and Marion Moran; [ch.] Joseph Taylor; [ed.] M.A. in Special Education 1980, U of Colorado Teacher for Denver Public schools, artist, observer; [occ.] Teacher; [hon.] M.A. U of Colorado, Dean's List, President's List; [oth. writ.] Stories, poems, newspaper articles.; [pers.] Skydive! Go for it anyway; [a.] Denver, CO

MORENO, ERICA A.
[pen.] Erica A. Moreno; [b.] August 18, 1960, Salford, England; [p.] Dr. Otto and Rosalinde Blum; [m.] George Moreno, November 27, 1992; [ch.] Katja T. Freeman, Nathaniel L. Wright; [ed.] Sisters of Notre Dame, Germany, Business Administration; [occ.] Collection Consultant with P.B.A., Long Beach, CA; [hon.] Col-

lection Award 5th Place in the U.S.; [oth. writ.] Collection Articles in the Healthcare Collector Short Stories; [pers.] "Why does not honor the penny, is not worth the dollar".; [a.] Carson, CA

MORGAN, READ
[pen.] Read Morgan; [b.] January 30, 1931, Chicago, IL; [p.] Don and Nina Morgan; [ed.] Grad. Northwestern Il., BA Speech School 1953; [occ.] Actor; [memb.] SAG Aftra; [hon.] High School City Basketball Champs 1940. Rufus King H. S. Milwaukee, Wis. Member 1950 U. of Kentucky Basketball Team. T.V. Costar with Henry Fonda 1960 the deputy - over 200 TV and 50 movies rules.; [oth. writ.] Several poems; [pers.] Have been greatly influenced by the ancient wisdom of east, west. I hope my work may aid personal growth for better living.; [a.] Los Angeles, CA

MORRIS, GAIL ROSE
[b.] March 7, 1958, Cadillac, MI; [p.] Max and Elaine Lee; [m.] John Christopher Morris, April 1, 1994; [ch.] Paul and Derick Morris; [ed.] BS in Education AAS in Commercial Art; [occ.] Pres-school teacher; [oth. writ.] Currently working on a fictional book for young teens titled the History Test. I hope to have it completed by next summer (1996).; [a.] Grandview, MO

MORRIS, KATHY A.
[b.] August 1, 1972, Paris, IL; [p.] Kathryn Morris, Bernie Morris; [ed.] Chrisman High, B.S. in Communications — Broadcast Journalism from the University of Illinois at Urbana-Champaign; [occ.] Aspiring Television News Reporter; [memb.] Society of Professional Journalists, Alpha Omicron Pi Fraternity Alumnae, Varsity "I" Association, University of Illinois Alumni Association, Women in Communications, Inc.; [hon.] George Huff Student-Athlete Academic Award, Member of Big Ten Championship Track and Field Teams 1992 and 1993, Varsity Letter Winner Cross Country, Track and Field '91-'94, Most Improved Runner '91, '93, 10th place 10,000 meters, 10th place 5,000 meters 1994 Big Ten Track and Field Championships; [pers.] Everything happens for a reason — but no matter how bad it seems, stand strong — you'll get through it.; [a.] Zionsville, IN

MORROW, SHIRLEY LEE
[pen.] S. L. Morrow; [b.] Medford, OR; [p.] Harry W. Morrow, Leila A. Baker Morrow; [ch.] Darrell W. Bohnert, Valorie L. Bohnert; [ed.] B.A. English/Classics, M.A. English, Calif. Comm. Colleges Instr. Credential in Language Arts and Literature, Humanities, Calif. Cert. Legal Assistant; [occ.] Teaching self computer, Russian Language. Study, read, write. Beginning Gaelic as I am Scottish. Doing Genealogy. Make jewelry-beads, wire work, etc.; [memb.] Past - LWV, NOW, AAUW, Dem. Pty. Worked pro bono publico in legal aid. Member Printer's Union - Commercial Proofreader. Unskilled laborer, teacher.; [hon.] Dean's List; [oth. writ.] Pub. 2 poems in coll. poetry books; [pers.] One must read in order to write. Physical surroundings can be limited - no matter. I try to draw from Chinese, Japanese, Buddhist local temple gardens serenity, reflection, austere thinking and integration of nature, water, stones. Museums provide wonder and knowledge.; [a.] Anaheim, CA

MORTON, JEROME
[pen.] Drake Lynn; [b.] August 20, 1973, Galesburg, IL; [p.] James and Patricia Morton; [ed.] Christian Liberty Academy, Carl Sandburg College; [hon.] Dean's List, Award of Achievement for being a President's Ambassador Club Award for Working with the club; [oth. writ.] Numerous unpublished works in short stories and poetry; [pers.] My time as a writer has been limited, but as with all writers I, one day hope to write the Great American Novel. To strive to be the best at all I do. My area of study has been business or law but writing has been my first love and like any who write I hope to one day be a published novelist.; [a.] Galesburg, IL

MOSLEY, CHANDRA
[b.] January 12, 1957, Richmond, VA; [m.] Divorced; [ch.] Rashida, Craig Mosley; [ed.] Leuzinger High School, California State University Los Angeles - "BA" Criminal Justice, Minor Sociology; [occ.] Principal Clerk Police II (Supervisor) LAPD - Chief's Office; [memb.] Zeta Phi Beta Sorority; [oth. writ.] Several of my poems have been written by request for special occasions, ie, speech meets and school graduations.; [pers.] Poetry reflects life journeys, seen and unseen. Experiences, wisdom and knowledge pouring from ones inner soul. Descriptive emotions changing gears as each new day evolved. My poetry is life, seen through my eyes.; [a.] Los Angeles, CA

MOTEN, TANESSA
[b.] December 7, 1978, Harrisburg, PA; [p.] Alfred and Eugenia Moten; [ed.] I am currently a junior, attending Central Dauphin East Sr. High School; [memb.] Member of Shiloh Church of God in Christ, a Girl Scout, Youth Choir, and a Member of East High's Indoor/ Outdoor Track Team, and Gospel Choir; [oth. writ.] Love Like An Ocean, Broken Hearted, What Do You See, The Black Man the King, True Love, Some Teardrops, Superior Woman, Don't Leave Me; [pers.] First and for most, I thank God, for giving me the ability and gift to write poetry. Secondly, I thank my mother, for instoring in me, that I can do any thing, through Christ Jesus, that strengthens me.; [a.] Harrisburg, PA

MOULTON, MARISSA
[pen.] Marissa Lynn Moulton; [b.] January 7, 1983, Las Vegas; [p.] Phillip C., Lynn L. Moulton; [ed.] Elementary Schools, Kindergarten - 2nd, Wengert Elem. Sch. - 3rd-5th, Kirk L. Adams - 6th-8th, O'Callaghan; [occ.] Full time student; [memb.] Art, Drama, Orchestra, and Visual Arts; [hon.] 1st place in reflection in Kindergarten for Primary art, 1st in Music (midi-board). Many awards from teachers for being helpful and polite.; [oth. writ.] Quarter Horse, Unicorn, Why Wilderbeast?, Autumn; [pers.] I'm only the age of 12 going 13 on Jan. 7, of 1996. Started writing poetry at age of 5 and 6. Continued with all arts of any types. Love computers. Dreams of becoming a writer.; [a.] Las Vegas, NV

MOUZAKITIS, ELENI
[b.] February 5, 1981, Cleveland, OH; [p.] Spiro and Betty Sue Mouzakitis; [ed.] St. Mary Byzantine Elem. grad., currently 9th gr. at Padua Franciscan High; [occ.] Student, volunteer as Candy Striper at Deaconess Hospital; [memb.] 4 yrs. Lil' Sewin' Sews 4-H Club, 5 yrs., St. Paul Greek Dance Group; [hon.] Also Consistently Honor Roll student, School Art Rep. to Case Western, 1st Award - School Science Fair, 1st Place (2x), School Young Authors Prog. 4-H State Fair Rep. Demo Speech (2x), 4-H State Rep. Creative Writing (poetry) Profiled in "Society of International Academic Excellence" volume currently in publication. School Rep. to Scripps - Howard Nat'l Spelling Bee. And now this honor.; [oth. writ.] None published to this point - but have written a couple of children's books and several poems; [pers.] I enjoy best writing about my feelings. I hope to pursue a career in pediatrics.; [a.] Cleveland, OH

MOY, STEPHEN
[pen.] Joshua Austin-Brown; [b.] January 9, 1951, Chicago, IL; [p.] Richard T. Moy, Ying Moy; [m.] Doris Moy, August 19, 1972; [ch.] Lauren Elizabeth; [ed.] Lindblom T.H.S. Wayne State University; [occ.] Mechanical Designer/CAD operator; [memb.] Good News, Via de Cristo; [oth. writ.] Poetry and letters of prose to hundreds of individuals as "jeremiah" and "Barnabas"; [pers.] By the grace and love of a awesome God who represents Father, Son and Holy Spirit. He gave me a gift.; [a.] Warren, MI

MUCCIO, MAUREEN
[b.] May 17, 1971, Milwaukee, WI; [p.] Ted and Rosemary Muccio; [ed.] University of Wisconsin Whitewater; [oth. writ.] Poems published by the American Poetry Association; [pers.] Writing is a reflection of my soul. My experiences in Alaska have been my greatest inspiration. It was there in the land of the midnight sun, that I found the true home of my soul and the nurturer of my spirit.; [a.] Milwaukee, WI

MUNSON, JOSETTE ROSE
[pen.] Josette Rose Munson; [b.] July 19, 1979, Toledo, OH; [p.] Mr. and Mrs. Luther Munson Jr.; [ed.] Junior at Tylertown, Ms. High School; [occ.] School and Carhop; [memb.] International Poet Society Union Baptist Church Youth French Club; [oth. writ.] Four poems published in National Library of Poetry; [pers.] I have been writing since eleven years old and have ever 200 poems in my portfolio. (I am 16 yrs. old) I like to write about pain love and death in this life we live.; [a.] Tylertown, MS

MURPHY, ROSEMARY
[b.] March 30, 1975, Drogheda, Ireland; [p.] Jimmy and Lena Murphy; [ed.] Loreto College Cavan; [occ.] Arts student studying English and History, St. Patrick's College Maynooth Ireland; [pers.] I feel an affinity with Irish poet Seamus Heaney who was a guest speaker at my college here in Maynooth. I admire his simplistic style of expression. He is a man of much charisma who despite his talent has no airs about him.; [a.] Ardee, Ireland

MURRAY, JAMES J.
[pen.] Jason James; [b.] June 17, 1950, Rockville Centre, NY; [p.] James and Adele Murray; [m.] Rebecca Murray, July 21, 1973; [ch.] Brian James, Jason Christopher; [ed.] A.S. Criminal Justice; [occ.] Police Sergeant City of Groton Police Department; [memb.] American Heart Association, National Association Underwater Instructors, Dive Rescue International; [hon.] US Coast Guard Meritorious Achievement Medal

MURRAY, ROBYN
[b.] July 27, 1961, Teaneck, NJ; [p.] Melva, Cortland Murray; [ed.] A.A.S. Nursing and A.A. Liberal Arts Humanities from Passaic County College; [occ.] Nurse, Registered in NJ; [memb.] National League of Nursing, National Dean's List, Phi Theta Kappa, National Honor Society; [hon.] "Spirit of Nursing" Award, U.S. Army Nurse Corps and National Student Nurse Association; [oth. writ.] I've written 300 poems, 40 songs. I'm just beginning to publish my work.; [pers.] Birds who cry when they try to sing, know the pain of freedom. Sing-

ing songs to those in chains ... People should hear and listen! (I love birds).; [a.] Paterson, NJ

MYERS, CALVIN SHANE
[pen.] Mountain; [b.] July 5, 1973, Salt Lake City, UT; [p.] Linda and Dave Myers; [ch.] LeeRoy Myers (Deceased); [ed.] Park City High School Graduate; [occ.] Incarcerated Construction Worker; [oth. writ.] Many other poems and stories, none published, but all important. At least to me.; [pers.] Pain is unescapable. It's a fact of life. How we deal with, and like with our pain shows our true colors. Also there is always joy, joy is in our hearts. Joy is stronger, and lifts us above our pain. It's unescapable.; [a.] Draper, UT

MYLES, ERICKA J.
[b.] November 22, 1972, Nashville, TN; [ed.] Senior, Tennessee State University; [occ.] Full-time Student; [memb.] Member of Delta Sigma Theta Sorority Inc. Member of Kappa Omicorn Nu Honor Society; [hon.] Who's Who Among College Students, 1995, Numerous Academic Awards; [oth. writ.] Illusions, Tribute to The Black Man and the Black Women, My Ebony Sister.

NANTAIS, JOSHUA
[b.] September 6, 1979, Bellflower, CA; [p.] Laurence and Lynette Nantais; [ed.] Junior in High School (will be a senior in Sept. '96); [occ.] Student; [hon.] Creative writing contest at school: 1st place in character sketch, 2nd place in place setting, 3rd in autobiographical incident and 3rd in short story; [oth. writ.] Several poems published in local papers, school papers, a few stories published in school year book; [pers.] Things are not always what they seem - phaedrus.; [a.] Garden Grove, CA

NASH, RICKY J.
[b.] July 1, 1958, Troy, NY; [p.] Juanita Passineau and Richard Nash; [m.] Velerie Lashway, May 26, 1995; [ch.] Ricky II, Melissa, (Step Children) Billy, Nadine, Nina; [ed.] High School G.E.D; [occ.] First Choice, Cleaning Division Foreman; [oth. writ.] Many unpublished poems; [pers.] When writing my poems. I strive to touch people with my words. To make them laugh with joy or warm with love and sometimes sad with life's bitter realities.; [a.] Hyde Park, NY

NAWMAN, AMANDA ROSHELLE
[b.] September 16, 1978, El Paso, TX; [p.] Jeff and Nancy Nawman; [ed.] I'm currently enrolled at Cibola High School, to graduate Spring '96 and have a scholarship to New Mexico Technical Institute, where I will obtain a Bachelor's degree in Engineering Mechanics; [occ.] Student; [memb.] MESA (Mathematical Engineering and Science Association) for Cibola, Spanish Honors Society for Cibola, and I am on the Literary Magazine staff at Cibola; [hon.] A presidential Scholarship to N.M. Tech, nominator and acceptance to Who's Who Among America's High School Students; [oth. writ.] Two poems and a short story published in the Cibola Literary Magazine; [pers.] A person can only write what he knows, but there are no limits to what he mind can learn.; [a.] Rio Rancho, NM

NAZELROD JR., DANIEL R.
[b.] May 20, 1947, Paw Paw, WV; [p.] Divorced; [ch.] Daniel Rap III, Nichole Danielle, Joshua Lee; [ed.] A.A. in electrical Engineering from Hagerstown Jr. College finishing B.S. in Mathematics/Physics applying to Kennedy Western Univ. to start M.S Mech. Eng.; [occ.] Senior Product Designer and Division Technical Instructor; [hon.] I received a Scholarship Award in High School. I graduated "With Honor" from Hagerstown Junior College. I consider having my poems published by The National Library of Poetry a special honor.; [oth. writ.] (Essays) "Water—Molecular Structure and Temperature Effect", Ancient Weapons", "Islam and the West", "Abraham's Sons, Ishmael nd Isaac", "The Chernobyl Catastrophe, Technical Aspects", I have also written numerous other essays and poems. (I have never submitted any of these for publication.); [a.] Saint Thomas, PA

NEAL, MELISSSA WALKER
[pen.] Shoelace; [b.] June 16, 1972, Hot Spring, AR; [p.] Johnny and Brenda Walker; [m.] Chuck Neal, January 11, 1991; [ch.] Christopher Lee 3, Emily Renea 5 months; [ed.] Magnet Cove High; [occ.] Full time mom; [oth. writ.] High School year book, advertisement in local newspaper and on local radio for the country garden,; [pers.] I love children, shoes and fishing. My writings come from within and gently tug at me to be released.; [a.] Bismarch, AR

NEMOCON, JAIRO H.
[b.] April 23, 1945, Santa Fe; [p.] Mr. V. M. Nemocon and Mrs. Mary Nemocon; [m.] Mrs. Maria Mercedes Nemocon, August 15, 1977; [ch.] Miss Alexandra Nemocon; [ed.] Elementary School, High School, UNiversity, Computer School, Hunter College for advanced French and English; [occ.] Teacher of a 10 year old child, father, husband, laborer, and poet; [hon.] Editor's Choice Award for outstanding achievement in poetry from the National Library of Poetry; [oth. writ.] In French (Poetry) in English (Poetry and Children's books), in Spanish (alphabet Book, book on Law, novels, and poetry); [pers.] May God and all the muses help me write incessantly on every conceivable topic.; [a.] Rutherford, NJ

NESBITT, THOMAS J.
[pen.] Lakota; [b.] October 13, 1943, Savanna, IL; [p.] Mr. and Mrs. Kenneth Nesbitt; [ch.] Two, Kimberly, Jamison; [ed.] B.S., M.S., Doctoral Candidate Adult Ed.; [occ.] Educational administration/Counseling; [memb.] Several professional educational Associations, pertinent to counseling, student services, and administration; [hon.] Univ. Nr. Dakota athletic Hall of Fame, several athletic and Academic Awards; [oth. writ.] Several Academic thesis, research papers, and studies; [pers.] Creativity and sensitivity are the "sou" of survival.; [a.] Gallup, NM

NICHOLS, JAMES J.
[pen.] Shamus; [b.] November 29, 1959, Brooklyn, NY; [p.] James and Joan Nichols; [ed.] Yorktown High School B.O.C.E.S. a course in data processing; [occ.] Superintendent of Senior Citizen Apt. bldg.; [oth. writ.] None at this time; [pers.] To live each day to the fullest. And if given the chance to help make the world a better place.; [a.] Yorktown Heights, NY

NICHOLSON, REBEKAH
[pen.] Beckie; [b.] June 20, 1981, WV; [p.] Pandy E. Cindy Nicholson; [ed.] Brookwood High School; [memb.] Bad Club, Key Club; [hon.] A&B Honor Roll; [oth. writ.] None have been published; [pers.] I would like to say that I put a lot of effort into my poems. They all come from my feelings and experiences.; [a.] Brookwood, AL

NIEDERLANDER, GERALYNN
[pen.] Geralynn; [b.] June 29, 1963, Utica, NY; [p.] Marilyn and Bill DeCrisci; [m.] Todd Niederlander, February 14, 1992; [ch.] Ashley and Brad; [ed.] High School U.F.A.; [occ.] Hair Stylist; [pers.] My poems come straight from my heart. I hope that anyone who reads them all will enjoy them, and maybe enlighten their lives, in some way. Thank you!; [a.] Utica, NY

NIEMCHAK, DANIEL M.
[b.] June 3, 1959, Detroit, MI; [p.] Marvin Niemchak, Patricia Niemchak; [m.] Rose Niemchak, July 3, 1995; [ed.] Fitzgerald High, Macomb Community College; [occ.] Customer Service Representative, Kennametal, Inc. Livonia, MI; [hon.] I was selected as an Honored Member of Who's Who in U.S. Executives in 1990, while working for Jessup Engineering, Inc.; [oth. writ.] Currently I have a collection of five poems being copyrighted under the title of "Rose". Titles of the poems include "A Rose Unlike Any Other", "Our day", "Land Called Love", "The Dream" and "The Gift"; [pers.] In life each individual owes themselves three things: Never take anything for granted... be happy... treat each and every moment you are here as it is special... because when you really think about it... every moment is special and deserves your entire focus. [a.] Livonia, MI

NOBERT SR., YVONNE M.
[pen.] Sr. Magdalen of Galilee C.S.C; [b.] June 30, 1905, Manchester, NH; [p.] Leopold Nobert, Laetitia Perron; [ch.] 2 Boys and 1 daughter; [ed.] First Commercial Business College, Theology Boston College, BA, MA; [occ.] Priest/Teacher; [memb.] The Round Robin I belonged to so they asked me to teach them all about poetry. They hired a weekly room at the YMCA and we had a fine lime for the year. Wherever I taught English subjects I also taught poetry had a book printed and sold 150 copies students' poems. Also wrote plays with students and put on 2-3 act plays for parents. So also as a Nun put on shows Sundays of all the funny happenings of the week; [hon.] So liked shows we put on the entire communities of nuns came and the boarders also! Most flattering, when I taught Religion in class gr. 10 all the High School would advanced their chairs, cup their chins over in their right and fall in love with Jesus, Mary, and Joseph. All my last years teaching adults school.; [oth. writ.] We had our own magazine "Echo" I wrote monthly poetry more than prose and came to states and belonged to NH Poetry Society. There at Nashua, N.H. Those in so I wrote good poems and knew rules etc.; [pers.] After a show one night. I told my helper. You did well so now I'm changing the saying: Jack of all trades a master of none to "Jack of all trades a matter of nuns.; [a.] Manchester, NH

NOBLE, THEODORE
[pen.] The perfect man; [b.] January 9, 1957, Greensboro; [p.] Rudulph and Theodosia Noble; [ed.] B.S. - Political Science 1981, MS - Adult Education 1986, MS - Educational Medical 1990, MLS - Candaite Master of Library Science; [occ.] Director of after Schow L. Bessermer School Program Hayestaylor YMCA; [memb.] National Teacher Association, National Media Association; [hon.] Employer of the year Hayestaylor YMCA; [pers.] I God went rust if you can dream it it can be come reality. Be relentless if you don't fail you will never succeed.; [a.] Greensboro, NC

NORFOLK, JAMES A.
[pen.] Skip Norfolk; [b.] June 1, 1950, Arlington, VA; [p.] James and Evelyn; [ed.] Univ. of VA; [occ.] Archi-

tect; [memb.] Omicron Delta, Kappa UVA, Raven Society UVA; [oth. writ.] Magazine article on San Francisco Victorian Architecture January, 1979; [pers.] My poetry most often bursts into my mind complete after an insight. I hastily transcribe it.; [a.] Corolla, NC

NORTHAGE, JOHN ROBERT PHILLIPS
[b.] September 12, 1919, Nottingham, England; [p.] John and Isabell Northage; [m.] Mary Jane Northage, July 11, 1987; [ch.] John, Victoria, Joan, Jennifer; [ed.] High School (FLI) and Technical School (Acme Inst.); [occ.] Retired Engr.; [memb.] Toast Masters International Club "578", Society Of Manufacturing Engineers Chapter #30 South Bend Ind; [hon.] LT Governor Of Year 1977-78 Of Northern Indiana (Toast Masters Intex.) President Chapter #30 1971-72; [oth. writ.] Sam And Stained Glass Windows (83 Verses), The Violet, The Dandelion Seed, The Old Carney Engine, My Thanks, Facts Of Life, Seasonal Action, Christmas Eve, Genevieve, Fantasy Of The Japanese Wind Chimes Birthday Day Present, and Others, The Scottish; [pers.] "Whatever moves me at the time."

NORTHCUTT, BETTY
[pen.] "Betty"; [b.] July 12, 1957, Texarkana, TX; [p.] H. V. Green, Dorothy Green; [m.] Carroll E. Northcutt, March 17, 1986; [ch.] Stepson - Christopher William Northcutt; [ed.] Linden-Kildare High School Linden, Texas; [occ.] Security Texas Eastman Chemical-Longview, TX; [oth. writ.] Personal poems dedicated and given to family and friends; [pers.] Forevermore, the country girl at heart.; [a.] Beckville, TX

NORWOOD, ELMA CLARK
[ed.] Sulphur and Durant High Moody Bible College; [occ.] Retired social worker and secretary; [memb.] K. St. Baptist Church International Society of Poets; [hon.] Salvation Army Distinguished Service Award; [oth. writ.] Newspaper articles and poems, articles in Arbuckle Historical Society's book, "Murray County Oklahoma II" Poem in "East of the Sunrise" and also in "Best Poems of 1996."; [pers.] "Love is patient, love is kind. It does not envy...it is not rude, it is not self-seeking, it is not easily angered, it keeps no record of wrongs.....Love never fails..." I Corinthians 13:4,5,5, and 8, NIV.; [a.] Ardmore, OK

NOWAK, KATHERINE KIERNAN
[pen.] Kassie Kiernan Nowak; [b.] March 3, 1949, Pittsburgh, PA; [p.] Arthur and Dolores Kiernan; [m.] Eugene Nowak, August 8, 1970; [ch.] Kenneth Eugene, Scott Kiernan, Daniel Anthony; [ed.] St. Joseph High, Penna College of Technology - pt-time; [occ.] Owner PP and LL Corp. DBA (doing business as) Dunkin Donuts franchise; [oth. writ.] This is the first poem I have ever submitted for publication.; [pers.] I rely on my feelings, "Gut Instinct" or personal experience for my poetry and children's book that I have written. My gifts to mankind flow from God.; [a.] Wellsboro, PA

NOWLAN, HELEN CHATBURN
[b.] January 4, 1935, Oklahoma City, OK; [p.] Thomas Struble Chatburn and Rebecca Smith Chatburn; [m.] William Taylor Nowlan, September 4, 1955; [ch.] Kathy Lynn Powell, Patrick Thomas Nowlan; [ed.] Classen High School Oklahoma City, OK, BS Phillips Univ., Enid, OK, MATM Webster College, St Louis, Ph.D. Univ Of Mississippi; [occ.] Retired Math Teacher; [memb.] Delta Kappa Gamma, AD-PEO; [hon.] Elder 1st Christian Church, Outstanding Teacher and Mentor By Kansas Univ., Who's Who Among American's Teacher, 1990, 1992, and 1994; [oth. writ.] Church Music; [a.] Lansing, KS

NUCKOLS, PEGGY LOIS
[pen.] Lois Palms; [b.] February 16, 1946, Charleston, SC; [p.] David and Marie Nuckols; [ed.] BS in Psychology ad Economics from MSCW in Columbus, MS some graduate work at Univ. of South Ala. and North Florida Univ.; [pers.] Seek a vision.; [a.] Jacksonville, FL

NUNER, JONATHAN
[pen.] Ian, Ben Mercury; [b.] September 21, 1972, South Bend, IN; [p.] Donald and Kathleen Nuner; [ed.] Washington High Wabash College - Bachelor of Arts, Psychology; [occ.] Photographer, Construction; [hon.] Dean's List, Golden Key award for Scholastic Art competition in Photography (1991), and subsequent publishing of photo in the book of knowledge. Awarded "Best Poem" from the Wabash Review (1994).; [oth. writ.] Several poems published in college literary magazine, the Wabash Review; [pers.] I try to perceive and expose things for what they truly are in my work, doing my best to not be fooled by experience and facades.; [a.] South Bend, IN

NURSE, ERICA
[pen.] Knight; [b.] October 10, 1979, Millington, TN; [p.] Veda Johnson and Arturo Nurse; [ed.] As of now I am in the process of completing my Junior year in High School; [occ.] Student; [memb.] Upward Bound, Chess Club, Pepsters, Acts Full Gospel Church; [hon.] 3.5 grade point Average (Upward Bound), best in Technical Art Expression; [oth. writ.] Poems published in the "Chicago Tribune"; [pers.] When I wrote "Observations", I was 14 years old.; [a.] Oakland, CA

NUSBAUM, JESSICA
[b.] February 4, 1979, Newton, MA; [p.] Marlene Nusbaum, Robert Nusbaum; [ed.] Newton North High School; [occ.] Student; [hon.] National merit semi-finalist, Smith College Book Award (Both 1995); [oth. writ.] Poems published in thought prints, school literary magazine; [pers.] I have always found my soul in the beauty of nature. In the words of St. Exupery's little prince, "come, let us go look at a sunset now."; [a.] Newton, MA

NWOKE, LUZ G. ALBARRACIN
[pen.] Baobablade; [b.] September 29, 1947, Cebu, Philippines; [p.] Librado and Anatolia Gabunada; [m.] Nicholas Chiezo Nwoke, April, 1987; [ch.] Bernabe G. Albarracin, Alexander G. Albarracin, Cynthia G. Albarracin Nicholas Akukwe G. Nwoke; [ed.] AB, BSE, MA in Urban and Regional Planning, M. Ed in ESL, M.A. in Educ'l. Media (Acad), MA in Guidance (Acad), Currently Matriculating For Ph.D. in Educ.; [occ.] Associate in Educ'l Improvement Services of New York State Educ. Dept; [hon.] Academic Scholar - University of the Philippines, UP-MEC Gent Scholar; [pers.] No child ever asks to be born.

O'CONNELL, DAVID
[b.] June 24, 1950, Providence, RI; [p.] Daniel and Marie; [m.] Manuela, June 4, 1977; [ch.] Brian David, Christopher Daniel; [ed.] La Salle Academy, Community College of RI; [occ.] Design Director of Sculpture, Hasbro Inc.; [memb.] International Sculpture Center; [hon.] 1st prize, Christian Artists Guild Members' show sculpture; [oth. writ.] Other poems unpublished; [pers.] The future has never been quite what I expected.; [a.] East Providence, RI

O'CONNOR, ERIN
[pen.] Erin O'Connor; [b.] November 5, 1945, Hollywood; [p.] Deceased; [ch.] 2 Sons, Donovan and Devin; [ed.] UCLA graduate Teacher 1969-1979; [occ.] Massage Therapist

O'HANLEY, CHARLOTTE
[b.] August 19, 1901, New Jersey; [p.] Charles and Emily Brodmerkel; [m.] John O'Hanley, April 7, 1926; [ch.] John Peter and Donald; [ed.] St Mary of the Woods, Ind., Immaculate Seminary, Wash D.C.; [occ.] Retired; [memb.] 3rd Order of St Francis, Our Lady of the Angels, Newport, RI; [oth. writ.] In process The Heartline to Heaven (1st pub of poetry); [pers.] I'm delighted with this and hope I win. Wish me luck!

O'HEARN, CATHY
[pen.] Cathy O'Connell; [b.] August 9, 1957, Louisville, KY; [p.] Michael O'Connell Sr, Dorothy O'Connell; [ch.] Charles M. Jr. and Ryan N. O'Hearn; [ed.] Our Lady Of Merry Academy, University of Kentucky; [occ.] Preschool Teacher, St Matthew UMC Day School Belleville, IL; [pers.] Through my poems my desire is to inspire others to have a personal relationship with Jesus Christ.; [a.] Shiloh, IL

OAKES, DAVE
[b.] September 5, 1954, Lockport, NY; [p.] Lester and Rosemary; [m.] LaDonna, March 31, 1983; [ch.] Chantil 18, Tiannall, David II and Joshua 8; [ed.] AA-Business Mgmt, Attending Senior Cal State San Bernadino; [occ.] Sr. Business Support Analyst; [memb.] APICS, United States Chess Federation; [hon.] Numerous academic and professional awards, listed in several Who's Who volumes; [oth. writ.] Have had about 20 poems published in various books and journals; [pers.] My poems are all the result of intense feeling in myself through my own life and observation and discussion with others. I write only what I feel and realize my poems may not evoke similar feelings in others.; [a.] Huntington, IN

ODUOLA, SARA LOUISE
[b.] August 19, 1986, Houston, TX; [p.] Zee and Esperanza Oduola; [ed.] Sneed Elementary, 4th grade; [occ.] Student; [memb.] Braeswood Assembly of God Church; [oth. writ.] Several unpublished stories and poems; [a.] Houston, TX

ODUOLA, ZEE
[pen.] Zee L. James; [b.] 1956, Lagos, Nigeria; [p.] James and Sarah Oduola; [m.] Esperanza, April 9, 1981; [ch.] Three daughters; [ed.] University of Houston, Houston, Texas, BA Jour. 1983, Master of Social Work, 1989; [occ.] Psychotherapist; [memb.] Braeswood Assembly of God Church, National Association of Social Workers; [pers.] In hindsight, it becomes clear that the greatest satisfaction lies not in the goal achievement, but in the course of striving towards that goal.; [a.] Houston, TX

OKON, JAYNAE
[b.] September 21, 1988, Newburgh, NY; [p.] Mr. and Mrs. John Okon; [ed.] Presently second grader in upstate New York; [hon.] Awards for Excellence in Reading and Writing, awarded for outstanding accomplishment in Sunday School; [oth. writ.] "I enjoy writing poetry very much"; [pers.] Newburgh, NY

OLADELL SR., MARCUS C.
[pen.] Marco Dell; [b.] January 16, 1917, Tampa, FL; [p.] Marcus and Ramona Oladell; [m.] Shirley Tanner Oladell, September 1, 1943; [ch.] Marcus Jr. and Christina Marie; [ed.] BA Degree from Colby College, 4 yrs. at the Hartford School of Music, course in Radio at Midland Radio in Mo., refresher course in Math at U Conn.; [occ.] Retired; [memb.] First Congregational Church of Harwinton, Ct. and Camden, Maine, American Legion, 50 yr member of The Grange, member of the Barber Shop Quartette; [hon.] Came out second in essay contest in Vermont, Dean's list; [oth. writ.] Poem - God's selection; [pers.] I believe if we loved our fellow man, regardless of color, religion, or status, this world would be a better place to live. As God said "Love thy neighbor as thy self".; [a.] Camden, ME

OLMSTEAD, JANE
[b.] June 5, 1954, Washington, DC; [p.] Jasper and Katherine (Boots) Olmstead; [ed.] University of Tennessee Knoxville, Tenn B.S. Accounting CPA; [occ.] Management Consulting Accounting and Tax Services; [memb.] AICPA for CPA degree; [hon.] CPA; [pers.] The best way to learn to write is to read. Always write from your heart and others will delight in your work if you write for yourself first.

OLSEN, BARBARA J.
[b.] May 5, 1936, Cortez, CO; [p.] Herald and Bernice Keown; [m.] George Olsen, July 16, 1961; [ch.] Loren George, Alan Wayne; [ed.] MA Psycho-Educational Studies University of Colorado Boulder, Co May 1979; [occ.] Retired teacher, Bureau of Indian Affairs, Tac Nos Pos, AZ; [memb.] Who's Who Among America's Teachers, Good Samaritan, Nurses Auxiliary

OLSEN, SUSAN ELIZABETH
[b.] August 5, 1962, Perth Amboy, NJ; [p.] Carl and Lucille Olsen; [pers.] The love of my parents has inspired me. I truly believe in the power of words. Writing is a gift which is meant to be shared.

OLSON, ZVELYN C.
[b.] July 13, 1925, Milwaukee, WI; [p.] Lorenzo and Margarita Farino; [m.] Clarence F. Olson, 1950; [ch.] Kathleen Gunta and Jeanette Olson (Three Grandsons); [ed.] St. Rose of Lima and West Division High School, Milwaukee, WI. Trained as a Dental Technician at Austenal Laboratories, Chicago, IL; [occ.] Dental Technician and Homemaker; [memb.] International Society of Poets, St. Raphael Catholic Church V.F.W. and American Legion Auxiliaries; [hon.] Editors Choice Award; [oth. writ.] Numerous poems and several humorous children's poems depicting good health and hygiene (Unpublished).; [pers.] I am inspired by the writings of the early Greek and Italian Poets and Philosophers. Some of my poetry reflects my husband's forty-two years of Military Service. My children's stories are based on the experiences of my children, nieces, nephews and grandsons.; [a.] Madison, WI

OROFINO, KIMBERLY A.
[b.] March 30, 1970, NY; [ed.] Hofstra University, NY Master of Science; [occ.] High School Teacher; [memb.] Kappa Delta Pi International Honor Society, Sigma Sigma Sigma Sorority; [hon.] Kettering Foundation Scholarship; [a.] Westbury, NY

ORSO, KENNY A.
[b.] July 26, 1957, Phoenix, AZ; [p.] Melvin, Orso Vermel Orso; [ch.] Katie, Marie Orso; [ed.] Carl Hayden High, Phoenix College; [occ.] Plumber; [oth. writ.] Drawings for Syn. books; [pers.] This poem is dedicated to someone I dreamed about then later met (Nancy); [a.] Phoenix, AZ

ORTIZ, MRS. TOMMIE J.
[pen.] Tommie Jefferson; [b.] June 3, 1947, Conroe, TX; [p.] My mother, Beate Stafford; [m.] Nickolas Ortiz Jr., June 27, 1969; [ch.] Nickolas Ortiz III and Terrie Pauline Ortiz; [ed.] Conroe High School; [occ.] Chiropractic Assistant to Dr. John C. Kelly for 17 years; [memb.] Washington Hospital Service League Volunteer, New Life Christian Church; [oth. writ.] "I was just a Little Girl from Trenton Street" poem, "Why Did You have to Hurt Me Dad" (book), "Sometimes" poem; [pers.] We must have Love and Hope in our lives. We must have Faith that it will all be alright. What we put out is what we will receive back. We must care about others as we care about ourself.; [a.] Union City, CA

OSBORNE, CAROL
[b.] November 24, 1977, Long Beach; [p.] Claudia Osborne, Earl Osborne; [ed.] Go to LBCC to become a teacher; [occ.] Teachers Aide at Jefferson Parent Center; [oth. writ.] Poem published in Anthology of Poetry; [a.] Long Beach, CA

OTT, GEORGIA LEA
[b.] March 7, 1940, Pueblo, CO; [p.] Lowell and Ada Day; [m.] Sunny Will Ott, August 24, 1967; [ch.] Heather Lea, Apryl, Anita and Craig; [ed.] Moran High, Pittsburgh College, Osawatomie State Hospital Psychiatric Aide II; [occ.] Housewife and Mother; [hon.] Honors for me have been having my poems published; [oth. writ.] Have poems published in Amateur Poet Volumes; [pers.] My love and admiration of friends, family and animals have inspired me. Special thanks to my husband for encouraging me.; [a.] Battlement Mesa, CO

PABICH, MAUREEN A.
[b.] February 5, 1957, Bay City, MI; [p.] Leonard and Bernadine Pabich; [ed.] All Saints H.S., Michigan Technological University; [occ.] Wage and Hour Compliance Specialist; [memb.] Art Institute of Chicago; [pers.] Poetry enables the reader to transcend time and place or be grounded in the here and now. What a wonderful and inspired format for the English Language. Love rules all!; [a.] Chicago, IL

PADGETT, RAY
[b.] April 3, 1941, Defunial Springs, FL; [p.] Mr and Mrs Hutch Padgett; [m.] Sandra Logan Duncan-Padgett, February 3, 1966; [ch.] 2 Duncan (29), Julia (25); [ed.] BS Mathematics, Physics; [occ.] Real Estate Developer; [pers.] Poetry is an outlet to deal with my otherwise "all business" world. This is the first poem that I have shared outside my "inner circle" of family and friends; [a.] Allanta, GA

PAIKAI, LAURA KAMALANI
[b.] May 23, 1956, Honolulu, HI; [p.] Alva Kamalani (Deceased), Susan (Campbell) Kamalani; [m.] Lee Jay Paikai, December 21, 1984; [ch.] Landen Daniel, Lacey Jaylene, Lindsay, Millicent, Lissane Cecilia, Lee Jay II; [ed.] Kailua High School, Cannon's Business College; [occ.] Parent Involver, Blanche Pope Elementary School; [pers.] The poems I write are a window to my soul and a mirror of the common experiences and emotions shared by all people, regardless of color.; [a.] Waimanalo, HI

PALAZZI, ARMAND R.
[b.] January 7, 1932, Union City, NJ; [p.] Benigno and Catherine Palazzi; [m.] Gloria Prince, May 26, 1957; [ch.] Robert, Kelly Ann, Kelly Gloria, Karla; [ed.] Memorial High, W.N.Y., Thomas Edison College; [occ.] Tax Assessor; [oth. writ.] Poems, short stories, I novel, all unpublished; [pers.] Use the least amount of descriptive words, get to the point as quickly and as flowingly as possible, unfold a meaningful story, then write "The End" and begin again.; [a.] South Hackensack, NJ

PAMIN, DIANA DOLHANCYK
[pen.] Diana Dolhancyk; [b.] December 13, Cleveland, OH; [p.] Peter Dolhancyk, Diana Dribus Dolhancyk; [m.] Leonard Pamin; [ch.] Louis Peter, Diana Anne; [ed.] West Tech High, Titus College of Cosmetology; [memb.] Arthritis Foundation, nominated into International Society of Poets (A distinguished member) and I've sponsored a young girl in India for the past 15 yrs.; [hon.] "Editors Choice Awards," for outstanding achievement in poetry, for "The Parting," in Journey of the Mind, published by the N.L.O.P. for "Stormy" in songs on the wind, also for "Shadow Side" in at Waters Edge. Received International Poet of Merit Award (plaque) from I.S.O.P. and was nominated poet of the year 1995 by I.S.O.P. accomplishment of Merit Award, for the poem "Rain" from creative Arts and Science, in Journey to our dreams; [oth. writ.] Honorable mention for the poem "The View," from Sparrow grass Poetry, in treasured poems of America. The poem "The Parting" was in the Sun Star Newspaper, along with a picture and write upon the front page. The poem "Love No More" will be in Best Poems of 1996. I will publish a book of my own poems soon.; [pers.] "Always give someone a smile, you'll never know whose heart you might lighten. I'm inspired by many things in life, a gamut of feelings and thoughts in regards to many things. Poets use words instead of paint brushes."; [a.] North Royalton, OH

PANK, ROBERTA
[pen.] Mimi Vanderpool; [b.] July 29, 1947, Greenville, OH; [p.] Walt and Rena Conley; [m.] Donald Pank, May 28, 1967; [ch.] (3) Barry, Joey, Jonathan; [ed.] High school; [occ.] Home maker; [oth. writ.] Unpublished children's books in poetry form including my two favorites: Clearlier and My Kind of Farm; [pers.] As a child, I was influenced by my brothers who where moving from a rented farm house, planted little poems in furniture drawers about mice running across the floor. God is not unhappy with me. Nor am I!; [a.] South Range, WI

PAQUETTE, MARJORIE
[pen.] Marge Paquette; [b.] March 20, 1922, MA; [p.] Mr. and Mrs. Ernest DeCoteau; [m.] Lawrence Paquette, July 27, 1946; [ch.] Larry, Ronald, Carol; [ed.] High School - Various College Courses - Writing and Extended Art and Music Studies Degree in Education; [occ.] Retired Music Teacher also Pianist and Organist; [memb.] Am. Music Teachers Assoc. Theater Organ Guild - USMC Reserves Organ Guild - Retired Teacher Assoc. H.A.R.P.; [hon.] Have won honors many times over the years for humanitarian actions! But most important philosophy is too just try to bring love and understanding wherever I could; [oth. writ.] "Tributes" - life experiences - observations - veterans - read in

minutes at State House, Boston, MA - VA Hospital tribute - Holyoke Mass - all Publ. Misc. Tributes to Notables; [pers.] We can never overestimate the basic goodness we find in life and mankind - At this particular time we all should be striving to give the "Hopeless, Hope" - The unloved - Love and People working to promote this.; [a.] Watsonville, CA

PARKER, ELIOT
[b.] May 9, 1980, Charleston, WV; [p.] Brent and Tonya Parker; [ed.] Currently enrolled at Capital High School - 10th grade; [occ.] Student; [memb.] Latin Club, Leo Club, National Honor Society, Student Council Member, WCHS - TV8 Explorer Club Member, Church Puppet Team Member, Church Choir Member; [hon.] Writing Award in 1994 (out of whole school), won the City of Charleston P.A.R.E. essay contest; [oth. writ.] (Help) publish a neighborhood newspaper called "The Maple Tree" - I'm senior writer. I founded the newspaper six years ago. We (staff and I) were featured on the front page of the Charleston Daily Mail newspaper; [pers.] I write from inside of me, I let my natural talents take over. Writing is something I truly cherish and love to do.; [a.] Charleston, WV

PARKER, JAIME
[b.] January 7, 1980, Beaumont, TX; [p.] Mable Harmon and Tom Parker; [ed.] Currently enrolled in West Brook Senior High; [occ.] (Plan to go to College and Major in Psychology); [hon.] (Small Awards throughout School Life); [oth. writ.] Personal poems, short stories, and so on - nothing published; [pers.] I have no secret to writing, I simply write what I feel.; [a.] Beaumont, TX

PARKER, MARK A. M.
[pen.] Dom'ny Parker, Azrael Mortis; [b.] May 6, 1974, Fort Wayne, IN; [p.] Larry and Janet Parker; [ed.] Bellmont High School, Rose - Hulman Institute of Technology (Chemical Engineering); [occ.] Undergraduate Student; [memb.] Alpha Chi Sigma, Aiche; [oth. writ.] Several poems for school literary magazines and a self-run emaling list, currently writing material for Dzound and Fyuhrie (song lyrics) and The Wanderer (Free-form prose/poetry); [pers.] My works tend to be too long for most contests, so this submission is a rarity. They are also highly personal, as I put a large part of my emotions into each of them.; [a.] Decatur, IN

PARKS, JENNIFER KAY
[pen.] Jenn; [b.] May 22, 1980, Huntsville, AL; [p.] Elizabeth and Larkin Parks; [ed.] J.O. Johnson High School, 10th Grade class of '92 Grade Point Average 3.78; [occ.] Softball Team, J.O.J. Marching Band, Concert Band; [memb.] A Member of the German Club, German Club Secretary, member of Omega Beta Upsilon, and the School Band; [hon.] Who's Who Among American High School Students, Presidential Academic Fitness Award, and Woodmen of the World for Proficiency in American History; [oth. writ.] Trying To Get Over You, To Think, Away From You, Day and Night, Valentines Day, and Peace and Love; [pers.] Most of my poems are about my everyday life. I instead of using violence I write my problems down on paper to calm my nerves. When people read my poems their responses are usually "That's true."; [a.] Huntsville, AL

PARKS, TANEESHA CHENILLE
[pen.] Neesha; [b.] February 25, 1980, Cook County; [p.] Willestine Parks; [ed.] Sophomore in High School; [hon.] Good Citizenship Swimming Trophy; [oth. writ.] Poems; [pers.] I only write about the truth and what goes or around me. Most of my writings are about my personal feelings. I get inspired by nature itself.; [a.] Forest Park, IL

PARLATO, KRISTY LYNN
[pen.] Kristy L. Parlato; [b.] March 20, 1977, Huntsville, TX; [p.] Sherry and Gene Stark; [ed.] Leander High School, Sam Houston State University; [occ.] Full time college student; [hon.] English award in high school; [oth. writ.] One other poem published in 1996 issue of a small magazine; [pers.] I love to write, and I appreciate the support I get from my family and friends of my writing. My high school English teachers have been a great influence for me. Thank you.; [a.] Leander, TX

PARR, ANNIE
[pen.] Annie Elizabeth Parr; [b.] July 24, 1980, Lincoln, NE; [p.] Carol and Denny Parr; [ed.] Sophomore in High School; [occ.] High School Student; [memb.] Hart High School Year Book Staff U.N.I.T.Y. Club, Hart High School; [pers.] I share my feelings with those who care enough to listen. I share my soul with those who care enough to read my poetry. I write for myself and for God, but I share my poetry with others for the spirit of the sky.; [a.] Valencia, CA

PARRISH, DARICK
[b.] April 24, 1971, GA; [ed.] John F. Kennedy High School Henry/Ford Community College; [occ.] Stage Manager for Television; [memb.] Member of the Directors Guild of America (DGA); [pers.] There is nothing like the fluid of poetry. Like a river joining two seas, it brings together the depths of man.; [a.] Anaheim Hills, CA

PATENTE, SUZETTE MICHELLE
[pen.] Maigret - Jensin; [b.] February 21, 1949, PA; [p.] Rose and Robert Marcel Patente; [ed.] George Washington High, The Jay Dash School of Dance (Certified of Teaching) The Community College of Philadelphia (Associates Degree in Library Science); [occ.] Story - Writer and Performing Artist; [memb.] Twenty-seven year member of Nichiren Shoshu of America, a Buddist organization for value creation for value creation and human revolution; [hon.] Royalties are for Drug and Alcohol Rehabilitation in America, especially Street alcoholism Prison System Reconstruction, Orphanayed Child Prostitution, Teenage Runaways and lastly - the shelter and protection of Street Prostitutes; [oth. writ.] (1) Umbrians Poetica, Poetry and Lyric Myth, (2) The Guards of Matilde, selected poems, (3) My Father was a frenchman, mystical short story and mine, (4) The Lollipop Man, selected mystical short stories and mines; [pers.] I should like to make an impact regarding social systems - their value and importance - social services in particular. It is imperative that they continue for the sake of our poor and underprivileged. I have lived my work. Fervently. I look forward to publishing my four books (20 years of writing) Romantic and Victorian poets, my pastime.; [a.] Philadelphia, PA

PATTERSON, BONNIE L.
[b.] December 12, 1948, Showlow, AZ; [p.] Clefford Reeves and Lavinia Truelock; [m.] Charles O. Patterson, June 7, 1968; [ch.] Shelly, Charles, Catherine and Falon; [occ.] Marketing Assistant, IDC, Carrollton, GA; [pers.] My Dad has been one of the greatest influences in my life. Through his eyes I have seen God's handiwork. Arizona fiery sunset and million and million of stars. Even though we are miles apart his love for me touches my heart.; [a.] Franklin, GA

PATTON, CLAUDIA
[b.] May 17, 1949, Tacoma, WA; [p.] Edmund and Eleanor Sayer; [m.] Michael Patton, July 31, 1970; [ed.] Sumner High School, Sumner WA; [occ.] Floral Designer/Wedding Consultant; [memb.] Destiny Cout No. 42, Order of the Amaranth, Warren Chapter No. 178 Order of the Eastern Star; [hon.] Grand Cross of Color International Order of the Rainbow for Girls, Lions Club Reg. Award Peace Essay Contest 1967, Past Royal Matron-Amaranth, Past Matron-Eastern Star; [oth. writ.] Poetry written for Fraternal Organizations, currently working on a collection of short stories for a Children's Book; [pers.] I try through my writing to reflect the hopes and dreams of children of all ages. A position attitude is one of the most important elements in my work.; [a.] Tacoma, WA

PAYNE, JACQUELYN
[pen.] Jackie; [b.] December 2, 1918, Brewton, AL; [p.] Thomas W. and Melissa Augusta Page; [m.] Seldon H. Payne, September 12, 1952; [ch.] Cherri Payne Graham; [ed.] High School, some non - Credit Courses American University; [occ.] Retired from D.C. Government - Laurel Maryland; [memb.] First Presbyterian Church, Church Circle - St. Peter, FL. Com. Committee - Leader of Prayer Chain at my church 11 years; [hon.] Two "outstanding performance ratings" while working D.C. Gov. many letters of commendation during working years. Worked with retarded children, volunteer cheer leading group several years; [oth. writ.] Poems for own enjoyment and given to friends and family members as a "hobby."; [pers.] Love to write poem "Off Toys of Head" and never change them. "Be Happy" is what I like to do and play country music.; [a.] Saint Petersburg, FL

PAYNE, MICHELLE LEE
[b.] August 2, 1978, Panama City, FL; [p.] Lee Payne, Georgette and Jim Brown (step father); [ed.] Ocean Springs High School, D'Iberville High School; [occ.] Student: Senior at D'Iberville High School in D'Iberville, MS; [memb.] Art Club, Baptist Church, Band- 6 years, Captain of flag team 95-96; [hon.] Who's Who Among American H.S. students, U.S Achievement Academy National Awards for Art, Honor roll student. Other poems have been published; [oth. writ.] Other poems have been published in a school newspaper and another anthology. They also have been in the final round of judging; [pers.] My feelings have influenced my poems. It's surprising to see a person can understand their feelings better after. They write a poem expressing their thoughts.; [a.] Biloxi, MS

PAYNE, MISTY
[b.] January 16, 1980, Dallas, TX; [p.] Pearl Payne and father unknown; [ed.] I'm a sophomore at H. Grady Spruce High School; [memb.] Youth Leadership Dallas, YW-Teens; [hon.] Several awards for poems I have written; [pers.] I express the kind of person I am in my writing. I am influenced by my friends, who is my true family; [a.] Dallas, TX

PEACE, DONNY BRUCE
[b.] November 14, 1974, Southern, CA; [p.] Doug and Linda Peace; [m.] Forthcoming; [ed.] Graduated High School in Southern Oregon; [occ.] Navy Medical Corpsman; [pers.] The time has come to talk of many things, shoes, ships, sealing wax, cabbages, and rings: Why the sea is boiling hot and whether pigs have wings. Lewis

Carrol.; [a.] Arants Pass, OR

PEACH, RUBYE D.
[b.] Tuscumbia, AL; [p.] Rev. and Mrs. John A. Doss; [m.] Matthew Peach; [ch.] 3 Adults (Clifford, Marc, Sheri); [ed.] Master's Degree in Reading Education Wayne State University Detroit, MI; [occ.] Retired Classroom Teacher; [memb.] Pi Lambda Theta Honor Society, American Federation of Teachers International Society of Poets, Bethel AME Church, Lesley Temple Christian Methodist Church; [hon.] Outstanding Woman of America Real Woman of the Year Award, National Honor Society, Distinguished Member of International Society of Poets; [pers.] I strongly believe that beauty, honesty, decency, truth and kindness are profound values and characteristics that all persons should be exposed to. The greatest tragedy of life is when one has not been touched by or shown this gifts.; [a.] Kansas City, MO

PEARCE-SHANE, DAVID
[b.] October 3, 1957, Glen Cove, NY; [m.] Sheree Pearce-Shane, September 3, 1993; [ed.] International School of Kuala Lumpor, Malaysia American Community School, Addis Ababa, Ethiopia, Adelphi University, Garden City, NY; [occ.] Branch Manager, Linosey Morden Clain Service; [hon.] Magna Cum Laude Graduate; [oth. writ.] Composer of over 100 songs; [pers.] "The secret of life is enjoying the passage of tine". "And in the end the love you take is equal to the love you make."; [a.] Forty Fort, PA

PEARSON, MARCIMEA MONIQUE
[pen.] Marcy; [b.] September 9, 1978, U.S. Army Landstuhl, Germany; [ed.] High School Senior Buffalo Academy of Visual and Performing Arts; [occ.] Music Teacher Consisting of Violin, and Piano, Flute; [hon.] Junior Miss America City Queen Buffalo New York, NAACP Act - So Awards in Drama, Contemporary and Classical Violin and Flute. Common Council Award, Omega, Phi Fraternity Talent Hunt Delta Jabberwock Award, Erie Country chapter of Limks Awards, Miss Prince of Peace 1992-1994 C.O.G.I.C.; [oth. writ.] 20 other poems; [pers.] As I climb I want others to climb with me. Only God and knowledge can make me admonish life for what it is. In my writing I strive to reach the mind, heart, and soul and every man, women, boy and girl. May God Bless.; [a.] Buffalo, NY

PEARSON, PATTI
[b.] January 2, 1956, Rennsalaer, IN; [p.] Ernest and Anita Howard; [m.] Rodney W. Pearson, September 2, 1977; [ch.] (2) Ryan (11), Hillary (8); [ed.] BSN - Bachelors Degree in Nursing; [occ.] (RN) Taking a Break from Nursing at this Time; [memb.] (1) St. Stephen Lutheran Church Council member, (2) Member of Sunday School Staff (5.6th grade teacher), (3) Rainbows Facilitator; [oth. writ.] I have written a children's book - yet to be published; [pers.] I write most of my poetry to express my deepest emotions. Many of my poems reflect tender memories of my childhood or of current moments with my children and husband.; [a.] Sylvania, OH

PEASE, RONALD
[b.] August 13, 1961, Revere, MA; [p.] Walter Pease, Helen Pease; [ed.] St. Mary's Regional High ITT Technical Institute; [occ.] Automotive Technician/Service Advisor; [pers.] Poems and writings are the expression of the human condition. Poems unmask the exterior, which allows ourselves to reflect upon and glimpse into the interior - the soul.; [a.] East Boston, MA

PEDICINI, MATT
[pen.] Infectious Soul; [b.] September 27, 1973, Long Island; [ed.] E. Meadow H.S., Nassau CC, Oneonta St., Cortland St.; [occ.] Home Improvements; [oth. writ.] Personal notebooks filled with knowledge about life; [pers.] One who is fulfilled can help another man become fulfilled. A person who listens can accomplish all that he wants.; [a.] East Meadow, NY

PENN, RICHETTA E.
[b.] July 7, 1971, Saylorsburg, PA; [p.] Richard W. Penn and Patricia E. Cooper; [m.] Frederick R. Curio Jr. (Significant other); [ed.] Pleasant Valley H.S., Northampton Community College; [occ.] Portrait Photographer; [oth. writ.] Several poems written for personal gratification and others printed in local literary papers and magazines; [pers.] I would like this opportunity to thank some very special people. First, Mother, I know at times it was hard for you to encourage me for various reasons. My deepest respect and gratitude. And, Fred, thank you for loving me. I will love you always.; [a.] Allentown, PA

PERCIVAL, KATHLEEN L.
[b.] October 20, 1953, Toledo, OH; [p.] Paul Neuser, Joan Neuser; [ch.] Gabriel, Kristina, Jesse; [ed.] Notre Dame Academy, The University of Toledo; [occ.] Elementary Teacher, Toledo Public Schools; [memb.] Toledo Federation of Teachers; [hon.] Graduated Cum Laude, President's List, Dean's List; [pers.] Writing is a creative process that I thoroughly enjoy, because through language I can express thoughts and emotions or paint word pictures to reflect the beauty and wonder in the world around me.; [a.] Toledo, OH

PEREIRA, MAUREEN O'NEAL
[b.] October 3, 1935, Yale, OK; [p.] John Wesley O'Neal, Audie Marie Corley; [m.] Mario Alberto Pereira; [ch.] Judy Lavonne Gammon, John Thomas Childs; [ed.] Bachelor of Liberal Studies, St. Edwards University, Austin, TX; [occ.] Data Systems Specialist, Lockheed Corp.; [oth. writ.] Short story, "Rancho Deo Volente"; [a.] Austin, TX

PERIFIMOS, MARY M.
[b.] Queens, NY; [p.] Harry and Georgia Perifimos (deceased); [ed.] BA-Hunter College; [occ.] Administrative Asst. to the Exec. Dir. of a Philanthropic Foundation; [hon.] Dean's List; [oth. writ.] "The Flame and the Fire" which is printed in "Reflections of Light" and an anthology of love poems entitled "Poems from the Heart"; [pers.] As I mentioned in "Reflections of Light" I like to express my feelings of joy and pain through my poems, and lyrics in both English and Greek.; [a.] New York, NY

PERREAULT, JOY
[b.] April 18, 1977, Davenport, IA; [p.] Jim and Sharon Perreault; [ed.] I graduated from Davenport Central High School in 1995 and am how attending Scott Community College; [occ.] Full time College Student; [memb.] I was a member of "Who's Who Among American High School Students"; [hon.] I was awarded with first honors upon graduation from high school, and I am now on the Dean's List in College; [oth. writ.] I have a large collection of writings that I hope will be published some day.; [pers.] I'd like to dedicate this poem, my first published poem, to my my sister, Robin, who is also my best friend.; [a.] Davenport, IA

PERRIN, VERONICA
[pen.] Miranda; [b.] August 12, 1972, Hammond; [p.] Rosalie Costanza - mother; [m.] Paul Brice Perrin, February 9, 1994; [ch.] Savannah Breeauna Perrin; [ed.] Completed high school, on Job Training Management; [occ.] Bookkeeper; [hon.] Poetry contests, working related awards; [oth. writ.] "The Other Side" - The Spirit Of The Age; [pers.] I have been greatly influenced by the past personal experiences of my life. I close my eyes and become another whom has suffered so greatly, wake-up, and begin to explore my imagination.; [a.] Tickfaw, LA

PERRY, DUANDOLYN CATHINA
[pen.] DJuan, London; [b.] May 12, 1962, San Diego, CA; [p.] Lillian Anderson-Temple, S./William C. Perry; [ch.] Isaac and Joseph Smith, Arial Pannell; [ed.] Bachelors of Arts degree, Journalism; [occ.] Aspiring Writer, Poet and Author; [memb.] Presidents, Founder, Enterprising Women's Organization, Toastmasters; [hon.] Public Speaking Honors, Educational Honors; [oth. writ.] Presently, an author to a host of poetry and mini novel; [pers.] As an African American woman who has overcome many obstacles - I endeavor to help, encourage and empower those in need through my writing and my success.; [a.] Sacramento, CA

PERRY, LORRAINE R.
[b.] October 8, 1926, Marshville, NC; [p.] James Arthur and Essie Bivens Russell; [m.] Joseph R. Perry Sr., February 12, 1945; [ch.] J. Richard Jr. and Lorenda Perry Thurman; [ed.] Apalachian State Teachers College, Boone, NC, Kings Business College, Charlotte, NC, Famous Writers School, Westport, CT, Various courses and seminars; [occ.] Word Processing Manager, National Court Reporters Assn., Vienna, VA; [memb.] Twin Lakes Baptist Mission of Fairfax Circle Bapt. Church Centreville, VA, former president and vice president in the Association for Children with Learning Disabilities (ACLD) in both NC and VA; [hon.] Listed in "Who's Who — Civic Leaders of the World"; [oth. writ.] Articles re hyperactive children in NC Edu. Journal other poems and newspapers published in a different anthology; [pers.] Celebrated 50th wedding anniversary February 12, 1995. I mainly use my poems as personal notes to friends and relatives, and I often create my own cards and Christmas cards.

PERRY, SHARLENE K.
[b.] January 4, 1960, Bethesda, MD; [p.] Leon E. and Beverly A. Perry; [m.] Divorced; [ch.] Trisha (8) and Melissa (10) two daughter; [ed.] RHAM High - Hebron, CT Manchester Community College Morse School of Business currently attending Springfield College; [occ.] Student - 40 Grade Average; [hon.] Certified in! Correctional Officer Home Health Aide; [oth. writ.] Blindness and Light The Male stripper Big White Pumpkins.

PERSON, LONNIE A.
[pen.] The Spectrum; [b.] January 16, 1950, Virginia; [p.] Joseph Person, Bernice Marable; [m.] Danita Ann Person, November 25, 1972; [ch.] Sharnell, Latefa, Rahman, Talisah, Marjarod; [ed.] Central High, University of Wisconsin Fox Valley Technical College, Kansas City Community College; [occ.] Chef, Show Case Eatery Atlanta, Georgia; [memb.] A.C. Society, Athletic Club; [hon.] Dean's List, Silver Medalist (Food Show Competition), Human Awareness Certificate; [oth. writ.] Several poems and essays published in "The Blue Biscuit" news letter and in "The Community Alliance Newspaper."; [pers.] It is my desire to share

words of wisdom on different schools of thought in understanding love, peace and happiness through the acceptance of life.; [a.] Atlanta, GA

PETERKE, CHARLETTE F.
[b.] October 12, 1975, Milwaukee; [p.] Lawrence and Theresa Peterke; [ch.] Dustin Christopher Peterke; [ed.] Wisconsin Lutheran High School, Redemption Lutheran, North Trinity Lutheran; [memb.] Redemption Lutheran Church; [oth. writ.] A poem published in the book shadows and light; [pers.] I enjoy writing very much. I am truly honored to be able to share my poem with others.; [a.] Milwaukee, WI

PETERS, NEOMA TOWNS
[pen.] (NTP) (Neoma); [b.] October 4, 1909, Walton County, GA; [p.] John Towns - Nellie Towns; [m.] R. S. Peters, November 11, 1929; [ch.] Evelyn Peters - Norman S. Peters; [ed.] A and M College Bostwick - High School; [occ.] Retired; [oth. writ.] Two short stories several poems (none published).

PETERSEN, DESIREE DAWN
[b.] March 9, 1983, Reno, NV; [p.] John and Virginia Petersen; [ed.] Currently in 7th Grade; [pers.] I enjoy writings about the things I write because of the straight and beauty of them.; [a.] Reno, NV

PETERSON, GAIL
[pen.] Gail Peterson; [b.] July 21, 1949; [p.] Martin and Mary Grantner; [m.] Roger D. Peterson, July 18, 1970; [ch.] James Allan, Mark Duane, Robert Martin; [ed.] Fenger High; [occ.] Domestic Technician; [oth. writ.] Several poems and a childrens book not yet submitted; [pers.] I enjoy writing very much. Often everyday occurrences or holidays inspire me. When asked to write for special occasions I usually comply, and enjoy the challenge. My desire is to bring honor and glory to God in my writing.; [a.] Chicago Heights, IL

PEVERLY, NINA SUE
[pen.] Sue Peverly; [b.] October 3, 1928, AR; [p.] Elvin and Ruth (Burroughs) King; [m.] John E. Peverly (Deceased April 12, 1992), June 29, 1946; [ch.] Sue Ann Walton, John Robert Peverly, Lanette Marie Wilcox: 6 grandchildren 6 greats; [ed.] Graduated Corona Adult School 1972 Business College Riverside Clerk Typist; [occ.] Retired Seamstress; [memb.] American Legion Ladies Auxiliary Post 328 (28 Yrs), Life Member Veteran of Foreign Wars Post 2924 Ladies Aux. Public Relations Chairman for, Dis-3 VWF Aux., Post 2924/ Ladies Aux., Hi-Desert Veteran Employment Committee. Past Sr. Vice President VFW Post 8583 Aux.; [hon.] Publicity Chairman for Topaz Post 363 o(Husband organized), Public Relations Chairman on Committee for Dept. NV VFW Convention, in Gardnewick, Co-P.R. for VFW Dept.' of CA Convention, in Ontario 1994, 1st Place certificate in our Div. for Public Relations in Dept. 1993-94 CA. 1st and 2nd place in Div. VFW for Dept. NV; [oth. writ.] Song recorded, The Golden Stairway copyrighted; [pers.] Poem dedicated to all veterans and my late husband for their sacrifices that gave us our Freedom.

PFAFF, DOROTHY C.
[pen.] Donna Lyon Rhose; [b.] February 2, 1954, Great Lakes, IL; [p.] Basil Pfaff, Dorothy Pfaff; [ed.] Irving Crown High, Elgin Community College; [occ.] Illustrator/Graphic Artist; [hon.] Who's Who American Jr. Colleges, Phi Theta Kappa, Dean's List; [oth. writ.] Edited and published newsletter 'Seasonal Silver', published small book 'Astral Pursuit,' several poems for small newsletter throughout US; [pers.] My poetry is most often my personal view of our spiritual connection to nature. My greatest influences have been shelley, WB Yeats and Poe.; [a.] Alpharetta, GA

PFEIFFER, ROBIN TIMOTHY
[pen.] P.S. Niemund; [b.] March 3, 1964, Flint, MI; [p.] Reta Lester and William Pfeiffer; [ed.] Grand Blanc High School, University of Michigan; [occ.] Client Service Representative; [memb.] Phi Alpha Theta National Honor Society; [hon.] U.S. Army Achievement Medal, U.S. Good Conduct Medal, Honors Graduate - University of Michigan, Phi Alpha Theta National Honor Society, Dean's List; [pers.] I search the inner self and society in my writings to express, explain, and help focus in on the important things of life. A person's writings - are ultimately a reflection on one's self - their personal history and their position in society; [a.] Flint, MI

PHELAN, MICHELLE
[b.] March 16, 1974, Pittsburgh, PA; [ed.] North Allegheny High School, Allegheny College, Meadville PA; [occ.] Student (Senior, Allegheny College); [memb.] Kappa Kappa Gamma Fraternity

PHILLIPS, AL HERMAN
[b.] October 4, 1929, Augusta, GA; [p.] Mae Belle and Forrest H. Phillips; [m.] Irene Lawson Phillips, December 29, 1950; [ch.] Alan Herman Phillips; [ed.] Academy of Richmond County, Hephzibah High School, Draugh's Business College, U.S. Army Clerk School, U.S. Army; [occ.] Retired from U.S. Postal Service; [memb.] Lyndon grove A.R.P. Church, Webb Mason, C Lodge, #166, American Guild of Hypnotherapists, 1995 Honorary Member Paralyzed Veterans of America, The American Legion; [hon.] Honorary Membership in several Charitable Organizations; [oth. writ.] Unpublished song lyrics and "Family Poems."; [pers.] I strike to help any organization or person who is in need of the help of God through another of his children, and to see the good in all "Brothers and sisters" on earth.; [a.] Augusta, GA

PHILLIPS, LUSCHENIA NICOLE
[b.] February 28, 1982, Tallahassee, AL; [p.] Sylvia and Eddie L. Phillips Jr.; [ed.] 8th Grade Student Southside Jr. High School Tallahassee, AL; [occ.] Student; [memb.] Oak Grove Baptist Church Strate; [hon.] Honor Roll Achievement in Band Softball All star (Dixie Youth); [oth. writ.] Numerous poems - none published; [pers.] My Motto: When evil lurks, avoid its powerful blow and be struck by its enemy.; [a.] Tallahassee, AL

PHILLIPS, TODD M.
[b.] January 7, 1972, Porotucket, RI; [p.] Patricia and Walter Phillips; [ed.] East Providence High University of RI, B.S. in English Education; [occ.] Secondary English Teacher; [memb.] Board of Directors Walden Forever Wild; [hon.] Dean's List 7 Semesters; [oth. writ.] Several poems published in local magazines, Walden Forever Wild Newsletter, Good 54 cigar; [pers.] My influences are numerous - the transcendentalist and Romanticists are perhaps my biggest ones.; [a.] Rumford, RI

PICKERING, PAT
[b.] March 8, 1952, Detroit; [p.] Norman and Adeline Pickering; [ed.] High School; [occ.] Sales Clerk; [a.] Waters, MI

PIERCE, NICK
[b.] October 13, 1979, DE; [p.] Rod and Cathy Pierce; [ed.] Sophomore in Bluffton High School, several Art Classes at IPFW College; [oth. writ.] The novel "Fiercest of Men," other short poems; [pers.] May the spirit of fierceness lie in all of US. Death is inescapable, so use your God-given talents to the most of their abilities.; [a.] Bluffton, IN

PIERRE, MICHELLE LOUISE
[b.] September 21, 1956, San Francisco, CA; [p.] Mary Louise Wright-Pierre and Robert Pierre; [ed.] Lowell High School-S.F., CA 1974, B.A. and M.A. 1979 and 1993 San Jose State Univ. in Speech Pathology and Audiology, Clinical Rehabilitative Services Credential - 1982, Licensed - Speech Pathologist, 1984; [occ.] Speech, Language and Hearing, East Side Union H.S.D., SJ Specialist - at Independence and Santa Teresa High Schools, concurrently; [memb.] Maranatha Christian Center: Adult Choir and the Drama Ministry in San Jose, CA, Planning Committee of the Daughters of Zion Dance Troup and Volunteer for Youth for Christ in the Santa Clara County Children's Shelter - both in San Jose, CA; [oth. writ.] Short non-fiction story entitled A Sister In Need, in the Dec. 14, 1995 issue of Woman's World Magazine. Current work in progress: A book of poetry entitled, Altars of Praise, Worship, Healing and Deliverance, which will be completed by the end of December of 1995.; [pers.] As a christian single woman in the 90's, I strive to remain faithful, on a daily basis, to my Lord. My desire is to have this also translate over in all that I do, as well as all that I write or create.; [a.] San Jose, CA

PIESZCHALA, TERRY
[b.] November 18, 1948, Hammond, IN; [p.] Andrew Pieszchala and Maxine Bussart Craig; [ed.] Hillsborough High Graduate; [occ.] Genealogical Researcher, Ex-Meatcutter Assistant, former Banker; [memb.] Church of the Nazarene, History Book Club, "Lost In Space" fan club (St. Louis, MO); [hon.] Award of merit, certificate for the poem "Bicentennial Review" written in 1976, from World of Poetry 1990, Golden Poet Award 1991 from World of Poetry, Editor's Choice Award 1995 from The National Library of Poetry; [oth. writ.] Several poems including Ancestors Of Long Ago (in the anthology "Edge Of Twilight"), Astor, John Jacob 4th, Chronicle Of A Fast, Halloween Night, Hot and Humid, Lezzie Borden (in the anthology "Best Poems of 1996"), Molasses and Honeysuckle Time, My Country Grandmother, Old Maid Washes Feet (in the anthology "A Moment In Time"), and Star Dust; [pers.] Good poetry is like a cool breeze of fresh air. Poems abound, but good ones are rare; [a.] Tampa, FL

PISANI, FRANK
[b.] November 18, 1960, Brooklyn, NY; [p.] Andrea and Filomena; [m.] Rosemarie, November 13, 1988; [ch.] Frank Jr. and Angela; [ed.] Sheepshead Bay High and Kingsborough College; [occ.] Manager, homeless Shelter for Women and Children; [oth. writ.] All my other poems have been written, and given, to those close to my heart; [pers.] God's gift of love, and pain, inspire me to write to others from within. In dedication to my dear father, and another to my beloved sister Teresa, all my Love!!; [a.] Brooklyn, NY

PITTS, DORIS STEDMIRE
[b.] April 23, 1946, Maines City, FL; [p.] Aldene Williams (deceased), Leola Williams; [m.] Tommy L. Pitts, April 20, 1990; [ch.] Cheryl, Sean, (Raphael deceased); [ed.] Haines City High - Florida Cleveland State Univ. OH; [occ.] Retiree - volunteer Legal Court Monitor - Domestic Violence; [memb.] United Way, Dreams Snatched Away, Raphael's Scholarship Committee, Mt. Sinai Baptist Church, NAACP, Women Community Society; [hon.] RTA United Way Award, Phi Beta Kappa; [pers.] "Accept" is the key word to your decisions - "Can I accept... change or changes in my life."; [a.] Cleveland Heights, OH

PIZZELLA, EDWARD G.
[b.] August 13, 1932, Hartford, CT; [ed.] Trinity College, Htfd, CT, Class of '54, cum laude, BA degree, Univ. of Conn., School of Law, Htfd., CT., Class of '57, LLB degree; [occ.] Lawyer; [memb.] Fr. Chairman, Ngtn. Zoning Board of Appeals, Fr. Pres., Ngtn. Chamber of Com., Fr. Grand Knight, Ngtn. K. of C., Fr. member, Ngtn. Town Council, Fr. candidate for Mayor and Probate Judge, Chairman, Cox Cable Advisory Council; [hon.] Nat'l. Honor Society, Civitan Award, Beatrice Auerbach Scholar, Law Review, K. of C. Grand Knight's Award, Rep. Town Com. Merit Award, Ngtn. Community TV Merit Award; [oth. writ.] Three articles published in Conn. Bar Journal, poems published in three prior N.L.P. anthologies, "A Delicate Balance" and "Sparkles on the Sand" and "The Voice Within"; [pers.] Poetry is the language of the soul. Only in art can the restless spirit of Man find fullness of expression and ultimate gratification.; [a.] Newington, CT

PLANDER, LYNETTE
[pen.] Lynette Lynch; [b.] August 18, 1962, Arlington, VA; [p.] Cleo Lynch, the late Cornelius Lynch; [m.] Jeff Plander, September 16, 1987; [ch.] Megan Elizabeth, Stephanie Lee, Jessica Christine; [ed.] Briar Cliff College; [occ.] Vocational Evaluator; [hon.] Who's Who of American College and University Students, Who's Who of American High School Students, National Dean's List; [pers.] I like to focus upon my view of society and interpersonal relationships in my writing.; [a.] Ames, IA

POCSIK, REAGEN
[b.] May 19, 1977, Akron, OH; [p.] John and Marianne Pocsik; [ed.] Holy Cross High School; [memb.] American Coaster Enthusiasts (A.C.E.); [oth. writ.] Articles in school newspaper as a journalist; [pers.] All of my poetry is based upon personal experiences and thoughts. My greatest influence is the people who hurt me most. Without them I would have never started writing poetry.; [a.] Cheshire, CT

POE, FLORENCE E.
[b.] January 28, 1943, Dade City, FL; [p.] Howard T. Wilson - Lena M. Wilson; [ch.] (1 one) 30 years old male; [ed.] 1-12 Grade 12 years Business College; [occ.] Work at GNC Nutrition Center - 2 Hills FL/ Weekend Musician; [oth. writ.] Thousands - unpublished in a book here in my home; [pers.] May I always find good in all that I meet.; [a.] San Antonio, FL

POINTER, SANDRA P.
[b.] February 7, Manhattan, NY; [p.] Hubert and Gloria Francis; [m.] The Late Emritt G. Pointer, December 17, 1995; [ch.] Debra M. Pointer, Kimberly A. Pointer; [ed.] N.C. A and T University, BS Atlanta Univ. School of Social Work, MS W; [occ.] Program Consultant, GA Dept. Human Resources and Public Speaker; [memb.] Leadership Albany Foundation Clark - Atlanta Alumni Association Black Womens National Health Project Links, Inc. Sigma Gamma Pho; [hon.] Gold Award - United Way Volunteer Leadership Award - March of Dimes Caring Hands Award Phoebe Putney Memorial Hospital; [oth. writ.] Numerous articles entitled "Sandys Pointers to Ponder" distributed but not submitted for publication; [pers.] People can easily identity with my writings as they are reflection of the innermost feelings, beliefs, and values that drive most of us.; [a.] Atlanta, GA

POLL, LAURA L.
[b.] April 24, 1971, Pueblo, CO; [p.] Leo and Theresa Poll; [pers.] I strongly believe that faith can be a valuable force in one's life. It can, undoubtedly, carry one through a trying today and allow one to see a better brighter tomorrow.; [a.] Pueblo, CO

POLLOCK, SIERRA
[b.] June 5, 1980, Humboldt County, CA; [p.] Barbara and Kent Pollock; [ed.] I'm a Sophomore in High School, currently attending Mira Loma High School in Sacramento; [oth. writ.] Many other poems never been published before; [pers.] "A day spent with one whom you love, shall never be considered wasted."; [a.] Carmichael, CA

PONCE DE LEON, REGAN A.
[b.] November 13, 1980, Harbor City, CA; [p.] Ramon Ponce de Leon and Sylvia Ponce de Leon; [ed.] Pacific Harbor Christian Jr. High, San Pedro High; [occ.] High School Student; [hon.] 6th grade - Yearly Citizenship, 9th grade - Science Fair and Principles Award, 8th and 9th grade Student Council Leadership-Knights for Christ; [pers.] When my poems are written, I am in a state of deep thought of how I'm feeling at that moment. I thank Jesus Christ my Savior, for this talent He has given me.; [a.] Carson, CA

POPOVICH, MARGUERITE
[b.] July 10, 1915, Saginaw, MI; [p.] George and Hannah Witt; [m.] Robert Popovich, February 14, 1958; [ed.] Bachelor of Arts, Alma, MI. Alma College, 1937. Mals - Master of Arts in Library Science, University of MI, Ann Arbor, MI, 1967; [occ.] Retired; [memb.] NEA-R., MEA-R, Kent Co., (MI) Humane Society, Humane Society of the W.S., D.E.L.T.A. rescue of CA, National Humane Education Society, Sils Alumni, Society, U. of MI; [hon.] Alpha Theta, Alma College, Golden Thistle Award, Alma, taught 43 years in Michigan public schools and in U. of M. 4 years; [oth. writ.] Occasional writings in newspapers; [pers.] No matter how hard "The Chips" may fall, there is some humor in life for all!; [a.] Grand Rapids, MI

PORINSKY, MICHAEL CHRIS
[b.] August 13, 1970, Cleveland, OH; [p.] Steve Porinsky and Sherry Dane; [ed.] South High School, Shoreline Community College; [occ.] Building Supply Representative; [memb.] Catholic Youth Organization Football League of Northeast OH, Big Brothers of America, Seattle WA. Chapter; [hon.] Honor and Merit Awards at South High, First Place in a Singing Contest, and a Drawing Display in High School; [oth. writ.] "Solace For A Malrock," "The Other Occupants," "Blind Waters" (These other writings are unpublished); [pers.] Influences: Arthur Rimbaud, Arthur Conan Doyle, David Bowie, Pat Conroy.; [a.] Newburg Heights, OH

POST, DEBORAH A.
[b.] August 17, 1962, Buffalo, NY; [ed.] Hamburg High School, B.S. in exceptional Education from Buffalo State College; [occ.] Owner and instructor of Color My world-a fine arts and crafts program for children and group homes located in Hamburg, NY; [memb.] Hamburg Chamber of Commerce, Hamburg Chamber Education Committee, Color My World, Scholarship Committee; [hon.] Army Commendation Medal for Active Duty, Southeast Asia Service Medal, Saudi Arabian Government Medal of Honor; [oth. writ.] Other poems published in college literary magazines; [pers.] In writing my poems, I try to bring out the mutual feelings that all people experience from many different situations. My inspiration comes from personal struggles and emotional courage.; [a.] Hamburg, NY

POTTER, JOSHUA
[b.] May 26, 1976, Baltimore, MD; [p.] Donald Potter Jr., Janet Potter; [ed.] Patapsco High, University of Maryland at Baltimore County; [occ.] Pharmacist Asst.; [pers.] My thoughts wander in aimless direction, looking for perfection, and only finding rejection.; [a.] Baltimore, MD

POTTER, PRISCILLA E.
[pen.] Pat - Potter; [b.] February 1, 1930, Trenton, NJ; [p.] Judy and Henry - Howerton; [ch.] 4 Patricia - Kathleen - Karen - Christine; [ed.] Dimond High School, Art - School - Elementary Schools F.R. MA. Secretary Wash. DC. School - and the school - of -Hard Knocks - common sence degree - got me through life - so far; [occ.] Retired; [oth. writ.] Many - poems over the years 2 books - black tie and tales - Lester the Christmas Easter Bunny) also some songs - never attempted to publish any - of it.; [pers.] My poem - says it - all as to my influence. God gave us all to preserve - but - man - with - wanting power and greed and wars are taking it all away. A tree a cloud an ocean should be inspiration enough for anyone I pray to these things - not churches. My inspirer - God of all.

POWELL, DEBORAH E.
[b.] September 25, 1964, Buffalo, NY; [p.] Susan S. Nagy and Raymond Worgo; [m.] Kenneth U. Powell, March 23, 1991; [ch.] Sam 8, Spencer 3, Jesse 1; [ed.] High School Diploma; [occ.] Homemaker; [memb.] Various community volunteer work; [oth. writ.] Many other poems which I keep for personal reading; [pers.] I try to live life to the fullest, I appreciate my family and friends. Remember, most folks are about as happy as they make up their minds to be. Don't look for bad in life.; [a.] Ashford, NY

POWERS, SANDRA L.
[b.] August 8, 1952, Eugene, OR; [p.] Alan and Lelah Powers; [ed.] B.S. Geology, Virginia Tech, M.S. Geology, Mackay School of Mines - Univ. NV, Reno; [occ.] Writer, Artist; [memb.] Audubon Society, Sierra Arts Foundation; [hon.] Phi Kappa Phi; [oth. writ.] In-house geologic reports, working on a book of dreams; [pers.] My writing reflects my mysterious workings of my inner being. I write for self-expression. I write to make a difference. I write to inspire, to teach, and to bring us together.; [a.] Reno, NV

PRICE, CHRISTINA
[b.] November 21, 1995, Plymouth, IN; [p.] Donald and Beverly Price; [ed.] Plymouth High School, plan to attend Indiana University of Bloomington; [occ.] Work part time at Price's Village Velet Cleaners; [memb.] Future Business Leaders of America, Student Against Drunk Driving, and the United States Tennis Association; [pers.] My junior year in high school I had an amazing English teacher who made everything we learned interesting. She introduced the early American poets like Walt Whitman and Ralph Waldo Emerson to me. These incredible authors have changed the way I look at things.; [a.] Plymouth, IN

PRICE, JASON R.
[b.] September 12, 1970, Norwich, CT; [p.] Willam and Katherine Price; [ed.] VA Tech, 1992 B.S. Biology; [occ.] Industrial Hygienist, John J. McMullen Associates, Inc.; [pers.] Ultimate Frisbee is good for the soul. Get horizontal.; [a.] Newport News, VA

PRICE, JOSEPH
[pen.] Joseph Price, Joe Price; [b.] January 2, 1979, Cleveland, OH; [ed.] Junior at Lakewood High School, Lakewood, Ohio; [occ.] Student; [memb.] Barnstormers (a theatrical group), Astronomy and Cinema; [hon.] Nominee for local chapter of National Thesbian Guild; [oth. writ.] Collaborating on an on-going political force with a number of my peers, co-wrote two short plays, I also write other, as yet unpublished, works of poetry; [pers.] In life's many journeys, there will be forks in the road. So listen t your heart, and choose the best path.; [a.] Lakewood, OH

PRINCE, MARCIA
[b.] July 12, 1965, Jamaica, West Indies; [m.] Peter Cuffe; [ed.] Currently pursuing a degree in Nursing; [occ.] Administrative Support for VHS of New York; [memb.] New York Christian Life Center, Pastor A.R. Bernard, Founder and Leader; [oth. writ.] Currently taking a writing course on writing for children; [pers.] My purpose in life is to represent the Lord Jesus Christ to the world, in everything that I do.; [a.] Brooklyn, NY

PRUDIC, JEREMY J.
[pen.] Broadway; [b.] May 24, 1977, Minot, ND; [p.] Mary and Larry Prudic; [ed.] Cholla High School c/o '95; [occ.] Actor/Tech for Arizona's Childrens Theatre CO; [hon.] Several Best Actor Awards; [pers.] I like to make people feel a certain feeling that I have in writing my poetry. They may see a different picture or thought, that's exactly what I want. For then to see different with the same feeling.; [a.] Tucson, AZ

PURCELLA, SUSAN M.
[pen.] S.A.A; [b.] March 11, 1949, Globe, AZ; [p.] Butch and Betty Smyers; [m.] Wayne Purcella, January 6, 1968; [ch.] William Scott and Elisha Dawn; [ed.] Globe High School, Rose-Mar Beauty College; [occ.] Office Nurse's Aide

QUAN, JOANNE P.
[pen.] Joane P. Quan; [b.] May 24, 1967, Vietnam; [p.] Kim K. Quan; [ed.] Alhambra High, Concordia University; [occ.] Teacher, Mt Calvary, Lutheran School; [oth. writ.] I do have other materials but never attempted to show others my work; [pers.] I use my passion as a driving force to paint pictures with words in which we can strive to understand the world of love, lust and acceptance.; [a.] San Dimas, CA

QUINTERO, MARGARET M. ABEL
[pen.] Margaret M. Abel-Quintero; [b.] January 20, 1957, Anderson, SC; [p.] Mary Sayre Abel and Arthur Harold Abel; [m.] Jose Luis Quintero, August 10, 1985; [ch.] (2) Nicolas Andres, Sebastian Abel; [ed.] PhD, MA Mispanic Languages and Literatures U of California Santa Barbara, B.A. University of Iowa; [occ.] Spanish Professor, Saint Mary's College of California, Moraga, CA; [memb.] M.L.A., A.C.T.F.L., Phi Beta Kappa, Sigma Delta Phi; [hon.] Teaching Assistant of the Year (UCSB, 1986), multiple recipient of Gulhenkian Award for Graduate study in Portuguese; [oth. writ.] "Sobre Ausencia y Presencia En Trilce" (article published in Cuadernos Hispanoamericanos), dissertation "Ega Beyond Realism: A Study of the Language of Flower in Os Maias"; [a.] Pittsbury, CA

RAGAN, SAMANTHA
[b.] January 2, 1980, St. Louis, MO; [p.] Steve and Bonnie Ragan, Cathy Williams; [ed.] McNeil High School (10th Grade); [memb.] German Club at McNeil High School and Trailblazer (Newspaper) at McNeil High School; [hon.] Honor classes a honor roll McNeil High School; [oth. writ.] Poem published in collections by the National Poetry Society; [pers.] When writing poetry I try to relay some of my own personal feelings. I write poetry mainly for personal release and for enjoyment.; [a.] Austin, TX

RAIGOSA, HEATHER E.
[b.] November 19, 1978; [p.] Olivia and Salvador Raigosa; [pers.] To love is to have and to have is to feel peace. Harmony is felt with the heart. To die for is to have been loved.; [a.] Lattabra, CA

RAJPATHAK, KATHERINE MEROSKY
[pen.] Kathy; [b.] NYC; [p.] Edu and John Merosky; [m.] Shirish S. Rajpathak, August 15, 1987; [ch.] Sarita-6 Timothy-5; [ed.] Manhattanville College Florida Atlantic University; [hon.] Dean's List and College Scholarship (Manhattanville College); [pers.] "Don't take life for granted". This poem was penned hastily @ 3:30 am the nite after my 1st nephew died: (13 days later, on 7-9-92) @ the NICU @ Columbia Pres. Med. Ctr. NYC Decision made to get off respirator (2 pm) Christian passed on-2:50 pm (1hr. later); [a.] Boca Raton, FL

RAMADAN, SUHAIR NAYIF
[b.] July 16, 1974, Richmond, VA; [p.] Mr. Nayif and Mrs. Hanan Ramadan; [ed.] Stephen Decatur High School Wor Wic Community College; [oth. writ.] Several poems published in local newspaper, and college poetic book.; [pers.] Having lived in Jerusalem and being a palestinian muslim it has reflected and influenced my writings. And finally a word to the wise: "Always and forever follow your dreams."; [a.] Bishopville, MD

RAMIREZ, OLGA E.
[pen.] Petrila Rabientz (later on); [b.] February 13, 1941, Cuba; [p.] Juvenal Ramirez, Petronila Bientz; [ch.] Frank, Theresa, Robert, William, and Evelyn; [ed.] Inst. #1, Havana, La Guardia C. Colleges, Academy of Beauty (Wilfred) NYC; [occ.] Elderly Care, Private Duty, N. Mia Beach, Fl. Free Lance Beauty Services; [memb.] Holy Family Catholic Church Choir Member, Pact: People Acting for the Community Together, (member); [hon.] Beauty Competition Most Professional Award, Clairol Coloring Award, No.1 Award for Styling Competition; [oth. writ.] A few more poems and inspirational sungs, and some non published articles focussing family difficulties or psychological problems; [pers.] I try hard to show the best and the beauty of people and things in my writing. Many times I am inspired by the Bible Teachings and some of the Great Saints, like St. Francis of Assissi and Teresa of Jesus; [a.] Hollywood, FL

RAMOS, LORETA
[pen.] Lo, Lolo; [b.] April 23, 1975, Brazil; [p.] Claudio and Carmen Ramos; [ed.] Grade 8 elementary school in Brazil, Hackettstown High, Warren College; [occ.] Waitress, Singer, Model; [oth. writ.] Read poems in coffee shops and radio station. Also few published in magazines; [pers.] Exercise your mind, your body and your soul. Always do what's right for nothing then can go wrong. Keep the faith real, and don't ever stop dreaming of your horizon.; [a.] Hackettstown, NJ

RAMSEY, JOEL
[pen.] Charles Cutsforth; [b.] March 1, 1975, Portage, WI; [p.] Robert and Josette Ramsey; [ed.] Poynette High, Edgewood College; [occ.] Student; [pers.] Never, never give up.; [a.] Poynette, WI

RAMSEY, JUDY
[b.] September 13, 1962, Canada; [m.] Jack Ramsey, May 18, 1985; [pers.] This poem was written for the most important person in my life, my husband Jack

RANK, DAGMAR
[pen.] Dee; [b.] September 5, 1971, Erlangen, Germany; [p.] Botho Meister, Renate Meister; [m.] Charles K. Rank Jr., September 17, 1993; [ch.] Christina-Ann, Kyle Alexander; [ed.] Spardorf High School Life; [occ.] Mother and Wife; [pers.] In order to see the world in its true unique colors you have to open both eyes, your heart and your mind and learn to accept.; [a.] New Haven, MI

RASHID, AZIZ AMIN
[pen.] Baksh, Brian; [b.] July 31, 1939, Guyana, South America; [p.] Rashid Abdul, Rashid Masudan; [m.] Rashid Nesha, March 10, 1968; [ch.] Sabina, Asiq, Ramona, Farisa, Nelissa; [ed.] St. Andrews Anglican, Guyana '44-'53, Guyana Sch. of Agriculture '76-'78; [occ.] Security Officer; [hon.] Guyana National Award in the field of Artificial Insemination; [oth. writ.] Six (600) hundred statements/quotations, as per sample below.; [pers.] In our quest for happiness and peace of mind, we must never lose sight of the fact that contentment holds the key to both.; [a.] Brooklyn, NY

RASMUSSEN, YVONNE
[b.] April 22, 1924, Rock Springs, WY; [p.] Joseph and Manie B. Fowkes; [m.] David Charles Rasmussen, Deceased, October 20, 1945; [ch.] 4 Noreen, Sharon, David and Rick; [ed.] High School, Medical Assistant College, Continuing Education; [occ.] Retired; [memb.] Church (LDS) Church of Jesus Christ of Latter day Saints DUP (Daughter of Utah Pioneers); [oth. writ.] Novel (unpublished) short stories (") many poems; [pers.] I am proud to be an American and worry about the road my countrymen may be following. I feel that "old fashioned" values and virtues are necessary to preserve our way of life, and I believe a strong family unit makes a strong matron.; [a.] Sandy, UT

RASO, CHRISTOPHER S.
[b.] April 17, 1966, NY; [p.] Anthony and Rachel Raso; [m.] Patricia Raso, March 11, 1995; [ch.] Kevin Raso; [ed.] Princess Anne High School, Phoenix College, Arizona State University; [occ.] Student Teacher; [memb.] Planetary Society; [hon.] Golden Key National Honor Society, National Dean's List, Maricopa College Writing Contest; [oth. writ.] Several short stories published in local anthologies. Currently I'm editing a collection of poetry.; [pers.] My poetry is written to speak to the souls of my fellow human beings.; [a.] Phoenix, AZ

RAYNE, CRICKETT R.
[pen.] C. L. Gordon; [b.] May 26, 1962, Lincoln, NE; [p.] Sharon Nellie and Donald Gordon Sr.; [ed.] University of Toledo, Lithographic Arts; [occ.] Printer; [memb.] MCC of God and Christ, Toledo, Ohio; [oth. writ.] 2 Books of Poetry 1) "They're Everywhere and 2) God Listens to All Children (both being printed, published by Feb. 1996); [pers.] My writings are influenced by experience and present surroundings. I enjoy spiritual and sexual poetry. There is no communication like written communication. Words speak louder than pictures.; [a.] Toledo, OH

RAZIEL, MICHAEL
[b.] May 1, 1946, New York, NY; [ed.] A.A.L. Beril Arts Colorado Mountain College, B.S Geology Ft. Lewis Cutlose; [occ.] Self-employed company ("Magma Minerals") Miner; [pers.] Poetry is an expression of my innermost thoughts and needs, the interface where my shadow can come out to play.

REAMY, DONALD G.
[pen.] Donnie Reamy; [b.] March 12, 1946, Alexandria, VA; [p.] Hazel Reamy, Harvey Reamy; [ed.] George Washington High; [occ.] Retired Fire-fighter, Vietnam Veteran; [memb.] American Lung Ass., Disabled American Vets.; [hon.] Won poetry contest, gave seminars to grade school students on poetry, and judged contests; [oth. writ.] Local newspapers, work newsletter, write poems since the 7th grade; [pers.] I write my own greeting, cards and also write for everyone who ask. Whenever I got the feeling, I sit and write.; [a.] Mechanicsville, VA

RECOTTA, CHARLIE
[b.] January 4, 1962, San Jose, CA; [p.] John and Lillian Recotta; [ed.] Willow Glen High School; [occ.] Artist/Craftsman; [memb.] Living Art Association; [hon.] Honors for charity work to the Child Abuse Prevention Counsel of San Joaquin Valley, 1st place awards for Crafts from the William James Art Council; [pers.] I feel art and poetry is a direct reflection of my inner being, I hope that all my works bring warmth and good feelings to all that experience it.; [a.] Bella Vista, CA

REESE, BERLYN
[b.] December 30, 1953, Cordele, GA; [p.] Mr. and Mrs. Herman Dean; [m.] Elaise R. Reese, April 2, 1977; [ch.] Ye'Ana S. and Jamal R.; [ed.] A.S. Clark High School; [pers.] I love writing very much, and to look around at God's beautiful creation, I will strive to write more.; [a.] Jacksonville, FL

REEVES, LATISHA D.
[b.] August 15, 1970, Knoxville; [p.] Vada E. Smith, Frank Reeves; [ch.] Shavada Dragg; [ed.] Austin-East High School, Knoxville College; [occ.] Case Manager; [memb.] Mt. Olive Baptist Church; [hon.] Ms. Black and Gold 1991 at Knoxville College, Mentor at Local High School; [pers.] Determination is the key to success. While many are appointed few are anointed. When we allow God to nurture our gifts and give them back we become anointed.; [a.] Knoxville, TN

REEVES, RUBY
[pen.] Jean Feathers; [b.] October 20, 1943, Indianola, MS; [p.] Bertha and Asberry Featherstone; [m.] James H. Reeves, March 11, 1972; [ch.] Bethany Reeves Lewis; [ed.] High school, some college Hyde Park Academy, Chicago, Ill. - Loop Jr. College, Chicago Ill.; [occ.] Wedding directing and consulting/Homemaker; [oth. writ.] I have written poems all my life but have not until now tried to publish any; [pers.] "Through the Storm" was written almost six years ago for a very dear friend who was very ill with cancer. She like my ship came through the storm and is today in good health. So I dedicate this poem to her, Mrs. Agnes Matlock.; [a.] Hermitage, TN

REHA, MAJELLA
[pen.] Majella Reha; [b.] December 14, 1946, Ireland; [p.] Thomas and Helena Clancy; [m.] Thomas Reha, October 28, 1966; [ch.] Kelly and Jason Reha; [occ.] Home Health Aid

REIFF, DAVID
[b.] February 5, 1977, Neptune, NJ; [p.] John and Carol Reiff; [ed.] High school graduate, 1st year college student; [occ.] Writer; [oth. writ.] 2 journals, 1 collection of poetry. The beginning works of a collection of short stories, nothing ready to publish as of yet.; [pers.] Never give up hope. Never let the pain control you. And always allow your soul to dance in the skies of tomorrow.; [a.] Wall, NJ

REIHL, MICHAEL A.
[b.] August 17, 1964, Upper Darby, PA; [p.] Joseph A. and Winifred H. Reihl; [m.] (Fiance) Nancy C. Dwyer; [ch.] Timothy M. and Charlotte E. Reihl; [occ.] Field Service Engineer Medical Linear Accelerators; [memb.] Bread of Life Assembles of God Church; [oth. writ.] Over 200 poems, songs, and short stories.; [pers.] Life is something never to be endured. It should be lived, loved, and embraced. This emotional disposition can only be obtained by achieving depth of characture, and depth of characture can only be achieved by focusing on the God of your understanding; [a.] Upper Darby, PA

REILLY, APRIL
[b.] June 5, 1976, Baltimore; [p.] Raymond and Roxanne Reilly; [ed.] Franklin High, Pursuing BA degree in psychology Carson-Newman College, TN; [memb.] BSU Gospel Choir; [hon.] Dean's List, Alpha Lambda Delta, Phi Eta Sigma; [pers.] Poetry is merely generating words for what the mouth is incapable of expressing.; [a.] Reisterstown, MD

REIMER, CHERYL ANN
[pen.] Cheryl Ann McCord; [b.] June 11, 1963, Fort Worth, TX; [p.] Bob McCord, Ann Anthony; [m.] David Wayne Reimer, September 3, 1994; [ch.] Matthew Wayne Reimer; [ed.] Crowley High School Torrant and County Junior College Court Reporting; [occ.] Housewife and Mom; [memb.] Birchman Baptist Church; [pers.] My desire is to help at least one person to know that there is always hope through Jesus Christ. And that every person does have a purpose.; [a.] Fortworth, TX

REISNER, LOUISE
[pen.] Mary Louise Farrar; [b.] August 22, 1932, Cameron, OK; [p.] Edna and Dolis J. Farrar; [ch.] Brooks, Thomas, Kenneth and Brenda; [ed.] 1 yr college University of Houston; [occ.] Retired; [memb.] Concordia Lutheran Church Ho., Tx. (Charter Member); [oth. writ.] C/W songs - Two being pitched for recording 1) Rest of My Life Loving You 2) Honey I Love You 3) Calcasieu Boogie 4) It's You 5) Blues Again Today 6) I Can't Live many others. I wrote and researched "Farrar Ancestry" for my family; [pers.] I wrote "Love" at a time in my life, after losing my husband. I felt it important to try to express the true meaning of God, who comes first in my life. In music I work very hard to select lyrics that has a dramatic impact on the listener. I hope it works.; [a.] Starks, LA

RENO, MEREDITH R.
[b.] May 21, 1951, Miami Beach, FL; [p.] Audrey and Frank Risorto; [ch.] Ryan P. Reno; [ed.] BA - Richmond College/CUNY; [occ.] Substitute Teacher for Duval County School Board; [memb.] American Cancer Society, Leukemia Society; [pers.] I write to attempt to teach people to see the sense and sensitivity, as well as the beauty, of the world around, and within us.; [a.] Jacksonville, FL

RENZULLO, BROOKE MARIAH
[b.] January 7, 1981, Torrington, CT; [p.] Choey Renzullo and Robert Renzullo; [ed.] Home schooled. I feel that life is the best teacher. The greatest lessons are learned from life's experiences.; [occ.] Vegetarian, student, christian; [memb.] Civil Air Patrol, an auxiliary of the United States Air Force; [hon.] Co-founder and publisher of Homeschoolers Journal, a homeschooling newsletter, various civil air patrol awards; [oth. writ.] Many different pieces of poetry; [pers.] I love life and everything it offers, family, friends, adventure and most of all God. I enjoy fun and excitement, but also enjoy little things like sitting outside while watching the stars and hearing the wind whisper to the trees.; [a.] East Machias, ME

REX, KENNETH JACKIE
[pen.] Jack Rex; [b.] March 17, 1939, Comanche, TX; [p.] Orville Rex, Jane Rex; [m.] Sara M. Rex, November 26, 1970; [ch.] Tawni, Todd, Stuart, William; [ed.] University of New Mexico, Power Plant Engineer, BS degree St. John's University - Police Science; [occ.] Power Plant Superintendent, New Mexico licensed Private Investigator; [memb.] First Baptist Church of Comanche, Texas, Private Investigators Association of New Mexico, Par Country Club; [hon.] Elected to the Albuquerque City Council, Member of United States Civil Defense Council; [oth. writ.] Published article on "Maximum Bodyguard" relating to trip on Bogata, Columbia. Now writing poems and a book.; [pers.] The writing of this poem was greatly influenced by my devotion to Jesus Christ and my God, love for our country, the West, and history, and my collection of 800 pieces of barbed wire. My sadness over the disappearance of the old west.; [a.] Comanche, TX

REYNOLDS, CORNELIOUS
[pen.] C. Reynolds; [b.] February 26, 1931, DeQueen, AR; [p.] Jessie and Frank Reynolds; [m.] Bertha Reynolds, March 22, 1982; [ed.] Manual Training High Muskogee, OK; [occ.] Retired; [memb.] Maria Regina, Catholic Church; [pers.] I strive to reflect love and understanding, with a religious view. I was influenced by Emerson and Omar and James Balwin; [a.]

Gardena, CA

REYNOLDS, DARREN J.
[b.] December 2, 1974, Los Alamitos, CA; [p.] Mom Lana Reynolds; [ed.] Green Valley High School Yucaipa CA. American River College Sacramento, CA.; [occ.] Software Distributor; [hon.] Merit Award for Poetry Writing; [oth. writ.] I continue to write; [pers.] I write to replace the loss of thought.; [a.] Fremont, CA

REYNOLDS, PERSHAUN
[b.] April 16, 1972, Denver, CO; [p.] Ruth Bryant White, Noe G. Reynolds; [ed.] Phineas Bauning High School, Undergraduate at Chapman University Major in Psychology; [occ.] Avionics Technician in the U.S. Marine Corps.; [memb.] A place for us Shaolin Kenpo Arts Ass. Black Karate Federation United States Achievement Academy ('87); [oth. writ.] Several I unpublished poems; [pers.] Writing and expressing myself is almost a necessity, but reading and learning the thoughts of others is a great pleasure; [a.] Los Angeles, CA

REYNOLDS, SHANTA
[pen.] Black Poet; [b.] January 16, 1978, Wilmington, DE; [p.] Lanora and Elbert Reynolds; [ed.] Graduate from high school in June 1996; [memb.] 9th, 10th and 11th grade I was a member of the basketball team, 12th grade I was a part of JDG (Job Delaware Graduate); [hon.] Honor Roll, basketball awards; [oth. writ.] Odyssey of Life, What is Love, Softly Killed, Anticipation Night, Mystery Girl, Mere Illusion, What It Means to be Young, Gifted and Black, Who are You?, Simple Man, A Lonely Heart, Real Feelings...none are published; [pers.] In order to write a poem you must put your heart in to it and you must feel the words you write.; [a.] Newark, DE

RHEA, LUCY M.
[p.] Sorrob and Marie Myrtle Ally (Both Deceased); [ch.] Terri Williams, Louis Rhea Jr. Rhea Cindy Bonnie Rhea/Scott and Lana Rhea; [ed.] Corpus Christi Catholic Elementary School of New Orleans; [occ.] Aerospace; [oth. writ.] Numerous poems; [pers.] The sound and smell of rain, the pulse of the ocean, the smell of wood burning fireplaces and fresh cut grass to my nostrils, are but a few of the fragrant perfumes of life than fill my senses and inspires my poetry.; [a.] Moreno Valley, CA

RICE, MIRANDA
[b.] July 2, 1982, Ann Arbor, MI; [p.] Patricia Petersen and stepdad Donald Petersen; [ed.] Tecumseh Elementary, Tecumseh Middle School 8th grade; [hon.] Educational honors from school; [oth. writ.] Many which I keep in a special diary; [pers.] I always write what I am feeling.; [a.] Tecumseh, MI

RICH, CRAIG L.
[pen.] Craig L. Rich; [b.] May 18, 1960, Akron, OH; [p.] Malcom E. Rich, Ethel Mae Rich; [ch.] Rizer and Rhoney (my cats); [ed.] Bachelor of Science, University of Akron. Doctor of Medicine Universidad Central del Este (Dominican Republic); [occ.] Psychiatrist; [memb.] Lanton Center for the Martial Arts; [oth. writ.] Scads of poems written for friends 10 yrs of journal writing.; [pers.] I strive to see life for what it really is rather then what I can conceptualize it as being in my mind. Ian Hunter, Stephen King, my imagination, my friends, people who have hurt me.; [a.] Lanton, OH

RICHARDS, AUDREY
[b.] September 10, 1972, Keen, NH; [p.] Susie A. Abbott Richards, William Richards Sr.; [ed.] Holyoke Community College - Associated degree, Granby Jr. Sr. High School; [occ.] Laundry Aide; [a.] South Deerfield, MA

RICHARDS, JENNIFER
[pen.] Super Girl, Alien Girl, Daisy Kid; [b.] August 24, 1977, Seattle, WA; [p.] Gayle Baker; [ed.] Graduated from High School March '96; [occ.] College student; [oth. writ.] This is my first published poem, but I am pursuing publication for my 3 volumes of poetry.; [pers.] My writing is all I feel. It pours out and I catch what I can. Greatly influenced by many feminist writers and musicians. Write to create changes. For Matt and Fran.; [a.] Salt Lake City, UT

RICHARDSON, FRANCES K.
[pen.] Frankie; [b.] April 29, 1936, SC; [p.] Mr. and Mrs. Robert K. Kea Sr.; [m.] Bob Richardson, December 1, 1962; [memb.] St. Paul United Methodist Church, Chesterfield SC, Woodman of the World, SC.

RICHARDSON, KRISTY
[b.] February 4, 1979, Renton, WA; [ed.] Federal Way High School; [hon.] Dec. 1994 Student of the Month, May 1995 Student of the Month; [pers.] I was influenced by my youth directors Jennifer Hille, and Kirk Hille; [a.] Federal Way, WA

RICHARDSON, ROY REX
[b.] February 10, 1959, Dickson, TN; [p.] Barney and Della Richardson; [m.] Lana Nicole Richardson (Nikki), December 4, 1993; [ch.] Justin Lee and Kayla Leeann; [ed.] Dickson County Senior High; [occ.] Builder, Carpenter; [oth. writ.] Include unpublished poems and songs; [pers.] I hope that everyone will frequently find and generously give a lifetime of love and happiness; [a.] Sugar Hill, GA

RICKETSON, ROBERT THAD
[b.] August 18, 1969, FL; [p.] Robert and Melanie Ricketson; [ed.] Attended Richland High school Currently Attending University of Texas at Arlington; [pers.] Poems are as thoughts... quick, clear, short lived, yet they can change ones perception of life... forever.... this poem is dedicated to my grandfather, Robert D. Ricketson; [a.] Arlington, TX

RICKETTS, ERIN RENEE
[b.] July 5, 1981, San Luis Obispo, CA; [p.] Paul and Sheree Ricketts; [ed.] Attending Atascadero High School, Atascadero, California; [memb.] Friday Night Live, Drama, Junior Kiwanis.; [hon.] Presidential Academic Fitness Award '92; [pers.] Being a freshman in High School writing professionally is one of my dreams. And because of this book my dreams seem to be one step closer to becoming a reality. Thank you.; [a.] Atascadero, CA

RIDENOUR, MICHAEL
[b.] March 29, 1943, Warrensberg, MO; [p.] Belle Ridenour, Herman Ridenour; [ed.] Formerly a BS in French, Math and Physics as well as a MA in English Lit.; [occ.] I teach (some Philosophy, some Literature, some Science), I work in a well-cluttered bookstore of Dickensonian ilk and I write; [memb.] Kappa Mu Epsilon Mathematics Fraternity. (I put that one down because I get a kick out of a poet belonging to a math frat.) Actually I don't belong to much. And nothing much belongs to me.; [hon.] I've been blessed by many unspeakable awards. I even survived Vietnam.; [oth. writ.] Some poems in small press mags. I'm currently at work on a poet's approach to teaching chemistry. Have a few poems in an anthology which came out this year called "Uncommon Ground."; [pers.] I belong to the Hamlet school of procrastinating prep and gradual progress toward a point where the readiness is all. That's probably why it's taken this long to get around to perfecting and polishing and finally publishing of a few poems.; [a.] Los Angeles, CA

RIGGS, KIMBERLY
[b.] April 5, 1979, Springfield, MO; [p.] Marion and Janice Riggs; [ed.] Public Schools of Van Buren, Arkansas; [occ.] Student; [memb.] Van Buren High School band; [hon.] No previous writing awards, numerous musical awards; [oth. writ.] Numerous unpublished poems; [pers.] I want to show the world what it's like to be a teen living in this age, what we feel, love, and strive to become. I want to give adults the chance to see inside the people who hold the future.; [a.] Van Buren, AR

RILEY, BETH ANN
[b.] July 30, 1971, Convoy, OH; [p.] Joseph Riley Jr., Margaret Riley; [pers.] "Let all that you do be done with love." I Cor. 16:14; [a.] Convoy State, OH

RILEY, KIMBERLY MARIE ANTOINETTE
[b.] March 8, 1973, Springville, NY; [p.] Allen and Dorothy Ellis; [m.] Brent Riley, November 18, 1995; [ed.] Nova High School, University of South Carolina completing requirements for a Masters of Arts and Teaching.; [memb.] Phi Theta Kappa Honor Society; [hon.] Phi Theta Kappa, Presidents List, Dean's List; [pers.] I have been greatly inspired by the Vietnam War, and most of my poetry surrounds this subject. The lives that were lost during the war should never be forgotten.; [a.] Columbia, SC

RILEY, TANYA P.
[pen.] Reyna; [b.] December 13, 1971, Lake Charles, LA; [p.] Roy Watson and Cassandra Watson; [m.] Ricardo Riley, November 2, 1991; [ch.] Sydni C. Watson-Riley; [ed.] Cool Spring Elementary; [occ.] Assistant Office Manager, Reliable References, Silver Spring, MD; [memb.] Student at the Institute of Children's Literature, Mount Olive Missionary Baptist Church; [hon.] Gold Cord from the National Honor Society; [oth. writ.] I'm Okay Now - a poem published in Atwater High's poetry notebook under a pseudonym, Reyna, in Atwater, California; [pers.] I write in the hope that my words evoke a very personal sense of empathy from each individual reader. My inspiration comes from God and my joy from my husband Rick and daughter Sydni. Strongly influenced by Langston Hughes.; [a.] Adelphi, MD

RINKENBERGER, IDA
[b.] January 2, 1939, Stewart, MS; [p.] Hobson Vaughn, Lydia Vaughn; [ch.] Douglas W. York, Angela D. York; [ed.] Cleveland High School, Cleveland, MS, Trevecca Nazarene College, Nashville, TN; [occ.] Office Administration, Independent Contractor; [oth. writ.] Calls to worship for church services, church school material for single adults; [pers.] Joy and peace - gifts from God to share with others.; [a.] Littleton, CO

RITCH, DIANE V.
[b.] January 6, 1960, Kingston, Jamaica; [p.] Timothy and Geraldine Ritch; [ed.] Hillsborough Community

College AA (Mass Communications) in process; [occ.] Proposal Coordinator; [hon.] National Dean's List, Dean's List (Hillsborough Community College - 4.0 GPA)

RITENBAUGH, STEPHANIE
[b.] February 16, 1982, Pittsburgh; [p.] David and Judith Ritenbaugh; [ed.] Attends 8th grade at Cheswick Christian Academy; [occ.] Student; [memb.] Youth Group at Dayspring Christian Center; [hon.] High honor student 4.0 average 7th grade, 1st place in Science Fair for Aircraft Flight in 5th grade, currently on honor roll 8th grade; [oth. writ.] Published in the Pittsburgh Health Journal, "Why Kids Should Not Take Drugs"; [a.] Brackenridge, PA

RITSEMA, KRISTEN
[pen.] Destiny; [b.] December 12, 1981, Kalamazoo, MI; [p.] Julie Collier and Rusty Ritsema; [occ.] Babysitter and Student; [memb.] Columbia House - Music Club, Harlinquin Book Club; [hon.] Perfect Attendants, Honor Roll, Honorable Mention, Student of the Week; [oth. writ.] The Haunted One, The Spooky Halloween, The Family; [pers.] I would like to thank my mom (Julie Collier) And My Stepfather (Chris Collier) and my brother (Dustin Ritsema). My family and relatives have given me opinions. Thanks everybody.; [a.] Lawrence, MI

RITT, CHRISTOPHER LYN
[b.] January 27, 1976, Richmond, VA; [p.] David Ritt, Janet Ritt; [ed.] King William High School, 2 sem. at Savannah College of Art and Design; [hon.] National Arts Honor Society; [oth. writ.] A poem in my High School's Literary Arts Magazine; [pers.] My greatest influences are mostly 90's musicians. My philosophical statement is a chinese saying "Sometimes life can be a bitter as dragon tears. But wether dragon as tears are bitter or sweet depends on how each man perceives the taste".; [a.] King William, VA

ROACH, LAVERNE
[b.] May 19, 1929, Gainsville, MO; [p.] Myrtle and Edgar Ragland; [m.] Billy Jose Roach, July 13, 1946; [ch.] 4 boys; [ed.] Just finished my degree in Journalism and Story Writing. (With International Corsp. School); [occ.] Retired - spend my time writing; [memb.] Poets of the Singing Hills; [oth. writ.] Haven't had time to get anything published but I have several about ready-/ article- hooked on automobiles-/two short stories and 1 book; [pers.] I quit the restaurant business when I was 65 and started back to school - I dearly want to be a writer.; [a.] Marshall, AR

ROBBINS, MARK A.
[b.] March 13, 1971, Evansville, IN; [p.] Dr. Jerry L. Robbins, Harriett B. Robbins; [m.] Elaine Denise Robbins, August 3, 1991; [ch.] Rebecca Denise Robbins; [ed.] BS in Accounting - Purdue University, passed CPA Exam; [occ.] Accountant, H.H. Gregg (Electronics/Appliance Retail) Indianapolis, IN, also Adjunct Professor in Accounting, Vincennes University Indianapolis; [memb.] Free Presbyterian Church of Indianapolis, Lawrence Township Republican Club, Vice Precinct Committeeman, Lawrence Co. Republicans; [hon.] Krannert Alumni Scholarship (Purdue), Hoosier Scholar Recipient (for Purdue); [oth. writ.] I have written church music which is in the process of being copyrighted and published.; [pers.] For this poem I looked within myself of the quandry of life, knowing what to do but not being able to do it. I find my hope in scripture which promises a new life to those who know Christ and His life.; [a.] Indianapolis, IN

ROBERTS, HEATHER LYNNE
[b.] March 2, 1983, New Hartford, NY; [p.] Mike and Lynne Roberts; [ed.] Clinton Middle School, 7th grade, Clinton, NY; [occ.] Student; [memb.] I took ballet for 9 years and was in the Nutcracker for 7 years. I am now involve in athletic activities such as basketball and field hockey.; [hon.] I was Clara - one of the main roles in the Nutcracker in 1992. I also got an All-star award for basketball. This here is also an honor!; [oth. writ.] I have never had anything published before but I like to write short stories and poems in my free time.; [pers.] My writing describes inner thoughts and feelings. I was influenced and inspired by the author of Anne of Green Gables, L. M. Montgomery.; [a.] Clinton, NY

ROBERTS-FRANCO, BARBARA
[b.] August 30, 1968, Medina, OH; [p.] Lyle and Doris Roberts; [m.] Larry J. Franco, May 28, 1994; [ch.] Jessica M. Franco; [ed.] Buckeye High School, Medina County Career Center; [occ.] Pharmacy Technician; [memb.] Waltz United Methodist Church; [pers.] This poem is dedicated to the memory of my grandfather, Addison W. Smith, who is the gardener in my writing.; [a.] Lodi, OH

ROBERTSON II, BURRELL L.
[pen.] Bud Robertson; [b.] September 25, 1965, New Kensington; [p.] Burrell Robertson, Ada Belle Robertson, September 1, 1989; [ch.] Shawna Marie, Jared Michael; [ed.] Valley High School, Penn State University; [occ.] Union Laborer; [hon.] Dedicated to my mother; [oth. writ.] several unpublished writings.; [pers.] I have always enjoyed and the way a person true thoughts and feelings come shining through as words for others to enjoy the experience of the imagination.; [a.] New Kensington, PA

ROBERTSON, SHANE
[pen.] Shane Roberson; [b.] February 7, 1974, Gadsden, AL; [p.] Robbie and Pam Robertson; [ed.] Coosa Christian High School, Luther Rice Bible College and Seminary; [occ.] Advance Auto Parts DC; [oth. writ.] Hail, King of the earth a empty heart, delighted by a touch, Gethsemane, a Psalm from the heart.; [pers.] I plan to finish my schooling in Dec 96. Where I will have my BA in Bible/Theology and Further Pusure my ministry as a pastor or whatever God has in store for me.; [a.] Gadsden, AL

ROBINSON, COREY L.
[b.] November 9, 1976, Lincoln Park, MI; [p.] Jesse, Robinson-Louise, Robinson; [ed.] MacKenzie High; [pers.] I tried to understand the goodness on the madness of are world as I walk down these aisle of life and hope; [a.] Detroit, MI

ROBINSON, EDDIE R.
[pen.] Eddie Ray; [b.] May 15, 1959, Davidson County; [p.] Eveline Baldwin; [m.] Rose M. Robinson, September 9, 1984; [ch.] Nicola, LeQuinta and Ebonee Robinson; [ed.] 11th grade education; [occ.] Forklift Operator; [oth. writ.] The Judgement, Your Brother's Keeper, and The Wicked Tongue; [pers.] Each poem is inspired by the Spirit of God and each one is written to encourage men and women in the end times. Thanks to the Almighty from whom all blessings flow.; [a.] Nashville, TN

ROBINSON, GWENDOLYN TRAVIS
[pen.] Pengwen; [b.] December 9, 1939, Greensboro, NC; [p.] Jacob Bethea, Mildred Oliphant; [m.] Divorced, June 11, 1976; [ed.] Support Staff (U.S. State Dept.) Foreign Service of U.S.A., Compton College, Anacosta High; [occ.] Retired Computer Graphics and Words Processing Business Owner Pengwen Poesies; [memb.] Veterans of Foreign Wars, Post 5394-Ladies Auxiliary (Chaplain-2yrs), YWCA Board Member Volunteer, Election Clerk for LA Country, Heritage Square HOA (Chair for 4 years), First Baptist Church of S. Los Angeles-Youth Committee, Deaconess; [hon.] National Philanthropic Ass'n Volunteer 1989, Camp Fire Council Volunteer 1990 Dominguez Brand Award for Volunteer 1991 Outstanding Employee 1986/1989 Award/City of Compton Graduated Compton College with High Honors; [oth. writ.] Lost of letters to family and friends regarding my travels and experiences abroad encouraged to go public with humorous writings.; [pers.] Human beings the world over desire the same things but the most important is "Love". I want to bring love to those who read my words, remind them of many ways we are loved and can love others.; [a.] Compton, CA

ROBINSON, LEE ROY
[pen.] Rob Boy; [b.] May 6, 1935, Oklahoma; [p.] Hartwell and Addie; [m.] Donna, May 5, 1955; [ch.] 5; [ed.] 10 Crd. Whittier High, 2 years Saddleback Comm. Coll., 1 yr. art school; [occ.] Retired Gen. Contractor; [memb.] SAG, AFTRA, BMI; [oth. writ.] Many poems none published, many songs one published and recorded Carry Me Back Home rec. Tom Willott; [pers.] Don't give living till you're dead; [a.] Hesperia, CA

ROBINSON, RENEE ANTONIA
[b.] May 18, 1960, Cleveland, OH; [p.] Loretta B. Tigner, Grady Saunders; [ed.] Working toward BA in Liberal Studies, Cabrillo Sr. High School; [occ.] (Communications) United States Air Force stationed at Andrews AFB, MD; [hon.] Achievement medal and other associated military ribbons and medals; [oth. writ.] Personal book of unpublished poems; [pers.] I have written my poetry based on my life's experiences. I believe no matter what happens, good or bad, one should live for today, because life is short.; [a.] Upper Marlboro, MD

ROBINSON, SUSAN LEIGH
[b.] June 11, 1981, South Carolina; [p.] Patti and Sam Robinson; [ed.] I am currently in the 9th grade; [pers.] I love animals, especially dogs and horses. I enjoy reading and writing. I enjoy singing and going to symphony concerts.; [a.] Duncan, SC

ROCHA, VERONICA SEGURA
[pen.] V.; [b.] May 6, 1958, Pueblo, CO; [p.] Filadelfio and Carmen Segura; [m.] David Rocha, July 23; [ch.] Matthew Andrew Rocha; [a.] Pueblo, CO

RODAK, JULIE ANNE
[b.] January 7, 1979, Clare, MI; [p.] Walter Rodak and Beverly Rodak; [ed.] I am currently a junior at Brighton High School and plan to attend Madonna University; [occ.] I am a full time High School Student; [memb.] Brighton H.S. Jazz Band, Brighton H.S. Concert Choir, Server at St. John the Baptist Church; [hon.] I have many awards and honors such as: Band, Choir, and Attendance; [oth. writ.] I have written many other poems but none have been published.; [pers.] I believe everyone has their own artistic talent, weather it be writing, music, art or dance. Some just have to find it

with in themselves; [a.] Brighton, MI

RODIN, PATRICK
[b.] July 8, 1972, Pennsauken, NJ; [p.] Jerry Rodin and Kathleen Rodio; [ed.] Pennsauken High School, Camden County College, Temple University (currently enrolled - Senior); [occ.] Film and Media Arts student at Temple University; [memb.] Greenpeace, TUSFVA (Temple University Film and Video Association; [hon.] Finalist in the Long Island Film and Video Festival, 1994, for "6". During various semesters, I've been in the Dean's List and the President's List while in college; [oth. writ.] Several screenplays, short stories and poems; [pers.] I've been influenced by many part and present films and writings. Peter Weir is my favorite film director, and Henry David Thoreau is my favorite writer. I feel that each and every one of us should make a positive impact in the world, whether through writing, film, or any other means.; [a.] Pennsauken, NJ

ROEMER, ALICIA A.
[b.] September 26, 1984, Houston, TX; [p.] Tonya Roemer and Doyle B. Roemer; [ed.] Edgewood Elementary 5th grade; [memb.] San Jacinto Girl Scout Troop #12061, S.P.J.S.T. Lodge #142, United States Gymnastics Federation, Spring Branch National Little League; [hon.] Honor Society; [pers.] I strive for humor and I hope that people will love poetry the way I do. I have been greatly influenced by the humor of Jack Prelutsky.; [a.] Houston, TX

ROGERS JR., CHARLIE
[pen.] RJ Harsey; [b.] July 9, 1978, Nashville, TN; [p.] Charlie Rogers, Dawn L. Rogers; [ed.] Wissahiclon Senior High School North Monteo Technical Career Center; [occ.] Electro Mechanical Engineer Apprentice/Student; [memb.] Boy Scouts of America US Army Reserve Horticulture Club; [hon.] Eagle Scout; [oth. writ.] In several poems published in school poetry journal called "Aura"; [pers.] I with about evils and wrong doings one does to the earth and other people. I am influence my past American authors especially the Transcendentalists.; [a.] Ambler, PA

ROLES, JERI
[b.] July 24, 1975, Tacoma, WA; [p.] Penny A Roles, Gary L. Roles; [ed.] Ashland High School; [oth. writ.] Through the eyes of me candlestick man this place royal beach book worm; [pers.] We can not escape the hardships of life, or the cruelty and bitterness caused by man. What we can do is learn from them and become strong enough to rise above the depressing atmosphere of these times. God bless everyone, our earth, and love.; [a.] Ashland, WI

ROMAN, DIANA
[b.] June 9, 1954, Limestone, ME; [ch.] David Roman Jr.; [occ.] Corp Collector and Cashier; [oth. writ.] The roses; [pers.] This poem is dedicated to Paul and Carol. Carol learned she had lung cancer at the age of 39. When they were looking into what kind of treatment, one of the places told her to get her things in order. That was 6 months ago. Treatment and with the help of the shrunk. Dr's have no explanation for it. God works in mysterious ways and Carol is living proof of it.; [a.] Newton, MA

ROMERO, MICHAEL
[b.] October 26, 1968, Fresno, CA; [p.] Ostelano (Tilo) Romero, Ida Romero; [m.] Sharee-Ann Romero, May 26, 1990; [ch.] Krystal, Michael; [ed.] West Mesa High; [occ.] Warehouse Foreman; [pers.] To my daughter and son whom I love so much. I am deeply blessed by the love they share, which keeps my dreams alive.; [a.] Albuquerque, NM

ROSARIO, MARK
[b.] February 11, 1974, Cleveland, OH; [p.] Jose and Julita Rosario; [ed.] Cleveland St. Ignatius High School, Cleveland State University; [occ.] Electrical Engineering Student; [memb.] Member of National Technical Assoc., former member of Cleveland Music Federation, former member of Junior Council of World Affairs; [hon.] Editor's Choice Award in the National Library of Poetry's Reflections of Light (1995), participated in 1992 Cuyahoga Community College Senior's Best Short Story and Poetry Competition; [oth. writ.] Published "A Magical Night" for The National Library of Poetry's Best Poems of 1995, published "An Untold Story" for the National Library of Poetry's Reflections of Light, Editor in Chief of Vista, high school literary magazine; [pers.] This poem is dedicated to Gina, Gale, Jane, Jocelyn, Nina, Myra and Joey. Thanks for inspiring me!; [a.] Cleveland, OH

ROSE, CAROLYN LYNN
[pen.] Carol or C. Rose; [b.] August 22, 1957, Carmel, CA; [p.] Myrtle B. Manigo and Ben A. Lott; [ch.] Michael Jude Armelin Jr., Richard Raymos Rose, Danielle Nickell Frederick; [ed.] High School early graduate, with honors, some college, and I'm trying to finish college now; [occ.] School Bus Driver/Teen Outreach Worker; [memb.] Girl Scouts of American, Seaside Junior Chamber of Commerce, "CSEA"; [hon.] Extra-Ordinary Individual Award for the State of California; [oth. writ.] Won an awards for my "God in my Life" essay for the State of California. There were 5,000 other people that were in the contest I was first place.; [pers.] I will always set goals, and once I reach that goal I will set another and work to reach it. This is one of my goal I have set and reached. Now I will keep reaching higher!; [a.] Seaside, CA

ROSE, CONNIE L.
[pen.] Connie L. Rose; [b.] December 5, 1940, Logansport, IN; [p.] Alvin A. and Lois M. Pursch; [ch.] 4 daughters April, Patty, Spring and Vicki; [ed.] Logansport High School, Ivy Tech.; [occ.] Factory worker; [memb.] V.F.W. - American Legion; [hon.] Being a mom and grandma - I realize they don't give honors/awards for this, but it is my honor and being published; [pers.] Try to make people see that there are good things even tho you wonder when things go wrong.

ROSE, GEORGE E.
[b.] March 16, 1972, Phila, PA; [p.] Sharon Quintieri, Joseph Quintieri; [ed.] Abraham Lincoln High - College Prep Classes; [occ.] Sampling director Cocoa Barry US Inc. Pennsauken, NJ; [hon.] Graduated with honors in top 5% of graduating class.; [oth. writ.] I have a collection of poems and few short stories that I wrote for my own personal enjoyment; [pers.] I love nature and wild life. I gather much of my inspiration from walking in the woods and watch nature. If we all take the time to preserve it, our children and their children can enjoy it as much as I do.; [a.] Philadelphia, PA

ROSE, JOYCE
[b.] October 27, 1927, Iowa; [p.] Orlando and Pearl Ball; [m.] William M. Rose, May 8, 1949; [ch.] 2 sons, 2 daughters; [ed.] Oaktown, Indiana High School, Famous Writers School, Westport, Conn., Beauty College, Terre Haute, Ind.; [occ.] Retired Featured Writer and Columnist for Indiana Newspaper and Oil Writer and Oil Editor of Standard Times Newspaper, San Angelo, TX - 24 yrs. as a journalist; [hon.] Award by International Reading Assoc., NARO Freedom Bell Award, Award by WECTOGA; [oth. writ.] Recently published book "Petals and Thorns" - humorous and serious stories of Great Depression, World War II and Post-War Days including family humor and trials; [pers.] I write to express the values this country was built upon - lest we all forget. I started writing poetry for my own enjoyment when I was nine years old.; [a.] San Angelo, TX

ROSNESS, BETTY J.
[b.] March 4, 1924, Oklahoma City, Ok; [p.] Harry and Margie Pyeatt; [m.] Joseph H. Rosness, Lt Col, USA (Ret), August 5, 1960; [ch.] 5; [ed.] H.S. Central High Okla. City College - OCU Ok. City; [occ.] Advertising Consultant; [memb.] Goleta Valley Community Hospital Board, Santa Barbara Rescue Mission Board, Founder Breast Care Center of Goleta Valley, Goleta Valley Chamber of Commerce, Channel City Club. (Recent to present memberships); [hon.] Santa Barbara Woman or year 1978, Who's Who America Women 1978 - (to date), Who's Who Finance and Industry, 1987-88, UCSB Affiliate of the year 1984-85, Woman of Distinction - Soroptomist Int. of Goleta - 1989; [oth. writ.] Collection of newspaper essays, spiritual and family verse - lyrics and music to jingles for broadcast commercials.; [pers.] With God's help, I strive to solve some of the problems around me - always available to listen, aid or find some kind of solution to pain and suffering - I want to make a difference!; [a.] Goleta, CA

ROSSER, C. ANGELA SCHILLER
[pen.] Angela C. Schiller/Marie Sergwin; [b.] August 15, 1935, Tacoma, WA; [p.] Joseph M. Schiller; [m.] Alfred E. Rosser, December 23, 1994; [ed.] GED/ 1yr. Collage/; [occ.] Housewife/Free Lance Writer Student NRI Continuing Education; [memb.] Blaine Christian Women Writer's Group; [oth. writ.] Requiem Dance of crows, 1980. The Spaghetti Factory Fire 1915, 1990. Soulmates Lovers Forever. 1994 Dreams, Dreams, A life come true, 1994.; [pers.] Find your life Dream. Begin by asking God Almighty, to show his plan. His are always best. He always answers and helps accomplish your hearts goal. Follow your dream. It is there for a reason.; [a.] Blaine, WA

ROTH, DOROTHY HUBBARD
[b.] August 2, 1929, Phebe, MS; [p.] Thomas and Ruth Hubbard; [m.] Robert F. Roth, MD, April 2, 1975; [ch.] Tom Roth, Laura Leiss, Joy Carroll; [ed.] BA - Millsaps College, MA in Biblical Studies at Northwestern University; [occ.] Retired Missionary Teacher at colleges in Korea; [memb.] United Methodist Church General Board of Global Ministries, Roanoke Sister Cities (in Korea, Kenya, Russia, Brazil, Poland, China); [hon.] Valedictorian of high school class, National Methodist Scholarship to Millsaps College; [oth. writ.] Numerous poems and feature stories of unforgettable persons and experiences (send to family and friends in newsletters from Korea); [pers.] I pray my writings may be seeds of World Peace - giving growth to God's Plan for all His human children to mutually care for one another within His Love.; [a.] Roanoke, VA

ROTH, MIRIAM SOLTZ
[b.] July 16, 1907, Philadelphia; [p.] Esther and Solmon; [m.] Isidore, 1930; [ch.] Two; [ed.] Graduated - Coombs

Conservatory - later also the Philadelphia Musical Academy - University of Penna.; [occ.] Violinist; [memb.] Past President of 5 organizations, established an opera series for Brandels women in Deerfield Beach project; [hon.] Cash prize and cameo pin for my play entitled "Sense and Non-Sense", I have completed a manuscript with photographs and art works entitled "Through the Years"; [oth. writ.] Wrote a prize winning play for B'nai Brith women - corroborated the 1st and only senior citizen Music Festival held in Wilmington, Del. the only one in the USA.; [pers.] I wrote a one hour lecture - entitled "The Similarity of Violin to Man", I conducted my own 14 all girl orchestra at seventeen years of age.

ROTH, ROBERT C.
[pen.] Bob; [b.] August 15, 1932, Alexandria, VA; [p.] Lois M. Cudney; [m.] Shirley Ann Roth, January 30, 1954; [ch.] Bob Jr., Debbie, Allison; [ed.] Lafayete HS Buffalo, NY and BS through Xerox (systems); [occ.] Retired from Xerox Production Audit Lab Supervisor; [memb.] Boy Scouts, Little League, Coach - 1 Meter Diving Board, Coach - taught swimming to mentally retarded; [hon.] Hi Cap Awards by my employer for excellence, recognition from YMCA and the mentally retarded group of Geneva, NY; [oth. writ.] Nine additional poems have been submitted; [pers.] There is a great need to teach (from a very young age) life and how it should be for all mankind.; [a.] Plant City, FL

ROTH, STEVEN F.
[b.] February 2, 1966, Philadelphia, PA; [p.] Robert and Patricia Browning Roth; [ed.] Washington and Lee University; [occ.] Developer; [memb.] GOP, Pi Kappa Alpha, NAHB, AMA; [oth. writ.] Editorials in local newspapers; [pers.] "I write this poem to my future wife."; [a.] Jacksonville, FL

ROUNTREE, THELMA T.
[b.] December 3, 1942, Howard Co., IN; [p.] Albert and Ica G. Tucker; [m.] Richard E. Rountree, May 24, 1969; [ch.] Kip, Kimberly (Dirk and Terri from former marr.); [ed.] Graduated: Pittsboro High School, FSU - Bach. Arts 4-27-91, TEC - AA 5-1-87; [occ.] Housewife, Freelance Writer; [memb.] BFS, Bible Believers Fellowship Ch.; [hon.] 1st place in Fiction 1986-87, Fla Com College Press Assoc., The Eyrie Award for Artistic or Literary Excellence 1986-87; [oth. writ.] TCC Jr. Coll - The Eyrie FSU; [pers.] I endeavor to accomplish what is sensitive to God and people and nature.; [a.] Tallahassee, FL

RUDD, JUNE E.
[b.] Michigan; [ed.] University of Detroit, NLP Learning Systems, Advanced Nuero Dynamics; [occ.] Writer, Marketing Specialist.; [pers.] Published poems, newspaper articles and editorial. Appeared on Cable TV: "Dial-a-Poet."

RUDENIS, STEPHEN
[pen.] Stevo, Steve R.; [b.] December 19, 1961, St. Petersburg, FL; [p.] David and Flora Jane Rudenis; [m.] Gina Rudenis, August 12, 1995; [ch.] Stephen Jr. and Owen Rudenis; [ed.] St. Pete Christian H.S. St. Pete Junior College; [occ.] Printer; [memb.] (1) United States Soccer Federation, (2) Pinellas Park Youth Soccer Association, (3) North American Fishing Club, (4) Literary Guild; [oth. writ.] Numerous poems and short stories; [pers.] To be different, is to be alive!; [a.] Pinellas Park, FL

RUIZ, DOREEN
[b.] September 17, 1975, Columbus, OH; [p.] Robert Ruiz, Veronica Ruiz; [ed.] Corandview Heights High School, The Ohio State University; [occ.] Student; [memb.] American Heart Association; [pers.] My poetry helps me express my true thoughts and feelings about life and its ingredients. You have your good ingredients and your bad, but when it comes down to the final product it all fits together perfectly.; [a.] Columbus, OH

RUIZ, DORIS
[b.] March 1, 1957, Newark, NJ; [p.] Jesus Ruiz, Angela Santana; [ch.] Andres Alejandro, David; [ed.] College of Staten Island BA Spanish, AAS Business Management; [occ.] Spanish Teacher, Monsignor Farrell HS SI, NY; [memb.] Latino Civic Association; [hon.] Foreign Language Teachers of Staten Island Asc.; [pers.] A writer is one who is able to use her heart as a means of communication, her pen as a vehicle, which is directed by her emotions and sincerity. A good writer sees and envisions where others see nothing.; [a.] Staten Island, NY

RUIZ, MANUEL ANGEL
[pen.] Angel; [b.] December 3, 1934, Puerto Rico; [p.] Angel and Rosa Ruiz; [m.] Carmen Carbonell, January 10, 1955; [ch.] Manuel - Pablo - Maria; [ed.] High School 12 years Manhattan Laboratory Medical Assistant School NYC Graduated 1957; [occ.] Baker; [hon.] Winner Several Poetry Contest in Homeland Puerto Rico; [oth. writ.] Many unedited songs in English and Spanish; [pers.] I believe that love is the essence of life in so many different ways.; [a.] Biloxi, MS

RUSHING, SHANNON COLLEEN
[b.] June 5, 1978, Albuquerque, NM; [p.] Charles and Diana Rushing; [ed.] Currently in High School at Grace Christian School finishing my Senior Year.; [occ.] High School Student; [memb.] National Honor Society, Editor-in-chief of the school year book, Alliance Bible Church member; [hon.] 2nd place, Inspirational Prose 1995 school contest, 1st place poetry 1992 Apache Junction school district 18th grade, highest honor roll, Who's Who in Americas Young People, National Speech and Drama Award, National History and Government Award, Scholastic Achievement Award; [oth. writ.] Poetry and Prose published in school anthologies and papers.; [pers.] My writing is meant to reflect the thoughts of the common man in uncommon way, to help them strive to become better. I enjoy writing about experiences understandable to all.; [a.] Anchorage, AK

RUSS, SANDRA LEE
[b.] May 20, 1942, Detroit, MI; [p.] Sanders English and Bernice Rucker; [m.] Lee Daniel Russ (Deceased), November 2, 1963; [ch.] Kirk Daniel, Kimberly Lynn, Kip Stacey and Kertia Renee Russ; [ed.] Central High School, Wayne Country Community College, Wayne State University and Spring Arbor College; [occ.] Clerical Specialist for Wayne County; [oth. writ.] I have written many poems, and I plan to publish a book of poems sometime in the future.; [pers.] I am constantly striving for spiritual growth, with the ultimate goal being that of self-actualization, becoming one with God and universe - God like, being a whole person, or maybe just being the best person that I can possibly be.; [a.] Detroit, MI

RUSSAMANO, MICHAEL JOHN
[b.] September 29, 1971, Davenport, IA; [p.] Dr and Mrs. Patrick J. Russamano; [m.] Spouse to be Chrislyn S. Smith, Oct 19, 1996; [ed.] Notre Dame High School Keystone Jr. College Kings College Palmer College of Chiropractic; [occ.] Student of Palmer College of Chiropractic; [pers.] If you look for the beauty in all that is around you an eternal fountain of inspiration and life will forever flow.; [a.] Easton, PA

RUSSEL, LINDA
[b.] July 24, 1979, Pittsburgh, PA; [p.] Mary Jo Townsend and David Russell; [ed.] Sophomore in High School, Gateway Senior High School in Monroeville, PA.

RUSSELL, EILEEN
[pen.] Truly Grateful; [b.] Newark, NJ; [ch.] Colleen, Trennen, Jestin and Nakia; [ed.] East Orange High, attended Fairleigh Dickinson University 1981-83, presently a sophomore student at the University of Akron; [occ.] Case Manager at Miller Community House; [memb.] Kent Housing Network, presently a volunteer at Kevin Coleman Center, Committee for Justice and Community Harmony; [hon.] Received certificates in volunteering Portage County Head Start Program, Kent Social Services, recognized at Miller Community House a homeless shelter, Record Courier Newspaper for Affordable Housing Forums; [oth. writ.] Poetry published in the Independent Black Student League Magazine at FDU, recognized for art and poetry at my first art show in Englewood, New Jersey; [pers.] I would like to dedicate this honor to my mother Rosemarie, Donna Speights, Trennen, my children and all of my family and friends.; [a.] Kent, OH

RUSSELL, LAUREN
[b.] December 9, 1983, Boston, MA; [p.] Albert and Claire Russell; [ed.] Grade 6, Sanborn Middle School, Concord, MA; [memb.] Mass. Audobon Society, Dolphin Research Center; [hon.] Certificate of Literary Merit from the Elementary School Writer, and an Honorary Mention from Cooperative Artists Institute; [oth. writ.] Published in local newspaper (The Boston Globe) Elementary School Writer, and Faces Magazine (Cobblestone Publishing Company); [pers.] My poem, "Champ," reflects my dog. He is a buff, 3 year old, cocker spaniel, and his pedigree name is Prince Champus Russell's Gold.; [a.] Concord, MA

RUSSELL, NORMA JEAN
[b.] April 7, 1936, Pella, IA; [p.] Henry and Dorothy Vander Horst (Both Deceased); [m.] Carl Dean Russell, April 7, 1952; [ch.] Daniel Lloyd, Thomas Glen, Larry Alan, also 15 grandchildren and 1 great grandson; [ed.] Pella Community Schools - Pella, Iowa, William Penn College - Oskaloosa, Iowa, The Institute of Children's Literature Redding Ridge, Connecticut; [occ.] Before illness - Office Manager at Midwest Legal Services, Inc., Des Moines, Iowa; [memb.] Society of Children's Book Writers (former member), First Assembly of God Church (current member), Des Moines, Iowa; [hon.] Writing presentation at an elementary school, Golden Globe Awards, Audio cassette of children's stories; [oth. writ.] Published poems: Only Hope, The View, The Year There was No Christmas, Life Dealt the Hand, Your Marriage Book, Just Yesterday, My Friend, Winter Birds, Peace and Beauty, Something Special, Why? And When? And Where?, I Write Poems, Early Springtime, When Lights Go Out, Silver Love, Siberian Cold Front; [pers.] My writing often follows a pattern of

hope and inspiration, dealing with pain and overcoming obstacles in life, sometimes as a therapy to express my thoughts. Crossings was written as an expression of encouragement to myself as I battle cancer. I probably will not live to see crossings in print, but always when I write from my voice within, I reach out to others as well.; [a.] Urbandale, IA

RUSSELL, VOLLIE R.
[b.] February 14, 1912, Lufkin, TX; [p.] Jesse, and Eva Russell (Deceased); [m.] Ann Harwood Russell (Deceased), October 9, 1940; [ed.] High-School; [occ.] Retired, and writing; [hon.] Numerous Military Discharges, Diploma—Non-Fictional Writing Course, From Writers Digest School, Cincinnatti, Ohio. Commandation from Chevron oil Co For Satisfactory work completed.; [oth. writ.] Numerous Newspaper pieces published, lots of poems, (unpublished) a Novel in Writing (The Sharecroppers) The book should be published in 96 "How To" Pieces, and Health articles, "Instructions For Living 100 Active Years" "Chemical Killers In Disguise"; [pers.] Attached, find a "Mini Copy" of My Biography" It may be too lengthy for the space you have available in the book. If this be the case, just condince it to fit anyway you see fit. From the heart, I sincerely thank your company for accepting my poem.; [a.] Brooksville, FL

RYBACKI, CHARLES E.
[pen.] Dan Karol; [b.] March 4, 1930, Johnstown, PA; [p.] Lenora and Stephen Rybacki; [ed.] BSci in Music Ed - State Teachers College, Indiana, PA, MA - NYU, 2 music/dance apprenticeships at Conn. College, New London, Language Studies in Lublin, Poland, Nerja, Puerto Santa Maria, Madrid, Spain, Cuernavaca, Mexico, Composer for the dance; [occ.] Retired Music Teacher and Pianist; [memb.] Church and Arts Performance Groups in various locations - have permitted memberships to lapse than the years - seem to be on "My Own" personal mission re: Understanding people and presenting my views; [hon.] High school: Alumni Award, College: Kappa Delta Pi Scholarship, apprenticeship to Am. Dance Festival School, Conn. College - was pianist for Master classes for dance celebs: Martha Graham, Jose Limon, Sophie Maslow, Jane Dudley, Margret Dietz, Murray Louis, etc.; [oth. writ.] "Strange Landscape" - for spoken voice, piano, solo dance, "The Last Meow" - novella, a spoof on Int'l Piano Competitions, "The Curse of Isadora" - short story (a nostalgic journey back to my youth, in Pa. and the Gene Kelly Dance Studio; [pers.] Still "scratchin' around", trying to find out what I am about and what it's all about! Have had public performances of some of my things, but have never had anything published, except for poetry at my college.; [a.] Mayfield Village, OH

RYMSHAW JR., RICHARD
[pen.] Rick Rymshaw; [b.] March 1, 1955, Reading, PA; [p.] Richard Sr. and Sally Rae; [m.] Divorced; [ch.] Son - Richard III; [ed.] Graduated High School Central Catholic H.S. Reading, PA in 1973; [occ.] Powder Tech at Morton Powder Coatings, Reading PA; [hon.] Won a Song Writing Contest in 1981 "One Wish" Song named "One Wish"; [oth. writ.] About 200 other poems and lyrics 2 novels on the life of Elvis Presley after 8/16/1977 been writing since 1969; [pers.] Dedicated to Cheryl Gassert; [a.] Reading, PA

SAENZ, CLAUDIA D.
[b.] April 19, 1979, El Paso, TX; [p.] Gloria A. Saenz, Salvador Saenz; [ed.] Go to school at Eastwood High, for about two years now. Like to study History, Science and English. Have an "AB" grade average.; [occ.] Student, Athlete.; [memb.] National Honor Society, East El Paso Soccer League; [hon.] A-B Honor Roll Awards, Soccer Tournament Award.; [oth. writ.] No other writings have been sent to no one else.; [pers.] To embrace life as much as possible and make the most of equipment.; [a.] El Paso, TX

SAGE, NYLA RAE
[pen.] Nyla Rae; [b.] October 26, 1971, Clarksburg, WV; [p.] Rita Rae Sage; [m.] Ruben Zavalza; [ch.] Cesar Zavalza; [ed.] Graduated from Valley High, Las Vegas, NV; [occ.] Self employed; [pers.] The writing of my poetry reflects personal experiences. Therefore, I am mostly influenced by my family and friends; [a.] Las Vegas, NV

SAGER, ROGER A.
[pen.] Josh; [b.] March 2, 1962, Bergton, VA; [p.] Joe and Alva Sager; [m.] R. Jean Sager, September 5, 1981; [ch.] Jessica and Misty Sager; [ed.] East Hardy High; [occ.] Gas compressor station operator; [memb.] Mathias Mennonite church, North American Hunting Club; [oth. writ.] Many more poems; [pers.] We can not bring back the past, but we must not forget our heritage or our ancestors; [a.] Lost River, WV

SAJETOWSKI, GERRY
[b.] December 7, 1943, Cleveland, OH; [p.] Frank and Emily Tatulinski; [m.] Mickey Sajetowski (Mitchell), October 3, 1968; [ch.] Laurel, Jonathan Musician and Writer; [ed.] BA in Communications HIRAM College Graduate 1994; [occ.] Budget Analyst; [memb.] St. Therese Renewal Community, PSR Teacher, Legion of Mary, Secy.; [pers.] This is the fist time I've submitted one of my poems. I truly love writing poetry and hope to help others find relaxation and peace of mind in this hurried world.; [a.] Cuyahoga Hts, OH

SALAZAR, MAYRA A.
[b.] April 5, 1978, Venezuela; [p.] Iris and Marcos Salazar Sr.; [ed.] Graduating Class of 1996 at Coconut Creek High School; [pers.] "The impossible is always possible." "You can do anything if you put your mind to it."; [a.] North Lauderdale, FL

SALDUTTI, MELISSA MICHELE
[b.] February 14, 1979, Edison, NJ; [p.] Joanne and Charlie Saldutti; [ed.] Currently a Junior at Woodbridge HS, Graduate in 1997; [occ.] Working for Zevinson, Axelrod, Wheaton and Grayzel Attorney's at Law; [hon.] Who's who among American High School Students; [pers.] All of my writings came from what I feel inside of my heart.

SAMUELSON, MATTHEW
[pen.] Seth Helm, R. Freeman; [b.] June 23, 1979, Corning, NY; [p.] Robert C. Lauglin Sr., and Marylou Laughlin Sr.; [ed.] 6 years at Carder Elementary School, 3 years at Corning Free Academy, 3 years at Corning Painted Post West High School; [occ.] Student; [memb.] Corning Interact Community Service Organization, International Thespian Society, Corning District Track Team West High Choir (Occidentals); [hon.] Freshman Musician of the year in the 93-94 school year.; [oth. writ.] Various poems published in school newspaper: "The West Wind"; [pers.] I am a great admirer of the works of Ralph Waldo Emmerson as well as T.S. Eliot, and William Butler Yeats. Music greatly influences my life. I admire the art of the Renaissance artists as well. I believe we should strive to be our best in everything.; [a.] Corning, NY

SANCHEZ, JULETTE M.
[pen.] Gina Sanchez; [b.] July 18, 1961, Kingston, Jamaica; [ed.] Lehman College City University of New York; [occ.] Full time student College Assistant, Lehman College; [memb.] Golden Key National Honors Society, American Association of University Women, The National Museum of Women in the Arts.; [hon.] Cuny-Pipeline Diamond Fellowship, Dean's List, Several Awards for writings in English and French; [oth. writ.] Several short stories and poems, 1 short story was published in college literary magazine.; [a.] Bronx, NY

SANDERS, CLYDE
[b.] May 19, 1940, Crenshaw; [p.] Jessie Sanders, Bessie L. Sanders; [m.] Earline B. Sanders, July 23, 1963; [ch.] Xavier Lovell, Tamra Marie; [ed.] Walton Chapel Voc High Sardis, Ms Park College, Kansas City, MO; [occ.] Retired from U.S. Air Force and U.S. Postal Service, over 30 yrs.; [memb.] Institute of Industrial Engineers Society of Manufacturing Engineer Society; [hon.] Air Force Commendation Medal, U.S. Postal Service Certificate Leadership Award, given by state Senator Roscoe Dixon; [oth. writ.] Poetry published in base news papers, poems to honor Federal Retirees, Weddings, Birthday's, and a Sunday of other occasions; [pers.] I seek topics of great impact on me and those I know or have known, also seek subjects that mirror experiences that help me understand myself and others.; [a.] Memphis, TN

SANDERS, WINNIE
[pen.] Win; [b.] February 3, 1965, Bronx, NY; [p.] Winston Sanders and Francine Rhodes; [occ.] Self-Employed; [oth. writ.] Due to encouragement from my father since my teen years I been writing for years I hope to continue to write for the public who may feel the same as me.; [pers.] Whether its a poem or story, if its a personal experience it has an extra accent to it. "Young child" was motivated by my grand parents, who eventually learned how to read and write thanks to some wonderful friends. Thank you.; [a.] Newport News, VA

SANDUSTY, STEVEN
[pen.] Steve, Steven Dean Sandusty; [b.] October 22, 1957, Louisville, KY; [p.] Willard and Catherine Sandusty; [m.] Deceased; [ed.] Ass. of Science in Computer Technologies; [occ.] Life; [memb.] American Legion, ISOP; [oth. writ.] Best poems of 1996, Down Peaceful Park Treasured poems of America fall edition selected works of worlds best poets best poems of 1995, listen with your heart all my tomorrows, whispers in the wind windows of the soul, treasured poems of America 1996 slimmer edition; [pers.] If we do not begin today to finish the destiny of the American dream our children will live in decay and corruption till the end.; [a.] Louisville, KY

SANFORD, CAROLYN
[pen.] Carolyn Sanford; [b.] Shelby, OH; [m.] Bill Sanford; [ch.] Five; [ed.] B.S. Ohio University; [occ.] Speech and Language Pathologist in Mansfield, Ohio Schools; [memb.] Set Forth Christian Writer's Guild, North Central Ohio Speech Therapy Association, Grace Fellowship Church; [hon.] First place award for non-fiction, set forth writer's Guild annual competition, 1995; [oth. writ.] A recent story to appear in Guideposts Angels On Earth May-June issue.; [pers.] I want to show how God works in the lives of people.; [a.]

Mansfield, OH

SANFORD, TAMYKA T.
[pen.] Tiffany Simmone; [b.] June 23, 1973, Boston, MA; [p.] Cheryl M. Sanford; [ed.] Madison Park High School Roxbury Community College (creative writing course); [occ.] Blue Cross Blue Shield Secretary; [memb.] Business Professionals of America Student Council; [hon.] National Honor Society Honor Roll Pride Award; [oth. writ.] Essence lost love several other poems, I am woman, body Jazz, on my own through the eyes of a child responder S'il vous plat black butterfly, missing link; [pers.] I believe everything happens for a reason, that frequently things happen in one's life that will change their future forever.; [a.] Dorchester, MA

SANTI, VICTORIA LYNN
[b.] May 4, 1949, Knoxville, TN; [p.] Deceased, Charles and Margaret Houser; [m.] David Michael Santi, January 22, 1982; [ch.] Jessica Julie Ann Mott, Michael Kuling Peter David Santi- Deceased; [ed.] Business College and Coursework at University of Tennessee, Numerous Real Estate Certifications, Affiliate Studied Holistic, Health from 1972 to 1989 with an Oriental Medicine Doctor Dr. Adano Ley.; [occ.] Co-owner of Santi Realty Affiliate Broker; [memb.] Knoxville Assoc of Realtors TN Association of Realtors, National Association of Realtors Women's Council of Realtors; [hon.] 1994, Presidential Appreciation Award for WCR, Volunteer Work with a Battered Women's Shelter; [oth. writ.] Technical for advertising properties. I sometimes write in personal journals. I have been keeping a gardening journal for the house we moved into 3 years ago. I enjoy keeping a diary of some sort.; [pers.] Life is a gift of journey.; [a.] Knoxville, TN

SANTIAGO, MARIA ERLINDA
[b.] March 17, 1979, Manila, Philippines; [p.] Resty Santiago and Priscila Santiago; [ed.] 11th grade-High School, Narbonne High School; [occ.] Student; [memb.] Member - Yearbook Staff-Carnegie, Middle School 1993-94, Member-Junior Statesmen of America, Narbonne Hi. Sch. 1994-95, President-Junior Class Narbonne Hi. Sch. 1995-96; [hon.] Young Leader Award-Narbonne Hi., Star Award- Carnegie Mid. School; [oth. writ.] Poems and essays entered in school and national contest; [pers.] Political gimmicks should end for the benefit of the masses.; [a.] Carson, CA

SANTORO, JENNIFER D.
[b.] April 19, 1965, Cleveland, OH; [p.] Ronald Mihalus, Connie Ogilvie; [m.] Michael Santoro, June 23, 1990; [ed.] Garfield Hts. High, MTI Business School; [occ.] Clerical supervisor; [pers.] This poems is in loving memory of blackjack, my faithful companion of 15 years.

SAULS SR., TERRY A.
[pen.] Papa Bean; [b.] May 14, 1955, New Orleans, LA; [p.] Shirley Graci and Edgar Sauls; [ch.] Christina Marie and Terry Jr.; [ed.] Bonnabel High, LSUNO, Delgado Jr. College; [occ.] Service Manager for Card Access Systems; [memb.] Slidell Elks Lodge, Lacombe Volunteer Fire Dept., American Legion, National Rifle Association; [hon.] Several Elk of the Month Awards, Grand Lodge Youth Activities Award; [a.] Lacombe, LA

SAWYER, DANIELLE KATHLEEN
[pen.] Danielle Kathleen Sawyer; [b.] August 19, 1971, Carson; [p.] Daniel George and Michele Amiel Sawyer; [ed.] Bachelor of Science, CSULB emphases: Environmental Health current student striving for Phd. emphasis: English; [occ.] Environmental Consultant/Student; [memb.] Surfrider, Greenpeace, Long Beach Chamber of Commerce; [hon.] Dean's List of CSULB 1989-1993, Associated student government at CSULB - student representative for CSULB campus recycling and campus recycling center (by vote); [oth. writ.] Some published short stories and poetry in college newspaper, coffee literature magazines and Local community newspaper. Journalist (for the Opinion section) for the Union at CSULPS ('93-95); [pers.] My writings reflect the pain and frustrations I have endured in hopes of helping others know that they are not alone and that we all have the strength to make it through.; [a.] Long Beach, CA

SCAFARU, ANDA
[b.] August 11, 1979, Bucharest, Romania; [p.] Serghel and Doina Scafaru; [occ.] Student in High School; [pers.] To be a poet entails more than writing poems, it demands a commitment to live, and die with great style and even greater sadness.; [a.] Phoenix, AZ

SCAGGS, LYNDA L.
[b.] November 17, 1946, Ashland, KY; [ed.] Hatcher Grade School and Putnam Jr. High both in Ashland, KY, move to Christiansburg while in 7th Grade and on through the 12th.; [occ.] Unemployed; [oth. writ.] I have other poems and songs too, none that has been published. I have one poem that wouldn't be acceptable because its 21 lines, about the Vietnam war.; [a.] Christiansburg, VA

SCHALL, MILDRED VIOLA
[pen.] Mill V S; [b.] August 3, 1924, Denver, CO; [p.] Deceased; [m.] Widow of John N. Schall Sr., November 23, 1950; [ch.] Joan N. Schall; [ed.] High School graduate from Denver, Colo. H.S., Coast to Coast and universal travel.; [occ.] Now resident of browning care center and author of "From The Pen Of". In monthly issues of "The Browning Bulletin".; [memb.] National Wildlife Federation, Audubon Society, Correspondence Friend Of The Late Lou Klewer and avid supporter of "Pilkingtons Persian Cattery"; [hon.] 3 merit awards 1990-1992 from "World Of Poetry" golden poet society, Sacramento, Calif. 2 blue ribbons for artwork at county fair, some sold to admirerors.; [oth. writ.] Many short stories and articles for several magazines, also selected 4th grade monitor because of excellence in poetry. Also many poems for monthly newsletters in bowling green, O, 1986-1990; [pers.] "The Lord is with us all, he helps me because I help myself, I firmly believe". Smile, and the others smile with you". ☺ ; [a.] Waterville, OH

SCHMIDT, VICTORIA
[b.] July 19, 1908, St. Louis, MO; [p.] Gottfried Schmidt, Christina Juenger Schmidt; [ed.] A.B. Harris Teachers College, St. Louis, MO, M.A. Teachers College, Columbia U., NY, NY Ed. D. U of Colorado, Boulder, CO Ran for Congress to learn politics taught 50 years, all levels, last 30 years, Prof. Harris Teachers College, St. Louis, MO; [occ.] Retired as teacher, 1978 Prof. Emeritus, Harris Stowe College, St. Louis Traveling and writing; [memb.] Parliamentarian St. Louis Library of Congress Assoc., Smithsonian Institution, American Museum of Natural History, World Wildlife Fund, Environmental Defense Fund, Polo Club, Explorers Club, International Society of Poets; [oth. writ.] Author of Victoria's Story Reincarnation God's love returned Vantage Press 1992 Bible Stories from heaven MS 1979 More Victoria's Story now in MS Still writing; [pers.] Have traveled all over the world including both polar regions and all five continents Survived a plane crash, two train wreck each day is a precious gift to be full lived. My writings carry a message to the world; [a.] Saint Louis, MO

SCHNEIDER, RICK
[b.] July 19, 1948, Sacramento, CA; [p.] Donald and Yolanda Schneider; [ch.] Heidi Schneider; [ed.] Pasadena High, Pasadena City College; [occ.] Taxidermy Business, Golden Chaparral Taxidermy; [oth. writ.] Many other poems and songs.; [a.] Alvord, TX

SCHOLTING, JACQUELINE LEE
[pen.] J. S.; [b.] June 3, 1953, Nebraska City, NE; [m.] September 24, 1980; [ch.] Chad David, Scott Allen, Rod J.; [ed.] I graduated from weeping Water High School. No further education. But would be interested in the field of art. A cartoonist perhaps.; [occ.] Truck driver for Installers Warehouse Service; [oth. writ.] I have had two poems published for the Texas Association against sexual assault. I'm waiting to see if I will have any poems published in the next book that will be coming out in the spring of 1995.; [pers.] I write about real life and hope others will benefits and understand that life can be better and you can go on. The fear of silence, I can not bear, The thought of not talking, And no one who cares.; [a.] Grapevine, TX

SCHULTZ, PAMELA K.
[b.] December 10, 1952, Sioux Falls, SD; [p.] Delores Doss; [m.] Larry A. Schultz, December 19, 1980; [ch.] Erik (Steve and Kris step kids); [ed.] Graduate of McKennan School of Respiratory Therapy 74 West Central High School Hartford SD; [occ.] Co-owner Ace Rentals and Equipment Sale, Inc; [memb.] Sweetwater Co. Hospice - board of Directors, P.E.O. Chapter AB, SSI Vice Pres Investment Club, Coordinator C.H.A.D.D. Chapter of R.S., Young Career Women SF, SD, 1974; [pers.] I am starting to write to reflect my inner assurance of good, love and enlightenment in all of us if we are aware of it. And believe in it. Have faith in it.; [a.] Rock Springs, WY

SCOGGINS, LILLIAN ADAMS
[b.] March 5, 1906, Newborn, GA; [p.] James Edward Adams, Lillian B. Adams; [m.] Deceased, June 3, 1924; [ch.] Mildred Inez Brown - deceased Dorothy Anne Gilbert; [ed.] Atlanta Girls High; [occ.] Retired Secretary; [memb.] Philadelphia Baptist Church 2 Senior Citizens Clubs; [hon.] Several stories and articles in Atlanta newspapers Oldest mother in church - last 2 yrs. Gold watch, as best around choir member; [oth. writ.] 165 Short Stories many poems. When Lewis Grizzard died, I wrote a letter to The Atlanta Journal and received many letters and phone calls, all compliments.; [pers.] I've been writing poems since I was fifteen years of age, but I never thought of publication, and just tossed them aside, or gave them to some friend. I findly began to write them in a book of black pages that was given to me by my grandson, to whom I gave the book.; [a.] Decatur, GA

SCOTT, ALICE
[pen.] Elizabeth Elia Emerson; [b.] February 13, 1943, Chicago, IL; [p.] Vernie Shores, Ruth Shores; [m.] Kenneth E. Scott, February 10, 1964; [ch.] Robert Terry, Janet Glorine and Jeffrey Norman; [ed.] Venice High, El Camino College and Denver Technical College of Colorado Spgs.; [occ.] Self-employed (Freelance

Writer, Desktop Publisher and Author); [memb.] Grace Fellowship Church, Morning Star Theatre Productions; [hon.] Dean's List; [oth. writ.] Writer for Colorado Christian News, Author of "The incredible power of cults", wrote for pikes peak messenger newspaper; [pers.] Using the written word to express who I am means that my thoughts, my passions and my inner soul will live on.; [a.] Colorado Springs, CO

SCOTT, BRENDA J.
[pen.] B. J. Scott; [b.] January 12, 1971, Madison, IN; [p.] Priscilla J. Johnson and Gilbert D. Scott; [ed.] Madison Consolidated High School; [pers.] Drink not the wine unless you care to dine.; [a.] Madison, IN

SCOTT, GARY EARL
[b.] May 23, 1955, Somers Point, NJ; [p.] Irene and Earl (deceased); [m.] Divorced; [ch.] Gary 17, Justin 9; [ed.] H. S. Diploma; [occ.] Trade Show Decorator, Custom Furniture Maker; [memb.] Local Union 831; [oth. writ.] Mother Speed, For what is a mother? "Intervulsions" (All not yet published).; [pers.] To dedicate this poem to Debbie whose love and understanding brought to me after years of writing to come forth and share.; [a.] Anaheim, CA

SCOTT, GERALDLYN
[pen.] Geraldlyn Scott; [b.] January 29, 1933, Ensley, AL; [p.] Edward, Mary Estelle McCary; [m.] Timothy D. Scott, May 23, 1959; [ch.] Karen, Deryl, Charles, Fern; [ed.] Southwestern High School, Adult Education, Poro Beauty College, Wayne County Community College Undergraduate - Major Liberal Arts; [occ.] Retired; [memb.] Literary Volunteers of America, Inc., First Missionary Baptist Church, Missionary Society, United Conference for women; [oth. writ.] Unpublished; [pers.] I truly love going to church, reading, music art, Theater plays, always willing to help someone in need.; [a.] Detroit, MI

SCOTT, MEL
[pen.] Mel Scott; [b.] Toronto; [p.] Frank and Pauline Scott; [occ.] Film writer; [memb.] Writer's Guild of America. International Society of Poets, Screen Actor's Guild of America; [hon.] 1995 National Library of Poetry "Editor's Choice Award" awardee.; [oth. writ.] Journalism, Poetry; [pers.] In our quests, it is desire which brings us to a reckoning with fate, not time. For time neither is nor is not, unless desire makes it so.; [a.] West Hollywood, CA

SCOTT, MICHAEL
[b.] September 24, 1945, Orange, CA; [ed.] M.A. in philosophy Calif. State Univ. Long Beach Claremont Graduate School (Doctorate Unfinished); [occ.] Professor of Philosophy; [memb.] Internat'l Society of Poets; [oth. writ.] Pigeon Feet Sand Extchings (Poetry) Dialectic: Platonic and Buddhist (Philosophical Essay) A Survey of Buddhist Logic (Essay) and some anthologized poems; [pers.] Our words are the mirrors of our souls; [a.] Huntington Beach, CA

SCOTT, PATREA LOIS
[pen.] The Stone, Rhea Williams; [b.] May 20, 1972, Baton Rouge, LA; [p.] Bonnie and David Williams; [m.] Jon Thomas Scott, August 9, 1992; [ed.] Glen Oak High School, T.C. Williams High, Woodbridge Sr. High School. Northern Virginia Community College University of Tennessee of Martin.; [oth. writ.] One poem in school poetry book. Glenacorns.; [pers.] Searching was done in response to a poem from my husband. I write what I feel the most about.; [a.] Martin, TN

SEATON, CLYDE C.
[pen.] Clyde C. Seaton; [b.] January 13, 1943, Trinidad; [p.] Roy and Thelma Seaton; [m.] Sadie D. Seaton, March 7, 1976; [ch.] Jermaine Tyrone Seaton; [ed.] Buniwick High School and PS 3; [occ.] Safe Deposit Clerk; [memb.] Trinity Community Assembly of God; [hon.] Berean College. The Police Department, Trinity Community Assembly of God; [oth. writ.] The key to the door a great numbers of others poems; [pers.] I like to reflect the goodness of human being with my poems.

SEATON, STACEY
[b.] July 29, 1965, Hibbing, MN; [p.] Sandra Lee Seaton and Richard Bruce Seaton; [ch.] Sean Ryan Seaton; [ed.] Pequot Lakes High School and Staples Area Vocational Technical Institute; [occ.] Sale, ABC Seamless, Sign Artist: Shafer Signs; [memb.] Member Community United Church of Christ; [pers.] My poetry is the mirror in which I see my soul. My true self is reflected in each and every new creation.; [a.] Saint Paul Park, MN

SEBES, TRICIA
[b.] April 26, 1980, Kankakee, IL; [p.] Phil and Donna Sebes; [ed.] Present sophomore in Girls Preparatory School; [hon.] Honor Roll, Terpsichord Dance Company; [oth. writ.] 2nd Place in Junior Division of Kosmos Woman's Club Poetry contest in 1991; [a.] Ooltewah, TN

SEBESTA, TAMARA
[b.] May 4, 1970, Altoona, PA; [p.] Fred Rentz, Patti Rentz; [m.] Paul Sebesta, August 3, 1990; [ch.] Jacob Sebesta; [ed.] Hollidaysburg High, U.S. Navy Jet Engine Mechanic; [occ.] Child Care Provider; [memb.] "We Care" support Group. Hearts United give strength and support (HUGSS) support group.; [oth. writ.] Several other poems about children with special needs, published in local support group newsletters.; [pers.] My poems come from my heart due to my son bring born with a serious heart condition. Through my poetry I try to help people understand what it's like to have a child with special needs.; [a.] Norfolk, VA

SEIDLER, MICHAEL ANTHONY
[pen.] Mas Anth; [b.] November 13, 1959, Louisville, KY; [p.] Jean Frances Schmitt and Fredrick William Seidler; [ed.] Valley High School, Jefferson Community College University of Kentucky, Arizona State University, Northern Arizona University; [occ.] Vocal Musician, Composer, Writer, Minister of Music, Eucharistic Minister; [memb.] Phi Mu Alpha Sinfonia Fraternity, American Legion, U.S. Navy Veteran, St. Joseph's Orphanage Alumnus, KIPWAC, Northern Arizona Aids Outreach, Flagstaff Master Chorale, Arizona Statesmen and Asu Blue Jackets Choir NRTC Great Lakes, IL; [hon.] Sea Service Ribbon U.S.N. 1982, 1989-90 Choral/Opera Scholarship and N.A.U., 1995-96 BF Foundation Scholarship and N.A.U. 1989 A.S.U. RHA Representative Award ACDA Men's Honor Choir 1992; [oth. writ.] "Dia de los Muertos": An Opera, "Orphans of the Marriage Wars", "Before I go"; [pers.] Leaders are those who act upon their ideas, do it don't just gripe, make a difference with positive action. If an idea can be formed in the mind, it can become reality. We are our stewards.; [a.] Louisville, KY

SENERES, WRIGHT B.
[b.] February 25, 1975, Butuan City, Philippines; [p.] Rey V. Seneres and Arlene B. Seneres; [ed.] Eastern Regional High, Rider University; [occ.] Student; [pers.] I write sometimes to get things out of my head. I feel better about it afterwards so it's all good.; [a.] Voorhees, NJ

SENN, VIOLET ROSS
[b.] February 25, 1922, Hopewell, OR; [p.] Orval Loyd and Winnie Carson Ross; [m.] Louie Edward Senn, February 28, 1942; [ch.] Carla 1948, Judy 1949, Ross 1951; [ed.] Lafayette High School, Adult Education Lane Community College, Computer Programming at Lane County Courthouse; [occ.] Retired Lane County Deputy, Clerk; [memb.] Business and Professional Women, International Toastmistress, National Association of Legal Secretaries, SDA Church, Lane County Democrats, Lincoln County Historical Society; [hon.] First president of AFSCME Union in Lane County (Assoc of Federal), State, County, Municipal Employees); [oth. writ.] Poem 1942 in Portland Newspaper, "My Army Heart" Family history books: Bones, Irish-Carson, Senn, Ross and Ward, Newspaper Editor: Laneco Capers, Newspaper General Mgr: The Phoenix News; [a.] Springfield, OR

SHADWICK, SHAYE
[b.] December 29, 1981, Dothan, AL; [p.] Julia and David Shadwick; [ed.] Centerville Elm. and Northside Middle School; [occ.] Student; [memb.] Student Council, and Chorus I'm also in the honors classes in my school; [oth. writ.] Several other poems and same short stories; [pers.] Just remember "Someday's your the wind shield and someday's your the bug."; [a.] Byron, GA

SHAFER, CAROLYN
[pen.] Carolyn Shafer; [b.] December 12, 1924, Norwood, MA; [p.] Dr. and Mrs. Herbert Gurnee; [m.] James F. Shafer, February 18, 1945; [ch.] James Jr, Julie, Joseph, Mary, Daniel, Grace, Paul, Thomas, Ruth Richard; [ed.] Cleveland Heights High School, Mather College, Western Reserve University, Arizona State University BA East Texas State University MS; [occ.] Retired; [memb.] AARP, Bethel Christian Church, Athens, Texas, International Society of Poets; [hon.] Magna Cum Laude, Arizona State University, International Poet of Merit Award, ISP; [oth. writ.] Poems for religious publications.; [pers.] I believe in Gods great love of mankind as reflected in all creation and in His Son's sacrifice. His glory is often best sun in everyday life and circumstances.; [a.] Athens, TX

SHAFFER, ROBERT
[b.] July 31, 1947, St. Joseph, MO; [p.] Gerold Shaffer and Leola Shaffer; [ed.] Ellsworth High; [occ.] Delivery man; [oth. writ.] I've written many poems, but this is my first to be published.; [pers.] I love writing and literature. I thank my mother, Leola Shaffer, and teachers Mabel Herzog, Phyllis Francis, and Al Farrington for this. They believed in my abilities.; [a.] McPherson, KS

SHANNON, MARYETT KAREN
[b.] September 1, 1943, Greenville, PA; [p.] Betty and Don Proud; [ed.] B.S.H.A.; [occ.] R.N. UPMC; [memb.] Jung Association; [a.] Pittsburgh, PA

SHARITZ, JOSEPHINE M.
[b.] June 29, 1912, Atlanta, Ga; [p.] Deceased; [m.] Deceased, World War II, 1st Lt. Thorold J. Sharitz, December 28, 1932; [ch.] Lst. Lt. Charles J. Sharitz

(Dec.), Mrs. Clyde Ray Ward, lives in Huntsville, Al, works for NASA and Army of Defense (Space) Librarian; [ed.] Florida State Univ., Tallahesse, LF, Univ. of Miami, Barry Univ., Skidmore Univ., History of Chinese Art, (taken course); [occ.] Artist, Write poetry, short stories; [memb.] Larramore Rader Poetry Group, Miami, FL; Prof. Membership in teaching art in schools in Miami, FL; [hon.] Anthology of Love Poems, "Remember Me," Florida State Literary Magazine 2 Clinquins. People ask me to read my poetry. They like my paintings; [oth. writ.] Talaria, Literary Magazine at Florida State Univ. in Tallahassee, FL; 3 poems honored in magazines; "Remember Me," published in World Anthology of Love Poems, 1983; other poems not listed; [pers.] I love nature and I am inspired by nature both in my poetry and painting. Poems sing to me in my mind, and I have to write them down. The sky, trees, birds and my love of people inspire me to write.; [a.] Atlanta, GA

SHARP, TERESA
[b.] November 11, 1979, Portsmouth, VA; [p.] Mary Sharp and Jeff Sharp; [ed.] Great Bridge High School, Governors School for Fine Art; [occ.] Student; [hon.] I recently received a $200 grant for the Chesapeake Fine Arts Commission, I won on Honorable Mention from the International Children's Art Exhibitation of the Turkisk Embassy; [pers.] In life, we walk around with veils n our eyes-a blind, closed-minded oblivion. But in poetry, it's like we can see and suddenly the world is such a beautiful and complicated place.; [a.] Chesapeake, VA

SHAWVER, JIMMY A.
[b.] March 27, 1948, Muncie, IN; [p.] Walter and Emagene Shawver; [ch.] Karyn Renee; [occ.] Serf; [memb.] Abate of Indiana, Motorcycle Riders Foundation; [oth. writ.] Poetry, prose and music shared with friends at campfires.; [pers.] Who among us can lift their head in pride and not be humbled by the sky; [a.] Newark, IN

SHAY, SHANNON
[pen.] Shannon Shay; [b.] September 14, 1976, Portales, NM; [p.] Veronica and Windsor Wright; [ch.] Draven Lee Shay; [ed.] Tucumcari High School, Clovis Community College; [occ.] Student; [hon.] Solo and ensemble Awards; [oth. writ.] Poem and story published in Clovis Community College Jaw Anthology; [pers.] Take time to hear the voice your heart deny's for the heart is scared to take a chance on what is whispered in the wind.; [a.] Tucumcari, NM

SHEA, PATRICIA
[pen.] Trish; [b.] July 29, 1981, Yonkers; [p.] Patrice and Joseph Shea; [ed.] Currently in the 9th grade; [occ.] Student; [memb.] I'm in numerous clubs and on the Fox Lane High School track team.; [hon.] I've never been recognized for my poetry. I am in Girl Scouts and I've earned my silver award.; [oth. writ.] I've written dozens of poems. To name them all would be a long list, too long to published.; [pers.] No matter where you are or what doing, you're not alone.; [a.] Bedford Hills, NY

SHEFFLER, BREANA
[pen.] Breana Sheffler; [b.] December 17, 1982, Huthchinson, KS; [p.] Vicky and Eric; [hon.] Honors in school

SHEPARD, AMY
[b.] May 15, 1964, Stockton, CA; [p.] Marian Williams-Sheffield; [ch.] Matthew Kenneth Pattison; [ed.] Colorado University at Boulder, Glendale College, San Joaquin Delta College; [occ.] Full-time student and Research Technician, Colorado University at Boulder, Boulder, CO; [pers.] In the words of a well-known poet, "The moment of change is the only poem." This poem was written for guy, who love inspired my biggest moment of change.; [a.] Broomfield, CO

SHEPHERD, SHANNON R.
[b.] November 2, 1978, Kankakee; [p.] Emma L. Shepherd, L. Shepherd; [ed.] Senior High School; [hon.] Grace N. Bongers School Award for overcoming great obstacles; [oth. writ.] 2 Unpublished poems. Titled the Innocence of the newborn and "My Quest."; [pers.] Man was built to love. Love defines man. If man kind embraces love peace and prosperity will ensue.; [a.] East Windsor, NJ

SHEPPARD, MARLENE S.
[b.] August 14, 1937, Edmonton, AB; [p.] Colin and Estella Wismer; [m.] Gary L. Sheppard, October 1, 1971; [ch.] Kim, Roger, Lisa; [ed.] Victoria Composite High 2 Semesters - 1972 - University of Alberta, Archaeology and Anthropology; [occ.] Retired Executive Secretary - Homemaker; [oth. writ.] Three stories in progress - 2 for children - 1 Semi-Autobiographical cannot complete them until have a hand surgery for joint deterioration from arthritis.; [pers.] Until several illnesses have limited my activities, I volunteered as a teacher's aide at our local Elementary School. I think everyone who has spare time should work with schools. I detest cruelty to children and animals and cannot fathom man's inhumanity to others.; [a.] Arcadia, CA

SHERWOOD, JOAN M.
[b.] July 30, 1942, Albany, NY; [p.] Thomas J. Dolan, Helen E. Dolan; [m.] Wrenn D. Sherwood, July 22, 1962; [ch.] Michael Scott, Thomas Ross, Kristina Rogers, Sandra Sherwood, Constance Sherwood (deceased); [ed.] Vincentian High School, College of St. Rose (2 years), courses at Siena College and Hudson Valley Community College; [occ.] Secretary - Receptionist, multiple Sclerosis College; [memb.] Church of St. Clare Hospitality Committee, Associate of the sisters of Mercy of the Americas, National Multiple Sclerosis Society, Aids Council of New York; [oth. writ.] Regular editorial contributor to local newspaper, poetry for the enjoyment of friends.; [pers.] Although diagnosed with multiple sclerosis 10 yrs. ago, I continue to lead an active life working, caring for 3 grandchildren and of course, writing poetry and stories whenever I can. I am not disabled, but rather, chronically inconvenienced!; [a.] Albany, NY

SHIELDS, RACHEL MAY
[b.] April 13, 1980, Salt Lake City, UT; [p.] Robert C. and Kathryn Shields; [ed.] Sophomore in Caldwell High School; [occ.] Student; [memb.] I am a member of the Caldwell High School Marching Band.; [hon.] My greatest honor is being my parents' daughter.; [oth. writ.] I have written other poems and short stories, none of which are published.; [pers.] I would like to dedicate "Dragons' Jubilee" to my brothers, Robert Jr. and Erik and my sister, Elizabeth.; [a.] Caldwell, ID

SHIELDS, SUSAN
[b.] August 18, 1950, Minneapolis, MN; [p.] W. Dayton Shields and Mildred Shields; [ch.] Karen Segrest, Richard Marks, Jr. granddaughter: Lauren Danielle Marks; [ed.] Mt. Eden High School, Hayward, CA; [occ.] Rural Mail Carrier, Tracy, CA; [oth. writ.] Teach the children, I'm a grandma; [pers.] My poetry reflects my true thoughts and feelings and I am able to express for others what they can't put into words.; [a.] Tracy, CA

SHONK, JOAN A.
[pen.] Joan Abigail; [b.] February 1, 1935, Honolulu, HI; [p.] Harvey and Mary Nobriga; [ed.] Roosevelt High School; [occ.] Retired; [oth. writ.] Nothing published; [pers.] I believe that like "The Silence" the written word is another treasure the almighty has gifted as with. Written expression allows me the luxury of defining a thought to it's acceptable meaning.; [a.] Honolulu, HI

SHORT, DION
[pen.] Dion Short; [b.] July 18, 1981, Queens, NY; [p.] Clevelette Short, Dr. Robby Short; [ed.] Friends Academy; [occ.] Student; [memb.] Diversity Committee, on your marks.; [hon.] Honorable mention in the Illiad Press Poetry Contest as well as publication; [pers.] I write what I feel in my heart and nothing less than that; [a.] Elmont, NY

SHOUDEL, BERTHA R.
[b.] February 28, 1924, Auburn, IN; [p.] Michael J., Alice L. Shoudel (Deceased); [ed.] Auburn High School Graduate; [occ.] Retired (34 years of service) from Renaissance Publishing Co., Inc., Auburn, IN; [oth. writ.] Two articles of prose and a poem "The Garden Lesson" were used on the back page of some religious calendars manufactured by Renaissance Publishing Company, Inc.; [pers.] I love poetry, and especially enjoy the writings of Helen Steiner Rice. I hope that many who read it will be blessed and inspired by the thoughts I have shared in the poem, "Calvary".; [a.] Auburn, IN

SHRAGAL, TINA
[b.] October 12, 1964, Galesburg, IL; [p.] Joe Shragal and Kay Shragal; [ed.] Methodist Medical Center School of Nursing; [occ.] RN; [oth. writ.] Poems published in newspaper and newsletters; [pers.] I believe people need and want to be inspired and this is why I write. Thanks to my many personal mentors.; [a.] Beaumont, TX

SHULZE JR., ROBERT B.
[pen.] Rob Shulze; [b.] January 8, 1973, Long Beach, CA; [p.] Diane Shulze, Robert B. Shulze Jr.; [ed.] Edmonds Woodway High 2 semesters Berklee College of Music; [occ.] Musician/Machinist, William Collins Co., Central Falls, RI; [hon.] National Merit Scholar; [pers.] I wish to connect with as many people as possible who may share my experiences and feelings. I wish to accomplish this musically and poetically. My main influence is my life.; [a.] Central Falls, RI

SIEWERT, LEATHIA R.
[b.] March 1, 1948, New Hampton, IA; [p.] William and Alice Jirak; [m.] Marlyn Donald Siewert, June 20, 1970; [ch.] Melvin A. Siewert, Florent Siewert; [ed.] Associate Degree in Nursing Rochester Community College Rochester, Minnesota; [occ.] Registered Nurse in Geriatric Psychiatry; [memb.] National Flute Society; [hon.] Wife and Mother; [oth. writ.] Several poems published including "World of Mystery", "Happy Donkey", "An Enrapturing Wind", "Sad Robin, Happy Robin" and more; [pers.] Poetry is so good. Poetry is a way to illustrate life's rhythm and mysticisms. Poetry is a sharing and reflecting on simple blessings and

fantasies.; [a.] Missouri City, TX

SILER, CHRISTIAN
[b.] October 15, 1966, Las Vegas, NV; [p.] Jim and Johnny Arrowood, Don Lofton; [ch.] Geoffrey Scott Siler; [ed.] Bach of Arts in Sociology from Southern California College, Costa Mesa, California; [occ.] Bartender for Applebee's, Grill and Bar in Las Vegas, NV; [hon.] Dean's List, Cum Laude, Sociology Club President; [oth. writ.] A personal book of poems and prose and several songs.; [a.] Las Vegas, NV

SIMMONS, DEBORAH K. VICKERY
[pen.] Debbi Simmons; [b.] November 19, 1950, Arkansas City, KS; [p.] Delbert and Carrie Vickery; [m.] Jimmie Lee Simmons, June 19, 1970; [ch.] Kristian, J. Shaun, Savannah, Courtney; [ed.] Ass. Degree in Art Cowley County Communities Cowley Arkansas City Kansas; [occ.] Working Artist, Self Employed, Grandmother; [memb.] Mu Alpha Theta Honor Math - Royal Neighbors of America - V.F.W. Womens Aux., - The First American Baptist Church Central Plains Artist of Kansas Who's Who in American Collegiate Scholars - College Honor Roll, High School Honor Roll; [hon.] Was officer in Student Governments Home Economics Club Office selected Artist of Month past January for Central Plains Artist Org. Office on Board of Directors Central Plains Artist exhibited my oil paintings in 5 of last Central Plain Artist Showing; [oth. writ.] "None Published" since I was a child but have submitted children's book and illustrated stories short stories; [pers.] God gave each of us a special talent or two - I love to experience as many new avenues to channel my desire to learn as much as I can to me an education is the most special gift you can give yourself and thank God at the same time I want to do or try everything God has to offer.; [a.] Arkansas City, KS

SIMMONS, HOPE CHRISTINA
[pen.] Hope Simmons; [b.] May 2, 1980, Arlington, VA; [p.] Mary Simmons, Clellan Simmons; [ed.] Osbourn Park High School; [occ.] Full-time Student; [memb.] U.S. Navy Leaque, Naval Junior Officer Training Corps, National Junior Honor Society; [hon.] Presidential Academic Fitness Award, Academic Letter; [oth. writ.] Montreal - a non-fiction book, 3rd place in young Author's Contest, many other unpublished poems; [pers.] Alot of people think that you can only express good things through the poetry medium, but you can express any feeling vividly through poetry, it's like music.; [a.] Manassas, VA

SIMMONS, ROBERT J.
[b.] August 24, 1925, Chicago, IL; [p.] William and Marie Simmons (Deceased); [m.] Geraldine M. Simons (Deceased), May 20, 1950; [ch.] Robert J., Mary C., Cathleen M., Stephen M., Daniel J., Christopher M.; [ed.] Associated of Science (with honors); [occ.] Retired; [memb.] Fleet Reserve Assn., Naval Institute, Int'l Society of Poets; [hon.] Associate honors degree, San Diego Community Colleges.; [oth. writ.] Five other poems published by NLP.; [pers.] I wrote the foregoing poem for my wife three years after her demise. It is a tribute to her and partial relief from my sorrows. After 45 years naval service many of my writings concern the sea, which I still love and miss as I do my wife.; [a.] San Diego, CA

SINGLETON, KEISHA
[b.] December 12, 1978, Washington, DC; [p.] Calvin and Queenie Singleton; [ed.] Senior-Surrattsville High Clinton, MD; [occ.] Student; [memb.] Pep Club, Female Coalition, Students High on Prevention, Student Government Association and National Honor Society; [hon.] 1st place in Alan Campbell Essay Contest, Honor Roll, Maryland Distinguished Scholar; [a.] Clinton, MD

SINGLETON, LURLEA
[pen.] "Coco Proud"; [occ.] "Ha Tha Yoga Instructor" "Psychic"; [memb.] Riverside Y.W.C.A. (Life Time Member), "University of California Riverside Womens Resource Center", UCR Student Program Board (Psychic Fair Fund Raising); [hon.] U.C.R. Grant, Riverside Y.W.C.A. Fund Raiser Award; [oth. writ.] I first started writing poetry as a "Ghost Writer" for my classmates in English/Literature class, in Francis Jr. High School, Washington D.C. The most impressive poem I wrote at that time, was dedicated to the "Fireside Girls". The subject was "Service" Y.W.C.A. Washington, D.C. Published in their year book.; [pers.] "Being positive will always work to our advantage"; [a.] Riverside, CA

SINGLETON, RICKEY LEE
[b.] April 21, 1955, Inglewood, CA; [p.] Leander Singleton, Rachel Singleton; [m.] Sandy Lynn Singleton, July 25, 1992; [ch.] Rikki Lyn, David John; [ed.] Lennox High, El Camino College; [occ.] Chauffer, Musician; [hon.] This specific poem was chosen and printed in my 1972 High School year book; [oth. writ.] I have written many poems throughout the years for family and friends as gifts; [pers.] I write from the soul, which God has renewed me of. My nights while a sleep, I'll awake, my head flooded with rhyme.; [a.] Riverside, CA

SISON, EVANGELINE A.
[pen.] Gee; [b.] Philippines; [ch.] Ching, Francis and Erich (Sison); [ed.] BA English, major in Journalism (Philippines), selected post graduate English courses at USF (University of San Francisco) CA; [occ.] Paralegal; [oth. writ.] Still awaiting a willing publisher for my first volume of 20 yrs. of poetry-writing.; [pers.] A writer touches people with pen. This allows the writer a satisfying freedom to express and the reader the choice to accept.; [a.] Concord, CA

SLAKE, EUGENE
[b.] December 7, 1960, Lubec, ME; [p.] William Slake, Rose Slake; [m.] Single; [ch.] Shawn Slake; [ed.] Lubec, High School; [occ.] Mechanic, Driver; [memb.] PADI Divemaster; [pers.] I strive to relay material that is simple and understandable. Material that will open ones mind and make one think.; [a.] Lubec, ME

SLATER, C. H.
[pen.] Naomi Slater; [b.] March 31, 1912, Florien, LA; [p.] J. E. Lilley and Lela Arthur Lilley; [m.] Clarence Hoy Slater, June 14, 1934; [ch.] Beverly Loraine; [ed.] M. Ed. University of Houston, Houston, Texas, Elementary School teacher thirty years in Houston I.S.D.; [occ.] Retired school teacher, Homemaker; [memb.] Retired Teachers Assn., Aimwell Baptist Church, S.S. Teacher, Women's Missionary Union, American Bible Society, Diabetes Ass'n., Salvation Army others; [hon.] Plaque for 30 years dedicated teaching on retirement from H.I.S.D.; [oth. writ.] Have had one poem published in local parish paper (Sabine Index) (not this poem); [pers.] I strive to reflect the goodness of God, the acceptance of Jesus as savior, his teachings in the bible, and Christian virtues.; [a.] Many, LA

SLAUGHTER, JANICE
[pen.] Jenny; [b.] October 3, 1936, Columbus, GA; [p.] Charles W. and Alice Cotton; [m.] Byrl Slaughter, June 14, 1968; [ch.] Stephen Thomas; [ed.] Jordan High School Columbus Tech. Early Childhood Courses.; [occ.] Owner, Director Armour Rd. Child Care Center; [oth. writ.] No other articles to date have been published. I am in the process of submitting six stories for publication of children's books.; [pers.] I enjoy writing stories that would interest children. Clean, violence free material. One of my favorite writers would be. "Helen Steiner Rice."; [a.] Columbus, GA

SLIMORITZ, ALBEN
[b.] October 7, 1941, Kealakekua, HI; [p.] Enrico Slimoritz, Kim Slimoritz; [m.] Desiree Slimoritz; [ch.] Caramel, Iodine, Bob; [occ.] Retired; [memb.] American Institute of Electrical Engineers, Association of Philippine Coconut Desiccators; [hon.] Melman Prize for Bicycle Safety, good posture award ninth grade King Kamehanda Jr. High, Don Ho Award for recording difference, father Damian Award for Beseless Optimism in the face of Adversity; [pers.] If you aren't part of the solution, you are part of the precipitate.; [a.] Minneapolis, MN

SMALLS, UNA
[b.] Jamaica, WI; [p.] Edith Smith, John Smith; [m.] Biggie Smalls, February 14, 1993; [ed.] Jose Marti High School - Spanish Town, Jamaica WI Dental Auxiliary School - Kingston, Jamaica WI; [occ.] Dental Hygienist; [pers.] If at first you don't succeed try and try and try again.; [a.] Bronx, NY

SMATHERS, ROXANNE A.
[pen.] Roxanne A. Smathers; [b.] January 30, 1963, Smyra, TN; [p.] Richard Talstrra and Alia Gorzoch; [m.] James R. Smathers, September 24, 1994; [ch.] Dirk and Garrett Smathers; [ed.] Brea-Olinda High School, Fullerton Community College, California State University Fullerton; [occ.] Wife and mother; [hon.] Deans List; [oth. writ.] Articles for the Hornet, and several poems published in anthologies.; [pers.] There is but one way that I can be assured to have those I love with me for eternity, that is also what leads me onward.; [a.] Mission Viejo, CA

SMELSER, JESSICA
[b.] March 19, 1983, Roanoke, VA; [p.] Rodney and Patrice Smelser; [ed.] I attend Northside Middle School; [occ.] Student; [hon.] Regional competition in Odessey of the mind, PTA reflections contest (first place); [oth. writ.] I have written several other poems and short stories, a few of which have been published in my schools newsletter.; [pers.] I try to use the talents God has given me o reveal to others the beauty of his creation.; [a.] Roanoke, VA

SMILLIE, GEORGE
[b.] October 12, 1930, New York, NY; [p.] Violet and Robert Smillie; [m.] Windower, June 22, 1958 to Phyllis; [ch.] Brenda Lee Smillie; [ed.] Stow College, School of Building and Allied Trades, Glasgow Scotland.; [occ.] Cabinet maker, Carpenter; [memb.] NRA, Wooden Canoe Heretage Assoc.; [hon.] USAF German Occ. ect 1951-55 Glasgow Camerounians 1945-6; [oth. writ.] About a handful; [pers.] Real poetry comes from life and the heart; [a.] Clearwater, FL

SMITH, ANNE GEORGIA
[b.] December 16, 1944, Raleigh, NC; [ed.] San Jose State University, B.A. Peperdine University Masters; [occ.] I am a retired special education teacher and wheelchair user. I taught on Guam.; [pers.] I wanted my students to know that it is okay to have a dream and to reach for their piece of the sky.; [a.] Honolulu, HI

SMITH, HELEN M.
[pen.] Helen Mitchell Smith; [b.] October 24, 1927, Leeds, AL; [p.] James Leo and Ruth Burns Mitchell; [m.] Don Carlos Smith, December 22, 1949; [ch.] Marsha Lynn, Nancy Ruth, Rebecca Jean; [ed.] Benjamin Franklin High School, B.A. from John Brown University; [occ.] Administrative Secretary for a church.; [oth. writ.] Radio scripts, various poems, composition of lyrics and music including recent wedding song for daughter's wedding, creative writing for public announcements in church bulletins on regular basis.; [pers.] I enjoy creative writing, writing poetry and composing music. Humor is an important element I use in my poetry. I have a fervent faith in God and His Son, Jesus Christ and a deep appreciation for the Bible. This is often emphasized in my poetry reflecting my love and devotion.; [a.] Los Angeles, CA

SMITH, JENNIFER
[b.] February 11, 1981, Canton, OH; [p.] Sam and Anita Smith; [ed.] Freshman at Canton South High School; [occ.] Student; [memb.] 4-H for horses, Marching Concert Band, previously in Girl Scouts, candy stripper at a local hospital; [hon.] Editor's Choice Award twice for poems published in, "A far off place" - The Dance "Best of 1995" - The Messenger; [oth. writ.] Poems published in "A Far Off Place" "Best of 1995"; [pers.] Play the hand that life has dealt you and play it well.; [a.] Canton, OH

SMITH, KATHRYN ANN
[b.] August 4, 1948, Houston, TX; [p.] Ann and J. B. Smith; [ed.] B.A., French and Spanish University of Texas, Austin Diploma D' Etudes, Sorbonne, Paris, France; [occ.] Artist, Writer; [hon.] Honor student, Memorial High School, honors program, UT Austin, entered as a sophomore, studied four languages, French, Spanish, Russian, German; [pers.] I hope that the young women, and men, in my family will pursue their own special gifts and abilities in life and see where it takes them.; [a.] Houston, TX

SMITH, PHILBERT KARL
[pen.] Philbert K.; [b.] January 5, 1995, Chicago; [p.] Catherine Bryant and John Adamson; [ed.] Lane Technical High Metropolitan State University; [occ.] UPS person/starving student; [memb.] New Hope Baptist Church; [hon.] Dean's List; [oth. writ.] "Wayward Rose", "Passages", "The Regrettables" and other various soul searching poems; [pers.] Poetry isn't just a frame of reference we use to look inside ourselves, it's a window into the soul.; [a.] Denver, CO

SMITH, RITA M.
[b.] March 16, 1927, Pontiac, MI; [p.] Leo J. and Mae Archambeau; [ch.] 3 Sons, and 5 grandchildren (Suzanne Terese, daughter); [ed.] Mercy College, Detroit, MI, MI State Univ. and continuous classes and workshops afterwards; [occ.] Owner: Rita M. Smith and Assoc. and Lagniappe Publishing, Poet, Author, International Speaker and Trainer, Storyteller, and Gerontologist.; [memb.] Nat'l Writers Assoc., Publishers Marketing Assoc. Co Independent Publishers, Christian Writers Assoc.,; [hon.] Women Leader's of CO 192-93. Took 5th Place at National Writers Assoc Conference, 1993 for poem, "Rainbows Come In Different Shapes."; [oth. writ.] Wrote and published poem book, and He said, "COME ONE/ALL and an audio cassette album, ADULT CHILDREN/AGING PARENTS, A common Sense Approach. Published in 2 Anthologies for Mile High Poetry Society and articles in newspapers; [pers.] ONE NIGHT, A LITTLE GIRL LOOKED UP was written to honor my daughter and to inspire young girls to follow their dreams. She has ben in aerospace for 20 yrs. She is a Physicist and Member of the Technical Staff in Optical Sciences.; [a.] Englewood, CO

SMITH, WILLIE CLAY
[pen.] The Forsaking One; [b.] July 21, 1962, Marked Tree, AR; [p.] Robert and Verlyn Smith; [ed.] G.E.D. In and from The school of life; [occ.] Seeking to be known as a poet seeking a publisher; [memb.] I.S.P.D. Member a Child of God Trinity Christian Church World Wide Prison Ministries; [hon.] I yet to achieve several poems published within the National Library of Poetry; [oth. writ.] To many to name I just write and write and write seeking a publisher to gists me in my goal of publishing a book of my works; [pers.] I am you and you are me and we yet to meet to know each other we are one but a one that is made into many we are our own mystery we are our own maze!; [a.] Marked Tree, AR

SNAUFFER, WILLIAM C.
[b.] July 15, 1940, Sunbury, PA; [p.] William, Edna; [m.] Single; [ed.] Albright College, West Virginia University, Penn State University; [occ.] CEO - Embreeville Center; [memb.] American Psychological Association, American Association on Mental Retardation, American Management Association, PGA of America, United States Golf Association.; [hon.] Dean's List; [oth. writ.] Professional Papers in Psychology, Behavior Management, Management, Organizational Strategies, Previous Publications by National Library of Poetry; [pers.] Poetry is Tension Reduction outlet for a troubled life writings are automatic, late night experiences; [a.] Coatesville, PA

SNEED, JENNIFER
[b.] November 16, 1981, Oxnard, CA; [p.] Mac and Linda Sneed; [ed.] Freshman at Santa Clara High School in Oxnard, CA; [occ.] Student; [memb.] Students Against Drunk Driving (SADD), Amateur Athletic Union (AAU), USA Track and Field Association; [hon.] 1st ever John R. Foster Scholar Athletic Award at Hueneme Christian School, Junior Olympian in Cross Country and Track and Field; [oth. writ.] Many unpublished poems and short stories; [a.] Oxnard, CA

SNOW, AMY
[b.] April 11, 1972, Ware, MA; [p.] Mary Ellen Snow and Mark Snow; [ed.] Quaboag Regional high UMASS - Amherst; [occ.] English teacher; [memb.] Mass teacher's Association; [hon.] Golden Key National Honor Society Dean's List; [oth. writ.] Currently working on a coming of age novel; [pers.] Each person creates and is responsible for their own destiny I try to write about and reflect on the struggles to reach that destiny, Maya Angela is an inspiration poet for me; [a.] Amherst, MA

SOBEL, HELEN FAY
[b.] Philadelphia; [p.] Morris and Lillian Fay; [m.] Arnold M, September 1, 1946; [ch.] 2 Females; [ed.] B.A. Hunter College, NYC MA Columbia University, MA Temple U. Elem. Ed. Secondary Ed.; [occ.] Retired give lectures on my travels; [oth. writ.] Articles on travels lectures on travel computer programs in Math, Language, Social Studies, Reading, etc. Plays for children including songs, choreography.; [pers.] I taught in N.Y. for 3 years, in cheltenham school district for 34 years both Elem. and Middle Schools. Many of my lessons have been incorporated into curriculum, wrote faculty programs every emotion I experience is always recorded

SOTO, EVANGELINA MARIA
[b.] December 6, 1979, Granada Hills, CA; [p.] Diomenda Maria Shane and Edward Soto; [ed.] I'm currently in 10th grade, but I'm above average in some of my classes.; [hon.] Reading contest when in kindergarden for hand books, parenting class, 40 hours of retailing and merchandising, training at my old place. Cutest smile, best artist, school for 21 good grams in a row.; [oth. writ.] I've written other ones but never published them. Some of them are, The Holy Virgin's Tears, Sweetie, a poem that's dedicated to my houses late kitten, sweetie, the wind, summer time, winter time.; [pers.] To all people out there you can do it if you try. I do my poems so people can do something else instead of killing, raping, and snatching violent movie, stop the violence. We could do it. Love all animals and pets.; [a.] Reseda, CA

SOTO, SAMUEL M.
[b.] October 5, 1925, Colorado, U.S.A.; [p.] Amado Soto and Ramona Soto; [m.] Mary Nieto Soto, August 29, 1947; [ch.] Christina, Amado, Arthur, Mark, and Zachary; [ed.] Bachelor of Arts in History California State University, Los Angeles December 10, 1983; [occ.] Retired; [memb.] Life member of the Military Order of the Purple Heart; [hon.] Honorable discharge U.S. Army purple heart medal and the bronze star medal September 1, 1943 to November 21, 1945.; [pers.] Perpetual Peace is a Universal Dream. Humanity must now come, to a universal conclusion that war is insanity itself.; [a.] Los Angeles, CA

SOWNEIDER, EIDER
[b.] July 11, 1969, Queens, NY; [p.] Theodore and Dominique; [ed.] Portledge School, Alfred Univ. and C. W. Post; [occ.] V.P. Eltron Supply; [memb.] Museum of Natural History, National Geographic, National Wildlife, Audobon Society.; [hon.] Phi Alpha Theta, Historical Honor Society.; [pers.] Be here now; [a.] New York, NY

SPAETH, MATTHEW
[b.] October 28, 1972, Hammond, IN; [p.] Roger and Meredith Spaeth; [ed.] Marian Catholic High School, B.S. in Geology from Northern Illinois University; [occ.] Environmental Contractor; [memb.] Golden Key National Honor Society, Illinois Groundwater Association; [oth. writ.] Several unpublished poems and short horror fiction stories; [pers.] Since early childhood, I've been fascinated by mythical beasts and monsters. These creatures represent the evils we se around us and in us, and are used both to express those evils, and to divorce them from out concepts of who we are.

SPARKS, CHELSEA A.
[pen.] Tiny, Lucky, Cheesy; [b.] November 1, 1980, Detroit; [p.] Celesta and Robert Sparks; [ed.] Denby Technical and Preparatory, High School Graduation 1999; [memb.] Jr. Key Club-We help the needy by passing out baskets and working in a soup kitchen.;

[hon.] I have won many awards for Chess.; [oth. writ.] I have several other writings; [pers.] I guess I can say that every one, and every thing in my life contributes to my writing. I write what I feel deep inside.; [a.] Detroit, MI

SPEHAR, VALERIE
[pen.] Valerie Spehar; [b.] May 7, 1959, Detroit, MI; [p.] Ralph and Joan Spehar; [m.] Single; [ed.] Taylor Center High; [occ.] Driver for Caterair International, Metro Airport, Detroit; [memb.] Paralyzed Veterans World Wildlife Fund; [pers.] I write what's in my heart.; [a.] Taylor, MI

SPERRY, DANIEL MARK
[b.] May 25, 1973, Royal Oak, MI; [p.] John and PJ Pryde, Tom Sperry; [m.] Klara Ruth Sperry, July 2, 1994; [ed.] Hazel Park High, Bob Jones University; [pers.] As a born again Christian, I give God all the credit for any talent I may have. My goal is to reflect themes that emphasize the destructiveness of hedonistic living and the benefits of morality. If my writings afford even one person the opportunity to learn of Christ's death and resurrection to save men, either through its content or through the testimony of the author, then I will be content.; [a.] Greenville, SC

SPRAGUE, DEVON
[b.] February 15, 1979, Bridgton, ME; [p.] Doreen and Glen Huntress, Don Sprague; [ed.] Junior at Lake Region High School, Naples, ME; [hon.] Honor student, English award, Sophomore year, Class treasurer Sophomore, Junior year; [oth. writ.] Essay published, 1992, Maine Council of English Language Arts.; [pers.] I believe poetry is a beautiful thing, even in its darkest tones.; [a.] Bridgton, ME

SPUHLER, TROY
[b.] Reading, PA, NYC; [p.] Deceased; [ed.] Reading Senior High, Pennsylvania State University; [occ.] Store Manager - General Nutrition Center; [memb.] Green peace; [hon.] National Honor Society; [pers.] I have seen a lot in my young life. I hope that my poems gives an individual insight to their souls and maybe, someday, make a different to the world we live in.; [a.] Drexel Hill, PA

SQUIRE, GWEN M.
[b.] August 22, 1966, Buffalo, NY; [p.] William and Lisa Squire; [ed.] Frontier Central High School, Erie Community College/South - Associates degree and Hilbert College - Bachelors Degree; [occ.] I will be graduating from Hilbert in May with my bachelor's degree; [memb.] Clubs in school include - Students with abilities Team (SWAT), Human Services Association and 23t club. Silver wheels wheelchair football Inc.; [hon.] Outstanding contribution to student with abilities team. Poem published in school magazine. Awards for silver wheels wheelchair football Inc.; [pers.] Being an Individual with Spina Bifida, I have tried to never let my disability get the better of me. I do this by living by the special Olympics Oath "Let me win but if I cannot win, let me be brave in the attempt."; [a.] Blasdell, NY

ST. CYR, GEMMA
[pen.] Gemma James, Tulips; [b.] September 26, 1950, Trinidad; [p.] Arthur-Paul and Ursula James; [m.] December 1973; [ch.] Tecla, Jeanine, Patrice, Marvin, Adelle; [ed.] Bishop Anstey High School Mausica Teachers Training College 1969-1971 (Trinidad) Elem. Teacher Trinidad 1971-1989; [occ.] Volunteer Services in Texas; [memb.] Travis Avenue Baptist Church - F. Worth; [hon.] Founder and P.R.O. for 'Faith Hope and Charity Mission School' on the site of the village dump in trinidad a place that lots of trinidadians are not aware of. May 1995 'Rose Award' for volunteer services at Plaza Medical Center F. Worth; [oth. writ.] In the making, religious, stories for children- unpublished; [pers.] 'Children are the wealth of the nations. God has an eternal destiny for every child'. My poem is dedicated to all children everywhere born into poverty, and my prayer is that. This cycle of poverty be broken in their lives.

STADELMAN, ANNE MARIE
[b.] January 22, 1982, Lockport, NY; [p.] Jerome and Mary Stadelman; [ed.] 8th Grade student at Royalton Hartland Jr./Sr. High School; [memb.] Jr. High Student Council, National Jr. Honor Society; [hon.] High honor roll student with several awards for academic achievements, band awards; [oth. writ.] Many other poems written in spare time as a hobby.; [pers.] I write many of my poems to show some kind of meaning. Someday I hope to write a poetry book, childrens' book, for a novel.; [a.] Lockport, NY

STALDER, WENDY
[b.] January 3, 1964, Canton, OH; [ed.] East Canton High School, 1982, New Mexico State University 1988; [occ.] Teacher, Coach El Paso, Texas; [memb.] Texas Association of Basketball Coaches. Texas Girls Coaches Association; [hon.] High School All American Athlete, all State Athlete (OH), Intercollegiate Athlete of the year.; [a.] El Paso, TX

STANFILL, MARY INGRAM
[b.] October 7, 1938, Port St. Joe, FL; [p.] Nina S. and Reginald M. Ingram; [m.] Billy Ray Stanfill Sr., February 7, 1959; [ch.] Millinea S. Johnson and Billy Ray Stanfill Jr.; [ed.] High School Diploma, Port St. Joe, Fl High School, Class of 1956 - Highest honors, American Institute of Banking; [occ.] Wife and homemaker, Ambassadress of the Lord Jesus Christ; [oth. writ.] Poems, songs and inspirational edifying writings shared in ministry with thanksgiving to God in the name of Jesus that the Father be glorified in the Son and people be helped by the Lord.; [pers.] I have received much mercy and grace by the love of God being poured out upon me in the name of Jesus and by the spirit of our God. The ability comes from God to be used for His glory and His pleasure for the good of all. God's will be done. Amen.; [a.] Huntsville, AL

STAPLETON, KRISTI
[b.] February 11, 1960, Springfield, MO; [p.] Virgil and Barbara Gray; [m.] Wilton Stapleton, June 20, 1992; [ed.] Forest Hill High School in Jackson, Ms. in 1978, two years at the University of south Alabama until a car accident (I was a passenger) left me with a teacup sized blood clot on my brain that put me in a 5 month long coma.; [occ.] Home maker; [memb.] I'm a proud member of old Spanish Fort Baptist Church in Spanish Fort, Alabama, where I'm a member of the Glory Choir; [hon.] I was in the National Honor Society in High School where I won 2nd place in a essay contest titled, 2001. How Today's Citizen can Ensure Freedom and Democracy for the 21st Century. I gave the Invocation at my graduation.; [oth. writ.] I've written poetry for 20 years and had one published in a Southern Baptist Sunday School book in 1978. One of my poems was put to music. My essay and a poem were published in my High School magazine, La Reflexion in 1978; [pers.] God left me here after the wreck for a steward of the talents he's given me. I want to tell the world about my precious Savior and how much he means to me, I think my writing is a way he can use; [a.] Bay Minette, AL

STARCHER, AMANDA C.
[b.] November 20, 1976, Parkersburg, WV; [p.] Pamela L. Starcher; [ed.] Parkersburg South High School, Salve Regina University; [occ.] Student at Salve Regina University; [memb.] Varsity Soccer and Sailing Teams, Bethel Baptist Church, 4-H, Salve Regina Theatre Company; [hon.] Publication in "Wood Whispers: (County writing magazine/contest): Participant in honors writing course project pen pals; [oth. writ.] "Acceptance", first place short story in Wood Whispers; [pers.] I have a tough time expressing myself vocally when I feel things too passionately. My writing reflects what I can't say or do, but need to.; [a.] Parkersburg, WV

STARKS, DOROTHY N.
[pen.] Dvo Iv' Starmancer; [b.] February 25, 1950, Montgomery, AL; [p.] Ed Starks Sr., Nellie Dillard; [ch.] James, Kate, Teka, Xeka, Tefa, Neal, Henrea Sherman; [ed.] George Washington Carver, Alabama State University (3 yrs) Trenholm Technical College (Nursing); [occ.] Home Health Care Nurse; [memb.] Holt Street Baptist Church.; [hon.] Two different parent award (Best Parent).; [oth. writ.] First writing.; [pers.] I speak from experience and everyday dealing, no matter how tough things may seem, always strive for the best (a star).; [a.] Montgomery, AL

STARNES, TREVOR
[b.] March 19, 1975, Rochester, MI; [p.] Rick and Steff Starnes; [ed.] Graduated as a Valedictorian at Eisenhower High School, Utica Community Schools - '93. Presently junior at Hope College, Holland, Michigan (Pre-Med student majoring in chemistry and Biology); [occ.] College student; [memb.] Mortar Board, Alpha Epsilon Delta, Phi Tau Nu Fraternity, Boy Scouts of America (Eagle Scout), Order of the Arrow, Hope College Football Team, Peace Lutheran Church, National Honor Society; [hon.] Dean's List, Presidential Scholar, Freshman Chemistry Student of the year, MIAA student athlete of the week, MIAA Academic honor roll, Jaecker Chemistry Scholar MHSAA Scholar Athlete 93, All-state '93 Academic Football and Soccer, All-County Acad.; [oth. writ.] Several poems published in junior and senior high creative writing magazines. Also participated in several essay contests in county.; [pers.] 'Always work to your full potential,' I enjoy writing about people in stressful or challenging situations!; [a.] Shelby Township, MI

STATHOPOULOS, ELLEN
[b.] June 29, 1982, Chicago, IL; [p.] George and Maureen Stathopoulos; [pers.] Homo sum-humani nihil a me alienum puto. (I am human nothing human is foreign to me.); [a.] Chicago, IL

STEEG, ANNA
[b.] December 13, 1902, Massachusetts; [p.] John, Amelia Pacewicz; [m.] Edwin W. Steeg; [ch.] Patricia Steeg Reynolds; [oth. writ.] For Senior Citizens meetings. Verse and worse from the Scape book of A.L.S.; [pers.] A compulsion to write long denied: Submission to nurture my soul.; [a.] Willsboro, NY

STEGER, CARIN ABRIA
[b.] August 22, 1976, Warwick, RI; [p.] Cynthia and Ron Steger; [ed.] Barrington High School, Penn State

University (currently attending); [occ.] Student - sophomore at P.S.U. majoring in Secondary Education English/Communications.; [memb.] Co-editor of Problem Child, Scholar's Literary Magazine, Recycling Coordinator for you my dorm, Volunteer with International Journeys Storyhour; [hon.] Deans List, University Scholar, Phi Eta Sigma Honor Society, National Honor Society; [oth. writ.] Published n Kalliope, P.S.U's literary magazine, and also on the World Wide Web! Address: hHP://www. ECNET., net/users/mudjh5/poetry.htm; [pers.] Thanks and much love to my parents and my dear Christopher for believing in me; [a.] Barrington, RI

STEINBRONER, JOHN D.
[b.] March 31, 1931, Los Angeles, CA; [p.] Arthur and Simone Steinbroner; [m.] Single; [ch.] Katherine Steinbroner, Maschler; [ed.] Mt. Carmel High, Loyola Uni. of LA; [occ.] Financial Credit Consultant; [oth. writ.] Out of the dark May 1985; [pers.] Take time to help others, the rewards are great; [a.] Los Angeles, CA

STEINBRONN, REUBEN
[b.] June 15, 1931, Iowa; [p.] Gottlob Steinbronn; [m.] Meta Steinbronn, June 23, 1954; [ch.] Anthony, Kevin, Rebecca, Jennie, Reuben D.; [ed.] Bachelors Degree, Wartburg College, Waverly, Iowa, Master of Divinity, Concordia Theological Seminary, Springfield, Ill., 1974; [occ.] Lutheran Pastor serving Trinity Lutheran Church, Albuquerque, NM; [hon.] Deans List; [oth. writ.] Poems published in parish newsletters, several meditational homilies in poetic format, numerous other poems.; [pers.] "To God be the glory" for talents and abilities; [a.] Albuquerque, NM

STEPHENS, MARY HAMILTON
[b.] Davidson, NC; [p.] Cornelia and Charles Hamilton; [m.] James Linley Stephens; [ch.] Richard Hamilton Stephens; [ed.] Davidson High School, Converse College, Columbia University Sorbonne; [occ.] Retired Teacher and Tour Director; [oth. writ.] Across the world with Mary and Martha; [a.] Lumberton, NC

STEPHENSON, TERESA
[b.] December 7, 1960, Detroit, MI; [p.] Bernard and Irene Bretz; [ch.] William J. Bieke Jr.; [ed.] Denby High, Macomb Community College; [occ.] Quality Engineer; [memb.] Right to Life; [pers.] I believe everything happens for a reason and no one enters your life on a whin. Thank you, MBP.; [a.] Eastpointe, MI

STERNBERG, SARA J.
[b.] July 11, 1980, New Haven, CT; [p.] Dr Robert J. Sternberg, Dr. Betty J. Sternberg; [ed.] Choate Rosemary Hall, Wallingfrod, CT. Class of 1988, Sedgwick Middle School, West Hartford, CT. Class of 1994, Braeburn Elementary School, West Hartford, CT. Class of 1991.; [occ.] Student; [memb.] United States Tennis Association, Hillel at Choate Rosemary Hall, Choate Rosemary Hall Band and Orchestra.; [hon.] Dean's List all terms, 2nd Place Connecticut Science Teacher's Association Award of the 1993 Connecticut Science fair, special Award from the American Heart Association and the Talcott Mountain Science Center, Presidential Academic Fitness Award, 1994.; [oth. writ.] Several poems and essays pending publication; [pers.] I would like to thank Mr. Ben Foster and Ms. Ann Nesslage, my English teachers at Chaote, for helping me explore various forms of writing through which I can express my inner thoughts.; [a.] West Hartford, CT

STEVENS, JAMIE L.
[b.] May 7, 1978, Garnett, KS; [p.] Bryan and Sandra Stevens; [ed.] Anderson County High School, Senior.; [oth. writ.] Various poems; [pers.] When I feel lost or alone, writing poems helps me relieve my stress and explain how I feel.; [a.] Garnett, KS

STEWARD, MARIE MARTA
[b.] September 29, 1962, Sonora, CA; [p.] Martha J. Steward, Donald G. Steward; [ed.] San Luis Obispo High School Santa Rosa Junior College Heald Business College; [occ.] Legal Secretary; [hon.] Dean's List, Perfect Attendance Award; [a.] Rohnert Park, CA

STEWART, DIANE LYNNE
[pen.] Dian Lynne; [b.] October 25, 1961, Haure de Grace, MD; [p.] Lewis Oliver Smith, Lynne Estelle Phelps Smith; [ch.] Amanda Elizabeth Stewart, Aaron Douglas King; [ed.] High School graduate (Aberdeen Sr. High Aberdeen, MD 21001) U.S. Navy Photography Class a school some college (Psychology, English); [occ.] Supply Technician for Dept. of Defense/Reservist, Sergeant, Maryland Army National Guards HQ-STARC (Det 1 and 2) Balt., Md 21201-2288; [memb.] St. John's Episcopal Church, Havre de Grace, Md 21078, Daughter's of the American Revolution, Windsor Historical Society (Connecticut); [hon.] Journalism Award - Senior (1979) year, Aberdeen Sr. High School, Naval Air Station Miramar Sailor-ofthe-Mouth Award, San Diego, CA 1982; [oth. writ.] Many poems! This is my first attempt at letting others hear them and I am so thankful and happy - it has given me the encouragement to go for it!; [pers.] The ability to learn from mistakes and take pain and sorrow, along with happiness, and transform the resulting energy into positivity, which is my writing. I like the thought that people may gain not only enjoyment, but compassion thru my poetry.; [a.] Havre de Grace, MD

STEWART, MANDI
[b.] August 12, 1981, Palacios, TX; [p.] Scott and Mona Stewart; [ed.] Tidehaven High School Freshman; [occ.] Tidehaven School Student; [pers.] I use my poetry to express my feelings.; [a.] Blessing, TX

STEWART, RITA MARIE
[b.] October 25, 1958, Johnstown, PA; [p.] James and Mary Frances Stewart; [ed.] Johnstown High School, Cambria Rowe Business College; [occ.] Legal Secretary; [oth. writ.] Several poems, yet unpublished; [pers.] In all things acknowledge God and He will direct your path.; [a.] Temple Hills, MD

STINGER, KIM
[b.] April 7, 1975, Darby, PA; [p.] Barbara Stinger, Raymond Stinger; [ed.] Springfield High, Berklee College of Music; [occ.] Music Business Student, Berklee College of Music; [memb.] National organization for Women; [hon.] Dean's List; [oth. writ.] A few poems published in music fanzines; [pers.] Because I'm shy, I have to find other ways to speak through dance, music and especially poetry. And if a poem of mine could touch someone's heart, and make them understand they're not alone, then I have accomplished my goal.; [a.] Springfield, PA

STOCK JR., GORDON J.
[b.] May 13, 1971, Richmond, VA; [p.] Gordon J. Stock, Sr., Judy W. Stock; [ed.] Midlothian High School, Yale University (BS 1993) University of Virginia (MA 1995); [occ.] Assistant Instructor for an Undergraduate Chemistry Laboratory, Yale University; [pers.] I believe that one should try to give one's life meaning. I am an ardent believer of the statement from the movie Barbacella that a life without cause is a life without effect!; [a.] New Haven, CT

STOCKMAL, SARABETH
[pen.] Sarabeth Stockmal; [b.] October 29, 1980, Bridgeport, CT; [p.] Richard Stockmal, Carol Stockmal; [ed.] Pomperaug Regional High School (Southbury, CT) 10th grade presently; [occ.] Student; [memb.] I actively collect stamps from around the world through the U.S. postal service and United nations, belong to the Adopt-A grand part club at school, and have sponsored many wolves through the National Wildlife Fed.; [hon.] Make High Honors at school, have won awards at dance competitions, won the Presidential Sports Award for dancing; [oth. writ.] Published quarterly for our church newsletters, am in the process of publishing a book with a company in California; [pers.] I believe the history of yesterday can be clearly seen in the future of tomorrow. Writers are here to bring that history to life.; [a.] Southbury, CT

STOKES, DANIEL ROBIN CHARLES
[pen.] Daniel Stokes Jr.; [b.] June 9, 1966, Dublin, Ireland; [p.] Daniel Stokes, Margaret Cassidy; [m.] Margaret Stokes, August 16, 1992; [ed.] Rath mines Senior College Dublin Ireland. Lewis Uni Joliet Ill; [occ.] Castle Builder/Writer Dreamer; [hon.] All awards and honors have been from sports. Which were National Diving and Trampoling Champion of Ireland.; [oth. writ.] All poetry which have yet to be published. Hopefully the National Library of Poetry will be the break that I've strived for these past nine years.; [pers.] I am incarcerated in pontiac prison I'll for murder. Being an Irish citizen I wish to see peace in Ireland United Ireland. Too many innocent lives ended by ignorance. I dedicate my work and life to my wife, she has given me rebirth.

STORLAZZI, MICHELLE
[b.] July 13, 1974, Quincy, MA; [p.] A. Michael and Elizabeth Storlazzi; [ed.] Bachelor of Science in Business Administration at Stonehill College, Braintree High School; [hon.] Awarded to attend a student seminar - one of 16 students across the county, Deans List; [oth. writ.] Several poems published in school magazines and other national anthologies; [pers.] I believe a person only lives once, so you must be willing to try everything, keep an open mind, and live each day as though it were the last.; [a.] Braintree, MA

STORY, JAMES MONROE
[b.] January 13, 1918, Purdy, VA; [m.] Widower of Alma Bishop, date of marriage 12-19-40; [ch.] Joyce, James Jr., John; [ed.] I am self taught and educated. I earned my GED certificate at age 72.; [occ.] Retired; [oth. writ.] Produced two booklets of poetry.; [pers.] I try to keep my poems simple, writing from the heart telling little rhyming stories. Most of these stories are true, telling of life on a farm in rural America of an era gone by. My writings consist of little love, religious, funny and sad stories about myself or people I know.; [a.] Mechanicsville, VA

STRANG, DOROTHY L.
[pen.] Louisa Dells; [b.] February 13, 1930, Los Angeles, CA; [p.] Dr. Theodore A. Strang and Dr. Pearl M. Sampson. They practiced OB and GYN in Long Beach, CA for 50 yrs. Dr. Pearl Sampson always used her

maiden name, although they had married on March 9, 1928.; [ch.] I have never married and children are not my cup of tea.; [ed.] B. A. in Latin America Affairs and English Lit. from U.C. Berkeley - 1952 M. L. S. (Library Science) U.C, Berkeley 1955; [occ.] Writer for own pleasure; [memb.] I am a loner. Belong to the Friends of the Nature Center at Idyllwild, CA., a small mountain community in the San Jacinto Mts.; [oth. writ.] Medicine, Mountains and Music, 2 Vos. plus their separate indexes, printed at Kinkos 1993, 1995. Biographical account of the year my parents were dating, 1927-1928, when they hiked the San Gabriel and San Bernardino Mts. of South CA. Books incorporate the history of the mountain areas and reveal their love of medicine, mountains and February 1995- Biographical classical music. Prose poem with picture of the life of my father.; [pers.] I believe in impersonal metaphysics and practical humanism. That is the intelligence and creative power of the universe is impersonal and we are temporary expressions of evolving ideas. Good and evil are human concepts, need to incorporate man's current scientific and technical knowledge and emphasize the importance of humans assuming the responsibility for what they think, say and do. Use their intelligence and practical sense I admire people who contribute towards humanity's scientific and technical knowledge and cultural refinement.; [a.] Long Beach, CA

STRANG, JOY
[pen.] J. P. Jordan; [b.] April 29, 1980, Richmond, VA; [p.] Jackie Reed, James Strang; [ed.] Colonial Heights High School Rising Junior; [occ.] Student at Colonial Heights High School; [memb.] Future Business Leaders of America Drama Club Spanish Club; [pers.] I find contentment in writing as I strive to reach the inner peace we all search for.; [a.] Colonial Heights, VA

STRATTMAN, PATRICIA
[pen.] Shalee Alisha; [b.] December 24, 1957, Poughkeepsie, NY; [p.] Mary E. Strattman; [ed.] Housatonic Valley Regional High School, Connecticut Business Institute; [occ.] Administrative Assistant Center Capital Corporation, Meriden, CT; [memb.] Fraternal Order of Eagles Womens Auxiliary, CT Red Cross, CT Salvation Army Volunteer; [hon.] High Honors, Dean's List; [oth. writ.] "The Wall Around My Heart", published in "The American Poetry Anthology", 1986, "Lady of Ladies", published in The Lakeville Journal, 1987 Several unpublished poems and short stories.; [pers.] I love life - I wake up in the morning and, like a 4 year old, look for the cookies. Most of my work is accomplished through the love I have for life, God and family. I am also greatly influenced by the works of Emily Dickenson and Mark Twain.; [a.] Winsted, CT

STRONG, JEFF
[b.] Salt Lake City, UT; [m.] Married for 9 years; [ch.] 1 daughter and 3 sons; [ed.] South High, University of Utah, Bringham Young University; [occ.] Police Officer/Sergeant, Brigham Young University; [memb.] The Church of Jesus Christ of Latter-Day Saints; [pers.] I am a realist that has really enjoyed watching people over the years. I try to govern my actions by the principles of basic common sense.; [a.] Sandy, UT

STRUNK, GORDON J.
[b.] October 20, 1963, St Charles, MO; [p.] Gordon and Iris Strunk; [ed.] St. Dominic High, Ranken Technical College; [occ.] Industrial Machine, Mechanic; [memb.] Knights of Columbus; [pers.] My aim when I write is to convey in a way the thought and concerns of the people today. High on my list of influence are, Ben Franklin, Thomas Jefferson, John Lennon, Ghandi, Jim Morrison and Beck.; [a.] O'fallon, MO

STUART, BRONWYN MARIE
[b.] December 29, 1974, Monterey Park, CA; [p.] Elaine and George Stuart; [ed.] San Gabriel High School Pasadena City College; [occ.] Student; [memb.] Church of Jesus Christ of Latter Day Saints, National Forensics League; [hon.] Young Womanhood Recognition Award, Camp Crafter Award, Miss T.E.E.N California Pageant.; [oth. writ.] Poetry, short stories and songs. Nothing published as yet.; [pers.] I have always been able to open myself up through my writing. I write on personal experiences and feelings, I hope my ordeals can help others out.; [a.] San Gabriel, GA

SUDLER, JULIE L.
[b.] September 19, 1959, Willow Grove, PA; [p.] Alonzo Sudler Jr., Winnifred Sudler; [ed.] Lesley College Graduate School Wellesley College (Undergrad), Abington High School; [occ.] Educator; [memb.] St. Anne's Episcopal Church Vestry Pennsylvania State Educator's Association (PSEA), National Educator's Association (NEA) various memberships with local Phila Museums and Phila Zoo; [hon.] Who's Who Among American High School Students, (1976-1977), National Merit Semi-Finalist; [oth. writ.] Several unpublished poems one published poem in Church newsletter; [pers.] Favorite poets Maya Angelou Langston Hughes, Robert Fast, Nikki Viovanni, Shel Silverstein, Robert Louis Stevenson, Mother Goose, Jack Prelutsky; [a.] Willow Grove, PA

SULLIVAN, GRACE LUCILLE
[b.] February 18, 1924, MI; [p.] Louise and Nelson McElmerry; [m.] Donald E. Sullivan, June 1, 1945; [ch.] Five; [ed.] High School; [occ.] Homemaker; [memb.] ARP and Senior Citizen member SDA Church pianist poet and song writer; [hon.] Publications of poetry in Grand Ledge Mr. Independent also in anthology books honorable mentions in "Talent" "American Poets and Songwriters" "Rhyme `n' Rhythm"; [oth. writ.] Jealousy, Mothers Day Tribute, Heartbroken The Ringing Bells, Music aiming High Baby Love Gods mysterious ways baby Love There's Laughter in your eyes; [pers.] I got published World War II song the world is dying for a little love; [a.] Dewitt, MI

SUMMERS, ESTHER ADAME
[pen.] Esther Summers; [b.] March 6, 1960, Houston, TX; [p.] Manuel and Alice Adame; [m.] Chris Summers, May 26, 1984; [ch.] Curtis Mitchell and Steven Michael; [ed.] Santa Fe High, B.A., Liberal Studies - California, State University, San Bernardino, Elementary Credential - CSU, Dominguez Hills; [occ.] 2nd Grade Teacher, Garretson Elementary; [oth. writ.] I have been writing prose and poetry since the age of fifteen.; [pers.] I have always believed before you can put something on paper you must believe in what you are writing. For this reason, everything I have been ever written has been from the heart.; [a.] Corona, CA

SUMMERS, KEYONNA MARIE
[b.] September 14, 1983, Detroit, MI; [p.] Shiela Summers, Donald Wesley; [ed.] Woodward Elementary McMichael Junior High; [occ.] 7th Grade student; [memb.] Angels of Praise choir, Kadesh Missionary Baptist Church; [hon.] 1994 Black Heroes Essay and Oratorical Contest (2nd place), 1994 Detroit Area B Spelling Bee Runner-up; [pers.] Hobbies - drawing, reading, writing, skating, playing piano; [a.] Detroit, MI

SUNDERMAN JR., JAMES PAUL
[pen.] Jim The Head, Grendel; [b.] December 21, 1963, Cincinnati, OH; [p.] Deacon Jim and Gracie; [m.] Enid Garcia-Warner, October 10, 1989; [ch.] Veronica Grace, Alexander James; [ed.] Elder High School, Xavier University; [occ.] Events and Promotions Specialist Cincinnati Zoo and Botanical Garden Sunderman; [memb.] Family and Humankind; [hon.] Presence at most wonderful events during to 80's. It's my start!; [oth. writ.] Unsubmitted; [pers.] I strive for truth in my life. I am influenced by all I have time to read.; [a.] Cincinnati, OH

SURAJ, MAYA
[b.] November 12, 1971, India; [ed.] B.A. in Psychology at Cal State Hayward in California; [occ.] Residential counselor for adolescents; [a.] San Mateo, CA

SUSKO, JANELLE
[b.] May 28, 1981, Pittsburgh, PA; [p.] Richard and Michele Susko; [ed.] Transfiguration School K-6 Our Lady of the Most Blessed Sacrament School 7-8 (9-12) St. Joseph's High School; [memb.] Transfiguration Youth Ministry and Civic Light Opera - Acting, Dance and Voice; [hon.] Honor Roll (7-8) Honors Band; [a.] Tarentum, PA

SUTHERLAND, FREDERICK
[pen.] Fred; [b.] December 7, 1974, Jamaica; [p.] Audrey Campbell; [ed.] Boys and Girls High School, Keystone College; [pers.] I am a man that writes to be a symbol for men, in hopes that they express to the women in our society the respect and admiration they so genuinely deserve.; [a.] Brooklyn, NY

SVENDSEN, SUSAN KRISTINE
[b.] October 19, 1973, Canal Zone, Panama; [p.] Don and Nancy Svendsen; [ed.] University of Rhode Island, B.S.B.A., (B.A.) Psychology - Magna Cum Laude, (B.S) Human Development, Counseling, and Family Studies - Summa Cum Laude; [occ.] Student working towards M.S. in Marriage and Family Therapy; [memb.] Student affiliate of the American Psychological Association; [hon.] National Honor Society, Phi Eta Sigma, Psi Chi, Golden Key, Phi Kappa Phi, Phi Beta Kappa, Deans List; [a.] East Greenwich, RI

SWAINSON, ANNIKA
[b.] February 13, 1977, Santa Clara, CA; [p.] Donald Swainson and Victoria Swainson; [ed.] Frontier High School; [hon.] 1995 Class Valedictorian, Carmen Camarillo Jones Award, 1995 Ventura, County Top Scholar Award and Leadership, Citation from the Noontime Optimist Club of Camarillo.; [pers.] Believe in the dreams of others as much as you would your own.; [a.] Oxnard, CA

SWALLEY, JAY
[pen.] Jay Charles; [occ.] Physical Therapist Assistant and Pro Wrestler; [memb.] Pi Lambda Phi Fraternity; [hon.] Phi Theta Kappa Honor Fraternity; [oth. writ.] None published yet.; [pers.] A real man can show his feelings and emotions and know that he is still a man.

SWAN, ZACH
[b.] April 4, 1975, S. L. C.; [p.] Tanya Henriod, Stephen Swan; [pers.] I am honored that my poem has been recognized; [a.] South Lake City, UT

SWANN, CHRISTOPHER P.
[pen.] Chris; [b.] January 10, 1980, Clinton, MD; [p.] Linda Daniel, and Skip Swann, S.D. Herb Daniel; [ed.] Currently a sophomore in High School, W.R.H.S.; [memb.] Debate Team, Hospital Volunteer, NEL (National Ferosnics League); [hon.] 50 Hours volunteer service, compl. of volunteer summer service; [oth. writ.] "Time" in Mists Of Enchantment; [pers.] C.S. 24 hours in a day should be the only restriction to what you do. "Age ain't nutt in but a thing."; [a.] Warner Robins, GA

SWANSON, JAMES TIMOTHY
[b.] February 1, 1977, Rhode Island; [p.] Roy Swanson, Pegg Swanson; [ed.] Warwick Veterans Memorial High, Community College of Rhode Island (CRRI); [occ.] United Parcel Service (UPS), Unload; [pers.] Be careful of who you let into your life, for cupid carries a shotgun; [a.] Warwick, RI

SWARD, ROBERT J.
[b.] March 14, 1923, Provo, UT; [p.] Robert I. and Goldie L. Sward; [m.] Louise C. Sward, March 6, 1946; [ch.] Wayne, Larry, David; [ed.] High School ICS: Aviaton Engines and Basic Electronics; [occ.] Mechanic (Retired); [memb.] Academy of Model Aeronautics Church of Jesus Christ of Latter Day Saints; [hon.] Math Medal in Junior High; [a.] Bountiful, UT

SWEGER, JESSICA L.
[b.] October 6, 1980, Harrisburg, PA; [p.] Robert L. II and Wendy L.; [ed.] 9th grade student Greenwood High School in Millerstown, PA; [memb.] Students Against Drunk Driving (SADD); Student Council; Art Club; Future Honor Roll Student; Jr. Varsity Cheerleader; Majorette in the Marching Band; Concert Band; [hon.] Honor Roll Student; [a.] Millerstown, PA

SWIFT, JOETTA
[b.] September 11, 1979, Mt. Vernon, MO; [p.] Glenda and Rusty Swift; [ed.] Currently a sophomore at Republic High School; [occ.] Student; [memb.] National Forensic League, Journalism Education Association, French Club, Speech Club, Hi-Step; [hon.] 2nd Place in school's reflections poetry contest, 3rd place in short story category of Lad Fair, 2nd place in poetry category of Lad Fair. 1st place in Bookworm's poetry contest.; [oth. writ.] Autumn Dream-poem, Revenge of the Irish-short Story; [a.] Republic, MO

SWINKS, WINOLA
[b.] May 11, 1947, Atlanta, GA; [ch.] A daughter and son; [ed.] College graduate; [occ.] Registered Nurse; [pers.] I find that nature in any form inspires my writings, which is a form of worship through script. My greatest influence and favorite poet is Robert Frost.; [a.] Atlanta, GA

SWYERS, MARJORIE ALYCE
[pen.] Margie; [b.] March 11, 1922, Detroit, MI; [p.] Arthur Lee and Alyce Leah; [m.] Archie Swyers, John M. Reeder, September 16, 1942, May 10, 1986; [ch.] Elizabeth, Thomas, Kenneth (Deceased) John, Nancy, Gregory, James; [ed.] High School Graduate; [occ.] Activity Assistant in a Nursing Home; [memb.] Salvation Army League of Mercy and Bethesda Dilworth Volunteer; [hon.] St. Louis Metropolitan Hospitals 1985 Gold Metal Award for Volunteering with the Salvation Army and Bethesda Dilworth a branch of Bethesda Hospital and Homes; [oth. writ.] I have written other poem but gave them away; [pers.] I have always been interested in poetry but if I don't write something down at the time it doesn't get done; [a.] Woodson Terr, MO

SYNNESTVEDT, STEVE
[b.] August 7, 1959, Bryn Athyn, PA; [p.] Sig, Nadine Synnestvedt; [ed.] Bachelor of English/Education Academy of the New Church College - High School Diploma A.N.C. High School; [occ.] Contractor; [memb.] To many groups to name - mostly charitable or conservation in nature; [oth. writ.] Various articles to editor published in Philadelphia Inquirer daily news; [pers.] My hope is that my writing both poetic and journalistic will outlive my body's time on this earth.; [a.] Bryn Athyn, PA

SZALA, DARLENE C.
[pen.] Dar; [b.] November 9, 1946, Chicago; [p.] George T. Warden, Martha Warden; [m.] Single; [ch.] Robert Todd, Shelly Ann, Jerome Jacob; [ed.] Woodrow Wilson - Wentworth Grammar and Jr. High, Thornton Fractional North High School, Thornton Community North High School, Thornton Community College Nursing Assist. Certificate.; [occ.] Certified Nursing Assistant, Monster Community Hospital; [memb.] American Cancer Society, North Shore Animal League, Disabled American Veterans; [pers.] I strive to put a smile on everyones face and to touch everyones heart in away to always be remembered.

TACKETT, DEBORAH ANN STERLING
[pen.] Debbie-Do; [b.] October 3, 1963, Baltimore, MD; [p.] Stella and James Sterling; [ed.] High School; [occ.] Office Assistant; [memb.] Long Ridge writers group; [oth. writ.] Country/Rock songs greeting cards, short stories all non-published!; [pers.] Writing stems from the heart, coincides with the mind and finishes with the pen in hand Influences: Stevie Nicks and Robert Frost.; [a.] Baltimore, MD

TALBOTT, PHYLLIS ANN
[pen.] Phyllis Yvonne; [b.] November 18, 1937, Louisville, KY; [p.] Carl Talbott and Henrietta Liveious; [m.] "Widow"; [ch.] Rhonda Martin, Toni Gasway, Sandra Talbott, Larry Talbott, Eric Talbott Sheila Talbott; [ed.] G.E.D. Sullivan Business School, Louisville, Kentucky; [occ.] Homemaker, Elder Serve, Inc. Louisville, Kentucky; [memb.] Little Flock Baptist Church; [hon.] "Homemaker Certificate" "First Aid and CPR" Certificates, G.E.D. certificate, (Business School Certificate); [oth. writ.] Several unpublished poems; [pers.] I strive to "uplift" mankind by writing informative and inspirational "poems". I have been greatly influenced by other people's sufferings and struggles in life as well as my own personal ones; [a.] Louisville, KY

TANKUS, HARRY
[b.] August 23, 1921, Polland; [m.] Lila, September 7, 1947; [ch.] Rolana (Deceased) and Ilyce; [ed.] 11T (Engineering); [occ.] Chmn. of the BD. (Retired); [memb.] Ill. Institute of Technology, Rush North Shore Medical Center, Rush North Shore Health Services, Chicago Lighthouse for the Blind, United Way of Stokie Valley, United Way of Suburban Chicago, United Way/ Crusader of Mercy, American Cancer Society, Turning Point Behavioral Health Care Center, Lutheran Social Services of Ill., Stokie Valley Rotary, Center East Inc. (for performing arts), Society for Tribology and Lubrication Engineers, National Conference on Fluid Power (NCFP), Oakton Community College (OCC); [hon.] North Shore Magazine. Top ten Volunteers, 1988, Boy Scout Community Service Award, 1985, LSSI Amicus Cirtus Award, 1988, JC Penney Golden Rule Award, 1990, Northwest Chicago Volunteer center Award, STLE P.M. KU Award (for contribution to tribology) 1986, STLE Fellow, 1977, Marquis Who's Who in the world, Marquis Who's Who in America Marquis Who's Who Midwest, Marquis Who's Who Finance and Industry, Who's Who in Engineering, Who's Who in Technology; [oth. writ.] Many technical papers on tribology (The Art and Science of Wear); [pers.] There's a dangerous attitude among too many citizens in this country that big government will take care of us from cradle to grave. The history of the birth, growth and personal initiative of the United States needs to be communicated on a constant basis especially as generations flee by.; [a.] Northfield, IL

TARASKA, DELLA
[b.] June 24, 1958, Cleveland, OH; [p.] Anna Webb and Raymond Lemasters (Deceased); [m.] Edward J. Taraska, October 21, 1980; [ch.] Diana and Daniel; [ed.] South High; [occ.] Housewife; [memb.] American Wild Life Federation a Member of the Coventry Poetry Association for the "Beat" scene; [hon.] High School Literature Awards. Poetry Contest in my senior year.; [oth. writ.] "I'm Blue", "Primal Scream", "My Room", "Confusion"; [pers.] I feel that if you can't be yourself then, be no one at all. I have been very inspired by Rod McKuen and Jack Keroug, Keats, Byron, Poe; [a.] Hudson, OH

TARLE, NAOMI
[b.] October 26, 1980, Santa Monica, CA; [p.] Marci and Norman Tarle; [ed.] Currently a sophomore at Santa Monica High School Graduating in 1998.; [occ.] Student; [memb.] Member of UCLA Junior Crew Team, member Delians at Santa Monica High School chapter of California Scholarship Federation; [hon.] Principal's Honor Roll 1994-1995; [oth. writ.] Short Story "Oatmeal Cookies", published in the magazine Young Voices.; [a.] Santa Monica, CA

TAYLOR, DEBRA
[b.] May 26, 1970, Spokane, WA; [p.] Lawrence Taylor, Carolyn Taylor; [ed.] Big Spring High School, Shippensburg University; [occ.] Marker; [memb.] St. Patricks Roman Catholic Church; [hon.] Dean's List, Fall semester of senior year in college; [pers.] I write from the heart.; [a.] Newville, PA

TAYLOR, LINDA L.
[b.] May 21, 1947, Beria, OH; [p.] Barbara and Stanley Larimer; [m.] William T. Taylor, April 2, 1974; [ch.] Three; [pers.] For momma was written from a deep feeling of grief and loss. Momma encouraged me all my life to write. This poem is for her, and my sisters, with much love.

TAYLOR, PEARLINE
[b.] April 2, 1930, Crowville, LA; [p.] Gus Wright Jr. and Addie Wright; [m.] Harry Taylor, August 14, 1955; [ch.] Denise Lynae, Sheila Eileen; [ed.] San Pedro High, Los Angeles Harbor College, Cerritos College; [occ.] Retired from the Insurance Industry; [memb.] Melchisedec Priest of The Universal World Church in Los Angeles, California; [pers.] Blessed is the nation whose God is the Lord, and the people (of all nationalities) whom he hath chosen for his own inheritance.; [a.] Cerritos, CA

TAYLOR, RON
[pen.] Ron Taylor; [b.] 1932, Windber, PA; [ed.] Lots of Education; [occ.] Retired Teacher/Librarian; [memb.] Amnesty International, Greenpeace, ACLU (American Civil liberties Union), PFLAG (Parents, Families and Friends of Lesbians and Gays), and MOG (Metropolitan Opera Guild).; [hon.] Eagle Scout; [oth. writ.] Several stories in progress; [pers.] "Live, live, live!"; [a.] State College, PA

TAYLOR, TERRI
[pen.] T. J. Taylor, Terri Burton Taylor; [b.] June 28, 1957, Aiken, SC; [p.] Lee and Jean Burton; [m.] Kenneth Earl Taylor, December 26, 1983; [ch.] Christopher Lee, Amber Noelle; [ed.] Greenwood High, Lander College Piedmont Tech; [occ.] Writer; [hon.] CDA in Child Development; [oth. writ.] Several children's books, One adult suspense, Non-fiction Articles, Dozens of poems; [pers.] I would like to thank God for all of his many blessings and ask that everyone offer up a special prayer for the many abused children, not only in our great nation, but the whole world.; [a.] Hodges, SC

TEDESCHI, THOMAS J.
[b.] November 16, 1969, Cleveland; [p.] Philemon J. and Louise Tedeschi; [ed.] Richmond Heights High School Cleveland Sate University; [occ.] Documentation/Training Specialist, Ecotran Corporation; [memb.] Society for Technical Communication; [hon.] Rotary Club Service Above self Scholarship (1988) Dean's List; [pers.] A true lover of the 18th century, I must give thanks to the outstanding scholarship in the English Department at Cleveland State.; [a.] Richmond Heights, OH

TENRREIRO, MARY A.
[pen.] Maria A. Tenrreiro; [b.] August 18, 1944, San Antonio, TX; [p.] Juan and Maria Huron; [ch.] Allison Kay Amador Kelly Diane Prettyman; [ed.] Southside High School Eastfield College; [occ.] Medical Records Coder; [oth. writ.] American Poetry Anthology 1984; [pers.] My life is poetic. Living, Loving and friendships are poems in progress.; [a.] Mesquite, TX

TETSELL, KIMBERLY
[b.] November 28, 1964, Cortez, CO; [p.] Nelda Burdett and Donald Tetsell; [ed.] BA in Communications from Southern CA. College Fresno Christian High School; [occ.] Assistant Office Manager for Ellison Educ Equip, Inc.; [hon.] Cum Laude, Dean's List, Best Supporting Actress (college prod. of You Can't Take It With You), Best Screen play '87 and '89, Best Radio Commercial '86 (SCC Communications Awards); [a.] Irvine, CA

THOMAS, BARBARA M.
[pen.] Ann Thomas; [b.] April 3, 1942, Banks County; [m.] John William Thomas, August 1963; [ch.] One; [ed.] Working on Bachelor's degree in Liberal Studies - am a junior at present time; [occ.] Administrative Secretary; [memb.] International Society of Poets; [hon.] Poem "Leaves of November" published in "Sound of Poetry" by Natl. Library of Poetry for Anthology East of Sunrise This poem placed Third in 1995 North American Open Poetry Contest and received Editor's Choice Award from National Library of Poetry; [oth. writ.] Will have poems, published by Creative Arts and Science, Inc. in Anthology Journey To Our Dreams; [pers.] Poetry is the window to one's soul.

THOMAS, BRENNAN
[b.] July 26, 1978, Dayton, OH; [p.] Jim and Cele Thomas; [occ.] Student, part-time actress; [memb.] National Honor Society, EHS Drama Club, The Way - Off Broadway Players; [hon.] Best Actress Award, 1993, Herman Zemmerman Memorial 1995, Voice of Democracy Award 1995; [oth. writ.] Poems published in the anthologies Best Poems of 1996, The Spirit of the Age, and East of the Sunrise. Also published in "Poetry Motel" magazine.; [pers.] I believe poetry to be God's fingers clasping the author's pages. In short, the ink we poets use is divine.; [a.] Eaton, OH

THOMPSON, BENNETT
[b.] December 14, 1947, Sumter, SC; [p.] Rosa Irick Whaley and Earl Whaley; [m.] Charles H. Thompson, June 16, 1687; [ch.] Sharron and Sheilah; [ed.] Vaux Jr High Fleet School of Business; [occ.] Homemaker; [memb.] Pleasantview Baptist Church, Choir and Mother's Board; [oth. writ.] 1 poem published; [pers.] The thinking of mankind is an awesome awareness of imagination, insight and accomplishment.; [a.] Scranton, PA

THOMPSON, GENE E.
[b.] I was Hatched, Barnyard; [p.] Two of course! What a question!; [m.] Overweight Female!, A day I'm trying to forget!; [ch.] One but he won't admit I'm his Dad!; [ed.] Streets and back alleys of South Chicago!; [occ.] Electrifying!; [memb.] One! the human race but very questionable!; [hon.] Kindergaten Valedictorian! Awards $1000 for whiplash! Yes my wife was driving!; [oth. writ.] Checks for my wife's spending spree's! also many funny poems and puns about everyday life, which I'm sure you wish I'd destroy after reading my answers to your above questions!; [pers.] Please don't take offense at my making light of the above bio-info questions you asked, as my Philosophical outlook on life is to bring a smile to one's face, without hurting anyone's feelings! My wife is not oops fat but enjoyed my spouse answer! She can also take a joke because she married one! A loser in life I'll never be, as I have my health and parents who cared for me!; [a.] Los Angeles, CA

THOMPSON, HEATHER MARIE
[b.] February 29, 1980, Omaha, NE; [p.] Robert and Debra Thompson; [ed.] Sophomore at Yutan High School in Yutan Nebraska.; [memb.] Senior Girl Scout, 6 years 4-H member, Co-Captain Cheer leader, Yutan R.A.V.E. Member (Responsible, Adolescents, Valuing, Education), Yutan Band; [hon.] '95 Band Letter, '93 State Champion Cat, Honor bands, Malcolm, Elkhorn, Districts Superior Flute Solos, Honor Roll of Destinction for Academics 91-92, 92-93, 93-94, 94-95, 95-96; [oth. writ.] "Lament for Life" poetic voices of America "How" poetic voices of America; [a.] Yutan, NE

THORNTON, LINDA M. J.
[pen.] Cokkie Jones; [b.] February 16, 1950, Williamsburg, VA; [p.] Charles and Hazel Jones; [ch.] Two and One grandchild; [ed.] Bruton Heights/Berkley High School, Norfolk State University and Pursuing Masters Degree at the University of Virginia School of Education; [occ.] 2nd Gr. Teacher, Greenbrier Primary School - Chesapeake, VA 23320; [memb.] First Lynnhaven Baptist Church, VA. Bch, VA and School PTA; [hon.] College Honor Graduate, Career Committment Teacher, 1st Year Sallie Mae Teacher Award Nominee, 1991/1992 Teacher of the Year at Greenbrier Primary in Chesapeake, VA.; [oth. writ.] Most of my writings have been poems of dedications for family, friends, colleagues and others. A favorite poem/song was written to the tune of "America" and dedicated to the desert storm troops in 1991/1992. Until now, I've had nothing published. Thank You!; [pers.] Take time to do what makes you happy! For me, writing helps me to unwind, and it's sooo - soothing to "my mind".; [a.] Virginia Beach, VA

TIDWELL, JOHN E.
[b.] May 28, 1973, Nauvoo, AL; [p.] Shirley and Terry Tidwell; [m.] Tracy Tidwell, June 17, 1993; [ch.] Kasey Diane Tidwell; [ed.] Victor Christian Academy; [occ.] Truck Driver; [oth. writ.] Life, Help Me O Lord, Thank You O Lord.; [a.] Nauvoo, AL

TILANUS, SAMANTHA
[b.] July 13, 1975, Johannesburg, Republic of South Africa; [p.] Jill and George Hefter, Bernard Tilanus; [ed.] Clay High, Oregon, Ohio Richland High, Richland, WA, Washington State University, Pullman, WA; [occ.] Student; [memb.] WSU Honor's Program President's Honor Roll; [hon.] Physical Fitness Awards many academic achievement awards senior award (French) Student of the month (Science and Foreign Language); [oth. writ.] Several other poems, one received honorable mention in local "Reflections" competition; [pers.] We all view life through different eyes but, I think, somehow, poetry seems to connect and, at the same time, explain these views.; [a.] Richland, WA

TIMBERLAKE, DORIS ANN
[b.] November 27, 1947, Portsmouth, OH; [p.] Doris and Bill Nuckols; [m.] Lester R. Timberlake, July 3, 1964; [ch.] Malinda and Randy; [ed.] GED; [occ.] Housewife helper for anyone in need.; [oth. writ.] Happy Birthday to me.

TIPTON, JAMI STINSON
[pen.] Jami Stinson; [b.] January 19, 1961, Fort Benning, GA; [p.] Retired Sgt. Major Robert E. Stinson and Mary E. Stinson; [m.] Divorced; [ch.] Misty Dawn, Barry Gene Jr.; [ed.] J. O. Johnson High, University of Alabama in Huntsville, North Alabama College of Commerce; [occ.] Lead Security Supervisor, Hunstville City Schools; [memb.] Central P.T.A., Boy Scouts of America (den leader), Forster Parenting Program; [hon.] Honor Roll, National Honor Society, Society of Distinguished American High School Students 1988 Employee of the Quarter - HSV. City Schools.; [oth. writ.] High School; [pers.] Writing is like finger painting... Pour your soul on the paper and spread it around. It will become whatever the reader perceives it to be.; [a.] Brownsboro, AL

TITUS, RON
[b.] February 16, 1968, Covina, CA; [ed.] B.S. Business Admin. Calif. St. Polytechnic Univ., Pomona; [occ.] Bookkeeper; [memb.] National Wildlife Federation, Defenders of Wildlife, Intl. Society of Poets; [oth. writ.] Several poems published in anthologies by Nat. Library of Poetry.; [pers.] A hope is for my writings to evoke images that stir the mind and touch the heart.; [a.] Pomona, CA

TOMCZYK, KEVIN S.
[pen.] K. Andrew Tomczyk; [b.] March 13, 1970, Chicago, IL; [ed.] Cornell University, Finch University of Health Sciences; [occ.] Biochemist; [a.] Downers Grove, IL

TORNABENE, DANIELLE
[b.] June 23, 1984, Staten Island, NY; [p.] Mariann and Joseph Tornabene; [ed.] 6th Grade St. Rita School.;

[occ.] Student; [memb.] Cheerleading Squad, (Captain) Brandy's Dancing Unique, St. Rita's Alter Serving; [hon.] Cheerleading Plaque, Reading Award, had poem published in anthology of poetry by young Americans; [oth. writ.] Can you hear them, you can help, a feeling and more; [pers.] My name is Danielle Tornabene. I come from a family of five with two brothers. I've been writing poetry for two years and am pretty well-known for it. I write to express myself, and how I feel.; [a.] Staten Island, NY

TORRES, CHRISTOPHER A.
[b.] January 11, 1964, Santa Maria, CA; [p.] Richard Torres and Mary Torres; [m.] Nicole Torres, August 27, 1994; [ch.] Richard, Stephanie, Brittanie; [ed.] Bella Vista High, Chicago City College (European Campus); [occ.] Claims/Contra Costa County Schools Insurance Group; [memb.] American Cancer Society; [oth. writ.] Numerous others, only this is the first poem I have ever let anyone examine.; [pers.] I wish I could devote all of my time to writing. To me, poetry is a compilation of thoughts and feelings, you can explain how you feel in detail, leaving enough for the imagination to finish the picture within.; [a.] Dixon, CA

TORRES, CLEMENTINA H.
[b.] September 11, 1953, Mexico; [p.] Avilia B. Hernandez and Antonio Hernandez; [m.] Esteban Torres, February 7, 1988; [ch.] Valeria, Alfredo and Esteban Jr.; [ed.] A.L. Mateos High School, State University, Chihuahua, Mexico, Eastern New Mexico University, Roswell NM, State University, Farmingdale, New York.; [occ.] Nursing Student; [hon.] Dean's List-State University at Roswell, National Dean's List.; [oth. writ.] Several unpublished poems and one song.; [pers.] I have been influenced by romantic poets in general, but especially by Spanish poets. I intend to touch the heart of those who read my writings by sending messages of love and understanding; [a.] Roswell, NM

TORRES, EDWARD
[pen.] Lalo; [b.] January 5, 1966, Mexico; [p.] Sobeyda and Emiliano; [m.] Kelly Torres, February 12, 1988; [ed.] High School and Phoenix Tech. Center; [occ.] (Dillards) Customer Service Rep. Bilingual; [memb.] Poisoned Pen Bookstore; [hon.] Young Authors Conf. Award Junior Achievement Award Presidential Phy. Fitness Award; [oth. writ.] Many other poems non-published.; [pers.] Music and books rule the world. Read, educate your mind and listen, to the music of your heart.; [a.] Glendale, AZ

TORRES, ESTEVAN IRIZARRY
[pen.] Steven Torres; [b.] December 23, 1961, Buffalo, NY; [p.] Jose Torres and Anna Irizarry; [m.] Kady Tran, July 4, 1985; [ch.] Enzo, Shao-Wan; [ed.] UCLA and USC; [occ.] Importer and Exporters of Creative World Communications; [memb.] Ferrain Owners Club, Aids Project Los Angeles, Aid For Aids, St. Finbar Church, Askew L.A. and Japan, L.A. Models, Stars Agency; [hon.] Estevan is my hero. Living with full blown Aids, he had demonstrated the quality of life. He deal with his illness courageously, Estevan deceased on July 26, 1995; [oth. writ.] "Set Me Free" poetry and to be published as poetry wearable under the clothing line of "Estevan I. Torres" in loving memory of Estevan I. Torres.; [pers.] Love never sees color or race. Love for a lifetime is love that has no boundaries, no conditions. If you don't risk in life, you'll never succeed. Follow your heart and success will follow.; [a.] West Hollywood, CA

TOWNLEY, JUDY E.
[b.] April 21, 1952, Swain Co, NC; [p.] Mr and Mrs M. H. Willis; [m.] Charles G. Townley, January 14, 1995; [ch.] Arron Willis, Charlie Townley; [ed.] High School Graduate two years College; [occ.] Housewife; [memb.] Ladies Auxiliary V.F.W.; [oth. writ.] Nothing published; [pers.] Each of us have stories or poetry within. We each chose wheather to write down what we feel or our dreams.; [a.] Whittier, NC

TOWNSEND, HOLLY
[b.] December 4, 1978, Flint, MI; [p.] Jim and Sue Townsend; [ed.] Junior in High School Currently (Goodrich High School); [occ.] Student, part-time job at Papa Romano's; [memb.] National Honor Society, Young American Bowling Alliance, "Word Up" staff for "The Flint Journal", School Quiz Bowl Team; [hon.] National Honor Society, Who's Who among American High School Students for two consecutive years; [oth. writ.] Several poems, articles, and reviews published in "Word Up" of "The Flint Journal", poem published in school literary magazine; [pers.] I personally believe that poetry is the greatest form of art, as it uses the power of words to express one's questions.; [a.] Atlas, MI

TRACY, ELIZABETH
[b.] October 9, 1909, Wisconsin, USA; [p.] Fred and Ida Reinke; [m.] Emilio Sartori, May 24, 1937, Joseph Tracy, February 10, 1966; [ch.] Edward Joseph, Robert Richard; [ed.] Elementary School; [occ.] Retired Sales Clerk; [memb.] Legacy of St. Joseph Cardinal Cooke Guild. Song Writers Club of America International Society of Poets; [hon.] For poetry Tear Drops for Heaven, The Earth's Blood, The Addicted Soul, Magnificent Dream, Earth's Bountiful Gifts, Tragic Day.; [oth. writ.] Fifteen songs with out success.; [a.] Yonkers, NY

TRAN, VINH Q.
[b.] September 22, 1946, Vietnam; [p.] Trung V. Tran and Dao T. Tran; [m.] Nhung T. Nguyen, September 16, 1970; [ch.] Thuy V. Q. and Heather T. H.; [ed.] BSC, BA, MBA, PhD.; [occ.] Global Fund Manager; [oth. writ.] Book Foreign Exchange Management in Multinational Firms (UMI Research Press, 1980); [pers.] I'd rather repent than regret; [a.] Greenwich, CT

TRAVERS, DENISE ANN MATTHEWS
[pen.] Sincerely Me; [b.] May 28, 1954, Baltimore, MD; [p.] Dewitt and Juanita Matthews; [m.] Rodney Travers, November 24, 1973; [ch.] Alicia Estelle Travers; [ed.] BS - Wayland Baptist University TX, AA - Eastern New Mexico University, AA - Community College of the Air Force, Graduated from Western High School; [occ.] Administrative Superintendent, United States Air Force presently assigned to Nellis Air Force Base, Nevada; [memb.] Business and Professional Womens Association (BPW), Air Force Sergeant's Association (AFSA), Air Force Association (AFA), Noncommissioned Officer's Association (NCOA), Dean's List; [hon.] Dean's List Two meritorious service medals, Three commendation Medals; [oth. writ.] Poems, short stories, songs, and kids computer learning projects in works; [pers.] My writings are a reflection of my obedience to do God's will and penetrate His divine love throughout the world; [a.] Las Vegas, NV

TRAVIS, SUSAN
[m.] Bruce Travis; [pers.] When my heart opens to the voice within, I am able to glimpse who I am.; [a.] Des Moines, IA

TREVINO, JOEL O.
[b.] November 13, 1956, Adrian, MO; [p.] Joe and Nina Trevino; [m.] Loretta L. Trevino, June, 16, 1978; [ch.] Five; [ed.] Madison High School, Michigan State University, B.S. Academy of Health Sciences U.S. Navy; [occ.] Material Quality Review Board Technician - Morton Int.; [memb.] Veterans of Foreign Wars; [hon.] Honors Graduate of U.S. Naval Academy of Health Sciences. Honorable Discharge from 10 years in U.S. Navy; [pers.] Always striving for excellence and helping others to do the same. Through my words and deeds, I hope I have helped someone along life's rocky road. My family and Edgar A. guest serve as my inspiration.; [a.] Brigham City, UT

TROHA, LEIGH
[b.] March 28, 1980, Dayton, OH; [p.] Frank and Gwen Troha; [ed.] Centerville High School, Miami Valley School; [occ.] Student; [memb.] 4 H Club; [oth. writ.] One other poem published in The Garden of Life "The Fog", Science publication in, Lafeber Friends of Bird Club, Vol. 2 1995; [a.] Dayton, OH

TROTTER JR., ROBERT
[pen.] Robert Trotter; [b.] August 24, 1978, Ann Arbor, MI; [p.] Eunice Trotter and Robert Trotter Sr.; [ed.] Father Gabriel Richard High School, Bishop Borgess High School; [occ.] Office Clerk; [memb.] New Hope Baptist Church Youth Group National Honor Society; [hon.] Rensselaer Award for Math and Science NAACP (Act- so competition) Honorable mention President of National Honor Society; [pers.] I constantly strive to use my writing as an outlet to express my ideas, thoughts, and emotions, I hope that through my writing I can touch some soul and make he or she feel better.; [a.] Ann Arbor, MI

TRUBEY, MARK DWIGHT
[pen.] Trubadour; [b.] February 16, 1955, Boston, MA; [p.] Marshall Trubey and Gabrielle Bergeron; [m.] Michelle L. Trubey, September 27, 1992; [ch.] Mason Gavin, William Joseph; [ed.] Salem High, LIFE; [oth. writ.] Numerous songs, both solo efforts, and collaborative works, lyrics, and music. Additional poems.; [pers.] There is nothing more valuable than wisdom, nothing more powerful than the truth, and, nothing as noble as love.; [a.] Pepperell, MA

TRUJILLO, MARTA C.
[b.] June 29, 1977, Cincinnati; [p.] Dr. Alfonso Trujillo, Mrs. Clara Trujillo; [ed.] McAuley High School University of Cincinnati; [occ.] Full time student at the university of Cincinnati; [memb.] Spanish Club, Chorus, Liturgical Committee; [hon.] Certificate of Recognition for outstanding Achievement in Spanish, Diploma of Merit for excellence in Spanish, National Spanish Honor Society, State Board of Education Award of Merit.; [oth. writ.] Other poems Kept in my Notebook, other poems have been published in the past.; [pers.] "To achieve all that is possible, we must attempt the impossible. To be as much as we can be, we must dream of being more."; [a.] Cincinnati, OH

TRUSIEWICZ, BRIAN
[b.] September 18, 1974, Waterbury, CT; [p.] Sandra and Edward Trusiewicz; [ed.] Currently attending Teikyo Post University; [hon.] National English Merit Award, NCTE Award (for writing), placed in various short story contests; [oth. writ.] Several short stories

published in Merlyn's Pen, Voices of Youth, and the CT Student Journal, Created, edited, and published The Tapestry: A scroll of student literature.; [pers.] Poetry is the most honest thing I know: A literary manifestation of the human experience. It is that honesty that helps me through life: It is sacred and real.; [a.] Waterbury, CT

TUCK, LISA
[pen.] Lisa Tuck; [b.] July 9, 1978, Bay City; [ed.] Currently, as of 1995-1996 School year, a Junior at Western High School.; [memb.] Volunteer Counselor at Camp Fowler, Camp for the mentally and physically handicapped (campers); [hon.] Student Council, Various school committees, Captain, Leadership conference participation; [oth. writ.] I have always written poetry, yet I have not had the chance to have them published.; [a.] Lindwood, MI

TUCKER, LEOTA M.
[b.] December 6, 1926, West Ledfond, IL; [p.] David H. Harrison and Emma Bean; [m.] F. Tucker Jr., April 11, 1947; [ch.] Two; [ed.] High School (Interior Design - Chicago) no degree, but many different studies; [occ.] Housewife - retired from Interior Design Field - Sales and Management.; [memb.] Ancient City Geneological Soc. not much time for outside memberships now - due to husbands illness.; [hon.] Published "The Ancient City Geneologist" for 2 years.; [oth. writ.] For "Springhouse" magazine - Herod, Illinois, short stories - "Old Leoford, a Mining Ghost Tacon" self published Poem "The Lord", Andurie Press to come out January 6, 1996; [pers.] I am reenly interested in seeing some real patriotism restored to our country, more progress toward ecological bolance, world peace, and above all, restoring healthy neighborhood climate for our children; [a.] Saint Augustine, FL

TURNER, EDDIE LEE
[b.] August 24, 1951, Jericho, KY; [p.] Ed Turner; [m.] Anna Belle Turner; [ed.] Graduated from Shelby County High; [occ.] Song Writer and poet; [memb.] Christiansburg Baptist Church Kentucky Colonel; [hon.] Deacon in The Church; [oth. writ.] Over 300 poems over 70 songs not published; [pers.] I write because I weed to, want to, and I love to. Thank you Jesus for allowing me to do what I love doing.; [a.] Bagdad, KY

TURNER, SANTINA BENEDETTI
[b.] February 28, 1948, Lexington, KY; [p.] Bernardine Benedetti and Louis Benedetti; [ch.] Holly Ann Turner; [occ.] Expanded Duty Dental Assistant, Pediatric Dentistry University of Kentucky and the family care center; [pers.] I once read somewhere "Life doesn't have to be perfect to be wonderful". It made me realize we need to count our blessings and be thankful for what we do have.; [a.] Lexington, KY

TURNGREN, MARIE ELIZABETH
[pen.] Bettie Alder Turngren; [b.] December 11, 1926, Loda, IL; [p.] Orville and Ethel Marie Alder; [m.] Elmer J. Turngren (Deceased), May 18, 1946; [ch.] Joyce, Keith, Melody, Kirk, Merri Angelie; [ed.] Loda (Journalist) High, 2 years at English and Art major, on Scholarship) Illinois State Normal, 2 years at Bellevue Com-College and AA degree, Ec. Ed. 1 year BCC and WU speech pathology, 1st Women's FBI Fingerprint School, at UW; [occ.] Retired, Taught in Learning Centers, Ident. Dept. and Disp. at local Police Dept. Secty. for Church and manpower assignments; [memb.] Rose Hill Presbyterian Church, Kirkland Women's Club, Volunteer at Seattle VA, Medical center, Bible study Fellowship; [hon.] Valedictorian and D.A.R. award, Balfour Medal, and Reader's Digest Awards High School, State and National Letter writing and Poem contest, 2nd Place 18th Cong. Dist. Pastel Arts at College.; [oth. writ.] Unpublished poems and plays mostly for church and friends, Radio play at ISNU, and for contests.; [pers.] To love and enjoy Jesus Christ, my country, my family, and my friends, to be sensitive to others, and to add "feet" to my prayers, (and to reflect this is my poetry and writings).; [a.] Kirkland, WA

TYSON, WYCLIFFE E.
[pen.] Wycliffe E. Tyson; [b.] January 12, 1953, Nevis, West Indies; [p.] Samuel Tyson and Margery Tyson; [ed.] Trinity International University Miami, FL. BSci Honor Resources Management, Biblical Studies, Miami Dale Community Collage, FL. Asci Dietitic Nutrition Care; [occ.] Student, Dr Naturopathy Clayton School of Natural Healing, Alabama; [memb.] First United Methodist Church Miami FL, International Society of Poets, MD; [hon.] Honorable Discharge U.S. Navy Vietnam Service National Defense Medal; [oth. writ.] Author of book titled "Messages, Prayers and Poetry"; [pers.] Life continues beyond life.; [a.] Miami Beach, FL

ULMER, DANA M.
[b.] February 8, 1970, Michigan; [p.] Linda and Jim Vaughn; [m.] Monte L. Ulmer, July 18, 1992; [ed.] Bachelor of Science in Psychology and a Masters in Social Work; [occ.] Social Worker; [memb.] National Association of Social Workers; [pers.] My poetry provides me with a sense of warmth and increased understanding of life. I hope it helps all who read it in some way. Poetry is my gift to the world.; [a.] Virginia Beach, VA

ULTAN, ROSLYE B.
[b.] Brooklyn, NY; [p.] Sarah Rubin, Philip Benson; [m.] Lloyd Ultan; [ch.] Wendy J., Alicia J., Jacqueline B. and Deborah K.; [ed.] Dickinson College B.A., American University M.A., University Minnesota. Post Graduate; [occ.] Hamline University Ass. Professor Graduate Liberal Studies; [memb.] The Loft: Writing and Literature College Art Association, Walker Art Center, Minneapolis Institute Art, Weisman Art Museum, National Museum of Women In the Arts; [hon.] Gaylord Patterson Award, Dickinson College Smithsonian Fellowship, Hirshhorn Mus. and Sculp. Garden, Rockfeller Foundation Associate Resident, Bellagio, Italy, 1944 Fall, Work in Progress: From the Last Supper to the Dinner Partnership, Sacred on Secular Feasts(Book); [oth. writ.] Sentinels Of Fire: Art of Jerane Tupa catalogue Minnesota Museum of American Art. 1990, Conticles. Jeruma Tupa catalogue. Walter Wickisel Gallery N.Y. N.Y. 1993, The Dialogue. Liberal Studies Journal. Hamline University St. Paul MN. 1989 (Numerous articles); [pers.] My poetry reflects my introspective nature...my deepest intimate emotions, thoughts, experience and memories. I perceive life as a spiral evolving and revolving through time past and present and beyond.; [a.] Minneapolis, MN

VAN DUYN, OTTO M.
[b.] August 29, 1942, San Francisco, CA; [p.] Otto and Adele Van Duyn; [ch.] David, Valerie, Kathryn, Emily; [pers.] I strive to reflect God's inspiration in my poetry. I have been greatly influenced by the love I have for my children and Billy Graham's book, Angels: God's Secret Messengers.; [a.] Lubbock, TX

VANDERSLICE, WILLIAM ROBERT
[b.] June 20, 1929, Coatesville, PA; [p.] George and Helen Vanderslice; [m.] Emily Martha Vanderslice, December 24, 1958; [ed.] Liberty High School, Bethlehem, Penna, Various Navy Courses; [occ.] Retired U.S. Navy and Harbour Master; [memb.] California Association Of Harbour Masters and Port Captains (Treasurer and Planks Owna), Scale Ship Modeler's Association of North America (treasurer), Fleet Reserve Association, Past Commodore Floating Realty Yacht Club of Walnut Creek, California, Chairman Board of Directors, ECA/Federal Credit of Antioch, CA.; [pers.] This poem was written in about 1942-43 While attending Sefton Jr High School, Hamilton a Suburb of Baltimore. It's intent was to get you to read-a pastime I still pursue. While not practicing a literary career, the call of the sea did become a mainstay. Perhaps now I will turn another page or character...; [a.] Pittsburg, CA

VANDERWOOD, DEBORAH M.
[b.] November 20, 1950, Ilion, NY; [p.] Frances Benson; [m.] Barry S. Vanderwood, March 7, 1967, Divorced; [ch.] Brandy A. Piotrowski, Dowen-Alan R. Piotrowski, Christopher M.J. Piotrowski; [ed.] Utica Free Academy Pikes Peaks Comm. College, Peterson Air Force Base Dental Assistant School, College of I.C.S. for Journalism.; [occ.] Current Writer, Poet, Songwriter, Prior-Dental Assistant, Preschool Teacher; [memb.] American Red Cross, Y.M.C.A., P.T.A., International Society Of Poets; [hon.] Certificate of Recognition for Preschool Teacher, Certificate of recognition from U.S.A.F. Space Command for Dental Assistant Program, Certificate of recognition from the American Red Cross for the Dental Assistant Program, Certificate of Appreciation from Defence Commissary Agency, Pikes Peak Community college for Dental Radiology and Math Science, Health division of Dental Assistant Program and Vertification, Certification of Degree for Journalism and short story writing from the college of I.C.S.; [oth. writ.] Several poems for-The National Libery Of Poetry Mile High Poetry Society 1. As Season's Change As We, In A sea of Treasures 2. To Every Thing There Is A Season, In A Sea Of Treasures 3. To Every Thing There Is A Season, In A Delicate Balance 4. Many Years Passed As I Waited For You, In The Rainbows End 5. Mother's, In The Book Of Piera 6. Grandparent's, In The Book Of Ariel 7. A Poet's Dream, In the Book Of Ariel 8. A Gift From Yesterday, Very Near To, In The Voice With In 9. There Are A Million Reasons Why I...I In A Muse To Follow; [pers.] As a new poet I hope that poet readers will feel the emotions in my poetry, and I hope to move their emotions with their souls, and their lives, as life is poetry. Though my poetry I leave a piece of myself when it is my time to move on. Than when someone reads me, they will think my what was she feeling or thinking or what message was she trying to give us? I have been greatly influenced by early romantic poets and Emily Dickerson.; [a.] Colorado Springs, CO

VANLANDINGHAM, VICTORIA
[b.] September 22, 1983, Lawton, OK; [p.] Peter and Sonia Vanlandingham; [ed.] I'm 12 years old and presently in the 16th grade at Horace Mann Elementary School; [a.] Duncan, OK

VARNEY, DENNY G.
[pen.] D. G. Varney; [b.] August 18, 1942, Hartford,

CT; [ch.] Lorna Valentine Varney; [ed.] William Hall High School, University Of Haltford; [occ.] Mail carrier, U.S. Postal Service; [memb.] Humane Society Of The U.S., ASPCA; [hon.] Evening Studies Honor Award, University Of Hartford, U.S. Air Force, Commendation Medal.; [oth. writ.] Personal journals and poetry collections.; [pers.] Poetry is the essence of the soul on its physical journey. I have been influenced and inspired by the poetry of Robert Frost, Walt Whitman and Edgar A. Poe.; [a.] Brooklyn, CT

VAUGHN, ELLI M.
[b.] May 5, 1933, Kingston, PA; [p.] Elsi I. Nieminen, James R. Ricker; [m.] Bruce Vaughn Sr.; [ch.] Elli Duplantis, Debbi Vitellard, Caye Liles, Bruce Vaughn Jr.; [ed.] Abington Sr. High School, Philadelphia museum school of Art.; [occ.] Sculptor, Designer; [hon.] Awarded 2 PA. College Art Scholarships. Awarded Best of Show and first place-Gulf Coast Ceramic Show, Houston, Texas. Works Show and sold Anaheim, California, Clear Lake, Texas Galleries, Astroworld, Astrodome Gift Shops, Houston, Texas.; [pers.] I write poetry for the joy and sorrow of my need to express feelings as a woman, artist, wife and mother.; [a.] Friendswood, TX

VAUGHN, GEOFFREY
[b.] January 23, 1970, Abilene, TX; [p.] Edgard D. and Doris Jo Vaughn; [m.] Melinda Myers Vaughn, September 17, 1993; [ed.] Bachelor Of Fine Arts, University Of Utah.; [occ.] Apprentice, Fraughton Foundry, Inc., South Jordan, UT.; [a.] Salt Lake City, UT

VAUGHN, LYNN
[b.] December 23, 1935, Ava, MO; [p.] Raymond and Dora Vaughn; [m.] Patricia Vaughn, October 20, 1993; [ch.] Kim Springsteud; [occ.] Retired; [memb.] American Legion; [oth. writ.] Poems - non published, Novel - non published; [pers.] I started writing poetry to free my soul of anger and hatred that I felt after my first wife's death 24 yrs. ago. This is the only way that I got rid of it. Now I can write more kind and loving things.; [a.] Olathe, KS

VENUTI, REBECCA
[pen.] Becky; [b.] November 1, 1978, Wellesly; [p.] Joseph and Barbara Venuti; [ed.] Currently a Junior at Bedford High School in Bedford, MA; [occ.] Student; [memb.] Drama club, SADD, Latin club, choir, yearbook, peer leadership; [hon.] Class President, Hugh O'Brian You Foundation, Creative Writing Award, Academic Achievement Award; [oth. writ.] Poems and short stories, but nothing that has ever been published before; [pers.] My writings are personal and express my innermost thoughts and feelings. The appreciation for my poetry may be lost in others, but I understand them and that is all that should matter.; [a.] Bedford, MA

VERLEY, DE ANNA Z.
[b.] January 26, 1978, Milwakee, WI; [p.] Liliane and Kenneth Verley; [ed.] Currently enrolled in Nathan Hale High School; [occ.] Student; [oth. writ.] A poem, called, "God You Are Beautiful" in the November 1st edition of the expressions Journal and some 69 completed short stories and poems awaiting finalization and publication.; [pers.] My works do not only express it. They are emotional and impulsive. They are that moment and change with the next. They are confused and a a little hard to understand. What you see is not always what you get for there are things hiding below the surface, praying against all their fears to be found. In short they are me.

VERMA, S. DEVENDORA K.
[pen.] Dev Verma; [b.] August 25, 1947, Siwan, India; [p.] Mr. Leksheni V., Mrs. Ganga D. Verma; [m.] Dr. Ratna Verma, May 3, 1978; [ed.] BEEE (Ranchi University), MSEE (Columbia University New York), MBA (Fairleigh Dicranson University, New Jersey); [occ.] MTS (Member of Technical Staff); [memb.] IEEE (Communication Society); [hon.] Member of several Educational and Social Organizations.; [oth. writ.] Several poems published I presented on: World Sisterhood and Brotherhood Precious Life, God's Creation So Beautiful, Baby's First Cry, Our Planet Earth-We Must Protect, Who Is He Who Am I?,—(GOD); [pers.] I believe in advocating for: "Shaping the world to have no war in the next century!" To build the new millennium with peace, prosperity and progress for generations to come, inviting full participations from all nations as world family members.; [a.] New York, NY

VERNA, KIMBERLY Q.
[pers.] This poem is dedicated to the memory of Michele Verna (1973-1991) without her this would not be possible. Taken from us too soon, she will forever remain in our hearts as a beloved daughter, sister, friend. She is greatly loved an dearly missed.

VERNON, DANIEL AARON
[b.] May 3, 1971, Salt Lake City, UT; [p.] Douglas A. and Karien B. Vernon; [ed.] Graduated from Skyline High School in '89. I played football and lettered twice. Jocks can write poems also, not all Jocks are dumb, people need at the man inside; [occ.] All Style Office products, I repair office furniture; [oth. writ.] I have written many poem unpublished; [pers.] I write poetry to help express myself, the way that I feel towards people. I hope that my poems will influence other to be kind to one another; [a.] Salt Lake City, UT

VERONIN, MICHAEL W.
[b.] June 24, 1932, California; [m.] Choung-Wen Liang; [ch.] Esther and Lara Veronin; [occ.] Private Investigator; [oth. writ.] Other poems, original songs, and drafts of novels.; [pers.] Strongly influenced by the writing and music of Bob Dylan, the Beatles, and other prominent artist of the 1960's and 1970's; [a.] Diamond Bar, CA

VIEIRA, JENNIFER A.
[b.] April 20, 1971, Long Beach, CA; [p.] Raymond and Nancy Vieira; [ed.] Monta Vista High School, Colorado Mtn. College, Regis University; [occ.] Student, Liberal Arts, Minor Elementary Education; [memb.] United States Figure Skating Association, Steamboat Springs Figure Skating Club; [hon.] Octoberfest Queen, 1989-1990, The National Student Government Award 1993-1994; [pers.] I have been influenced by my own experiences in life.; [a.] Steamboat Springs, CO

VINSANT, CONNIE S.
[b.] November 22, 1964, Southbend; [p.] Howard and Mary Ottman; [m.] Ronald Visant, March 21, 1980; [ch.] Brandon, Brandi, Brent; [memb.] (Considering) Corresponding classes with Long Ridge Writers Group.; [oth. writ.] Compilation of poetry entitled "Holy Images"; [pers.] I truly believe that we are the most-blessed out of all of God's Creation, for we are given the ability to communicate: Our emotions, idea's and our word. "If one can open the door of communication, another can gain an heart to understand".; [a.] Bristol, IN

VOGELPOHL, JASON NELS
[b.] March 9, 1972, Portland, OR; [p.] Marcia and William; [ed.] University of California at Santa Barbara. Georg-August University in Goettingen, Germany; [occ.] Penniless Poet; [pers.] I do not fear to feel: this is my gift.; [a.] Carmel, CA

VOIGT, ALLAN
[b.] August 13, 1935; [m.] Judith Voigt; [ed.] BSEE; [occ.] Technical Writer; [memb.] Society of Technical Communicators, Society for the Preservation and Encouragement of Barbershop Quartet Singing in America; [pers.] "Dear Bill" was written in memory of Bill George, a fellow barbershop quartet singer who was not only a great joke teller, but also had such an outstanding bass voice that upon his arrival in heaven must certainly have been put in charge of thunder.; [a.] Mentor, OH

VON LINDERN SR., DONOVAN RAY
[b.] July 17, 1954, Coeur D'Alene, ID; [p.] Donald and Beverly Von Lindern; [m.] June Lee McCall, Von Lindern, October 28, 1993; [ch.] Donovan Ray Jr; [ed.] Westmont High School Graduate 12th grade; [occ.] Commercial Painter, Wallcovering installer; [hon.] Being chosen by National Library of Poetry for publication; [oth. writ.] I have numerous other poems which I have written over last 15 years which I've compiled but never tried to published; [pers.] I wish to thank my wife. My poetry is written to instill thought happiness, and joy to those who enjoy poetry-mostly written from life's trials and tribulations; [a.] Stockton, CA

VOYLES, PAMELA K.
[b.] February 5, 1965, Corpus Christi, TX; [p.] Mr. and Mrs. L. Wallace and B. Regmund; [m.] Robert Voyles, December 27, 1987; [ch.] Katherine Voyles; [ed.] Bachelor of Science; [occ.] Teacher; [pers.] I wrote this poem for a friend. Now I use it for anyone having a baby.; [a.] Corpus Christi, TX

WADAS, STEVEN
[b.] May 16, 1955, Ludlow, MA; [p.] Walter E., Sophie B.; [pers.] My poetry's purpose is to illuminate the Stillness within us as it informs our actions in this edifice of Reason we call reality. Prose is unfit for the task, each sentence is built upon its predecessor, a tool facile for creating worlds, but inappropriate for recording the truth of this one. For that we need poetry, which by its nature it stops our sailing across the surface, and, like the pearl divers of Japan, drops us into the Deep, returning to the surface with pearls commensurate with our courage and our integrity.; [a.] Concord, CA

WAGNER, BETTY H.
[pen.] Betty H. Wagner; [b.] May 21, 1933, Dublin, VA; [p.] Pauline Bane Harrell, Bassler (Deceased 1970); [m.] Donald J. Wagner Sr. (Deceased) 1995, April 28, 1952; [ch.] Sharon, Donna, Alex, Jimmy, Jeff, Tammy; [ed.] Dublin High School Graduate 1951; [occ.] Healthcare Giver/House keeper retired Endoscopy Tech. Prince William Hospital 1988; [memb.] AARP; [hon.] Prince William Hospital Award for 16 years of service.; [oth. writ.] Poem: published in 1979 Young Publications, Knoxville, TN, Book title: Lyrical Voices an International Poetry Anthology; [pers.] I like to read and I try to write about my feelings concerning the things I see around me. I have been working on my first book that I started in 1993. It is a mystery fiction. I have

14 grandchildren and 3 great grandchildren. They are all special to me.; [a.] Manassas, VA

WAGNER, JULIE ANNE

[b.] May 10, 1966; [p.] Barbara M. Vikre; [m.] Reese Lynn Wagner, May 13, 1995; [ed.] B.S. Fishery Biology, Colorado State University; [hon.] Xi Sigma Pi; [pers.] I am grateful to those who have encouraged me to reach for goals I didn't realize I could achieve; [a.] Cedaredge, CO

WAGNER, PATRICK

[b.] July 20, 1973, Pennsylvania; [p.] Bernard and Helen Wagner; [ed.] Salesianum High School, University of Delaware, BA in English Literature; [hon.] Dean's List; [pers.] I am influenced by the works of Poe, Nietzsche, Nagokov, Genet, BauDelaire, and Rimband. This poem was written in genetian fashion as a metaphysical love poem so that the characters and their actions could be given greater weight and mobility w/ out actually defining them; [a.] Wilmington, DE

WAHLEN, DAO NGUYEN

[b.] March 15, 1967, Vietnam; [p.] Ky and Lo Nguyen; [m.] Tom Wahlen, September 8, 1990; [ed.] B.A. English; [occ.] Manager - The Gap; [memb.] Earth Share and United Way; [oth. writ.] I'm currently working on two books; [pers.] I'm constantly strive to be true to myself and not letting the society dictate the course of my behavior. I'm learning to be happy and at peace with myself by living life from moment to moment; [a.] Salt Lake, UT

WAINWRIGHT, TERRI

[b.] August 6, 1950, Baltimore; [p.] John and Georgia Carrick; [m.] Wm. Wainwright, Jr., 1971; [ch.] Katie and Jonathan; [ed.] B.S. Johns Hopkins University, MLA Johns Hopkins University; [occ.] English and Creative writing Instructor, Bel Air HS,Bel Air, MD; [memb.] NEA, MSTA, NCTE, Delta Kappa Gamma; [oth. writ.] Several poems published in local magazines, newsletters; [pers.] Thanks to the hundreds of students who have in the past and continue to inspire me daily; [a.] Fallston, MD

WAKELY, JACQUELINE JACKSON

[b.] July 6, 1928, Detroit, MI; [p.] Harold Jackson, Velma Jackson; [m.] Donald J. Wakely, February 5, 1949; [ch.] Randall Wm, Allen James; [ed.] Lincoln High Sch. Eastern Mich. University Wayne State University; [occ.] Retired Artist, Interior Designer; [hon.] 1st, 2nd and 3rd place awards in Juried Art Shows Mt. Pleasant Art Assoc. Saginaw Artist and Craftsman Midland Art Association; [a.] Oldsmar, FL

WALKER, LATORIA S.

[b.] August 2, 1976, Poughkeepsie, NY; [p.] Jesse and Frances Walker; [ed.] Franklin D. Roosevelt High School Marist College; [occ.] Teller at First Union Bank; [hon.] 4 year honor roll student, Dean's List; [pers.] So Unique is one of my favorite poems because it reflects my feelings about the women in my family who are all truly unique. There are women who I love, Cherish and admire; [a.] Hyde Park, NY

WALLACE, ARVELLA S.

[pen.] Arvella S. Wallace; [b.] June 9, 1979, Dodge City; [p.] Mark and Charlotte Wallace; [ed.] I am a junior in high school at Cimarron Jr/Sr High; [occ.] School; [memb.] Cimarron 1st Church of the Nazarene; [hon.] District 5 honor choir Sophomore/Junior year; [oth. writ.] I am in the process of trying to get a song published. "The Lost" - it hasn't been sent in yet, but I'm working on it.; [pers.] Job 8:9 (KJV) (For we are but of yesterday, and know nothing, because our days upon earth are a shadow.); [a.] Cimarron, KS

WALLACE, HUGH

[b.] January 5, 1923, Grove, OK; [occ.] Retired; [memb.] Republican inner circle and medal of freedom. Golden poet 1950-51. Editor's choice awards 1993-94-95. Several merit certificates; [hon.] Life membership inter motion society of poets- who's in poetry - National Library of Poetry; [a.] Okmulgee, OK

WALLACE, RONALD A.

[b.] June 28, 1975, Bastrop, LA; [p.] John and Lucy Wallace; [ed.] Spring Woods Sr. High Community College of the Air Force; [occ.] Aircraft armament systems specialist - United States Air Force; [memb.] Church of the Lord Jesus Christ 4209 Rosemary Lane Houston, Texas 77093; [oth. writ.] Senior High School Publications; [pers.] If I have a talent I believe it was given to me by God only. I give thanks in return by using this God-gives talent for a service to him in Jesus name.; [a.] Houston, TX

WALSH, PATRICIA HOWAY

[p.] Kenneth W. Walsh; [ch.] Nicholas, Amber, Stephen, Renee and Joseph; [ed.] Tarrant County Junior College Texas Wesleyan University; [occ.] Bureau of Engraving and Printing, Secretary; [memb.] Saint Patrick's Cathedral - Forth Worth, Adopt-A-School, Guest Speaker for local Civic Organizations.; [hon.] Award for Patriotic Service, Recognition of Excellence for exemplifying Performance, Fairness and Integrity; [oth. writ.] Over ten years of journal entries are a source of rich reminders and gives hope for the future and joy to those who read of themselves. Wrote/Illustrated book promoting the Children's Museum in Flint, MI. and carried the book to daycares reading to the children, leaving them a copy.; [pers.] Everyday there is someone whose life might be touched by God's human hands. His gift to me to reach people through my writing is precious. I simply cannot write!; [a.] Fort Worth, TX

WALTMAN, LINDA J.

[b.] September 5, 1945, Homestead, FL; [p.] Lavelle and Margaret Kirkwood; [ch.] Paul Waltman; [ed.] South Dade High School, Homestead, Fla, Spencer Bus. Col. New Orleans, La.; [occ.] Disability from Cherron Refinery, Pascagoula, MS; [memb.] God's Kingdom, Wade Baptist Church, East Central Order of Eastern Star; [oth. writ.] Approximately 20 poems glorifying God and acknowledging His leadership in our lives; [pers.] The only things we will carry from this world into eternity that will count, are the things we do that glorify God and bring honor to His son, Jesus Christ; [a.] Pascagoula, MS

WAN, QIAN ELYSA

[b.] July 13, 1985, Columbus, OH; [p.] Xiaoming Wan, Yeging Song; [ed.] 5th grade (Mathematics in 6-7th grade, Gifted and Talented Program); [occ.] 5th grade student at West Windsor-Plainsboro Upper Elementary School, NJ; [pers.] I wish everyone peace in the heart and that all people were judged equally regardless of their race of gender.; [a.] Cranbury, NJ

WANGBERG, ELIZABETH L.

[pen.] Elizabeth Wangberg; [b.] March 14, 1964, North Dakota; [p.] Peter J. Wangberg, Neva J. Wangberg; [m.] Happily Divorced, March 28, 1981; [ch.] Dallas, Eric and Rebecca Duncan; [ed.] Oatville Haysville Jr. High, Campus High, Mulvane High, GED Derby night school, College- Central Hair Design. College - I.C.S. Journalism Course; [occ.] Homemaker, Mother, Journalist in training, new Author.; [hon.] Jr. Golf Pro. at 13 years old Hole-in-one at Rolling Hills Country Club, G.E.D. at 26 Semi-Finalist in 1995 North American Open Poetry Contest.; [oth. writ.] In 4th grade at Oatville School, a book of children's Poems done by a friend and myself, was put in the Library there. I am working on a line of children's books now. Also, a book of Poems, and a Novel on Life with an Abusive Alcoholic, The Hard Facts.; [pers.] I am just really beginning as an Author but began writing at an early age. I am a Perfectionist and am working towards being the best I can be as an author. My books will hopefully be a learning experience for all that read them. I was inspired by my children to carry out my dream and to let the abused women of the world know, they're not alone.; [a.] Mulvane, KS

WARD, MRS. CLEONE M.

[pen.] Margaret Ward; [b.] October 11, 1932, Fond Du Lac, WI; [m.] James Ward, August 23, 1994; [ch.] Barbara J. Ostrander, Jack J. Nutter; [ed.] Goodrich Senior High, WI; [occ.] Receptionist/Office Manager for acupuncture doctor. Formerly bank accounting clerk for 20 year Lancaster WI; [memb.] United Methodist Church, WI; [oth. writ.] "Signs of Winter", "Ignored Beauty" and other such poems for personal pleasure.; [pers.] Mostly influenced by the beauty all around us that is ignored by most because of busy schedules.; [a.] Las Vegas, NV

WARREN, KAREN

[pen.] Ana Weatherton; [b.] February 23, 1977, Waycross, GA; [p.] Bobby and Kathy Warren; [ed.] Graduated from Brantley County High School - Currently attending Georgia College in Milledgeville, GA; [occ.] Third Key Claire's Boutiques, milledgeville, GA; [memb.] Brantley Explorer Club-Law enforcement, American Cancer Society, SADD America Heart Association, Models US; [hon.] Who's Who Among American High School Students, National Foreign Language Award: Spanish; [oth. writ.] Had a column in the Brantley Enterprise, several works printed in "The Peacock's Feet"; [pers.] Every letter, word, sentence, and phrase has a meaning in my life. It all comes from within.; [a.] Nahunta, GA

WARREN, KATHERINE O.

[b.] Seneca, SC; [p.] James T. and Kathlyn L. Owens; [ch.] Two daughters and John; [ed.] The School of Life; [occ.] Poet; [memb.] Brotherhood of man and woman; [hon.] Letter of commendation from the President of Oglethorpe University...Atlanta, GA; [oth. writ.] "This I Pray" (Self- Published Book)...45 pages selected form the hundreds and hundreds of writings channed by spirit thru this poet...; [pers.] I believe our sole purpose is to love God...and to love and help one another; [a.] Chamblee, GA

WASHINGTON, JANET ELAINE WEAVER

[b.] August 15, 1931, Newark, NJ; [p.] Enos and Kathleen Weaver; [ch.] Julia, Jevan, Johnathan; [occ.] Retired

WASHINGTON, WILMA B.

[b.] Birmingham, AL; [p.] Major and Willie Lee Bozman; [m.] Alvin Washington, November 22, 1980;

[ch.] Allison Monshae and Alvin Jr.; [ed.] Western High, Ala. A and M University; [occ.] Teacher Gate City Elementary School - Birmingham, AL

WASSIL, PATRICIA A.
[b.] May 10, 1960, Lewiston, ME; [p.] Thomas and Rachel Dempe; [m.] Keith R. Wassil, October 22, 1993; [ch.] Justin T. Dempe; [occ.] Assistant Branch Manager, First Savings Bank; [oth. writ.] Several poems that remain unseen and unpublished; [pers.] At the most difficult times when I could not share with anyone, I shared with myself in the form of a poem. Its been a great comfort to know I can always count on me. I have been greatly influenced by the musical talents of my husband.; [a.] Laurence Harbor, NJ

WATKINS, DAVID A.
[pen.] Heartbreak Kid; [b.] January 4, 1970, Good Sam, SJ; [p.] Al and Elaine Watkins; [m.] Lisa Arnold, Sometime in 1997; [ed.] Lynbrook High, De Anza, Bethany Bible College, and Nation University; [occ.] Nob Hill Employee; [hon.] Two first place lip sync awards: "When I'm 64" by the Beatles; [oth. writ.] Many poems published in school newspapers, church, and in a music magazine. (If only this was a career); [pers.] When friends turn you and there is nowhere to run then call upon my friends (who is true) Jesus Christ, Gods son; [a.] San Jose, CA

WEAVER, NANCY J.
[b.] June 17, 1948, La Junta, CO; [p.] Wm. and Edith Griffin; [m.] Leland Weaver, May 21, 1967; [ch.] Lori and Dana; [ed.] Diploma from Paramount High Paramount, California; [occ.] Housewife, Grandmother; [memb.] ISP; [hon.] Another poem published in "Garden of Life" by National Library of Poetry.; [oth. writ.] "Through The Wearer's Needle," printed and sold locally.; [pers.] I want to praise God through my writings, and express my love for him, and nature that he created. I know it's only through him that I write.; [a.] Wichita, KS

WEAVER, RHONDA
[b.] September 25, 1951, Denver, CO; [p.] Chester and Jody Weaver; [ed.] BA English, University of Northern Colorado MA Reading, University of Colorado; [occ.] Reading Teacher; [memb.] International Reading Association; [hon.] Delta Kappa Gamma; [pers.] I wish to convey the pleasures, memories and sadness of the human experience.; [a.] Estes Park, CO

WEBB, KENDRA
[pen.] Kendra Casewell; [b.] March 10, 1980, Alameda, CA; [p.] Jim and Cheryle Webb; [ed.] Castro Valley High School; [pers.] Some things have to be believed to be seen. "I am the owner of the sphere, of the seven stars and the solar year, ...of Caesar's hand and Plato's brain. Of Lord Christ's heart and Shakespeare's strain".; [a.] Castro Valley, CA

WEBER, AOLELHEID HEIOLI
[b.] May 19, 1934, Berlin, Germany; [p.] Ernst Weber and Grete Weber (Deceased); [ed.] 8 Volks sohule in Berlin graduate in 48 during the Blocorde of Berlin, 1 year work in Martin Luther Hospital, Spandau, Magarete; [occ.] Stitcher in Shoe Foc - Heimtory Frankli Shoe Co; [memb.] Lifetime membership of Maine poets; [hon.] For guilts from early American Society; [oth. writ.] Write children story, using dolls or Teddy bears to act out the part, I win published yet, also write songs-poem, but can't while the notes, also in German or translate into english old Christmas Carols; [pers.] According to my father, we Weber one decent from Karl - Manie Von Weber, his grand father was a grandson he never knew born in 1844 for Karl-Monie died in 1826, I am 6th in time but it ends with me do old to have children; [a.] Wilton, ME

WECHSELBERGER, JOHN B.
[pen.] JB Wex; [b.] November 7, 1956, Hawthorne, CA; [p.] JW Wechselberger, Jeannette Hofmann; [ed.] Upland High School, Upland California Practical Schools - Anaheim, CA, New Horizons - Santa Anna, CA; [occ.] Computer Technician Network Engineer; [memb.] Calvary Chapel Fellowship of Hemet; [oth. writ.] Several other poems not yet published; [pers.] I give thanks to the Lord - Jesus Christ for all He has done for me.; [a.] Hemet, CA

WEINSTEIN, WHITNEY
[b.] November 27, 1948, Lake Charles, LA; [p.] Adolphus and Nettie Ferguson; [ed.] LaGrange Sr. High, Los Angeles Trade Technical College; [occ.] Designer of women's clothing; [hon.] Dean's list, 1st place award in fashion illustration competition, 1st in both sportswear and town and travel categories of the "Gold Thimble" graduates design competition; [pers.] I wrote "Eternal Flower Child" for my beloved sister, whom I only truly discovered in this last decade, and who has helped me to learn the paramount importance of love for each other and the world around us; [a.] Los Angeles, CA

WELLS, BETTY J.
[b.] September 29, 1921, Effingham, IL; [p.] Deceased Abigail and Frederich W.; [m.] Deceased Howard I. Wells, Jr., May 16, 1948; [ch.] Annette Z. Wells, Howard T. Wells, III; [ed.] College - same courses short of degree. Numerous and varied studies - audited and seminars/workshops/Katharine Gibbs Graduate; [occ.] Retired writer, freelance; [memb.] None current I am nearly blind. My participation in outside organization is self limited. I am written a novel the finish of which has heard. A race between my fail eyesight and the last time of the story. Throughout the years of poetry writing I was published in many small "mags" most of which are now out of print.; [oth. writ.] Free lance writer for years - suitable credit for much done for others. Too numerous to list. Rating and "ghost" write speeches in Professional in health field, etc.; [pers.] I am is a writer, to write is to live. All future self-discovery and personal philosophy will be found in one's words no matter the forms.; [a.] Cincinnati, OH

WELTZ, MIKE
[b.] February 25, 1976, Washington, DC; [p.] Dr. and Mrs. Weltz; [ed.] McDonogh, The George Washington University pursuing A.B.S. in Biology; [occ.] Student; [memb.] The Creative Alliance; [oth. writ.] Tyranny of the majority Pooka press release date: Early 1996; [pers.] I would like to take this opportunity to thank my mother and father for their undying support over the years. I would also like to thank Renee and Sharon Randazzo for their encouragement.; [a.] Washington, DC

WENINGER, MICHELLE
[b.] July 13, 1967, Sterling, KS; [ed.] Associate of Arts Degree; [a.] Burrton, KS

WETZEL, REBECCA
[b.] February 13, 1978, Lebanon, PA; [p.] David Wetzel, Linda Wetzel; [ed.] Senior at Northern Lebanon Jr./Sr. High School; [pers.] Pressure is the difference between a lump of coal and a precious diamond.

WHITE, FRANK
[b.] Ithaca, NY; [m.] Dora; [occ.] Also a music student on piano and voice, he left home to travel with bands and trios. Later he switched to a single act as Frankie Valentine; [memb.] American Federation of Musicians; [oth. writ.] Includes newsletters and articles; [pers.] Frank desires to spend more time writing all kinds of material. He resides in the Las Vegas area with his wife, Dora, a Queensland Heeler and a cat with a face like a Panda; [a.] Henderson, NV

WHITMAN, ARTHUR JACOB
[b.] February 17, 1979, Philadelphia, PA; [p.] Dr. Glenn and Anna Whitman; [ed.] William Penn Charter School; [occ.] Student; [oth. writ.] I have many other writings (unfortunately more than 20 lines), however, none are published in any recognized text. I also write lyrics for my brother, a pianist composer. Together, we are trying to make it a career.; [pers.] It is our own personal relationship to love that determines the way we judge beauty. When love is lost, beauty fades. However, it is the wonder of the human spirit that we can find love within the gloomiest and most violent storms.; [a.] Philadelphia, PA

WHITMAN, CARLENE M.
[pen.] Pumpkin; [b.] October 5, 1968, Detroit, MI; [p.] Beverly Houston and Larry D. Wilson; [ch.] Na'Kyra Monise and Deven Marie; [ed.] Finney High, Wayne County Community College; [occ.] Clerk II; [memb.] Children's Center Backbone Committee; [oth. writ.] Several poems written for church anniversaries, birthdays and conventions; [pers.] The art of poetry comes from within we color ourselves with shades in which we feel; [a.] Detroit, MI

WHITMAN, CRYSTAL AILEEN
[b.] June 30, 1978, Midland, MI; [p.] Christine and William Whitman (Divorced); [ed.] I am currently in 11th grade after completing my high school education I plan to get a bachelors degree in acheology; [occ.] Student; [memb.] High School Choir; [hon.] Art award; [oth. writ.] I am currently writing a book of poetry; [pers.] I try to bring the things to light that many people would rather forget, through my poetry.; [a.] Sanford, MI

WHITMAN, MATTHEW EDWARD
[b.] Northampton; [p.] Robert and Christine Whitman; [ed.] Northamptom High, Westfield State College; [occ.] Transportation Planner Pioneer Valley Planning Commission; [memb.] Benevolent and protective order of elks; [hon.] Who's Who in American Universities and Colleges, Outstanding Senior, Dean's List; [oth. writ.] Numerous unpublished poems; [pers.] This was inspired by someone who I will always love, that move west. Cynthia D.B. thank you for giving me the best times of my life.; [a.] Northampton, MA

WHITTINGTON, PAMELA L.
[pen.] PLW; [b.] October 19, 1950, Hamilton, OH; [p.] Thelma, Grover Gabbard; [ch.] Steven, Barry, Brian and Kellie; [ed.] Frankfurst High, Frankfurst, Germany, Hazel Park Adult Ed, Oakland Community College; [occ.] CENA Certified Nursing Assistant; [memb.] Church of God Teacher, member Troy Cathedral of Praise; [hon.] Outstanding Science Award 1987, Hazel

Park Adult Ed., MCLA Scholarship; [oth. writ.] Nothing published to date; [pers.] Just as an artist splashes colors on a canvas to touch the senses and "tell" what he sees, it has been my life long dream to bless others with the same beauty "painted" with words.; [a.] Ferndale, MI

WIBBERLEY, JOANN
[b.] May 24, 1931, Toledo, OH; [p.] Harry and Vera Mulholland; [m.] Clarence R. Wibberley, June 9, 1956; [ch.] Two; [ed.] High School; [occ.] Homemaker; [oth. writ.] Other poems, such as these (and one song).; [pers.] Through struggles, and trials in life, my only source of Strength and Security was my Lord Jesus Christ, who has been with me through it all. Without Him, for me, there is no Life at all. All Praise and Honor for any talent that I have goes to Him.; [a.] Tallahassee, FL

WICKHAM, MAUREEN
[b.] February 28, 1955, Pocatelo, ID; [p.] Lynn C and Irene E. Simmons; [ch.] Brock Wickham; [ed.] Is 16 year old in school in Hillsborough, Oregon now with his Dad and and new family in Oregon until X-mas voc. I get him and all summer.; [oth. writ.] "It Shows On Your Face", Memory Lane", "Passing Years" and "Snake River"; [pers.] I've reflected on my life and the trials I've been through that all the Simmons family has been very much a helping part, of this and I dedicate it to them and Brock; [a.] Idaho Falls, ID

WIENER, ADAM LEWIS
[pen.] "Buzz" Wiener, Piano Legs Hickman; [b.] July 29, 1969, New York, NY; [p.] Joseph and Judy Wiener; [ed.] BA in English-University of Michigan Juris Doctoris - Washington University School of Law in St. Louis; [occ.] Attorney; [memb.] Jewish Captain of St. Bedes Softball Team, original member of "The Adam Gang", Attorney in St. Louis City Public Defender Office; [hon.] Voted best entry for poem "The Magician" in high School Anthology Etchings, Univ. of Michigan "Hopwood Award" winner for book "The Hired Gun", Selected "Mojoite of the Year" 1984, Runner-up Carter Tedrow Award, 1993 Batting Leader-St. Bedes softball Team; [oth. writ.] Co-Wrote weekly "DNA Column" in Mosher-Jordan's "John Door Weekly" Newspaper 1983-85; [pers.] My friends are family, my family members are my friends.; [a.] Royal Oak, MI

WIGGINS, TERRI L. K.
[b.] September 14, 1957, Chas., SC; [p.] Marvin and Harriette Kirkland; [m.] Michael S. Wiggins, May 8, 1982; [ch.] Michael S. Wiggins Jr.; [ed.] St. Andrews Parish High School; [occ.] House Wife; [memb.] Grace United Methodist Church; [pers.] Being a military wife, I have lived many different places, I liked to write about the cities and surrounding areas.; [a.] Charleston, SC

WILAND, ARTHUR
[pen.] Jonathan W. Smith; [b.] August 3, 1909, New York City; [p.] Mary and Harry; [m.] Faye (Deceased December 7, 1991), September 6, 1944; [ed.] B.S. D.D.S. FICD FACD EGNYAP; [occ.] Retired; [memb.] Fellow International College of Dentists, Fellow American College of Dentists, Fellow Greater New York Academy of Prosthodontics; [hon.] Speyer Experimental Junior High School Arista, Ommicron Kappa Upsilon Professor N.Y.U. College of Dentistry; [oth. writ.] "I Want To Cry Uncle" a humorous family ongoing situation.; [pers.] "Retirement is not doing nothing. It's doing all the things you always wanted to do but never had the time". So - I have been painting and making fine gold jewelry; [a.] Delray Beach, FL

WILBERT, DWAYNE L.
[pen.] Dwayne L. Wilbert; [b.] January 20, 1956, Los Angeles, CA; [p.] Lillie and Vernett Wilbert; [m.] Carla D. Neal-Wilbert, August 23, 1987; [ch.] Marla, Christopher and Darla; [ed.] Attain Leroy Locke Hi School L.A. L.A.T.T.C.; [occ.] Plumber-Parent; [memb.] Macedonia Baptist Church Denver, Co Los Angeles, CA; [hon.] Hi School Honor Graduate outstanding school spirit award H.S.; [oth. writ.] Passion - Windows - sisters (Beauty Under Oppression) To each his own; [pers.] Life is so diverse-so complex- and yet so simple -tomorrow is never seem, but only a time frame for starting a new; [a.] Denver, CO

WILCOX, JENIFER V. M.
[b.] January 27, 1924, Seattle, WA; [p.] Mary GM and Roy A. Raymond; [m.] Elmer 'Bud' Wilcox, April 22, 1947; [ch.] Russ, Roger, Rebecca, Ross; [ed.] Lincoln High St Elizabeth School of Nursing; [occ.] Surgical Nurse - Director now retired; [memb.] Ana WSNA VFW-AORN from which I am also retired; [oth. writ.] Poems - short children's tales - after the death of my 1 year old granddaughter I wrote a few things re sorrow and the grief of grand parents.; [pers.] Give unto others that which self would like to receive as we each traverse our own hills and valleys of life here upon earth.; [a.] Monroe, WA

WILCOX, SHERYL L.
[b.] July 12, 1948, Warren, PA; [p.] Gerald and Nellie Vorse; [m.] Frank C. Wilcox, June 8, 1979; [ch.] Cyndi, Matthew, Mike, Shelly and Andy; [ed.] Associate in Arts Jamestown Community College Currently-Senior-Writing Major University of Pittsburgh-Bradford; [occ.] College Student; [hon.] Phi Theta Kappa Society Dean's List; [oth. writ.] Feature Article published in local newspaper; [pers.] Everyone should dream and, if possible, follow those dreams; [a.] Russell, PA

WILKINS, LOUISE IRENE
[b.] August 26, 1977, Secaucus, NJ; [occ.] I would like to be a private investigator, I am currently in high school.; [oth. writ.] I wrote the poem I sent in at age 17. I am now 18 and have over 20 other poems; [pers.] I write what I feel and believe in. Reading my work will give you a good understanding of who I am and what I believe in. People should do what they feel is right not what others think; [a.] Watkins Glen, NY

WILLIAMS, CAROL K.
[b.] September 6, 1942, Franklin CO, IL; [p.] Mrs. Billie Guff and Late Kenneth Golf; [m.] Donald R. Williams, October 21, 1960; [ch.] Christopher Dee Williams and Roxanna Lyn Davis; [ed.] Benton Consolidated High School -Grad- 1960; [occ.] Retired Computer Operator; [memb.] Minier Assembly of God Church; [oth. writ.] Several poems and children's stories. Have not pursued getting published yet; [pers.] I want to reflect my love for God, family and country.; [a.] Benton, IL

WILLIAMS, DEBORAH E.
[b.] July 10, 1956, Byron, GA; [p.] Ella F. Richardson and Robert Smith; [m.] Larry Williams, July 9, 1977; [ch.] Larry, Tevares and Tamarcus; [ed.] Peach Co, High, Crandall College; [occ.] Homemaker; [memb.] President of WWC, (Church), Chairman Program Committee (Church); [oth. writ.] Written special dedications for weddings, anniversaries, any occasions requested by community, writes skits/plays for church, creates cards with writings of poetry.; [pers.] When I became totally blind, different circumstances occurring around me whether through others with problems or even my own motivated me to start writing as a means of reaching out to others.; [a.] Warner Robins, GA

WILLIAMS, GENA L.
[pen.] CatWoman; [b.] February 17, 1957, Columbia, SC; [p.] Fred and Linda H. Williams; [m.] Separated, April 10, 1980; [ch.] Monic F. Wms and Lee C. C. Turner; [ed.] A.C. Flora High, S.C. Cola College P.T.C. Nursing School D.C.; [occ.] Writer (Poetry, spiritual plays, choreographer and Gina's Catering Retired Instrument - Tech; [memb.] Saint James AME, Church S.C. The Way Of The Cross Church Of Christ D.C. National Theatre Hospitality Committee Saturday Morning at the National Red Cross Nursing Association, Renown Creative Dancer, Sunshine Dancer. Institute for Cosmic Consciousness; [hon.] Elen Hayes Gallery Award, Dean List Community Services, National Nursing Assoc. National poet society, Employee of the month, Employee of the year, The Christian Association for Nursing Services; [oth. writ.] Reflection of the light 35 plus 1; [pers.] 'You hold the key' an "You can make it"; [a.] Washington, DC

WILLIAMS, HATTIE
[pen.] Hattie Williams; [b.] October 19, 1962, Philadelphia; [p.] Marie Williams; [ch.] Quianna, Sirron, Nicole and Jazmine; [ed.] Daysha Kingsingten High; [occ.] Senior Aide Maintenance Central Maintenance; [oth. writ.] None of my writings been publish this first of my many poems; [pers.] I only write what I know and what I see and what I feel as part of my life and the life that lives around me; [a.] Philadelphia, PA

WILLIAMS, MICHAEL T.
[pen.] W. M. Deverreaux; [b.] March 30, 1971, Brooklyn, NY; [p.] Betty J. Williams; [ed.] Far Rockaway HS Amherst College; [occ.] Teacher/Tutor; [hon.] Third-place winner of the New York City Poetry Contest (1989), Magna cum laude honors from Amherst College (1993), United Federation of Teachers Scholarship (1989-1993); [oth. writ.] Poem collection in the Amherst College archives, a memoriam plaque dedicated to an high school English teacher.; [pers.] I attempt to illustrate and reconcile poetically the essential tension in man between has rational and animal natures. My influences include the romantic and meta-physical English poets and Albert Camus; [a.] Detroit, MI

WILLIAMS, MILDRED L.
[b.] August 9, 1954, Henderson, NC; [ed.] I year post graduate training; [occ.] LPN; [pers.] My desire, my dream to write a work - that would bring the world to its knees, weeping for what it has been, see it raised up again into compassion, hope, and joy, that can only come through "Perfect - Love"; [a.] Cincinnati, OH

WILLIAMS, O. EMILY
[pen.] O. Emily; [b.] November 15, 1935, Kissimmee, FL; [p.] George F. and Pauline E. Lucas; [ch.] Jamee Marie, Domda LuAnne, David A. Andy Williams, Baby Austin James Williams, Lucas Hunter, Katherine W., Emily R., Sarah E., Kelsey L., and Justin E,; [occ.] Yard and lap children; [pers.] Augusta, GA

WILLIAMS, STAN
[b.] October 15, 1933, California; [m.] Dana, May 10, 1986; [ch.] Lyn, Deb, Allison and George; [ed.] University of Tennessee; [occ.] Dentist, Philosopher and Observer of life; [pers.] My writings reflect personal experiences of life. I gain satisfaction when one reads my work and relates in some way to a similar experience. Writing and life. They are best when kept simple!; [a.] Greenville, SC

WILLIAMS, VIRGINIA DALE
[pen.] Dale; [b.] December 1, 1946, Caldwell County; [p.] Mr. and Mrs. Joe and Rosalee Patterson; [m.] Separated; [ch.] Five; [ed.] 11 Grade Freedmon High School; [occ.] Brayhill furniture Caldwell Memorial Hospital; [memb.] Dula Town Presbyterian Church the cancer society; [hon.] I recall an awards from the National Library of Poet in the fall of 95 the Gordon of life, some one, spedal several ordical publish in the Lenoir new topic; [oth. writ.] I have a lots of poem written and hope to soon publish my own book, if it the Lord will; [pers.] The words come straight from my heart. I have had hard time in my life. And the Lord has always been their for me, so all most every poem I write I include him, because he is my strength; [a.] Lenoir, NC

WILLIS, RICHARD LEE
[pen.] Rick Wallace; [b.] October 1, 1931, Geneva, IL; [p.] Mr. and Mrs. Fred L. Willis; [ed.] Glenbard High School Glen Ellyn IL; [occ.] Retired; [oth. writ.] Song "Best Bookie Ever"; [pers.] Leaving Dupage County IL, I simply stated "I don't miss". Modesty is now abandoned. Circumstances became "Anything goes" poetry inspired to the recipient to bring intrigue could lead to finished songs, a movie, the completion of my book, and the introduction of a unique game called "Givers and takers." Your bet!; [a.] Tampa, FL

WILLY, SHANGRILA
[b.] November 10, 1980, Houston, TX; [p.] George Willy and Shanti Willy; [ed.] Duchesne Academy Clements High School; [occ.] High - School student at Clements High School; [memb.] Global Awareness, Junior Achievement, Literary Magazine, Odessy of the Mind, Democratic Youth of Clements, Yearbook, Choir; [hon.] 1st place in the 3rd annual art of caring essay contest, National School Spelling Bee Winner, 3rd place in Science fair; [pers.] "We are the music-makers and we are the dreamers of dreams." My role models are my mother and father who have supported me through everything I've done; [a.] Sugarland, TX

WILSON, IVORY
[b.] March 1, 1969, Cherokee County Hospital; [p.] Mr. and Mrs. Billy Wilson; [m.] Tracie Wilson, September 22, 1995; [ch.] Derrick Wilson; [ed.] Gaffney Senior High School Limestone College - BA in History Converse Graduate Program - Currently majoring in Ele./Sec. Education; [occ.] Sub. Teacher; [memb.] International Reading Association; [hon.] Limestone Honor Roll Spring '94; [oth. writ.] Working on collection of poetry for publication; [pers.] I write about my experiences and my inner-most feelings.; [a.] Gaffney, SC

WILSON, LARRY M.
[b.] August 19, 1965, Muleshoe, TX; [p.] Lois Carter; [ch.] Anthony, Myles Wilson Shayla More Wilson; [oth. writ.] Several poems and short stories also Lyric's to songs. This is my first official publication; [pers.] In life, above all, we must love!; [a.] Guymon, OK

WILSON, LEO CLEMENT
[b.] November 16, 1935, Galveston, TX; [p.] Clement Leo Wilson and Irma Wilson; [m.] Syble Marie Wilson, March 26, 1983; [ch.] Sheryl, Vincent, Rene, Robert, Natalie, Joseph, Marie, Michael, and Kimberly; [ed.] GED., BST Univ of Houston, MST Univ of Houston; [occ.] Retired U.S. Navy Chief Petty Officer Retired Teacher San Jacinto College, Houston, TX; [memb.] DAV, FRA, VFW, Amplegio Vietnam Vets; [hon.] Navy Commendation Medal for Leadership 1971, Phi Kappa Phi, Dean's List; [oth. writ.] "You've Seen Him A Thousand Times" published in creative Writing annual - "Mother never told me" published in newspaper, "Veteran's Day" published in VVA publication; [pers.] I write to Express my most inner feelings at that moment, most of my work is based on powerful emotions of the time; [a.] Galveston, TX

WILSON, MAC A.
[pen.] Mac A. Wilson; [b.] November 2, 1929, Bradenton, FL; [p.] A. E. Bud and Thora Wilson (Deceased); [m.] Lucille G. Wilson, November 1, 1952; [ch.] David and Lucille Lee; [ed.] Pensacola High School, University of Florida, USAF Officer and Pilot Training; [occ.] President, Marketing Services of Al. Inc and Dale Carnegie Trainer; [memb.] Cathedral Church of the Advent (Episcopal), Vestavia Country Club, Rotary, MGMA, HFMA, Sales and Marketing Executives, Chamber of Commerce, Assistant Professor, Univ. of Alabama B'ham; [hon.] U of Dean's List, American Spirit Honor Medal - USAF, Jet Pilot Officer - USAF, National Sales Trainer - I.B.M. Corp, Manager of the year - 1965, Christian - saved by Grace; [oth. writ.] National Sales Training Course for I.B.M. Educational T.V. sales course for U.A.B. and S.M.E. "For the Love of Selling" in writing to be published many unpublished poems and writings; [pers.] Your title "The Voice Within" says it all. There are times, events, and people, who stir the spirit inside me (usually around 3 o'clock A.M.) struggling to be free, in song, word or poetry.; [a.] Birmingham, AL

WILSON, SYLVIA W.
[pen.] Ashmor Wilson; [b.] January 26, 1964, Houston, TX; [p.] Elmo and Ida Weaver; [m.] Damon J. Wilson, May 12, 1990; [ch.] Ashley Elaine and Morgan Elizabeth; [ed.] High School for Health Professions, Houston, TX, University of Texas C Austin; [occ.] Interior Designer; [oth. writ.] Monthly articles for sophisticated woman magazine's distinctive living section; [pers.] My writings reflect the unpredictable path of human experiences. The inspiration to put these experiences into words comes from the things seen and heard in my natural surroundings.; [a.] Detroit, MI

WILSON, WILMA
[b.] May 14, 1920, Taunton, MA; [m.] Harvey W. Wilson Jr., April 24, 1948; [ch.] William, Patricia, Joanne, Bonnie, Terri, James; [occ.] Housewife; [memb.] No Taunton Baptist Church Charity Madd (Mother's against drunk driving Just Say No (to drugs) Charity Special Olympics Charity; [hon.] Award of Merit Certificate Honorable Mention for poem entered in "World of Poetry" contest; [oth. writ.] Many entered in our local Newspaper the Taunton Daily Gazette; [pers.] My poems are my inward thoughts of everyday life, some happy, some sad when I am writing poems, it relaxes me, and I block out all my surrounding, like I am in outer-space - just me and my thoughts, purely paradise.; [a.] Taunton, MA

WIMBERLY, GLORIA
[pen.] Riordan Winds; [b.] December 1, 1953, Chelsea, MA; [p.] Robert E. Hebrank Sr. and Dorothy Davis; [m.] John Fayne Wimberly, December 12, 1992; [ch.] Jeremy, Leah and Joann Hendrix; [ed.] San Jacinto Jr. College, University of Houston; [occ.] Cosmetology instructor, consultant; [hon.] Phi Theta Kappa Who's Who in American Jr. Colleges 1987 Top 12 students on campus San Jacinto Jr. College 1988, Dean's Honor List 1981, 9187; [oth. writ.] Riordan (Ree-or-dan) Winds has many complications being readied for print at this time along with art pieces that will accompany.; [pers.] I have allowed my creator, the God of all Ages to reflect himself through my hand as write. It is for His Glory that these writings will come forth and bless His people; [a.] Houston, TX

WIMBERLY JR., STEVEN P.
[b.] October 21, 1972, Pauls Valley, OK; [p.] Steven P. Wimberly Sr., Penny J. Bell; [ed.] Wynnewood High School, University of Science and Arts of Oklahoma; [occ.] Fuel Jockey at the local gas station; [pers.] To dreamers such as I. Who in these infinite search for the realm of human possibility, the world is lacking and I'm left unimpressed, unenthusiased and undaunted within my hopes and dreams.; [a.] Davis, OK

WINBERG, MAUREEN
[b.] May 13, 1951, Red Wing, MN; [p.] Lester Frazier and Margaret Frazier; [m.] Paul, October 25, 1975; [ch.] Bridget Amara, and Christine Margaret; [ed.] Red Wing Central High School Rochester Tech. College, Red Wing-Winona Tech. College; [occ.] Burnside School Learning aide, Library aide; [memb.] St. Joseph's Catholic Church, M.A.D.D., Humane Society; [oth. writ.] The Dream The Lady Jane; [pers.] Writing is meditation for the soul. It emptys the mind and body and spirit and makes us whole again. Writing is my memory for gladness and escape from sadness.; [a.] Red Wing, MN

WINSTON, MARCIA B.
[pen.] Firebrand; [b.] November 17, 1961, Atlanta, GA; [p.] Margaret Winston; [ed.] Archer High Georgia State University; [occ.] Claims Reviewer, Metropolitan Life Insurance; [hon.] Class Valedictorian; [pers.] My inspiration is to light the souls of others with my words.; [a.] Atlanta, GA

WITMER, LOIS ANN
[b.] March 13, 1938, Mechanicsburg; [p.] R. Stanley Witmer and Irma Witmer; [ed.] Mechanicsburg High; [occ.] Accounting/Clerical Capital Recovery Associates; [oth. writ.] A poem published in the Harrisburg Evening News; [pers.] My poetry has been inspired by experiences throughout my life. The words can only be written when feelings are intertwined with the heart, mind and soul.; [a.] Harrisburg, PA

WOHLFORD, CHARLES R.
[pen.] Christian Wohlf; [b.] May 2, Knoxville, TN; [p.] Nina Jackie Heath, Charles Wohlford; [ed.] Attended L.S.U. (Louisiana State Uni.); [occ.] Self employed; [memb.] United States Marine Corps (honorably - discharged) (Debating Team) M.G.C.J.C. - Goutier, Miss; [oth. writ.] Compilation of poetry short story presently working on a novel; [pers.] In the midst of chaos, it's my one true shelter, this ink, this immortal blood, maybe, in spite of myself, I call leave a small flicker of light, as I, someday, fade into my own darkness; [a.] Mobile, AL

WOICEK, MICHAEL S.
[pen.] Mic Woicek; [occ.] Writer, Actor and Director; [oth. writ.] Plays "The Wait" "The Bird"; [a.] Madison, WI

WOLFE, ALLENE C.
[pen.] Homer Wolfe; [b.] November 23, 1944, Amarillo, TX; [p.] Jack Robinson Culp and Marjorie Louis Fisk Culp; [m.] John F. Wolfe, December 20, 1963; [ch.] Fred, John, Alvin and Bill; [ed.] Wolfin Elementary Radford School for Girls, Barstow School for young Ladies Amarillo High School; [occ.] DELI worker, cook and cross trained dept. associate at super-k mart; [memb.] National Poetry Society - WIBC, National Assn. of Pat Boone Fan Clubs.; [hon.] Bowling - Scouts - Church - School parents awards - Riflery - Archery Editor Choice - Painting; [oth. writ.] News papers - school publications tomorrow never knows (anthology)- Pat Boone Publications - Work Newsletter; [pers.] I have been blessed in many ways and expressing my feelings with pen and brush are among those blessings - If I can share the love, laughter and moving feeling with others, then that's the talent God has wished for me and I am grateful to do so.; [a.] Thornton, CO

WOLLAM, ASHLEY SUSANNE
[b.] October 21, 1984, Webster, TX; [p.] Tim and Susan Wollam; [ed.] Currently in 6th grade, I am educated at home by my parents; [occ.] Student; [memb.] First Baptist Church of Alta Loma, Girls in Action mission organization, Torch (Galveston County home school group); [hon.] Superior Achievement Rating at Texas State Bible Drill; [pers.] I'm grateful to God for the talent to write. I hope that in the years to come you will read much more of my writing and will find pleasure in doing so.; [a.] Santa Fe, TX

WOLLINGER, NANCI S.
[b.] September 4, 1963, Cudahy, WI; [p.] Lloyd Bigger Sr., LaVerne Bigger; [m.] David T. Wollinger, September 10, 1982; [ch.] Joshua David, Alicia Irene; [ed.] Jefferson High, Madison Area Technical College; [occ.] Laboratory Technician; [memb.] Johnson Creek Library Board Member, National Registry Emergency Medical Technician; [oth. writ.] "Alicia's Poem" and many other poems that have not been sent in for publication; [pers.] This poem "Bless The Special Children" was inspired by my daughters illness in July of 1990. She is now a cancer survivor and it is my wish that we all "Bless The Special Children" and pray that they may stay.; [a.] Johnson Creek, WI

WONG, ERIC
[pen.] Eric Wong; [b.] May 3, 1978, Van Nuys; [p.] Wanda Wong and Chan K. Wong; [ed.] Diamond Bar High; [occ.] Student; [memb.] Diamond Bar Key Club TKC Church, Diamond Bar High School Yearbook Staff; [oth. writ.] Diamond Bar High Yearbook articles; [pers.] I don't think there are any bad people in the world. Just a bunch of misdirected ones; [a.] Diamond Bar, CA

WOODARD, ALBERT E.
[b.] October 19, 1933, Lula, MS; [p.] Thomas C. and Annie M. Woodard; [m.] Ruth A. Woodard, October 20, 1951; [ch.] Sheryl Harrison; [ed.] Crenshaw, MS High School, BBA, Accounting, MS, Management University of Memphis; [occ.] Credit Manager, Oil Distributor; [memb.] Calvary Church of the Nazarene, American Diabetes Association, United We Stand America, Southwest Credit Association; [hon.] Honorable discharge, U.S. Army, Who's Who in TN, 1973; [pers.] The outer person is known by all who see you. The inner person is known by you and God. Only you can decide which is most important. Be sure you make the right decision.; [a.] Memphis, TN

WOODS, JOHN T.
[pen.] John Terry Woods; [b.] August 20, 1950, Roanoke; [p.] John and Eleanor Woods; [ed.] Livingstone College BA Degree in History; [occ.] Interviewer with the State of VA; [oth. writ.] "Snow", "When The Fox Guards The Hen House", "Forgotten", "True Love", "Friends".; [pers.] I have been influenced by the earlier poet's, I wish someday to publish my own book on life and love; [a.] Rocky Mount, VA

WOOLRIDGE, SUMMER LYNN
[b.] May 22, 1979, Alameda County; [p.] Bunny and Dave Woolridge; [ed.] Jr in High School at Bishop O Dowd; [hon.] 1991 James Logan Speech Invitational - 1st place interpretation, poem 1990 poem contest in Jr High "Where The Sky Ends", 1989 Kevin Webb award - scholar 1989 Eagle Award scholar, Bancroft Jr. Hish 1993 PT Award, 1995 - Miss Jr. Teen San Francisco 1995 MAII - Talent of America - 1st place, monologue, 2nd place commercial 3rd runaway and photo; [oth. writ.] I love to write poems. I have been writing them since I was 9 years old.; [pers.] Poetry is always there to use as an escape goat for honesty to be let out. Robert Frost once said, "you may read it a hundred times: it will forever keep it's freshness as a petal keeps its fragrance.; [a.] San Leandro, CA

WORLEY, NATALIE
[b.] November 13, 1979, Los Gatos Community Hospital; [ed.] Leigh High School; [occ.] Student; [memb.] Key Club, Interact Club; [hon.] Honors English; [oth. writ.] Nothing that has been published, but I have written numerous poems and I am beginning a book.; [a.] San Jose, CA

WORWOOD, JANICE KAY
[b.] November 6, 1940, Northwood, ND; [p.] Joseph and Adelaide Vonesh; [m.] Keith A. Worwood, August 21, 1993; [ch.] Linda, Kevin, Aaron, Preston; [ed.] Masters in Elementary Education; [occ.] Teacher at Mt. View Elementary School; [pers.] I believe the words of this poem came as an answer to the sudden death of my daughter, Linda. These words have always brought comfort to me.; [a.] Las Vegas, NV

WRIGHT, JUDY
[b.] November 7, 1960, West Bend, WI; [p.] Lorraine Rosenthal, Wilbert Rosenthal; [ch.] Jennifer Jean; [ed.] Ozaukee High, Fredonia WI Northcentral Technical College Wausau WI; [occ.] Laborer, J.W. Window Component, Merrill, WI; [oth. writ.] Several poems unpublished, "Voice"; [pers.] I write poems so that someday people across the world can read and enjoy them too.; [a.] Irma, WI

WRIGHT, STACI D.
[b.] May 9, 1975, Bakersfield; [p.] Willie and Debra Wright; [ed.] Sophomore at Bakersfield College South High School '93; [occ.] Courtesy Clerk (Box Girl) Vons Co, Inc.; [pers.] Trust in the Lord with all thine heart, and lean not unto thine own understanding, Proverbs 3:5; [a.] Bakersfield, CA

YANIS, SYLVIA CRUZ
[pen.] Sylvia Diaz Cruz; [b.] March 18, 1958, Tinian, MI; [p.] Juan and Conception D. Cruz; [m.] Edward Steven Yanis, September 22, 1984; [ch.] Nicholas Steven, Natalie Gloria and Nydia Conception; [ed.] John F. Kennedy High Kelsey-Jenney College; [occ.] Legal Secretary; [hon.] Outstanding Graduate of 1991 Kelsey-Jenney College, Honor Roll; [oth. writ.] Several articles for the "Success Express Paper" of Kelsey-Jenney College

YOKOYAMA, JUNKO
[pen.] Junko Kuroda; [b.] March 4, 1936, Japan; [p.] Shoichiro Yokoyama (Deceased), Hanako Yokoyama; [m.] Divorced; [ch.] Arthur Kuroda, Mabelle Kuroda; [ed.] Kanto Gakuin College, Japan College of Marine, Marine County in California (one year), California Beauty Culture, San Francisco (one year); [occ.] Chairman of the Board of Director, Century and Co., Ltd., Tokyo, Japan; [memb.] Junior Chamber of Commerce of Tokyo, Senior Chamber of Commerce of Tokyo; [hon.] Medal for Merit from Red Cross (1989), Medal Dark Blue Ribbon from the Prime Minister of Japan (1989); [oth. writ.] Book (Non-fiction) Title: "No More Japanese Style"; [pers.] After I will be retired I want to be writing the novel, the poem, the scenario with my experience. "My Philosophical Statement is what ever I want to do, I will try and challenging.; [a.] Honolulu, HI

YOUNG, ALMA
[b.] August 7, 1953, Grayson, KY; [p.] Ellis and Muddanie Blevins; [m.] Divorced; [ch.] Sandora Humphrey; [ed.] East Carter High New Opportunity School for Women Berea College Ashland K.Y. Community College; [occ.] Domestic Engineer; [memb.] Women for Women Organization Kanawha Valley Emmaus Community Bagby Memorial United Methodist Church Carter Co. Humane Society; [oth. writ.] Editorial for the homeless in 1988 in the Ashland Daily Independent Newspaper; [pers.] I strive to reflect my Lord God creator's Love and respect for all animals and people.; [a.] Grayson, KY

YOUNG, BILL
[pen.] Trace Hunter; [b.] March 11, 1933, KY; [p.] Deceased; [m.] Divorced; [ed.] High School, IBM Center of New York; [occ.] Painting contractor; [memb.] Christian Coalition, Baptist Church; [oth. writ.] Other types of poetry; [pers.] The purpose of my writing is to acknowledge what God has given me: "The expression of his love to all mankind, with a call to each individual heart".; [a.] Muncie, IN

YOUNG, RHONDA GILLEY J.
[pen.] Rhonda J. Gilley; [b.] February 27, 1953, Texas; [p.] E. R. Gilley; [m.] Broadley D. Young, June 26, 1993; [ch.] Shaun, Nathan; [ed.] GED 1971 Vocational Nurse and Liscensure 1975; [occ.] Disabled; [hon.] Graduated Highest in Nursing Class; [oth. writ.] Several more unpublished poems; [pers.] I am no better than anyone else, but there is no one better than me. The only person I have to be better than, is the person I am today.; [a.] San Dimas, CA

ZAJAC, JOHN
[b.] February 4, 1971; [pers.] Life in modern day, industrialized society has promoted certain values over mankinds truest substance, love. We as individuals become so wrapped up in the survival and economic advancement of ourselves that we often lose perspective

on the basic feelings of love, and what these feelings mean towards our personal enrichment. It is my goal to help as many people as possible realize this, bettering our society in the process.; [a.] Palm Harbor, FL

ZAMBITO, ELIZABETH
[b.] April 22, 1975, Waltham, MA; [p.] John and Beverly Zambito; [ed.] South Carroll High School Towson State University; [occ.] Full-time Student; [memb.] National Honor Society National Wildlife Society National Geographic Society; [hon.] Dean's List - Frostburg State University; [oth. writ.] Creative writing portfolio in high school. Copy for yearbook in high school. Several writings for college classes.; [pers.] Writing poetry is a positive outlet for emotions that are difficult to otherwise express. Everyone needs some way to vent their feelings.; [a.] Eldersburg, MD

ZANELOTTI, NICOLE
[b.] July 21, 1979, Silver Spring, MD; [p.] Stephanie and James Zanelotti; [ed.] Currently a Junior at Calvert High School in Prince Frederick, MD - Calvert County; [occ.] Student; [memb.] Captain, Calvert H.S. Pom Squad; [pers.] My poems reflect true life situations inspired by the growing pains of today's teenagers. My greatest influence is my inner spiritual growth.; [a.] Chesapeake Beach, MD

ZDENEK, VIOLET
[b.] June 4, 1930, Chicago; [p.] Mirko and Violet Popovic; [m.] James A. Zdenek, May 18, 1957; [ch.] Violet and Jim; [ed.] High School - Farragut Jan Neruda - Bohemian School; [occ.] Retired; [hon.] National Honor Society; [oth. writ.] "Age" and "My Son, My Son" - published in the National Library of Poetry; [pers.] Family is the key to riches.

ZIMARDO, NATOSHA A.
[b.] December 29, 1972, Seattle, WA; [p.] Michel Zimardo, Sheila Zimardo; [ed.] Everett High School currently a student at ECC; [hon.] Music scholar award; [oth. writ.] Two poems published in a local Newsletter, Three published in a book entitled "Illuminati NW"; [a.] Everett, WA

ZIMMER JR., KARL
[b.] September 5, 1926, Kalamazoo, MI; [p.] Karl and Lorena Zimmer; [m.] Barbara Zimmer, March 19, 1949; [ch.] Kaarina, Karl III, Erik; [ed.] A.B., Univ of Chicago, Cand. Mag., Univ. of Copenhagen (Denmark); [occ.] Chairman, Zimmer Paper Inc.; [memb.] Common Foreign Relations, Athenaeum Foundation, Confreriedes Chevaliers du Tastevin, etc.; [hon.] Short story prizes from the Univ. of Chicago and Indiana University (Indianapolis), order of the Lion of Finland; [oth. writ.] Former Columnist, Danish and American Newspapers; [pers.] Ideas have consequences - and each of us is responsible for our actions.; [a.] Indianapolis, IN

ZUBLENA, KIMBERLEY
[b.] December 30, 1965, Aberdeen, WA; [p.] Ken and Geraldine Ketola; [ch.] Mikala and McKenzie; [ed.] Wethenvax H.S. Adene's Beauty College; [occ.] Cosmetologist; [pers.] My poem was inspired by the love I had for my mother and the worst pain I have ever felt in the loss of my mother. I pray for a cure for cancer and an end to all the suffering this disease causes everyone it touches.; [a.] Gig Harbor, WA

ZUIDERVEEN, J. A.
[b.] July 17, 1961, Kalamazoo, MI; [m.] K. J. Zuiderveen, August 18, 1984; [ch.] Caleb Nathaneal, Lydia Joy; [ed.] Allegan High School Western Michigan Univ. - B.S. (Chemistry) University of Kentucky - Ph. D. (Toxicology); [occ.] Biology Professor - Columbus College, Columbus, GA; [memb.] Society of Environmental Toxicology and Chemistry North American Benthological Society American Chemical Society American Association for the Advancement of Science; [hon.] Beta Beta Beta Biological Honor Society, Who's Who Environmental Registry, open competition fellowship - University of Kentucky; [a.] Cataula, GA

ZURAWSKI, KAREN
[pen.] Firehawk; [b.] February 1953, Liberty, NY; [ed.] BA English Literature and Secondary Education continuing Education in Computer Sciences. Lifetime independent studies of Philosophy and Sociology; [occ.] Author, Artist, Philosopher; [oth. writ.] Various articles, poems and essays over the past decades have been published in local journals. Projects at present include a book of philosophy, a self-healing book and a collaborative book of art and poetry.; [a.] Santa Fe, NM

INDEX